A FLEETWAY LIBRARY

BATTLE PICTURE LIBRARY COLLECTION No 2

LET EM HAVE IT

The publishers would like to thank the team at IPC Media Ltd
and DC Comics for their help in compiling this book, particularly
David Abbott and Linda Lee.

Published in 2008 by Prion
An imprint of the Carlton Publishing Group
20 Mortimer Street
London W1T 3JW

A catalogue record for this book is available from the British Library.

ISBN 978-1-85375-671-9

Printed and bound in Thailand

10 9 8 7 6 5 4 3 2 1

A FLEETWAY LIBRARY

BATTLE PICTURE LIBRARY COLLECTION No 2

LET EM HAVE IT

12 OF THE BEST BATTLE PICTURE LIBRARY COMIC BOOKS EVER!

GENERAL EDITOR:
STEVE HOLLAND

CARLTON
BOOKS

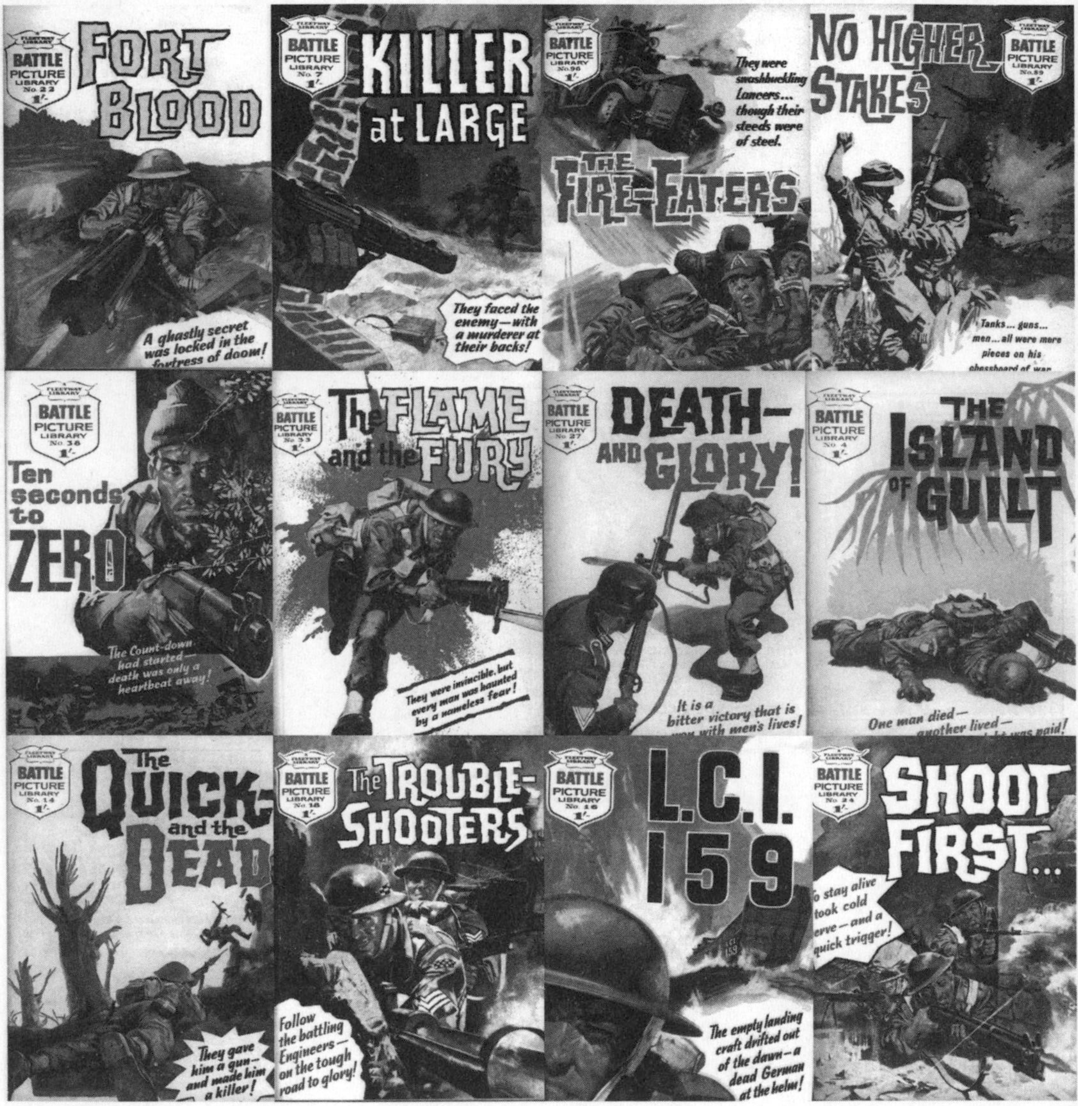

BATTLE PICTURE LIBRARY No. 22 1/-
FORT BLOOD
A ghastly secret was locked in the fortress of doom!
BATTLE PICTURE LIBRARY No. 7 1/-
KILLER at LARGE
They faced the enemy—with a murderer at their backs!
BATTLE PICTURE LIBRARY No. 96
They were swashbuckling Lancers... though their steeds were of steel.
THE FIRE-EATERS
NO HIGHER STAKES
BATTLE PICTURE LIBRARY
Tanks... guns... men... all were more pieces on his
BATTLE PICTURE LIBRARY No. 36 1/-
Ten seconds to ZERO
The Count-down had started—death was only a heartbeat away!
BATTLE PICTURE LIBRARY
The FLAME and the FURY
They were invincible, but every man was haunted by a nameless fear!
BATTLE PICTURE LIBRARY No. 27 1/-
DEATH—AND GLORY!
It is a bitter victory that is
BATTLE PICTURE LIBRARY No. 4 1/-
THE ISLAND OF GUILT
One man died—another lived—
BATTLE PICTURE LIBRARY No. 14 1/-
The QUICK—and the DEAD
They gave him a gun—and made him a killer!
BATTLE PICTURE LIBRARY No. 18 1/-
The TROUBLE-SHOOTERS
Follow the battling Engineers—on the tough road to glory!
BATTLE PICTURE LIBRARY No. 16 1/-
L.C.I. 159
The empty landing craft drifted out of the dawn—a dead German at the helm!
BATTLE PICTURE LIBRARY No. 24 1/-
SHOOT FIRST...
quick trigger!

CONTENTS

INTRODUCTION

Fifteen years ago I had the good fortune to talk to Ted Bensberg, then in his seventies and living on the south coast, about his years as editor of the famous Fleetway Publications' war libraries, including every issue of *Battle Picture Library* from whose pages these stories have been selected. Ted had no doubts that their success ("and they were successful," he proudly stated) was "due to the high quality of the script. We aimed for strong, believable human stories set against a background of realistic and exciting action."

Each script earned its author fifty guineas (a good wage for the time and probably worth around £2,000 nowadays) so it was in the author's best interest to tell the best stories he could and keep the commissions for new yarns coming in month after month. If you could put together the 135 or so frames required in a week—and authors like Donne Avenell, Ken Bulmer and A. Carney Allan could do so with ease—you would be earn yourself nearly four times the average wage (below £15 in the early 1960s).

The rewards attracted good writers, many of them veterans of the war themselves. Bensberg had been called up for the Territorials in 1939 and served as a sergeant in the Royal Signals. One of his most prolific writers on *Battle Picture Library*, Ken Bulmer, had also served with the Royal Signals in Africa, Sicily and Italy, which gave his stories a verisimilitude lacking in many of the war stories that most of us grew up on in the 1970s. The stars of *Battle Picture Library* were rarely the gung-ho super-soldiers portrayed in Hollywood movies; they were the often the Tommies on the front line: fragile and fearful who would have to face up to their mortality, finding in a corner their hearts the courage to do their duty in the face of terrifying odds. Some of the Tommies of *Battle Picture Library* were as far from heroes as you could get.

By the time *Battle Picture Library* began publication, it already had two companion titles, including *Air Ace Picture Library,* which meant that the new series avoided tales of war in the air. Not that

Battle Picture Library found that limiting: there was plenty of action to go around in the burning deserts of North Africa and Somaliland; the steaming jungles of Burma and New Guinea; the fight for the Aegean Islands in the Mediterranean and the Island of Raka in the Pacific; the landings in Italy and the March on Rome; and the landing in Normandy and the advance that would eventually take the Allied armies to Berlin. No theatre of war was ignored.

The names of the characters may have been made up, but the stories themselves revolved around the real situations that the fathers and grandfathers of the readers had faced in battle. Time has distanced us from the Second World War, but these little slices of history can bring us closer to the action.

Steve Holland

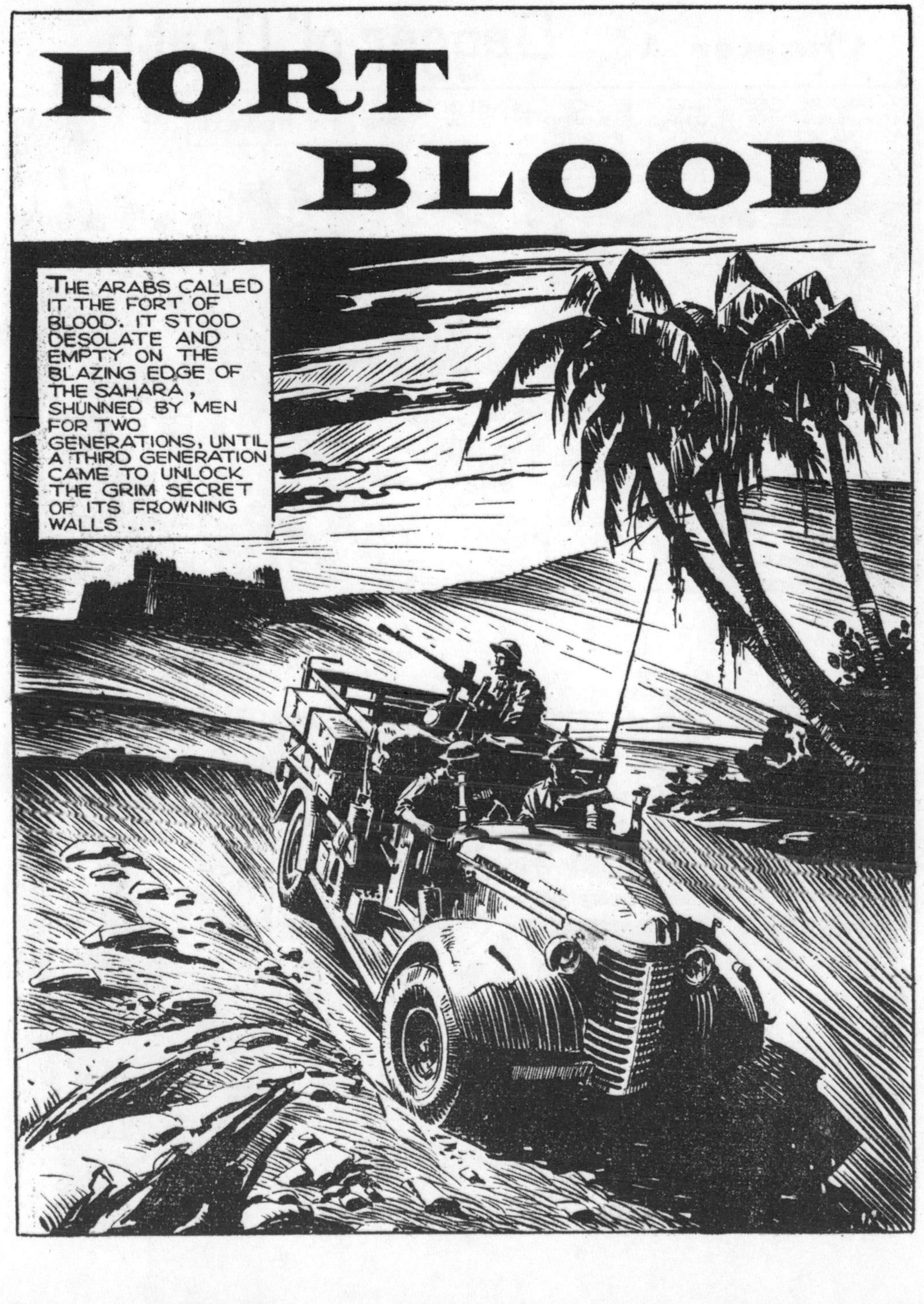
FORT BLOOD
THE ARABS CALLED IT THE FORT OF BLOOD. IT STOOD DESOLATE AND EMPTY ON THE BLAZING EDGE OF THE SAHARA, SHUNNED BY MEN FOR TWO GENERATIONS, UNTIL A THIRD GENERATION CAME TO UNLOCK THE GRIM SECRET OF ITS FROWNING WALLS ...

Chapter 1. Dagger of Death

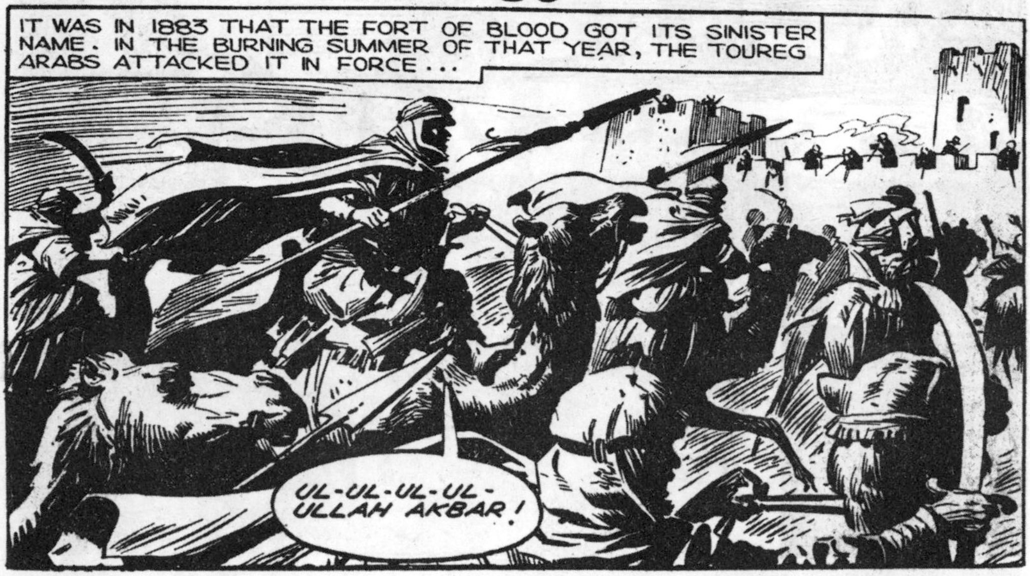
IT WAS IN 1883 THAT THE FORT OF BLOOD GOT ITS SINISTER NAME. IN THE BURNING SUMMER OF THAT YEAR, THE TOUREG ARABS ATTACKED IT IN FORCE...
UL-UL-UL-UL-ULLAH AKBAR!

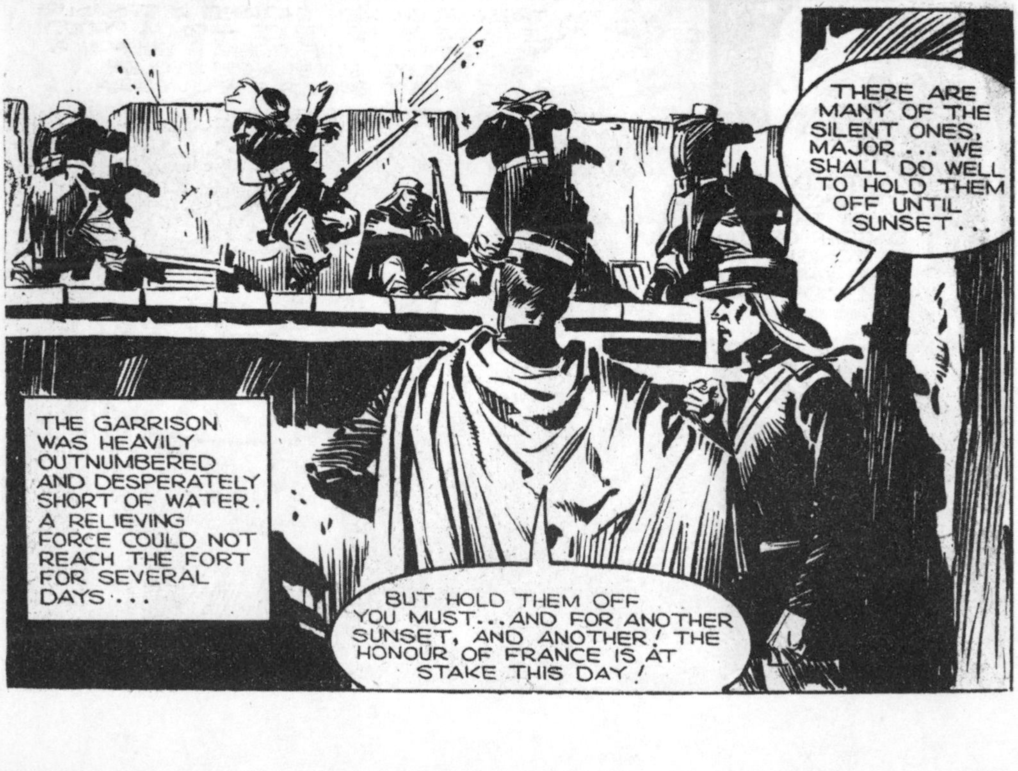
THERE ARE MANY OF THE SILENT ONES, MAJOR ... WE SHALL DO WELL TO HOLD THEM OFF UNTIL SUNSET...
THE GARRISON WAS HEAVILY OUTNUMBERED AND DESPERATELY SHORT OF WATER. A RELIEVING FORCE COULD NOT REACH THE FORT FOR SEVERAL DAYS...
BUT HOLD THEM OFF YOU MUST...AND FOR ANOTHER SUNSET, AND ANOTHER! THE HONOUR OF FRANCE IS AT STAKE THIS DAY!

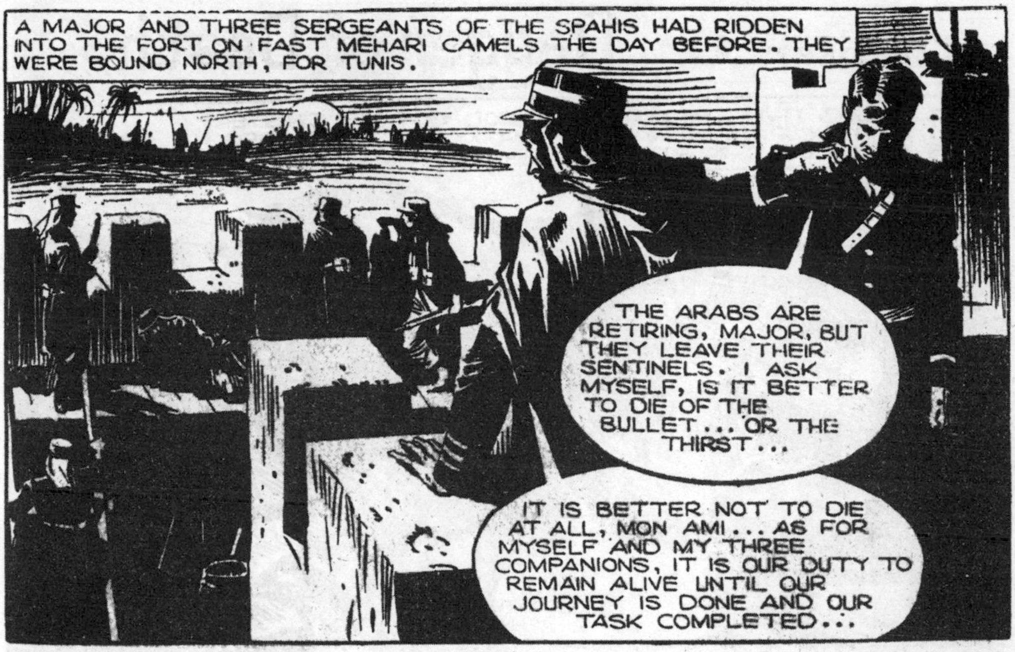
A MAJOR AND THREE SERGEANTS OF THE SPAHIS HAD RIDDEN INTO THE FORT ON FAST MEHARI CAMELS THE DAY BEFORE. THEY WERE BOUND NORTH, FOR TUNIS.
THE ARABS ARE RETIRING, MAJOR, BUT THEY LEAVE THEIR SENTINELS. I ASK MYSELF, IS IT BETTER TO DIE OF THE BULLET ... OR THE THIRST ...
IT IS BETTER NOT TO DIE AT ALL, MON AMI ... AS FOR MYSELF AND MY THREE COMPANIONS, IT IS OUR DUTY TO REMAIN ALIVE UNTIL OUR JOURNEY IS DONE AND OUR TASK COMPLETED ...

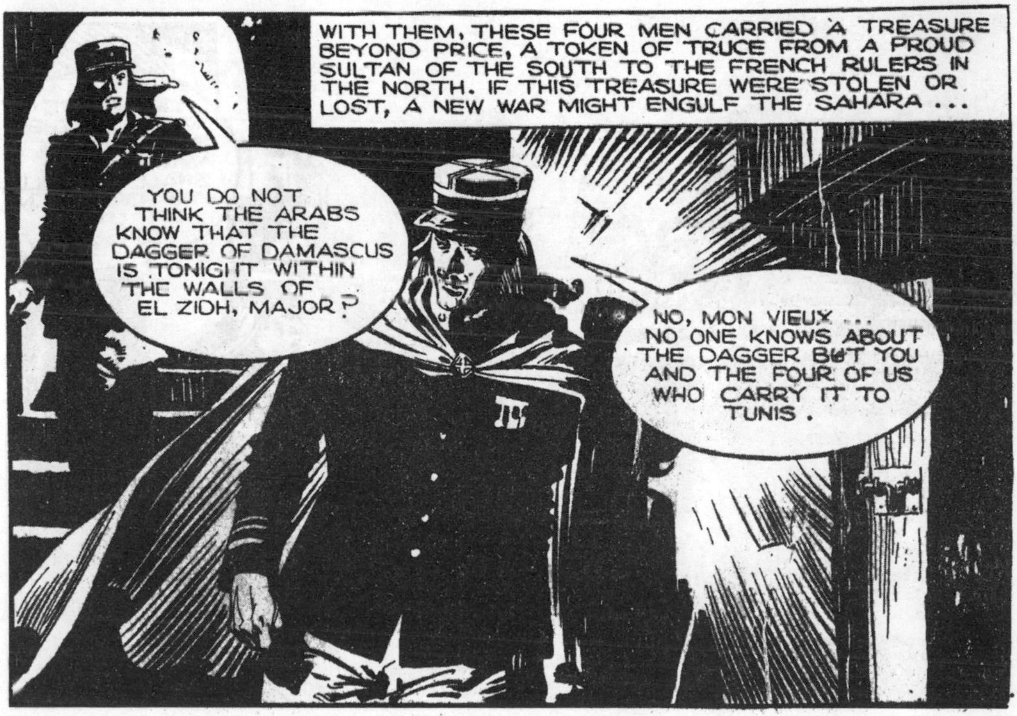
WITH THEM, THESE FOUR MEN CARRIED A TREASURE BEYOND PRICE, A TOKEN OF TRUCE FROM A PROUD SULTAN OF THE SOUTH TO THE FRENCH RULERS IN THE NORTH. IF THIS TREASURE WERE STOLEN OR LOST, A NEW WAR MIGHT ENGULF THE SAHARA ...
YOU DO NOT THINK THE ARABS KNOW THAT THE DAGGER OF DAMASCUS IS TONIGHT WITHIN THE WALLS OF EL ZIDH, MAJOR?
NO, MON VIEUX ... NO ONE KNOWS ABOUT THE DAGGER BUT YOU AND THE FOUR OF US WHO CARRY IT TO TUNIS .

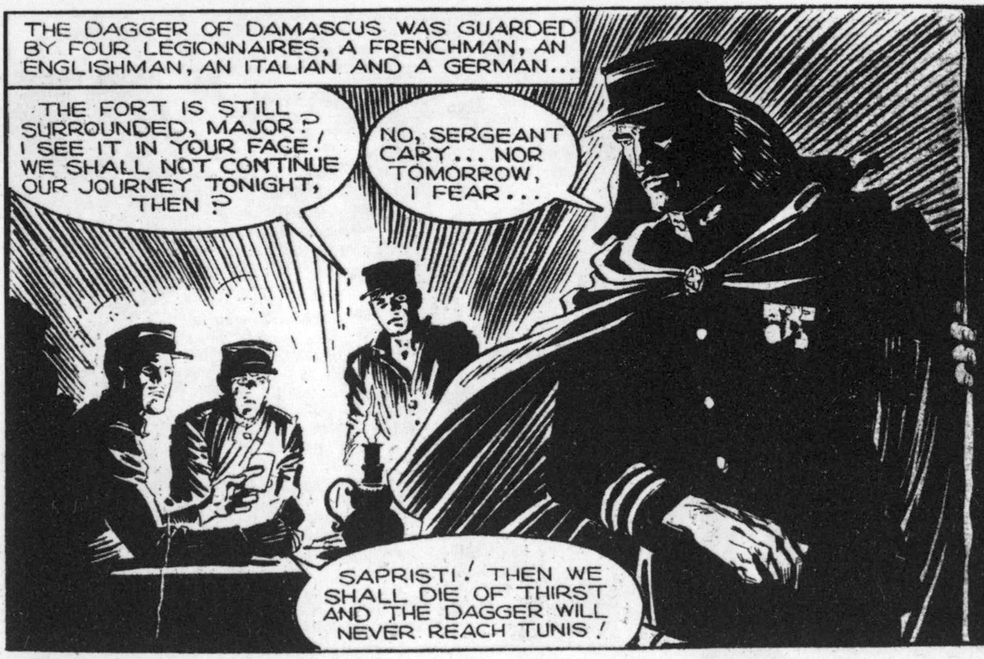
THE DAGGER OF DAMASCUS WAS GUARDED BY FOUR LEGIONNAIRES, A FRENCHMAN, AN ENGLISHMAN, AN ITALIAN AND A GERMAN...
THE FORT IS STILL SURROUNDED, MAJOR? I SEE IT IN YOUR FACE! WE SHALL NOT CONTINUE OUR JOURNEY TONIGHT, THEN?
NO, SERGEANT CARY... NOR TOMORROW, I FEAR...
SAPRISTI! THEN WE SHALL DIE OF THIRST AND THE DAGGER WILL NEVER REACH TUNIS!

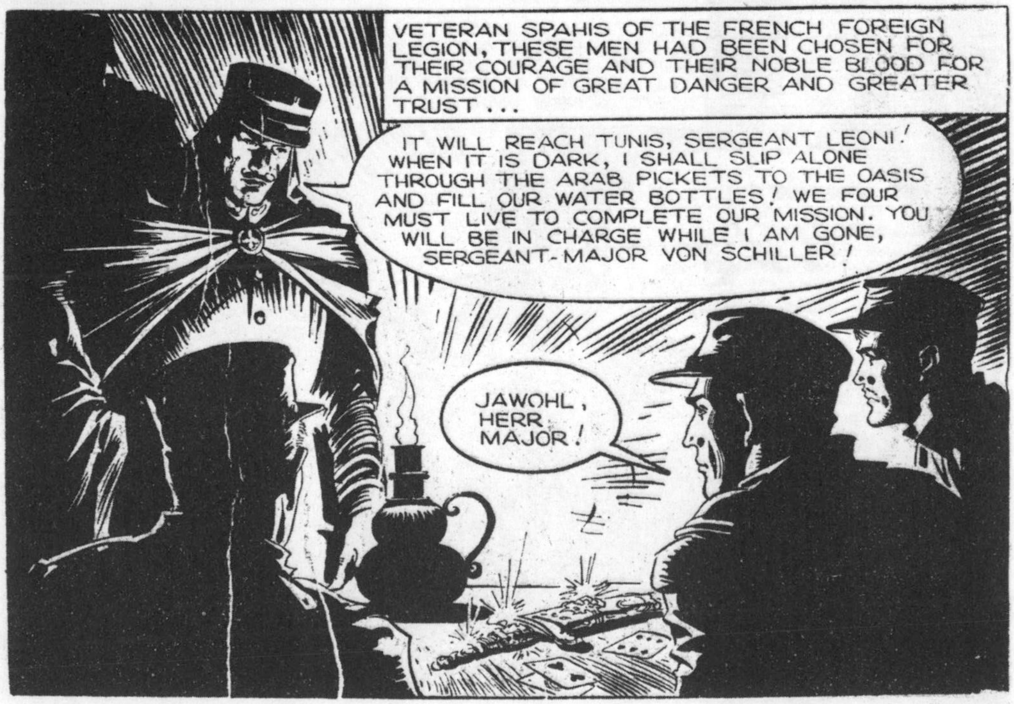
VETERAN SPAHIS OF THE FRENCH FOREIGN LEGION, THESE MEN HAD BEEN CHOSEN FOR THEIR COURAGE AND THEIR NOBLE BLOOD FOR A MISSION OF GREAT DANGER AND GREATER TRUST...
IT WILL REACH TUNIS, SERGEANT LEONI! WHEN IT IS DARK, I SHALL SLIP ALONE THROUGH THE ARAB PICKETS TO THE OASIS AND FILL OUR WATER BOTTLES! WE FOUR MUST LIVE TO COMPLETE OUR MISSION. YOU WILL BE IN CHARGE WHILE I AM GONE, SERGEANT-MAJOR VON SCHILLER!
JAWOHL, HERR MAJOR!

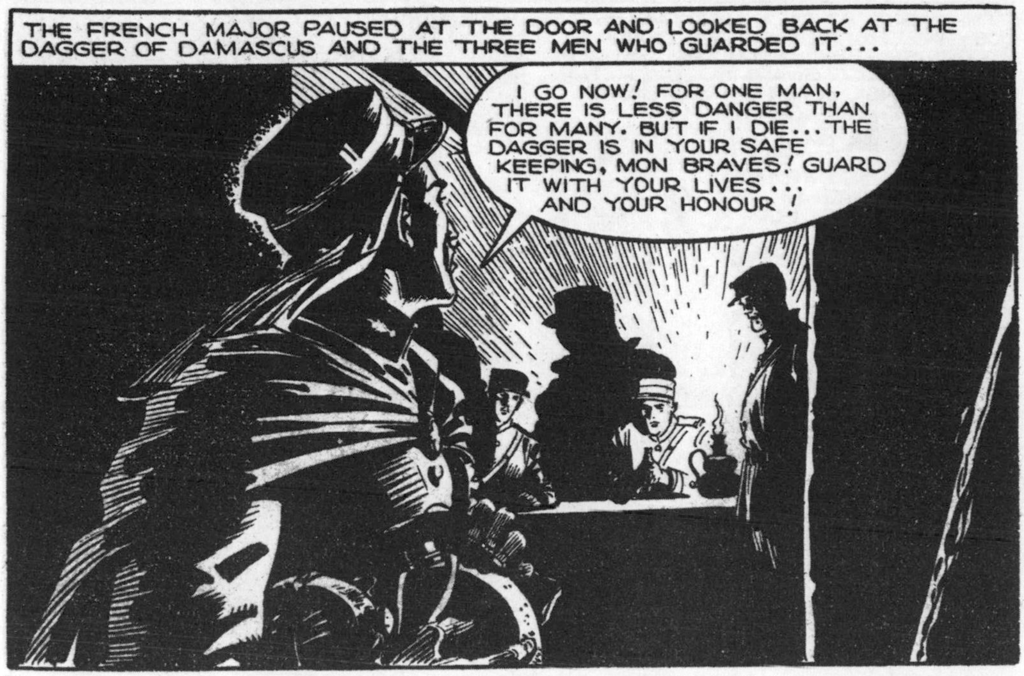
THE FRENCH MAJOR PAUSED AT THE DOOR AND LOOKED BACK AT THE DAGGER OF DAMASCUS AND THE THREE MEN WHO GUARDED IT ...
I GO NOW! FOR ONE MAN, THERE IS LESS DANGER THAN FOR MANY. BUT IF I DIE... THE DAGGER IS IN YOUR SAFE KEEPING, MON BRAVES! GUARD IT WITH YOUR LIVES ... AND YOUR HONOUR!

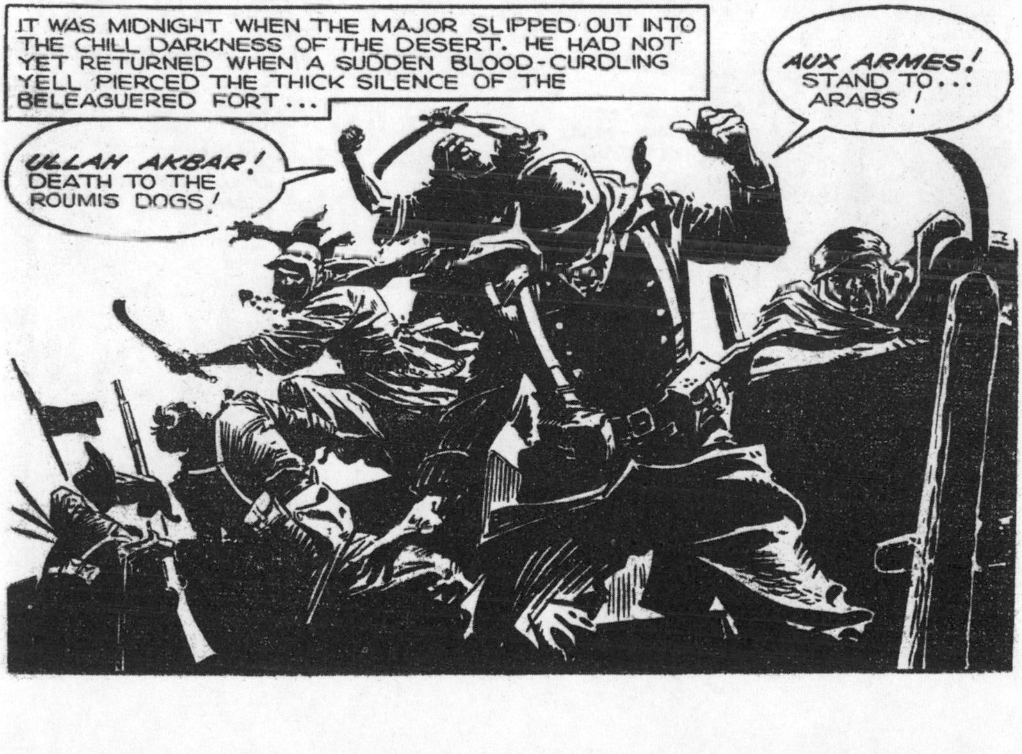
IT WAS MIDNIGHT WHEN THE MAJOR SLIPPED OUT INTO THE CHILL DARKNESS OF THE DESERT. HE HAD NOT YET RETURNED WHEN A SUDDEN BLOOD-CURDLING YELL PIERCED THE THICK SILENCE OF THE BELEAGUERED FORT...
ULLAH AKBAR! DEATH TO THE ROUMIS DOGS!
AUX ARMES! STAND TO... ARABS!

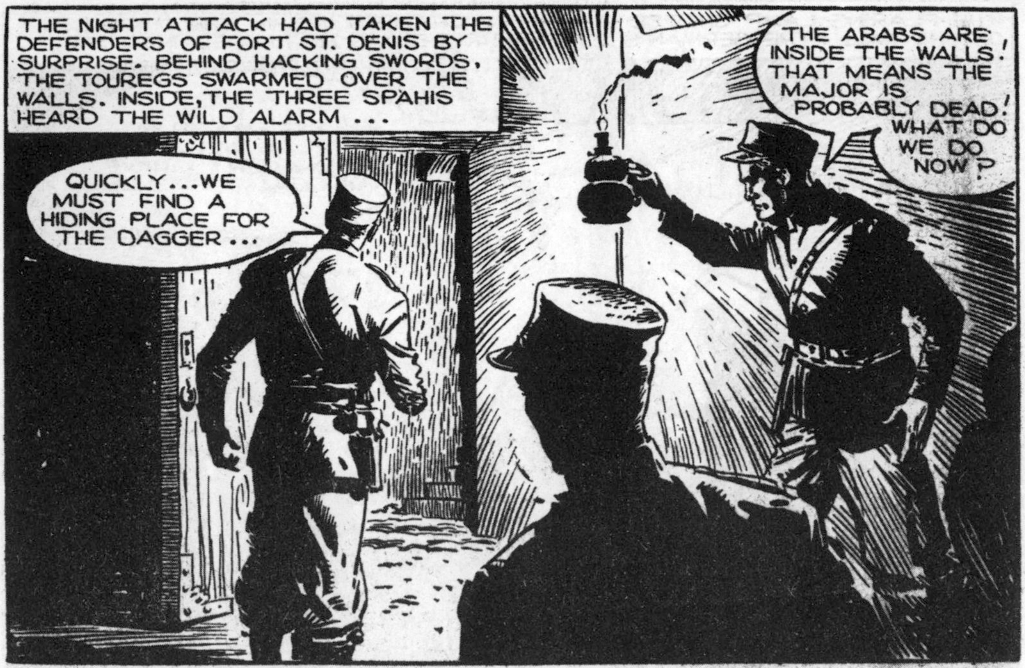
THE NIGHT ATTACK HAD TAKEN THE DEFENDERS OF FORT ST. DENIS BY SURPRISE. BEHIND HACKING SWORDS, THE TOUREGS SWARMED OVER THE WALLS. INSIDE, THE THREE SPAHIS HEARD THE WILD ALARM ...
THE ARABS ARE INSIDE THE WALLS! THAT MEANS THE MAJOR IS PROBABLY DEAD! WHAT DO WE DO NOW?
QUICKLY...WE MUST FIND A HIDING PLACE FOR THE DAGGER...

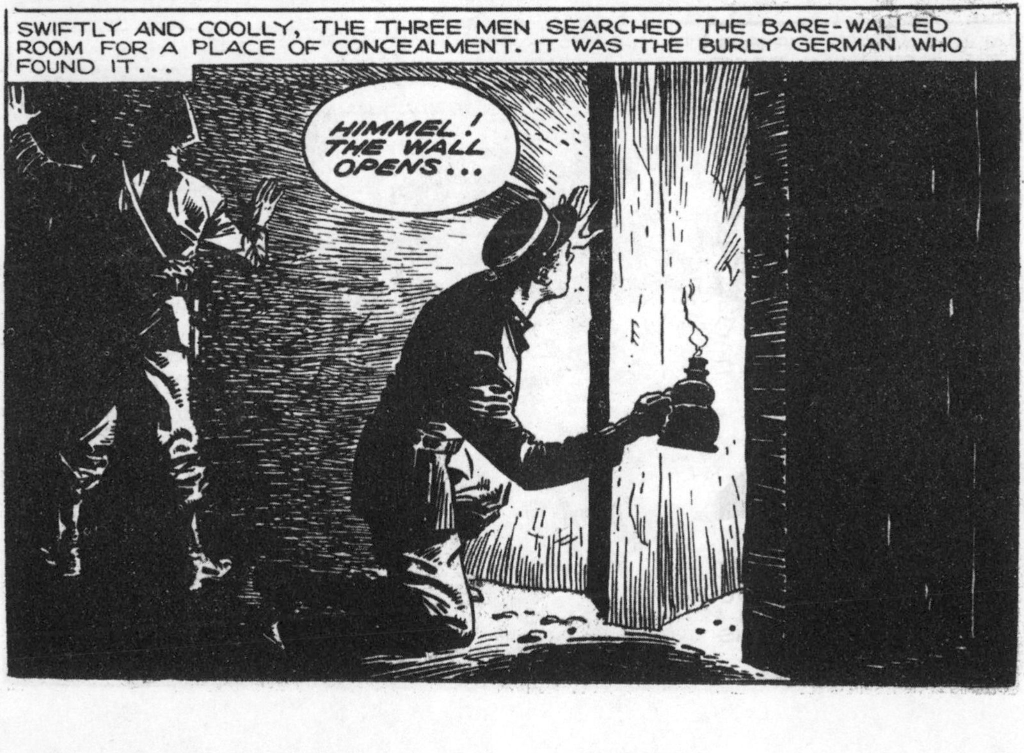
SWIFTLY AND COOLLY, THE THREE MEN SEARCHED THE BARE-WALLED ROOM FOR A PLACE OF CONCEALMENT. IT WAS THE BURLY GERMAN WHO FOUND IT...
HIMMEL! THE WALL OPENS...

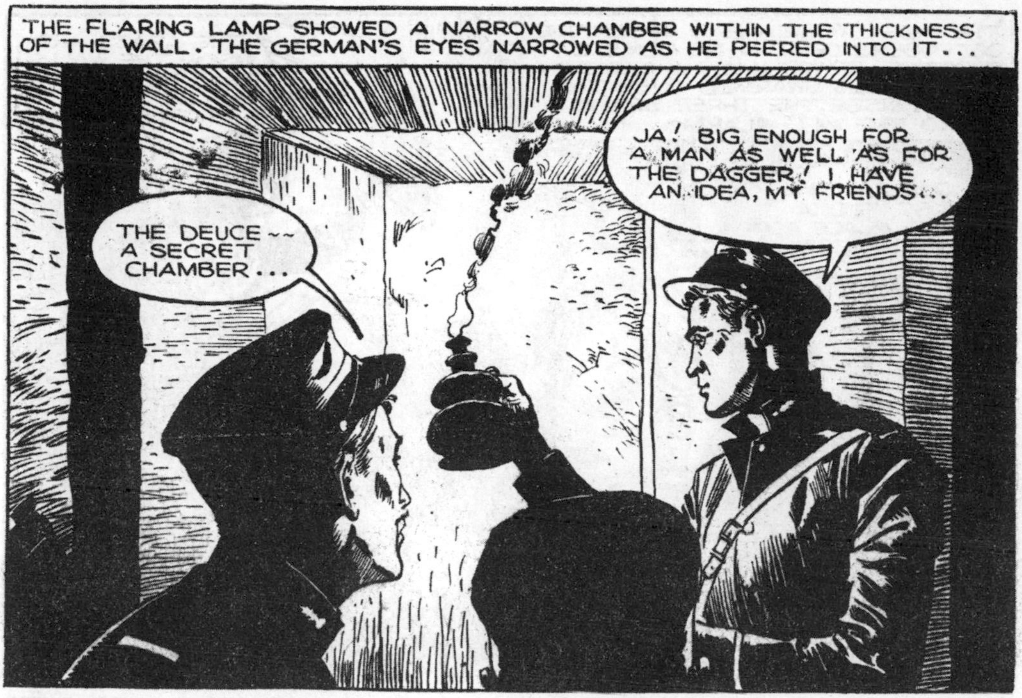
THE FLARING LAMP SHOWED A NARROW CHAMBER WITHIN THE THICKNESS OF THE WALL. THE GERMAN'S EYES NARROWED AS HE PEERED INTO IT...
THE DEUCE -- A SECRET CHAMBER...
JA! BIG ENOUGH FOR A MAN AS WELL AS FOR THE DAGGER! I HAVE AN IDEA, MY FRIENDS...

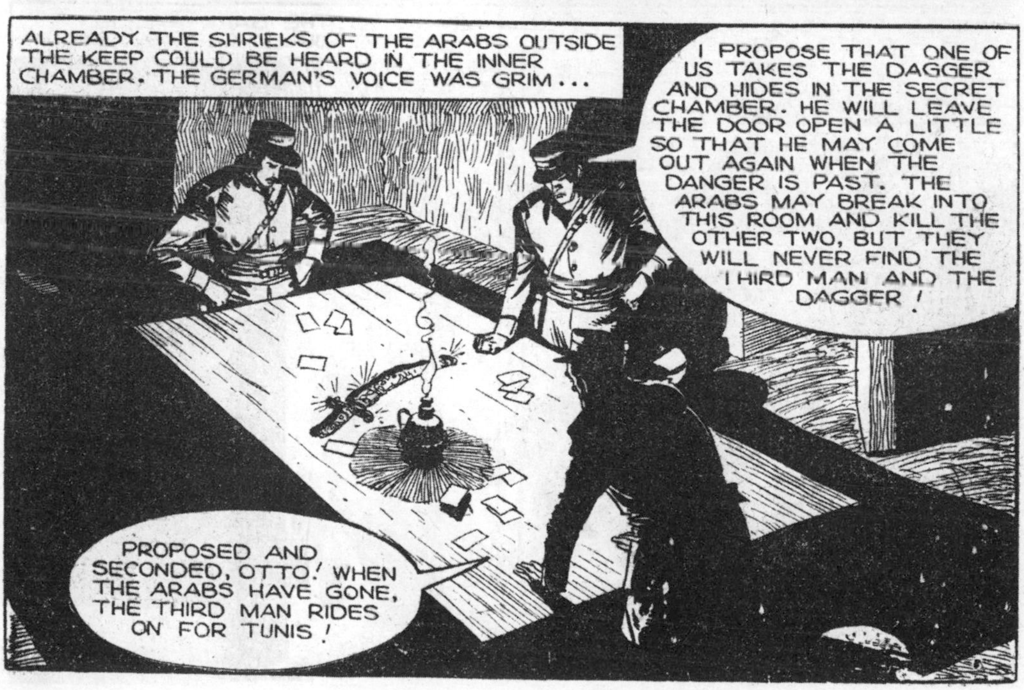
ALREADY THE SHRIEKS OF THE ARABS OUTSIDE THE KEEP COULD BE HEARD IN THE INNER CHAMBER. THE GERMAN'S VOICE WAS GRIM...
I PROPOSE THAT ONE OF US TAKES THE DAGGER AND HIDES IN THE SECRET CHAMBER. HE WILL LEAVE THE DOOR OPEN A LITTLE SO THAT HE MAY COME OUT AGAIN WHEN THE DANGER IS PAST. THE ARABS MAY BREAK INTO THIS ROOM AND KILL THE OTHER TWO, BUT THEY WILL NEVER FIND THE THIRD MAN AND THE DAGGER!
PROPOSED AND SECONDED, OTTO! WHEN THE ARABS HAVE GONE, THE THIRD MAN RIDES ON FOR TUNIS!

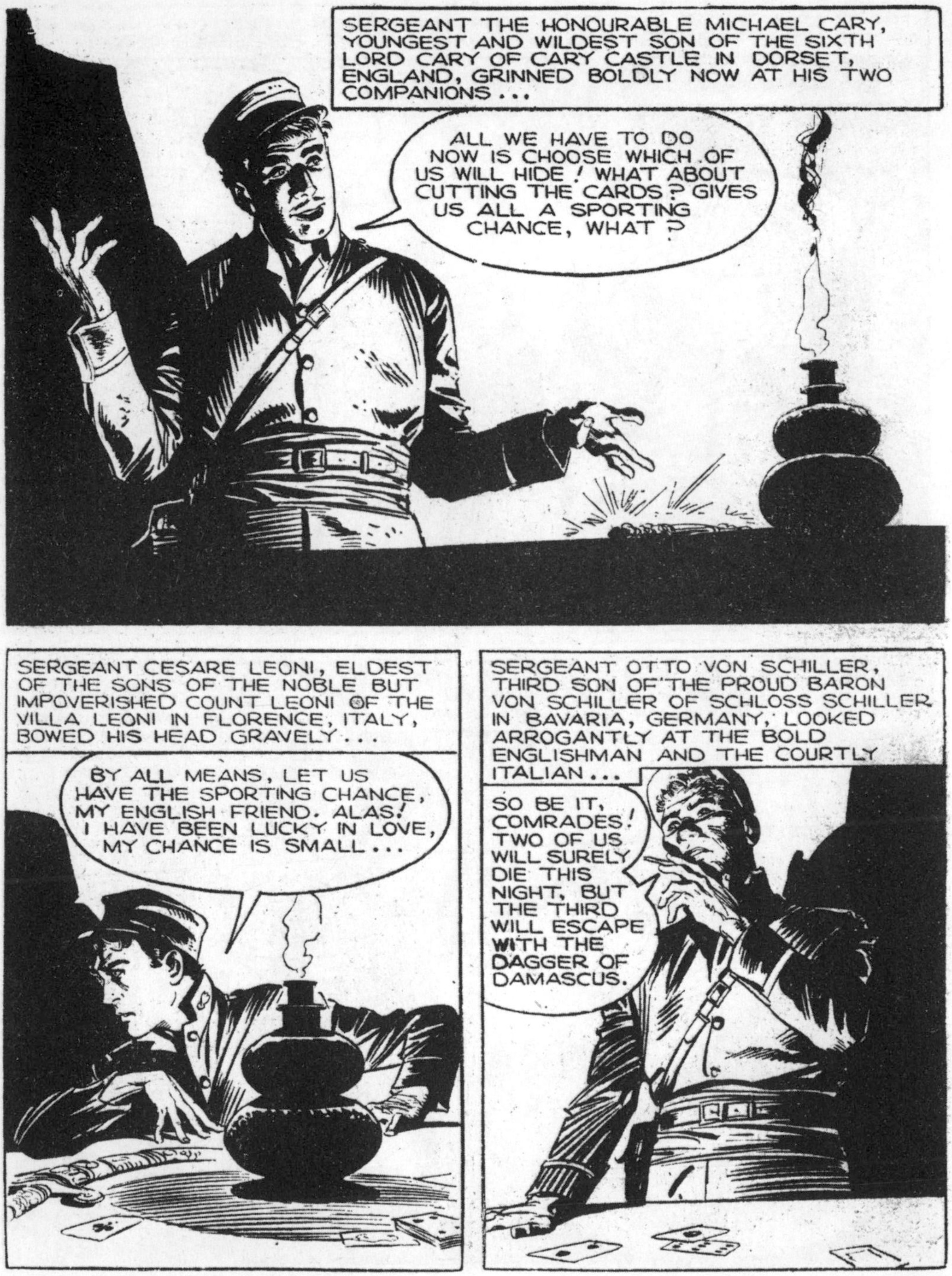
SERGEANT THE HONOURABLE MICHAEL CARY, YOUNGEST AND WILDEST SON OF THE SIXTH LORD CARY OF CARY CASTLE IN DORSET, ENGLAND, GRINNED BOLDLY NOW AT HIS TWO COMPANIONS ...
ALL WE HAVE TO DO NOW IS CHOOSE WHICH OF US WILL HIDE! WHAT ABOUT CUTTING THE CARDS? GIVES US ALL A SPORTING CHANCE, WHAT?
SERGEANT CESARE LEONI, ELDEST OF THE SONS OF THE NOBLE BUT IMPOVERISHED COUNT LEONI OF THE VILLA LEONI IN FLORENCE, ITALY, BOWED HIS HEAD GRAVELY ...
BY ALL MEANS, LET US HAVE THE SPORTING CHANCE, MY ENGLISH FRIEND. ALAS! I HAVE BEEN LUCKY IN LOVE, MY CHANCE IS SMALL ...
SERGEANT OTTO VON SCHILLER, THIRD SON OF THE PROUD BARON VON SCHILLER OF SCHLOSS SCHILLER IN BAVARIA, GERMANY, LOOKED ARROGANTLY AT THE BOLD ENGLISHMAN AND THE COURTLY ITALIAN ...
SO BE IT, COMRADES! TWO OF US WILL SURELY DIE THIS NIGHT, BUT THE THIRD WILL ESCAPE WITH THE DAGGER OF DAMASCUS.

THE THREE MEN CAME OF ANCIENT AND NOBLE STOCK. HONOUR HAD BEEN THEIR INHERITANCE. BUT ONE OF THEM WAS A THIEF AND A TRAITOR AND A MURDERER...

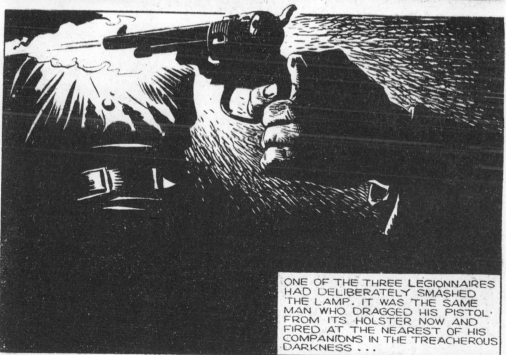

ONE OF THE THREE LEGIONNAIRES HAD DELIBERATELY SMASHED THE LAMP. IT WAS THE SAME MAN WHO DRAGGED HIS PISTOL FROM ITS HOLSTER NOW AND FIRED AT THE NEAREST OF HIS COMPANIONS IN THE TREACHEROUS DARKNESS...

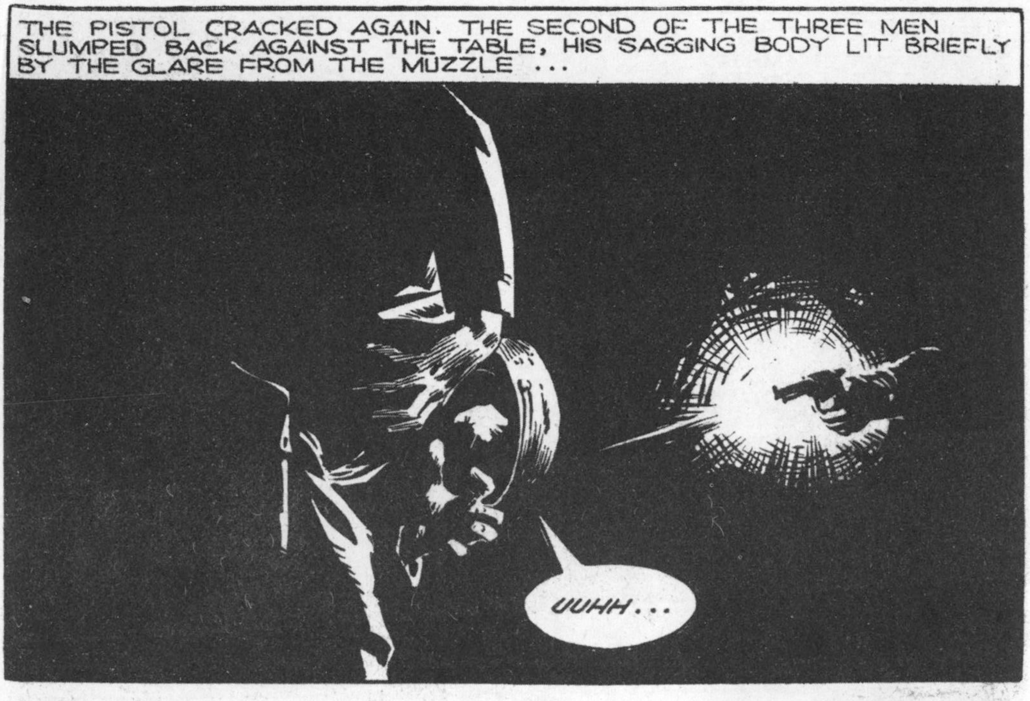
THE PISTOL CRACKED AGAIN. THE SECOND OF THE THREE MEN SLUMPED BACK AGAINST THE TABLE, HIS SAGGING BODY LIT BRIEFLY BY THE GLARE FROM THE MUZZLE ...
UUHH ...

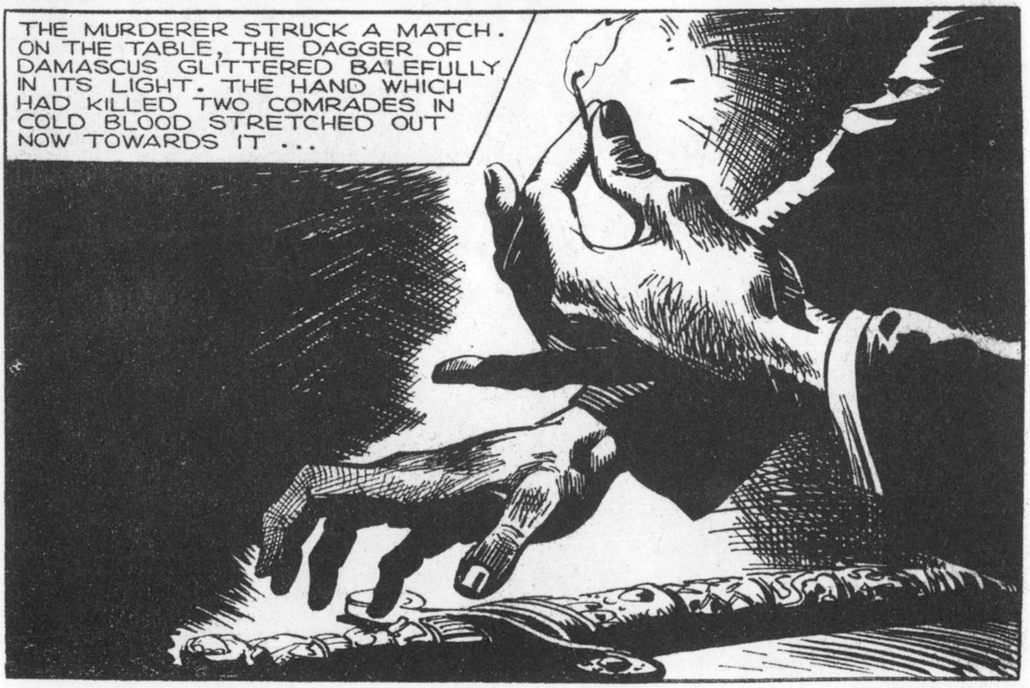
THE MURDERER STRUCK A MATCH. ON THE TABLE, THE DAGGER OF DAMASCUS GLITTERED BALEFULLY IN ITS LIGHT. THE HAND WHICH HAD KILLED TWO COMRADES IN COLD BLOOD STRETCHED OUT NOW TOWARDS IT ...

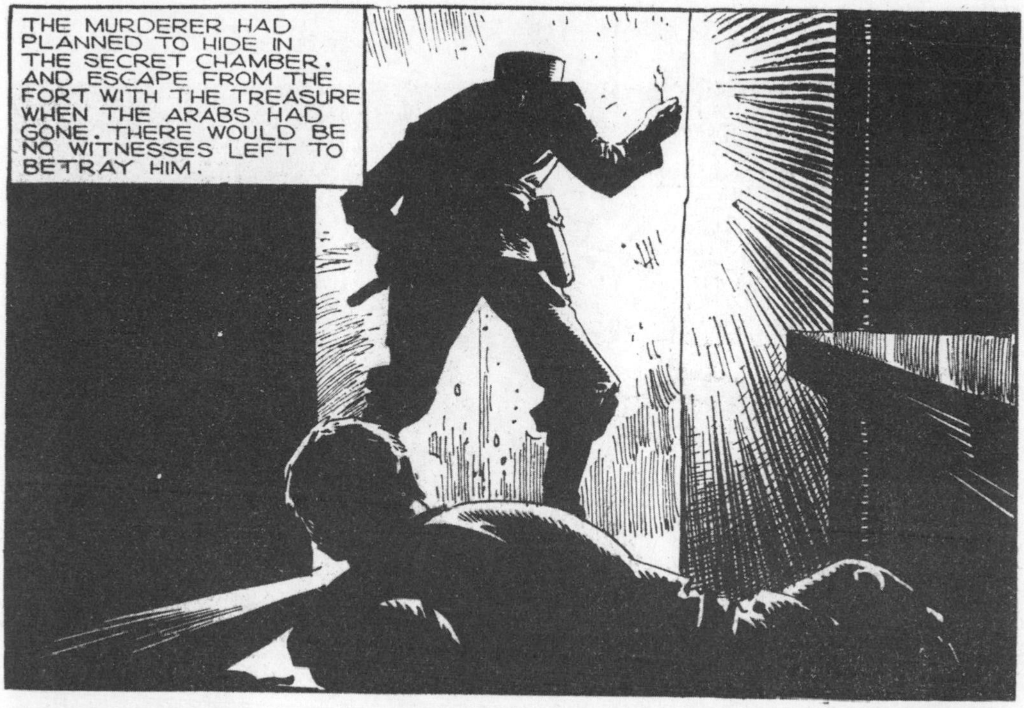
THE MURDERER HAD PLANNED TO HIDE IN THE SECRET CHAMBER. AND ESCAPE FROM THE FORT WITH THE TREASURE WHEN THE ARABS HAD GONE. THERE WOULD BE NO WITNESSES LEFT TO BETRAY HIM.

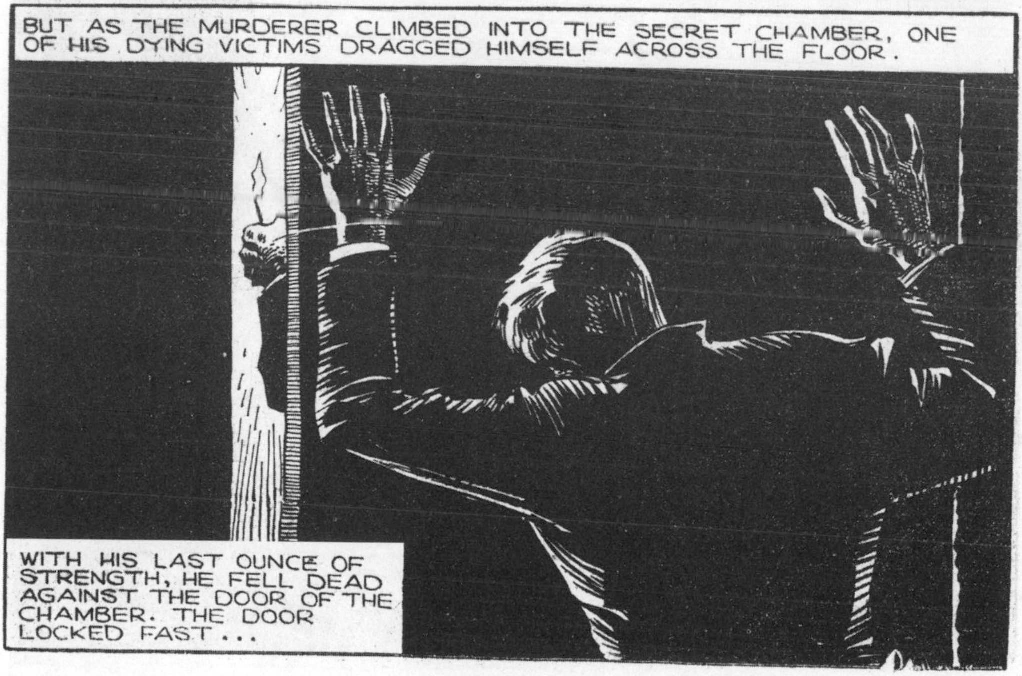
BUT AS THE MURDERER CLIMBED INTO THE SECRET CHAMBER, ONE OF HIS DYING VICTIMS DRAGGED HIMSELF ACROSS THE FLOOR.
WITH HIS LAST OUNCE OF STRENGTH, HE FELL DEAD AGAINST THE DOOR OF THE CHAMBER. THE DOOR LOCKED FAST ...

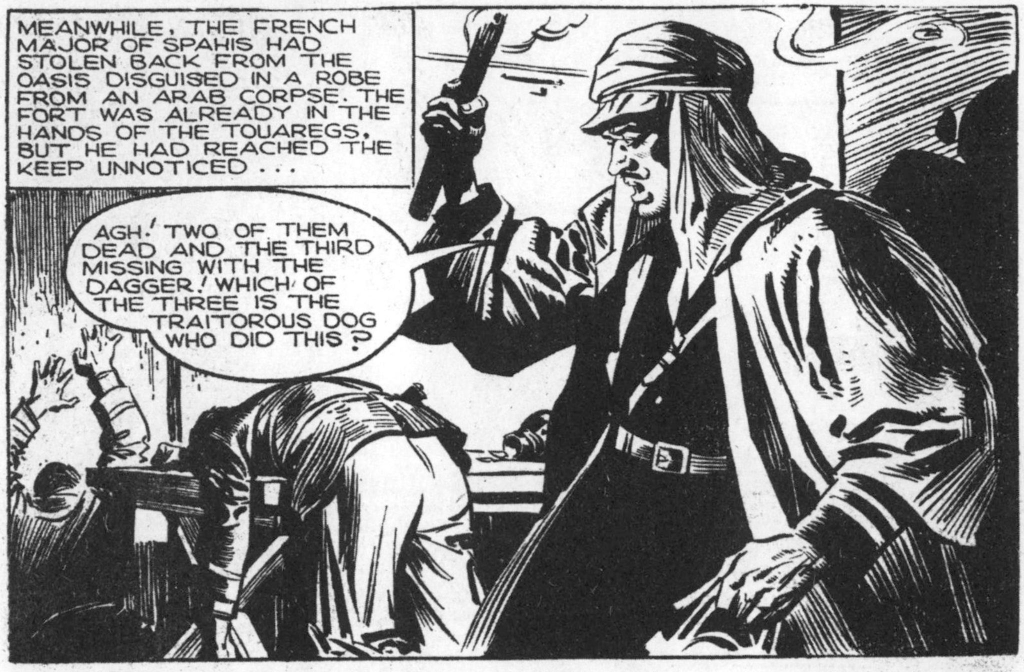
MEANWHILE, THE FRENCH MAJOR OF SPAHIS HAD STOLEN BACK FROM THE OASIS DISGUISED IN A ROBE FROM AN ARAB CORPSE. THE FORT WAS ALREADY IN THE HANDS OF THE TOUAREGS, BUT HE HAD REACHED THE KEEP UNNOTICED . . .
AGH! TWO OF THEM DEAD AND THE THIRD MISSING WITH THE DAGGER! WHICH OF THE THREE IS THE TRAITOROUS DOG WHO DID THIS?

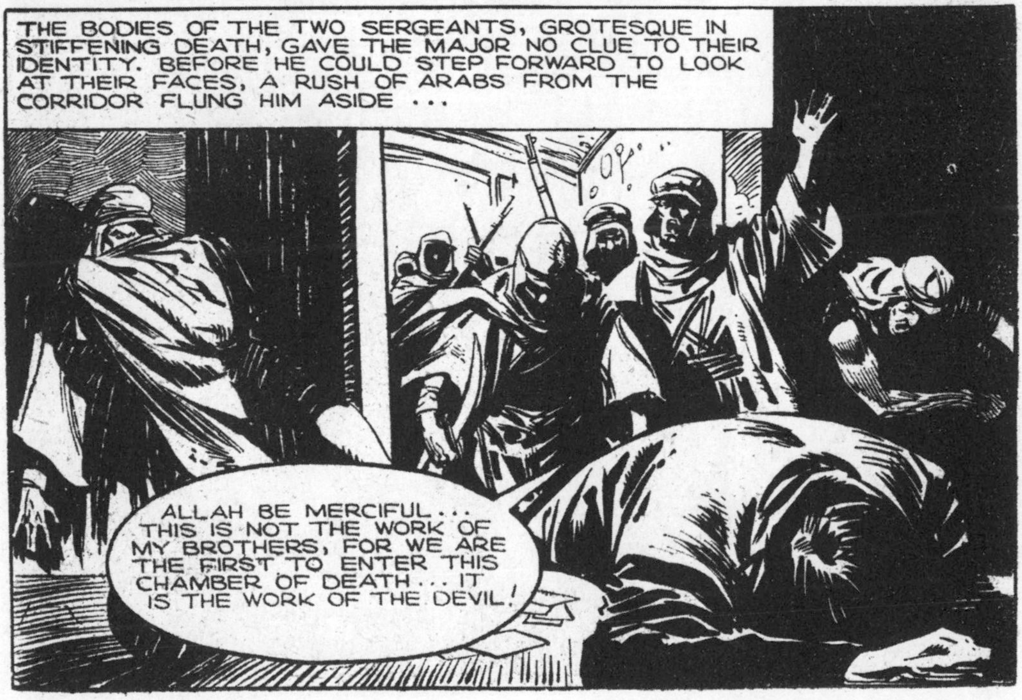
THE BODIES OF THE TWO SERGEANTS, GROTESQUE IN STIFFENING DEATH, GAVE THE MAJOR NO CLUE TO THEIR IDENTITY. BEFORE HE COULD STEP FORWARD TO LOOK AT THEIR FACES, A RUSH OF ARABS FROM THE CORRIDOR FLUNG HIM ASIDE . . .
ALLAH BE MERCIFUL . . . THIS IS NOT THE WORK OF MY BROTHERS, FOR WE ARE THE FIRST TO ENTER THIS CHAMBER OF DEATH . . . IT IS THE WORK OF THE DEVIL!

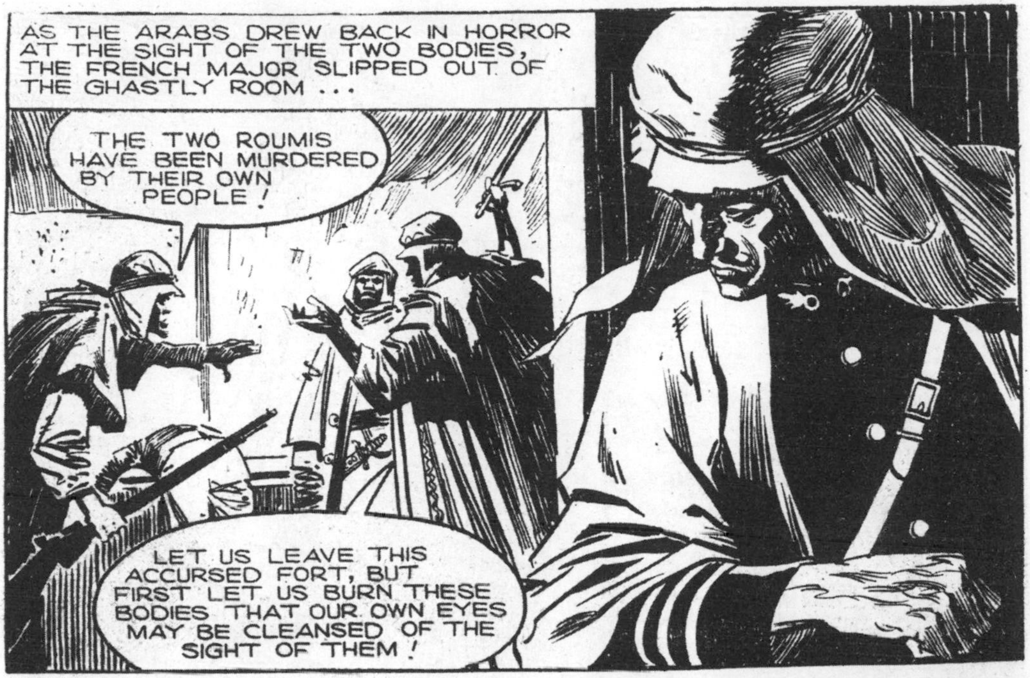
AS THE ARABS DREW BACK IN HORROR AT THE SIGHT OF THE TWO BODIES, THE FRENCH MAJOR SLIPPED OUT OF THE GHASTLY ROOM ...
THE TWO ROUMIS HAVE BEEN MURDERED BY THEIR OWN PEOPLE!
LET US LEAVE THIS ACCURSED FORT, BUT FIRST LET US BURN THESE BODIES THAT OUR OWN EYES MAY BE CLEANSED OF THE SIGHT OF THEM!

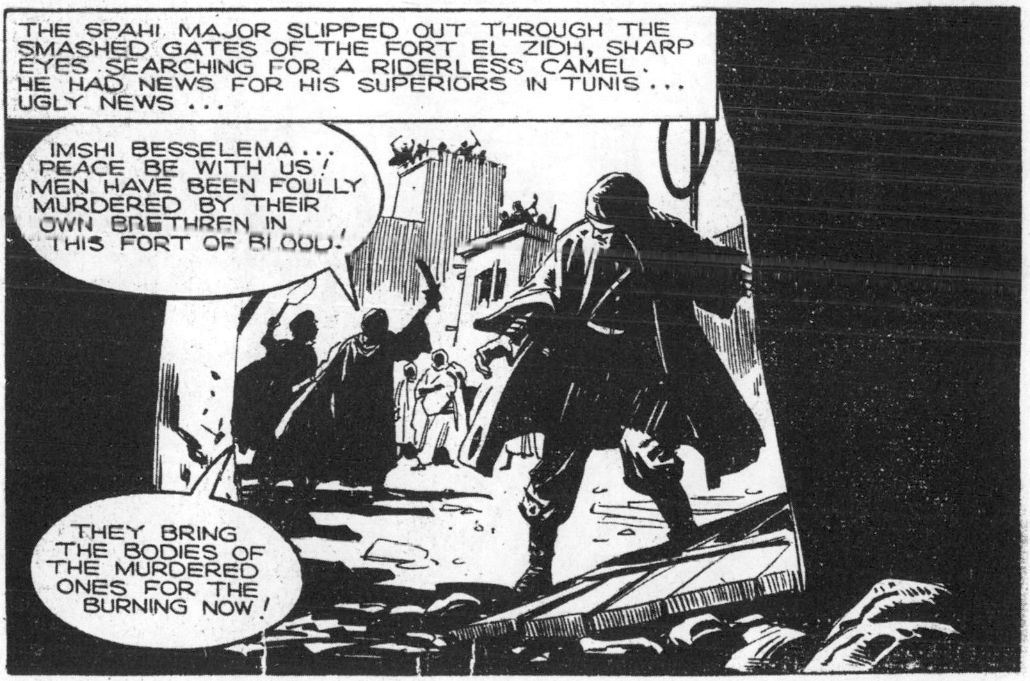
THE SPAHI MAJOR SLIPPED OUT THROUGH THE SMASHED GATES OF THE FORT EL ZIDH, SHARP EYES SEARCHING FOR A RIDERLESS CAMEL. HE HAD NEWS FOR HIS SUPERIORS IN TUNIS ... UGLY NEWS ...
IMSHI BESSELEMA ... PEACE BE WITH US! MEN HAVE BEEN FOULLY MURDERED BY THEIR OWN BRETHREN IN THIS FORT OF BLOOD!
THEY BRING THE BODIES OF THE MURDERED ONES FOR THE BURNING NOW!

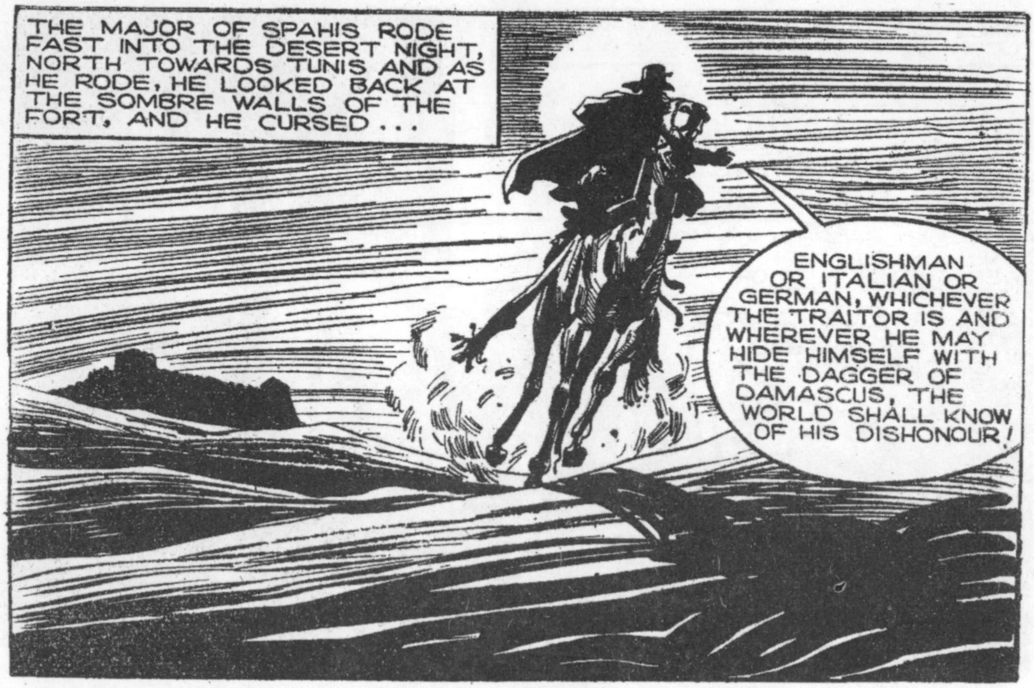
THE MAJOR OF SPAHIS RODE FAST INTO THE DESERT NIGHT, NORTH TOWARDS TUNIS AND AS HE RODE, HE LOOKED BACK AT THE SOMBRE WALLS OF THE FORT, AND HE CURSED ...
ENGLISHMAN OR ITALIAN OR GERMAN, WHICHEVER THE TRAITOR IS AND WHEREVER HE MAY HIDE HIMSELF WITH THE DAGGER OF DAMASCUS, THE WORLD SHALL KNOW OF HIS DISHONOUR!

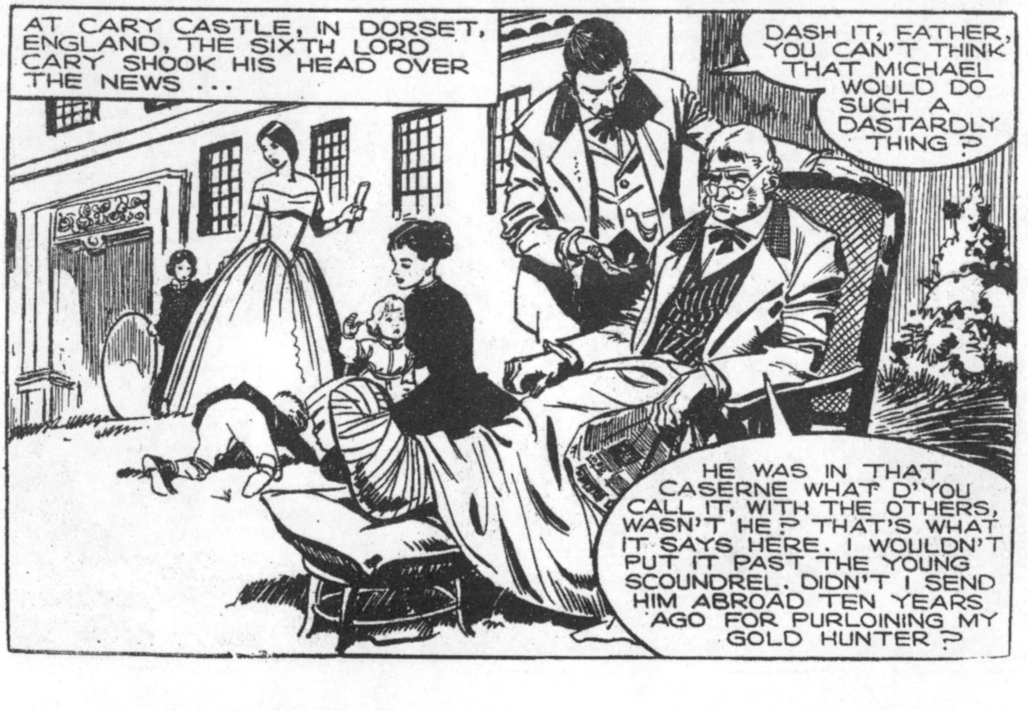
AT CARY CASTLE, IN DORSET, ENGLAND, THE SIXTH LORD CARY SHOOK HIS HEAD OVER THE NEWS ...
DASH IT, FATHER, YOU CAN'T THINK THAT MICHAEL WOULD DO SUCH A DASTARDLY THING?
HE WAS IN THAT CASERNE WHAT D'YOU CALL IT, WITH THE OTHERS, WASN'T HE? THAT'S WHAT IT SAYS HERE. I WOULDN'T PUT IT PAST THE YOUNG SCOUNDREL. DIDN'T I SEND HIM ABROAD TEN YEARS AGO FOR PURLOINING MY GOLD HUNTER?

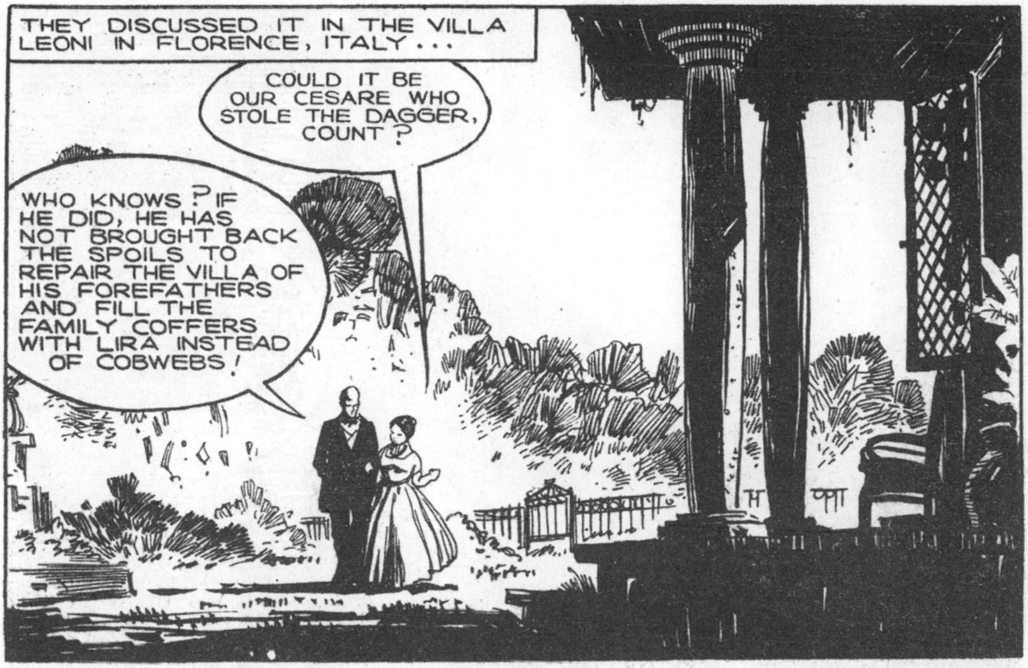
THEY DISCUSSED IT IN THE VILLA LEONI IN FLORENCE, ITALY . . .
COULD IT BE OUR CESARE WHO STOLE THE DAGGER, COUNT?
WHO KNOWS? IF HE DID, HE HAS NOT BROUGHT BACK THE SPOILS TO REPAIR THE VILLA OF HIS FOREFATHERS AND FILL THE FAMILY COFFERS WITH LIRA INSTEAD OF COBWEBS!

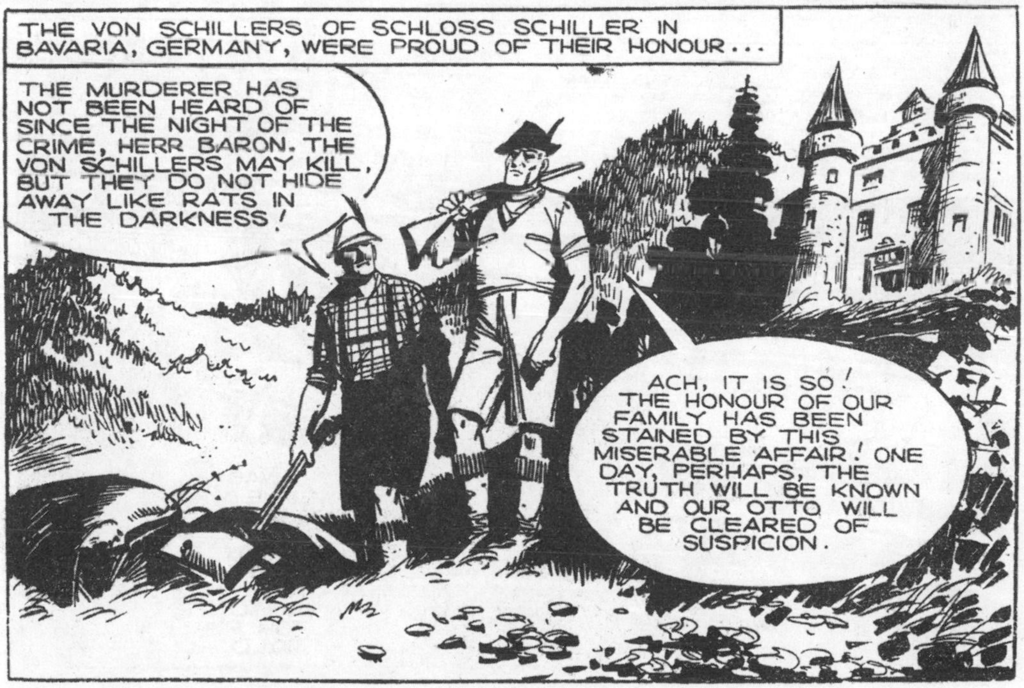
THE VON SCHILLERS OF SCHLOSS SCHILLER IN BAVARIA, GERMANY, WERE PROUD OF THEIR HONOUR . . .
THE MURDERER HAS NOT BEEN HEARD OF SINCE THE NIGHT OF THE CRIME, HERR BARON. THE VON SCHILLERS MAY KILL, BUT THEY DO NOT HIDE AWAY LIKE RATS IN THE DARKNESS!
ACH, IT IS SO! THE HONOUR OF OUR FAMILY HAS BEEN STAINED BY THIS MISERABLE AFFAIR! ONE DAY, PERHAPS, THE TRUTH WILL BE KNOWN AND OUR OTTO WILL BE CLEARED OF SUSPICION.

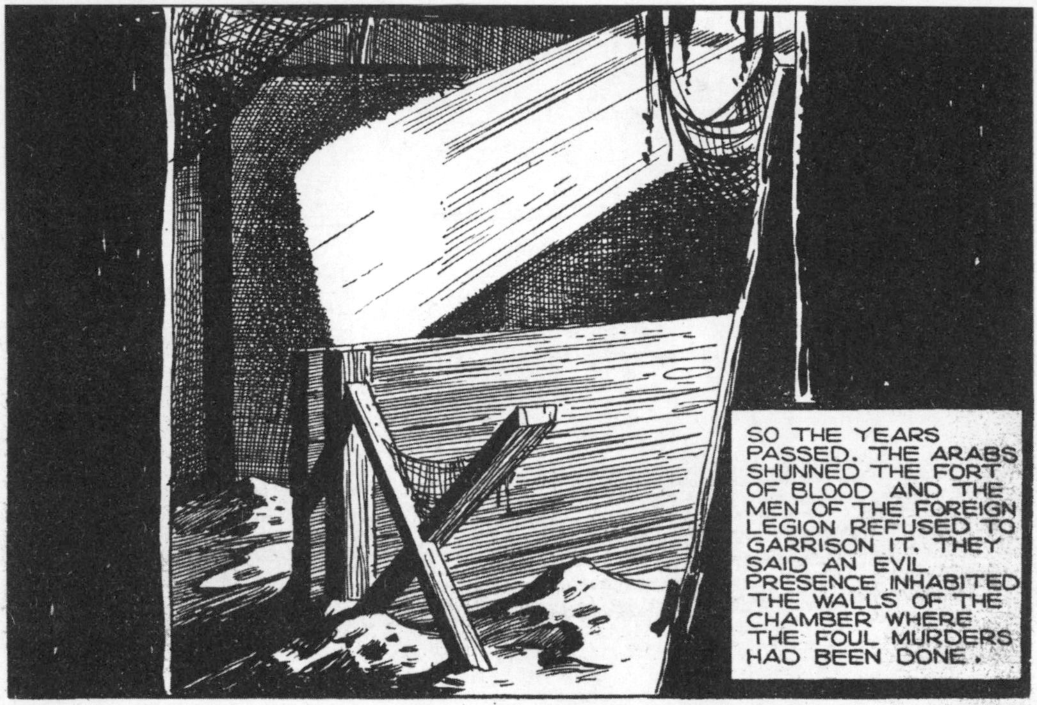
SO THE YEARS PASSED. THE ARABS SHUNNED THE FORT OF BLOOD AND THE MEN OF THE FOREIGN LEGION REFUSED TO GARRISON IT. THEY SAID AN EVIL PRESENCE INHABITED THE WALLS OF THE CHAMBER WHERE THE FOUL MURDERS HAD BEEN DONE.

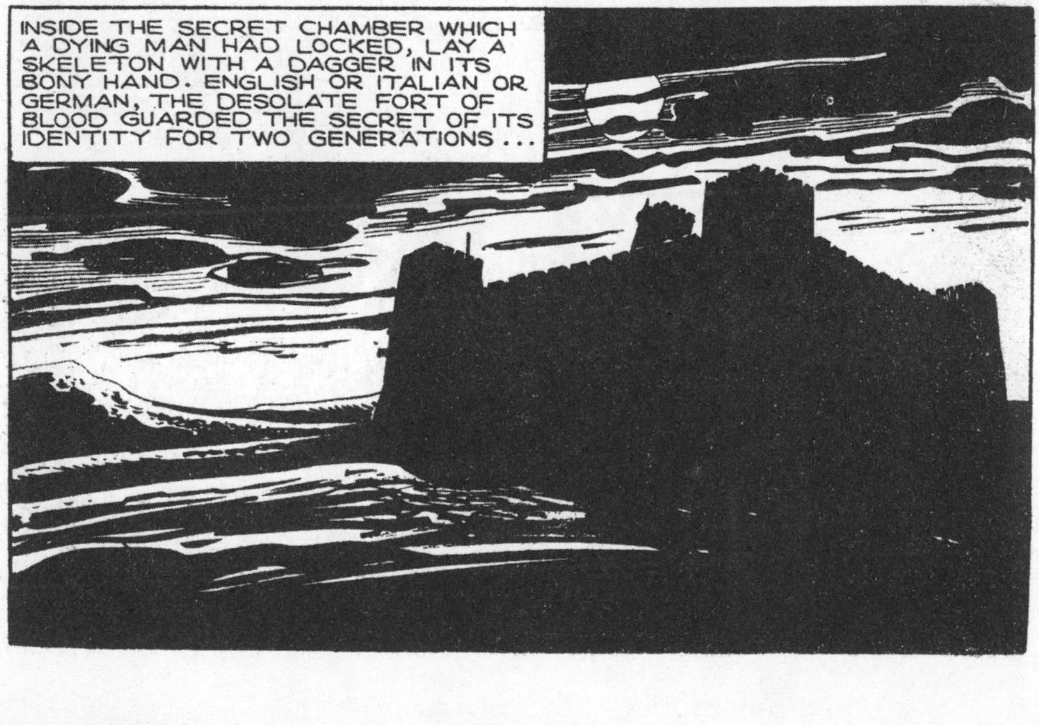
INSIDE THE SECRET CHAMBER WHICH A DYING MAN HAD LOCKED, LAY A SKELETON WITH A DAGGER IN ITS BONY HAND. ENGLISH OR ITALIAN OR GERMAN, THE DESOLATE FORT OF BLOOD GUARDED THE SECRET OF ITS IDENTITY FOR TWO GENERATIONS...

Chapter 2. Strange Encounter

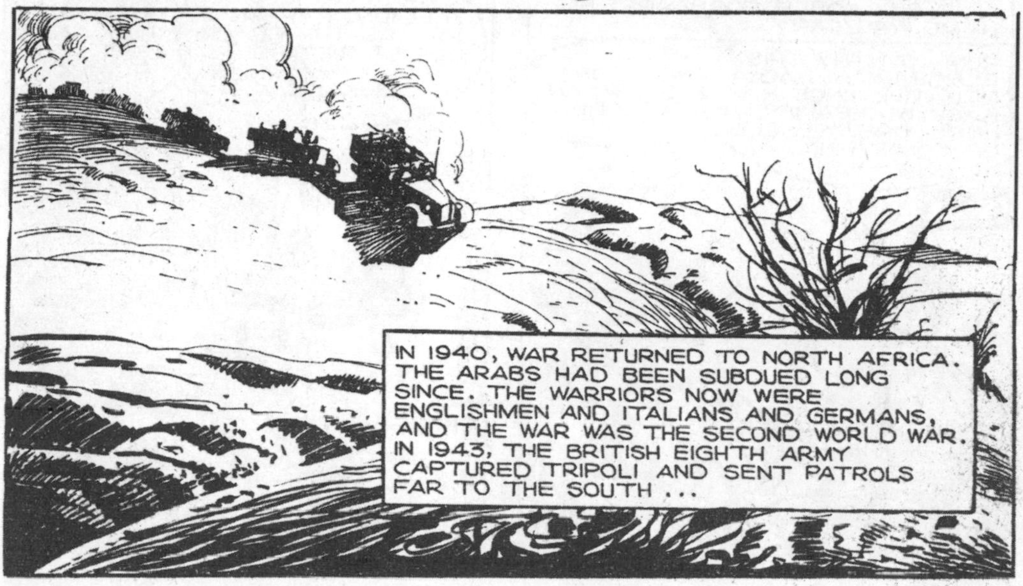
IN 1940, WAR RETURNED TO NORTH AFRICA. THE ARABS HAD BEEN SUBDUED LONG SINCE. THE WARRIORS NOW WERE ENGLISHMEN AND ITALIANS AND GERMANS, AND THE WAR WAS THE SECOND WORLD WAR. IN 1943, THE BRITISH EIGHTH ARMY CAPTURED TRIPOLI AND SENT PATROLS FAR TO THE SOUTH ...

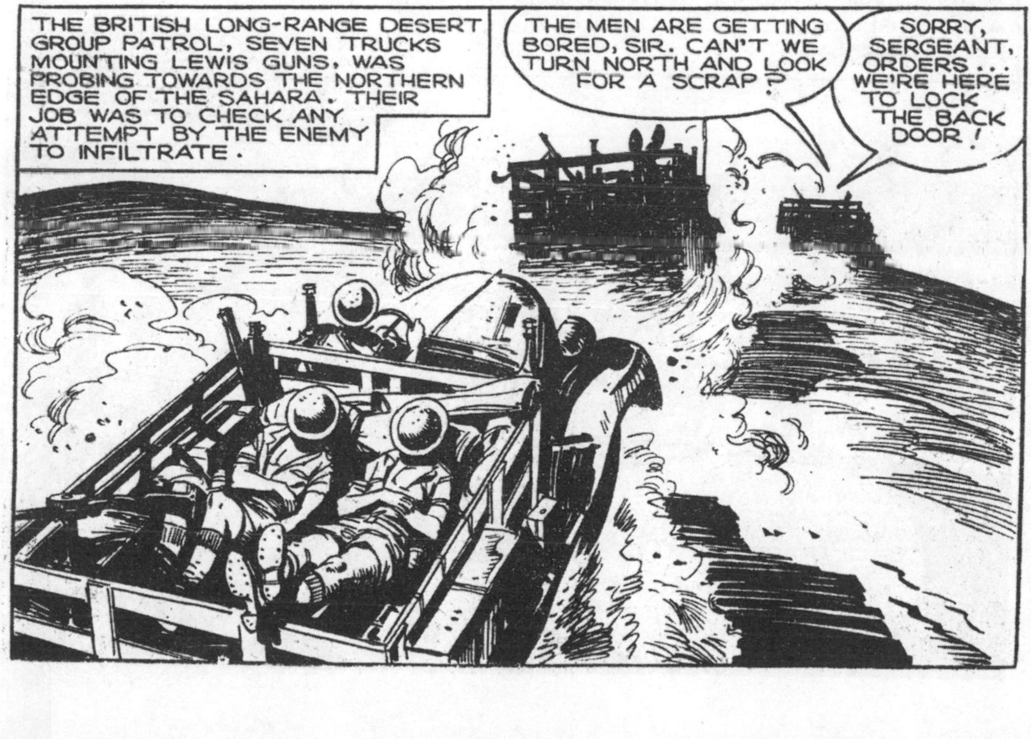
THE BRITISH LONG-RANGE DESERT GROUP PATROL, SEVEN TRUCKS MOUNTING LEWIS GUNS, WAS PROBING TOWARDS THE NORTHERN EDGE OF THE SAHARA. THEIR JOB WAS TO CHECK ANY ATTEMPT BY THE ENEMY TO INFILTRATE.
THE MEN ARE GETTING BORED, SIR. CAN'T WE TURN NORTH AND LOOK FOR A SCRAP?
SORRY, SERGEANT, ORDERS ... WE'RE HERE TO LOCK THE BACK DOOR!

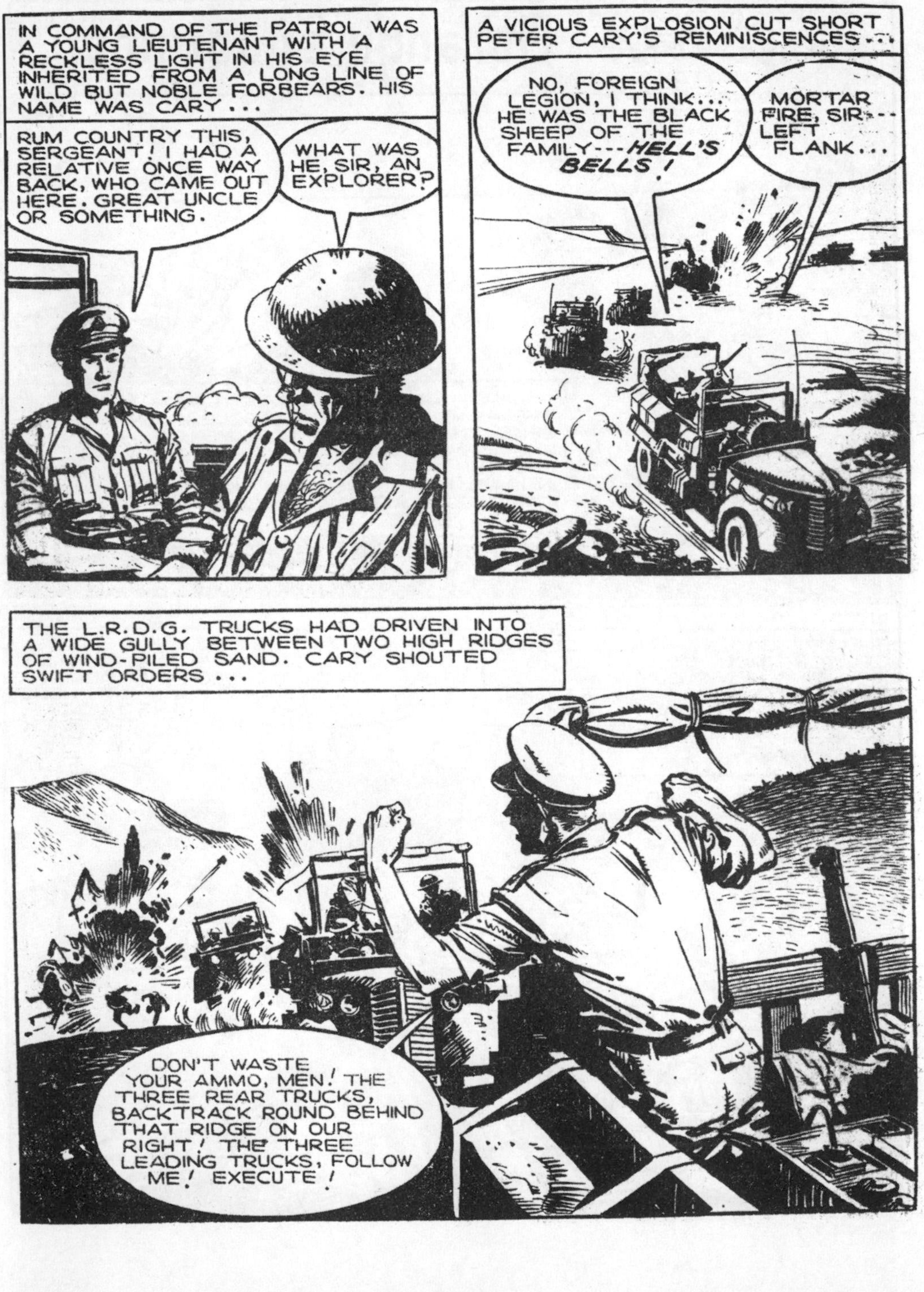
IN COMMAND OF THE PATROL WAS A YOUNG LIEUTENANT WITH A RECKLESS LIGHT IN HIS EYE INHERITED FROM A LONG LINE OF WILD BUT NOBLE FORBEARS. HIS NAME WAS CARY ...
RUM COUNTRY THIS, SERGEANT! I HAD A RELATIVE ONCE WAY BACK, WHO CAME OUT HERE. GREAT UNCLE OR SOMETHING.
WHAT WAS HE, SIR, AN EXPLORER?
A VICIOUS EXPLOSION CUT SHORT PETER CARY'S REMINISCENCES ...
NO, FOREIGN LEGION, I THINK... HE WAS THE BLACK SHEEP OF THE FAMILY---HELL'S BELLS!
MORTAR FIRE, SIR--- LEFT FLANK...
THE L.R.D.G. TRUCKS HAD DRIVEN INTO A WIDE GULLY BETWEEN TWO HIGH RIDGES OF WIND-PILED SAND. CARY SHOUTED SWIFT ORDERS ...
DON'T WASTE YOUR AMMO, MEN! THE THREE REAR TRUCKS, BACKTRACK ROUND BEHIND THAT RIDGE ON OUR RIGHT! THE THREE LEADING TRUCKS, FOLLOW ME! EXECUTE!

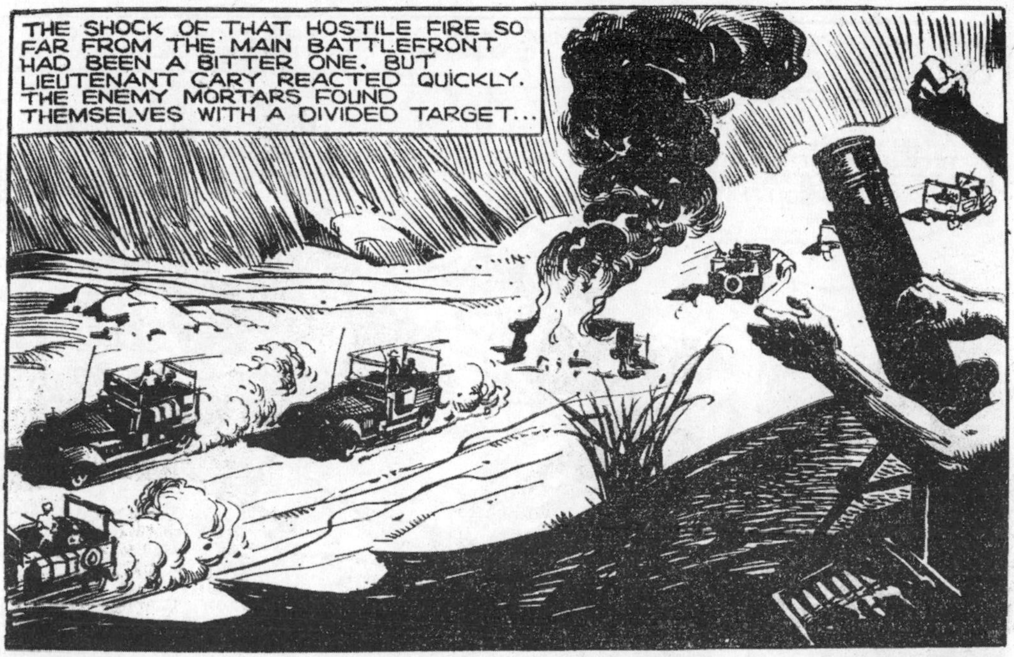
THE SHOCK OF THAT HOSTILE FIRE SO FAR FROM THE MAIN BATTLEFRONT HAD BEEN A BITTER ONE. BUT LIEUTENANT CARY REACTED QUICKLY. THE ENEMY MORTARS FOUND THEMSELVES WITH A DIVIDED TARGET...

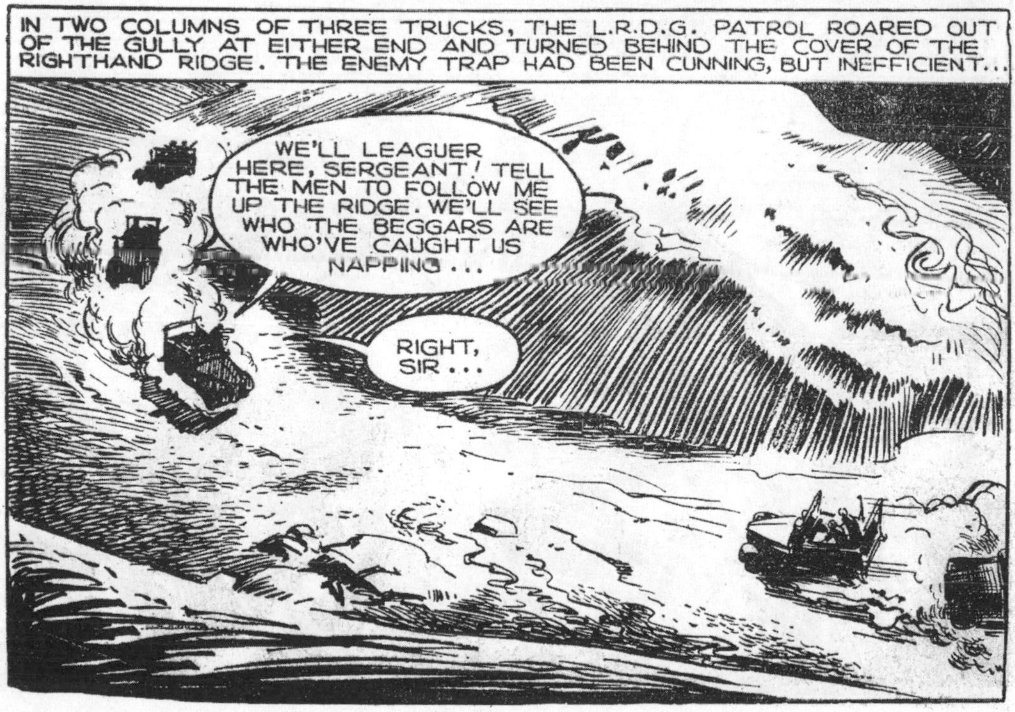
IN TWO COLUMNS OF THREE TRUCKS, THE L.R.D.G. PATROL ROARED OUT OF THE GULLY AT EITHER END AND TURNED BEHIND THE COVER OF THE RIGHTHAND RIDGE. THE ENEMY TRAP HAD BEEN CUNNING, BUT INEFFICIENT...
WE'LL LEAGUER HERE, SERGEANT! TELL THE MEN TO FOLLOW ME UP THE RIDGE. WE'LL SEE WHO THE BEGGARS ARE WHO'VE CAUGHT US NAPPING...
RIGHT, SIR...

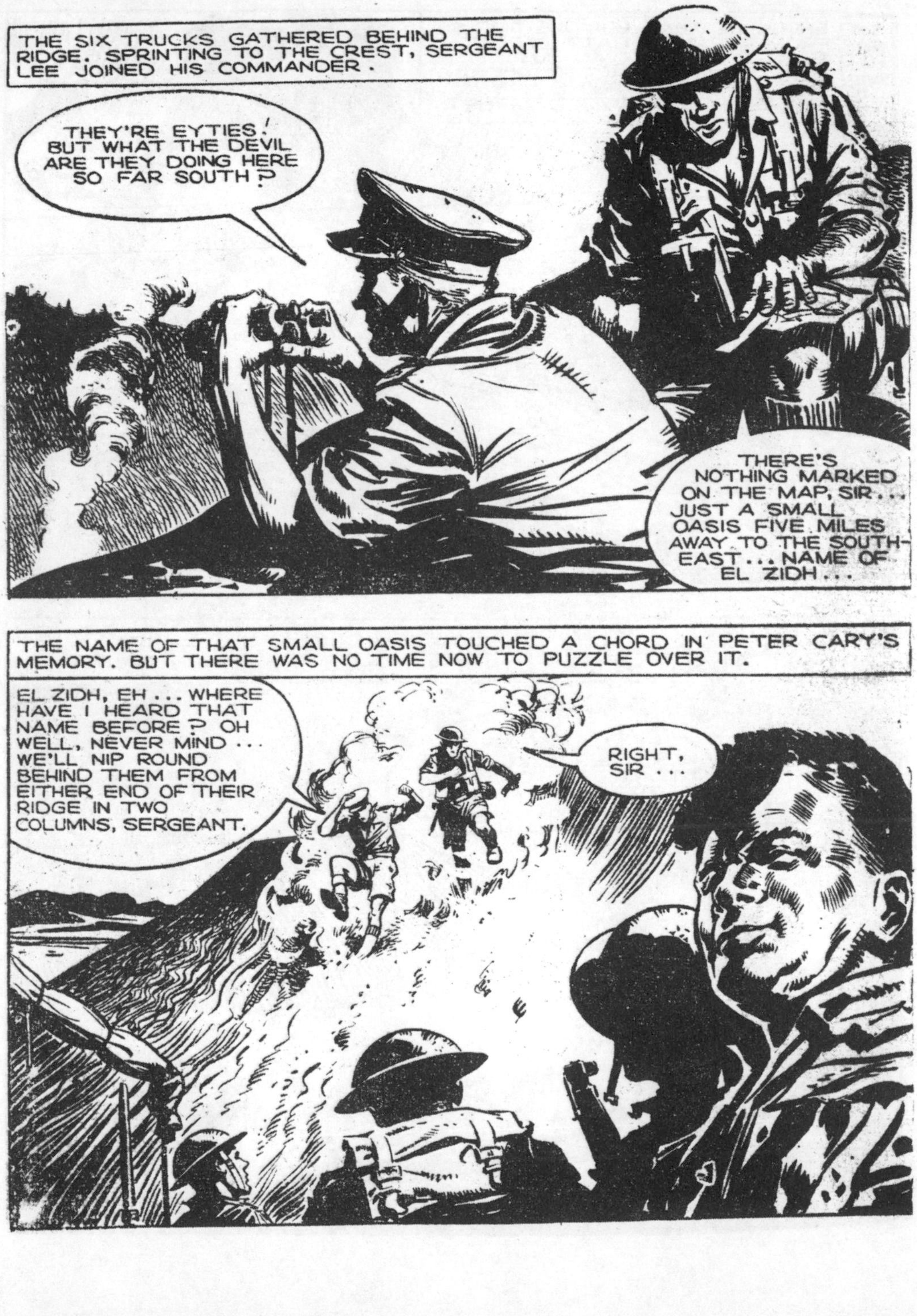
THE SIX TRUCKS GATHERED BEHIND THE RIDGE. SPRINTING TO THE CREST, SERGEANT LEE JOINED HIS COMMANDER.
THEY'RE EYTIES! BUT WHAT THE DEVIL ARE THEY DOING HERE SO FAR SOUTH?
THERE'S NOTHING MARKED ON THE MAP, SIR... JUST A SMALL OASIS FIVE MILES AWAY TO THE SOUTH-EAST... NAME OF EL ZIDH...
THE NAME OF THAT SMALL OASIS TOUCHED A CHORD IN PETER CARY'S MEMORY. BUT THERE WAS NO TIME NOW TO PUZZLE OVER IT.
EL ZIDH, EH... WHERE HAVE I HEARD THAT NAME BEFORE? OH WELL, NEVER MIND... WE'LL NIP ROUND BEHIND THEM FROM EITHER END OF THEIR RIDGE IN TWO COLUMNS, SERGEANT.
RIGHT, SIR...

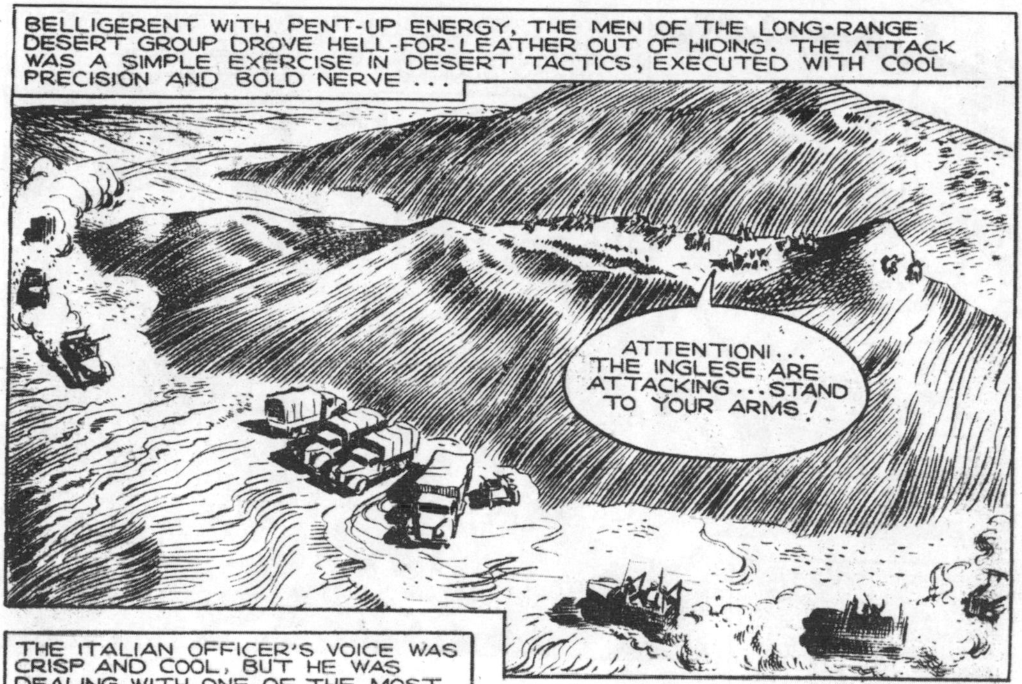
BELLIGERENT WITH PENT-UP ENERGY, THE MEN OF THE LONG-RANGE DESERT GROUP DROVE HELL-FOR-LEATHER OUT OF HIDING. THE ATTACK WAS A SIMPLE EXERCISE IN DESERT TACTICS, EXECUTED WITH COOL PRECISION AND BOLD NERVE ...
ATTENTIONI ... THE INGLESE ARE ATTACKING ... STAND TO YOUR ARMS!

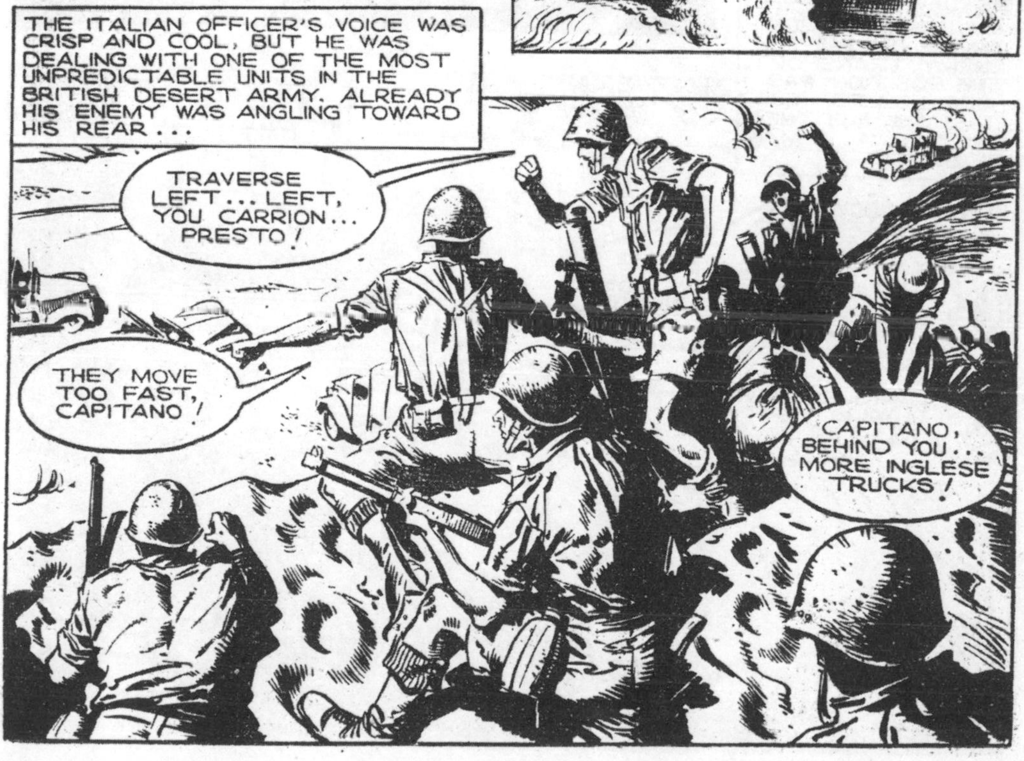
THE ITALIAN OFFICER'S VOICE WAS CRISP AND COOL, BUT HE WAS DEALING WITH ONE OF THE MOST UNPREDICTABLE UNITS IN THE BRITISH DESERT ARMY. ALREADY HIS ENEMY WAS ANGLING TOWARD HIS REAR ...
TRAVERSE LEFT ... LEFT, YOU CARRION ... PRESTO!
THEY MOVE TOO FAST, CAPITANO!
CAPITANO, BEHIND YOU ... MORE INGLESE TRUCKS!

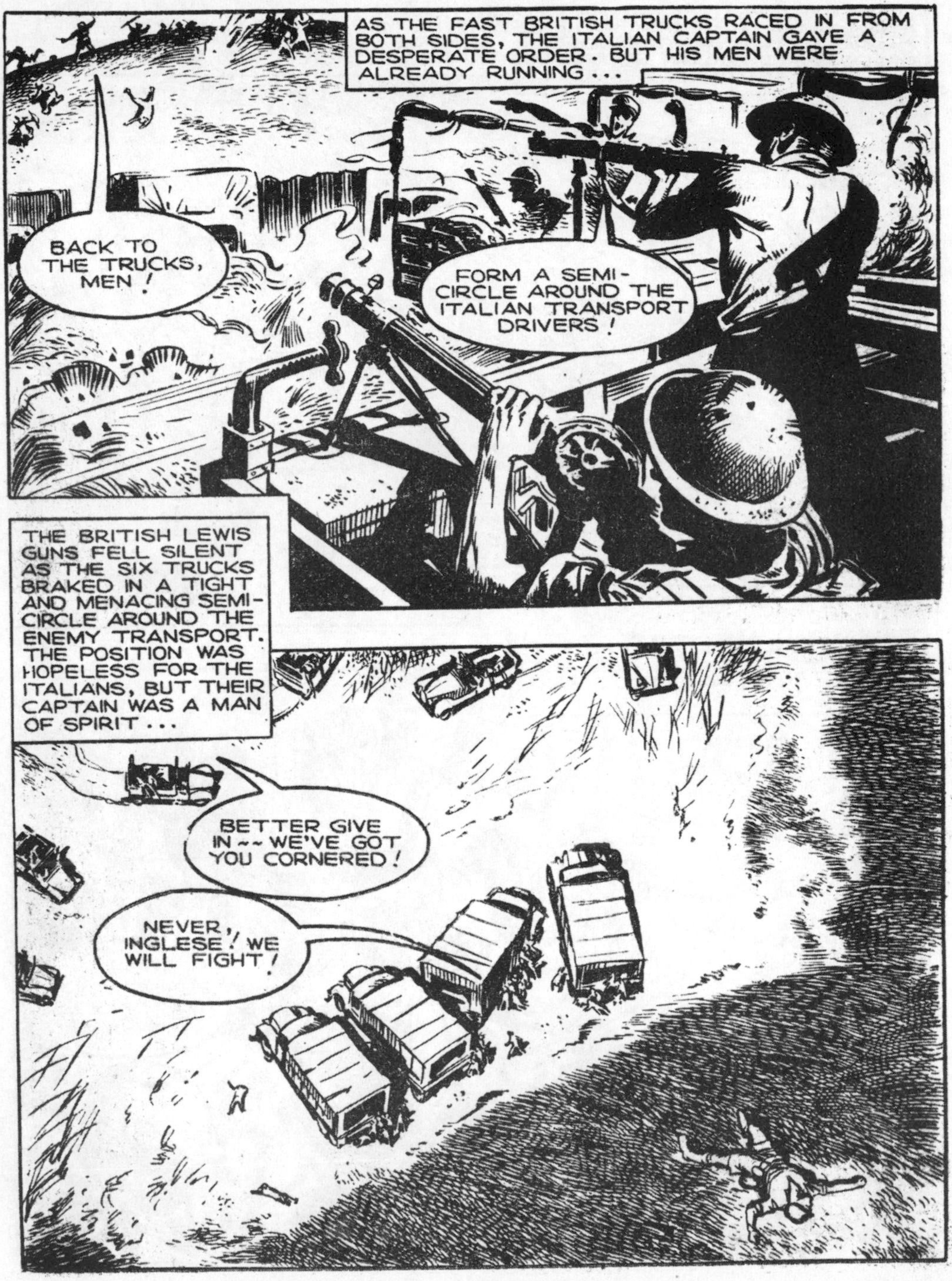
AS THE FAST BRITISH TRUCKS RACED IN FROM BOTH SIDES, THE ITALIAN CAPTAIN GAVE A DESPERATE ORDER. BUT HIS MEN WERE ALREADY RUNNING...
BACK TO THE TRUCKS, MEN!
FORM A SEMI-CIRCLE AROUND THE ITALIAN TRANSPORT DRIVERS!
THE BRITISH LEWIS GUNS FELL SILENT AS THE SIX TRUCKS BRAKED IN A TIGHT AND MENACING SEMI-CIRCLE AROUND THE ENEMY TRANSPORT. THE POSITION WAS HOPELESS FOR THE ITALIANS, BUT THEIR CAPTAIN WAS A MAN OF SPIRIT...
BETTER GIVE IN -- WE'VE GOT YOU CORNERED!
NEVER, INGLESE! WE WILL FIGHT!

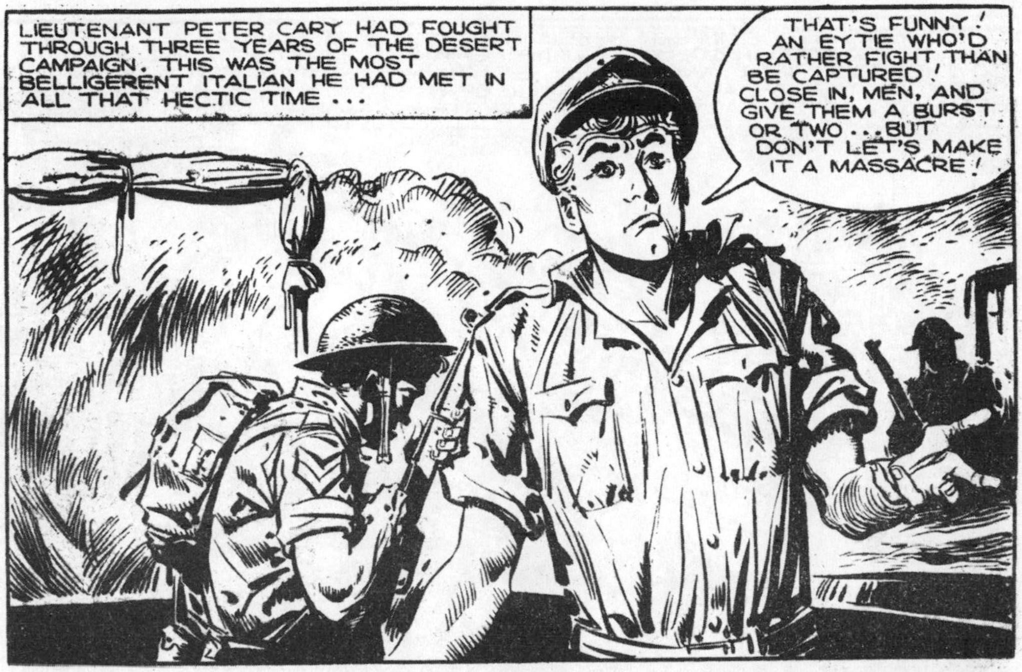
LIEUTENANT PETER CARY HAD FOUGHT THROUGH THREE YEARS OF THE DESERT CAMPAIGN. THIS WAS THE MOST BELLIGERENT ITALIAN HE HAD MET IN ALL THAT HECTIC TIME ...
THAT'S FUNNY! AN EYTIE WHO'D RATHER FIGHT THAN BE CAPTURED! CLOSE IN, MEN, AND GIVE THEM A BURST OR TWO ... BUT DON'T LET'S MAKE IT A MASSACRE!

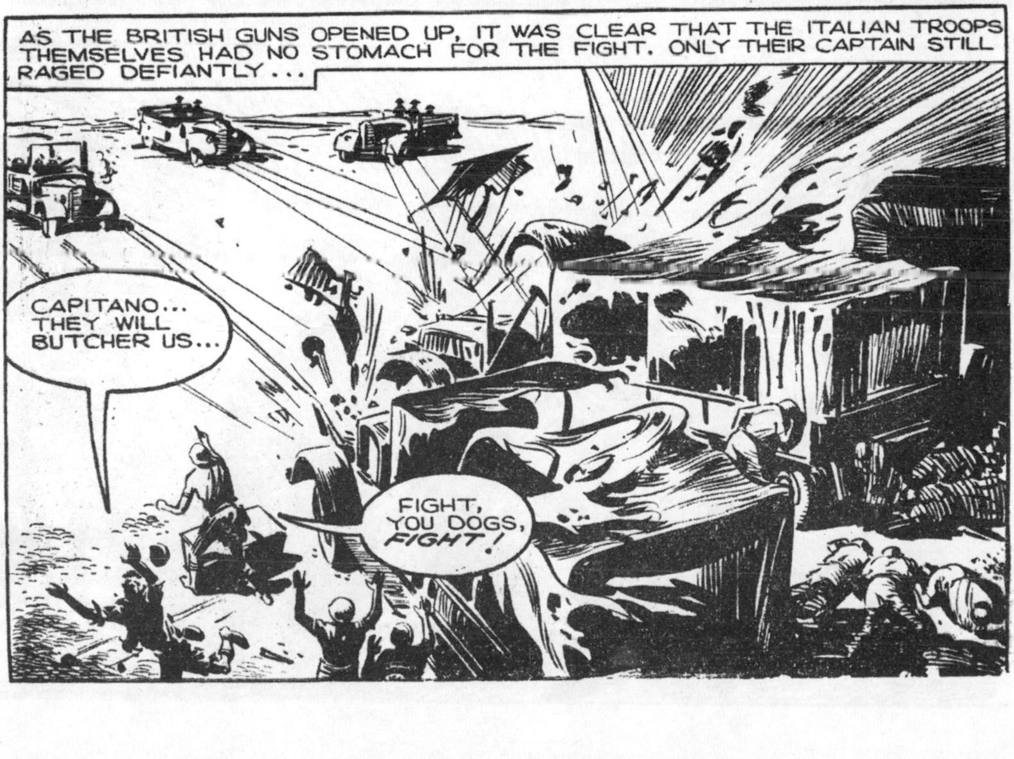
AS THE BRITISH GUNS OPENED UP, IT WAS CLEAR THAT THE ITALIAN TROOPS THEMSELVES HAD NO STOMACH FOR THE FIGHT. ONLY THEIR CAPTAIN STILL RAGED DEFIANTLY ...
CAPITANO... THEY WILL BUTCHER US...
FIGHT, YOU DOGS, *FIGHT*!

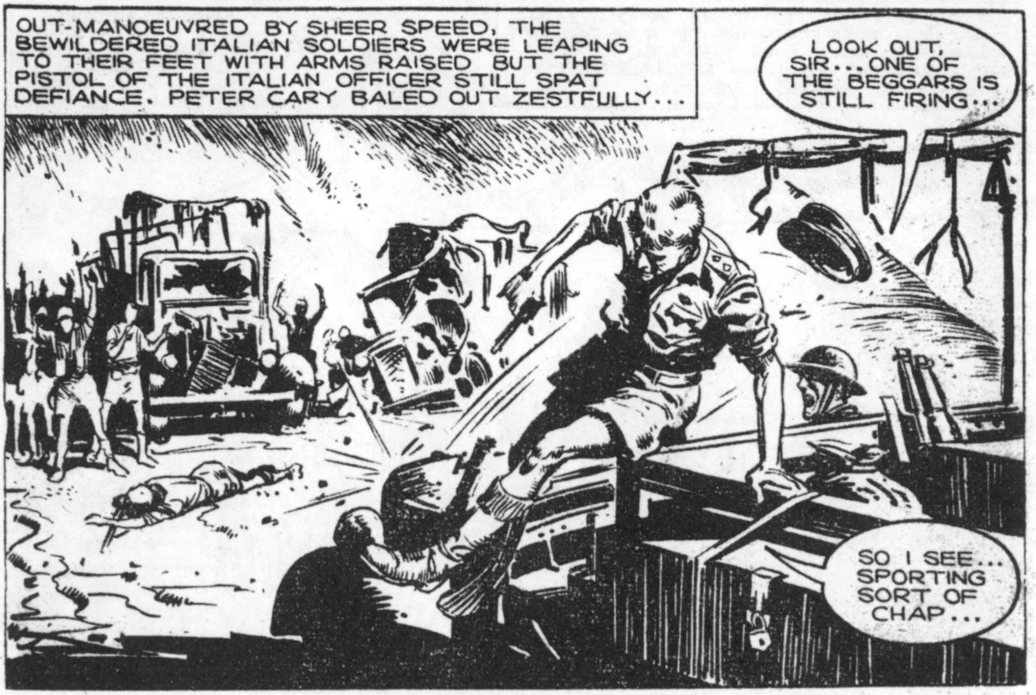
OUT-MANOEUVRED BY SHEER SPEED, THE BEWILDERED ITALIAN SOLDIERS WERE LEAPING TO THEIR FEET WITH ARMS RAISED BUT THE PISTOL OF THE ITALIAN OFFICER STILL SPAT DEFIANCE. PETER CARY BALED OUT ZESTFULLY...
LOOK OUT, SIR...ONE OF THE BEGGARS IS STILL FIRING...
SO I SEE... SPORTING SORT OF CHAP...

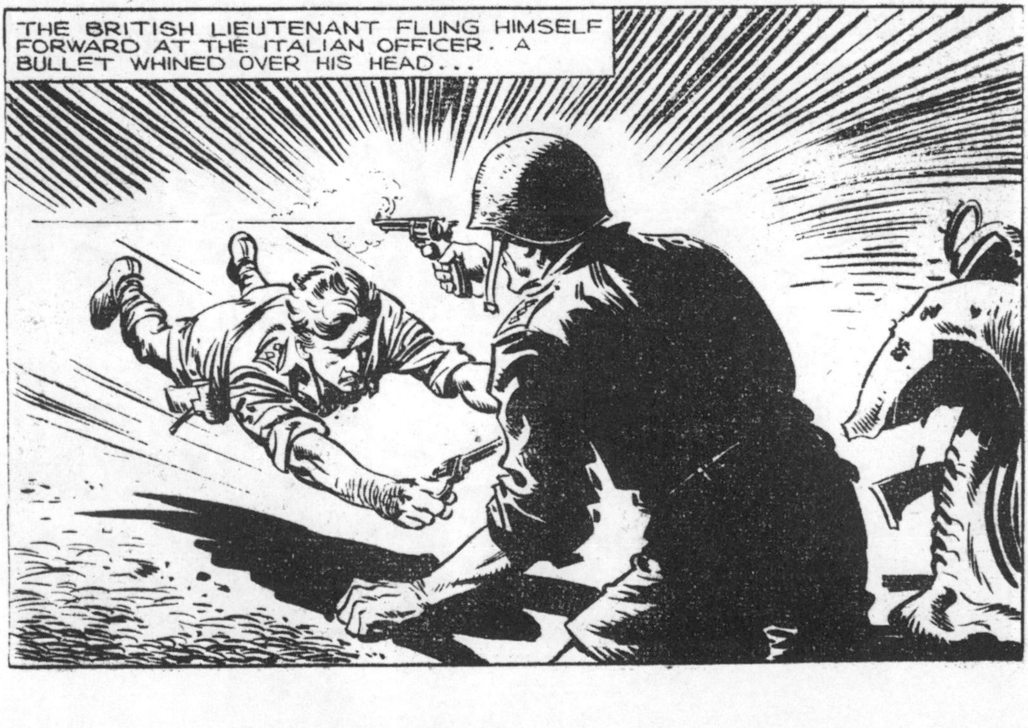
THE BRITISH LIEUTENANT FLUNG HIMSELF FORWARD AT THE ITALIAN OFFICER. A BULLET WHINED OVER HIS HEAD...

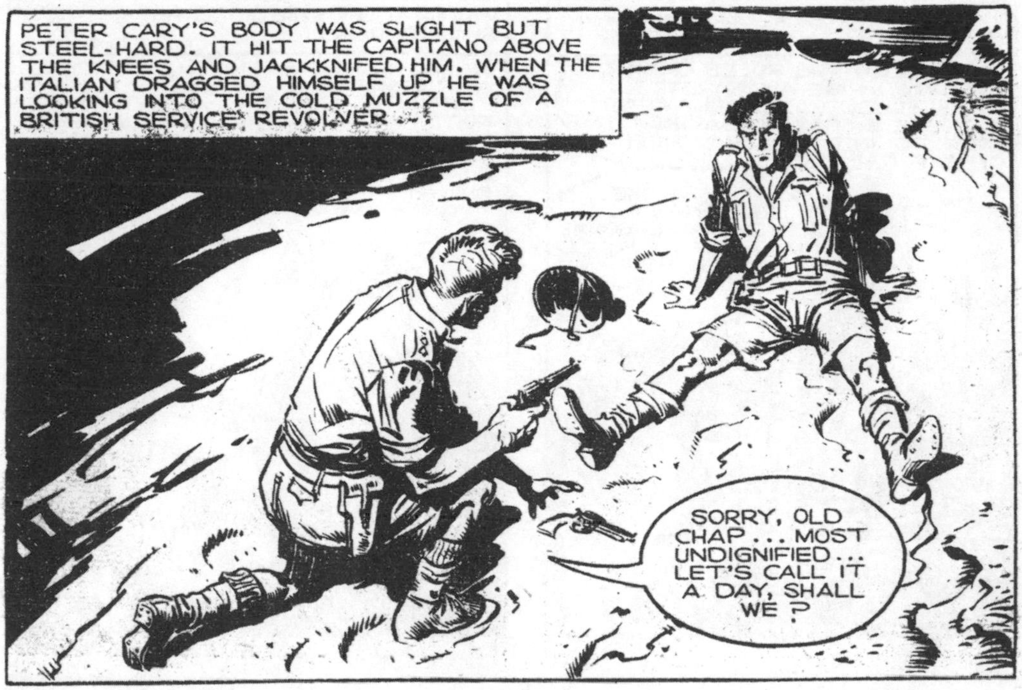
PETER CARY'S BODY WAS SLIGHT BUT STEEL-HARD. IT HIT THE CAPITANO ABOVE THE KNEES AND JACKKNIFED HIM. WHEN THE ITALIAN DRAGGED HIMSELF UP HE WAS LOOKING INTO THE COLD MUZZLE OF A BRITISH SERVICE REVOLVER ...
SORRY, OLD CHAP ... MOST UNDIGNIFIED ... LET'S CALL IT A DAY, SHALL WE ?

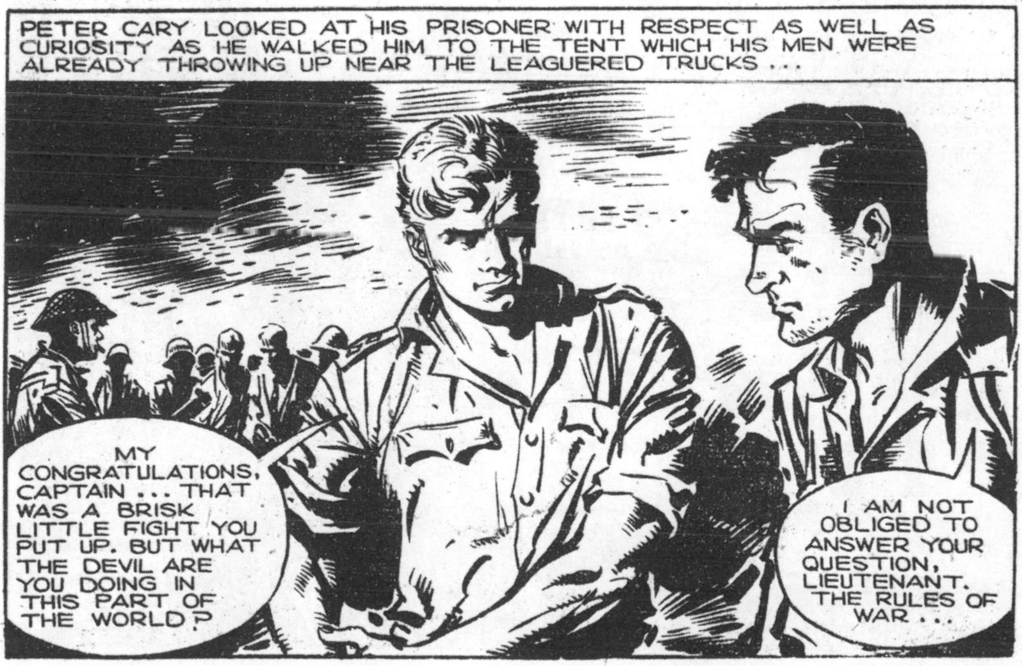
PETER CARY LOOKED AT HIS PRISONER WITH RESPECT AS WELL AS CURIOSITY AS HE WALKED HIM TO THE TENT WHICH HIS MEN WERE ALREADY THROWING UP NEAR THE LEAGUERED TRUCKS ...
MY CONGRATULATIONS, CAPTAIN ... THAT WAS A BRISK LITTLE FIGHT YOU PUT UP. BUT WHAT THE DEVIL ARE YOU DOING IN THIS PART OF THE WORLD?
I AM NOT OBLIGED TO ANSWER YOUR QUESTION, LIEUTENANT. THE RULES OF WAR ...

THE ITALIAN SEATED HIMSELF WITH DIGNITY.

LOOK, BLOW THE RULES OF WAR, CAPTAIN... HAVE A CIGARETTE... I'M CURIOUS, THAT'S ALL! WHAT IS THERE IN THIS FORSAKEN SPOT TO ATTRACT AN OFFICER OF YOUR CALIBRE?

FORGIVE ME, LIEUTENANT... THIS IS A PERSONAL MATTER... I WOULD RATHER NOT DISCUSS IT...

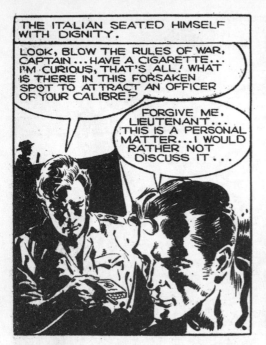

PETER CARY SHRUGGED HIS SHOULDERS...

AS YOU WISH, CAPTAIN. IN THE MORNING I SHALL BE CIRCLING NORTH AGAIN... I SHALL BE ABLE TO OFFER YOU BETTER QUARTERS IN TRIPOLI. OH... BY THE WAY... YOUR NAME...

MY NAME IS *LEONI*... CAPITANO MARIO LEONI, AT YOUR SERVICE...

LIKE THE NAME OF THE OASIS ON THE SERGEANT'S MAP, THE NAME OF THIS ITALIAN OFFICER TOUCHED A CHORD IN PETER CARY'S MEMORY. FIVE HOURS LATER, LONG AFTER MIDNIGHT, HE WAS STILL PUZZLING OVER THE PROBLEM OUTSIDE HIS TENT...

IT'S DEUCED ODD, BUT THOSE TWO NAMES SEEM TO GO TOGETHER. EL ZIDH... LEONI... BUT WHERE THE DICKENS COULD I HAVE HEARD THEM BEFORE?

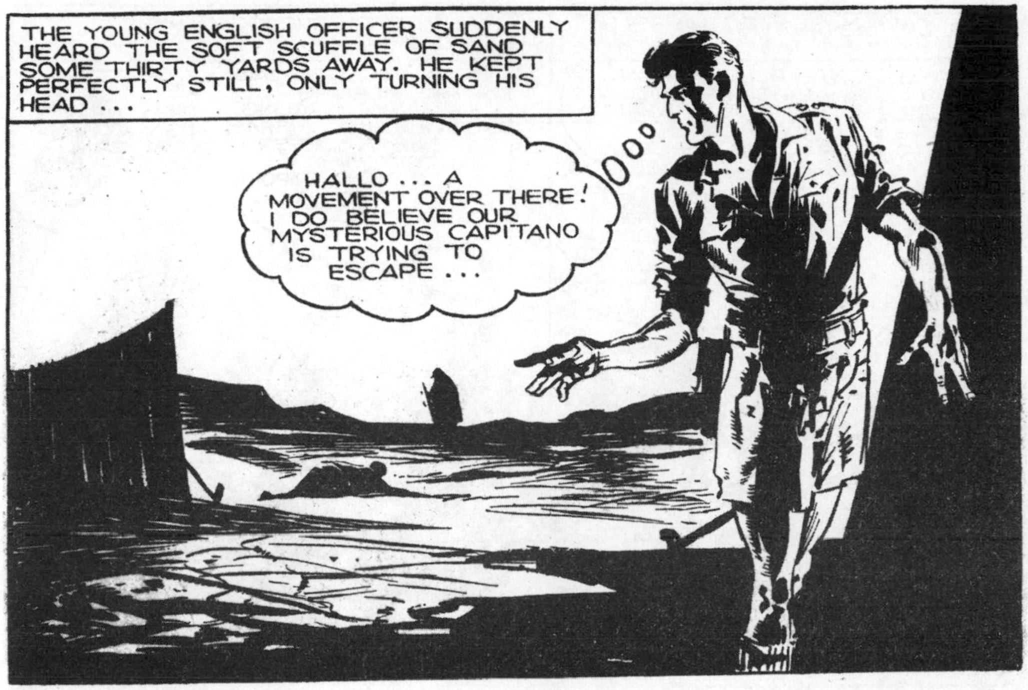
THE YOUNG ENGLISH OFFICER SUDDENLY HEARD THE SOFT SCUFFLE OF SAND SOME THIRTY YARDS AWAY. HE KEPT PERFECTLY STILL, ONLY TURNING HIS HEAD ...
HALLO ... A MOVEMENT OVER THERE! I DO BELIEVE OUR MYSTERIOUS CAPITANO IS TRYING TO ESCAPE ...

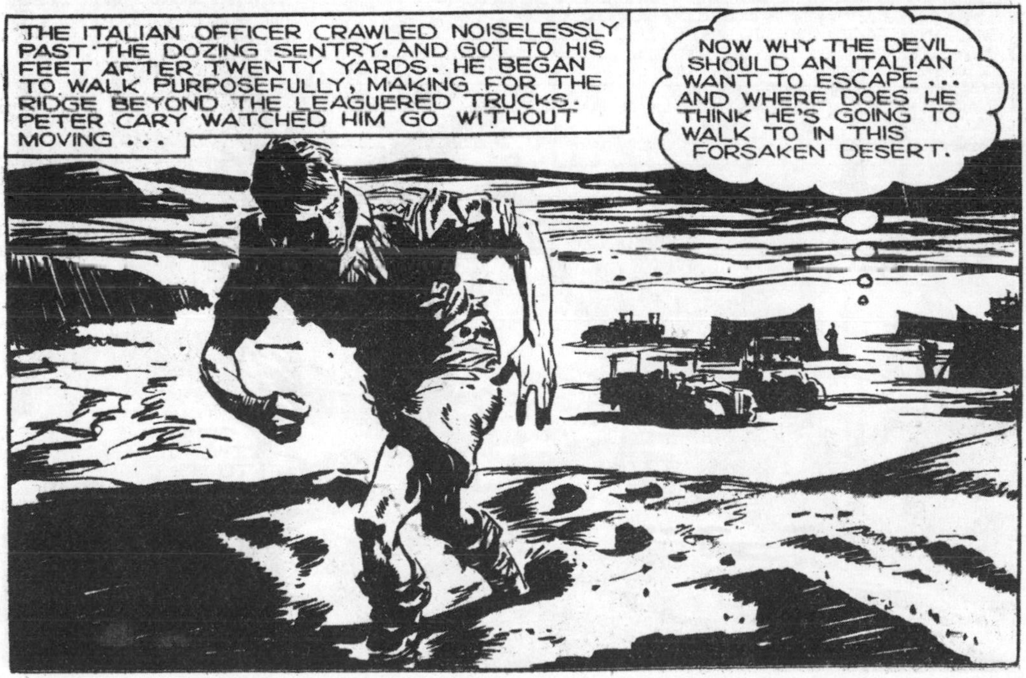
THE ITALIAN OFFICER CRAWLED NOISELESSLY PAST THE DOZING SENTRY. AND GOT TO HIS FEET AFTER TWENTY YARDS. HE BEGAN TO WALK PURPOSEFULLY, MAKING FOR THE RIDGE BEYOND THE LEAGUERED TRUCKS. PETER CARY WATCHED HIM GO WITHOUT MOVING ...
NOW WHY THE DEVIL SHOULD AN ITALIAN WANT TO ESCAPE ... AND WHERE DOES HE THINK HE'S GOING TO WALK TO IN THIS FORSAKEN DESERT.

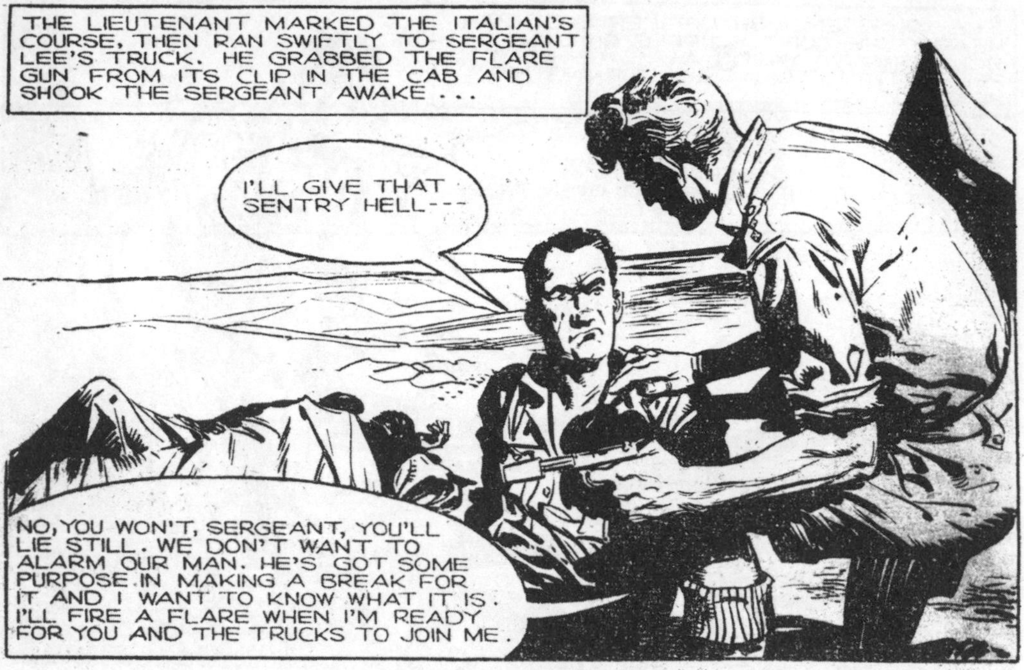
THE LIEUTENANT MARKED THE ITALIAN'S COURSE, THEN RAN SWIFTLY TO SERGEANT LEE'S TRUCK. HE GRABBED THE FLARE GUN FROM ITS CLIP IN THE CAB AND SHOOK THE SERGEANT AWAKE ...
I'LL GIVE THAT SENTRY HELL---
NO, YOU WON'T, SERGEANT, YOU'LL LIE STILL. WE DON'T WANT TO ALARM OUR MAN. HE'S GOT SOME PURPOSE IN MAKING A BREAK FOR IT AND I WANT TO KNOW WHAT IT IS. I'LL FIRE A FLARE WHEN I'M READY FOR YOU AND THE TRUCKS TO JOIN ME.

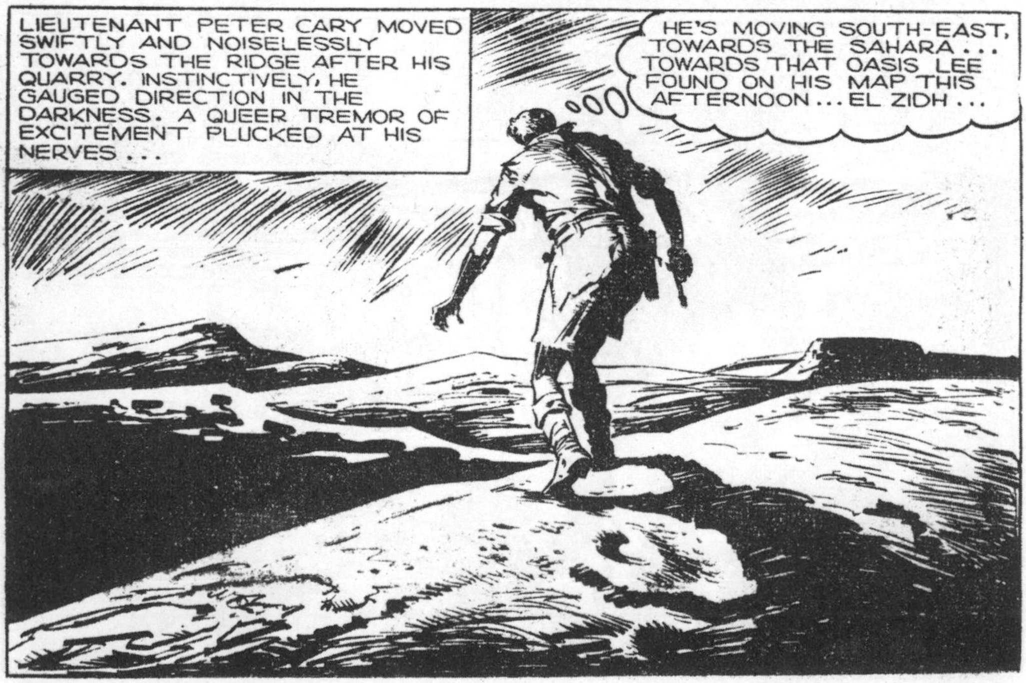
LIEUTENANT PETER CARY MOVED SWIFTLY AND NOISELESSLY TOWARDS THE RIDGE AFTER HIS QUARRY. INSTINCTIVELY, HE GAUGED DIRECTION IN THE DARKNESS. A QUEER TREMOR OF EXCITEMENT PLUCKED AT HIS NERVES ...
HE'S MOVING SOUTH-EAST, TOWARDS THE SAHARA ... TOWARDS THAT OASIS LEE FOUND ON HIS MAP THIS AFTERNOON ... EL ZIDH ...

Chapter 3. The Deserted Fort

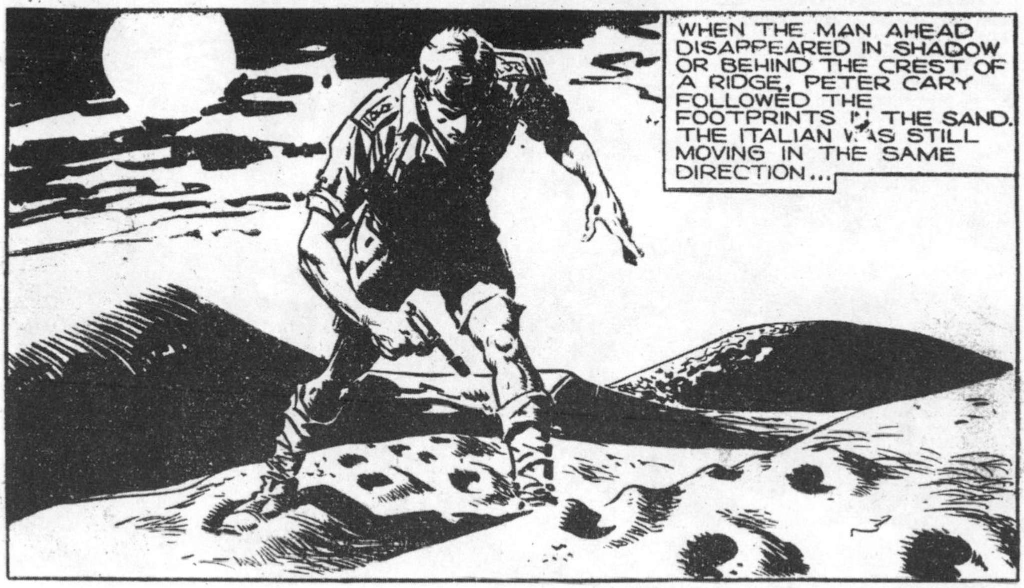
WHEN THE MAN AHEAD DISAPPEARED IN SHADOW OR BEHIND THE CREST OF A RIDGE, PETER CARY FOLLOWED THE FOOTPRINTS IN THE SAND. THE ITALIAN WAS STILL MOVING IN THE SAME DIRECTION...

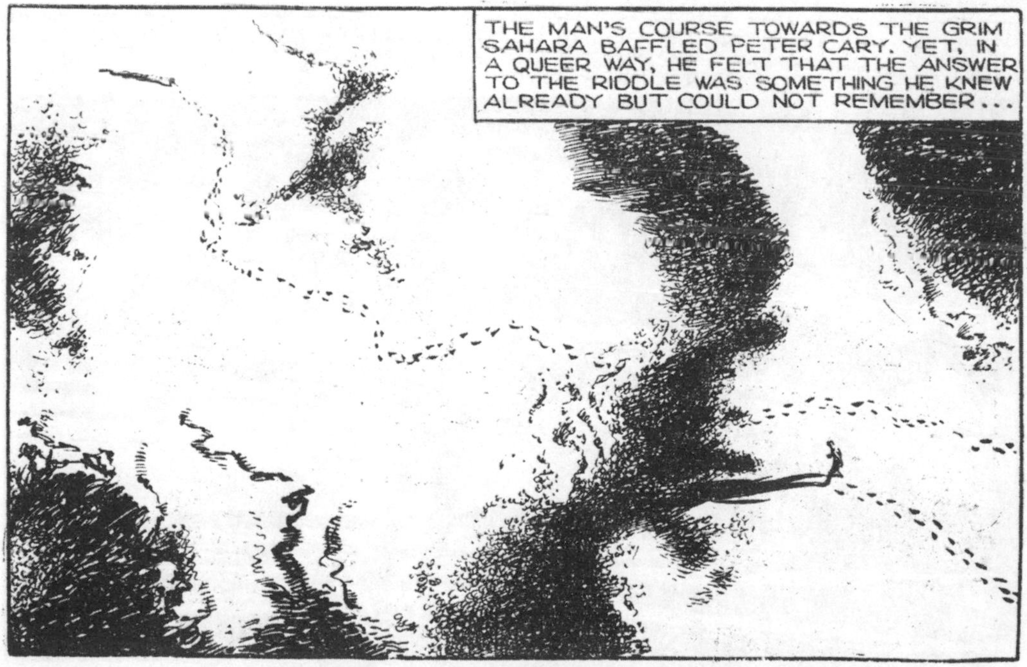
THE MAN'S COURSE TOWARDS THE GRIM SAHARA BAFFLED PETER CARY. YET, IN A QUEER WAY, HE FELT THAT THE ANSWER TO THE RIDDLE WAS SOMETHING HE KNEW ALREADY BUT COULD NOT REMEMBER...

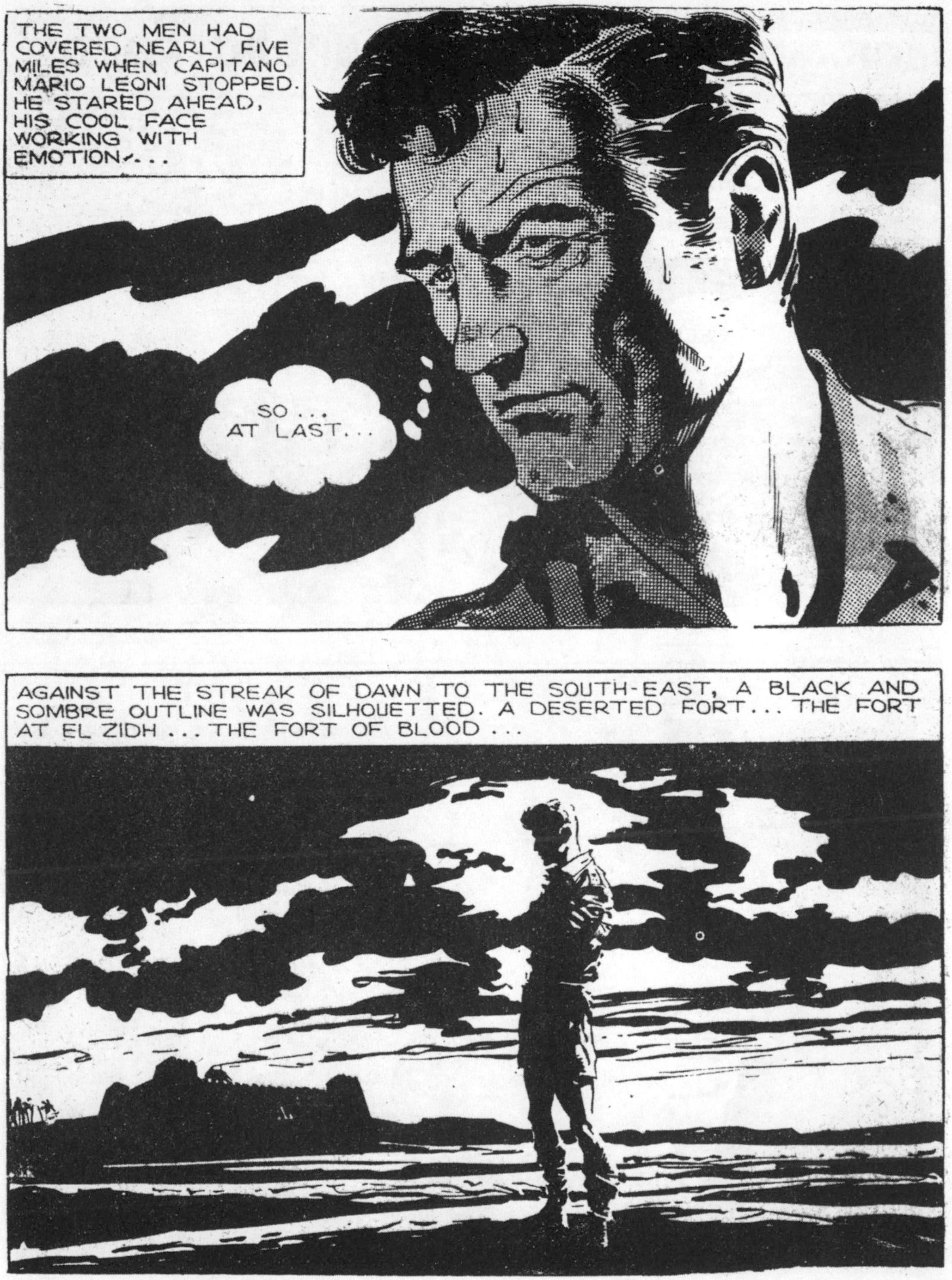
THE TWO MEN HAD COVERED NEARLY FIVE MILES WHEN CAPITANO MARIO LEONI STOPPED. HE STARED AHEAD, HIS COOL FACE WORKING WITH EMOTION . . .
SO . . . AT LAST . . .
AGAINST THE STREAK OF DAWN TO THE SOUTH-EAST, A BLACK AND SOMBRE OUTLINE WAS SILHOUETTED. A DESERTED FORT . . . THE FORT AT EL ZIDH . . . THE FORT OF BLOOD . . .

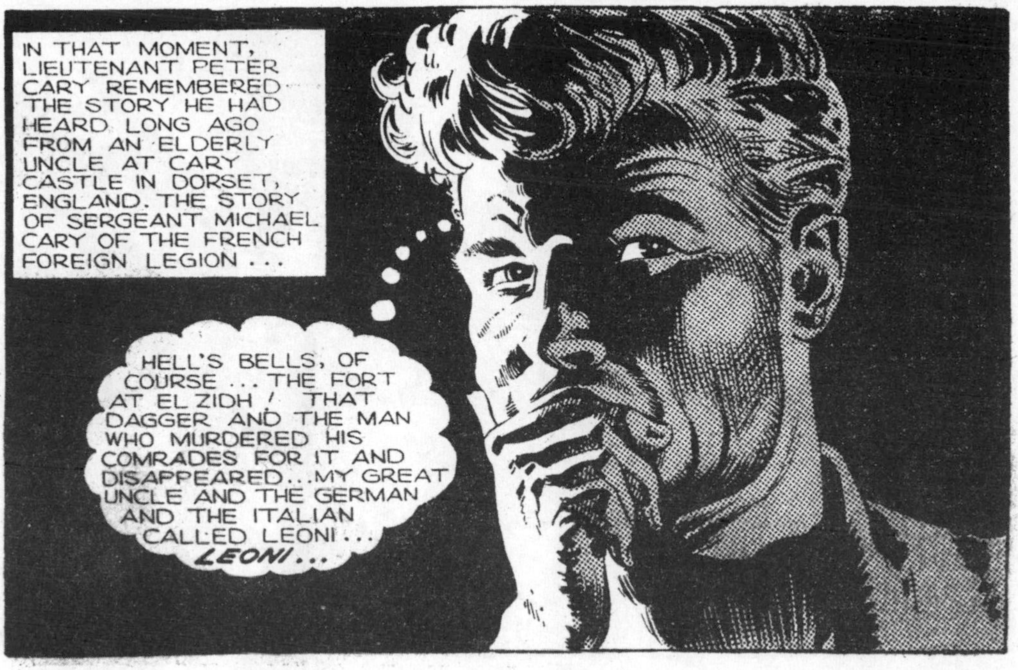
IN THAT MOMENT, LIEUTENANT PETER CARY REMEMBERED THE STORY HE HAD HEARD LONG AGO FROM AN ELDERLY UNCLE AT CARY CASTLE IN DORSET, ENGLAND. THE STORY OF SERGEANT MICHAEL CARY OF THE FRENCH FOREIGN LEGION ...
HELL'S BELLS, OF COURSE ... THE FORT AT EL ZIDH ! THAT DAGGER AND THE MAN WHO MURDERED HIS COMRADES FOR IT AND DISAPPEARED... MY GREAT UNCLE AND THE GERMAN AND THE ITALIAN CALLED LEONI ... LEONI ...

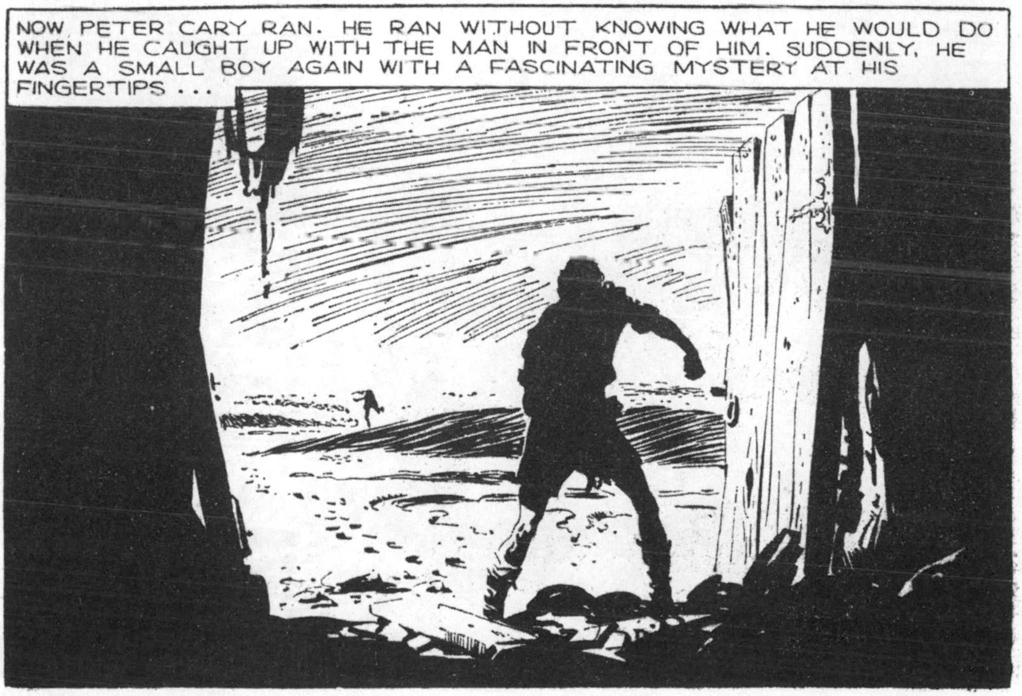
NOW PETER CARY RAN. HE RAN WITHOUT KNOWING WHAT HE WOULD DO WHEN HE CAUGHT UP WITH THE MAN IN FRONT OF HIM. SUDDENLY, HE WAS A SMALL BOY AGAIN WITH A FASCINATING MYSTERY AT HIS FINGERTIPS ...

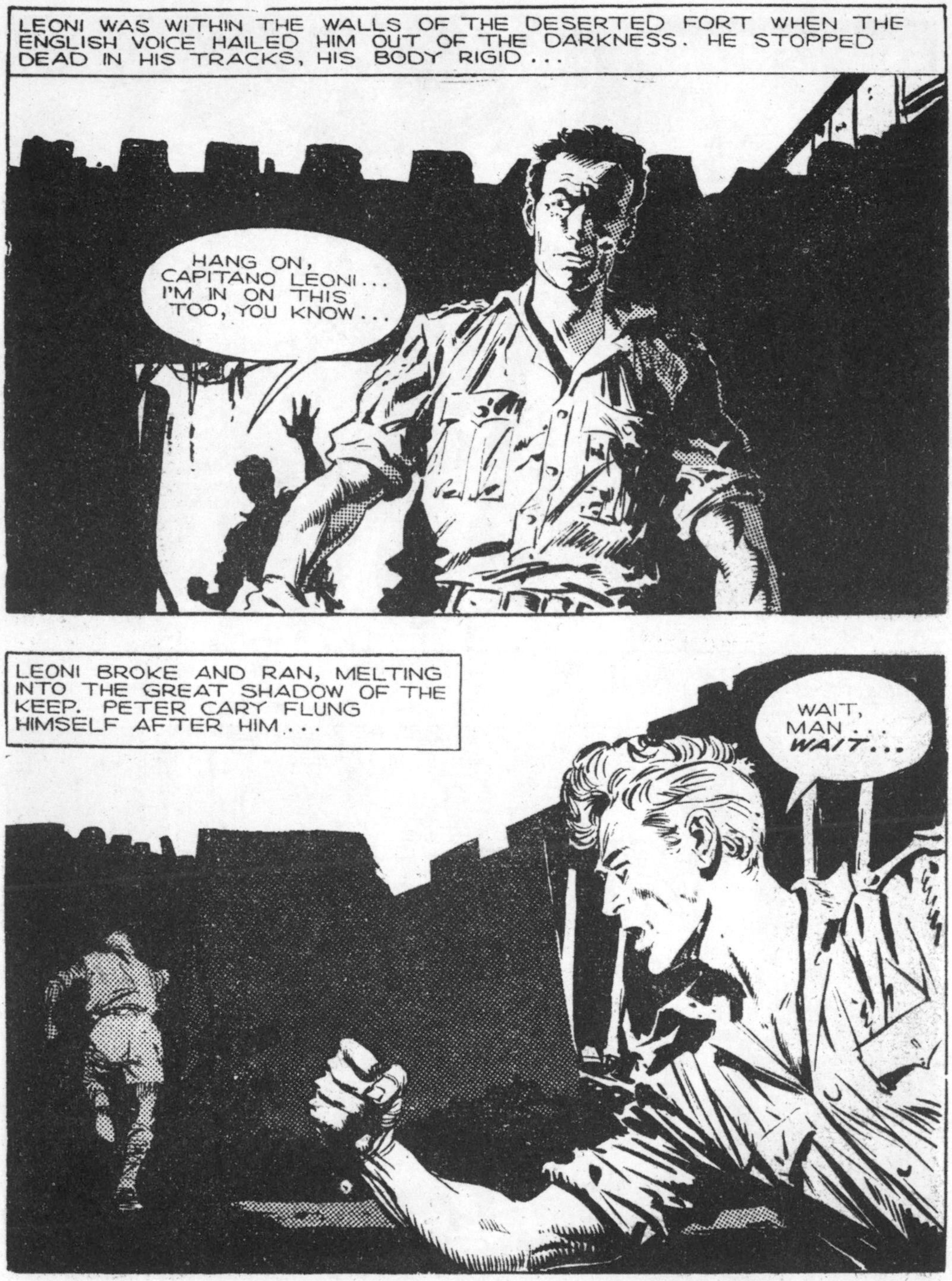
LEONI WAS WITHIN THE WALLS OF THE DESERTED FORT WHEN THE ENGLISH VOICE HAILED HIM OUT OF THE DARKNESS. HE STOPPED DEAD IN HIS TRACKS, HIS BODY RIGID . . .
HANG ON, CAPITANO LEONI . . . I'M IN ON THIS TOO, YOU KNOW . . .
LEONI BROKE AND RAN, MELTING INTO THE GREAT SHADOW OF THE KEEP. PETER CARY FLUNG HIMSELF AFTER HIM . . .
WAIT, MAN . . . WAIT . . .

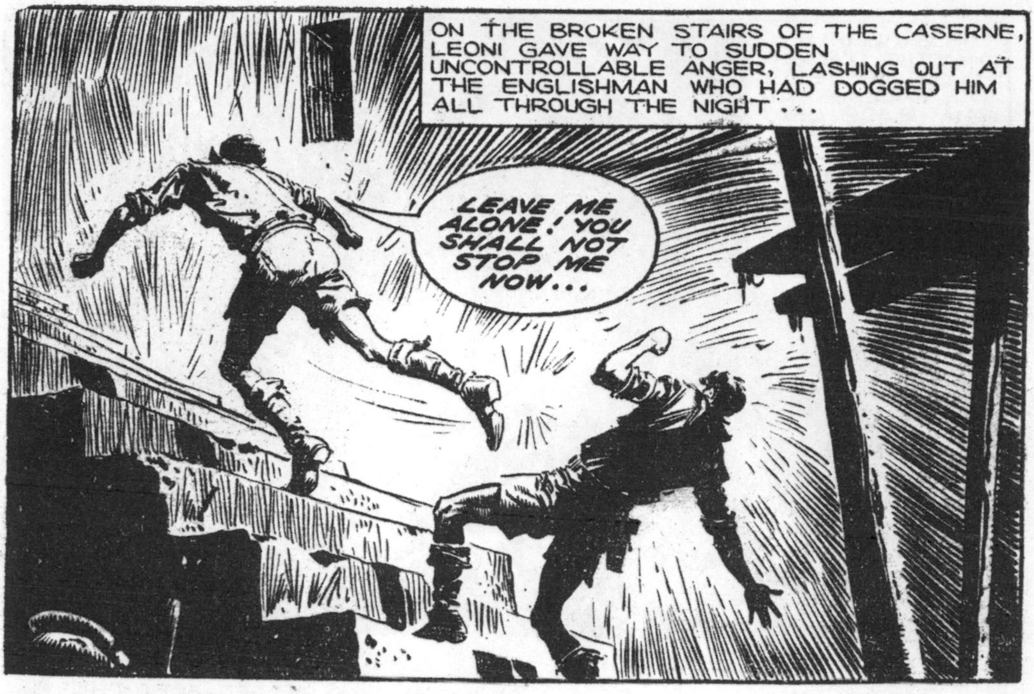
ON THE BROKEN STAIRS OF THE CASERNE, LEONI GAVE WAY TO SUDDEN UNCONTROLLABLE ANGER, LASHING OUT AT THE ENGLISHMAN WHO HAD DOGGED HIM ALL THROUGH THE NIGHT . . .
LEAVE ME ALONE! YOU SHALL NOT STOP ME NOW...

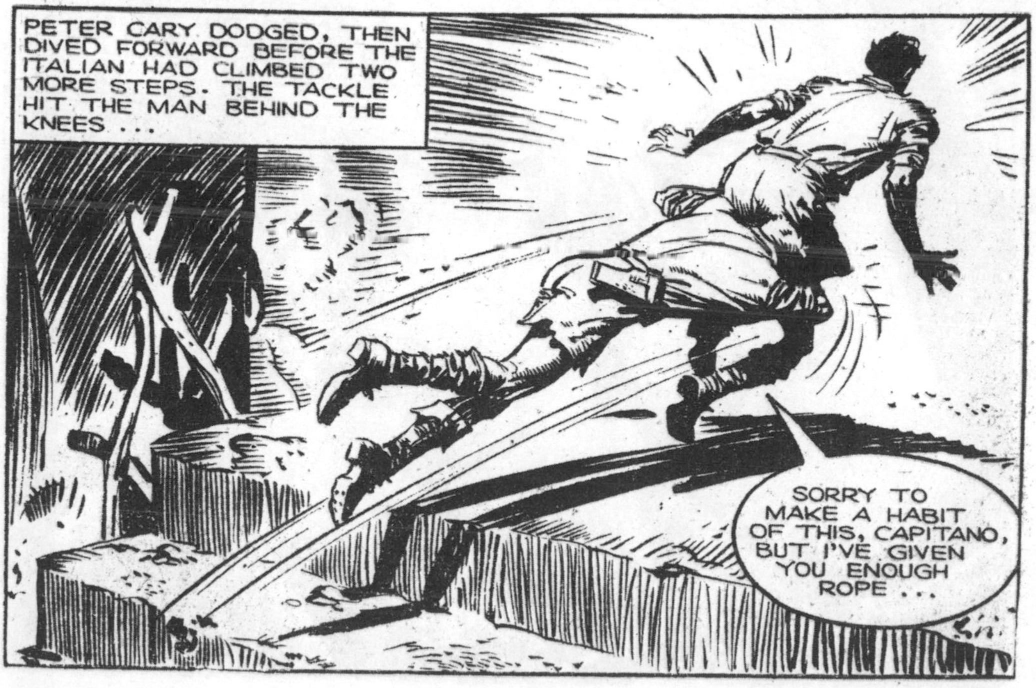
PETER CARY DODGED, THEN DIVED FORWARD BEFORE THE ITALIAN HAD CLIMBED TWO MORE STEPS. THE TACKLE HIT THE MAN BEHIND THE KNEES . . .
SORRY TO MAKE A HABIT OF THIS, CAPITANO, BUT I'VE GIVEN YOU ENOUGH ROPE . . .

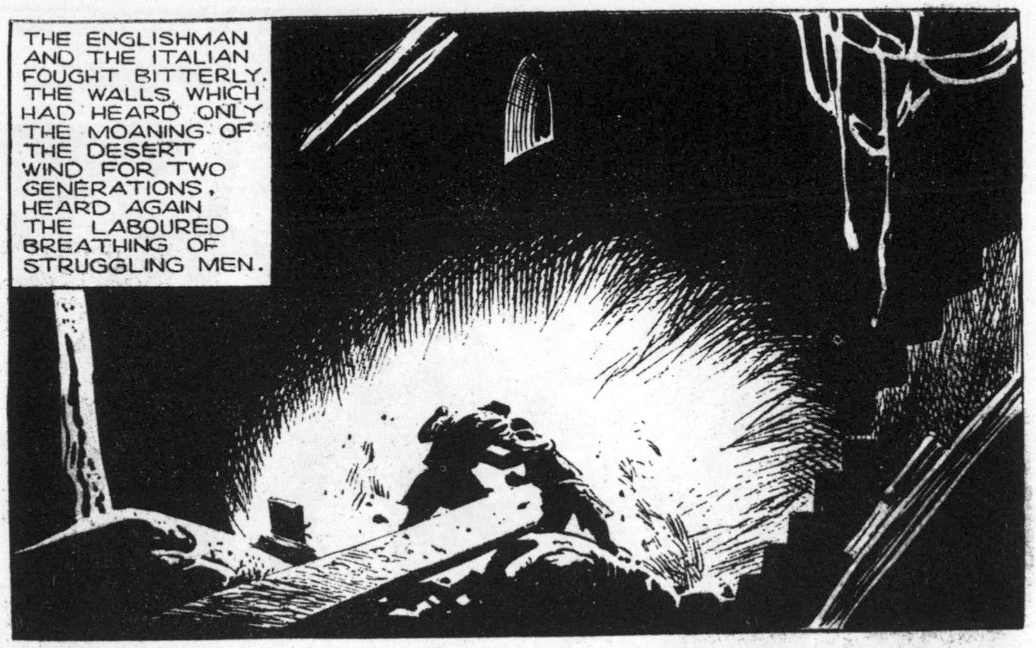
THE ENGLISHMAN AND THE ITALIAN FOUGHT BITTERLY. THE WALLS WHICH HAD HEARD ONLY THE MOANING OF THE DESERT WIND FOR TWO GENERATIONS, HEARD AGAIN THE LABOURED BREATHING OF STRUGGLING MEN.

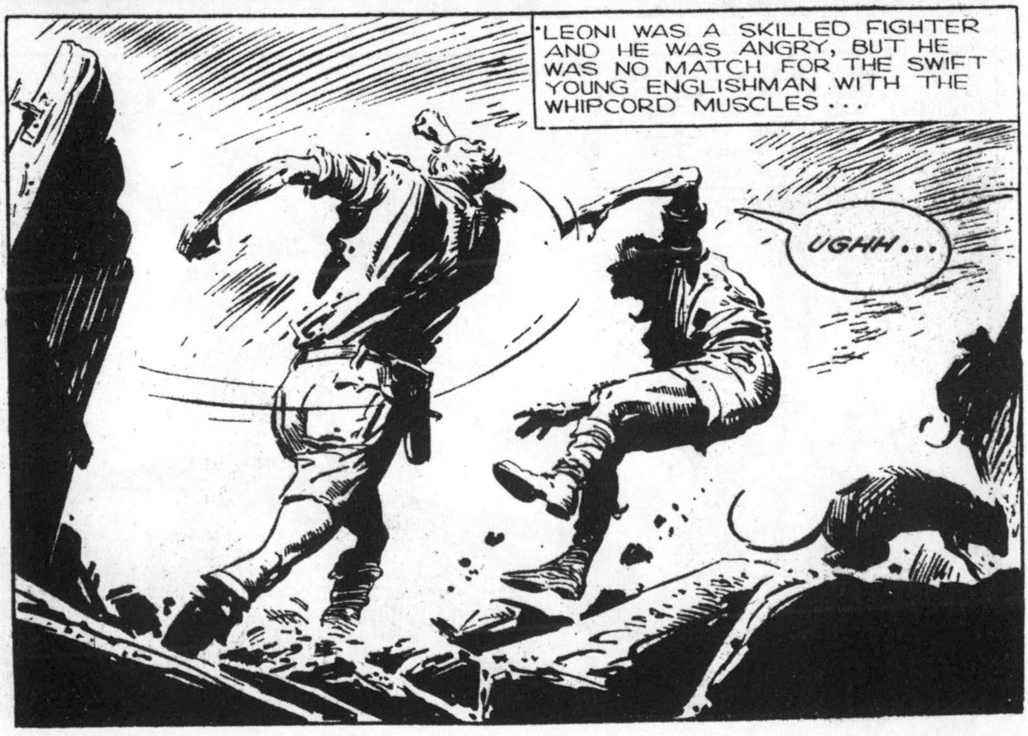
LEONI WAS A SKILLED FIGHTER AND HE WAS ANGRY, BUT HE WAS NO MATCH FOR THE SWIFT YOUNG ENGLISHMAN WITH THE WHIPCORD MUSCLES...
UGHH...

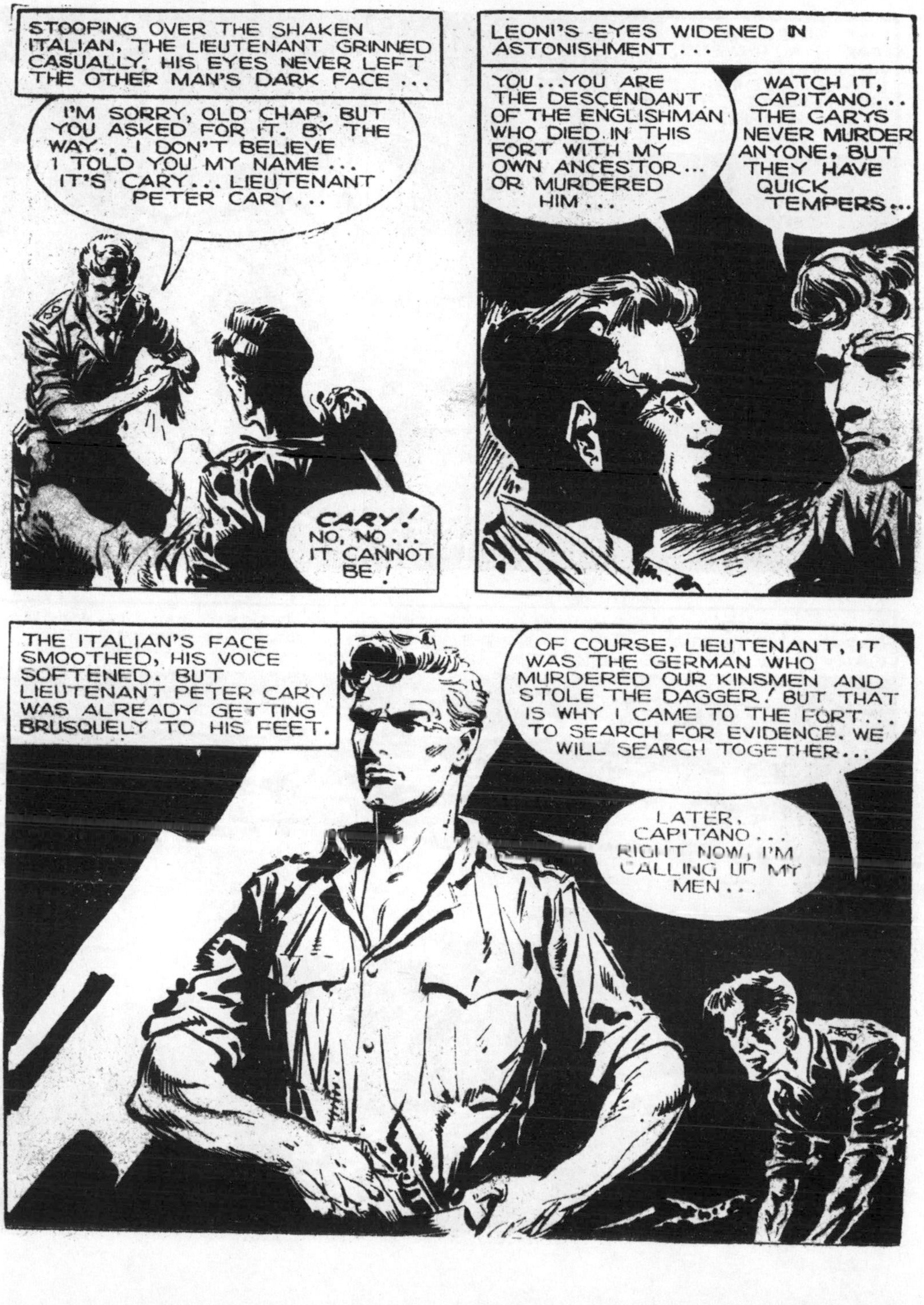
STOOPING OVER THE SHAKEN ITALIAN, THE LIEUTENANT GRINNED CASUALLY. HIS EYES NEVER LEFT THE OTHER MAN'S DARK FACE ...
I'M SORRY, OLD CHAP, BUT YOU ASKED FOR IT. BY THE WAY... I DON'T BELIEVE I TOLD YOU MY NAME ... IT'S CARY... LIEUTENANT PETER CARY ...
CARY! NO, NO ... IT CANNOT BE!
LEONI'S EYES WIDENED IN ASTONISHMENT ...
YOU... YOU ARE THE DESCENDANT OF THE ENGLISHMAN WHO DIED IN THIS FORT WITH MY OWN ANCESTOR ... OR MURDERED HIM ...
WATCH IT, CAPITANO ... THE CARYS NEVER MURDER ANYONE, BUT THEY HAVE QUICK TEMPERS ...
THE ITALIAN'S FACE SMOOTHED, HIS VOICE SOFTENED. BUT LIEUTENANT PETER CARY WAS ALREADY GETTING BRUSQUELY TO HIS FEET.
OF COURSE, LIEUTENANT, IT WAS THE GERMAN WHO MURDERED OUR KINSMEN AND STOLE THE DAGGER! BUT THAT IS WHY I CAME TO THE FORT... TO SEARCH FOR EVIDENCE. WE WILL SEARCH TOGETHER ...
LATER, CAPITANO ... RIGHT NOW, I'M CALLING UP MY MEN ...

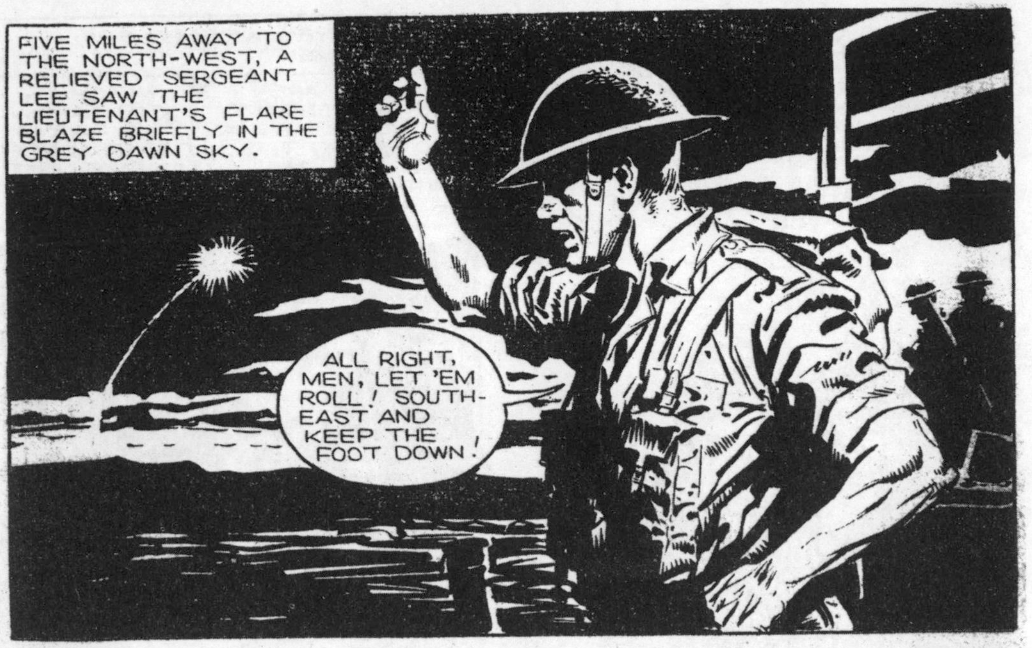
FIVE MILES AWAY TO THE NORTH-WEST, A RELIEVED SERGEANT LEE SAW THE LIEUTENANT'S FLARE BLAZE BRIEFLY IN THE GREY DAWN SKY.
ALL RIGHT, MEN, LET 'EM ROLL! SOUTH-EAST AND KEEP THE FOOT DOWN!

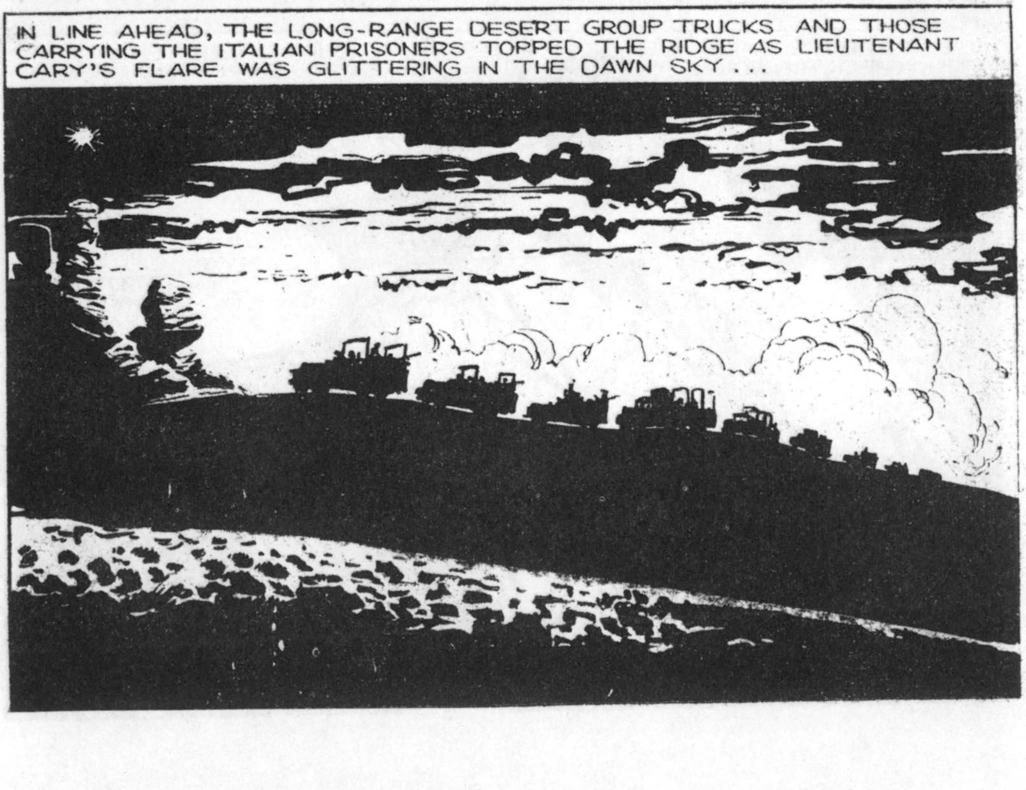
IN LINE AHEAD, THE LONG-RANGE DESERT GROUP TRUCKS AND THOSE CARRYING THE ITALIAN PRISONERS TOPPED THE RIDGE AS LIEUTENANT CARY'S FLARE WAS GLITTERING IN THE DAWN SKY ...

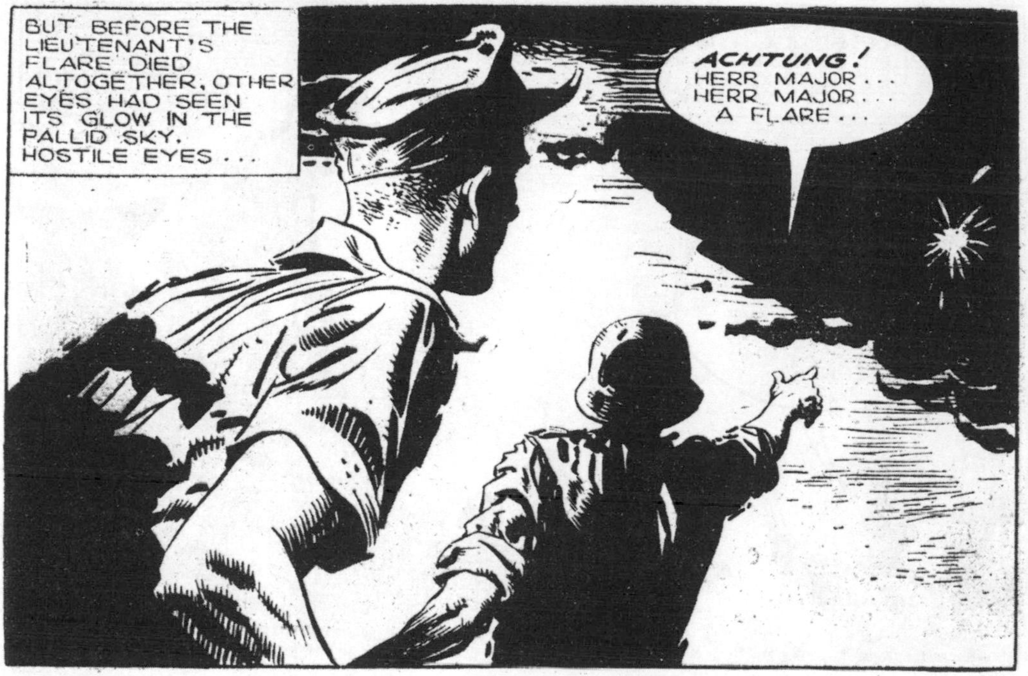
BUT BEFORE THE LIEUTENANT'S FLARE DIED ALTOGETHER, OTHER EYES HAD SEEN ITS GLOW IN THE PALLID SKY. HOSTILE EYES ...
ACHTUNG! HERR MAJOR ... HERR MAJOR ... A FLARE ...

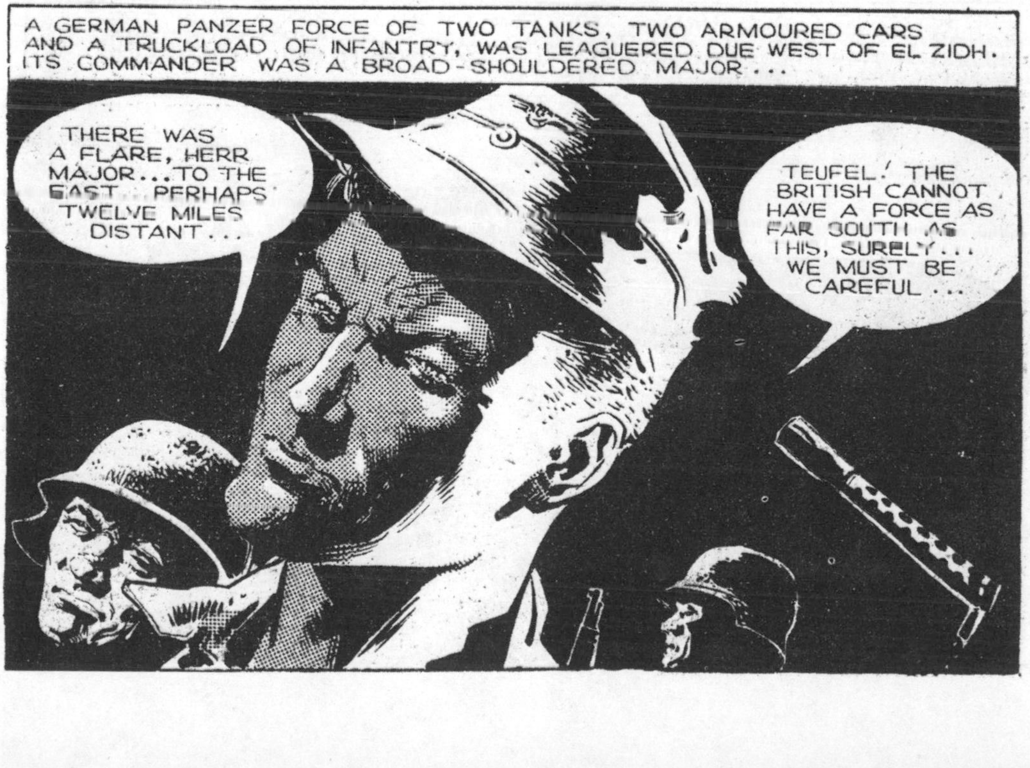
A GERMAN PANZER FORCE OF TWO TANKS, TWO ARMOURED CARS AND A TRUCKLOAD OF INFANTRY, WAS LEAGUERED DUE WEST OF EL ZIDH. ITS COMMANDER WAS A BROAD-SHOULDERED MAJOR ...
THERE WAS A FLARE, HERR MAJOR ... TO THE EAST ... PERHAPS TWELVE MILES DISTANT ...
TEUFEL! THE BRITISH CANNOT HAVE A FORCE AS FAR SOUTH AS THIS, SURELY ... WE MUST BE CAREFUL ...

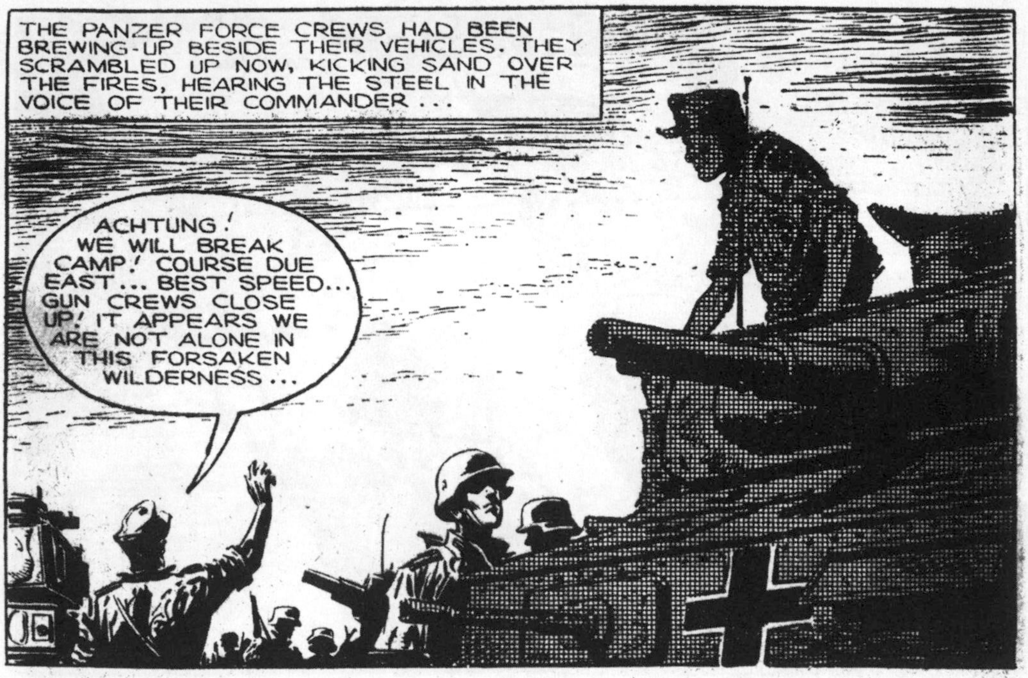
THE PANZER FORCE CREWS HAD BEEN BREWING-UP BESIDE THEIR VEHICLES. THEY SCRAMBLED UP NOW, KICKING SAND OVER THE FIRES, HEARING THE STEEL IN THE VOICE OF THEIR COMMANDER ...
ACHTUNG! WE WILL BREAK CAMP! COURSE DUE EAST... BEST SPEED... GUN CREWS CLOSE UP! IT APPEARS WE ARE NOT ALONE IN THIS FORSAKEN WILDERNESS ...

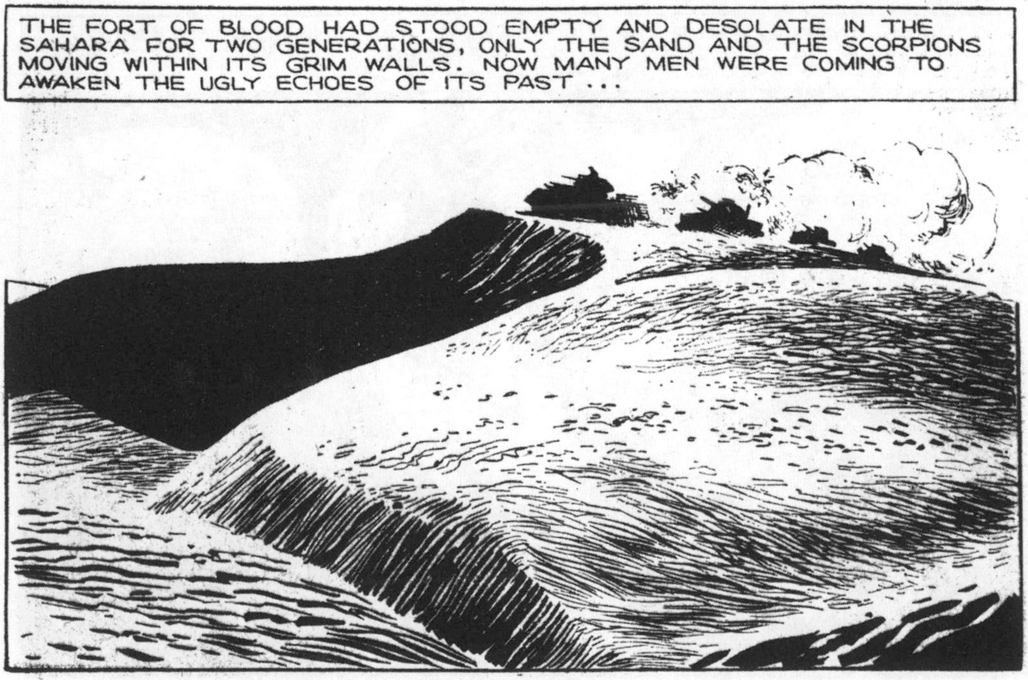
THE FORT OF BLOOD HAD STOOD EMPTY AND DESOLATE IN THE SAHARA FOR TWO GENERATIONS, ONLY THE SAND AND THE SCORPIONS MOVING WITHIN ITS GRIM WALLS. NOW MANY MEN WERE COMING TO AWAKEN THE UGLY ECHOES OF ITS PAST ...

Chapter 4. The Searchers

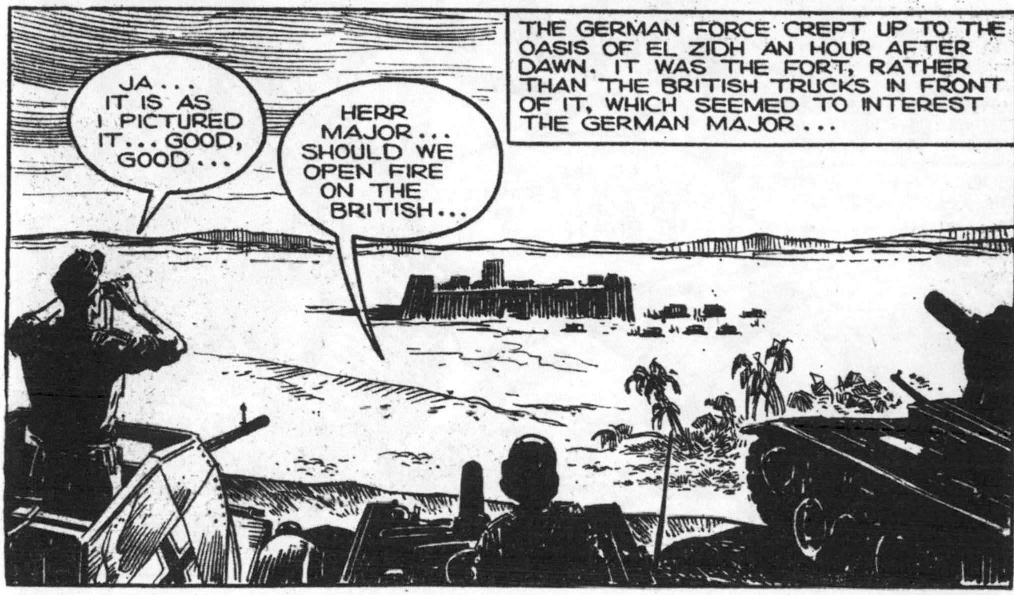
THE GERMAN FORCE CREPT UP TO THE OASIS OF EL ZIDH AN HOUR AFTER DAWN. IT WAS THE FORT, RATHER THAN THE BRITISH TRUCKS IN FRONT OF IT, WHICH SEEMED TO INTEREST THE GERMAN MAJOR ...
JA ... IT IS AS I PICTURED IT ... GOOD, GOOD ...
HERR MAJOR ... SHOULD WE OPEN FIRE ON THE BRITISH ...

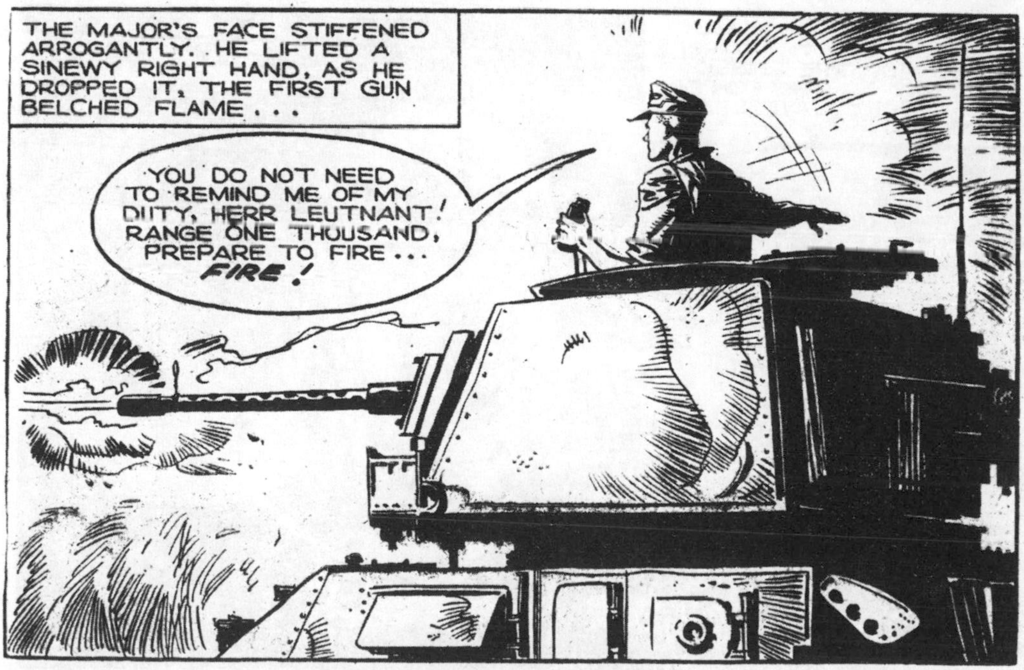
THE MAJOR'S FACE STIFFENED ARROGANTLY. HE LIFTED A SINEWY RIGHT HAND, AS HE DROPPED IT, THE FIRST GUN BELCHED FLAME ...
YOU DO NOT NEED TO REMIND ME OF MY DUTY, HERR LEUTNANT! RANGE ONE THOUSAND, PREPARE TO FIRE ... FIRE!

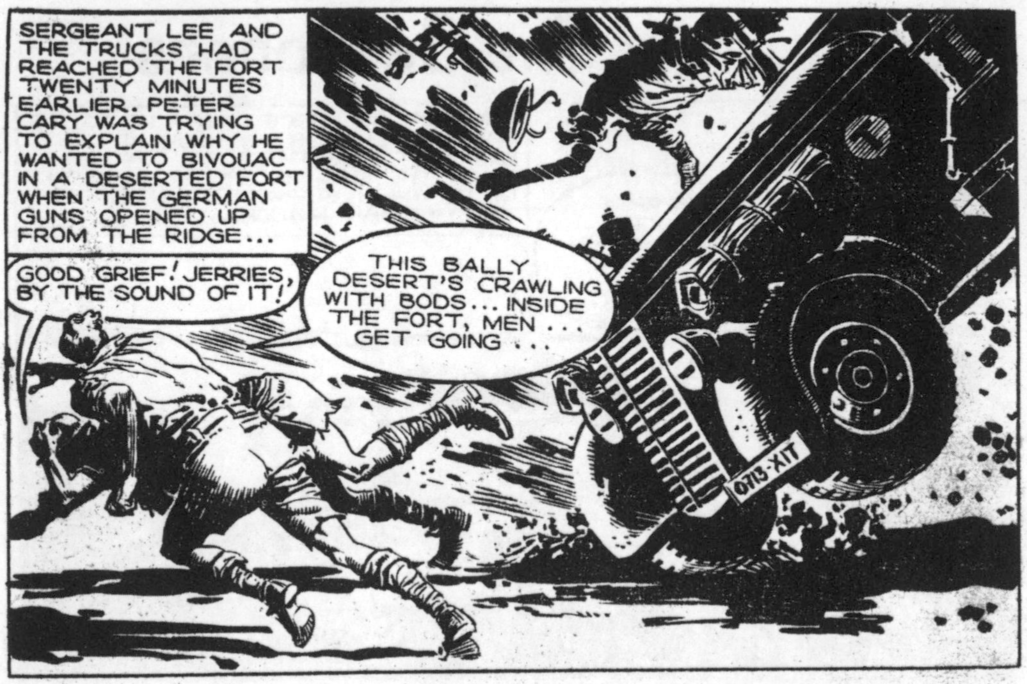
SERGEANT LEE AND THE TRUCKS HAD REACHED THE FORT TWENTY MINUTES EARLIER. PETER CARY WAS TRYING TO EXPLAIN WHY HE WANTED TO BIVOUAC IN A DESERTED FORT WHEN THE GERMAN GUNS OPENED UP FROM THE RIDGE...
GOOD GRIEF! JERRIES, BY THE SOUND OF IT!
THIS BALLY DESERT'S CRAWLING WITH BODS... INSIDE THE FORT, MEN... GET GOING...
0713-X17

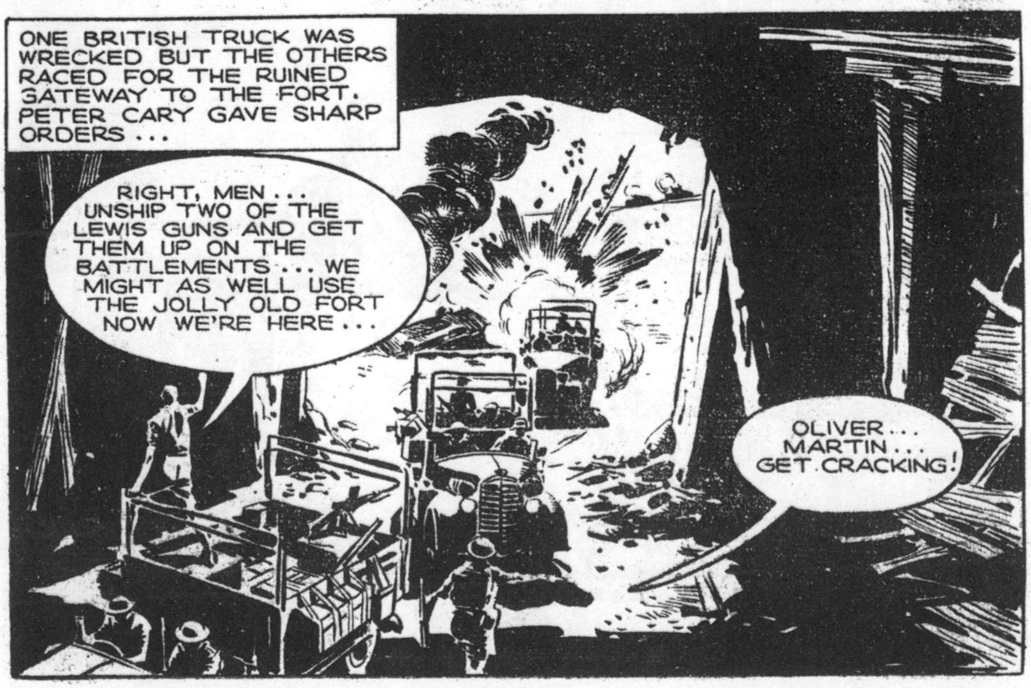
ONE BRITISH TRUCK WAS WRECKED BUT THE OTHERS RACED FOR THE RUINED GATEWAY TO THE FORT. PETER CARY GAVE SHARP ORDERS...
RIGHT, MEN... UNSHIP TWO OF THE LEWIS GUNS AND GET THEM UP ON THE BATTLEMENTS... WE MIGHT AS WELL USE THE JOLLY OLD FORT NOW WE'RE HERE...
OLIVER... MARTIN... GET CRACKING!

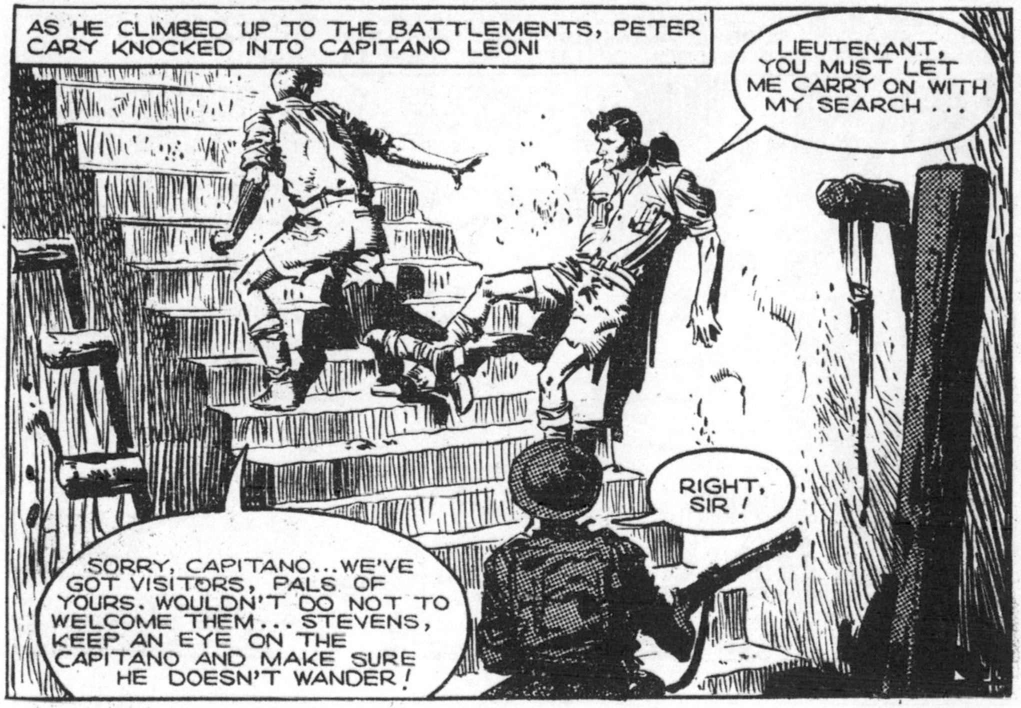
AS HE CLIMBED UP TO THE BATTLEMENTS, PETER CARY KNOCKED INTO CAPITANO LEONI
LIEUTENANT, YOU MUST LET ME CARRY ON WITH MY SEARCH . . .
SORRY, CAPITANO...WE'VE GOT VISITORS, PALS OF YOURS. WOULDN'T DO NOT TO WELCOME THEM . . . STEVENS, KEEP AN EYE ON THE CAPITANO AND MAKE SURE HE DOESN'T WANDER!
RIGHT, SIR!

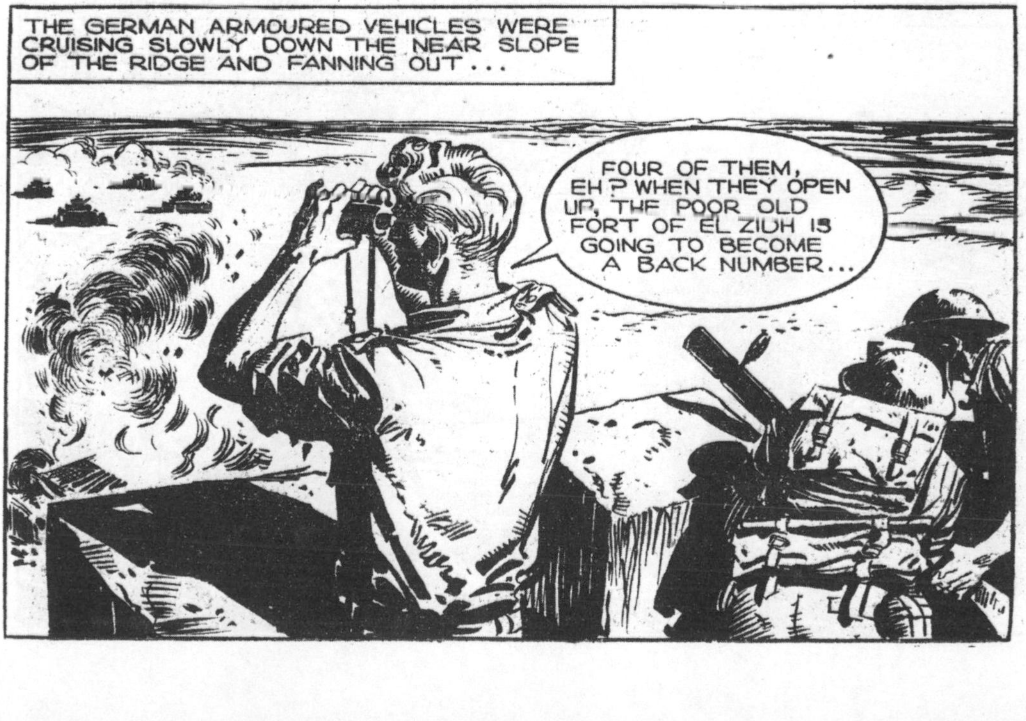
THE GERMAN ARMOURED VEHICLES WERE CRUISING SLOWLY DOWN THE NEAR SLOPE OF THE RIDGE AND FANNING OUT . . .
FOUR OF THEM, EH? WHEN THEY OPEN UP, THE POOR OLD FORT OF EL ZIUH IS GOING TO BECOME A BACK NUMBER...

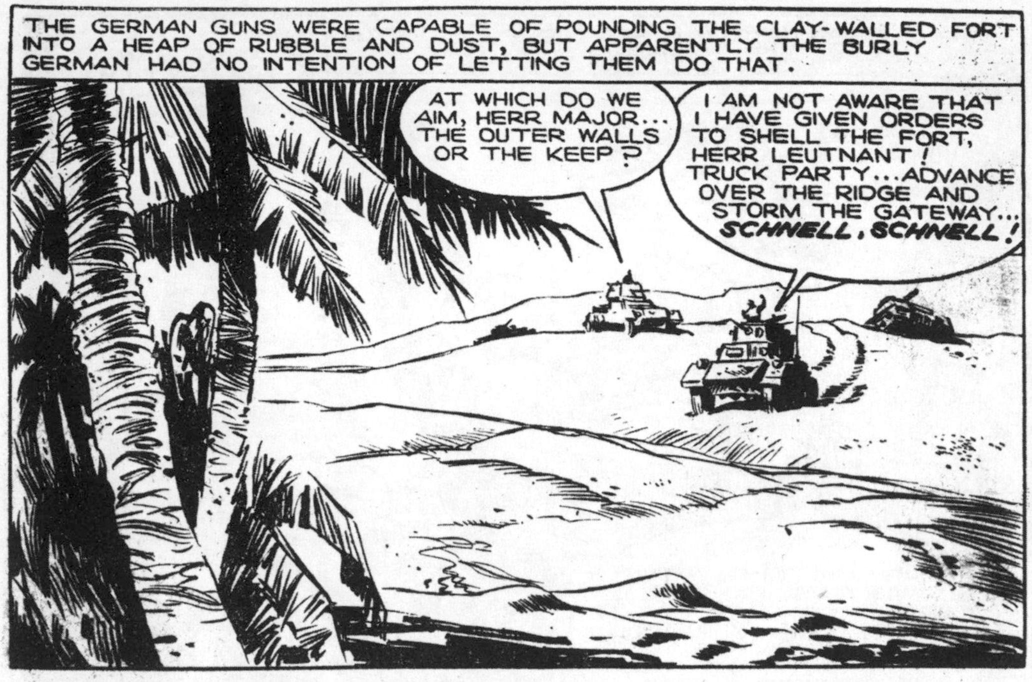
THE GERMAN GUNS WERE CAPABLE OF POUNDING THE CLAY-WALLED FORT INTO A HEAP OF RUBBLE AND DUST, BUT APPARENTLY THE BURLY GERMAN HAD NO INTENTION OF LETTING THEM DO THAT.
AT WHICH DO WE AIM, HERR MAJOR... THE OUTER WALLS OR THE KEEP?
I AM NOT AWARE THAT I HAVE GIVEN ORDERS TO SHELL THE FORT, HERR LEUTNANT! TRUCK PARTY...ADVANCE OVER THE RIDGE AND STORM THE GATEWAY... SCHNELL, SCHNELL!

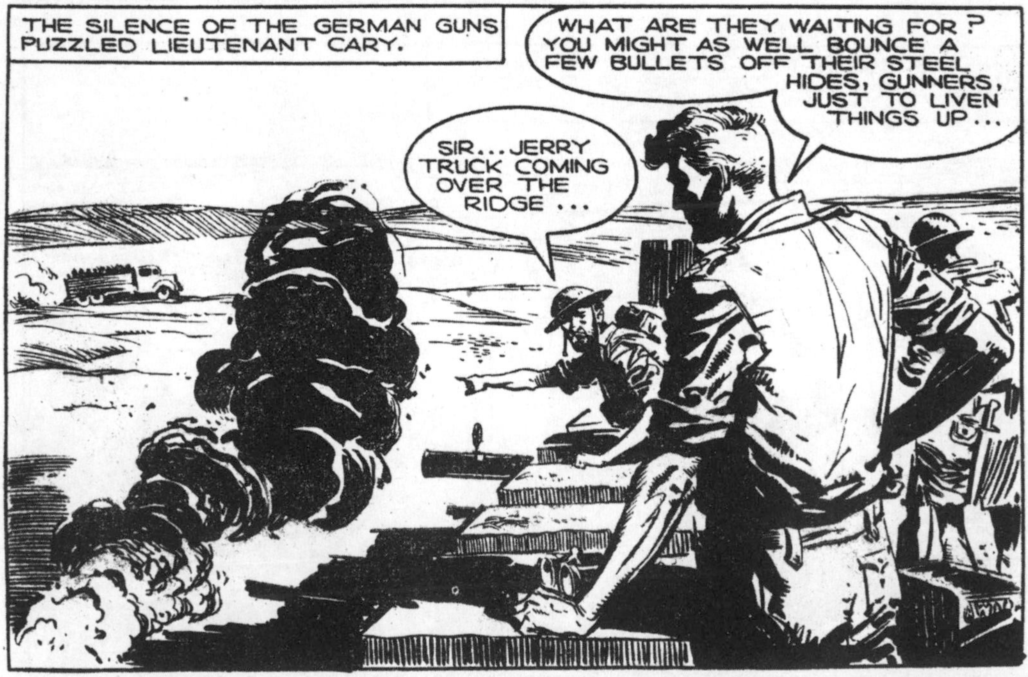
THE SILENCE OF THE GERMAN GUNS PUZZLED LIEUTENANT CARY.
WHAT ARE THEY WAITING FOR? YOU MIGHT AS WELL BOUNCE A FEW BULLETS OFF THEIR STEEL HIDES, GUNNERS, JUST TO LIVEN THINGS UP...
SIR... JERRY TRUCK COMING OVER THE RIDGE ...

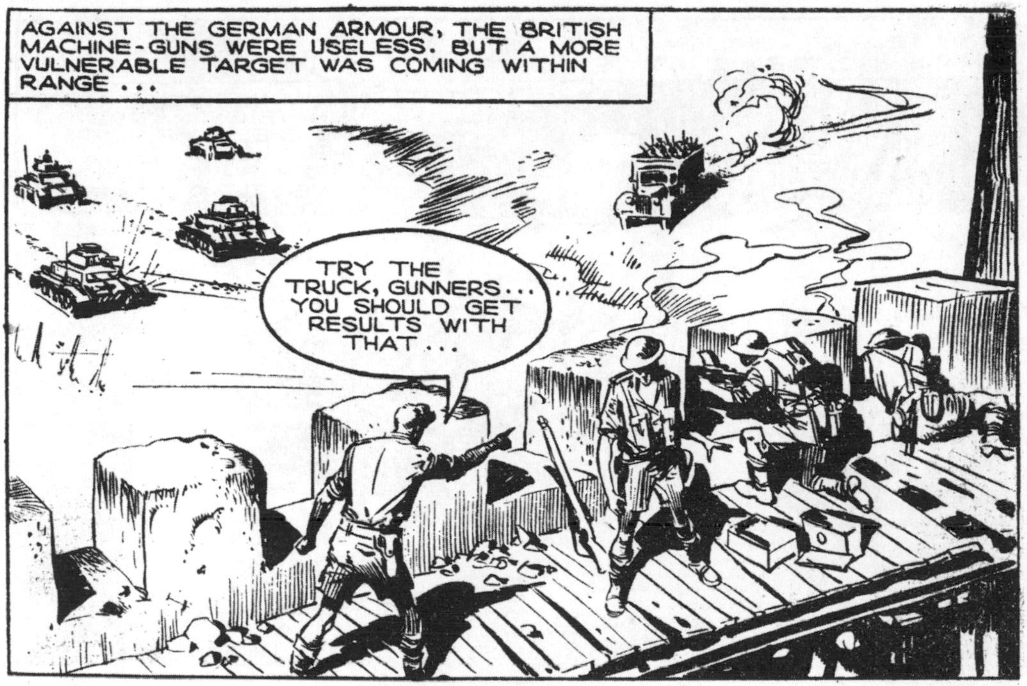
AGAINST THE GERMAN ARMOUR, THE BRITISH MACHINE-GUNS WERE USELESS. BUT A MORE VULNERABLE TARGET WAS COMING WITHIN RANGE ...
TRY THE TRUCK, GUNNERS... YOU SHOULD GET RESULTS WITH THAT ...

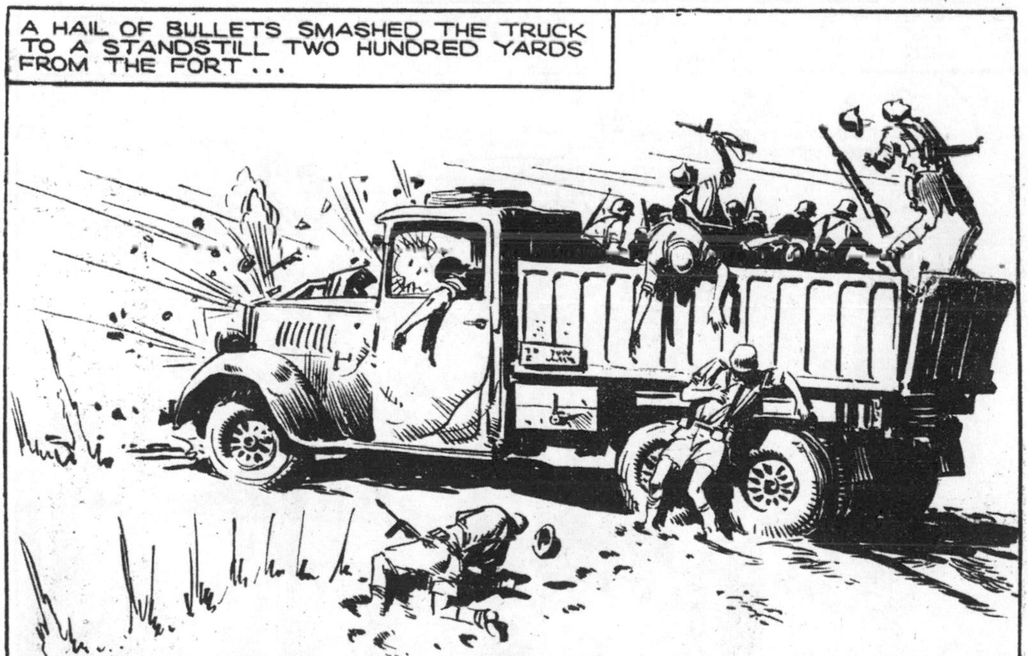
A HAIL OF BULLETS SMASHED THE TRUCK TO A STANDSTILL TWO HUNDRED YARDS FROM THE FORT ...

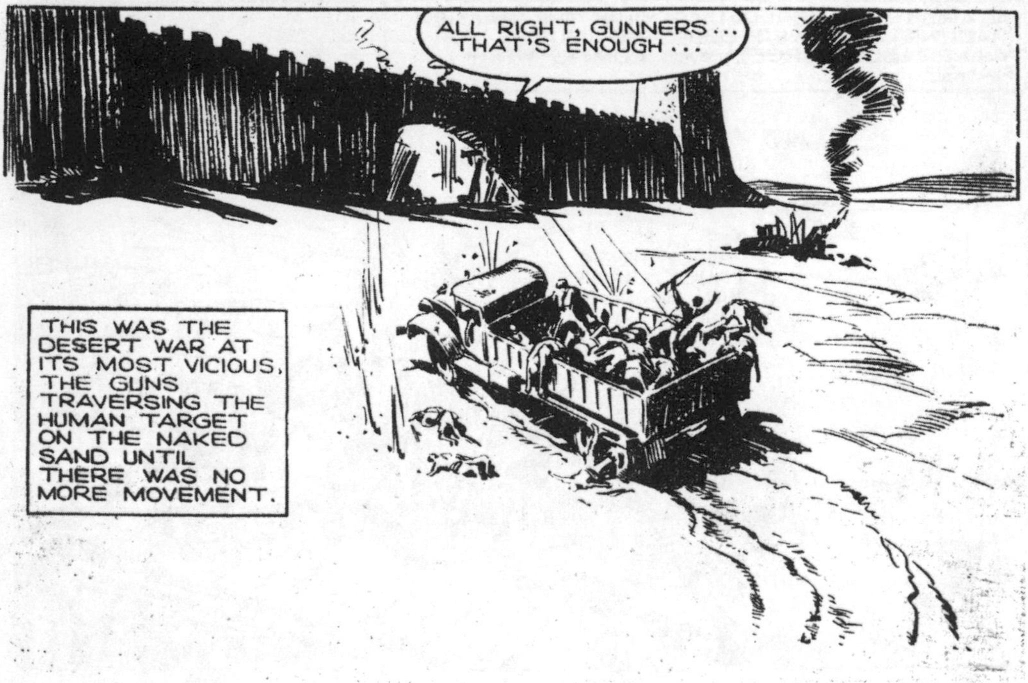
ALL RIGHT, GUNNERS... THAT'S ENOUGH...
THIS WAS THE DESERT WAR AT ITS MOST VICIOUS, THE GUNS TRAVERSING THE HUMAN TARGET ON THE NAKED SAND UNTIL THERE WAS NO MORE MOVEMENT.

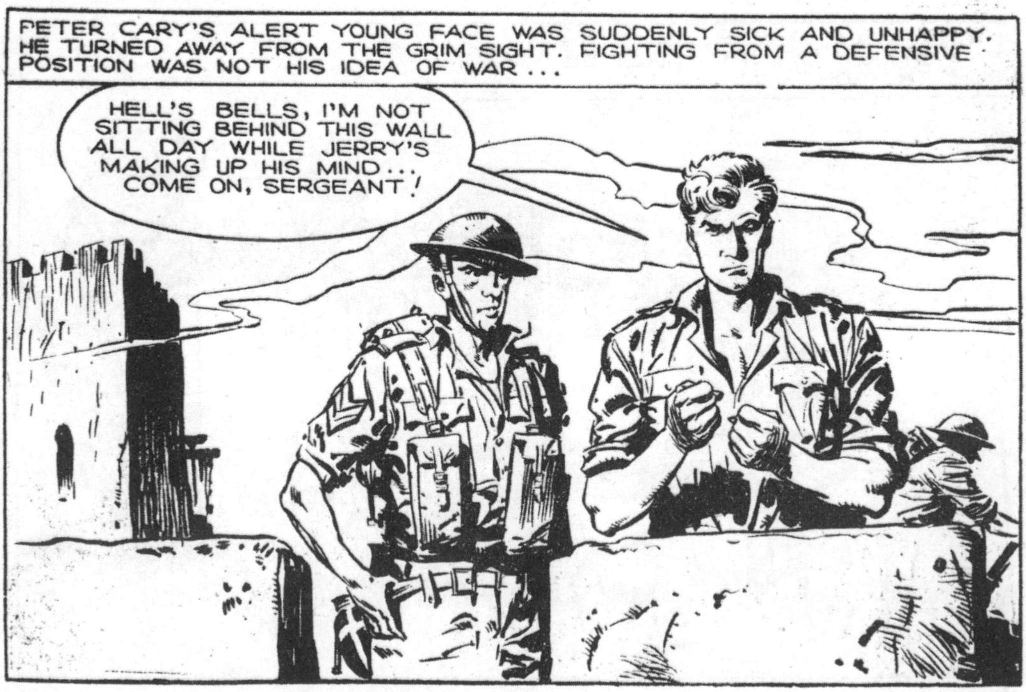
PETER CARY'S ALERT YOUNG FACE WAS SUDDENLY SICK AND UNHAPPY. HE TURNED AWAY FROM THE GRIM SIGHT. FIGHTING FROM A DEFENSIVE POSITION WAS NOT HIS IDEA OF WAR...
HELL'S BELLS, I'M NOT SITTING BEHIND THIS WALL ALL DAY WHILE JERRY'S MAKING UP HIS MIND... COME ON, SERGEANT!

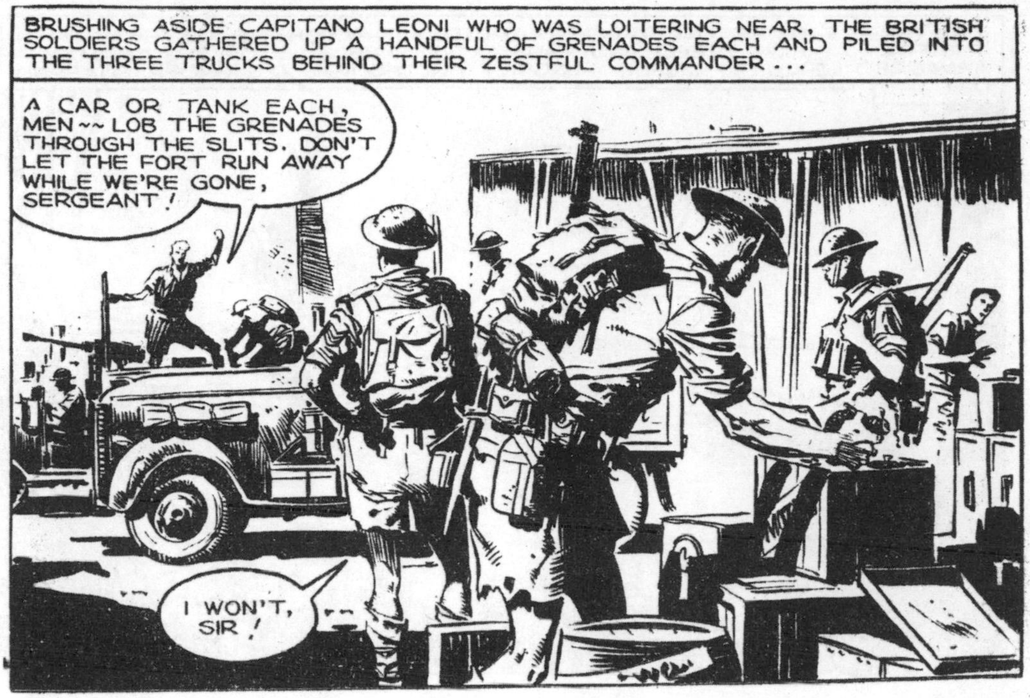
BRUSHING ASIDE CAPITANO LEONI WHO WAS LOITERING NEAR, THE BRITISH SOLDIERS GATHERED UP A HANDFUL OF GRENADES EACH AND PILED INTO THE THREE TRUCKS BEHIND THEIR ZESTFUL COMMANDER ...
A CAR OR TANK EACH, MEN ~~ LOB THE GRENADES THROUGH THE SLITS. DON'T LET THE FORT RUN AWAY WHILE WE'RE GONE, SERGEANT !
I WON'T, SIR !

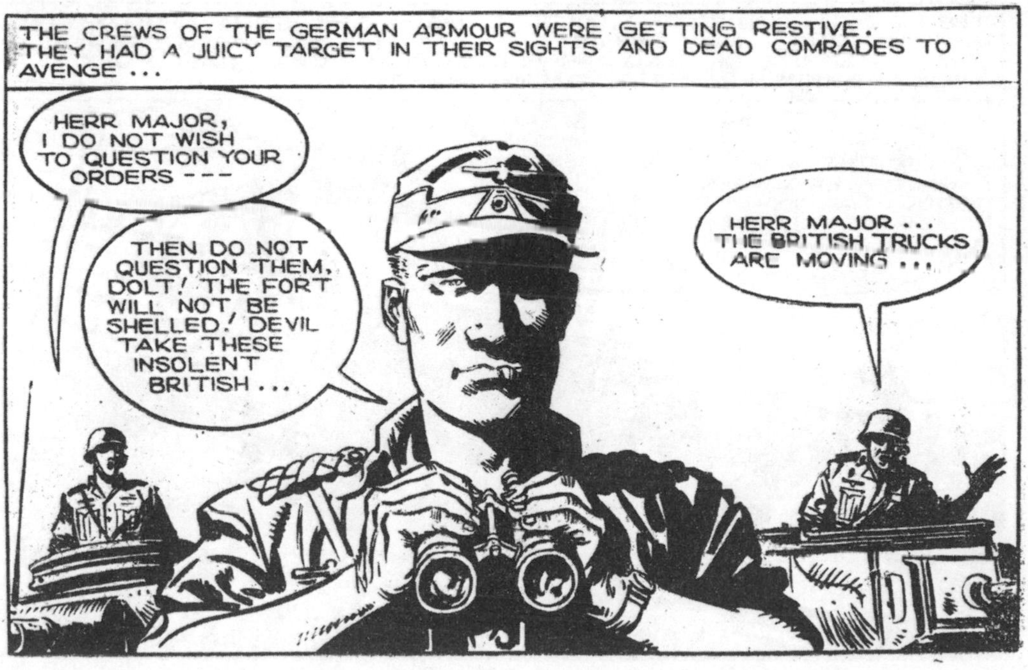
THE CREWS OF THE GERMAN ARMOUR WERE GETTING RESTIVE. THEY HAD A JUICY TARGET IN THEIR SIGHTS AND DEAD COMRADES TO AVENGE ...
HERR MAJOR, I DO NOT WISH TO QUESTION YOUR ORDERS ---
THEN DO NOT QUESTION THEM, DOLT! THE FORT WILL NOT BE SHELLED! DEVIL TAKE THESE INSOLENT BRITISH ...
HERR MAJOR ... THE BRITISH TRUCKS ARE MOVING ...

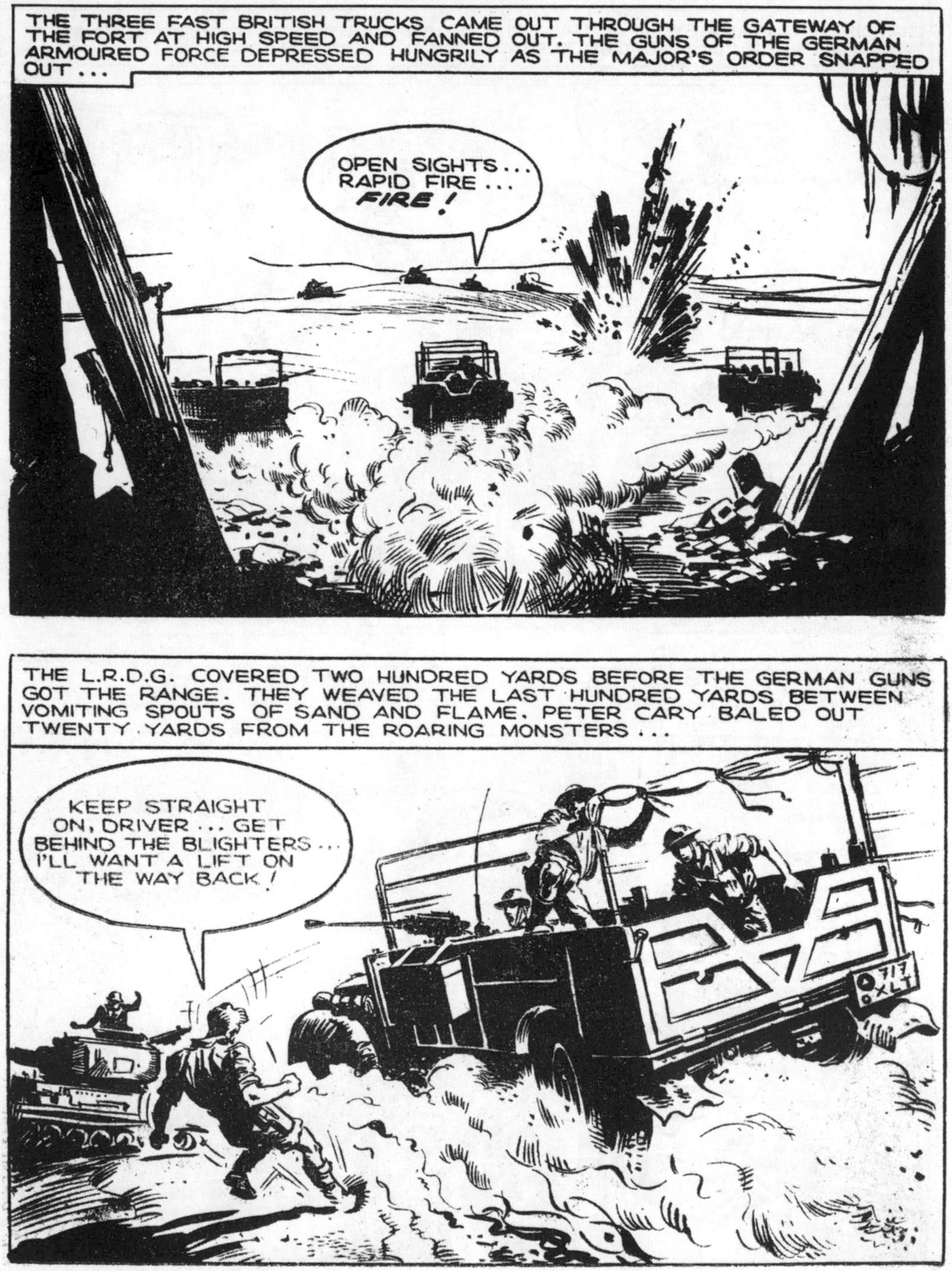
THE THREE FAST BRITISH TRUCKS CAME OUT THROUGH THE GATEWAY OF THE FORT AT HIGH SPEED AND FANNED OUT. THE GUNS OF THE GERMAN ARMOURED FORCE DEPRESSED HUNGRILY AS THE MAJOR'S ORDER SNAPPED OUT . . .
OPEN SIGHTS . . . RAPID FIRE . . . FIRE !
THE L.R.D.G. COVERED TWO HUNDRED YARDS BEFORE THE GERMAN GUNS GOT THE RANGE. THEY WEAVED THE LAST HUNDRED YARDS BETWEEN VOMITING SPOUTS OF SAND AND FLAME. PETER CARY BALED OUT TWENTY YARDS FROM THE ROARING MONSTERS . . .
KEEP STRAIGHT ON, DRIVER . . . GET BEHIND THE BLIGHTERS . . . I'LL WANT A LIFT ON THE WAY BACK !

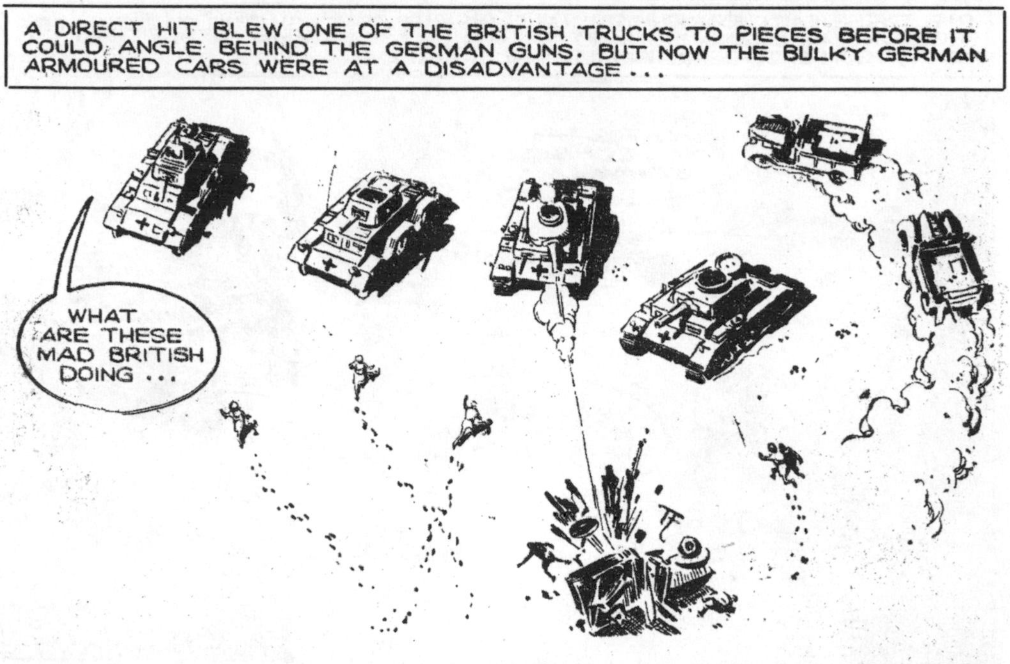
A DIRECT HIT BLEW ONE OF THE BRITISH TRUCKS TO PIECES BEFORE IT COULD ANGLE BEHIND THE GERMAN GUNS. BUT NOW THE BULKY GERMAN ARMOURED CARS WERE AT A DISADVANTAGE . . .
WHAT ARE THESE MAD BRITISH DOING . . .

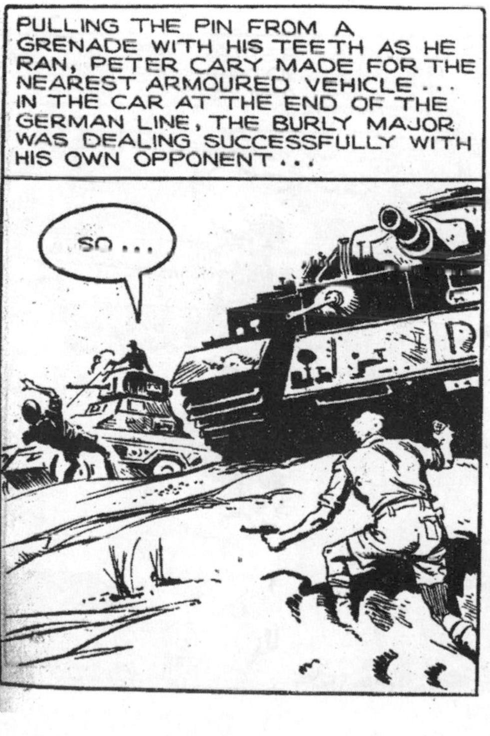
PULLING THE PIN FROM A GRENADE WITH HIS TEETH AS HE RAN, PETER CARY MADE FOR THE NEAREST ARMOURED VEHICLE . . . IN THE CAR AT THE END OF THE GERMAN LINE, THE BURLY MAJOR WAS DEALING SUCCESSFULLY WITH HIS OWN OPPONENT . . .
SO . . .

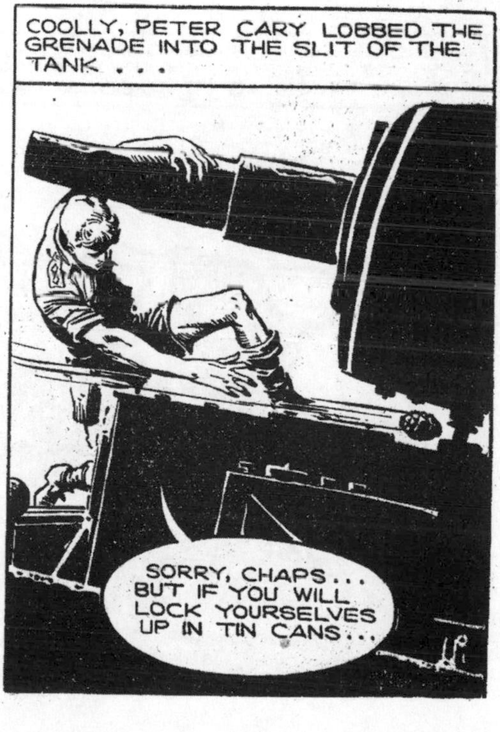
COOLLY, PETER CARY LOBBED THE GRENADE INTO THE SLIT OF THE TANK . . .
SORRY, CHAPS . . . BUT IF YOU WILL LOCK YOURSELVES UP IN TIN CANS . . .

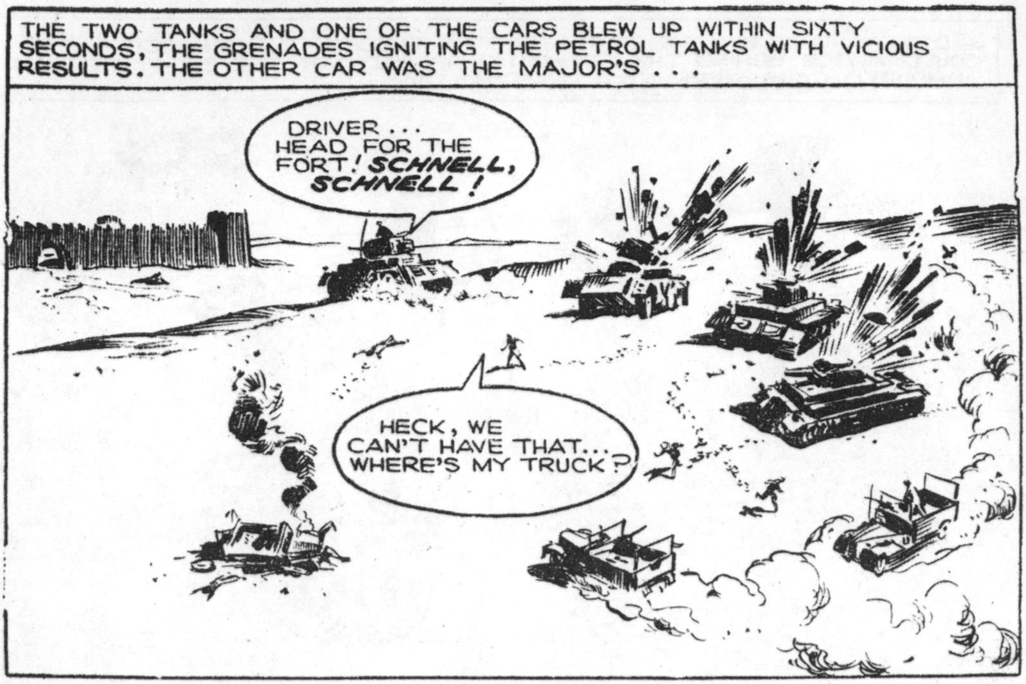
THE TWO TANKS AND ONE OF THE CARS BLEW UP WITHIN SIXTY SECONDS, THE GRENADES IGNITING THE PETROL TANKS WITH VICIOUS RESULTS. THE OTHER CAR WAS THE MAJOR'S . . .
DRIVER ... HEAD FOR THE FORT! SCHNELL, SCHNELL!
HECK, WE CAN'T HAVE THAT... WHERE'S MY TRUCK?

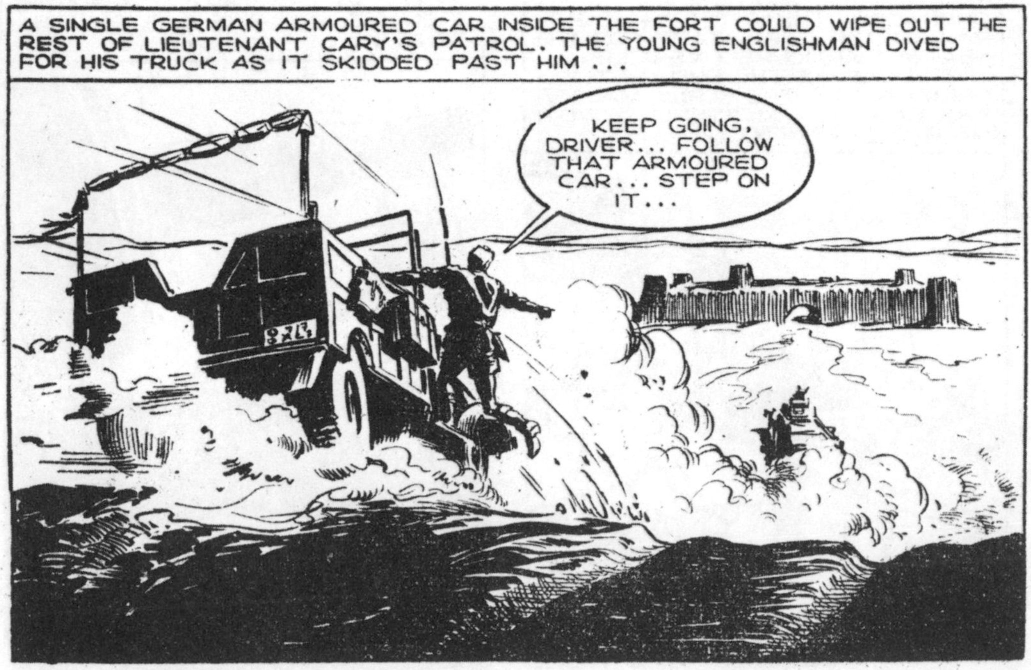
A SINGLE GERMAN ARMOURED CAR INSIDE THE FORT COULD WIPE OUT THE REST OF LIEUTENANT CARY'S PATROL. THE YOUNG ENGLISHMAN DIVED FOR HIS TRUCK AS IT SKIDDED PAST HIM . . .
KEEP GOING, DRIVER... FOLLOW THAT ARMOURED CAR... STEP ON IT...

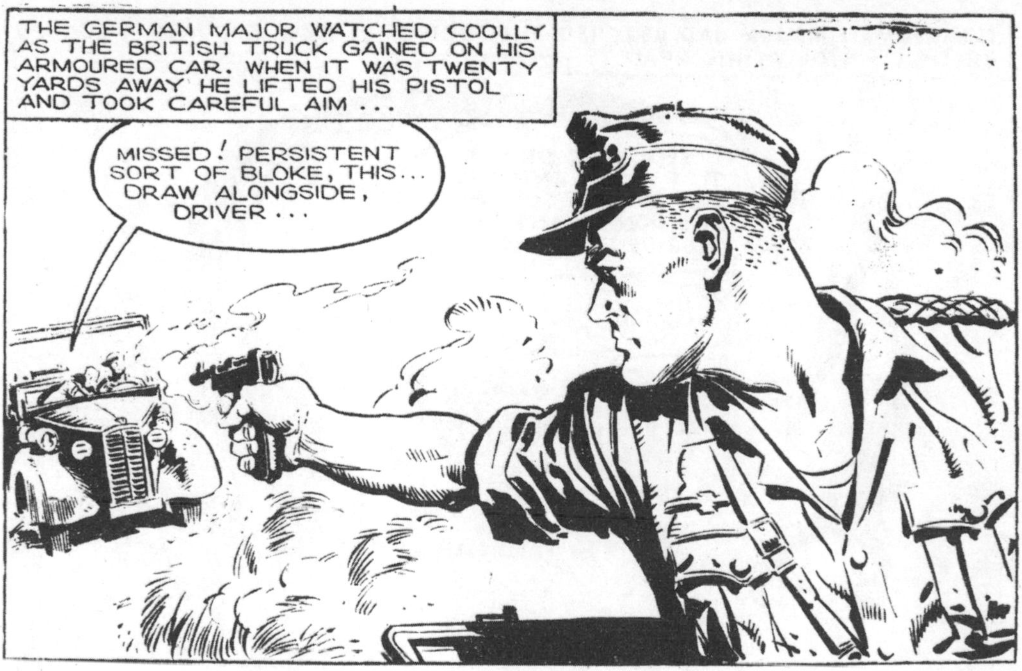
THE GERMAN MAJOR WATCHED COOLLY AS THE BRITISH TRUCK GAINED ON HIS ARMOURED CAR. WHEN IT WAS TWENTY YARDS AWAY HE LIFTED HIS PISTOL AND TOOK CAREFUL AIM ...
MISSED! PERSISTENT SORT OF BLOKE, THIS... DRAW ALONGSIDE, DRIVER ...

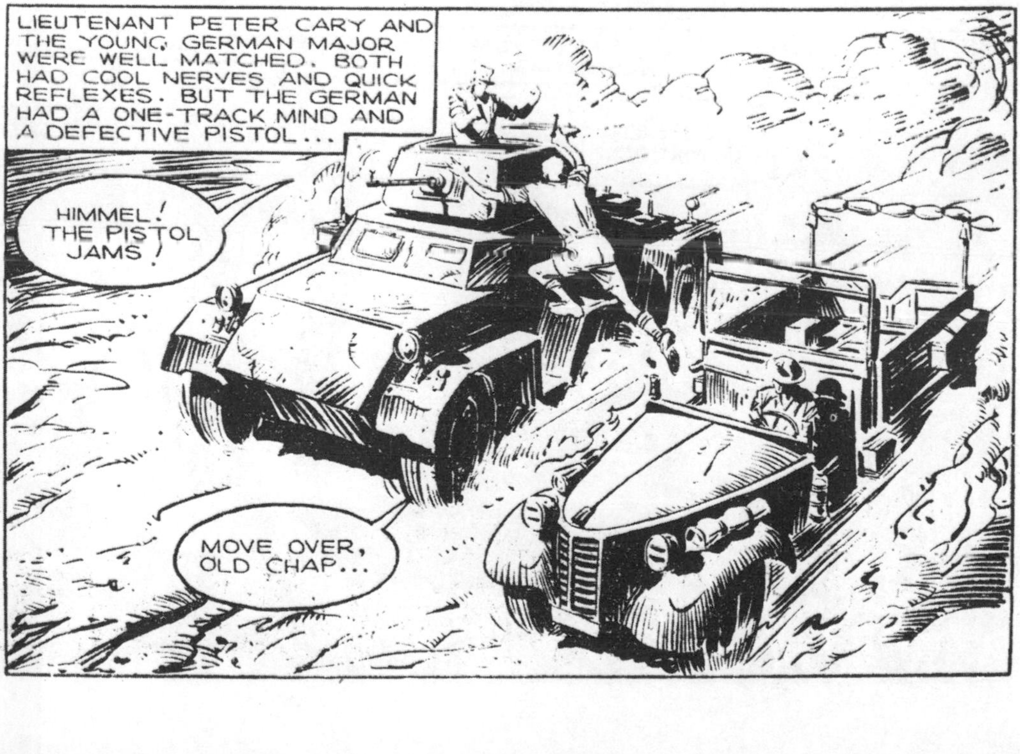
LIEUTENANT PETER CARY AND THE YOUNG GERMAN MAJOR WERE WELL MATCHED. BOTH HAD COOL NERVES AND QUICK REFLEXES. BUT THE GERMAN HAD A ONE-TRACK MIND AND A DEFECTIVE PISTOL...
HIMMEL! THE PISTOL JAMS!
MOVE OVER, OLD CHAP...

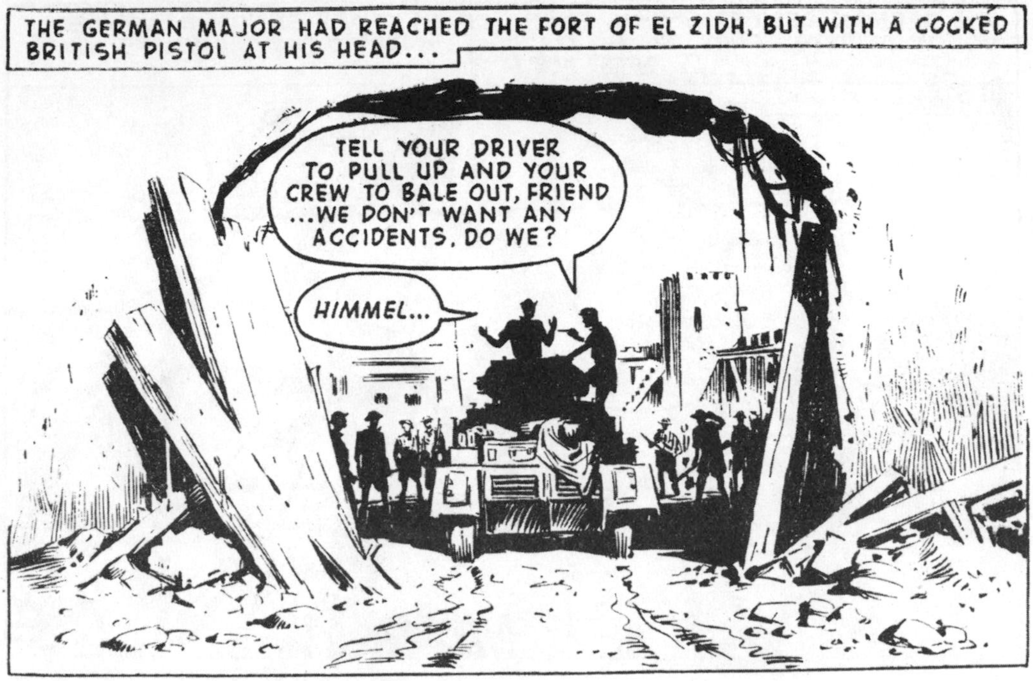
THE GERMAN MAJOR HAD REACHED THE FORT OF EL ZIDH, BUT WITH A COCKED BRITISH PISTOL AT HIS HEAD...
TELL YOUR DRIVER TO PULL UP AND YOUR CREW TO BALE OUT, FRIEND ...WE DON'T WANT ANY ACCIDENTS, DO WE?
HIMMEL...

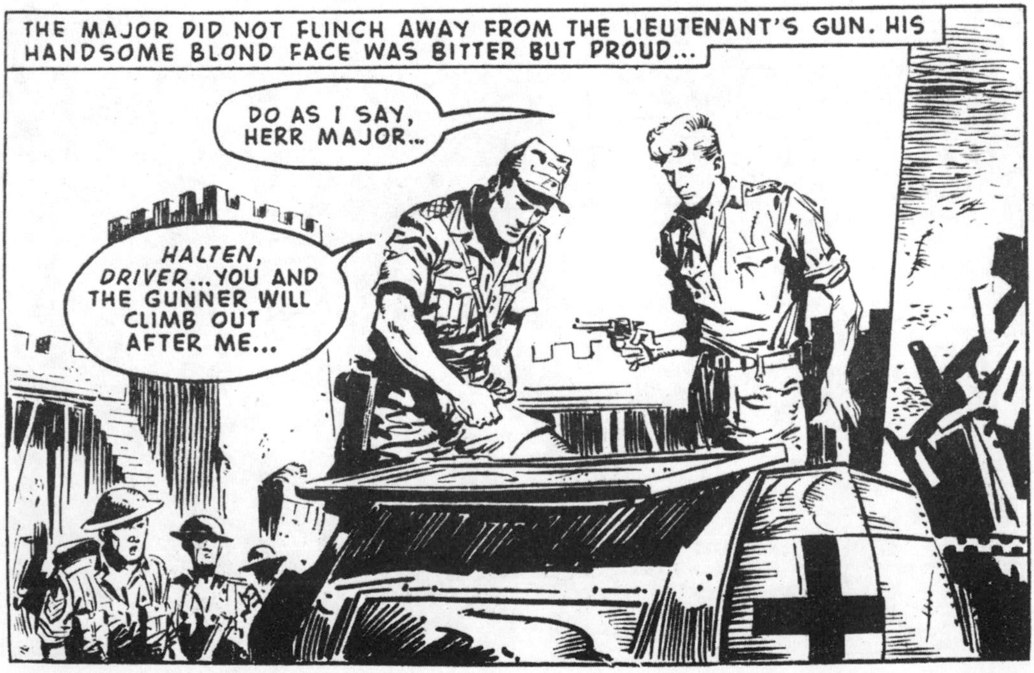
THE MAJOR DID NOT FLINCH AWAY FROM THE LIEUTENANT'S GUN. HIS HANDSOME BLOND FACE WAS BITTER BUT PROUD...
DO AS I SAY, HERR MAJOR...
HALTEN, DRIVER...YOU AND THE GUNNER WILL CLIMB OUT AFTER ME...

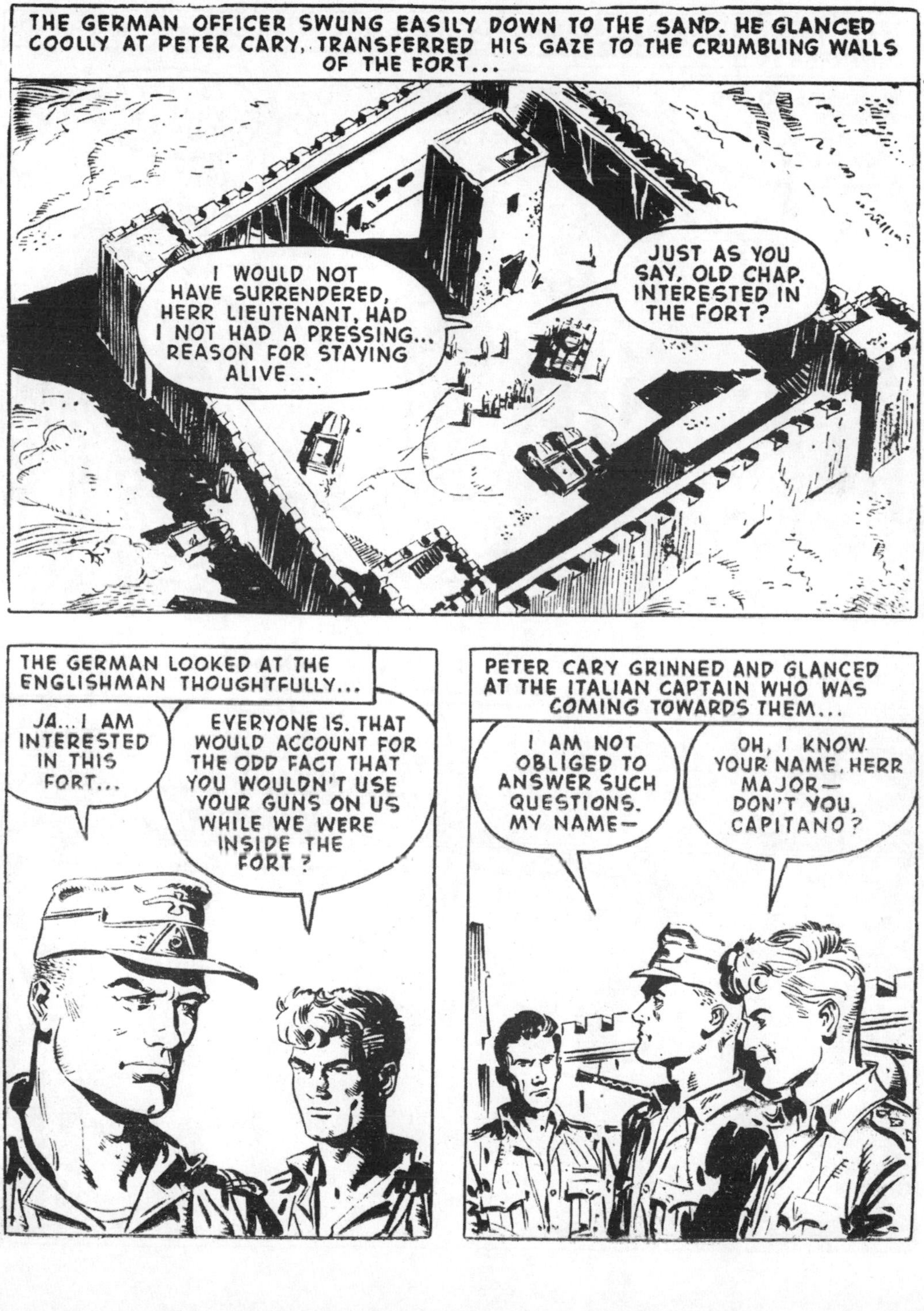
THE GERMAN OFFICER SWUNG EASILY DOWN TO THE SAND. HE GLANCED COOLLY AT PETER CARY, TRANSFERRED HIS GAZE TO THE CRUMBLING WALLS OF THE FORT...
I WOULD NOT HAVE SURRENDERED, HERR LIEUTENANT, HAD I NOT HAD A PRESSING... REASON FOR STAYING ALIVE...
JUST AS YOU SAY, OLD CHAP. INTERESTED IN THE FORT?
THE GERMAN LOOKED AT THE ENGLISHMAN THOUGHTFULLY...
JA... I AM INTERESTED IN THIS FORT...
EVERYONE IS. THAT WOULD ACCOUNT FOR THE ODD FACT THAT YOU WOULDN'T USE YOUR GUNS ON US WHILE WE WERE INSIDE THE FORT?
PETER CARY GRINNED AND GLANCED AT THE ITALIAN CAPTAIN WHO WAS COMING TOWARDS THEM...
I AM NOT OBLIGED TO ANSWER SUCH QUESTIONS. MY NAME—
OH, I KNOW YOUR NAME, HERR MAJOR— DON'T YOU, CAPITANO?

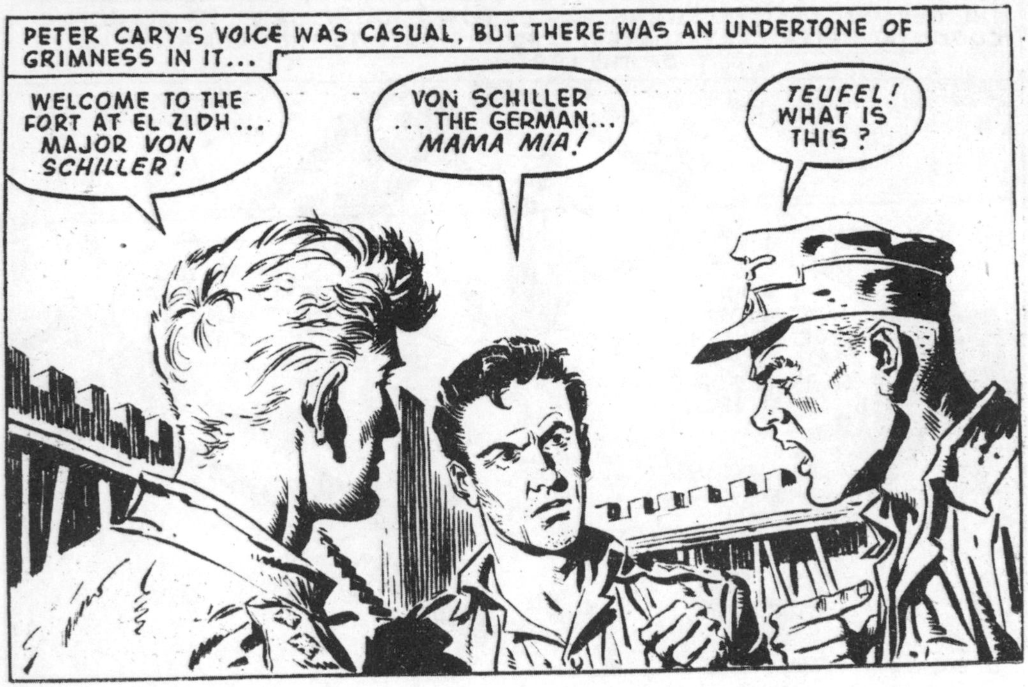
PETER CARY'S VOICE WAS CASUAL, BUT THERE WAS AN UNDERTONE OF GRIMNESS IN IT...
WELCOME TO THE FORT AT EL ZIDH... MAJOR VON SCHILLER!
VON SCHILLER ... THE GERMAN... MAMA MIA!
TEUFEL! WHAT IS THIS?

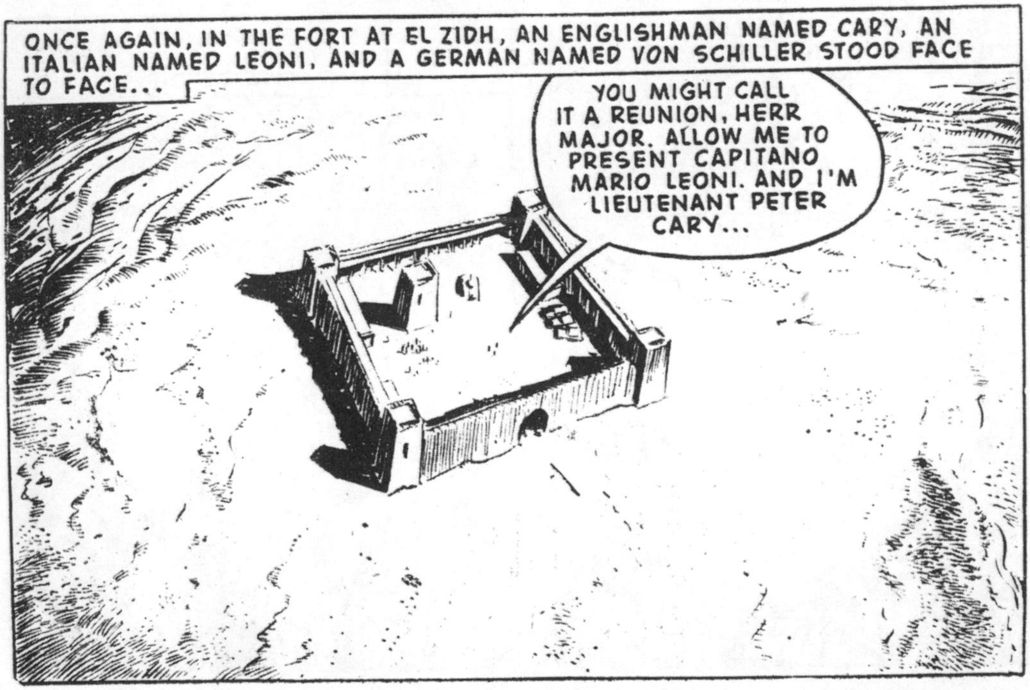
ONCE AGAIN, IN THE FORT AT EL ZIDH, AN ENGLISHMAN NAMED CARY, AN ITALIAN NAMED LEONI, AND A GERMAN NAMED VON SCHILLER STOOD FACE TO FACE...
YOU MIGHT CALL IT A REUNION, HERR MAJOR. ALLOW ME TO PRESENT CAPITANO MARIO LEONI. AND I'M LIEUTENANT PETER CARY...

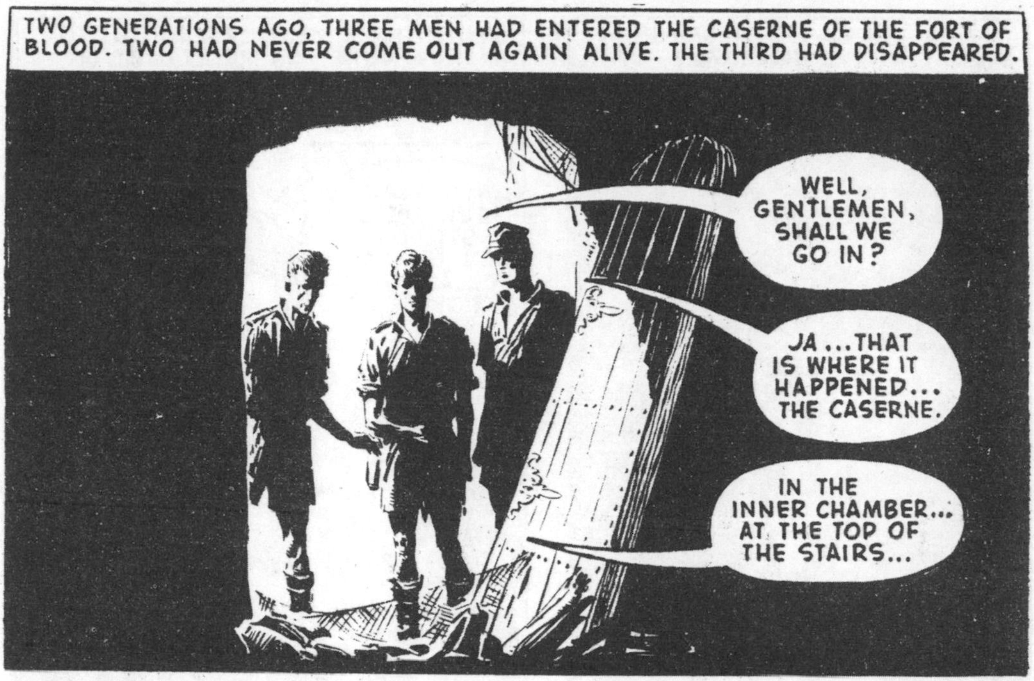
TWO GENERATIONS AGO, THREE MEN HAD ENTERED THE CASERNE OF THE FORT OF BLOOD. TWO HAD NEVER COME OUT AGAIN ALIVE. THE THIRD HAD DISAPPEARED.
WELL, GENTLEMEN, SHALL WE GO IN?
JA...THAT IS WHERE IT HAPPENED... THE CASERNE.
IN THE INNER CHAMBER... AT THE TOP OF THE STAIRS...

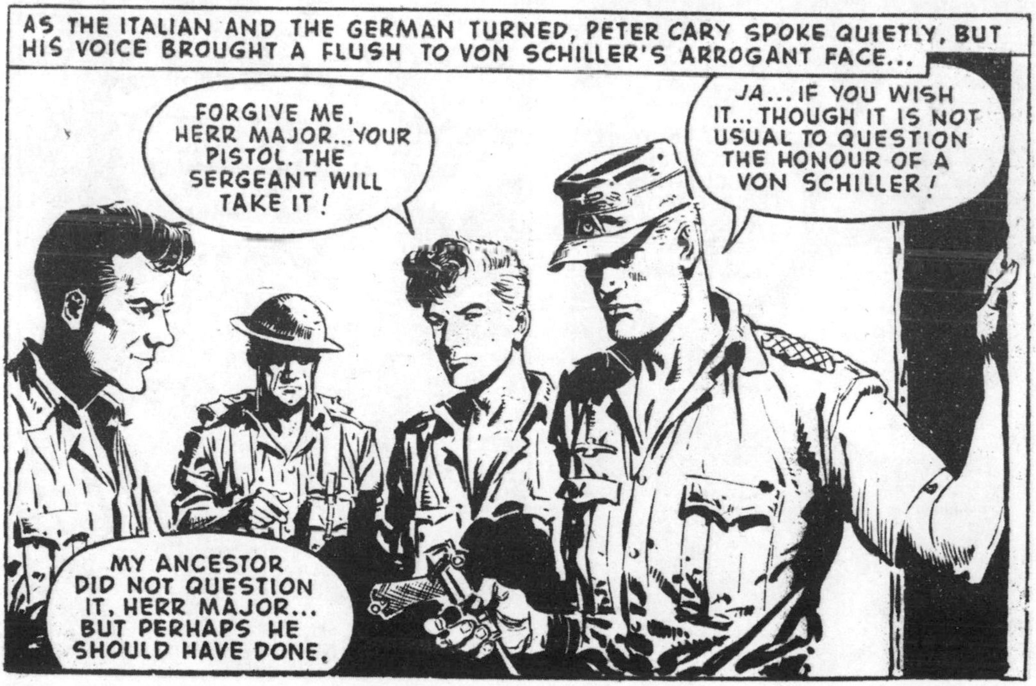
AS THE ITALIAN AND THE GERMAN TURNED, PETER CARY SPOKE QUIETLY, BUT HIS VOICE BROUGHT A FLUSH TO VON SCHILLER'S ARROGANT FACE...
FORGIVE ME, HERR MAJOR...YOUR PISTOL. THE SERGEANT WILL TAKE IT!
JA...IF YOU WISH IT...THOUGH IT IS NOT USUAL TO QUESTION THE HONOUR OF A VON SCHILLER!
MY ANCESTOR DID NOT QUESTION IT, HERR MAJOR... BUT PERHAPS HE SHOULD HAVE DONE.

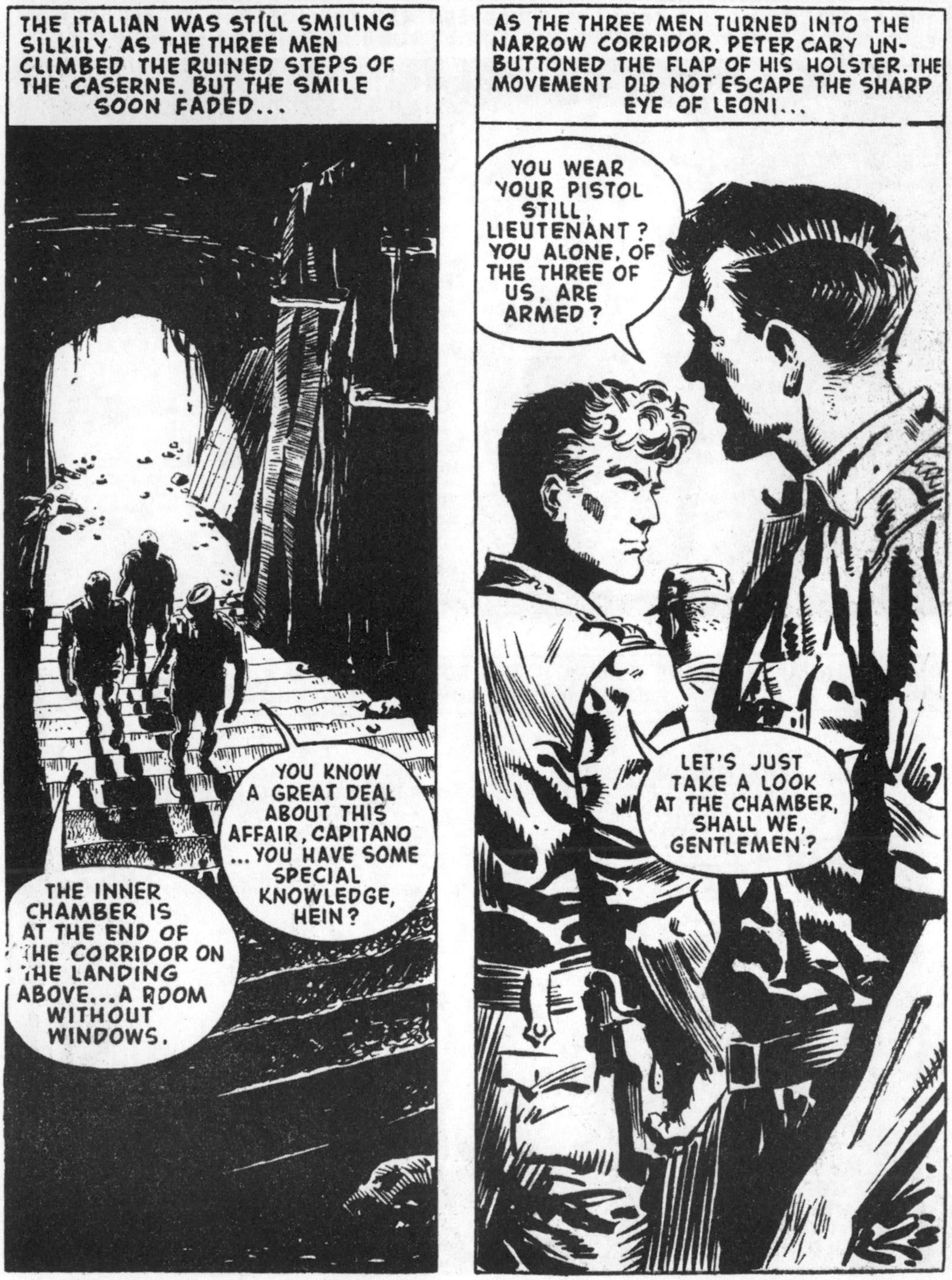
THE ITALIAN WAS STILL SMILING SILKILY AS THE THREE MEN CLIMBED THE RUINED STEPS OF THE CASERNE. BUT THE SMILE SOON FADED...
THE INNER CHAMBER IS AT THE END OF THE CORRIDOR ON THE LANDING ABOVE...A ROOM WITHOUT WINDOWS.
YOU KNOW A GREAT DEAL ABOUT THIS AFFAIR, CAPITANO ...YOU HAVE SOME SPECIAL KNOWLEDGE, HEIN?
AS THE THREE MEN TURNED INTO THE NARROW CORRIDOR, PETER CARY UNBUTTONED THE FLAP OF HIS HOLSTER. THE MOVEMENT DID NOT ESCAPE THE SHARP EYE OF LEONI...
YOU WEAR YOUR PISTOL STILL, LIEUTENANT? YOU ALONE, OF THE THREE OF US, ARE ARMED?
LET'S JUST TAKE A LOOK AT THE CHAMBER, SHALL WE, GENTLEMEN?

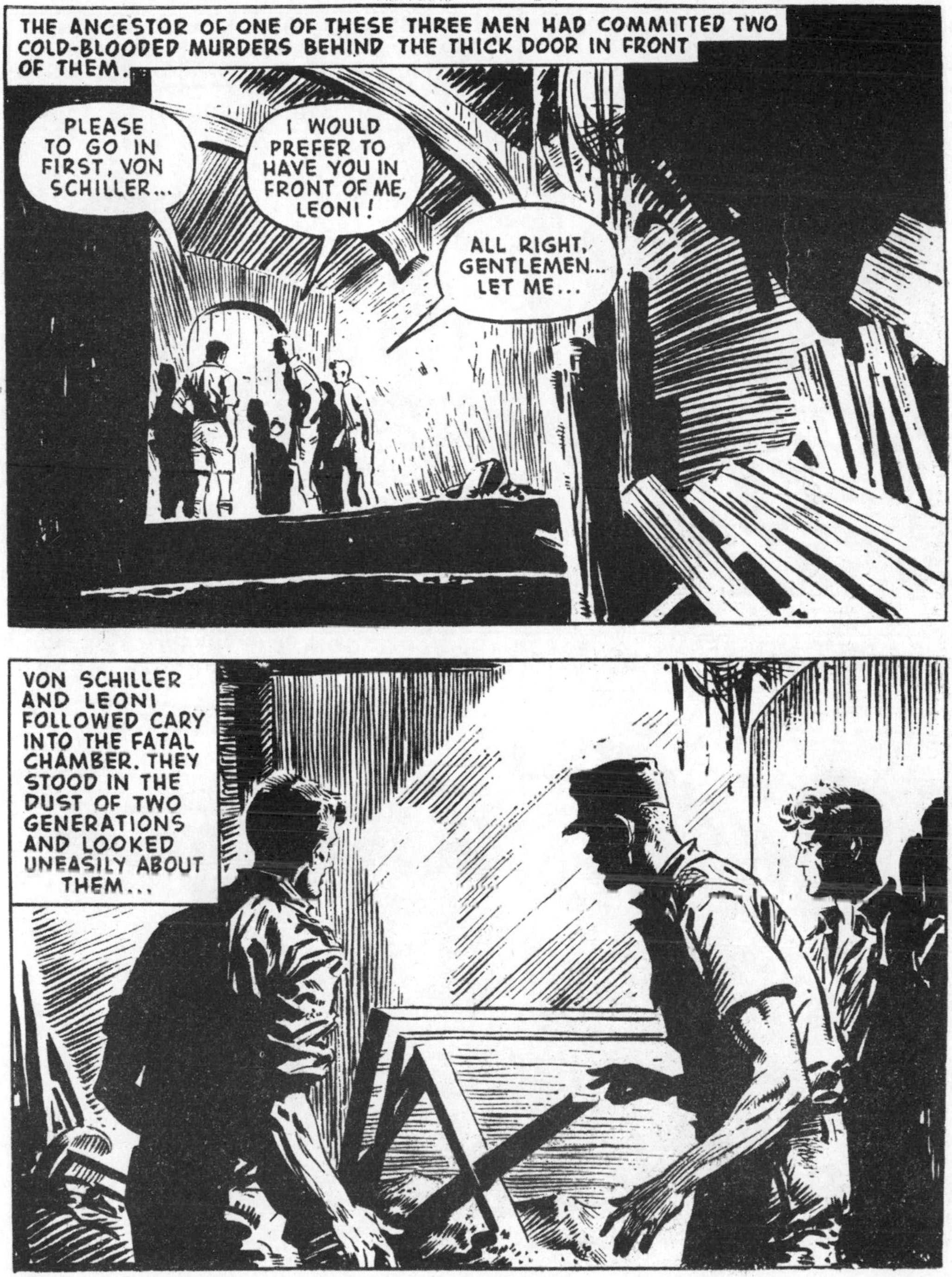
THE ANCESTOR OF ONE OF THESE THREE MEN HAD COMMITTED TWO COLD-BLOODED MURDERS BEHIND THE THICK DOOR IN FRONT OF THEM.
PLEASE TO GO IN FIRST, VON SCHILLER...
I WOULD PREFER TO HAVE YOU IN FRONT OF ME, LEONI!
ALL RIGHT, GENTLEMEN... LET ME...
VON SCHILLER AND LEONI FOLLOWED CARY INTO THE FATAL CHAMBER. THEY STOOD IN THE DUST OF TWO GENERATIONS AND LOOKED UNEASILY ABOUT THEM...

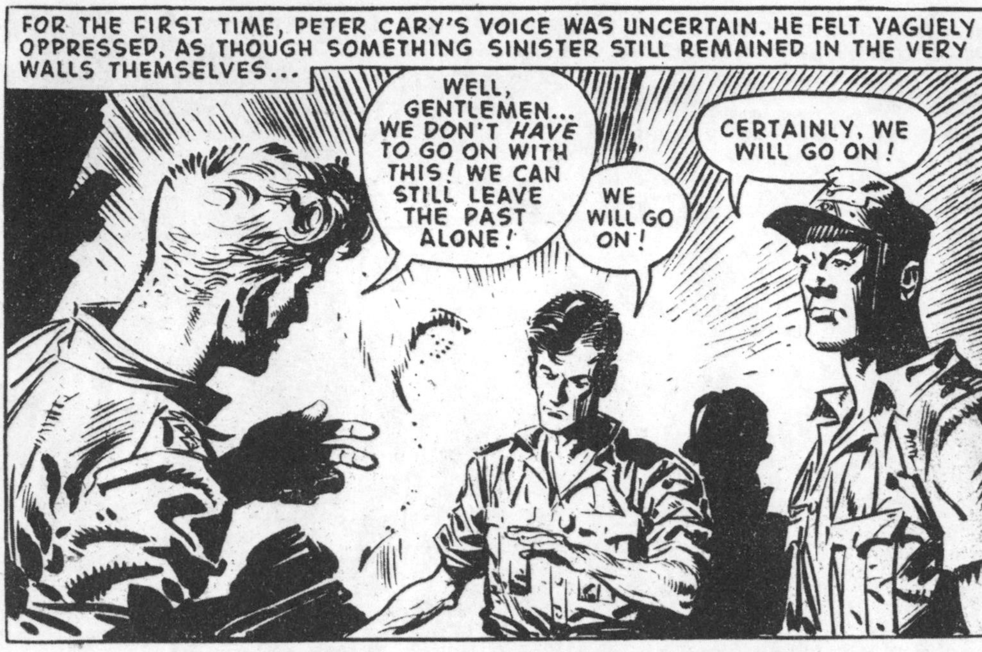
FOR THE FIRST TIME, PETER CARY'S VOICE WAS UNCERTAIN. HE FELT VAGUELY OPPRESSED, AS THOUGH SOMETHING SINISTER STILL REMAINED IN THE VERY WALLS THEMSELVES...
WELL, GENTLEMEN... WE DON'T *HAVE* TO GO ON WITH THIS! WE CAN STILL LEAVE THE PAST ALONE!
WE WILL GO ON!
CERTAINLY, WE WILL GO ON!

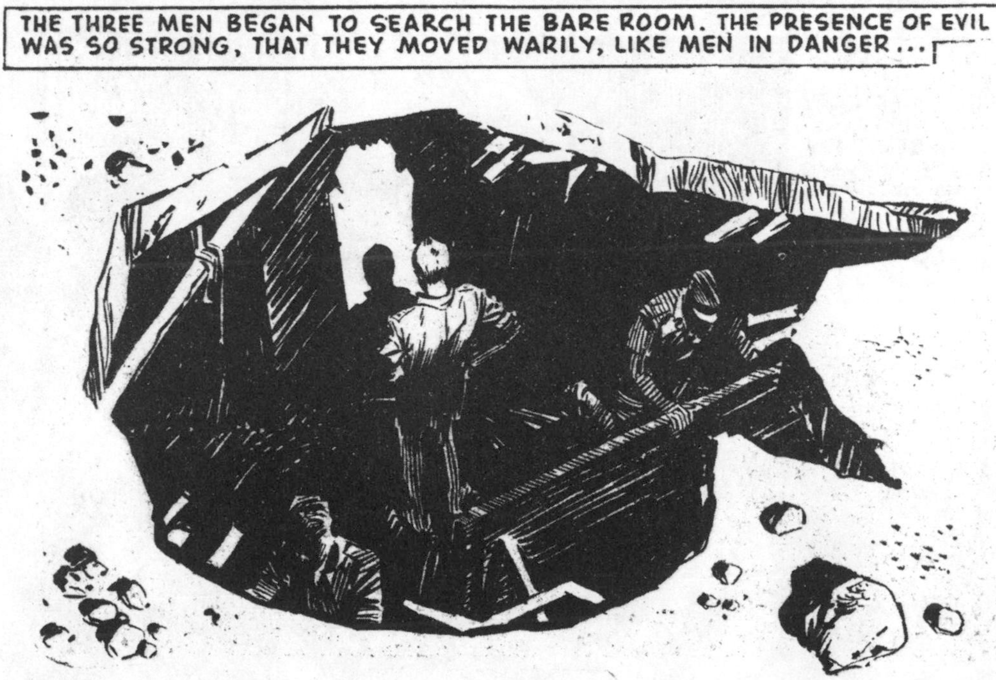
THE THREE MEN BEGAN TO SEARCH THE BARE ROOM. THE PRESENCE OF EVIL WAS SO STRONG, THAT THEY MOVED WARILY, LIKE MEN IN DANGER...

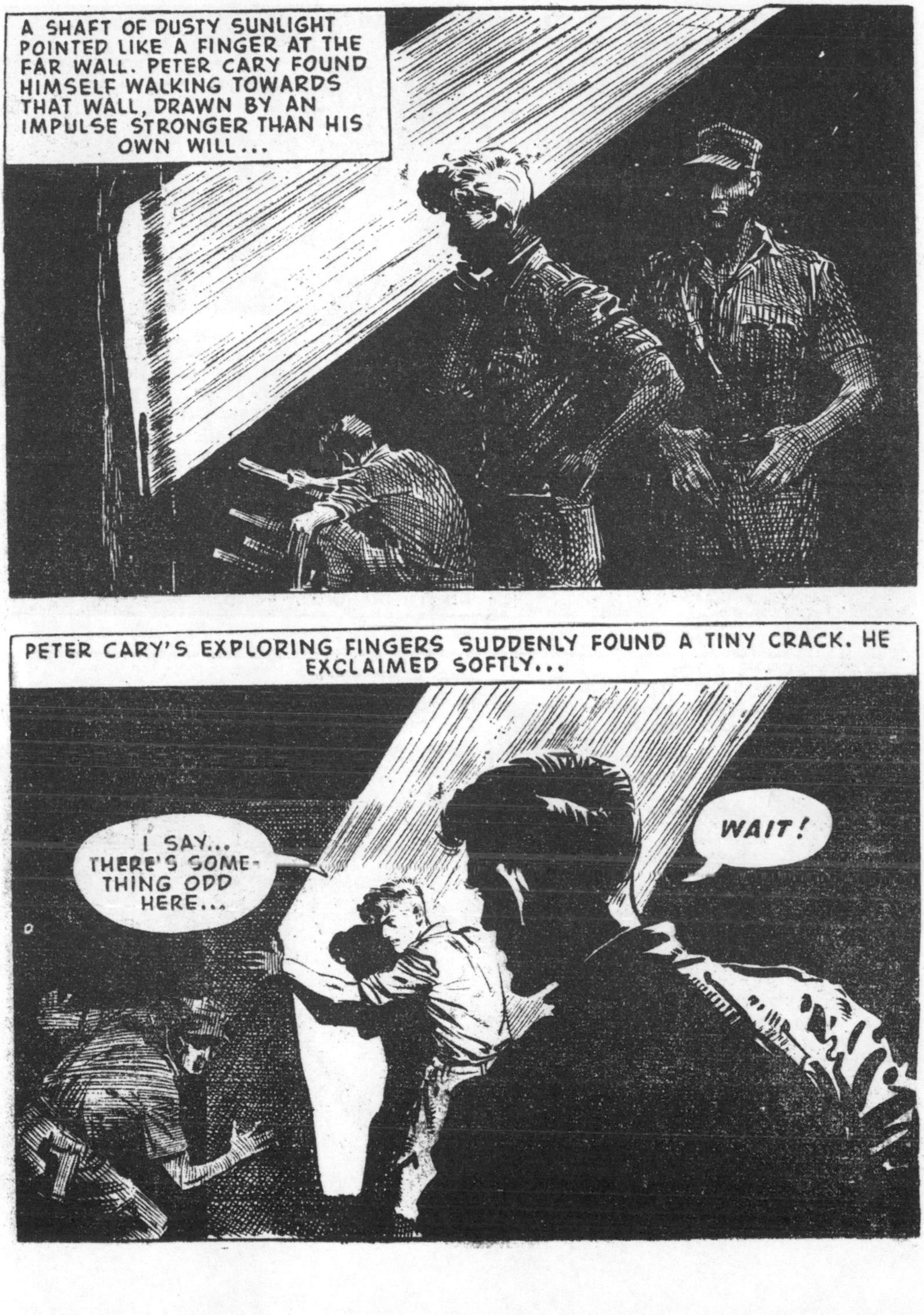
A SHAFT OF DUSTY SUNLIGHT POINTED LIKE A FINGER AT THE FAR WALL. PETER CARY FOUND HIMSELF WALKING TOWARDS THAT WALL, DRAWN BY AN IMPULSE STRONGER THAN HIS OWN WILL...
PETER CARY'S EXPLORING FINGERS SUDDENLY FOUND A TINY CRACK. HE EXCLAIMED SOFTLY...
I SAY... THERE'S SOMETHING ODD HERE...
WAIT!

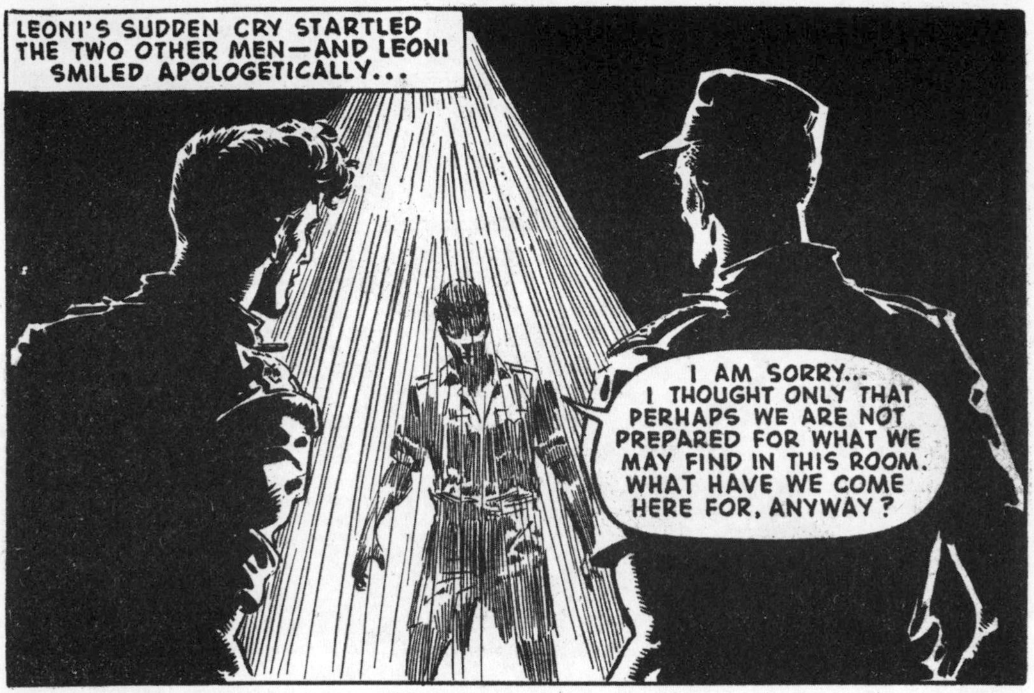
LEONI'S SUDDEN CRY STARTLED THE TWO OTHER MEN—AND LEONI SMILED APOLOGETICALLY...
I AM SORRY... I THOUGHT ONLY THAT PERHAPS WE ARE NOT PREPARED FOR WHAT WE MAY FIND IN THIS ROOM. WHAT HAVE WE COME HERE FOR, ANYWAY?

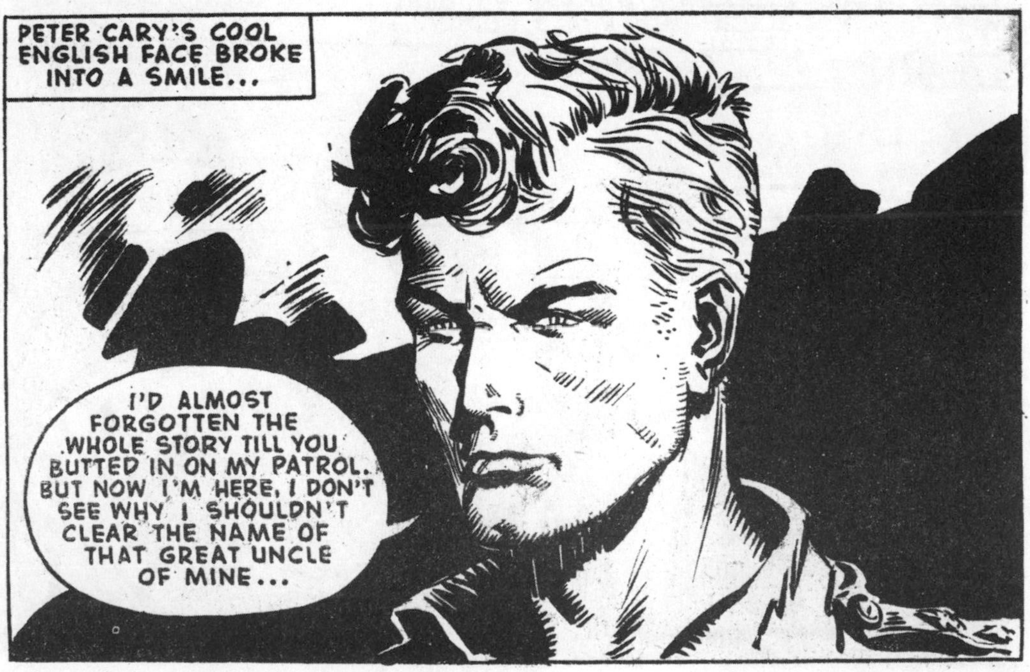
PETER CARY'S COOL ENGLISH FACE BROKE INTO A SMILE...
I'D ALMOST FORGOTTEN THE WHOLE STORY TILL YOU BUTTED IN ON MY PATROL. BUT NOW I'M HERE, I DON'T SEE WHY I SHOULDN'T CLEAR THE NAME OF THAT GREAT UNCLE OF MINE...

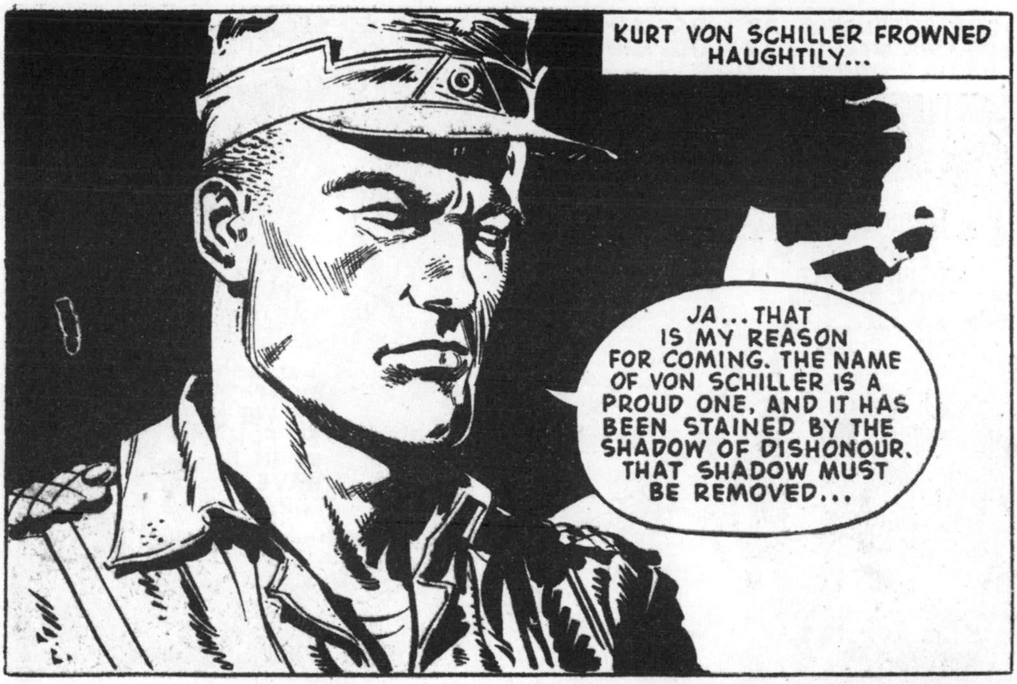
KURT VON SCHILLER FROWNED HAUGHTILY...
JA... THAT IS MY REASON FOR COMING. THE NAME OF VON SCHILLER IS A PROUD ONE, AND IT HAS BEEN STAINED BY THE SHADOW OF DISHONOUR. THAT SHADOW MUST BE REMOVED...

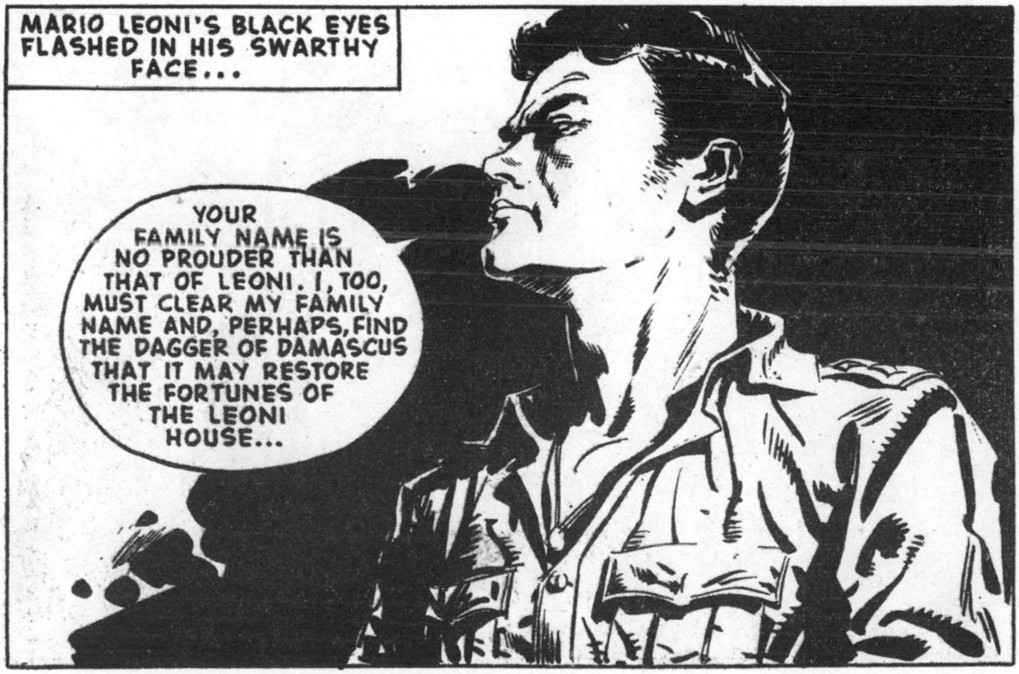
MARIO LEONI'S BLACK EYES FLASHED IN HIS SWARTHY FACE...
YOUR FAMILY NAME IS NO PROUDER THAN THAT OF LEONI. I, TOO, MUST CLEAR MY FAMILY NAME AND, PERHAPS, FIND THE DAGGER OF DAMASCUS THAT IT MAY RESTORE THE FORTUNES OF THE LEONI HOUSE...

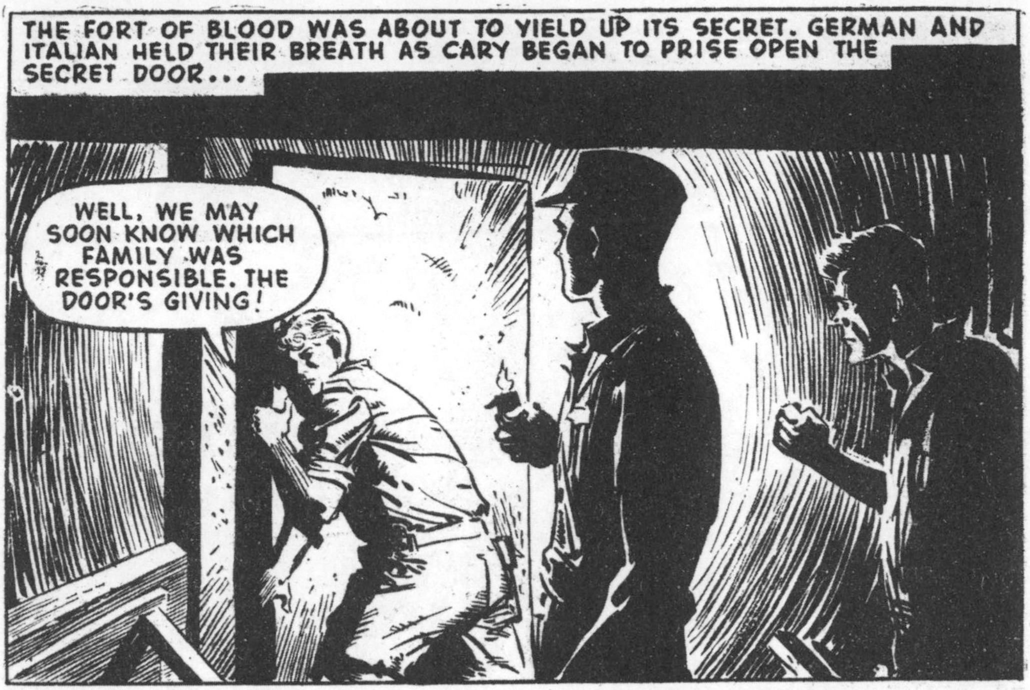
THE FORT OF BLOOD WAS ABOUT TO YIELD UP ITS SECRET. GERMAN AND ITALIAN HELD THEIR BREATH AS CARY BEGAN TO PRISE OPEN THE SECRET DOOR...
WELL, WE MAY SOON KNOW WHICH FAMILY WAS RESPONSIBLE. THE DOOR'S GIVING!

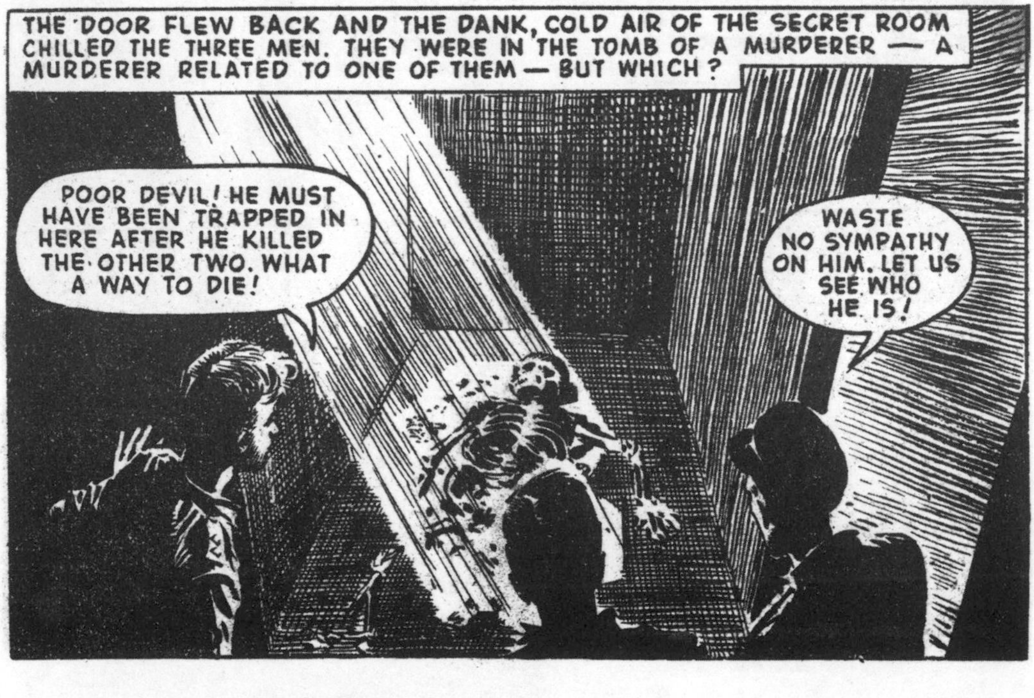
THE DOOR FLEW BACK AND THE DANK, COLD AIR OF THE SECRET ROOM CHILLED THE THREE MEN. THEY WERE IN THE TOMB OF A MURDERER — A MURDERER RELATED TO ONE OF THEM — BUT WHICH?
POOR DEVIL! HE MUST HAVE BEEN TRAPPED IN HERE AFTER HE KILLED THE OTHER TWO. WHAT A WAY TO DIE!
WASTE NO SYMPATHY ON HIM. LET US SEE WHO HE IS!

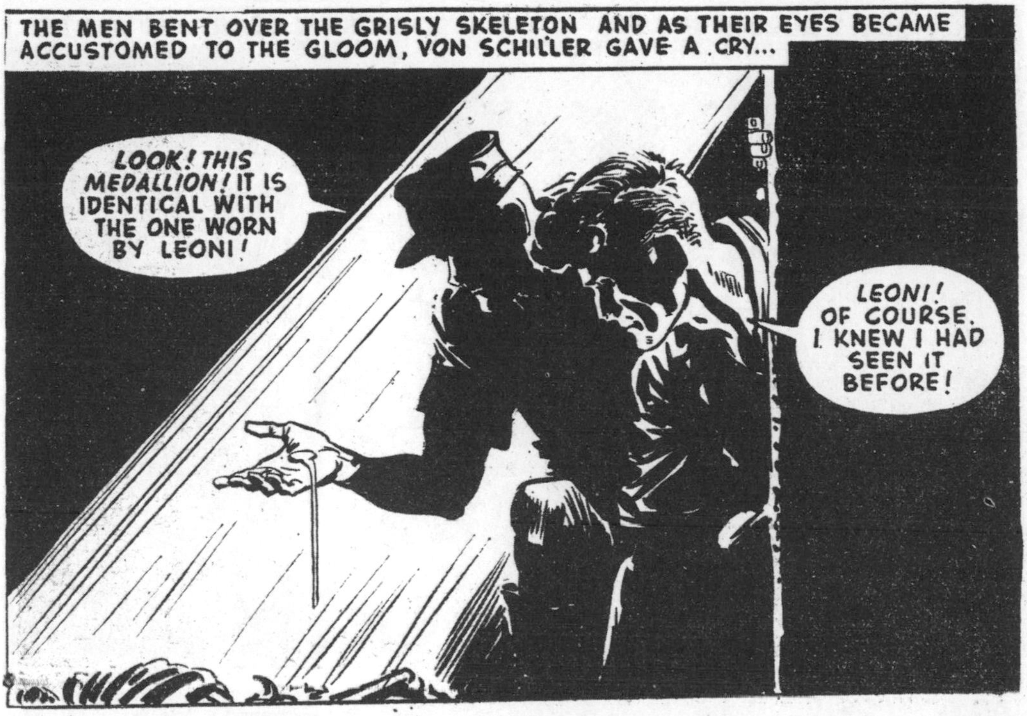
THE MEN BENT OVER THE GRISLY SKELETON AND AS THEIR EYES BECAME ACCUSTOMED TO THE GLOOM, VON SCHILLER GAVE A CRY...
LOOK! THIS MEDALLION! IT IS IDENTICAL WITH THE ONE WORN BY LEONI!
LEONI! OF COURSE. I KNEW I HAD SEEN IT BEFORE!

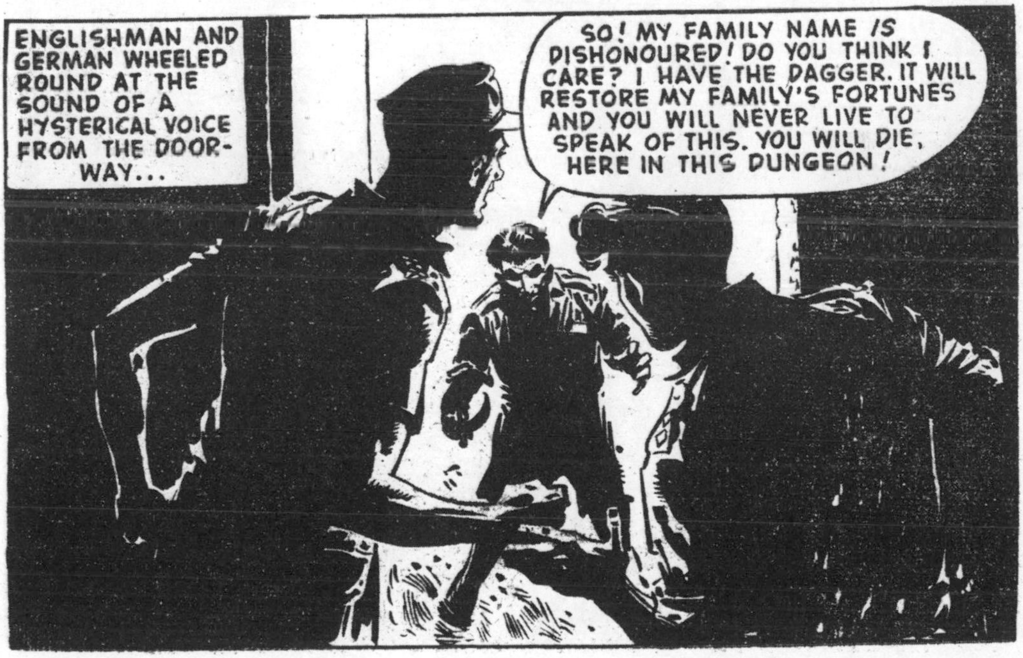
ENGLISHMAN AND GERMAN WHEELED ROUND AT THE SOUND OF A HYSTERICAL VOICE FROM THE DOOR-WAY...
SO! MY FAMILY NAME IS DISHONOURED! DO YOU THINK I CARE? I HAVE THE DAGGER. IT WILL RESTORE MY FAMILY'S FORTUNES AND YOU WILL NEVER LIVE TO SPEAK OF THIS. YOU WILL DIE, HERE IN THIS DUNGEON!

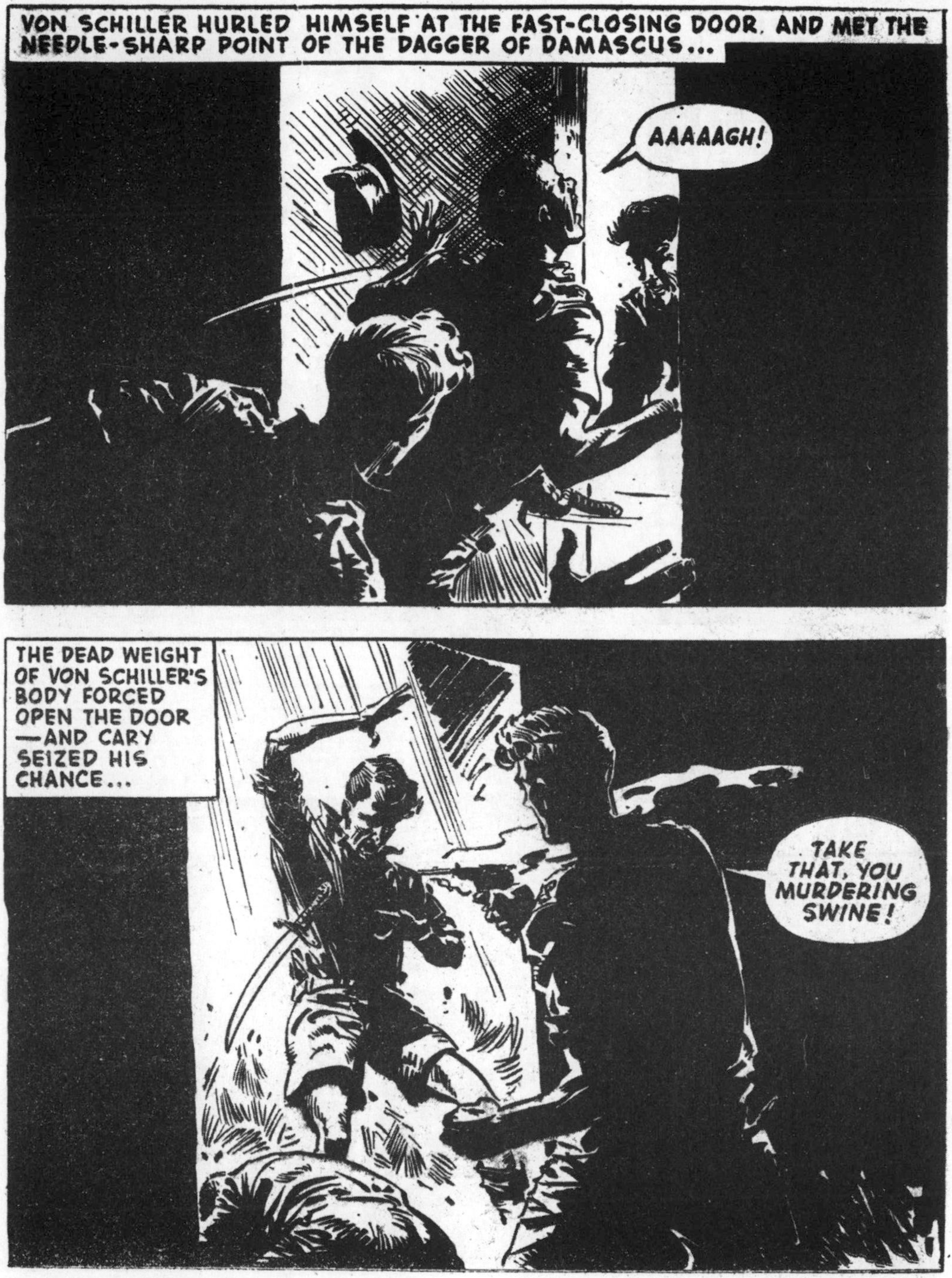
VON SCHILLER HURLED HIMSELF AT THE FAST-CLOSING DOOR. AND MET THE NEEDLE-SHARP POINT OF THE DAGGER OF DAMASCUS...
AAAAAGH!
THE DEAD WEIGHT OF VON SCHILLER'S BODY FORCED OPEN THE DOOR —AND CARY SEIZED HIS CHANCE...
TAKE THAT, YOU MURDERING SWINE!

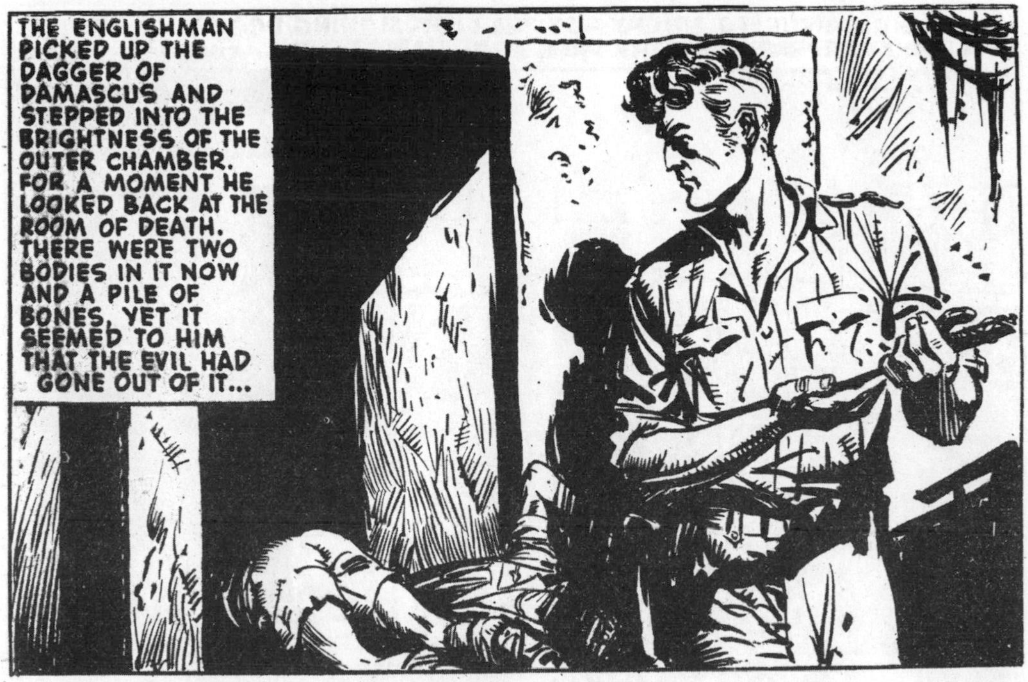
THE ENGLISHMAN PICKED UP THE DAGGER OF DAMASCUS AND STEPPED INTO THE BRIGHTNESS OF THE OUTER CHAMBER. FOR A MOMENT HE LOOKED BACK AT THE ROOM OF DEATH. THERE WERE TWO BODIES IN IT NOW AND A PILE OF BONES, YET IT SEEMED TO HIM THAT THE EVIL HAD GONE OUT OF IT...

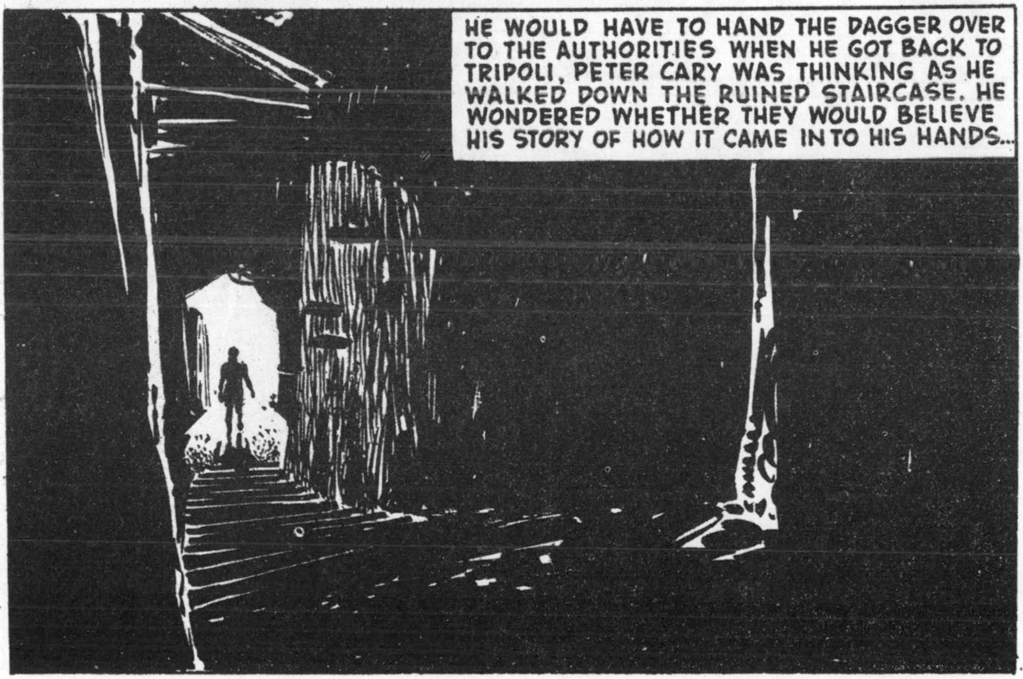
HE WOULD HAVE TO HAND THE DAGGER OVER TO THE AUTHORITIES WHEN HE GOT BACK TO TRIPOLI, PETER CARY WAS THINKING AS HE WALKED DOWN THE RUINED STAIRCASE. HE WONDERED WHETHER THEY WOULD BELIEVE HIS STORY OF HOW IT CAME IN TO HIS HANDS...

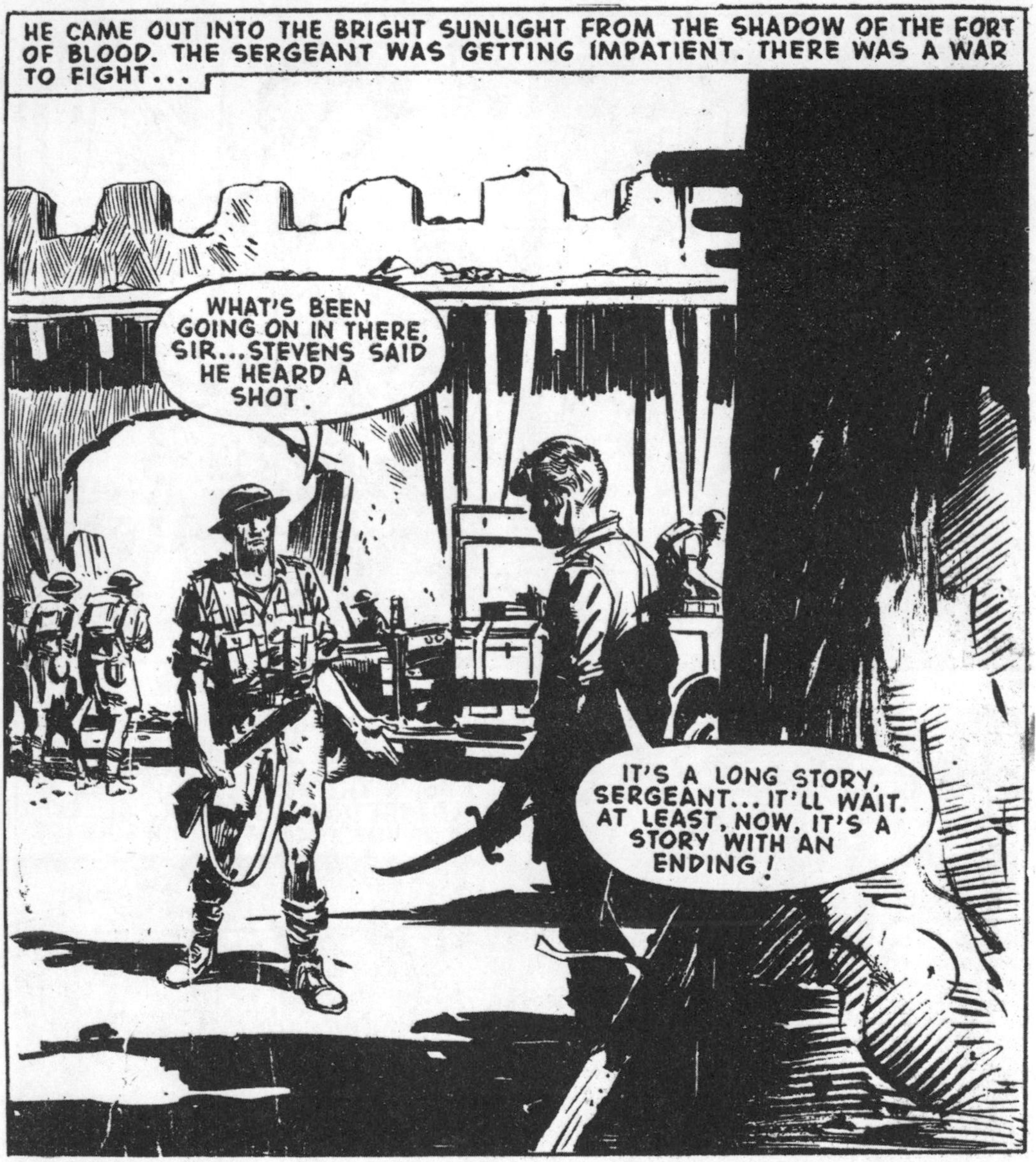
HE CAME OUT INTO THE BRIGHT SUNLIGHT FROM THE SHADOW OF THE FORT OF BLOOD. THE SERGEANT WAS GETTING IMPATIENT. THERE WAS A WAR TO FIGHT...
WHAT'S BEEN GOING ON IN THERE, SIR...STEVENS SAID HE HEARD A SHOT.
IT'S A LONG STORY, SERGEANT... IT'LL WAIT. AT LEAST, NOW, IT'S A STORY WITH AN ENDING!

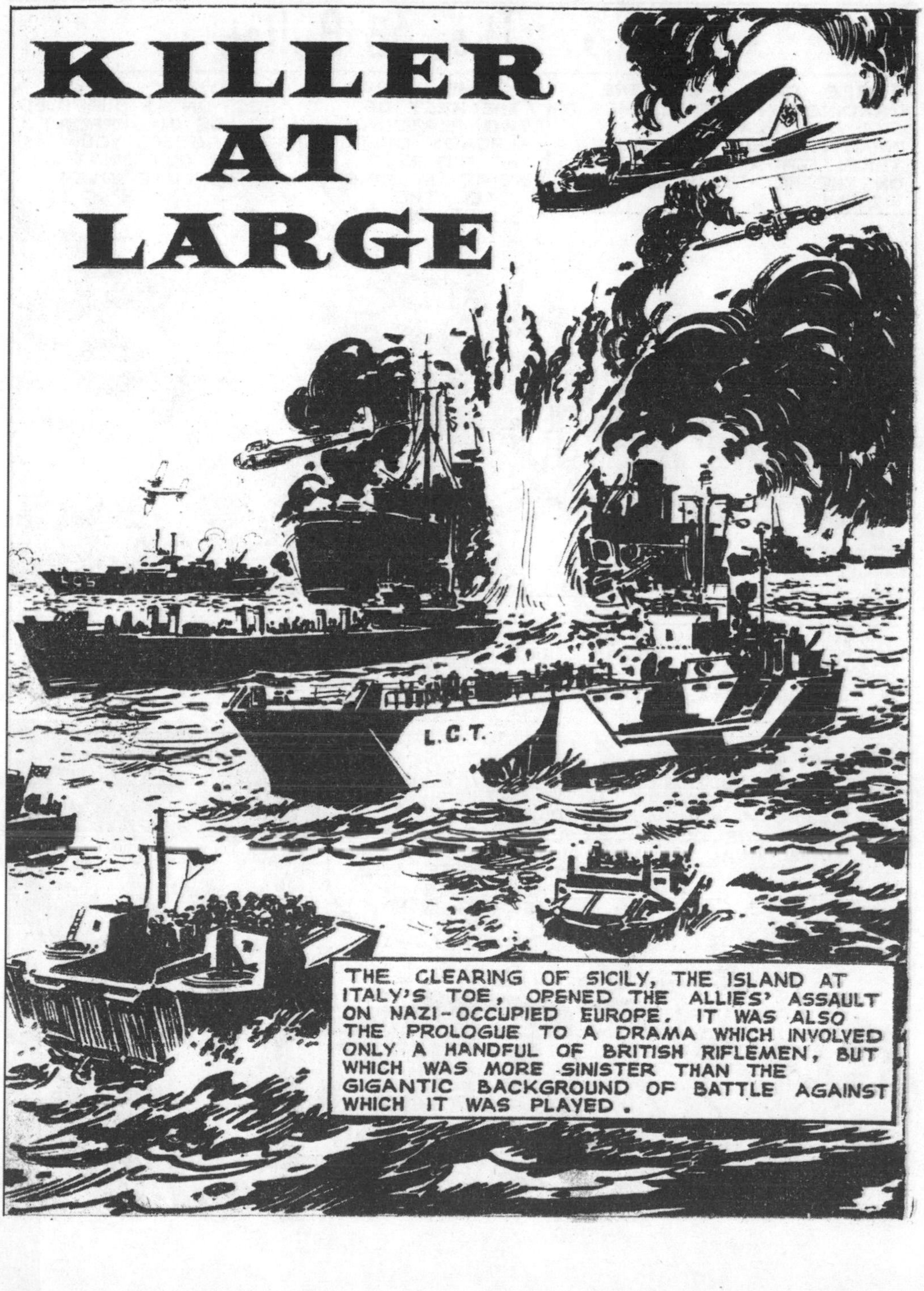
KILLER AT LARGE
L.C.T.
THE CLEARING OF SICILY, THE ISLAND AT ITALY'S TOE, OPENED THE ALLIES' ASSAULT ON NAZI-OCCUPIED EUROPE. IT WAS ALSO THE PROLOGUE TO A DRAMA WHICH INVOLVED ONLY A HANDFUL OF BRITISH RIFLEMEN, BUT WHICH WAS MORE SINISTER THAN THE GIGANTIC BACKGROUND OF BATTLE AGAINST WHICH IT WAS PLAYED.

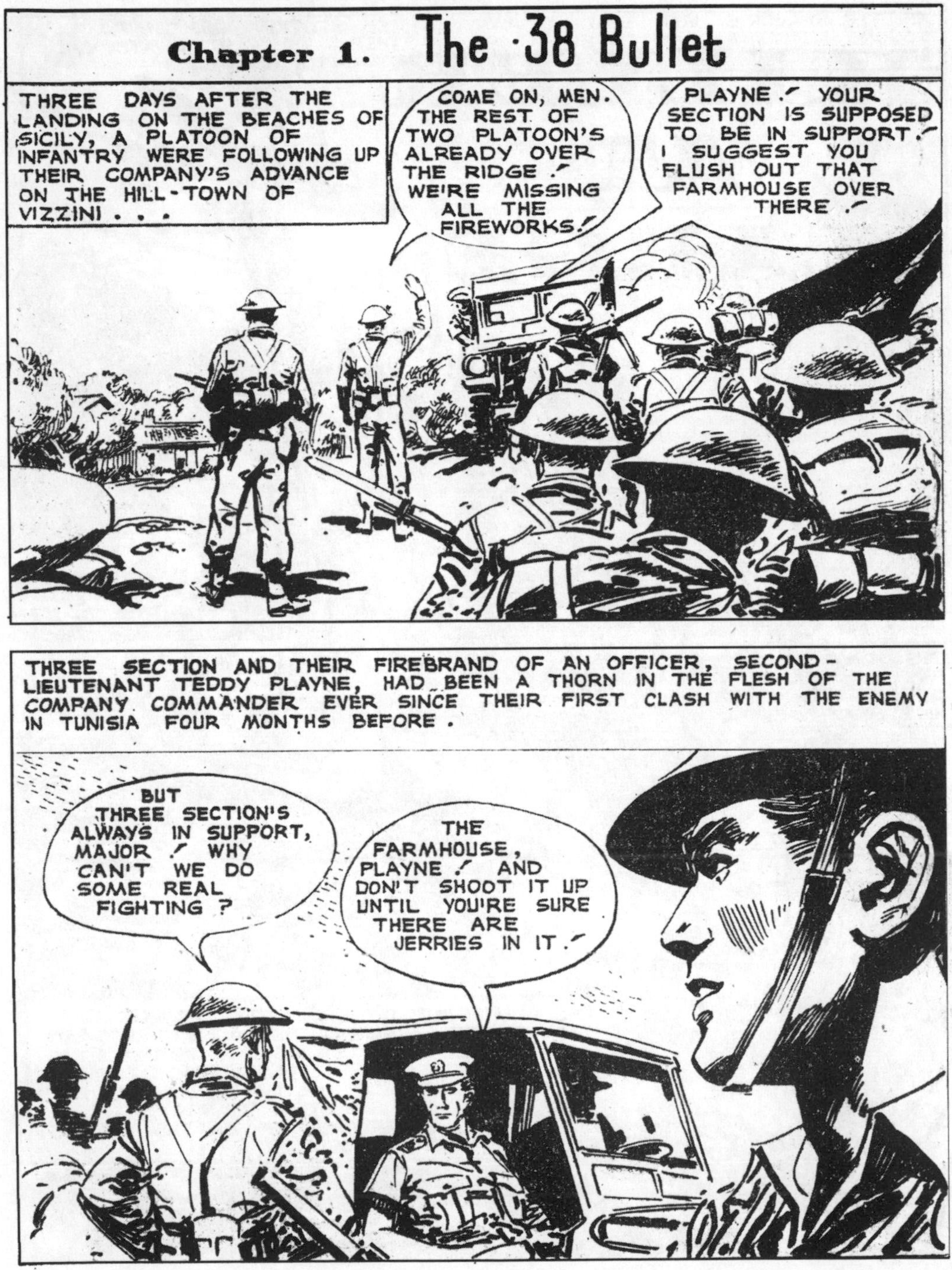
Chapter 1. The ·38 Bullet
THREE DAYS AFTER THE LANDING ON THE BEACHES OF SICILY, A PLATOON OF INFANTRY WERE FOLLOWING UP THEIR COMPANY'S ADVANCE ON THE HILL-TOWN OF VIZZINI . . .
COME ON, MEN. THE REST OF TWO PLATOON'S ALREADY OVER THE RIDGE! WE'RE MISSING ALL THE FIREWORKS!
PLAYNE! YOUR SECTION IS SUPPOSED TO BE IN SUPPORT! I SUGGEST YOU FLUSH OUT THAT FARMHOUSE OVER THERE!
THREE SECTION AND THEIR FIREBRAND OF AN OFFICER, SECOND-LIEUTENANT TEDDY PLAYNE, HAD BEEN A THORN IN THE FLESH OF THE COMPANY COMMANDER EVER SINCE THEIR FIRST CLASH WITH THE ENEMY IN TUNISIA FOUR MONTHS BEFORE.
BUT THREE SECTION'S ALWAYS IN SUPPORT, MAJOR! WHY CAN'T WE DO SOME REAL FIGHTING?
THE FARMHOUSE, PLAYNE! AND DON'T SHOOT IT UP UNTIL YOU'RE SURE THERE ARE JERRIES IN IT!

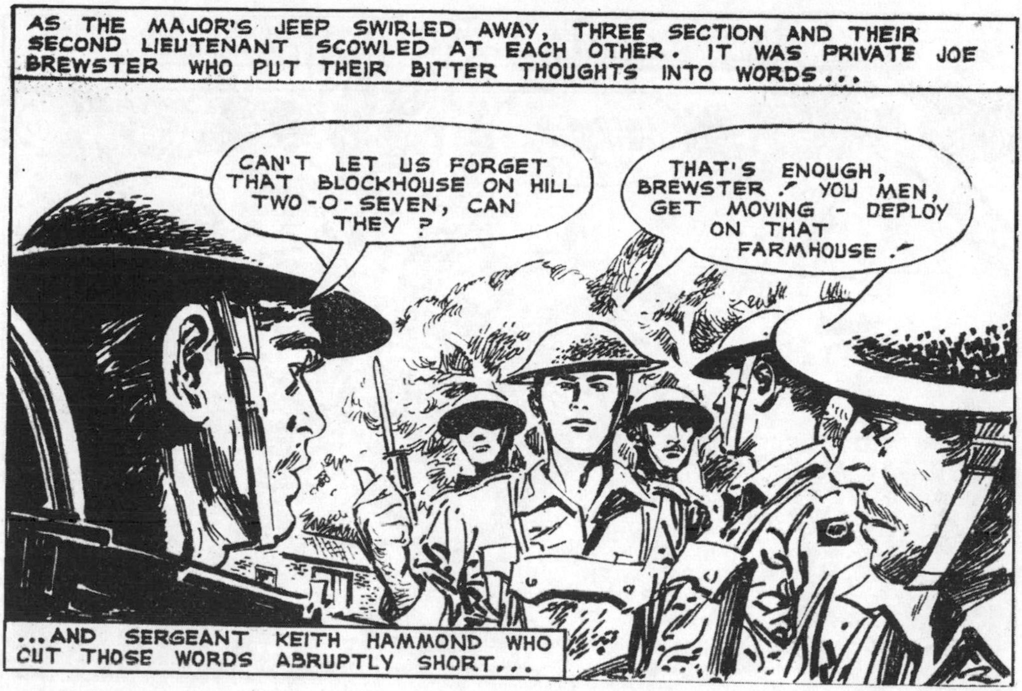
AS THE MAJOR'S JEEP SWIRLED AWAY, THREE SECTION AND THEIR SECOND LIEUTENANT SCOWLED AT EACH OTHER. IT WAS PRIVATE JOE BREWSTER WHO PUT THEIR BITTER THOUGHTS INTO WORDS...
CAN'T LET US FORGET THAT BLOCKHOUSE ON HILL TWO-O-SEVEN, CAN THEY ?
THAT'S ENOUGH, BREWSTER ! YOU MEN, GET MOVING - DEPLOY ON THAT FARMHOUSE !
...AND SERGEANT KEITH HAMMOND WHO CUT THOSE WORDS ABRUPTLY SHORT...

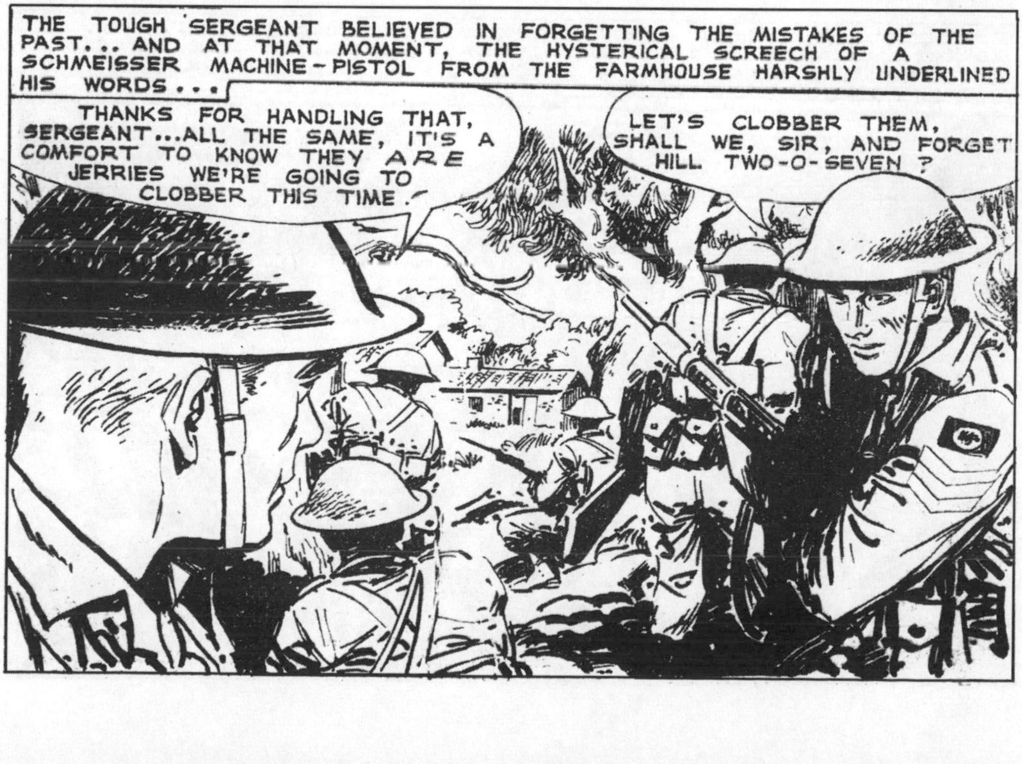
THE TOUGH SERGEANT BELIEVED IN FORGETTING THE MISTAKES OF THE PAST... AND AT THAT MOMENT, THE HYSTERICAL SCREECH OF A SCHMEISSER MACHINE-PISTOL FROM THE FARMHOUSE HARSHLY UNDERLINED HIS WORDS...
THANKS FOR HANDLING THAT, SERGEANT...ALL THE SAME, IT'S A COMFORT TO KNOW THEY ARE JERRIES WE'RE GOING TO CLOBBER THIS TIME !
LET'S CLOBBER THEM, SHALL WE, SIR, AND FORGET HILL TWO-O-SEVEN ?

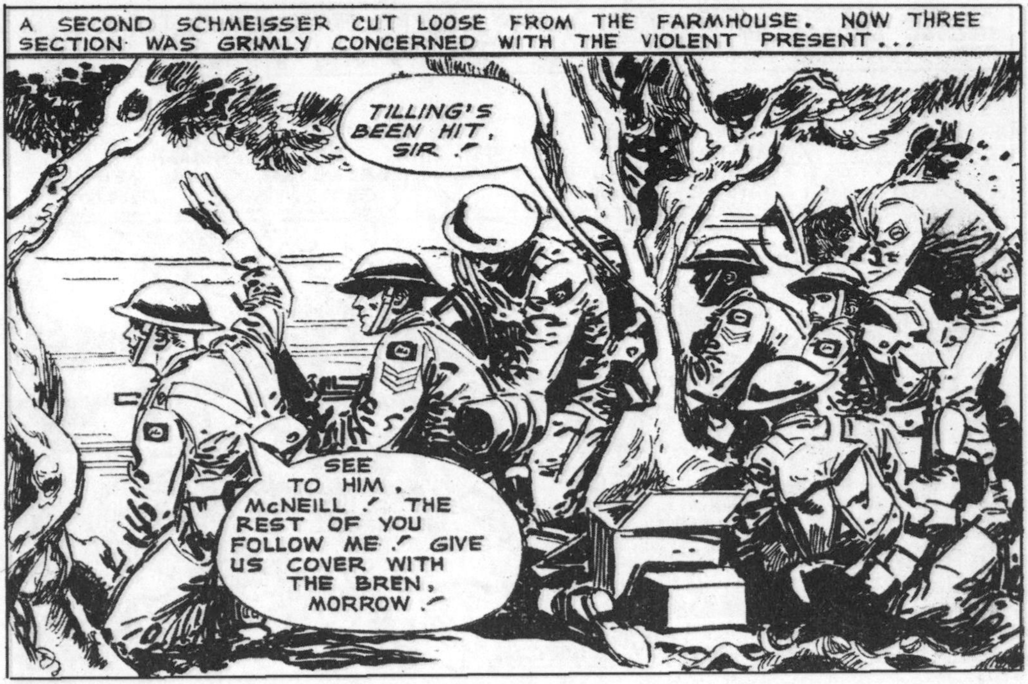
A SECOND SCHMEISSER CUT LOOSE FROM THE FARMHOUSE. NOW THREE SECTION WAS GRIMLY CONCERNED WITH THE VIOLENT PRESENT...
TILLING'S BEEN HIT, SIR!
SEE TO HIM, McNEILL! THE REST OF YOU FOLLOW ME! GIVE US COVER WITH THE BREN, MORROW!

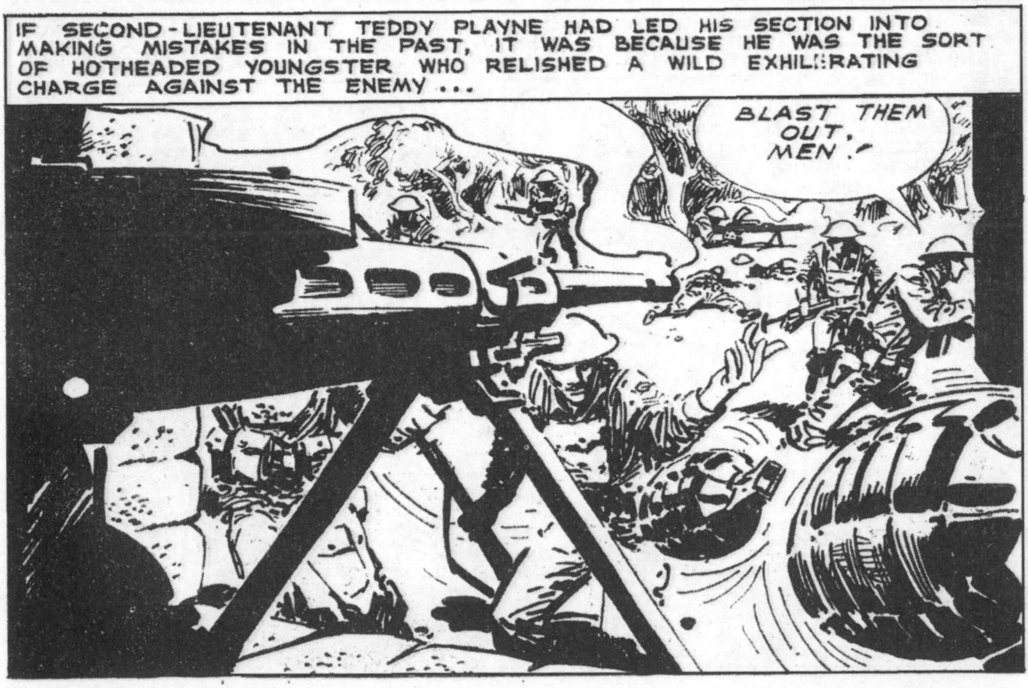
IF SECOND-LIEUTENANT TEDDY PLAYNE HAD LED HIS SECTION INTO MAKING MISTAKES IN THE PAST, IT WAS BECAUSE HE WAS THE SORT OF HOTHEADED YOUNGSTER WHO RELISHED A WILD EXHILARATING CHARGE AGAINST THE ENEMY...
BLAST THEM OUT, MEN!

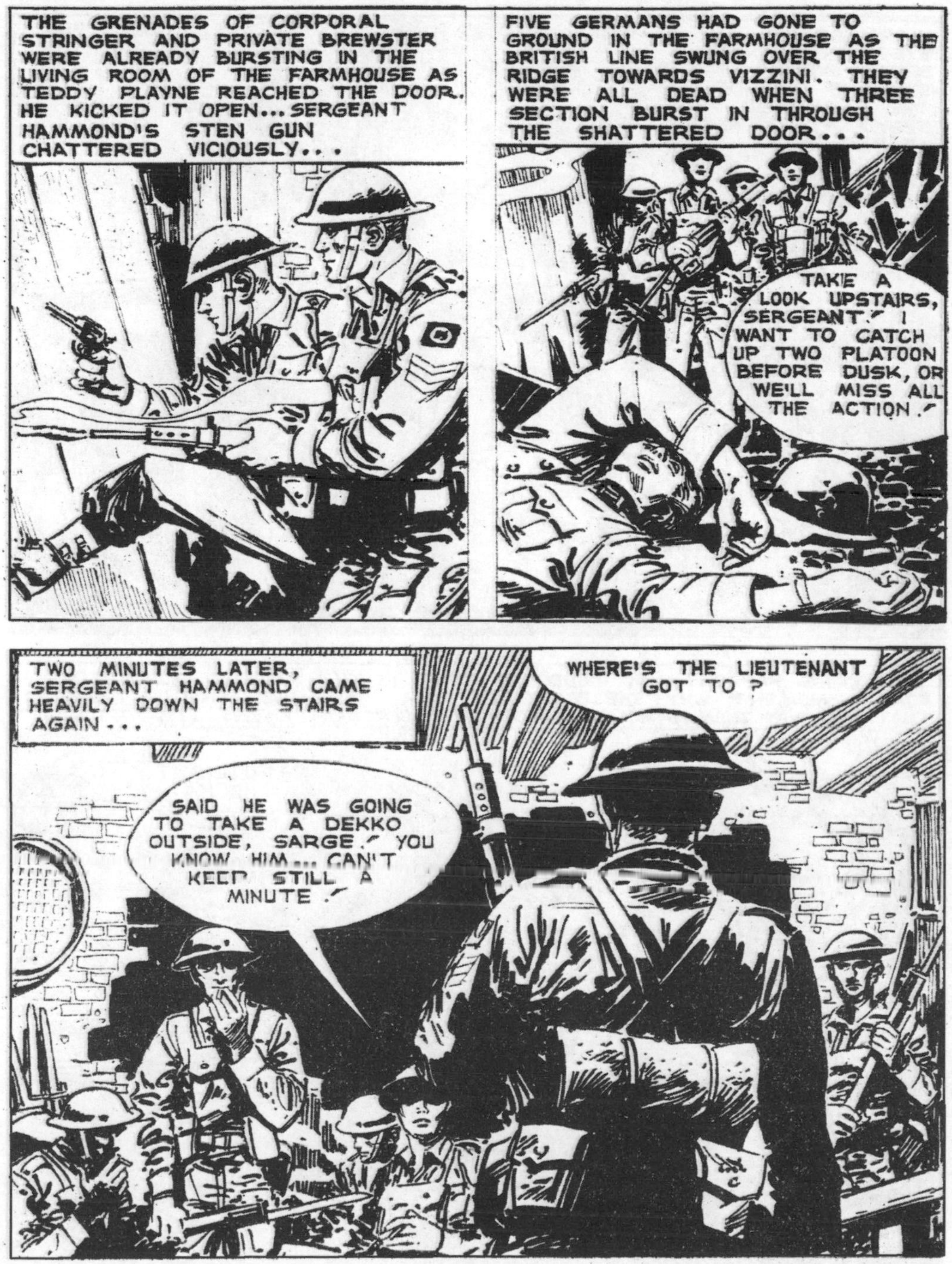
THE GRENADES OF CORPORAL STRINGER AND PRIVATE BREWSTER WERE ALREADY BURSTING IN THE LIVING ROOM OF THE FARMHOUSE AS TEDDY PLAYNE REACHED THE DOOR. HE KICKED IT OPEN... SERGEANT HAMMOND'S STEN GUN CHATTERED VICIOUSLY...
FIVE GERMANS HAD GONE TO GROUND IN THE FARMHOUSE AS THE BRITISH LINE SWUNG OVER THE RIDGE TOWARDS VIZZINI. THEY WERE ALL DEAD WHEN THREE SECTION BURST IN THROUGH THE SHATTERED DOOR...
TAKE A LOOK UPSTAIRS, SERGEANT! I WANT TO CATCH UP TWO PLATOON BEFORE DUSK, OR WE'LL MISS ALL THE ACTION!
TWO MINUTES LATER, SERGEANT HAMMOND CAME HEAVILY DOWN THE STAIRS AGAIN...
WHERE'S THE LIEUTENANT GOT TO?
SAID HE WAS GOING TO TAKE A DEKKO OUTSIDE, SARGE! YOU KNOW HIM... CAN'T KEEP 'M STILL A MINUTE!

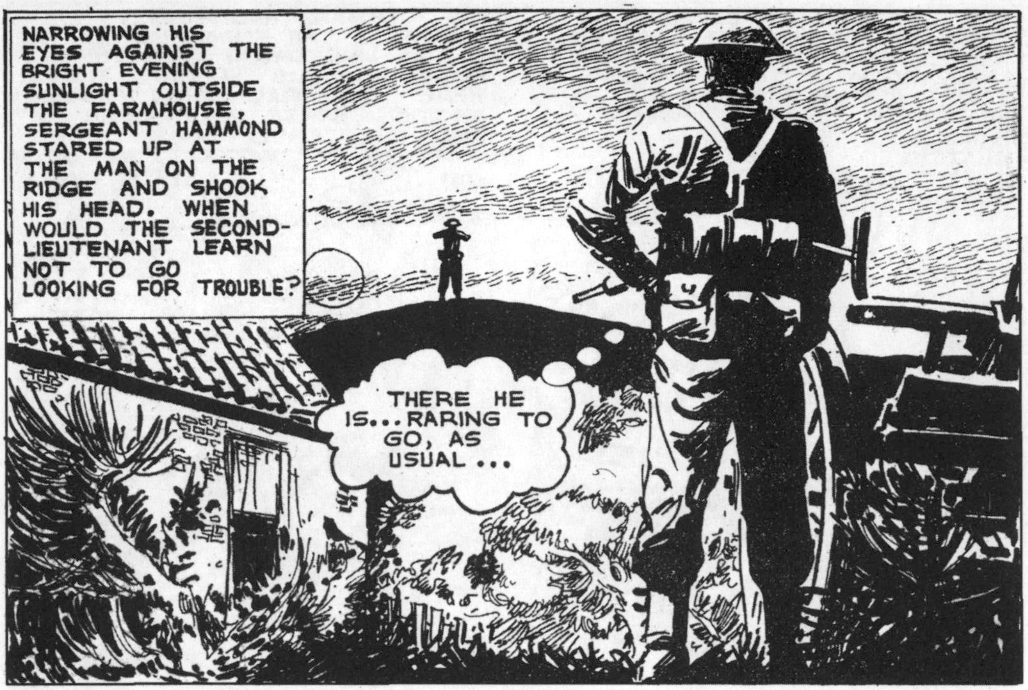
NARROWING HIS EYES AGAINST THE BRIGHT EVENING SUNLIGHT OUTSIDE THE FARMHOUSE, SERGEANT HAMMOND STARED UP AT THE MAN ON THE RIDGE AND SHOOK HIS HEAD. WHEN WOULD THE SECOND-LIEUTENANT LEARN NOT TO GO LOOKING FOR TROUBLE?
THERE HE IS... RARING TO GO, AS USUAL ...

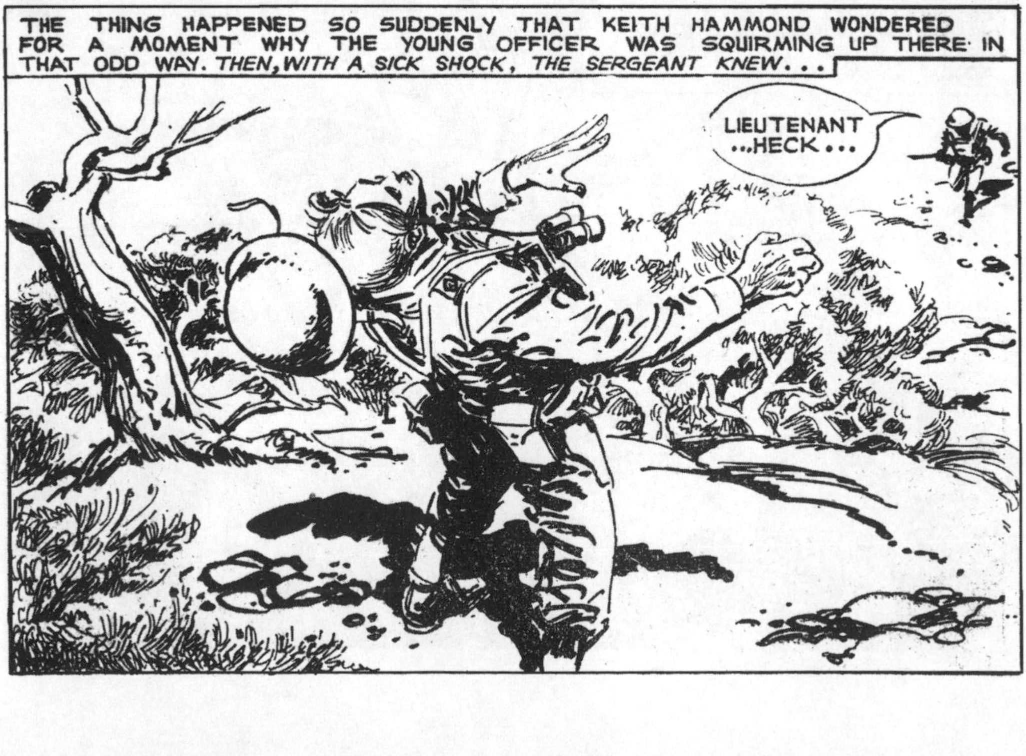
THE THING HAPPENED SO SUDDENLY THAT KEITH HAMMOND WONDERED FOR A MOMENT WHY THE YOUNG OFFICER WAS SQUIRMING UP THERE IN THAT ODD WAY. THEN, WITH A SICK SHOCK, THE SERGEANT KNEW...
LIEUTENANT ...HECK...

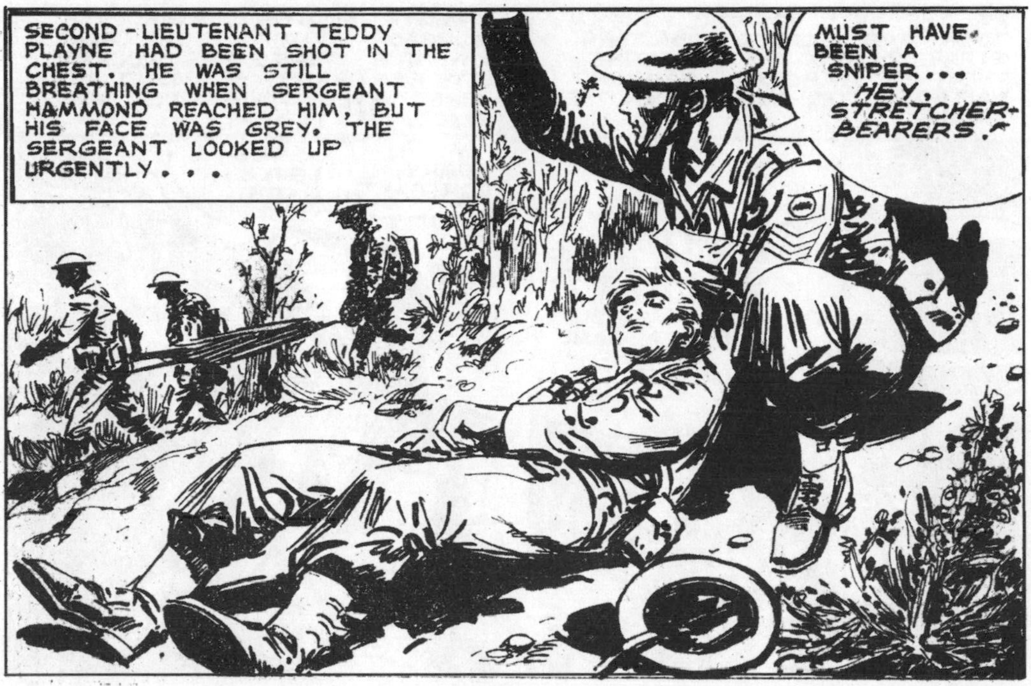
SECOND-LIEUTENANT TEDDY PLAYNE HAD BEEN SHOT IN THE CHEST. HE WAS STILL BREATHING WHEN SERGEANT HAMMOND REACHED HIM, BUT HIS FACE WAS GREY. THE SERGEANT LOOKED UP URGENTLY . . .
MUST HAVE BEEN A SNIPER... HEY, STRETCHER-BEARERS!

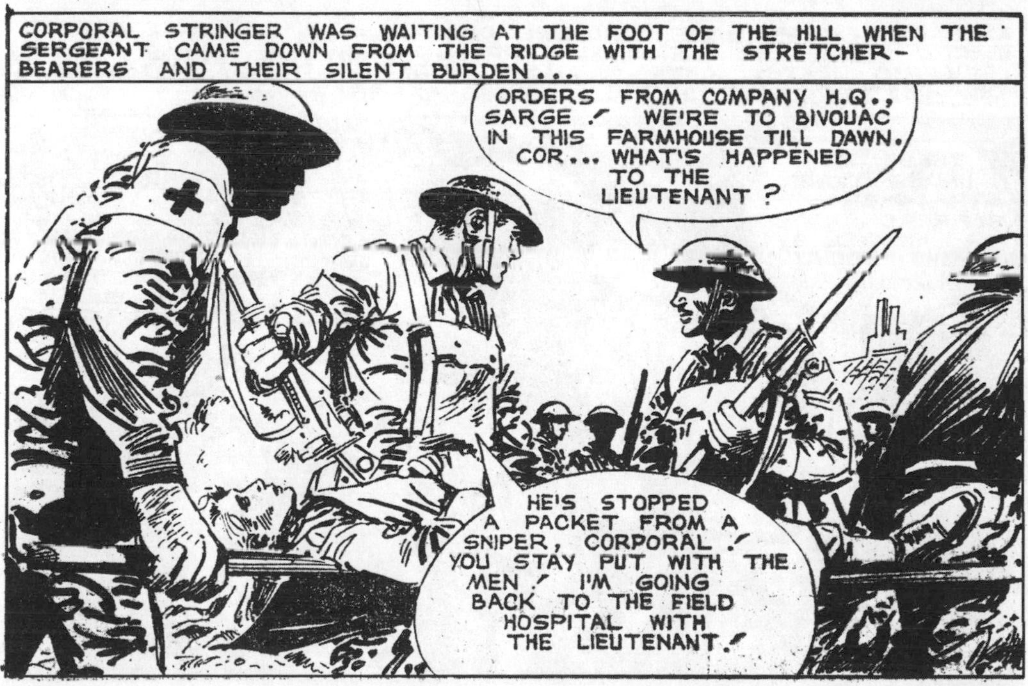
CORPORAL STRINGER WAS WAITING AT THE FOOT OF THE HILL WHEN THE SERGEANT CAME DOWN FROM THE RIDGE WITH THE STRETCHER-BEARERS AND THEIR SILENT BURDEN...
ORDERS FROM COMPANY H.Q., SARGE! WE'RE TO BIVOUAC IN THIS FARMHOUSE TILL DAWN. COR... WHAT'S HAPPENED TO THE LIEUTENANT?
HE'S STOPPED A PACKET FROM A SNIPER, CORPORAL! YOU STAY PUT WITH THE MEN! I'M GOING BACK TO THE FIELD HOSPITAL WITH THE LIEUTENANT!

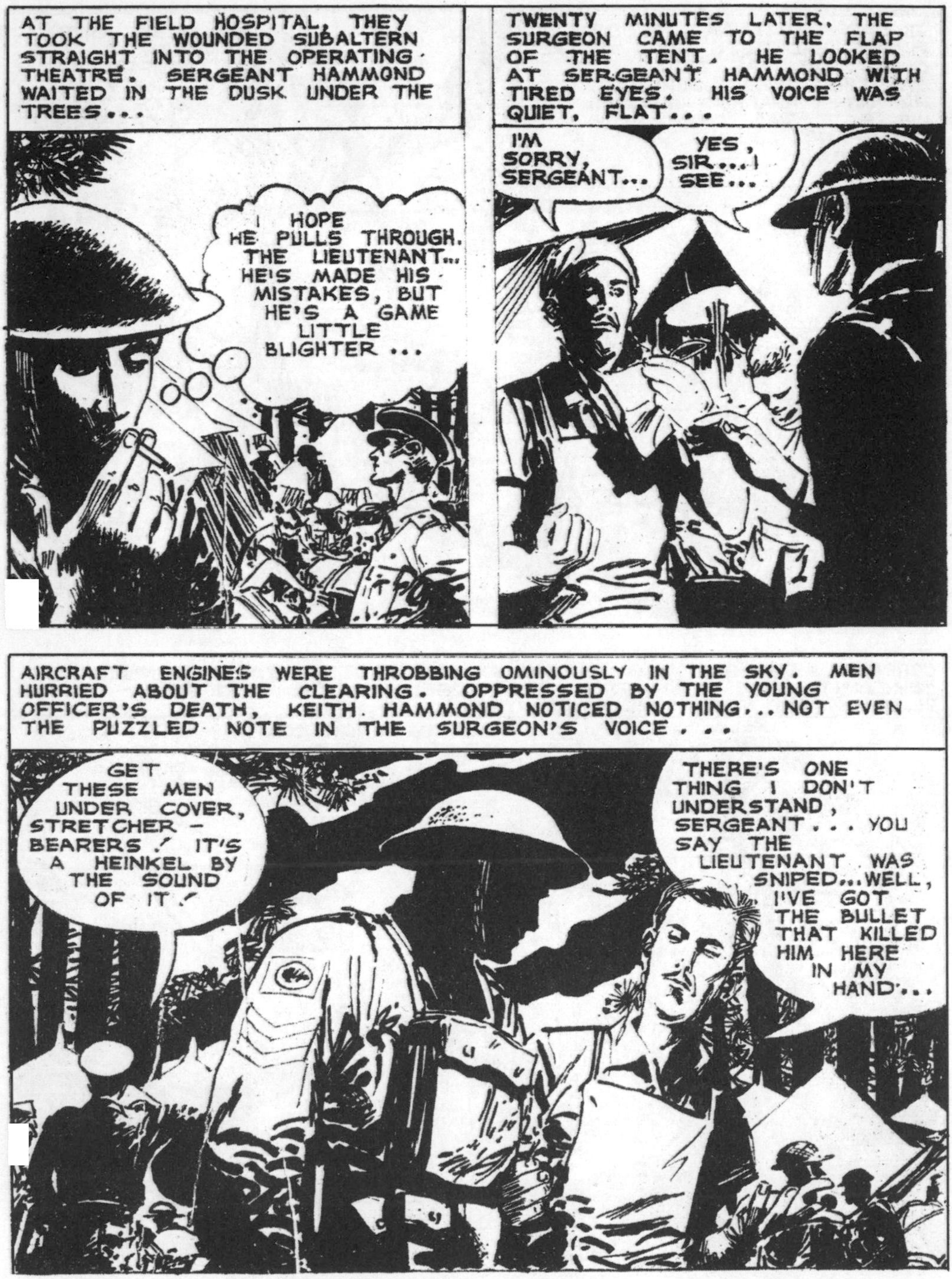
AT THE FIELD HOSPITAL, THEY TOOK THE WOUNDED SUBALTERN STRAIGHT INTO THE OPERATING THEATRE. SERGEANT HAMMOND WAITED IN THE DUSK UNDER THE TREES...
I HOPE HE PULLS THROUGH. THE LIEUTENANT... HE'S MADE HIS MISTAKES, BUT HE'S A GAME LITTLE BLIGHTER ...
TWENTY MINUTES LATER, THE SURGEON CAME TO THE FLAP OF THE TENT. HE LOOKED AT SERGEANT HAMMOND WITH TIRED EYES. HIS VOICE WAS QUIET, FLAT...
I'M SORRY, SERGEANT...
YES, SIR... I SEE...
AIRCRAFT ENGINES WERE THROBBING OMINOUSLY IN THE SKY. MEN HURRIED ABOUT THE CLEARING. OPPRESSED BY THE YOUNG OFFICER'S DEATH, KEITH HAMMOND NOTICED NOTHING... NOT EVEN THE PUZZLED NOTE IN THE SURGEON'S VOICE...
GET THESE MEN UNDER COVER, STRETCHER-BEARERS! IT'S A HEINKEL BY THE SOUND OF IT!
THERE'S ONE THING I DON'T UNDERSTAND, SERGEANT... YOU SAY THE LIEUTENANT WAS SNIPED... WELL, I'VE GOT THE BULLET THAT KILLED HIM HERE IN MY HAND...

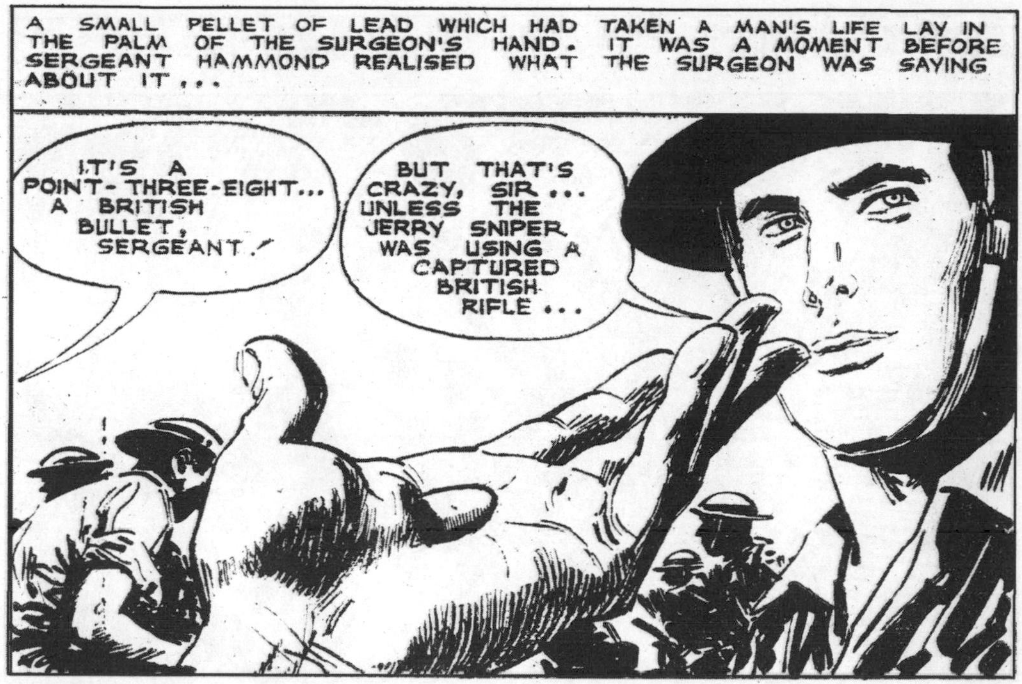
A SMALL PELLET OF LEAD WHICH HAD TAKEN A MAN'S LIFE LAY IN THE PALM OF THE SURGEON'S HAND. IT WAS A MOMENT BEFORE SERGEANT HAMMOND REALISED WHAT THE SURGEON WAS SAYING ABOUT IT...
IT'S A POINT-THREE-EIGHT... A BRITISH BULLET, SERGEANT!
BUT THAT'S CRAZY, SIR... UNLESS THE JERRY SNIPER WAS USING A CAPTURED BRITISH RIFLE...

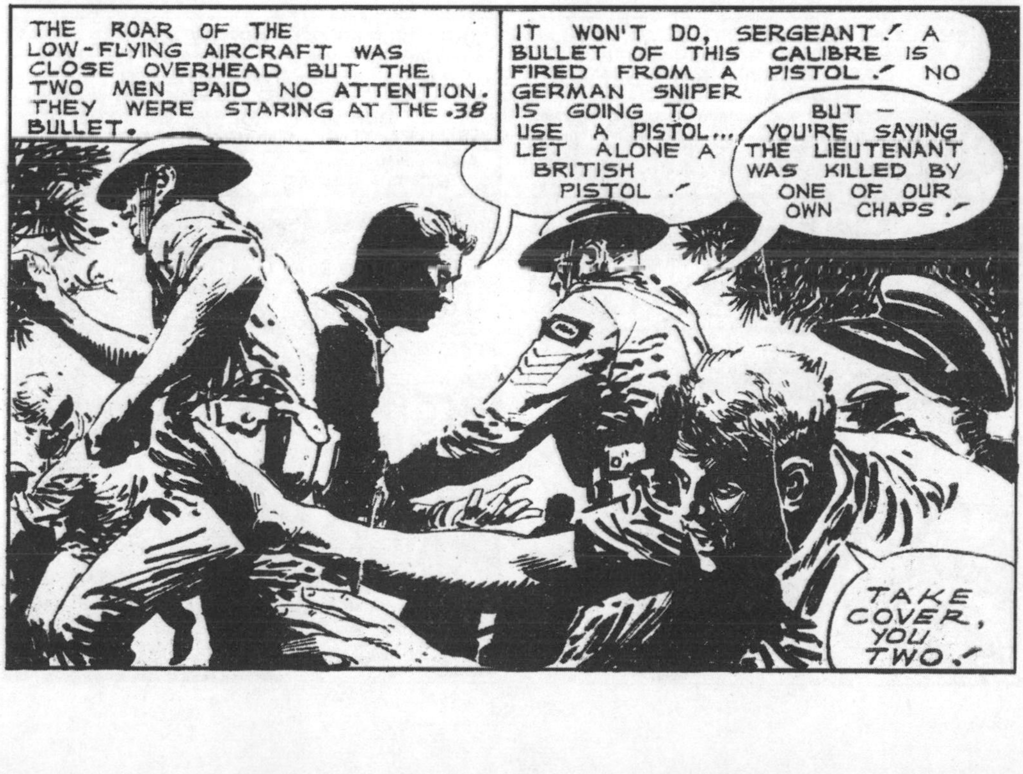
THE ROAR OF THE LOW-FLYING AIRCRAFT WAS CLOSE OVERHEAD BUT THE TWO MEN PAID NO ATTENTION. THEY WERE STARING AT THE .38 BULLET.
IT WON'T DO, SERGEANT! A BULLET OF THIS CALIBRE IS FIRED FROM A PISTOL! NO GERMAN SNIPER IS GOING TO USE A PISTOL... LET ALONE A BRITISH PISTOL!
BUT — YOU'RE SAYING THE LIEUTENANT WAS KILLED BY ONE OF OUR OWN CHAPS!
TAKE COVER, YOU TWO!

SERGEANT HAMMOND NEVER HEARD THE BOMB FALL. A FLASH OF LIGHT BLINDED HIM... THE EARTH HEAVED UNDER HIS FEET...

WHEN THE SERGEANT CAME TO, HIS EYES STILL ACHED WITH LIGHT, HIS BRAIN WAS NUMB. THEN HE REMEMBERED...

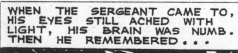

THE BULLET...

THE SURGEON SERGEANT HAMMOND WAS TALKING TO WAS DEAD. BUT THE GHASTLY WORDS HE HAD SPOKEN WERE STILL BURNING HOLES IN THE SERGEANT'S SHOCKED BRAIN...

ARE YOU ALL RIGHT, SARGE?

YES... YES... LEAVE ME ALONE! I'VE GOT TO SEE THE MAJOR!

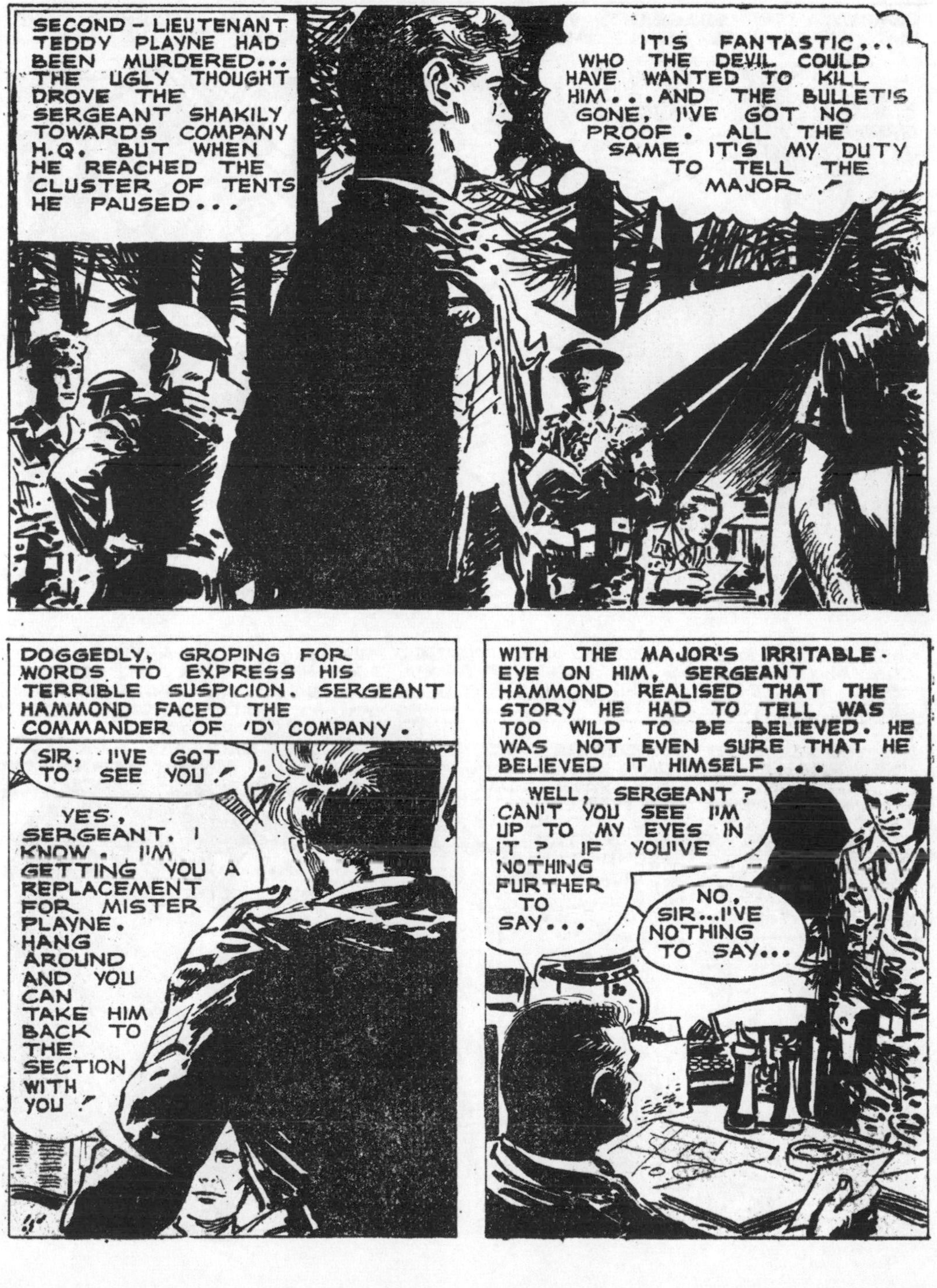
SECOND - LIEUTENANT TEDDY PLAYNE HAD BEEN MURDERED... THE UGLY THOUGHT DROVE THE SERGEANT SHAKILY TOWARDS COMPANY H.Q. BUT WHEN HE REACHED THE CLUSTER OF TENTS HE PAUSED...
IT'S FANTASTIC... WHO THE DEVIL COULD HAVE WANTED TO KILL HIM...AND THE BULLET'S GONE, I'VE GOT NO PROOF. ALL THE SAME IT'S MY DUTY TO TELL THE MAJOR!
DOGGEDLY, GROPING FOR WORDS TO EXPRESS HIS TERRIBLE SUSPICION, SERGEANT HAMMOND FACED THE COMMANDER OF 'D' COMPANY.
SIR, I'VE GOT TO SEE YOU!
YES, SERGEANT, I KNOW. I'M GETTING YOU A REPLACEMENT FOR MISTER PLAYNE. HANG AROUND AND YOU CAN TAKE HIM BACK TO THE SECTION WITH YOU!
WITH THE MAJOR'S IRRITABLE EYE ON HIM, SERGEANT HAMMOND REALISED THAT THE STORY HE HAD TO TELL WAS TOO WILD TO BE BELIEVED. HE WAS NOT EVEN SURE THAT HE BELIEVED IT HIMSELF...
WELL, SERGEANT? CAN'T YOU SEE I'M UP TO MY EYES IN IT? IF YOU'VE NOTHING FURTHER TO SAY...
NO, SIR...I'VE NOTHING TO SAY...

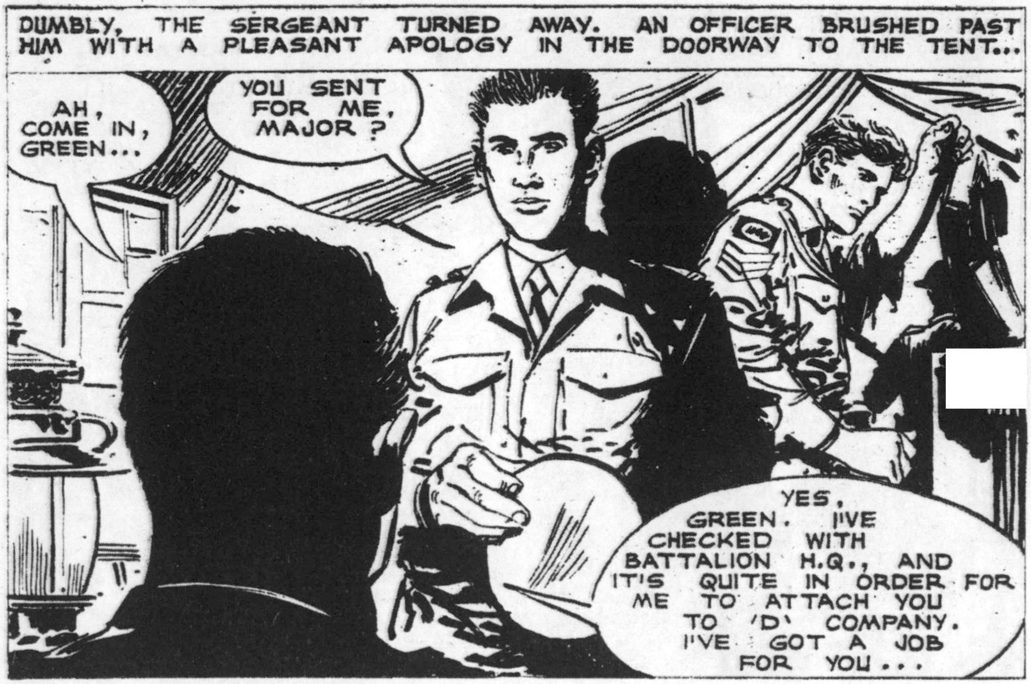
DUMBLY, THE SERGEANT TURNED AWAY. AN OFFICER BRUSHED PAST HIM WITH A PLEASANT APOLOGY IN THE DOORWAY TO THE TENT...
AH, COME IN, GREEN...
YOU SENT FOR ME, MAJOR?
YES, GREEN. I'VE CHECKED WITH BATTALION H.Q., AND IT'S QUITE IN ORDER FOR ME TO ATTACH YOU TO 'D' COMPANY. I'VE GOT A JOB FOR YOU...

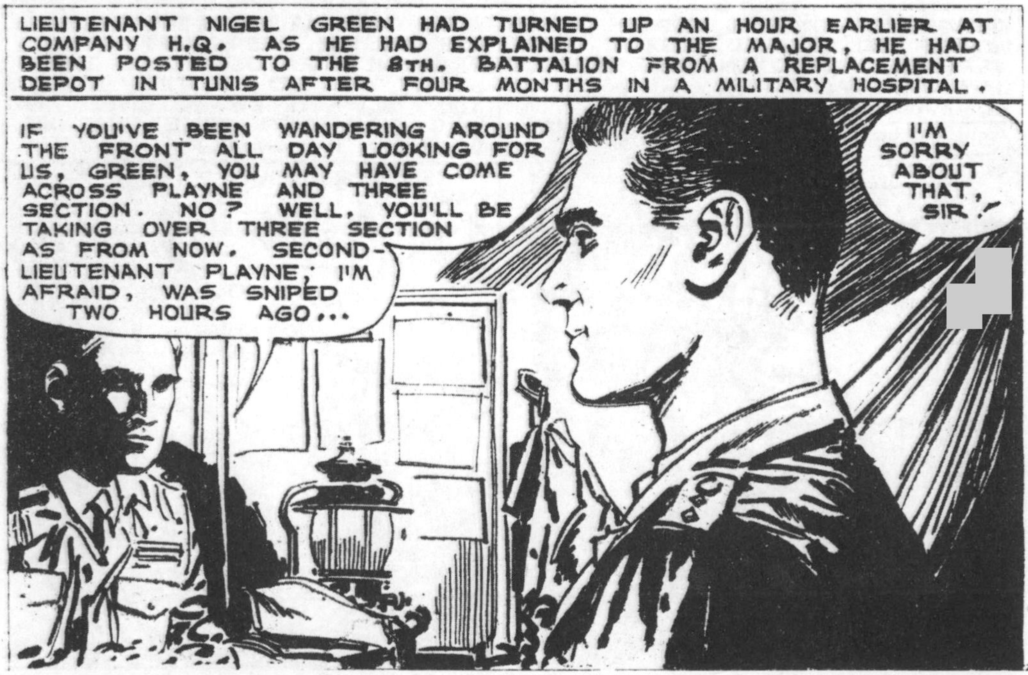
LIEUTENANT NIGEL GREEN HAD TURNED UP AN HOUR EARLIER AT COMPANY H.Q. AS HE HAD EXPLAINED TO THE MAJOR, HE HAD BEEN POSTED TO THE 8TH. BATTALION FROM A REPLACEMENT DEPOT IN TUNIS AFTER FOUR MONTHS IN A MILITARY HOSPITAL.
IF YOU'VE BEEN WANDERING AROUND THE FRONT ALL DAY LOOKING FOR US, GREEN, YOU MAY HAVE COME ACROSS PLAYNE AND THREE SECTION. NO? WELL, YOU'LL BE TAKING OVER THREE SECTION AS FROM NOW. SECOND-LIEUTENANT PLAYNE, I'M AFRAID, WAS SNIPED TWO HOURS AGO...
I'M SORRY ABOUT THAT, SIR.

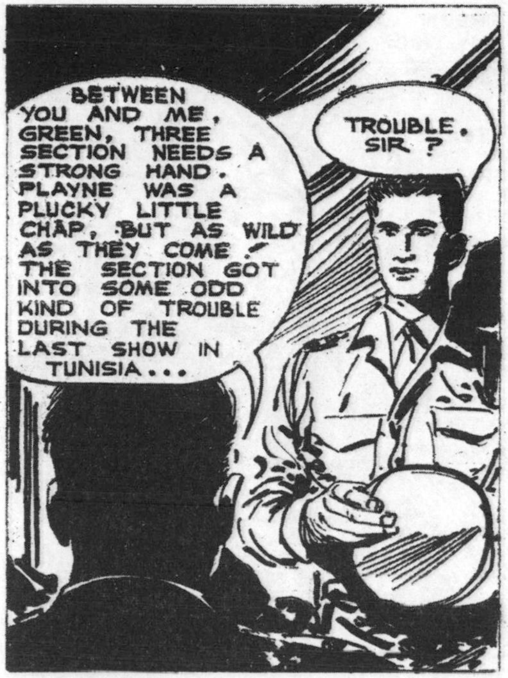
BETWEEN YOU AND ME, GREEN, THREE SECTION NEEDS A STRONG HAND. PLAYNE WAS A PLUCKY LITTLE CHAP, BUT AS WILD AS THEY COME! THE SECTION GOT INTO SOME ODD KIND OF TROUBLE DURING THE LAST SHOW IN TUNISIA...
TROUBLE, SIR?

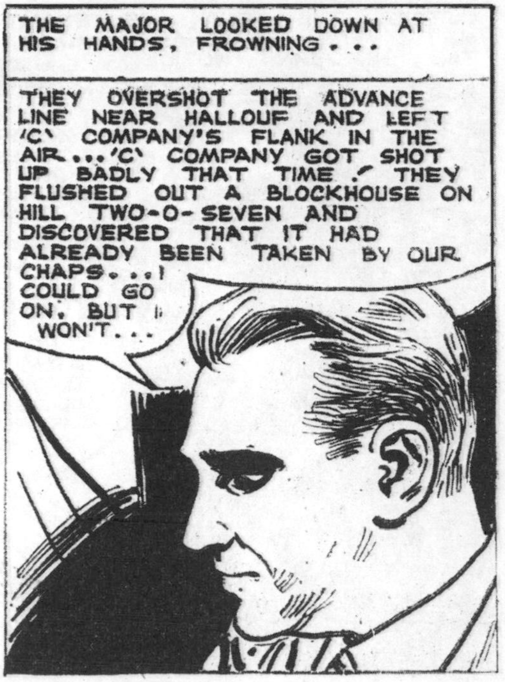
THE MAJOR LOOKED DOWN AT HIS HANDS, FROWNING...
THEY OVERSHOT THE ADVANCE LINE NEAR HALLOUF AND LEFT 'C' COMPANY'S FLANK IN THE AIR... 'C' COMPANY GOT SHOT UP BADLY THAT TIME! THEY FLUSHED OUT A BLOCKHOUSE ON HILL TWO-O-SEVEN AND DISCOVERED THAT IT HAD ALREADY BEEN TAKEN BY OUR CHAPS...I COULD GO ON. BUT I WON'T...

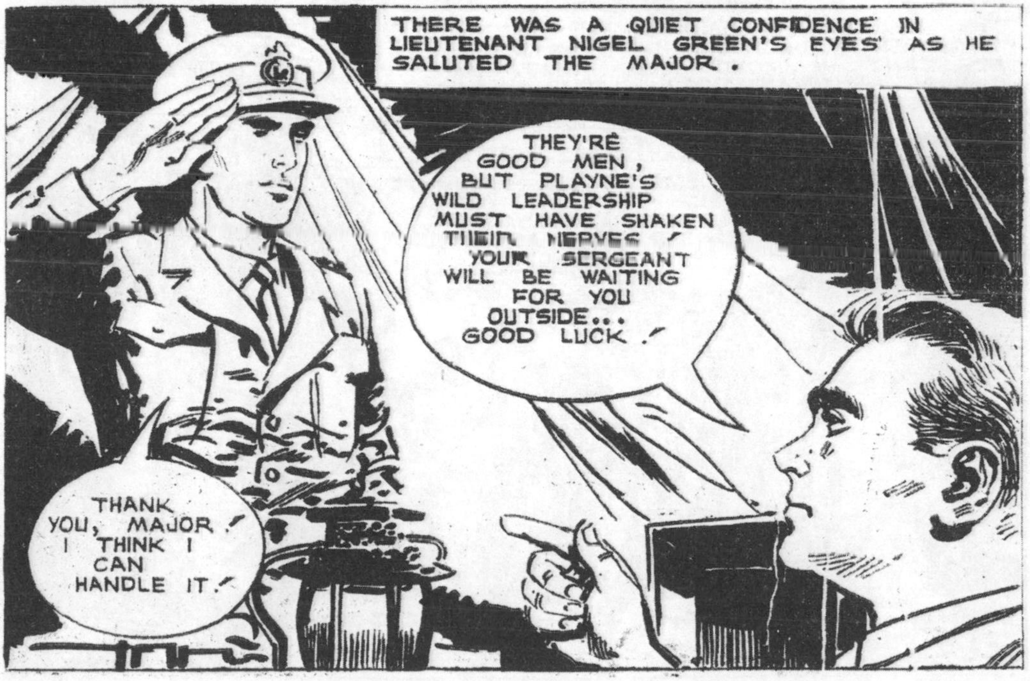
THERE WAS A QUIET CONFIDENCE IN LIEUTENANT NIGEL GREEN'S EYES AS HE SALUTED THE MAJOR.
THEY'RE GOOD MEN, BUT PLAYNE'S WILD LEADERSHIP MUST HAVE SHAKEN THEIR NERVES! YOUR SERGEANT WILL BE WAITING FOR YOU OUTSIDE... GOOD LUCK!
THANK YOU, MAJOR! I THINK I CAN HANDLE IT!

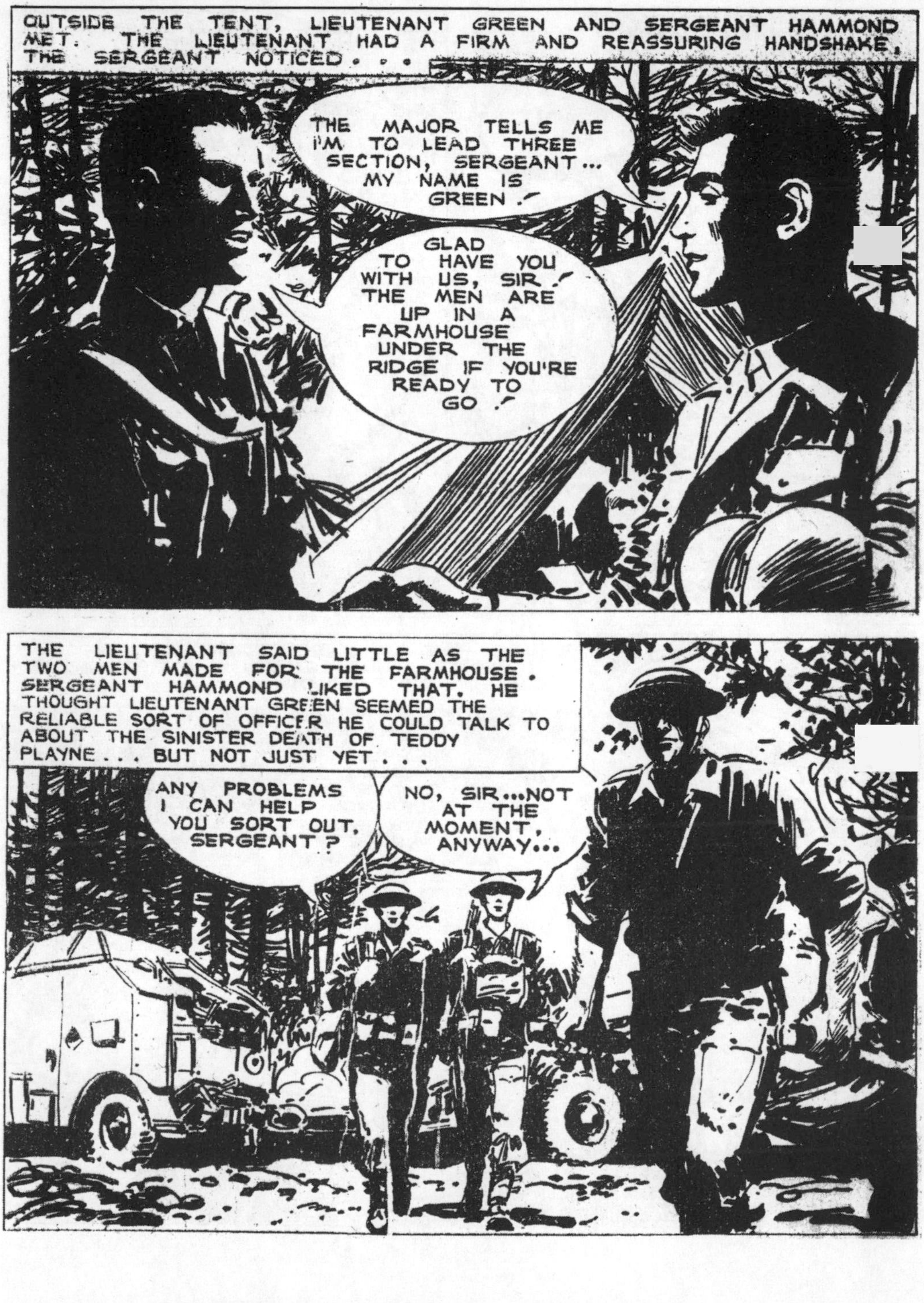
OUTSIDE THE TENT, LIEUTENANT GREEN AND SERGEANT HAMMOND MET. THE LIEUTENANT HAD A FIRM AND REASSURING HANDSHAKE, THE SERGEANT NOTICED . . .
THE MAJOR TELLS ME I'M TO LEAD THREE SECTION, SERGEANT... MY NAME IS GREEN!
GLAD TO HAVE YOU WITH US, SIR! THE MEN ARE UP IN A FARMHOUSE UNDER THE RIDGE IF YOU'RE READY TO GO!
THE LIEUTENANT SAID LITTLE AS THE TWO MEN MADE FOR THE FARMHOUSE. SERGEANT HAMMOND LIKED THAT. HE THOUGHT LIEUTENANT GREEN SEEMED THE RELIABLE SORT OF OFFICER HE COULD TALK TO ABOUT THE SINISTER DEATH OF TEDDY PLAYNE . . . BUT NOT JUST YET . . .
ANY PROBLEMS I CAN HELP YOU SORT OUT, SERGEANT?
NO, SIR...NOT AT THE MOMENT, ANYWAY...

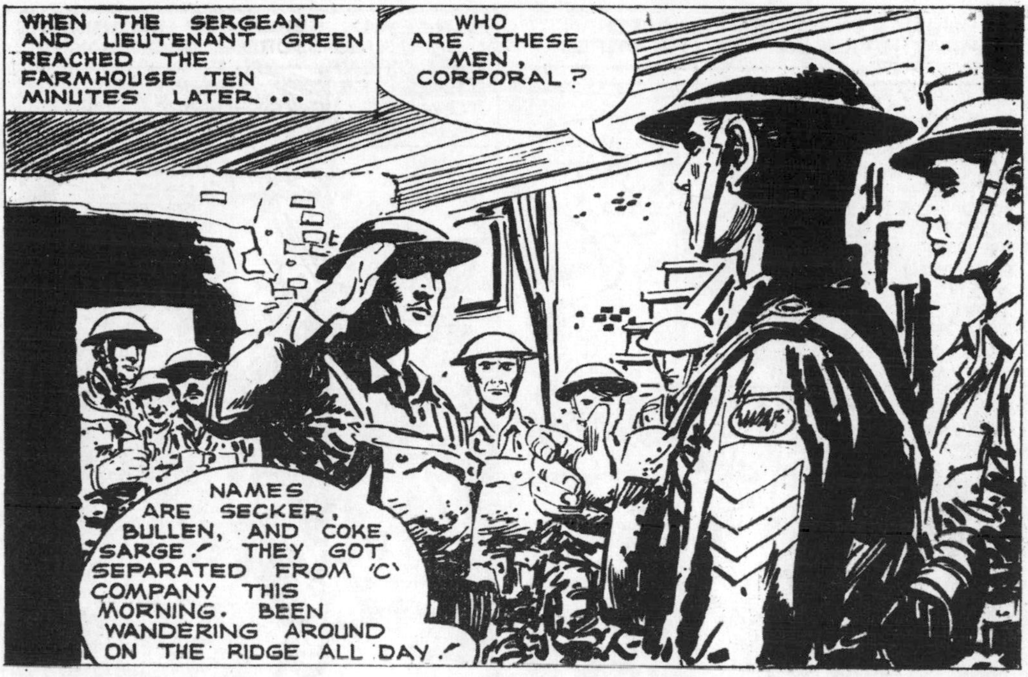
WHEN THE SERGEANT AND LIEUTENANT GREEN REACHED THE FARMHOUSE TEN MINUTES LATER ...
WHO ARE THESE MEN, CORPORAL?
NAMES ARE SECKER, BULLEN, AND COKE, SARGE! THEY GOT SEPARATED FROM 'C' COMPANY THIS MORNING. BEEN WANDERING AROUND ON THE RIDGE ALL DAY!

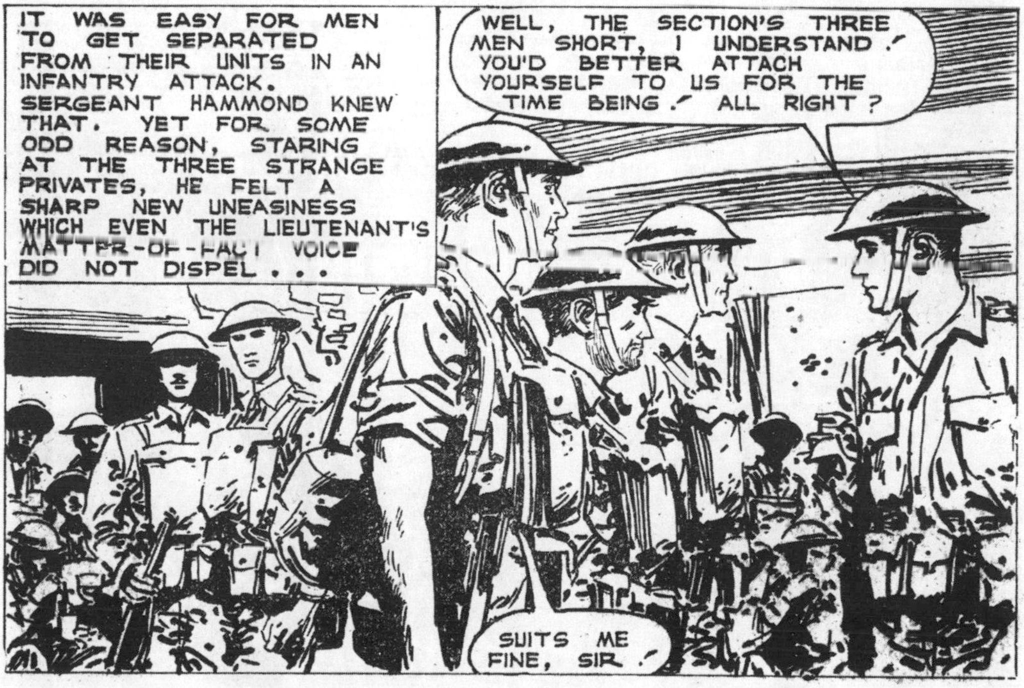
IT WAS EASY FOR MEN TO GET SEPARATED FROM THEIR UNITS IN AN INFANTRY ATTACK. SERGEANT HAMMOND KNEW THAT. YET FOR SOME ODD REASON, STARING AT THE THREE STRANGE PRIVATES, HE FELT A SHARP NEW UNEASINESS WHICH EVEN THE LIEUTENANT'S MATTER-OF-FACT VOICE DID NOT DISPEL ...
WELL, THE SECTION'S THREE MEN SHORT, I UNDERSTAND! YOU'D BETTER ATTACH YOURSELF TO US FOR THE TIME BEING! ALL RIGHT?
SUITS ME FINE, SIR!

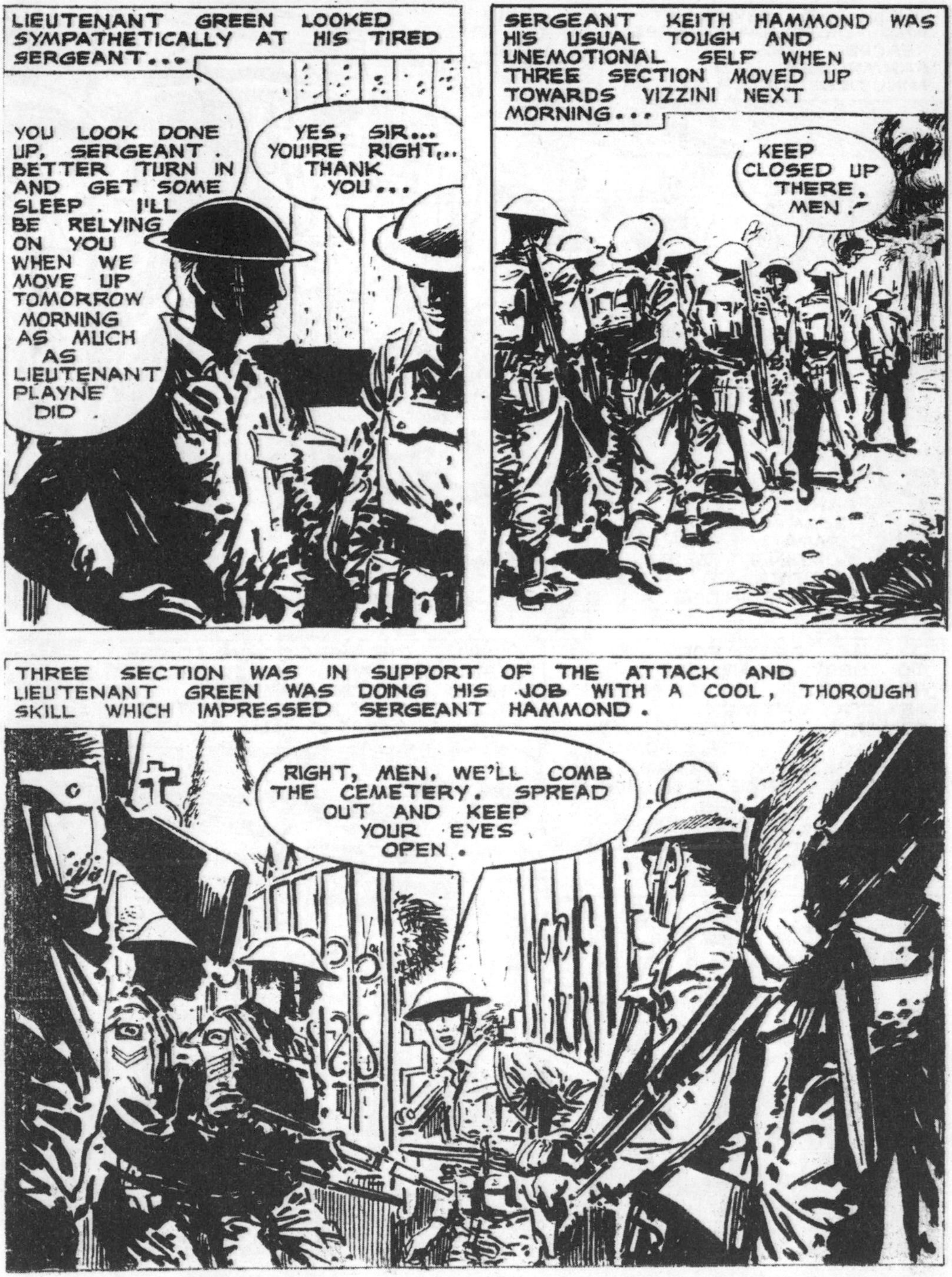
LIEUTENANT GREEN LOOKED SYMPATHETICALLY AT HIS TIRED SERGEANT...
YOU LOOK DONE UP, SERGEANT. BETTER TURN IN AND GET SOME SLEEP. I'LL BE RELYING ON YOU WHEN WE MOVE UP TOMORROW MORNING AS MUCH AS LIEUTENANT PLAYNE DID.
YES, SIR... YOU'RE RIGHT... THANK YOU...
SERGEANT KEITH HAMMOND WAS HIS USUAL TOUGH AND UNEMOTIONAL SELF WHEN THREE SECTION MOVED UP TOWARDS VIZZINI NEXT MORNING...
KEEP CLOSED UP THERE, MEN.
THREE SECTION WAS IN SUPPORT OF THE ATTACK AND LIEUTENANT GREEN WAS DOING HIS JOB WITH A COOL, THOROUGH SKILL WHICH IMPRESSED SERGEANT HAMMOND.
RIGHT, MEN. WE'LL COMB THE CEMETERY. SPREAD OUT AND KEEP YOUR EYES OPEN.

THEY WOULD FIND NO SNIPERS HERE, SERGEANT HAMMOND THOUGHT, BUT THE LIEUTENANT WAS RIGHT TO COMB THE PLACE. TEDDY PLAYNE WOULD HAVE GONE CHARGING STRAIGHT UP THE ROAD...

SERGEANT HAMMOND GRINNED AT THE MEMORY OF THE FIRE-EATING PLAYNE. HE WAS JUST WONDERING HOW HE COULD HAVE SERIOUSLY BELIEVED THAT ANYONE WOULD MURDER THE YOUNG OFFICER WHEN A SHOT AND A CHOKING CRY BROKE THE DUSTY SILENCE OF THE CEMETERY...

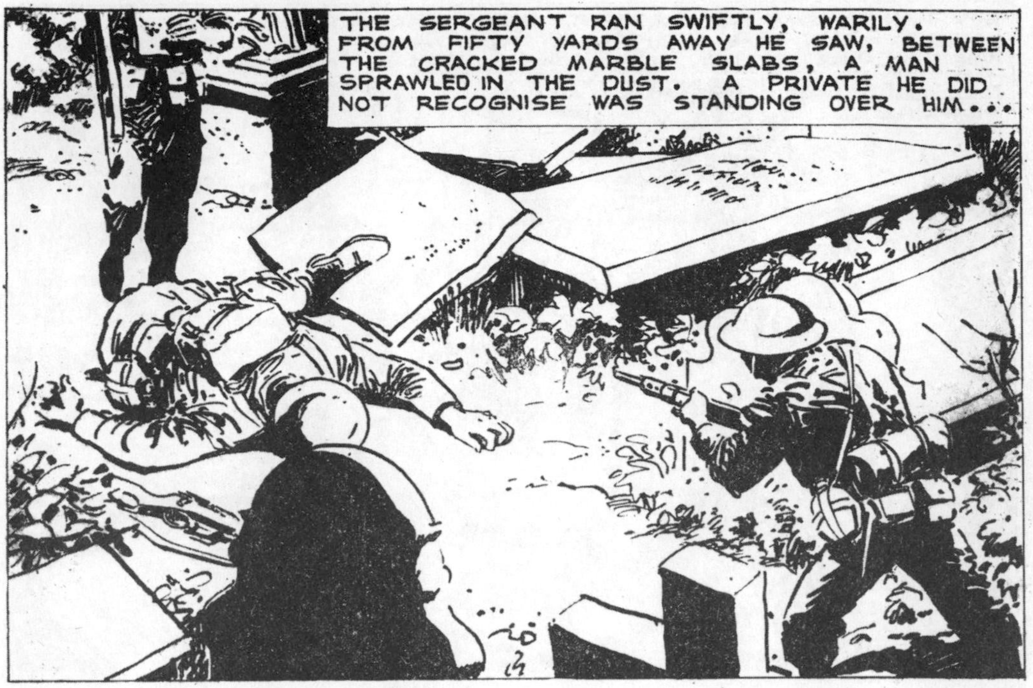
THE SERGEANT RAN SWIFTLY, WARILY. FROM FIFTY YARDS AWAY HE SAW, BETWEEN THE CRACKED MARBLE SLABS, A MAN SPRAWLED IN THE DUST. A PRIVATE HE DID NOT RECOGNISE WAS STANDING OVER HIM...

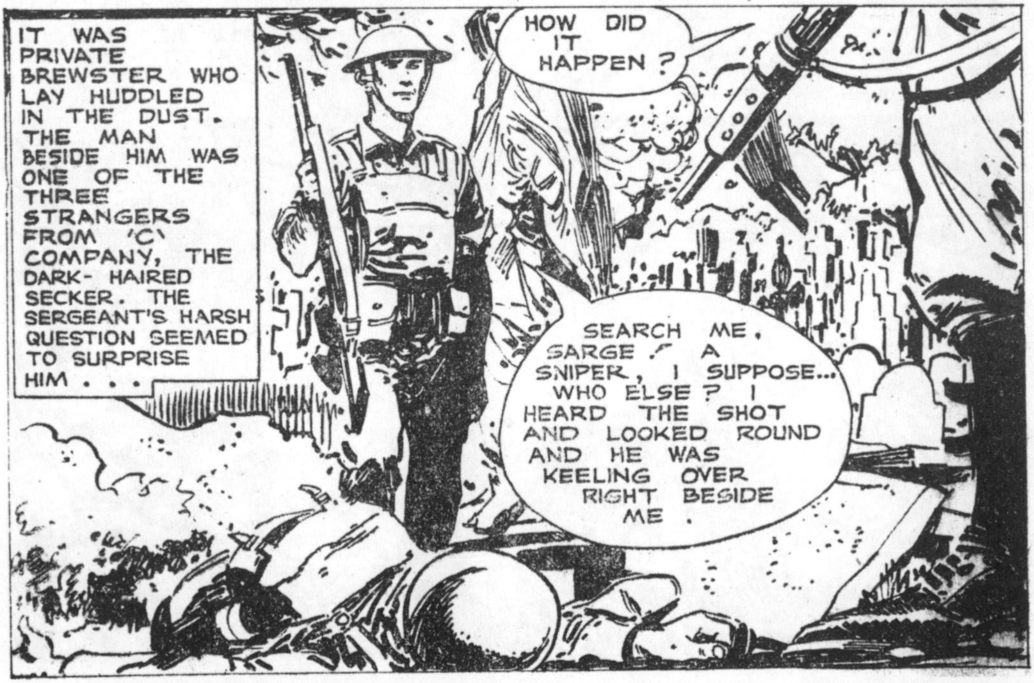
IT WAS PRIVATE BREWSTER WHO LAY HUDDLED IN THE DUST. THE MAN BESIDE HIM WAS ONE OF THE THREE STRANGERS FROM 'C' COMPANY, THE DARK-HAIRED SECKER. THE SERGEANT'S HARSH QUESTION SEEMED TO SURPRISE HIM...
HOW DID IT HAPPEN?
SEARCH ME, SARGE! A SNIPER, I SUPPOSE... WHO ELSE? I HEARD THE SHOT AND LOOKED ROUND AND HE WAS KEELING OVER RIGHT BESIDE ME.

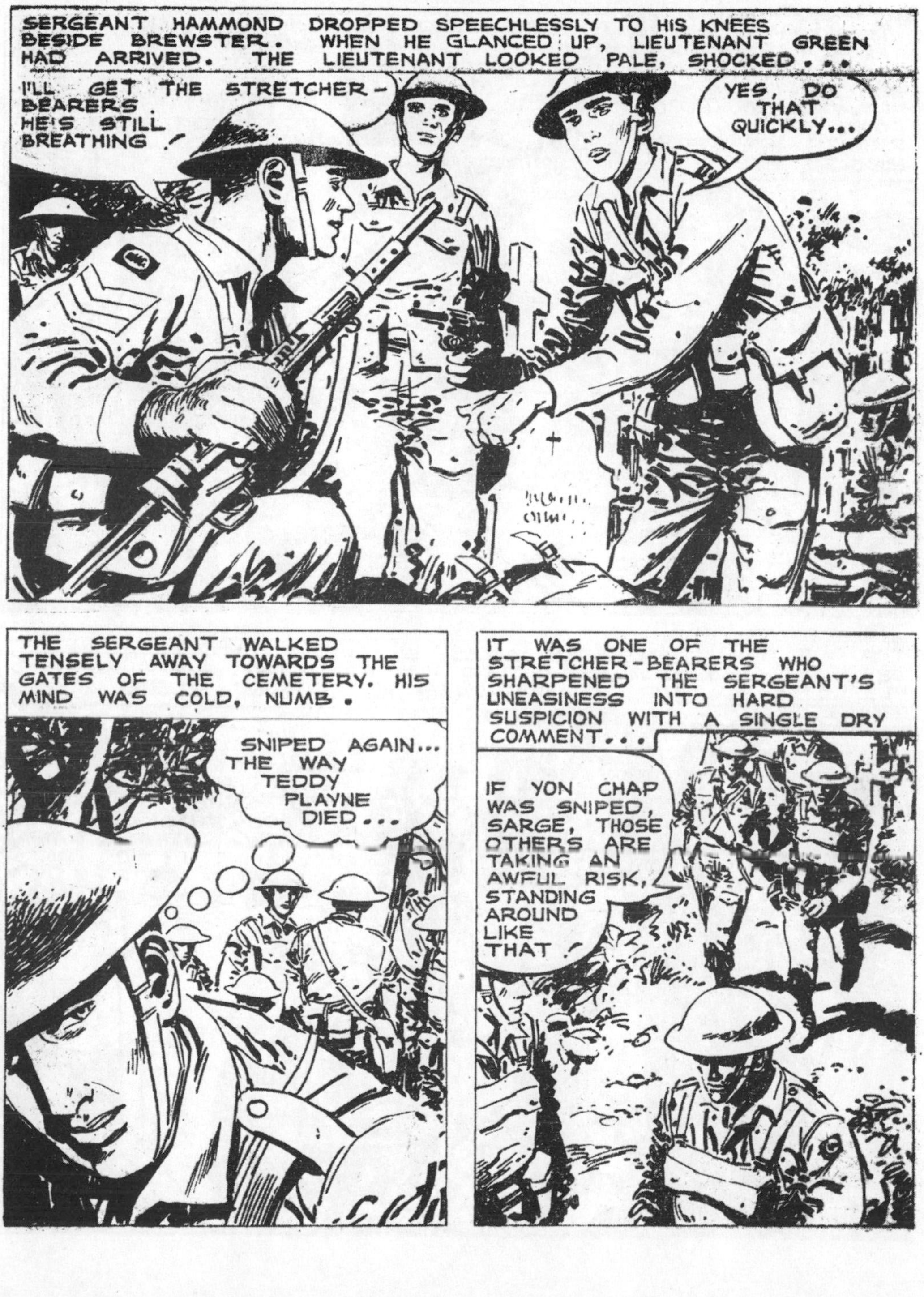
SERGEANT HAMMOND DROPPED SPEECHLESSLY TO HIS KNEES BESIDE BREWSTER. WHEN HE GLANCED UP, LIEUTENANT GREEN HAD ARRIVED. THE LIEUTENANT LOOKED PALE, SHOCKED . . .
I'LL GET THE STRETCHER-BEARERS HE'S STILL BREATHING
YES, DO THAT QUICKLY...
THE SERGEANT WALKED TENSELY AWAY TOWARDS THE GATES OF THE CEMETERY. HIS MIND WAS COLD, NUMB.
SNIPED AGAIN... THE WAY TEDDY PLAYNE DIED...
IT WAS ONE OF THE STRETCHER-BEARERS WHO SHARPENED THE SERGEANT'S UNEASINESS INTO HARD SUSPICION WITH A SINGLE DRY COMMENT...
IF YON CHAP WAS SNIPED, SARGE, THOSE OTHERS ARE TAKING AN AWFUL RISK, STANDING AROUND LIKE THAT

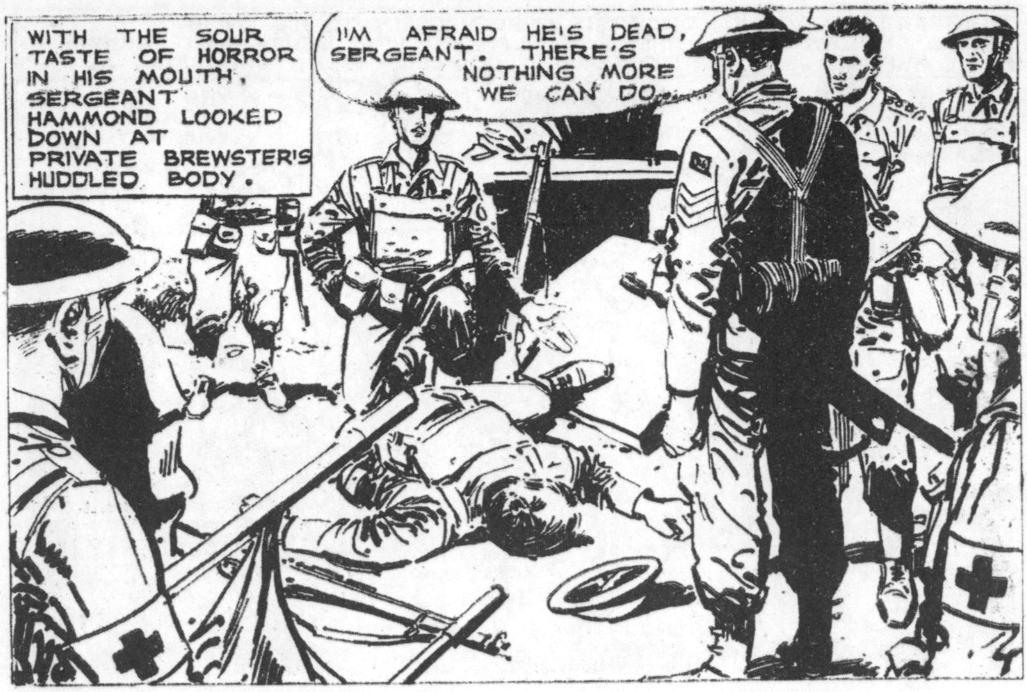
WITH THE SOUR TASTE OF HORROR IN HIS MOUTH, SERGEANT HAMMOND LOOKED DOWN AT PRIVATE BREWSTER'S HUDDLED BODY.
I'M AFRAID HE'S DEAD, SERGEANT. THERE'S NOTHING MORE WE CAN DO.

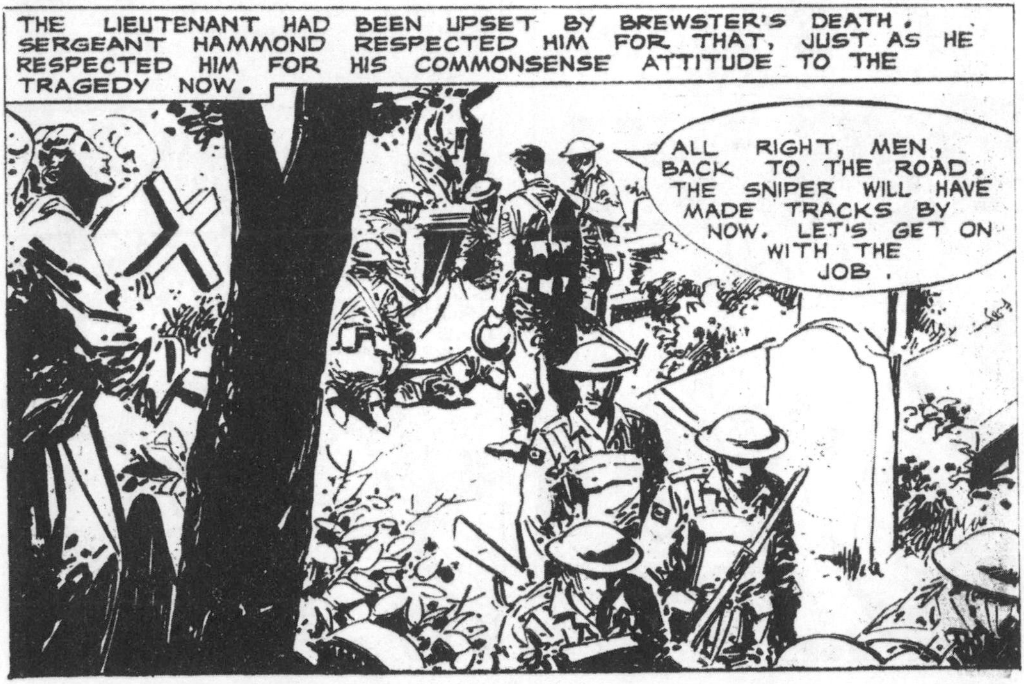
THE LIEUTENANT HAD BEEN UPSET BY BREWSTER'S DEATH. SERGEANT HAMMOND RESPECTED HIM FOR THAT, JUST AS HE RESPECTED HIM FOR HIS COMMONSENSE ATTITUDE TO THE TRAGEDY NOW.
ALL RIGHT, MEN, BACK TO THE ROAD. THE SNIPER WILL HAVE MADE TRACKS BY NOW. LET'S GET ON WITH THE JOB.

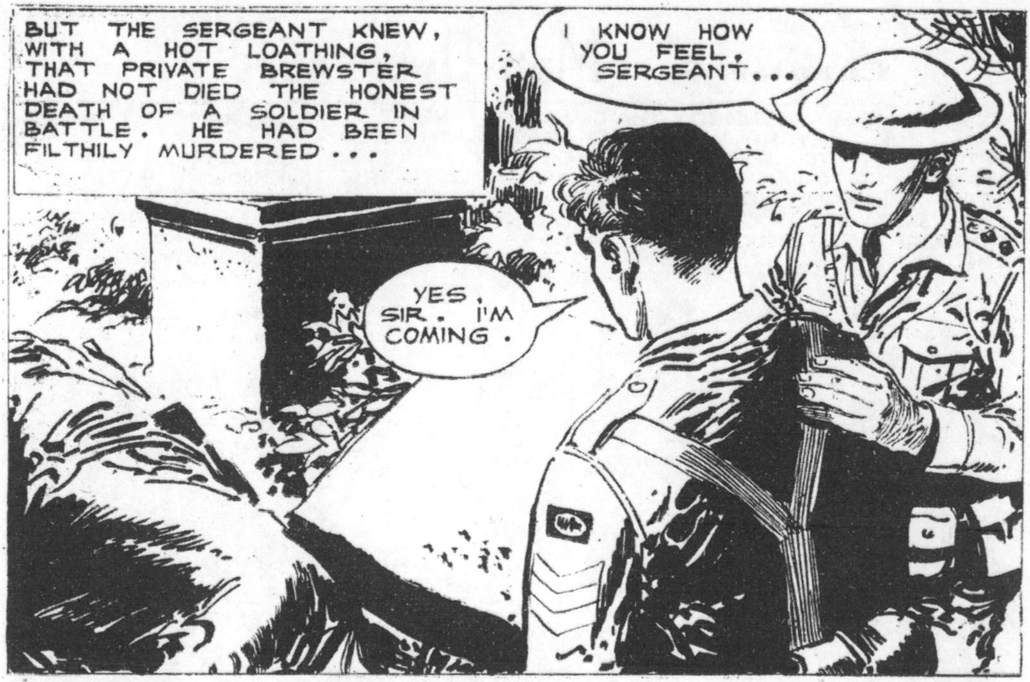
BUT THE SERGEANT KNEW, WITH A HOT LOATHING, THAT PRIVATE BREWSTER HAD NOT DIED THE HONEST DEATH OF A SOLDIER IN BATTLE. HE HAD BEEN FILTHILY MURDERED...
I KNOW HOW YOU FEEL, SERGEANT...
YES, SIR. I'M COMING.

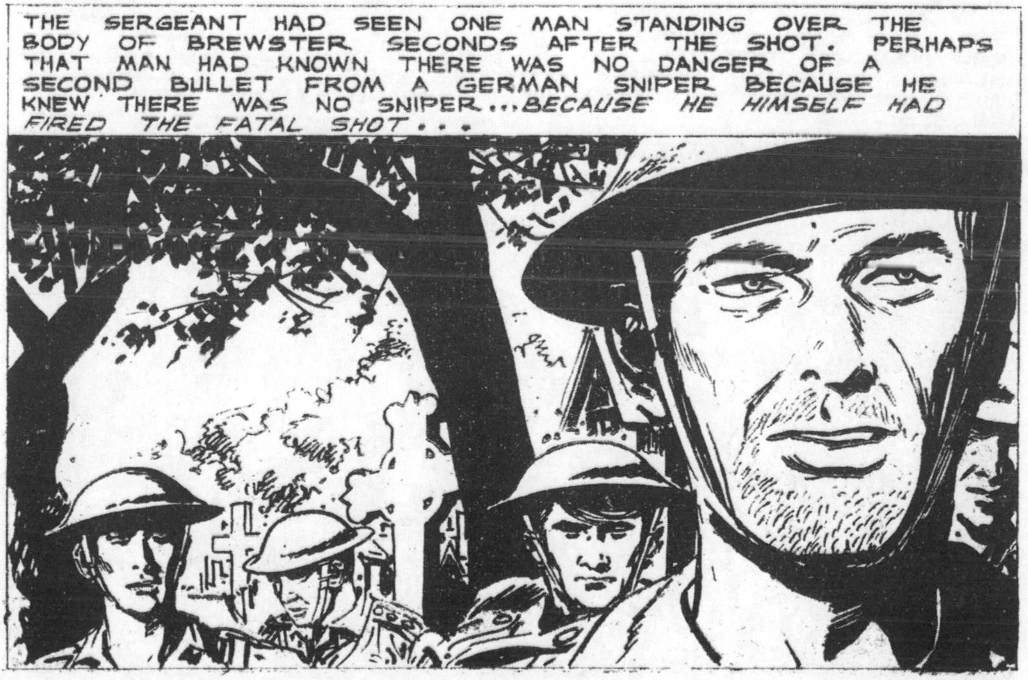
THE SERGEANT HAD SEEN ONE MAN STANDING OVER THE BODY OF BREWSTER SECONDS AFTER THE SHOT. PERHAPS THAT MAN HAD KNOWN THERE WAS NO DANGER OF A SECOND BULLET FROM A GERMAN SNIPER BECAUSE HE KNEW THERE WAS NO SNIPER... *BECAUSE HE HIMSELF HAD FIRED THE FATAL SHOT...*

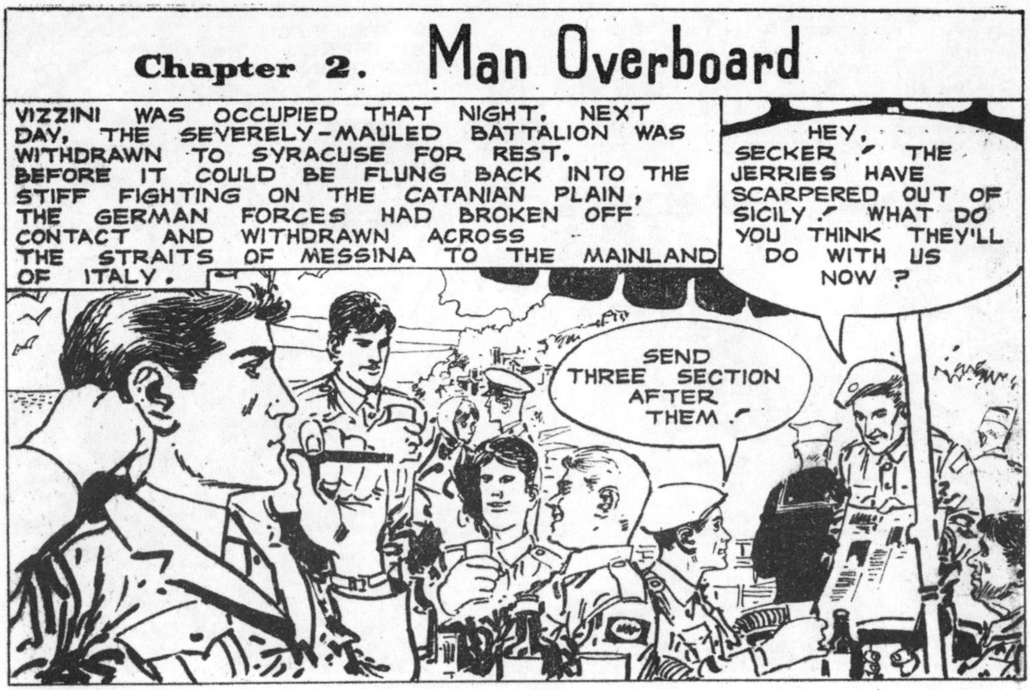
Chapter 2. Man Overboard
VIZZINI WAS OCCUPIED THAT NIGHT. NEXT DAY, THE SEVERELY-MAULED BATTALION WAS WITHDRAWN TO SYRACUSE FOR REST. BEFORE IT COULD BE FLUNG BACK INTO THE STIFF FIGHTING ON THE CATANIAN PLAIN, THE GERMAN FORCES HAD BROKEN OFF CONTACT AND WITHDRAWN ACROSS THE STRAITS OF MESSINA TO THE MAINLAND OF ITALY.
HEY, SECKER! THE JERRIES HAVE SCARPERED OUT OF SICILY! WHAT DO YOU THINK THEY'LL DO WITH US NOW?
SEND THREE SECTION AFTER THEM!

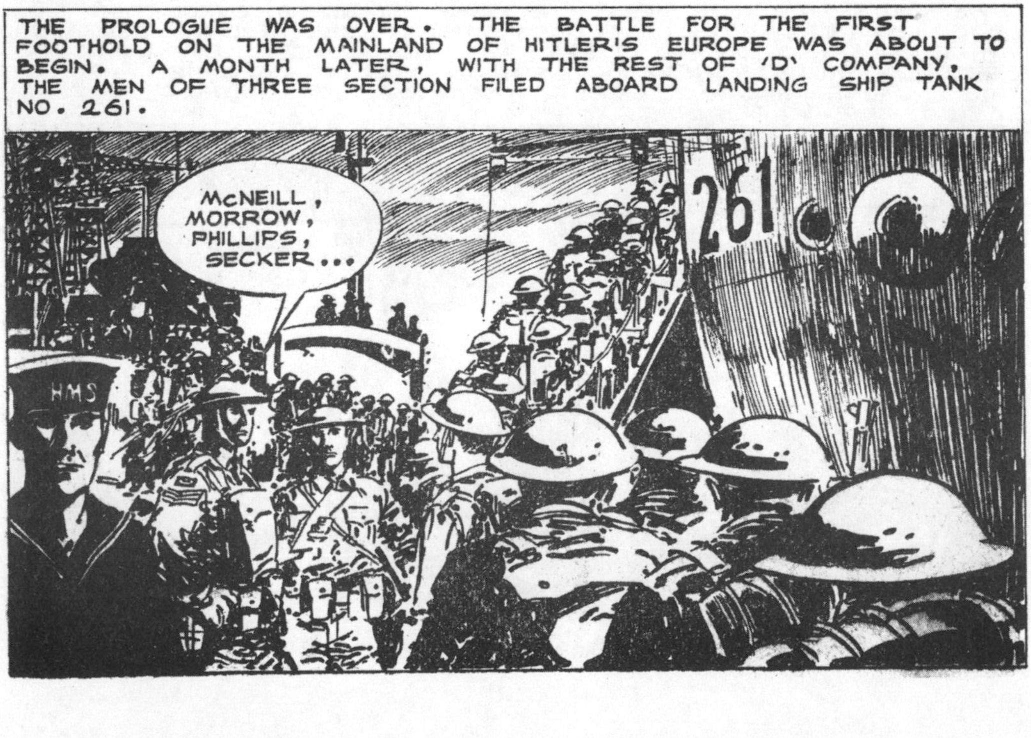
THE PROLOGUE WAS OVER. THE BATTLE FOR THE FIRST FOOTHOLD ON THE MAINLAND OF HITLER'S EUROPE WAS ABOUT TO BEGIN. A MONTH LATER, WITH THE REST OF 'D' COMPANY, THE MEN OF THREE SECTION FILED ABOARD LANDING SHIP TANK NO. 261.
McNEILL, MORROW, PHILLIPS, SECKER...
261
HMS

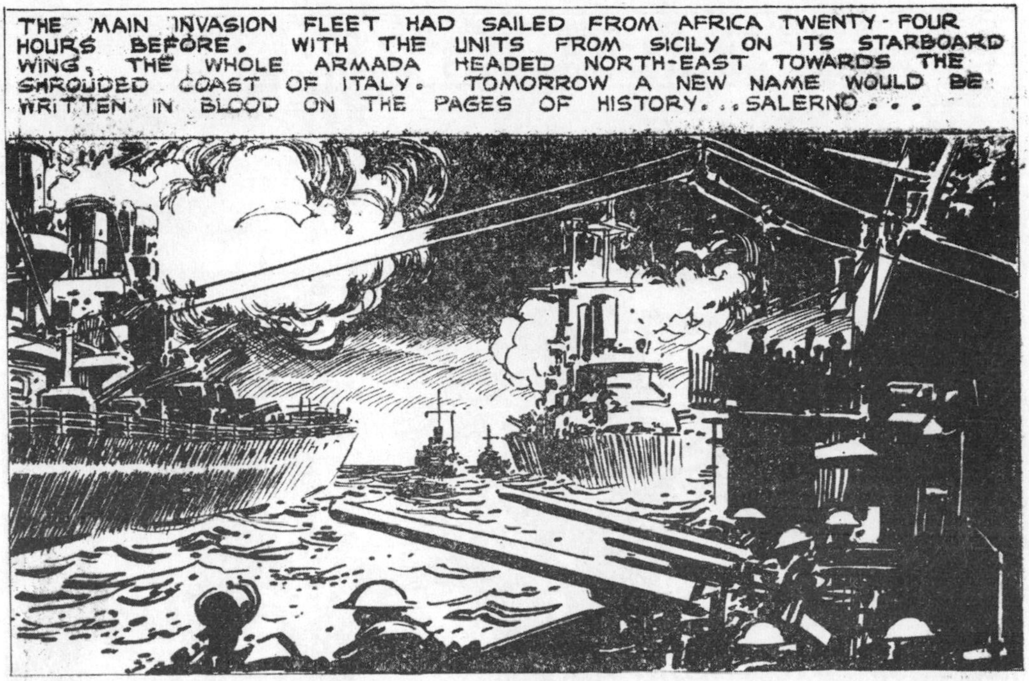
THE MAIN INVASION FLEET HAD SAILED FROM AFRICA TWENTY-FOUR HOURS BEFORE. WITH THE UNITS FROM SICILY ON ITS STARBOARD WING, THE WHOLE ARMADA HEADED NORTH-EAST TOWARDS THE SHROUDED COAST OF ITALY. TOMORROW A NEW NAME WOULD BE WRITTEN IN BLOOD ON THE PAGES OF HISTORY...SALERNO...

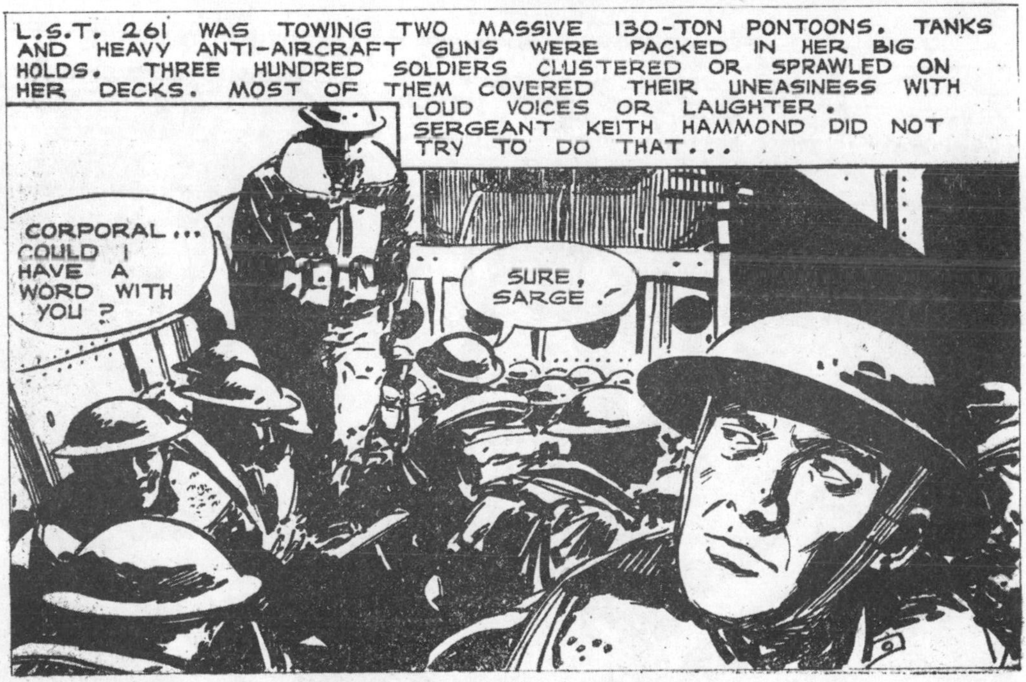
L.S.T. 261 WAS TOWING TWO MASSIVE 130-TON PONTOONS. TANKS AND HEAVY ANTI-AIRCRAFT GUNS WERE PACKED IN HER BIG HOLDS. THREE HUNDRED SOLDIERS CLUSTERED OR SPRAWLED ON HER DECKS. MOST OF THEM COVERED THEIR UNEASINESS WITH LOUD VOICES OR LAUGHTER. SERGEANT KEITH HAMMOND DID NOT TRY TO DO THAT...
CORPORAL... COULD I HAVE A WORD WITH YOU?
SURE, SARGE!

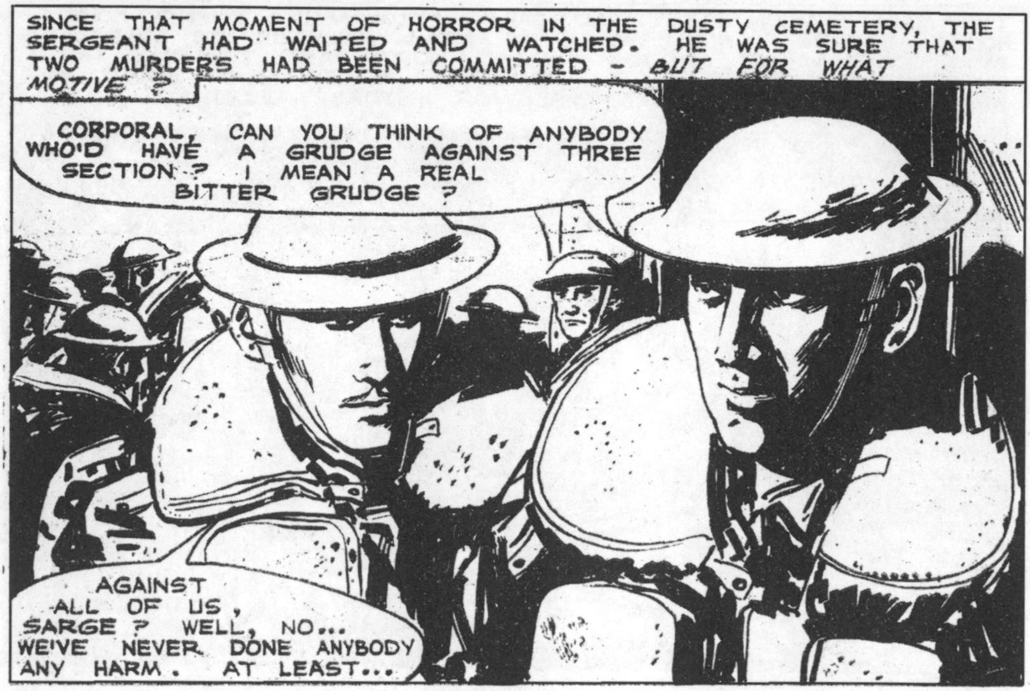
SINCE THAT MOMENT OF HORROR IN THE DUSTY CEMETERY, THE SERGEANT HAD WAITED AND WATCHED. HE WAS SURE THAT TWO MURDERS HAD BEEN COMMITTED - BUT FOR WHAT MOTIVE ?
CORPORAL, CAN YOU THINK OF ANYBODY WHO'D HAVE A GRUDGE AGAINST THREE SECTION ? I MEAN A REAL BITTER GRUDGE ?
AGAINST ALL OF US, SARGE ? WELL, NO... WE'VE NEVER DONE ANYBODY ANY HARM. AT LEAST...

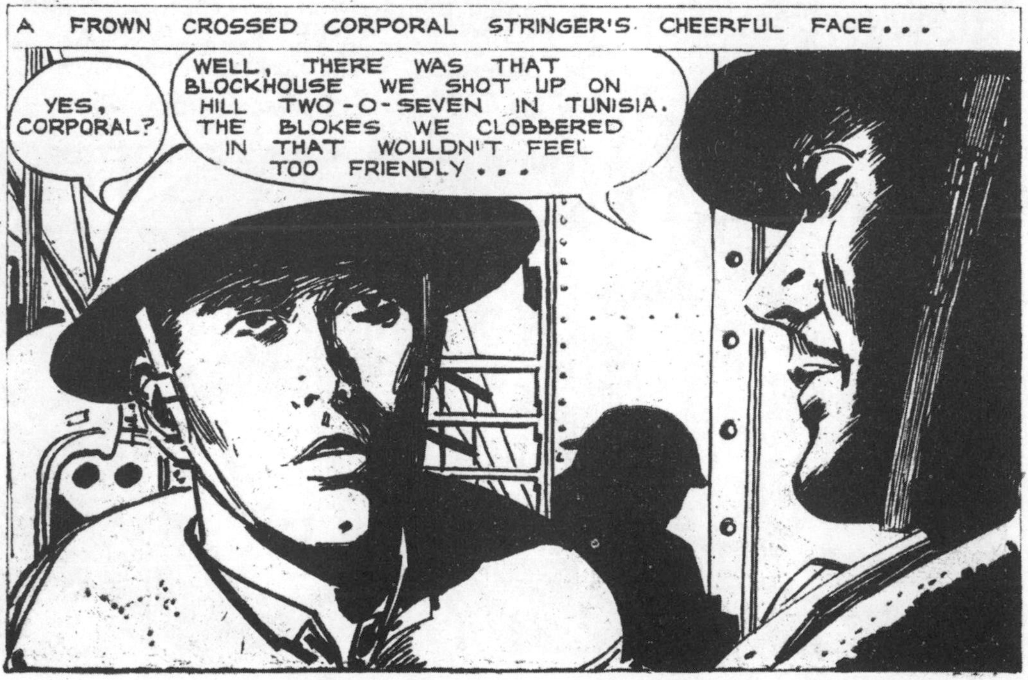
A FROWN CROSSED CORPORAL STRINGER'S CHEERFUL FACE...
YES, CORPORAL?
WELL, THERE WAS THAT BLOCKHOUSE WE SHOT UP ON HILL TWO-O-SEVEN IN TUNISIA. THE BLOKES WE CLOBBERED IN THAT WOULDN'T FEEL TOO FRIENDLY...

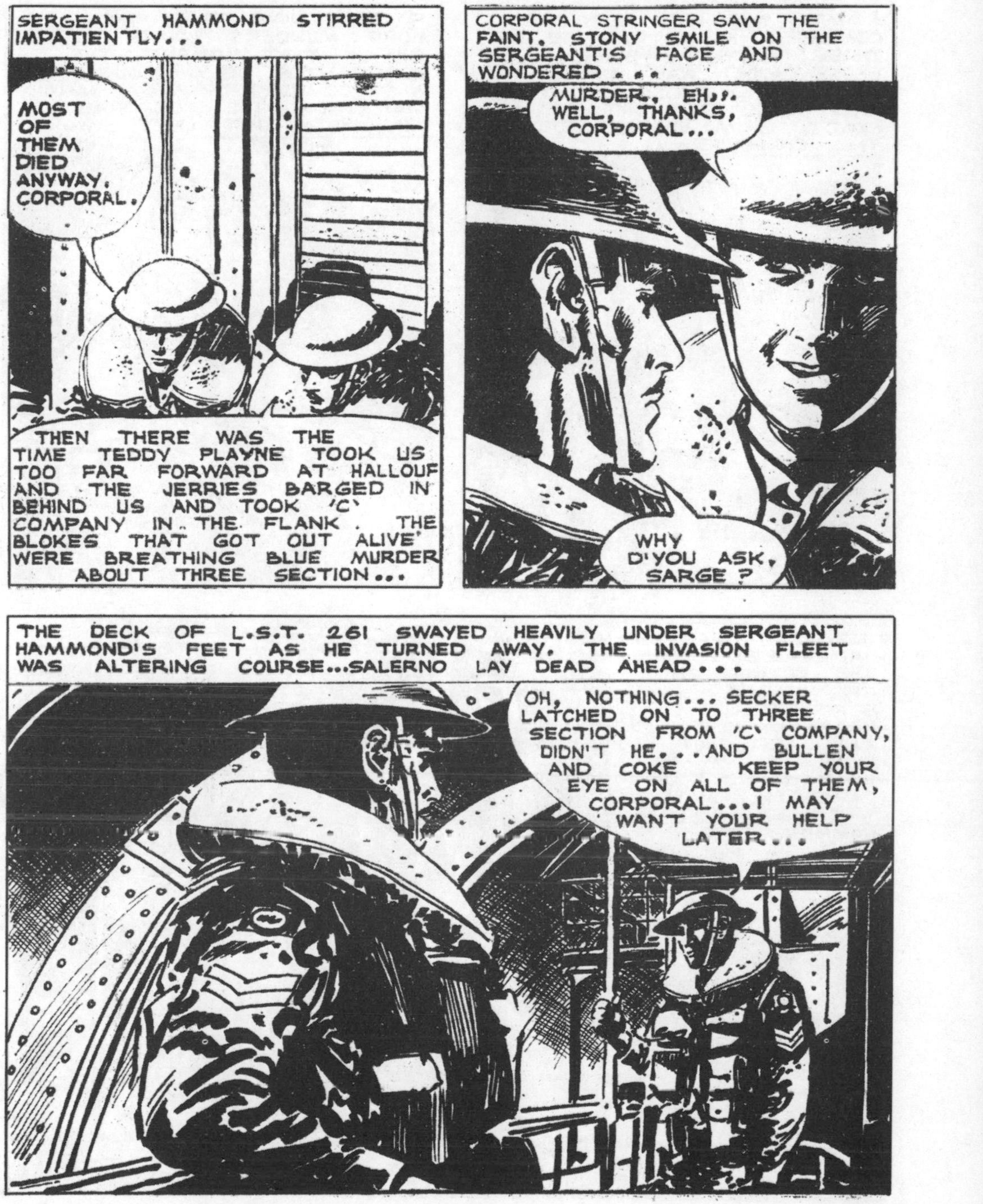
SERGEANT HAMMOND STIRRED IMPATIENTLY...
MOST OF THEM DIED ANYWAY, CORPORAL.
THEN THERE WAS THE TIME TEDDY PLAYNE TOOK US TOO FAR FORWARD AT HALLOUF AND THE JERRIES BARGED IN BEHIND US AND TOOK 'C' COMPANY IN THE FLANK. THE BLOKES THAT GOT OUT ALIVE WERE BREATHING BLUE MURDER ABOUT THREE SECTION...
CORPORAL STRINGER SAW THE FAINT, STONY SMILE ON THE SERGEANT'S FACE AND WONDERED...
MURDER, EH... WELL, THANKS, CORPORAL...
WHY D'YOU ASK, SARGE?
THE DECK OF L.S.T. 261 SWAYED HEAVILY UNDER SERGEANT HAMMOND'S FEET AS HE TURNED AWAY. THE INVASION FLEET WAS ALTERING COURSE...SALERNO LAY DEAD AHEAD...
OH, NOTHING... SECKER LATCHED ON TO THREE SECTION FROM 'C' COMPANY, DIDN'T HE...AND BULLEN AND COKE KEEP YOUR EYE ON ALL OF THEM, CORPORAL...I MAY WANT YOUR HELP LATER...

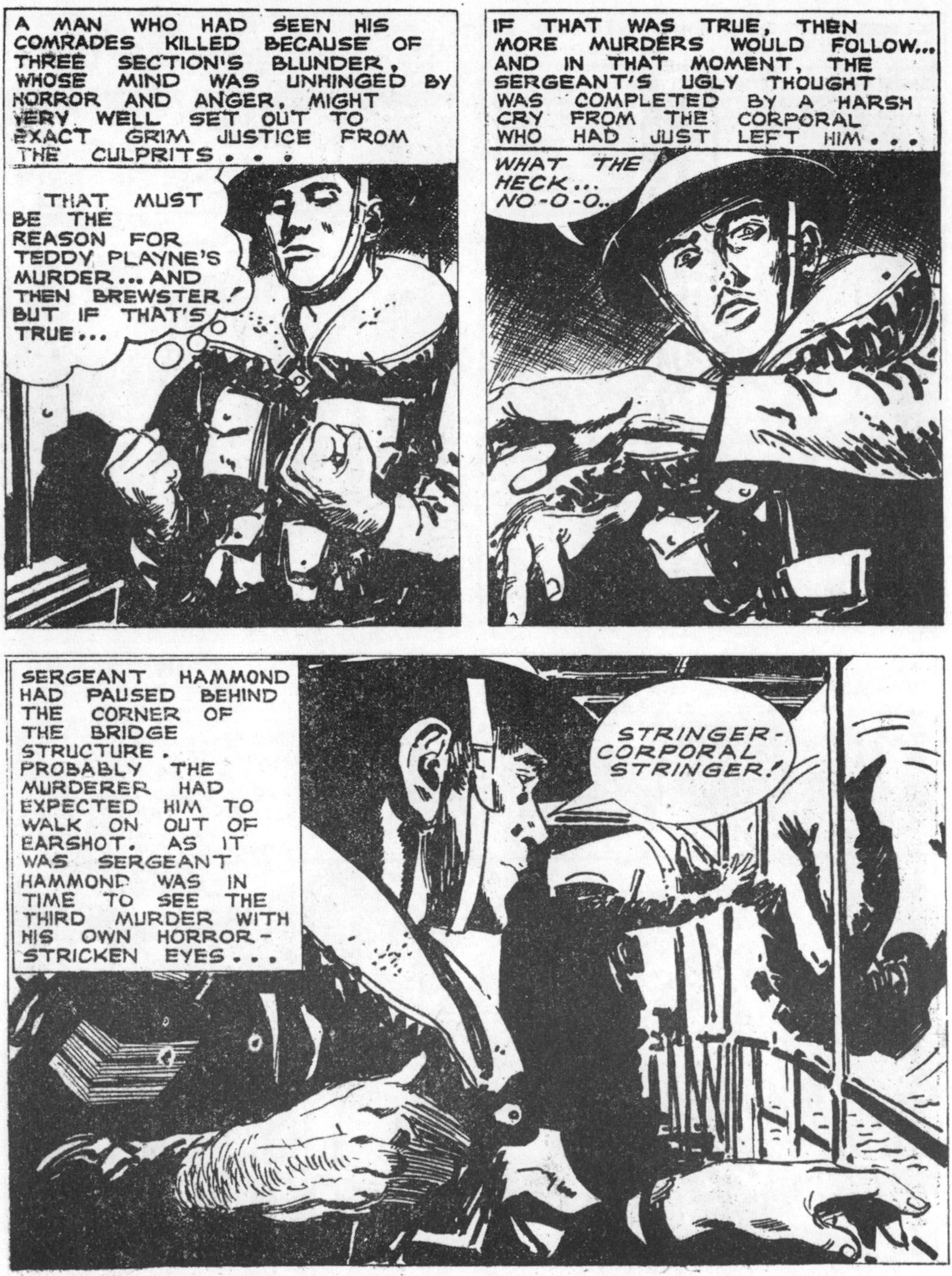
A MAN WHO HAD SEEN HIS COMRADES KILLED BECAUSE OF THREE SECTION'S BLUNDER, WHOSE MIND WAS UNHINGED BY HORROR AND ANGER, MIGHT VERY WELL SET OUT TO EXACT GRIM JUSTICE FROM THE CULPRITS . . .
THAT MUST BE THE REASON FOR TEDDY PLAYNE'S MURDER... AND THEN BREWSTER! BUT IF THAT'S TRUE...
IF THAT WAS TRUE, THEN MORE MURDERS WOULD FOLLOW... AND IN THAT MOMENT, THE SERGEANT'S UGLY THOUGHT WAS COMPLETED BY A HARSH CRY FROM THE CORPORAL WHO HAD JUST LEFT HIM . . .
WHAT THE HECK... NO-O-O..
SERGEANT HAMMOND HAD PAUSED BEHIND THE CORNER OF THE BRIDGE STRUCTURE. PROBABLY THE MURDERER HAD EXPECTED HIM TO WALK ON OUT OF EARSHOT. AS IT WAS SERGEANT HAMMOND WAS IN TIME TO SEE THE THIRD MURDER WITH HIS OWN HORROR-STRICKEN EYES . . .
STRINGER-CORPORAL STRINGER!

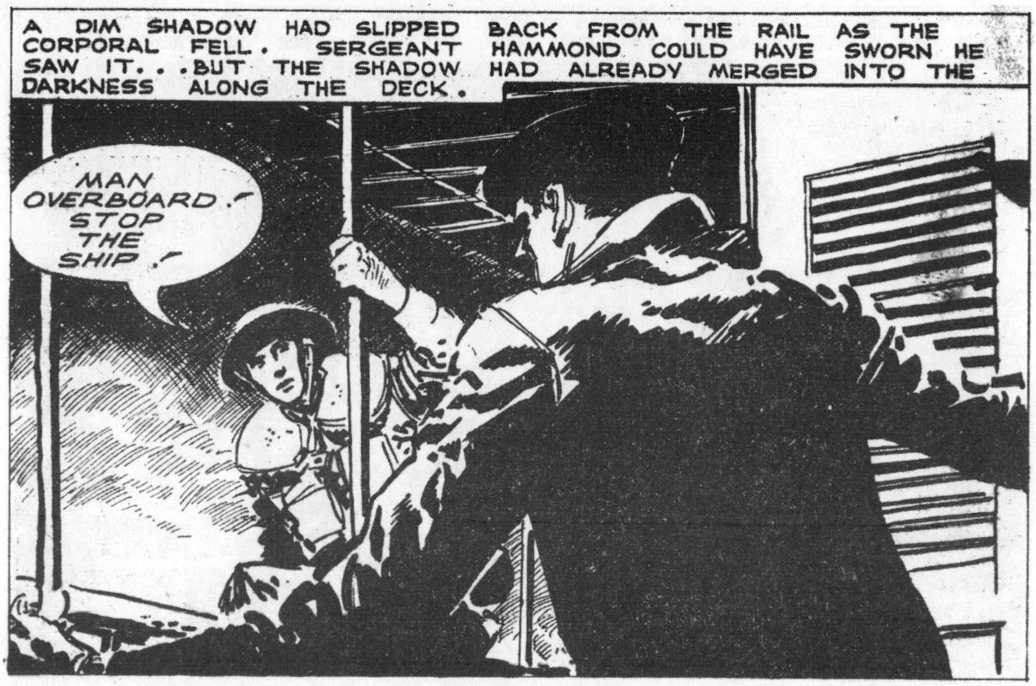
A DIM SHADOW HAD SLIPPED BACK FROM THE RAIL AS THE CORPORAL FELL. SERGEANT HAMMOND COULD HAVE SWORN HE SAW IT...BUT THE SHADOW HAD ALREADY MERGED INTO THE DARKNESS ALONG THE DECK.
MAN OVERBOARD! STOP THE SHIP!

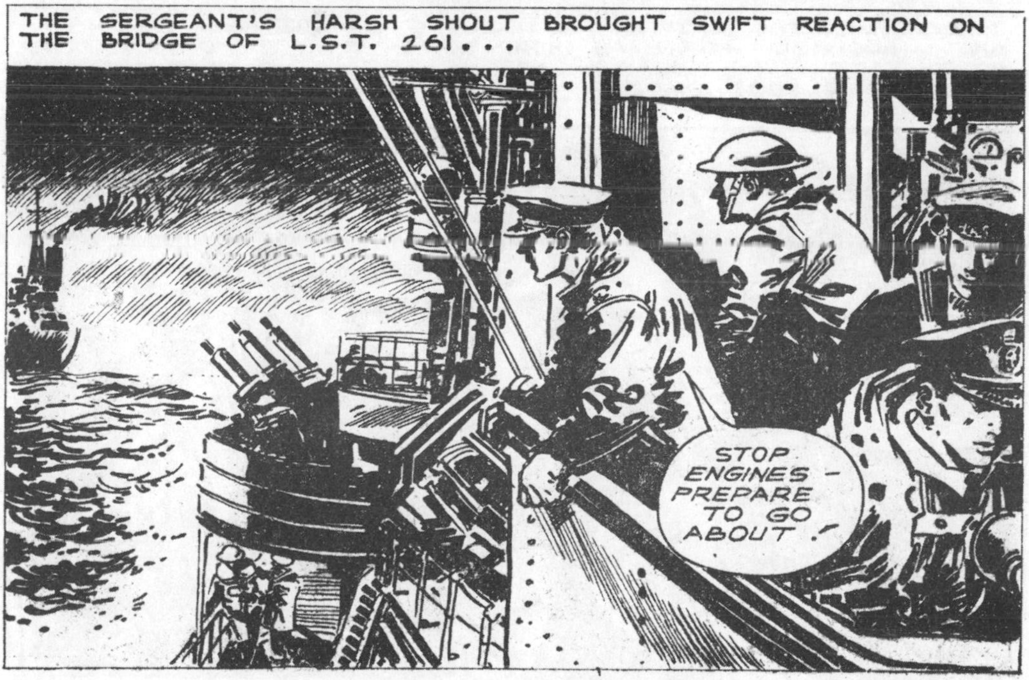
THE SERGEANT'S HARSH SHOUT BROUGHT SWIFT REACTION ON THE BRIDGE OF L.S.T. 261...
STOP ENGINES - PREPARE TO GO ABOUT!

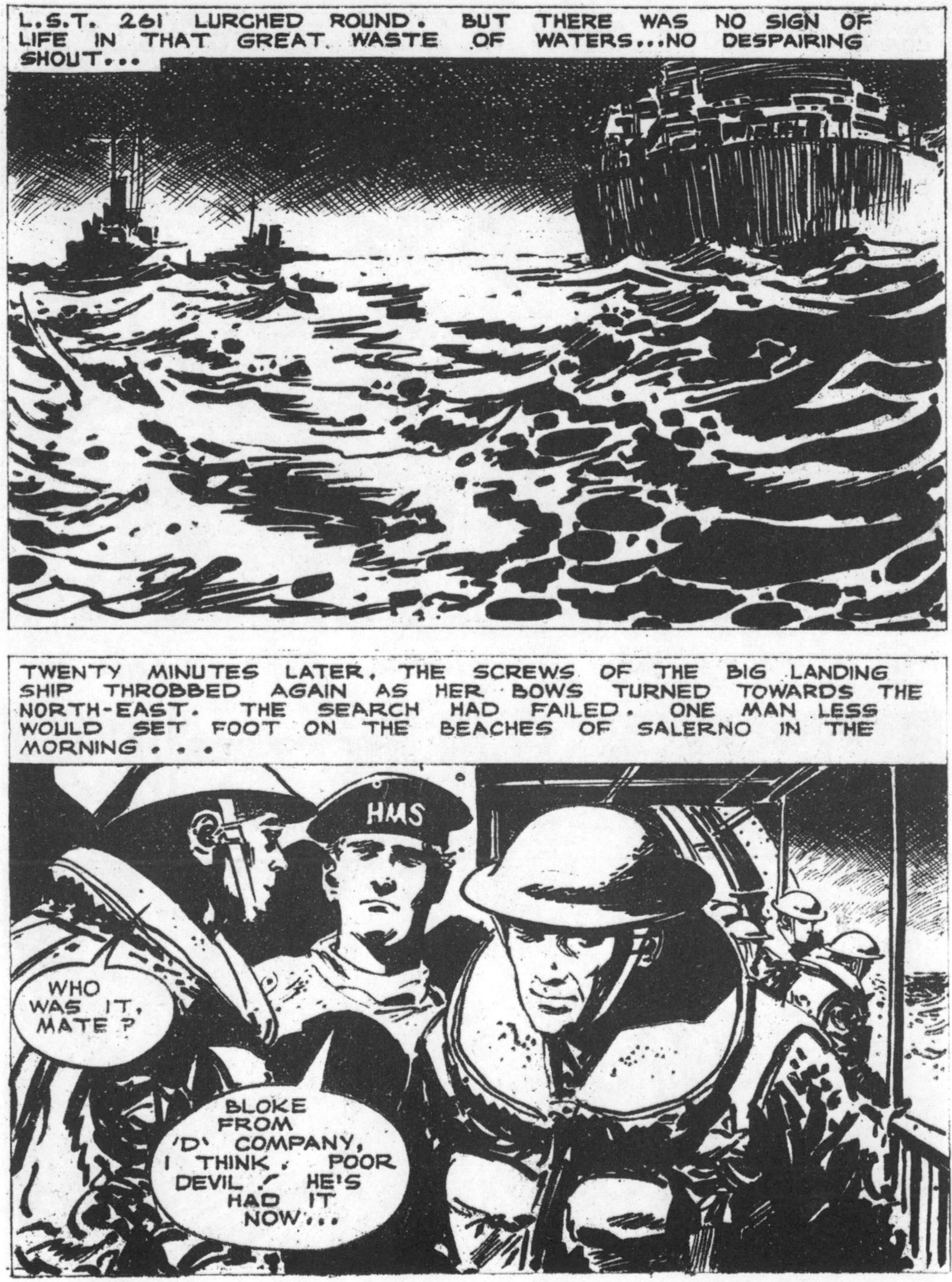
L.S.T. 261 LURCHED ROUND. BUT THERE WAS NO SIGN OF LIFE IN THAT GREAT WASTE OF WATERS...NO DESPAIRING SHOUT...
TWENTY MINUTES LATER, THE SCREWS OF THE BIG LANDING SHIP THROBBED AGAIN AS HER BOWS TURNED TOWARDS THE NORTH-EAST. THE SEARCH HAD FAILED. ONE MAN LESS WOULD SET FOOT ON THE BEACHES OF SALERNO IN THE MORNING . . .
HMS
WHO WAS IT, MATE ?
BLOKE FROM 'D' COMPANY, I THINK. POOR DEVIL ! HE'S HAD IT NOW...

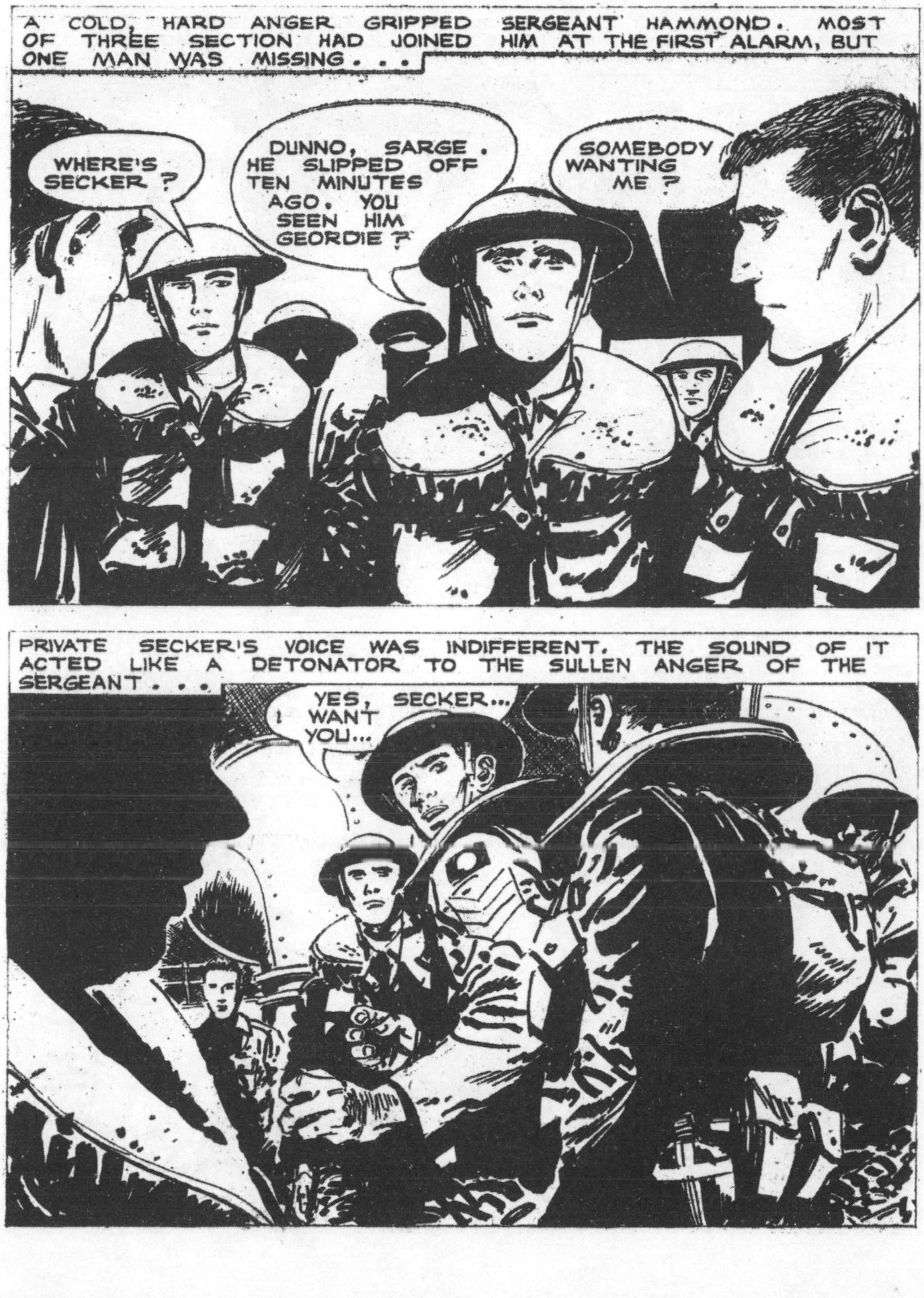
A COLD, HARD ANGER GRIPPED SERGEANT HAMMOND. MOST OF THREE SECTION HAD JOINED HIM AT THE FIRST ALARM, BUT ONE MAN WAS MISSING . . .
WHERE'S SECKER ?
DUNNO, SARGE. HE SLIPPED OFF TEN MINUTES AGO. YOU SEEN HIM GEORDIE ?
SOMEBODY WANTING ME ?
PRIVATE SECKER'S VOICE WAS INDIFFERENT. THE SOUND OF IT ACTED LIKE A DETONATOR TO THE SULLEN ANGER OF THE SERGEANT . . .
YES, SECKER... I WANT YOU...

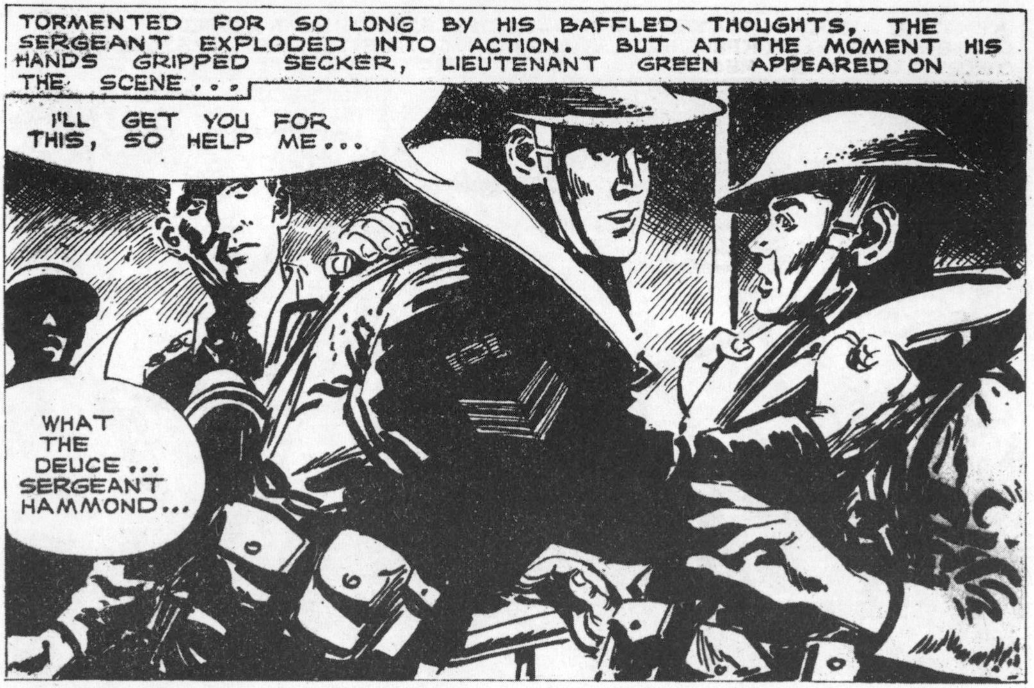
TORMENTED FOR SO LONG BY HIS BAFFLED THOUGHTS, THE SERGEANT EXPLODED INTO ACTION. BUT AT THE MOMENT HIS HANDS GRIPPED SECKER, LIEUTENANT GREEN APPEARED ON THE SCENE...
I'LL GET YOU FOR THIS, SO HELP ME...
WHAT THE DEUCE... SERGEANT HAMMOND...

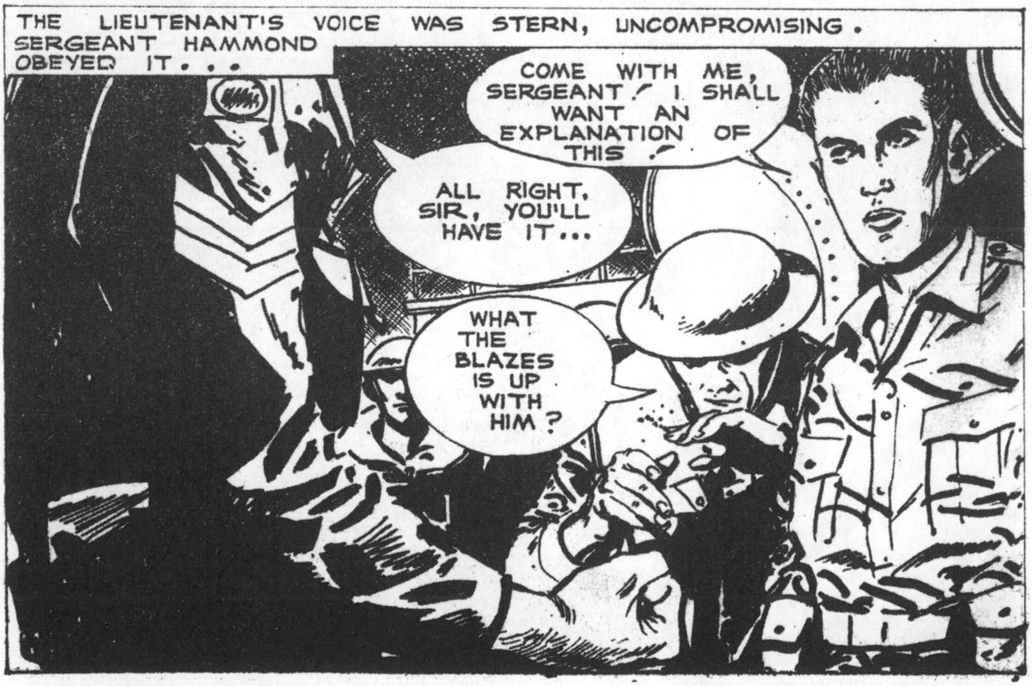
THE LIEUTENANT'S VOICE WAS STERN, UNCOMPROMISING. SERGEANT HAMMOND OBEYED IT...
COME WITH ME, SERGEANT! I SHALL WANT AN EXPLANATION OF THIS!
ALL RIGHT, SIR, YOU'LL HAVE IT...
WHAT THE BLAZES IS UP WITH HIM?

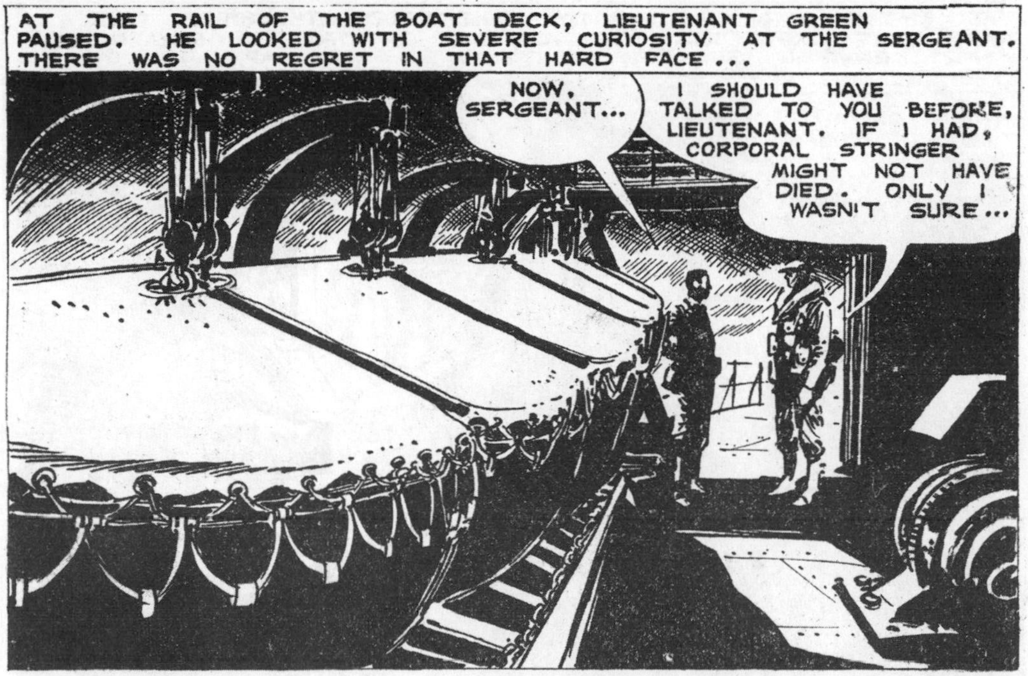
AT THE RAIL OF THE BOAT DECK, LIEUTENANT GREEN PAUSED. HE LOOKED WITH SEVERE CURIOSITY AT THE SERGEANT. THERE WAS NO REGRET IN THAT HARD FACE...
NOW, SERGEANT...
I SHOULD HAVE TALKED TO YOU BEFORE, LIEUTENANT. IF I HAD, CORPORAL STRINGER MIGHT NOT HAVE DIED. ONLY I WASN'T SURE...

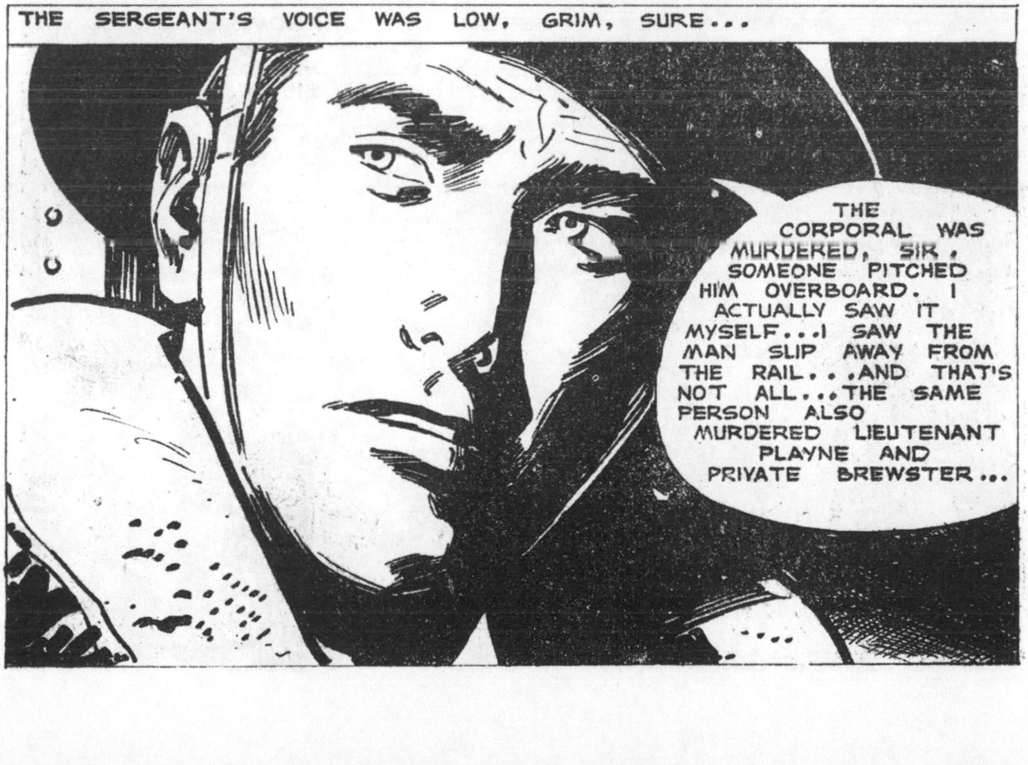
THE SERGEANT'S VOICE WAS LOW, GRIM, SURE...
THE CORPORAL WAS MURDERED, SIR. SOMEONE PITCHED HIM OVERBOARD. I ACTUALLY SAW IT MYSELF...I SAW THE MAN SLIP AWAY FROM THE RAIL...AND THAT'S NOT ALL...THE SAME PERSON ALSO MURDERED LIEUTENANT PLAYNE AND PRIVATE BREWSTER...

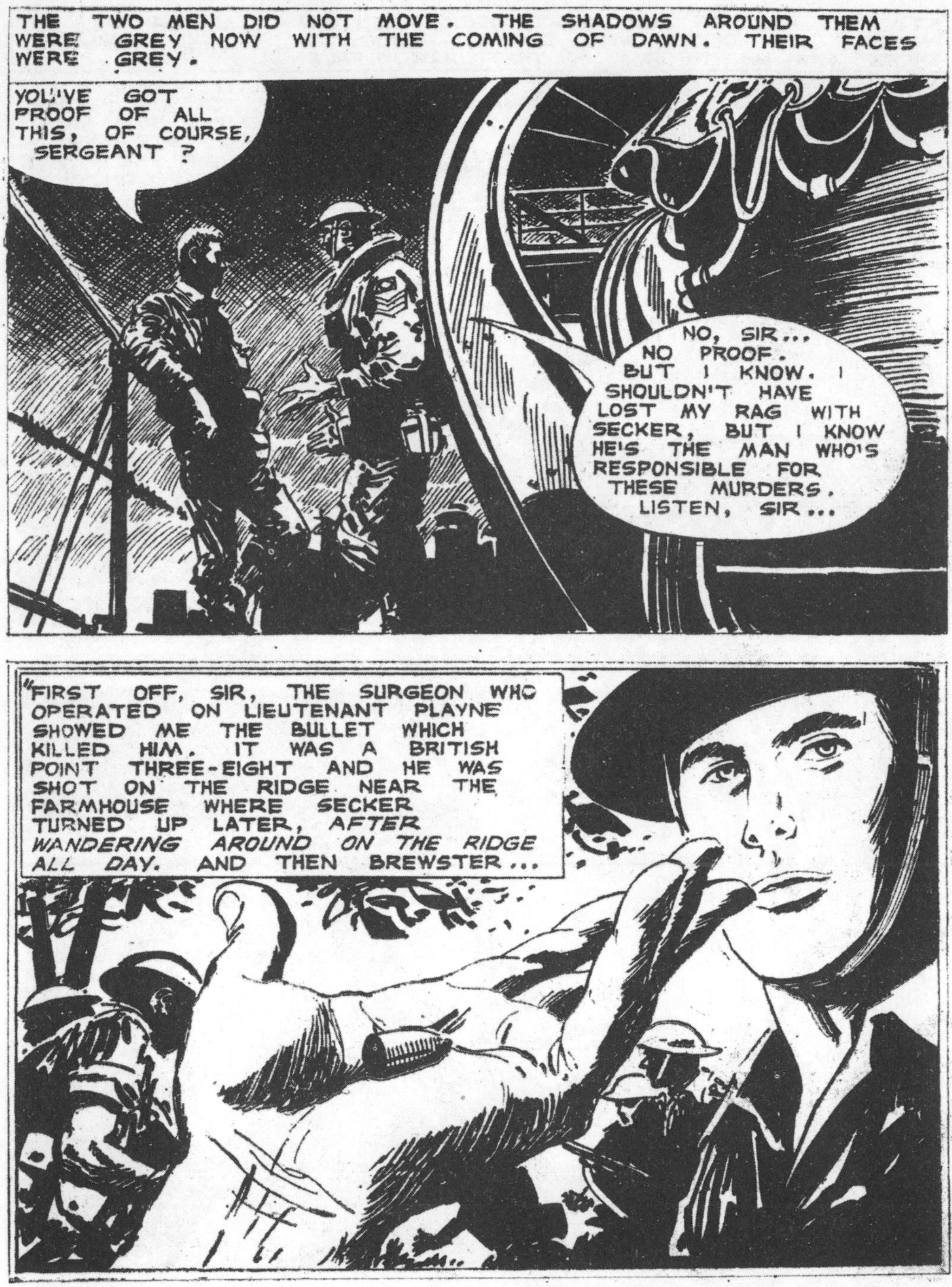
THE TWO MEN DID NOT MOVE. THE SHADOWS AROUND THEM WERE GREY NOW WITH THE COMING OF DAWN. THEIR FACES WERE GREY.
YOU'VE GOT PROOF OF ALL THIS, OF COURSE, SERGEANT ?
NO, SIR... NO PROOF. BUT I KNOW. I SHOULDN'T HAVE LOST MY RAG WITH SECKER, BUT I KNOW HE'S THE MAN WHO'S RESPONSIBLE FOR THESE MURDERS. LISTEN, SIR...
"FIRST OFF, SIR, THE SURGEON WHO OPERATED ON LIEUTENANT PLAYNE SHOWED ME THE BULLET WHICH KILLED HIM. IT WAS A BRITISH POINT THREE-EIGHT AND HE WAS SHOT ON THE RIDGE NEAR THE FARMHOUSE WHERE SECKER TURNED UP LATER, AFTER WANDERING AROUND ON THE RIDGE ALL DAY. AND THEN BREWSTER...

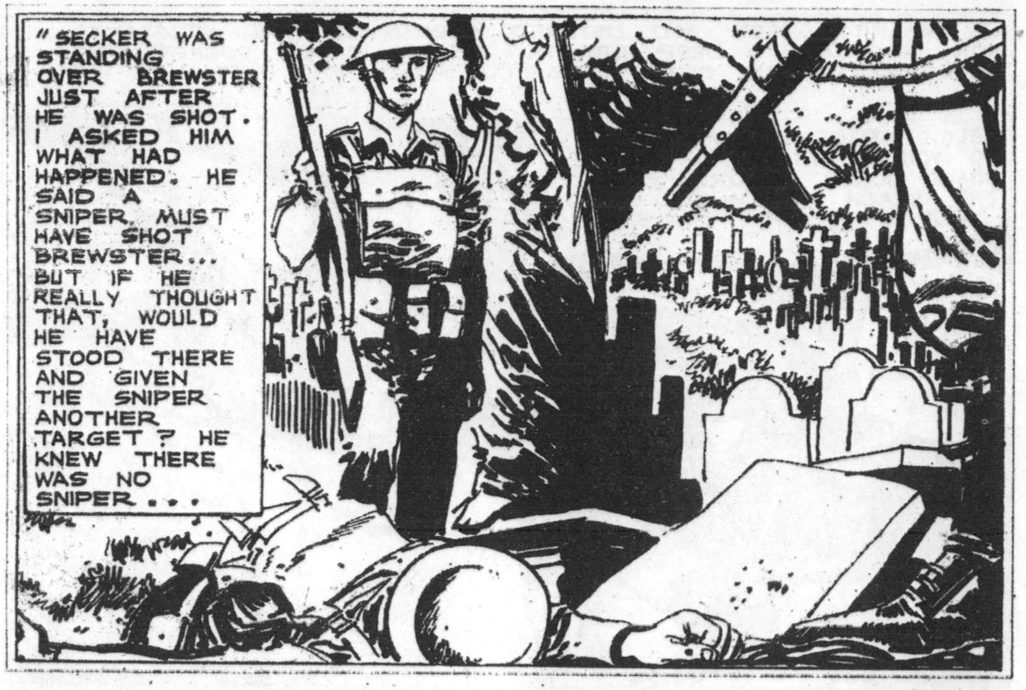
"SECKER WAS STANDING OVER BREWSTER JUST AFTER HE WAS SHOT. I ASKED HIM WHAT HAD HAPPENED. HE SAID A SNIPER MUST HAVE SHOT BREWSTER... BUT IF HE REALLY THOUGHT THAT, WOULD HE HAVE STOOD THERE AND GIVEN THE SNIPER ANOTHER TARGET? HE KNEW THERE WAS NO SNIPER...

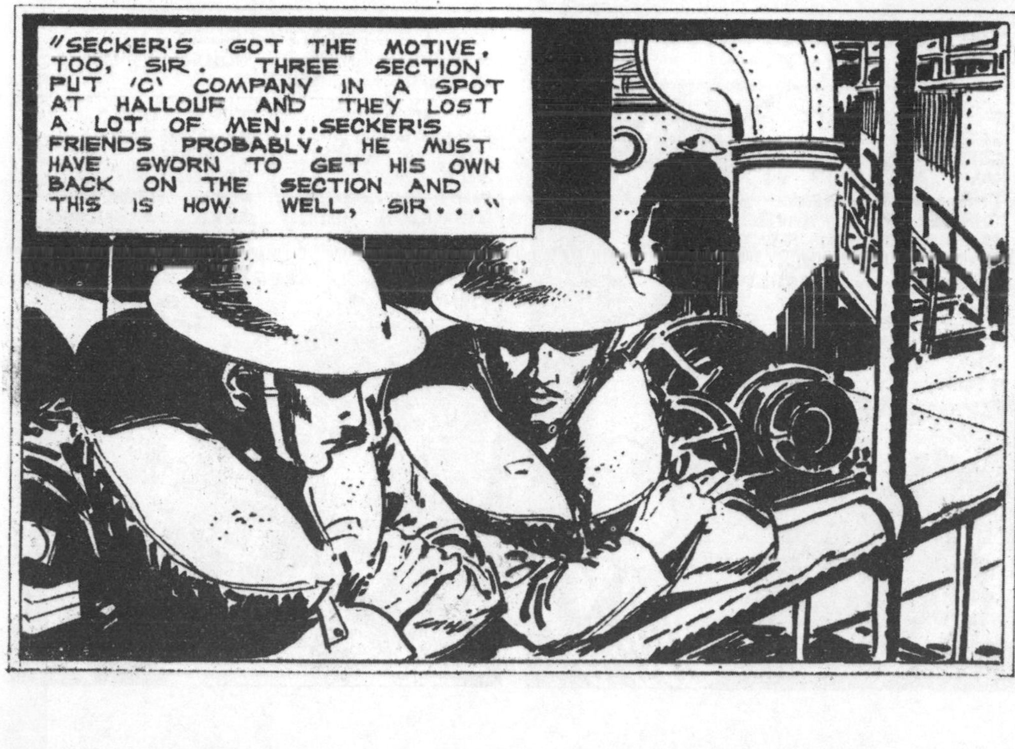
"SECKER'S GOT THE MOTIVE, TOO, SIR. THREE SECTION PUT 'C' COMPANY IN A SPOT AT HALLOUF AND THEY LOST A LOT OF MEN...SECKER'S FRIENDS PROBABLY. HE MUST HAVE SWORN TO GET HIS OWN BACK ON THE SECTION AND THIS IS HOW. WELL, SIR..."

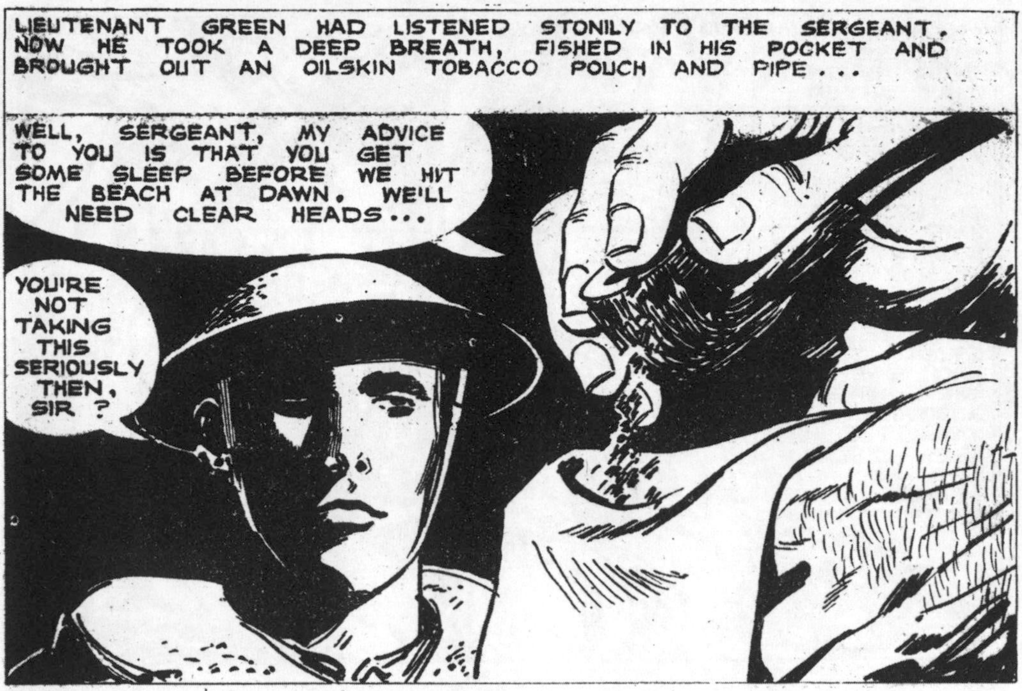
LIEUTENANT GREEN HAD LISTENED STONILY TO THE SERGEANT. NOW HE TOOK A DEEP BREATH, FISHED IN HIS POCKET AND BROUGHT OUT AN OILSKIN TOBACCO POUCH AND PIPE...
WELL, SERGEANT, MY ADVICE TO YOU IS THAT YOU GET SOME SLEEP BEFORE WE HIT THE BEACH AT DAWN. WE'LL NEED CLEAR HEADS...
YOU'RE NOT TAKING THIS SERIOUSLY THEN, SIR ?

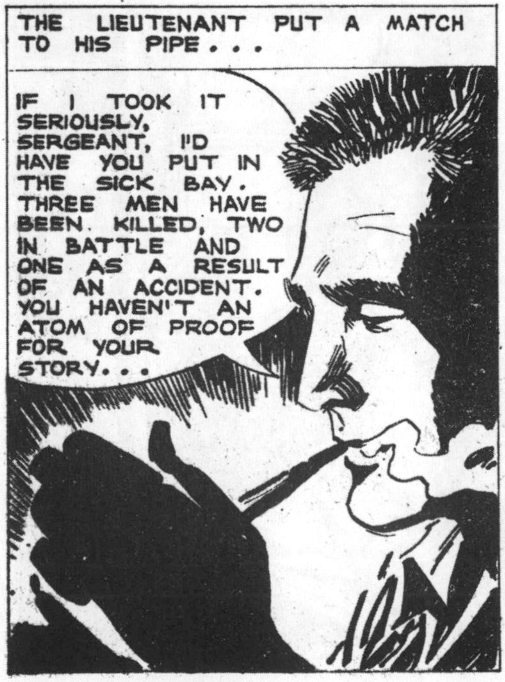
THE LIEUTENANT PUT A MATCH TO HIS PIPE...
IF I TOOK IT SERIOUSLY, SERGEANT, I'D HAVE YOU PUT IN THE SICK BAY. THREE MEN HAVE BEEN KILLED, TWO IN BATTLE AND ONE AS A RESULT OF AN ACCIDENT. YOU HAVEN'T AN ATOM OF PROOF FOR YOUR STORY...

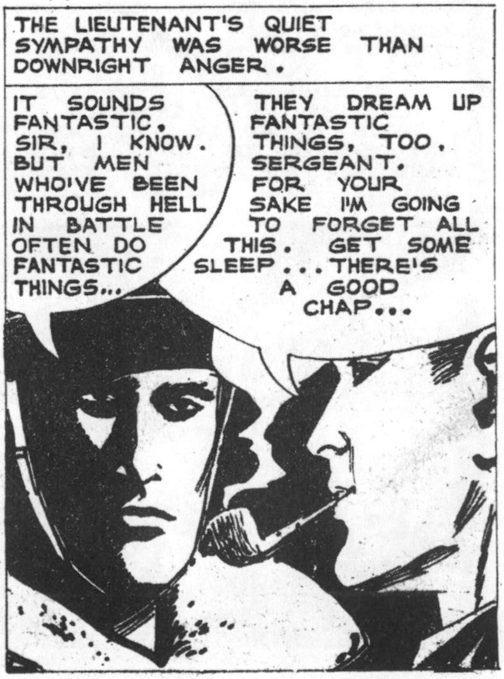
THE LIEUTENANT'S QUIET SYMPATHY WAS WORSE THAN DOWNRIGHT ANGER.
IT SOUNDS FANTASTIC, SIR, I KNOW. BUT MEN WHO'VE BEEN THROUGH HELL IN BATTLE OFTEN DO FANTASTIC THINGS...
THEY DREAM UP FANTASTIC THINGS, TOO, SERGEANT. FOR YOUR SAKE I'M GOING TO FORGET ALL THIS. GET SOME SLEEP... THERE'S A GOOD CHAP...

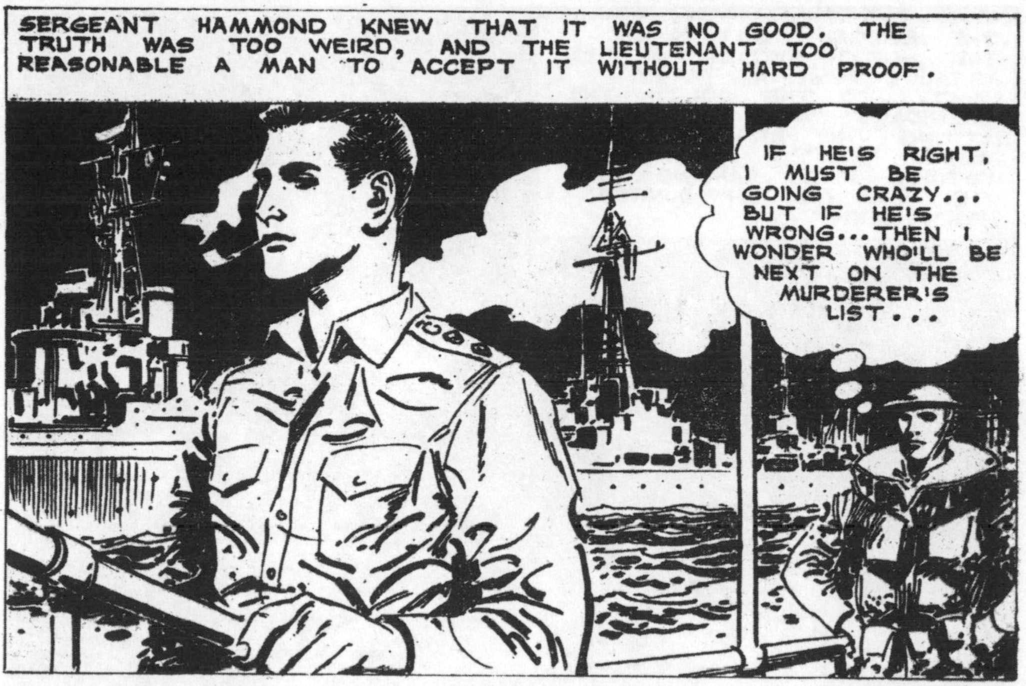
SERGEANT HAMMOND KNEW THAT IT WAS NO GOOD. THE TRUTH WAS TOO WEIRD, AND THE LIEUTENANT TOO REASONABLE A MAN TO ACCEPT IT WITHOUT HARD PROOF.
IF HE'S RIGHT, I MUST BE GOING CRAZY... BUT IF HE'S WRONG...THEN I WONDER WHO'LL BE NEXT ON THE MURDERER'S LIST...

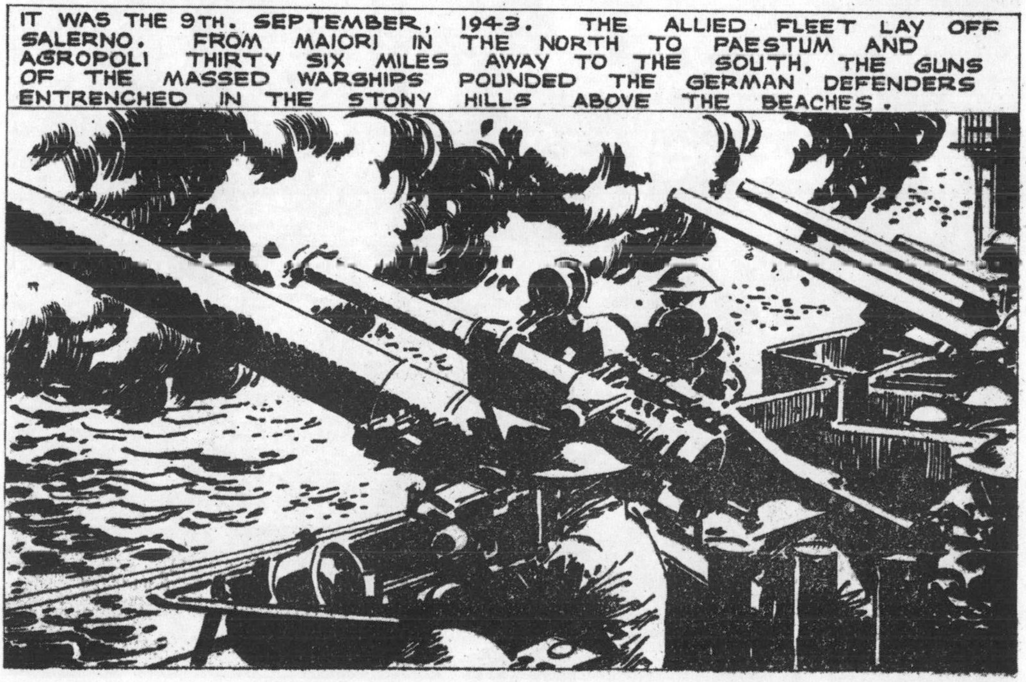
IT WAS THE 9TH. SEPTEMBER, 1943. THE ALLIED FLEET LAY OFF SALERNO. FROM MAIORI IN THE NORTH TO PAESTUM AND AGROPOLI THIRTY SIX MILES AWAY TO THE SOUTH, THE GUNS OF THE MASSED WARSHIPS POUNDED THE GERMAN DEFENDERS ENTRENCHED IN THE STONY HILLS ABOVE THE BEACHES.

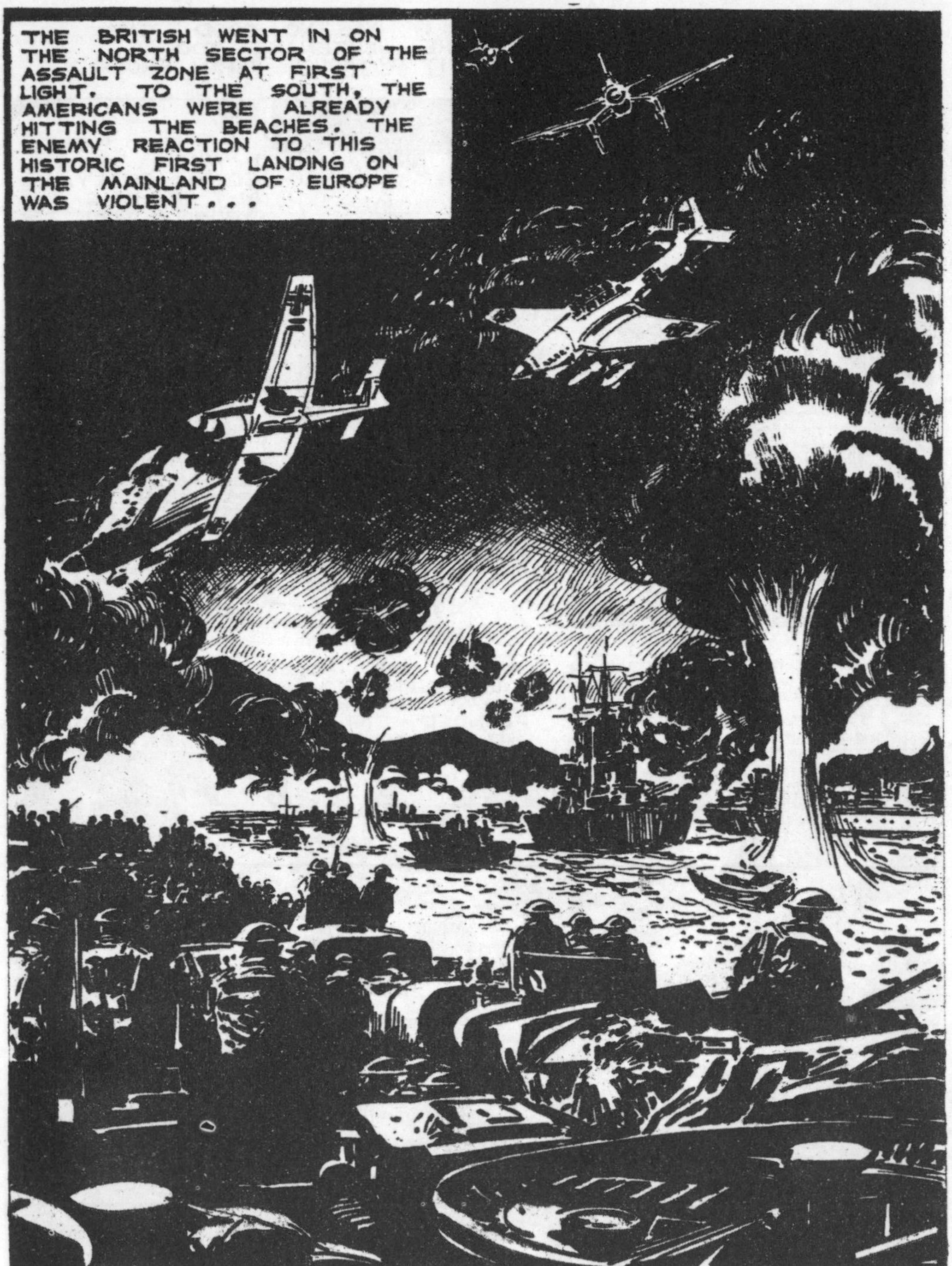
THE BRITISH WENT IN ON THE NORTH SECTOR OF THE ASSAULT ZONE AT FIRST LIGHT. TO THE SOUTH, THE AMERICANS WERE ALREADY HITTING THE BEACHES. THE ENEMY REACTION TO THIS HISTORIC FIRST LANDING ON THE MAINLAND OF EUROPE WAS VIOLENT . . .

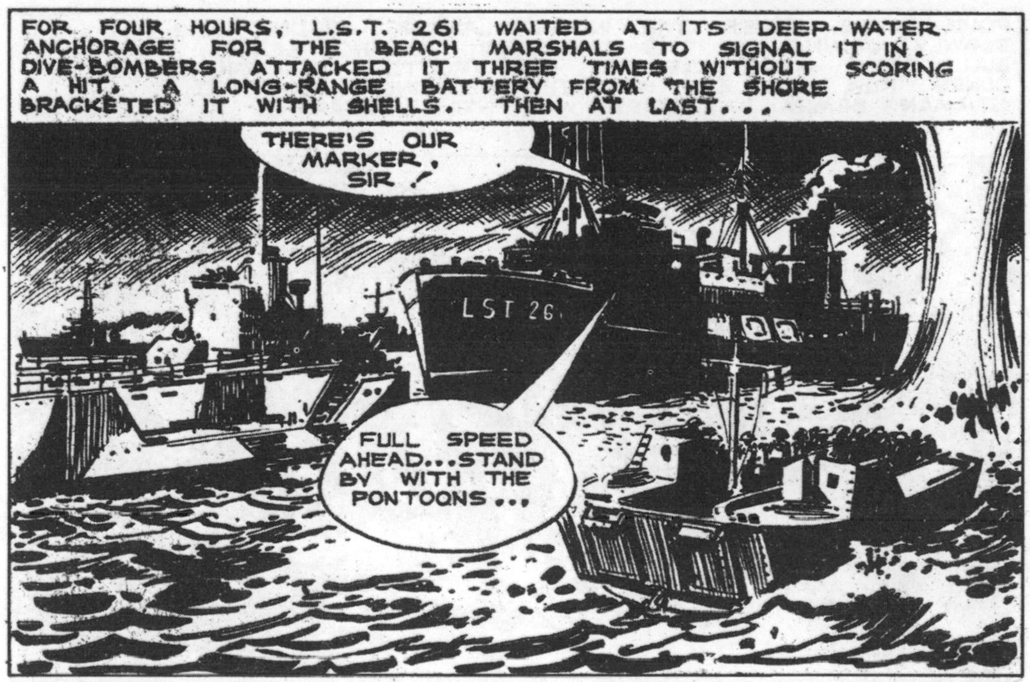
FOR FOUR HOURS, L.S.T. 261 WAITED AT ITS DEEP-WATER ANCHORAGE FOR THE BEACH MARSHALS TO SIGNAL IT IN. DIVE-BOMBERS ATTACKED IT THREE TIMES WITHOUT SCORING A HIT. A LONG-RANGE BATTERY FROM THE SHORE BRACKETED IT WITH SHELLS. THEN AT LAST...
THERE'S OUR MARKER, SIR!
LST 26
FULL SPEED AHEAD...STAND BY WITH THE PONTOONS...

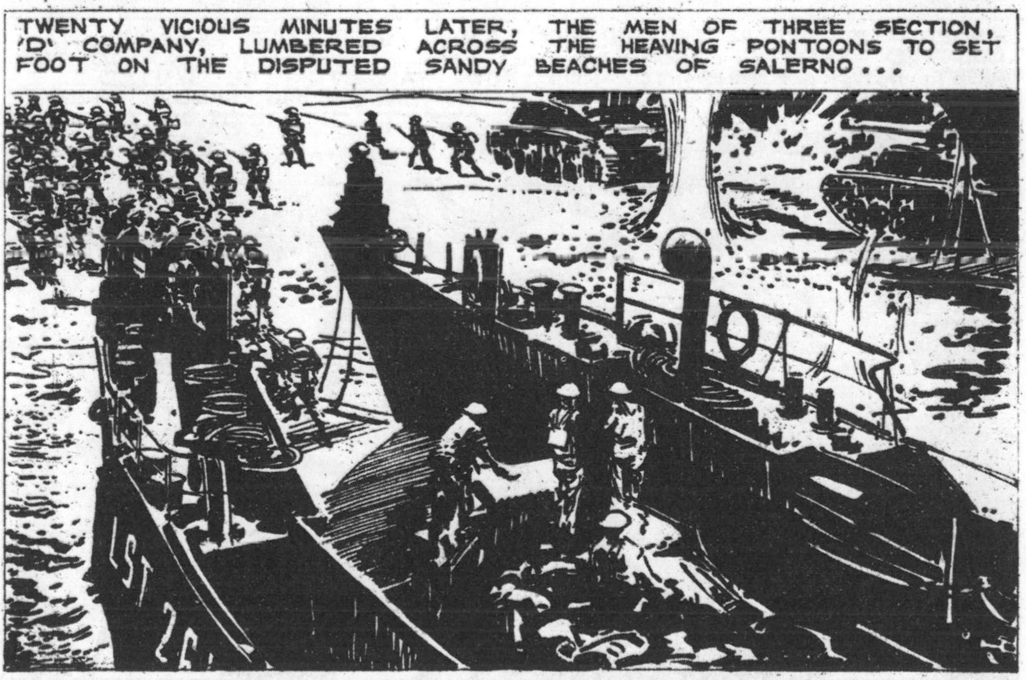
TWENTY VICIOUS MINUTES LATER, THE MEN OF THREE SECTION, 'D' COMPANY, LUMBERED ACROSS THE HEAVING PONTOONS TO SET FOOT ON THE DISPUTED SANDY BEACHES OF SALERNO...

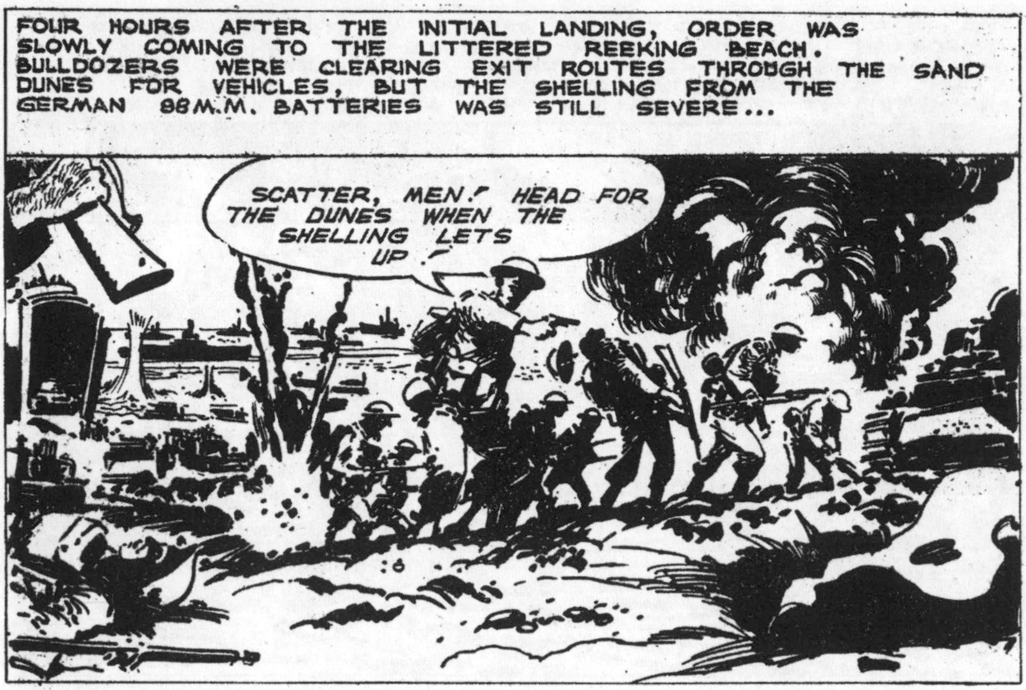
FOUR HOURS AFTER THE INITIAL LANDING, ORDER WAS SLOWLY COMING TO THE LITTERED REEKING BEACH. BULLDOZERS WERE CLEARING EXIT ROUTES THROUGH THE SAND DUNES FOR VEHICLES, BUT THE SHELLING FROM THE GERMAN 88M.M. BATTERIES WAS STILL SEVERE...
SCATTER, MEN! HEAD FOR THE DUNES WHEN THE SHELLING LETS UP!

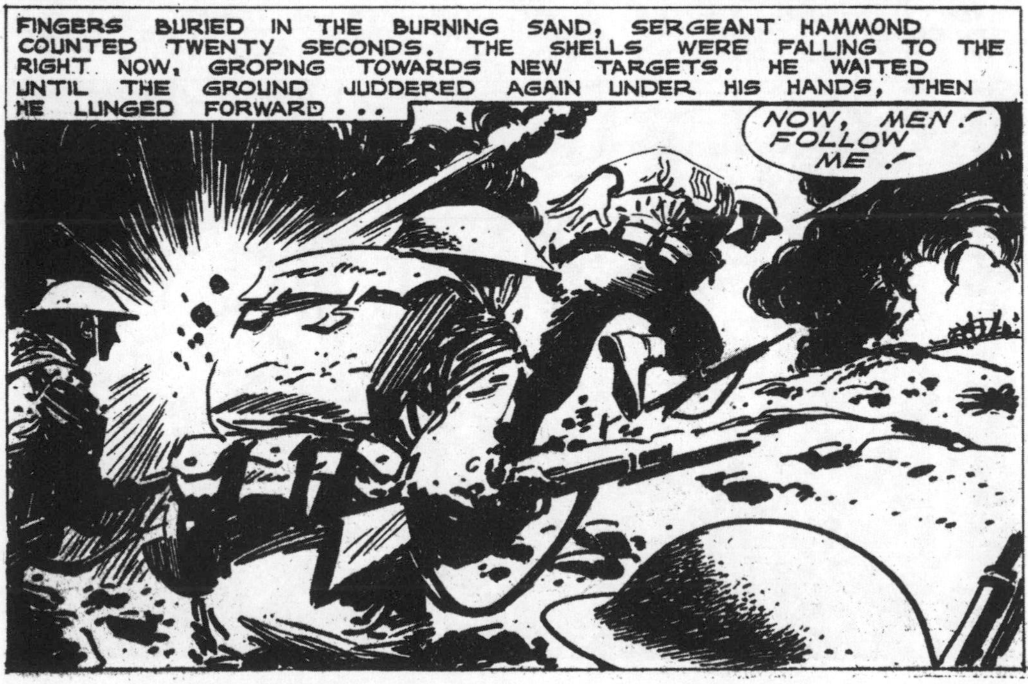
FINGERS BURIED IN THE BURNING SAND, SERGEANT HAMMOND COUNTED TWENTY SECONDS. THE SHELLS WERE FALLING TO THE RIGHT NOW, GROPING TOWARDS NEW TARGETS. HE WAITED UNTIL THE GROUND JUDDERED AGAIN UNDER HIS HANDS, THEN HE LUNGED FORWARD...
NOW, MEN! FOLLOW ME!

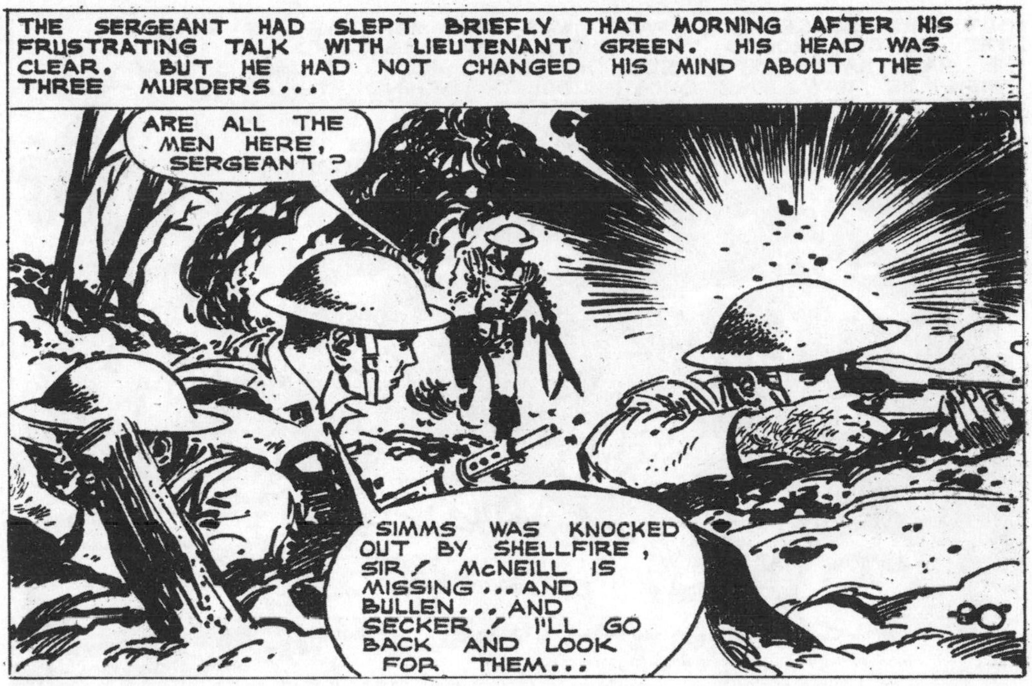
THE SERGEANT HAD SLEPT BRIEFLY THAT MORNING AFTER HIS FRUSTRATING TALK WITH LIEUTENANT GREEN. HIS HEAD WAS CLEAR. BUT HE HAD NOT CHANGED HIS MIND ABOUT THE THREE MURDERS...
ARE ALL THE MEN HERE, SERGEANT?
SIMMS WAS KNOCKED OUT BY SHELLFIRE, SIR! McNEILL IS MISSING...AND BULLEN...AND SECKER! I'LL GO BACK AND LOOK FOR THEM...

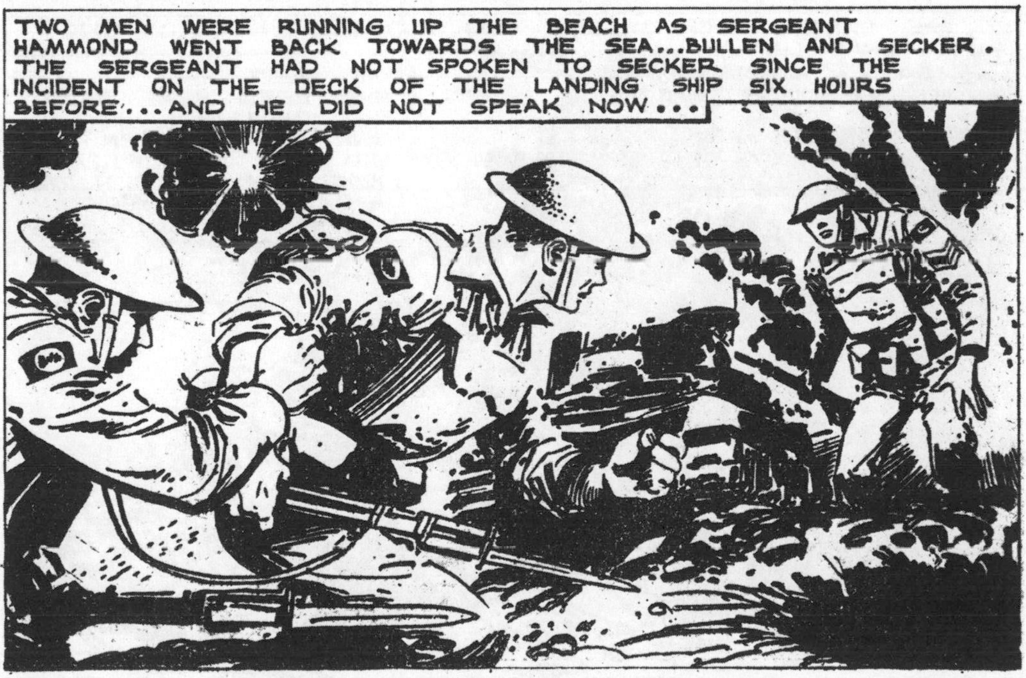
TWO MEN WERE RUNNING UP THE BEACH AS SERGEANT HAMMOND WENT BACK TOWARDS THE SEA...BULLEN AND SECKER. THE SERGEANT HAD NOT SPOKEN TO SECKER SINCE THE INCIDENT ON THE DECK OF THE LANDING SHIP SIX HOURS BEFORE...AND HE DID NOT SPEAK NOW...

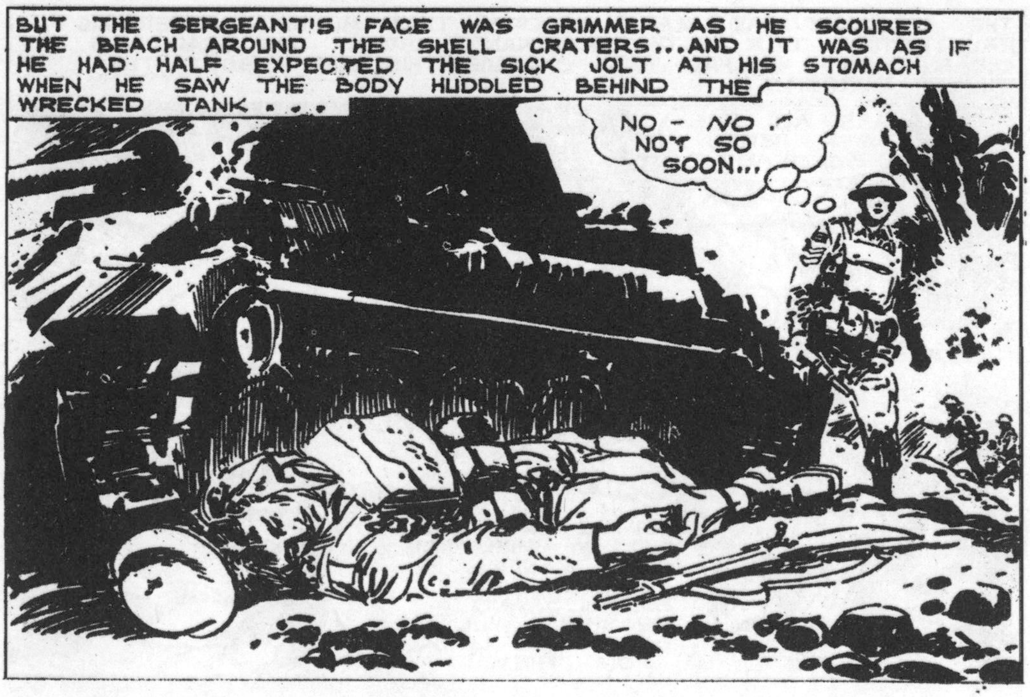
BUT THE SERGEANT'S FACE WAS GRIMMER AS HE SCOURED THE BEACH AROUND THE SHELL CRATERS...AND IT WAS AS IF HE HAD HALF EXPECTED THE SICK JOLT AT HIS STOMACH WHEN HE SAW THE BODY HUDDLED BEHIND THE WRECKED TANK...
NO - NO - NOT SO SOON...

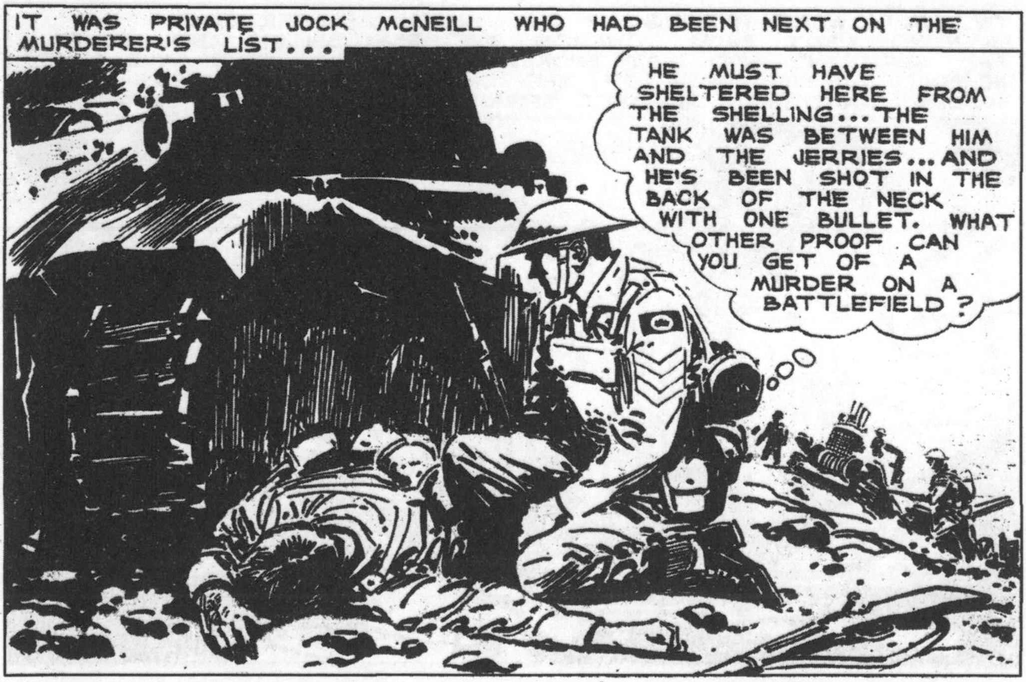
IT WAS PRIVATE JOCK McNEILL WHO HAD BEEN NEXT ON THE MURDERER'S LIST...
HE MUST HAVE SHELTERED HERE FROM THE SHELLING... THE TANK WAS BETWEEN HIM AND THE JERRIES... AND HE'S BEEN SHOT IN THE BACK OF THE NECK WITH ONE BULLET. WHAT OTHER PROOF CAN YOU GET OF A MURDER ON A BATTLEFIELD?

Chapter 3. Murderer Unmasked

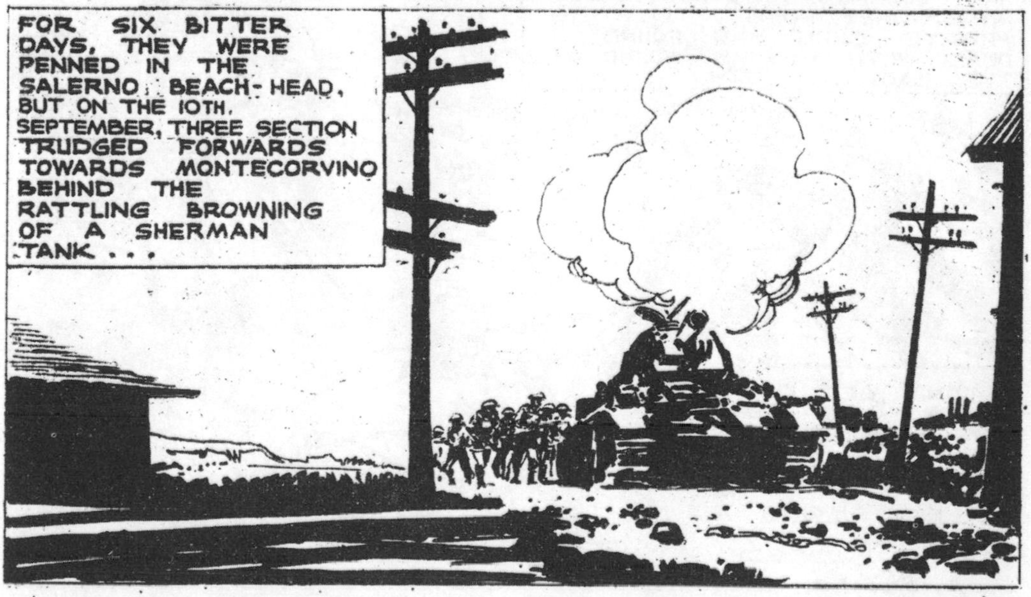
FOR SIX BITTER DAYS, THEY WERE PENNED IN THE SALERNO BEACH-HEAD, BUT ON THE 10TH SEPTEMBER, THREE SECTION TRUDGED FORWARDS TOWARDS MONTECORVINO BEHIND THE RATTLING BROWNING OF A SHERMAN TANK . . .

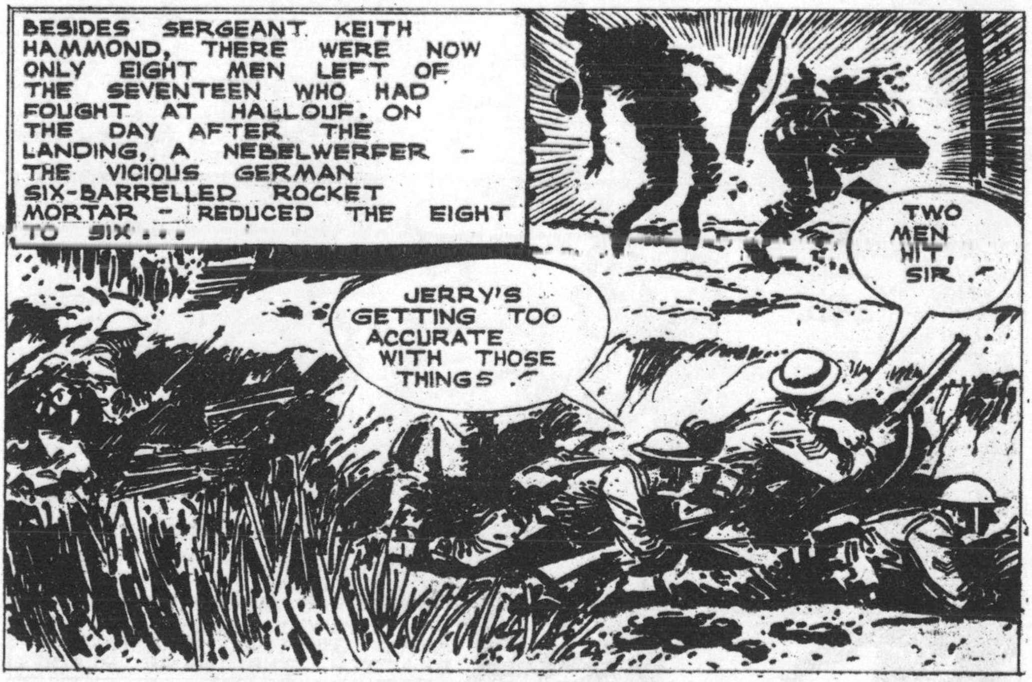
BESIDES SERGEANT KEITH HAMMOND, THERE WERE NOW ONLY EIGHT MEN LEFT OF THE SEVENTEEN WHO HAD FOUGHT AT HALLOUF. ON THE DAY AFTER THE LANDING, A NEBELWERFER – THE VICIOUS GERMAN SIX-BARRELLED ROCKET MORTAR – REDUCED THE EIGHT TO SIX . . .
TWO MEN HIT, SIR.
JERRY'S GETTING TOO ACCURATE WITH THOSE THINGS.

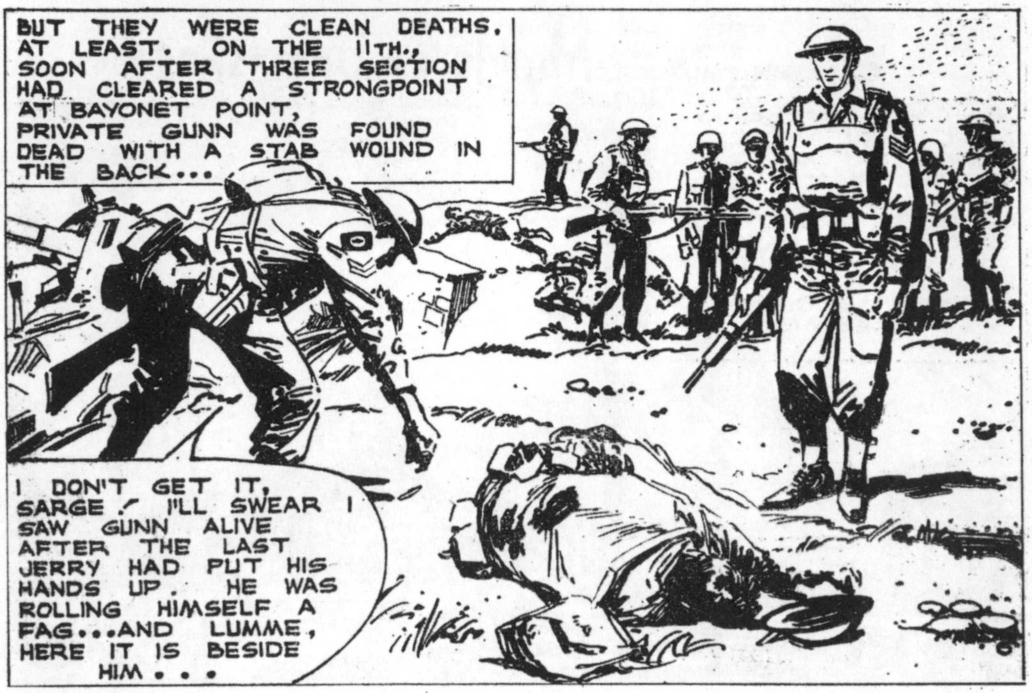
BUT THEY WERE CLEAN DEATHS, AT LEAST. ON THE 11TH., SOON AFTER THREE SECTION HAD CLEARED A STRONGPOINT AT BAYONET POINT, PRIVATE GUNN WAS FOUND DEAD WITH A STAB WOUND IN THE BACK...
I DON'T GET IT, SARGE! I'LL SWEAR I SAW GUNN ALIVE AFTER THE LAST JERRY HAD PUT HIS HANDS UP. HE WAS ROLLING HIMSELF A FAG...AND LUMME, HERE IT IS BESIDE HIM...

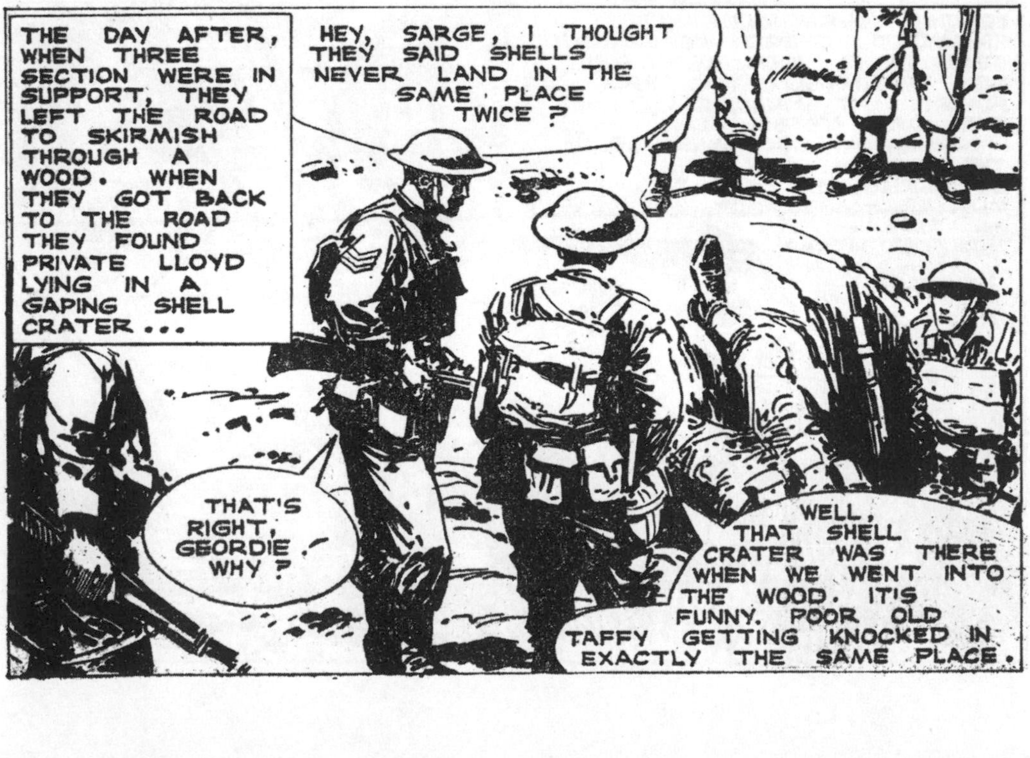
THE DAY AFTER, WHEN THREE SECTION WERE IN SUPPORT, THEY LEFT THE ROAD TO SKIRMISH THROUGH A WOOD. WHEN THEY GOT BACK TO THE ROAD THEY FOUND PRIVATE LLOYD LYING IN A GAPING SHELL CRATER...
HEY, SARGE, I THOUGHT THEY SAID SHELLS NEVER LAND IN THE SAME PLACE TWICE?
THAT'S RIGHT, GEORDIE. WHY?
WELL, THAT SHELL CRATER WAS THERE WHEN WE WENT INTO THE WOOD. IT'S FUNNY. POOR OLD TAFFY GETTING KNOCKED IN EXACTLY THE SAME PLACE.

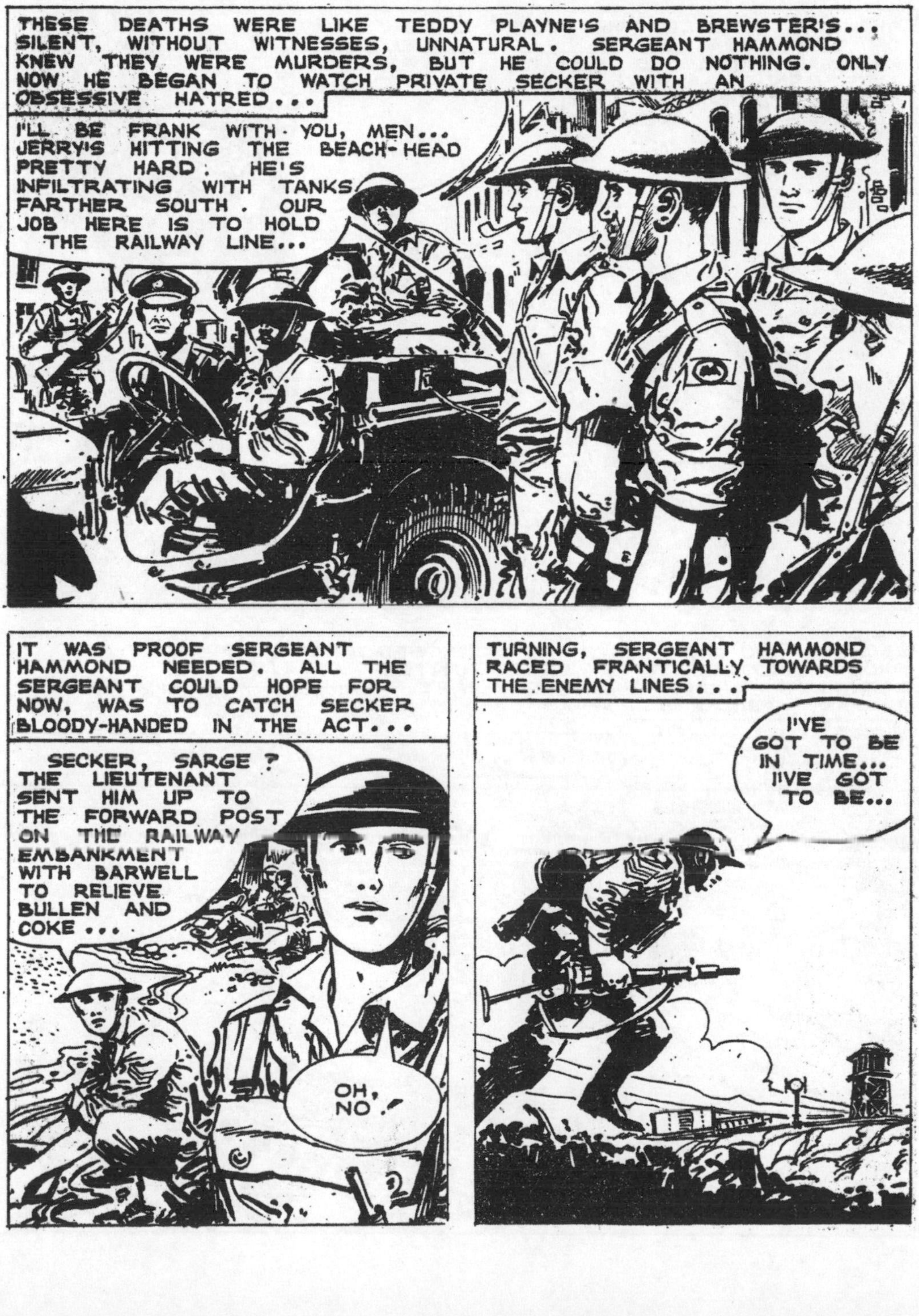
THESE DEATHS WERE LIKE TEDDY PLAYNE'S AND BREWSTER'S... SILENT, WITHOUT WITNESSES, UNNATURAL. SERGEANT HAMMOND KNEW THEY WERE MURDERS, BUT HE COULD DO NOTHING. ONLY NOW HE BEGAN TO WATCH PRIVATE SECKER WITH AN OBSESSIVE HATRED...
I'LL BE FRANK WITH YOU, MEN... JERRY'S HITTING THE BEACH-HEAD PRETTY HARD. HE'S INFILTRATING WITH TANKS FARTHER SOUTH. OUR JOB HERE IS TO HOLD THE RAILWAY LINE...
IT WAS PROOF SERGEANT HAMMOND NEEDED. ALL THE SERGEANT COULD HOPE FOR NOW, WAS TO CATCH SECKER BLOODY-HANDED IN THE ACT...
SECKER, SARGE? THE LIEUTENANT SENT HIM UP TO THE FORWARD POST ON THE RAILWAY EMBANKMENT WITH BARWELL TO RELIEVE BULLEN AND COKE...
OH, NO!
TURNING, SERGEANT HAMMOND RACED FRANTICALLY TOWARDS THE ENEMY LINES...
I'VE GOT TO BE IN TIME... I'VE GOT TO BE...

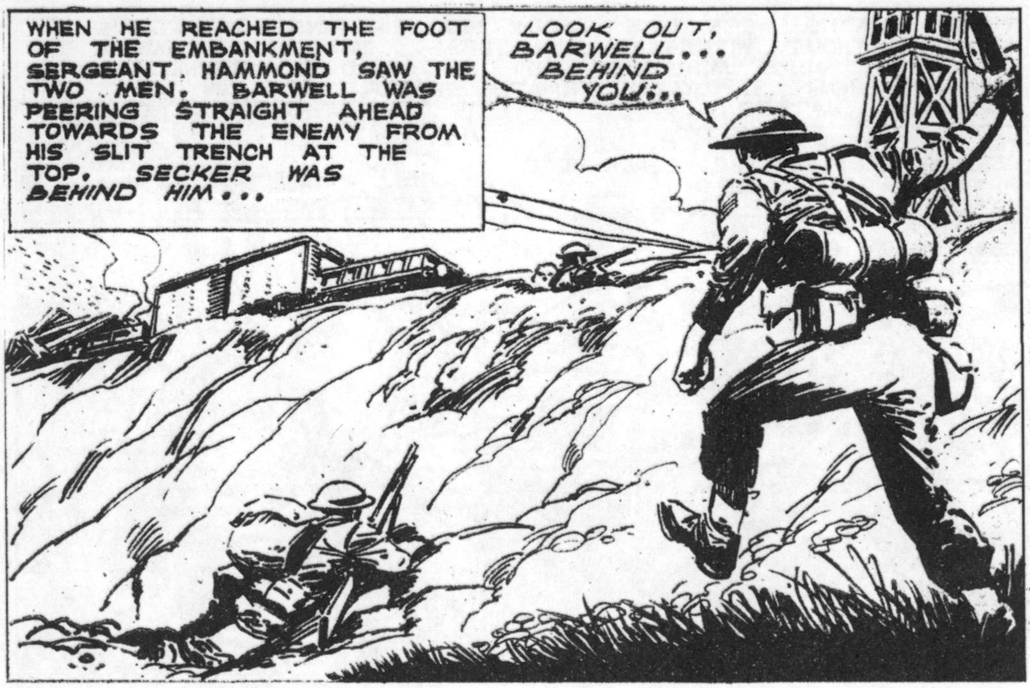
WHEN HE REACHED THE FOOT OF THE EMBANKMENT, SERGEANT HAMMOND SAW THE TWO MEN. BARWELL WAS PEERING STRAIGHT AHEAD TOWARDS THE ENEMY FROM HIS SLIT TRENCH AT THE TOP. SECKER WAS BEHIND HIM...
LOOK OUT, BARWELL... BEHIND YOU!...

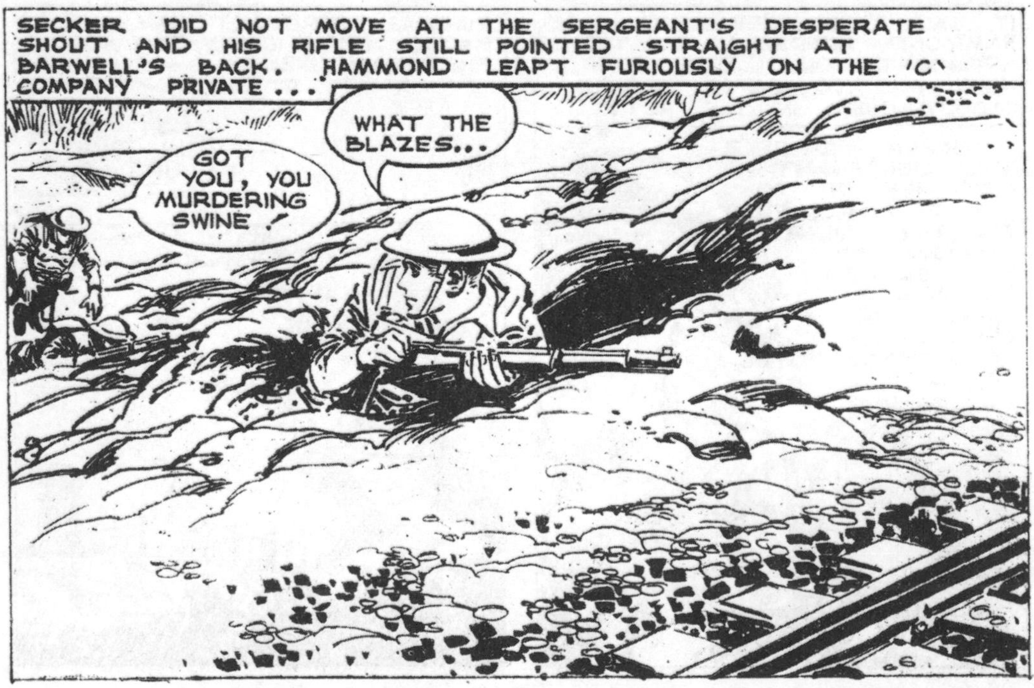
SECKER DID NOT MOVE AT THE SERGEANT'S DESPERATE SHOUT AND HIS RIFLE STILL POINTED STRAIGHT AT BARWELL'S BACK. HAMMOND LEAPT FURIOUSLY ON THE 'C' COMPANY PRIVATE...
GOT YOU, YOU MURDERING SWINE!
WHAT THE BLAZES...

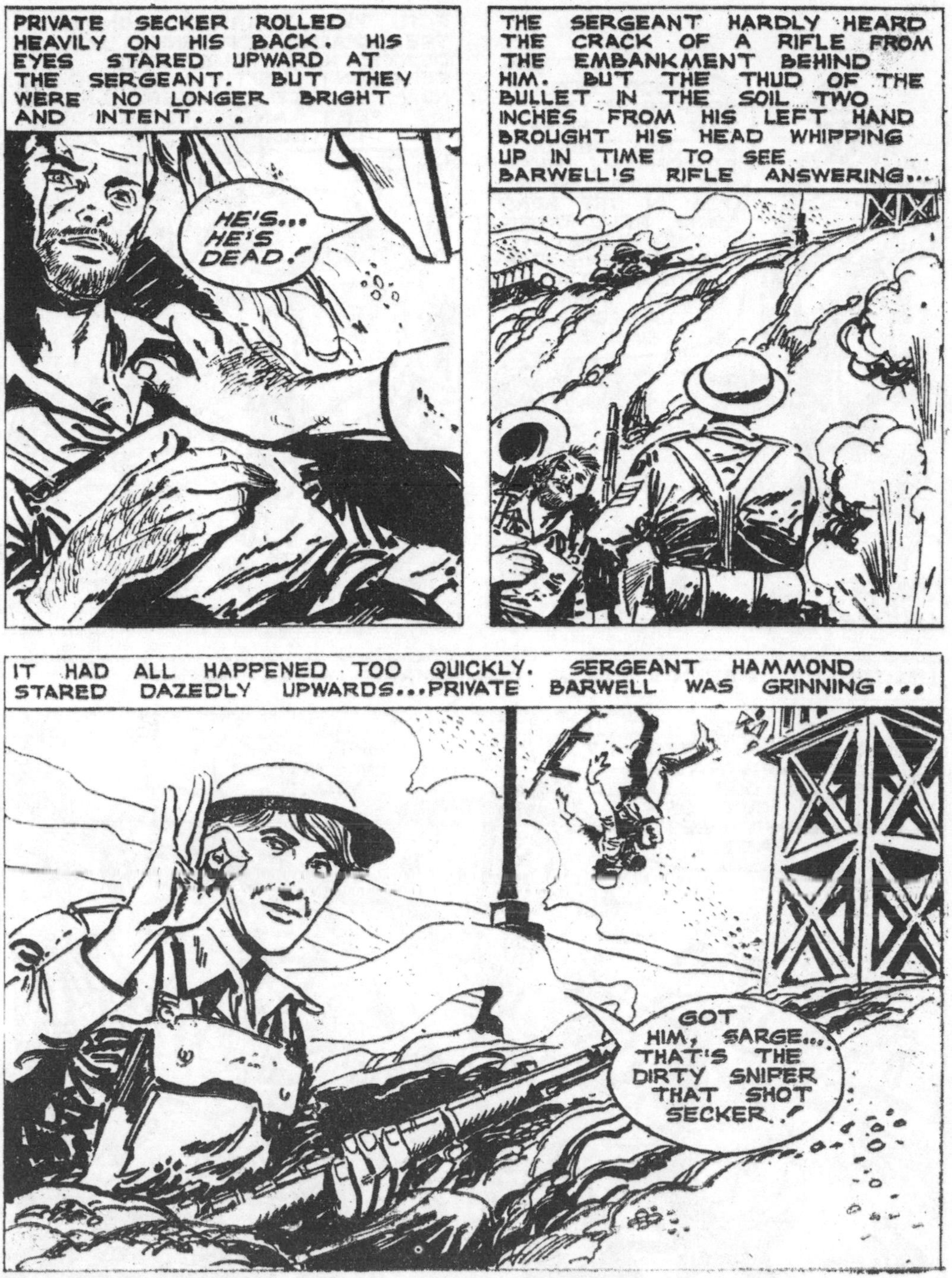
PRIVATE SECKER ROLLED HEAVILY ON HIS BACK. HIS EYES STARED UPWARD AT THE SERGEANT. BUT THEY WERE NO LONGER BRIGHT AND INTENT...
HE'S... HE'S DEAD.!
THE SERGEANT HARDLY HEARD THE CRACK OF A RIFLE FROM THE EMBANKMENT BEHIND HIM. BUT THE THUD OF THE BULLET IN THE SOIL TWO INCHES FROM HIS LEFT HAND BROUGHT HIS HEAD WHIPPING UP IN TIME TO SEE BARWELL'S RIFLE ANSWERING...
IT HAD ALL HAPPENED TOO QUICKLY. SERGEANT HAMMOND STARED DAZEDLY UPWARDS...PRIVATE BARWELL WAS GRINNING...
GOT HIM, SARGE... THAT'S THE DIRTY SNIPER THAT SHOT SECKER.!

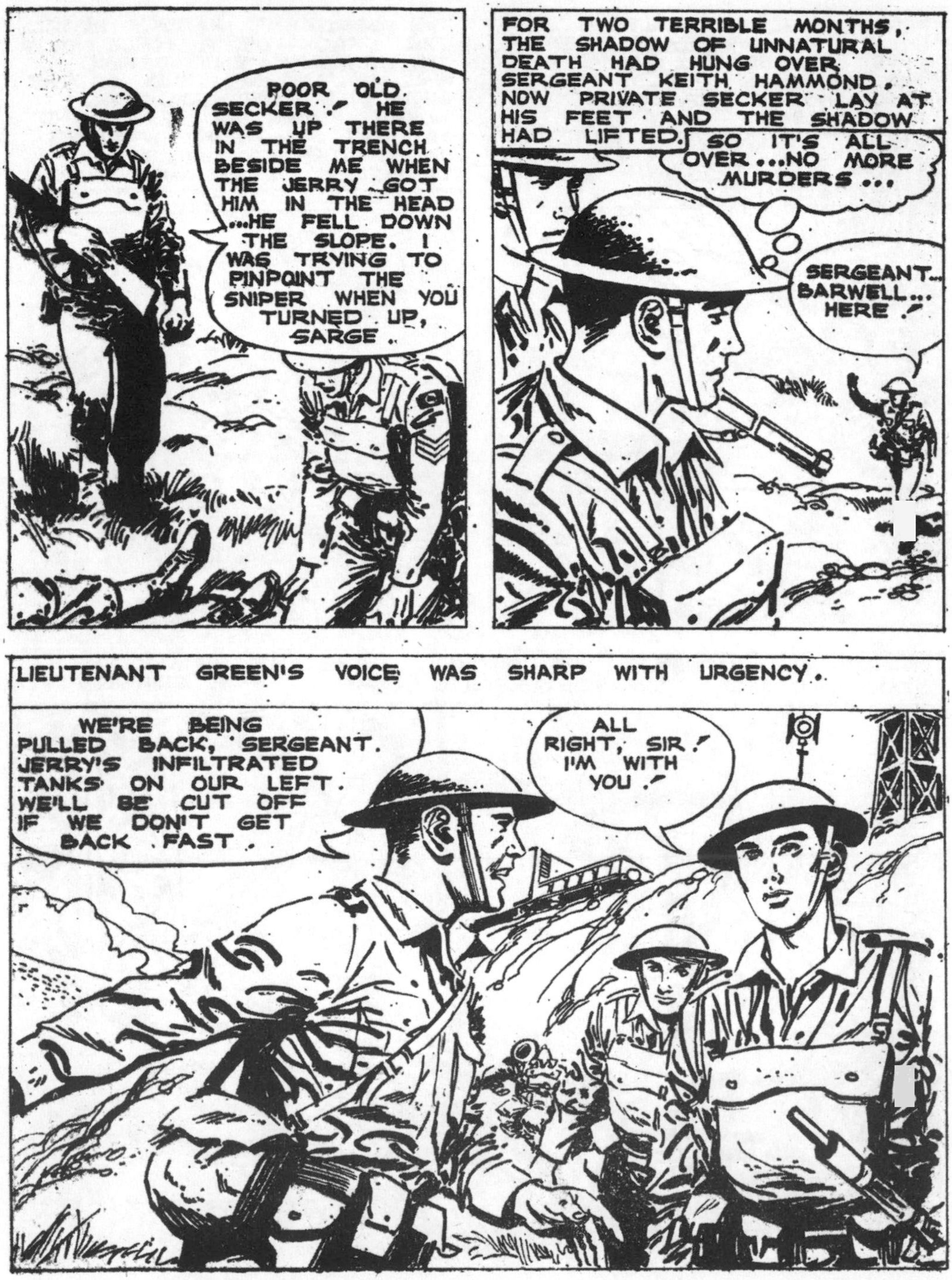
POOR OLD SECKER! HE WAS UP THERE IN THE TRENCH BESIDE ME WHEN THE JERRY GOT HIM IN THE HEAD ...HE FELL DOWN THE SLOPE. I WAS TRYING TO PINPOINT THE SNIPER WHEN YOU TURNED UP, SARGE.
FOR TWO TERRIBLE MONTHS, THE SHADOW OF UNNATURAL DEATH HAD HUNG OVER SERGEANT KEITH HAMMOND. NOW PRIVATE SECKER LAY AT HIS FEET AND THE SHADOW HAD LIFTED.
SO IT'S ALL OVER...NO MORE MURDERS...
SERGEANT... BARWELL... HERE!
LIEUTENANT GREEN'S VOICE WAS SHARP WITH URGENCY.
WE'RE BEING PULLED BACK, SERGEANT. JERRY'S INFILTRATED TANKS ON OUR LEFT. WE'LL BE CUT OFF IF WE DON'T GET BACK FAST.
ALL RIGHT, SIR! I'M WITH YOU!

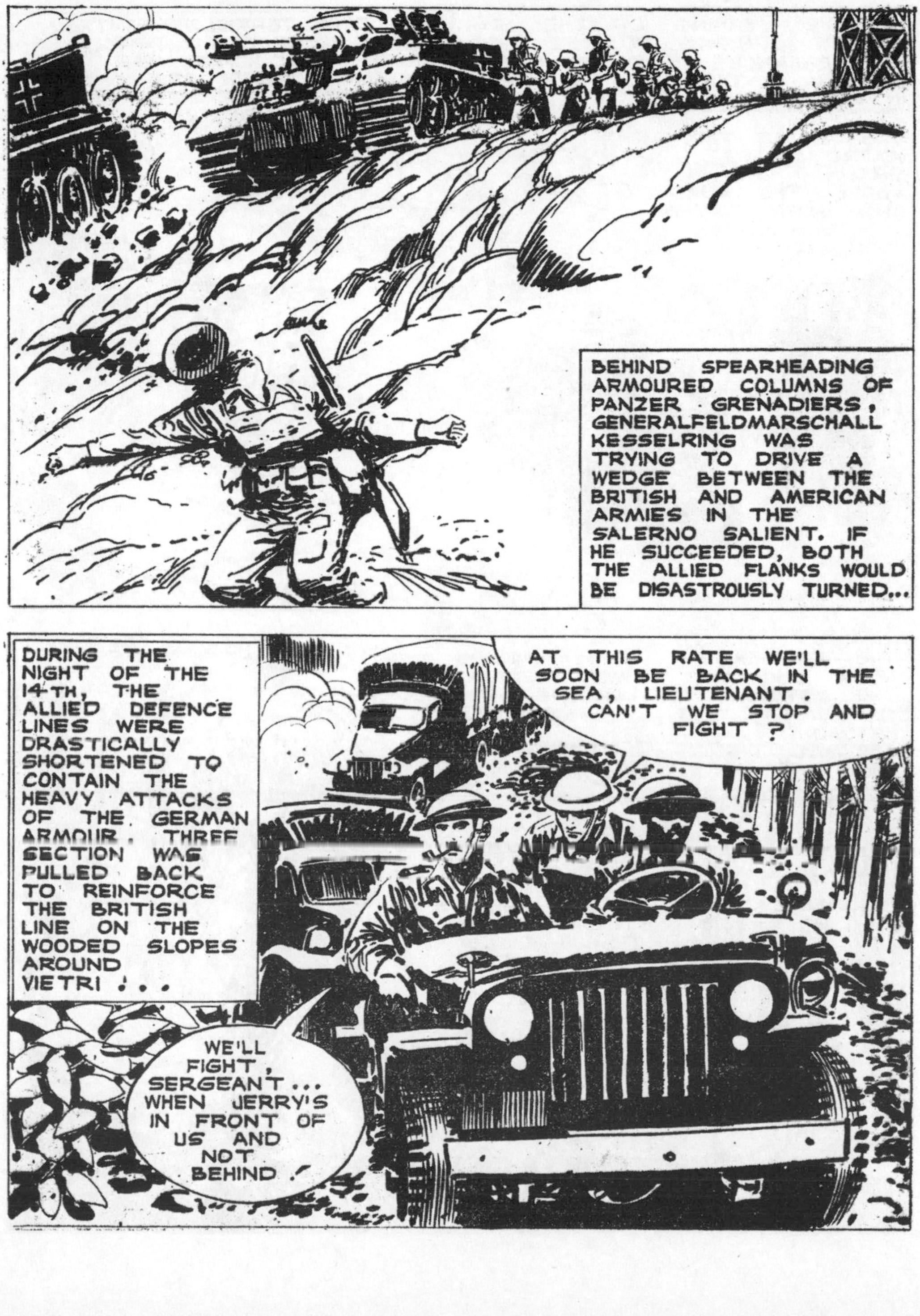
BEHIND SPEARHEADING ARMOURED COLUMNS OF PANZER GRENADIERS, GENERALFELDMARSCHALL KESSELRING WAS TRYING TO DRIVE A WEDGE BETWEEN THE BRITISH AND AMERICAN ARMIES IN THE SALERNO SALIENT. IF HE SUCCEEDED, BOTH THE ALLIED FLANKS WOULD BE DISASTROUSLY TURNED...
DURING THE NIGHT OF THE 14TH, THE ALLIED DEFENCE LINES WERE DRASTICALLY SHORTENED TO CONTAIN THE HEAVY ATTACKS OF THE GERMAN ARMOUR. THREE SECTION WAS PULLED BACK TO REINFORCE THE BRITISH LINE ON THE WOODED SLOPES AROUND VIETRI ! . . .
AT THIS RATE WE'LL SOON BE BACK IN THE SEA, LIEUTENANT. CAN'T WE STOP AND FIGHT ?
WE'LL FIGHT, SERGEANT... WHEN JERRY'S IN FRONT OF US AND NOT BEHIND !

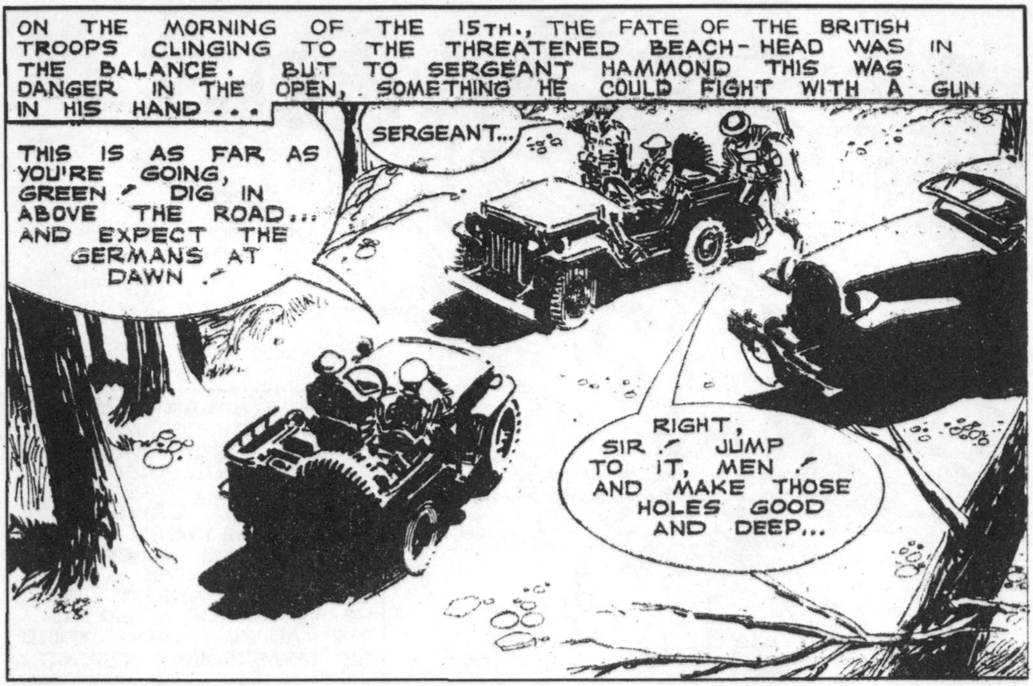
ON THE MORNING OF THE 15TH., THE FATE OF THE BRITISH TROOPS CLINGING TO THE THREATENED BEACH-HEAD WAS IN THE BALANCE. BUT TO SERGEANT HAMMOND THIS WAS DANGER IN THE OPEN, SOMETHING HE COULD FIGHT WITH A GUN IN HIS HAND...
SERGEANT...
THIS IS AS FAR AS YOU'RE GOING, GREEN! DIG IN ABOVE THE ROAD... AND EXPECT THE GERMANS AT DAWN!
RIGHT, SIR! JUMP TO IT, MEN! AND MAKE THOSE HOLES GOOD AND DEEP...

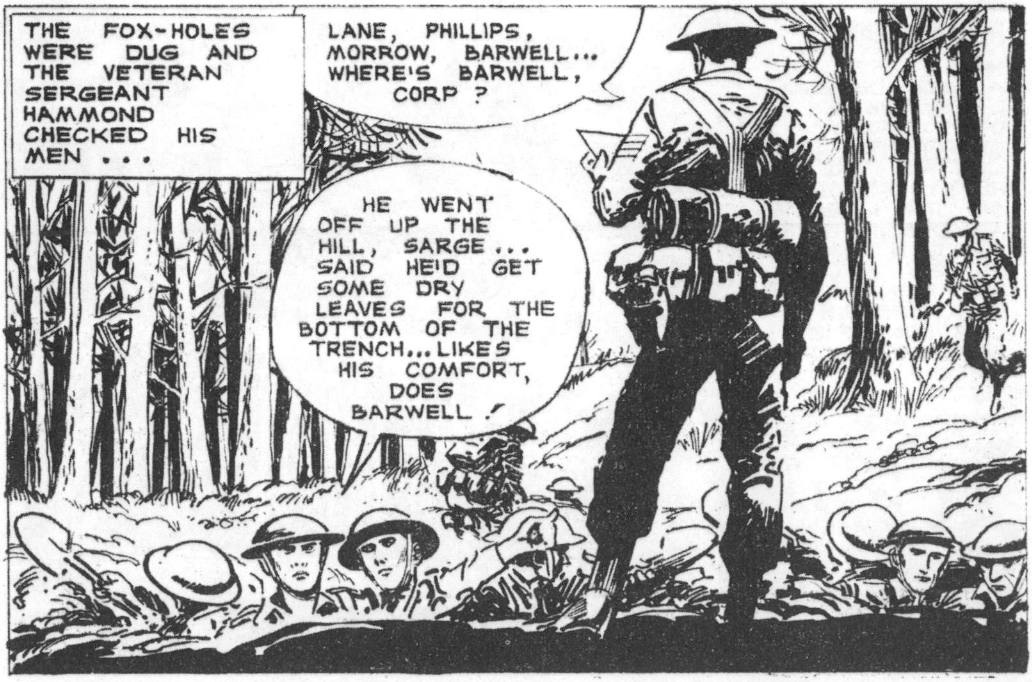
THE FOX-HOLES WERE DUG AND THE VETERAN SERGEANT HAMMOND CHECKED HIS MEN...
LANE, PHILLIPS, MORROW, BARWELL... WHERE'S BARWELL, CORP?
HE WENT OFF UP THE HILL, SARGE... SAID HE'D GET SOME DRY LEAVES FOR THE BOTTOM OF THE TRENCH... LIKES HIS COMFORT, DOES BARWELL!

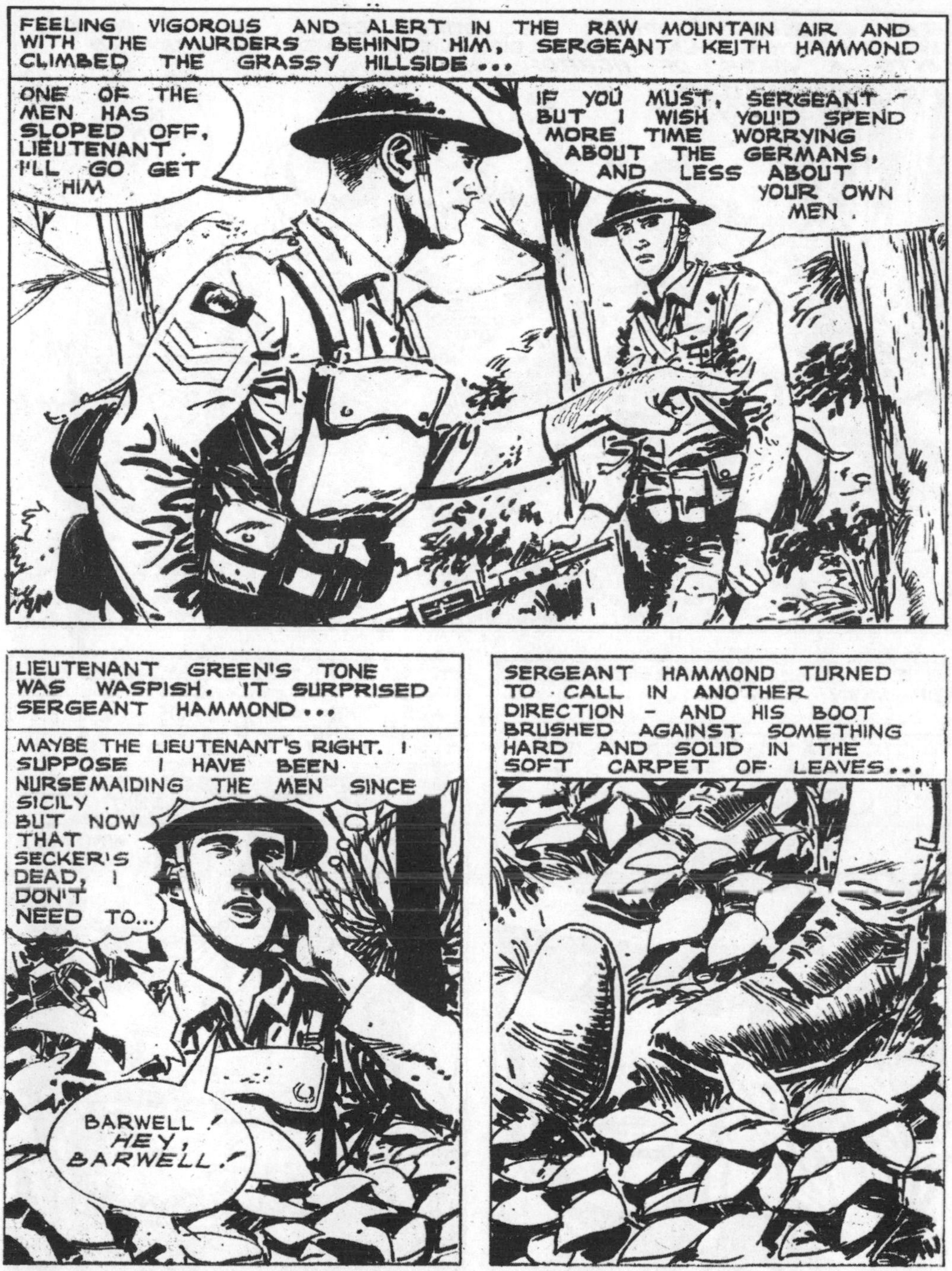
FEELING VIGOROUS AND ALERT IN THE RAW MOUNTAIN AIR AND WITH THE MURDERS BEHIND HIM, SERGEANT KEITH HAMMOND CLIMBED THE GRASSY HILLSIDE ...
ONE OF THE MEN HAS SLOPED OFF, LIEUTENANT. I'LL GO GET HIM
IF YOU MUST, SERGEANT - BUT I WISH YOU'D SPEND MORE TIME WORRYING ABOUT THE GERMANS, AND LESS ABOUT YOUR OWN MEN.
LIEUTENANT GREEN'S TONE WAS WASPISH. IT SURPRISED SERGEANT HAMMOND ...
MAYBE THE LIEUTENANT'S RIGHT. I SUPPOSE I HAVE BEEN NURSEMAIDING THE MEN SINCE SICILY. BUT NOW THAT SECKER'S DEAD, I DON'T NEED TO...
BARWELL! HEY, BARWELL!
SERGEANT HAMMOND TURNED TO CALL IN ANOTHER DIRECTION - AND HIS BOOT BRUSHED AGAINST SOMETHING HARD AND SOLID IN THE SOFT CARPET OF LEAVES...

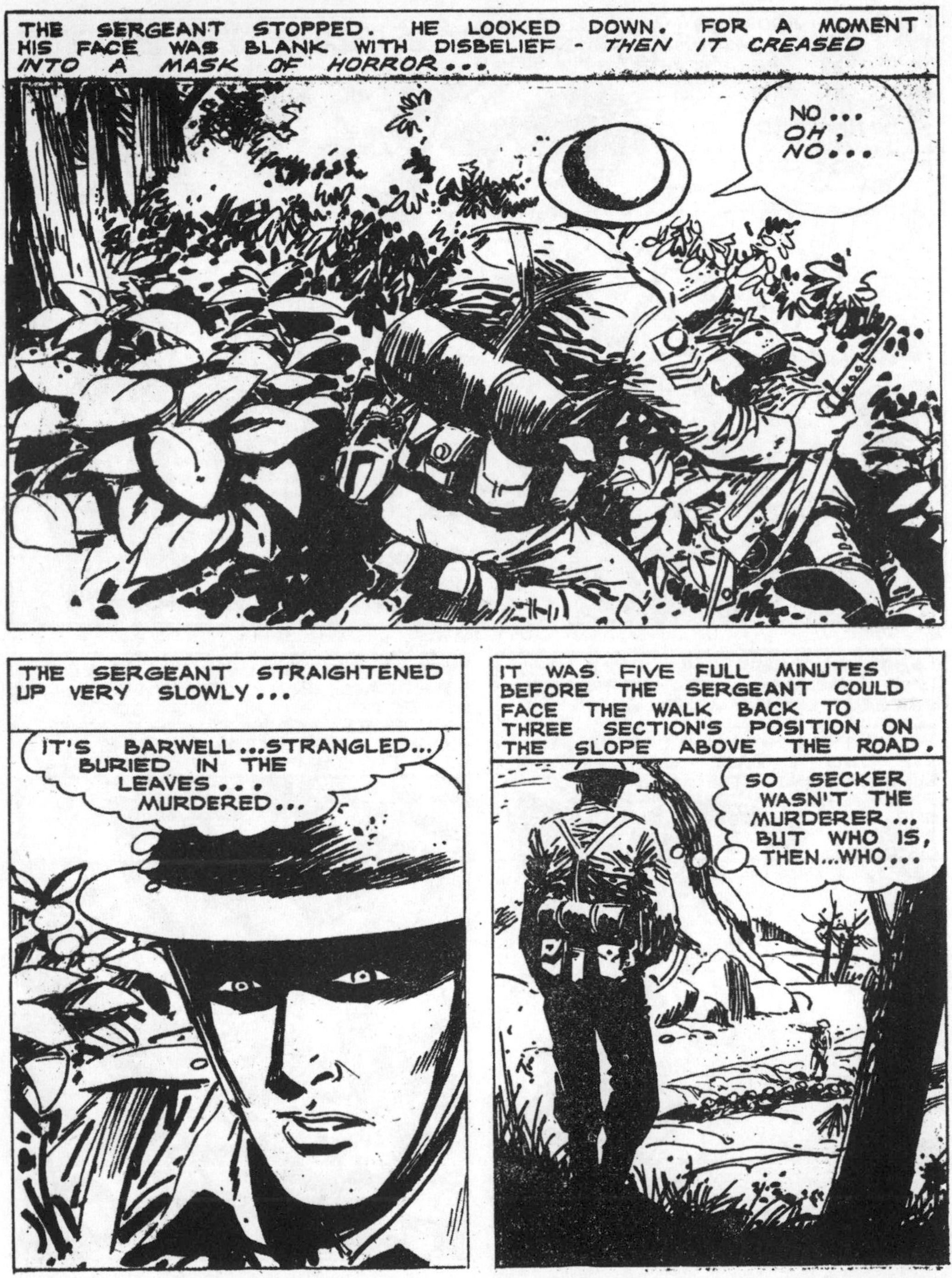
THE SERGEANT STOPPED. HE LOOKED DOWN. FOR A MOMENT HIS FACE WAS BLANK WITH DISBELIEF - THEN IT CREASED INTO A MASK OF HORROR...
NO... OH, NO...
THE SERGEANT STRAIGHTENED UP VERY SLOWLY...
IT'S BARWELL...STRANGLED... BURIED IN THE LEAVES... MURDERED...
IT WAS FIVE FULL MINUTES BEFORE THE SERGEANT COULD FACE THE WALK BACK TO THREE SECTION'S POSITION ON THE SLOPE ABOVE THE ROAD.
SO SECKER WASN'T THE MURDERER... BUT WHO IS, THEN...WHO...

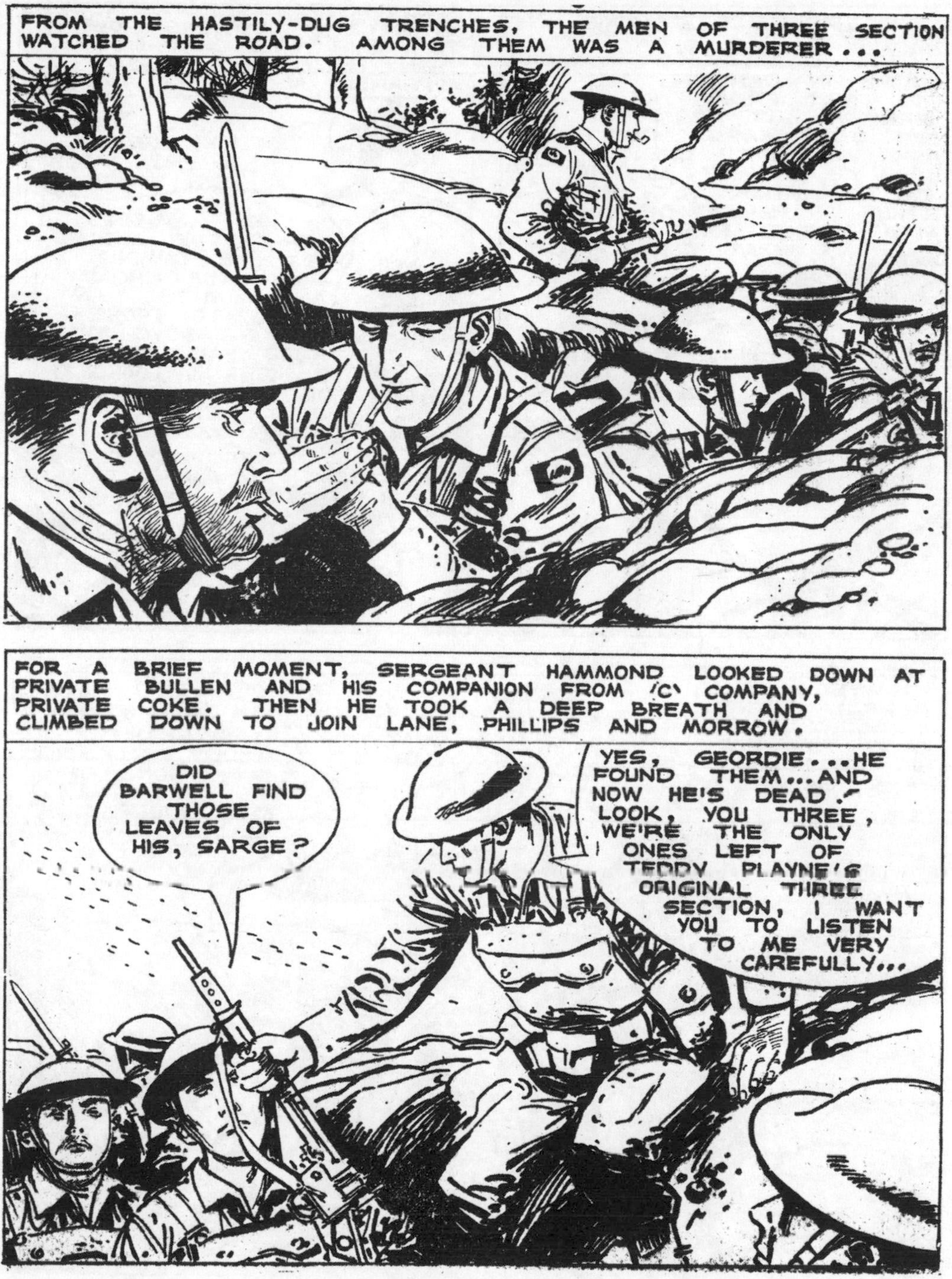
FROM THE HASTILY-DUG TRENCHES, THE MEN OF THREE SECTION WATCHED THE ROAD. AMONG THEM WAS A MURDERER...
FOR A BRIEF MOMENT, SERGEANT HAMMOND LOOKED DOWN AT PRIVATE BULLEN AND HIS COMPANION FROM 'C' COMPANY, PRIVATE COKE. THEN HE TOOK A DEEP BREATH AND CLIMBED DOWN TO JOIN LANE, PHILLIPS AND MORROW.
DID BARWELL FIND THOSE LEAVES OF HIS, SARGE?
YES, GEORDIE...HE FOUND THEM...AND NOW HE'S DEAD. LOOK, YOU THREE, WE'RE THE ONLY ONES LEFT OF TEDDY PLAYNE'S ORIGINAL THREE SECTION, I WANT YOU TO LISTEN TO ME VERY CAREFULLY...

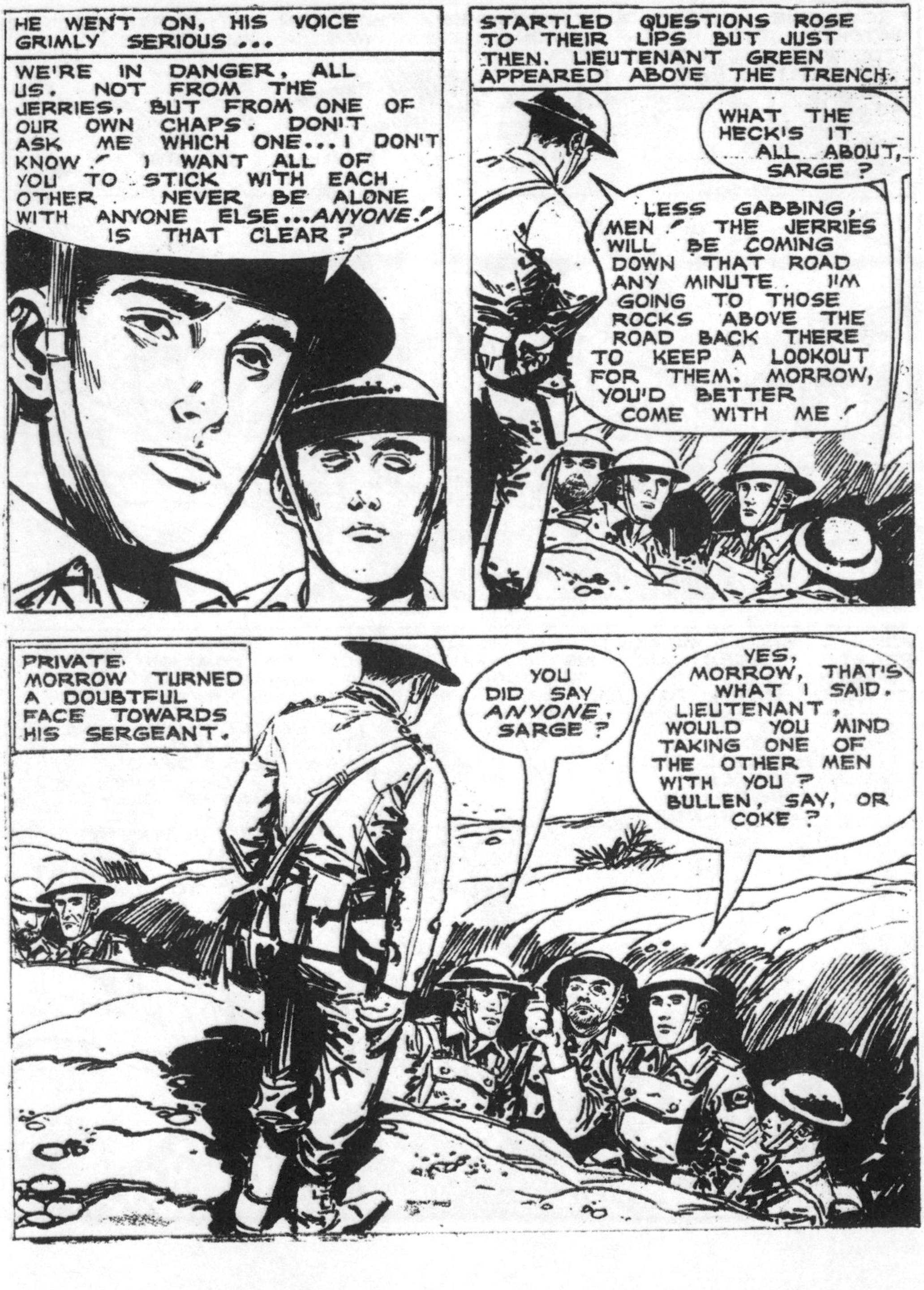
HE WENT ON, HIS VOICE GRIMLY SERIOUS ...
WE'RE IN DANGER, ALL US. NOT FROM THE JERRIES, BUT FROM ONE OF OUR OWN CHAPS. DON'T ASK ME WHICH ONE... I DON'T KNOW! I WANT ALL OF YOU TO STICK WITH EACH OTHER. NEVER BE ALONE WITH ANYONE ELSE... ANYONE! IS THAT CLEAR?
STARTLED QUESTIONS ROSE TO THEIR LIPS BUT JUST THEN, LIEUTENANT GREEN APPEARED ABOVE THE TRENCH.
WHAT THE HECK'S IT ALL ABOUT, SARGE?
LESS GABBING, MEN! THE JERRIES WILL BE COMING DOWN THAT ROAD ANY MINUTE. I'M GOING TO THOSE ROCKS ABOVE THE ROAD BACK THERE TO KEEP A LOOKOUT FOR THEM. MORROW, YOU'D BETTER COME WITH ME!
PRIVATE MORROW TURNED A DOUBTFUL FACE TOWARDS HIS SERGEANT.
YOU DID SAY ANYONE, SARGE?
YES, MORROW, THAT'S WHAT I SAID. LIEUTENANT, WOULD YOU MIND TAKING ONE OF THE OTHER MEN WITH YOU? BULLEN, SAY, OR COKE?

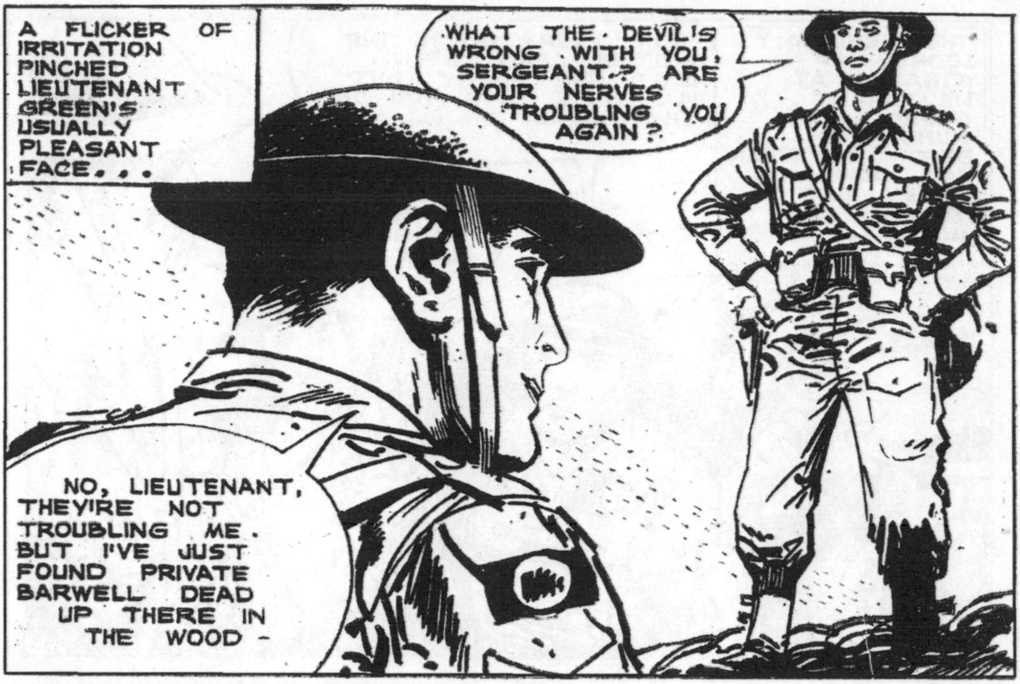
A FLICKER OF IRRITATION PINCHED LIEUTENANT GREEN'S USUALLY PLEASANT FACE...
WHAT THE DEVIL'S WRONG WITH YOU, SERGEANT? ARE YOUR NERVES TROUBLING YOU AGAIN?
NO, LIEUTENANT, THEY'RE NOT TROUBLING ME. BUT I'VE JUST FOUND PRIVATE BARWELL DEAD UP THERE IN THE WOOD -

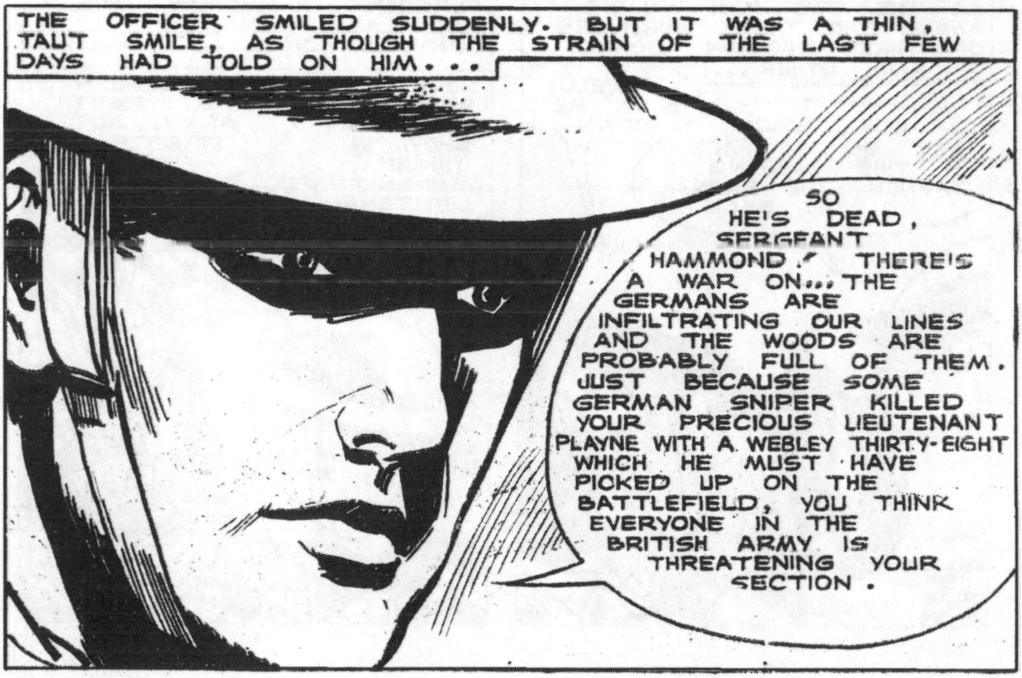
THE OFFICER SMILED SUDDENLY. BUT IT WAS A THIN, TAUT SMILE, AS THOUGH THE STRAIN OF THE LAST FEW DAYS HAD TOLD ON HIM...
SO HE'S DEAD, SERGEANT HAMMOND! THERE'S A WAR ON... THE GERMANS ARE INFILTRATING OUR LINES AND THE WOODS ARE PROBABLY FULL OF THEM. JUST BECAUSE SOME GERMAN SNIPER KILLED YOUR PRECIOUS LIEUTENANT PLAYNE WITH A WEBLEY THIRTY-EIGHT WHICH HE MUST HAVE PICKED UP ON THE BATTLEFIELD, YOU THINK EVERYONE IN THE BRITISH ARMY IS THREATENING YOUR SECTION.

THE SERGEANT LOOKED UP STEADILY AT LIEUTENANT GREEN. THE GUNS HAD BEGUN TO SPEAK FAR DOWN THE VALLEY, BUT NEITHER MAN MOVED...

NOT EVERYONE IN THE BRITISH ARMY, SIR... JUST ONE MAN! BUT I'LL COME WITH YOU TO THE ROCKS, IF I'LL DO!

YOU... WHY NOT... YES, SERGEANT HAMMOND, YOU'LL DO!

AS THE TWO MEN WALKED AWAY, THE THREE SURVIVORS OF THREE SECTION LOOKED AT EACH OTHER...

WELL, BLOW ME DOWN.

COR, WHICH WAY DO WE FACE IN THIS BLINKING TRENCH... THE FRONT OR THE BACK?

SERGEANT HAMMOND'S VOICE WAS LAZY NOW, CONVERSATIONAL...

YOU WERE IN THE LAST SHOW IN TUNISIA, WEREN'T YOU, LIEUTENANT?

YES, SERGEANT, I WAS. EIGHTH ARMY, NOT FIRST!

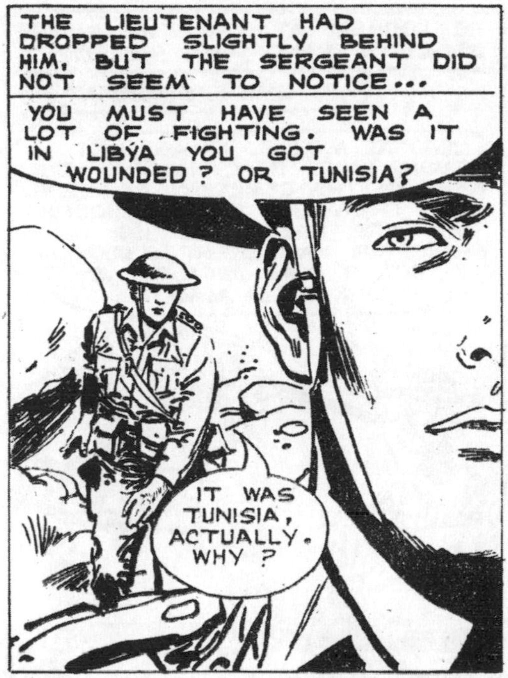
THE LIEUTENANT HAD DROPPED SLIGHTLY BEHIND HIM, BUT THE SERGEANT DID NOT SEEM TO NOTICE...
YOU MUST HAVE SEEN A LOT OF FIGHTING. WAS IT IN LIBYA YOU GOT WOUNDED? OR TUNISIA?
IT WAS TUNISIA, ACTUALLY. WHY?

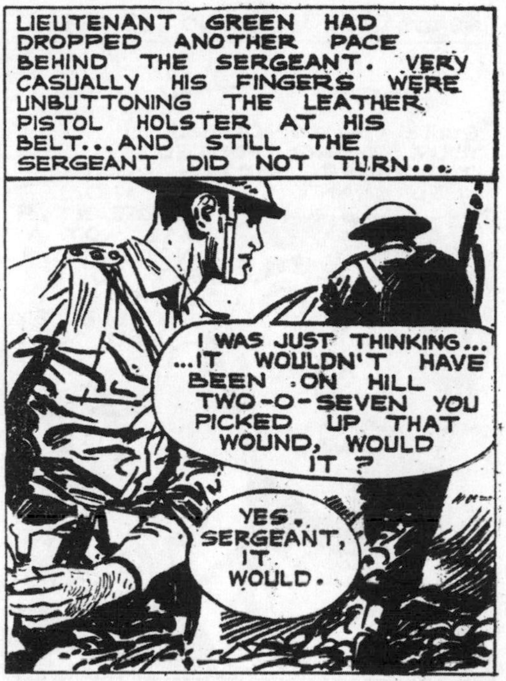
LIEUTENANT GREEN HAD DROPPED ANOTHER PACE BEHIND THE SERGEANT. VERY CASUALLY HIS FINGERS WERE UNBUTTONING THE LEATHER PISTOL HOLSTER AT HIS BELT...AND STILL THE SERGEANT DID NOT TURN...
I WAS JUST THINKING... ...IT WOULDN'T HAVE BEEN ON HILL TWO-O-SEVEN YOU PICKED UP THAT WOUND, WOULD IT?
YES, SERGEANT, IT WOULD.

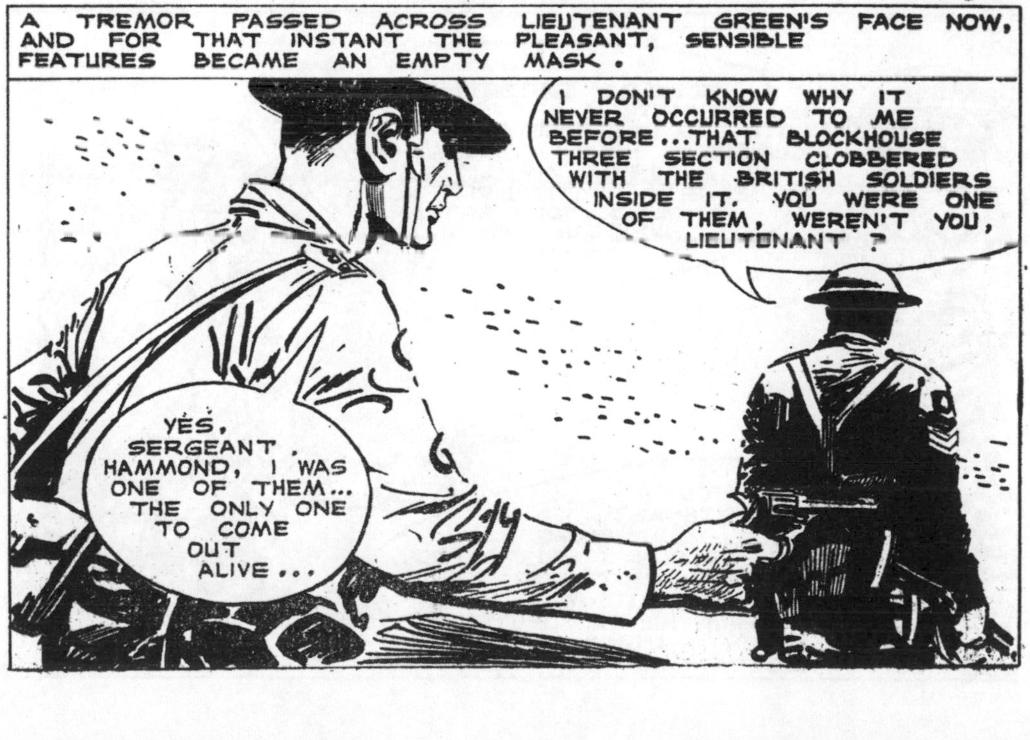
A TREMOR PASSED ACROSS LIEUTENANT GREEN'S FACE NOW, AND FOR THAT INSTANT THE PLEASANT, SENSIBLE FEATURES BECAME AN EMPTY MASK.
I DON'T KNOW WHY IT NEVER OCCURRED TO ME BEFORE...THAT BLOCKHOUSE THREE SECTION CLOBBERED WITH THE BRITISH SOLDIERS INSIDE IT. YOU WERE ONE OF THEM, WEREN'T YOU, LIEUTENANT?
YES, SERGEANT. HAMMOND, I WAS ONE OF THEM... THE ONLY ONE TO COME OUT ALIVE...

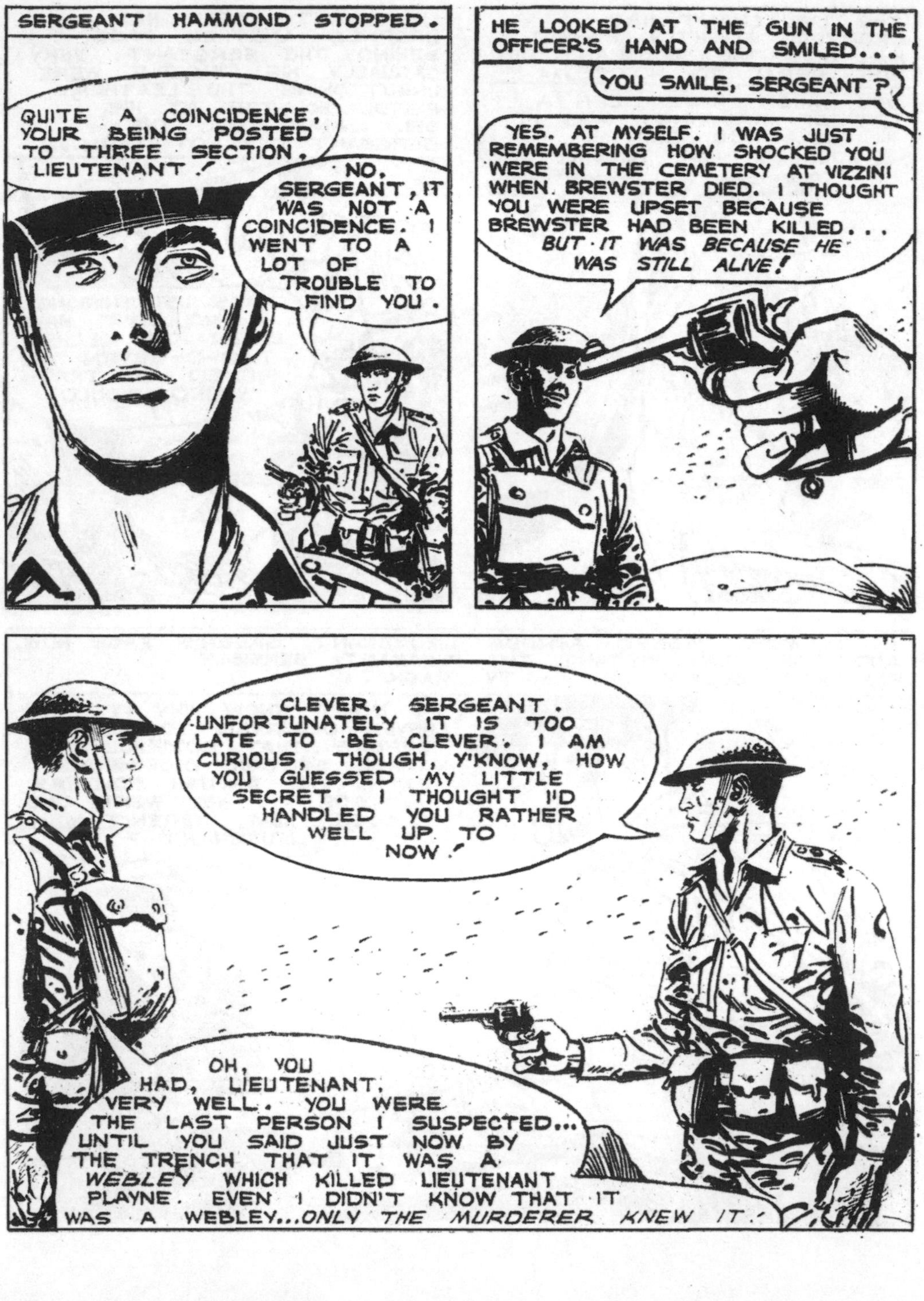
SERGEANT HAMMOND STOPPED.
QUITE A COINCIDENCE, YOUR BEING POSTED TO THREE SECTION, LIEUTENANT!
NO. SERGEANT, IT WAS NOT A COINCIDENCE. I WENT TO A LOT OF TROUBLE TO FIND YOU.
HE LOOKED AT THE GUN IN THE OFFICER'S HAND AND SMILED...
YOU SMILE, SERGEANT?
YES. AT MYSELF. I WAS JUST REMEMBERING HOW SHOCKED YOU WERE IN THE CEMETERY AT VIZZINI WHEN BREWSTER DIED. I THOUGHT YOU WERE UPSET BECAUSE BREWSTER HAD BEEN KILLED... *BUT IT WAS BECAUSE HE WAS STILL ALIVE!*
CLEVER, SERGEANT. UNFORTUNATELY IT IS TOO LATE TO BE CLEVER. I AM CURIOUS, THOUGH, Y'KNOW, HOW YOU GUESSED MY LITTLE SECRET. I THOUGHT I'D HANDLED YOU RATHER WELL UP TO NOW!
OH, YOU HAD, LIEUTENANT, VERY WELL. YOU WERE THE LAST PERSON I SUSPECTED... UNTIL YOU SAID JUST NOW BY THE TRENCH THAT IT WAS A *WEBLEY* WHICH KILLED LIEUTENANT PLAYNE. EVEN I DIDN'T KNOW THAT IT WAS A WEBLEY... *ONLY THE MURDERER KNEW IT.*

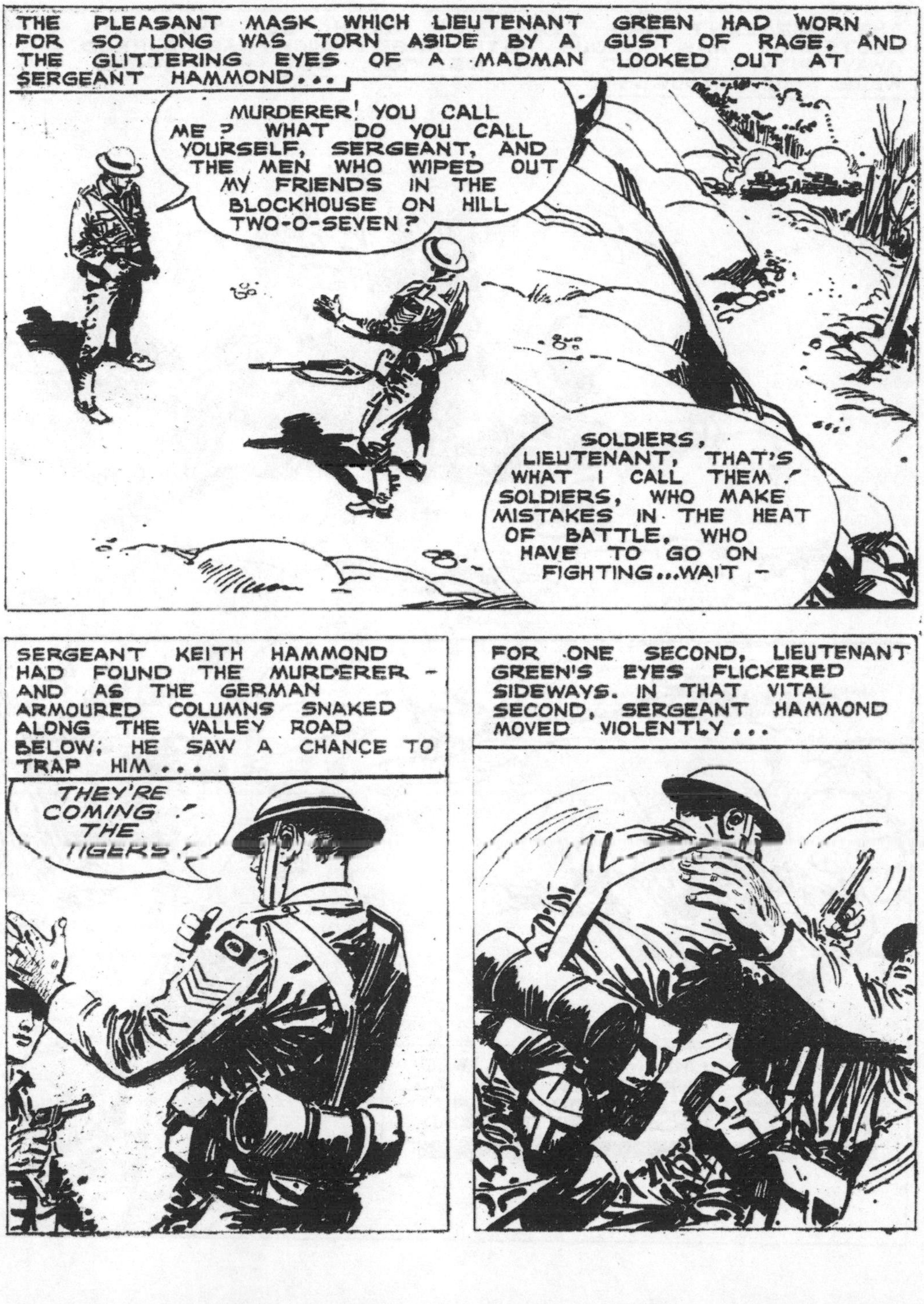
THE PLEASANT MASK WHICH LIEUTENANT GREEN HAD WORN FOR SO LONG WAS TORN ASIDE BY A GUST OF RAGE, AND THE GLITTERING EYES OF A MADMAN LOOKED OUT AT SERGEANT HAMMOND...
MURDERER! YOU CALL ME? WHAT DO YOU CALL YOURSELF, SERGEANT, AND THE MEN WHO WIPED OUT MY FRIENDS IN THE BLOCKHOUSE ON HILL TWO-O-SEVEN?
SOLDIERS, LIEUTENANT, THAT'S WHAT I CALL THEM! SOLDIERS, WHO MAKE MISTAKES IN THE HEAT OF BATTLE, WHO HAVE TO GO ON FIGHTING...WAIT –
SERGEANT KEITH HAMMOND HAD FOUND THE MURDERER – AND AS THE GERMAN ARMOURED COLUMNS SNAKED ALONG THE VALLEY ROAD BELOW, HE SAW A CHANCE TO TRAP HIM...
THEY'RE COMING! THE TIGERS!
FOR ONE SECOND, LIEUTENANT GREEN'S EYES FLICKERED SIDEWAYS. IN THAT VITAL SECOND, SERGEANT HAMMOND MOVED VIOLENTLY...

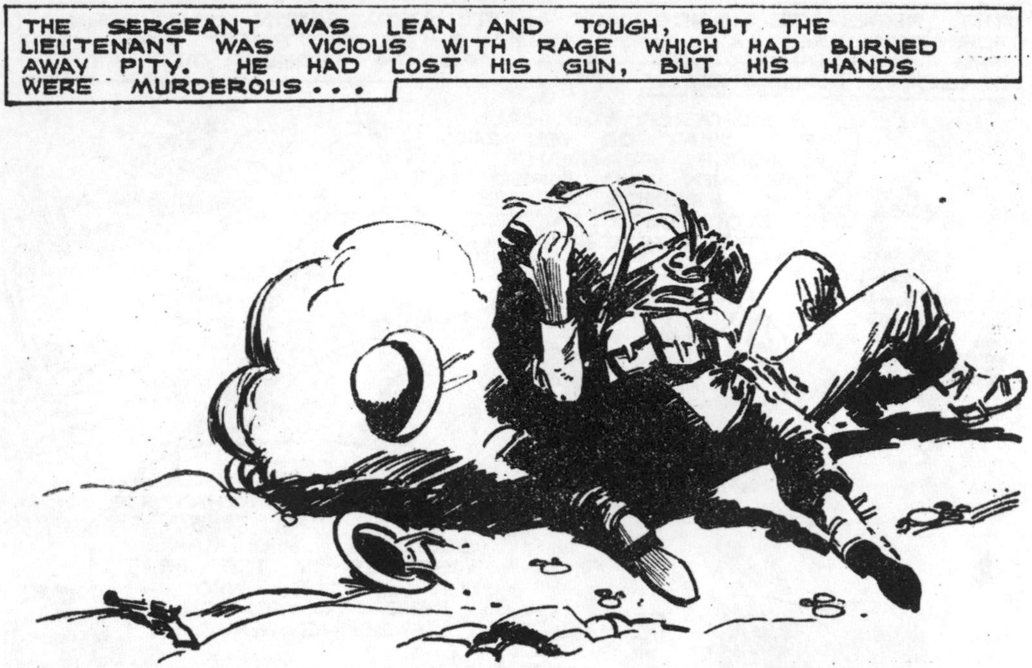
THE SERGEANT WAS LEAN AND TOUGH, BUT THE LIEUTENANT WAS VICIOUS WITH RAGE WHICH HAD BURNED AWAY PITY. HE HAD LOST HIS GUN, BUT HIS HANDS WERE MURDEROUS . . .

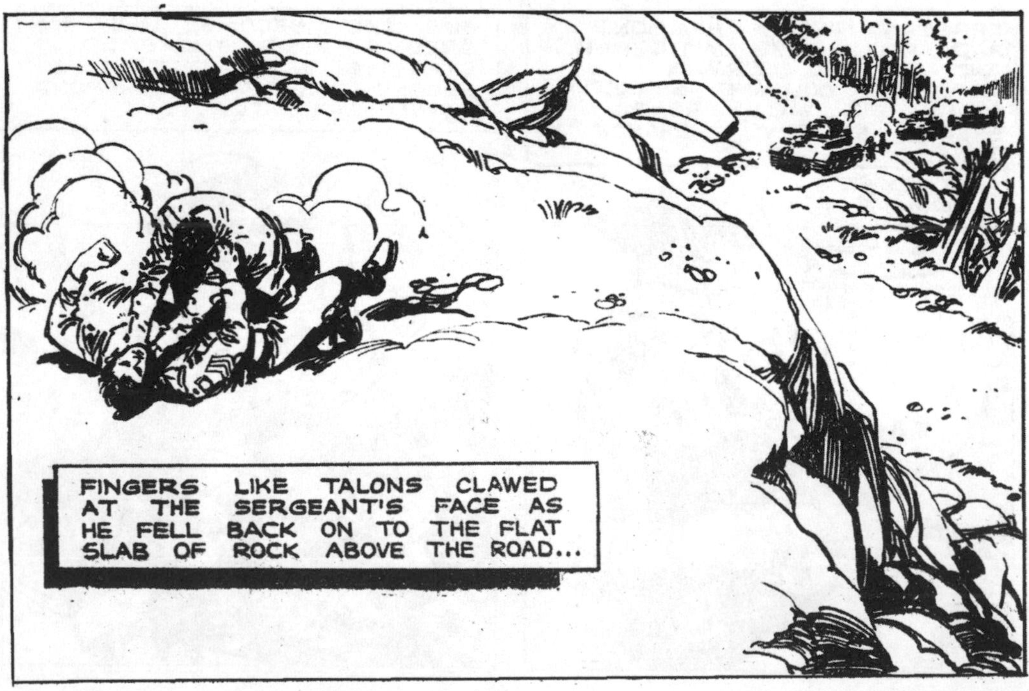
FINGERS LIKE TALONS CLAWED AT THE SERGEANT'S FACE AS HE FELL BACK ON TO THE FLAT SLAB OF ROCK ABOVE THE ROAD...

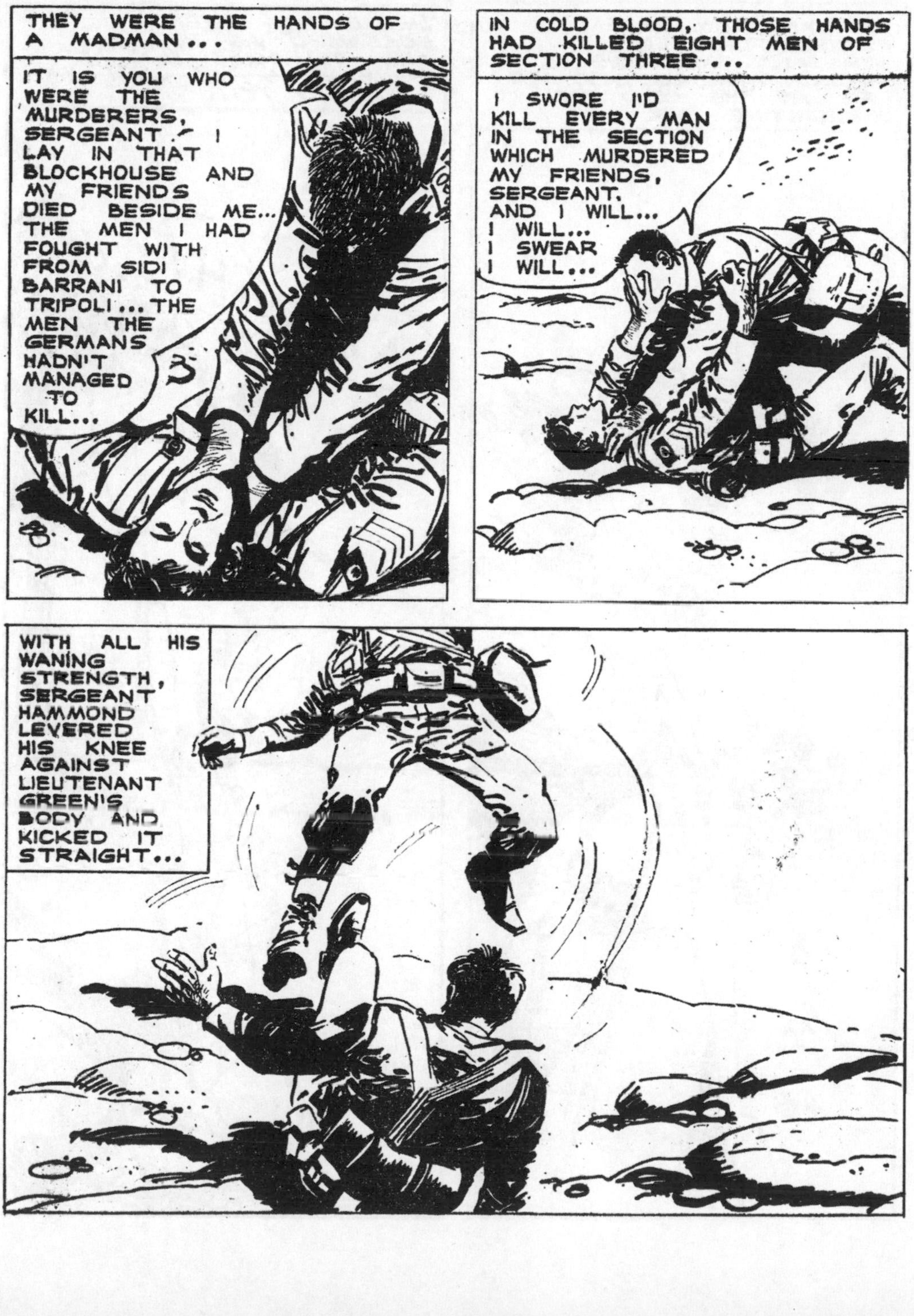
THEY WERE THE HANDS OF A MADMAN...
IT IS YOU WHO WERE THE MURDERERS, SERGEANT - I LAY IN THAT BLOCKHOUSE AND MY FRIENDS DIED BESIDE ME... THE MEN I HAD FOUGHT WITH FROM SIDI BARRANI TO TRIPOLI... THE MEN THE GERMANS HADN'T MANAGED TO KILL...
IN COLD BLOOD, THOSE HANDS HAD KILLED EIGHT MEN OF SECTION THREE...
I SWORE I'D KILL EVERY MAN IN THE SECTION WHICH MURDERED MY FRIENDS, SERGEANT. AND I WILL... I WILL... I SWEAR I WILL...
WITH ALL HIS WANING STRENGTH, SERGEANT HAMMOND LEVERED HIS KNEE AGAINST LIEUTENANT GREEN'S BODY AND KICKED IT STRAIGHT...

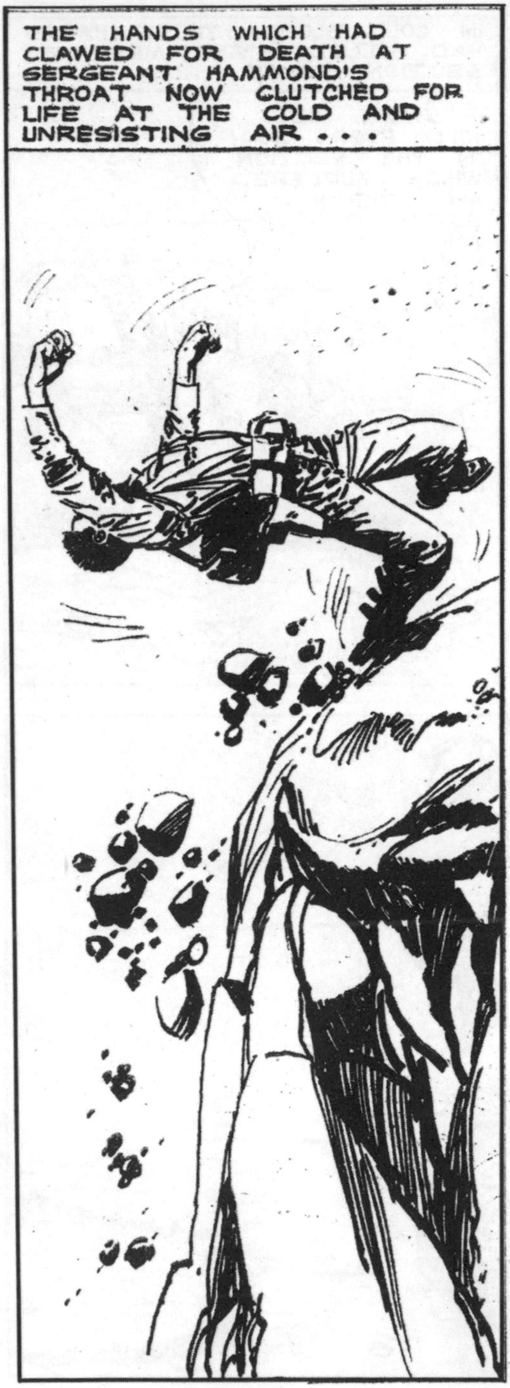
THE HANDS WHICH HAD CLAWED FOR DEATH AT SERGEANT HAMMOND'S THROAT NOW CLUTCHED FOR LIFE AT THE COLD AND UNRESISTING AIR . . .

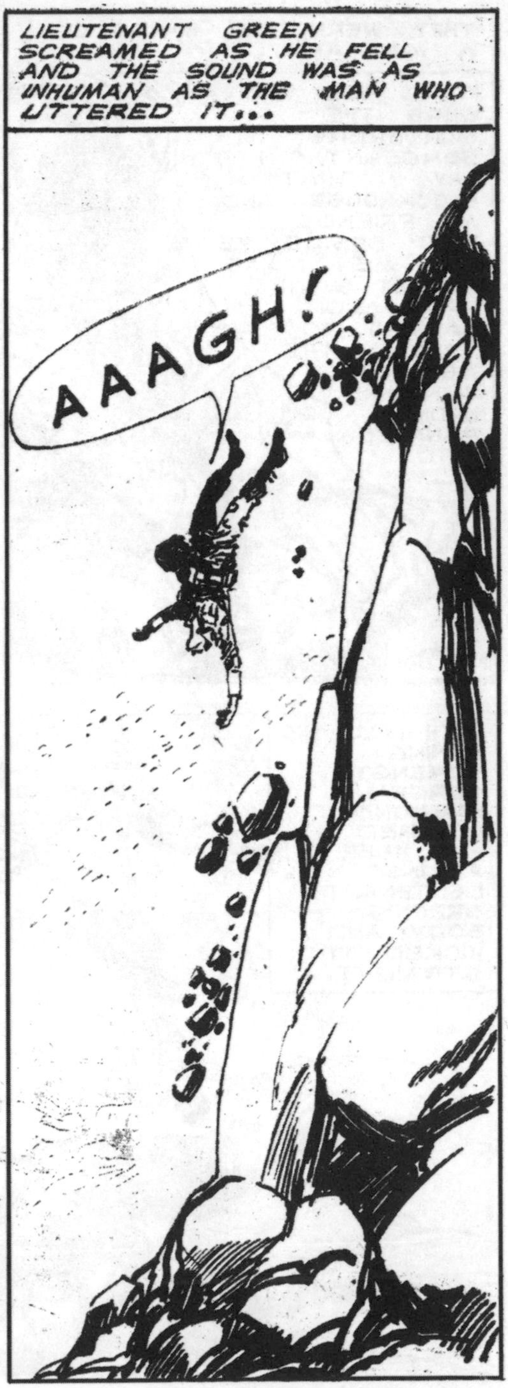
LIEUTENANT GREEN SCREAMED AS HE FELL AND THE SOUND WAS AS INHUMAN AS THE MAN WHO UTTERED IT...
AAAGH!

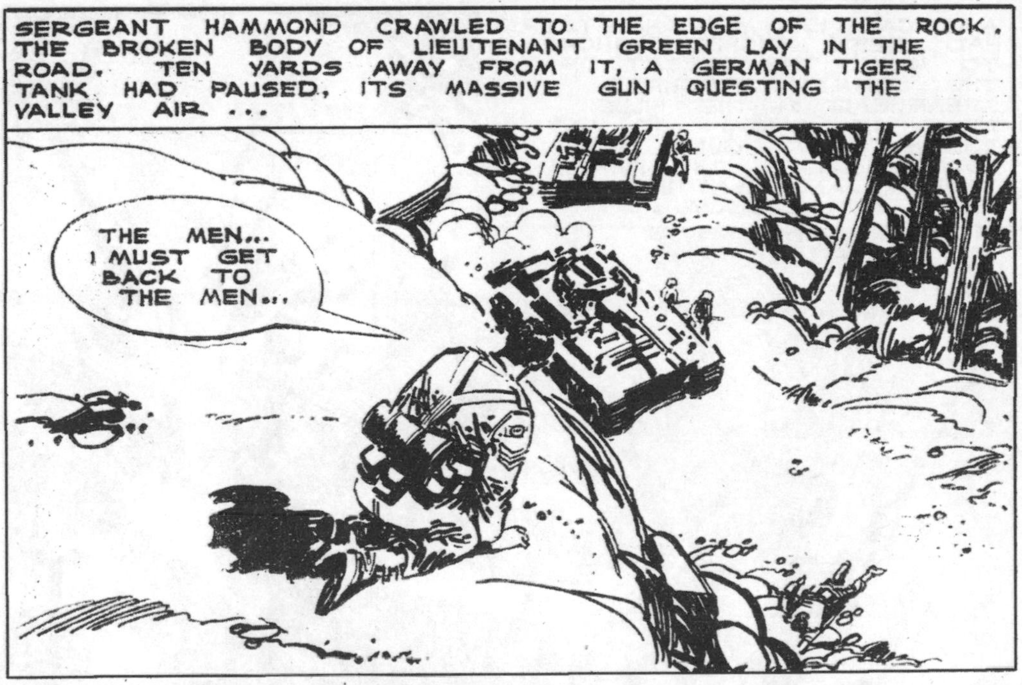
SERGEANT HAMMOND CRAWLED TO THE EDGE OF THE ROCK. THE BROKEN BODY OF LIEUTENANT GREEN LAY IN THE ROAD. TEN YARDS AWAY FROM IT, A GERMAN TIGER TANK HAD PAUSED, ITS MASSIVE GUN QUESTING THE VALLEY AIR ...
THE MEN... I MUST GET BACK TO THE MEN...

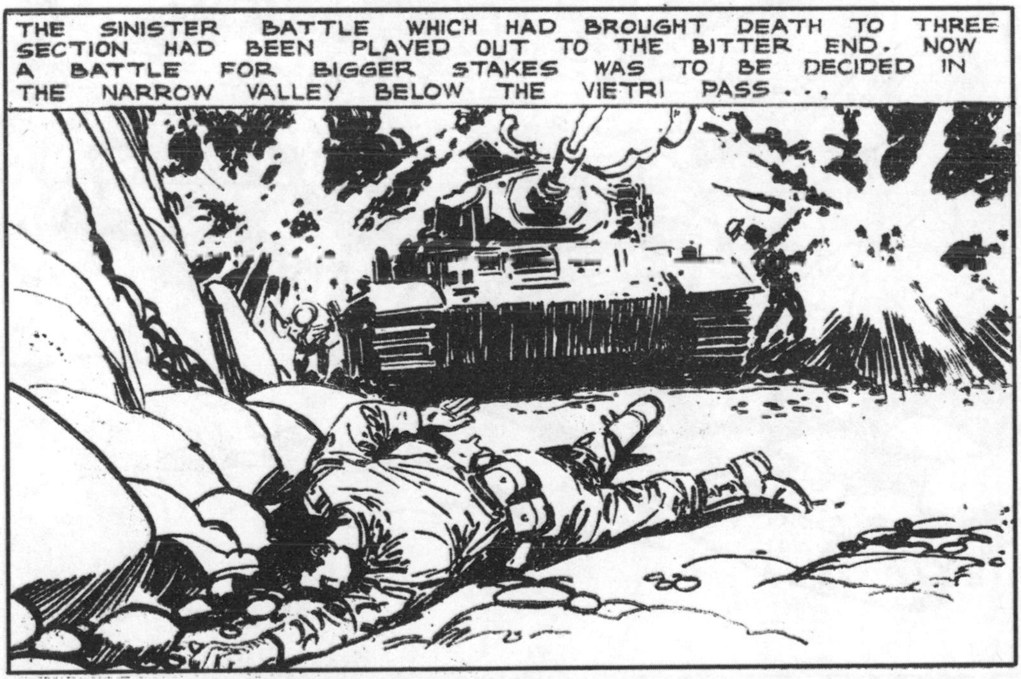
THE SINISTER BATTLE WHICH HAD BROUGHT DEATH TO THREE SECTION HAD BEEN PLAYED OUT TO THE BITTER END. NOW A BATTLE FOR BIGGER STAKES WAS TO BE DECIDED IN THE NARROW VALLEY BELOW THE VIETRI PASS ...

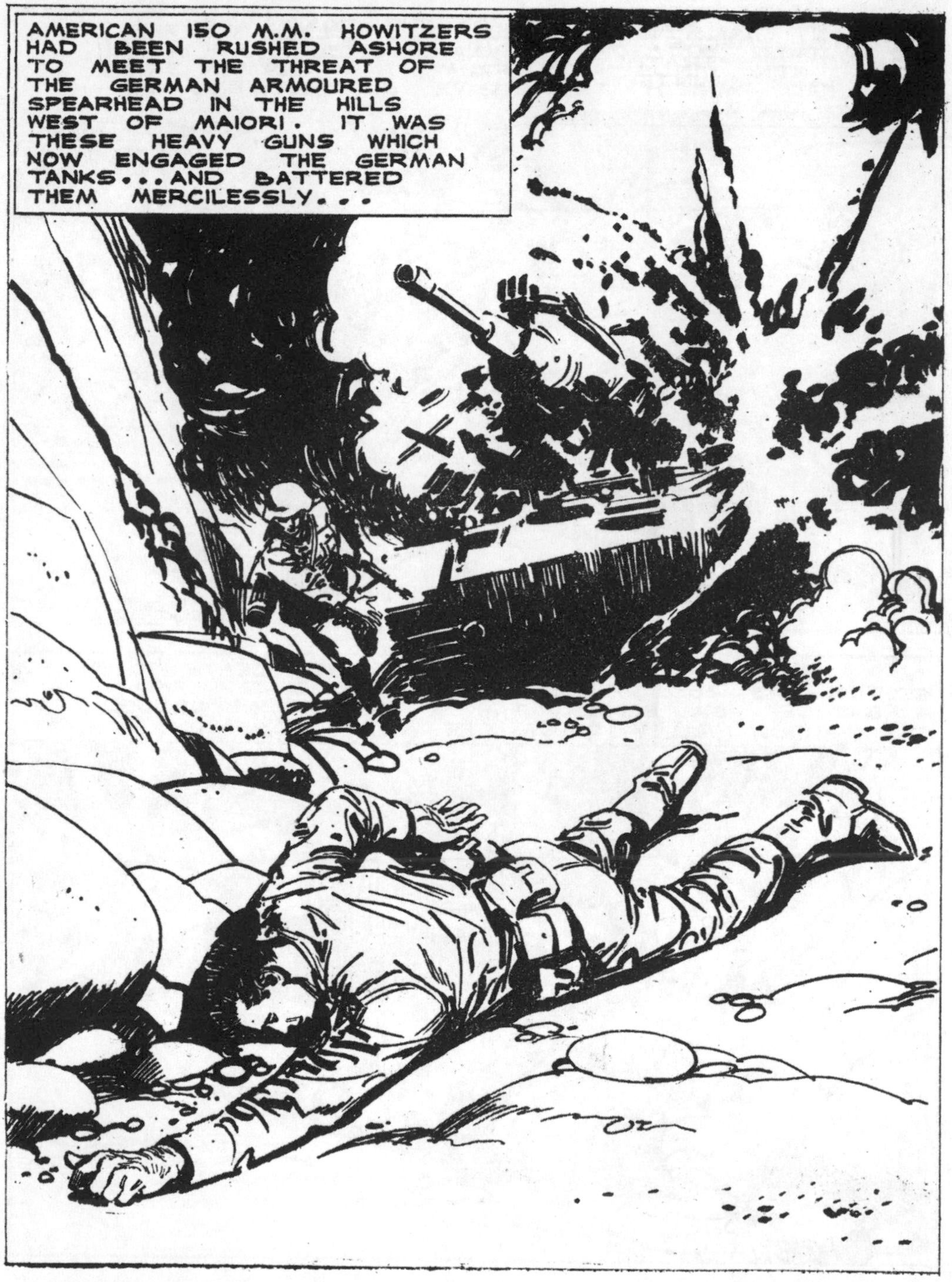
AMERICAN 150 M.M. HOWITZERS HAD BEEN RUSHED ASHORE TO MEET THE THREAT OF THE GERMAN ARMOURED SPEARHEAD IN THE HILLS WEST OF MAIORI. IT WAS THESE HEAVY GUNS WHICH NOW ENGAGED THE GERMAN TANKS...AND BATTERED THEM MERCILESSLY...

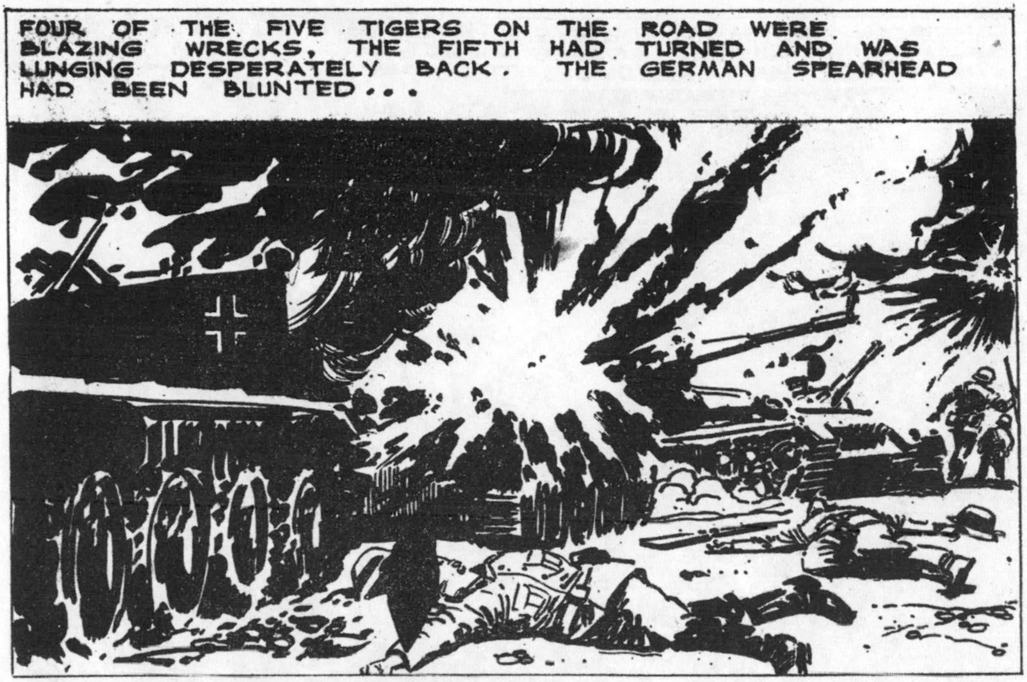
FOUR OF THE FIVE TIGERS ON THE ROAD WERE BLAZING WRECKS, THE FIFTH HAD TURNED AND WAS LUNGING DESPERATELY BACK. THE GERMAN SPEARHEAD HAD BEEN BLUNTED...

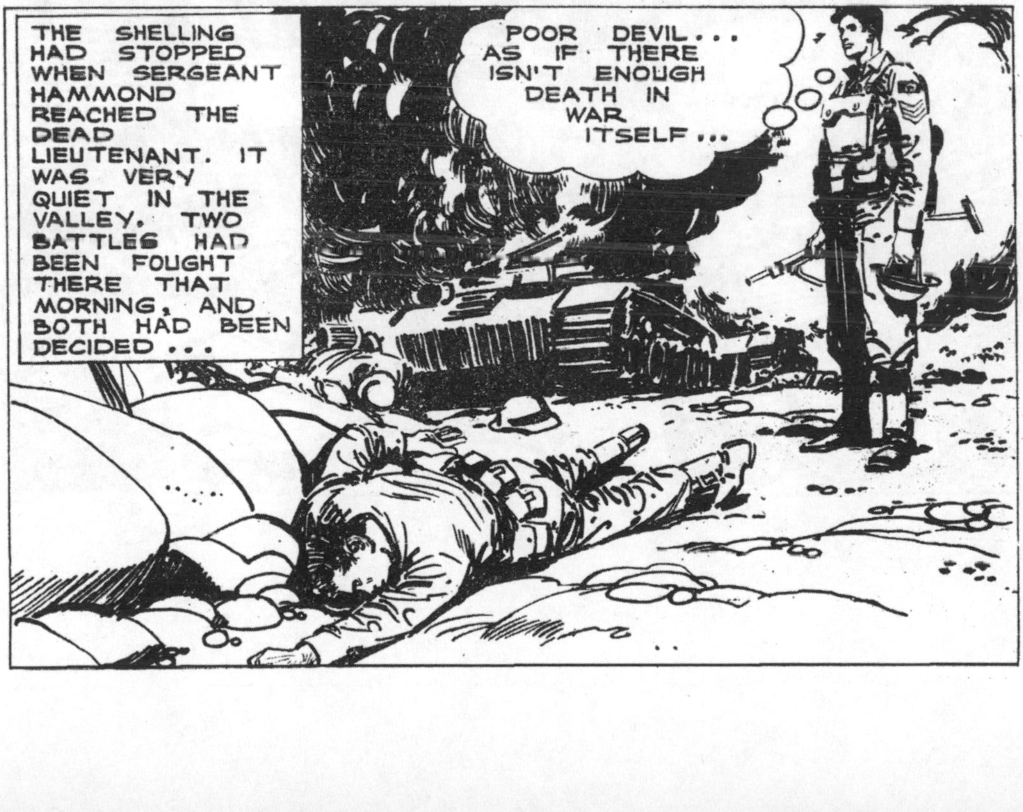
THE SHELLING HAD STOPPED WHEN SERGEANT HAMMOND REACHED THE DEAD LIEUTENANT. IT WAS VERY QUIET IN THE VALLEY. TWO BATTLES HAD BEEN FOUGHT THERE THAT MORNING, AND BOTH HAD BEEN DECIDED...
POOR DEVIL... AS IF THERE ISN'T ENOUGH DEATH IN WAR ITSELF...

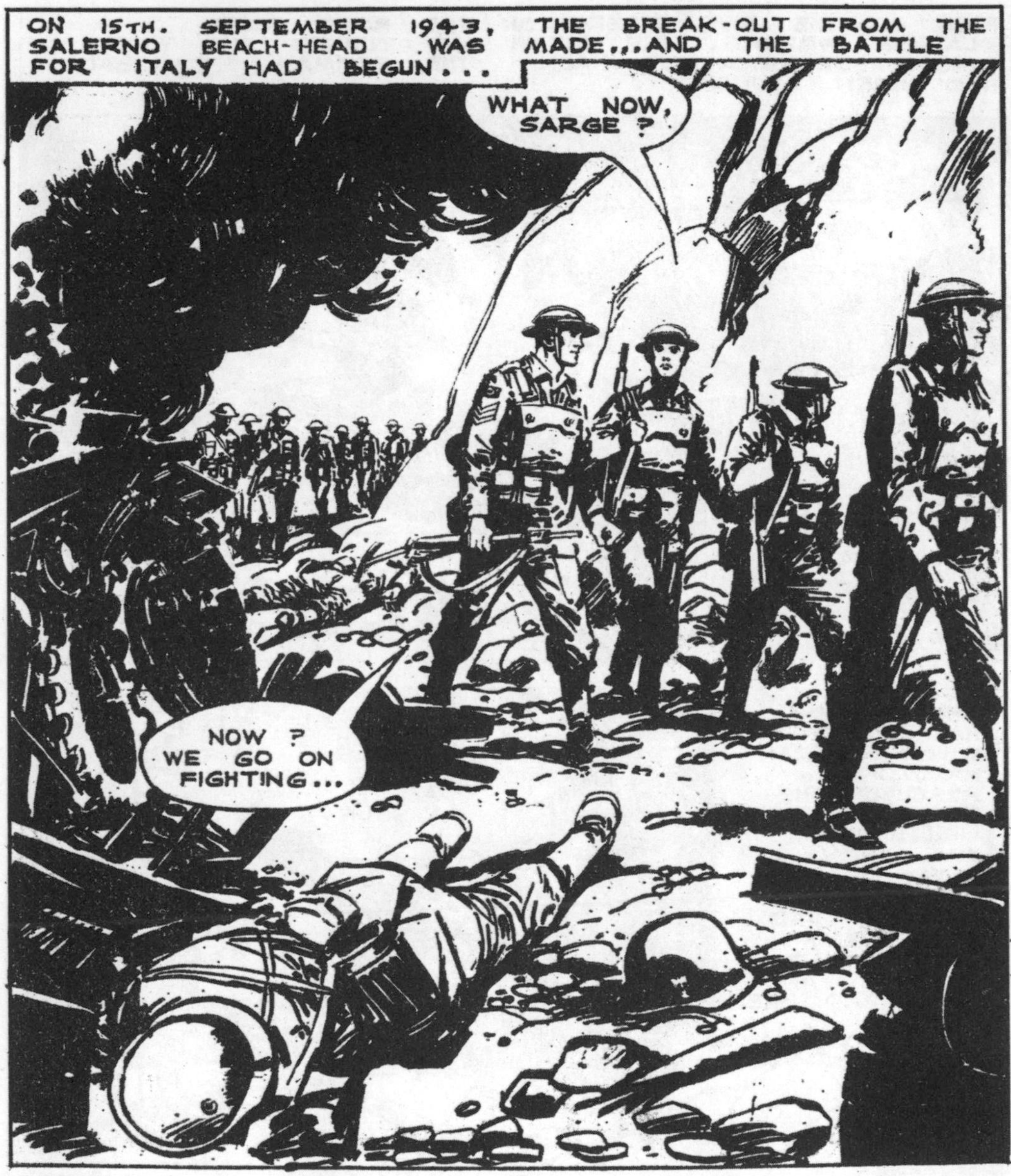
ON 15TH. SEPTEMBER 1943, THE BREAK-OUT FROM THE SALERNO BEACH-HEAD WAS MADE...AND THE BATTLE FOR ITALY HAD BEGUN...
WHAT NOW, SARGE?
NOW? WE GO ON FIGHTING...

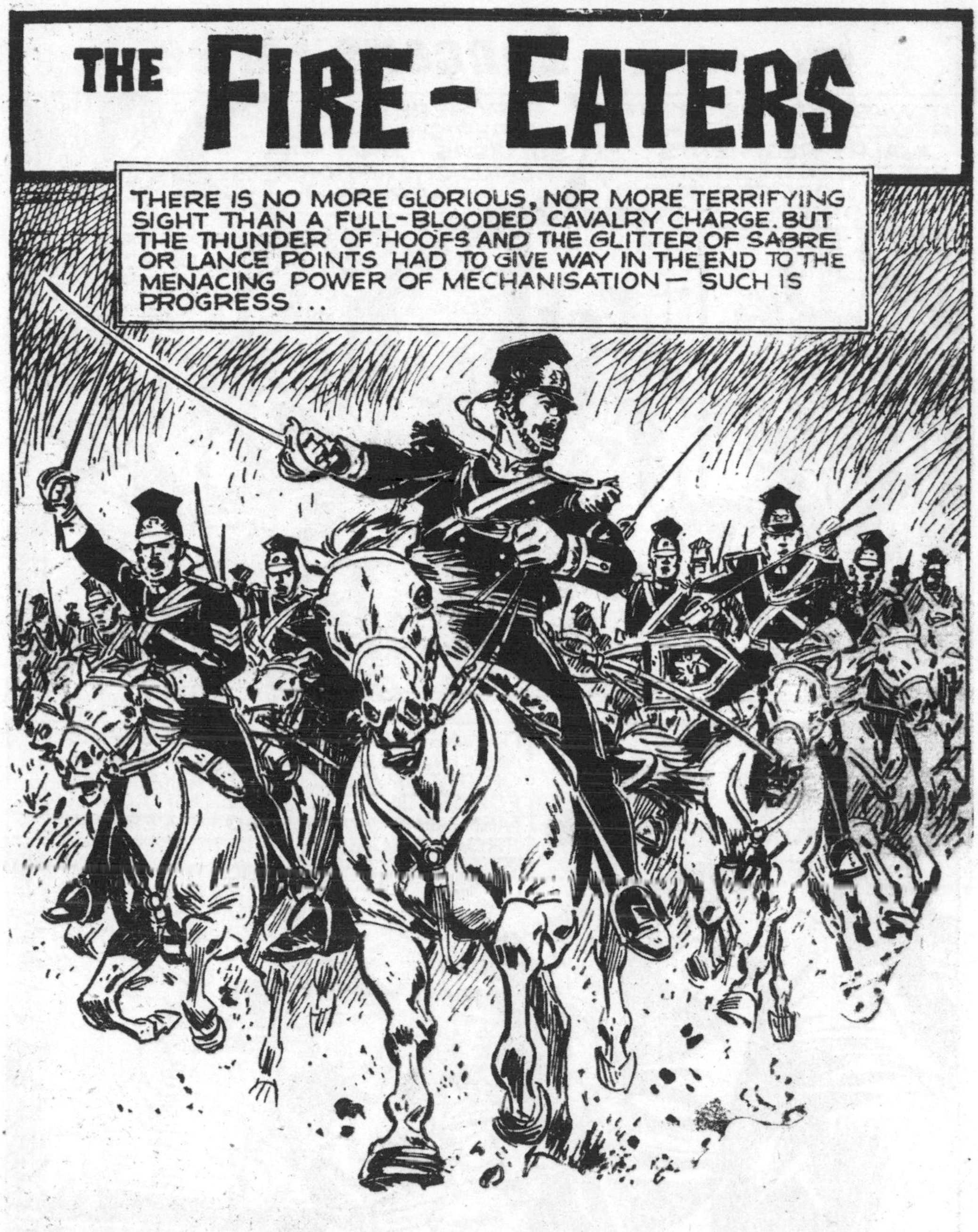
THE FIRE-EATERS
THERE IS NO MORE GLORIOUS, NOR MORE TERRIFYING SIGHT THAN A FULL-BLOODED CAVALRY CHARGE. BUT THE THUNDER OF HOOFS AND THE GLITTER OF SABRE OR LANCE POINTS HAD TO GIVE WAY IN THE END TO THE MENACING POWER OF MECHANISATION — SUCH IS PROGRESS...

Chapter 1. Lancers Three

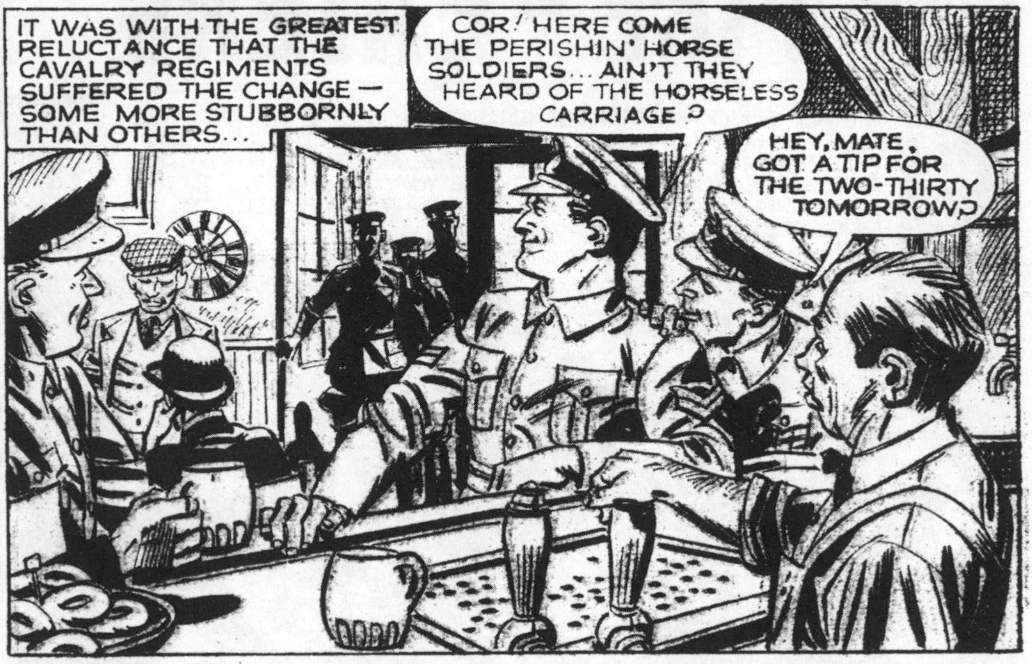
IT WAS WITH THE GREATEST RELUCTANCE THAT THE CAVALRY REGIMENTS SUFFERED THE CHANGE — SOME MORE STUBBORNLY THAN OTHERS...
COR! HERE COME THE PERISHIN' HORSE SOLDIERS... AIN'T THEY HEARD OF THE HORSELESS CARRIAGE?
HEY, MATE, GOT A TIP FOR THE TWO-THIRTY TOMORROW?

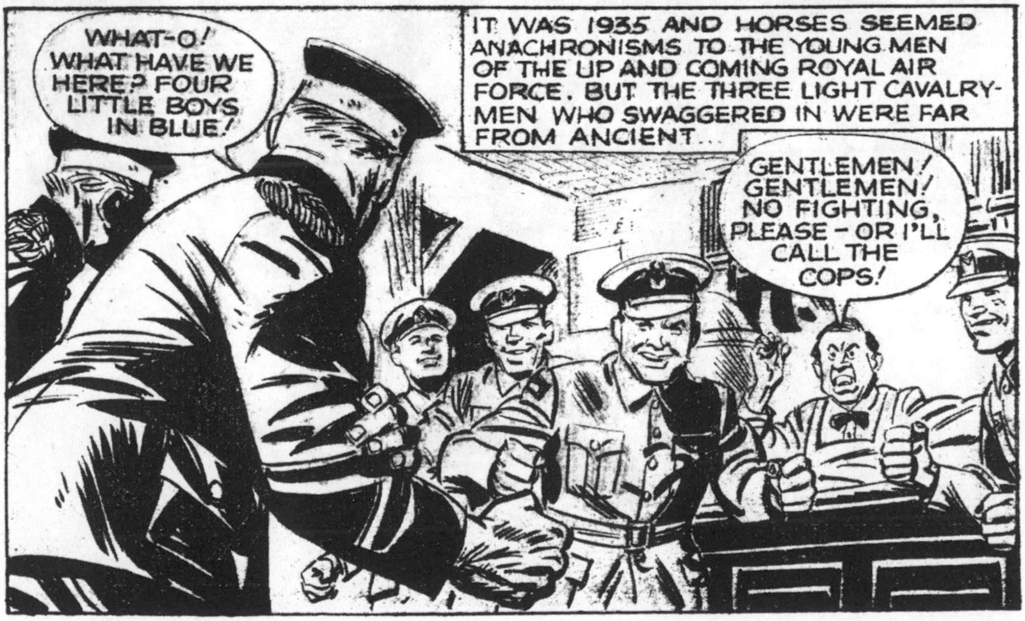
IT WAS 1935 AND HORSES SEEMED ANACHRONISMS TO THE YOUNG MEN OF THE UP AND COMING ROYAL AIR FORCE. BUT THE THREE LIGHT CAVALRYMEN WHO SWAGGERED IN WERE FAR FROM ANCIENT...
WHAT-O! WHAT HAVE WE HERE? FOUR LITTLE BOYS IN BLUE!
GENTLEMEN! GENTLEMEN! NO FIGHTING, PLEASE - OR I'LL CALL THE COPS!

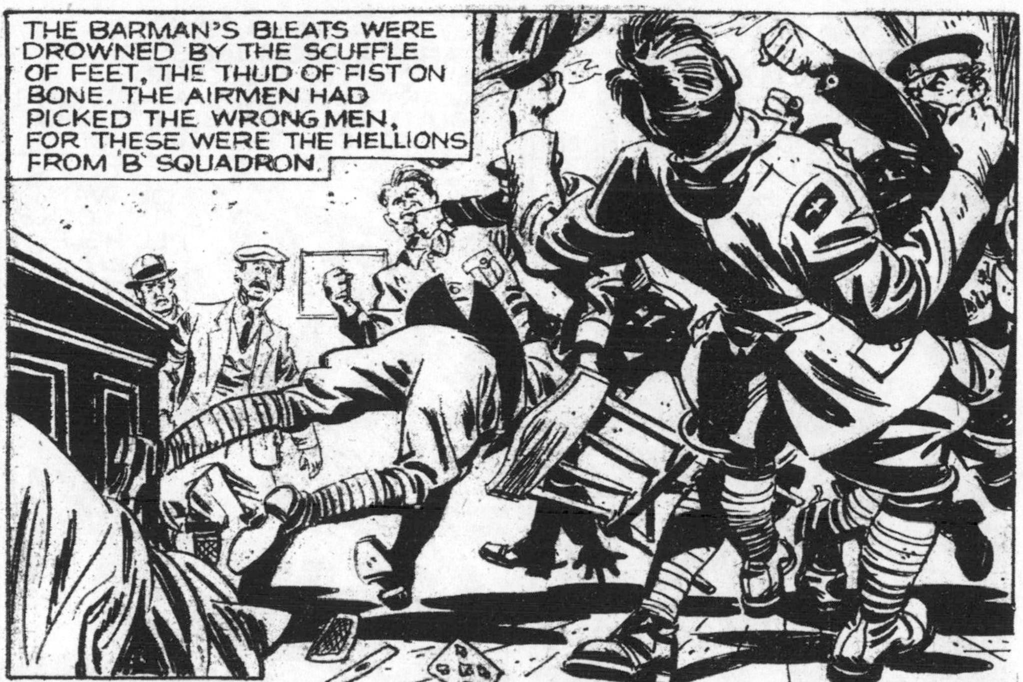
THE BARMAN'S BLEATS WERE DROWNED BY THE SCUFFLE OF FEET, THE THUD OF FIST ON BONE. THE AIRMEN HAD PICKED THE WRONG MEN, FOR THESE WERE THE HELLIONS FROM 'B' SQUADRON.

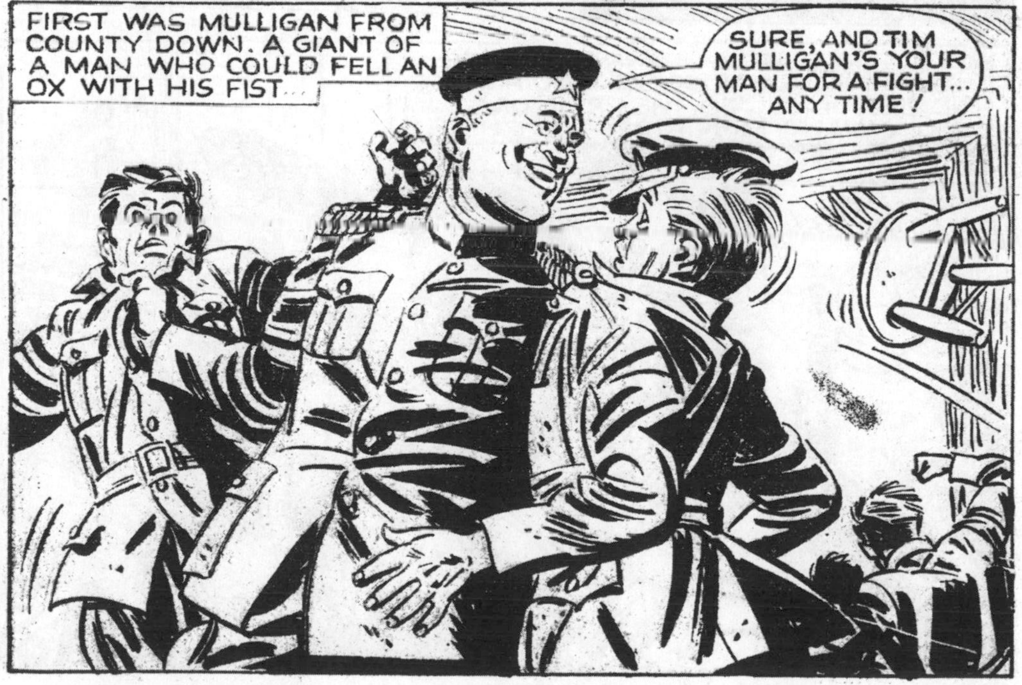
FIRST WAS MULLIGAN FROM COUNTY DOWN. A GIANT OF A MAN WHO COULD FELL AN OX WITH HIS FIST...
SURE, AND TIM MULLIGAN'S YOUR MAN FOR A FIGHT... ANY TIME!

THE SECOND WAS D'ARCY— HUGH EGREMONT D'ARCY FROM NOWHERE. AN ELEGANT GENTLEMAN RANKER, A MAN WHO DID NOT SPEAK LIKE HIS COMRADES AND YET COMMANDED THEIR RESPECT...

HORSES ARE A NOBLE CREATION, FRIEND. UNLIKE YOUR FOUL FLYING CONTRAPTIONS!

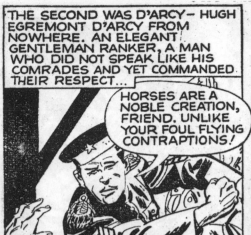

AND THE THIRD WAS SPARROW— SPARROW FROM THE ELEPHANT AND CASTLE. A COCKNEY, A SMART OPERATOR, A MAN WHO COULD FIND DRY BILLETS AND HOT FOOD IN THE MIDST OF DESOLATION...

YOU WANT TO FLY, COCK? I'LL HELP YOU!

MULLIGAN, D'ARCY, SPARROW. THREE INSEPARABLES WHOSE BELOVED HORSES HAD BEEN INSULTED. THE PRIDE OF A LIGHT CAVALRYMAN RIDES VERY HIGH.

COPS! RUN FOR IT, MATES!

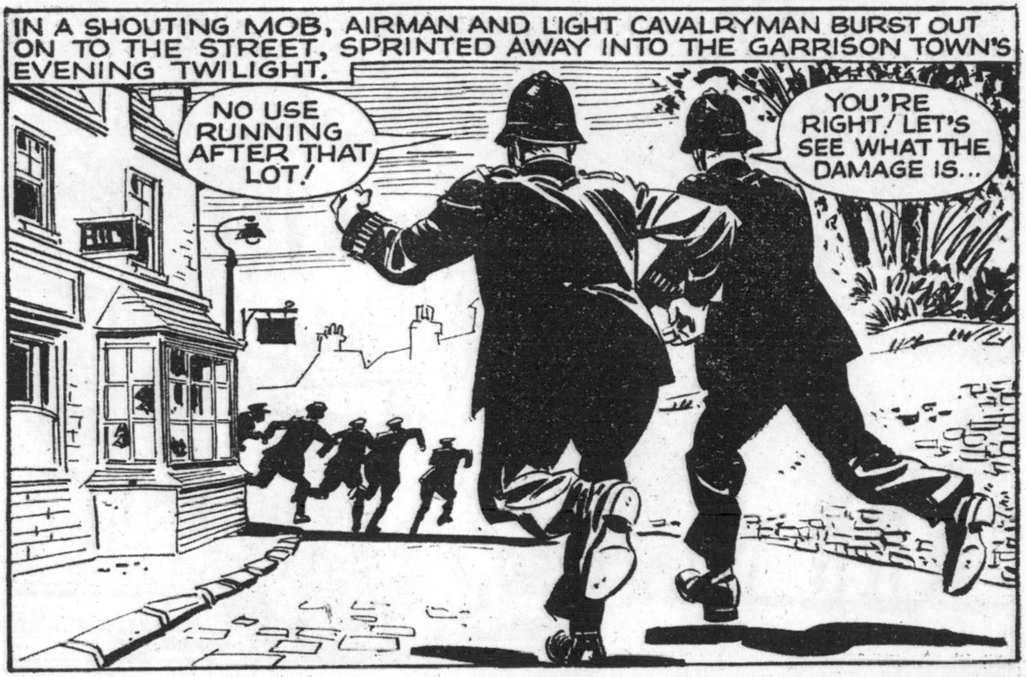
IN A SHOUTING MOB, AIRMAN AND LIGHT CAVALRYMAN BURST OUT ON TO THE STREET, SPRINTED AWAY INTO THE GARRISON TOWN'S EVENING TWILIGHT.
NO USE RUNNING AFTER THAT LOT!
YOU'RE RIGHT! LET'S SEE WHAT THE DAMAGE IS...

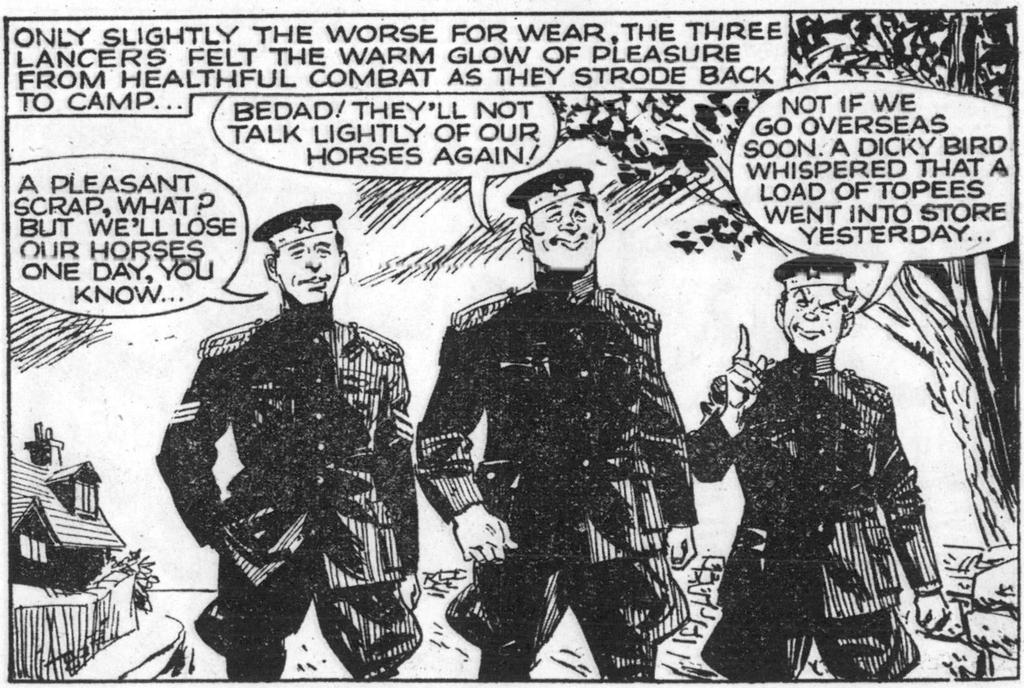
ONLY SLIGHTLY THE WORSE FOR WEAR, THE THREE LANCERS FELT THE WARM GLOW OF PLEASURE FROM HEALTHFUL COMBAT AS THEY STRODE BACK TO CAMP...
A PLEASANT SCRAP, WHAT? BUT WE'LL LOSE OUR HORSES ONE DAY, YOU KNOW...
BEDAD! THEY'LL NOT TALK LIGHTLY OF OUR HORSES AGAIN!
NOT IF WE GO OVERSEAS SOON. A DICKY BIRD WHISPERED THAT A LOAD OF TOPEES WENT INTO STORE YESTERDAY...

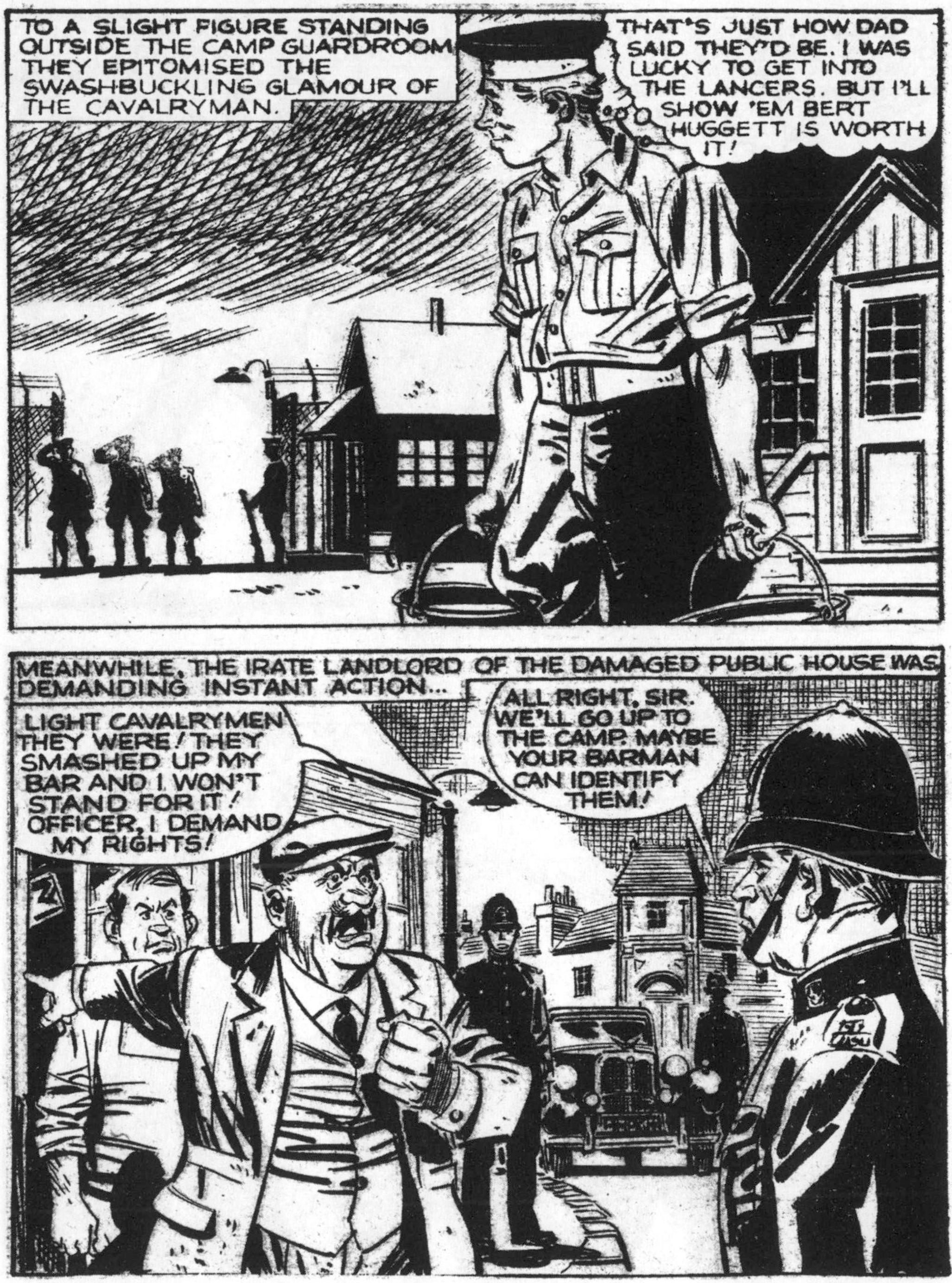
TO A SLIGHT FIGURE STANDING OUTSIDE THE CAMP GUARDROOM THEY EPITOMISED THE SWASHBUCKLING GLAMOUR OF THE CAVALRYMAN.
THAT'S JUST HOW DAD SAID THEY'D BE. I WAS LUCKY TO GET INTO THE LANCERS. BUT I'LL SHOW 'EM BERT HUGGETT IS WORTH IT!
MEANWHILE, THE IRATE LANDLORD OF THE DAMAGED PUBLIC HOUSE WAS DEMANDING INSTANT ACTION...
LIGHT CAVALRYMEN THEY WERE! THEY SMASHED UP MY BAR AND I WON'T STAND FOR IT! OFFICER, I DEMAND MY RIGHTS!
ALL RIGHT, SIR. WE'LL GO UP TO THE CAMP. MAYBE YOUR BARMAN CAN IDENTIFY THEM!

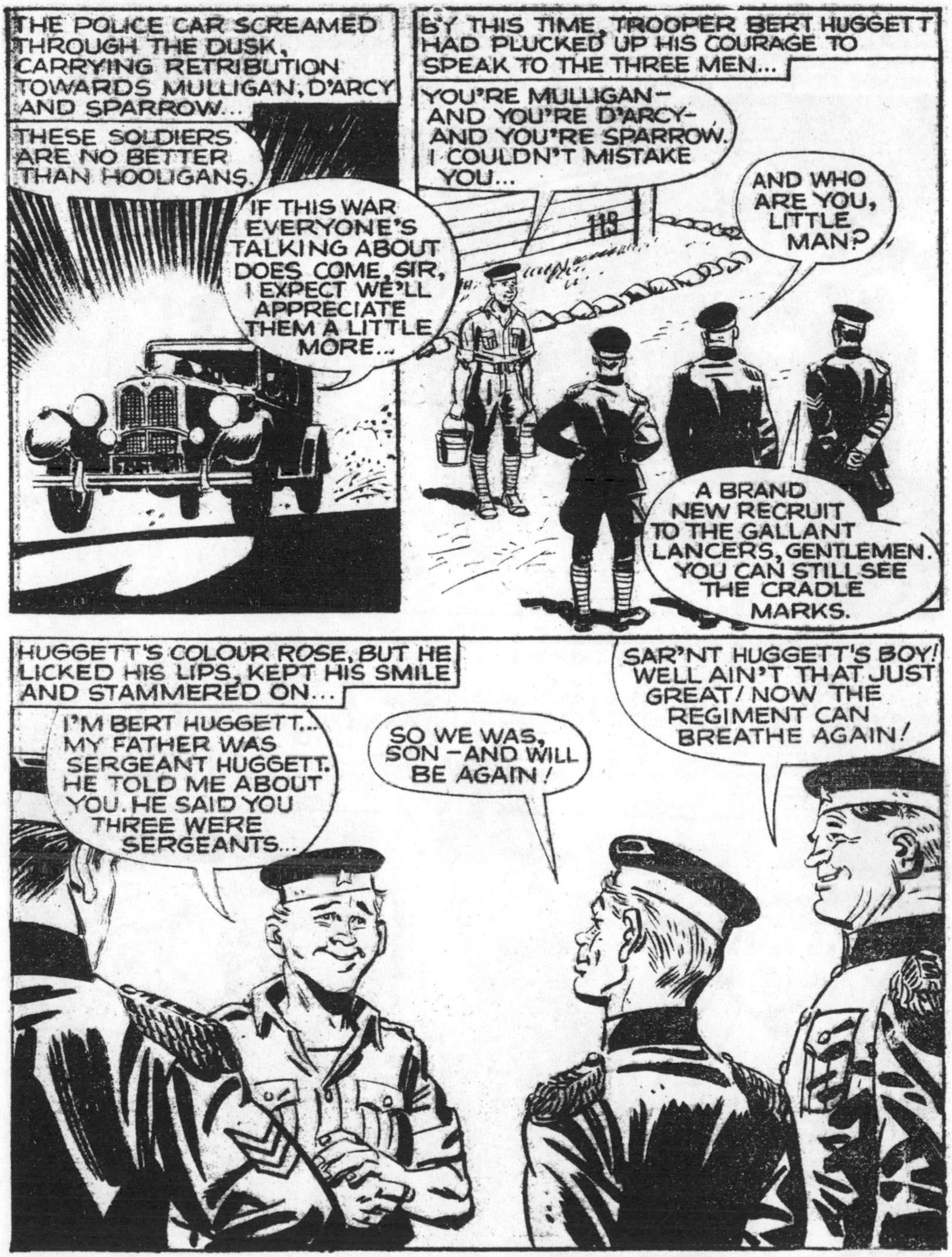
THE POLICE CAR SCREAMED THROUGH THE DUSK, CARRYING RETRIBUTION TOWARDS MULLIGAN, D'ARCY AND SPARROW...
THESE SOLDIERS ARE NO BETTER THAN HOOLIGANS.
IF THIS WAR EVERYONE'S TALKING ABOUT DOES COME, SIR, I EXPECT WE'LL APPRECIATE THEM A LITTLE MORE...
BY THIS TIME, TROOPER BERT HUGGETT HAD PLUCKED UP HIS COURAGE TO SPEAK TO THE THREE MEN...
YOU'RE MULLIGAN— AND YOU'RE D'ARCY— AND YOU'RE SPARROW. I COULDN'T MISTAKE YOU...
AND WHO ARE YOU, LITTLE MAN?
A BRAND NEW RECRUIT TO THE GALLANT LANCERS, GENTLEMEN. YOU CAN STILL SEE THE CRADLE MARKS.
HUGGETT'S COLOUR ROSE, BUT HE LICKED HIS LIPS, KEPT HIS SMILE AND STAMMERED ON...
I'M BERT HUGGETT... MY FATHER WAS SERGEANT HUGGETT. HE TOLD ME ABOUT YOU. HE SAID YOU THREE WERE SERGEANTS...
SO WE WAS, SON —AND WILL BE AGAIN!
SAR'NT HUGGETT'S BOY! WELL AIN'T THAT JUST GREAT! NOW THE REGIMENT CAN BREATHE AGAIN!

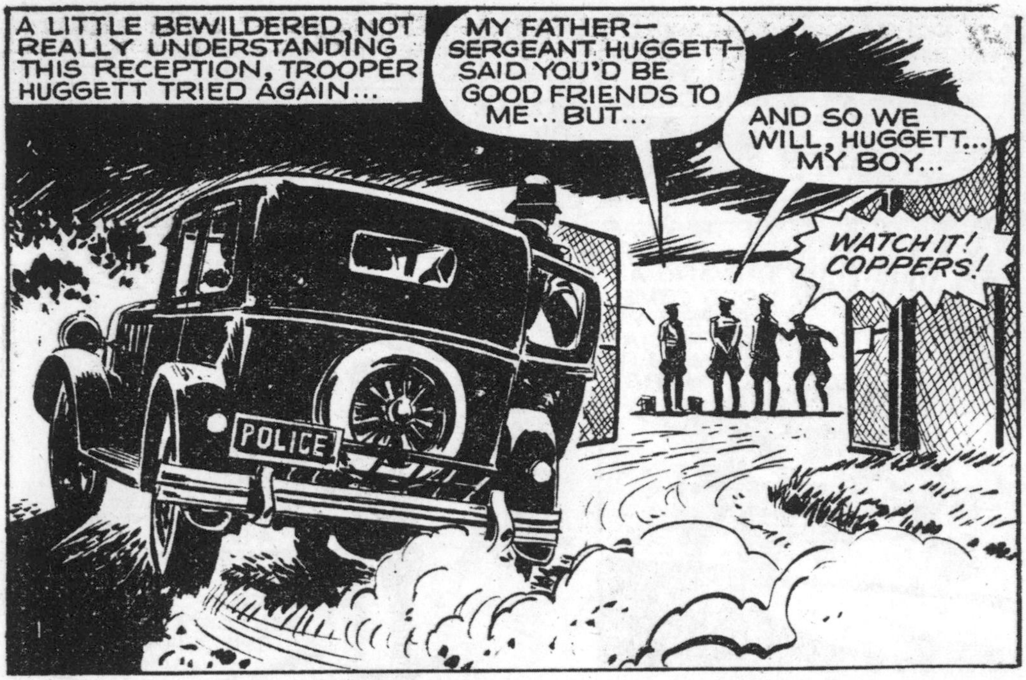
A LITTLE BEWILDERED, NOT REALLY UNDERSTANDING THIS RECEPTION, TROOPER HUGGETT TRIED AGAIN...
MY FATHER— SERGEANT HUGGETT— SAID YOU'D BE GOOD FRIENDS TO ME... BUT...
AND SO WE WILL, HUGGETT... MY BOY...
WATCH IT! COPPERS!
POLICE

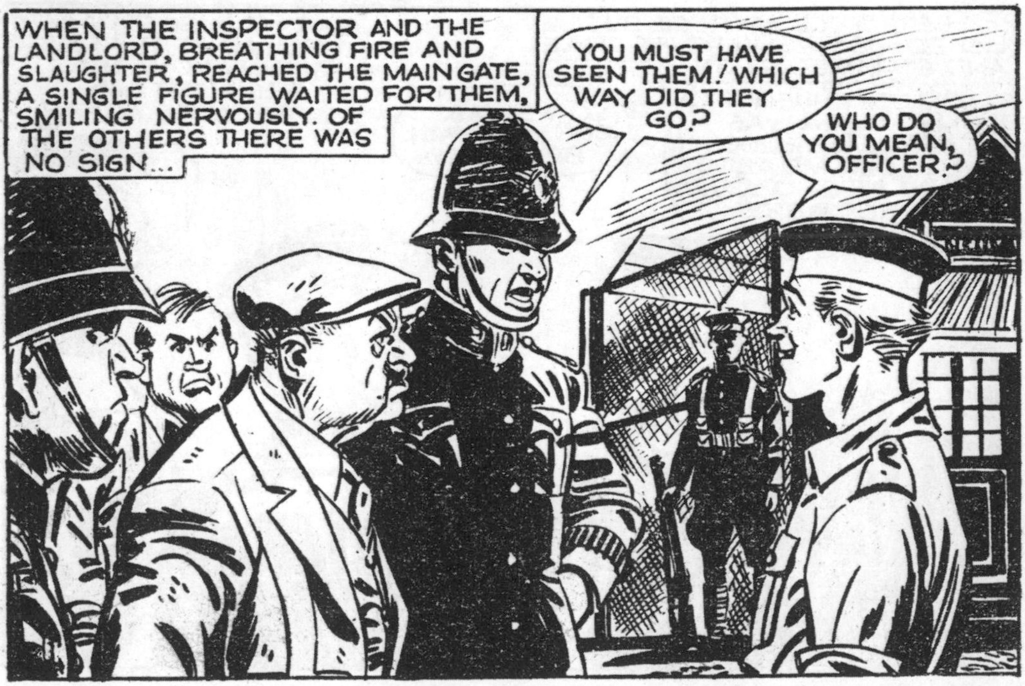
WHEN THE INSPECTOR AND THE LANDLORD, BREATHING FIRE AND SLAUGHTER, REACHED THE MAIN GATE, A SINGLE FIGURE WAITED FOR THEM, SMILING NERVOUSLY. OF THE OTHERS THERE WAS NO SIGN...
YOU MUST HAVE SEEN THEM! WHICH WAY DID THEY GO?
WHO DO YOU MEAN, OFFICER?

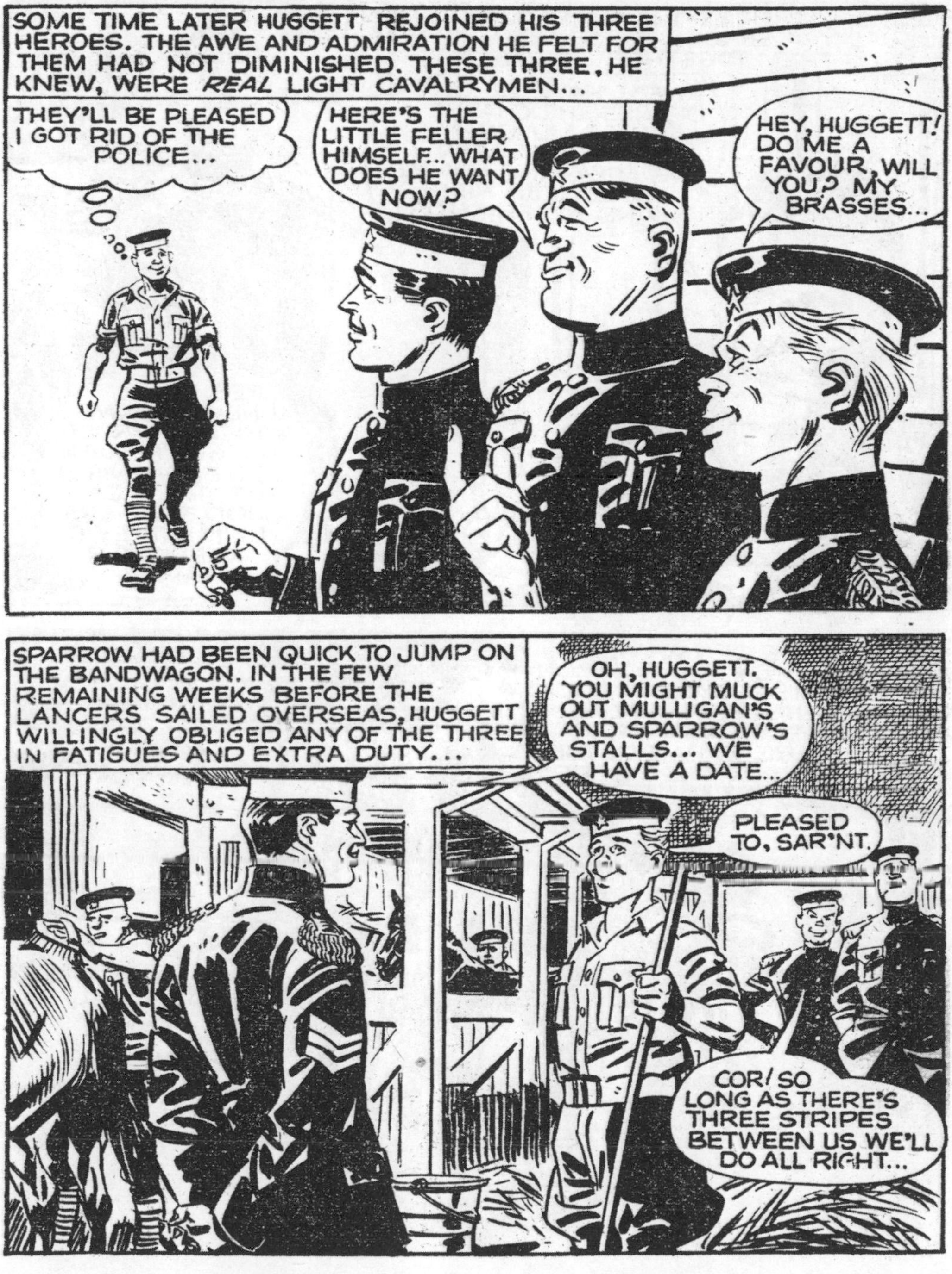
SOME TIME LATER HUGGETT REJOINED HIS THREE HEROES. THE AWE AND ADMIRATION HE FELT FOR THEM HAD NOT DIMINISHED. THESE THREE, HE KNEW, WERE *REAL* LIGHT CAVALRYMEN...
THEY'LL BE PLEASED I GOT RID OF THE POLICE...
HERE'S THE LITTLE FELLER HIMSELF... WHAT DOES HE WANT NOW?
HEY, HUGGETT! DO ME A FAVOUR, WILL YOU? MY BRASSES...
SPARROW HAD BEEN QUICK TO JUMP ON THE BANDWAGON. IN THE FEW REMAINING WEEKS BEFORE THE LANCERS SAILED OVERSEAS, HUGGETT WILLINGLY OBLIGED ANY OF THE THREE IN FATIGUES AND EXTRA DUTY...
OH, HUGGETT. YOU MIGHT MUCK OUT MULLIGAN'S AND SPARROW'S STALLS... WE HAVE A DATE...
PLEASED TO, SAR'NT.
COR! SO LONG AS THERE'S THREE STRIPES BETWEEN US WE'LL DO ALL RIGHT...

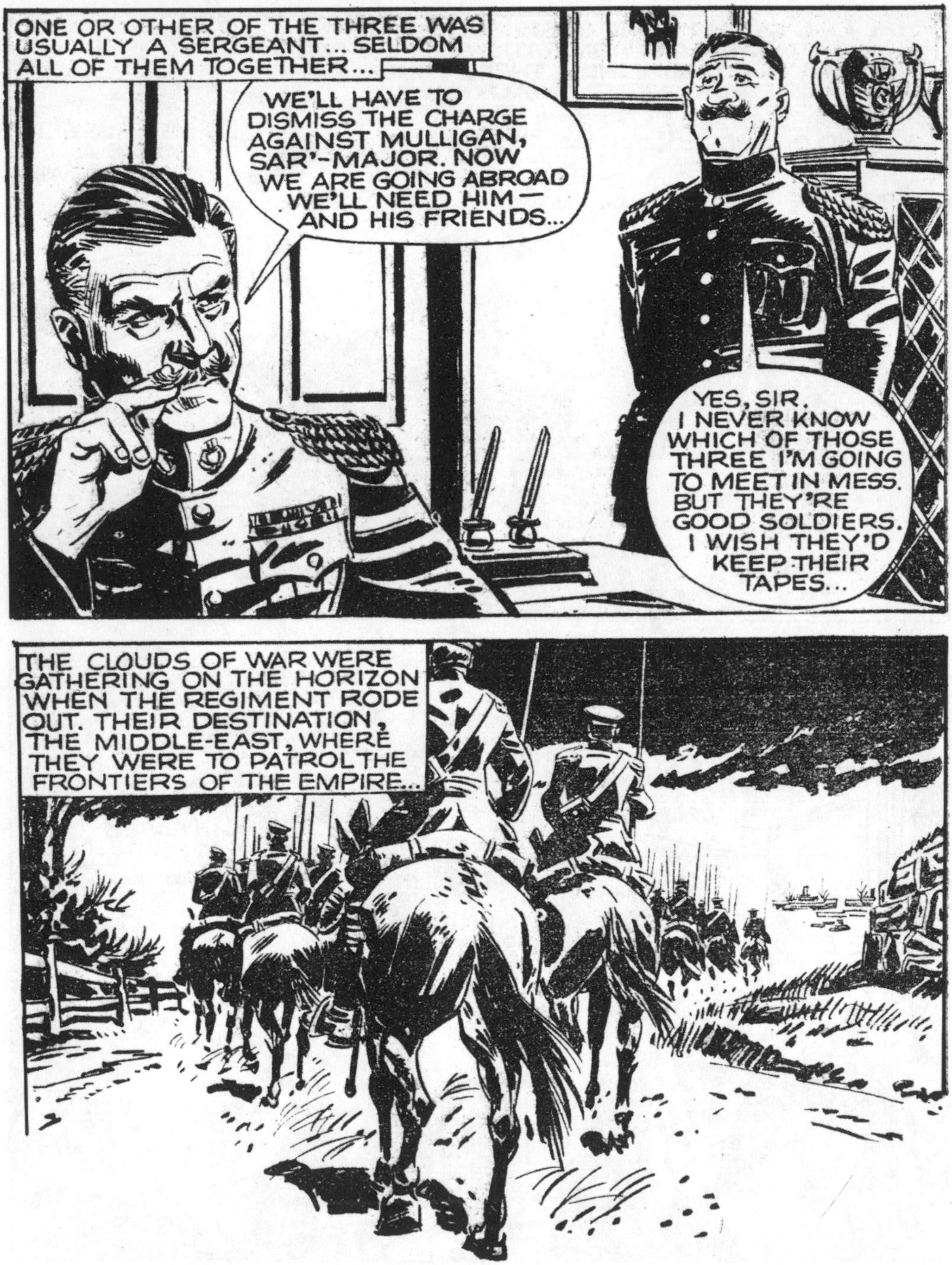
ONE OR OTHER OF THE THREE WAS USUALLY A SERGEANT... SELDOM ALL OF THEM TOGETHER...
WE'LL HAVE TO DISMISS THE CHARGE AGAINST MULLIGAN, SAR'-MAJOR. NOW WE ARE GOING ABROAD WE'LL NEED HIM — AND HIS FRIENDS...
YES, SIR. I NEVER KNOW WHICH OF THOSE THREE I'M GOING TO MEET IN MESS. BUT THEY'RE GOOD SOLDIERS. I WISH THEY'D KEEP THEIR TAPES...
THE CLOUDS OF WAR WERE GATHERING ON THE HORIZON WHEN THE REGIMENT RODE OUT. THEIR DESTINATION, THE MIDDLE-EAST, WHERE THEY WERE TO PATROL THE FRONTIERS OF THE EMPIRE...

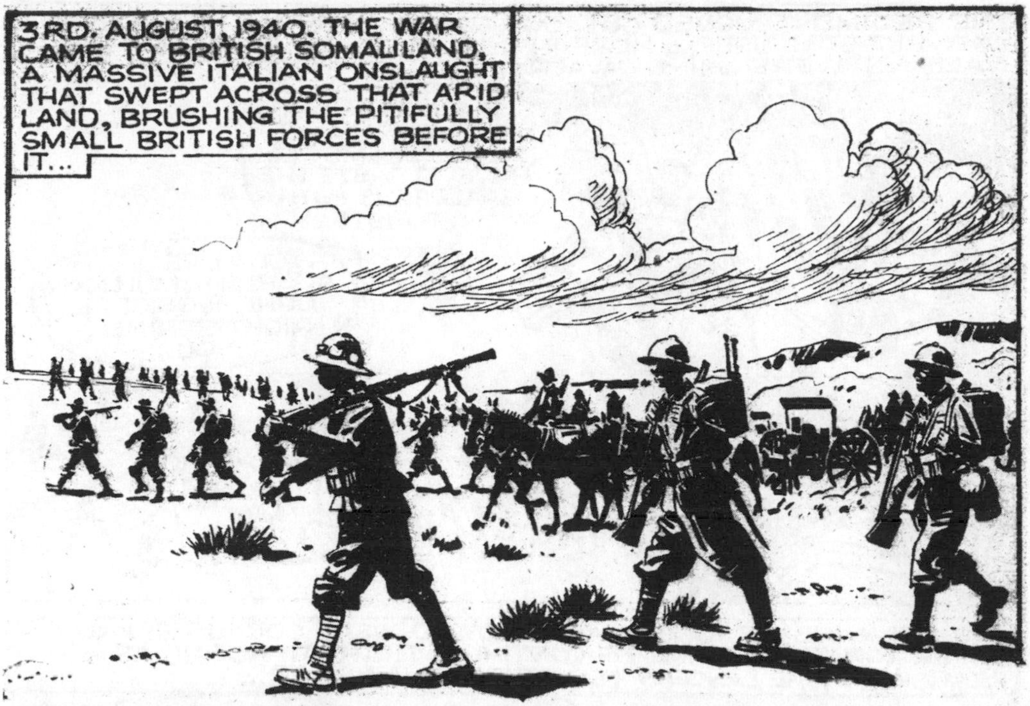
3RD. AUGUST, 1940. THE WAR CAME TO BRITISH SOMALILAND, A MASSIVE ITALIAN ONSLAUGHT THAT SWEPT ACROSS THAT ARID LAND, BRUSHING THE PITIFULLY SMALL BRITISH FORCES BEFORE IT...

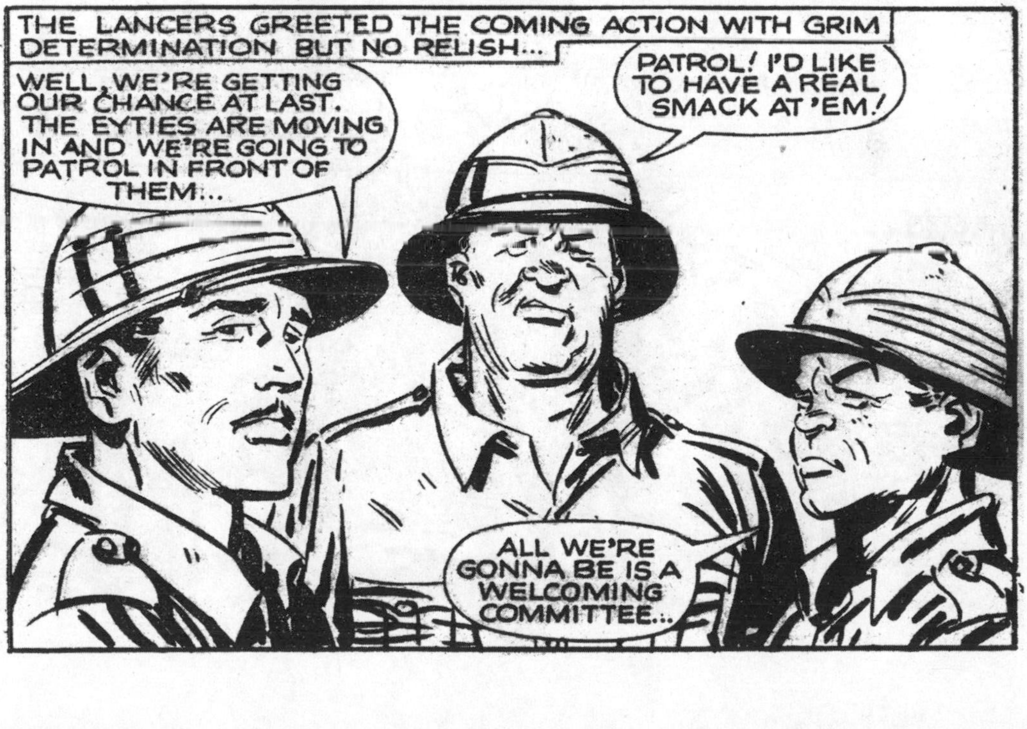
THE LANCERS GREETED THE COMING ACTION WITH GRIM DETERMINATION BUT NO RELISH...
WELL, WE'RE GETTING OUR CHANCE AT LAST. THE EYTIES ARE MOVING IN AND WE'RE GOING TO PATROL IN FRONT OF THEM...
PATROL! I'D LIKE TO HAVE A REAL SMACK AT 'EM!
ALL WE'RE GONNA BE IS A WELCOMING COMMITTEE...

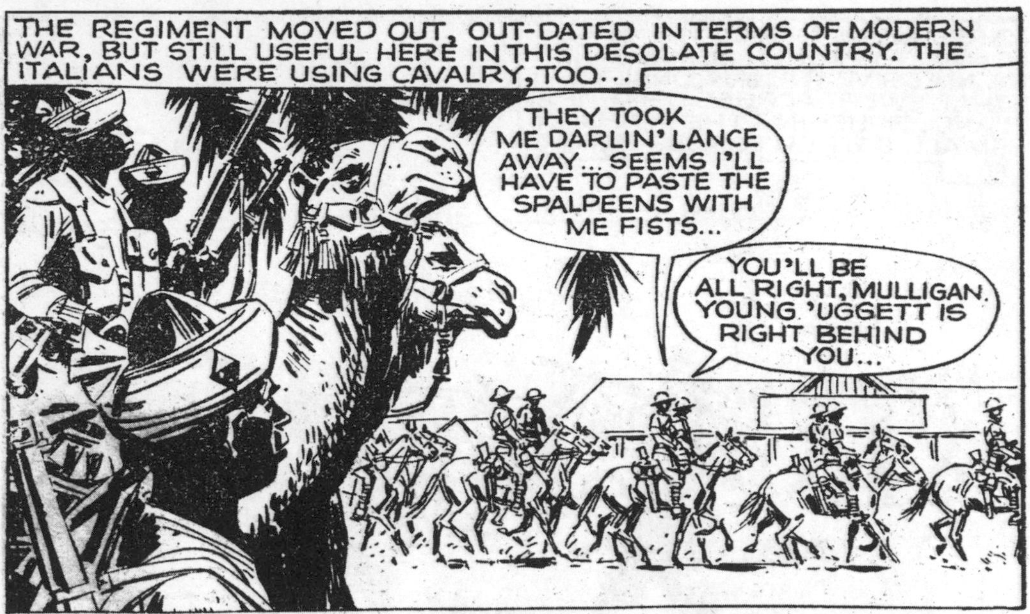
THE REGIMENT MOVED OUT, OUT-DATED IN TERMS OF MODERN WAR, BUT STILL USEFUL HERE IN THIS DESOLATE COUNTRY. THE ITALIANS WERE USING CAVALRY, TOO...
THEY TOOK ME DARLIN' LANCE AWAY... SEEMS I'LL HAVE TO PASTE THE SPALPEENS WITH ME FISTS...
YOU'LL BE ALL RIGHT, MULLIGAN. YOUNG 'UGGETT IS RIGHT BEHIND YOU...

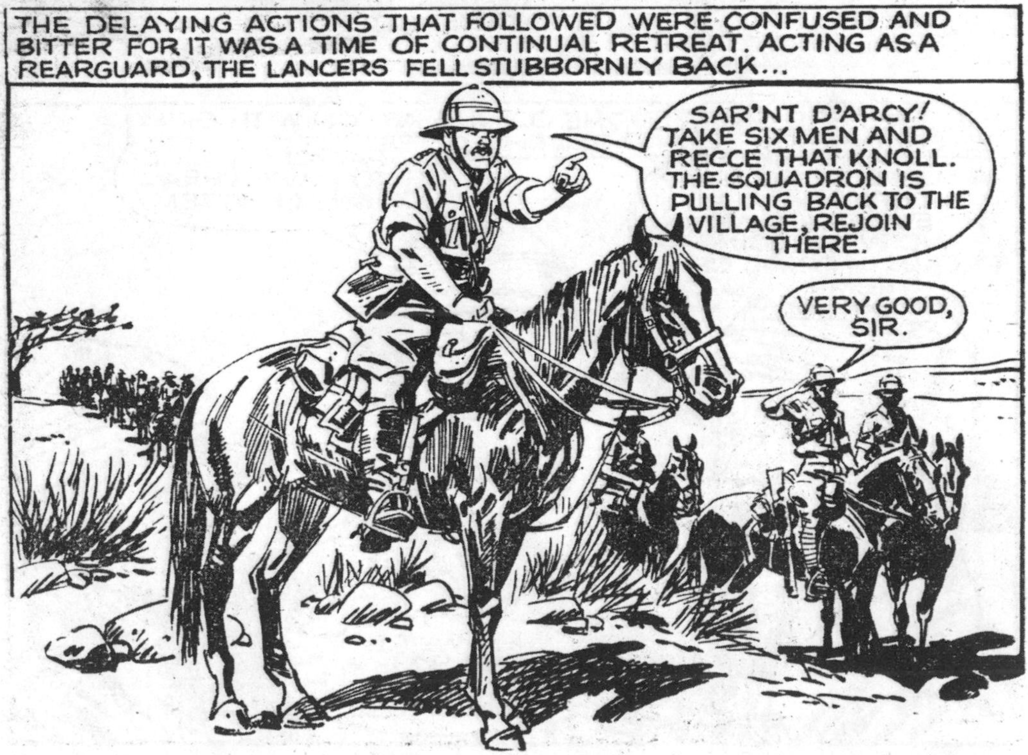
THE DELAYING ACTIONS THAT FOLLOWED WERE CONFUSED AND BITTER FOR IT WAS A TIME OF CONTINUAL RETREAT. ACTING AS A REARGUARD, THE LANCERS FELL STUBBORNLY BACK...
SAR'NT D'ARCY! TAKE SIX MEN AND RECCE THAT KNOLL. THE SQUADRON IS PULLING BACK TO THE VILLAGE, REJOIN THERE.
VERY GOOD, SIR.

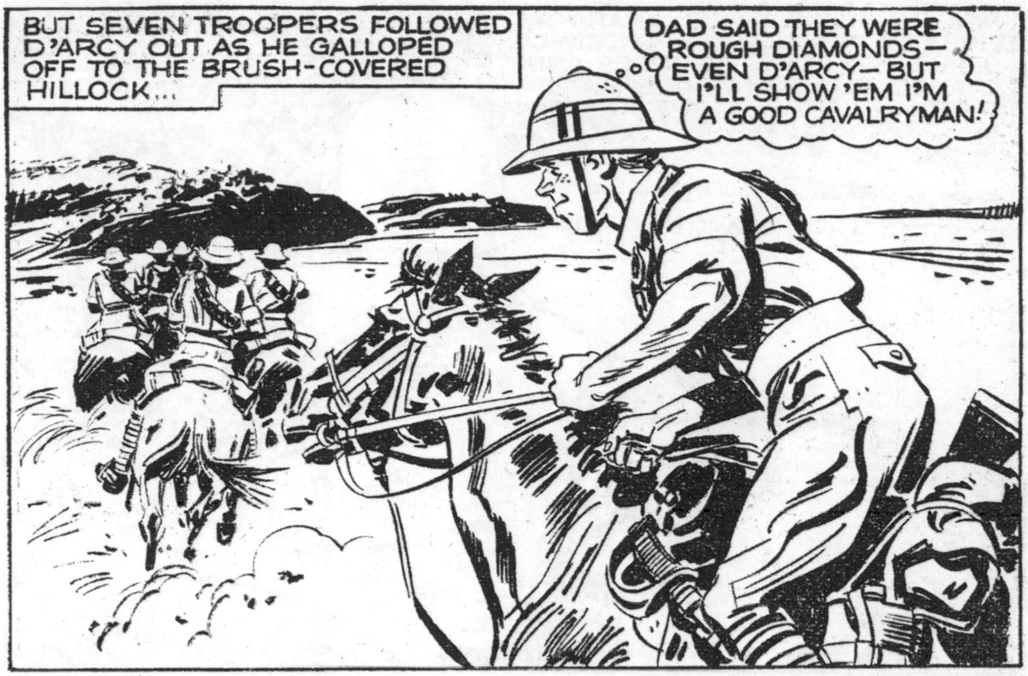
BUT SEVEN TROOPERS FOLLOWED D'ARCY OUT AS HE GALLOPED OFF TO THE BRUSH-COVERED HILLOCK...
DAD SAID THEY WERE ROUGH DIAMONDS— EVEN D'ARCY— BUT I'LL SHOW 'EM I'M A GOOD CAVALRYMAN!

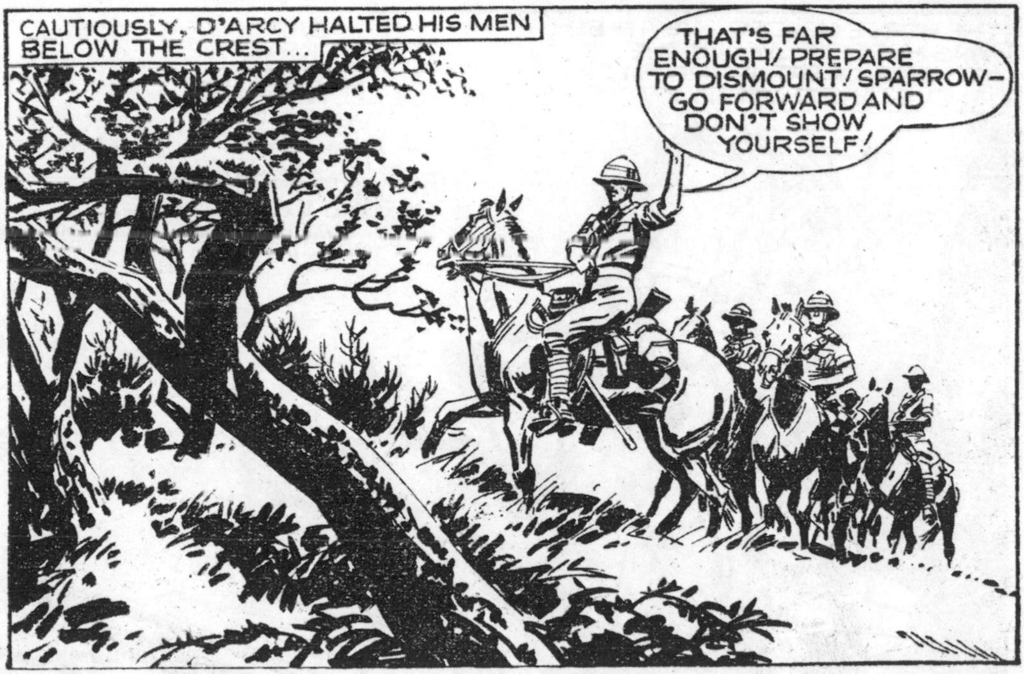
CAUTIOUSLY, D'ARCY HALTED HIS MEN BELOW THE CREST...
THAT'S FAR ENOUGH! PREPARE TO DISMOUNT! SPARROW— GO FORWARD AND DON'T SHOW YOURSELF!

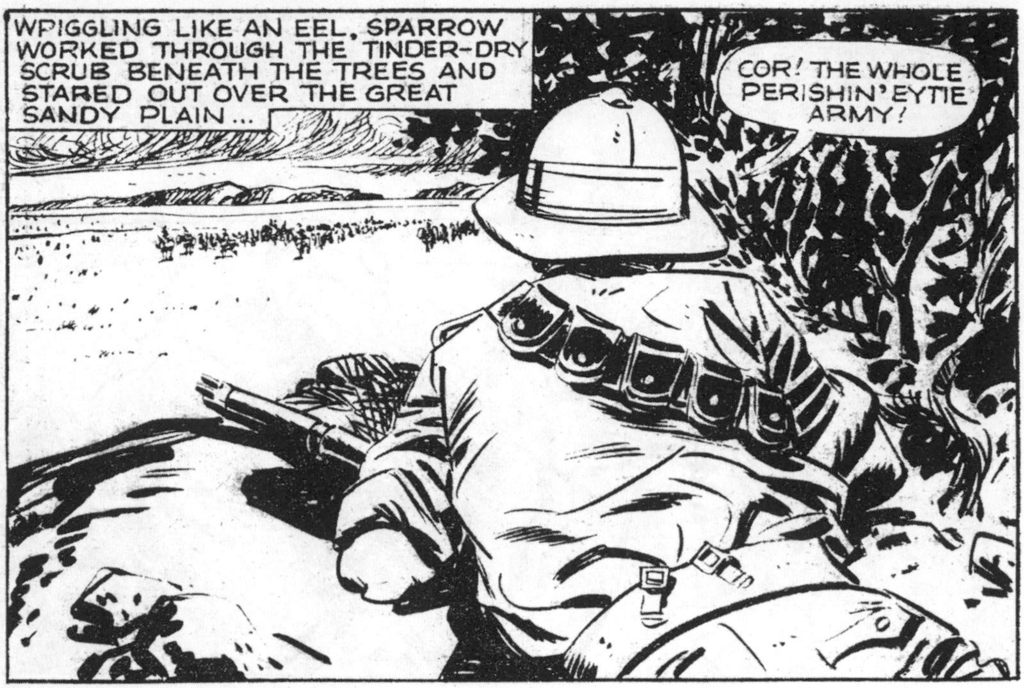
WRIGGLING LIKE AN EEL, SPARROW WORKED THROUGH THE TINDER-DRY SCRUB BENEATH THE TREES AND STARED OUT OVER THE GREAT SANDY PLAIN...
COR! THE WHOLE PERISHIN' EYTIE ARMY!

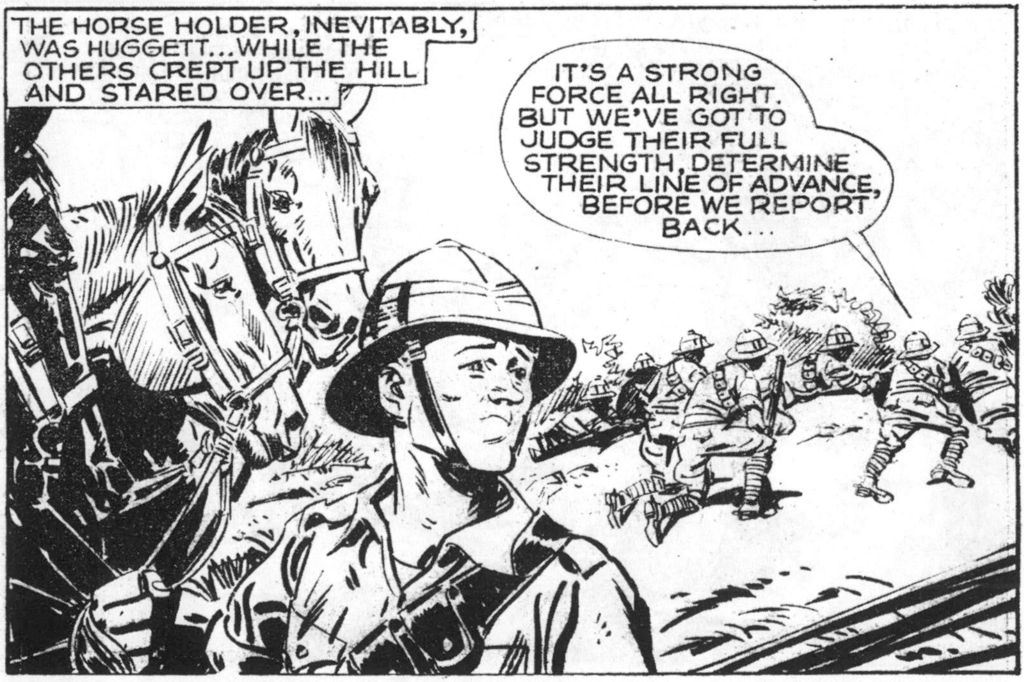
THE HORSE HOLDER, INEVITABLY, WAS HUGGETT...WHILE THE OTHERS CREPT UP THE HILL AND STARED OVER...
IT'S A STRONG FORCE ALL RIGHT. BUT WE'VE GOT TO JUDGE THEIR FULL STRENGTH, DETERMINE THEIR LINE OF ADVANCE, BEFORE WE REPORT BACK...

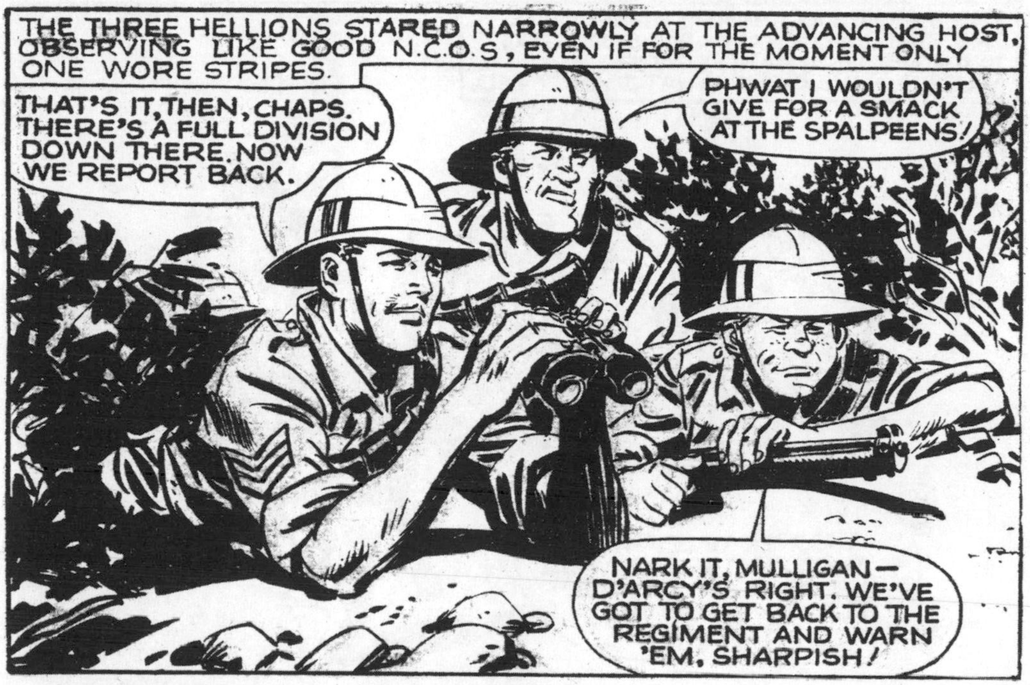
THE THREE HELLIONS STARED NARROWLY AT THE ADVANCING HOST, OBSERVING LIKE GOOD N.C.O.S, EVEN IF FOR THE MOMENT ONLY ONE WORE STRIPES.
THAT'S IT, THEN, CHAPS. THERE'S A FULL DIVISION DOWN THERE. NOW WE REPORT BACK.
PHWAT I WOULDN'T GIVE FOR A SMACK AT THE SPALPEENS!
NARK IT, MULLIGAN — D'ARCY'S RIGHT. WE'VE GOT TO GET BACK TO THE REGIMENT AND WARN 'EM, SHARPISH!

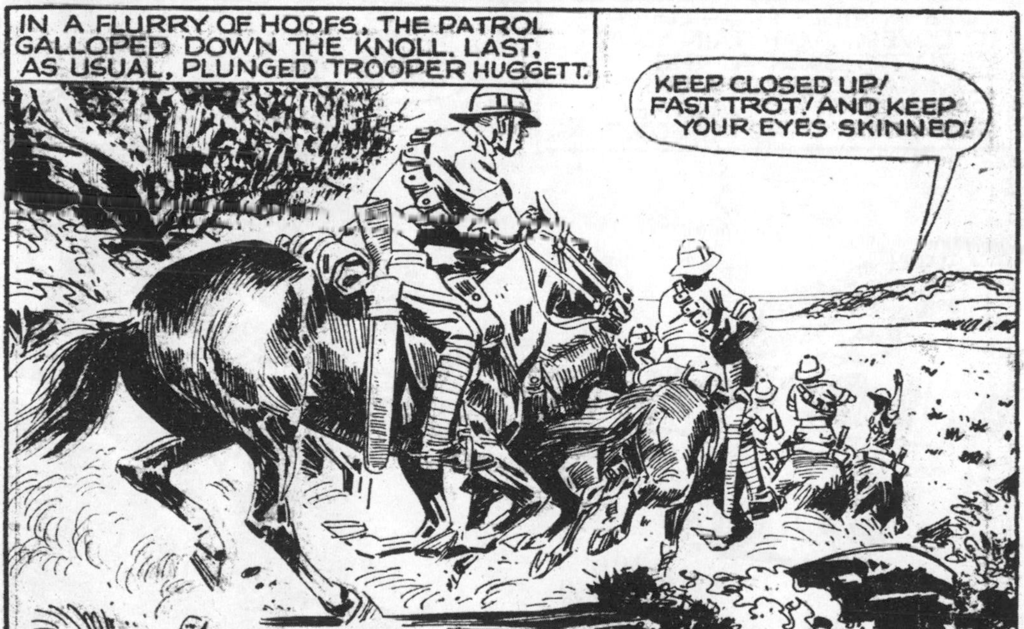
IN A FLURRY OF HOOFS, THE PATROL GALLOPED DOWN THE KNOLL. LAST, AS USUAL, PLUNGED TROOPER HUGGETT.
KEEP CLOSED UP! FAST TROT! AND KEEP YOUR EYES SKINNED!

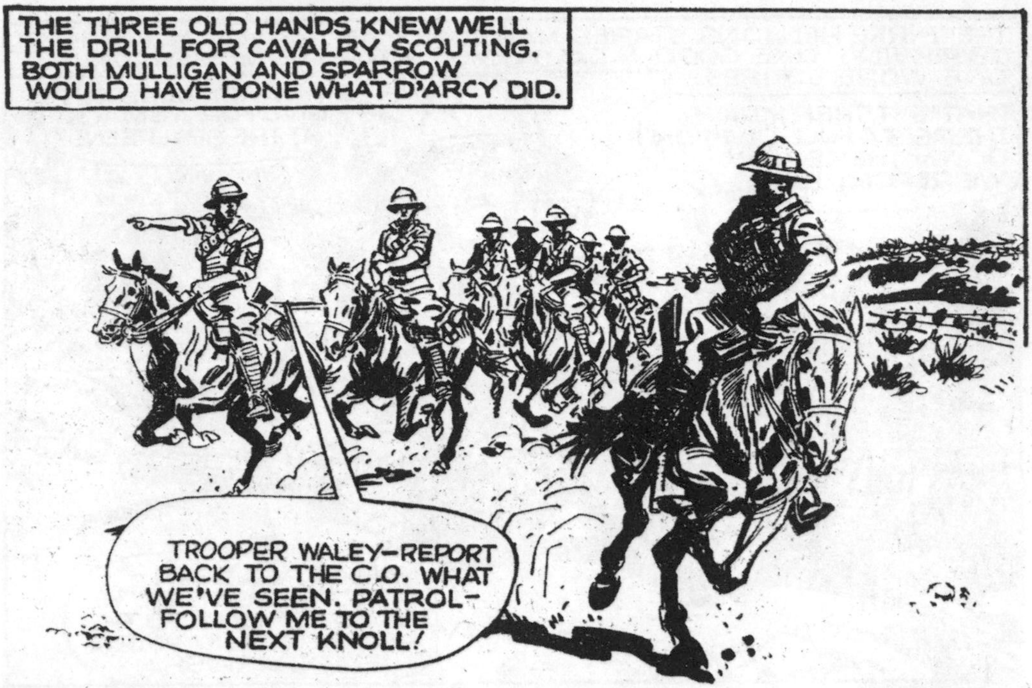
THE THREE OLD HANDS KNEW WELL THE DRILL FOR CAVALRY SCOUTING. BOTH MULLIGAN AND SPARROW WOULD HAVE DONE WHAT D'ARCY DID.
TROOPER WALEY–REPORT BACK TO THE C.O. WHAT WE'VE SEEN. PATROL–FOLLOW ME TO THE NEXT KNOLL!

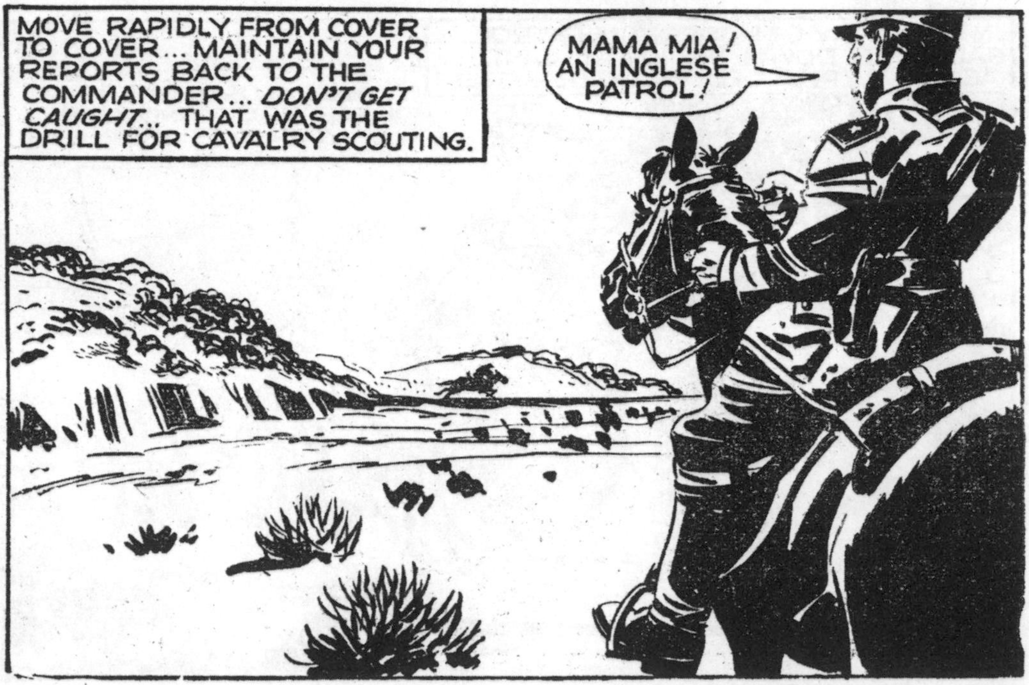
MOVE RAPIDLY FROM COVER TO COVER... MAINTAIN YOUR REPORTS BACK TO THE COMMANDER... *DON'T GET CAUGHT*... THAT WAS THE DRILL FOR CAVALRY SCOUTING.
MAMA MIA! AN INGLESE PATROL!

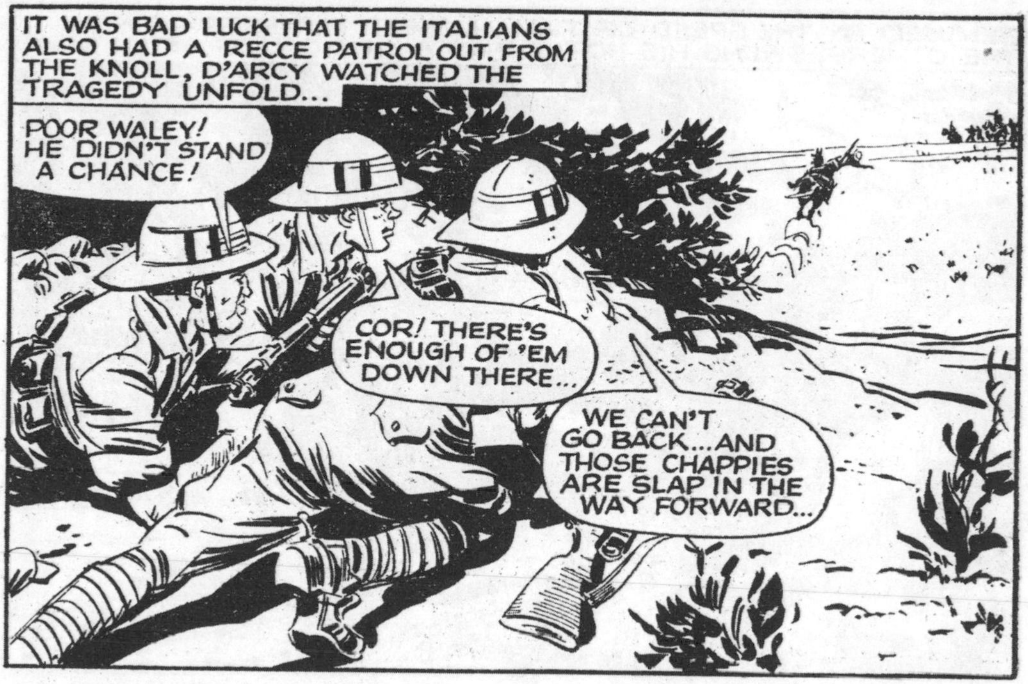
IT WAS BAD LUCK THAT THE ITALIANS ALSO HAD A RECCE PATROL OUT. FROM THE KNOLL, D'ARCY WATCHED THE TRAGEDY UNFOLD...
POOR WALEY! HE DIDN'T STAND A CHANCE!
COR! THERE'S ENOUGH OF 'EM DOWN THERE...
WE CAN'T GO BACK...AND THOSE CHAPPIES ARE SLAP IN THE WAY FORWARD...

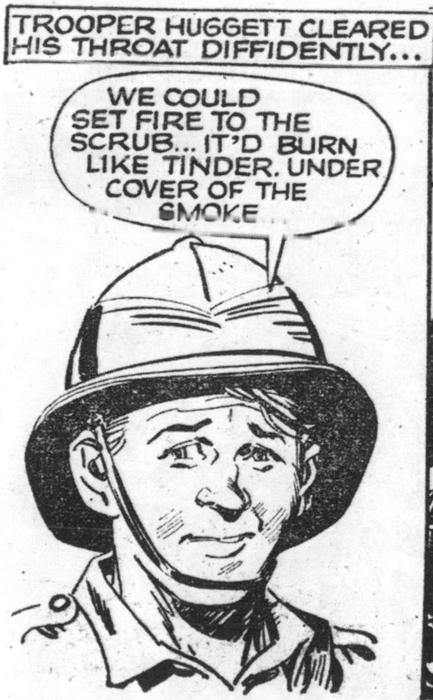
TROOPER HUGGETT CLEARED HIS THROAT DIFFIDENTLY...
WE COULD SET FIRE TO THE SCRUB... IT'D BURN LIKE TINDER. UNDER COVER OF THE SMOKE

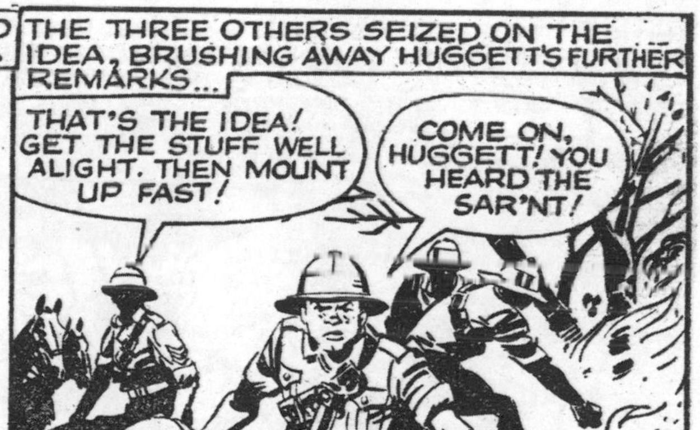
THE THREE OTHERS SEIZED ON THE IDEA, BRUSHING AWAY HUGGETT'S FURTHER REMARKS...
THAT'S THE IDEA! GET THE STUFF WELL ALIGHT. THEN MOUNT UP FAST!
COME ON, HUGGETT! YOU HEARD THE SAR'NT!

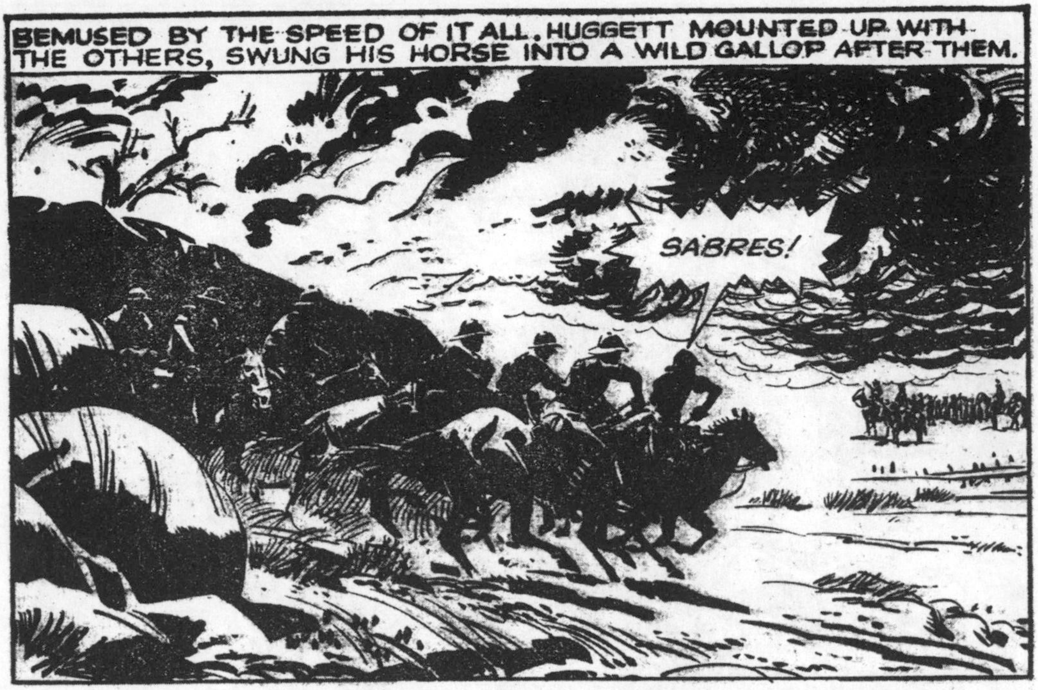
BEMUSED BY THE SPEED OF IT ALL, HUGGETT MOUNTED UP WITH THE OTHERS, SWUNG HIS HORSE INTO A WILD GALLOP AFTER THEM.
SABRES!

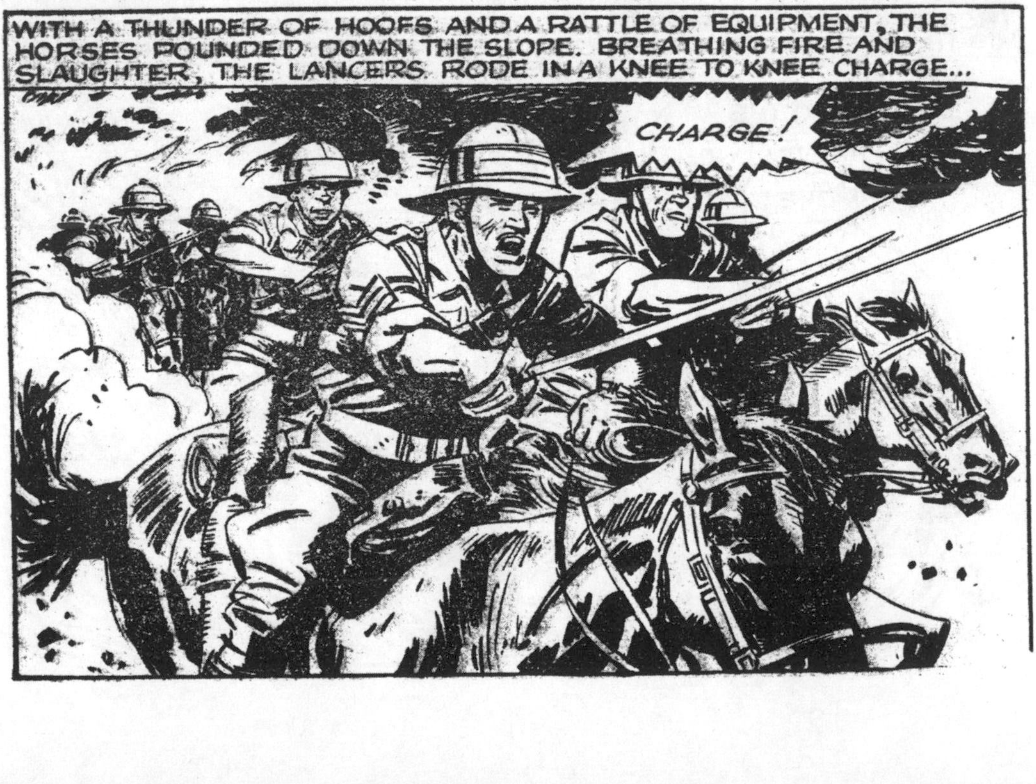
WITH A THUNDER OF HOOFS AND A RATTLE OF EQUIPMENT, THE HORSES POUNDED DOWN THE SLOPE. BREATHING FIRE AND SLAUGHTER, THE LANCERS RODE IN A KNEE TO KNEE CHARGE...
CHARGE!

LIKE THE IRON RAM OF A BATTLESHIP, THE LANCERS PIERCED DEEPLY INTO THE ITALIAN CAVALRY LINE, SABRES FLASHING IN THE BRASSY SUNLIGHT.

WITH A BLOOD-THRILLING YELL, THEY BURST CLEAN THROUGH THE ENEMY CAVALRY TROOP...

WE'RE THROUGH! RIDE!

THE FIRE DID THE TRICK!

THEY DIDN'T KNOW WHAT HIT THEM, BEGORRAH!

IT WAS A SMALL BUT SUCCESSFUL SKIRMISH, BUT THE DAYS OF THE LIGHT CAVALRY WERE NUMBERED.

Chapter 2. Front-Line Desert

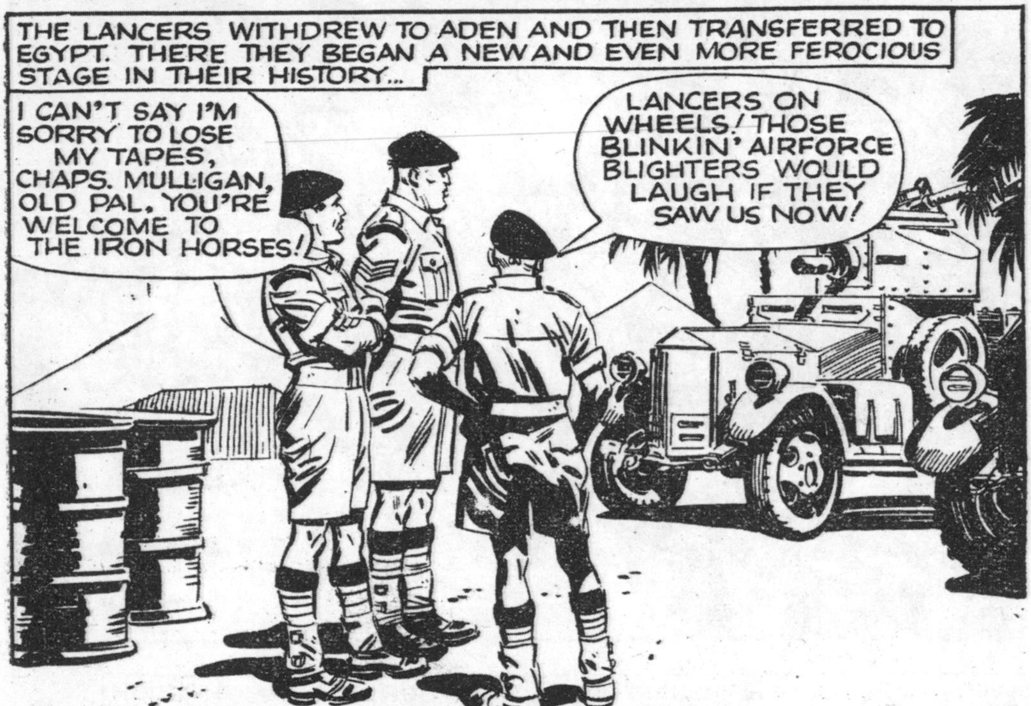
THE LANCERS WITHDREW TO ADEN AND THEN TRANSFERRED TO EGYPT. THERE THEY BEGAN A NEW AND EVEN MORE FEROCIOUS STAGE IN THEIR HISTORY...
I CAN'T SAY I'M SORRY TO LOSE MY TAPES, CHAPS. MULLIGAN, OLD PAL, YOU'RE WELCOME TO THE IRON HORSES!
LANCERS ON WHEELS! THOSE BLINKIN' AIRFORCE BLIGHTERS WOULD LAUGH IF THEY SAW US NOW!

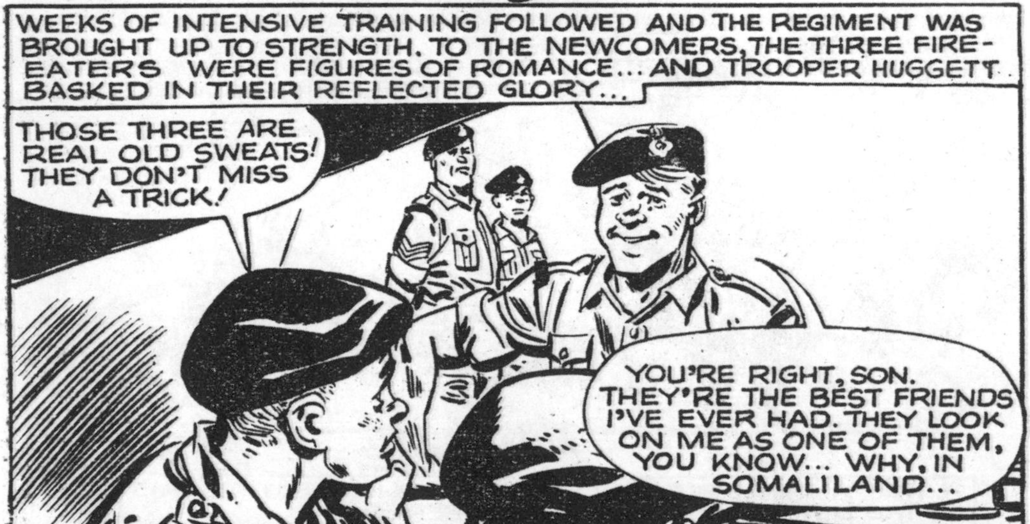
WEEKS OF INTENSIVE TRAINING FOLLOWED AND THE REGIMENT WAS BROUGHT UP TO STRENGTH. TO THE NEWCOMERS, THE THREE FIRE-EATERS WERE FIGURES OF ROMANCE... AND TROOPER HUGGETT BASKED IN THEIR REFLECTED GLORY...
THOSE THREE ARE REAL OLD SWEATS! THEY DON'T MISS A TRICK!
YOU'RE RIGHT, SON. THEY'RE THE BEST FRIENDS I'VE EVER HAD. THEY LOOK ON ME AS ONE OF THEM, YOU KNOW... WHY, IN SOMALILAND...

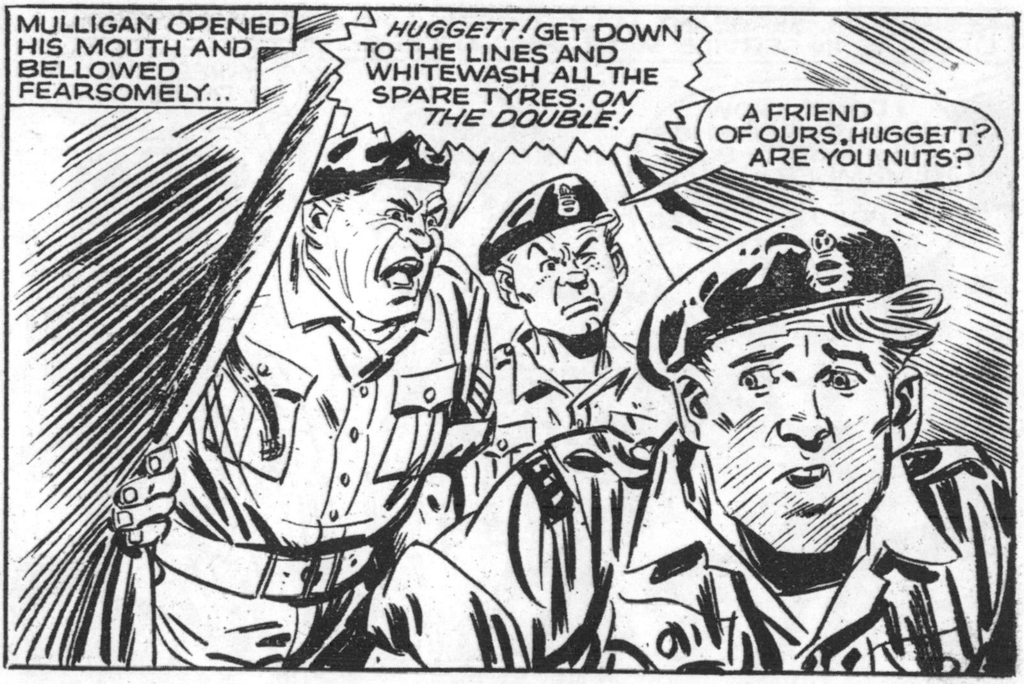
MULLIGAN OPENED HIS MOUTH AND BELLOWED FEARSOMELY...
HUGGETT! GET DOWN TO THE LINES AND WHITEWASH ALL THE SPARE TYRES. ON THE DOUBLE!
A FRIEND OF OURS, HUGGETT? ARE YOU NUTS?

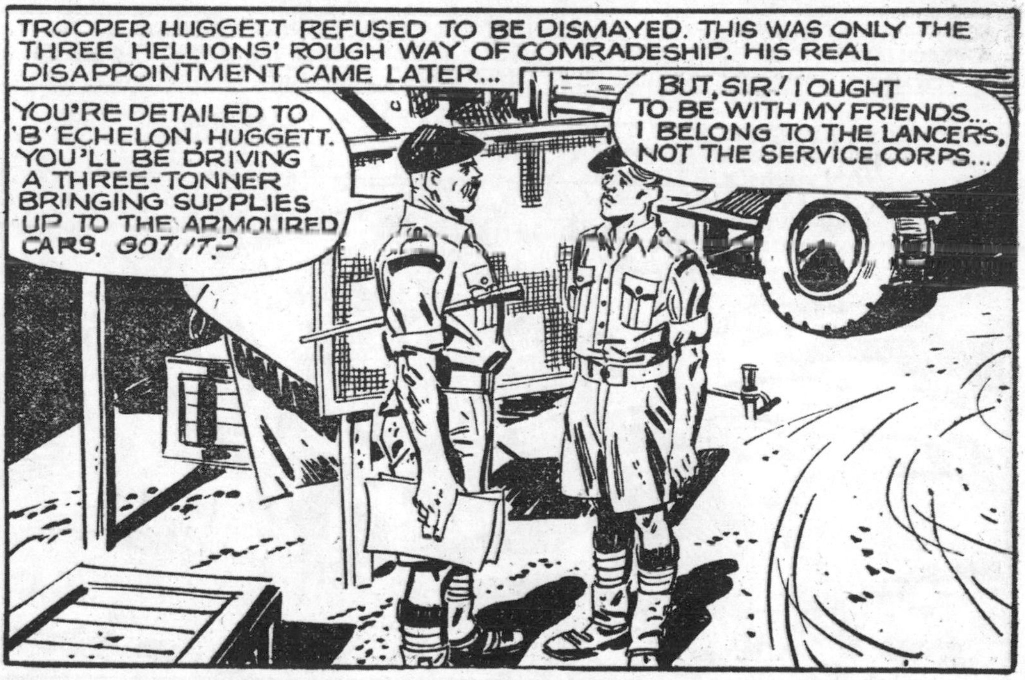
TROOPER HUGGETT REFUSED TO BE DISMAYED. THIS WAS ONLY THE THREE HELLIONS' ROUGH WAY OF COMRADESHIP. HIS REAL DISAPPOINTMENT CAME LATER...
YOU'RE DETAILED TO 'B' ECHELON, HUGGETT. YOU'LL BE DRIVING A THREE-TONNER BRINGING SUPPLIES UP TO THE ARMOURED CARS. GOT IT?
BUT, SIR! I OUGHT TO BE WITH MY FRIENDS... I BELONG TO THE LANCERS, NOT THE SERVICE CORPS...

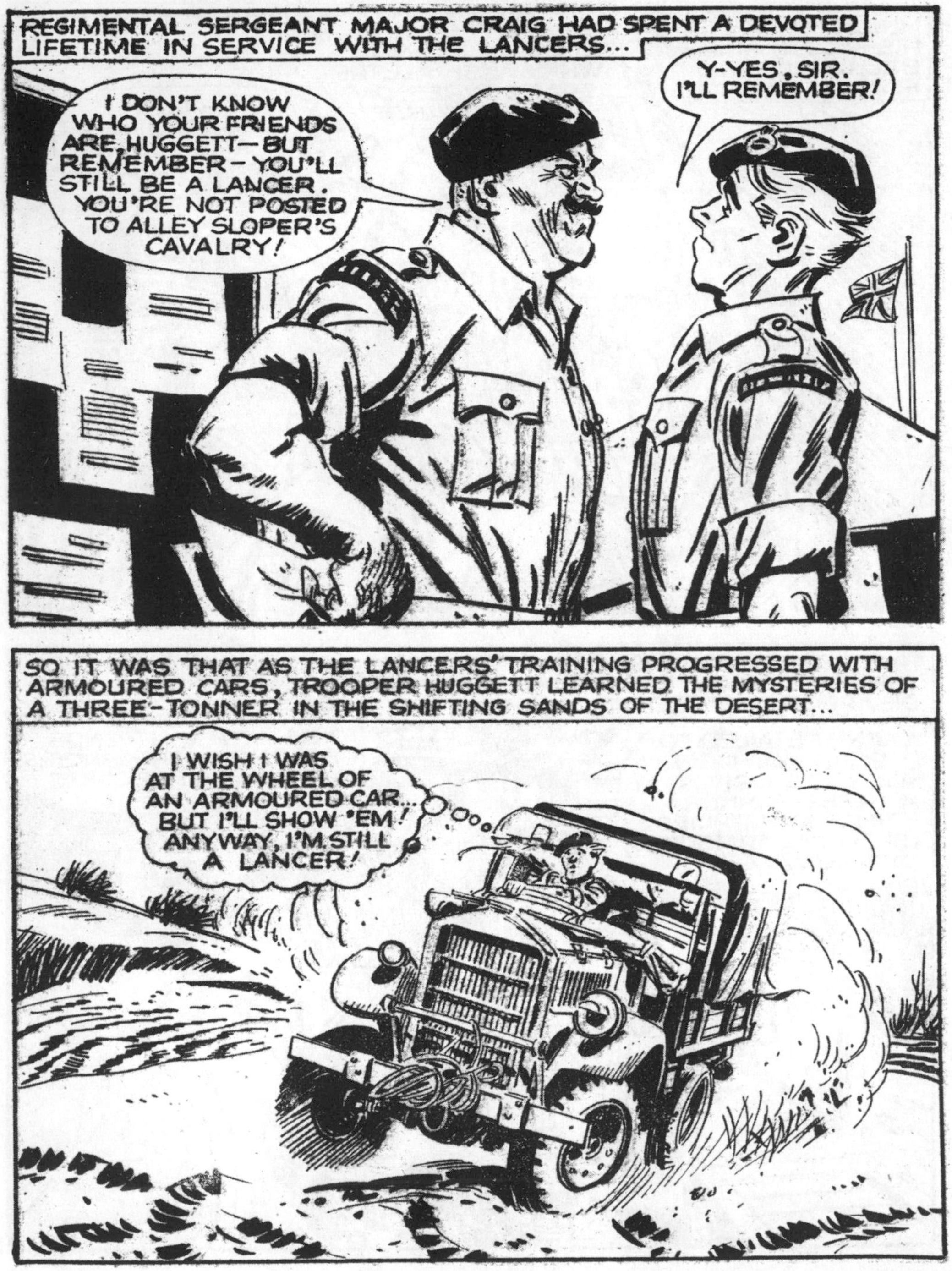
REGIMENTAL SERGEANT MAJOR CRAIG HAD SPENT A DEVOTED LIFETIME IN SERVICE WITH THE LANCERS...
I DON'T KNOW WHO YOUR FRIENDS ARE, HUGGETT—BUT REMEMBER—YOU'LL STILL BE A LANCER. YOU'RE NOT POSTED TO ALLEY SLOPER'S CAVALRY!
Y-YES, SIR. I'LL REMEMBER!
SO IT WAS THAT AS THE LANCERS' TRAINING PROGRESSED WITH ARMOURED CARS, TROOPER HUGGETT LEARNED THE MYSTERIES OF A THREE-TONNER IN THE SHIFTING SANDS OF THE DESERT...
I WISH I WAS AT THE WHEEL OF AN ARMOURED CAR... BUT I'LL SHOW 'EM! ANYWAY, I'M STILL A LANCER!

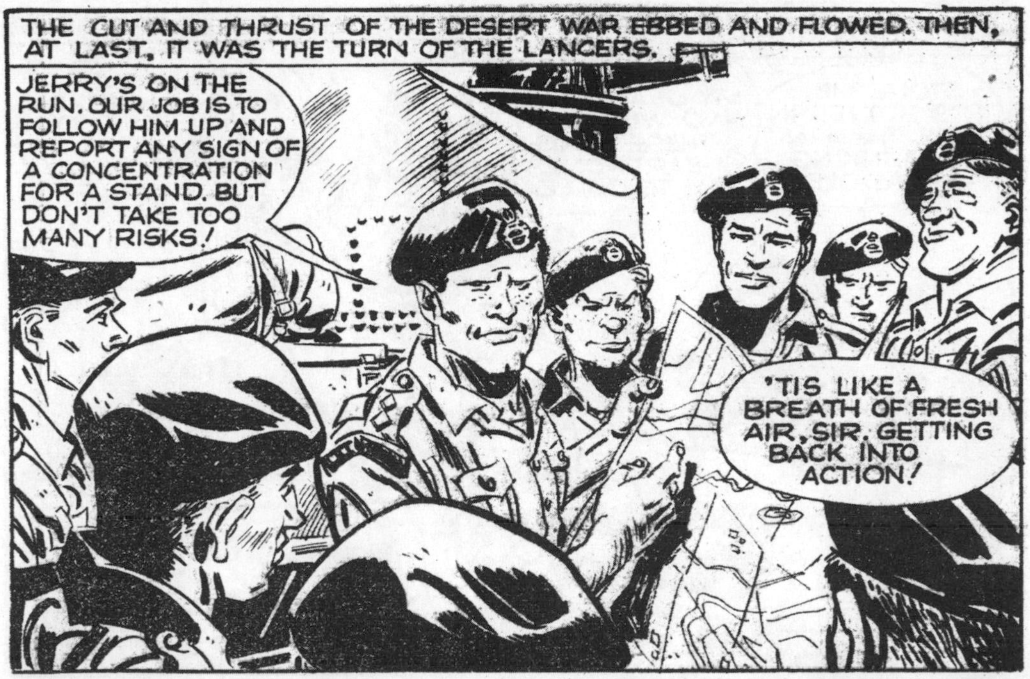
THE CUT AND THRUST OF THE DESERT WAR EBBED AND FLOWED. THEN, AT LAST, IT WAS THE TURN OF THE LANCERS.
JERRY'S ON THE RUN. OUR JOB IS TO FOLLOW HIM UP AND REPORT ANY SIGN OF A CONCENTRATION FOR A STAND. BUT DON'T TAKE TOO MANY RISKS!
'TIS LIKE A BREATH OF FRESH AIR, SIR. GETTING BACK INTO ACTION!

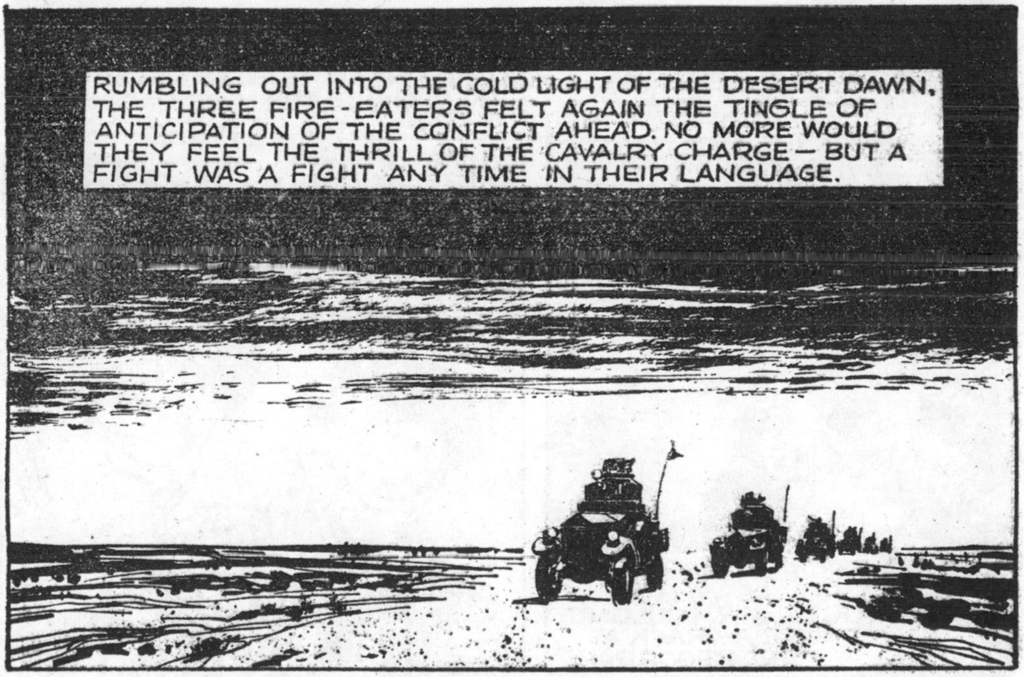
RUMBLING OUT INTO THE COLD LIGHT OF THE DESERT DAWN, THE THREE FIRE-EATERS FELT AGAIN THE TINGLE OF ANTICIPATION OF THE CONFLICT AHEAD. NO MORE WOULD THEY FEEL THE THRILL OF THE CAVALRY CHARGE — BUT A FIGHT WAS A FIGHT ANY TIME IN THEIR LANGUAGE.

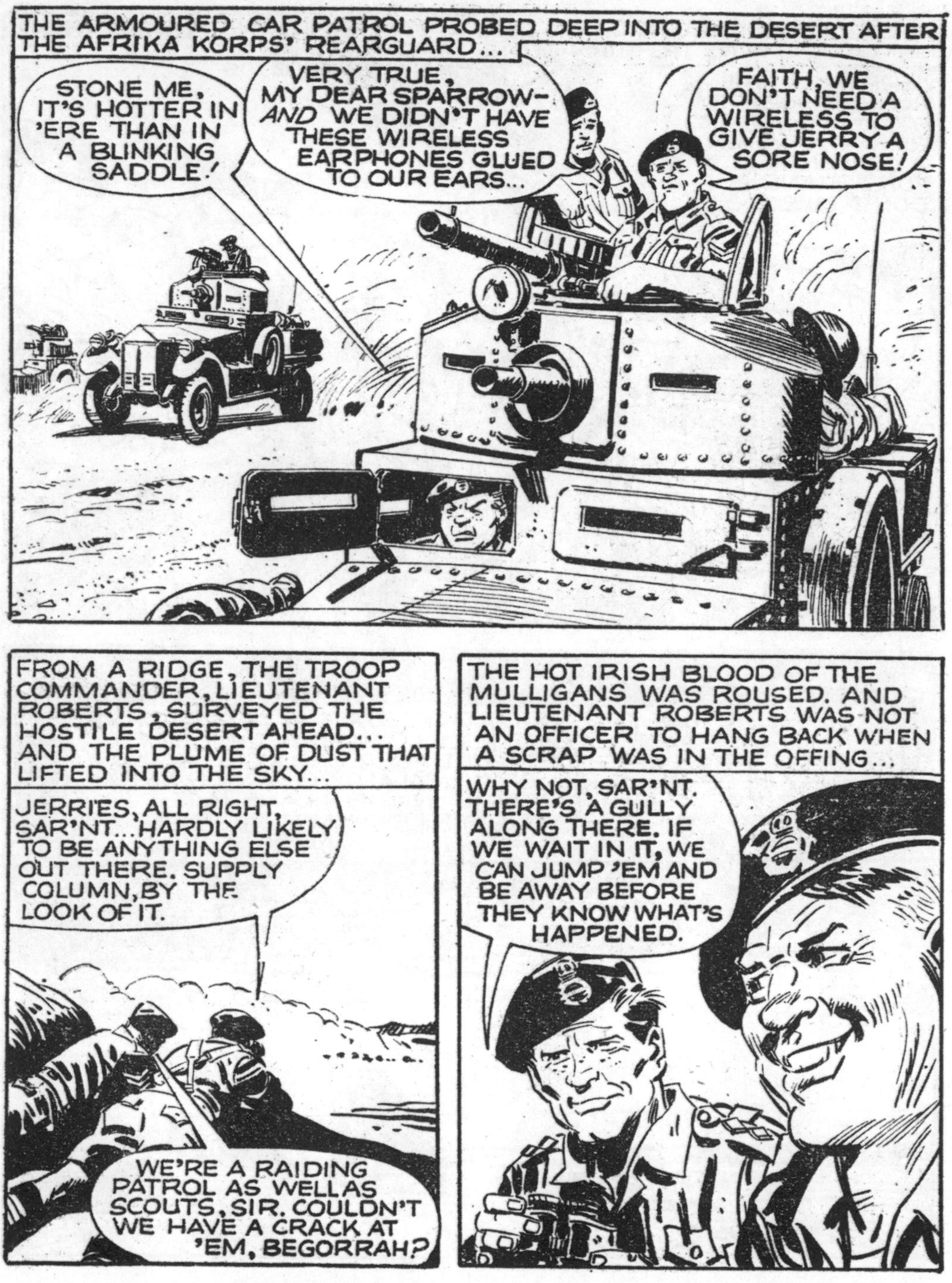
THE ARMOURED CAR PATROL PROBED DEEP INTO THE DESERT AFTER THE AFRIKA KORPS' REARGUARD...
STONE ME, IT'S HOTTER IN 'ERE THAN IN A BLINKING SADDLE!
VERY TRUE, MY DEAR SPARROW– *AND* WE DIDN'T HAVE THESE WIRELESS EARPHONES GLUED TO OUR EARS...
FAITH, WE DON'T NEED A WIRELESS TO GIVE JERRY A SORE NOSE!
FROM A RIDGE, THE TROOP COMMANDER, LIEUTENANT ROBERTS, SURVEYED THE HOSTILE DESERT AHEAD... AND THE PLUME OF DUST THAT LIFTED INTO THE SKY...
JERRIES, ALL RIGHT, SAR'NT... HARDLY LIKELY TO BE ANYTHING ELSE OUT THERE. SUPPLY COLUMN, BY THE LOOK OF IT.
WE'RE A RAIDING PATROL AS WELL AS SCOUTS, SIR. COULDN'T WE HAVE A CRACK AT 'EM, BEGORRAH?
THE HOT IRISH BLOOD OF THE MULLIGANS WAS ROUSED. AND LIEUTENANT ROBERTS WAS NOT AN OFFICER TO HANG BACK WHEN A SCRAP WAS IN THE OFFING...
WHY NOT, SAR'NT. THERE'S A GULLY ALONG THERE. IF WE WAIT IN IT, WE CAN JUMP 'EM AND BE AWAY BEFORE THEY KNOW WHAT'S HAPPENED.

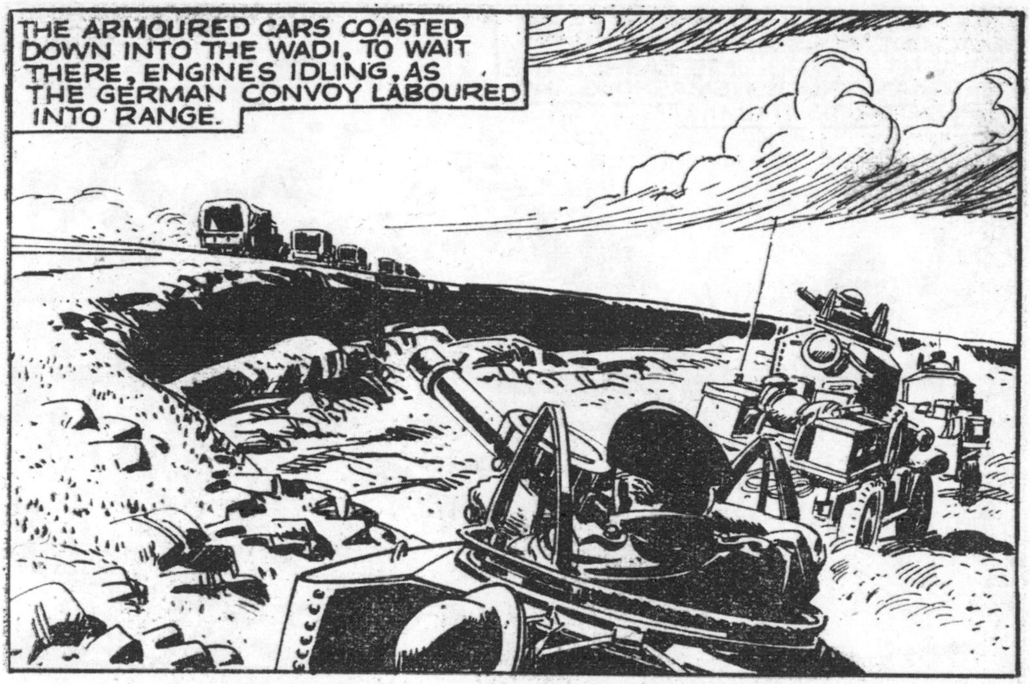
THE ARMOURED CARS COASTED DOWN INTO THE WADI, TO WAIT THERE, ENGINES IDLING, AS THE GERMAN CONVOY LABOURED INTO RANGE.

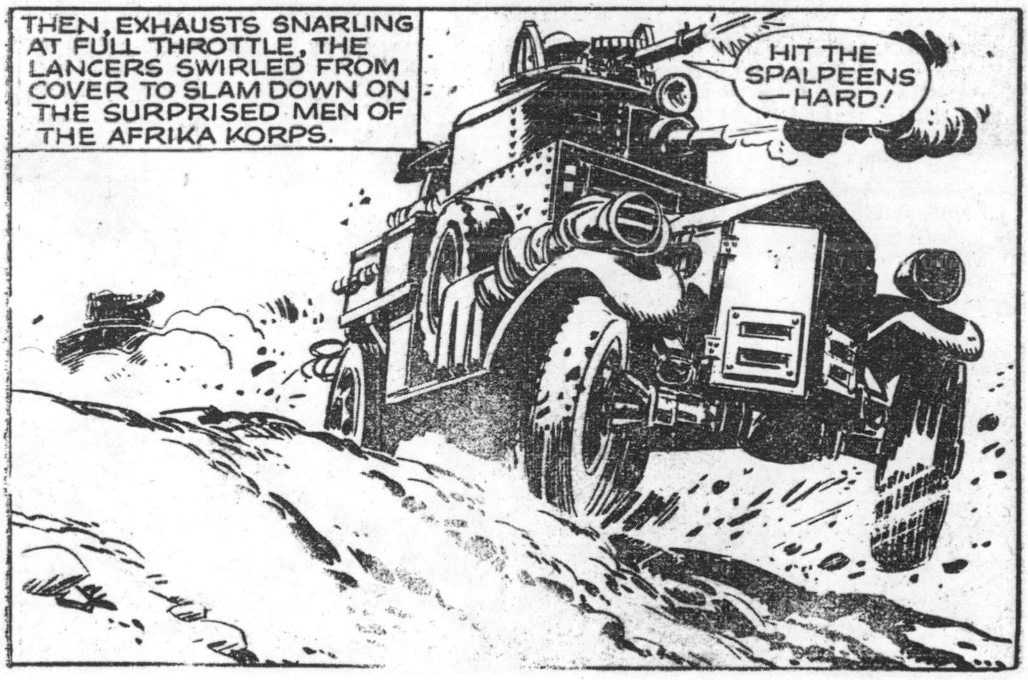
THEN, EXHAUSTS SNARLING AT FULL THROTTLE, THE LANCERS SWIRLED FROM COVER TO SLAM DOWN ON THE SURPRISED MEN OF THE AFRIKA KORPS.
HIT THE SPALPEENS —HARD!

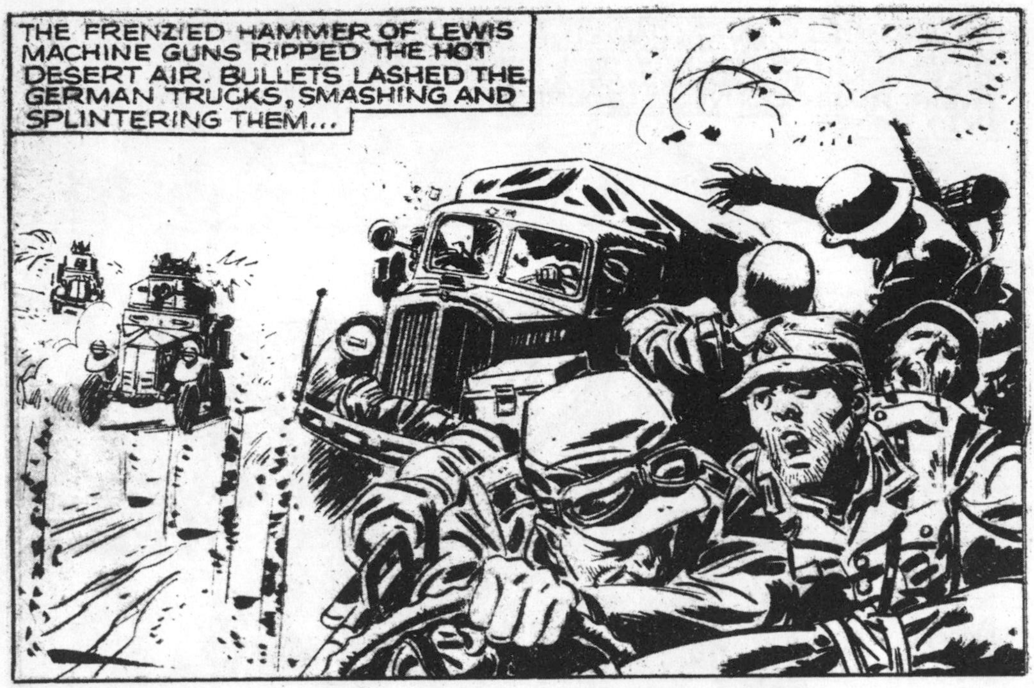
THE FRENZIED HAMMER OF LEWIS MACHINE GUNS RIPPED THE HOT DESERT AIR. BULLETS LASHED THE GERMAN TRUCKS, SMASHING AND SPLINTERING THEM...

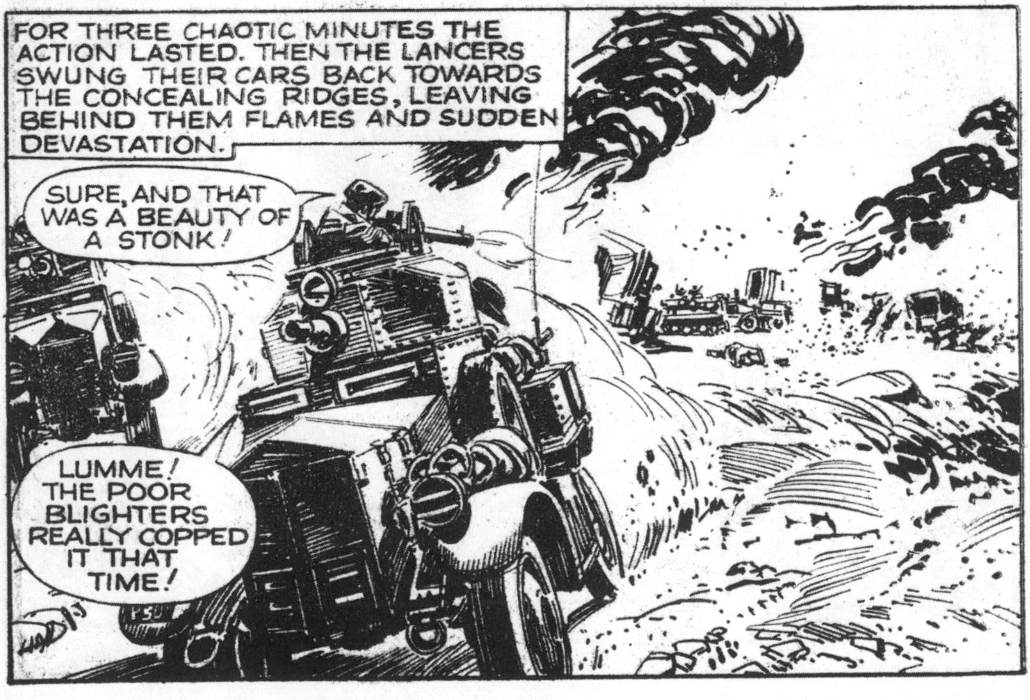
FOR THREE CHAOTIC MINUTES THE ACTION LASTED. THEN THE LANCERS SWUNG THEIR CARS BACK TOWARDS THE CONCEALING RIDGES, LEAVING BEHIND THEM FLAMES AND SUDDEN DEVASTATION.
SURE, AND THAT WAS A BEAUTY OF A STONK!
LUMME! THE POOR BLIGHTERS REALLY COPPED IT THAT TIME!

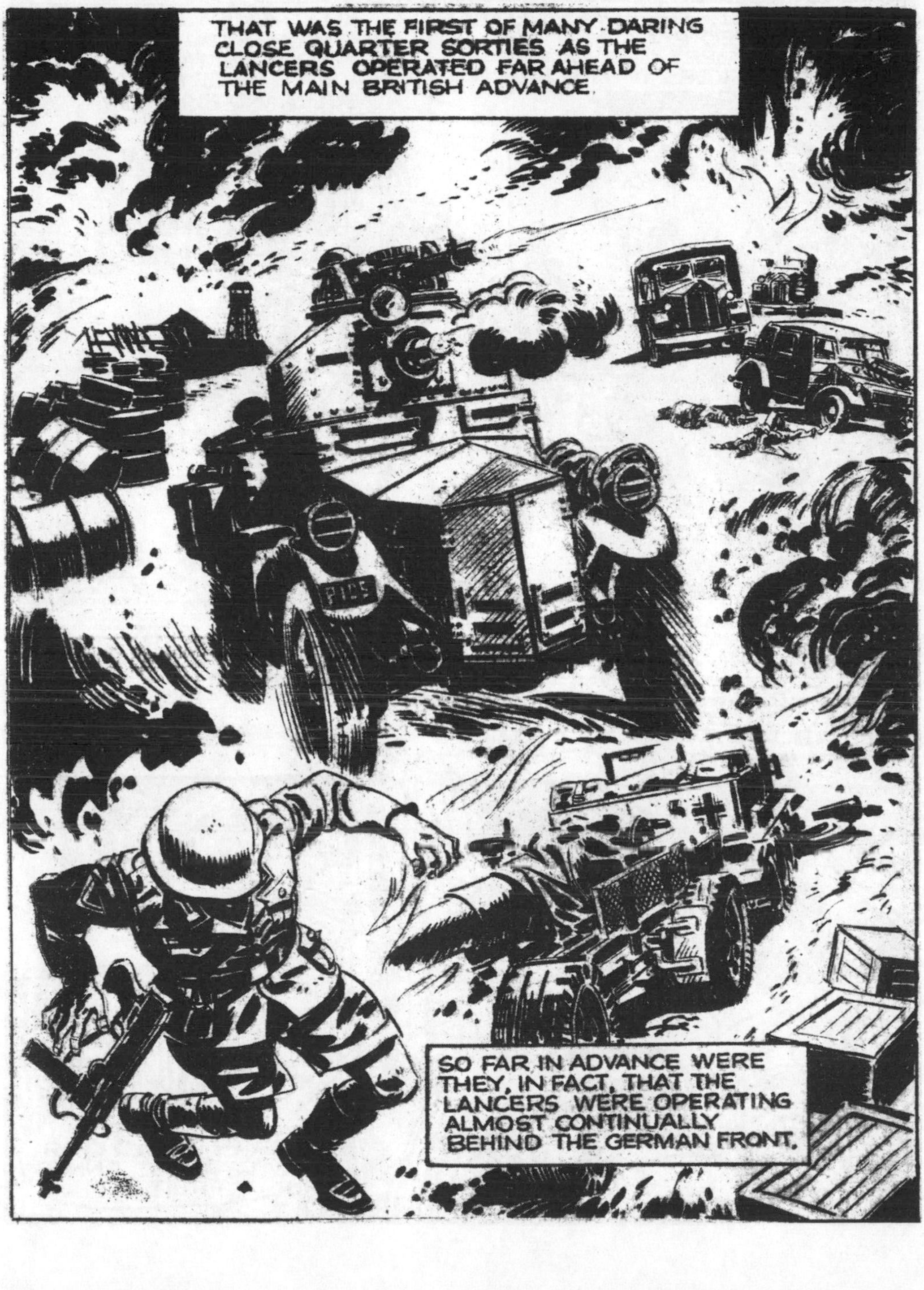
THAT WAS THE FIRST OF MANY DARING CLOSE QUARTER SORTIES AS THE LANCERS OPERATED FAR AHEAD OF THE MAIN BRITISH ADVANCE.
SO FAR IN ADVANCE WERE THEY, IN FACT, THAT THE LANCERS WERE OPERATING ALMOST CONTINUALLY BEHIND THE GERMAN FRONT.

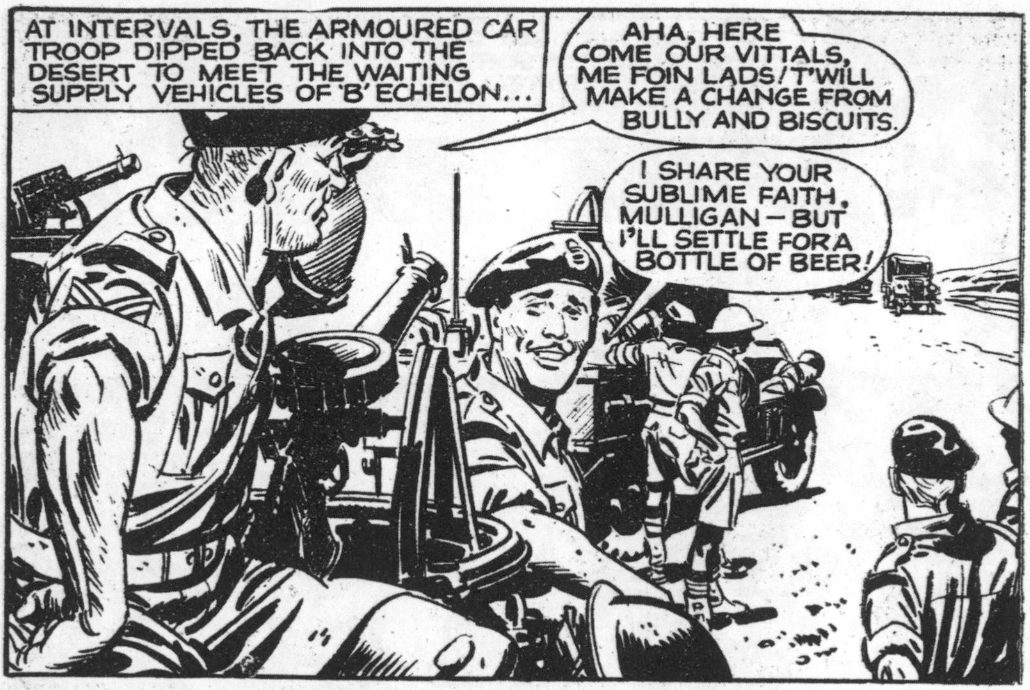
AT INTERVALS, THE ARMOURED CAR TROOP DIPPED BACK INTO THE DESERT TO MEET THE WAITING SUPPLY VEHICLES OF 'B' ECHELON...
AHA, HERE COME OUR VITTALS, ME FOIN LADS! T'WILL MAKE A CHANGE FROM BULLY AND BISCUITS.
I SHARE YOUR SUBLIME FAITH, MULLIGAN — BUT I'LL SETTLE FOR A BOTTLE OF BEER!

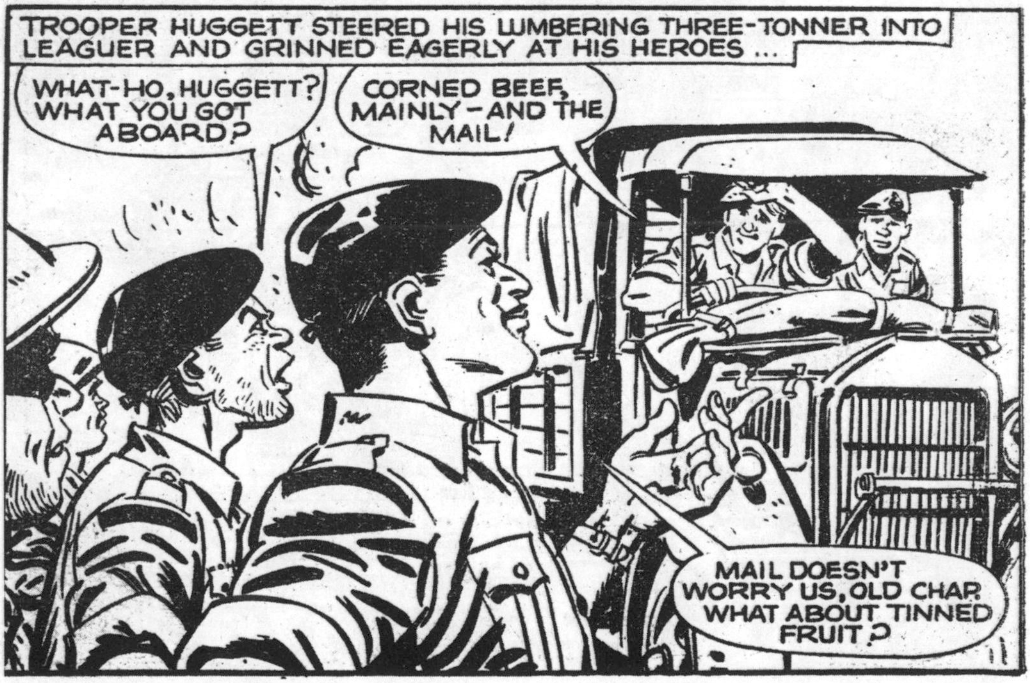
TROOPER HUGGETT STEERED HIS LUMBERING THREE-TONNER INTO LEAGUER AND GRINNED EAGERLY AT HIS HEROES ...
WHAT-HO, HUGGETT? WHAT YOU GOT ABOARD?
CORNED BEEF, MAINLY — AND THE MAIL!
MAIL DOESN'T WORRY US, OLD CHAP. WHAT ABOUT TINNED FRUIT?

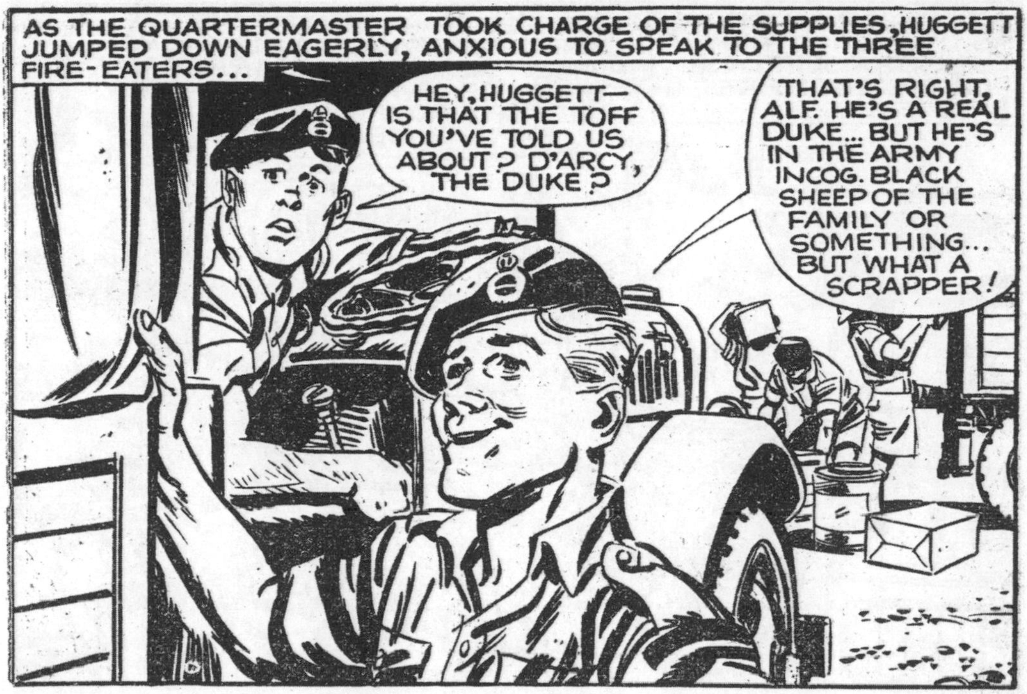
AS THE QUARTERMASTER TOOK CHARGE OF THE SUPPLIES, HUGGETT JUMPED DOWN EAGERLY, ANXIOUS TO SPEAK TO THE THREE FIRE-EATERS...
HEY, HUGGETT— IS THAT THE TOFF YOU'VE TOLD US ABOUT? D'ARCY, THE DUKE?
THAT'S RIGHT, ALF. HE'S A REAL DUKE... BUT HE'S IN THE ARMY INCOG. BLACK SHEEP OF THE FAMILY OR SOMETHING... BUT WHAT A SCRAPPER!

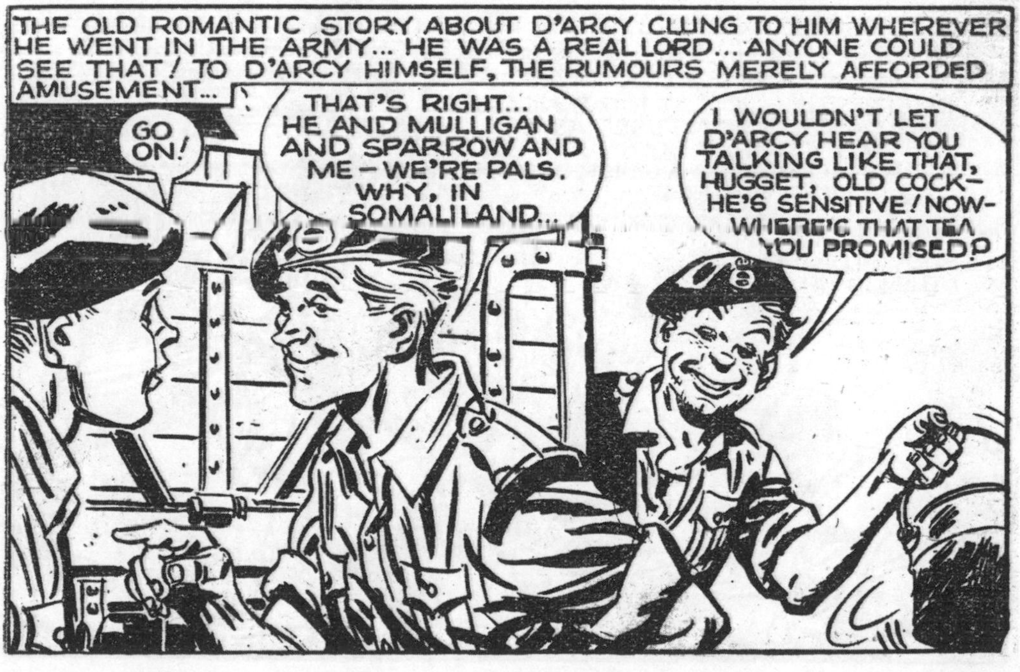
THE OLD ROMANTIC STORY ABOUT D'ARCY CLUNG TO HIM WHEREVER HE WENT IN THE ARMY... HE WAS A REAL LORD... ANYONE COULD SEE THAT! TO D'ARCY HIMSELF, THE RUMOURS MERELY AFFORDED AMUSEMENT...
GO ON!
THAT'S RIGHT... HE AND MULLIGAN AND SPARROW AND ME – WE'RE PALS. WHY, IN SOMALILAND...
I WOULDN'T LET D'ARCY HEAR YOU TALKING LIKE THAT, HUGGET, OLD COCK— HE'S SENSITIVE! NOW– WHERE'S THAT TEA YOU PROMISED?

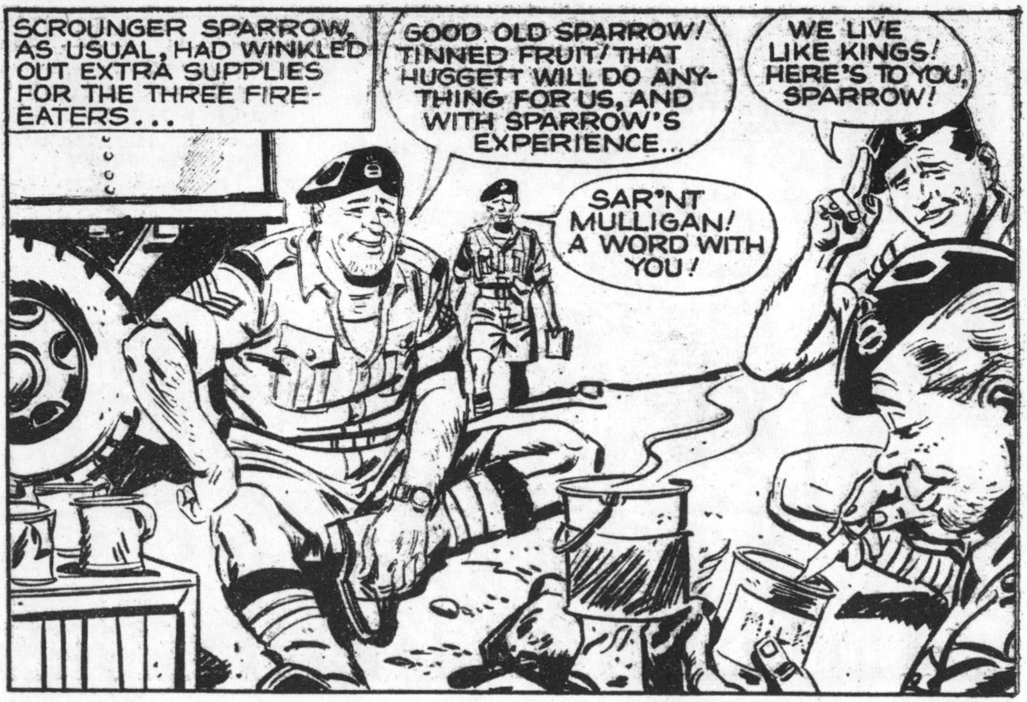
SCROUNGER SPARROW, AS USUAL, HAD WINKLED OUT EXTRA SUPPLIES FOR THE THREE FIRE-EATERS...
GOOD OLD SPARROW! TINNED FRUIT! THAT HUGGETT WILL DO ANYTHING FOR US, AND WITH SPARROW'S EXPERIENCE...
WE LIVE LIKE KINGS! HERE'S TO YOU, SPARROW!
SAR'NT MULLIGAN! A WORD WITH YOU!
MILK

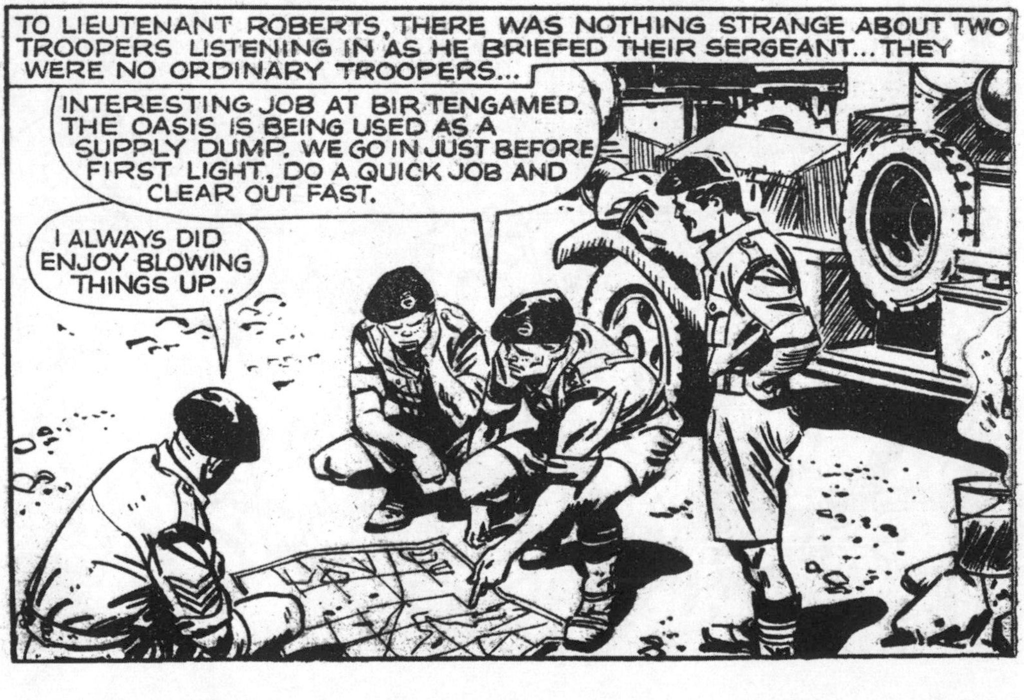
TO LIEUTENANT ROBERTS, THERE WAS NOTHING STRANGE ABOUT TWO TROOPERS LISTENING IN AS HE BRIEFED THEIR SERGEANT... THEY WERE NO ORDINARY TROOPERS...
INTERESTING JOB AT BIR TENGAMED. THE OASIS IS BEING USED AS A SUPPLY DUMP. WE GO IN JUST BEFORE FIRST LIGHT, DO A QUICK JOB AND CLEAR OUT FAST.
I ALWAYS DID ENJOY BLOWING THINGS UP...

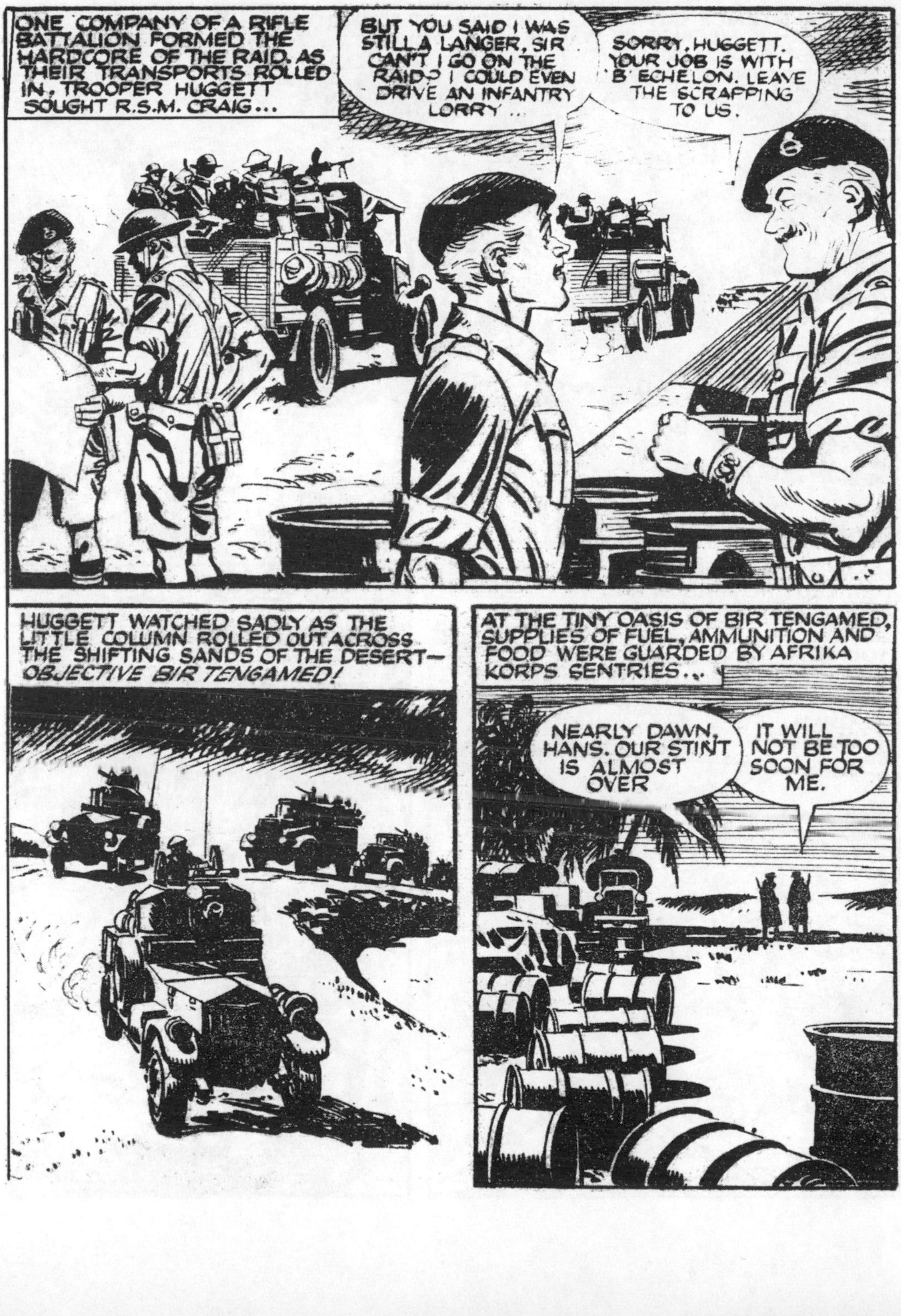
ONE COMPANY OF A RIFLE BATTALION FORMED THE HARDCORE OF THE RAID. AS THEIR TRANSPORTS ROLLED IN, TROOPER HUGGETT SOUGHT R.S.M. CRAIG...
BUT YOU SAID I WAS STILL A LANGER, SIR CAN'T I GO ON THE RAID? I COULD EVEN DRIVE AN INFANTRY LORRY...
SORRY, HUGGETT. YOUR JOB IS WITH 'B' ECHELON. LEAVE THE SCRAPPING TO US.
HUGGETT WATCHED SADLY AS THE LITTLE COLUMN ROLLED OUT ACROSS THE SHIFTING SANDS OF THE DESERT— *OBJECTIVE BIR TENGAMED!*
AT THE TINY OASIS OF BIR TENGAMED, SUPPLIES OF FUEL, AMMUNITION AND FOOD WERE GUARDED BY AFRIKA KORPS SENTRIES...
NEARLY DAWN, HANS. OUR STINT IS ALMOST OVER
IT WILL NOT BE TOO SOON FOR ME.

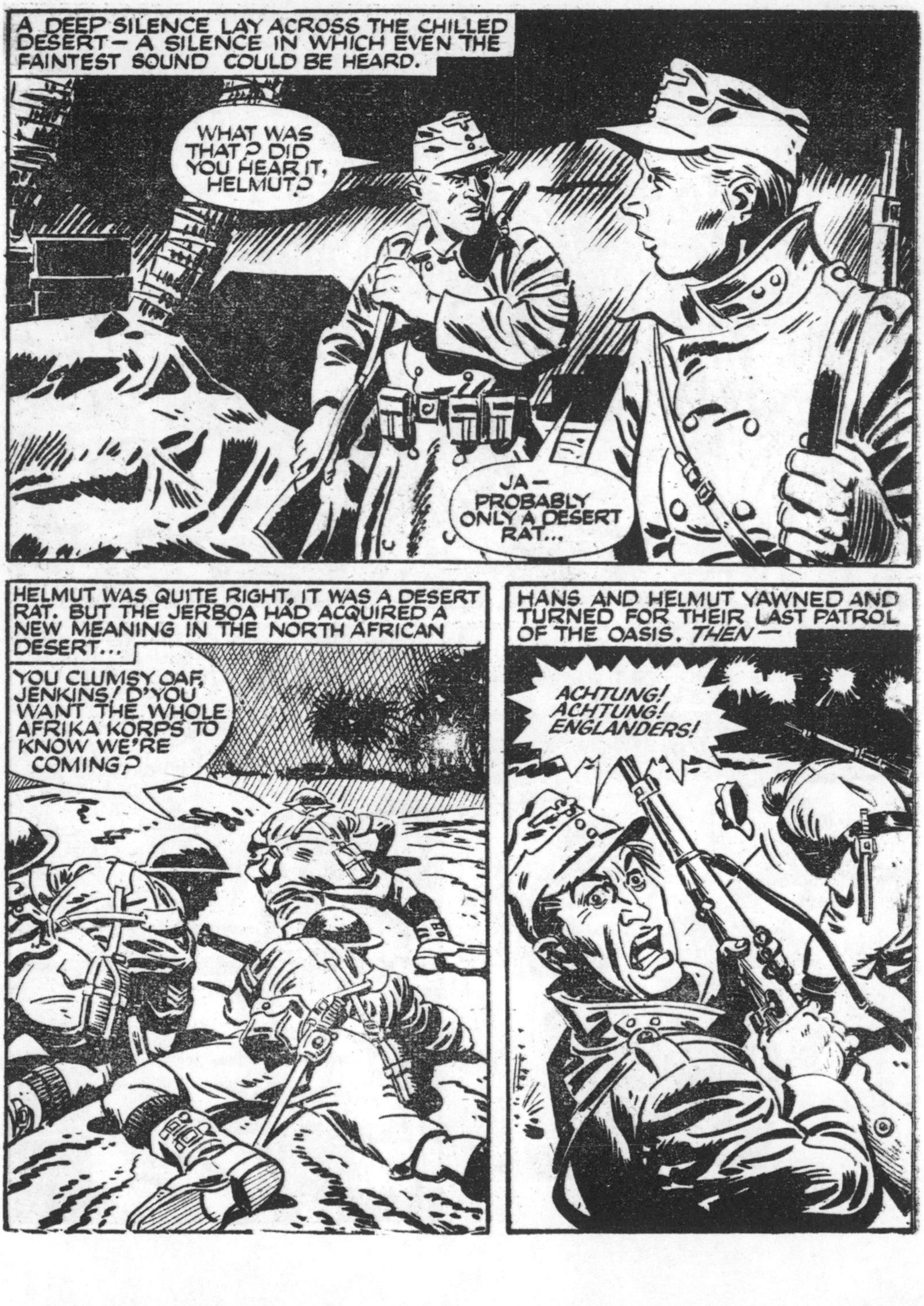
A DEEP SILENCE LAY ACROSS THE CHILLED DESERT — A SILENCE IN WHICH EVEN THE FAINTEST SOUND COULD BE HEARD.
WHAT WAS THAT? DID YOU HEAR IT, HELMUT?
JA — PROBABLY ONLY A DESERT RAT...
HELMUT WAS QUITE RIGHT, IT WAS A DESERT RAT. BUT THE JERBOA HAD ACQUIRED A NEW MEANING IN THE NORTH AFRICAN DESERT...
YOU CLUMSY OAF, JENKINS! D'YOU WANT THE WHOLE AFRIKA KORPS TO KNOW WE'RE COMING?
HANS AND HELMUT YAWNED AND TURNED FOR THEIR LAST PATROL OF THE OASIS. THEN —
ACHTUNG! ACHTUNG! ENGLANDERS!

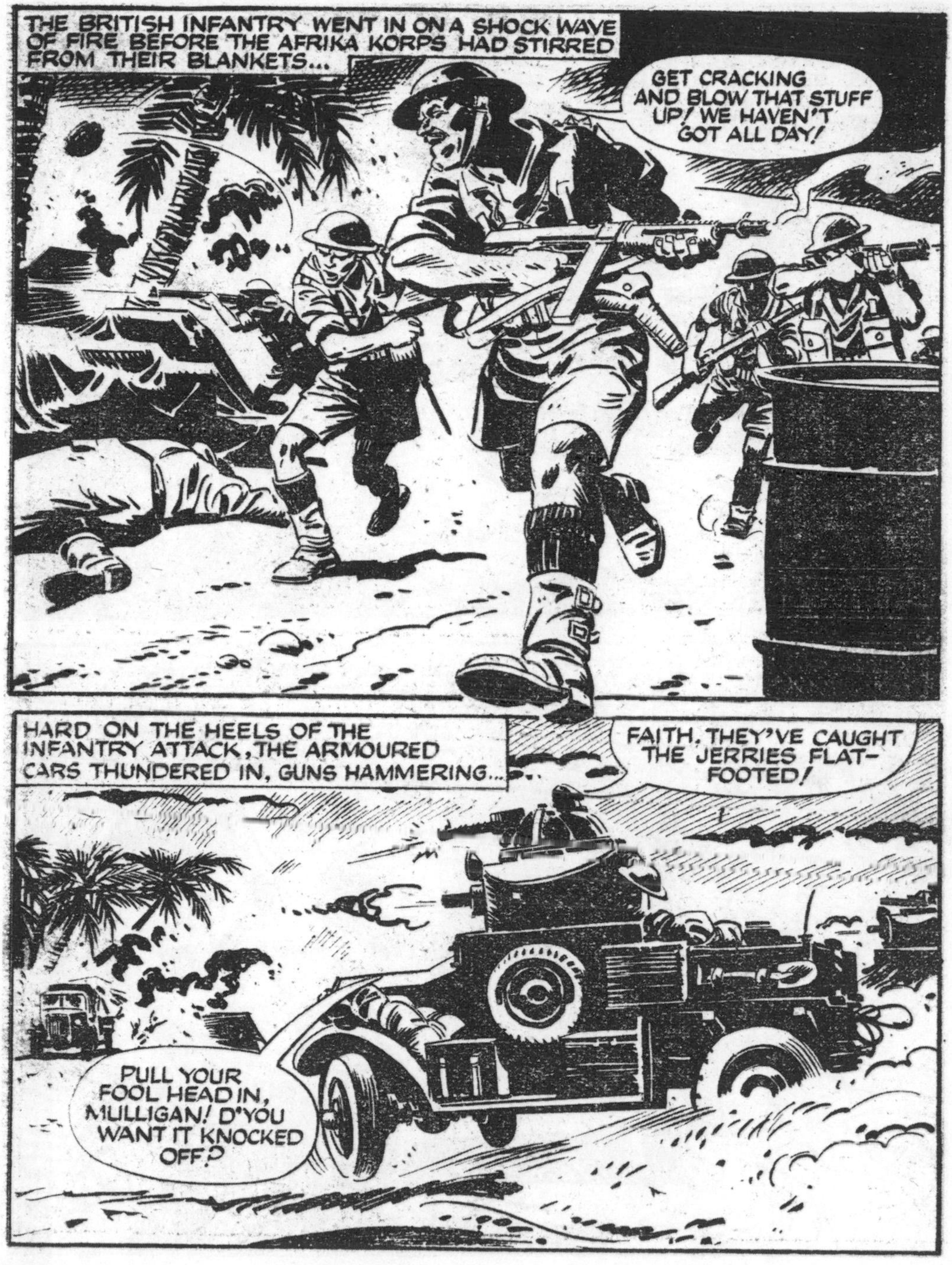
THE BRITISH INFANTRY WENT IN ON A SHOCK WAVE OF FIRE BEFORE THE AFRIKA KORPS HAD STIRRED FROM THEIR BLANKETS...
GET CRACKING AND BLOW THAT STUFF UP! WE HAVEN'T GOT ALL DAY!
HARD ON THE HEELS OF THE INFANTRY ATTACK, THE ARMOURED CARS THUNDERED IN, GUNS HAMMERING...
FAITH, THEY'VE CAUGHT THE JERRIES FLAT-FOOTED!
PULL YOUR FOOL HEAD IN, MULLIGAN! D'YOU WANT IT KNOCKED OFF?

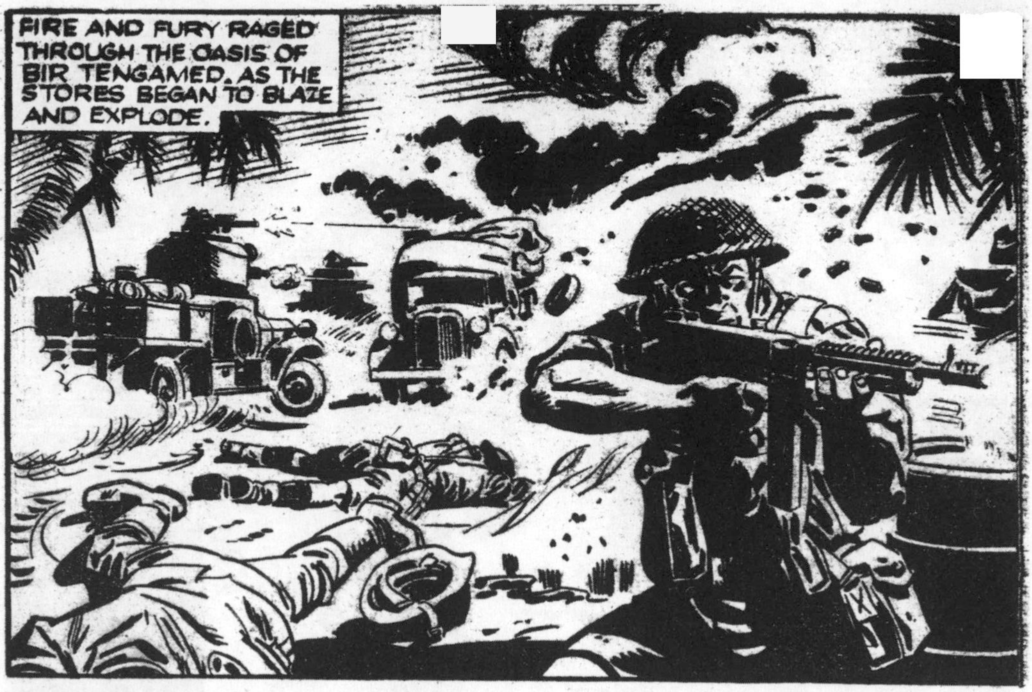
FIRE AND FURY RAGED THROUGH THE OASIS OF BIR TENGAMED, AS THE STORES BEGAN TO BLAZE AND EXPLODE.

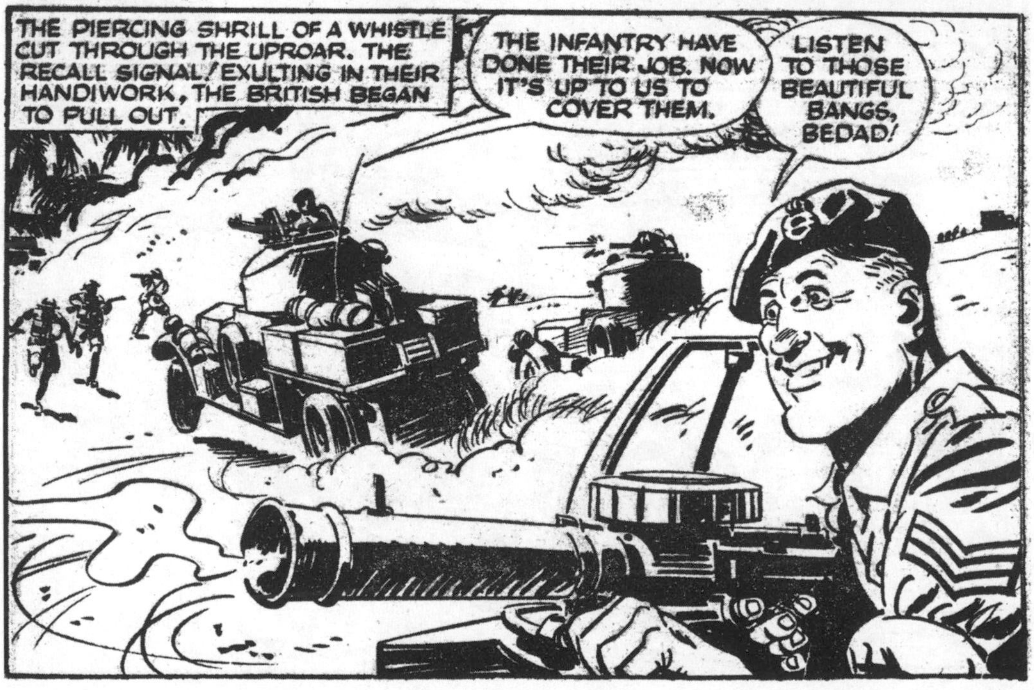
THE PIERCING SHRILL OF A WHISTLE CUT THROUGH THE UPROAR. THE RECALL SIGNAL! EXULTING IN THEIR HANDIWORK, THE BRITISH BEGAN TO PULL OUT.
THE INFANTRY HAVE DONE THEIR JOB. NOW IT'S UP TO US TO COVER THEM.
LISTEN TO THOSE BEAUTIFUL BANGS, BEDAD!

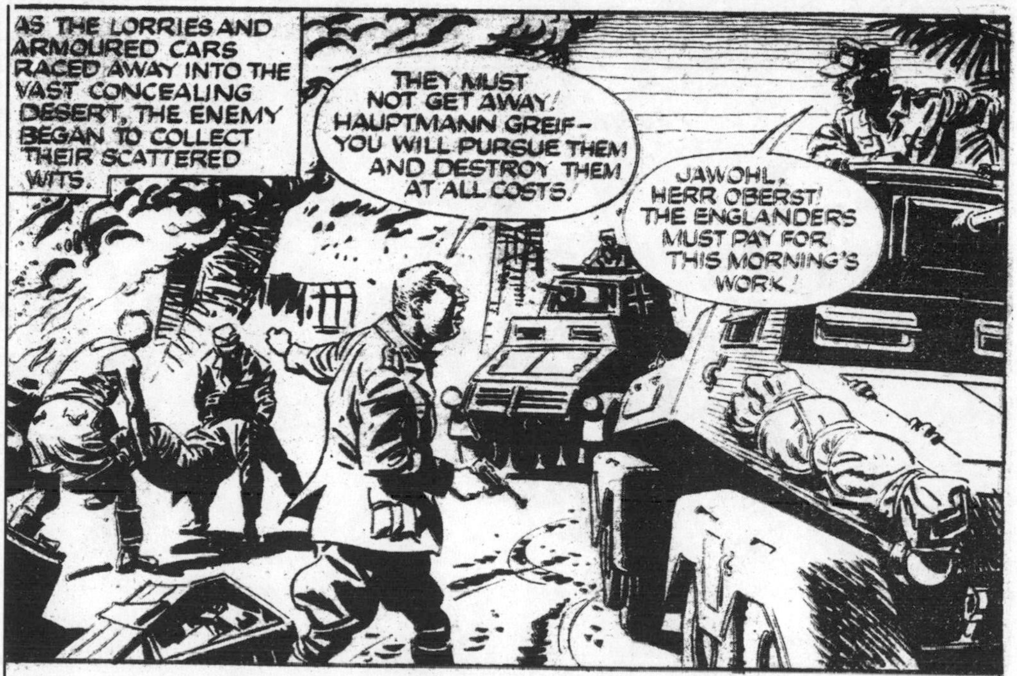
AS THE LORRIES AND ARMOURED CARS RACED AWAY INTO THE VAST CONCEALING DESERT, THE ENEMY BEGAN TO COLLECT THEIR SCATTERED WITS.
THEY MUST NOT GET AWAY! HAUPTMANN GREIF– YOU WILL PURSUE THEM AND DESTROY THEM AT ALL COSTS!
JAWOHL, HERR OBERST! THE ENGLANDERS MUST PAY FOR THIS MORNING'S WORK!

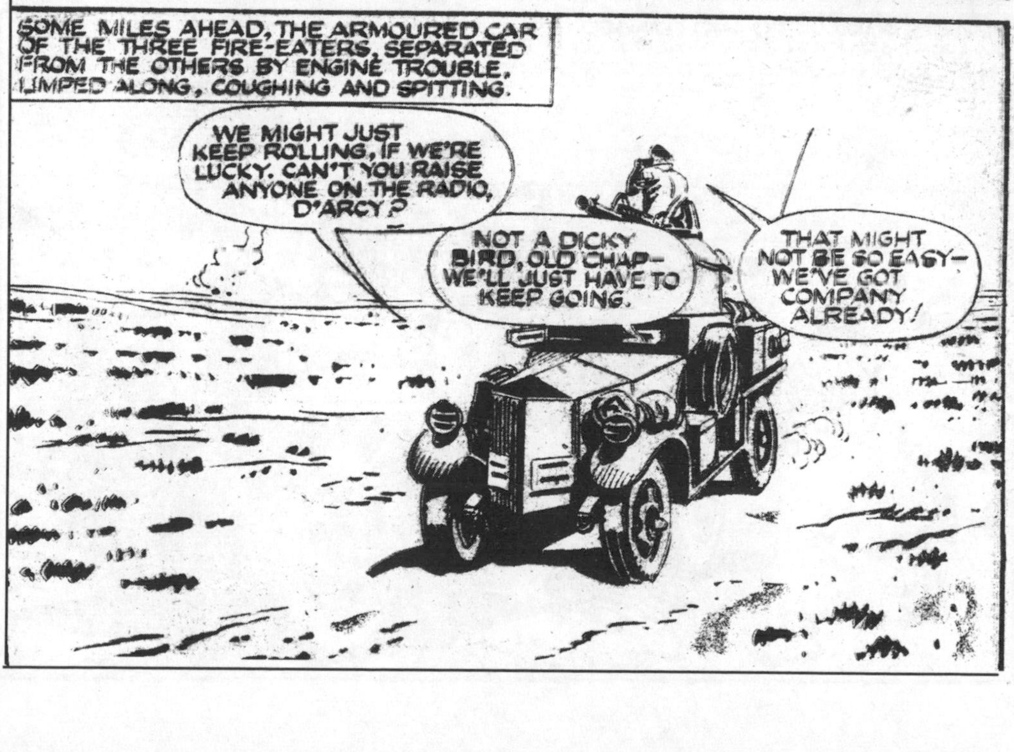
SOME MILES AHEAD, THE ARMOURED CAR OF THE THREE FIRE-EATERS, SEPARATED FROM THE OTHERS BY ENGINE TROUBLE, LIMPED ALONG, COUGHING AND SPITTING.
WE MIGHT JUST KEEP ROLLING, IF WE'RE LUCKY. CAN'T YOU RAISE ANYONE ON THE RADIO, D'ARCY?
NOT A DICKY BIRD, OLD CHAP– WE'LL JUST HAVE TO KEEP GOING.
THAT MIGHT NOT BE SO EASY– WE'VE GOT COMPANY ALREADY!

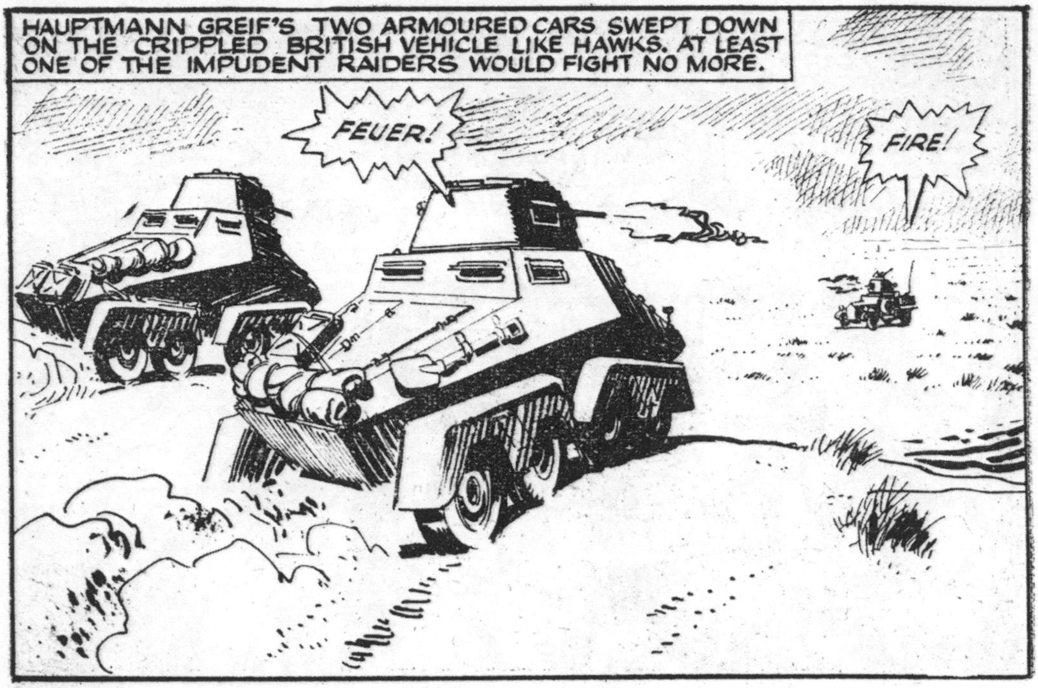
HAUPTMANN GREIF'S TWO ARMOURED CARS SWEPT DOWN ON THE CRIPPLED BRITISH VEHICLE LIKE HAWKS. AT LEAST ONE OF THE IMPUDENT RAIDERS WOULD FIGHT NO MORE.
FEUER!
FIRE!

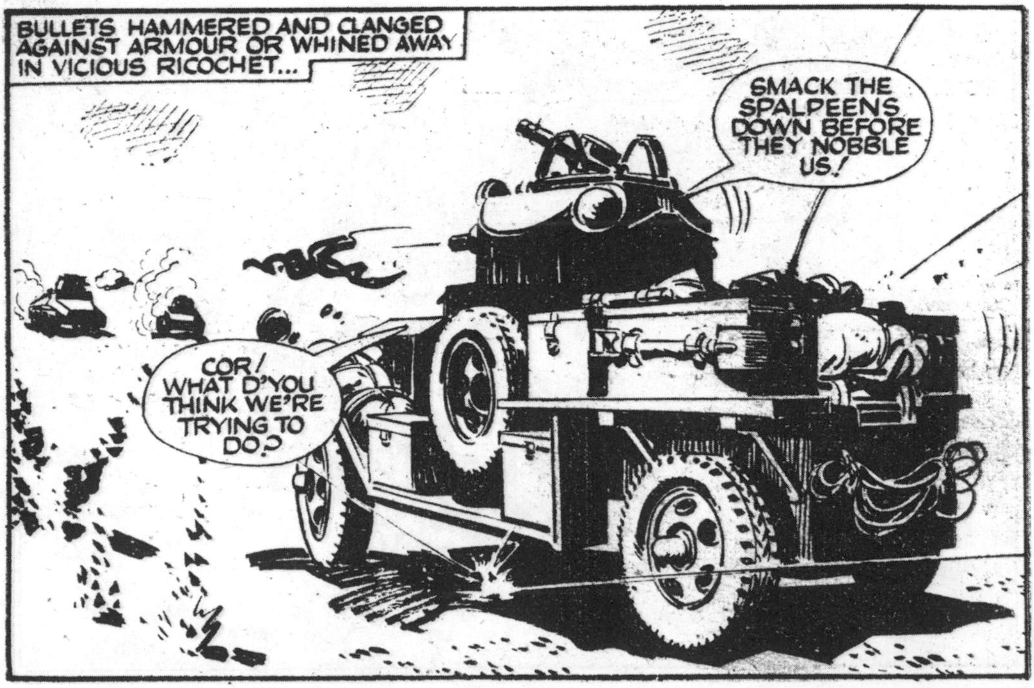
BULLETS HAMMERED AND CLANGED AGAINST ARMOUR OR WHINED AWAY IN VICIOUS RICOCHET...
SMACK THE SPALPEENS DOWN BEFORE THEY NOBBLE US!
COR! WHAT D'YOU THINK WE'RE TRYING TO DO?

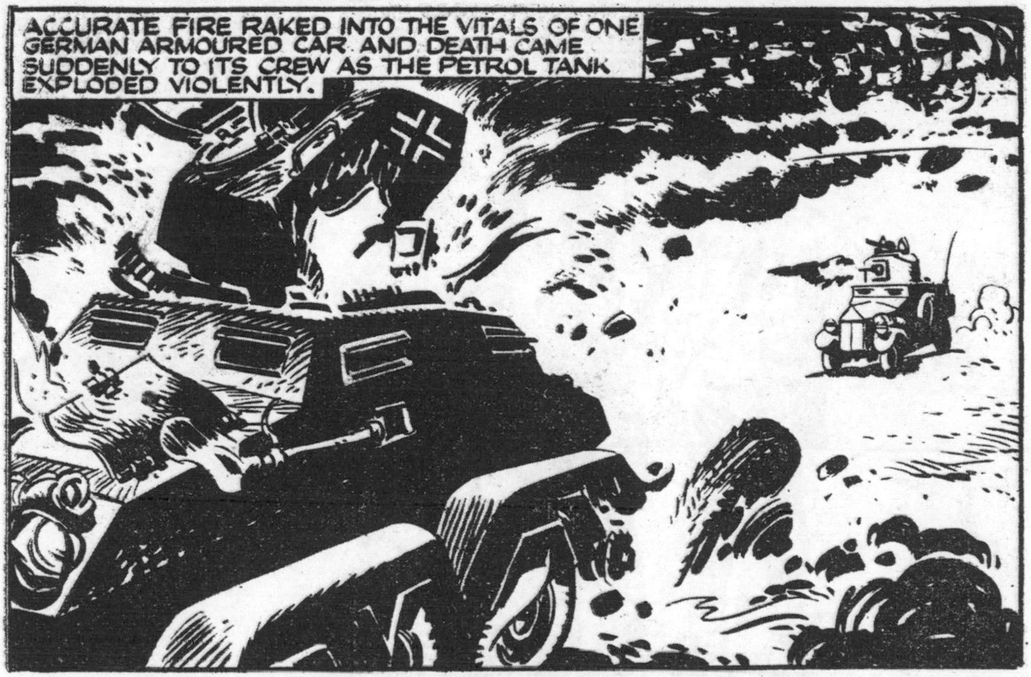
ACCURATE FIRE RAKED INTO THE VITALS OF ONE GERMAN ARMOURED CAR AND DEATH CAME SUDDENLY TO ITS CREW AS THE PETROL TANK EXPLODED VIOLENTLY.

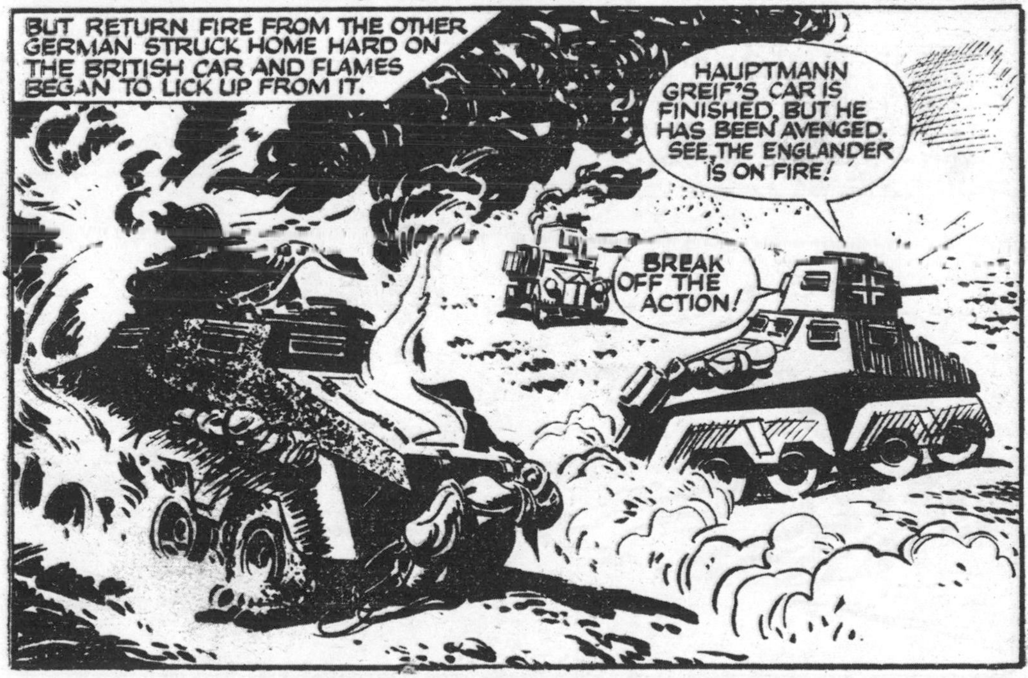
BUT RETURN FIRE FROM THE OTHER GERMAN STRUCK HOME HARD ON THE BRITISH CAR AND FLAMES BEGAN TO LICK UP FROM IT.
HAUPTMANN GREIF'S CAR IS FINISHED, BUT HE HAS BEEN AVENGED. SEE, THE ENGLANDER IS ON FIRE!
BREAK OFF THE ACTION!

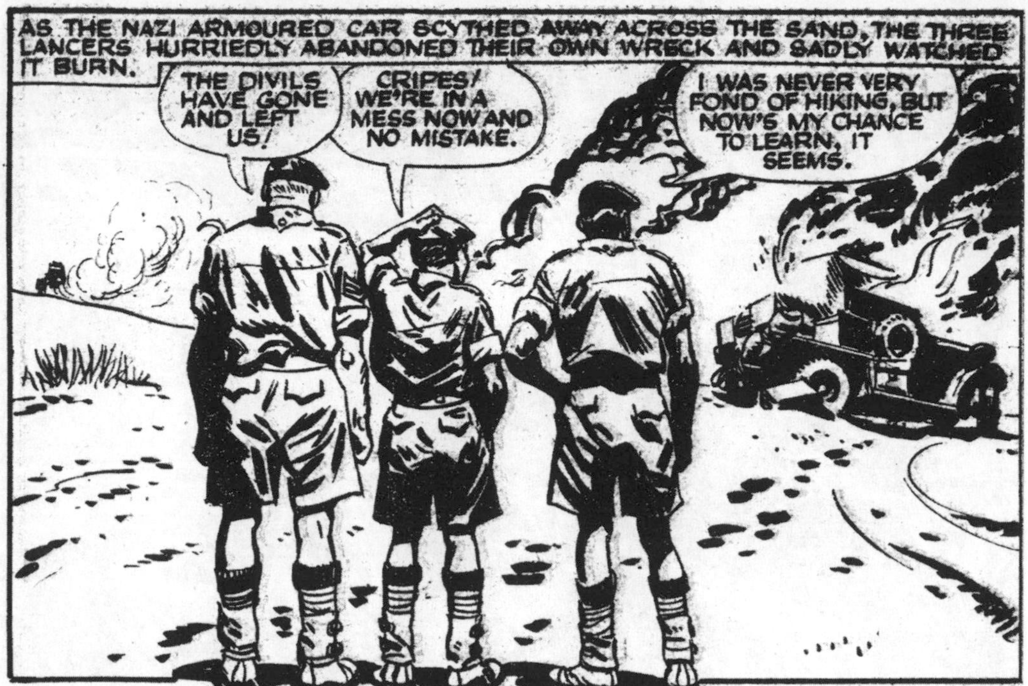
AS THE NAZI ARMOURED CAR SCYTHED AWAY ACROSS THE SAND, THE THREE LANCERS HURRIEDLY ABANDONED THEIR OWN WRECK AND SADLY WATCHED IT BURN.
THE DIVILS HAVE GONE AND LEFT US!
CRIPES! WE'RE IN A MESS NOW AND NO MISTAKE.
I WAS NEVER VERY FOND OF HIKING, BUT NOW'S MY CHANCE TO LEARN, IT SEEMS.

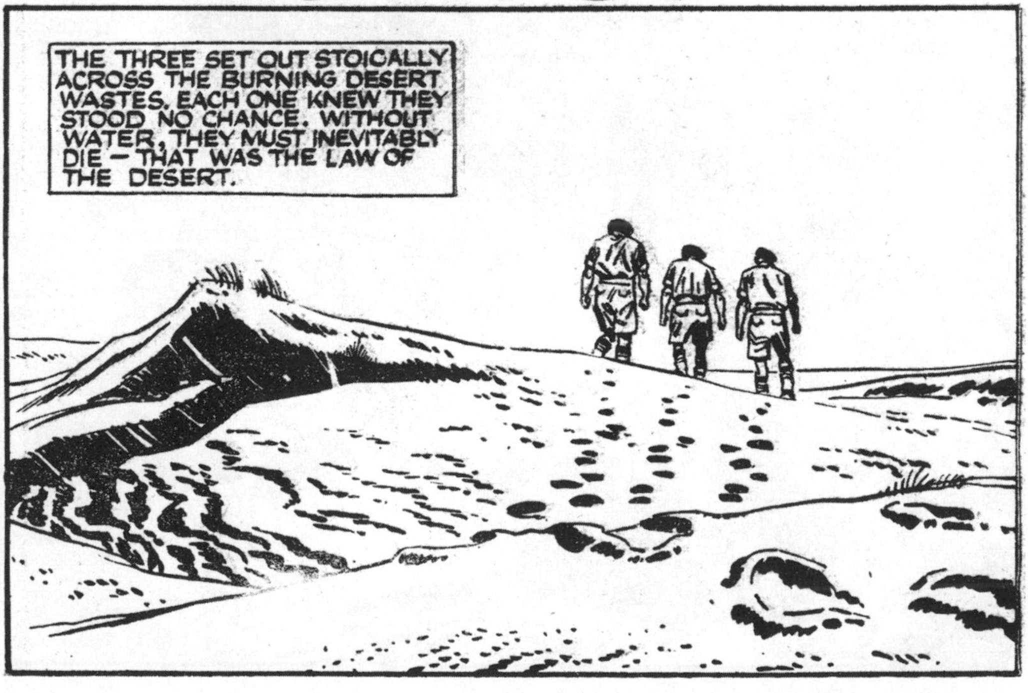
THE THREE SET OUT STOICALLY ACROSS THE BURNING DESERT WASTES. EACH ONE KNEW THEY STOOD NO CHANCE. WITHOUT WATER, THEY MUST INEVITABLY DIE — THAT WAS THE LAW OF THE DESERT.

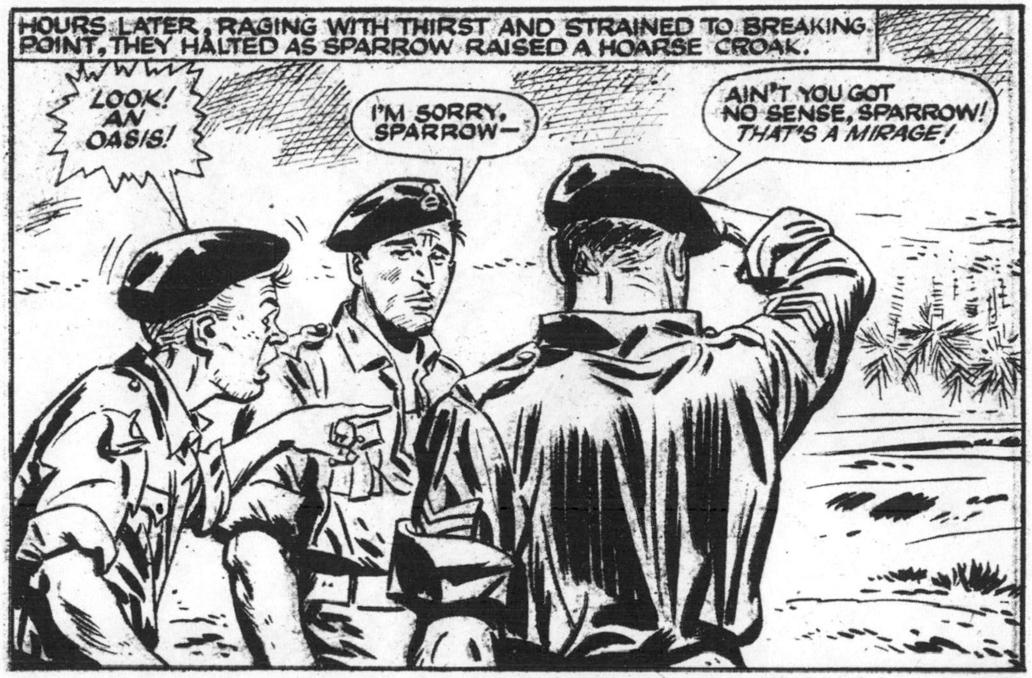
HOURS LATER, RAGING WITH THIRST AND STRAINED TO BREAKING POINT, THEY HALTED AS SPARROW RAISED A HOARSE CROAK.
LOOK! AN OASIS!
I'M SORRY, SPARROW—
AIN'T YOU GOT NO SENSE, SPARROW! THAT'S A MIRAGE!

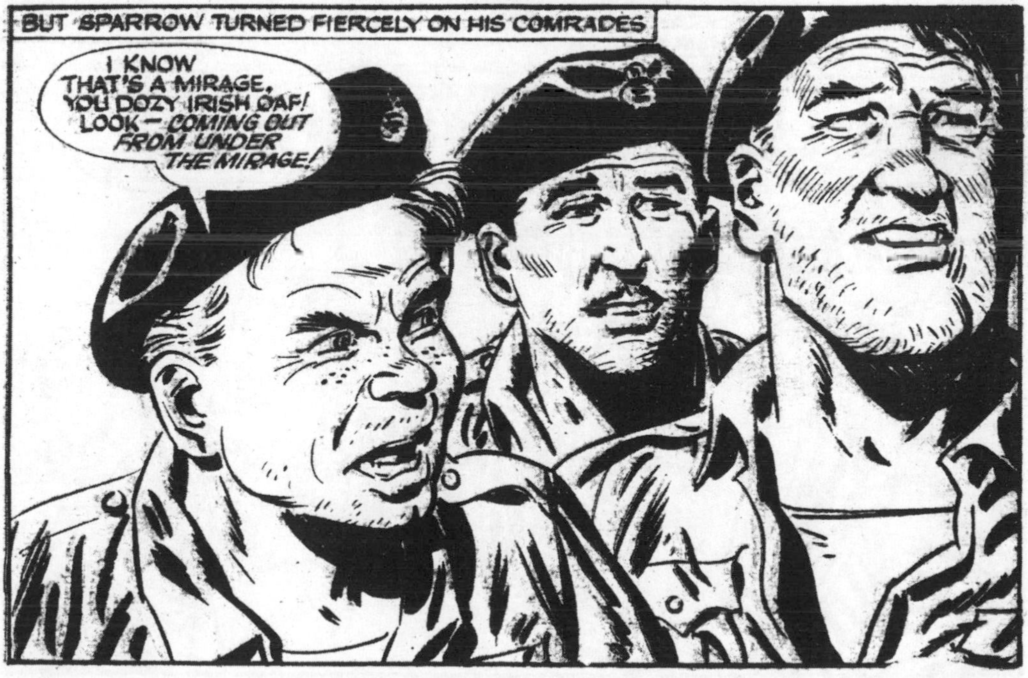
BUT SPARROW TURNED FIERCELY ON HIS COMRADES
I KNOW THAT'S A MIRAGE, YOU DOZY IRISH OAF! LOOK—COMING OUT FROM UNDER THE MIRAGE!

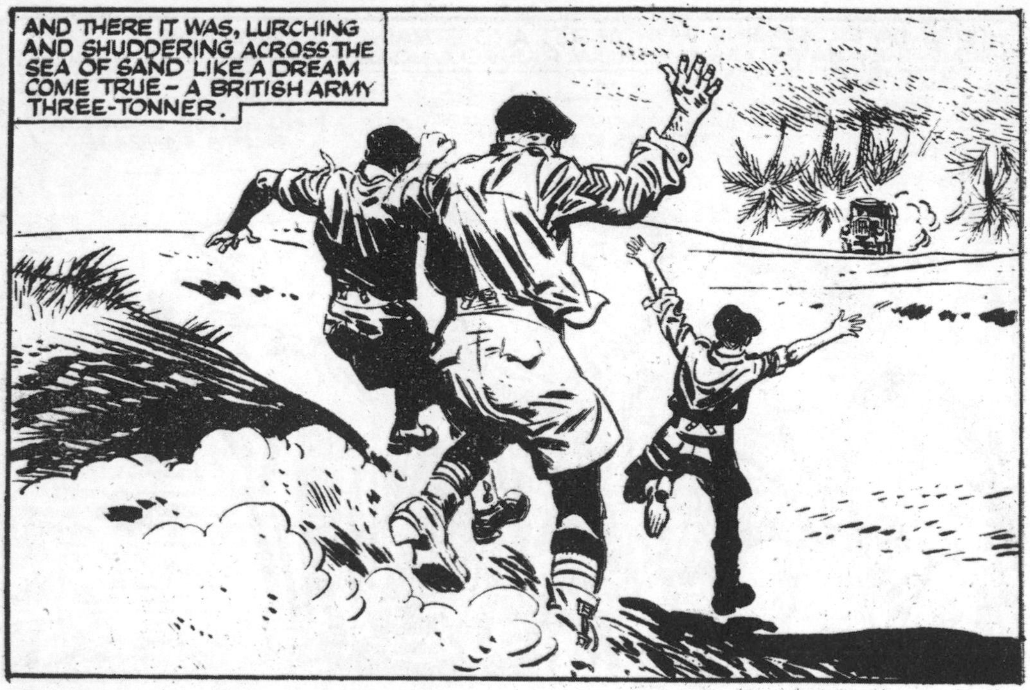
AND THERE IT WAS, LURCHING AND SHUDDERING ACROSS THE SEA OF SAND LIKE A DREAM COME TRUE – A BRITISH ARMY THREE-TONNER.

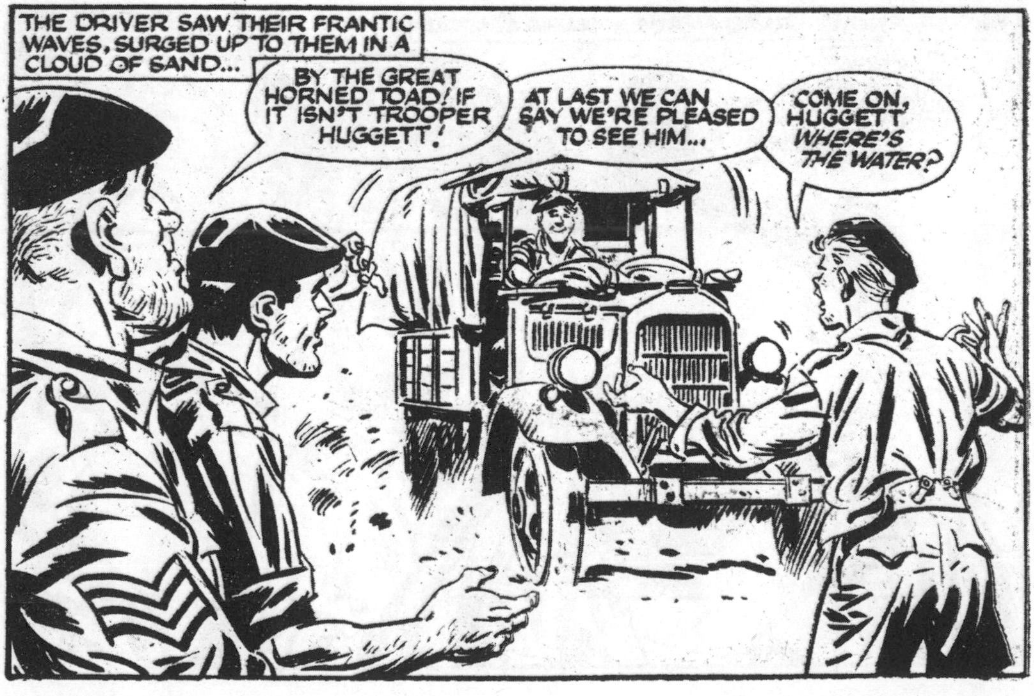
THE DRIVER SAW THEIR FRANTIC WAVES, SURGED UP TO THEM IN A CLOUD OF SAND...
BY THE GREAT HORNED TOAD! IF IT ISN'T TROOPER HUGGETT!
AT LAST WE CAN SAY WE'RE PLEASED TO SEE HIM...
COME ON, HUGGETT! *WHERE'S THE WATER?*

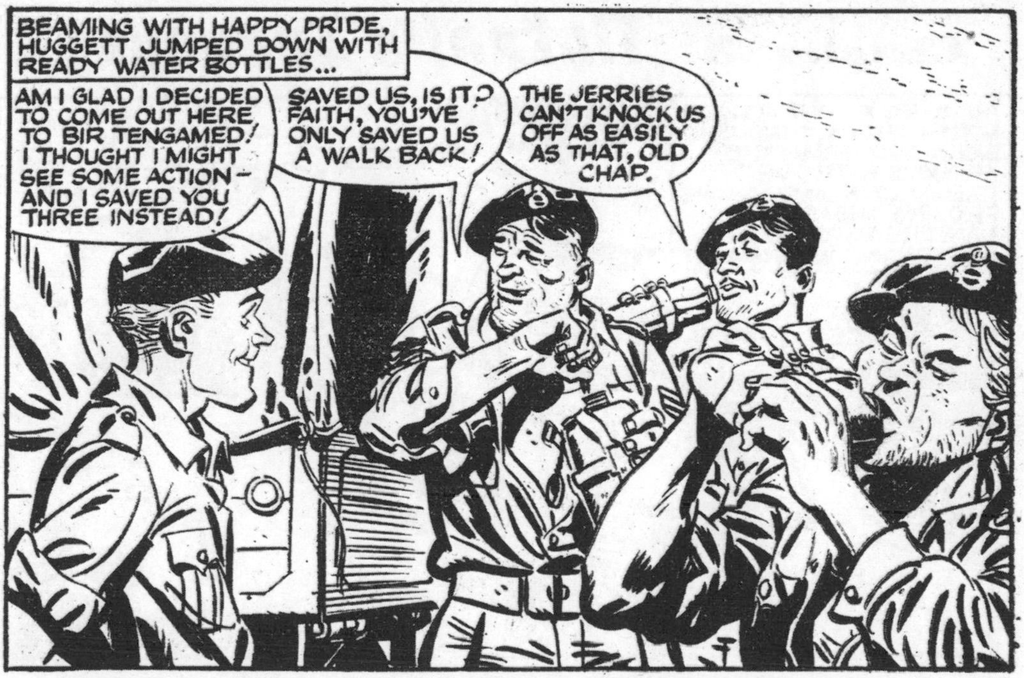
BEAMING WITH HAPPY PRIDE, HUGGETT JUMPED DOWN WITH READY WATER BOTTLES...
AM I GLAD I DECIDED TO COME OUT HERE TO BIR TENGAMED! I THOUGHT I MIGHT SEE SOME ACTION — AND I SAVED YOU THREE INSTEAD!
SAVED US, IS IT? FAITH, YOU'VE ONLY SAVED US A WALK BACK!
THE JERRIES CAN'T KNOCK US OFF AS EASILY AS THAT, OLD CHAP.

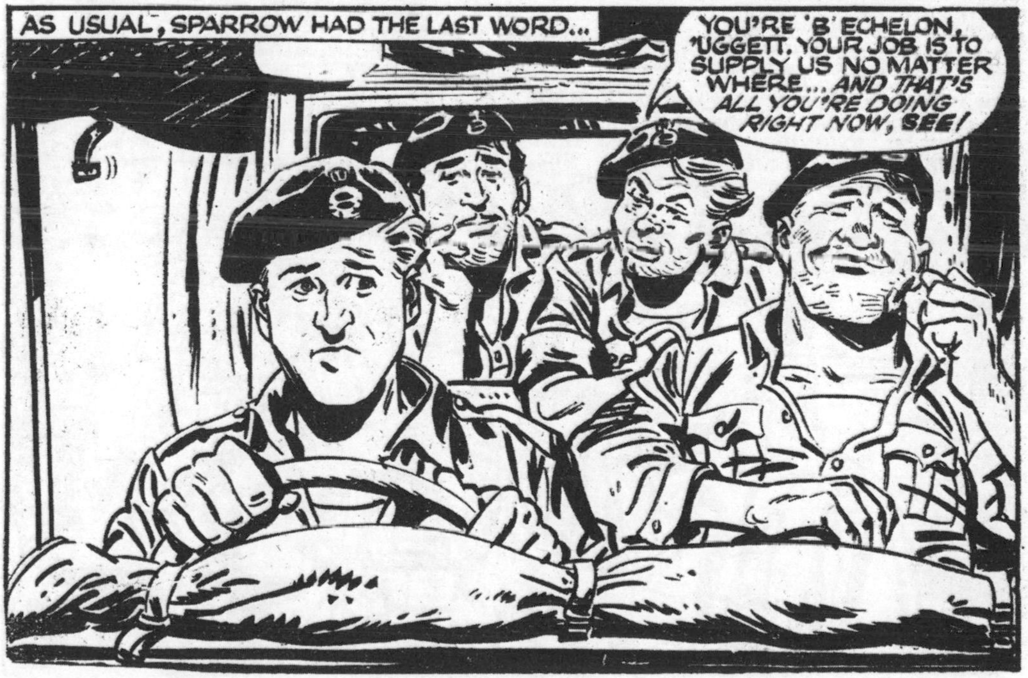
AS USUAL, SPARROW HAD THE LAST WORD...
YOU'RE 'B' ECHELON, 'UGGETT. YOUR JOB IS TO SUPPLY US NO MATTER WHERE... *AND THAT'S ALL YOU'RE DOING RIGHT NOW,* **SEE!**

Chapter 3. Tinfani's Treasure

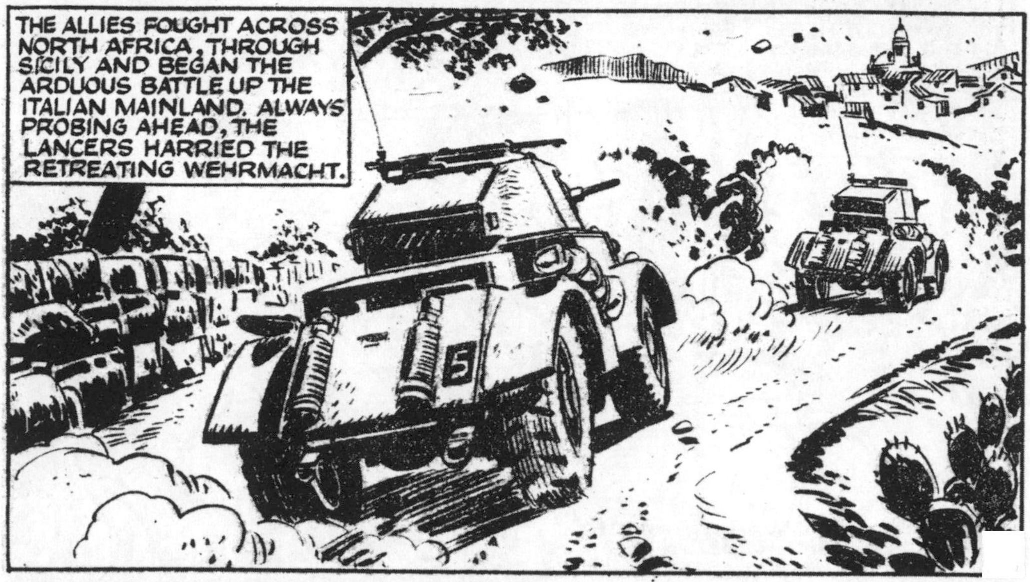
THE ALLIES FOUGHT ACROSS NORTH AFRICA, THROUGH SICILY AND BEGAN THE ARDUOUS BATTLE UP THE ITALIAN MAINLAND. ALWAYS PROBING AHEAD, THE LANCERS HARRIED THE RETREATING WEHRMACHT.
5

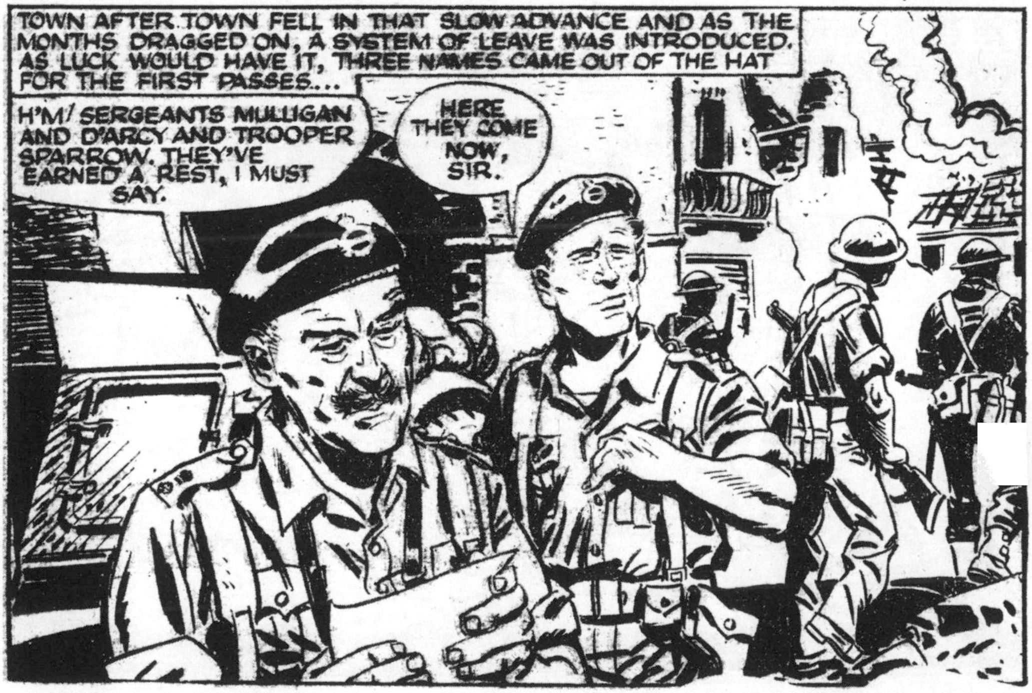
TOWN AFTER TOWN FELL IN THAT SLOW ADVANCE AND AS THE MONTHS DRAGGED ON, A SYSTEM OF LEAVE WAS INTRODUCED. AS LUCK WOULD HAVE IT, THREE NAMES CAME OUT OF THE HAT FOR THE FIRST PASSES...
H'M! SERGEANTS MULLIGAN AND D'ARCY AND TROOPER SPARROW. THEY'VE EARNED A REST, I MUST SAY.
HERE THEY COME NOW, SIR.

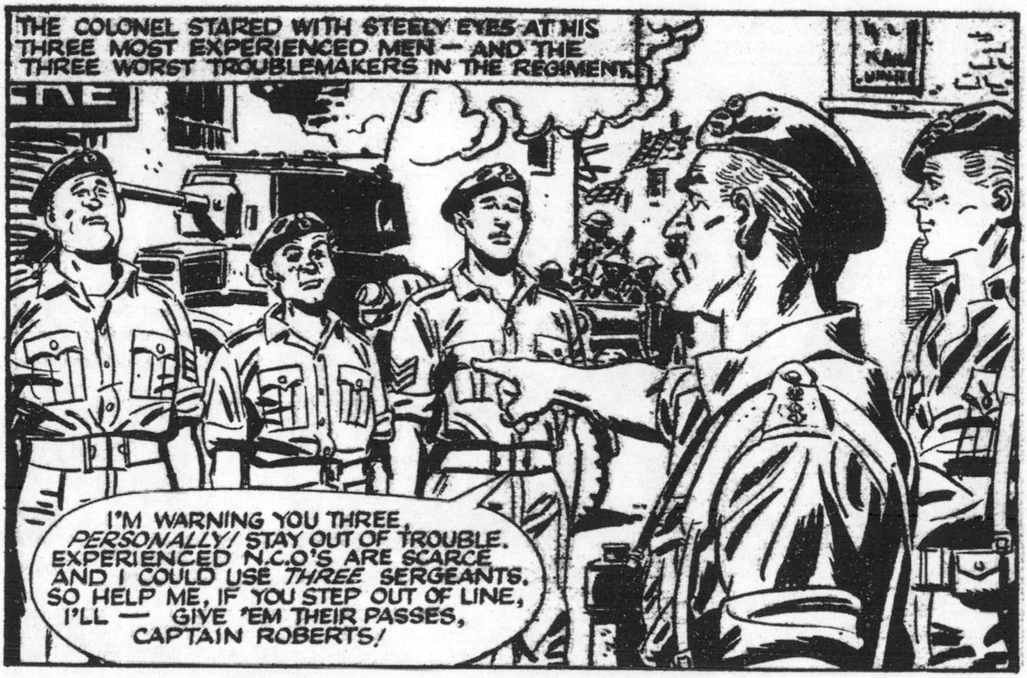
THE COLONEL STARED WITH STEELY EYES AT HIS THREE MOST EXPERIENCED MEN — AND THE THREE WORST TROUBLEMAKERS IN THE REGIMENT.
I'M WARNING YOU THREE, *PERSONALLY!* STAY OUT OF TROUBLE. EXPERIENCED N.C.O'S ARE SCARCE AND I COULD USE *THREE* SERGEANTS. SO HELP ME, IF YOU STEP OUT OF LINE, I'LL — GIVE 'EM THEIR PASSES, CAPTAIN ROBERTS!

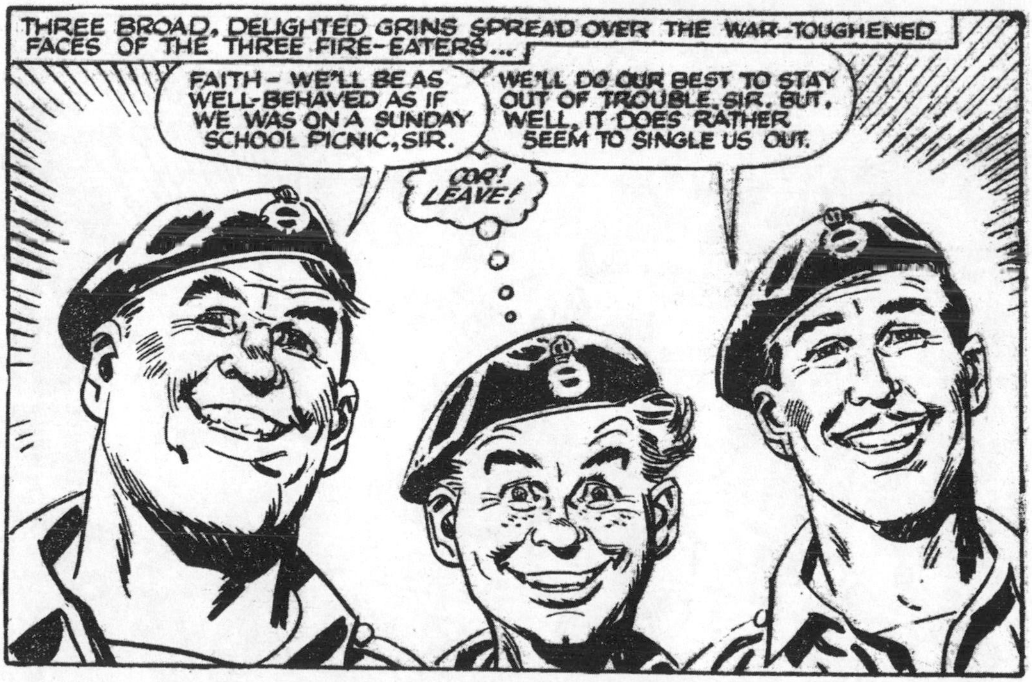
THREE BROAD, DELIGHTED GRINS SPREAD OVER THE WAR-TOUGHENED FACES OF THE THREE FIRE-EATERS...
FAITH - WE'LL BE AS WELL-BEHAVED AS IF WE WAS ON A SUNDAY SCHOOL PICNIC, SIR.
COR! LEAVE!
WE'LL DO OUR BEST TO STAY OUT OF TROUBLE, SIR. BUT, WELL, IT DOES RATHER SEEM TO SINGLE US OUT.

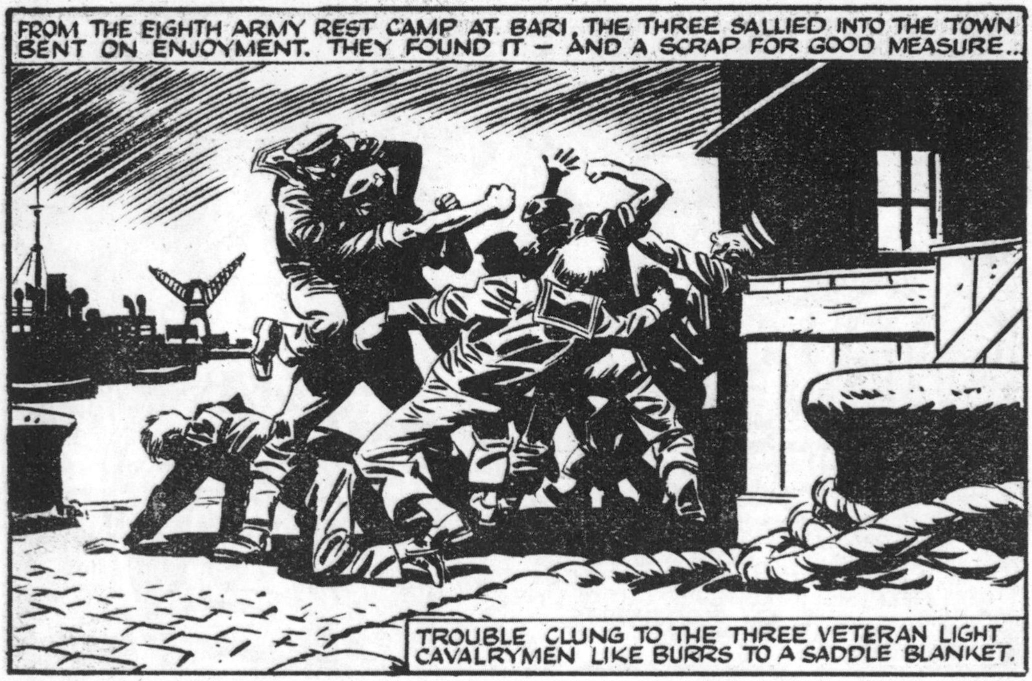
FROM THE EIGHTH ARMY REST CAMP AT BARI, THE THREE SALLIED INTO THE TOWN BENT ON ENJOYMENT. THEY FOUND IT – AND A SCRAP FOR GOOD MEASURE...
TROUBLE CLUNG TO THE THREE VETERAN LIGHT CAVALRYMEN LIKE BURRS TO A SADDLE BLANKET.

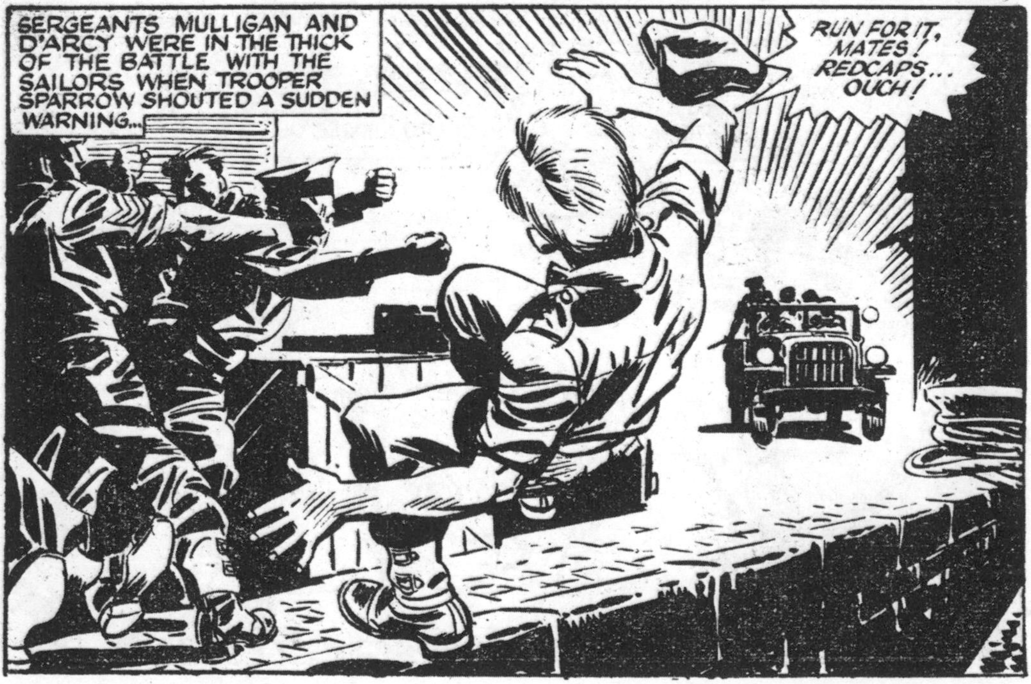
SERGEANTS MULLIGAN AND D'ARCY WERE IN THE THICK OF THE BATTLE WITH THE SAILORS WHEN TROOPER SPARROW SHOUTED A SUDDEN WARNING...
RUN FOR IT, MATES! REDCAPS... OUCH!

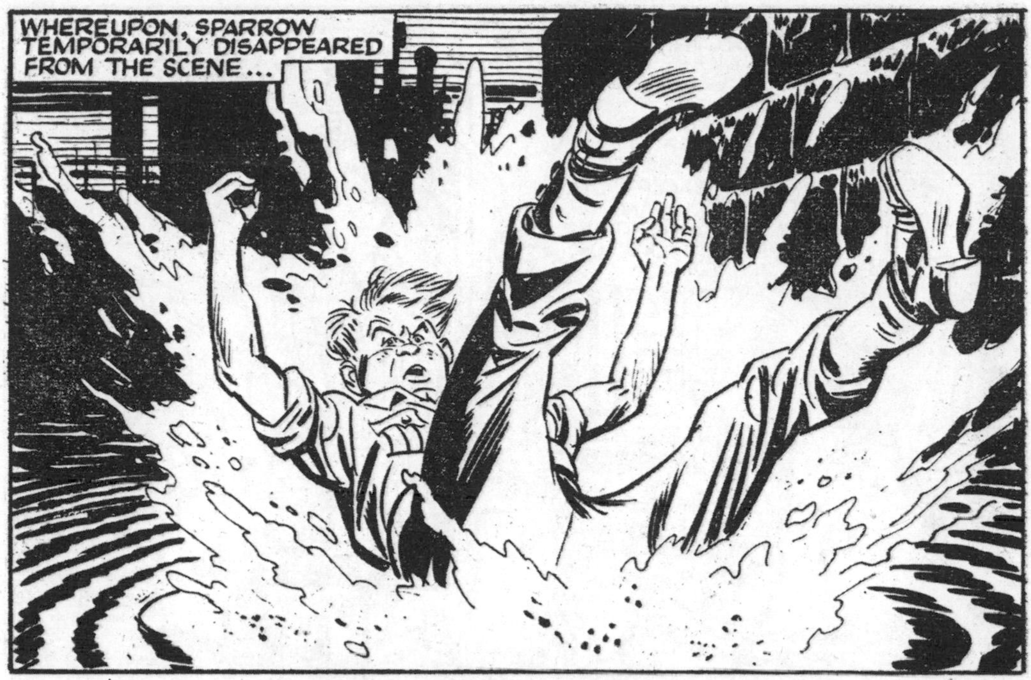
WHEREUPON, SPARROW TEMPORARILY DISAPPEARED FROM THE SCENE...

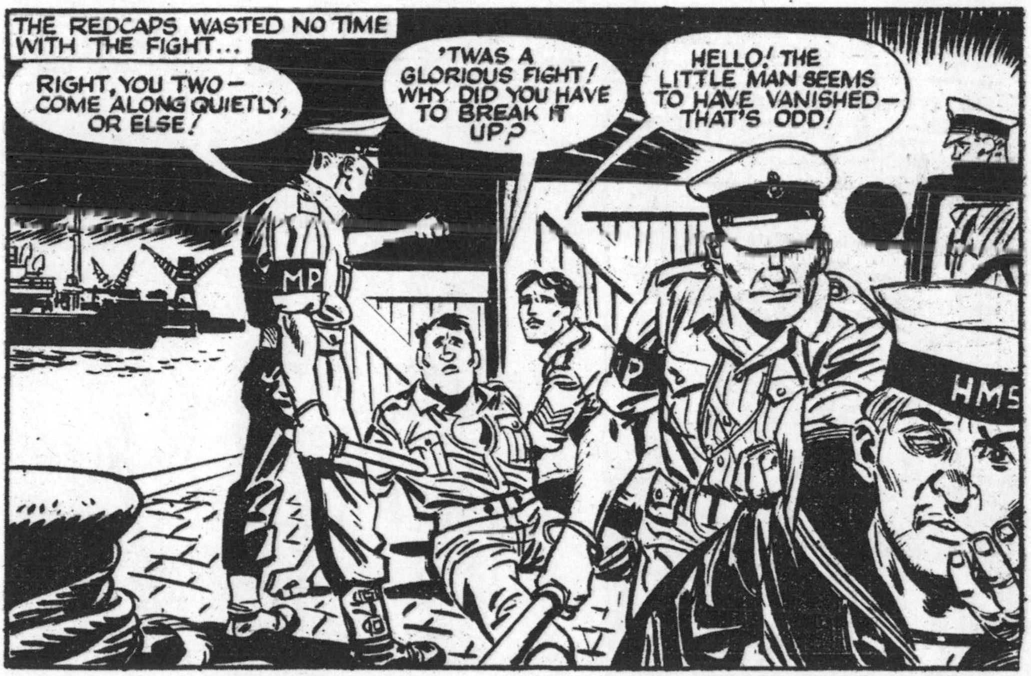
THE REDCAPS WASTED NO TIME WITH THE FIGHT...
RIGHT, YOU TWO—COME ALONG QUIETLY, OR ELSE!
'TWAS A GLORIOUS FIGHT! WHY DID YOU HAVE TO BREAK IT UP?
HELLO! THE LITTLE MAN SEEMS TO HAVE VANISHED—THAT'S ODD!
MP
P
HMS

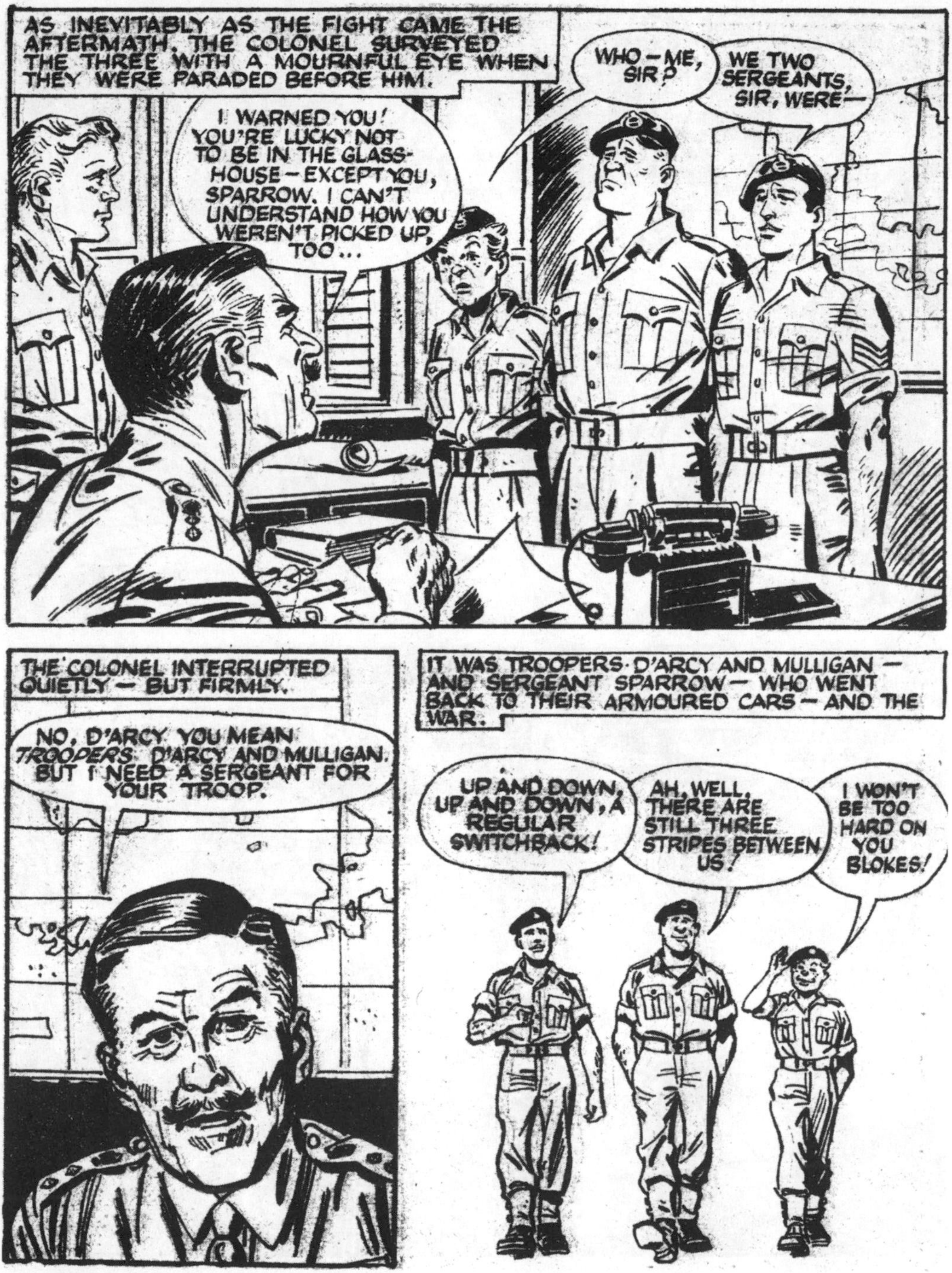
AS INEVITABLY AS THE FIGHT CAME THE AFTERMATH. THE COLONEL SURVEYED THE THREE WITH A MOURNFUL EYE WHEN THEY WERE PARADED BEFORE HIM.
I WARNED YOU! YOU'RE LUCKY NOT TO BE IN THE GLASS-HOUSE — EXCEPT YOU, SPARROW. I CAN'T UNDERSTAND HOW YOU WEREN'T PICKED UP, TOO...
WHO — ME, SIR?
WE TWO SERGEANTS, SIR, WERE—
THE COLONEL INTERRUPTED QUIETLY — BUT FIRMLY.
NO, D'ARCY. YOU MEAN *TROOPERS* D'ARCY AND MULLIGAN. BUT I NEED A SERGEANT FOR YOUR TROOP.
IT WAS TROOPERS D'ARCY AND MULLIGAN — AND SERGEANT SPARROW — WHO WENT BACK TO THEIR ARMOURED CARS — AND THE WAR.
UP AND DOWN, UP AND DOWN, A REGULAR SWITCHBACK!
AH, WELL, THERE ARE STILL THREE STRIPES BETWEEN US!
I WON'T BE TOO HARD ON YOU BLOKES!

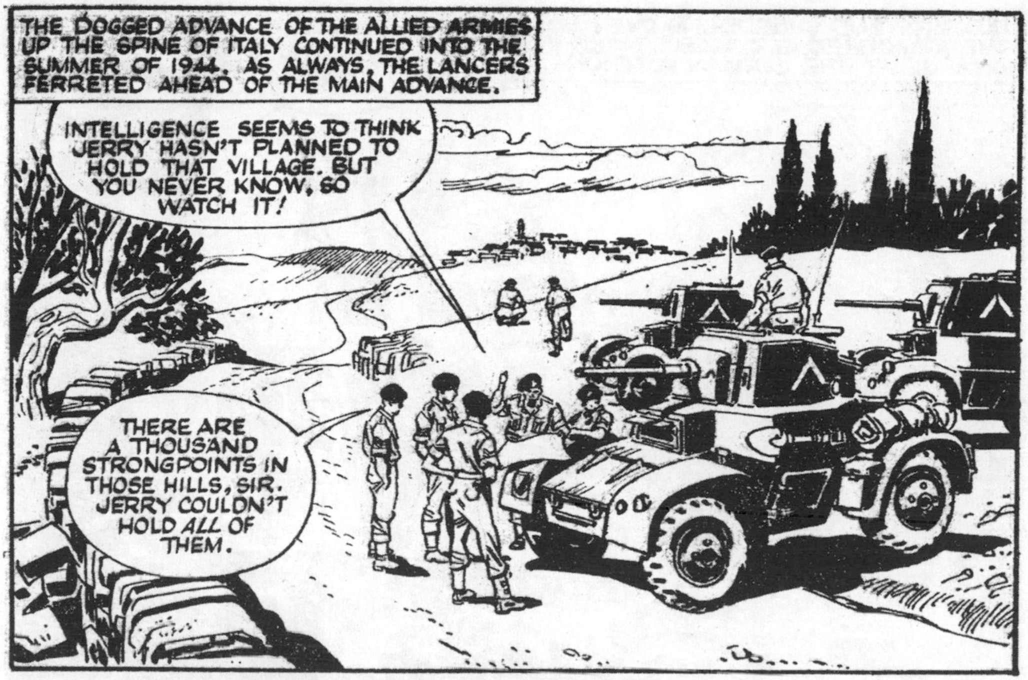
THE DOGGED ADVANCE OF THE ALLIED ARMIES UP THE SPINE OF ITALY CONTINUED INTO THE SUMMER OF 1944. AS ALWAYS, THE LANCERS FERRETED AHEAD OF THE MAIN ADVANCE.
INTELLIGENCE SEEMS TO THINK JERRY HASN'T PLANNED TO HOLD THAT VILLAGE. BUT YOU NEVER KNOW, SO WATCH IT!
THERE ARE A THOUSAND STRONGPOINTS IN THOSE HILLS, SIR. JERRY COULDN'T HOLD *ALL* OF THEM.

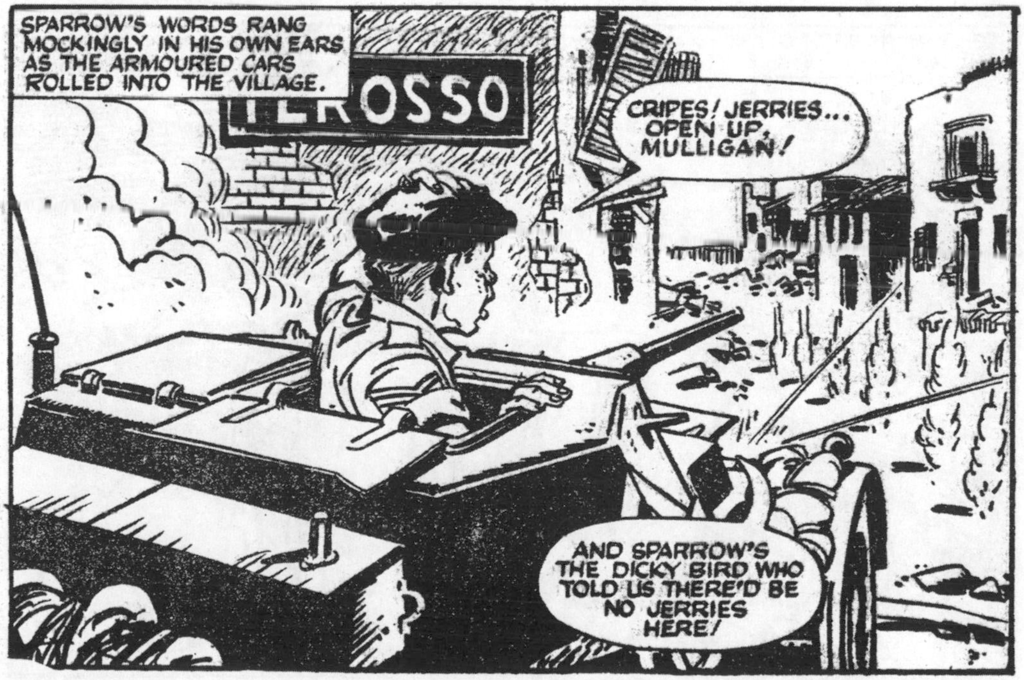
SPARROW'S WORDS RANG MOCKINGLY IN HIS OWN EARS AS THE ARMOURED CARS ROLLED INTO THE VILLAGE.
OSSO
CRIPES! JERRIES... OPEN UP, MULLIGAN!
AND SPARROW'S THE DICKY BIRD WHO TOLD US THERE'D BE NO JERRIES HERE!

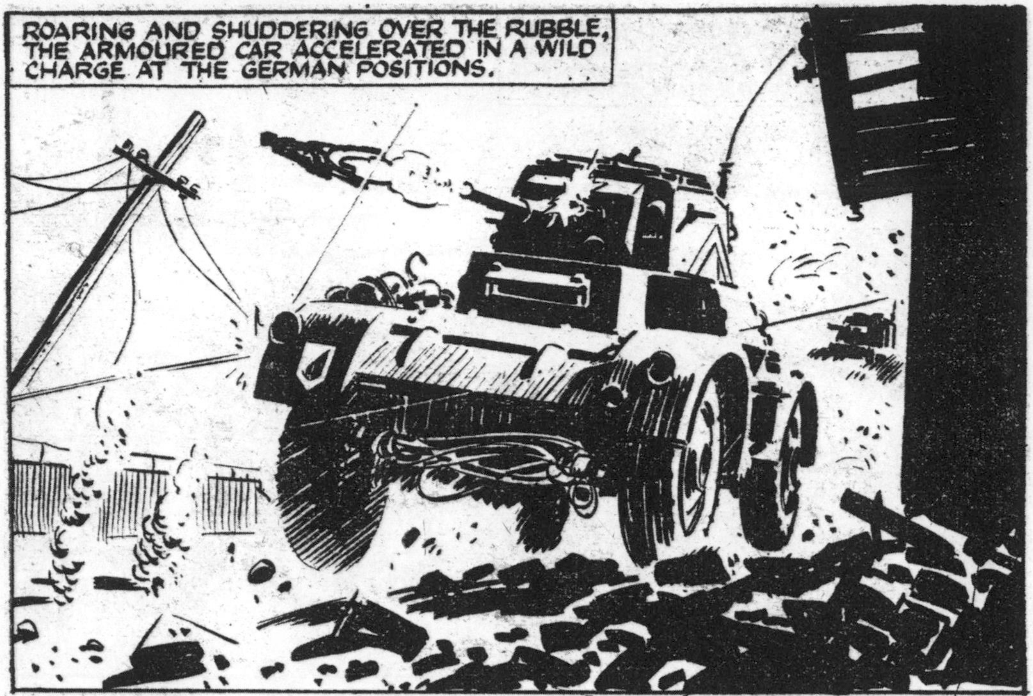
ROARING AND SHUDDERING OVER THE RUBBLE, THE ARMOURED CAR ACCELERATED IN A WILD CHARGE AT THE GERMAN POSITIONS.

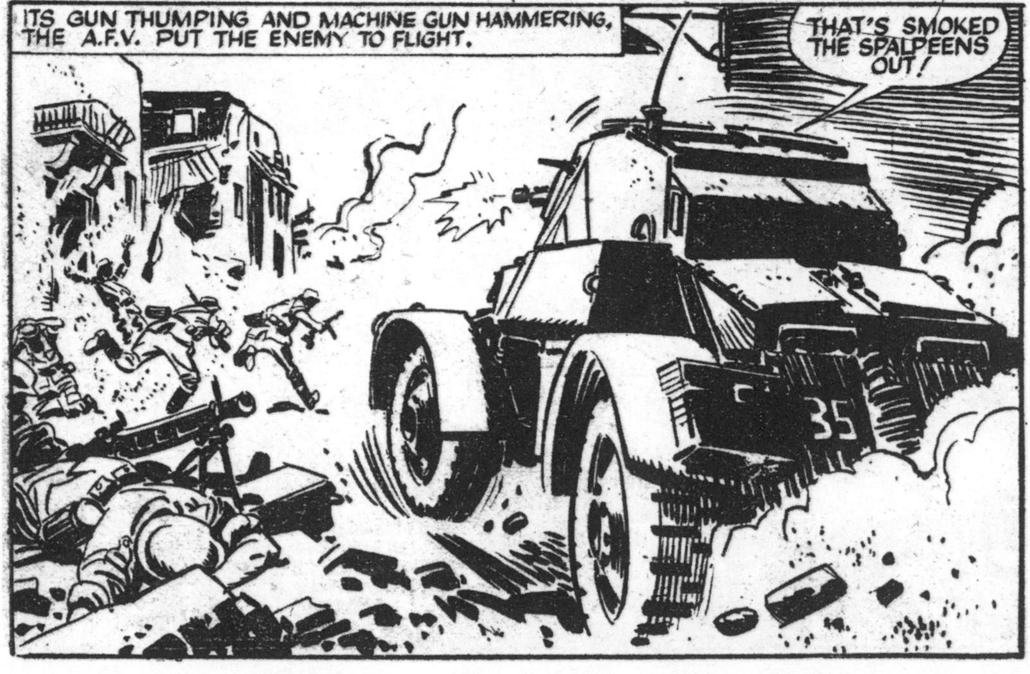
ITS GUN THUMPING AND MACHINE GUN HAMMERING, THE A.F.V. PUT THE ENEMY TO FLIGHT.
THAT'S SMOKED THE SPALPEENS OUT!

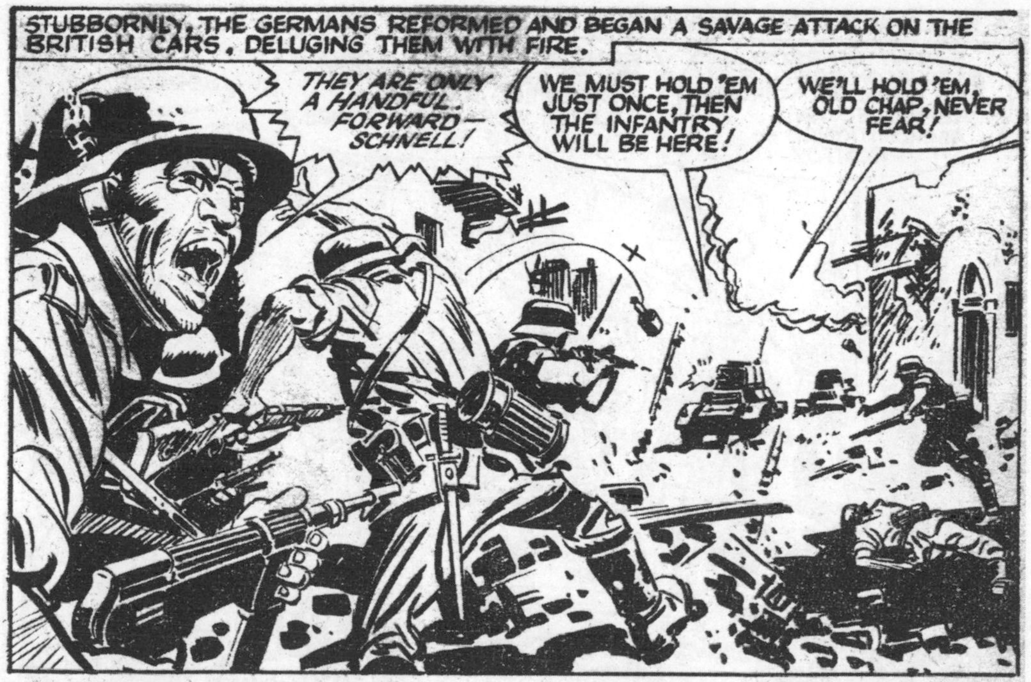
STUBBORNLY, THE GERMANS REFORMED AND BEGAN A SAVAGE ATTACK ON THE BRITISH CARS, DELUGING THEM WITH FIRE.
THEY ARE ONLY A HANDFUL. FORWARD— SCHNELL!
WE MUST HOLD 'EM JUST ONCE, THEN THE INFANTRY WILL BE HERE!
WE'LL HOLD 'EM, OLD CHAP, NEVER FEAR!

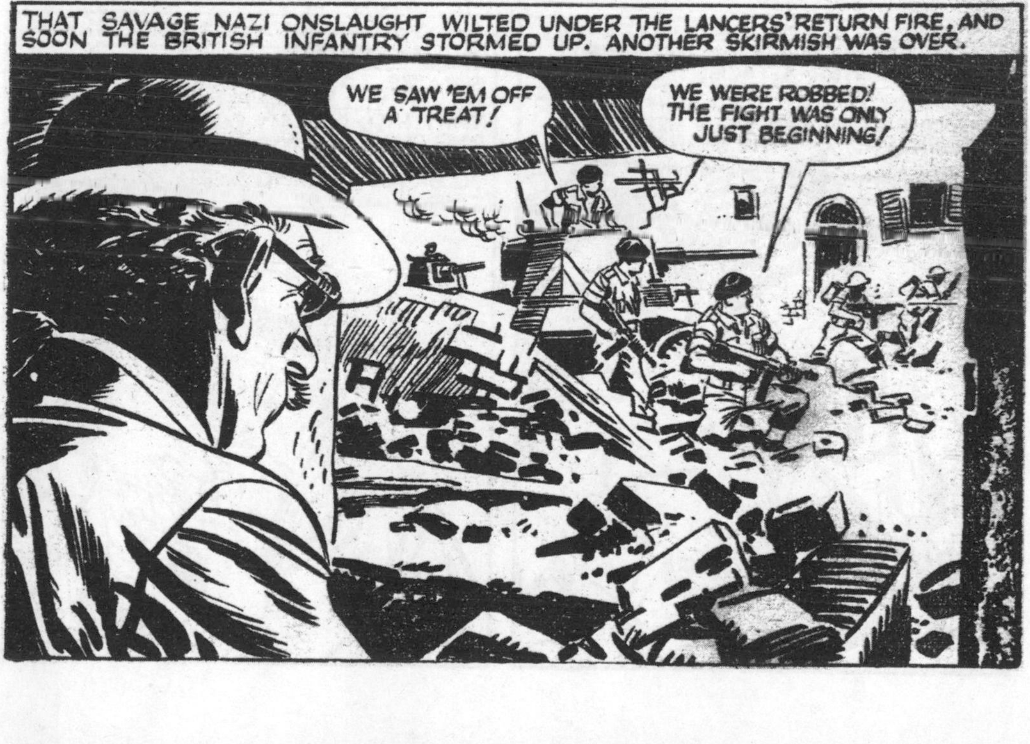
THAT SAVAGE NAZI ONSLAUGHT WILTED UNDER THE LANCERS' RETURN FIRE, AND SOON THE BRITISH INFANTRY STORMED UP. ANOTHER SKIRMISH WAS OVER.
WE SAW 'EM OFF A TREAT!
WE WERE ROBBED! THE FIGHT WAS ONLY JUST BEGINNING!

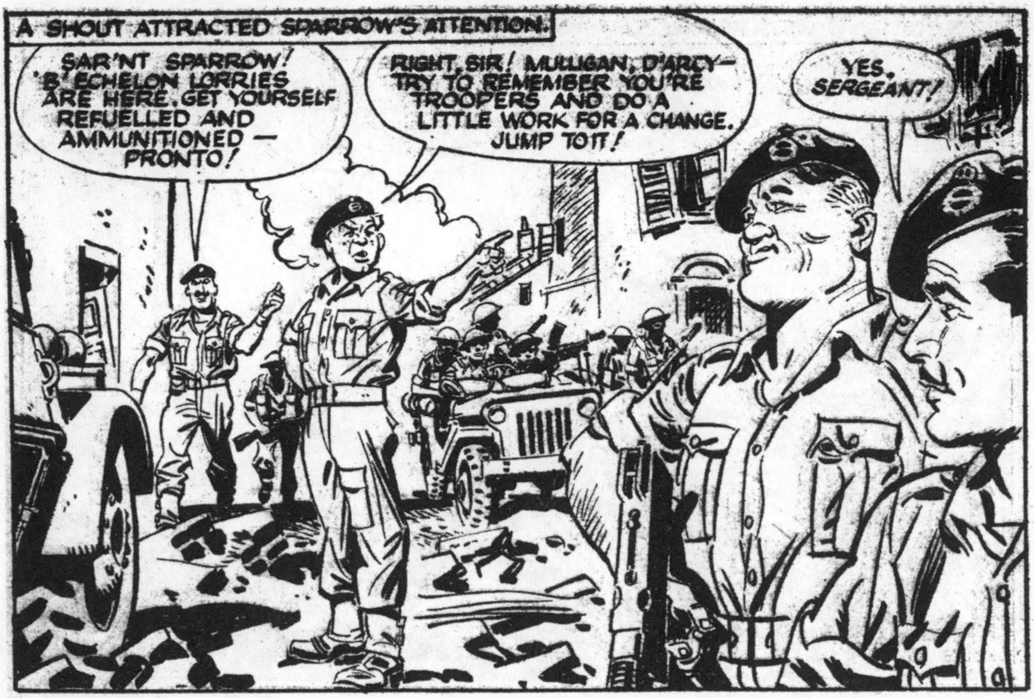
A SHOUT ATTRACTED SPARROW'S ATTENTION.
SAR'NT SPARROW! 'B' ECHELON LORRIES ARE HERE. GET YOURSELF REFUELLED AND AMMUNITIONED — PRONTO!
RIGHT, SIR! MULLIGAN, D'ARCY— TRY TO REMEMBER YOU'RE TROOPERS AND DO A LITTLE WORK FOR A CHANGE. JUMP TO IT!
YES, SERGEANT!

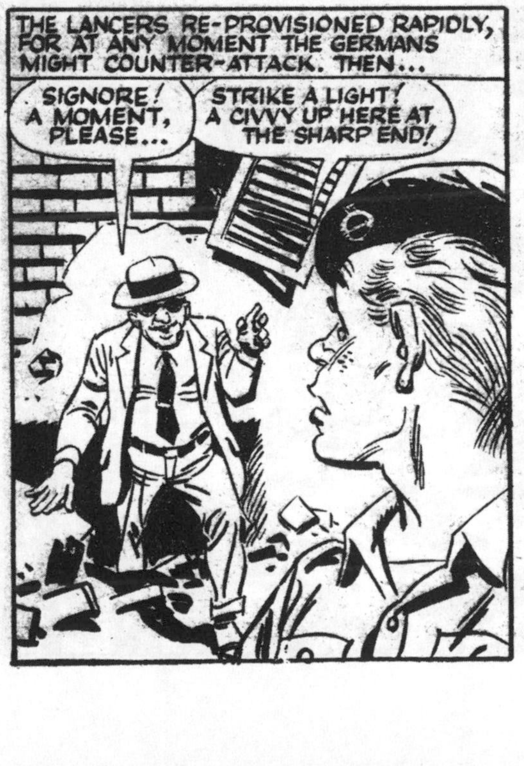
THE LANCERS RE-PROVISIONED RAPIDLY, FOR AT ANY MOMENT THE GERMANS MIGHT COUNTER-ATTACK. THEN...
SIGNORE! A MOMENT, PLEASE...
STRIKE A LIGHT! A CIVVY UP HERE AT THE SHARP END!

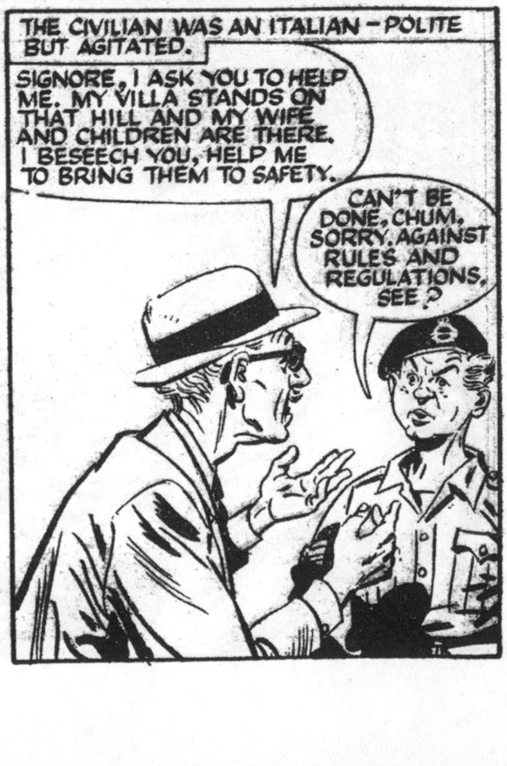
THE CIVILIAN WAS AN ITALIAN — POLITE BUT AGITATED.
SIGNORE, I ASK YOU TO HELP ME. MY VILLA STANDS ON THAT HILL AND MY WIFE AND CHILDREN ARE THERE. I BESEECH YOU, HELP ME TO BRING THEM TO SAFETY.
CAN'T BE DONE, CHUM. SORRY. AGAINST RULES AND REGULATIONS, SEE?

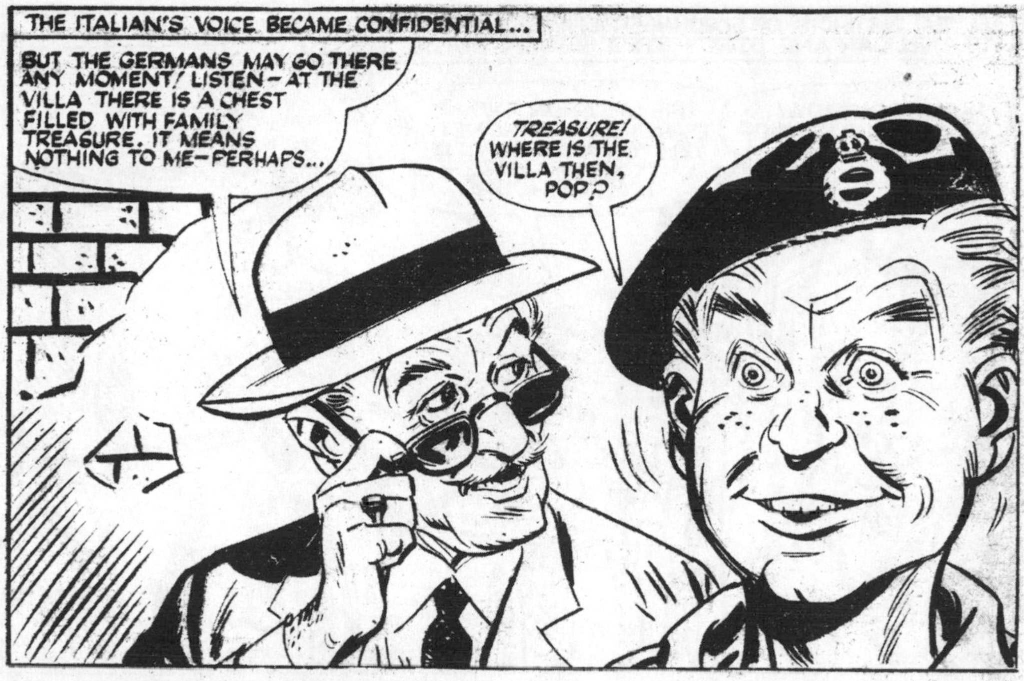
THE ITALIAN'S VOICE BECAME CONFIDENTIAL...
BUT THE GERMANS MAY GO THERE ANY MOMENT! LISTEN—AT THE VILLA THERE IS A CHEST FILLED WITH FAMILY TREASURE. IT MEANS NOTHING TO ME—PERHAPS...
TREASURE! WHERE IS THE VILLA THEN, POP?

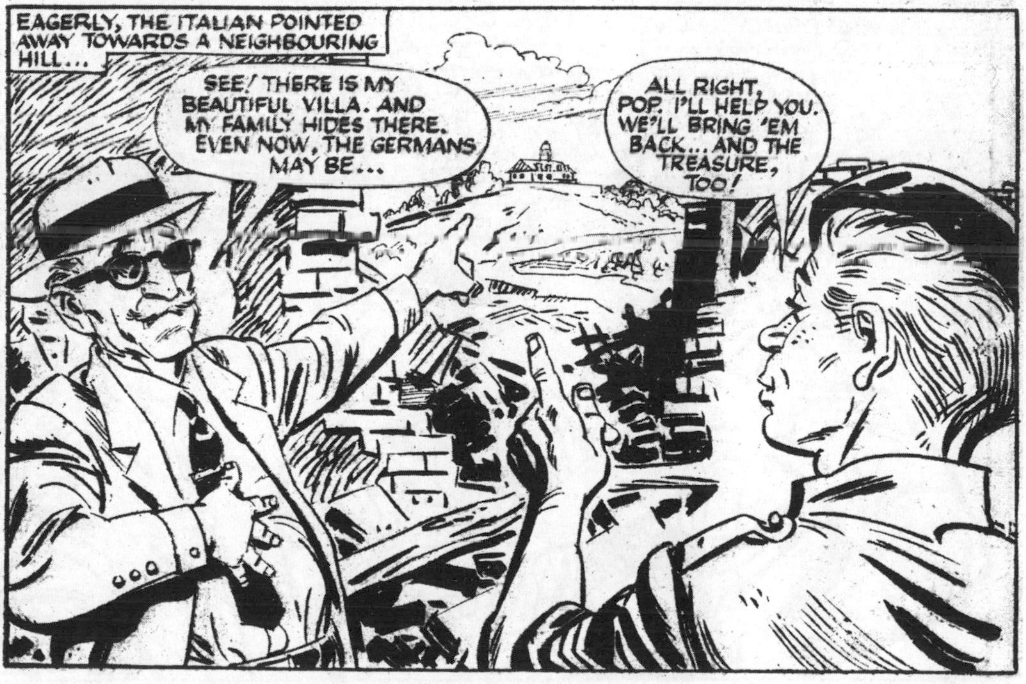
EAGERLY, THE ITALIAN POINTED AWAY TOWARDS A NEIGHBOURING HILL...
SEE! THERE IS MY BEAUTIFUL VILLA. AND MY FAMILY HIDES THERE. EVEN NOW, THE GERMANS MAY BE...
ALL RIGHT, POP. I'LL HELP YOU. WE'LL BRING 'EM BACK... AND THE TREASURE, TOO!

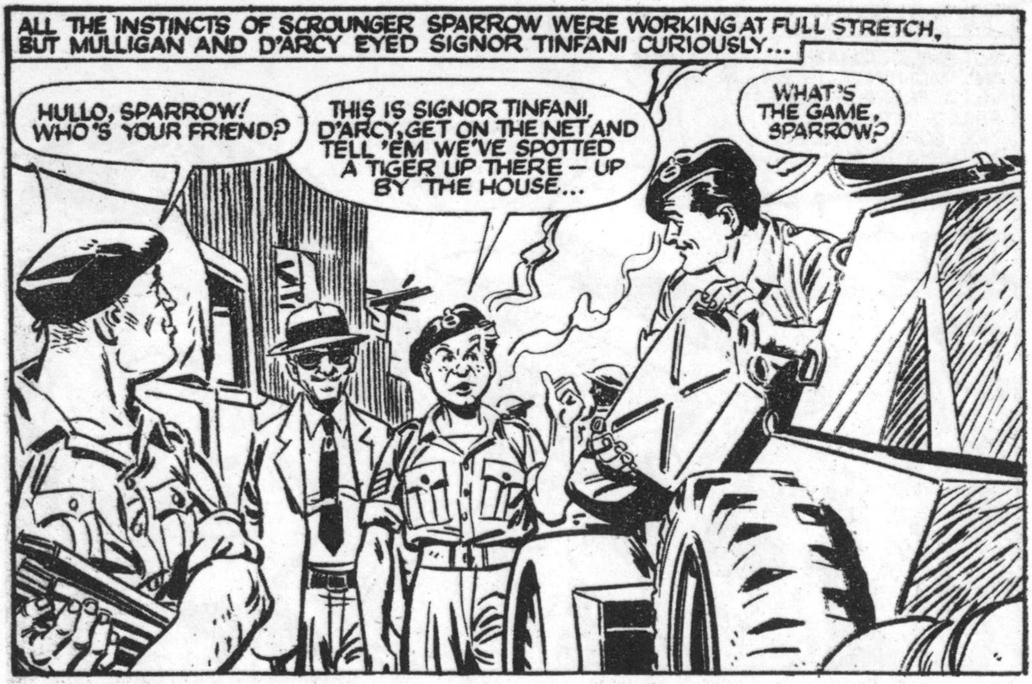
ALL THE INSTINCTS OF SCROUNGER SPARROW WERE WORKING AT FULL STRETCH, BUT MULLIGAN AND D'ARCY EYED SIGNOR TINFANI CURIOUSLY...
HULLO, SPARROW! WHO'S YOUR FRIEND?
THIS IS SIGNOR TINFANI. D'ARCY, GET ON THE NET AND TELL 'EM WE'VE SPOTTED A TIGER UP THERE — UP BY THE HOUSE...
WHAT'S THE GAME, SPARROW?

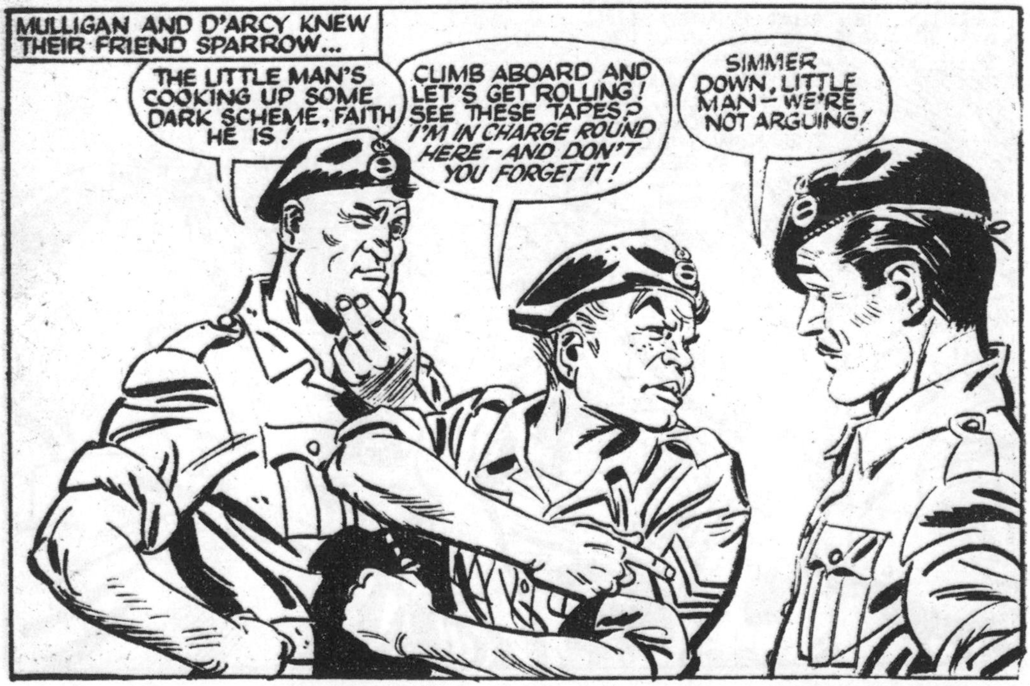
MULLIGAN AND D'ARCY KNEW THEIR FRIEND SPARROW...
THE LITTLE MAN'S COOKING UP SOME DARK SCHEME, FAITH HE IS!
CLIMB ABOARD AND LET'S GET ROLLING! SEE THESE TAPES? I'M IN CHARGE ROUND HERE — AND DON'T YOU FORGET IT!
SIMMER DOWN, LITTLE MAN — WE'RE NOT ARGUING!

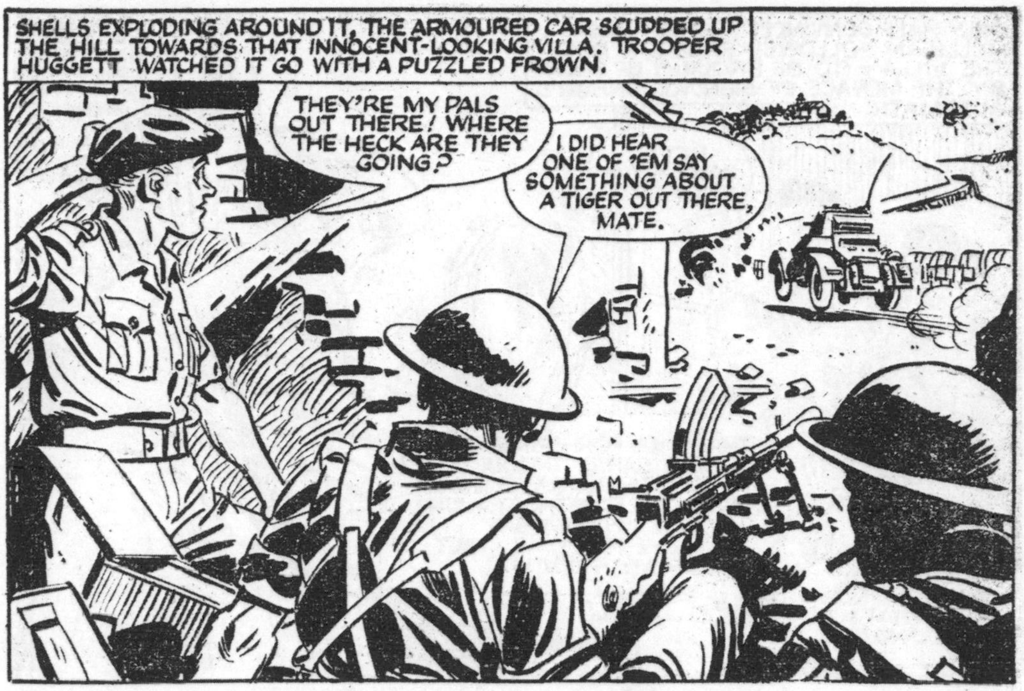
SHELLS EXPLODING AROUND IT, THE ARMOURED CAR SCUDDED UP THE HILL TOWARDS THAT INNOCENT-LOOKING VILLA. TROOPER HUGGETT WATCHED IT GO WITH A PUZZLED FROWN.
THEY'RE MY PALS OUT THERE! WHERE THE HECK ARE THEY GOING?
I DID HEAR ONE OF 'EM SAY SOMETHING ABOUT A TIGER OUT THERE, MATE.

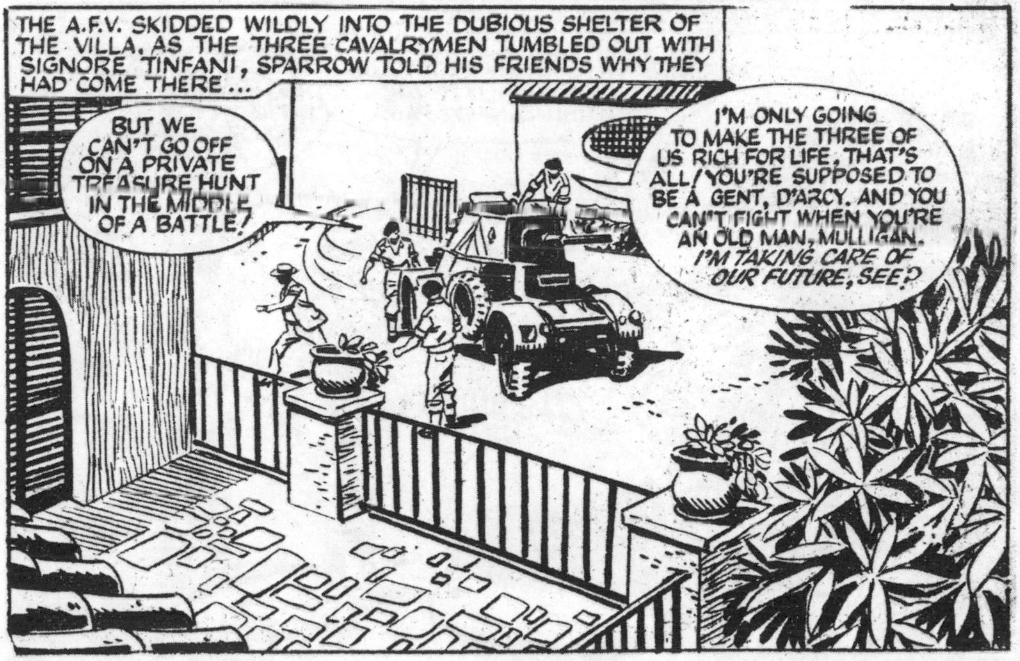
THE A.F.V. SKIDDED WILDLY INTO THE DUBIOUS SHELTER OF THE VILLA. AS THE THREE CAVALRYMEN TUMBLED OUT WITH SIGNORE TINFANI, SPARROW TOLD HIS FRIENDS WHY THEY HAD COME THERE...
BUT WE CAN'T GO OFF ON A PRIVATE TREASURE HUNT IN THE MIDDLE OF A BATTLE!
I'M ONLY GOING TO MAKE THE THREE OF US RICH FOR LIFE, THAT'S ALL! YOU'RE SUPPOSED TO BE A GENT, D'ARCY. AND YOU CAN'T FIGHT WHEN YOU'RE AN OLD MAN, MULLIGAN. I'M TAKING CARE OF OUR FUTURE, SEE?

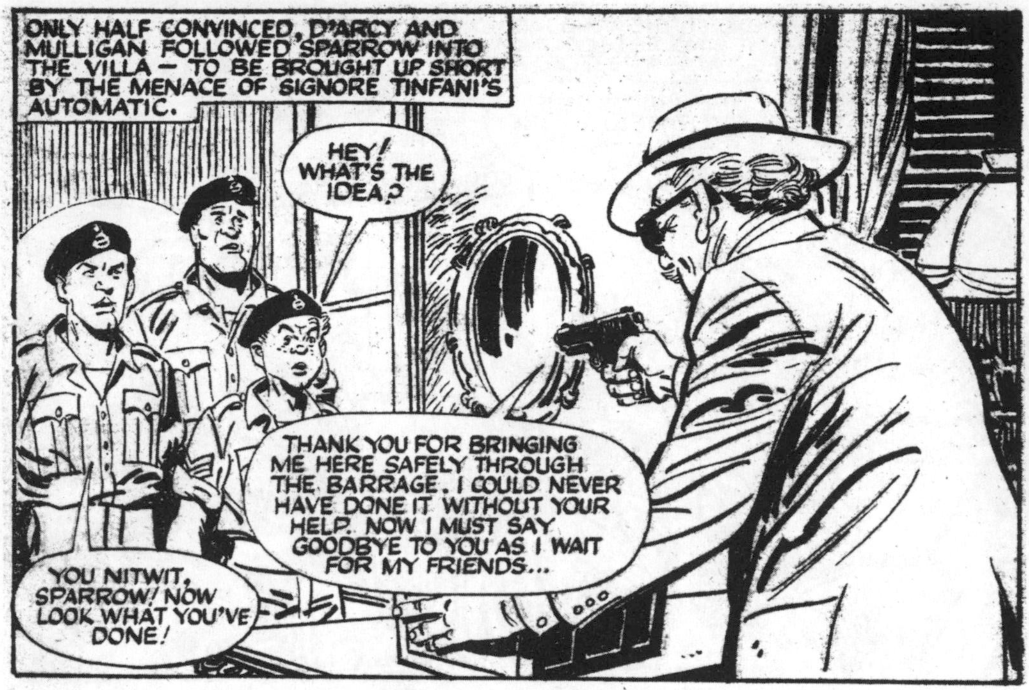
ONLY HALF CONVINCED, D'ARCY AND MULLIGAN FOLLOWED SPARROW INTO THE VILLA — TO BE BROUGHT UP SHORT BY THE MENACE OF SIGNORE TINFANI'S AUTOMATIC.
HEY! WHAT'S THE IDEA?
THANK YOU FOR BRINGING ME HERE SAFELY THROUGH THE BARRAGE. I COULD NEVER HAVE DONE IT WITHOUT YOUR HELP. NOW I MUST SAY GOODBYE TO YOU AS I WAIT FOR MY FRIENDS...
YOU NITWIT, SPARROW! NOW LOOK WHAT YOU'VE DONE!

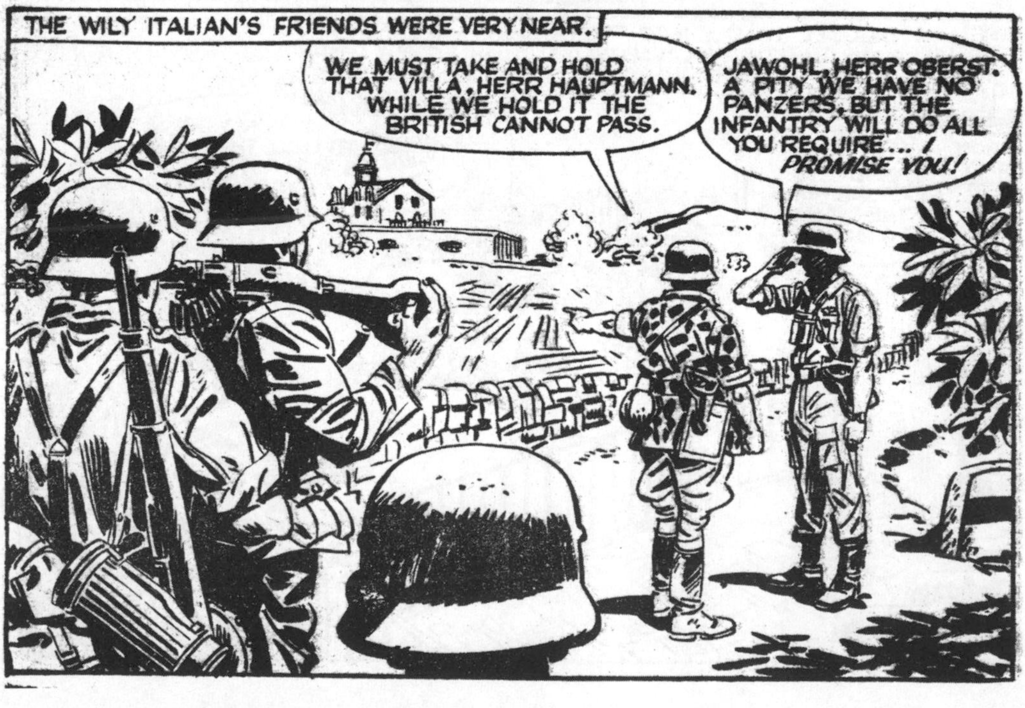
THE WILY ITALIAN'S FRIENDS WERE VERY NEAR.
WE MUST TAKE AND HOLD THAT VILLA, HERR HAUPTMANN. WHILE WE HOLD IT THE BRITISH CANNOT PASS.
JAWOHL, HERR OBERST. A PITY WE HAVE NO PANZERS, BUT THE INFANTRY WILL DO ALL YOU REQUIRE... I PROMISE YOU!

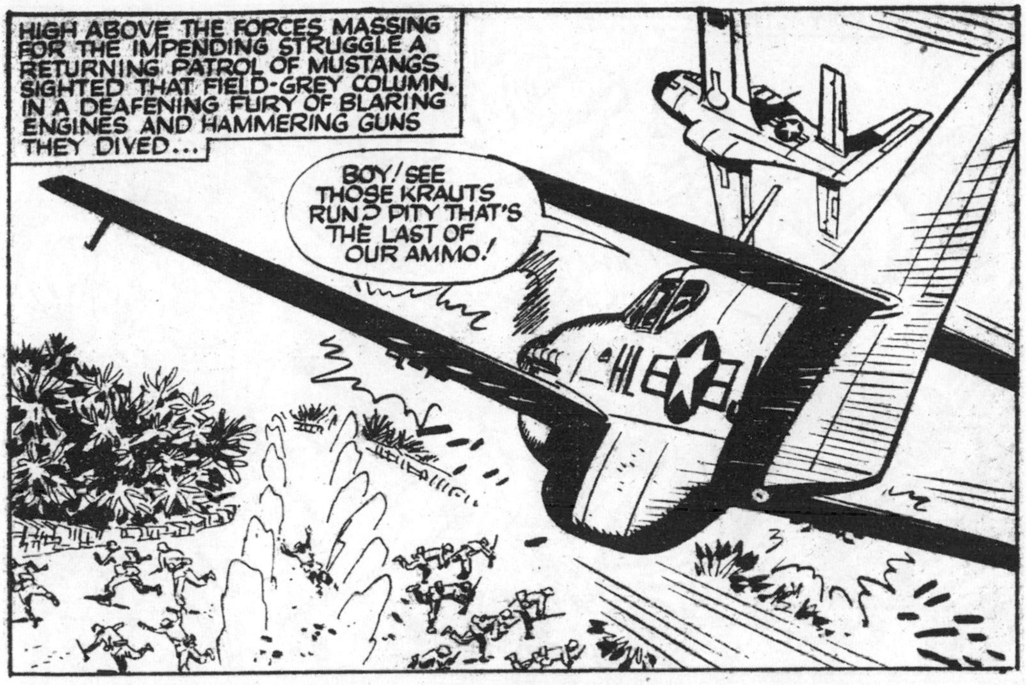
HIGH ABOVE THE FORCES MASSING FOR THE IMPENDING STRUGGLE A RETURNING PATROL OF MUSTANGS SIGHTED THAT FIELD-GREY COLUMN. IN A DEAFENING FURY OF BLARING ENGINES AND HAMMERING GUNS THEY DIVED...
BOY! SEE THOSE KRAUTS RUN? PITY THAT'S THE LAST OF OUR AMMO!

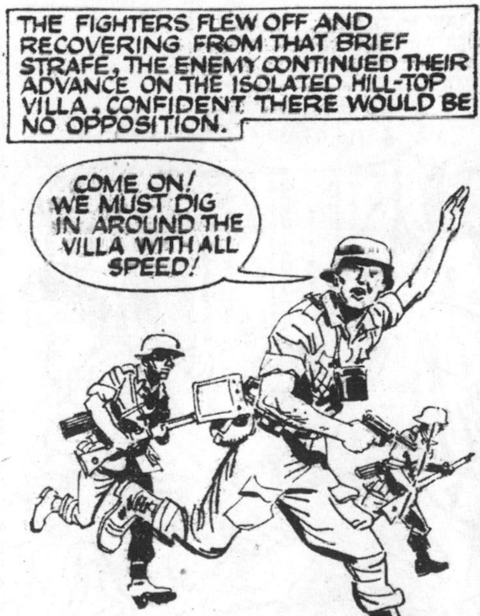
THE FIGHTERS FLEW OFF AND RECOVERING FROM THAT BRIEF STRAFE, THE ENEMY CONTINUED THEIR ADVANCE ON THE ISOLATED HILL-TOP VILLA, CONFIDENT THERE WOULD BE NO OPPOSITION.
COME ON! WE MUST DIG IN AROUND THE VILLA WITH ALL SPEED!

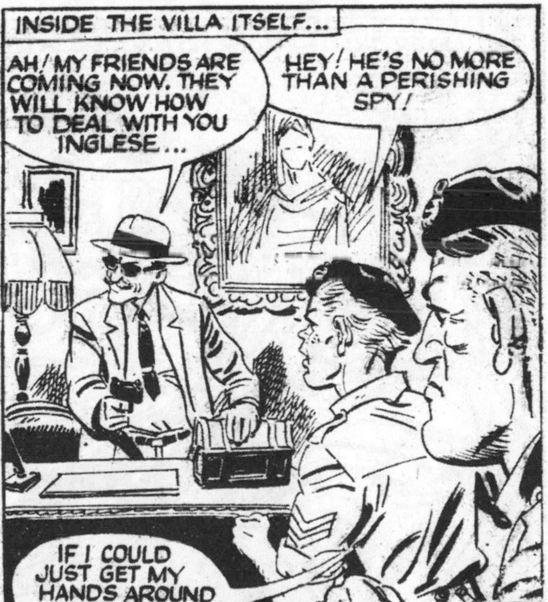
INSIDE THE VILLA ITSELF...
AH! MY FRIENDS ARE COMING NOW. THEY WILL KNOW HOW TO DEAL WITH YOU INGLESE...
HEY! HE'S NO MORE THAN A PERISHING SPY!
IF I COULD JUST GET MY HANDS AROUND HIS SCRAWNY NECK!

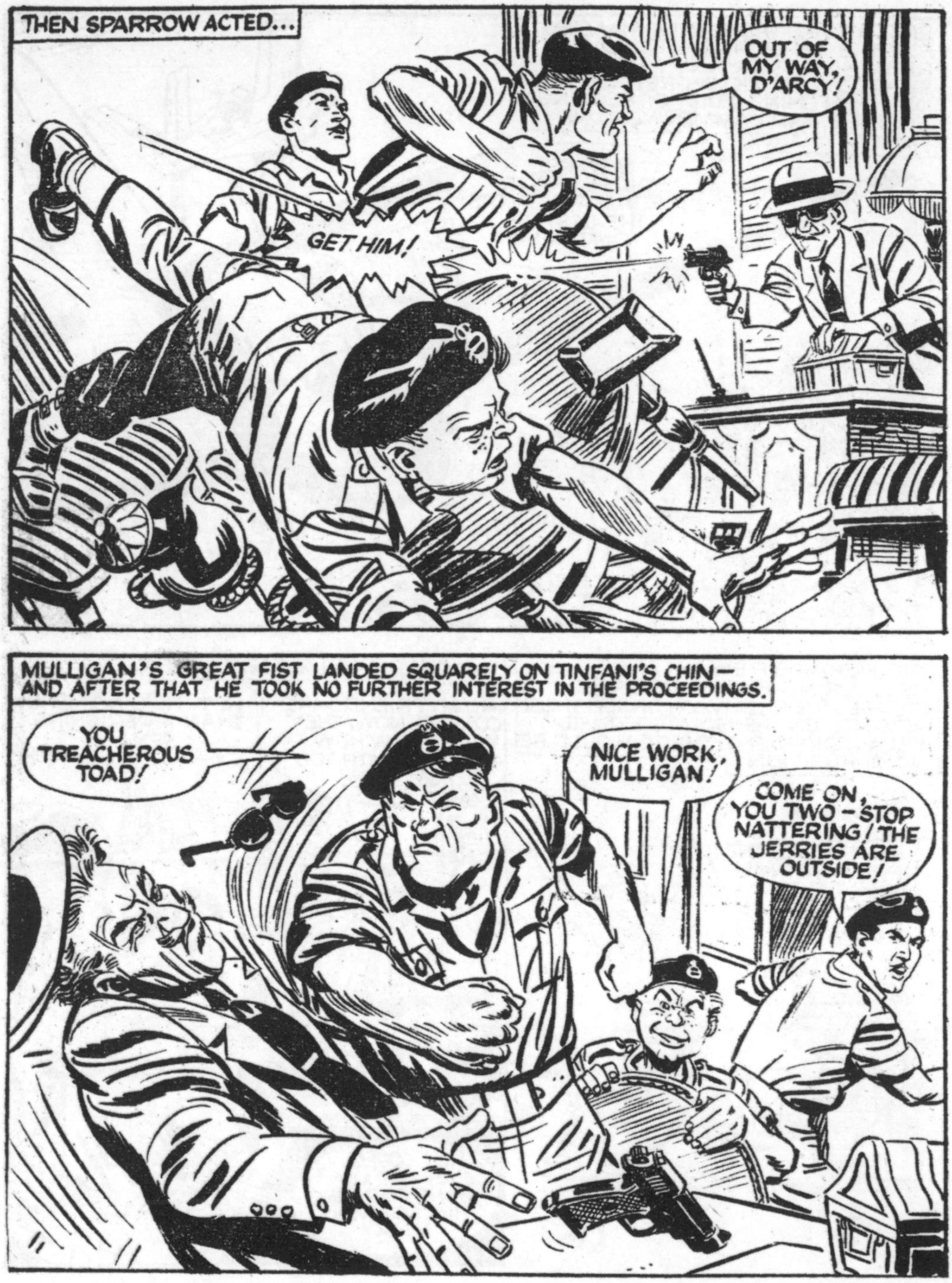
THEN SPARROW ACTED...
OUT OF MY WAY, D'ARCY!
GET HIM!
MULLIGAN'S GREAT FIST LANDED SQUARELY ON TINFANI'S CHIN— AND AFTER THAT HE TOOK NO FURTHER INTEREST IN THE PROCEEDINGS.
YOU TREACHEROUS TOAD!
NICE WORK, MULLIGAN!
COME ON, YOU TWO – STOP NATTERING! THE JERRIES ARE OUTSIDE!

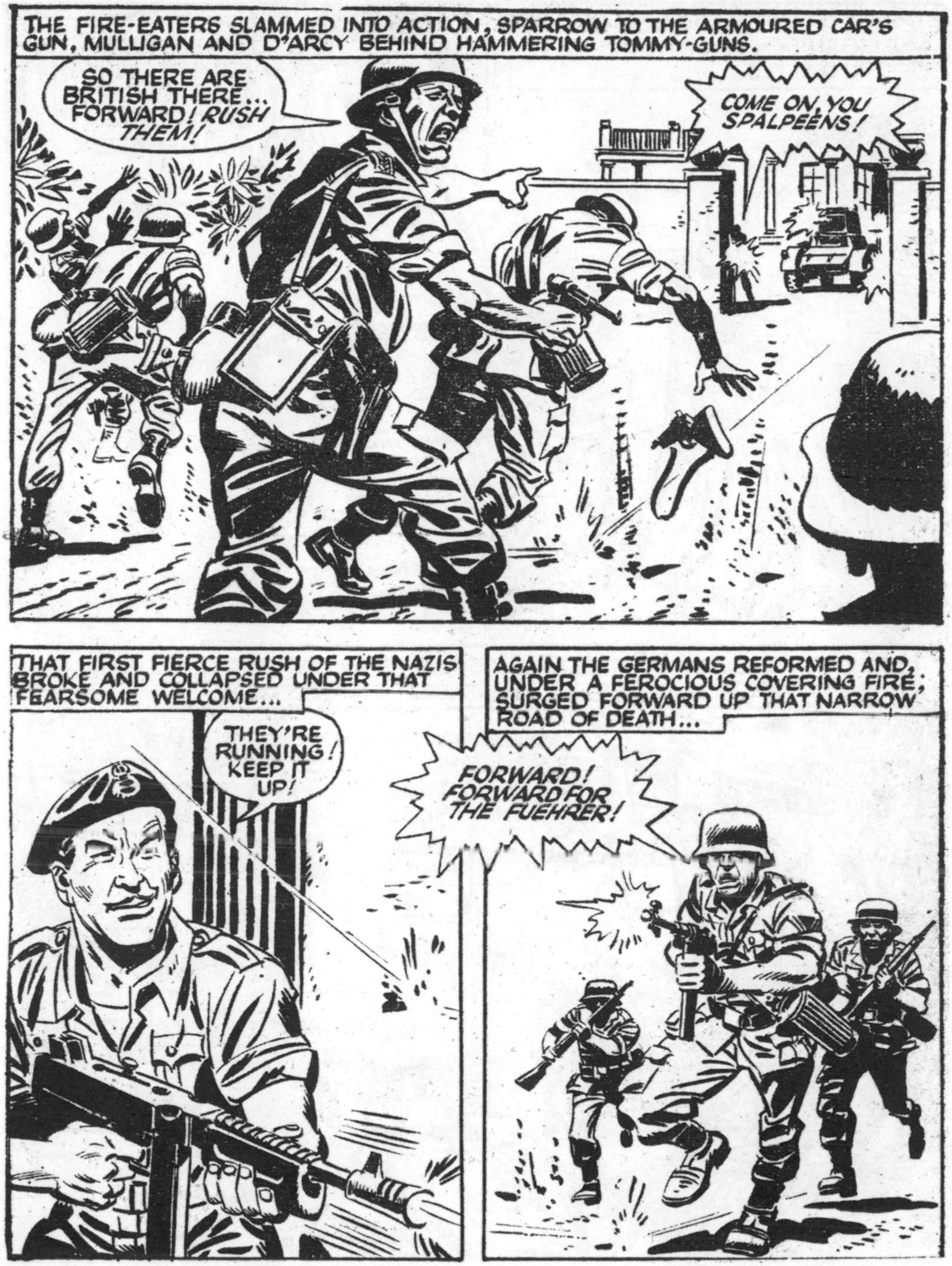
THE FIRE-EATERS SLAMMED INTO ACTION, SPARROW TO THE ARMOURED CAR'S GUN, MULLIGAN AND D'ARCY BEHIND HAMMERING TOMMY-GUNS.
SO THERE ARE BRITISH THERE... FORWARD! RUSH THEM!
COME ON, YOU SPALPEENS!
THAT FIRST FIERCE RUSH OF THE NAZIS BROKE AND COLLAPSED UNDER THAT FEARSOME WELCOME...
THEY'RE RUNNING! KEEP IT UP!
AGAIN THE GERMANS REFORMED AND, UNDER A FEROCIOUS COVERING FIRE, SURGED FORWARD UP THAT NARROW ROAD OF DEATH...
FORWARD! FORWARD FOR THE FUEHRER!

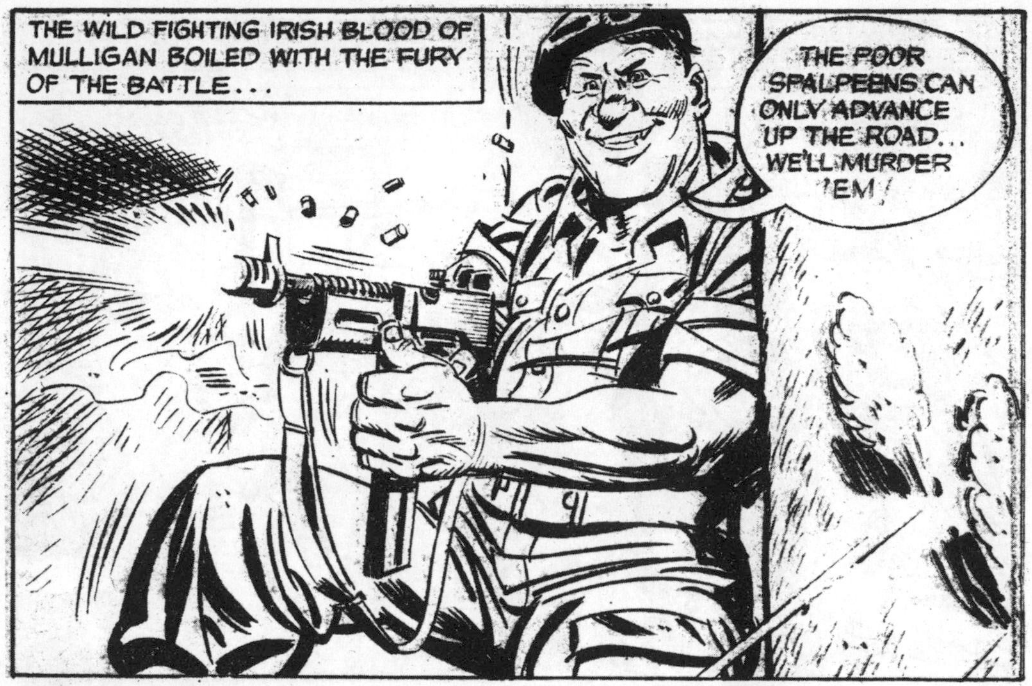
THE WILD FIGHTING IRISH BLOOD OF MULLIGAN BOILED WITH THE FURY OF THE BATTLE...
THE POOR SPALPEENS CAN ONLY ADVANCE UP THE ROAD... WE'LL MURDER 'EM!

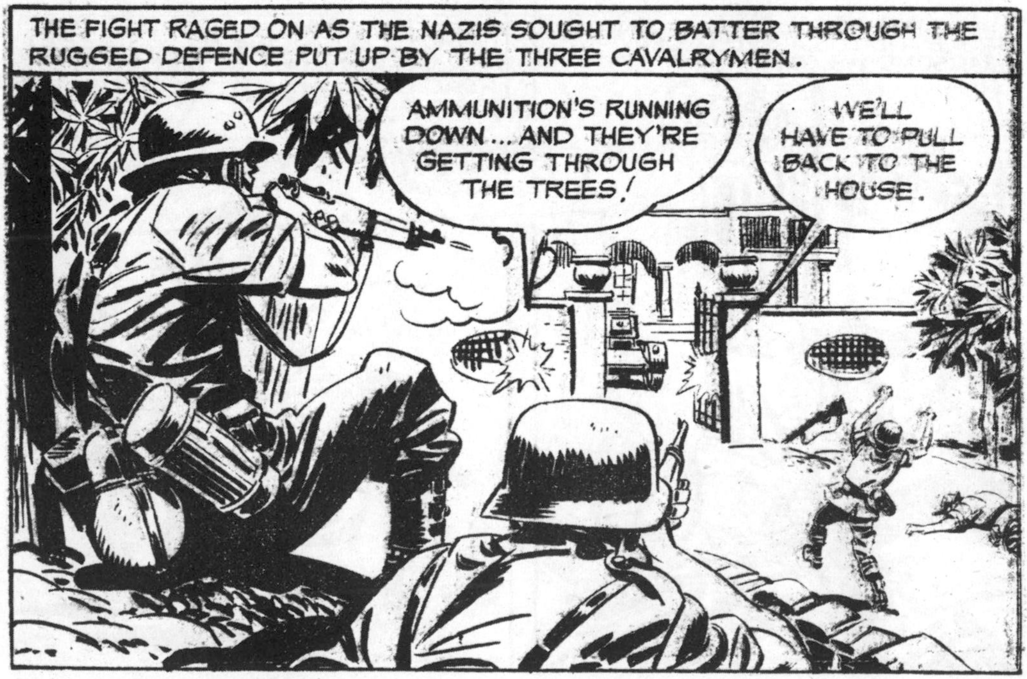
THE FIGHT RAGED ON AS THE NAZIS SOUGHT TO BATTER THROUGH THE RUGGED DEFENCE PUT UP BY THE THREE CAVALRYMEN.
AMMUNITION'S RUNNING DOWN... AND THEY'RE GETTING THROUGH THE TREES!
WE'LL HAVE TO PULL BACK TO THE HOUSE.

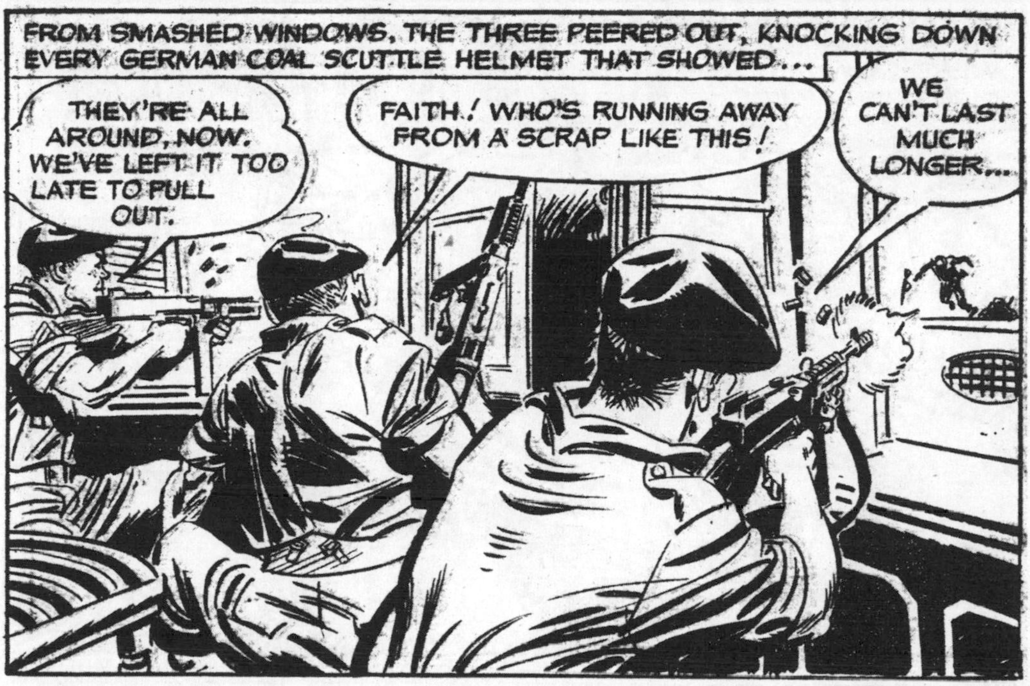
FROM SMASHED WINDOWS, THE THREE PEERED OUT, KNOCKING DOWN EVERY GERMAN COAL SCUTTLE HELMET THAT SHOWED...
THEY'RE ALL AROUND, NOW. WE'VE LEFT IT TOO LATE TO PULL OUT.
FAITH! WHO'S RUNNING AWAY FROM A SCRAP LIKE THIS!
WE CAN'T LAST MUCH LONGER...

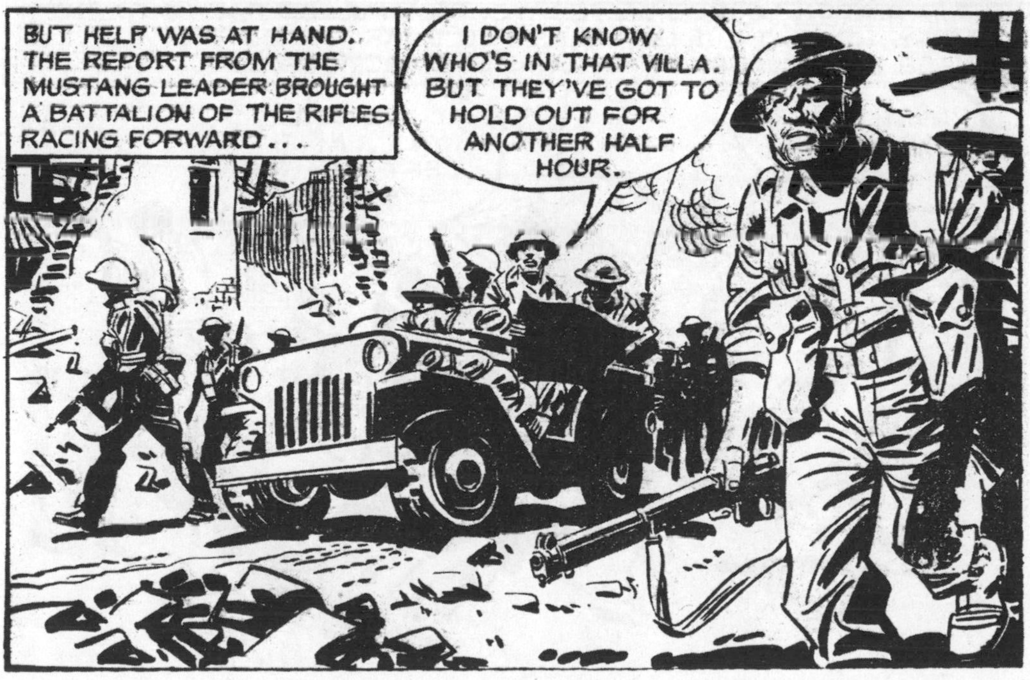
BUT HELP WAS AT HAND. THE REPORT FROM THE MUSTANG LEADER BROUGHT A BATTALION OF THE RIFLES RACING FORWARD...
I DON'T KNOW WHO'S IN THAT VILLA. BUT THEY'VE GOT TO HOLD OUT FOR ANOTHER HALF HOUR.

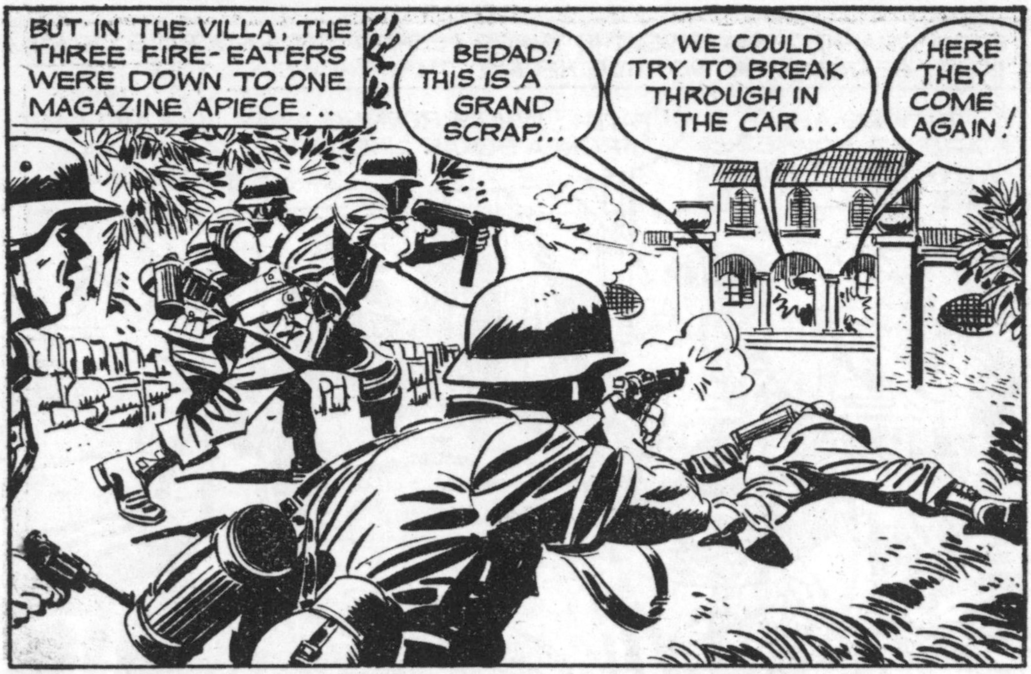
BUT IN THE VILLA, THE THREE FIRE-EATERS WERE DOWN TO ONE MAGAZINE APIECE...
BEDAD! THIS IS A GRAND SCRAP...
WE COULD TRY TO BREAK THROUGH IN THE CAR...
HERE THEY COME AGAIN!

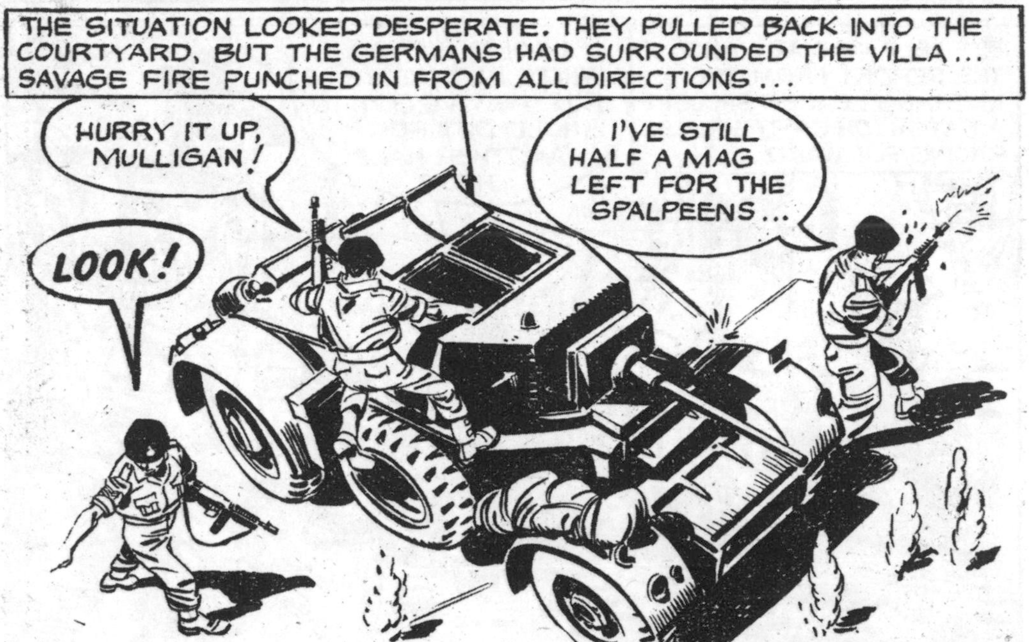
THE SITUATION LOOKED DESPERATE. THEY PULLED BACK INTO THE COURTYARD, BUT THE GERMANS HAD SURROUNDED THE VILLA... SAVAGE FIRE PUNCHED IN FROM ALL DIRECTIONS...
HURRY IT UP, MULLIGAN!
I'VE STILL HALF A MAG LEFT FOR THE SPALPEENS...
LOOK!

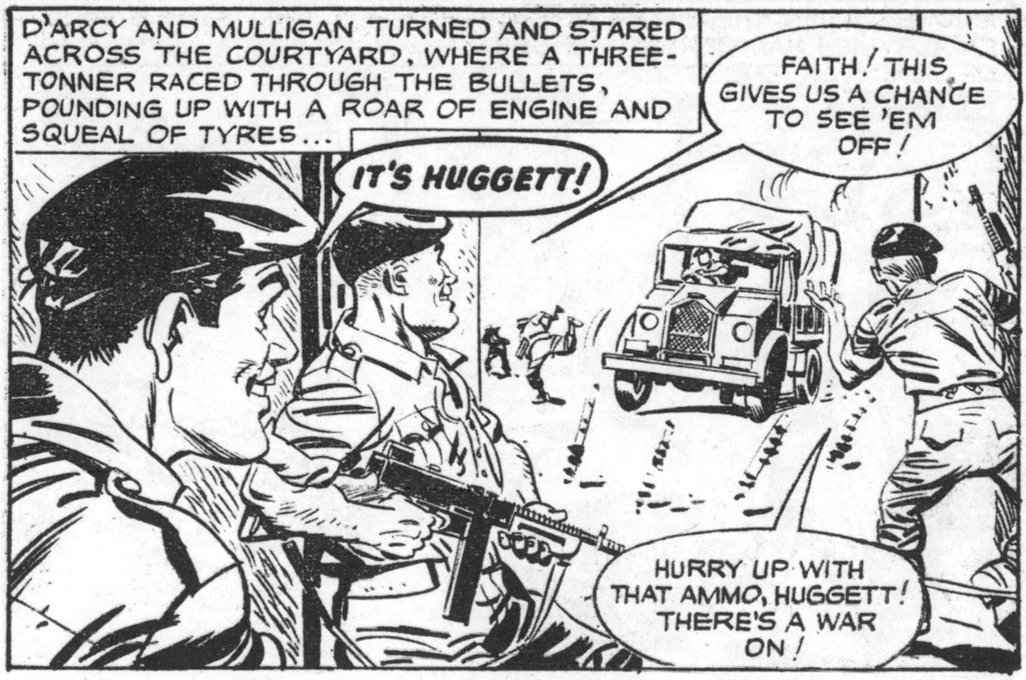
D'ARCY AND MULLIGAN TURNED AND STARED ACROSS THE COURTYARD, WHERE A THREE-TONNER RACED THROUGH THE BULLETS, POUNDING UP WITH A ROAR OF ENGINE AND SQUEAL OF TYRES...
IT'S HUGGETT!
FAITH! THIS GIVES US A CHANCE TO SEE 'EM OFF!
HURRY UP WITH THAT AMMO, HUGGETT! THERE'S A WAR ON!

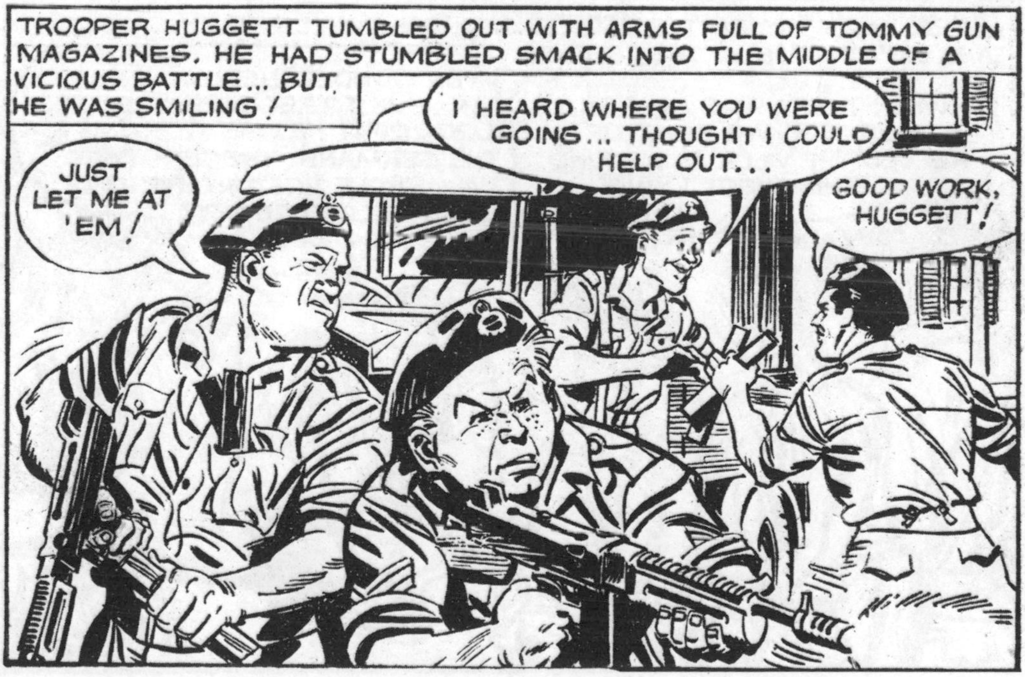
TROOPER HUGGETT TUMBLED OUT WITH ARMS FULL OF TOMMY GUN MAGAZINES. HE HAD STUMBLED SMACK INTO THE MIDDLE OF A VICIOUS BATTLE... BUT HE WAS SMILING!
I HEARD WHERE YOU WERE GOING... THOUGHT I COULD HELP OUT...
JUST LET ME AT 'EM!
GOOD WORK, HUGGETT!

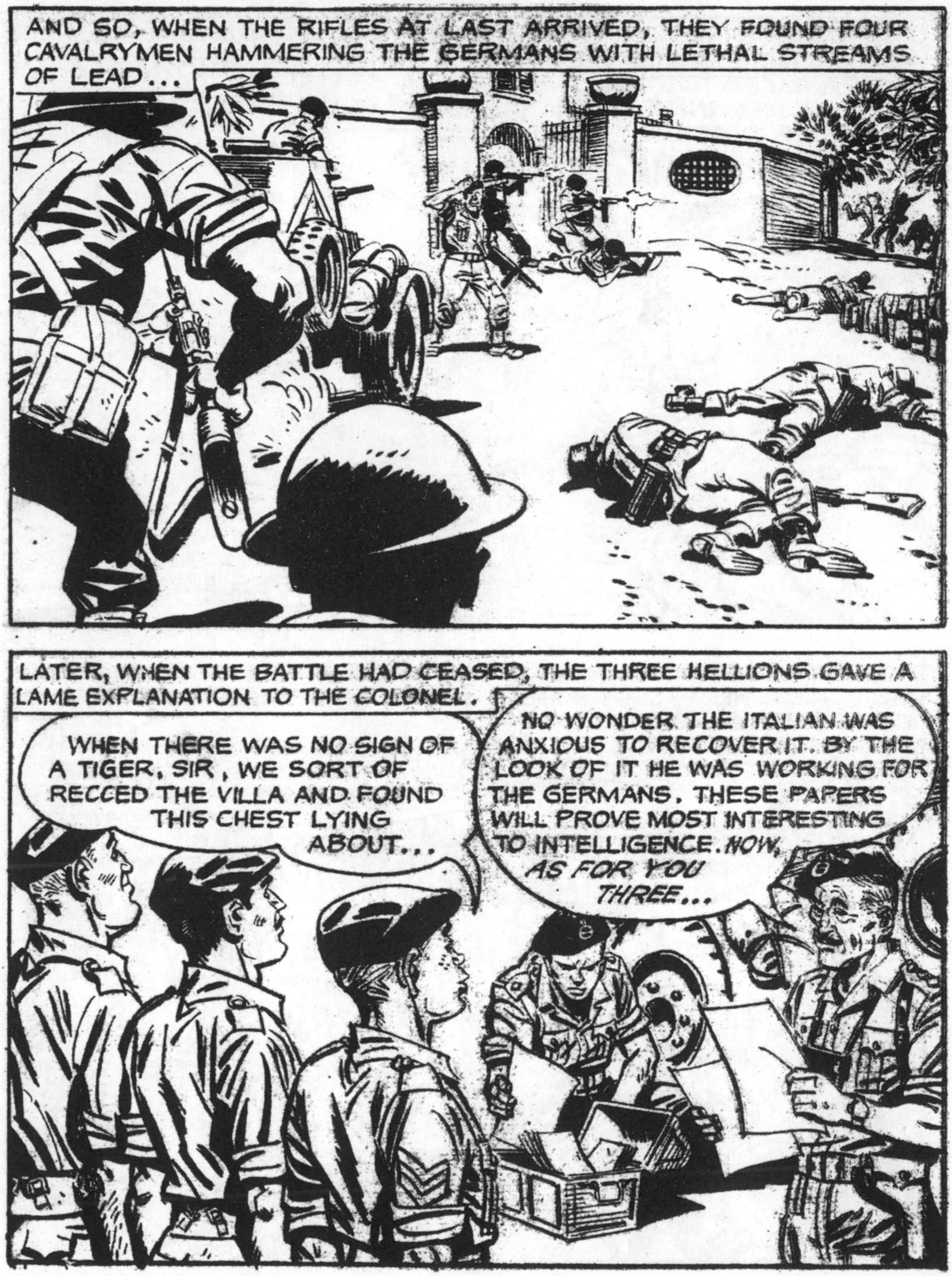
AND SO, WHEN THE RIFLES AT LAST ARRIVED, THEY FOUND FOUR CAVALRYMEN HAMMERING THE GERMANS WITH LETHAL STREAMS OF LEAD...
LATER, WHEN THE BATTLE HAD CEASED, THE THREE HELLIONS GAVE A LAME EXPLANATION TO THE COLONEL.
WHEN THERE WAS NO SIGN OF A TIGER, SIR, WE SORT OF RECCED THE VILLA AND FOUND THIS CHEST LYING ABOUT...
NO WONDER THE ITALIAN WAS ANXIOUS TO RECOVER IT. BY THE LOOK OF IT HE WAS WORKING FOR THE GERMANS. THESE PAPERS WILL PROVE MOST INTERESTING TO INTELLIGENCE. NOW, AS FOR YOU THREE...

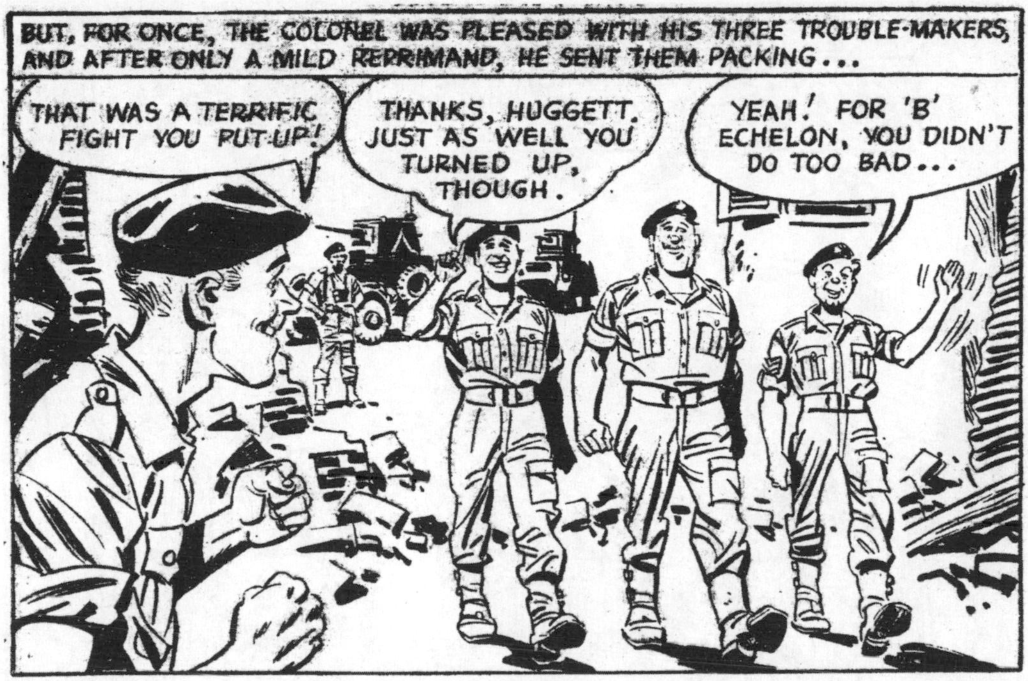
BUT, FOR ONCE, THE COLONEL WAS PLEASED WITH HIS THREE TROUBLE-MAKERS, AND AFTER ONLY A MILD REPRIMAND, HE SENT THEM PACKING...
THAT WAS A TERRIFIC FIGHT YOU PUT UP!
THANKS, HUGGETT. JUST AS WELL YOU TURNED UP, THOUGH.
YEAH! FOR 'B' ECHELON, YOU DIDN'T DO TOO BAD...

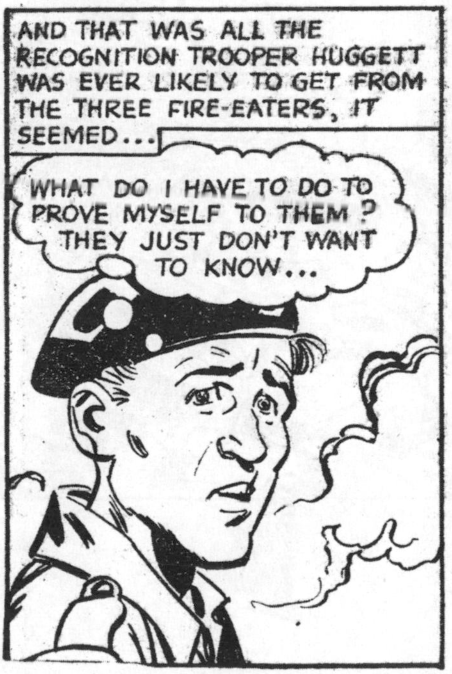
AND THAT WAS ALL THE RECOGNITION TROOPER HUGGETT WAS EVER LIKELY TO GET FROM THE THREE FIRE-EATERS, IT SEEMED...
WHAT DO I HAVE TO DO TO PROVE MYSELF TO THEM? THEY JUST DON'T WANT TO KNOW...

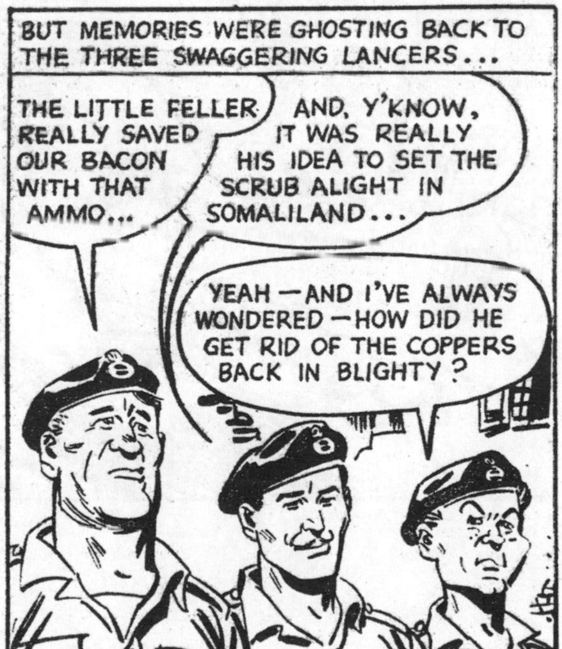
BUT MEMORIES WERE GHOSTING BACK TO THE THREE SWAGGERING LANCERS...
THE LITTLE FELLER REALLY SAVED OUR BACON WITH THAT AMMO...
AND, Y'KNOW, IT WAS REALLY HIS IDEA TO SET THE SCRUB ALIGHT IN SOMALILAND...
YEAH — AND I'VE ALWAYS WONDERED — HOW DID HE GET RID OF THE COPPERS BACK IN BLIGHTY?

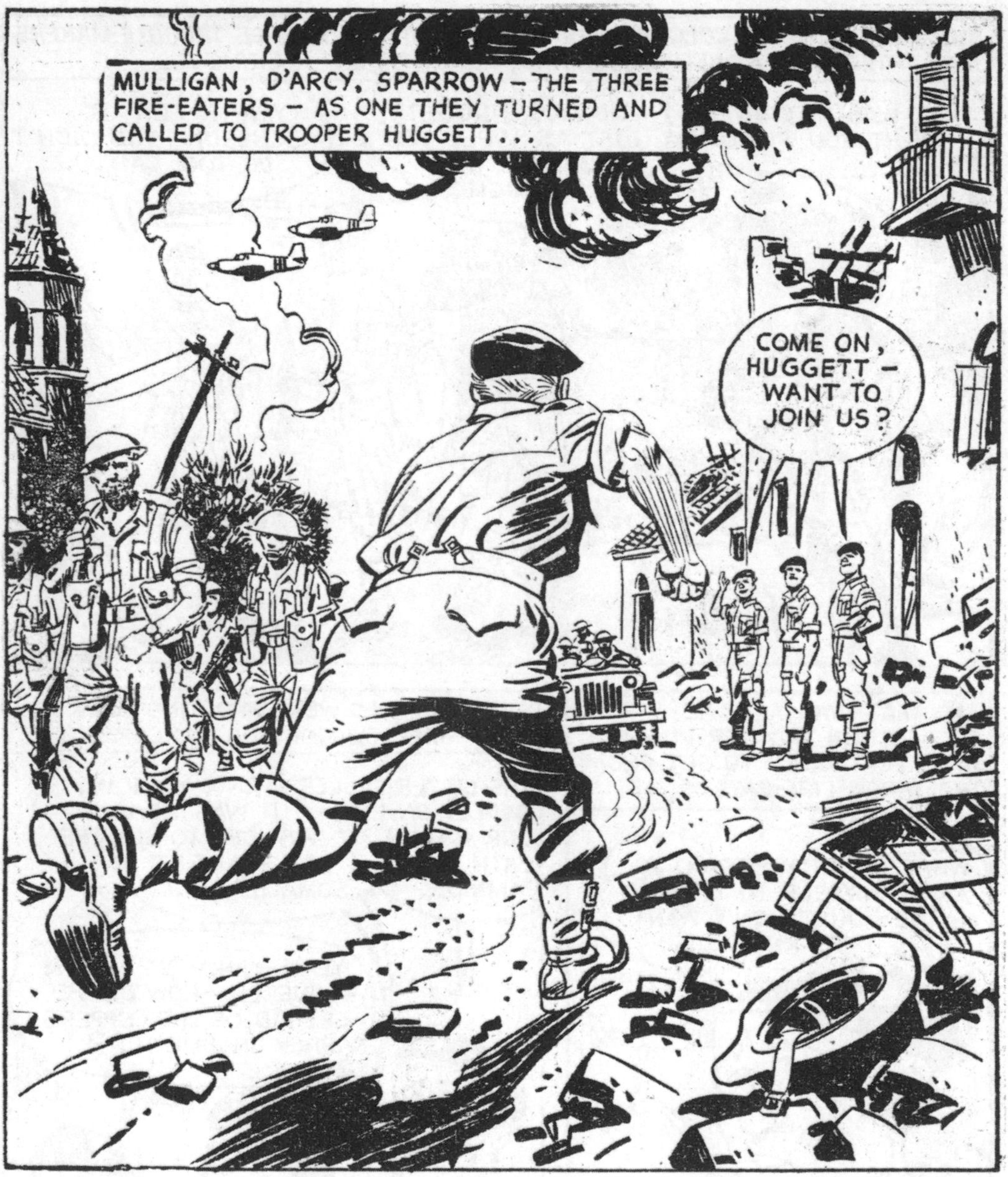
MULLIGAN, D'ARCY, SPARROW – THE THREE FIRE-EATERS – AS ONE THEY TURNED AND CALLED TO TROOPER HUGGETT...
COME ON, HUGGETT – WANT TO JOIN US?

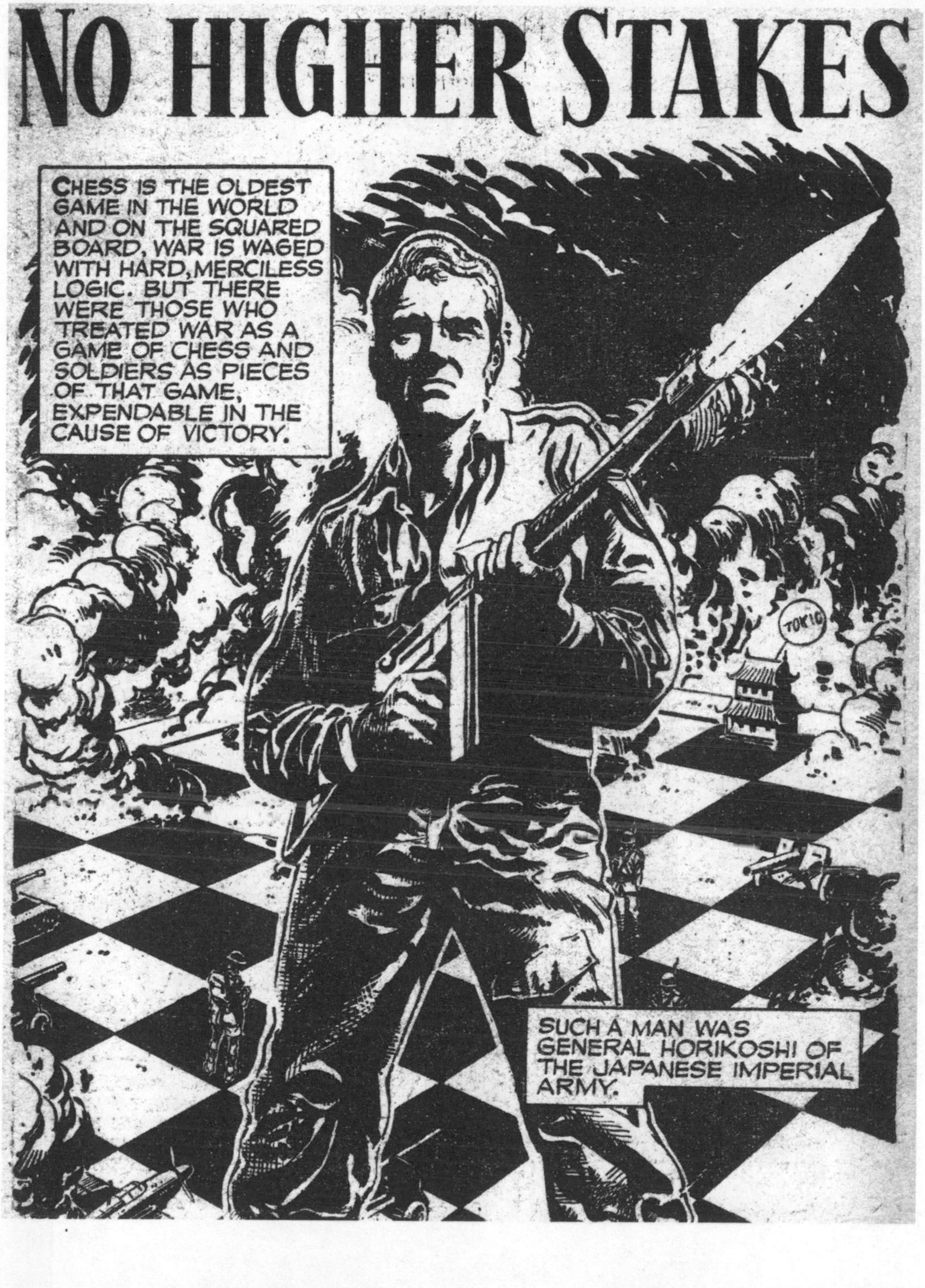
NO HIGHER STAKES
CHESS IS THE OLDEST GAME IN THE WORLD AND ON THE SQUARED BOARD, WAR IS WAGED WITH HARD, MERCILESS LOGIC. BUT THERE WERE THOSE WHO TREATED WAR AS A GAME OF CHESS AND SOLDIERS AS PIECES OF THAT GAME, EXPENDABLE IN THE CAUSE OF VICTORY.
TOKIO
SUCH A MAN WAS GENERAL HORIKOSHI OF THE JAPANESE IMPERIAL ARMY.

Chapter 1. The Chess Player

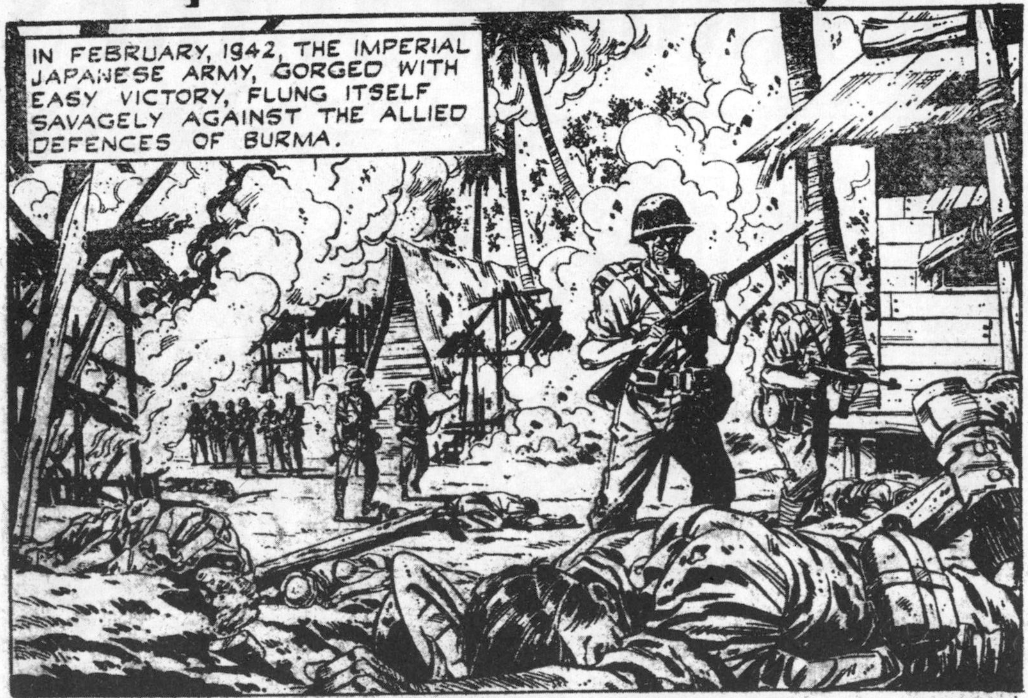
IN FEBRUARY, 1942, THE IMPERIAL JAPANESE ARMY, GORGED WITH EASY VICTORY, FLUNG ITSELF SAVAGELY AGAINST THE ALLIED DEFENCES OF BURMA.

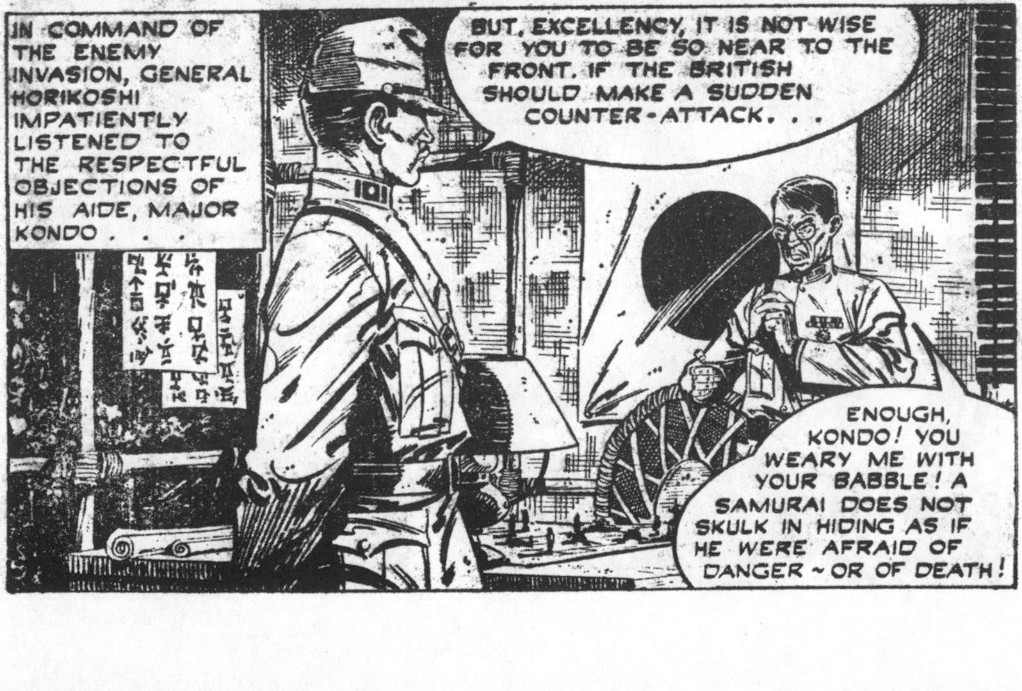
IN COMMAND OF THE ENEMY INVASION, GENERAL HORIKOSHI IMPATIENTLY LISTENED TO THE RESPECTFUL OBJECTIONS OF HIS AIDE, MAJOR KONDO . . .
BUT, EXCELLENCY, IT IS NOT WISE FOR YOU TO BE SO NEAR TO THE FRONT. IF THE BRITISH SHOULD MAKE A SUDDEN COUNTER-ATTACK. . .
ENOUGH, KONDO! YOU WEARY ME WITH YOUR BABBLE! A SAMURAI DOES NOT SKULK IN HIDING AS IF HE WERE AFRAID OF DANGER ~ OR OF DEATH!

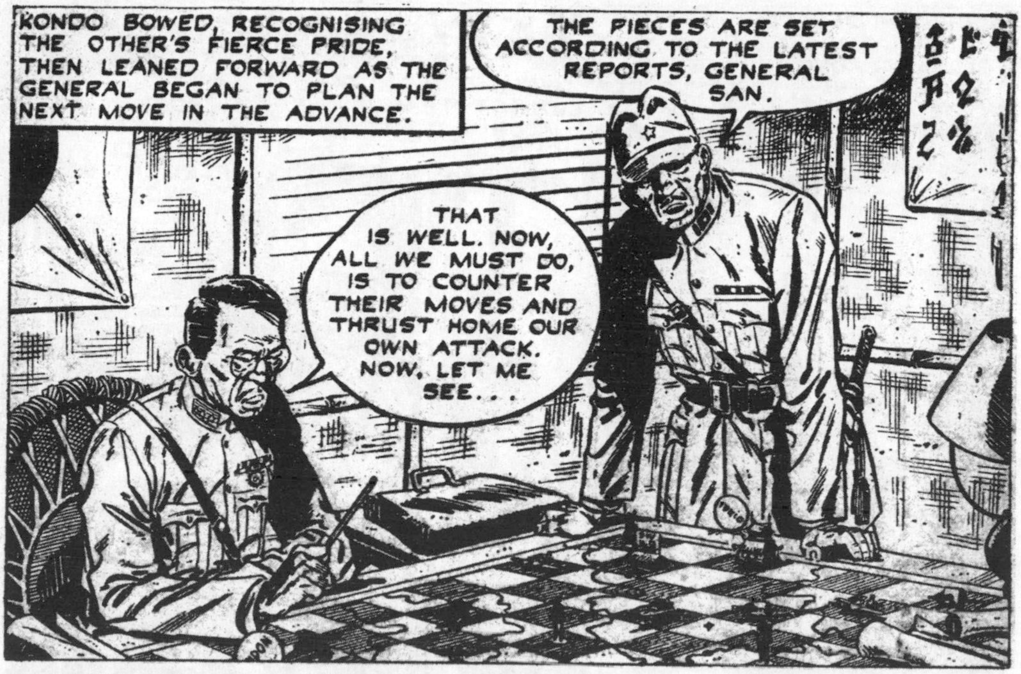
KONDO BOWED, RECOGNISING THE OTHER'S FIERCE PRIDE, THEN LEANED FORWARD AS THE GENERAL BEGAN TO PLAN THE NEXT MOVE IN THE ADVANCE.
THE PIECES ARE SET ACCORDING TO THE LATEST REPORTS, GENERAL SAN.
THAT IS WELL. NOW, ALL WE MUST DO, IS TO COUNTER THEIR MOVES AND THRUST HOME OUR OWN ATTACK. NOW, LET ME SEE...

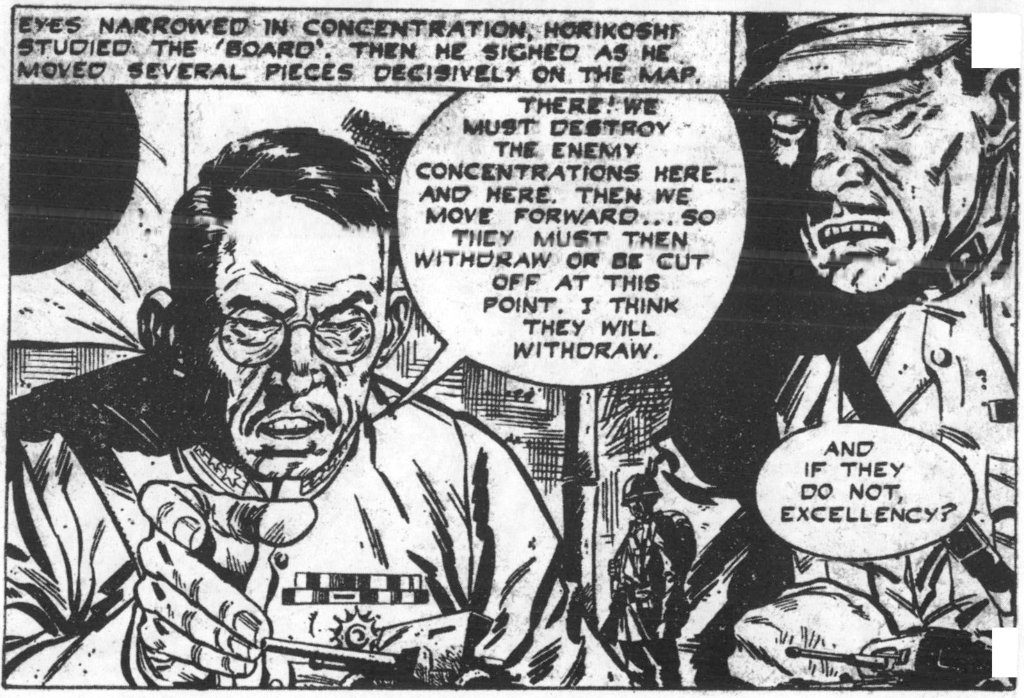
EYES NARROWED IN CONCENTRATION, HORIKOSHI STUDIED THE 'BOARD'. THEN HE SIGHED AS HE MOVED SEVERAL PIECES DECISIVELY ON THE MAP.
THERE! WE MUST DESTROY THE ENEMY CONCENTRATIONS HERE... AND HERE. THEN WE MOVE FORWARD... SO THEY MUST THEN WITHDRAW OR BE CUT OFF AT THIS POINT. I THINK THEY WILL WITHDRAW.
AND IF THEY DO NOT, EXCELLENCY?

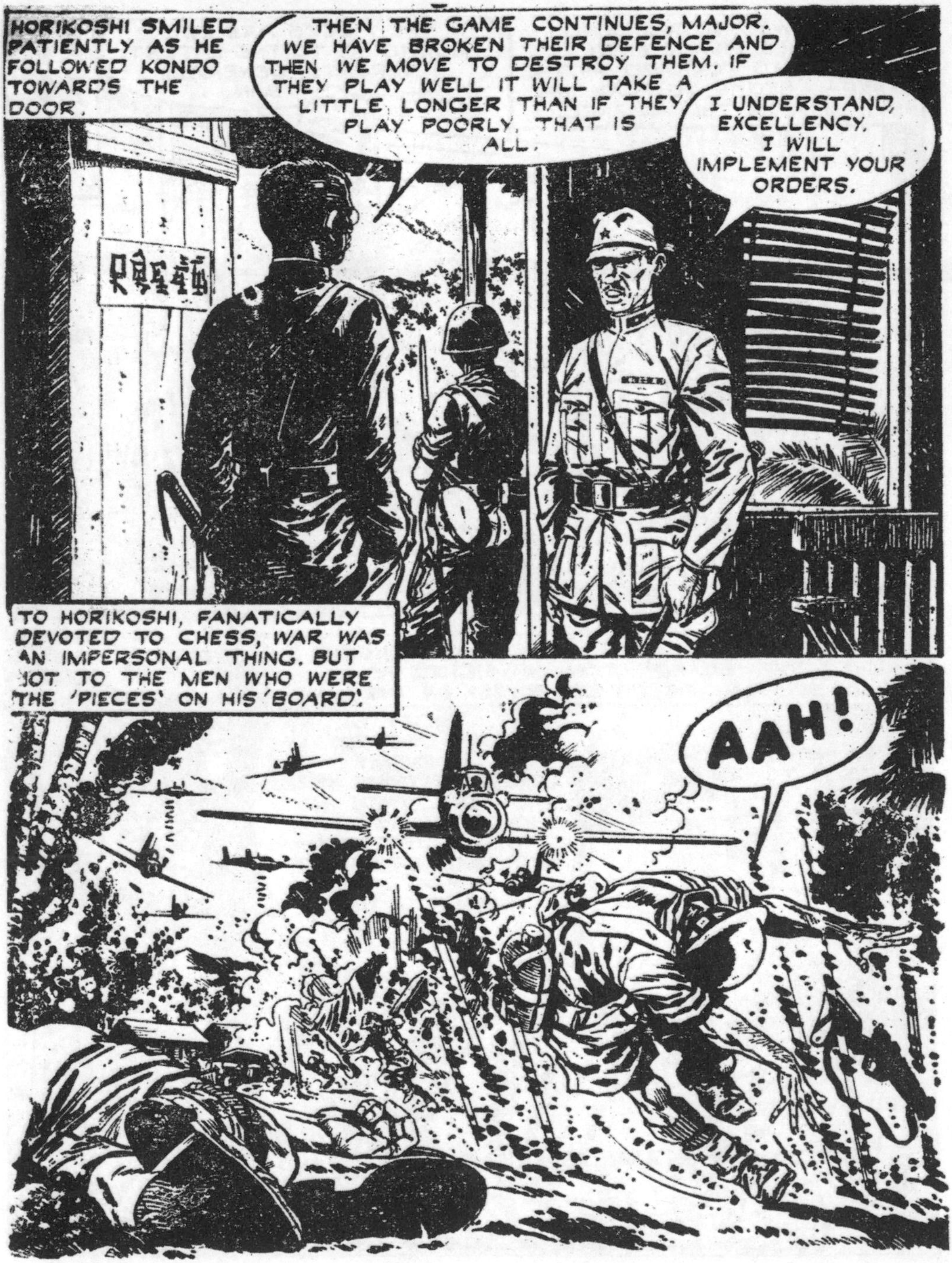
HORIKOSHI SMILED PATIENTLY AS HE FOLLOWED KONDO TOWARDS THE DOOR.
THEN THE GAME CONTINUES, MAJOR. WE HAVE BROKEN THEIR DEFENCE AND THEN WE MOVE TO DESTROY THEM. IF THEY PLAY WELL IT WILL TAKE A LITTLE LONGER THAN IF THEY PLAY POORLY, THAT IS ALL.
I UNDERSTAND, EXCELLENCY. I WILL IMPLEMENT YOUR ORDERS.
TO HORIKOSHI, FANATICALLY DEVOTED TO CHESS, WAR WAS AN IMPERSONAL THING. BUT NOT TO THE MEN WHO WERE THE 'PIECES' ON HIS 'BOARD'.
AAH!

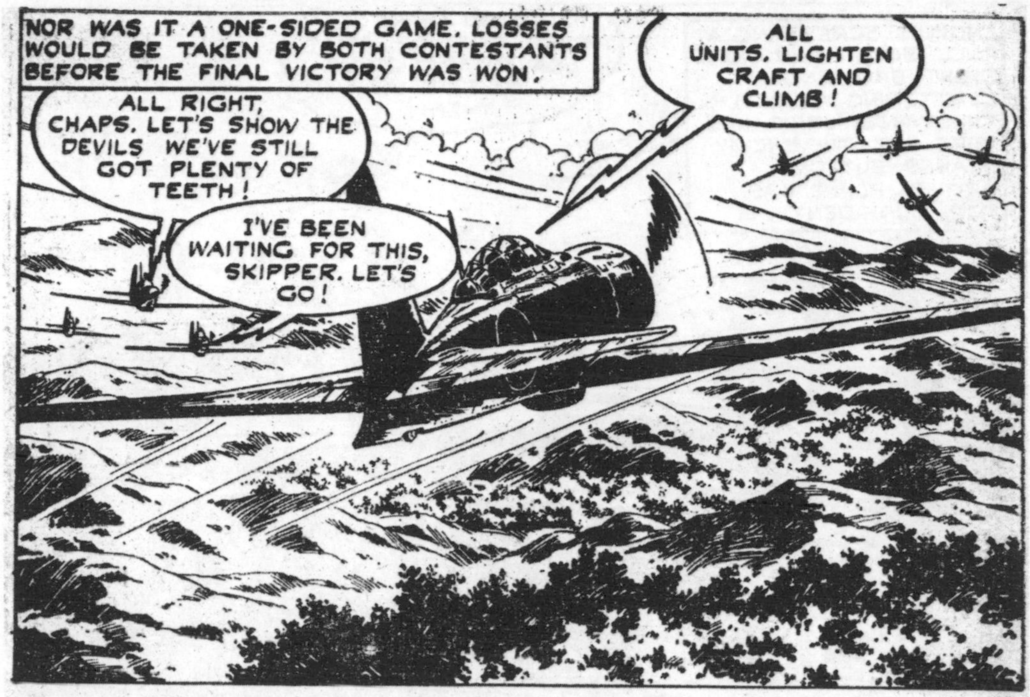
NOR WAS IT A ONE-SIDED GAME. LOSSES WOULD BE TAKEN BY BOTH CONTESTANTS BEFORE THE FINAL VICTORY WAS WON.
ALL RIGHT, CHAPS. LET'S SHOW THE DEVILS WE'VE STILL GOT PLENTY OF TEETH!
ALL UNITS. LIGHTEN CRAFT AND CLIMB!
I'VE BEEN WAITING FOR THIS, SKIPPER. LET'S GO!

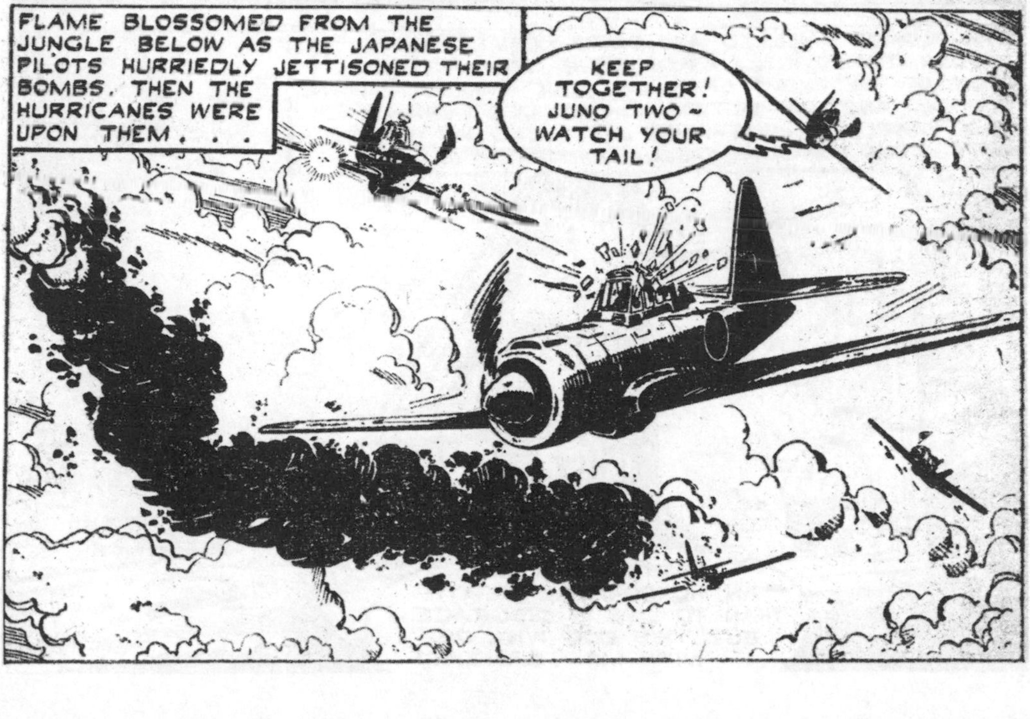
FLAME BLOSSOMED FROM THE JUNGLE BELOW AS THE JAPANESE PILOTS HURRIEDLY JETTISONED THEIR BOMBS. THEN THE HURRICANES WERE UPON THEM . . .
KEEP TOGETHER! JUNO TWO ~ WATCH YOUR TAIL!

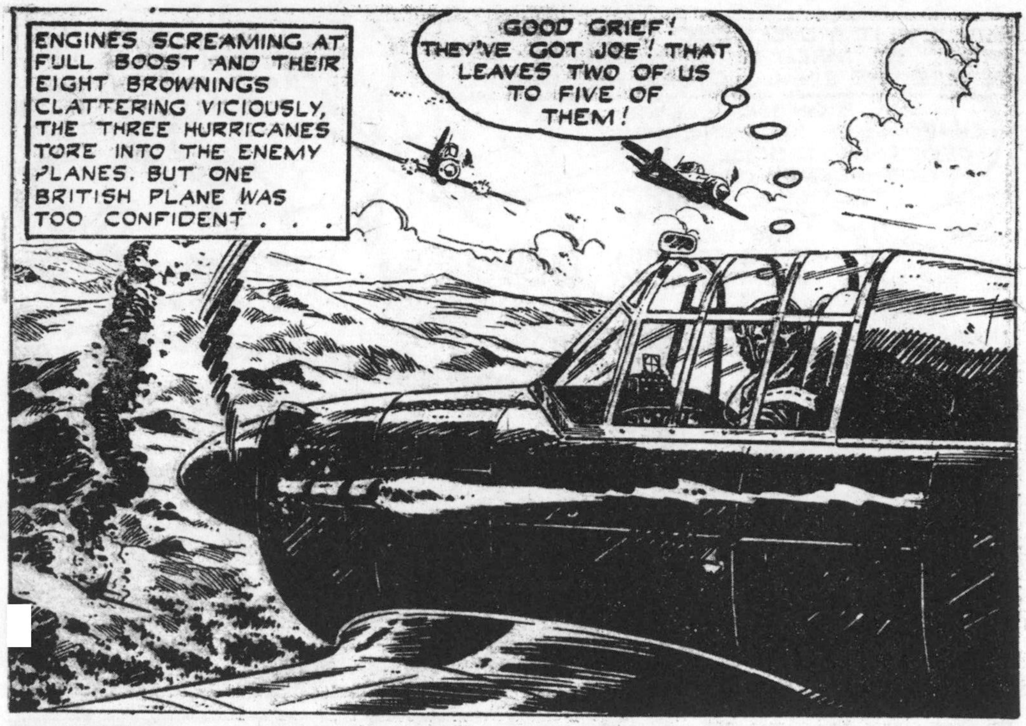
ENGINES SCREAMING AT FULL BOOST AND THEIR EIGHT BROWNINGS CLATTERING VICIOUSLY, THE THREE HURRICANES TORE INTO THE ENEMY PLANES. BUT ONE BRITISH PLANE WAS TOO CONFIDENT . . .
GOOD GRIEF! THEY'VE GOT JOE! THAT LEAVES TWO OF US TO FIVE OF THEM!

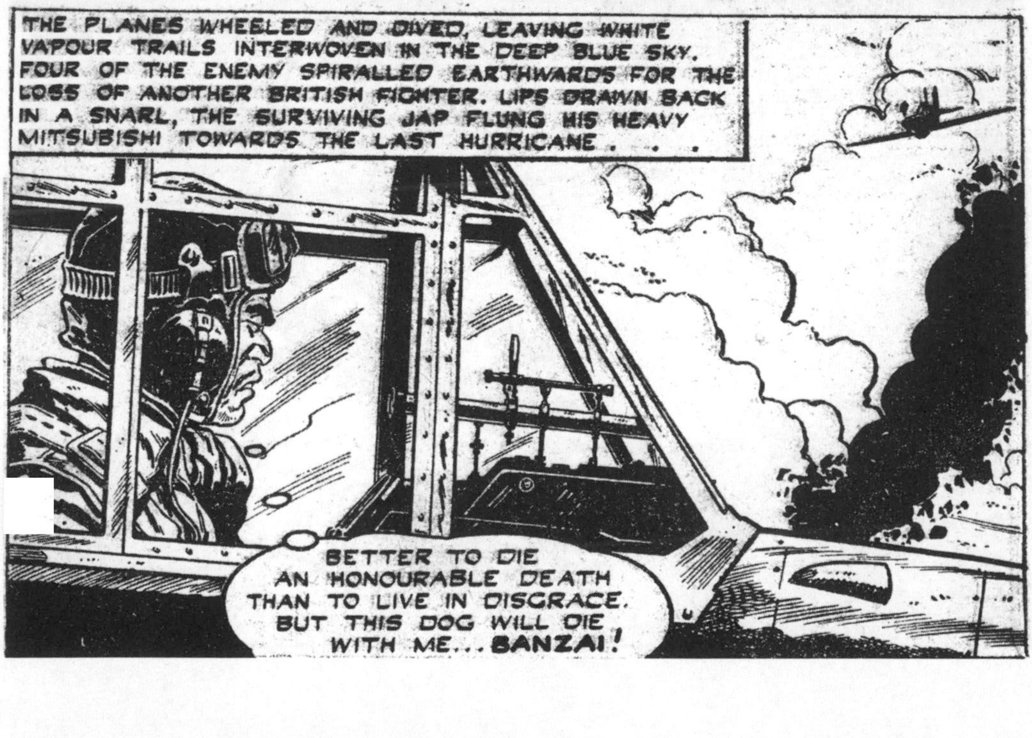
THE PLANES WHEELED AND DIVED, LEAVING WHITE VAPOUR TRAILS INTERWOVEN IN THE DEEP BLUE SKY. FOUR OF THE ENEMY SPIRALLED EARTHWARDS FOR THE LOSS OF ANOTHER BRITISH FIGHTER. LIPS DRAWN BACK IN A SNARL, THE SURVIVING JAP FLUNG HIS HEAVY MITSUBISHI TOWARDS THE LAST HURRICANE . . .
BETTER TO DIE AN HONOURABLE DEATH THAN TO LIVE IN DISGRACE. BUT THIS DOG WILL DIE WITH ME... BANZAI!

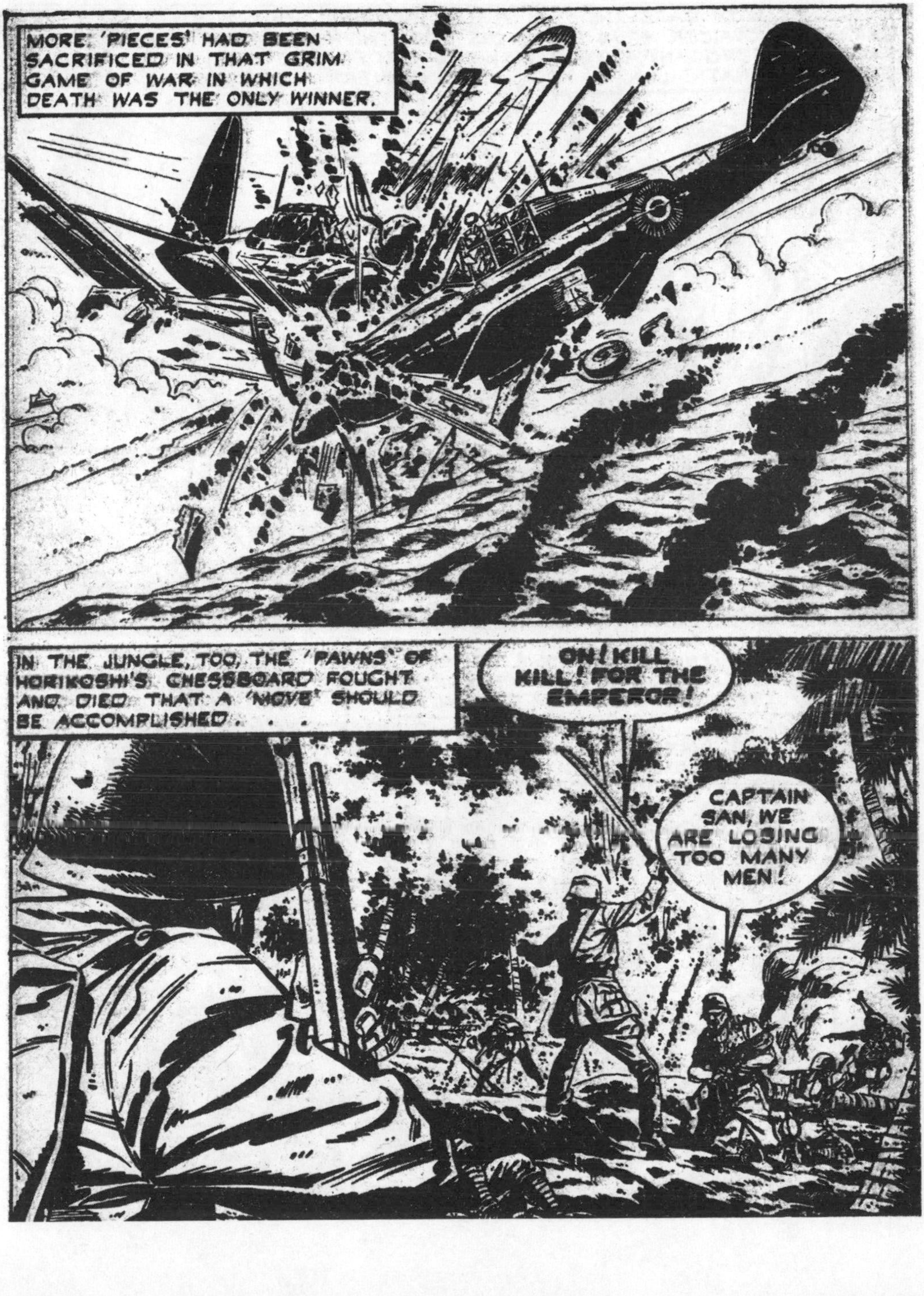
MORE 'PIECES' HAD BEEN SACRIFICED IN THAT GRIM GAME OF WAR IN WHICH DEATH WAS THE ONLY WINNER.
IN THE JUNGLE, TOO, THE 'PAWNS' OF HORIKOSHI'S CHESSBOARD FOUGHT AND DIED THAT A 'MOVE' SHOULD BE ACCOMPLISHED . . .
ON! KILL KILL! FOR THE EMPEROR!
CAPTAIN SAN, WE ARE LOSING TOO MANY MEN!

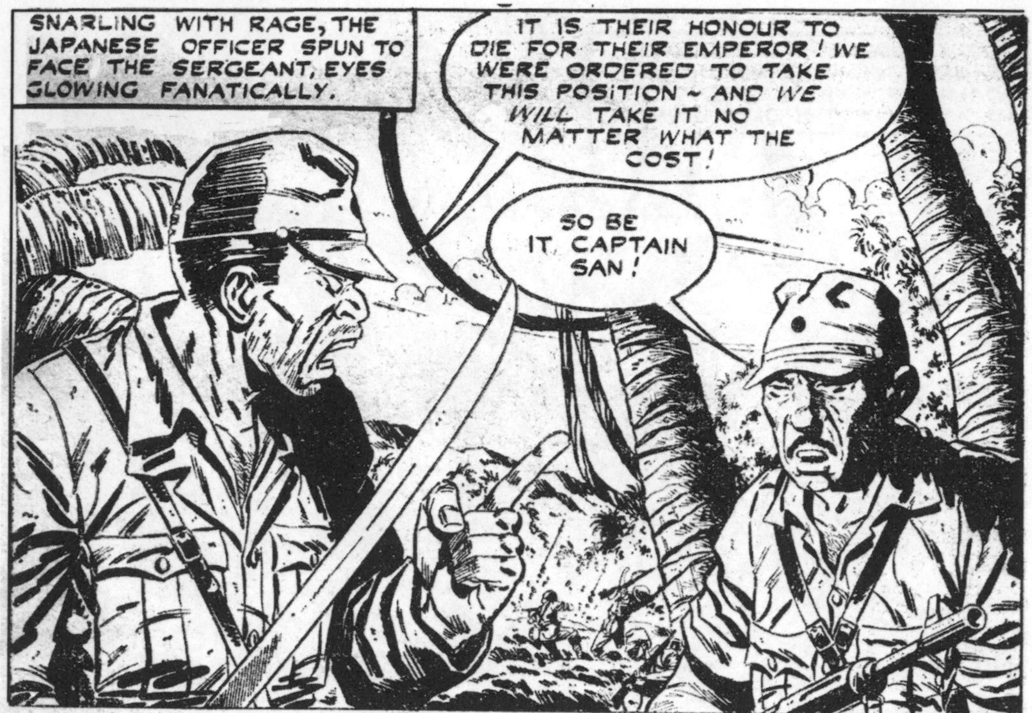
SNARLING WITH RAGE, THE JAPANESE OFFICER SPUN TO FACE THE SERGEANT, EYES GLOWING FANATICALLY.
IT IS THEIR HONOUR TO DIE FOR THEIR EMPEROR! WE WERE ORDERED TO TAKE THIS POSITION ~ AND WE WILL TAKE IT NO MATTER WHAT THE COST!
SO BE IT, CAPTAIN SAN!

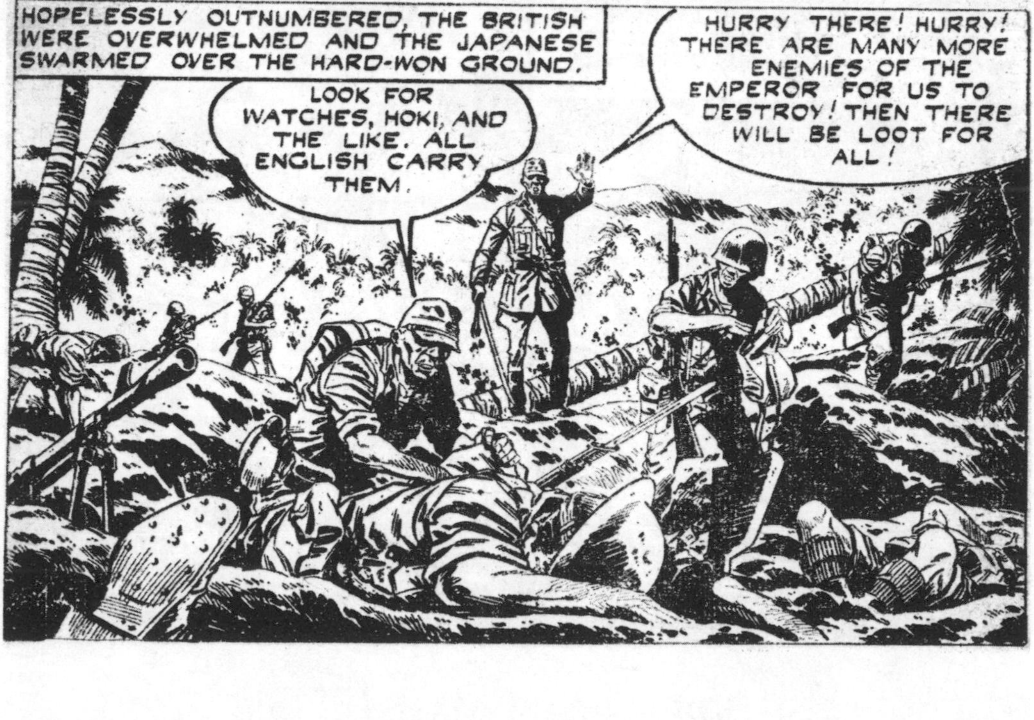
HOPELESSLY OUTNUMBERED, THE BRITISH WERE OVERWHELMED AND THE JAPANESE SWARMED OVER THE HARD-WON GROUND.
HURRY THERE! HURRY! THERE ARE MANY MORE ENEMIES OF THE EMPEROR FOR US TO DESTROY! THEN THERE WILL BE LOOT FOR ALL!
LOOK FOR WATCHES, HOKI, AND THE LIKE. ALL ENGLISH CARRY THEM.

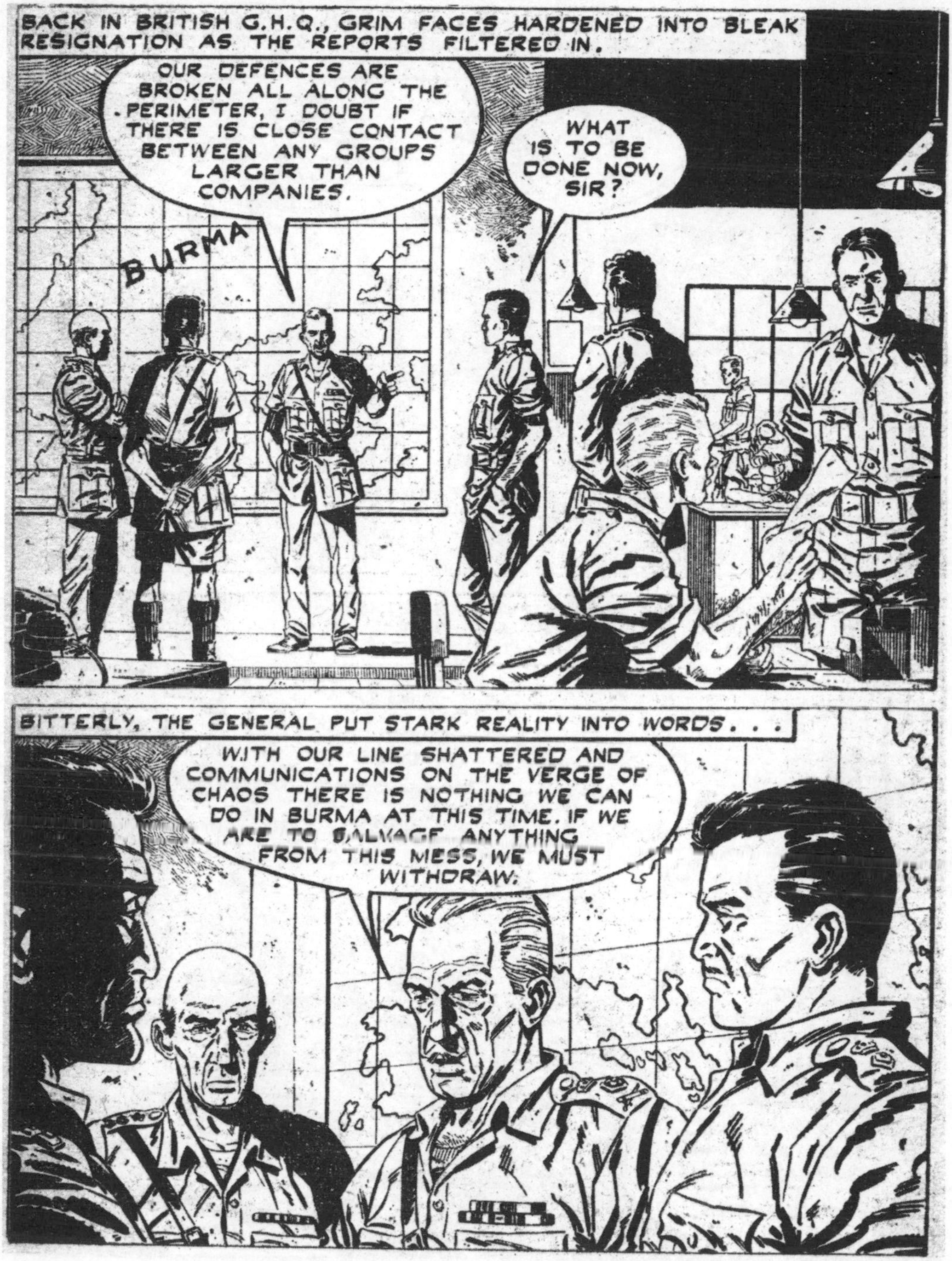
BACK IN BRITISH G.H.Q., GRIM FACES HARDENED INTO BLEAK RESIGNATION AS THE REPORTS FILTERED IN.
OUR DEFENCES ARE BROKEN ALL ALONG THE PERIMETER, I DOUBT IF THERE IS CLOSE CONTACT BETWEEN ANY GROUPS LARGER THAN COMPANIES.
WHAT IS TO BE DONE NOW, SIR?
BURMA
BITTERLY, THE GENERAL PUT STARK REALITY INTO WORDS. . .
WITH OUR LINE SHATTERED AND COMMUNICATIONS ON THE VERGE OF CHAOS THERE IS NOTHING WE CAN DO IN BURMA AT THIS TIME. IF WE ARE TO SALVAGE ANYTHING FROM THIS MESS, WE MUST WITHDRAW.

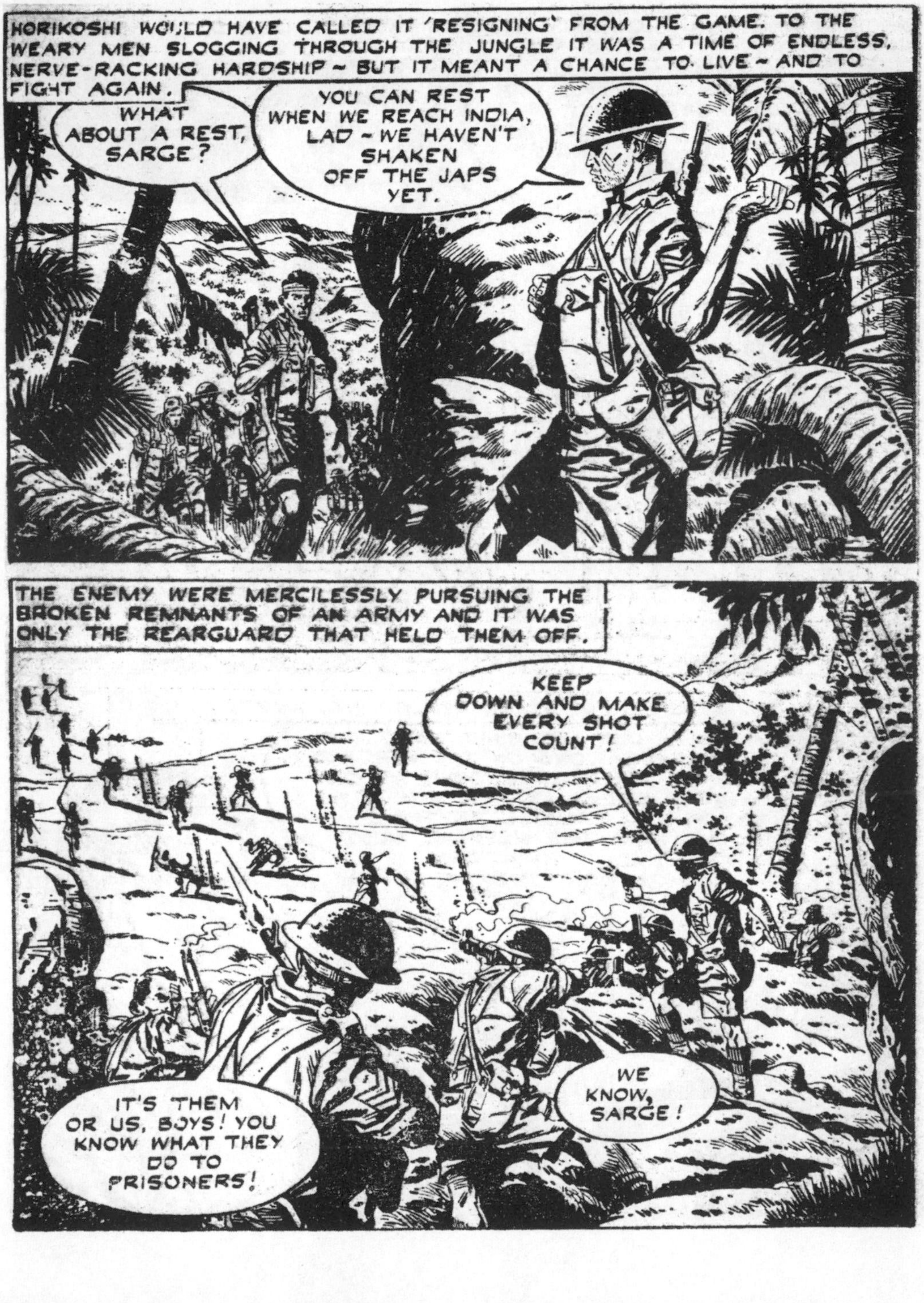
HORIKOSHI WOULD HAVE CALLED IT 'RESIGNING' FROM THE GAME. TO THE WEARY MEN SLOGGING THROUGH THE JUNGLE IT WAS A TIME OF ENDLESS, NERVE-RACKING HARDSHIP ~ BUT IT MEANT A CHANCE TO LIVE ~ AND TO FIGHT AGAIN.
WHAT ABOUT A REST, SARGE?
YOU CAN REST WHEN WE REACH INDIA, LAD ~ WE HAVEN'T SHAKEN OFF THE JAPS YET.
THE ENEMY WERE MERCILESSLY PURSUING THE BROKEN REMNANTS OF AN ARMY AND IT WAS ONLY THE REARGUARD THAT HELD THEM OFF.
KEEP DOWN AND MAKE EVERY SHOT COUNT!
IT'S THEM OR US, BOYS! YOU KNOW WHAT THEY DO TO PRISONERS!
WE KNOW, SARGE!

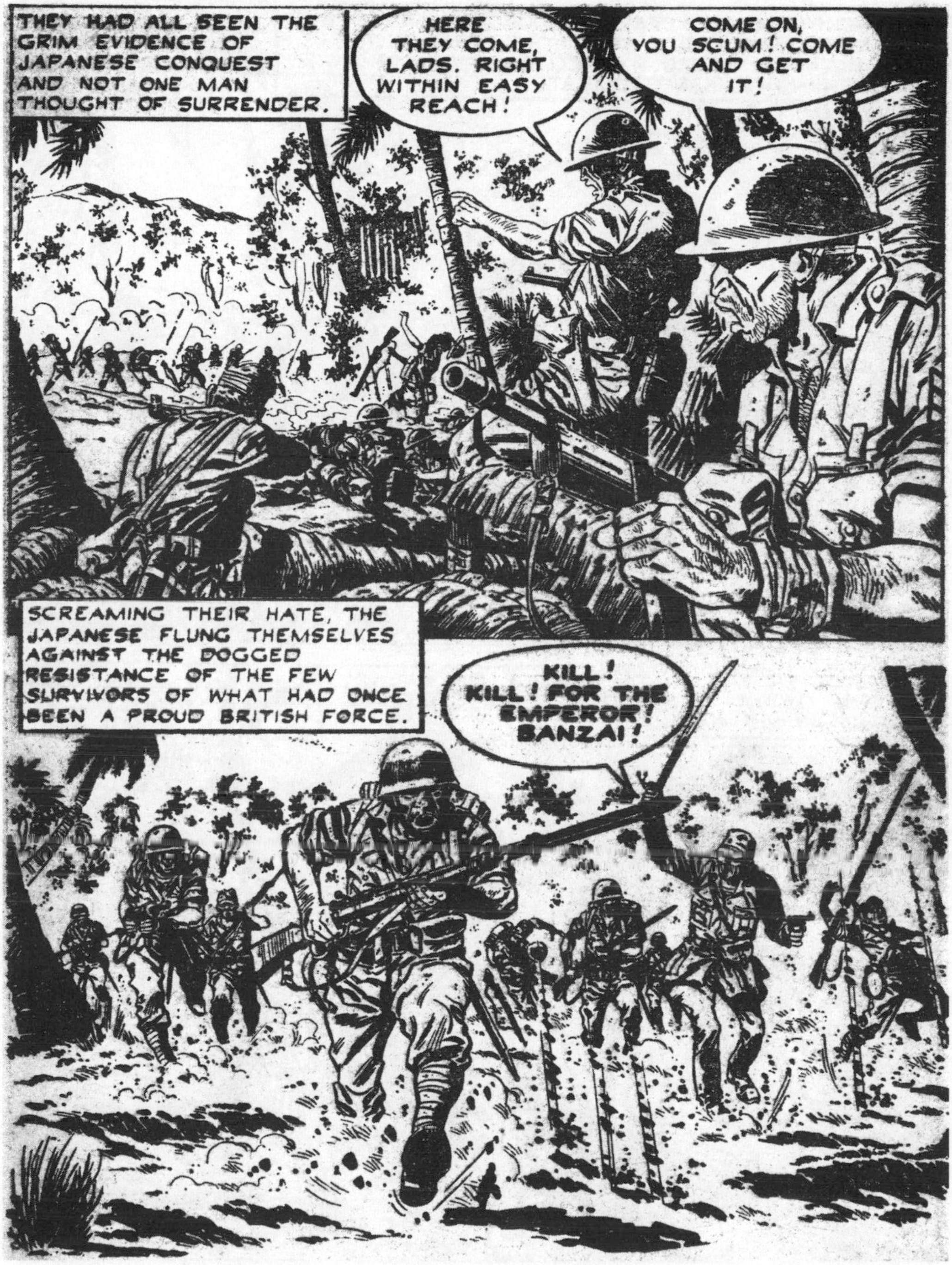
THEY HAD ALL SEEN THE GRIM EVIDENCE OF JAPANESE CONQUEST AND NOT ONE MAN THOUGHT OF SURRENDER.
HERE THEY COME, LADS. RIGHT WITHIN EASY REACH!
COME ON, YOU SCUM! COME AND GET IT!
SCREAMING THEIR HATE, THE JAPANESE FLUNG THEMSELVES AGAINST THE DOGGED RESISTANCE OF THE FEW SURVIVORS OF WHAT HAD ONCE BEEN A PROUD BRITISH FORCE.
KILL! KILL! FOR THE EMPEROR! BANZAI!

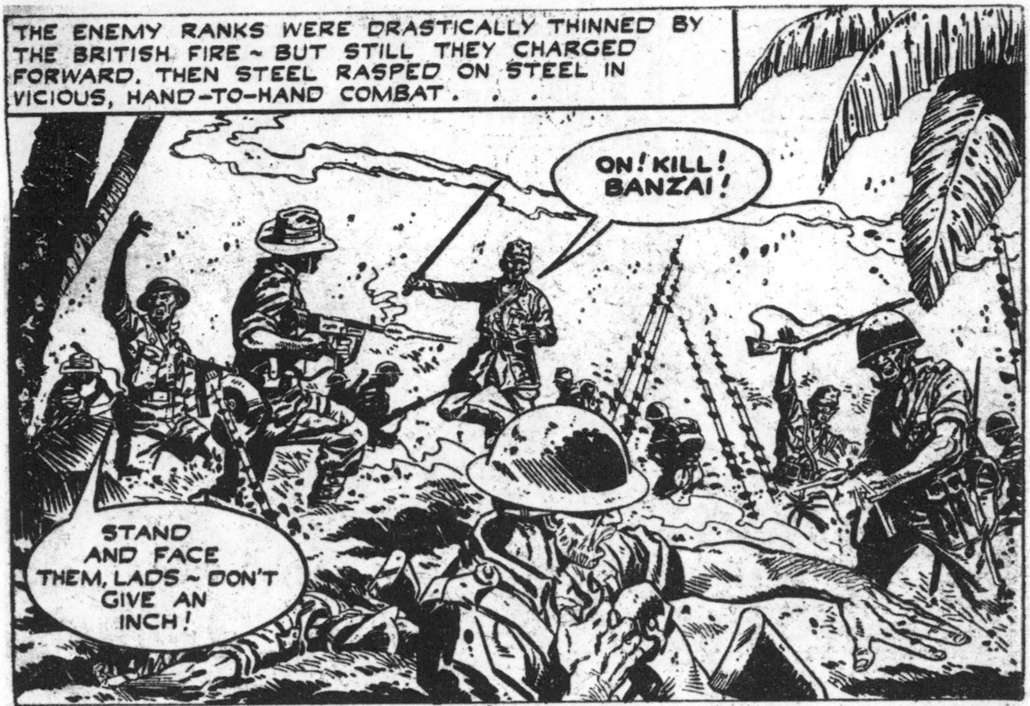
THE ENEMY RANKS WERE DRASTICALLY THINNED BY THE BRITISH FIRE ~ BUT STILL THEY CHARGED FORWARD. THEN STEEL RASPED ON STEEL IN VICIOUS, HAND-TO-HAND COMBAT . . .
ON! KILL! BANZAI!
STAND AND FACE THEM, LADS ~ DON'T GIVE AN INCH!

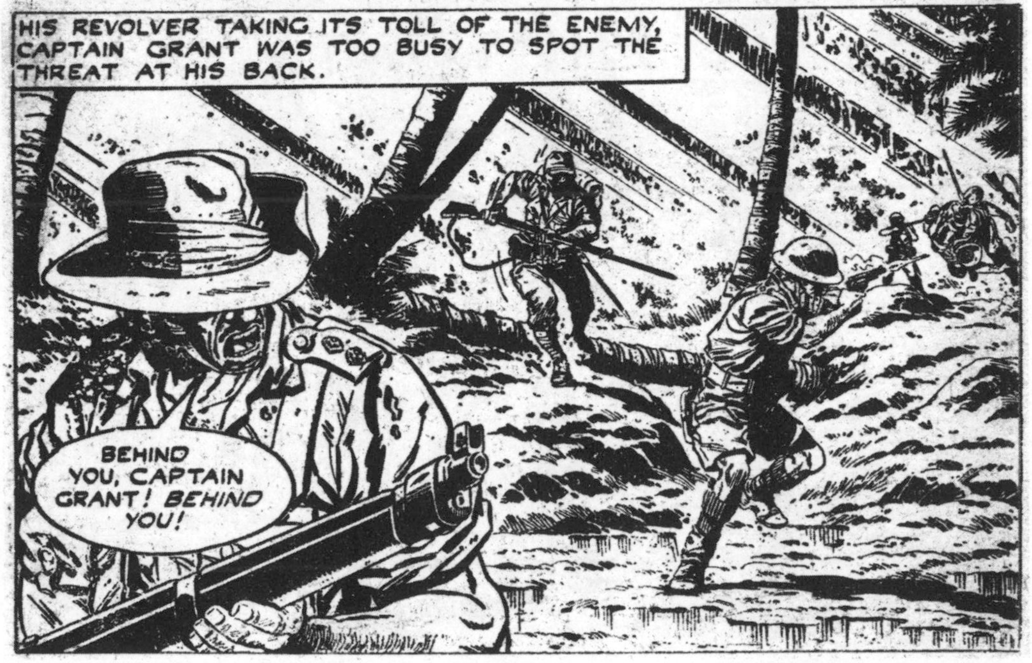
HIS REVOLVER TAKING ITS TOLL OF THE ENEMY, CAPTAIN GRANT WAS TOO BUSY TO SPOT THE THREAT AT HIS BACK.
BEHIND YOU, CAPTAIN GRANT! BEHIND YOU!

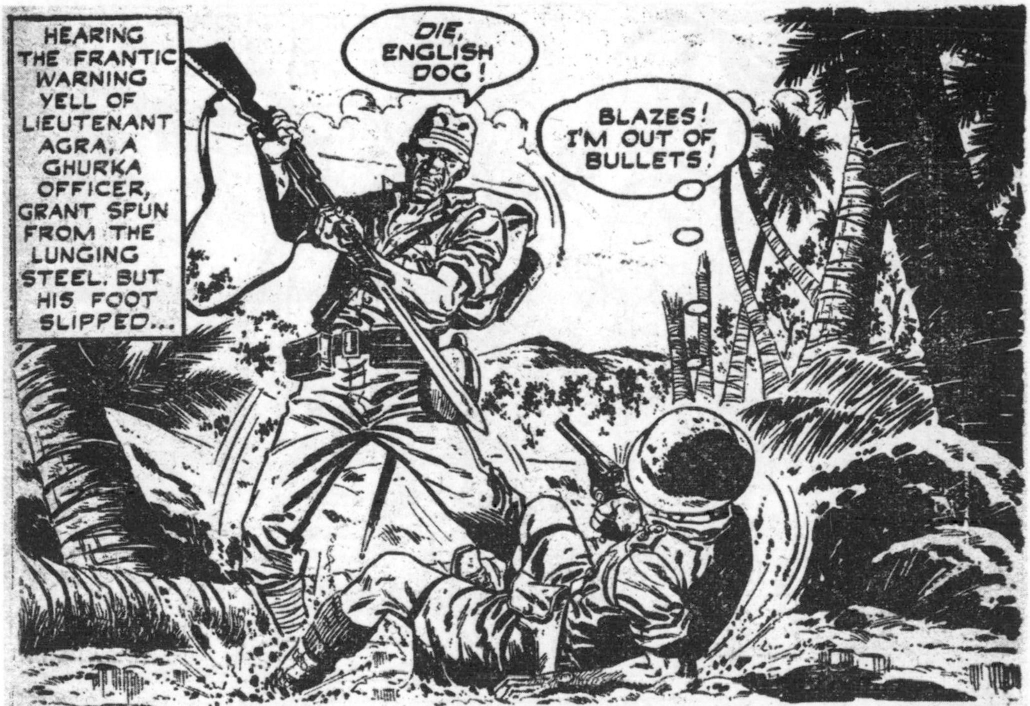
HEARING THE FRANTIC WARNING YELL OF LIEUTENANT AGRA, A GHURKA OFFICER, GRANT SPUN FROM THE LUNGING STEEL. BUT HIS FOOT SLIPPED...
DIE, ENGLISH DOG!
BLAZES! I'M OUT OF BULLETS!

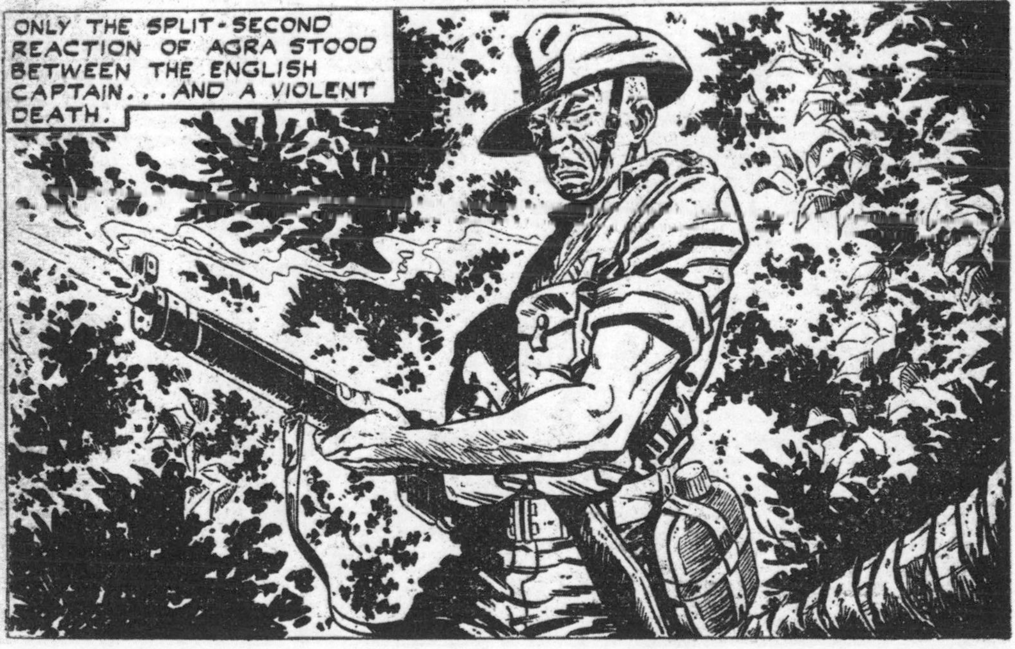
ONLY THE SPLIT-SECOND REACTION OF AGRA STOOD BETWEEN THE ENGLISH CAPTAIN. . .AND A VIOLENT DEATH.

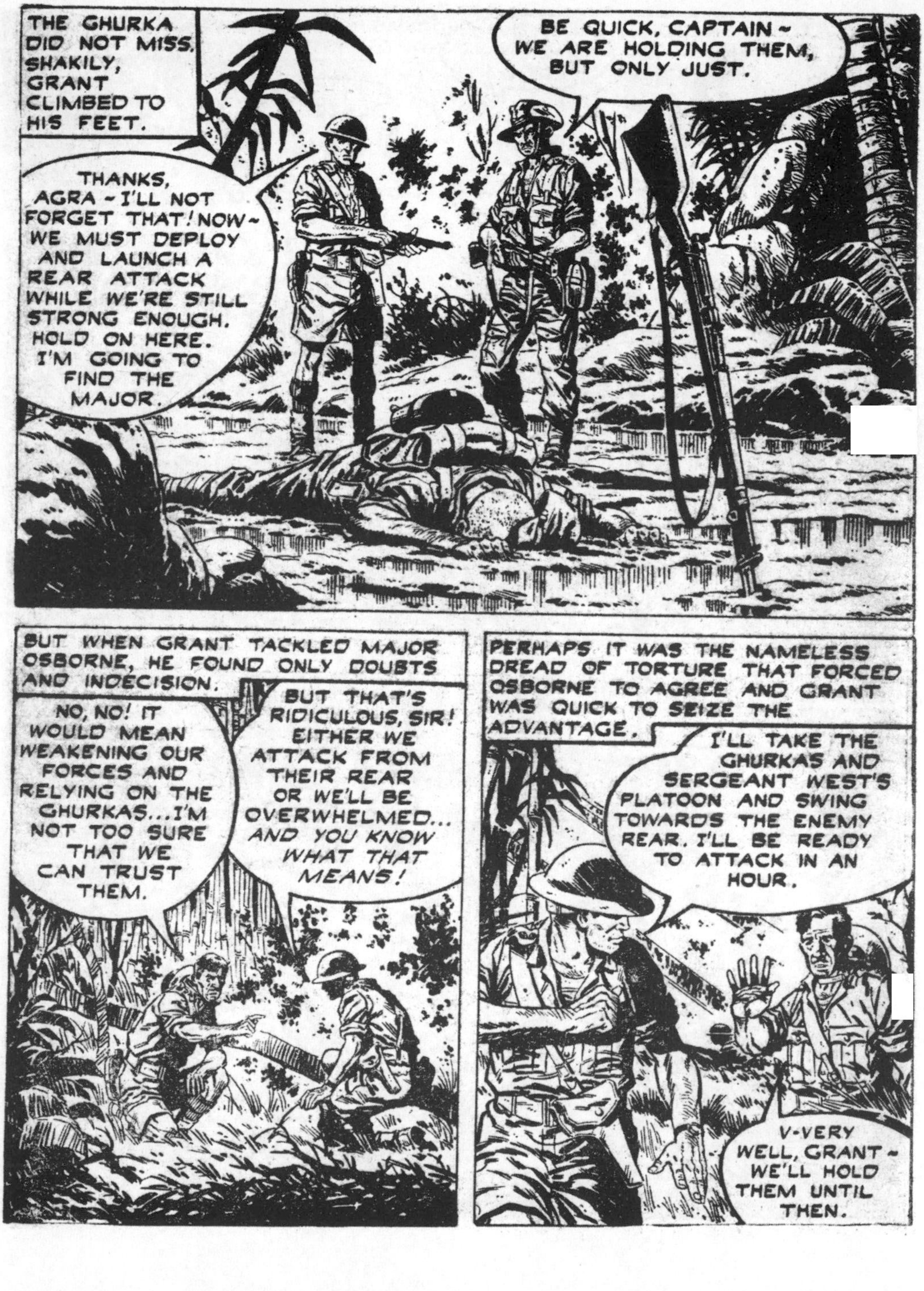
THE GHURKA DID NOT MISS. SHAKILY, GRANT CLIMBED TO HIS FEET.
BE QUICK, CAPTAIN ~ WE ARE HOLDING THEM, BUT ONLY JUST.
THANKS, AGRA ~ I'LL NOT FORGET THAT! NOW ~ WE MUST DEPLOY AND LAUNCH A REAR ATTACK WHILE WE'RE STILL STRONG ENOUGH. HOLD ON HERE. I'M GOING TO FIND THE MAJOR.
BUT WHEN GRANT TACKLED MAJOR OSBORNE, HE FOUND ONLY DOUBTS AND INDECISION.
NO, NO! IT WOULD MEAN WEAKENING OUR FORCES AND RELYING ON THE GHURKAS...I'M NOT TOO SURE THAT WE CAN TRUST THEM.
BUT THAT'S RIDICULOUS, SIR! EITHER WE ATTACK FROM THEIR REAR OR WE'LL BE OVERWHELMED... AND YOU KNOW WHAT THAT MEANS!
PERHAPS IT WAS THE NAMELESS DREAD OF TORTURE THAT FORCED OSBORNE TO AGREE AND GRANT WAS QUICK TO SEIZE THE ADVANTAGE.
I'LL TAKE THE GHURKAS AND SERGEANT WEST'S PLATOON AND SWING TOWARDS THE ENEMY REAR. I'LL BE READY TO ATTACK IN AN HOUR.
V-VERY WELL, GRANT ~ WE'LL HOLD THEM UNTIL THEN.

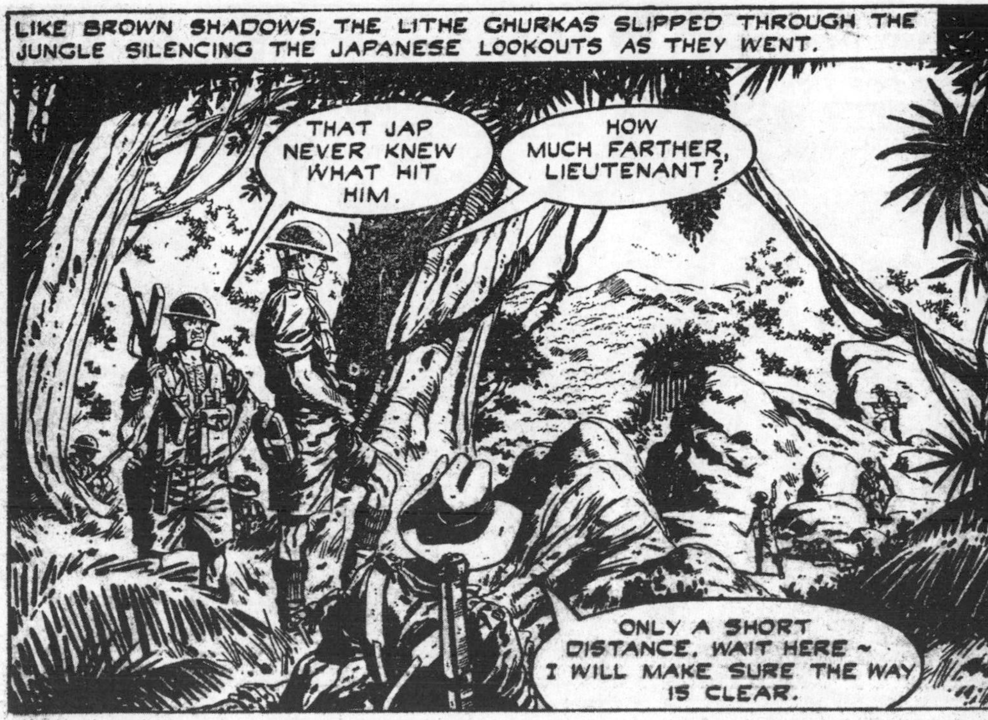
LIKE BROWN SHADOWS, THE LITHE GHURKAS SLIPPED THROUGH THE JUNGLE SILENCING THE JAPANESE LOOKOUTS AS THEY WENT.
THAT JAP NEVER KNEW WHAT HIT HIM.
HOW MUCH FARTHER, LIEUTENANT?
ONLY A SHORT DISTANCE. WAIT HERE ~ I WILL MAKE SURE THE WAY IS CLEAR.

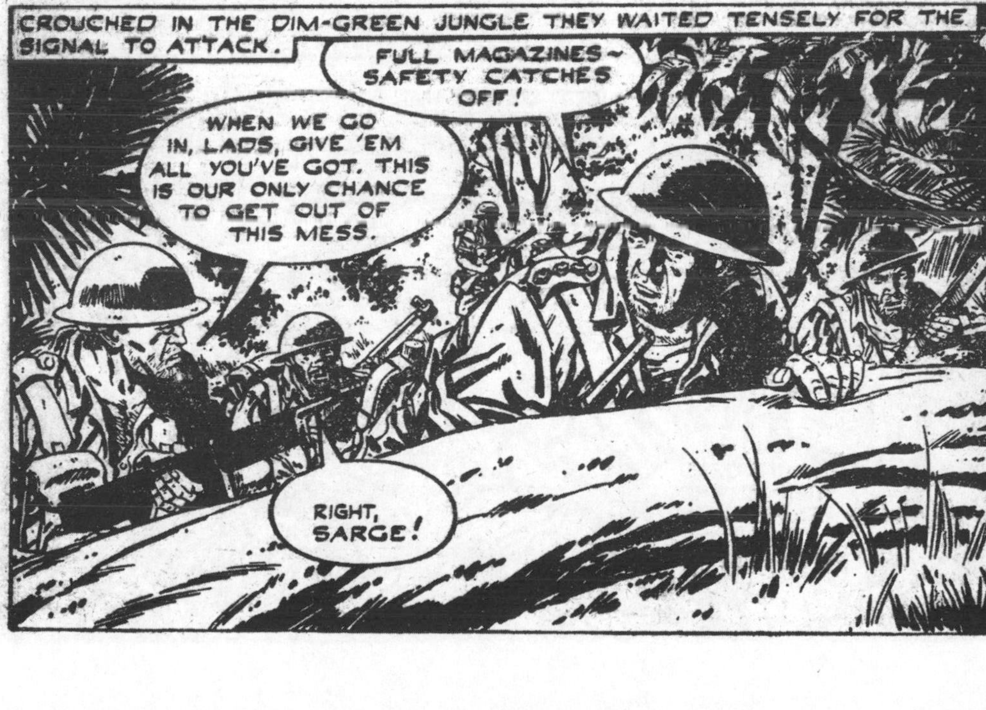
CROUCHED IN THE DIM-GREEN JUNGLE THEY WAITED TENSELY FOR THE SIGNAL TO ATTACK.
FULL MAGAZINES ~ SAFETY CATCHES OFF!
WHEN WE GO IN, LADS, GIVE 'EM ALL YOU'VE GOT. THIS IS OUR ONLY CHANCE TO GET OUT OF THIS MESS.
RIGHT, SARGE!

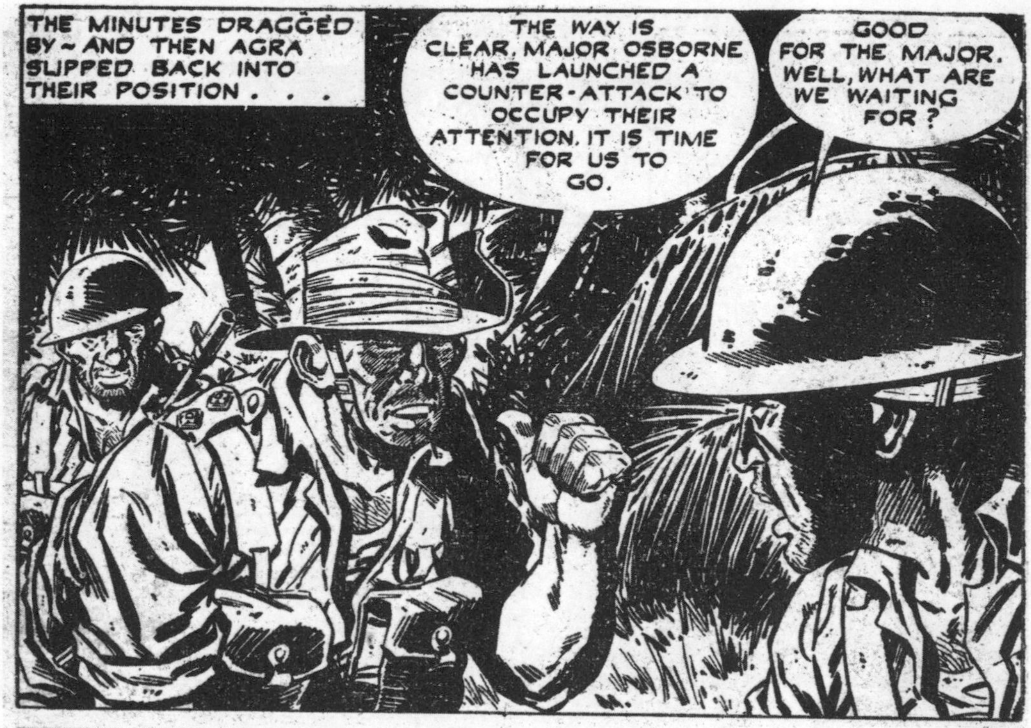
THE MINUTES DRAGGED BY ~ AND THEN AGRA SLIPPED BACK INTO THEIR POSITION . . .
THE WAY IS CLEAR. MAJOR OSBORNE HAS LAUNCHED A COUNTER-ATTACK TO OCCUPY THEIR ATTENTION. IT IS TIME FOR US TO GO.
GOOD FOR THE MAJOR. WELL, WHAT ARE WE WAITING FOR?

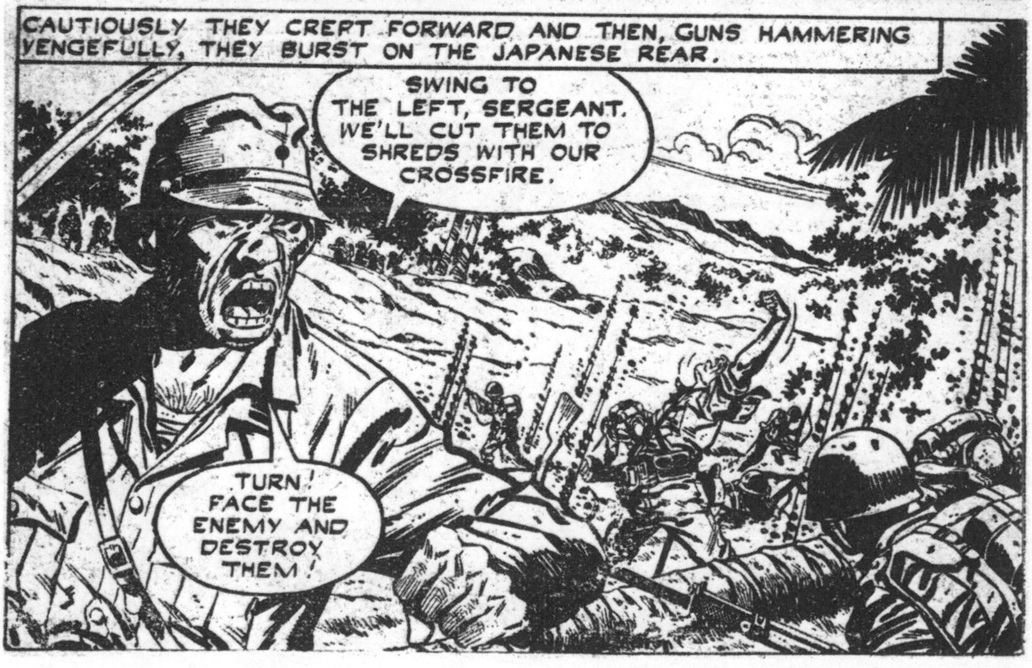
CAUTIOUSLY THEY CREPT FORWARD AND THEN, GUNS HAMMERING VENGEFULLY, THEY BURST ON THE JAPANESE REAR.
SWING TO THE LEFT, SERGEANT. WE'LL CUT THEM TO SHREDS WITH OUR CROSSFIRE.
TURN! FACE THE ENEMY AND DESTROY THEM!

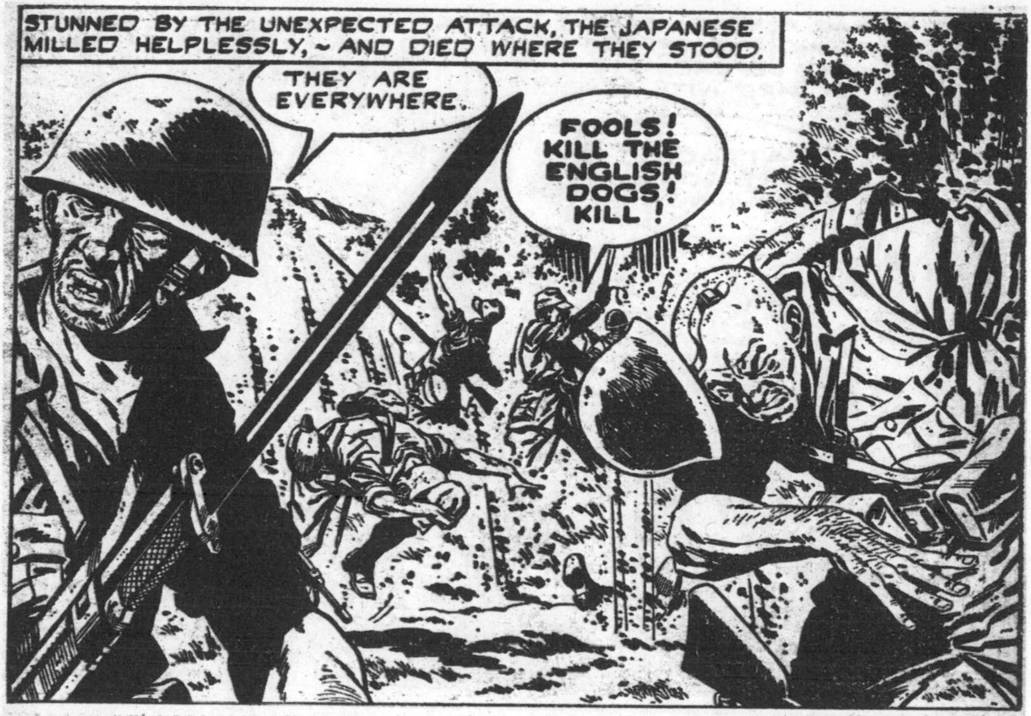
STUNNED BY THE UNEXPECTED ATTACK, THE JAPANESE MILLED HELPLESSLY, ~ AND DIED WHERE THEY STOOD.
THEY ARE EVERYWHERE.
FOOLS! KILL THE ENGLISH DOGS! KILL!

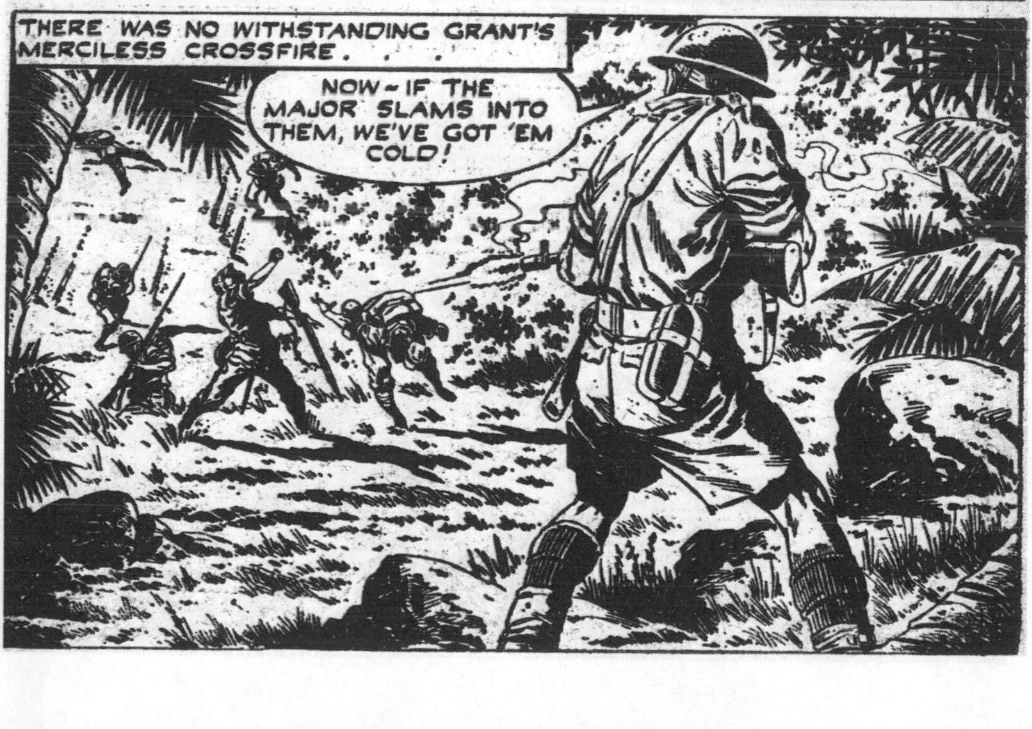
THERE WAS NO WITHSTANDING GRANT'S MERCILESS CROSSFIRE . . .
NOW ~ IF THE MAJOR SLAMS INTO THEM, WE'VE GOT 'EM COLD!

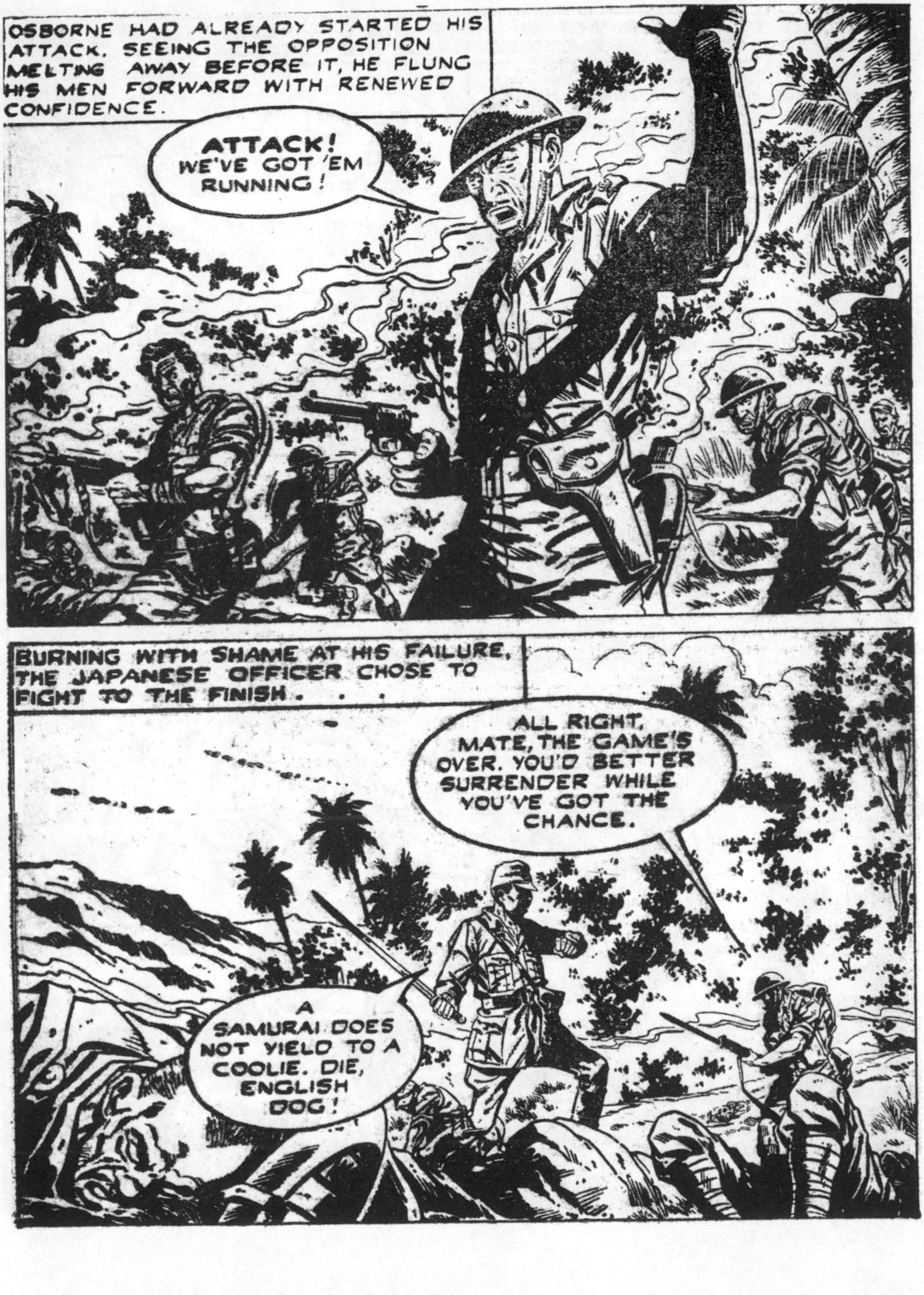
OSBORNE HAD ALREADY STARTED HIS ATTACK. SEEING THE OPPOSITION MELTING AWAY BEFORE IT, HE FLUNG HIS MEN FORWARD WITH RENEWED CONFIDENCE.
ATTACK! WE'VE GOT 'EM RUNNING!
BURNING WITH SHAME AT HIS FAILURE, THE JAPANESE OFFICER CHOSE TO FIGHT TO THE FINISH . . .
ALL RIGHT, MATE, THE GAME'S OVER. YOU'D BETTER SURRENDER WHILE YOU'VE GOT THE CHANCE.
A SAMURAI DOES NOT YIELD TO A COOLIE. DIE, ENGLISH DOG!

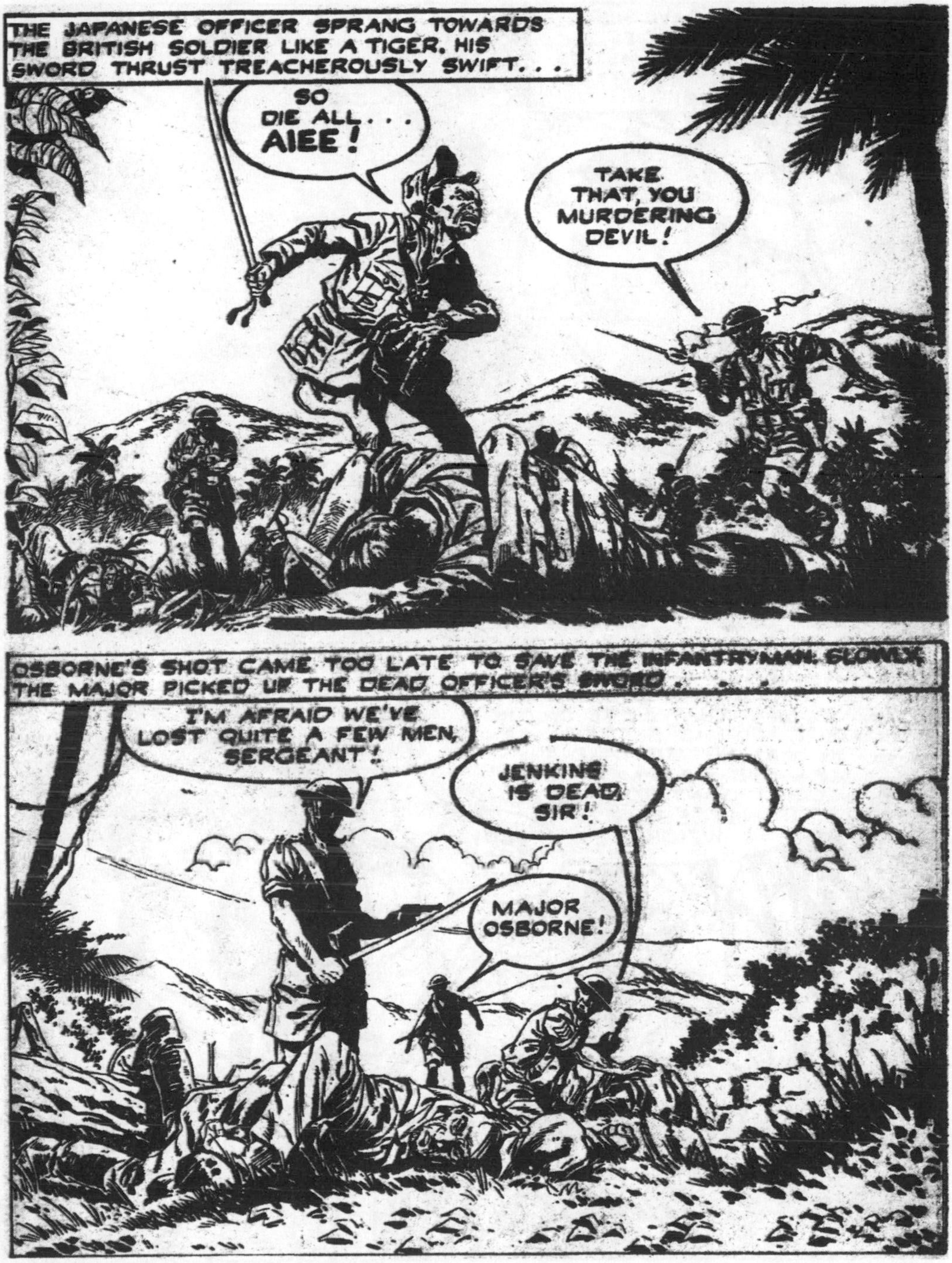
THE JAPANESE OFFICER SPRANG TOWARDS THE BRITISH SOLDIER LIKE A TIGER. HIS SWORD THRUST TREACHEROUSLY SWIFT. . .
SO DIE ALL. . . AIEE!
TAKE THAT, YOU MURDERING DEVIL!
OSBORNE'S SHOT CAME TOO LATE TO SAVE THE INFANTRYMAN. SLOWLY THE MAJOR PICKED UP THE DEAD OFFICER'S SWORD . . .
I'M AFRAID WE'VE LOST QUITE A FEW MEN, SERGEANT!
JENKINS IS DEAD SIR!
MAJOR OSBORNE!

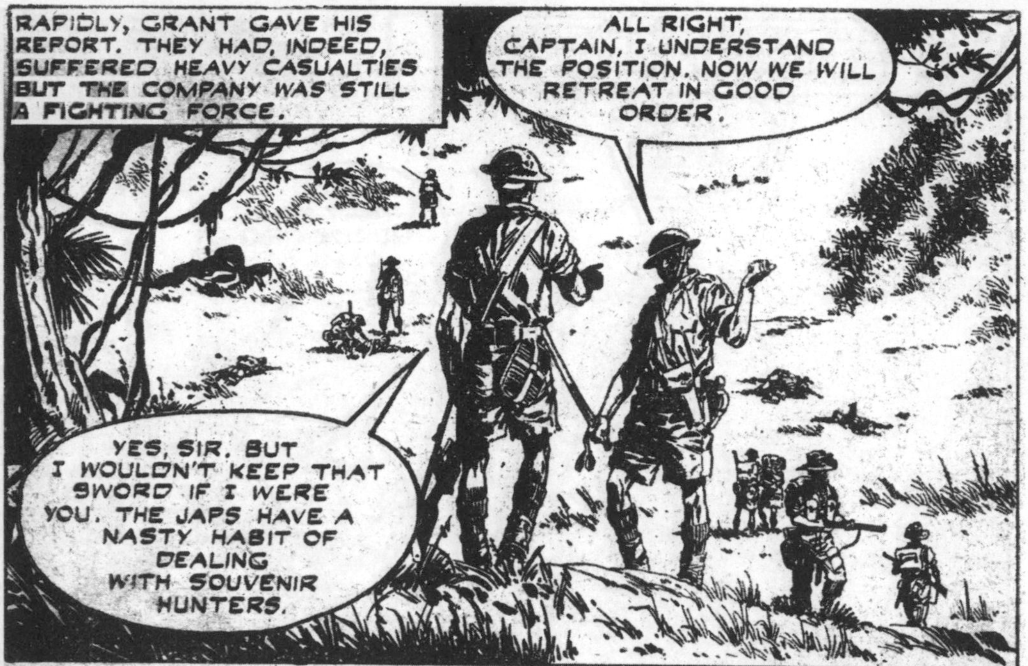
RAPIDLY, GRANT GAVE HIS REPORT. THEY HAD, INDEED, SUFFERED HEAVY CASUALTIES BUT THE COMPANY WAS STILL A FIGHTING FORCE.
ALL RIGHT, CAPTAIN, I UNDERSTAND THE POSITION. NOW WE WILL RETREAT IN GOOD ORDER.
YES, SIR. BUT I WOULDN'T KEEP THAT SWORD IF I WERE YOU. THE JAPS HAVE A NASTY HABIT OF DEALING WITH SOUVENIR HUNTERS.

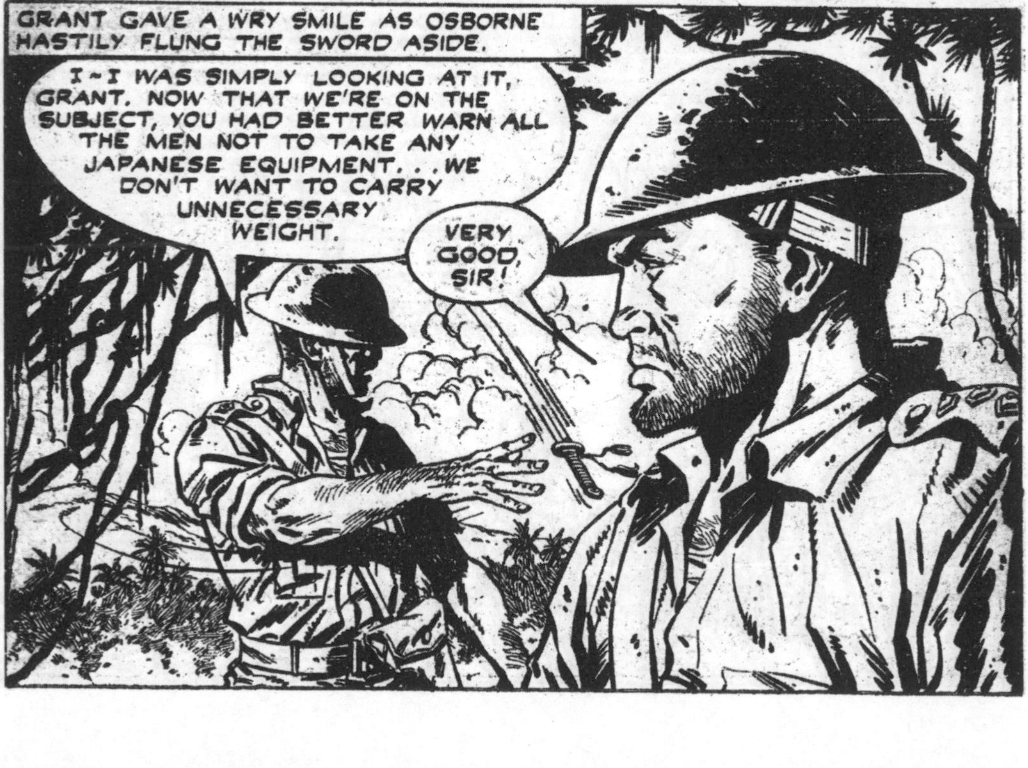
GRANT GAVE A WRY SMILE AS OSBORNE HASTILY FLUNG THE SWORD ASIDE.
I-I WAS SIMPLY LOOKING AT IT, GRANT. NOW THAT WE'RE ON THE SUBJECT, YOU HAD BETTER WARN ALL THE MEN NOT TO TAKE ANY JAPANESE EQUIPMENT. . .WE DON'T WANT TO CARRY UNNECESSARY WEIGHT.
VERY GOOD, SIR!

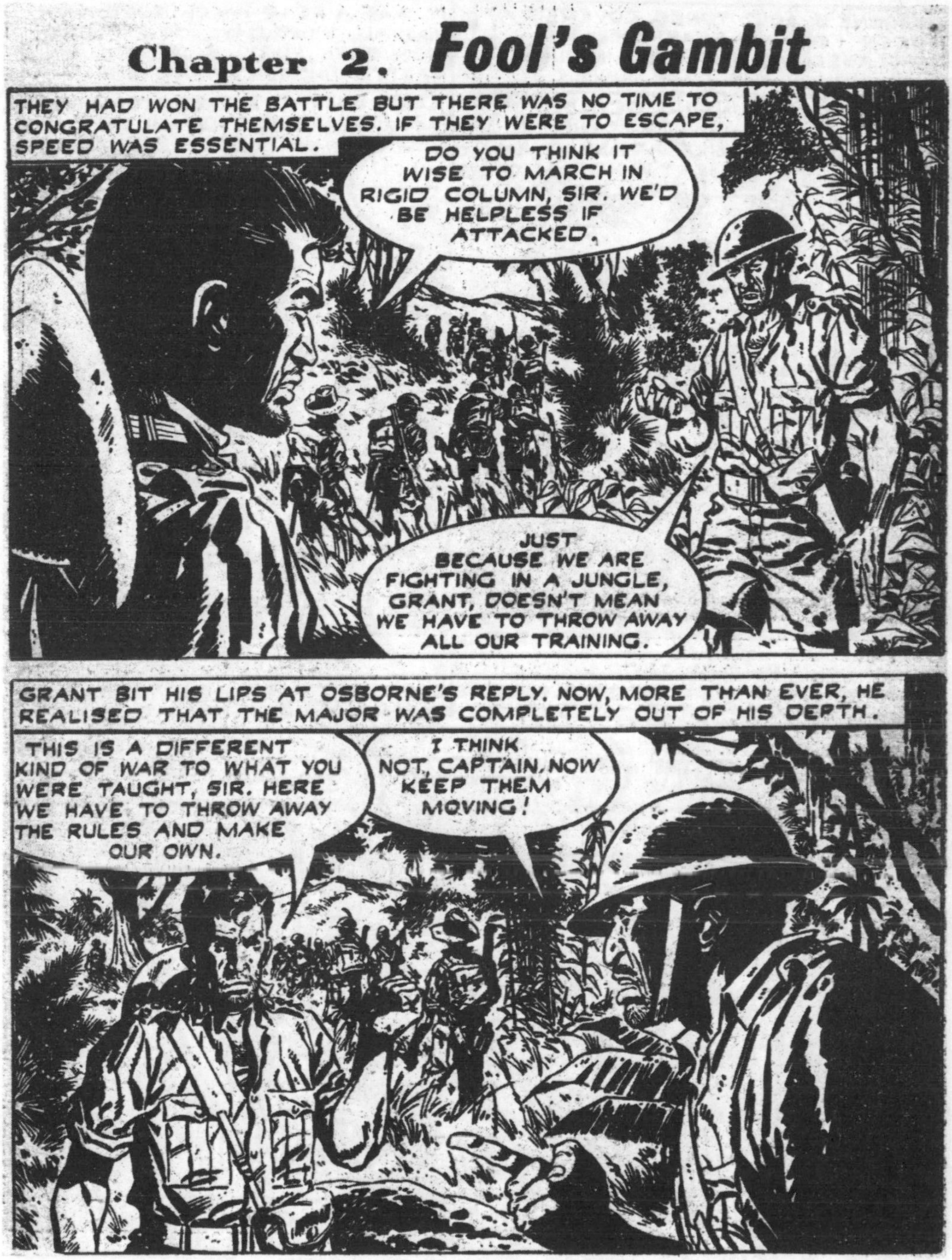
Chapter 2. Fool's Gambit
THEY HAD WON THE BATTLE BUT THERE WAS NO TIME TO CONGRATULATE THEMSELVES. IF THEY WERE TO ESCAPE, SPEED WAS ESSENTIAL.
DO YOU THINK IT WISE TO MARCH IN RIGID COLUMN, SIR. WE'D BE HELPLESS IF ATTACKED.
JUST BECAUSE WE ARE FIGHTING IN A JUNGLE, GRANT, DOESN'T MEAN WE HAVE TO THROW AWAY ALL OUR TRAINING.
GRANT BIT HIS LIPS AT OSBORNE'S REPLY. NOW, MORE THAN EVER, HE REALISED THAT THE MAJOR WAS COMPLETELY OUT OF HIS DEPTH.
THIS IS A DIFFERENT KIND OF WAR TO WHAT YOU WERE TAUGHT, SIR. HERE WE HAVE TO THROW AWAY THE RULES AND MAKE OUR OWN.
I THINK NOT, CAPTAIN. NOW KEEP THEM MOVING!

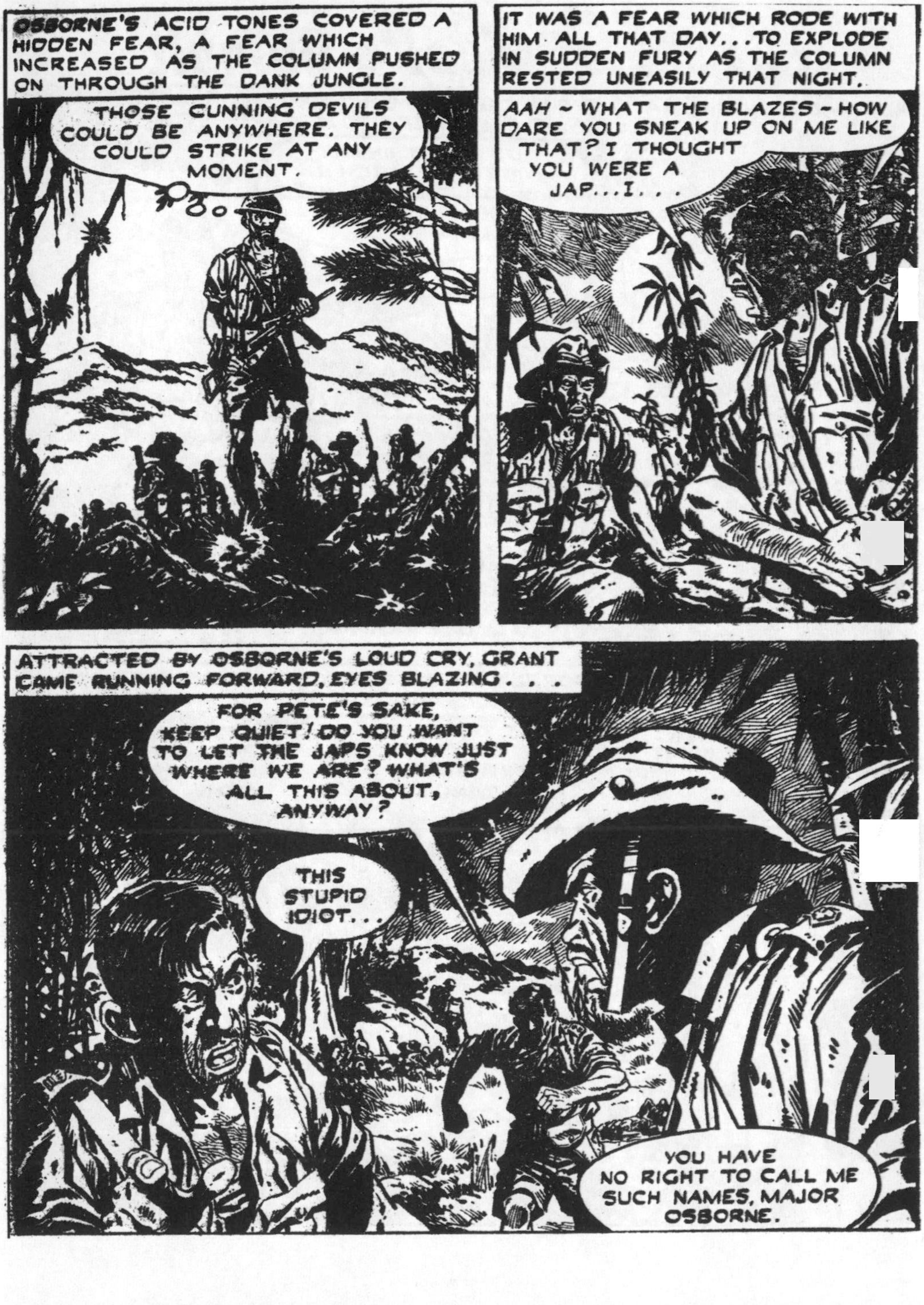
OSBORNE'S ACID TONES COVERED A HIDDEN FEAR, A FEAR WHICH INCREASED AS THE COLUMN PUSHED ON THROUGH THE DANK JUNGLE.
THOSE CUNNING DEVILS COULD BE ANYWHERE. THEY COULD STRIKE AT ANY MOMENT.
IT WAS A FEAR WHICH RODE WITH HIM ALL THAT DAY...TO EXPLODE IN SUDDEN FURY AS THE COLUMN RESTED UNEASILY THAT NIGHT.
AAH ~ WHAT THE BLAZES - HOW DARE YOU SNEAK UP ON ME LIKE THAT? I THOUGHT YOU WERE A JAP...I...
ATTRACTED BY OSBORNE'S LOUD CRY, GRANT CAME RUNNING FORWARD, EYES BLAZING . . .
FOR PETE'S SAKE, KEEP QUIET! DO YOU WANT TO LET THE JAPS KNOW JUST WHERE WE ARE? WHAT'S ALL THIS ABOUT, ANYWAY?
THIS STUPID IDIOT...
YOU HAVE NO RIGHT TO CALL ME SUCH NAMES, MAJOR OSBORNE.

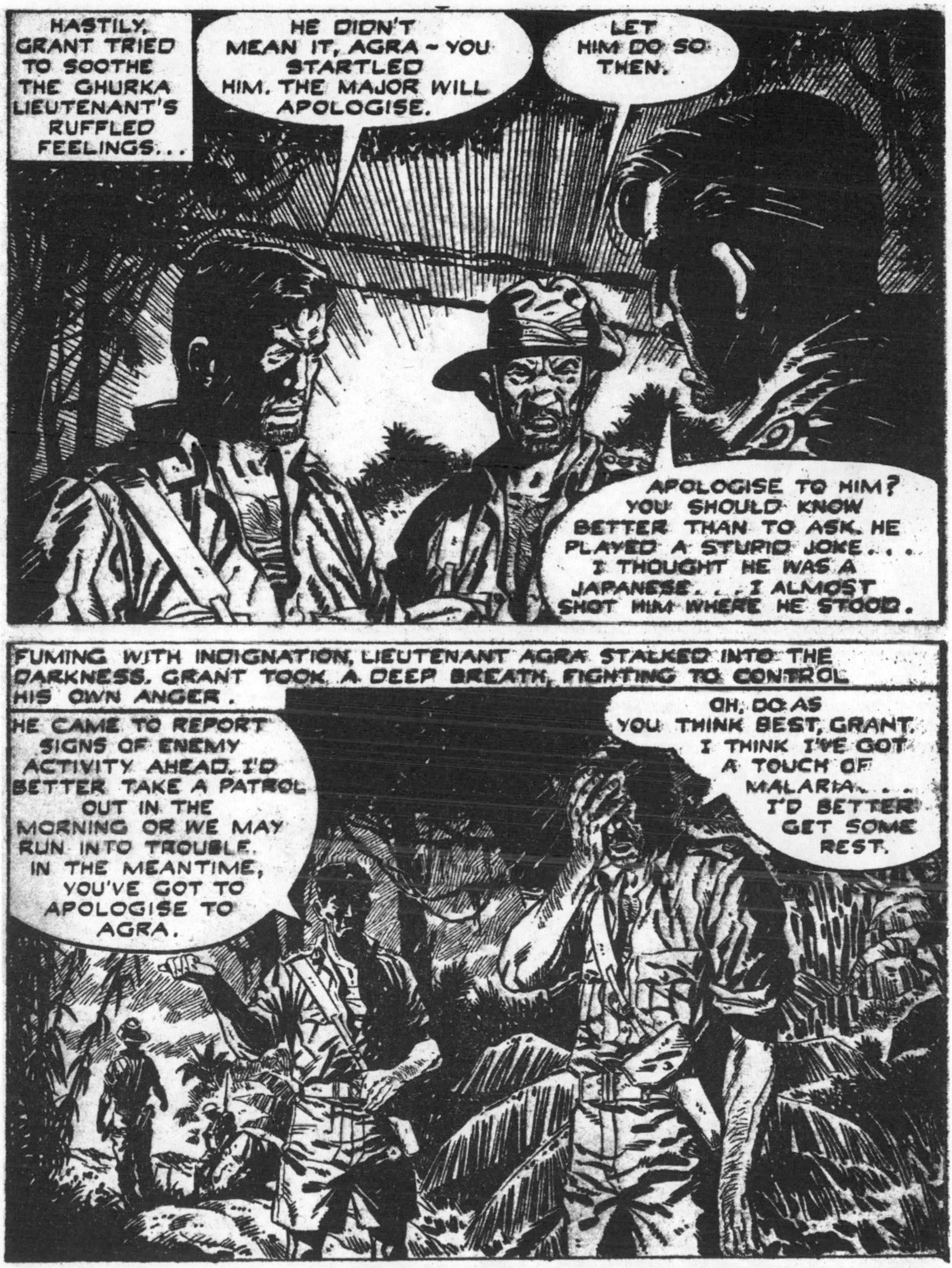
HASTILY, GRANT TRIED TO SOOTHE THE GHURKA LIEUTENANT'S RUFFLED FEELINGS...
HE DIDN'T MEAN IT, AGRA – YOU STARTLED HIM. THE MAJOR WILL APOLOGISE.
LET HIM DO SO THEN.
APOLOGISE TO HIM? YOU SHOULD KNOW BETTER THAN TO ASK. HE PLAYED A STUPID JOKE... I THOUGHT HE WAS A JAPANESE... I ALMOST SHOT HIM WHERE HE STOOD.
FUMING WITH INDIGNATION, LIEUTENANT AGRA STALKED INTO THE DARKNESS. GRANT TOOK A DEEP BREATH, FIGHTING TO CONTROL HIS OWN ANGER.
HE CAME TO REPORT SIGNS OF ENEMY ACTIVITY AHEAD. I'D BETTER TAKE A PATROL OUT IN THE MORNING OR WE MAY RUN INTO TROUBLE. IN THE MEANTIME, YOU'VE GOT TO APOLOGISE TO AGRA.
OH, DO AS YOU THINK BEST, GRANT. I THINK I'VE GOT A TOUCH OF MALARIA... I'D BETTER GET SOME REST.

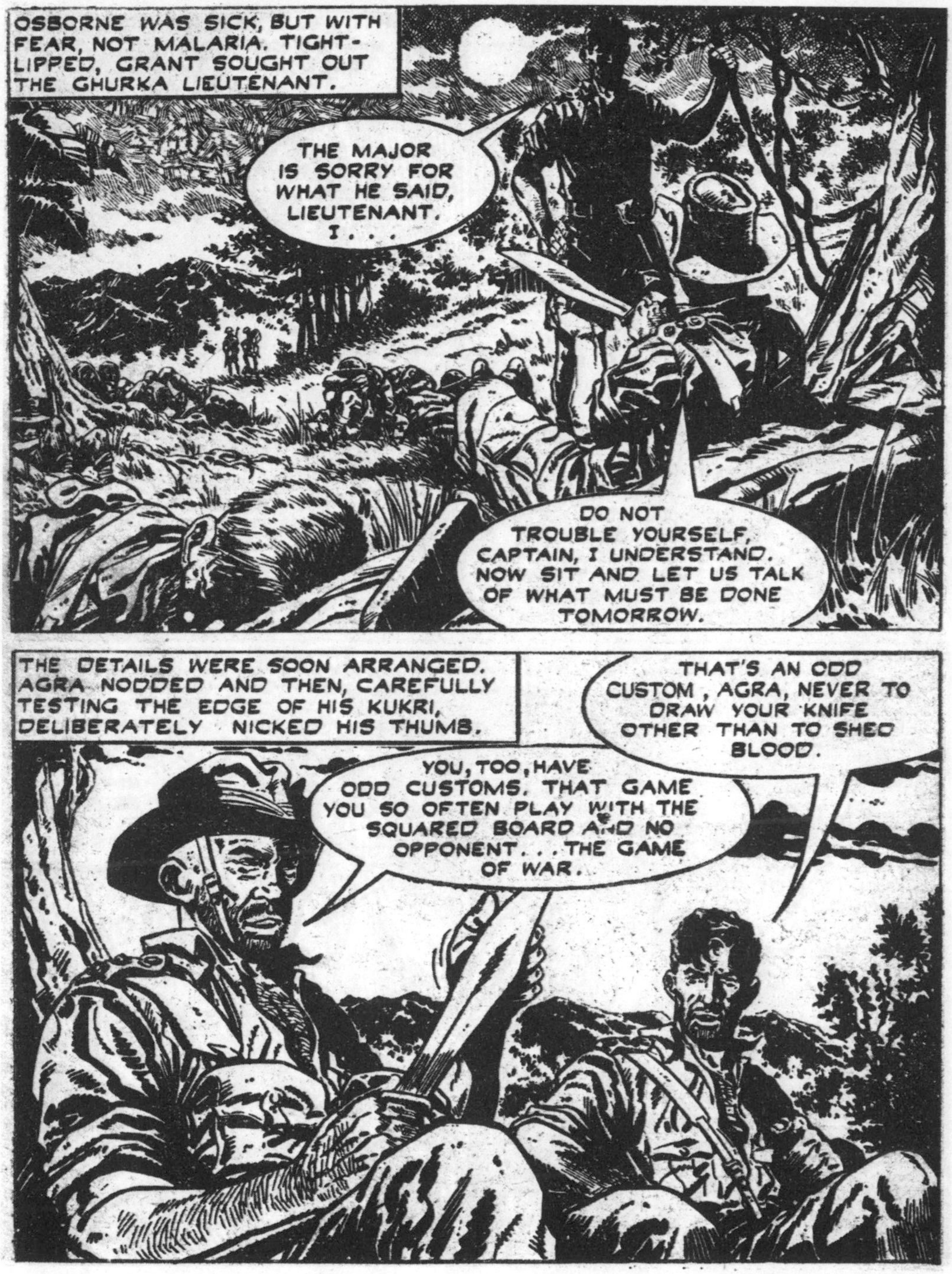
OSBORNE WAS SICK, BUT WITH FEAR, NOT MALARIA. TIGHT-LIPPED, GRANT SOUGHT OUT THE GHURKA LIEUTENANT.
THE MAJOR IS SORRY FOR WHAT HE SAID, LIEUTENANT. I . . .
DO NOT TROUBLE YOURSELF, CAPTAIN, I UNDERSTAND. NOW SIT AND LET US TALK OF WHAT MUST BE DONE TOMORROW.
THE DETAILS WERE SOON ARRANGED. AGRA NODDED AND THEN, CAREFULLY TESTING THE EDGE OF HIS KUKRI, DELIBERATELY NICKED HIS THUMB.
THAT'S AN ODD CUSTOM , AGRA, NEVER TO DRAW YOUR KNIFE OTHER THAN TO SHED BLOOD.
YOU, TOO, HAVE ODD CUSTOMS. THAT GAME YOU SO OFTEN PLAY WITH THE SQUARED BOARD AND NO OPPONENT . . . THE GAME OF WAR.

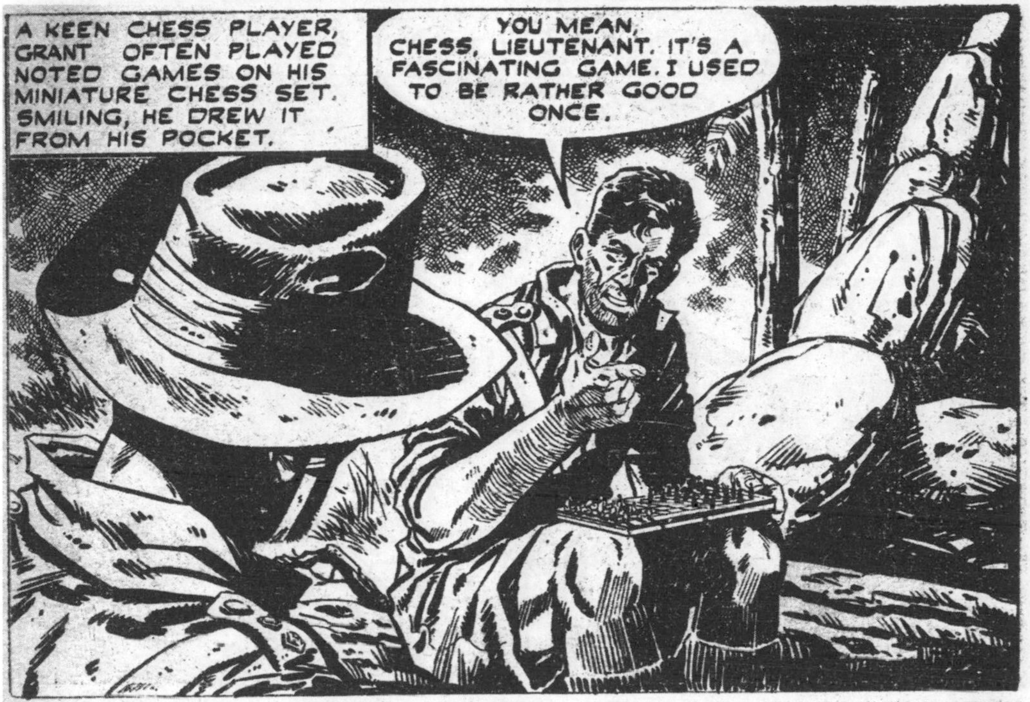
A KEEN CHESS PLAYER, GRANT OFTEN PLAYED NOTED GAMES ON HIS MINIATURE CHESS SET. SMILING, HE DREW IT FROM HIS POCKET.
YOU MEAN, CHESS, LIEUTENANT. IT'S A FASCINATING GAME. I USED TO BE RATHER GOOD ONCE.

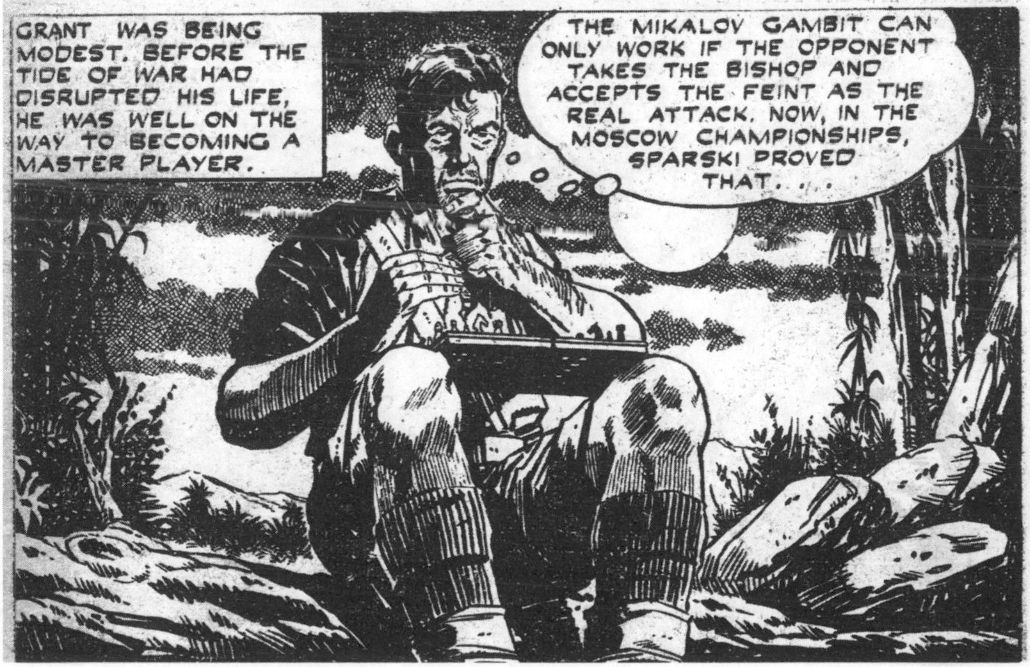
GRANT WAS BEING MODEST. BEFORE THE TIDE OF WAR HAD DISRUPTED HIS LIFE, HE WAS WELL ON THE WAY TO BECOMING A MASTER PLAYER.
THE MIKALOV GAMBIT CAN ONLY WORK IF THE OPPONENT TAKES THE BISHOP AND ACCEPTS THE FEINT AS THE REAL ATTACK. NOW, IN THE MOSCOW CHAMPIONSHIPS, SPARSKI PROVED THAT. . .

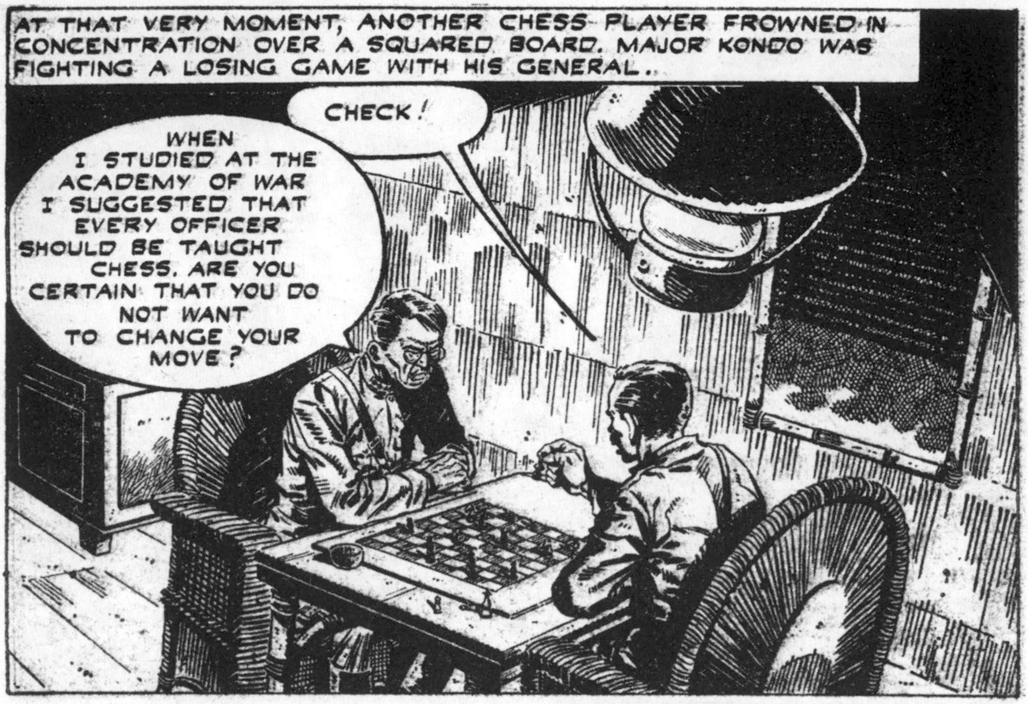
AT THAT VERY MOMENT, ANOTHER CHESS PLAYER FROWNED IN CONCENTRATION OVER A SQUARED BOARD. MAJOR KONDO WAS FIGHTING A LOSING GAME WITH HIS GENERAL.
CHECK!
WHEN I STUDIED AT THE ACADEMY OF WAR I SUGGESTED THAT EVERY OFFICER SHOULD BE TAUGHT CHESS. ARE YOU CERTAIN THAT YOU DO NOT WANT TO CHANGE YOUR MOVE?

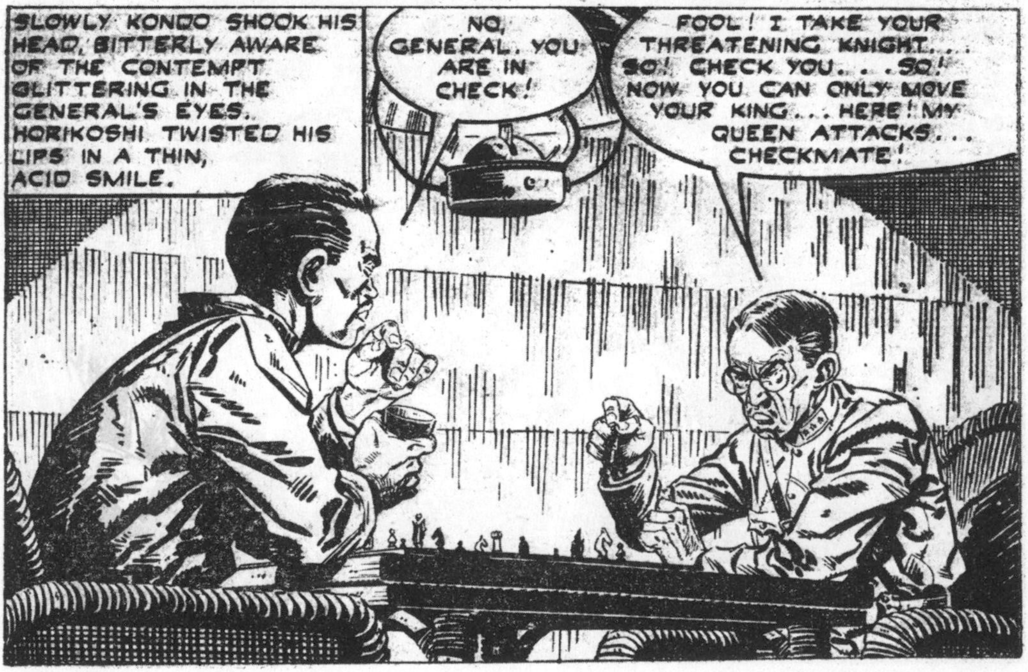
SLOWLY KONDO SHOOK HIS HEAD, BITTERLY AWARE OF THE CONTEMPT GLITTERING IN THE GENERAL'S EYES. HORIKOSHI TWISTED HIS LIPS IN A THIN, ACID SMILE.
NO, GENERAL. YOU ARE IN CHECK!
FOOL! I TAKE YOUR THREATENING KNIGHT... SO! CHECK YOU... SO! NOW YOU CAN ONLY MOVE YOUR KING... HERE! MY QUEEN ATTACKS... CHECKMATE!

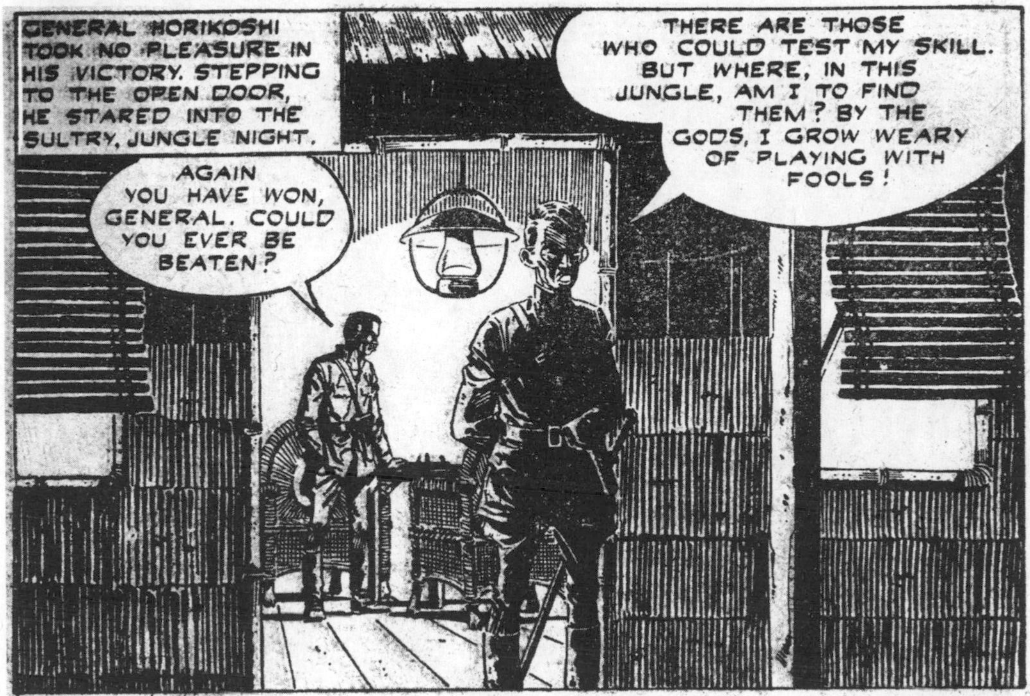
GENERAL HORIKOSHI TOOK NO PLEASURE IN HIS VICTORY. STEPPING TO THE OPEN DOOR, HE STARED INTO THE SULTRY, JUNGLE NIGHT.
AGAIN YOU HAVE WON, GENERAL. COULD YOU EVER BE BEATEN?
THERE ARE THOSE WHO COULD TEST MY SKILL. BUT WHERE, IN THIS JUNGLE, AM I TO FIND THEM? BY THE GODS, I GROW WEARY OF PLAYING WITH FOOLS!

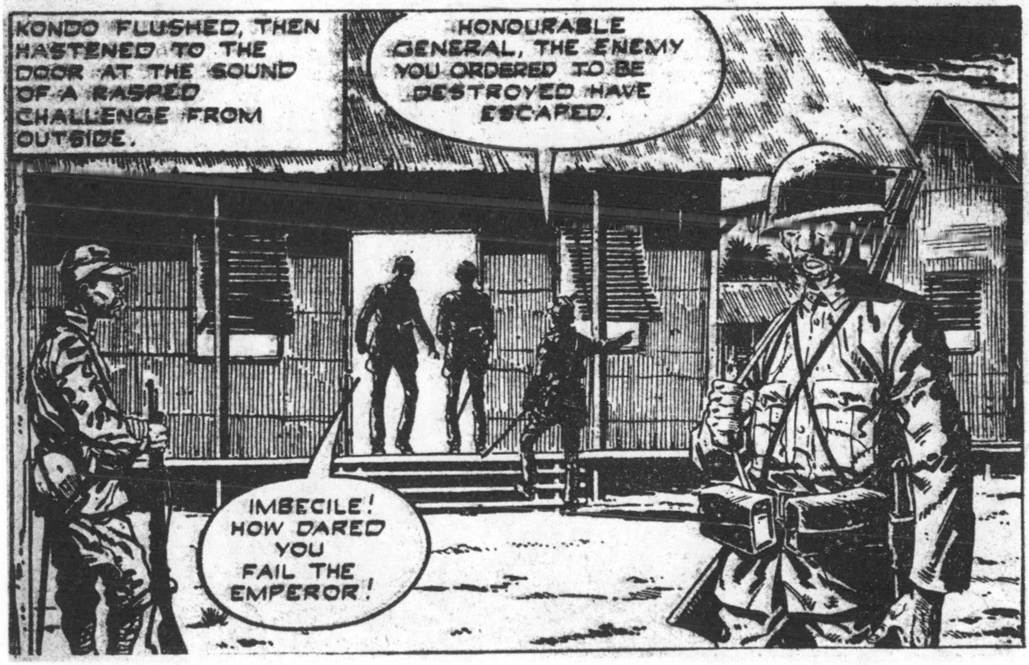
KONDO FLUSHED, THEN HASTENED TO THE DOOR AT THE SOUND OF A RASPED CHALLENGE FROM OUTSIDE.
HONOURABLE GENERAL, THE ENEMY YOU ORDERED TO BE DESTROYED HAVE ESCAPED.
IMBECILE! HOW DARED YOU FAIL THE EMPEROR!

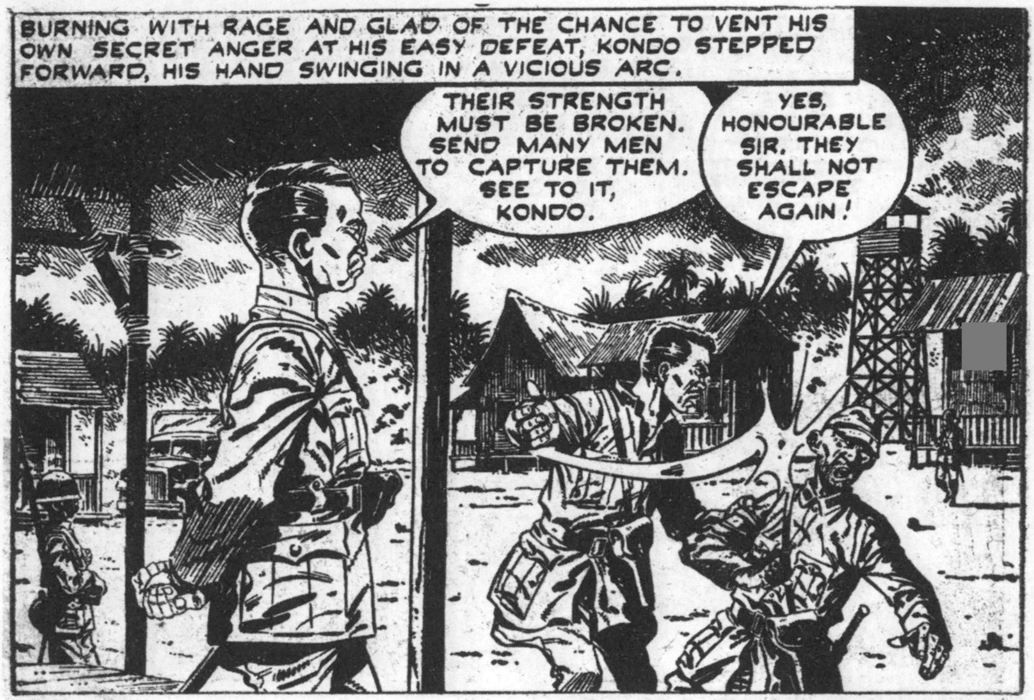
BURNING WITH RAGE AND GLAD OF THE CHANCE TO VENT HIS OWN SECRET ANGER AT HIS EASY DEFEAT, KONDO STEPPED FORWARD, HIS HAND SWINGING IN A VICIOUS ARC.
THEIR STRENGTH MUST BE BROKEN. SEND MANY MEN TO CAPTURE THEM. SEE TO IT, KONDO.
YES, HONOURABLE SIR. THEY SHALL NOT ESCAPE AGAIN!

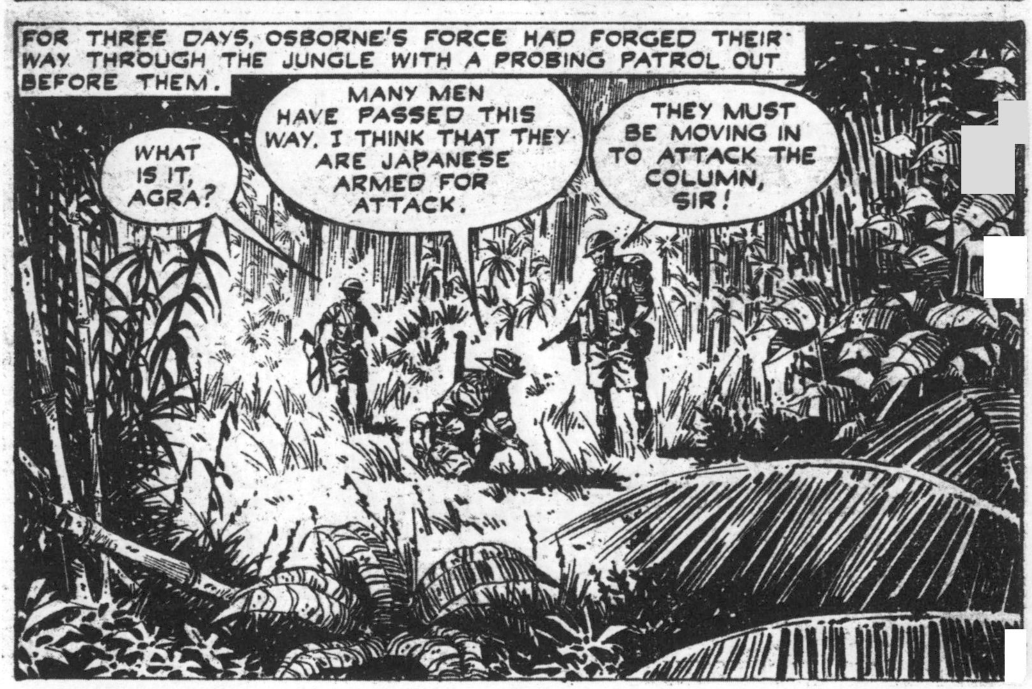
FOR THREE DAYS, OSBORNE'S FORCE HAD FORGED THEIR WAY THROUGH THE JUNGLE WITH A PROBING PATROL OUT BEFORE THEM.
WHAT IS IT, AGRA?
MANY MEN HAVE PASSED THIS WAY. I THINK THAT THEY ARE JAPANESE ARMED FOR ATTACK.
THEY MUST BE MOVING IN TO ATTACK THE COLUMN, SIR!

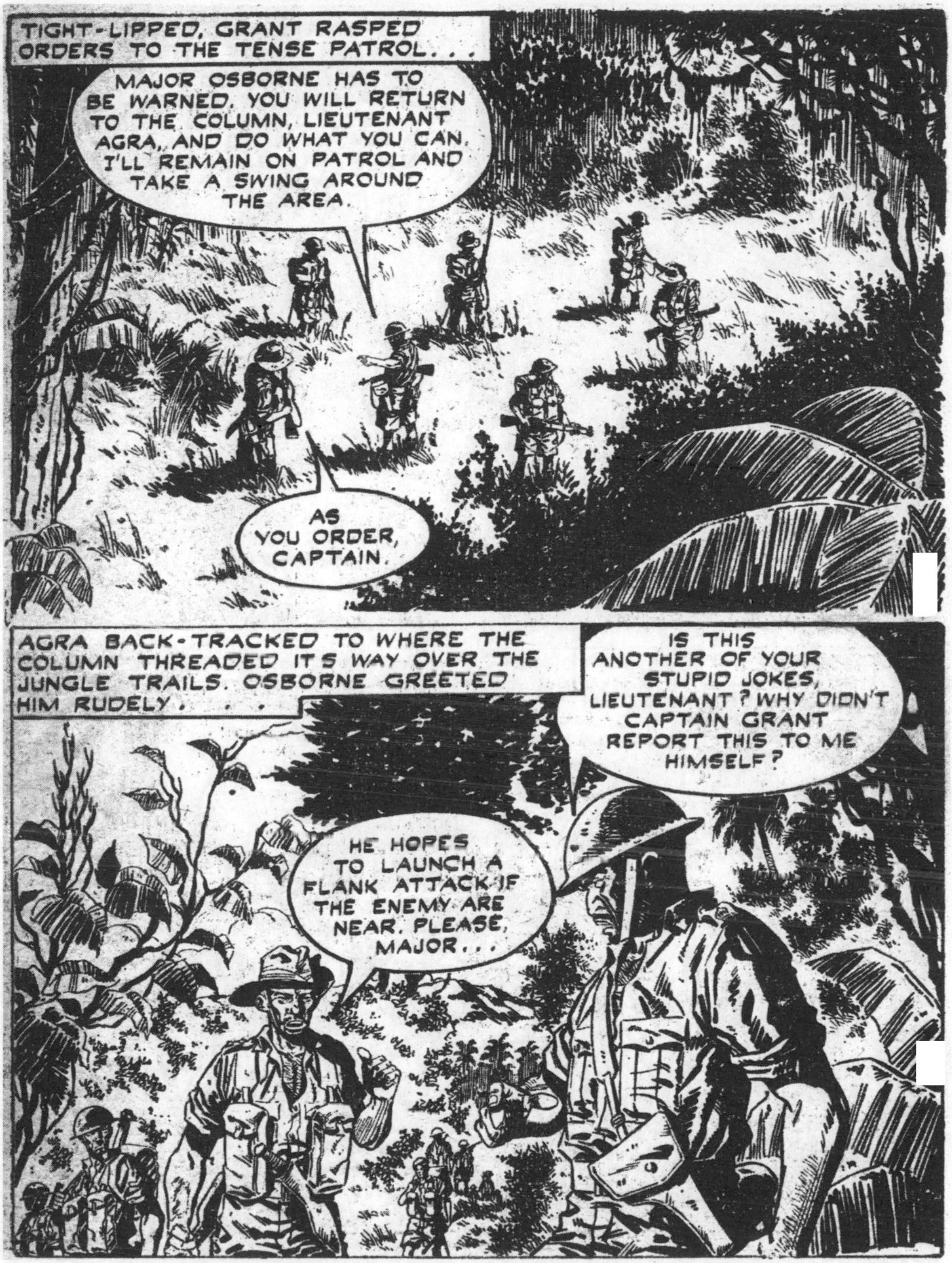
TIGHT-LIPPED, GRANT RASPED ORDERS TO THE TENSE PATROL. . .
MAJOR OSBORNE HAS TO BE WARNED. YOU WILL RETURN TO THE COLUMN, LIEUTENANT AGRA, AND DO WHAT YOU CAN. I'LL REMAIN ON PATROL AND TAKE A SWING AROUND THE AREA.
AS YOU ORDER, CAPTAIN.
AGRA BACK-TRACKED TO WHERE THE COLUMN THREADED IT'S WAY OVER THE JUNGLE TRAILS. OSBORNE GREETED HIM RUDELY. . .
IS THIS ANOTHER OF YOUR STUPID JOKES, LIEUTENANT? WHY DIDN'T CAPTAIN GRANT REPORT THIS TO ME HIMSELF?
HE HOPES TO LAUNCH A FLANK ATTACK IF THE ENEMY ARE NEAR. PLEASE, MAJOR. . .

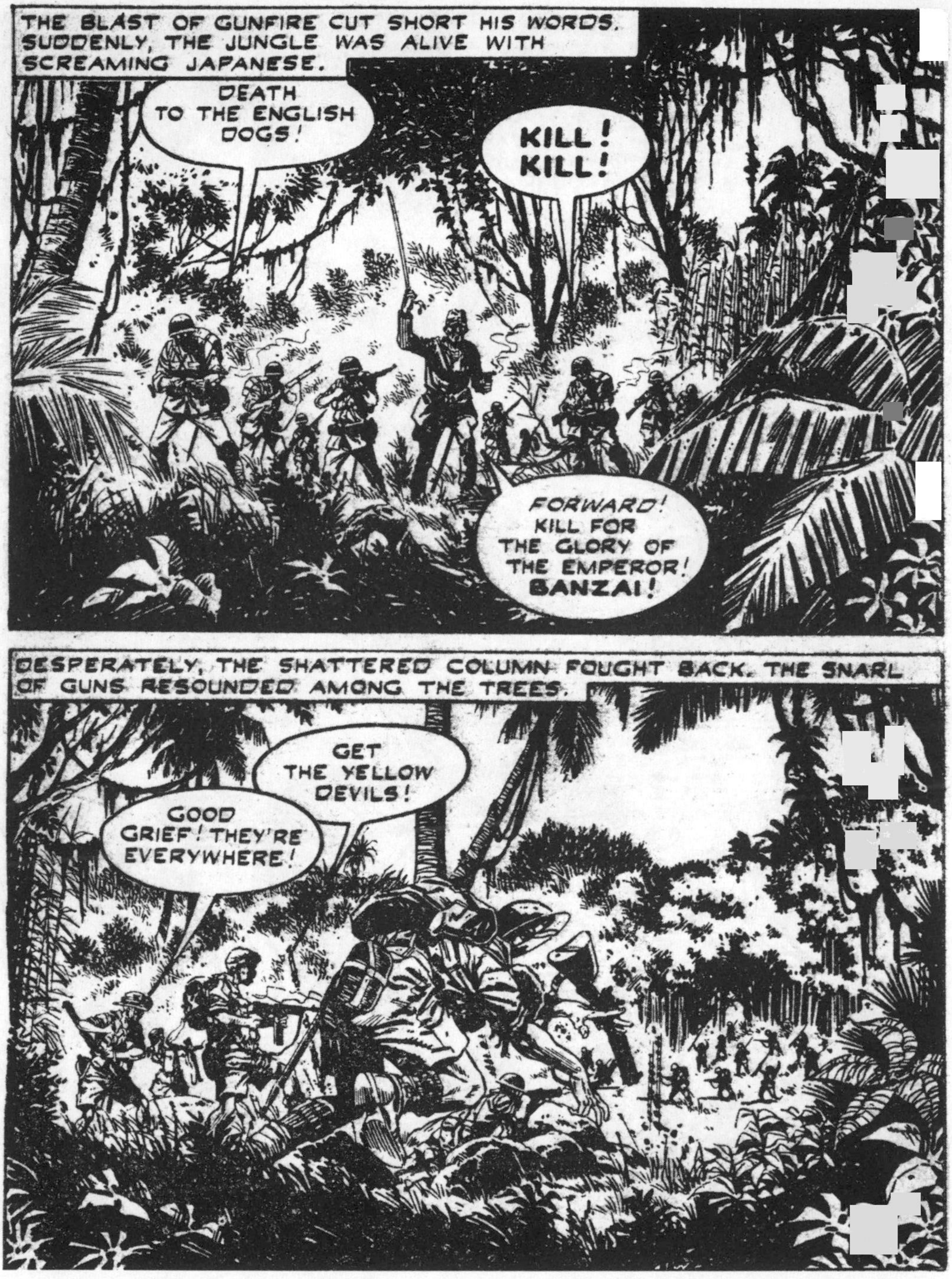
THE BLAST OF GUNFIRE CUT SHORT HIS WORDS. SUDDENLY, THE JUNGLE WAS ALIVE WITH SCREAMING JAPANESE.
DEATH TO THE ENGLISH DOGS!
KILL! KILL!
FORWARD! KILL FOR THE GLORY OF THE EMPEROR! BANZAI!
DESPERATELY, THE SHATTERED COLUMN FOUGHT BACK. THE SNARL OF GUNS RESOUNDED AMONG THE TREES.
GOOD GRIEF! THEY'RE EVERYWHERE!
GET THE YELLOW DEVILS!

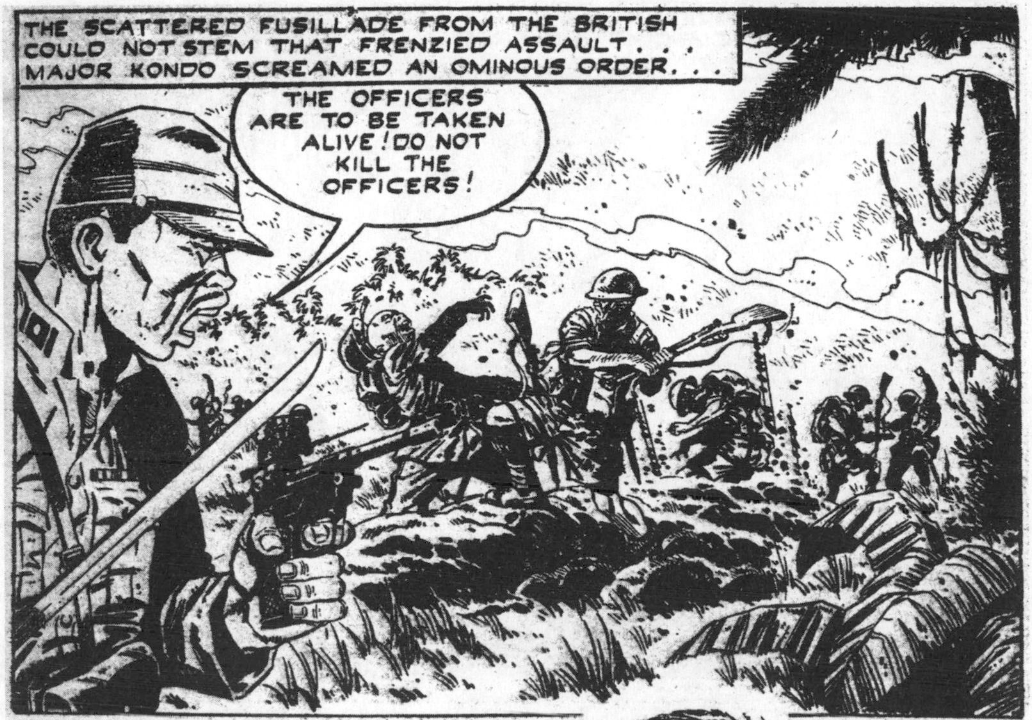
THE SCATTERED FUSILLADE FROM THE BRITISH COULD NOT STEM THAT FRENZIED ASSAULT . . . MAJOR KONDO SCREAMED AN OMINOUS ORDER . . .
THE OFFICERS ARE TO BE TAKEN ALIVE! DO NOT KILL THE OFFICERS!

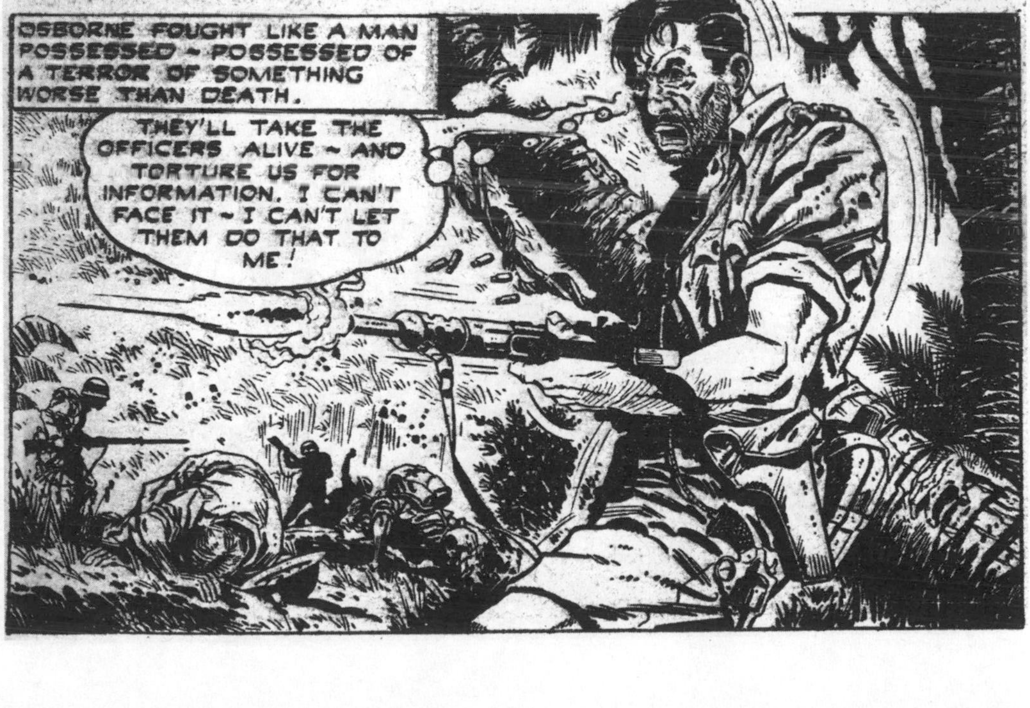
OSBORNE FOUGHT LIKE A MAN POSSESSED ~ POSSESSED OF A TERROR OF SOMETHING WORSE THAN DEATH.
THEY'LL TAKE THE OFFICERS ALIVE ~ AND TORTURE US FOR INFORMATION. I CAN'T FACE IT ~ I CAN'T LET THEM DO THAT TO ME!

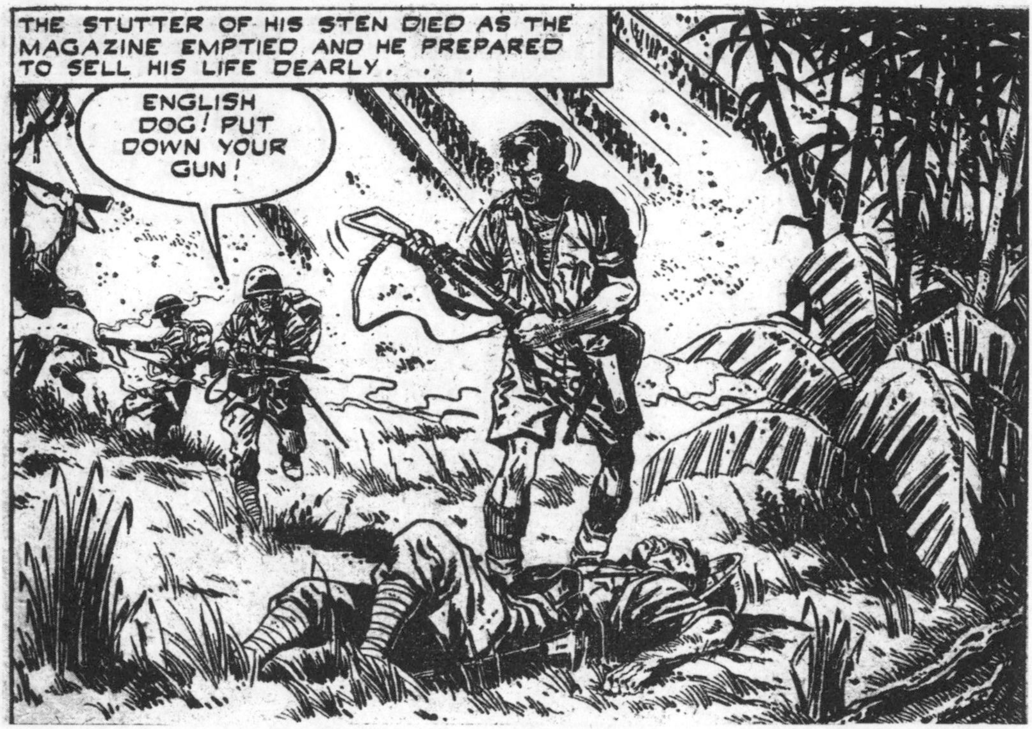
THE STUTTER OF HIS STEN DIED AS THE MAGAZINE EMPTIED AND HE PREPARED TO SELL HIS LIFE DEARLY. . .
ENGLISH DOG! PUT DOWN YOUR GUN!

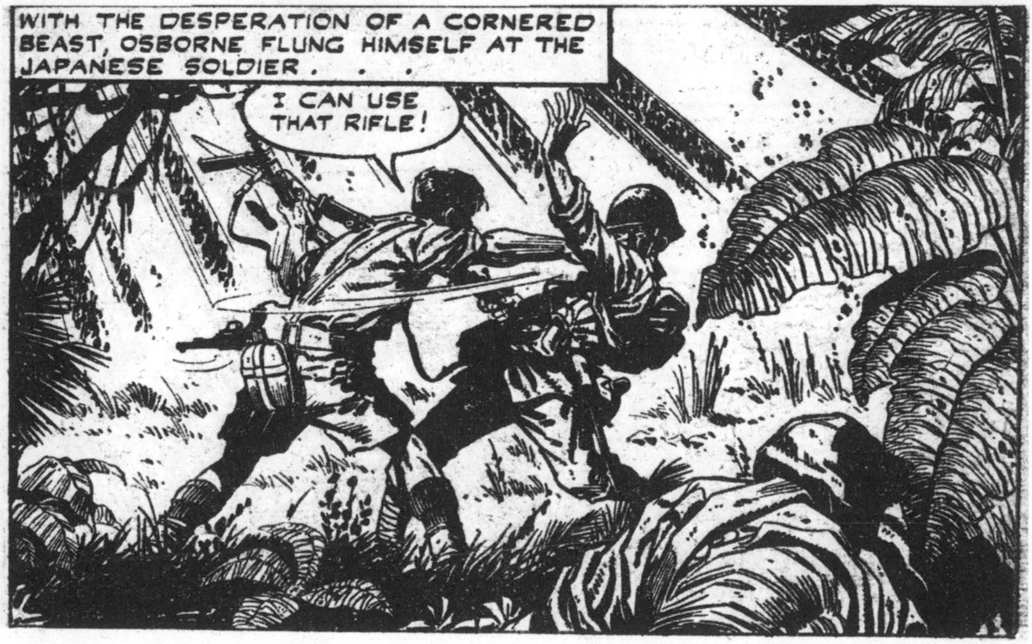
WITH THE DESPERATION OF A CORNERED BEAST, OSBORNE FLUNG HIMSELF AT THE JAPANESE SOLDIER. . .
I CAN USE THAT RIFLE!

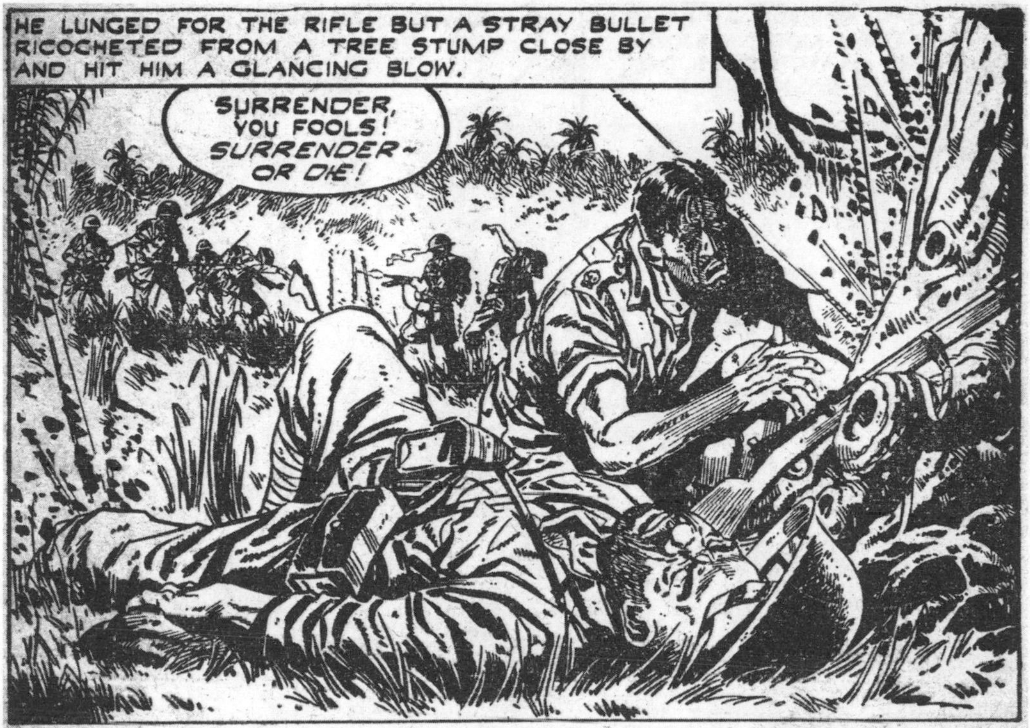
HE LUNGED FOR THE RIFLE BUT A STRAY BULLET RICOCHETED FROM A TREE STUMP CLOSE BY AND HIT HIM A GLANCING BLOW.
SURRENDER, YOU FOOLS! SURRENDER~ OR DIE!

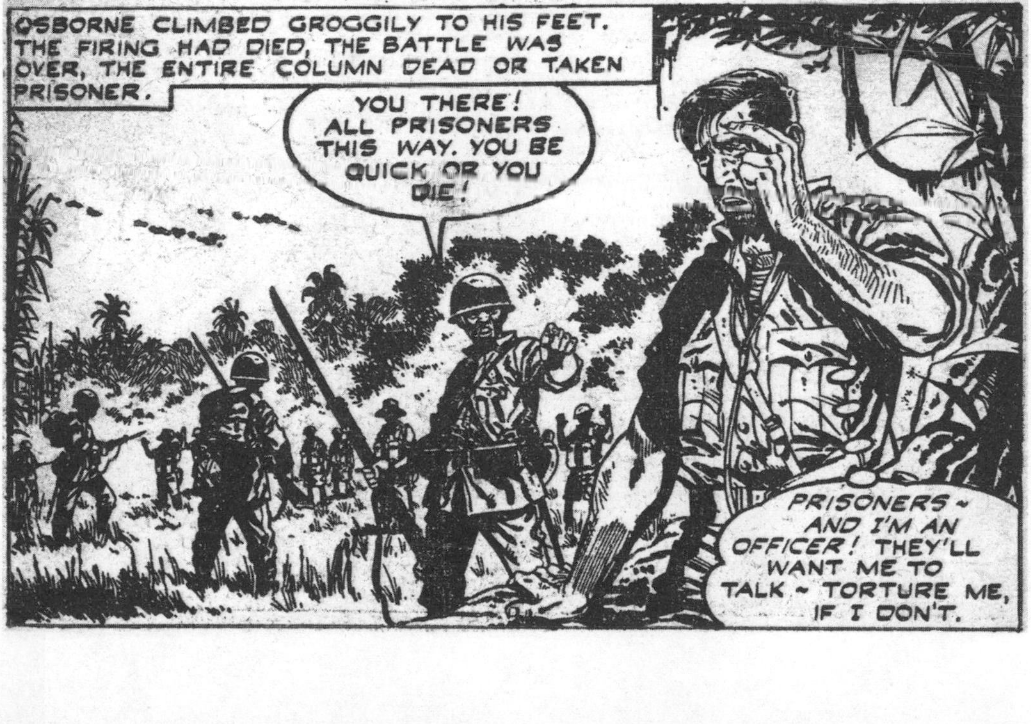
OSBORNE CLIMBED GROGGILY TO HIS FEET. THE FIRING HAD DIED, THE BATTLE WAS OVER, THE ENTIRE COLUMN DEAD OR TAKEN PRISONER.
YOU THERE! ALL PRISONERS THIS WAY. YOU BE QUICK OR YOU DIE!
PRISONERS~ AND I'M AN OFFICER! THEY'LL WANT ME TO TALK ~ TORTURE ME, IF I DON'T.

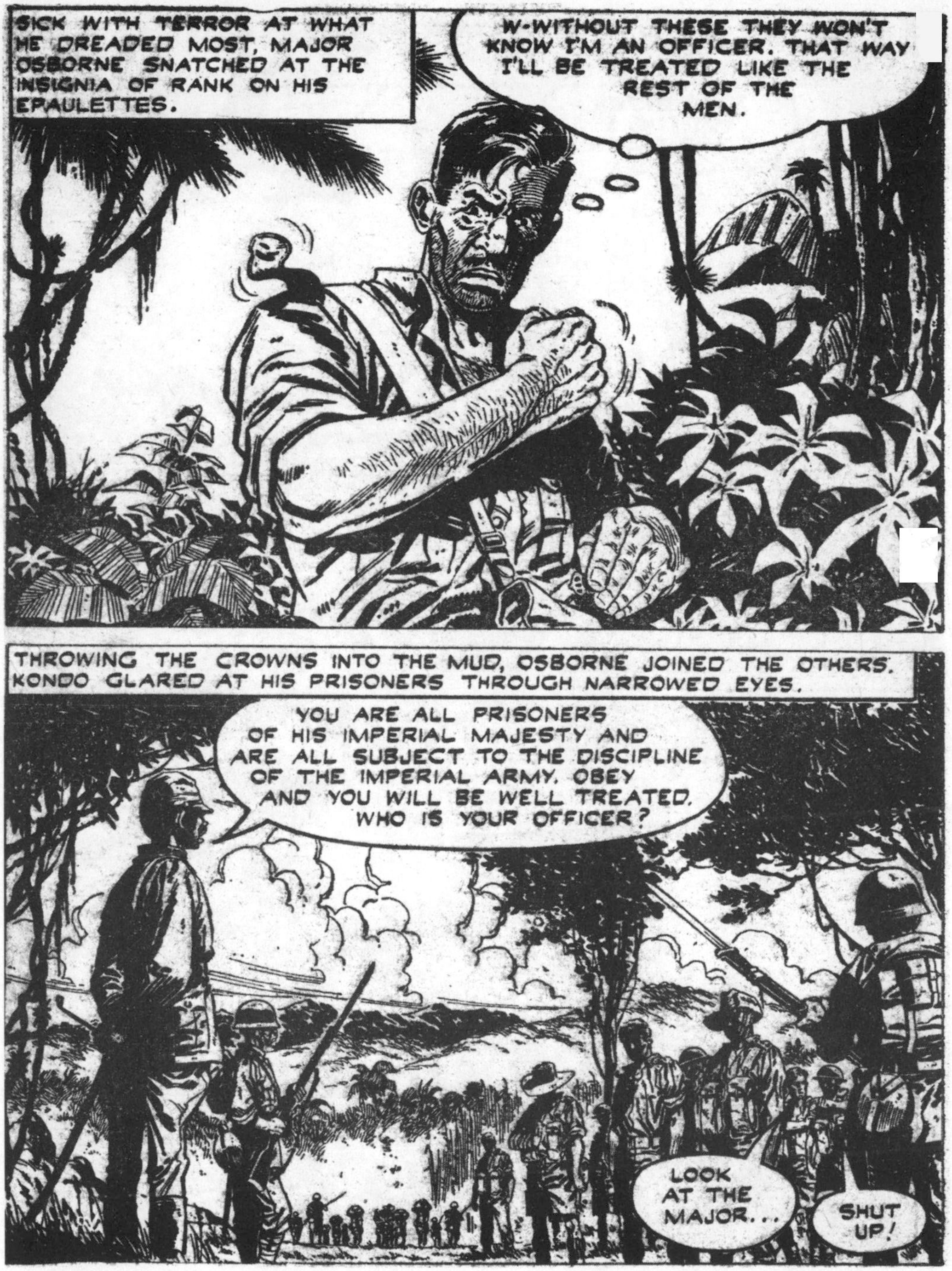
SICK WITH TERROR AT WHAT HE DREADED MOST, MAJOR OSBORNE SNATCHED AT THE INSIGNIA OF RANK ON HIS EPAULETTES.
W-WITHOUT THESE THEY WON'T KNOW I'M AN OFFICER. THAT WAY I'LL BE TREATED LIKE THE REST OF THE MEN.
THROWING THE CROWNS INTO THE MUD, OSBORNE JOINED THE OTHERS. KONDO GLARED AT HIS PRISONERS THROUGH NARROWED EYES.
YOU ARE ALL PRISONERS OF HIS IMPERIAL MAJESTY AND ARE ALL SUBJECT TO THE DISCIPLINE OF THE IMPERIAL ARMY. OBEY AND YOU WILL BE WELL TREATED. WHO IS YOUR OFFICER?
LOOK AT THE MAJOR...
SHUT UP!

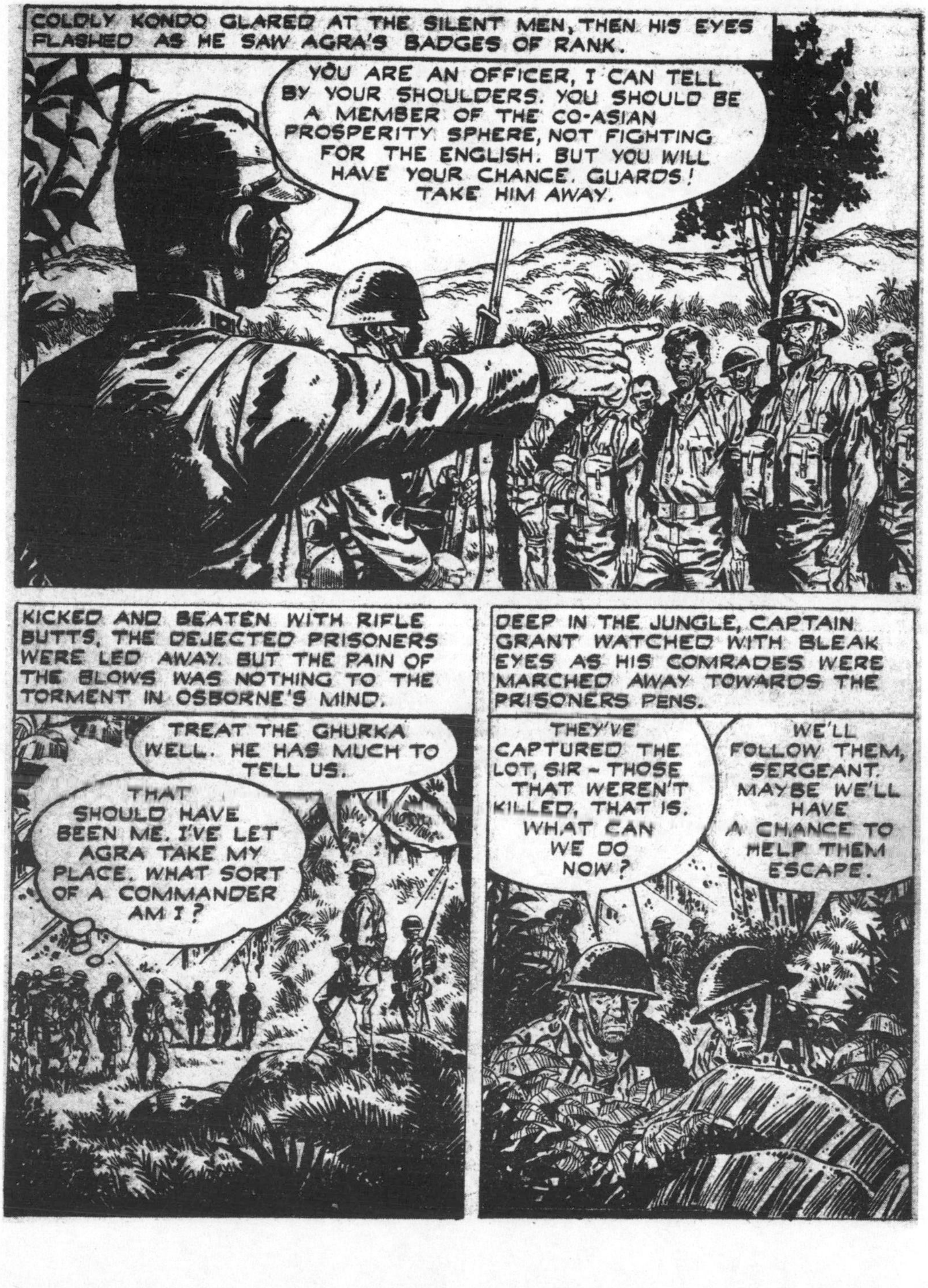
COLDLY KONDO GLARED AT THE SILENT MEN, THEN HIS EYES FLASHED AS HE SAW AGRA'S BADGES OF RANK.
YOU ARE AN OFFICER, I CAN TELL BY YOUR SHOULDERS. YOU SHOULD BE A MEMBER OF THE CO-ASIAN PROSPERITY SPHERE, NOT FIGHTING FOR THE ENGLISH. BUT YOU WILL HAVE YOUR CHANCE. GUARDS! TAKE HIM AWAY.
KICKED AND BEATEN WITH RIFLE BUTTS, THE DEJECTED PRISONERS WERE LED AWAY. BUT THE PAIN OF THE BLOWS WAS NOTHING TO THE TORMENT IN OSBORNE'S MIND.
TREAT THE GHURKA WELL. HE HAS MUCH TO TELL US.
THAT SHOULD HAVE BEEN ME. I'VE LET AGRA TAKE MY PLACE. WHAT SORT OF A COMMANDER AM I?
DEEP IN THE JUNGLE, CAPTAIN GRANT WATCHED WITH BLEAK EYES AS HIS COMRADES WERE MARCHED AWAY TOWARDS THE PRISONERS PENS.
THEY'VE CAPTURED THE LOT, SIR – THOSE THAT WEREN'T KILLED, THAT IS. WHAT CAN WE DO NOW?
WE'LL FOLLOW THEM, SERGEANT. MAYBE WE'LL HAVE A CHANCE TO HELP THEM ESCAPE.

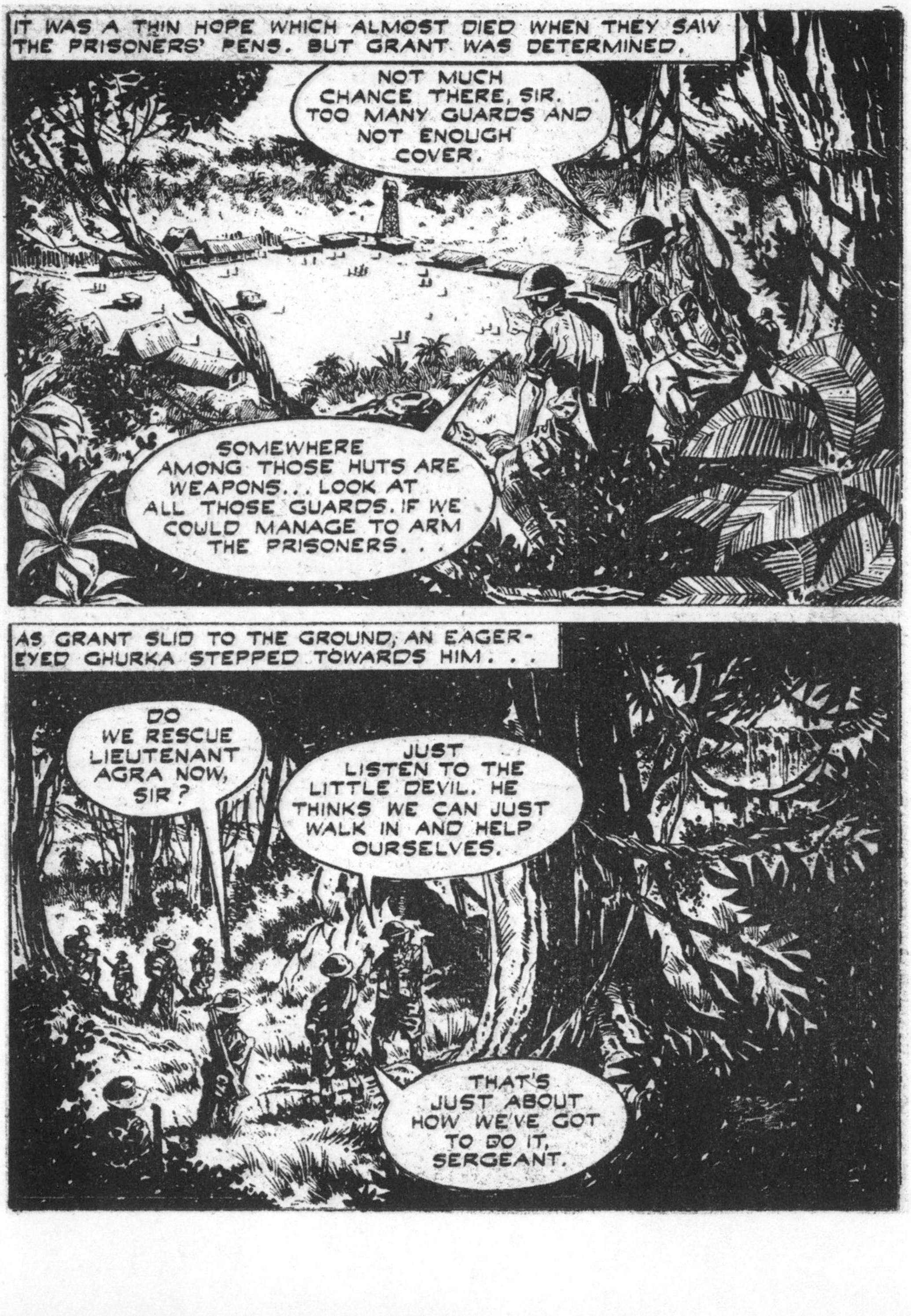
IT WAS A THIN HOPE WHICH ALMOST DIED WHEN THEY SAW THE PRISONERS' PENS. BUT GRANT WAS DETERMINED.
NOT MUCH CHANCE THERE, SIR. TOO MANY GUARDS AND NOT ENOUGH COVER.
SOMEWHERE AMONG THOSE HUTS ARE WEAPONS... LOOK AT ALL THOSE GUARDS. IF WE COULD MANAGE TO ARM THE PRISONERS. .
AS GRANT SLID TO THE GROUND, AN EAGER-EYED GHURKA STEPPED TOWARDS HIM. . .
DO WE RESCUE LIEUTENANT AGRA NOW, SIR?
JUST LISTEN TO THE LITTLE DEVIL. HE THINKS WE CAN JUST WALK IN AND HELP OURSELVES.
THAT'S JUST ABOUT HOW WE'VE GOT TO DO IT, SERGEANT.

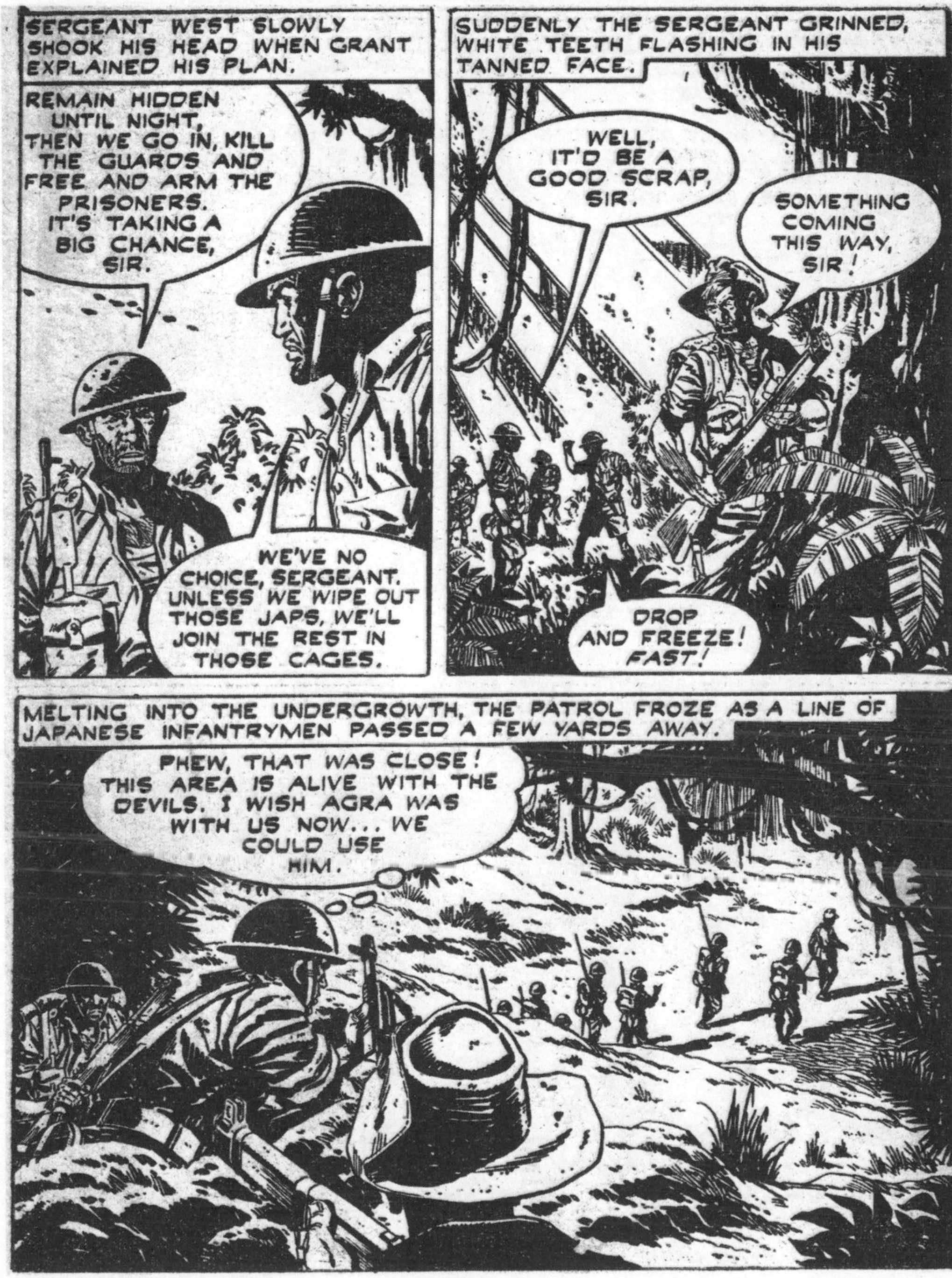
SERGEANT WEST SLOWLY SHOOK HIS HEAD WHEN GRANT EXPLAINED HIS PLAN.
REMAIN HIDDEN UNTIL NIGHT, THEN WE GO IN, KILL THE GUARDS AND FREE AND ARM THE PRISONERS. IT'S TAKING A BIG CHANCE, SIR.
WE'VE NO CHOICE, SERGEANT. UNLESS WE WIPE OUT THOSE JAPS, WE'LL JOIN THE REST IN THOSE CAGES.
SUDDENLY THE SERGEANT GRINNED, WHITE TEETH FLASHING IN HIS TANNED FACE.
WELL, IT'D BE A GOOD SCRAP, SIR.
SOMETHING COMING THIS WAY, SIR!
DROP AND FREEZE! FAST!
MELTING INTO THE UNDERGROWTH, THE PATROL FROZE AS A LINE OF JAPANESE INFANTRYMEN PASSED A FEW YARDS AWAY.
PHEW, THAT WAS CLOSE! THIS AREA IS ALIVE WITH THE DEVILS. I WISH AGRA WAS WITH US NOW... WE COULD USE HIM.

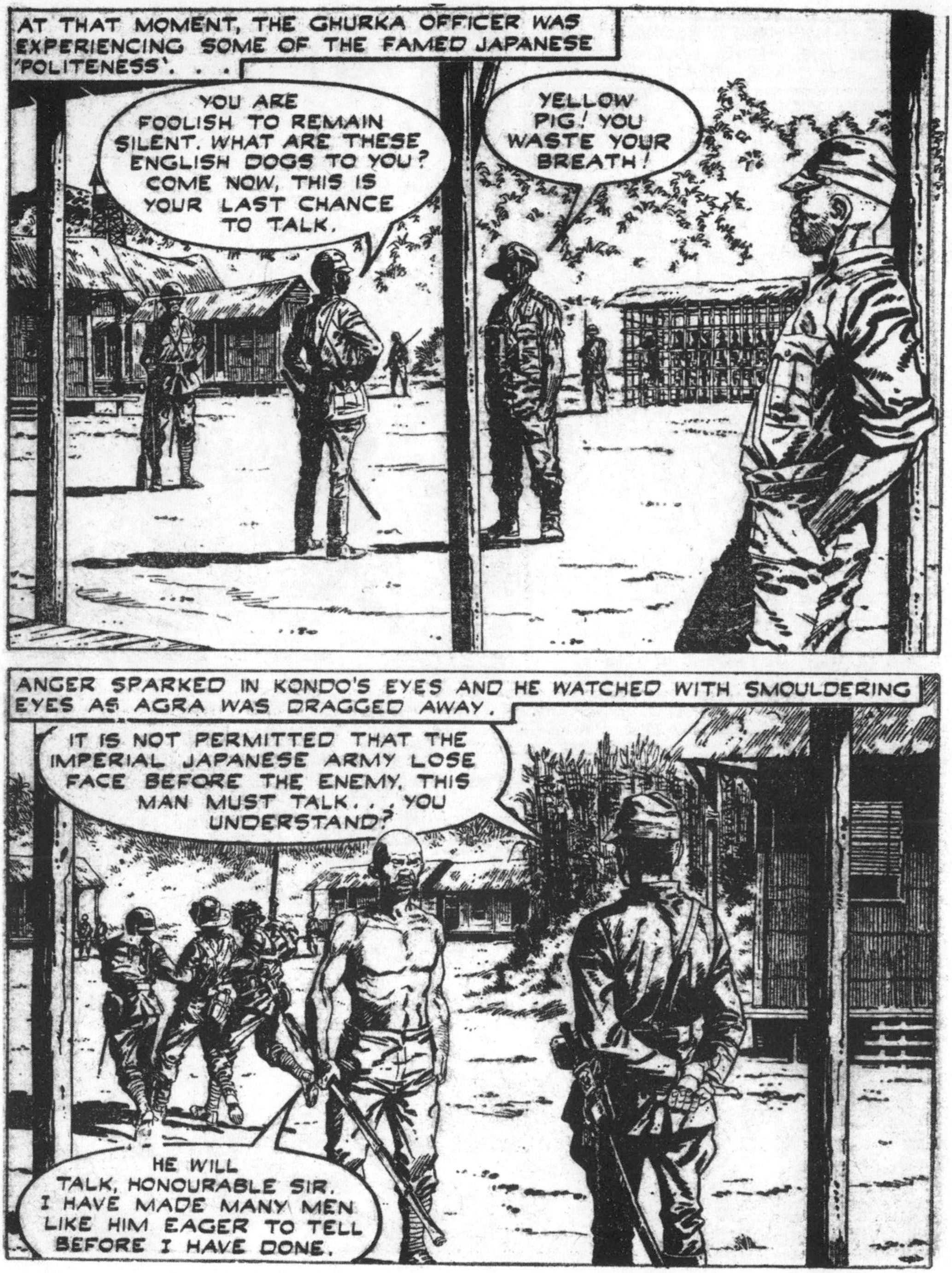
AT THAT MOMENT, THE GHURKA OFFICER WAS EXPERIENCING SOME OF THE FAMED JAPANESE 'POLITENESS'. . .
YOU ARE FOOLISH TO REMAIN SILENT. WHAT ARE THESE ENGLISH DOGS TO YOU? COME NOW, THIS IS YOUR LAST CHANCE TO TALK.
YELLOW PIG! YOU WASTE YOUR BREATH!
ANGER SPARKED IN KONDO'S EYES AND HE WATCHED WITH SMOULDERING EYES AS AGRA WAS DRAGGED AWAY.
IT IS NOT PERMITTED THAT THE IMPERIAL JAPANESE ARMY LOSE FACE BEFORE THE ENEMY. THIS MAN MUST TALK. . . YOU UNDERSTAND?
HE WILL TALK, HONOURABLE SIR. I HAVE MADE MANY MEN LIKE HIM EAGER TO TELL BEFORE I HAVE DONE.

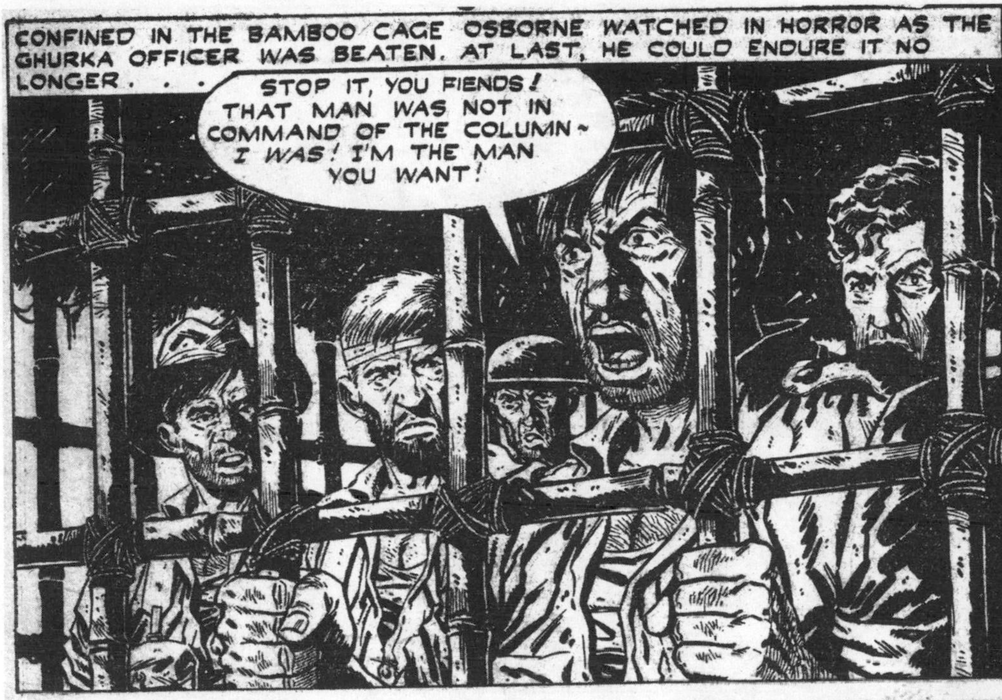
CONFINED IN THE BAMBOO CAGE OSBORNE WATCHED IN HORROR AS THE GHURKA OFFICER WAS BEATEN. AT LAST, HE COULD ENDURE IT NO LONGER . . .
STOP IT, YOU FIENDS! THAT MAN WAS NOT IN COMMAND OF THE COLUMN ~ I WAS! I'M THE MAN YOU WANT!

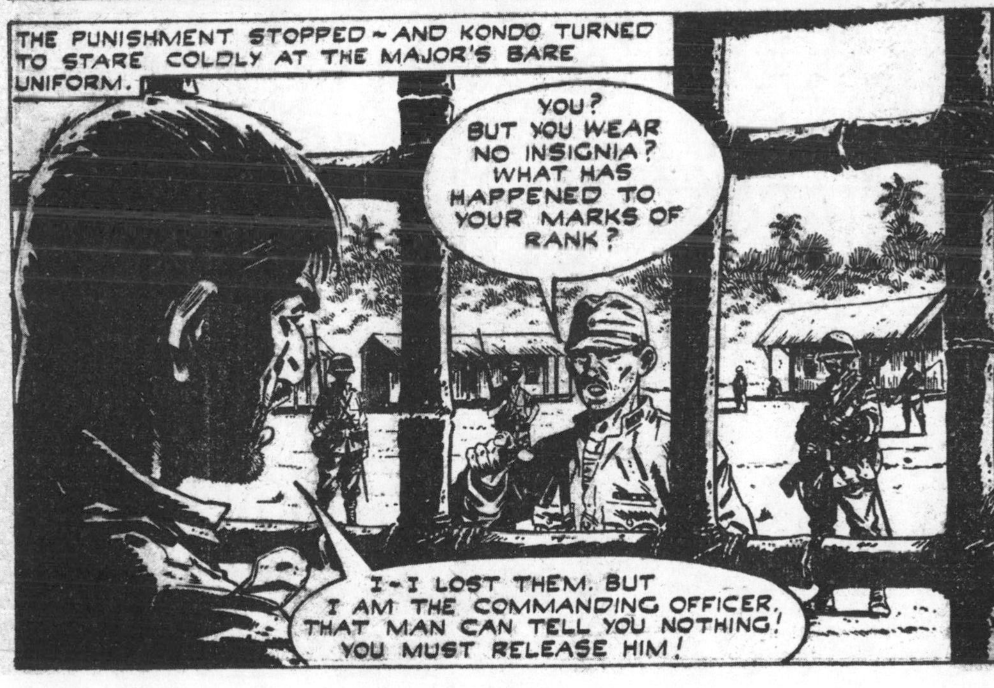
THE PUNISHMENT STOPPED ~ AND KONDO TURNED TO STARE COLDLY AT THE MAJOR'S BARE UNIFORM.
YOU? BUT YOU WEAR NO INSIGNIA? WHAT HAS HAPPENED TO YOUR MARKS OF RANK?
I ~ I LOST THEM. BUT I AM THE COMMANDING OFFICER. THAT MAN CAN TELL YOU NOTHING! YOU MUST RELEASE HIM!

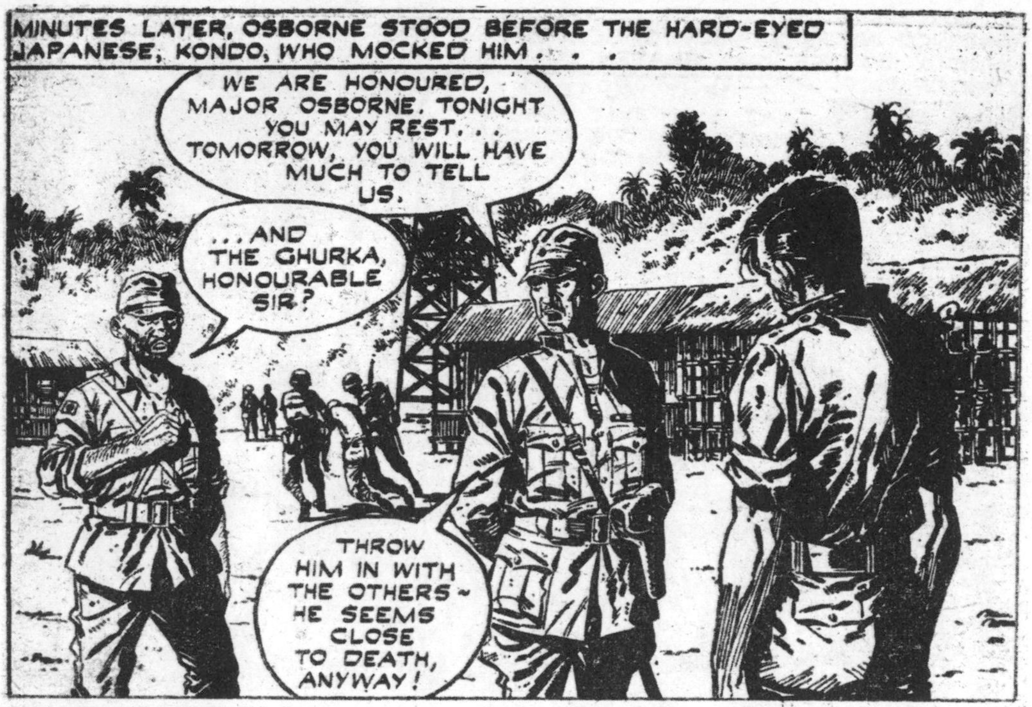
MINUTES LATER, OSBORNE STOOD BEFORE THE HARD-EYED JAPANESE, KONDO, WHO MOCKED HIM . . .
WE ARE HONOURED, MAJOR OSBORNE. TONIGHT YOU MAY REST. . . TOMORROW, YOU WILL HAVE MUCH TO TELL US.
. . . AND THE GHURKA, HONOURABLE SIR?
THROW HIM IN WITH THE OTHERS ~ HE SEEMS CLOSE TO DEATH, ANYWAY!

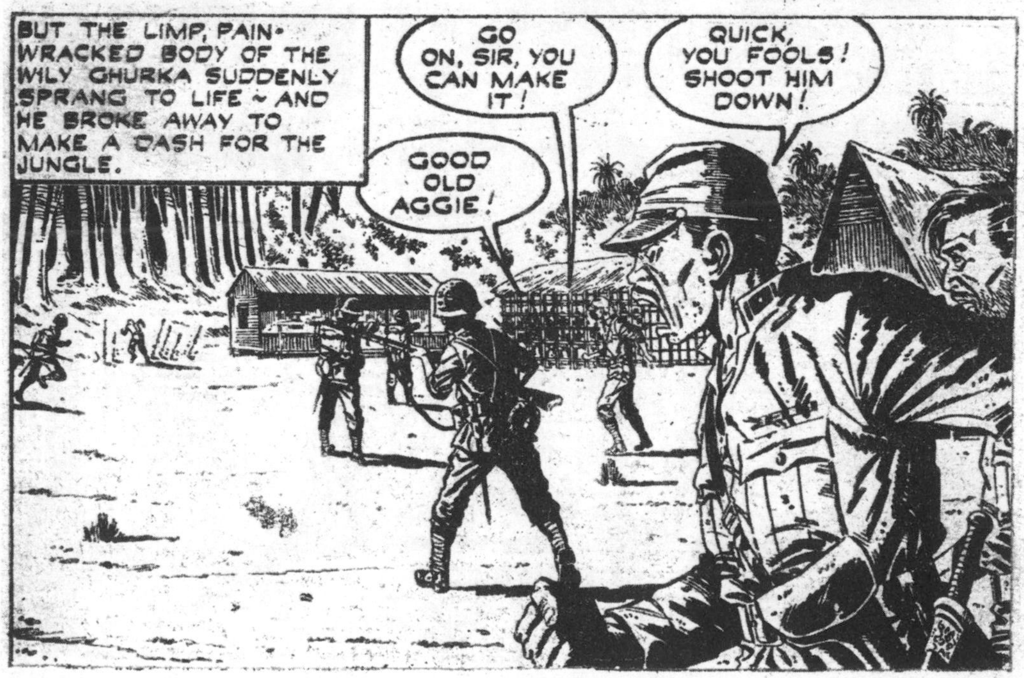
BUT THE LIMP, PAIN-WRACKED BODY OF THE WILY GHURKA SUDDENLY SPRANG TO LIFE ~ AND HE BROKE AWAY TO MAKE A DASH FOR THE JUNGLE.
GO ON, SIR, YOU CAN MAKE IT!
GOOD OLD AGGIE!
QUICK, YOU FOOLS! SHOOT HIM DOWN!

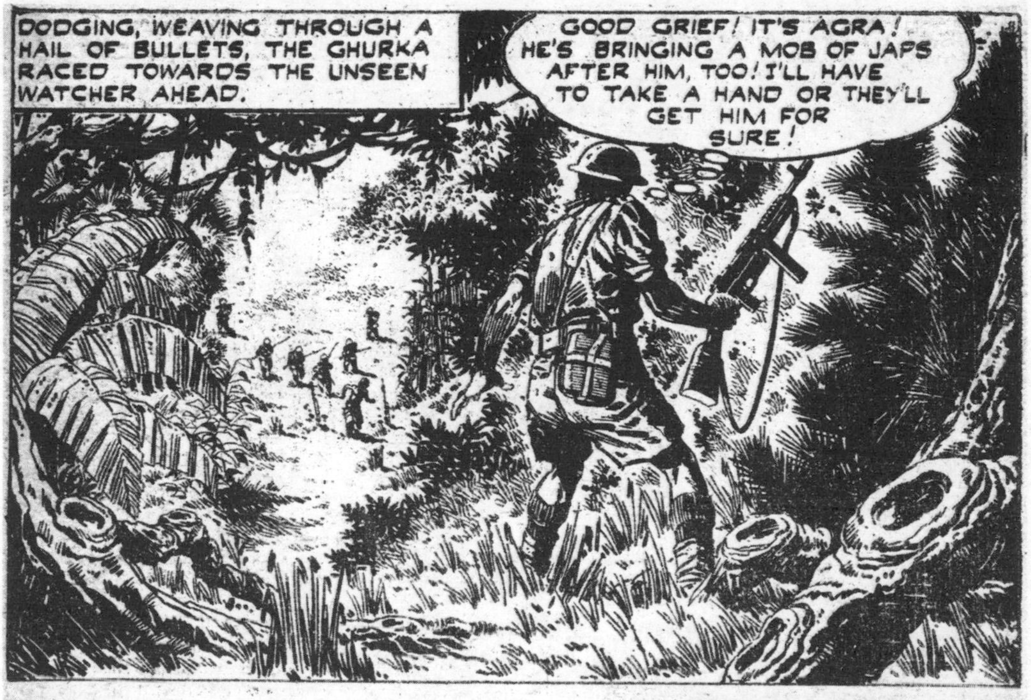
DODGING, WEAVING THROUGH A HAIL OF BULLETS, THE GHURKA RACED TOWARDS THE UNSEEN WATCHER AHEAD.
GOOD GRIEF! IT'S AGRA! HE'S BRINGING A MOB OF JAPS AFTER HIM, TOO! I'LL HAVE TO TAKE A HAND OR THEY'LL GET HIM FOR SURE!

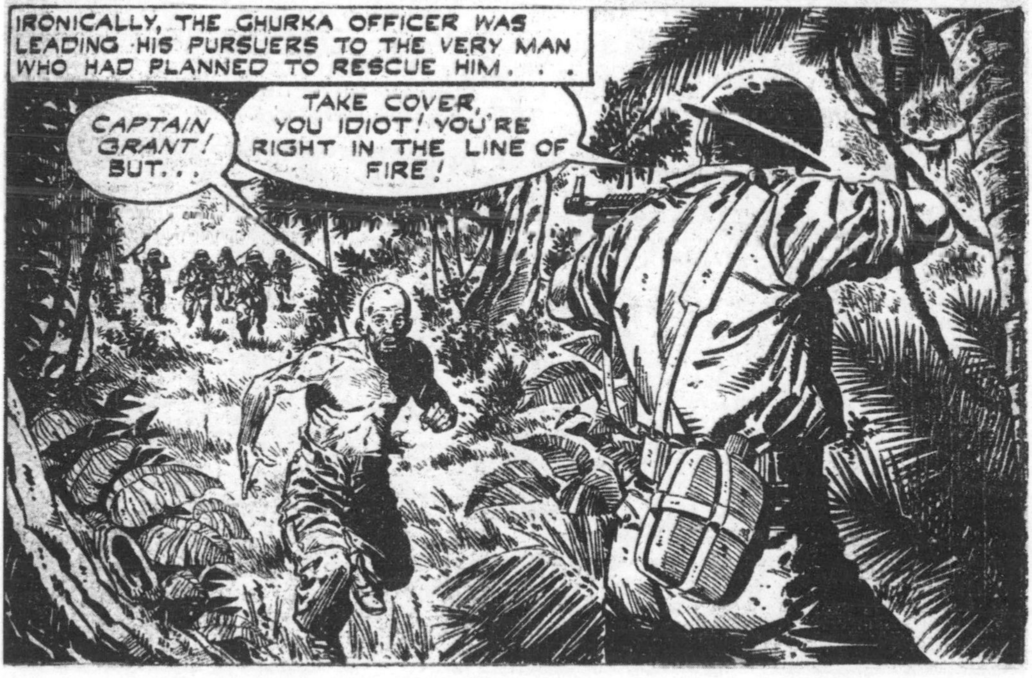
IRONICALLY, THE GHURKA OFFICER WAS LEADING HIS PURSUERS TO THE VERY MAN WHO HAD PLANNED TO RESCUE HIM. . .
CAPTAIN GRANT! BUT. . .
TAKE COVER, YOU IDIOT! YOU'RE RIGHT IN THE LINE OF FIRE!

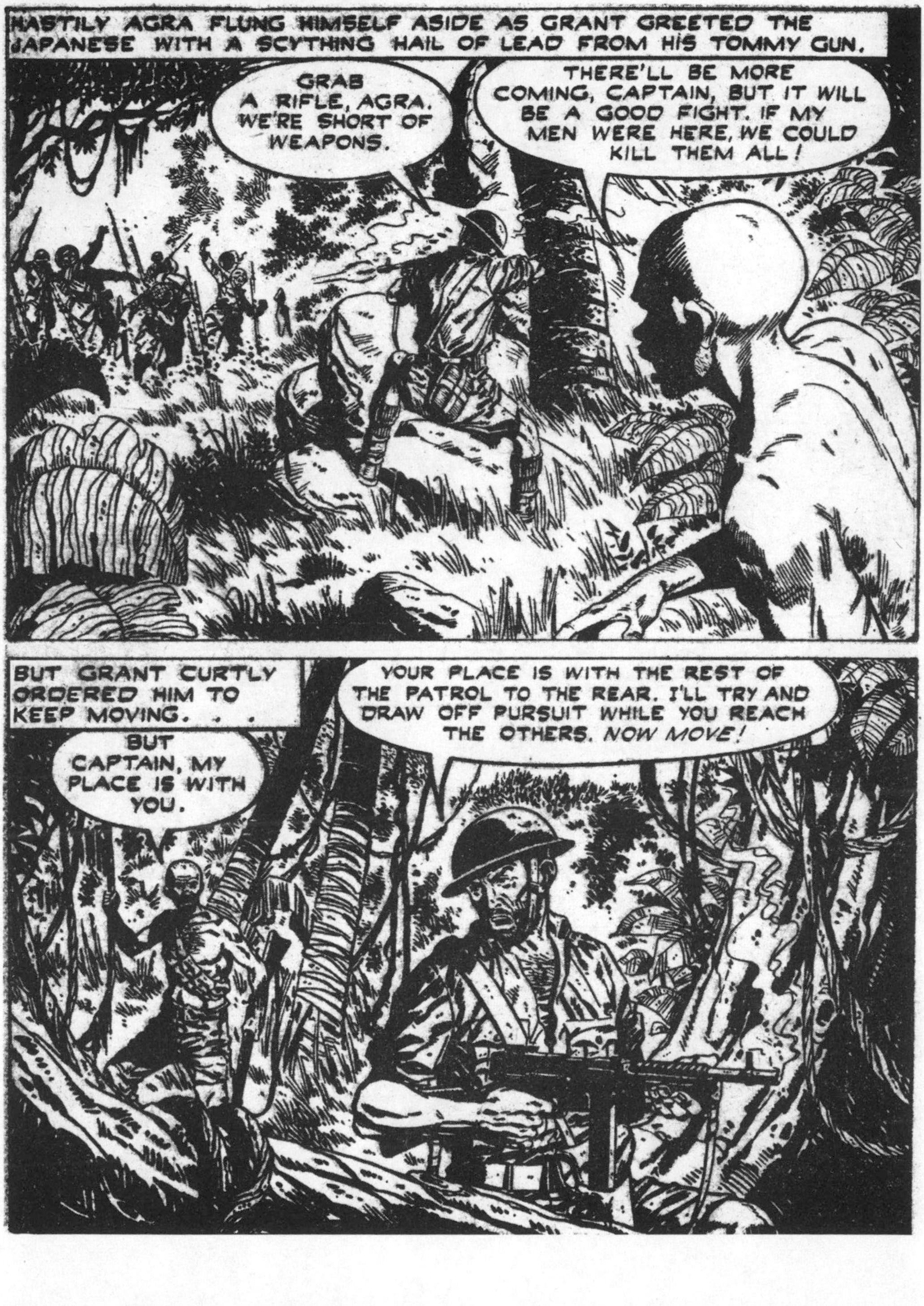
HASTILY AGRA FLUNG HIMSELF ASIDE AS GRANT GREETED THE JAPANESE WITH A SCYTHING HAIL OF LEAD FROM HIS TOMMY GUN.
GRAB A RIFLE, AGRA. WE'RE SHORT OF WEAPONS.
THERE'LL BE MORE COMING, CAPTAIN, BUT IT WILL BE A GOOD FIGHT. IF MY MEN WERE HERE, WE COULD KILL THEM ALL!
BUT GRANT CURTLY ORDERED HIM TO KEEP MOVING. . .
BUT CAPTAIN, MY PLACE IS WITH YOU.
YOUR PLACE IS WITH THE REST OF THE PATROL TO THE REAR. I'LL TRY AND DRAW OFF PURSUIT WHILE YOU REACH THE OTHERS. *NOW MOVE!*

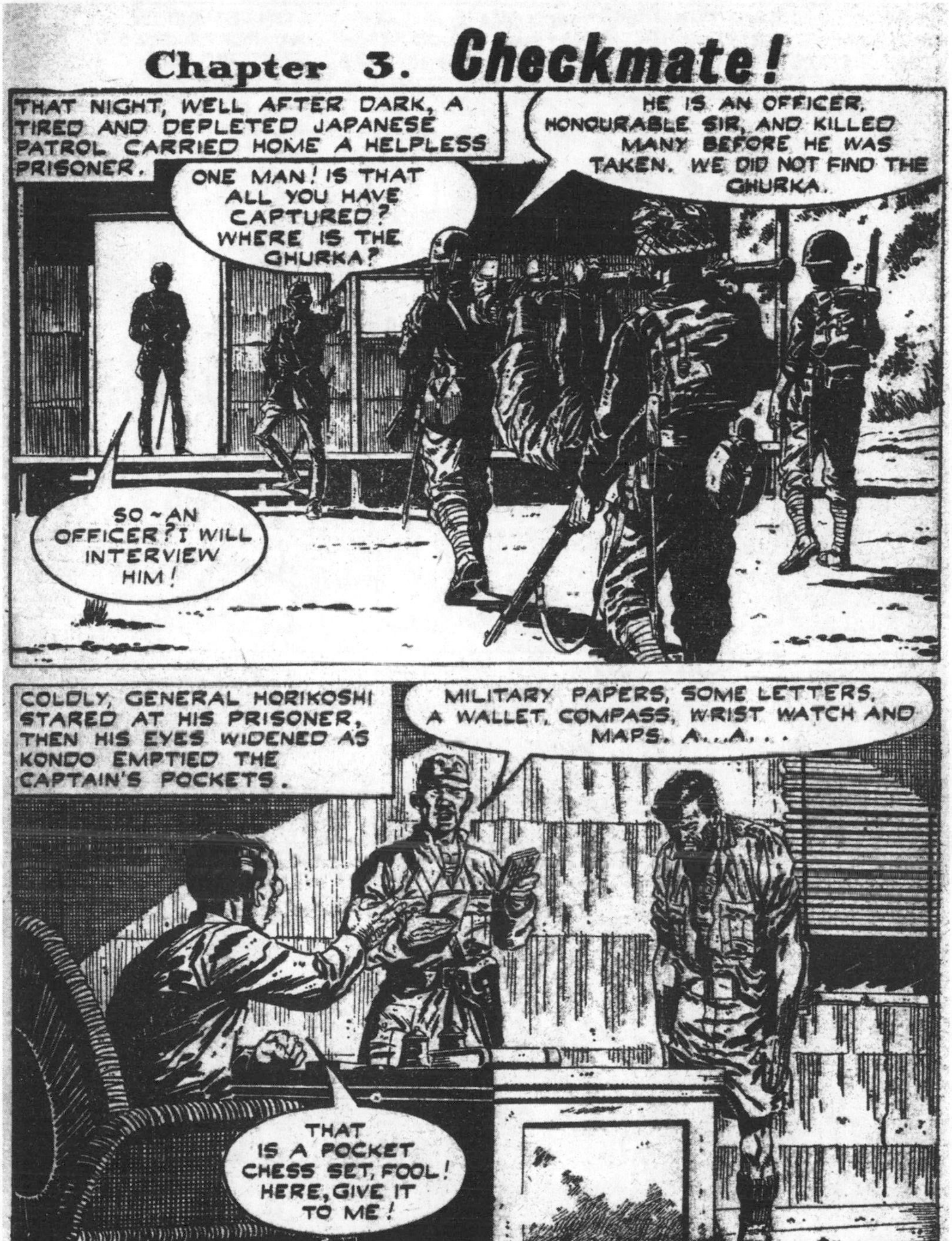
Chapter 3. Checkmate!
THAT NIGHT, WELL AFTER DARK, A TIRED AND DEPLETED JAPANESE PATROL CARRIED HOME A HELPLESS PRISONER.
ONE MAN! IS THAT ALL YOU HAVE CAPTURED? WHERE IS THE GHURKA?
HE IS AN OFFICER, HONOURABLE SIR, AND KILLED MANY BEFORE HE WAS TAKEN. WE DID NOT FIND THE GHURKA.
SO ~ AN OFFICER? I WILL INTERVIEW HIM!
COLDLY, GENERAL HORIKOSHI STARED AT HIS PRISONER, THEN HIS EYES WIDENED AS KONDO EMPTIED THE CAPTAIN'S POCKETS.
MILITARY PAPERS, SOME LETTERS, A WALLET, COMPASS, WRIST WATCH AND MAPS. A...A. . .
THAT IS A POCKET CHESS SET, FOOL! HERE, GIVE IT TO ME!

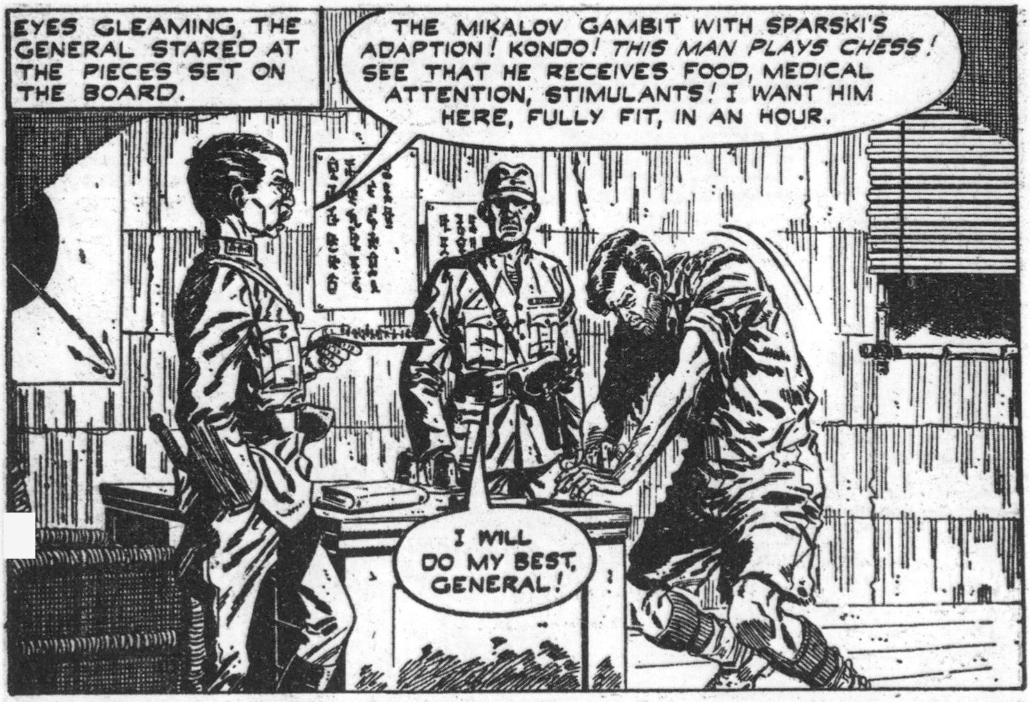
EYES GLEAMING, THE GENERAL STARED AT THE PIECES SET ON THE BOARD.
THE MIKALOV GAMBIT WITH SPARSKI'S ADAPTION! KONDO! *THIS MAN PLAYS CHESS!* SEE THAT HE RECEIVES FOOD, MEDICAL ATTENTION, STIMULANTS! I WANT HIM HERE, FULLY FIT, IN AN HOUR.
I WILL DO MY BEST, GENERAL!

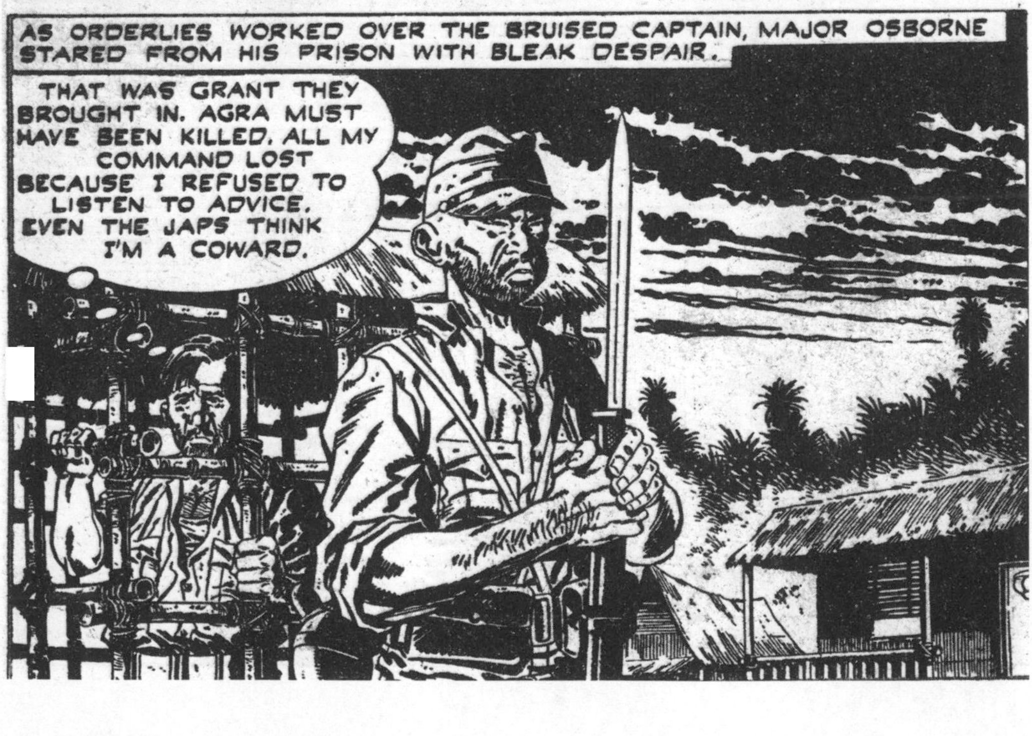
AS ORDERLIES WORKED OVER THE BRUISED CAPTAIN, MAJOR OSBORNE STARED FROM HIS PRISON WITH BLEAK DESPAIR.
THAT WAS GRANT THEY BROUGHT IN. AGRA MUST HAVE BEEN KILLED. ALL MY COMMAND LOST BECAUSE I REFUSED TO LISTEN TO ADVICE. EVEN THE JAPS THINK I'M A COWARD.

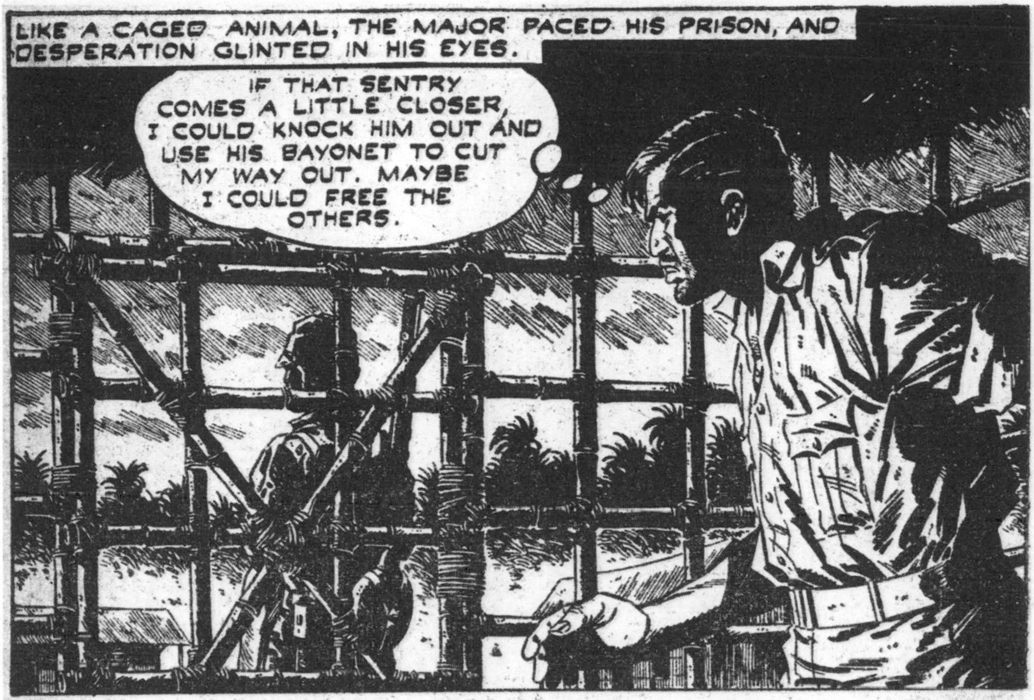
LIKE A CAGED ANIMAL, THE MAJOR PACED HIS PRISON, AND DESPERATION GLINTED IN HIS EYES.
IF THAT SENTRY COMES A LITTLE CLOSER, I COULD KNOCK HIM OUT AND USE HIS BAYONET TO CUT MY WAY OUT. MAYBE I COULD FREE THE OTHERS.

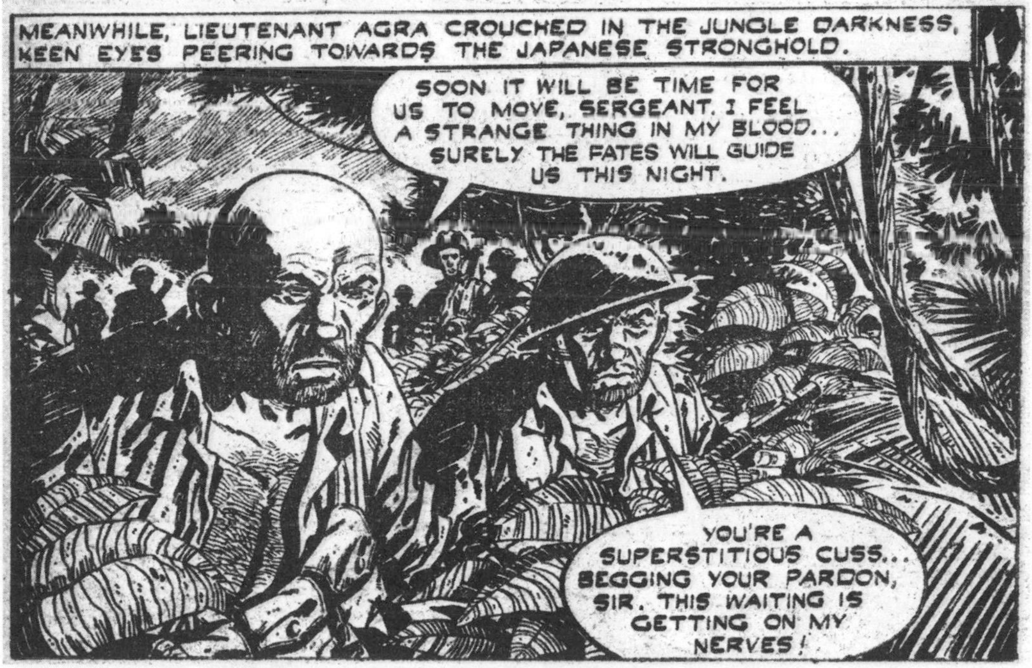
MEANWHILE, LIEUTENANT AGRA CROUCHED IN THE JUNGLE DARKNESS, KEEN EYES PEERING TOWARDS THE JAPANESE STRONGHOLD.
SOON IT WILL BE TIME FOR US TO MOVE, SERGEANT. I FEEL A STRANGE THING IN MY BLOOD... SURELY THE FATES WILL GUIDE US THIS NIGHT.
YOU'RE A SUPERSTITIOUS CUSS... BEGGING YOUR PARDON, SIR. THIS WAITING IS GETTING ON MY NERVES!

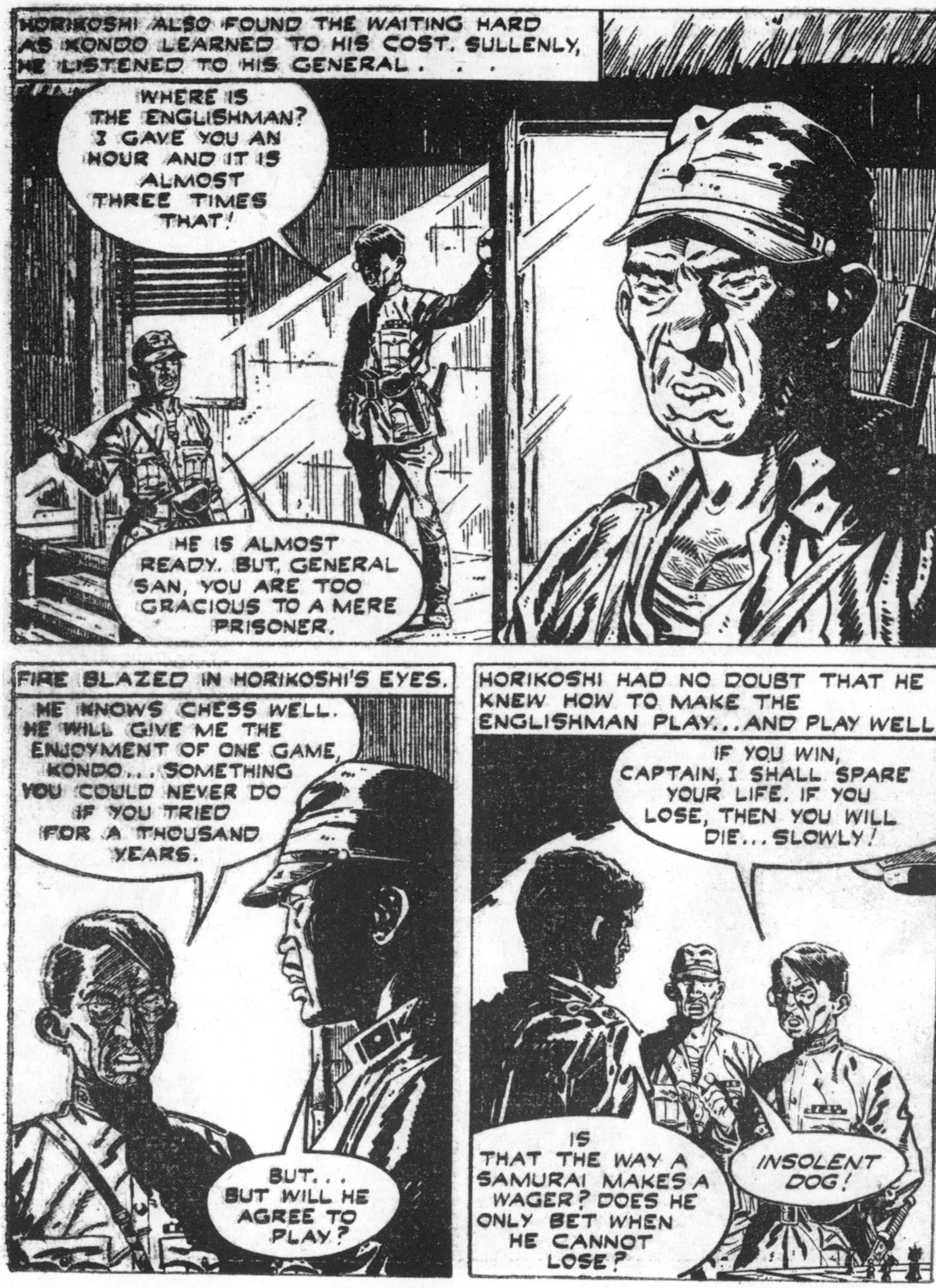
HORIKOSHI ALSO FOUND THE WAITING HARD AS KONDO LEARNED TO HIS COST. SULLENLY, HE LISTENED TO HIS GENERAL . . .
WHERE IS THE ENGLISHMAN? I GAVE YOU AN HOUR AND IT IS ALMOST THREE TIMES THAT!
HE IS ALMOST READY. BUT, GENERAL SAN, YOU ARE TOO GRACIOUS TO A MERE PRISONER.
FIRE BLAZED IN HORIKOSHI'S EYES.
HE KNOWS CHESS WELL. HE WILL GIVE ME THE ENJOYMENT OF ONE GAME, KONDO... SOMETHING YOU COULD NEVER DO IF YOU TRIED FOR A THOUSAND YEARS.
BUT... BUT WILL HE AGREE TO PLAY?
HORIKOSHI HAD NO DOUBT THAT HE KNEW HOW TO MAKE THE ENGLISHMAN PLAY...AND PLAY WELL
IF YOU WIN, CAPTAIN, I SHALL SPARE YOUR LIFE. IF YOU LOSE, THEN YOU WILL DIE... SLOWLY!
IS THAT THE WAY A SAMURAI MAKES A WAGER? DOES HE ONLY BET WHEN HE CANNOT LOSE?
INSOLENT DOG!

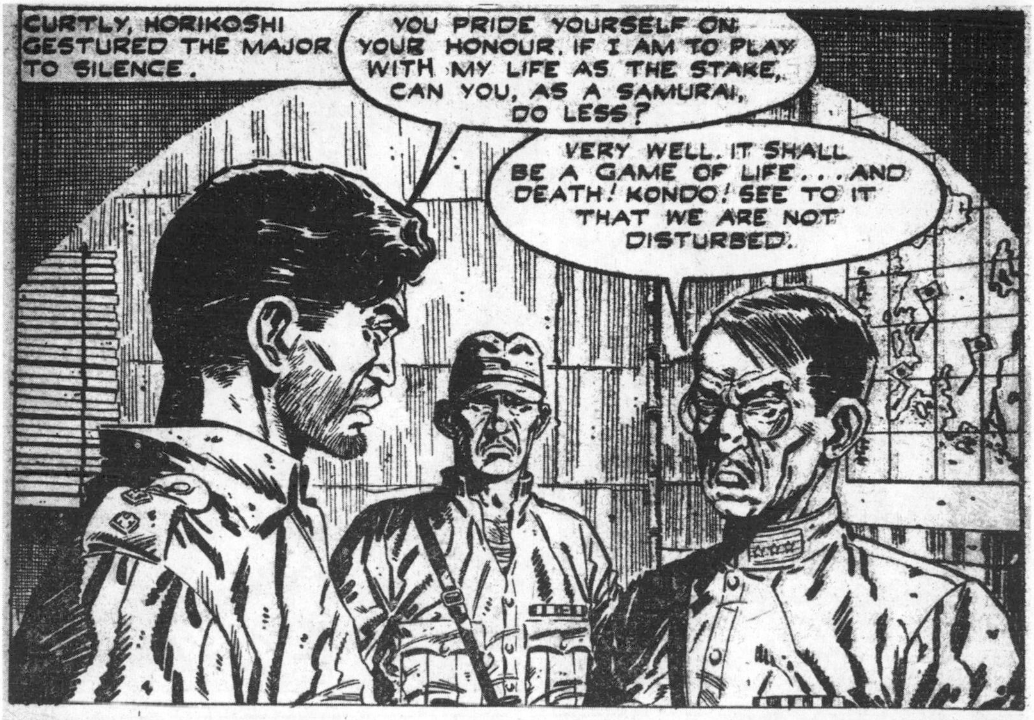
CURTLY, HORIKOSHI GESTURED THE MAJOR TO SILENCE.
YOU PRIDE YOURSELF ON YOUR HONOUR. IF I AM TO PLAY WITH MY LIFE AS THE STAKE, CAN YOU, AS A SAMURAI, DO LESS?
VERY WELL. IT SHALL BE A GAME OF LIFE. . . AND DEATH! KONDO! SEE TO IT THAT WE ARE NOT DISTURBED.

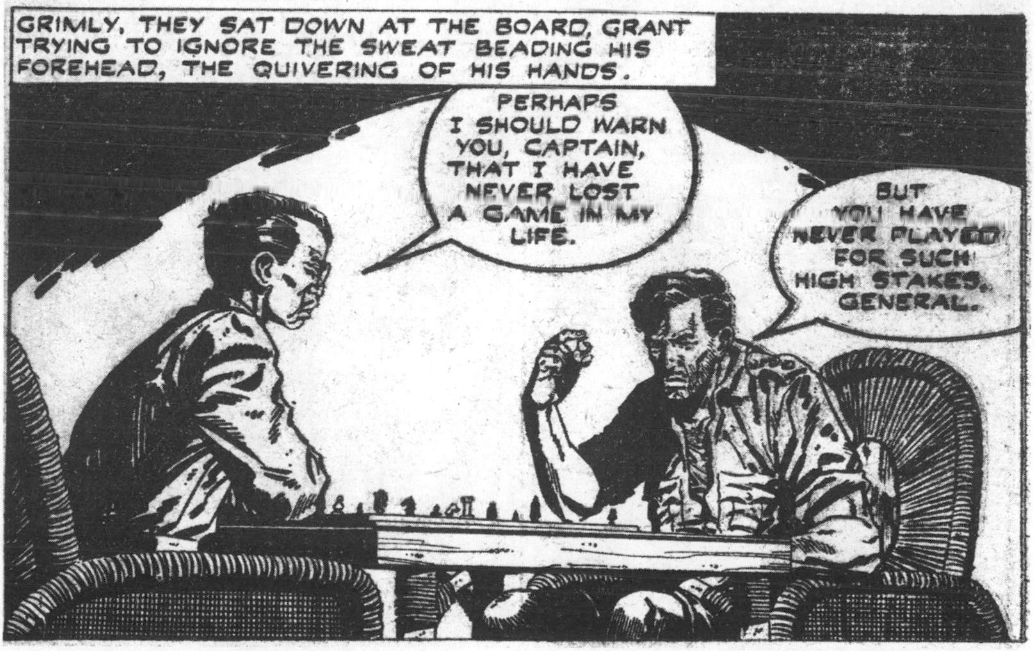
GRIMLY, THEY SAT DOWN AT THE BOARD, GRANT TRYING TO IGNORE THE SWEAT BEADING HIS FOREHEAD, THE QUIVERING OF HIS HANDS.
PERHAPS I SHOULD WARN YOU, CAPTAIN, THAT I HAVE NEVER LOST A GAME IN MY LIFE.
BUT YOU HAVE NEVER PLAYED FOR SUCH HIGH STAKES, GENERAL.

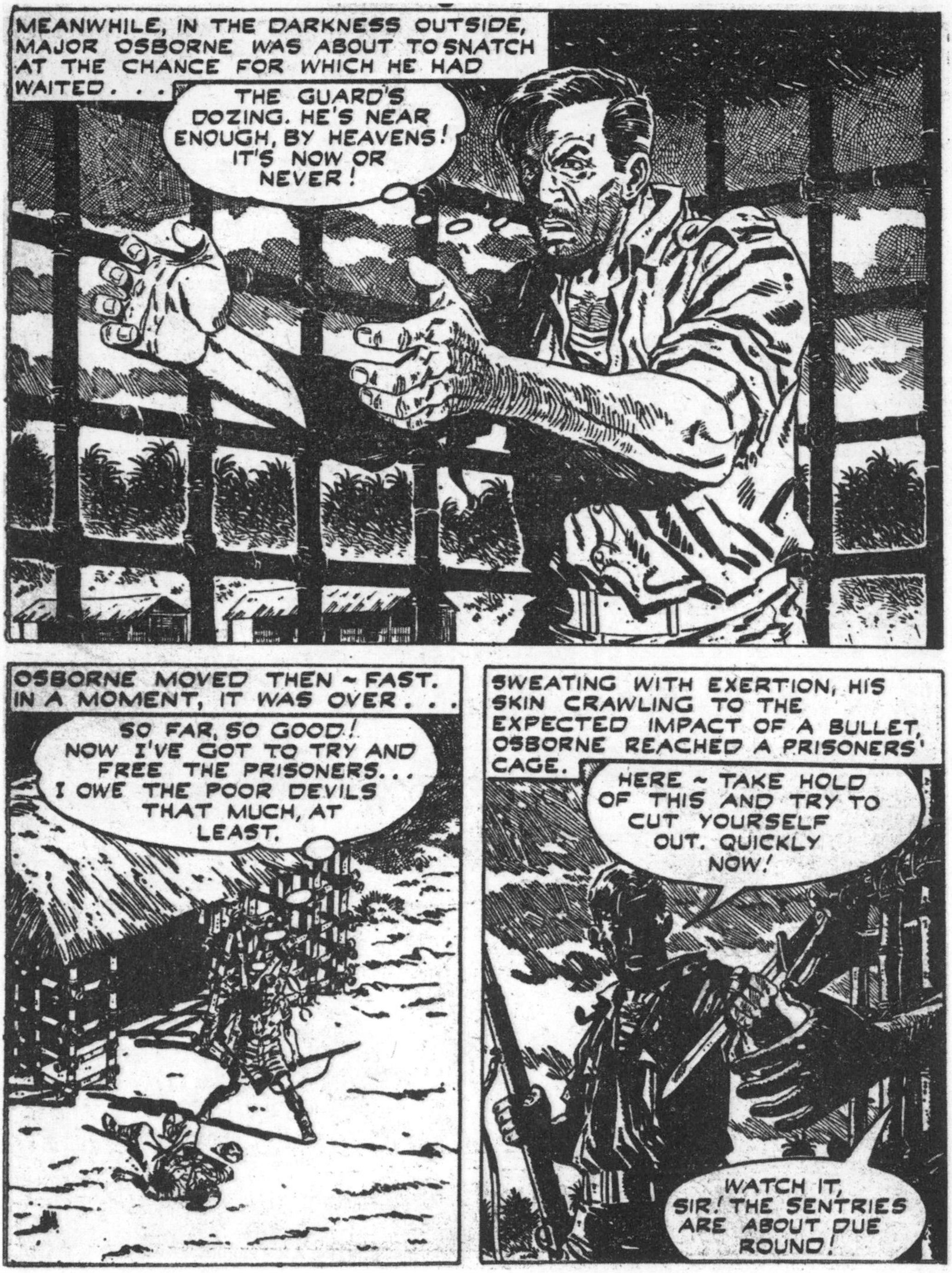
MEANWHILE, IN THE DARKNESS OUTSIDE, MAJOR OSBORNE WAS ABOUT TO SNATCH AT THE CHANCE FOR WHICH HE HAD WAITED . . .
THE GUARD'S DOZING. HE'S NEAR ENOUGH, BY HEAVENS! IT'S NOW OR NEVER!
OSBORNE MOVED THEN ~ FAST. IN A MOMENT, IT WAS OVER . . .
SO FAR, SO GOOD! NOW I'VE GOT TO TRY AND FREE THE PRISONERS... I OWE THE POOR DEVILS THAT MUCH, AT LEAST.
SWEATING WITH EXERTION, HIS SKIN CRAWLING TO THE EXPECTED IMPACT OF A BULLET, OSBORNE REACHED A PRISONERS' CAGE.
HERE ~ TAKE HOLD OF THIS AND TRY TO CUT YOURSELF OUT. QUICKLY NOW!
WATCH IT, SIR! THE SENTRIES ARE ABOUT DUE ROUND!

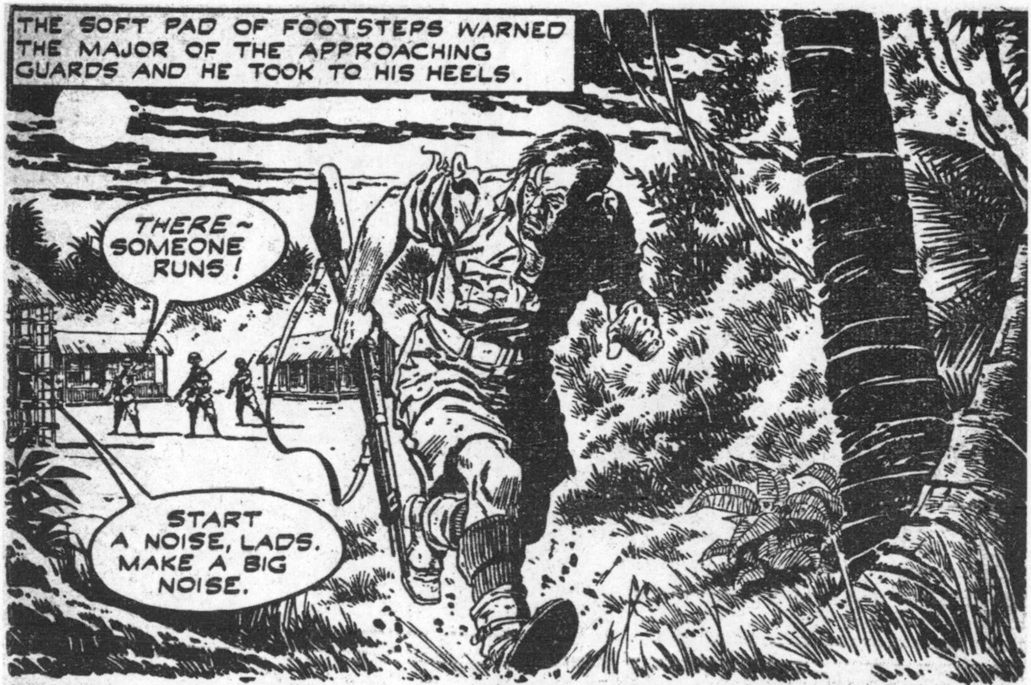
THE SOFT PAD OF FOOTSTEPS WARNED THE MAJOR OF THE APPROACHING GUARDS AND HE TOOK TO HIS HEELS.
THERE~ SOMEONE RUNS!
START A NOISE, LADS. MAKE A BIG NOISE.

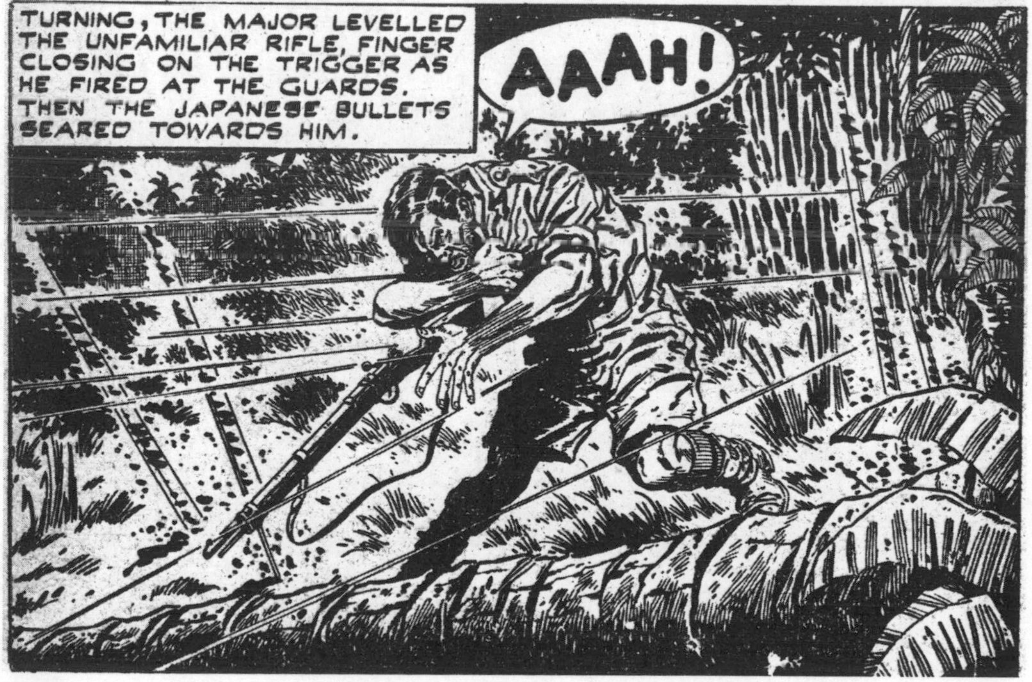
TURNING, THE MAJOR LEVELLED THE UNFAMILIAR RIFLE, FINGER CLOSING ON THE TRIGGER AS HE FIRED AT THE GUARDS. THEN THE JAPANESE BULLETS SEARED TOWARDS HIM.
AAAH!

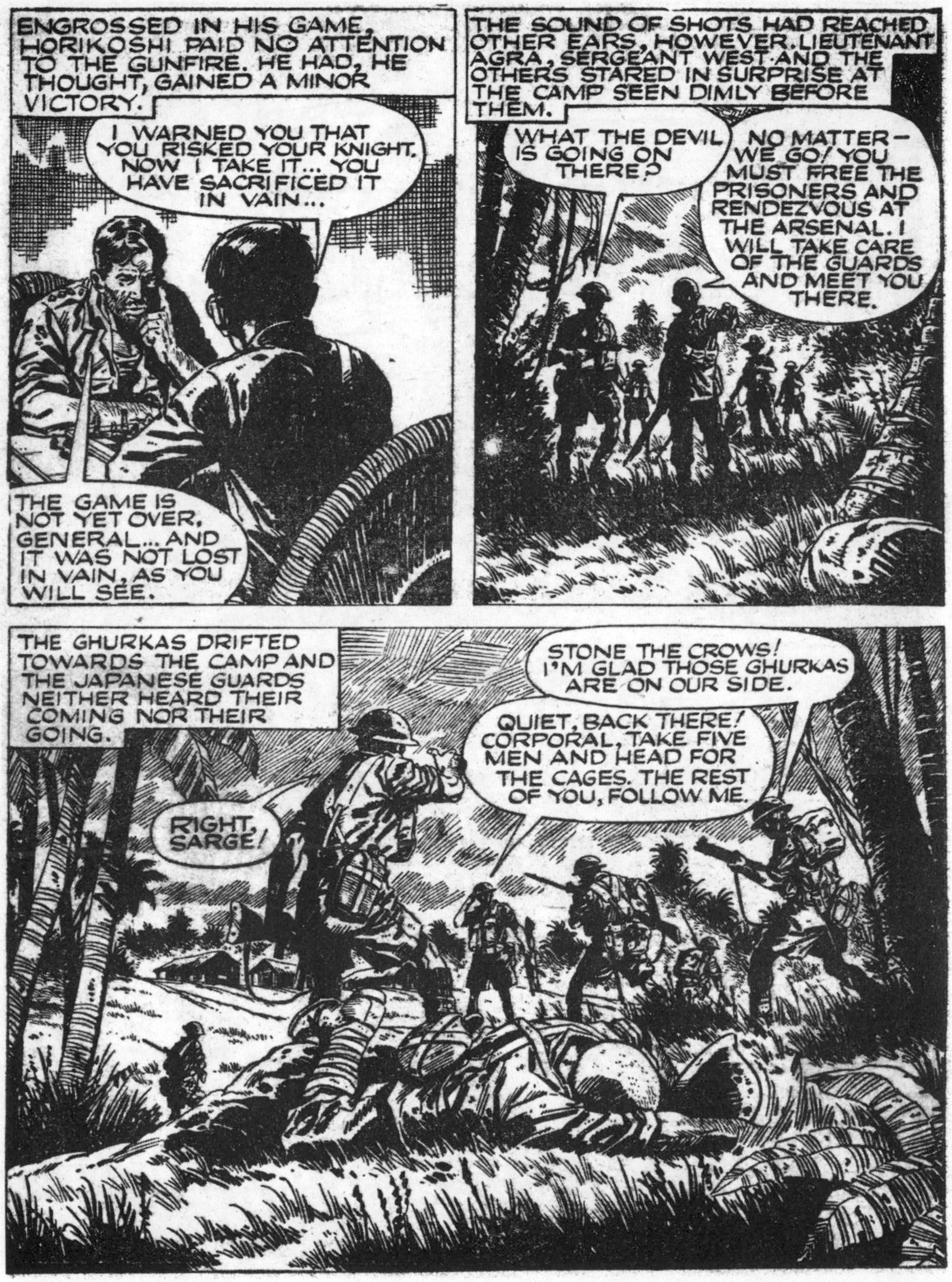
ENGROSSED IN HIS GAME, HORIKOSHI PAID NO ATTENTION TO THE GUNFIRE. HE HAD, HE THOUGHT, GAINED A MINOR VICTORY.
I WARNED YOU THAT YOU RISKED YOUR KNIGHT. NOW I TAKE IT... YOU HAVE SACRIFICED IT IN VAIN...
THE GAME IS NOT YET OVER, GENERAL... AND IT WAS NOT LOST IN VAIN, AS YOU WILL SEE.
THE SOUND OF SHOTS HAD REACHED OTHER EARS, HOWEVER. LIEUTENANT AGRA, SERGEANT WEST AND THE OTHERS STARED IN SURPRISE AT THE CAMP SEEN DIMLY BEFORE THEM.
WHAT THE DEVIL IS GOING ON THERE?
NO MATTER – WE GO! YOU MUST FREE THE PRISONERS AND RENDEZVOUS AT THE ARSENAL. I WILL TAKE CARE OF THE GUARDS AND MEET YOU THERE.
THE GHURKAS DRIFTED TOWARDS THE CAMP AND THE JAPANESE GUARDS NEITHER HEARD THEIR COMING NOR THEIR GOING.
STONE THE CROWS! I'M GLAD THOSE GHURKAS ARE ON OUR SIDE.
QUIET, BACK THERE! CORPORAL, TAKE FIVE MEN AND HEAD FOR THE CAGES. THE REST OF YOU, FOLLOW ME.
RIGHT, SARGE!

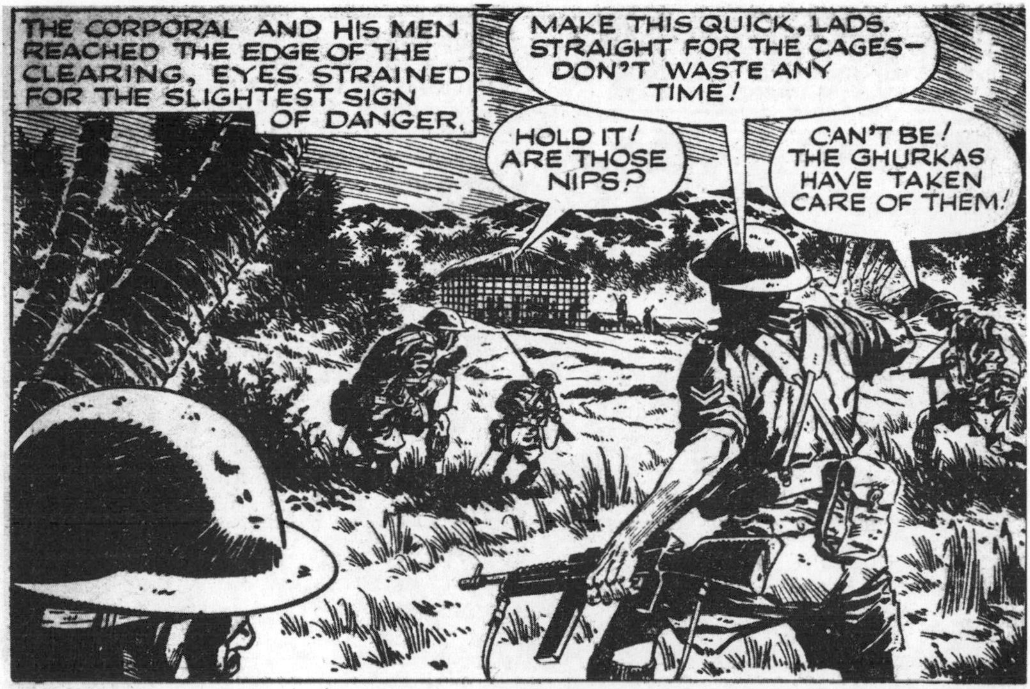
THE CORPORAL AND HIS MEN REACHED THE EDGE OF THE CLEARING, EYES STRAINED FOR THE SLIGHTEST SIGN OF DANGER.
MAKE THIS QUICK, LADS. STRAIGHT FOR THE CAGES— DON'T WASTE ANY TIME!
HOLD IT! ARE THOSE NIPS?
CAN'T BE! THE GHURKAS HAVE TAKEN CARE OF THEM!

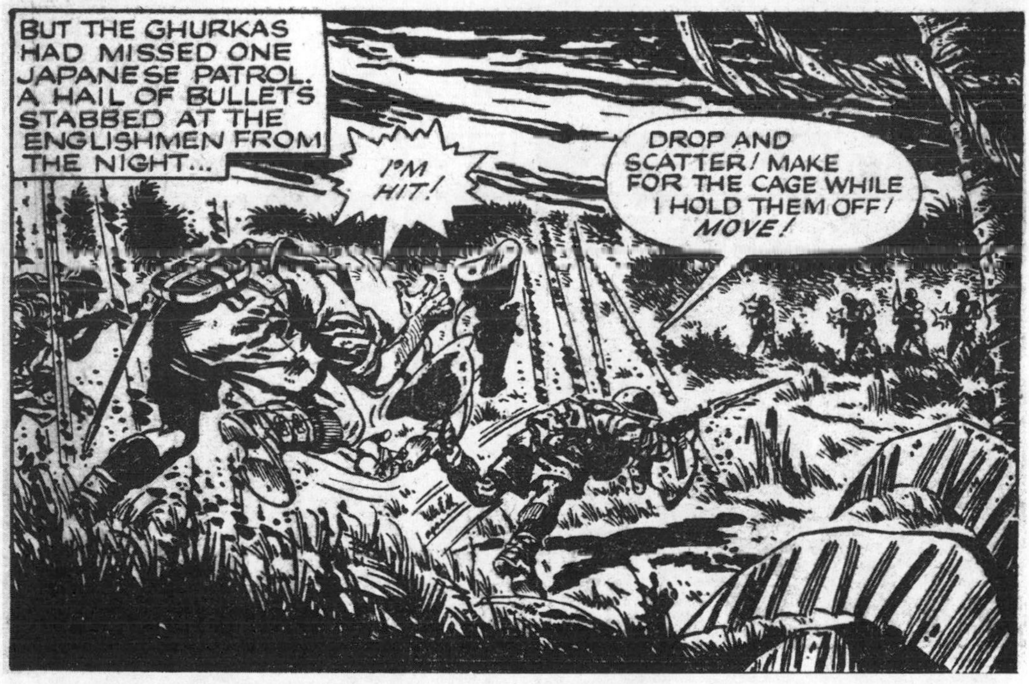
BUT THE GHURKAS HAD MISSED ONE JAPANESE PATROL. A HAIL OF BULLETS STABBED AT THE ENGLISHMEN FROM THE NIGHT...
I'M HIT!
DROP AND SCATTER! MAKE FOR THE CAGE WHILE I HOLD THEM OFF! MOVE!

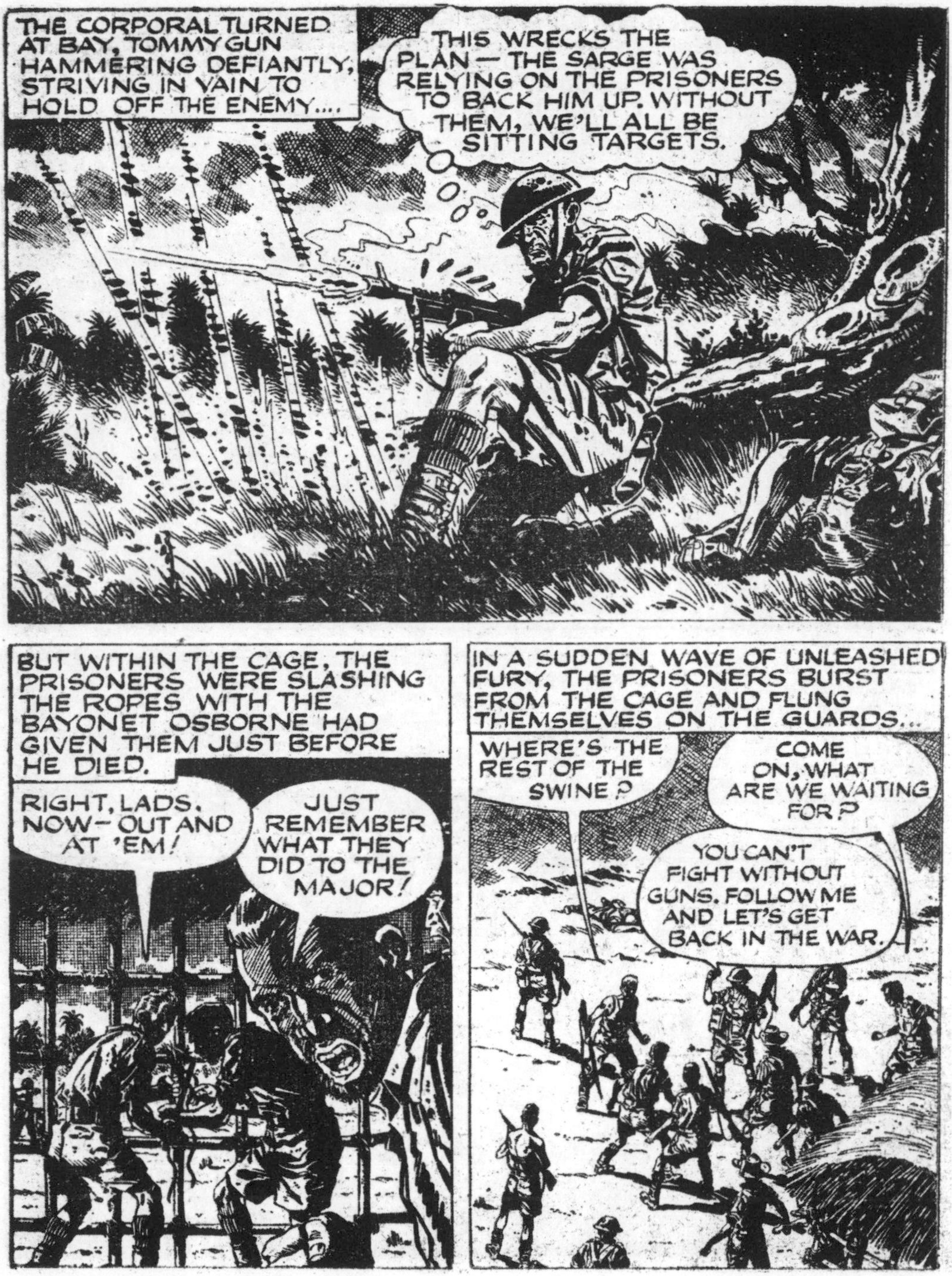
THE CORPORAL TURNED AT BAY, TOMMY GUN HAMMERING DEFIANTLY, STRIVING IN VAIN TO HOLD OFF THE ENEMY....
THIS WRECKS THE PLAN — THE SARGE WAS RELYING ON THE PRISONERS TO BACK HIM UP. WITHOUT THEM, WE'LL ALL BE SITTING TARGETS.
BUT WITHIN THE CAGE, THE PRISONERS WERE SLASHING THE ROPES WITH THE BAYONET OSBORNE HAD GIVEN THEM JUST BEFORE HE DIED.
RIGHT, LADS. NOW – OUT AND AT 'EM!
JUST REMEMBER WHAT THEY DID TO THE MAJOR!
IN A SUDDEN WAVE OF UNLEASHED FURY, THE PRISONERS BURST FROM THE CAGE AND FLUNG THEMSELVES ON THE GUARDS...
WHERE'S THE REST OF THE SWINE?
COME ON, WHAT ARE WE WAITING FOR?
YOU CAN'T FIGHT WITHOUT GUNS. FOLLOW ME AND LET'S GET BACK IN THE WAR.

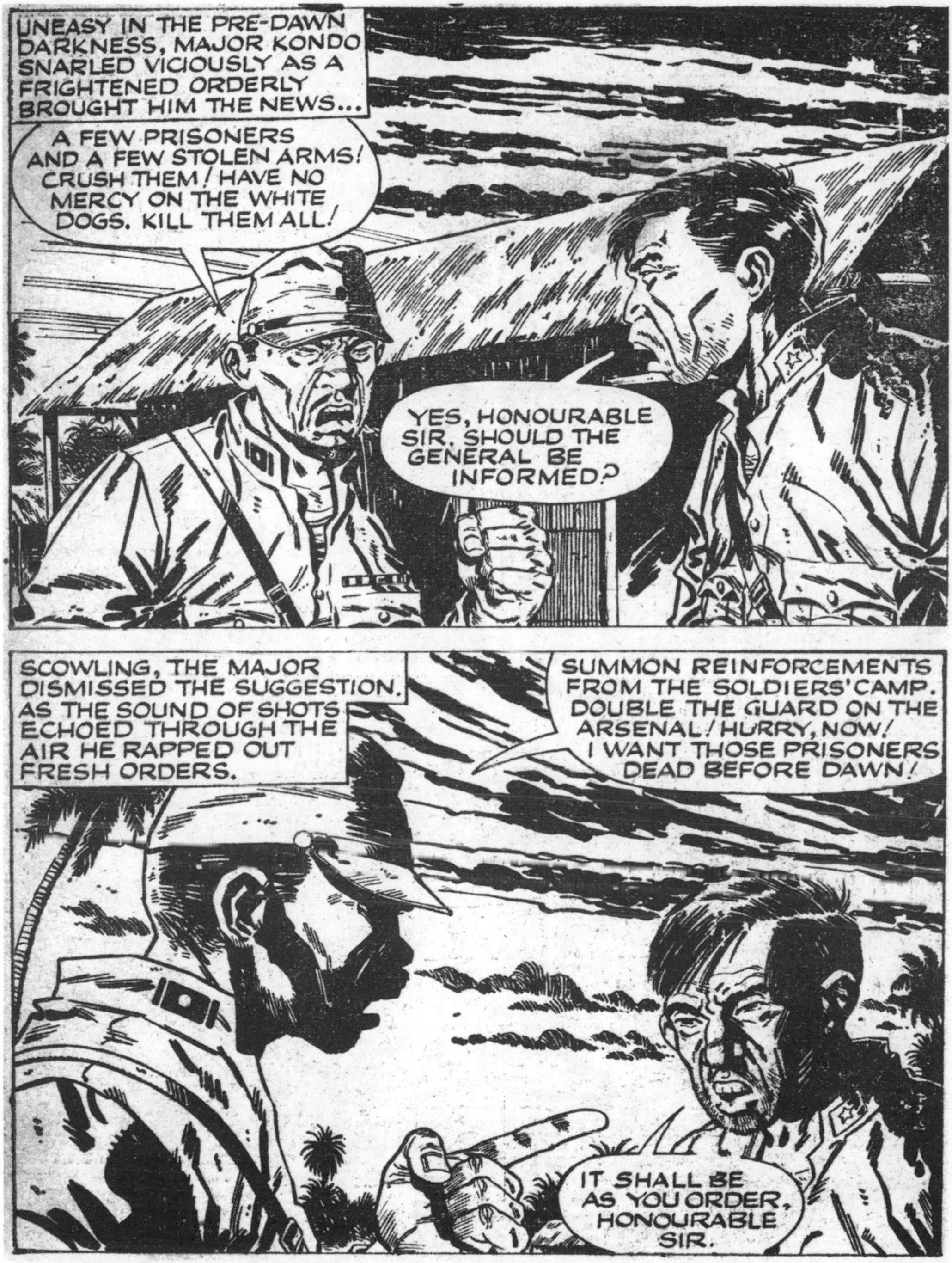
UNEASY IN THE PRE-DAWN DARKNESS, MAJOR KONDO SNARLED VICIOUSLY AS A FRIGHTENED ORDERLY BROUGHT HIM THE NEWS...
A FEW PRISONERS AND A FEW STOLEN ARMS! CRUSH THEM! HAVE NO MERCY ON THE WHITE DOGS. KILL THEM ALL!
YES, HONOURABLE SIR. SHOULD THE GENERAL BE INFORMED?
SCOWLING, THE MAJOR DISMISSED THE SUGGESTION. AS THE SOUND OF SHOTS ECHOED THROUGH THE AIR HE RAPPED OUT FRESH ORDERS.
SUMMON REINFORCEMENTS FROM THE SOLDIERS' CAMP. DOUBLE THE GUARD ON THE ARSENAL! HURRY, NOW! I WANT THOSE PRISONERS DEAD BEFORE DAWN!
IT SHALL BE AS YOU ORDER, HONOURABLE SIR.

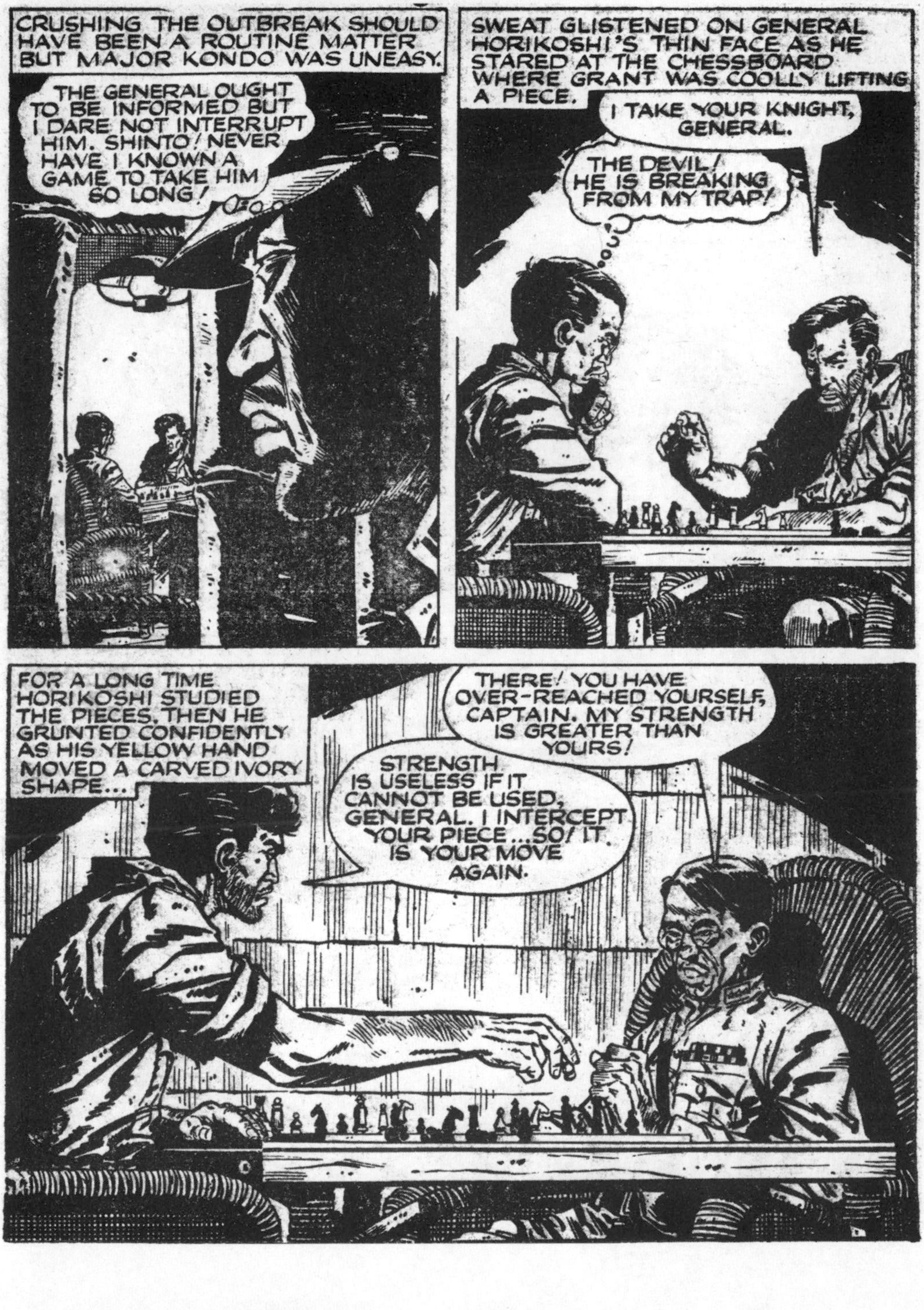
CRUSHING THE OUTBREAK SHOULD HAVE BEEN A ROUTINE MATTER BUT MAJOR KONDO WAS UNEASY.
THE GENERAL OUGHT TO BE INFORMED BUT I DARE NOT INTERRUPT HIM. SHINTO! NEVER HAVE I KNOWN A GAME TO TAKE HIM SO LONG!
SWEAT GLISTENED ON GENERAL HORIKOSHI'S THIN FACE AS HE STARED AT THE CHESSBOARD WHERE GRANT WAS COOLLY LIFTING A PIECE.
I TAKE YOUR KNIGHT, GENERAL.
THE DEVIL! HE IS BREAKING FROM MY TRAP!
FOR A LONG TIME HORIKOSHI STUDIED THE PIECES. THEN HE GRUNTED CONFIDENTLY AS HIS YELLOW HAND MOVED A CARVED IVORY SHAPE...
THERE! YOU HAVE OVER-REACHED YOURSELF, CAPTAIN. MY STRENGTH IS GREATER THAN YOURS!
STRENGTH IS USELESS IF IT CANNOT BE USED, GENERAL. I INTERCEPT YOUR PIECE...SO! IT IS YOUR MOVE AGAIN.

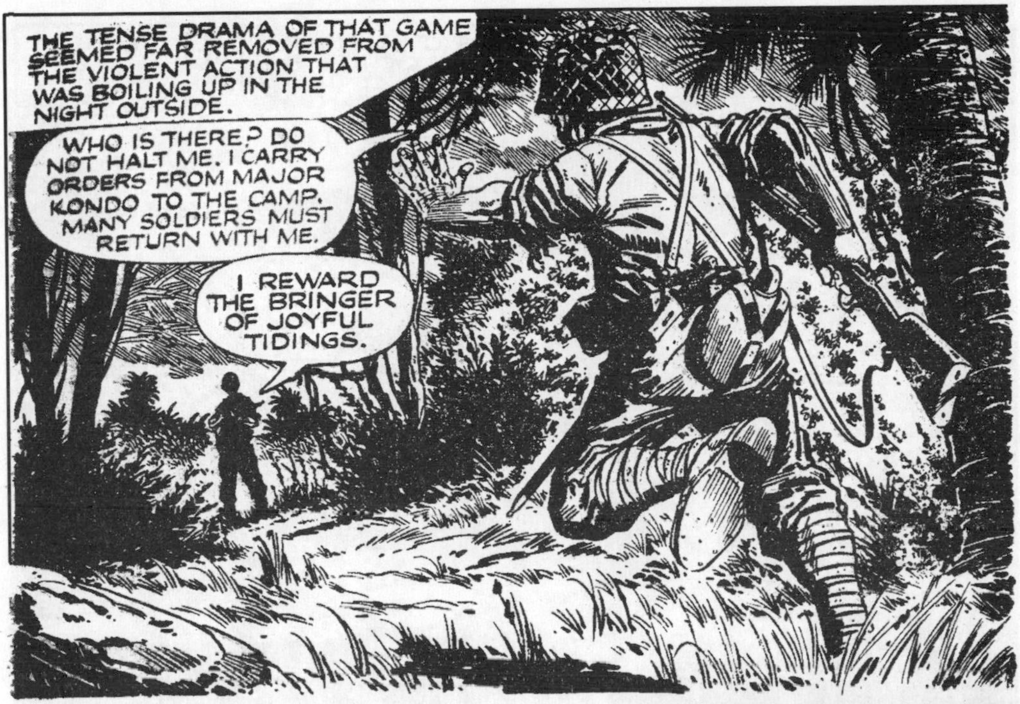
THE TENSE DRAMA OF THAT GAME SEEMED FAR REMOVED FROM THE VIOLENT ACTION THAT WAS BOILING UP IN THE NIGHT OUTSIDE.
WHO IS THERE? DO NOT HALT ME. I CARRY ORDERS FROM MAJOR KONDO TO THE CAMP. MANY SOLDIERS MUST RETURN WITH ME.
I REWARD THE BRINGER OF JOYFUL TIDINGS.

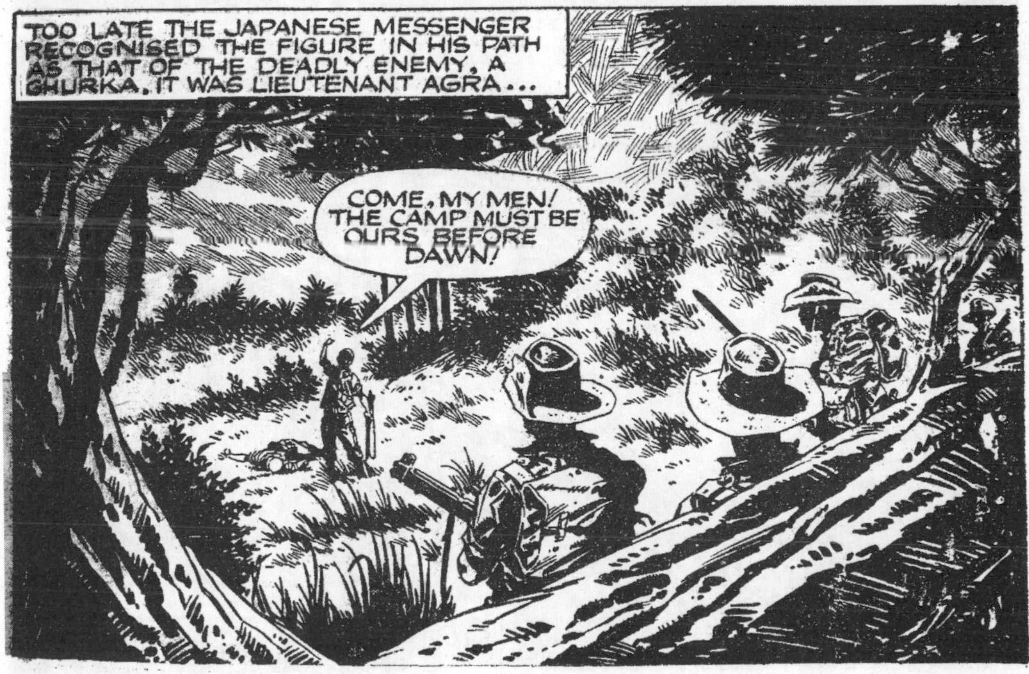
TOO LATE THE JAPANESE MESSENGER RECOGNISED THE FIGURE IN HIS PATH AS THAT OF THE DEADLY ENEMY, A GHURKA. IT WAS LIEUTENANT AGRA...
COME, MY MEN! THE CAMP MUST BE OURS BEFORE DAWN!

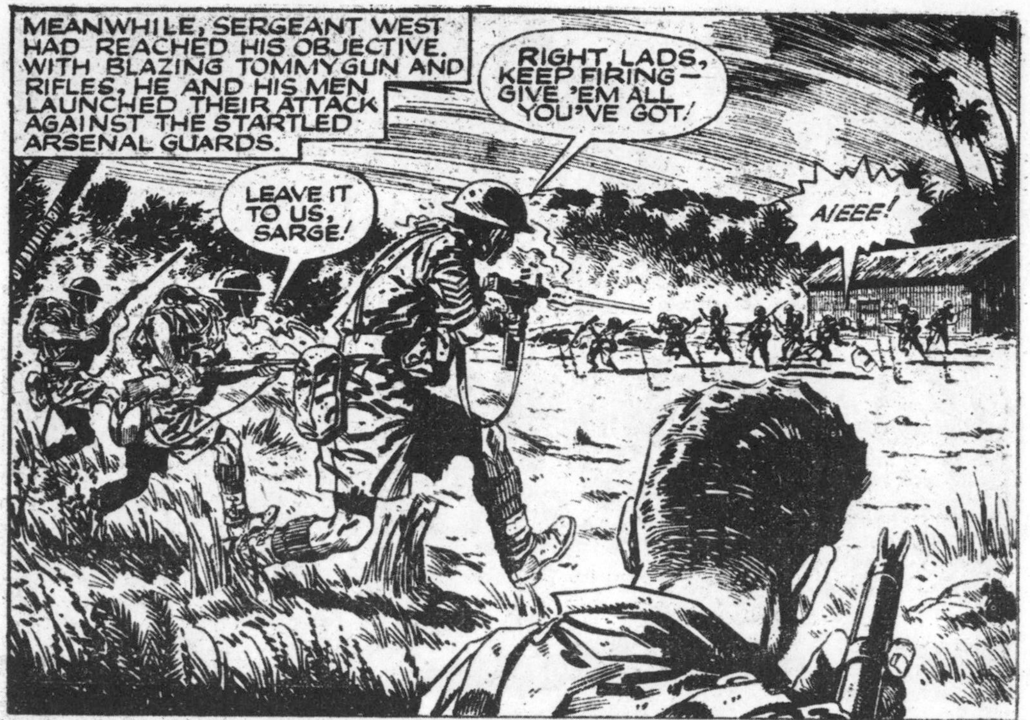
MEANWHILE, SERGEANT WEST HAD REACHED HIS OBJECTIVE. WITH BLAZING TOMMYGUN AND RIFLES, HE AND HIS MEN LAUNCHED THEIR ATTACK AGAINST THE STARTLED ARSENAL GUARDS.
RIGHT, LADS, KEEP FIRING — GIVE 'EM ALL YOU'VE GOT!
LEAVE IT TO US, SARGE!
AIEEE!

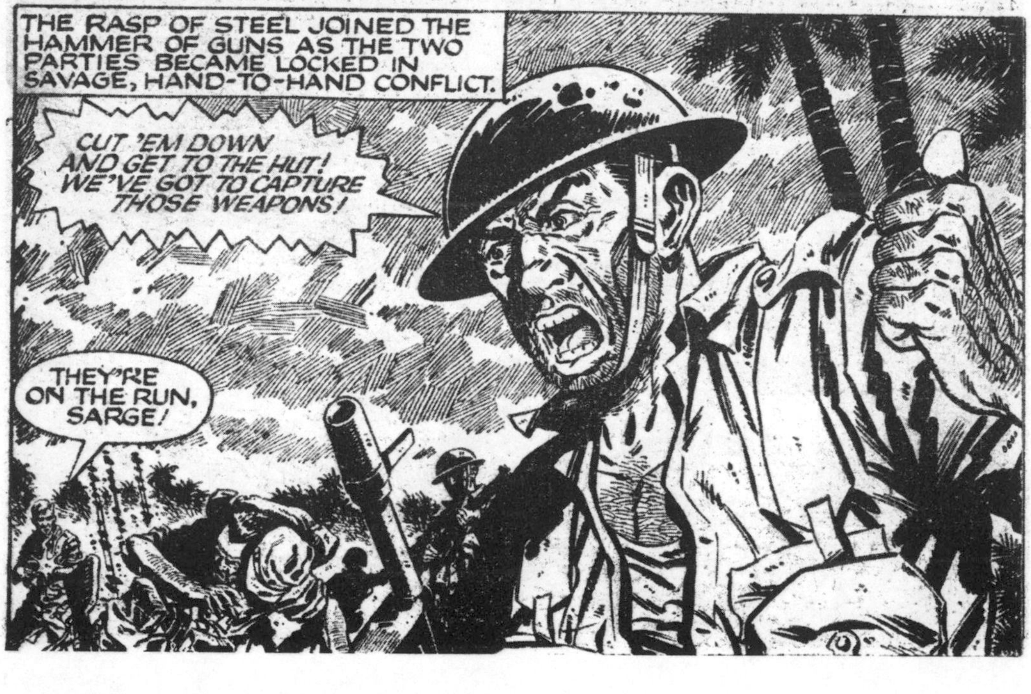
THE RASP OF STEEL JOINED THE HAMMER OF GUNS AS THE TWO PARTIES BECAME LOCKED IN SAVAGE, HAND-TO-HAND CONFLICT.
CUT 'EM DOWN AND GET TO THE HUT! WE'VE GOT TO CAPTURE THOSE WEAPONS!
THEY'RE ON THE RUN, SARGE!

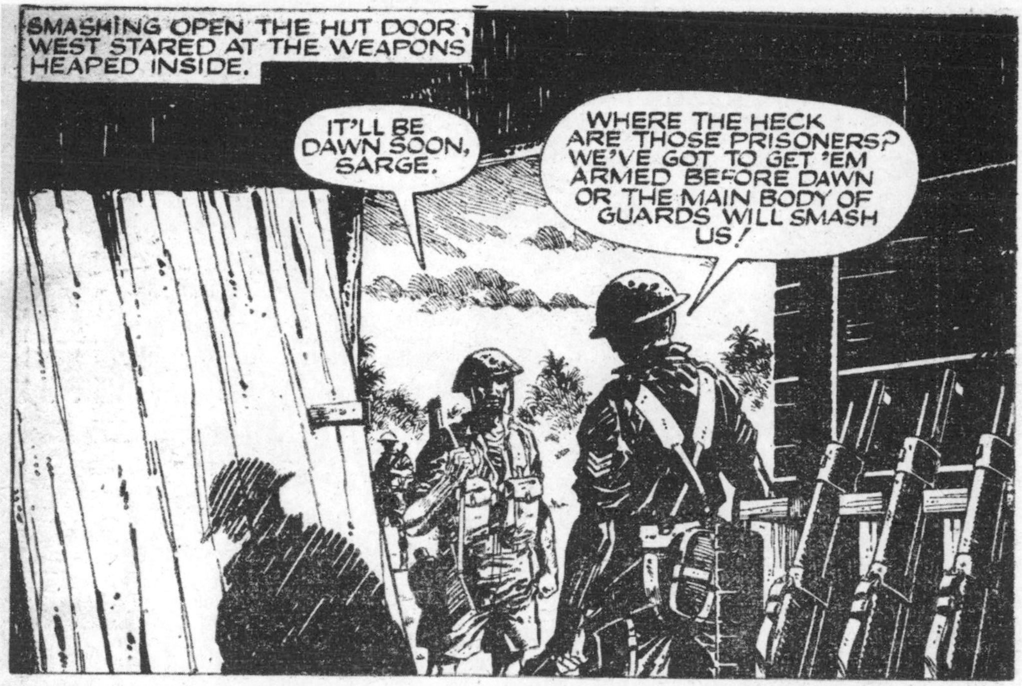
SMASHING OPEN THE HUT DOOR, WEST STARED AT THE WEAPONS HEAPED INSIDE.
IT'LL BE DAWN SOON, SARGE.
WHERE THE HECK ARE THOSE PRISONERS? WE'VE GOT TO GET 'EM ARMED BEFORE DAWN OR THE MAIN BODY OF GUARDS WILL SMASH US!

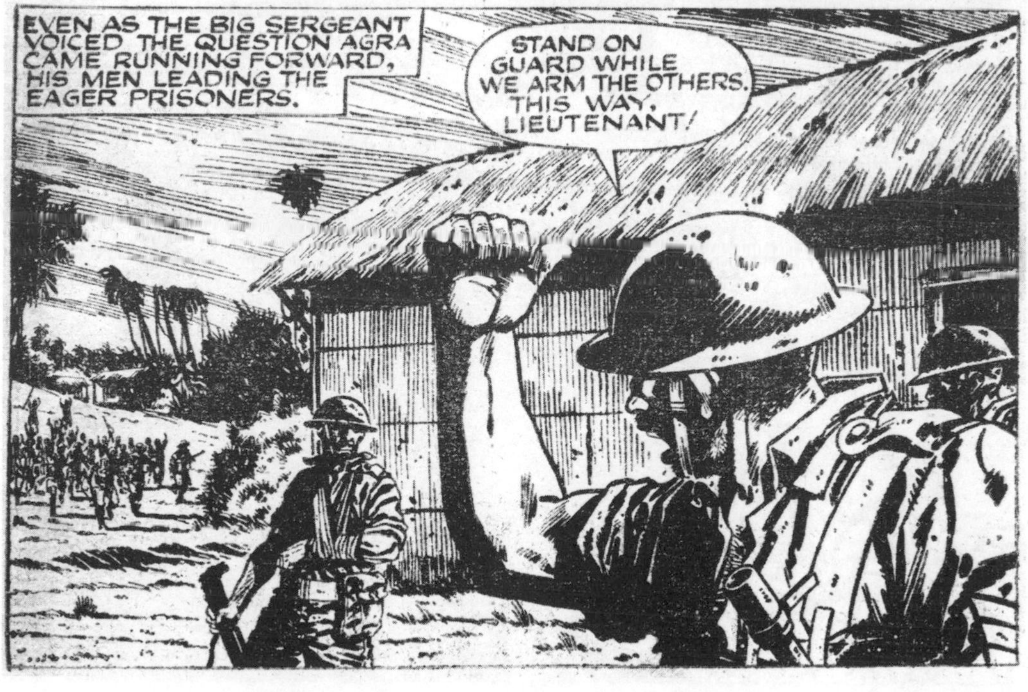
EVEN AS THE BIG SERGEANT VOICED THE QUESTION AGRA CAME RUNNING FORWARD, HIS MEN LEADING THE EAGER PRISONERS.
STAND ON GUARD WHILE WE ARM THE OTHERS. THIS WAY, LIEUTENANT!

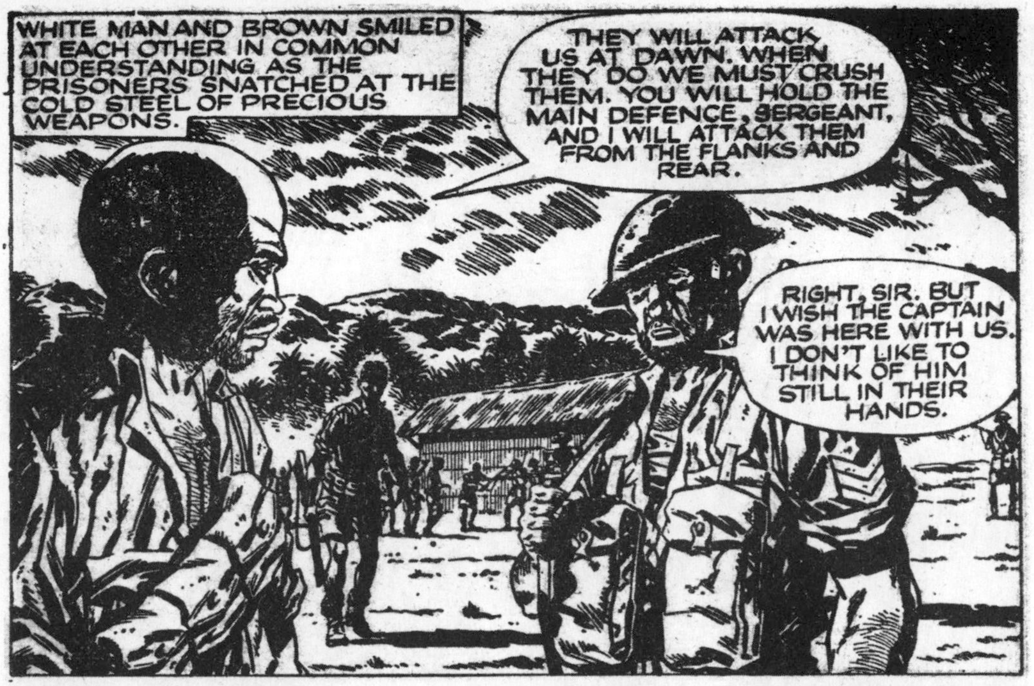
WHITE MAN AND BROWN SMILED AT EACH OTHER IN COMMON UNDERSTANDING AS THE PRISONERS SNATCHED AT THE COLD STEEL OF PRECIOUS WEAPONS.
THEY WILL ATTACK US AT DAWN. WHEN THEY DO WE MUST CRUSH THEM. YOU WILL HOLD THE MAIN DEFENCE, SERGEANT, AND I WILL ATTACK THEM FROM THE FLANKS AND REAR.
RIGHT, SIR. BUT I WISH THE CAPTAIN WAS HERE WITH US. I DON'T LIKE TO THINK OF HIM STILL IN THEIR HANDS.

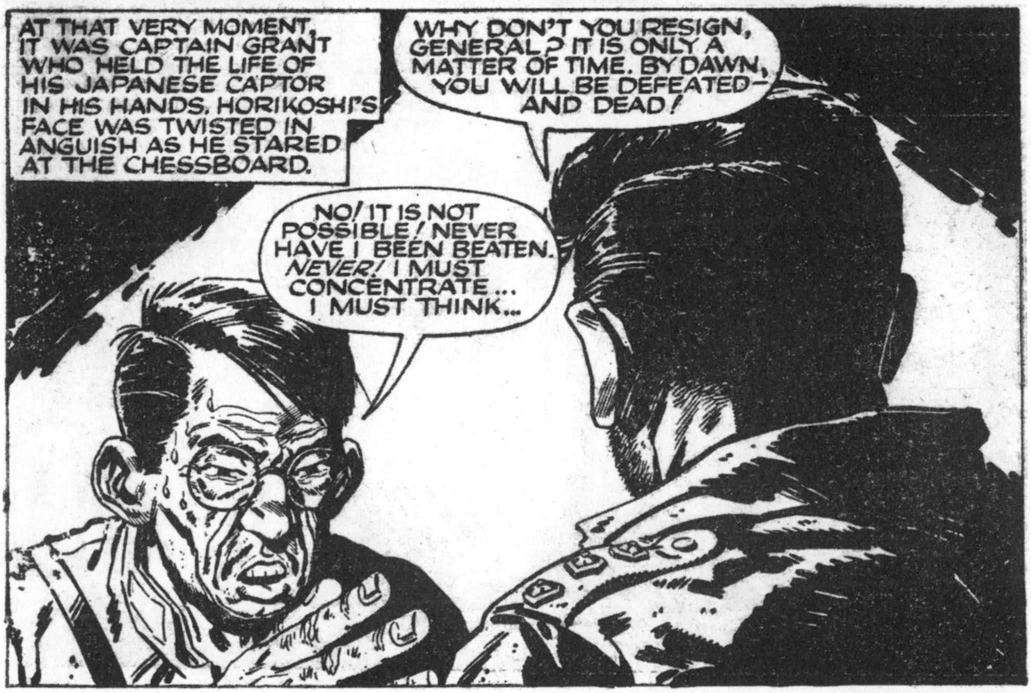
AT THAT VERY MOMENT, IT WAS CAPTAIN GRANT WHO HELD THE LIFE OF HIS JAPANESE CAPTOR IN HIS HANDS. HORIKOSHI'S FACE WAS TWISTED IN ANGUISH AS HE STARED AT THE CHESSBOARD.
WHY DON'T YOU RESIGN, GENERAL? IT IS ONLY A MATTER OF TIME. BY DAWN, YOU WILL BE DEFEATED— AND DEAD!
NO! IT IS NOT POSSIBLE! NEVER HAVE I BEEN BEATEN. *NEVER!* I MUST CONCENTRATE... I MUST THINK...

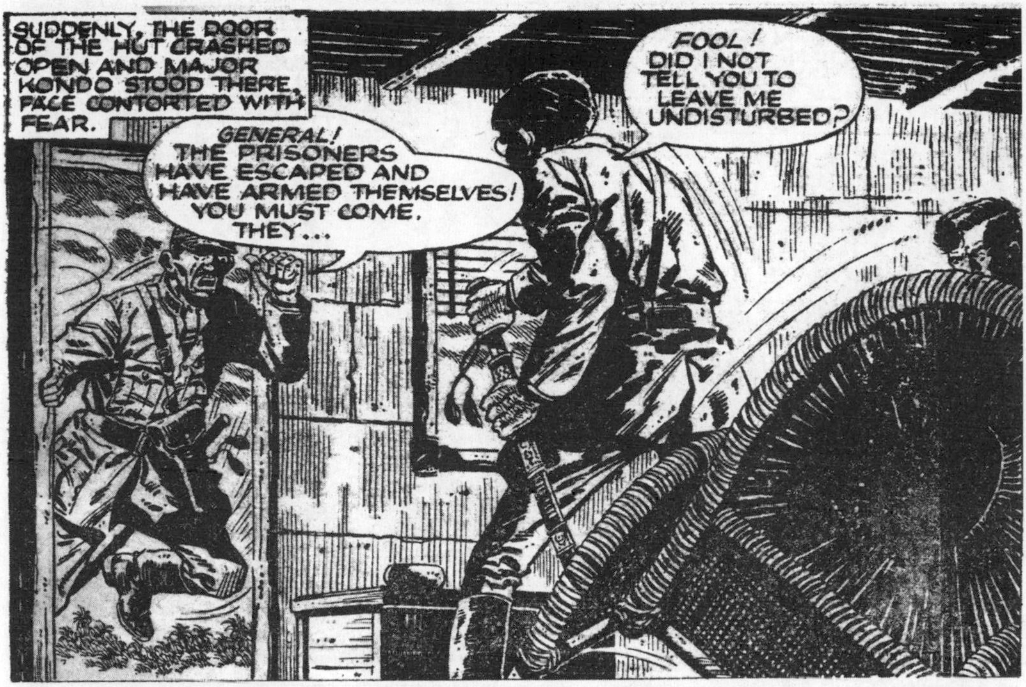
SUDDENLY, THE DOOR OF THE HUT CRASHED OPEN AND MAJOR KONDO STOOD THERE, FACE CONTORTED WITH FEAR.
GENERAL! THE PRISONERS HAVE ESCAPED AND HAVE ARMED THEMSELVES! YOU MUST COME. THEY...
FOOL! DID I NOT TELL YOU TO LEAVE ME UNDISTURBED?

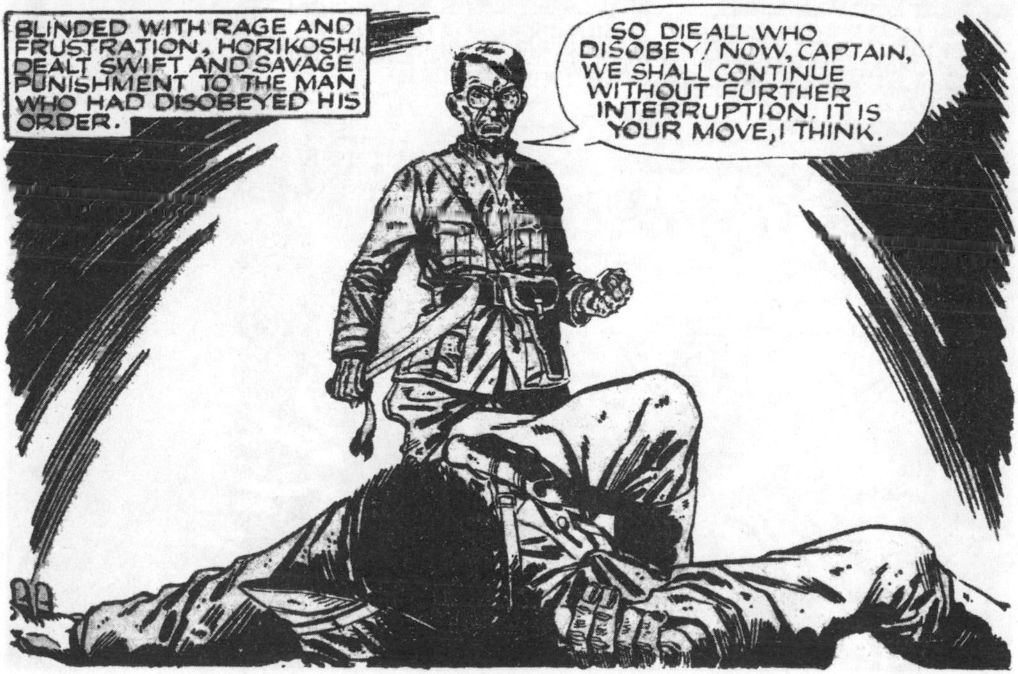
BLINDED WITH RAGE AND FRUSTRATION, HORIKOSHI DEALT SWIFT AND SAVAGE PUNISHMENT TO THE MAN WHO HAD DISOBEYED HIS ORDER.
SO DIE ALL WHO DISOBEY! NOW, CAPTAIN, WE SHALL CONTINUE WITHOUT FURTHER INTERRUPTION. IT IS YOUR MOVE, I THINK.

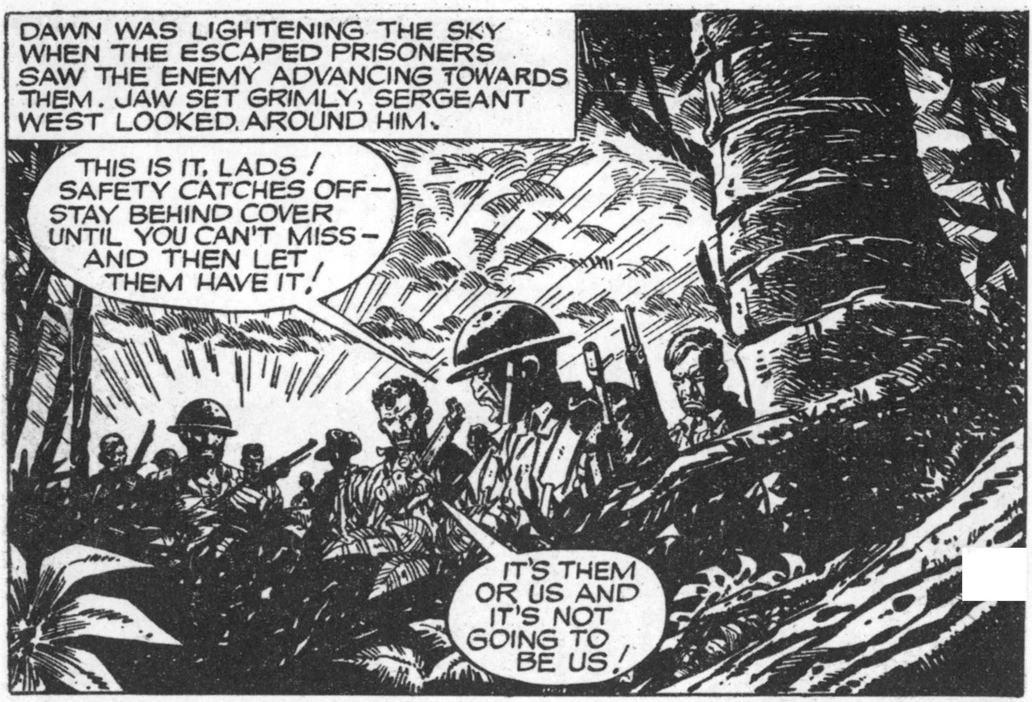
DAWN WAS LIGHTENING THE SKY WHEN THE ESCAPED PRISONERS SAW THE ENEMY ADVANCING TOWARDS THEM. JAW SET GRIMLY, SERGEANT WEST LOOKED AROUND HIM.
THIS IS IT, LADS! SAFETY CATCHES OFF— STAY BEHIND COVER UNTIL YOU CAN'T MISS— AND THEN LET THEM HAVE IT!
IT'S THEM OR US AND IT'S NOT GOING TO BE US!

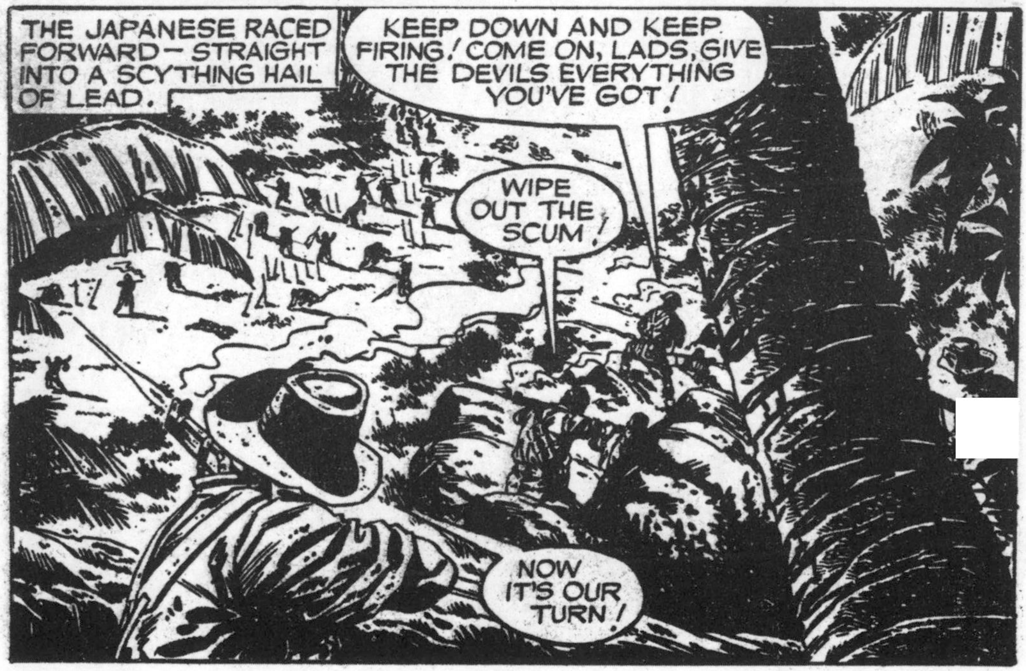
THE JAPANESE RACED FORWARD— STRAIGHT INTO A SCYTHING HAIL OF LEAD.
KEEP DOWN AND KEEP FIRING! COME ON, LADS, GIVE THE DEVILS EVERYTHING YOU'VE GOT!
WIPE OUT THE SCUM!
NOW IT'S OUR TURN!

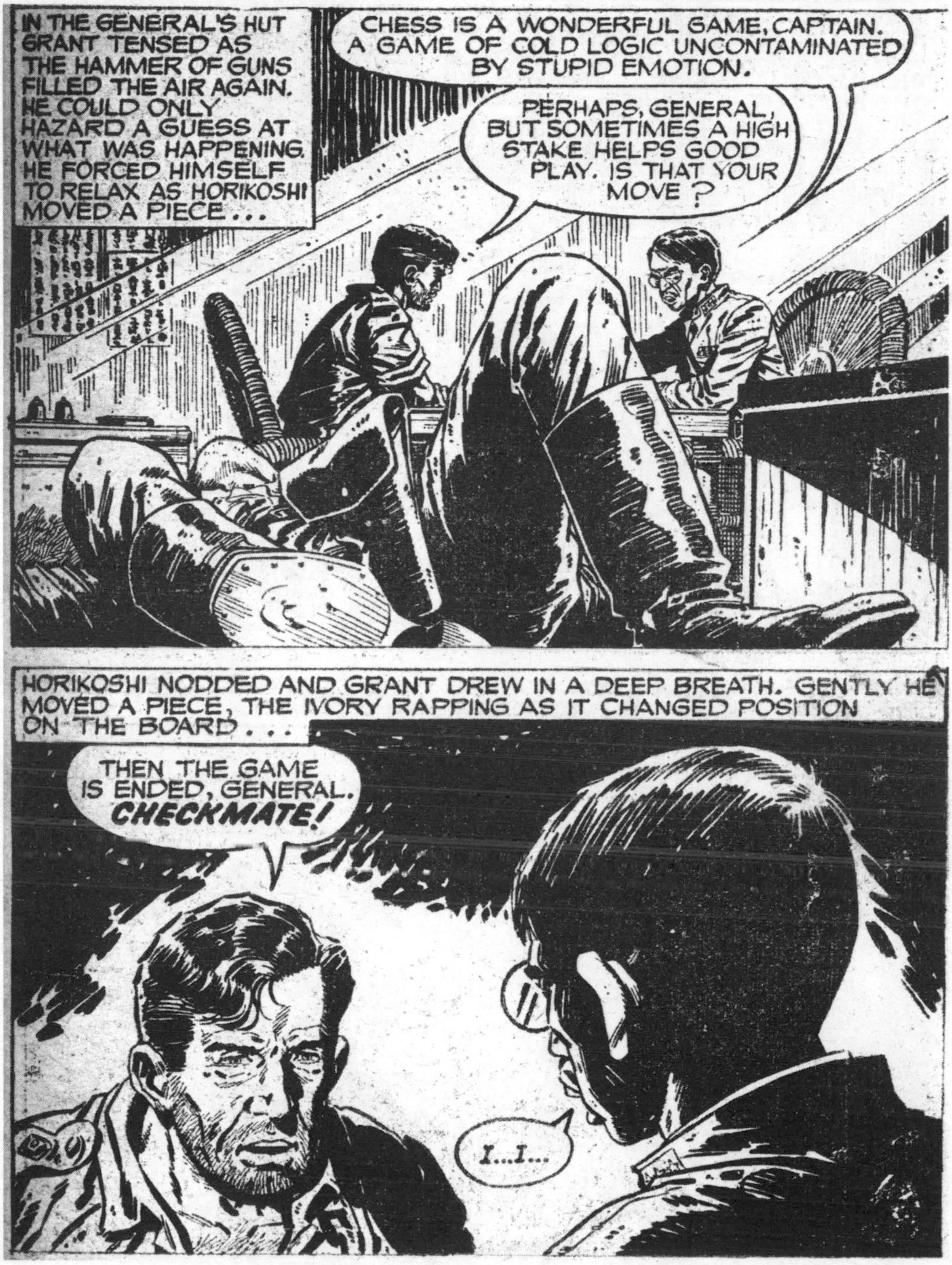
IN THE GENERAL'S HUT GRANT TENSED AS THE HAMMER OF GUNS FILLED THE AIR AGAIN. HE COULD ONLY HAZARD A GUESS AT WHAT WAS HAPPENING. HE FORCED HIMSELF TO RELAX AS HORIKOSHI MOVED A PIECE . . .
CHESS IS A WONDERFUL GAME, CAPTAIN. A GAME OF COLD LOGIC UNCONTAMINATED BY STUPID EMOTION.
PERHAPS, GENERAL, BUT SOMETIMES A HIGH STAKE HELPS GOOD PLAY. IS THAT YOUR MOVE ?
HORIKOSHI NODDED AND GRANT DREW IN A DEEP BREATH. GENTLY HE MOVED A PIECE, THE IVORY RAPPING AS IT CHANGED POSITION ON THE BOARD . . .
THEN THE GAME IS ENDED, GENERAL. CHECKMATE!
I...I...

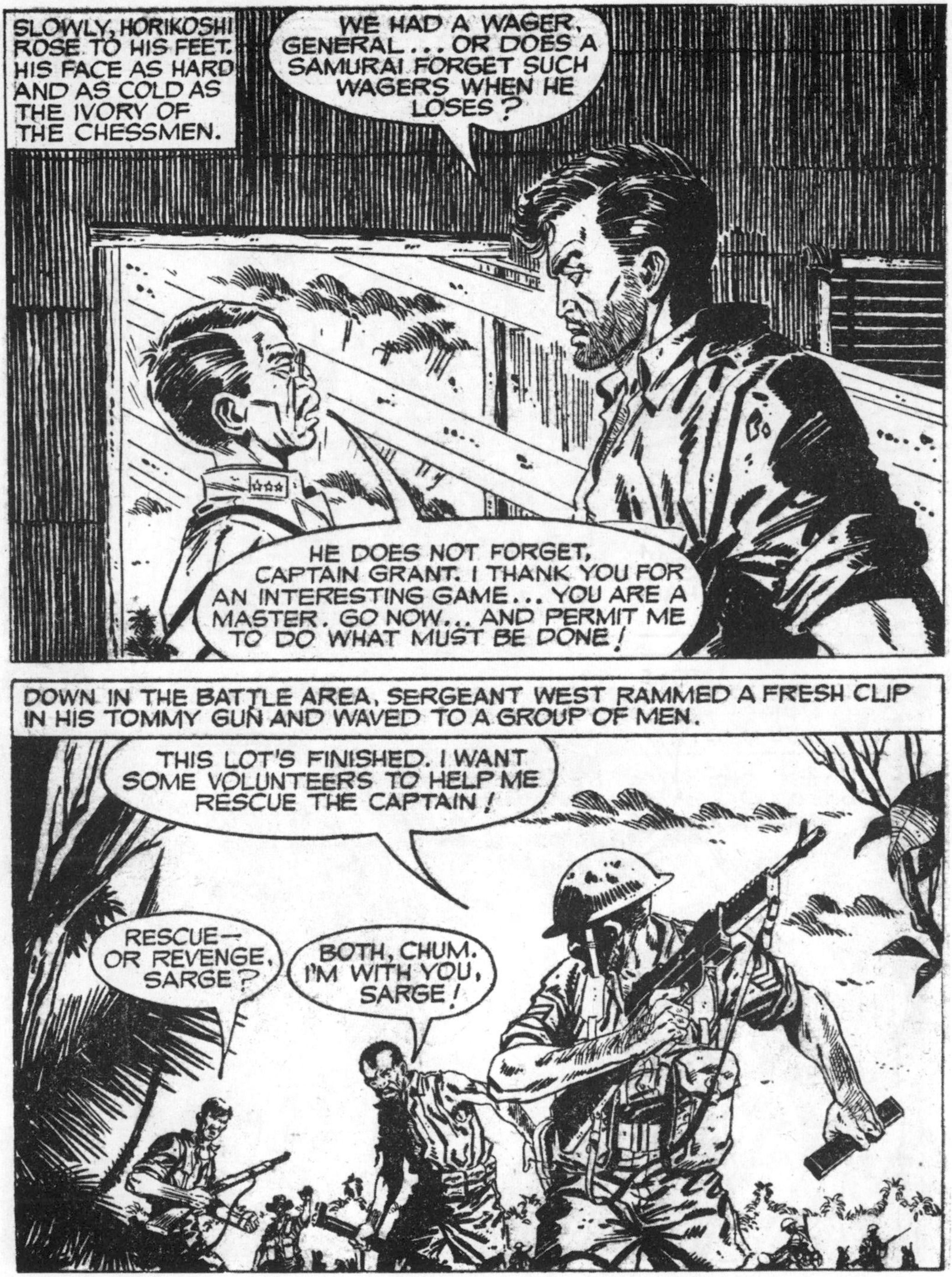
SLOWLY, HORIKOSHI ROSE TO HIS FEET. HIS FACE AS HARD AND AS COLD AS THE IVORY OF THE CHESSMEN.
WE HAD A WAGER, GENERAL ... OR DOES A SAMURAI FORGET SUCH WAGERS WHEN HE LOSES?
HE DOES NOT FORGET, CAPTAIN GRANT. I THANK YOU FOR AN INTERESTING GAME ... YOU ARE A MASTER. GO NOW ... AND PERMIT ME TO DO WHAT MUST BE DONE!
DOWN IN THE BATTLE AREA, SERGEANT WEST RAMMED A FRESH CLIP IN HIS TOMMY GUN AND WAVED TO A GROUP OF MEN.
THIS LOT'S FINISHED. I WANT SOME VOLUNTEERS TO HELP ME RESCUE THE CAPTAIN!
RESCUE— OR REVENGE, SARGE?
BOTH, CHUM. I'M WITH YOU, SARGE!

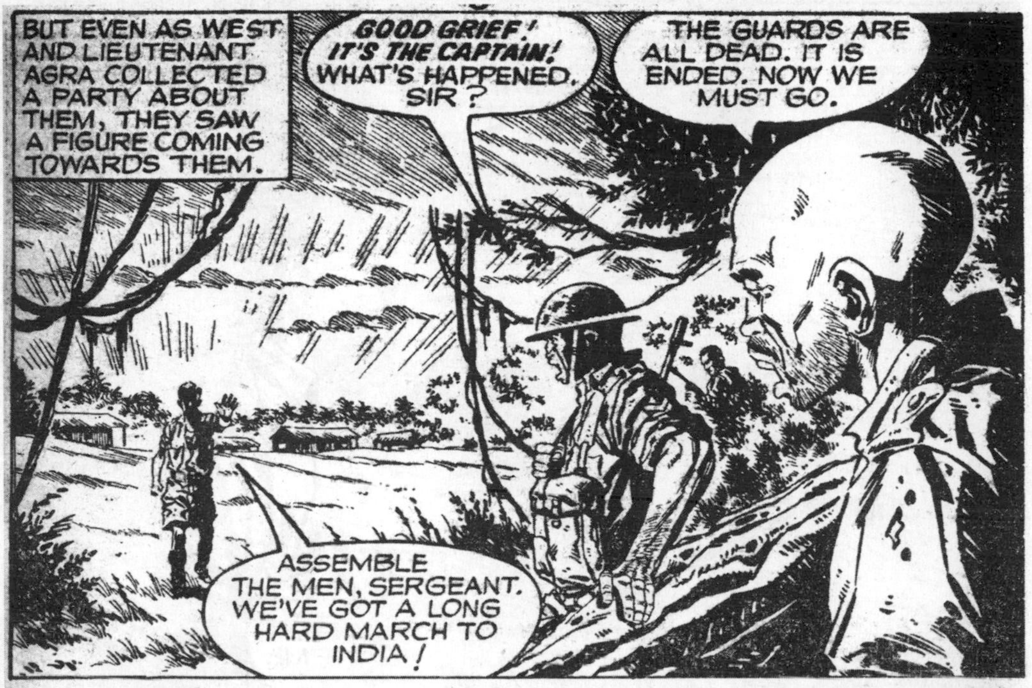
BUT EVEN AS WEST AND LIEUTENANT AGRA COLLECTED A PARTY ABOUT THEM, THEY SAW A FIGURE COMING TOWARDS THEM.
GOOD GRIEF! IT'S THE CAPTAIN! WHAT'S HAPPENED, SIR?
THE GUARDS ARE ALL DEAD. IT IS ENDED. NOW WE MUST GO.
ASSEMBLE THE MEN, SERGEANT. WE'VE GOT A LONG HARD MARCH TO INDIA!

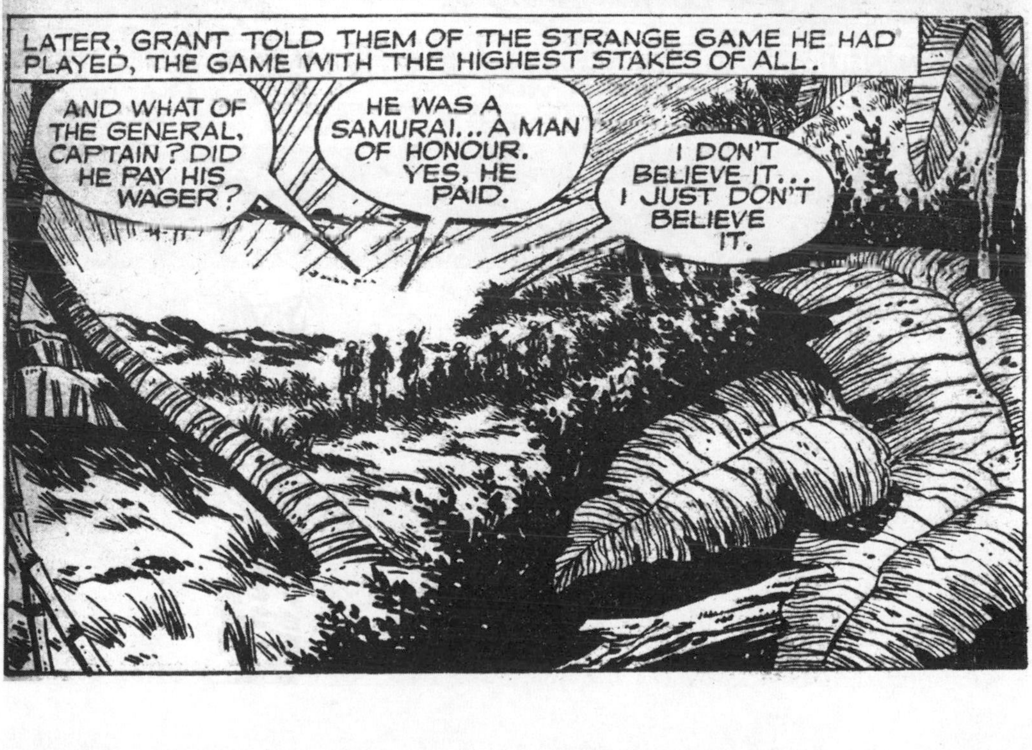
LATER, GRANT TOLD THEM OF THE STRANGE GAME HE HAD PLAYED, THE GAME WITH THE HIGHEST STAKES OF ALL.
AND WHAT OF THE GENERAL, CAPTAIN? DID HE PAY HIS WAGER?
HE WAS A SAMURAI... A MAN OF HONOUR. YES, HE PAID.
I DON'T BELIEVE IT... I JUST DON'T BELIEVE IT.

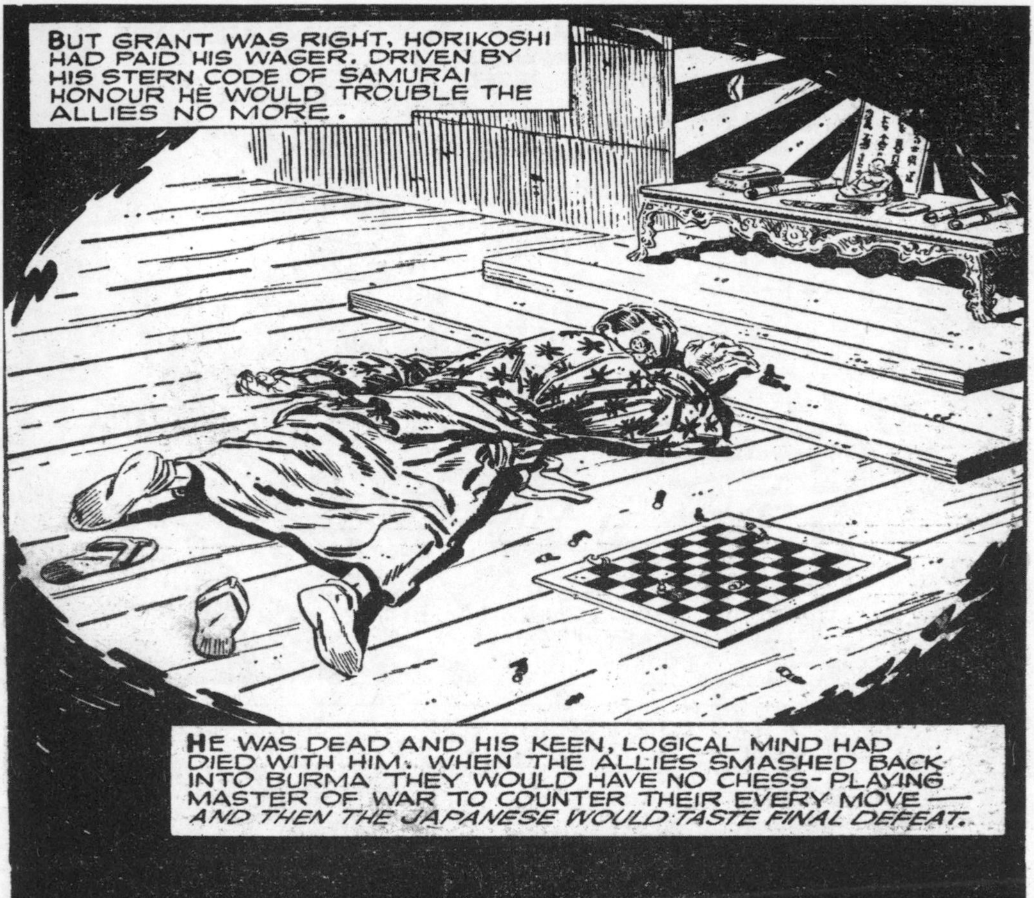
BUT GRANT WAS RIGHT, HORIKOSHI HAD PAID HIS WAGER. DRIVEN BY HIS STERN CODE OF SAMURAI HONOUR HE WOULD TROUBLE THE ALLIES NO MORE.
HE WAS DEAD AND HIS KEEN, LOGICAL MIND HAD DIED WITH HIM. WHEN THE ALLIES SMASHED BACK INTO BURMA THEY WOULD HAVE NO CHESS-PLAYING MASTER OF WAR TO COUNTER THEIR EVERY MOVE — AND THEN THE JAPANESE WOULD TASTE FINAL DEFEAT.

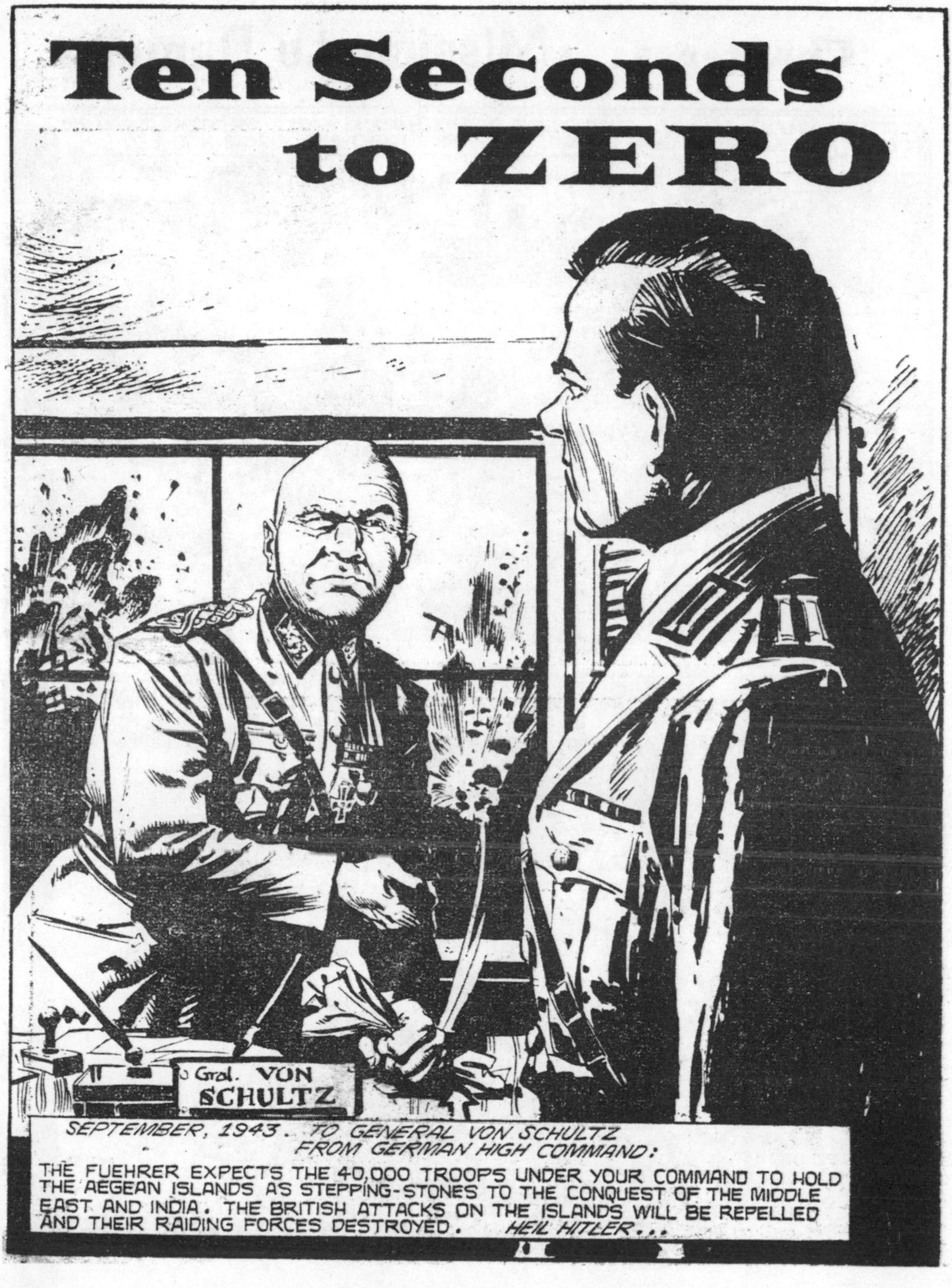
Ten Seconds to ZERO
Gral. VON SCHULTZ
SEPTEMBER, 1943. TO GENERAL VON SCHULTZ FROM GERMAN HIGH COMMAND:
THE FUEHRER EXPECTS THE 40,000 TROOPS UNDER YOUR COMMAND TO HOLD THE AEGEAN ISLANDS AS STEPPING-STONES TO THE CONQUEST OF THE MIDDLE EAST AND INDIA. THE BRITISH ATTACKS ON THE ISLANDS WILL BE REPELLED AND THEIR RAIDING FORCES DESTROYED. HEIL HITLER...

Chapter 1. Mission to Damos

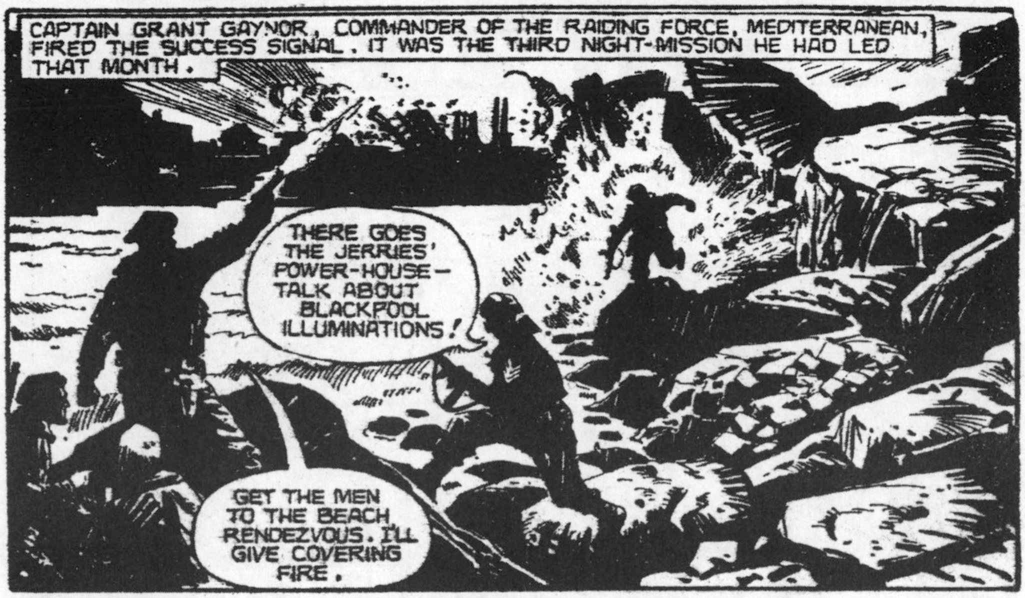
CAPTAIN GRANT GAYNOR, COMMANDER OF THE RAIDING FORCE, MEDITERRANEAN, FIRED THE SUCCESS SIGNAL. IT WAS THE THIRD NIGHT-MISSION HE HAD LED THAT MONTH.
THERE GOES THE JERRIES' POWER-HOUSE — TALK ABOUT BLACKPOOL ILLUMINATIONS!
GET THE MEN TO THE BEACH RENDEZVOUS. I'LL GIVE COVERING FIRE.

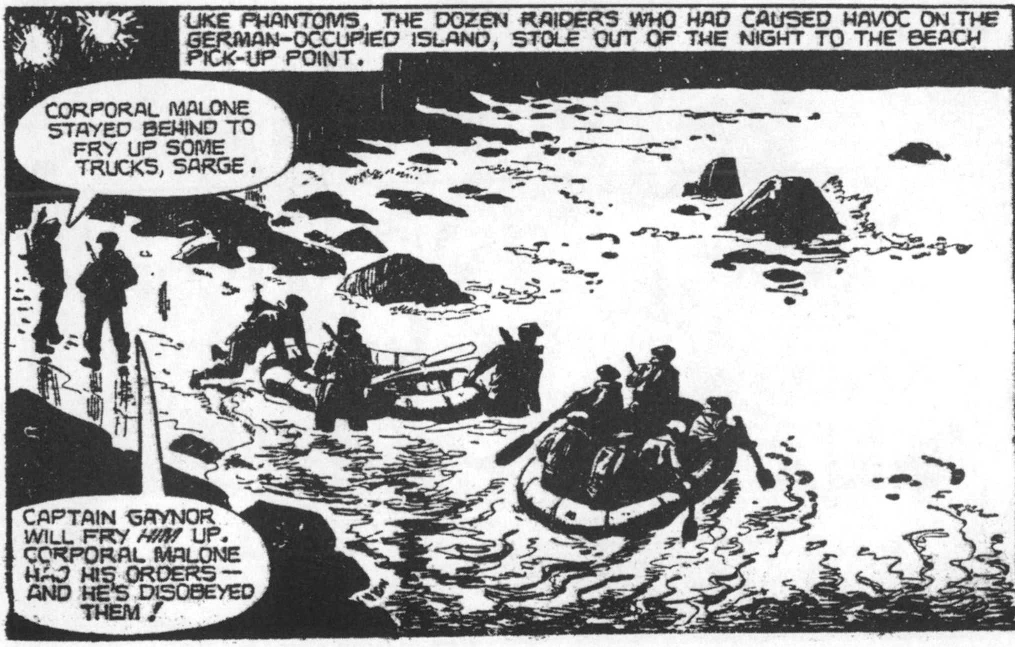
LIKE PHANTOMS, THE DOZEN RAIDERS WHO HAD CAUSED HAVOC ON THE GERMAN-OCCUPIED ISLAND, STOLE OUT OF THE NIGHT TO THE BEACH PICK-UP POINT.
CORPORAL MALONE STAYED BEHIND TO FRY UP SOME TRUCKS, SARGE.
CAPTAIN GAYNOR WILL FRY HIM UP. CORPORAL MALONE HAD HIS ORDERS — AND HE'S DISOBEYED THEM!

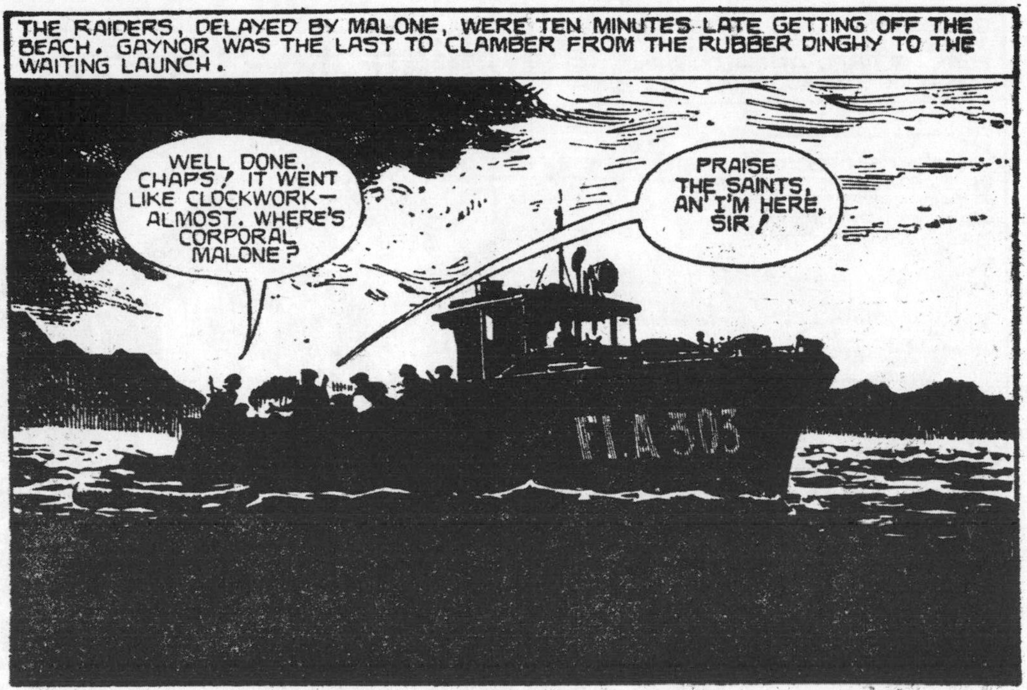
THE RAIDERS, DELAYED BY MALONE, WERE TEN MINUTES LATE GETTING OFF THE BEACH. GAYNOR WAS THE LAST TO CLAMBER FROM THE RUBBER DINGHY TO THE WAITING LAUNCH.
WELL DONE, CHAPS! IT WENT LIKE CLOCKWORK— ALMOST. WHERE'S CORPORAL MALONE?
PRAISE THE SAINTS, AN' I'M HERE, SIR!

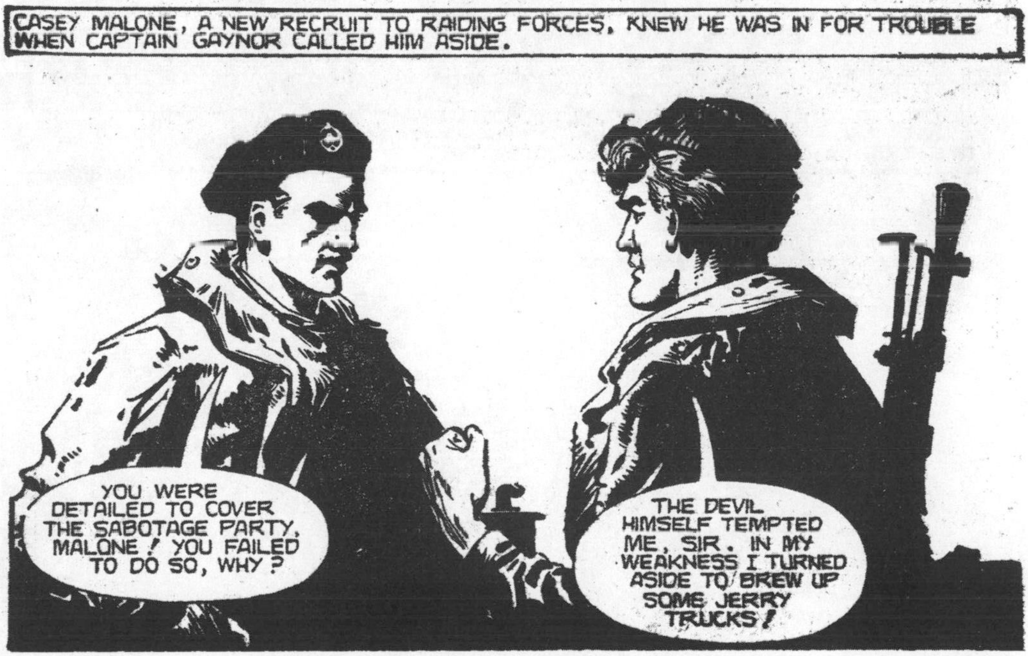
CASEY MALONE, A NEW RECRUIT TO RAIDING FORCES, KNEW HE WAS IN FOR TROUBLE WHEN CAPTAIN GAYNOR CALLED HIM ASIDE.
YOU WERE DETAILED TO COVER THE SABOTAGE PARTY, MALONE! YOU FAILED TO DO SO, WHY?
THE DEVIL HIMSELF TEMPTED ME, SIR. IN MY WEAKNESS I TURNED ASIDE TO BREW UP SOME JERRY TRUCKS!

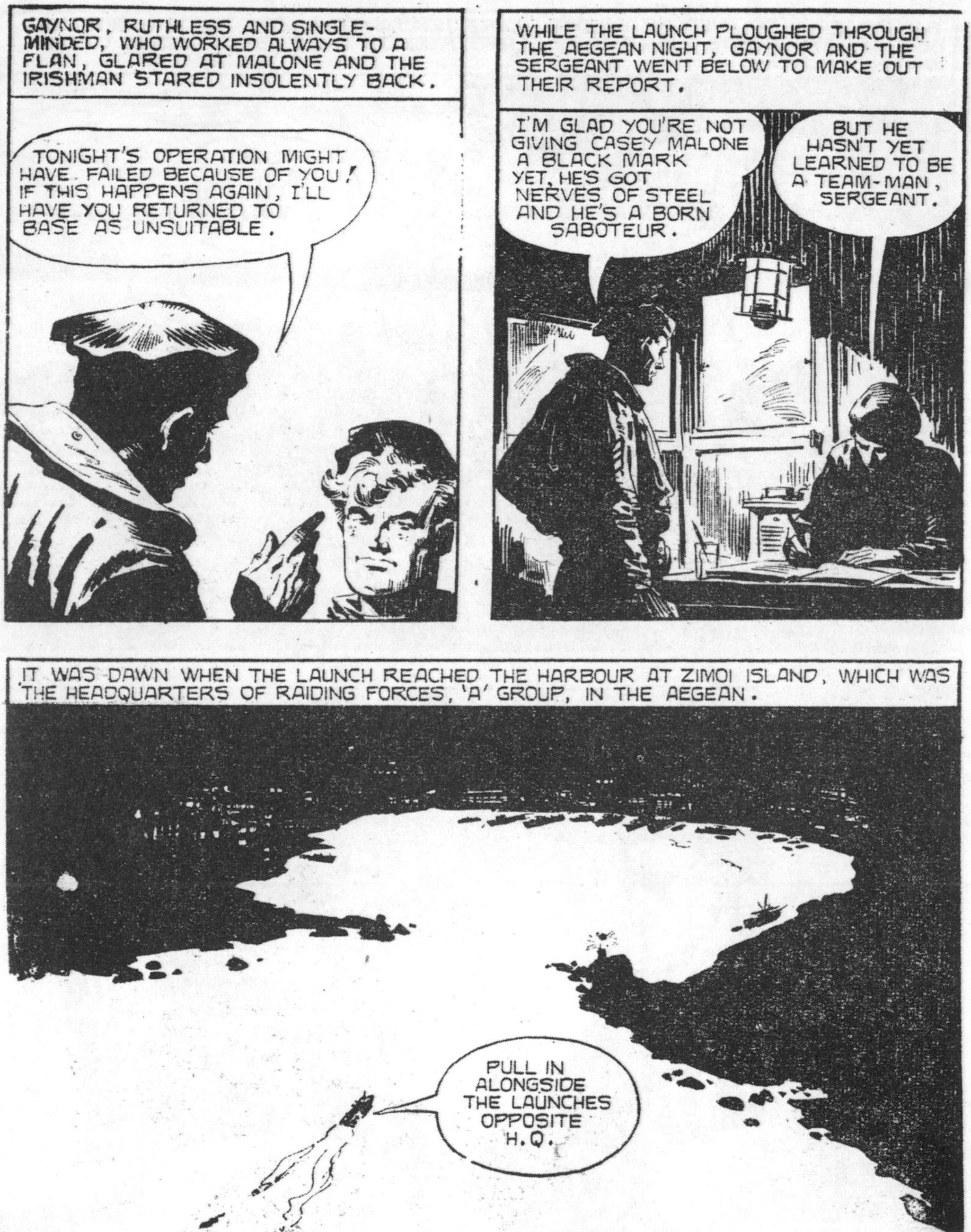
GAYNOR, RUTHLESS AND SINGLE-MINDED, WHO WORKED ALWAYS TO A PLAN, GLARED AT MALONE AND THE IRISHMAN STARED INSOLENTLY BACK.
TONIGHT'S OPERATION MIGHT HAVE FAILED BECAUSE OF YOU! IF THIS HAPPENS AGAIN, I'LL HAVE YOU RETURNED TO BASE AS UNSUITABLE.
WHILE THE LAUNCH PLOUGHED THROUGH THE AEGEAN NIGHT, GAYNOR AND THE SERGEANT WENT BELOW TO MAKE OUT THEIR REPORT.
I'M GLAD YOU'RE NOT GIVING CASEY MALONE A BLACK MARK YET. HE'S GOT NERVES OF STEEL AND HE'S A BORN SABOTEUR.
BUT HE HASN'T YET LEARNED TO BE A TEAM-MAN, SERGEANT.
IT WAS DAWN WHEN THE LAUNCH REACHED THE HARBOUR AT ZIMOI ISLAND, WHICH WAS THE HEADQUARTERS OF RAIDING FORCES, 'A' GROUP, IN THE AEGEAN.
PULL IN ALONGSIDE THE LAUNCHES OPPOSITE H.Q.

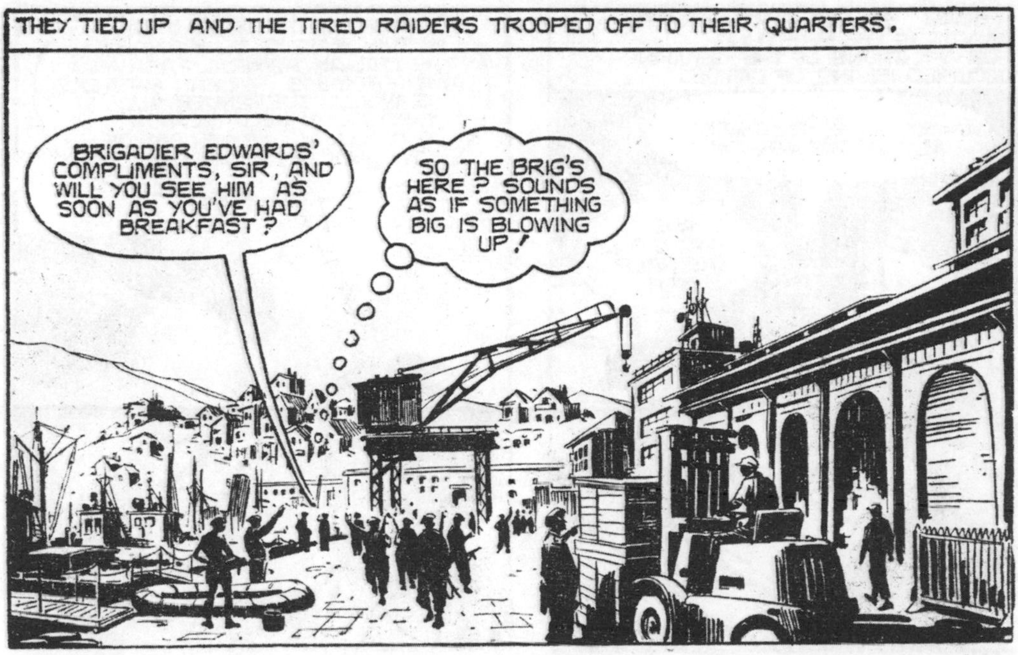
THEY TIED UP AND THE TIRED RAIDERS TROOPED OFF TO THEIR QUARTERS.
BRIGADIER EDWARDS' COMPLIMENTS, SIR, AND WILL YOU SEE HIM AS SOON AS YOU'VE HAD BREAKFAST?
SO THE BRIG'S HERE? SOUNDS AS IF SOMETHING BIG IS BLOWING UP!

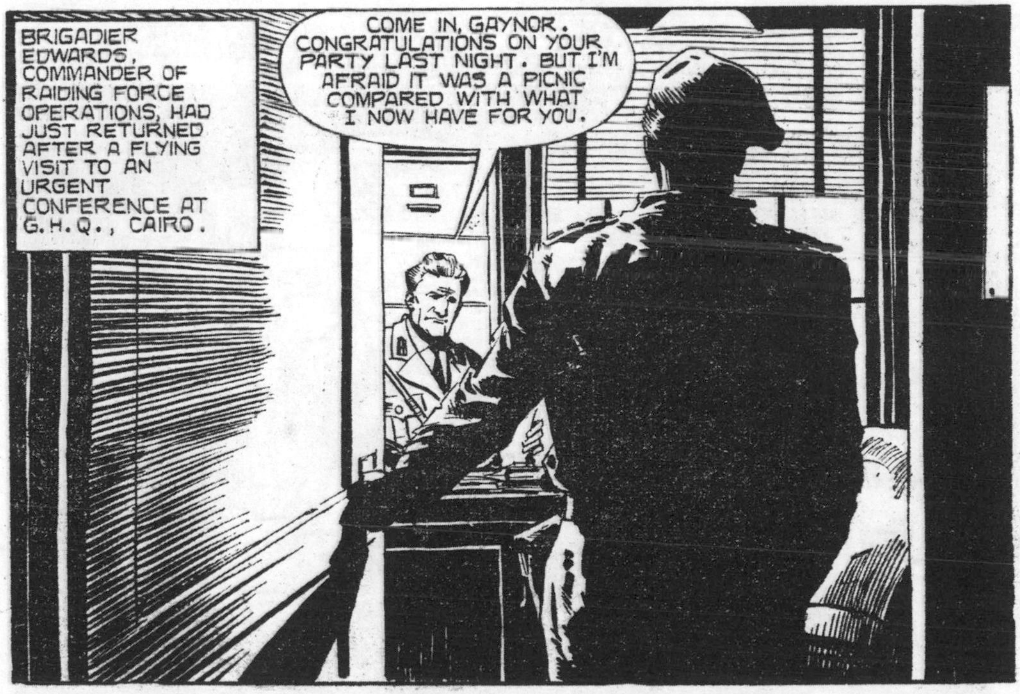
BRIGADIER EDWARDS, COMMANDER OF RAIDING FORCE OPERATIONS, HAD JUST RETURNED AFTER A FLYING VISIT TO AN URGENT CONFERENCE AT G.H.Q., CAIRO.
COME IN, GAYNOR. CONGRATULATIONS ON YOUR PARTY LAST NIGHT. BUT I'M AFRAID IT WAS A PICNIC COMPARED WITH WHAT I NOW HAVE FOR YOU.

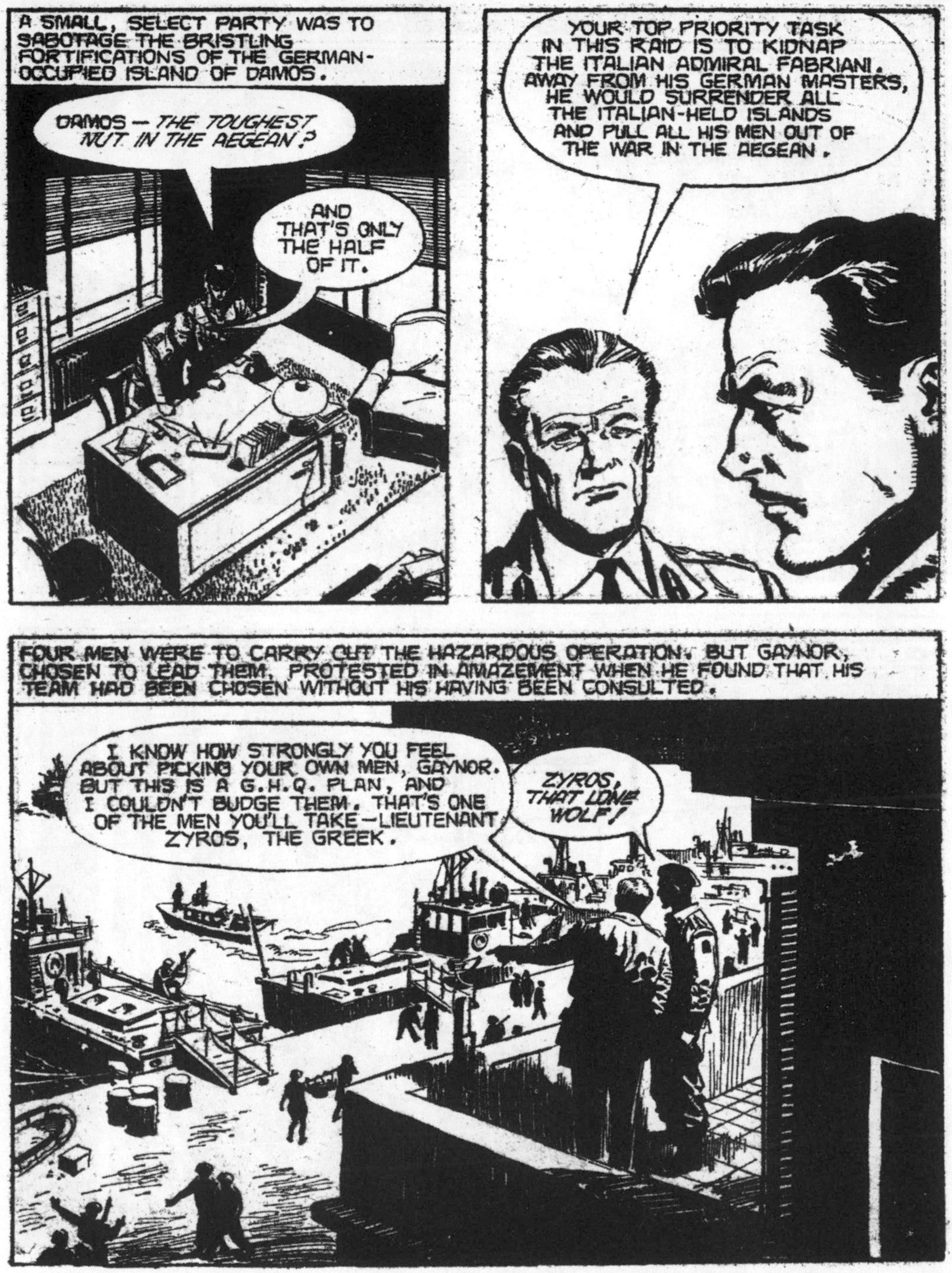
A SMALL, SELECT PARTY WAS TO SABOTAGE THE BRISTLING FORTIFICATIONS OF THE GERMAN-OCCUPIED ISLAND OF DAMOS.
DAMOS — THE TOUGHEST NUT IN THE AEGEAN?
AND THAT'S ONLY THE HALF OF IT.
YOUR TOP PRIORITY TASK IN THIS RAID IS TO KIDNAP THE ITALIAN ADMIRAL FABRIANI. AWAY FROM HIS GERMAN MASTERS, HE WOULD SURRENDER ALL THE ITALIAN-HELD ISLANDS AND PULL ALL HIS MEN OUT OF THE WAR IN THE AEGEAN.
FOUR MEN WERE TO CARRY OUT THE HAZARDOUS OPERATION. BUT GAYNOR, CHOSEN TO LEAD THEM, PROTESTED IN AMAZEMENT WHEN HE FOUND THAT HIS TEAM HAD BEEN CHOSEN WITHOUT HIS HAVING BEEN CONSULTED.
I KNOW HOW STRONGLY YOU FEEL ABOUT PICKING YOUR OWN MEN, GAYNOR. BUT THIS IS A G.H.Q. PLAN, AND I COULDN'T BUDGE THEM. THAT'S ONE OF THE MEN YOU'LL TAKE—LIEUTENANT ZYROS, THE GREEK.
ZYROS, THAT LONE WOLF!

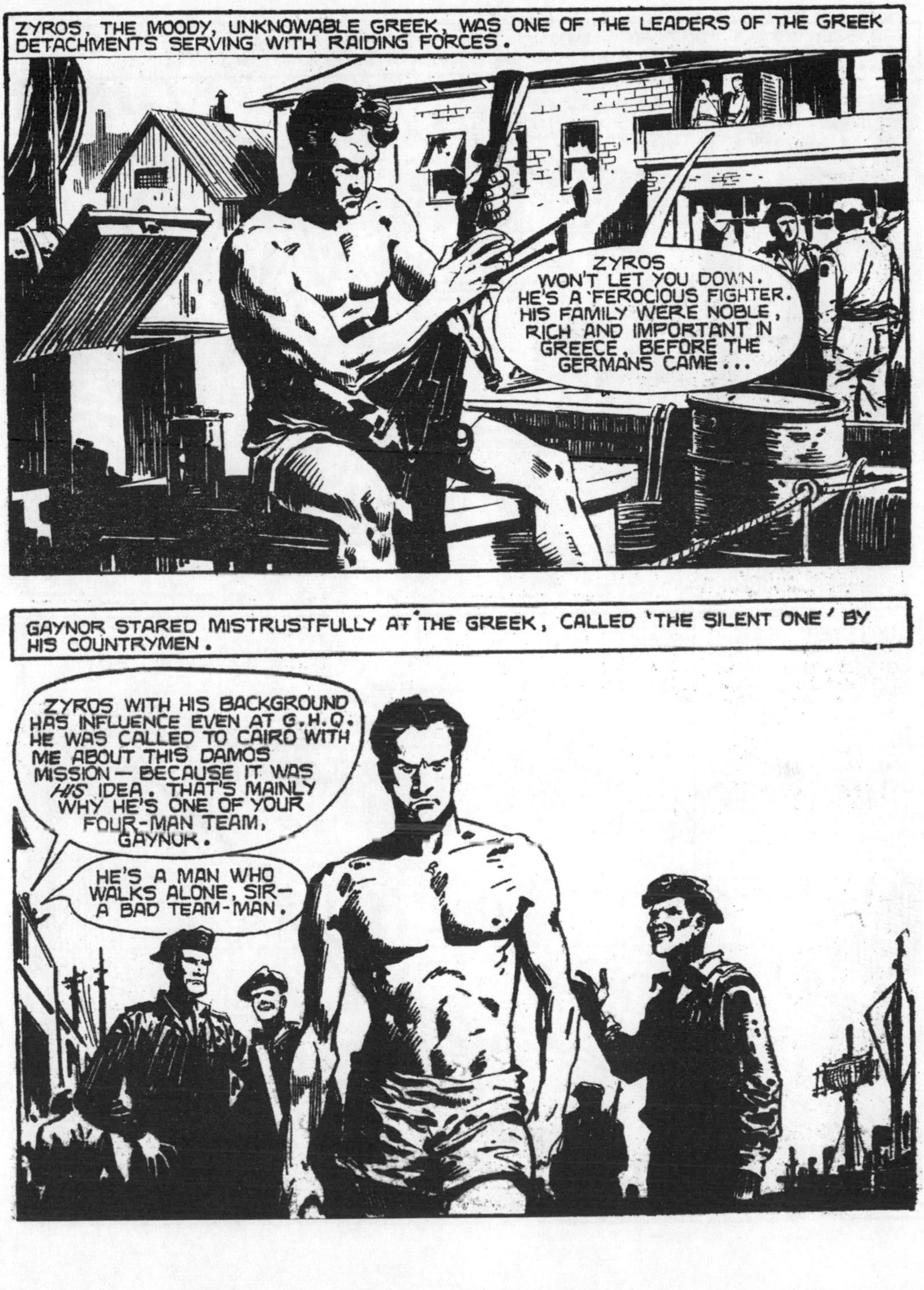
ZYROS, THE MOODY, UNKNOWABLE GREEK, WAS ONE OF THE LEADERS OF THE GREEK DETACHMENTS SERVING WITH RAIDING FORCES.
ZYROS WON'T LET YOU DOWN. HE'S A FEROCIOUS FIGHTER. HIS FAMILY WERE NOBLE, RICH AND IMPORTANT IN GREECE, BEFORE THE GERMANS CAME...
GAYNOR STARED MISTRUSTFULLY AT THE GREEK, CALLED 'THE SILENT ONE' BY HIS COUNTRYMEN.
ZYROS WITH HIS BACKGROUND HAS INFLUENCE EVEN AT G.H.Q. HE WAS CALLED TO CAIRO WITH ME ABOUT THIS DAMOS MISSION — BECAUSE IT WAS *HIS* IDEA. THAT'S MAINLY WHY HE'S ONE OF YOUR FOUR-MAN TEAM, GAYNOR.
HE'S A MAN WHO WALKS ALONE, SIR— A BAD TEAM-MAN.

THAT AFTERNOON, ALL BUT ONE OF THE OPERATIONAL PARTY, CODE-NAMED 'FUN FAIR' HAD BEEN DRAWN TOGETHER. ANOTHER DISTASTEFUL SURPRISE AWAITED GAYNOR, WHEN THEY ASSEMBLED IN WHAT HAD ONCE BEEN A SCHOOL-ROOM.

CORPORAL MALONE — HOW THE DEVIL DID *YOU* GET IN THIS TEAM?

'TIS ME KNOWLEDGE OF EXPLOSIVES, SIR.

WHATEVER HE THOUGHT OF HIS MEN, GAYNOR KNEW HE MUST WELD THEM INTO A TEAM. THE REMAINING MEMBER OF OPERATION FUN-FAIR WAS TO JOIN THE EXPEDITION BEFORE IT STARTED. MEANWHILE, GAYNOR WENT OVER THE PLAN WITH THE OTHERS.

LANDING POINT
KOSSIN POINT
TEMPLE OF DIANA
BISHOPS SUMMER PALACE
DAMO
PORT OF SARPHIA

WE SHALL BE LANDED AT KOSSIN POINT IN THE NORTH, AN HOUR BEFORE DAWN ON SATURDAY. BY MIDNIGHT, SUNDAY, WE MUST BE IN POSITION TO MAKE OUR BID ON THE JERRY H.Q. AT SARPHIA. THIS IS HOW IT WILL BE DONE...

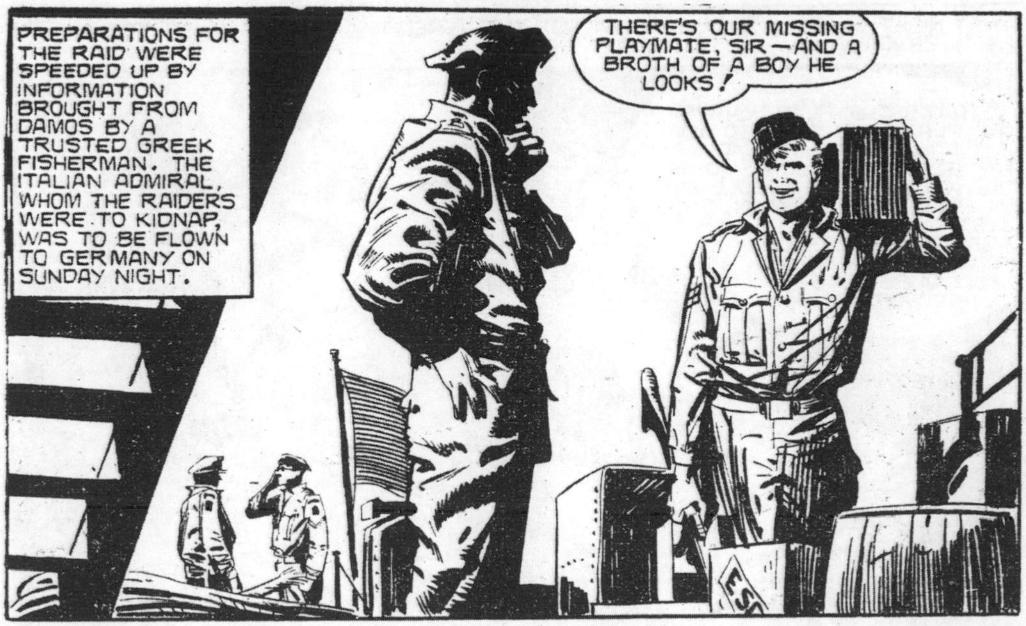
PREPARATIONS FOR THE RAID WERE SPEEDED UP BY INFORMATION BROUGHT FROM DAMOS BY A TRUSTED GREEK FISHERMAN. THE ITALIAN ADMIRAL, WHOM THE RAIDERS WERE TO KIDNAP, WAS TO BE FLOWN TO GERMANY ON SUNDAY NIGHT.
THERE'S OUR MISSING PLAYMATE, SIR—AND A BROTH OF A BOY HE LOOKS!

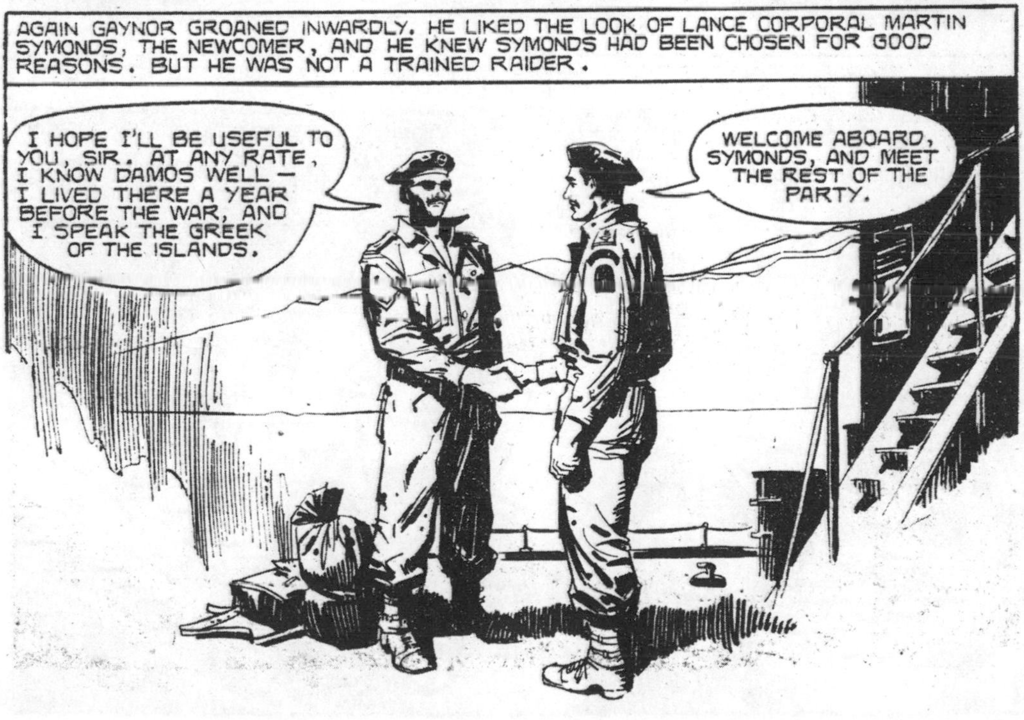
AGAIN GAYNOR GROANED INWARDLY. HE LIKED THE LOOK OF LANCE CORPORAL MARTIN SYMONDS, THE NEWCOMER, AND HE KNEW SYMONDS HAD BEEN CHOSEN FOR GOOD REASONS. BUT HE WAS NOT A TRAINED RAIDER.
I HOPE I'LL BE USEFUL TO YOU, SIR. AT ANY RATE, I KNOW DAMOS WELL — I LIVED THERE A YEAR BEFORE THE WAR, AND I SPEAK THE GREEK OF THE ISLANDS.
WELCOME ABOARD, SYMONDS, AND MEET THE REST OF THE PARTY.

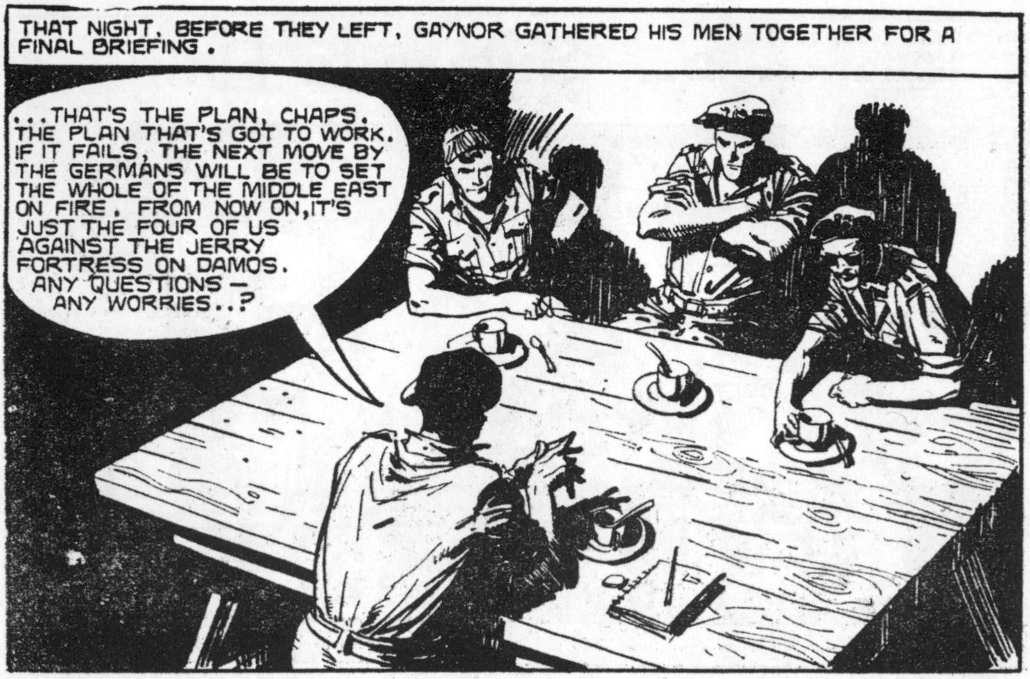
THAT NIGHT, BEFORE THEY LEFT, GAYNOR GATHERED HIS MEN TOGETHER FOR A FINAL BRIEFING.
...THAT'S THE PLAN, CHAPS. THE PLAN THAT'S GOT TO WORK. IF IT FAILS, THE NEXT MOVE BY THE GERMANS WILL BE TO SET THE WHOLE OF THE MIDDLE EAST ON FIRE. FROM NOW ON, IT'S JUST THE FOUR OF US AGAINST THE JERRY FORTRESS ON DAMOS. ANY QUESTIONS — ANY WORRIES..?

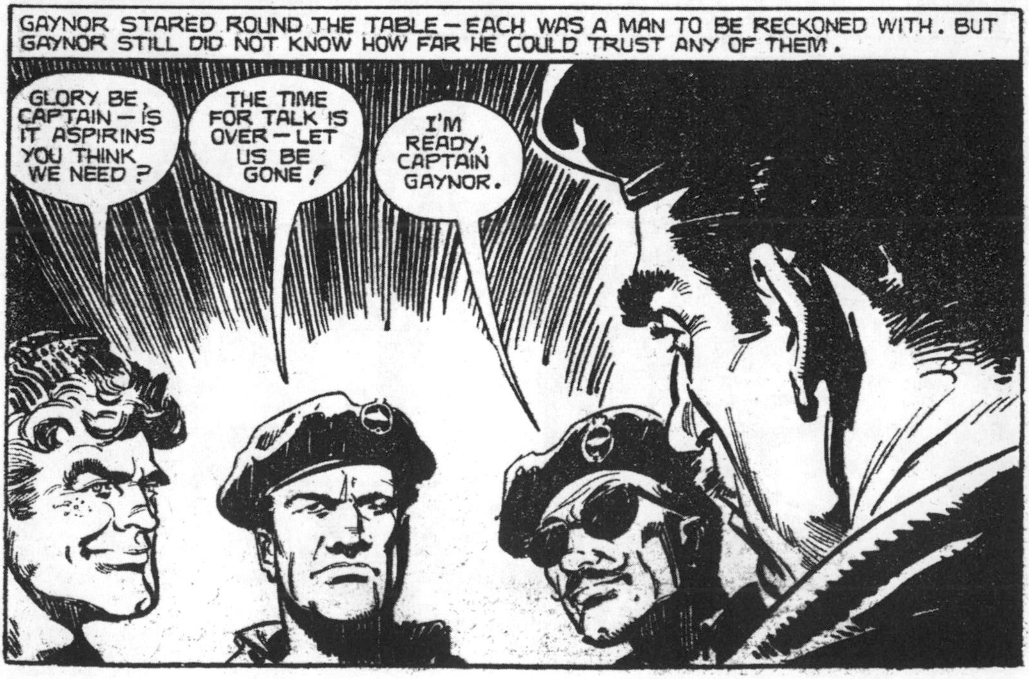
GAYNOR STARED ROUND THE TABLE — EACH WAS A MAN TO BE RECKONED WITH. BUT GAYNOR STILL DID NOT KNOW HOW FAR HE COULD TRUST ANY OF THEM.
GLORY BE, CAPTAIN — IS IT ASPIRINS YOU THINK WE NEED?
THE TIME FOR TALK IS OVER — LET US BE GONE!
I'M READY, CAPTAIN GAYNOR.

Chapter 2. Symonds Folly

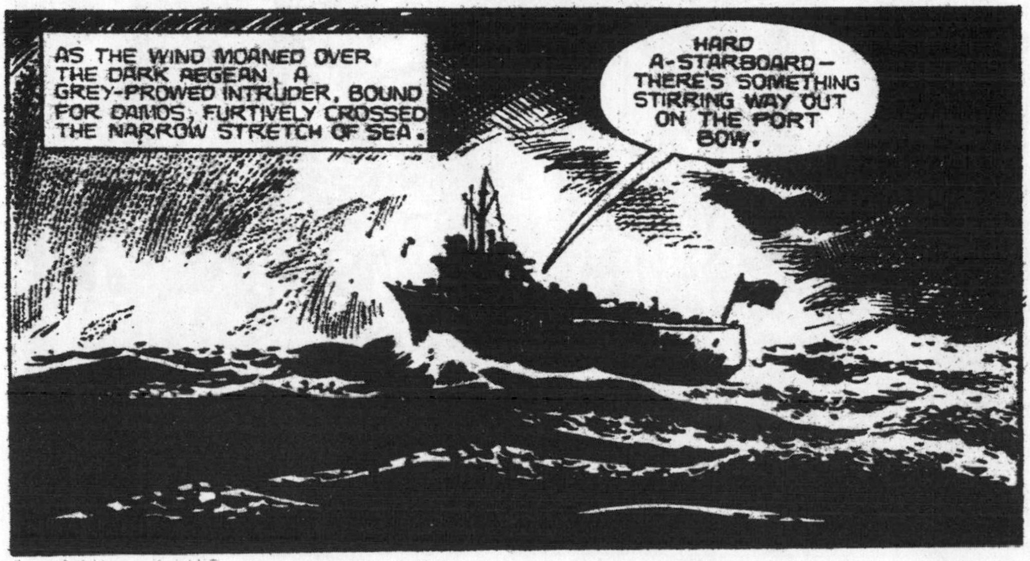
AS THE WIND MOANED OVER THE DARK AEGEAN, A GREY-PROWED INTRUDER, BOUND FOR DAMOS, FURTIVELY CROSSED THE NARROW STRETCH OF SEA.
HARD A-STARBOARD— THERE'S SOMETHING STIRRING WAY OUT ON THE PORT BOW.

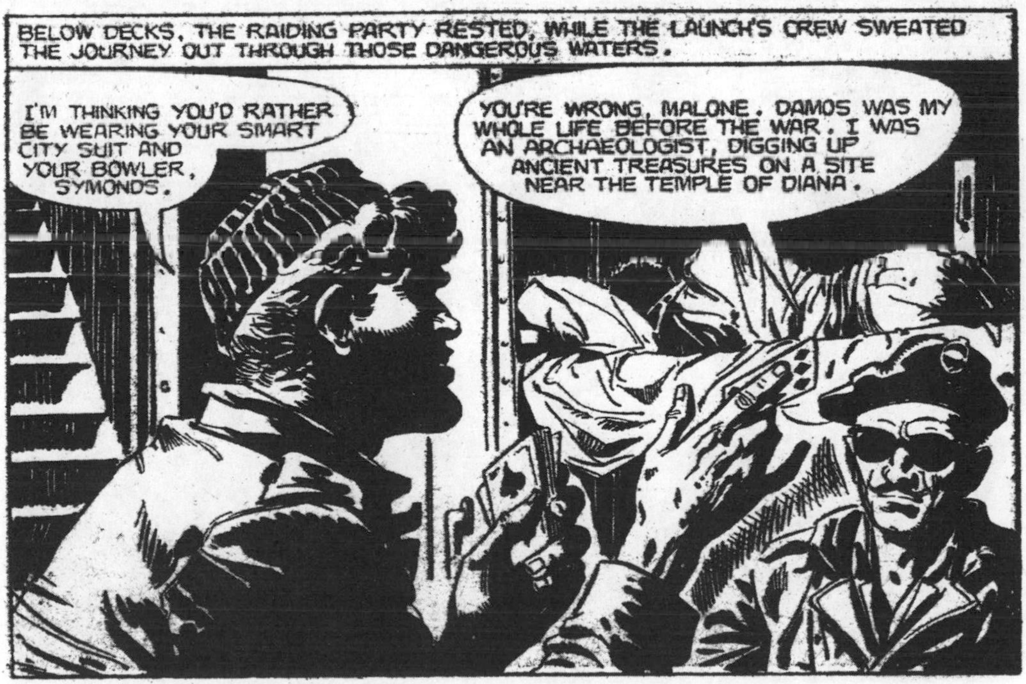
BELOW DECKS, THE RAIDING PARTY RESTED, WHILE THE LAUNCH'S CREW SWEATED THE JOURNEY OUT THROUGH THOSE DANGEROUS WATERS.
I'M THINKING YOU'D RATHER BE WEARING YOUR SMART CITY SUIT AND YOUR BOWLER, SYMONDS.
YOU'RE WRONG, MALONE. DAMOS WAS MY WHOLE LIFE BEFORE THE WAR. I WAS AN ARCHAEOLOGIST, DIGGING UP ANCIENT TREASURES ON A SITE NEAR THE TEMPLE OF DIANA.

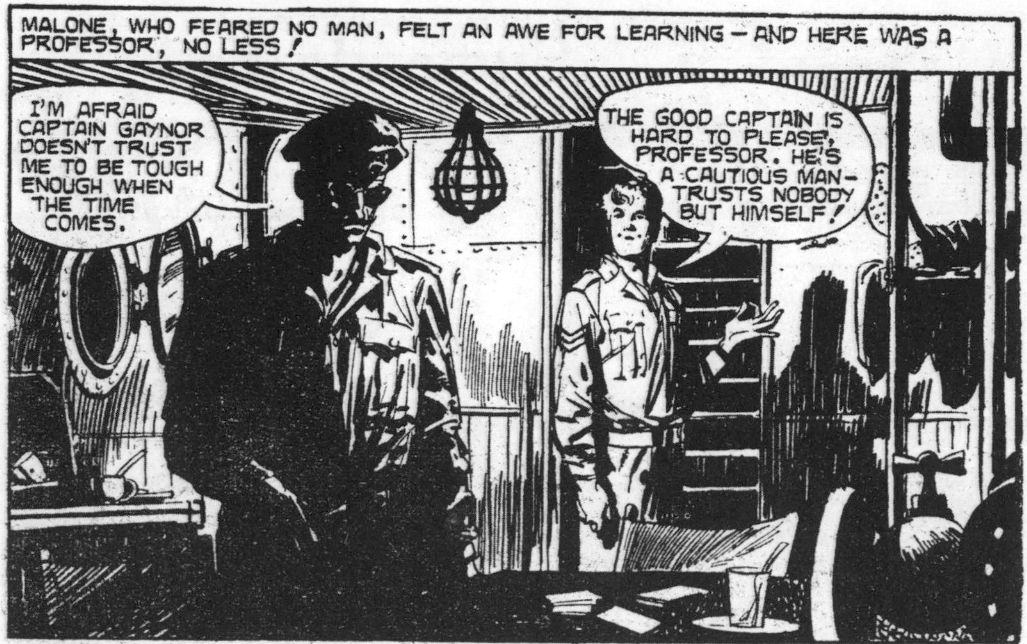
MALONE, WHO FEARED NO MAN, FELT AN AWE FOR LEARNING — AND HERE WAS A PROFESSOR, NO LESS!
I'M AFRAID CAPTAIN GAYNOR DOESN'T TRUST ME TO BE TOUGH ENOUGH WHEN THE TIME COMES.
THE GOOD CAPTAIN IS HARD TO PLEASE, PROFESSOR. HE'S A CAUTIOUS MAN — TRUSTS NOBODY BUT HIMSELF!

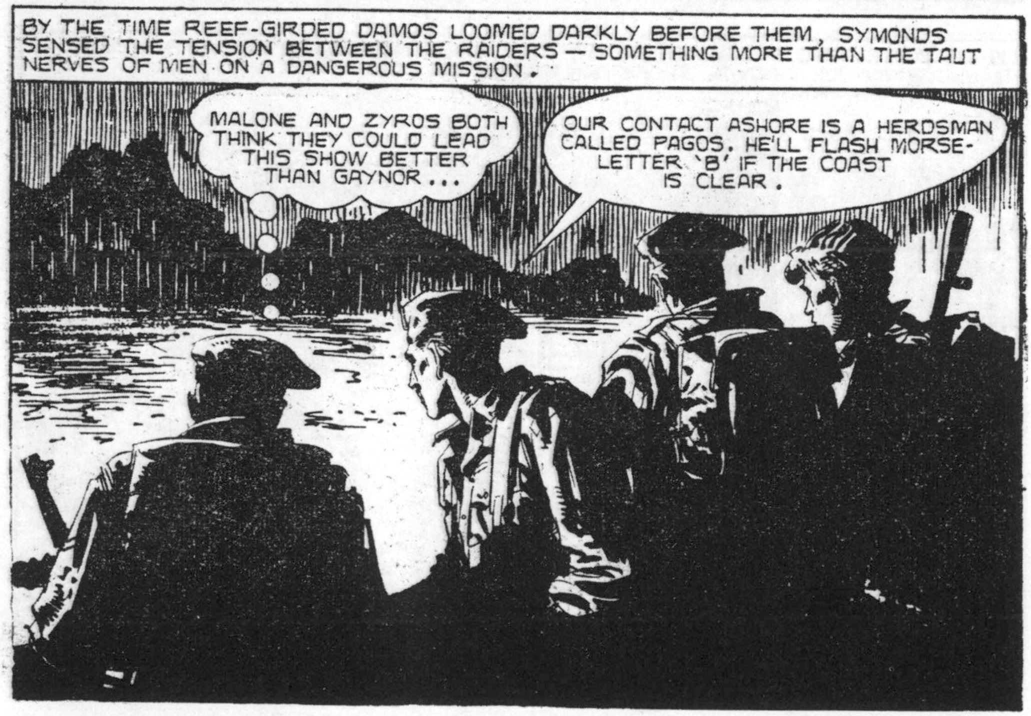
BY THE TIME REEF-GIRDED DAMOS LOOMED DARKLY BEFORE THEM, SYMONDS SENSED THE TENSION BETWEEN THE RAIDERS — SOMETHING MORE THAN THE TAUT NERVES OF MEN ON A DANGEROUS MISSION.
MALONE AND ZYROS BOTH THINK THEY COULD LEAD THIS SHOW BETTER THAN GAYNOR...
OUR CONTACT ASHORE IS A HERDSMAN CALLED PAGOS. HE'LL FLASH MORSE-LETTER 'B' IF THE COAST IS CLEAR.

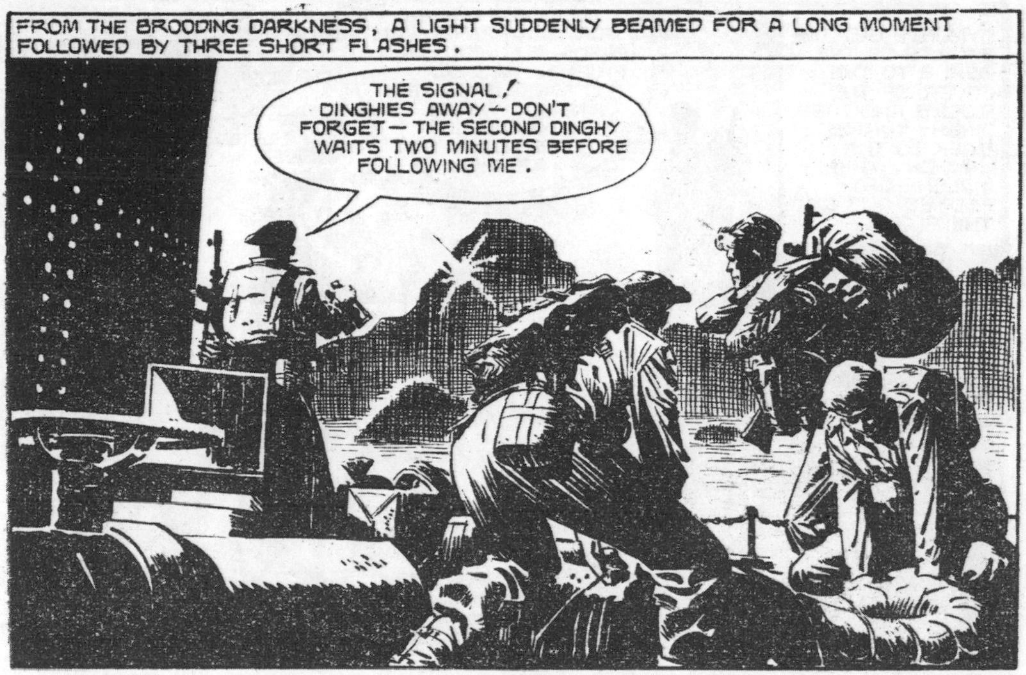
FROM THE BROODING DARKNESS, A LIGHT SUDDENLY BEAMED FOR A LONG MOMENT FOLLOWED BY THREE SHORT FLASHES.
THE SIGNAL! DINGHIES AWAY—DON'T FORGET—THE SECOND DINGHY WAITS TWO MINUTES BEFORE FOLLOWING ME.

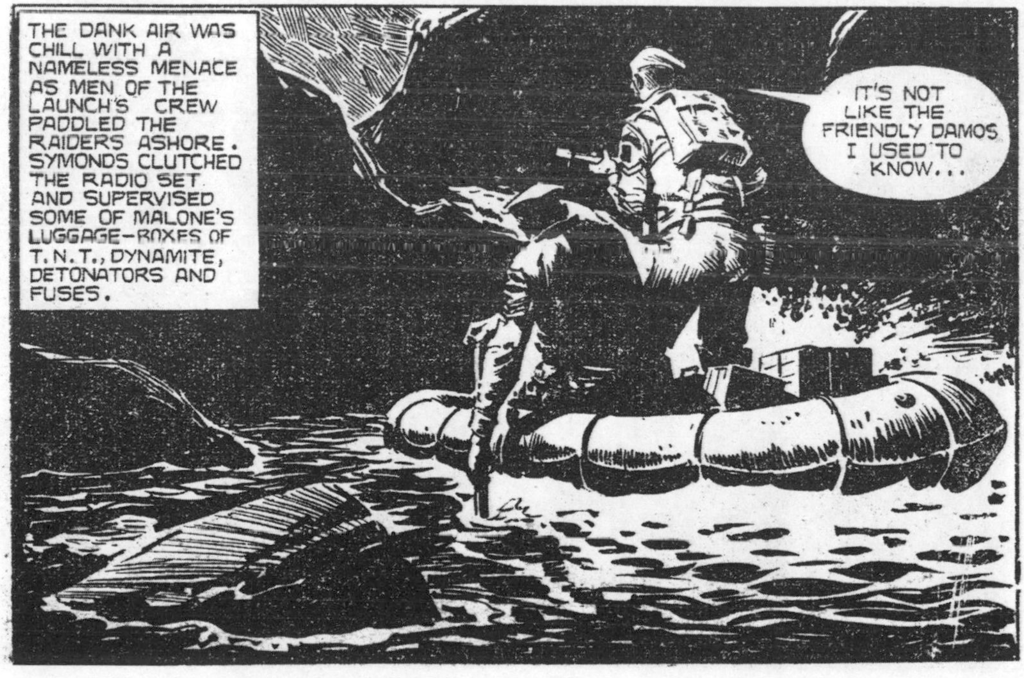
THE DANK AIR WAS CHILL WITH A NAMELESS MENACE AS MEN OF THE LAUNCH'S CREW PADDLED THE RAIDERS ASHORE. SYMONDS CLUTCHED THE RADIO SET AND SUPERVISED SOME OF MALONE'S LUGGAGE—BOXES OF T.N.T., DYNAMITE, DETONATORS AND FUSES.
IT'S NOT LIKE THE FRIENDLY DAMOS I USED TO KNOW...

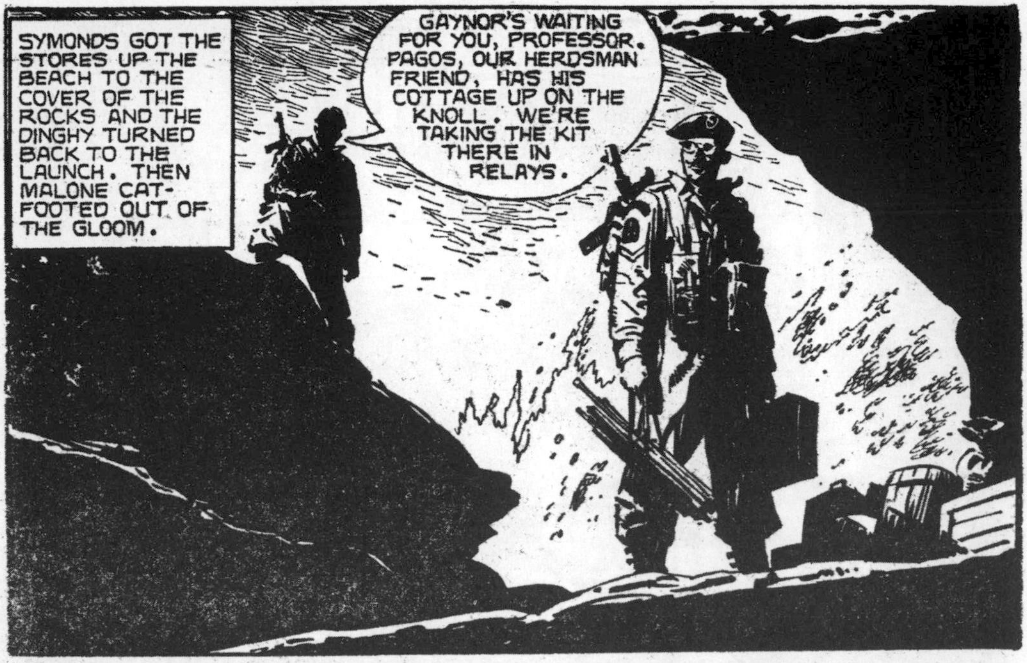
SYMONDS GOT THE STORES UP THE BEACH TO THE COVER OF THE ROCKS AND THE DINGHY TURNED BACK TO THE LAUNCH. THEN MALONE CAT-FOOTED OUT OF THE GLOOM.
GAYNOR'S WAITING FOR YOU, PROFESSOR. PAGOS, OUR HERDSMAN FRIEND, HAS HIS COTTAGE UP ON THE KNOLL. WE'RE TAKING THE KIT THERE IN RELAYS.

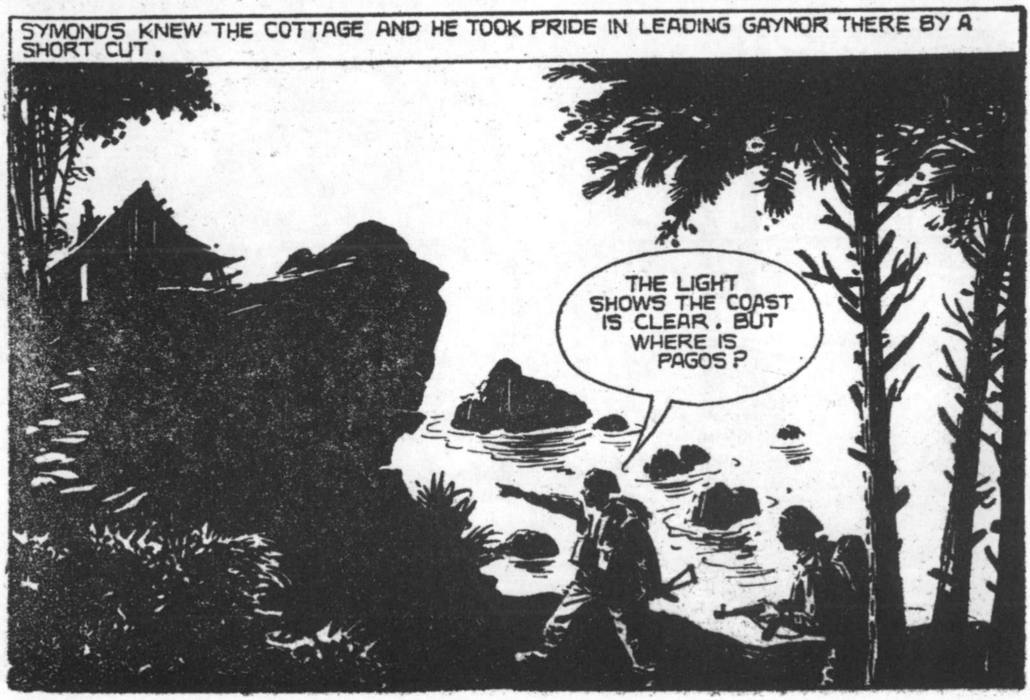
SYMONDS KNEW THE COTTAGE AND HE TOOK PRIDE IN LEADING GAYNOR THERE BY A SHORT CUT.
THE LIGHT SHOWS THE COAST IS CLEAR. BUT WHERE IS PAGOS?

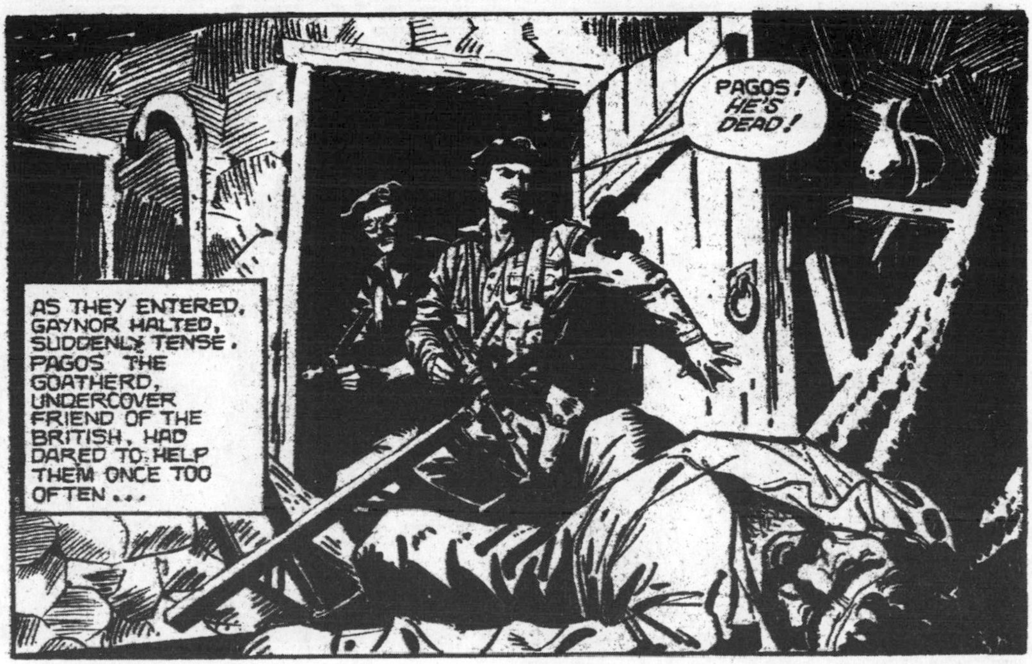
AS THEY ENTERED, GAYNOR HALTED, SUDDENLY TENSE. PAGOS THE GOATHERD, UNDERCOVER FRIEND OF THE BRITISH, HAD DARED TO HELP THEM ONCE TOO OFTEN...
PAGOS! HE'S DEAD!

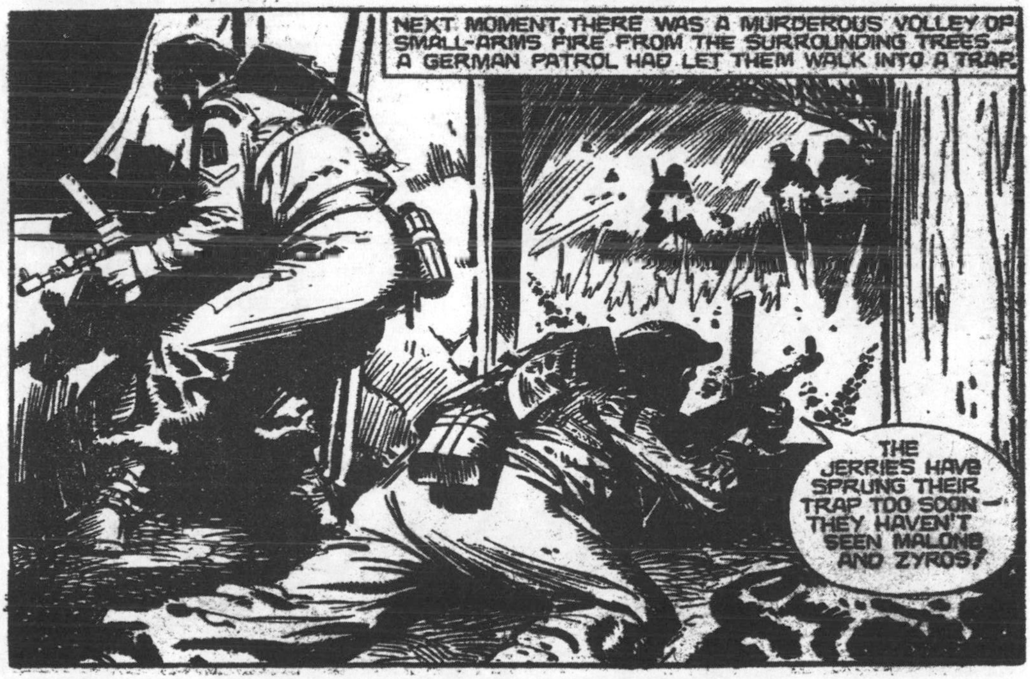
NEXT MOMENT, THERE WAS A MURDEROUS VOLLEY OF SMALL-ARMS FIRE FROM THE SURROUNDING TREES—A GERMAN PATROL HAD LET THEM WALK INTO A TRAP.
THE JERRIES HAVE SPRUNG THEIR TRAP TOO SOON—THEY HAVEN'T SEEN MALONE AND ZYROS!

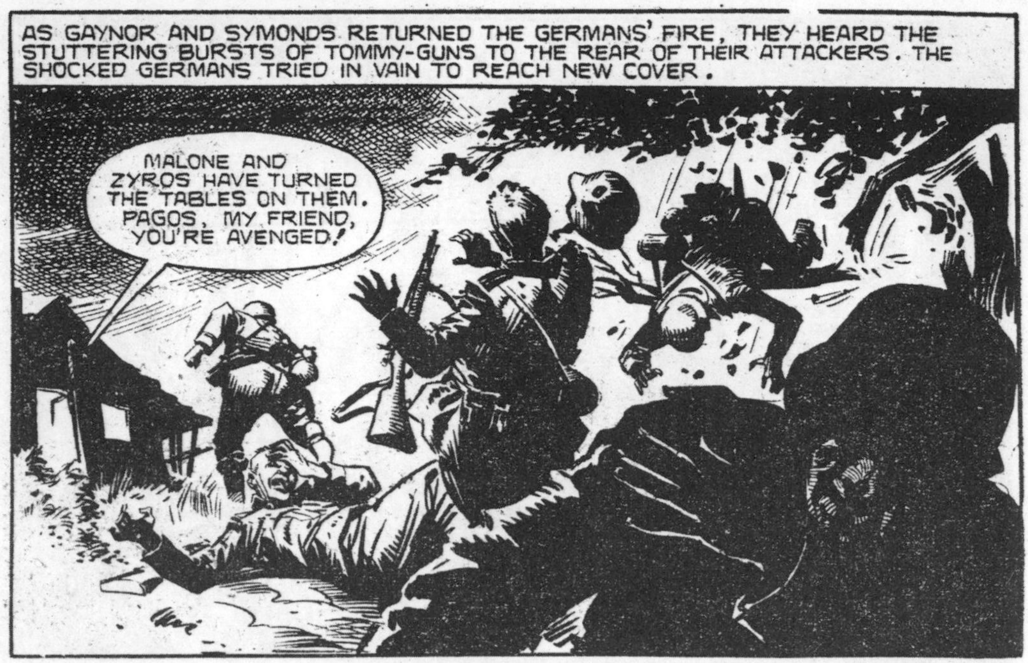
AS GAYNOR AND SYMONDS RETURNED THE GERMANS' FIRE, THEY HEARD THE STUTTERING BURSTS OF TOMMY-GUNS TO THE REAR OF THEIR ATTACKERS. THE SHOCKED GERMANS TRIED IN VAIN TO REACH NEW COVER.
MALONE AND ZYROS HAVE TURNED THE TABLES ON THEM. PAGOS, MY FRIEND, YOU'RE AVENGED!

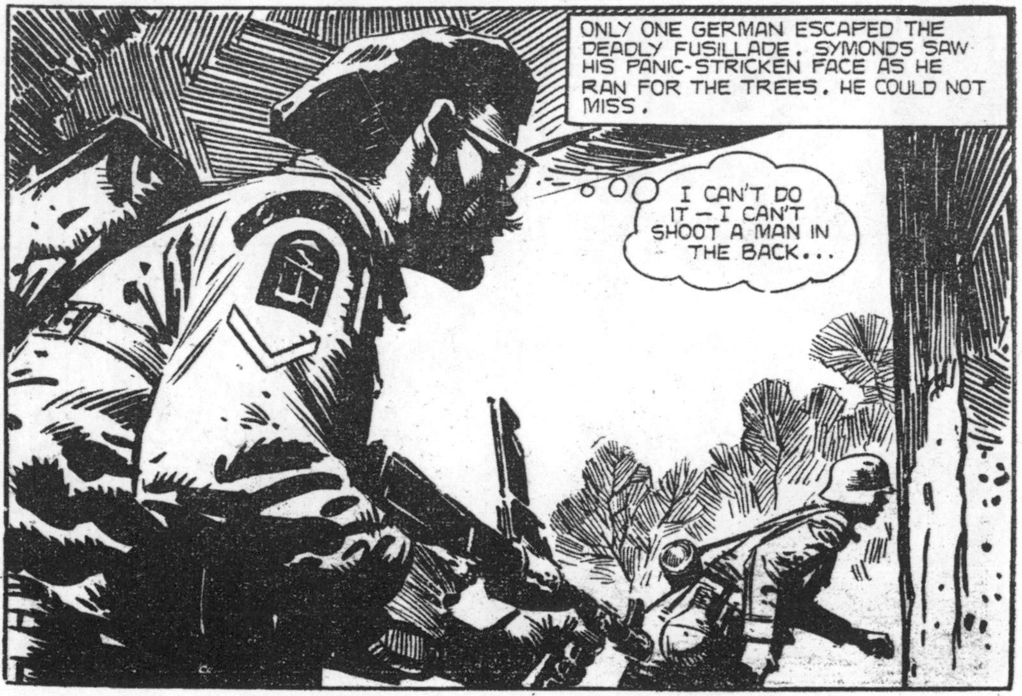
ONLY ONE GERMAN ESCAPED THE DEADLY FUSILLADE. SYMONDS SAW HIS PANIC-STRICKEN FACE AS HE RAN FOR THE TREES. HE COULD NOT MISS.
I CAN'T DO IT — I CAN'T SHOOT A MAN IN THE BACK...

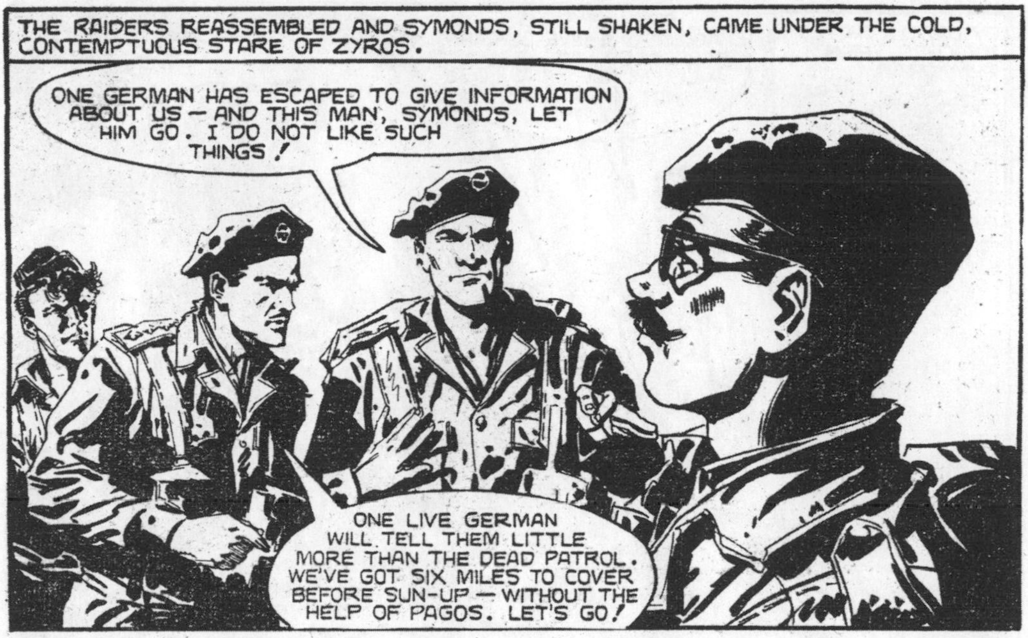
THE RAIDERS REASSEMBLED AND SYMONDS, STILL SHAKEN, CAME UNDER THE COLD, CONTEMPTUOUS STARE OF ZYROS.
ONE GERMAN HAS ESCAPED TO GIVE INFORMATION ABOUT US — AND THIS MAN, SYMONDS, LET HIM GO. I DO NOT LIKE SUCH THINGS!
ONE LIVE GERMAN WILL TELL THEM LITTLE MORE THAN THE DEAD PATROL. WE'VE GOT SIX MILES TO COVER BEFORE SUN-UP — WITHOUT THE HELP OF PAGOS. LET'S GO!

THEIR NEXT STAGING POINT WAS IN THE CRAGGY APPROACHES TO THE KARGA HILLS, WHICH BARRED THE WAY TO THEIR TARGET IN THE SOUTH OF THE ISLAND.

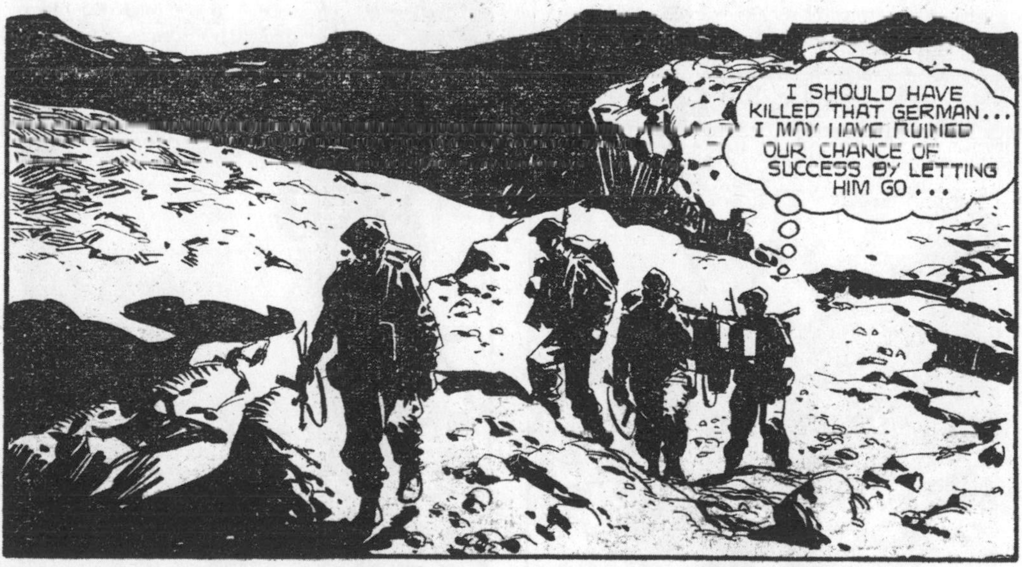
I SHOULD HAVE KILLED THAT GERMAN... I MAY HAVE RUINED OUR CHANCE OF SUCCESS BY LETTING HIM GO...

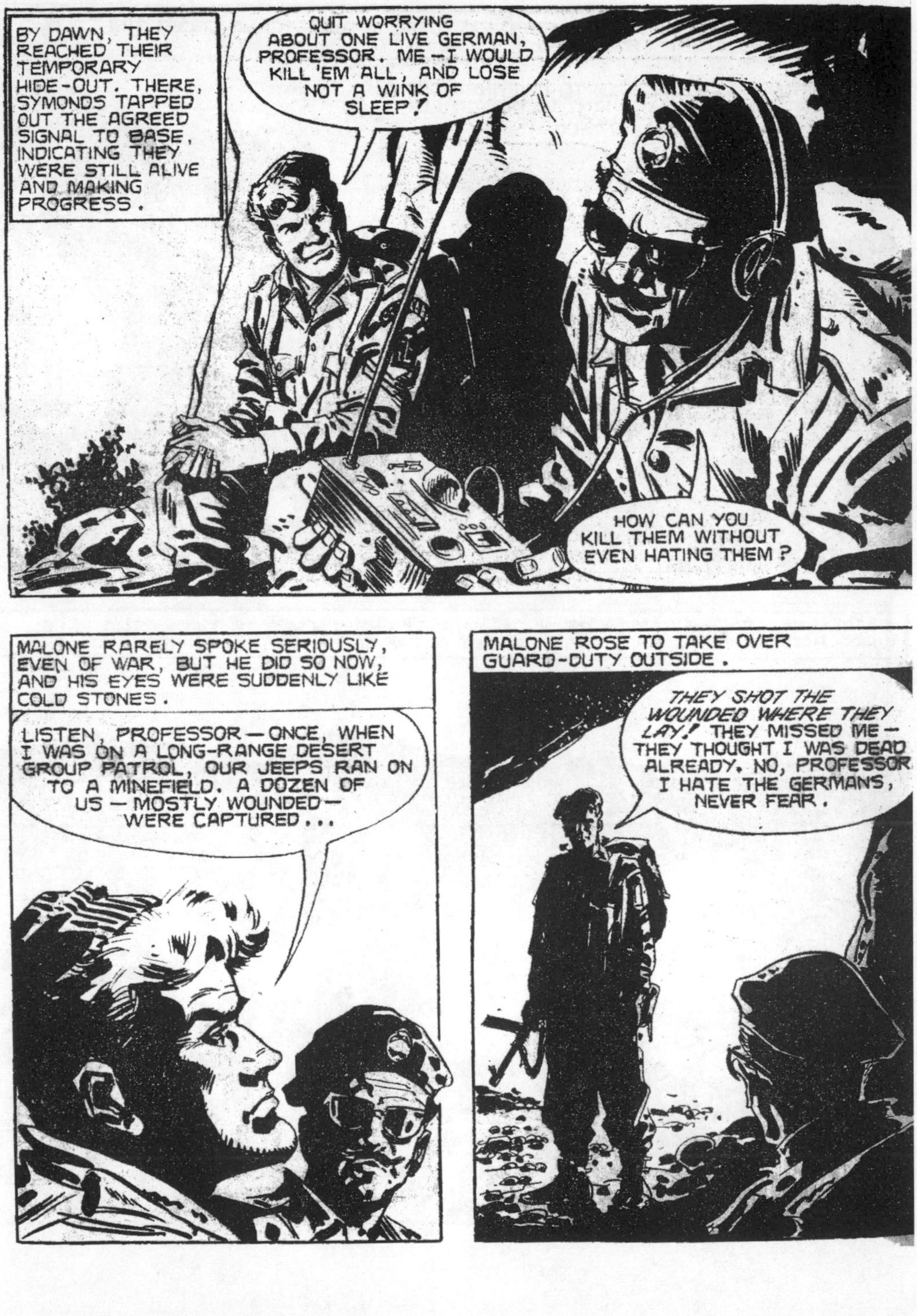
BY DAWN, THEY REACHED THEIR TEMPORARY HIDE-OUT. THERE, SYMONDS TAPPED OUT THE AGREED SIGNAL TO BASE, INDICATING THEY WERE STILL ALIVE AND MAKING PROGRESS.
QUIT WORRYING ABOUT ONE LIVE GERMAN, PROFESSOR. ME—I WOULD KILL 'EM ALL, AND LOSE NOT A WINK OF SLEEP!
HOW CAN YOU KILL THEM WITHOUT EVEN HATING THEM?
MALONE RARELY SPOKE SERIOUSLY, EVEN OF WAR, BUT HE DID SO NOW, AND HIS EYES WERE SUDDENLY LIKE COLD STONES.
LISTEN, PROFESSOR—ONCE, WHEN I WAS ON A LONG-RANGE DESERT GROUP PATROL, OUR JEEPS RAN ON TO A MINEFIELD. A DOZEN OF US—MOSTLY WOUNDED—WERE CAPTURED...
MALONE ROSE TO TAKE OVER GUARD-DUTY OUTSIDE.
THEY SHOT THE WOUNDED WHERE THEY LAY! THEY MISSED ME—THEY THOUGHT I WAS DEAD ALREADY. NO, PROFESSOR, I HATE THE GERMANS, NEVER FEAR.

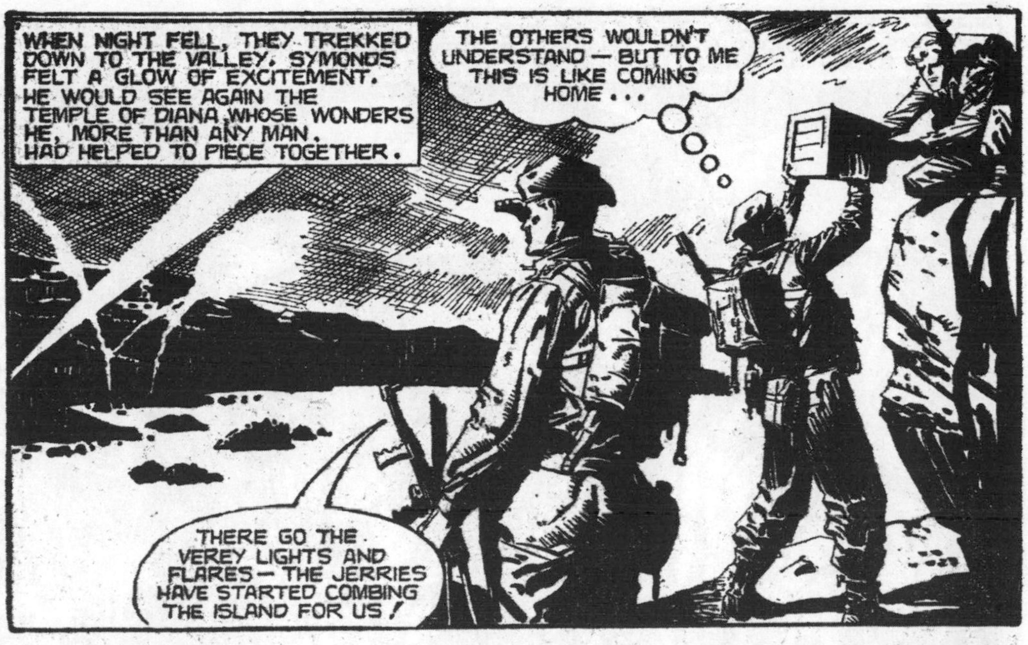
WHEN NIGHT FELL, THEY TREKKED DOWN TO THE VALLEY. SYMONDS FELT A GLOW OF EXCITEMENT. HE WOULD SEE AGAIN THE TEMPLE OF DIANA WHOSE WONDERS HE, MORE THAN ANY MAN, HAD HELPED TO PIECE TOGETHER.
THE OTHERS WOULDN'T UNDERSTAND — BUT TO ME THIS IS LIKE COMING HOME...
THERE GO THE VEREY LIGHTS AND FLARES — THE JERRIES HAVE STARTED COMBING THE ISLAND FOR US!

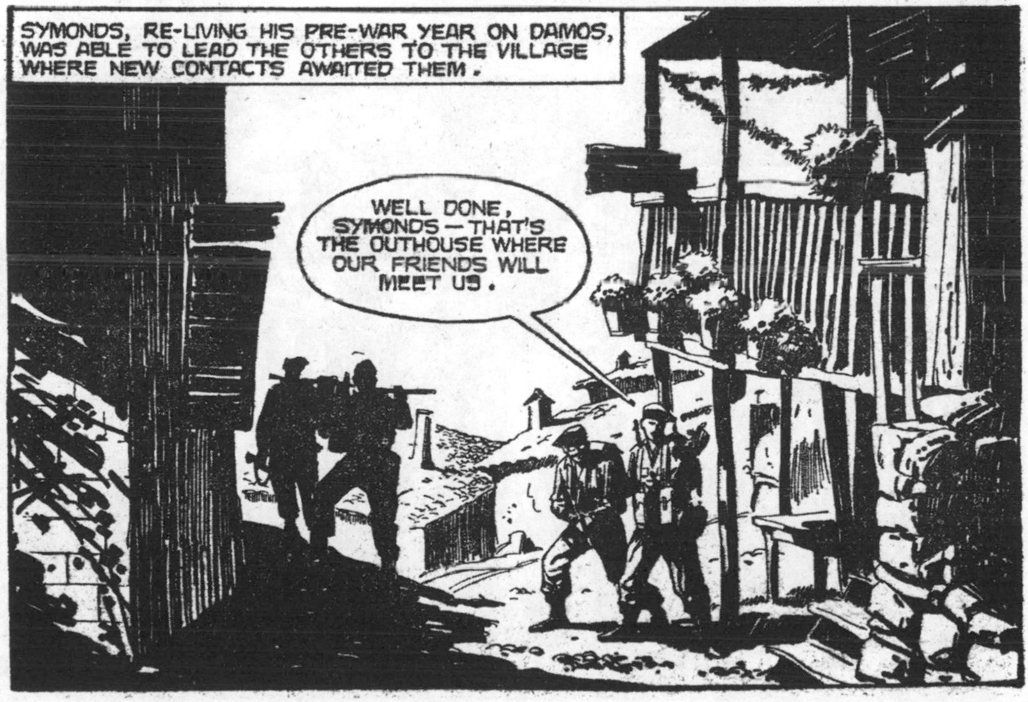
SYMONDS, RE-LIVING HIS PRE-WAR YEAR ON DAMOS, WAS ABLE TO LEAD THE OTHERS TO THE VILLAGE WHERE NEW CONTACTS AWAITED THEM.
WELL DONE, SYMONDS — THAT'S THE OUTHOUSE WHERE OUR FRIENDS WILL MEET US.

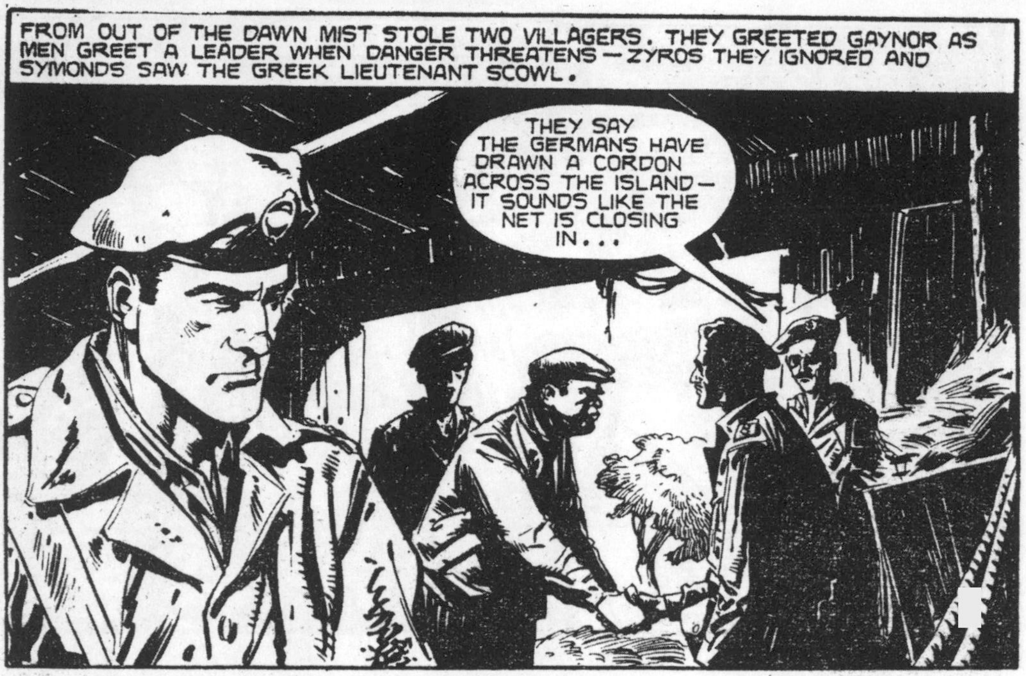
FROM OUT OF THE DAWN MIST STOLE TWO VILLAGERS. THEY GREETED GAYNOR AS MEN GREET A LEADER WHEN DANGER THREATENS — ZYROS THEY IGNORED AND SYMONDS SAW THE GREEK LIEUTENANT SCOWL.
THEY SAY THE GERMANS HAVE DRAWN A CORDON ACROSS THE ISLAND — IT SOUNDS LIKE THE NET IS CLOSING IN...

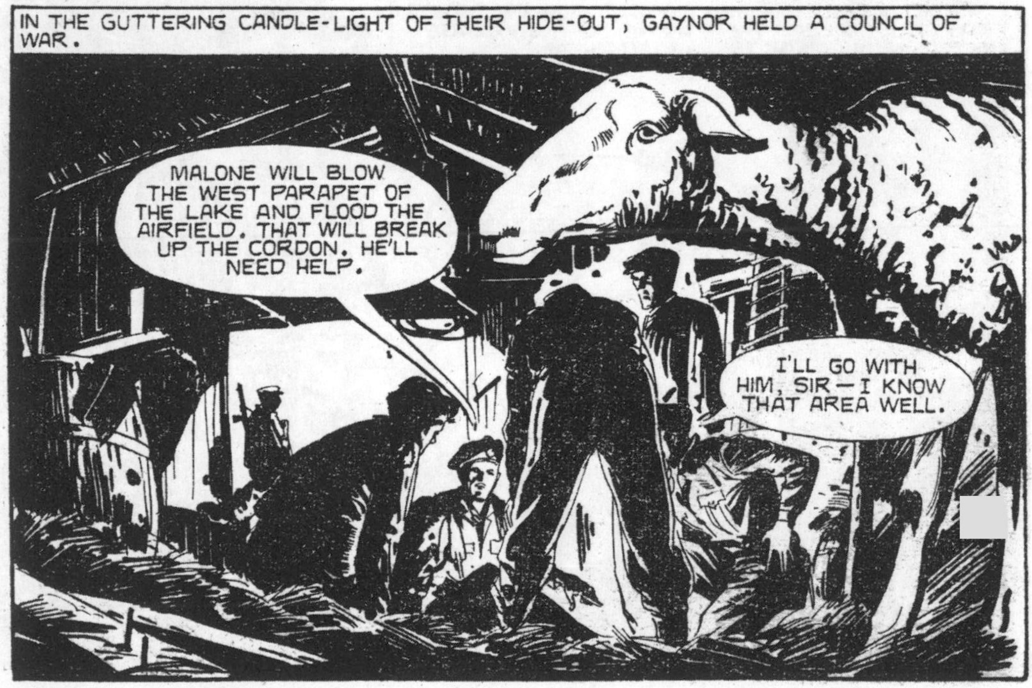
IN THE GUTTERING CANDLE-LIGHT OF THEIR HIDE-OUT, GAYNOR HELD A COUNCIL OF WAR.
MALONE WILL BLOW THE WEST PARAPET OF THE LAKE AND FLOOD THE AIRFIELD. THAT WILL BREAK UP THE CORDON. HE'LL NEED HELP.
I'LL GO WITH HIM, SIR — I KNOW THAT AREA WELL.

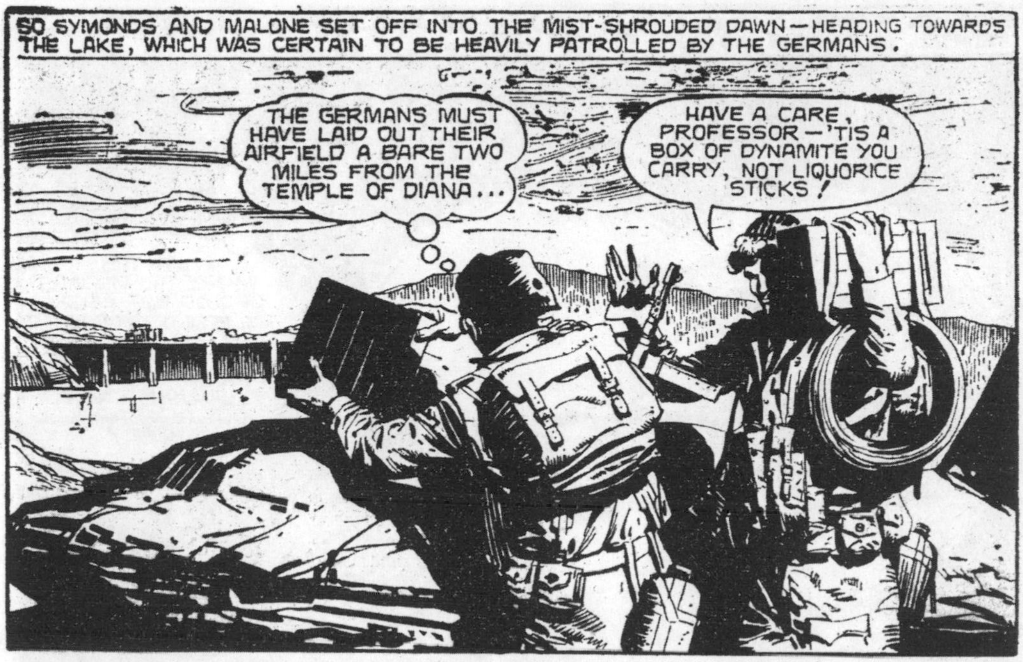
SO SYMONDS AND MALONE SET OFF INTO THE MIST-SHROUDED DAWN—HEADING TOWARDS THE LAKE, WHICH WAS CERTAIN TO BE HEAVILY PATROLLED BY THE GERMANS.
THE GERMANS MUST HAVE LAID OUT THEIR AIRFIELD A BARE TWO MILES FROM THE TEMPLE OF DIANA...
HAVE A CARE, PROFESSOR—'TIS A BOX OF DYNAMITE YOU CARRY, NOT LIQUORICE STICKS!

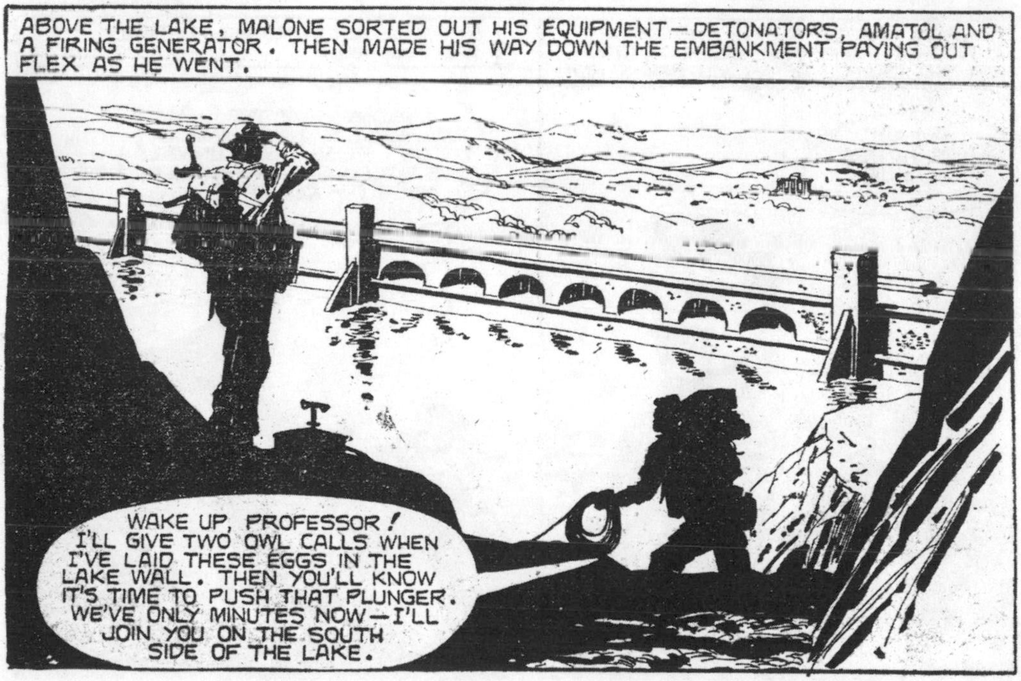
ABOVE THE LAKE, MALONE SORTED OUT HIS EQUIPMENT—DETONATORS, AMATOL AND A FIRING GENERATOR. THEN MADE HIS WAY DOWN THE EMBANKMENT PAYING OUT FLEX AS HE WENT.
WAKE UP, PROFESSOR! I'LL GIVE TWO OWL CALLS WHEN I'VE LAID THESE EGGS IN THE LAKE WALL. THEN YOU'LL KNOW IT'S TIME TO PUSH THAT PLUNGER. WE'VE ONLY MINUTES NOW—I'LL JOIN YOU ON THE SOUTH SIDE OF THE LAKE.

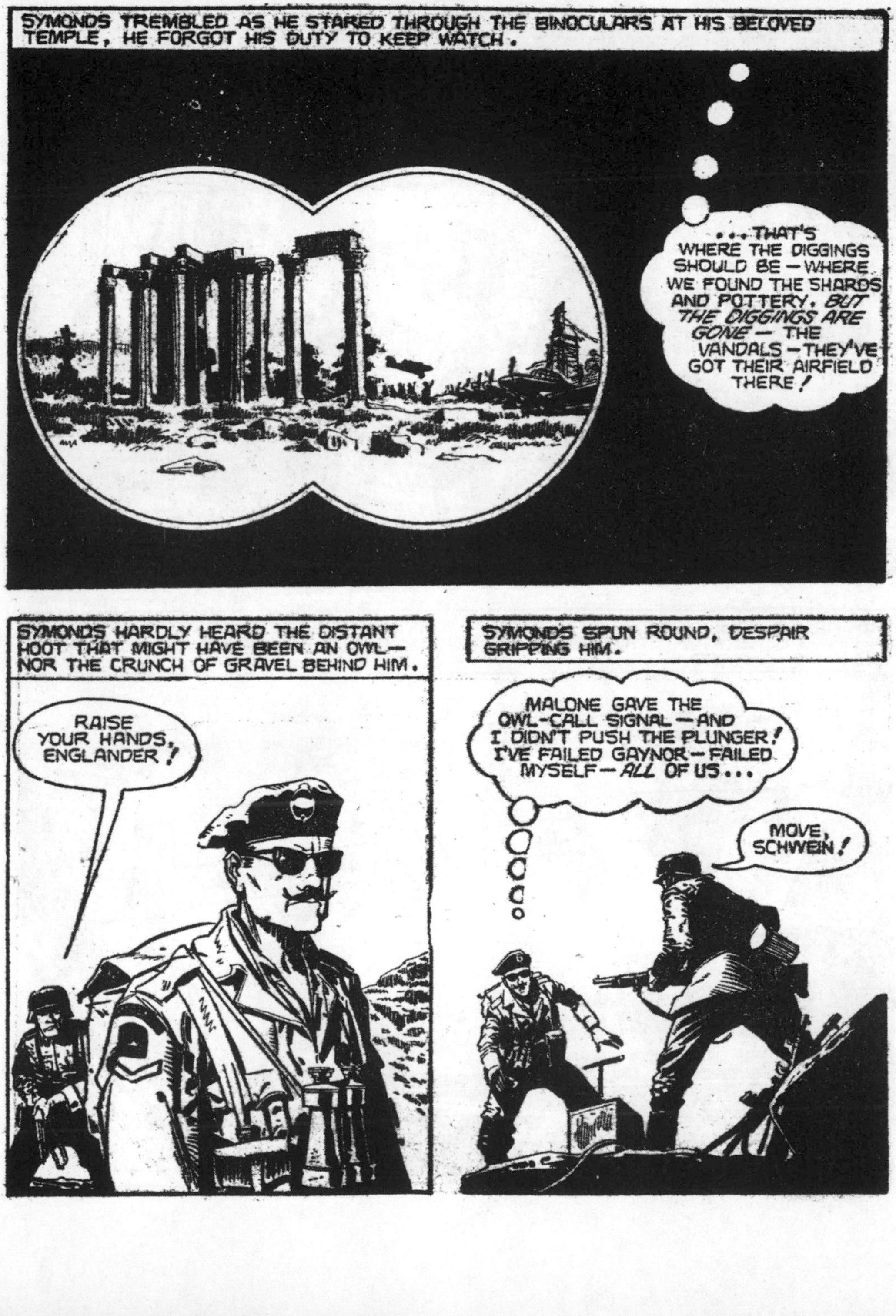
SYMONDS TREMBLED AS HE STARED THROUGH THE BINOCULARS AT HIS BELOVED TEMPLE, HE FORGOT HIS DUTY TO KEEP WATCH.
...THAT'S WHERE THE DIGGINGS SHOULD BE—WHERE WE FOUND THE SHARDS AND POTTERY. *BUT THE DIGGINGS ARE GONE*—THE VANDALS—THEY'VE GOT THEIR AIRFIELD THERE!
SYMONDS HARDLY HEARD THE DISTANT HOOT THAT MIGHT HAVE BEEN AN OWL—NOR THE CRUNCH OF GRAVEL BEHIND HIM.
RAISE YOUR HANDS, ENGLANDER!
SYMONDS SPUN ROUND, DESPAIR GRIPPING HIM.
MALONE GAVE THE OWL-CALL SIGNAL—AND I DIDN'T PUSH THE PLUNGER! I'VE FAILED GAYNOR—FAILED MYSELF—*ALL* OF US...
MOVE, SCHWEIN!

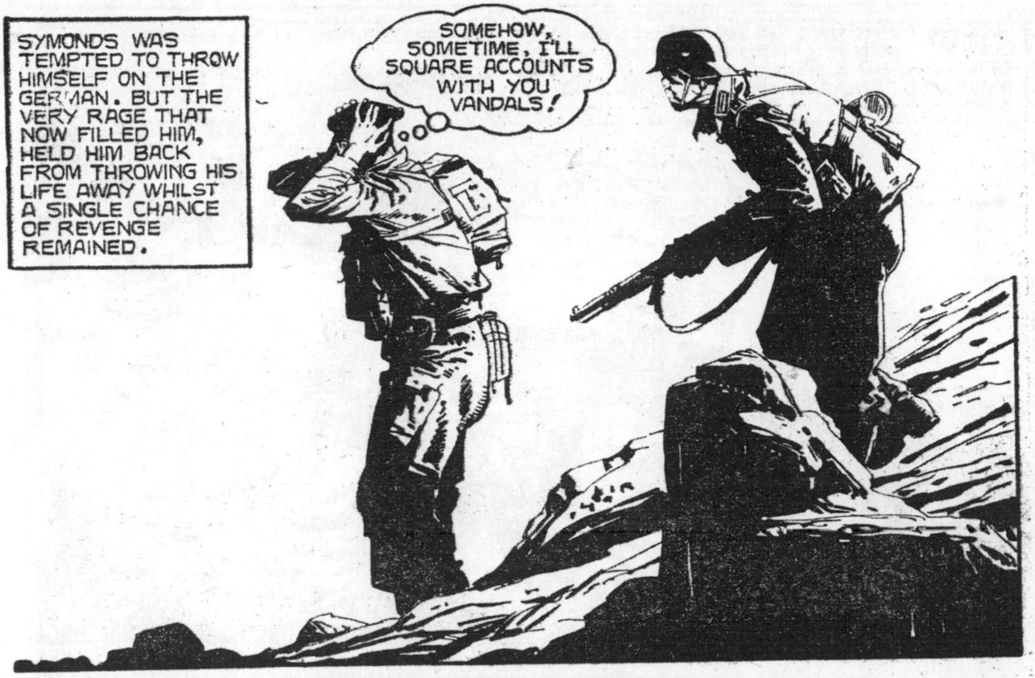
SYMONDS WAS TEMPTED TO THROW HIMSELF ON THE GERMAN. BUT THE VERY RAGE THAT NOW FILLED HIM, HELD HIM BACK FROM THROWING HIS LIFE AWAY WHILST A SINGLE CHANCE OF REVENGE REMAINED.
SOMEHOW, SOMETIME, I'LL SQUARE ACCOUNTS WITH YOU VANDALS!

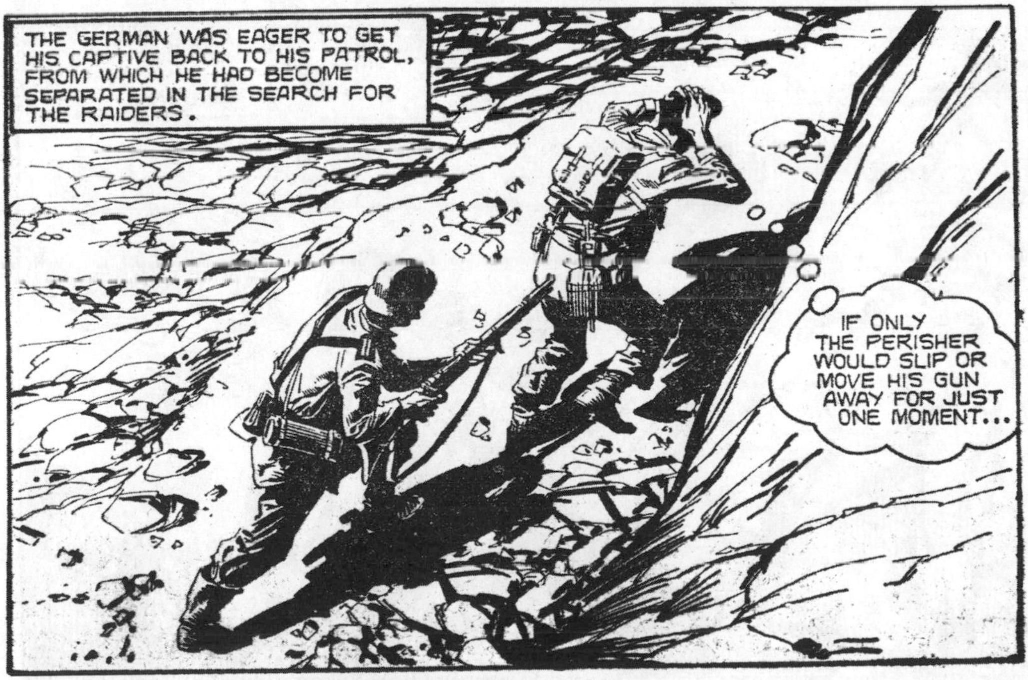
THE GERMAN WAS EAGER TO GET HIS CAPTIVE BACK TO HIS PATROL, FROM WHICH HE HAD BECOME SEPARATED IN THE SEARCH FOR THE RAIDERS.
IF ONLY THE PERISHER WOULD SLIP OR MOVE HIS GUN AWAY FOR JUST ONE MOMENT...

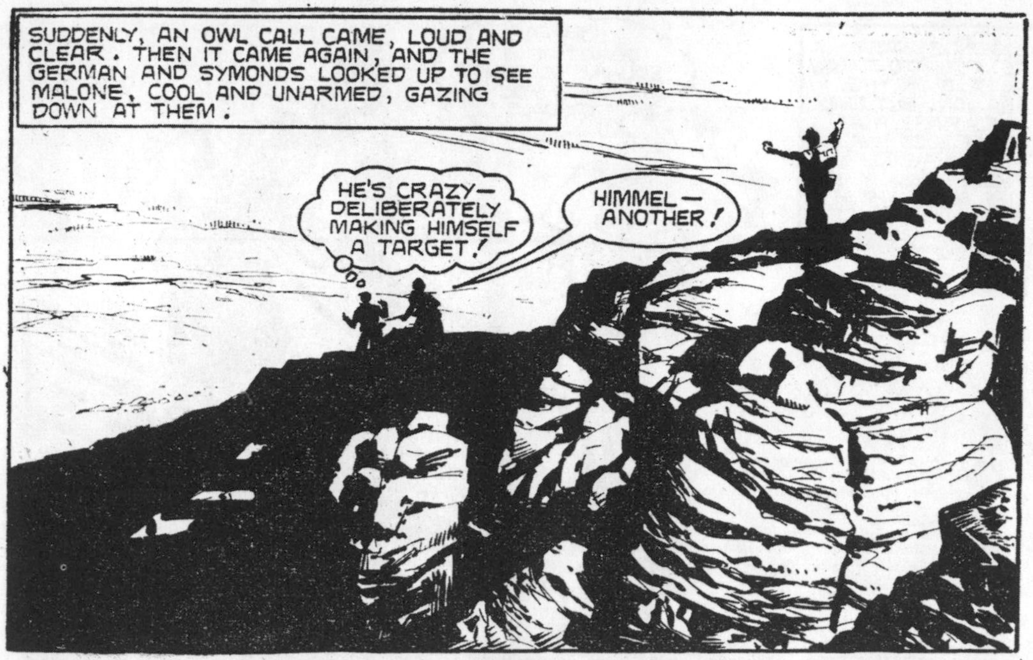
SUDDENLY, AN OWL CALL CAME, LOUD AND CLEAR. THEN IT CAME AGAIN, AND THE GERMAN AND SYMONDS LOOKED UP TO SEE MALONE, COOL AND UNARMED, GAZING DOWN AT THEM.
HE'S CRAZY—DELIBERATELY MAKING HIMSELF A TARGET!
HIMMEL—ANOTHER!

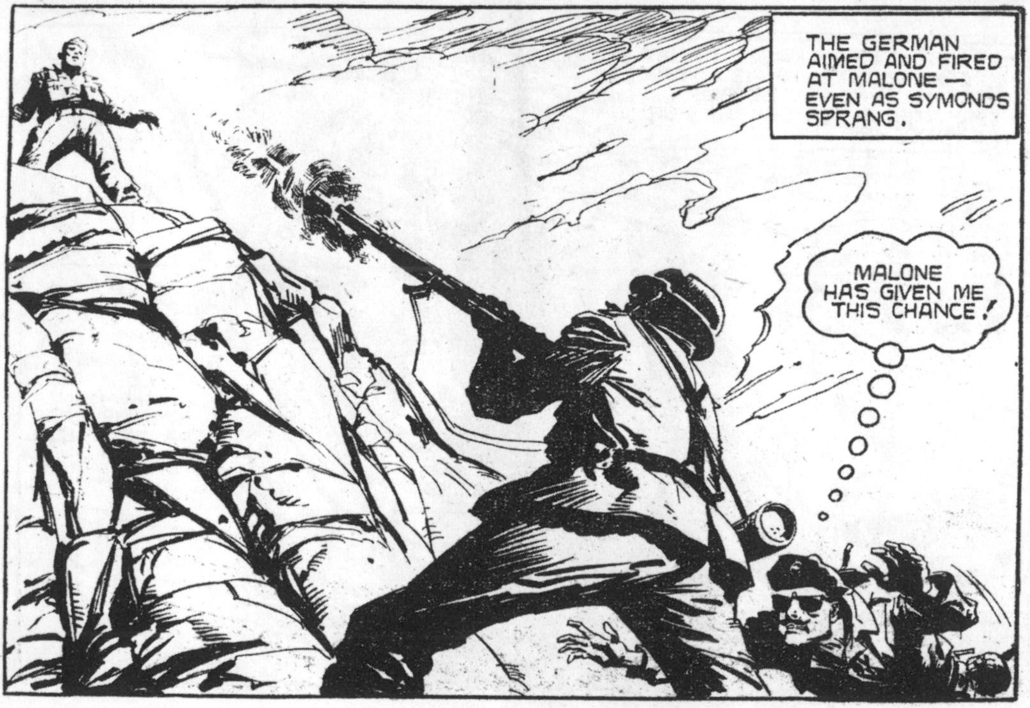
THE GERMAN AIMED AND FIRED AT MALONE—EVEN AS SYMONDS SPRANG.
MALONE HAS GIVEN ME THIS CHANCE!

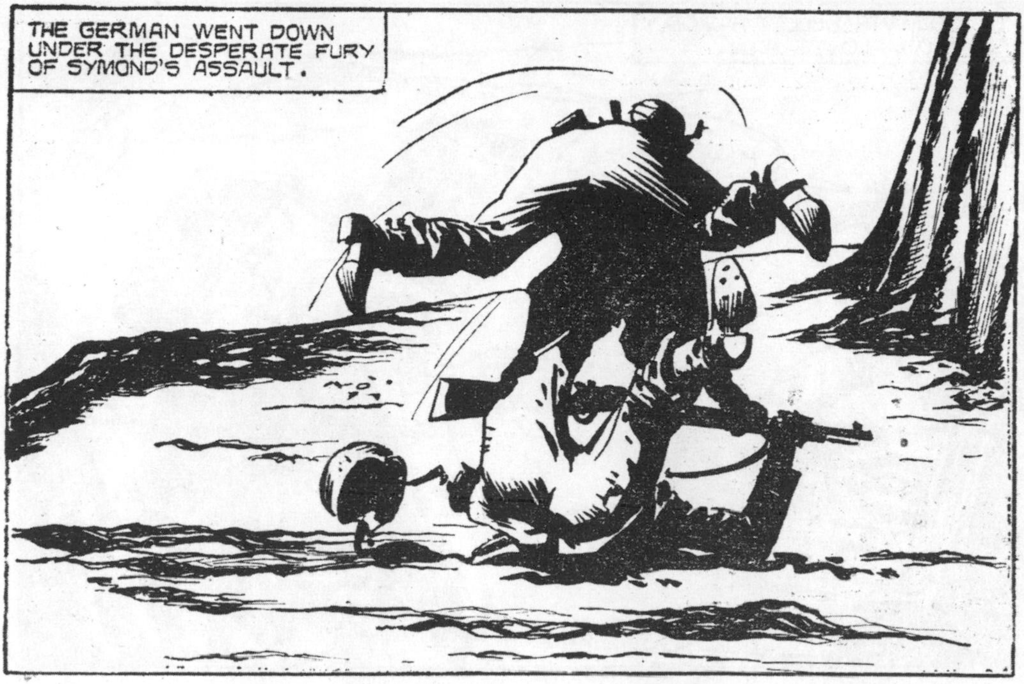
THE GERMAN WENT DOWN UNDER THE DESPERATE FURY OF SYMOND'S ASSAULT.

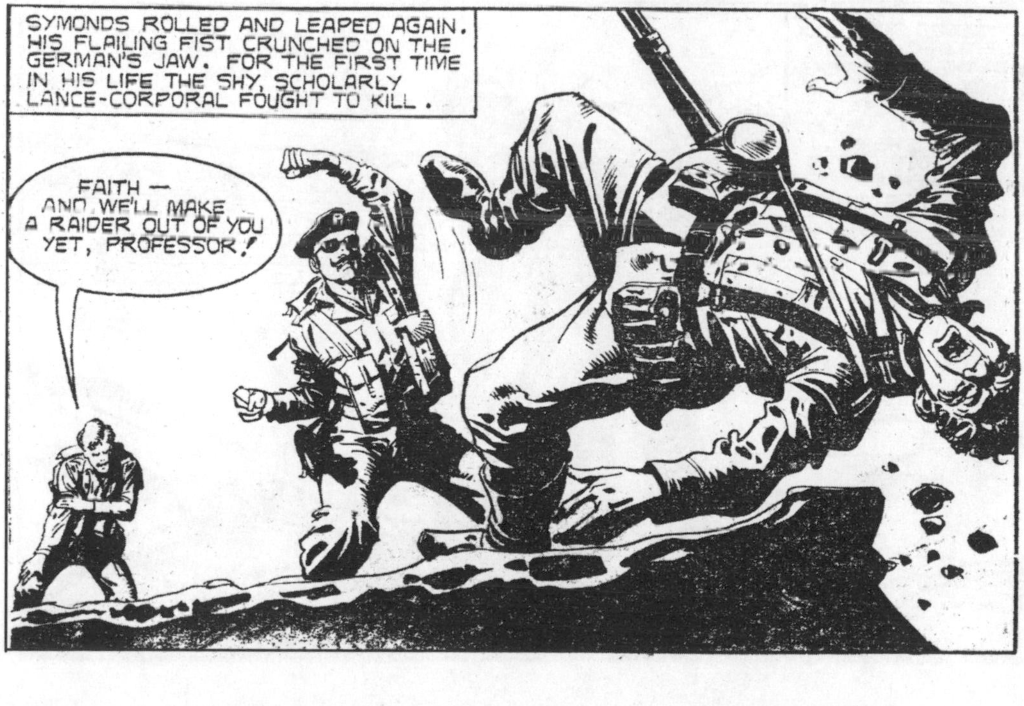
SYMONDS ROLLED AND LEAPED AGAIN. HIS FLAILING FIST CRUNCHED ON THE GERMAN'S JAW. FOR THE FIRST TIME IN HIS LIFE THE SHY, SCHOLARLY LANCE-CORPORAL FOUGHT TO KILL.
FAITH — AND WE'LL MAKE A RAIDER OUT OF YOU YET, PROFESSOR!

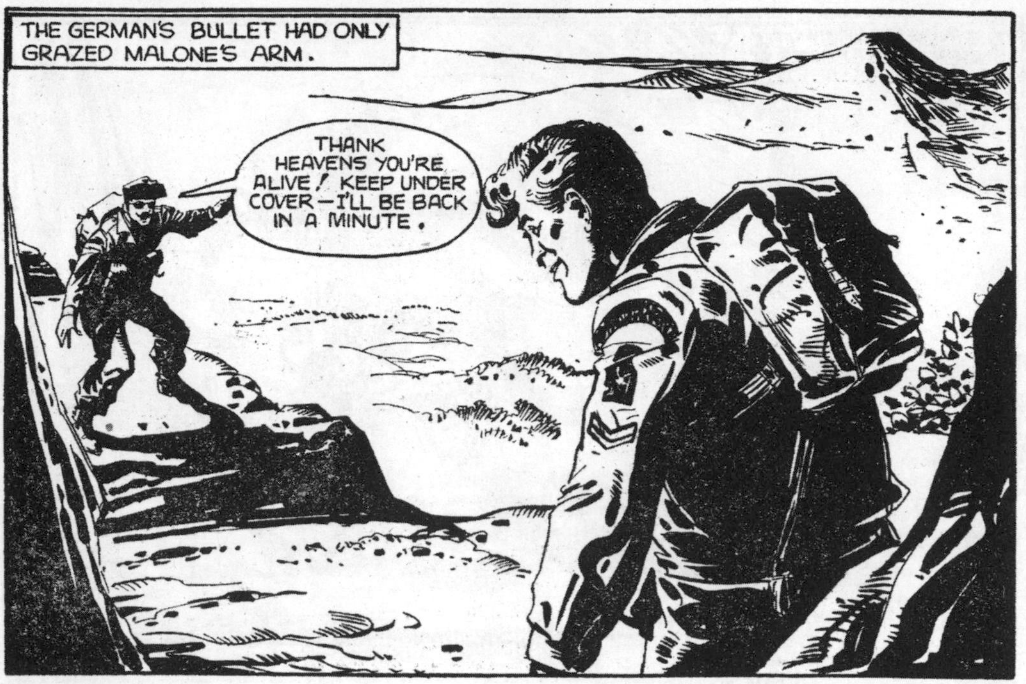
THE GERMAN'S BULLET HAD ONLY GRAZED MALONE'S ARM.
THANK HEAVENS YOU'RE ALIVE! KEEP UNDER COVER—I'LL BE BACK IN A MINUTE.

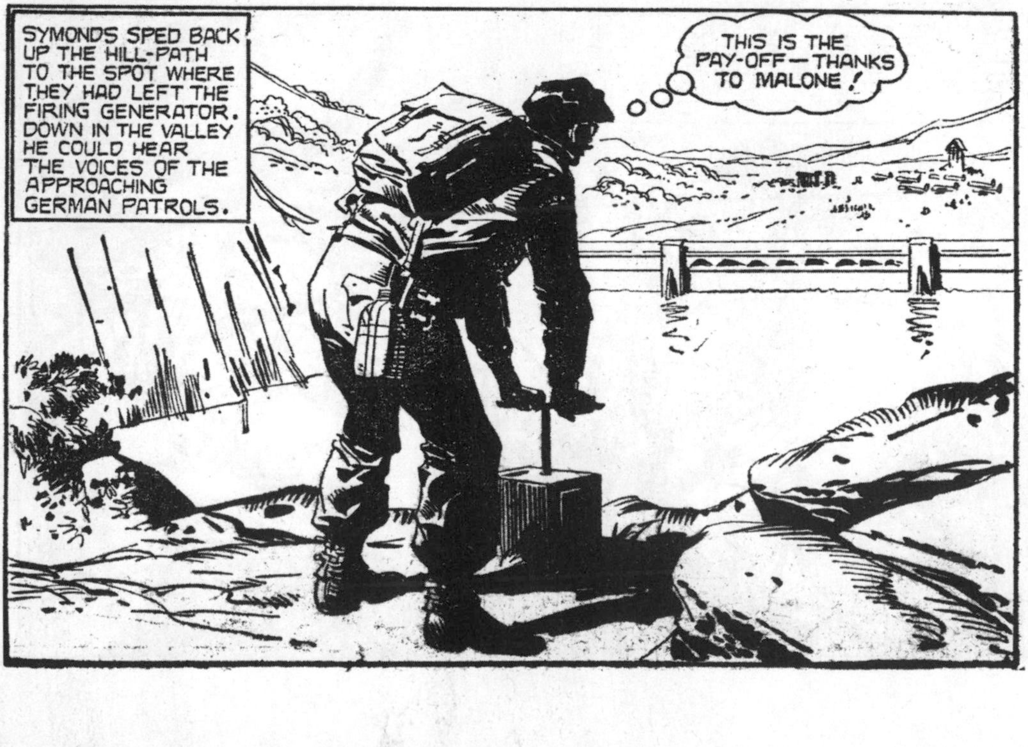
SYMONDS SPED BACK UP THE HILL-PATH TO THE SPOT WHERE THEY HAD LEFT THE FIRING GENERATOR. DOWN IN THE VALLEY HE COULD HEAR THE VOICES OF THE APPROACHING GERMAN PATROLS.
THIS IS THE PAY-OFF—THANKS TO MALONE!

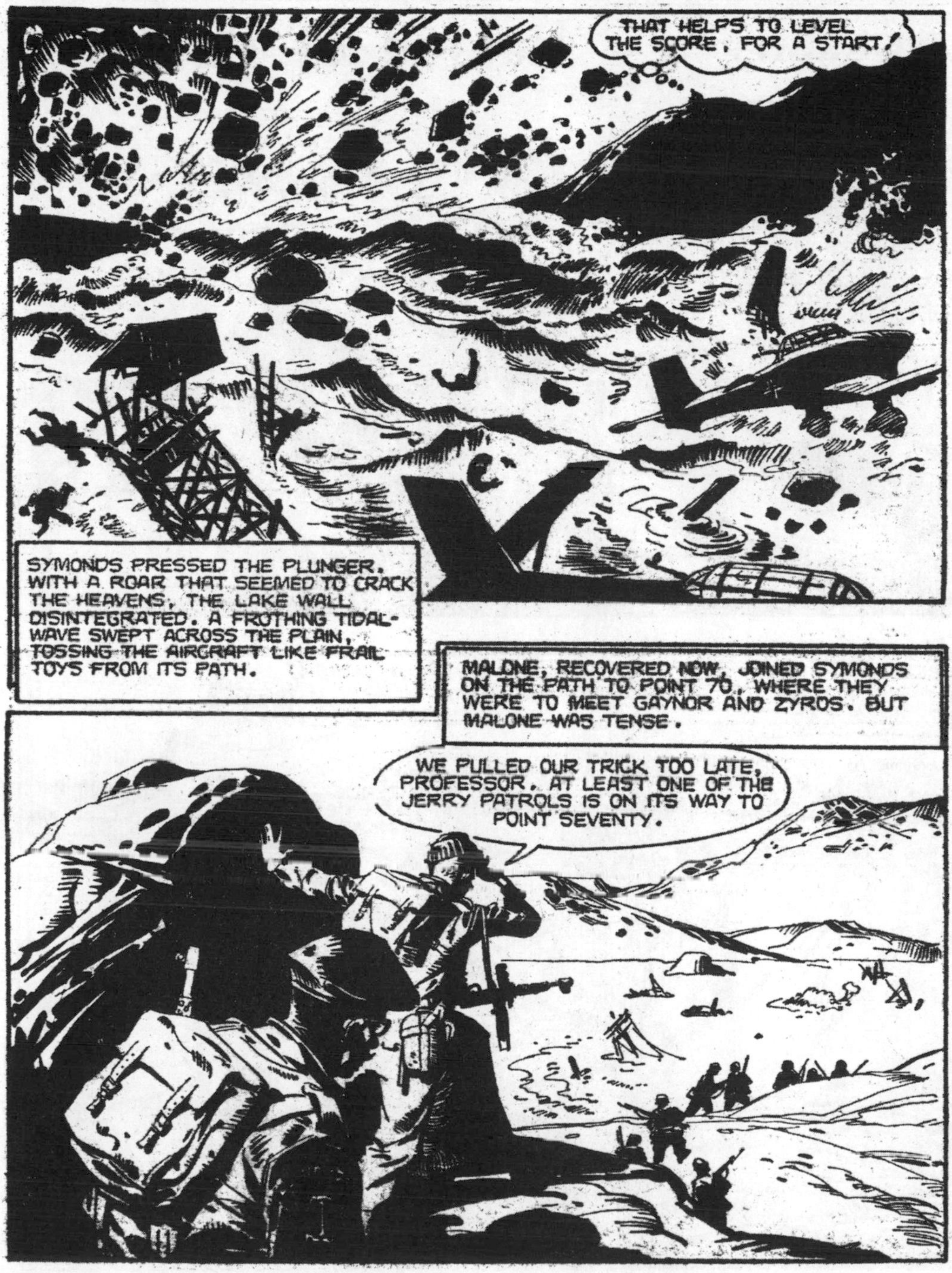
THAT HELPS TO LEVEL THE SCORE, FOR A START!
SYMONDS PRESSED THE PLUNGER. WITH A ROAR THAT SEEMED TO CRACK THE HEAVENS, THE LAKE WALL DISINTEGRATED. A FROTHING TIDAL-WAVE SWEPT ACROSS THE PLAIN, TOSSING THE AIRCRAFT LIKE FRAIL TOYS FROM ITS PATH.
MALONE, RECOVERED NOW, JOINED SYMONDS ON THE PATH TO POINT 70, WHERE THEY WERE TO MEET GAYNOR AND ZYROS. BUT MALONE WAS TENSE.
WE PULLED OUR TRICK TOO LATE, PROFESSOR. AT LEAST ONE OF THE JERRY PATROLS IS ON ITS WAY TO POINT SEVENTY.

Chapter 3. Palace of Death

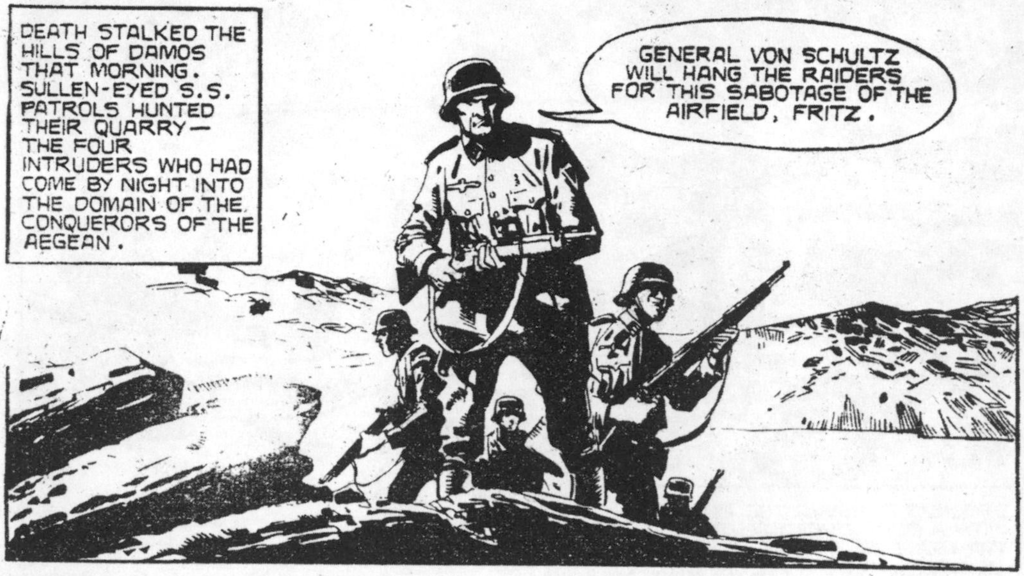
DEATH STALKED THE HILLS OF DAMOS THAT MORNING. SULLEN-EYED S.S. PATROLS HUNTED THEIR QUARRY— THE FOUR INTRUDERS WHO HAD COME BY NIGHT INTO THE DOMAIN OF THE CONQUERORS OF THE AEGEAN.
GENERAL VON SCHULTZ WILL HANG THE RAIDERS FOR THIS SABOTAGE OF THE AIRFIELD, FRITZ.

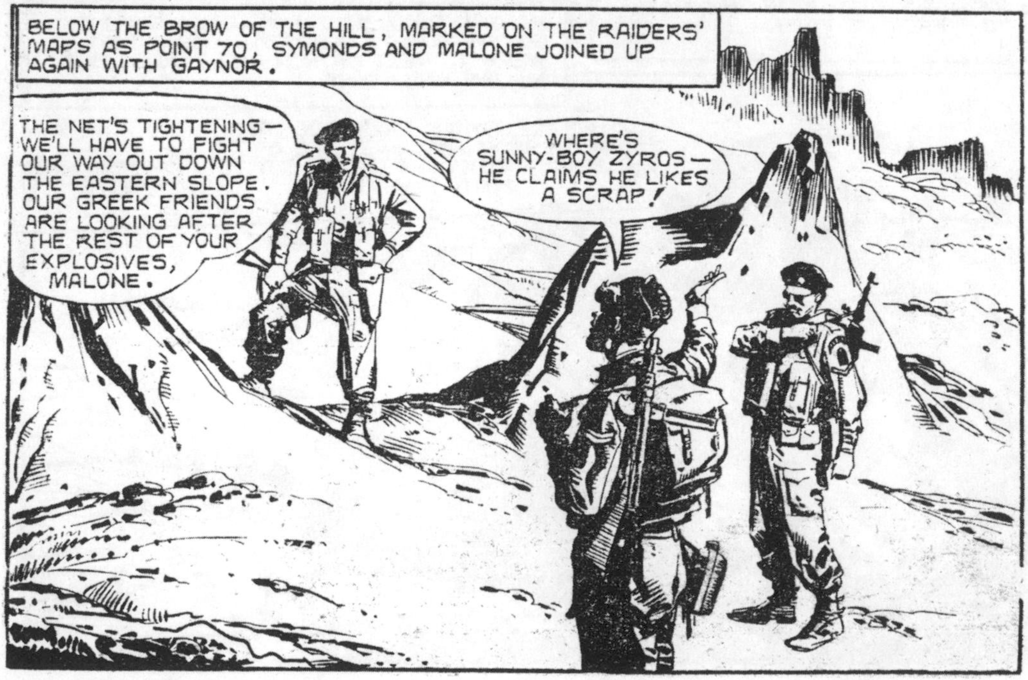
BELOW THE BROW OF THE HILL, MARKED ON THE RAIDERS' MAPS AS POINT 70, SYMONDS AND MALONE JOINED UP AGAIN WITH GAYNOR.
THE NET'S TIGHTENING— WE'LL HAVE TO FIGHT OUR WAY OUT DOWN THE EASTERN SLOPE. OUR GREEK FRIENDS ARE LOOKING AFTER THE REST OF YOUR EXPLOSIVES, MALONE.
WHERE'S SUNNY-BOY ZYROS— HE CLAIMS HE LIKES A SCRAP!

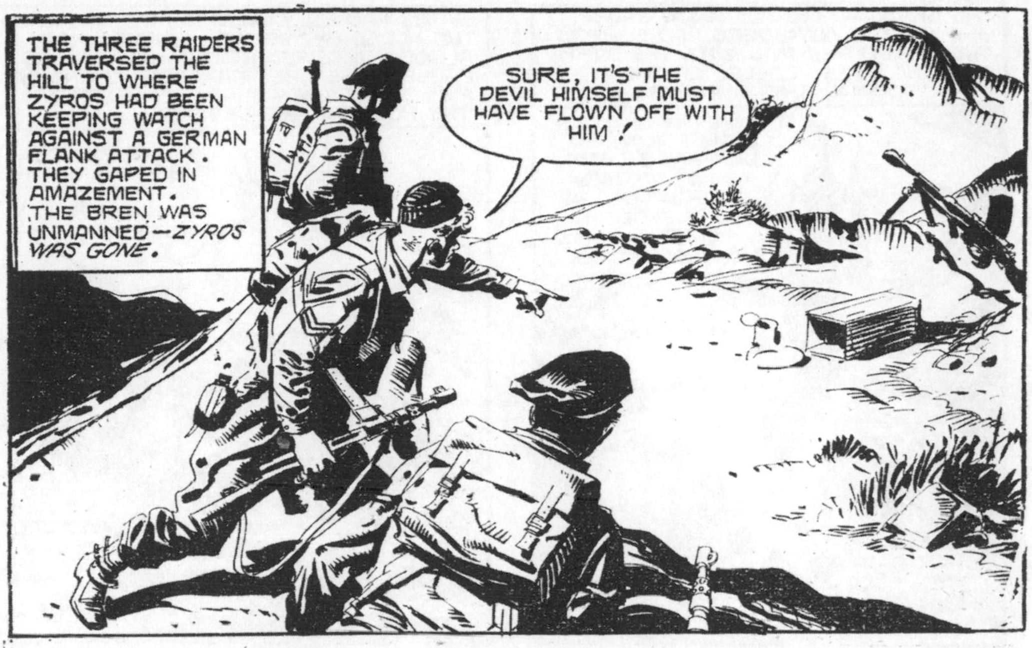
THE THREE RAIDERS TRAVERSED THE HILL TO WHERE ZYROS HAD BEEN KEEPING WATCH AGAINST A GERMAN FLANK ATTACK. THEY GAPED IN AMAZEMENT. THE BREN WAS UNMANNED—ZYROS WAS GONE.
SURE, IT'S THE DEVIL HIMSELF MUST HAVE FLOWN OFF WITH HIM!

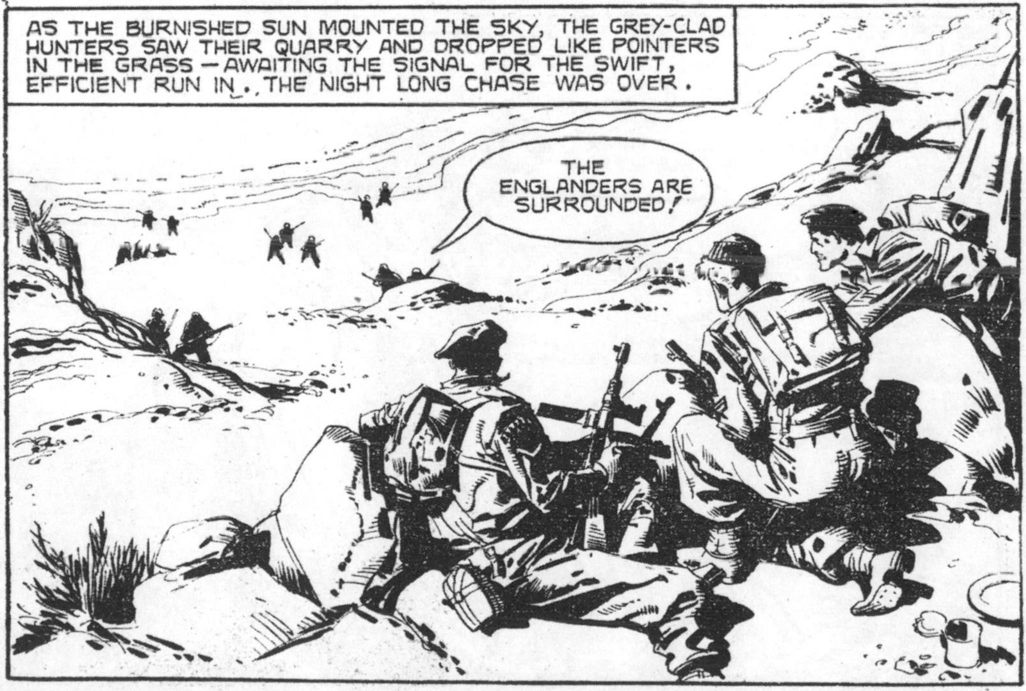
AS THE BURNISHED SUN MOUNTED THE SKY, THE GREY-CLAD HUNTERS SAW THEIR QUARRY AND DROPPED LIKE POINTERS IN THE GRASS—AWAITING THE SIGNAL FOR THE SWIFT, EFFICIENT RUN IN.. THE NIGHT LONG CHASE WAS OVER.
THE ENGLANDERS ARE SURROUNDED!

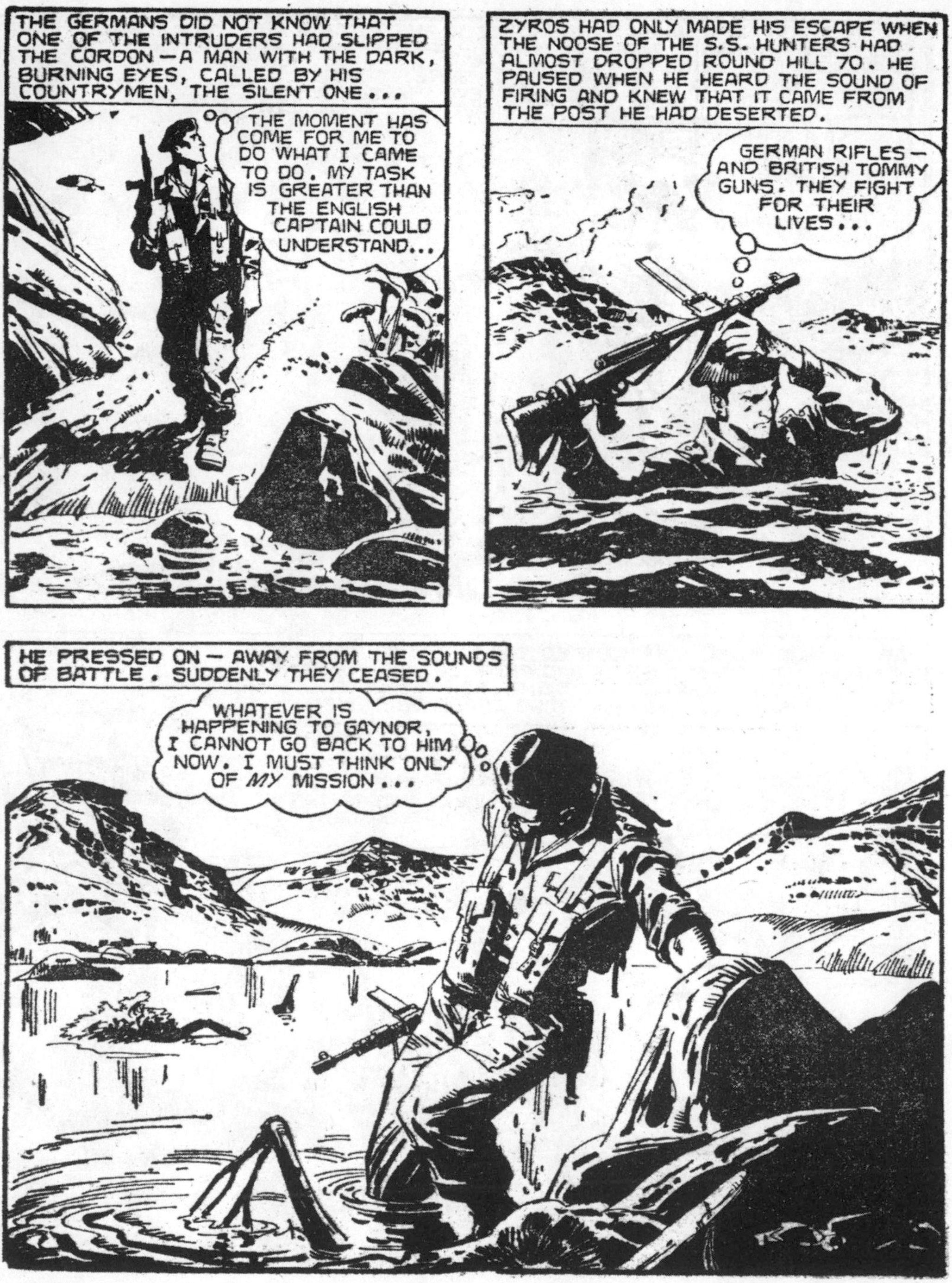
THE GERMANS DID NOT KNOW THAT ONE OF THE INTRUDERS HAD SLIPPED THE CORDON — A MAN WITH THE DARK, BURNING EYES, CALLED BY HIS COUNTRYMEN, THE SILENT ONE...
THE MOMENT HAS COME FOR ME TO DO WHAT I CAME TO DO. MY TASK IS GREATER THAN THE ENGLISH CAPTAIN COULD UNDERSTAND...
ZYROS HAD ONLY MADE HIS ESCAPE WHEN THE NOOSE OF THE S.S. HUNTERS HAD ALMOST DROPPED ROUND HILL 70. HE PAUSED WHEN HE HEARD THE SOUND OF FIRING AND KNEW THAT IT CAME FROM THE POST HE HAD DESERTED.
GERMAN RIFLES — AND BRITISH TOMMY GUNS. THEY FIGHT FOR THEIR LIVES...
HE PRESSED ON — AWAY FROM THE SOUNDS OF BATTLE. SUDDENLY THEY CEASED.
WHATEVER IS HAPPENING TO GAYNOR, I CANNOT GO BACK TO HIM NOW. I MUST THINK ONLY OF *MY* MISSION...

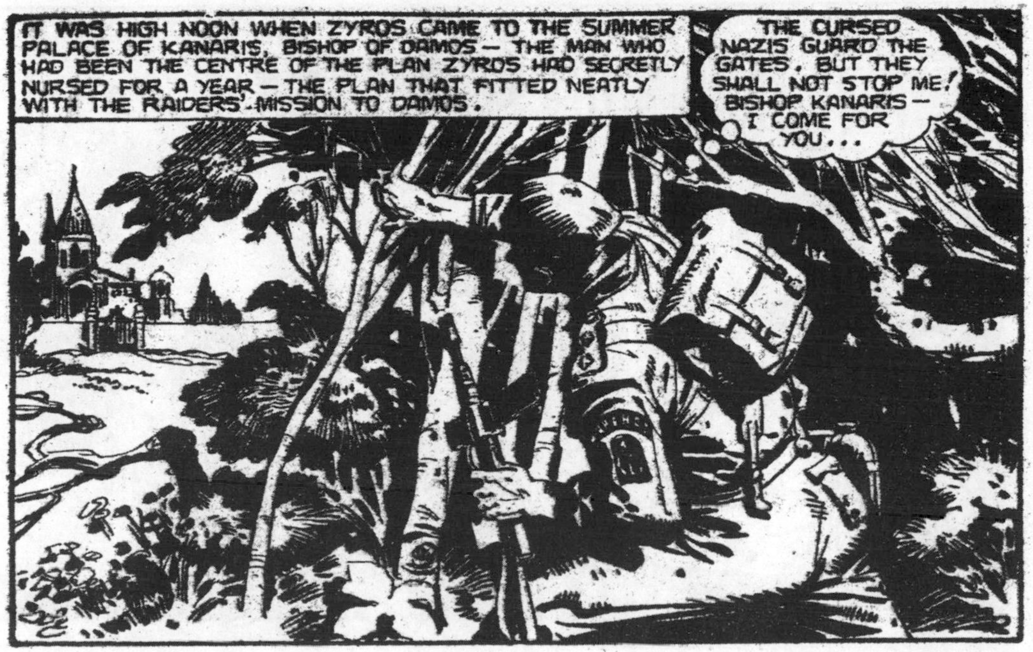
IT WAS HIGH NOON WHEN ZYROS CAME TO THE SUMMER PALACE OF KANARIS, BISHOP OF DAMOS — THE MAN WHO HAD BEEN THE CENTRE OF THE PLAN ZYROS HAD SECRETLY NURSED FOR A YEAR — THE PLAN THAT FITTED NEATLY WITH THE RAIDERS' MISSION TO DAMOS.
THE CURSED NAZIS GUARD THE GATES. BUT THEY SHALL NOT STOP ME! BISHOP KANARIS — I COME FOR YOU...

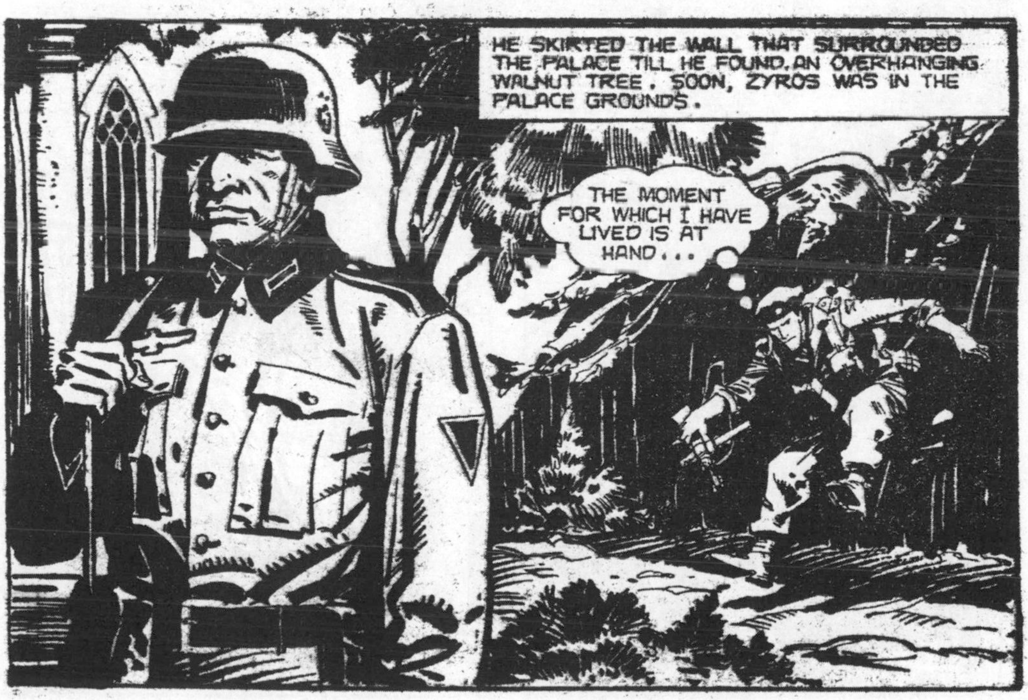
HE SKIRTED THE WALL THAT SURROUNDED THE PALACE TILL HE FOUND AN OVERHANGING WALNUT TREE. SOON, ZYROS WAS IN THE PALACE GROUNDS.
THE MOMENT FOR WHICH I HAVE LIVED IS AT HAND...

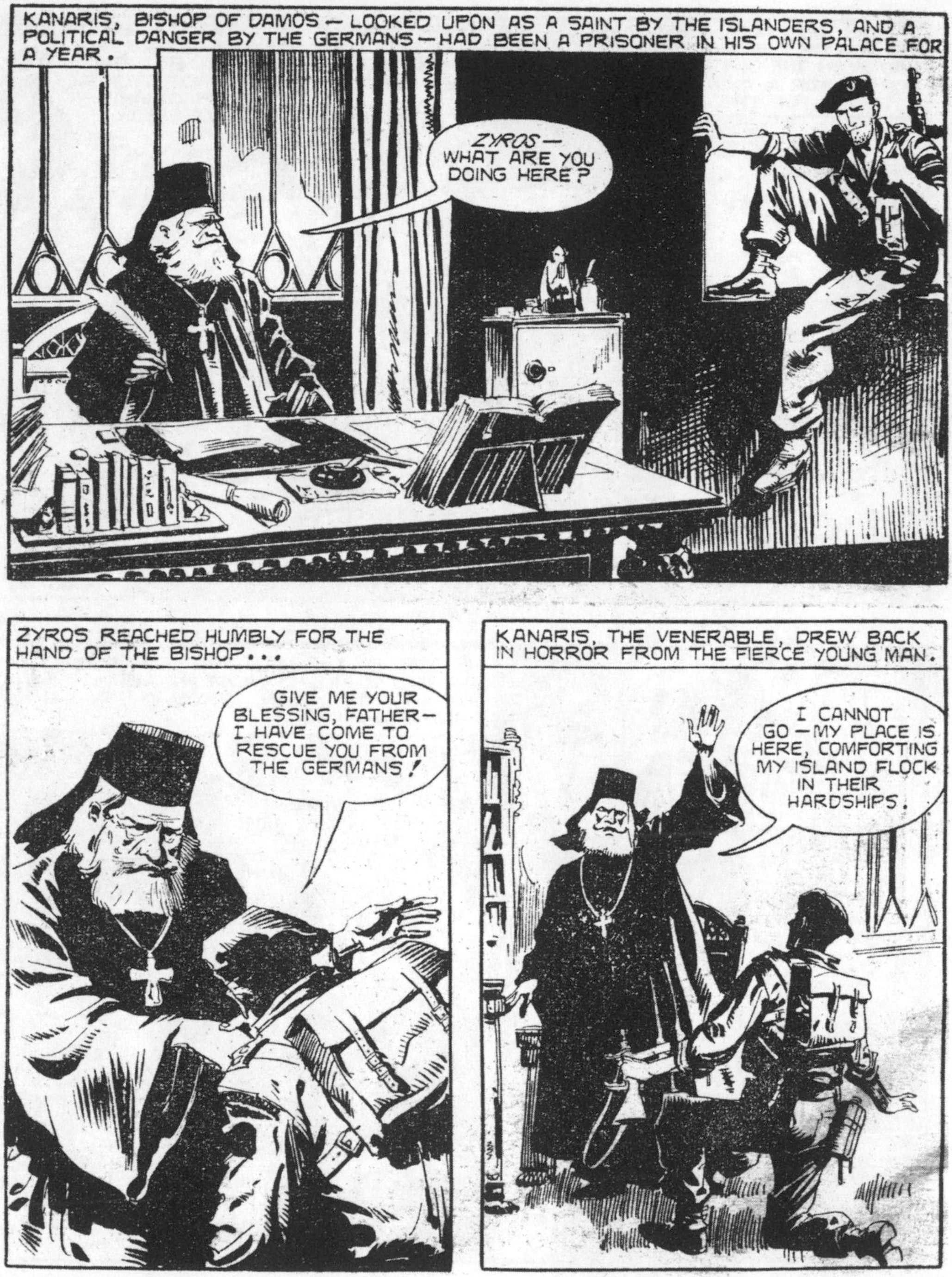
KANARIS, BISHOP OF DAMOS — LOOKED UPON AS A SAINT BY THE ISLANDERS, AND A POLITICAL DANGER BY THE GERMANS — HAD BEEN A PRISONER IN HIS OWN PALACE FOR A YEAR.
ZYROS — WHAT ARE YOU DOING HERE?
ZYROS REACHED HUMBLY FOR THE HAND OF THE BISHOP...
GIVE ME YOUR BLESSING, FATHER — I HAVE COME TO RESCUE YOU FROM THE GERMANS!
KANARIS, THE VENERABLE, DREW BACK IN HORROR FROM THE FIERCE YOUNG MAN.
I CANNOT GO — MY PLACE IS HERE, COMFORTING MY ISLAND FLOCK IN THEIR HARDSHIPS.

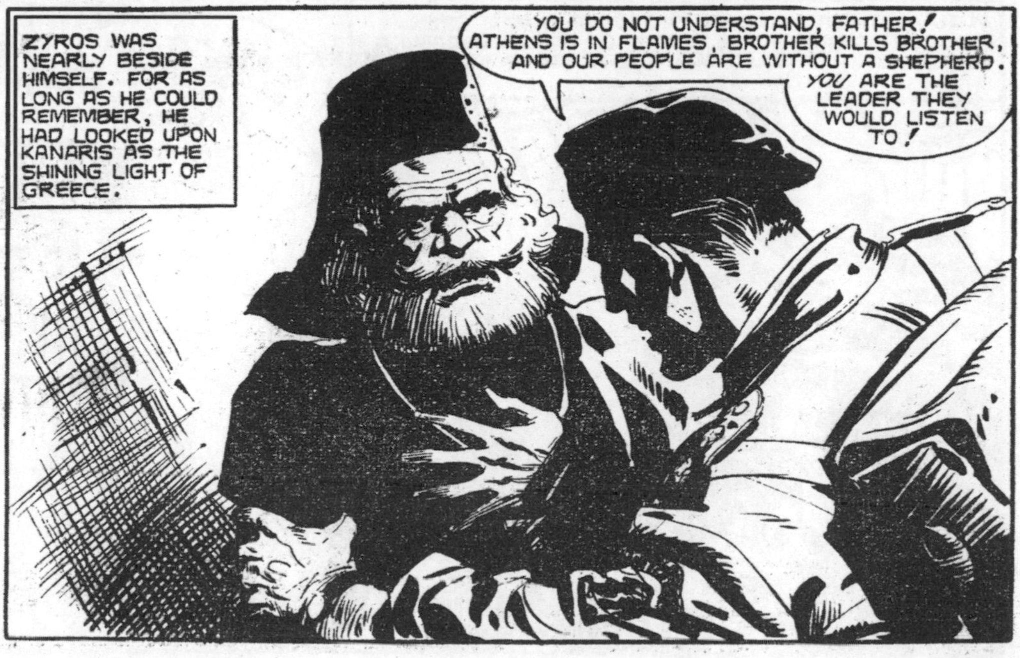
ZYROS WAS NEARLY BESIDE HIMSELF. FOR AS LONG AS HE COULD REMEMBER, HE HAD LOOKED UPON KANARIS AS THE SHINING LIGHT OF GREECE.
YOU DO NOT UNDERSTAND, FATHER! ATHENS IS IN FLAMES, BROTHER KILLS BROTHER, AND OUR PEOPLE ARE WITHOUT A SHEPHERD. YOU ARE THE LEADER THEY WOULD LISTEN TO!

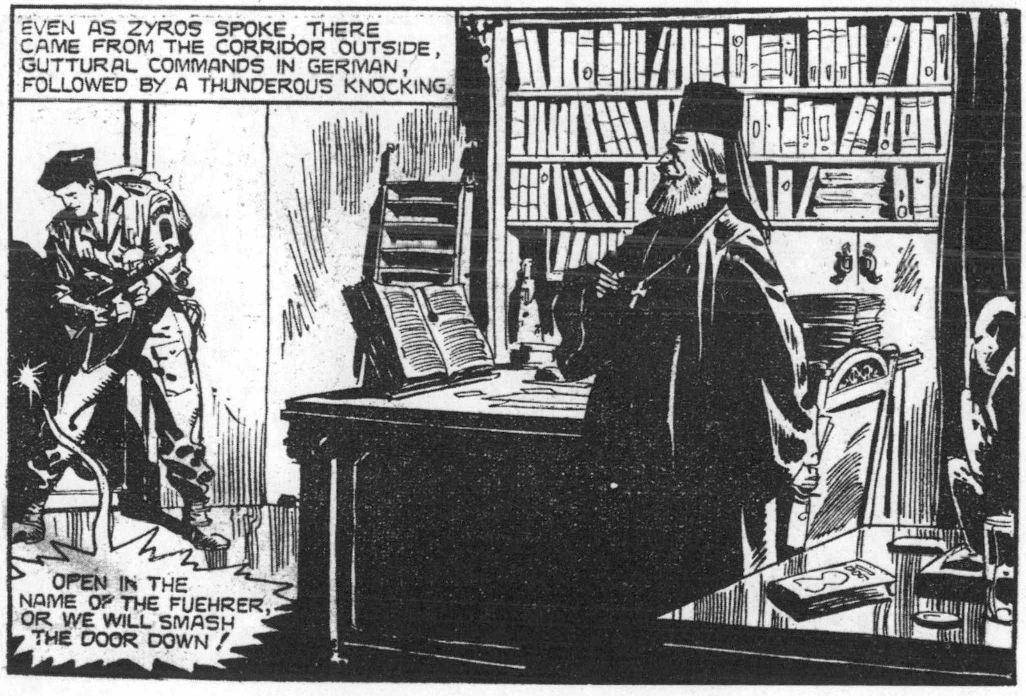
EVEN AS ZYROS SPOKE, THERE CAME FROM THE CORRIDOR OUTSIDE, GUTTURAL COMMANDS IN GERMAN, FOLLOWED BY A THUNDEROUS KNOCKING.
OPEN IN THE NAME OF THE FUEHRER, OR WE WILL SMASH THE DOOR DOWN!

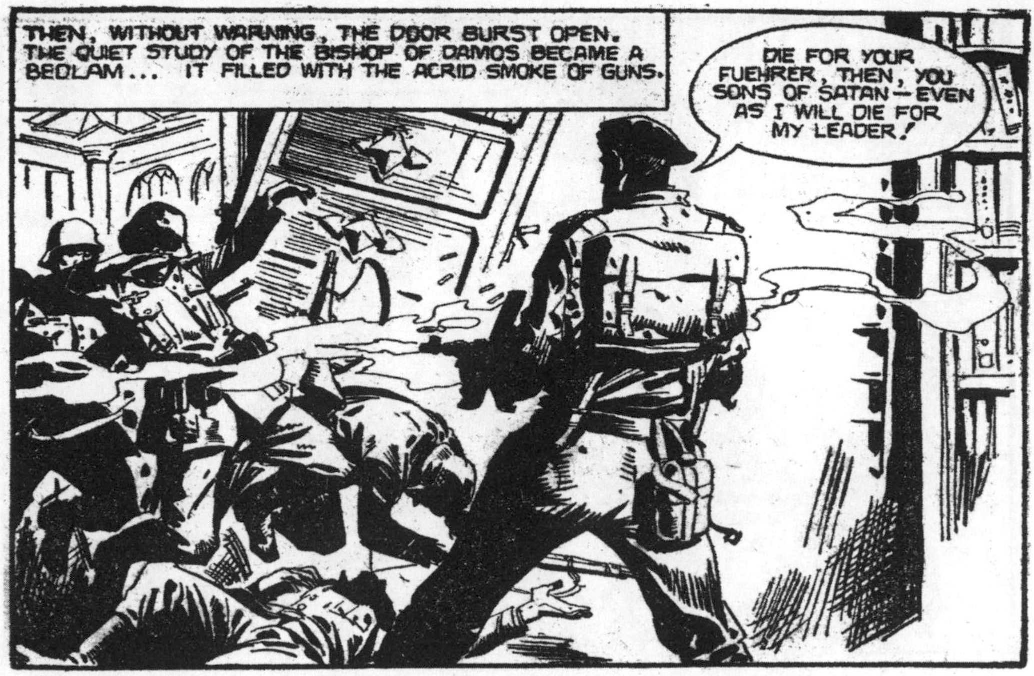
THEN, WITHOUT WARNING, THE DOOR BURST OPEN. THE QUIET STUDY OF THE BISHOP OF DAMOS BECAME A BEDLAM ... IT FILLED WITH THE ACRID SMOKE OF GUNS.
DIE FOR YOUR FUEHRER, THEN, YOU SONS OF SATAN — EVEN AS I WILL DIE FOR MY LEADER!

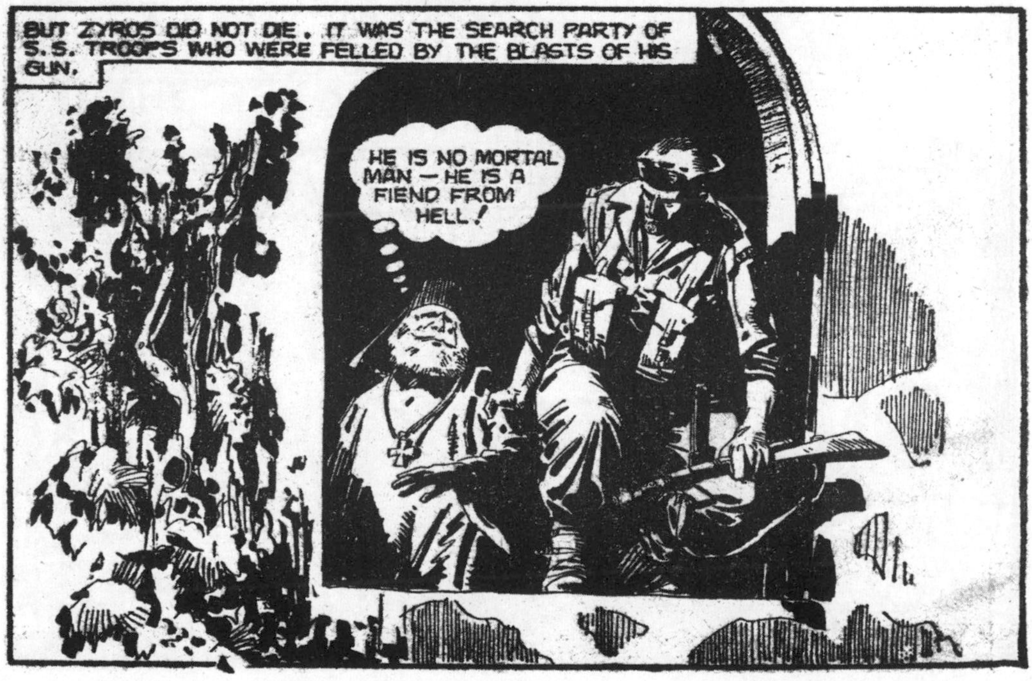
BUT ZYROS DID NOT DIE. IT WAS THE SEARCH PARTY OF S.S. TROOPS WHO WERE FELLED BY THE BLASTS OF HIS GUN.
HE IS NO MORTAL MAN — HE IS A FIEND FROM HELL!

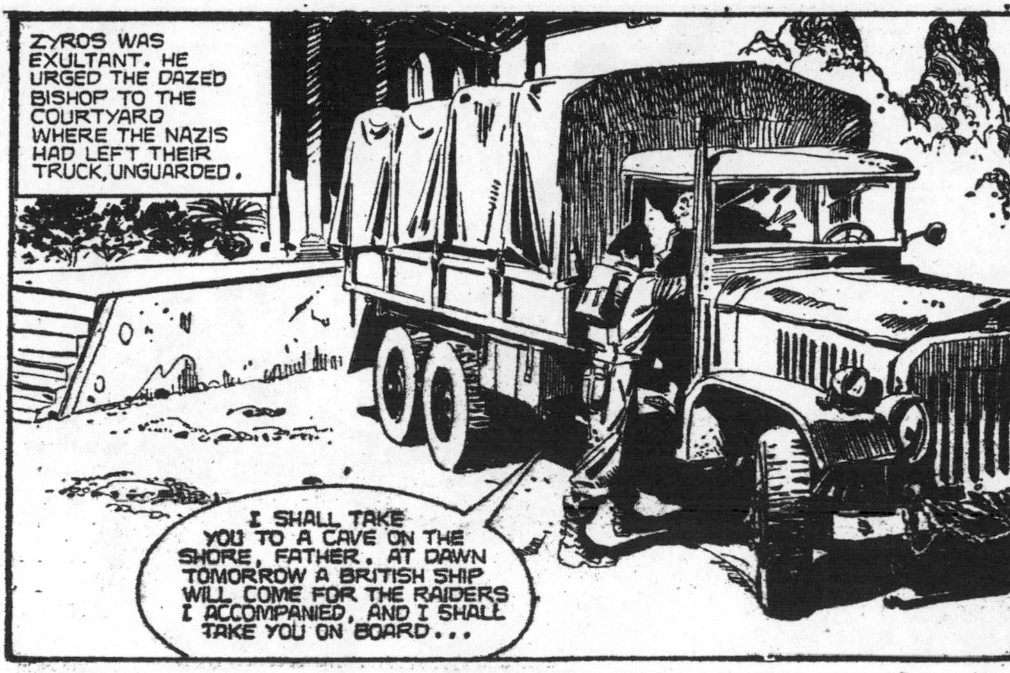
ZYROS WAS EXULTANT. HE URGED THE DAZED BISHOP TO THE COURTYARD WHERE THE NAZIS HAD LEFT THEIR TRUCK, UNGUARDED.
I SHALL TAKE YOU TO A CAVE ON THE SHORE, FATHER. AT DAWN TOMORROW A BRITISH SHIP WILL COME FOR THE RAIDERS I ACCOMPANIED, AND I SHALL TAKE YOU ON BOARD...

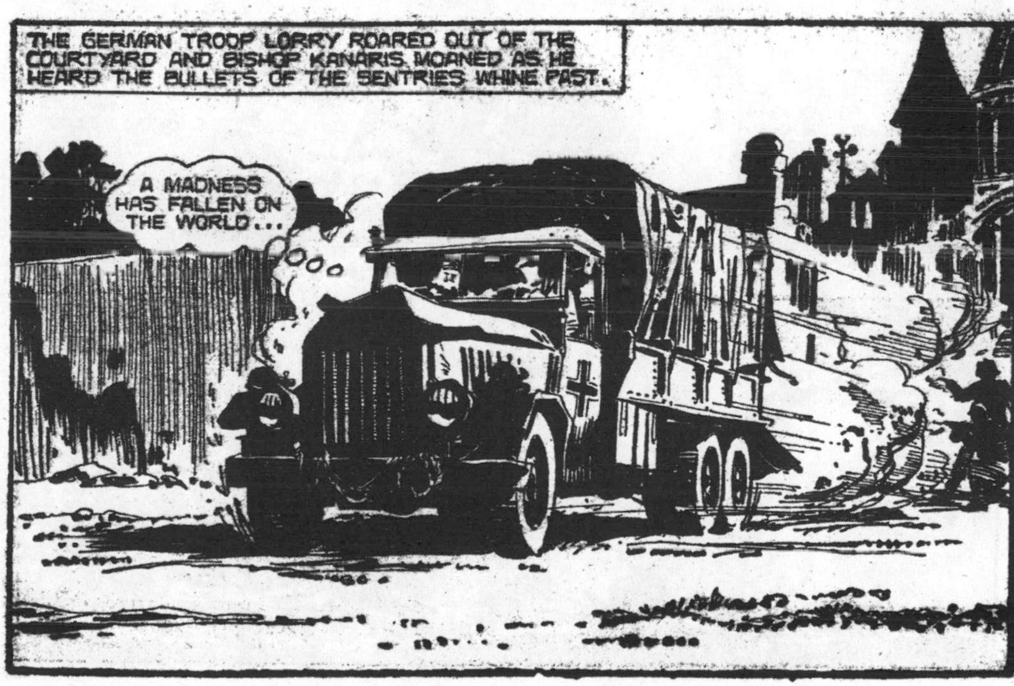
THE GERMAN TROOP LORRY ROARED OUT OF THE COURTYARD AND BISHOP KANARIS MOANED AS HE HEARD THE BULLETS OF THE SENTRIES WHINE PAST.
A MADNESS HAS FALLEN ON THE WORLD...

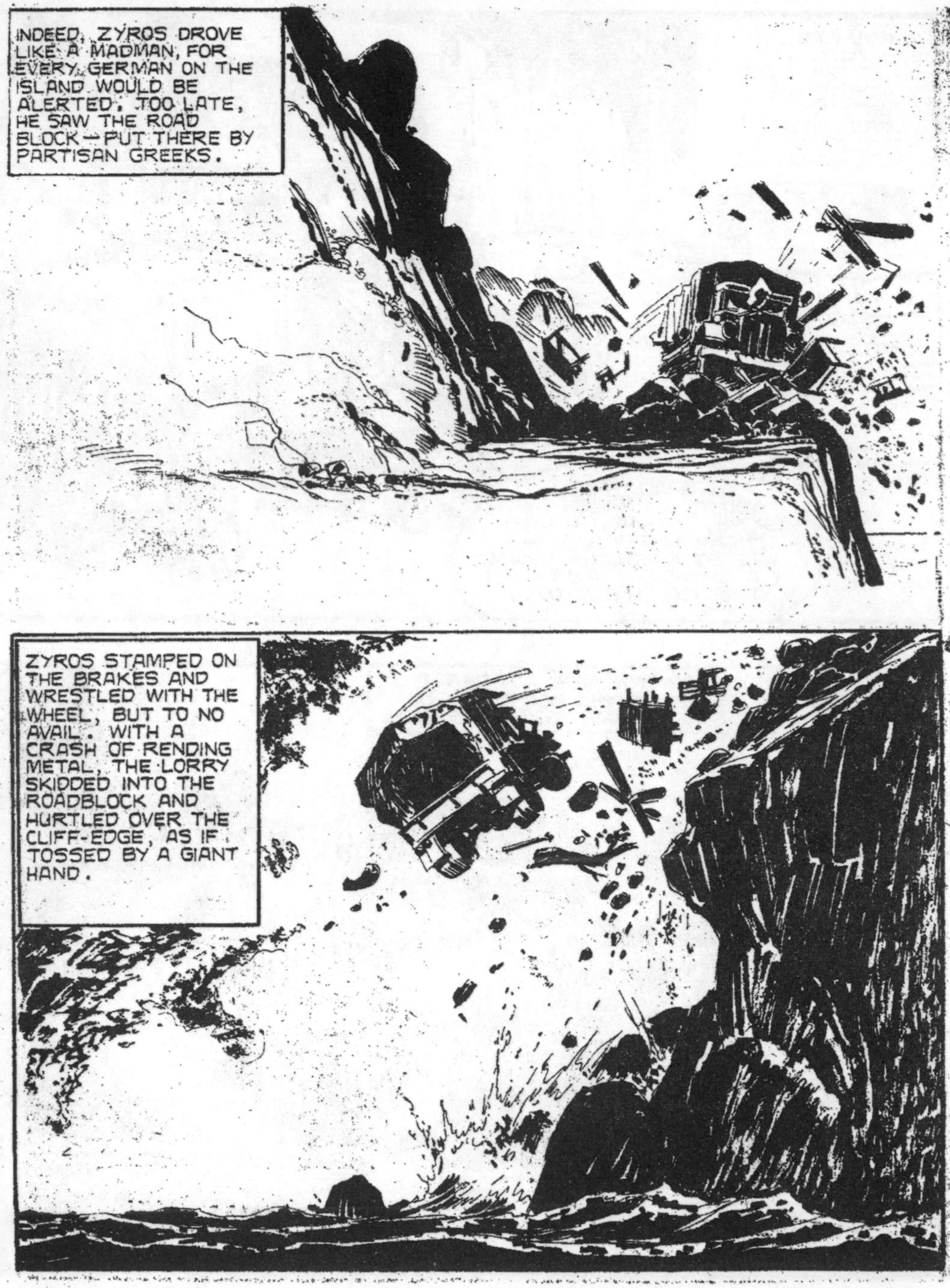
INDEED, ZYROS DROVE LIKE A MADMAN, FOR EVERY GERMAN ON THE ISLAND WOULD BE ALERTED. TOO LATE, HE SAW THE ROAD BLOCK—PUT THERE BY PARTISAN GREEKS.
ZYROS STAMPED ON THE BRAKES AND WRESTLED WITH THE WHEEL, BUT TO NO AVAIL. WITH A CRASH OF RENDING METAL, THE LORRY SKIDDED INTO THE ROADBLOCK AND HURTLED OVER THE CLIFF-EDGE, AS IF TOSSED BY A GIANT HAND.

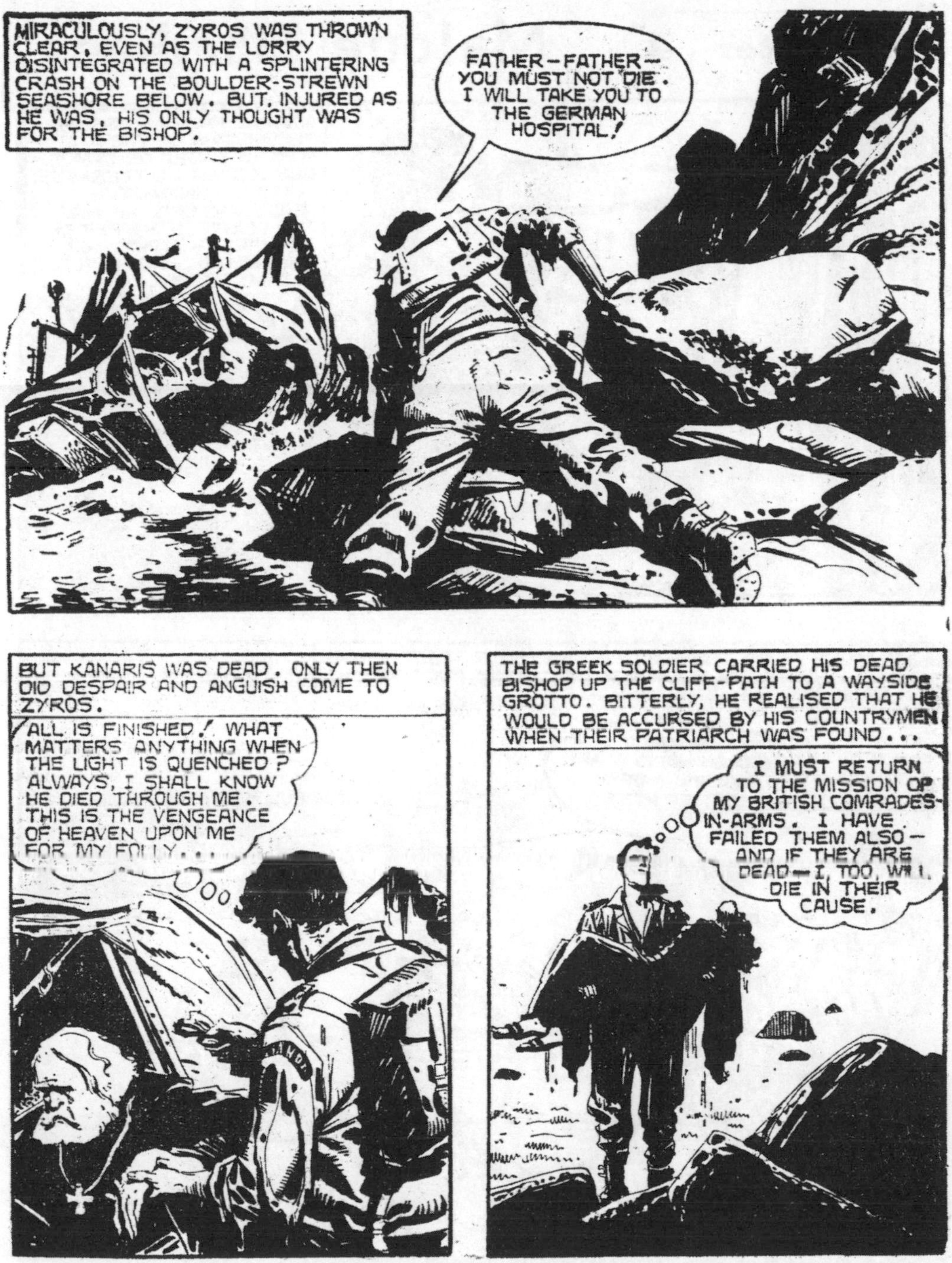
MIRACULOUSLY, ZYROS WAS THROWN CLEAR, EVEN AS THE LORRY DISINTEGRATED WITH A SPLINTERING CRASH ON THE BOULDER-STREWN SEASHORE BELOW. BUT, INJURED AS HE WAS, HIS ONLY THOUGHT WAS FOR THE BISHOP.
FATHER—FATHER—YOU MUST NOT DIE. I WILL TAKE YOU TO THE GERMAN HOSPITAL!
BUT KANARIS WAS DEAD. ONLY THEN DID DESPAIR AND ANGUISH COME TO ZYROS.
ALL IS FINISHED! WHAT MATTERS ANYTHING WHEN THE LIGHT IS QUENCHED? ALWAYS, I SHALL KNOW HE DIED THROUGH ME. THIS IS THE VENGEANCE OF HEAVEN UPON ME FOR MY FOLLY...
THE GREEK SOLDIER CARRIED HIS DEAD BISHOP UP THE CLIFF-PATH TO A WAYSIDE GROTTO. BITTERLY, HE REALISED THAT HE WOULD BE ACCURSED BY HIS COUNTRYMEN WHEN THEIR PATRIARCH WAS FOUND...
I MUST RETURN TO THE MISSION OF MY BRITISH COMRADES-IN-ARMS. I HAVE FAILED THEM ALSO—AND IF THEY ARE DEAD—I, TOO, WILL DIE IN THEIR CAUSE.

Chapter 4. Malone Strikes

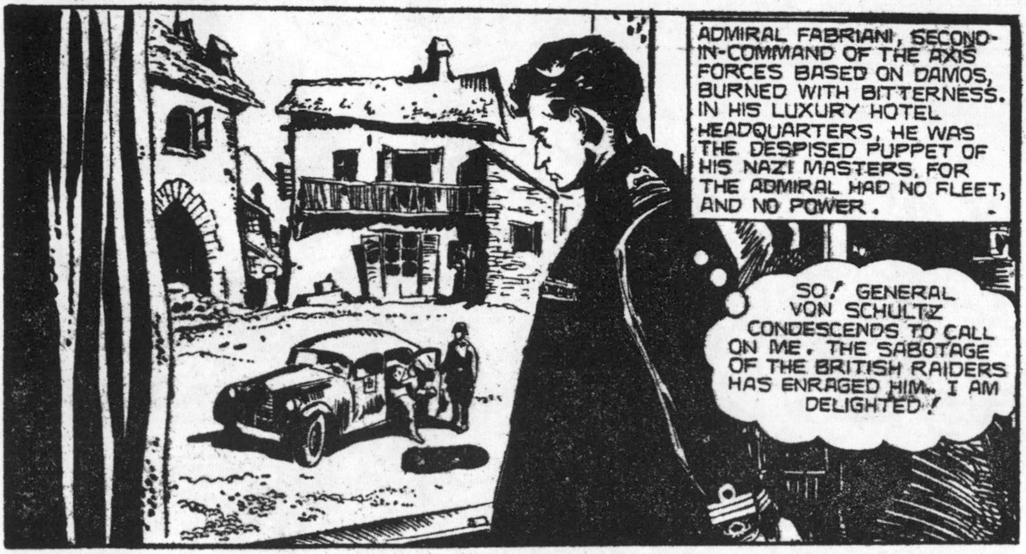
ADMIRAL FABRIANI, SECOND-IN-COMMAND OF THE AXIS FORCES BASED ON DAMOS, BURNED WITH BITTERNESS. IN HIS LUXURY HOTEL HEADQUARTERS, HE WAS THE DESPISED PUPPET OF HIS NAZI MASTERS, FOR THE ADMIRAL HAD NO FLEET, AND NO POWER.
SO! GENERAL VON SCHULTZ CONDESCENDS TO CALL ON ME. THE SABOTAGE OF THE BRITISH RAIDERS HAS ENRAGED HIM. I AM DELIGHTED!

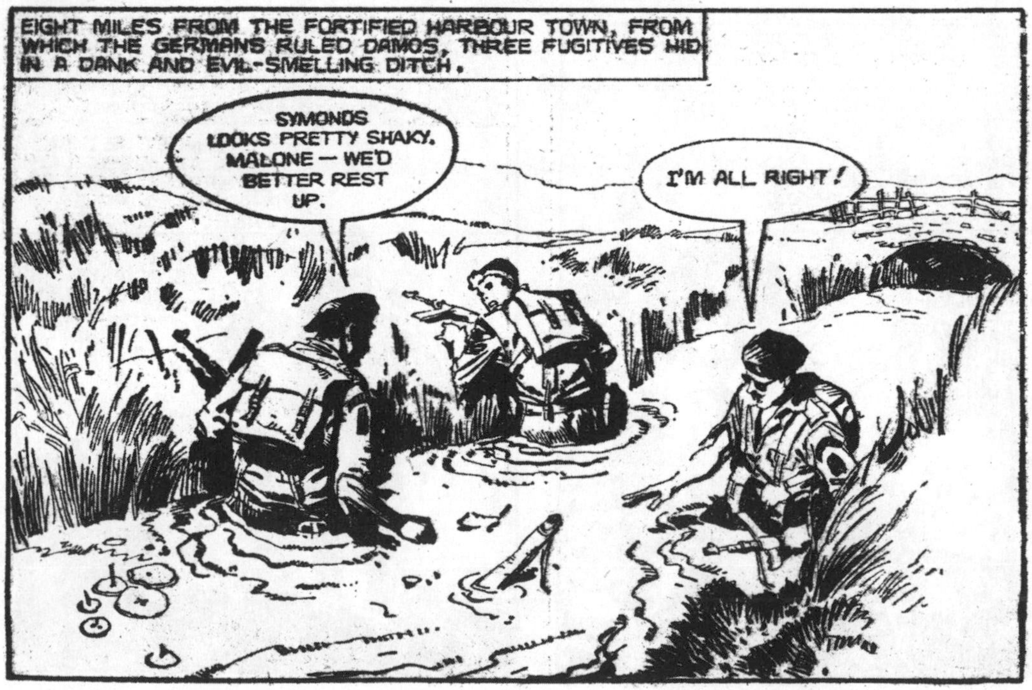
EIGHT MILES FROM THE FORTIFIED HARBOUR TOWN, FROM WHICH THE GERMANS RULED DAMOS, THREE FUGITIVES HID IN A DANK AND EVIL-SMELLING DITCH.
SYMONDS LOOKS PRETTY SHAKY, MALONE — WE'D BETTER REST UP.
I'M ALL RIGHT!

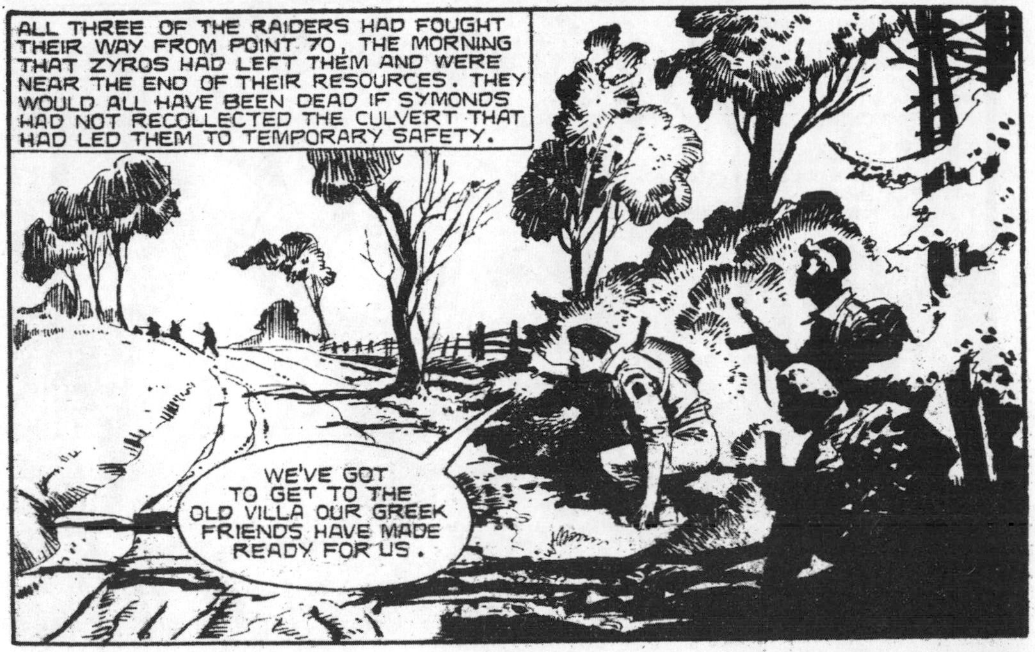
ALL THREE OF THE RAIDERS HAD FOUGHT THEIR WAY FROM POINT 70, THE MORNING THAT ZYROS HAD LEFT THEM AND WERE NEAR THE END OF THEIR RESOURCES. THEY WOULD ALL HAVE BEEN DEAD IF SYMONDS HAD NOT RECOLLECTED THE CULVERT THAT HAD LED THEM TO TEMPORARY SAFETY.
WE'VE GOT TO GET TO THE OLD VILLA OUR GREEK FRIENDS HAVE MADE READY FOR US.

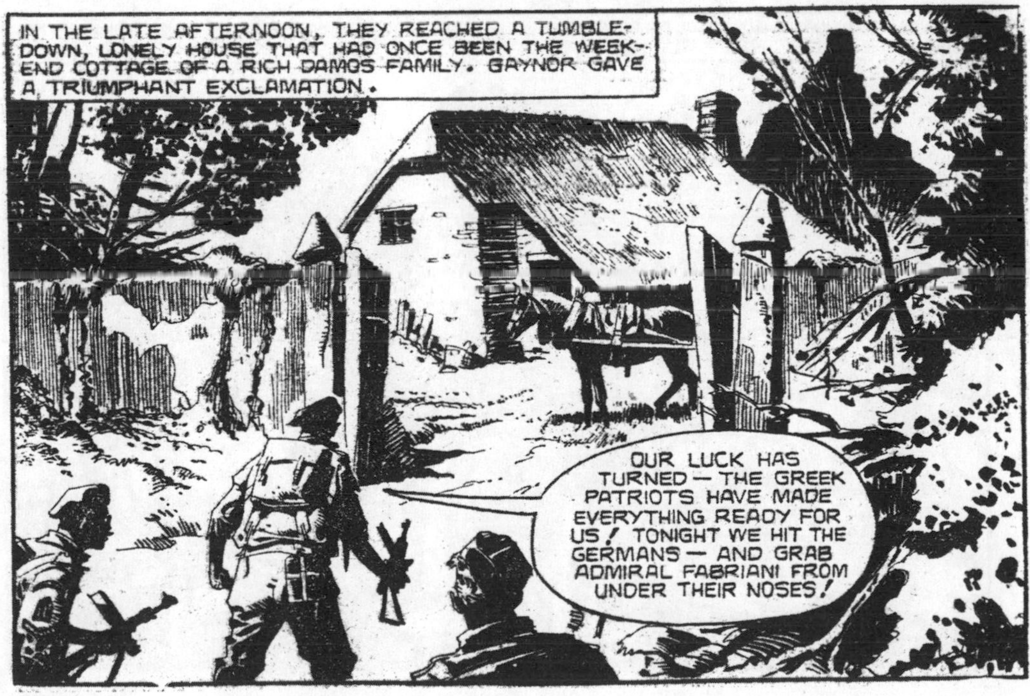
IN THE LATE AFTERNOON, THEY REACHED A TUMBLE-DOWN, LONELY HOUSE THAT HAD ONCE BEEN THE WEEK-END COTTAGE OF A RICH DAMOS FAMILY. GAYNOR GAVE A TRIUMPHANT EXCLAMATION.
OUR LUCK HAS TURNED — THE GREEK PATRIOTS HAVE MADE EVERYTHING READY FOR US! TONIGHT WE HIT THE GERMANS — AND GRAB ADMIRAL FABRIANI FROM UNDER THEIR NOSES!

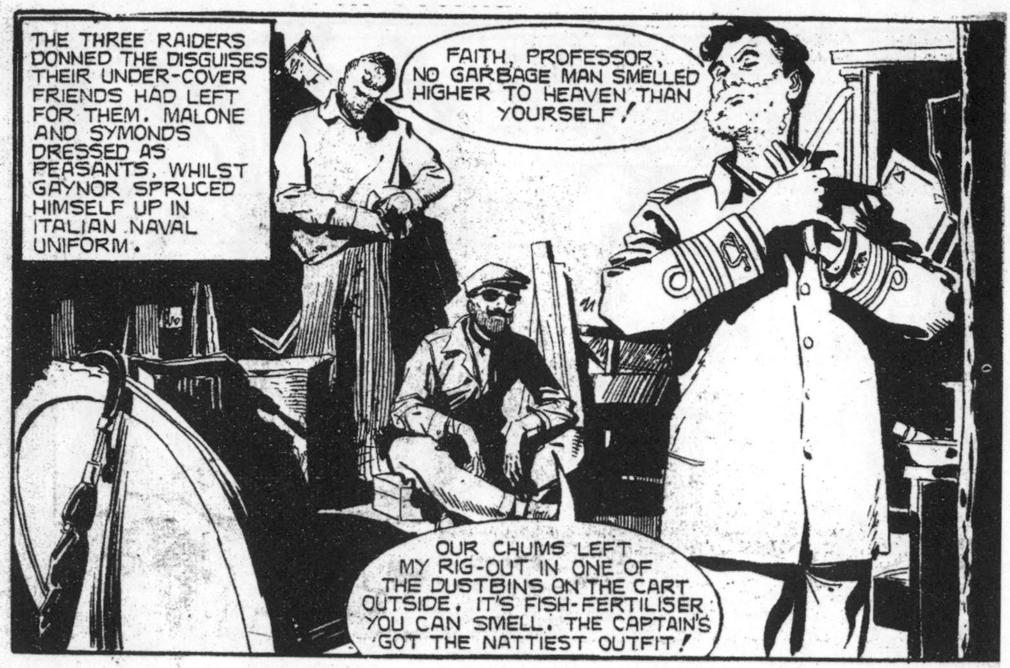
THE THREE RAIDERS DONNED THE DISGUISES THEIR UNDER-COVER FRIENDS HAD LEFT FOR THEM. MALONE AND SYMONDS DRESSED AS PEASANTS, WHILST GAYNOR SPRUCED HIMSELF UP IN ITALIAN NAVAL UNIFORM.
FAITH, PROFESSOR, NO GARBAGE MAN SMELLED HIGHER TO HEAVEN THAN YOURSELF!
OUR CHUMS LEFT MY RIG-OUT IN ONE OF THE DUSTBINS ON THE CART OUTSIDE. IT'S FISH-FERTILISER YOU CAN SMELL. THE CAPTAIN'S GOT THE NATTIEST OUTFIT!

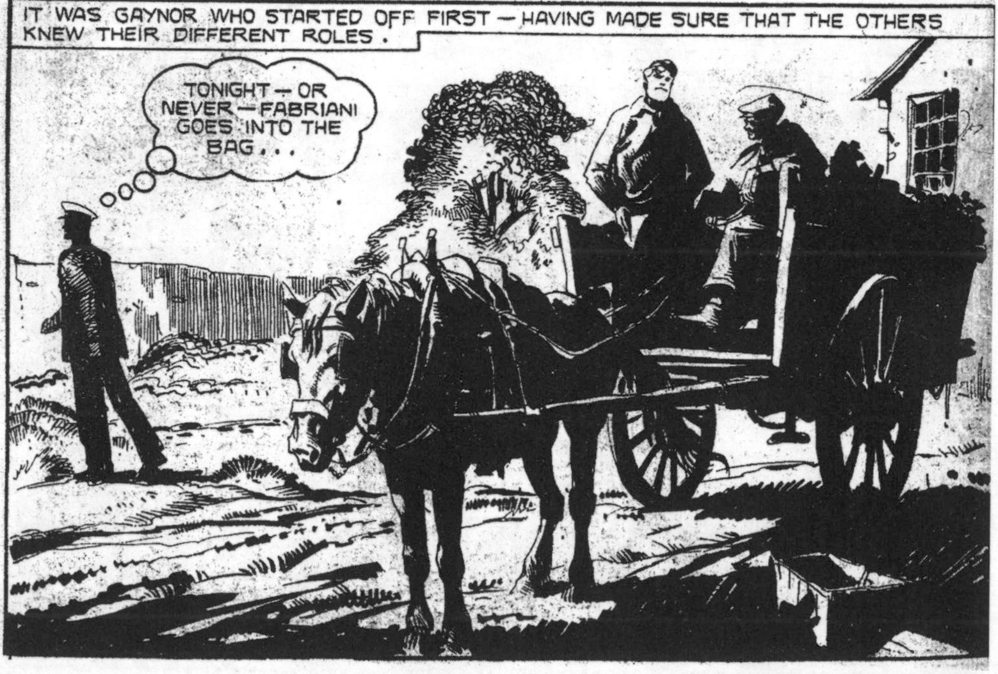
IT WAS GAYNOR WHO STARTED OFF FIRST — HAVING MADE SURE THAT THE OTHERS KNEW THEIR DIFFERENT ROLES.
TONIGHT — OR NEVER — FABRIANI GOES INTO THE BAG...

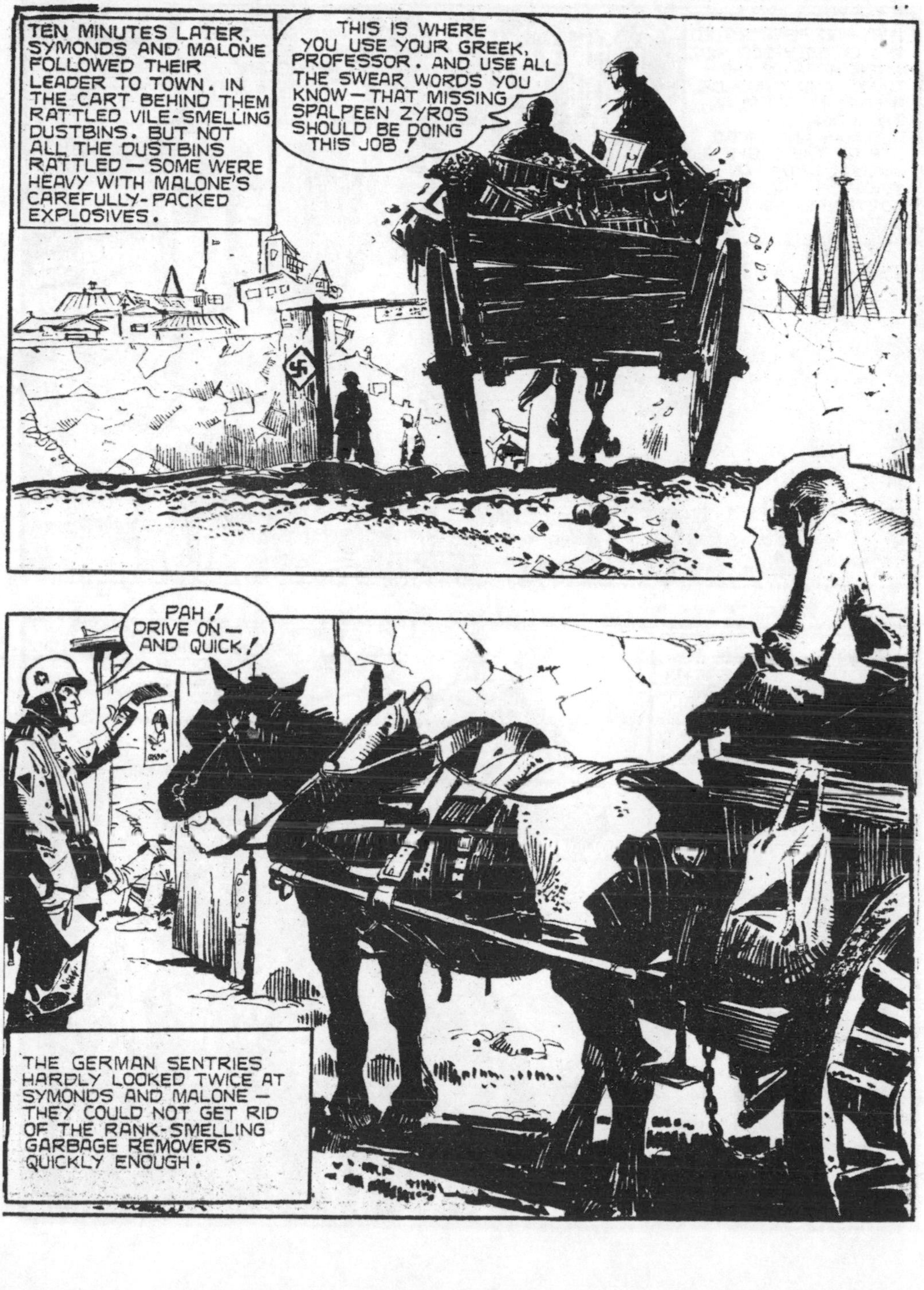
TEN MINUTES LATER, SYMONDS AND MALONE FOLLOWED THEIR LEADER TO TOWN. IN THE CART BEHIND THEM RATTLED VILE-SMELLING DUSTBINS. BUT NOT ALL THE DUSTBINS RATTLED — SOME WERE HEAVY WITH MALONE'S CAREFULLY-PACKED EXPLOSIVES.
THIS IS WHERE YOU USE YOUR GREEK, PROFESSOR. AND USE ALL THE SWEAR WORDS YOU KNOW — THAT MISSING SPALPEEN ZYROS SHOULD BE DOING THIS JOB!
PAH! DRIVE ON — AND QUICK!
THE GERMAN SENTRIES HARDLY LOOKED TWICE AT SYMONDS AND MALONE — THEY COULD NOT GET RID OF THE RANK-SMELLING GARBAGE REMOVERS QUICKLY ENOUGH.

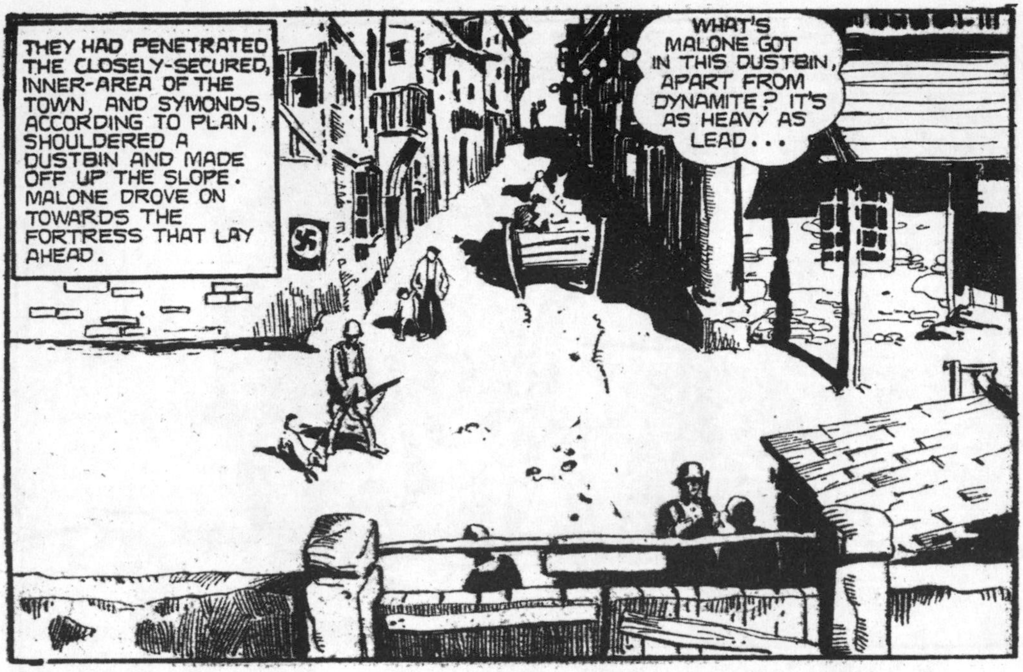
THEY HAD PENETRATED THE CLOSELY-SECURED, INNER-AREA OF THE TOWN, AND SYMONDS, ACCORDING TO PLAN, SHOULDERED A DUSTBIN AND MADE OFF UP THE SLOPE. MALONE DROVE ON TOWARDS THE FORTRESS THAT LAY AHEAD.
WHAT'S MALONE GOT IN THIS DUSTBIN, APART FROM DYNAMITE? IT'S AS HEAVY AS LEAD...

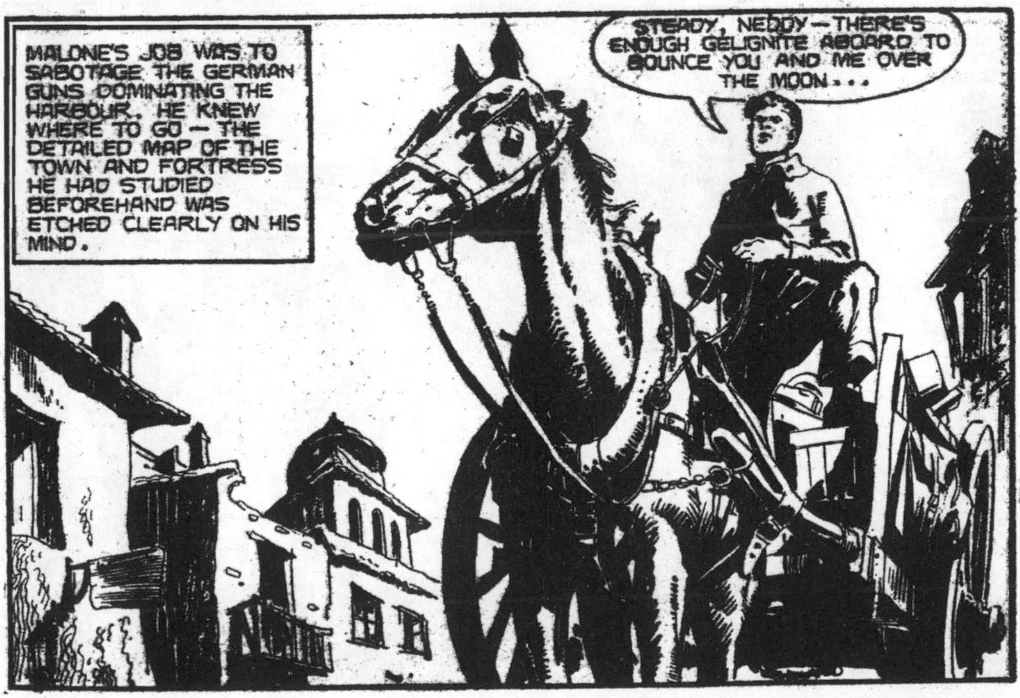
MALONE'S JOB WAS TO SABOTAGE THE GERMAN GUNS DOMINATING THE HARBOUR. HE KNEW WHERE TO GO — THE DETAILED MAP OF THE TOWN AND FORTRESS HE HAD STUDIED BEFOREHAND WAS ETCHED CLEARLY ON HIS MIND.
STEADY, NEDDY — THERE'S ENOUGH GELIGNITE ABOARD TO BOUNCE YOU AND ME OVER THE MOON...

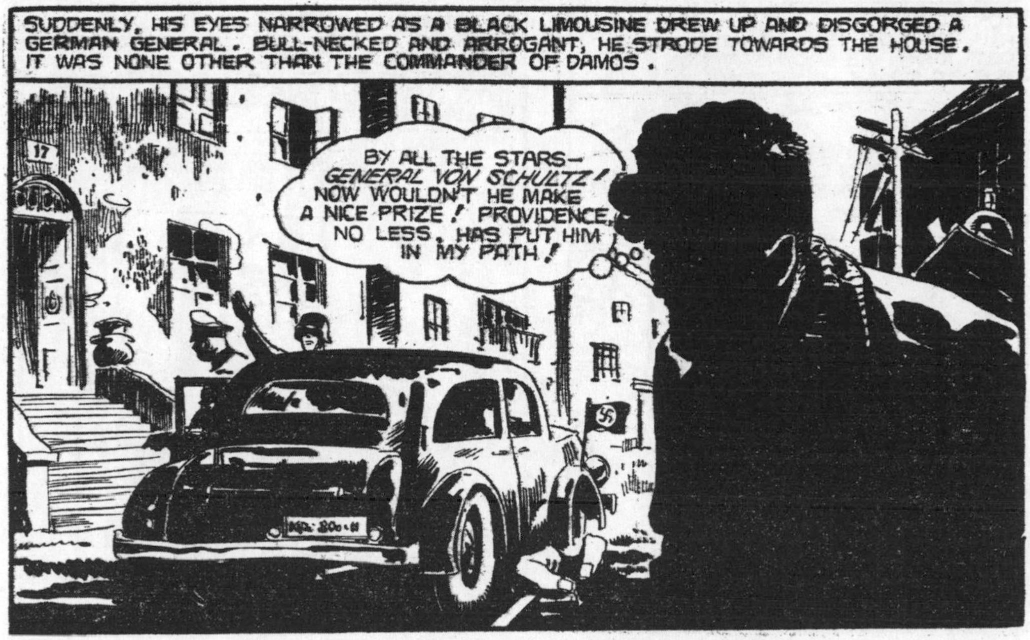
SUDDENLY, HIS EYES NARROWED AS A BLACK LIMOUSINE DREW UP AND DISGORGED A GERMAN GENERAL. BULL-NECKED AND ARROGANT, HE STRODE TOWARDS THE HOUSE. IT WAS NONE OTHER THAN THE COMMANDER OF DAMOS.
BY ALL THE STARS— GENERAL VON SCHULTZ! NOW WOULDN'T HE MAKE A NICE PRIZE! PROVIDENCE, NO LESS, HAS PUT HIM IN MY PATH!

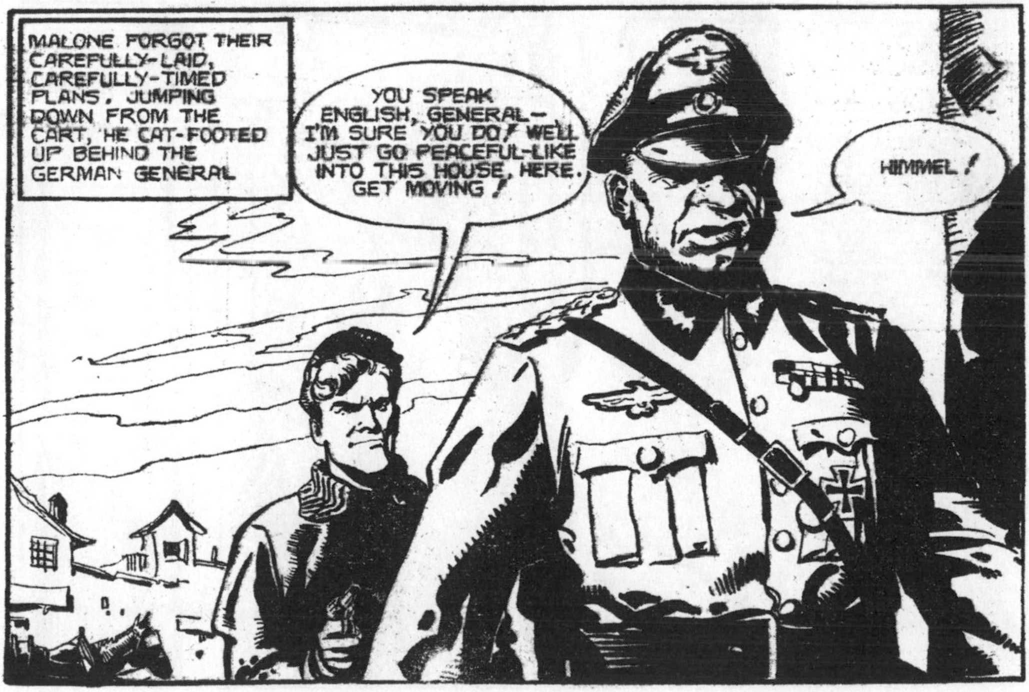
MALONE FORGOT THEIR CAREFULLY-LAID, CAREFULLY-TIMED PLANS. JUMPING DOWN FROM THE CART, HE CAT-FOOTED UP BEHIND THE GERMAN GENERAL
YOU SPEAK ENGLISH, GENERAL— I'M SURE YOU DO! WELL JUST GO PEACEFUL-LIKE INTO THIS HOUSE, HERE. GET MOVING!
HIMMEL!

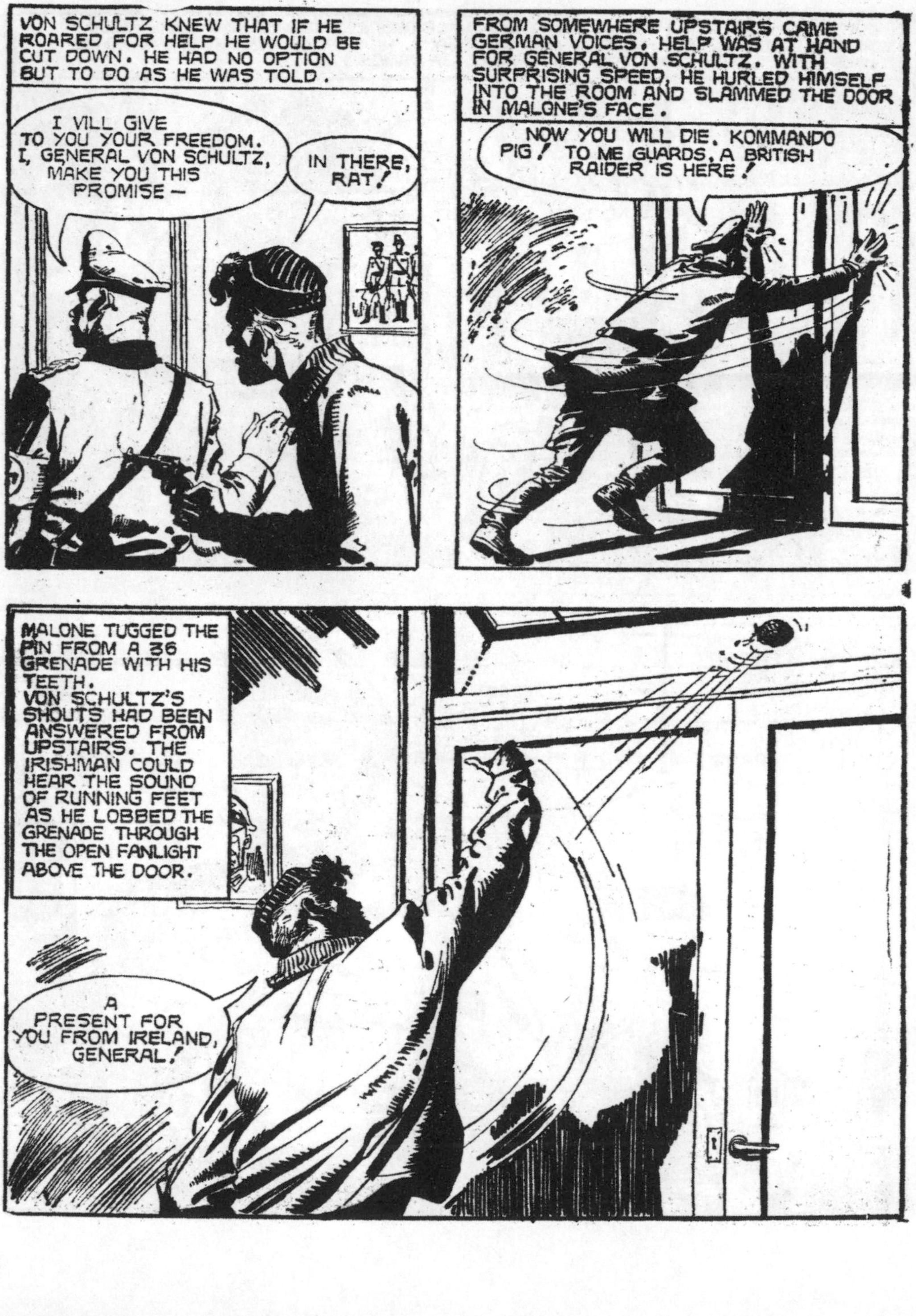
VON SCHULTZ KNEW THAT IF HE ROARED FOR HELP HE WOULD BE CUT DOWN. HE HAD NO OPTION BUT TO DO AS HE WAS TOLD.
I VILL GIVE TO YOU YOUR FREEDOM. I, GENERAL VON SCHULTZ, MAKE YOU THIS PROMISE—
IN THERE, RAT!
FROM SOMEWHERE UPSTAIRS CAME GERMAN VOICES. HELP WAS AT HAND FOR GENERAL VON SCHULTZ. WITH SURPRISING SPEED, HE HURLED HIMSELF INTO THE ROOM AND SLAMMED THE DOOR IN MALONE'S FACE.
NOW YOU WILL DIE, KOMMANDO PIG! TO ME GUARDS, A BRITISH RAIDER IS HERE!
MALONE TUGGED THE PIN FROM A 36 GRENADE WITH HIS TEETH. VON SCHULTZ'S SHOUTS HAD BEEN ANSWERED FROM UPSTAIRS. THE IRISHMAN COULD HEAR THE SOUND OF RUNNING FEET AS HE LOBBED THE GRENADE THROUGH THE OPEN FANLIGHT ABOVE THE DOOR.
A PRESENT FOR YOU FROM IRELAND, GENERAL!

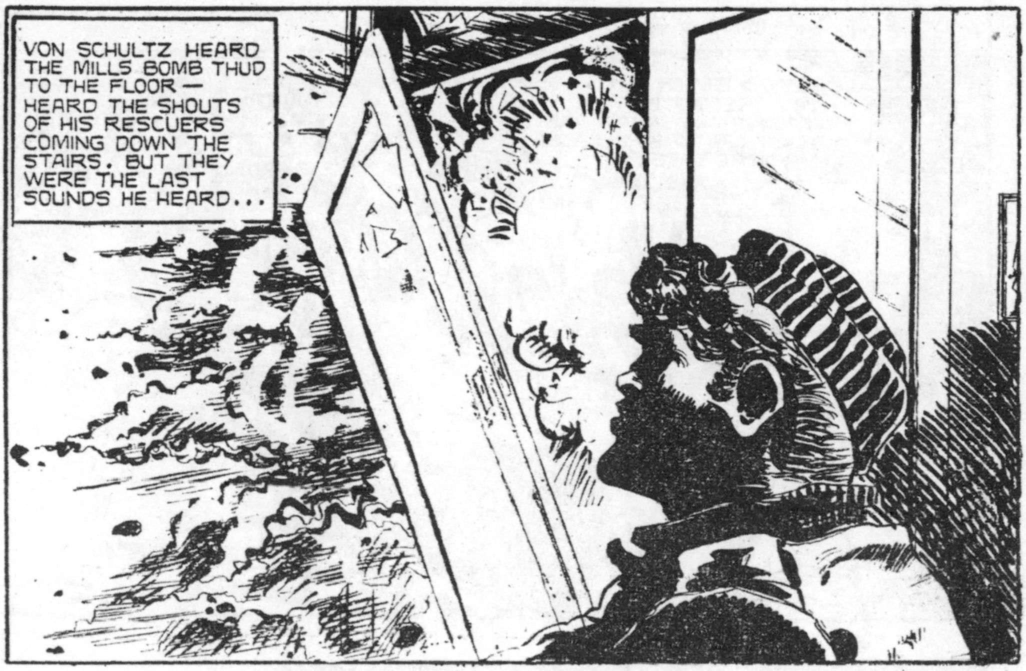
VON SCHULTZ HEARD THE MILLS BOMB THUD TO THE FLOOR — HEARD THE SHOUTS OF HIS RESCUERS COMING DOWN THE STAIRS. BUT THEY WERE THE LAST SOUNDS HE HEARD...

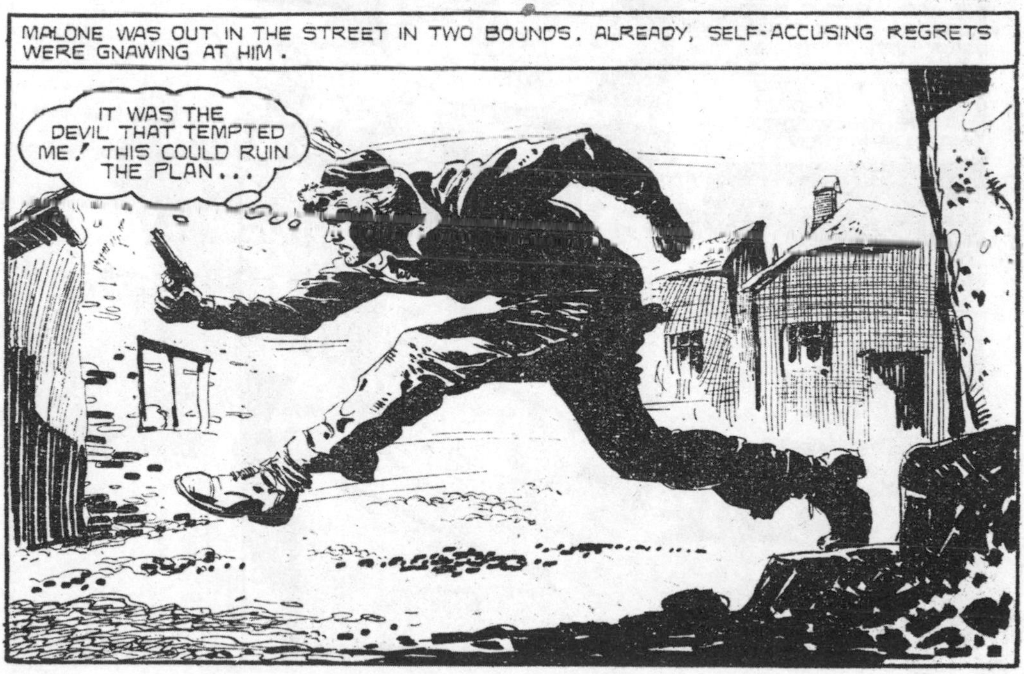
MALONE WAS OUT IN THE STREET IN TWO BOUNDS. ALREADY, SELF-ACCUSING REGRETS WERE GNAWING AT HIM.
IT WAS THE DEVIL THAT TEMPTED ME! THIS COULD RUIN THE PLAN...

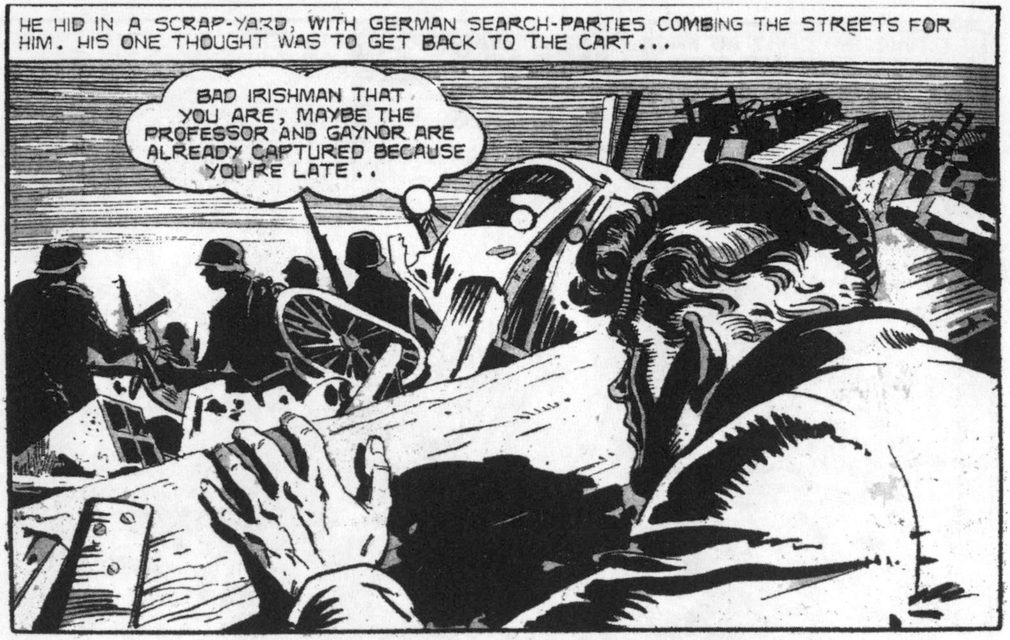
HE HID IN A SCRAP-YARD, WITH GERMAN SEARCH-PARTIES COMBING THE STREETS FOR HIM. HIS ONE THOUGHT WAS TO GET BACK TO THE CART...
BAD IRISHMAN THAT YOU ARE, MAYBE THE PROFESSOR AND GAYNOR ARE ALREADY CAPTURED BECAUSE YOU'RE LATE..

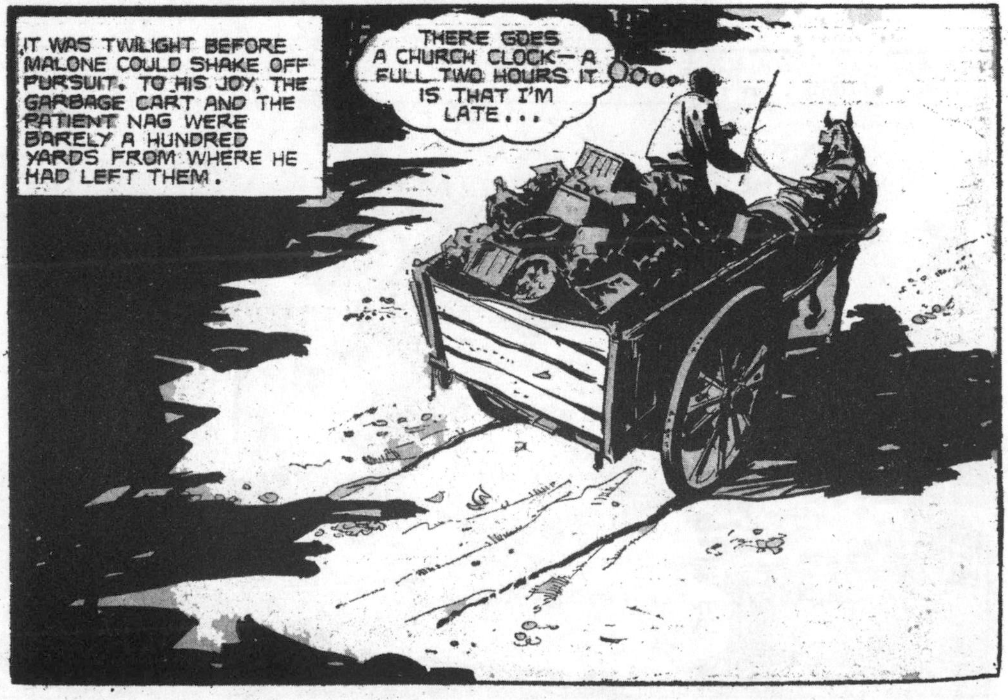
IT WAS TWILIGHT BEFORE MALONE COULD SHAKE OFF PURSUIT. TO HIS JOY, THE GARBAGE CART AND THE PATIENT NAG WERE BARELY A HUNDRED YARDS FROM WHERE HE HAD LEFT THEM.
THERE GOES A CHURCH CLOCK—A FULL TWO HOURS IT IS THAT I'M LATE...

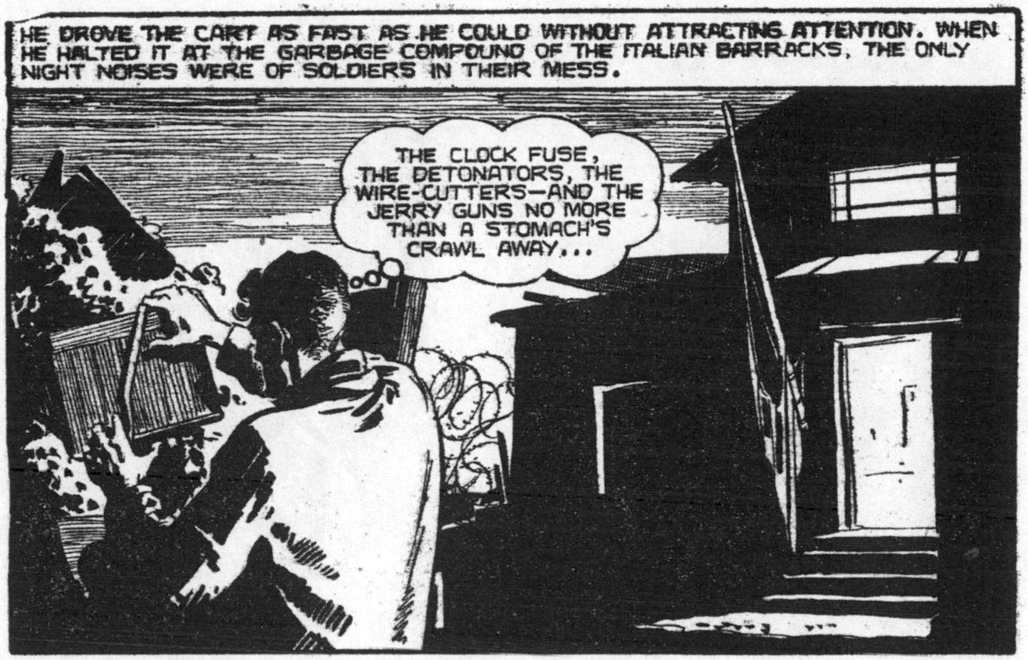
HE DROVE THE CART AS FAST AS HE COULD WITHOUT ATTRACTING ATTENTION. WHEN HE HALTED IT AT THE GARBAGE COMPOUND OF THE ITALIAN BARRACKS, THE ONLY NIGHT NOISES WERE OF SOLDIERS IN THEIR MESS.
THE CLOCK FUSE, THE DETONATORS, THE WIRE-CUTTERS—AND THE JERRY GUNS NO MORE THAN A STOMACH'S CRAWL AWAY...

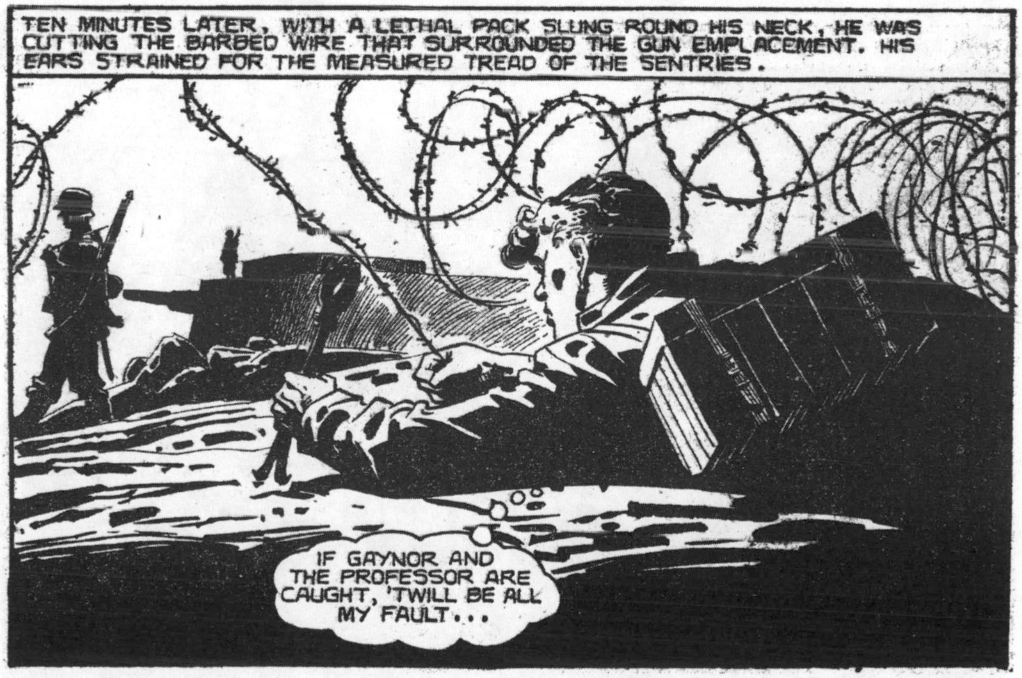
TEN MINUTES LATER, WITH A LETHAL PACK SLUNG ROUND HIS NECK, HE WAS CUTTING THE BARBED WIRE THAT SURROUNDED THE GUN EMPLACEMENT. HIS EARS STRAINED FOR THE MEASURED TREAD OF THE SENTRIES.
IF GAYNOR AND THE PROFESSOR ARE CAUGHT, 'TWILL BE ALL MY FAULT...

Chapter 5 Night of Blood

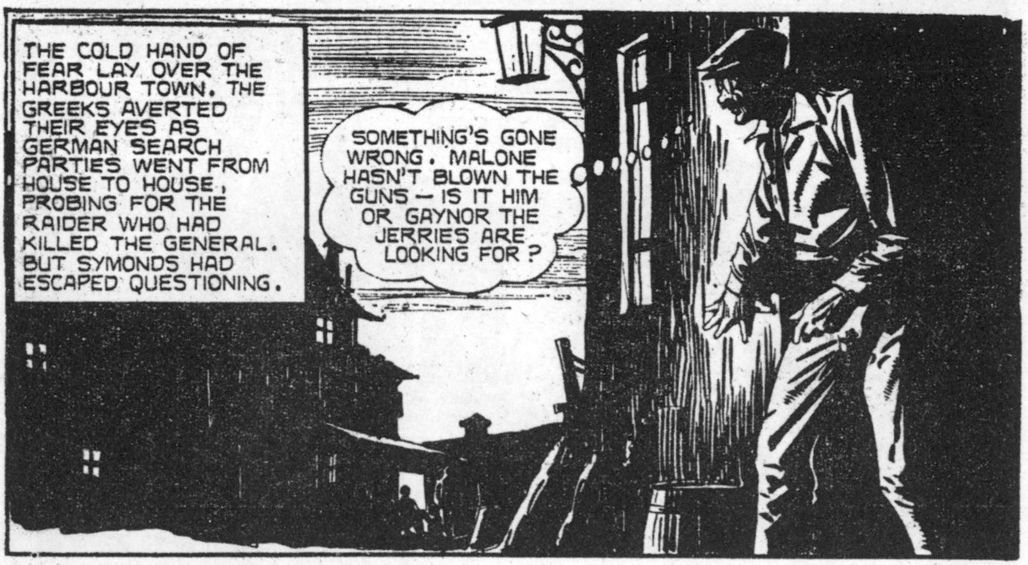
THE COLD HAND OF FEAR LAY OVER THE HARBOUR TOWN. THE GREEKS AVERTED THEIR EYES AS GERMAN SEARCH PARTIES WENT FROM HOUSE TO HOUSE, PROBING FOR THE RAIDER WHO HAD KILLED THE GENERAL. BUT SYMONDS HAD ESCAPED QUESTIONING.
SOMETHING'S GONE WRONG. MALONE HASN'T BLOWN THE GUNS — IS IT HIM OR GAYNOR THE JERRIES ARE LOOKING FOR?

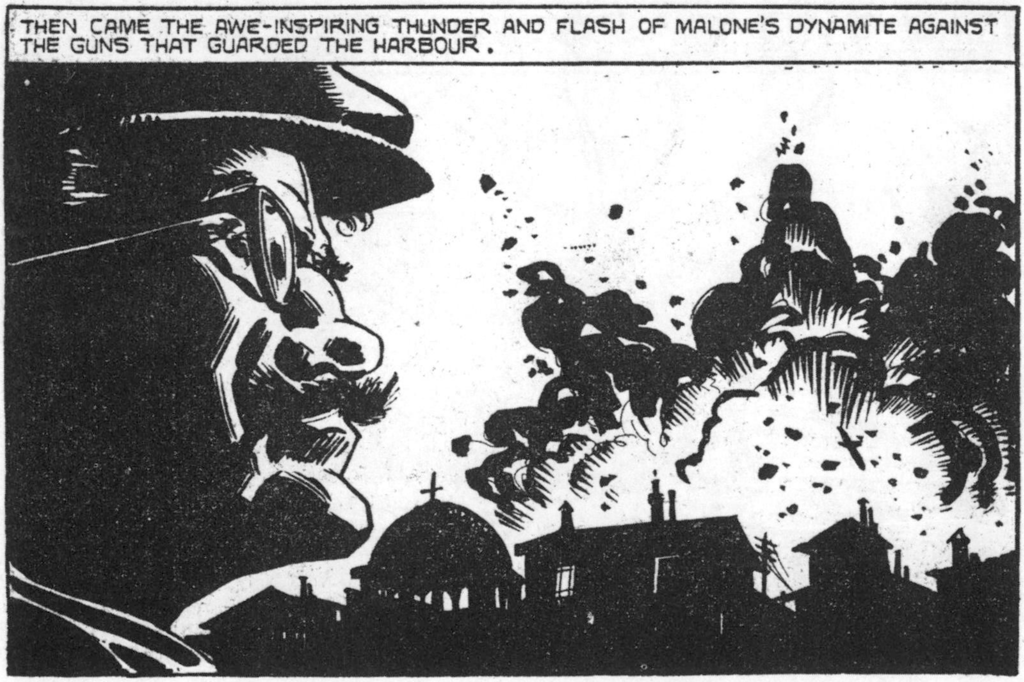
THEN CAME THE AWE-INSPIRING THUNDER AND FLASH OF MALONE'S DYNAMITE AGAINST THE GUNS THAT GUARDED THE HARBOUR.

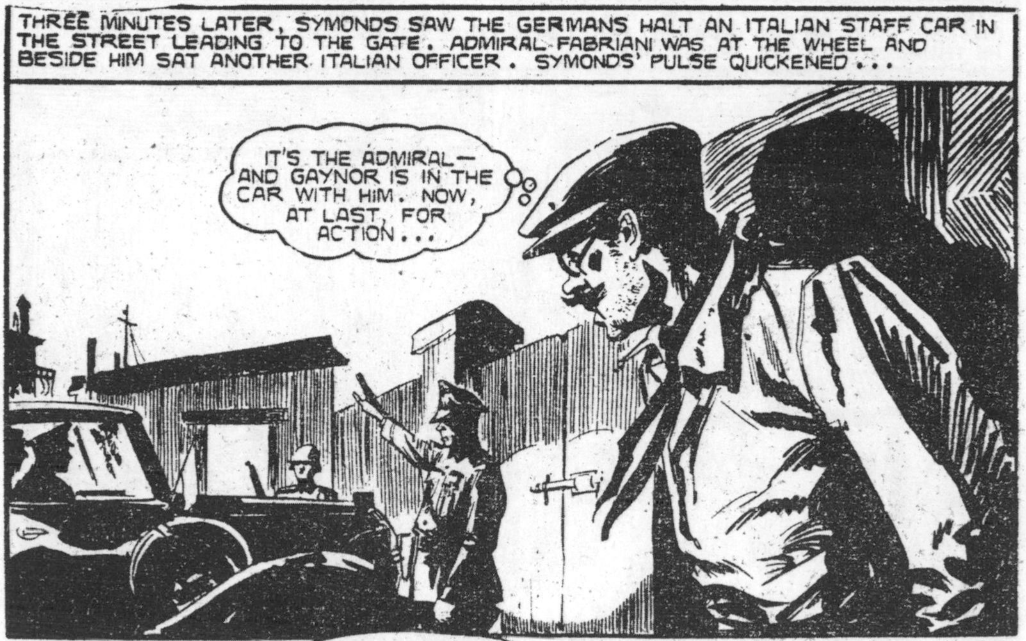
THREE MINUTES LATER, SYMONDS SAW THE GERMANS HALT AN ITALIAN STAFF CAR IN THE STREET LEADING TO THE GATE. ADMIRAL FABRIANI WAS AT THE WHEEL AND BESIDE HIM SAT ANOTHER ITALIAN OFFICER. SYMONDS' PULSE QUICKENED...
IT'S THE ADMIRAL— AND GAYNOR IS IN THE CAR WITH HIM. NOW, AT LAST, FOR ACTION...

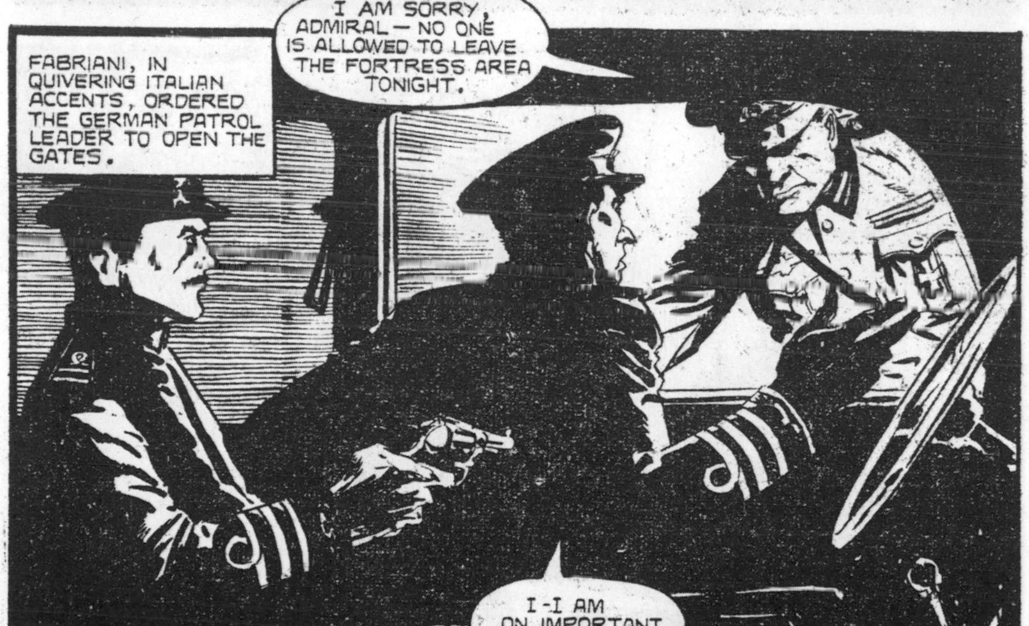
FABRIANI, IN QUIVERING ITALIAN ACCENTS, ORDERED THE GERMAN PATROL LEADER TO OPEN THE GATES.
I AM SORRY, ADMIRAL— NO ONE IS ALLOWED TO LEAVE THE FORTRESS AREA TONIGHT.
I-I AM ON IMPORTANT BUSINESS!

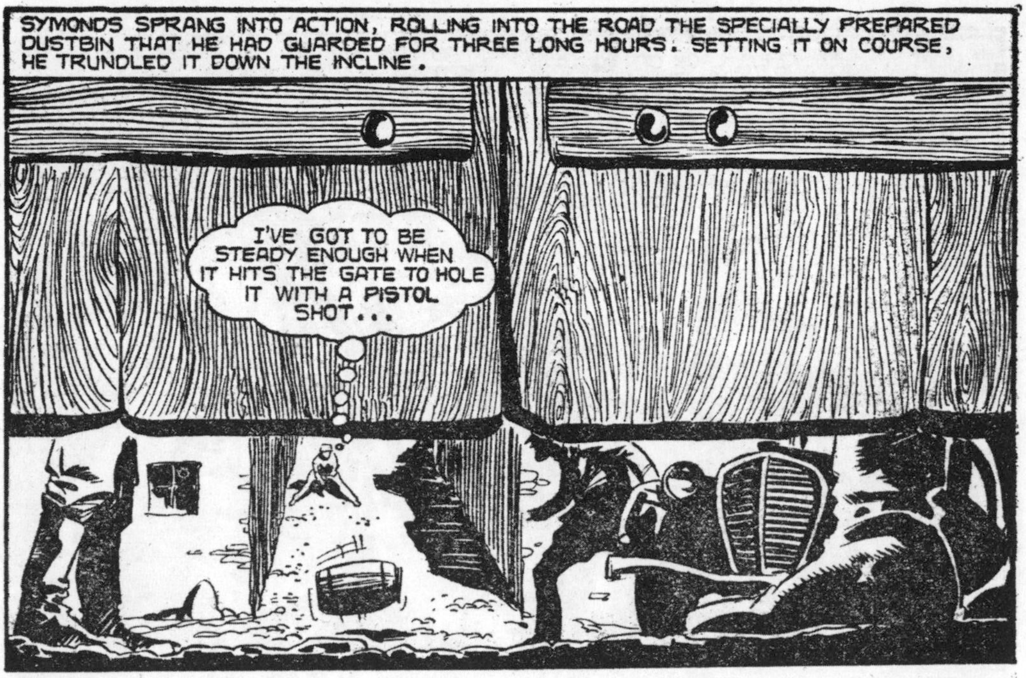
SYMONDS SPRANG INTO ACTION, ROLLING INTO THE ROAD THE SPECIALLY PREPARED DUSTBIN THAT HE HAD GUARDED FOR THREE LONG HOURS. SETTING IT ON COURSE, HE TRUNDLED IT DOWN THE INCLINE.
I'VE GOT TO BE STEADY ENOUGH WHEN IT HITS THE GATE TO HOLE IT WITH A PISTOL SHOT...

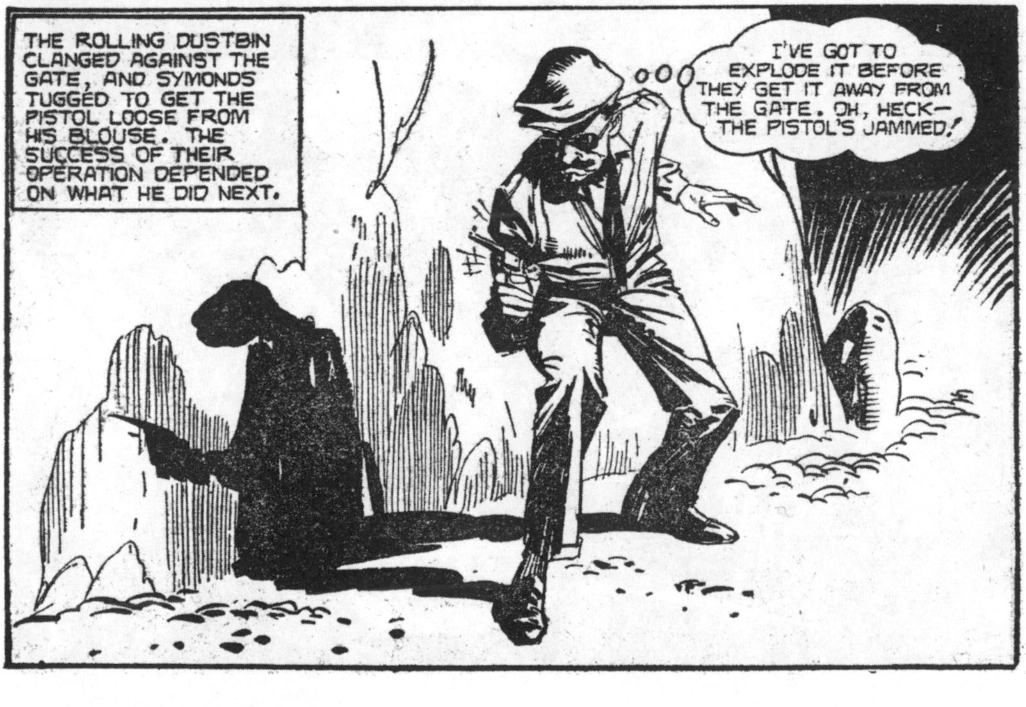
THE ROLLING DUSTBIN CLANGED AGAINST THE GATE, AND SYMONDS TUGGED TO GET THE PISTOL LOOSE FROM HIS BLOUSE. THE SUCCESS OF THEIR OPERATION DEPENDED ON WHAT HE DID NEXT.
I'VE GOT TO EXPLODE IT BEFORE THEY GET IT AWAY FROM THE GATE. OH, HECK— THE PISTOL'S JAMMED!

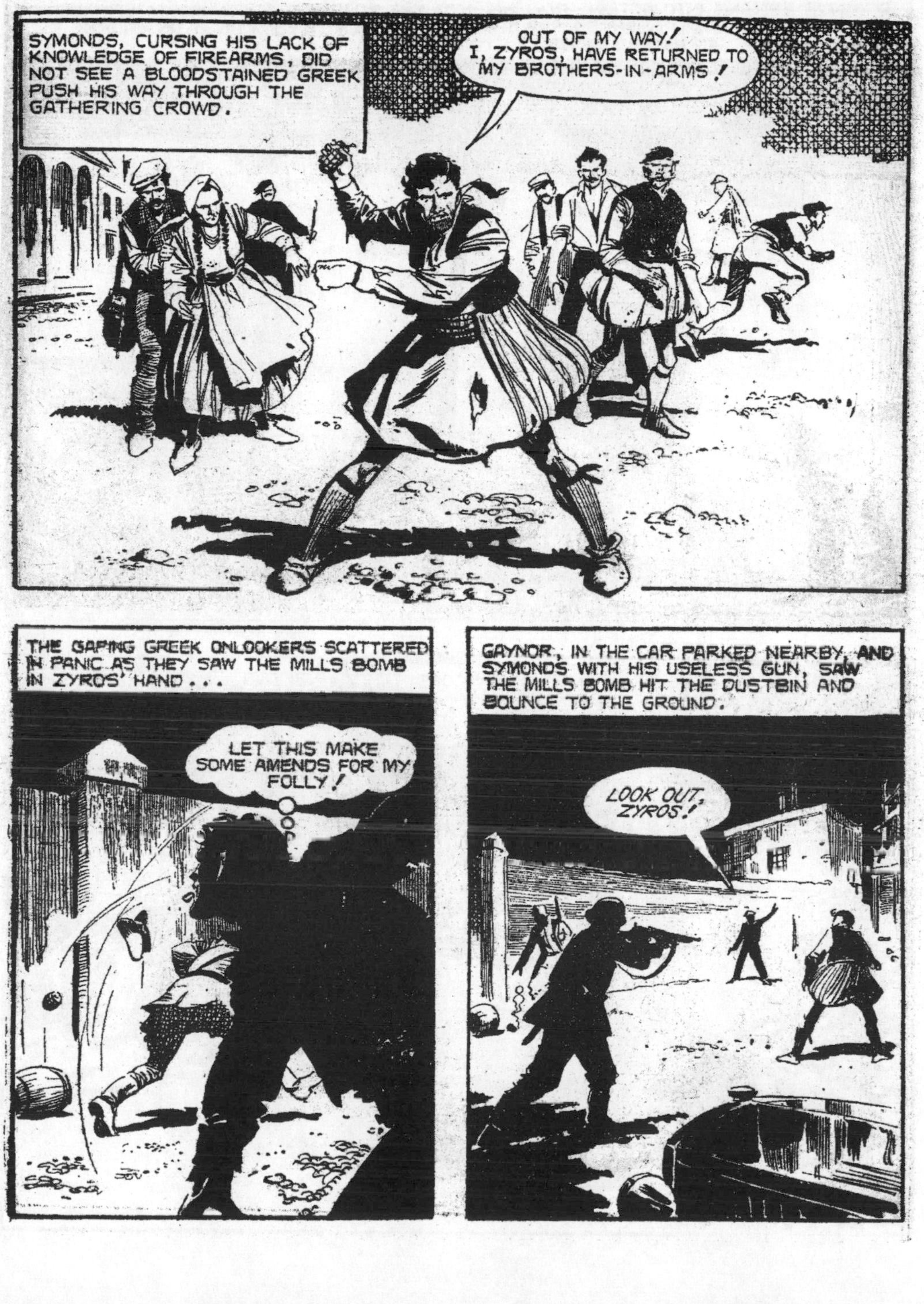
SYMONDS, CURSING HIS LACK OF KNOWLEDGE OF FIREARMS, DID NOT SEE A BLOODSTAINED GREEK PUSH HIS WAY THROUGH THE GATHERING CROWD.
OUT OF MY WAY! I, ZYROS, HAVE RETURNED TO MY BROTHERS-IN-ARMS!
THE GAPING GREEK ONLOOKERS SCATTERED IN PANIC AS THEY SAW THE MILLS BOMB IN ZYROS' HAND . . .
LET THIS MAKE SOME AMENDS FOR MY FOLLY!
GAYNOR, IN THE CAR PARKED NEARBY, AND SYMONDS WITH HIS USELESS GUN, SAW THE MILLS BOMB HIT THE DUSTBIN AND BOUNCE TO THE GROUND.
LOOK OUT, ZYROS!

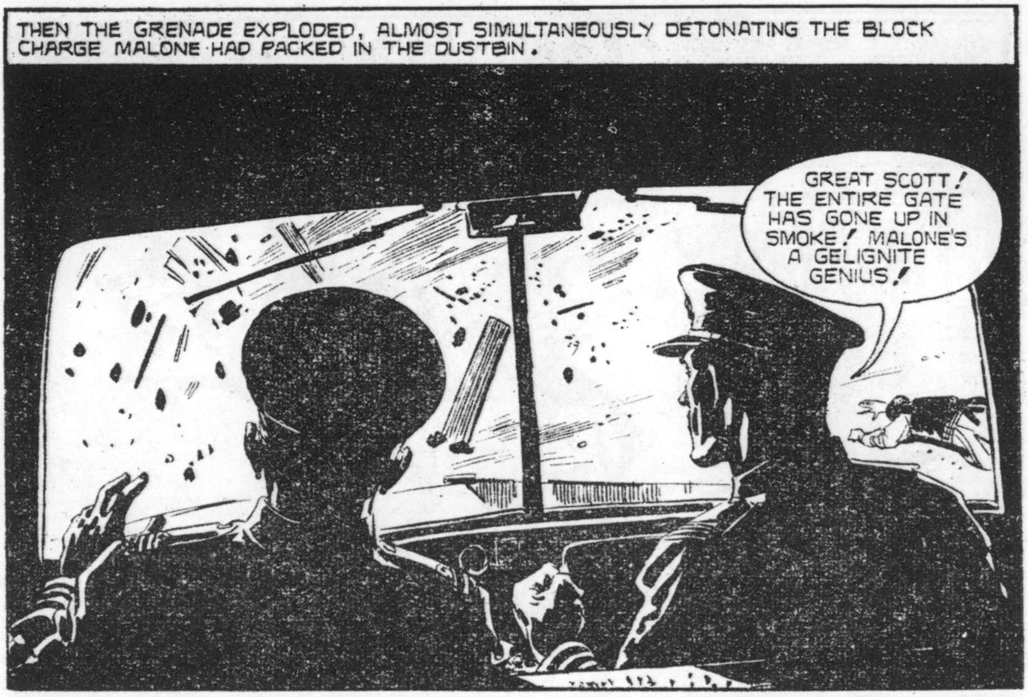
THEN THE GRENADE EXPLODED, ALMOST SIMULTANEOUSLY DETONATING THE BLOCK CHARGE MALONE HAD PACKED IN THE DUSTBIN.
GREAT SCOTT! THE ENTIRE GATE HAS GONE UP IN SMOKE! MALONE'S A GELIGNITE GENIUS!

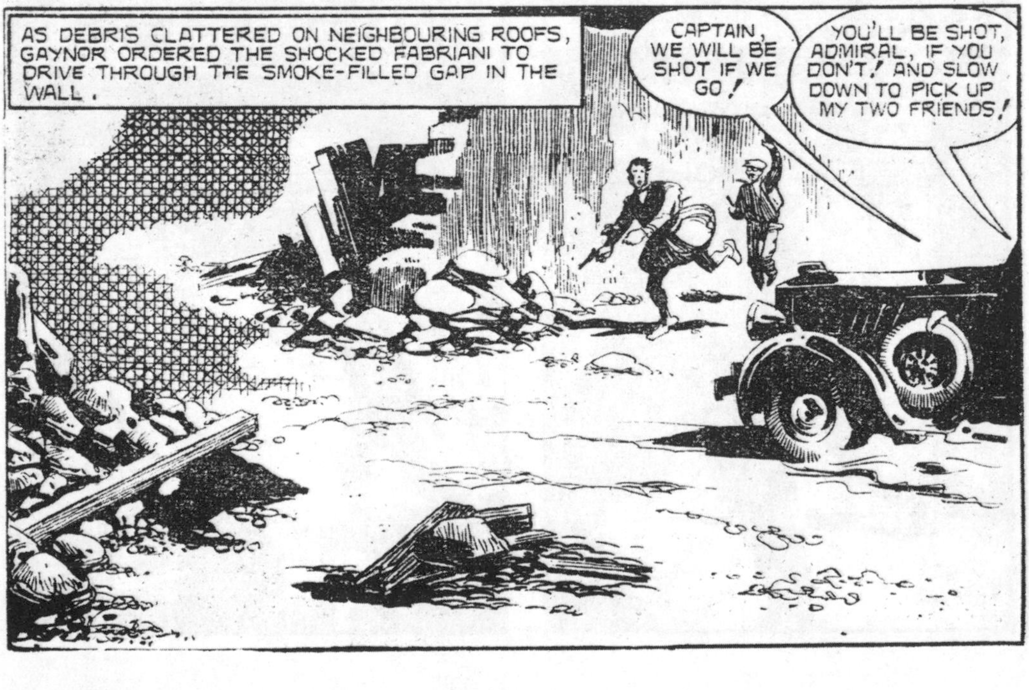
AS DEBRIS CLATTERED ON NEIGHBOURING ROOFS, GAYNOR ORDERED THE SHOCKED FABRIANI TO DRIVE THROUGH THE SMOKE-FILLED GAP IN THE WALL.
CAPTAIN, WE WILL BE SHOT IF WE GO!
YOU'LL BE SHOT, ADMIRAL, IF YOU DON'T! AND SLOW DOWN TO PICK UP MY TWO FRIENDS!

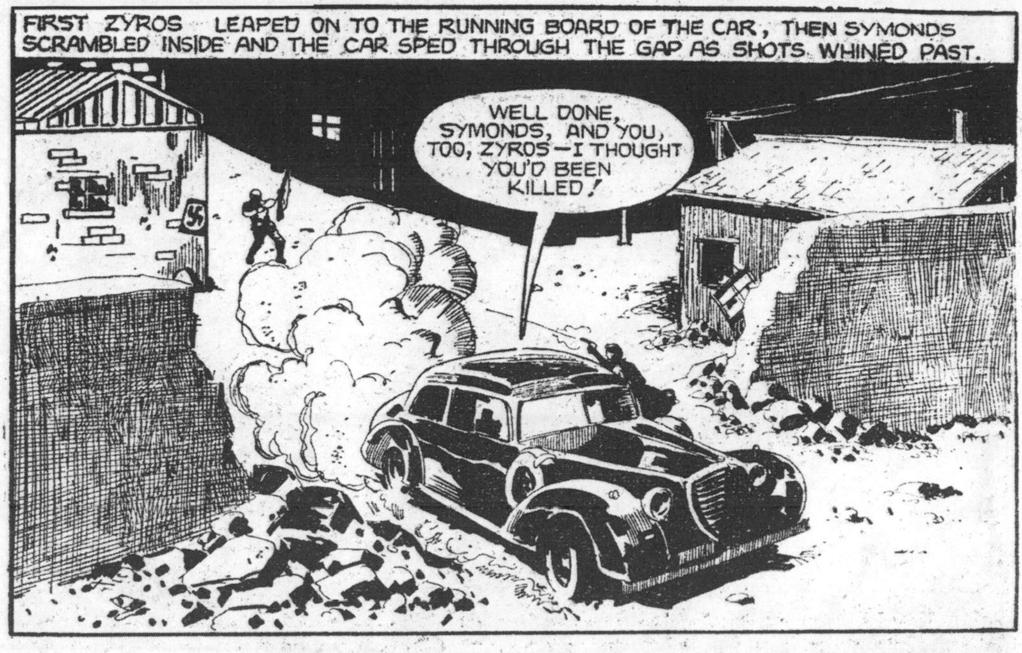
FIRST ZYROS LEAPED ON TO THE RUNNING BOARD OF THE CAR, THEN SYMONDS SCRAMBLED INSIDE AND THE CAR SPED THROUGH THE GAP AS SHOTS WHINED PAST.
WELL DONE, SYMONDS, AND YOU, TOO, ZYROS—I THOUGHT YOU'D BEEN KILLED!

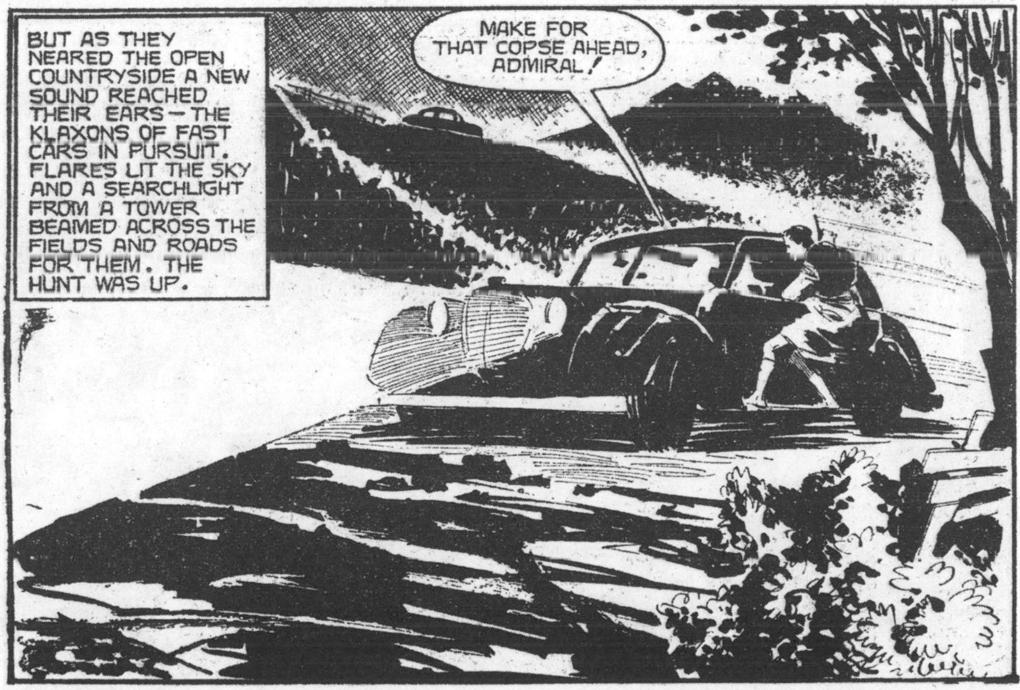
BUT AS THEY NEARED THE OPEN COUNTRYSIDE A NEW SOUND REACHED THEIR EARS—THE KLAXONS OF FAST CARS IN PURSUIT. FLARES LIT THE SKY AND A SEARCHLIGHT FROM A TOWER BEAMED ACROSS THE FIELDS AND ROADS FOR THEM. THE HUNT WAS UP.
MAKE FOR THAT COPSE AHEAD, ADMIRAL!

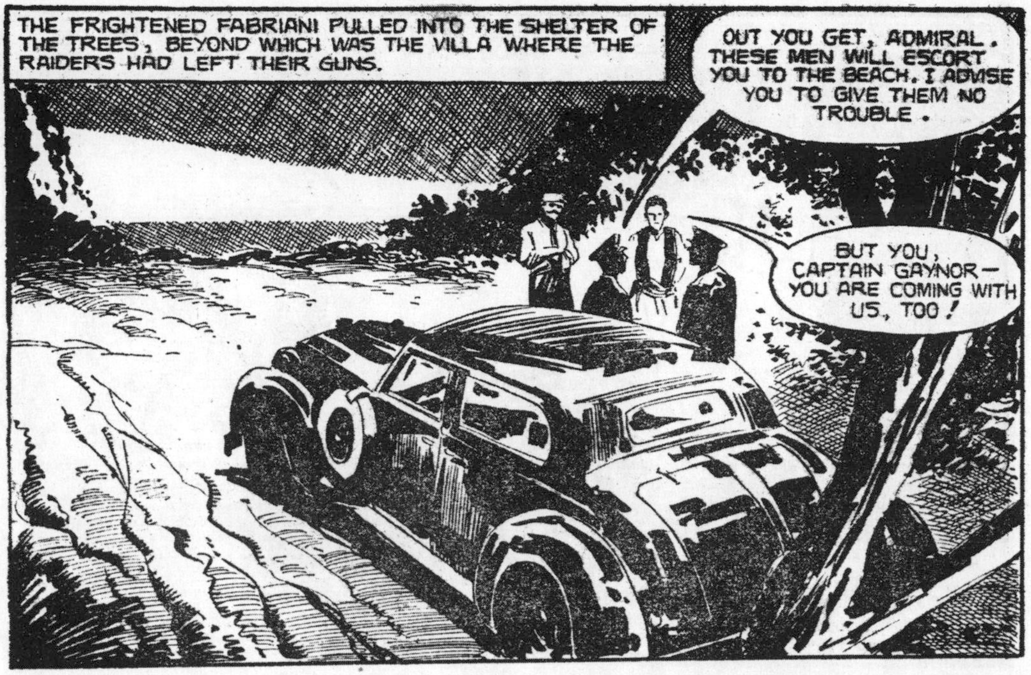
THE FRIGHTENED FABRIANI PULLED INTO THE SHELTER OF THE TREES, BEYOND WHICH WAS THE VILLA WHERE THE RAIDERS HAD LEFT THEIR GUNS.
OUT YOU GET, ADMIRAL. THESE MEN WILL ESCORT YOU TO THE BEACH. I ADVISE YOU TO GIVE THEM NO TROUBLE.
BUT YOU, CAPTAIN GAYNOR— YOU ARE COMING WITH US, TOO!

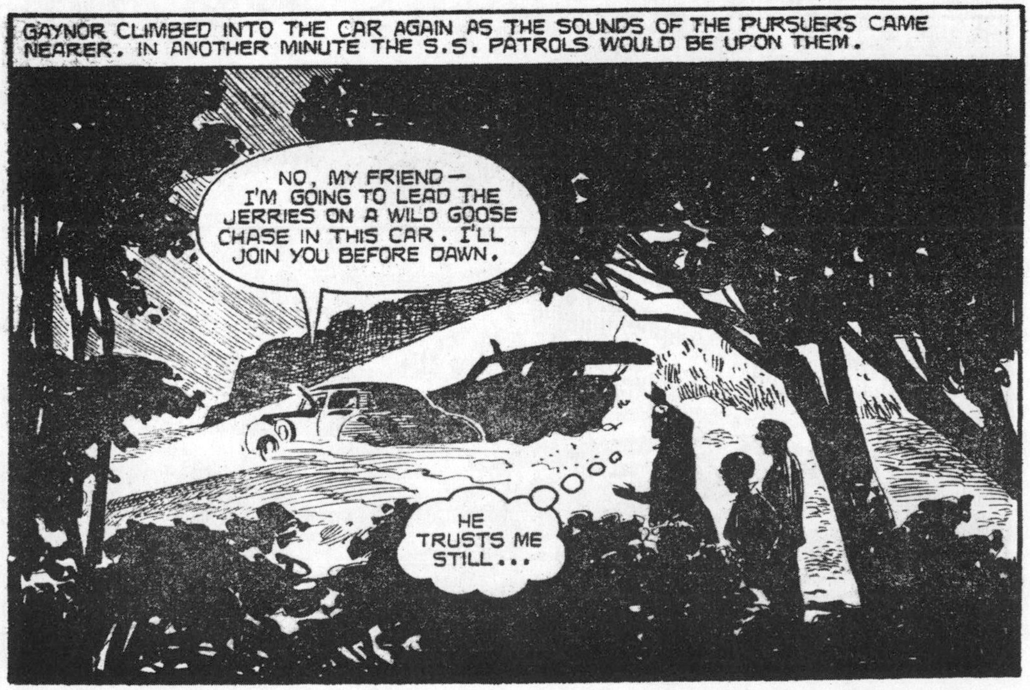
GAYNOR CLIMBED INTO THE CAR AGAIN AS THE SOUNDS OF THE PURSUERS CAME NEARER. IN ANOTHER MINUTE THE S.S. PATROLS WOULD BE UPON THEM.
NO, MY FRIEND— I'M GOING TO LEAD THE JERRIES ON A WILD GOOSE CHASE IN THIS CAR. I'LL JOIN YOU BEFORE DAWN.
HE TRUSTS ME STILL...

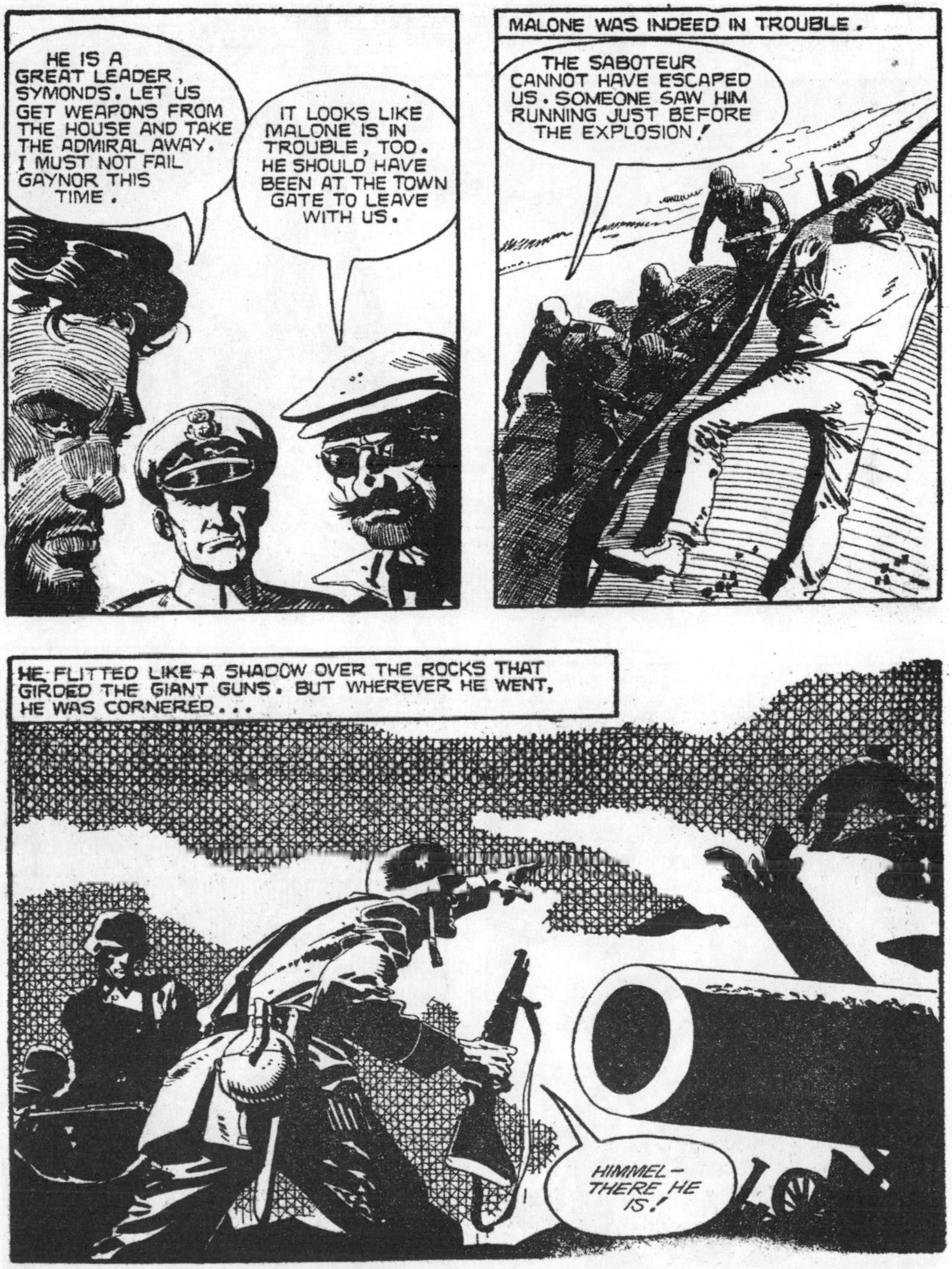
HE IS A GREAT LEADER, SYMONDS. LET US GET WEAPONS FROM THE HOUSE AND TAKE THE ADMIRAL AWAY. I MUST NOT FAIL GAYNOR THIS TIME.
IT LOOKS LIKE MALONE IS IN TROUBLE, TOO. HE SHOULD HAVE BEEN AT THE TOWN GATE TO LEAVE WITH US.
MALONE WAS INDEED IN TROUBLE.
THE SABOTEUR CANNOT HAVE ESCAPED US. SOMEONE SAW HIM RUNNING JUST BEFORE THE EXPLOSION!
HE FLITTED LIKE A SHADOW OVER THE ROCKS THAT GIRDED THE GIANT GUNS. BUT WHEREVER HE WENT, HE WAS CORNERED...
HIMMEL– THERE HE IS!

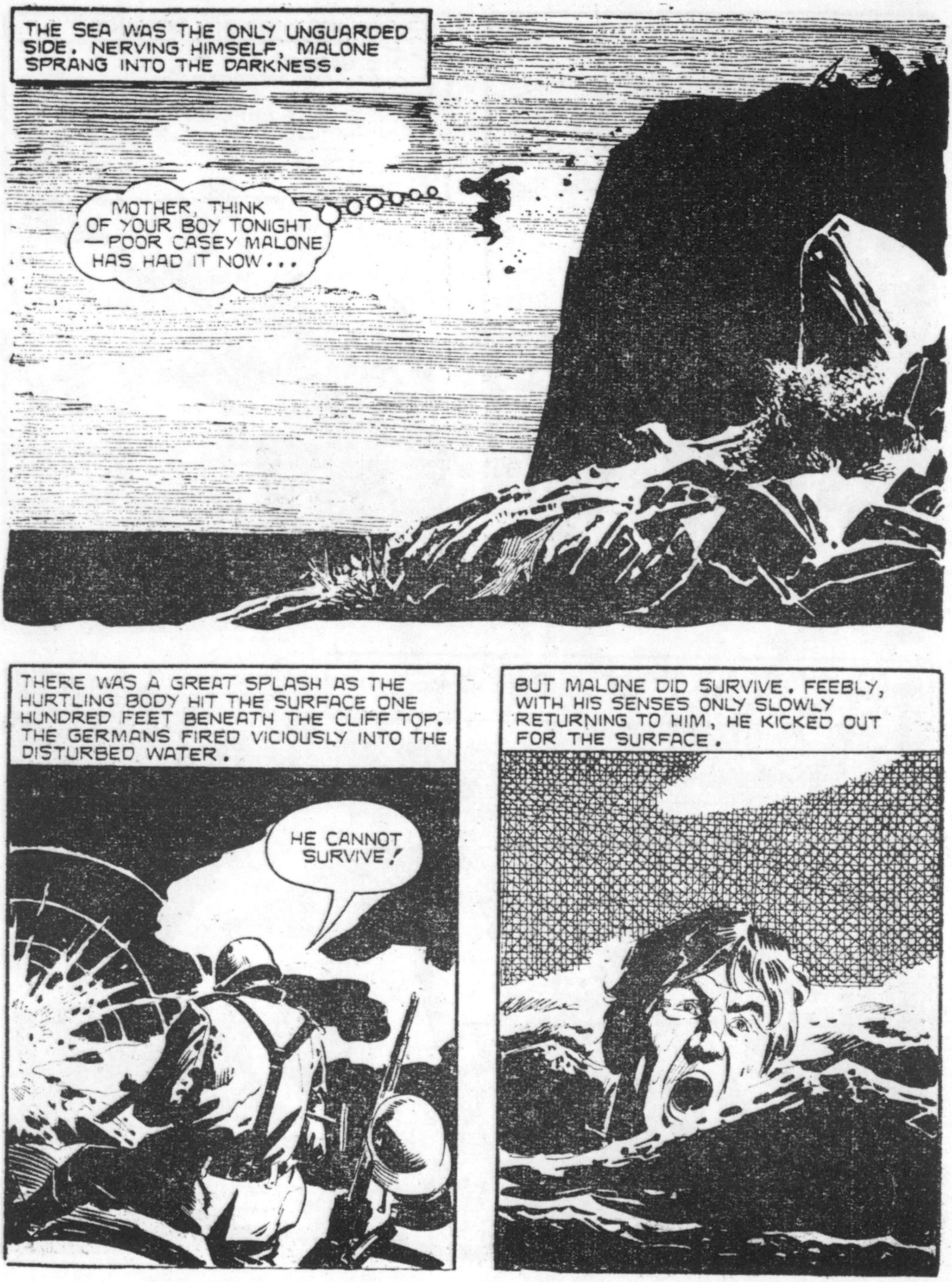
THE SEA WAS THE ONLY UNGUARDED SIDE. NERVING HIMSELF, MALONE SPRANG INTO THE DARKNESS.
MOTHER, THINK OF YOUR BOY TONIGHT —POOR CASEY MALONE HAS HAD IT NOW...
THERE WAS A GREAT SPLASH AS THE HURTLING BODY HIT THE SURFACE ONE HUNDRED FEET BENEATH THE CLIFF TOP. THE GERMANS FIRED VICIOUSLY INTO THE DISTURBED WATER.
HE CANNOT SURVIVE!
BUT MALONE DID SURVIVE. FEEBLY, WITH HIS SENSES ONLY SLOWLY RETURNING TO HIM, HE KICKED OUT FOR THE SURFACE.

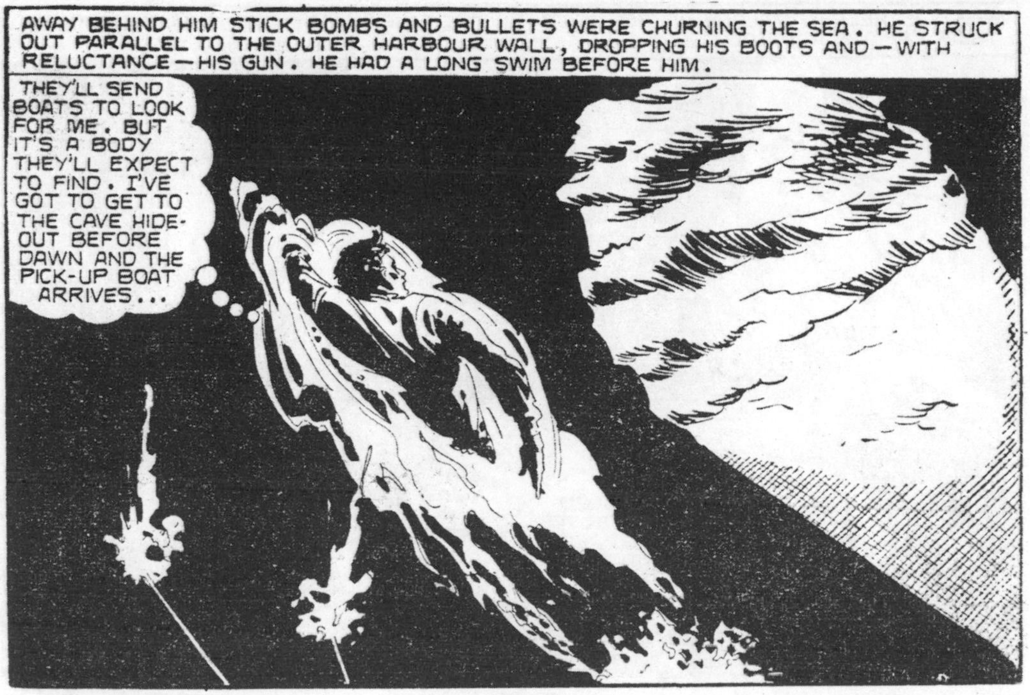
AWAY BEHIND HIM STICK BOMBS AND BULLETS WERE CHURNING THE SEA. HE STRUCK OUT PARALLEL TO THE OUTER HARBOUR WALL, DROPPING HIS BOOTS AND—WITH RELUCTANCE—HIS GUN. HE HAD A LONG SWIM BEFORE HIM.
THEY'LL SEND BOATS TO LOOK FOR ME. BUT IT'S A BODY THEY'LL EXPECT TO FIND. I'VE GOT TO GET TO THE CAVE HIDE-OUT BEFORE DAWN AND THE PICK-UP BOAT ARRIVES...

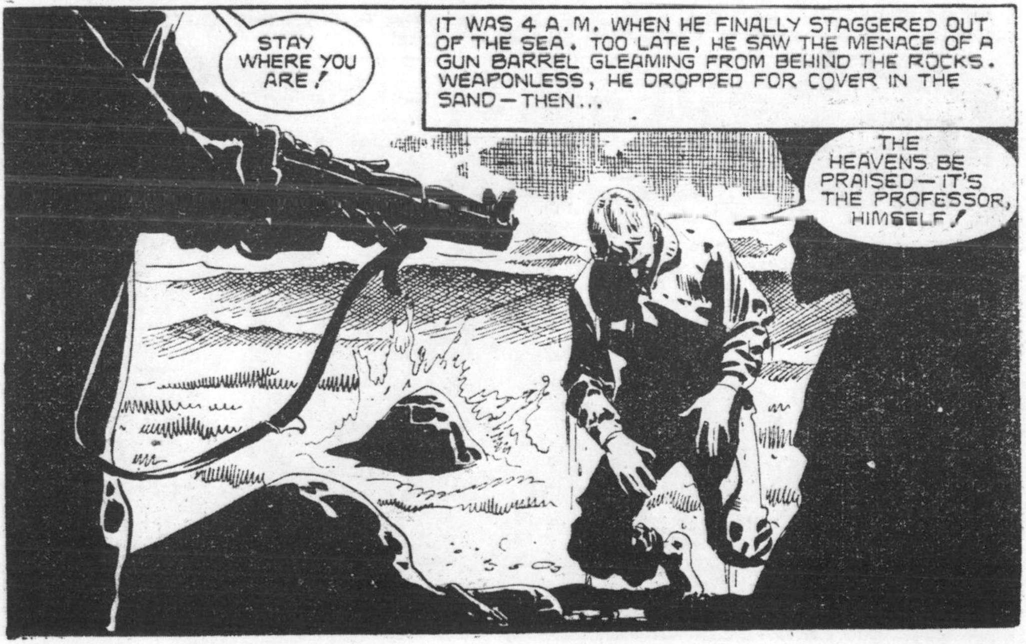
IT WAS 4 A.M. WHEN HE FINALLY STAGGERED OUT OF THE SEA. TOO LATE, HE SAW THE MENACE OF A GUN BARREL GLEAMING FROM BEHIND THE ROCKS. WEAPONLESS, HE DROPPED FOR COVER IN THE SAND—THEN...
STAY WHERE YOU ARE!
THE HEAVENS BE PRAISED—IT'S THE PROFESSOR, HIMSELF!

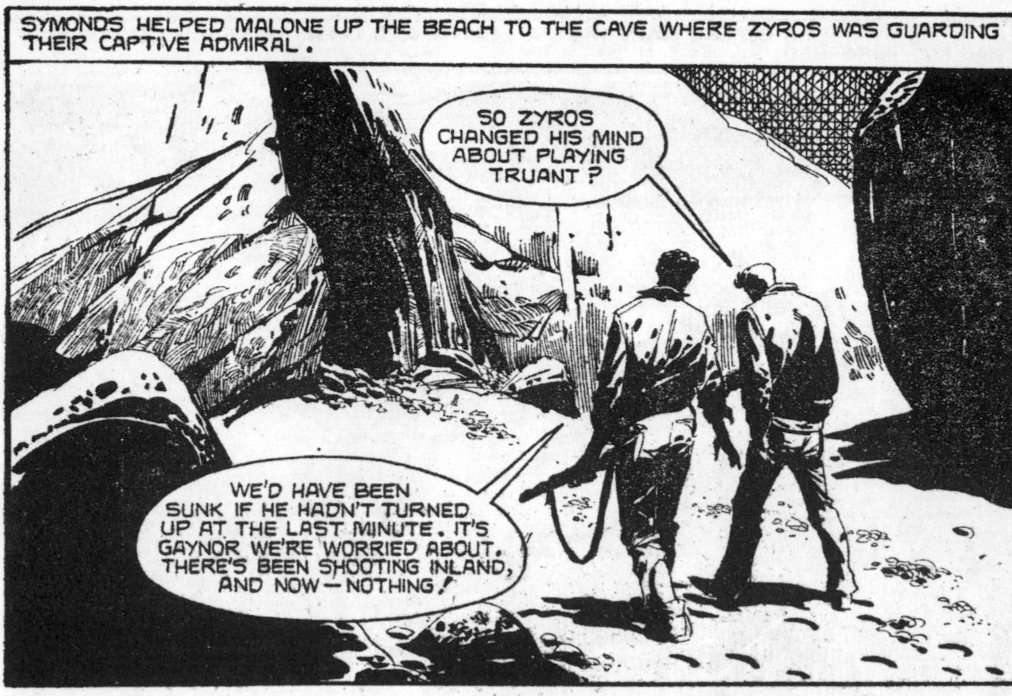
SYMONDS HELPED MALONE UP THE BEACH TO THE CAVE WHERE ZYROS WAS GUARDING THEIR CAPTIVE ADMIRAL.
SO ZYROS CHANGED HIS MIND ABOUT PLAYING TRUANT?
WE'D HAVE BEEN SUNK IF HE HADN'T TURNED UP AT THE LAST MINUTE. IT'S GAYNOR WE'RE WORRIED ABOUT. THERE'S BEEN SHOOTING INLAND, AND NOW—NOTHING!

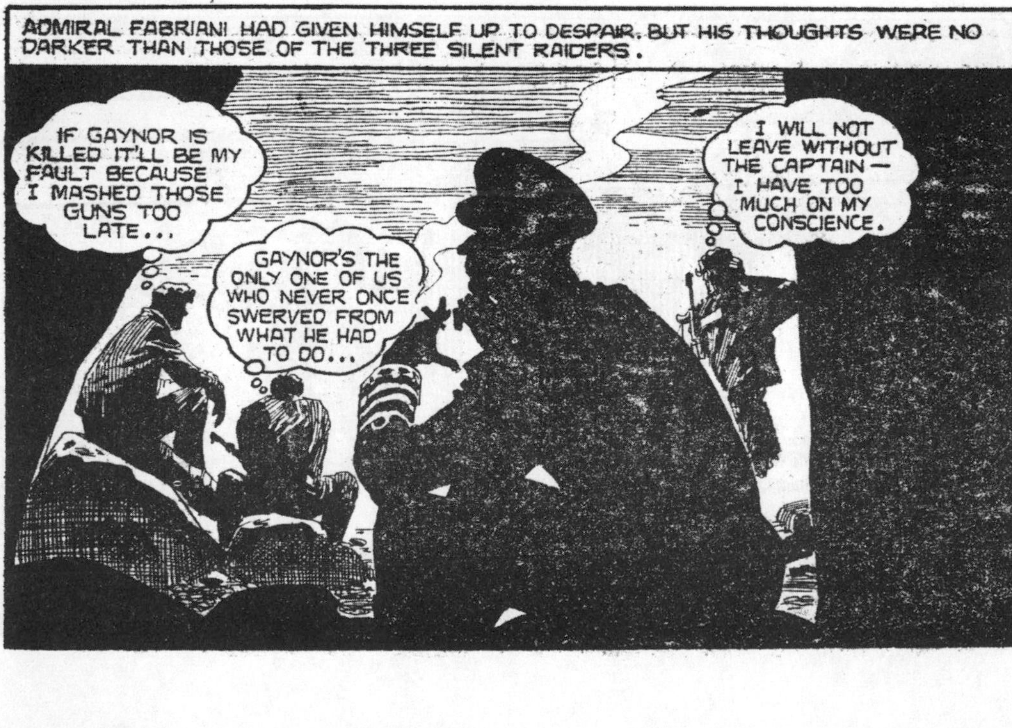
ADMIRAL FABRIANI HAD GIVEN HIMSELF UP TO DESPAIR. BUT HIS THOUGHTS WERE NO DARKER THAN THOSE OF THE THREE SILENT RAIDERS.
IF GAYNOR IS KILLED IT'LL BE MY FAULT BECAUSE I MASHED THOSE GUNS TOO LATE...
GAYNOR'S THE ONLY ONE OF US WHO NEVER ONCE SWERVED FROM WHAT HE HAD TO DO...
I WILL NOT LEAVE WITHOUT THE CAPTAIN—I HAVE TOO MUCH ON MY CONSCIENCE.

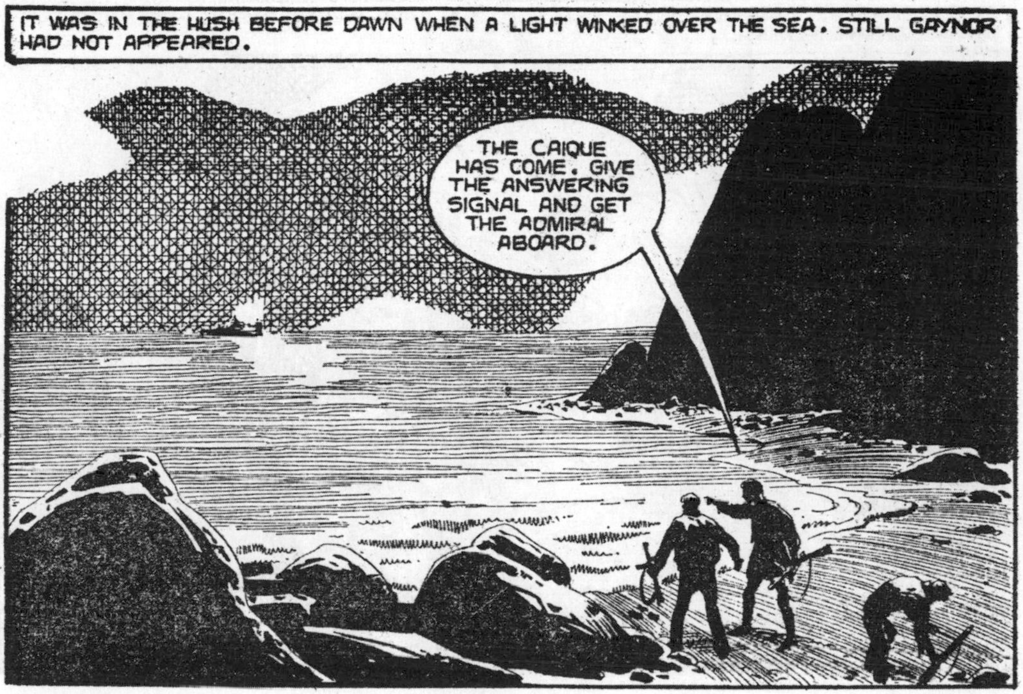
IT WAS IN THE HUSH BEFORE DAWN WHEN A LIGHT WINKED OVER THE SEA. STILL GAYNOR HAD NOT APPEARED.
THE CAIQUE HAS COME. GIVE THE ANSWERING SIGNAL AND GET THE ADMIRAL ABOARD.

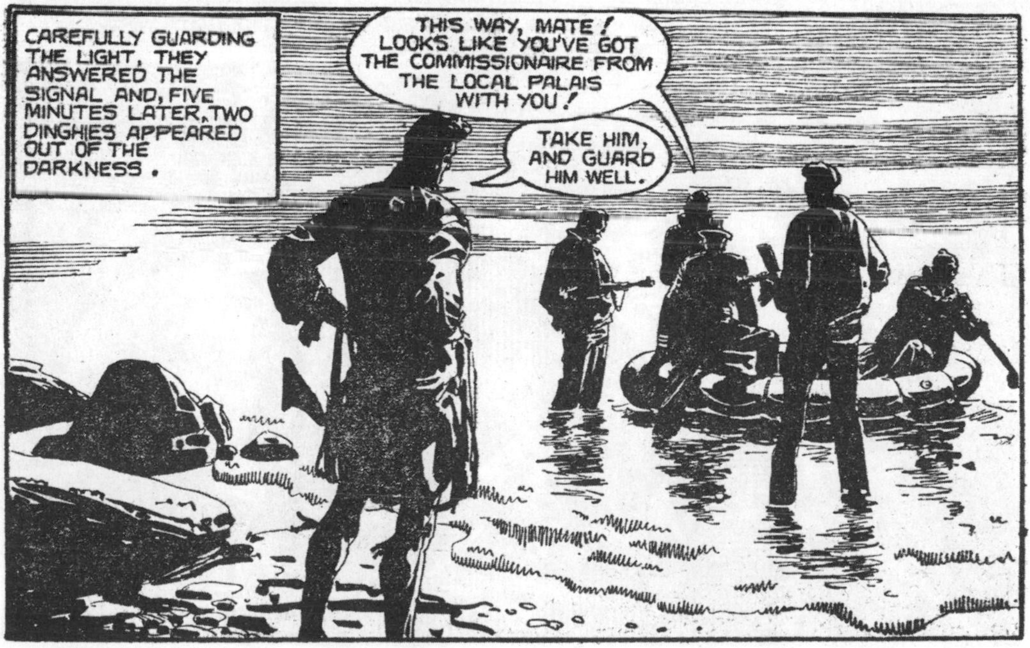
CAREFULLY GUARDING THE LIGHT, THEY ANSWERED THE SIGNAL AND, FIVE MINUTES LATER, TWO DINGHIES APPEARED OUT OF THE DARKNESS.
THIS WAY, MATE! LOOKS LIKE YOU'VE GOT THE COMMISSIONAIRE FROM THE LOCAL PALAIS WITH YOU!
TAKE HIM, AND GUARD HIM WELL.

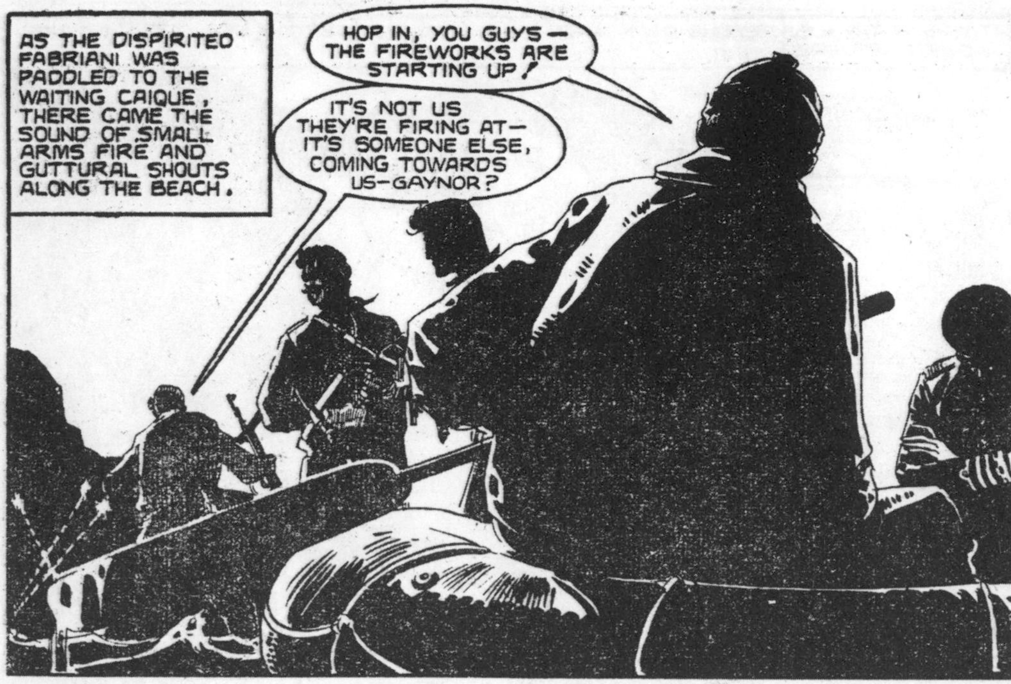
AS THE DISPIRITED FABRIANI WAS PADDLED TO THE WAITING CAIQUE, THERE CAME THE SOUND OF SMALL ARMS FIRE AND GUTTURAL SHOUTS ALONG THE BEACH.
HOP IN, YOU GUYS — THE FIREWORKS ARE STARTING UP!
IT'S NOT US THEY'RE FIRING AT — IT'S SOMEONE ELSE, COMING TOWARDS US — GAYNOR?

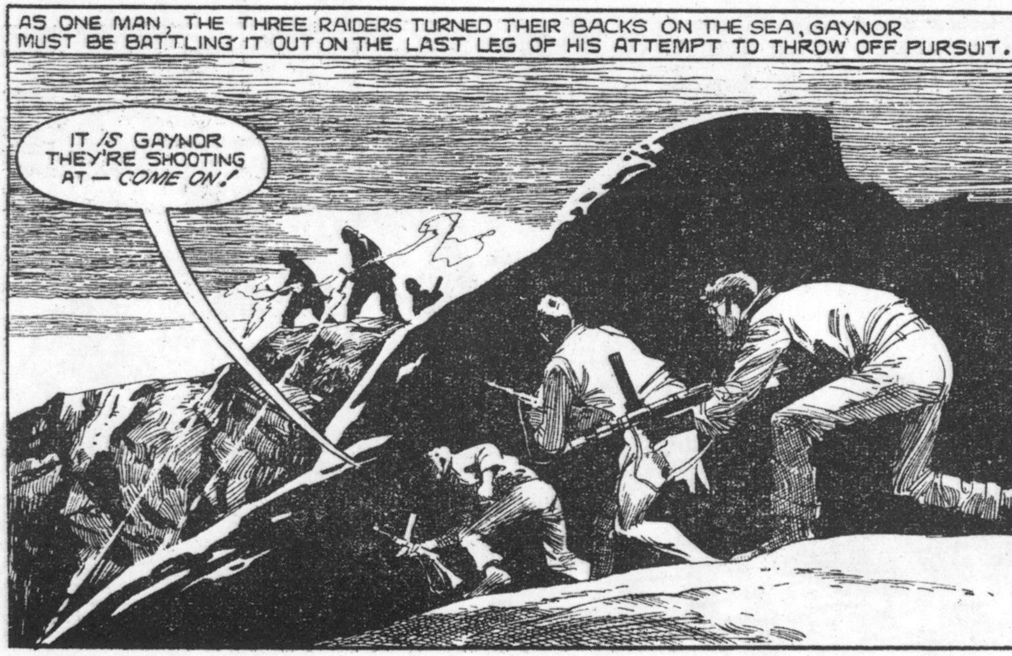
AS ONE MAN, THE THREE RAIDERS TURNED THEIR BACKS ON THE SEA, GAYNOR MUST BE BATTLING IT OUT ON THE LAST LEG OF HIS ATTEMPT TO THROW OFF PURSUIT.
IT *IS* GAYNOR THEY'RE SHOOTING AT — *COME ON!*

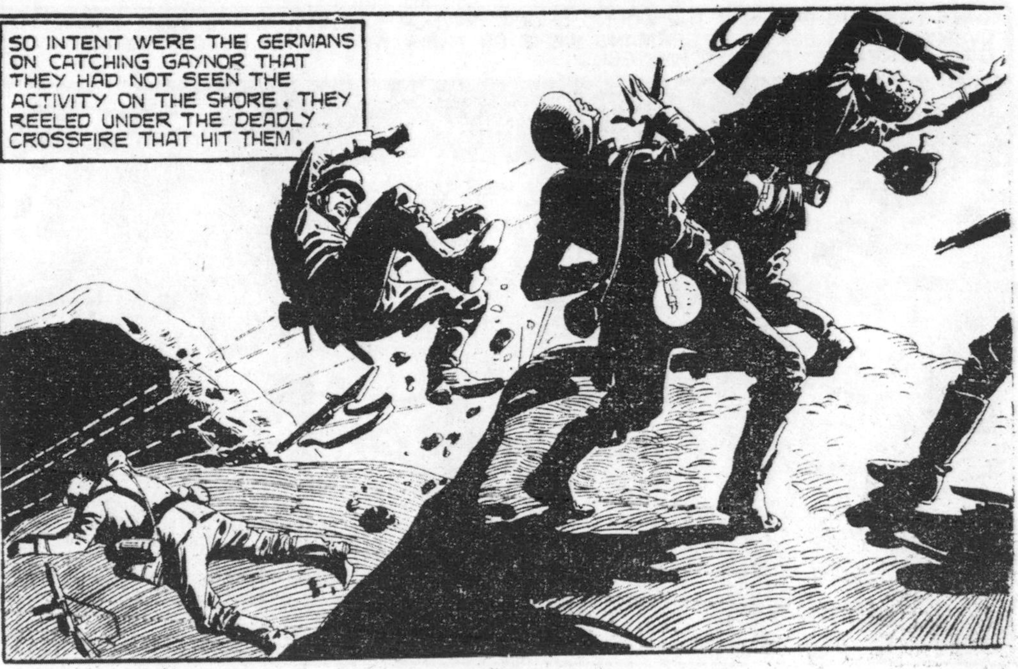
SO INTENT WERE THE GERMANS ON CATCHING GAYNOR THAT THEY HAD NOT SEEN THE ACTIVITY ON THE SHORE. THEY REELED UNDER THE DEADLY CROSSFIRE THAT HIT THEM.

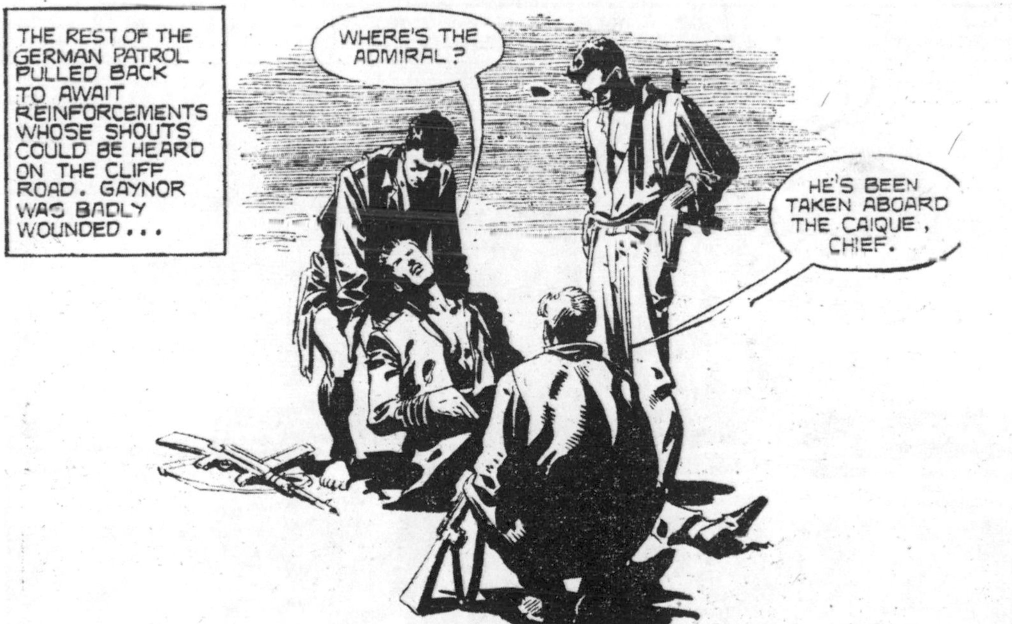
THE REST OF THE GERMAN PATROL PULLED BACK TO AWAIT REINFORCEMENTS WHOSE SHOUTS COULD BE HEARD ON THE CLIFF ROAD. GAYNOR WAS BADLY WOUNDED...
WHERE'S THE ADMIRAL?
HE'S BEEN TAKEN ABOARD THE CAIQUE, CHIEF.

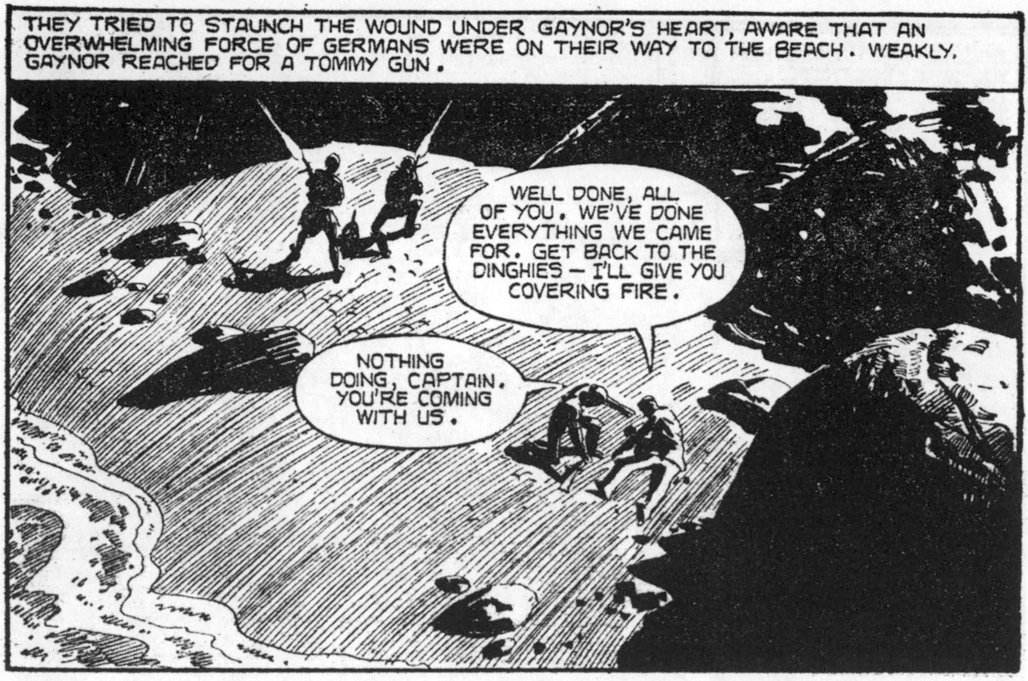
THEY TRIED TO STAUNCH THE WOUND UNDER GAYNOR'S HEART, AWARE THAT AN OVERWHELMING FORCE OF GERMANS WERE ON THEIR WAY TO THE BEACH. WEAKLY, GAYNOR REACHED FOR A TOMMY GUN.
WELL DONE, ALL OF YOU. WE'VE DONE EVERYTHING WE CAME FOR. GET BACK TO THE DINGHIES — I'LL GIVE YOU COVERING FIRE.
NOTHING DOING, CAPTAIN. YOU'RE COMING WITH US.

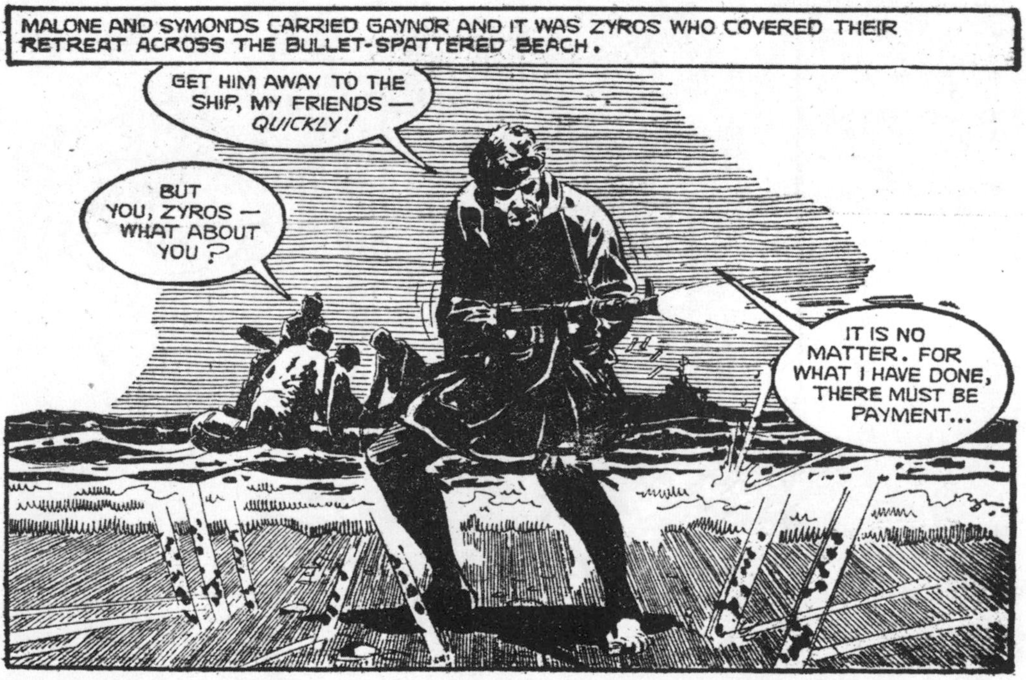
MALONE AND SYMONDS CARRIED GAYNOR AND IT WAS ZYROS WHO COVERED THEIR RETREAT ACROSS THE BULLET-SPATTERED BEACH.
GET HIM AWAY TO THE SHIP, MY FRIENDS — QUICKLY!
BUT YOU, ZYROS — WHAT ABOUT YOU?
IT IS NO MATTER. FOR WHAT I HAVE DONE, THERE MUST BE PAYMENT...

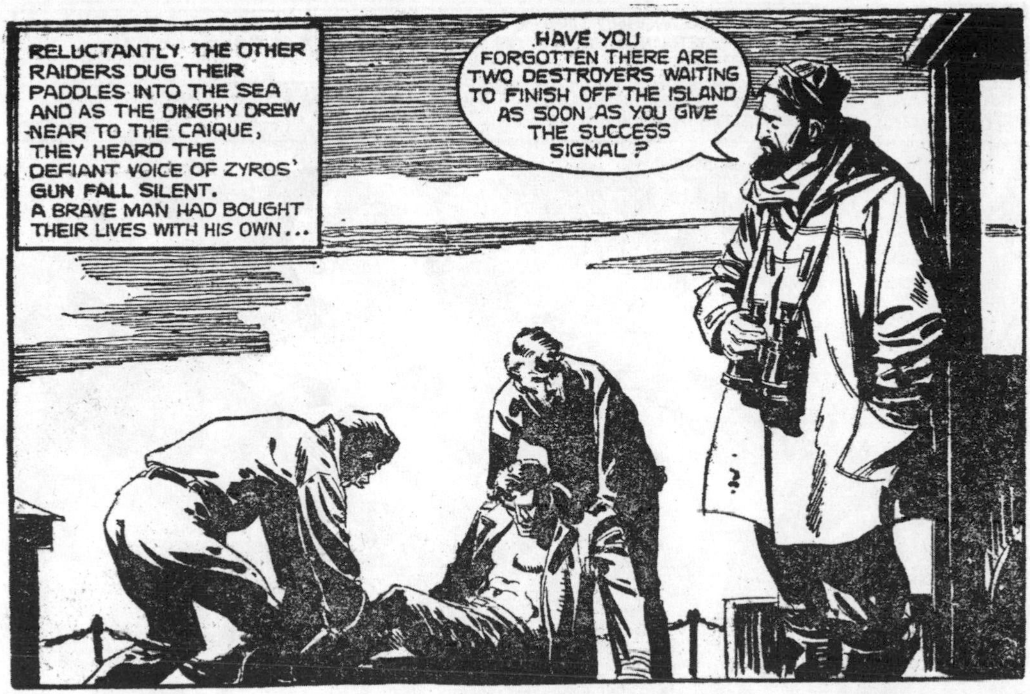
RELUCTANTLY THE OTHER RAIDERS DUG THEIR PADDLES INTO THE SEA AND AS THE DINGHY DREW NEAR TO THE CAIQUE, THEY HEARD THE DEFIANT VOICE OF ZYROS' GUN FALL SILENT. A BRAVE MAN HAD BOUGHT THEIR LIVES WITH HIS OWN...
HAVE YOU FORGOTTEN THERE ARE TWO DESTROYERS WAITING TO FINISH OFF THE ISLAND AS SOON AS YOU GIVE THE SUCCESS SIGNAL?

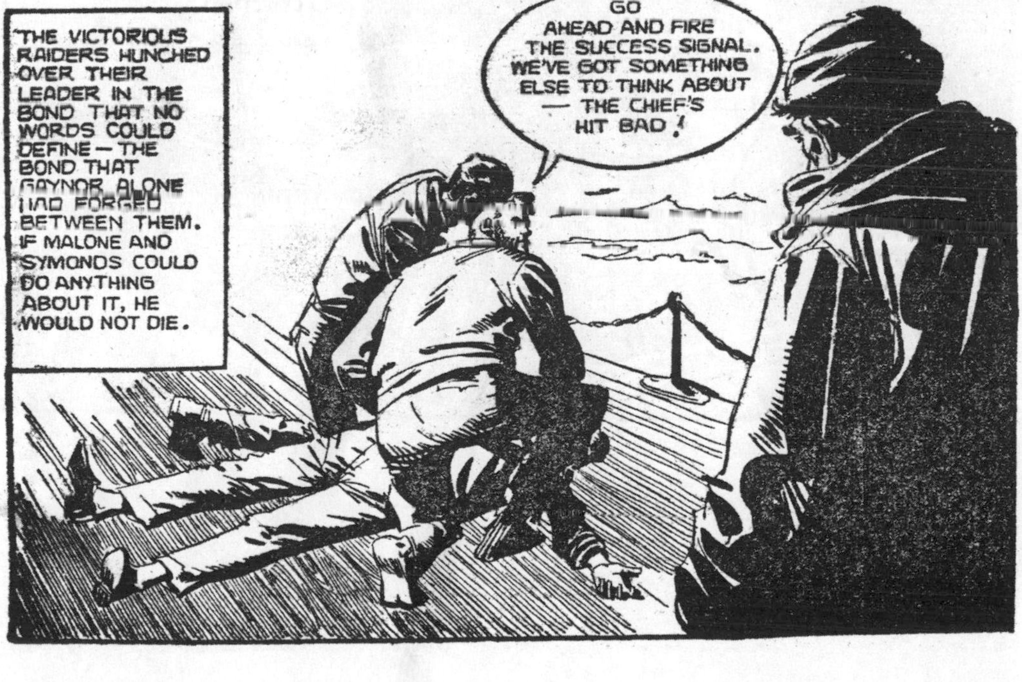
THE VICTORIOUS RAIDERS HUNCHED OVER THEIR LEADER IN THE BOND THAT NO WORDS COULD DEFINE — THE BOND THAT GAYNOR ALONE HAD FORGED BETWEEN THEM. IF MALONE AND SYMONDS COULD DO ANYTHING ABOUT IT, HE WOULD NOT DIE.
GO AHEAD AND FIRE THE SUCCESS SIGNAL. WE'VE GOT SOMETHING ELSE TO THINK ABOUT — THE CHIEF'S HIT BAD!

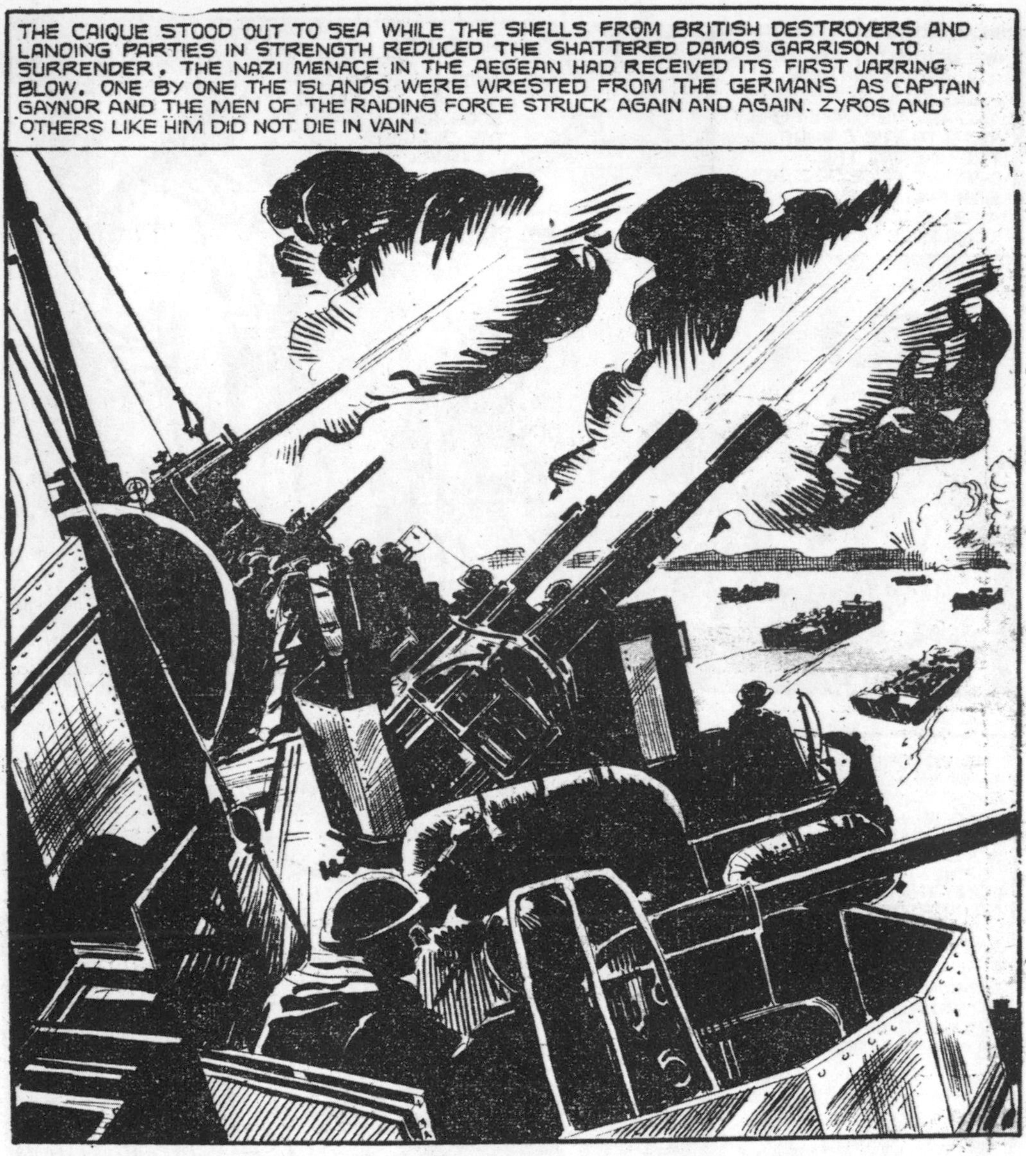
THE CAIQUE STOOD OUT TO SEA WHILE THE SHELLS FROM BRITISH DESTROYERS AND LANDING PARTIES IN STRENGTH REDUCED THE SHATTERED DAMOS GARRISON TO SURRENDER. THE NAZI MENACE IN THE AEGEAN HAD RECEIVED ITS FIRST JARRING BLOW. ONE BY ONE THE ISLANDS WERE WRESTED FROM THE GERMANS AS CAPTAIN GAYNOR AND THE MEN OF THE RAIDING FORCE STRUCK AGAIN AND AGAIN. ZYROS AND OTHERS LIKE HIM DID NOT DIE IN VAIN.

The FLAME and the FURY

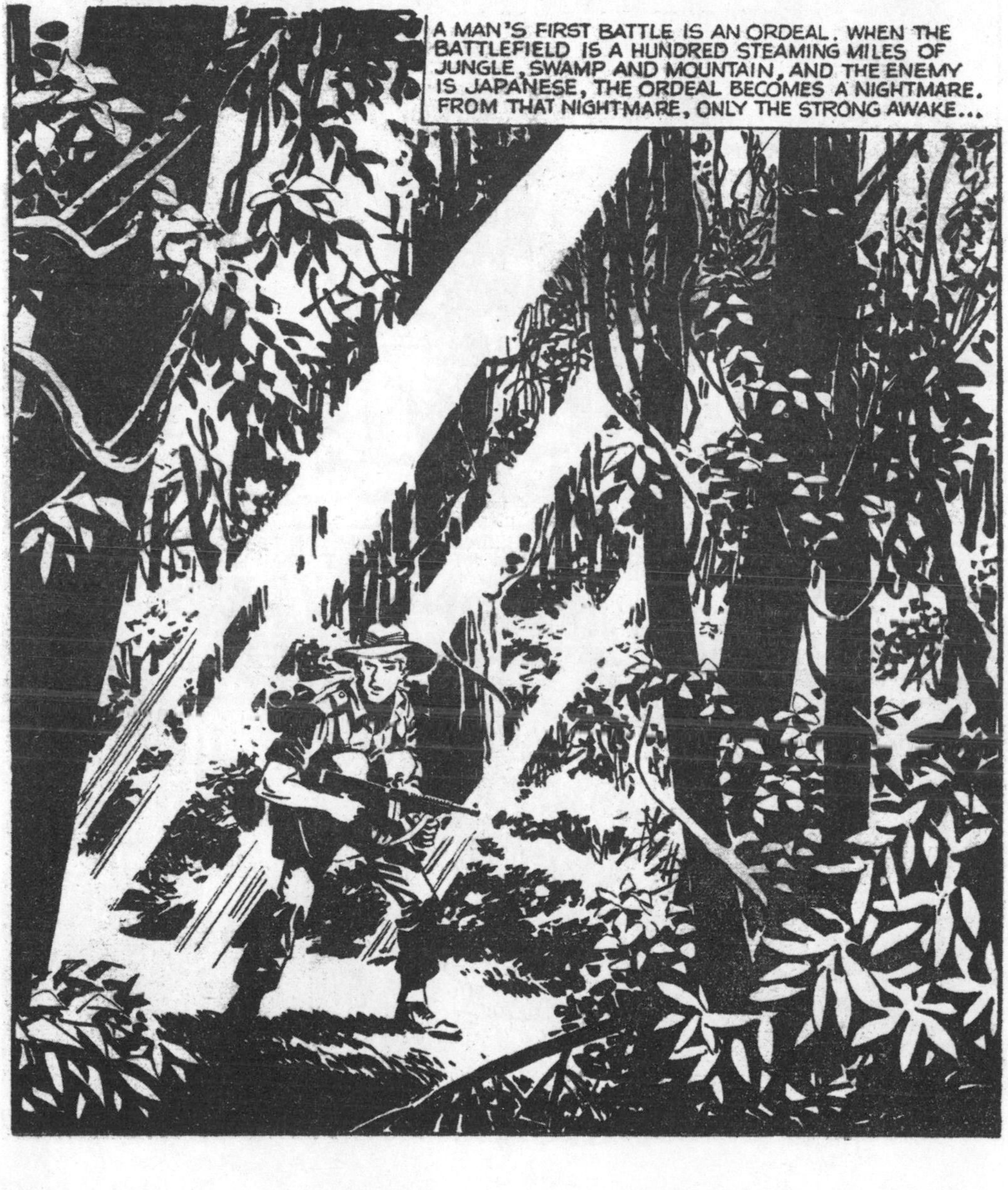
A MAN'S FIRST BATTLE IS AN ORDEAL. WHEN THE BATTLEFIELD IS A HUNDRED STEAMING MILES OF JUNGLE, SWAMP AND MOUNTAIN, AND THE ENEMY IS JAPANESE, THE ORDEAL BECOMES A NIGHTMARE. FROM THAT NIGHTMARE, ONLY THE STRONG AWAKE...

Chapter 1. Panic

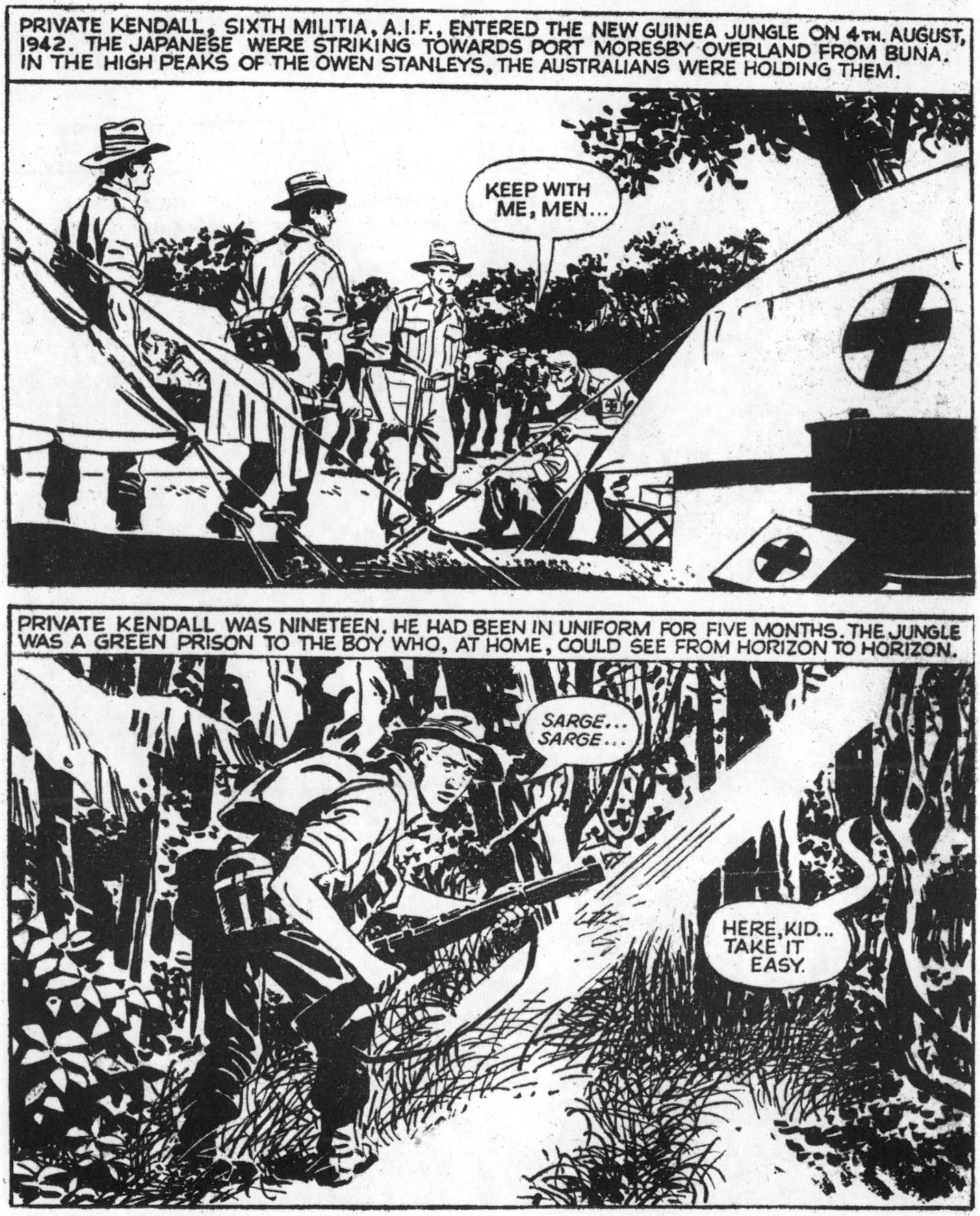
PRIVATE KENDALL, SIXTH MILITIA, A.I.F., ENTERED THE NEW GUINEA JUNGLE ON 4TH. AUGUST, 1942. THE JAPANESE WERE STRIKING TOWARDS PORT MORESBY OVERLAND FROM BUNA. IN THE HIGH PEAKS OF THE OWEN STANLEYS, THE AUSTRALIANS WERE HOLDING THEM.
KEEP WITH ME, MEN...
PRIVATE KENDALL WAS NINETEEN. HE HAD BEEN IN UNIFORM FOR FIVE MONTHS. THE JUNGLE WAS A GREEN PRISON TO THE BOY WHO, AT HOME, COULD SEE FROM HORIZON TO HORIZON.
SARGE... SARGE...
HERE, KID... TAKE IT EASY.

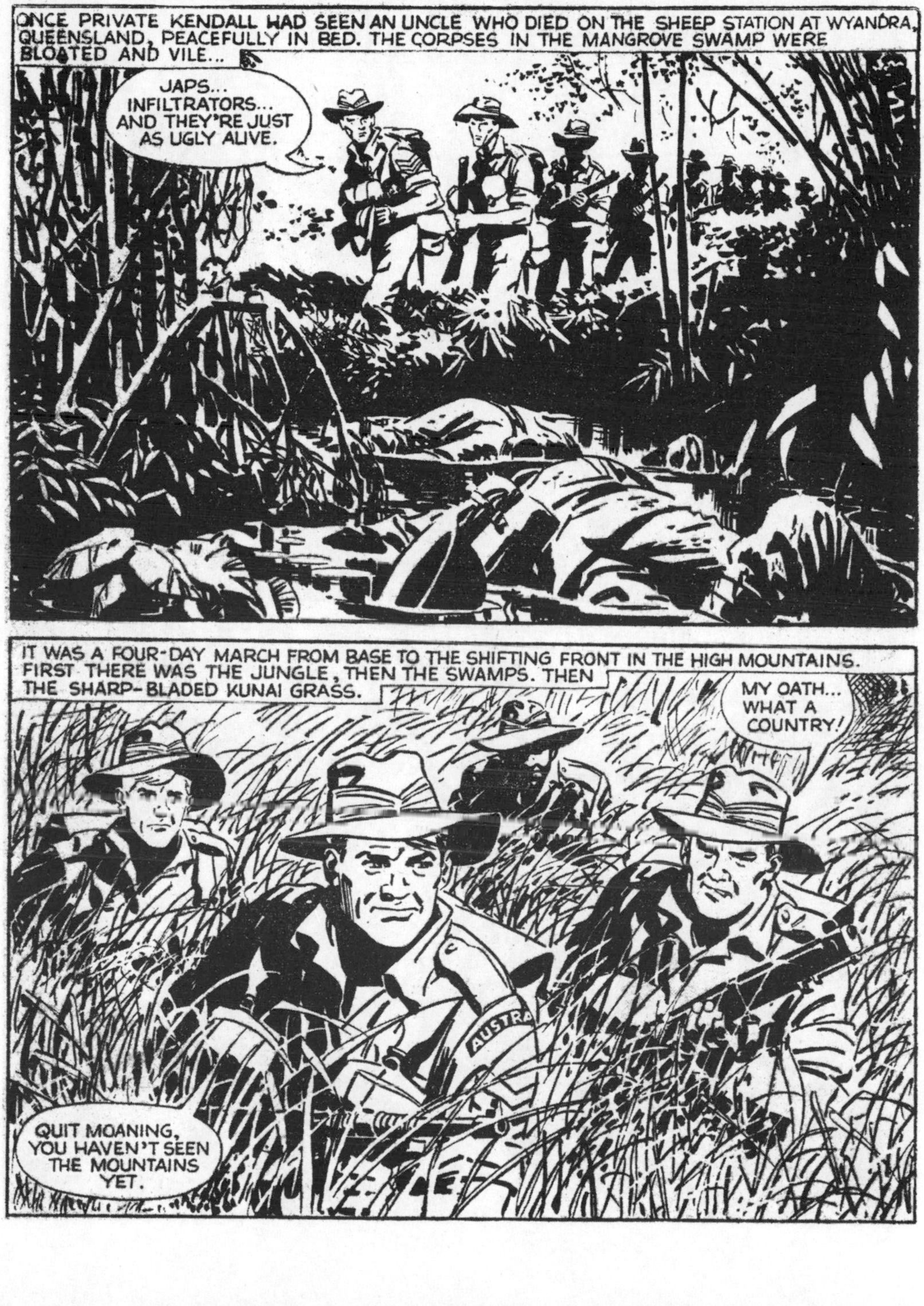
ONCE PRIVATE KENDALL HAD SEEN AN UNCLE WHO DIED ON THE SHEEP STATION AT WYANDRA, QUEENSLAND, PEACEFULLY IN BED. THE CORPSES IN THE MANGROVE SWAMP WERE BLOATED AND VILE...
JAPS... INFILTRATORS... AND THEY'RE JUST AS UGLY ALIVE.
IT WAS A FOUR-DAY MARCH FROM BASE TO THE SHIFTING FRONT IN THE HIGH MOUNTAINS. FIRST THERE WAS THE JUNGLE, THEN THE SWAMPS. THEN THE SHARP-BLADED KUNAI GRASS.
MY OATH... WHAT A COUNTRY!
QUIT MOANING, YOU HAVEN'T SEEN THE MOUNTAINS YET.

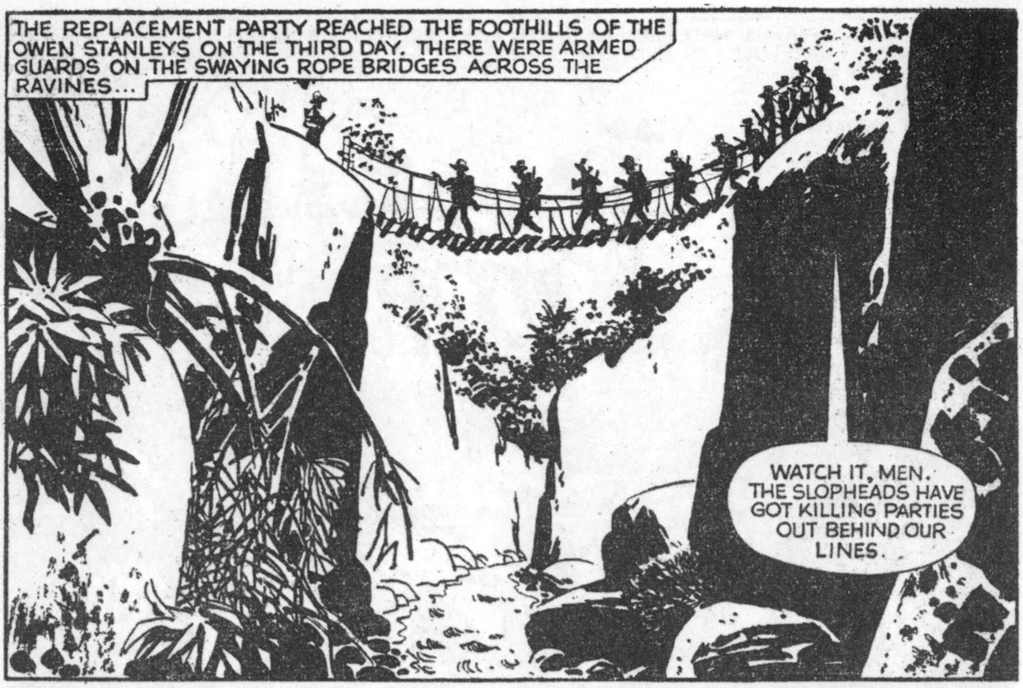
THE REPLACEMENT PARTY REACHED THE FOOTHILLS OF THE OWEN STANLEYS ON THE THIRD DAY. THERE WERE ARMED GUARDS ON THE SWAYING ROPE BRIDGES ACROSS THE RAVINES...
WATCH IT, MEN. THE SLOPHEADS HAVE GOT KILLING PARTIES OUT BEHIND OUR LINES.

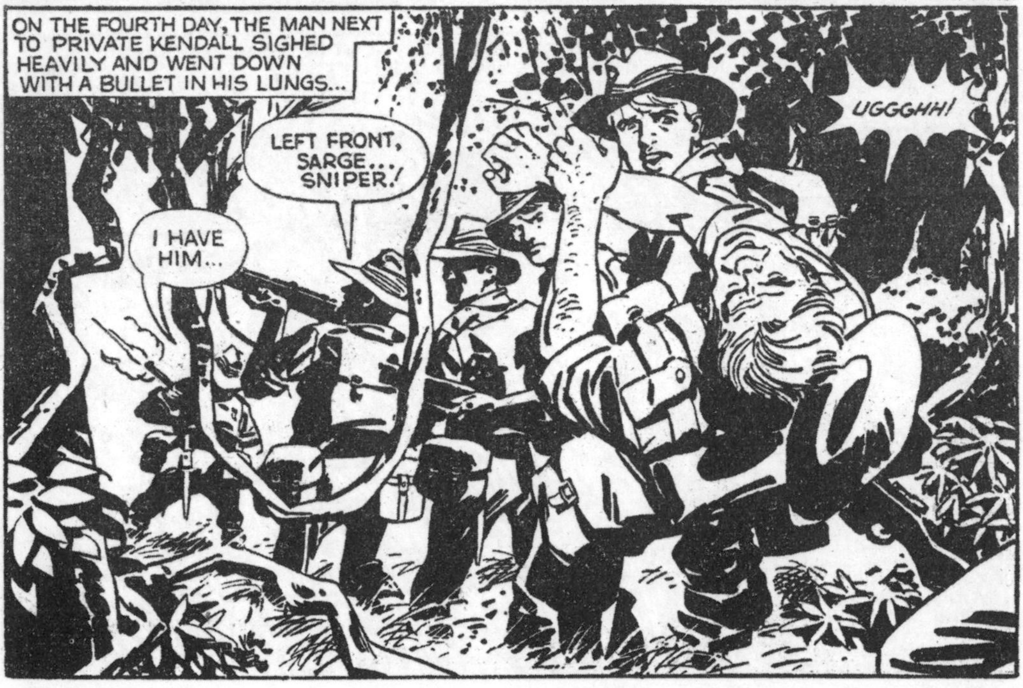
ON THE FOURTH DAY, THE MAN NEXT TO PRIVATE KENDALL SIGHED HEAVILY AND WENT DOWN WITH A BULLET IN HIS LUNGS...
UGGGHH!
LEFT FRONT, SARGE... SNIPER!
I HAVE HIM...

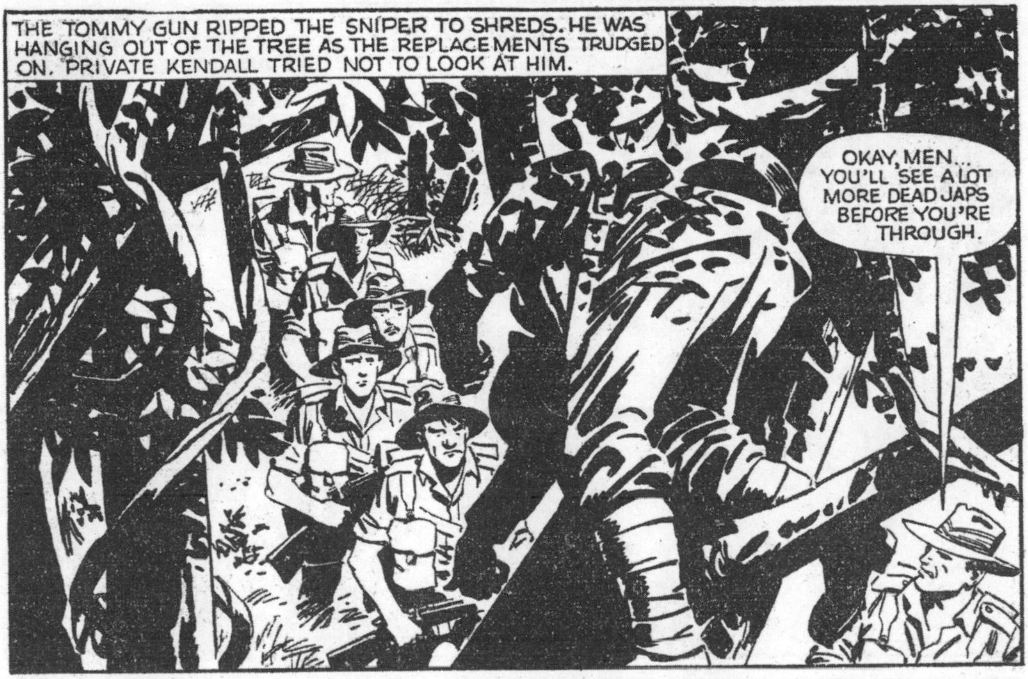
THE TOMMY GUN RIPPED THE SNIPER TO SHREDS. HE WAS HANGING OUT OF THE TREE AS THE REPLACEMENTS TRUDGED ON. PRIVATE KENDALL TRIED NOT TO LOOK AT HIM.
OKAY, MEN... YOU'LL SEE A LOT MORE DEAD JAPS BEFORE YOU'RE THROUGH.

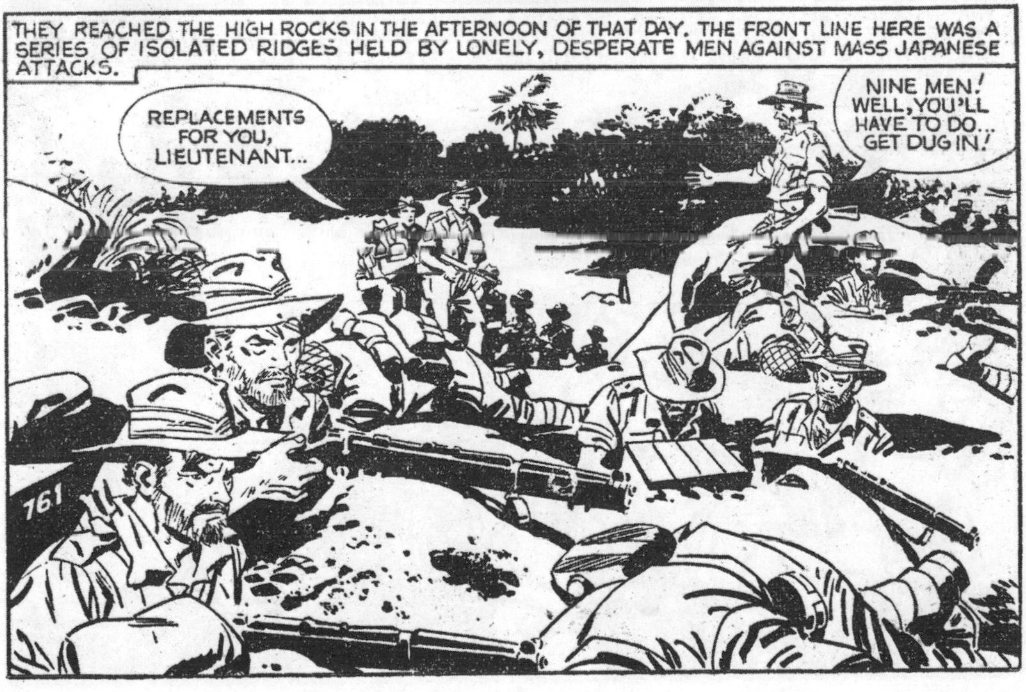
THEY REACHED THE HIGH ROCKS IN THE AFTERNOON OF THAT DAY. THE FRONT LINE HERE WAS A SERIES OF ISOLATED RIDGES HELD BY LONELY, DESPERATE MEN AGAINST MASS JAPANESE ATTACKS.
REPLACEMENTS FOR YOU, LIEUTENANT...
NINE MEN! WELL, YOU'LL HAVE TO DO... GET DUG IN!
761

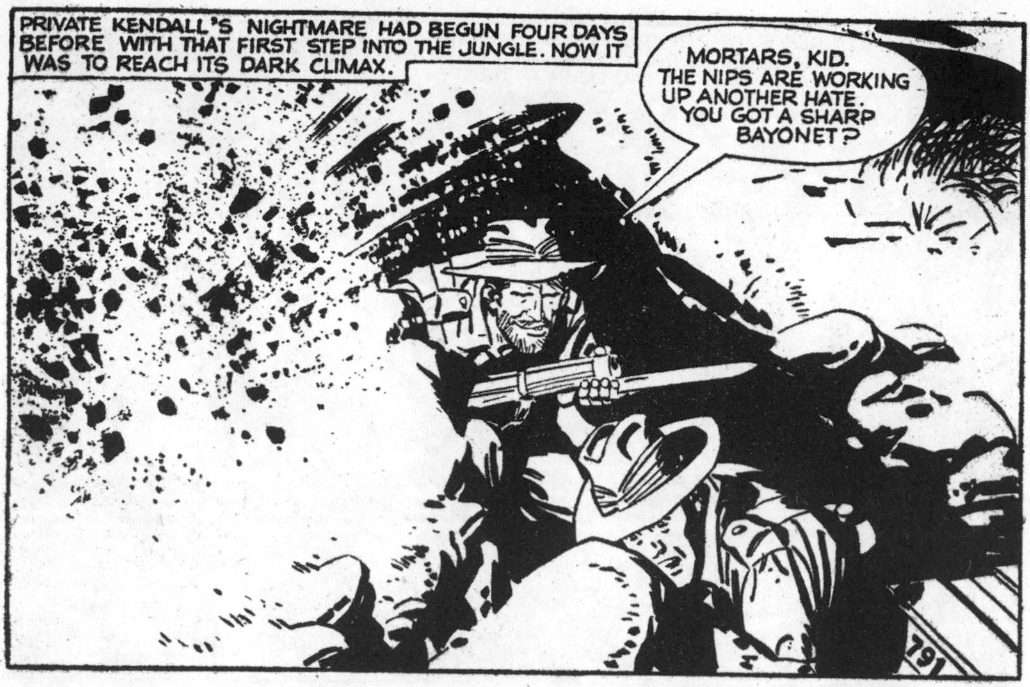
PRIVATE KENDALL'S NIGHTMARE HAD BEGUN FOUR DAYS BEFORE WITH THAT FIRST STEP INTO THE JUNGLE. NOW IT WAS TO REACH ITS DARK CLIMAX.
MORTARS, KID. THE NIPS ARE WORKING UP ANOTHER HATE. YOU GOT A SHARP BAYONET?
791

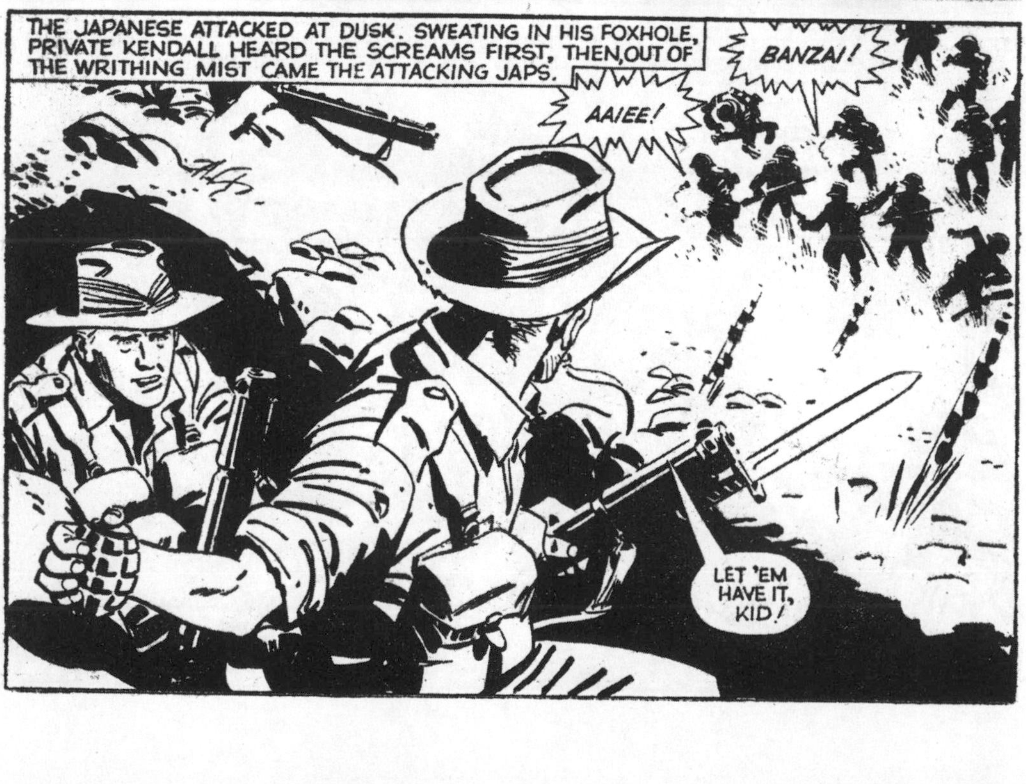
THE JAPANESE ATTACKED AT DUSK. SWEATING IN HIS FOXHOLE, PRIVATE KENDALL HEARD THE SCREAMS FIRST, THEN, OUT OF THE WRITHING MIST CAME THE ATTACKING JAPS.
BANZAI!
AAIEE!
LET 'EM HAVE IT, KID!

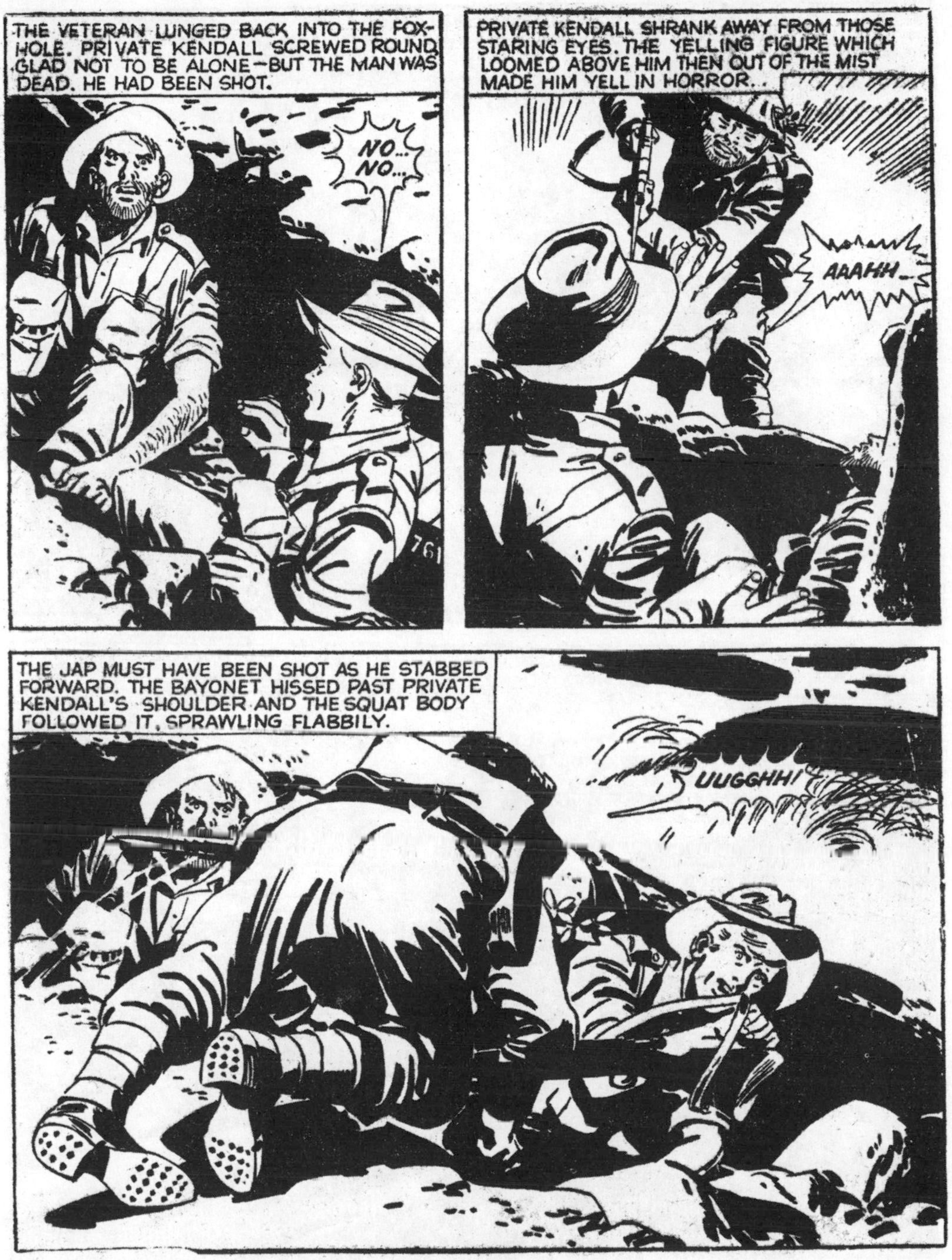
THE VETERAN LUNGED BACK INTO THE FOX-HOLE. PRIVATE KENDALL SCREWED ROUND, GLAD NOT TO BE ALONE—BUT THE MAN WAS DEAD. HE HAD BEEN SHOT.
NO... NO...
PRIVATE KENDALL SHRANK AWAY FROM THOSE STARING EYES. THE YELLING FIGURE WHICH LOOMED ABOVE HIM THEN OUT OF THE MIST MADE HIM YELL IN HORROR...
AAAHH...
THE JAP MUST HAVE BEEN SHOT AS HE STABBED FORWARD. THE BAYONET HISSED PAST PRIVATE KENDALL'S SHOULDER AND THE SQUAT BODY FOLLOWED IT, SPRAWLING FLABBILY.
UUGGHH!

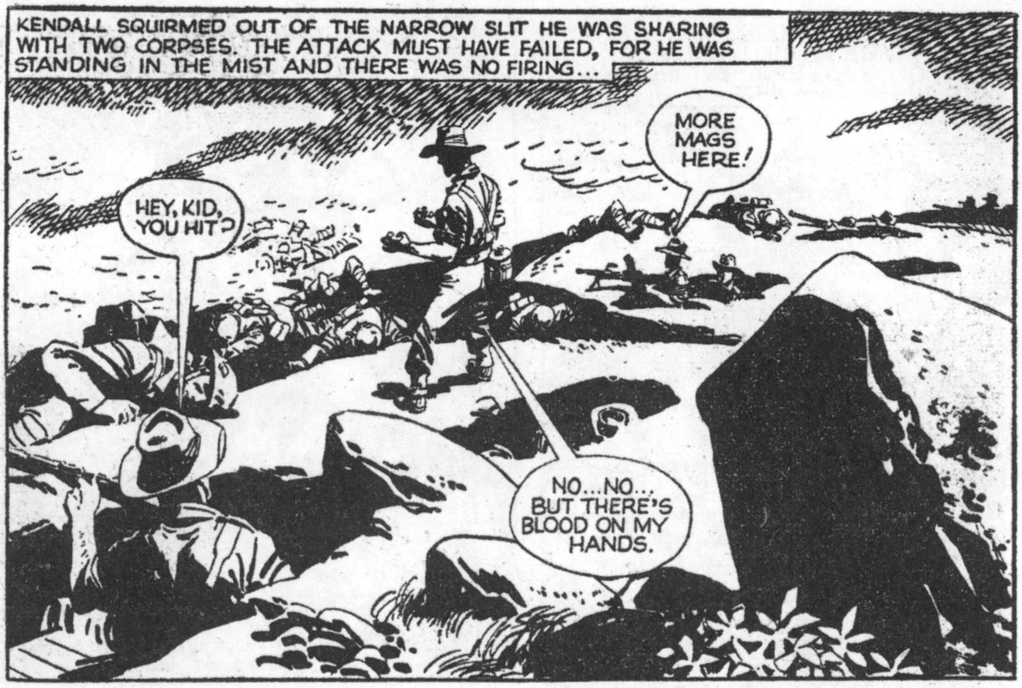
KENDALL SQUIRMED OUT OF THE NARROW SLIT HE WAS SHARING WITH TWO CORPSES. THE ATTACK MUST HAVE FAILED, FOR HE WAS STANDING IN THE MIST AND THERE WAS NO FIRING...
HEY, KID, YOU HIT?
MORE MAGS HERE!
NO...NO... BUT THERE'S BLOOD ON MY HANDS.

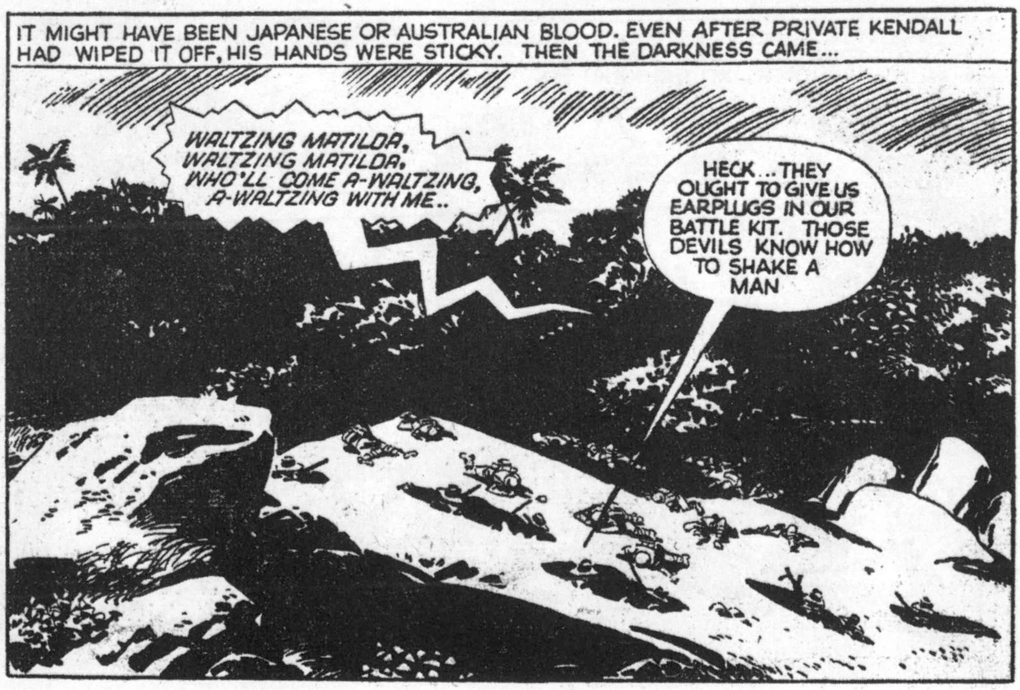
IT MIGHT HAVE BEEN JAPANESE OR AUSTRALIAN BLOOD. EVEN AFTER PRIVATE KENDALL HAD WIPED IT OFF, HIS HANDS WERE STICKY. THEN THE DARKNESS CAME...
WALTZING MATILDA, WALTZING MATILDA, WHO'LL COME A-WALTZING, A-WALTZING WITH ME..
HECK...THEY OUGHT TO GIVE US EARPLUGS IN OUR BATTLE KIT. THOSE DEVILS KNOW HOW TO SHAKE A MAN

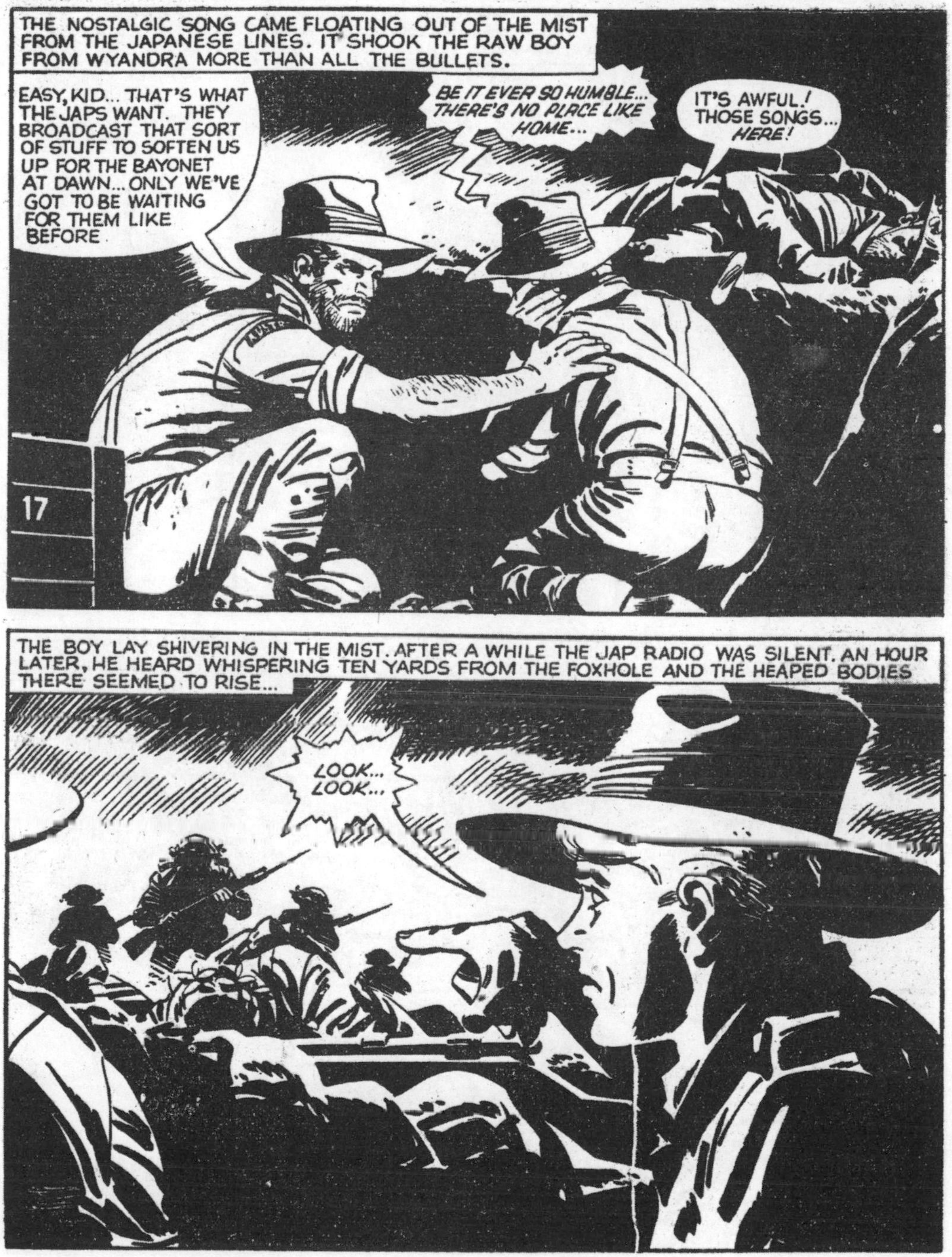
THE NOSTALGIC SONG CAME FLOATING OUT OF THE MIST FROM THE JAPANESE LINES. IT SHOOK THE RAW BOY FROM WYANDRA MORE THAN ALL THE BULLETS.
EASY, KID... THAT'S WHAT THE JAPS WANT. THEY BROADCAST THAT SORT OF STUFF TO SOFTEN US UP FOR THE BAYONET AT DAWN... ONLY WE'VE GOT TO BE WAITING FOR THEM LIKE BEFORE
BE IT EVER SO HUMBLE... THERE'S NO PLACE LIKE HOME...
IT'S AWFUL! THOSE SONGS... HERE!
17
THE BOY LAY SHIVERING IN THE MIST. AFTER A WHILE THE JAP RADIO WAS SILENT. AN HOUR LATER, HE HEARD WHISPERING TEN YARDS FROM THE FOXHOLE AND THE HEAPED BODIES THERE SEEMED TO RISE...
LOOK... LOOK...

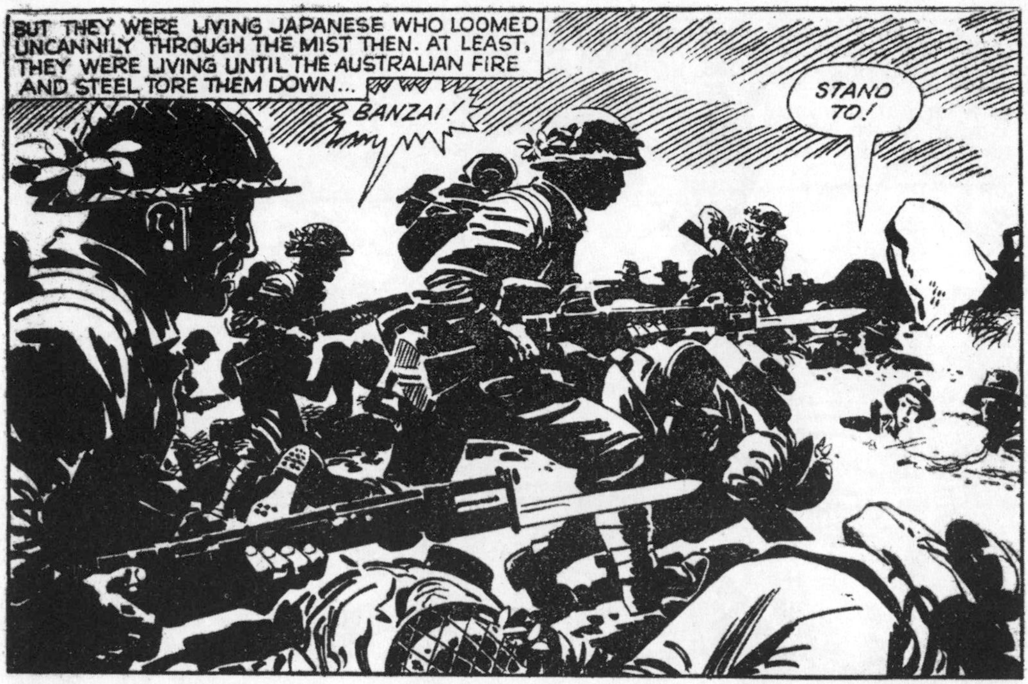
BUT THEY WERE LIVING JAPANESE WHO LOOMED UNCANNILY THROUGH THE MIST THEN. AT LEAST, THEY WERE LIVING UNTIL THE AUSTRALIAN FIRE AND STEEL TORE THEM DOWN...
BANZAI!
STAND TO!

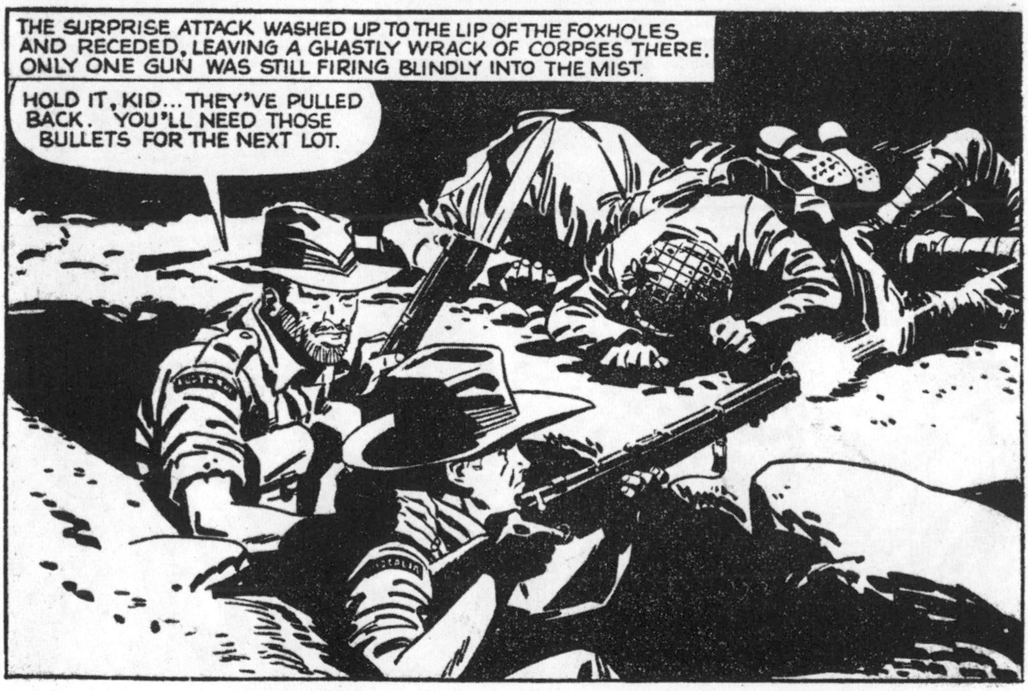
THE SURPRISE ATTACK WASHED UP TO THE LIP OF THE FOXHOLES AND RECEDED, LEAVING A GHASTLY WRACK OF CORPSES THERE. ONLY ONE GUN WAS STILL FIRING BLINDLY INTO THE MIST.
HOLD IT, KID... THEY'VE PULLED BACK. YOU'LL NEED THOSE BULLETS FOR THE NEXT LOT.

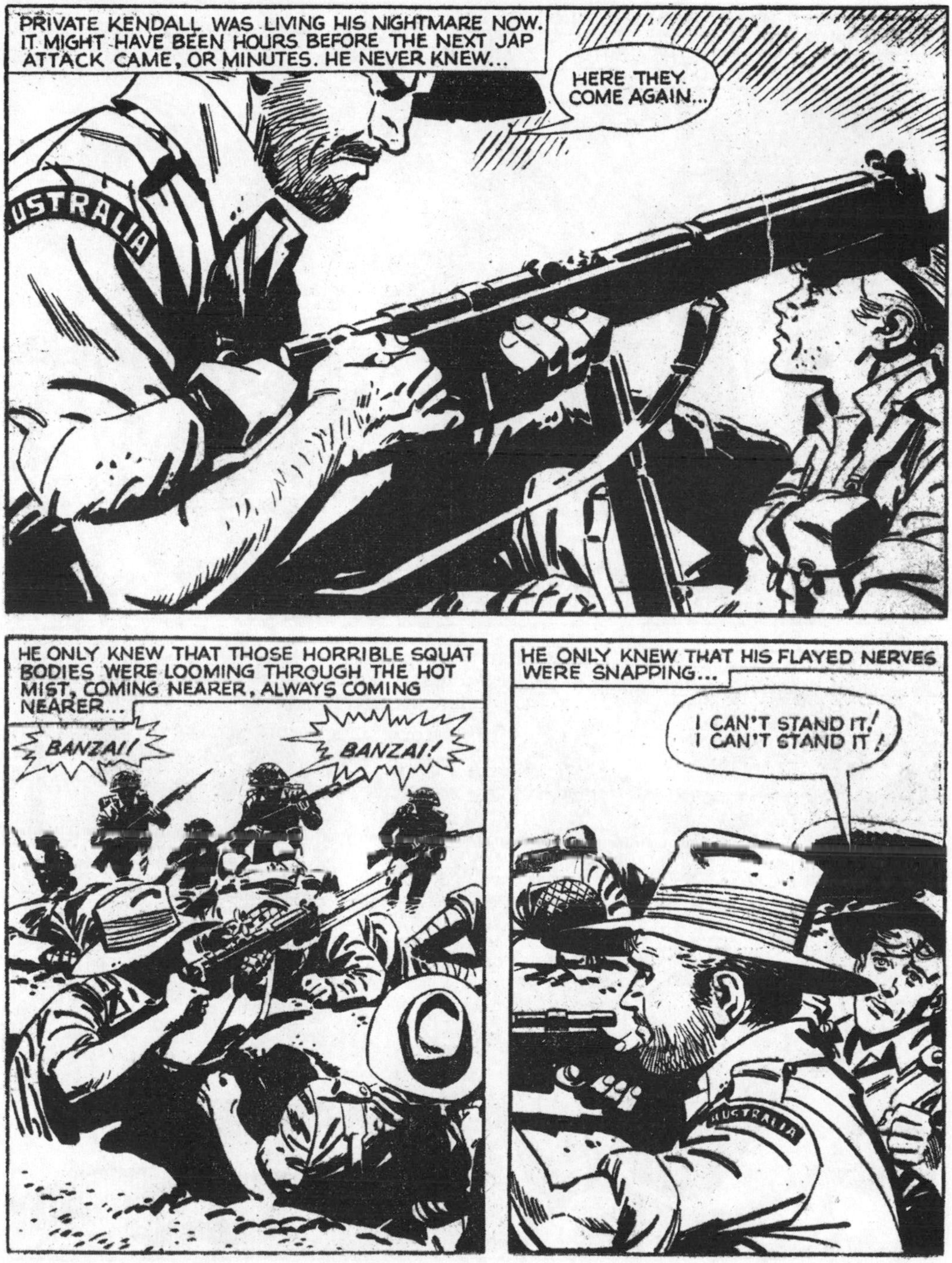
PRIVATE KENDALL WAS LIVING HIS NIGHTMARE NOW. IT MIGHT HAVE BEEN HOURS BEFORE THE NEXT JAP ATTACK CAME, OR MINUTES. HE NEVER KNEW...
HERE THEY COME AGAIN...
AUSTRALIA
HE ONLY KNEW THAT THOSE HORRIBLE SQUAT BODIES WERE LOOMING THROUGH THE HOT MIST, COMING NEARER, ALWAYS COMING NEARER...
BANZAI!
BANZAI!
HE ONLY KNEW THAT HIS FLAYED NERVES WERE SNAPPING...
I CAN'T STAND IT! I CAN'T STAND IT!
AUSTRALIA

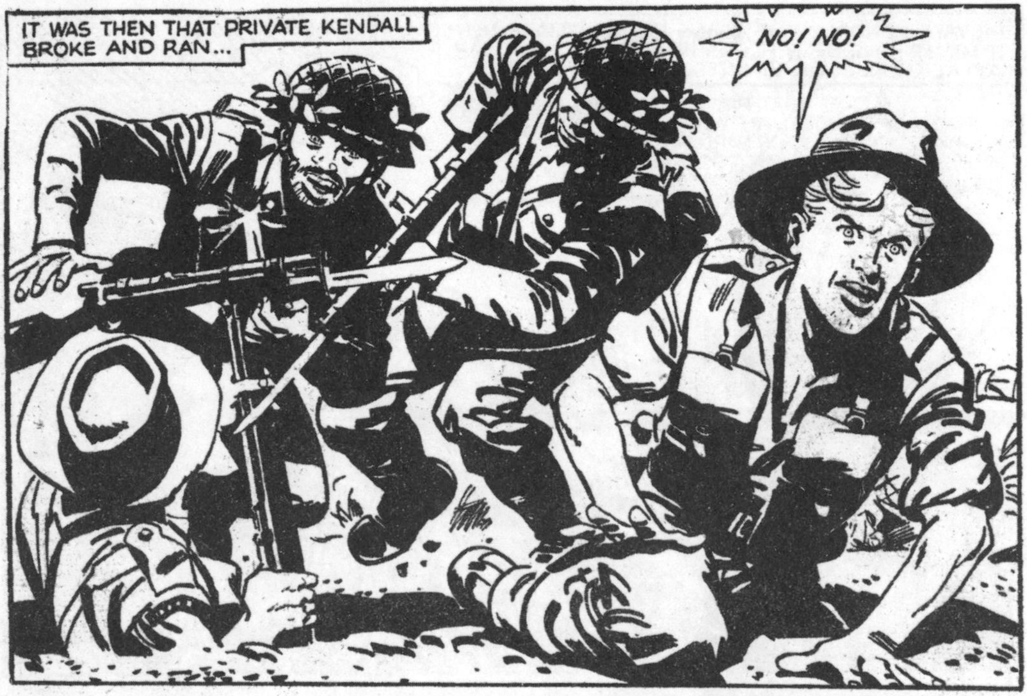
IT WAS THEN THAT PRIVATE KENDALL BROKE AND RAN...
NO! NO!

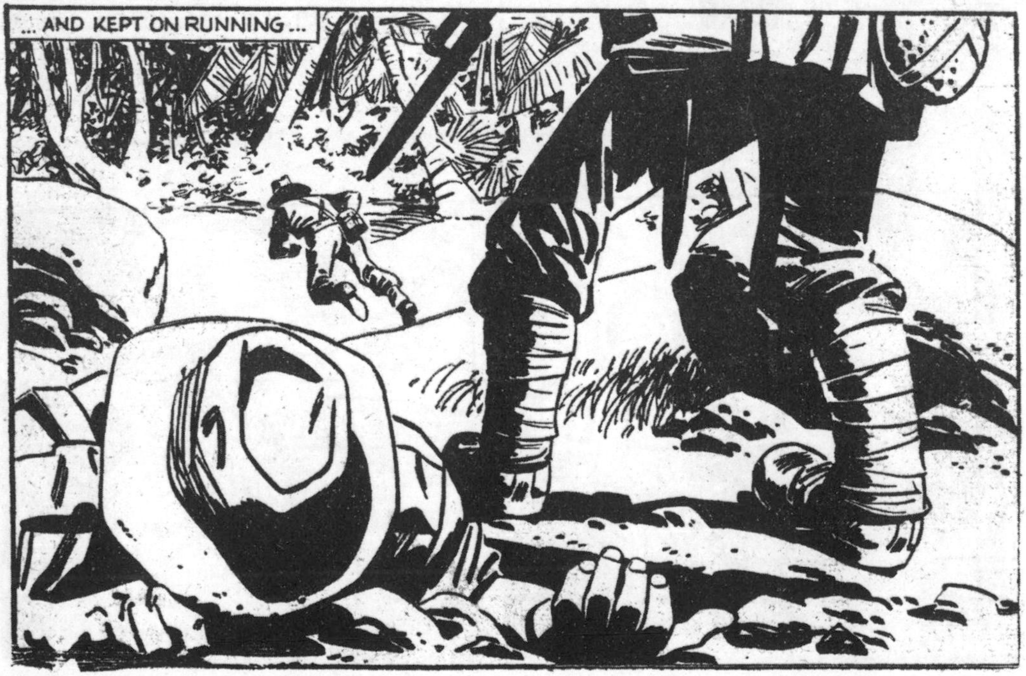
... AND KEPT ON RUNNING ...

Chapter 2. Trek

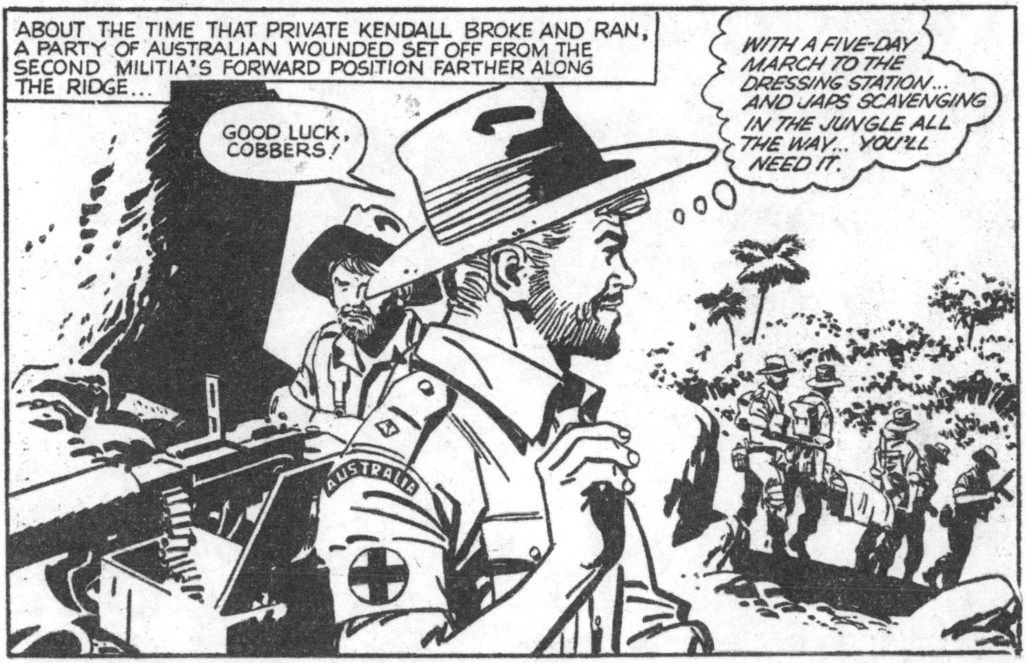
ABOUT THE TIME THAT PRIVATE KENDALL BROKE AND RAN, A PARTY OF AUSTRALIAN WOUNDED SET OFF FROM THE SECOND MILITIA'S FORWARD POSITION FARTHER ALONG THE RIDGE...
GOOD LUCK, COBBERS!
WITH A FIVE-DAY MARCH TO THE DRESSING STATION... AND JAPS SCAVENGING IN THE JUNGLE ALL THE WAY... YOU'LL NEED IT.
AUSTRALIA

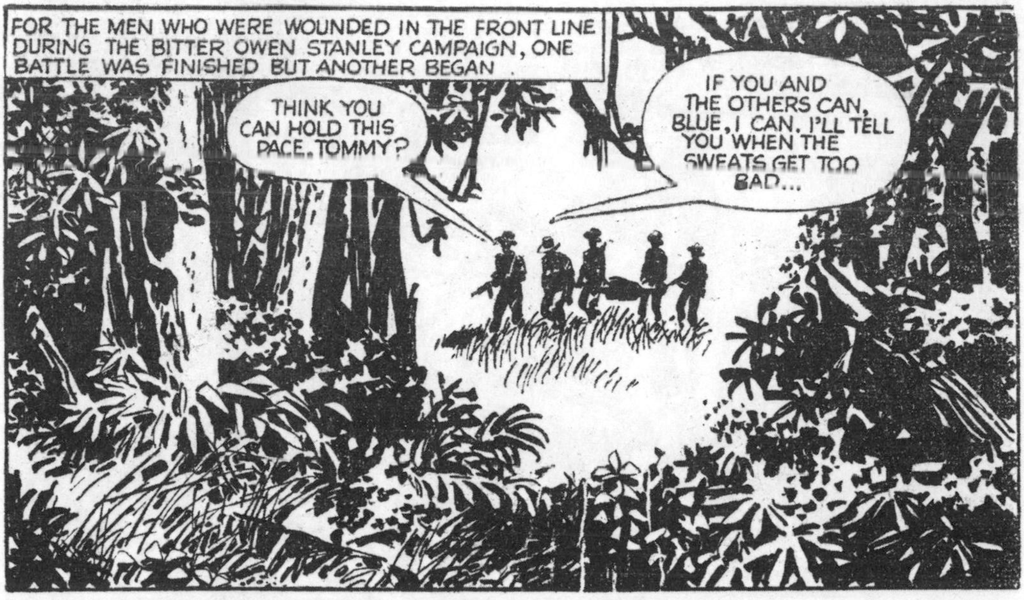
FOR THE MEN WHO WERE WOUNDED IN THE FRONT LINE DURING THE BITTER OWEN STANLEY CAMPAIGN, ONE BATTLE WAS FINISHED BUT ANOTHER BEGAN
THINK YOU CAN HOLD THIS PACE, TOMMY?
IF YOU AND THE OTHERS CAN, BLUE, I CAN. I'LL TELL YOU WHEN THE SWEATS GET TOO BAD...

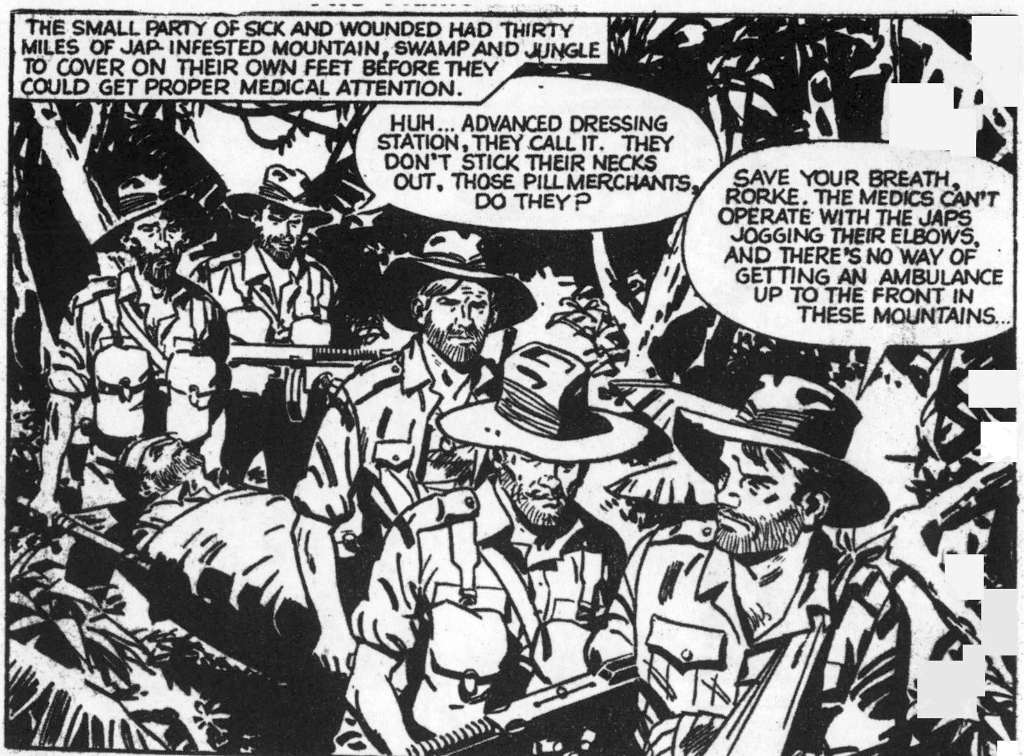
THE SMALL PARTY OF SICK AND WOUNDED HAD THIRTY MILES OF JAP-INFESTED MOUNTAIN, SWAMP AND JUNGLE TO COVER ON THEIR OWN FEET BEFORE THEY COULD GET PROPER MEDICAL ATTENTION.
HUH... ADVANCED DRESSING STATION, THEY CALL IT. THEY DON'T STICK THEIR NECKS OUT, THOSE PILL MERCHANTS, DO THEY?
SAVE YOUR BREATH, RORKE. THE MEDICS CAN'T OPERATE WITH THE JAPS JOGGING THEIR ELBOWS, AND THERE'S NO WAY OF GETTING AN AMBULANCE UP TO THE FRONT IN THESE MOUNTAINS...

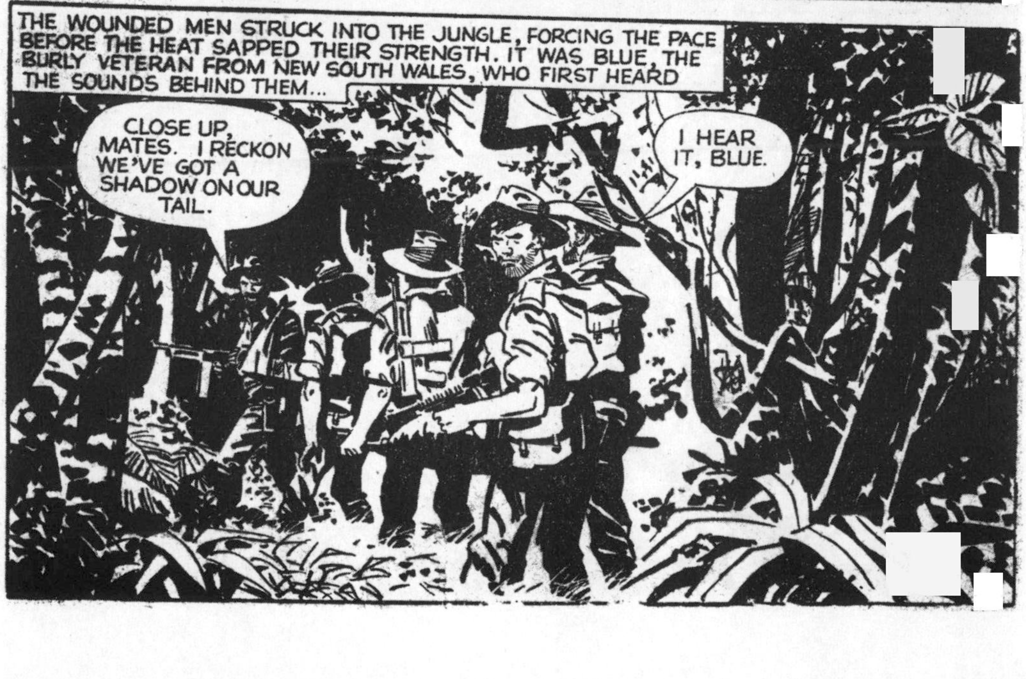
THE WOUNDED MEN STRUCK INTO THE JUNGLE, FORCING THE PACE BEFORE THE HEAT SAPPED THEIR STRENGTH. IT WAS BLUE, THE BURLY VETERAN FROM NEW SOUTH WALES, WHO FIRST HEARD THE SOUNDS BEHIND THEM...
CLOSE UP, MATES. I RECKON WE'VE GOT A SHADOW ON OUR TAIL.
I HEAR IT, BLUE.

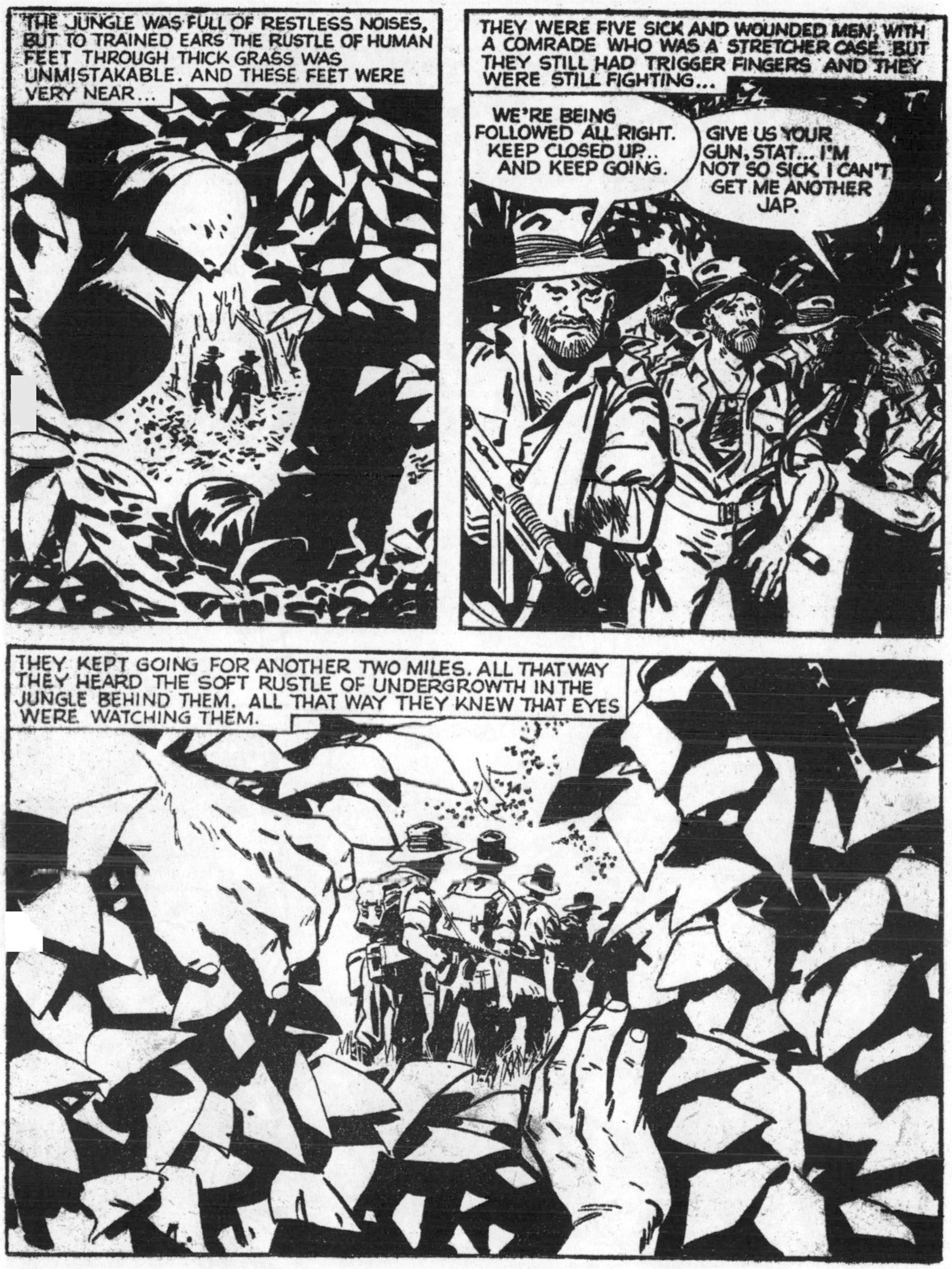
THE JUNGLE WAS FULL OF RESTLESS NOISES, BUT TO TRAINED EARS THE RUSTLE OF HUMAN FEET THROUGH THICK GRASS WAS UNMISTAKABLE. AND THESE FEET WERE VERY NEAR...
THEY WERE FIVE SICK AND WOUNDED MEN, WITH A COMRADE WHO WAS A STRETCHER CASE. BUT THEY STILL HAD TRIGGER FINGERS AND THEY WERE STILL FIGHTING...
WE'RE BEING FOLLOWED ALL RIGHT. KEEP CLOSED UP.. AND KEEP GOING.
GIVE US YOUR GUN, STAT... I'M NOT SO SICK I CAN'T GET ME ANOTHER JAP.
THEY KEPT GOING FOR ANOTHER TWO MILES. ALL THAT WAY THEY HEARD THE SOFT RUSTLE OF UNDERGROWTH IN THE JUNGLE BEHIND THEM. ALL THAT WAY THEY KNEW THAT EYES WERE WATCHING THEM.

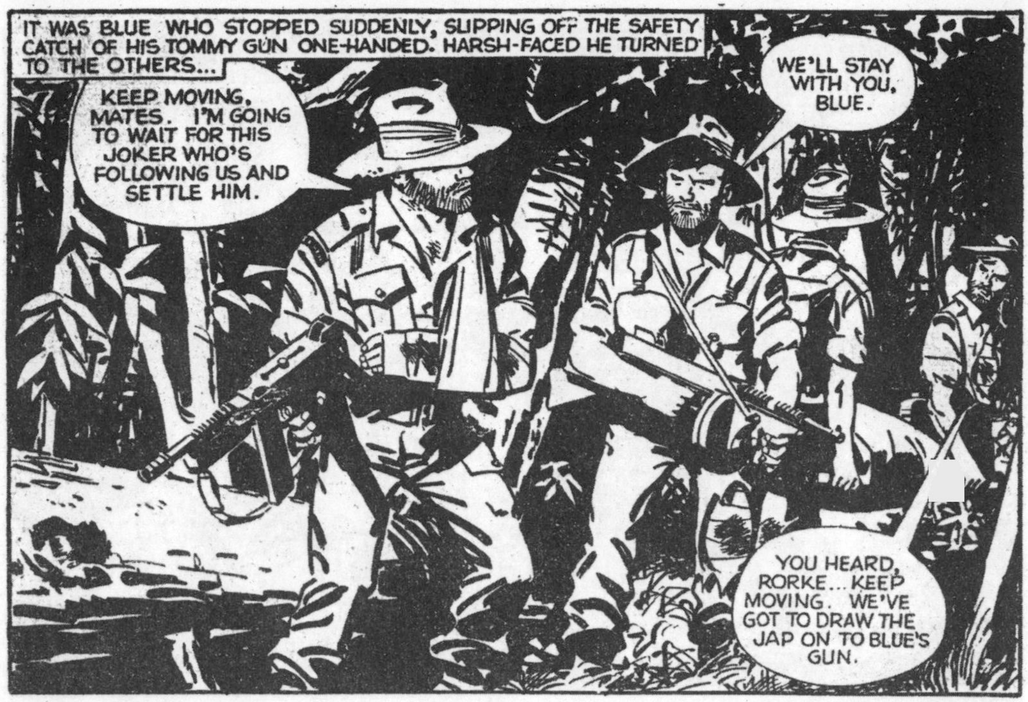
IT WAS BLUE WHO STOPPED SUDDENLY, SLIPPING OFF THE SAFETY CATCH OF HIS TOMMY GUN ONE-HANDED. HARSH-FACED HE TURNED TO THE OTHERS...
KEEP MOVING, MATES. I'M GOING TO WAIT FOR THIS JOKER WHO'S FOLLOWING US AND SETTLE HIM.
WE'LL STAY WITH YOU, BLUE.
YOU HEARD, RORKE... KEEP MOVING. WE'VE GOT TO DRAW THE JAP ON TO BLUE'S GUN.

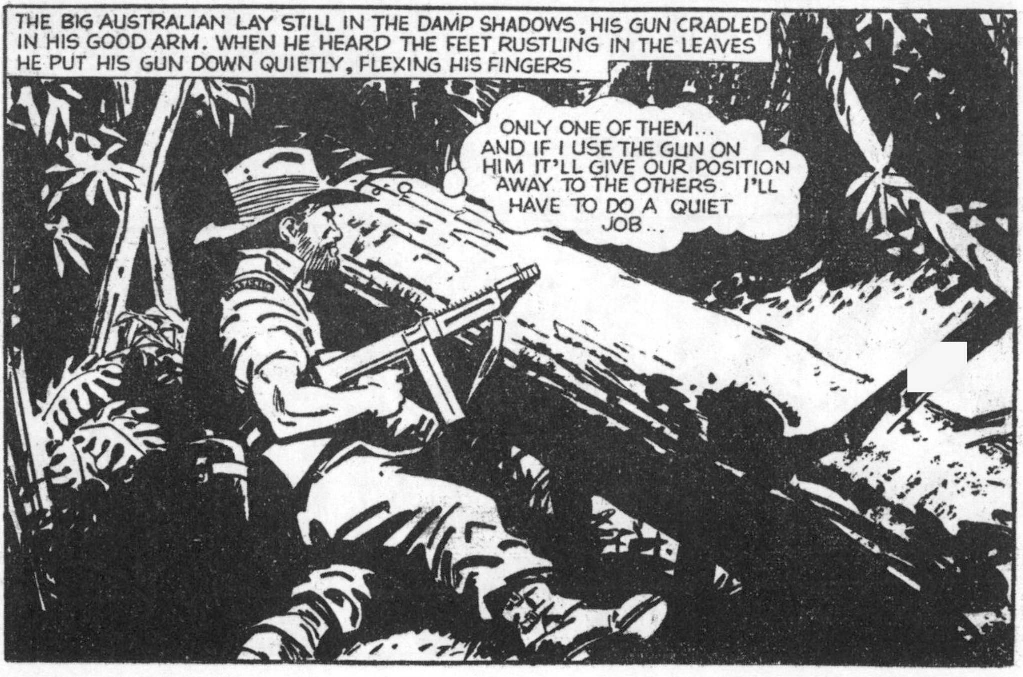
THE BIG AUSTRALIAN LAY STILL IN THE DAMP SHADOWS, HIS GUN CRADLED IN HIS GOOD ARM. WHEN HE HEARD THE FEET RUSTLING IN THE LEAVES HE PUT HIS GUN DOWN QUIETLY, FLEXING HIS FINGERS.
ONLY ONE OF THEM... AND IF I USE THE GUN ON HIM IT'LL GIVE OUR POSITION AWAY TO THE OTHERS. I'LL HAVE TO DO A QUIET JOB...

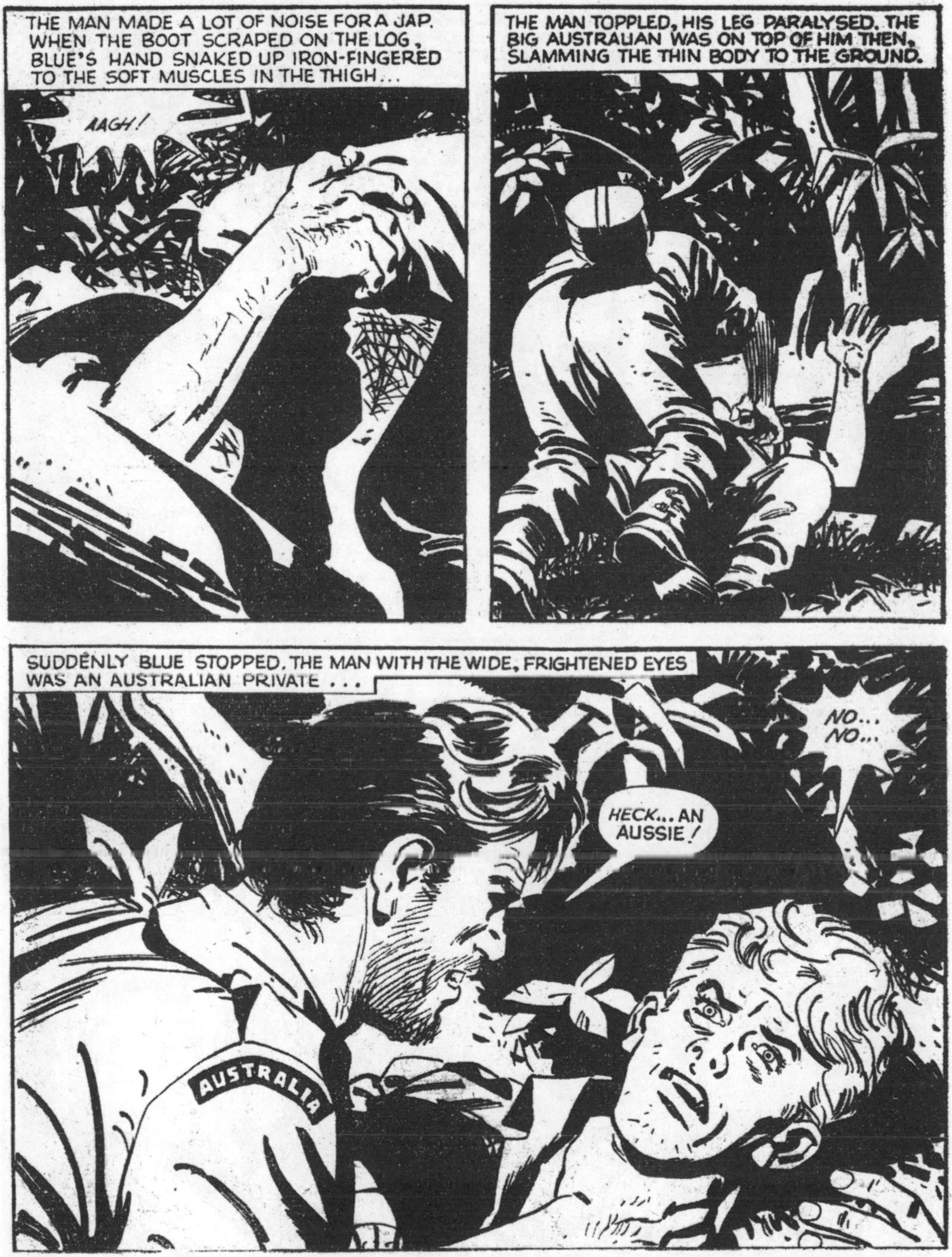
THE MAN MADE A LOT OF NOISE FOR A JAP. WHEN THE BOOT SCRAPED ON THE LOG, BLUE'S HAND SNAKED UP IRON-FINGERED TO THE SOFT MUSCLES IN THE THIGH...
AAGH!
THE MAN TOPPLED, HIS LEG PARALYSED. THE BIG AUSTRALIAN WAS ON TOP OF HIM THEN, SLAMMING THE THIN BODY TO THE GROUND.
SUDDENLY BLUE STOPPED. THE MAN WITH THE WIDE, FRIGHTENED EYES WAS AN AUSTRALIAN PRIVATE ...
NO... NO...
HECK... AN AUSSIE!
AUSTRALIA

YOUNG KENDALL HAD BEEN RUNNING IN PANIC THROUGH THE JUNGLE WHEN HE HAD STUMBLED ACROSS THE PARTY OF AUSTRALIAN WOUNDED TWO HOURS BEFORE AND FOLLOWED THEM. THE PANIC WAS EBBING NOW. SHAME WAS TAKING ITS PLACE...
YOU PLAYED THAT KIND OF TRICKY, KID.
YEAH... WHY SIT ON OUR TAIL LIKE THAT...
I .. I WAS SCARED TO JOIN UP WITH YOU. . BUT I WAS ALONE .. LOST. I HAD TO KEEP NEAR YOU
IT WAS THE OLDER MAN, THE ONE WITH THE SICK FACE, WHO KNELT BESIDE THE BOY. HE HAD WASHED-OUT BLUE EYES, LIKE THE SKY AT WYANDRA AFTER RAIN.
YOU'RE NOT WOUNDED, KID?
NO... I.. I GOT CUT OFF FROM MY UNIT. THE JAPS WERE ATTACKING US. THEY KEPT ON COMING. THEY KEPT ON. IT WAS HORRIBLE.

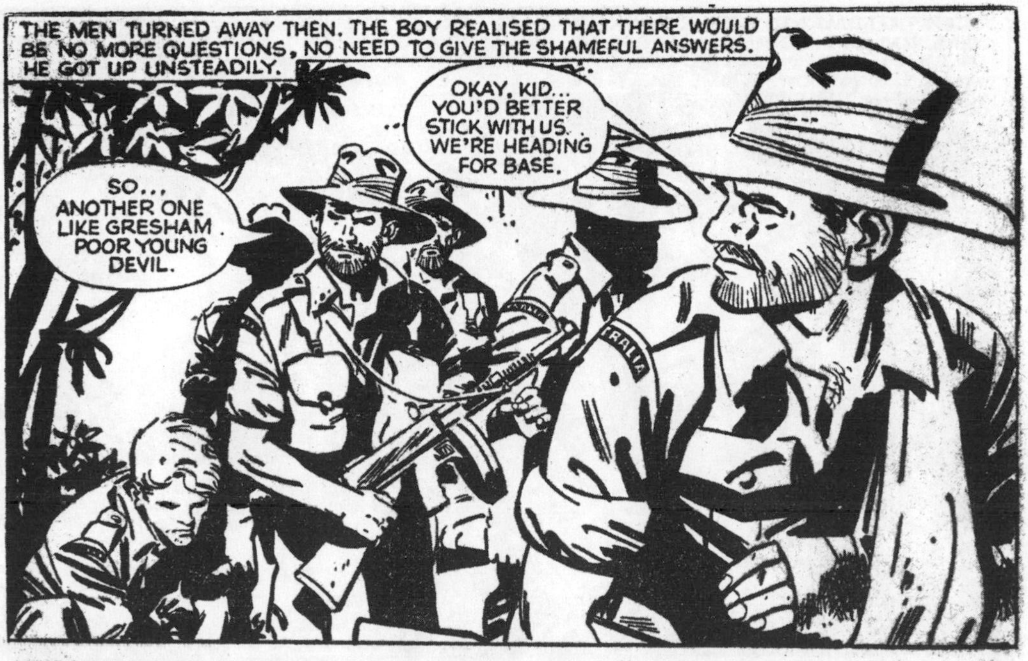
THE MEN TURNED AWAY THEN. THE BOY REALISED THAT THERE WOULD BE NO MORE QUESTIONS, NO NEED TO GIVE THE SHAMEFUL ANSWERS. HE GOT UP UNSTEADILY.
SO... ANOTHER ONE LIKE GRESHAM POOR YOUNG DEVIL.
OKAY, KID... YOU'D BETTER STICK WITH US. WE'RE HEADING FOR BASE.

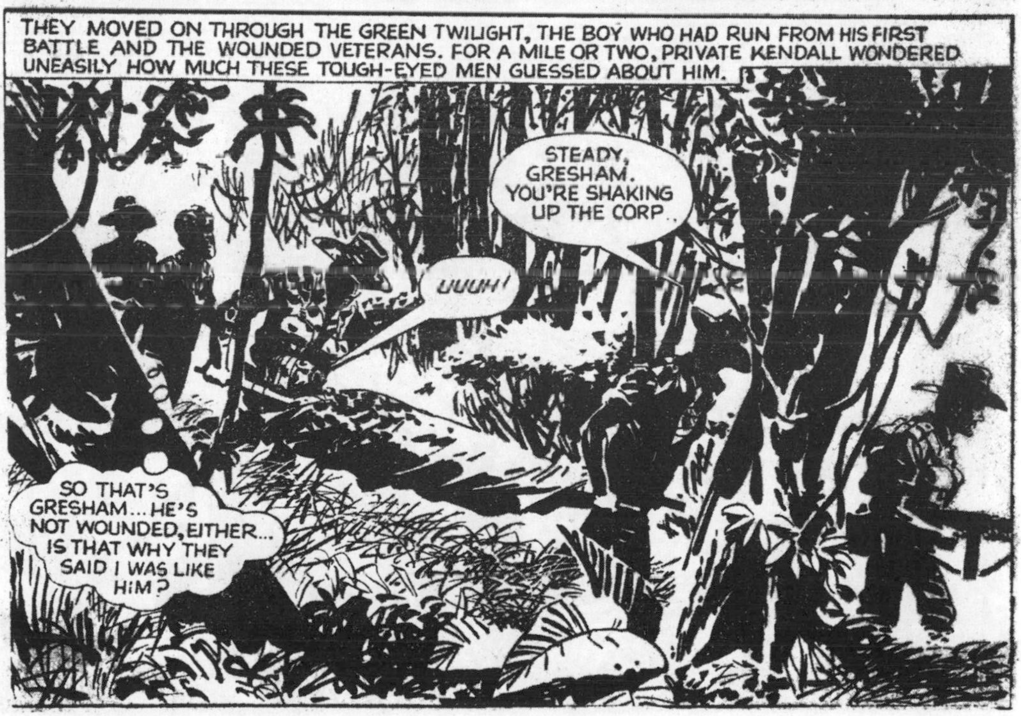
THEY MOVED ON THROUGH THE GREEN TWILIGHT, THE BOY WHO HAD RUN FROM HIS FIRST BATTLE AND THE WOUNDED VETERANS. FOR A MILE OR TWO, PRIVATE KENDALL WONDERED UNEASILY HOW MUCH THESE TOUGH-EYED MEN GUESSED ABOUT HIM.
STEADY, GRESHAM. YOU'RE SHAKING UP THE CORP.
UUUH!
SO THAT'S GRESHAM... HE'S NOT WOUNDED, EITHER... IS THAT WHY THEY SAID I WAS LIKE HIM?

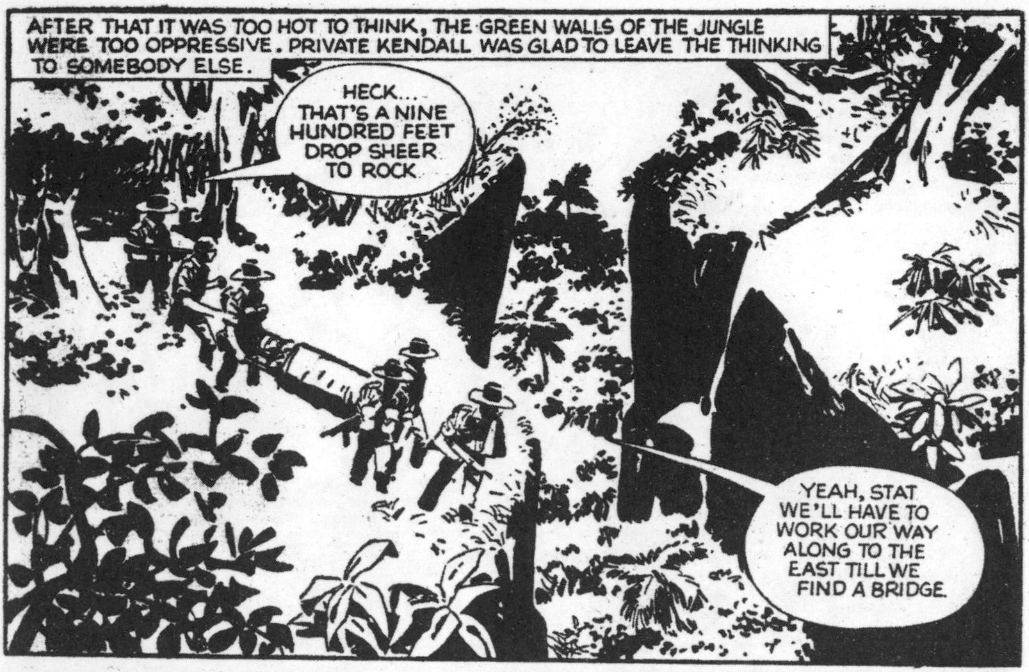
AFTER THAT IT WAS TOO HOT TO THINK, THE GREEN WALLS OF THE JUNGLE WERE TOO OPPRESSIVE. PRIVATE KENDALL WAS GLAD TO LEAVE THE THINKING TO SOMEBODY ELSE.
HECK... THAT'S A NINE HUNDRED FEET DROP SHEER TO ROCK.
YEAH, STAT WE'LL HAVE TO WORK OUR WAY ALONG TO THE EAST TILL WE FIND A BRIDGE.

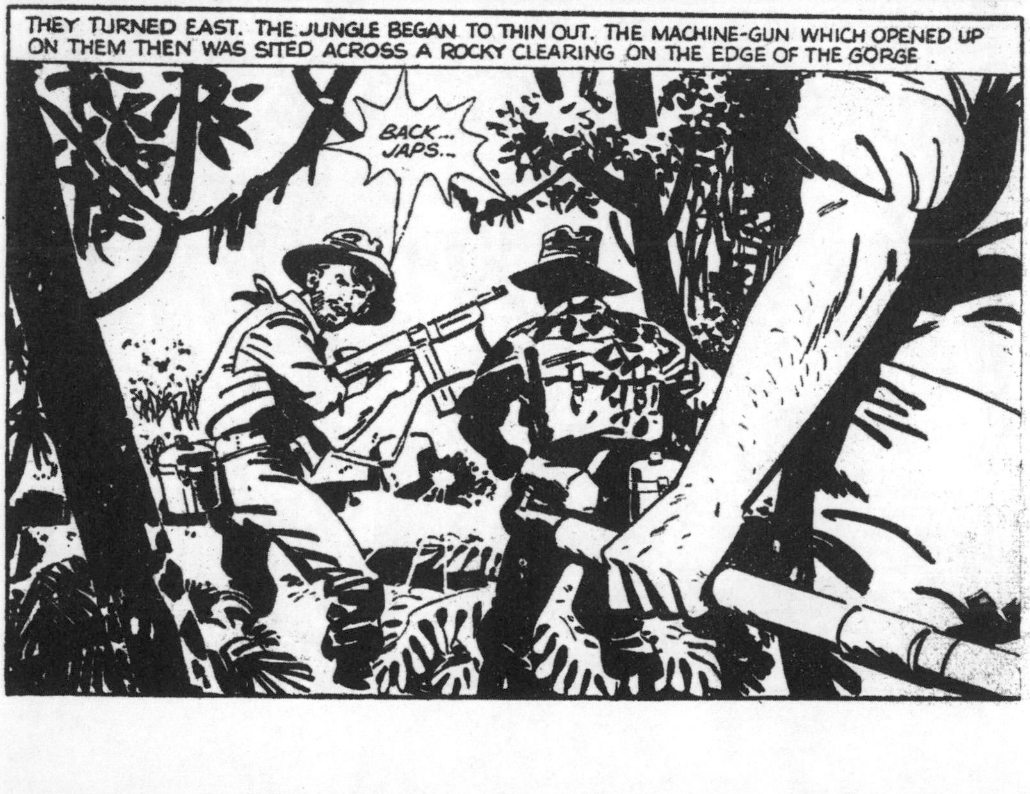
THEY TURNED EAST. THE JUNGLE BEGAN TO THIN OUT. THE MACHINE-GUN WHICH OPENED UP ON THEM THEN WAS SITED ACROSS A ROCKY CLEARING ON THE EDGE OF THE GORGE.
BACK... JAPS...

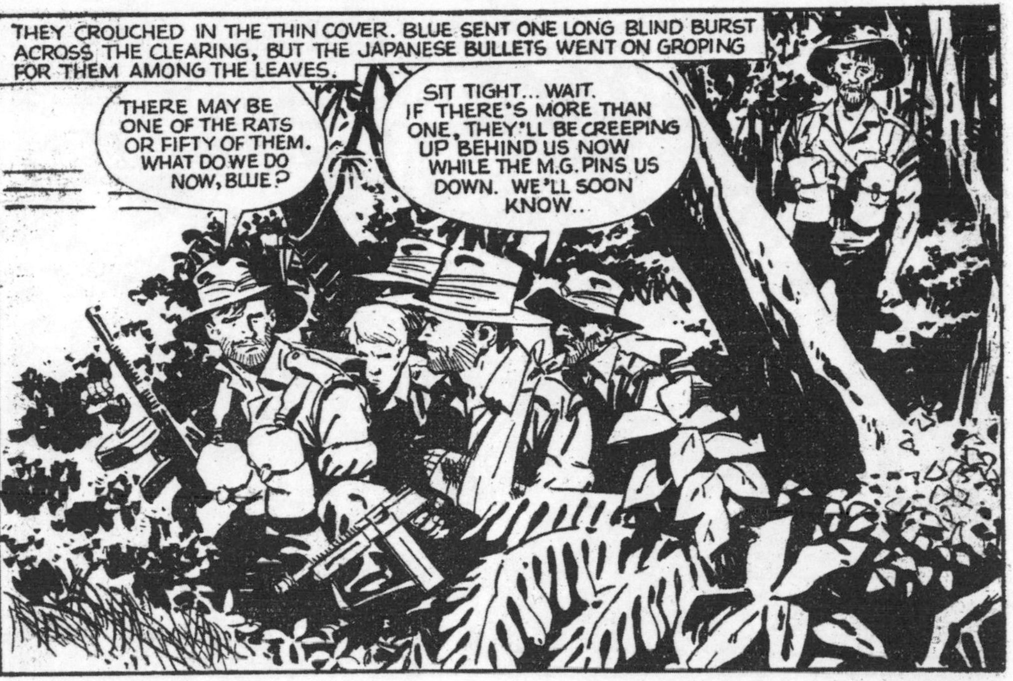
THEY CROUCHED IN THE THIN COVER. BLUE SENT ONE LONG BLIND BURST ACROSS THE CLEARING, BUT THE JAPANESE BULLETS WENT ON GROPING FOR THEM AMONG THE LEAVES.
THERE MAY BE ONE OF THE RATS OR FIFTY OF THEM. WHAT DO WE DO NOW, BLUE?
SIT TIGHT... WAIT. IF THERE'S MORE THAN ONE, THEY'LL BE CREEPING UP BEHIND US NOW WHILE THE M.G. PINS US DOWN. WE'LL SOON KNOW...

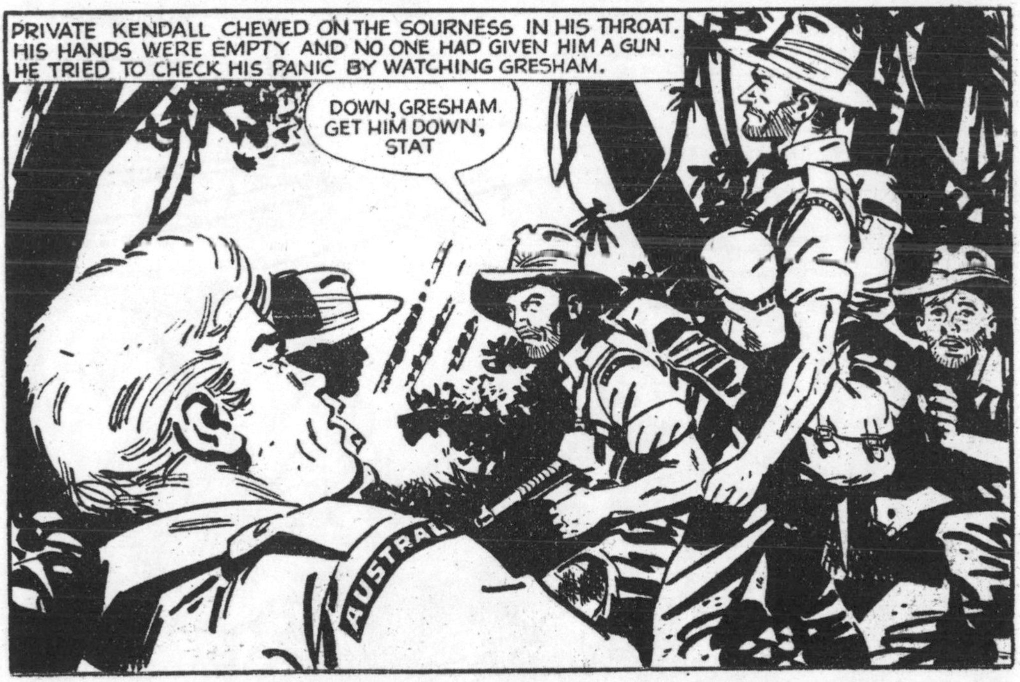
PRIVATE KENDALL CHEWED ON THE SOURNESS IN HIS THROAT. HIS HANDS WERE EMPTY AND NO ONE HAD GIVEN HIM A GUN. HE TRIED TO CHECK HIS PANIC BY WATCHING GRESHAM.
DOWN, GRESHAM. GET HIM DOWN, STAT

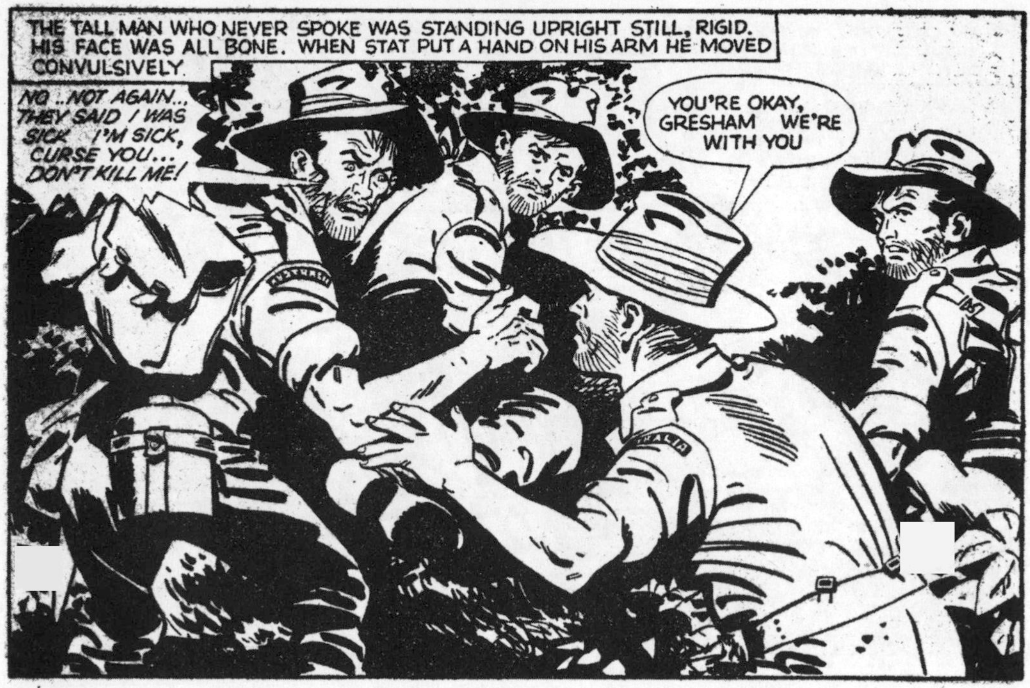
THE TALL MAN WHO NEVER SPOKE WAS STANDING UPRIGHT STILL, RIGID. HIS FACE WAS ALL BONE. WHEN STAT PUT A HAND ON HIS ARM HE MOVED CONVULSIVELY.
NO ..NOT AGAIN... THEY SAID I WAS SICK I'M SICK, CURSE YOU... DON'T KILL ME!
YOU'RE OKAY, GRESHAM WE'RE WITH YOU

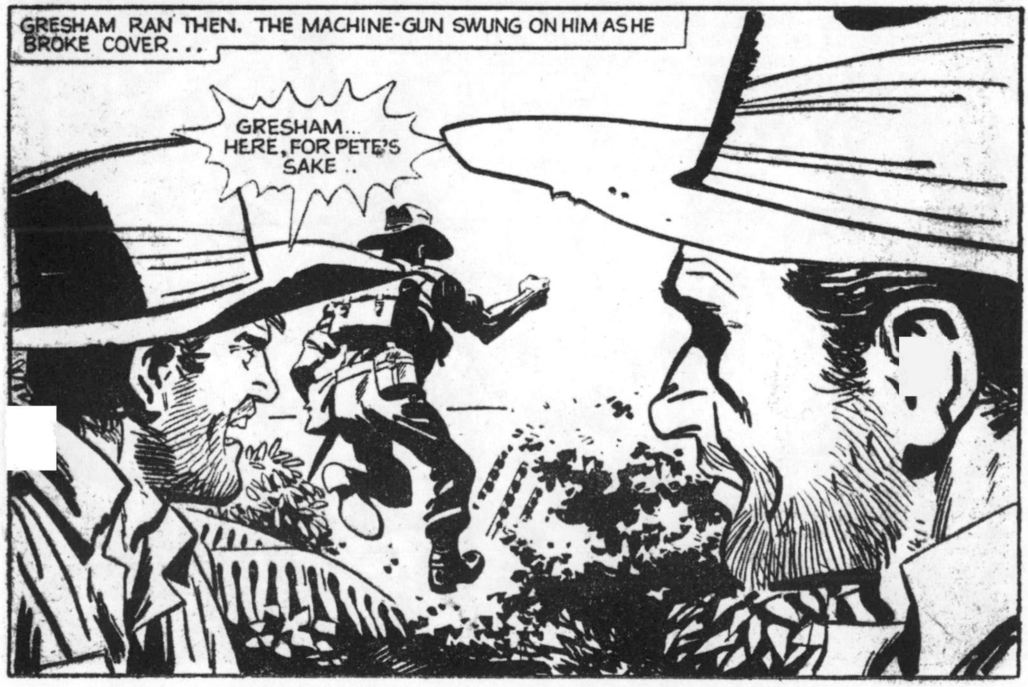
GRESHAM RAN THEN. THE MACHINE-GUN SWUNG ON HIM AS HE BROKE COVER...
GRESHAM... HERE, FOR PETE'S SAKE ..

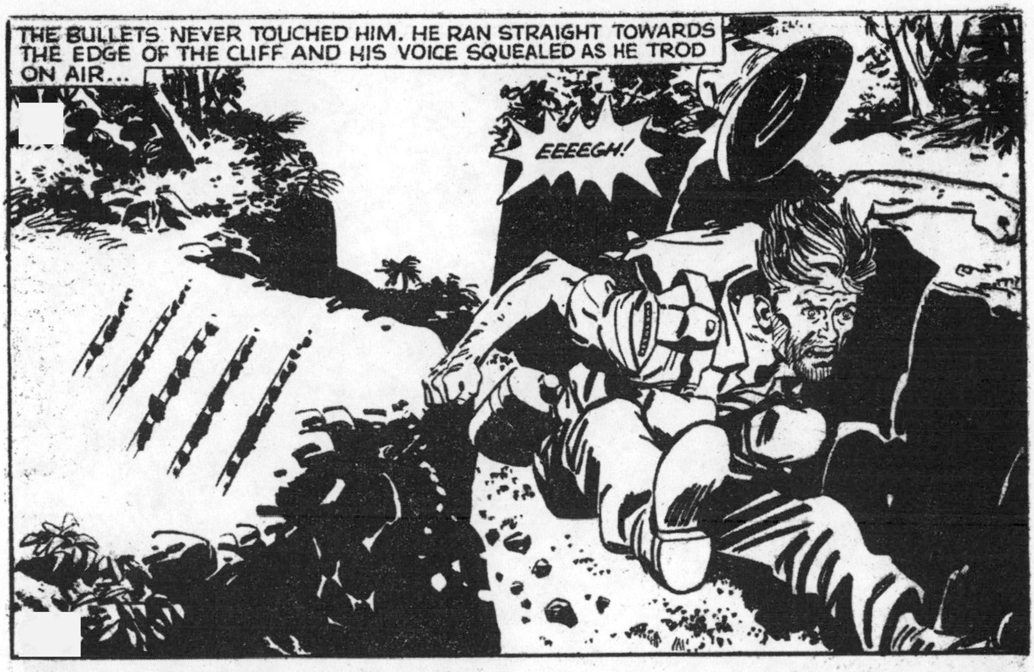
THE BULLETS NEVER TOUCHED HIM. HE RAN STRAIGHT TOWARDS THE EDGE OF THE CLIFF AND HIS VOICE SQUEALED AS HE TROD ON AIR...
EEEEGH!

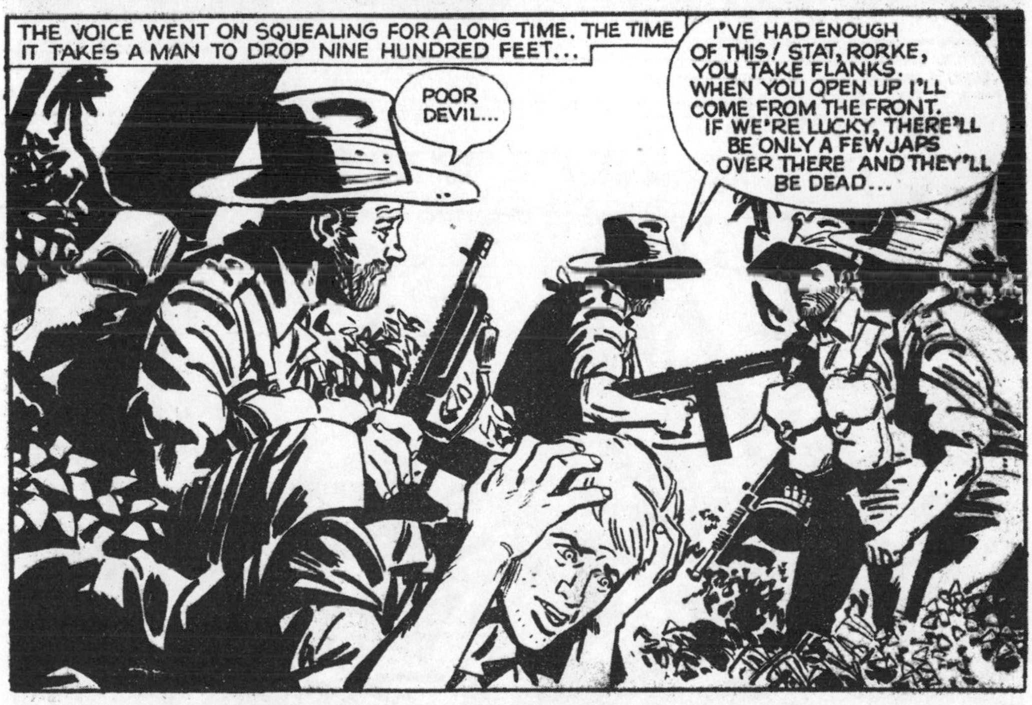
THE VOICE WENT ON SQUEALING FOR A LONG TIME. THE TIME IT TAKES A MAN TO DROP NINE HUNDRED FEET...
POOR DEVIL...
I'VE HAD ENOUGH OF THIS! STAT, RORKE, YOU TAKE FLANKS. WHEN YOU OPEN UP I'LL COME FROM THE FRONT. IF WE'RE LUCKY, THERE'LL BE ONLY A FEW JAPS OVER THERE AND THEY'LL BE DEAD...

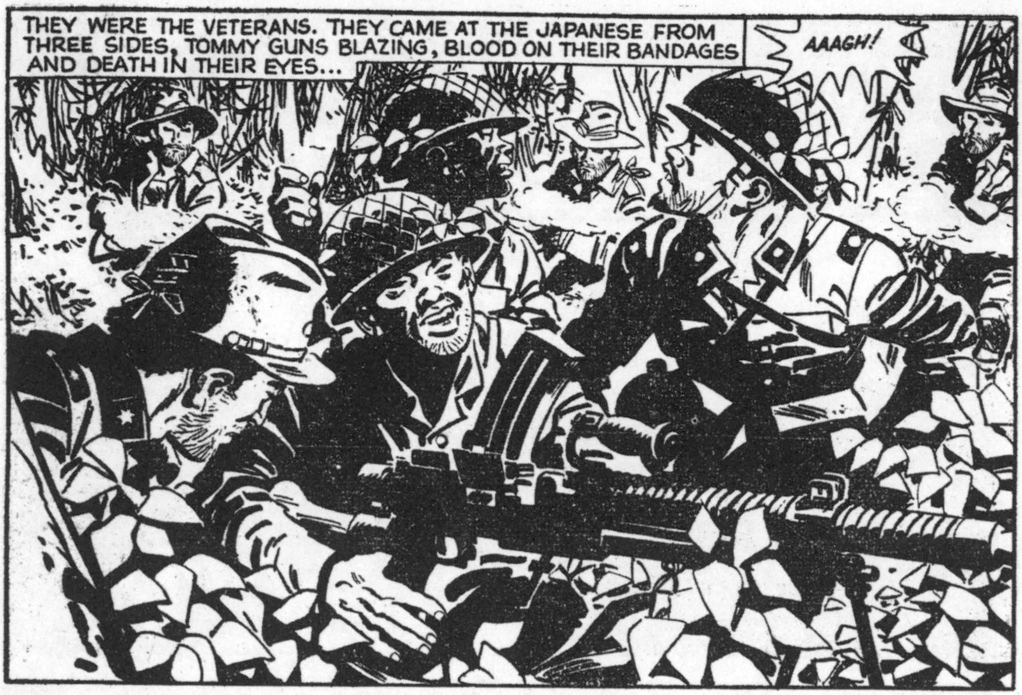
THEY WERE THE VETERANS. THEY CAME AT THE JAPANESE FROM THREE SIDES, TOMMY GUNS BLAZING, BLOOD ON THEIR BANDAGES AND DEATH IN THEIR EYES...
AAAGH!

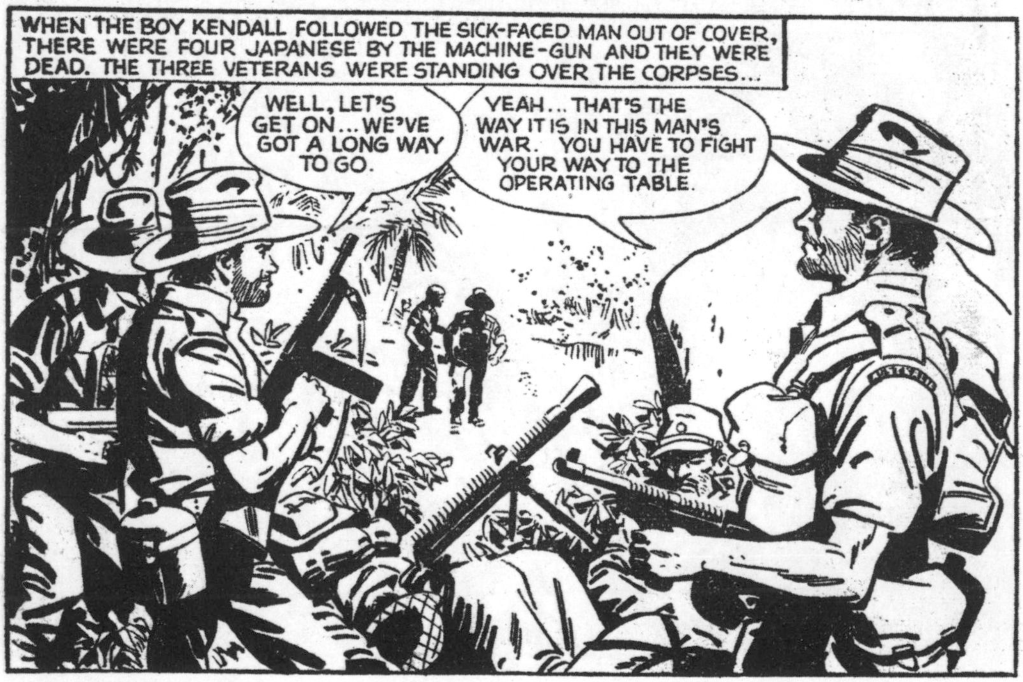
WHEN THE BOY KENDALL FOLLOWED THE SICK-FACED MAN OUT OF COVER, THERE WERE FOUR JAPANESE BY THE MACHINE-GUN AND THEY WERE DEAD. THE THREE VETERANS WERE STANDING OVER THE CORPSES...
WELL, LET'S GET ON... WE'VE GOT A LONG WAY TO GO.
YEAH... THAT'S THE WAY IT IS IN THIS MAN'S WAR. YOU HAVE TO FIGHT YOUR WAY TO THE OPERATING TABLE.

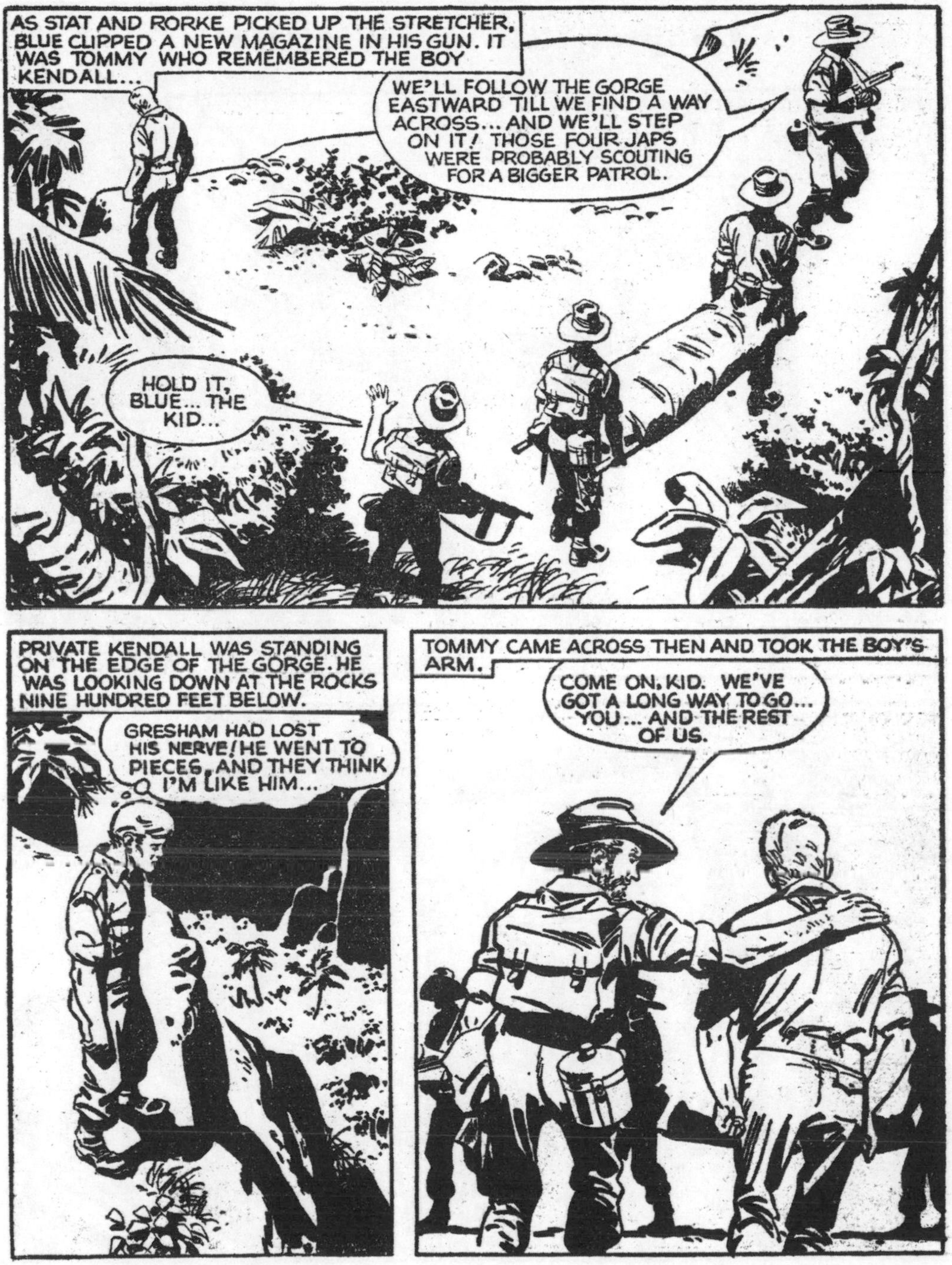
AS STAT AND RORKE PICKED UP THE STRETCHER, BLUE CLIPPED A NEW MAGAZINE IN HIS GUN. IT WAS TOMMY WHO REMEMBERED THE BOY KENDALL...
WE'LL FOLLOW THE GORGE EASTWARD TILL WE FIND A WAY ACROSS... AND WE'LL STEP ON IT! THOSE FOUR JAPS WERE PROBABLY SCOUTING FOR A BIGGER PATROL.
HOLD IT, BLUE... THE KID...
PRIVATE KENDALL WAS STANDING ON THE EDGE OF THE GORGE. HE WAS LOOKING DOWN AT THE ROCKS NINE HUNDRED FEET BELOW.
GRESHAM HAD LOST HIS NERVE! HE WENT TO PIECES, AND THEY THINK I'M LIKE HIM...
TOMMY CAME ACROSS THEN AND TOOK THE BOY'S ARM.
COME ON, KID. WE'VE GOT A LONG WAY TO GO... YOU... AND THE REST OF US.

Chapter 3. Anger

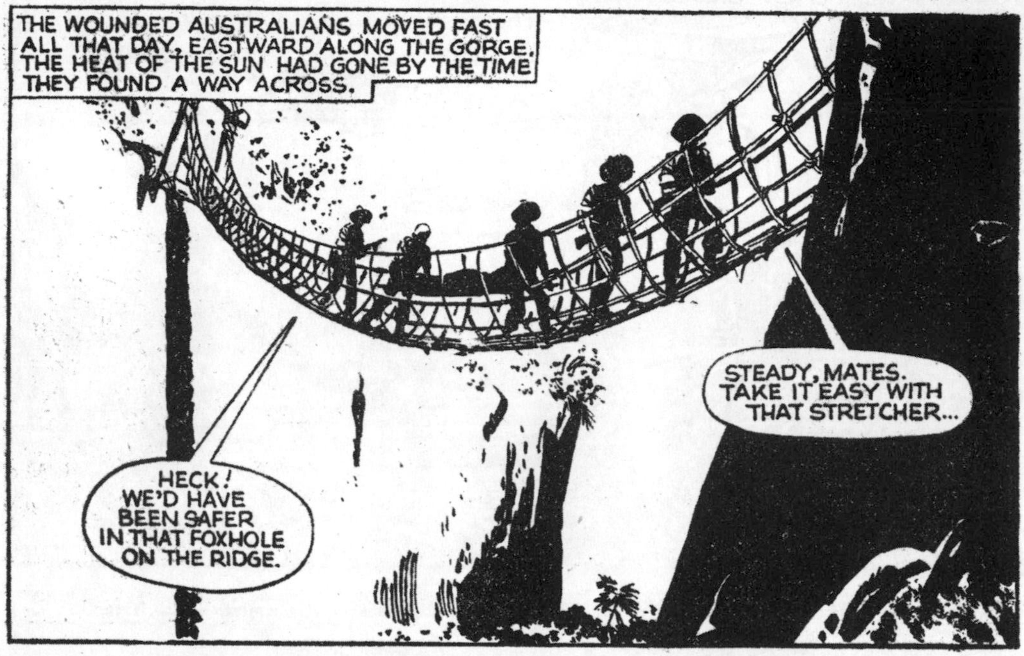
THE WOUNDED AUSTRALIANS MOVED FAST ALL THAT DAY, EASTWARD ALONG THE GORGE. THE HEAT OF THE SUN HAD GONE BY THE TIME THEY FOUND A WAY ACROSS.
HECK! WE'D HAVE BEEN SAFER IN THAT FOXHOLE ON THE RIDGE.
STEADY, MATES. TAKE IT EASY WITH THAT STRETCHER...

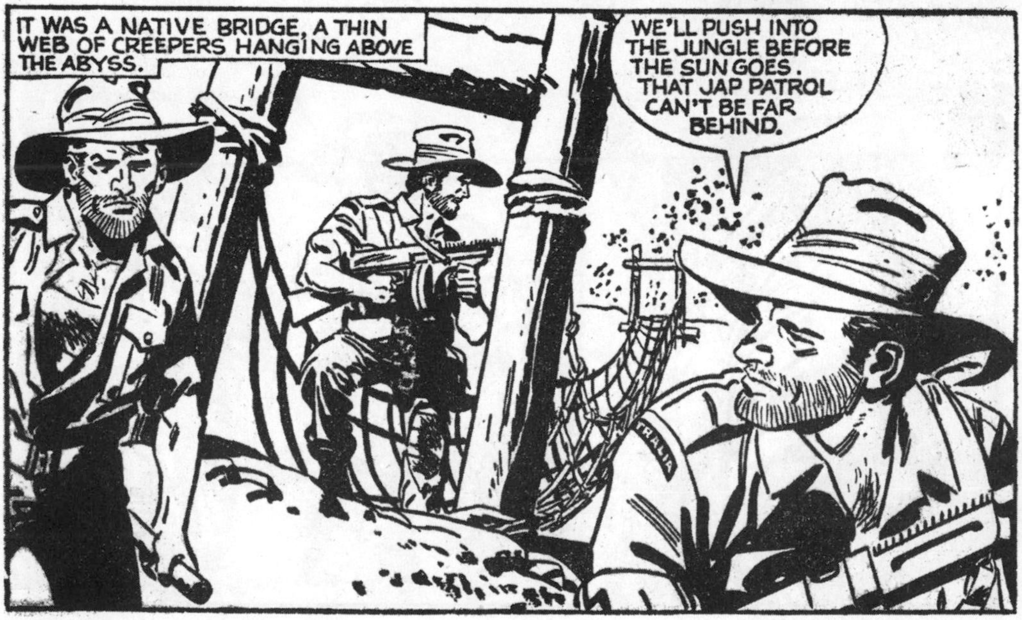
IT WAS A NATIVE BRIDGE, A THIN WEB OF CREEPERS HANGING ABOVE THE ABYSS.
WE'LL PUSH INTO THE JUNGLE BEFORE THE SUN GOES. THAT JAP PATROL CAN'T BE FAR BEHIND.

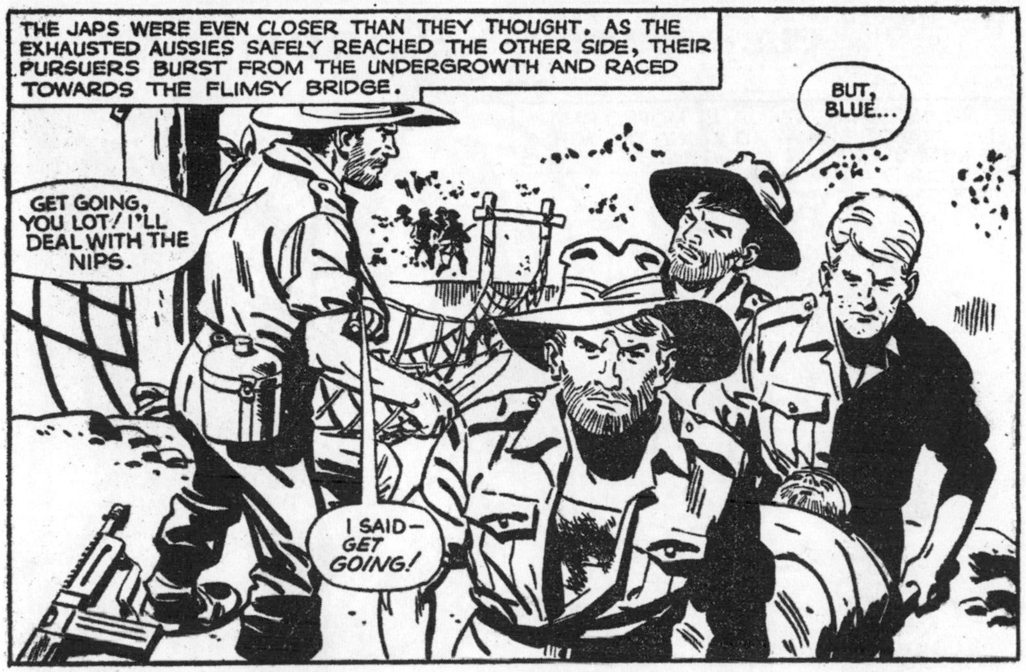
THE JAPS WERE EVEN CLOSER THAN THEY THOUGHT. AS THE EXHAUSTED AUSSIES SAFELY REACHED THE OTHER SIDE, THEIR PURSUERS BURST FROM THE UNDERGROWTH AND RACED TOWARDS THE FLIMSY BRIDGE.
GET GOING, YOU LOT! I'LL DEAL WITH THE NIPS.
BUT, BLUE...
I SAID— GET GOING!

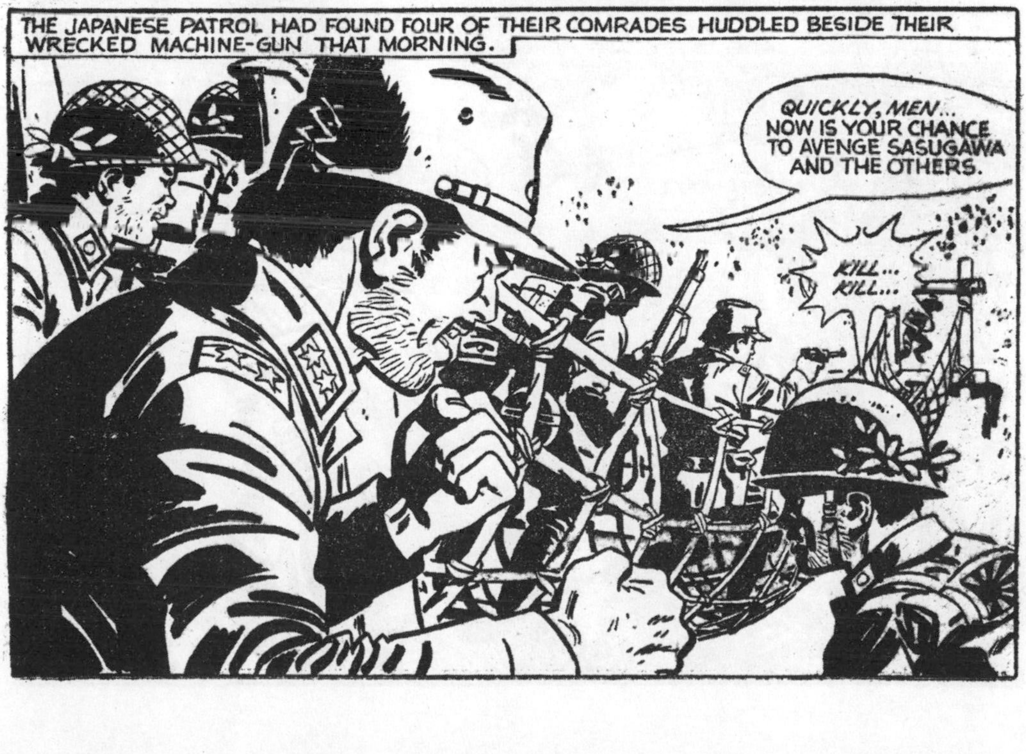
THE JAPANESE PATROL HAD FOUND FOUR OF THEIR COMRADES HUDDLED BESIDE THEIR WRECKED MACHINE-GUN THAT MORNING.
QUICKLY, MEN... NOW IS YOUR CHANCE TO AVENGE SASUGAWA AND THE OTHERS.
KILL... KILL...

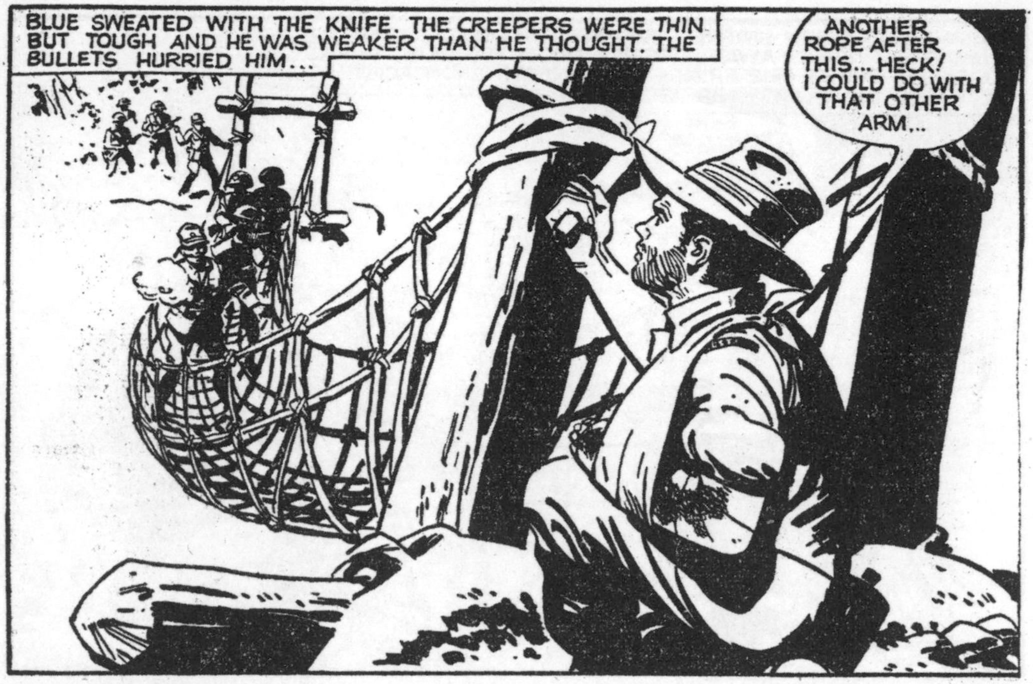
BLUE SWEATED WITH THE KNIFE. THE CREEPERS WERE THIN BUT TOUGH AND HE WAS WEAKER THAN HE THOUGHT. THE BULLETS HURRIED HIM...
ANOTHER ROPE AFTER THIS... HECK! I COULD DO WITH THAT OTHER ARM...

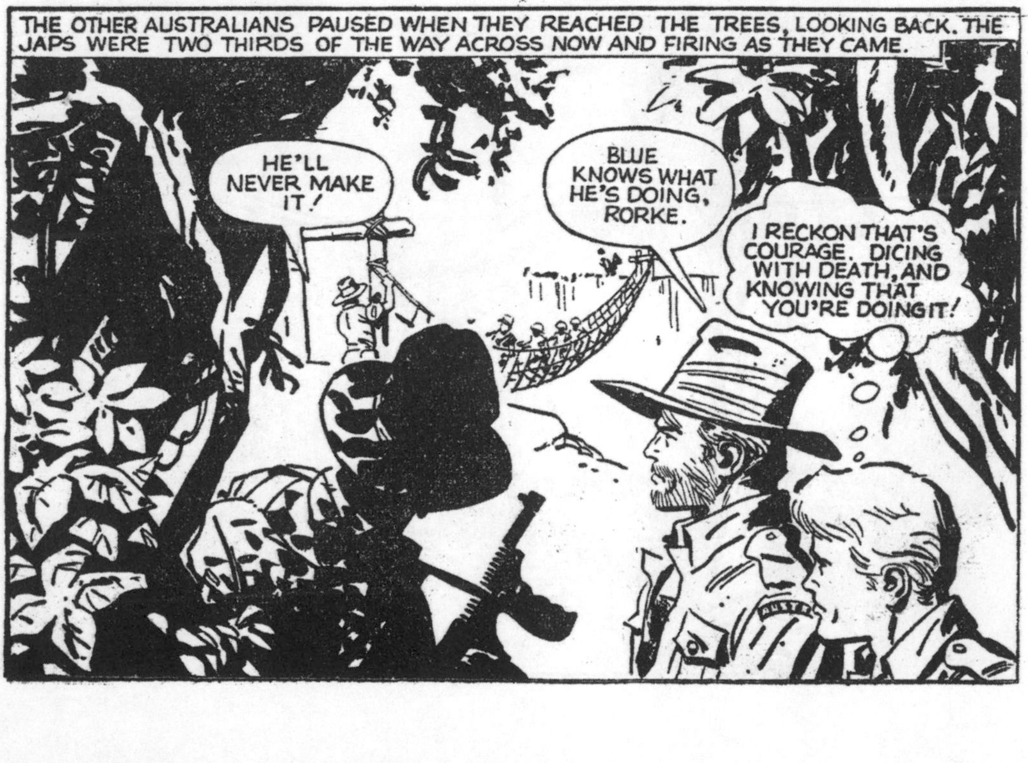
THE OTHER AUSTRALIANS PAUSED WHEN THEY REACHED THE TREES, LOOKING BACK. THE JAPS WERE TWO THIRDS OF THE WAY ACROSS NOW AND FIRING AS THEY CAME.
HE'LL NEVER MAKE IT!
BLUE KNOWS WHAT HE'S DOING, RORKE.
I RECKON THAT'S COURAGE. DICING WITH DEATH, AND KNOWING THAT YOU'RE DOING IT!

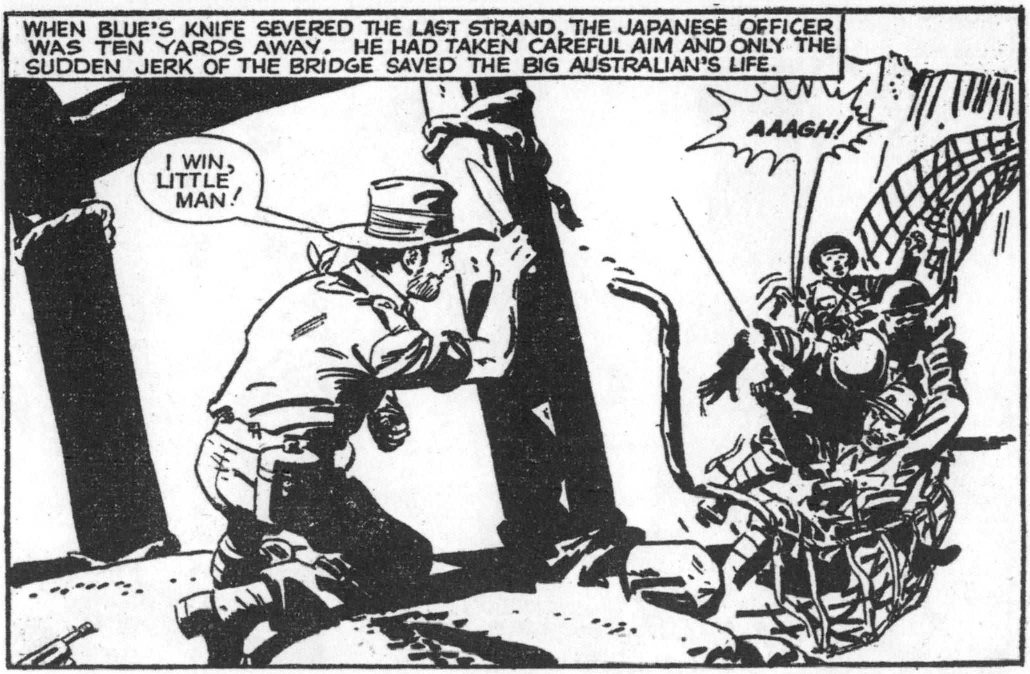
WHEN BLUE'S KNIFE SEVERED THE LAST STRAND, THE JAPANESE OFFICER WAS TEN YARDS AWAY. HE HAD TAKEN CAREFUL AIM AND ONLY THE SUDDEN JERK OF THE BRIDGE SAVED THE BIG AUSTRALIAN'S LIFE.
I WIN, LITTLE MAN!
AAAGH!

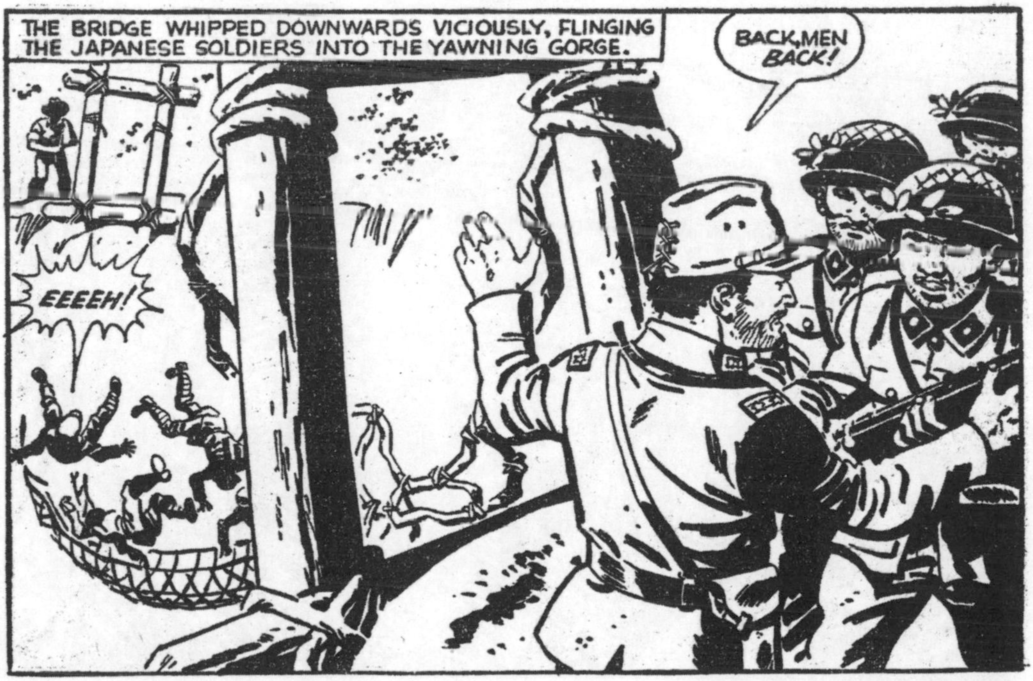
THE BRIDGE WHIPPED DOWNWARDS VICIOUSLY, FLINGING THE JAPANESE SOLDIERS INTO THE YAWNING GORGE.
BACK, MEN BACK!
EEEEH!

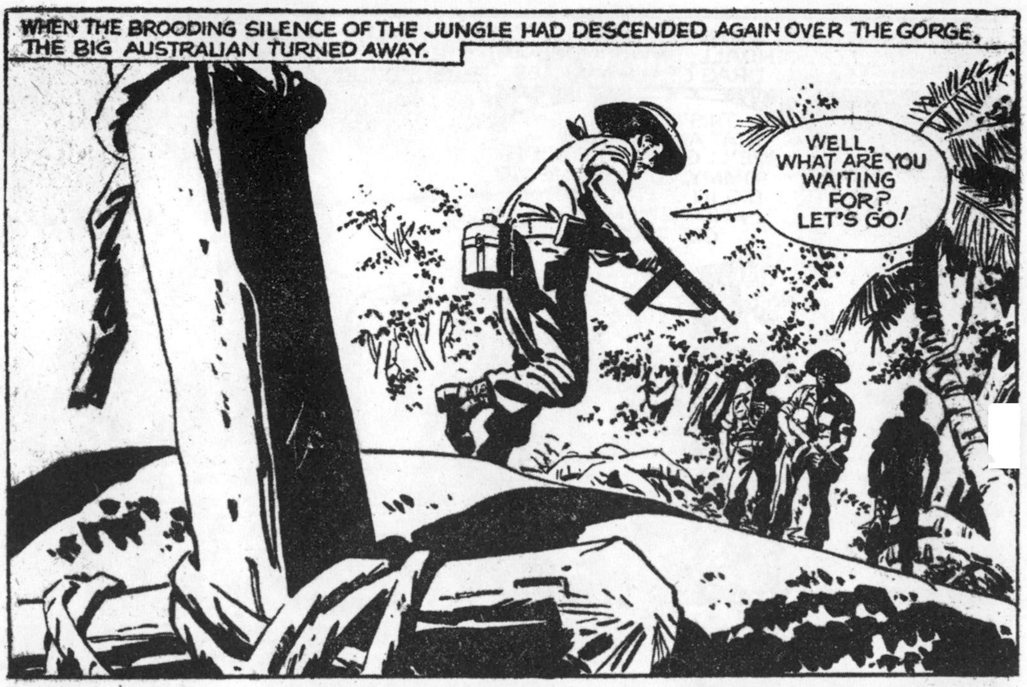
WHEN THE BROODING SILENCE OF THE JUNGLE HAD DESCENDED AGAIN OVER THE GORGE, THE BIG AUSTRALIAN TURNED AWAY.
WELL, WHAT ARE YOU WAITING FOR? LET'S GO!

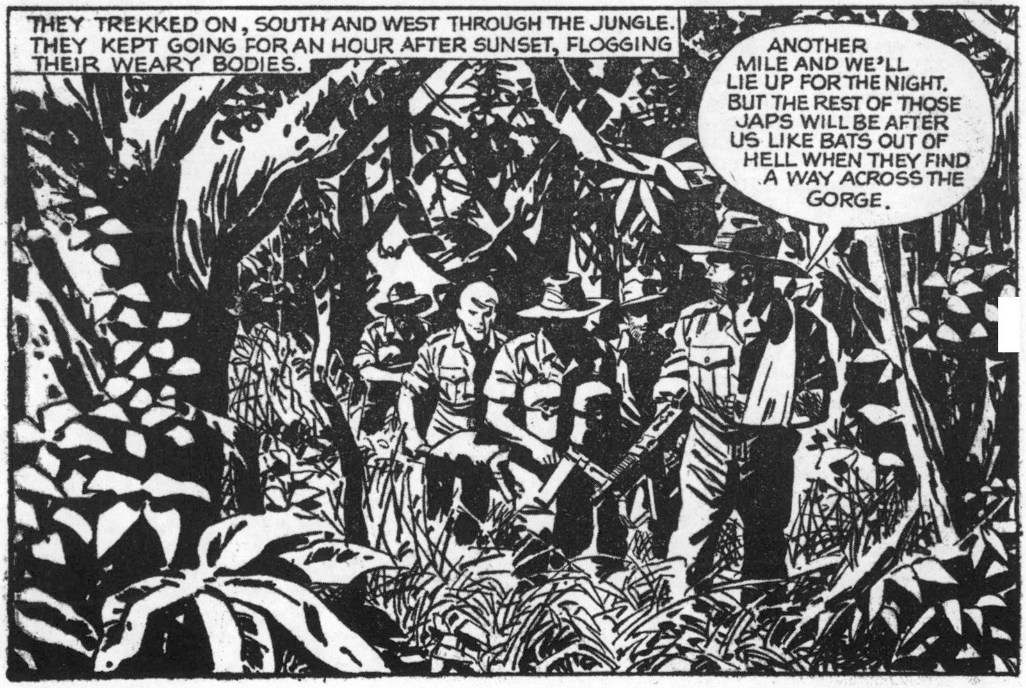
THEY TREKKED ON, SOUTH AND WEST THROUGH THE JUNGLE. THEY KEPT GOING FOR AN HOUR AFTER SUNSET, FLOGGING THEIR WEARY BODIES.
ANOTHER MILE AND WE'LL LIE UP FOR THE NIGHT. BUT THE REST OF THOSE JAPS WILL BE AFTER US LIKE BATS OUT OF HELL WHEN THEY FIND A WAY ACROSS THE GORGE.

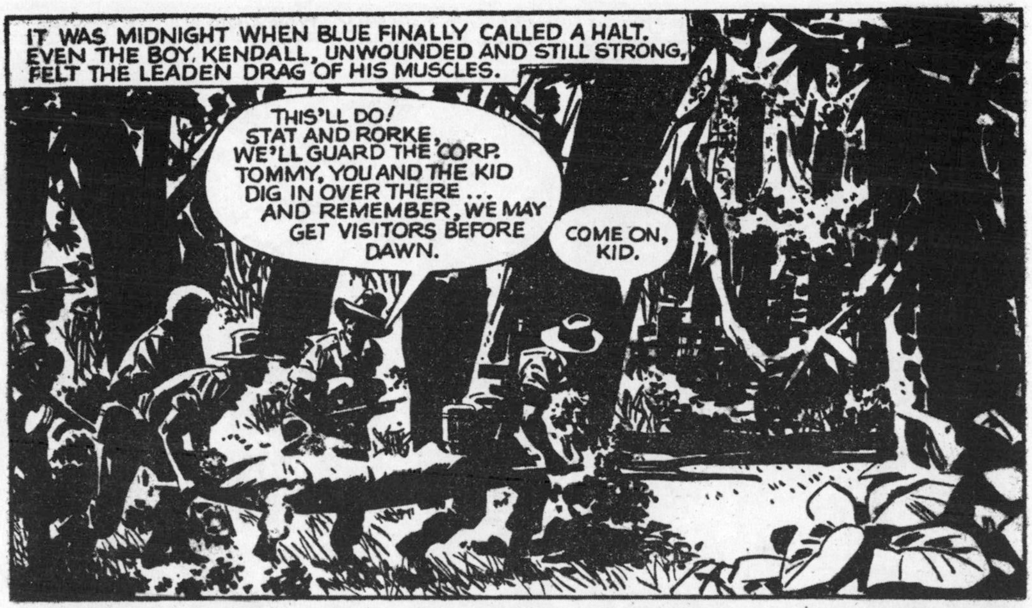
IT WAS MIDNIGHT WHEN BLUE FINALLY CALLED A HALT. EVEN THE BOY, KENDALL, UNWOUNDED AND STILL STRONG, FELT THE LEADEN DRAG OF HIS MUSCLES.
THIS'LL DO! STAT AND RORKE, WE'LL GUARD THE CORP. TOMMY, YOU AND THE KID DIG IN OVER THERE ... AND REMEMBER, WE MAY GET VISITORS BEFORE DAWN.
COME ON, KID.

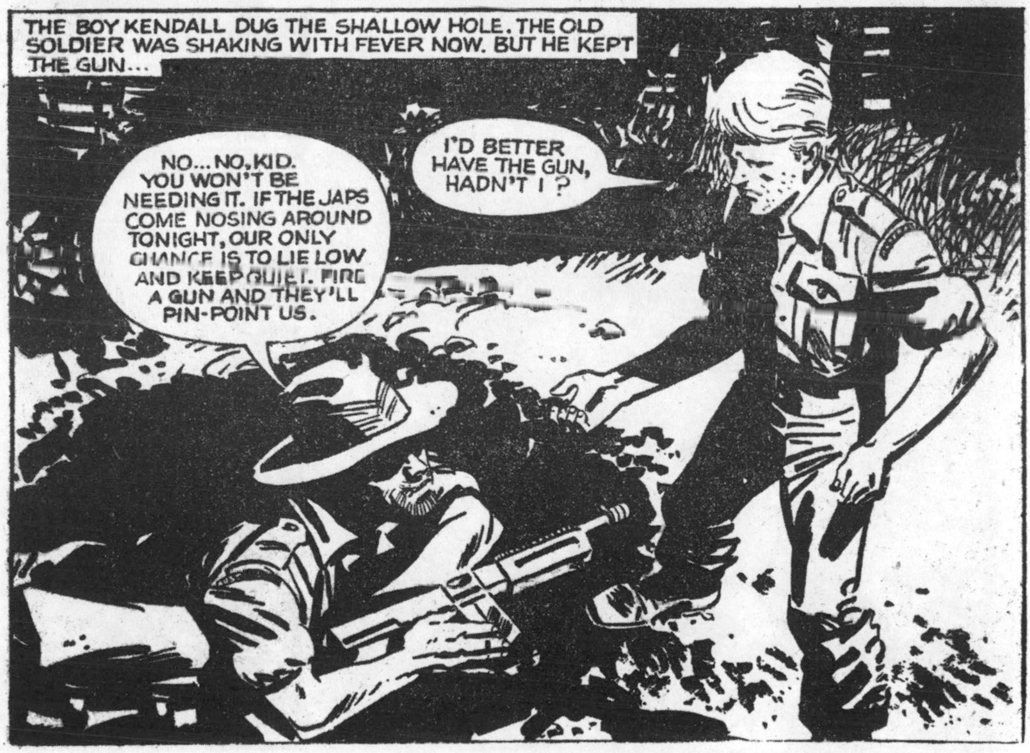
THE BOY KENDALL DUG THE SHALLOW HOLE. THE OLD SOLDIER WAS SHAKING WITH FEVER NOW. BUT HE KEPT THE GUN...
I'D BETTER HAVE THE GUN, HADN'T I ?
NO... NO, KID. YOU WON'T BE NEEDING IT. IF THE JAPS COME NOSING AROUND TONIGHT, OUR ONLY CHANCE IS TO LIE LOW AND KEEP QUIET. FIRE A GUN AND THEY'LL PIN-POINT US.

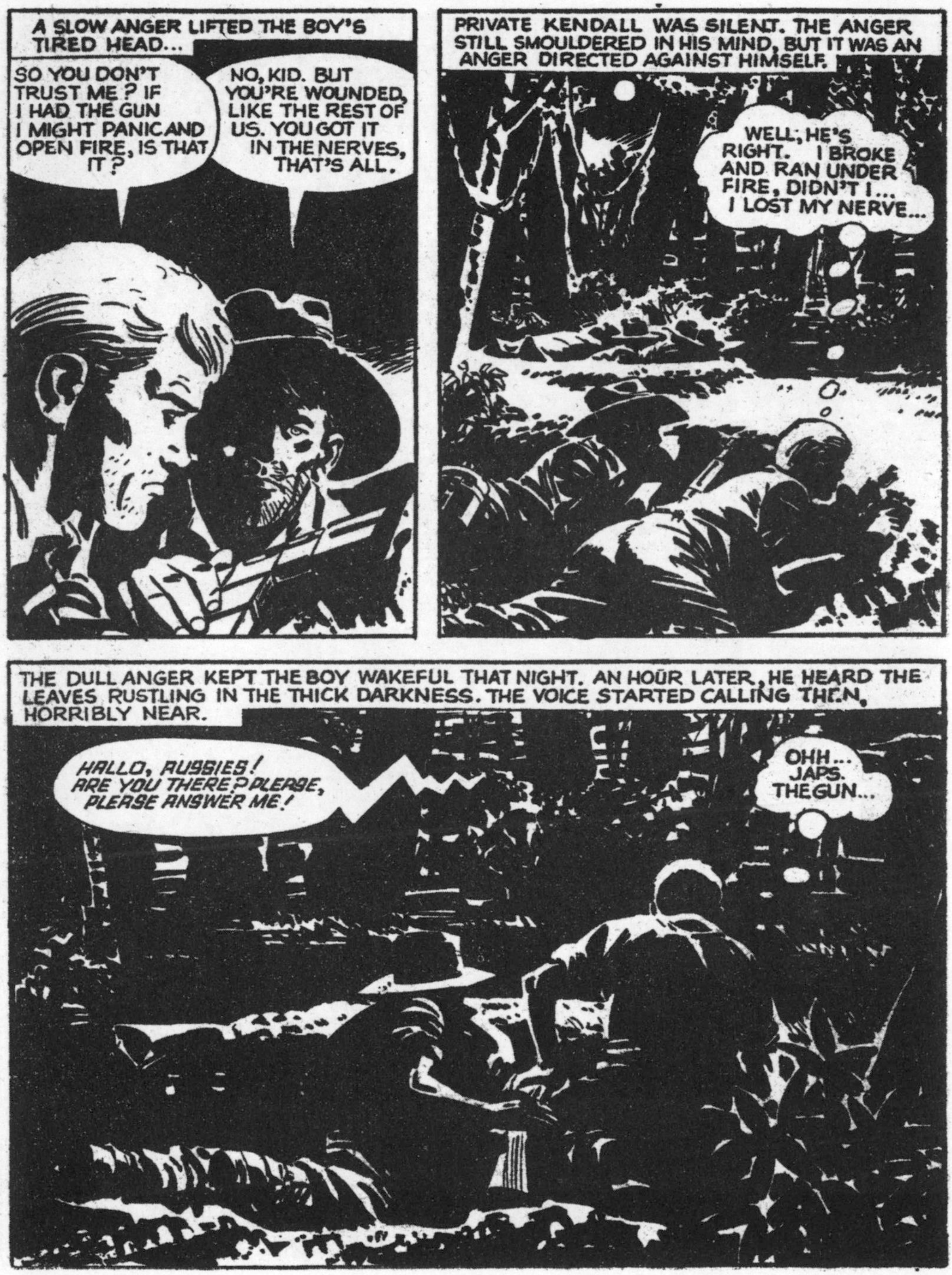
A SLOW ANGER LIFTED THE BOY'S TIRED HEAD...
SO YOU DON'T TRUST ME? IF I HAD THE GUN I MIGHT PANIC AND OPEN FIRE, IS THAT IT?
NO, KID. BUT YOU'RE WOUNDED, LIKE THE REST OF US. YOU GOT IT IN THE NERVES, THAT'S ALL.
PRIVATE KENDALL WAS SILENT. THE ANGER STILL SMOULDERED IN HIS MIND, BUT IT WAS AN ANGER DIRECTED AGAINST HIMSELF.
WELL, HE'S RIGHT. I BROKE AND RAN UNDER FIRE, DIDN'T I... I LOST MY NERVE...
THE DULL ANGER KEPT THE BOY WAKEFUL THAT NIGHT. AN HOUR LATER, HE HEARD THE LEAVES RUSTLING IN THE THICK DARKNESS. THE VOICE STARTED CALLING THEN, HORRIBLY NEAR.
HALLO, AUSSIES! ARE YOU THERE? PLEASE, PLEASE ANSWER ME!
OHH... JAPS. THE GUN...

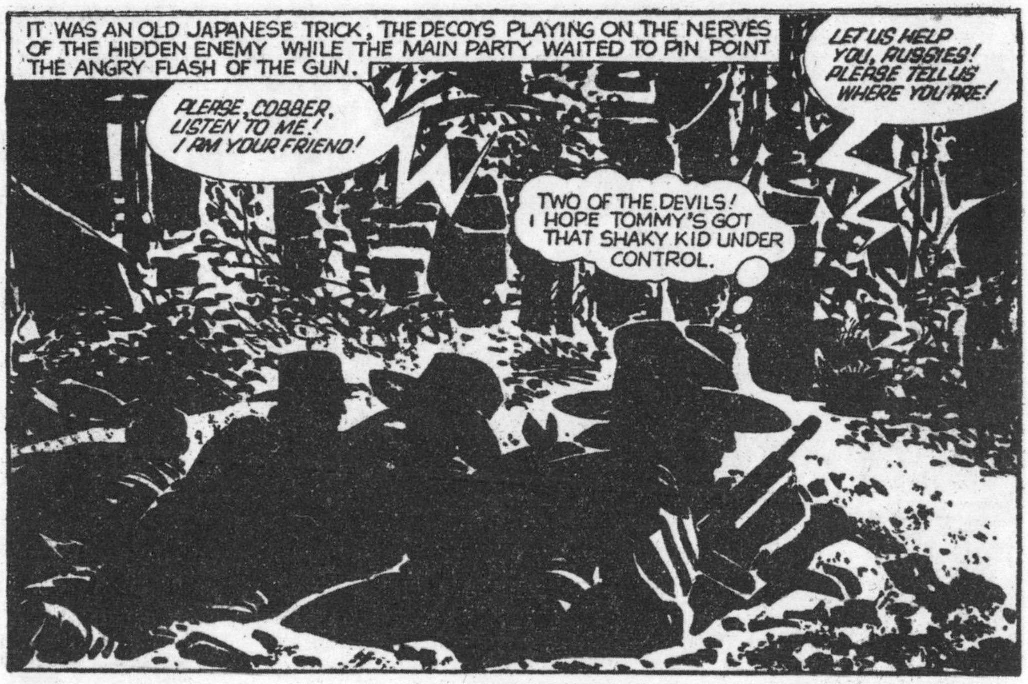
IT WAS AN OLD JAPANESE TRICK, THE DECOYS PLAYING ON THE NERVES OF THE HIDDEN ENEMY WHILE THE MAIN PARTY WAITED TO PIN POINT THE ANGRY FLASH OF THE GUN.
PLEASE, COBBER, LISTEN TO ME! I AM YOUR FRIEND!
LET US HELP YOU, AUSSIES! PLEASE TELL US WHERE YOU ARE!
TWO OF THE DEVILS! I HOPE TOMMY'S GOT THAT SHAKY KID UNDER CONTROL.

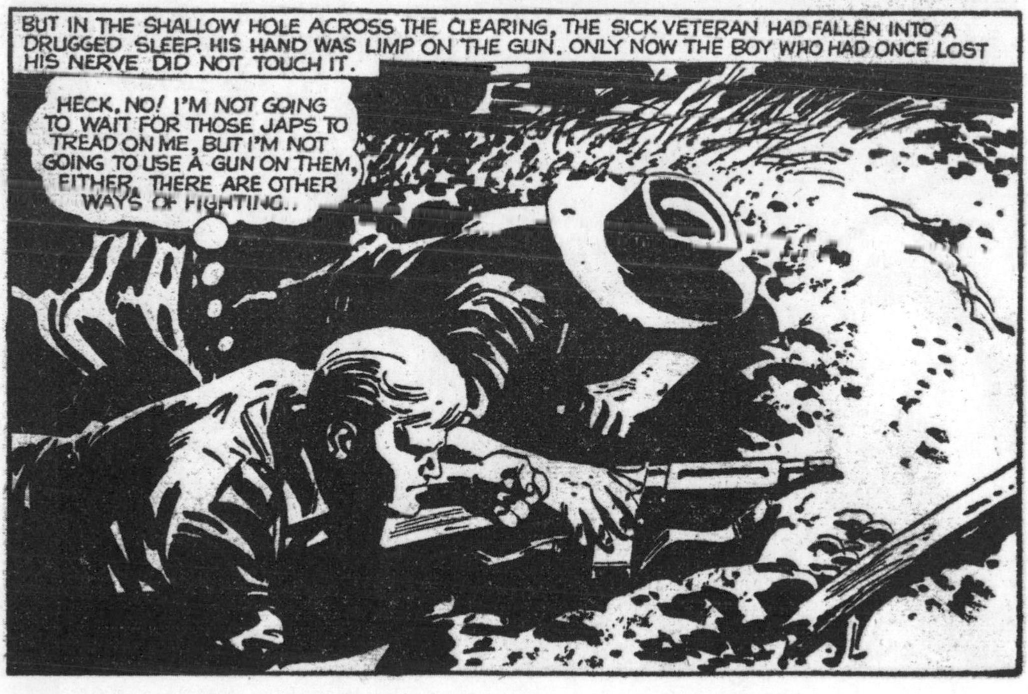
BUT IN THE SHALLOW HOLE ACROSS THE CLEARING, THE SICK VETERAN HAD FALLEN INTO A DRUGGED SLEEP. HIS HAND WAS LIMP ON THE GUN. ONLY NOW THE BOY WHO HAD ONCE LOST HIS NERVE DID NOT TOUCH IT.
HECK, NO! I'M NOT GOING TO WAIT FOR THOSE JAPS TO TREAD ON ME, BUT I'M NOT GOING TO USE A GUN ON THEM, EITHER. THERE ARE OTHER WAYS OF FIGHTING..

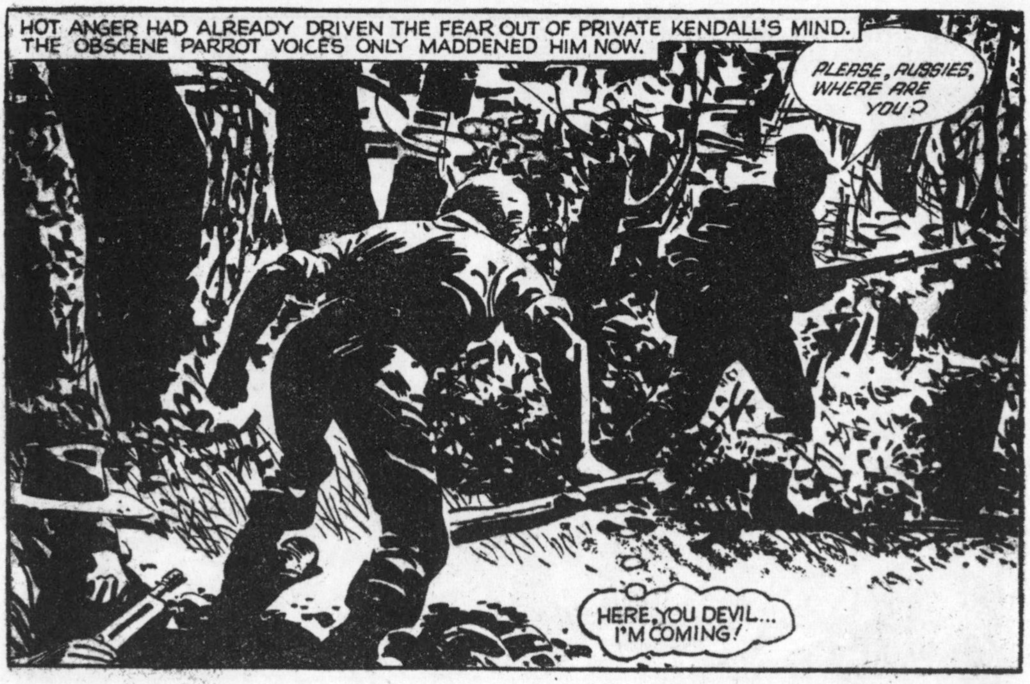
HOT ANGER HAD ALREADY DRIVEN THE FEAR OUT OF PRIVATE KENDALL'S MIND. THE OBSCENE PARROT VOICES ONLY MADDENED HIM NOW.
PLEASE, RUSSIES, WHERE ARE YOU?
HERE, YOU DEVIL... I'M COMING!

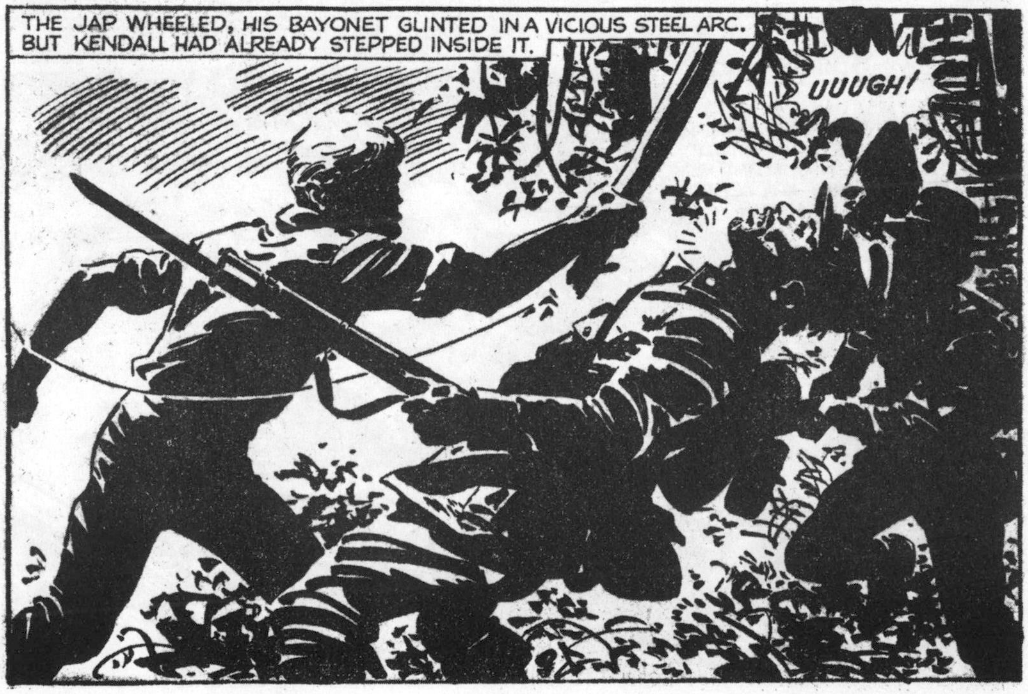
THE JAP WHEELED, HIS BAYONET GLINTED IN A VICIOUS STEEL ARC. BUT KENDALL HAD ALREADY STEPPED INSIDE IT.
UUUGH!

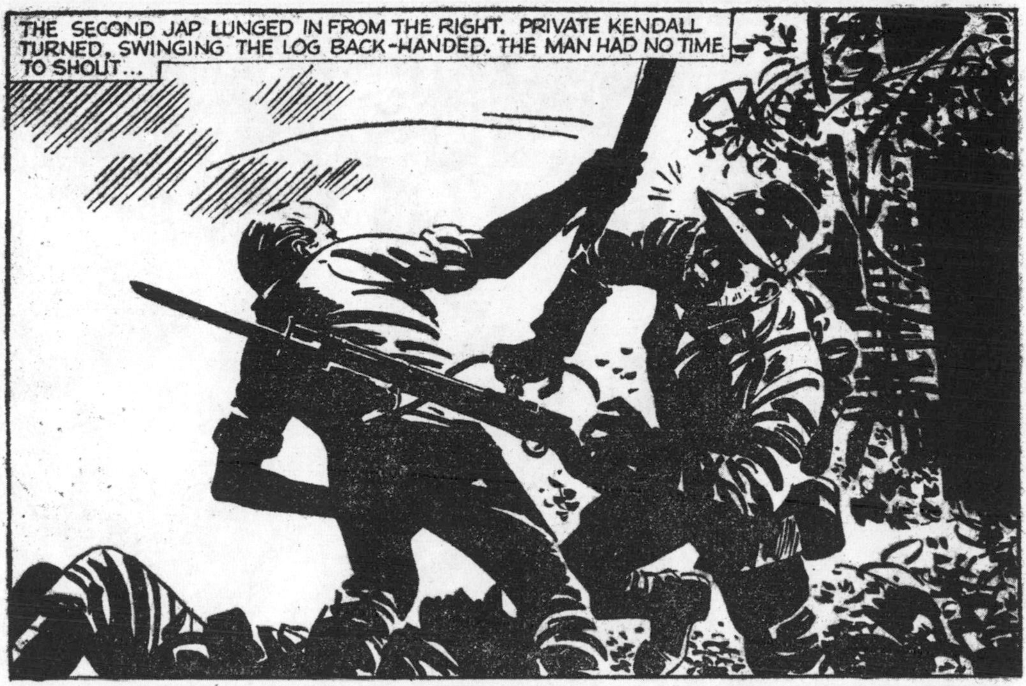
THE SECOND JAP LUNGED IN FROM THE RIGHT. PRIVATE KENDALL TURNED, SWINGING THE LOG BACK-HANDED. THE MAN HAD NO TIME TO SHOUT...

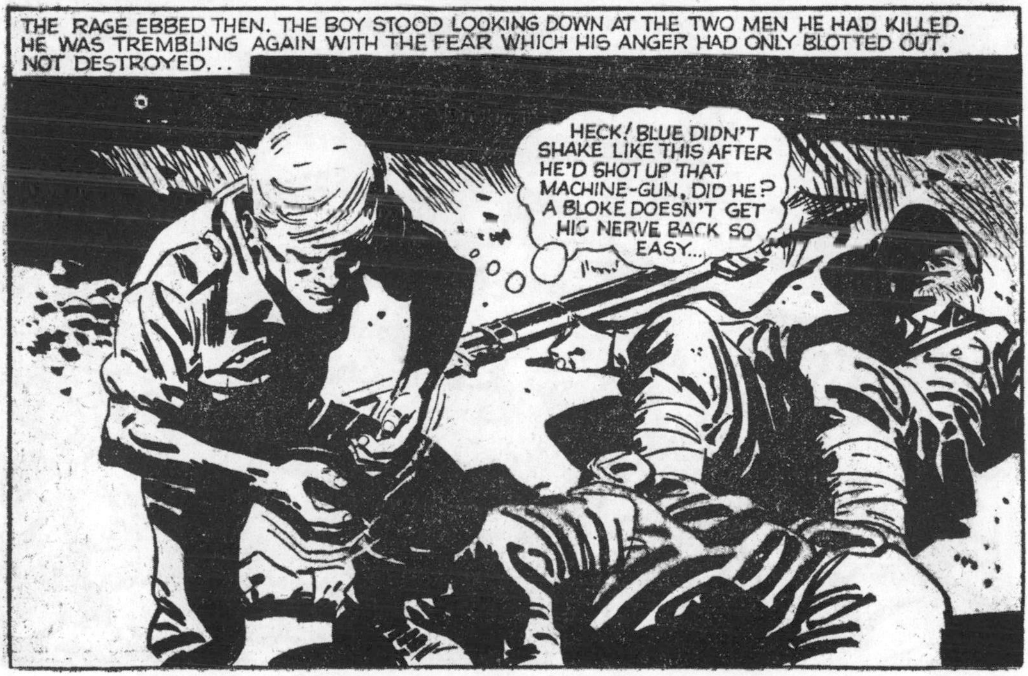
THE RAGE EBBED THEN. THE BOY STOOD LOOKING DOWN AT THE TWO MEN HE HAD KILLED. HE WAS TREMBLING AGAIN WITH THE FEAR WHICH HIS ANGER HAD ONLY BLOTTED OUT, NOT DESTROYED...
HECK! BLUE DIDN'T SHAKE LIKE THIS AFTER HE'D SHOT UP THAT MACHINE-GUN, DID HE? A BLOKE DOESN'T GET HIS NERVE BACK SO EASY...

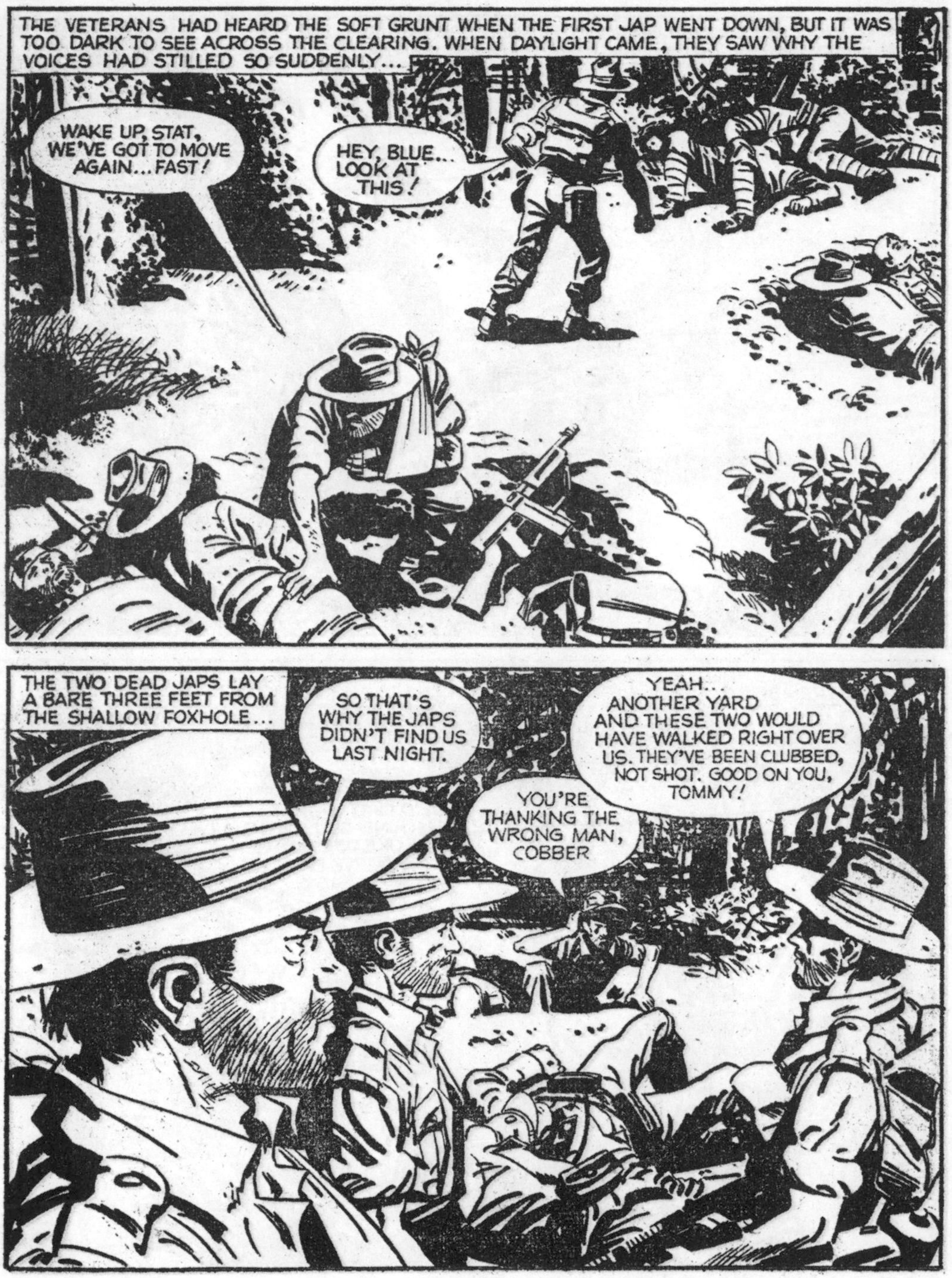
THE VETERANS HAD HEARD THE SOFT GRUNT WHEN THE FIRST JAP WENT DOWN, BUT IT WAS TOO DARK TO SEE ACROSS THE CLEARING. WHEN DAYLIGHT CAME, THEY SAW WHY THE VOICES HAD STILLED SO SUDDENLY...
WAKE UP, STAT, WE'VE GOT TO MOVE AGAIN... FAST!
HEY, BLUE... LOOK AT THIS!
THE TWO DEAD JAPS LAY A BARE THREE FEET FROM THE SHALLOW FOXHOLE...
SO THAT'S WHY THE JAPS DIDN'T FIND US LAST NIGHT.
YEAH... ANOTHER YARD AND THESE TWO WOULD HAVE WALKED RIGHT OVER US. THEY'VE BEEN CLUBBED, NOT SHOT. GOOD ON YOU, TOMMY!
YOU'RE THANKING THE WRONG MAN, COBBER

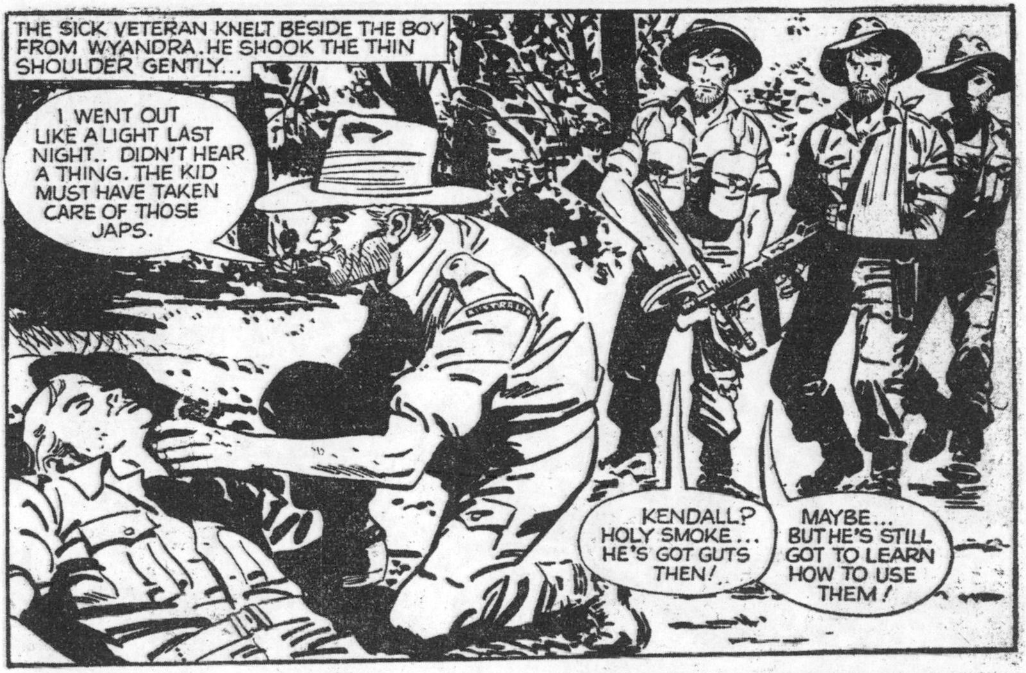
THE SICK VETERAN KNELT BESIDE THE BOY FROM WYANDRA. HE SHOOK THE THIN SHOULDER GENTLY...
I WENT OUT LIKE A LIGHT LAST NIGHT.. DIDN'T HEAR A THING. THE KID MUST HAVE TAKEN CARE OF THOSE JAPS.
KENDALL? HOLY SMOKE... HE'S GOT GUTS THEN!
MAYBE... BUT HE'S STILL GOT TO LEARN HOW TO USE THEM!

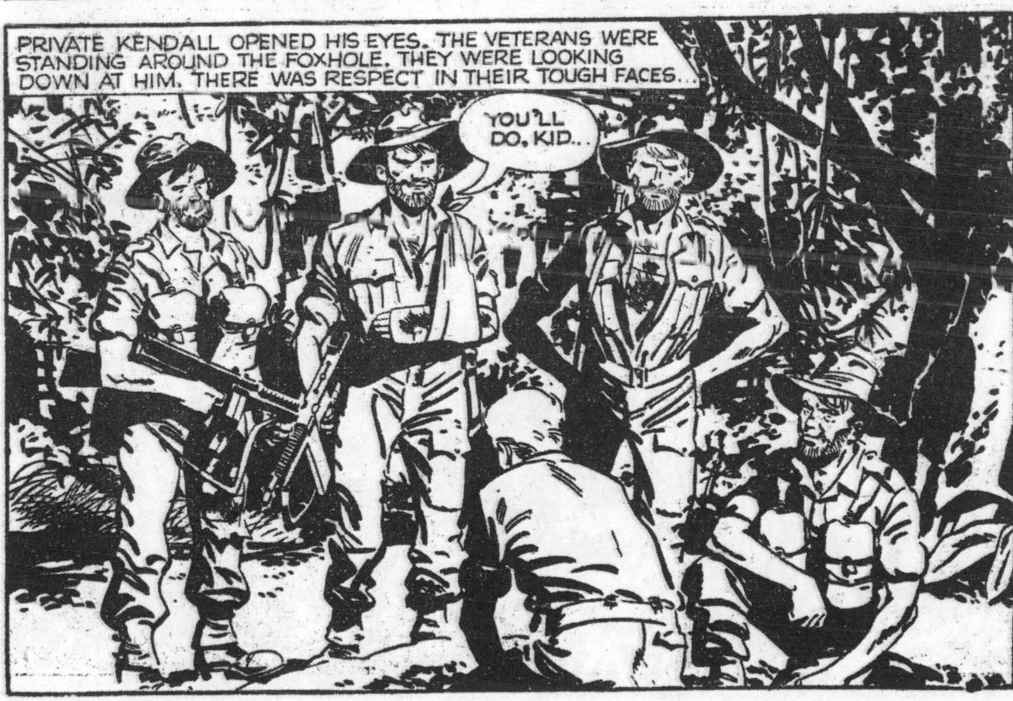
PRIVATE KENDALL OPENED HIS EYES. THE VETERANS WERE STANDING AROUND THE FOXHOLE. THEY WERE LOOKING DOWN AT HIM. THERE WAS RESPECT IN THEIR TOUGH FACES...
YOU'LL DO, KID...

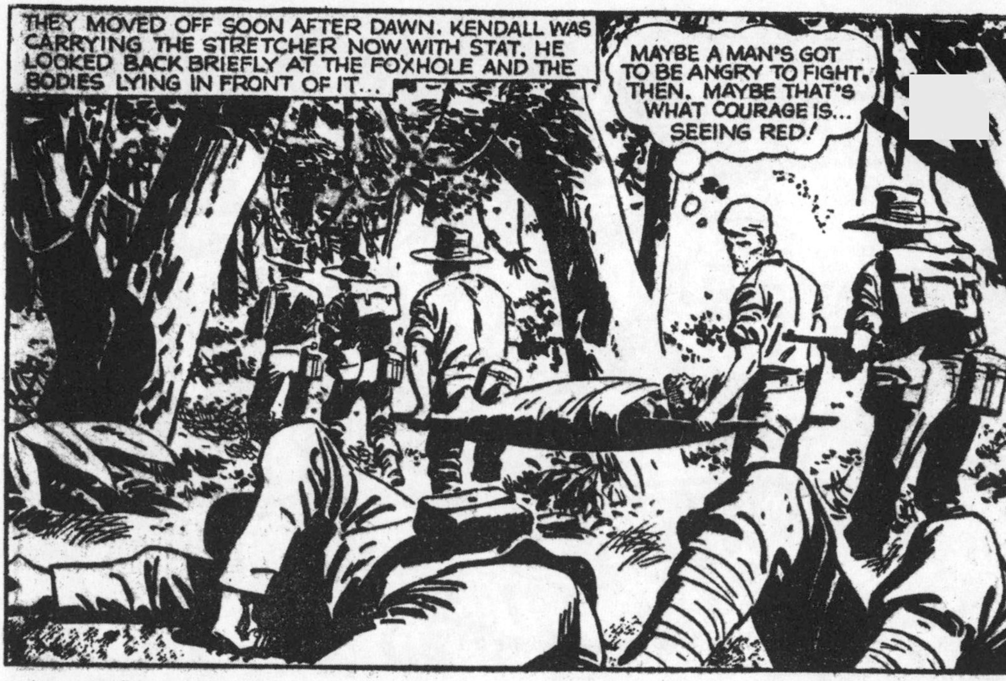
THEY MOVED OFF SOON AFTER DAWN. KENDALL WAS CARRYING THE STRETCHER NOW WITH STAT. HE LOOKED BACK BRIEFLY AT THE FOXHOLE AND THE BODIES LYING IN FRONT OF IT...
MAYBE A MAN'S GOT TO BE ANGRY TO FIGHT, THEN. MAYBE THAT'S WHAT COURAGE IS... SEEING RED!

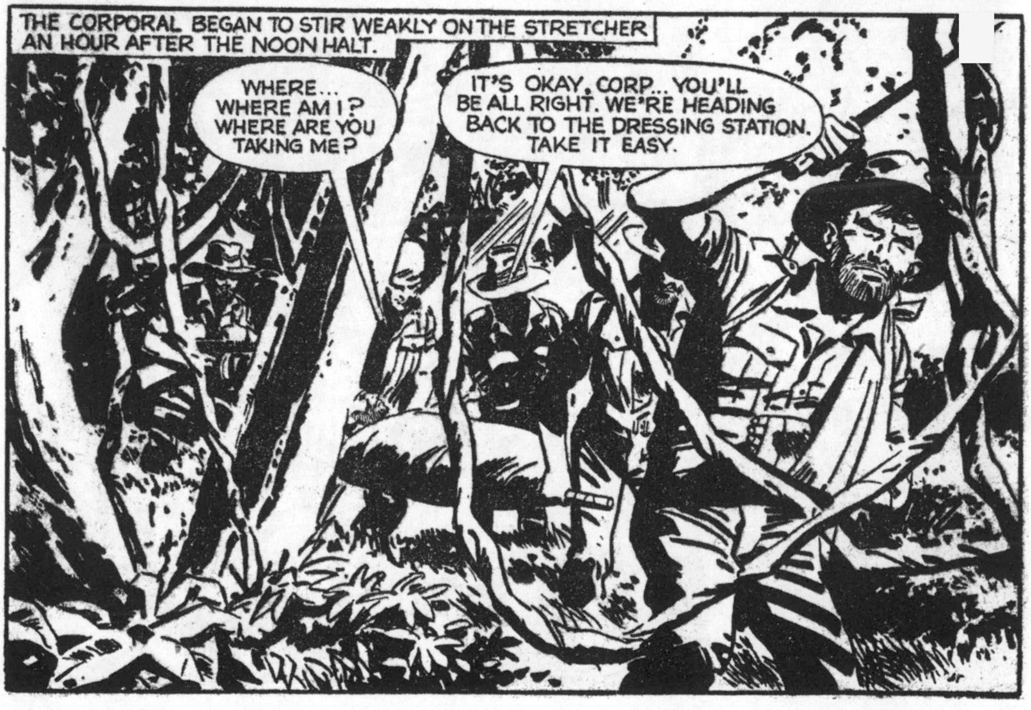
THE CORPORAL BEGAN TO STIR WEAKLY ON THE STRETCHER AN HOUR AFTER THE NOON HALT.
WHERE... WHERE AM I? WHERE ARE YOU TAKING ME?
IT'S OKAY, CORP... YOU'LL BE ALL RIGHT. WE'RE HEADING BACK TO THE DRESSING STATION. TAKE IT EASY.

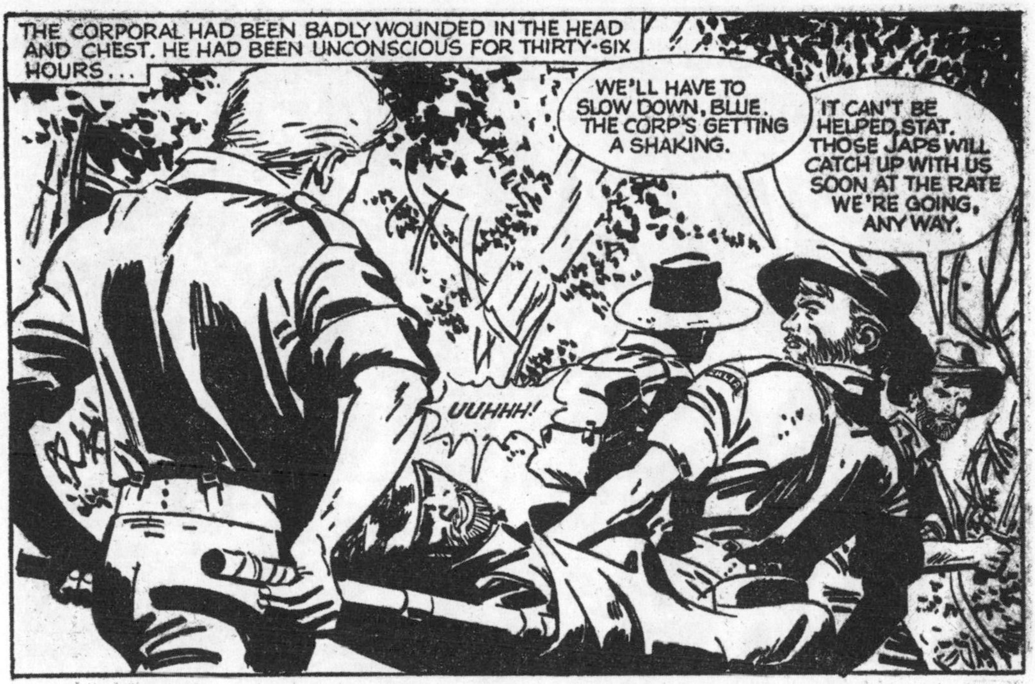
THE CORPORAL HAD BEEN BADLY WOUNDED IN THE HEAD AND CHEST. HE HAD BEEN UNCONSCIOUS FOR THIRTY-SIX HOURS...
WE'LL HAVE TO SLOW DOWN, BLUE. THE CORP'S GETTING A SHAKING.
IT CAN'T BE HELPED, STAT. THOSE JAPS WILL CATCH UP WITH US SOON AT THE RATE WE'RE GOING, ANY WAY.
UUHHH!

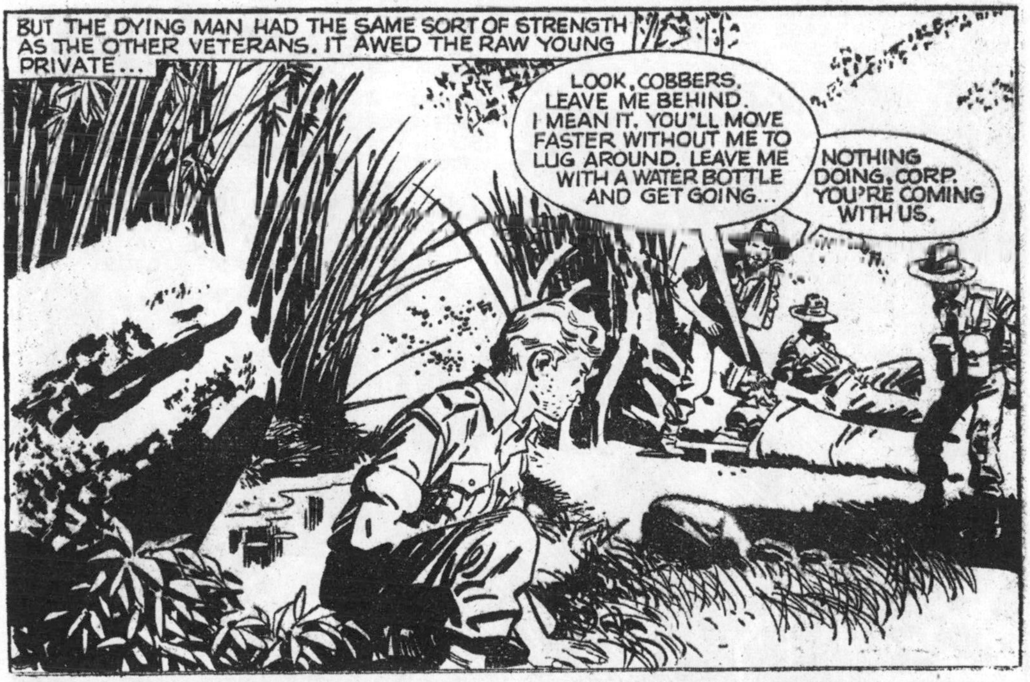
BUT THE DYING MAN HAD THE SAME SORT OF STRENGTH AS THE OTHER VETERANS. IT AWED THE RAW YOUNG PRIVATE...
LOOK, COBBERS, LEAVE ME BEHIND. I MEAN IT. YOU'LL MOVE FASTER WITHOUT ME TO LUG AROUND. LEAVE ME WITH A WATER BOTTLE AND GET GOING...
NOTHING DOING, CORP. YOU'RE COMING WITH US.

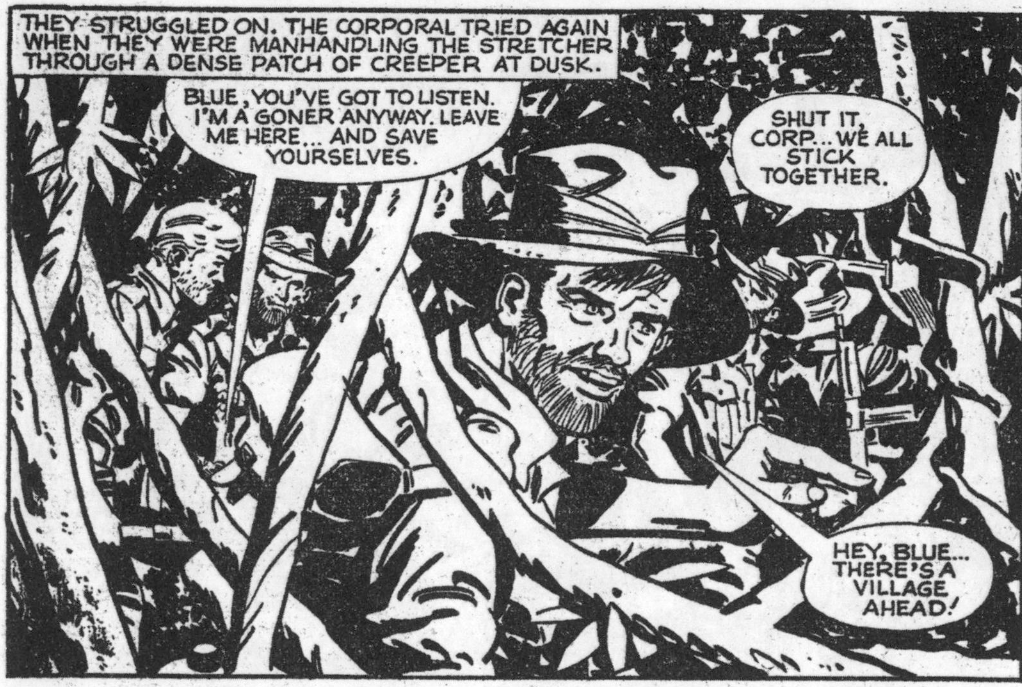
THEY STRUGGLED ON. THE CORPORAL TRIED AGAIN WHEN THEY WERE MANHANDLING THE STRETCHER THROUGH A DENSE PATCH OF CREEPER AT DUSK.
BLUE, YOU'VE GOT TO LISTEN. I'M A GONER ANYWAY. LEAVE ME HERE... AND SAVE YOURSELVES.
SHUT IT, CORP... WE ALL STICK TOGETHER.
HEY, BLUE... THERE'S A VILLAGE AHEAD!

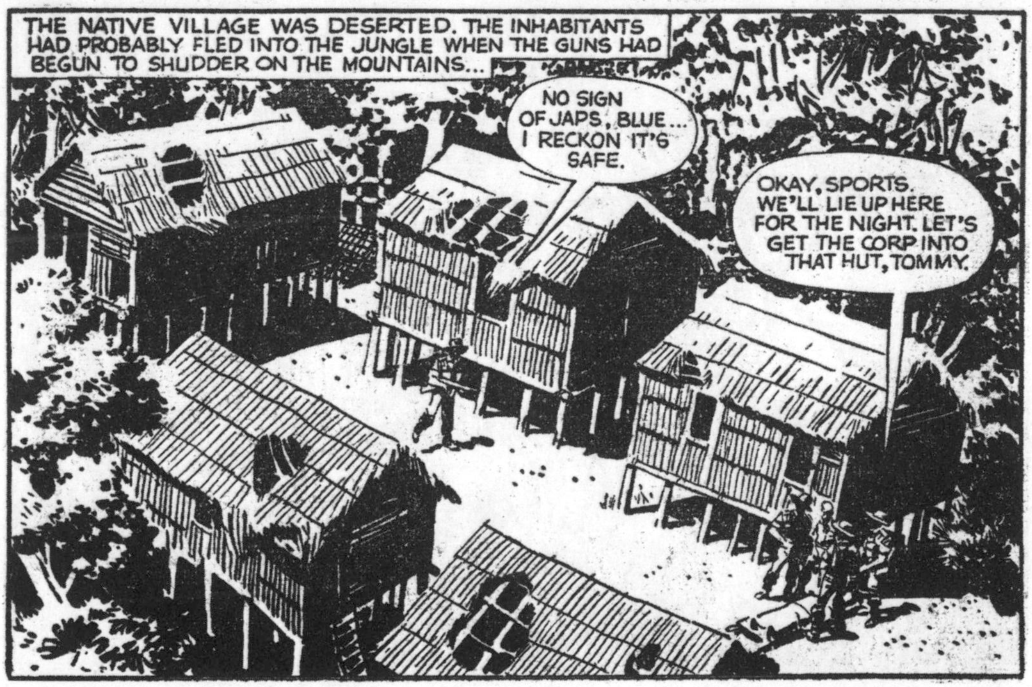
THE NATIVE VILLAGE WAS DESERTED. THE INHABITANTS HAD PROBABLY FLED INTO THE JUNGLE WHEN THE GUNS HAD BEGUN TO SHUDDER ON THE MOUNTAINS...
NO SIGN OF JAPS, BLUE... I RECKON IT'S SAFE.
OKAY, SPORTS. WE'LL LIE UP HERE FOR THE NIGHT. LET'S GET THE CORP INTO THAT HUT, TOMMY.

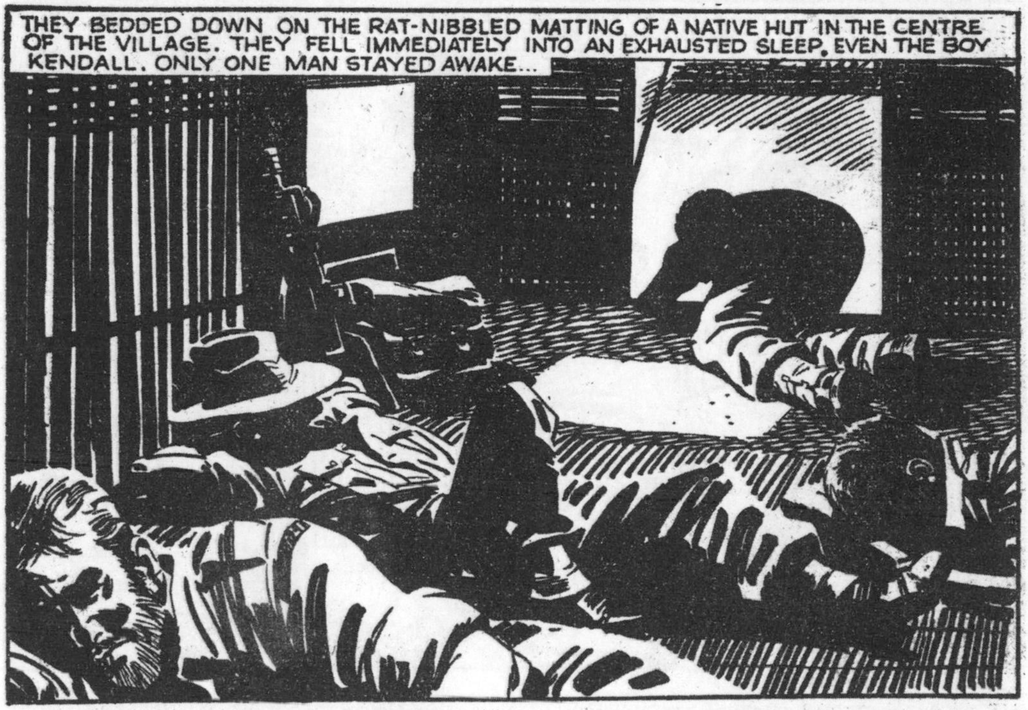
THEY BEDDED DOWN ON THE RAT-NIBBLED MATTING OF A NATIVE HUT IN THE CENTRE OF THE VILLAGE. THEY FELL IMMEDIATELY INTO AN EXHAUSTED SLEEP, EVEN THE BOY KENDALL. ONLY ONE MAN STAYED AWAKE...

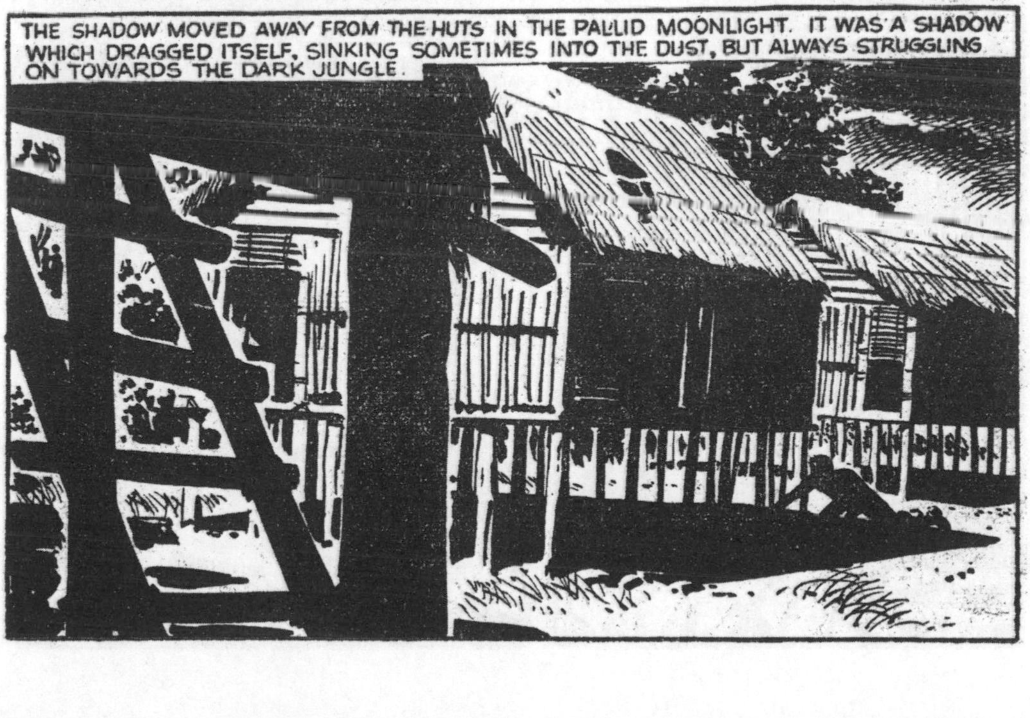
THE SHADOW MOVED AWAY FROM THE HUTS IN THE PALLID MOONLIGHT. IT WAS A SHADOW WHICH DRAGGED ITSELF, SINKING SOMETIMES INTO THE DUST, BUT ALWAYS STRUGGLING ON TOWARDS THE DARK JUNGLE.

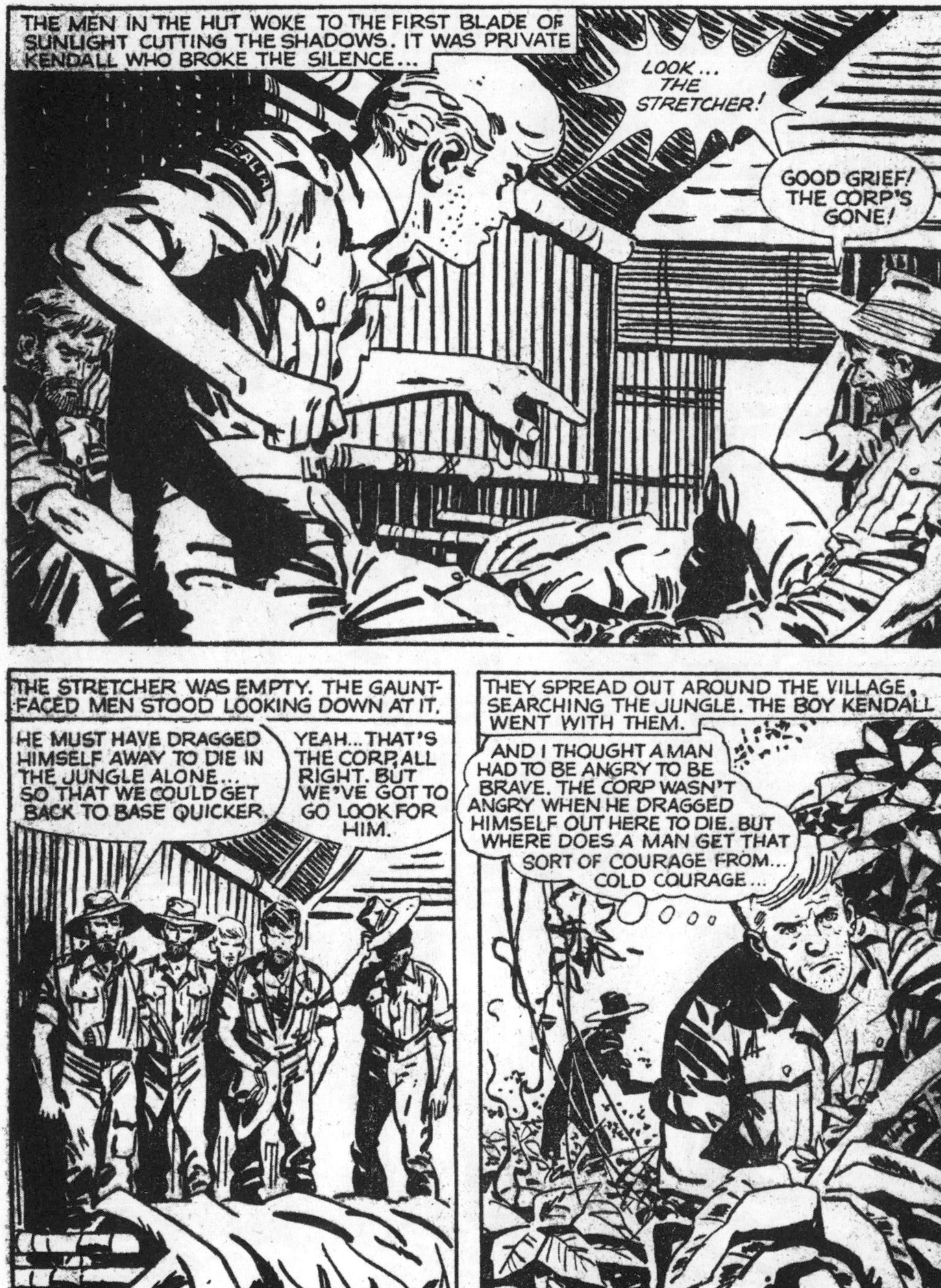
THE MEN IN THE HUT WOKE TO THE FIRST BLADE OF SUNLIGHT CUTTING THE SHADOWS. IT WAS PRIVATE KENDALL WHO BROKE THE SILENCE...
LOOK... THE STRETCHER!
GOOD GRIEF! THE CORP'S GONE!
THE STRETCHER WAS EMPTY. THE GAUNT-FACED MEN STOOD LOOKING DOWN AT IT.
HE MUST HAVE DRAGGED HIMSELF AWAY TO DIE IN THE JUNGLE ALONE... SO THAT WE COULD GET BACK TO BASE QUICKER.
YEAH... THAT'S THE CORP, ALL RIGHT. BUT WE'VE GOT TO GO LOOK FOR HIM.
THEY SPREAD OUT AROUND THE VILLAGE, SEARCHING THE JUNGLE. THE BOY KENDALL WENT WITH THEM.
AND I THOUGHT A MAN HAD TO BE ANGRY TO BE BRAVE. THE CORP WASN'T ANGRY WHEN HE DRAGGED HIMSELF OUT HERE TO DIE. BUT WHERE DOES A MAN GET THAT SORT OF COURAGE FROM... COLD COURAGE...

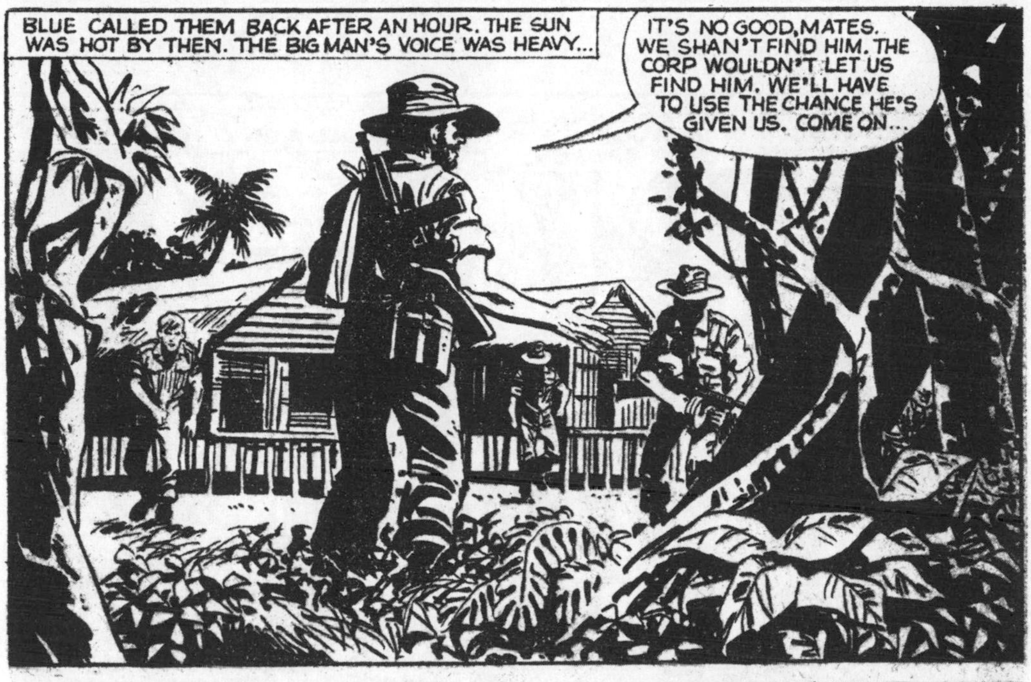
BLUE CALLED THEM BACK AFTER AN HOUR. THE SUN WAS HOT BY THEN. THE BIG MAN'S VOICE WAS HEAVY...
IT'S NO GOOD, MATES. WE SHAN'T FIND HIM. THE CORP WOULDN'T LET US FIND HIM. WE'LL HAVE TO USE THE CHANCE HE'S GIVEN US. COME ON...

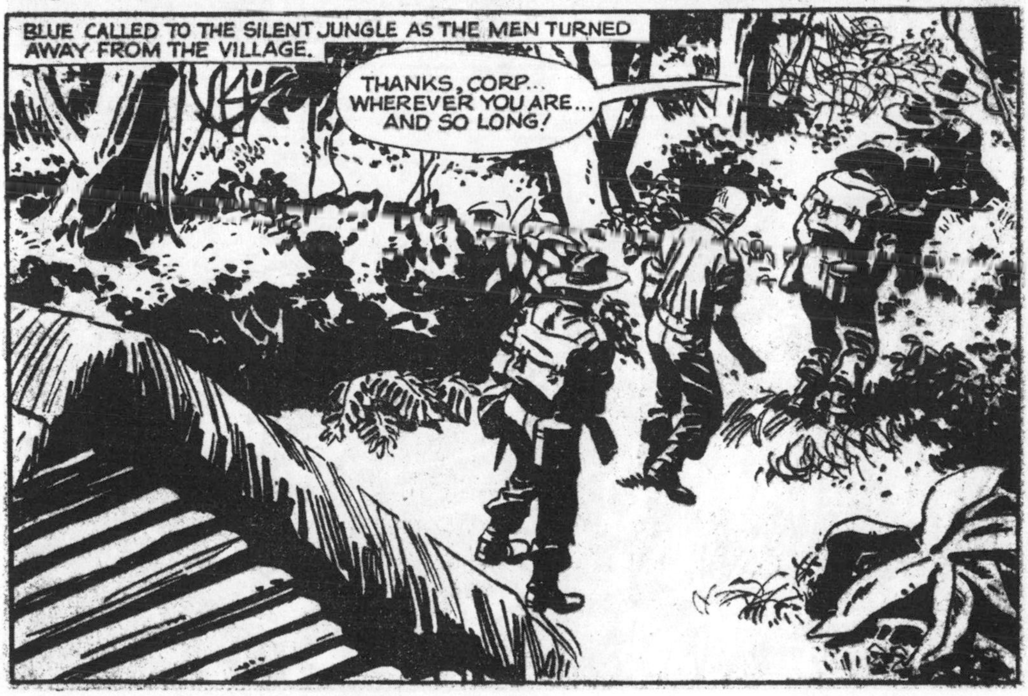
BLUE CALLED TO THE SILENT JUNGLE AS THE MEN TURNED AWAY FROM THE VILLAGE.
THANKS, CORP... WHEREVER YOU ARE... AND SO LONG!

Chapter 4. Courage

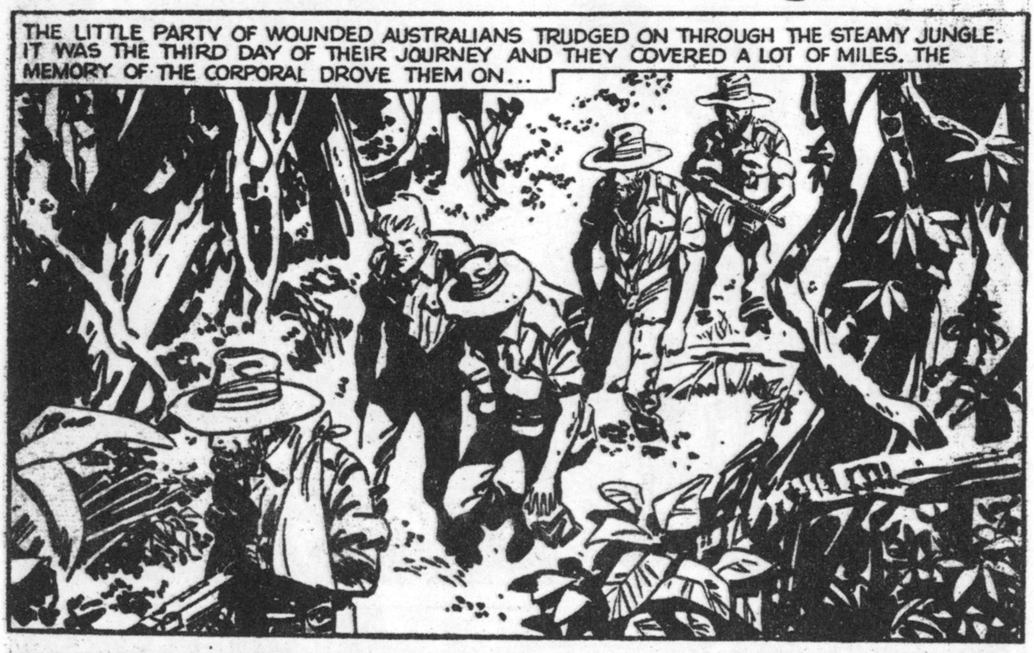
THE LITTLE PARTY OF WOUNDED AUSTRALIANS TRUDGED ON THROUGH THE STEAMY JUNGLE. IT WAS THE THIRD DAY OF THEIR JOURNEY AND THEY COVERED A LOT OF MILES. THE MEMORY OF THE CORPORAL DROVE THEM ON...

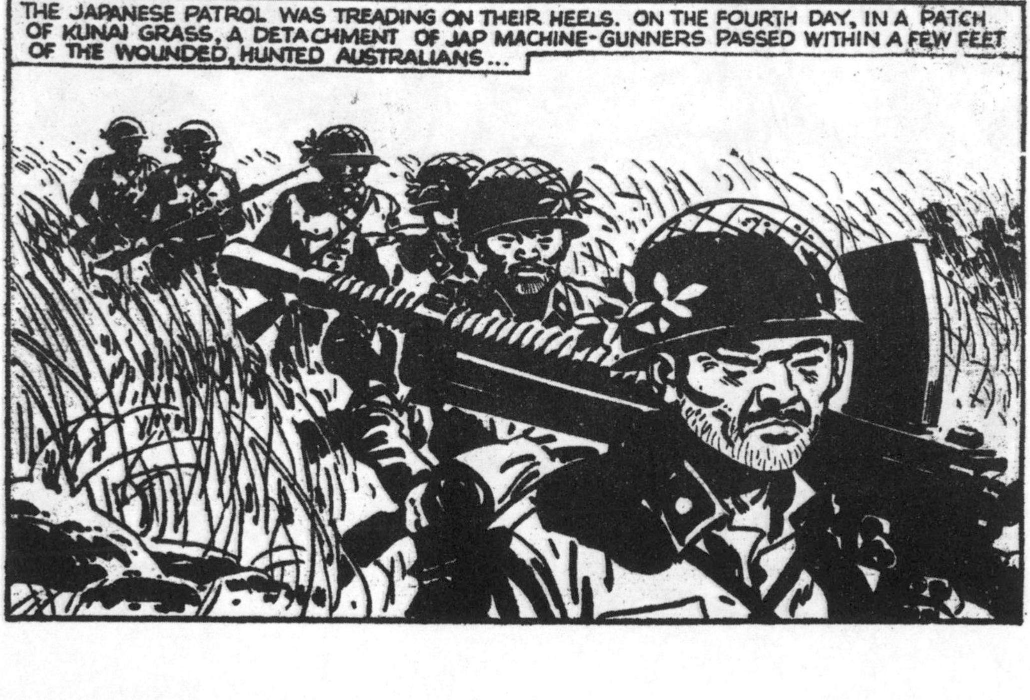
THE JAPANESE PATROL WAS TREADING ON THEIR HEELS. ON THE FOURTH DAY, IN A PATCH OF KUNAI GRASS, A DETACHMENT OF JAP MACHINE-GUNNERS PASSED WITHIN A FEW FEET OF THE WOUNDED, HUNTED AUSTRALIANS...

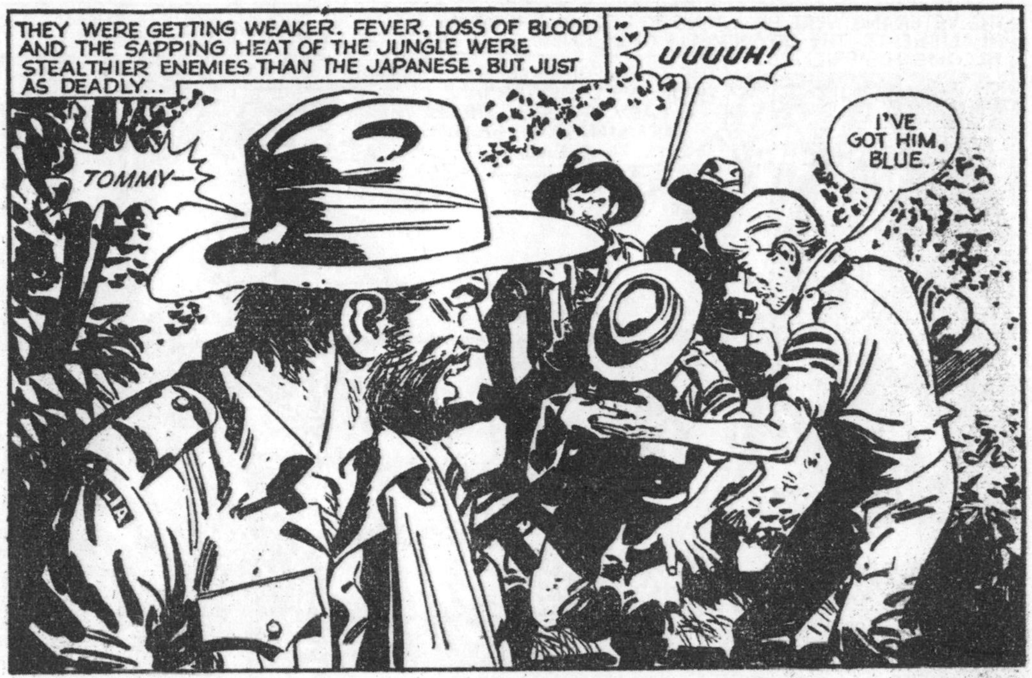
THEY WERE GETTING WEAKER. FEVER, LOSS OF BLOOD AND THE SAPPING HEAT OF THE JUNGLE WERE STEALTHIER ENEMIES THAN THE JAPANESE, BUT JUST AS DEADLY...
UUUUH!
I'VE GOT HIM, BLUE.
TOMMY–

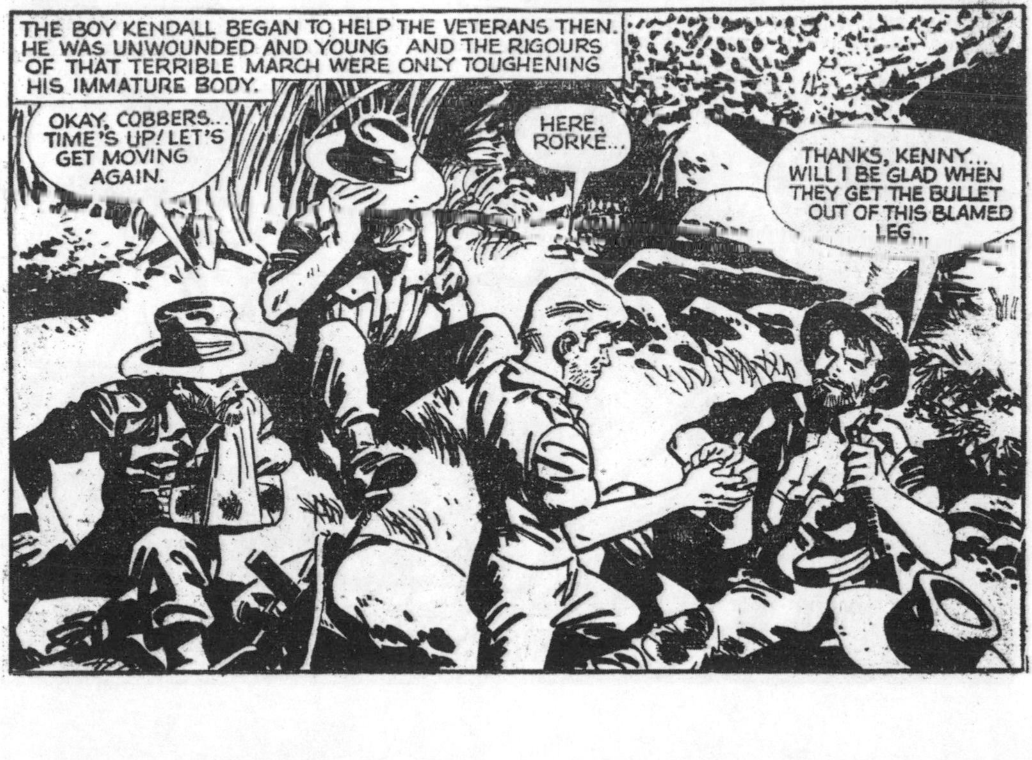
THE BOY KENDALL BEGAN TO HELP THE VETERANS THEN. HE WAS UNWOUNDED AND YOUNG AND THE RIGOURS OF THAT TERRIBLE MARCH WERE ONLY TOUGHENING HIS IMMATURE BODY.
OKAY, COBBERS... TIME'S UP! LET'S GET MOVING AGAIN.
HERE, RORKE...
THANKS, KENNY... WILL I BE GLAD WHEN THEY GET THE BULLET OUT OF THIS BLAMED LEG...

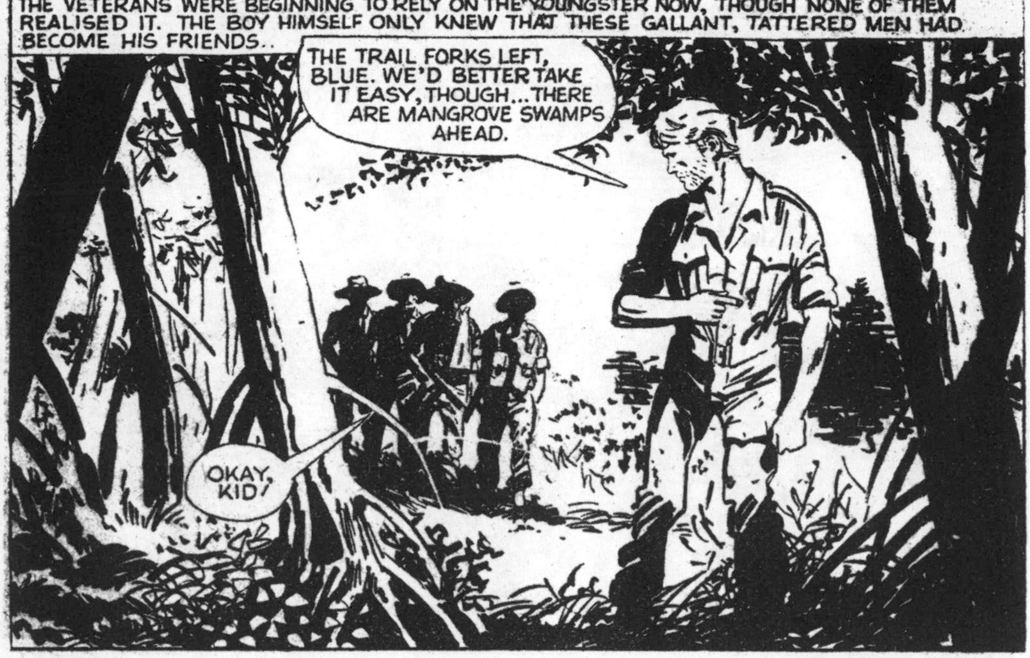
THE VETERANS WERE BEGINNING TO RELY ON THE YOUNGSTER NOW, THOUGH NONE OF THEM REALISED IT. THE BOY HIMSELF ONLY KNEW THAT THESE GALLANT, TATTERED MEN HAD BECOME HIS FRIENDS..
THE TRAIL FORKS LEFT, BLUE. WE'D BETTER TAKE IT EASY, THOUGH... THERE ARE MANGROVE SWAMPS AHEAD.
OKAY, KID!

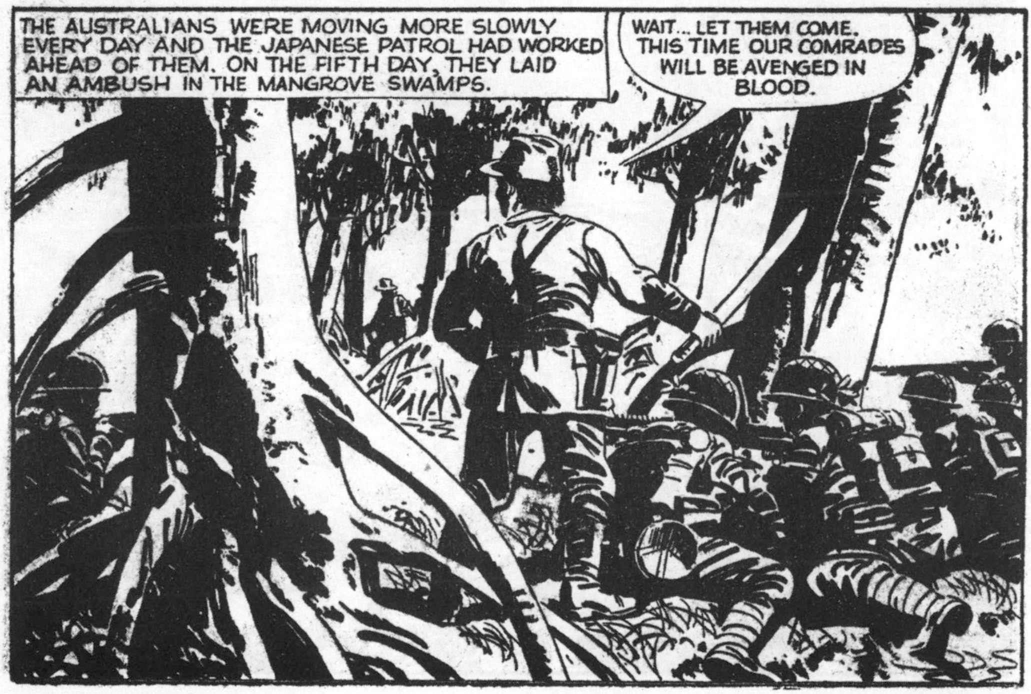
THE AUSTRALIANS WERE MOVING MORE SLOWLY EVERY DAY AND THE JAPANESE PATROL HAD WORKED AHEAD OF THEM. ON THE FIFTH DAY, THEY LAID AN AMBUSH IN THE MANGROVE SWAMPS.
WAIT... LET THEM COME. THIS TIME OUR COMRADES WILL BE AVENGED IN BLOOD.

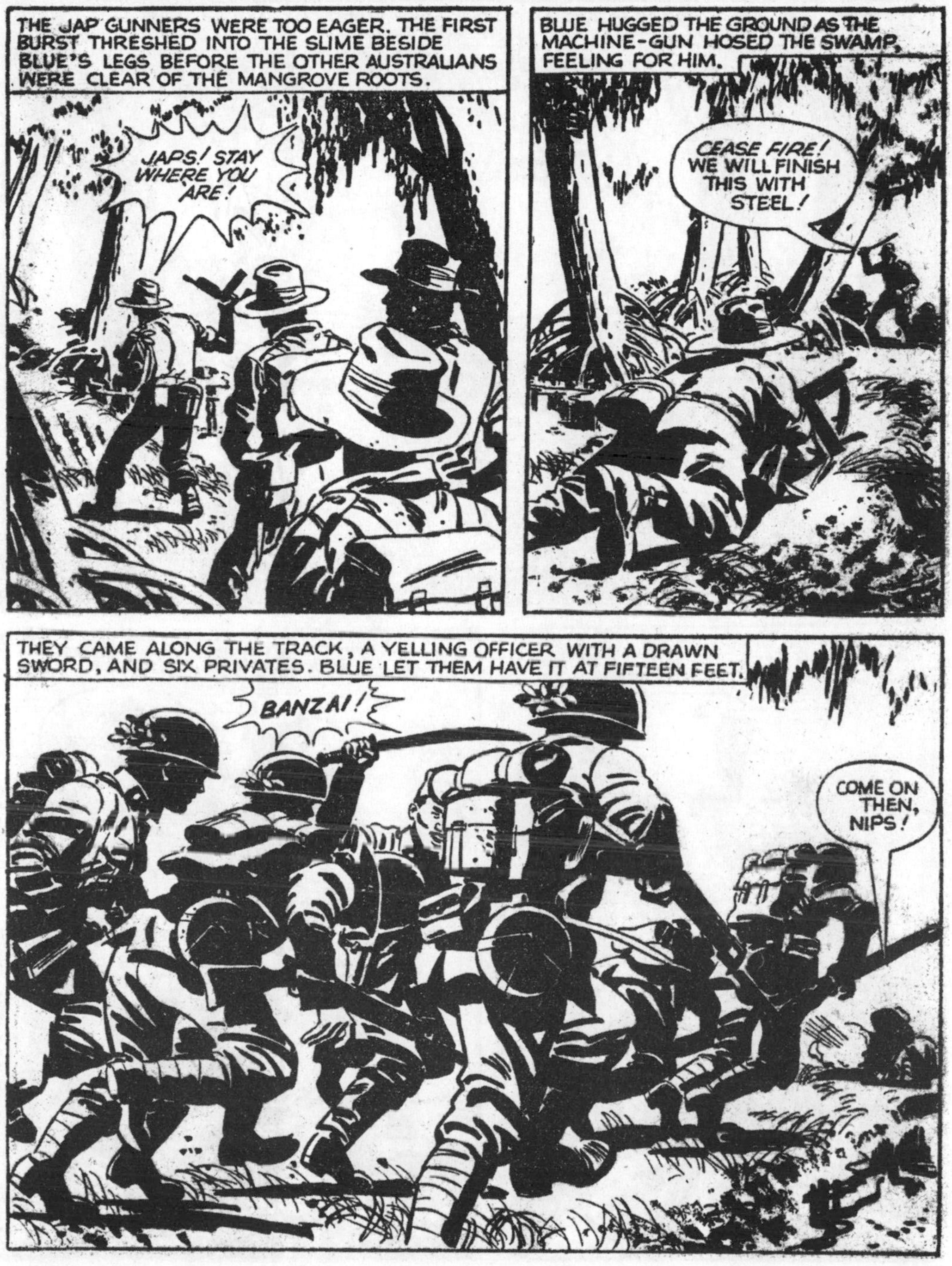
THE JAP GUNNERS WERE TOO EAGER. THE FIRST BURST THRESHED INTO THE SLIME BESIDE BLUE'S LEGS BEFORE THE OTHER AUSTRALIANS WERE CLEAR OF THE MANGROVE ROOTS.
JAPS! STAY WHERE YOU ARE!
BLUE HUGGED THE GROUND AS THE MACHINE-GUN HOSED THE SWAMP, FEELING FOR HIM.
CEASE FIRE! WE WILL FINISH THIS WITH STEEL!
THEY CAME ALONG THE TRACK, A YELLING OFFICER WITH A DRAWN SWORD, AND SIX PRIVATES. BLUE LET THEM HAVE IT AT FIFTEEN FEET.
BANZAI!
COME ON THEN, NIPS!

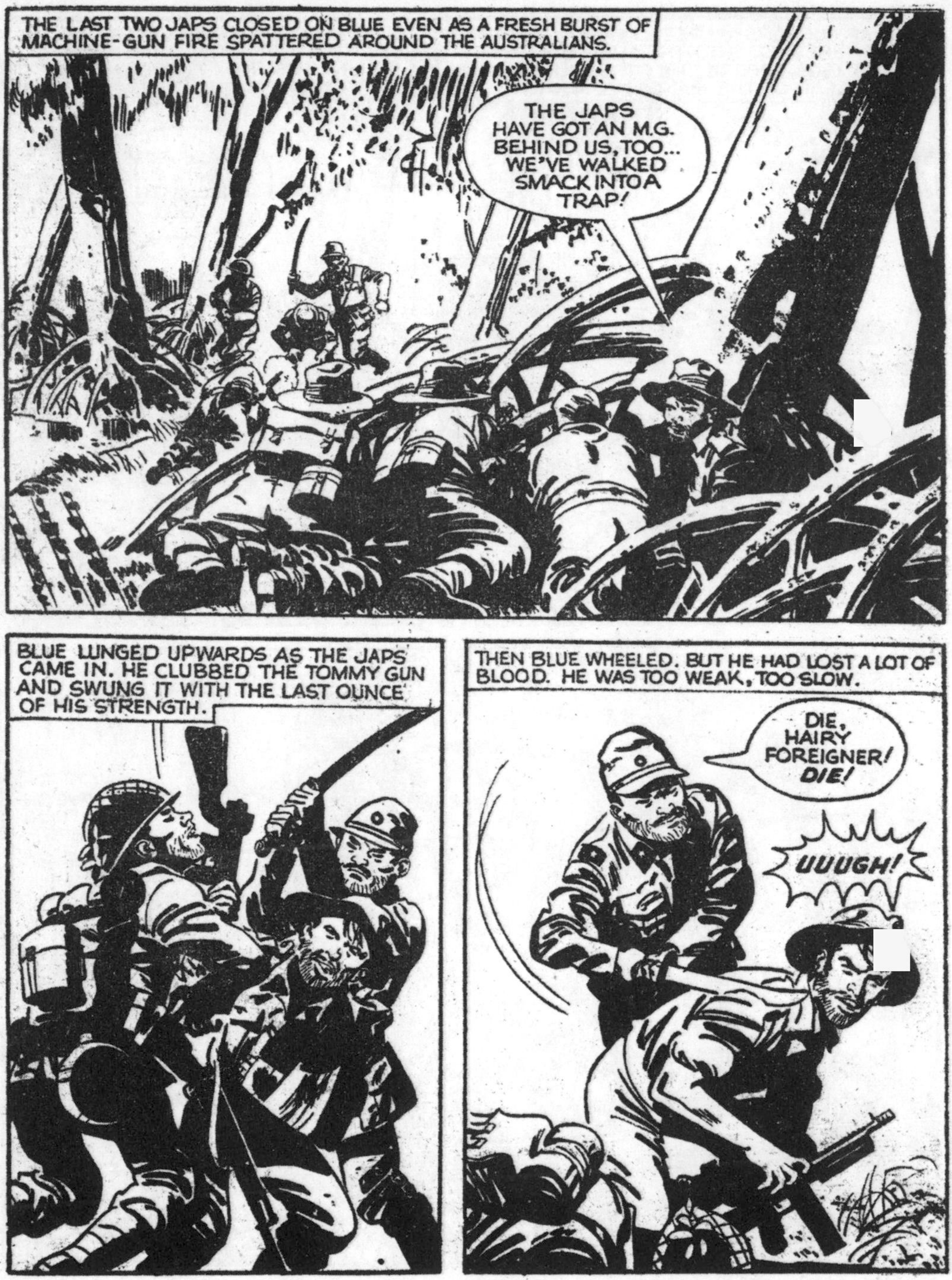
THE LAST TWO JAPS CLOSED ON BLUE EVEN AS A FRESH BURST OF MACHINE-GUN FIRE SPATTERED AROUND THE AUSTRALIANS.
THE JAPS HAVE GOT AN M.G. BEHIND US, TOO... WE'VE WALKED SMACK INTO A TRAP!
BLUE LUNGED UPWARDS AS THE JAPS CAME IN. HE CLUBBED THE TOMMY GUN AND SWUNG IT WITH THE LAST OUNCE OF HIS STRENGTH.
THEN BLUE WHEELED. BUT HE HAD LOST A LOT OF BLOOD. HE WAS TOO WEAK, TOO SLOW.
DIE, HAIRY FOREIGNER! DIE!
UUUGH!

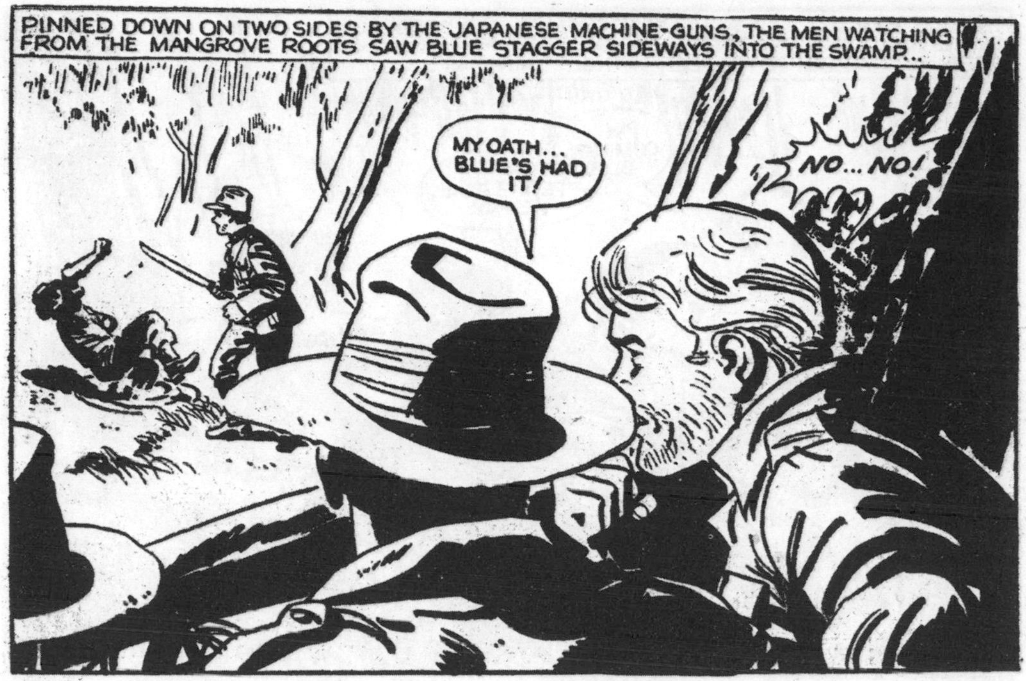
PINNED DOWN ON TWO SIDES BY THE JAPANESE MACHINE-GUNS, THE MEN WATCHING FROM THE MANGROVE ROOTS SAW BLUE STAGGER SIDEWAYS INTO THE SWAMP...
MY OATH... BLUE'S HAD IT!
NO... NO!

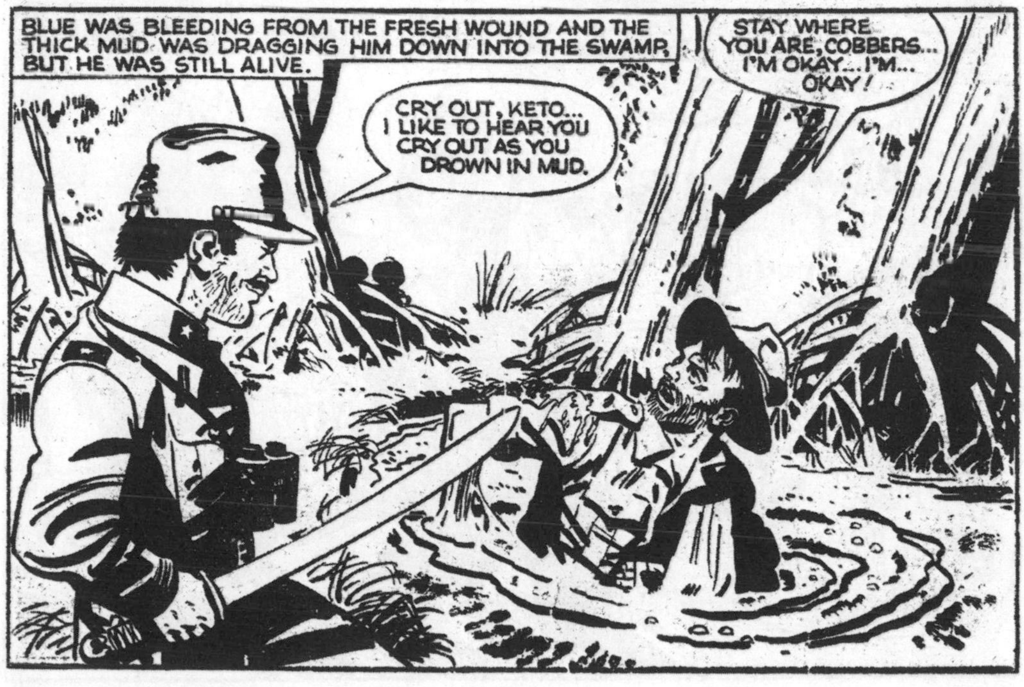
BLUE WAS BLEEDING FROM THE FRESH WOUND AND THE THICK MUD WAS DRAGGING HIM DOWN INTO THE SWAMP, BUT HE WAS STILL ALIVE.
STAY WHERE YOU ARE, COBBERS... I'M OKAY... I'M... OKAY!
CRY OUT, KETO... I LIKE TO HEAR YOU CRY OUT AS YOU DROWN IN MUD.

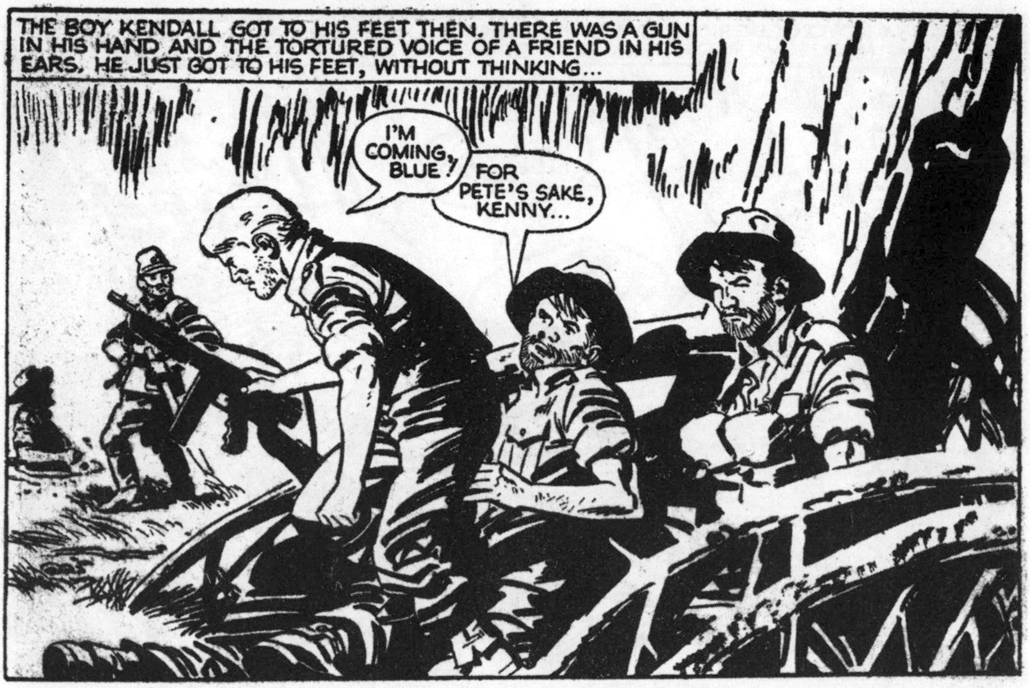
THE BOY KENDALL GOT TO HIS FEET THEN. THERE WAS A GUN IN HIS HAND AND THE TORTURED VOICE OF A FRIEND IN HIS EARS. HE JUST GOT TO HIS FEET, WITHOUT THINKING...
I'M COMING, BLUE!
FOR PETE'S SAKE, KENNY...

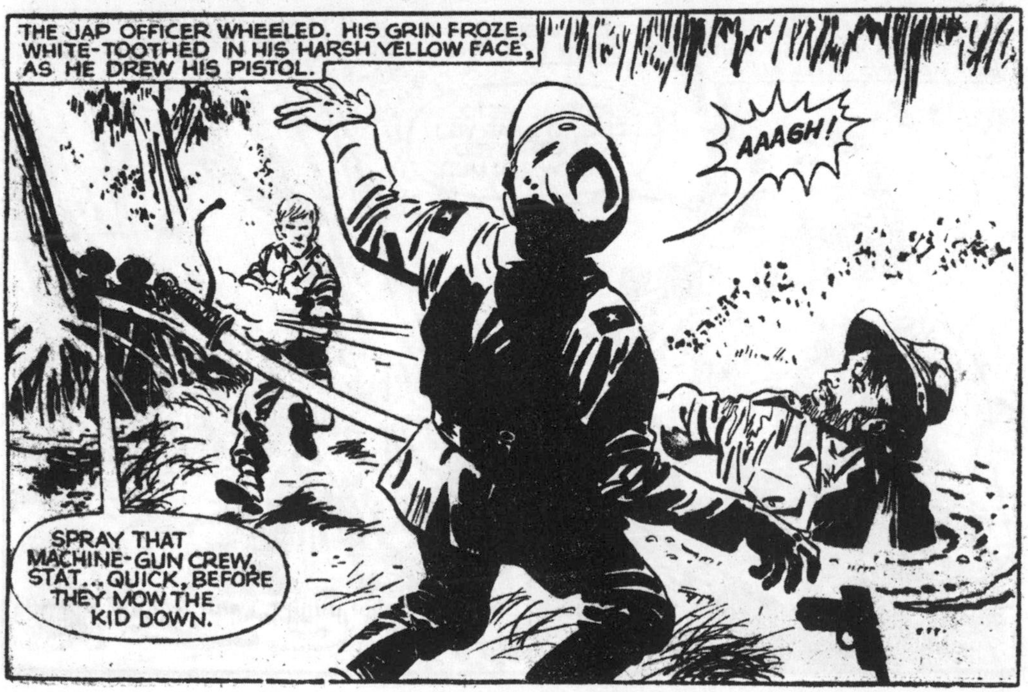
THE JAP OFFICER WHEELED. HIS GRIN FROZE, WHITE-TOOTHED IN HIS HARSH YELLOW FACE, AS HE DREW HIS PISTOL.
AAAGH!
SPRAY THAT MACHINE-GUN CREW, STAT... QUICK, BEFORE THEY MOW THE KID DOWN.

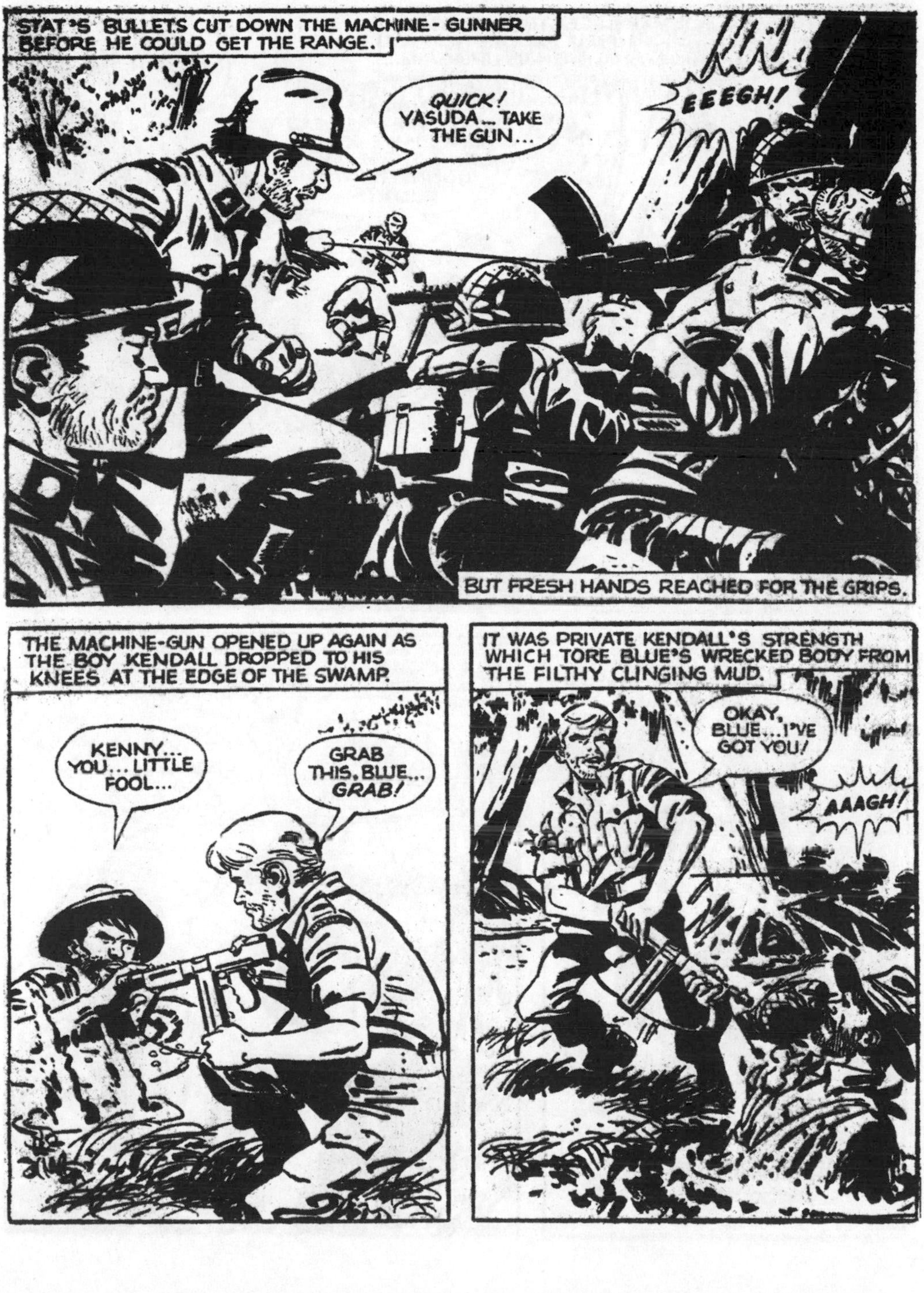
STAT'S BULLETS CUT DOWN THE MACHINE-GUNNER BEFORE HE COULD GET THE RANGE.
QUICK! YASUDA... TAKE THE GUN...
EEEGH!
BUT FRESH HANDS REACHED FOR THE GRIPS.
THE MACHINE-GUN OPENED UP AGAIN AS THE BOY KENDALL DROPPED TO HIS KNEES AT THE EDGE OF THE SWAMP.
KENNY... YOU... LITTLE FOOL...
GRAB THIS, BLUE... GRAB!
IT WAS PRIVATE KENDALL'S STRENGTH WHICH TORE BLUE'S WRECKED BODY FROM THE FILTHY CLINGING MUD.
OKAY, BLUE... I'VE GOT YOU!
AAAGH!

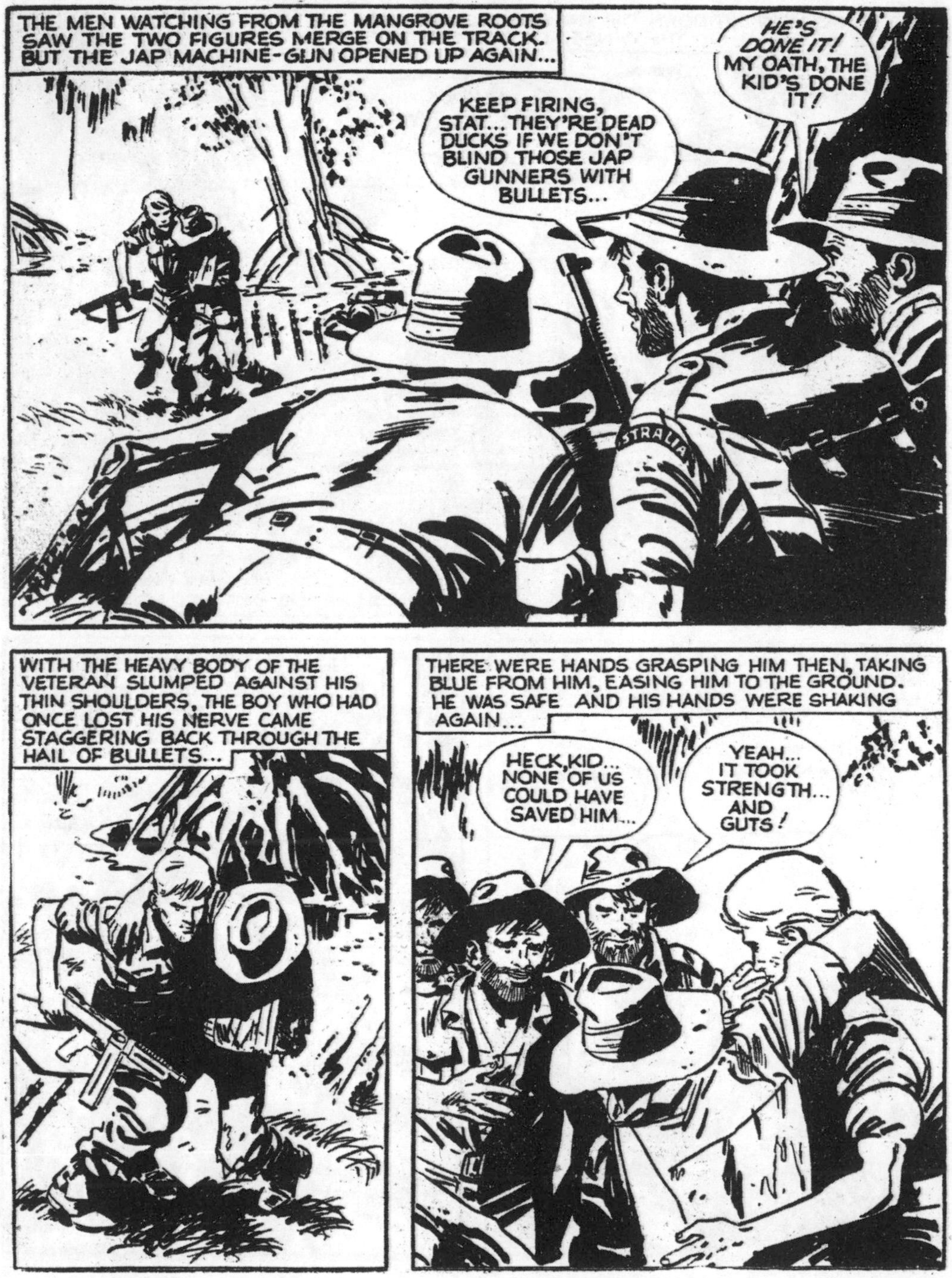
THE MEN WATCHING FROM THE MANGROVE ROOTS SAW THE TWO FIGURES MERGE ON THE TRACK. BUT THE JAP MACHINE-GUN OPENED UP AGAIN...
KEEP FIRING, STAT... THEY'RE DEAD DUCKS IF WE DON'T BLIND THOSE JAP GUNNERS WITH BULLETS...
HE'S DONE IT! MY OATH, THE KID'S DONE IT!
STRALIA
WITH THE HEAVY BODY OF THE VETERAN SLUMPED AGAINST HIS THIN SHOULDERS, THE BOY WHO HAD ONCE LOST HIS NERVE CAME STAGGERING BACK THROUGH THE HAIL OF BULLETS...
THERE WERE HANDS GRASPING HIM THEN, TAKING BLUE FROM HIM, EASING HIM TO THE GROUND. HE WAS SAFE AND HIS HANDS WERE SHAKING AGAIN...
HECK, KID... NONE OF US COULD HAVE SAVED HIM...
YEAH... IT TOOK STRENGTH... AND GUTS!

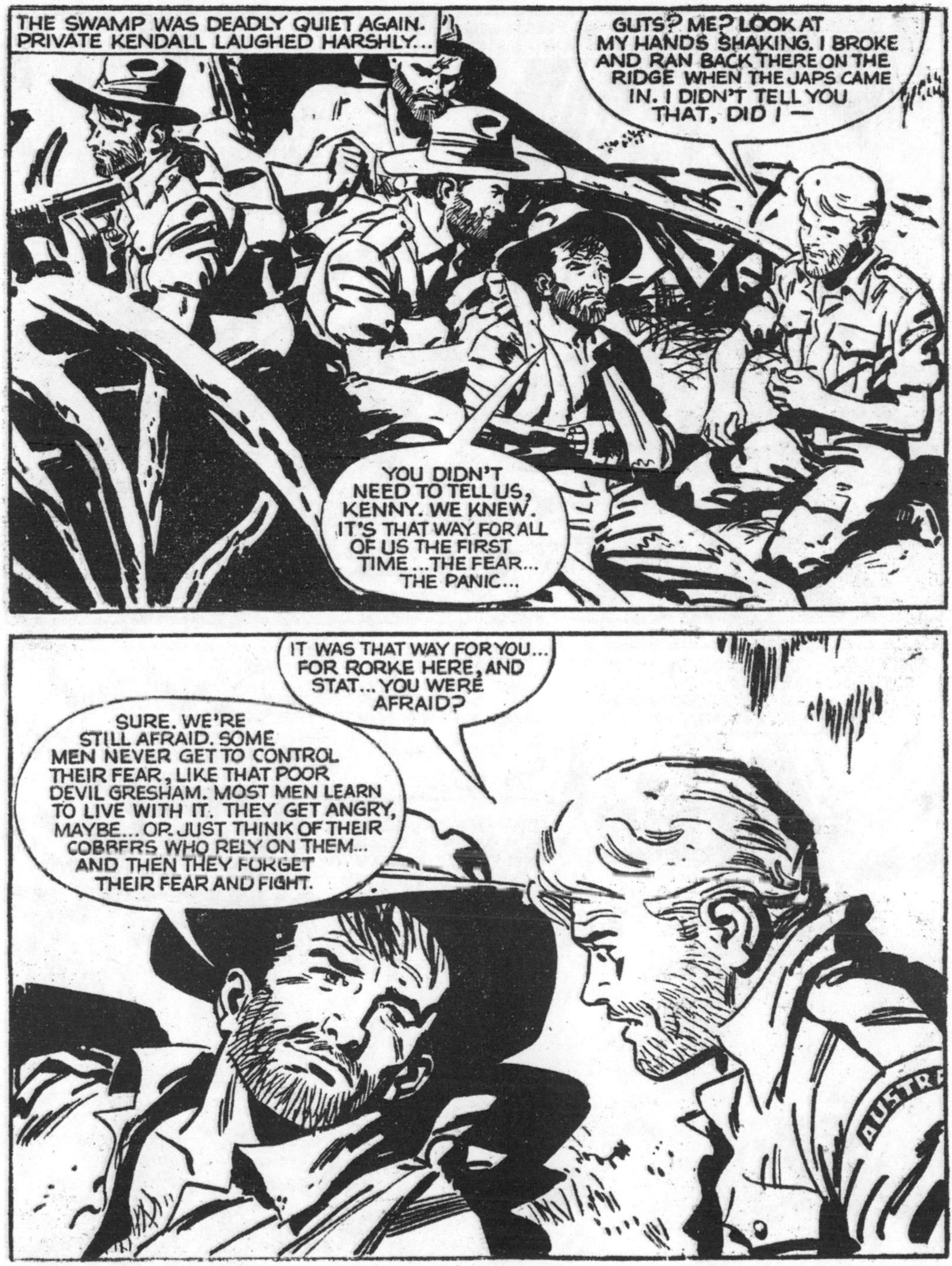
THE SWAMP WAS DEADLY QUIET AGAIN. PRIVATE KENDALL LAUGHED HARSHLY...
GUTS? ME? LOOK AT MY HANDS SHAKING. I BROKE AND RAN BACK THERE ON THE RIDGE WHEN THE JAPS CAME IN. I DIDN'T TELL YOU THAT, DID I —
YOU DIDN'T NEED TO TELL US, KENNY. WE KNEW. IT'S THAT WAY FOR ALL OF US THE FIRST TIME...THE FEAR... THE PANIC...
IT WAS THAT WAY FOR YOU... FOR RORKE HERE, AND STAT... YOU WERE AFRAID?
SURE. WE'RE STILL AFRAID. SOME MEN NEVER GET TO CONTROL THEIR FEAR, LIKE THAT POOR DEVIL GRESHAM. MOST MEN LEARN TO LIVE WITH IT. THEY GET ANGRY, MAYBE... OR JUST THINK OF THEIR COBBERS WHO RELY ON THEM... AND THEN THEY FORGET THEIR FEAR AND FIGHT.

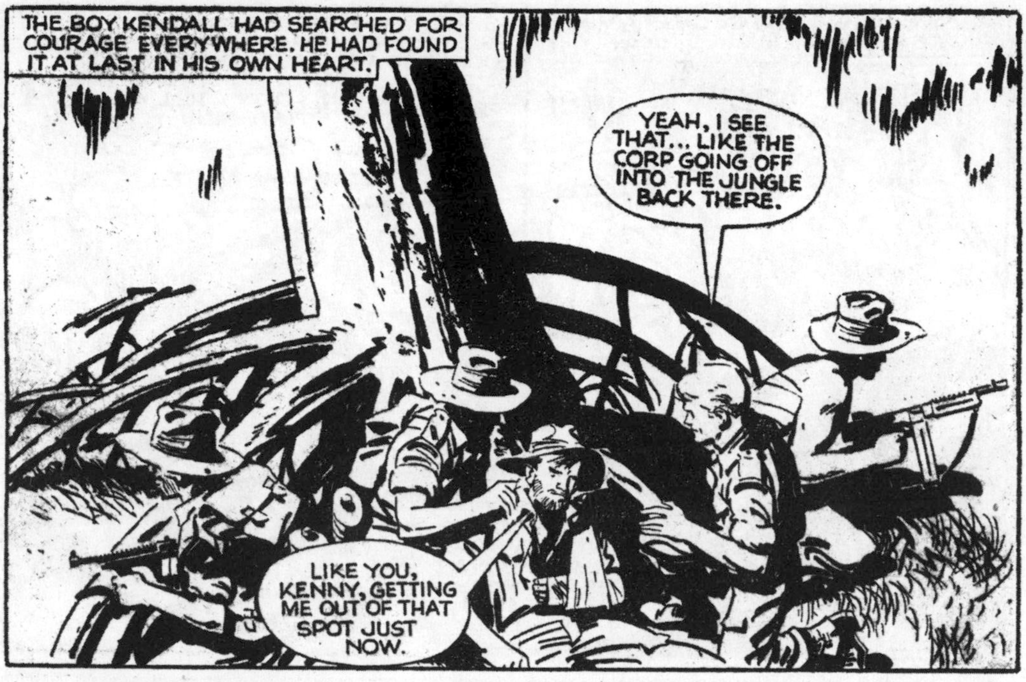
THE BOY KENDALL HAD SEARCHED FOR COURAGE EVERYWHERE. HE HAD FOUND IT AT LAST IN HIS OWN HEART.
YEAH, I SEE THAT... LIKE THE CORP GOING OFF INTO THE JUNGLE BACK THERE.
LIKE YOU, KENNY, GETTING ME OUT OF THAT SPOT JUST NOW.

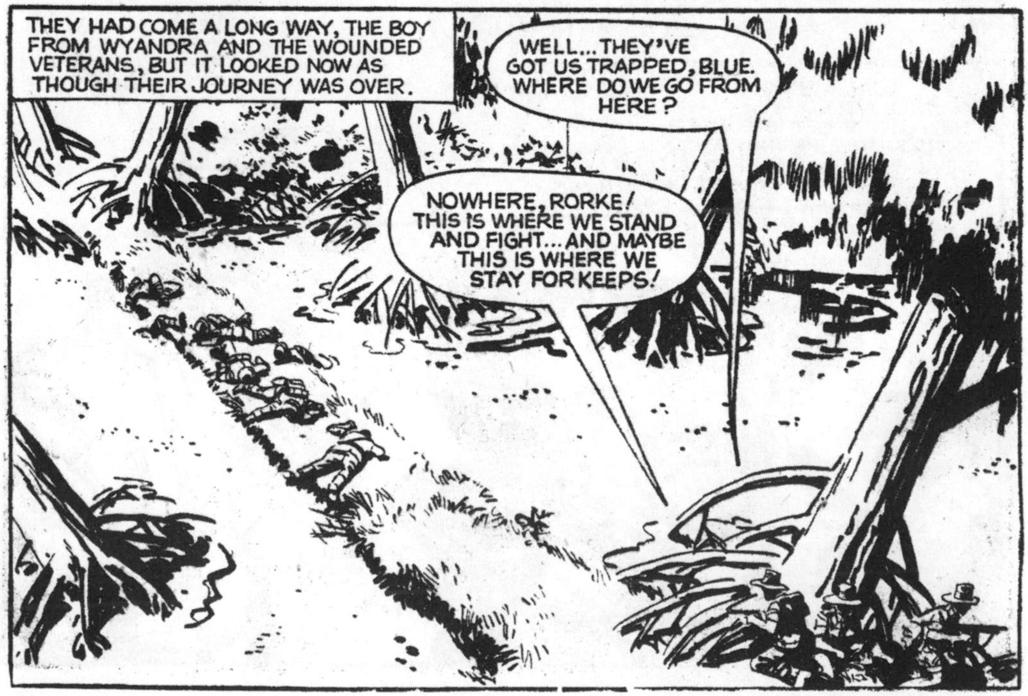
THEY HAD COME A LONG WAY, THE BOY FROM WYANDRA AND THE WOUNDED VETERANS, BUT IT LOOKED NOW AS THOUGH THEIR JOURNEY WAS OVER.
WELL... THEY'VE GOT US TRAPPED, BLUE. WHERE DO WE GO FROM HERE?
NOWHERE, RORKE! THIS IS WHERE WE STAND AND FIGHT... AND MAYBE THIS IS WHERE WE STAY FOR KEEPS!

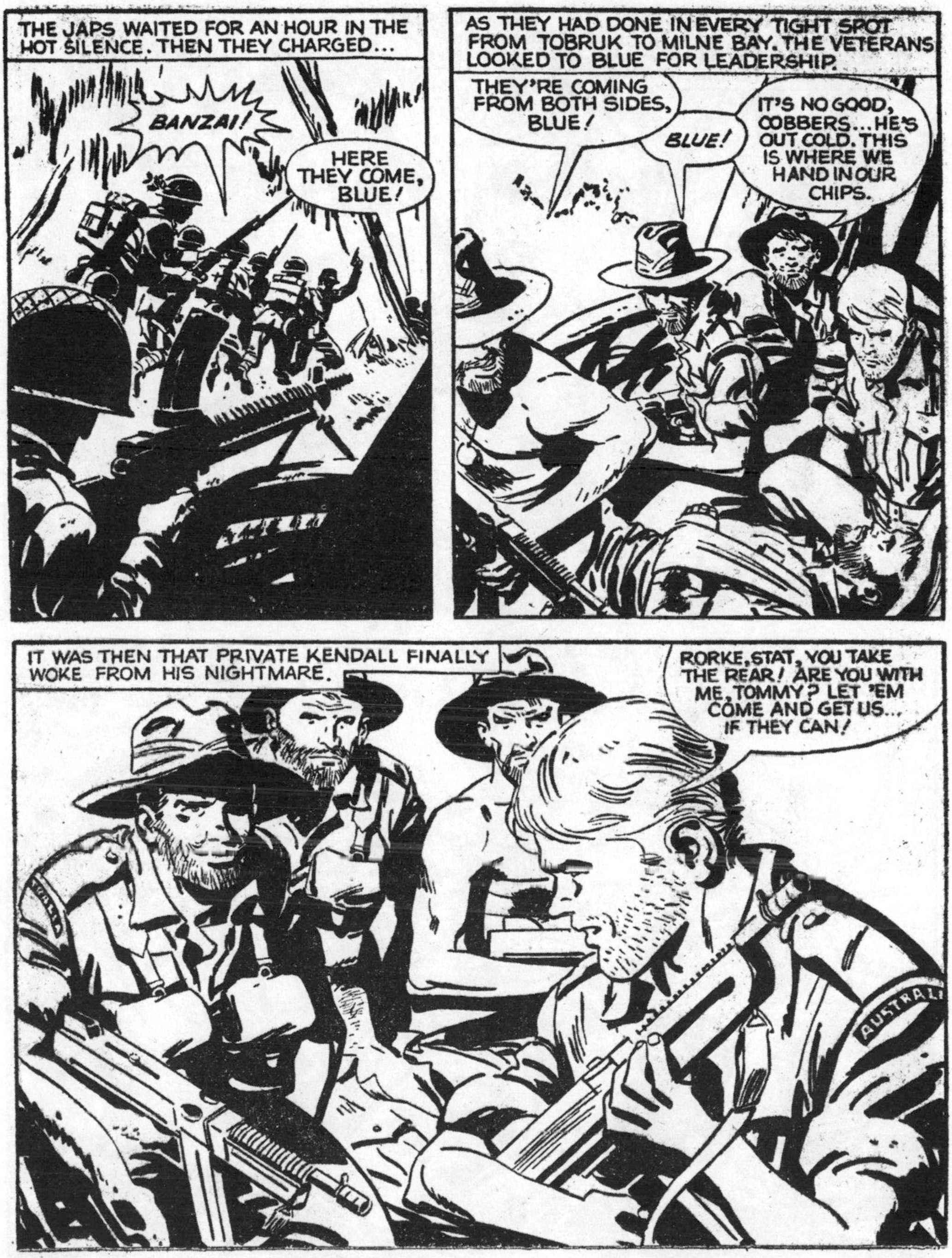
THE JAPS WAITED FOR AN HOUR IN THE HOT SILENCE. THEN THEY CHARGED...
BANZAI!
HERE THEY COME, BLUE!
AS THEY HAD DONE IN EVERY TIGHT SPOT FROM TOBRUK TO MILNE BAY. THE VETERANS LOOKED TO BLUE FOR LEADERSHIP.
THEY'RE COMING FROM BOTH SIDES, BLUE!
BLUE!
IT'S NO GOOD, COBBERS... HE'S OUT COLD. THIS IS WHERE WE HAND IN OUR CHIPS.
IT WAS THEN THAT PRIVATE KENDALL FINALLY WOKE FROM HIS NIGHTMARE.
RORKE, STAT, YOU TAKE THE REAR! ARE YOU WITH ME, TOMMY? LET 'EM COME AND GET US... IF THEY CAN!
AUSTRALIA

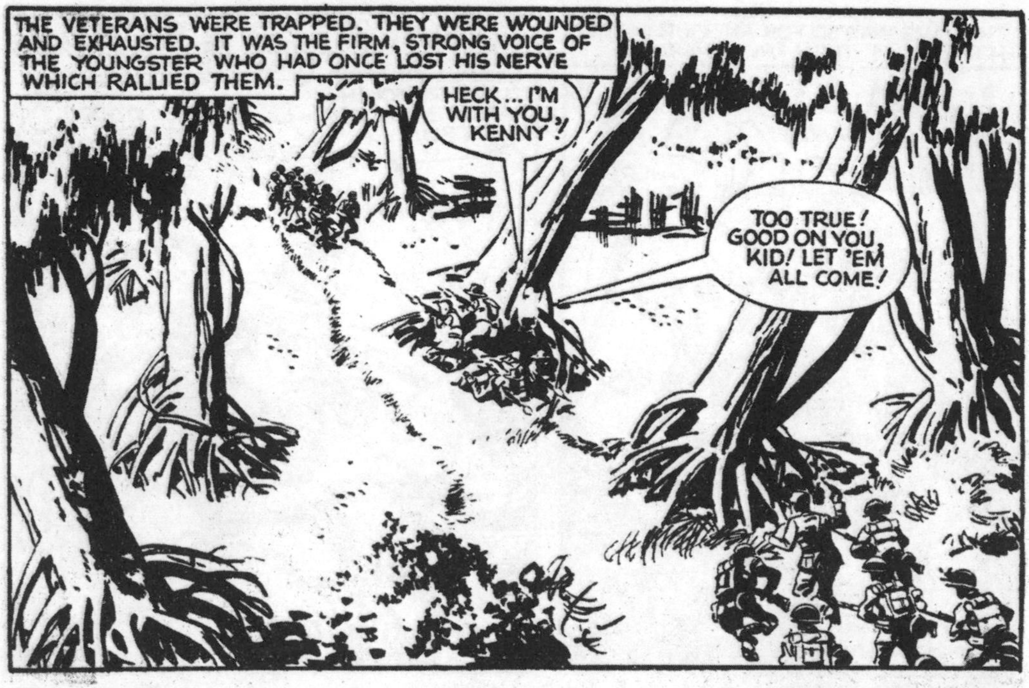
THE VETERANS WERE TRAPPED. THEY WERE WOUNDED AND EXHAUSTED. IT WAS THE FIRM, STRONG VOICE OF THE YOUNGSTER WHO HAD ONCE LOST HIS NERVE WHICH RALLIED THEM.
HECK... I'M WITH YOU, KENNY!
TOO TRUE! GOOD ON YOU, KID! LET 'EM ALL COME!

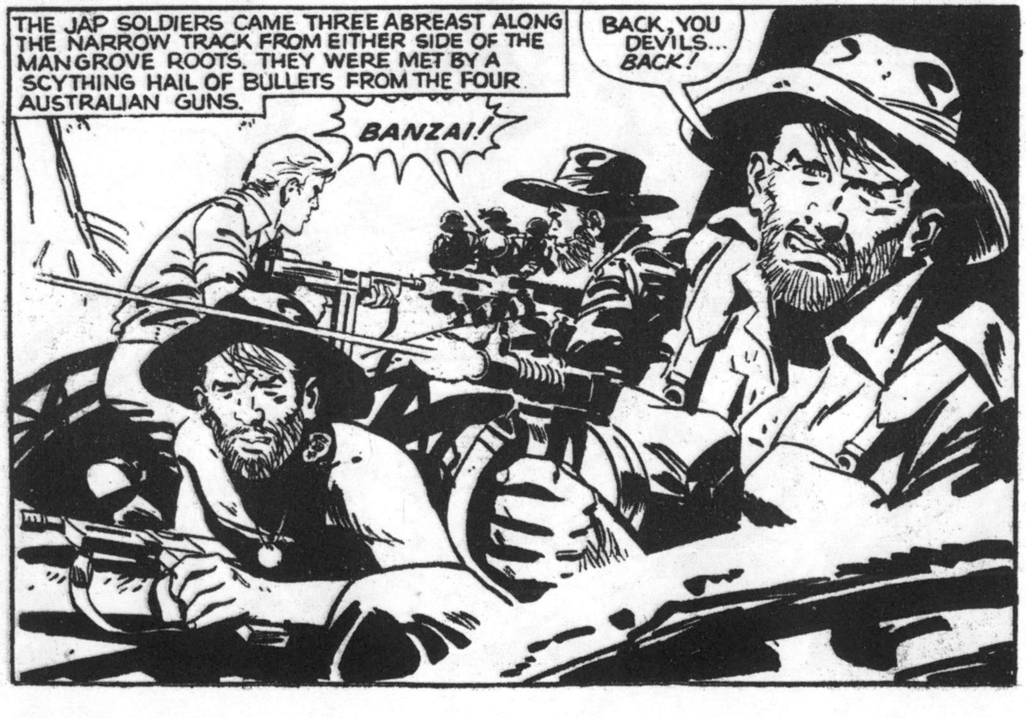
THE JAP SOLDIERS CAME THREE ABREAST ALONG THE NARROW TRACK FROM EITHER SIDE OF THE MANGROVE ROOTS. THEY WERE MET BY A SCYTHING HAIL OF BULLETS FROM THE FOUR AUSTRALIAN GUNS.
BACK, YOU DEVILS... BACK!
BANZAI!

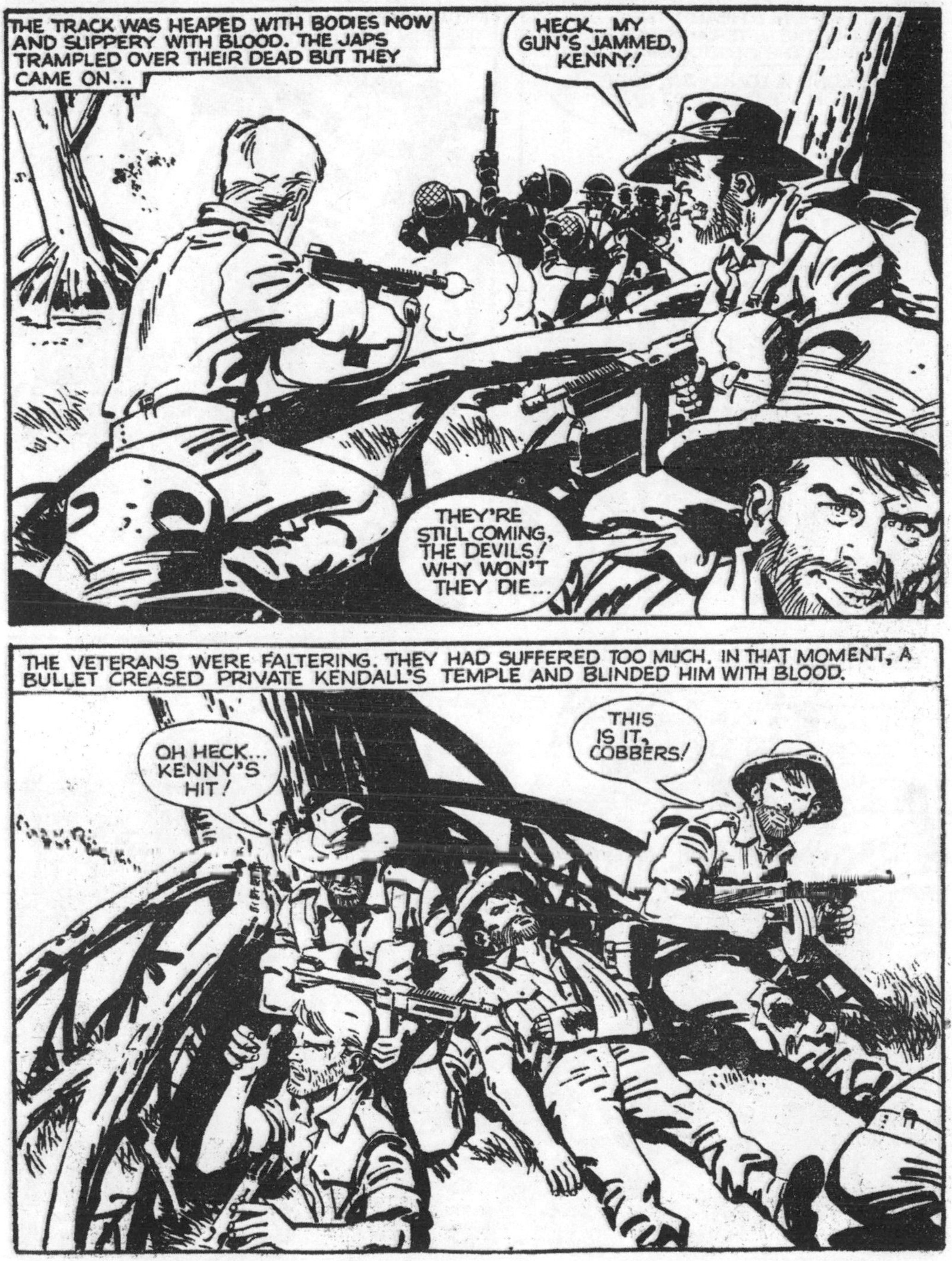
THE TRACK WAS HEAPED WITH BODIES NOW AND SLIPPERY WITH BLOOD. THE JAPS TRAMPLED OVER THEIR DEAD BUT THEY CAME ON...
HECK... MY GUN'S JAMMED, KENNY!
THEY'RE STILL COMING, THE DEVILS! WHY WON'T THEY DIE...
THE VETERANS WERE FALTERING. THEY HAD SUFFERED TOO MUCH. IN THAT MOMENT, A BULLET CREASED PRIVATE KENDALL'S TEMPLE AND BLINDED HIM WITH BLOOD.
OH HECK... KENNY'S HIT!
THIS IS IT, COBBERS!

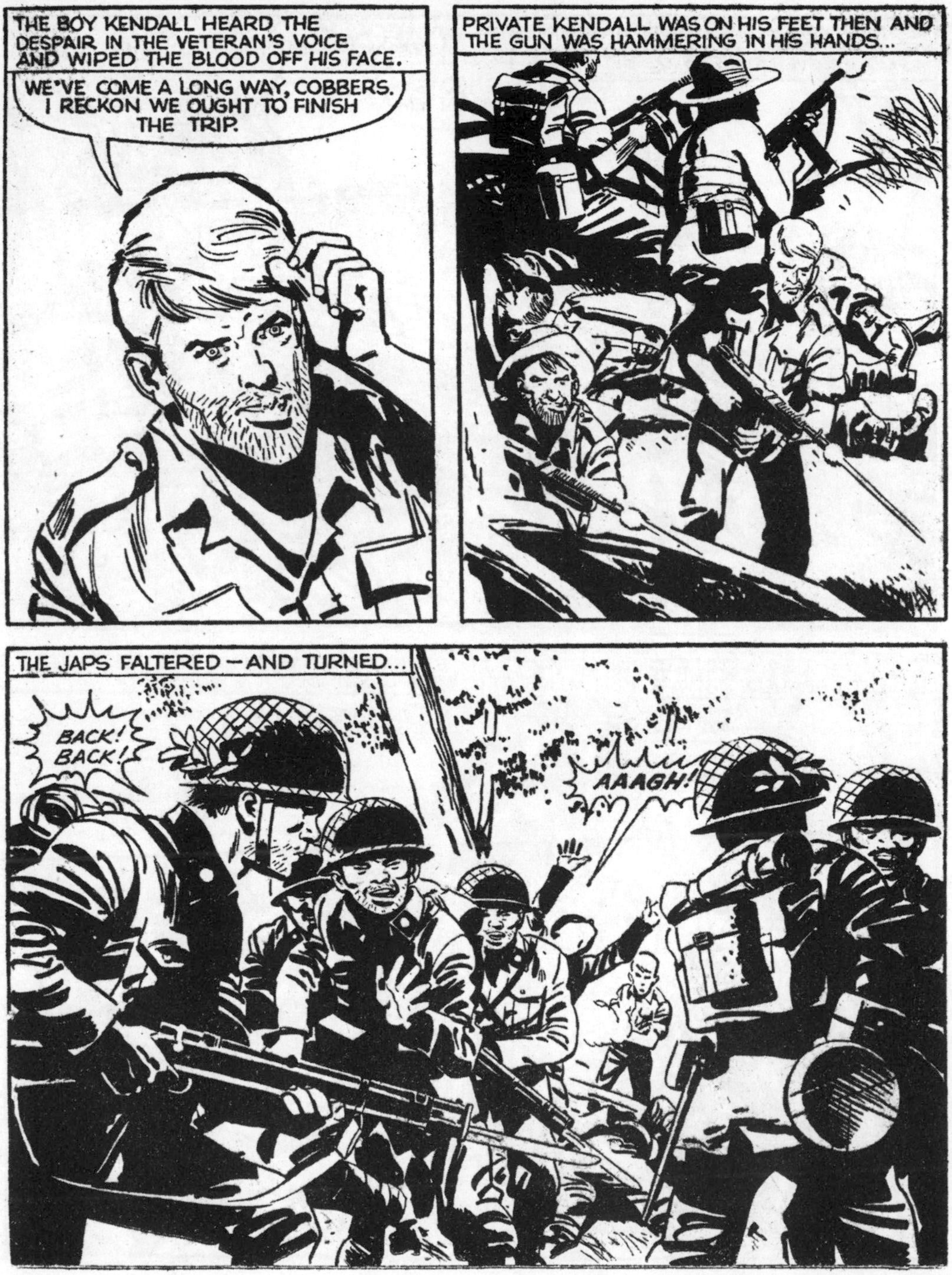
THE BOY KENDALL HEARD THE DESPAIR IN THE VETERAN'S VOICE AND WIPED THE BLOOD OFF HIS FACE.
WE'VE COME A LONG WAY, COBBERS. I RECKON WE OUGHT TO FINISH THE TRIP.
PRIVATE KENDALL WAS ON HIS FEET THEN AND THE GUN WAS HAMMERING IN HIS HANDS...
THE JAPS FALTERED — AND TURNED...
BACK! BACK!
AAAGH!

PRIVATE KENDALL FOLLOWED THE JAPS, STIFF-LEGGED, THE GUN LEAPING AT HIS HIP. BEHIND HIM, THE VETERANS EASED OFF ON THEIR TRIGGERS...

THE KID'S BEATEN 'EM!

YEAH...AND THERE ARE NO MORE TO COME ON THIS SIDE EITHER, COBBERS!

HE STOOD ALONE ON THE TRACK ABOVE THE SWAMP. A BOY WITH BLOOD ON HIS FACE AND THE KNOWLEDGE OF DEATH IN HIS EYES. HIS HANDS WERE NOT SHAKING...

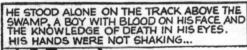

PRIVATE KENDALL TURNED AND LOOKED AT THE VETERANS. THEY WAITED FOR WHAT HE HAD TO SAY...

OKAY, COBBERS... THAT'S IT! LET'S BE ON OUR WAY.

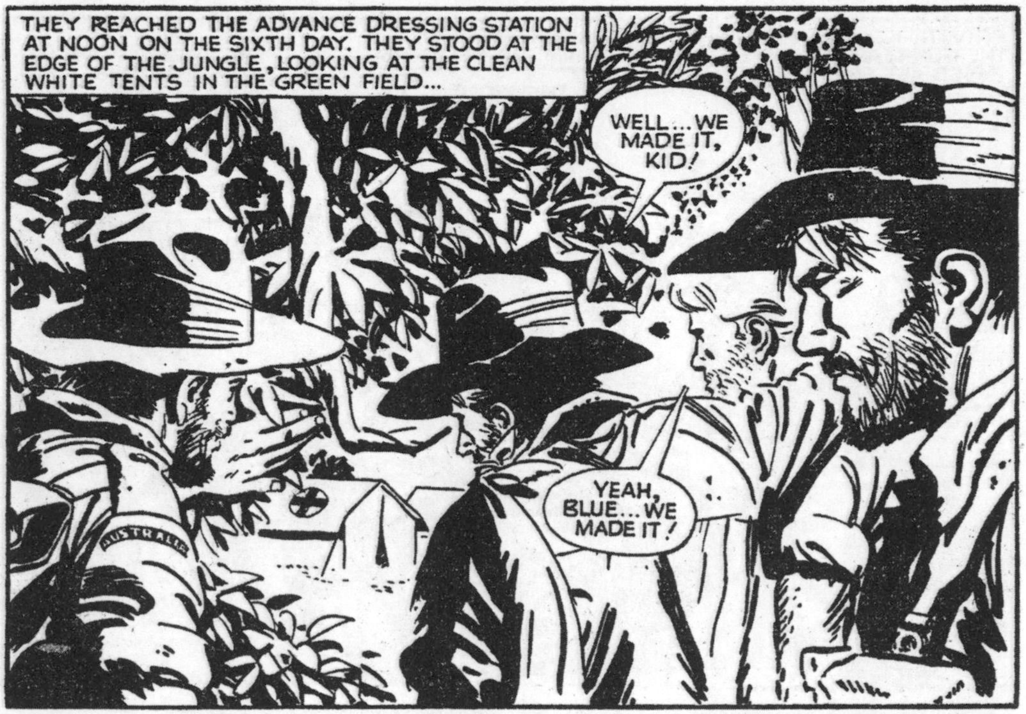
THEY REACHED THE ADVANCE DRESSING STATION AT NOON ON THE SIXTH DAY. THEY STOOD AT THE EDGE OF THE JUNGLE, LOOKING AT THE CLEAN WHITE TENTS IN THE GREEN FIELD...
WELL... WE MADE IT, KID!
YEAH, BLUE... WE MADE IT!

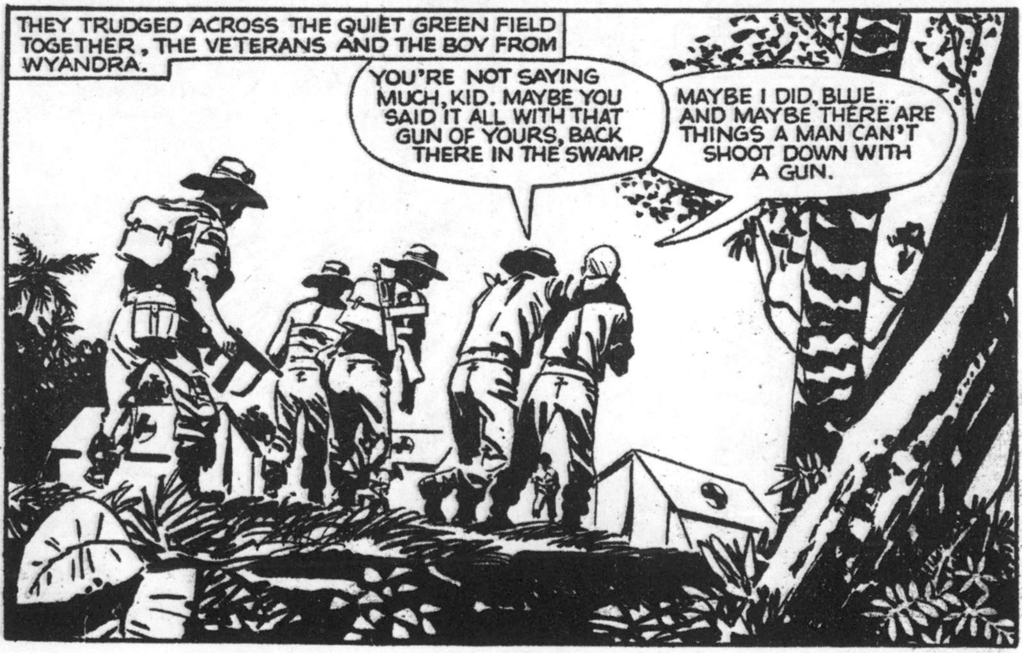
THEY TRUDGED ACROSS THE QUIET GREEN FIELD TOGETHER, THE VETERANS AND THE BOY FROM WYANDRA.
YOU'RE NOT SAYING MUCH, KID. MAYBE YOU SAID IT ALL WITH THAT GUN OF YOURS, BACK THERE IN THE SWAMP.
MAYBE I DID, BLUE... AND MAYBE THERE ARE THINGS A MAN CAN'T SHOOT DOWN WITH A GUN.

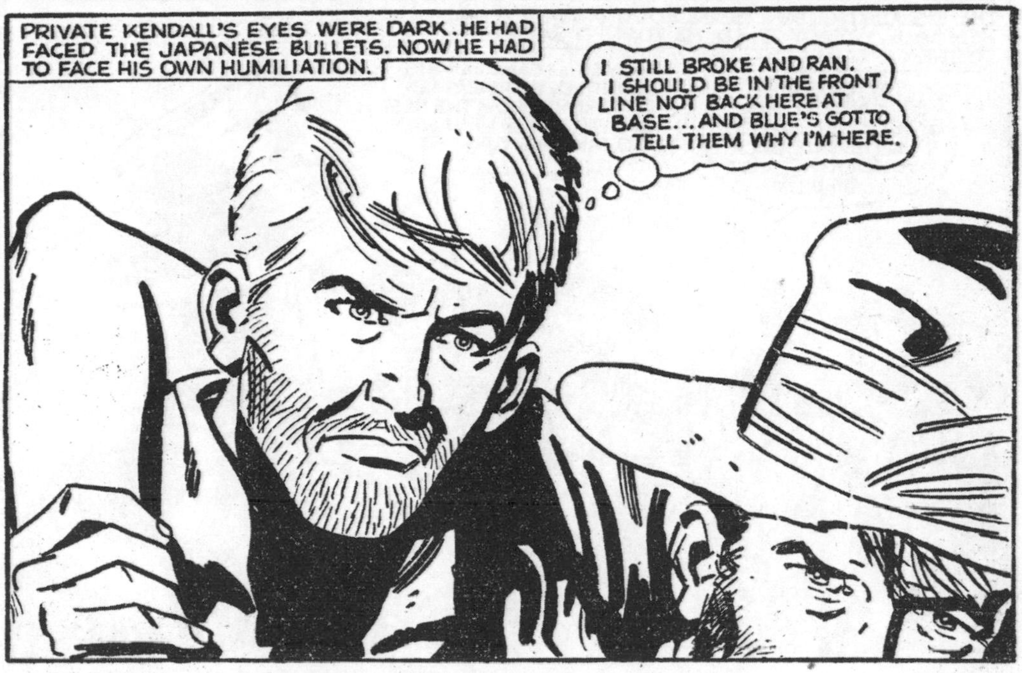
PRIVATE KENDALL'S EYES WERE DARK. HE HAD FACED THE JAPANESE BULLETS. NOW HE HAD TO FACE HIS OWN HUMILIATION.
I STILL BROKE AND RAN. I SHOULD BE IN THE FRONT LINE NOT BACK HERE AT BASE... AND BLUE'S GOT TO TELL THEM WHY I'M HERE.

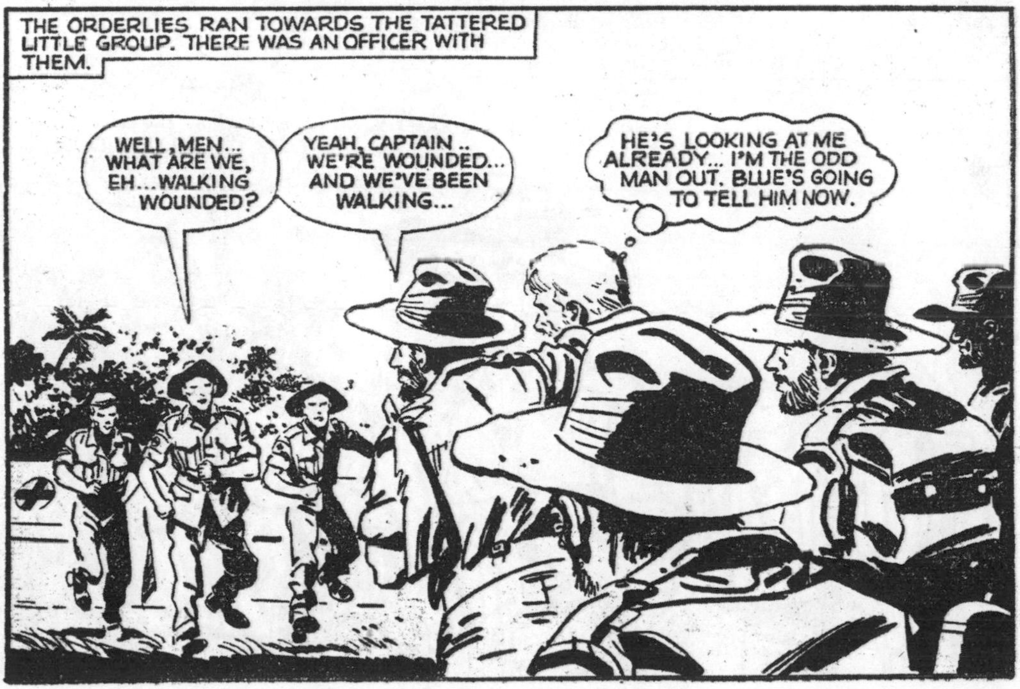
THE ORDERLIES RAN TOWARDS THE TATTERED LITTLE GROUP. THERE WAS AN OFFICER WITH THEM.
WELL, MEN... WHAT ARE WE, EH... WALKING WOUNDED?
YEAH, CAPTAIN .. WE'RE WOUNDED... AND WE'VE BEEN WALKING...
HE'S LOOKING AT ME ALREADY... I'M THE ODD MAN OUT. BLUE'S GOING TO TELL HIM NOW.

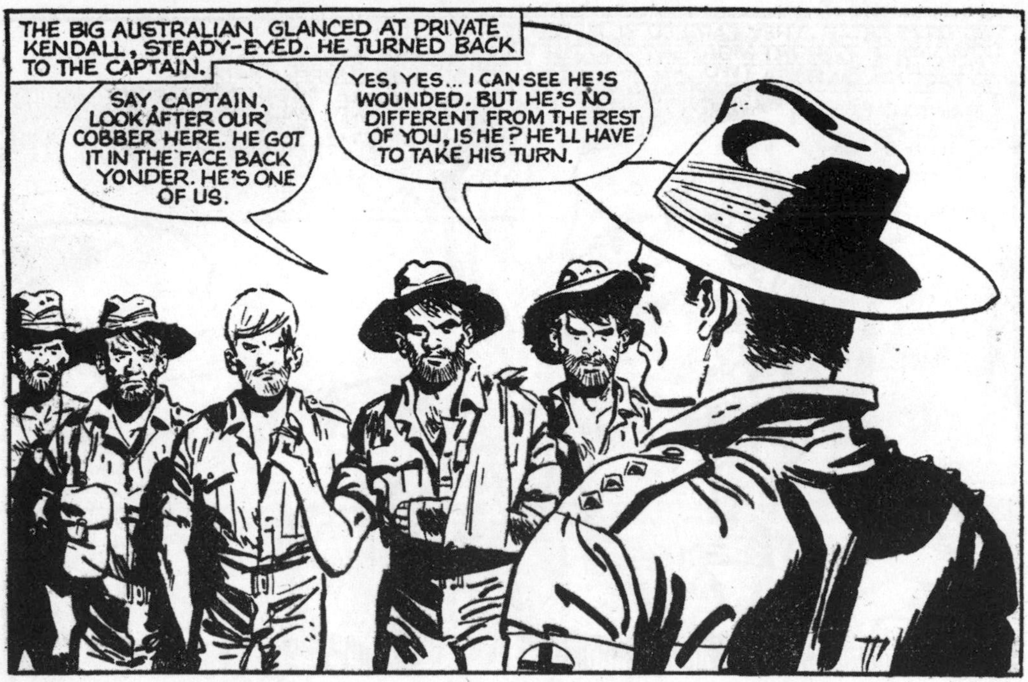
THE BIG AUSTRALIAN GLANCED AT PRIVATE KENDALL, STEADY-EYED. HE TURNED BACK TO THE CAPTAIN.
SAY, CAPTAIN, LOOK AFTER OUR COBBER HERE. HE GOT IT IN THE FACE BACK YONDER. HE'S ONE OF US.
YES, YES... I CAN SEE HE'S WOUNDED. BUT HE'S NO DIFFERENT FROM THE REST OF YOU, IS HE? HE'LL HAVE TO TAKE HIS TURN.

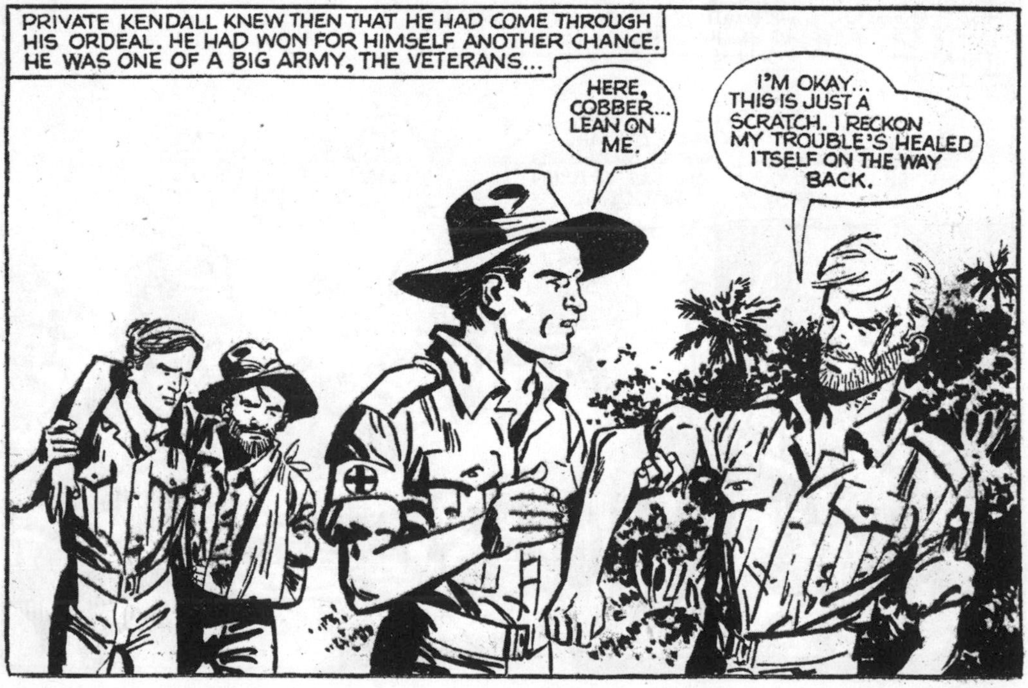
PRIVATE KENDALL KNEW THEN THAT HE HAD COME THROUGH HIS ORDEAL. HE HAD WON FOR HIMSELF ANOTHER CHANCE. HE WAS ONE OF A BIG ARMY, THE VETERANS...
HERE, COBBER... LEAN ON ME.
I'M OKAY... THIS IS JUST A SCRATCH. I RECKON MY TROUBLE'S HEALED ITSELF ON THE WAY BACK.

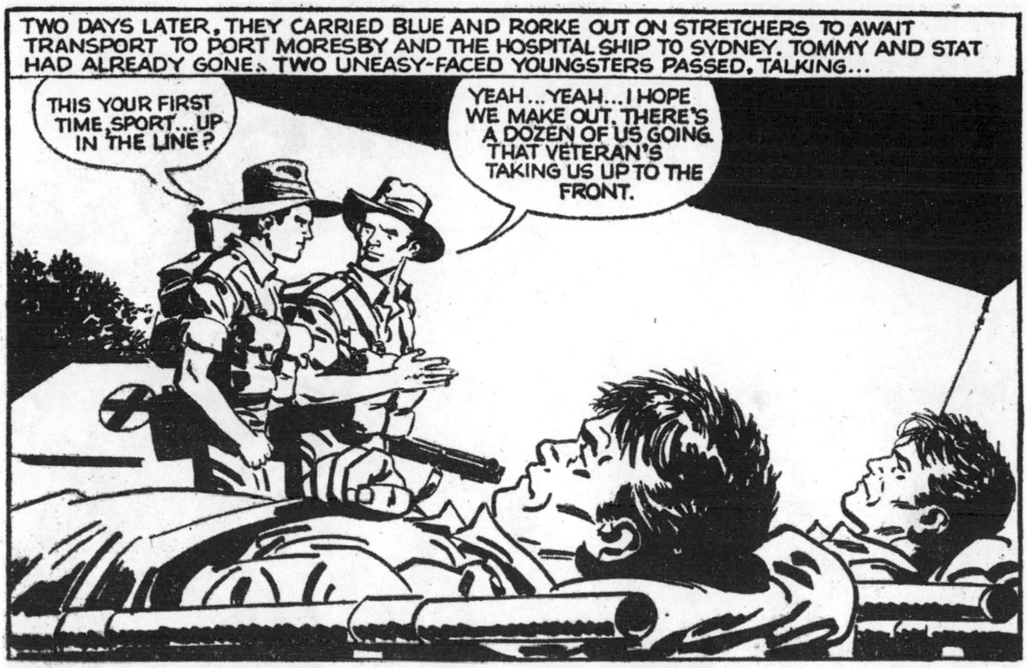
TWO DAYS LATER, THEY CARRIED BLUE AND RORKE OUT ON STRETCHERS TO AWAIT TRANSPORT TO PORT MORESBY AND THE HOSPITAL SHIP TO SYDNEY. TOMMY AND STAT HAD ALREADY GONE. TWO UNEASY-FACED YOUNGSTERS PASSED, TALKING...
THIS YOUR FIRST TIME, SPORT... UP IN THE LINE?
YEAH... YEAH... I HOPE WE MAKE OUT. THERE'S A DOZEN OF US GOING. THAT VETERAN'S TAKING US UP TO THE FRONT.

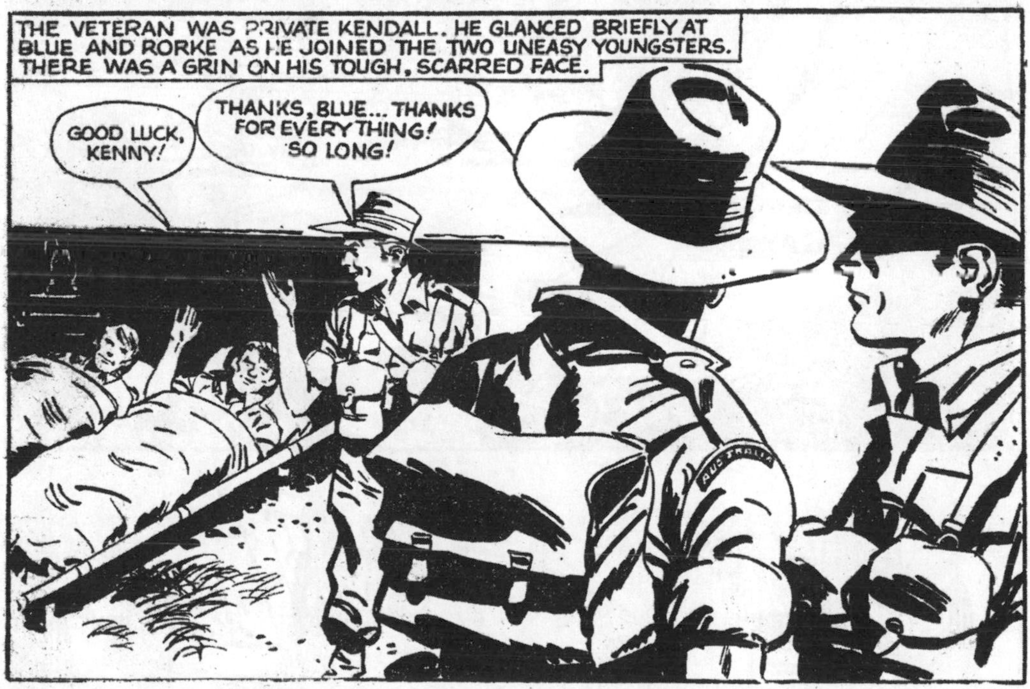
THE VETERAN WAS PRIVATE KENDALL. HE GLANCED BRIEFLY AT BLUE AND RORKE AS HE JOINED THE TWO UNEASY YOUNGSTERS. THERE WAS A GRIN ON HIS TOUGH, SCARRED FACE.
GOOD LUCK, KENNY!
THANKS, BLUE... THANKS FOR EVERYTHING! SO LONG!

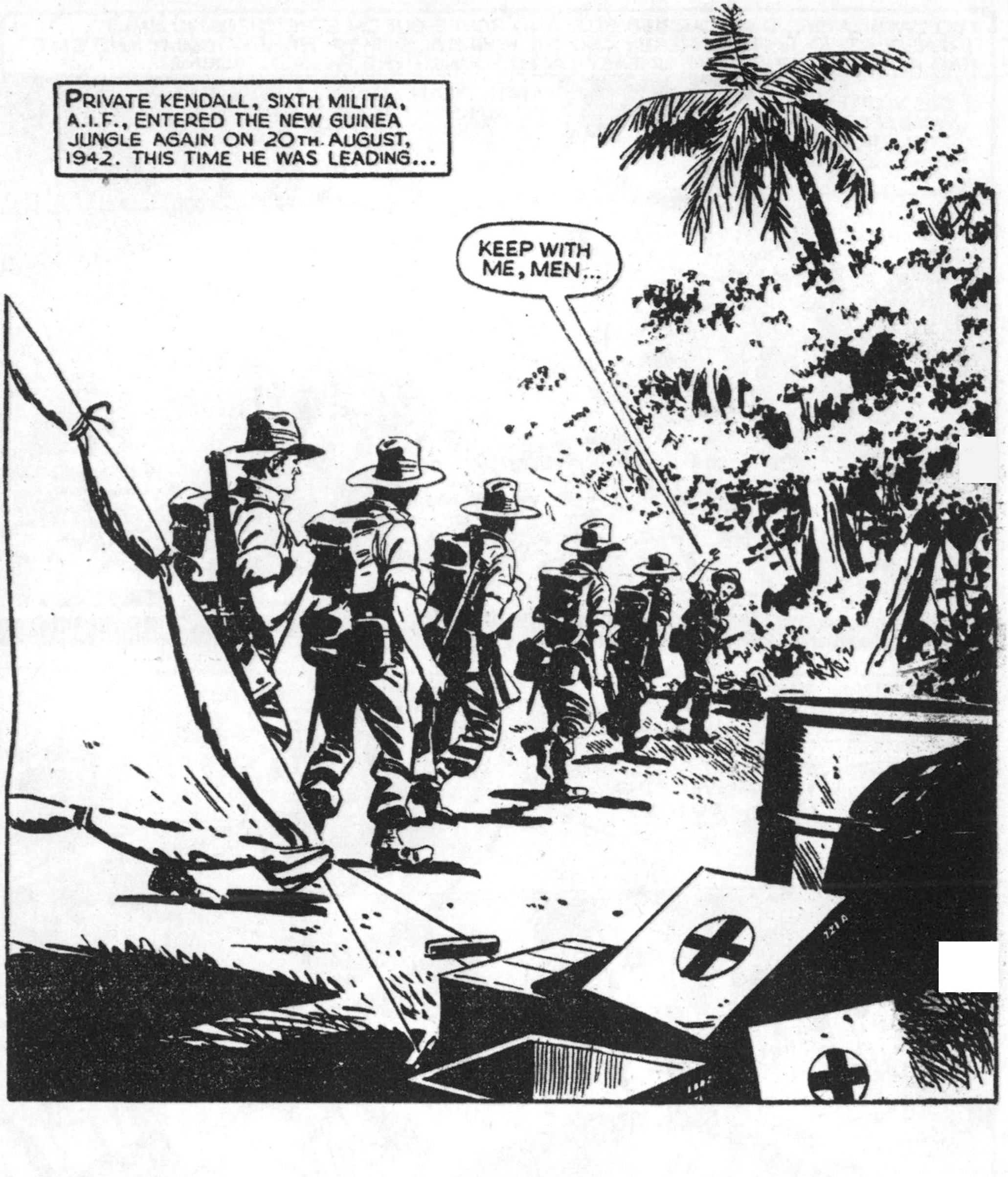
PRIVATE KENDALL, SIXTH MILITIA, A.I.F., ENTERED THE NEW GUINEA JUNGLE AGAIN ON 20TH. AUGUST, 1942. THIS TIME HE WAS LEADING...
KEEP WITH ME, MEN...

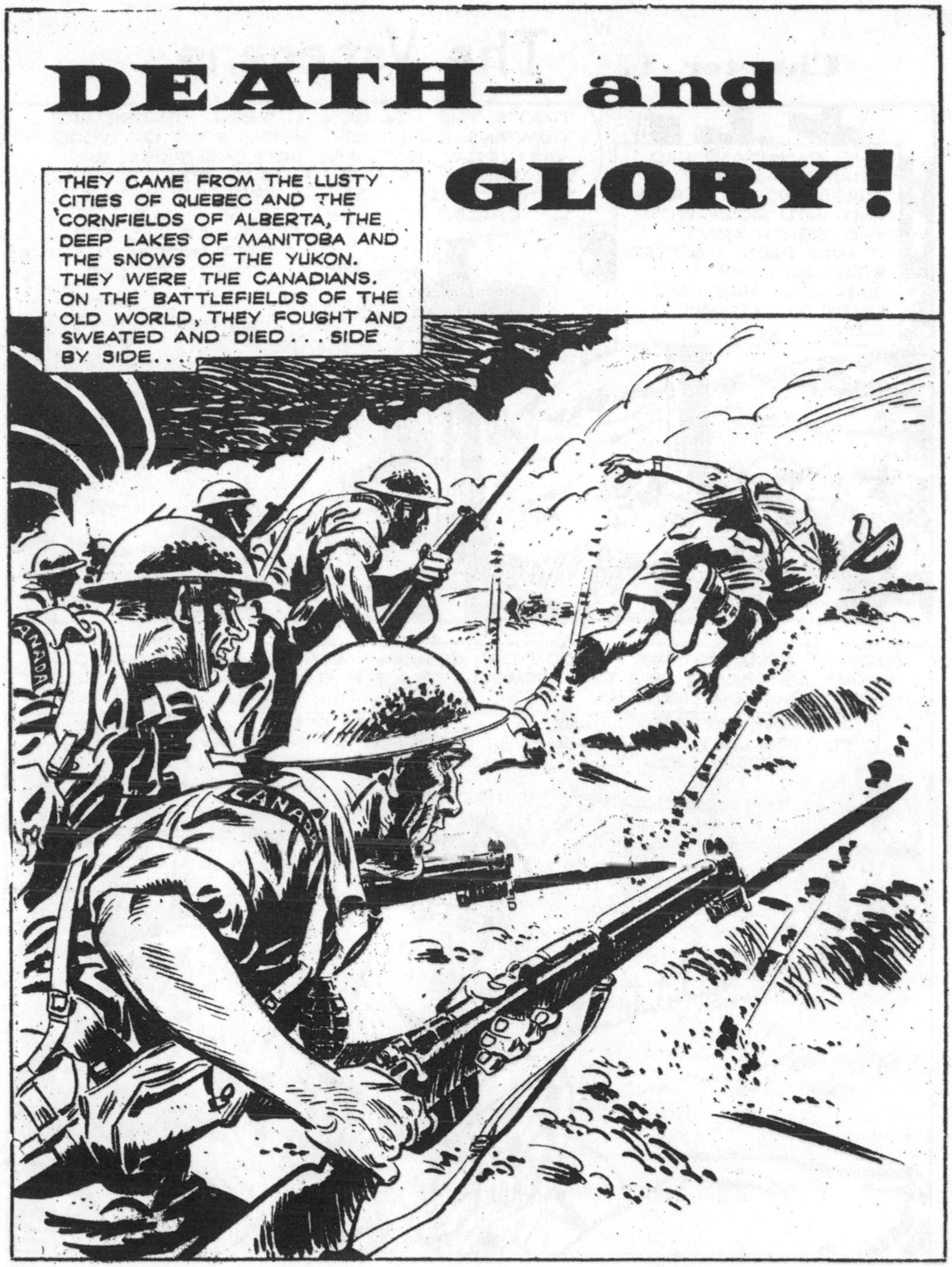
DEATH—and GLORY!
THEY CAME FROM THE LUSTY CITIES OF QUEBEC AND THE CORNFIELDS OF ALBERTA, THE DEEP LAKES OF MANITOBA AND THE SNOWS OF THE YUKON. THEY WERE THE CANADIANS. ON THE BATTLEFIELDS OF THE OLD WORLD, THEY FOUGHT AND SWEATED AND DIED . . . SIDE BY SIDE . . .
CANADA

Chapter 1. The Veterans

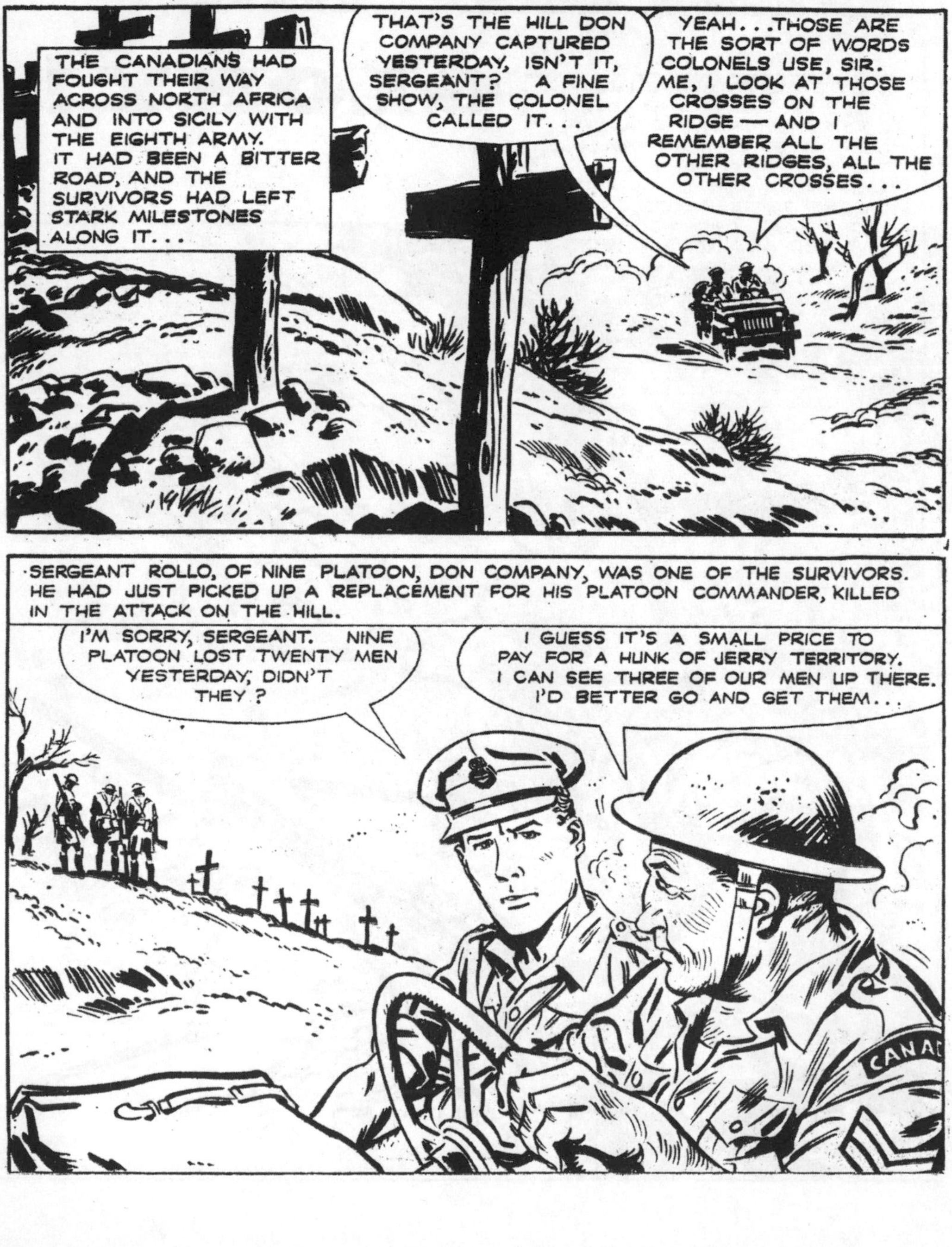
THE CANADIANS HAD FOUGHT THEIR WAY ACROSS NORTH AFRICA AND INTO SICILY WITH THE EIGHTH ARMY. IT HAD BEEN A BITTER ROAD, AND THE SURVIVORS HAD LEFT STARK MILESTONES ALONG IT...
THAT'S THE HILL DON COMPANY CAPTURED YESTERDAY, ISN'T IT, SERGEANT? A FINE SHOW, THE COLONEL CALLED IT...
YEAH...THOSE ARE THE SORT OF WORDS COLONELS USE, SIR. ME, I LOOK AT THOSE CROSSES ON THE RIDGE — AND I REMEMBER ALL THE OTHER RIDGES, ALL THE OTHER CROSSES...
SERGEANT ROLLO, OF NINE PLATOON, DON COMPANY, WAS ONE OF THE SURVIVORS. HE HAD JUST PICKED UP A REPLACEMENT FOR HIS PLATOON COMMANDER, KILLED IN THE ATTACK ON THE HILL.
I'M SORRY, SERGEANT. NINE PLATOON LOST TWENTY MEN YESTERDAY, DIDN'T THEY?
I GUESS IT'S A SMALL PRICE TO PAY FOR A HUNK OF JERRY TERRITORY. I CAN SEE THREE OF OUR MEN UP THERE. I'D BETTER GO AND GET THEM...

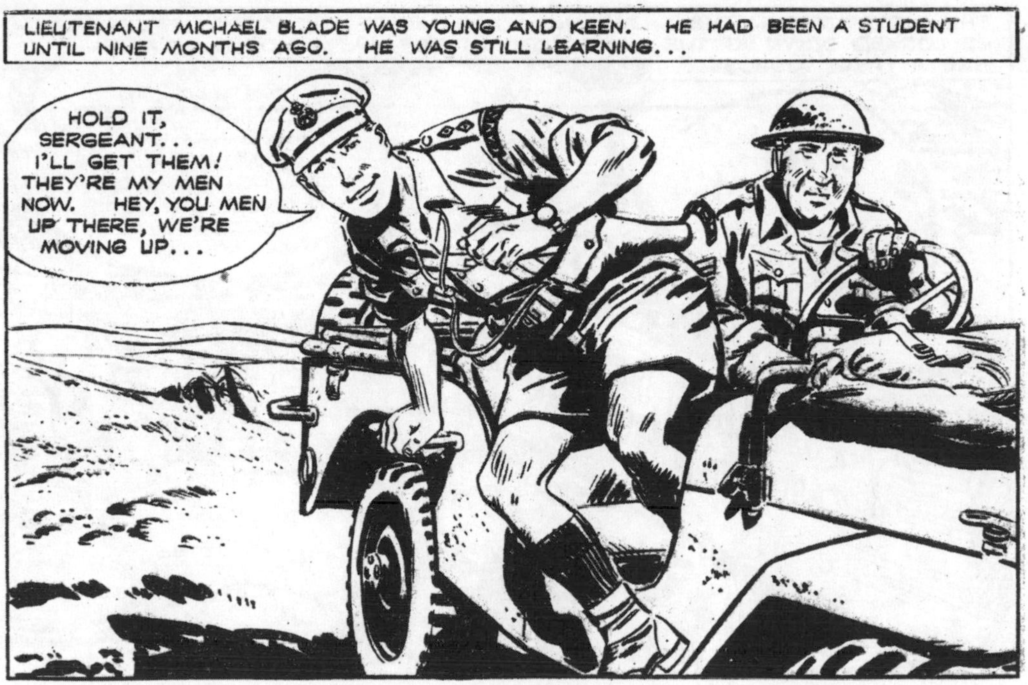
LIEUTENANT MICHAEL BLADE WAS YOUNG AND KEEN. HE HAD BEEN A STUDENT UNTIL NINE MONTHS AGO. HE WAS STILL LEARNING...
HOLD IT, SERGEANT... I'LL GET THEM! THEY'RE MY MEN NOW. HEY, YOU MEN UP THERE, WE'RE MOVING UP...

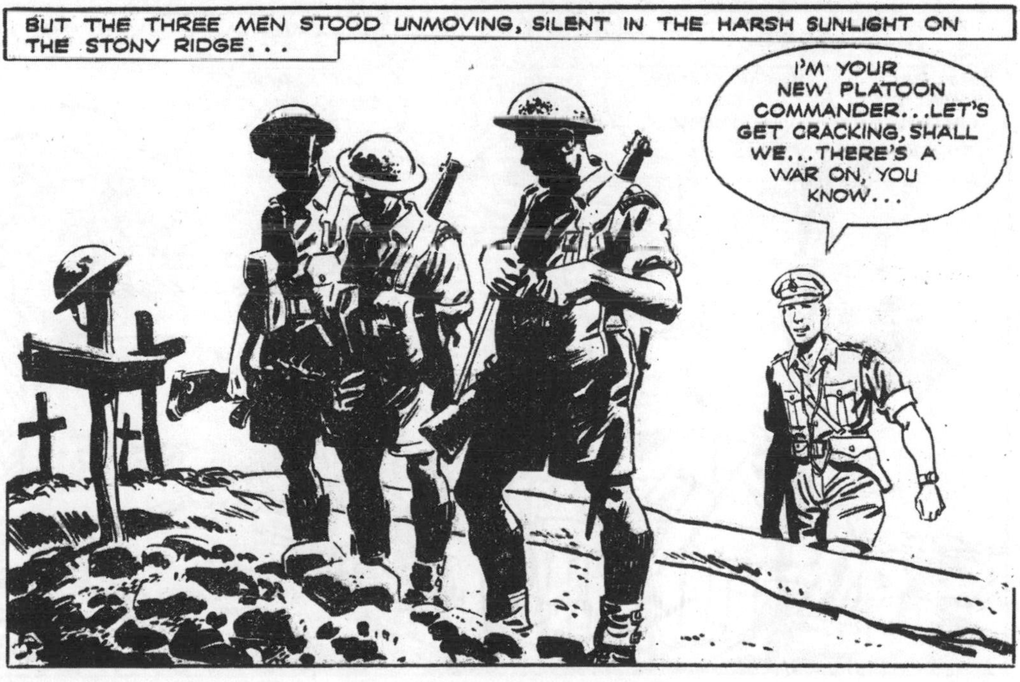
BUT THE THREE MEN STOOD UNMOVING, SILENT IN THE HARSH SUNLIGHT ON THE STONY RIDGE...
I'M YOUR NEW PLATOON COMMANDER...LET'S GET CRACKING, SHALL WE...THERE'S A WAR ON, YOU KNOW...

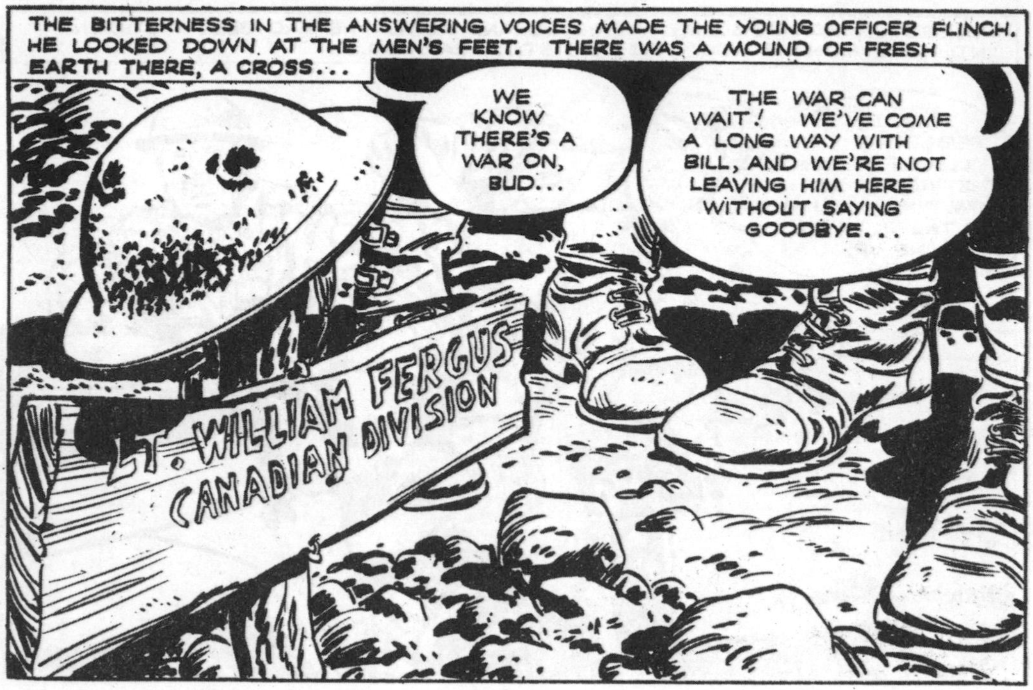
THE BITTERNESS IN THE ANSWERING VOICES MADE THE YOUNG OFFICER FLINCH. HE LOOKED DOWN AT THE MEN'S FEET. THERE WAS A MOUND OF FRESH EARTH THERE, A CROSS...
WE KNOW THERE'S A WAR ON, BUD...
THE WAR CAN WAIT! WE'VE COME A LONG WAY WITH BILL, AND WE'RE NOT LEAVING HIM HERE WITHOUT SAYING GOODBYE...
LT. WILLIAM FERGUS
CANADIAN DIVISION

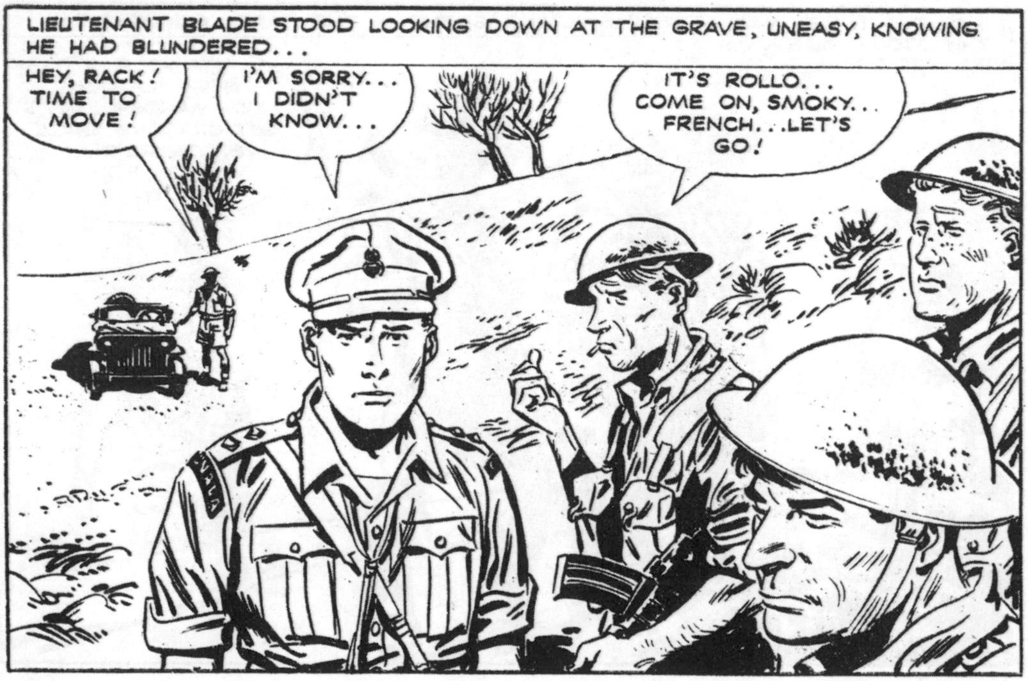
LIEUTENANT BLADE STOOD LOOKING DOWN AT THE GRAVE, UNEASY, KNOWING HE HAD BLUNDERED...
HEY, RACK! TIME TO MOVE!
I'M SORRY... I DIDN'T KNOW...
IT'S ROLLO... COME ON, SMOKY... FRENCH... LET'S GO!

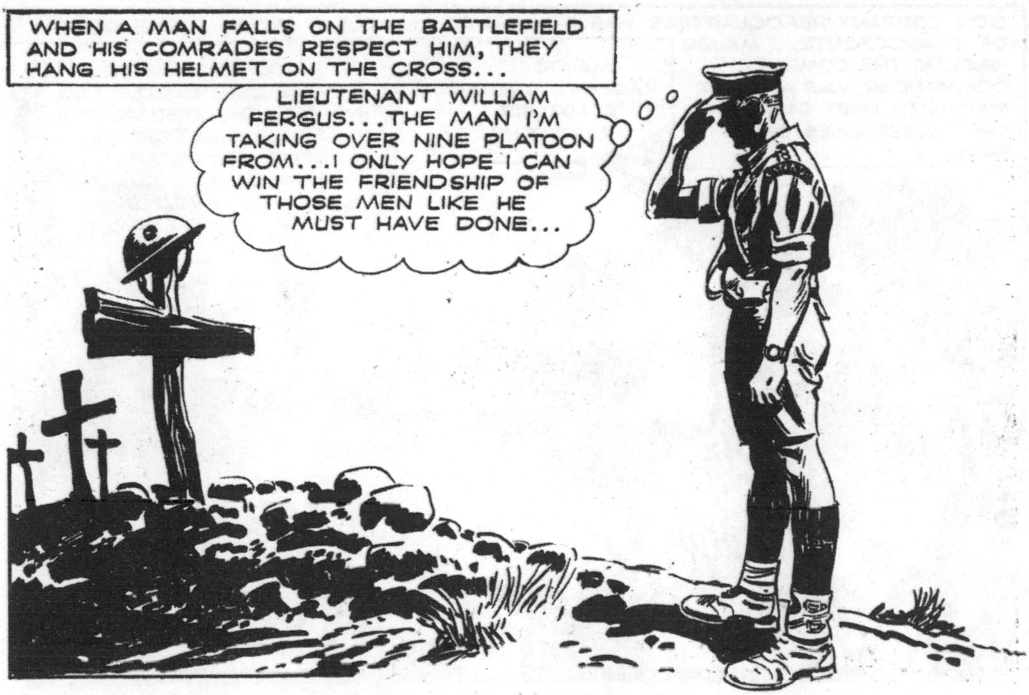
WHEN A MAN FALLS ON THE BATTLEFIELD AND HIS COMRADES RESPECT HIM, THEY HANG HIS HELMET ON THE CROSS...
LIEUTENANT WILLIAM FERGUS...THE MAN I'M TAKING OVER NINE PLATOON FROM...I ONLY HOPE I CAN WIN THE FRIENDSHIP OF THOSE MEN LIKE HE MUST HAVE DONE...

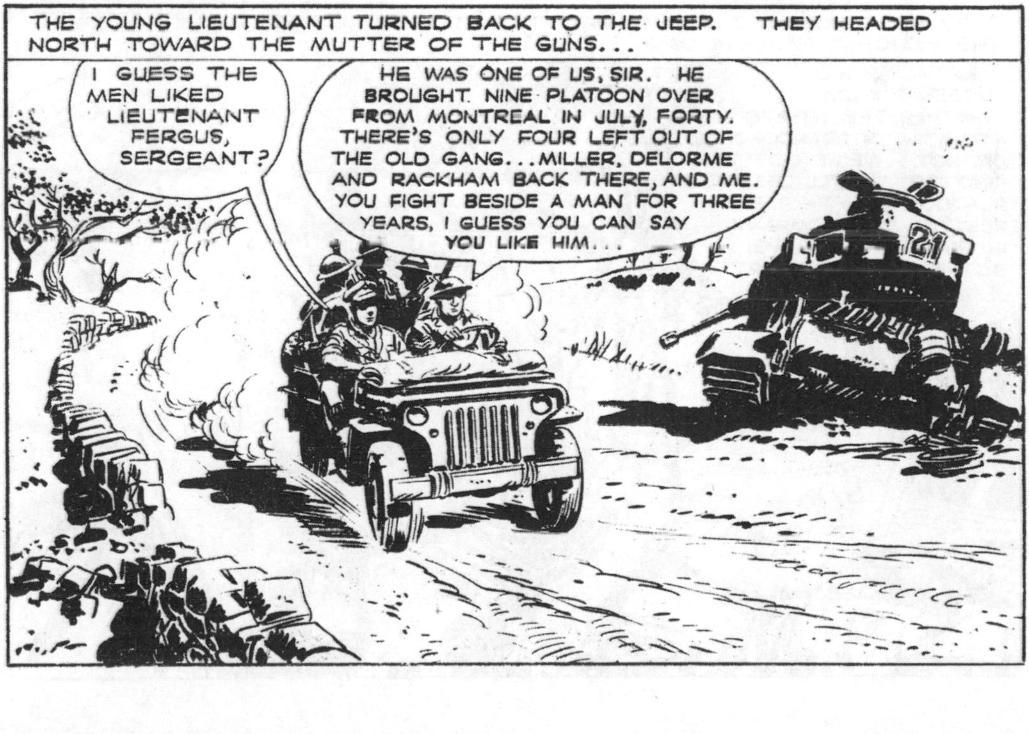
THE YOUNG LIEUTENANT TURNED BACK TO THE JEEP. THEY HEADED NORTH TOWARD THE MUTTER OF THE GUNS...
I GUESS THE MEN LIKED LIEUTENANT FERGUS, SERGEANT?
HE WAS ONE OF US, SIR. HE BROUGHT NINE PLATOON OVER FROM MONTREAL IN JULY, FORTY. THERE'S ONLY FOUR LEFT OUT OF THE OLD GANG...MILLER, DELORME AND RACKHAM BACK THERE, AND ME. YOU FIGHT BESIDE A MAN FOR THREE YEARS, I GUESS YOU CAN SAY YOU LIKE HIM...
21

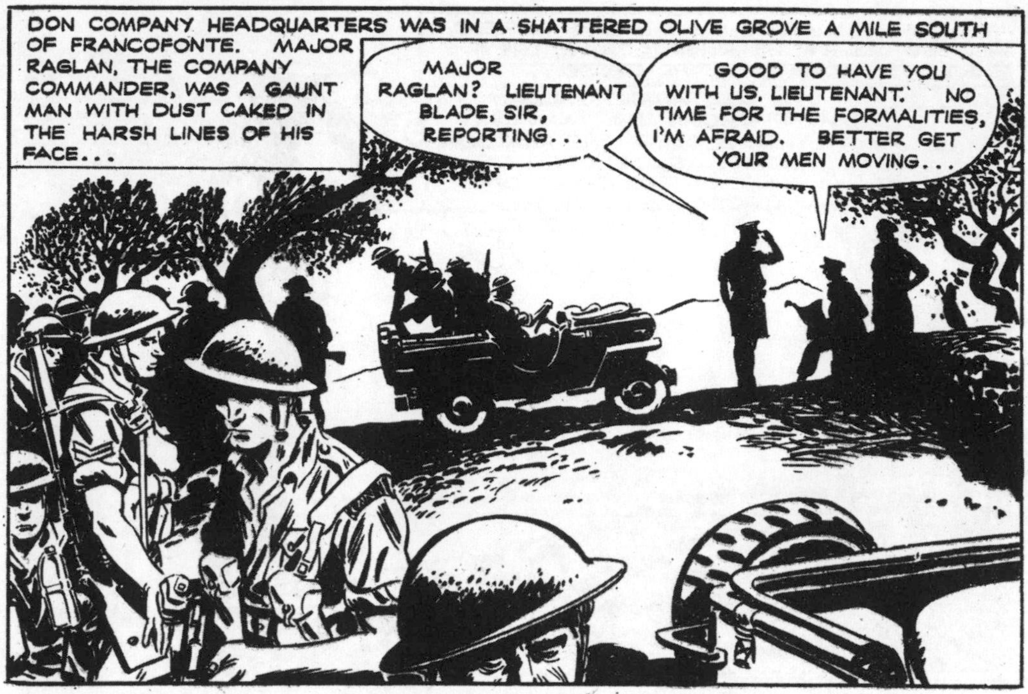
DON COMPANY HEADQUARTERS WAS IN A SHATTERED OLIVE GROVE A MILE SOUTH OF FRANCOFONTE. MAJOR RAGLAN, THE COMPANY COMMANDER, WAS A GAUNT MAN WITH DUST CAKED IN THE HARSH LINES OF HIS FACE...
MAJOR RAGLAN? LIEUTENANT BLADE, SIR, REPORTING...
GOOD TO HAVE YOU WITH US, LIEUTENANT. NO TIME FOR THE FORMALITIES, I'M AFRAID. BETTER GET YOUR MEN MOVING...

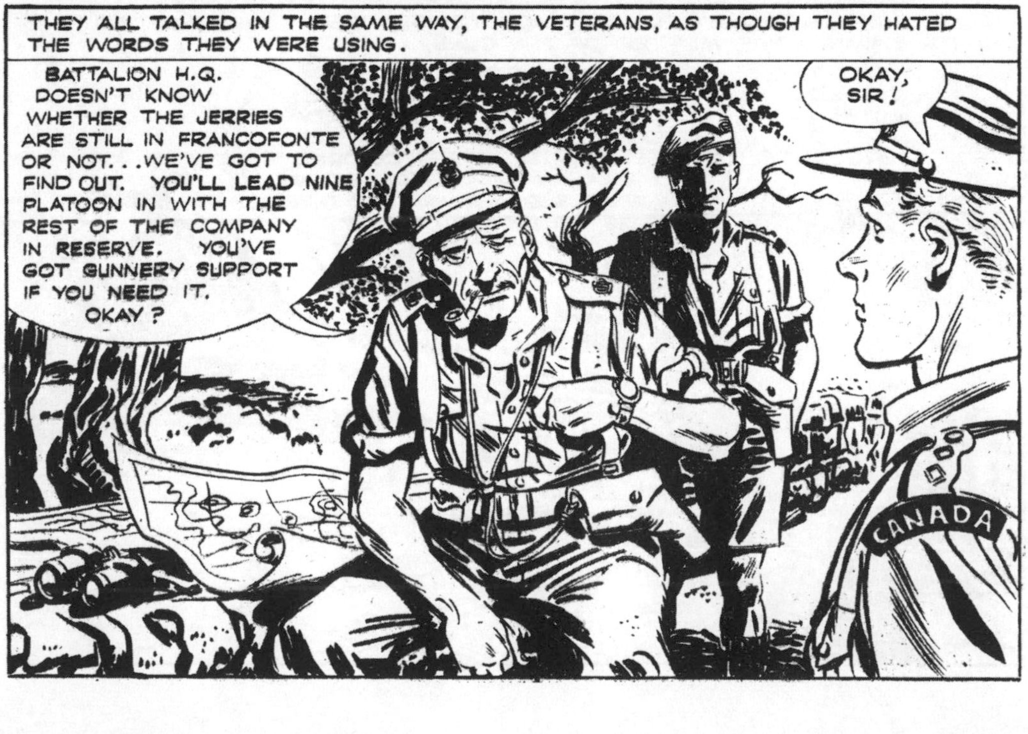
THEY ALL TALKED IN THE SAME WAY, THE VETERANS, AS THOUGH THEY HATED THE WORDS THEY WERE USING.
BATTALION H.Q. DOESN'T KNOW WHETHER THE JERRIES ARE STILL IN FRANCOFONTE OR NOT...WE'VE GOT TO FIND OUT. YOU'LL LEAD NINE PLATOON IN WITH THE REST OF THE COMPANY IN RESERVE. YOU'VE GOT GUNNERY SUPPORT IF YOU NEED IT. OKAY?
OKAY, SIR!
CANADA

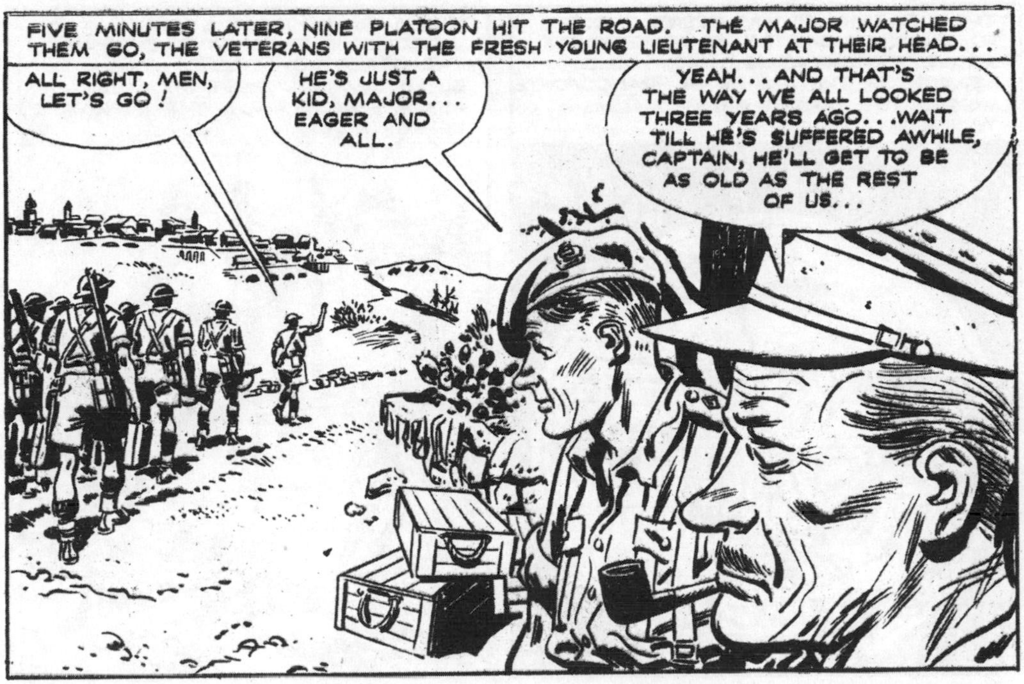
FIVE MINUTES LATER, NINE PLATOON HIT THE ROAD. THE MAJOR WATCHED THEM GO, THE VETERANS WITH THE FRESH YOUNG LIEUTENANT AT THEIR HEAD...
ALL RIGHT, MEN, LET'S GO!
HE'S JUST A KID, MAJOR... EAGER AND ALL.
YEAH... AND THAT'S THE WAY WE ALL LOOKED THREE YEARS AGO...WAIT TILL HE'S SUFFERED AWHILE, CAPTAIN, HE'LL GET TO BE AS OLD AS THE REST OF US...

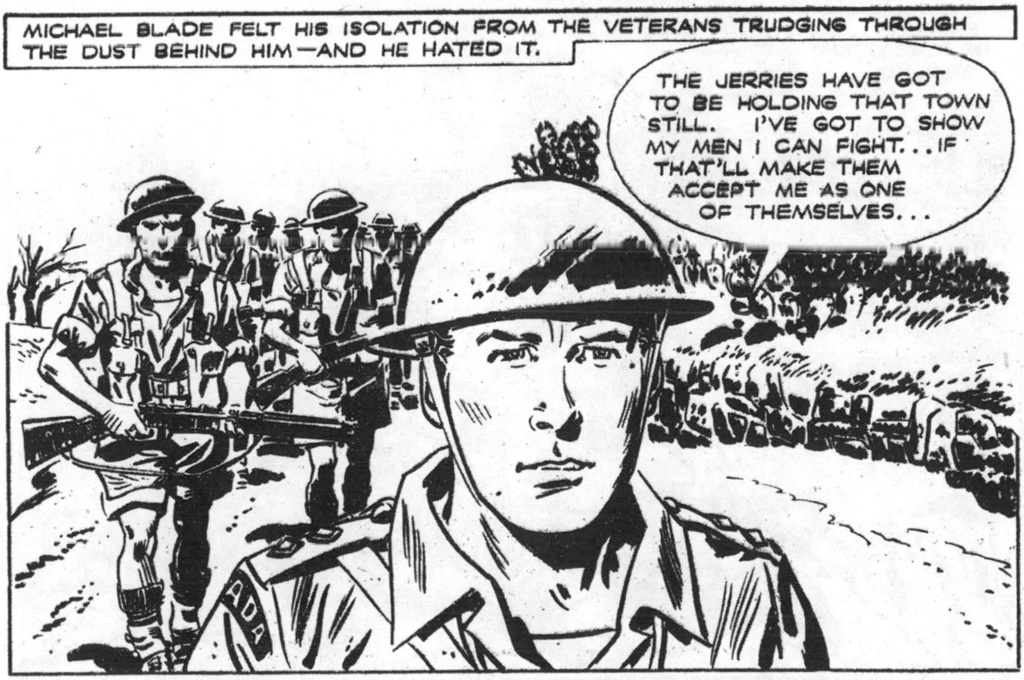
MICHAEL BLADE FELT HIS ISOLATION FROM THE VETERANS TRUDGING THROUGH THE DUST BEHIND HIM—AND HE HATED IT.
THE JERRIES HAVE GOT TO BE HOLDING THAT TOWN STILL. I'VE GOT TO SHOW MY MEN I CAN FIGHT...IF THAT'LL MAKE THEM ACCEPT ME AS ONE OF THEMSELVES...

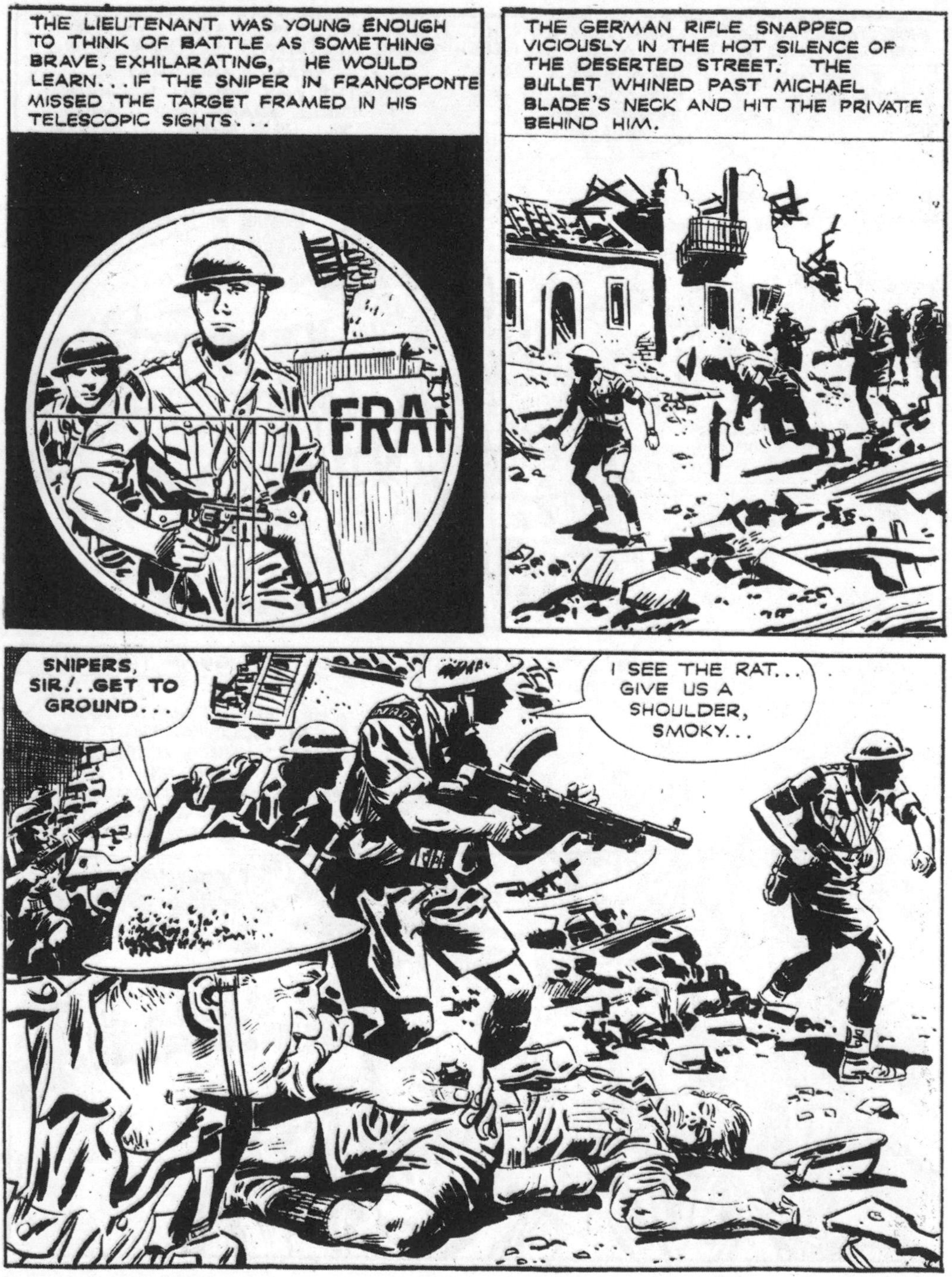
THE LIEUTENANT WAS YOUNG ENOUGH TO THINK OF BATTLE AS SOMETHING BRAVE, EXHILARATING. HE WOULD LEARN. . . IF THE SNIPER IN FRANCOFONTE MISSED THE TARGET FRAMED IN HIS TELESCOPIC SIGHTS. . .
FRAI
THE GERMAN RIFLE SNAPPED VICIOUSLY IN THE HOT SILENCE OF THE DESERTED STREET. THE BULLET WHINED PAST MICHAEL BLADE'S NECK AND HIT THE PRIVATE BEHIND HIM.
SNIPERS, SIR!..GET TO GROUND...
I SEE THE RAT... GIVE US A SHOULDER, SMOKY...

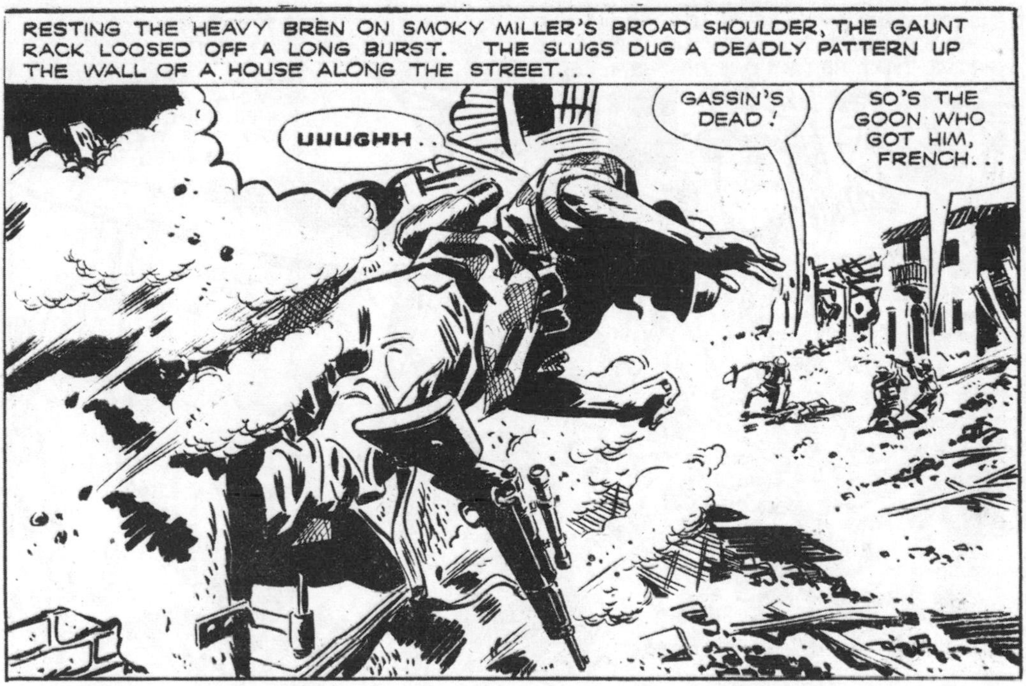
RESTING THE HEAVY BREN ON SMOKY MILLER'S BROAD SHOULDER, THE GAUNT RACK LOOSED OFF A LONG BURST. THE SLUGS DUG A DEADLY PATTERN UP THE WALL OF A HOUSE ALONG THE STREET...
UUUGHH..
GASSIN'S DEAD!
SO'S THE GOON WHO GOT HIM, FRENCH...

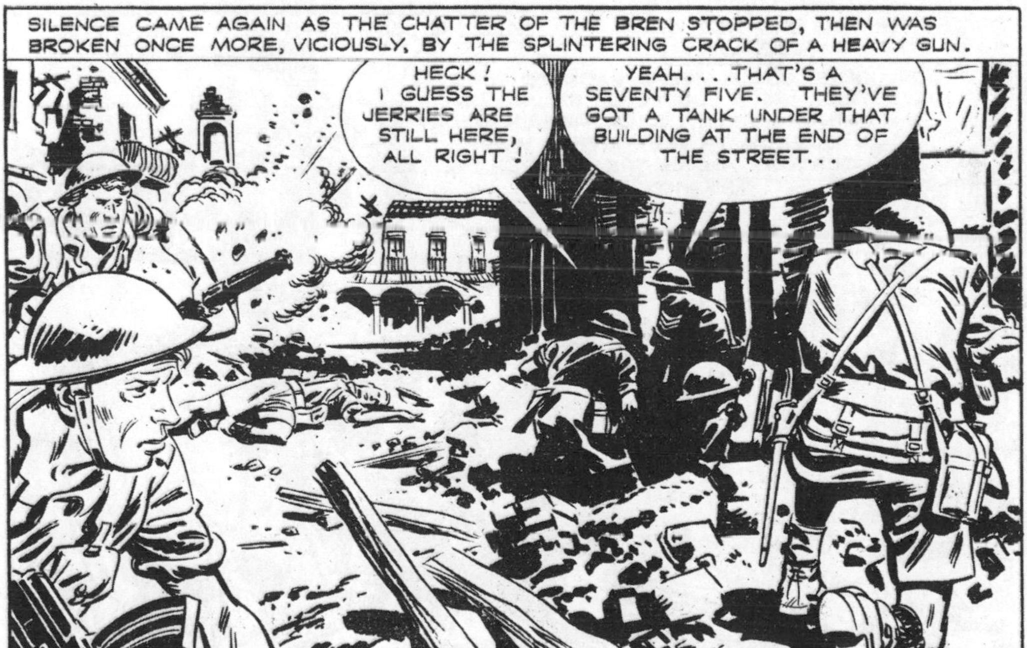
SILENCE CAME AGAIN AS THE CHATTER OF THE BREN STOPPED, THEN WAS BROKEN ONCE MORE, VICIOUSLY, BY THE SPLINTERING CRACK OF A HEAVY GUN.
HECK! I GUESS THE JERRIES ARE STILL HERE, ALL RIGHT!
YEAH....THAT'S A SEVENTY FIVE. THEY'VE GOT A TANK UNDER THAT BUILDING AT THE END OF THE STREET...

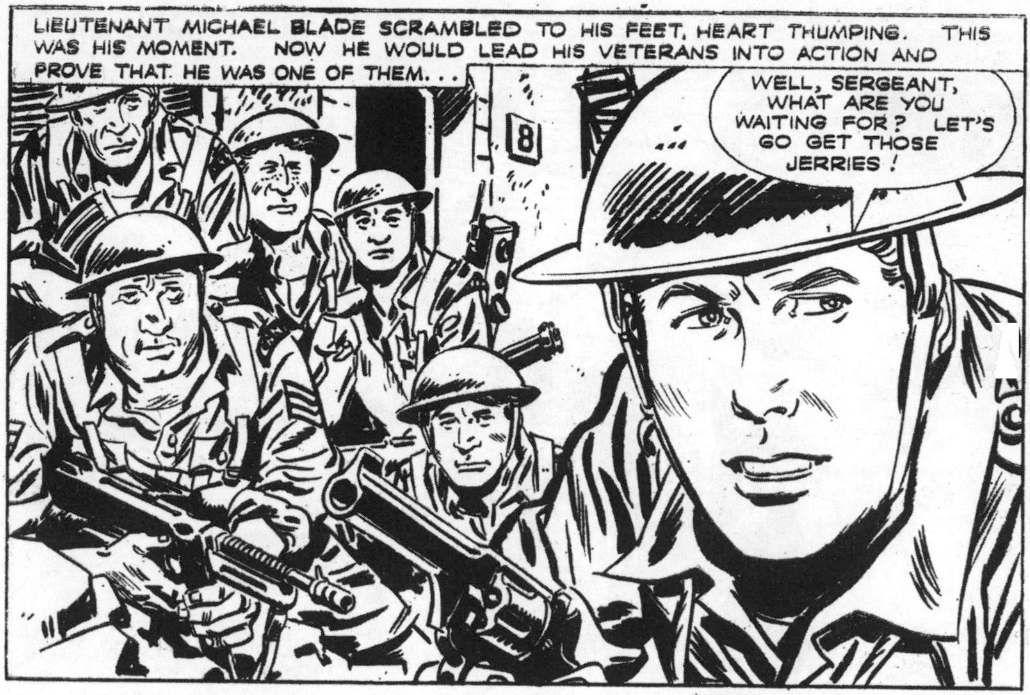
LIEUTENANT MICHAEL BLADE SCRAMBLED TO HIS FEET, HEART THUMPING. THIS WAS HIS MOMENT. NOW HE WOULD LEAD HIS VETERANS INTO ACTION AND PROVE THAT HE WAS ONE OF THEM...
WELL, SERGEANT, WHAT ARE YOU WAITING FOR? LET'S GO GET THOSE JERRIES!
8

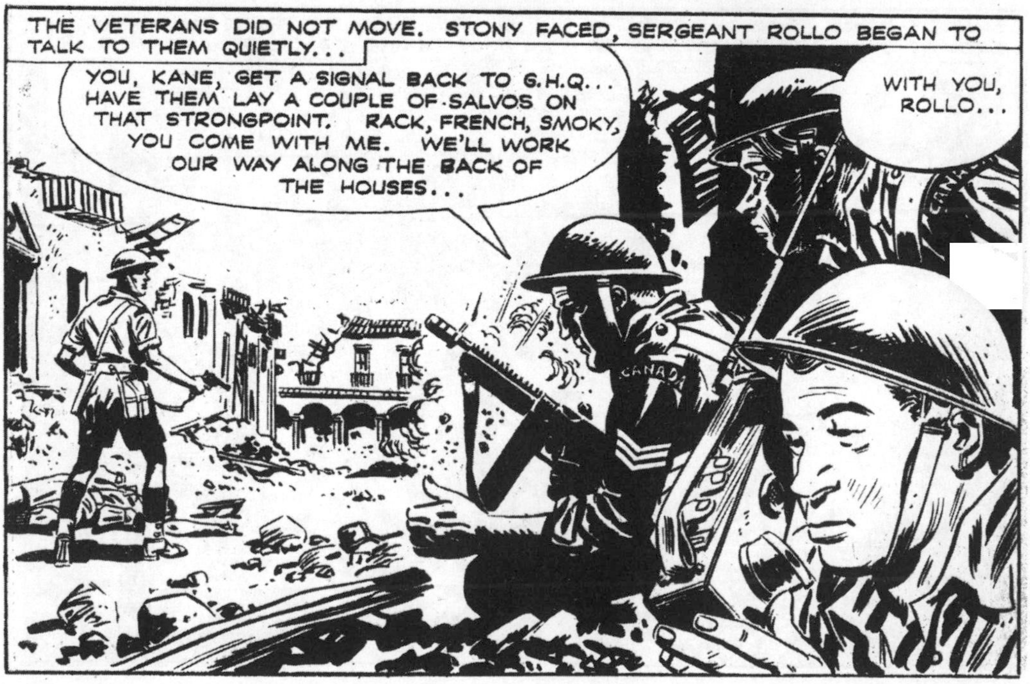
THE VETERANS DID NOT MOVE. STONY FACED, SERGEANT ROLLO BEGAN TO TALK TO THEM QUIETLY...
YOU, KANE, GET A SIGNAL BACK TO G.H.Q... HAVE THEM LAY A COUPLE OF SALVOS ON THAT STRONGPOINT. RACK, FRENCH, SMOKY, YOU COME WITH ME. WE'LL WORK OUR WAY ALONG THE BACK OF THE HOUSES...
WITH YOU, ROLLO...
CANADA

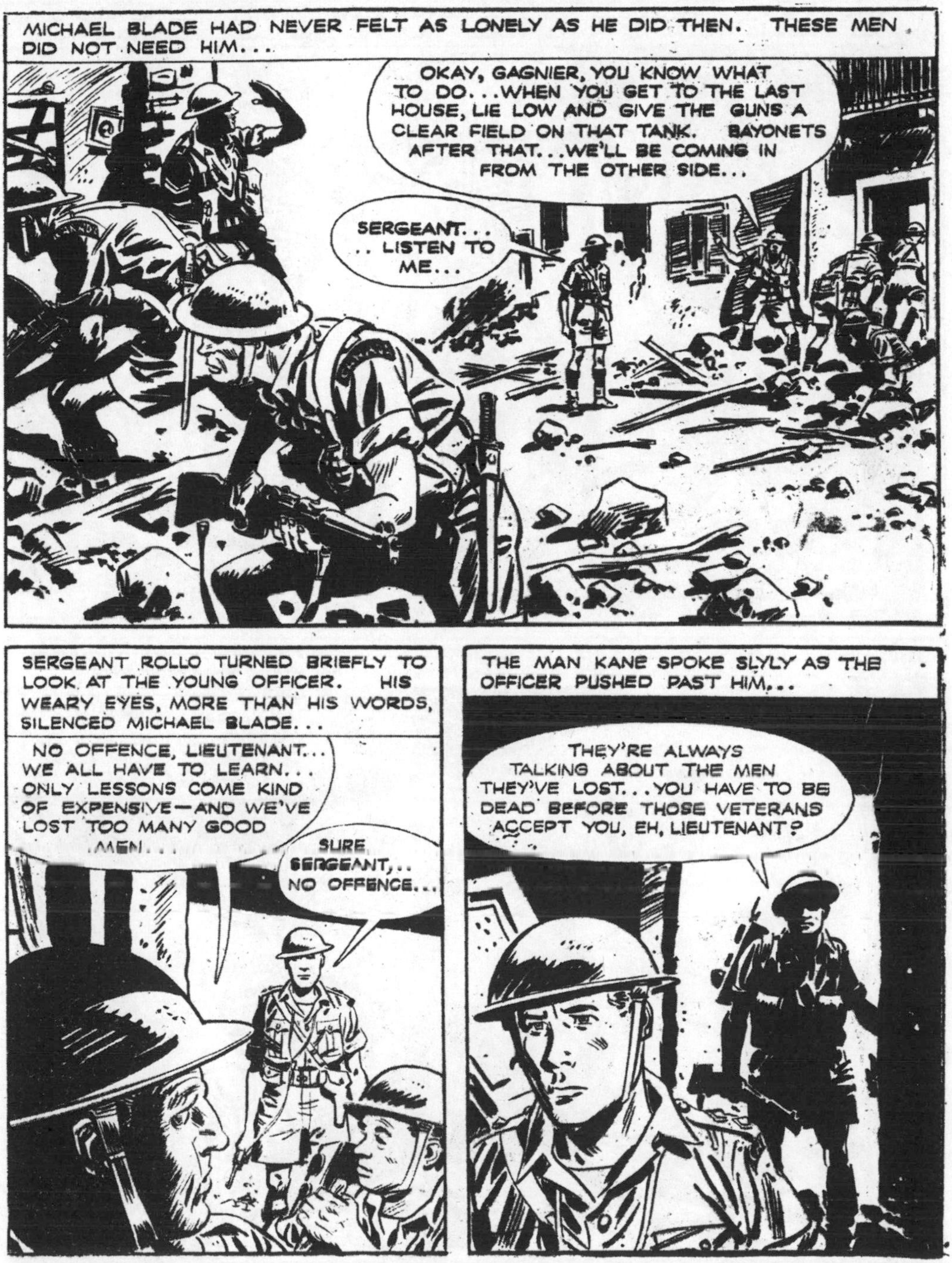
MICHAEL BLADE HAD NEVER FELT AS LONELY AS HE DID THEN. THESE MEN DID NOT NEED HIM...
OKAY, GAGNIER, YOU KNOW WHAT TO DO...WHEN YOU GET TO THE LAST HOUSE, LIE LOW AND GIVE THE GUNS A CLEAR FIELD ON THAT TANK. BAYONETS AFTER THAT...WE'LL BE COMING IN FROM THE OTHER SIDE...
SERGEANT... ..LISTEN TO ME...
SERGEANT ROLLO TURNED BRIEFLY TO LOOK AT THE YOUNG OFFICER. HIS WEARY EYES, MORE THAN HIS WORDS, SILENCED MICHAEL BLADE...
NO OFFENCE, LIEUTENANT... WE ALL HAVE TO LEARN... ONLY LESSONS COME KIND OF EXPENSIVE—AND WE'VE LOST TOO MANY GOOD MEN...
SURE, SERGEANT,.. NO OFFENCE...
THE MAN KANE SPOKE SLYLY AS THE OFFICER PUSHED PAST HIM...
THEY'RE ALWAYS TALKING ABOUT THE MEN THEY'VE LOST...YOU HAVE TO BE DEAD BEFORE THOSE VETERANS ACCEPT YOU, EH, LIEUTENANT?

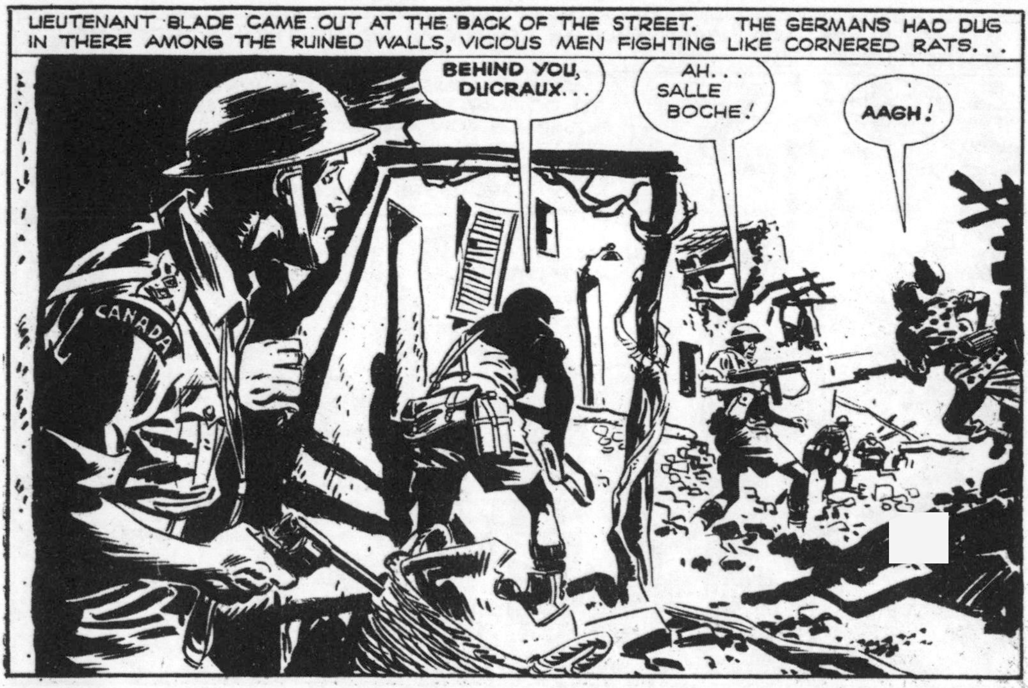
LIEUTENANT BLADE CAME OUT AT THE BACK OF THE STREET. THE GERMANS HAD DUG IN THERE AMONG THE RUINED WALLS, VICIOUS MEN FIGHTING LIKE CORNERED RATS...
BEHIND YOU, DUCRAUX...
AH... SALLE BOCHE!
AAGH!
CANADA

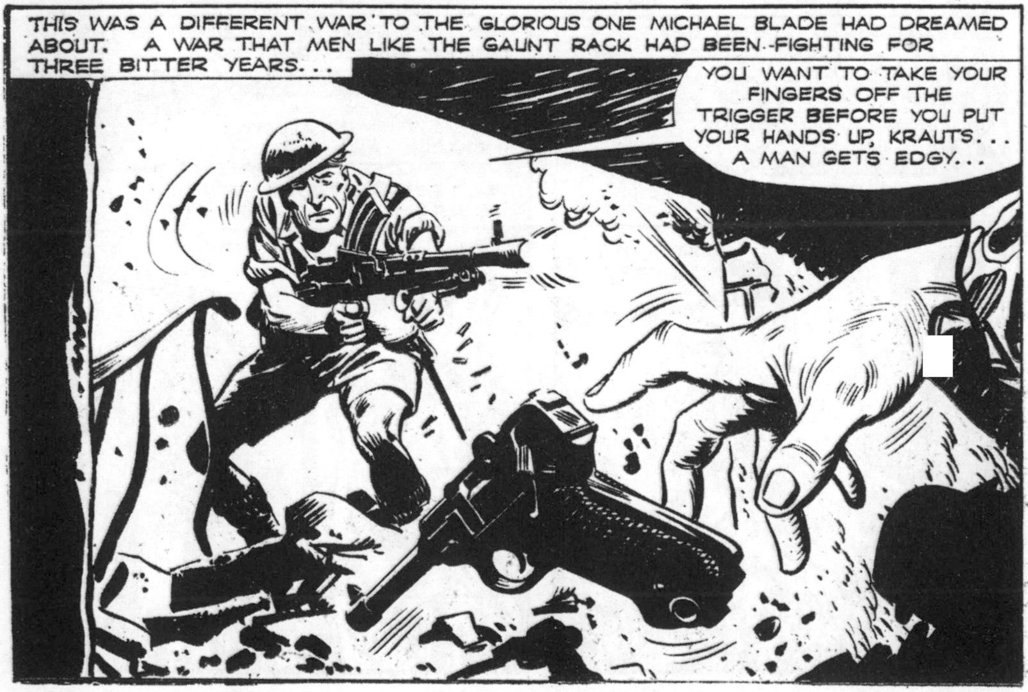
THIS WAS A DIFFERENT WAR TO THE GLORIOUS ONE MICHAEL BLADE HAD DREAMED ABOUT. A WAR THAT MEN LIKE THE GAUNT RACK HAD BEEN FIGHTING FOR THREE BITTER YEARS...
YOU WANT TO TAKE YOUR FINGERS OFF THE TRIGGER BEFORE YOU PUT YOUR HANDS UP, KRAUTS... A MAN GETS EDGY...

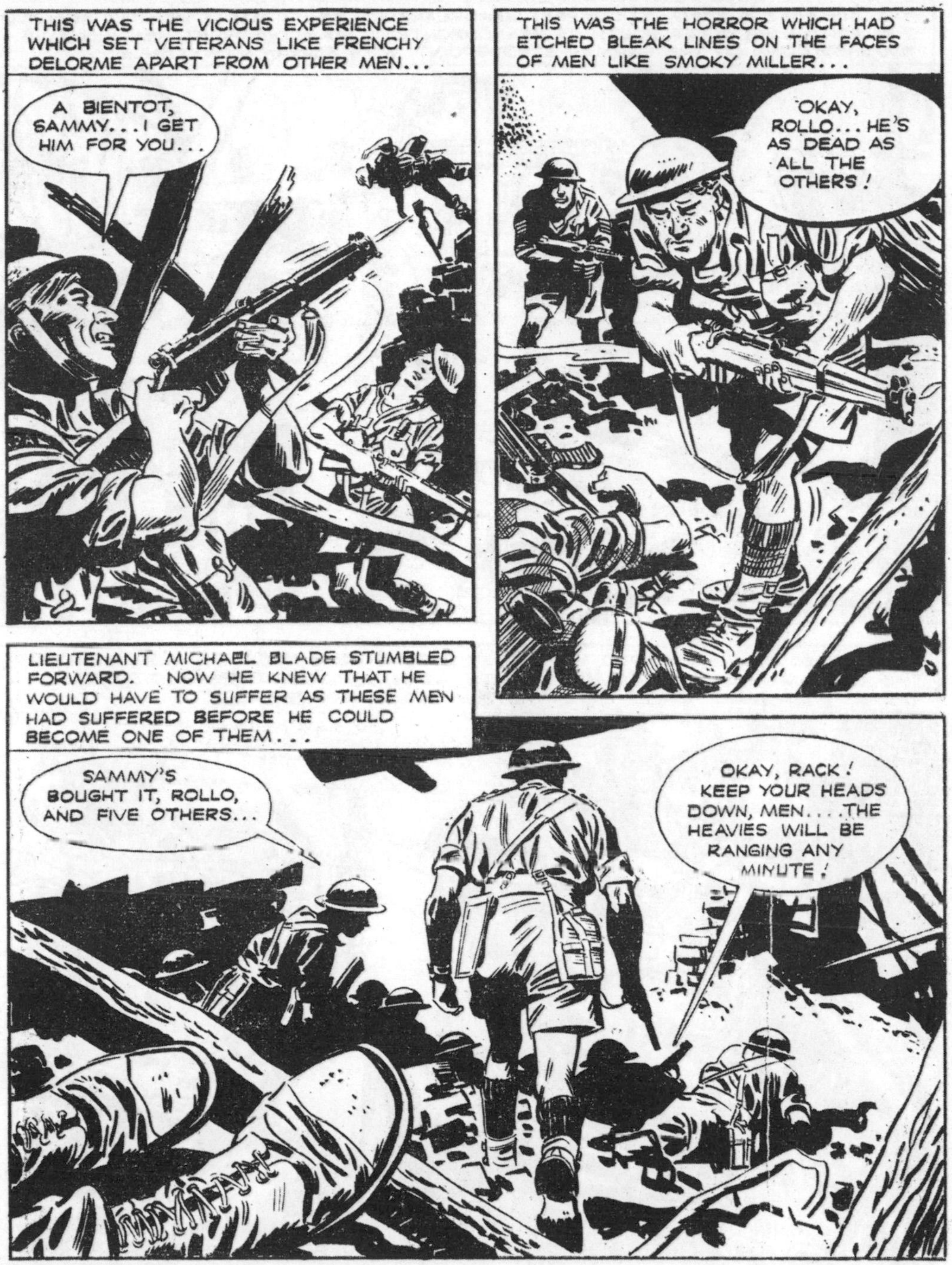
THIS WAS THE VICIOUS EXPERIENCE WHICH SET VETERANS LIKE FRENCHY DELORME APART FROM OTHER MEN...
A BIENTOT, SAMMY...I GET HIM FOR YOU...
THIS WAS THE HORROR WHICH HAD ETCHED BLEAK LINES ON THE FACES OF MEN LIKE SMOKY MILLER...
OKAY, ROLLO...HE'S AS DEAD AS ALL THE OTHERS!
LIEUTENANT MICHAEL BLADE STUMBLED FORWARD. NOW HE KNEW THAT HE WOULD HAVE TO SUFFER AS THESE MEN HAD SUFFERED BEFORE HE COULD BECOME ONE OF THEM...
SAMMY'S BOUGHT IT, ROLLO, AND FIVE OTHERS...
OKAY, RACK! KEEP YOUR HEADS DOWN, MEN....THE HEAVIES WILL BE RANGING ANY MINUTE!

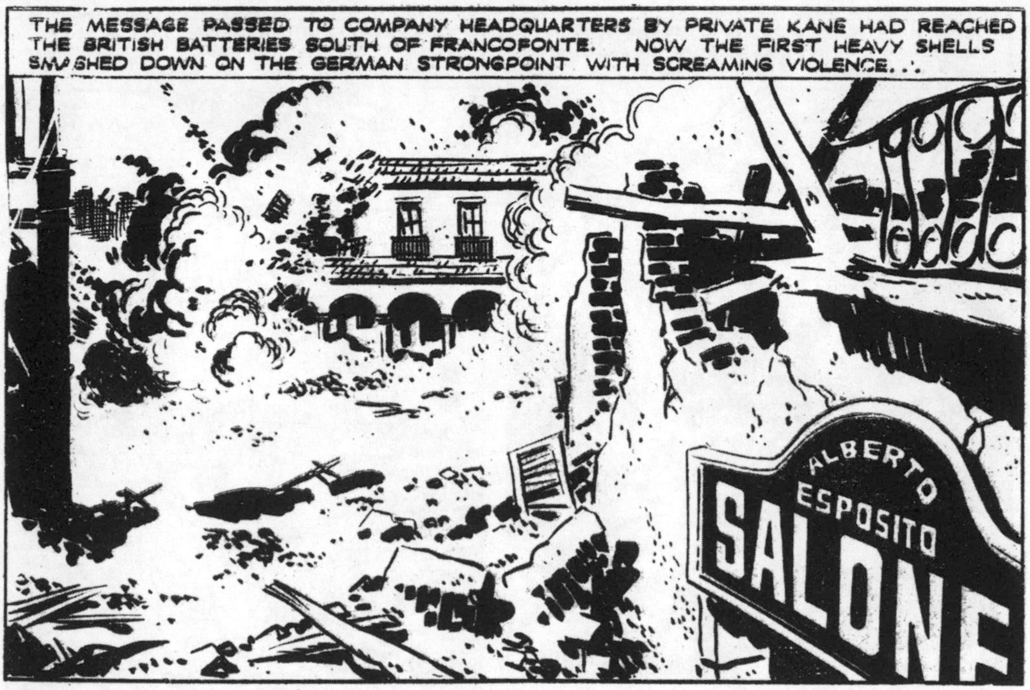
THE MESSAGE PASSED TO COMPANY HEADQUARTERS BY PRIVATE KANE HAD REACHED THE BRITISH BATTERIES SOUTH OF FRANCOFONTE. NOW THE FIRST HEAVY SHELLS SMASHED DOWN ON THE GERMAN STRONGPOINT WITH SCREAMING VIOLENCE...
ALBERTO
ESPOSITO
SALONE

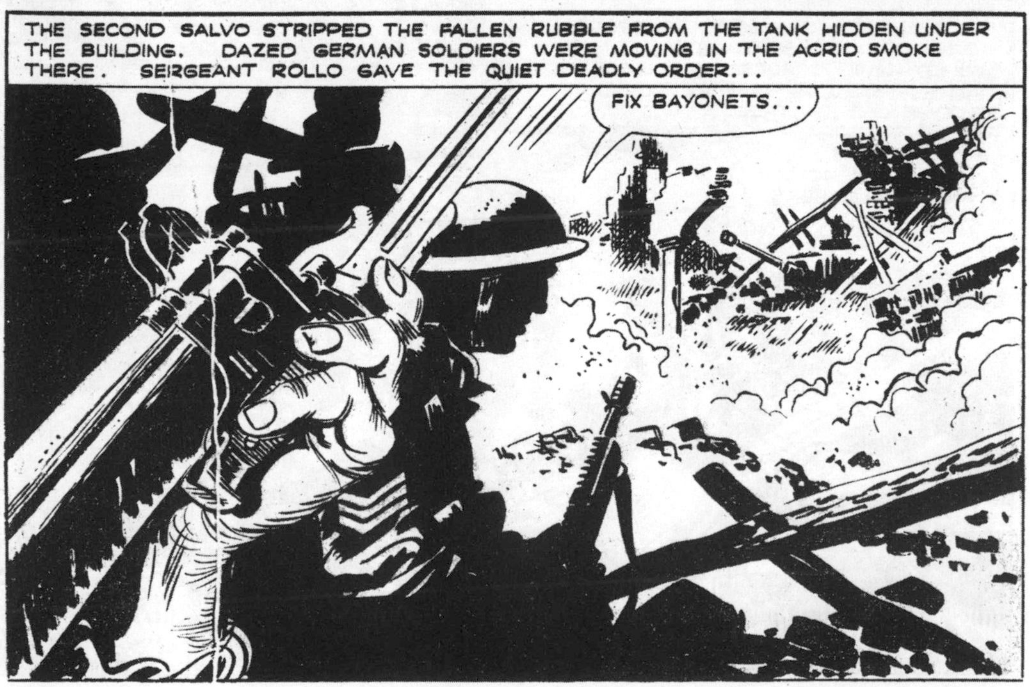
THE SECOND SALVO STRIPPED THE FALLEN RUBBLE FROM THE TANK HIDDEN UNDER THE BUILDING. DAZED GERMAN SOLDIERS WERE MOVING IN THE ACRID SMOKE THERE. SEIRGEANT ROLLO GAVE THE QUIET DEADLY ORDER...
FIX BAYONETS...

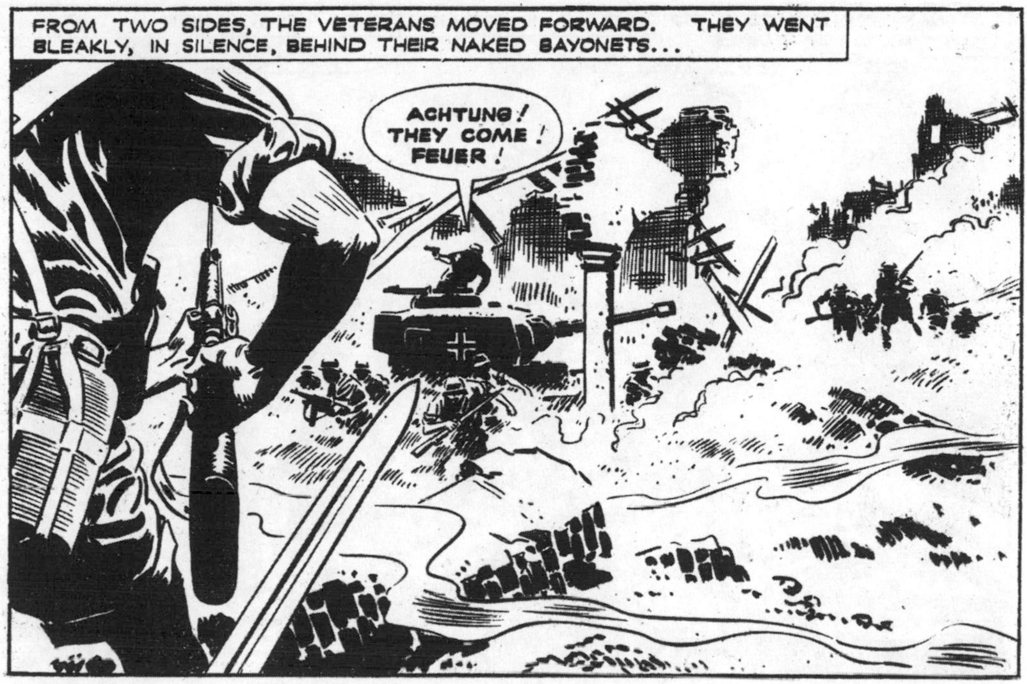
FROM TWO SIDES, THE VETERANS MOVED FORWARD. THEY WENT BLEAKLY, IN SILENCE, BEHIND THEIR NAKED BAYONETS...
ACHTUNG! THEY COME! FEUER!

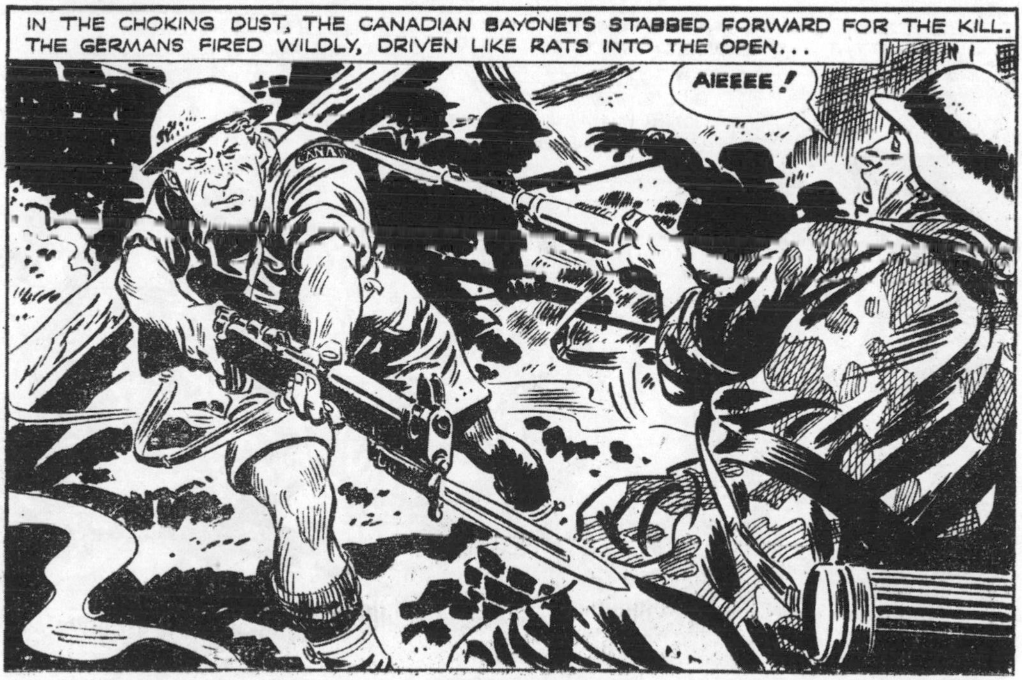
IN THE CHOKING DUST, THE CANADIAN BAYONETS STABBED FORWARD FOR THE KILL. THE GERMANS FIRED WILDLY, DRIVEN LIKE RATS INTO THE OPEN...
AIEEEE!

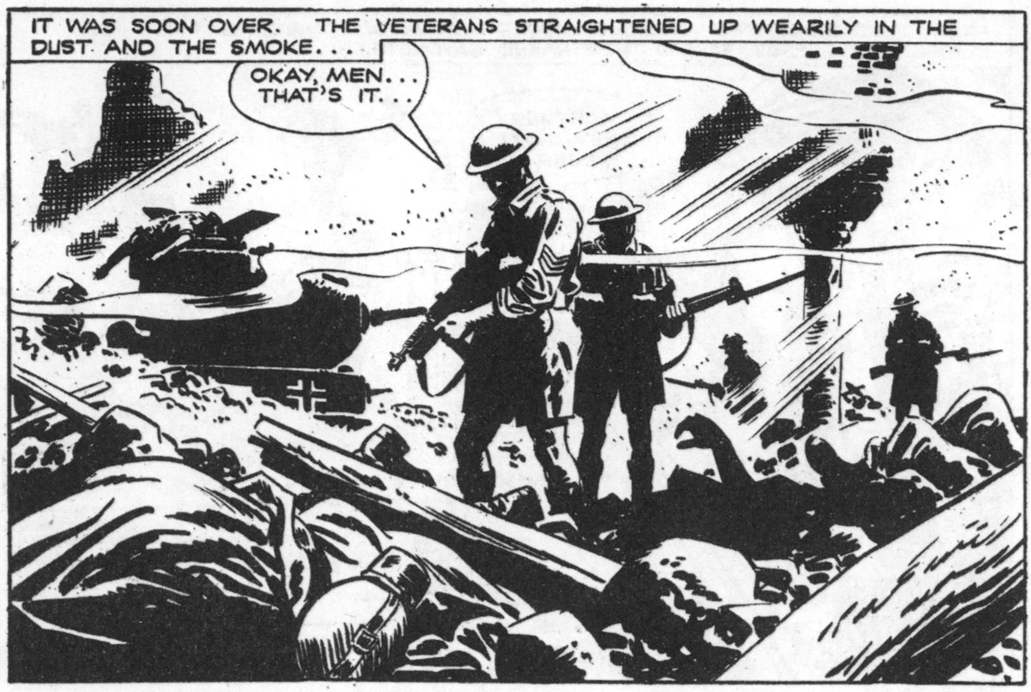
IT WAS SOON OVER. THE VETERANS STRAIGHTENED UP WEARILY IN THE DUST AND THE SMOKE...
OKAY, MEN... THAT'S IT...

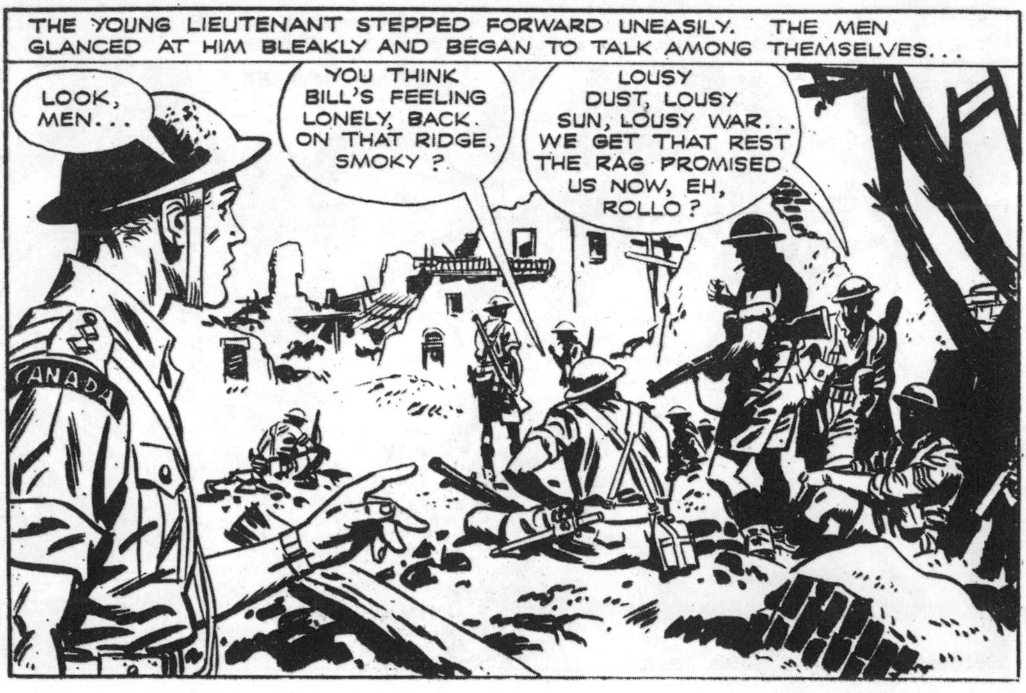
THE YOUNG LIEUTENANT STEPPED FORWARD UNEASILY. THE MEN GLANCED AT HIM BLEAKLY AND BEGAN TO TALK AMONG THEMSELVES...
LOOK, MEN...
YOU THINK BILL'S FEELING LONELY, BACK ON THAT RIDGE, SMOKY ?
LOUSY DUST, LOUSY SUN, LOUSY WAR... WE GET THAT REST THE RAG PROMISED US NOW, EH, ROLLO ?
CANADA

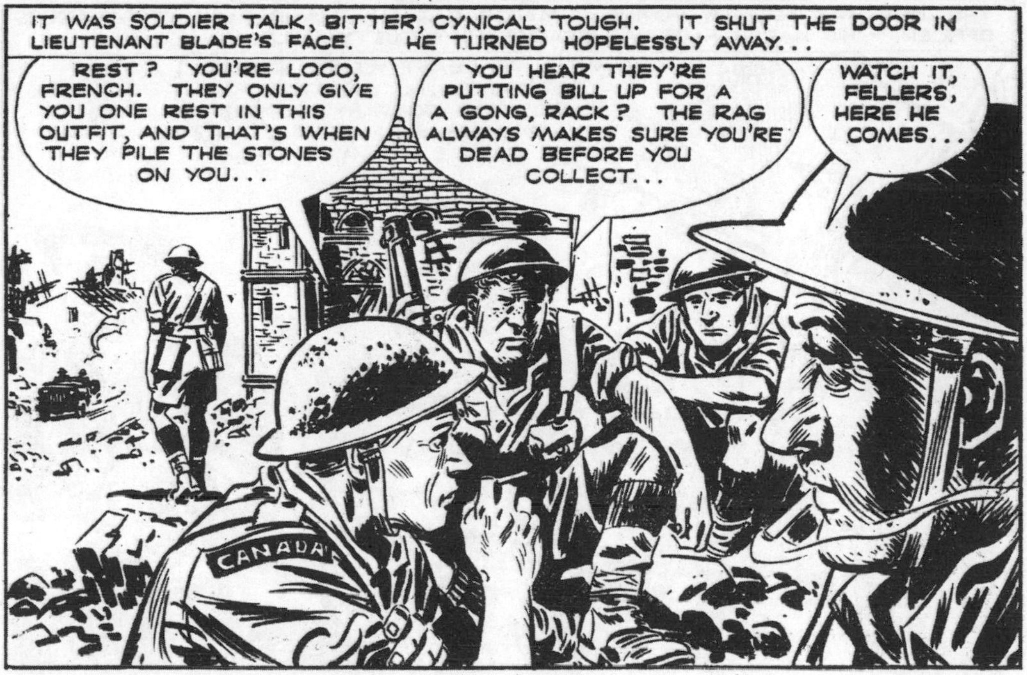
IT WAS SOLDIER TALK, BITTER, CYNICAL, TOUGH. IT SHUT THE DOOR IN LIEUTENANT BLADE'S FACE. HE TURNED HOPELESSLY AWAY...
REST? YOU'RE LOCO, FRENCH. THEY ONLY GIVE YOU ONE REST IN THIS OUTFIT, AND THAT'S WHEN THEY PILE THE STONES ON YOU...
YOU HEAR THEY'RE PUTTING BILL UP FOR A A GONG, RACK? THE RAG ALWAYS MAKES SURE YOU'RE DEAD BEFORE YOU COLLECT...
WATCH IT, FELLERS, HERE HE COMES...
CANADA

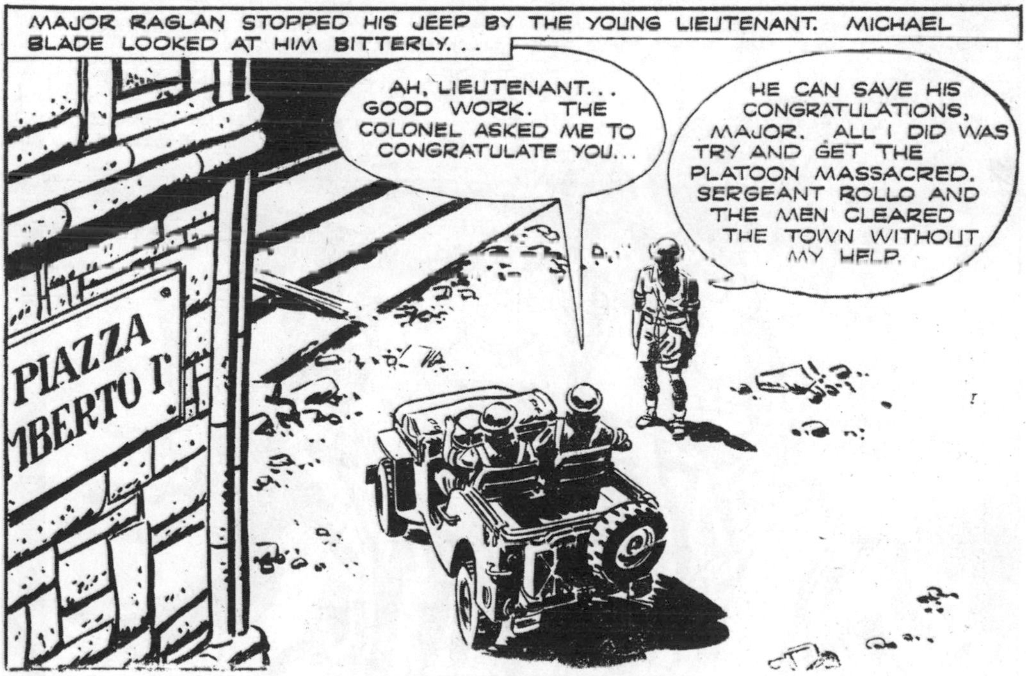
MAJOR RAGLAN STOPPED HIS JEEP BY THE YOUNG LIEUTENANT. MICHAEL BLADE LOOKED AT HIM BITTERLY...
AH, LIEUTENANT... GOOD WORK. THE COLONEL ASKED ME TO CONGRATULATE YOU...
HE CAN SAVE HIS CONGRATULATIONS, MAJOR. ALL I DID WAS TRY AND GET THE PLATOON MASSACRED. SERGEANT ROLLO AND THE MEN CLEARED THE TOWN WITHOUT MY HELP.
PIAZZA
MBERTO I°

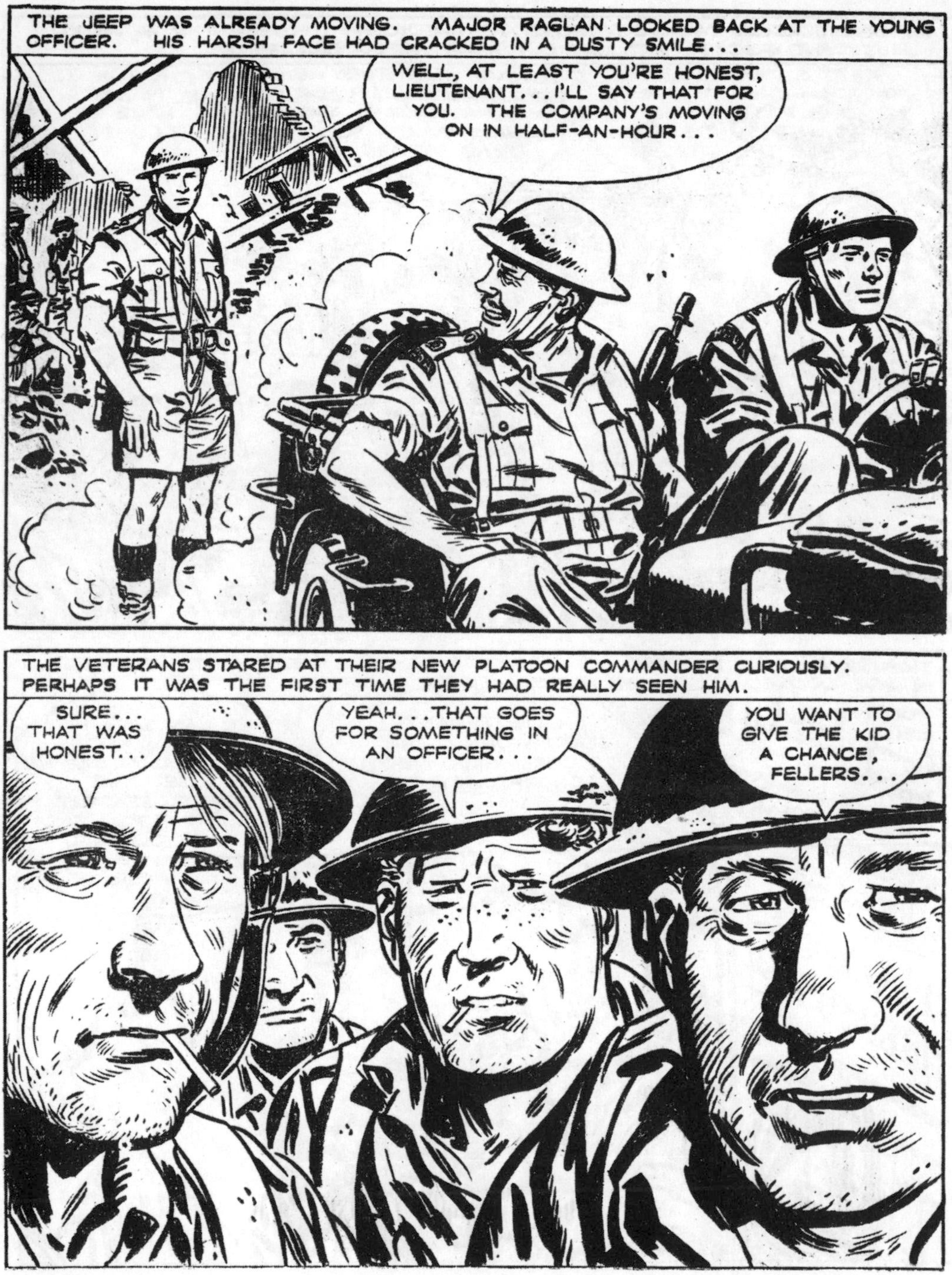
THE JEEP WAS ALREADY MOVING. MAJOR RAGLAN LOOKED BACK AT THE YOUNG OFFICER. HIS HARSH FACE HAD CRACKED IN A DUSTY SMILE...
WELL, AT LEAST YOU'RE HONEST, LIEUTENANT... I'LL SAY THAT FOR YOU. THE COMPANY'S MOVING ON IN HALF-AN-HOUR...
THE VETERANS STARED AT THEIR NEW PLATOON COMMANDER CURIOUSLY. PERHAPS IT WAS THE FIRST TIME THEY HAD REALLY SEEN HIM.
SURE... THAT WAS HONEST...
YEAH... THAT GOES FOR SOMETHING IN AN OFFICER...
YOU WANT TO GIVE THE KID A CHANCE, FELLERS...

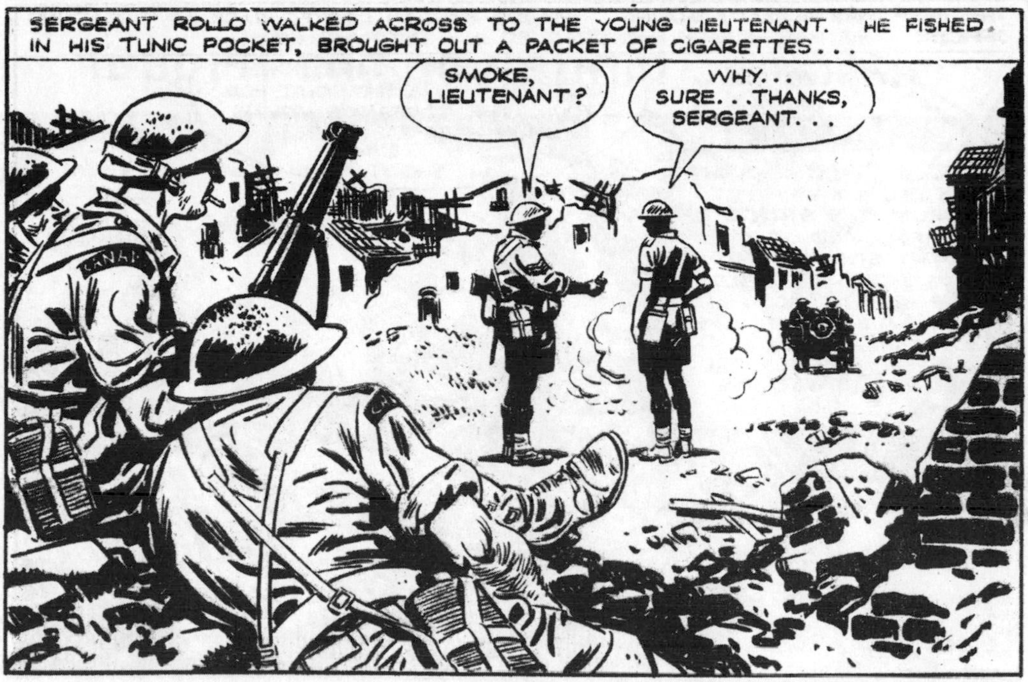
SERGEANT ROLLO WALKED ACROSS TO THE YOUNG LIEUTENANT. HE FISHED IN HIS TUNIC POCKET, BROUGHT OUT A PACKET OF CIGARETTES . . .
SMOKE, LIEUTENANT?
WHY . . . SURE. . .THANKS, SERGEANT. . .

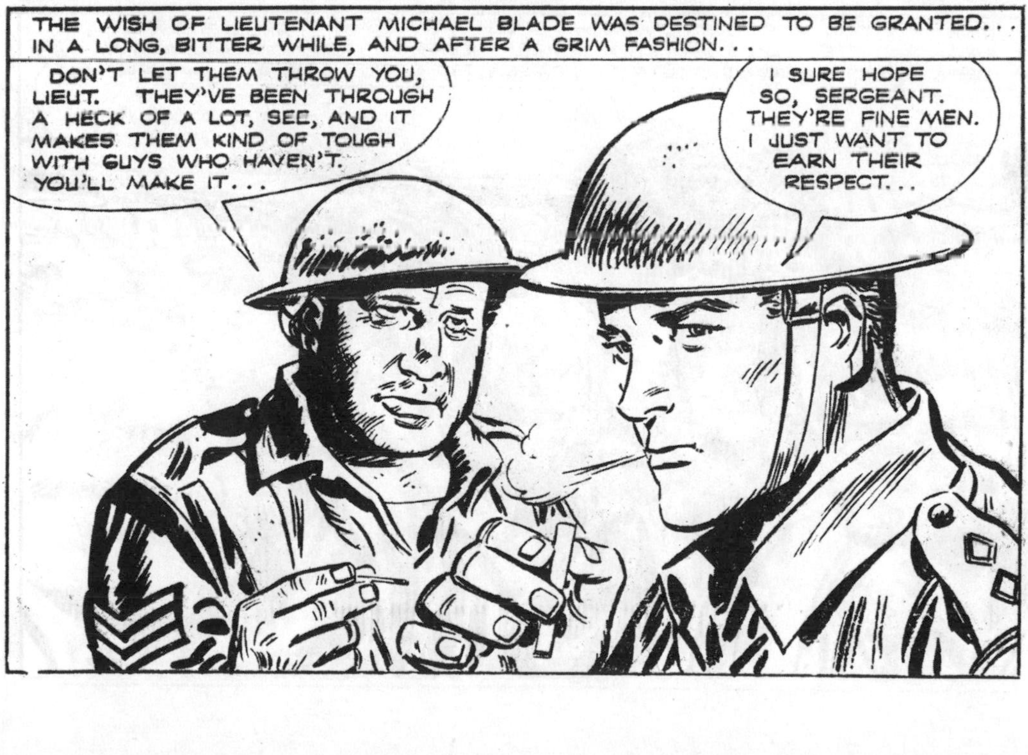
THE WISH OF LIEUTENANT MICHAEL BLADE WAS DESTINED TO BE GRANTED. . . IN A LONG, BITTER WHILE, AND AFTER A GRIM FASHION. . .
DON'T LET THEM THROW YOU, LIEUT. THEY'VE BEEN THROUGH A HECK OF A LOT, SEE, AND IT MAKES THEM KIND OF TOUGH WITH GUYS WHO HAVEN'T. YOU'LL MAKE IT. . .
I SURE HOPE SO, SERGEANT. THEY'RE FINE MEN. I JUST WANT TO EARN THEIR RESPECT. . .

Chapter 2. Finger on the Trigger

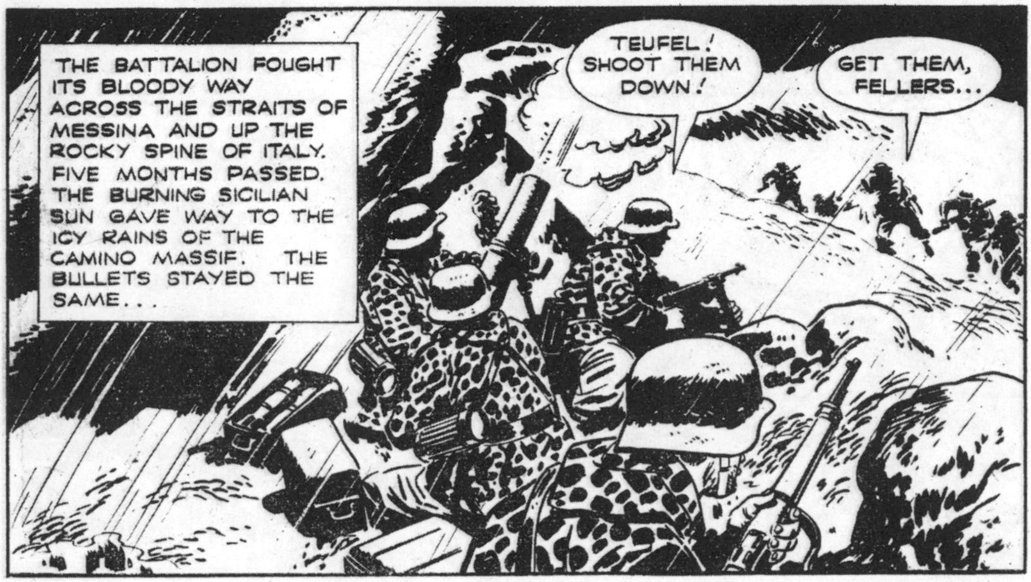
THE BATTALION FOUGHT ITS BLOODY WAY ACROSS THE STRAITS OF MESSINA AND UP THE ROCKY SPINE OF ITALY. FIVE MONTHS PASSED. THE BURNING SICILIAN SUN GAVE WAY TO THE ICY RAINS OF THE CAMINO MASSIF. THE BULLETS STAYED THE SAME...
TEUFEL! SHOOT THEM DOWN!
GET THEM, FELLERS...

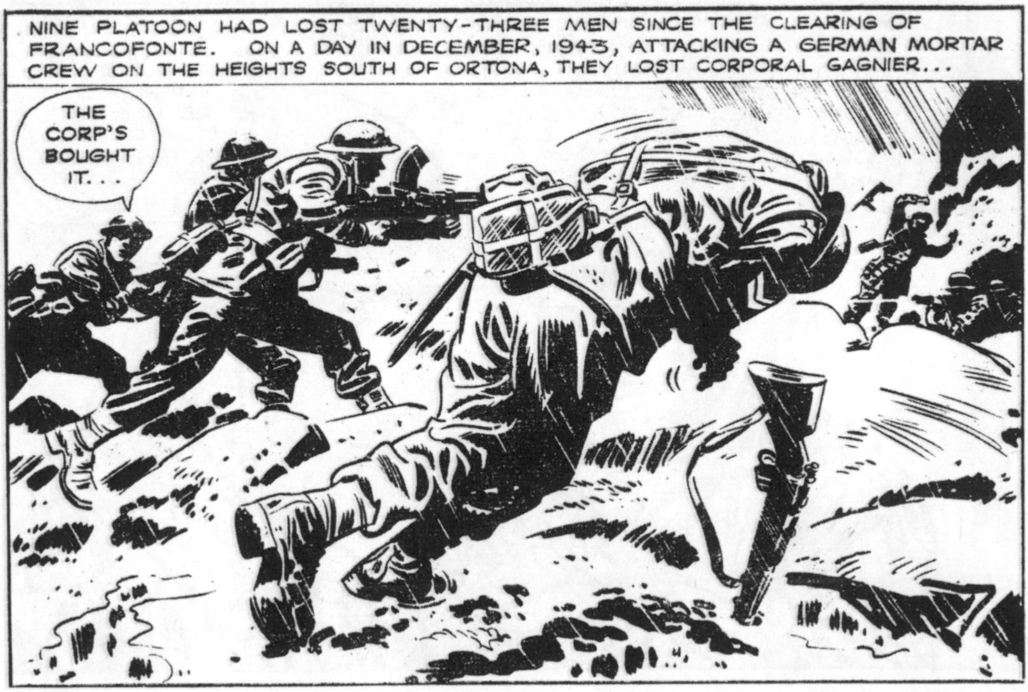
NINE PLATOON HAD LOST TWENTY-THREE MEN SINCE THE CLEARING OF FRANCOFONTE. ON A DAY IN DECEMBER, 1943, ATTACKING A GERMAN MORTAR CREW ON THE HEIGHTS SOUTH OF ORTONA, THEY LOST CORPORAL GAGNIER...
THE CORP'S BOUGHT IT...

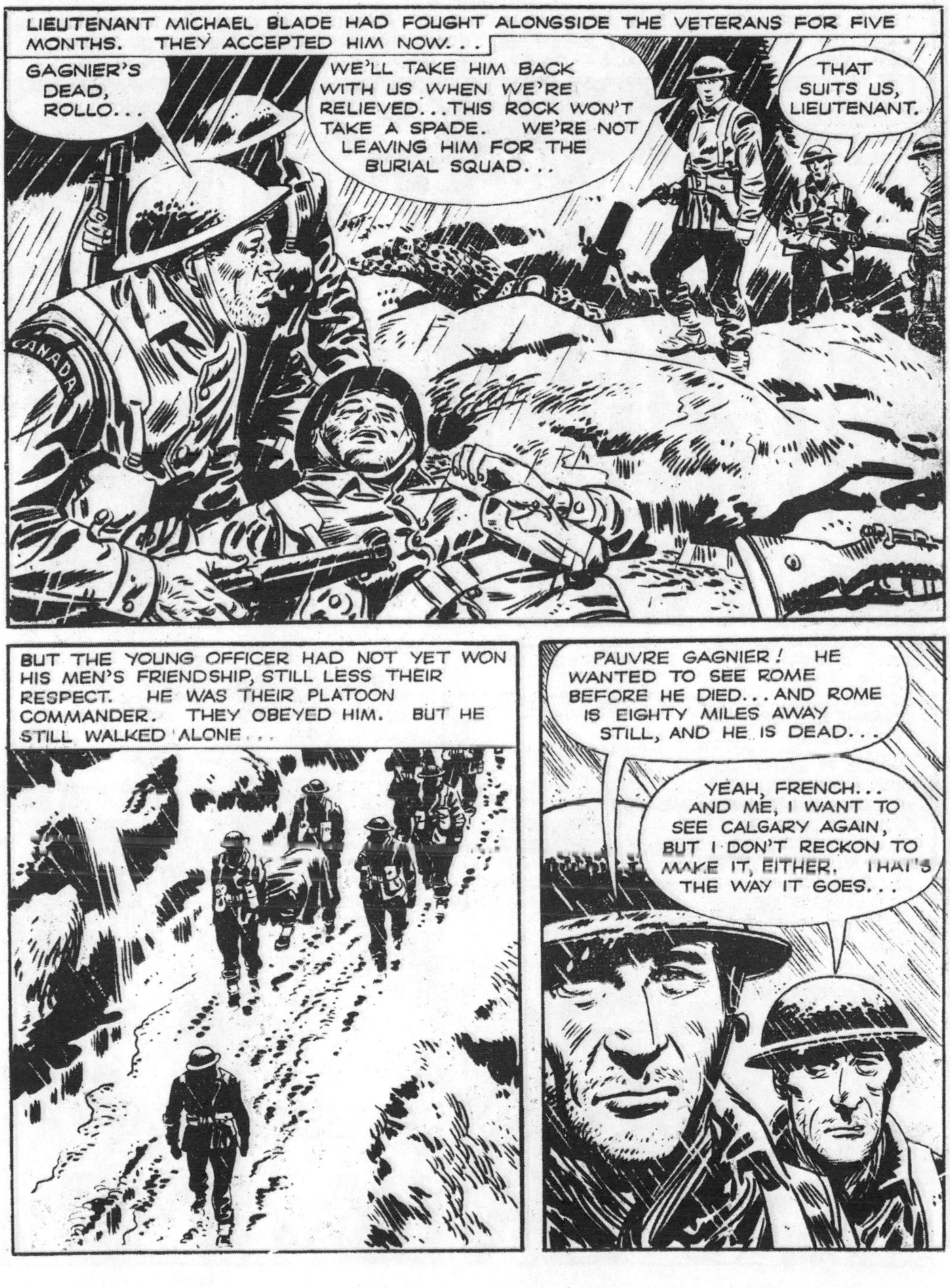
LIEUTENANT MICHAEL BLADE HAD FOUGHT ALONGSIDE THE VETERANS FOR FIVE MONTHS. THEY ACCEPTED HIM NOW...
GAGNIER'S DEAD, ROLLO...
WE'LL TAKE HIM BACK WITH US WHEN WE'RE RELIEVED...THIS ROCK WON'T TAKE A SPADE. WE'RE NOT LEAVING HIM FOR THE BURIAL SQUAD...
THAT SUITS US, LIEUTENANT.
CANADA
BUT THE YOUNG OFFICER HAD NOT YET WON HIS MEN'S FRIENDSHIP, STILL LESS THEIR RESPECT. HE WAS THEIR PLATOON COMMANDER. THEY OBEYED HIM. BUT HE STILL WALKED ALONE...
PAUVRE GAGNIER! HE WANTED TO SEE ROME BEFORE HE DIED...AND ROME IS EIGHTY MILES AWAY STILL, AND HE IS DEAD...
YEAH, FRENCH... AND ME, I WANT TO SEE CALGARY AGAIN, BUT I DON'T RECKON TO MAKE IT, EITHER. THAT'S THE WAY IT GOES...

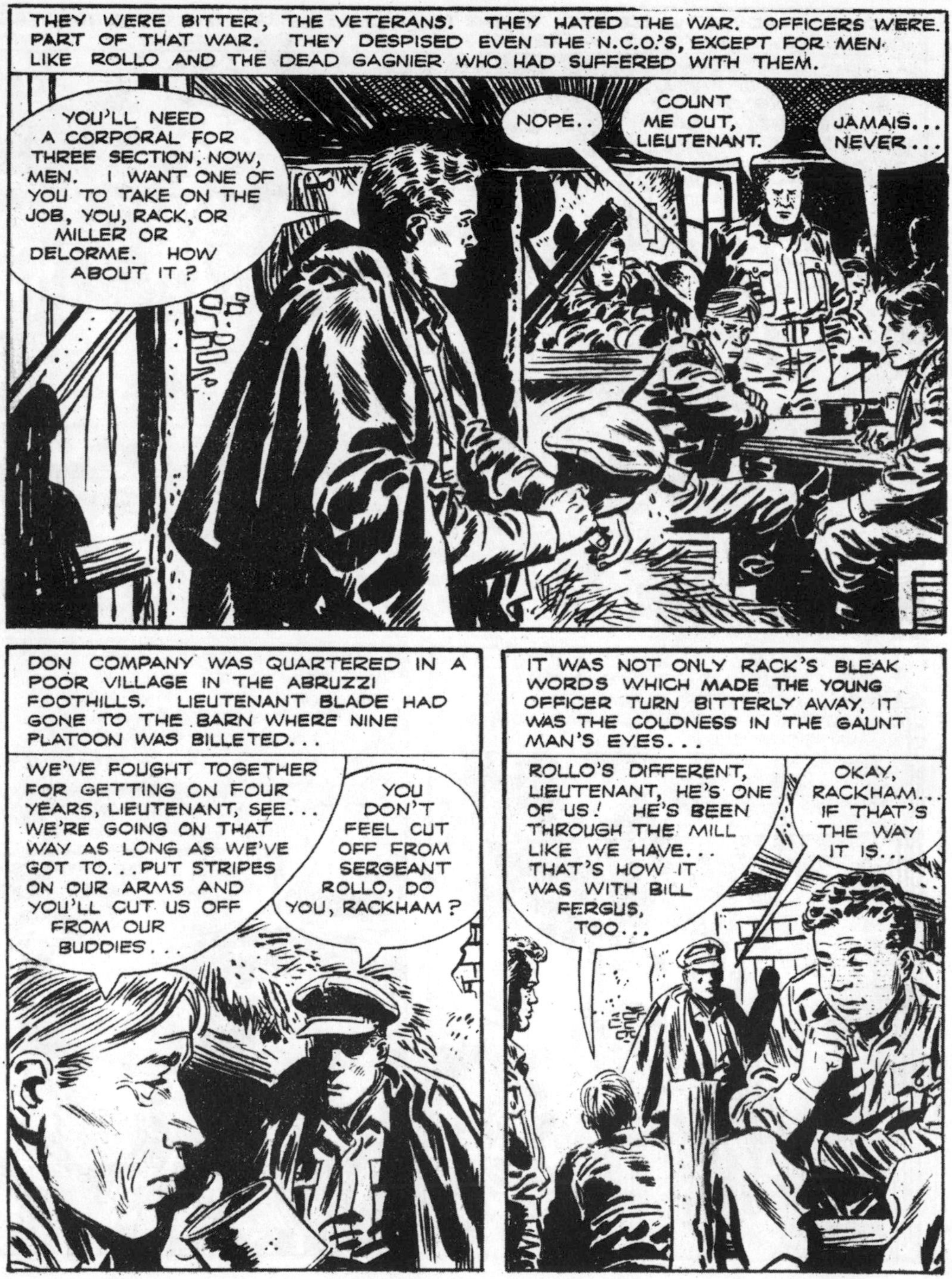
THEY WERE BITTER, THE VETERANS. THEY HATED THE WAR. OFFICERS WERE PART OF THAT WAR. THEY DESPISED EVEN THE N.C.O.'S, EXCEPT FOR MEN LIKE ROLLO AND THE DEAD GAGNIER WHO HAD SUFFERED WITH THEM.
YOU'LL NEED A CORPORAL FOR THREE SECTION, NOW, MEN. I WANT ONE OF YOU TO TAKE ON THE JOB, YOU, RACK, OR MILLER OR DELORME. HOW ABOUT IT?
NOPE..
COUNT ME OUT, LIEUTENANT.
JAMAIS... NEVER...
DON COMPANY WAS QUARTERED IN A POOR VILLAGE IN THE ABRUZZI FOOTHILLS. LIEUTENANT BLADE HAD GONE TO THE BARN WHERE NINE PLATOON WAS BILLETED...
WE'VE FOUGHT TOGETHER FOR GETTING ON FOUR YEARS, LIEUTENANT, SEE... WE'RE GOING ON THAT WAY AS LONG AS WE'VE GOT TO... PUT STRIPES ON OUR ARMS AND YOU'LL CUT US OFF FROM OUR BUDDIES...
YOU DON'T FEEL CUT OFF FROM SERGEANT ROLLO, DO YOU, RACKHAM?
IT WAS NOT ONLY RACK'S BLEAK WORDS WHICH MADE THE YOUNG OFFICER TURN BITTERLY AWAY, IT WAS THE COLDNESS IN THE GAUNT MAN'S EYES...
ROLLO'S DIFFERENT, LIEUTENANT, HE'S ONE OF US! HE'S BEEN THROUGH THE MILL LIKE WE HAVE... THAT'S HOW IT WAS WITH BILL FERGUS, TOO...
OKAY, RACKHAM... IF THAT'S THE WAY IT IS...

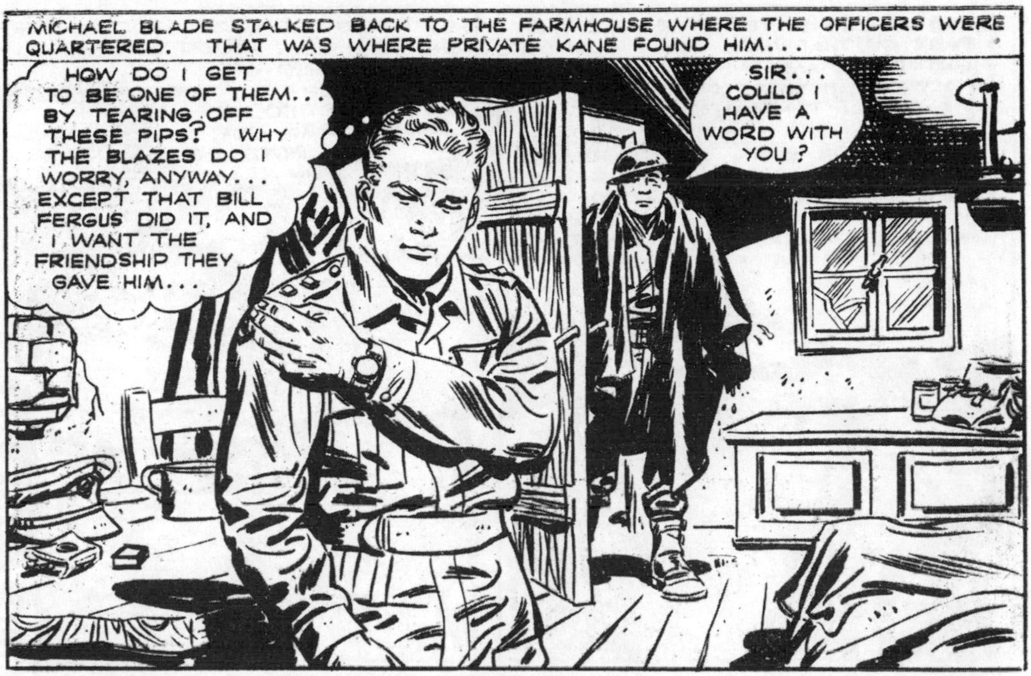
MICHAEL BLADE STALKED BACK TO THE FARMHOUSE WHERE THE OFFICERS WERE QUARTERED. THAT WAS WHERE PRIVATE KANE FOUND HIM...
HOW DO I GET TO BE ONE OF THEM... BY TEARING OFF THESE PIPS? WHY THE BLAZES DO I WORRY, ANYWAY... EXCEPT THAT BILL FERGUS DID IT, AND I WANT THE FRIENDSHIP THEY GAVE HIM...
SIR... COULD I HAVE A WORD WITH YOU?

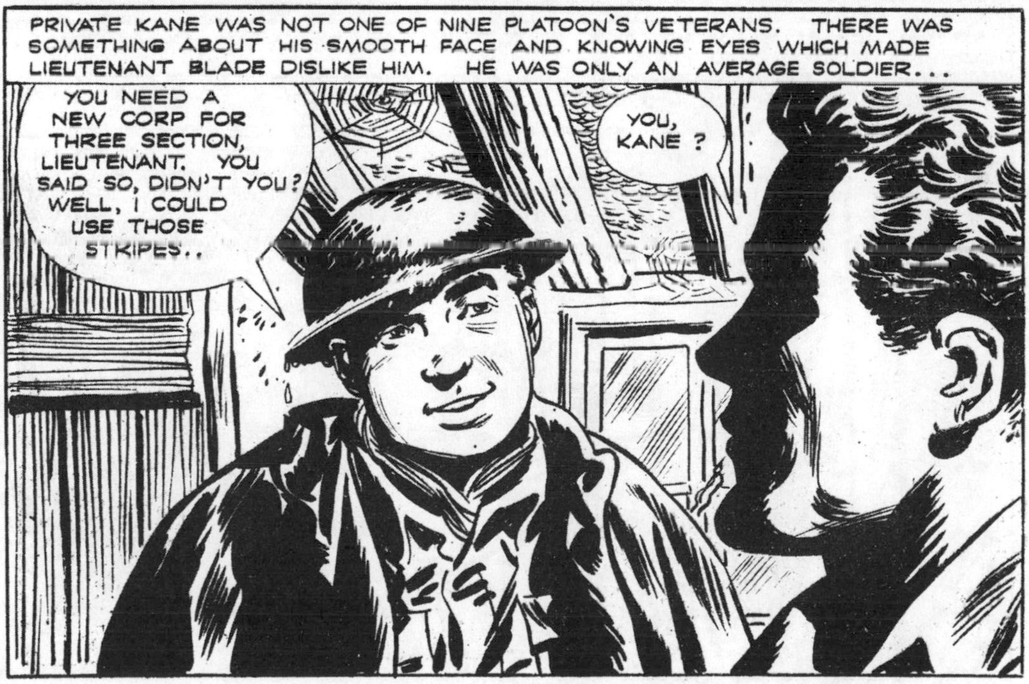
PRIVATE KANE WAS NOT ONE OF NINE PLATOON'S VETERANS. THERE WAS SOMETHING ABOUT HIS SMOOTH FACE AND KNOWING EYES WHICH MADE LIEUTENANT BLADE DISLIKE HIM. HE WAS ONLY AN AVERAGE SOLDIER...
YOU NEED A NEW CORP FOR THREE SECTION, LIEUTENANT. YOU SAID SO, DIDN'T YOU? WELL, I COULD USE THOSE STRIPES..
YOU, KANE ?

KANE WAS THE TYPE OF MAN YOU NEVER NOTICE WHEN MEN ARE FIGHTING FOR THEIR LIVES, BUT WHO IS ALWAYS THERE AFTER THE KILL WITH A FREE-HANDED PACKET OF CIGARETTES AND A LOUD MOUTH.

WHY NOT ME, SIR? I ONLY JOINED THE PLATOON AT TRIPOLI, SURE, BUT I'VE KILLED MY SHARE OF KRAUTS. I COULD LEAD THE SECTION AS WELL AS RACK OR THE OTHERS.

YOU HEARD WHAT RACKHAM SAID TO ME IN THE BILLET, KANE... THAT DOESN'T BOTHER YOU?

THEY AREN'T MY BUDDIES, SIR. JUST BECAUSE I HAVEN'T BEEN SWEATING IT OUT WITH THEM FOR THREE YEARS, THEY ACT LIKE I DON'T EXIST. **YOU** KNOW HOW IT IS, LIEUT...

OKAY, KANE, THAT'LL DO! I'LL THINK ABOUT IT...

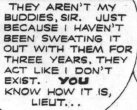

COMING FROM A SHIFTY LOUDMOUTH LIKE KANE, THE TRUTH HURT. RESTLESS, BITTER, MICHAEL BLADE WENT DOWN TO THE MUDDY YARD. MAJOR RAGLAN WAS SHOUTING FOR HIM THERE...

SURE...THAT'S ALL I AM TO THOSE MEN... AN OUTSIDER LIKE KANE...

HEY, MICHAEL...I'VE GOT A RECCE JOB FOR NINE PLATOON... COME OVER TO THE OFFICE...

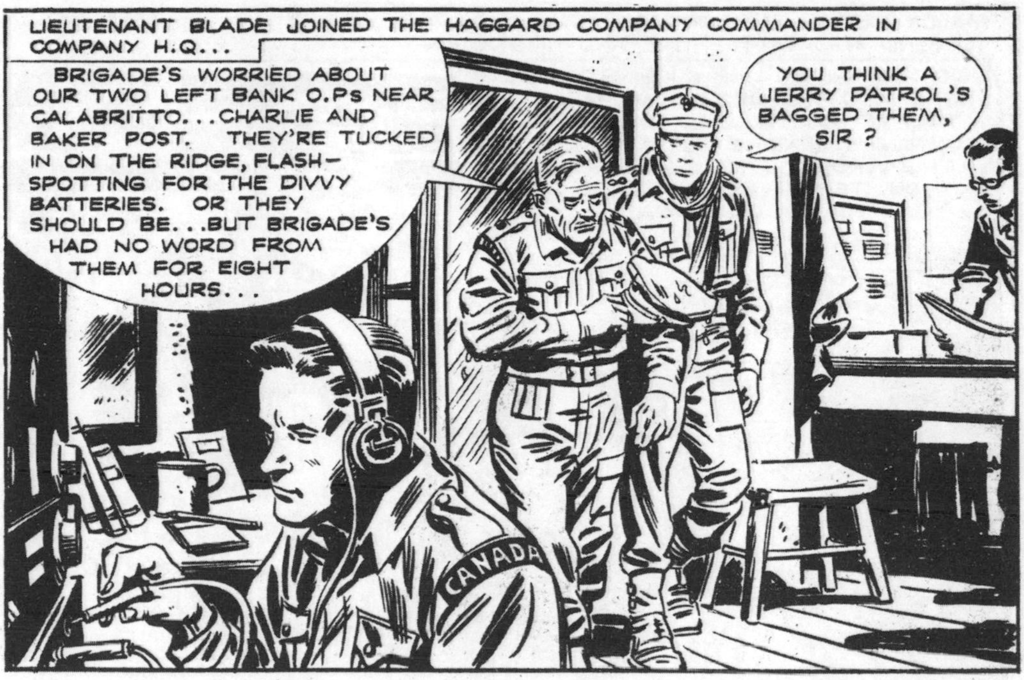
LIEUTENANT BLADE JOINED THE HAGGARD COMPANY COMMANDER IN COMPANY H.Q...
BRIGADE'S WORRIED ABOUT OUR TWO LEFT BANK O.Ps NEAR CALABRITTO...CHARLIE AND BAKER POST. THEY'RE TUCKED IN ON THE RIDGE, FLASH-SPOTTING FOR THE DIVVY BATTERIES. OR THEY SHOULD BE...BUT BRIGADE'S HAD NO WORD FROM THEM FOR EIGHT HOURS...
YOU THINK A JERRY PATROL'S BAGGED THEM, SIR ?
CANADA

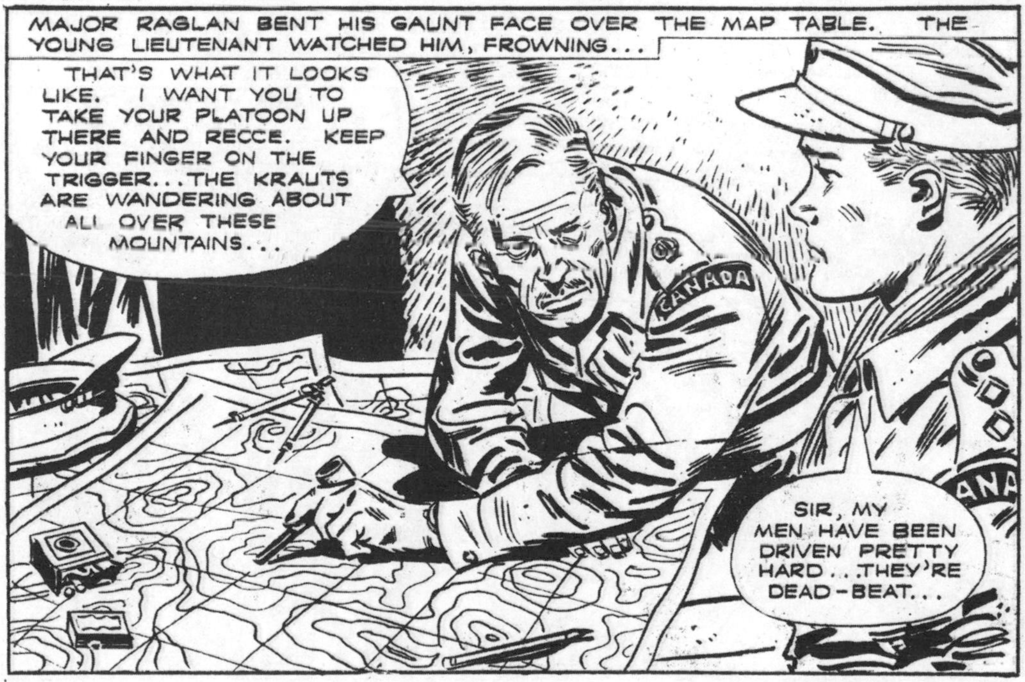
MAJOR RAGLAN BENT HIS GAUNT FACE OVER THE MAP TABLE. THE YOUNG LIEUTENANT WATCHED HIM, FROWNING...
THAT'S WHAT IT LOOKS LIKE. I WANT YOU TO TAKE YOUR PLATOON UP THERE AND RECCE. KEEP YOUR FINGER ON THE TRIGGER...THE KRAUTS ARE WANDERING ABOUT ALL OVER THESE MOUNTAINS...
CANADA
SIR, MY MEN HAVE BEEN DRIVEN PRETTY HARD...THEY'RE DEAD-BEAT...

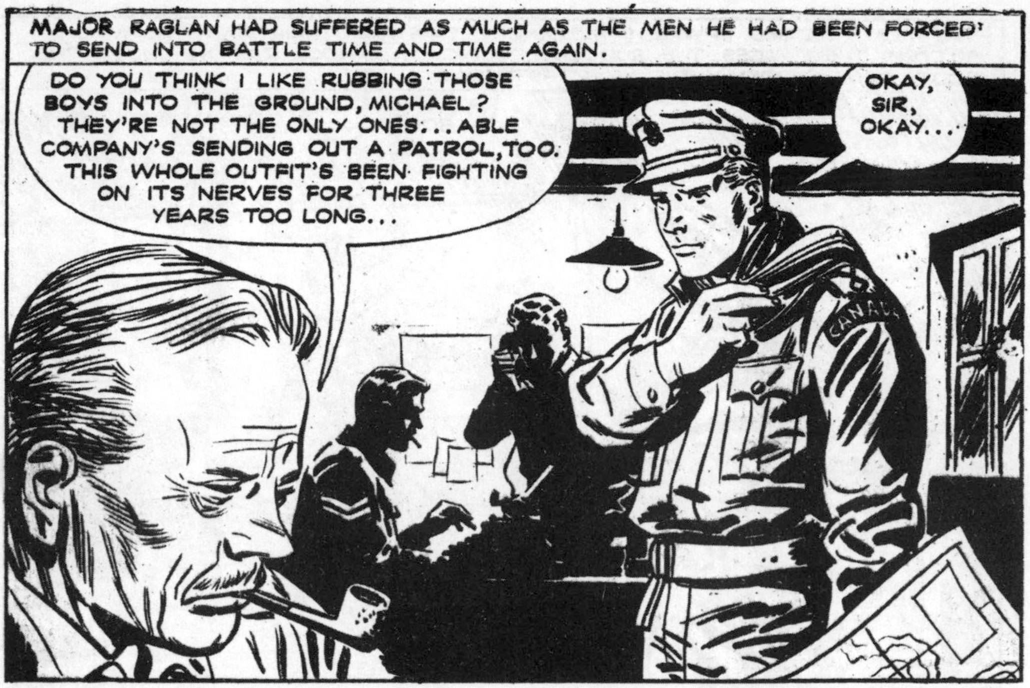
MAJOR RAGLAN HAD SUFFERED AS MUCH AS THE MEN HE HAD BEEN FORCED TO SEND INTO BATTLE TIME AND TIME AGAIN.
DO YOU THINK I LIKE RUBBING THOSE BOYS INTO THE GROUND, MICHAEL? THEY'RE NOT THE ONLY ONES...ABLE COMPANY'S SENDING OUT A PATROL, TOO. THIS WHOLE OUTFIT'S BEEN FIGHTING ON ITS NERVES FOR THREE YEARS TOO LONG...
OKAY, SIR, OKAY...

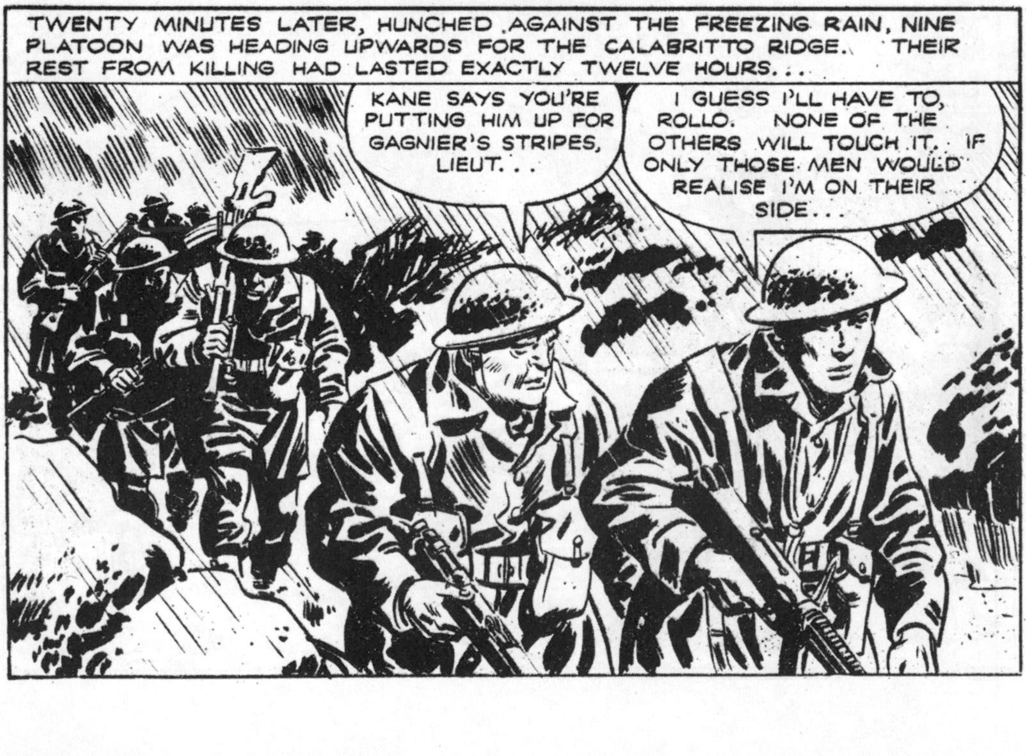
TWENTY MINUTES LATER, HUNCHED AGAINST THE FREEZING RAIN, NINE PLATOON WAS HEADING UPWARDS FOR THE CALABRITTO RIDGE. THEIR REST FROM KILLING HAD LASTED EXACTLY TWELVE HOURS...
KANE SAYS YOU'RE PUTTING HIM UP FOR GAGNIER'S STRIPES, LIEUT...
I GUESS I'LL HAVE TO, ROLLO. NONE OF THE OTHERS WILL TOUCH IT. IF ONLY THOSE MEN WOULD REALISE I'M ON THEIR SIDE...

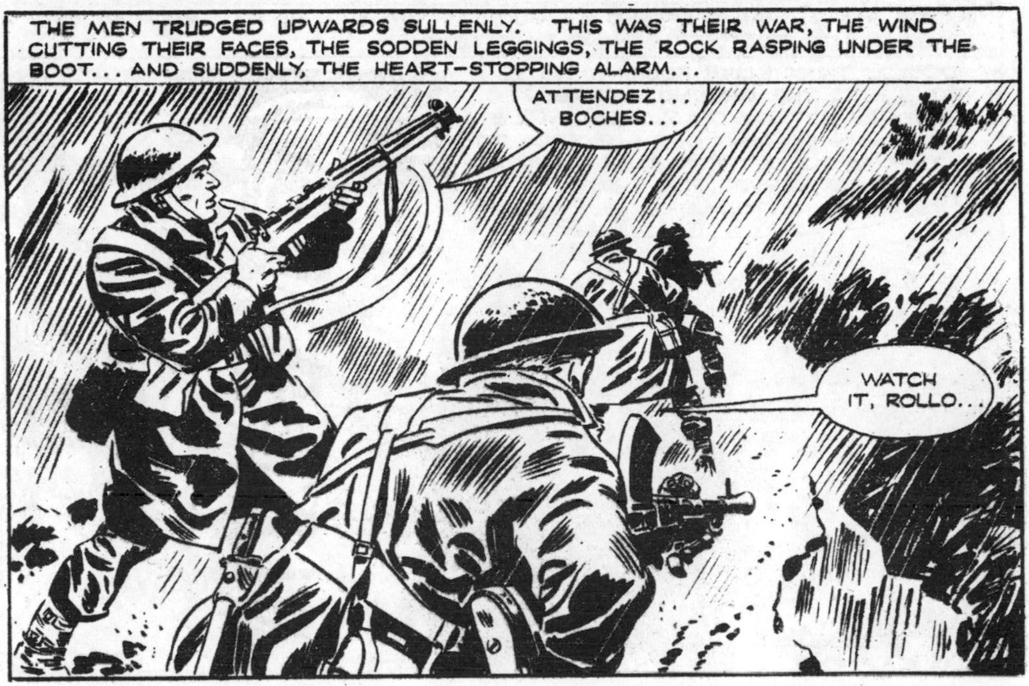
THE MEN TRUDGED UPWARDS SULLENLY. THIS WAS THEIR WAR, THE WIND CUTTING THEIR FACES, THE SODDEN LEGGINGS, THE ROCK RASPING UNDER THE BOOT... AND SUDDENLY, THE HEART-STOPPING ALARM...
ATTENDEZ... BOCHES...
WATCH IT, ROLLO...

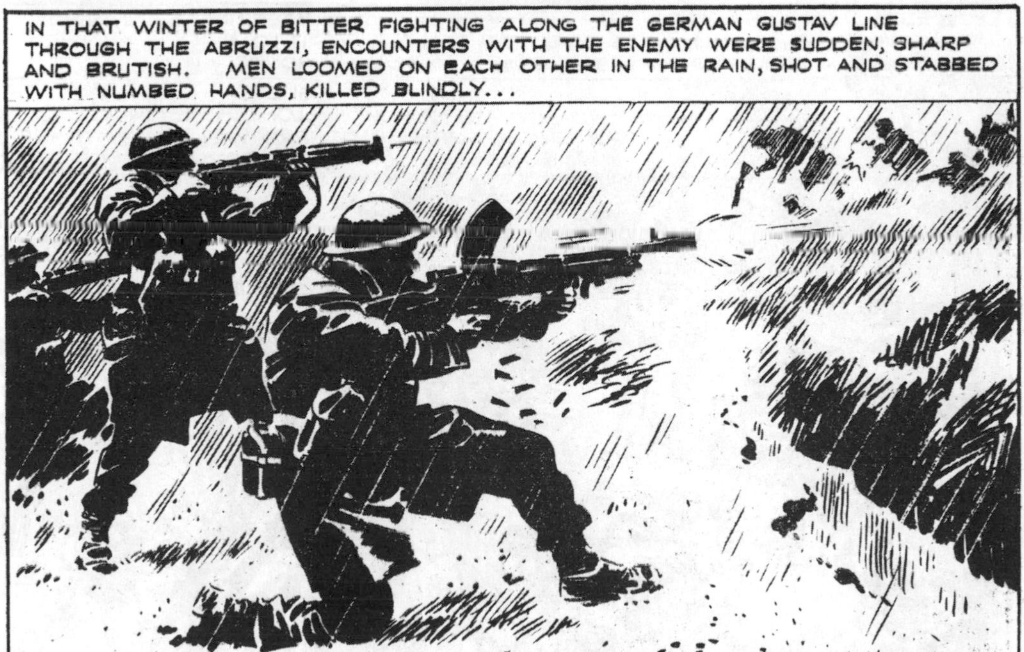
IN THAT WINTER OF BITTER FIGHTING ALONG THE GERMAN GUSTAV LINE THROUGH THE ABRUZZI, ENCOUNTERS WITH THE ENEMY WERE SUDDEN, SHARP AND BRUTISH. MEN LOOMED ON EACH OTHER IN THE RAIN, SHOT AND STABBED WITH NUMBED HANDS, KILLED BLINDLY...

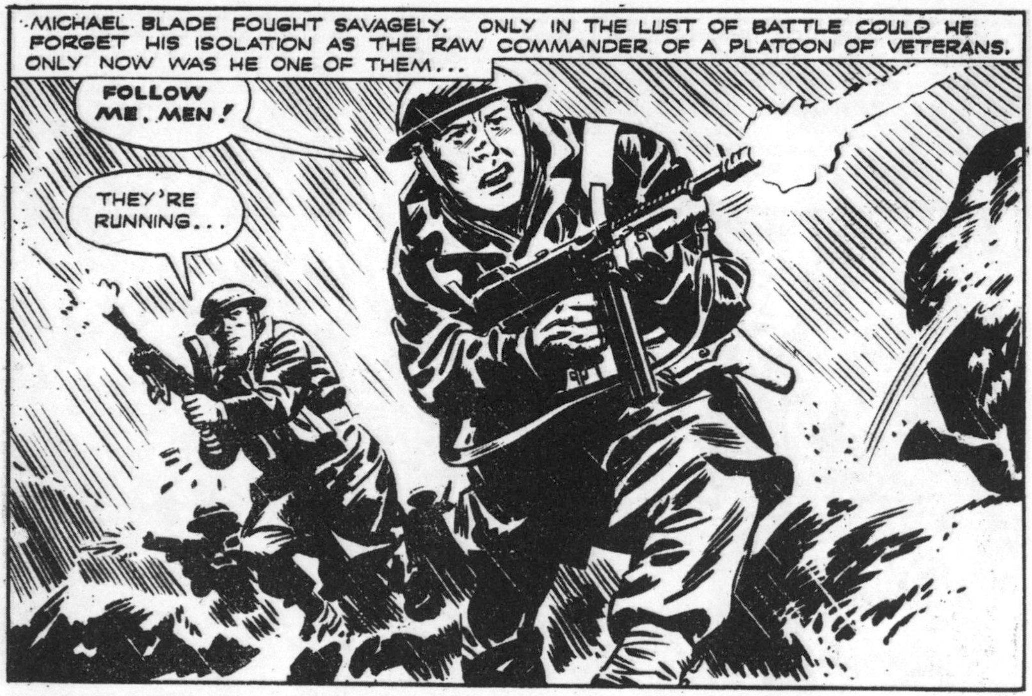
MICHAEL BLADE FOUGHT SAVAGELY. ONLY IN THE LUST OF BATTLE COULD HE FORGET HIS ISOLATION AS THE RAW COMMANDER OF A PLATOON OF VETERANS. ONLY NOW WAS HE ONE OF THEM...
FOLLOW ME, MEN!
THEY'RE RUNNING...

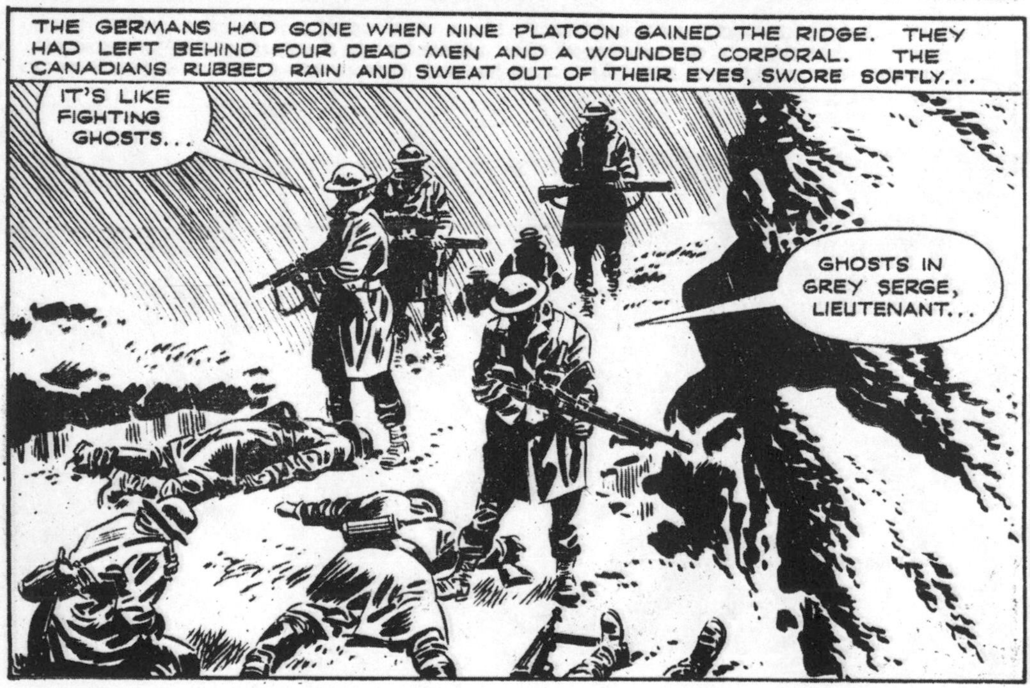
THE GERMANS HAD GONE WHEN NINE PLATOON GAINED THE RIDGE. THEY HAD LEFT BEHIND FOUR DEAD MEN AND A WOUNDED CORPORAL. THE CANADIANS RUBBED RAIN AND SWEAT OUT OF THEIR EYES, SWORE SOFTLY...
IT'S LIKE FIGHTING GHOSTS...
GHOSTS IN GREY SERGE, LIEUTENANT...

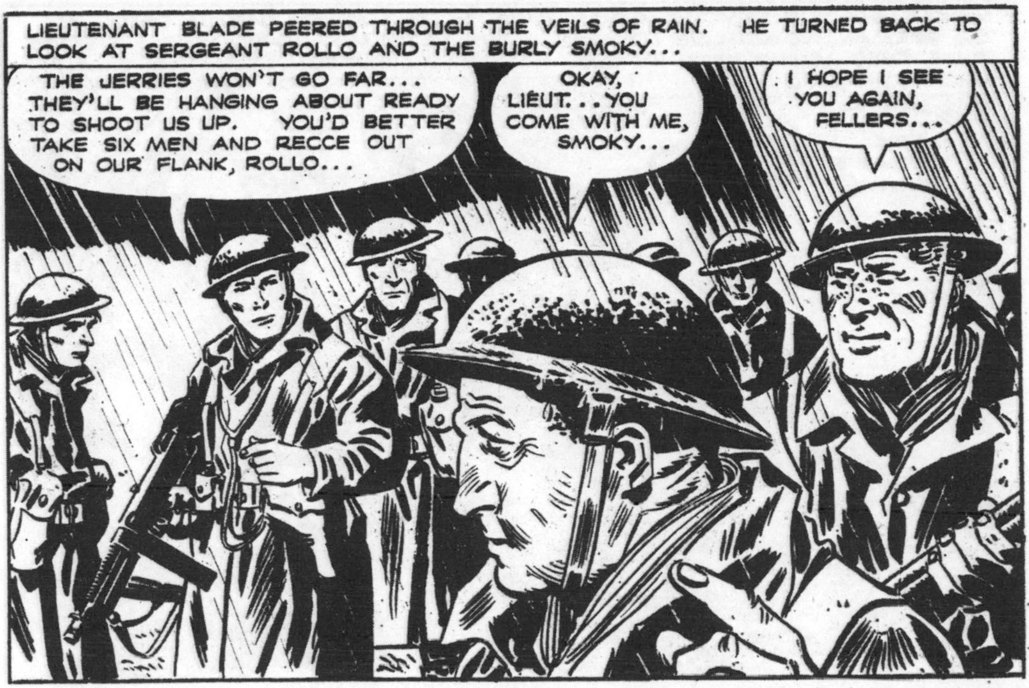
LIEUTENANT BLADE PEERED THROUGH THE VEILS OF RAIN. HE TURNED BACK TO LOOK AT SERGEANT ROLLO AND THE BURLY SMOKY...
THE JERRIES WON'T GO FAR... THEY'LL BE HANGING ABOUT READY TO SHOOT US UP. YOU'D BETTER TAKE SIX MEN AND RECCE OUT ON OUR FLANK, ROLLO...
OKAY, LIEUT...YOU COME WITH ME, SMOKY...
I HOPE I SEE YOU AGAIN, FELLERS...

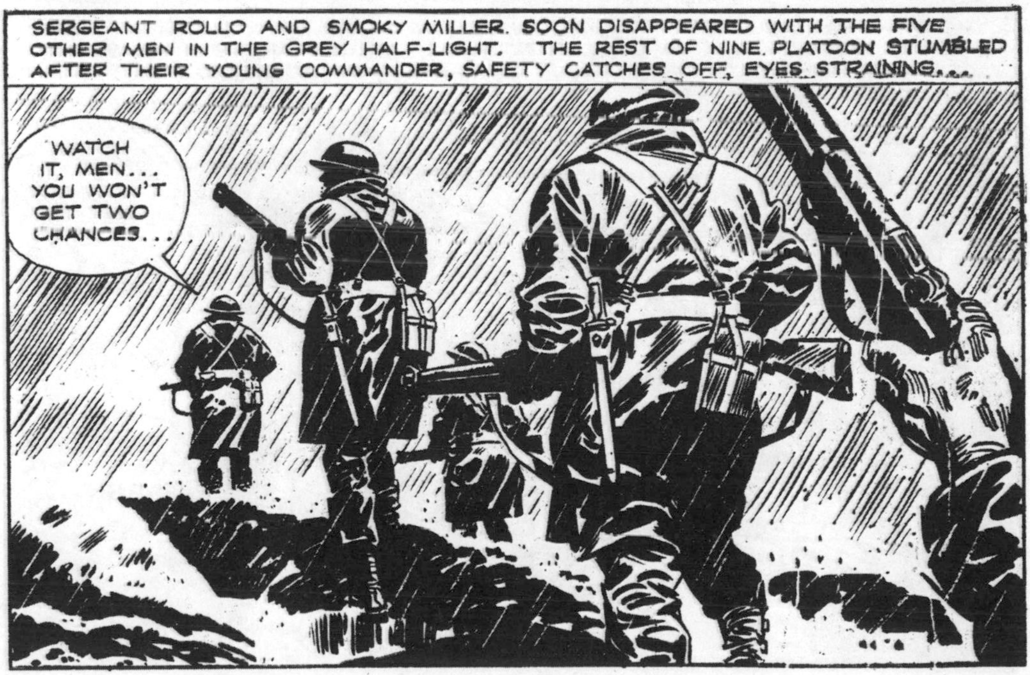
SERGEANT ROLLO AND SMOKY MILLER SOON DISAPPEARED WITH THE FIVE OTHER MEN IN THE GREY HALF-LIGHT. THE REST OF NINE PLATOON STUMBLED AFTER THEIR YOUNG COMMANDER, SAFETY CATCHES OFF, EYES STRAINING...
WATCH IT, MEN... YOU WON'T GET TWO CHANCES...

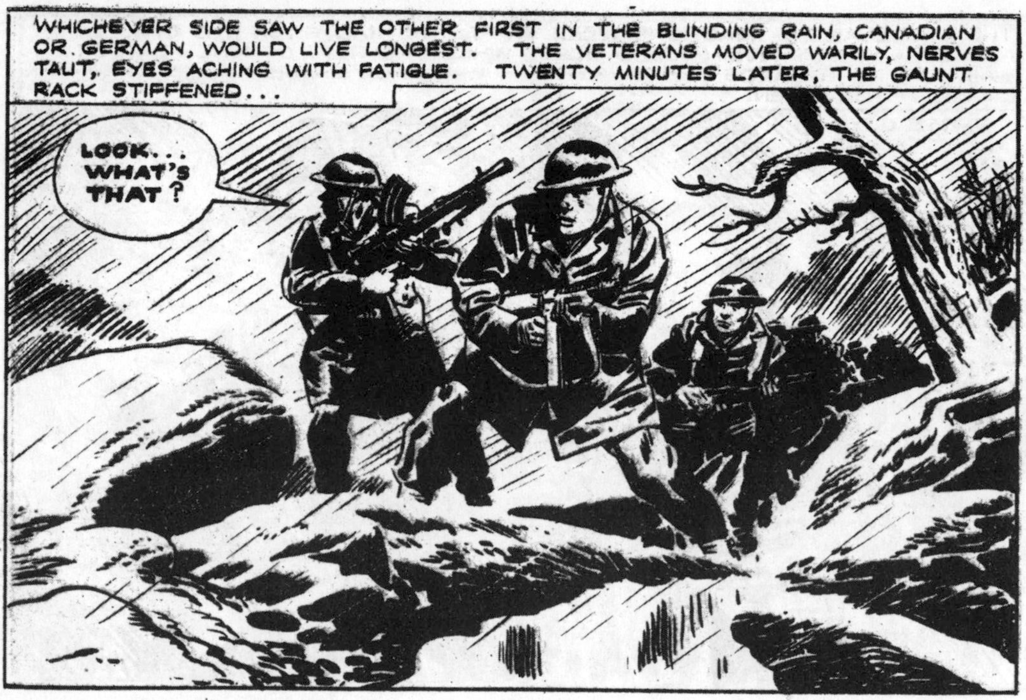
WHICHEVER SIDE SAW THE OTHER FIRST IN THE BLINDING RAIN, CANADIAN OR GERMAN, WOULD LIVE LONGEST. THE VETERANS MOVED WARILY, NERVES TAUT, EYES ACHING WITH FATIGUE. TWENTY MINUTES LATER, THE GAUNT RACK STIFFENED...
LOOK... WHAT'S THAT?

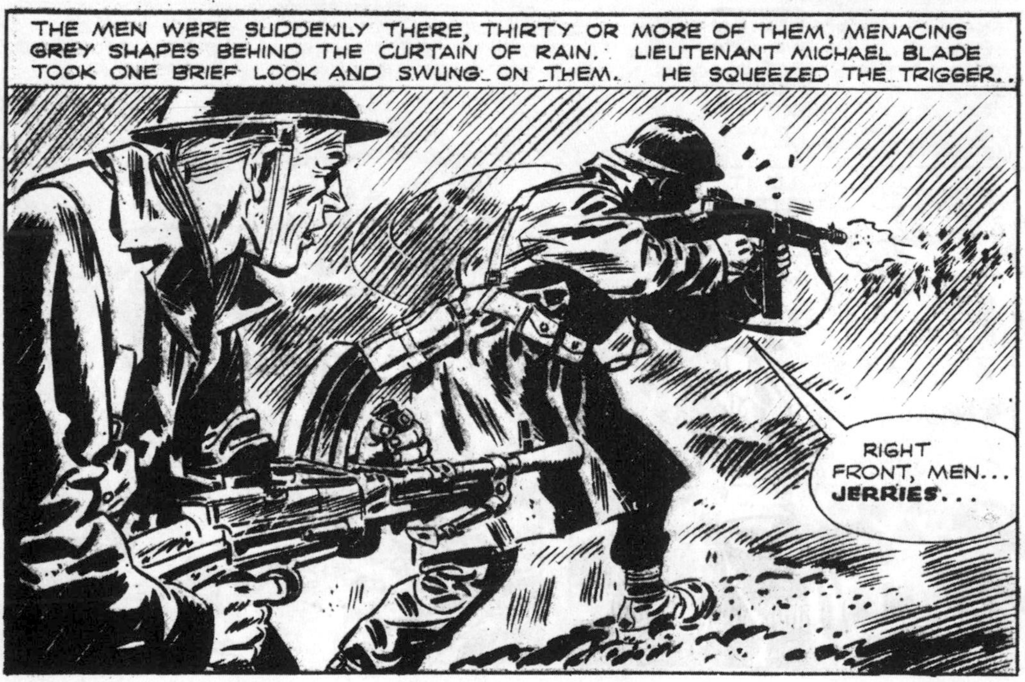
THE MEN WERE SUDDENLY THERE, THIRTY OR MORE OF THEM, MENACING GREY SHAPES BEHIND THE CURTAIN OF RAIN. LIEUTENANT MICHAEL BLADE TOOK ONE BRIEF LOOK AND SWUNG ON THEM. HE SQUEEZED THE TRIGGER..
RIGHT FRONT, MEN... **JERRIES**...

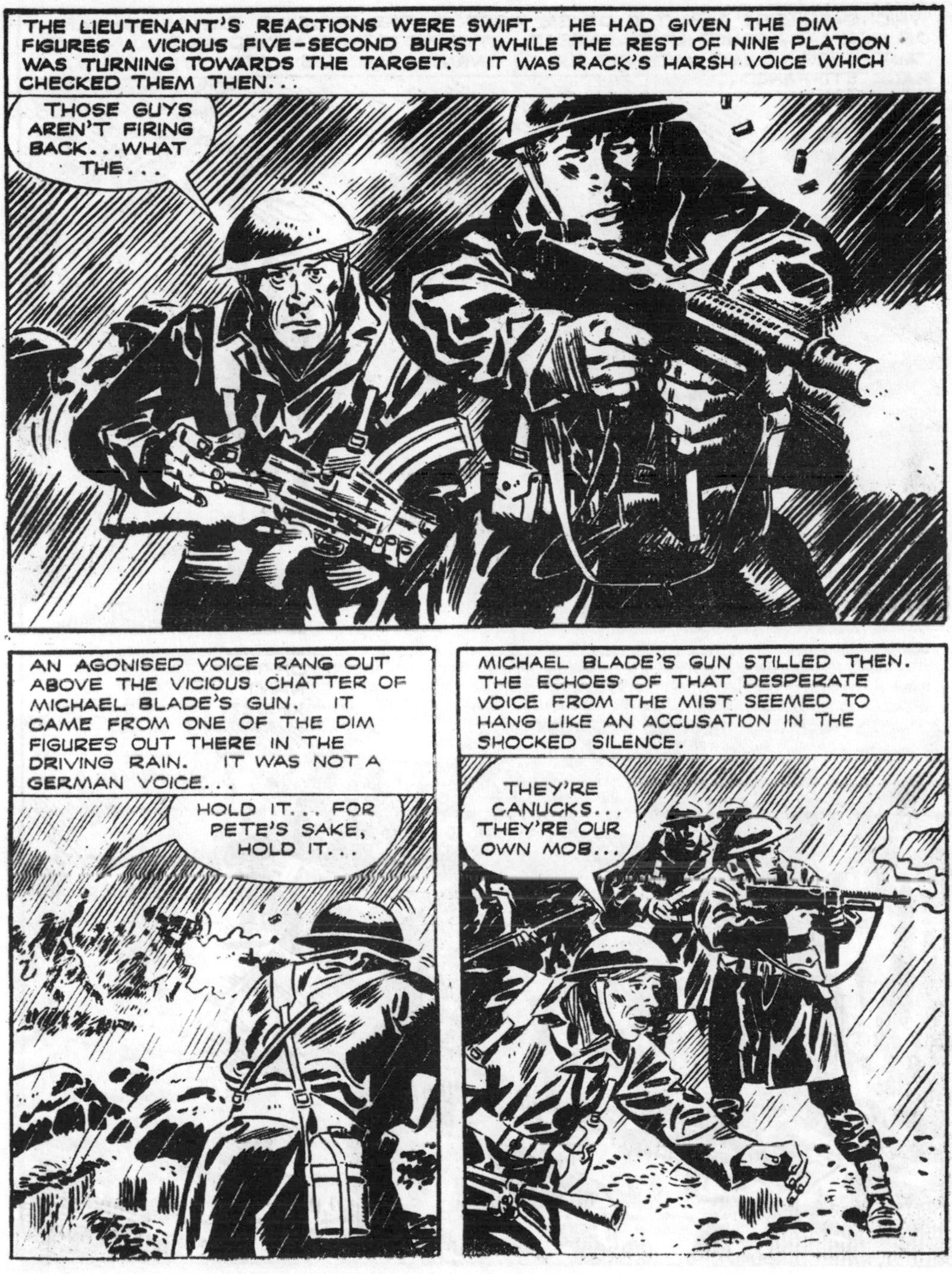
THE LIEUTENANT'S REACTIONS WERE SWIFT. HE HAD GIVEN THE DIM FIGURES A VICIOUS FIVE-SECOND BURST WHILE THE REST OF NINE PLATOON WAS TURNING TOWARDS THE TARGET. IT WAS RACK'S HARSH VOICE WHICH CHECKED THEM THEN...
THOSE GUYS AREN'T FIRING BACK...WHAT THE...
AN AGONISED VOICE RANG OUT ABOVE THE VICIOUS CHATTER OF MICHAEL BLADE'S GUN. IT CAME FROM ONE OF THE DIM FIGURES OUT THERE IN THE DRIVING RAIN. IT WAS NOT A GERMAN VOICE...
HOLD IT... FOR PETE'S SAKE, HOLD IT...
MICHAEL BLADE'S GUN STILLED THEN. THE ECHOES OF THAT DESPERATE VOICE FROM THE MIST SEEMED TO HANG LIKE AN ACCUSATION IN THE SHOCKED SILENCE.
THEY'RE CANUCKS... THEY'RE OUR OWN MOB...

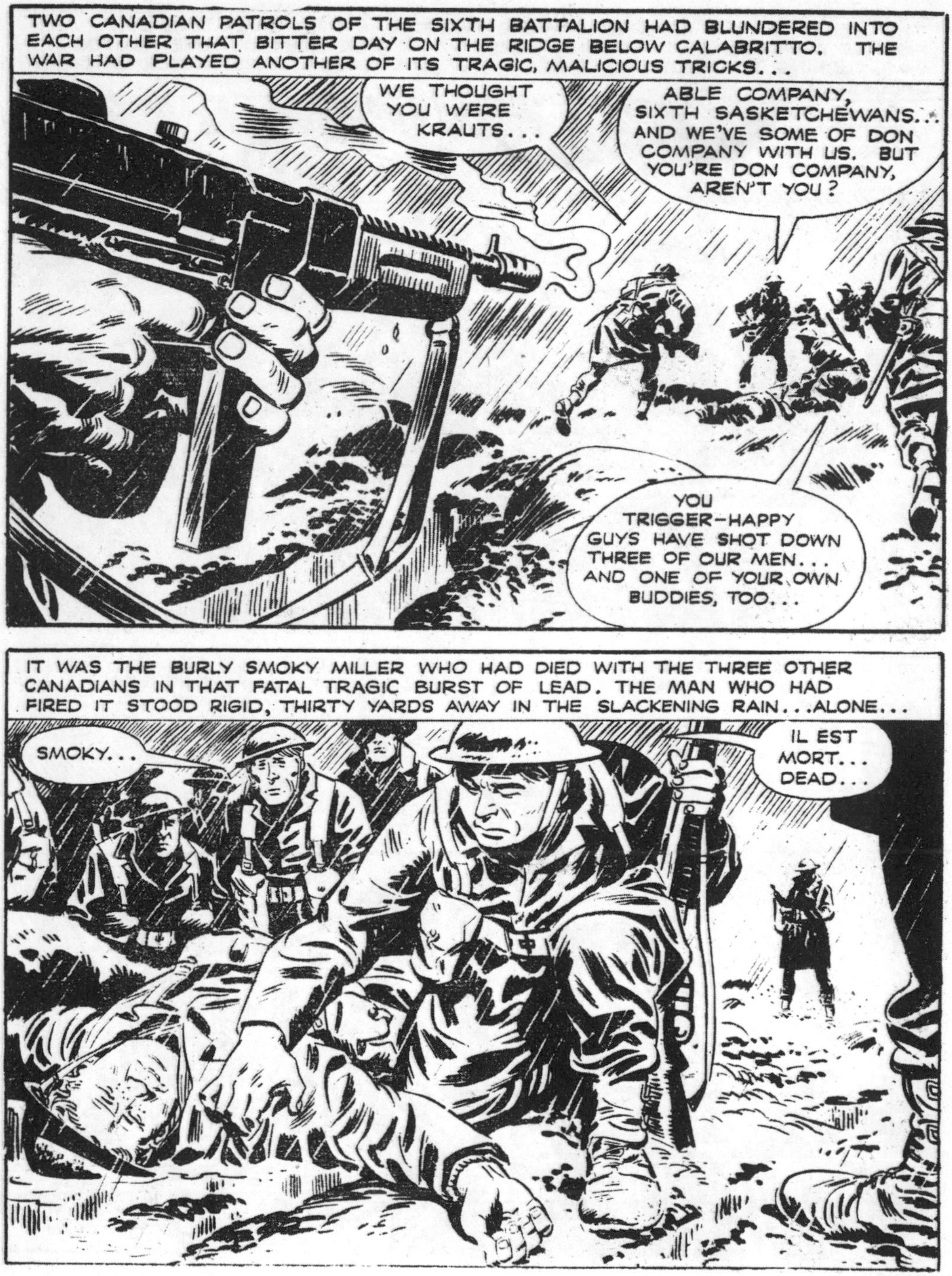
TWO CANADIAN PATROLS OF THE SIXTH BATTALION HAD BLUNDERED INTO EACH OTHER THAT BITTER DAY ON THE RIDGE BELOW CALABRITTO. THE WAR HAD PLAYED ANOTHER OF ITS TRAGIC, MALICIOUS TRICKS...
WE THOUGHT YOU WERE KRAUTS...
ABLE COMPANY, SIXTH SASKETCHEWANS... AND WE'VE SOME OF DON COMPANY WITH US. BUT YOU'RE DON COMPANY, AREN'T YOU?
YOU TRIGGER-HAPPY GUYS HAVE SHOT DOWN THREE OF OUR MEN... AND ONE OF YOUR OWN BUDDIES, TOO...
IT WAS THE BURLY SMOKY MILLER WHO HAD DIED WITH THE THREE OTHER CANADIANS IN THAT FATAL TRAGIC BURST OF LEAD. THE MAN WHO HAD FIRED IT STOOD RIGID, THIRTY YARDS AWAY IN THE SLACKENING RAIN...ALONE...
SMOKY...
IL EST MORT... DEAD...

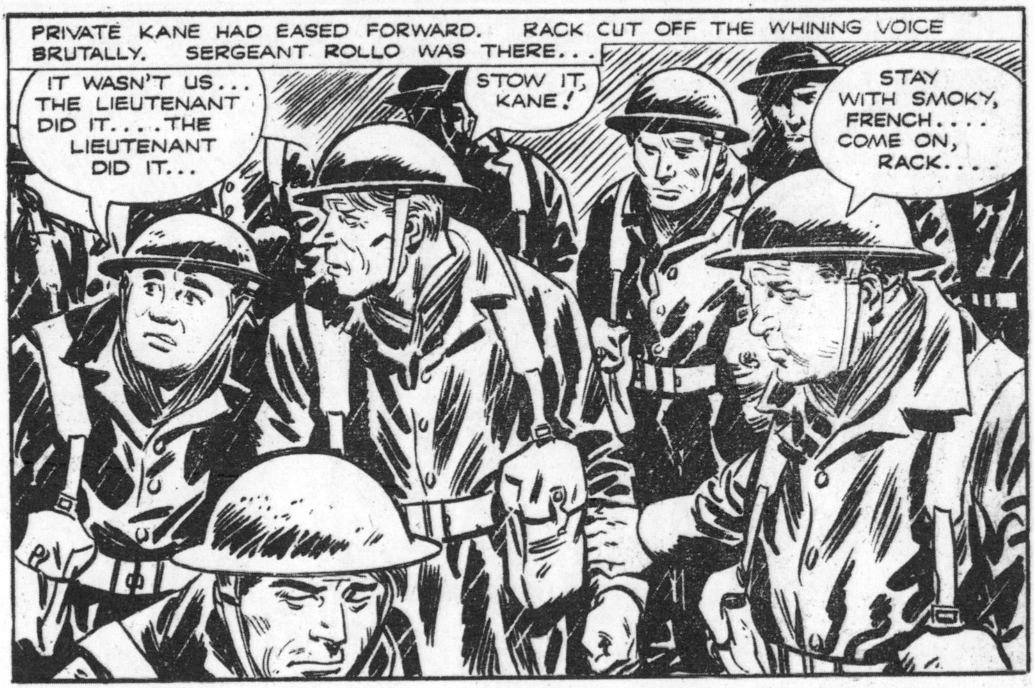
PRIVATE KANE HAD EASED FORWARD. RACK CUT OFF THE WHINING VOICE BRUTALLY. SERGEANT ROLLO WAS THERE...
IT WASN'T US... THE LIEUTENANT DID IT.... THE LIEUTENANT DID IT...
STOW IT, KANE!
STAY WITH SMOKY, FRENCH.... COME ON, RACK....

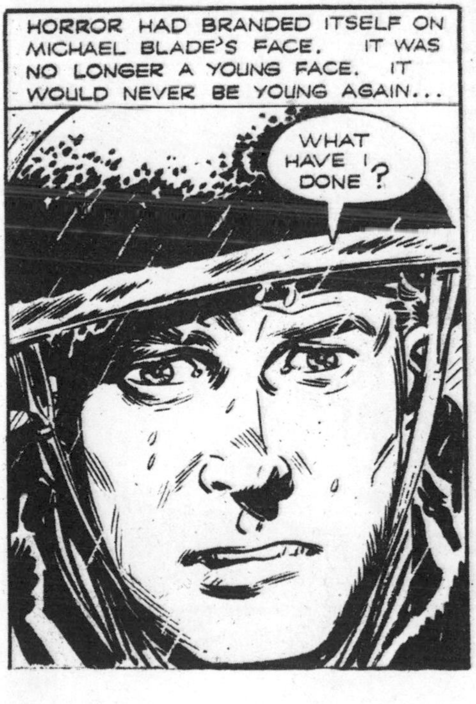
HORROR HAD BRANDED ITSELF ON MICHAEL BLADE'S FACE. IT WAS NO LONGER A YOUNG FACE. IT WOULD NEVER BE YOUNG AGAIN...
WHAT HAVE I DONE?

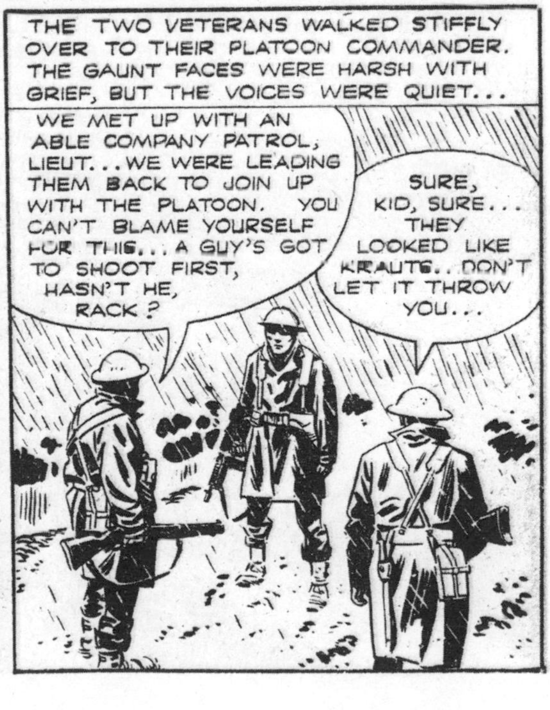
THE TWO VETERANS WALKED STIFFLY OVER TO THEIR PLATOON COMMANDER. THE GAUNT FACES WERE HARSH WITH GRIEF, BUT THE VOICES WERE QUIET...
WE MET UP WITH AN ABLE COMPANY PATROL, LIEUT... WE WERE LEADING THEM BACK TO JOIN UP WITH THE PLATOON. YOU CAN'T BLAME YOURSELF FOR THIS... A GUY'S GOT TO SHOOT FIRST, HASN'T HE, RACK?
SURE, KID, SURE... THEY LOOKED LIKE KRAUTS... DON'T LET IT THROW YOU...

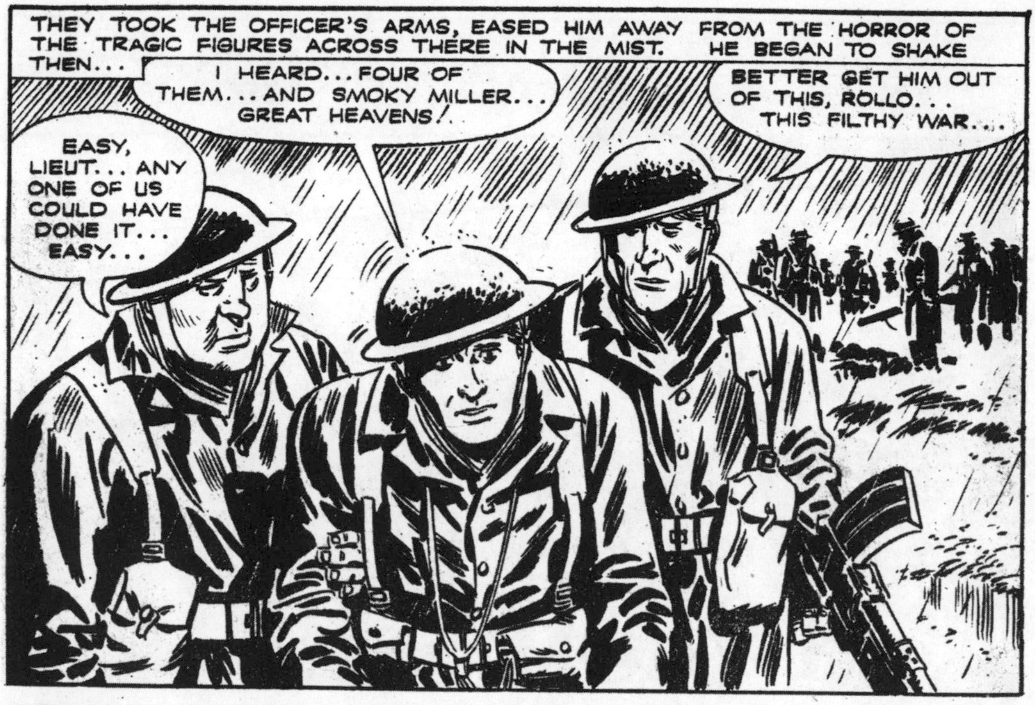
THEY TOOK THE OFFICER'S ARMS, EASED HIM AWAY FROM THE HORROR OF THE TRAGIC FIGURES ACROSS THERE IN THE MIST. HE BEGAN TO SHAKE THEN...
EASY, LIEUT... ANY ONE OF US COULD HAVE DONE IT... EASY...
I HEARD... FOUR OF THEM... AND SMOKY MILLER... GREAT HEAVENS!
BETTER GET HIM OUT OF THIS, ROLLO... THIS FILTHY WAR...

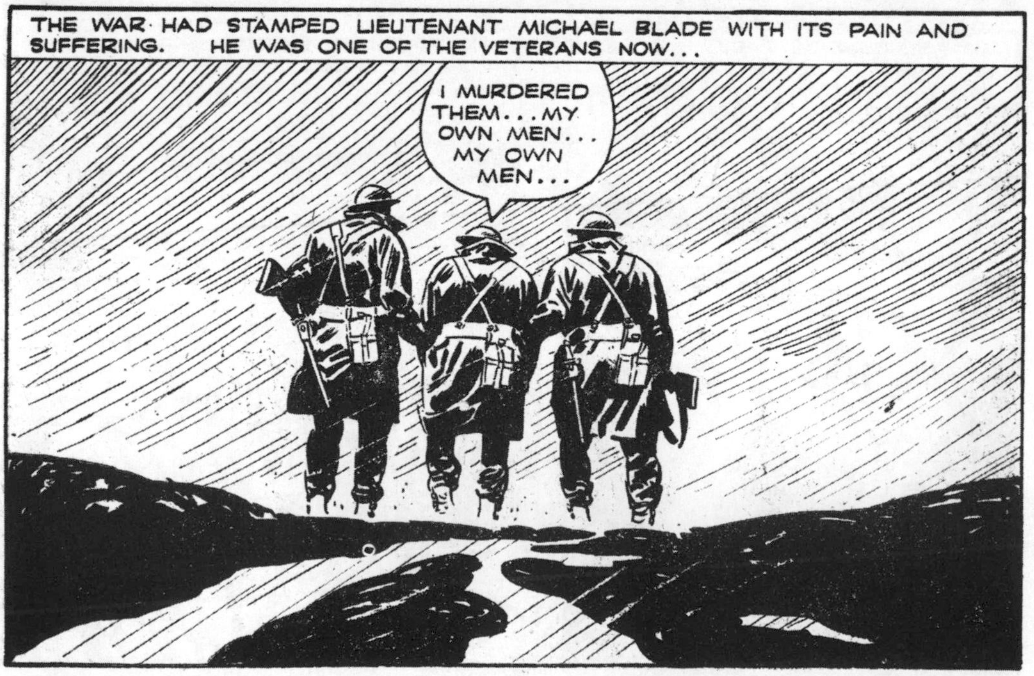
THE WAR HAD STAMPED LIEUTENANT MICHAEL BLADE WITH ITS PAIN AND SUFFERING. HE WAS ONE OF THE VETERANS NOW...
I MURDERED THEM... MY OWN MEN... MY OWN MEN...

Chapter 3. Burden of Guilt

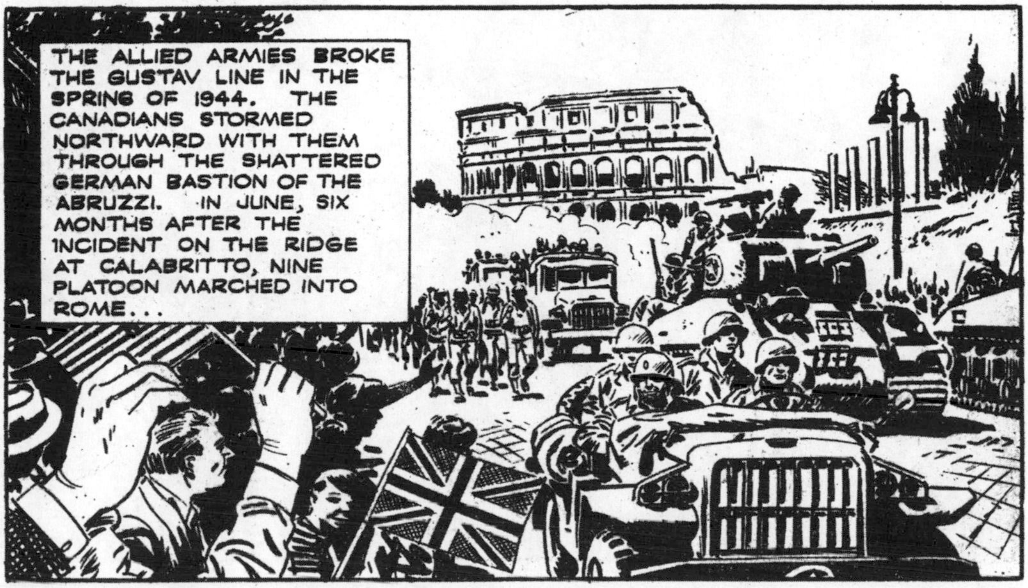
THE ALLIED ARMIES BROKE THE GUSTAV LINE IN THE SPRING OF 1944. THE CANADIANS STORMED NORTHWARD WITH THEM THROUGH THE SHATTERED GERMAN BASTION OF THE ABRUZZI. IN JUNE, SIX MONTHS AFTER THE INCIDENT ON THE RIDGE AT CALABRITTO, NINE PLATOON MARCHED INTO ROME...

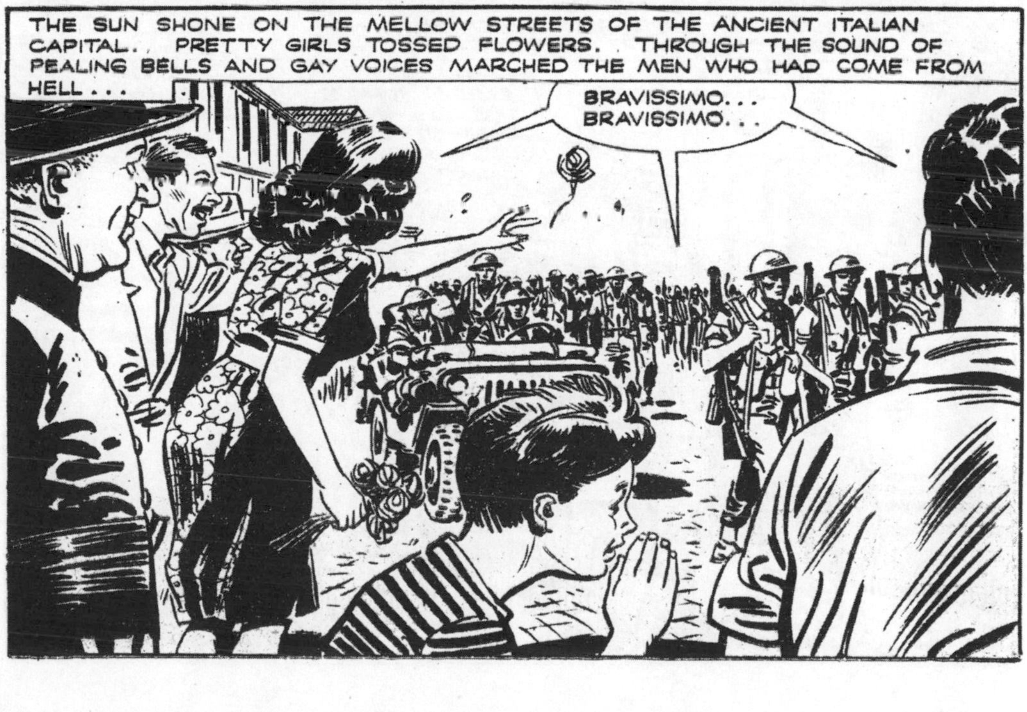
THE SUN SHONE ON THE MELLOW STREETS OF THE ANCIENT ITALIAN CAPITAL. PRETTY GIRLS TOSSED FLOWERS. THROUGH THE SOUND OF PEALING BELLS AND GAY VOICES MARCHED THE MEN WHO HAD COME FROM HELL...
BRAVISSIMO... BRAVISSIMO...

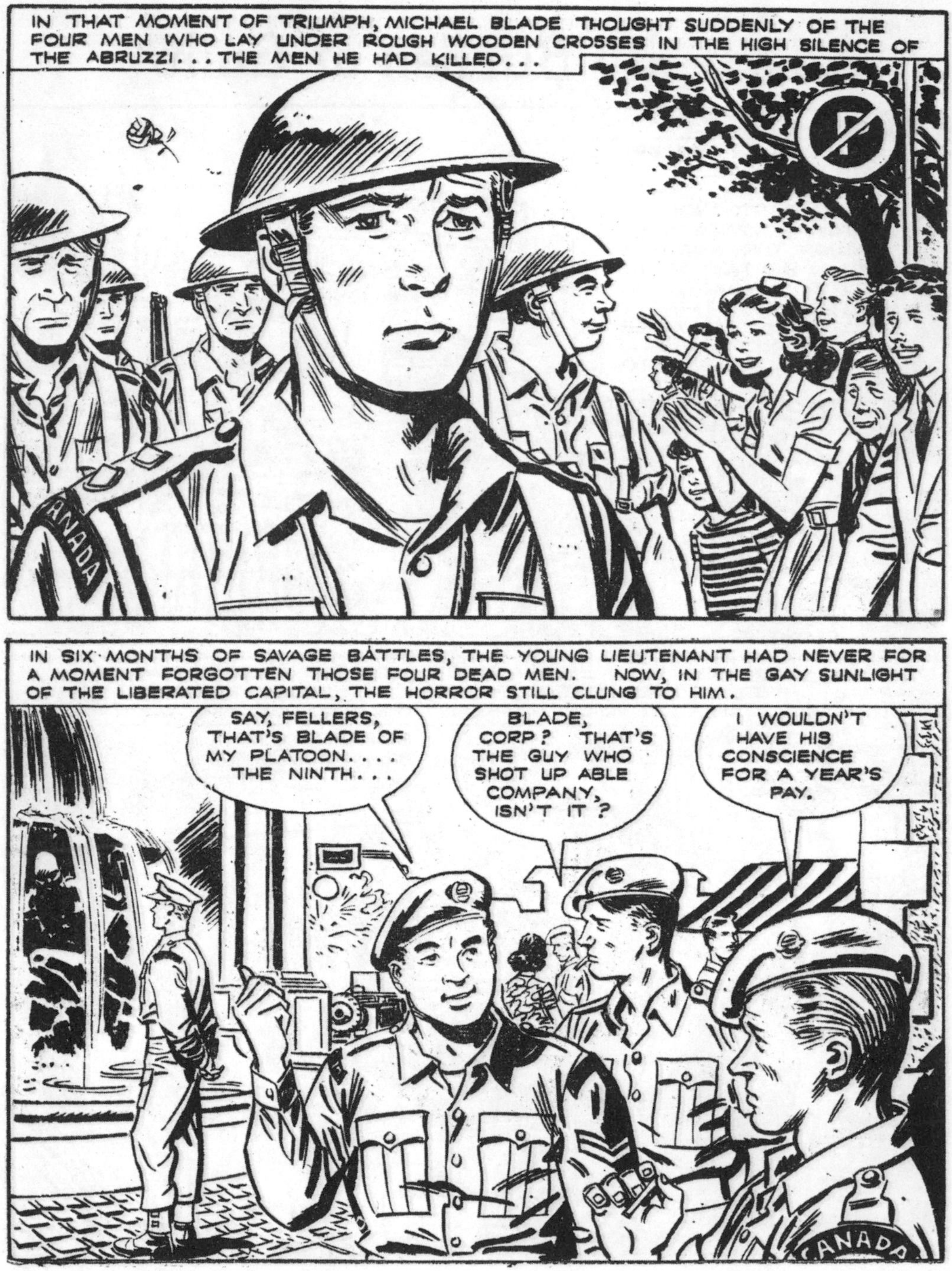
IN THAT MOMENT OF TRIUMPH, MICHAEL BLADE THOUGHT SUDDENLY OF THE FOUR MEN WHO LAY UNDER ROUGH WOODEN CROSSES IN THE HIGH SILENCE OF THE ABRUZZI... THE MEN HE HAD KILLED...
IN SIX MONTHS OF SAVAGE BATTLES, THE YOUNG LIEUTENANT HAD NEVER FOR A MOMENT FORGOTTEN THOSE FOUR DEAD MEN. NOW, IN THE GAY SUNLIGHT OF THE LIBERATED CAPITAL, THE HORROR STILL CLUNG TO HIM.
SAY, FELLERS, THAT'S BLADE OF MY PLATOON.... THE NINTH...
BLADE, CORP? THAT'S THE GUY WHO SHOT UP ABLE COMPANY, ISN'T IT?
I WOULDN'T HAVE HIS CONSCIENCE FOR A YEAR'S PAY.

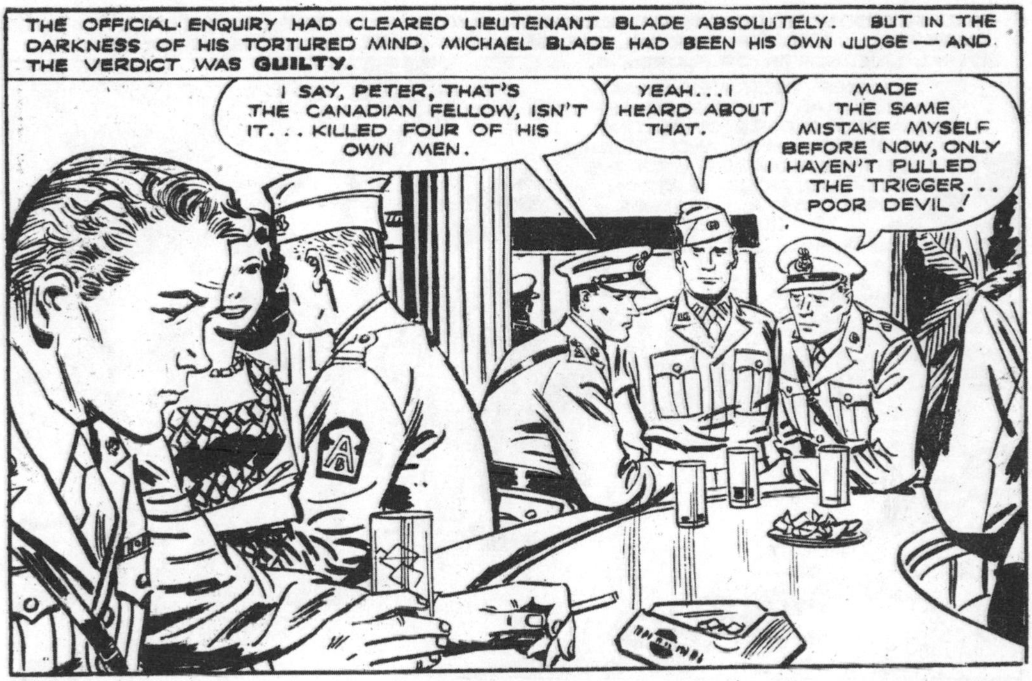
THE OFFICIAL ENQUIRY HAD CLEARED LIEUTENANT BLADE ABSOLUTELY. BUT IN THE DARKNESS OF HIS TORTURED MIND, MICHAEL BLADE HAD BEEN HIS OWN JUDGE — AND THE VERDICT WAS **GUILTY.**
I SAY, PETER, THAT'S THE CANADIAN FELLOW, ISN'T IT. . . KILLED FOUR OF HIS OWN MEN.
YEAH. . . I HEARD ABOUT THAT.
MADE THE SAME MISTAKE MYSELF BEFORE NOW, ONLY I HAVEN'T PULLED THE TRIGGER. . . POOR DEVIL!

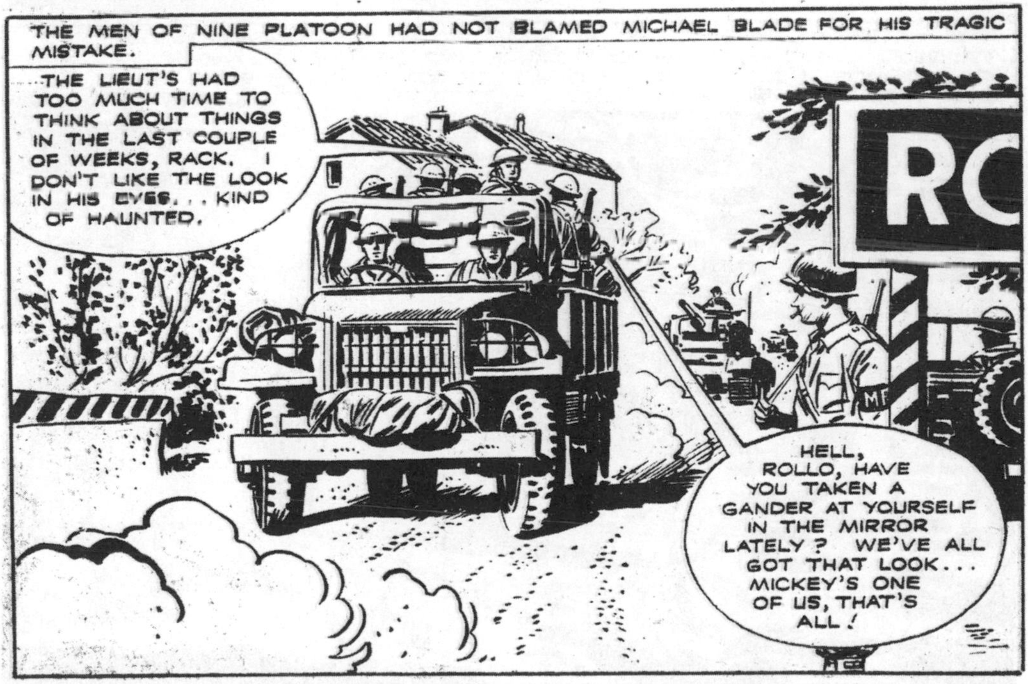
THE MEN OF NINE PLATOON HAD NOT BLAMED MICHAEL BLADE FOR HIS TRAGIC MISTAKE.
THE LIEUT'S HAD TOO MUCH TIME TO THINK ABOUT THINGS IN THE LAST COUPLE OF WEEKS, RACK. I DON'T LIKE THE LOOK IN HIS EYES. . . KIND OF HAUNTED.
RO
MP
HELL, ROLLO, HAVE YOU TAKEN A GANDER AT YOURSELF IN THE MIRROR LATELY? WE'VE ALL GOT THAT LOOK. . . MICKEY'S ONE OF US, THAT'S ALL!

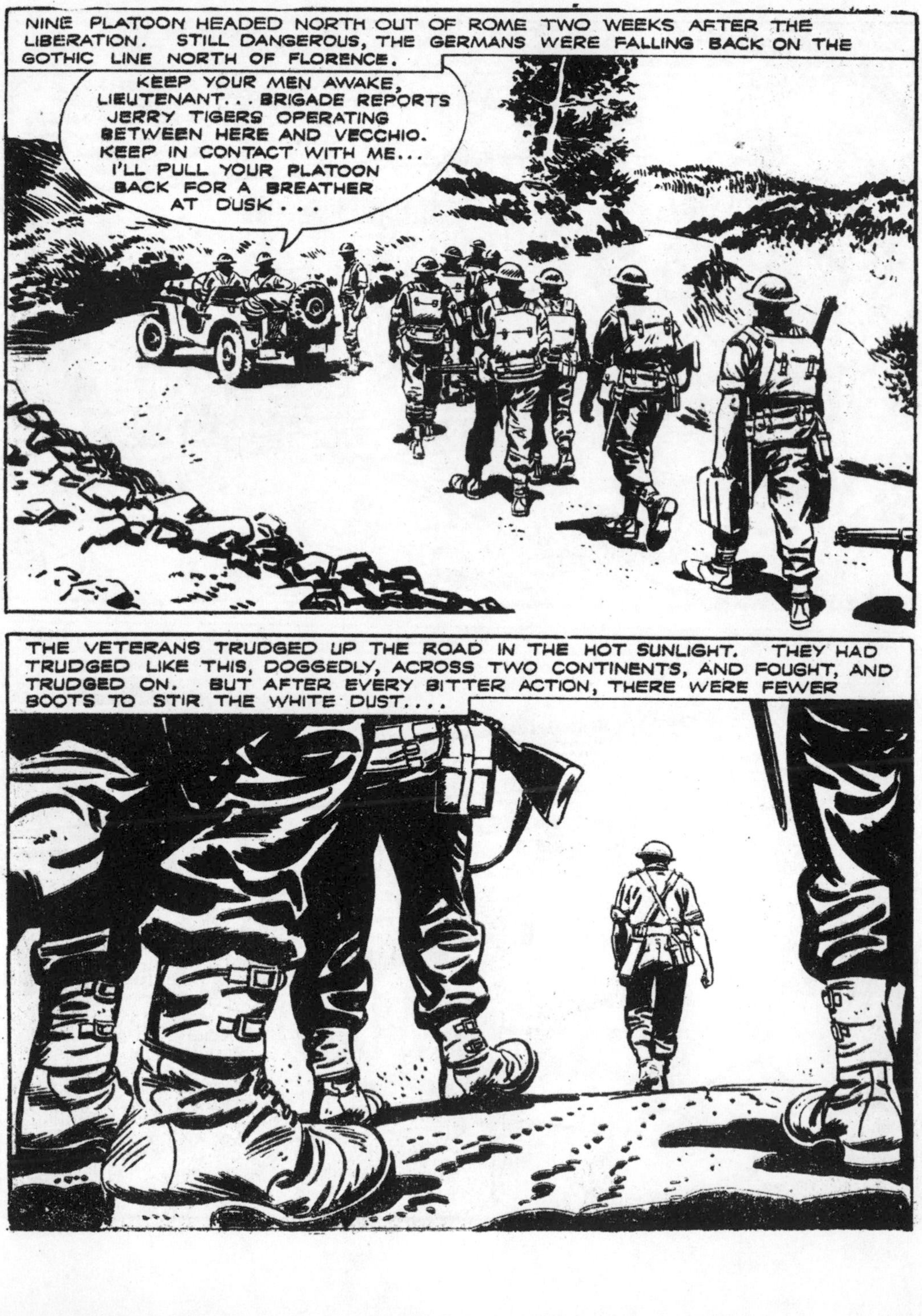
NINE PLATOON HEADED NORTH OUT OF ROME TWO WEEKS AFTER THE LIBERATION. STILL DANGEROUS, THE GERMANS WERE FALLING BACK ON THE GOTHIC LINE NORTH OF FLORENCE.
KEEP YOUR MEN AWAKE, LIEUTENANT... BRIGADE REPORTS JERRY TIGERS OPERATING BETWEEN HERE AND VECCHIO. KEEP IN CONTACT WITH ME... I'LL PULL YOUR PLATOON BACK FOR A BREATHER AT DUSK...
THE VETERANS TRUDGED UP THE ROAD IN THE HOT SUNLIGHT. THEY HAD TRUDGED LIKE THIS, DOGGEDLY, ACROSS TWO CONTINENTS, AND FOUGHT, AND TRUDGED ON. BUT AFTER EVERY BITTER ACTION, THERE WERE FEWER BOOTS TO STIR THE WHITE DUST....

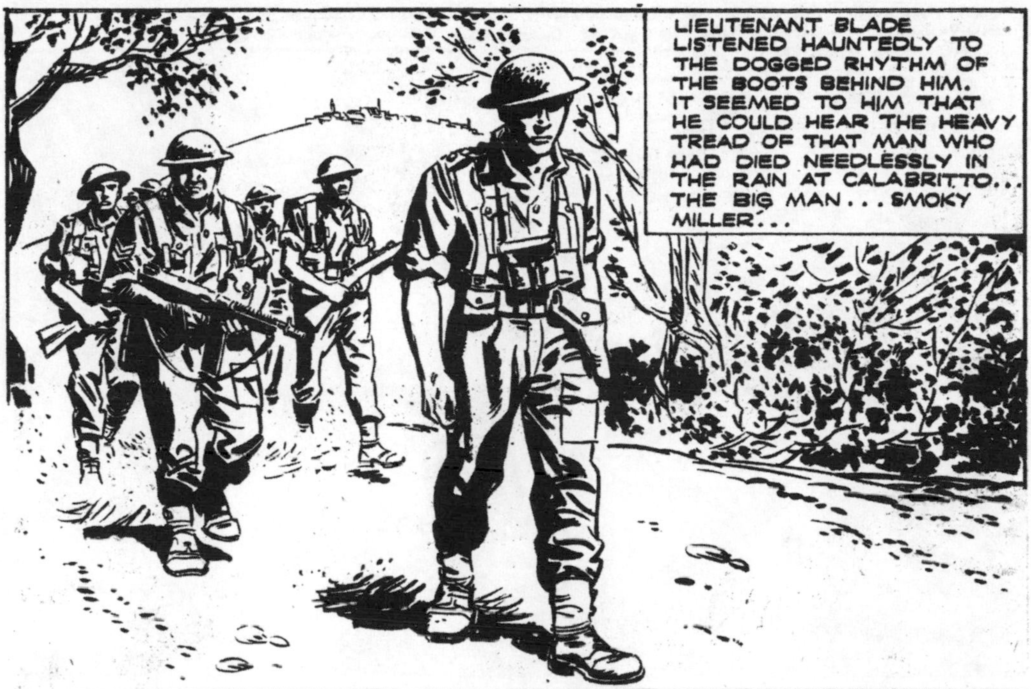
LIEUTENANT BLADE LISTENED HAUNTEDLY TO THE DOGGED RHYTHM OF THE BOOTS BEHIND HIM. IT SEEMED TO HIM THAT HE COULD HEAR THE HEAVY TREAD OF THAT MAN WHO HAD DIED NEEDLESSLY IN THE RAIN AT CALABRITTO... THE BIG MAN . . . SMOKY MILLER . . .

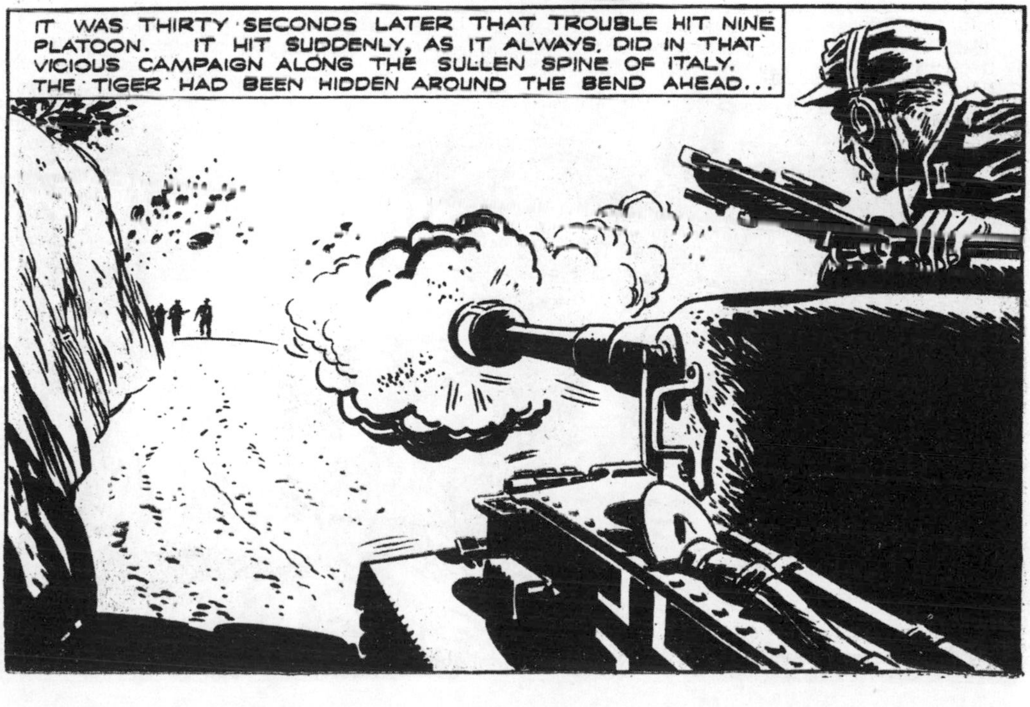
IT WAS THIRTY SECONDS LATER THAT TROUBLE HIT NINE PLATOON. IT HIT SUDDENLY, AS IT ALWAYS, DID IN THAT VICIOUS CAMPAIGN ALONG THE SULLEN SPINE OF ITALY. THE TIGER HAD BEEN HIDDEN AROUND THE BEND AHEAD...

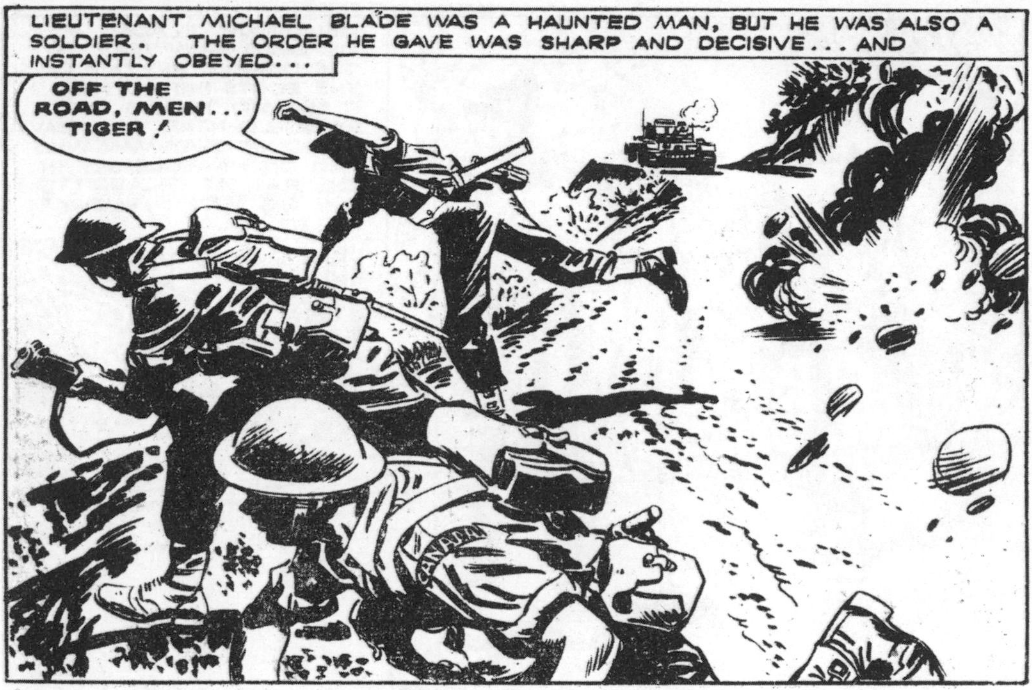
LIEUTENANT MICHAEL BLADE WAS A HAUNTED MAN, BUT HE WAS ALSO A SOLDIER. THE ORDER HE GAVE WAS SHARP AND DECISIVE... AND INSTANTLY OBEYED...
OFF THE ROAD, MEN... TIGER!

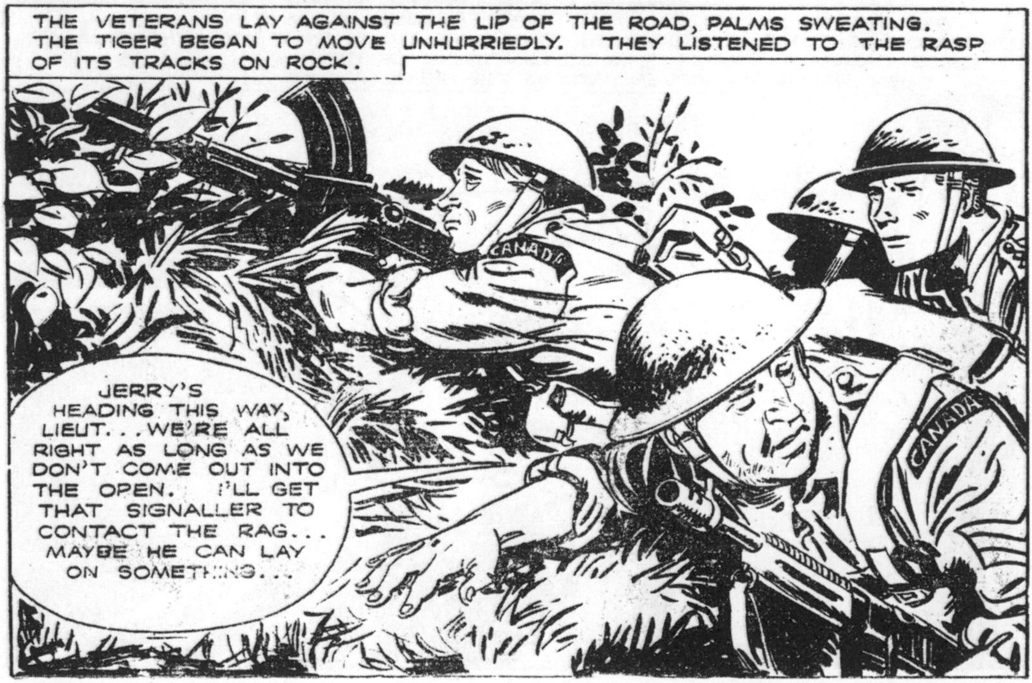
THE VETERANS LAY AGAINST THE LIP OF THE ROAD, PALMS SWEATING. THE TIGER BEGAN TO MOVE UNHURRIEDLY. THEY LISTENED TO THE RASP OF ITS TRACKS ON ROCK.
JERRY'S HEADING THIS WAY, LIEUT... WE'RE ALL RIGHT AS LONG AS WE DON'T COME OUT INTO THE OPEN. I'LL GET THAT SIGNALLER TO CONTACT THE RAG... MAYBE HE CAN LAY ON SOMETHING...

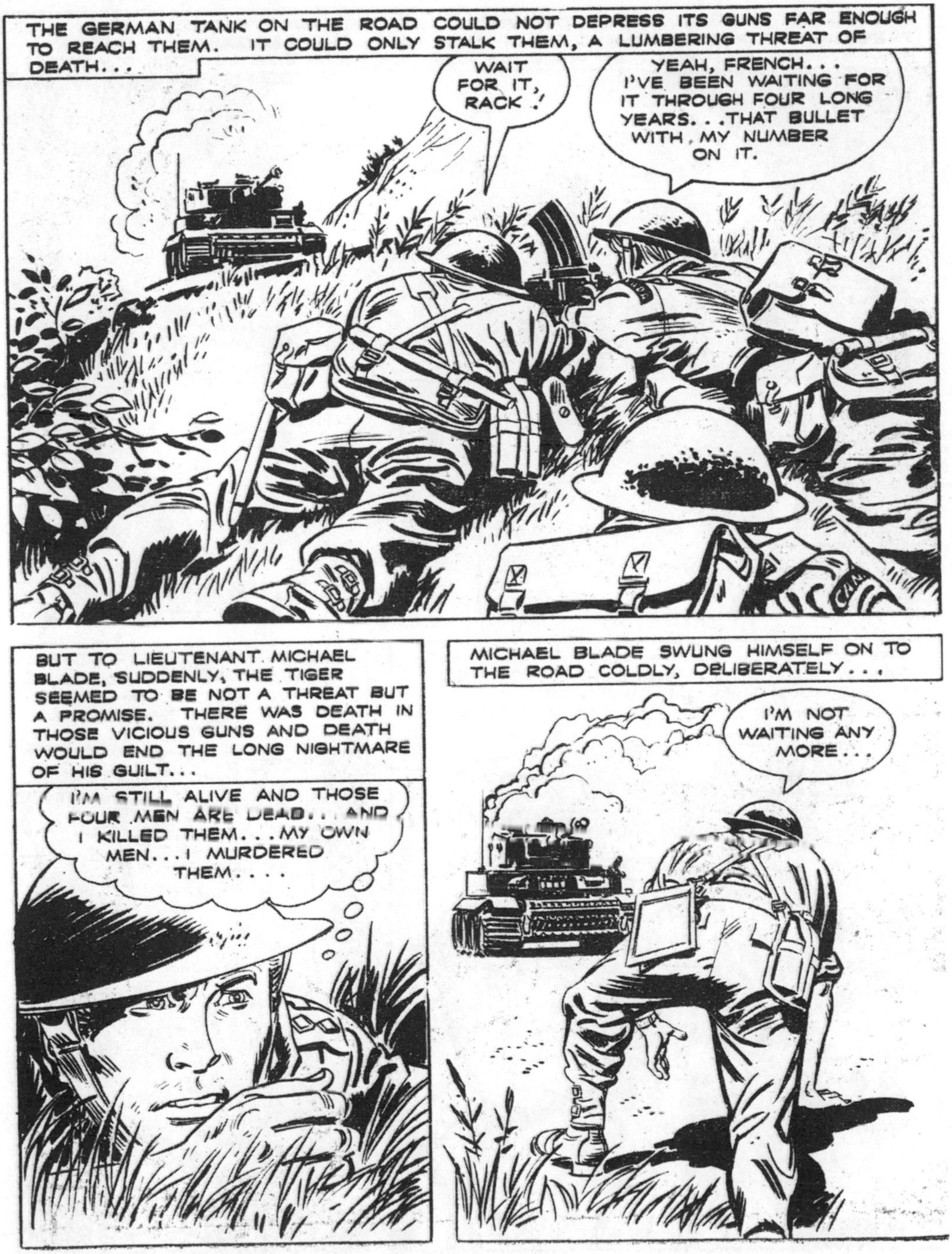
THE GERMAN TANK ON THE ROAD COULD NOT DEPRESS ITS GUNS FAR ENOUGH TO REACH THEM. IT COULD ONLY STALK THEM, A LUMBERING THREAT OF DEATH...
WAIT FOR IT, RACK.
YEAH, FRENCH... I'VE BEEN WAITING FOR IT THROUGH FOUR LONG YEARS...THAT BULLET WITH MY NUMBER ON IT.
BUT TO LIEUTENANT MICHAEL BLADE, SUDDENLY, THE TIGER SEEMED TO BE NOT A THREAT BUT A PROMISE. THERE WAS DEATH IN THOSE VICIOUS GUNS AND DEATH WOULD END THE LONG NIGHTMARE OF HIS GUILT...
I'M STILL ALIVE AND THOSE FOUR MEN ARE DEAD... AND I KILLED THEM...MY OWN MEN...I MURDERED THEM....
MICHAEL BLADE SWUNG HIMSELF ON TO THE ROAD COLDLY, DELIBERATELY...
I'M NOT WAITING ANY MORE...

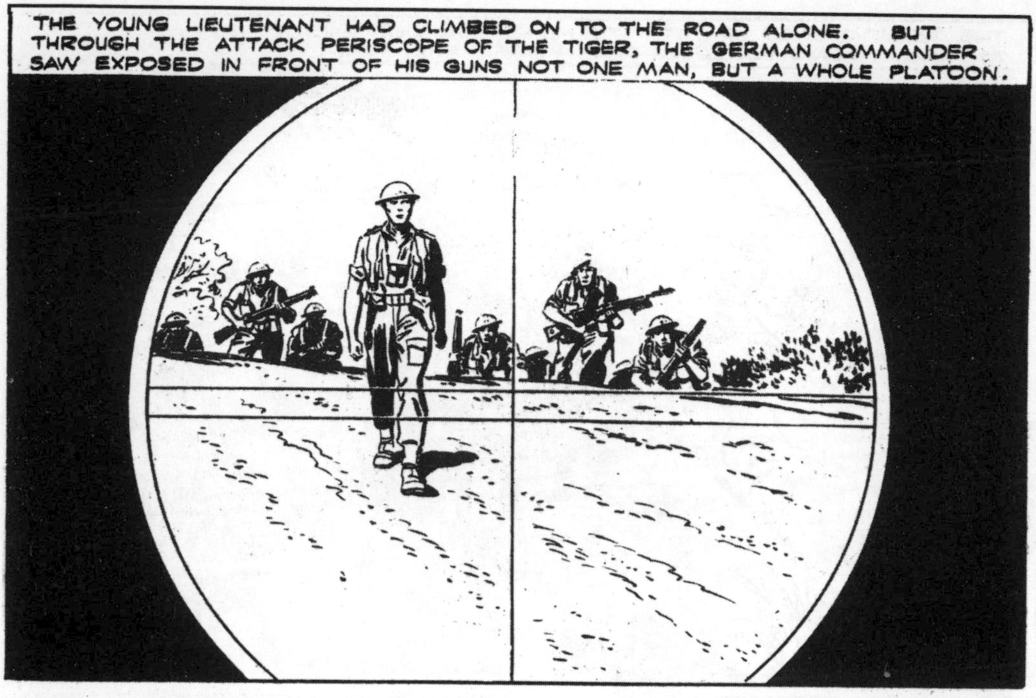
THE YOUNG LIEUTENANT HAD CLIMBED ON TO THE ROAD ALONE. BUT THROUGH THE ATTACK PERISCOPE OF THE TIGER, THE GERMAN COMMANDER SAW EXPOSED IN FRONT OF HIS GUNS NOT ONE MAN, BUT A WHOLE PLATOON.

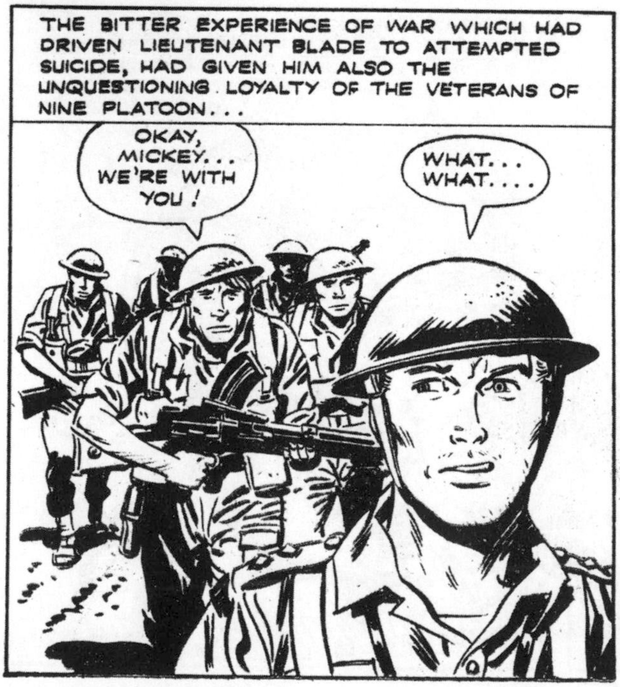
THE BITTER EXPERIENCE OF WAR WHICH HAD DRIVEN LIEUTENANT BLADE TO ATTEMPTED SUICIDE, HAD GIVEN HIM ALSO THE UNQUESTIONING LOYALTY OF THE VETERANS OF NINE PLATOON...
OKAY, MICKEY... WE'RE WITH YOU!
WHAT... WHAT....

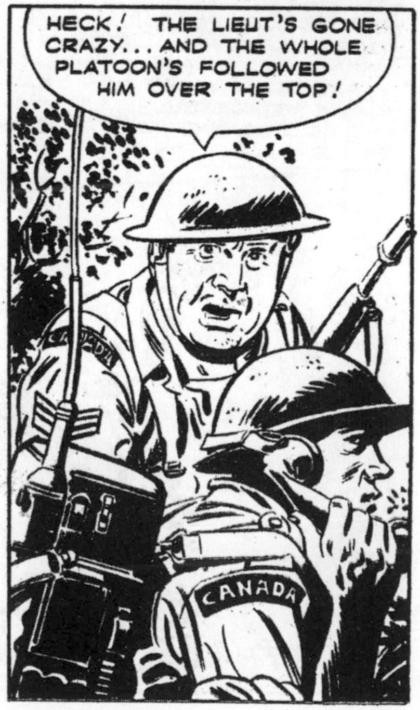
HECK! THE LIEUT'S GONE CRAZY... AND THE WHOLE PLATOON'S FOLLOWED HIM OVER THE TOP!
CANADA

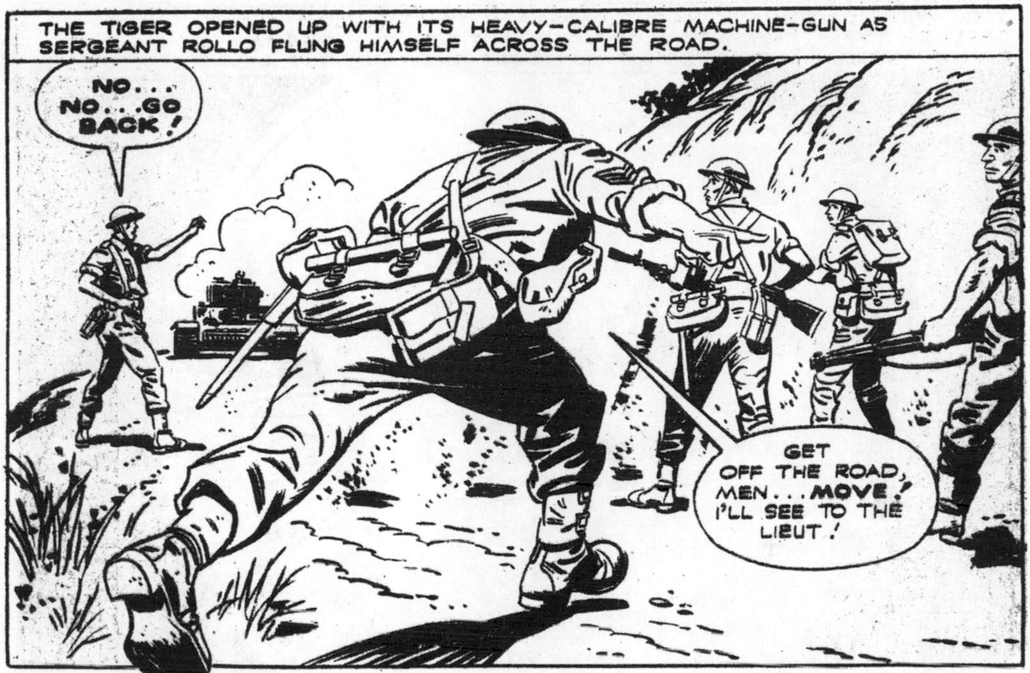
THE TIGER OPENED UP WITH ITS HEAVY-CALIBRE MACHINE-GUN AS SERGEANT ROLLO FLUNG HIMSELF ACROSS THE ROAD.
NO... NO...GO BACK!
GET OFF THE ROAD, MEN... MOVE! I'LL SEE TO THE LIEUT!

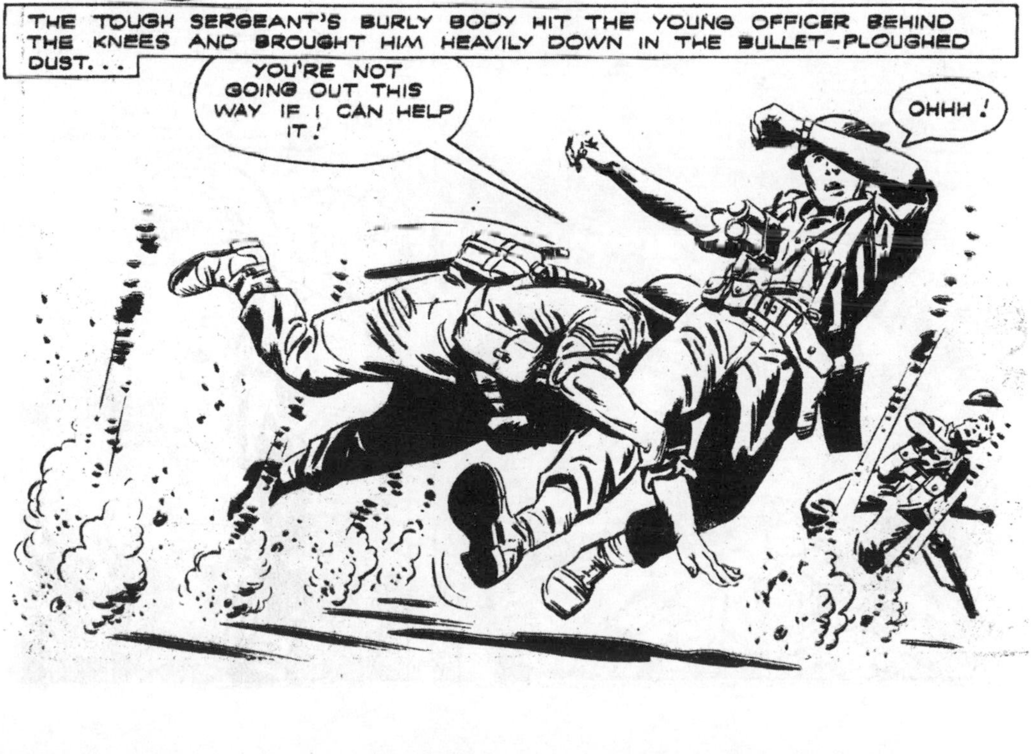
THE TOUGH SERGEANT'S BURLY BODY HIT THE YOUNG OFFICER BEHIND THE KNEES AND BROUGHT HIM HEAVILY DOWN IN THE BULLET-PLOUGHED DUST...
YOU'RE NOT GOING OUT THIS WAY IF I CAN HELP IT!
OHHH!

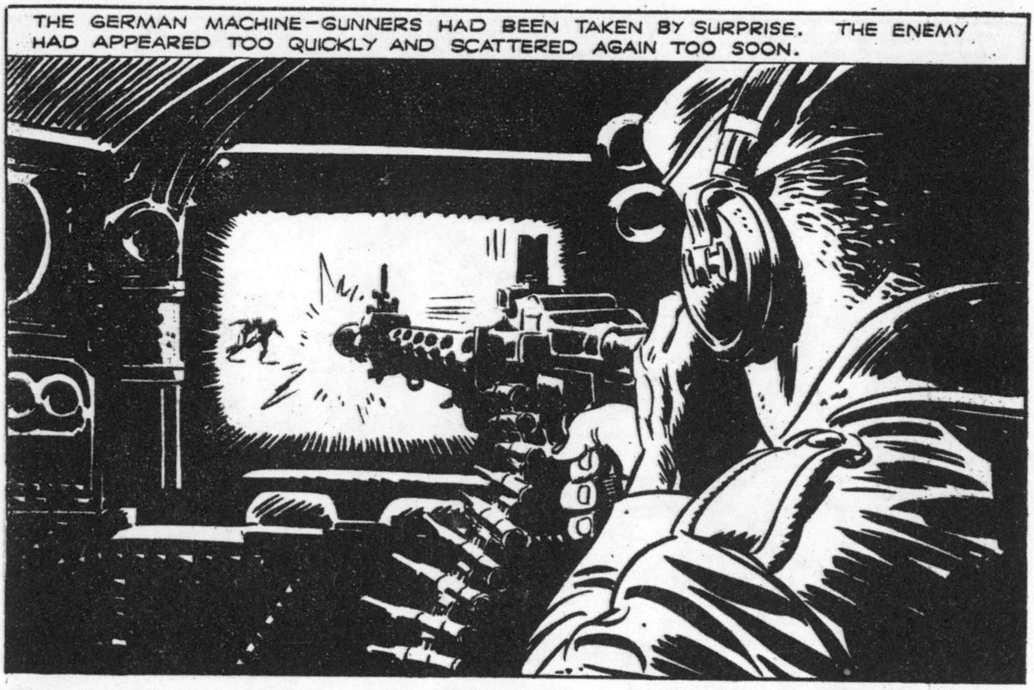
THE GERMAN MACHINE-GUNNERS HAD BEEN TAKEN BY SURPRISE. THE ENEMY HAD APPEARED TOO QUICKLY AND SCATTERED AGAIN TOO SOON.

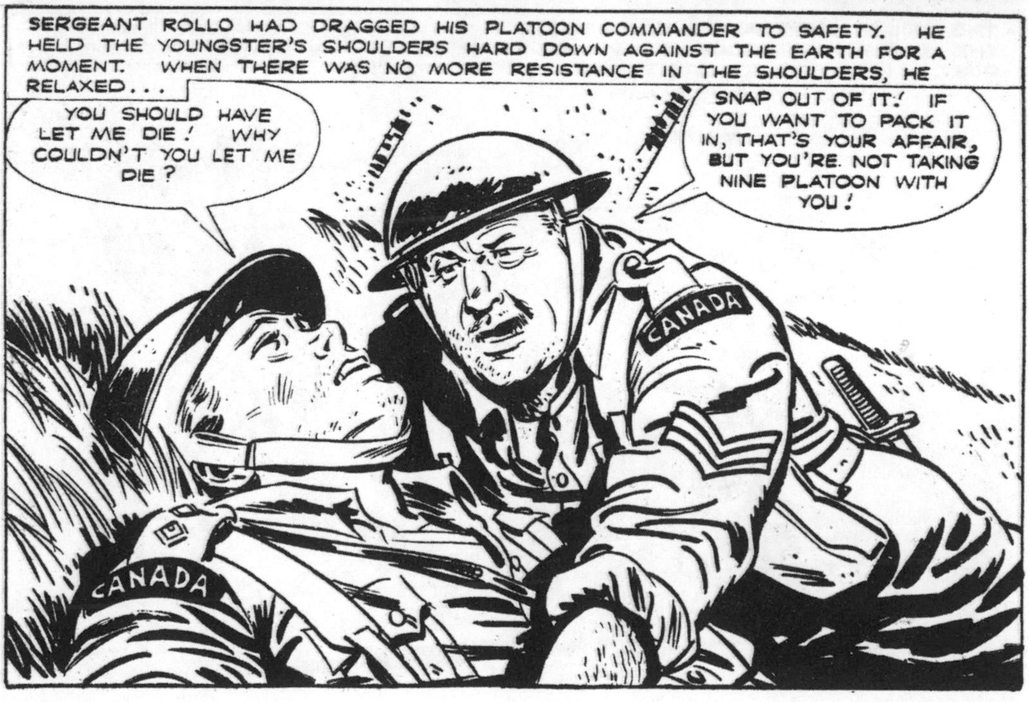
SERGEANT ROLLO HAD DRAGGED HIS PLATOON COMMANDER TO SAFETY. HE HELD THE YOUNGSTER'S SHOULDERS HARD DOWN AGAINST THE EARTH FOR A MOMENT. WHEN THERE WAS NO MORE RESISTANCE IN THE SHOULDERS, HE RELAXED...
YOU SHOULD HAVE LET ME DIE! WHY COULDN'T YOU LET ME DIE?
SNAP OUT OF IT! IF YOU WANT TO PACK IT IN, THAT'S YOUR AFFAIR, BUT YOU'RE. NOT TAKING NINE PLATOON WITH YOU!
CANADA
CANADA

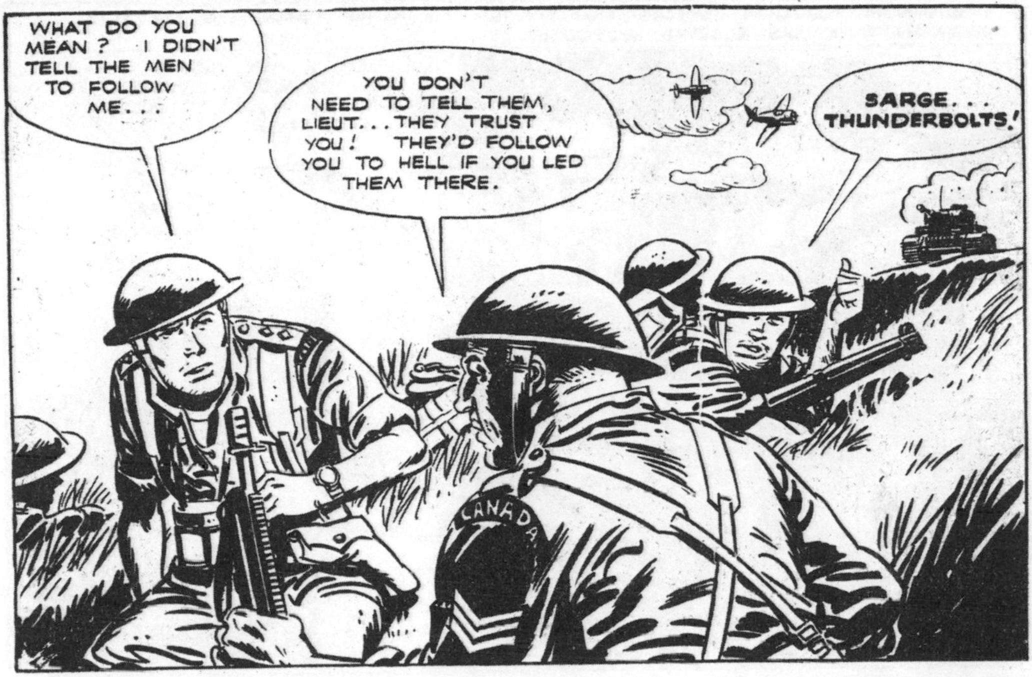
WHAT DO YOU MEAN ? I DIDN'T TELL THE MEN TO FOLLOW ME...
YOU DON'T NEED TO TELL THEM, LIEUT...THEY TRUST YOU! THEY'D FOLLOW YOU TO HELL IF YOU LED THEM THERE.
SARGE... THUNDERBOLTS!
CANADA

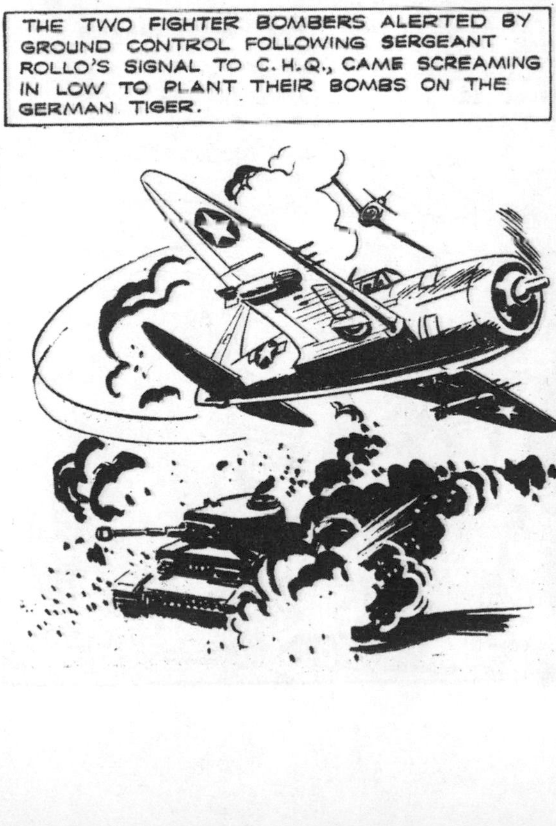
THE TWO FIGHTER BOMBERS ALERTED BY GROUND CONTROL FOLLOWING SERGEANT ROLLO'S SIGNAL TO C.H.Q., CAME SCREAMING IN LOW TO PLANT THEIR BOMBS ON THE GERMAN TIGER.

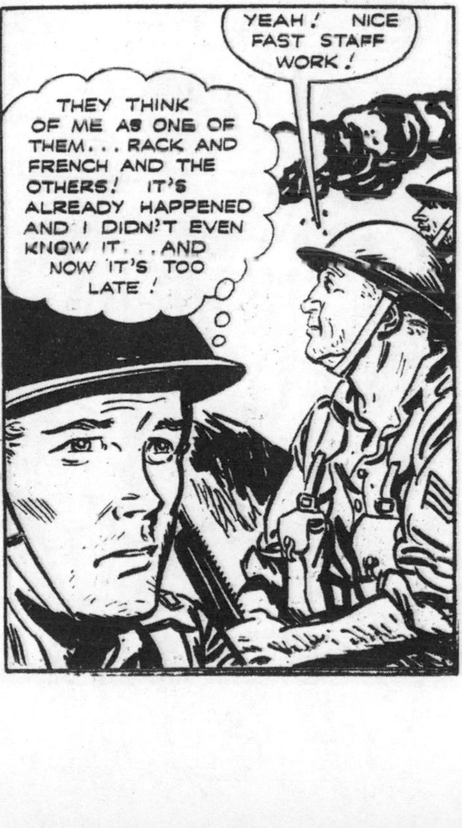
YEAH! NICE FAST STAFF WORK!
THEY THINK OF ME AS ONE OF THEM...RACK AND FRENCH AND THE OTHERS! IT'S ALREADY HAPPENED AND I DIDN'T EVEN KNOW IT...AND NOW IT'S TOO LATE!

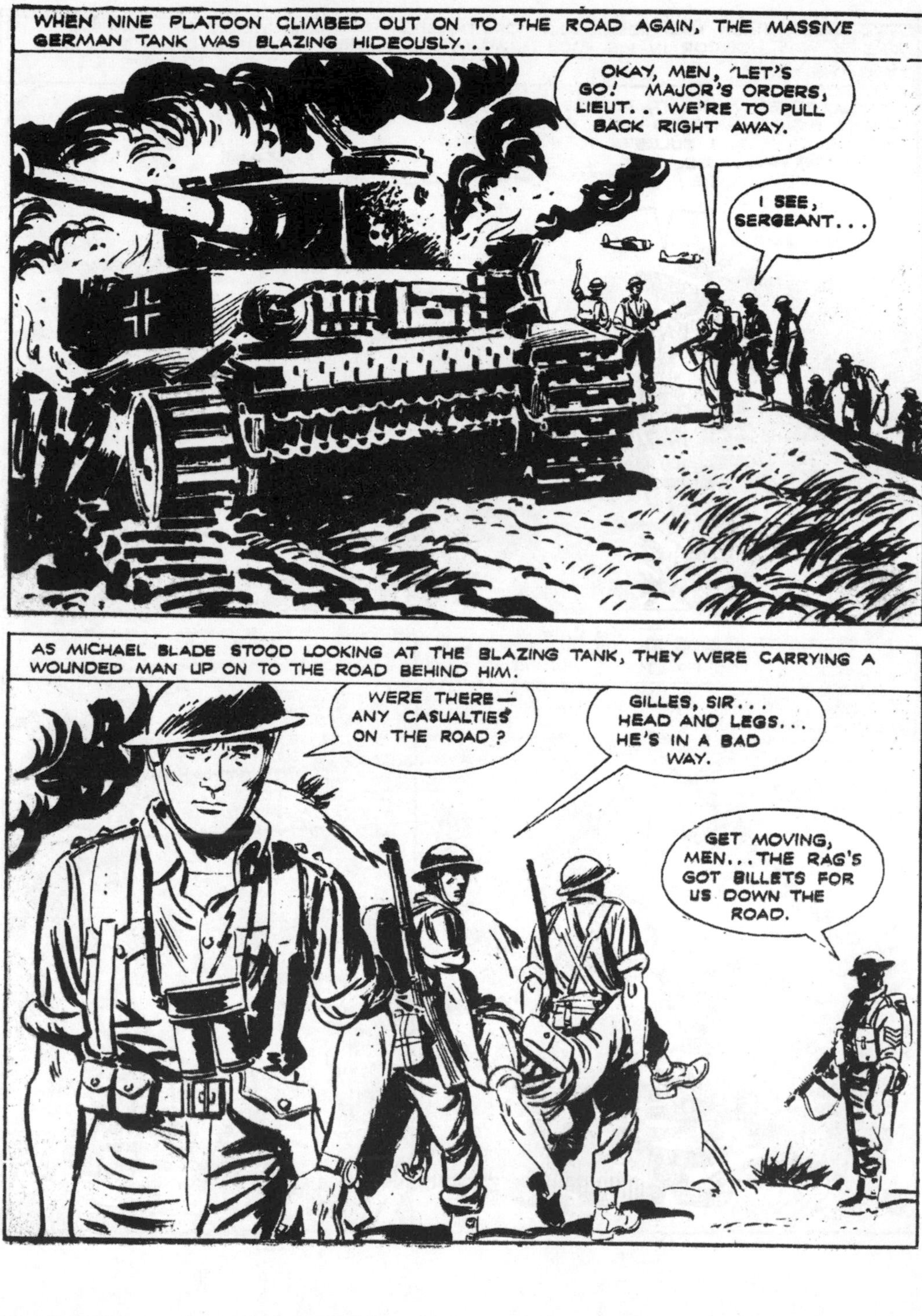
WHEN NINE PLATOON CLIMBED OUT ON TO THE ROAD AGAIN, THE MASSIVE GERMAN TANK WAS BLAZING HIDEOUSLY...
OKAY, MEN, LET'S GO! MAJOR'S ORDERS, LIEUT... WE'RE TO PULL BACK RIGHT AWAY.
I SEE, SERGEANT...
AS MICHAEL BLADE STOOD LOOKING AT THE BLAZING TANK, THEY WERE CARRYING A WOUNDED MAN UP ON TO THE ROAD BEHIND HIM.
WERE THERE— ANY CASUALTIES ON THE ROAD?
GILLES, SIR... HEAD AND LEGS... HE'S IN A BAD WAY.
GET MOVING, MEN... THE RAG'S GOT BILLETS FOR US DOWN THE ROAD.

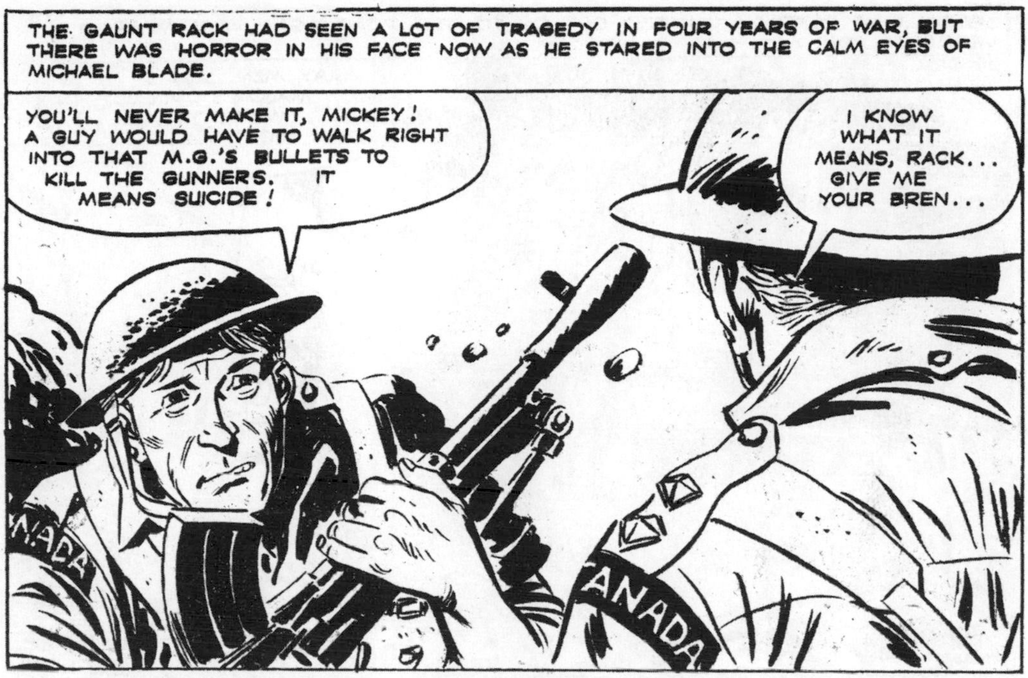
THE GAUNT RACK HAD SEEN A LOT OF TRAGEDY IN FOUR YEARS OF WAR, BUT THERE WAS HORROR IN HIS FACE NOW AS HE STARED INTO THE CALM EYES OF MICHAEL BLADE.
YOU'LL NEVER MAKE IT, MICKEY! A GUY WOULD HAVE TO WALK RIGHT INTO THAT M.G.'S BULLETS TO KILL THE GUNNERS. IT MEANS SUICIDE!
I KNOW WHAT IT MEANS, RACK... GIVE ME YOUR BREN...
CANADA
CANADA

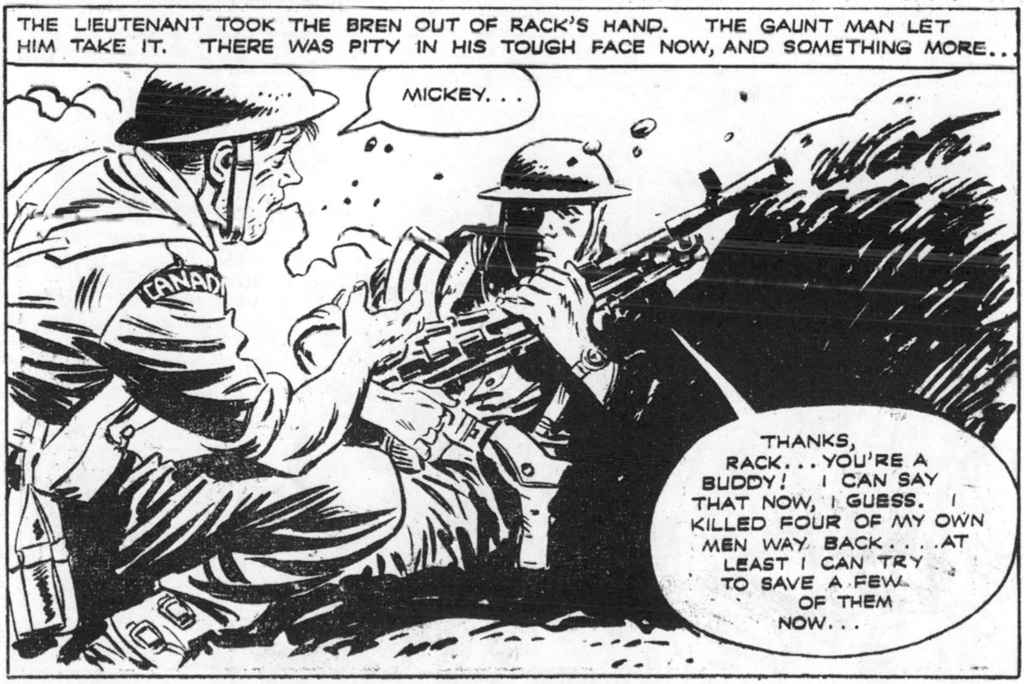
THE LIEUTENANT TOOK THE BREN OUT OF RACK'S HAND. THE GAUNT MAN LET HIM TAKE IT. THERE WAS PITY IN HIS TOUGH FACE NOW, AND SOMETHING MORE..
MICKEY...
THANKS, RACK... YOU'RE A BUDDY! I CAN SAY THAT NOW, I GUESS. I KILLED FOUR OF MY OWN MEN WAY BACK... AT LEAST I CAN TRY TO SAVE A FEW OF THEM NOW...

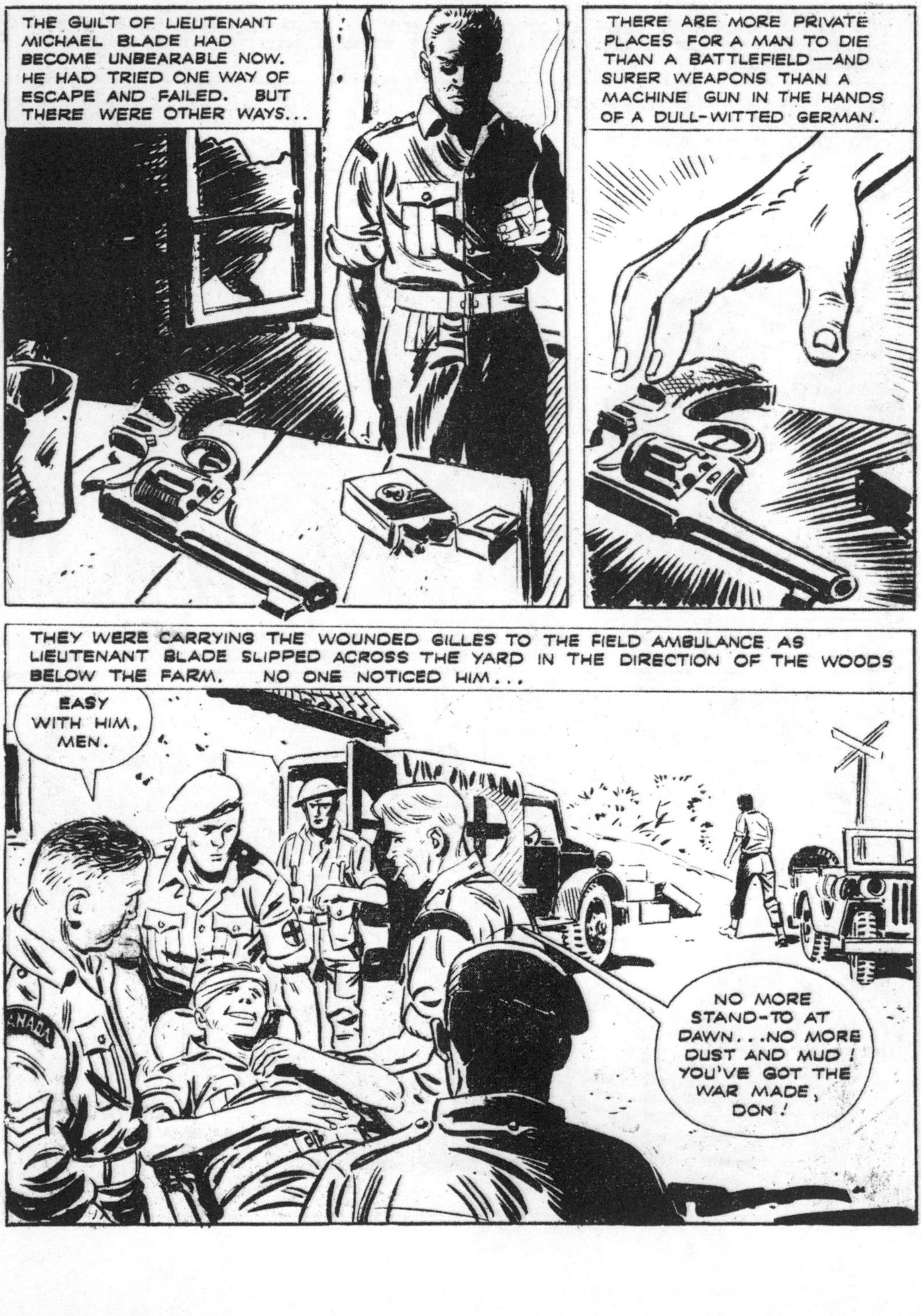
THE GUILT OF LIEUTENANT MICHAEL BLADE HAD BECOME UNBEARABLE NOW. HE HAD TRIED ONE WAY OF ESCAPE AND FAILED. BUT THERE WERE OTHER WAYS...
THERE ARE MORE PRIVATE PLACES FOR A MAN TO DIE THAN A BATTLEFIELD—AND SURER WEAPONS THAN A MACHINE GUN IN THE HANDS OF A DULL-WITTED GERMAN.
THEY WERE CARRYING THE WOUNDED GILLES TO THE FIELD AMBULANCE AS LIEUTENANT BLADE SLIPPED ACROSS THE YARD IN THE DIRECTION OF THE WOODS BELOW THE FARM. NO ONE NOTICED HIM...
EASY WITH HIM, MEN.
NO MORE STAND-TO AT DAWN...NO MORE DUST AND MUD! YOU'VE GOT THE WAR MADE, DON!

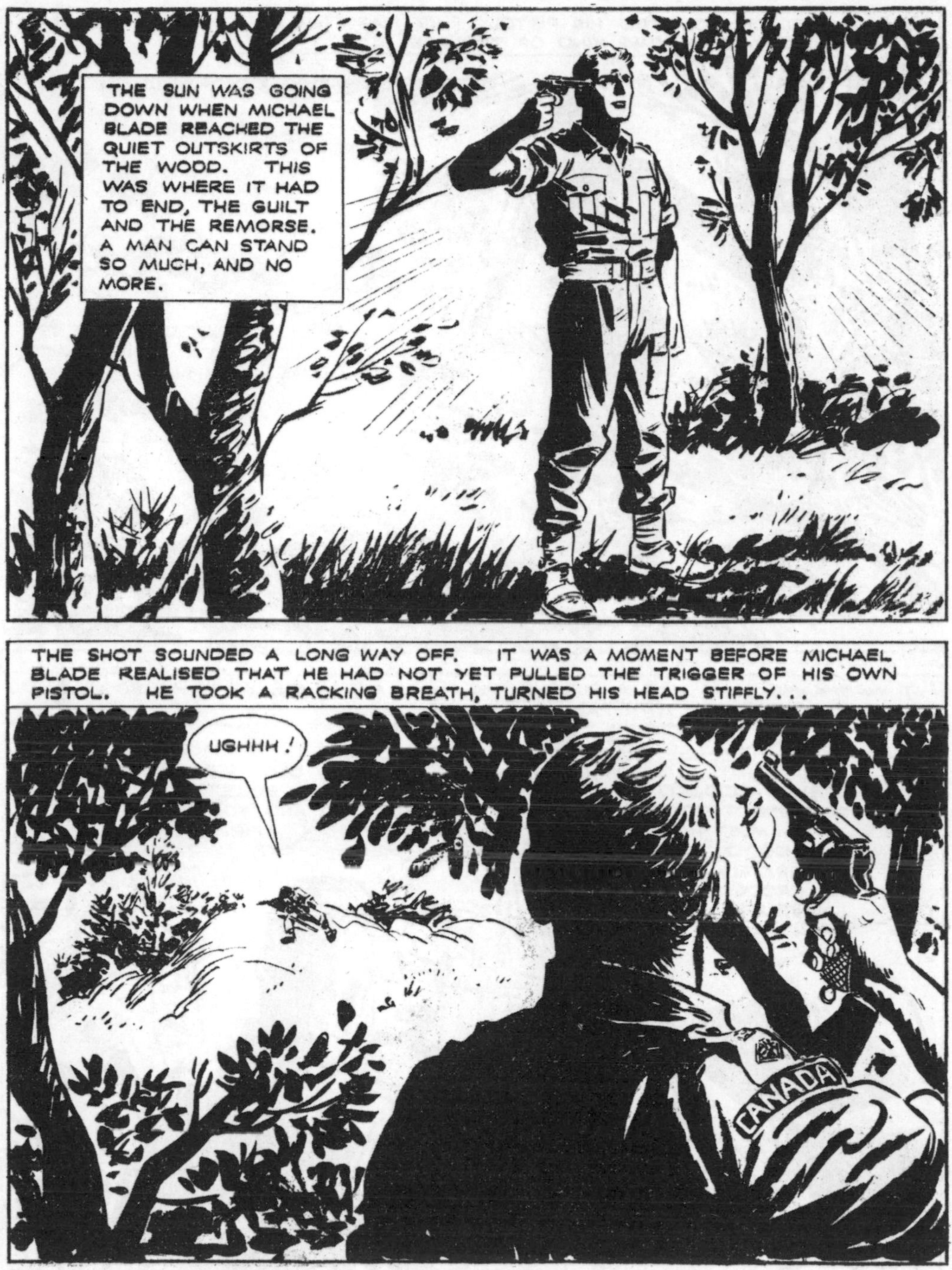
THE SUN WAS GOING DOWN WHEN MICHAEL BLADE REACHED THE QUIET OUTSKIRTS OF THE WOOD. THIS WAS WHERE IT HAD TO END, THE GUILT AND THE REMORSE. A MAN CAN STAND SO MUCH, AND NO MORE.
THE SHOT SOUNDED A LONG WAY OFF. IT WAS A MOMENT BEFORE MICHAEL BLADE REALISED THAT HE HAD NOT YET PULLED THE TRIGGER OF HIS OWN PISTOL. HE TOOK A RACKING BREATH, TURNED HIS HEAD STIFFLY...
UGHHH!
CANADA

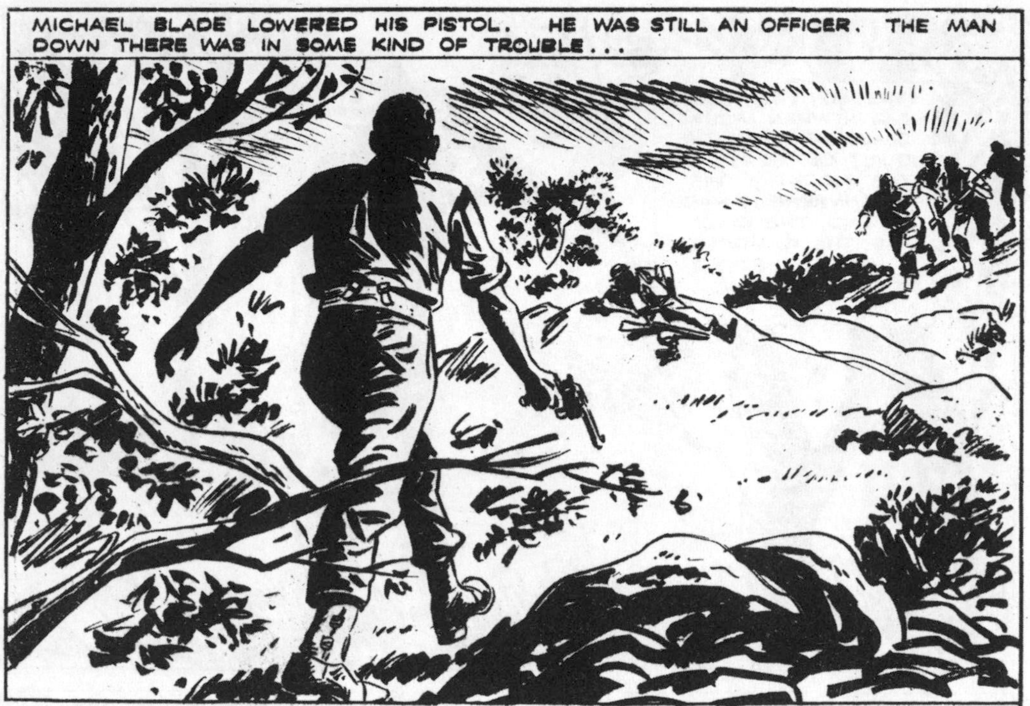
MICHAEL BLADE LOWERED HIS PISTOL. HE WAS STILL AN OFFICER. THE MAN DOWN THERE WAS IN SOME KIND OF TROUBLE...

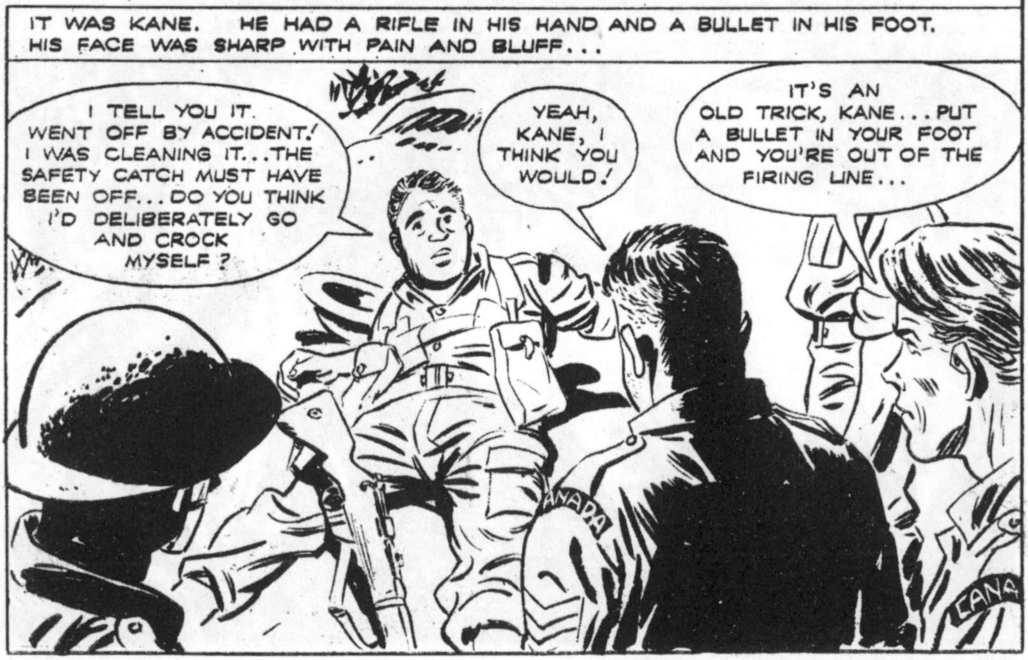
IT WAS KANE. HE HAD A RIFLE IN HIS HAND AND A BULLET IN HIS FOOT. HIS FACE WAS SHARP WITH PAIN AND BLUFF...
I TELL YOU IT WENT OFF BY ACCIDENT! I WAS CLEANING IT...THE SAFETY CATCH MUST HAVE BEEN OFF...DO YOU THINK I'D DELIBERATELY GO AND CROCK MYSELF?
YEAH, KANE, I THINK YOU WOULD!
IT'S AN OLD TRICK, KANE...PUT A BULLET IN YOUR FOOT AND YOU'RE OUT OF THE FIRING LINE...

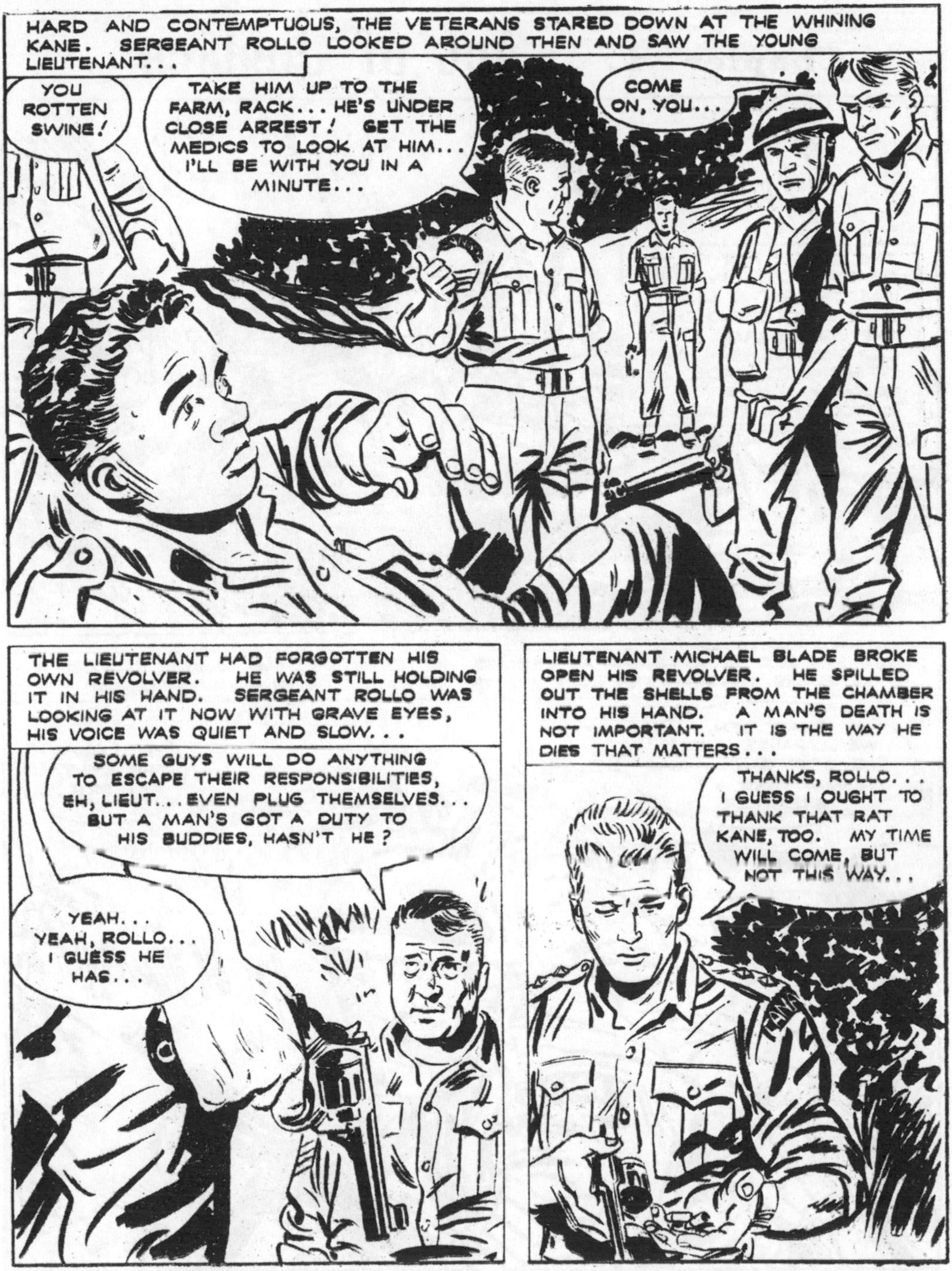
HARD AND CONTEMPTUOUS, THE VETERANS STARED DOWN AT THE WHINING KANE. SERGEANT ROLLO LOOKED AROUND THEN AND SAW THE YOUNG LIEUTENANT...
YOU ROTTEN SWINE!
TAKE HIM UP TO THE FARM, RACK... HE'S UNDER CLOSE ARREST! GET THE MEDICS TO LOOK AT HIM... I'LL BE WITH YOU IN A MINUTE...
COME ON, YOU...
THE LIEUTENANT HAD FORGOTTEN HIS OWN REVOLVER. HE WAS STILL HOLDING IT IN HIS HAND. SERGEANT ROLLO WAS LOOKING AT IT NOW WITH GRAVE EYES, HIS VOICE WAS QUIET AND SLOW...
SOME GUYS WILL DO ANYTHING TO ESCAPE THEIR RESPONSIBILITIES, EH, LIEUT... EVEN PLUG THEMSELVES... BUT A MAN'S GOT A DUTY TO HIS BUDDIES, HASN'T HE?
YEAH... YEAH, ROLLO... I GUESS HE HAS...
LIEUTENANT MICHAEL BLADE BROKE OPEN HIS REVOLVER. HE SPILLED OUT THE SHELLS FROM THE CHAMBER INTO HIS HAND. A MAN'S DEATH IS NOT IMPORTANT. IT IS THE WAY HE DIES THAT MATTERS...
THANKS, ROLLO... I GUESS I OUGHT TO THANK THAT RAT KANE, TOO. MY TIME WILL COME, BUT NOT THIS WAY...

Chapter 4. Act of Justice

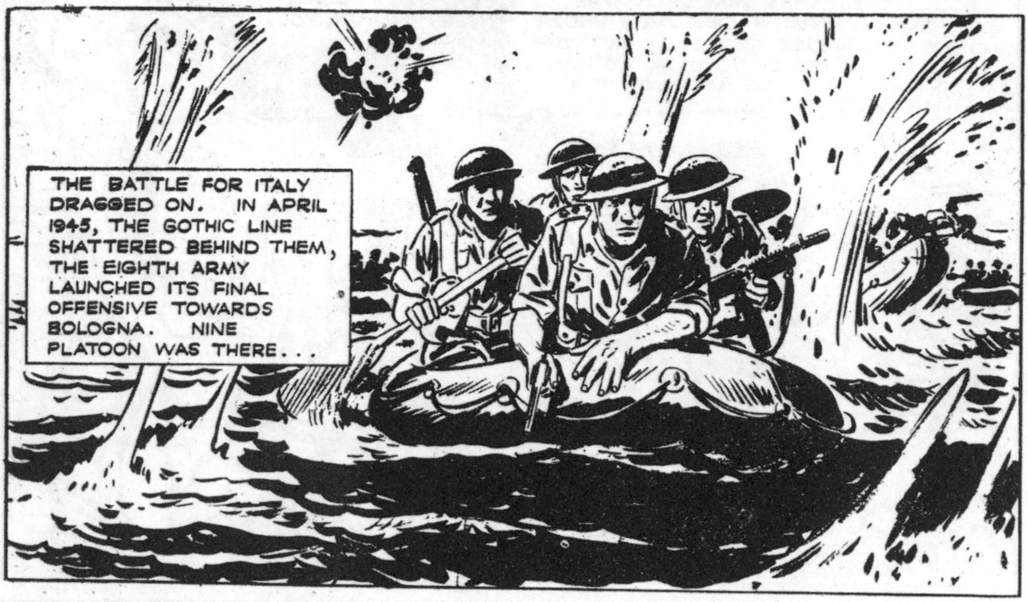
THE BATTLE FOR ITALY DRAGGED ON. IN APRIL 1945, THE GOTHIC LINE SHATTERED BEHIND THEM, THE EIGHTH ARMY LAUNCHED ITS FINAL OFFENSIVE TOWARDS BOLOGNA. NINE PLATOON WAS THERE...

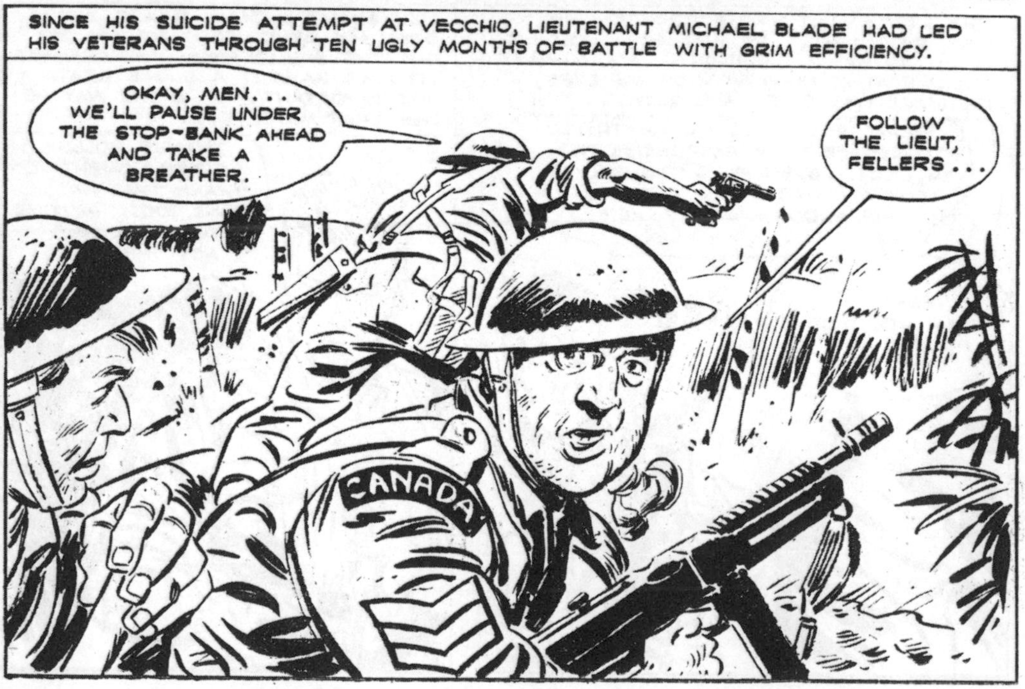
SINCE HIS SUICIDE ATTEMPT AT VECCHIO, LIEUTENANT MICHAEL BLADE HAD LED HIS VETERANS THROUGH TEN UGLY MONTHS OF BATTLE WITH GRIM EFFICIENCY.
OKAY, MEN... WE'LL PAUSE UNDER THE STOP-BANK AHEAD AND TAKE A BREATHER.
FOLLOW THE LIEUT, FELLERS...
CANADA

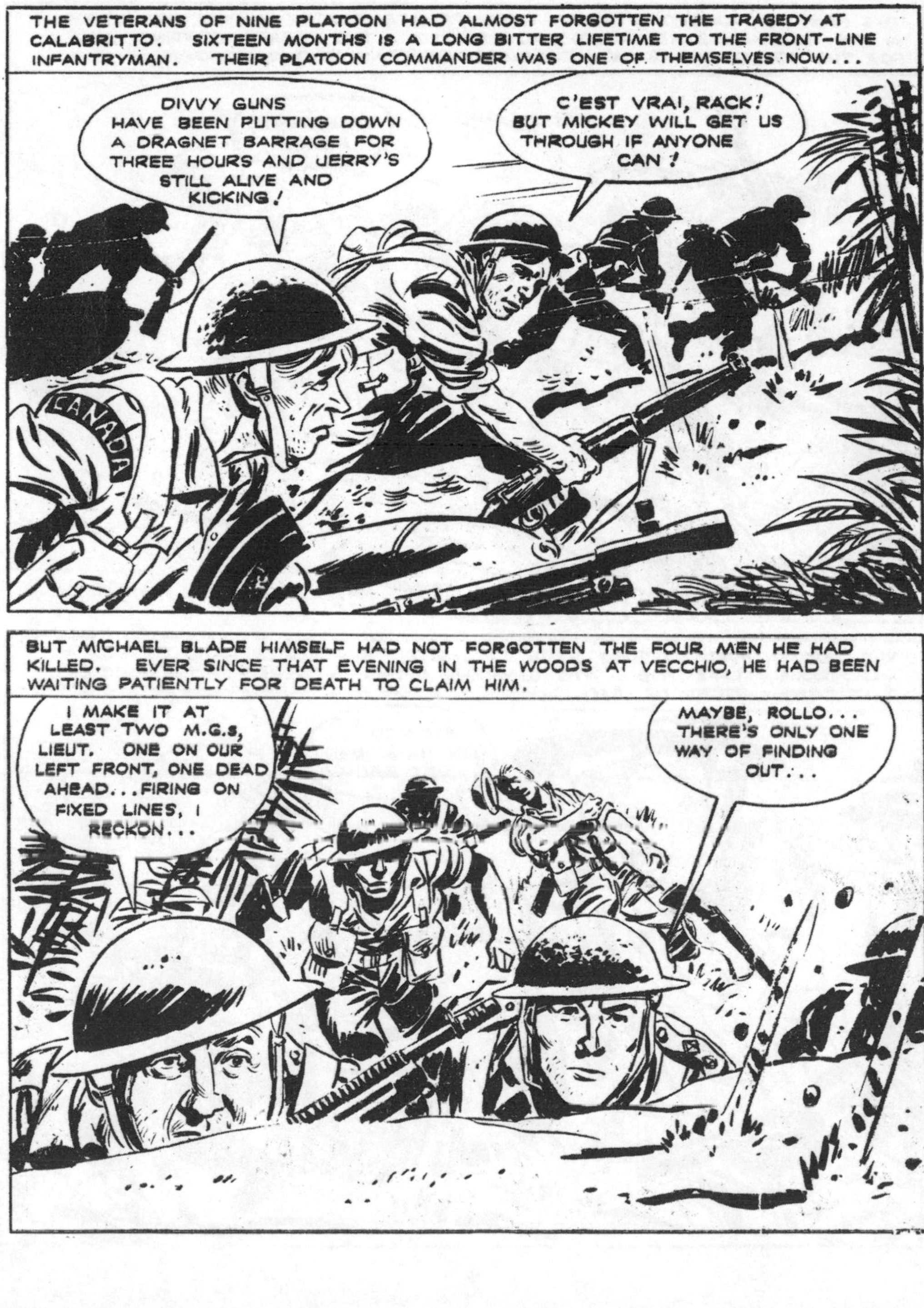
THE VETERANS OF NINE PLATOON HAD ALMOST FORGOTTEN THE TRAGEDY AT CALABRITTO. SIXTEEN MONTHS IS A LONG BITTER LIFETIME TO THE FRONT-LINE INFANTRYMAN. THEIR PLATOON COMMANDER WAS ONE OF THEMSELVES NOW...
DIVVY GUNS HAVE BEEN PUTTING DOWN A DRAGNET BARRAGE FOR THREE HOURS AND JERRY'S STILL ALIVE AND KICKING!
C'EST VRAI, RACK! BUT MICKEY WILL GET US THROUGH IF ANYONE CAN!
CANADA
BUT MICHAEL BLADE HIMSELF HAD NOT FORGOTTEN THE FOUR MEN HE HAD KILLED. EVER SINCE THAT EVENING IN THE WOODS AT VECCHIO, HE HAD BEEN WAITING PATIENTLY FOR DEATH TO CLAIM HIM.
I MAKE IT AT LEAST TWO M.G.s, LIEUT. ONE ON OUR LEFT FRONT, ONE DEAD AHEAD...FIRING ON FIXED LINES, I RECKON...
MAYBE, ROLLO... THERE'S ONLY ONE WAY OF FINDING OUT...

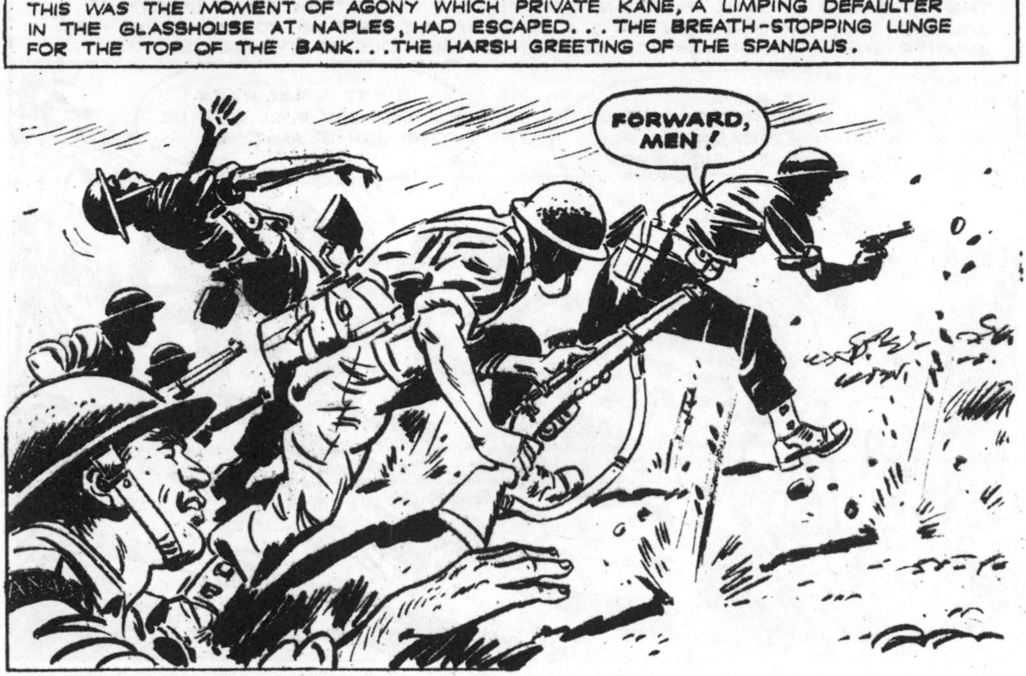
THIS WAS THE MOMENT OF AGONY WHICH PRIVATE KANE, A LIMPING DEFAULTER IN THE GLASSHOUSE AT NAPLES, HAD ESCAPED. . . THE BREATH-STOPPING LUNGE FOR THE TOP OF THE BANK. . .THE HARSH GREETING OF THE SPANDAUS.
FORWARD, MEN!

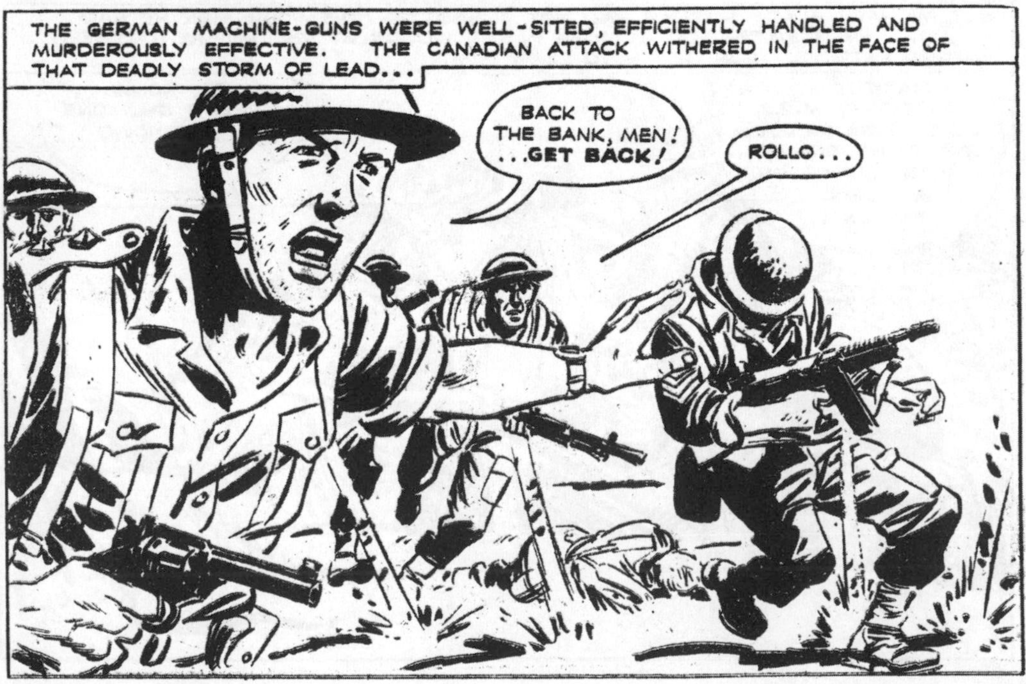
THE GERMAN MACHINE-GUNS WERE WELL-SITED, EFFICIENTLY HANDLED AND MURDEROUSLY EFFECTIVE. THE CANADIAN ATTACK WITHERED IN THE FACE OF THAT DEADLY STORM OF LEAD...
BACK TO THE BANK, MEN! ...GET BACK!
ROLLO...

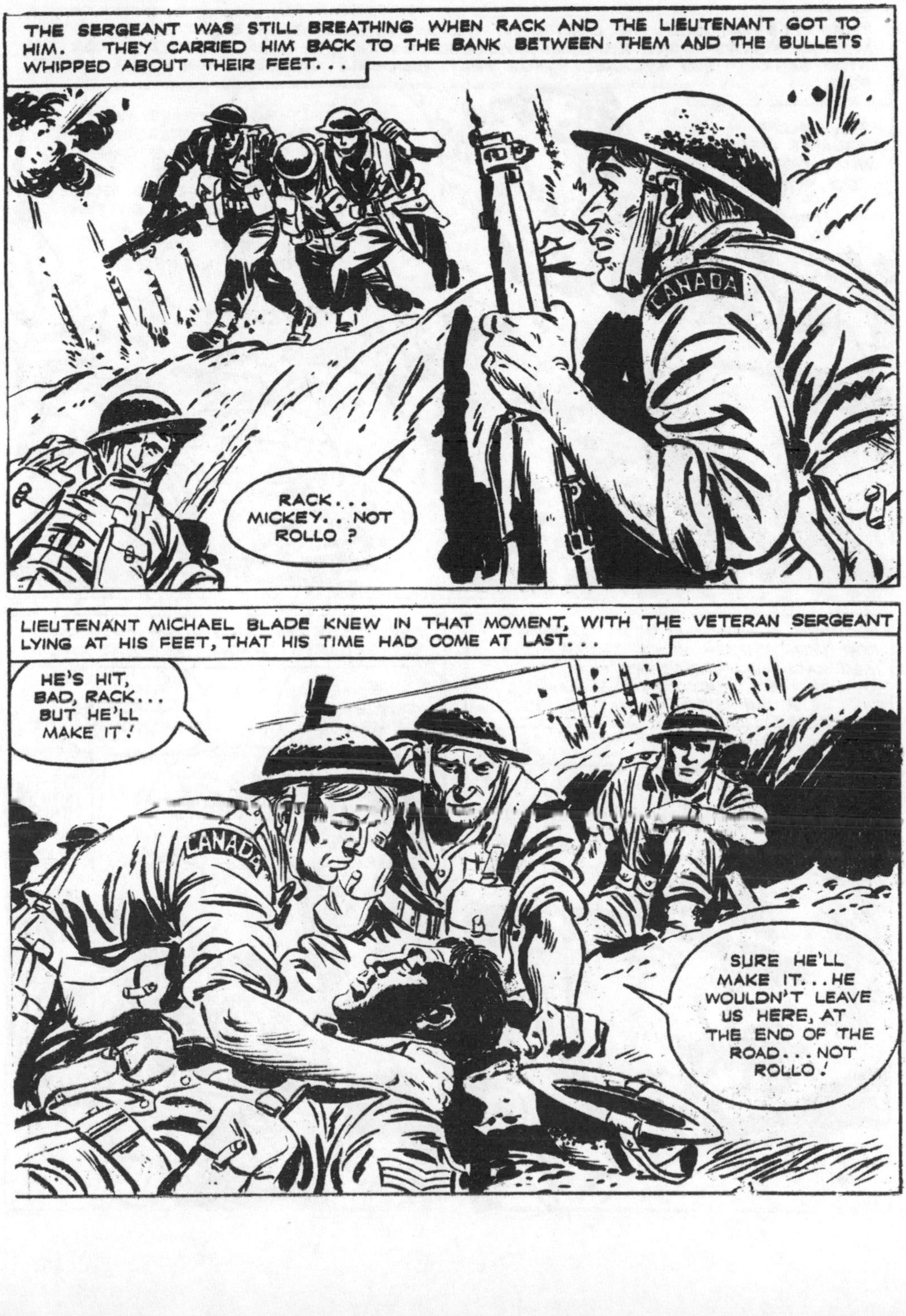
THE SERGEANT WAS STILL BREATHING WHEN RACK AND THE LIEUTENANT GOT TO HIM. THEY CARRIED HIM BACK TO THE BANK BETWEEN THEM AND THE BULLETS WHIPPED ABOUT THEIR FEET...
CANADA
RACK... MICKEY... NOT ROLLO ?
LIEUTENANT MICHAEL BLADE KNEW IN THAT MOMENT, WITH THE VETERAN SERGEANT LYING AT HIS FEET, THAT HIS TIME HAD COME AT LAST...
HE'S HIT, BAD, RACK... BUT HE'LL MAKE IT !
CANADA
SURE HE'LL MAKE IT... HE WOULDN'T LEAVE US HERE, AT THE END OF THE ROAD... NOT ROLLO !

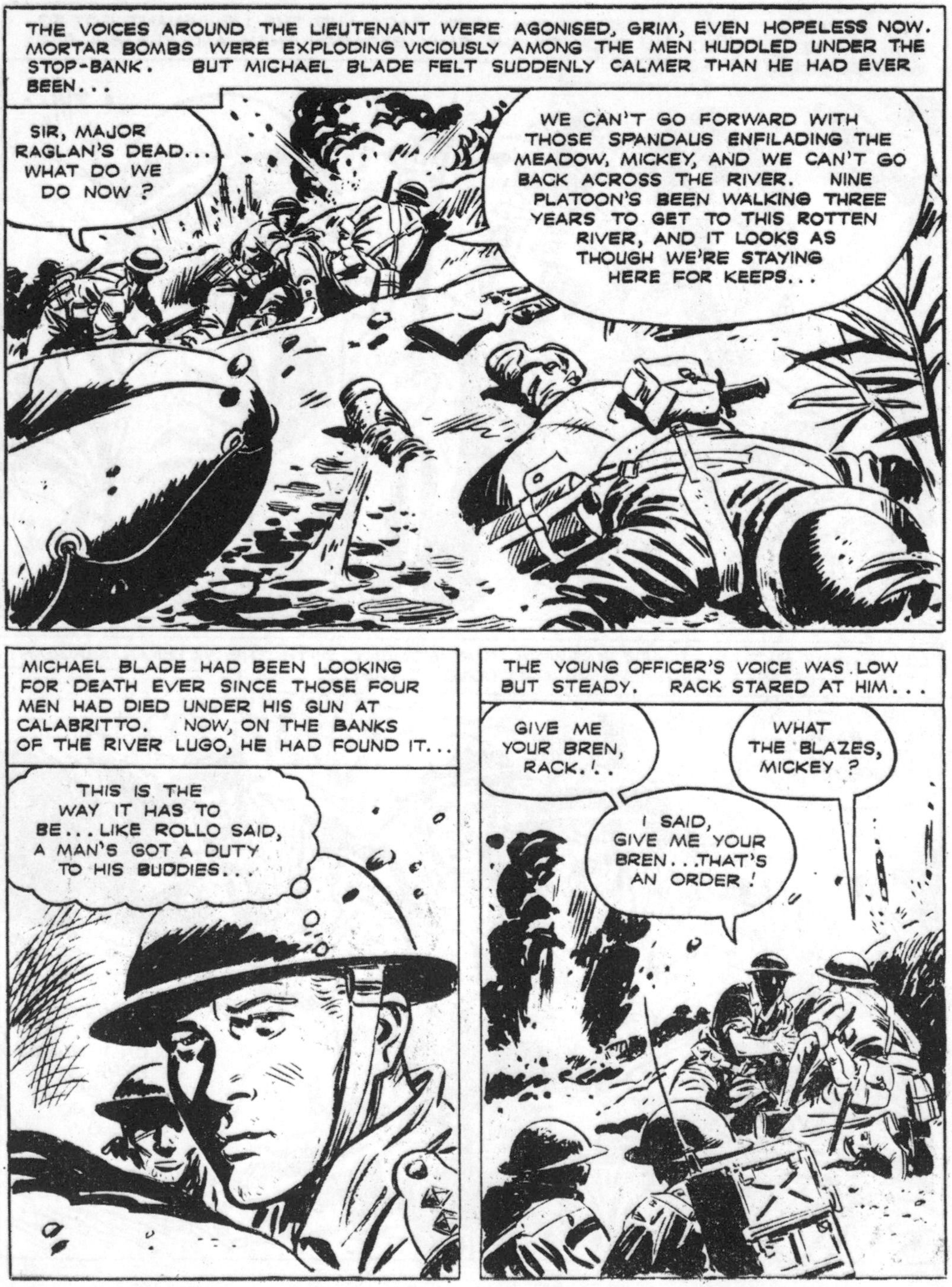
THE VOICES AROUND THE LIEUTENANT WERE AGONISED, GRIM, EVEN HOPELESS NOW. MORTAR BOMBS WERE EXPLODING VICIOUSLY AMONG THE MEN HUDDLED UNDER THE STOP-BANK. BUT MICHAEL BLADE FELT SUDDENLY CALMER THAN HE HAD EVER BEEN...
SIR, MAJOR RAGLAN'S DEAD... WHAT DO WE DO NOW ?
WE CAN'T GO FORWARD WITH THOSE SPANDAUS ENFILADING THE MEADOW, MICKEY, AND WE CAN'T GO BACK ACROSS THE RIVER. NINE PLATOON'S BEEN WALKING THREE YEARS TO GET TO THIS ROTTEN RIVER, AND IT LOOKS AS THOUGH WE'RE STAYING HERE FOR KEEPS...
MICHAEL BLADE HAD BEEN LOOKING FOR DEATH EVER SINCE THOSE FOUR MEN HAD DIED UNDER HIS GUN AT CALABRITTO. NOW, ON THE BANKS OF THE RIVER LUGO, HE HAD FOUND IT...
THIS IS THE WAY IT HAS TO BE... LIKE ROLLO SAID, A MAN'S GOT A DUTY TO HIS BUDDIES...
THE YOUNG OFFICER'S VOICE WAS LOW BUT STEADY. RACK STARED AT HIM...
GIVE ME YOUR BREN, RACK...
WHAT THE BLAZES, MICKEY ?
I SAID, GIVE ME YOUR BREN... THAT'S AN ORDER !

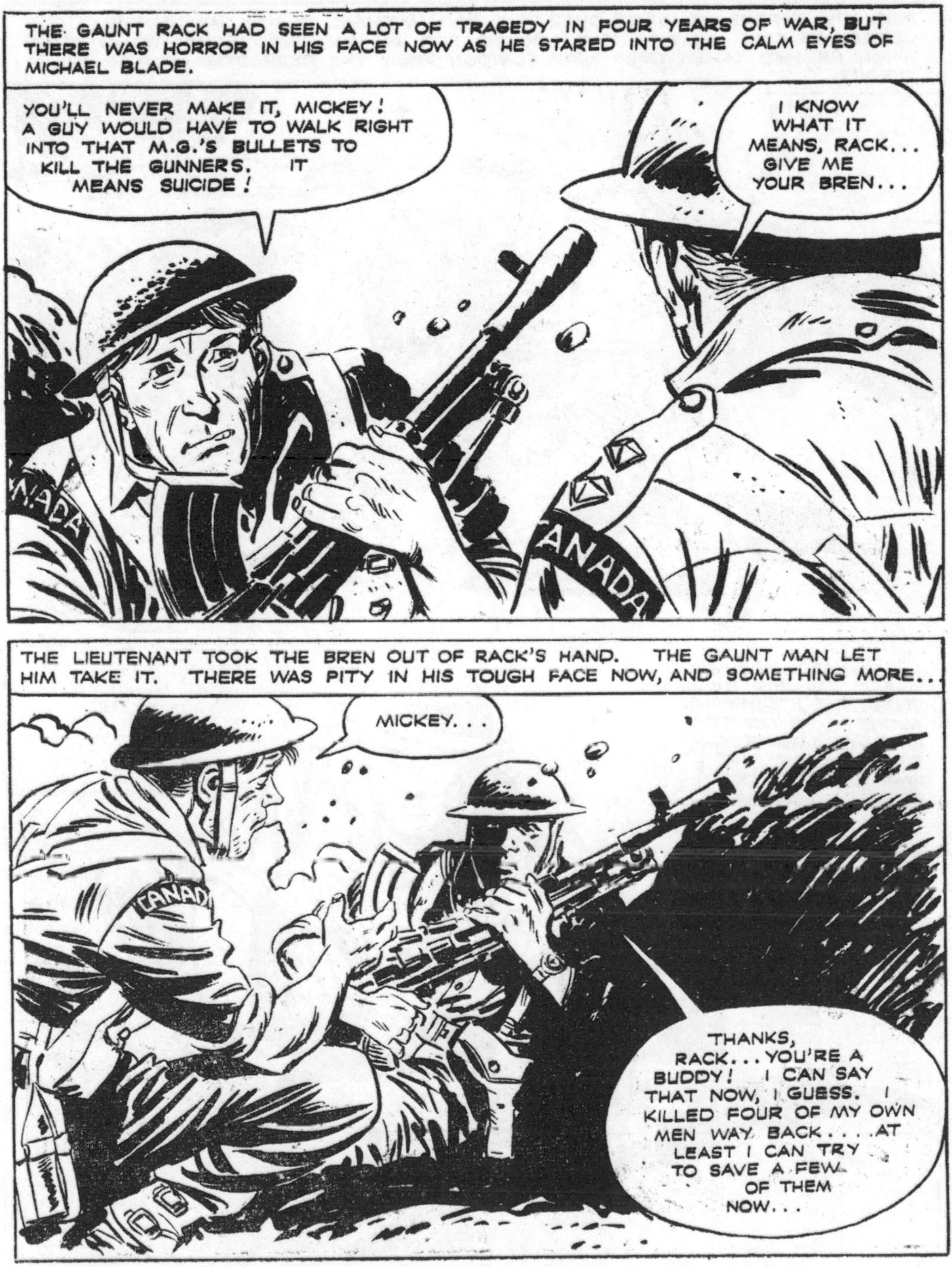
THE GAUNT RACK HAD SEEN A LOT OF TRAGEDY IN FOUR YEARS OF WAR, BUT THERE WAS HORROR IN HIS FACE NOW AS HE STARED INTO THE CALM EYES OF MICHAEL BLADE.
YOU'LL NEVER MAKE IT, MICKEY! A GUY WOULD HAVE TO WALK RIGHT INTO THAT M.G.'S BULLETS TO KILL THE GUNNERS. IT MEANS SUICIDE!
I KNOW WHAT IT MEANS, RACK... GIVE ME YOUR BREN...
CANADA
CANADA
THE LIEUTENANT TOOK THE BREN OUT OF RACK'S HAND. THE GAUNT MAN LET HIM TAKE IT. THERE WAS PITY IN HIS TOUGH FACE NOW, AND SOMETHING MORE...
MICKEY...
THANKS, RACK... YOU'RE A BUDDY! I CAN SAY THAT NOW, I GUESS. I KILLED FOUR OF MY OWN MEN WAY BACK... AT LEAST I CAN TRY TO SAVE A FEW OF THEM NOW...
CANADA

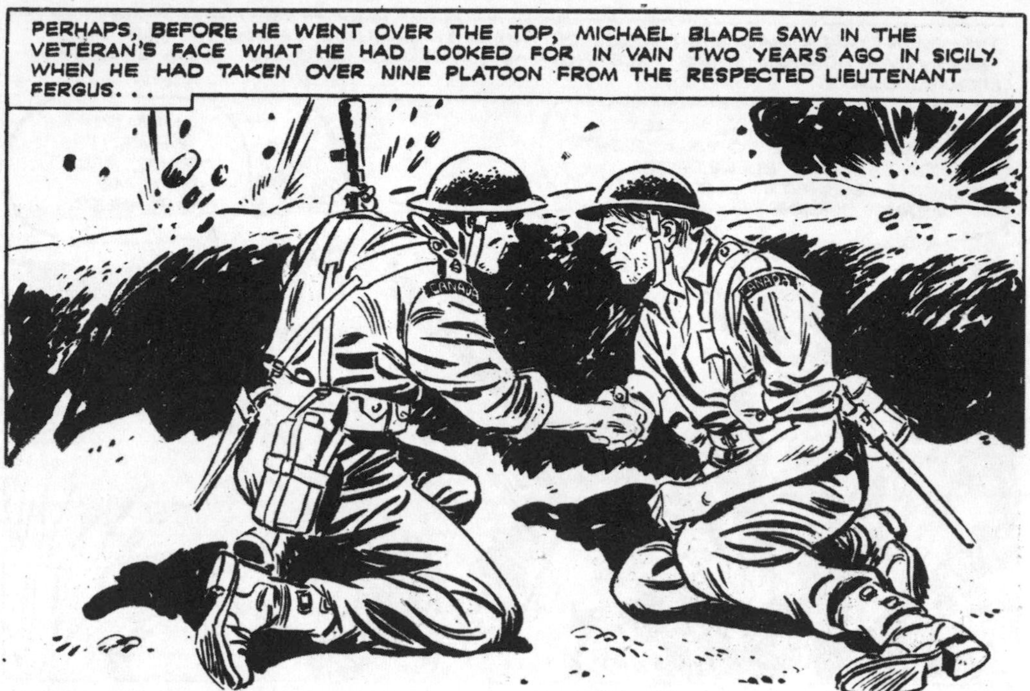
PERHAPS, BEFORE HE WENT OVER THE TOP, MICHAEL BLADE SAW IN THE VETERAN'S FACE WHAT HE HAD LOOKED FOR IN VAIN TWO YEARS AGO IN SICILY, WHEN HE HAD TAKEN OVER NINE PLATOON FROM THE RESPECTED LIEUTENANT FERGUS. . .
CANADA
CANADA

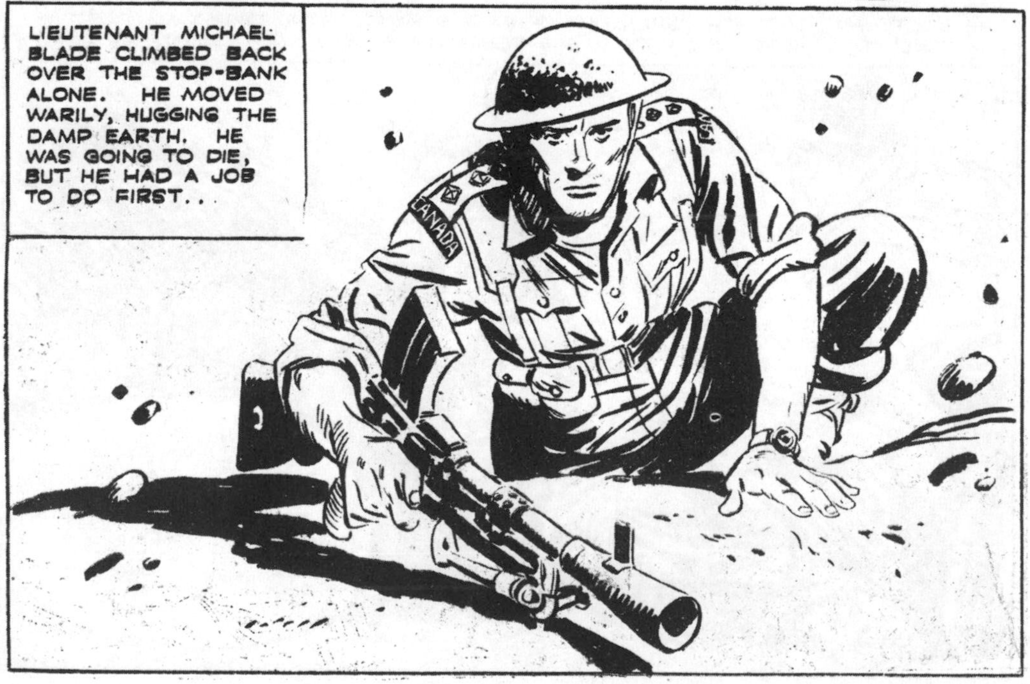
LIEUTENANT MICHAEL BLADE CLIMBED BACK OVER THE STOP-BANK ALONE. HE MOVED WARILY, HUGGING THE DAMP EARTH. HE WAS GOING TO DIE, BUT HE HAD A JOB TO DO FIRST. .
CANADA

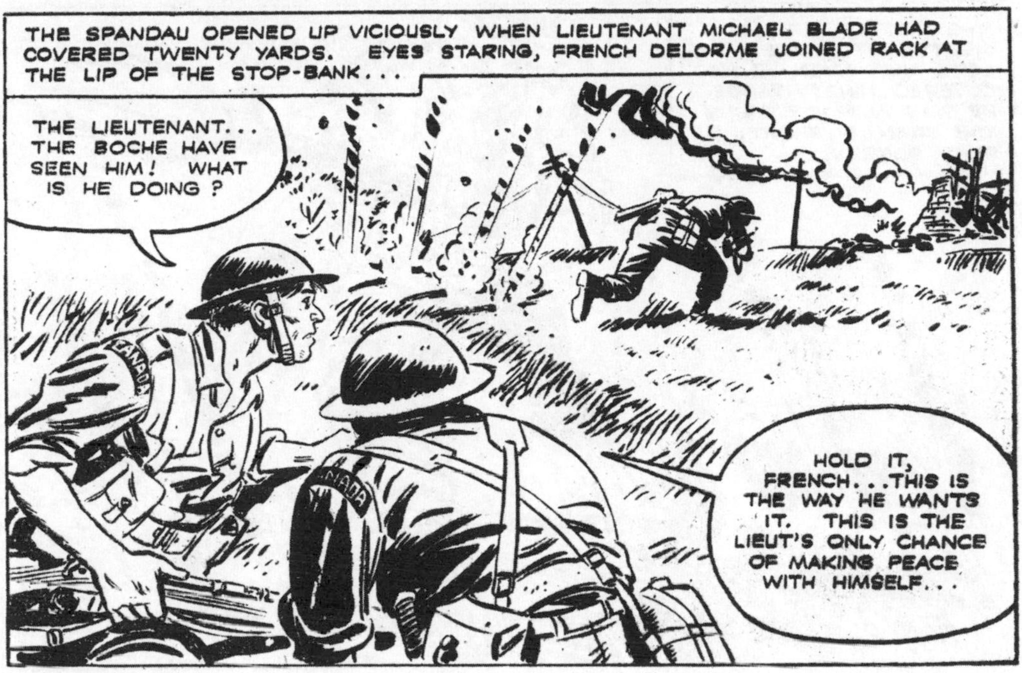
THE SPANDAU OPENED UP VICIOUSLY WHEN LIEUTENANT MICHAEL BLADE HAD COVERED TWENTY YARDS. EYES STARING, FRENCH DELORME JOINED RACK AT THE LIP OF THE STOP-BANK...
THE LIEUTENANT... THE BOCHE HAVE SEEN HIM! WHAT IS HE DOING?
HOLD IT, FRENCH...THIS IS THE WAY HE WANTS IT. THIS IS THE LIEUT'S ONLY CHANCE OF MAKING PEACE WITH HIMSELF...

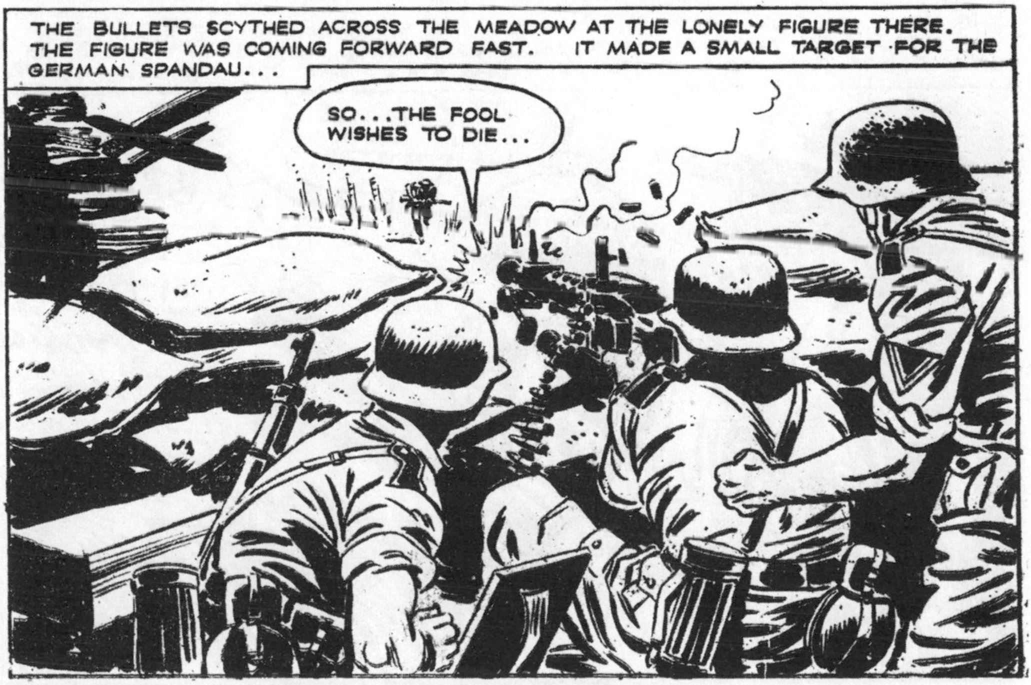
THE BULLETS SCYTHED ACROSS THE MEADOW AT THE LONELY FIGURE THERE. THE FIGURE WAS COMING FORWARD FAST. IT MADE A SMALL TARGET FOR THE GERMAN SPANDAU...
SO...THE FOOL WISHES TO DIE...

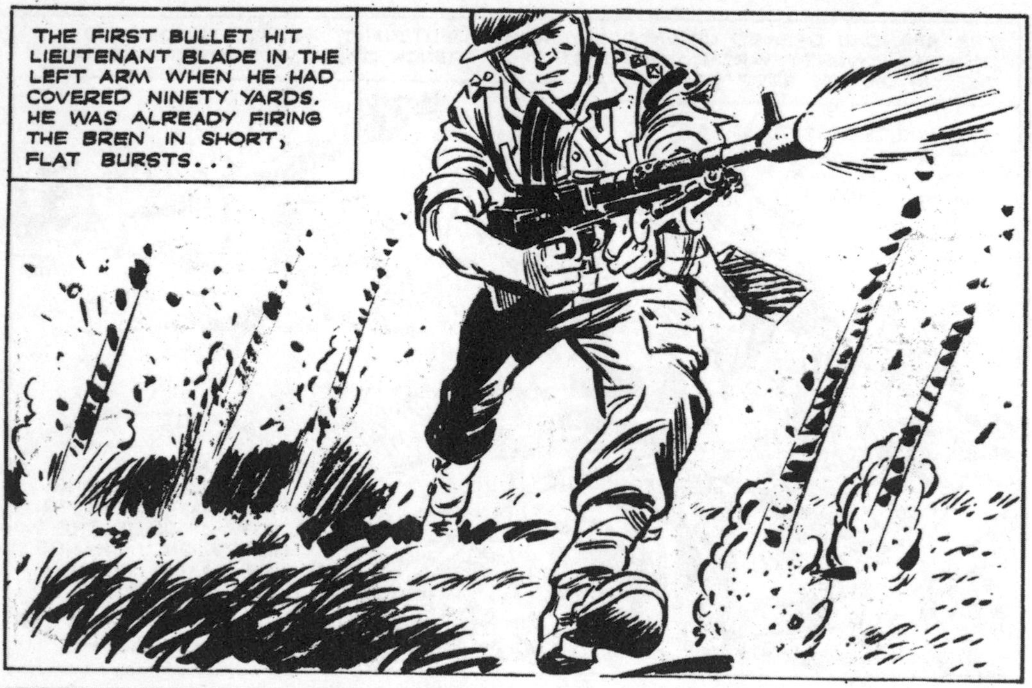
THE FIRST BULLET HIT LIEUTENANT BLADE IN THE LEFT ARM WHEN HE HAD COVERED NINETY YARDS. HE WAS ALREADY FIRING THE BREN IN SHORT, FLAT BURSTS...

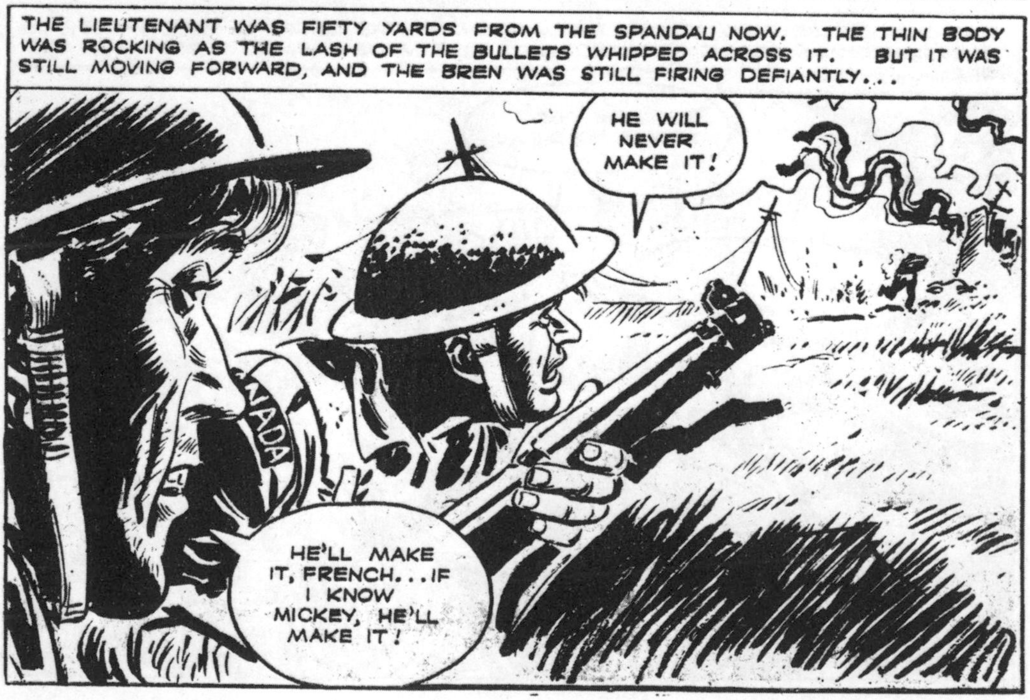
THE LIEUTENANT WAS FIFTY YARDS FROM THE SPANDAU NOW. THE THIN BODY WAS ROCKING AS THE LASH OF THE BULLETS WHIPPED ACROSS IT. BUT IT WAS STILL MOVING FORWARD, AND THE BREN WAS STILL FIRING DEFIANTLY...
HE WILL NEVER MAKE IT!
HE'LL MAKE IT, FRENCH...IF I KNOW MICKEY, HE'LL MAKE IT!

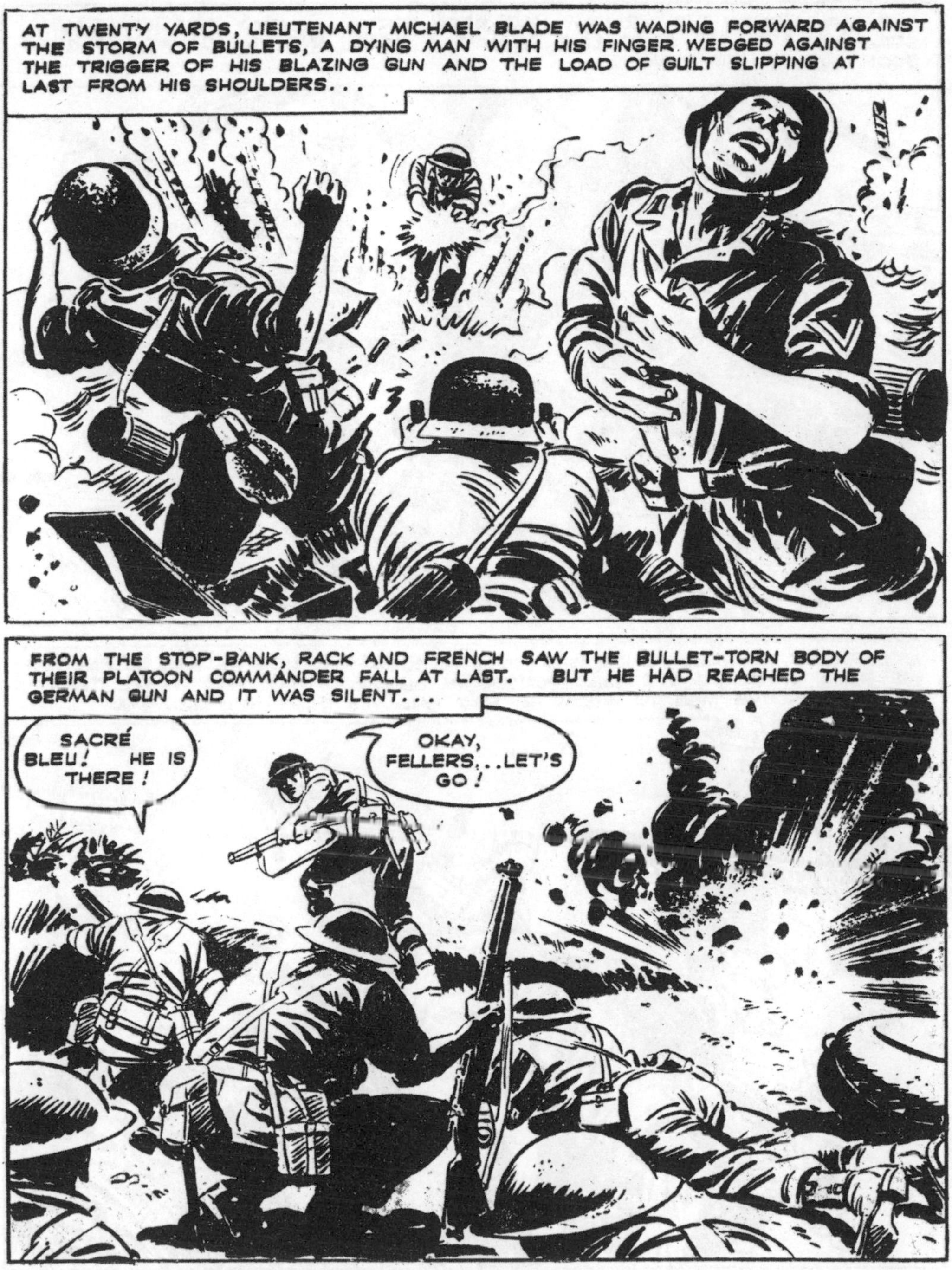
AT TWENTY YARDS, LIEUTENANT MICHAEL BLADE WAS WADING FORWARD AGAINST THE STORM OF BULLETS, A DYING MAN WITH HIS FINGER WEDGED AGAINST THE TRIGGER OF HIS BLAZING GUN AND THE LOAD OF GUILT SLIPPING AT LAST FROM HIS SHOULDERS...
FROM THE STOP-BANK, RACK AND FRENCH SAW THE BULLET-TORN BODY OF THEIR PLATOON COMMANDER FALL AT LAST. BUT HE HAD REACHED THE GERMAN GUN AND IT WAS SILENT...
SACRÉ BLEU! HE IS THERE!
OKAY, FELLERS...LET'S GO!

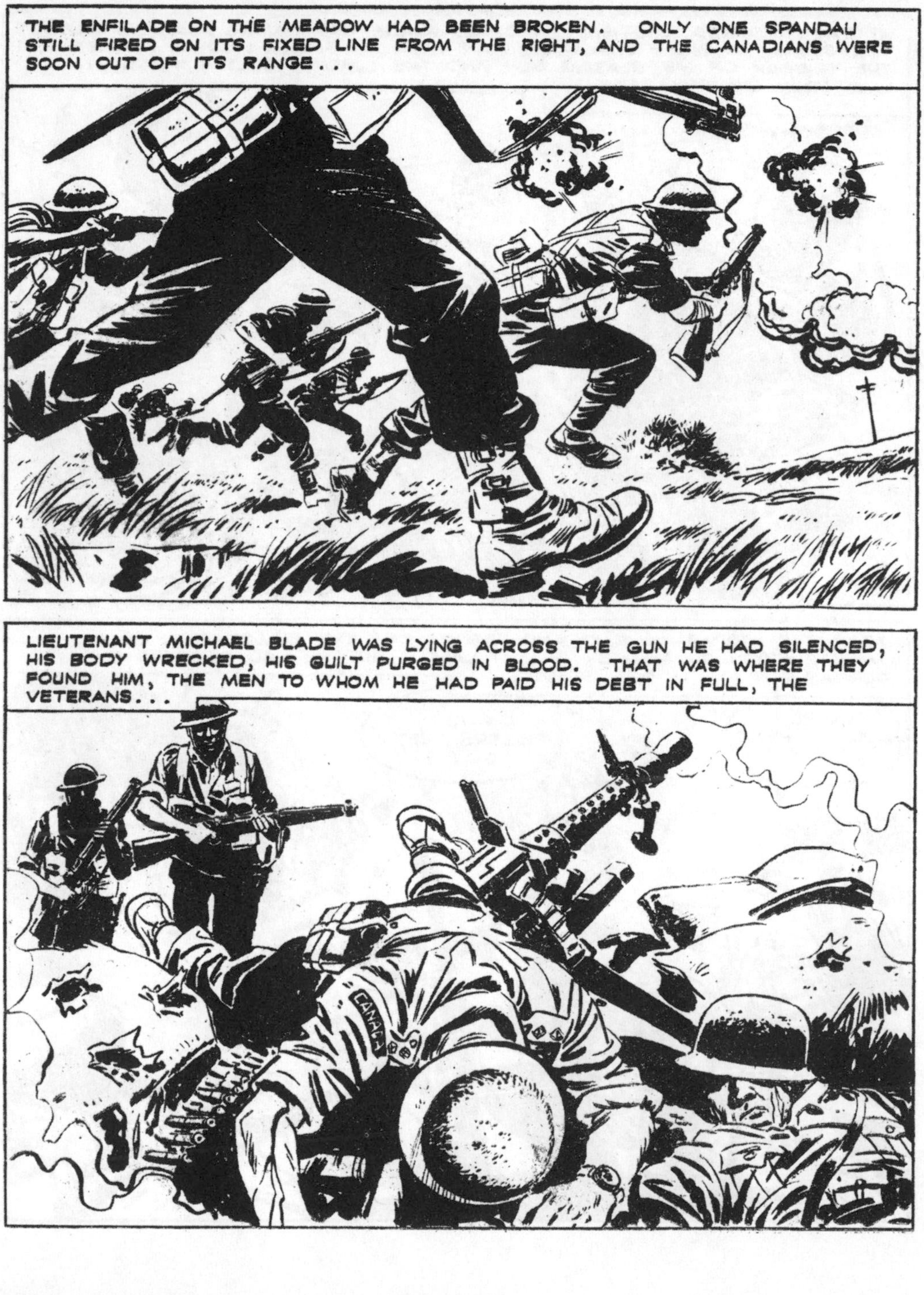
THE ENFILADE ON THE MEADOW HAD BEEN BROKEN. ONLY ONE SPANDAU STILL FIRED ON ITS FIXED LINE FROM THE RIGHT, AND THE CANADIANS WERE SOON OUT OF ITS RANGE...
LIEUTENANT MICHAEL BLADE WAS LYING ACROSS THE GUN HE HAD SILENCED, HIS BODY WRECKED, HIS GUILT PURGED IN BLOOD. THAT WAS WHERE THEY FOUND HIM, THE MEN TO WHOM HE HAD PAID HIS DEBT IN FULL, THE VETERANS...
CANADA

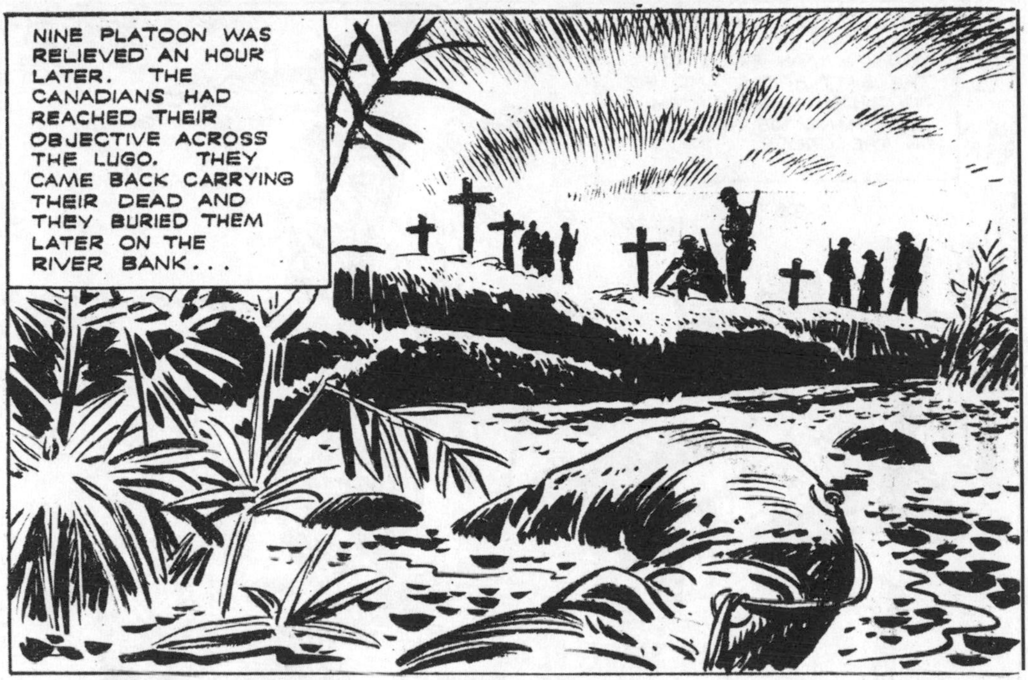
NINE PLATOON WAS RELIEVED AN HOUR LATER. THE CANADIANS HAD REACHED THEIR OBJECTIVE ACROSS THE LUGO. THEY CAME BACK CARRYING THEIR DEAD AND THEY BURIED THEM LATER ON THE RIVER BANK . . .

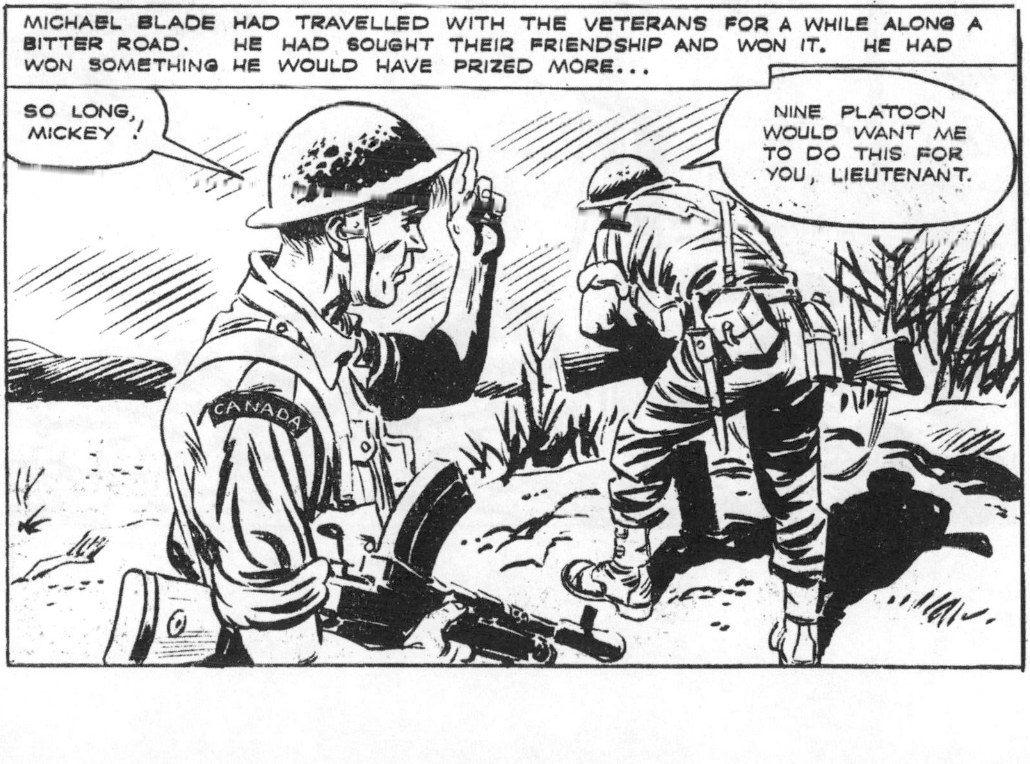
MICHAEL BLADE HAD TRAVELLED WITH THE VETERANS FOR A WHILE ALONG A BITTER ROAD. HE HAD SOUGHT THEIR FRIENDSHIP AND WON IT. HE HAD WON SOMETHING HE WOULD HAVE PRIZED MORE...
SO LONG, MICKEY !
NINE PLATOON WOULD WANT ME TO DO THIS FOR YOU, LIEUTENANT.
CANADA

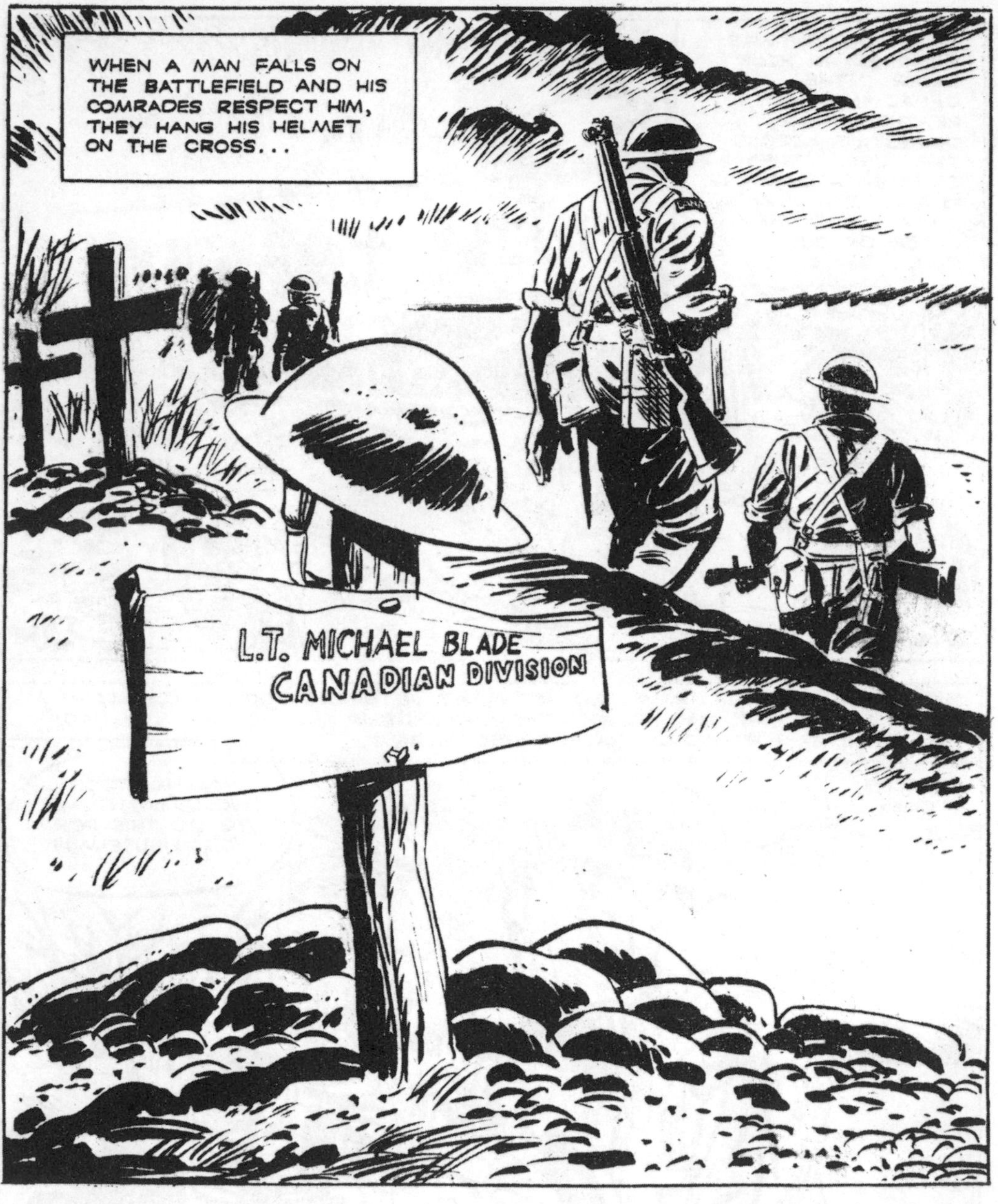
WHEN A MAN FALLS ON THE BATTLEFIELD AND HIS COMRADES RESPECT HIM, THEY HANG HIS HELMET ON THE CROSS...
L.T. MICHAEL BLADE
CANADIAN DIVISION

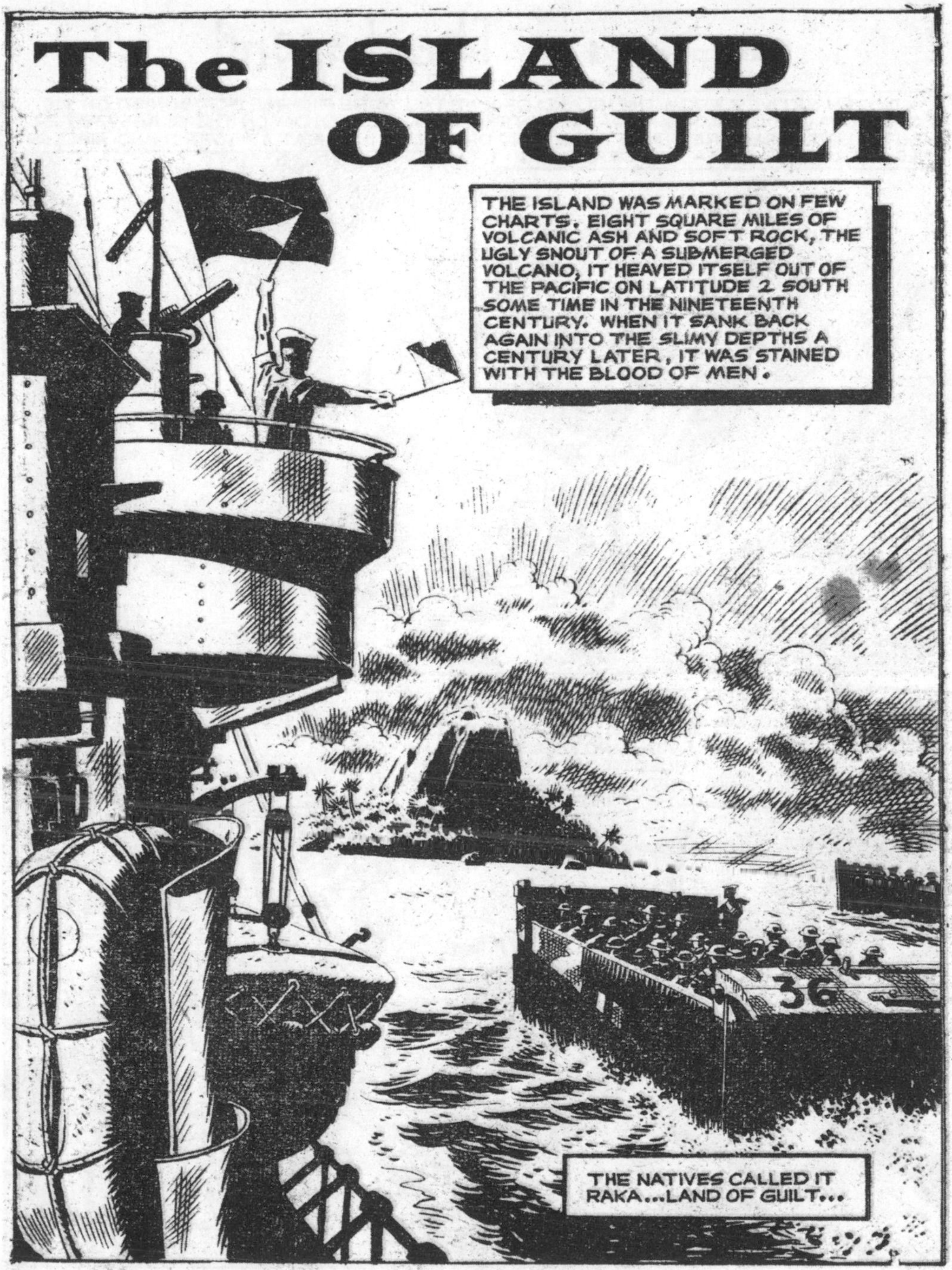
The ISLAND OF GUILT
THE ISLAND WAS MARKED ON FEW CHARTS. EIGHT SQUARE MILES OF VOLCANIC ASH AND SOFT ROCK, THE UGLY SNOUT OF A SUBMERGED VOLCANO, IT HEAVED ITSELF OUT OF THE PACIFIC ON LATITUDE 2 SOUTH SOME TIME IN THE NINETEENTH CENTURY. WHEN IT SANK BACK AGAIN INTO THE SLIMY DEPTHS A CENTURY LATER, IT WAS STAINED WITH THE BLOOD OF MEN.
36
THE NATIVES CALLED IT RAKA...LAND OF GUILT...

Chapter 1. The Legend

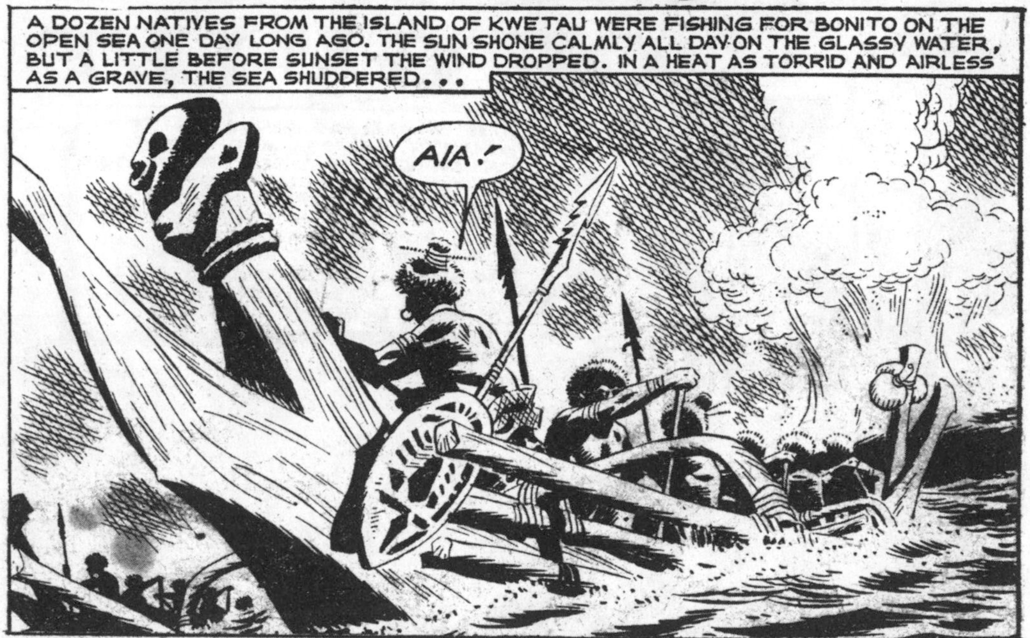
A DOZEN NATIVES FROM THE ISLAND OF KWETAU WERE FISHING FOR BONITO ON THE OPEN SEA ONE DAY LONG AGO. THE SUN SHONE CALMLY ALL DAY ON THE GLASSY WATER, BUT A LITTLE BEFORE SUNSET THE WIND DROPPED. IN A HEAT AS TORRID AND AIRLESS AS A GRAVE, THE SEA SHUDDERED...
AIA!

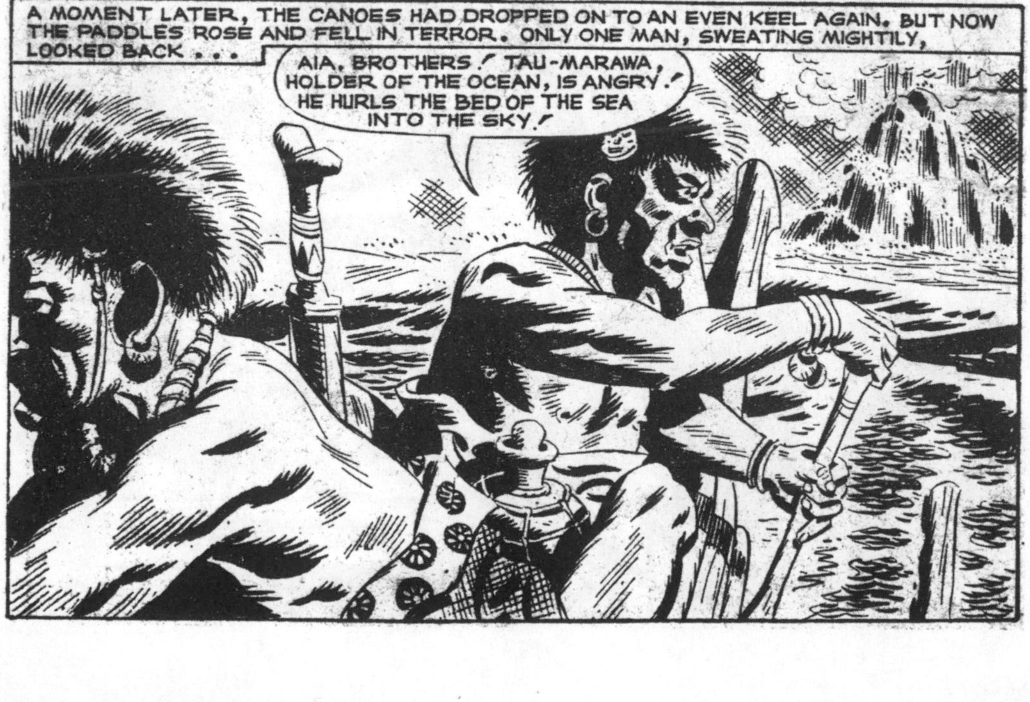
A MOMENT LATER, THE CANOES HAD DROPPED ON TO AN EVEN KEEL AGAIN. BUT NOW THE PADDLES ROSE AND FELL IN TERROR. ONLY ONE MAN, SWEATING MIGHTILY, LOOKED BACK...
AIA, BROTHERS! TAU-MARAWA, HOLDER OF THE OCEAN, IS ANGRY! HE HURLS THE BED OF THE SEA INTO THE SKY!

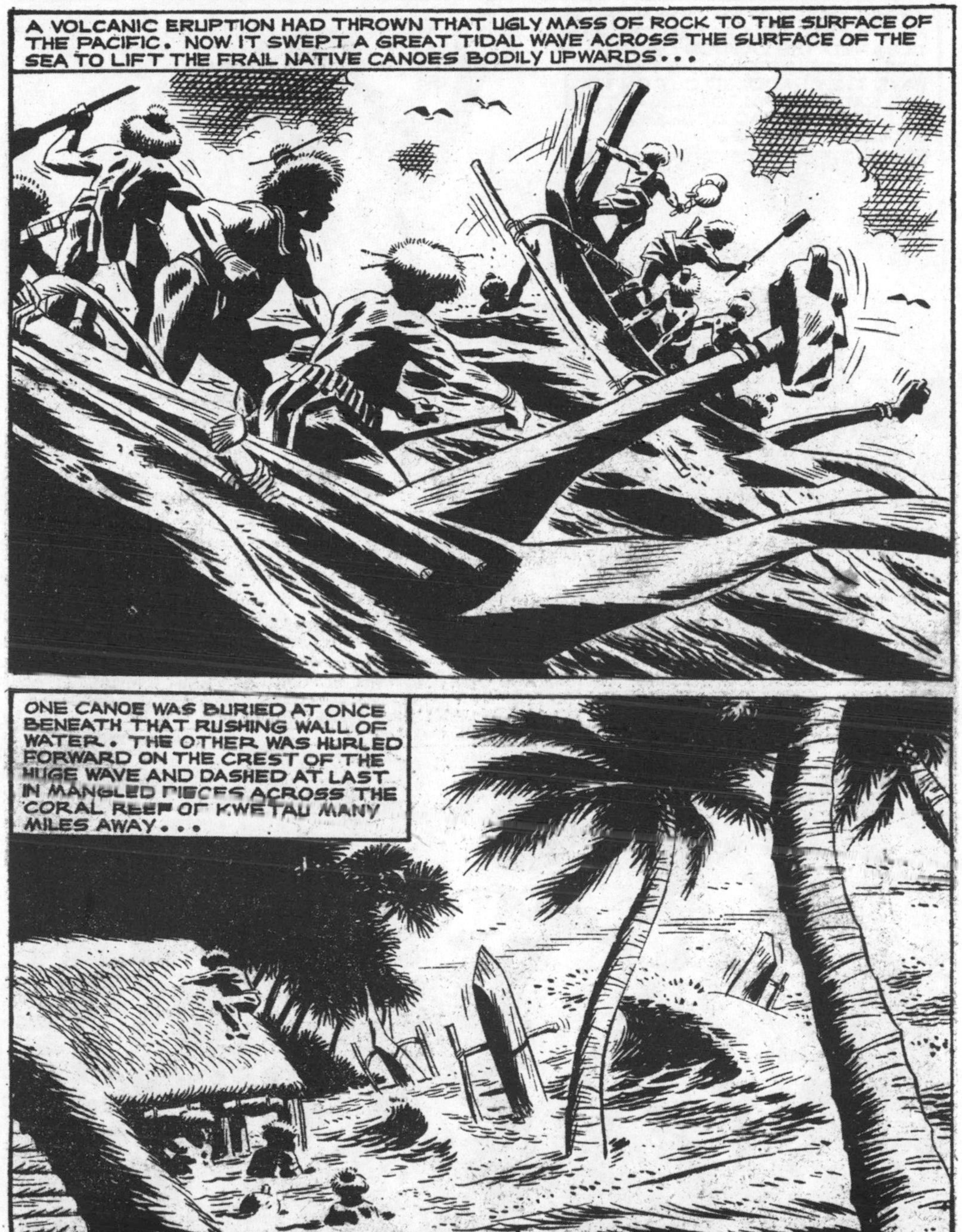
A VOLCANIC ERUPTION HAD THROWN THAT UGLY MASS OF ROCK TO THE SURFACE OF THE PACIFIC. NOW IT SWEPT A GREAT TIDAL WAVE ACROSS THE SURFACE OF THE SEA TO LIFT THE FRAIL NATIVE CANOES BODILY UPWARDS...
ONE CANOE WAS BURIED AT ONCE BENEATH THAT RUSHING WALL OF WATER. THE OTHER WAS HURLED FORWARD ON THE CREST OF THE HUGE WAVE AND DASHED AT LAST IN MANGLED PIECES ACROSS THE CORAL REEF OF KWETAU MANY MILES AWAY...

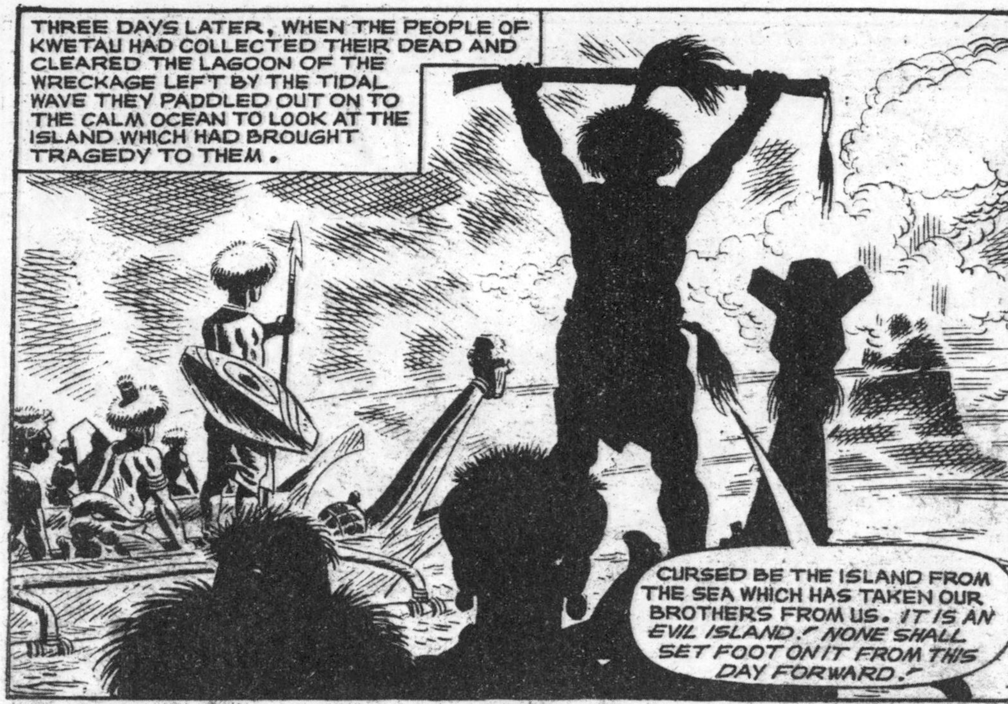
THREE DAYS LATER, WHEN THE PEOPLE OF KWETAU HAD COLLECTED THEIR DEAD AND CLEARED THE LAGOON OF THE WRECKAGE LEFT BY THE TIDAL WAVE THEY PADDLED OUT ON TO THE CALM OCEAN TO LOOK AT THE ISLAND WHICH HAD BROUGHT TRAGEDY TO THEM.
CURSED BE THE ISLAND FROM THE SEA WHICH HAS TAKEN OUR BROTHERS FROM US. IT IS AN EVIL ISLAND! NONE SHALL SET FOOT ON IT FROM THIS DAY FORWARD!

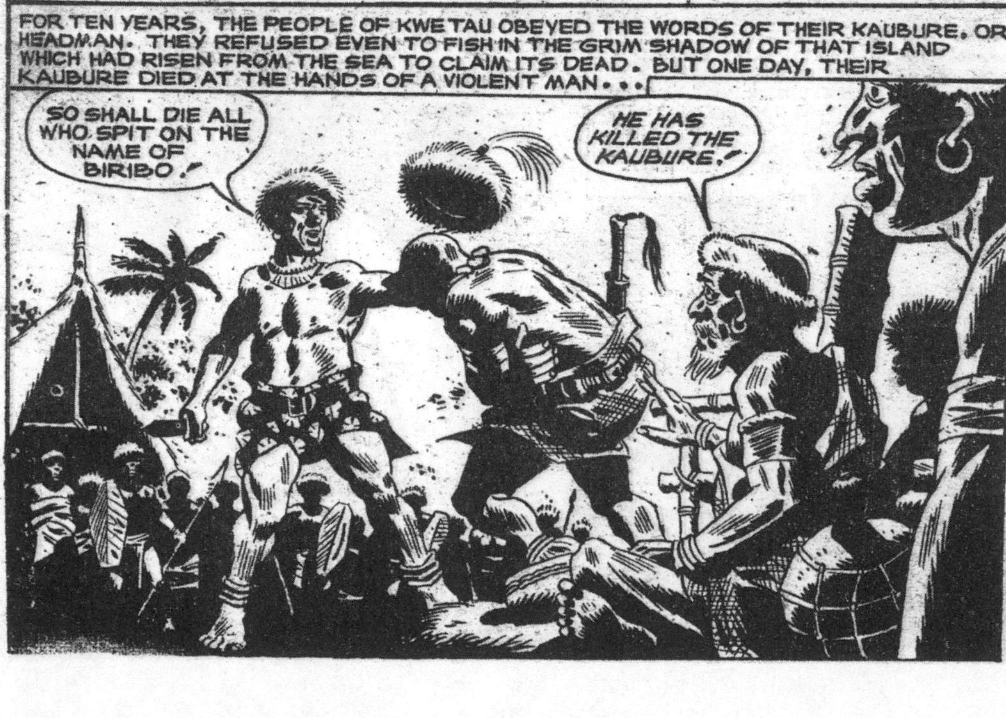
FOR TEN YEARS, THE PEOPLE OF KWETAU OBEYED THE WORDS OF THEIR KAUBURE, OR HEADMAN. THEY REFUSED EVEN TO FISH IN THE GRIM SHADOW OF THAT ISLAND WHICH HAD RISEN FROM THE SEA TO CLAIM ITS DEAD. BUT ONE DAY, THEIR KAUBURE DIED AT THE HANDS OF A VIOLENT MAN...
SO SHALL DIE ALL WHO SPIT ON THE NAME OF BIRIBO!
HE HAS KILLED THE KAUBURE!

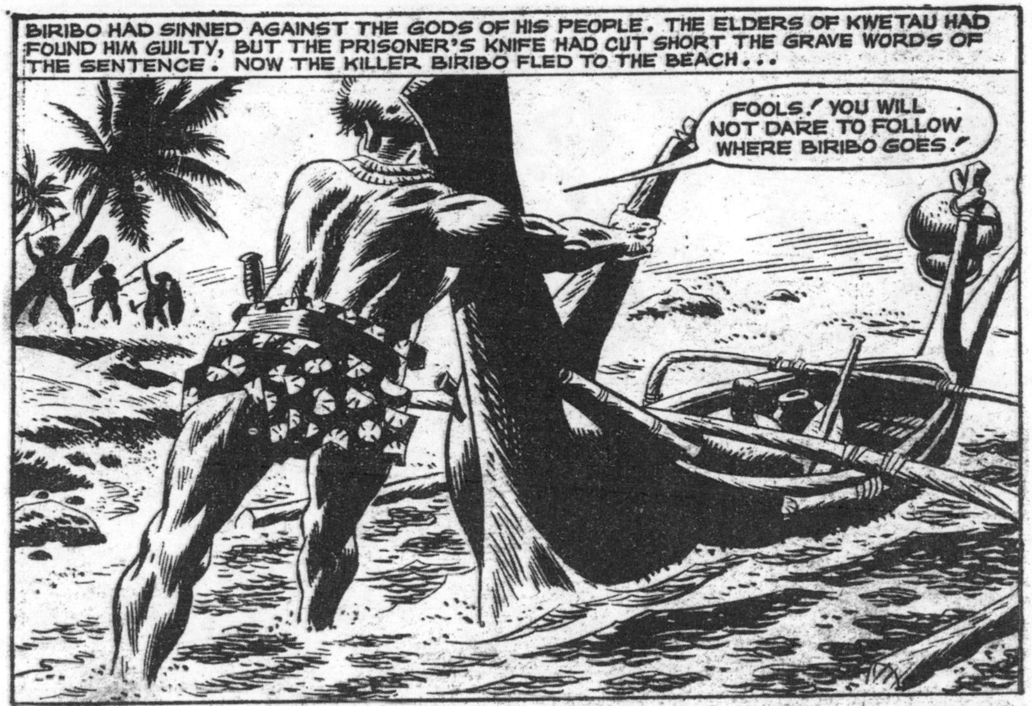
BIRIBO HAD SINNED AGAINST THE GODS OF HIS PEOPLE. THE ELDERS OF KWETAU HAD FOUND HIM GUILTY, BUT THE PRISONER'S KNIFE HAD CUT SHORT THE GRAVE WORDS OF THE SENTENCE. NOW THE KILLER BIRIBO FLED TO THE BEACH...
FOOLS! YOU WILL NOT DARE TO FOLLOW WHERE BIRIBO GOES!

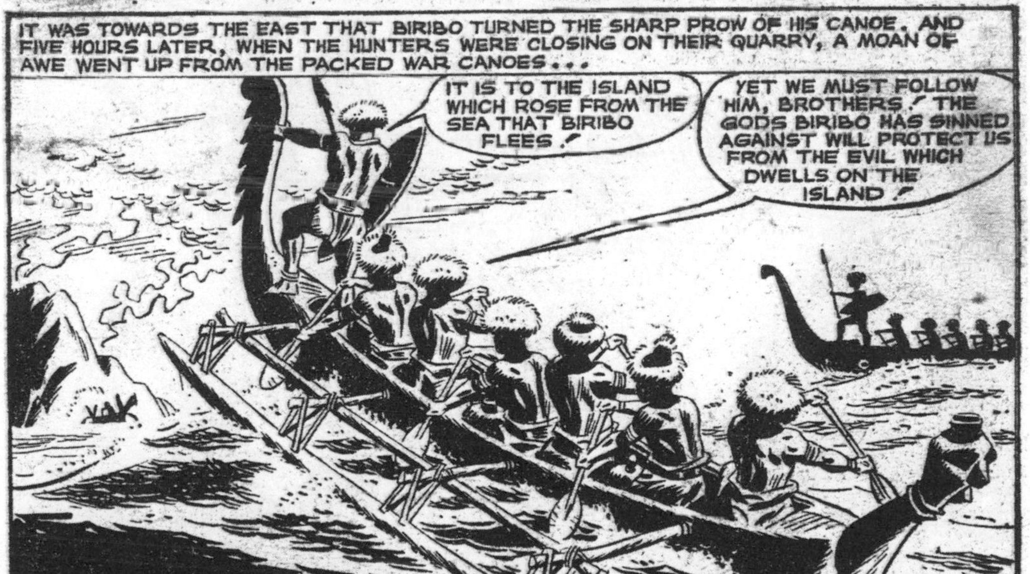
IT WAS TOWARDS THE EAST THAT BIRIBO TURNED THE SHARP PROW OF HIS CANOE. AND FIVE HOURS LATER, WHEN THE HUNTERS WERE CLOSING ON THEIR QUARRY, A MOAN OF AWE WENT UP FROM THE PACKED WAR CANOES...
IT IS TO THE ISLAND WHICH ROSE FROM THE SEA THAT BIRIBO FLEES!
YET WE MUST FOLLOW HIM, BROTHERS! THE GODS BIRIBO HAS SINNED AGAINST WILL PROTECT US FROM THE EVIL WHICH DWELLS ON THE ISLAND!

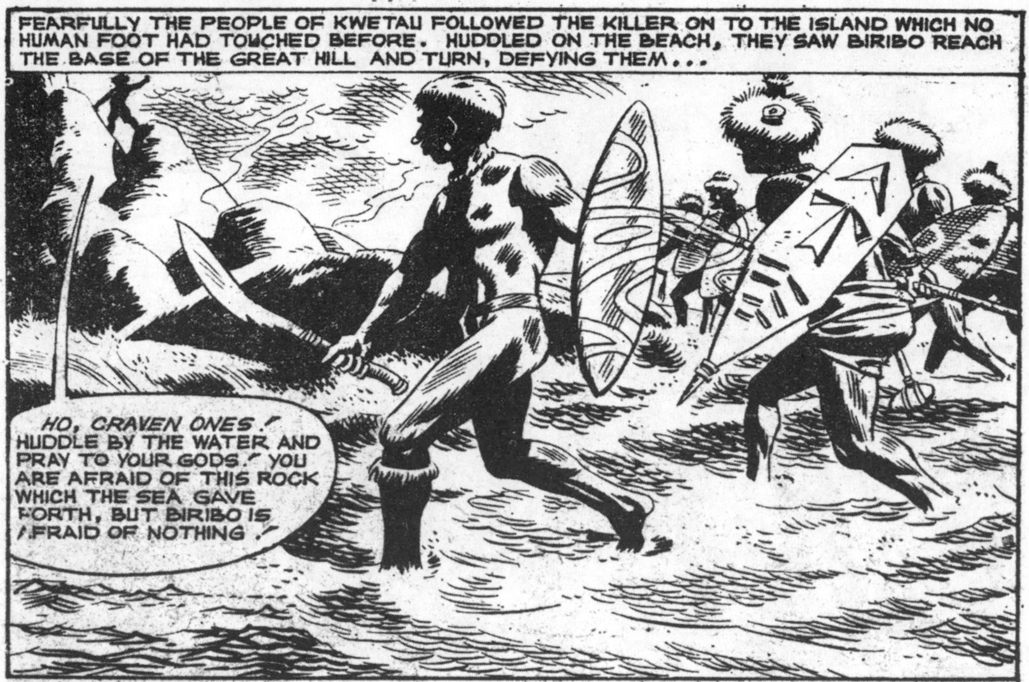
FEARFULLY THE PEOPLE OF KWETAU FOLLOWED THE KILLER ON TO THE ISLAND WHICH NO HUMAN FOOT HAD TOUCHED BEFORE. HUDDLED ON THE BEACH, THEY SAW BIRIBO REACH THE BASE OF THE GREAT HILL AND TURN, DEFYING THEM...
HO, CRAVEN ONES! HUDDLE BY THE WATER AND PRAY TO YOUR GODS! YOU ARE AFRAID OF THIS ROCK WHICH THE SEA GAVE FORTH, BUT BIRIBO IS AFRAID OF NOTHING!

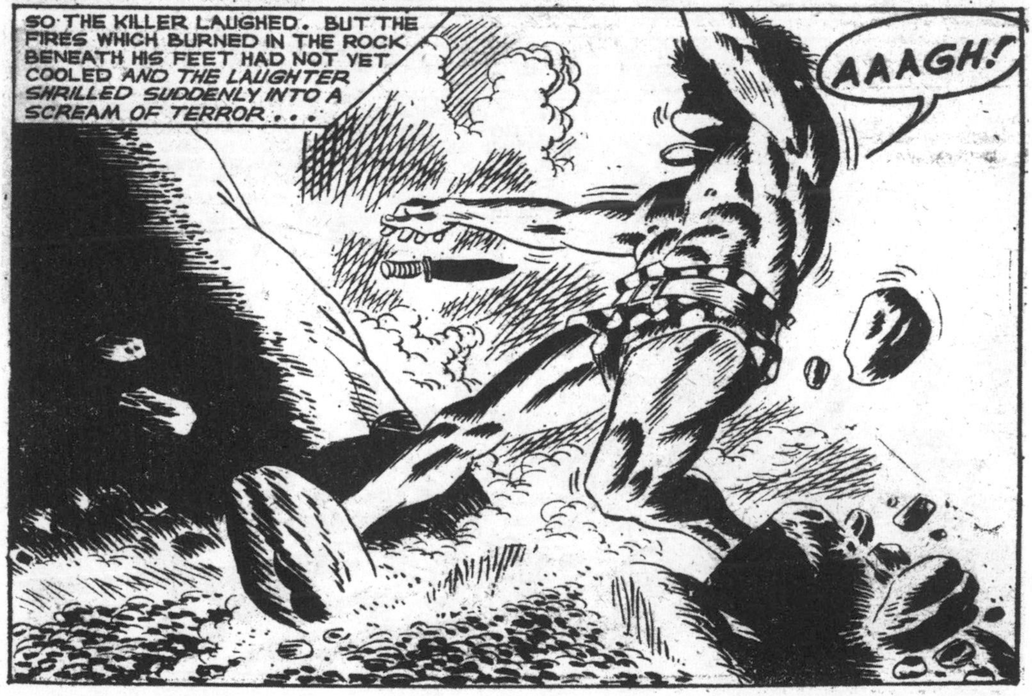
SO THE KILLER LAUGHED. BUT THE FIRES WHICH BURNED IN THE ROCK BENEATH HIS FEET HAD NOT YET COOLED AND THE LAUGHTER SHRILLED SUDDENLY INTO A SCREAM OF TERROR...
AAAGH!

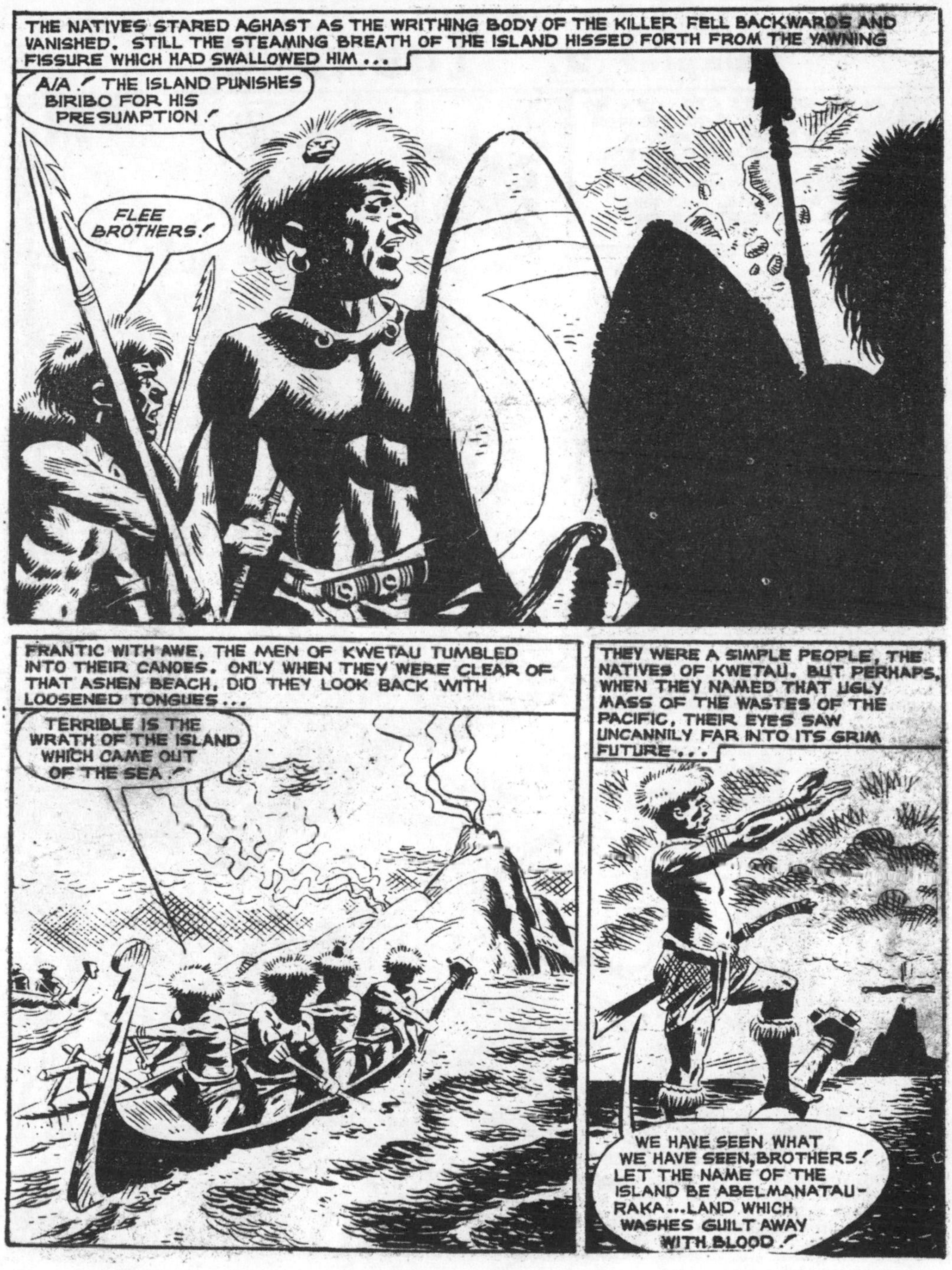
THE NATIVES STARED AGHAST AS THE WRITHING BODY OF THE KILLER FELL BACKWARDS AND VANISHED. STILL THE STEAMING BREATH OF THE ISLAND HISSED FORTH FROM THE YAWNING FISSURE WHICH HAD SWALLOWED HIM ...
A/A! THE ISLAND PUNISHES BIRIBO FOR HIS PRESUMPTION!
FLEE BROTHERS!
FRANTIC WITH AWE, THE MEN OF KWETAU TUMBLED INTO THEIR CANOES. ONLY WHEN THEY WERE CLEAR OF THAT ASHEN BEACH, DID THEY LOOK BACK WITH LOOSENED TONGUES ...
TERRIBLE IS THE WRATH OF THE ISLAND WHICH CAME OUT OF THE SEA!
THEY WERE A SIMPLE PEOPLE, THE NATIVES OF KWETAU. BUT PERHAPS, WHEN THEY NAMED THAT UGLY MASS OF THE WASTES OF THE PACIFIC, THEIR EYES SAW UNCANNILY FAR INTO ITS GRIM FUTURE ...
WE HAVE SEEN WHAT WE HAVE SEEN, BROTHERS! LET THE NAME OF THE ISLAND BE ABELMANATAU-RAKA...LAND WHICH WASHES GUILT AWAY WITH BLOOD!

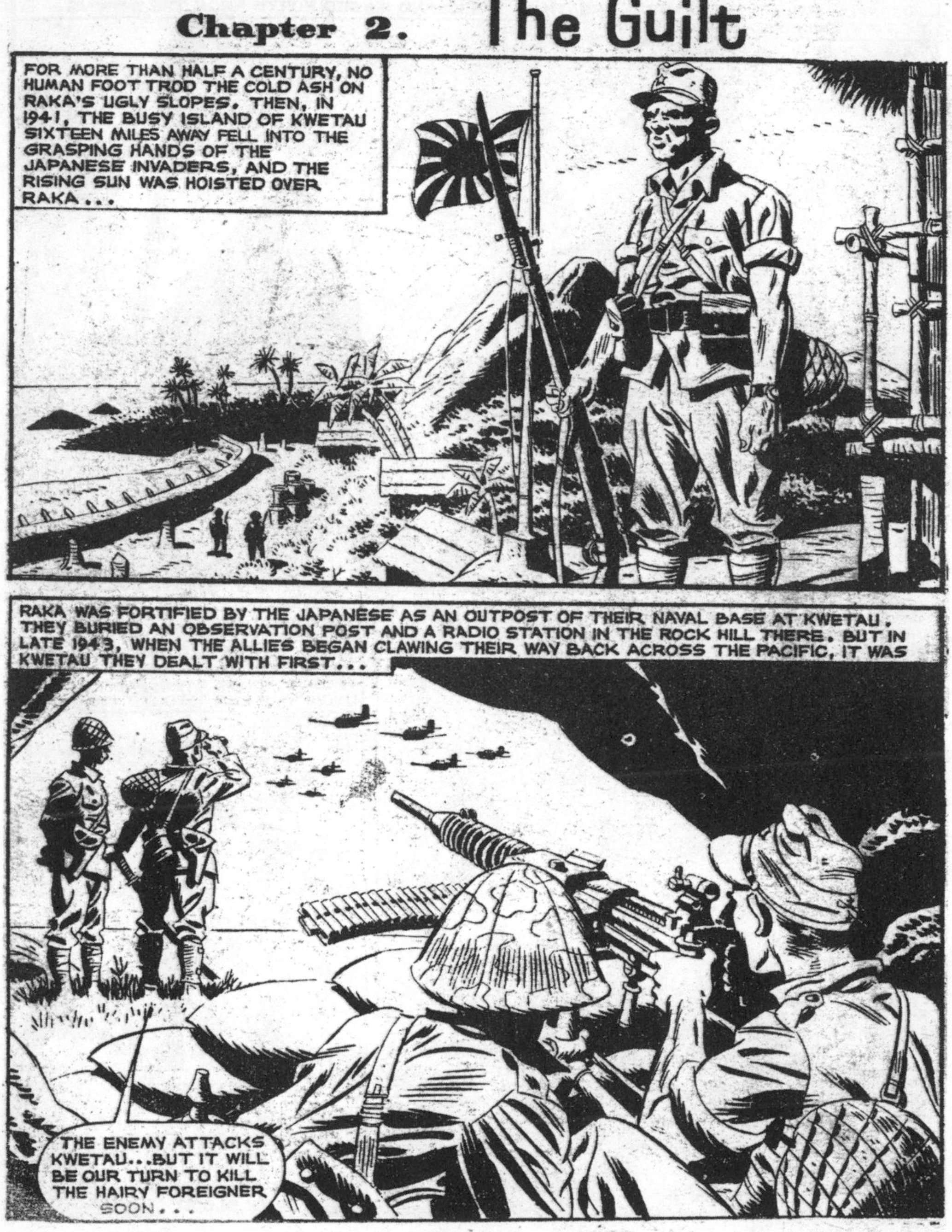
Chapter 2. The Guilt
FOR MORE THAN HALF A CENTURY, NO HUMAN FOOT TROD THE COLD ASH ON RAKA'S UGLY SLOPES. THEN, IN 1941, THE BUSY ISLAND OF KWETAU SIXTEEN MILES AWAY FELL INTO THE GRASPING HANDS OF THE JAPANESE INVADERS, AND THE RISING SUN WAS HOISTED OVER RAKA...
RAKA WAS FORTIFIED BY THE JAPANESE AS AN OUTPOST OF THEIR NAVAL BASE AT KWETAU. THEY BURIED AN OBSERVATION POST AND A RADIO STATION IN THE ROCK HILL THERE. BUT IN LATE 1943, WHEN THE ALLIES BEGAN CLAWING THEIR WAY BACK ACROSS THE PACIFIC, IT WAS KWETAU THEY DEALT WITH FIRST...
THE ENEMY ATTACKS KWETAU...BUT IT WILL BE OUR TURN TO KILL THE HAIRY FOREIGNER SOON...

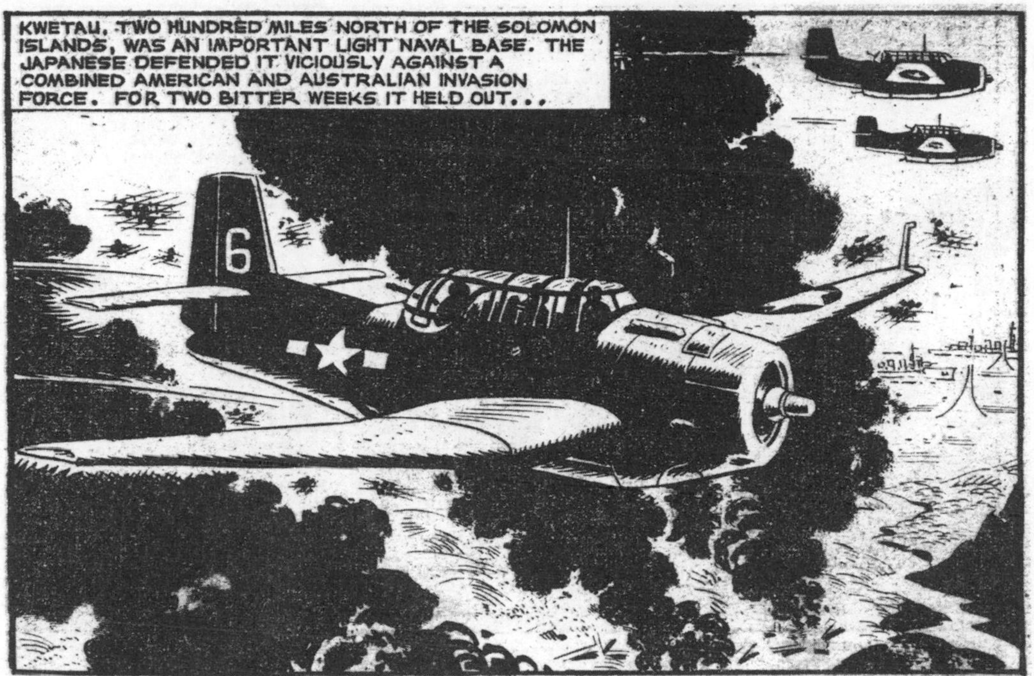
KWETAU, TWO HUNDRED MILES NORTH OF THE SOLOMON ISLANDS, WAS AN IMPORTANT LIGHT NAVAL BASE. THE JAPANESE DEFENDED IT VICIOUSLY AGAINST A COMBINED AMERICAN AND AUSTRALIAN INVASION FORCE. FOR TWO BITTER WEEKS IT HELD OUT...
6

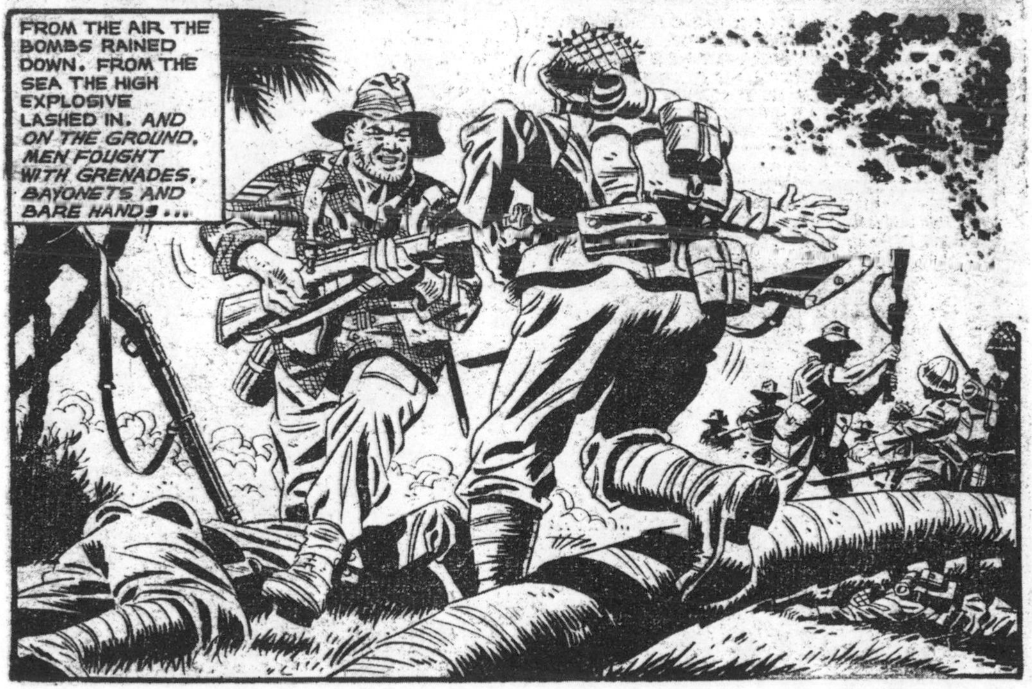
FROM THE AIR THE BOMBS RAINED DOWN. FROM THE SEA THE HIGH EXPLOSIVE LASHED IN. AND ON THE GROUND, MEN FOUGHT WITH GRENADES, BAYONETS AND BARE HANDS...

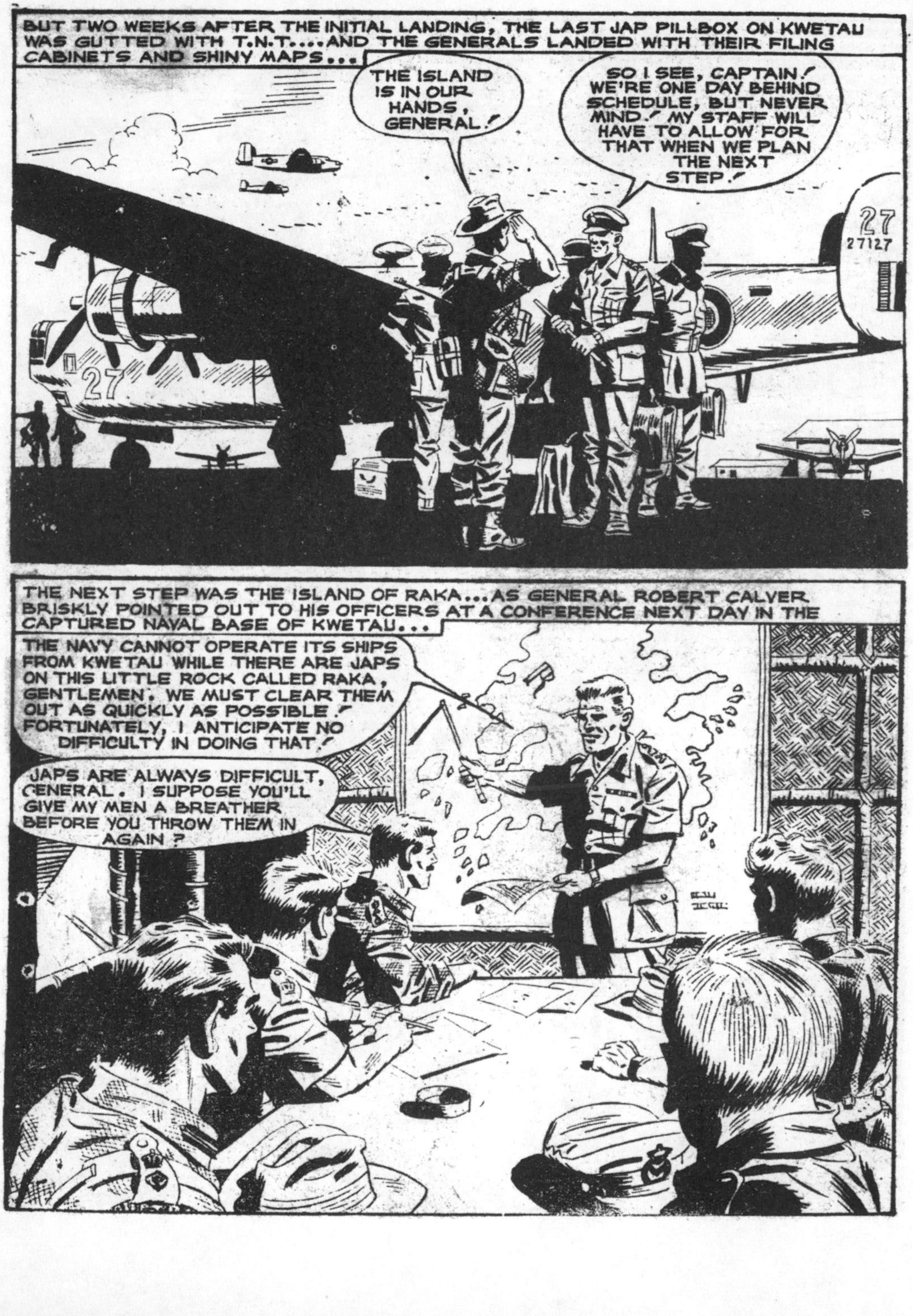
BUT TWO WEEKS AFTER THE INITIAL LANDING, THE LAST JAP PILLBOX ON KWETAU WAS GUTTED WITH T.N.T....AND THE GENERALS LANDED WITH THEIR FILING CABINETS AND SHINY MAPS...
THE ISLAND IS IN OUR HANDS, GENERAL!
SO I SEE, CAPTAIN! WE'RE ONE DAY BEHIND SCHEDULE, BUT NEVER MIND! MY STAFF WILL HAVE TO ALLOW FOR THAT WHEN WE PLAN THE NEXT STEP!
27
27127
27
THE NEXT STEP WAS THE ISLAND OF RAKA...AS GENERAL ROBERT CALVER BRISKLY POINTED OUT TO HIS OFFICERS AT A CONFERENCE NEXT DAY IN THE CAPTURED NAVAL BASE OF KWETAU...
THE NAVY CANNOT OPERATE ITS SHIPS FROM KWETAU WHILE THERE ARE JAPS ON THIS LITTLE ROCK CALLED RAKA, GENTLEMEN. WE MUST CLEAR THEM OUT AS QUICKLY AS POSSIBLE! FORTUNATELY, I ANTICIPATE NO DIFFICULTY IN DOING THAT!
JAPS ARE ALWAYS DIFFICULT, GENERAL. I SUPPOSE YOU'LL GIVE MY MEN A BREATHER BEFORE YOU THROW THEM IN AGAIN?

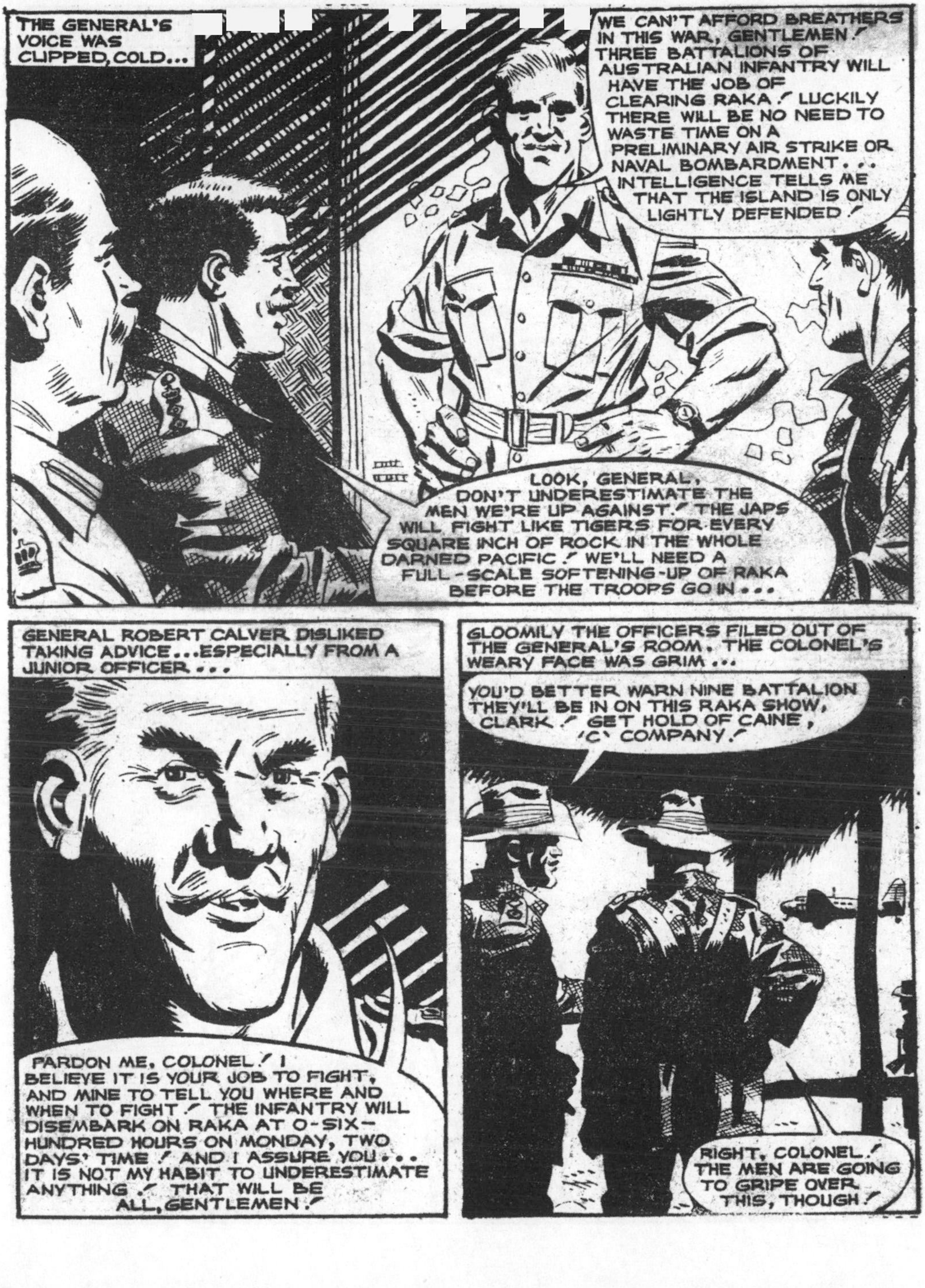
THE GENERAL'S VOICE WAS CLIPPED, COLD...
WE CAN'T AFFORD BREATHERS IN THIS WAR, GENTLEMEN! THREE BATTALIONS OF AUSTRALIAN INFANTRY WILL HAVE THE JOB OF CLEARING RAKA! LUCKILY THERE WILL BE NO NEED TO WASTE TIME ON A PRELIMINARY AIR STRIKE OR NAVAL BOMBARDMENT... INTELLIGENCE TELLS ME THAT THE ISLAND IS ONLY LIGHTLY DEFENDED!
LOOK, GENERAL, DON'T UNDERESTIMATE THE MEN WE'RE UP AGAINST! THE JAPS WILL FIGHT LIKE TIGERS FOR EVERY SQUARE INCH OF ROCK IN THE WHOLE DARNED PACIFIC! WE'LL NEED A FULL-SCALE SOFTENING-UP OF RAKA BEFORE THE TROOPS GO IN...
GENERAL ROBERT CALVER DISLIKED TAKING ADVICE...ESPECIALLY FROM A JUNIOR OFFICER...
PARDON ME, COLONEL! I BELIEVE IT IS YOUR JOB TO FIGHT, AND MINE TO TELL YOU WHERE AND WHEN TO FIGHT! THE INFANTRY WILL DISEMBARK ON RAKA AT O-SIX-HUNDRED HOURS ON MONDAY, TWO DAYS' TIME! AND I ASSURE YOU... IT IS NOT MY HABIT TO UNDERESTIMATE ANYTHING! THAT WILL BE ALL, GENTLEMEN!
GLOOMILY THE OFFICERS FILED OUT OF THE GENERAL'S ROOM. THE COLONEL'S WEARY FACE WAS GRIM...
YOU'D BETTER WARN NINE BATTALION THEY'LL BE IN ON THIS RAKA SHOW, CLARK! GET HOLD OF CAINE, 'C' COMPANY!
RIGHT, COLONEL! THE MEN ARE GOING TO GRIPE OVER THIS, THOUGH!

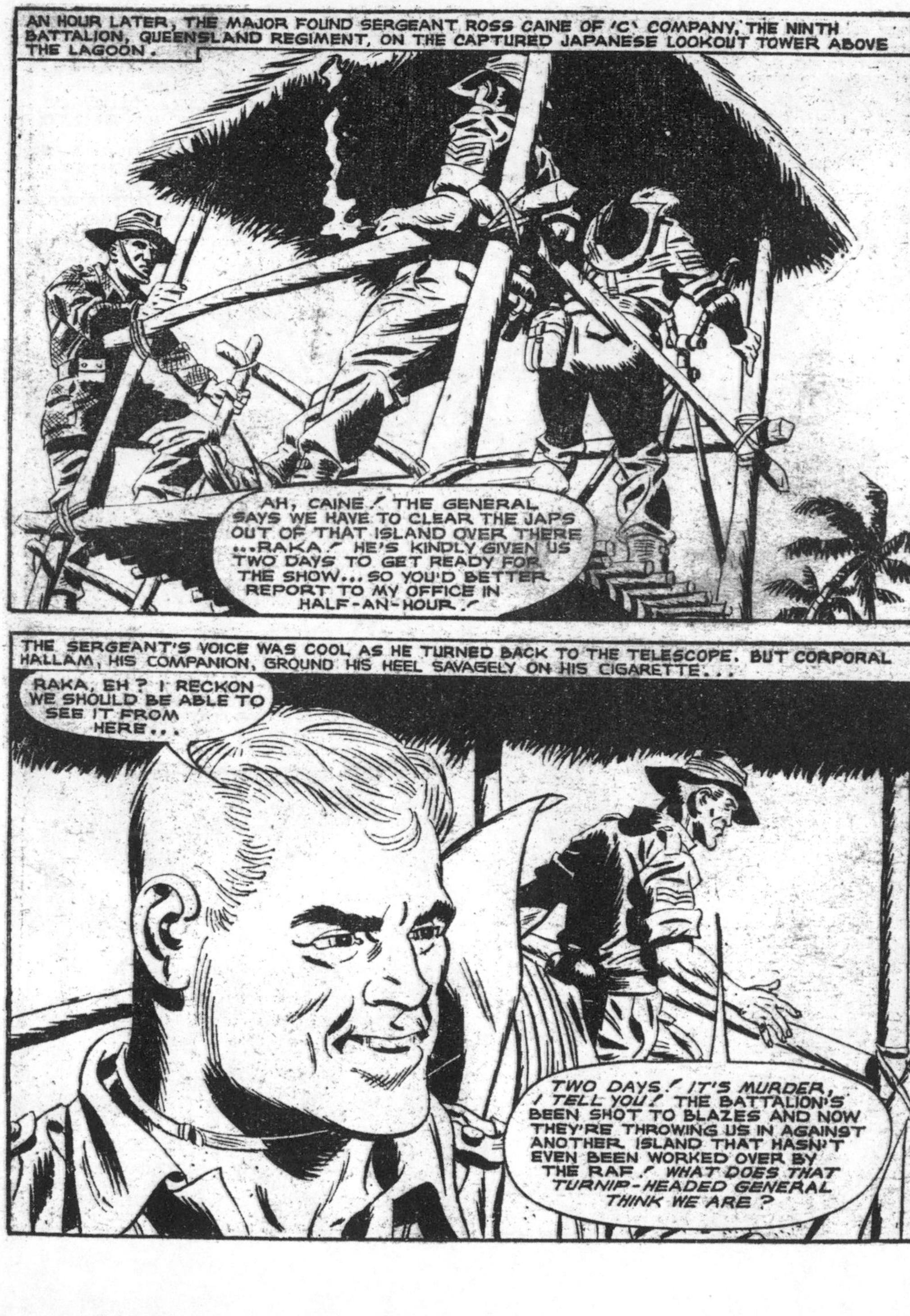
AN HOUR LATER, THE MAJOR FOUND SERGEANT ROSS CAINE OF 'C' COMPANY, THE NINTH BATTALION, QUEENSLAND REGIMENT, ON THE CAPTURED JAPANESE LOOKOUT TOWER ABOVE THE LAGOON.
AH, CAINE! THE GENERAL SAYS WE HAVE TO CLEAR THE JAPS OUT OF THAT ISLAND OVER THERE ...RAKA! HE'S KINDLY GIVEN US TWO DAYS TO GET READY FOR THE SHOW... SO YOU'D BETTER REPORT TO MY OFFICE IN HALF-AN-HOUR!
THE SERGEANT'S VOICE WAS COOL AS HE TURNED BACK TO THE TELESCOPE. BUT CORPORAL HALLAM, HIS COMPANION, GROUND HIS HEEL SAVAGELY ON HIS CIGARETTE...
RAKA, EH? I RECKON WE SHOULD BE ABLE TO SEE IT FROM HERE...
TWO DAYS! IT'S MURDER, I TELL YOU! THE BATTALION'S BEEN SHOT TO BLAZES AND NOW THEY'RE THROWING US IN AGAINST ANOTHER ISLAND THAT HASN'T EVEN BEEN WORKED OVER BY THE RAF! WHAT DOES THAT TURNIP-HEADED GENERAL THINK WE ARE?

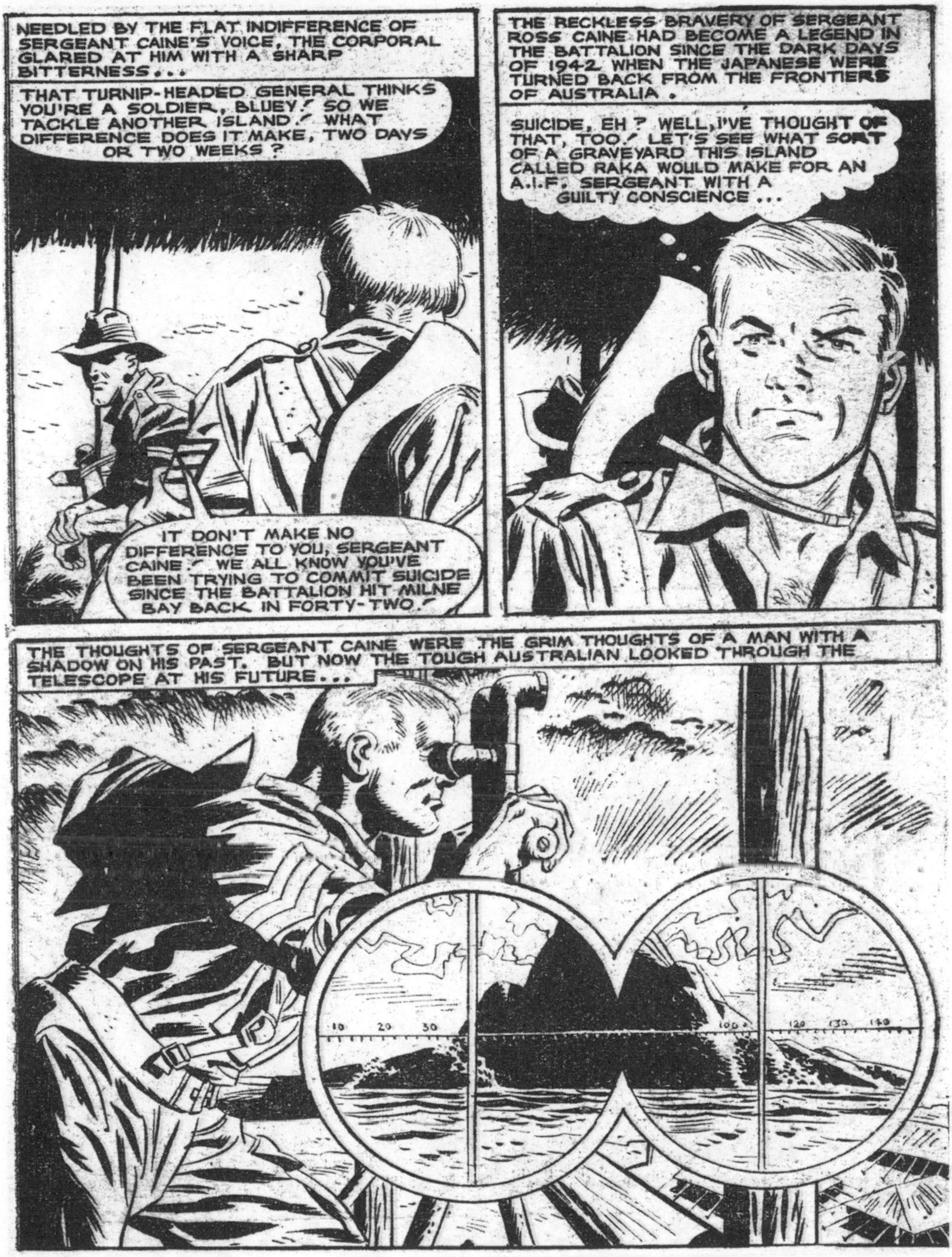
NEEDLED BY THE FLAT INDIFFERENCE OF SERGEANT CAINE'S VOICE, THE CORPORAL GLARED AT HIM WITH A SHARP BITTERNESS...
THAT TURNIP-HEADED GENERAL THINKS YOU'RE A SOLDIER, BLUEY! SO WE TACKLE ANOTHER ISLAND! WHAT DIFFERENCE DOES IT MAKE, TWO DAYS OR TWO WEEKS?
IT DON'T MAKE NO DIFFERENCE TO YOU, SERGEANT CAINE! WE ALL KNOW YOU'VE BEEN TRYING TO COMMIT SUICIDE SINCE THE BATTALION HIT MILNE BAY BACK IN FORTY-TWO!
THE RECKLESS BRAVERY OF SERGEANT ROSS CAINE HAD BECOME A LEGEND IN THE BATTALION SINCE THE DARK DAYS OF 1942 WHEN THE JAPANESE WERE TURNED BACK FROM THE FRONTIERS OF AUSTRALIA.
SUICIDE, EH? WELL, I'VE THOUGHT OF THAT, TOO! LET'S SEE WHAT SORT OF A GRAVEYARD THIS ISLAND CALLED RAKA WOULD MAKE FOR AN A.I.F. SERGEANT WITH A GUILTY CONSCIENCE...
THE THOUGHTS OF SERGEANT CAINE WERE THE GRIM THOUGHTS OF A MAN WITH A SHADOW ON HIS PAST. BUT NOW THE TOUGH AUSTRALIAN LOOKED THROUGH THE TELESCOPE AT HIS FUTURE...

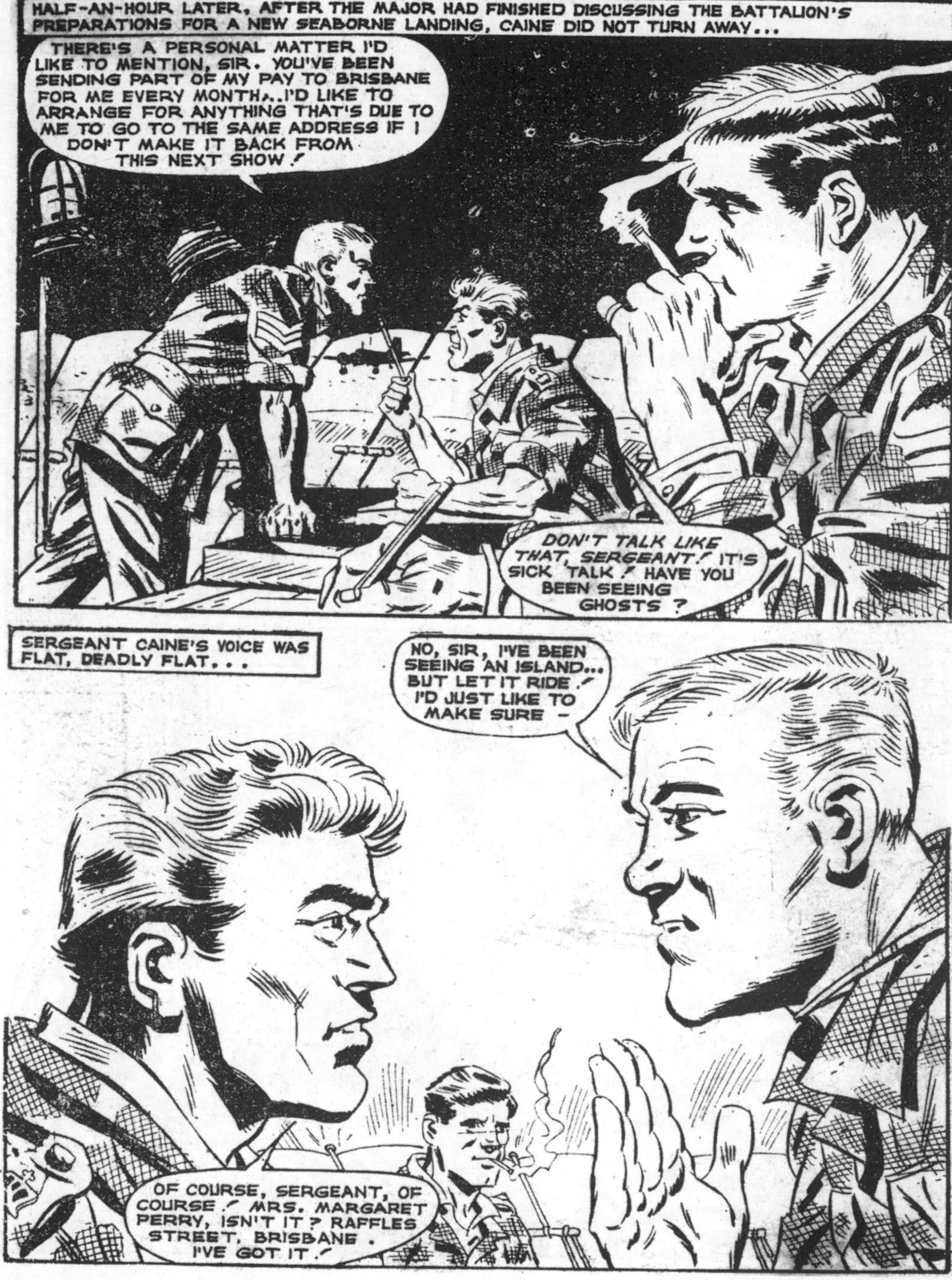
HALF-AN-HOUR LATER, AFTER THE MAJOR HAD FINISHED DISCUSSING THE BATTALION'S PREPARATIONS FOR A NEW SEABORNE LANDING, CAINE DID NOT TURN AWAY...
THERE'S A PERSONAL MATTER I'D LIKE TO MENTION, SIR. YOU'VE BEEN SENDING PART OF MY PAY TO BRISBANE FOR ME EVERY MONTH...I'D LIKE TO ARRANGE FOR ANYTHING THAT'S DUE TO ME TO GO TO THE SAME ADDRESS IF I DON'T MAKE IT BACK FROM THIS NEXT SHOW!
DON'T TALK LIKE THAT, SERGEANT! IT'S SICK TALK! HAVE YOU BEEN SEEING GHOSTS?
SERGEANT CAINE'S VOICE WAS FLAT, DEADLY FLAT...
NO, SIR, I'VE BEEN SEEING AN ISLAND... BUT LET IT RIDE! I'D JUST LIKE TO MAKE SURE –
OF COURSE, SERGEANT, OF COURSE! MRS. MARGARET PERRY, ISN'T IT? RAFFLES STREET, BRISBANE. I'VE GOT IT!

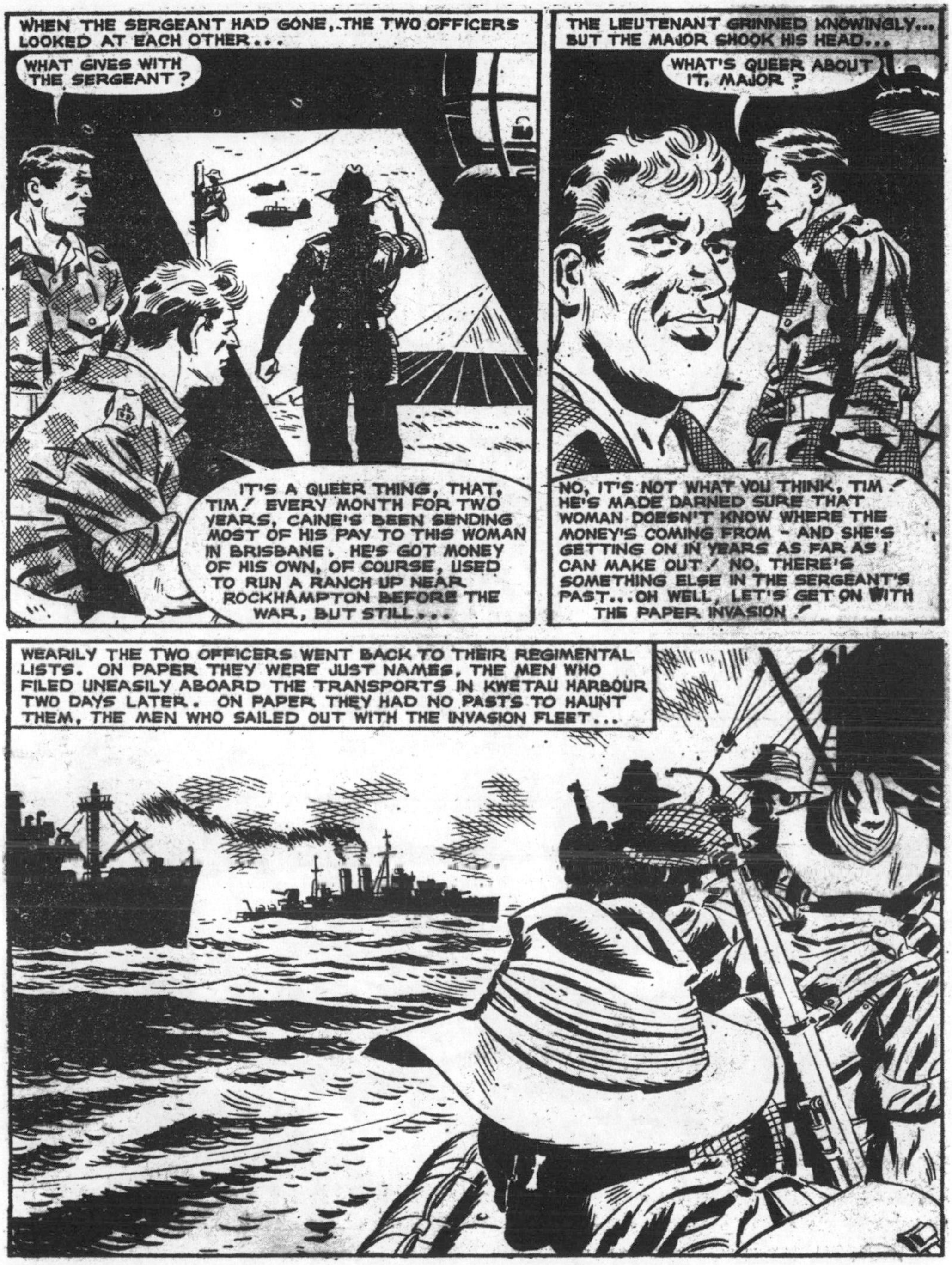
WHEN THE SERGEANT HAD GONE, THE TWO OFFICERS LOOKED AT EACH OTHER...
WHAT GIVES WITH THE SERGEANT?
IT'S A QUEER THING, THAT, TIM! EVERY MONTH FOR TWO YEARS, CAINE'S BEEN SENDING MOST OF HIS PAY TO THIS WOMAN IN BRISBANE. HE'S GOT MONEY OF HIS OWN, OF COURSE, USED TO RUN A RANCH UP NEAR ROCKHAMPTON BEFORE THE WAR, BUT STILL...
THE LIEUTENANT GRINNED KNOWINGLY... BUT THE MAJOR SHOOK HIS HEAD...
WHAT'S QUEER ABOUT IT, MAJOR?
NO, IT'S NOT WHAT YOU THINK, TIM! HE'S MADE DARNED SURE THAT WOMAN DOESN'T KNOW WHERE THE MONEY'S COMING FROM - AND SHE'S GETTING ON IN YEARS AS FAR AS I CAN MAKE OUT! NO, THERE'S SOMETHING ELSE IN THE SERGEANT'S PAST...OH WELL, LET'S GET ON WITH THE PAPER INVASION!
WEARILY THE TWO OFFICERS WENT BACK TO THEIR REGIMENTAL LISTS. ON PAPER THEY WERE JUST NAMES, THE MEN WHO FILED UNEASILY ABOARD THE TRANSPORTS IN KWETAU HARBOUR TWO DAYS LATER. ON PAPER THEY HAD NO PASTS TO HAUNT THEM, THE MEN WHO SAILED OUT WITH THE INVASION FLEET...

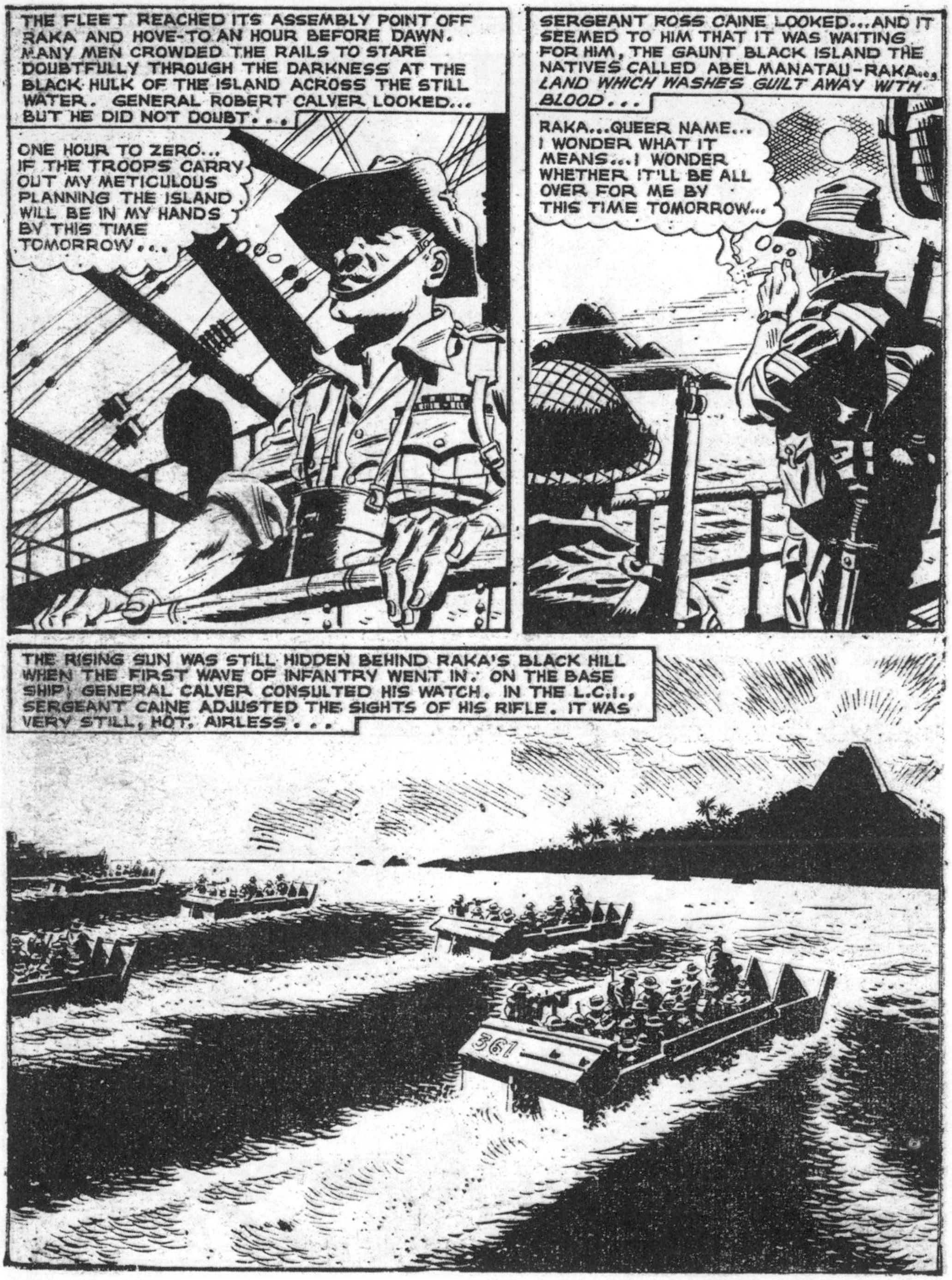
THE FLEET REACHED ITS ASSEMBLY POINT OFF RAKA AND HOVE-TO AN HOUR BEFORE DAWN. MANY MEN CROWDED THE RAILS TO STARE DOUBTFULLY THROUGH THE DARKNESS AT THE BLACK HULK OF THE ISLAND ACROSS THE STILL WATER. GENERAL ROBERT CALVER LOOKED... BUT HE DID NOT DOUBT...
ONE HOUR TO ZERO... IF THE TROOPS CARRY OUT MY METICULOUS PLANNING THE ISLAND WILL BE IN MY HANDS BY THIS TIME TOMORROW...
SERGEANT ROSS CAINE LOOKED... AND IT SEEMED TO HIM THAT IT WAS WAITING FOR HIM, THE GAUNT BLACK ISLAND THE NATIVES CALLED ABELMANATAU-RAKA... *LAND WHICH WASHES GUILT AWAY WITH BLOOD*...
RAKA... QUEER NAME... I WONDER WHAT IT MEANS... I WONDER WHETHER IT'LL BE ALL OVER FOR ME BY THIS TIME TOMORROW...
THE RISING SUN WAS STILL HIDDEN BEHIND RAKA'S BLACK HILL WHEN THE FIRST WAVE OF INFANTRY WENT IN. ON THE BASE SHIP, GENERAL CALVER CONSULTED HIS WATCH. IN THE L.C.I., SERGEANT CAINE ADJUSTED THE SIGHTS OF HIS RIFLE. IT WAS VERY STILL, HOT, AIRLESS...
361

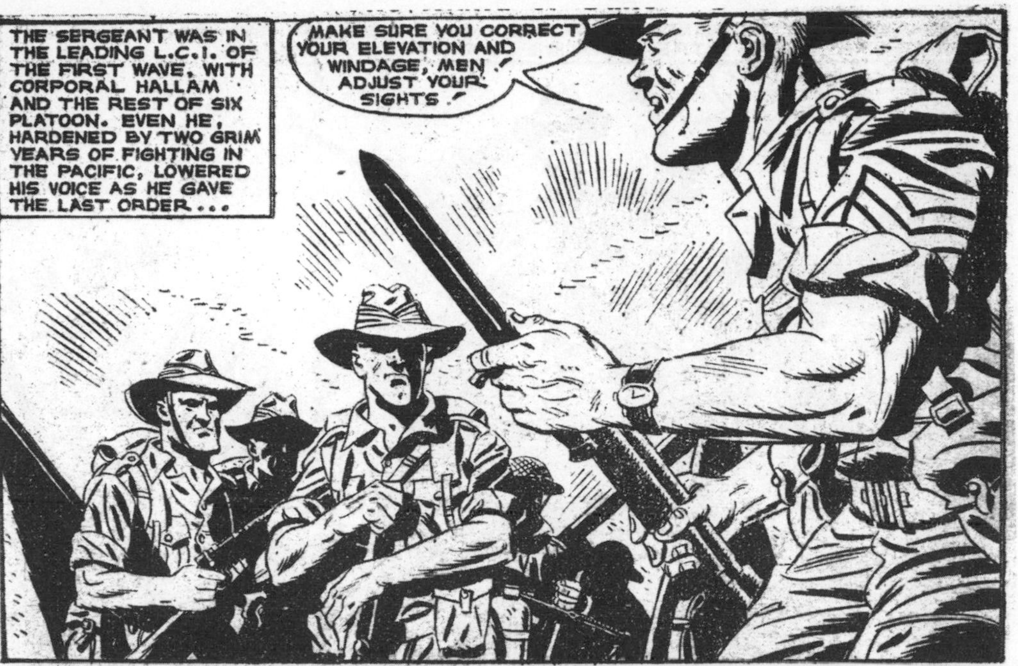
THE SERGEANT WAS IN THE LEADING L.C.I. OF THE FIRST WAVE, WITH CORPORAL HALLAM AND THE REST OF SIX PLATOON. EVEN HE, HARDENED BY TWO GRIM YEARS OF FIGHTING IN THE PACIFIC, LOWERED HIS VOICE AS HE GAVE THE LAST ORDER...
MAKE SURE YOU CORRECT YOUR ELEVATION AND WINDAGE, MEN! ADJUST YOUR SIGHTS!

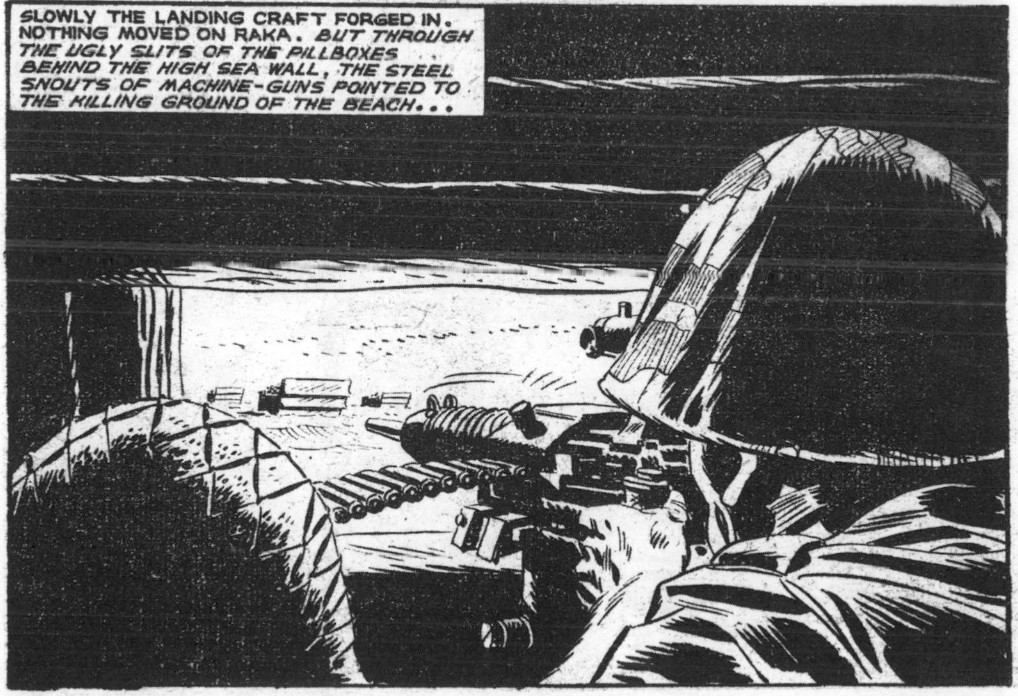
SLOWLY THE LANDING CRAFT FORGED IN. NOTHING MOVED ON RAKA. BUT THROUGH THE UGLY SLITS OF THE PILLBOXES BEHIND THE HIGH SEA WALL, THE STEEL SNOUTS OF MACHINE-GUNS POINTED TO THE KILLING GROUND OF THE BEACH...

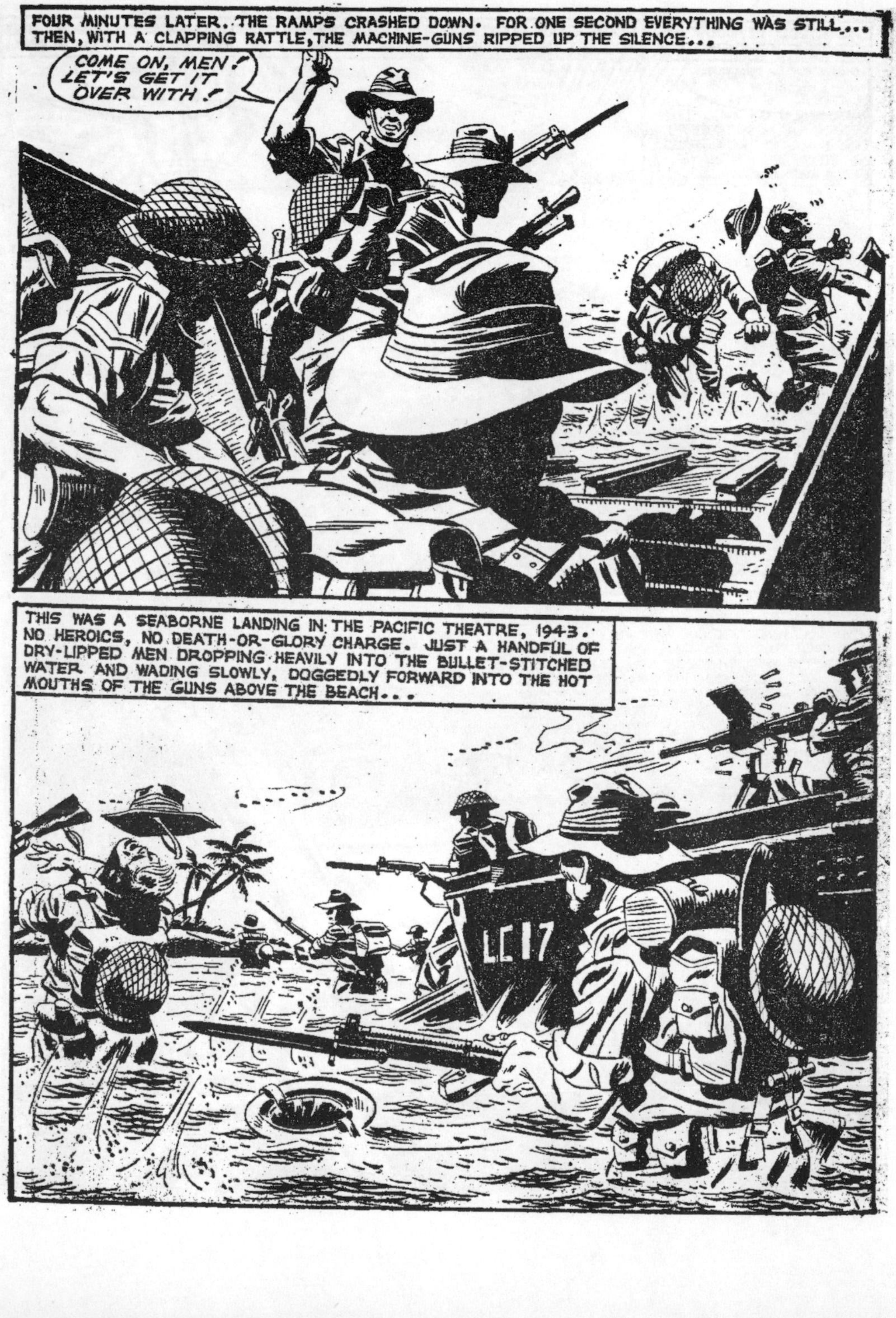
FOUR MINUTES LATER. THE RAMPS CRASHED DOWN. FOR ONE SECOND EVERYTHING WAS STILL... THEN, WITH A CLAPPING RATTLE, THE MACHINE-GUNS RIPPED UP THE SILENCE...
COME ON, MEN! LET'S GET IT OVER WITH!
THIS WAS A SEABORNE LANDING IN THE PACIFIC THEATRE, 1943. NO HEROICS, NO DEATH-OR-GLORY CHARGE. JUST A HANDFUL OF DRY-LIPPED MEN DROPPING HEAVILY INTO THE BULLET-STITCHED WATER AND WADING SLOWLY, DOGGEDLY FORWARD INTO THE HOT MOUTHS OF THE GUNS ABOVE THE BEACH...
LC17

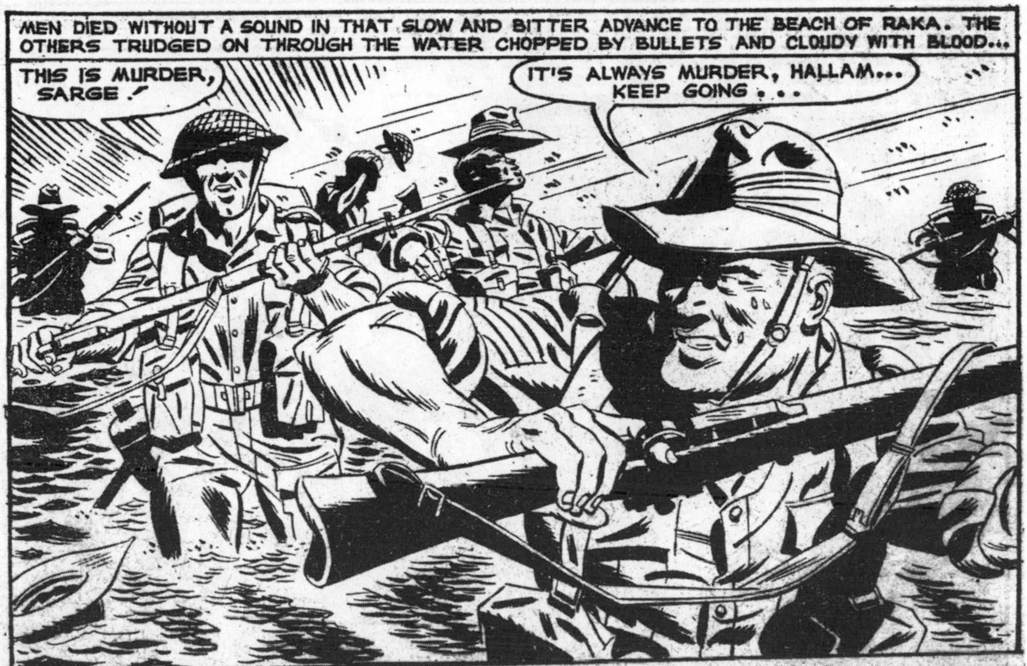
MEN DIED WITHOUT A SOUND IN THAT SLOW AND BITTER ADVANCE TO THE BEACH OF RAKA. THE OTHERS TRUDGED ON THROUGH THE WATER CHOPPED BY BULLETS AND CLOUDY WITH BLOOD...
THIS IS MURDER, SARGE!
IT'S ALWAYS MURDER, HALLAM... KEEP GOING...

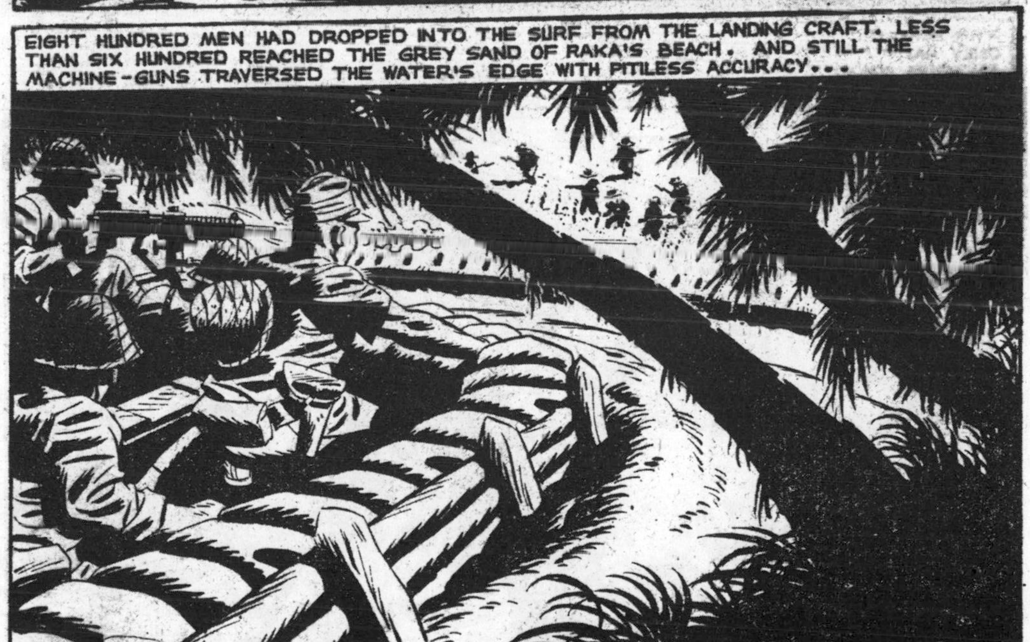
EIGHT HUNDRED MEN HAD DROPPED INTO THE SURF FROM THE LANDING CRAFT. LESS THAN SIX HUNDRED REACHED THE GREY SAND OF RAKA'S BEACH. AND STILL THE MACHINE-GUNS TRAVERSED THE WATER'S EDGE WITH PITILESS ACCURACY...

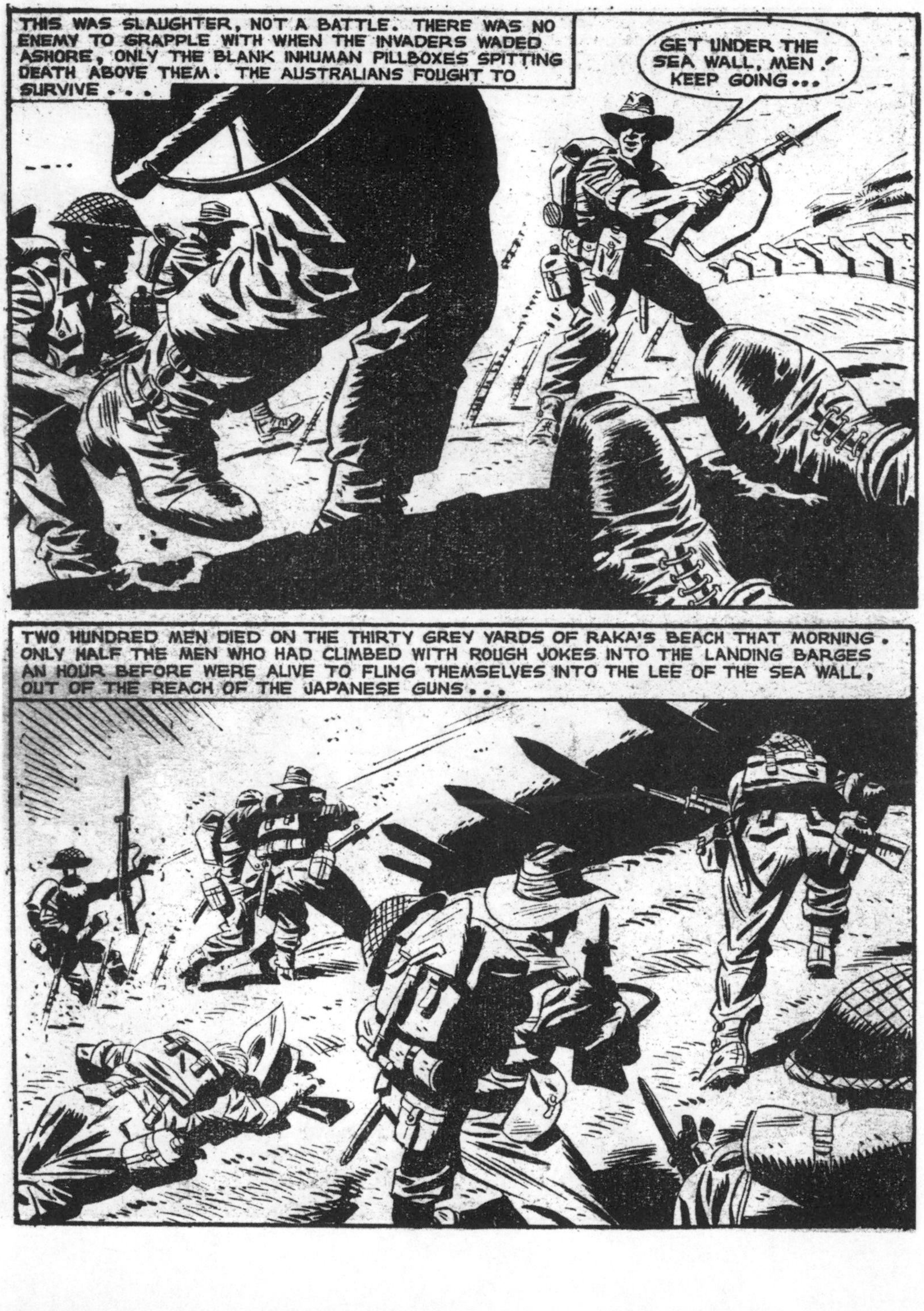
THIS WAS SLAUGHTER, NOT A BATTLE. THERE WAS NO ENEMY TO GRAPPLE WITH WHEN THE INVADERS WADED ASHORE, ONLY THE BLANK INHUMAN PILLBOXES SPITTING DEATH ABOVE THEM. THE AUSTRALIANS FOUGHT TO SURVIVE . . .
GET UNDER THE SEA WALL, MEN. KEEP GOING...
TWO HUNDRED MEN DIED ON THE THIRTY GREY YARDS OF RAKA'S BEACH THAT MORNING. ONLY HALF THE MEN WHO HAD CLIMBED WITH ROUGH JOKES INTO THE LANDING BARGES AN HOUR BEFORE WERE ALIVE TO FLING THEMSELVES INTO THE LEE OF THE SEA WALL, OUT OF THE REACH OF THE JAPANESE GUNS . . .

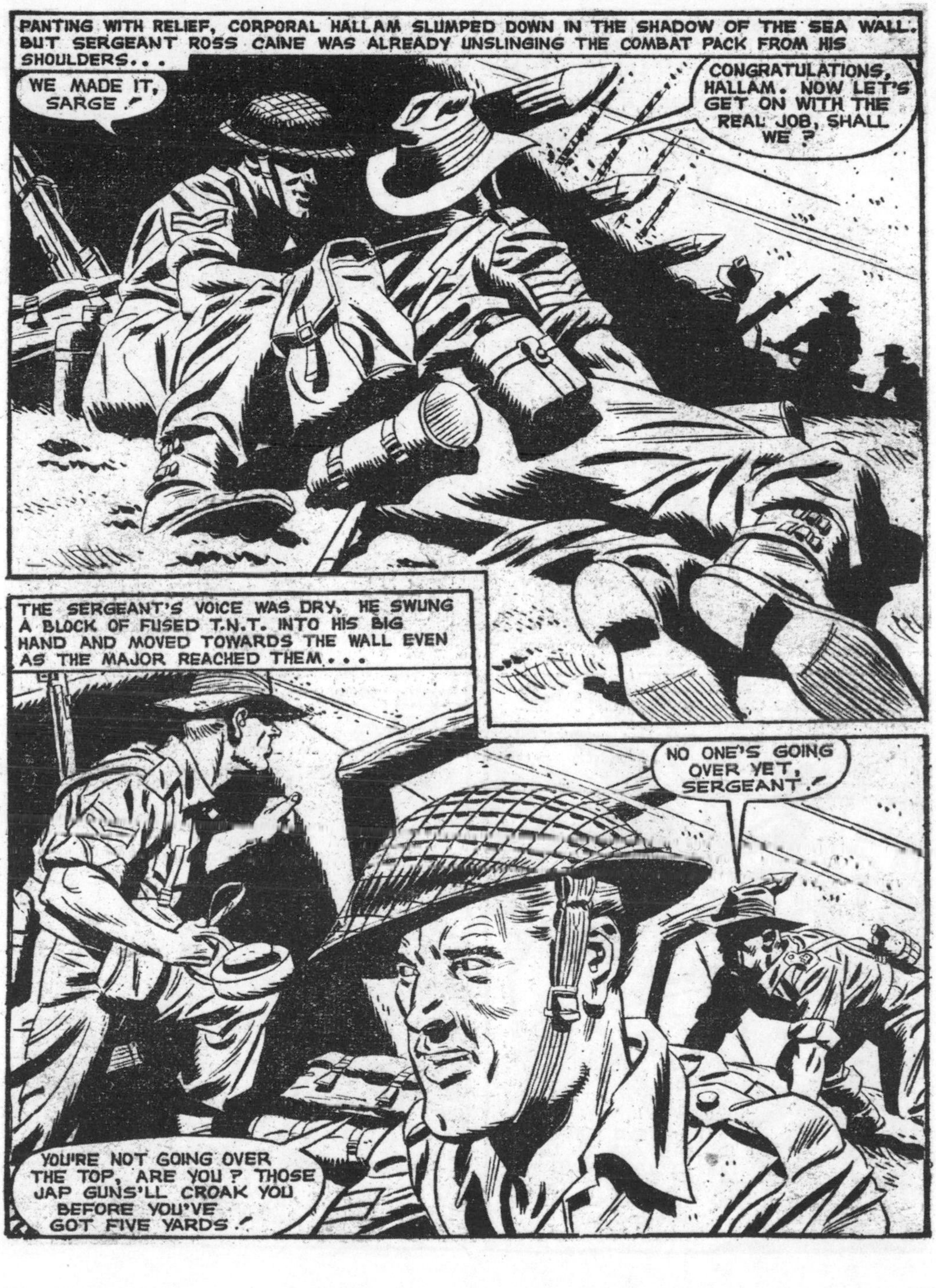
PANTING WITH RELIEF, CORPORAL HALLAM SLUMPED DOWN IN THE SHADOW OF THE SEA WALL. BUT SERGEANT ROSS CAINE WAS ALREADY UNSLINGING THE COMBAT PACK FROM HIS SHOULDERS...
WE MADE IT, SARGE!
CONGRATULATIONS, HALLAM. NOW LET'S GET ON WITH THE REAL JOB, SHALL WE?
THE SERGEANT'S VOICE WAS DRY. HE SWUNG A BLOCK OF FUSED T.N.T. INTO HIS BIG HAND AND MOVED TOWARDS THE WALL EVEN AS THE MAJOR REACHED THEM...
NO ONE'S GOING OVER YET, SERGEANT!
YOU'RE NOT GOING OVER THE TOP, ARE YOU? THOSE JAP GUNS'LL CROAK YOU BEFORE YOU'VE GOT FIVE YARDS!

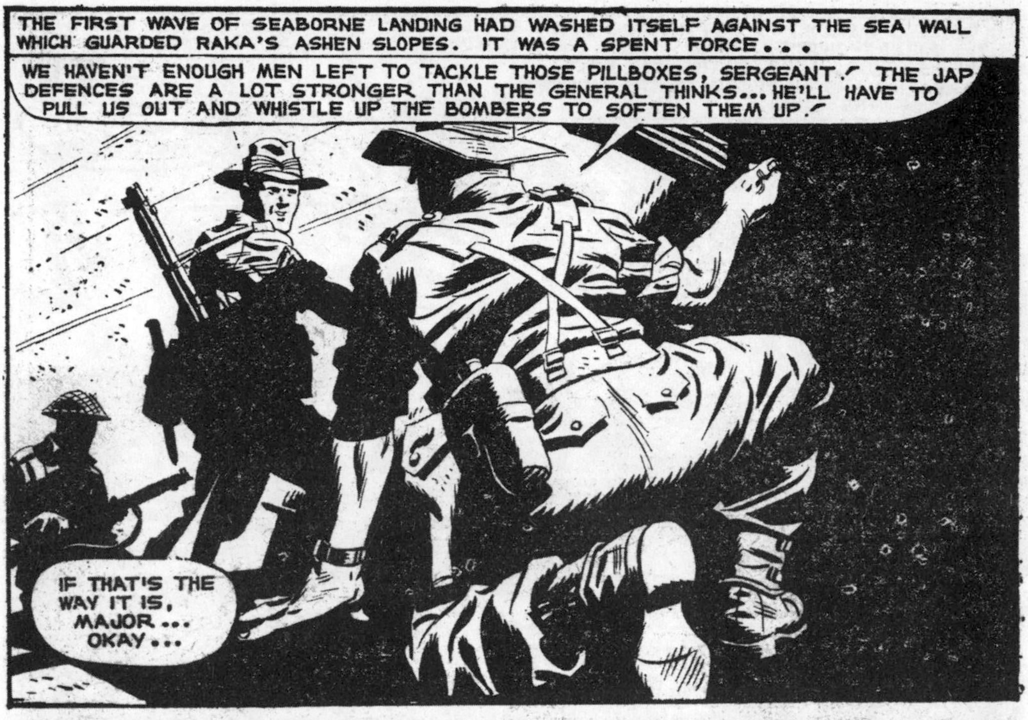
THE FIRST WAVE OF SEABORNE LANDING HAD WASHED ITSELF AGAINST THE SEA WALL WHICH GUARDED RAKA'S ASHEN SLOPES. IT WAS A SPENT FORCE...
WE HAVEN'T ENOUGH MEN LEFT TO TACKLE THOSE PILLBOXES, SERGEANT! THE JAP DEFENCES ARE A LOT STRONGER THAN THE GENERAL THINKS... HE'LL HAVE TO PULL US OUT AND WHISTLE UP THE BOMBERS TO SOFTEN THEM UP!
IF THAT'S THE WAY IT IS, MAJOR... OKAY...

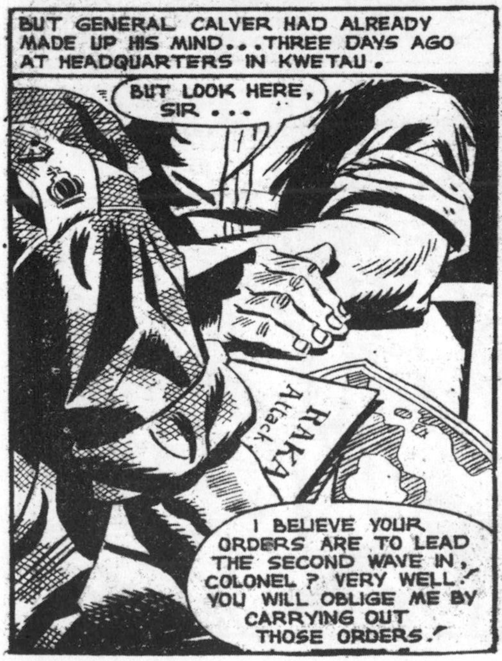
BUT GENERAL CALVER HAD ALREADY MADE UP HIS MIND... THREE DAYS AGO AT HEADQUARTERS IN KWETAU.
BUT LOOK HERE, SIR...
RAKA Attack
I BELIEVE YOUR ORDERS ARE TO LEAD THE SECOND WAVE IN, COLONEL? VERY WELL! YOU WILL OBLIGE ME BY CARRYING OUT THOSE ORDERS!

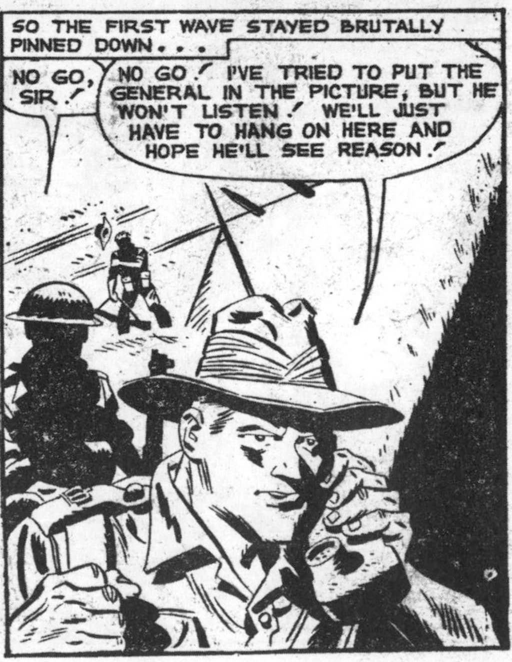
SO THE FIRST WAVE STAYED BRUTALLY PINNED DOWN...
NO GO, SIR!
NO GO! I'VE TRIED TO PUT THE GENERAL IN THE PICTURE, BUT HE WON'T LISTEN! WE'LL JUST HAVE TO HANG ON HERE AND HOPE HE'LL SEE REASON!

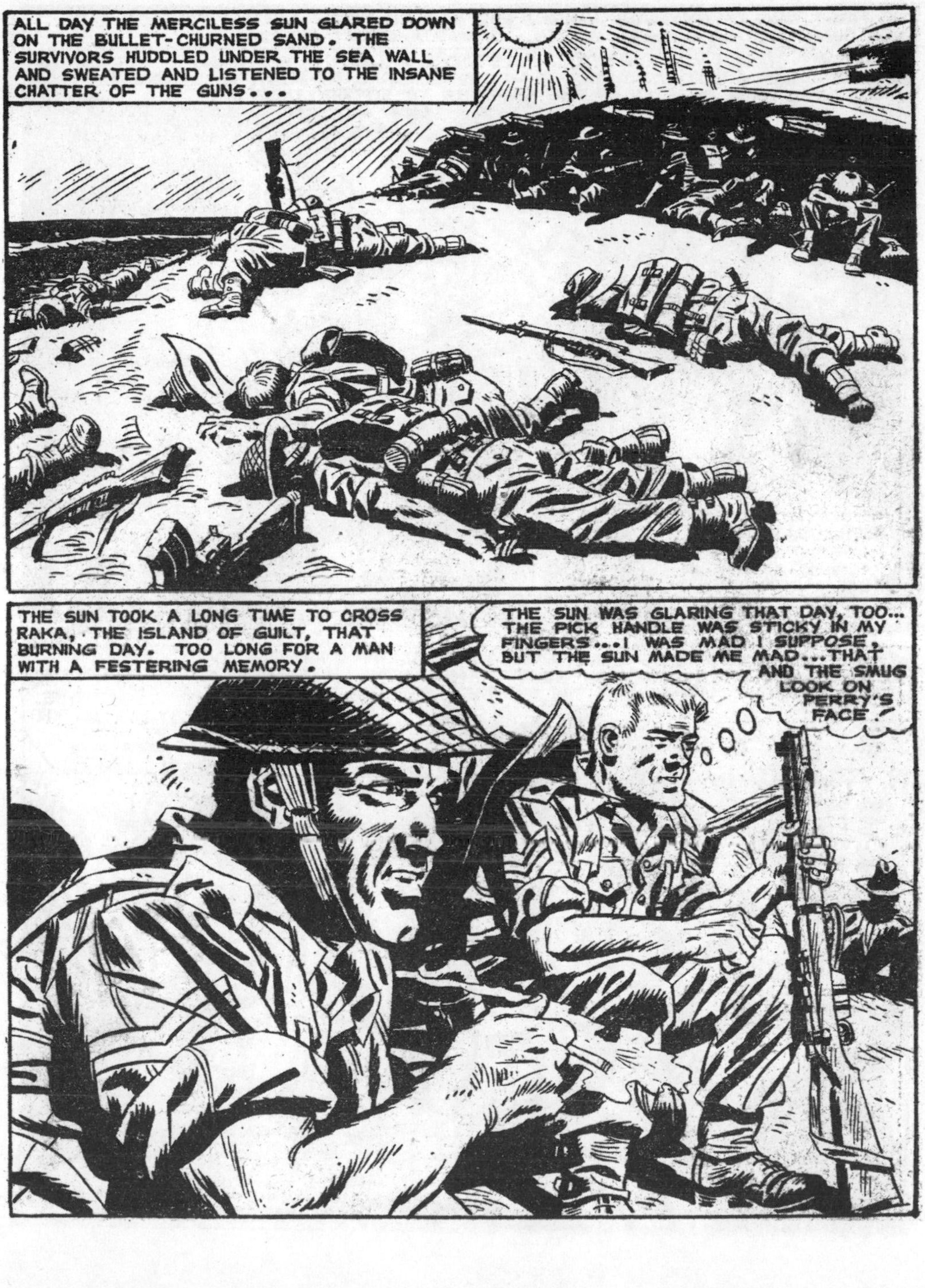
ALL DAY THE MERCILESS SUN GLARED DOWN ON THE BULLET-CHURNED SAND. THE SURVIVORS HUDDLED UNDER THE SEA WALL AND SWEATED AND LISTENED TO THE INSANE CHATTER OF THE GUNS...
THE SUN TOOK A LONG TIME TO CROSS RAKA, THE ISLAND OF GUILT, THAT BURNING DAY. TOO LONG FOR A MAN WITH A FESTERING MEMORY.
THE SUN WAS GLARING THAT DAY, TOO... THE PICK HANDLE WAS STICKY IN MY FINGERS...I WAS MAD I SUPPOSE, BUT THE SUN MADE ME MAD...THAT AND THE SMUG LOOK ON PERRY'S FACE.

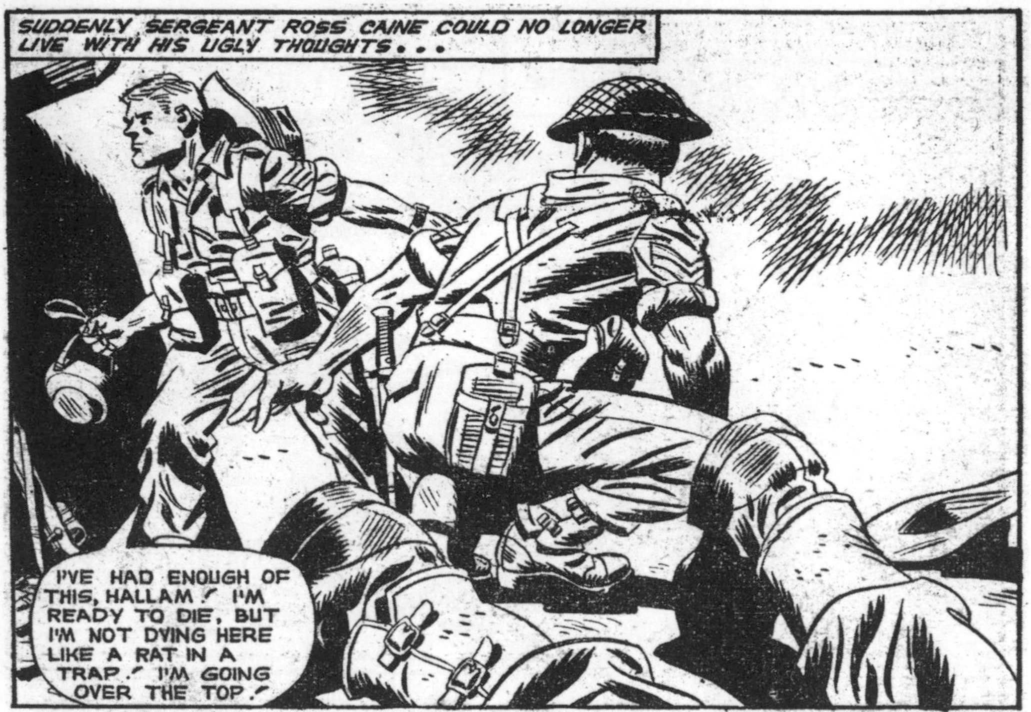
SUDDENLY SERGEANT ROSS CAINE COULD NO LONGER LIVE WITH HIS UGLY THOUGHTS...
I'VE HAD ENOUGH OF THIS, HALLAM! I'M READY TO DIE, BUT I'M NOT DYING HERE LIKE A RAT IN A TRAP! I'M GOING OVER THE TOP!

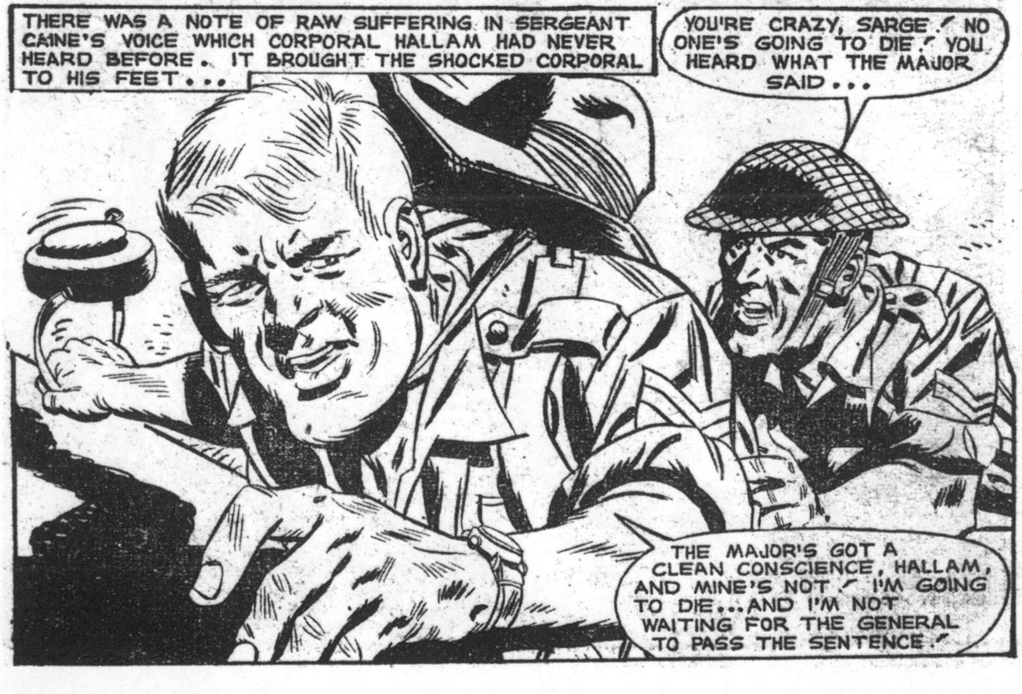
THERE WAS A NOTE OF RAW SUFFERING IN SERGEANT CAINE'S VOICE WHICH CORPORAL HALLAM HAD NEVER HEARD BEFORE. IT BROUGHT THE SHOCKED CORPORAL TO HIS FEET...
YOU'RE CRAZY, SARGE! NO ONE'S GOING TO DIE! YOU HEARD WHAT THE MAJOR SAID...
THE MAJOR'S GOT A CLEAN CONSCIENCE, HALLAM, AND MINE'S NOT! I'M GOING TO DIE...AND I'M NOT WAITING FOR THE GENERAL TO PASS THE SENTENCE!

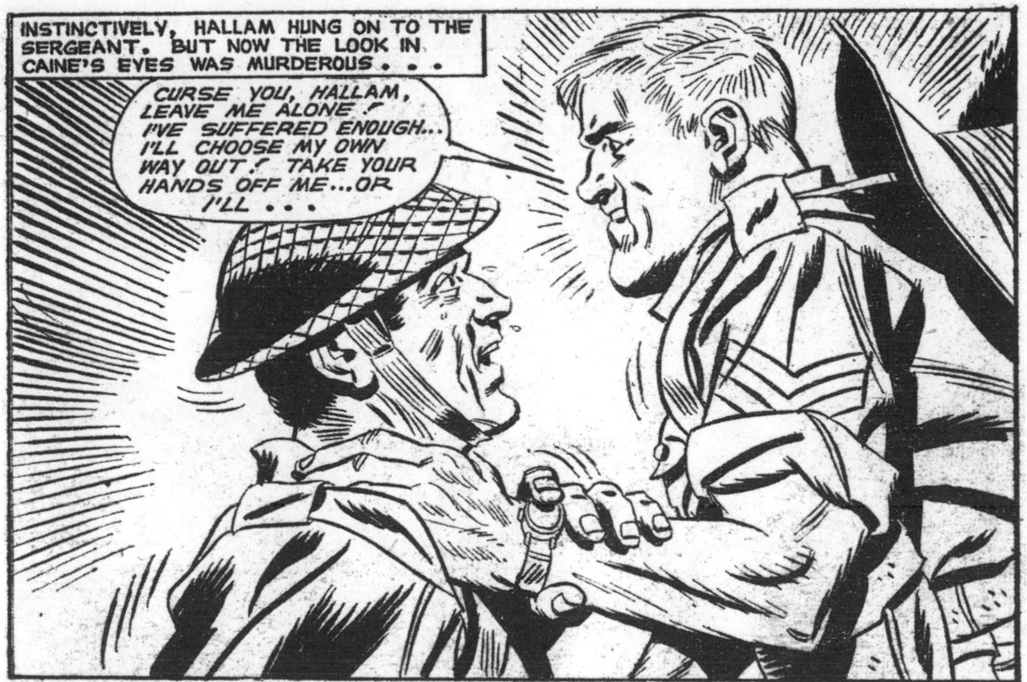
INSTINCTIVELY, HALLAM HUNG ON TO THE SERGEANT. BUT NOW THE LOOK IN CAINE'S EYES WAS MURDEROUS . . .
CURSE YOU, HALLAM, LEAVE ME ALONE! I'VE SUFFERED ENOUGH... I'LL CHOOSE MY OWN WAY OUT! TAKE YOUR HANDS OFF ME...OR I'LL . . .

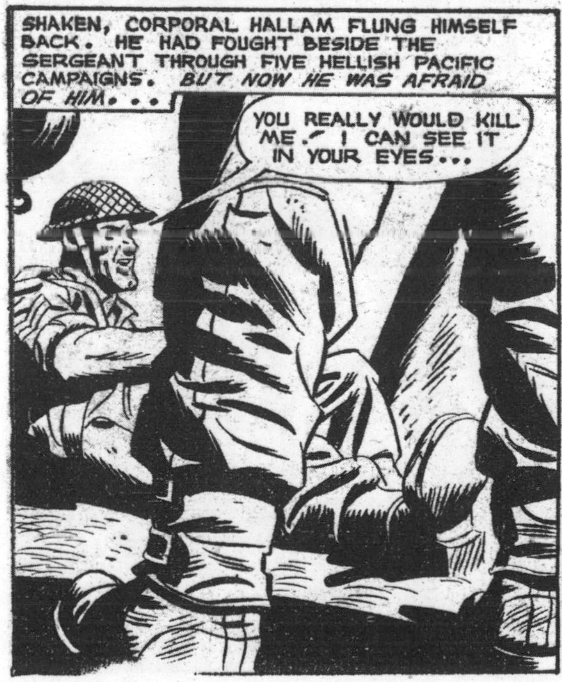
SHAKEN, CORPORAL HALLAM FLUNG HIMSELF BACK. HE HAD FOUGHT BESIDE THE SERGEANT THROUGH FIVE HELLISH PACIFIC CAMPAIGNS. BUT NOW HE WAS AFRAID OF HIM. . .
YOU REALLY WOULD KILL ME! I CAN SEE IT IN YOUR EYES...

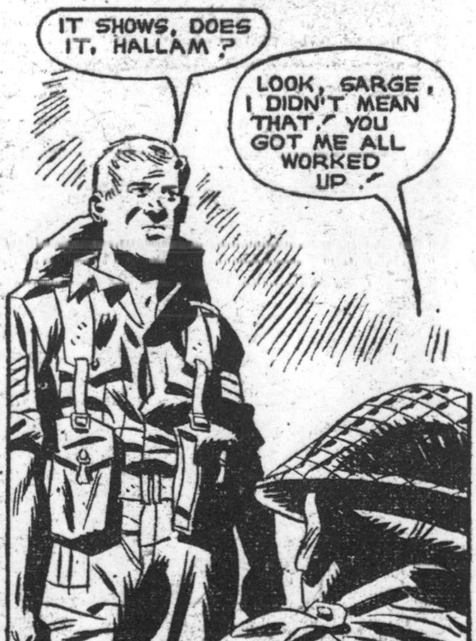
IT SHOWS, DOES IT, HALLAM?
LOOK, SARGE, I DIDN'T MEAN THAT! YOU GOT ME ALL WORKED UP!

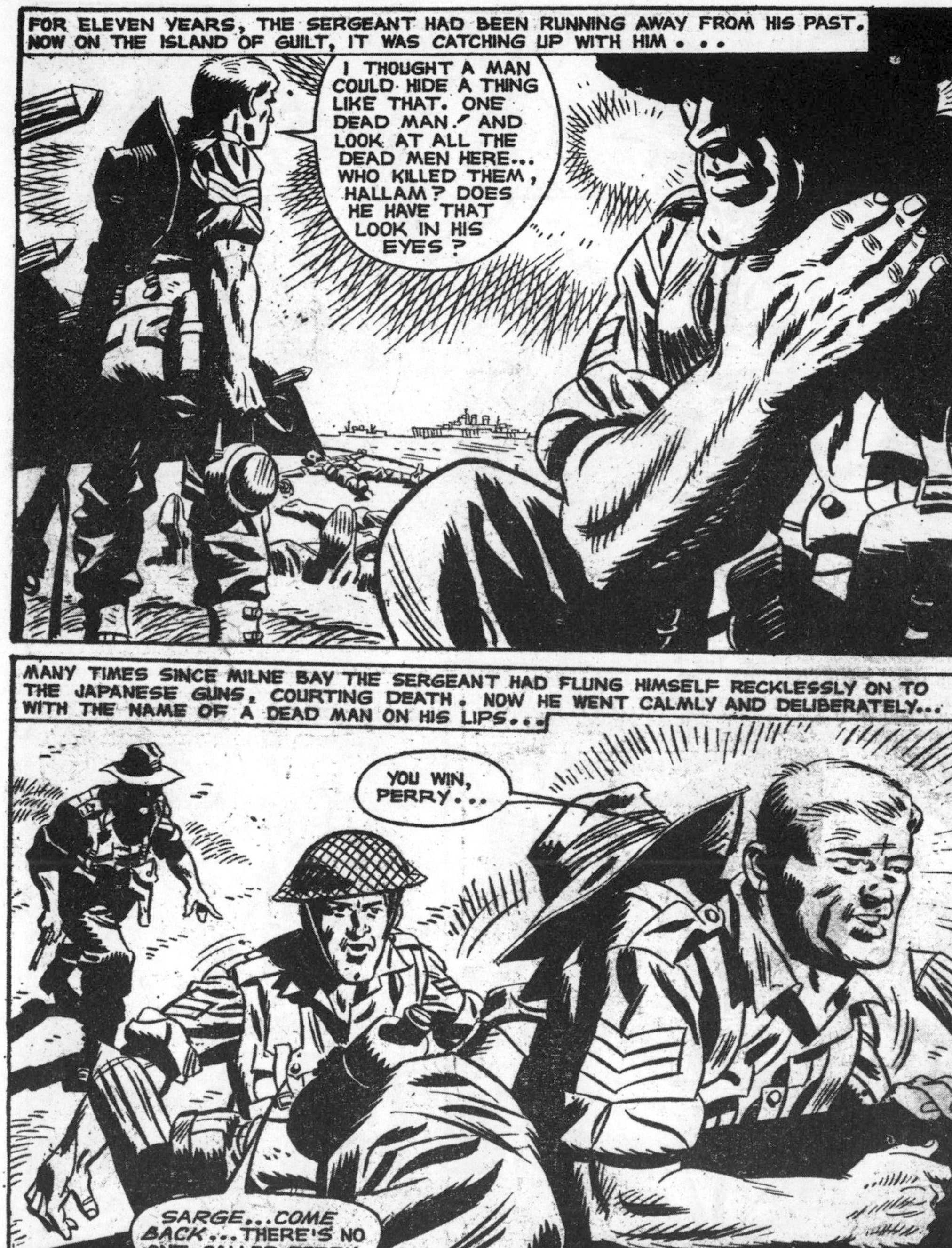
FOR ELEVEN YEARS, THE SERGEANT HAD BEEN RUNNING AWAY FROM HIS PAST. NOW ON THE ISLAND OF GUILT, IT WAS CATCHING UP WITH HIM . . .
I THOUGHT A MAN COULD HIDE A THING LIKE THAT. ONE DEAD MAN! AND LOOK AT ALL THE DEAD MEN HERE... WHO KILLED THEM, HALLAM? DOES HE HAVE THAT LOOK IN HIS EYES?
MANY TIMES SINCE MILNE BAY THE SERGEANT HAD FLUNG HIMSELF RECKLESSLY ON TO THE JAPANESE GUNS, COURTING DEATH. NOW HE WENT CALMLY AND DELIBERATELY... WITH THE NAME OF A DEAD MAN ON HIS LIPS...
YOU WIN, PERRY...
SARGE...COME BACK...THERE'S NO ONE CALLED PERRY HERE...

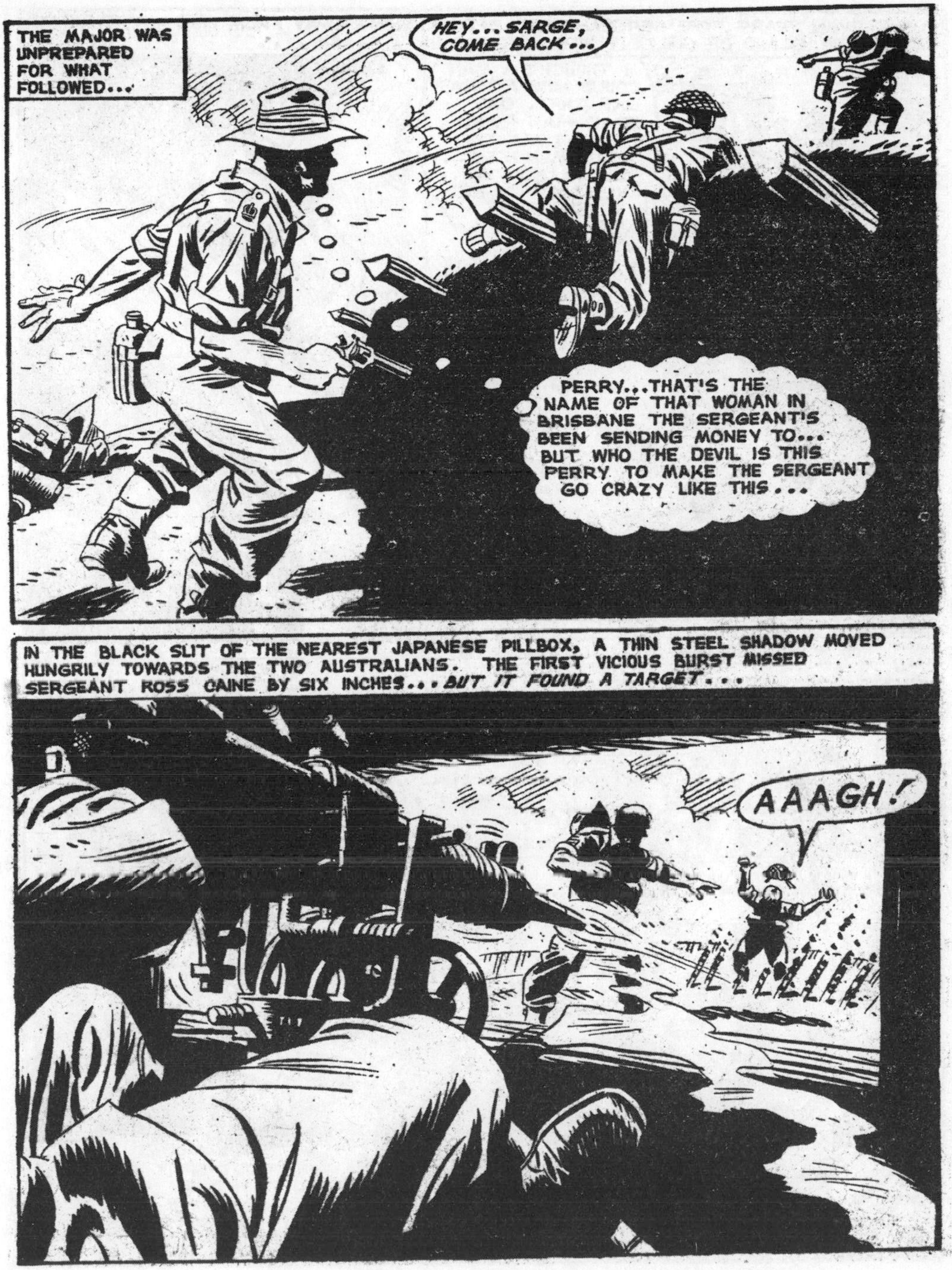
THE MAJOR WAS UNPREPARED FOR WHAT FOLLOWED...
HEY... SARGE, COME BACK...
PERRY...THAT'S THE NAME OF THAT WOMAN IN BRISBANE THE SERGEANT'S BEEN SENDING MONEY TO... BUT WHO THE DEVIL IS THIS PERRY TO MAKE THE SERGEANT GO CRAZY LIKE THIS...
IN THE BLACK SLIT OF THE NEAREST JAPANESE PILLBOX, A THIN STEEL SHADOW MOVED HUNGRILY TOWARDS THE TWO AUSTRALIANS. THE FIRST VICIOUS BURST MISSED SERGEANT ROSS CAINE BY SIX INCHES... BUT IT FOUND A TARGET...
AAAGH!

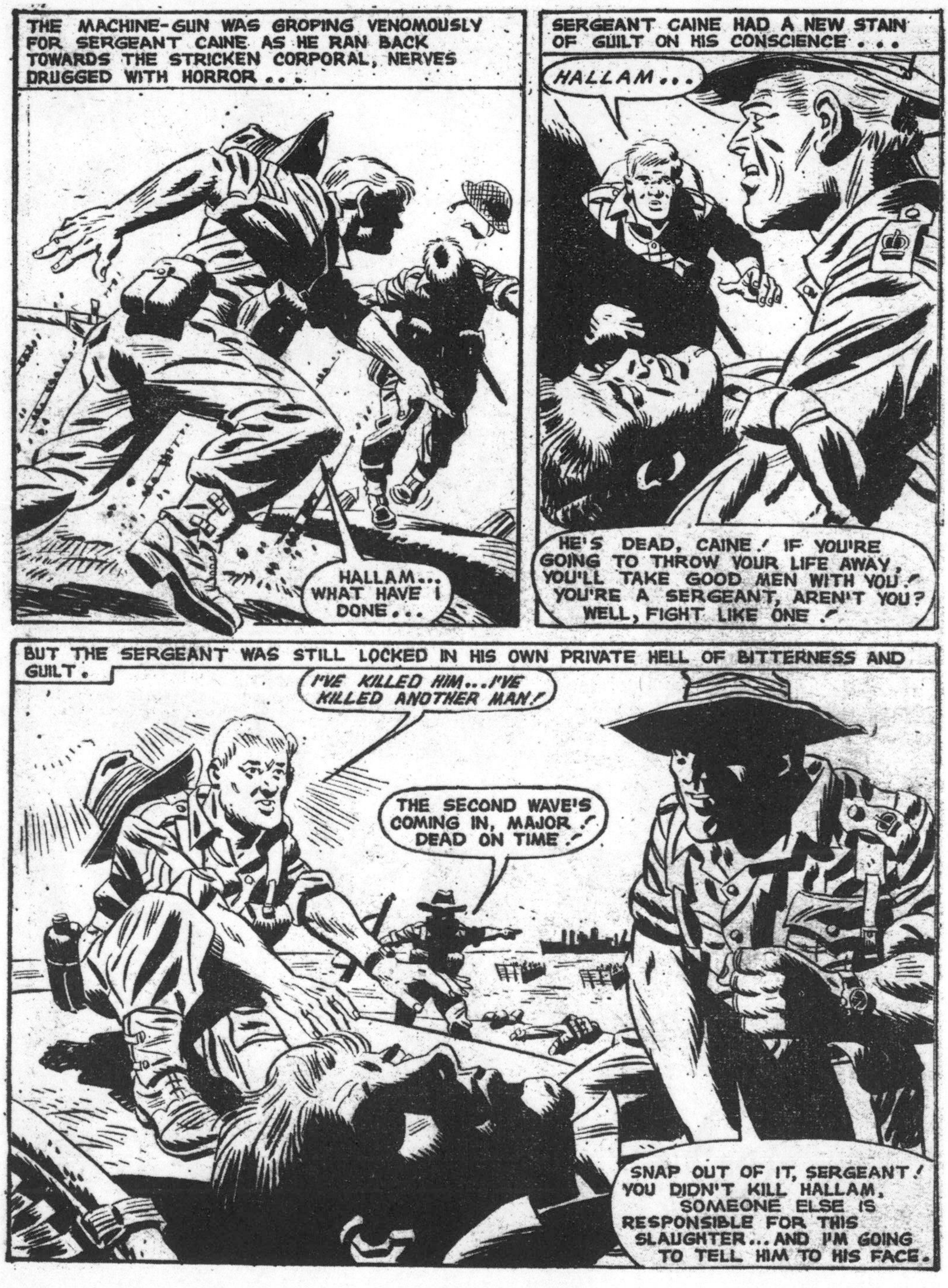
THE MACHINE-GUN WAS GROPING VENOMOUSLY FOR SERGEANT CAINE AS HE RAN BACK TOWARDS THE STRICKEN CORPORAL, NERVES DRUGGED WITH HORROR . . .
HALLAM... WHAT HAVE I DONE...
SERGEANT CAINE HAD A NEW STAIN OF GUILT ON HIS CONSCIENCE . . .
HALLAM...
HE'S DEAD, CAINE! IF YOU'RE GOING TO THROW YOUR LIFE AWAY, YOU'LL TAKE GOOD MEN WITH YOU! YOU'RE A SERGEANT, AREN'T YOU? WELL, FIGHT LIKE ONE!
BUT THE SERGEANT WAS STILL LOCKED IN HIS OWN PRIVATE HELL OF BITTERNESS AND GUILT.
I'VE KILLED HIM...I'VE KILLED ANOTHER MAN!
THE SECOND WAVE'S COMING IN, MAJOR! DEAD ON TIME!
SNAP OUT OF IT, SERGEANT! YOU DIDN'T KILL HALLAM, SOMEONE ELSE IS RESPONSIBLE FOR THIS SLAUGHTER... AND I'M GOING TO TELL HIM TO HIS FACE.

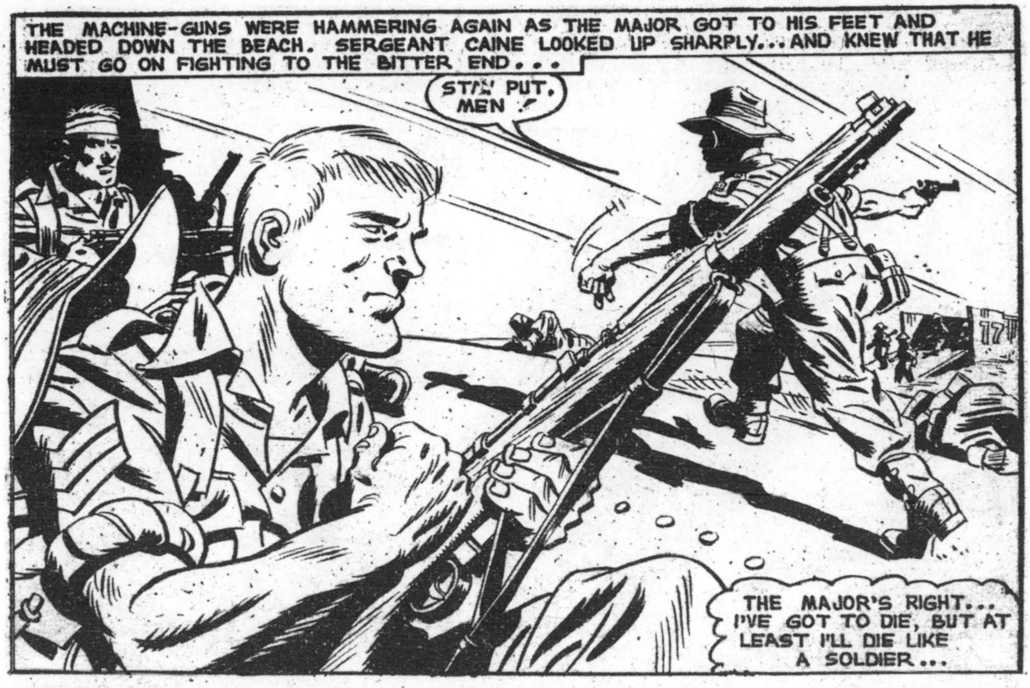
THE MACHINE-GUNS WERE HAMMERING AGAIN AS THE MAJOR GOT TO HIS FEET AND HEADED DOWN THE BEACH. SERGEANT CAINE LOOKED UP SHARPLY... AND KNEW THAT HE MUST GO ON FIGHTING TO THE BITTER END...
STAY PUT, MEN !
THE MAJOR'S RIGHT... I'VE GOT TO DIE, BUT AT LEAST I'LL DIE LIKE A SOLDIER...

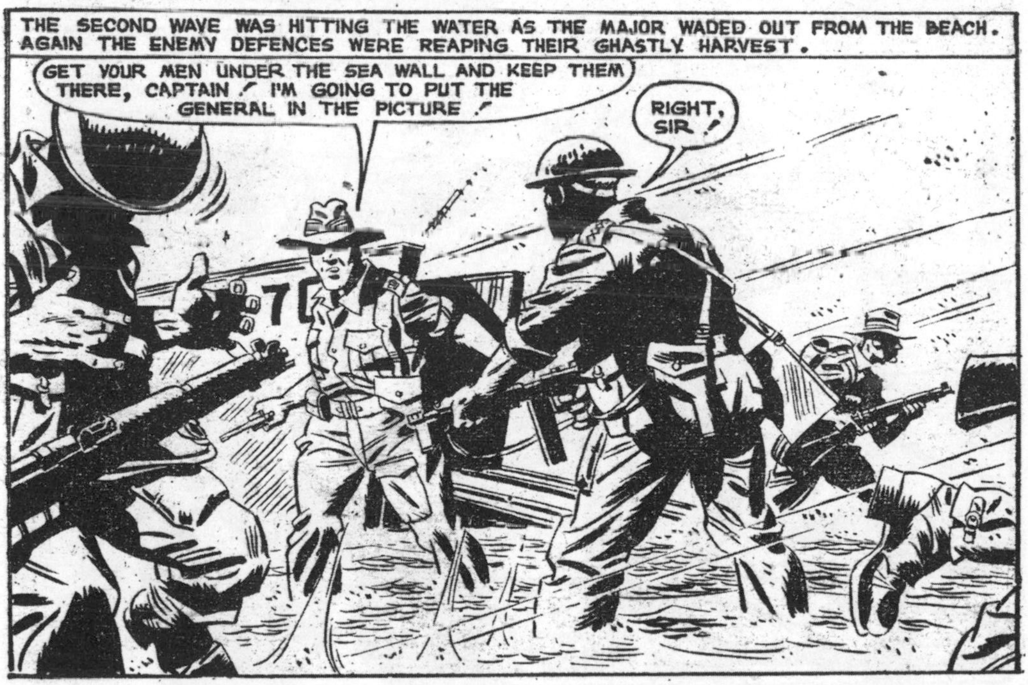
THE SECOND WAVE WAS HITTING THE WATER AS THE MAJOR WADED OUT FROM THE BEACH. AGAIN THE ENEMY DEFENCES WERE REAPING THEIR GHASTLY HARVEST.
GET YOUR MEN UNDER THE SEA WALL AND KEEP THEM THERE, CAPTAIN ! I'M GOING TO PUT THE GENERAL IN THE PICTURE !
RIGHT, SIR !

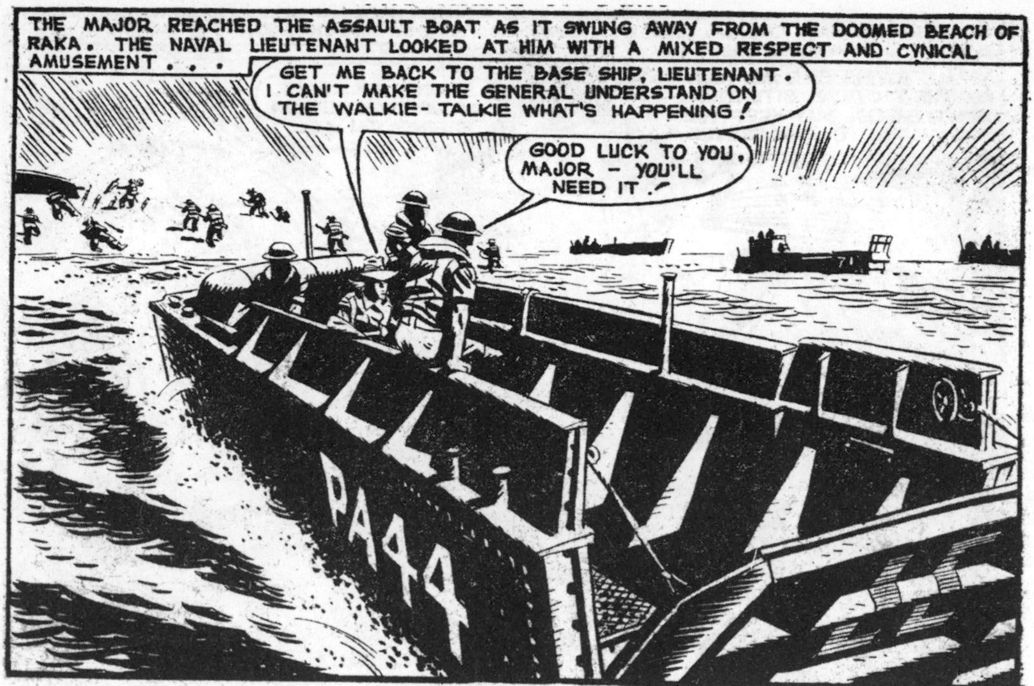
THE MAJOR REACHED THE ASSAULT BOAT AS IT SWUNG AWAY FROM THE DOOMED BEACH OF RAKA. THE NAVAL LIEUTENANT LOOKED AT HIM WITH A MIXED RESPECT AND CYNICAL AMUSEMENT . . .
GET ME BACK TO THE BASE SHIP, LIEUTENANT. I CAN'T MAKE THE GENERAL UNDERSTAND ON THE WALKIE-TALKIE WHAT'S HAPPENING!
GOOD LUCK TO YOU, MAJOR - YOU'LL NEED IT.
PA44

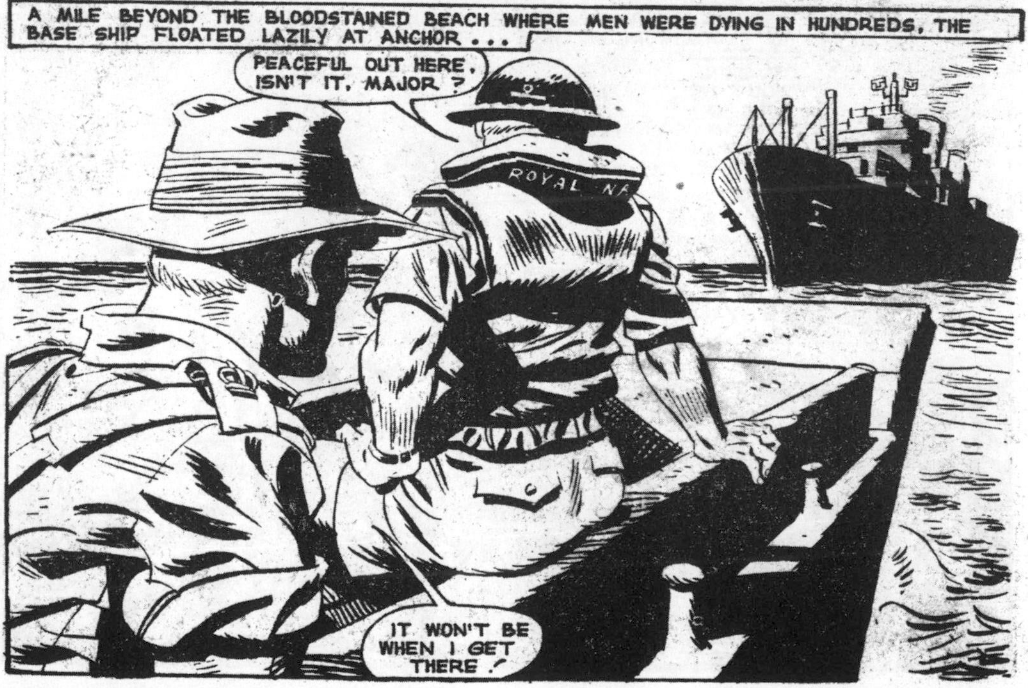
A MILE BEYOND THE BLOODSTAINED BEACH WHERE MEN WERE DYING IN HUNDREDS, THE BASE SHIP FLOATED LAZILY AT ANCHOR ...
PEACEFUL OUT HERE, ISN'T IT, MAJOR?
IT WON'T BE WHEN I GET THERE!

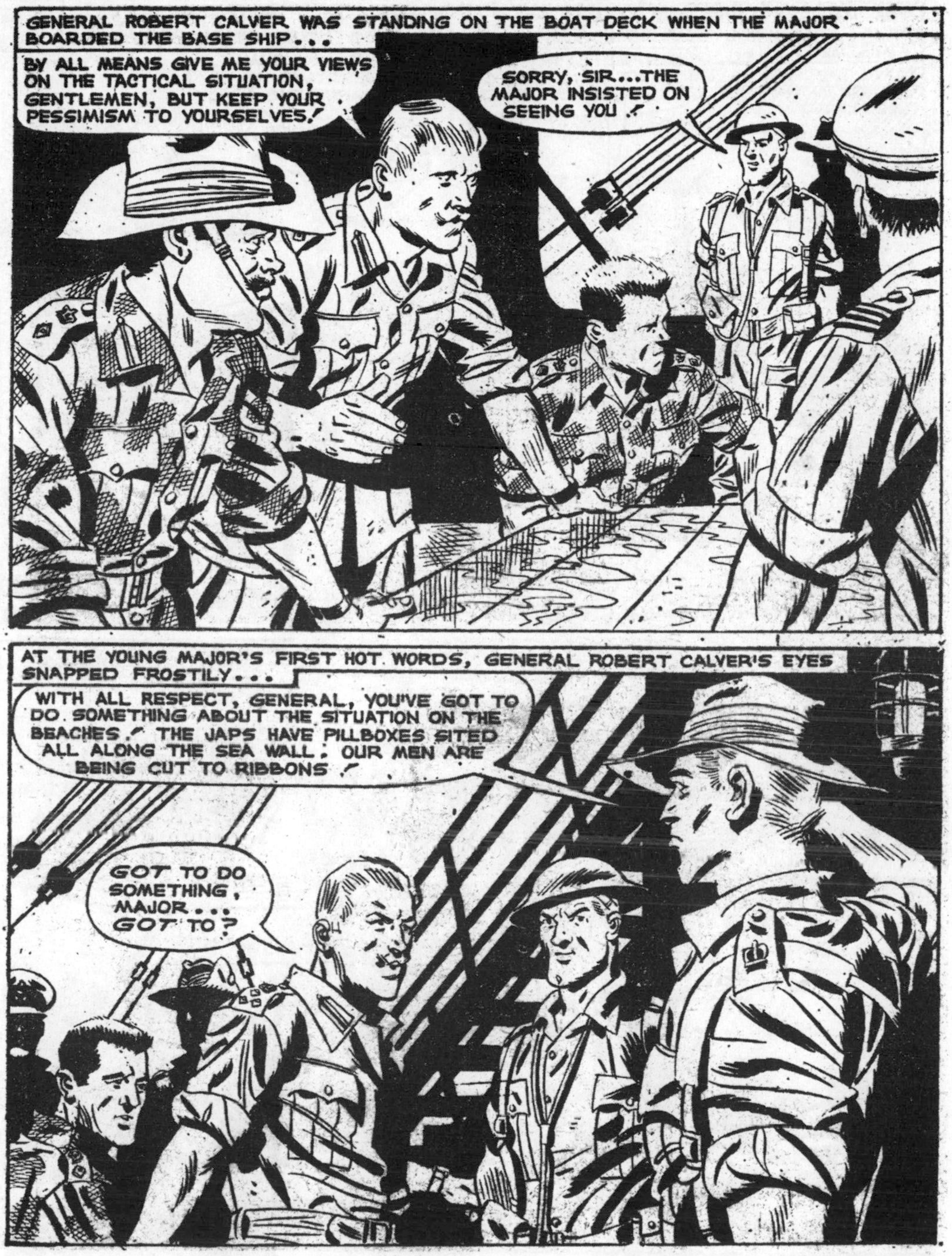
GENERAL ROBERT CALVER WAS STANDING ON THE BOAT DECK WHEN THE MAJOR BOARDED THE BASE SHIP...
BY ALL MEANS GIVE ME YOUR VIEWS ON THE TACTICAL SITUATION, GENTLEMEN, BUT KEEP YOUR PESSIMISM TO YOURSELVES!
SORRY, SIR...THE MAJOR INSISTED ON SEEING YOU!
AT THE YOUNG MAJOR'S FIRST HOT WORDS, GENERAL ROBERT CALVER'S EYES SNAPPED FROSTILY...
WITH ALL RESPECT, GENERAL, YOU'VE GOT TO DO SOMETHING ABOUT THE SITUATION ON THE BEACHES! THE JAPS HAVE PILLBOXES SITED ALL ALONG THE SEA WALL. OUR MEN ARE BEING CUT TO RIBBONS!
GOT TO DO SOMETHING, MAJOR... GOT TO?

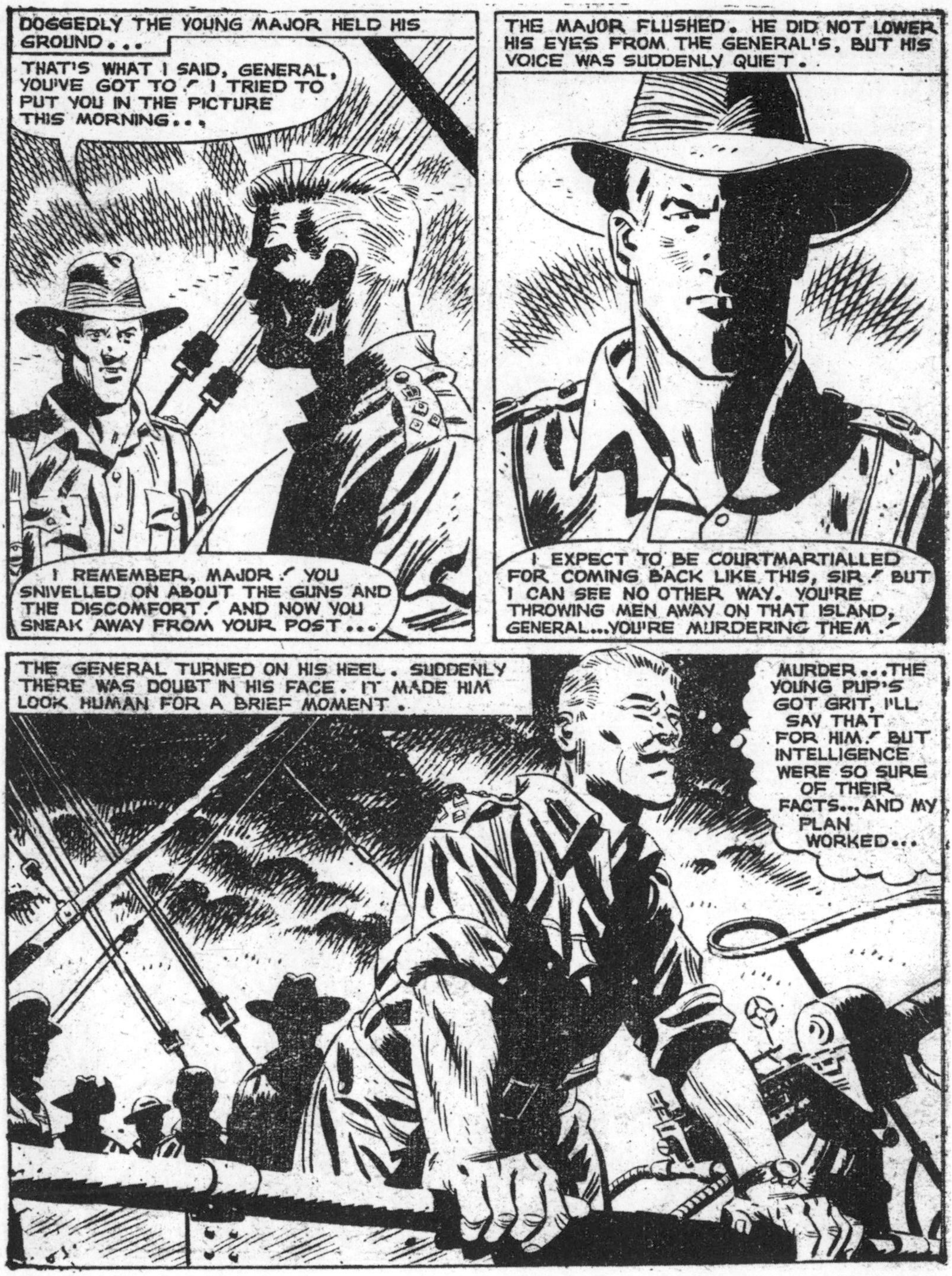
DOGGEDLY THE YOUNG MAJOR HELD HIS GROUND...
THAT'S WHAT I SAID, GENERAL, YOU'VE GOT TO! I TRIED TO PUT YOU IN THE PICTURE THIS MORNING...
I REMEMBER, MAJOR! YOU SNIVELLED ON ABOUT THE GUNS AND THE DISCOMFORT! AND NOW YOU SNEAK AWAY FROM YOUR POST...
THE MAJOR FLUSHED. HE DID NOT LOWER HIS EYES FROM THE GENERAL'S, BUT HIS VOICE WAS SUDDENLY QUIET..
I EXPECT TO BE COURTMARTIALLED FOR COMING BACK LIKE THIS, SIR! BUT I CAN SEE NO OTHER WAY. YOU'RE THROWING MEN AWAY ON THAT ISLAND, GENERAL...YOU'RE MURDERING THEM!
THE GENERAL TURNED ON HIS HEEL. SUDDENLY THERE WAS DOUBT IN HIS FACE. IT MADE HIM LOOK HUMAN FOR A BRIEF MOMENT.
MURDER...THE YOUNG PUP'S GOT GRIT, I'LL SAY THAT FOR HIM! BUT INTELLIGENCE WERE SO SURE OF THEIR FACTS...AND MY PLAN WORKED...

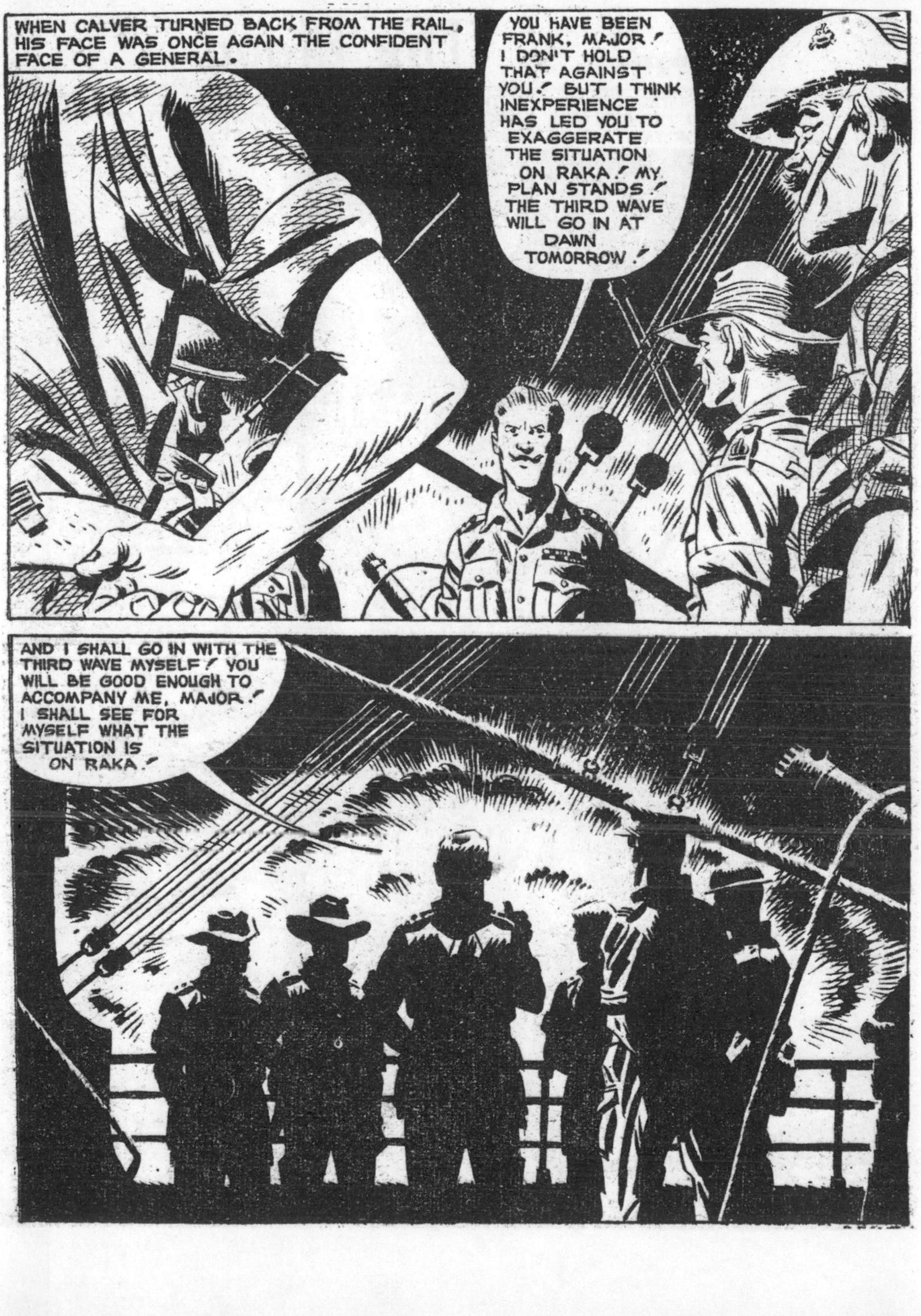
WHEN CALVER TURNED BACK FROM THE RAIL, HIS FACE WAS ONCE AGAIN THE CONFIDENT FACE OF A GENERAL.
YOU HAVE BEEN FRANK, MAJOR! I DON'T HOLD THAT AGAINST YOU! BUT I THINK INEXPERIENCE HAS LED YOU TO EXAGGERATE THE SITUATION ON RAKA! MY PLAN STANDS! THE THIRD WAVE WILL GO IN AT DAWN TOMORROW!
AND I SHALL GO IN WITH THE THIRD WAVE MYSELF! YOU WILL BE GOOD ENOUGH TO ACCOMPANY ME, MAJOR! I SHALL SEE FOR MYSELF WHAT THE SITUATION IS ON RAKA!

Chapter 3. The Blood

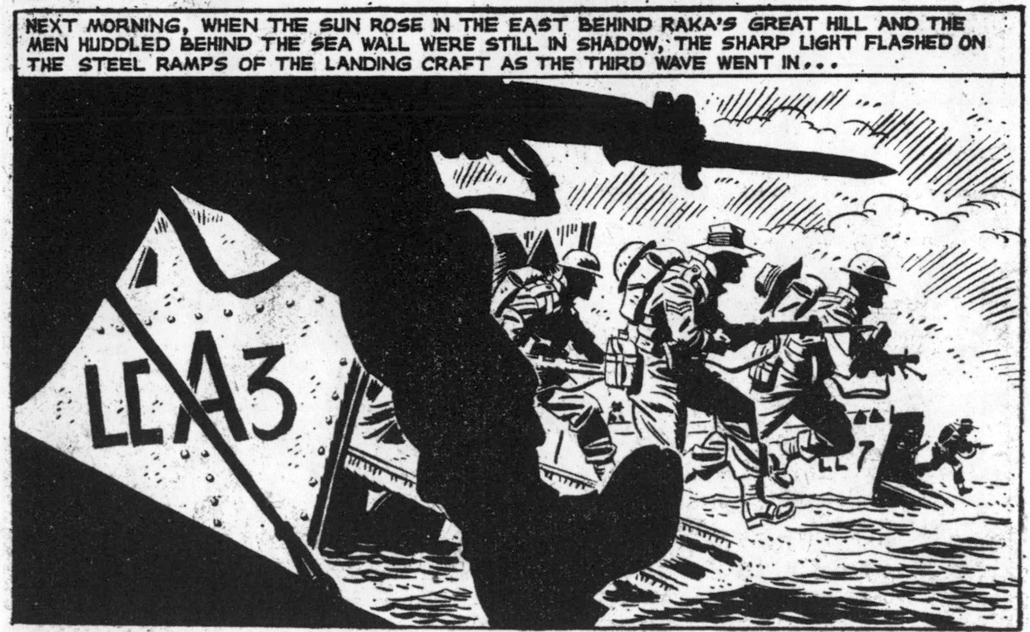
NEXT MORNING, WHEN THE SUN ROSE IN THE EAST BEHIND RAKA'S GREAT HILL AND THE MEN HUDDLED BEHIND THE SEA WALL WERE STILL IN SHADOW, THE SHARP LIGHT FLASHED ON THE STEEL RAMPS OF THE LANDING CRAFT AS THE THIRD WAVE WENT IN...
LCA3

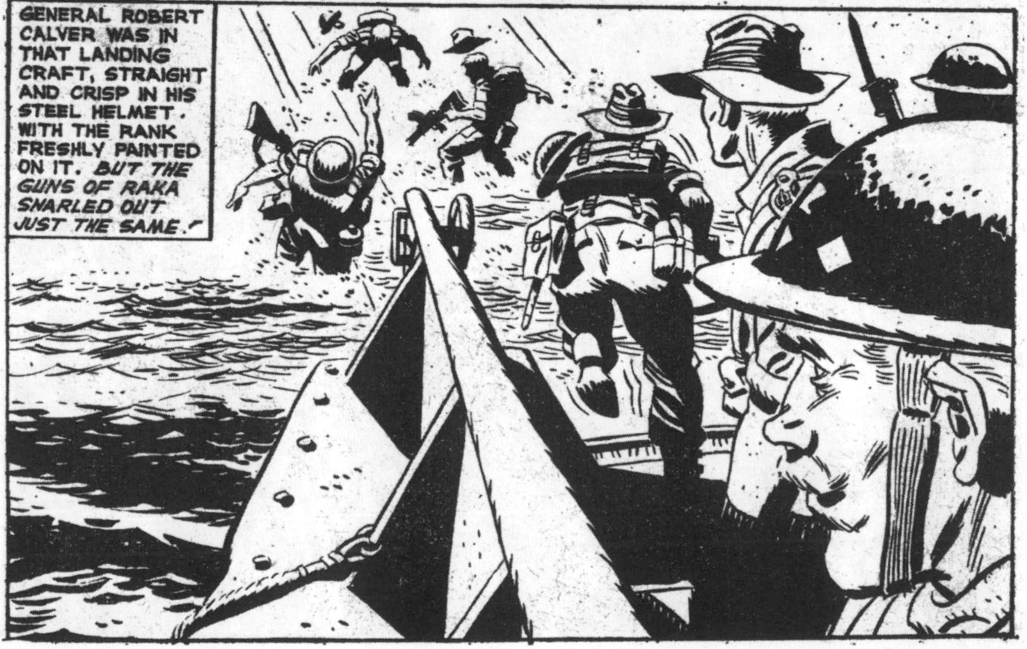
GENERAL ROBERT CALVER WAS IN THAT LANDING CRAFT, STRAIGHT AND CRISP IN HIS STEEL HELMET. WITH THE RANK FRESHLY PAINTED ON IT. *BUT THE GUNS OF RAKA SNARLED OUT JUST THE SAME!*

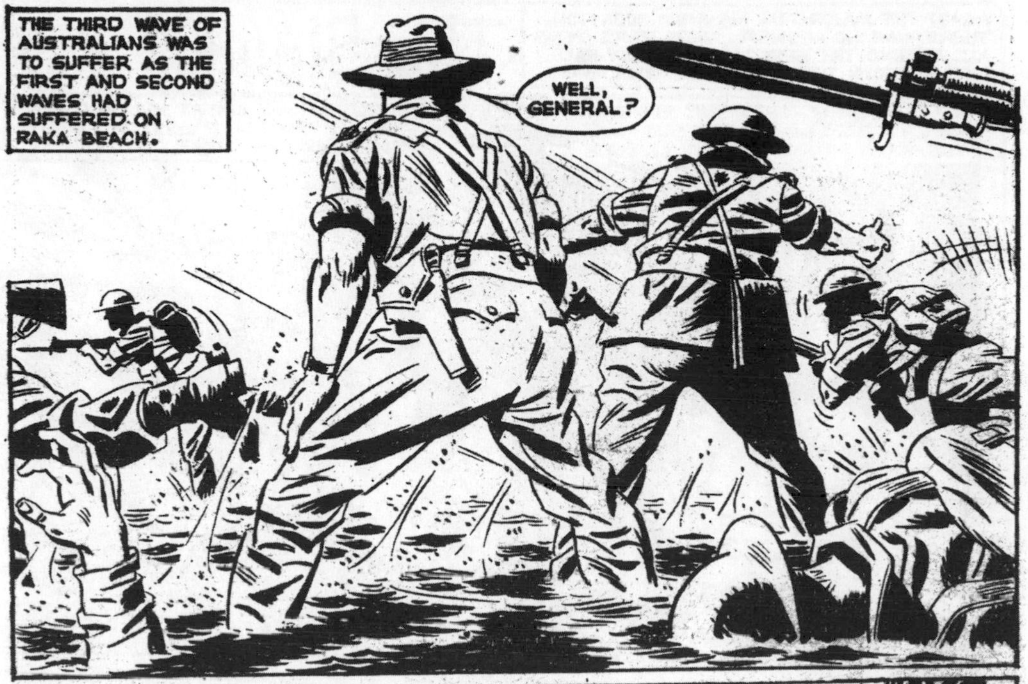
THE THIRD WAVE OF AUSTRALIANS WAS TO SUFFER AS THE FIRST AND SECOND WAVES HAD SUFFERED ON RAKA BEACH.
WELL, GENERAL?

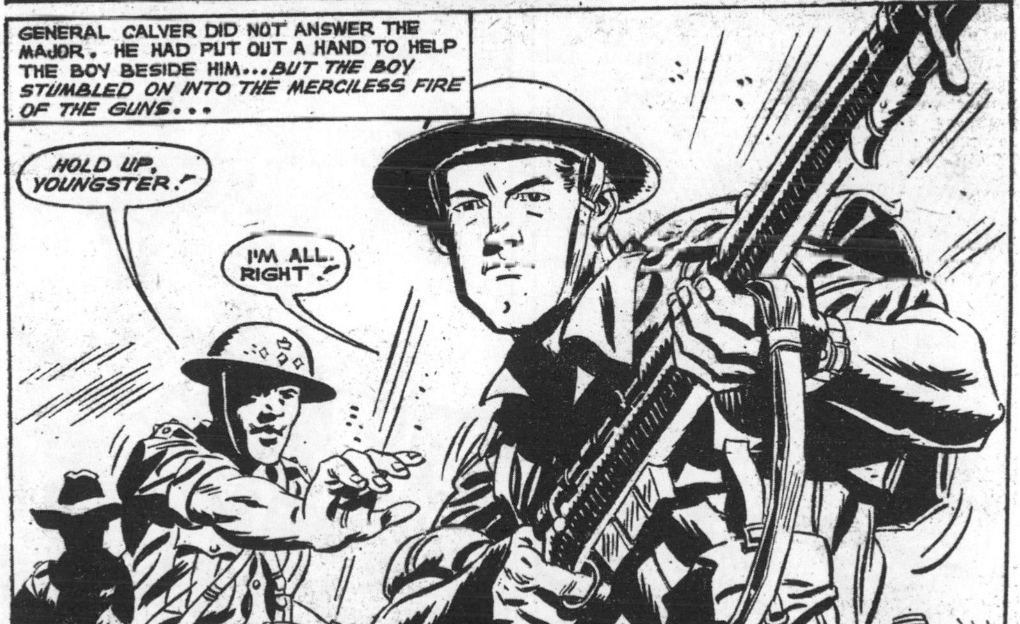
GENERAL CALVER DID NOT ANSWER THE MAJOR. HE HAD PUT OUT A HAND TO HELP THE BOY BESIDE HIM...BUT THE BOY STUMBLED ON INTO THE MERCILESS FIRE OF THE GUNS...
HOLD UP, YOUNGSTER!
I'M ALL RIGHT!

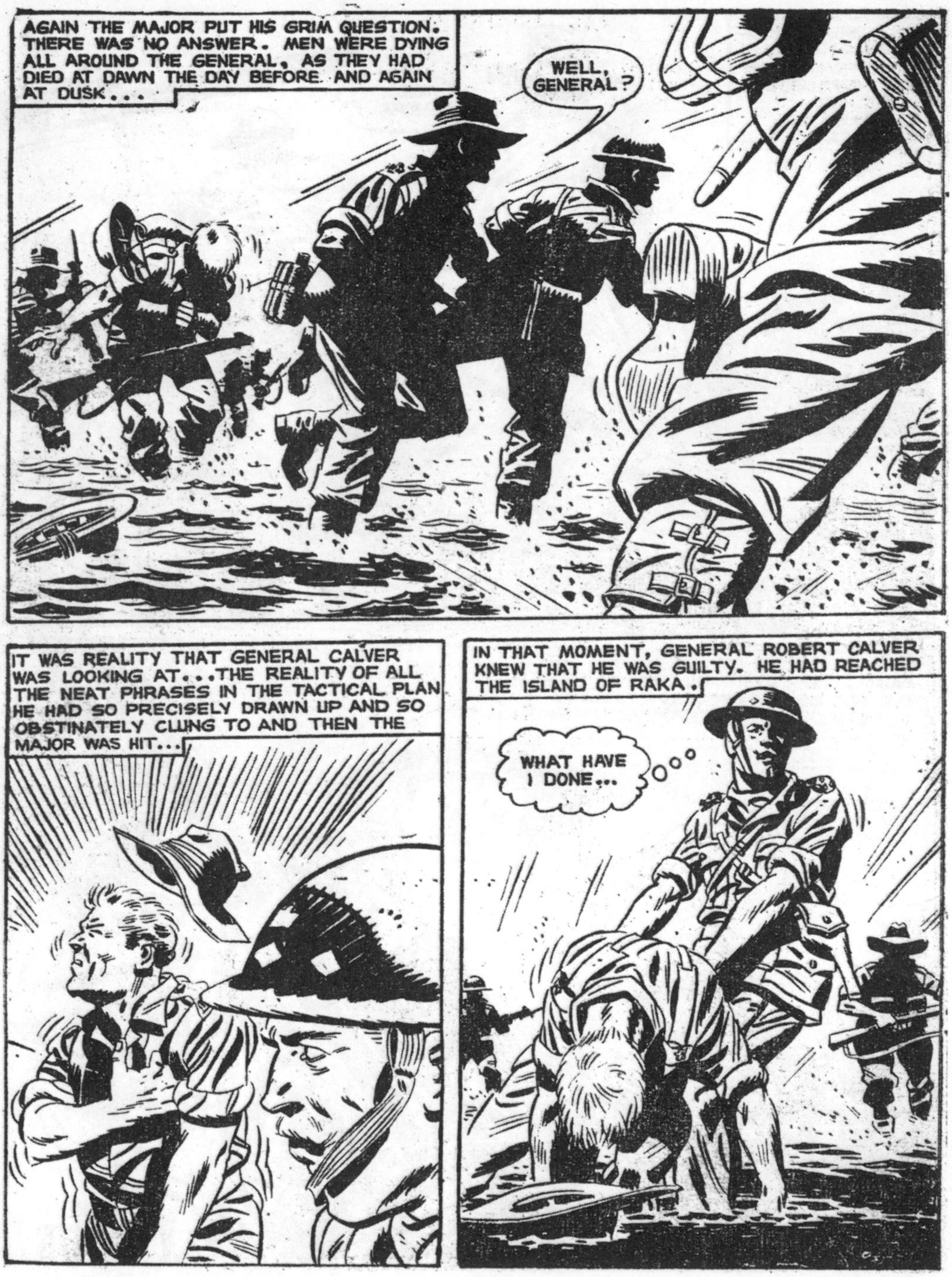
AGAIN THE MAJOR PUT HIS GRIM QUESTION. THERE WAS NO ANSWER. MEN WERE DYING ALL AROUND THE GENERAL, AS THEY HAD DIED AT DAWN THE DAY BEFORE AND AGAIN AT DUSK...
WELL, GENERAL?
IT WAS REALITY THAT GENERAL CALVER WAS LOOKING AT...THE REALITY OF ALL THE NEAT PHRASES IN THE TACTICAL PLAN HE HAD SO PRECISELY DRAWN UP AND SO OBSTINATELY CLUNG TO AND THEN THE MAJOR WAS HIT...
IN THAT MOMENT, GENERAL ROBERT CALVER KNEW THAT HE WAS GUILTY. HE HAD REACHED THE ISLAND OF RAKA.
WHAT HAVE I DONE...

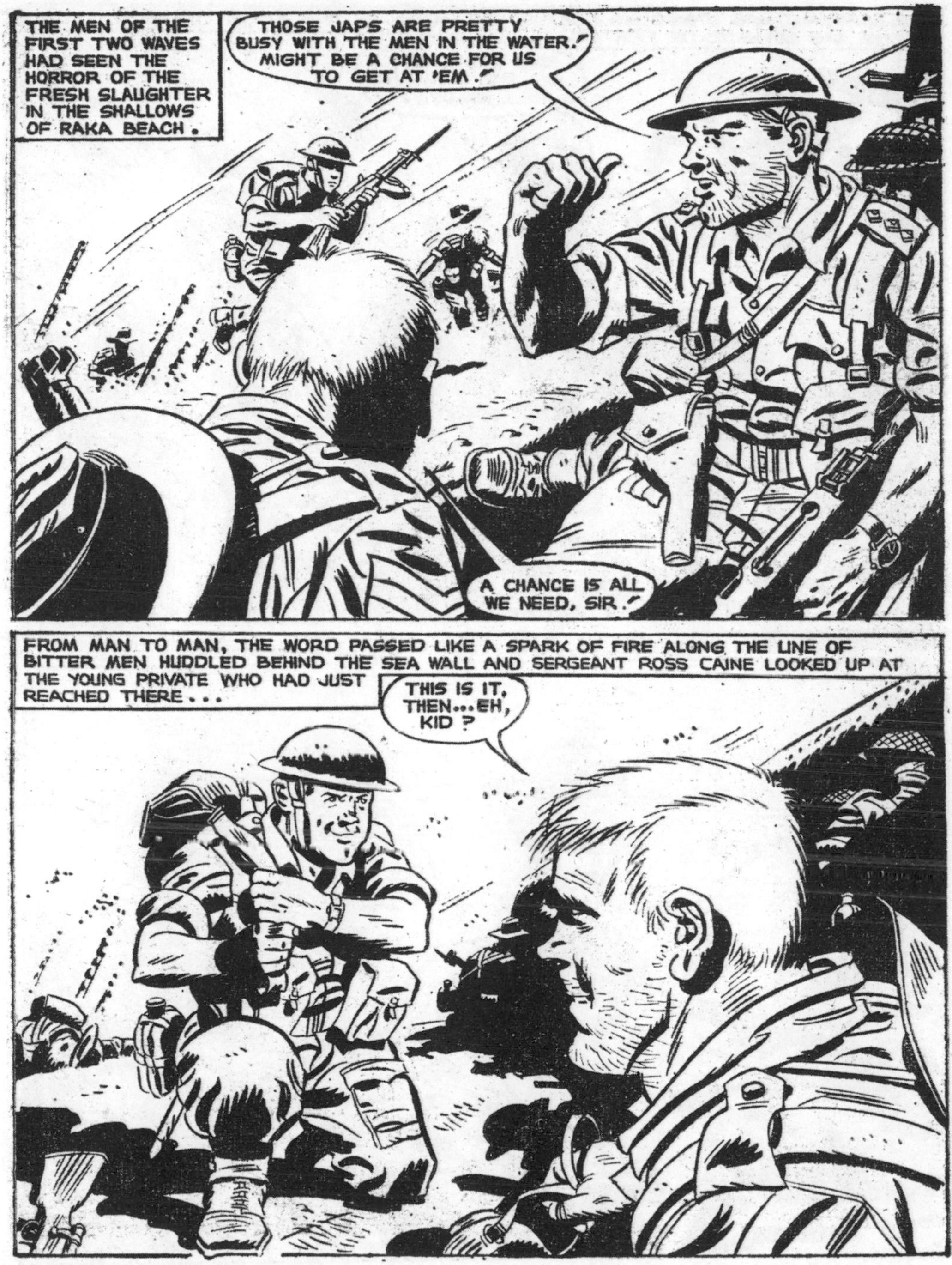
THE MEN OF THE FIRST TWO WAVES HAD SEEN THE HORROR OF THE FRESH SLAUGHTER IN THE SHALLOWS OF RAKA BEACH.
THOSE JAPS ARE PRETTY BUSY WITH THE MEN IN THE WATER! MIGHT BE A CHANCE FOR US TO GET AT 'EM!
A CHANCE IS ALL WE NEED, SIR!
FROM MAN TO MAN, THE WORD PASSED LIKE A SPARK OF FIRE ALONG THE LINE OF BITTER MEN HUDDLED BEHIND THE SEA WALL AND SERGEANT ROSS CAINE LOOKED UP AT THE YOUNG PRIVATE WHO HAD JUST REACHED THERE...
THIS IS IT, THEN...EH, KID?

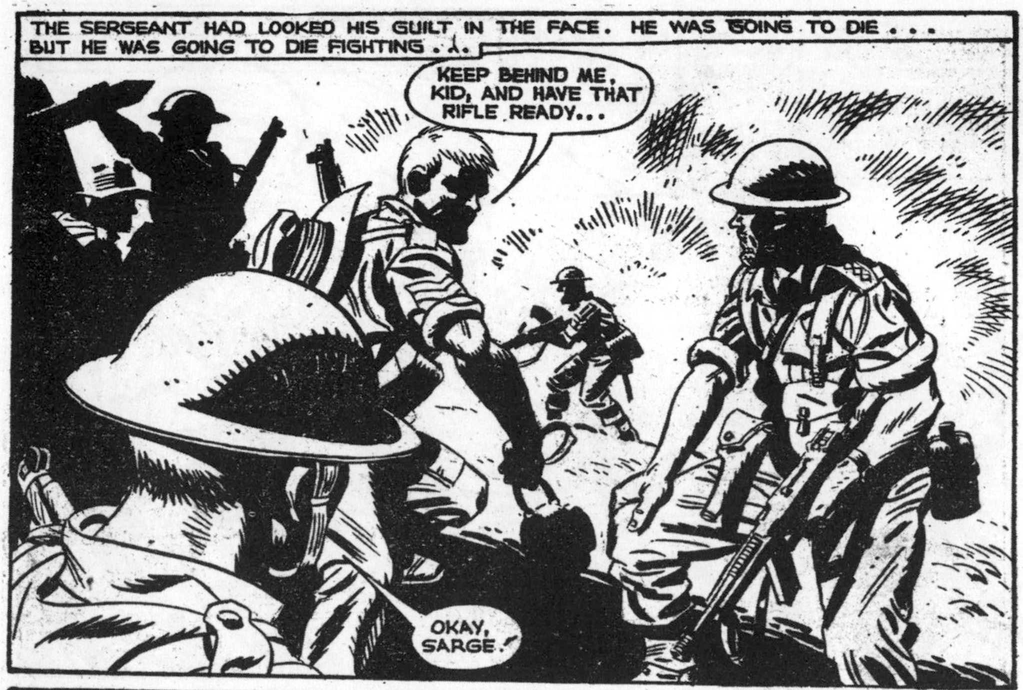
THE SERGEANT HAD LOOKED HIS GUILT IN THE FACE. HE WAS GOING TO DIE . . . BUT HE WAS GOING TO DIE FIGHTING . . .
KEEP BEHIND ME, KID, AND HAVE THAT RIFLE READY...
OKAY, SARGE.

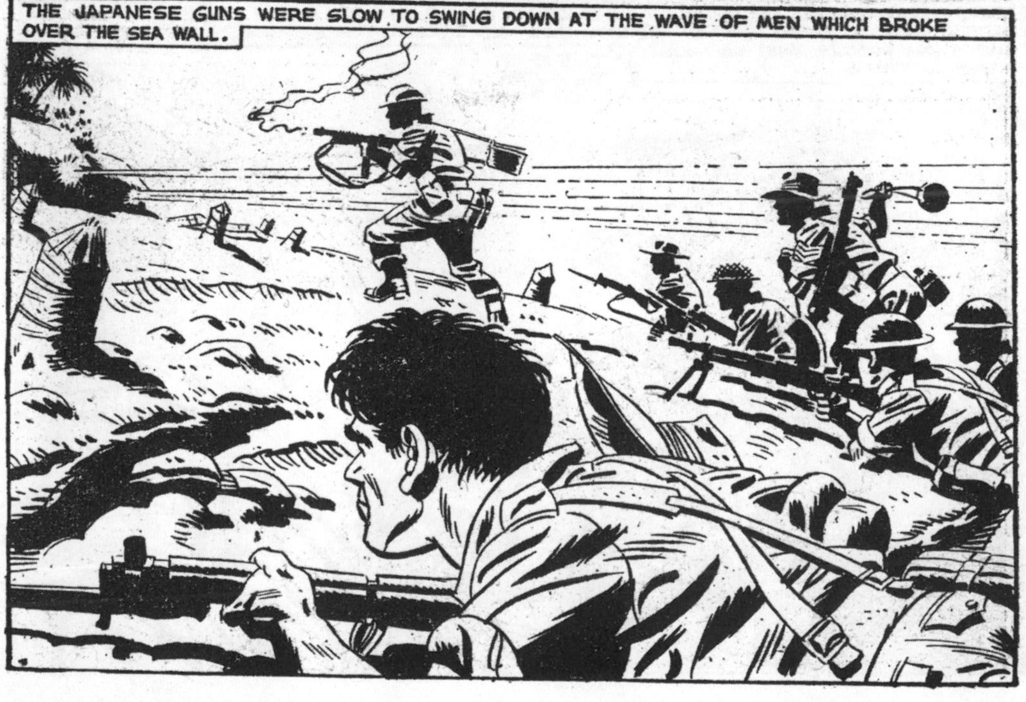
THE JAPANESE GUNS WERE SLOW TO SWING DOWN AT THE WAVE OF MEN WHICH BROKE OVER THE SEA WALL.

SOON THE MACHINE-GUNS FOUND THEM AND RAGGED HOLES WERE TORN IN THE THIN LINE OF MEN... *BUT THE SURVIVORS WENT ON...*

BULLETS KICKED UP AT THE FEET OF SERGEANT CAINE AS HE FLUNG HIMSELF FORWARD AGAINST THE ROUGH WALL OF THE PILLBOX. HE TOOK A DEEP BREATH...

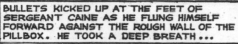

COVER THAT DOOR AT THE SIDE OF THE BOX, KID!

HE SWUNG THE BLOCK OF FUSED EXPLOSIVE TOWARDS THE GAPING SLIT IN THE STRONGPOINT... AND LET GO...

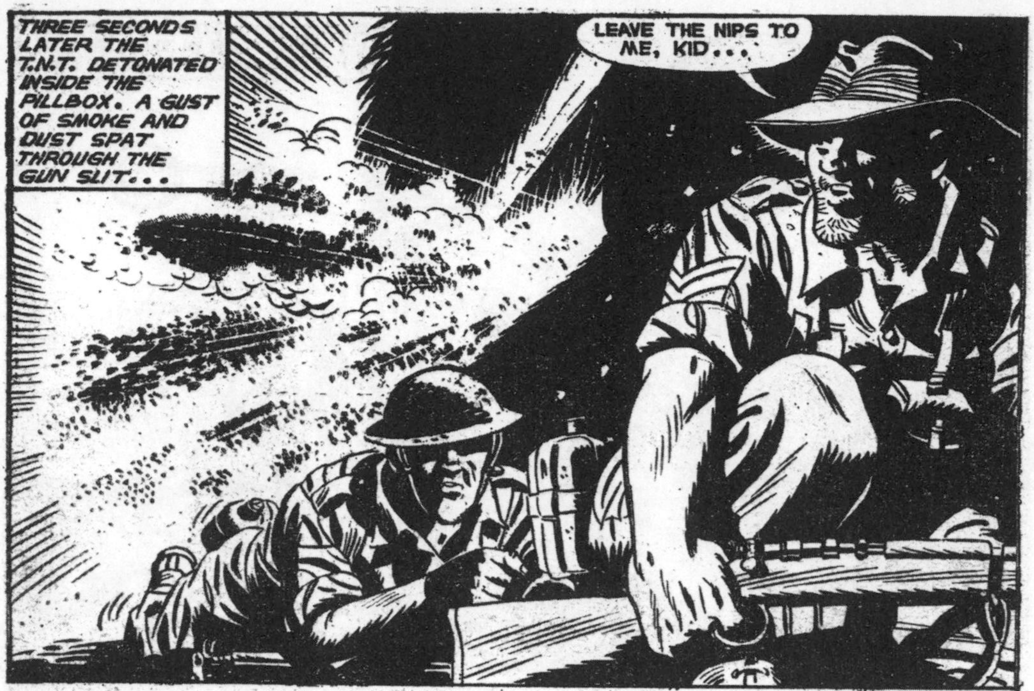
THREE SECONDS LATER THE T.N.T. DETONATED INSIDE THE PILLBOX. A GUST OF SMOKE AND DUST SPAT THROUGH THE GUN SLIT...
LEAVE THE NIPS TO ME, KID...

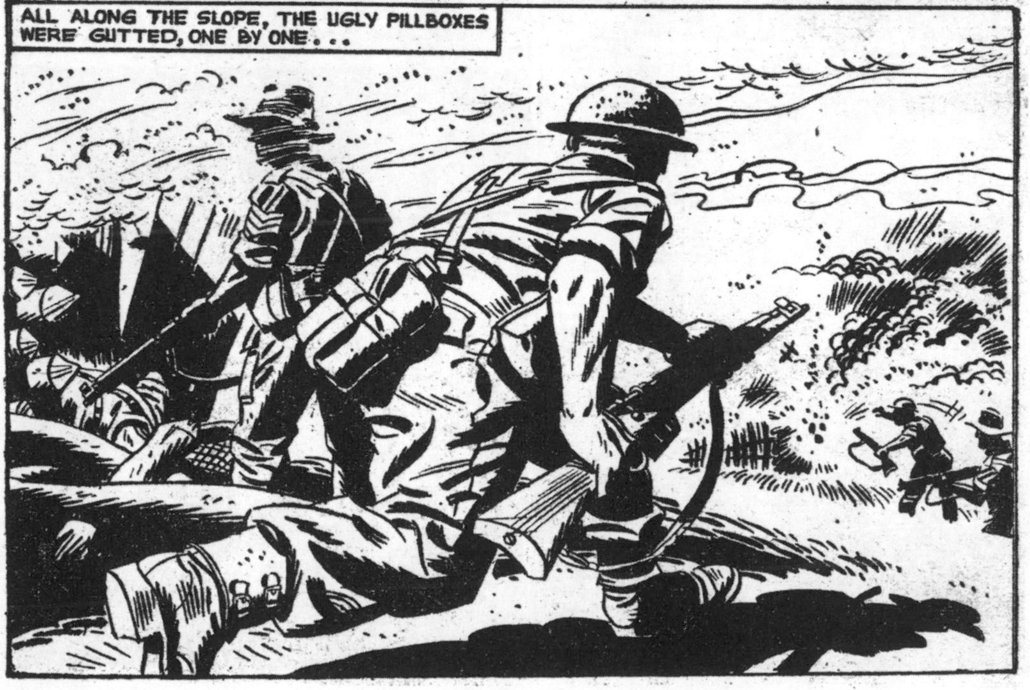
ALL ALONG THE SLOPE, THE UGLY PILLBOXES WERE GUTTED, ONE BY ONE...

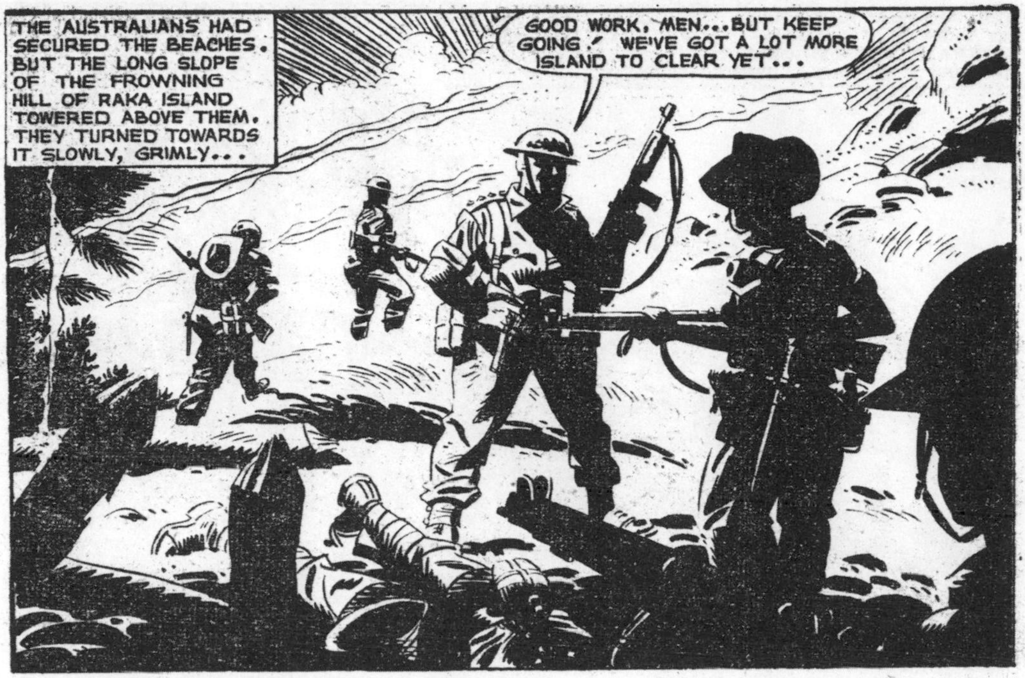
THE AUSTRALIANS HAD SECURED THE BEACHES. BUT THE LONG SLOPE OF THE FROWNING HILL OF RAKA ISLAND TOWERED ABOVE THEM. THEY TURNED TOWARDS IT SLOWLY, GRIMLY...
GOOD WORK, MEN...BUT KEEP GOING! WE'VE GOT A LOT MORE ISLAND TO CLEAR YET...

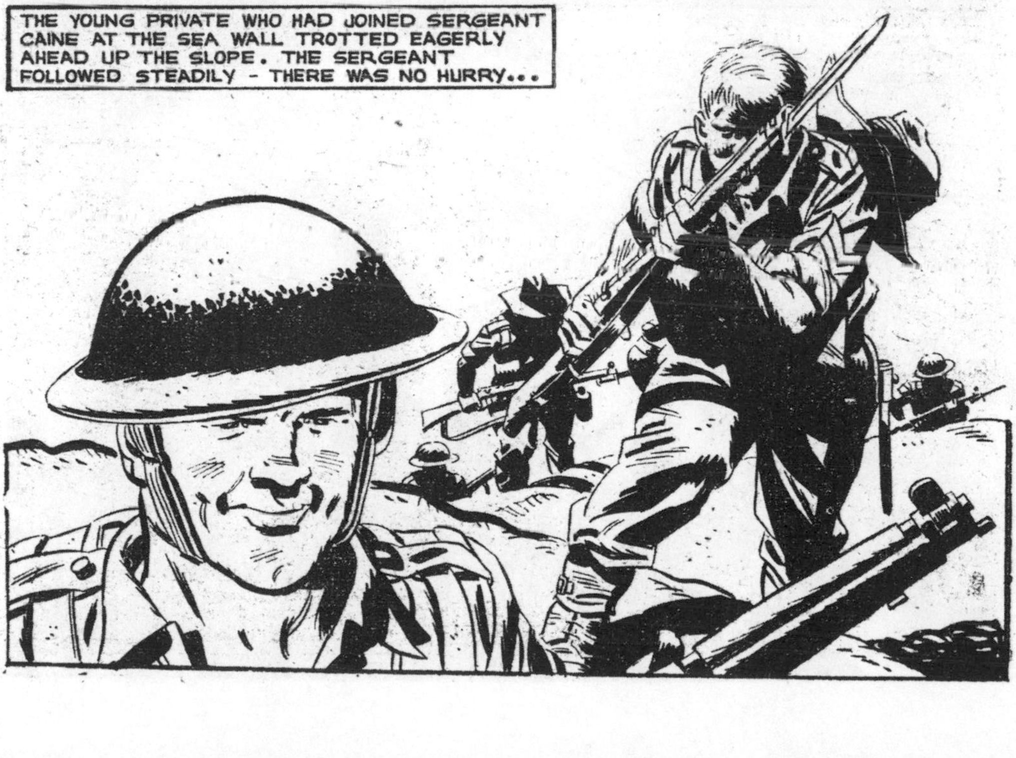
THE YOUNG PRIVATE WHO HAD JOINED SERGEANT CAINE AT THE SEA WALL TROTTED EAGERLY AHEAD UP THE SLOPE. THE SERGEANT FOLLOWED STEADILY - THERE WAS NO HURRY...

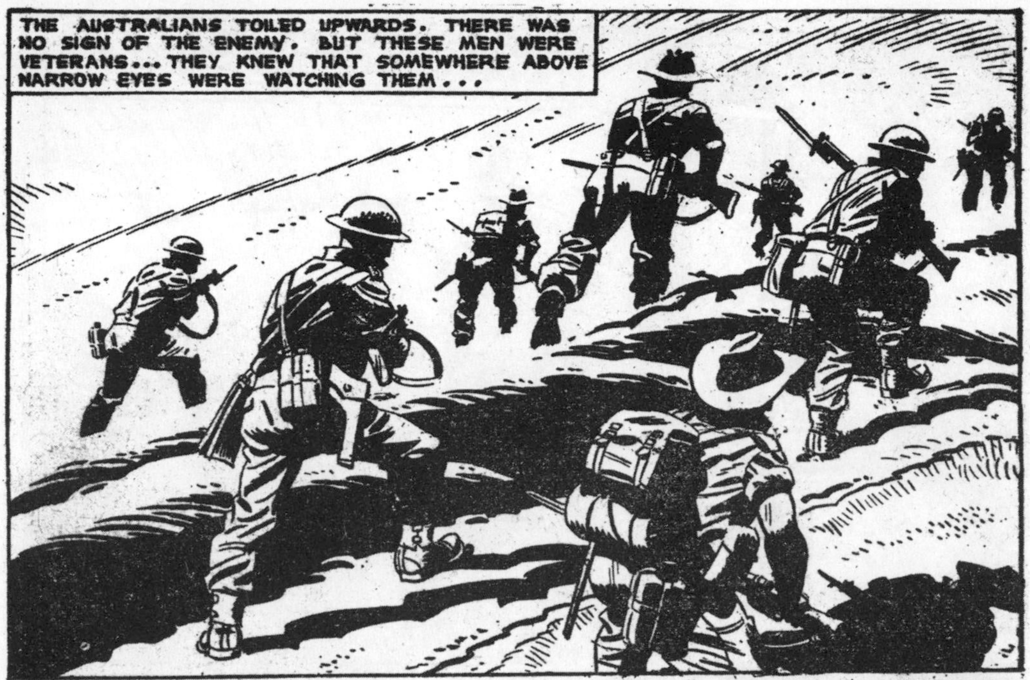
THE AUSTRALIANS TOILED UPWARDS. THERE WAS NO SIGN OF THE ENEMY. BUT THESE MEN WERE VETERANS... THEY KNEW THAT SOMEWHERE ABOVE NARROW EYES WERE WATCHING THEM...

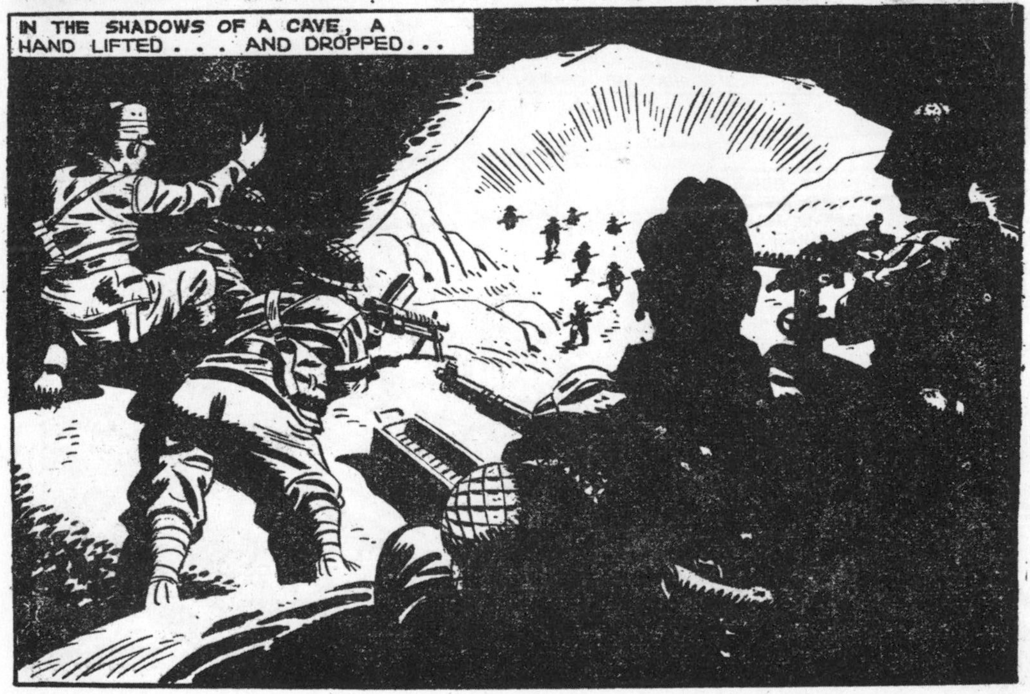
IN THE SHADOWS OF A CAVE, A HAND LIFTED . . . AND DROPPED...

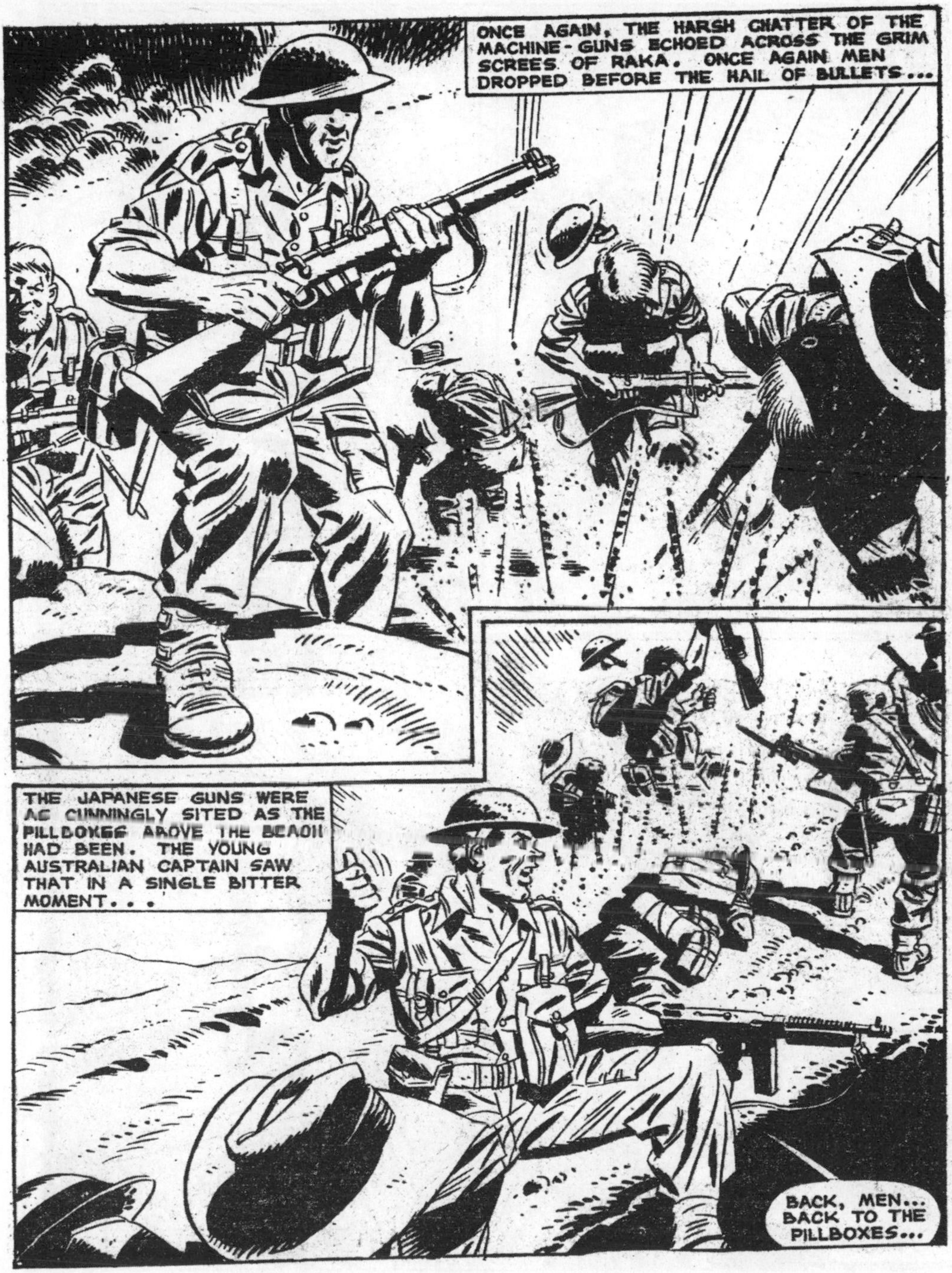
ONCE AGAIN, THE HARSH CHATTER OF THE MACHINE-GUNS ECHOED ACROSS THE GRIM SCREES OF RAKA. ONCE AGAIN MEN DROPPED BEFORE THE HAIL OF BULLETS...
THE JAPANESE GUNS WERE AS CUNNINGLY SITED AS THE PILLBOXES ABOVE THE BEACH HAD BEEN. THE YOUNG AUSTRALIAN CAPTAIN SAW THAT IN A SINGLE BITTER MOMENT...
BACK, MEN... BACK TO THE PILLBOXES...

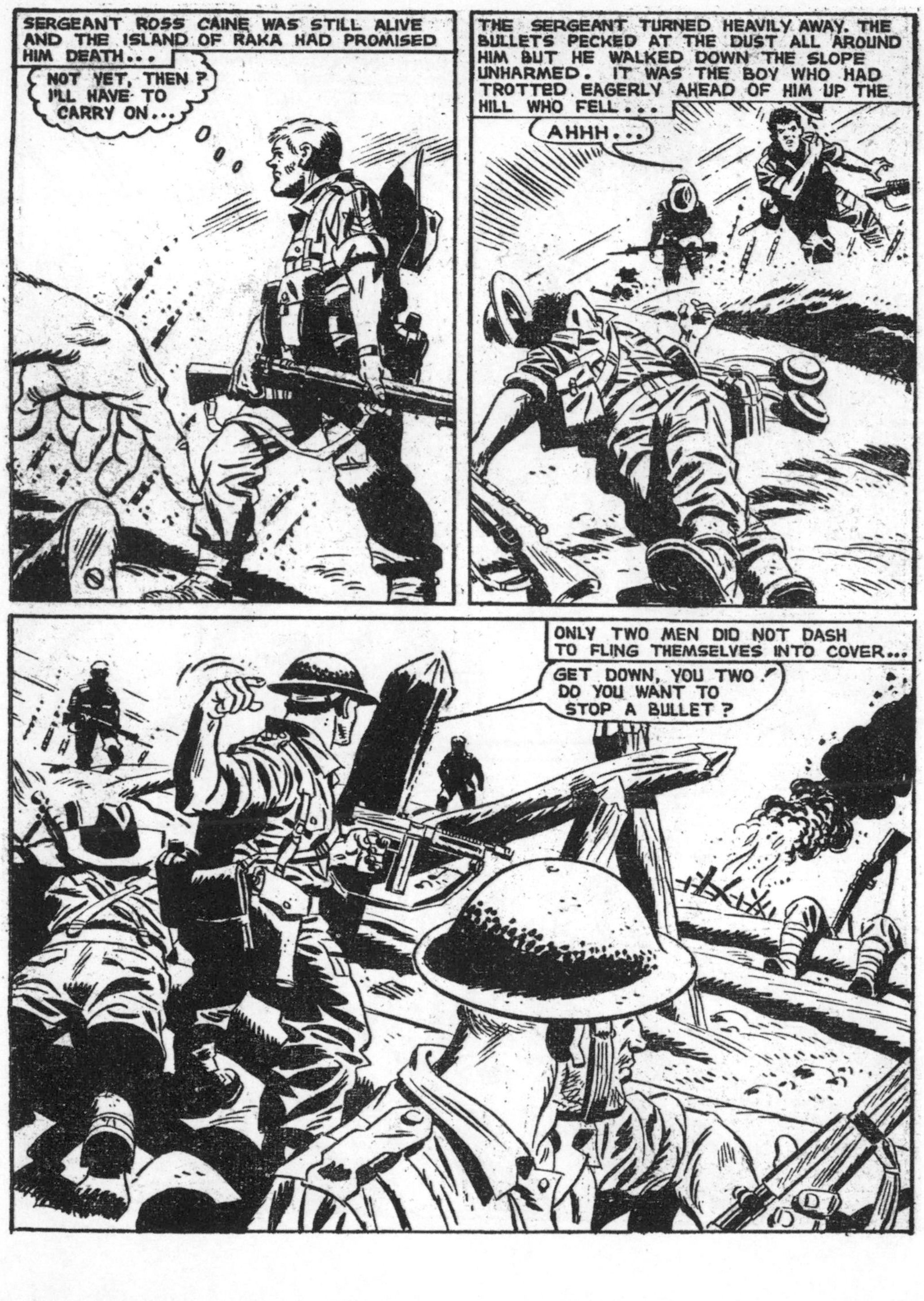
SERGEANT ROSS CAINE WAS STILL ALIVE AND THE ISLAND OF RAKA HAD PROMISED HIM DEATH...
NOT YET, THEN? I'LL HAVE TO CARRY ON...
THE SERGEANT TURNED HEAVILY AWAY. THE BULLETS PECKED AT THE DUST ALL AROUND HIM BUT HE WALKED DOWN THE SLOPE UNHARMED. IT WAS THE BOY WHO HAD TROTTED EAGERLY AHEAD OF HIM UP THE HILL WHO FELL...
AHHH...
ONLY TWO MEN DID NOT DASH TO FLING THEMSELVES INTO COVER...
GET DOWN, YOU TWO! DO YOU WANT TO STOP A BULLET?

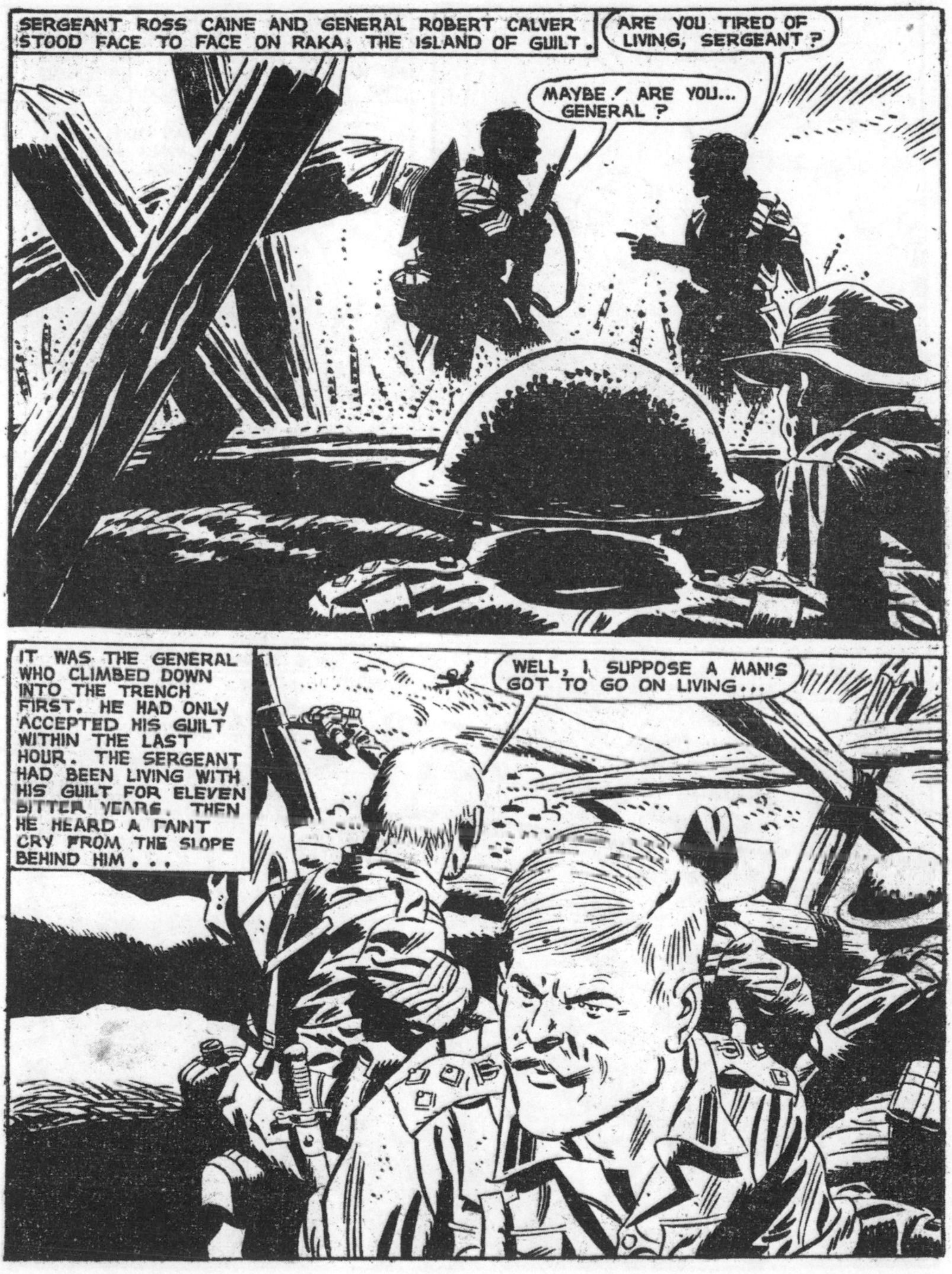
SERGEANT ROSS CAINE AND GENERAL ROBERT CALVER STOOD FACE TO FACE ON RAKA, THE ISLAND OF GUILT.
ARE YOU TIRED OF LIVING, SERGEANT?
MAYBE! ARE YOU... GENERAL?
IT WAS THE GENERAL WHO CLIMBED DOWN INTO THE TRENCH FIRST. HE HAD ONLY ACCEPTED HIS GUILT WITHIN THE LAST HOUR. THE SERGEANT HAD BEEN LIVING WITH HIS GUILT FOR ELEVEN BITTER YEARS. THEN HE HEARD A FAINT CRY FROM THE SLOPE BEHIND HIM...
WELL, I SUPPOSE A MAN'S GOT TO GO ON LIVING...

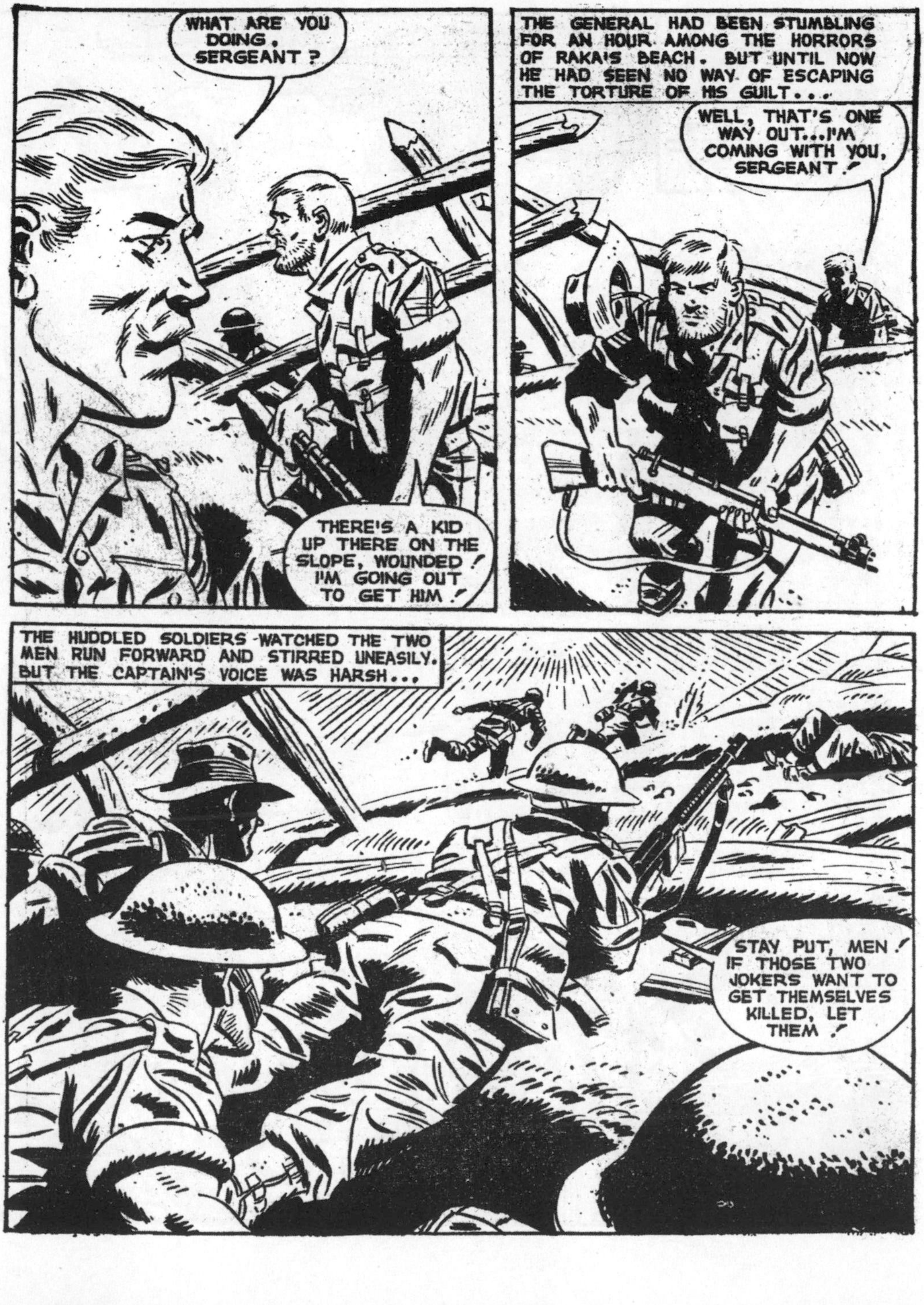
WHAT ARE YOU DOING, SERGEANT?
THERE'S A KID UP THERE ON THE SLOPE, WOUNDED! I'M GOING OUT TO GET HIM!
THE GENERAL HAD BEEN STUMBLING FOR AN HOUR AMONG THE HORRORS OF RAKA'S BEACH. BUT UNTIL NOW HE HAD SEEN NO WAY OF ESCAPING THE TORTURE OF HIS GUILT...
WELL, THAT'S ONE WAY OUT...I'M COMING WITH YOU, SERGEANT!
THE HUDDLED SOLDIERS WATCHED THE TWO MEN RUN FORWARD AND STIRRED UNEASILY. BUT THE CAPTAIN'S VOICE WAS HARSH...
STAY PUT, MEN! IF THOSE TWO JOKERS WANT TO GET THEMSELVES KILLED, LET THEM!

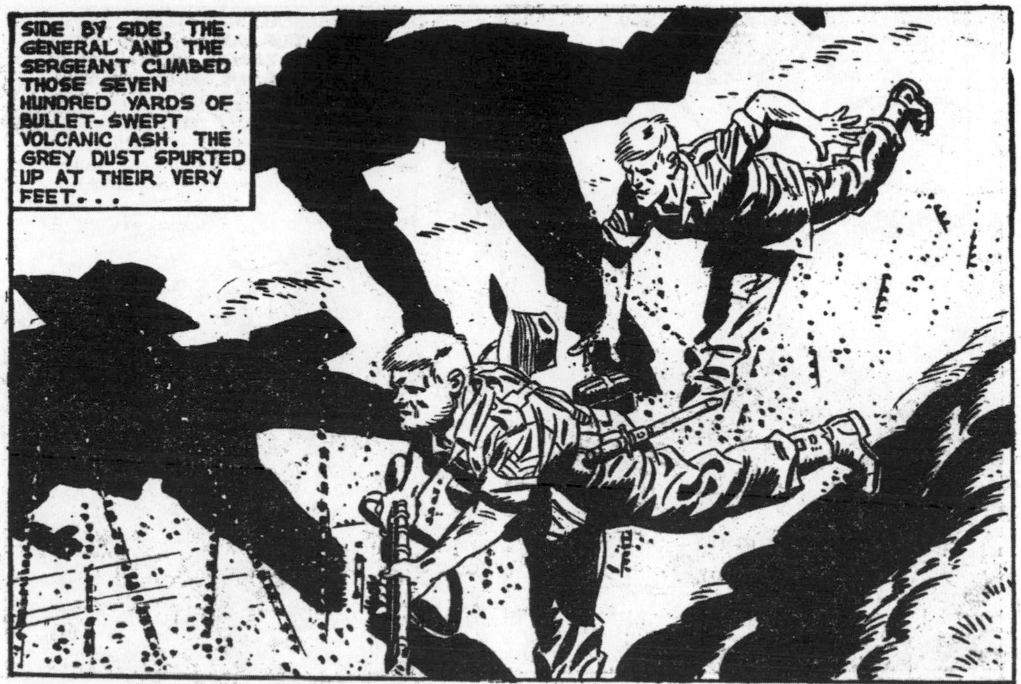
SIDE BY SIDE, THE GENERAL AND THE SERGEANT CLIMBED THOSE SEVEN HUNDRED YARDS OF BULLET-SWEPT VOLCANIC ASH. THE GREY DUST SPURTED UP AT THEIR VERY FEET...

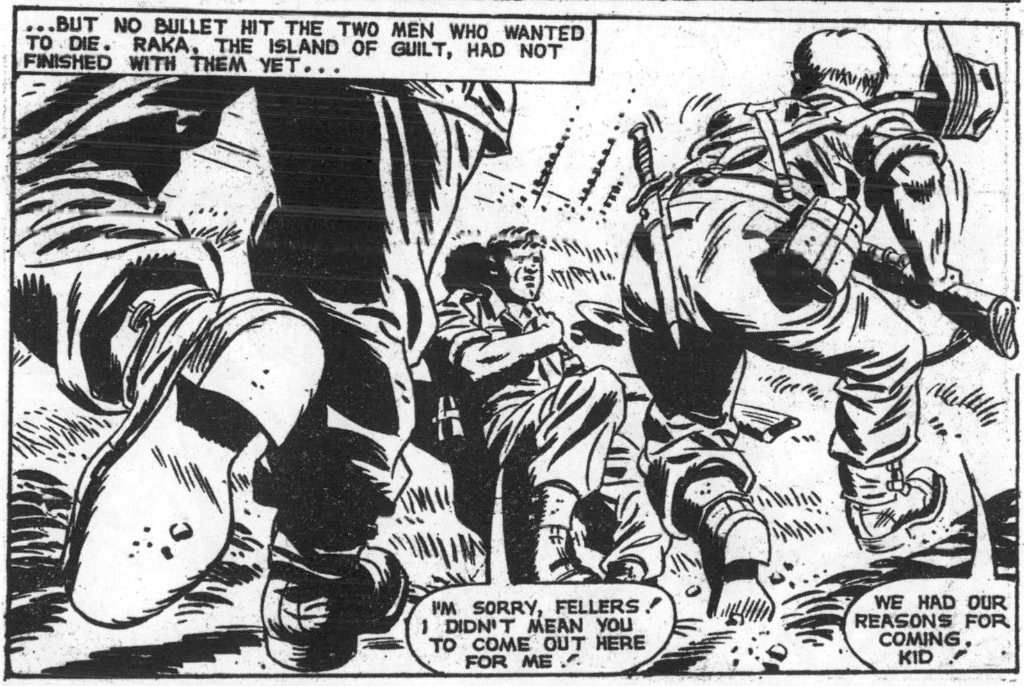
...BUT NO BULLET HIT THE TWO MEN WHO WANTED TO DIE. RAKA, THE ISLAND OF GUILT, HAD NOT FINISHED WITH THEM YET...
I'M SORRY, FELLERS! I DIDN'T MEAN YOU TO COME OUT HERE FOR ME!
WE HAD OUR REASONS FOR COMING, KID!

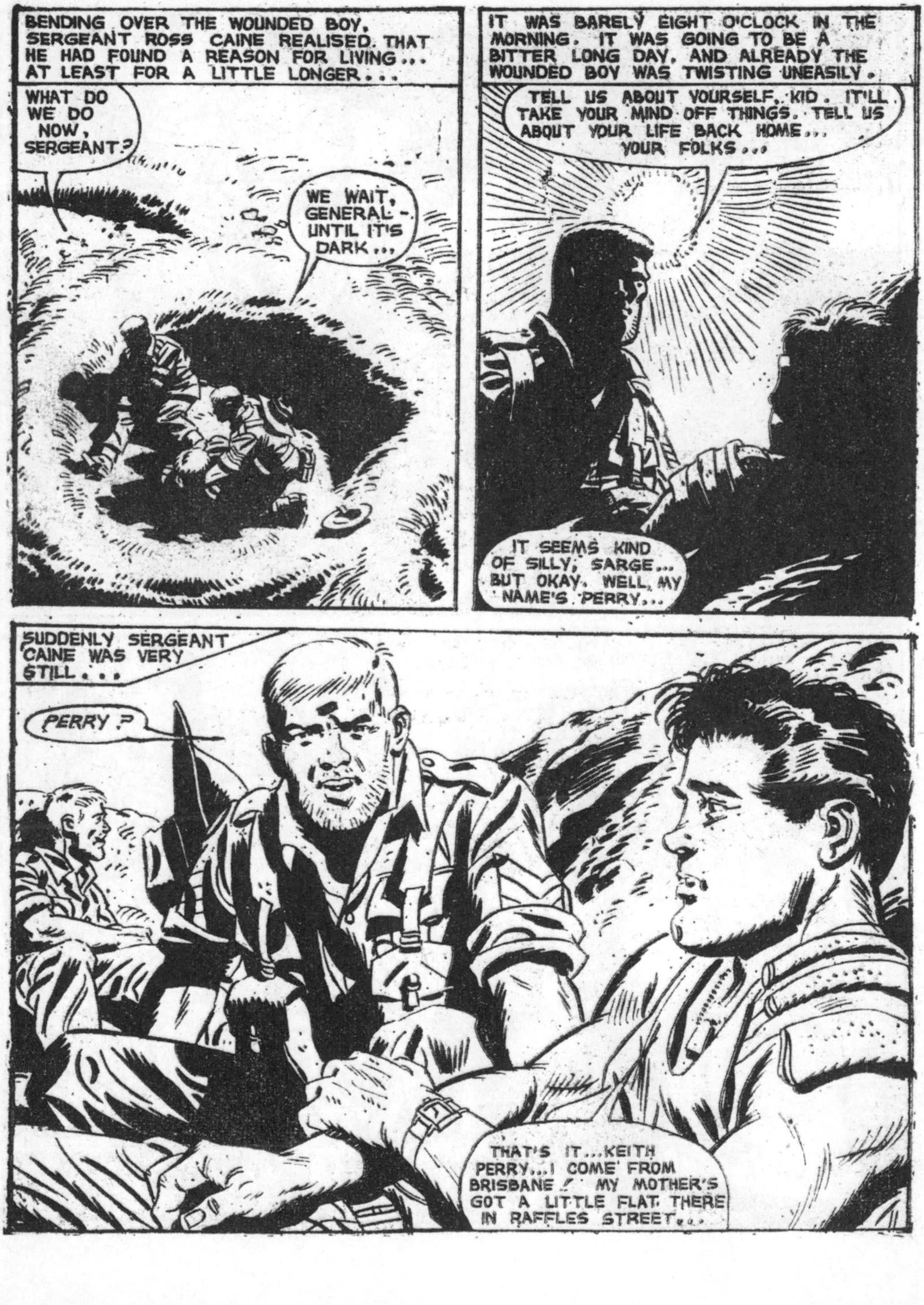
BENDING OVER THE WOUNDED BOY, SERGEANT ROSS CAINE REALISED THAT HE HAD FOUND A REASON FOR LIVING... AT LEAST FOR A LITTLE LONGER...
WHAT DO WE DO NOW, SERGEANT?
WE WAIT, GENERAL - UNTIL IT'S DARK...
IT WAS BARELY EIGHT O'CLOCK IN THE MORNING. IT WAS GOING TO BE A BITTER LONG DAY, AND ALREADY THE WOUNDED BOY WAS TWISTING UNEASILY.
TELL US ABOUT YOURSELF, KID. IT'LL TAKE YOUR MIND OFF THINGS. TELL US ABOUT YOUR LIFE BACK HOME... YOUR FOLKS...
IT SEEMS KIND OF SILLY, SARGE... BUT OKAY. WELL, MY NAME'S PERRY...
SUDDENLY SERGEANT CAINE WAS VERY STILL...
PERRY?
THAT'S IT...KEITH PERRY...I COME FROM BRISBANE! MY MOTHER'S GOT A LITTLE FLAT THERE IN RAFFLES STREET...

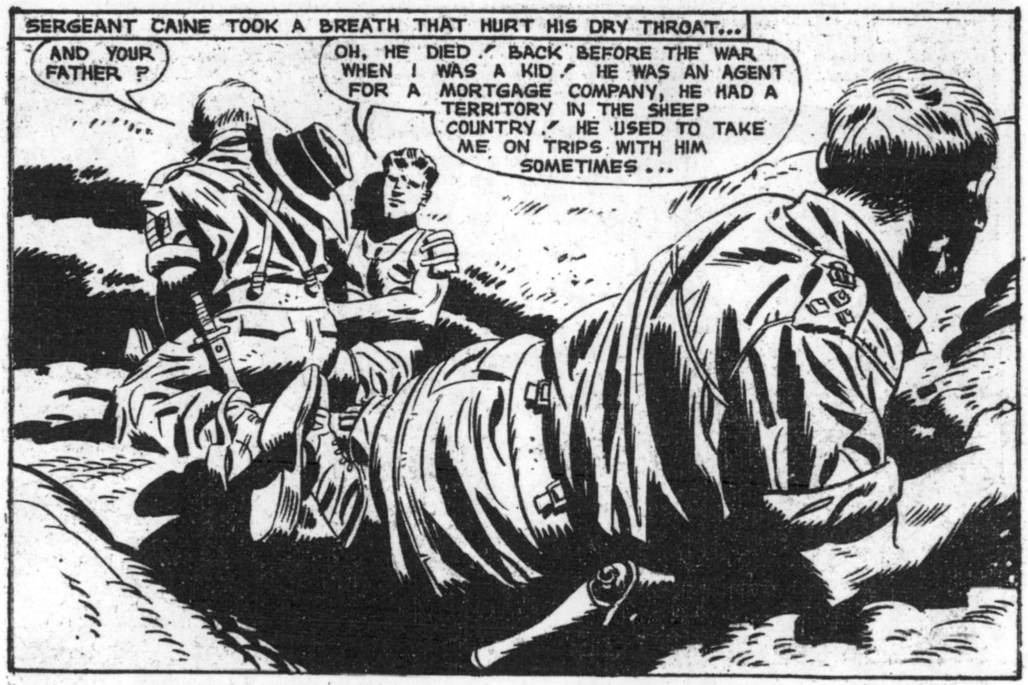
SERGEANT CAINE TOOK A BREATH THAT HURT HIS DRY THROAT...
AND YOUR FATHER ?
OH, HE DIED! BACK BEFORE THE WAR WHEN I WAS A KID! HE WAS AN AGENT FOR A MORTGAGE COMPANY, HE HAD A TERRITORY IN THE SHEEP COUNTRY! HE USED TO TAKE ME ON TRIPS WITH HIM SOMETIMES...

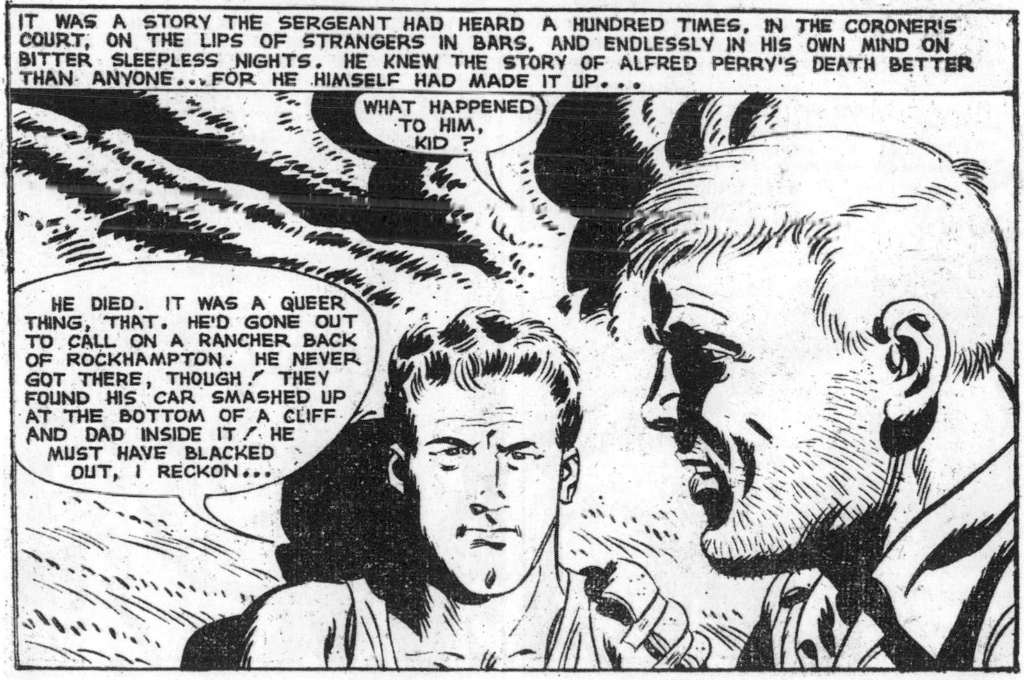
IT WAS A STORY THE SERGEANT HAD HEARD A HUNDRED TIMES, IN THE CORONER'S COURT, ON THE LIPS OF STRANGERS IN BARS, AND ENDLESSLY IN HIS OWN MIND ON BITTER SLEEPLESS NIGHTS. HE KNEW THE STORY OF ALFRED PERRY'S DEATH BETTER THAN ANYONE...FOR HE HIMSELF HAD MADE IT UP...
WHAT HAPPENED TO HIM, KID ?
HE DIED. IT WAS A QUEER THING, THAT. HE'D GONE OUT TO CALL ON A RANCHER BACK OF ROCKHAMPTON. HE NEVER GOT THERE, THOUGH! THEY FOUND HIS CAR SMASHED UP AT THE BOTTOM OF A CLIFF AND DAD INSIDE IT! HE MUST HAVE BLACKED OUT, I RECKON...

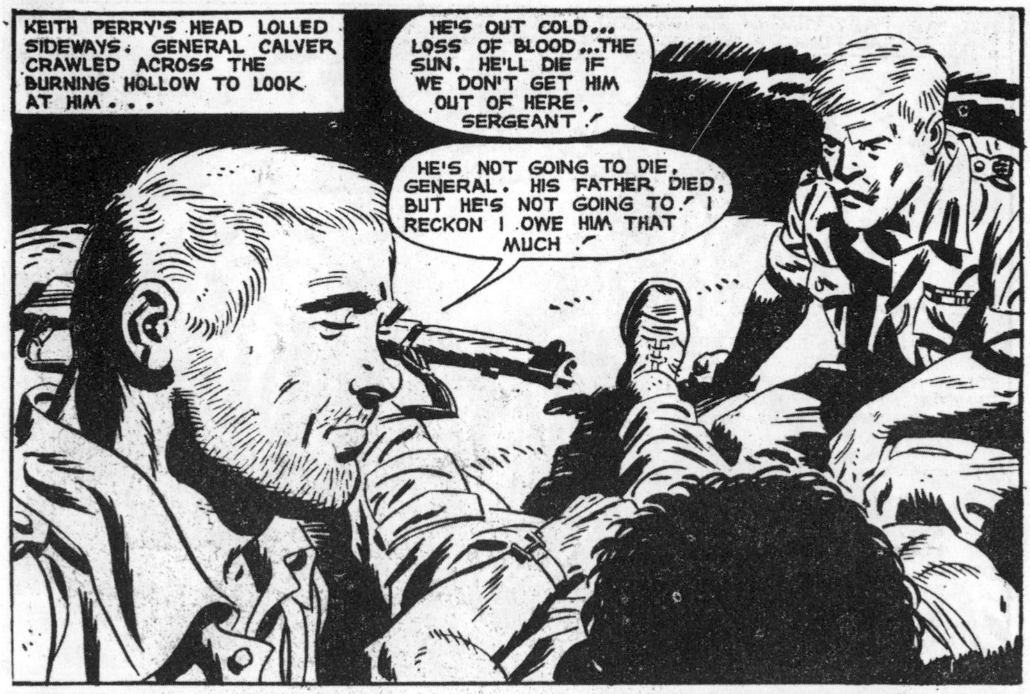
KEITH PERRY'S HEAD LOLLED SIDEWAYS. GENERAL CALVER CRAWLED ACROSS THE BURNING HOLLOW TO LOOK AT HIM . . .
HE'S OUT COLD... LOSS OF BLOOD...THE SUN. HE'LL DIE IF WE DON'T GET HIM OUT OF HERE, SERGEANT!
HE'S NOT GOING TO DIE, GENERAL. HIS FATHER DIED, BUT HE'S NOT GOING TO! I RECKON I OWE HIM THAT MUCH!

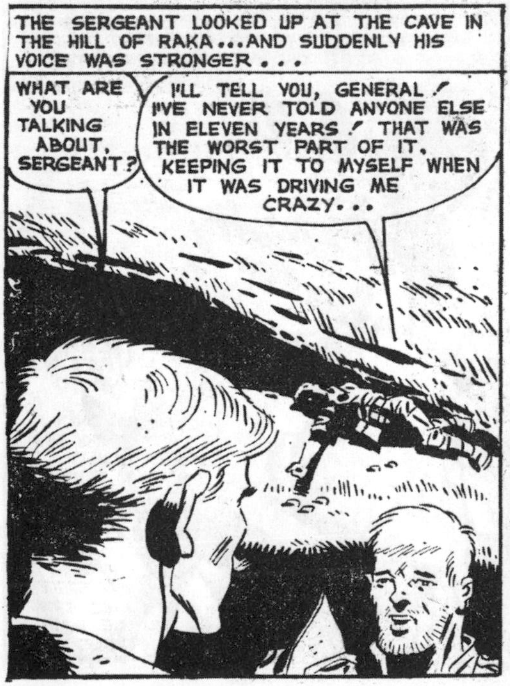
THE SERGEANT LOOKED UP AT THE CAVE IN THE HILL OF RAKA...AND SUDDENLY HIS VOICE WAS STRONGER . . .
WHAT ARE YOU TALKING ABOUT, SERGEANT?
I'LL TELL YOU, GENERAL! I'VE NEVER TOLD ANYONE ELSE IN ELEVEN YEARS! THAT WAS THE WORST PART OF IT, KEEPING IT TO MYSELF WHEN IT WAS DRIVING ME CRAZY. . .

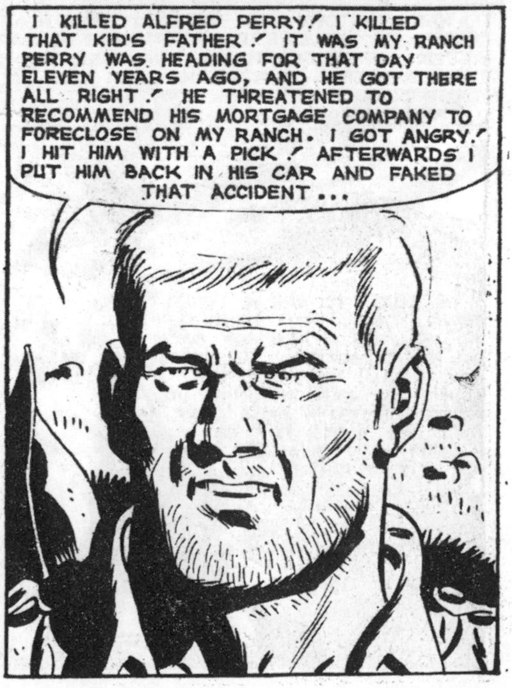
I KILLED ALFRED PERRY! I KILLED THAT KID'S FATHER! IT WAS MY RANCH PERRY WAS HEADING FOR THAT DAY ELEVEN YEARS AGO, AND HE GOT THERE ALL RIGHT! HE THREATENED TO RECOMMEND HIS MORTGAGE COMPANY TO FORECLOSE ON MY RANCH. I GOT ANGRY! I HIT HIM WITH A PICK! AFTERWARDS I PUT HIM BACK IN HIS CAR AND FAKED THAT ACCIDENT...

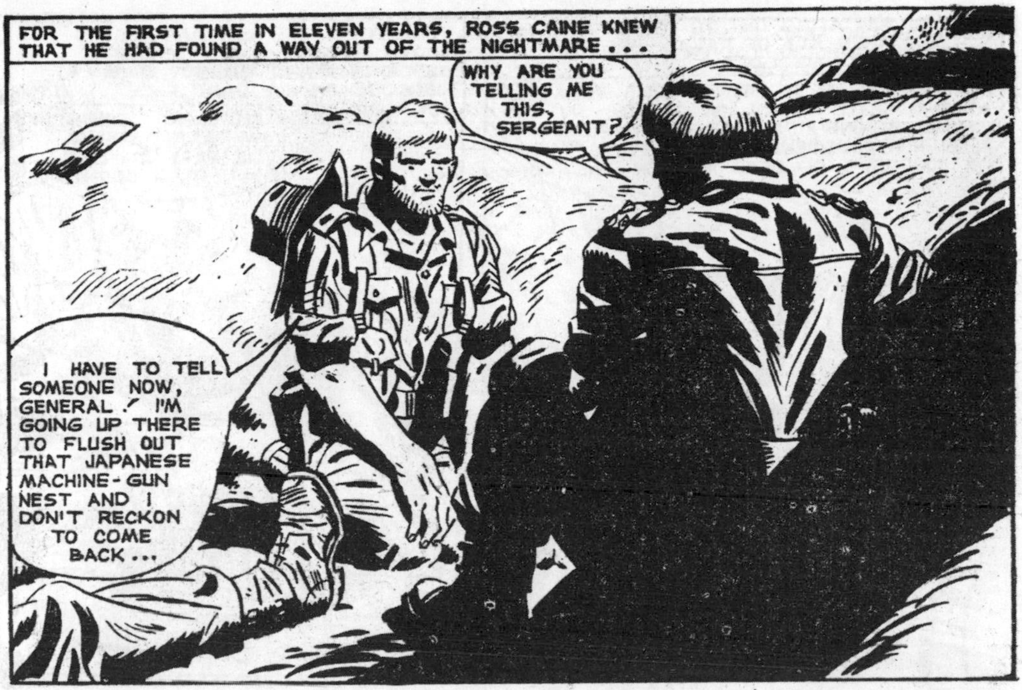
FOR THE FIRST TIME IN ELEVEN YEARS, ROSS CAINE KNEW THAT HE HAD FOUND A WAY OUT OF THE NIGHTMARE...
WHY ARE YOU TELLING ME THIS, SERGEANT?
I HAVE TO TELL SOMEONE NOW, GENERAL! I'M GOING UP THERE TO FLUSH OUT THAT JAPANESE MACHINE-GUN NEST AND I DON'T RECKON TO COME BACK...

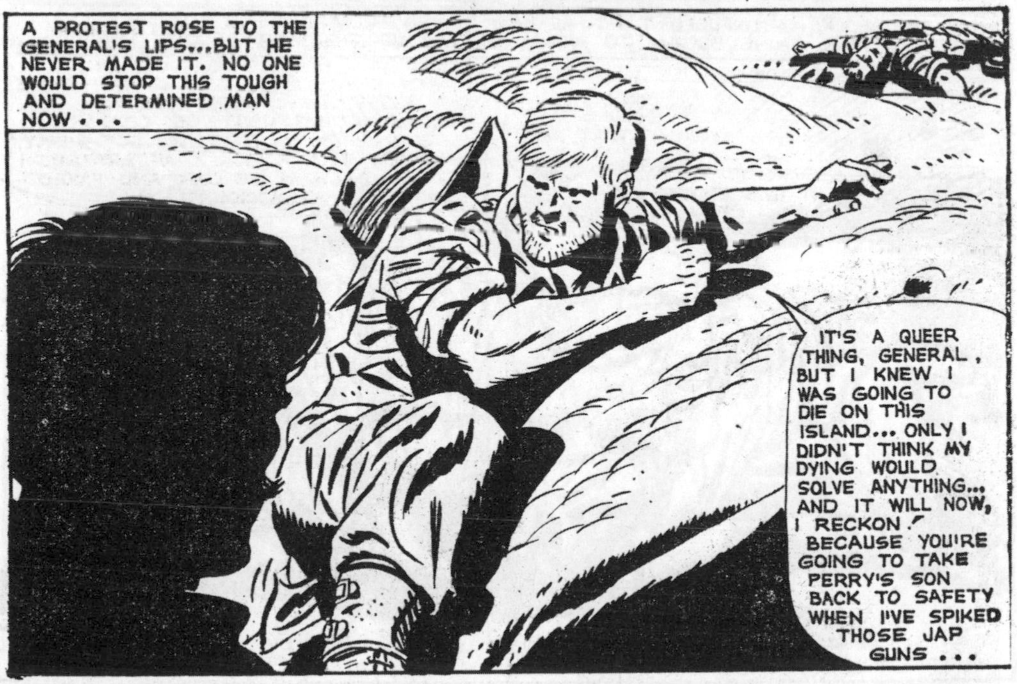
A PROTEST ROSE TO THE GENERAL'S LIPS...BUT HE NEVER MADE IT. NO ONE WOULD STOP THIS TOUGH AND DETERMINED MAN NOW...
IT'S A QUEER THING, GENERAL, BUT I KNEW I WAS GOING TO DIE ON THIS ISLAND... ONLY I DIDN'T THINK MY DYING WOULD SOLVE ANYTHING... AND IT WILL NOW, I RECKON! BECAUSE YOU'RE GOING TO TAKE PERRY'S SON BACK TO SAFETY WHEN I'VE SPIKED THOSE JAP GUNS...

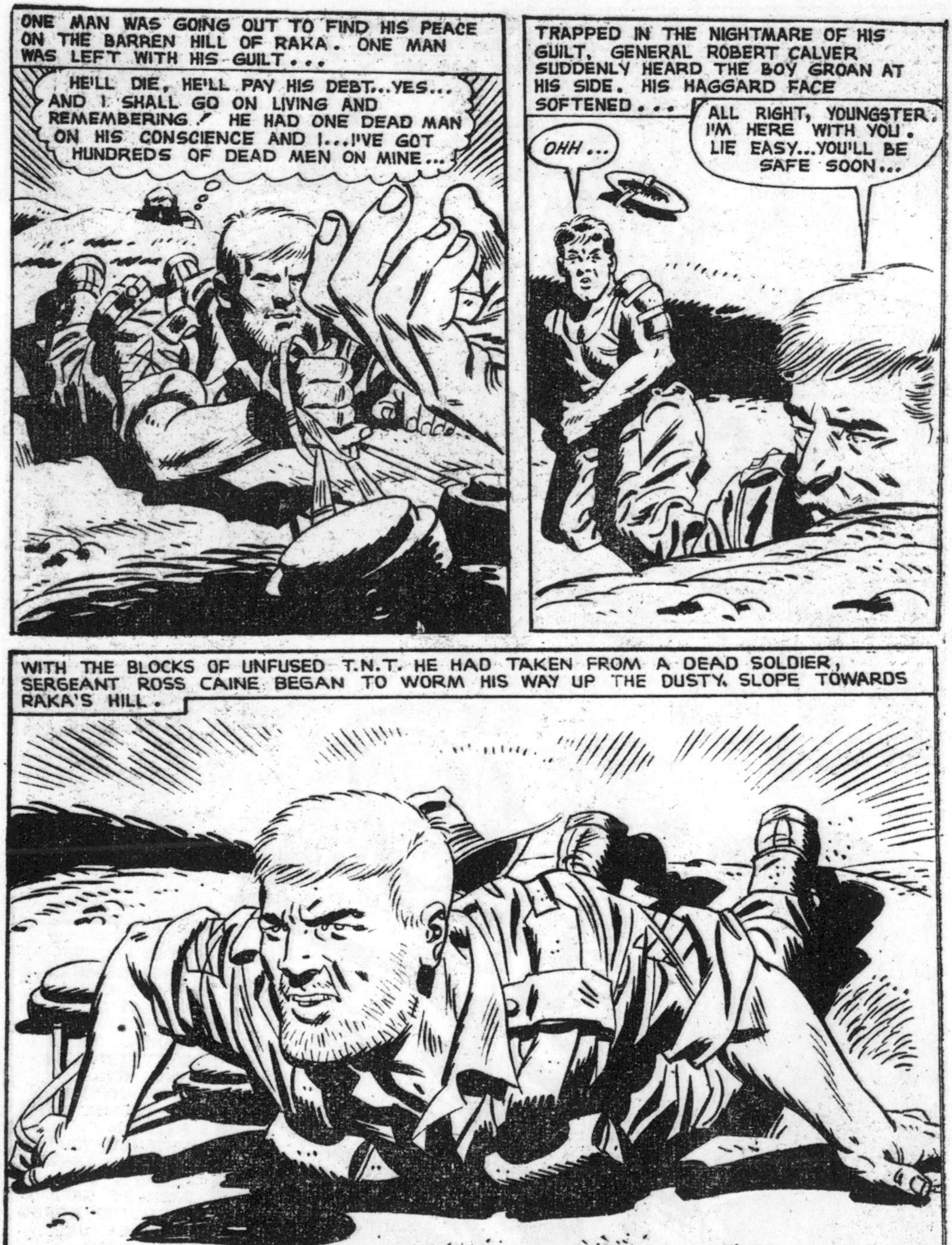
ONE MAN WAS GOING OUT TO FIND HIS PEACE ON THE BARREN HILL OF RAKA. ONE MAN WAS LEFT WITH HIS GUILT...
HE'LL DIE, HE'LL PAY HIS DEBT...YES... AND I SHALL GO ON LIVING AND REMEMBERING! HE HAD ONE DEAD MAN ON HIS CONSCIENCE AND I...I'VE GOT HUNDREDS OF DEAD MEN ON MINE...
TRAPPED IN THE NIGHTMARE OF HIS GUILT, GENERAL ROBERT CALVER SUDDENLY HEARD THE BOY GROAN AT HIS SIDE. HIS HAGGARD FACE SOFTENED...
OHH...
ALL RIGHT, YOUNGSTER. I'M HERE WITH YOU. LIE EASY...YOU'LL BE SAFE SOON...
WITH THE BLOCKS OF UNFUSED T.N.T. HE HAD TAKEN FROM A DEAD SOLDIER, SERGEANT ROSS CAINE BEGAN TO WORM HIS WAY UP THE DUSTY SLOPE TOWARDS RAKA'S HILL.

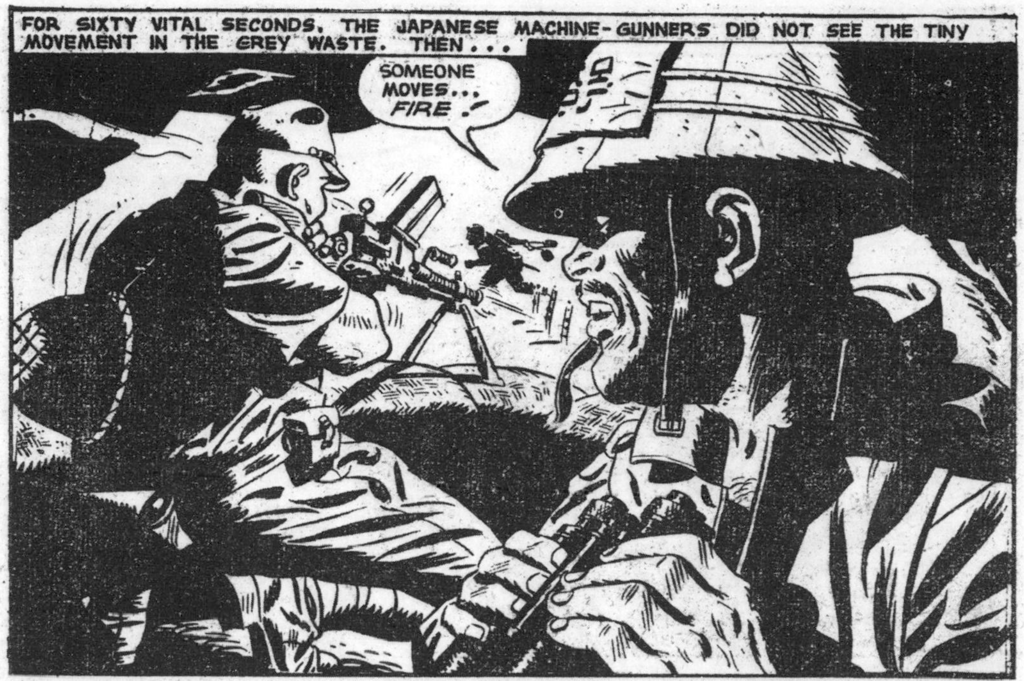
FOR SIXTY VITAL SECONDS, THE JAPANESE MACHINE-GUNNERS DID NOT SEE THE TINY MOVEMENT IN THE GREY WASTE. THEN...
SOMEONE MOVES... FIRE!

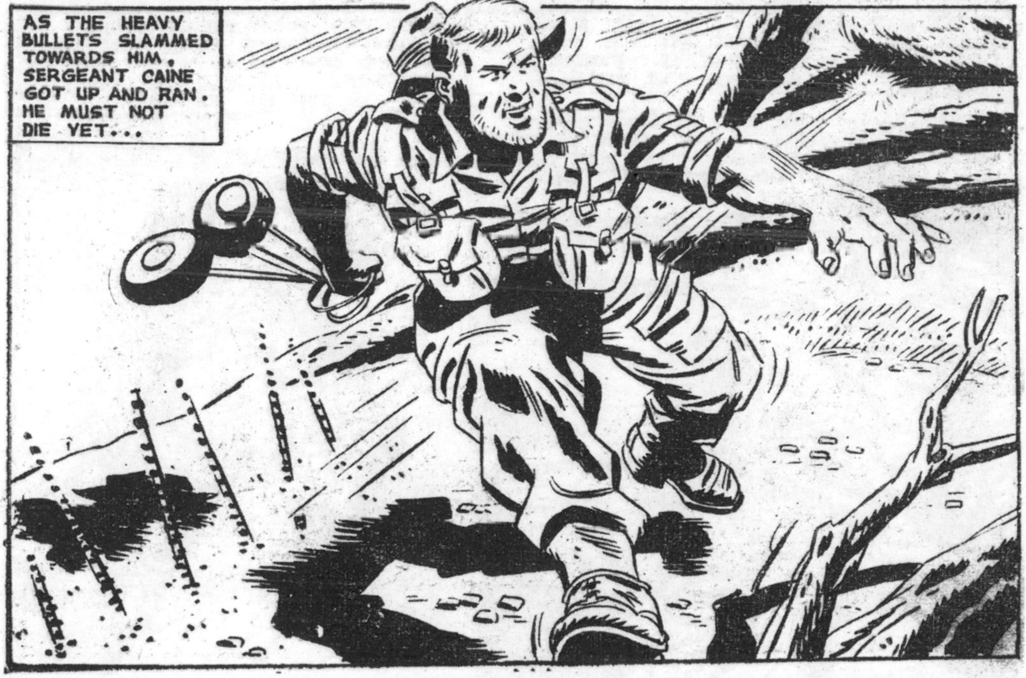
AS THE HEAVY BULLETS SLAMMED TOWARDS HIM, SERGEANT CAINE GOT UP AND RAN. HE MUST NOT DIE YET...

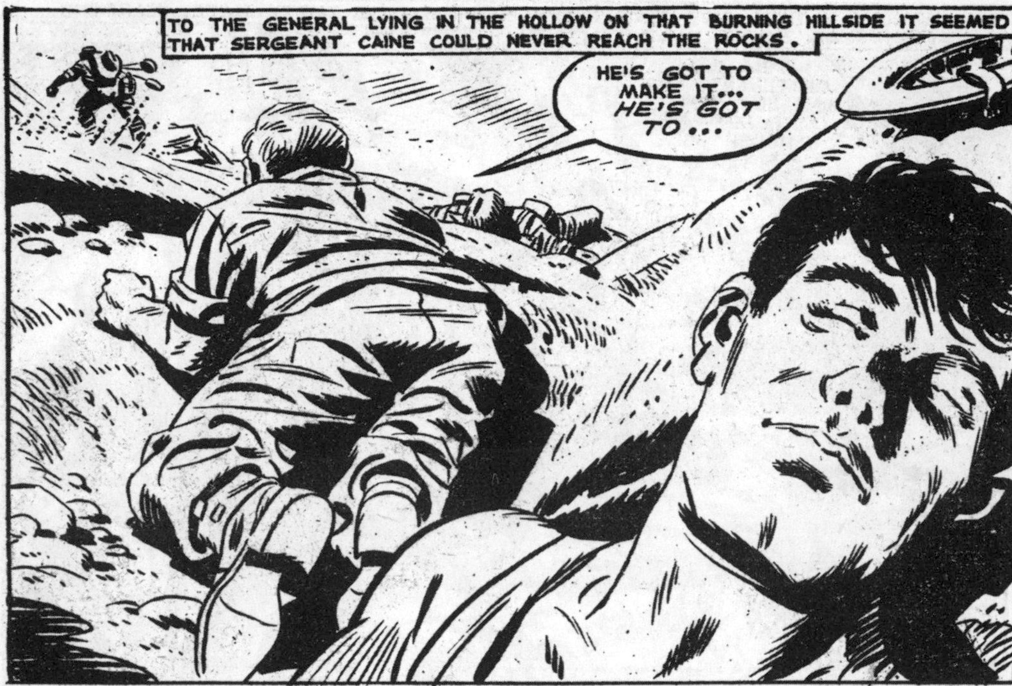
TO THE GENERAL LYING IN THE HOLLOW ON THAT BURNING HILLSIDE IT SEEMED THAT SERGEANT CAINE COULD NEVER REACH THE ROCKS.
HE'S GOT TO MAKE IT... HE'S GOT TO...

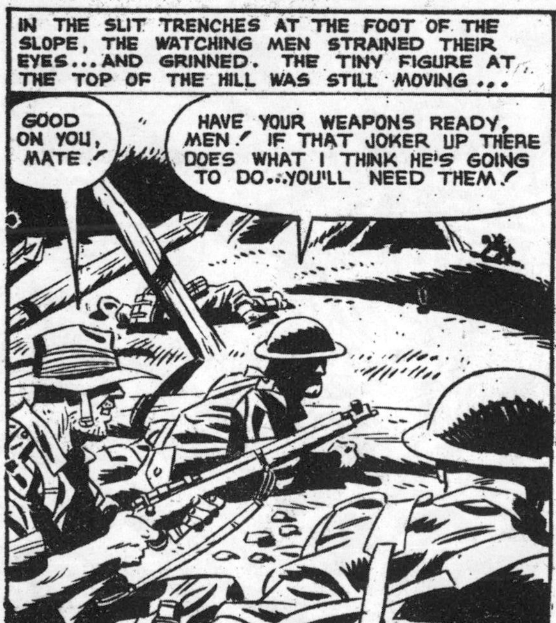
IN THE SLIT TRENCHES AT THE FOOT OF THE SLOPE, THE WATCHING MEN STRAINED THEIR EYES... AND GRINNED. THE TINY FIGURE AT THE TOP OF THE HILL WAS STILL MOVING...
GOOD ON YOU, MATE!
HAVE YOUR WEAPONS READY, MEN! IF THAT JOKER UP THERE DOES WHAT I THINK HE'S GOING TO DO...YOU'LL NEED THEM!

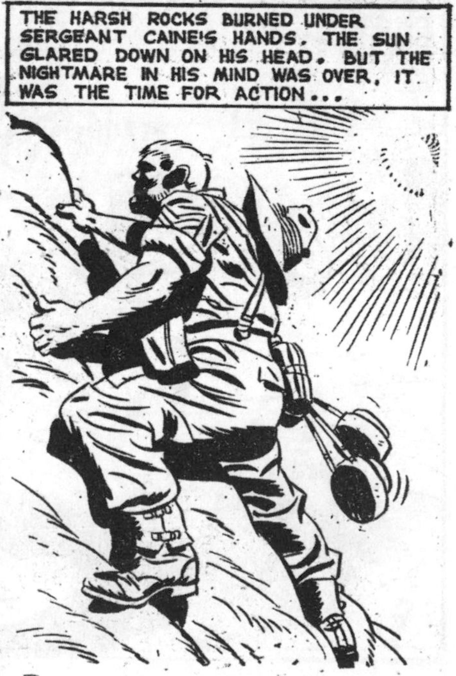
THE HARSH ROCKS BURNED UNDER SERGEANT CAINE'S HANDS. THE SUN GLARED DOWN ON HIS HEAD. BUT THE NIGHTMARE IN HIS MIND WAS OVER. IT WAS THE TIME FOR ACTION...

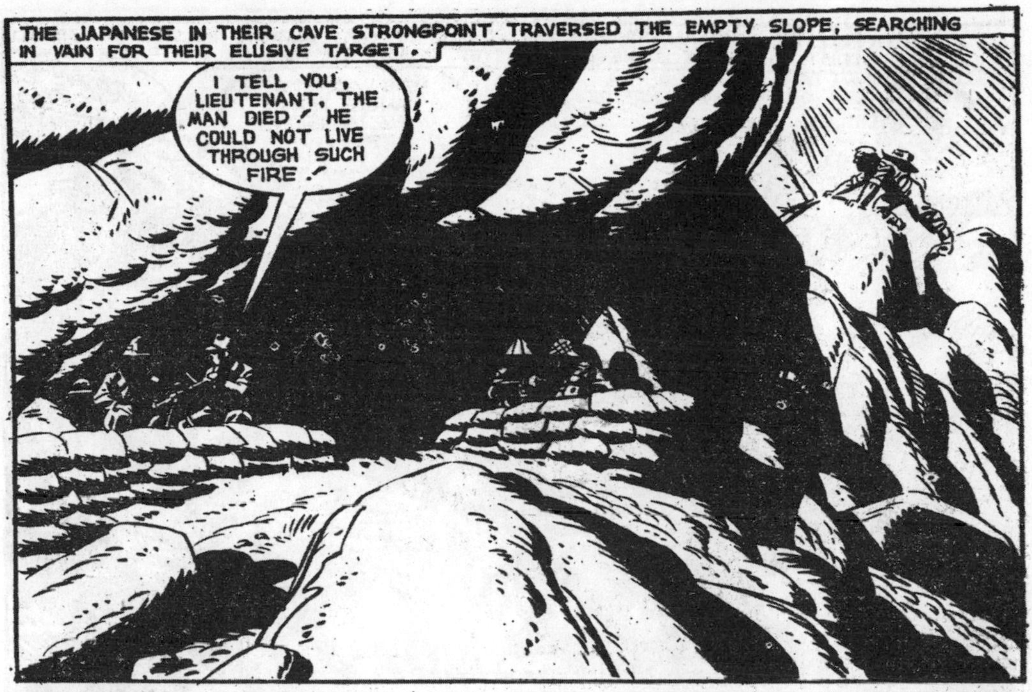
THE JAPANESE IN THEIR CAVE STRONGPOINT TRAVERSED THE EMPTY SLOPE, SEARCHING IN VAIN FOR THEIR ELUSIVE TARGET.
I TELL YOU, LIEUTENANT, THE MAN DIED! HE COULD NOT LIVE THROUGH SUCH FIRE!

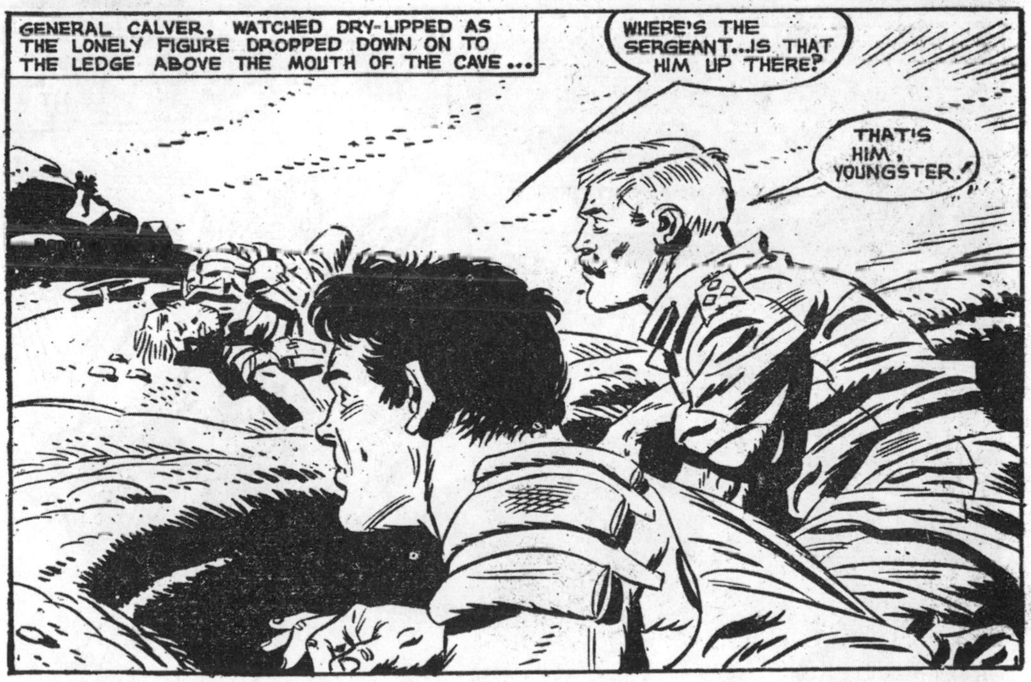
GENERAL CALVER, WATCHED DRY-LIPPED AS THE LONELY FIGURE DROPPED DOWN ON TO THE LEDGE ABOVE THE MOUTH OF THE CAVE...
WHERE'S THE SERGEANT...IS THAT HIM UP THERE?
THAT'S HIM, YOUNGSTER!

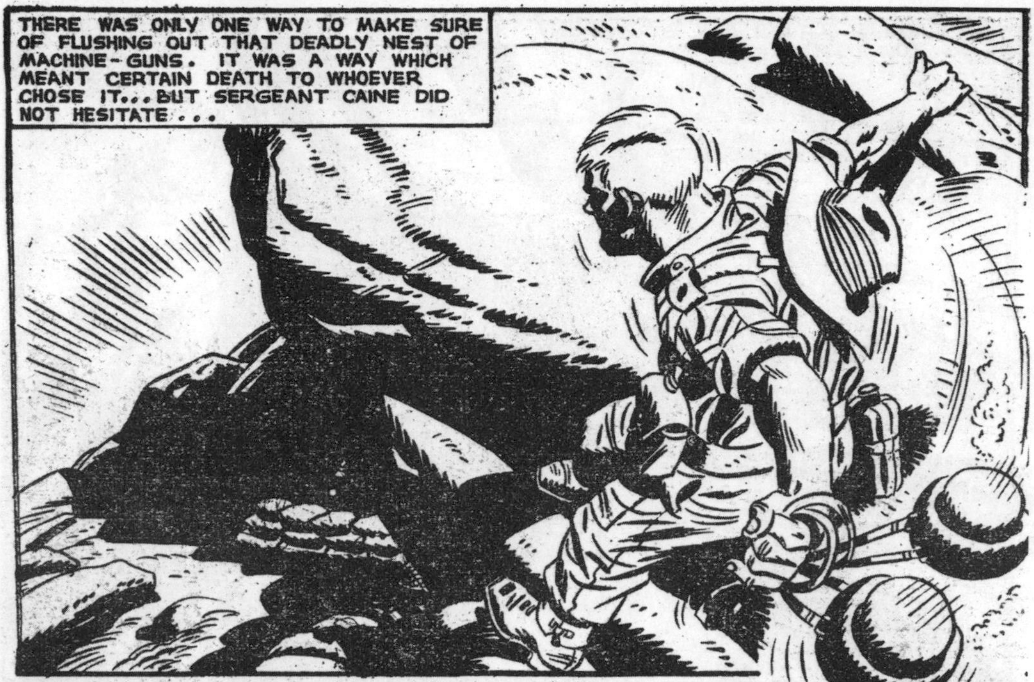
THERE WAS ONLY ONE WAY TO MAKE SURE OF FLUSHING OUT THAT DEADLY NEST OF MACHINE-GUNS. IT WAS A WAY WHICH MEANT CERTAIN DEATH TO WHOEVER CHOSE IT...BUT SERGEANT CAINE DID NOT HESITATE...

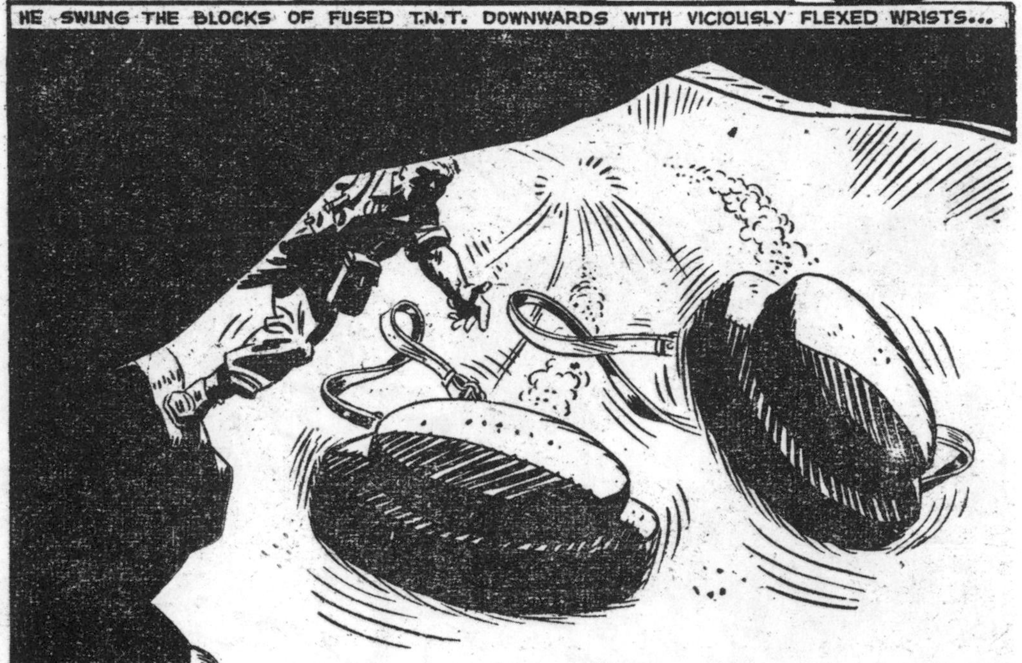
HE SWUNG THE BLOCKS OF FUSED T.N.T. DOWNWARDS WITH VICIOUSLY FLEXED WRISTS...

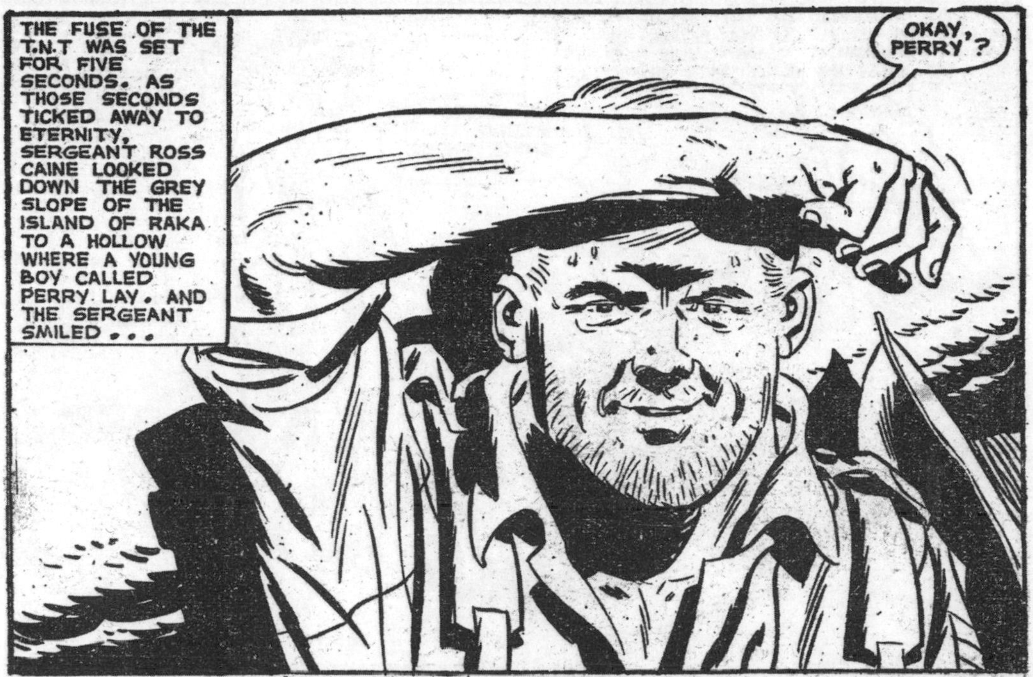
THE FUSE OF THE T.N.T WAS SET FOR FIVE SECONDS. AS THOSE SECONDS TICKED AWAY TO ETERNITY, SERGEANT ROSS CAINE LOOKED DOWN THE GREY SLOPE OF THE ISLAND OF RAKA TO A HOLLOW WHERE A YOUNG BOY CALLED PERRY LAY. AND THE SERGEANT SMILED...
OKAY, PERRY?

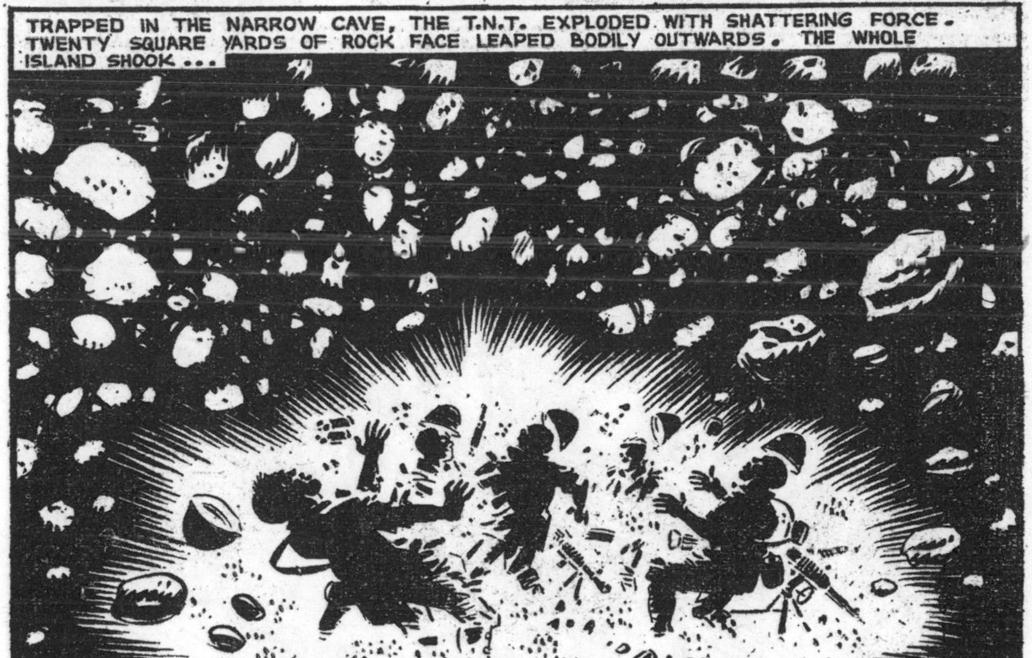
TRAPPED IN THE NARROW CAVE, THE T.N.T. EXPLODED WITH SHATTERING FORCE. TWENTY SQUARE YARDS OF ROCK FACE LEAPED BODILY OUTWARDS. THE WHOLE ISLAND SHOOK...

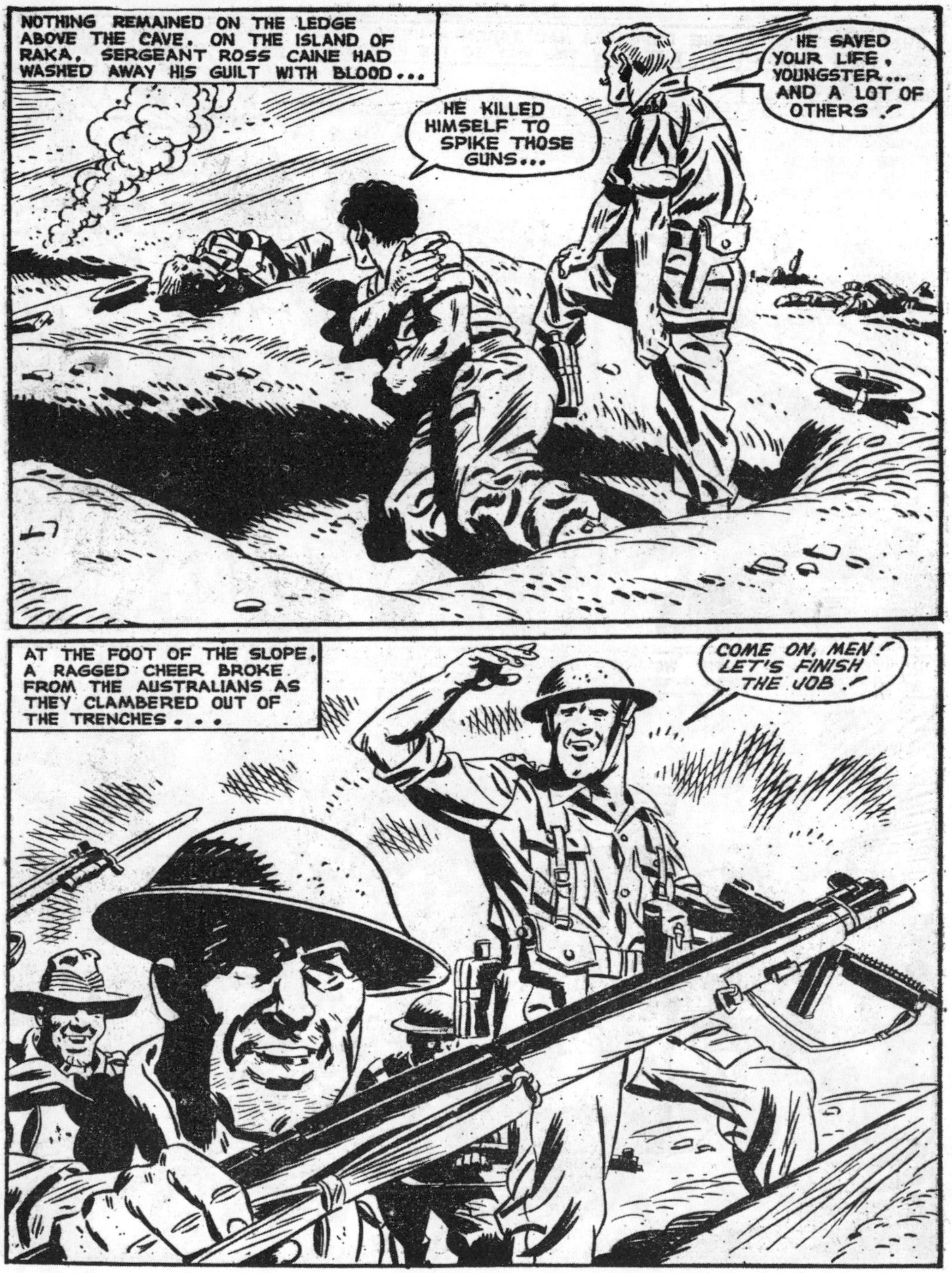
NOTHING REMAINED ON THE LEDGE ABOVE THE CAVE. ON THE ISLAND OF RAKA, SERGEANT ROSS CAINE HAD WASHED AWAY HIS GUILT WITH BLOOD...
HE KILLED HIMSELF TO SPIKE THOSE GUNS...
HE SAVED YOUR LIFE, YOUNGSTER... AND A LOT OF OTHERS!
AT THE FOOT OF THE SLOPE, A RAGGED CHEER BROKE FROM THE AUSTRALIANS AS THEY CLAMBERED OUT OF THE TRENCHES...
COME ON, MEN! LET'S FINISH THE JOB!

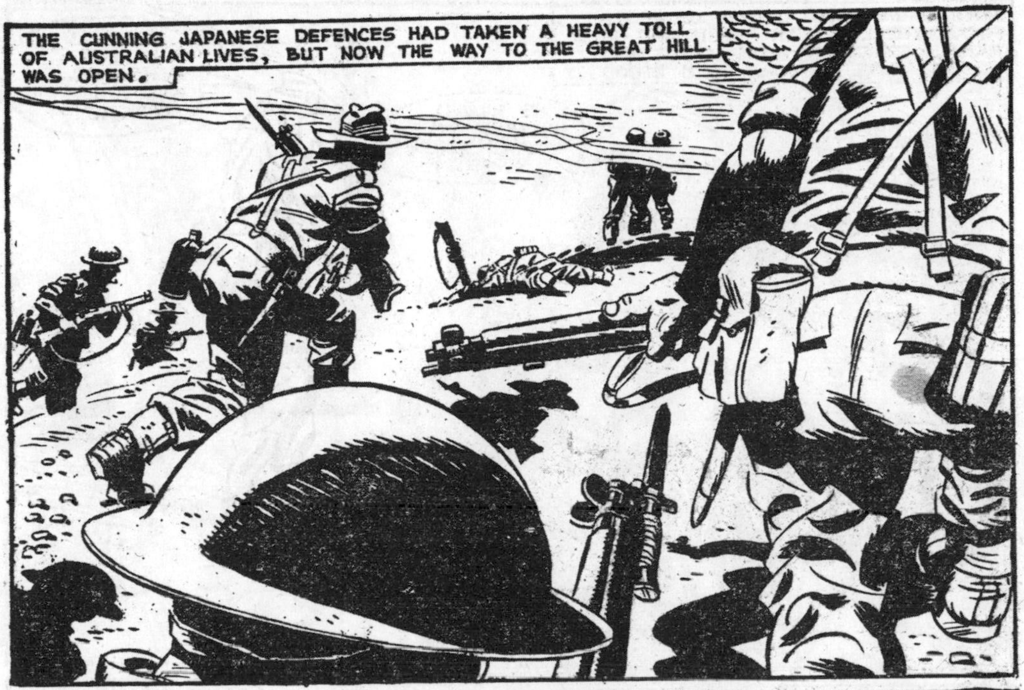
THE CUNNING JAPANESE DEFENCES HAD TAKEN A HEAVY TOLL OF AUSTRALIAN LIVES, BUT NOW THE WAY TO THE GREAT HILL WAS OPEN.

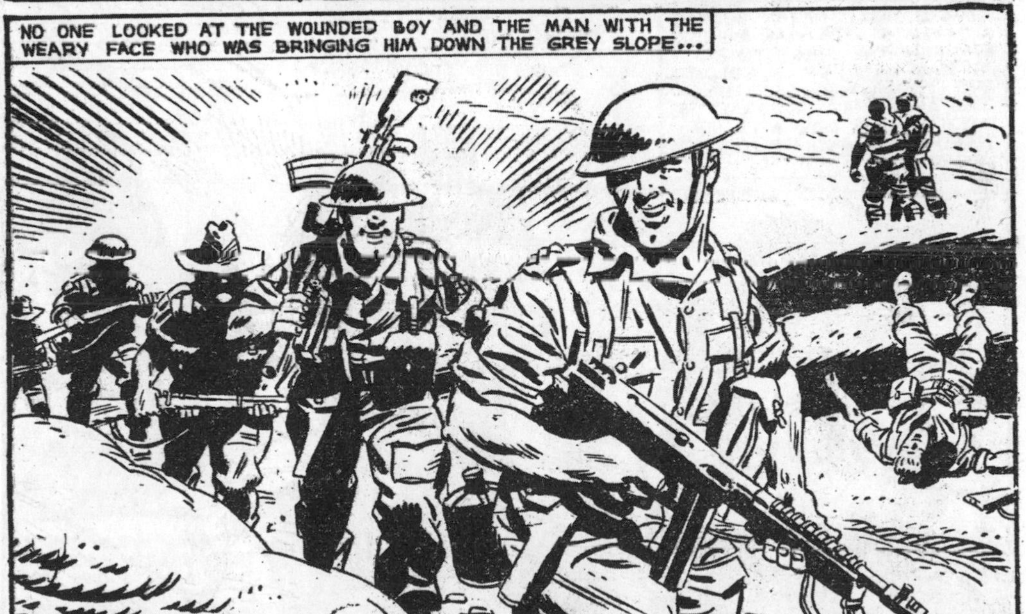
NO ONE LOOKED AT THE WOUNDED BOY AND THE MAN WITH THE WEARY FACE WHO WAS BRINGING HIM DOWN THE GREY SLOPE...

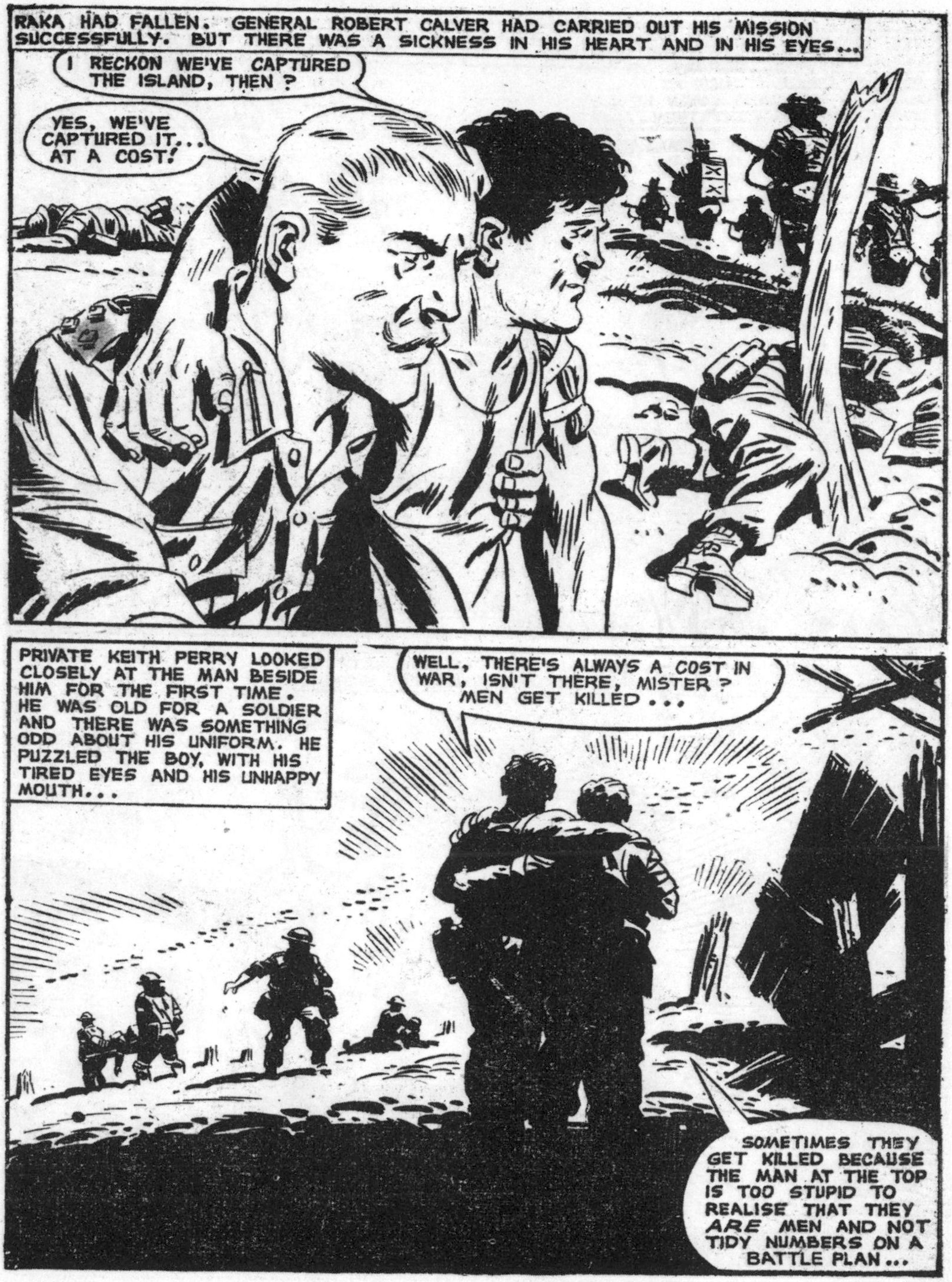
RAKA HAD FALLEN. GENERAL ROBERT CALVER HAD CARRIED OUT HIS MISSION SUCCESSFULLY. BUT THERE WAS A SICKNESS IN HIS HEART AND IN HIS EYES...
I RECKON WE'VE CAPTURED THE ISLAND, THEN?
YES, WE'VE CAPTURED IT... AT A COST!
PRIVATE KEITH PERRY LOOKED CLOSELY AT THE MAN BESIDE HIM FOR THE FIRST TIME. HE WAS OLD FOR A SOLDIER AND THERE WAS SOMETHING ODD ABOUT HIS UNIFORM. HE PUZZLED THE BOY, WITH HIS TIRED EYES AND HIS UNHAPPY MOUTH...
WELL, THERE'S ALWAYS A *COST* IN WAR, ISN'T THERE, MISTER? MEN GET KILLED...
SOMETIMES THEY GET KILLED BECAUSE THE MAN AT THE TOP IS TOO STUPID TO REALISE THAT THEY *ARE* MEN AND NOT TIDY NUMBERS ON A BATTLE PLAN...

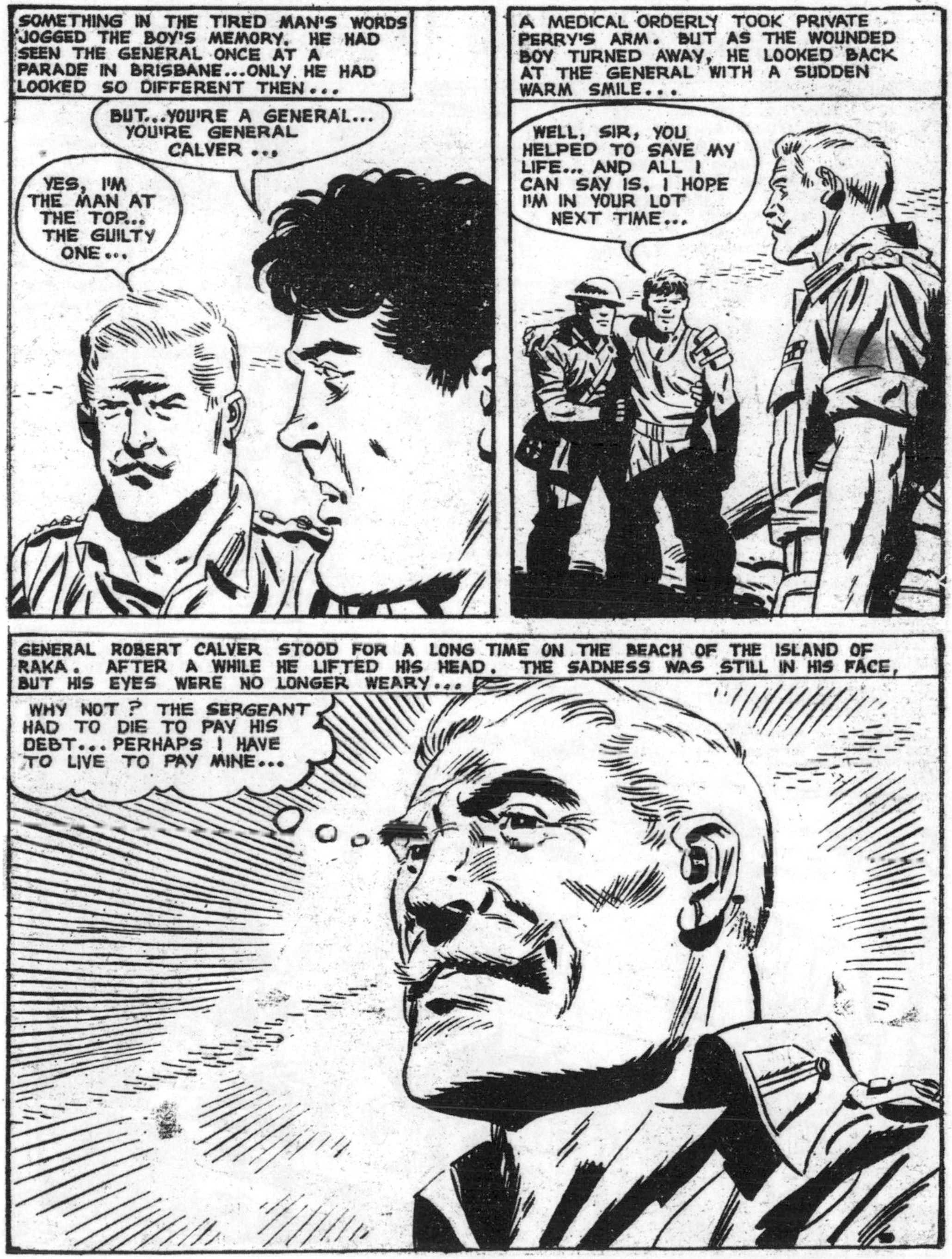
SOMETHING IN THE TIRED MAN'S WORDS JOGGED THE BOY'S MEMORY. HE HAD SEEN THE GENERAL ONCE AT A PARADE IN BRISBANE...ONLY HE HAD LOOKED SO DIFFERENT THEN...
BUT...YOU'RE A GENERAL... YOU'RE GENERAL CALVER...
YES, I'M THE MAN AT THE TOP... THE GUILTY ONE...
A MEDICAL ORDERLY TOOK PRIVATE PERRY'S ARM. BUT AS THE WOUNDED BOY TURNED AWAY, HE LOOKED BACK AT THE GENERAL WITH A SUDDEN WARM SMILE...
WELL, SIR, YOU HELPED TO SAVE MY LIFE... AND ALL I CAN SAY IS, I HOPE I'M IN YOUR LOT NEXT TIME...
GENERAL ROBERT CALVER STOOD FOR A LONG TIME ON THE BEACH OF THE ISLAND OF RAKA. AFTER A WHILE HE LIFTED HIS HEAD. THE SADNESS WAS STILL IN HIS FACE, BUT HIS EYES WERE NO LONGER WEARY...
WHY NOT? THE SERGEANT HAD TO DIE TO PAY HIS DEBT... PERHAPS I HAVE TO LIVE TO PAY MINE...

Chapter 4. The Legend Dies

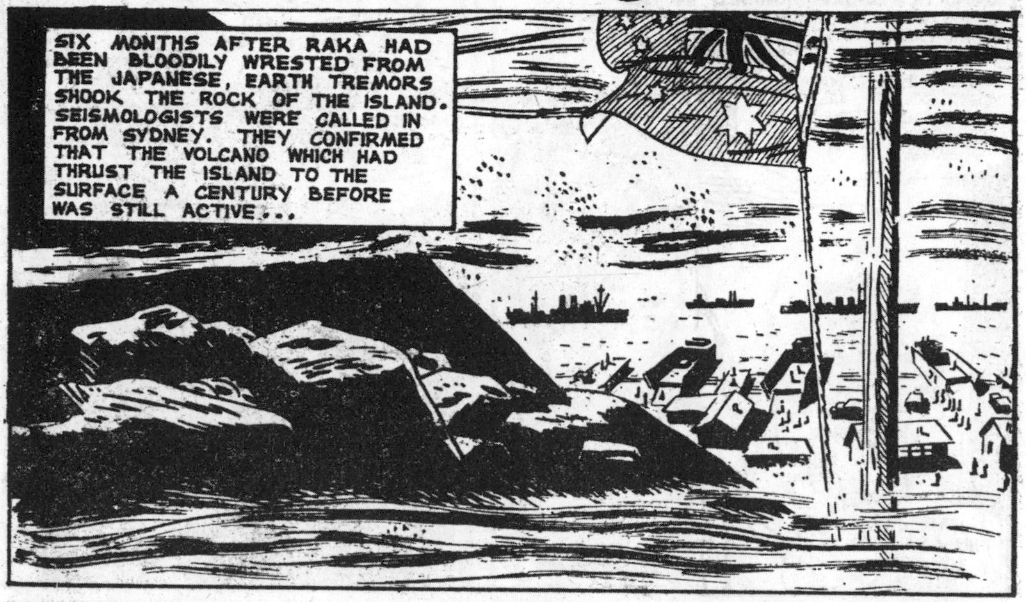
SIX MONTHS AFTER RAKA HAD BEEN BLOODILY WRESTED FROM THE JAPANESE, EARTH TREMORS SHOOK THE ROCK OF THE ISLAND. SEISMOLOGISTS WERE CALLED IN FROM SYDNEY. THEY CONFIRMED THAT THE VOLCANO WHICH HAD THRUST THE ISLAND TO THE SURFACE A CENTURY BEFORE WAS STILL ACTIVE...

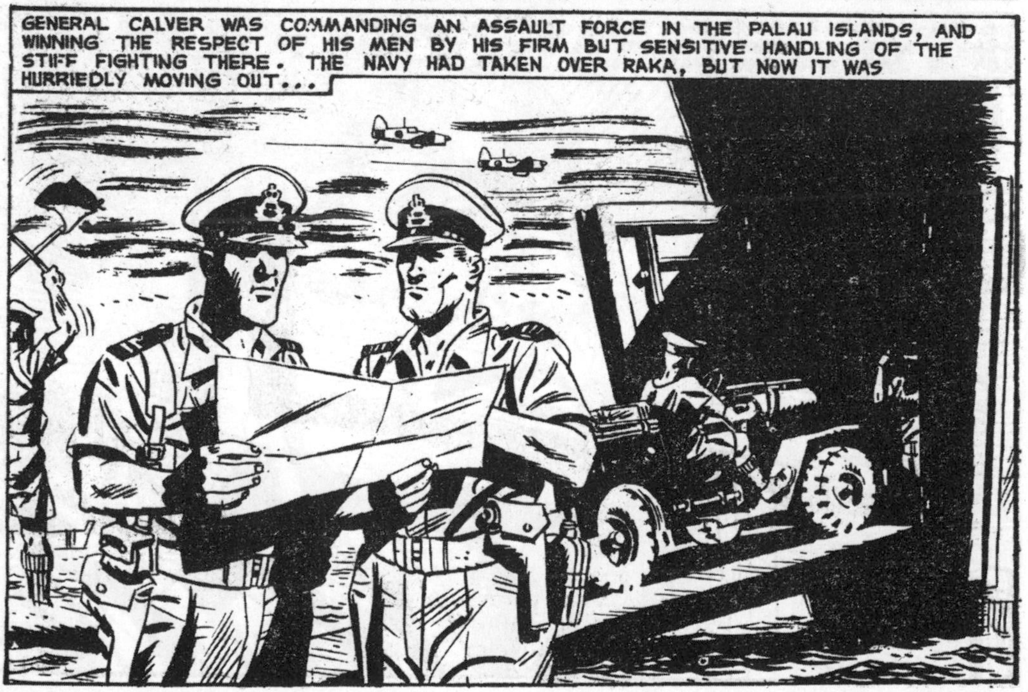
GENERAL CALVER WAS COMMANDING AN ASSAULT FORCE IN THE PALAU ISLANDS, AND WINNING THE RESPECT OF HIS MEN BY HIS FIRM BUT SENSITIVE HANDLING OF THE STIFF FIGHTING THERE. THE NAVY HAD TAKEN OVER RAKA, BUT NOW IT WAS HURRIEDLY MOVING OUT...

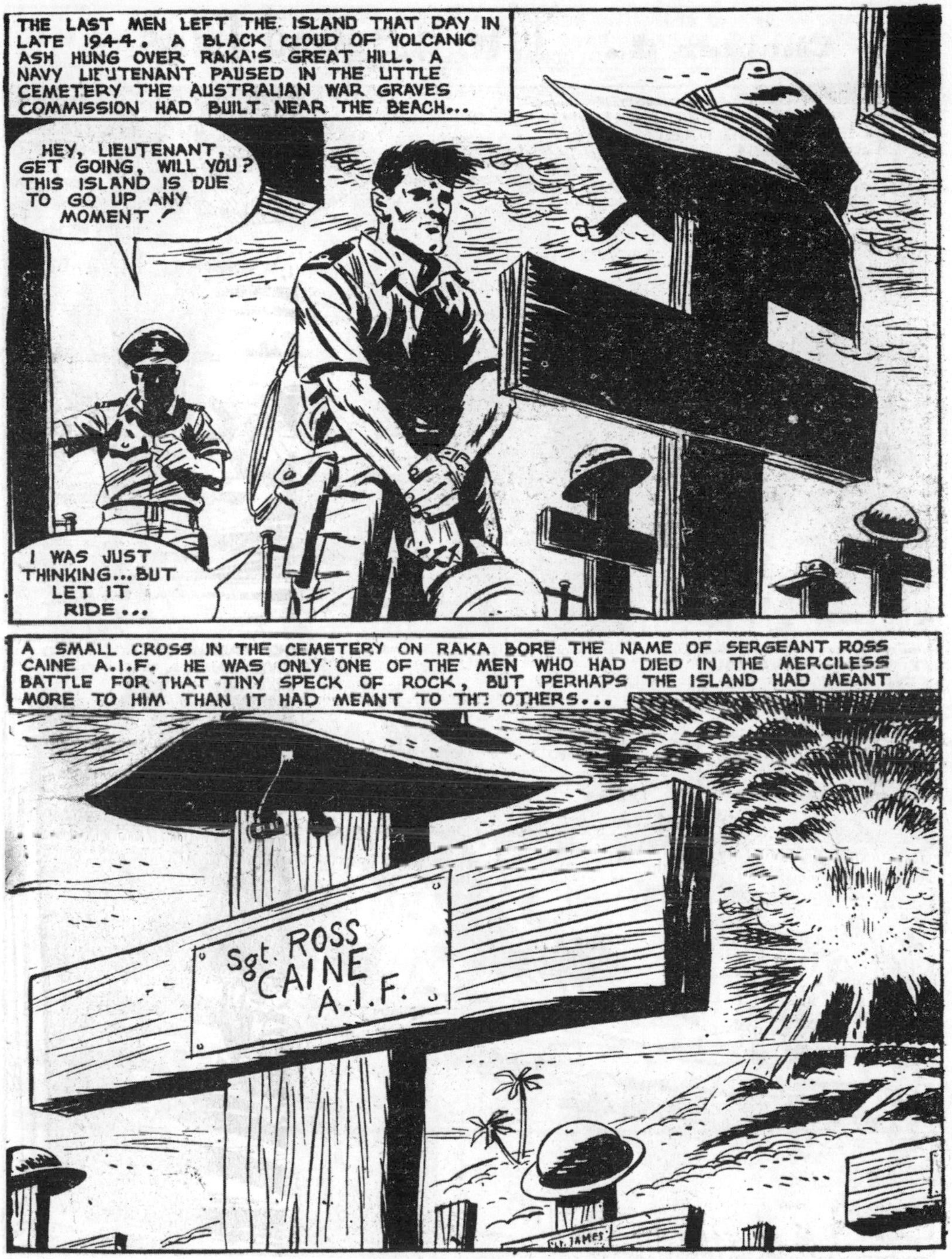
THE LAST MEN LEFT THE ISLAND THAT DAY IN LATE 1944. A BLACK CLOUD OF VOLCANIC ASH HUNG OVER RAKA'S GREAT HILL. A NAVY LIEUTENANT PAUSED IN THE LITTLE CEMETERY THE AUSTRALIAN WAR GRAVES COMMISSION HAD BUILT NEAR THE BEACH...
HEY, LIEUTENANT, GET GOING, WILL YOU? THIS ISLAND IS DUE TO GO UP ANY MOMENT!
I WAS JUST THINKING... BUT LET IT RIDE...
A SMALL CROSS IN THE CEMETERY ON RAKA BORE THE NAME OF SERGEANT ROSS CAINE A.I.F. HE WAS ONLY ONE OF THE MEN WHO HAD DIED IN THE MERCILESS BATTLE FOR THAT TINY SPECK OF ROCK, BUT PERHAPS THE ISLAND HAD MEANT MORE TO HIM THAN IT HAD MEANT TO THE OTHERS...
Sgt. ROSS CAINE A.I.F.

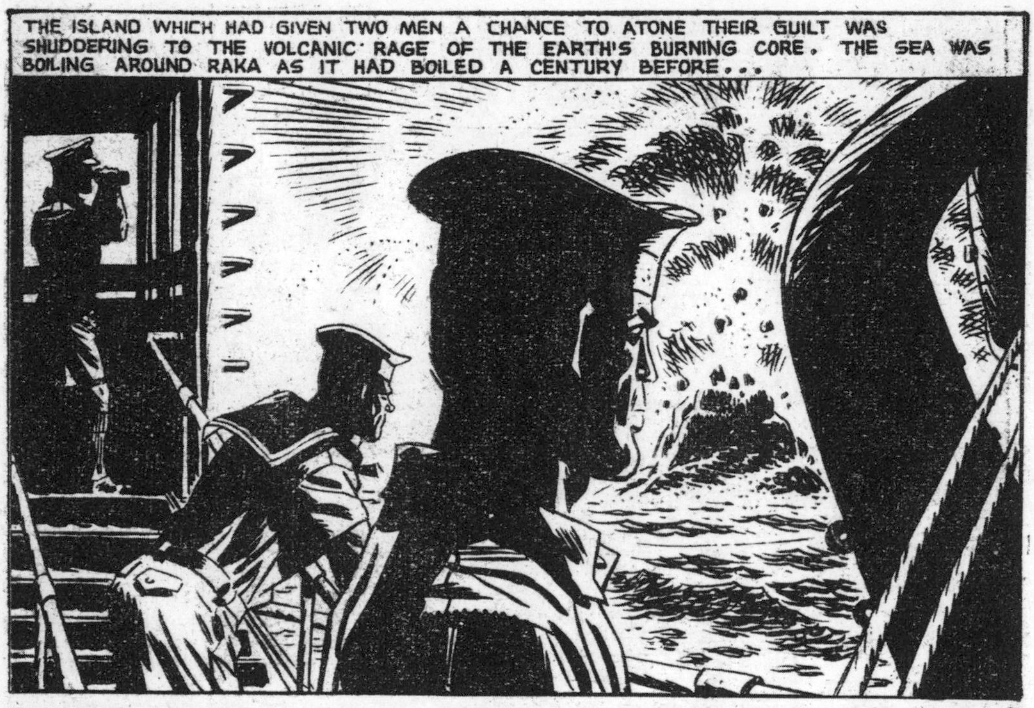
THE ISLAND WHICH HAD GIVEN TWO MEN A CHANCE TO ATONE THEIR GUILT WAS SHUDDERING TO THE VOLCANIC RAGE OF THE EARTH'S BURNING CORE. THE SEA WAS BOILING AROUND RAKA AS IT HAD BOILED A CENTURY BEFORE...

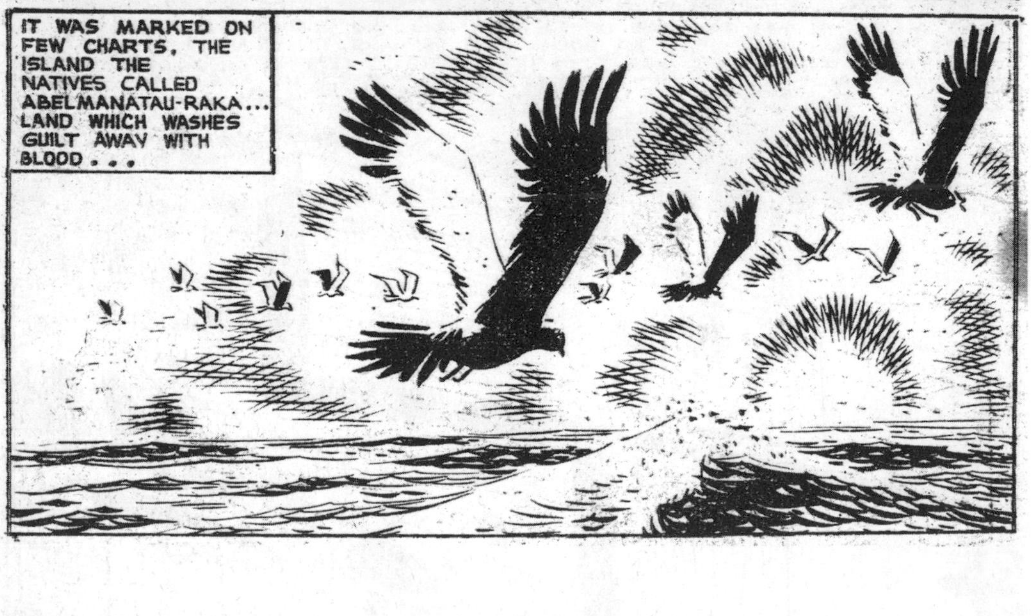
IT WAS MARKED ON FEW CHARTS, THE ISLAND THE NATIVES CALLED ABELMANATAU-RAKA... LAND WHICH WASHES GUILT AWAY WITH BLOOD...

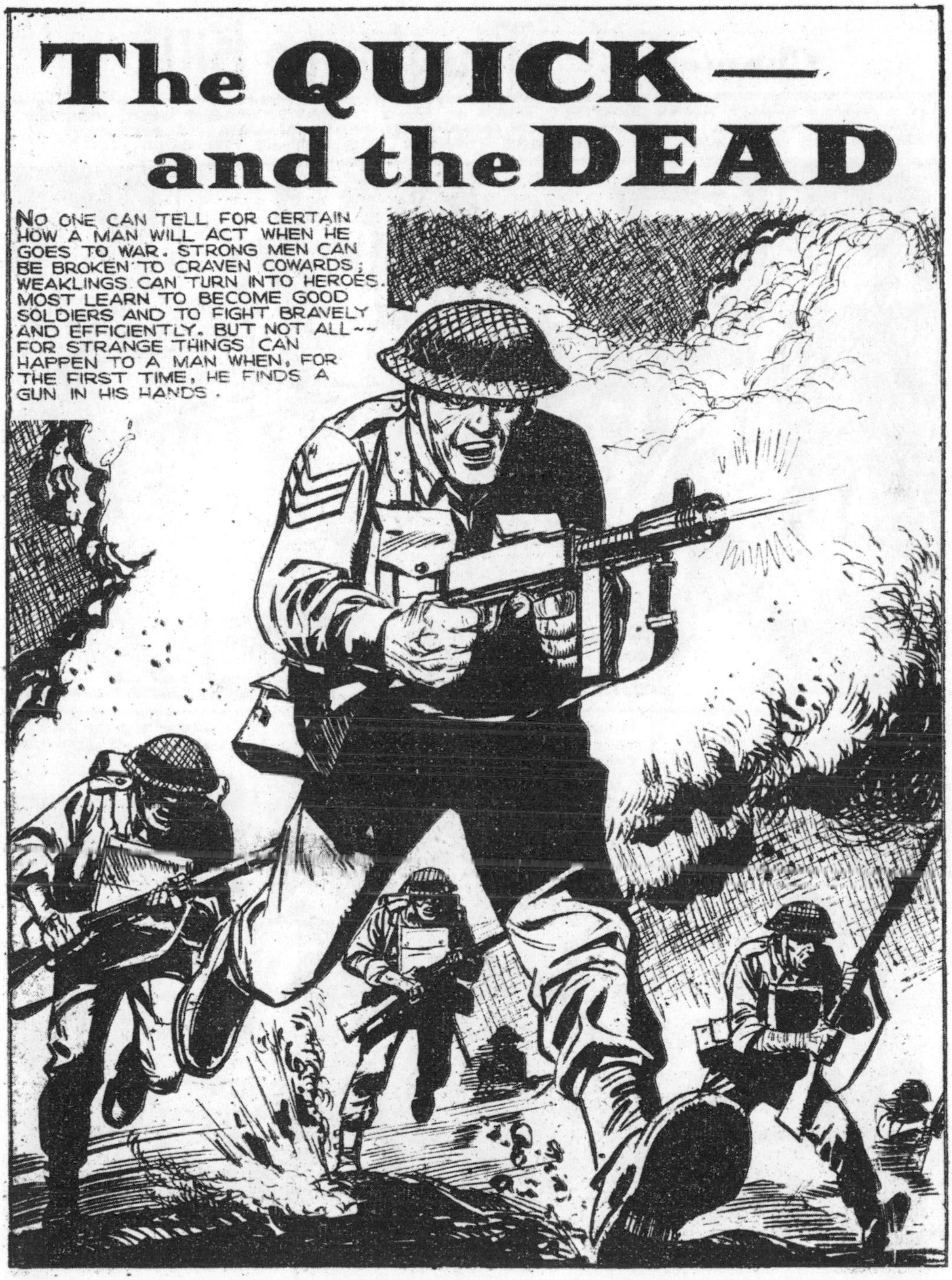
The QUICK—
and the DEAD
NO ONE CAN TELL FOR CERTAIN HOW A MAN WILL ACT WHEN HE GOES TO WAR. STRONG MEN CAN BE BROKEN TO CRAVEN COWARDS; WEAKLINGS CAN TURN INTO HEROES. MOST LEARN TO BECOME GOOD SOLDIERS AND TO FIGHT BRAVELY AND EFFICIENTLY. BUT NOT ALL~~ FOR STRANGE THINGS CAN HAPPEN TO A MAN WHEN, FOR THE FIRST TIME, HE FINDS A GUN IN HIS HANDS.

Chapter 1. Taught to Kill

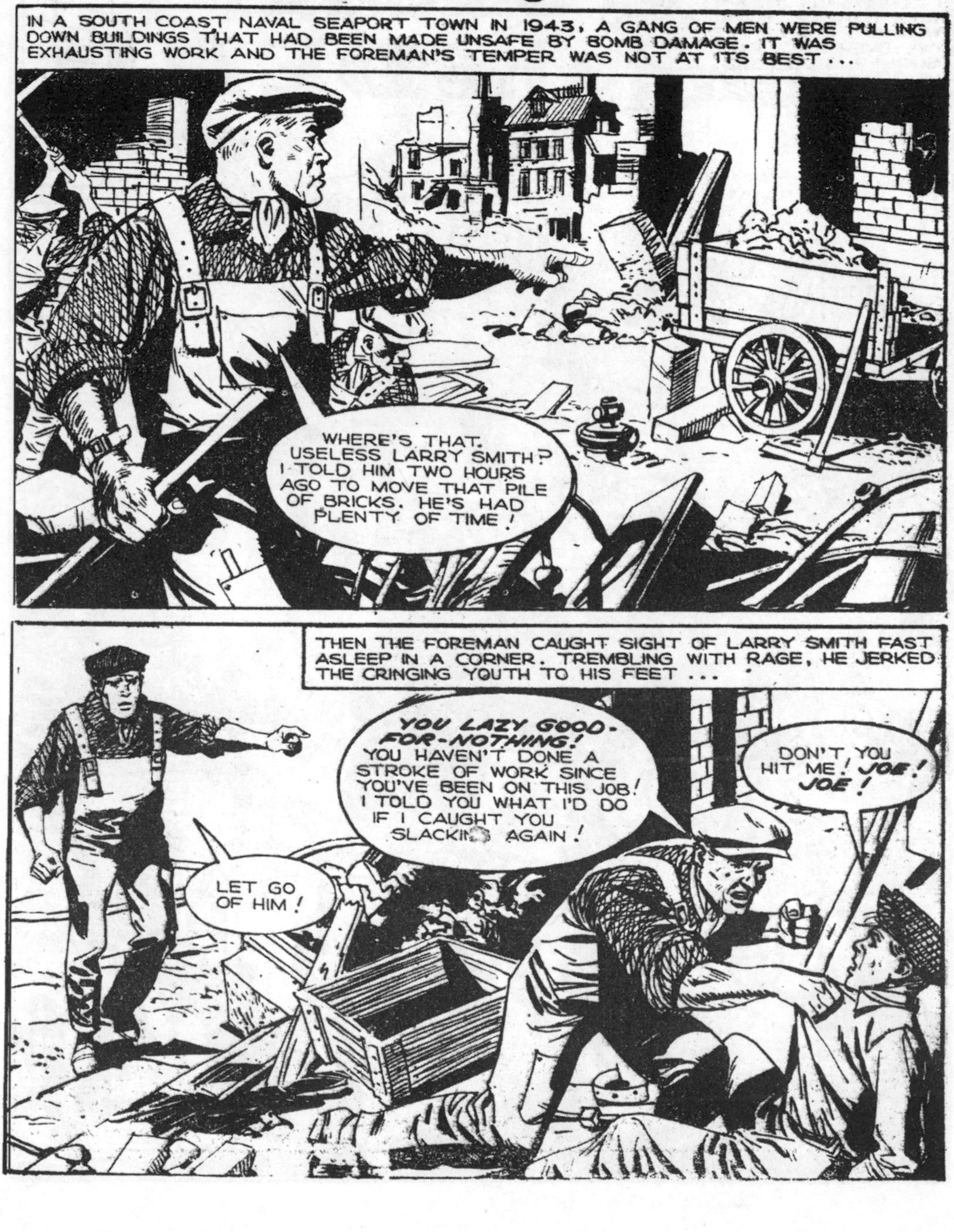
IN A SOUTH COAST NAVAL SEAPORT TOWN IN 1943, A GANG OF MEN WERE PULLING DOWN BUILDINGS THAT HAD BEEN MADE UNSAFE BY BOMB DAMAGE. IT WAS EXHAUSTING WORK AND THE FOREMAN'S TEMPER WAS NOT AT ITS BEST ...
WHERE'S THAT USELESS LARRY SMITH? I TOLD HIM TWO HOURS AGO TO MOVE THAT PILE OF BRICKS. HE'S HAD PLENTY OF TIME!
THEN THE FOREMAN CAUGHT SIGHT OF LARRY SMITH FAST ASLEEP IN A CORNER. TREMBLING WITH RAGE, HE JERKED THE CRINGING YOUTH TO HIS FEET ...
YOU LAZY GOOD-FOR-NOTHING! YOU HAVEN'T DONE A STROKE OF WORK SINCE YOU'VE BEEN ON THIS JOB! I TOLD YOU WHAT I'D DO IF I CAUGHT YOU SLACKING AGAIN!
DON'T YOU HIT ME! JOE! JOE!
LET GO OF HIM!

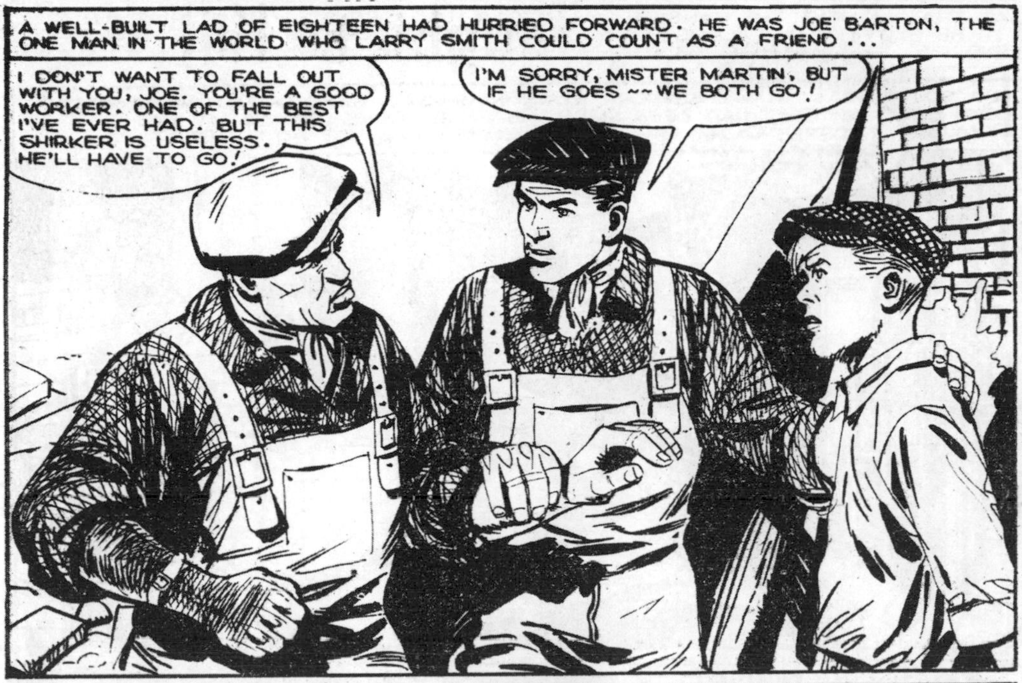
A WELL-BUILT LAD OF EIGHTEEN HAD HURRIED FORWARD. HE WAS JOE BARTON, THE ONE MAN IN THE WORLD WHO LARRY SMITH COULD COUNT AS A FRIEND ...
I DON'T WANT TO FALL OUT WITH YOU, JOE. YOU'RE A GOOD WORKER. ONE OF THE BEST I'VE EVER HAD. BUT THIS SHIRKER IS USELESS. HE'LL HAVE TO GO!
I'M SORRY, MISTER MARTIN, BUT IF HE GOES ~~ WE BOTH GO!

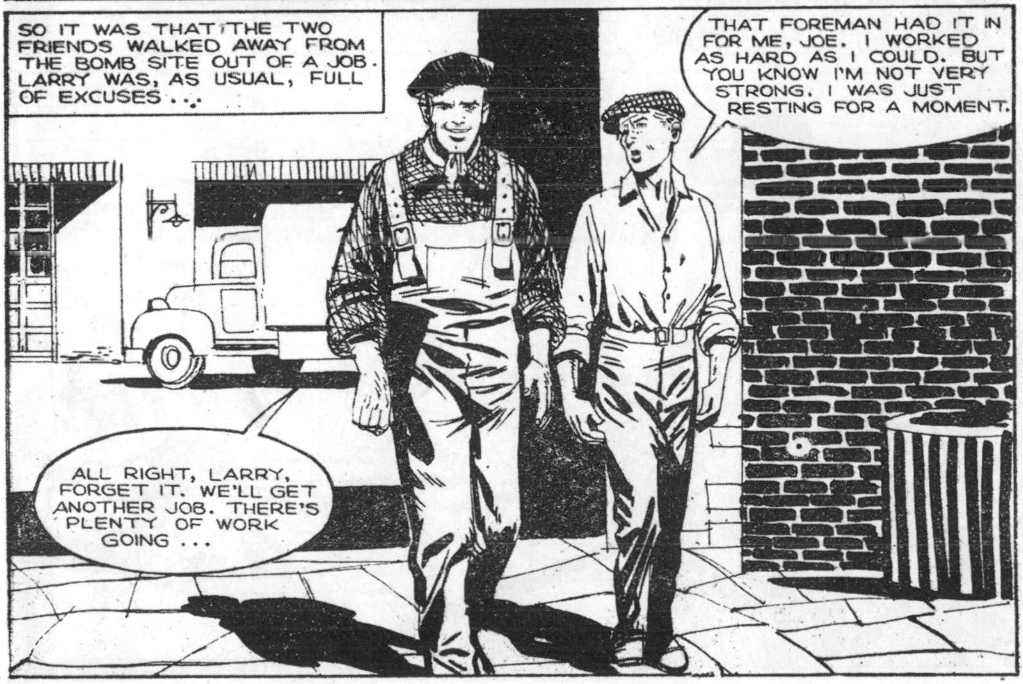
SO IT WAS THAT THE TWO FRIENDS WALKED AWAY FROM THE BOMB SITE OUT OF A JOB. LARRY WAS, AS USUAL, FULL OF EXCUSES ...
THAT FOREMAN HAD IT IN FOR ME, JOE. I WORKED AS HARD AS I COULD. BUT YOU KNOW I'M NOT VERY STRONG. I WAS JUST RESTING FOR A MOMENT.
ALL RIGHT, LARRY, FORGET IT. WE'LL GET ANOTHER JOB. THERE'S PLENTY OF WORK GOING ...

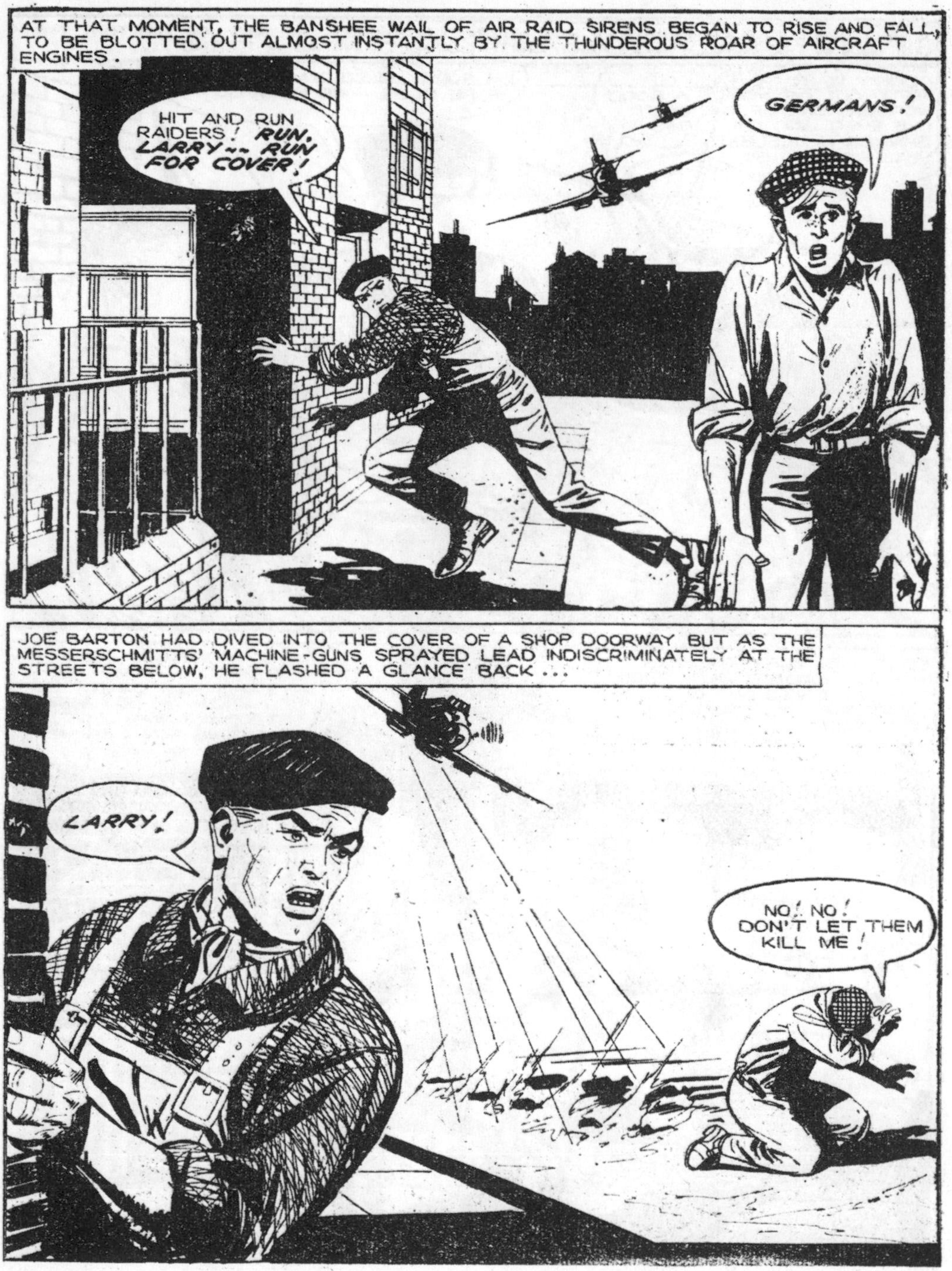
AT THAT MOMENT, THE BANSHEE WAIL OF AIR RAID SIRENS BEGAN TO RISE AND FALL, TO BE BLOTTED OUT ALMOST INSTANTLY BY THE THUNDEROUS ROAR OF AIRCRAFT ENGINES.
HIT AND RUN RAIDERS! RUN, LARRY -- RUN FOR COVER!
GERMANS!
JOE BARTON HAD DIVED INTO THE COVER OF A SHOP DOORWAY BUT AS THE MESSERSCHMITTS' MACHINE-GUNS SPRAYED LEAD INDISCRIMINATELY AT THE STREETS BELOW, HE FLASHED A GLANCE BACK ...
LARRY!
NO! NO! DON'T LET THEM KILL ME!

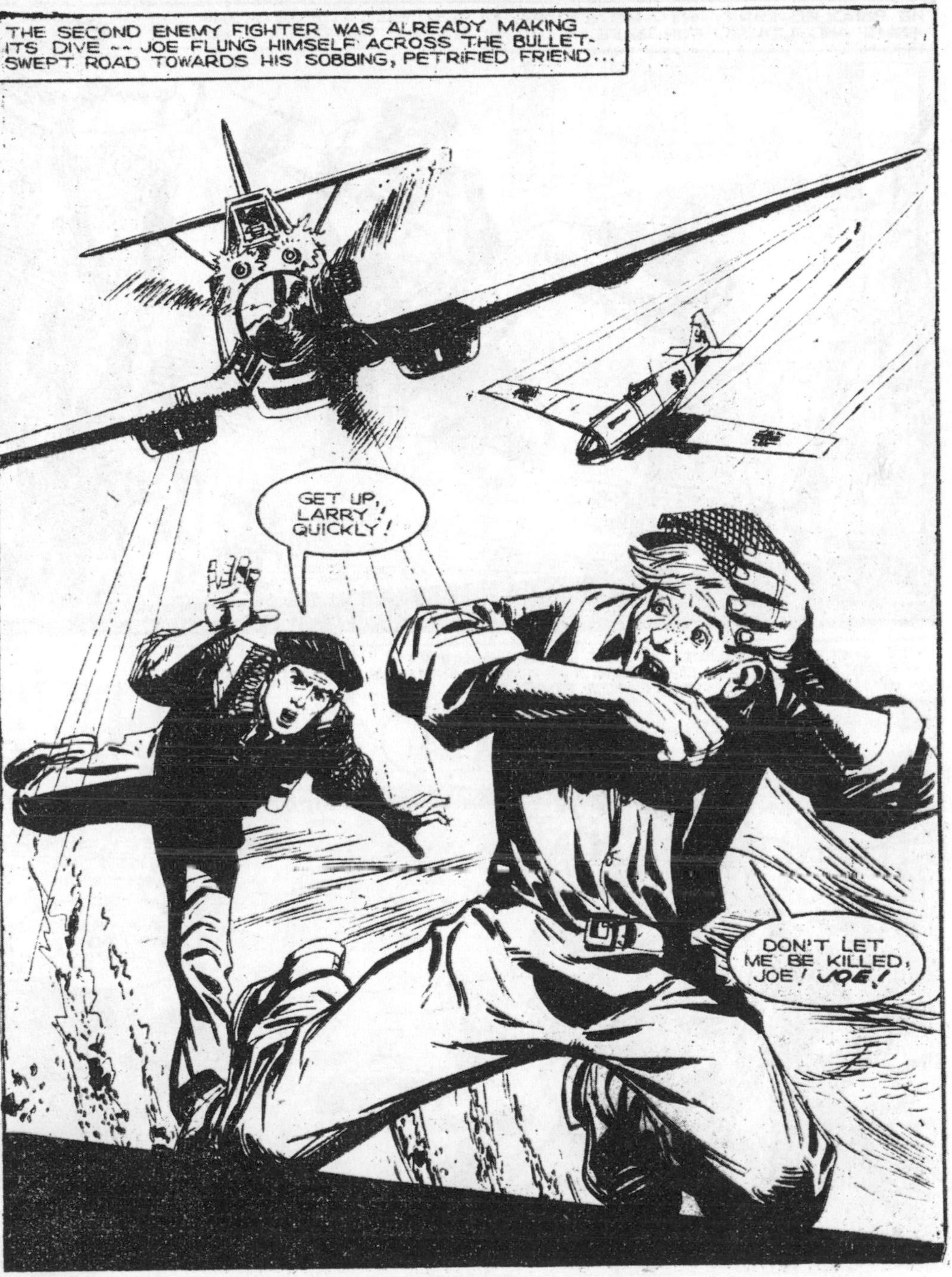
THE SECOND ENEMY FIGHTER WAS ALREADY MAKING ITS DIVE -- JOE FLUNG HIMSELF ACROSS THE BULLET-SWEPT ROAD TOWARDS HIS SOBBING, PETRIFIED FRIEND...
GET UP, LARRY! QUICKLY!
DON'T LET ME BE KILLED, JOE! JOE!

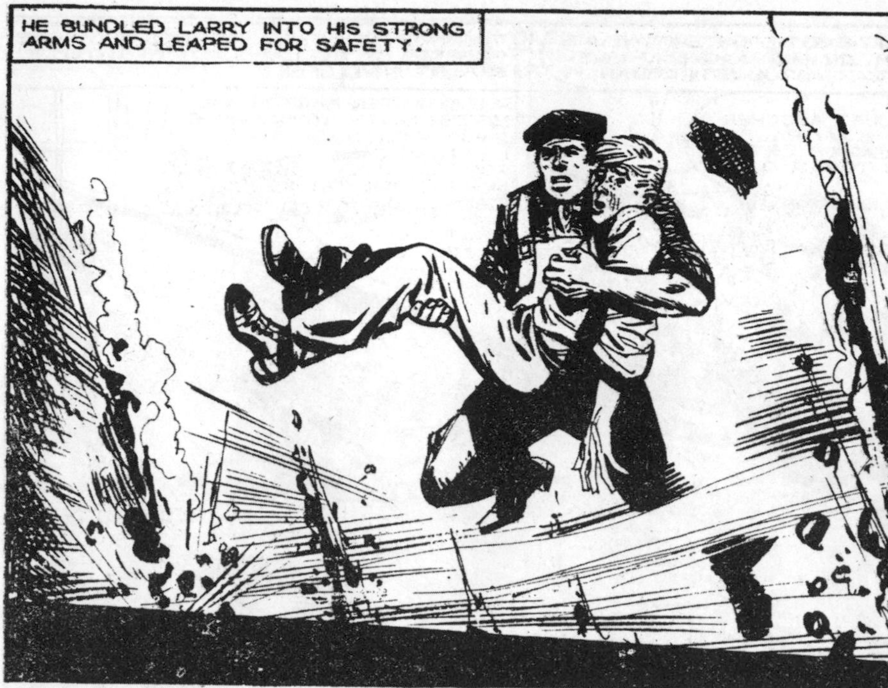
HE BUNDLED LARRY INTO HIS STRONG ARMS AND LEAPED FOR SAFETY.

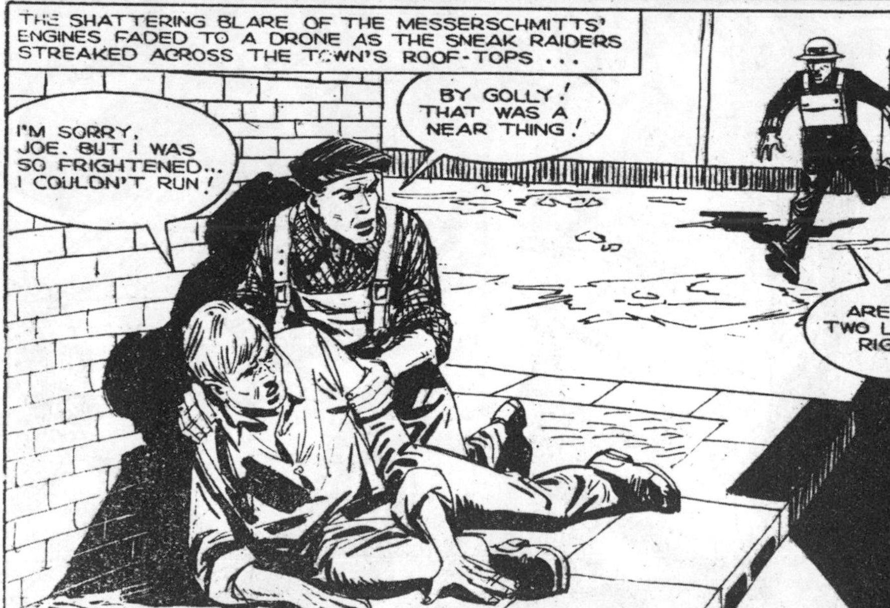
THE SHATTERING BLARE OF THE MESSERSCHMITTS' ENGINES FADED TO A DRONE AS THE SNEAK RAIDERS STREAKED ACROSS THE TOWN'S ROOF-TOPS ...
I'M SORRY, JOE. BUT I WAS SO FRIGHTENED... I COULDN'T RUN!
BY GOLLY! THAT WAS A NEAR THING!
ARE YOU TWO LADS ALL RIGHT?

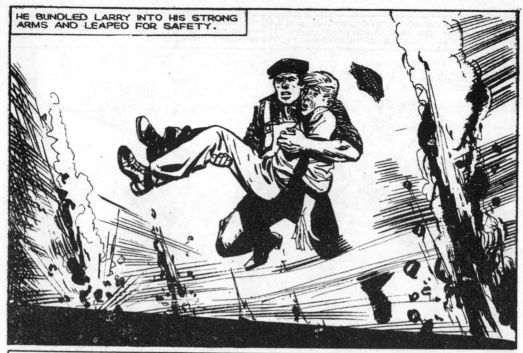

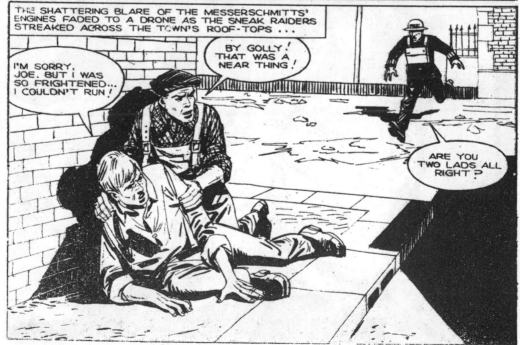

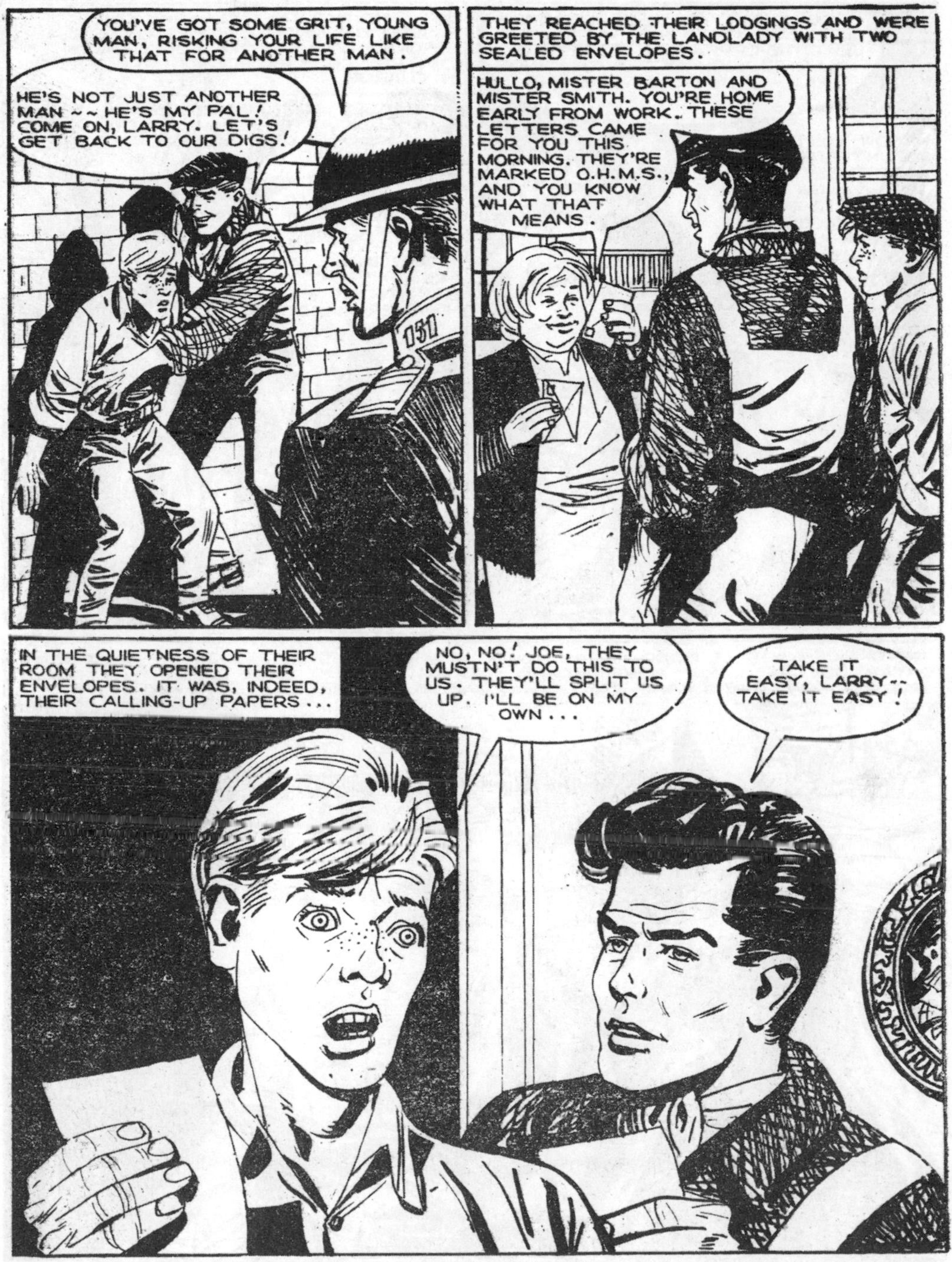
YOU'VE GOT SOME GRIT, YOUNG MAN, RISKING YOUR LIFE LIKE THAT FOR ANOTHER MAN.
HE'S NOT JUST ANOTHER MAN ~~ HE'S MY PAL! COME ON, LARRY. LET'S GET BACK TO OUR DIGS!
THEY REACHED THEIR LODGINGS AND WERE GREETED BY THE LANDLADY WITH TWO SEALED ENVELOPES.
HULLO, MISTER BARTON AND MISTER SMITH. YOU'RE HOME EARLY FROM WORK. THESE LETTERS CAME FOR YOU THIS MORNING. THEY'RE MARKED O.H.M.S., AND YOU KNOW WHAT THAT MEANS.
IN THE QUIETNESS OF THEIR ROOM THEY OPENED THEIR ENVELOPES. IT WAS, INDEED, THEIR CALLING-UP PAPERS...
NO, NO! JOE, THEY MUSTN'T DO THIS TO US. THEY'LL SPLIT US UP. I'LL BE ON MY OWN...
TAKE IT EASY, LARRY-- TAKE IT EASY!

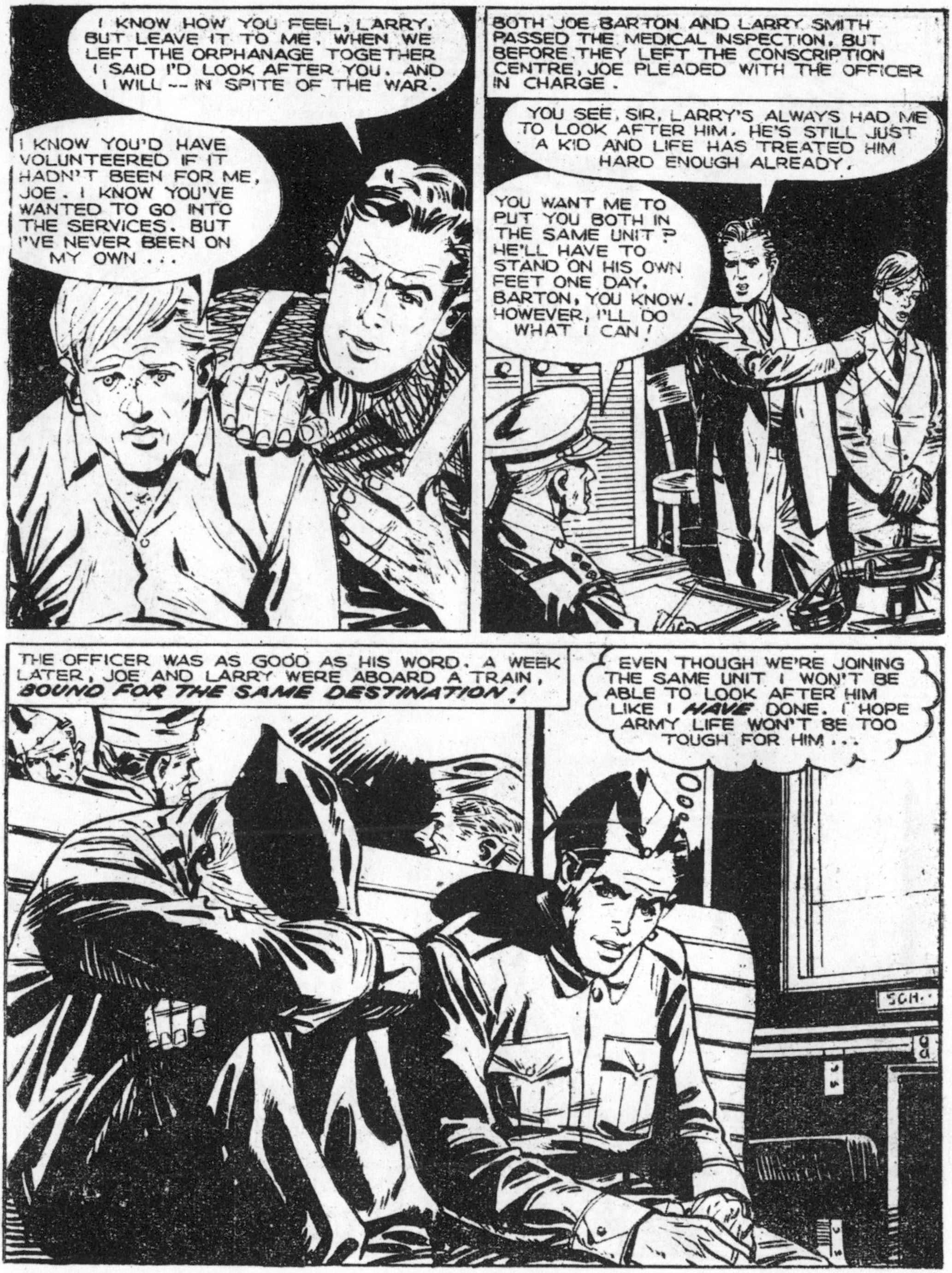
I KNOW HOW YOU FEEL, LARRY, BUT LEAVE IT TO ME. WHEN WE LEFT THE ORPHANAGE TOGETHER I SAID I'D LOOK AFTER YOU. AND I WILL -- IN SPITE OF THE WAR.
I KNOW YOU'D HAVE VOLUNTEERED IF IT HADN'T BEEN FOR ME, JOE. I KNOW YOU'VE WANTED TO GO INTO THE SERVICES. BUT I'VE NEVER BEEN ON MY OWN . . .
BOTH JOE BARTON AND LARRY SMITH PASSED THE MEDICAL INSPECTION, BUT BEFORE THEY LEFT THE CONSCRIPTION CENTRE, JOE PLEADED WITH THE OFFICER IN CHARGE.
YOU SEE, SIR, LARRY'S ALWAYS HAD ME TO LOOK AFTER HIM. HE'S STILL JUST A KID AND LIFE HAS TREATED HIM HARD ENOUGH ALREADY.
YOU WANT ME TO PUT YOU BOTH IN THE SAME UNIT? HE'LL HAVE TO STAND ON HIS OWN FEET ONE DAY, BARTON, YOU KNOW. HOWEVER, I'LL DO WHAT I CAN!
THE OFFICER WAS AS GOOD AS HIS WORD. A WEEK LATER, JOE AND LARRY WERE ABOARD A TRAIN, BOUND FOR THE SAME DESTINATION!
EVEN THOUGH WE'RE JOINING THE SAME UNIT I WON'T BE ABLE TO LOOK AFTER HIM LIKE I HAVE DONE. I HOPE ARMY LIFE WON'T BE TOO TOUGH FOR HIM . . .
SCH.

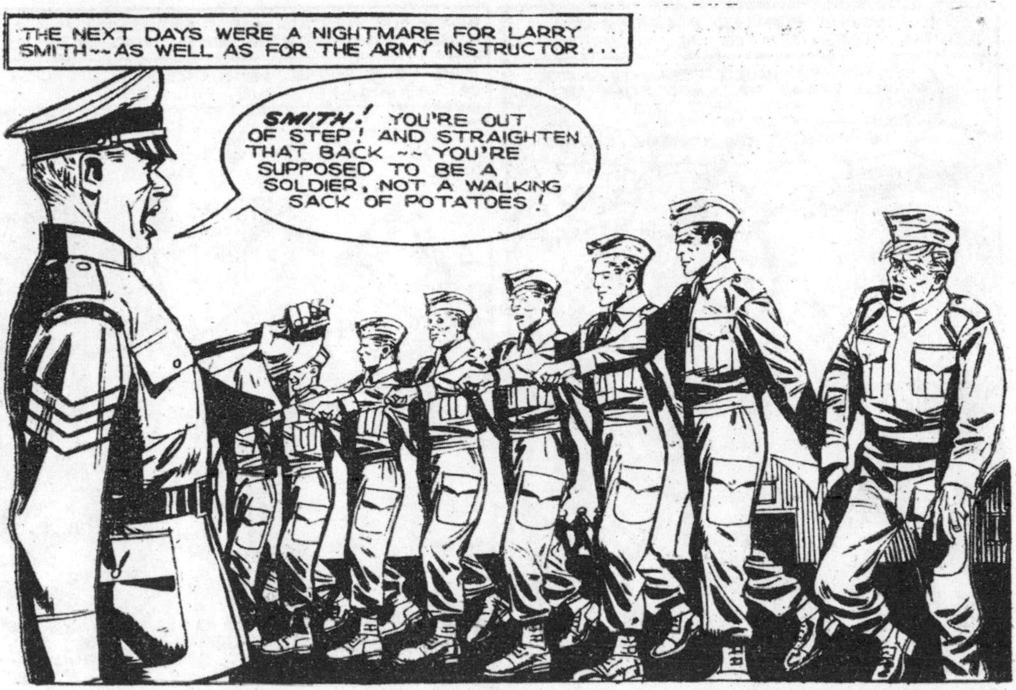
THE NEXT DAYS WERE A NIGHTMARE FOR LARRY SMITH--AS WELL AS FOR THE ARMY INSTRUCTOR ...
SMITH! YOU'RE OUT OF STEP! AND STRAIGHTEN THAT BACK -- YOU'RE SUPPOSED TO BE A SOLDIER, NOT A WALKING SACK OF POTATOES!

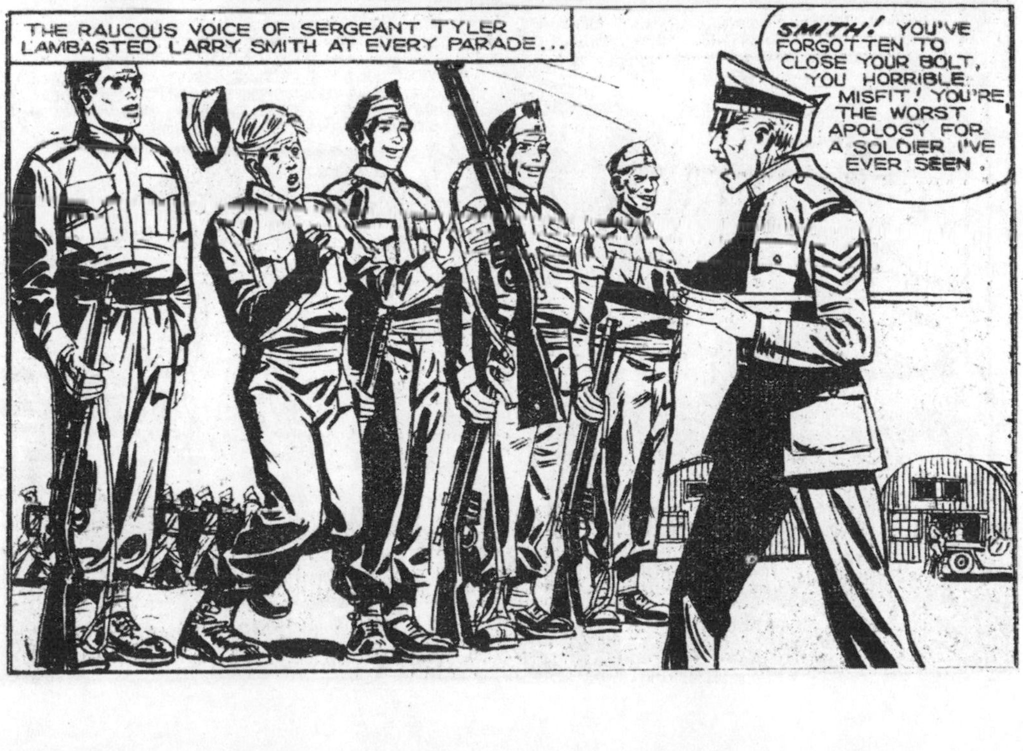
THE RAUCOUS VOICE OF SERGEANT TYLER LAMBASTED LARRY SMITH AT EVERY PARADE...
SMITH! YOU'VE FORGOTTEN TO CLOSE YOUR BOLT, YOU HORRIBLE MISFIT! YOU'RE THE WORST APOLOGY FOR A SOLDIER I'VE EVER SEEN.

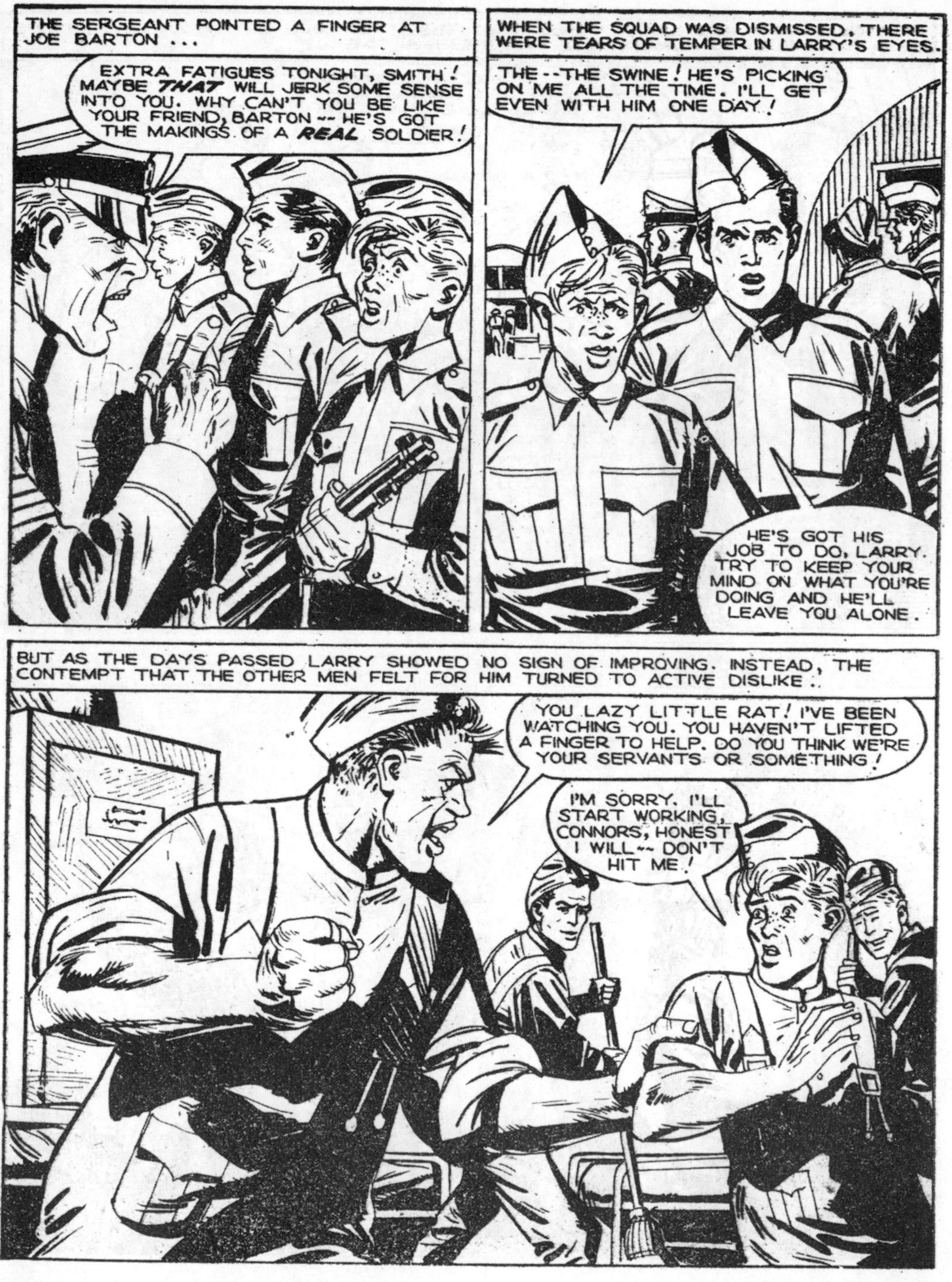
THE SERGEANT POINTED A FINGER AT JOE BARTON ...
EXTRA FATIGUES TONIGHT, SMITH! MAYBE THAT WILL JERK SOME SENSE INTO YOU. WHY CAN'T YOU BE LIKE YOUR FRIEND, BARTON -- HE'S GOT THE MAKINGS OF A REAL SOLDIER!
WHEN THE SQUAD WAS DISMISSED, THERE WERE TEARS OF TEMPER IN LARRY'S EYES.
THE--THE SWINE! HE'S PICKING ON ME ALL THE TIME. I'LL GET EVEN WITH HIM ONE DAY!
HE'S GOT HIS JOB TO DO, LARRY. TRY TO KEEP YOUR MIND ON WHAT YOU'RE DOING AND HE'LL LEAVE YOU ALONE.
BUT AS THE DAYS PASSED LARRY SHOWED NO SIGN OF IMPROVING. INSTEAD, THE CONTEMPT THAT THE OTHER MEN FELT FOR HIM TURNED TO ACTIVE DISLIKE.
YOU LAZY LITTLE RAT! I'VE BEEN WATCHING YOU. YOU HAVEN'T LIFTED A FINGER TO HELP. DO YOU THINK WE'RE YOUR SERVANTS OR SOMETHING!
I'M SORRY. I'LL START WORKING, CONNORS, HONEST I WILL -- DON'T HIT ME!

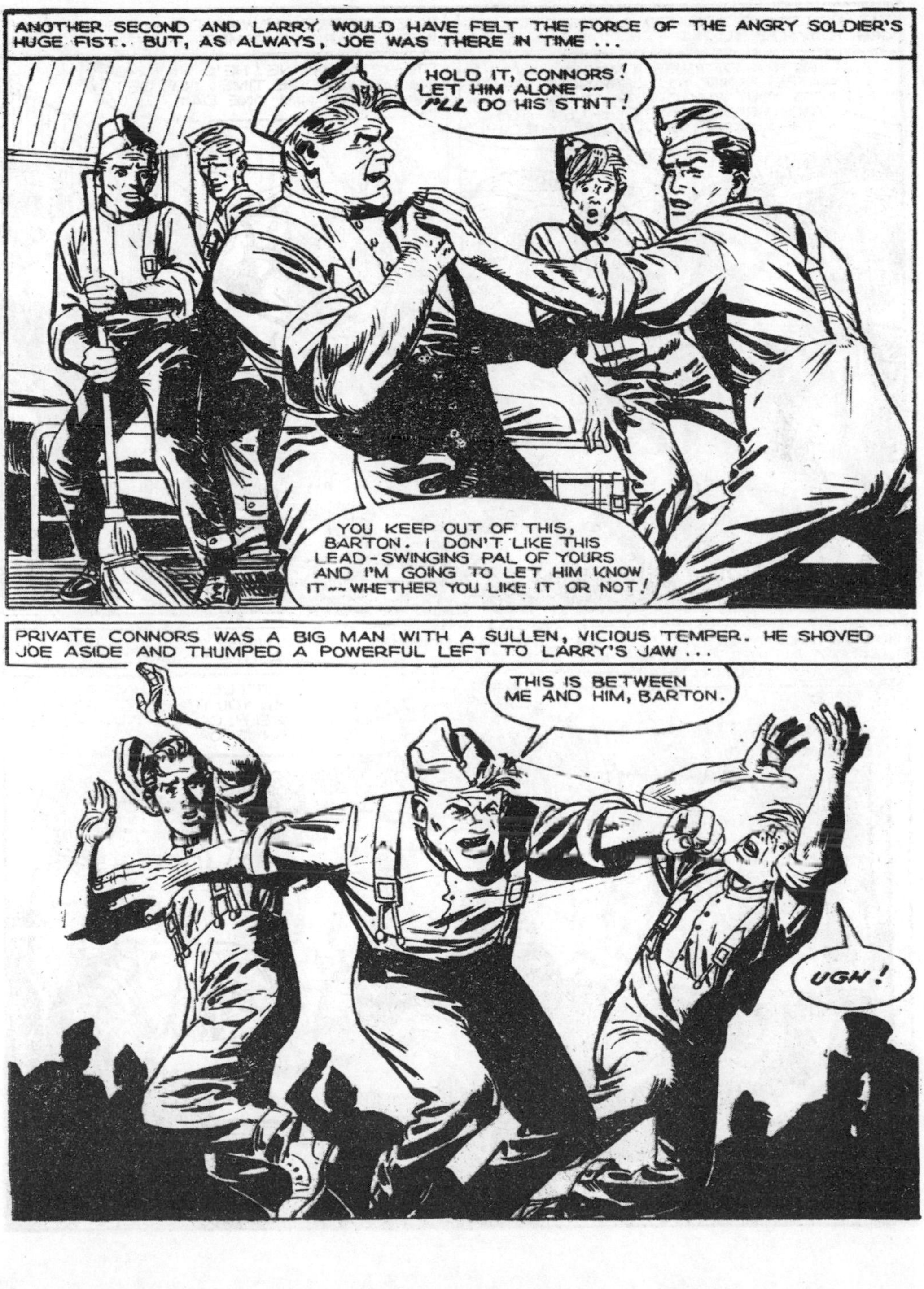
ANOTHER SECOND AND LARRY WOULD HAVE FELT THE FORCE OF THE ANGRY SOLDIER'S HUGE FIST. BUT, AS ALWAYS, JOE WAS THERE IN TIME ...
HOLD IT, CONNORS! LET HIM ALONE -- I'LL DO HIS STINT!
YOU KEEP OUT OF THIS, BARTON. I DON'T LIKE THIS LEAD-SWINGING PAL OF YOURS AND I'M GOING TO LET HIM KNOW IT -- WHETHER YOU LIKE IT OR NOT!
PRIVATE CONNORS WAS A BIG MAN WITH A SULLEN, VICIOUS TEMPER. HE SHOVED JOE ASIDE AND THUMPED A POWERFUL LEFT TO LARRY'S JAW ...
THIS IS BETWEEN ME AND HIM, BARTON.
UGH!

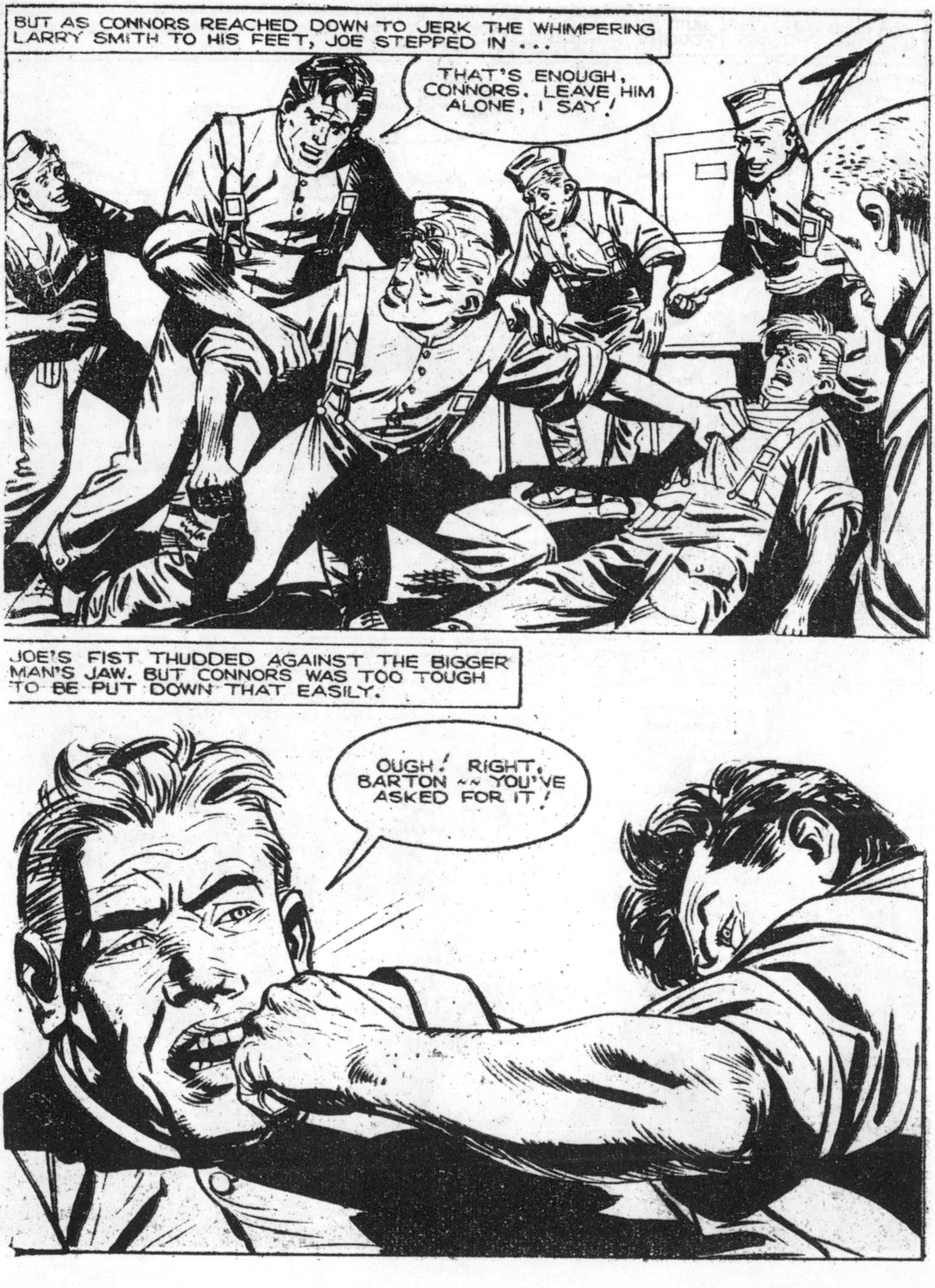
BUT AS CONNORS REACHED DOWN TO JERK THE WHIMPERING LARRY SMITH TO HIS FEET, JOE STEPPED IN ...
THAT'S ENOUGH, CONNORS. LEAVE HIM ALONE, I SAY!
JOE'S FIST THUDDED AGAINST THE BIGGER MAN'S JAW. BUT CONNORS WAS TOO TOUGH TO BE PUT DOWN THAT EASILY.
OUGH! RIGHT, BARTON -- YOU'VE ASKED FOR IT!

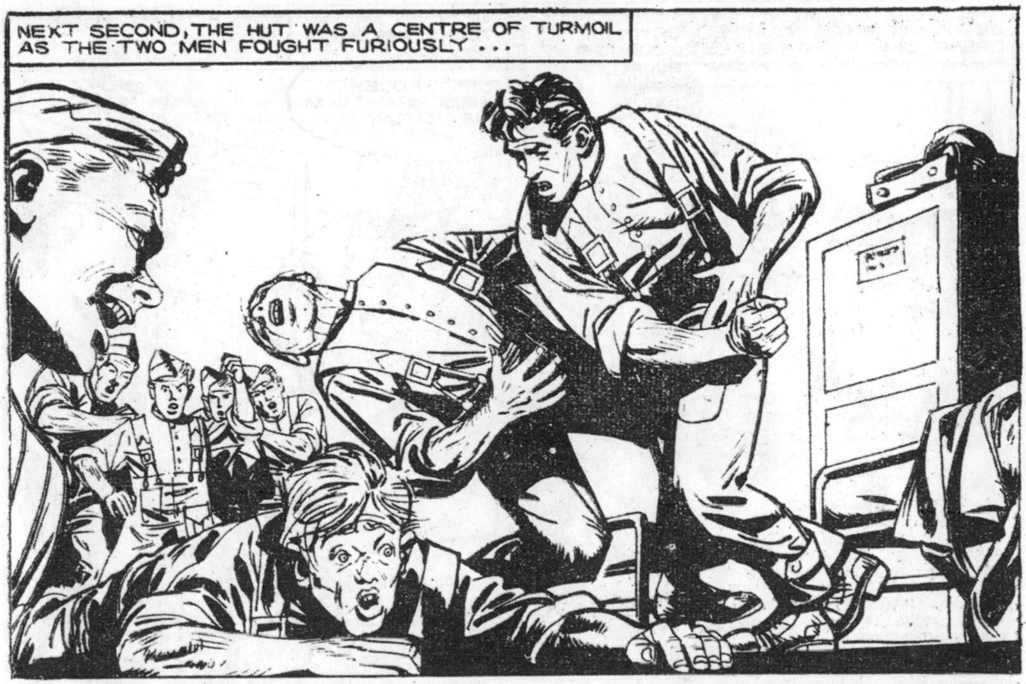
NEXT SECOND, THE HUT WAS A CENTRE OF TURMOIL AS THE TWO MEN FOUGHT FURIOUSLY ...

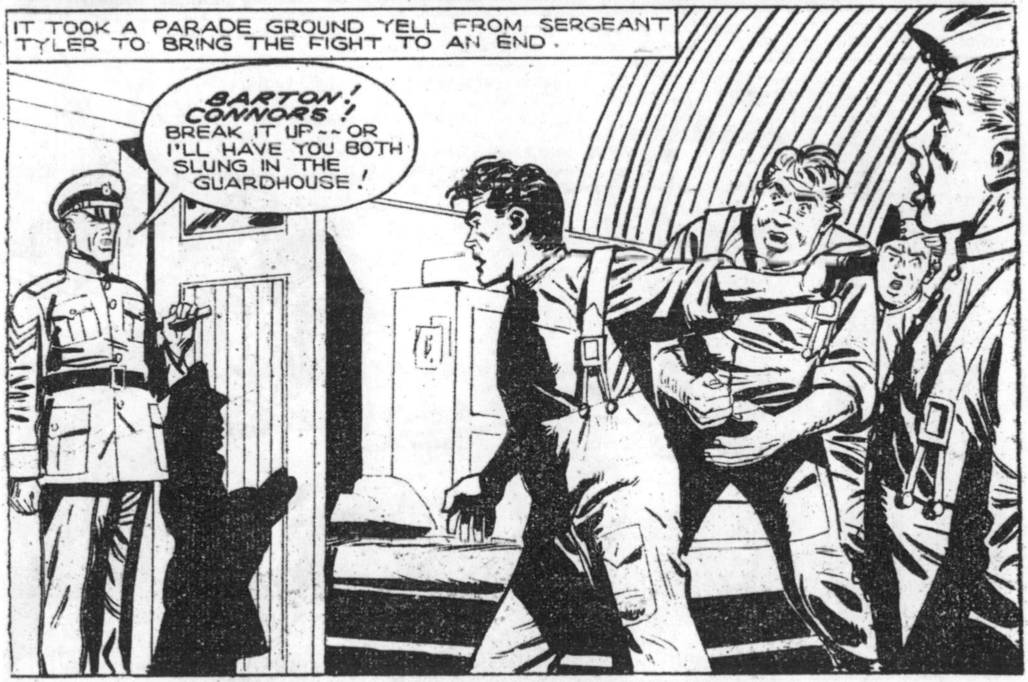
IT TOOK A PARADE GROUND YELL FROM SERGEANT TYLER TO BRING THE FIGHT TO AN END.
BARTON! CONNORS! BREAK IT UP -- OR I'LL HAVE YOU BOTH SLUNG IN THE GUARDHOUSE!

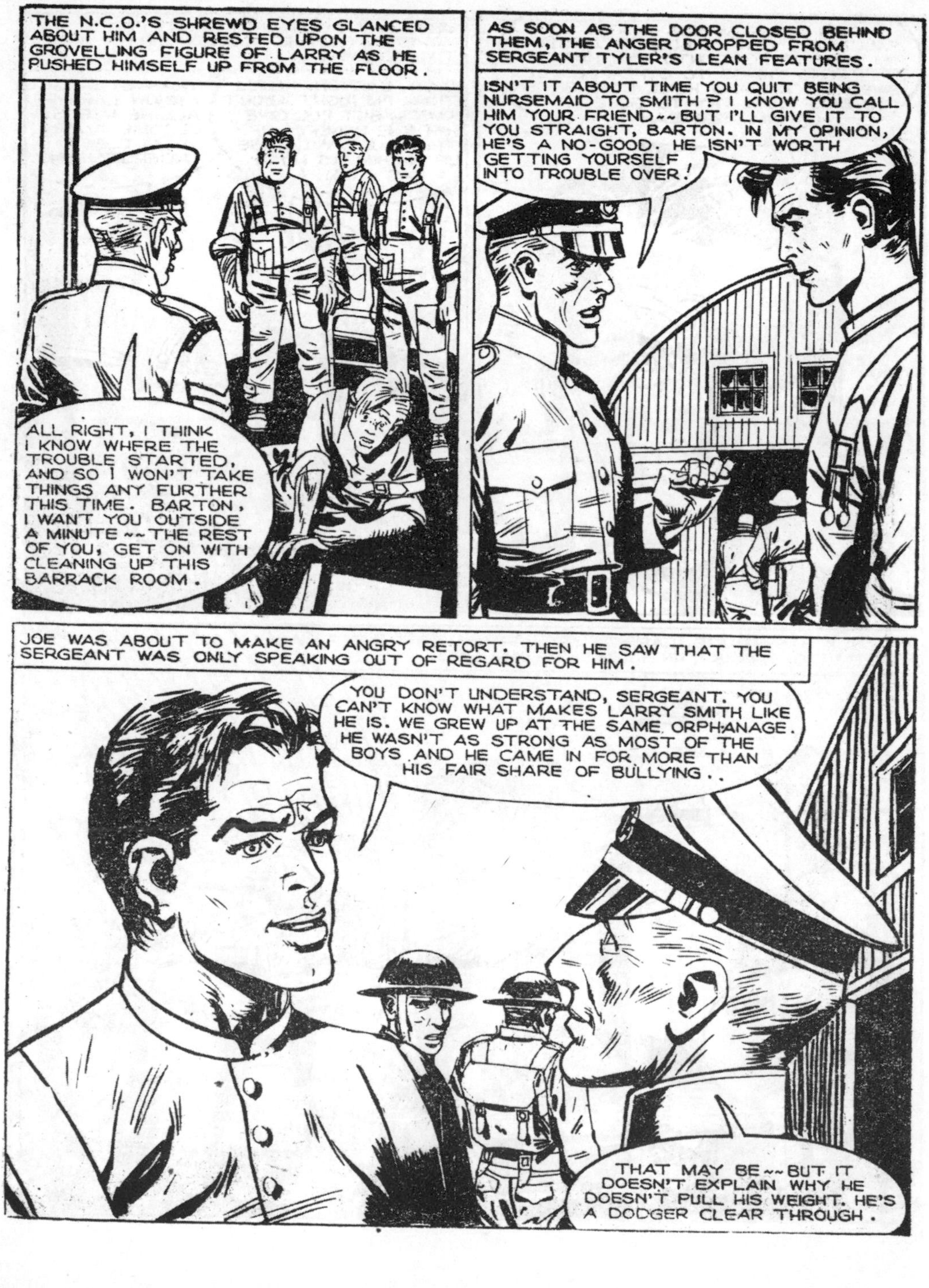
THE N.C.O.'S SHREWD EYES GLANCED ABOUT HIM AND RESTED UPON THE GROVELLING FIGURE OF LARRY AS HE PUSHED HIMSELF UP FROM THE FLOOR.
ALL RIGHT, I THINK I KNOW WHERE THE TROUBLE STARTED, AND SO I WON'T TAKE THINGS ANY FURTHER THIS TIME. BARTON, I WANT YOU OUTSIDE A MINUTE -- THE REST OF YOU, GET ON WITH CLEANING UP THIS BARRACK ROOM.
AS SOON AS THE DOOR CLOSED BEHIND THEM, THE ANGER DROPPED FROM SERGEANT TYLER'S LEAN FEATURES.
ISN'T IT ABOUT TIME YOU QUIT BEING NURSEMAID TO SMITH? I KNOW YOU CALL HIM YOUR FRIEND -- BUT I'LL GIVE IT TO YOU STRAIGHT, BARTON. IN MY OPINION, HE'S A NO-GOOD. HE ISN'T WORTH GETTING YOURSELF INTO TROUBLE OVER!
JOE WAS ABOUT TO MAKE AN ANGRY RETORT. THEN HE SAW THAT THE SERGEANT WAS ONLY SPEAKING OUT OF REGARD FOR HIM.
YOU DON'T UNDERSTAND, SERGEANT. YOU CAN'T KNOW WHAT MAKES LARRY SMITH LIKE HE IS. WE GREW UP AT THE SAME ORPHANAGE. HE WASN'T AS STRONG AS MOST OF THE BOYS AND HE CAME IN FOR MORE THAN HIS FAIR SHARE OF BULLYING..
THAT MAY BE -- BUT IT DOESN'T EXPLAIN WHY HE DOESN'T PULL HIS WEIGHT. HE'S A DODGER CLEAR THROUGH.

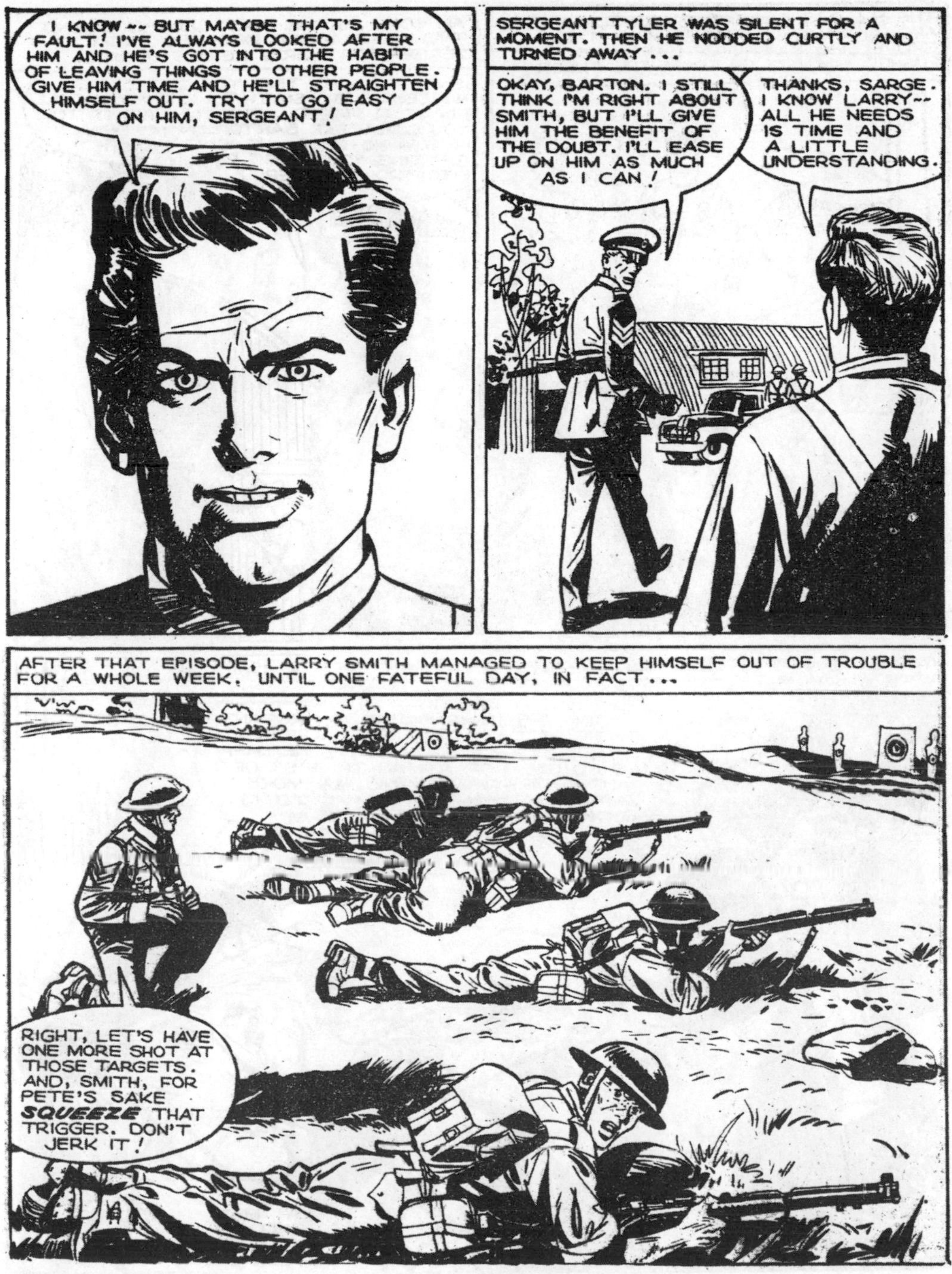
I KNOW -- BUT MAYBE THAT'S MY FAULT! I'VE ALWAYS LOOKED AFTER HIM AND HE'S GOT INTO THE HABIT OF LEAVING THINGS TO OTHER PEOPLE. GIVE HIM TIME AND HE'LL STRAIGHTEN HIMSELF OUT. TRY TO GO EASY ON HIM, SERGEANT!
SERGEANT TYLER WAS SILENT FOR A MOMENT. THEN HE NODDED CURTLY AND TURNED AWAY ...
OKAY, BARTON. I STILL THINK I'M RIGHT ABOUT SMITH, BUT I'LL GIVE HIM THE BENEFIT OF THE DOUBT. I'LL EASE UP ON HIM AS MUCH AS I CAN!
THANKS, SARGE. I KNOW LARRY-- ALL HE NEEDS IS TIME AND A LITTLE UNDERSTANDING.
AFTER THAT EPISODE, LARRY SMITH MANAGED TO KEEP HIMSELF OUT OF TROUBLE FOR A WHOLE WEEK, UNTIL ONE FATEFUL DAY, IN FACT...
RIGHT, LET'S HAVE ONE MORE SHOT AT THOSE TARGETS. AND, SMITH, FOR PETE'S SAKE SQUEEZE THAT TRIGGER. DON'T JERK IT!

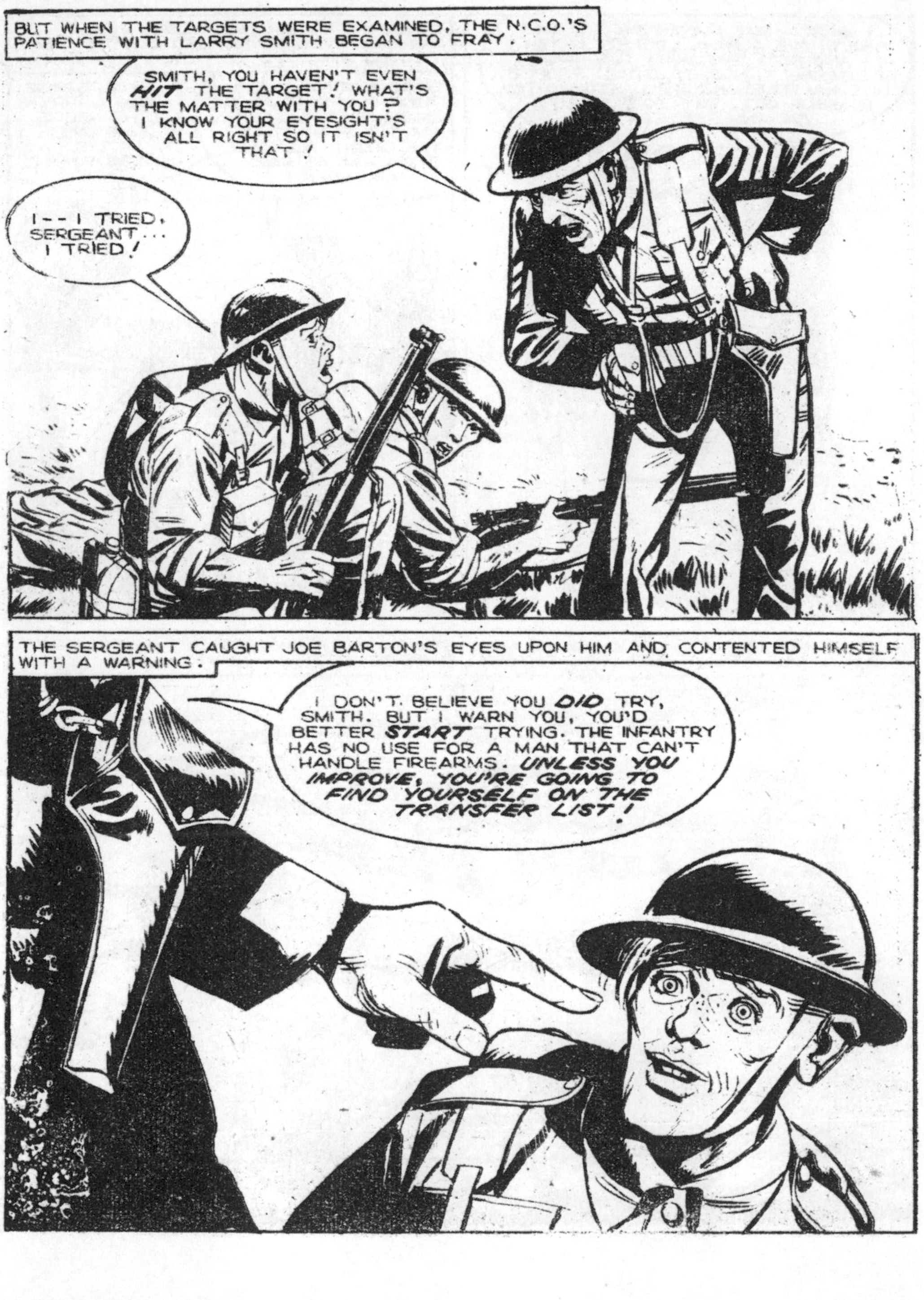
BUT WHEN THE TARGETS WERE EXAMINED, THE N.C.O.'S PATIENCE WITH LARRY SMITH BEGAN TO FRAY.
SMITH, YOU HAVEN'T EVEN HIT THE TARGET! WHAT'S THE MATTER WITH YOU? I KNOW YOUR EYESIGHT'S ALL RIGHT SO IT ISN'T THAT!
I -- I TRIED, SERGEANT... I TRIED!
THE SERGEANT CAUGHT JOE BARTON'S EYES UPON HIM AND CONTENTED HIMSELF WITH A WARNING.
I DON'T BELIEVE YOU DID TRY, SMITH. BUT I WARN YOU, YOU'D BETTER START TRYING. THE INFANTRY HAS NO USE FOR A MAN THAT CAN'T HANDLE FIREARMS. UNLESS YOU IMPROVE, YOU'RE GOING TO FIND YOURSELF ON THE TRANSFER LIST!

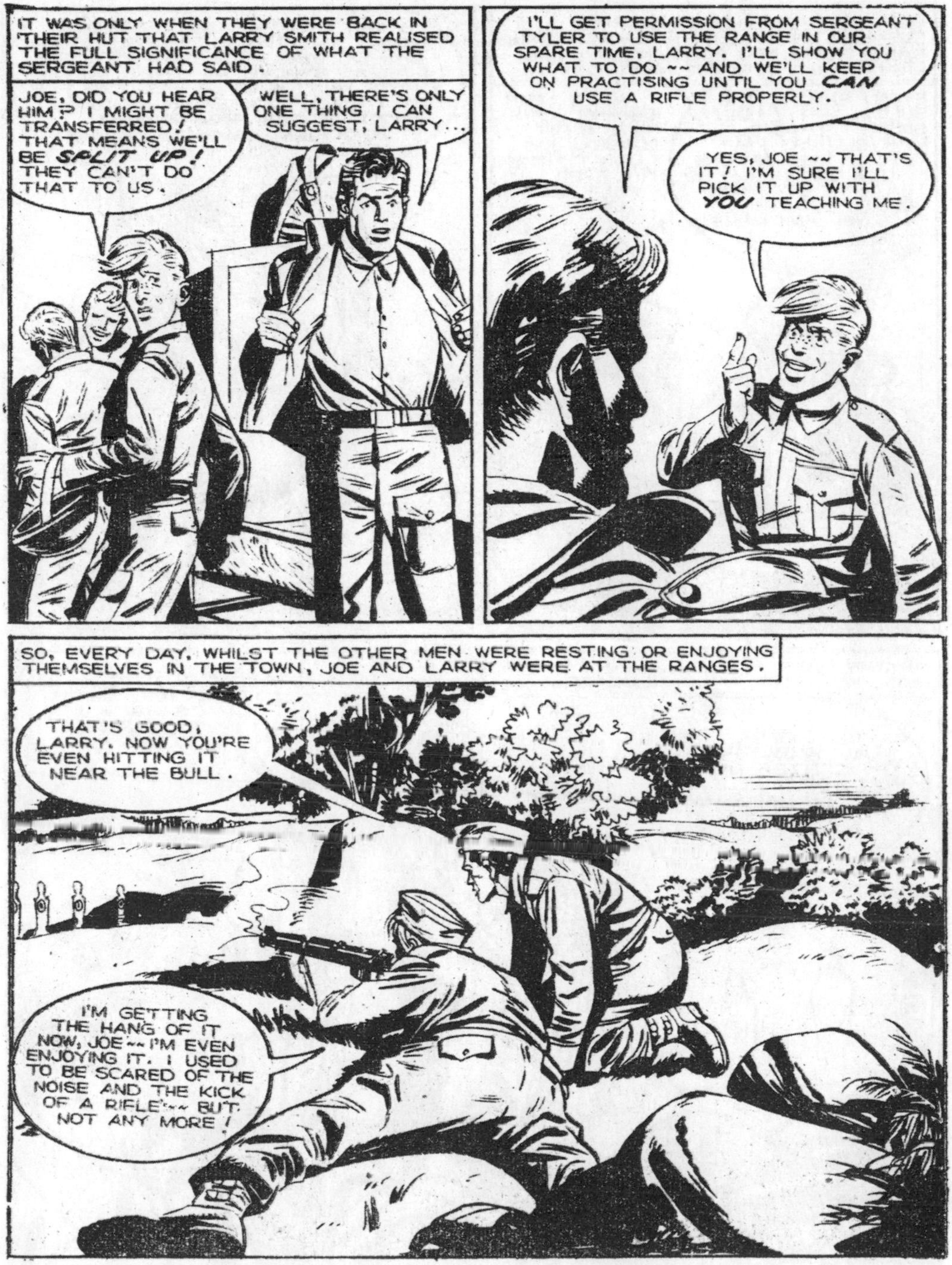
IT WAS ONLY WHEN THEY WERE BACK IN THEIR HUT THAT LARRY SMITH REALISED THE FULL SIGNIFICANCE OF WHAT THE SERGEANT HAD SAID.
JOE, DID YOU HEAR HIM?! I MIGHT BE TRANSFERRED! THAT MEANS WE'LL BE SPLIT UP! THEY CAN'T DO THAT TO US.
WELL, THERE'S ONLY ONE THING I CAN SUGGEST, LARRY...
I'LL GET PERMISSION FROM SERGEANT TYLER TO USE THE RANGE IN OUR SPARE TIME, LARRY. I'LL SHOW YOU WHAT TO DO ~~ AND WE'LL KEEP ON PRACTISING UNTIL YOU CAN USE A RIFLE PROPERLY.
YES, JOE ~~ THAT'S IT! I'M SURE I'LL PICK IT UP WITH YOU TEACHING ME.
SO, EVERY DAY, WHILST THE OTHER MEN WERE RESTING OR ENJOYING THEMSELVES IN THE TOWN, JOE AND LARRY WERE AT THE RANGES.
THAT'S GOOD, LARRY. NOW YOU'RE EVEN HITTING IT NEAR THE BULL.
I'M GETTING THE HANG OF IT NOW, JOE ~~ I'M EVEN ENJOYING IT. I USED TO BE SCARED OF THE NOISE AND THE KICK OF A RIFLE ~~ BUT NOT ANY MORE!

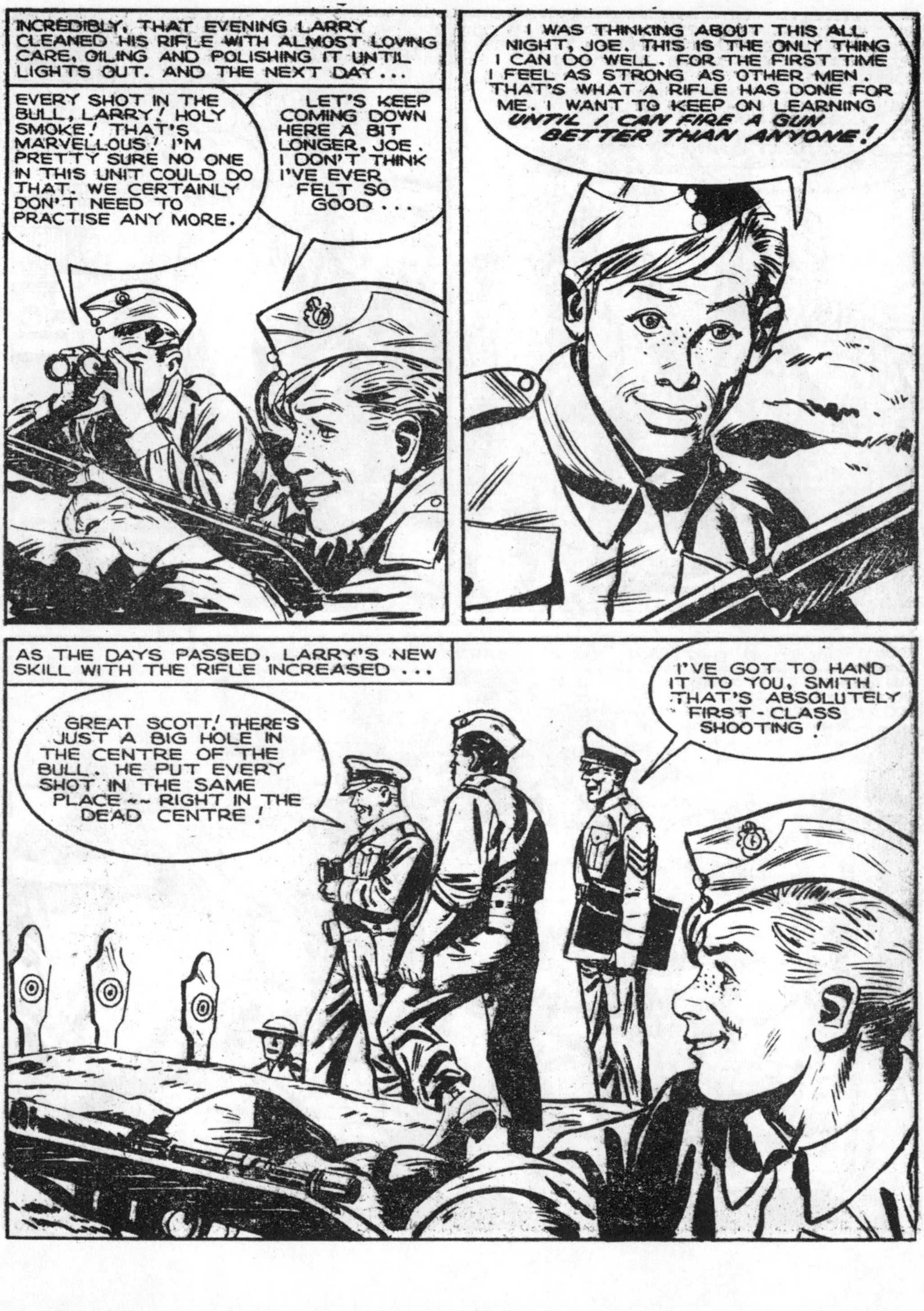
INCREDIBLY, THAT EVENING LARRY CLEANED HIS RIFLE WITH ALMOST LOVING CARE, OILING AND POLISHING IT UNTIL LIGHTS OUT. AND THE NEXT DAY...
EVERY SHOT IN THE BULL, LARRY! HOLY SMOKE! THAT'S MARVELLOUS! I'M PRETTY SURE NO ONE IN THIS UNIT COULD DO THAT. WE CERTAINLY DON'T NEED TO PRACTISE ANY MORE.
LET'S KEEP COMING DOWN HERE A BIT LONGER, JOE. I DON'T THINK I'VE EVER FELT SO GOOD...
I WAS THINKING ABOUT THIS ALL NIGHT, JOE. THIS IS THE ONLY THING I CAN DO WELL. FOR THE FIRST TIME I FEEL AS STRONG AS OTHER MEN. THAT'S WHAT A RIFLE HAS DONE FOR ME. I WANT TO KEEP ON LEARNING UNTIL I CAN FIRE A GUN BETTER THAN ANYONE!
AS THE DAYS PASSED, LARRY'S NEW SKILL WITH THE RIFLE INCREASED...
GREAT SCOTT! THERE'S JUST A BIG HOLE IN THE CENTRE OF THE BULL. HE PUT EVERY SHOT IN THE SAME PLACE -- RIGHT IN THE DEAD CENTRE!
I'VE GOT TO HAND IT TO YOU, SMITH. THAT'S ABSOLUTELY FIRST-CLASS SHOOTING!

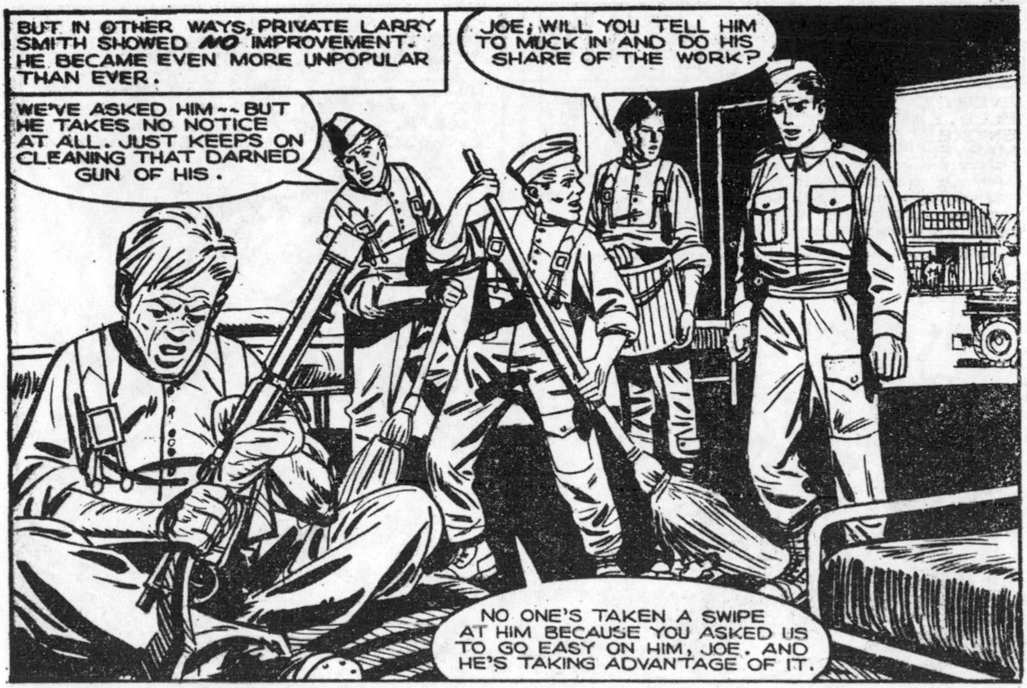
BUT IN OTHER WAYS, PRIVATE LARRY SMITH SHOWED NO IMPROVEMENT. HE BECAME EVEN MORE UNPOPULAR THAN EVER.
JOE, WILL YOU TELL HIM TO MUCK IN AND DO HIS SHARE OF THE WORK?
WE'VE ASKED HIM -- BUT HE TAKES NO NOTICE AT ALL. JUST KEEPS ON CLEANING THAT DARNED GUN OF HIS.
NO ONE'S TAKEN A SWIPE AT HIM BECAUSE YOU ASKED US TO GO EASY ON HIM, JOE. AND HE'S TAKING ADVANTAGE OF IT.

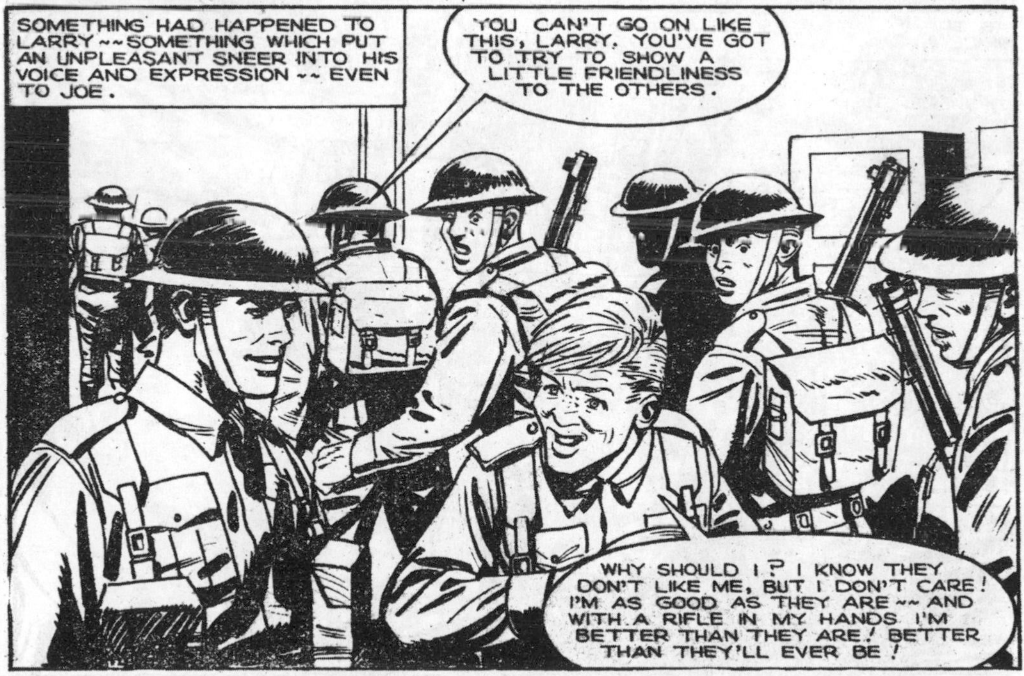
SOMETHING HAD HAPPENED TO LARRY -- SOMETHING WHICH PUT AN UNPLEASANT SNEER INTO HIS VOICE AND EXPRESSION -- EVEN TO JOE.
YOU CAN'T GO ON LIKE THIS, LARRY. YOU'VE GOT TO TRY TO SHOW A LITTLE FRIENDLINESS TO THE OTHERS.
WHY SHOULD I? I KNOW THEY DON'T LIKE ME, BUT I DON'T CARE! I'M AS GOOD AS THEY ARE -- AND WITH A RIFLE IN MY HANDS I'M BETTER THAN THEY ARE! BETTER THAN THEY'LL EVER BE!

Chapter 2. The Lesson Learned

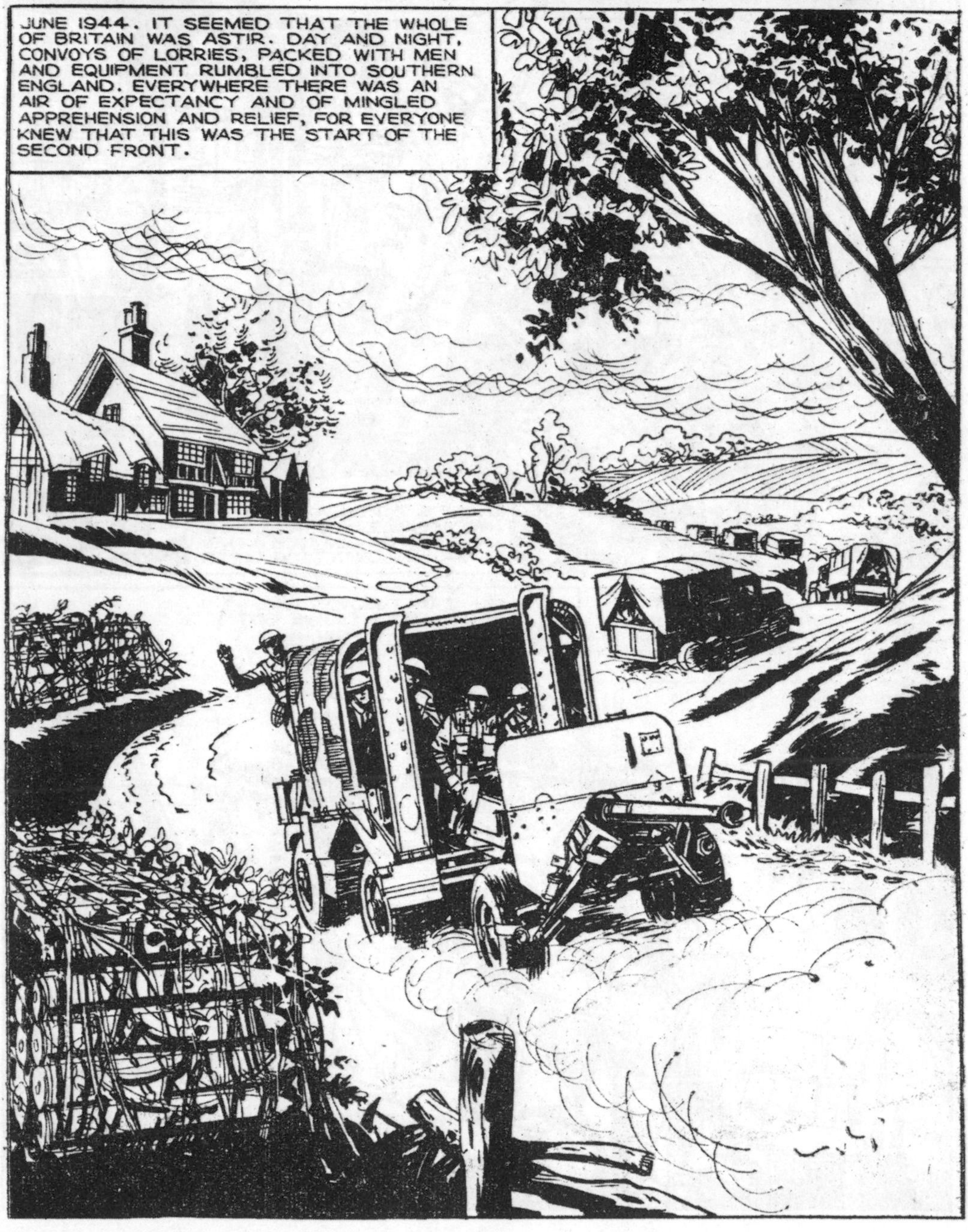
JUNE 1944. IT SEEMED THAT THE WHOLE OF BRITAIN WAS ASTIR. DAY AND NIGHT, CONVOYS OF LORRIES, PACKED WITH MEN AND EQUIPMENT RUMBLED INTO SOUTHERN ENGLAND. EVERYWHERE THERE WAS AN AIR OF EXPECTANCY AND OF MINGLED APPREHENSION AND RELIEF, FOR EVERYONE KNEW THAT THIS WAS THE START OF THE SECOND FRONT.

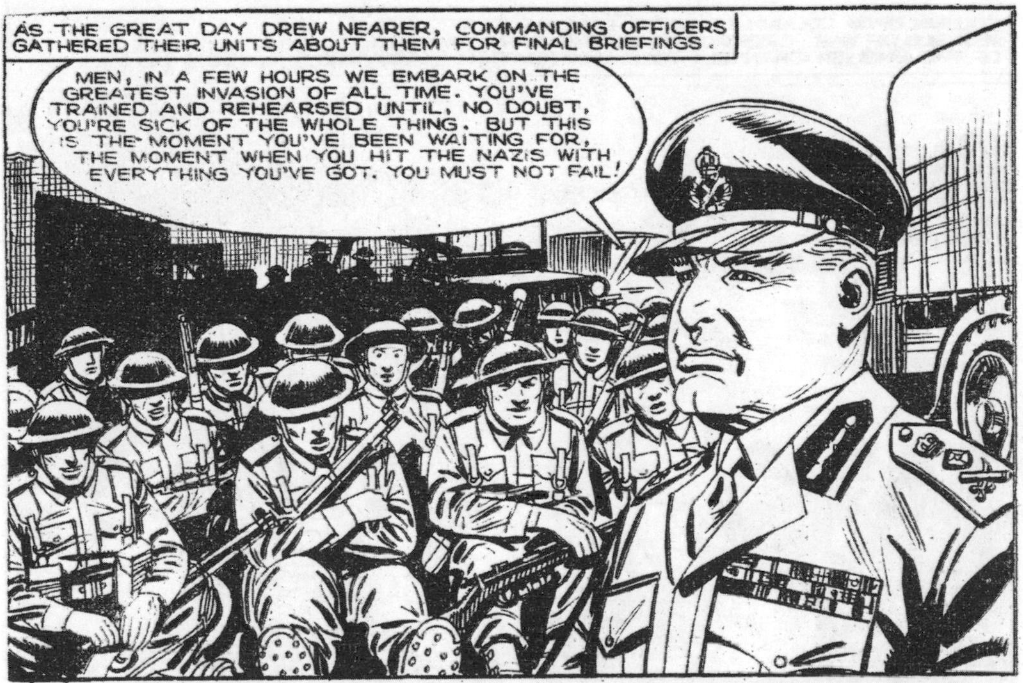
AS THE GREAT DAY DREW NEARER, COMMANDING OFFICERS GATHERED THEIR UNITS ABOUT THEM FOR FINAL BRIEFINGS.
MEN, IN A FEW HOURS WE EMBARK ON THE GREATEST INVASION OF ALL TIME. YOU'VE TRAINED AND REHEARSED UNTIL, NO DOUBT, YOU'RE SICK OF THE WHOLE THING. BUT THIS IS THE MOMENT YOU'VE BEEN WAITING FOR, THE MOMENT WHEN YOU HIT THE NAZIS WITH EVERYTHING YOU'VE GOT. YOU MUST NOT FAIL!

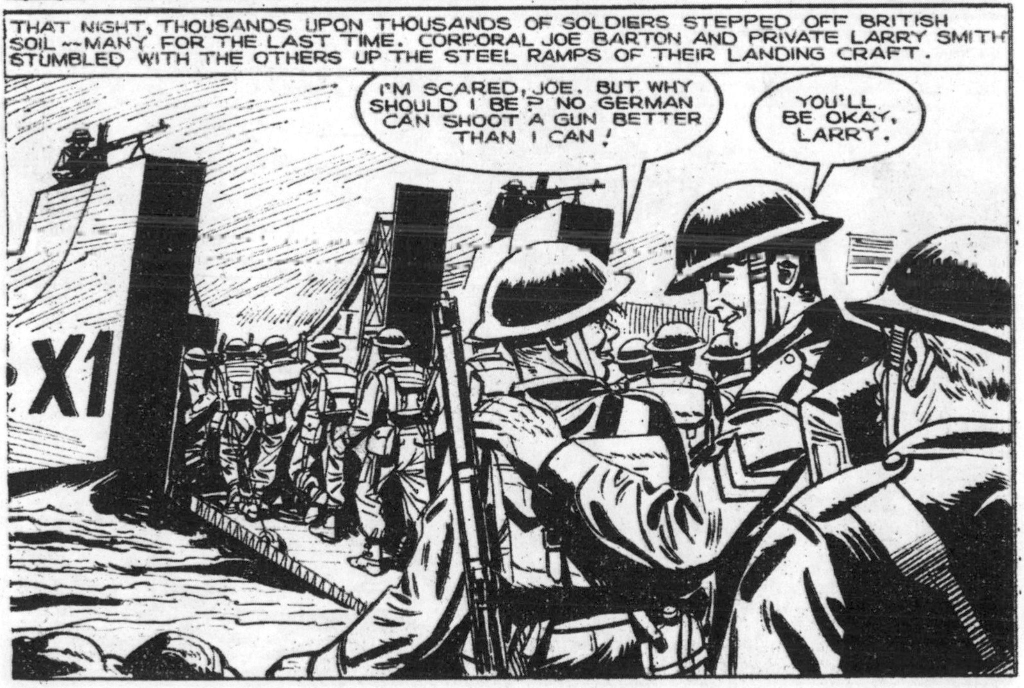
THAT NIGHT, THOUSANDS UPON THOUSANDS OF SOLDIERS STEPPED OFF BRITISH SOIL--MANY FOR THE LAST TIME. CORPORAL JOE BARTON AND PRIVATE LARRY SMITH STUMBLED WITH THE OTHERS UP THE STEEL RAMPS OF THEIR LANDING CRAFT.
I'M SCARED, JOE. BUT WHY SHOULD I BE? NO GERMAN CAN SHOOT A GUN BETTER THAN I CAN!
YOU'LL BE OKAY, LARRY.
X1

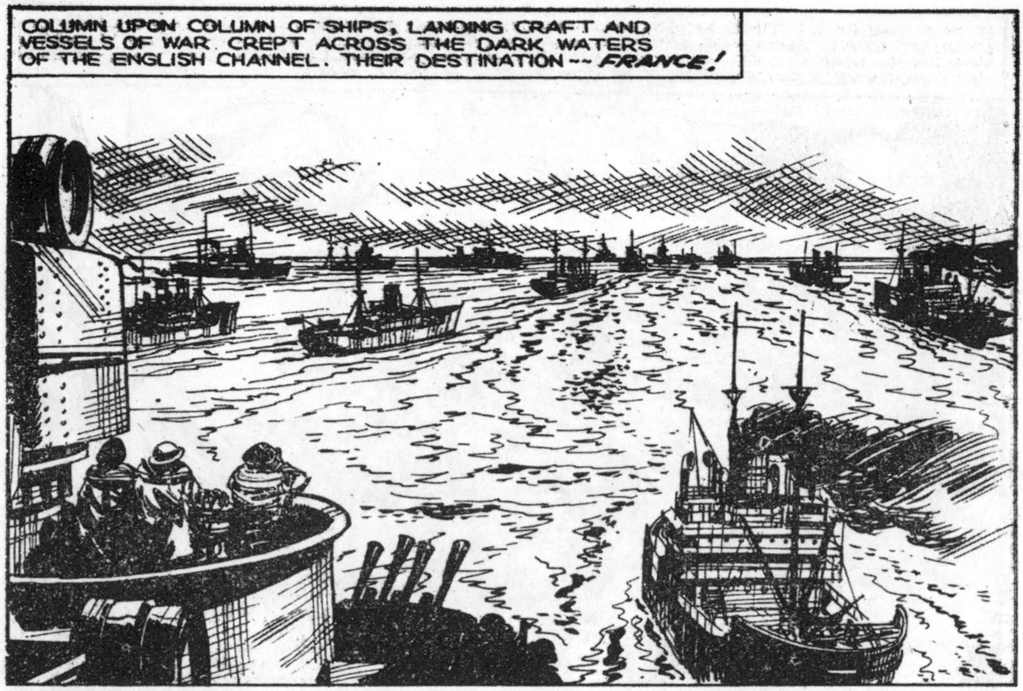
COLUMN UPON COLUMN OF SHIPS, LANDING CRAFT AND VESSELS OF WAR CREPT ACROSS THE DARK WATERS OF THE ENGLISH CHANNEL. THEIR DESTINATION -- FRANCE!

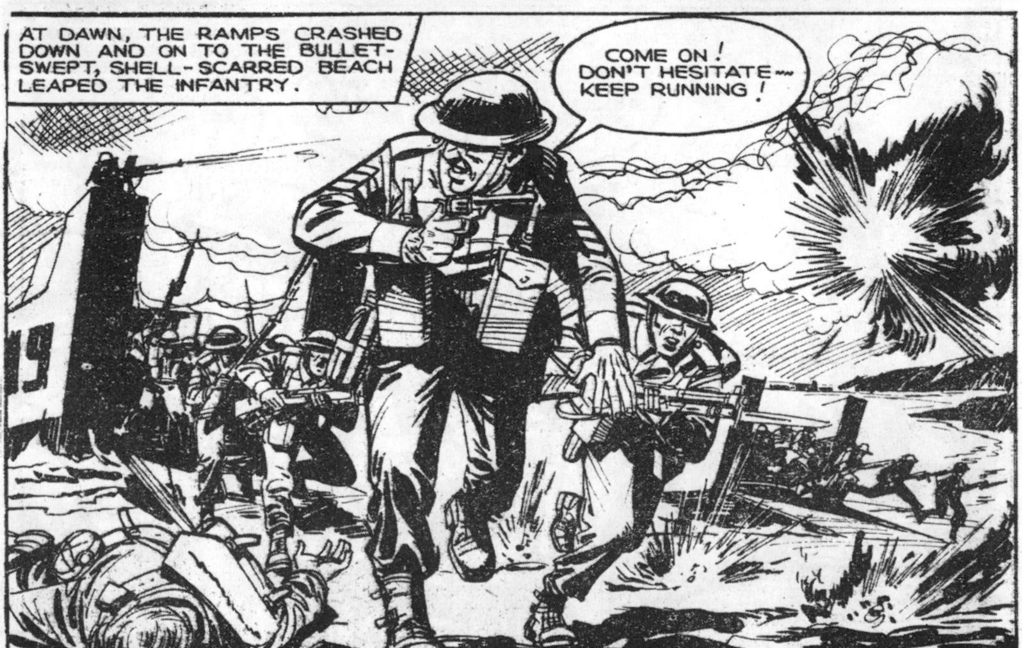
AT DAWN, THE RAMPS CRASHED DOWN AND ON TO THE BULLET-SWEPT, SHELL-SCARRED BEACH LEAPED THE INFANTRY.
COME ON! DON'T HESITATE -- KEEP RUNNING!

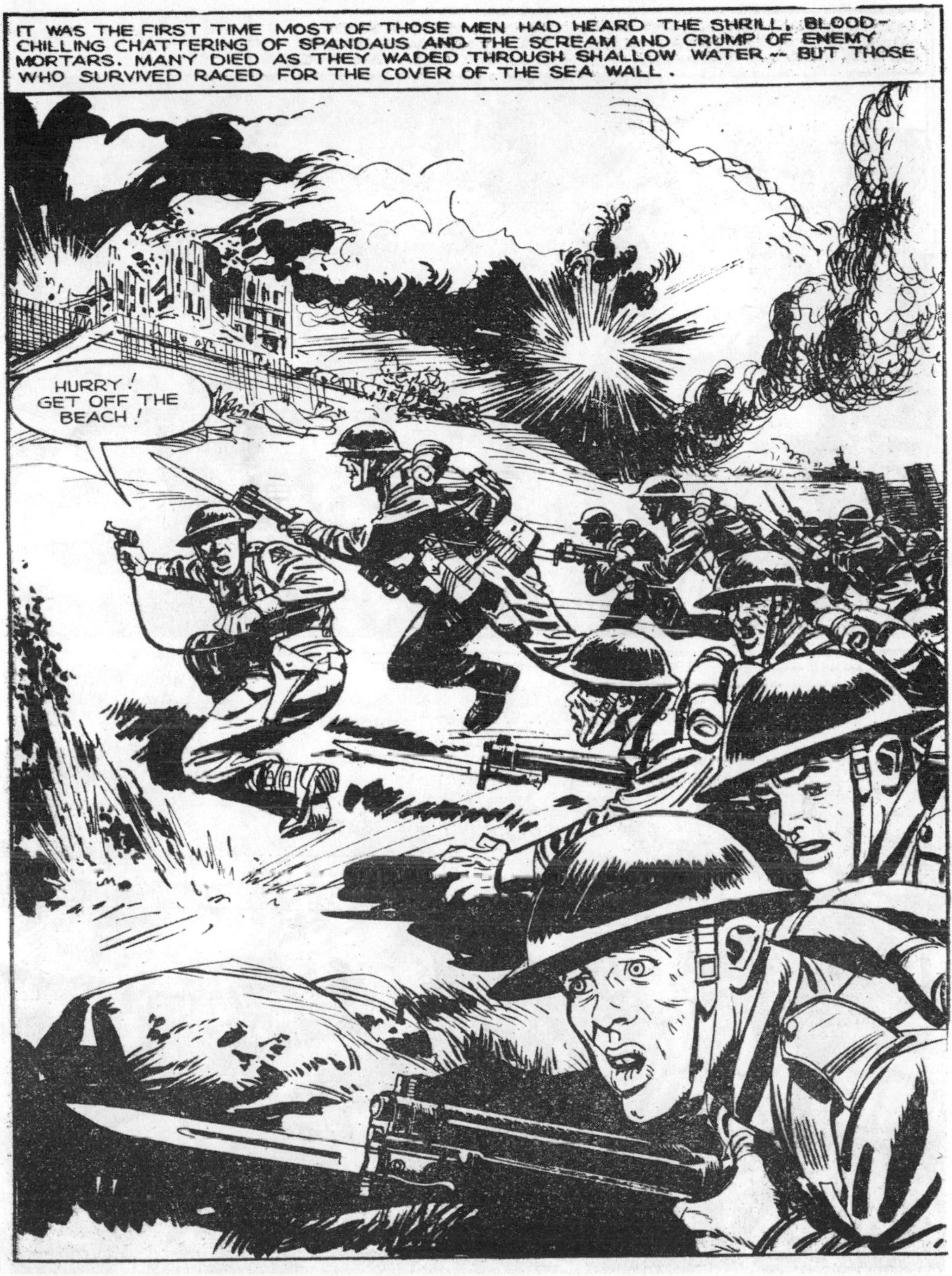
IT WAS THE FIRST TIME MOST OF THOSE MEN HAD HEARD THE SHRILL, BLOOD-CHILLING CHATTERING OF SPANDAUS AND THE SCREAM AND CRUMP OF ENEMY MORTARS. MANY DIED AS THEY WADED THROUGH SHALLOW WATER -- BUT THOSE WHO SURVIVED RACED FOR THE COVER OF THE SEA WALL.
HURRY! GET OFF THE BEACH!

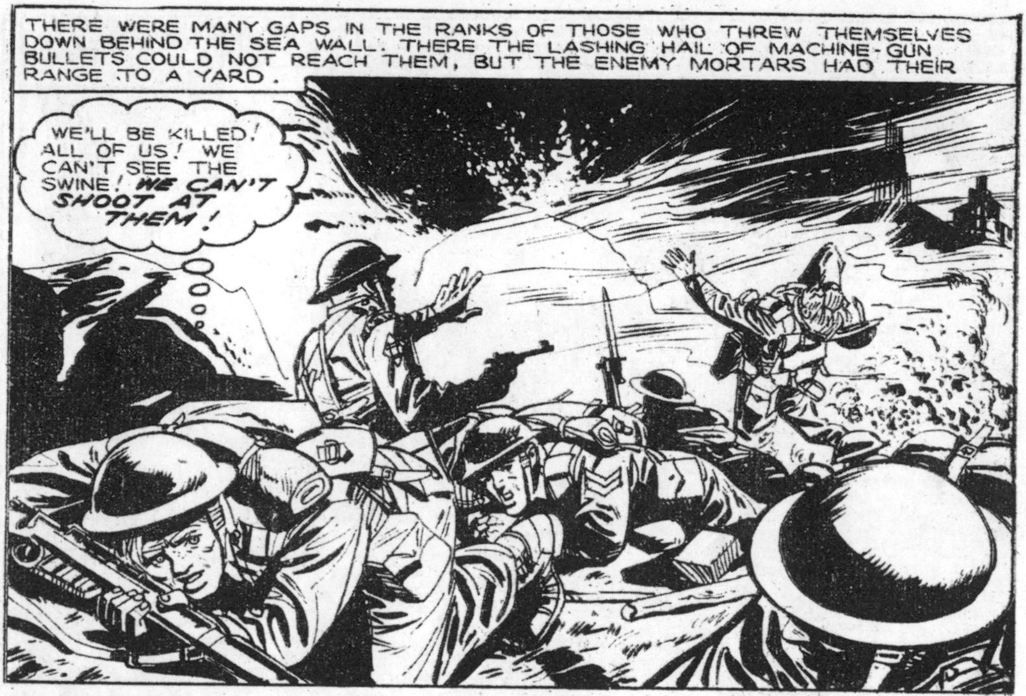
THERE WERE MANY GAPS IN THE RANKS OF THOSE WHO THREW THEMSELVES DOWN BEHIND THE SEA WALL. THERE THE LASHING HAIL OF MACHINE-GUN BULLETS COULD NOT REACH THEM, BUT THE ENEMY MORTARS HAD THEIR RANGE TO A YARD.
WE'LL BE KILLED! ALL OF US! WE CAN'T SEE THE SWINE! WE CAN'T SHOOT AT THEM!

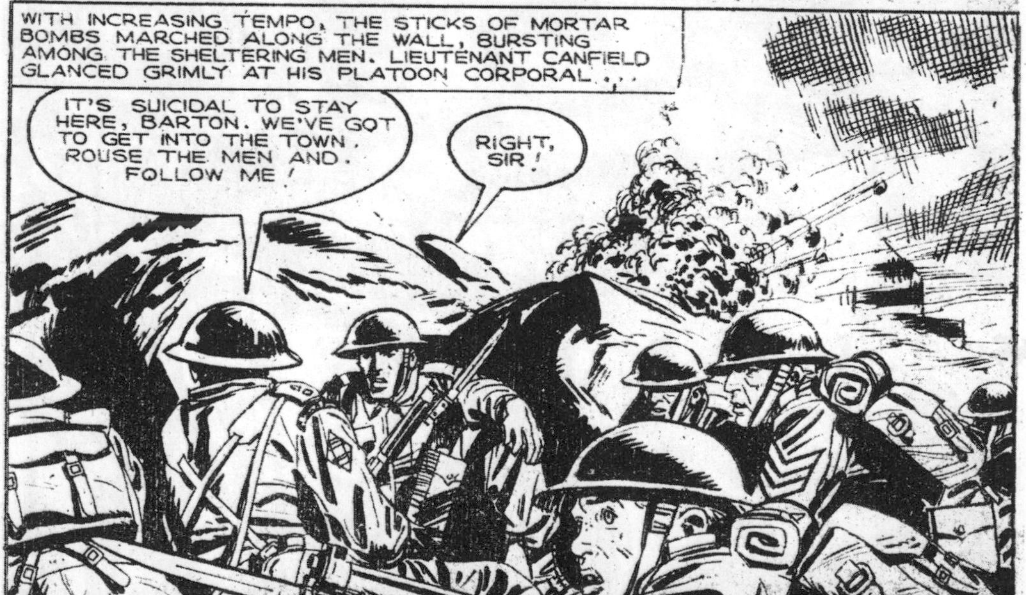
WITH INCREASING TEMPO, THE STICKS OF MORTAR BOMBS MARCHED ALONG THE WALL, BURSTING AMONG THE SHELTERING MEN. LIEUTENANT CANFIELD GLANCED GRIMLY AT HIS PLATOON CORPORAL...
IT'S SUICIDAL TO STAY HERE, BARTON. WE'VE GOT TO GET INTO THE TOWN. ROUSE THE MEN AND FOLLOW ME!
RIGHT, SIR!

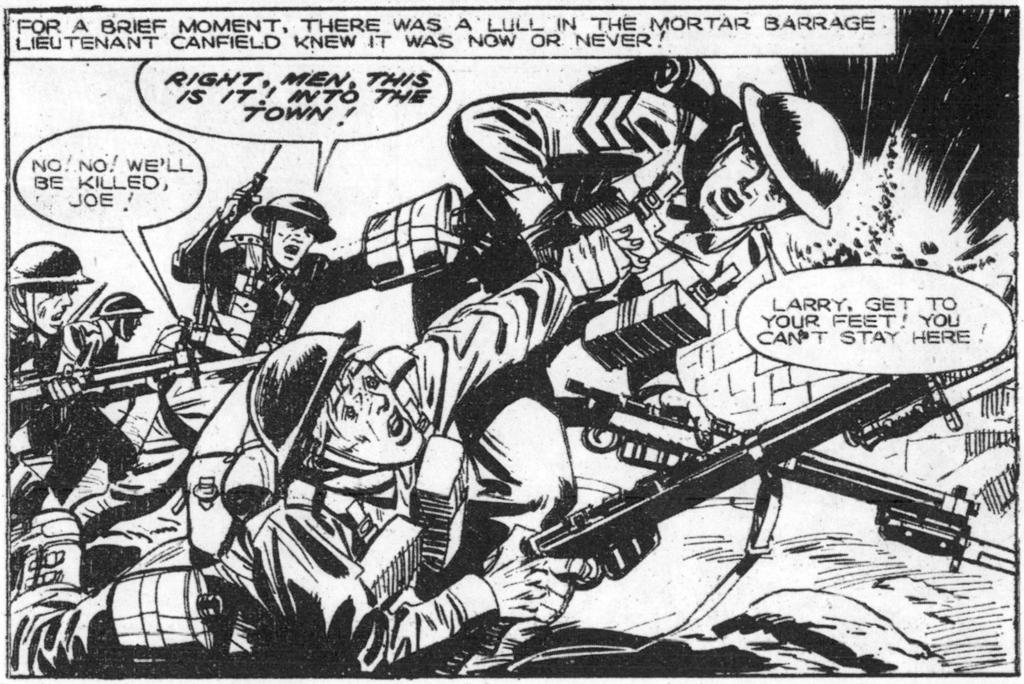
FOR A BRIEF MOMENT, THERE WAS A LULL IN THE MORTAR BARRAGE. LIEUTENANT CANFIELD KNEW IT WAS NOW OR NEVER!
RIGHT, MEN, THIS IS IT! INTO THE TOWN!
NO! NO! WE'LL BE KILLED, JOE!
LARRY, GET TO YOUR FEET! YOU CAN'T STAY HERE!

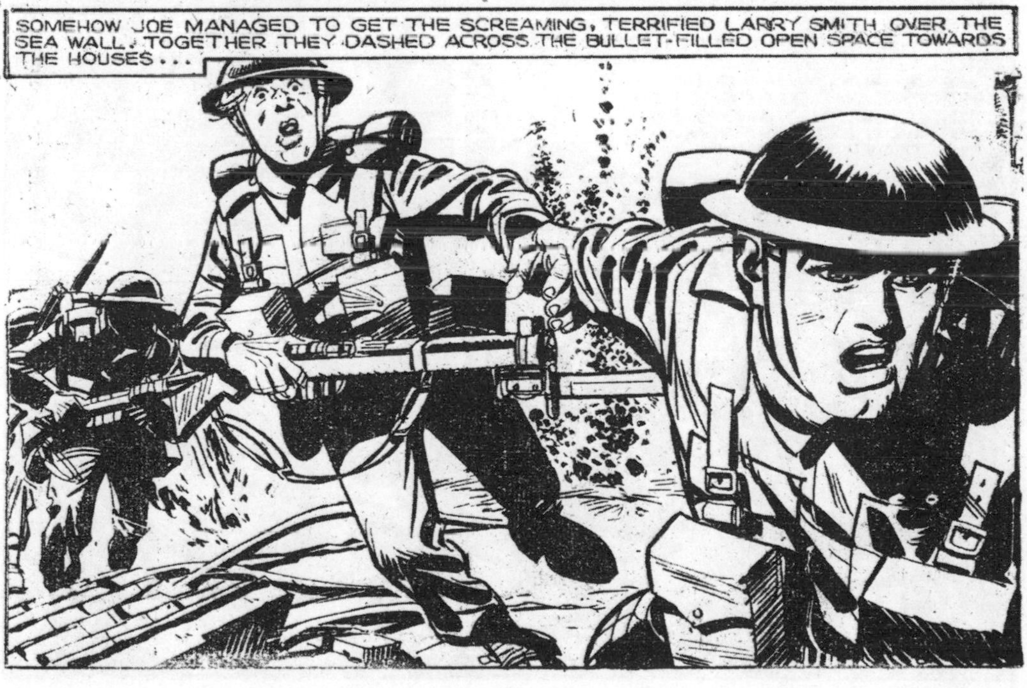
SOMEHOW JOE MANAGED TO GET THE SCREAMING, TERRIFIED LARRY SMITH OVER THE SEA WALL. TOGETHER THEY DASHED ACROSS THE BULLET-FILLED OPEN SPACE TOWARDS THE HOUSES...

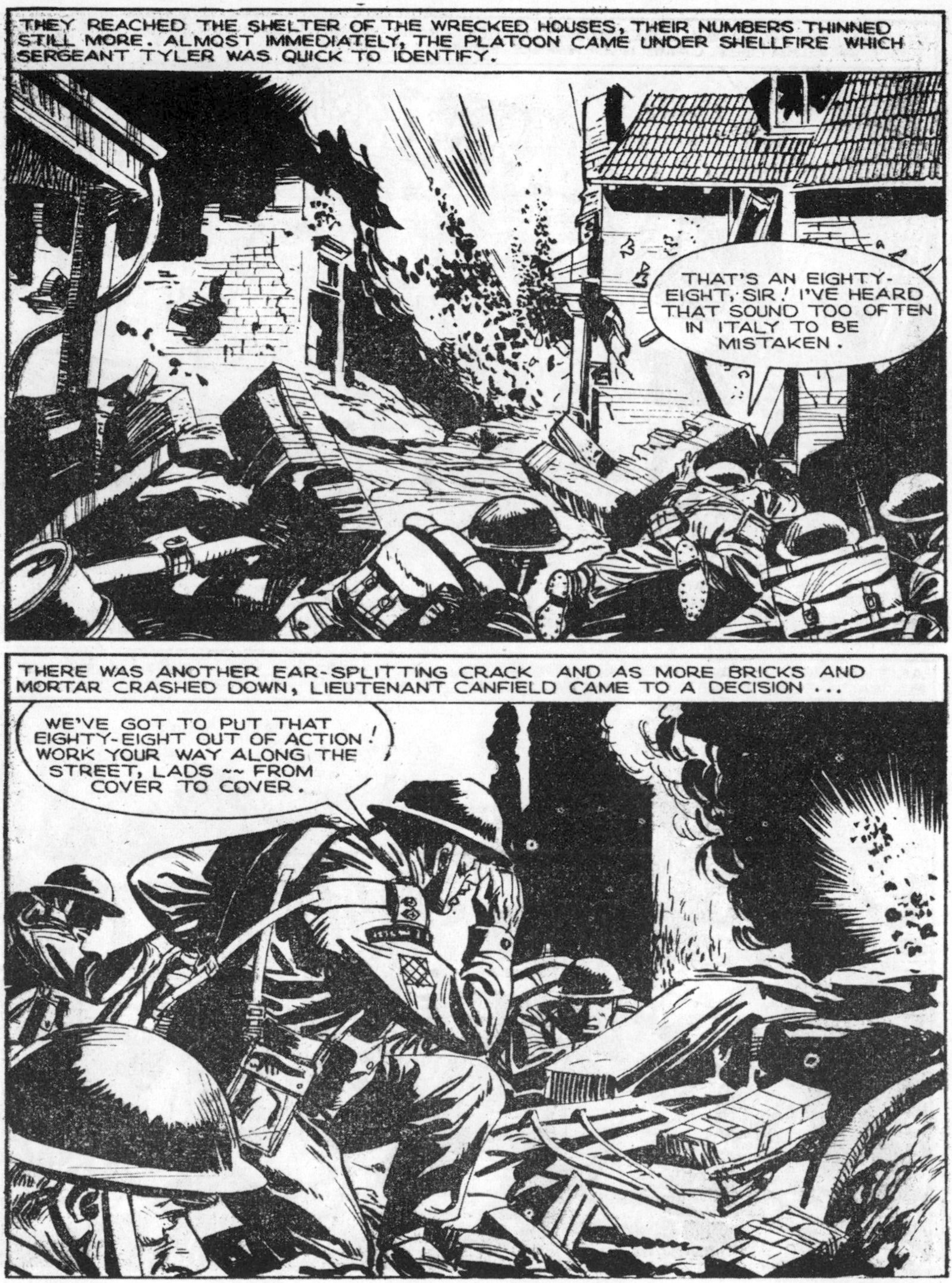
THEY REACHED THE SHELTER OF THE WRECKED HOUSES, THEIR NUMBERS THINNED STILL MORE. ALMOST IMMEDIATELY, THE PLATOON CAME UNDER SHELLFIRE WHICH SERGEANT TYLER WAS QUICK TO IDENTIFY.
THAT'S AN EIGHTY-EIGHT, SIR! I'VE HEARD THAT SOUND TOO OFTEN IN ITALY TO BE MISTAKEN.
THERE WAS ANOTHER EAR-SPLITTING CRACK AND AS MORE BRICKS AND MORTAR CRASHED DOWN, LIEUTENANT CANFIELD CAME TO A DECISION ...
WE'VE GOT TO PUT THAT EIGHTY-EIGHT OUT OF ACTION! WORK YOUR WAY ALONG THE STREET, LADS -- FROM COVER TO COVER.

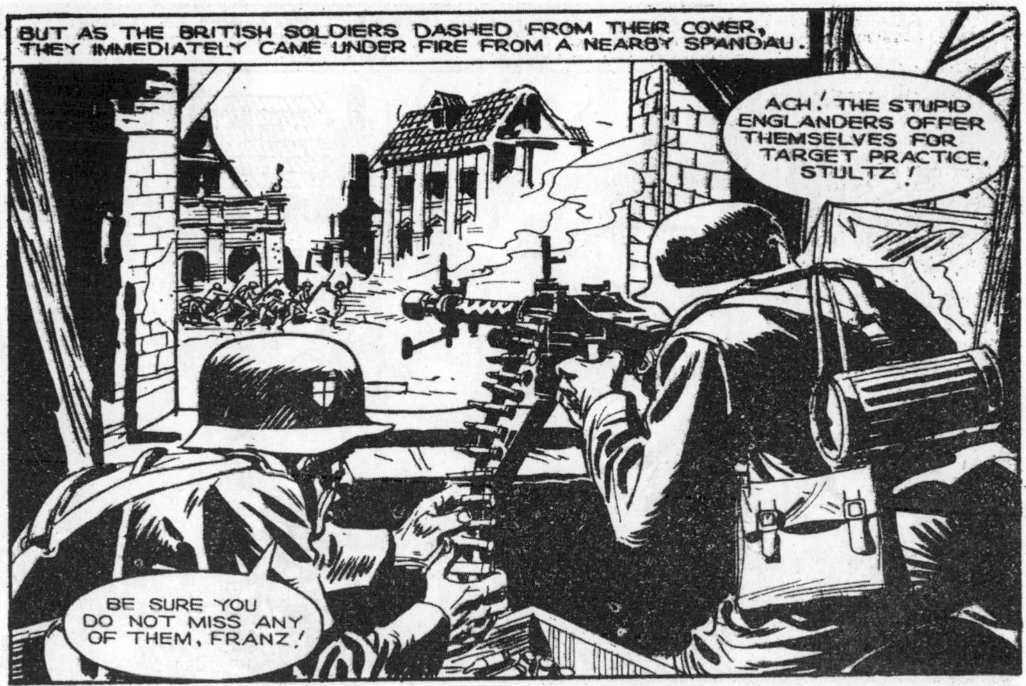
BUT AS THE BRITISH SOLDIERS DASHED FROM THEIR COVER, THEY IMMEDIATELY CAME UNDER FIRE FROM A NEARBY SPANDAU.
ACH! THE STUPID ENGLANDERS OFFER THEMSELVES FOR TARGET PRACTICE, STULTZ!
BE SURE YOU DO NOT MISS ANY OF THEM, FRANZ!

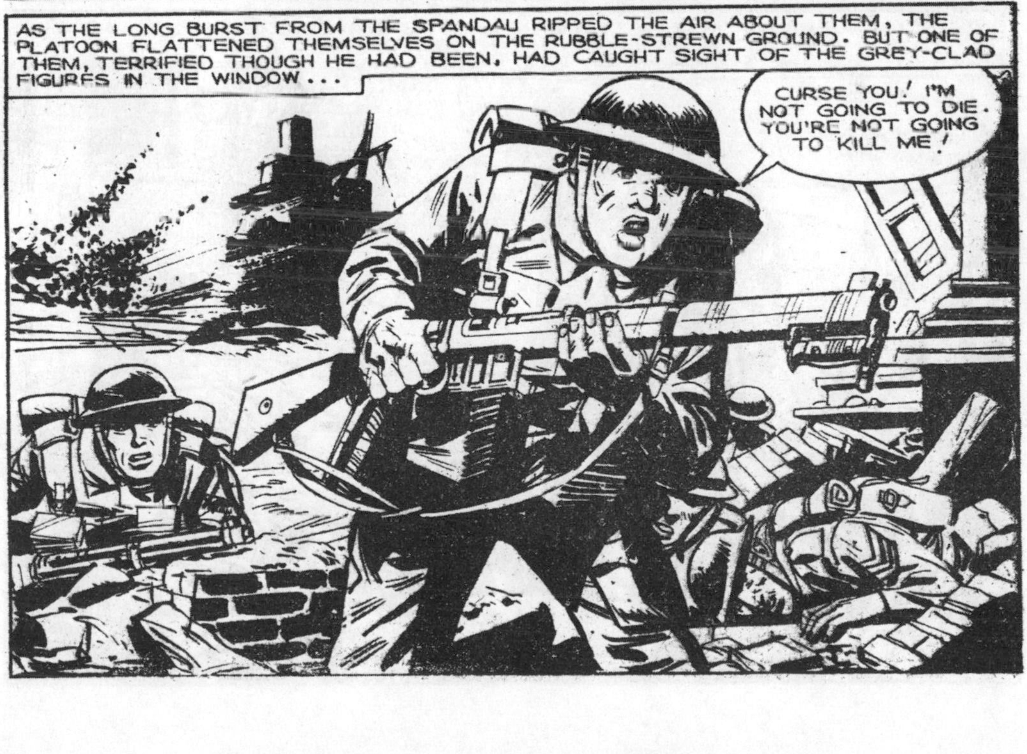
AS THE LONG BURST FROM THE SPANDAU RIPPED THE AIR ABOUT THEM, THE PLATOON FLATTENED THEMSELVES ON THE RUBBLE-STREWN GROUND. BUT ONE OF THEM, TERRIFIED THOUGH HE HAD BEEN, HAD CAUGHT SIGHT OF THE GREY-CLAD FIGURES IN THE WINDOW...
CURSE YOU! I'M NOT GOING TO DIE. YOU'RE NOT GOING TO KILL ME!

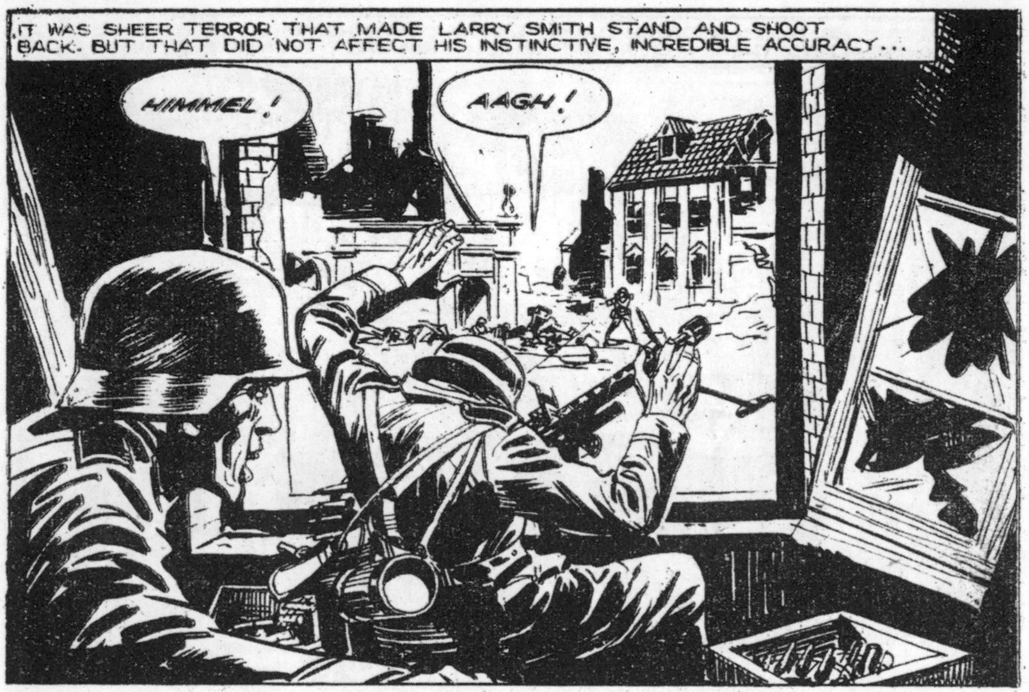
IT WAS SHEER TERROR THAT MADE LARRY SMITH STAND AND SHOOT BACK. BUT THAT DID NOT AFFECT HIS INSTINCTIVE, INCREDIBLE ACCURACY...
HIMMEL!
AAGH!

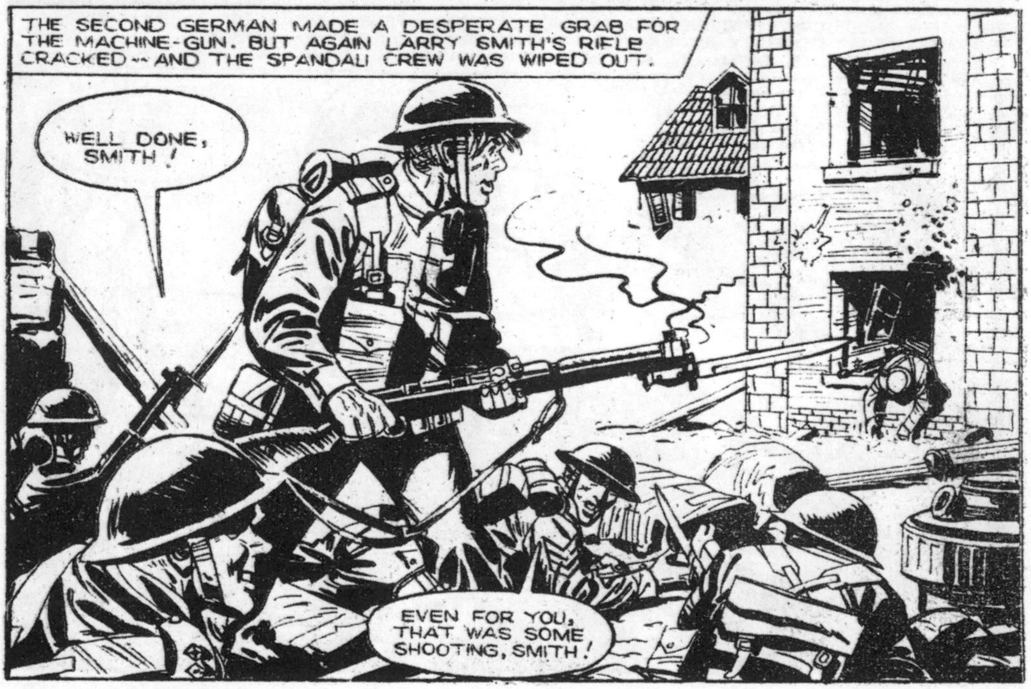
THE SECOND GERMAN MADE A DESPERATE GRAB FOR THE MACHINE-GUN. BUT AGAIN LARRY SMITH'S RIFLE CRACKED -- AND THE SPANDAU CREW WAS WIPED OUT.
WELL DONE, SMITH!
EVEN FOR YOU, THAT WAS SOME SHOOTING, SMITH!

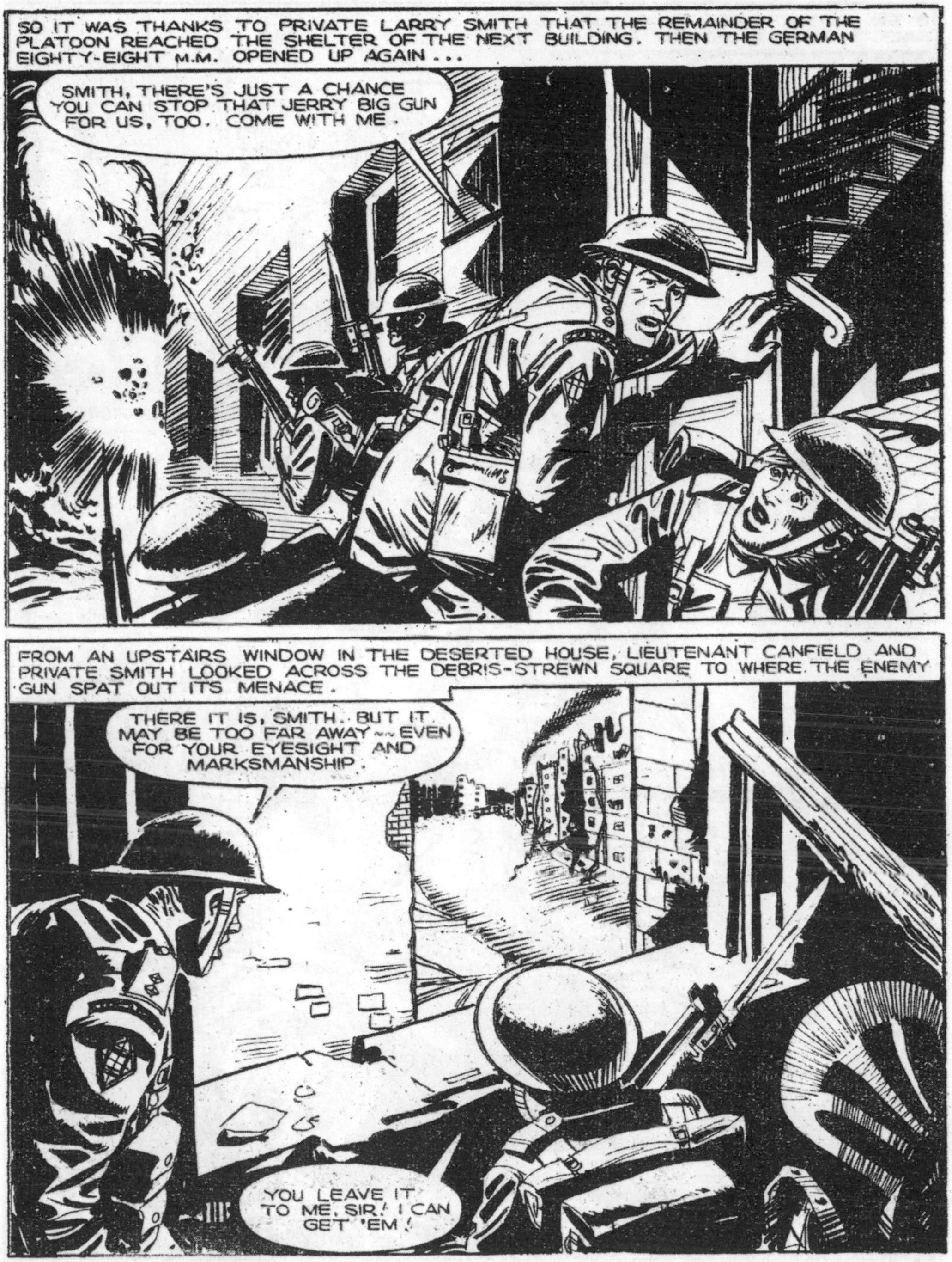
SO IT WAS THANKS TO PRIVATE LARRY SMITH THAT THE REMAINDER OF THE PLATOON REACHED THE SHELTER OF THE NEXT BUILDING. THEN THE GERMAN EIGHTY-EIGHT M.M. OPENED UP AGAIN ...
SMITH, THERE'S JUST A CHANCE YOU CAN STOP THAT JERRY BIG GUN FOR US, TOO. COME WITH ME.
FROM AN UPSTAIRS WINDOW IN THE DESERTED HOUSE, LIEUTENANT CANFIELD AND PRIVATE SMITH LOOKED ACROSS THE DEBRIS-STREWN SQUARE TO WHERE THE ENEMY GUN SPAT OUT ITS MENACE.
THERE IT IS, SMITH. BUT IT MAY BE TOO FAR AWAY -- EVEN FOR YOUR EYESIGHT AND MARKSMANSHIP.
YOU LEAVE IT TO ME, SIR! I CAN GET 'EM!

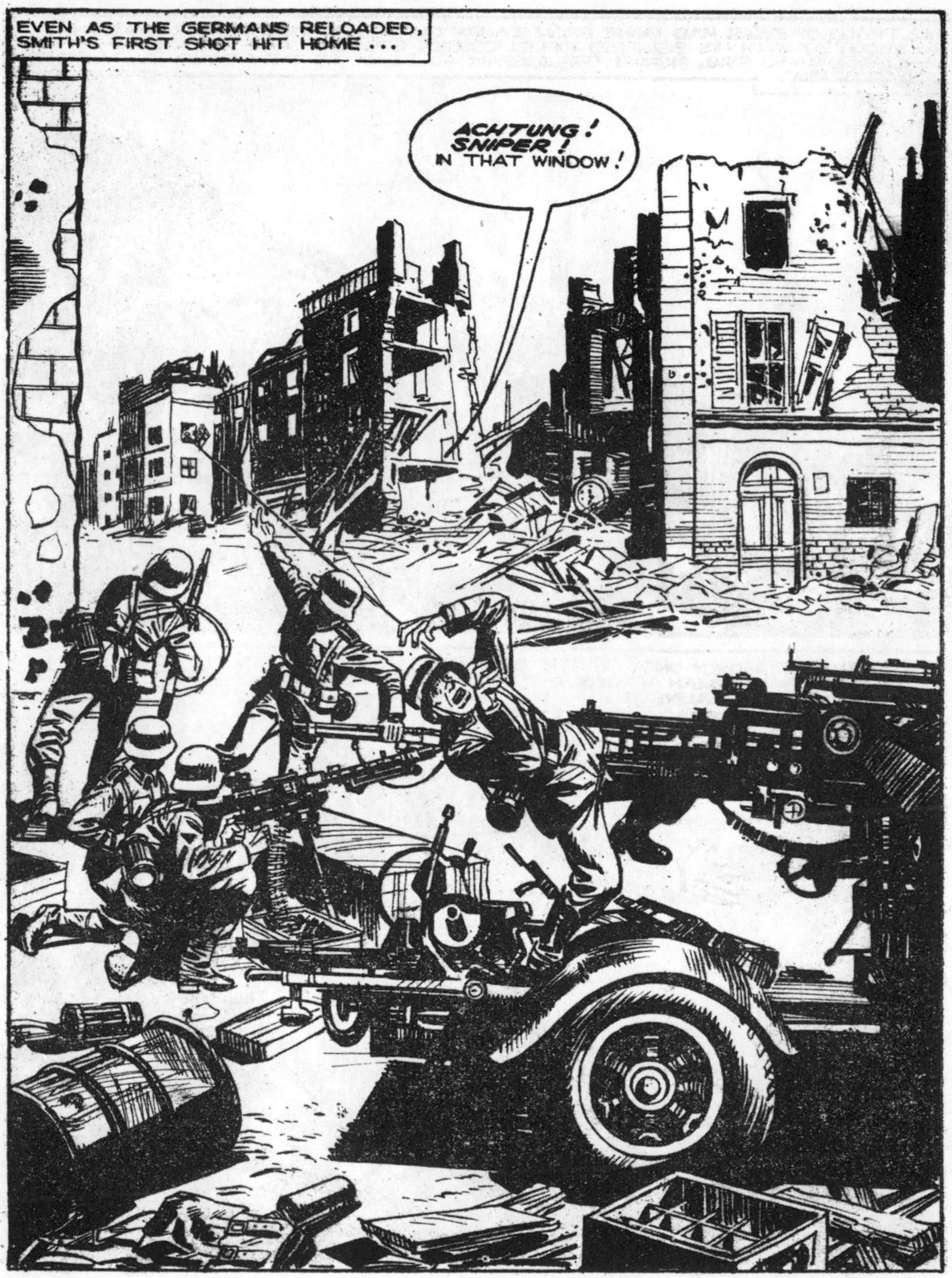
EVEN AS THE GERMANS RELOADED, SMITH'S FIRST SHOT HIT HOME ...
ACHTUNG! SNIPER! IN THAT WINDOW!

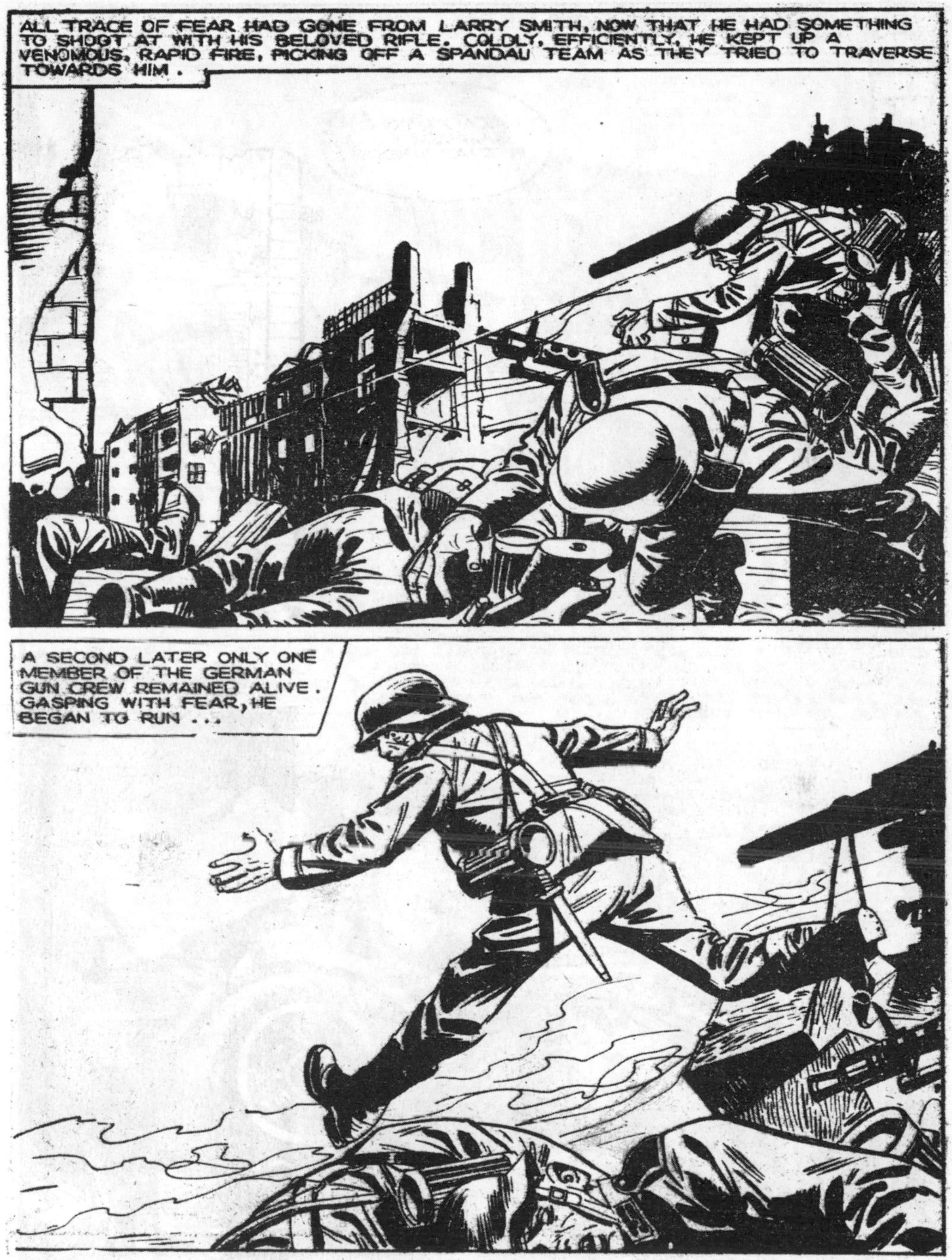
ALL TRACE OF FEAR HAD GONE FROM LARRY SMITH, NOW THAT HE HAD SOMETHING TO SHOOT AT WITH HIS BELOVED RIFLE. COLDLY, EFFICIENTLY, HE KEPT UP A VENOMOUS, RAPID FIRE, PICKING OFF A SPANDAU TEAM AS THEY TRIED TO TRAVERSE TOWARDS HIM.
A SECOND LATER ONLY ONE MEMBER OF THE GERMAN GUN CREW REMAINED ALIVE. GASPING WITH FEAR, HE BEGAN TO RUN ...

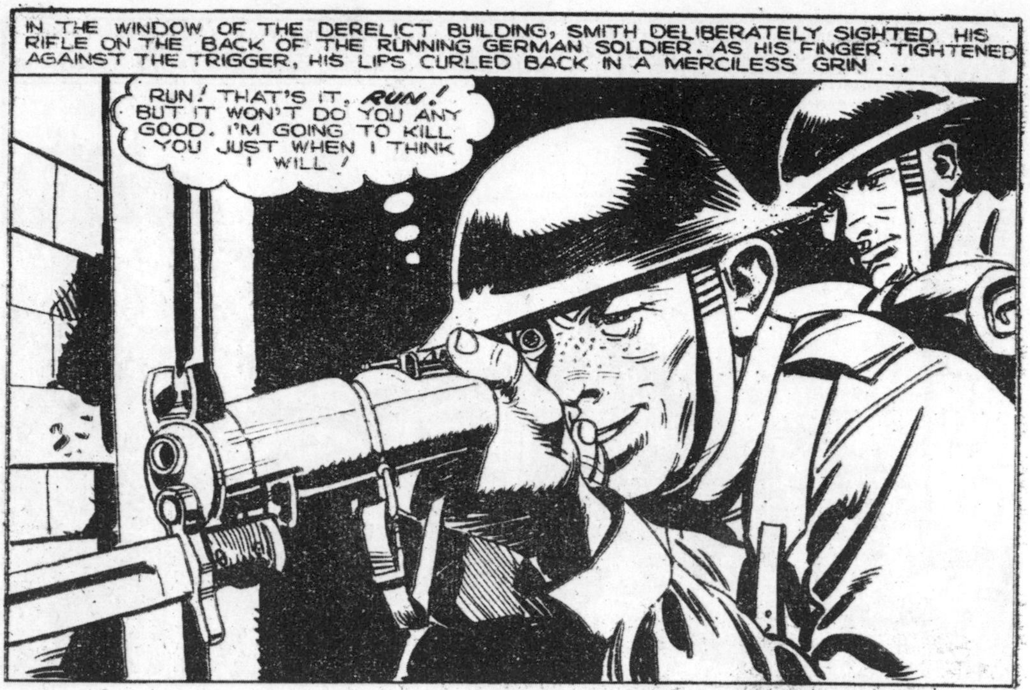
IN THE WINDOW OF THE DERELICT BUILDING, SMITH DELIBERATELY SIGHTED HIS RIFLE ON THE BACK OF THE RUNNING GERMAN SOLDIER. AS HIS FINGER TIGHTENED AGAINST THE TRIGGER, HIS LIPS CURLED BACK IN A MERCILESS GRIN . . .
RUN! THAT'S IT, RUN! BUT IT WON'T DO YOU ANY GOOD. I'M GOING TO KILL YOU JUST WHEN I THINK I WILL!

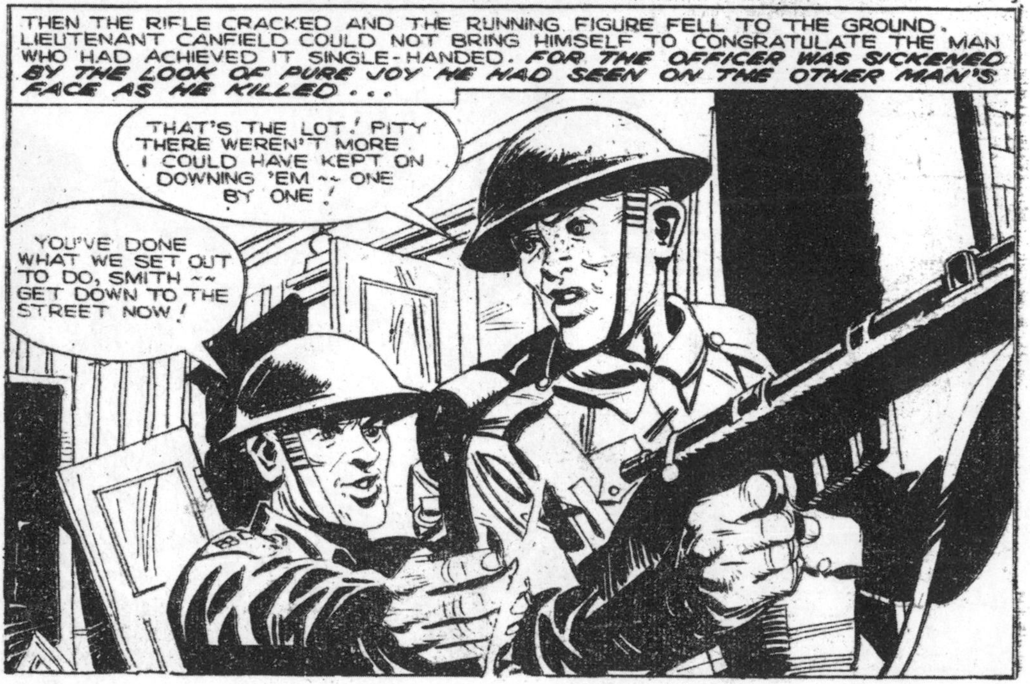
THEN THE RIFLE CRACKED AND THE RUNNING FIGURE FELL TO THE GROUND. LIEUTENANT CANFIELD COULD NOT BRING HIMSELF TO CONGRATULATE THE MAN WHO HAD ACHIEVED IT SINGLE-HANDED. FOR THE OFFICER WAS SICKENED BY THE LOOK OF PURE JOY HE HAD SEEN ON THE OTHER MAN'S FACE AS HE KILLED . . .
THAT'S THE LOT! PITY THERE WEREN'T MORE I COULD HAVE KEPT ON DOWNING 'EM -- ONE BY ONE!
YOU'VE DONE WHAT WE SET OUT TO DO, SMITH -- GET DOWN TO THE STREET NOW!

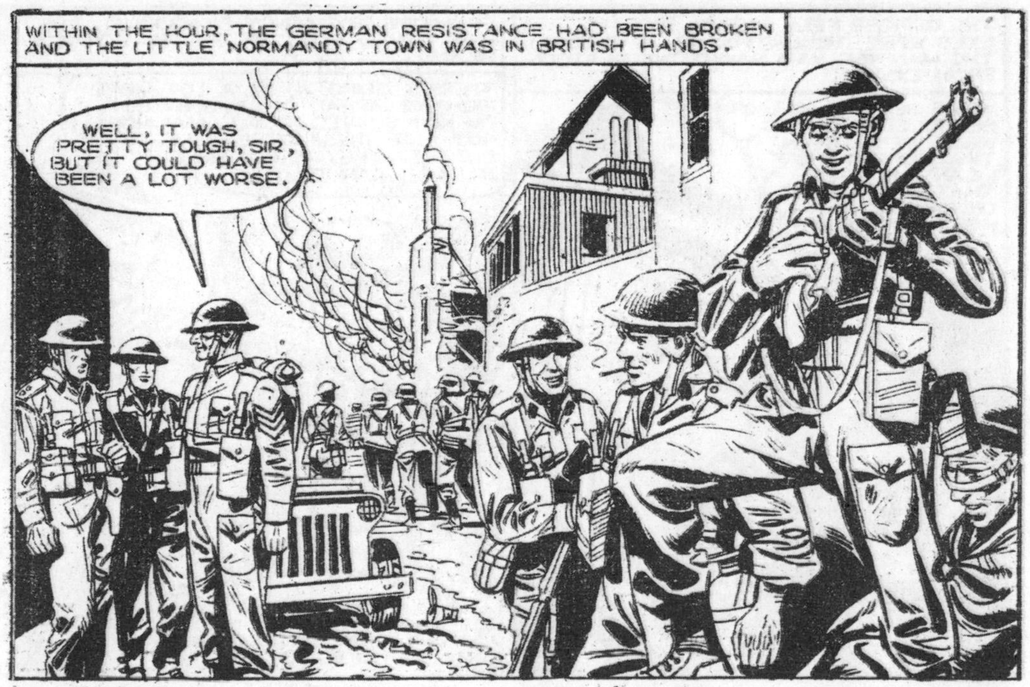
WITHIN THE HOUR, THE GERMAN RESISTANCE HAD BEEN BROKEN AND THE LITTLE NORMANDY TOWN WAS IN BRITISH HANDS.
WELL, IT WAS PRETTY TOUGH, SIR, BUT IT COULD HAVE BEEN A LOT WORSE.

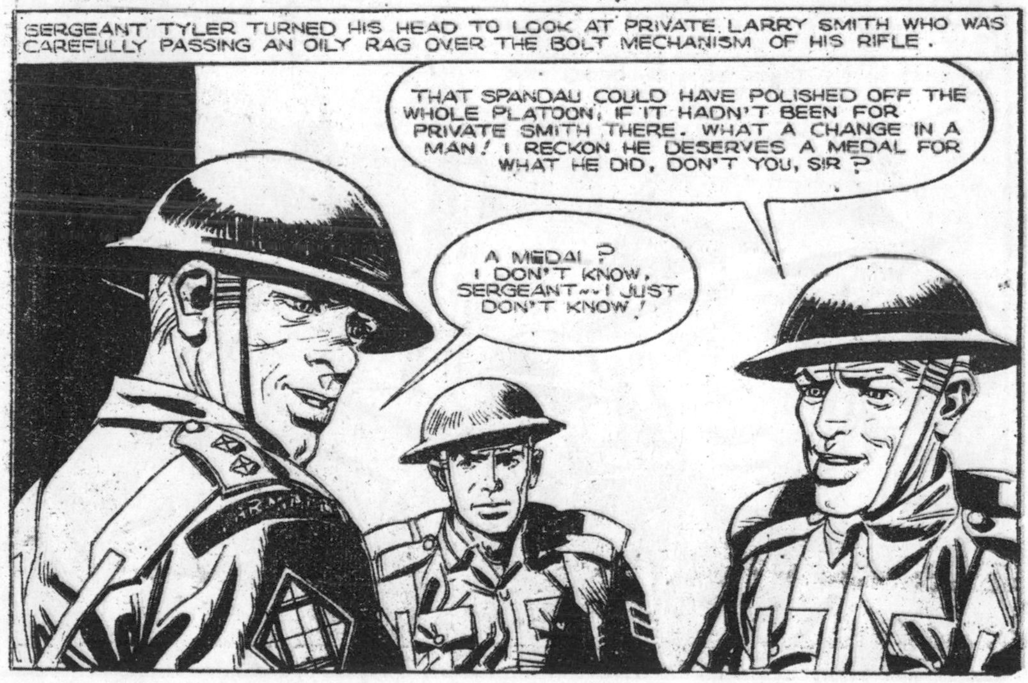
SERGEANT TYLER TURNED HIS HEAD TO LOOK AT PRIVATE LARRY SMITH WHO WAS CAREFULLY PASSING AN OILY RAG OVER THE BOLT MECHANISM OF HIS RIFLE.
THAT SPANDAU COULD HAVE POLISHED OFF THE WHOLE PLATOON, IF IT HADN'T BEEN FOR PRIVATE SMITH THERE. WHAT A CHANGE IN A MAN! I RECKON HE DESERVES A MEDAL FOR WHAT HE DID, DON'T YOU, SIR?
A MEDAL? I DON'T KNOW, SERGEANT-- I JUST DON'T KNOW!

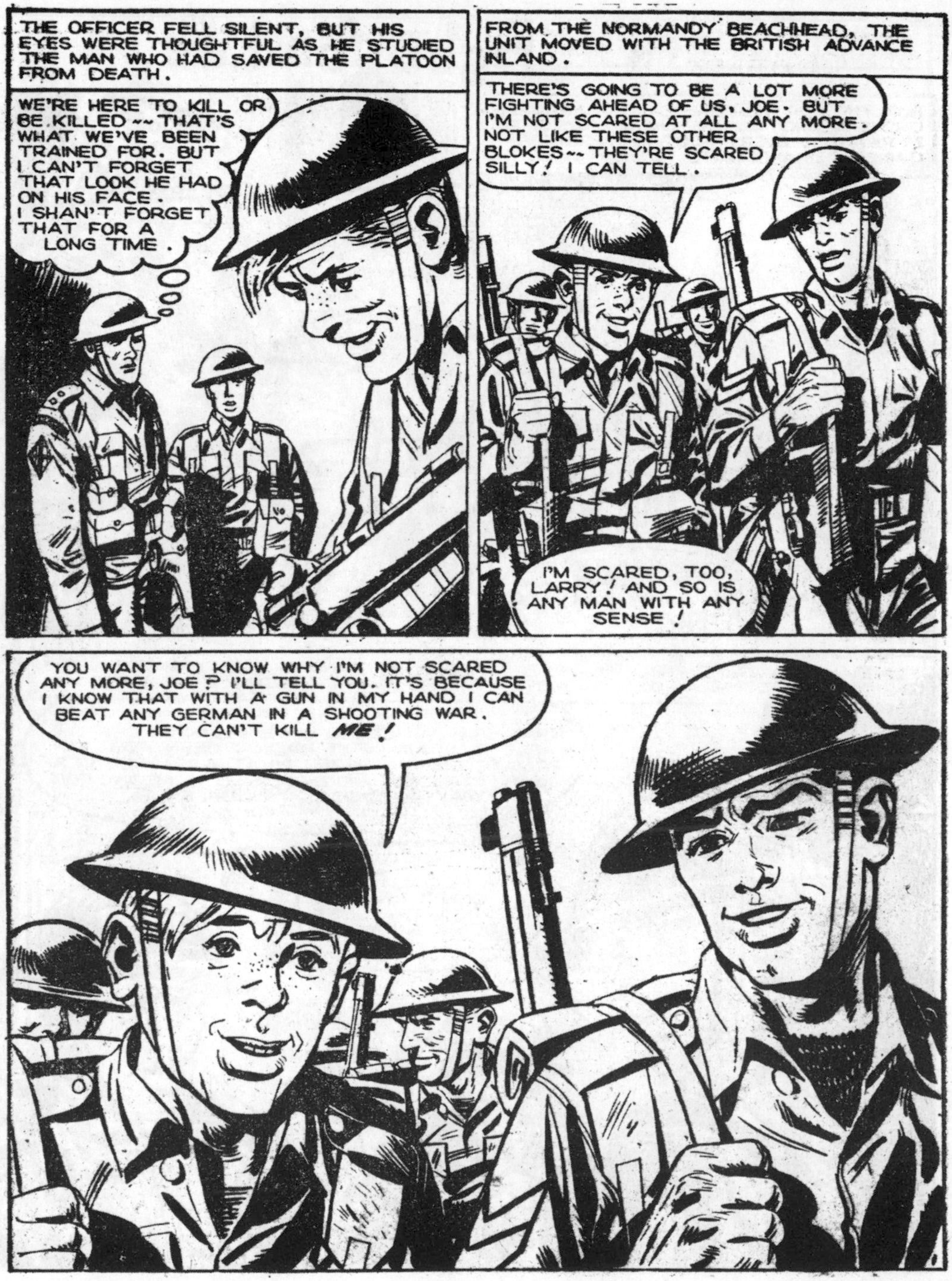
THE OFFICER FELL SILENT, BUT HIS EYES WERE THOUGHTFUL AS HE STUDIED THE MAN WHO HAD SAVED THE PLATOON FROM DEATH.
WE'RE HERE TO KILL OR BE KILLED -- THAT'S WHAT WE'VE BEEN TRAINED FOR. BUT I CAN'T FORGET THAT LOOK HE HAD ON HIS FACE. I SHAN'T FORGET THAT FOR A LONG TIME.
FROM THE NORMANDY BEACHHEAD, THE UNIT MOVED WITH THE BRITISH ADVANCE INLAND.
THERE'S GOING TO BE A LOT MORE FIGHTING AHEAD OF US, JOE. BUT I'M NOT SCARED AT ALL ANY MORE. NOT LIKE THESE OTHER BLOKES -- THEY'RE SCARED SILLY! I CAN TELL.
I'M SCARED, TOO, LARRY! AND SO IS ANY MAN WITH ANY SENSE!
YOU WANT TO KNOW WHY I'M NOT SCARED ANY MORE, JOE? I'LL TELL YOU. IT'S BECAUSE I KNOW THAT WITH A GUN IN MY HAND I CAN BEAT ANY GERMAN IN A SHOOTING WAR. THEY CAN'T KILL ME!

Chapter 3. Fight for Life

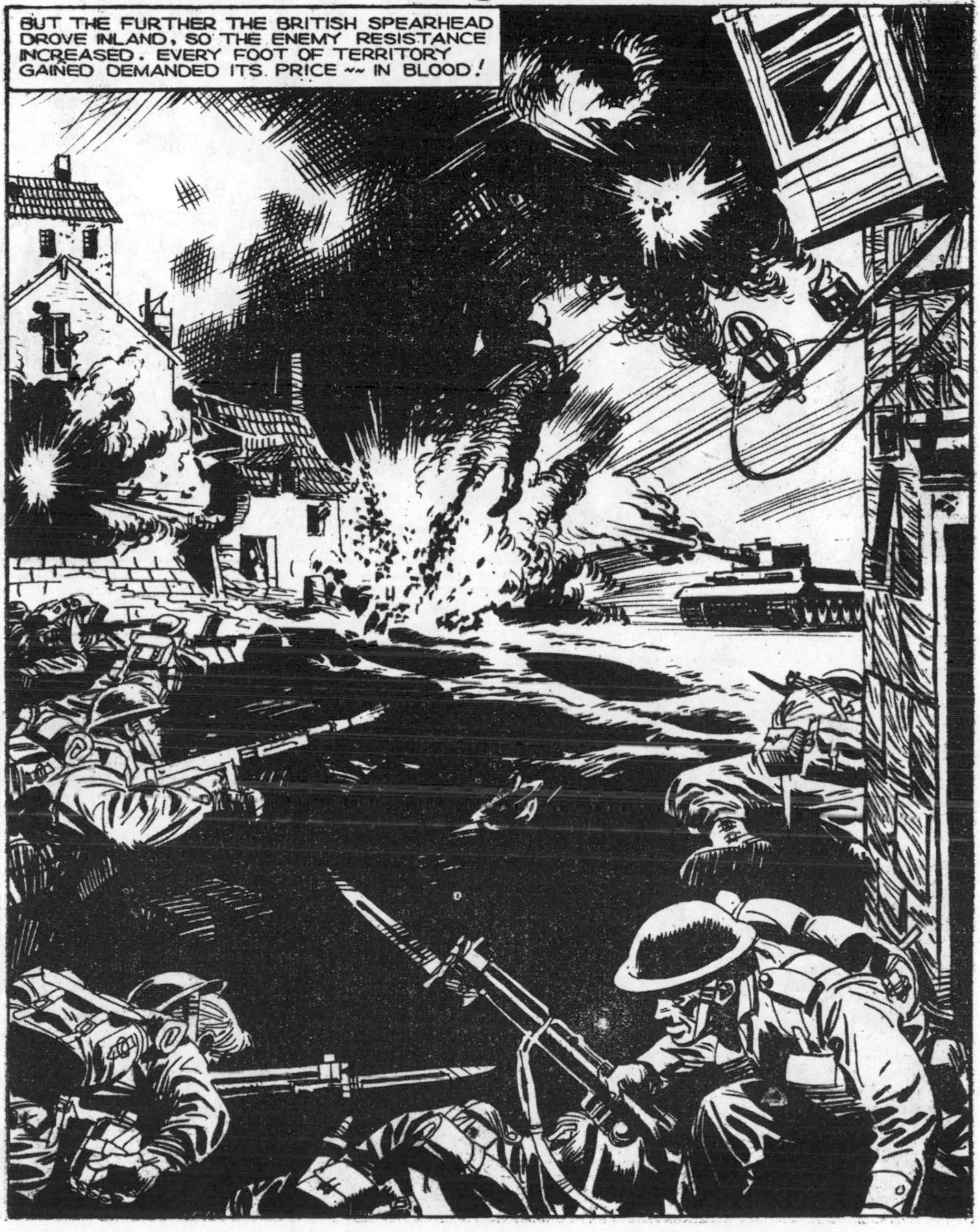
BUT THE FURTHER THE BRITISH SPEARHEAD DROVE INLAND, SO THE ENEMY RESISTANCE INCREASED. EVERY FOOT OF TERRITORY GAINED DEMANDED ITS PRICE ~~ IN BLOOD!

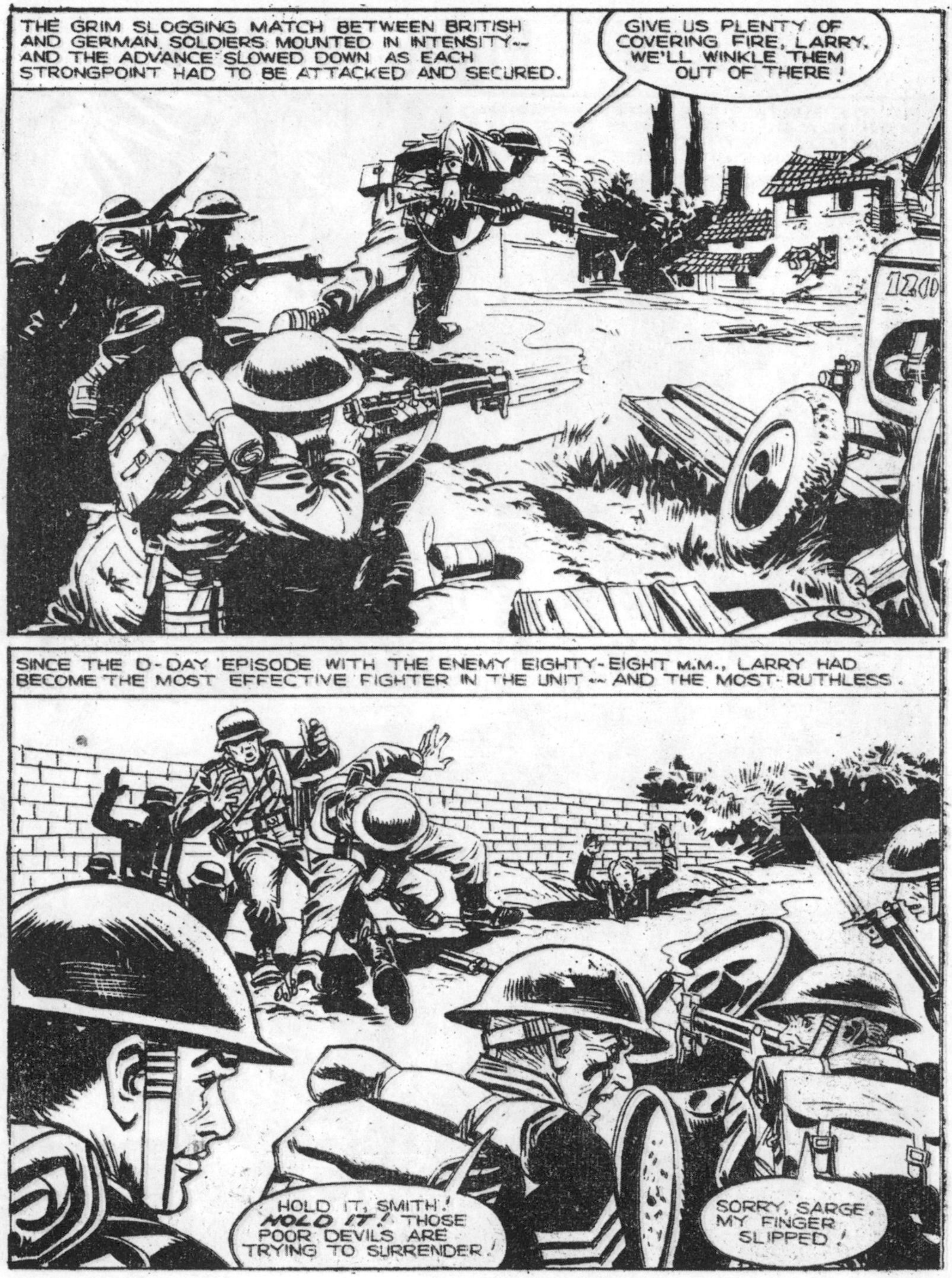
THE GRIM SLOGGING MATCH BETWEEN BRITISH AND GERMAN SOLDIERS MOUNTED IN INTENSITY-- AND THE ADVANCE SLOWED DOWN AS EACH STRONGPOINT HAD TO BE ATTACKED AND SECURED.
GIVE US PLENTY OF COVERING FIRE, LARRY. WE'LL WINKLE THEM OUT OF THERE !
SINCE THE D-DAY EPISODE WITH THE ENEMY EIGHTY-EIGHT M.M., LARRY HAD BECOME THE MOST EFFECTIVE FIGHTER IN THE UNIT -- AND THE MOST RUTHLESS.
HOLD IT, SMITH! HOLD IT! THOSE POOR DEVILS ARE TRYING TO SURRENDER.
SORRY, SARGE. MY FINGER SLIPPED !

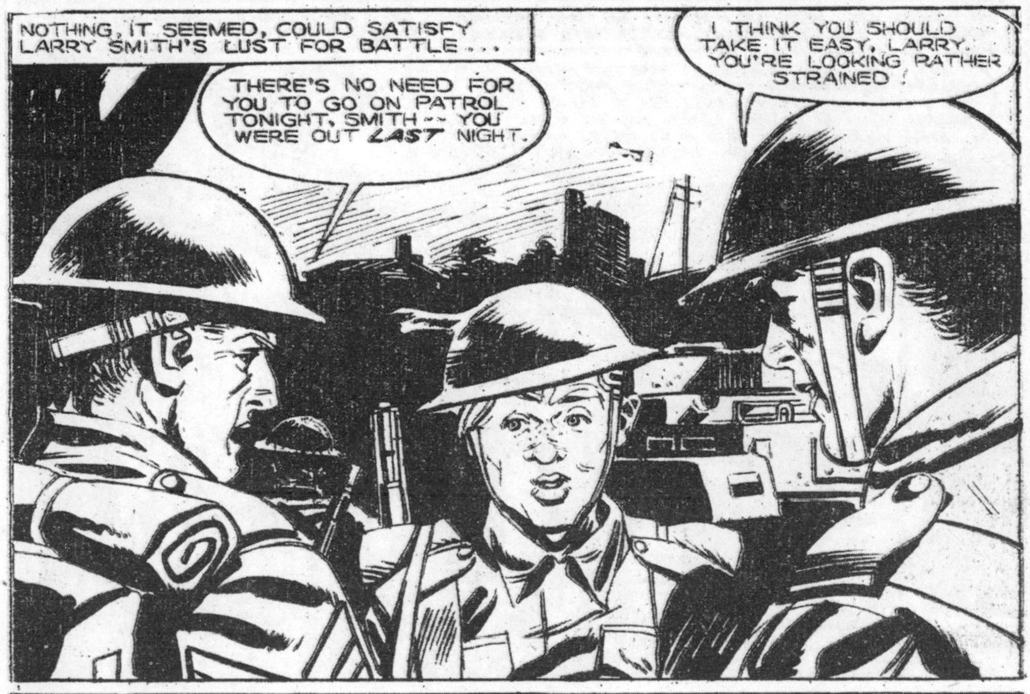
NOTHING, IT SEEMED, COULD SATISFY LARRY SMITH'S LUST FOR BATTLE ...
THERE'S NO NEED FOR YOU TO GO ON PATROL TONIGHT, SMITH -- YOU WERE OUT LAST NIGHT.
I THINK YOU SHOULD TAKE IT EASY, LARRY. YOU'RE LOOKING RATHER STRAINED!

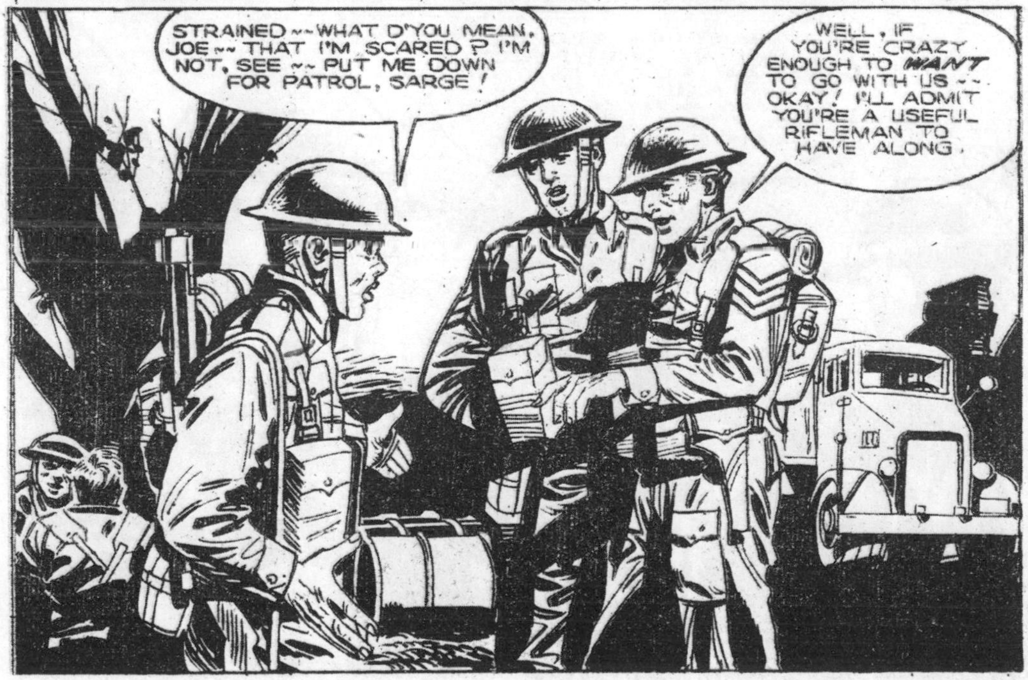
STRAINED -- WHAT D'YOU MEAN, JOE -- THAT I'M SCARED? I'M NOT, SEE -- PUT ME DOWN FOR PATROL, SARGE!
WELL, IF YOU'RE CRAZY ENOUGH TO WANT TO GO WITH US -- OKAY! I'LL ADMIT YOU'RE A USEFUL RIFLEMAN TO HAVE ALONG.

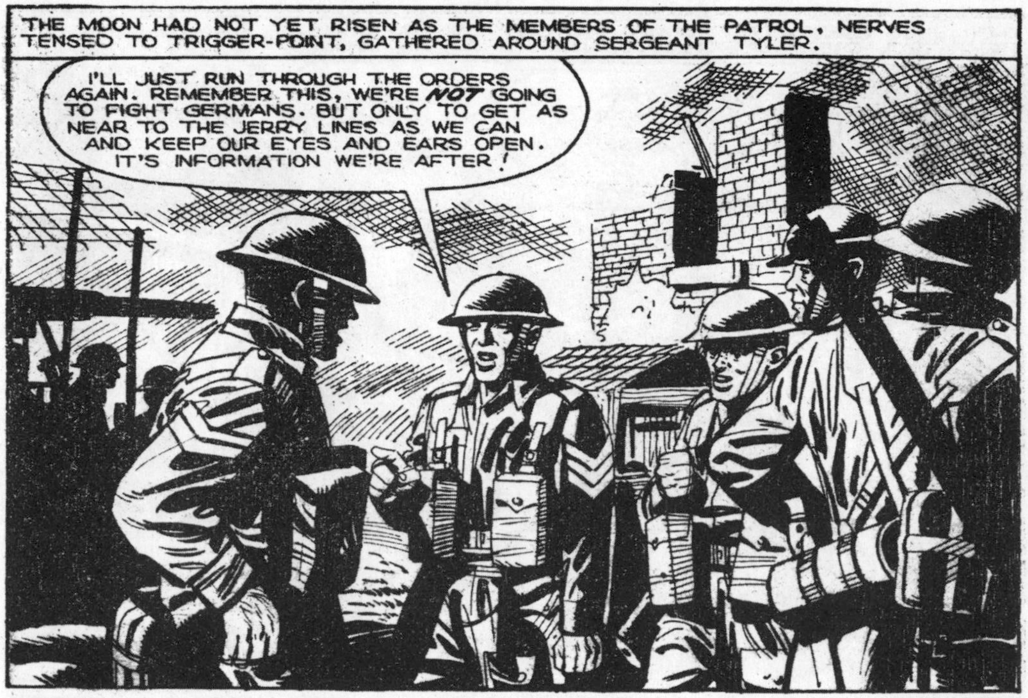
THE MOON HAD NOT YET RISEN AS THE MEMBERS OF THE PATROL, NERVES TENSED TO TRIGGER-POINT, GATHERED AROUND SERGEANT TYLER.
I'LL JUST RUN THROUGH THE ORDERS AGAIN. REMEMBER THIS, WE'RE NOT GOING TO FIGHT GERMANS. BUT ONLY TO GET AS NEAR TO THE JERRY LINES AS WE CAN AND KEEP OUR EYES AND EARS OPEN. IT'S INFORMATION WE'RE AFTER!

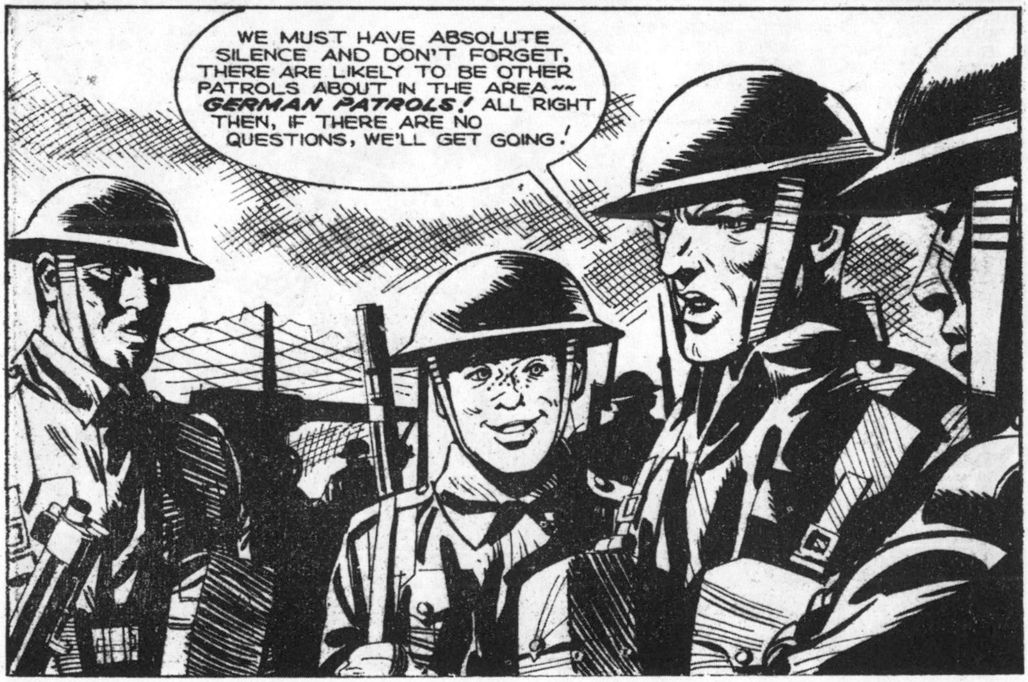
WE MUST HAVE ABSOLUTE SILENCE AND DON'T FORGET, THERE ARE LIKELY TO BE OTHER PATROLS ABOUT IN THE AREA~~ GERMAN PATROLS! ALL RIGHT THEN, IF THERE ARE NO QUESTIONS, WE'LL GET GOING!

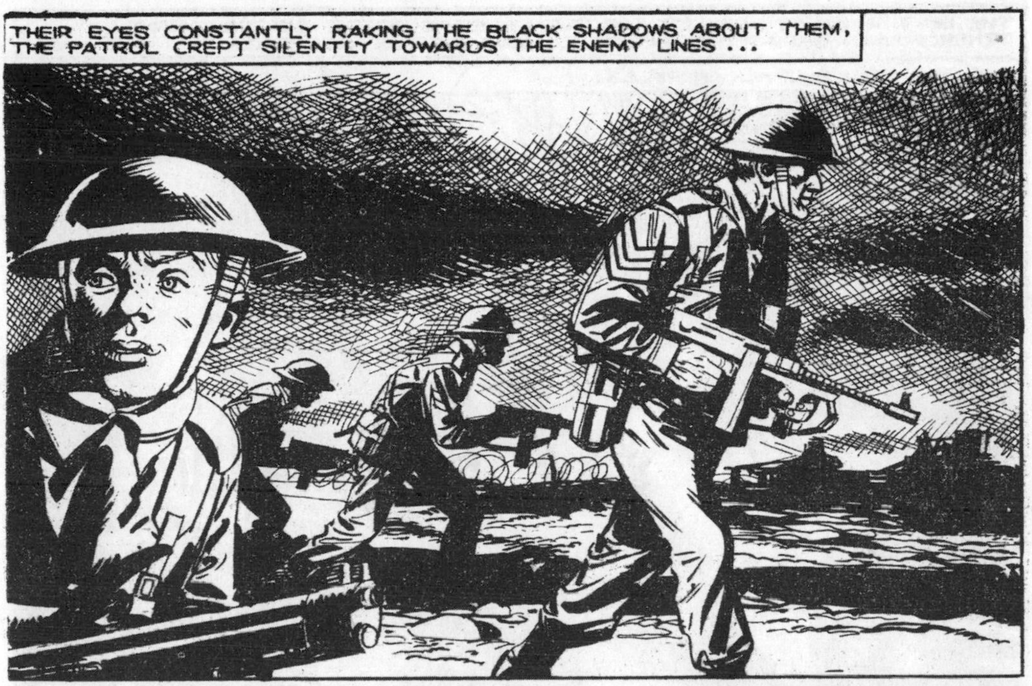
THEIR EYES CONSTANTLY RAKING THE BLACK SHADOWS ABOUT THEM, THE PATROL CREPT SILENTLY TOWARDS THE ENEMY LINES ...

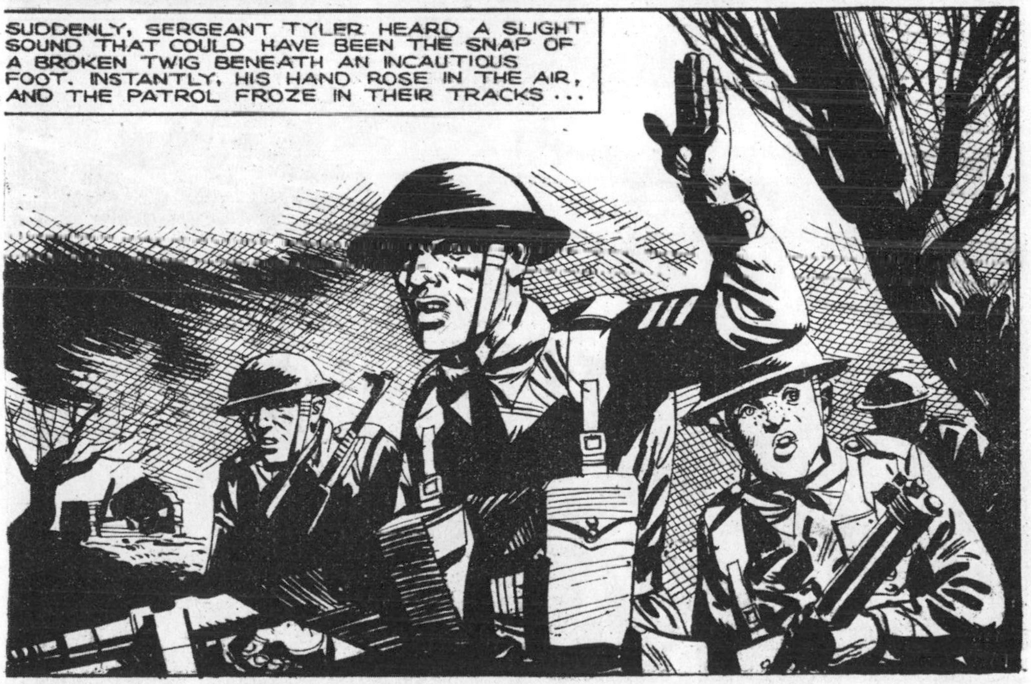
SUDDENLY, SERGEANT TYLER HEARD A SLIGHT SOUND THAT COULD HAVE BEEN THE SNAP OF A BROKEN TWIG BENEATH AN INCAUTIOUS FOOT. INSTANTLY, HIS HAND ROSE IN THE AIR, AND THE PATROL FROZE IN THEIR TRACKS ...

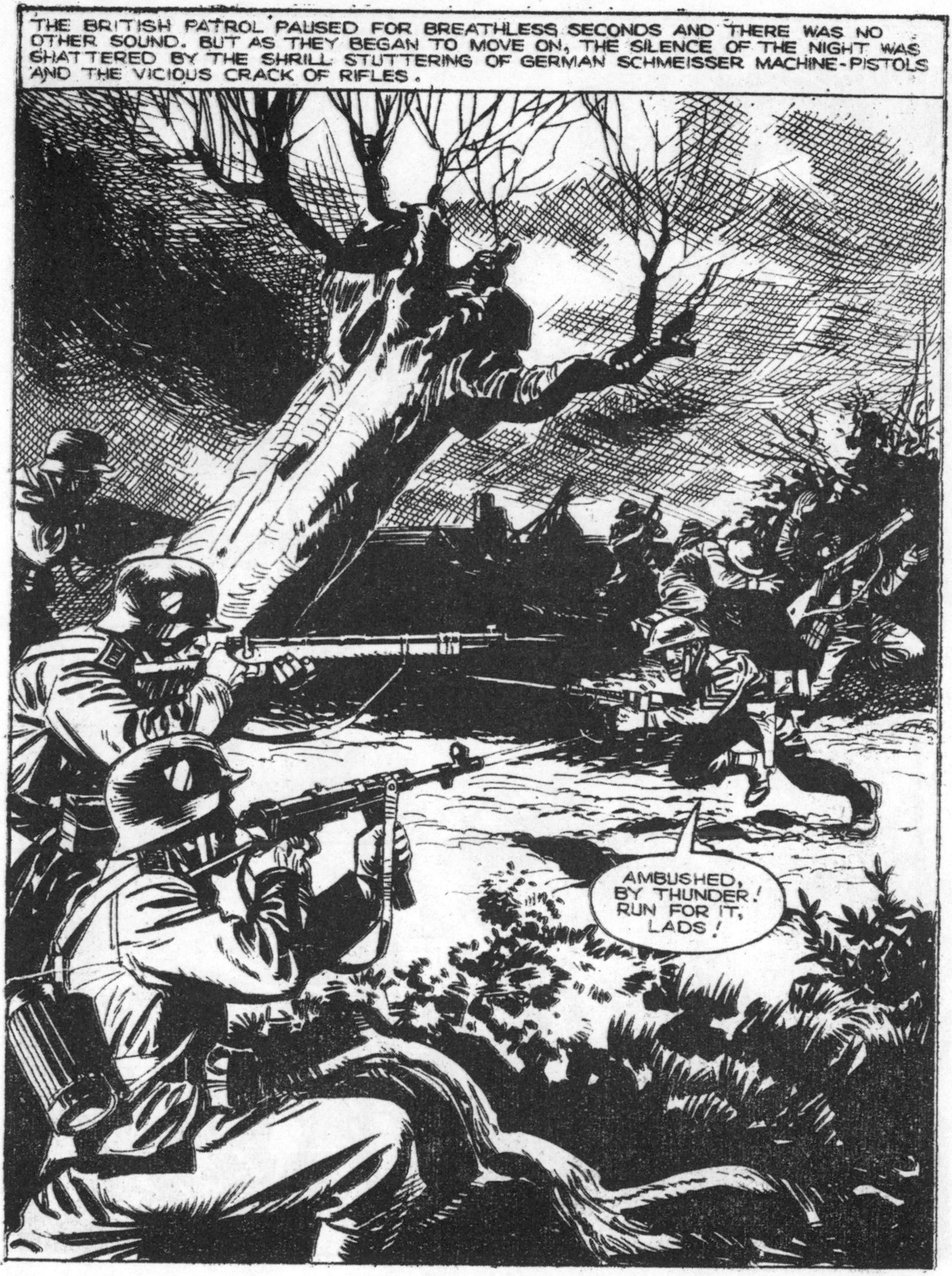
THE BRITISH PATROL PAUSED FOR BREATHLESS SECONDS AND THERE WAS NO OTHER SOUND. BUT AS THEY BEGAN TO MOVE ON, THE SILENCE OF THE NIGHT WAS SHATTERED BY THE SHRILL STUTTERING OF GERMAN SCHMEISSER MACHINE-PISTOLS AND THE VICIOUS CRACK OF RIFLES.
AMBUSHED, BY THUNDER! RUN FOR IT, LADS!

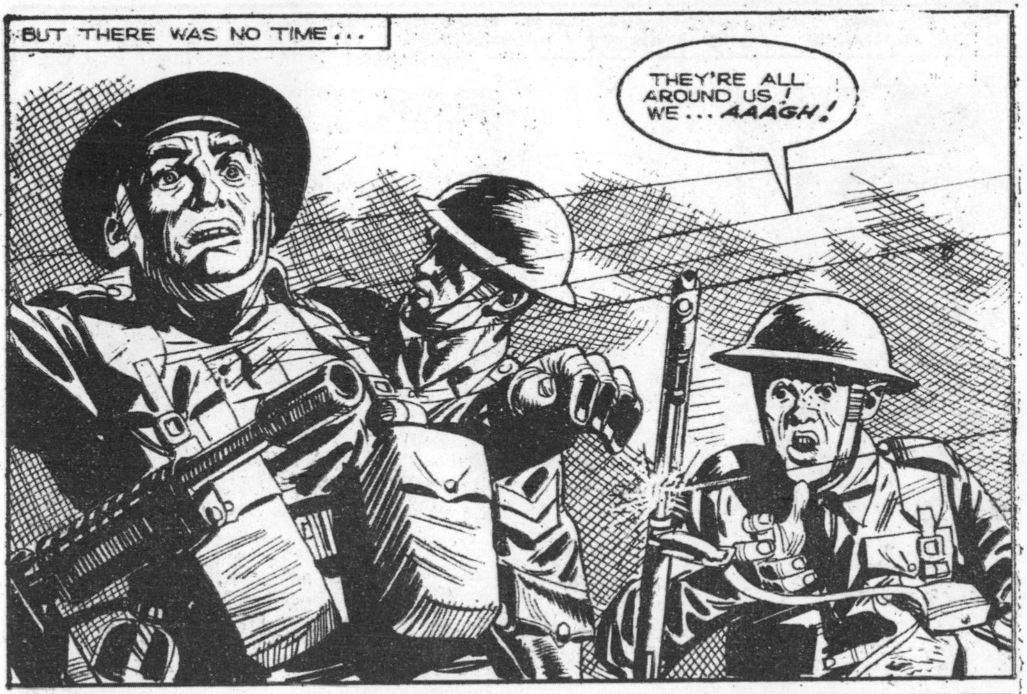
BUT THERE WAS NO TIME...
THEY'RE ALL AROUND US! WE... AAAGH!

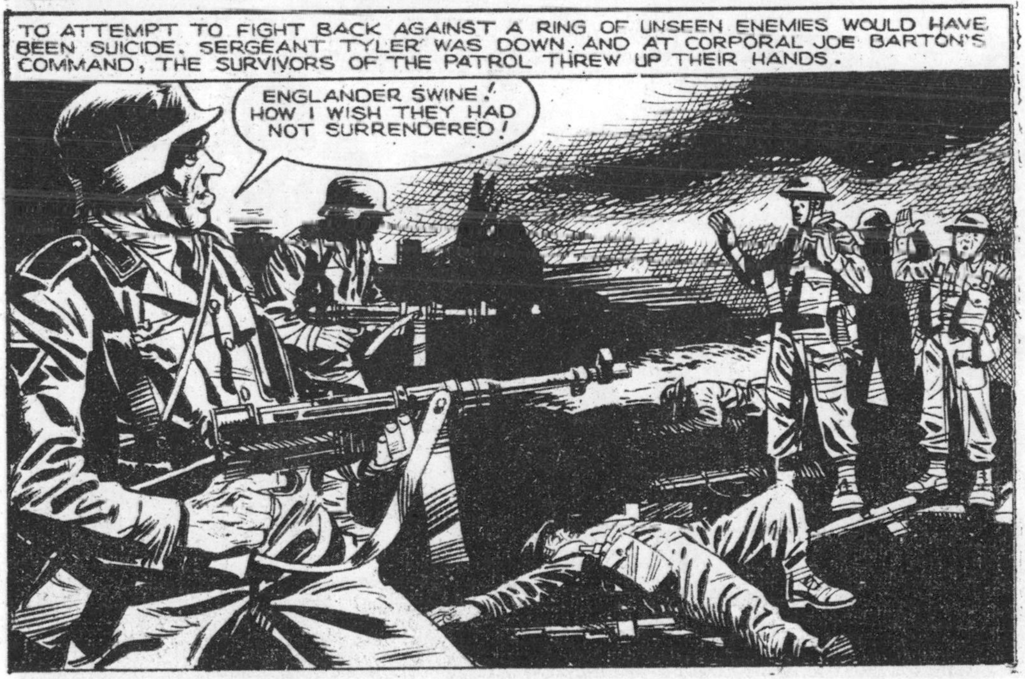
TO ATTEMPT TO FIGHT BACK AGAINST A RING OF UNSEEN ENEMIES WOULD HAVE BEEN SUICIDE. SERGEANT TYLER WAS DOWN. AND AT CORPORAL JOE BARTON'S COMMAND, THE SURVIVORS OF THE PATROL THREW UP THEIR HANDS.
ENGLANDER SWINE! HOW I WISH THEY HAD NOT SURRENDERED!

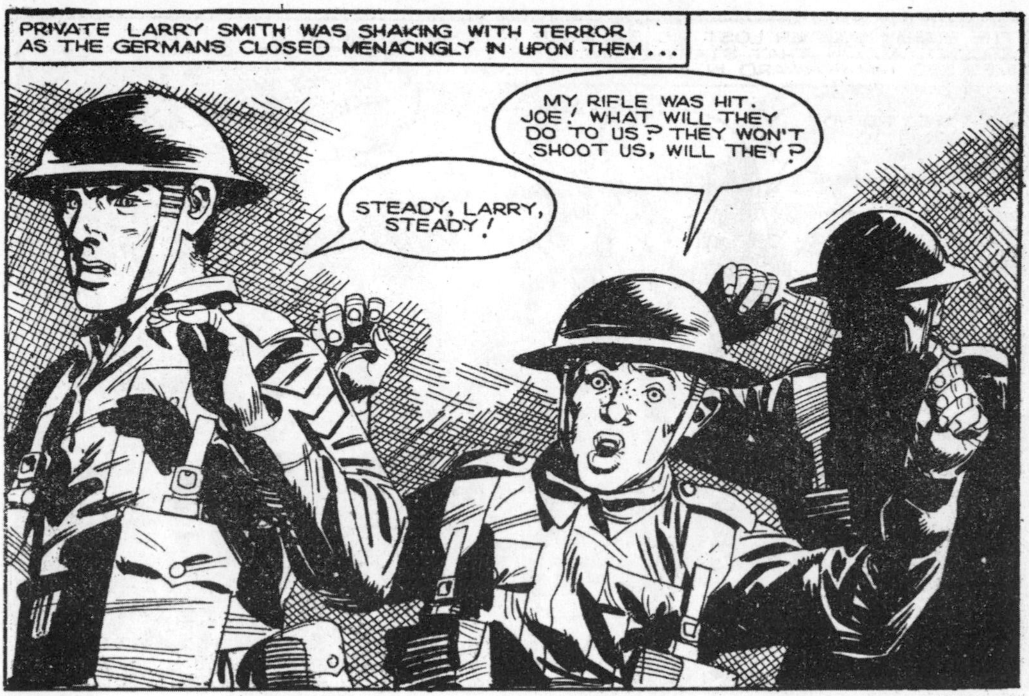
PRIVATE LARRY SMITH WAS SHAKING WITH TERROR AS THE GERMANS CLOSED MENACINGLY IN UPON THEM...
MY RIFLE WAS HIT. JOE! WHAT WILL THEY DO TO US? THEY WON'T SHOOT US, WILL THEY?
STEADY, LARRY, STEADY!

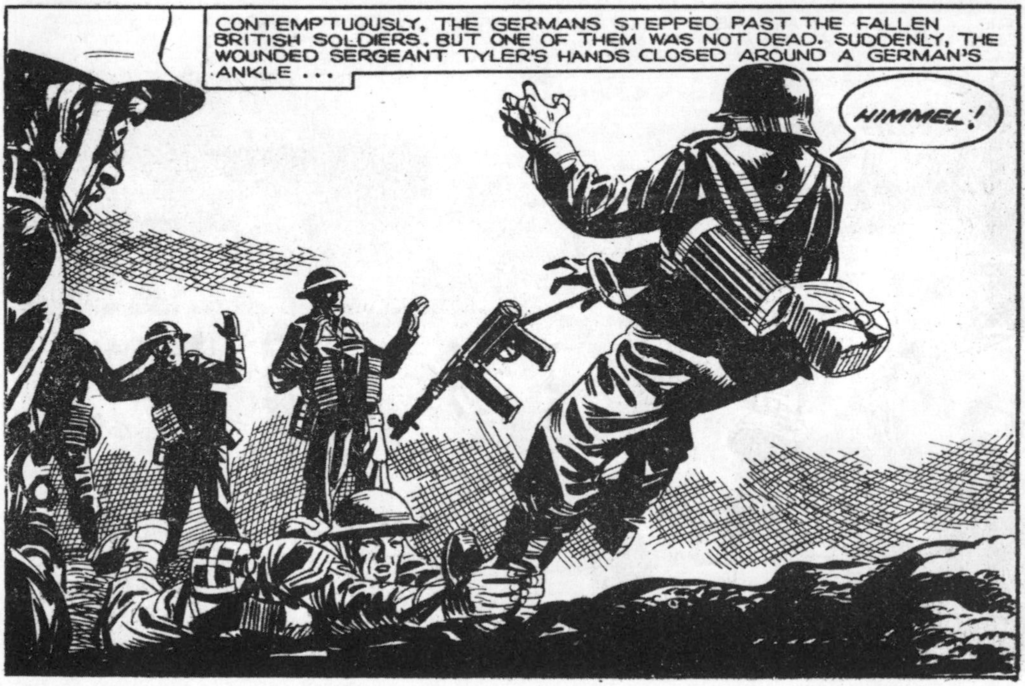
CONTEMPTUOUSLY, THE GERMANS STEPPED PAST THE FALLEN BRITISH SOLDIERS. BUT ONE OF THEM WAS NOT DEAD. SUDDENLY, THE WOUNDED SERGEANT TYLER'S HANDS CLOSED AROUND A GERMAN'S ANKLE...
HIMMEL!

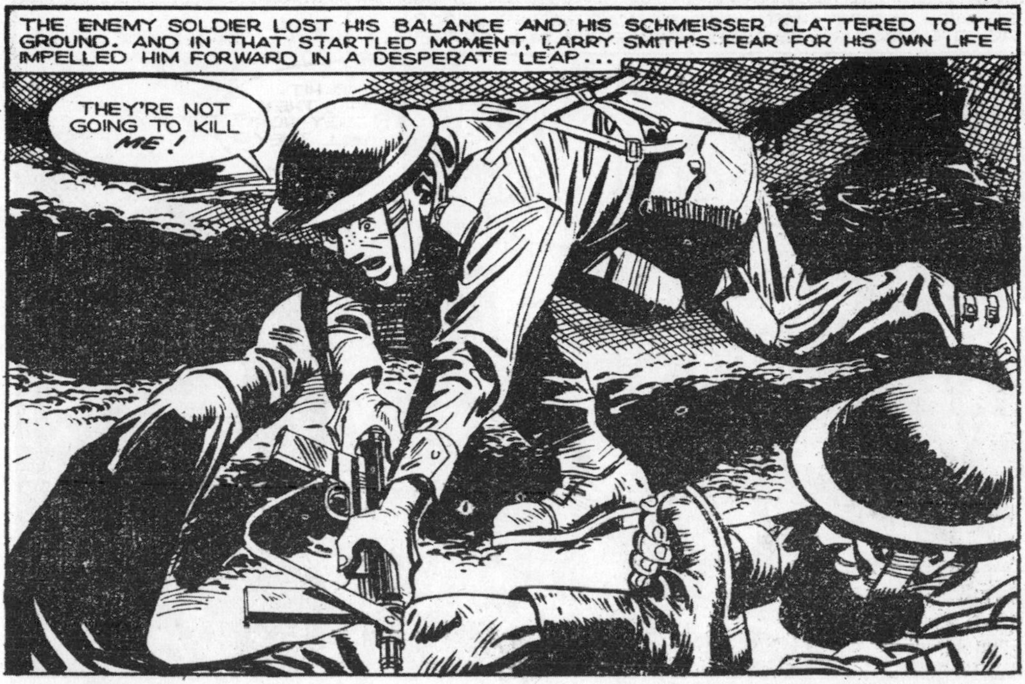
THE ENEMY SOLDIER LOST HIS BALANCE AND HIS SCHMEISSER CLATTERED TO THE GROUND. AND IN THAT STARTLED MOMENT, LARRY SMITH'S FEAR FOR HIS OWN LIFE IMPELLED HIM FORWARD IN A DESPERATE LEAP...
THEY'RE NOT GOING TO KILL *ME!*

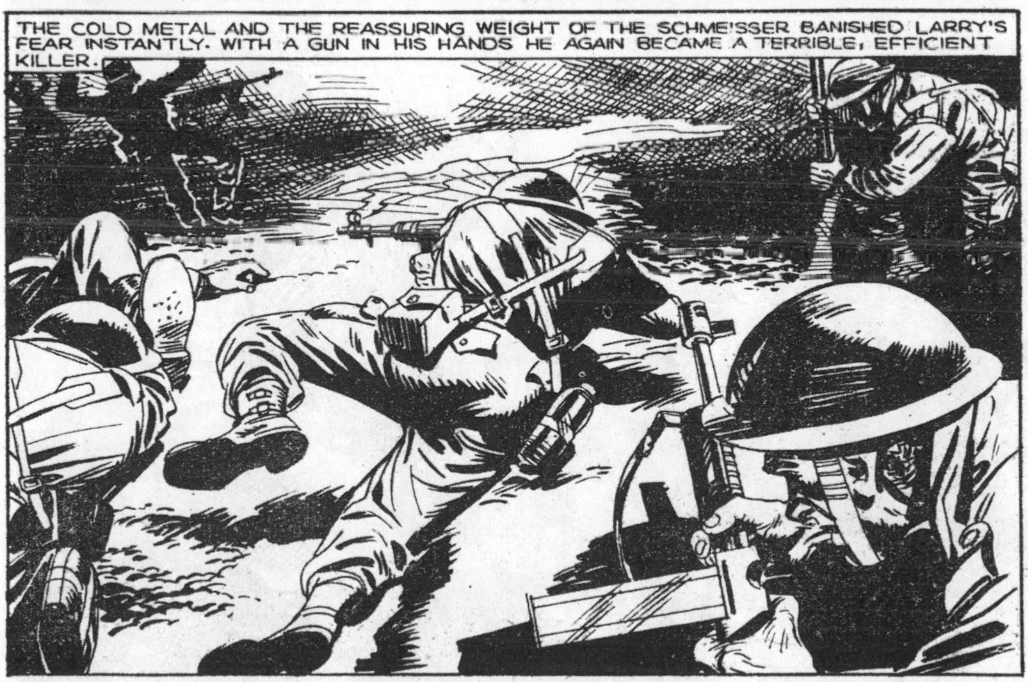
THE COLD METAL AND THE REASSURING WEIGHT OF THE SCHMEISSER BANISHED LARRY'S FEAR INSTANTLY. WITH A GUN IN HIS HANDS HE AGAIN BECAME A TERRIBLE, EFFICIENT KILLER.

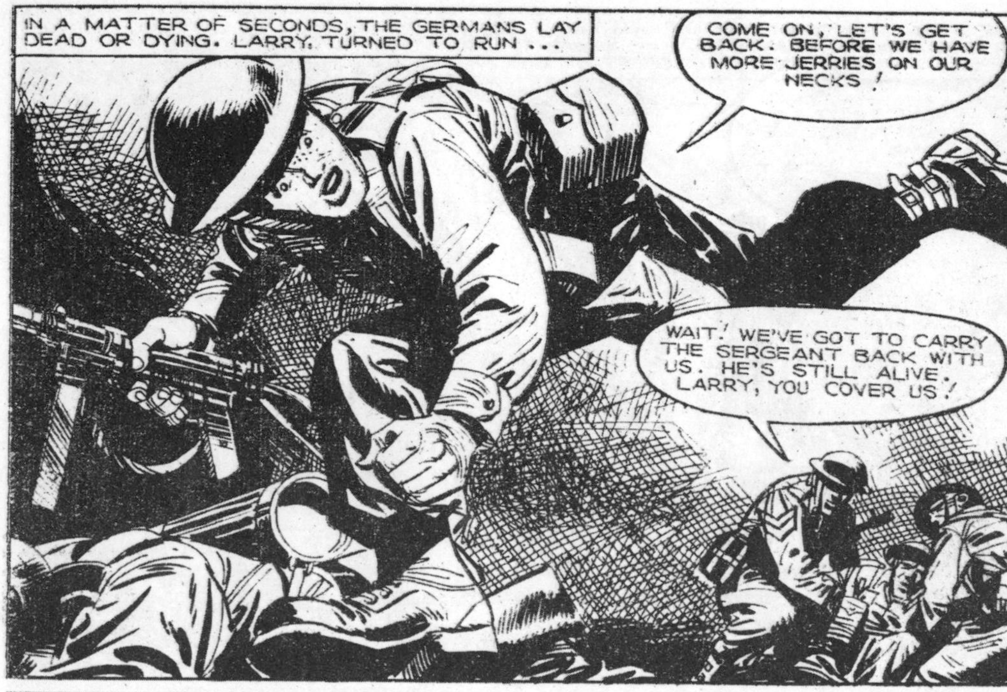
IN A MATTER OF SECONDS, THE GERMANS LAY DEAD OR DYING. LARRY TURNED TO RUN ...
COME ON, LET'S GET BACK. BEFORE WE HAVE MORE JERRIES ON OUR NECKS!
WAIT! WE'VE GOT TO CARRY THE SERGEANT BACK WITH US. HE'S STILL ALIVE. LARRY, YOU COVER US!

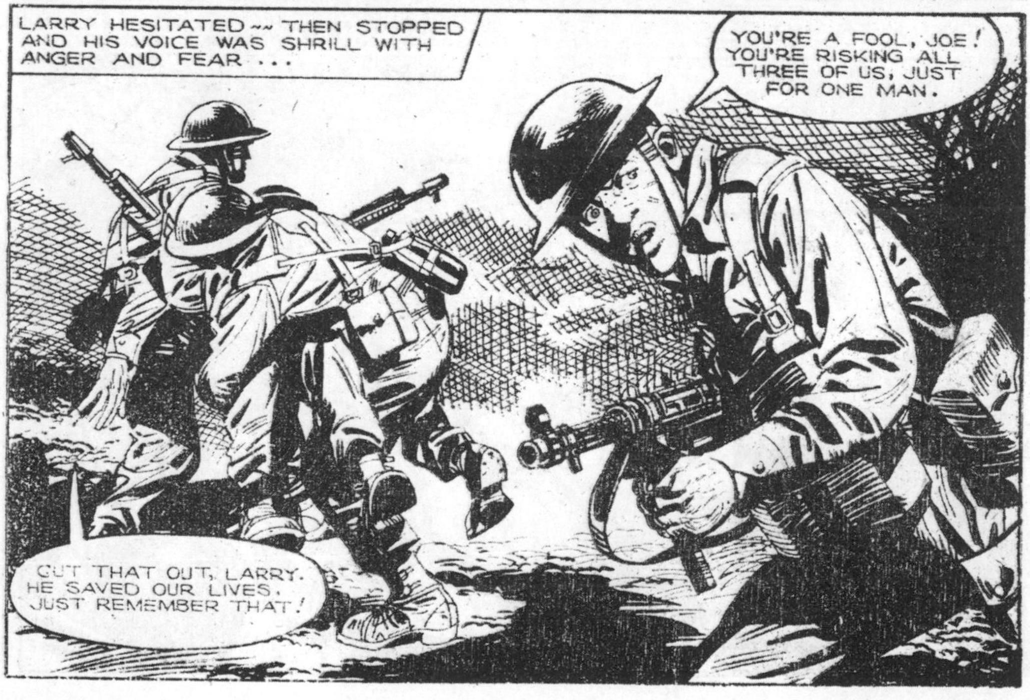
LARRY HESITATED -- THEN STOPPED AND HIS VOICE WAS SHRILL WITH ANGER AND FEAR ...
YOU'RE A FOOL, JOE! YOU'RE RISKING ALL THREE OF US, JUST FOR ONE MAN.
CUT THAT OUT, LARRY. HE SAVED OUR LIVES. JUST REMEMBER THAT!

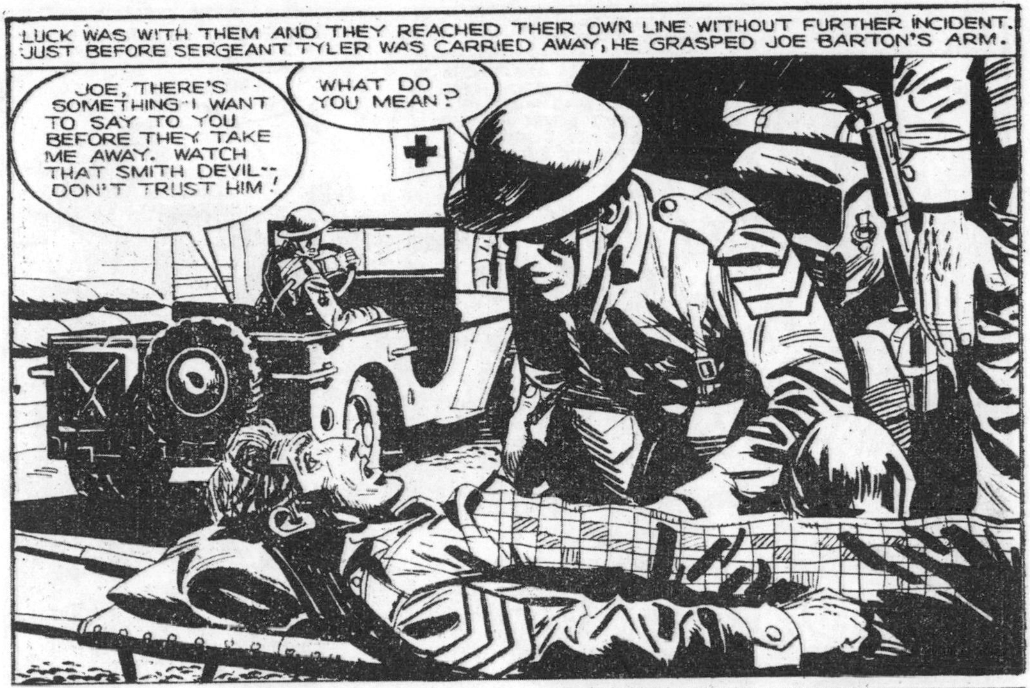
LUCK WAS WITH THEM AND THEY REACHED THEIR OWN LINE WITHOUT FURTHER INCIDENT. JUST BEFORE SERGEANT TYLER WAS CARRIED AWAY, HE GRASPED JOE BARTON'S ARM.
JOE, THERE'S SOMETHING I WANT TO SAY TO YOU BEFORE THEY TAKE ME AWAY. WATCH THAT SMITH DEVIL-- DON'T TRUST HIM!
WHAT DO YOU MEAN?

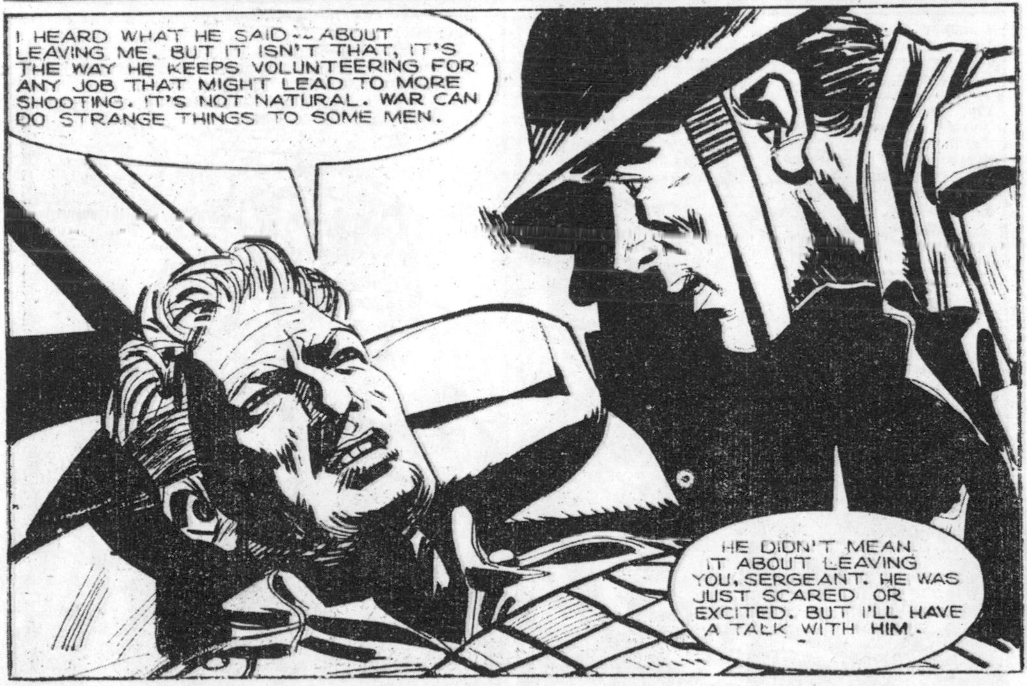
I HEARD WHAT HE SAID -- ABOUT LEAVING ME. BUT IT ISN'T THAT, IT'S THE WAY HE KEEPS VOLUNTEERING FOR ANY JOB THAT MIGHT LEAD TO MORE SHOOTING. IT'S NOT NATURAL. WAR CAN DO STRANGE THINGS TO SOME MEN.
HE DIDN'T MEAN IT ABOUT LEAVING YOU, SERGEANT. HE WAS JUST SCARED OR EXCITED. BUT I'LL HAVE A TALK WITH HIM.

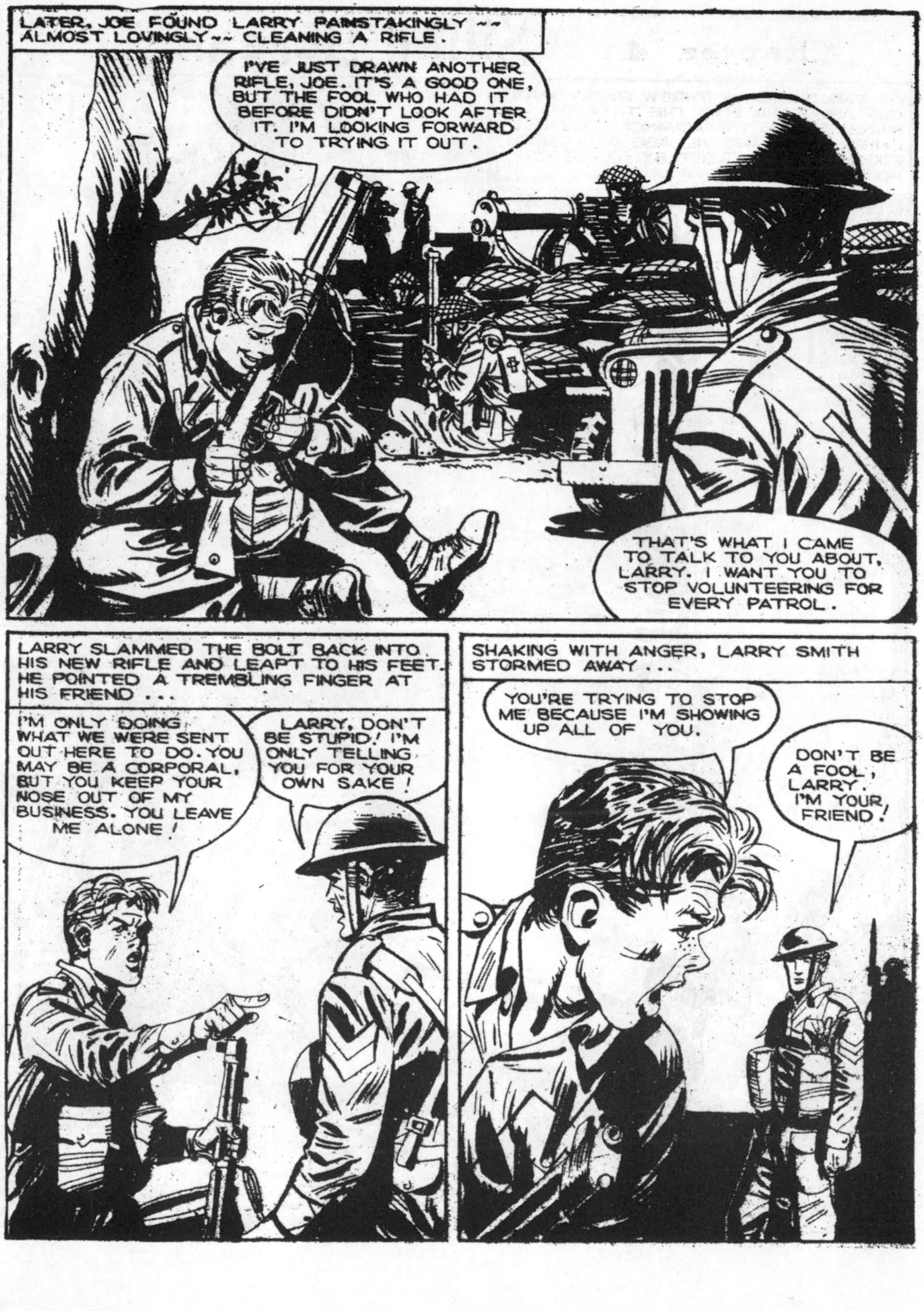
LATER, JOE FOUND LARRY PAINSTAKINGLY -- ALMOST LOVINGLY -- CLEANING A RIFLE.
I'VE JUST DRAWN ANOTHER RIFLE, JOE. IT'S A GOOD ONE, BUT THE FOOL WHO HAD IT BEFORE DIDN'T LOOK AFTER IT. I'M LOOKING FORWARD TO TRYING IT OUT.
THAT'S WHAT I CAME TO TALK TO YOU ABOUT, LARRY. I WANT YOU TO STOP VOLUNTEERING FOR EVERY PATROL.
LARRY SLAMMED THE BOLT BACK INTO HIS NEW RIFLE AND LEAPT TO HIS FEET. HE POINTED A TREMBLING FINGER AT HIS FRIEND ...
I'M ONLY DOING WHAT WE WERE SENT OUT HERE TO DO. YOU MAY BE A CORPORAL, BUT YOU KEEP YOUR NOSE OUT OF MY BUSINESS. YOU LEAVE ME ALONE!
LARRY, DON'T BE STUPID! I'M ONLY TELLING YOU FOR YOUR OWN SAKE!
SHAKING WITH ANGER, LARRY SMITH STORMED AWAY ...
YOU'RE TRYING TO STOP ME BECAUSE I'M SHOWING UP ALL OF YOU.
DON'T BE A FOOL, LARRY. I'M YOUR FRIEND!

Chapter 4. Killer Streak

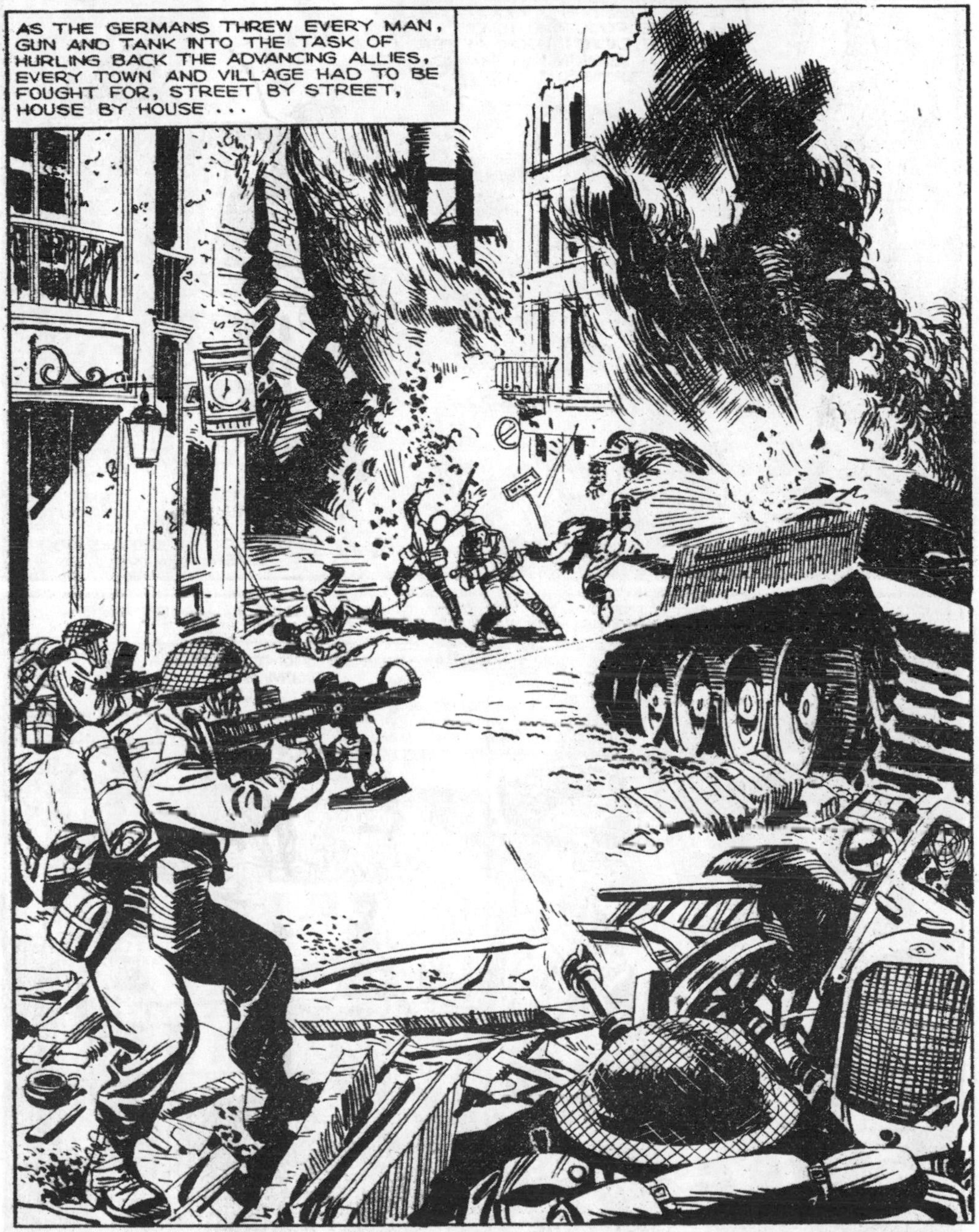
AS THE GERMANS THREW EVERY MAN, GUN AND TANK INTO THE TASK OF HURLING BACK THE ADVANCING ALLIES, EVERY TOWN AND VILLAGE HAD TO BE FOUGHT FOR, STREET BY STREET, HOUSE BY HOUSE ...

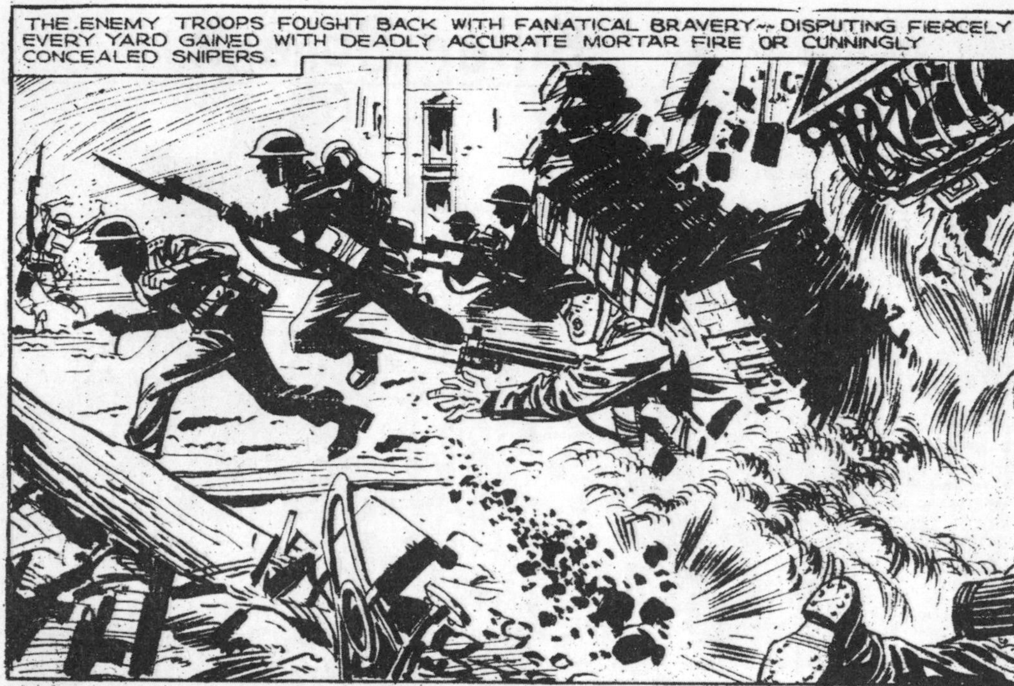
THE ENEMY TROOPS FOUGHT BACK WITH FANATICAL BRAVERY -- DISPUTING FIERCELY EVERY YARD GAINED WITH DEADLY ACCURATE MORTAR FIRE OR CUNNINGLY CONCEALED SNIPERS.

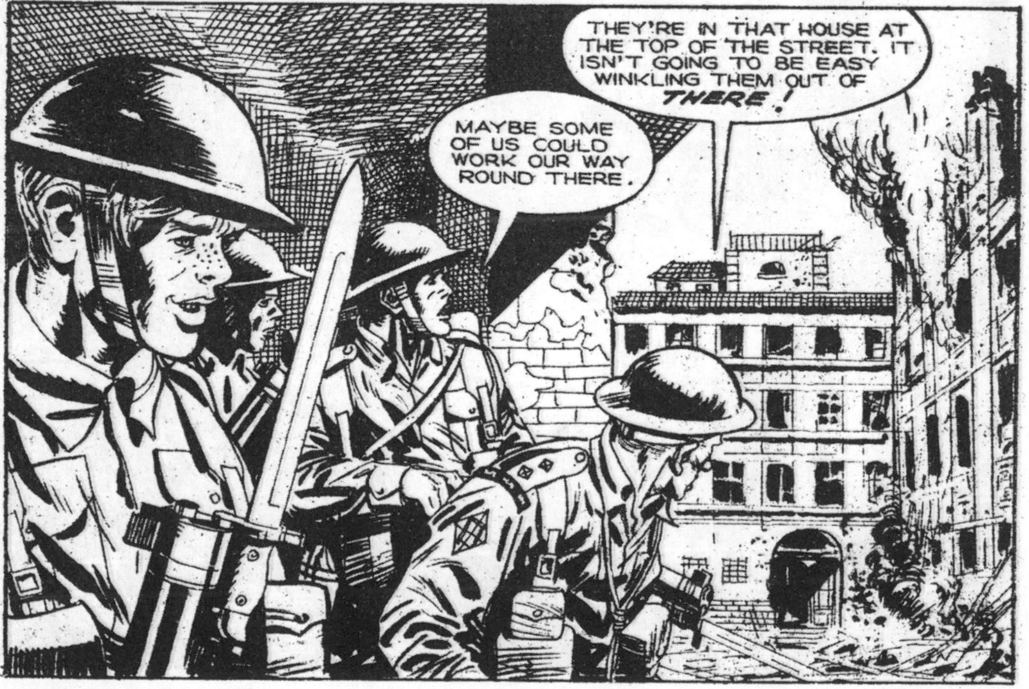
THEY'RE IN THAT HOUSE AT THE TOP OF THE STREET. IT ISN'T GOING TO BE EASY WINKLING THEM OUT OF THERE!
MAYBE SOME OF US COULD WORK OUR WAY ROUND THERE.

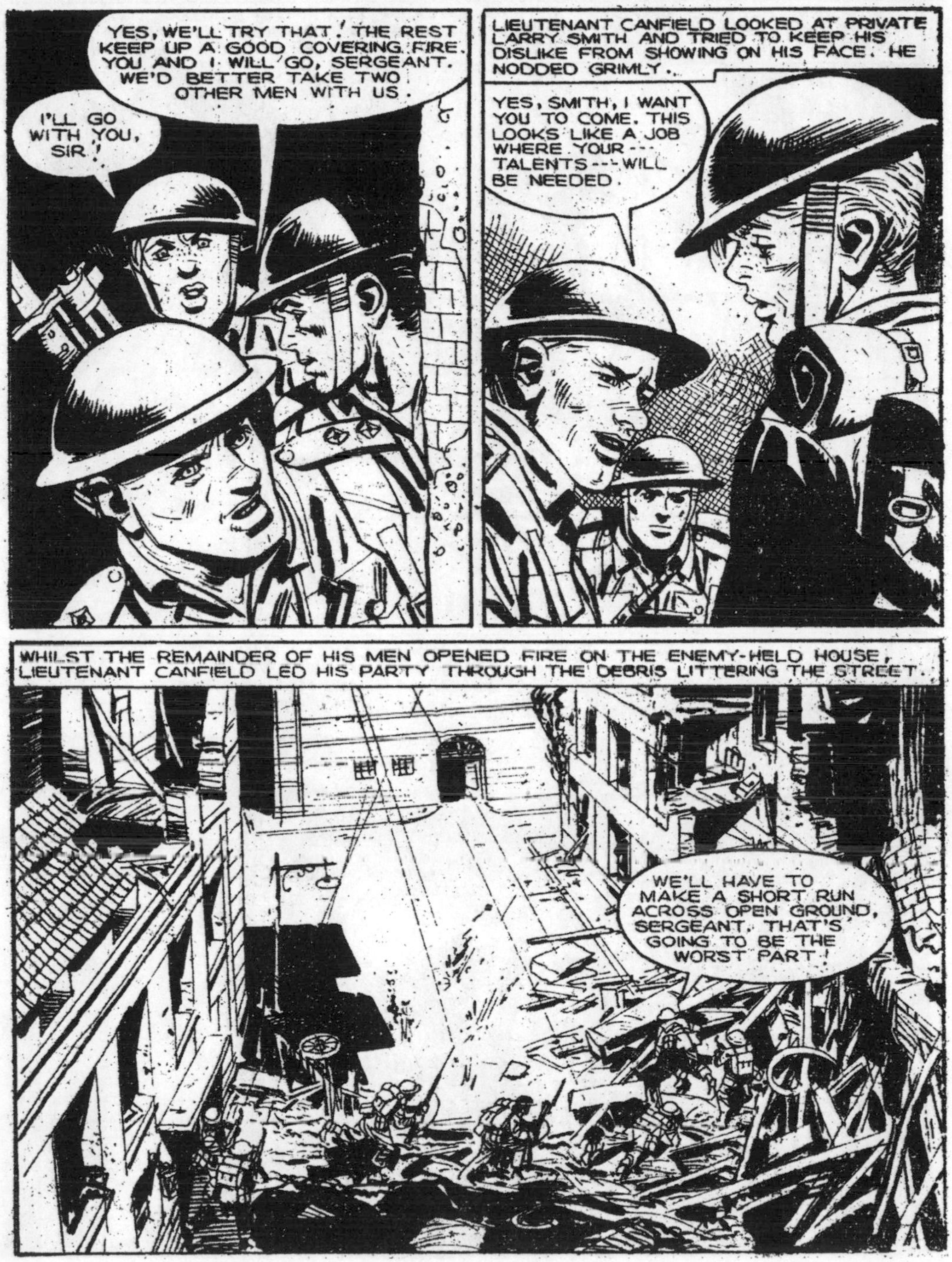
YES, WE'LL TRY THAT! THE REST KEEP UP A GOOD COVERING FIRE. YOU AND I WILL GO, SERGEANT. WE'D BETTER TAKE TWO OTHER MEN WITH US.
I'LL GO WITH YOU, SIR!
LIEUTENANT CANFIELD LOOKED AT PRIVATE LARRY SMITH AND TRIED TO KEEP HIS DISLIKE FROM SHOWING ON HIS FACE. HE NODDED GRIMLY.
YES, SMITH, I WANT YOU TO COME. THIS LOOKS LIKE A JOB WHERE YOUR--- TALENTS---WILL BE NEEDED.
WHILST THE REMAINDER OF HIS MEN OPENED FIRE ON THE ENEMY-HELD HOUSE, LIEUTENANT CANFIELD LED HIS PARTY THROUGH THE DEBRIS LITTERING THE STREET.
WE'LL HAVE TO MAKE A SHORT RUN ACROSS OPEN GROUND, SERGEANT. THAT'S GOING TO BE THE WORST PART!

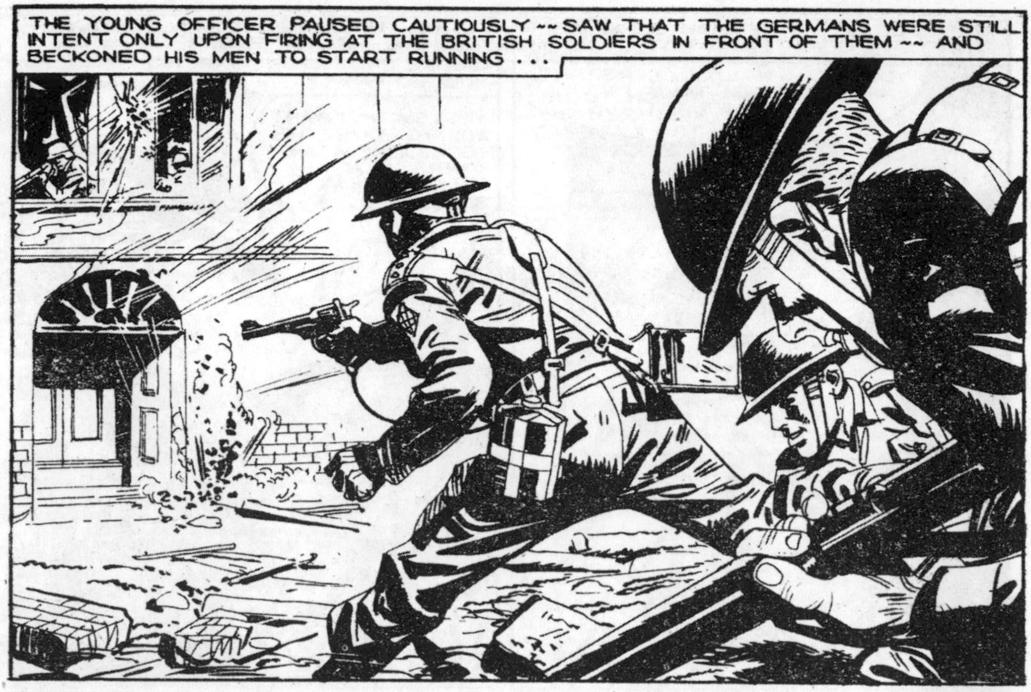
THE YOUNG OFFICER PAUSED CAUTIOUSLY -- SAW THAT THE GERMANS WERE STILL INTENT ONLY UPON FIRING AT THE BRITISH SOLDIERS IN FRONT OF THEM -- AND BECKONED HIS MEN TO START RUNNING ...

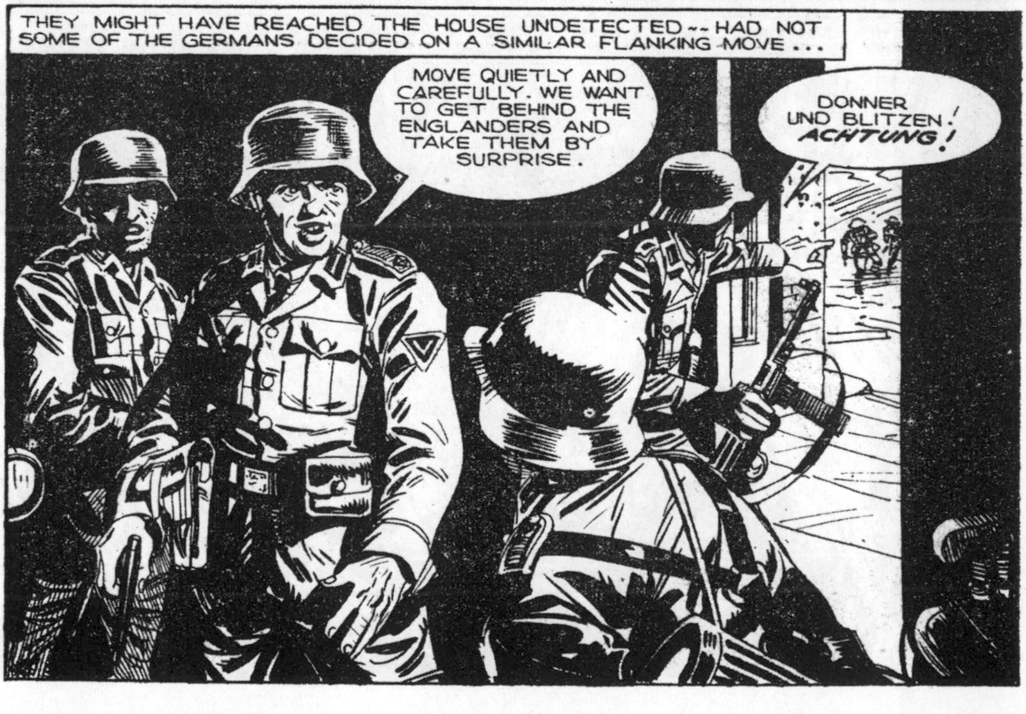
THEY MIGHT HAVE REACHED THE HOUSE UNDETECTED -- HAD NOT SOME OF THE GERMANS DECIDED ON A SIMILAR FLANKING MOVE ...
MOVE QUIETLY AND CAREFULLY. WE WANT TO GET BEHIND THE ENGLANDERS AND TAKE THEM BY SURPRISE.
DONNER UND BLITZEN! ACHTUNG!

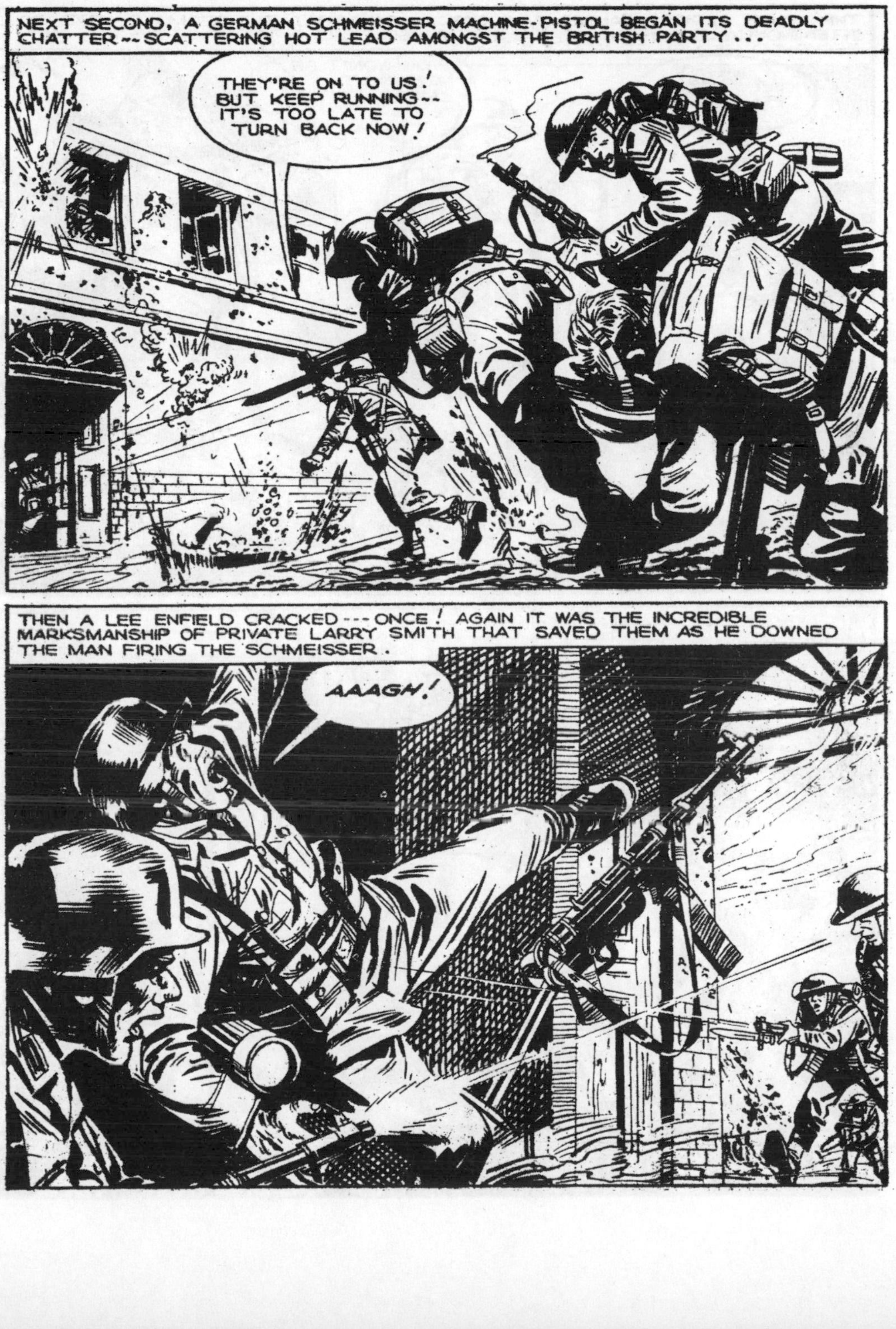
NEXT SECOND, A GERMAN SCHMEISSER MACHINE-PISTOL BEGAN ITS DEADLY CHATTER--SCATTERING HOT LEAD AMONGST THE BRITISH PARTY...
THEY'RE ON TO US! BUT KEEP RUNNING-- IT'S TOO LATE TO TURN BACK NOW!
THEN A LEE ENFIELD CRACKED---ONCE! AGAIN IT WAS THE INCREDIBLE MARKSMANSHIP OF PRIVATE LARRY SMITH THAT SAVED THEM AS HE DOWNED THE MAN FIRING THE SCHMEISSER.
AAAGH!

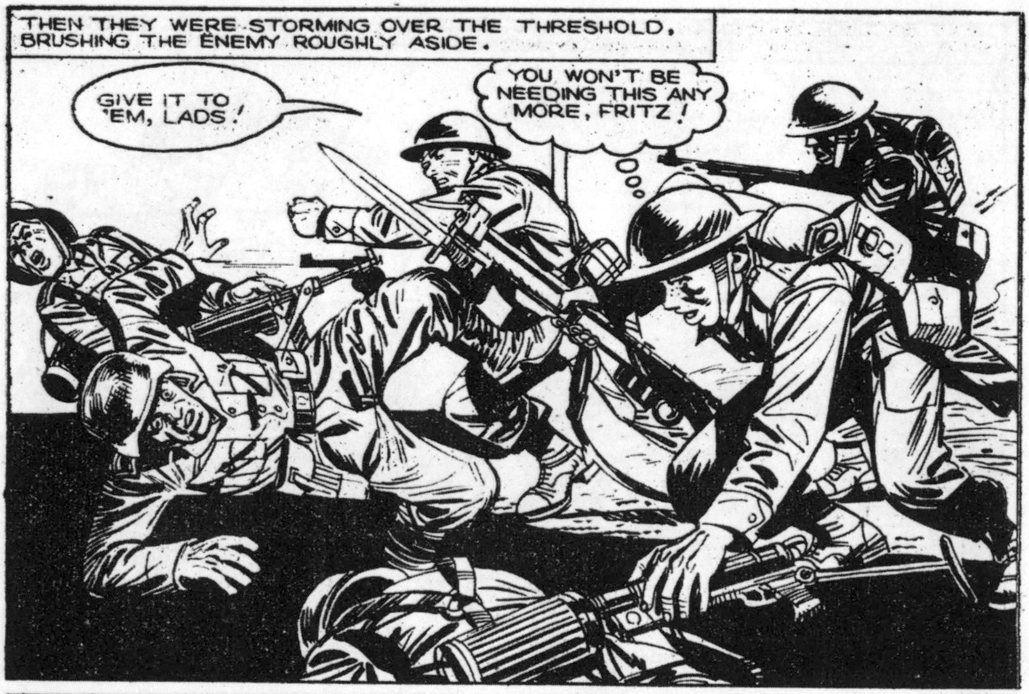
THEN THEY WERE STORMING OVER THE THRESHOLD, BRUSHING THE ENEMY ROUGHLY ASIDE.
GIVE IT TO 'EM, LADS!
YOU WON'T BE NEEDING THIS ANY MORE, FRITZ!

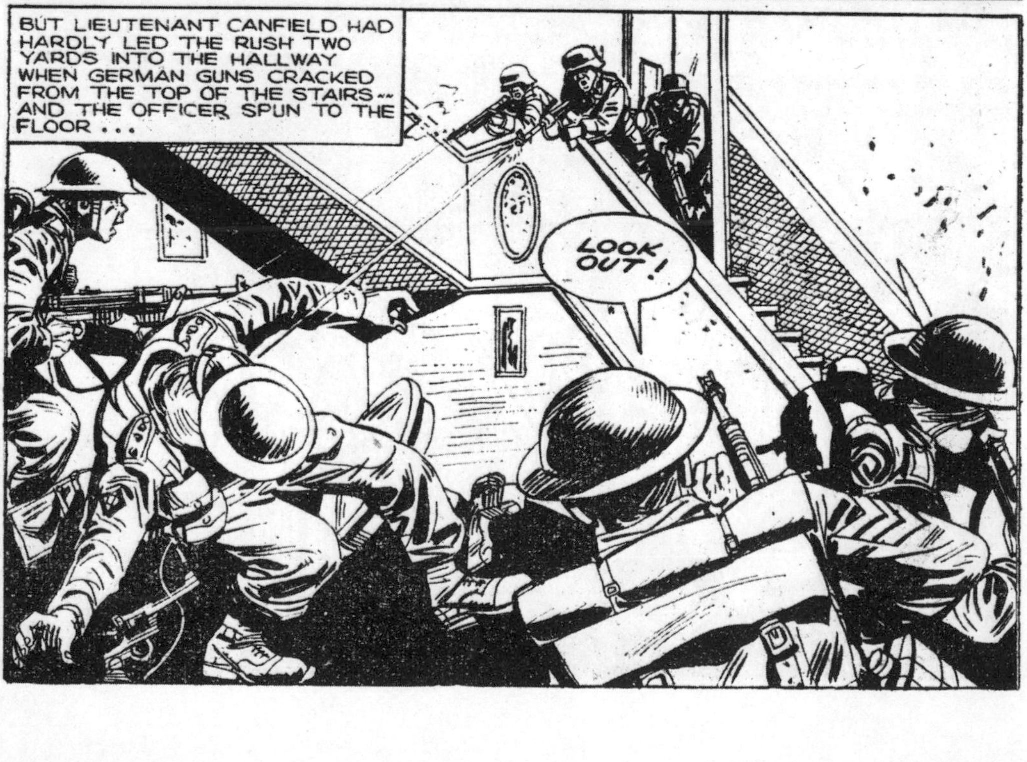
BUT LIEUTENANT CANFIELD HAD HARDLY LED THE RUSH TWO YARDS INTO THE HALLWAY WHEN GERMAN GUNS CRACKED FROM THE TOP OF THE STAIRS -- AND THE OFFICER SPUN TO THE FLOOR ...
LOOK OUT!

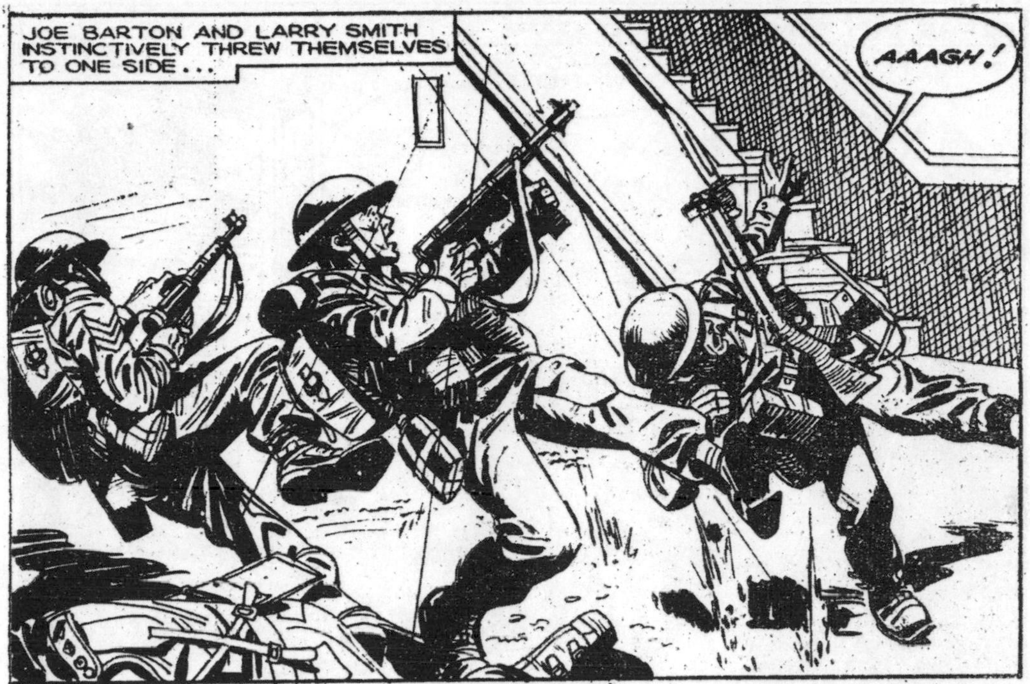
JOE BARTON AND LARRY SMITH INSTINCTIVELY THREW THEMSELVES TO ONE SIDE...
AAAGH!

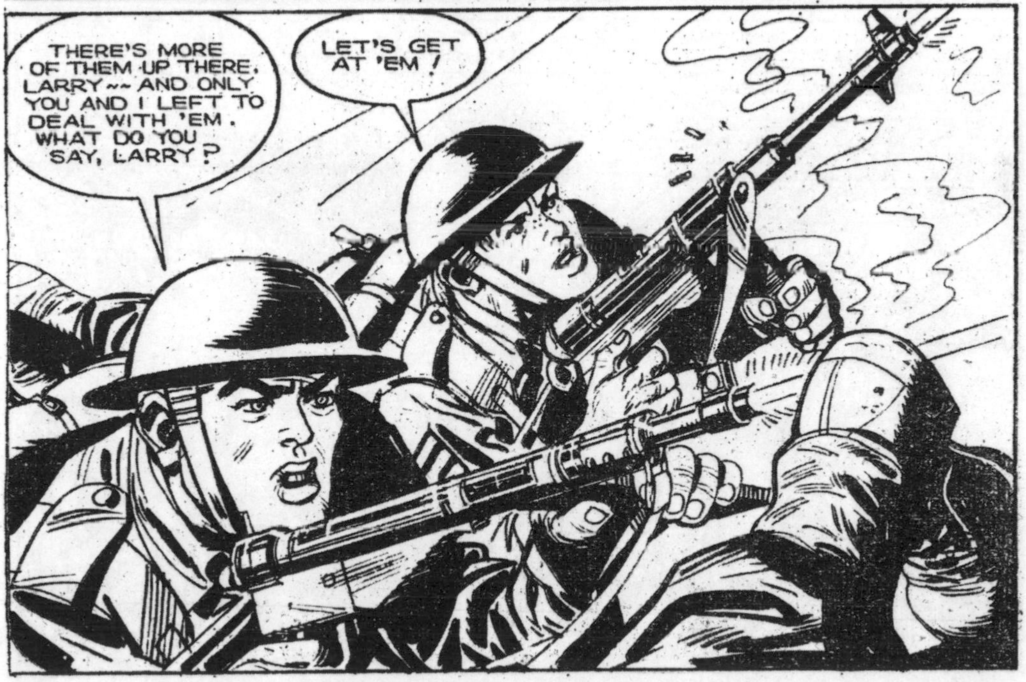
THERE'S MORE OF THEM UP THERE, LARRY~~ AND ONLY YOU AND I LEFT TO DEAL WITH 'EM. WHAT DO YOU SAY, LARRY?
LET'S GET AT 'EM!

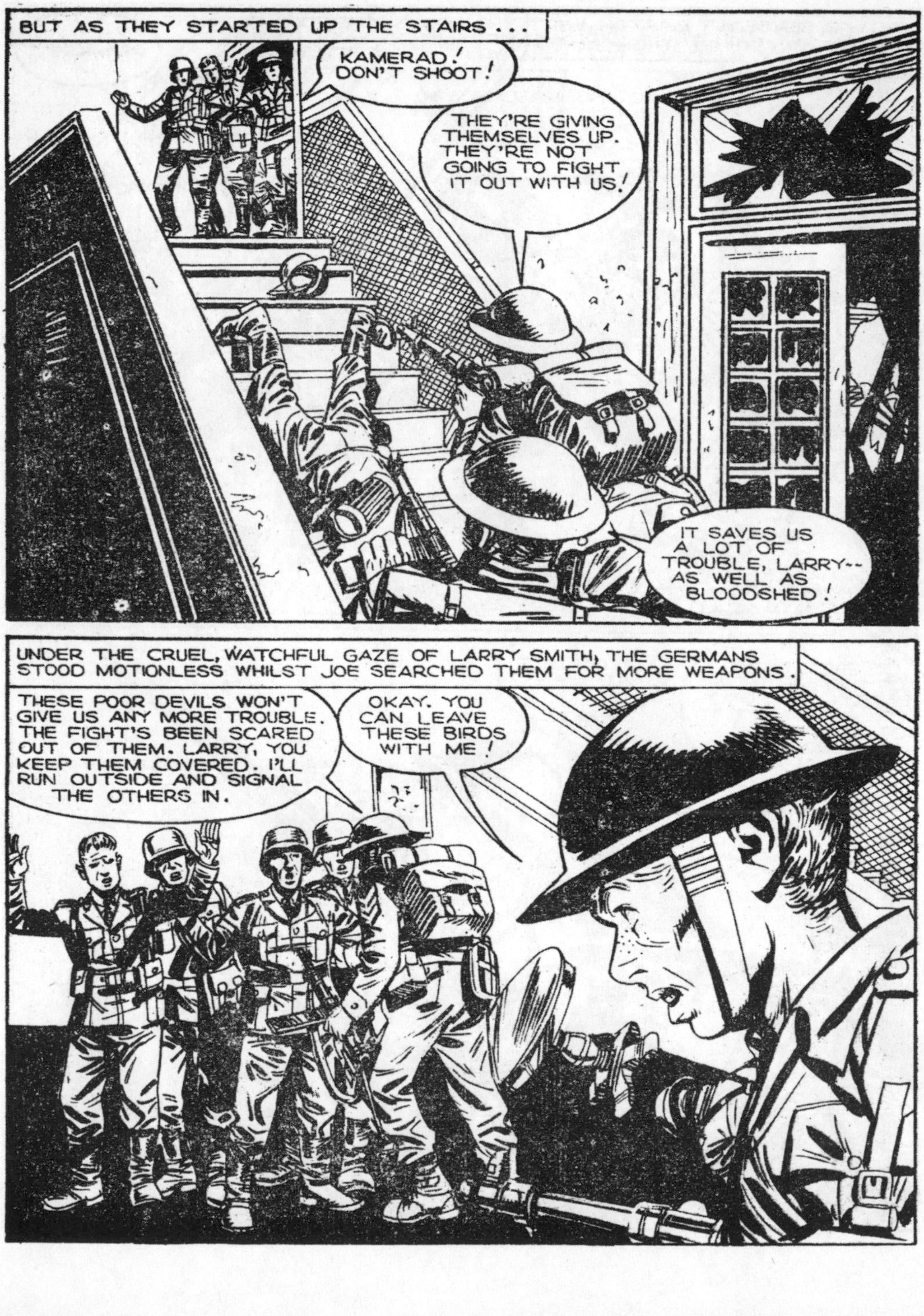
BUT AS THEY STARTED UP THE STAIRS ...
KAMERAD! DON'T SHOOT!
THEY'RE GIVING THEMSELVES UP. THEY'RE NOT GOING TO FIGHT IT OUT WITH US!
IT SAVES US A LOT OF TROUBLE, LARRY-- AS WELL AS BLOODSHED!
UNDER THE CRUEL, WATCHFUL GAZE OF LARRY SMITH, THE GERMANS STOOD MOTIONLESS WHILST JOE SEARCHED THEM FOR MORE WEAPONS.
THESE POOR DEVILS WON'T GIVE US ANY MORE TROUBLE. THE FIGHT'S BEEN SCARED OUT OF THEM. LARRY, YOU KEEP THEM COVERED. I'LL RUN OUTSIDE AND SIGNAL THE OTHERS IN.
OKAY. YOU CAN LEAVE THESE BIRDS WITH ME!

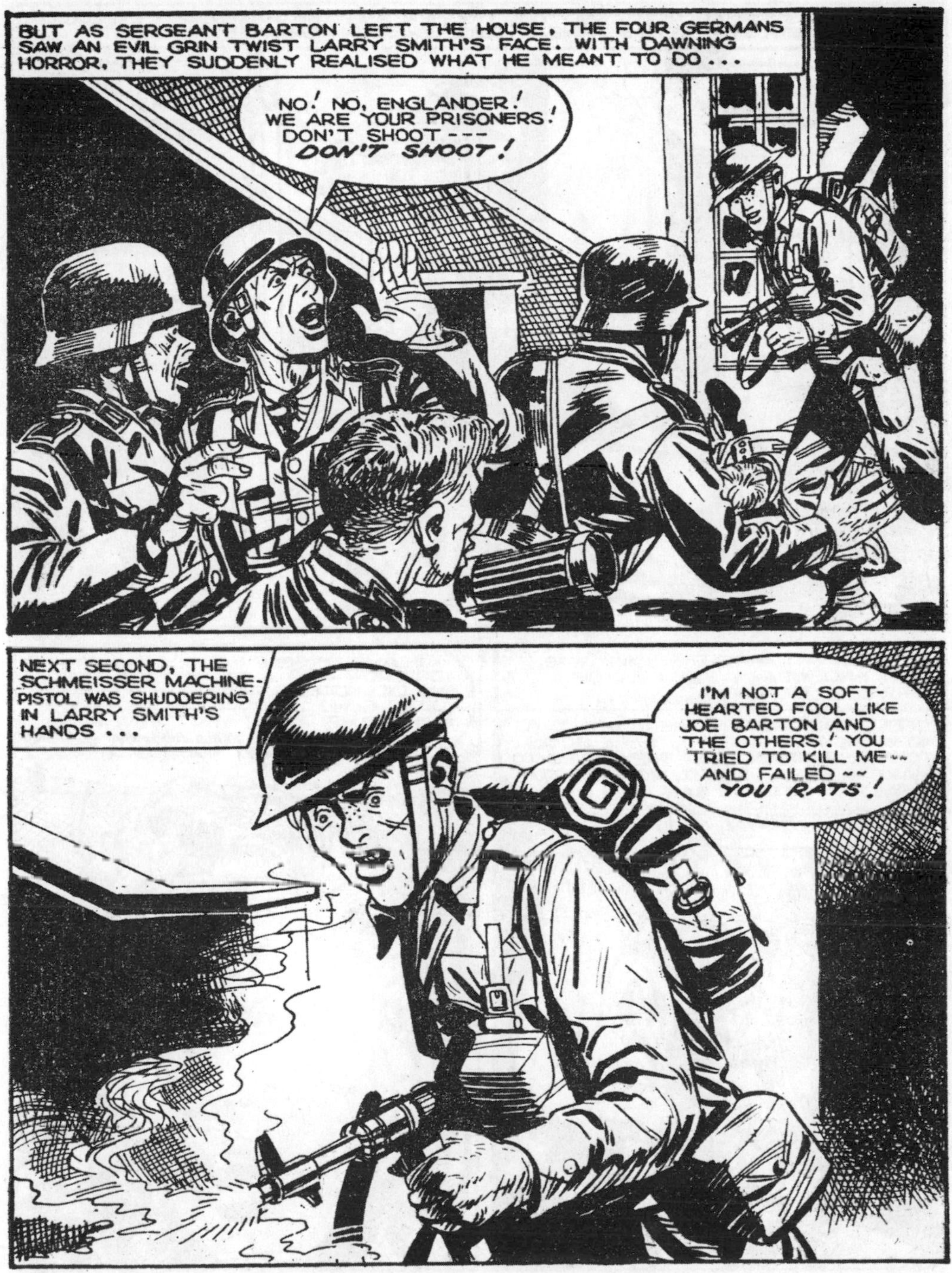
BUT AS SERGEANT BARTON LEFT THE HOUSE, THE FOUR GERMANS SAW AN EVIL GRIN TWIST LARRY SMITH'S FACE. WITH DAWNING HORROR, THEY SUDDENLY REALISED WHAT HE MEANT TO DO...
NO! NO, ENGLANDER! WE ARE YOUR PRISONERS! DON'T SHOOT --- DON'T SHOOT!
NEXT SECOND, THE SCHMEISSER MACHINE-PISTOL WAS SHUDDERING IN LARRY SMITH'S HANDS...
I'M NOT A SOFT-HEARTED FOOL LIKE JOE BARTON AND THE OTHERS! YOU TRIED TO KILL ME -- AND FAILED -- YOU RATS!

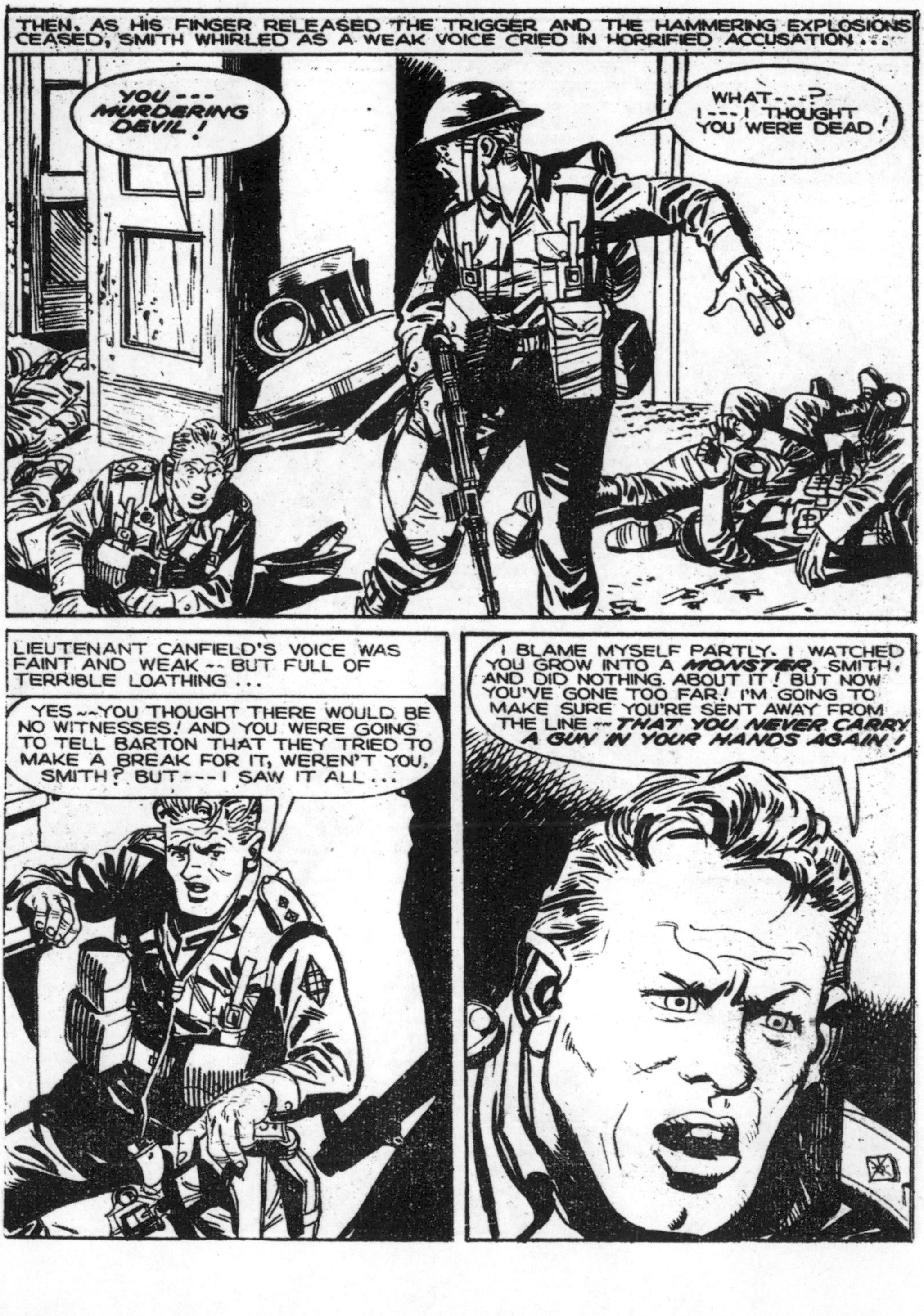
THEN, AS HIS FINGER RELEASED THE TRIGGER AND THE HAMMERING EXPLOSIONS CEASED, SMITH WHIRLED AS A WEAK VOICE CRIED IN HORRIFIED ACCUSATION . . .
YOU --- MURDERING DEVIL!
WHAT---? I---I THOUGHT YOU WERE DEAD!
LIEUTENANT CANFIELD'S VOICE WAS FAINT AND WEAK -- BUT FULL OF TERRIBLE LOATHING . . .
YES -- YOU THOUGHT THERE WOULD BE NO WITNESSES! AND YOU WERE GOING TO TELL BARTON THAT THEY TRIED TO MAKE A BREAK FOR IT, WEREN'T YOU, SMITH? BUT---I SAW IT ALL . . .
I BLAME MYSELF PARTLY. I WATCHED YOU GROW INTO A MONSTER, SMITH, AND DID NOTHING ABOUT IT! BUT NOW YOU'VE GONE TOO FAR! I'M GOING TO MAKE SURE YOU'RE SENT AWAY FROM THE LINE -- THAT YOU NEVER CARRY A GUN IN YOUR HANDS AGAIN!

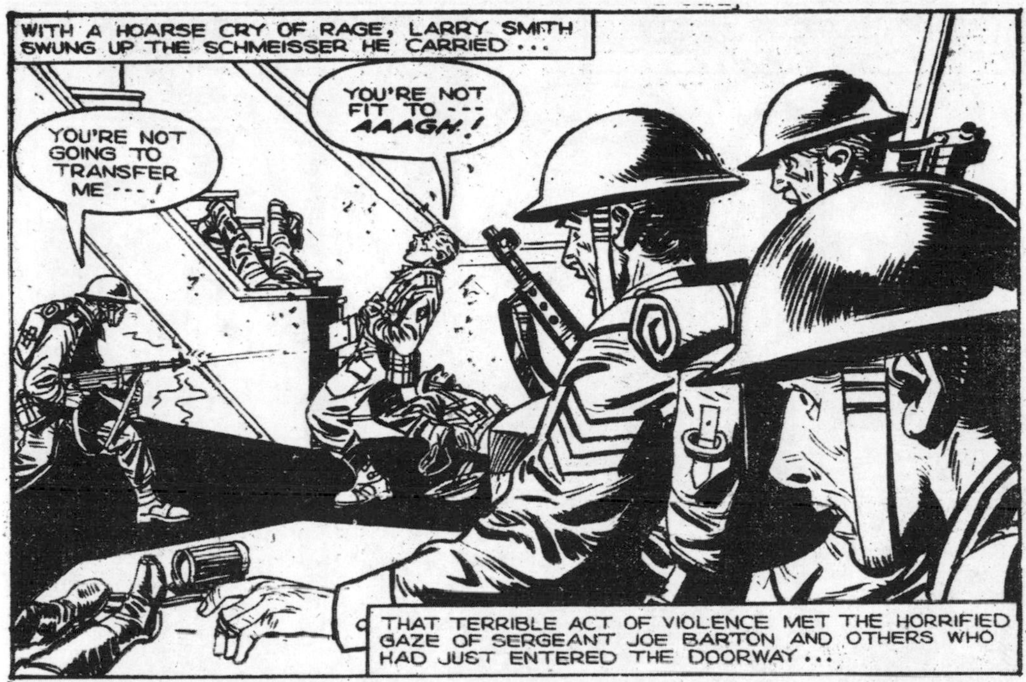
WITH A HOARSE CRY OF RAGE, LARRY SMITH SWUNG UP THE SCHMEISSER HE CARRIED ...
YOU'RE NOT GOING TO TRANSFER ME ---!
YOU'RE NOT FIT TO --- AAAGH!
THAT TERRIBLE ACT OF VIOLENCE MET THE HORRIFIED GAZE OF SERGEANT JOE BARTON AND OTHERS WHO HAD JUST ENTERED THE DOORWAY ...

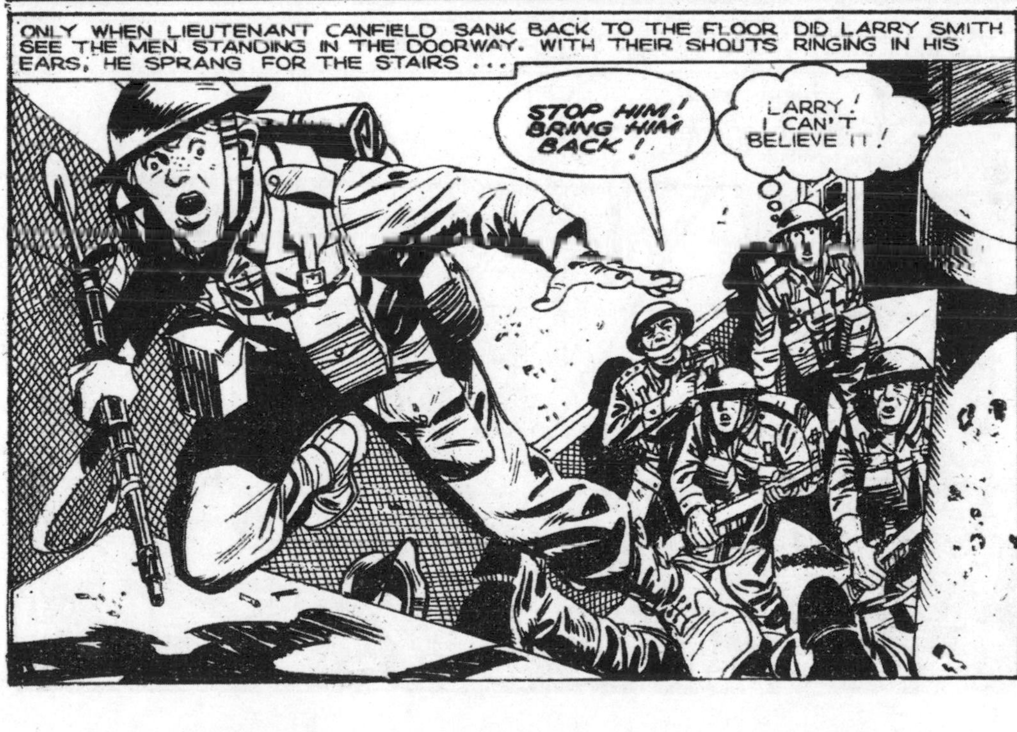
ONLY WHEN LIEUTENANT CANFIELD SANK BACK TO THE FLOOR DID LARRY SMITH SEE THE MEN STANDING IN THE DOORWAY. WITH THEIR SHOUTS RINGING IN HIS EARS, HE SPRANG FOR THE STAIRS ...
STOP HIM! BRING HIM BACK!
LARRY! I CAN'T BELIEVE IT!

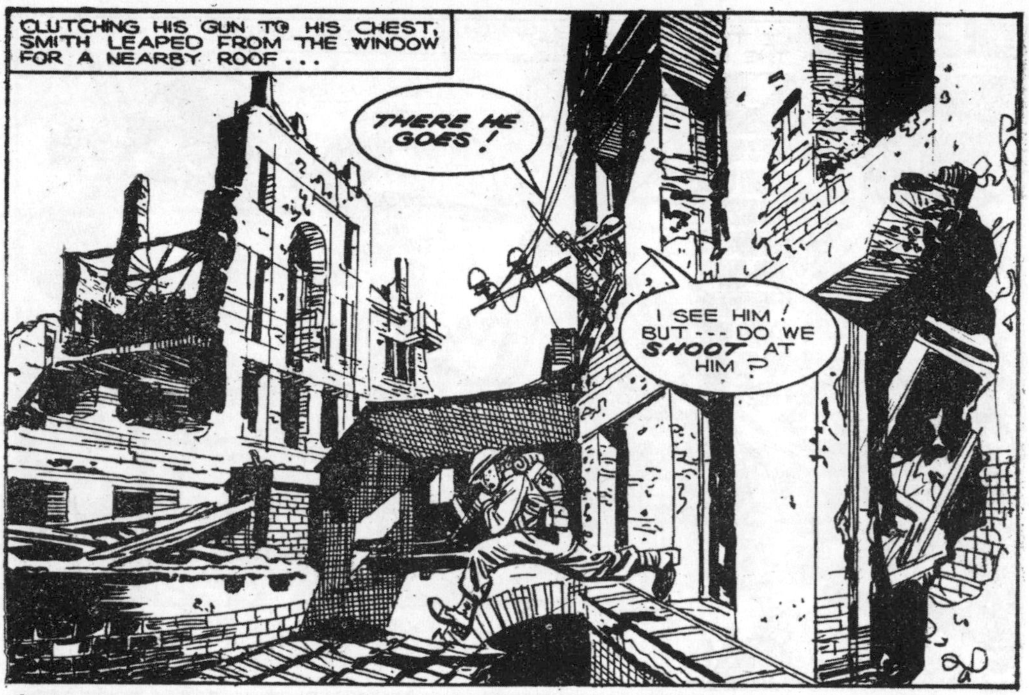
CLUTCHING HIS GUN TO HIS CHEST, SMITH LEAPED FROM THE WINDOW FOR A NEARBY ROOF . . .
THERE HE GOES !
I SEE HIM ! BUT - - - DO WE SHOOT AT HIM ?

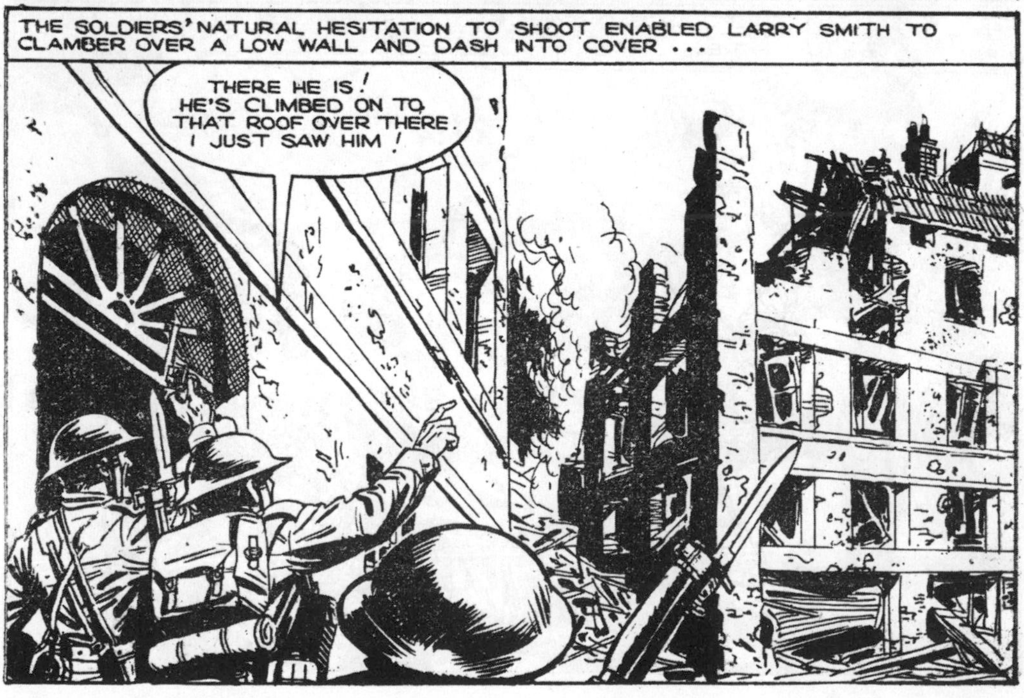
THE SOLDIERS' NATURAL HESITATION TO SHOOT ENABLED LARRY SMITH TO CLAMBER OVER A LOW WALL AND DASH INTO COVER . . .
THERE HE IS ! HE'S CLIMBED ON TO THAT ROOF OVER THERE. I JUST SAW HIM !

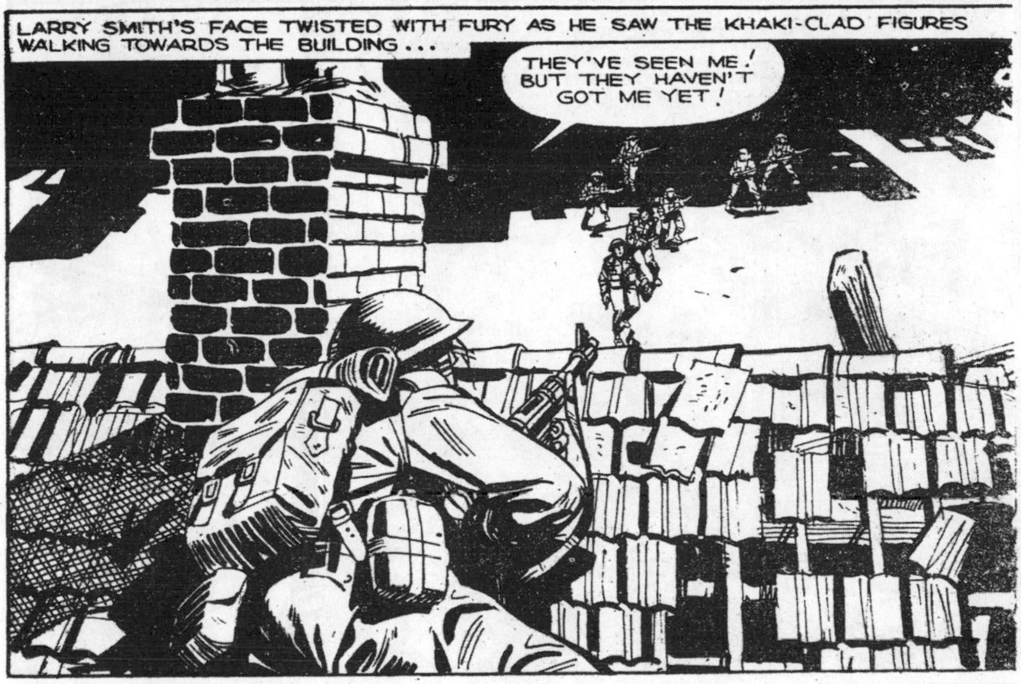
LARRY SMITH'S FACE TWISTED WITH FURY AS HE SAW THE KHAKI-CLAD FIGURES WALKING TOWARDS THE BUILDING...
THEY'VE SEEN ME! BUT THEY HAVEN'T GOT ME YET!

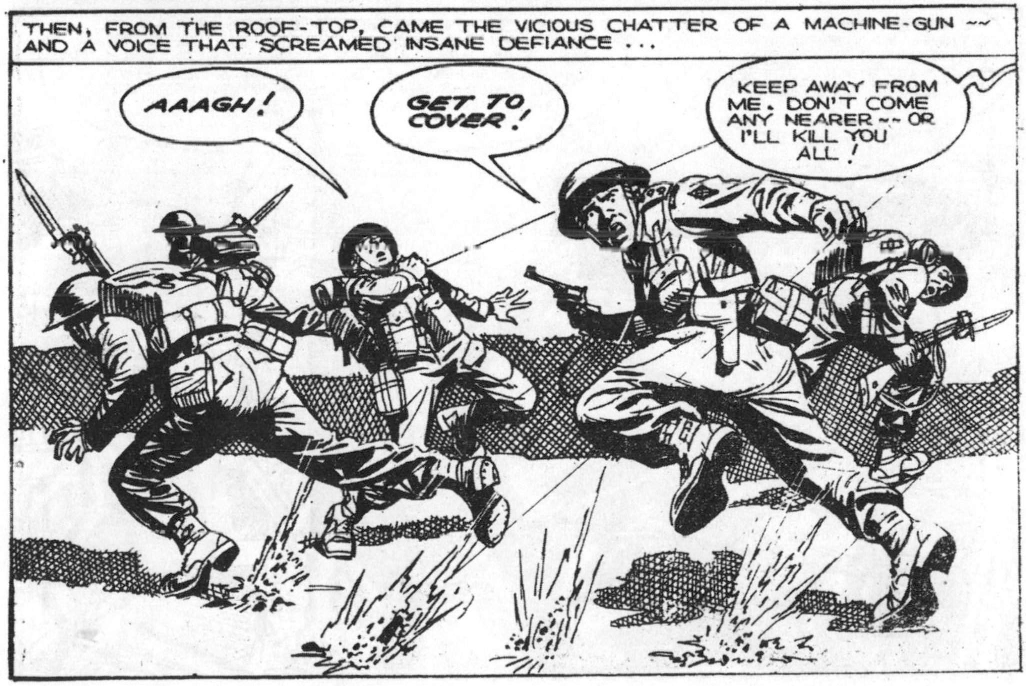
THEN, FROM THE ROOF-TOP, CAME THE VICIOUS CHATTER OF A MACHINE-GUN -- AND A VOICE THAT SCREAMED INSANE DEFIANCE...
AAAGH!
GET TO COVER!
KEEP AWAY FROM ME. DON'T COME ANY NEARER -- OR I'LL KILL YOU ALL!

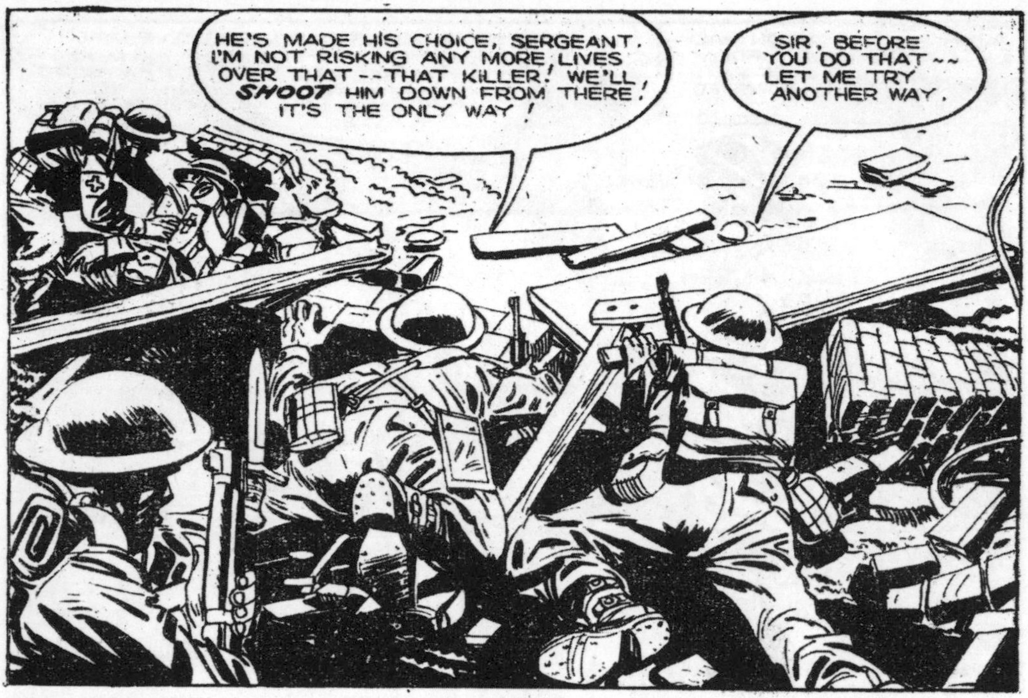
HE'S MADE HIS CHOICE, SERGEANT. I'M NOT RISKING ANY MORE LIVES OVER THAT--THAT KILLER! WE'LL SHOOT HIM DOWN FROM THERE! IT'S THE ONLY WAY!
SIR, BEFORE YOU DO THAT-- LET ME TRY ANOTHER WAY.

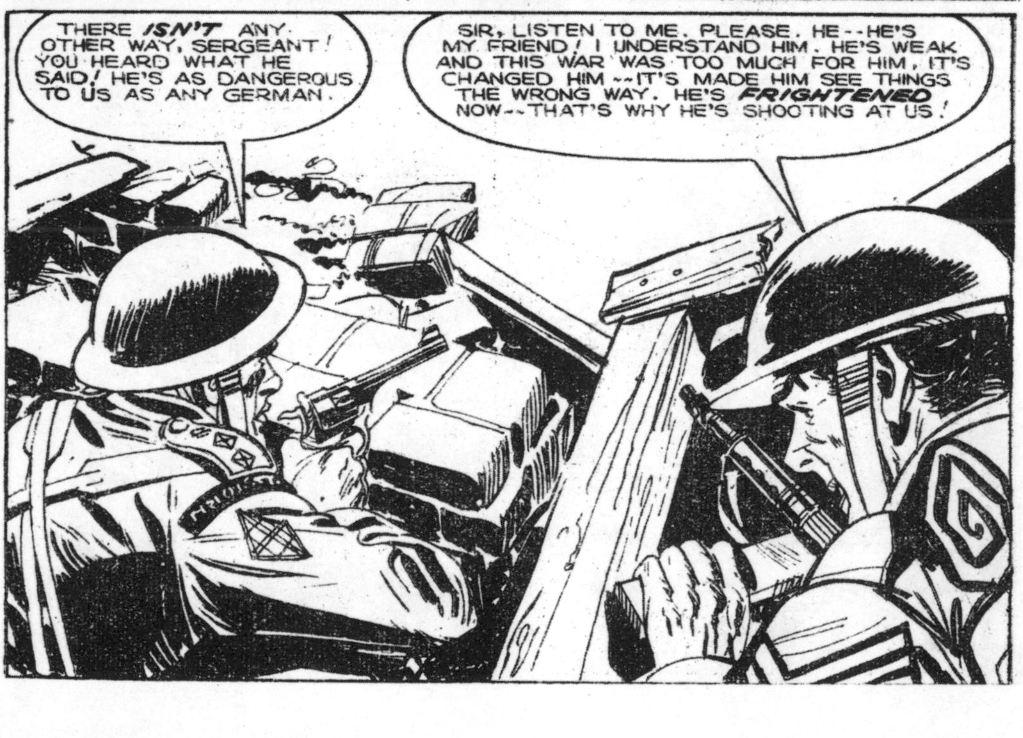
THERE ISN'T ANY OTHER WAY, SERGEANT! YOU HEARD WHAT HE SAID! HE'S AS DANGEROUS TO US AS ANY GERMAN.
SIR, LISTEN TO ME. PLEASE. HE--HE'S MY FRIEND! I UNDERSTAND HIM. HE'S WEAK AND THIS WAR WAS TOO MUCH FOR HIM. IT'S CHANGED HIM--IT'S MADE HIM SEE THINGS THE WRONG WAY. HE'S FRIGHTENED NOW--THAT'S WHY HE'S SHOOTING AT US!

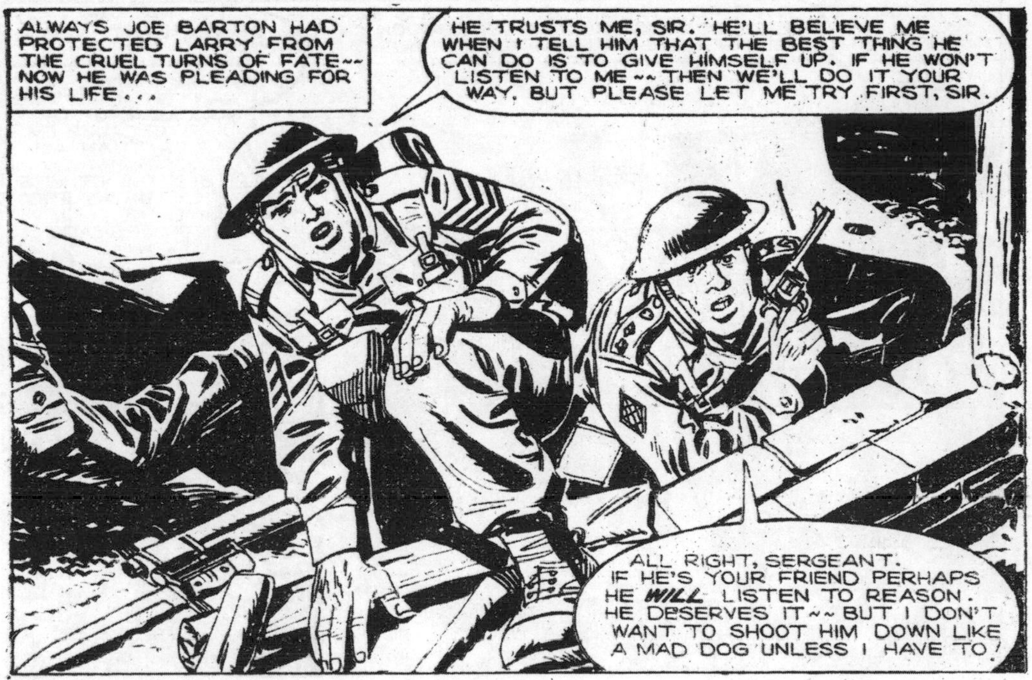
ALWAYS JOE BARTON HAD PROTECTED LARRY FROM THE CRUEL TURNS OF FATE~~ NOW HE WAS PLEADING FOR HIS LIFE...
HE TRUSTS ME, SIR. HE'LL BELIEVE ME WHEN I TELL HIM THAT THE BEST THING HE CAN DO IS TO GIVE HIMSELF UP. IF HE WON'T LISTEN TO ME~~THEN WE'LL DO IT YOUR WAY. BUT PLEASE LET ME TRY FIRST, SIR.
ALL RIGHT, SERGEANT. IF HE'S YOUR FRIEND PERHAPS HE WILL LISTEN TO REASON. HE DESERVES IT~~BUT I DON'T WANT TO SHOOT HIM DOWN LIKE A MAD DOG UNLESS I HAVE TO!

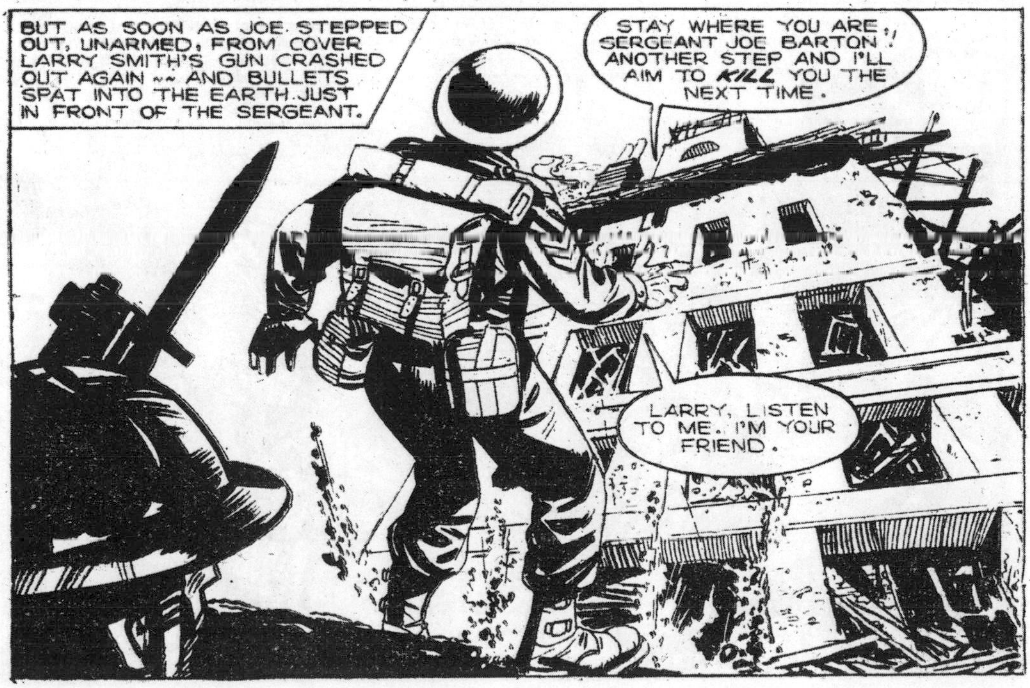
BUT AS SOON AS JOE STEPPED OUT, UNARMED, FROM COVER LARRY SMITH'S GUN CRASHED OUT AGAIN~~AND BULLETS SPAT INTO THE EARTH JUST IN FRONT OF THE SERGEANT.
STAY WHERE YOU ARE, SERGEANT JOE BARTON! ANOTHER STEP AND I'LL AIM TO KILL YOU THE NEXT TIME.
LARRY, LISTEN TO ME. I'M YOUR FRIEND.

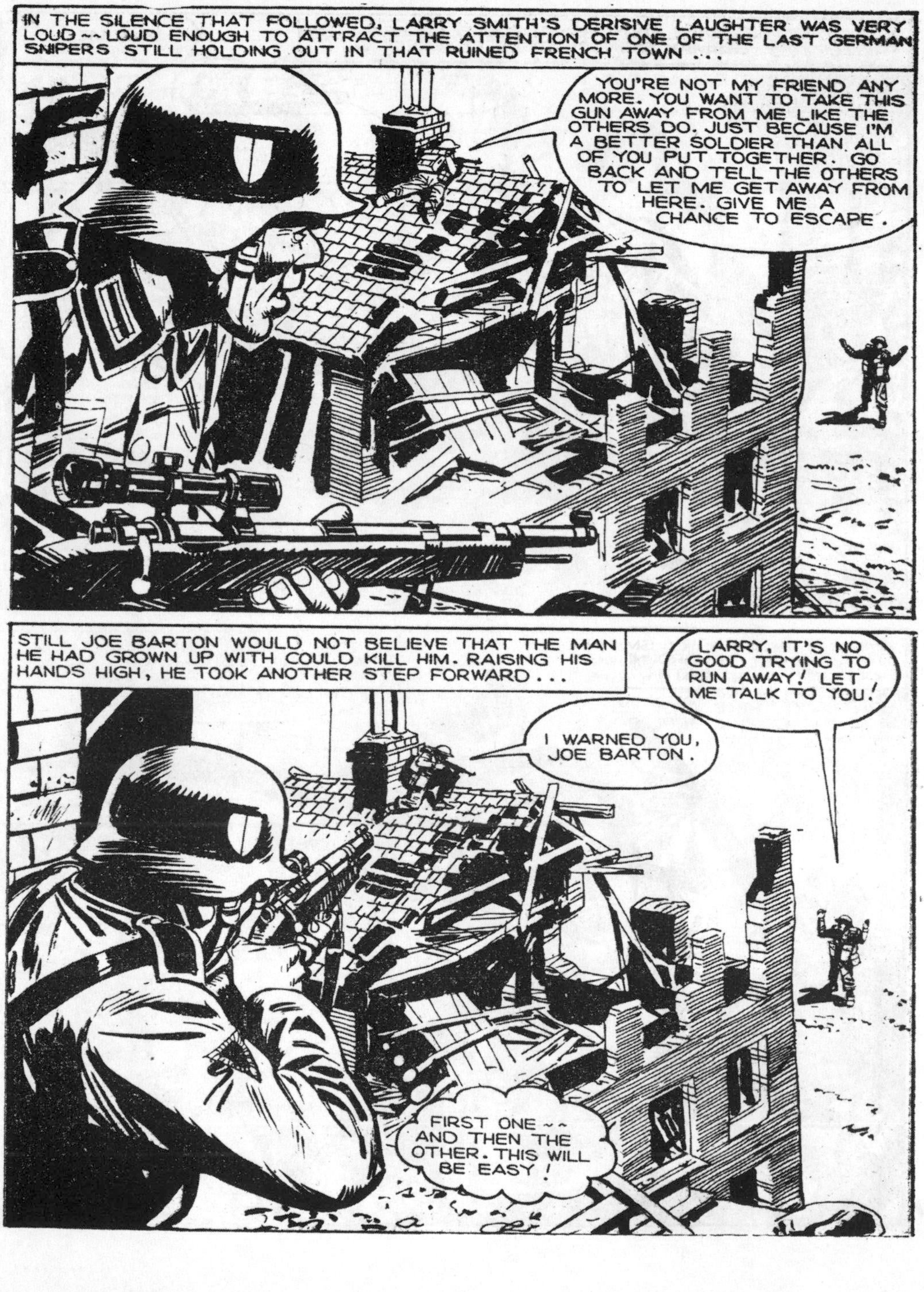
IN THE SILENCE THAT FOLLOWED, LARRY SMITH'S DERISIVE LAUGHTER WAS VERY LOUD -- LOUD ENOUGH TO ATTRACT THE ATTENTION OF ONE OF THE LAST GERMAN SNIPERS STILL HOLDING OUT IN THAT RUINED FRENCH TOWN ...
YOU'RE NOT MY FRIEND ANY MORE. YOU WANT TO TAKE THIS GUN AWAY FROM ME LIKE THE OTHERS DO. JUST BECAUSE I'M A BETTER SOLDIER THAN ALL OF YOU PUT TOGETHER. GO BACK AND TELL THE OTHERS TO LET ME GET AWAY FROM HERE. GIVE ME A CHANCE TO ESCAPE.
STILL JOE BARTON WOULD NOT BELIEVE THAT THE MAN HE HAD GROWN UP WITH COULD KILL HIM. RAISING HIS HANDS HIGH, HE TOOK ANOTHER STEP FORWARD ...
LARRY, IT'S NO GOOD TRYING TO RUN AWAY! LET ME TALK TO YOU!
I WARNED YOU, JOE BARTON.
FIRST ONE -- AND THEN THE OTHER. THIS WILL BE EASY!

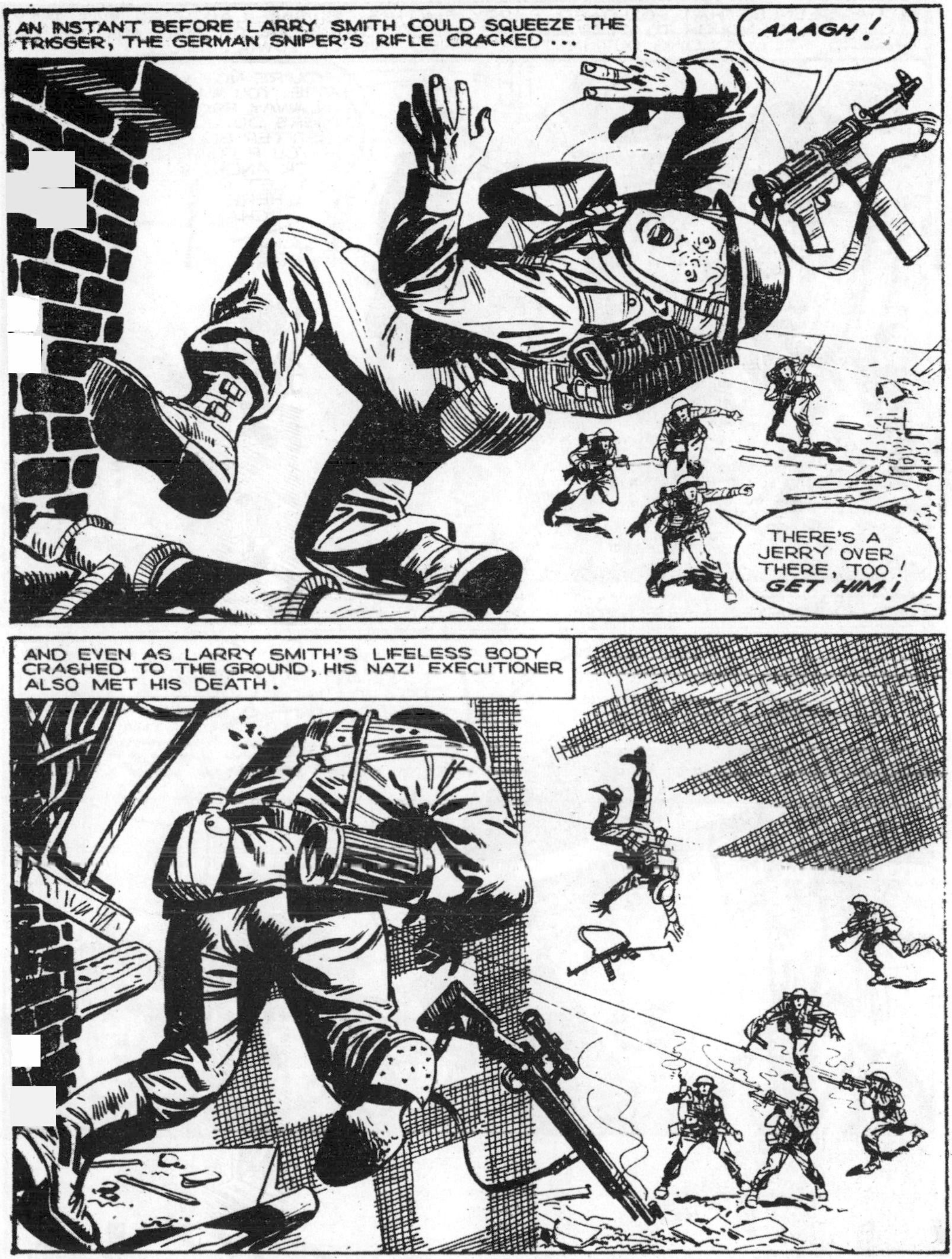
AN INSTANT BEFORE LARRY SMITH COULD SQUEEZE THE TRIGGER, THE GERMAN SNIPER'S RIFLE CRACKED ...
AAAGH!
THERE'S A JERRY OVER THERE, TOO! GET HIM!
AND EVEN AS LARRY SMITH'S LIFELESS BODY CRASHED TO THE GROUND, HIS NAZI EXECUTIONER ALSO MET HIS DEATH.

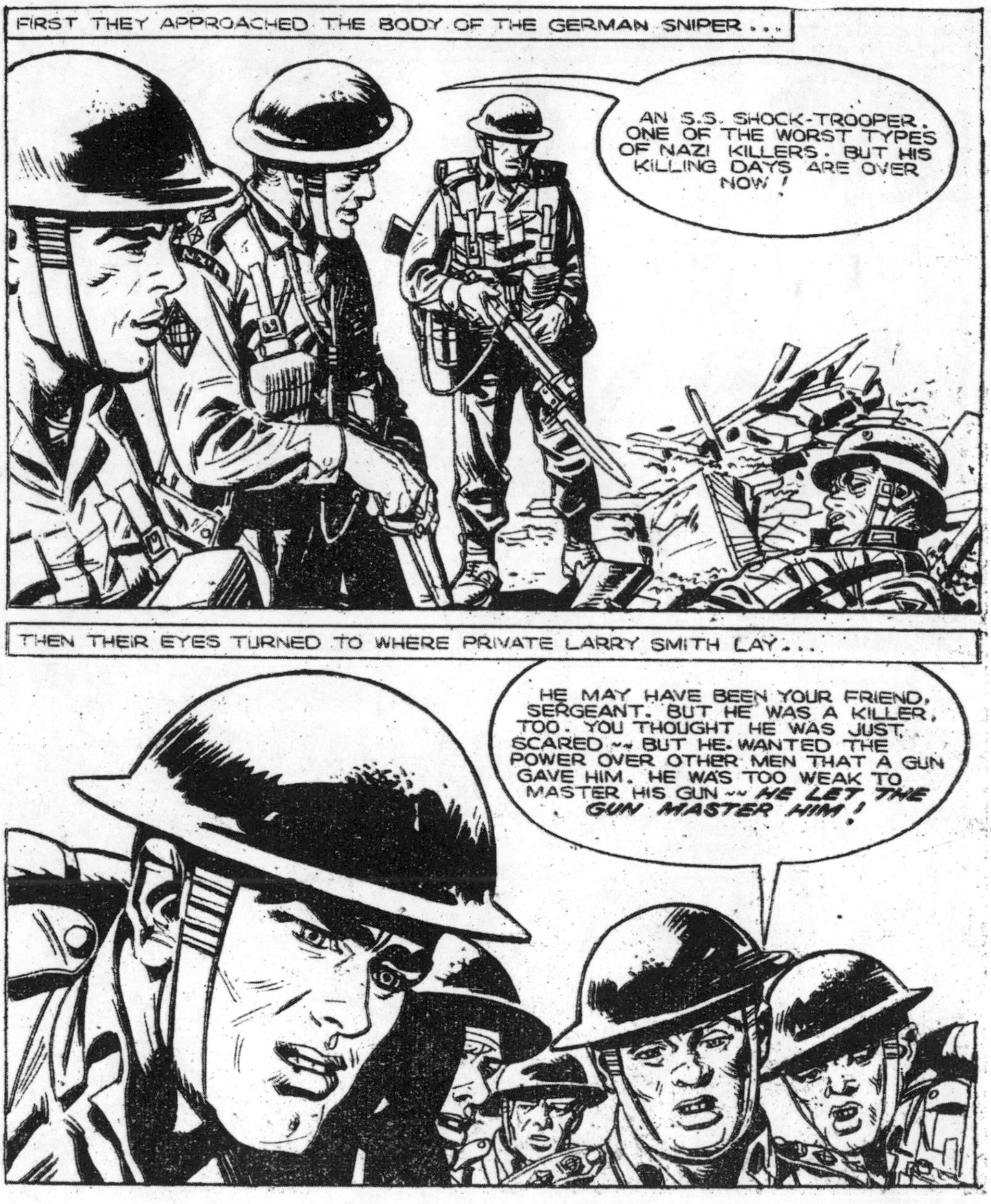
FIRST THEY APPROACHED THE BODY OF THE GERMAN SNIPER ...
AN S.S. SHOCK-TROOPER. ONE OF THE WORST TYPES OF NAZI KILLERS. BUT HIS KILLING DAYS ARE OVER NOW!
THEN THEIR EYES TURNED TO WHERE PRIVATE LARRY SMITH LAY ...
HE MAY HAVE BEEN YOUR FRIEND, SERGEANT. BUT HE WAS A KILLER, TOO. YOU THOUGHT HE WAS JUST SCARED -- BUT HE WANTED THE POWER OVER OTHER MEN THAT A GUN GAVE HIM. HE WAS TOO WEAK TO MASTER HIS GUN -- HE LET THE GUN MASTER HIM!

The TROUBLE-SHOOTERS

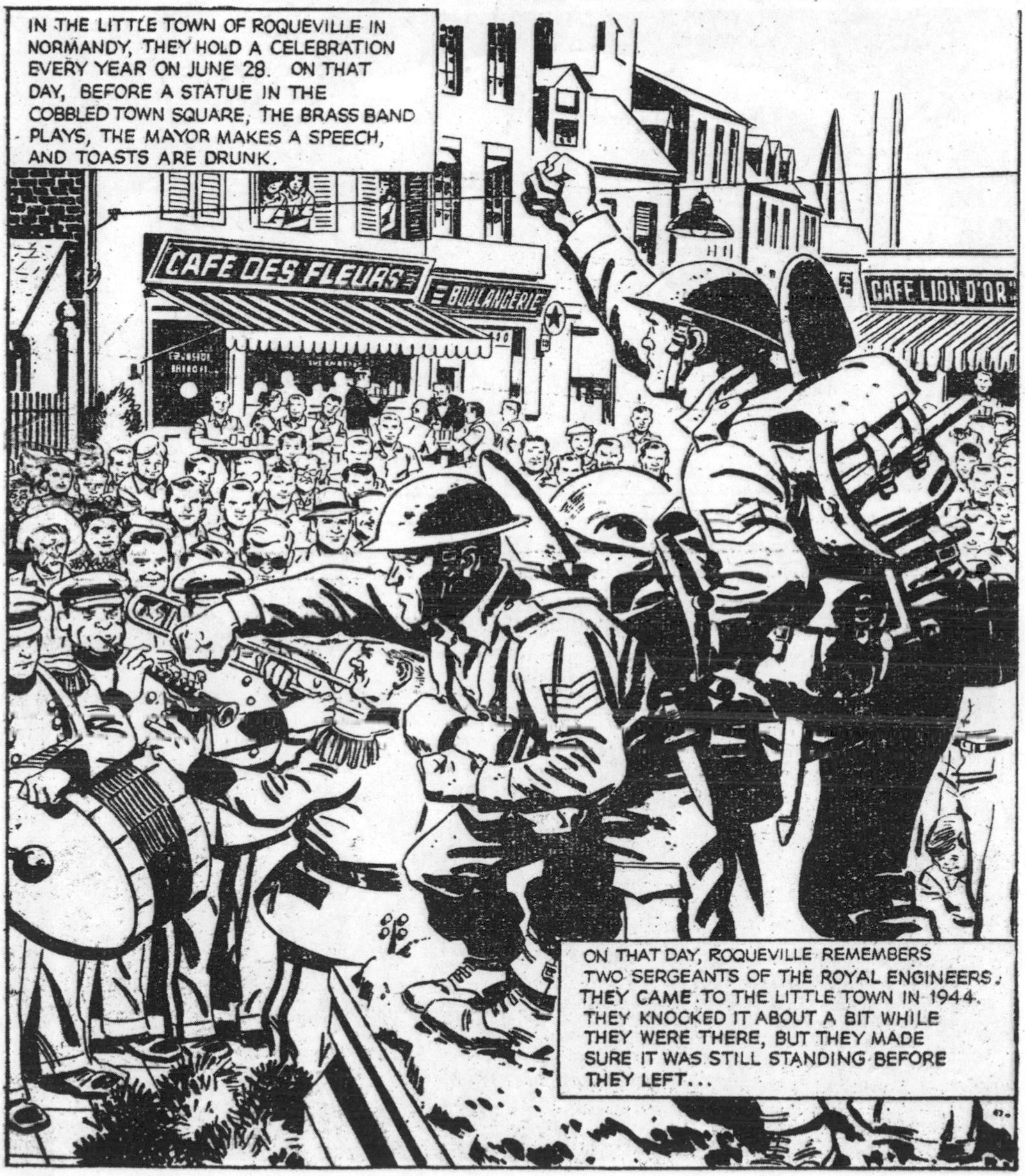
IN THE LITTLE TOWN OF ROQUEVILLE IN NORMANDY, THEY HOLD A CELEBRATION EVERY YEAR ON JUNE 28. ON THAT DAY, BEFORE A STATUE IN THE COBBLED TOWN SQUARE, THE BRASS BAND PLAYS, THE MAYOR MAKES A SPEECH, AND TOASTS ARE DRUNK.
CAFE DES FLEURS
BOULANGERIE
CAFE LION D'OR
ON THAT DAY, ROQUEVILLE REMEMBERS TWO SERGEANTS OF THE ROYAL ENGINEERS. THEY CAME TO THE LITTLE TOWN IN 1944. THEY KNOCKED IT ABOUT A BIT WHILE THEY WERE THERE, BUT THEY MADE SURE IT WAS STILL STANDING BEFORE THEY LEFT...

Chapter 1. The Lost Stripes

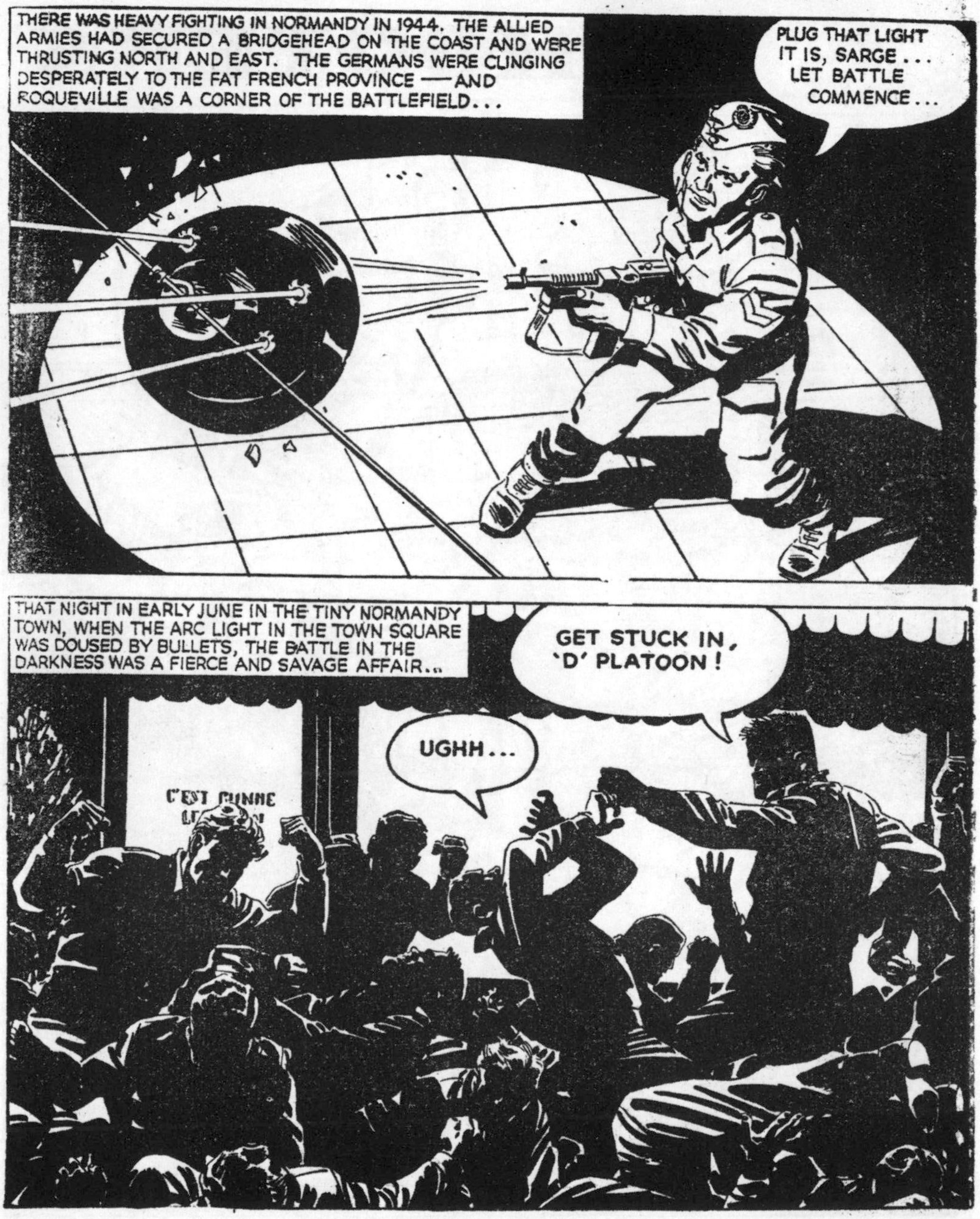
THERE WAS HEAVY FIGHTING IN NORMANDY IN 1944. THE ALLIED ARMIES HAD SECURED A BRIDGEHEAD ON THE COAST AND WERE THRUSTING NORTH AND EAST. THE GERMANS WERE CLINGING DESPERATELY TO THE FAT FRENCH PROVINCE — AND ROQUEVILLE WAS A CORNER OF THE BATTLEFIELD...
PLUG THAT LIGHT IT IS, SARGE... LET BATTLE COMMENCE...
THAT NIGHT IN EARLY JUNE IN THE TINY NORMANDY TOWN, WHEN THE ARC LIGHT IN THE TOWN SQUARE WAS DOUSED BY BULLETS, THE BATTLE IN THE DARKNESS WAS A FIERCE AND SAVAGE AFFAIR...
GET STUCK IN, 'D' PLATOON!
UGHH...

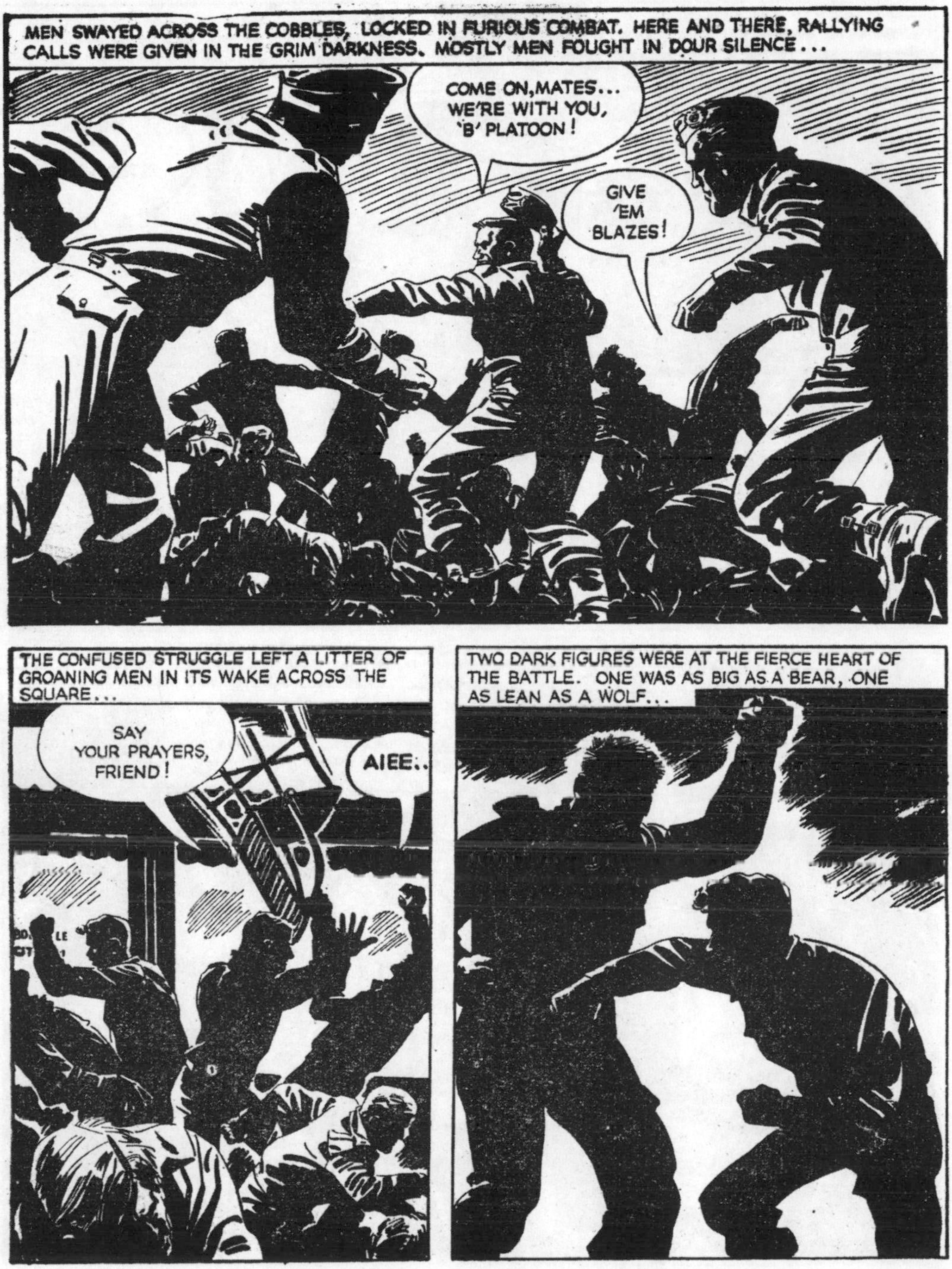
MEN SWAYED ACROSS THE COBBLES, LOCKED IN FURIOUS COMBAT. HERE AND THERE, RALLYING CALLS WERE GIVEN IN THE GRIM DARKNESS. MOSTLY MEN FOUGHT IN DOUR SILENCE...
COME ON, MATES... WE'RE WITH YOU, 'B' PLATOON!
GIVE 'EM BLAZES!
THE CONFUSED STRUGGLE LEFT A LITTER OF GROANING MEN IN ITS WAKE ACROSS THE SQUARE...
SAY YOUR PRAYERS, FRIEND!
AIEE...
TWO DARK FIGURES WERE AT THE FIERCE HEART OF THE BATTLE. ONE WAS AS BIG AS A BEAR, ONE AS LEAN AS A WOLF...

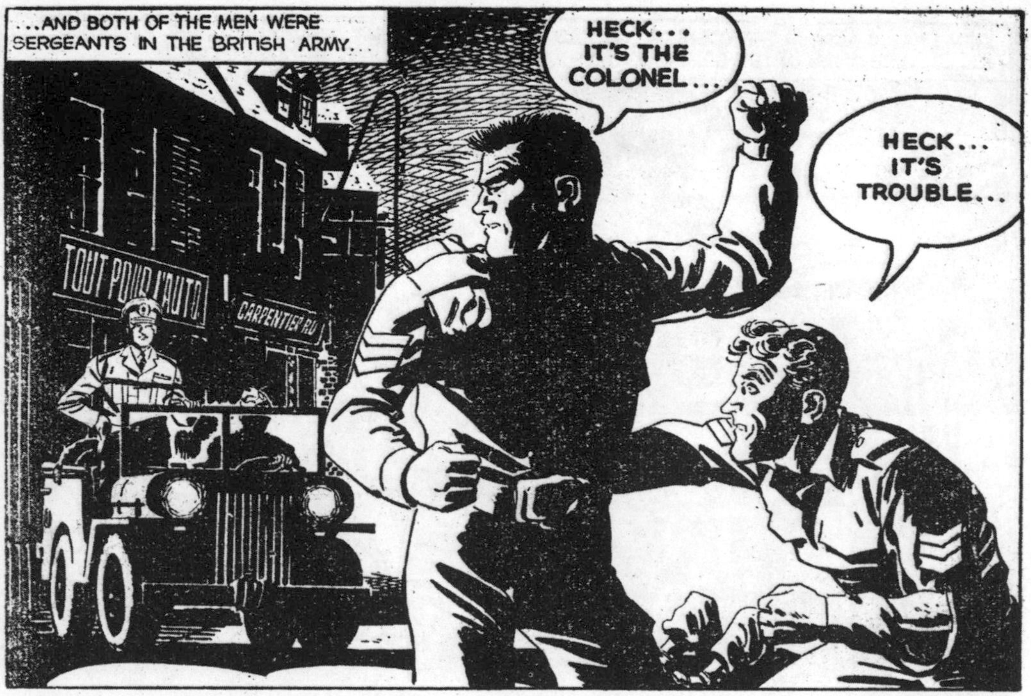
...AND BOTH OF THE MEN WERE SERGEANTS IN THE BRITISH ARMY...
HECK... IT'S THE COLONEL...
HECK... IT'S TROUBLE...
TOUT POUR L'AUTO
CARPENTIER RU

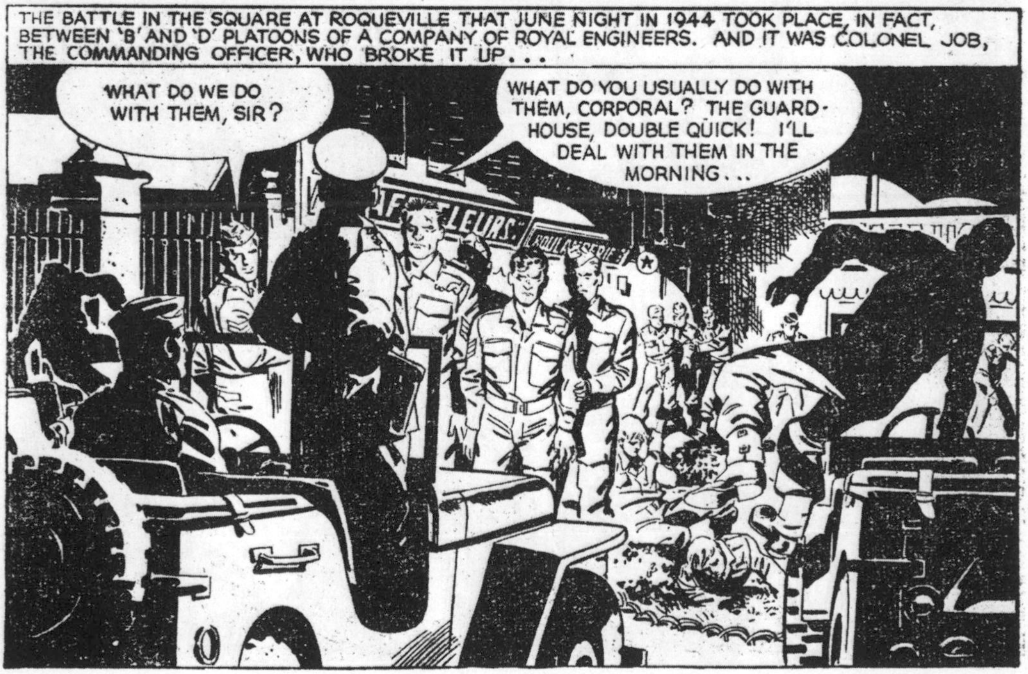
THE BATTLE IN THE SQUARE AT ROQUEVILLE THAT JUNE NIGHT IN 1944 TOOK PLACE, IN FACT, BETWEEN 'B' AND 'D' PLATOONS OF A COMPANY OF ROYAL ENGINEERS. AND IT WAS COLONEL JOB, THE COMMANDING OFFICER, WHO BROKE IT UP...
WHAT DO WE DO WITH THEM, SIR?
WHAT DO YOU USUALLY DO WITH THEM, CORPORAL? THE GUARD-HOUSE, DOUBLE QUICK! I'LL DEAL WITH THEM IN THE MORNING...

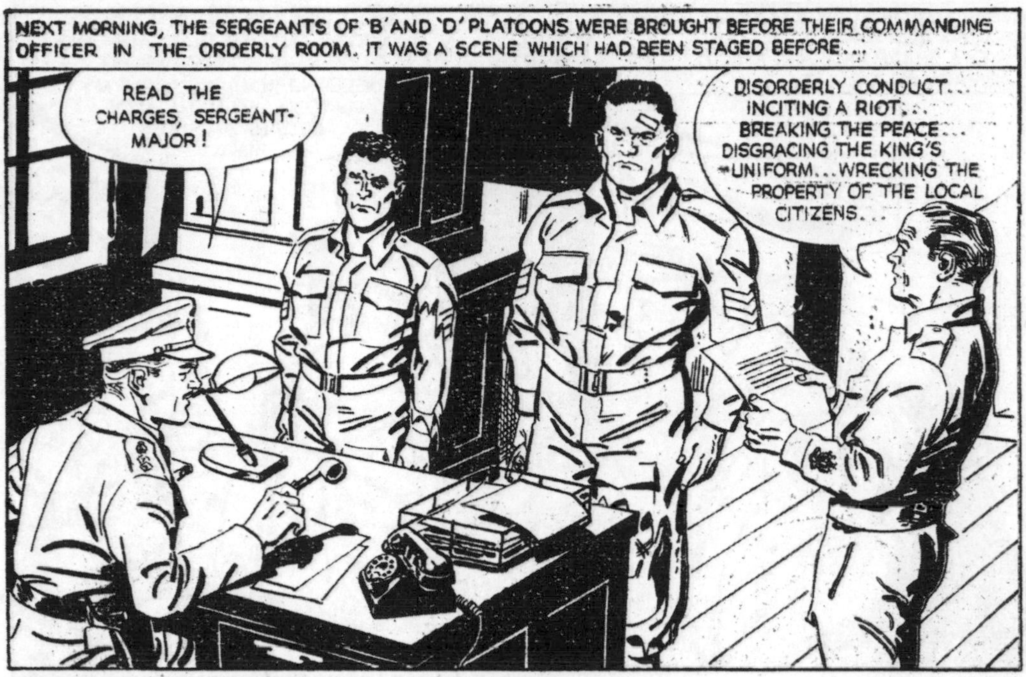
NEXT MORNING, THE SERGEANTS OF 'B' AND 'D' PLATOONS WERE BROUGHT BEFORE THEIR COMMANDING OFFICER IN THE ORDERLY ROOM. IT WAS A SCENE WHICH HAD BEEN STAGED BEFORE...
READ THE CHARGES, SERGEANT-MAJOR!
DISORDERLY CONDUCT... INCITING A RIOT... BREAKING THE PEACE... DISGRACING THE KING'S UNIFORM... WRECKING THE PROPERTY OF THE LOCAL CITIZENS...

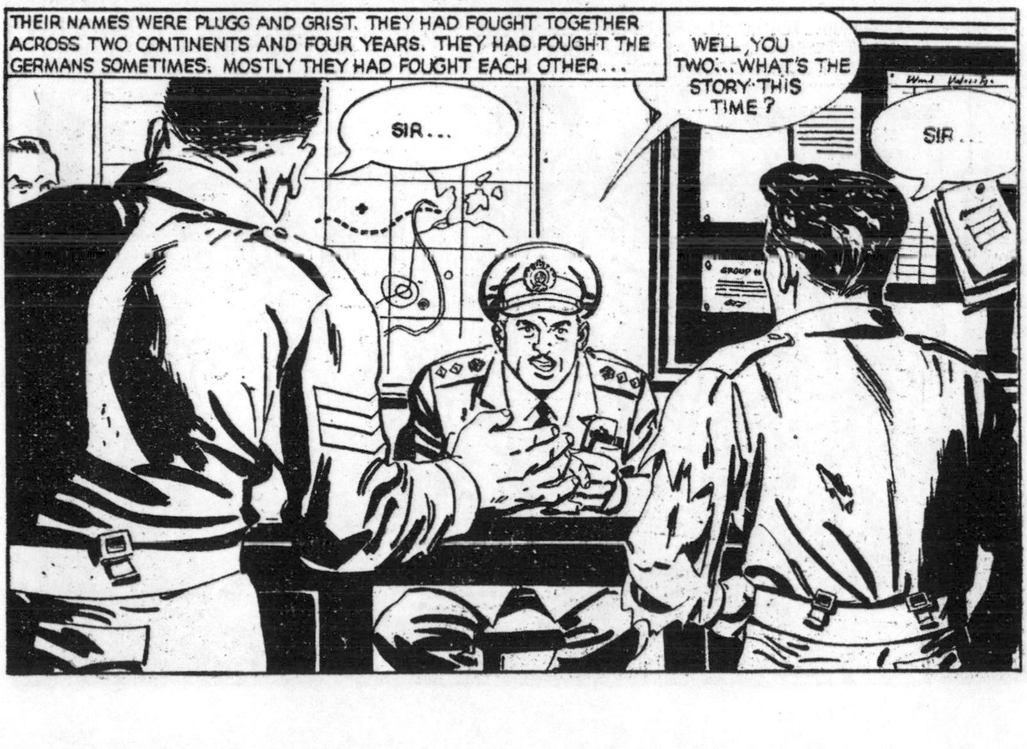
THEIR NAMES WERE PLUGG AND GRIST. THEY HAD FOUGHT TOGETHER ACROSS TWO CONTINENTS AND FOUR YEARS. THEY HAD FOUGHT THE GERMANS SOMETIMES. MOSTLY THEY HAD FOUGHT EACH OTHER...
WELL, YOU TWO... WHAT'S THE STORY THIS TIME?
SIR...
SIR...

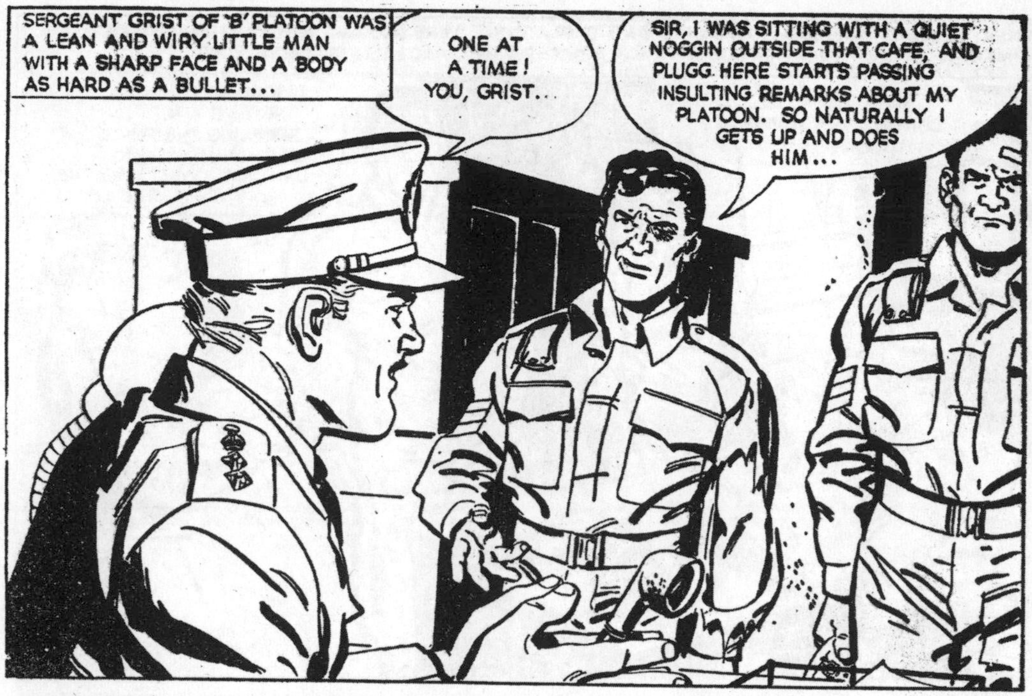
SERGEANT GRIST OF 'B' PLATOON WAS A LEAN AND WIRY LITTLE MAN WITH A SHARP FACE AND A BODY AS HARD AS A BULLET...
ONE AT A TIME! YOU, GRIST...
SIR, I WAS SITTING WITH A QUIET NOGGIN OUTSIDE THAT CAFE, AND PLUGG HERE STARTS PASSING INSULTING REMARKS ABOUT MY PLATOON. SO NATURALLY I GETS UP AND DOES HIM...

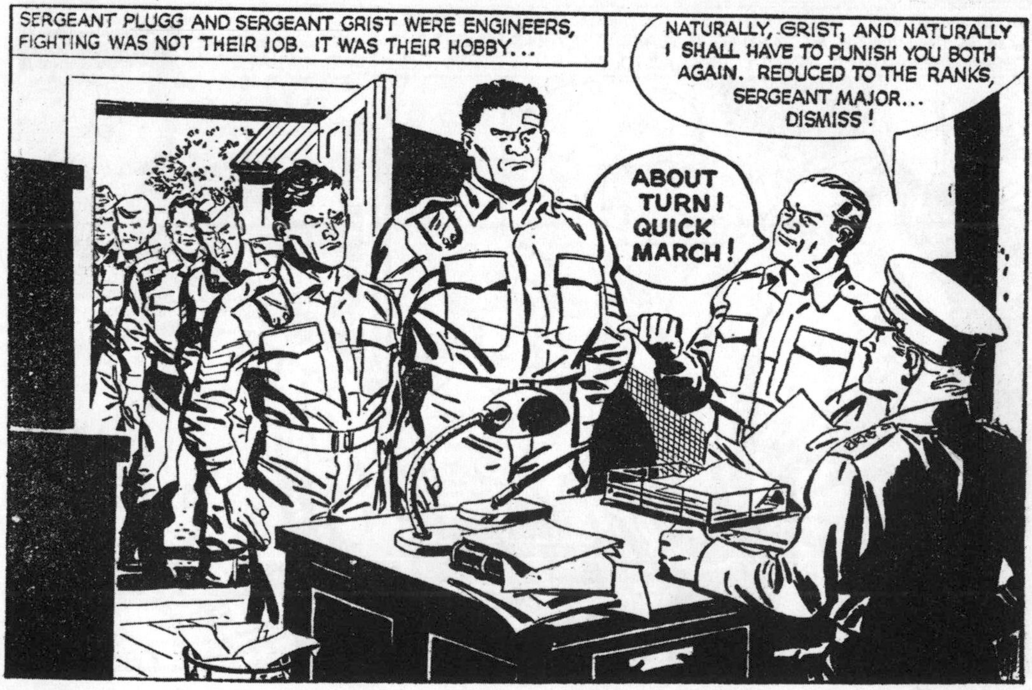
SERGEANT PLUGG AND SERGEANT GRIST WERE ENGINEERS, FIGHTING WAS NOT THEIR JOB. IT WAS THEIR HOBBY...
NATURALLY, GRIST, AND NATURALLY I SHALL HAVE TO PUNISH YOU BOTH AGAIN. REDUCED TO THE RANKS, SERGEANT MAJOR... DISMISS!
ABOUT TURN! QUICK MARCH!

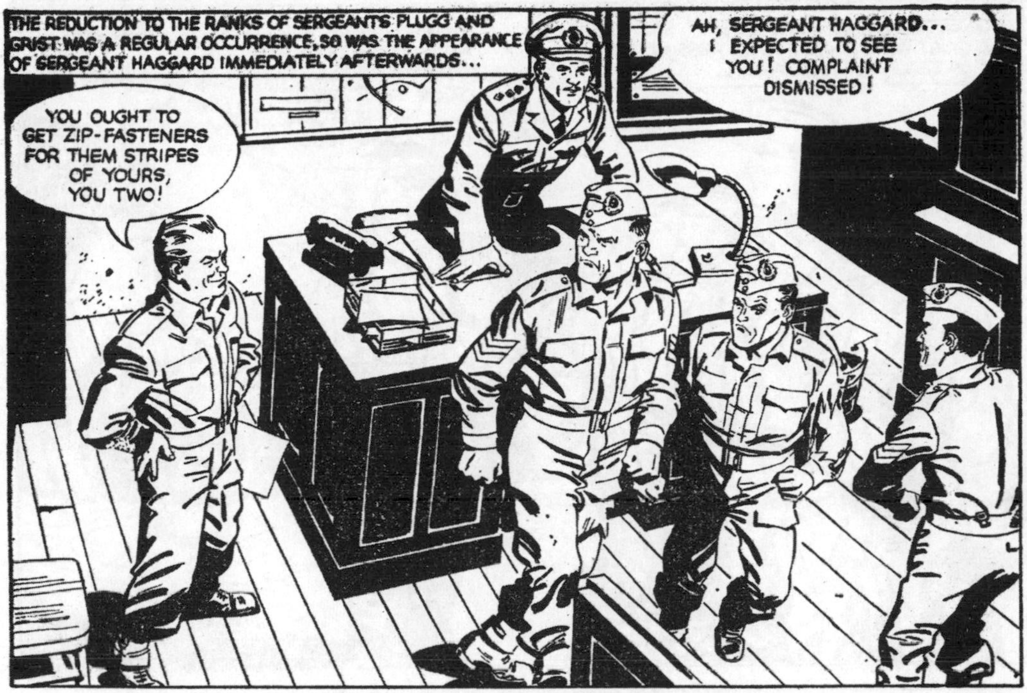
THE REDUCTION TO THE RANKS OF SERGEANTS PLUGG AND GRIST WAS A REGULAR OCCURRENCE, SO WAS THE APPEARANCE OF SERGEANT HAGGARD IMMEDIATELY AFTERWARDS...
AH, SERGEANT HAGGARD... I EXPECTED TO SEE YOU! COMPLAINT DISMISSED!
YOU OUGHT TO GET ZIP-FASTENERS FOR THEM STRIPES OF YOURS, YOU TWO!

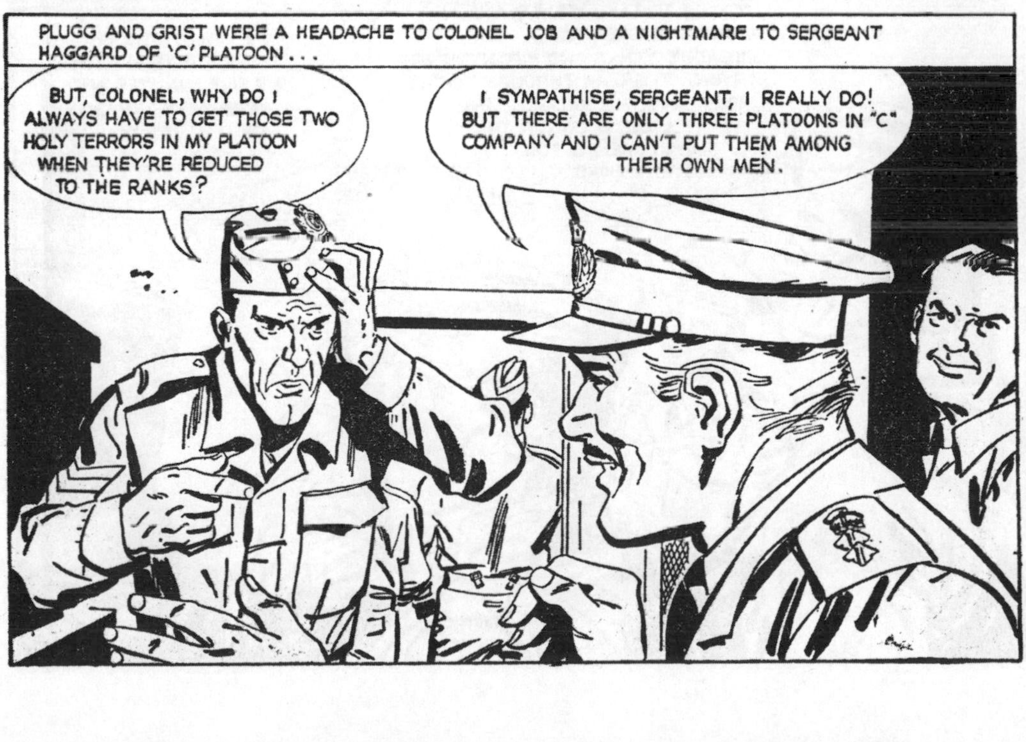
PLUGG AND GRIST WERE A HEADACHE TO COLONEL JOB AND A NIGHTMARE TO SERGEANT HAGGARD OF 'C' PLATOON...
BUT, COLONEL, WHY DO I ALWAYS HAVE TO GET THOSE TWO HOLY TERRORS IN MY PLATOON WHEN THEY'RE REDUCED TO THE RANKS?
I SYMPATHISE, SERGEANT, I REALLY DO! BUT THERE ARE ONLY THREE PLATOONS IN "C" COMPANY AND I CAN'T PUT THEM AMONG THEIR OWN MEN.

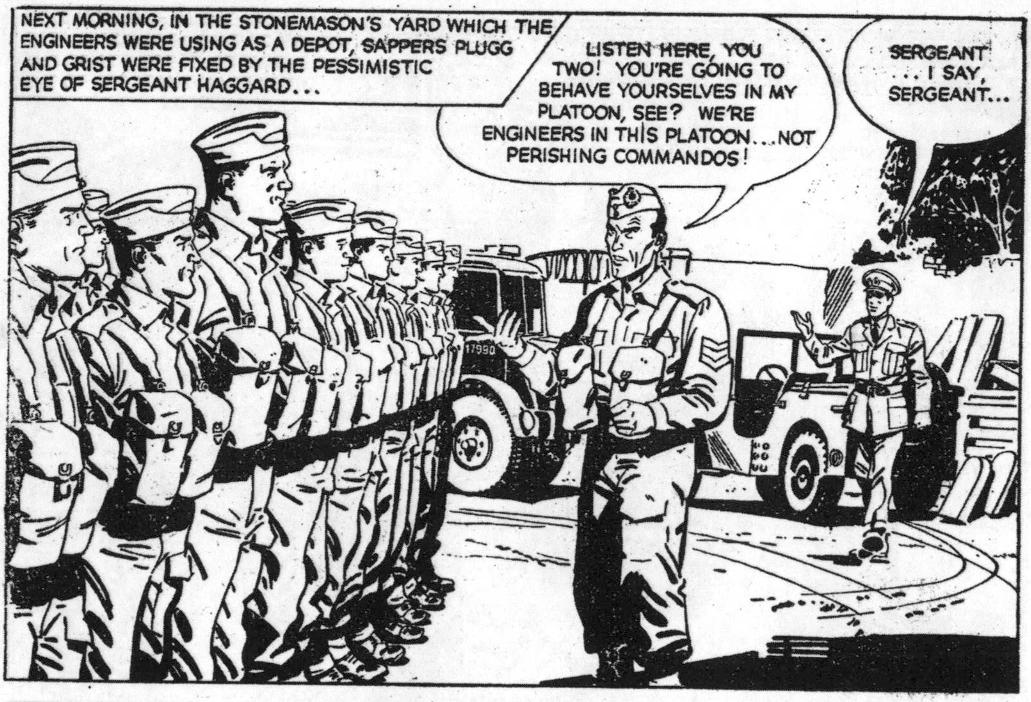
NEXT MORNING, IN THE STONEMASON'S YARD WHICH THE ENGINEERS WERE USING AS A DEPOT, SAPPERS PLUGG AND GRIST WERE FIXED BY THE PESSIMISTIC EYE OF SERGEANT HAGGARD...
LISTEN HERE, YOU TWO! YOU'RE GOING TO BEHAVE YOURSELVES IN MY PLATOON, SEE? WE'RE ENGINEERS IN THIS PLATOON...NOT PERISHING COMMANDOS!
SERGEANT ... I SAY, SERGEANT...

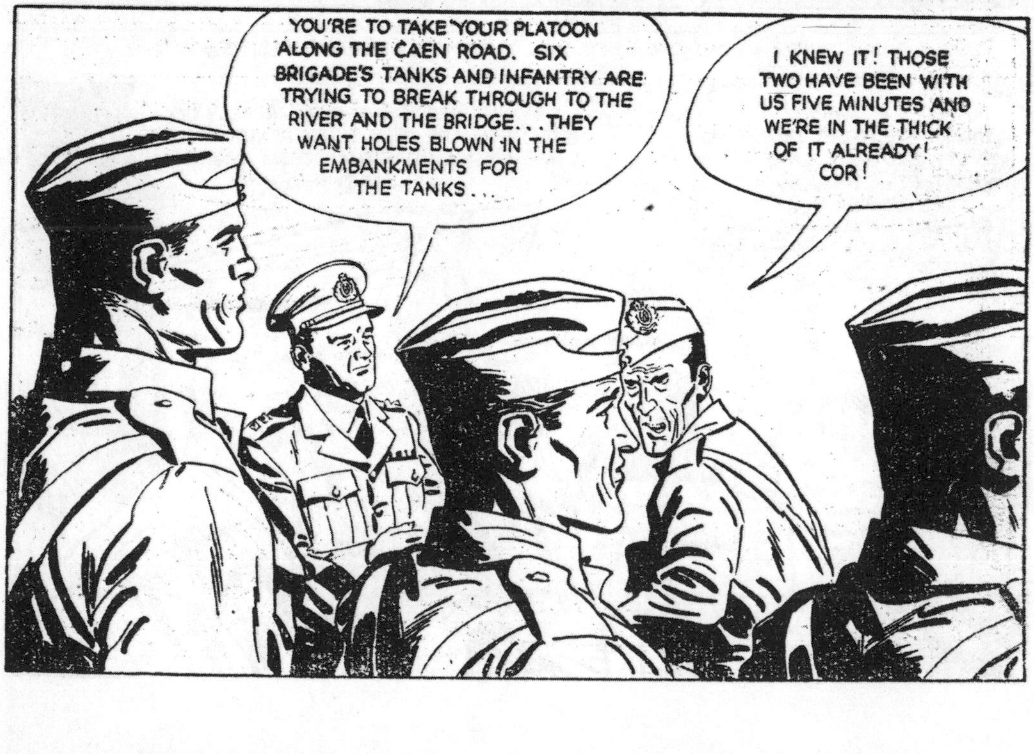
YOU'RE TO TAKE YOUR PLATOON ALONG THE CAEN ROAD. SIX BRIGADE'S TANKS AND INFANTRY ARE TRYING TO BREAK THROUGH TO THE RIVER AND THE BRIDGE...THEY WANT HOLES BLOWN IN THE EMBANKMENTS FOR THE TANKS...
I KNEW IT! THOSE TWO HAVE BEEN WITH US FIVE MINUTES AND WE'RE IN THE THICK OF IT ALREADY! COR!

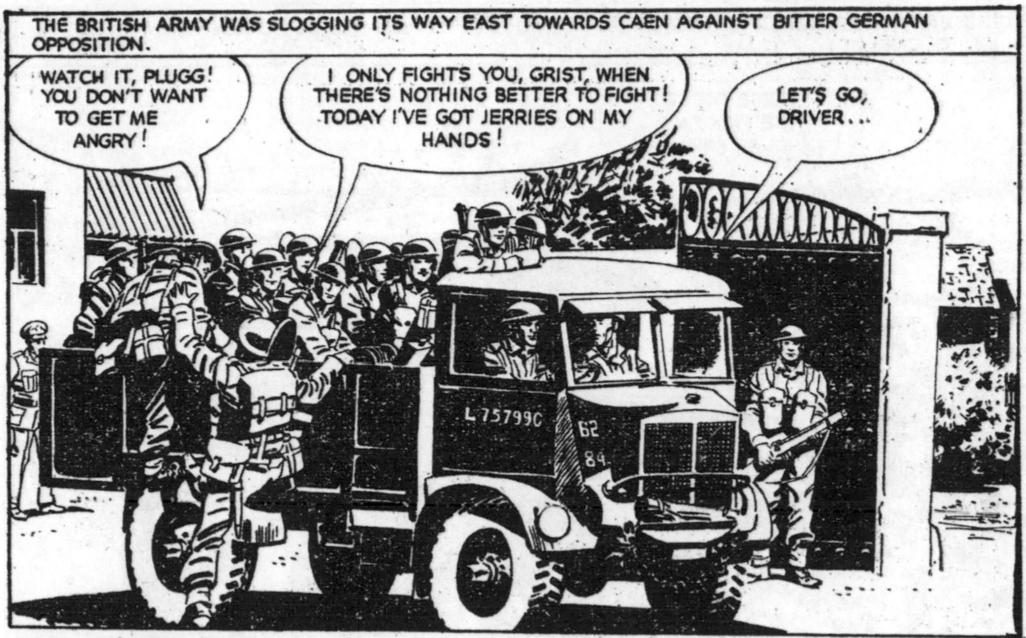
THE BRITISH ARMY WAS SLOGGING ITS WAY EAST TOWARDS CAEN AGAINST BITTER GERMAN OPPOSITION.
WATCH IT, PLUGG! YOU DON'T WANT TO GET ME ANGRY!
I ONLY FIGHTS YOU, GRIST, WHEN THERE'S NOTHING BETTER TO FIGHT! TODAY I'VE GOT JERRIES ON MY HANDS!
LET'S GO, DRIVER...
L 757990
62
84

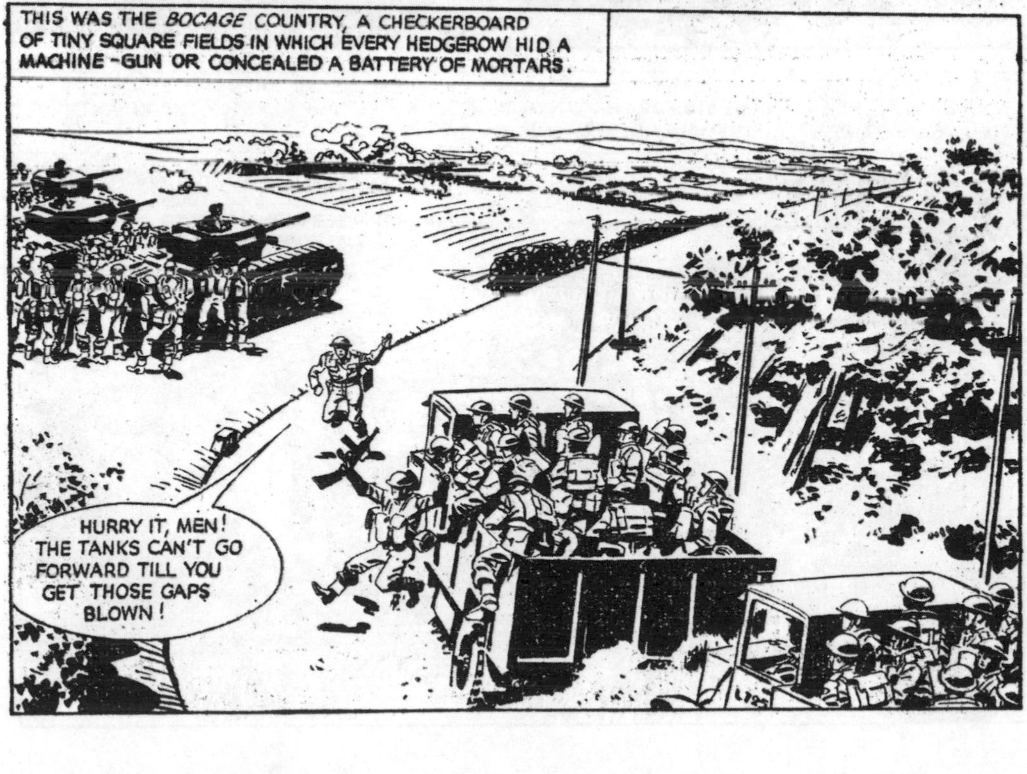
THIS WAS THE *BOCAGE* COUNTRY, A CHECKERBOARD OF TINY SQUARE FIELDS IN WHICH EVERY HEDGEROW HID A MACHINE-GUN OR CONCEALED A BATTERY OF MORTARS.
HURRY IT, MEN! THE TANKS CAN'T GO FORWARD TILL YOU GET THOSE GAPS BLOWN!

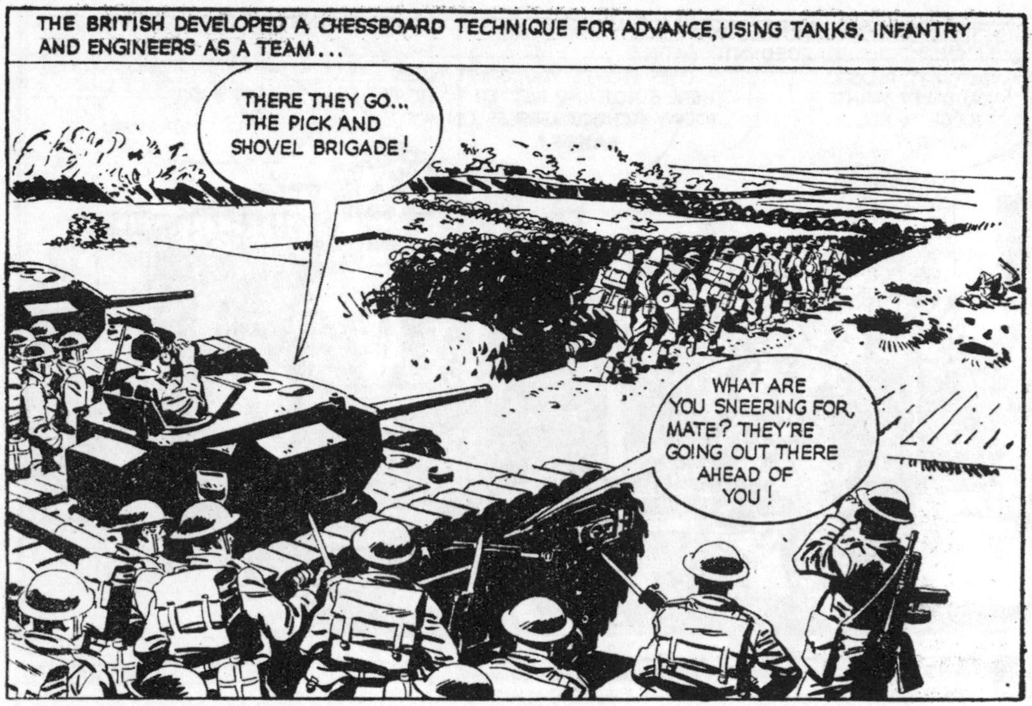
THE BRITISH DEVELOPED A CHESSBOARD TECHNIQUE FOR ADVANCE, USING TANKS, INFANTRY AND ENGINEERS AS A TEAM...
THERE THEY GO... THE PICK AND SHOVEL BRIGADE!
WHAT ARE YOU SNEERING FOR, MATE? THEY'RE GOING OUT THERE AHEAD OF YOU!

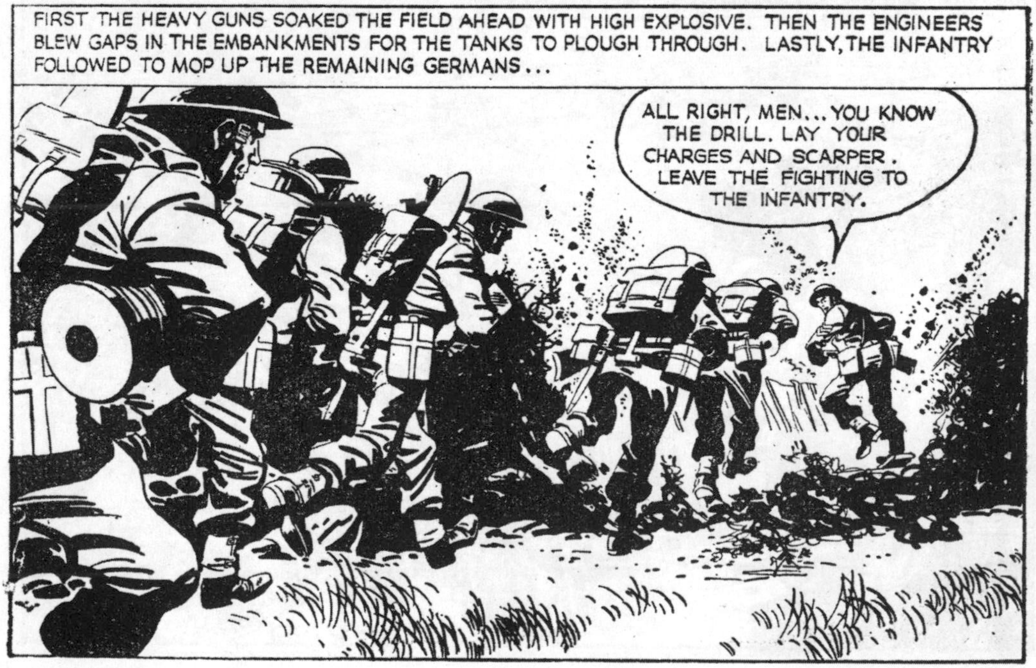
FIRST THE HEAVY GUNS SOAKED THE FIELD AHEAD WITH HIGH EXPLOSIVE. THEN THE ENGINEERS BLEW GAPS IN THE EMBANKMENTS FOR THE TANKS TO PLOUGH THROUGH. LASTLY, THE INFANTRY FOLLOWED TO MOP UP THE REMAINING GERMANS...
ALL RIGHT, MEN... YOU KNOW THE DRILL. LAY YOUR CHARGES AND SCARPER. LEAVE THE FIGHTING TO THE INFANTRY.

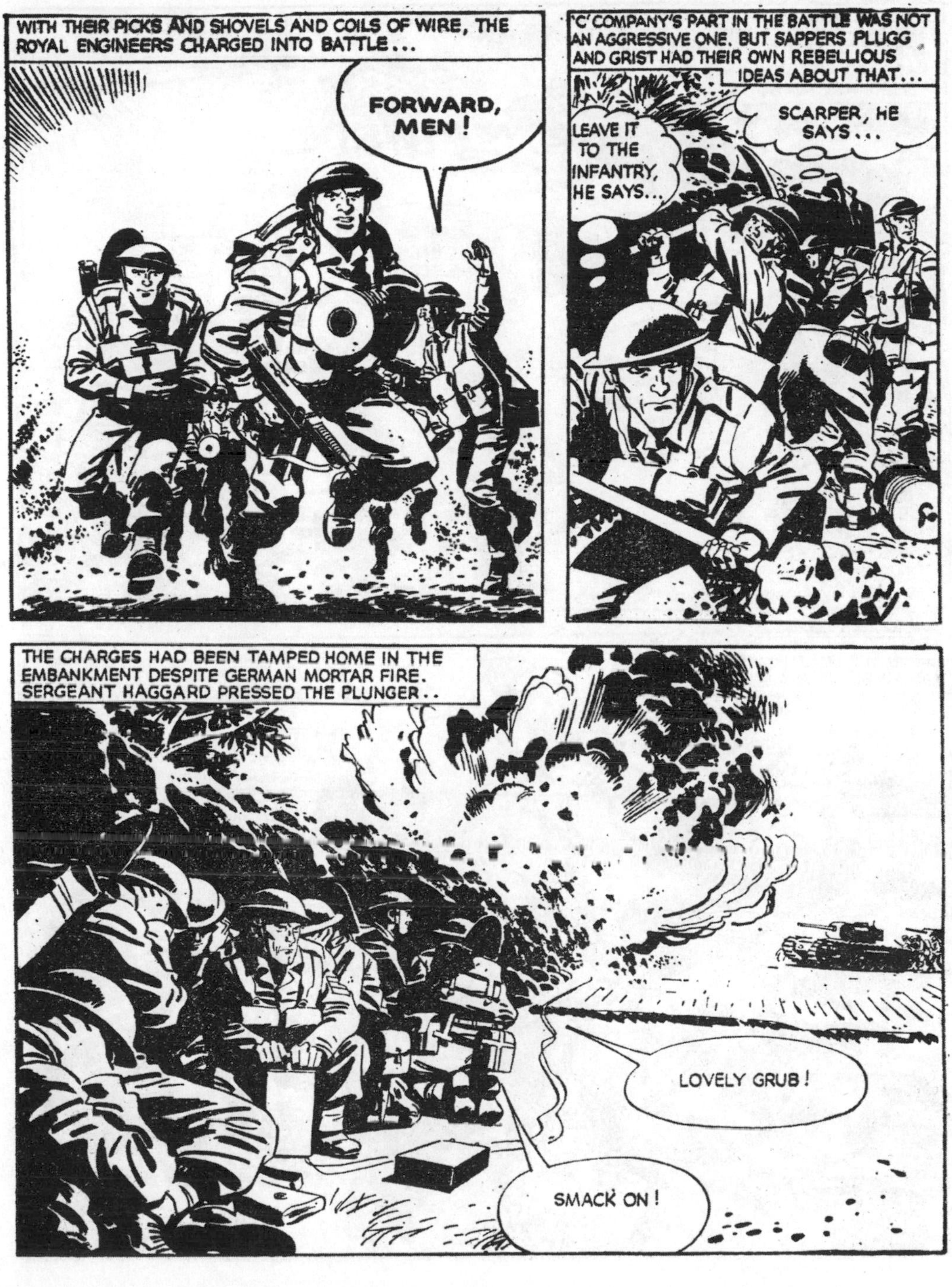
WITH THEIR PICKS AND SHOVELS AND COILS OF WIRE, THE ROYAL ENGINEERS CHARGED INTO BATTLE...
FORWARD, MEN!
'C' COMPANY'S PART IN THE BATTLE WAS NOT AN AGGRESSIVE ONE. BUT SAPPERS PLUGG AND GRIST HAD THEIR OWN REBELLIOUS IDEAS ABOUT THAT...
LEAVE IT TO THE INFANTRY, HE SAYS...
SCARPER, HE SAYS...
THE CHARGES HAD BEEN TAMPED HOME IN THE EMBANKMENT DESPITE GERMAN MORTAR FIRE. SERGEANT HAGGARD PRESSED THE PLUNGER..
LOVELY GRUB!
SMACK ON!

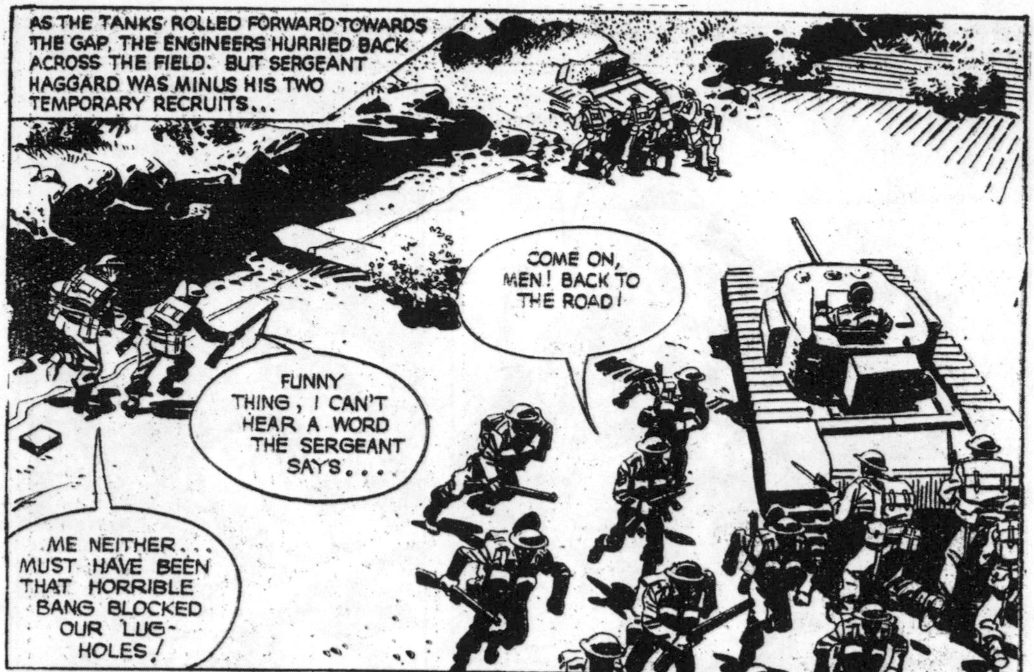
AS THE TANKS ROLLED FORWARD TOWARDS THE GAP, THE ENGINEERS HURRIED BACK ACROSS THE FIELD. BUT SERGEANT HAGGARD WAS MINUS HIS TWO TEMPORARY RECRUITS...
COME ON, MEN! BACK TO THE ROAD!
FUNNY THING, I CAN'T HEAR A WORD THE SERGEANT SAYS...
ME NEITHER... MUST HAVE BEEN THAT HORRIBLE BANG BLOCKED OUR LUG-HOLES!

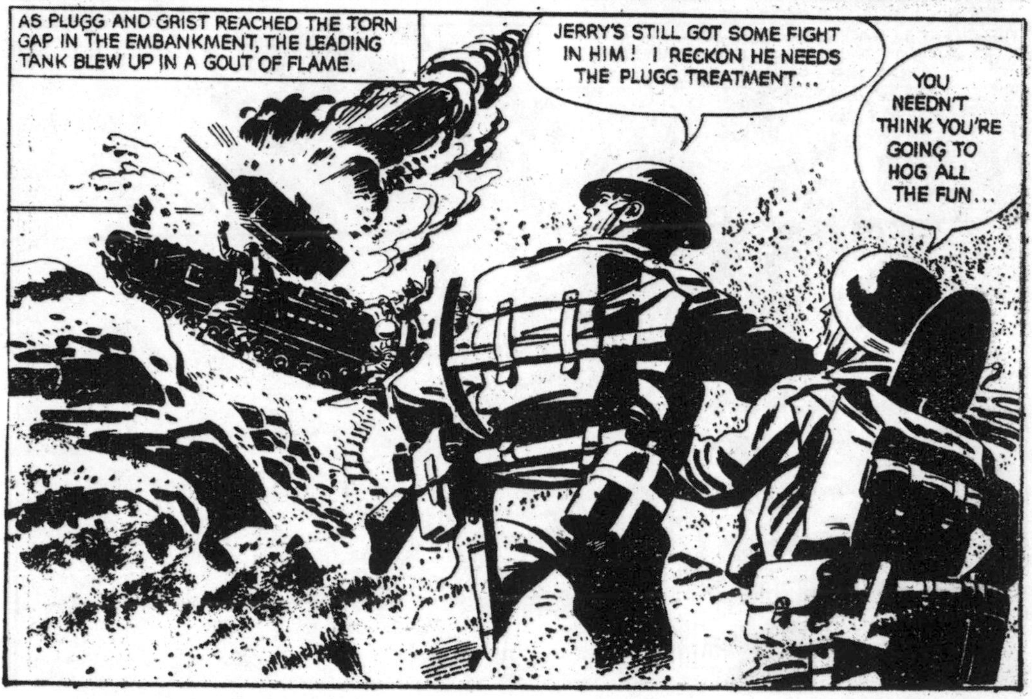
AS PLUGG AND GRIST REACHED THE TORN GAP IN THE EMBANKMENT, THE LEADING TANK BLEW UP IN A GOUT OF FLAME.
JERRY'S STILL GOT SOME FIGHT IN HIM! I RECKON HE NEEDS THE PLUGG TREATMENT...
YOU NEEDN'T THINK YOU'RE GOING TO HOG ALL THE FUN...

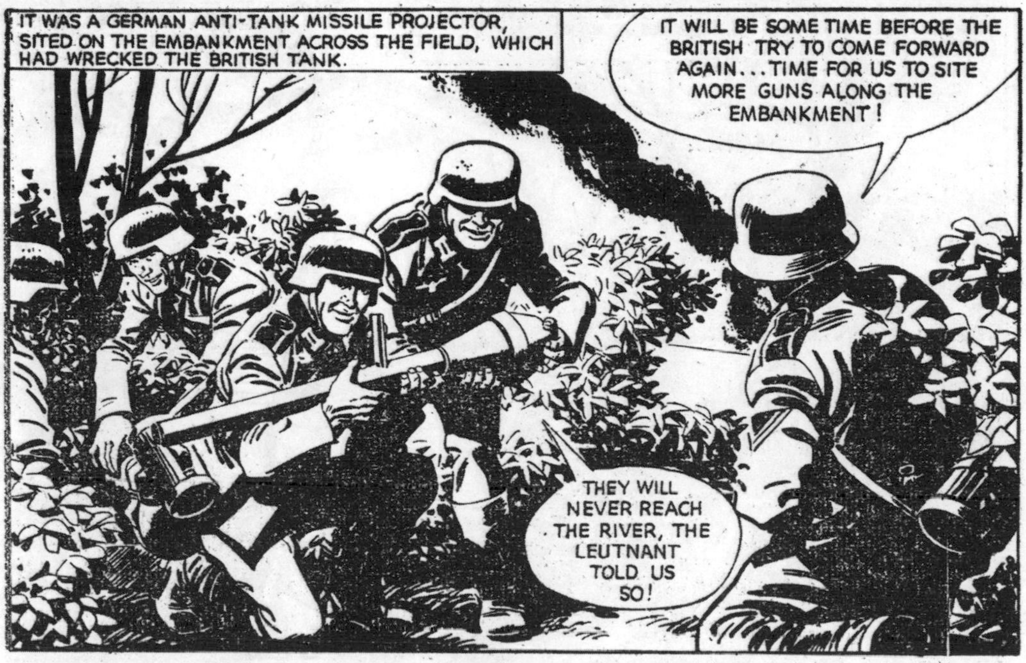
IT WAS A GERMAN ANTI-TANK MISSILE PROJECTOR, SITED ON THE EMBANKMENT ACROSS THE FIELD, WHICH HAD WRECKED THE BRITISH TANK.
IT WILL BE SOME TIME BEFORE THE BRITISH TRY TO COME FORWARD AGAIN...TIME FOR US TO SITE MORE GUNS ALONG THE EMBANKMENT!
THEY WILL NEVER REACH THE RIVER, THE LEUTNANT TOLD US SO!

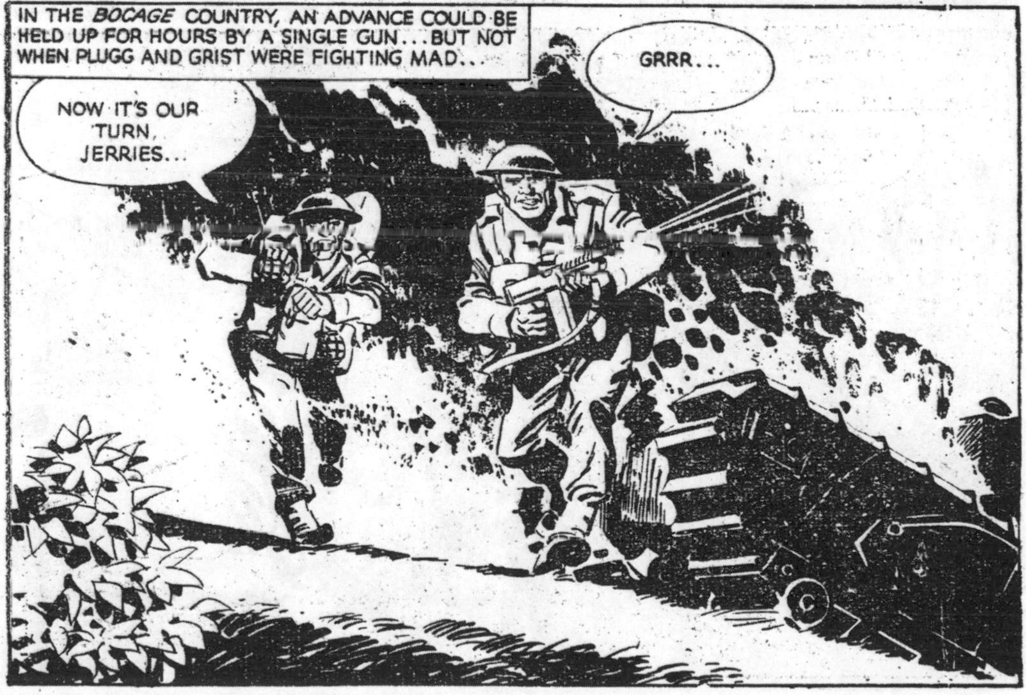
IN THE *BOCAGE* COUNTRY, AN ADVANCE COULD BE HELD UP FOR HOURS BY A SINGLE GUN...BUT NOT WHEN PLUGG AND GRIST WERE FIGHTING MAD...
NOW IT'S OUR TURN, JERRIES...
GRRR...

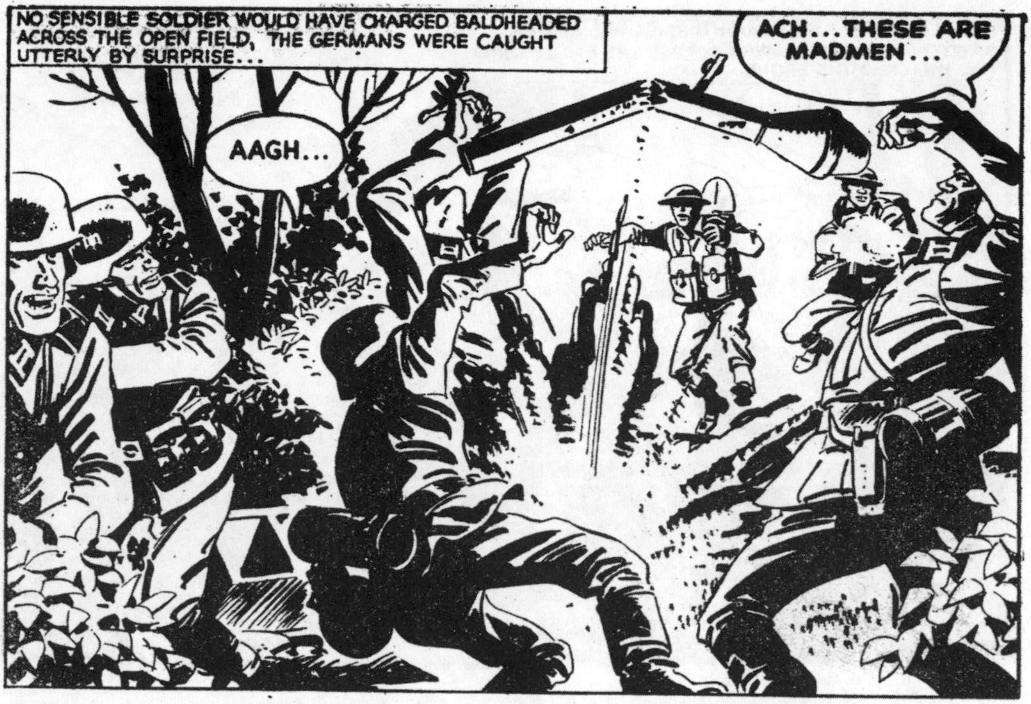
NO SENSIBLE SOLDIER WOULD HAVE CHARGED BALDHEADED ACROSS THE OPEN FIELD, THE GERMANS WERE CAUGHT UTTERLY BY SURPRISE...
ACH...THESE ARE MADMEN...
AAGH...

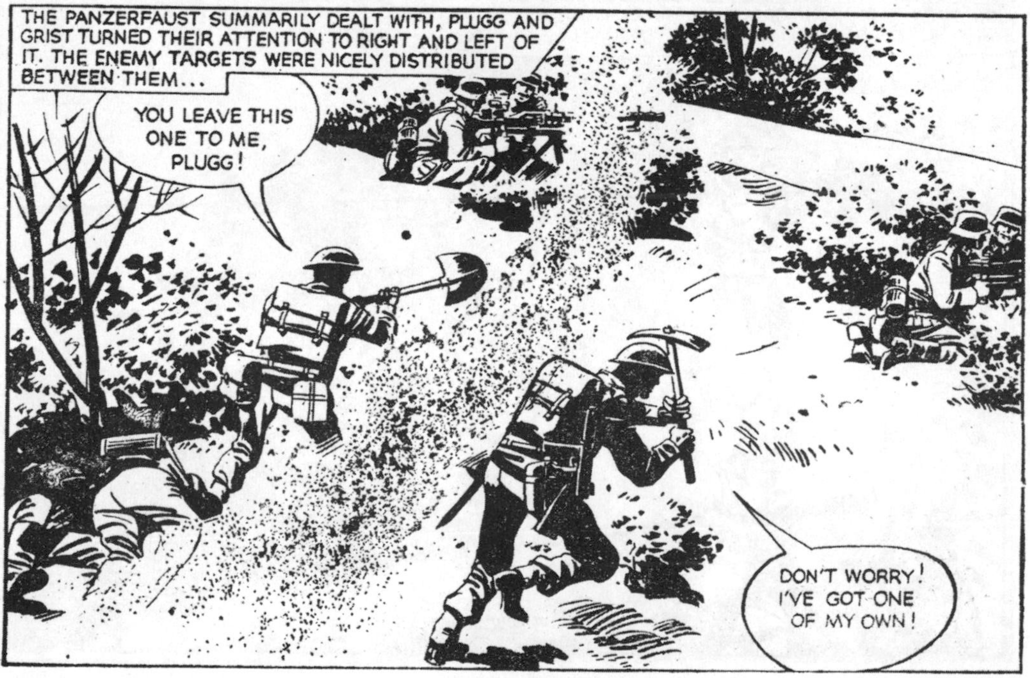
THE PANZERFAUST SUMMARILY DEALT WITH, PLUGG AND GRIST TURNED THEIR ATTENTION TO RIGHT AND LEFT OF IT. THE ENEMY TARGETS WERE NICELY DISTRIBUTED BETWEEN THEM...
YOU LEAVE THIS ONE TO ME, PLUGG!
DON'T WORRY! I'VE GOT ONE OF MY OWN!

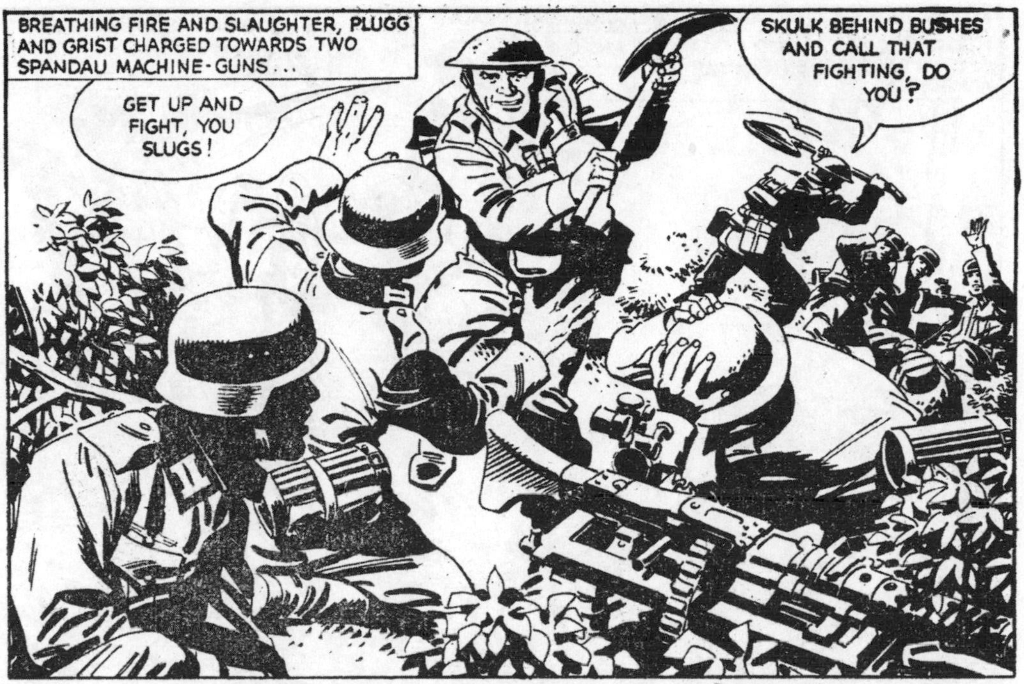
BREATHING FIRE AND SLAUGHTER, PLUGG AND GRIST CHARGED TOWARDS TWO SPANDAU MACHINE-GUNS...
GET UP AND FIGHT, YOU SLUGS!
SKULK BEHIND BUSHES AND CALL THAT FIGHTING, DO YOU?

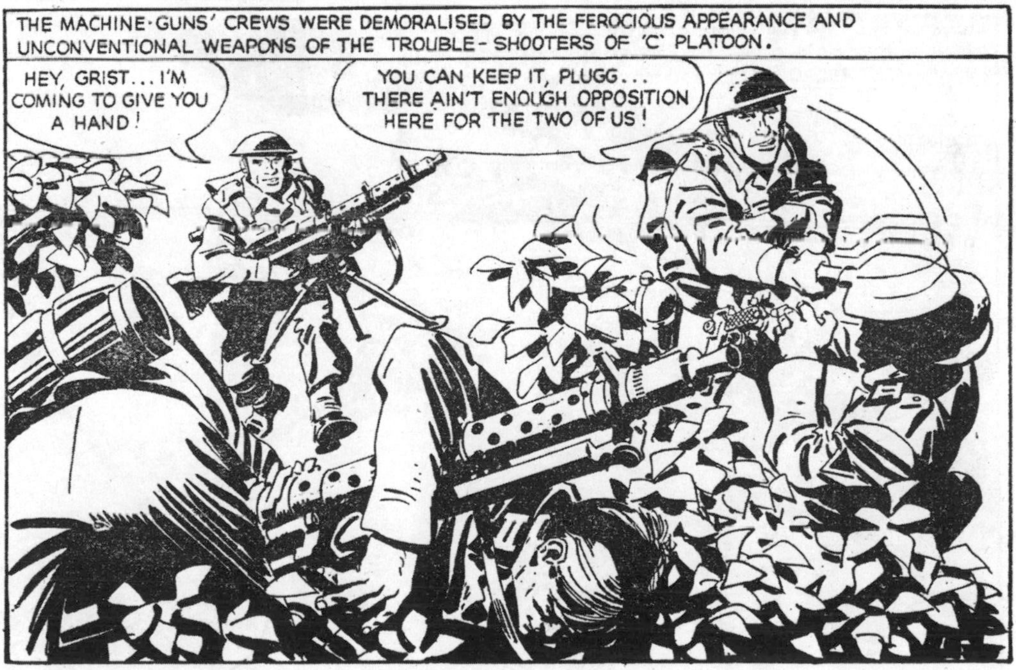
THE MACHINE-GUNS' CREWS WERE DEMORALISED BY THE FEROCIOUS APPEARANCE AND UNCONVENTIONAL WEAPONS OF THE TROUBLE-SHOOTERS OF 'C' PLATOON.
HEY, GRIST... I'M COMING TO GIVE YOU A HAND!
YOU CAN KEEP IT, PLUGG... THERE AIN'T ENOUGH OPPOSITION HERE FOR THE TWO OF US!

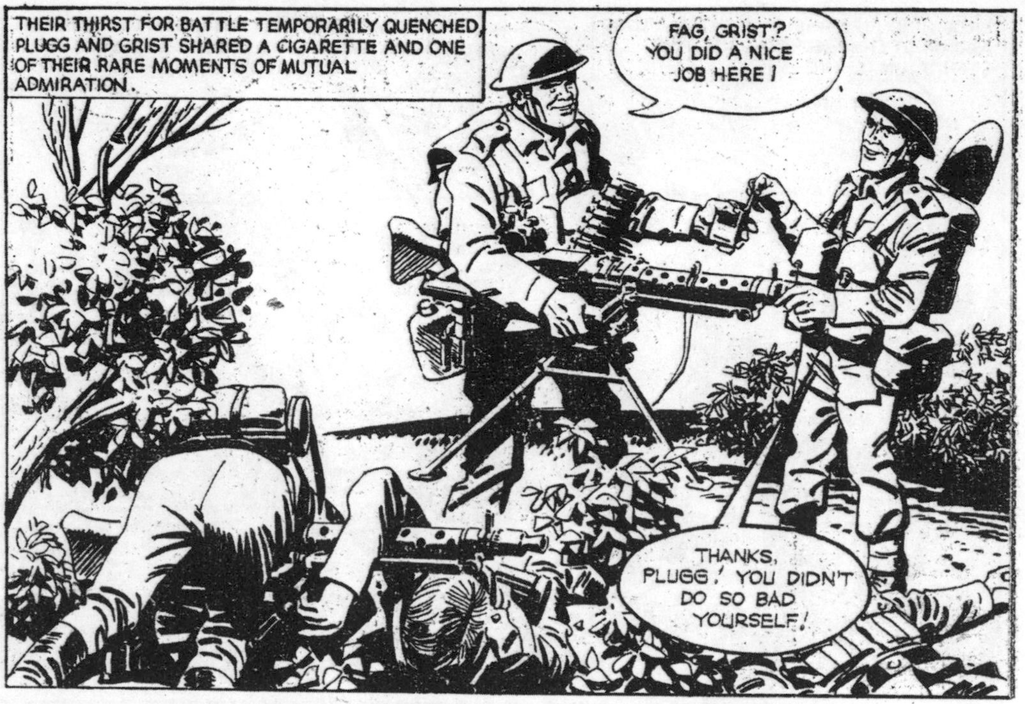
THEIR THIRST FOR BATTLE TEMPORARILY QUENCHED, PLUGG AND GRIST SHARED A CIGARETTE AND ONE OF THEIR RARE MOMENTS OF MUTUAL ADMIRATION.
FAG, GRIST? YOU DID A NICE JOB HERE!
THANKS, PLUGG! YOU DIDN'T DO SO BAD YOURSELF!

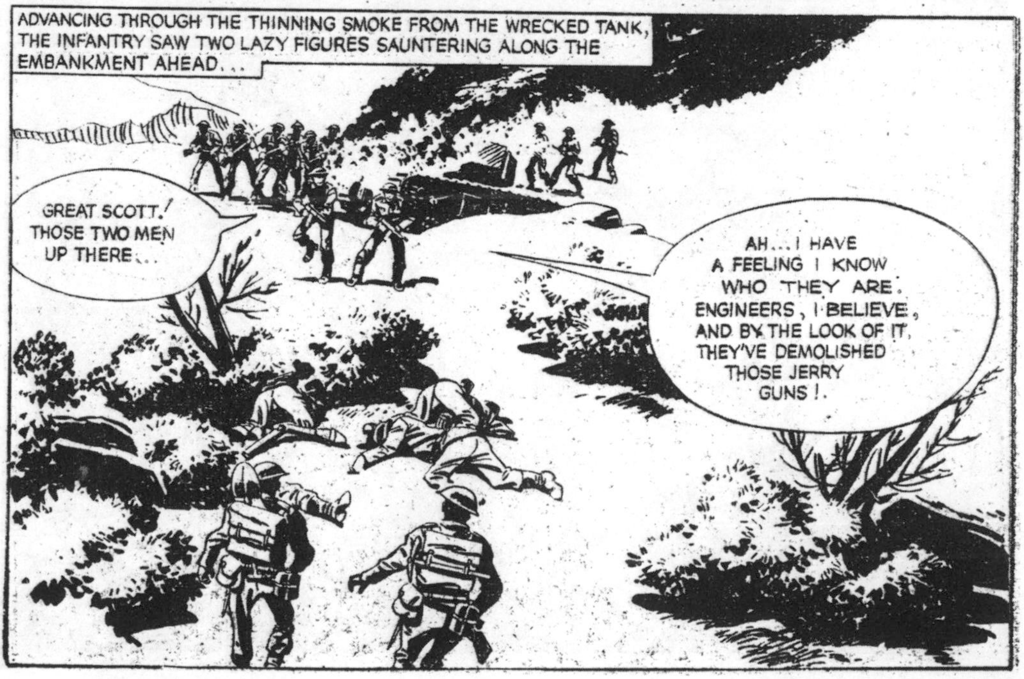
ADVANCING THROUGH THE THINNING SMOKE FROM THE WRECKED TANK, THE INFANTRY SAW TWO LAZY FIGURES SAUNTERING ALONG THE EMBANKMENT AHEAD...
GREAT SCOTT! THOSE TWO MEN UP THERE...
AH... I HAVE A FEELING I KNOW WHO THEY ARE. ENGINEERS, I BELIEVE, AND BY THE LOOK OF IT, THEY'VE DEMOLISHED THOSE JERRY GUNS!

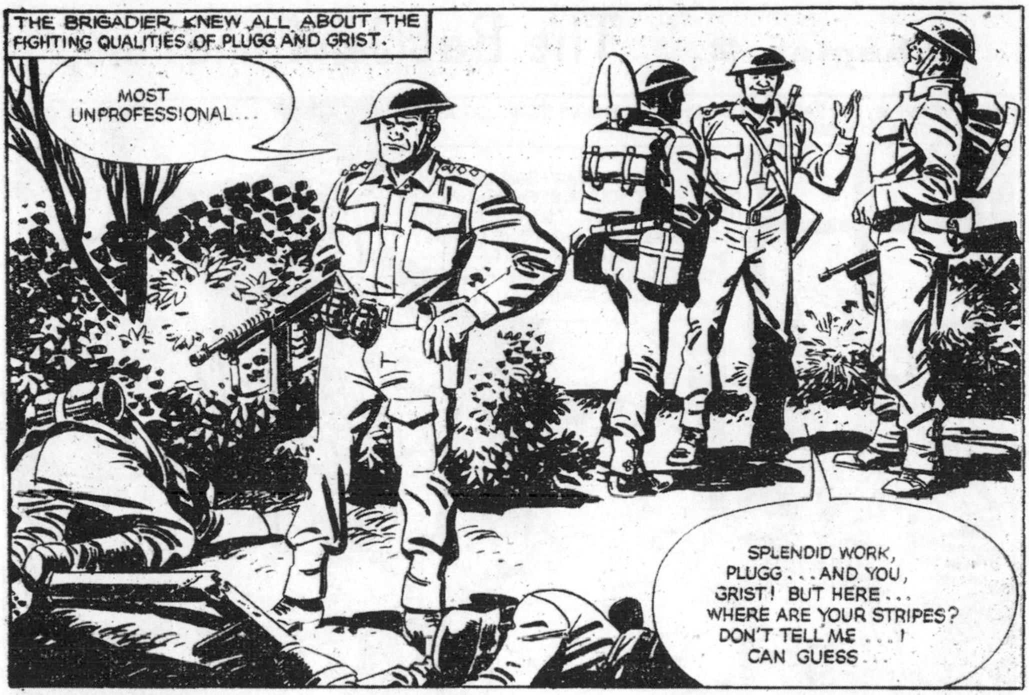
THE BRIGADIER KNEW ALL ABOUT THE FIGHTING QUALITIES OF PLUGG AND GRIST.
MOST UNPROFESSIONAL...
SPLENDID WORK, PLUGG...AND YOU, GRIST! BUT HERE... WHERE ARE YOUR STRIPES? DON'T TELL ME...I CAN GUESS...

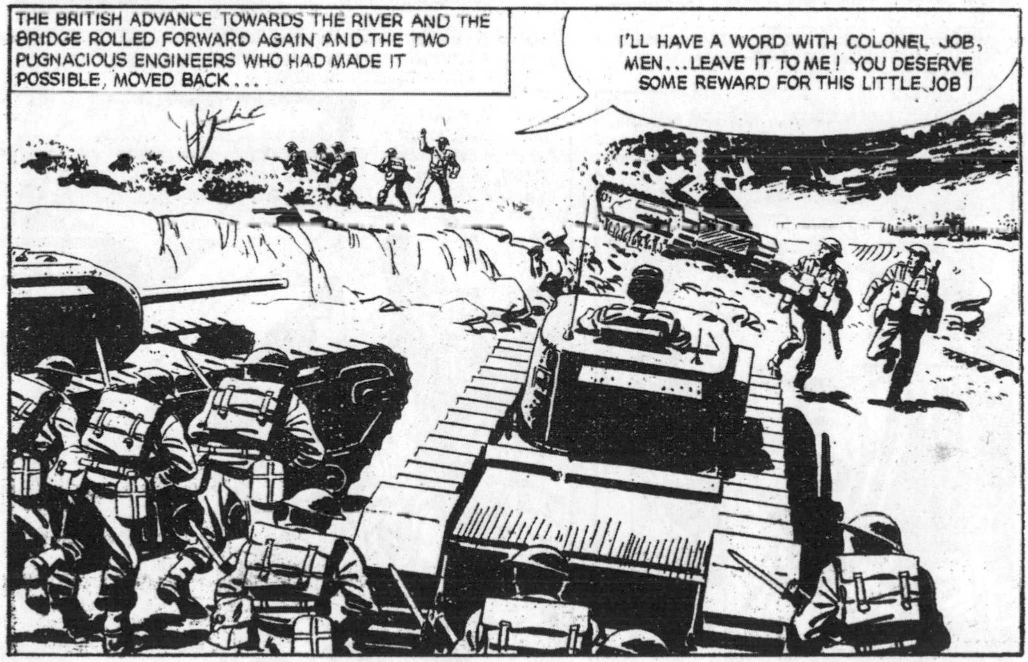
THE BRITISH ADVANCE TOWARDS THE RIVER AND THE BRIDGE ROLLED FORWARD AGAIN AND THE TWO PUGNACIOUS ENGINEERS WHO HAD MADE IT POSSIBLE, MOVED BACK...
I'LL HAVE A WORD WITH COLONEL JOB, MEN...LEAVE IT TO ME! YOU DESERVE SOME REWARD FOR THIS LITTLE JOB!

Chapter 2. The Battle of the Pump

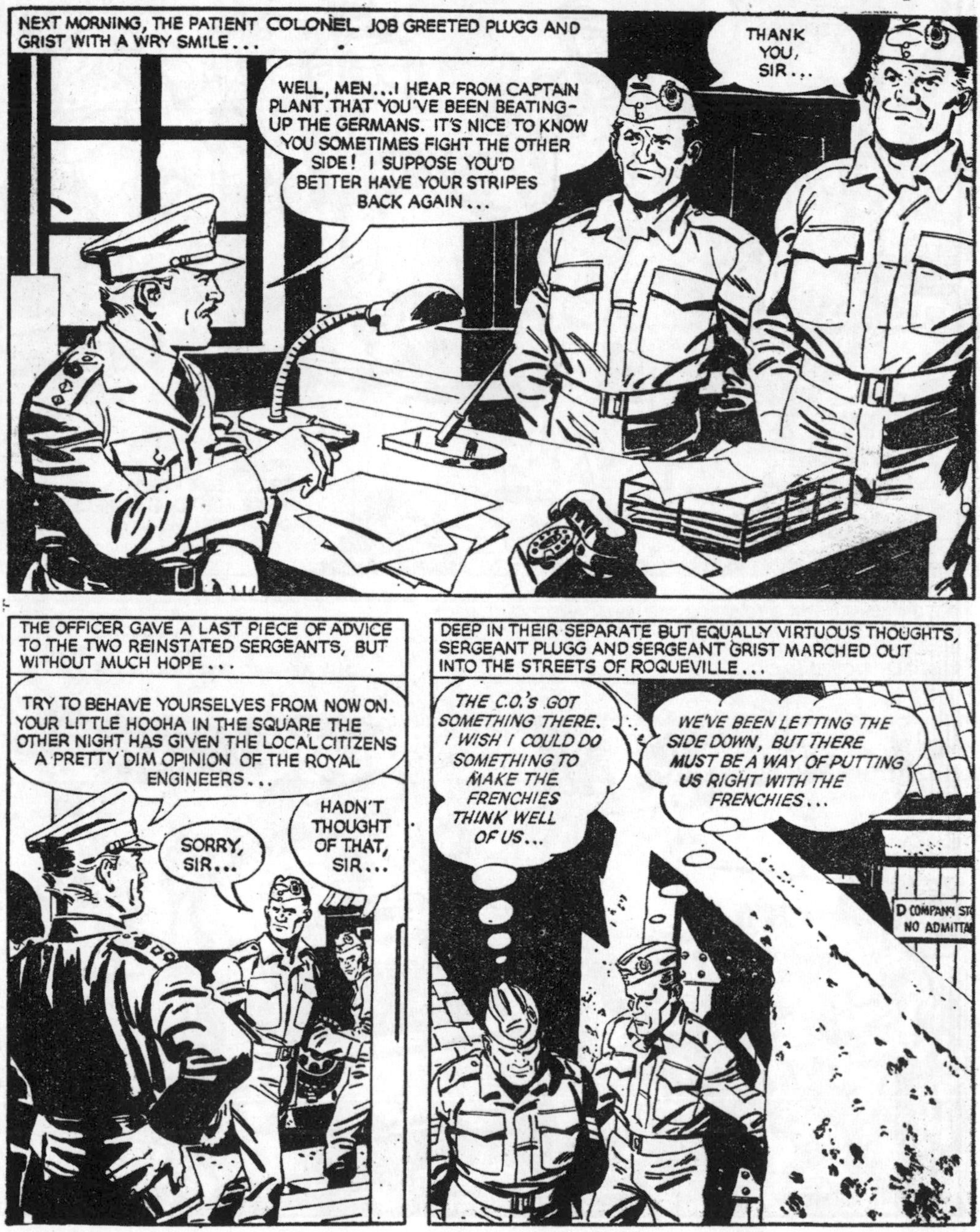
NEXT MORNING, THE PATIENT COLONEL JOB GREETED PLUGG AND GRIST WITH A WRY SMILE...
WELL, MEN...I HEAR FROM CAPTAIN PLANT THAT YOU'VE BEEN BEATING-UP THE GERMANS. IT'S NICE TO KNOW YOU SOMETIMES FIGHT THE OTHER SIDE! I SUPPOSE YOU'D BETTER HAVE YOUR STRIPES BACK AGAIN...
THANK YOU, SIR...
THE OFFICER GAVE A LAST PIECE OF ADVICE TO THE TWO REINSTATED SERGEANTS, BUT WITHOUT MUCH HOPE...
TRY TO BEHAVE YOURSELVES FROM NOW ON. YOUR LITTLE HOOHA IN THE SQUARE THE OTHER NIGHT HAS GIVEN THE LOCAL CITIZENS A PRETTY DIM OPINION OF THE ROYAL ENGINEERS...
SORRY, SIR...
HADN'T THOUGHT OF THAT, SIR...
DEEP IN THEIR SEPARATE BUT EQUALLY VIRTUOUS THOUGHTS, SERGEANT PLUGG AND SERGEANT GRIST MARCHED OUT INTO THE STREETS OF ROQUEVILLE...
THE C.O.'s GOT SOMETHING THERE. I WISH I COULD DO SOMETHING TO MAKE THE FRENCHIES THINK WELL OF US...
WE'VE BEEN LETTING THE SIDE DOWN, BUT THERE MUST BE A WAY OF PUTTING US RIGHT WITH THE FRENCHIES...

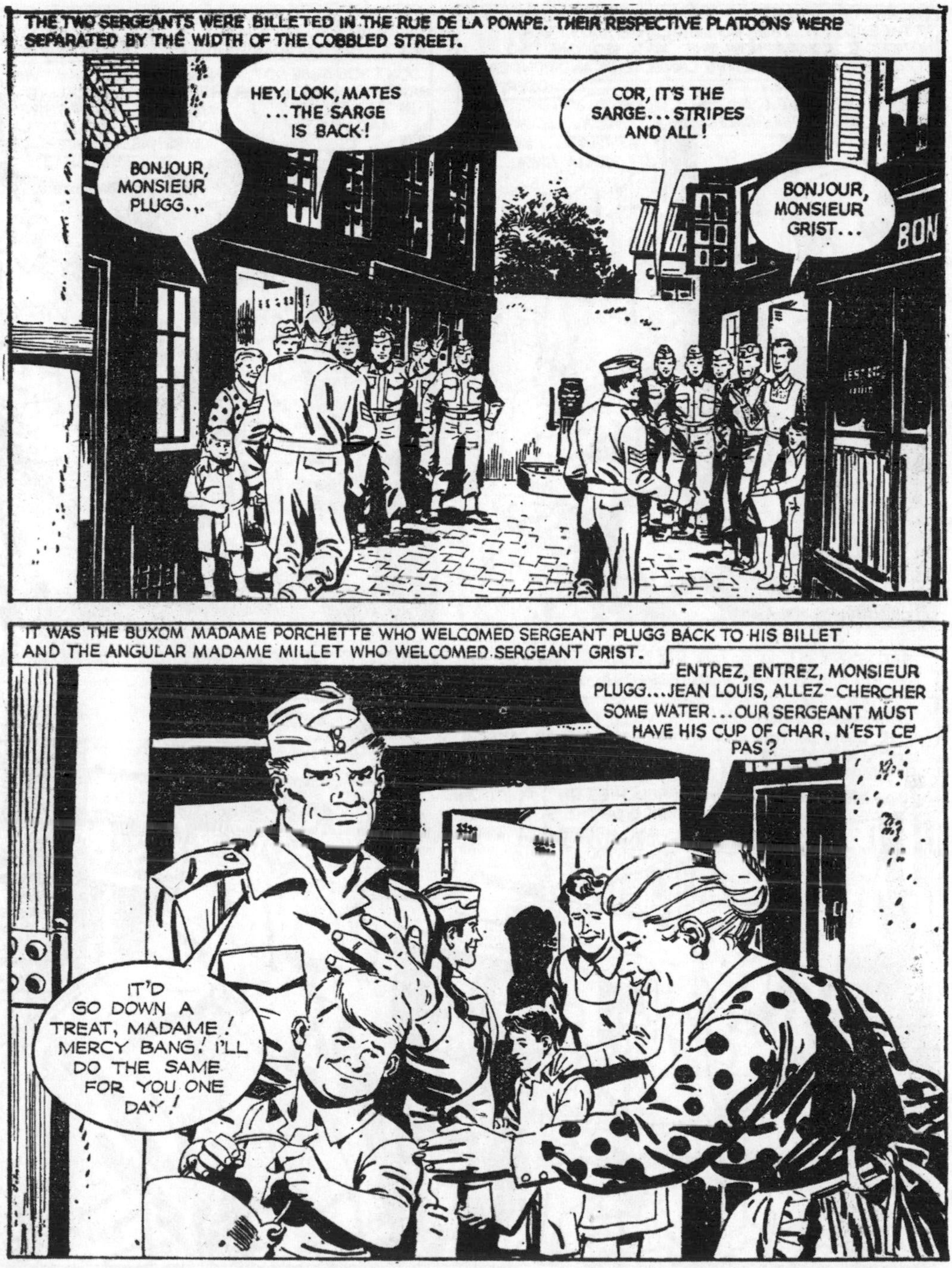
THE TWO SERGEANTS WERE BILLETED IN THE RUE DE LA POMPE. THEIR RESPECTIVE PLATOONS WERE SEPARATED BY THE WIDTH OF THE COBBLED STREET.
BONJOUR, MONSIEUR PLUGG...
HEY, LOOK, MATES ...THE SARGE IS BACK!
COR, IT'S THE SARGE...STRIPES AND ALL!
BONJOUR, MONSIEUR GRIST...
BON
IT WAS THE BUXOM MADAME PORCHETTE WHO WELCOMED SERGEANT PLUGG BACK TO HIS BILLET AND THE ANGULAR MADAME MILLET WHO WELCOMED SERGEANT GRIST.
ENTREZ, ENTREZ, MONSIEUR PLUGG...JEAN LOUIS, ALLEZ-CHERCHER SOME WATER...OUR SERGEANT MUST HAVE HIS CUP OF CHAR, N'EST CE PAS?
IT'D GO DOWN A TREAT, MADAME! MERCY BANG! I'LL DO THE SAME FOR YOU ONE DAY!

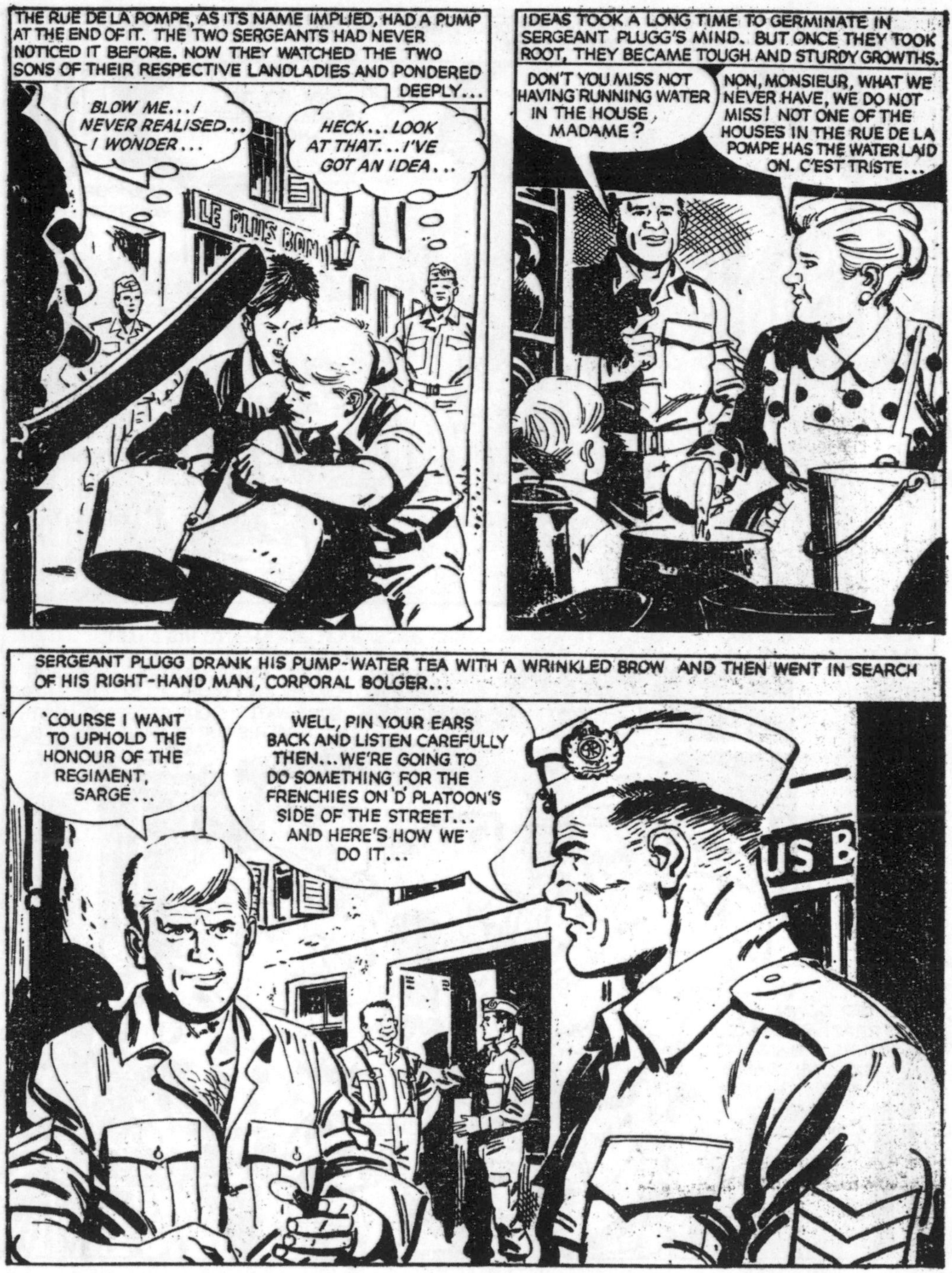
THE RUE DE LA POMPE, AS ITS NAME IMPLIED, HAD A PUMP AT THE END OF IT. THE TWO SERGEANTS HAD NEVER NOTICED IT BEFORE. NOW THEY WATCHED THE TWO SONS OF THEIR RESPECTIVE LANDLADIES AND PONDERED DEEPLY...
BLOW ME...! NEVER REALISED... I WONDER...
HECK... LOOK AT THAT... I'VE GOT AN IDEA...
LE PLUS BON
IDEAS TOOK A LONG TIME TO GERMINATE IN SERGEANT PLUGG'S MIND. BUT ONCE THEY TOOK ROOT, THEY BECAME TOUGH AND STURDY GROWTHS.
DON'T YOU MISS NOT HAVING RUNNING WATER IN THE HOUSE, MADAME?
NON, MONSIEUR, WHAT WE NEVER HAVE, WE DO NOT MISS! NOT ONE OF THE HOUSES IN THE RUE DE LA POMPE HAS THE WATER LAID ON. C'EST TRISTE...
SERGEANT PLUGG DRANK HIS PUMP-WATER TEA WITH A WRINKLED BROW AND THEN WENT IN SEARCH OF HIS RIGHT-HAND MAN, CORPORAL BOLGER...
'COURSE I WANT TO UPHOLD THE HONOUR OF THE REGIMENT, SARGE...
WELL, PIN YOUR EARS BACK AND LISTEN CAREFULLY THEN... WE'RE GOING TO DO SOMETHING FOR THE FRENCHIES ON 'D' PLATOON'S SIDE OF THE STREET... AND HERE'S HOW WE DO IT...
US B

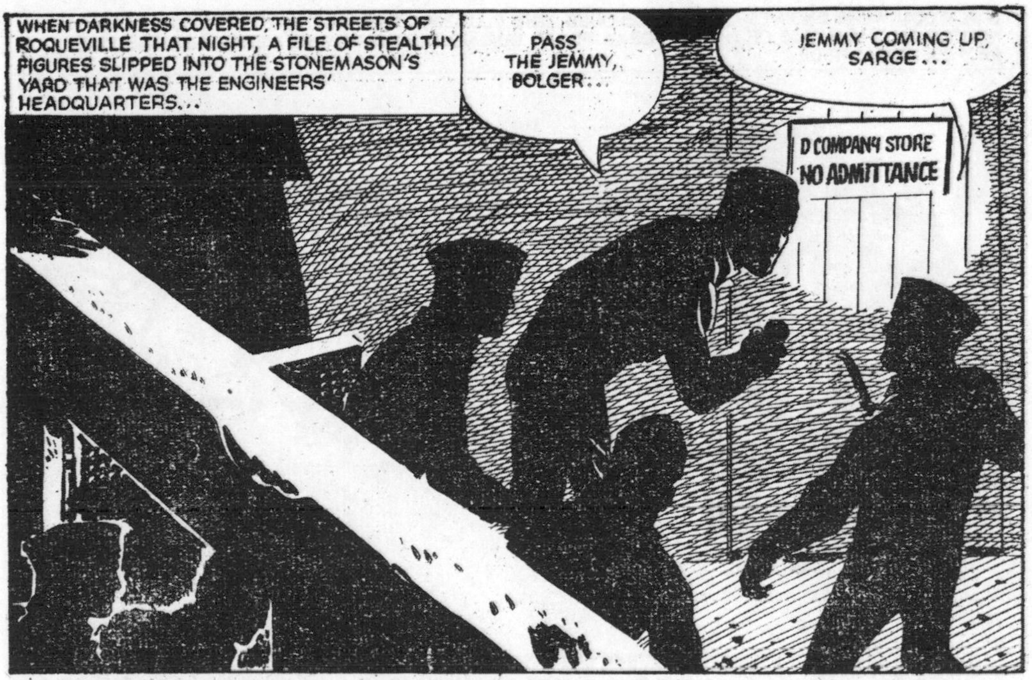
WHEN DARKNESS COVERED THE STREETS OF ROQUEVILLE THAT NIGHT, A FILE OF STEALTHY FIGURES SLIPPED INTO THE STONEMASON'S YARD THAT WAS THE ENGINEERS' HEADQUARTERS...
PASS THE JEMMY, BOLGER...
JEMMY COMING UP, SARGE...
D COMPANY STORE
NO ADMITTANCE

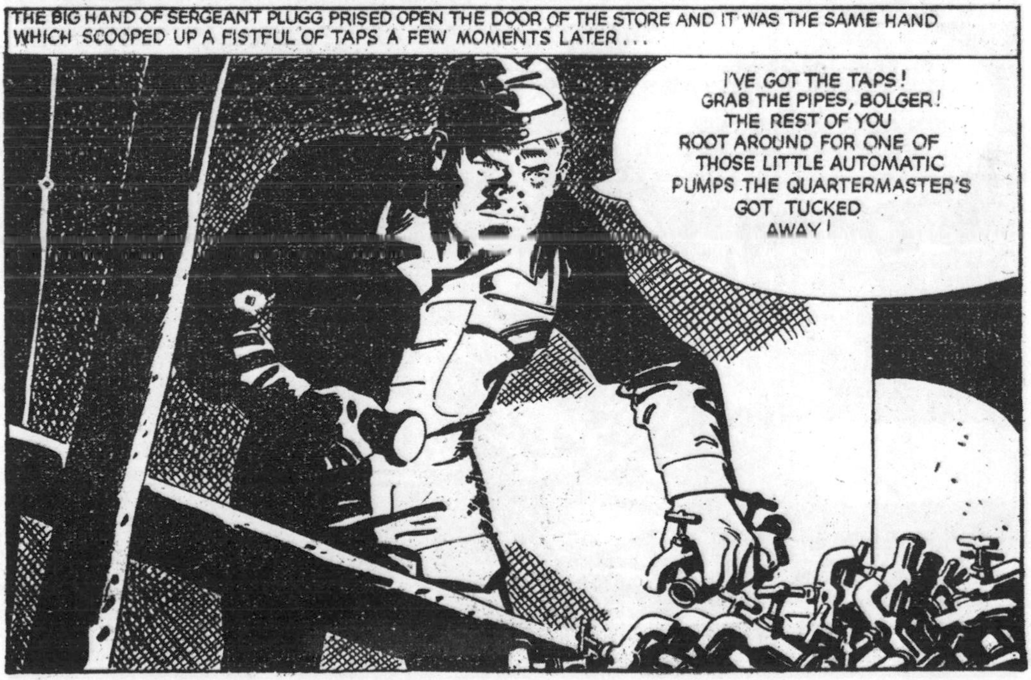
THE BIG HAND OF SERGEANT PLUGG PRISED OPEN THE DOOR OF THE STORE AND IT WAS THE SAME HAND WHICH SCOOPED UP A FISTFUL OF TAPS A FEW MOMENTS LATER...
I'VE GOT THE TAPS! GRAB THE PIPES, BOLGER! THE REST OF YOU ROOT AROUND FOR ONE OF THOSE LITTLE AUTOMATIC PUMPS THE QUARTERMASTER'S GOT TUCKED AWAY!

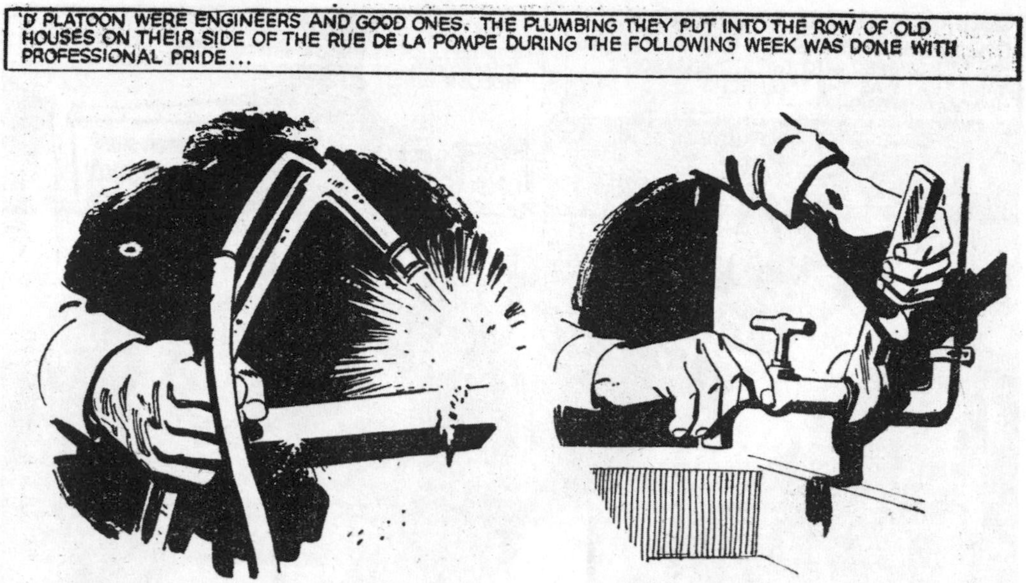
'D' PLATOON WERE ENGINEERS AND GOOD ONES. THE PLUMBING THEY PUT INTO THE ROW OF OLD HOUSES ON THEIR SIDE OF THE RUE DE LA POMPE DURING THE FOLLOWING WEEK WAS DONE WITH PROFESSIONAL PRIDE...

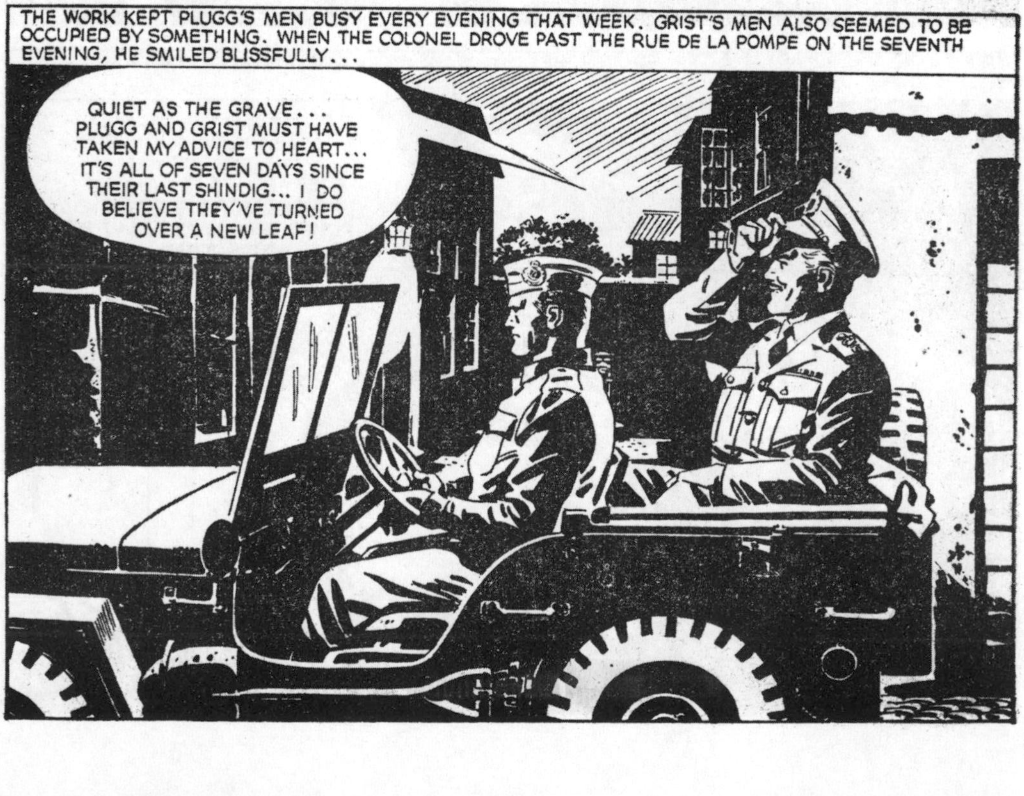
THE WORK KEPT PLUGG'S MEN BUSY EVERY EVENING THAT WEEK. GRIST'S MEN ALSO SEEMED TO BE OCCUPIED BY SOMETHING. WHEN THE COLONEL DROVE PAST THE RUE DE LA POMPE ON THE SEVENTH EVENING, HE SMILED BLISSFULLY...
QUIET AS THE GRAVE... PLUGG AND GRIST MUST HAVE TAKEN MY ADVICE TO HEART... IT'S ALL OF SEVEN DAYS SINCE THEIR LAST SHINDIG... I DO BELIEVE THEY'VE TURNED OVER A NEW LEAF!

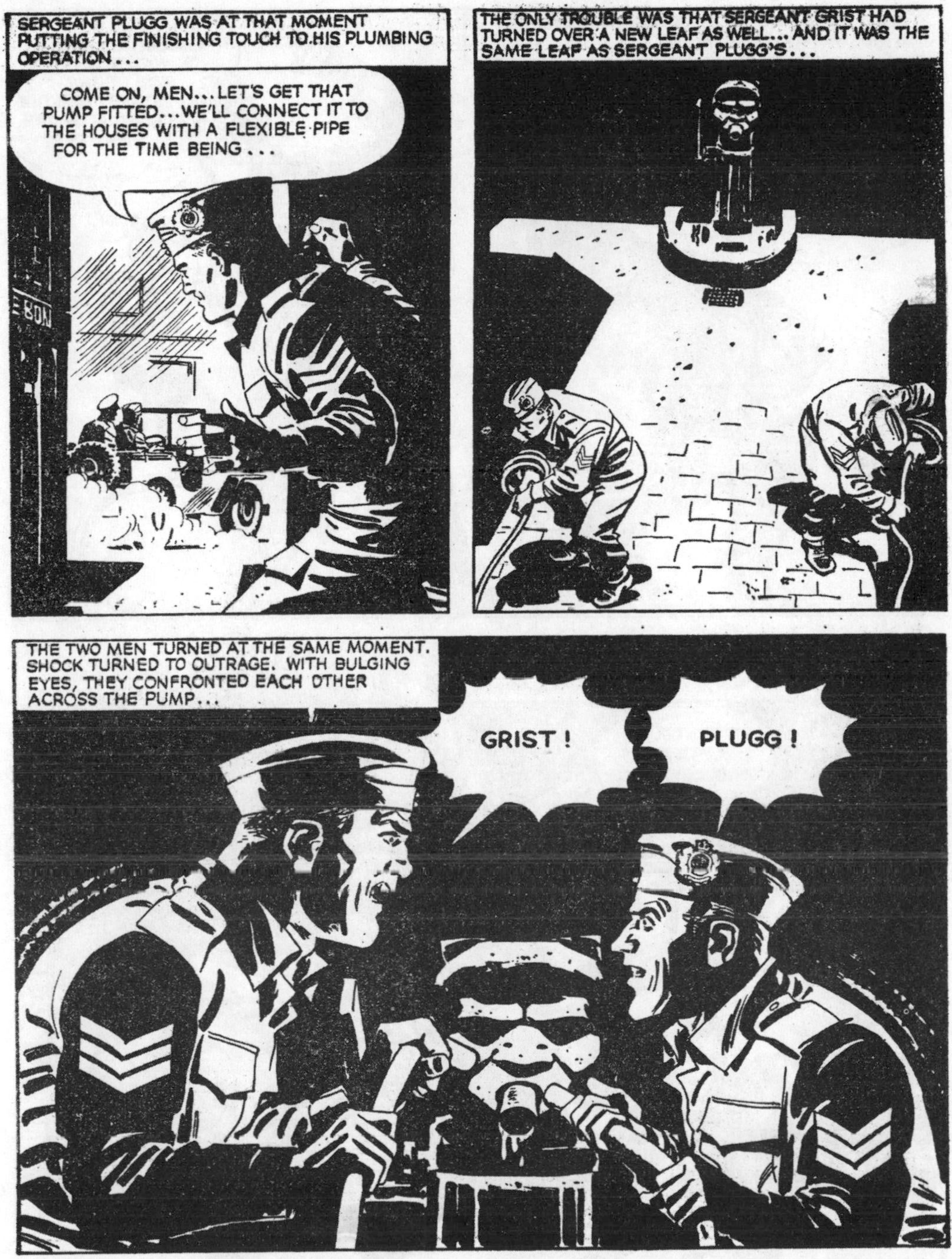
SERGEANT PLUGG WAS AT THAT MOMENT PUTTING THE FINISHING TOUCH TO HIS PLUMBING OPERATION...
COME ON, MEN...LET'S GET THAT PUMP FITTED...WE'LL CONNECT IT TO THE HOUSES WITH A FLEXIBLE PIPE FOR THE TIME BEING...
THE ONLY TROUBLE WAS THAT SERGEANT GRIST HAD TURNED OVER A NEW LEAF AS WELL... AND IT WAS THE SAME LEAF AS SERGEANT PLUGG'S...
THE TWO MEN TURNED AT THE SAME MOMENT. SHOCK TURNED TO OUTRAGE. WITH BULGING EYES, THEY CONFRONTED EACH OTHER ACROSS THE PUMP...
GRIST!
PLUGG!

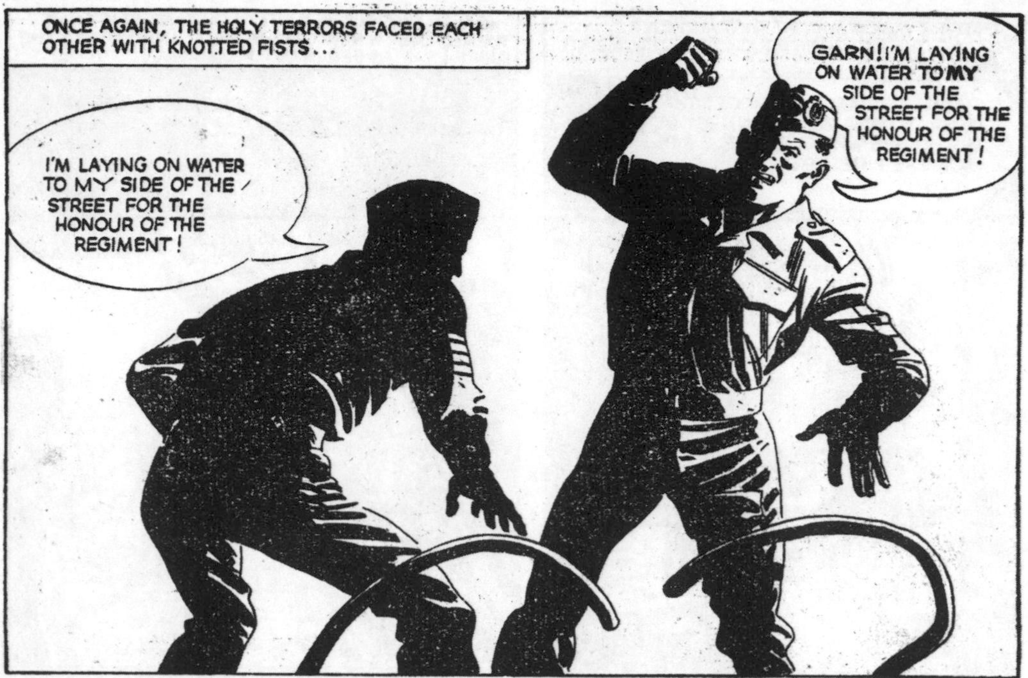
ONCE AGAIN, THE HOLY TERRORS FACED EACH OTHER WITH KNOTTED FISTS...
GARN! I'M LAYING ON WATER TO MY SIDE OF THE STREET FOR THE HONOUR OF THE REGIMENT!
I'M LAYING ON WATER TO MY SIDE OF THE STREET FOR THE HONOUR OF THE REGIMENT!

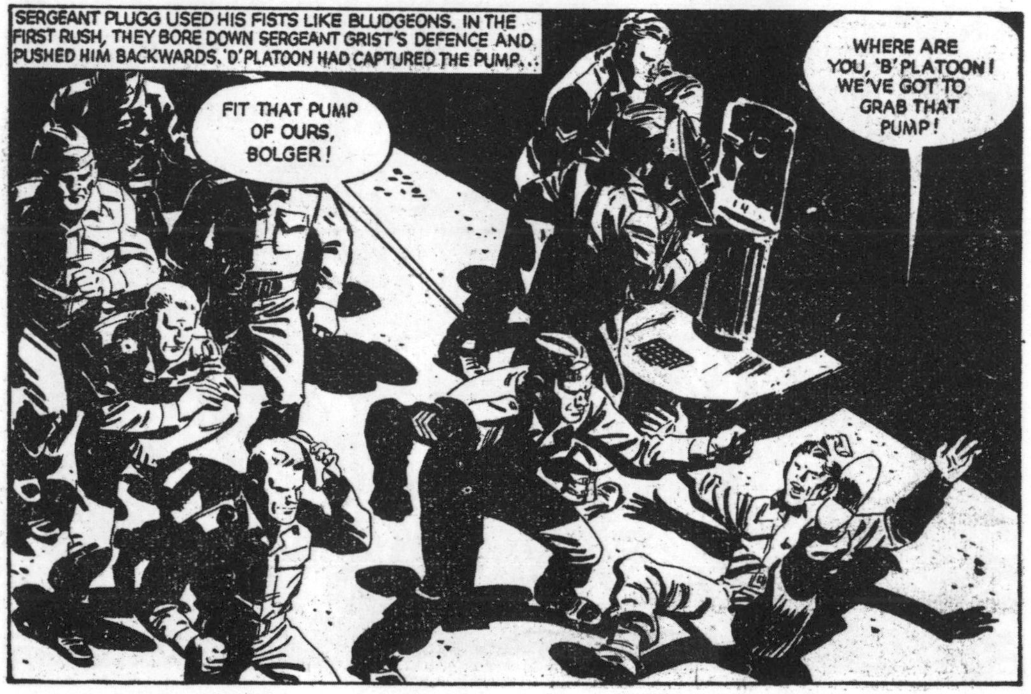
SERGEANT PLUGG USED HIS FISTS LIKE BLUDGEONS. IN THE FIRST RUSH, THEY BORE DOWN SERGEANT GRIST'S DEFENCE AND PUSHED HIM BACKWARDS. 'D' PLATOON HAD CAPTURED THE PUMP...
FIT THAT PUMP OF OURS, BOLGER!
WHERE ARE YOU, 'B' PLATOON! WE'VE GOT TO GRAB THAT PUMP!

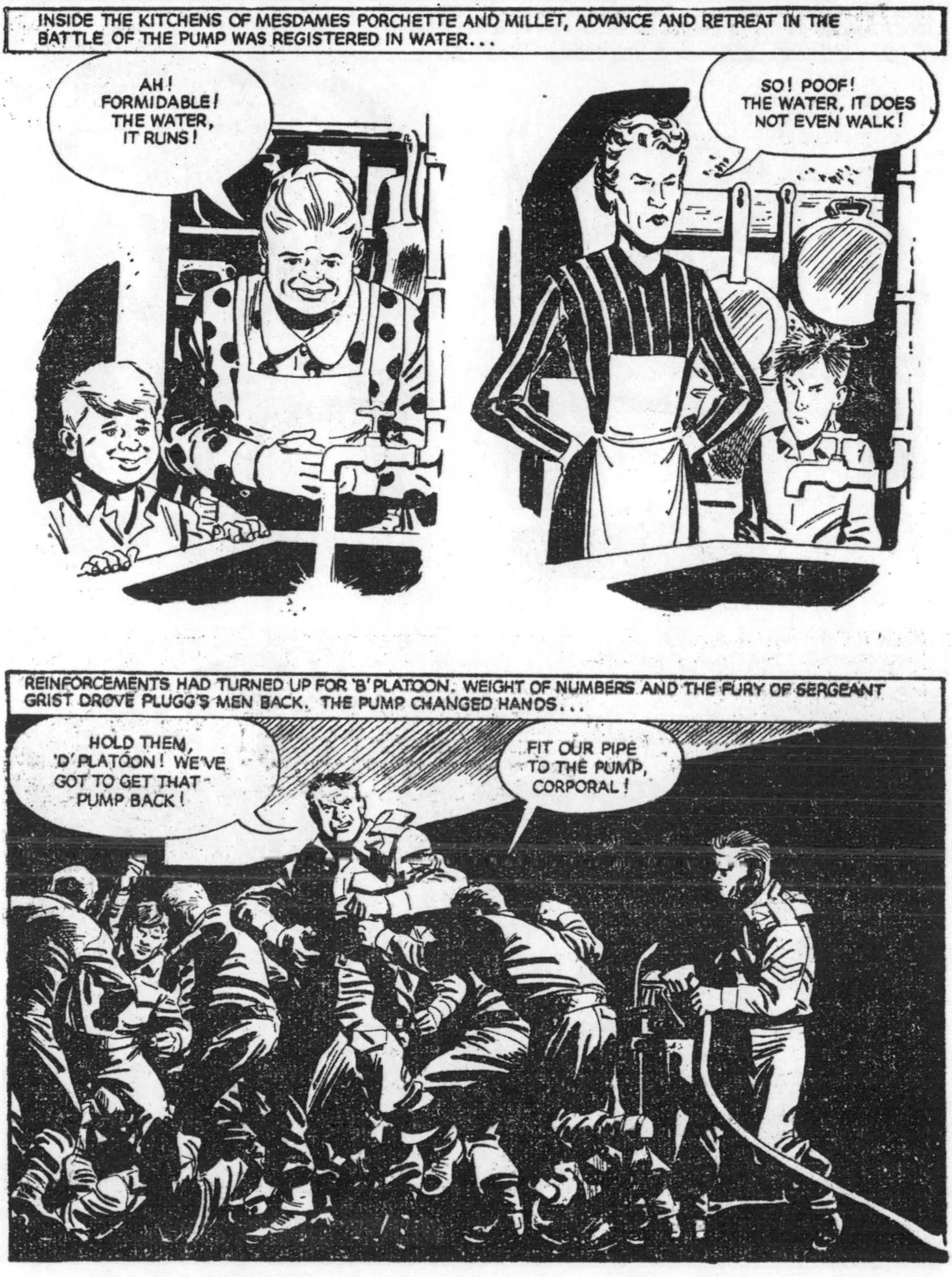
INSIDE THE KITCHENS OF MESDAMES PORCHETTE AND MILLET, ADVANCE AND RETREAT IN THE BATTLE OF THE PUMP WAS REGISTERED IN WATER...
AH! FORMIDABLE! THE WATER, IT RUNS!
SO! POOF! THE WATER, IT DOES NOT EVEN WALK!
REINFORCEMENTS HAD TURNED UP FOR 'B' PLATOON. WEIGHT OF NUMBERS AND THE FURY OF SERGEANT GRIST DROVE PLUGG'S MEN BACK. THE PUMP CHANGED HANDS...
HOLD THEM, 'D' PLATOON! WE'VE GOT TO GET THAT PUMP BACK!
FIT OUR PIPE TO THE PUMP, CORPORAL!

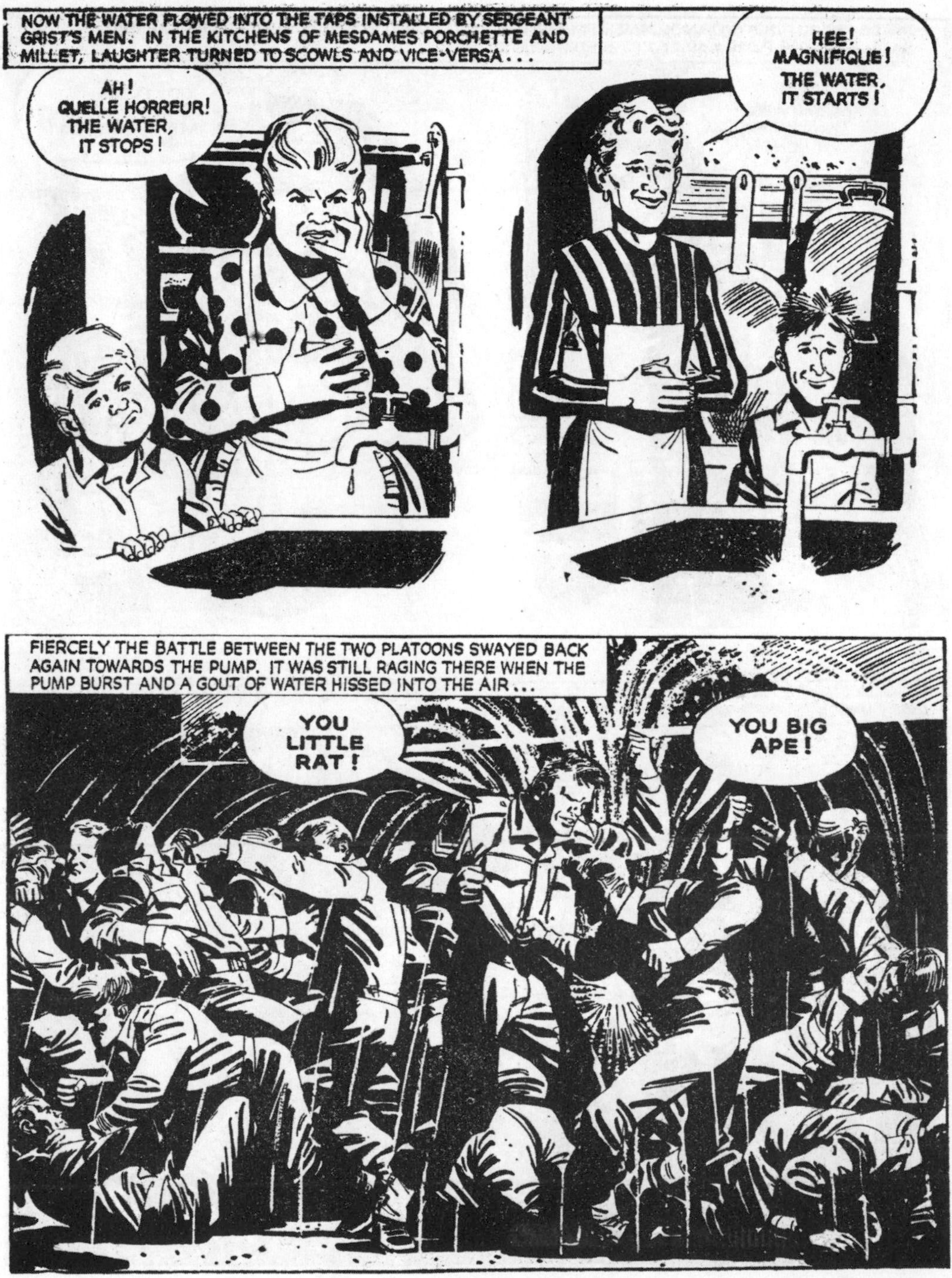
NOW THE WATER FLOWED INTO THE TAPS INSTALLED BY SERGEANT GRIST'S MEN. IN THE KITCHENS OF MESDAMES PORCHETTE AND MILLET, LAUGHTER TURNED TO SCOWLS AND VICE-VERSA...
AH! QUELLE HORREUR! THE WATER, IT STOPS!
HEE! MAGNIFIQUE! THE WATER, IT STARTS!
FIERCELY THE BATTLE BETWEEN THE TWO PLATOONS SWAYED BACK AGAIN TOWARDS THE PUMP. IT WAS STILL RAGING THERE WHEN THE PUMP BURST AND A GOUT OF WATER HISSED INTO THE AIR...
YOU LITTLE RAT!
YOU BIG APE!

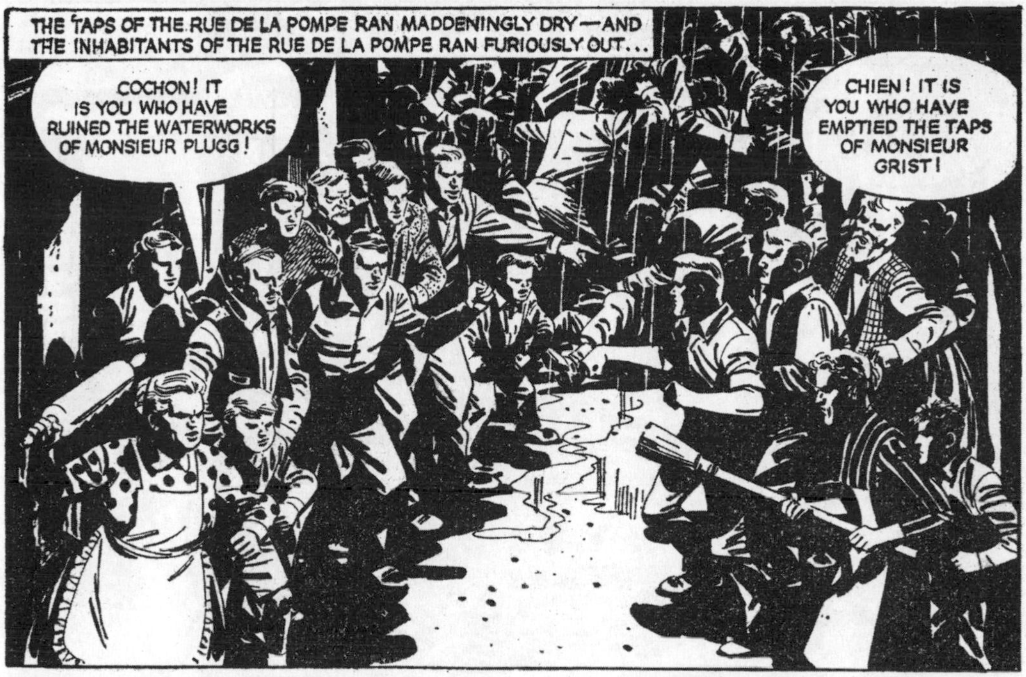
THE TAPS OF THE RUE DE LA POMPE RAN MADDENINGLY DRY—AND THE INHABITANTS OF THE RUE DE LA POMPE RAN FURIOUSLY OUT...
COCHON! IT IS YOU WHO HAVE RUINED THE WATERWORKS OF MONSIEUR PLUGG!
CHIEN! IT IS YOU WHO HAVE EMPTIED THE TAPS OF MONSIEUR GRIST!

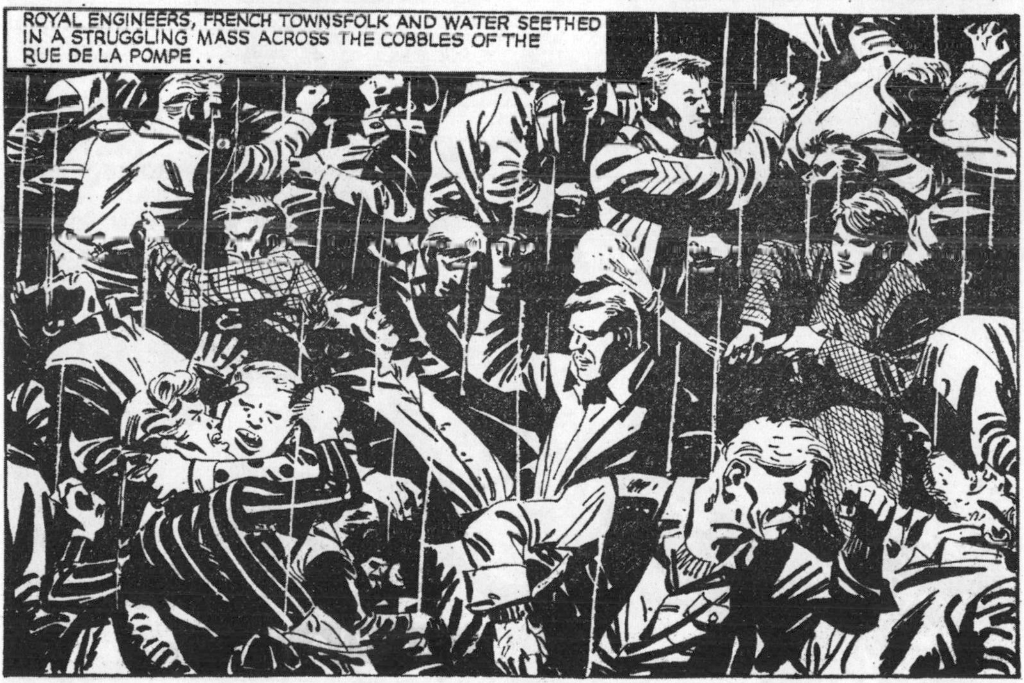
ROYAL ENGINEERS, FRENCH TOWNSFOLK AND WATER SEETHED IN A STRUGGLING MASS ACROSS THE COBBLES OF THE RUE DE LA POMPE...

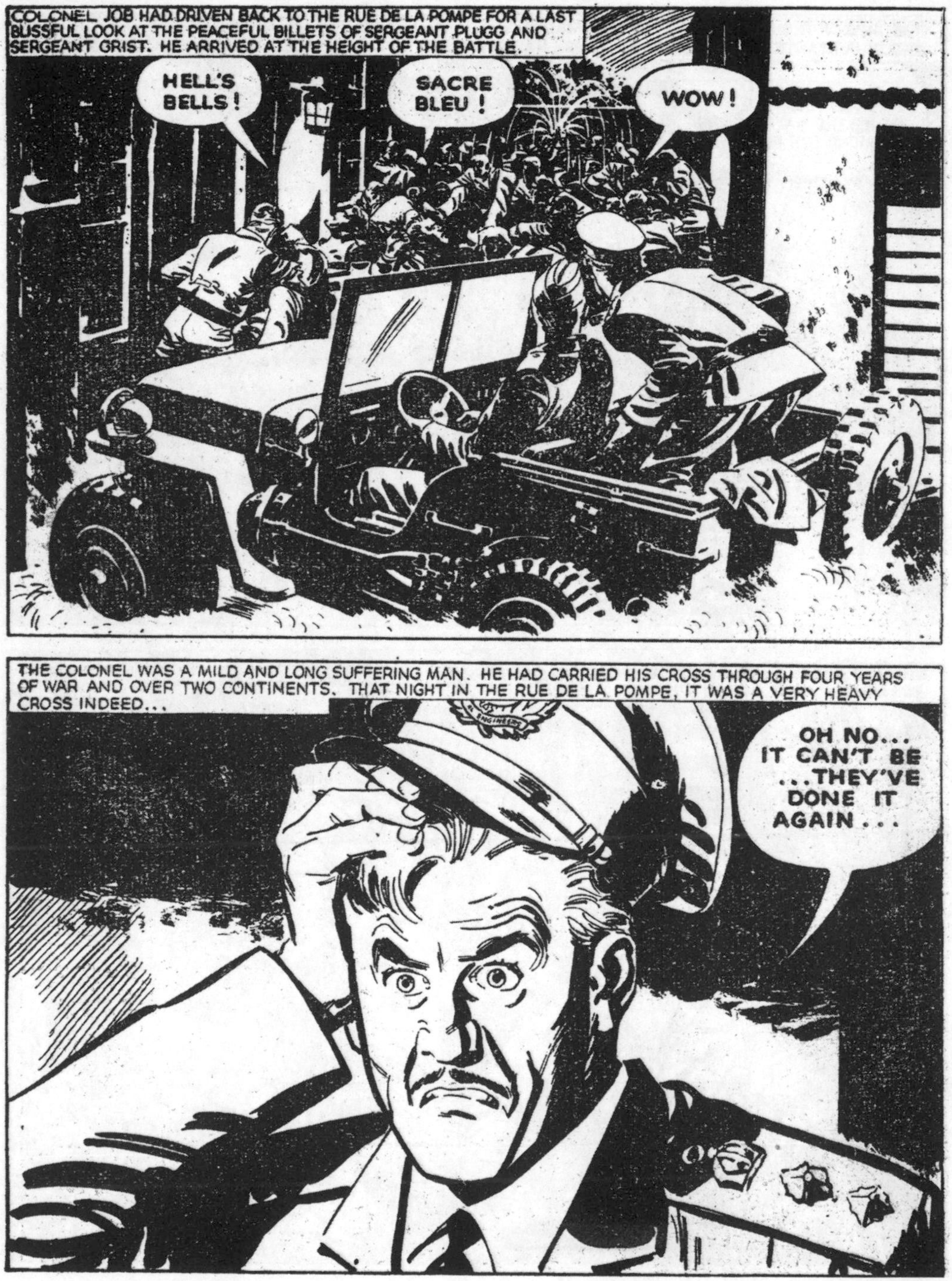
COLONEL JOB HAD DRIVEN BACK TO THE RUE DE LA POMPE FOR A LAST BLISSFUL LOOK AT THE PEACEFUL BILLETS OF SERGEANT PLUGG AND SERGEANT GRIST. HE ARRIVED AT THE HEIGHT OF THE BATTLE.
HELL'S BELLS!
SACRE BLEU!
WOW!
THE COLONEL WAS A MILD AND LONG SUFFERING MAN. HE HAD CARRIED HIS CROSS THROUGH FOUR YEARS OF WAR AND OVER TWO CONTINENTS. THAT NIGHT IN THE RUE DE LA POMPE, IT WAS A VERY HEAVY CROSS INDEED...
OH NO... IT CAN'T BE ...THEY'VE DONE IT AGAIN...

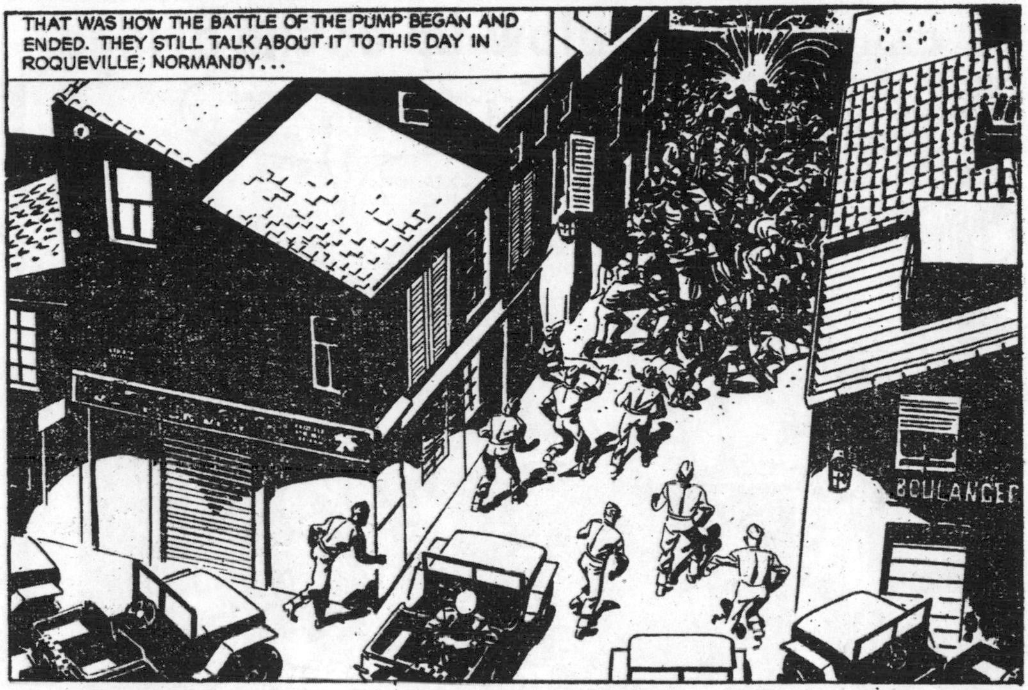
THAT WAS HOW THE BATTLE OF THE PUMP BEGAN AND ENDED. THEY STILL TALK ABOUT IT TO THIS DAY IN ROQUEVILLE; NORMANDY...
BOULANGER

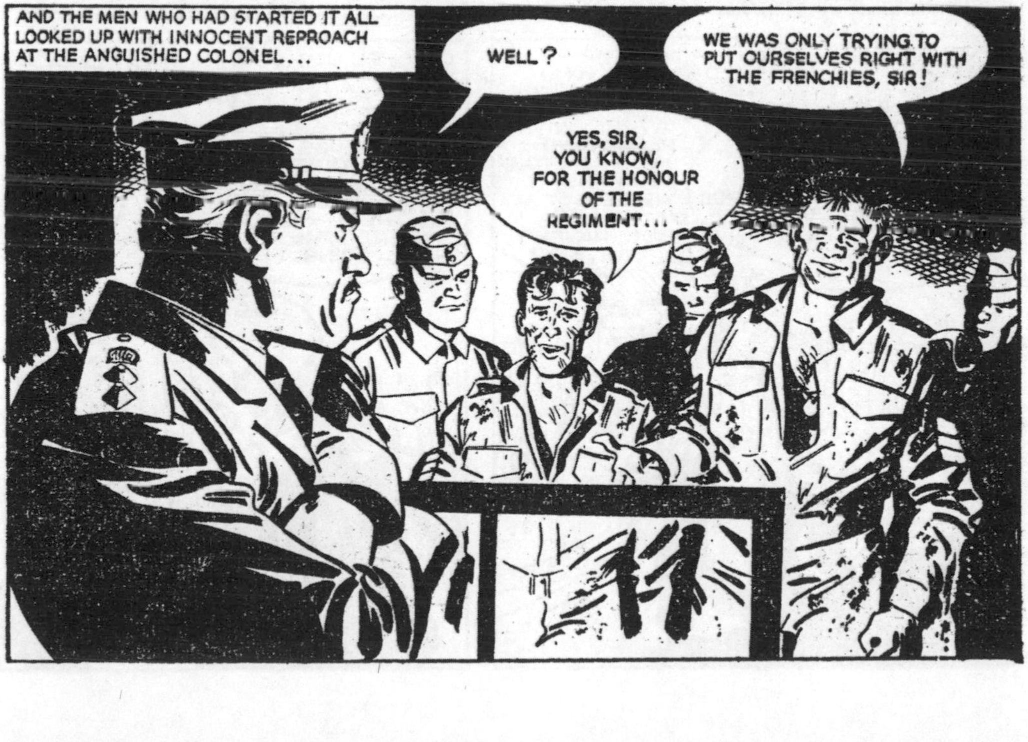
AND THE MEN WHO HAD STARTED IT ALL LOOKED UP WITH INNOCENT REPROACH AT THE ANGUISHED COLONEL...
WELL?
WE WAS ONLY TRYING TO PUT OURSELVES RIGHT WITH THE FRENCHIES, SIR!
YES, SIR, YOU KNOW, FOR THE HONOUR OF THE REGIMENT...

Chapter 3. Blow Up at the Bridge

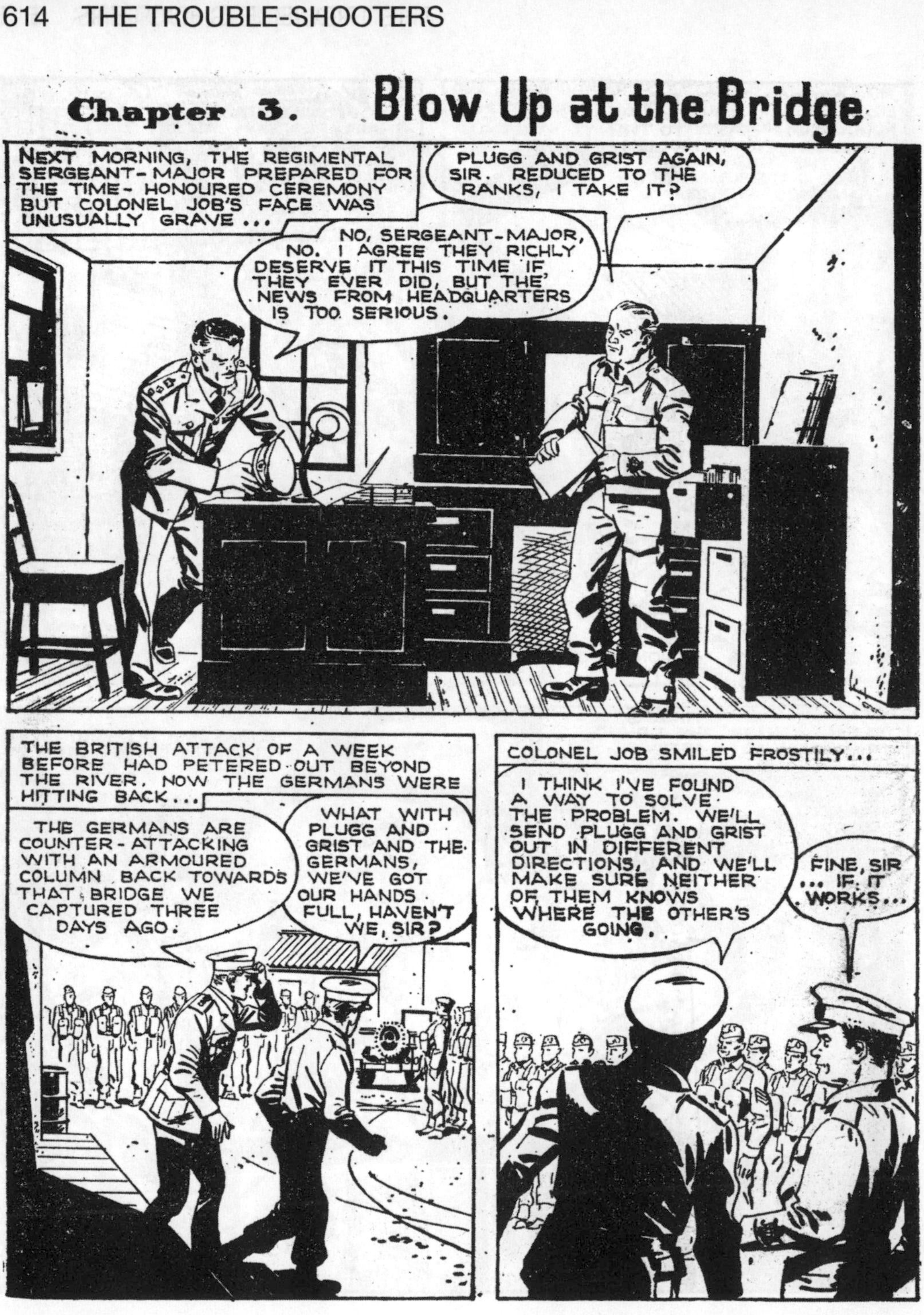
NEXT MORNING, THE REGIMENTAL SERGEANT-MAJOR PREPARED FOR THE TIME-HONOURED CEREMONY BUT COLONEL JOB'S FACE WAS UNUSUALLY GRAVE...
PLUGG AND GRIST AGAIN, SIR. REDUCED TO THE RANKS, I TAKE IT?
NO, SERGEANT-MAJOR, NO. I AGREE THEY RICHLY DESERVE IT THIS TIME IF THEY EVER DID, BUT THE NEWS FROM HEADQUARTERS IS TOO SERIOUS.
THE BRITISH ATTACK OF A WEEK BEFORE HAD PETERED OUT BEYOND THE RIVER. NOW THE GERMANS WERE HITTING BACK...
THE GERMANS ARE COUNTER-ATTACKING WITH AN ARMOURED COLUMN BACK TOWARDS THAT BRIDGE WE CAPTURED THREE DAYS AGO.
WHAT WITH PLUGG AND GRIST AND THE GERMANS, WE'VE GOT OUR HANDS FULL, HAVEN'T WE, SIR?
COLONEL JOB SMILED FROSTILY...
I THINK I'VE FOUND A WAY TO SOLVE THE PROBLEM. WE'LL SEND PLUGG AND GRIST OUT IN DIFFERENT DIRECTIONS, AND WE'LL MAKE SURE NEITHER OF THEM KNOWS WHERE THE OTHER'S GOING.
FINE, SIR ... IF IT WORKS...

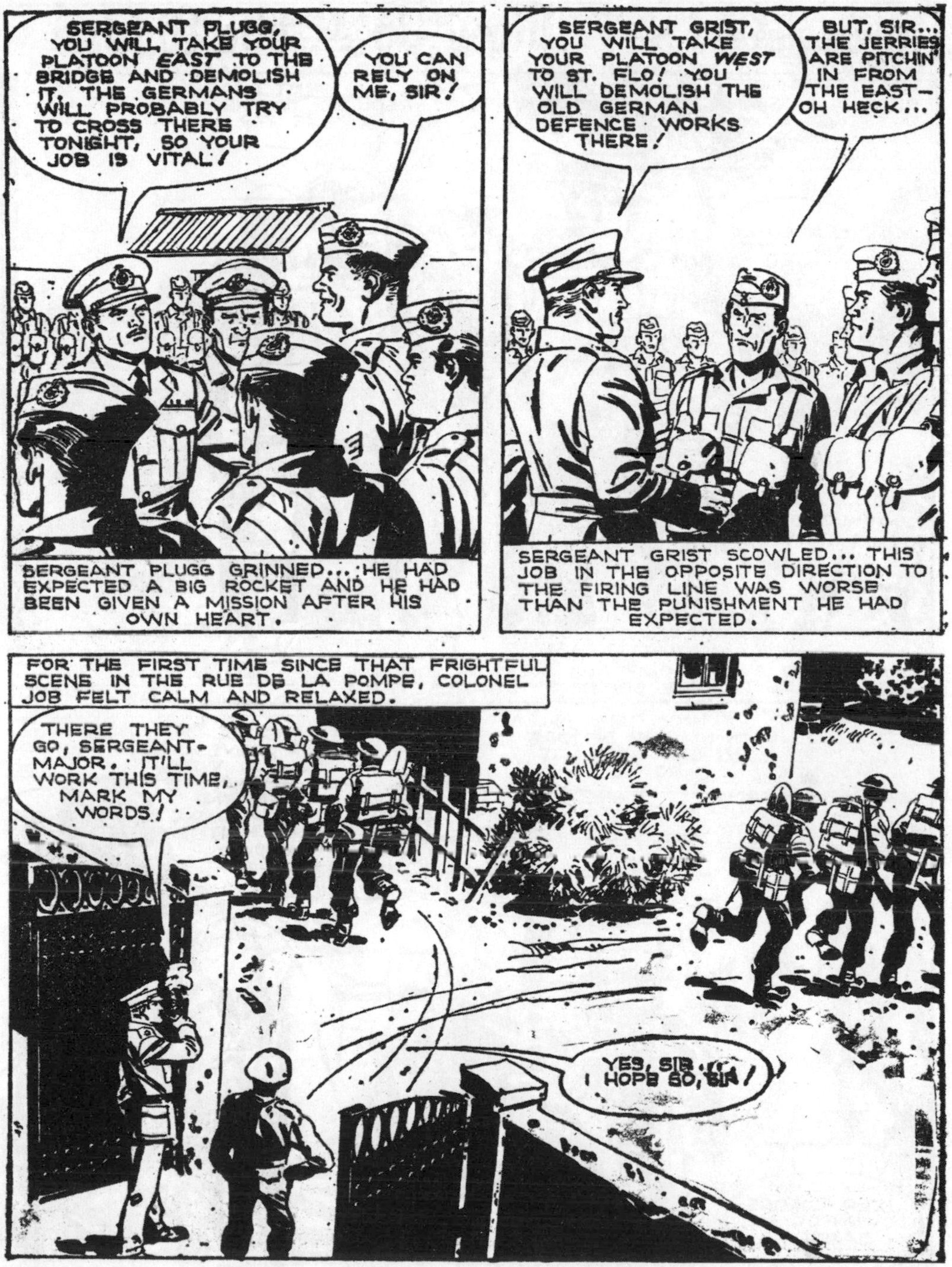
SERGEANT PLUGG, YOU WILL TAKE YOUR PLATOON *EAST* TO THE BRIDGE AND DEMOLISH IT. THE GERMANS WILL PROBABLY TRY TO CROSS THERE TONIGHT, SO YOUR JOB IS VITAL!
YOU CAN RELY ON ME, SIR!
SERGEANT PLUGG GRINNED... HE HAD EXPECTED A BIG ROCKET AND HE HAD BEEN GIVEN A MISSION AFTER HIS OWN HEART.
SERGEANT GRIST, YOU WILL TAKE YOUR PLATOON *WEST* TO ST. FLO! YOU WILL DEMOLISH THE OLD GERMAN DEFENCE WORKS THERE!
BUT, SIR... THE JERRIES ARE PITCHIN' IN FROM THE EAST— OH HECK...
SERGEANT GRIST SCOWLED... THIS JOB IN THE OPPOSITE DIRECTION TO THE FIRING LINE WAS WORSE THAN THE PUNISHMENT HE HAD EXPECTED.
FOR THE FIRST TIME SINCE THAT FRIGHTFUL SCENE IN THE RUE DE LA POMPE, COLONEL JOB FELT CALM AND RELAXED.
THERE THEY GO, SERGEANT-MAJOR. IT'LL WORK THIS TIME, MARK MY WORDS!
YES, SIR... I HOPE SO, SIR!

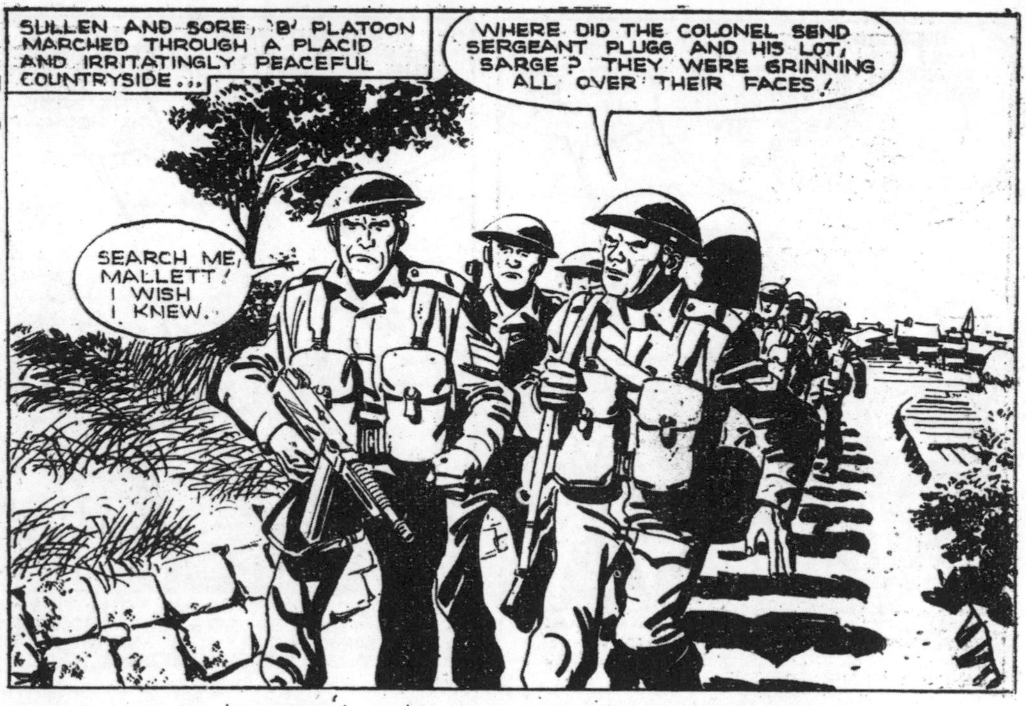
SULLEN AND SORE, 'B' PLATOON MARCHED THROUGH A PLACID AND IRRITATINGLY PEACEFUL COUNTRYSIDE...
WHERE DID THE COLONEL SEND SERGEANT PLUGG AND HIS LOT, SARGE? THEY WERE GRINNING ALL OVER THEIR FACES!
SEARCH ME, MALLETT! I WISH I KNEW.

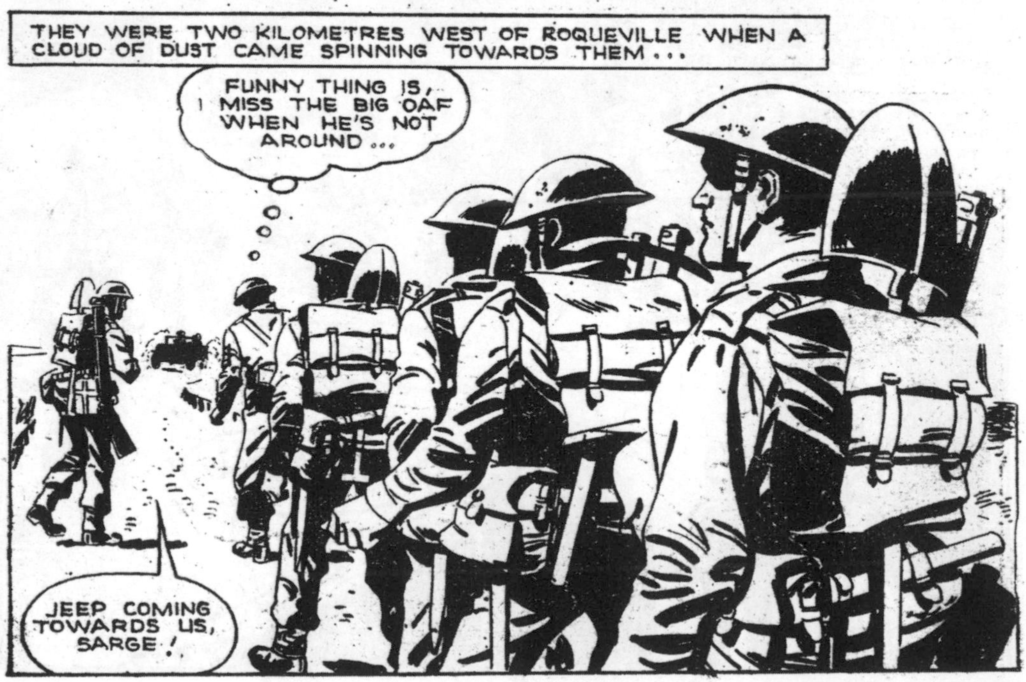
THEY WERE TWO KILOMETRES WEST OF ROQUEVILLE WHEN A CLOUD OF DUST CAME SPINNING TOWARDS THEM...
FUNNY THING IS, I MISS THE BIG OAF WHEN HE'S NOT AROUND...
JEEP COMING TOWARDS US, SARGE!

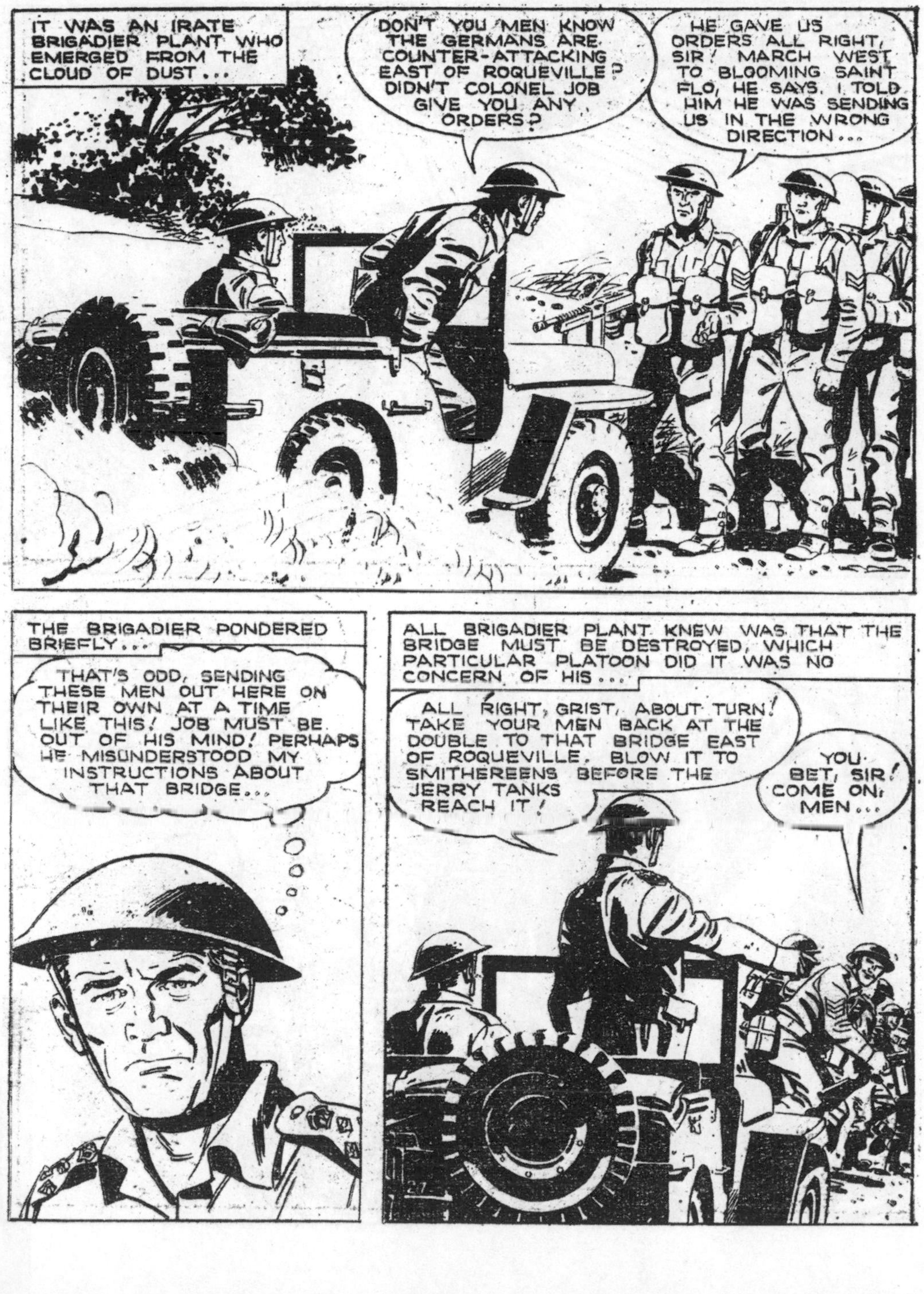
IT WAS AN IRATE BRIGADIER PLANT WHO EMERGED FROM THE CLOUD OF DUST...
DON'T YOU MEN KNOW THE GERMANS ARE COUNTER-ATTACKING EAST OF ROQUEVILLE? DIDN'T COLONEL JOB GIVE YOU ANY ORDERS?
HE GAVE US ORDERS ALL RIGHT, SIR! MARCH WEST TO BLOOMING SAINT FLO, HE SAYS. I TOLD HIM HE WAS SENDING US IN THE WRONG DIRECTION...
THE BRIGADIER PONDERED BRIEFLY...
THAT'S ODD, SENDING THESE MEN OUT HERE ON THEIR OWN AT A TIME LIKE THIS! JOB MUST BE OUT OF HIS MIND! PERHAPS HE MISUNDERSTOOD MY INSTRUCTIONS ABOUT THAT BRIDGE...
ALL BRIGADIER PLANT KNEW WAS THAT THE BRIDGE MUST BE DESTROYED, WHICH PARTICULAR PLATOON DID IT WAS NO CONCERN OF HIS...
ALL RIGHT, GRIST, ABOUT TURN! TAKE YOUR MEN BACK AT THE DOUBLE TO THAT BRIDGE EAST OF ROQUEVILLE. BLOW IT TO SMITHEREENS BEFORE THE JERRY TANKS REACH IT!
YOU BET, SIR! COME ON, MEN...

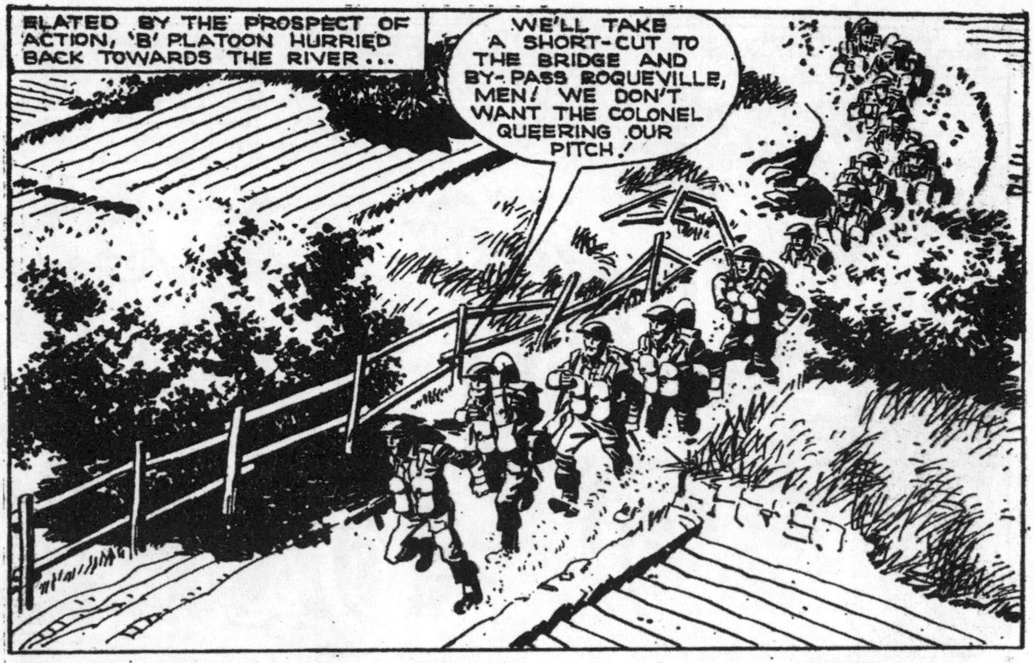
ELATED BY THE PROSPECT OF ACTION, 'B' PLATOON HURRIED BACK TOWARDS THE RIVER ...
WE'LL TAKE A SHORT-CUT TO THE BRIDGE AND BY-PASS ROQUEVILLE, MEN! WE DON'T WANT THE COLONEL QUEERING OUR PITCH!

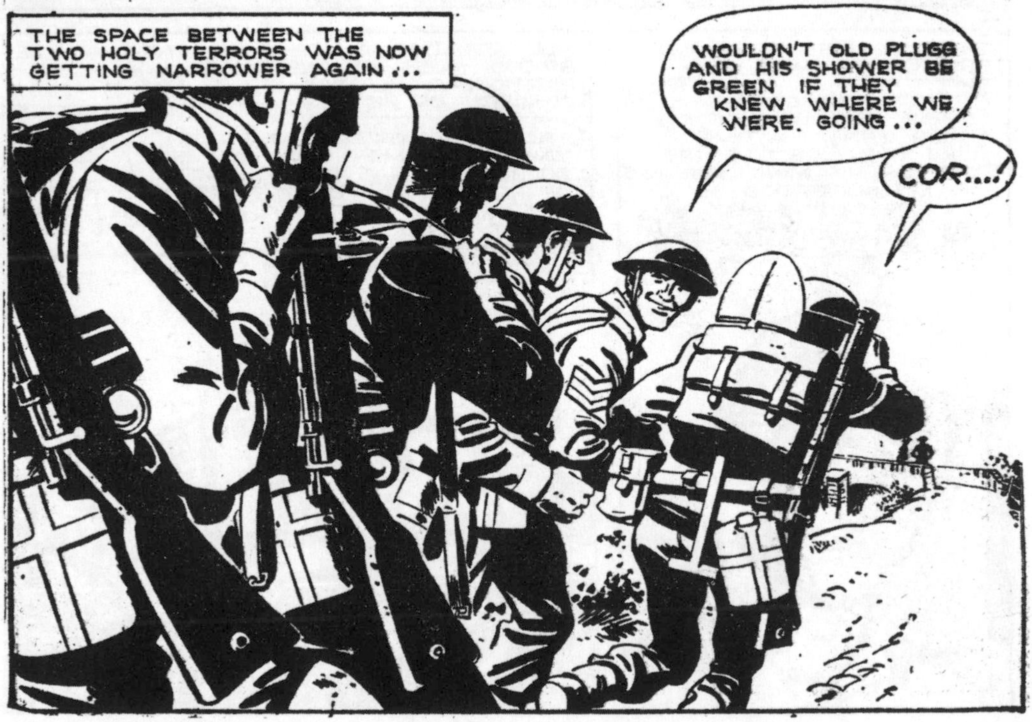
THE SPACE BETWEEN THE TWO HOLY TERRORS WAS NOW GETTING NARROWER AGAIN ...
WOULDN'T OLD PLUGG AND HIS SHOWER BE GREEN IF THEY KNEW WHERE WE WERE GOING ...
COR...!

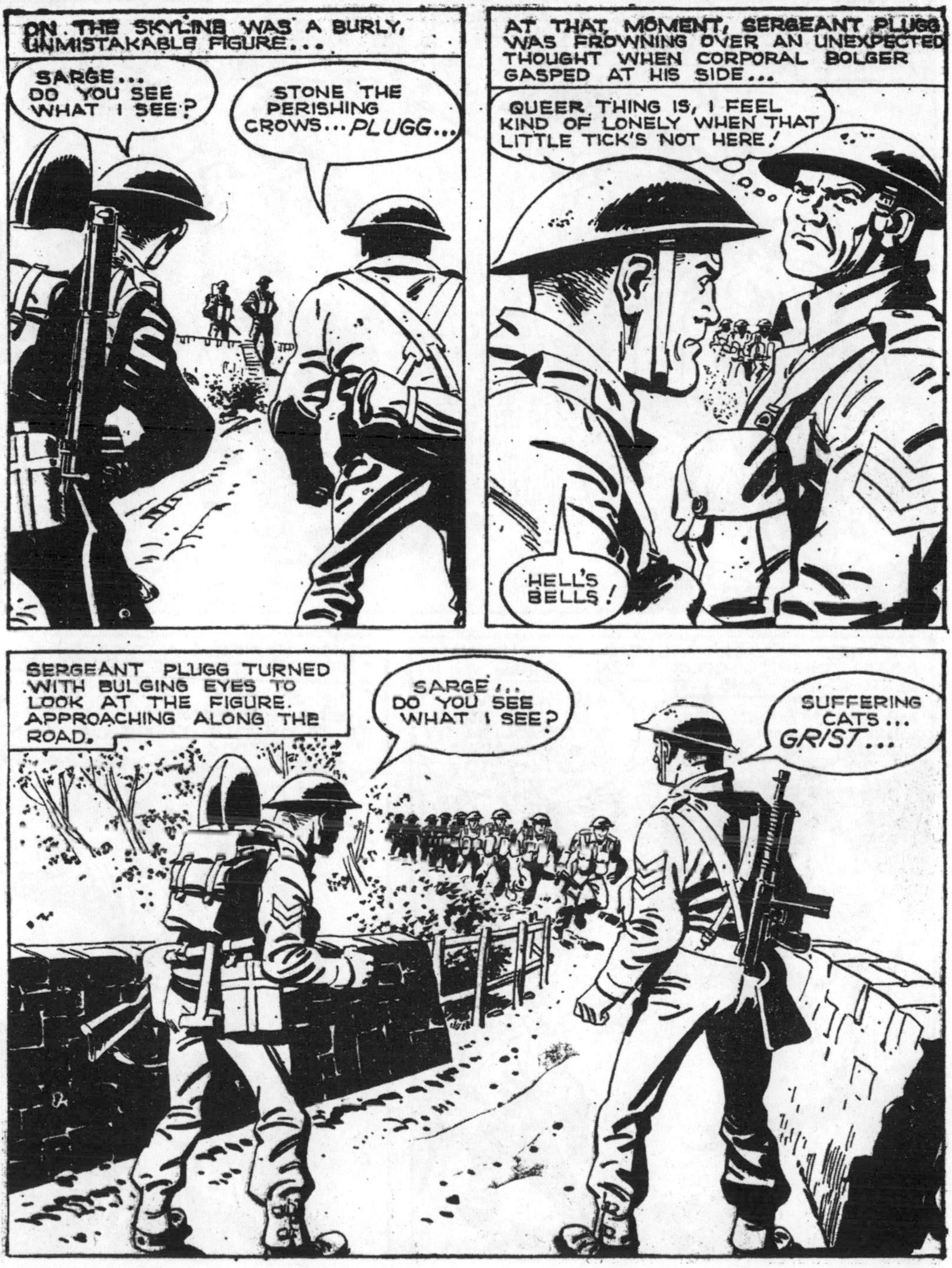
ON THE SKYLINE WAS A BURLY, UNMISTAKABLE FIGURE...
SARGE... DO YOU SEE WHAT I SEE?
STONE THE PERISHING CROWS... PLUGG...
AT THAT MOMENT, SERGEANT PLUGG WAS FROWNING OVER AN UNEXPECTED THOUGHT WHEN CORPORAL BOLGER GASPED AT HIS SIDE...
QUEER THING IS, I FEEL KIND OF LONELY WHEN THAT LITTLE TICK'S NOT HERE!
HELL'S BELLS!
SERGEANT PLUGG TURNED WITH BULGING EYES TO LOOK AT THE FIGURE. APPROACHING ALONG THE ROAD.
SARGE... DO YOU SEE WHAT I SEE?
SUFFERING CATS... GRIST...

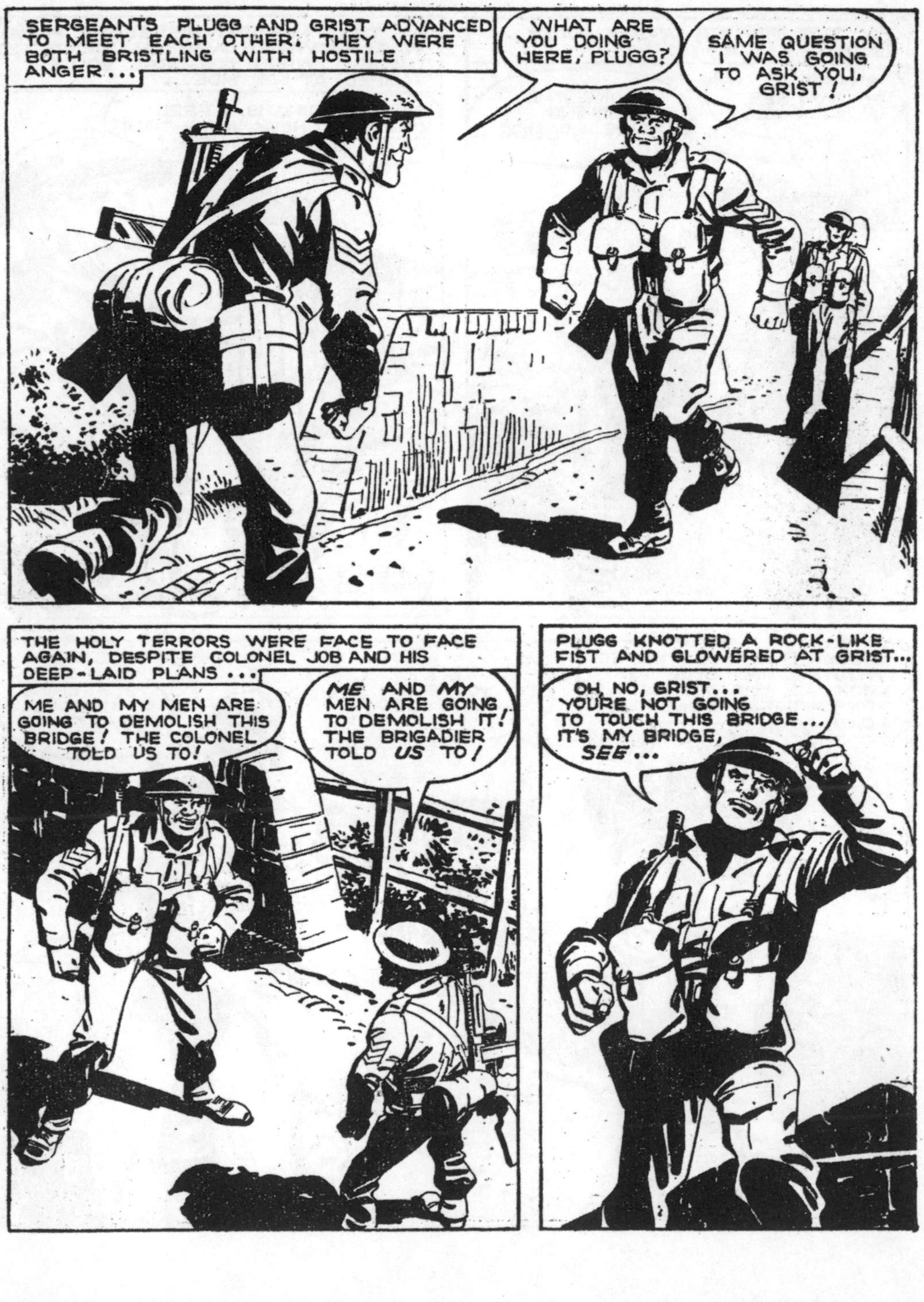
SERGEANTS PLUGG AND GRIST ADVANCED TO MEET EACH OTHER. THEY WERE BOTH BRISTLING WITH HOSTILE ANGER...
WHAT ARE YOU DOING HERE, PLUGG?
SAME QUESTION I WAS GOING TO ASK YOU, GRIST!
THE HOLY TERRORS WERE FACE TO FACE AGAIN, DESPITE COLONEL JOB AND HIS DEEP-LAID PLANS...
ME AND MY MEN ARE GOING TO DEMOLISH THIS BRIDGE! THE COLONEL TOLD US TO!
ME AND MY MEN ARE GOING TO DEMOLISH IT! THE BRIGADIER TOLD US TO!
PLUGG KNOTTED A ROCK-LIKE FIST AND GLOWERED AT GRIST...
OH, NO, GRIST... YOU'RE NOT GOING TO TOUCH THIS BRIDGE... IT'S MY BRIDGE, SEE...

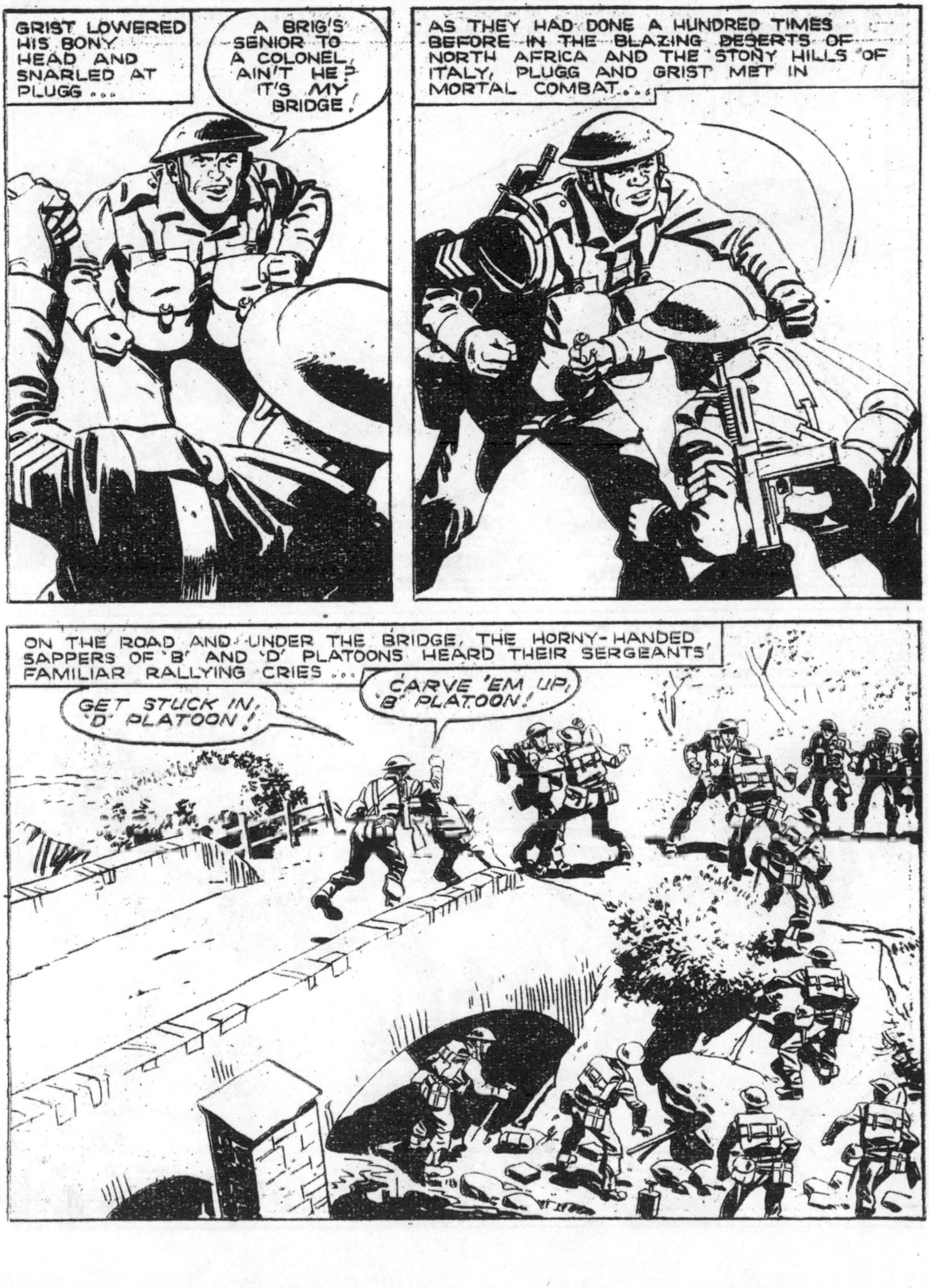
GRIST LOWERED HIS BONY HEAD AND SNARLED AT PLUGG ...
A BRIG'S SENIOR TO A COLONEL, AIN'T HE? IT'S MY BRIDGE!
AS THEY HAD DONE A HUNDRED TIMES BEFORE IN THE BLAZING DESERTS OF NORTH AFRICA AND THE STONY HILLS OF ITALY, PLUGG AND GRIST MET IN MORTAL COMBAT...
ON THE ROAD AND UNDER THE BRIDGE, THE HORNY-HANDED SAPPERS OF 'B' AND 'D' PLATOONS HEARD THEIR SERGEANTS' FAMILIAR RALLYING CRIES ...
GET STUCK IN, 'D' PLATOON!
CARVE 'EM UP, 'B' PLATOON!

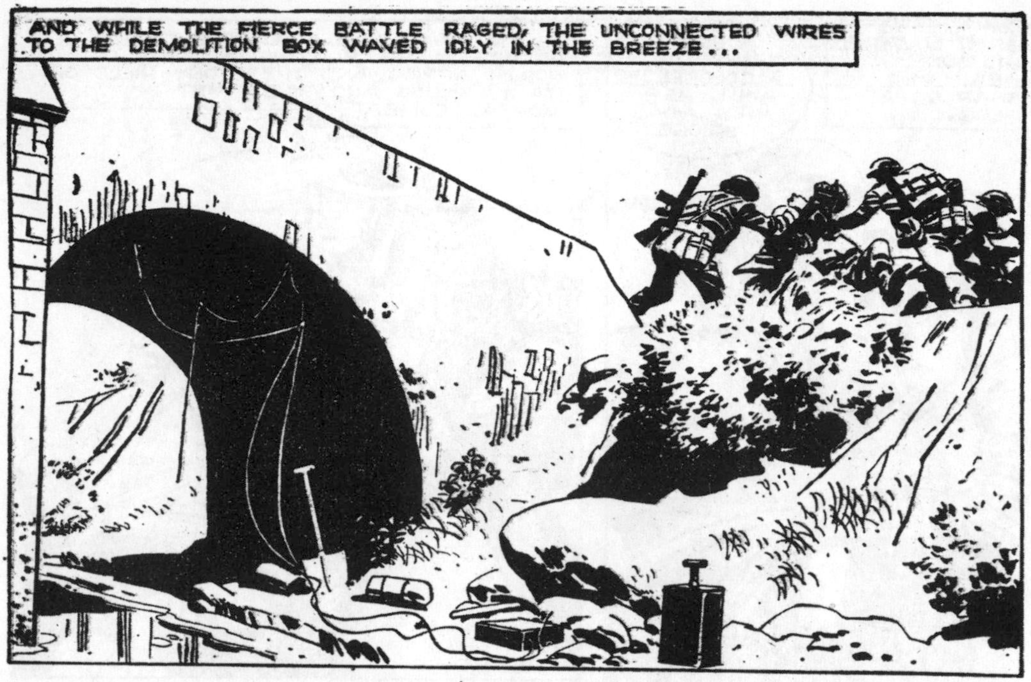
AND WHILE THE FIERCE BATTLE RAGED, THE UNCONNECTED WIRES TO THE DEMOLITION BOX WAVED IDLY IN THE BREEZE...

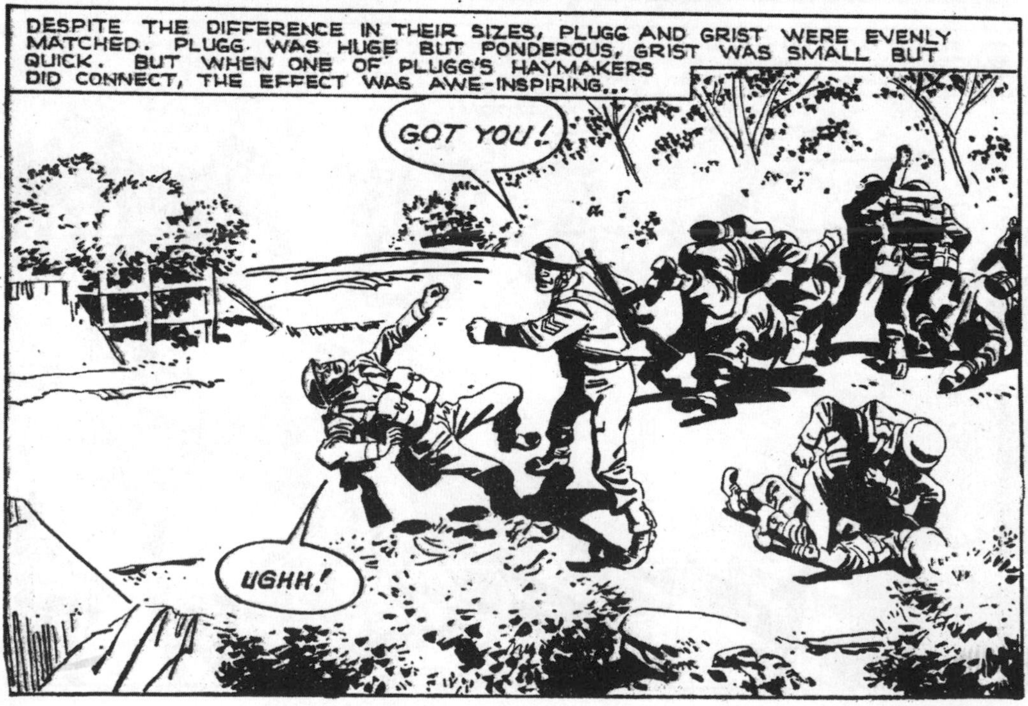
DESPITE THE DIFFERENCE IN THEIR SIZES, PLUGG AND GRIST WERE EVENLY MATCHED. PLUGG WAS HUGE BUT PONDEROUS, GRIST WAS SMALL BUT QUICK. BUT WHEN ONE OF PLUGG'S HAYMAKERS DID CONNECT, THE EFFECT WAS AWE-INSPIRING...
GOT YOU!
UGHH!

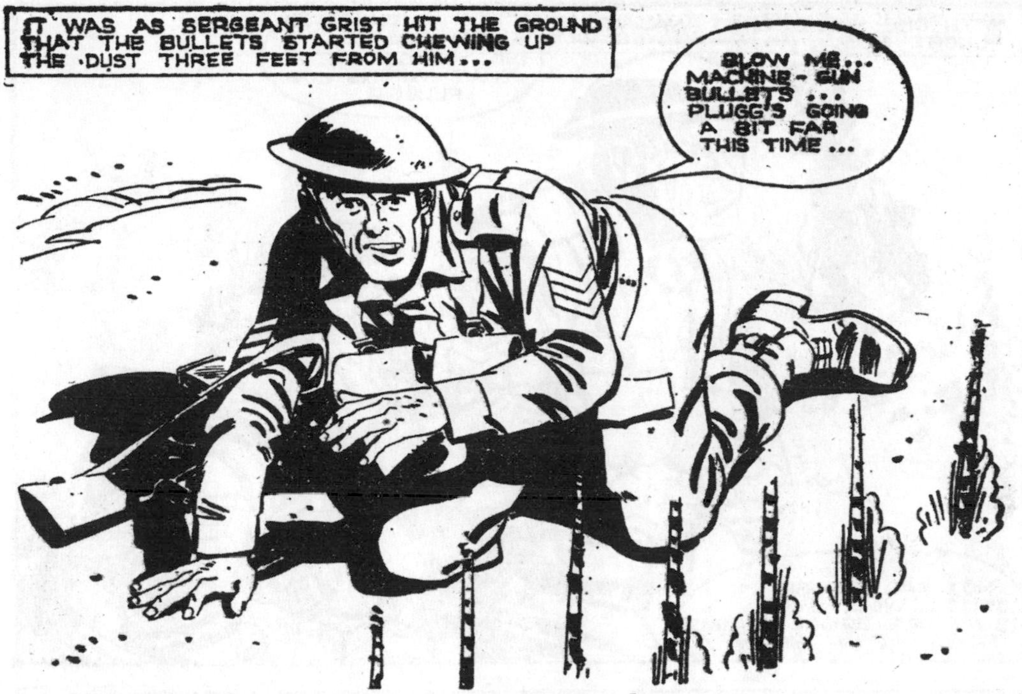
IT WAS AS SERGEANT GRIST HIT THE GROUND THAT THE BULLETS STARTED CHEWING UP THE DUST THREE FEET FROM HIM...
BLOW ME... MACHINE-GUN BULLETS... PLUGG'S GOING A BIT FAR THIS TIME...

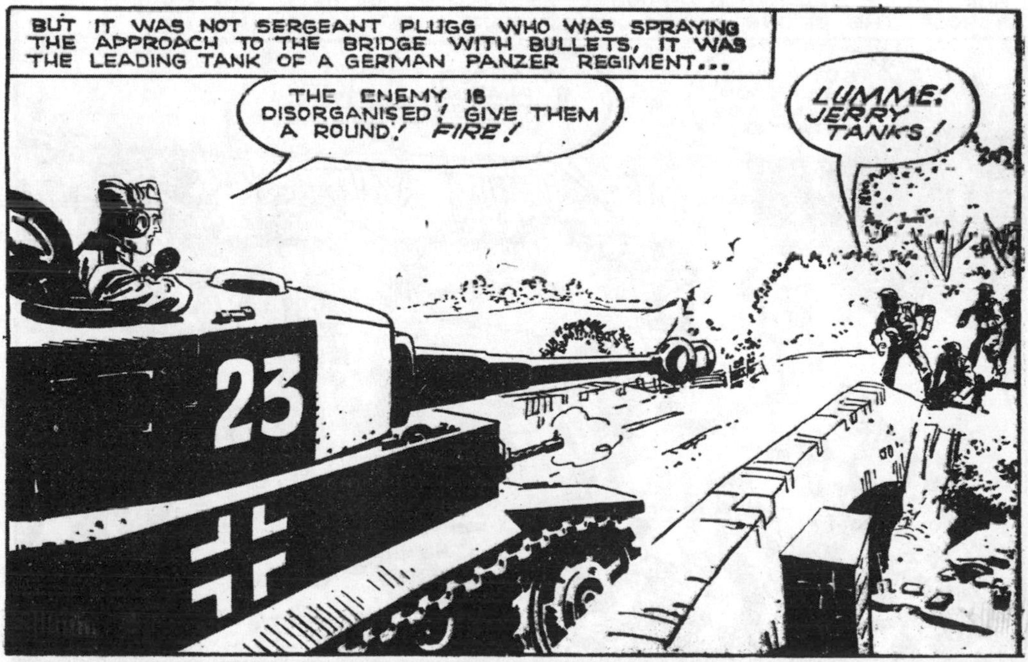
BUT IT WAS NOT SERGEANT PLUGG WHO WAS SPRAYING THE APPROACH TO THE BRIDGE WITH BULLETS, IT WAS THE LEADING TANK OF A GERMAN PANZER REGIMENT...
THE ENEMY IS DISORGANISED! GIVE THEM A ROUND! FIRE!
LUMME! JERRY TANKS!
23

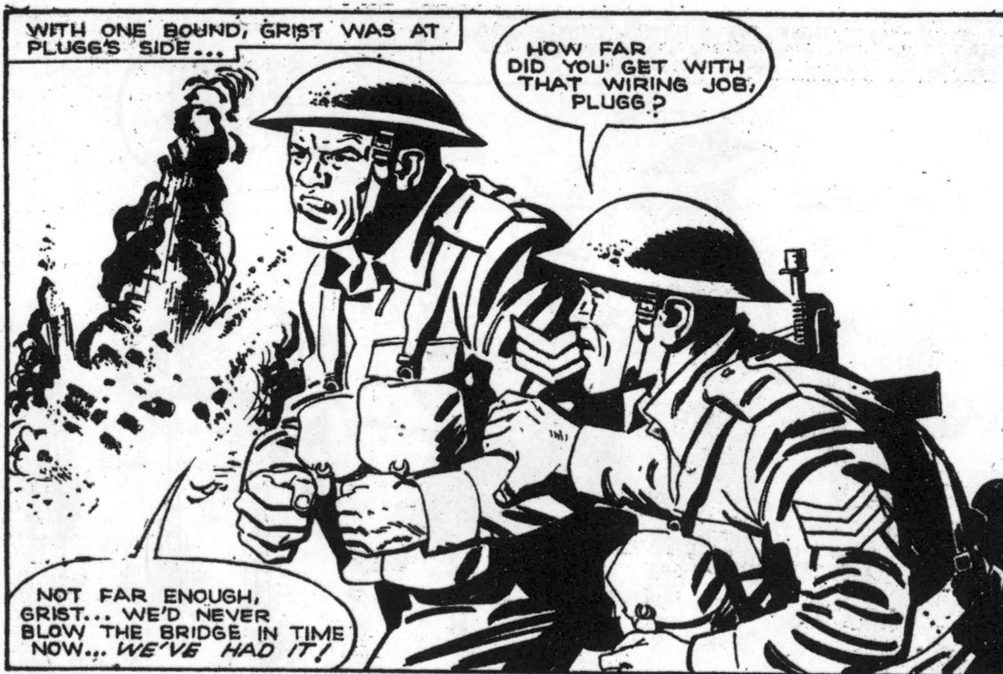
WITH ONE BOUND, GRIST WAS AT PLUGG'S SIDE...
HOW FAR DID YOU GET WITH THAT WIRING JOB, PLUGG?
NOT FAR ENOUGH, GRIST... WE'D NEVER BLOW THE BRIDGE IN TIME NOW... WE'VE HAD IT!

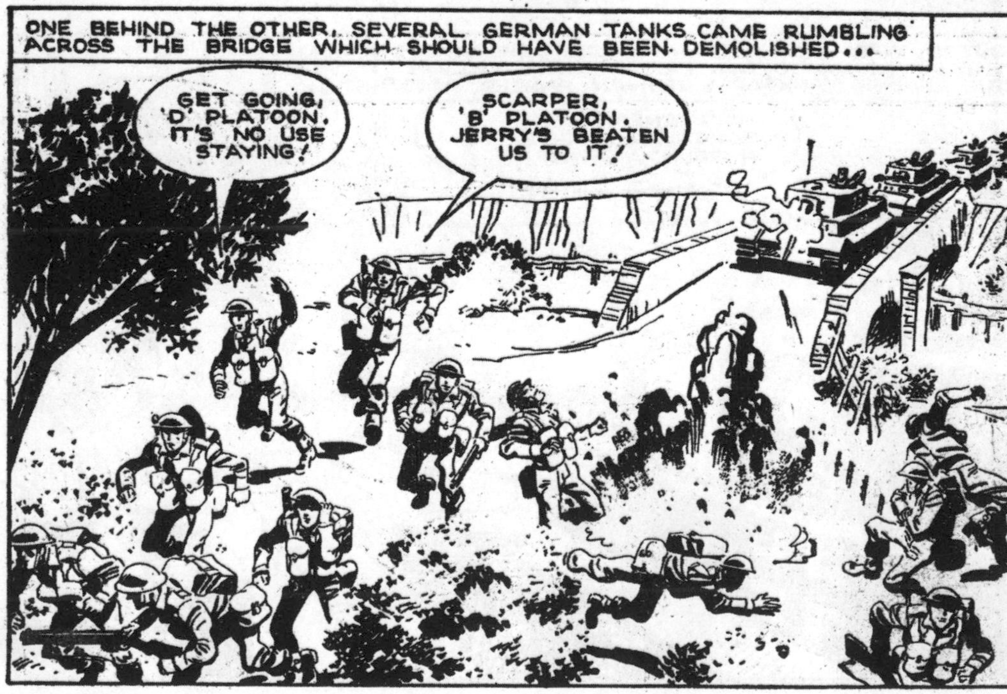
ONE BEHIND THE OTHER, SEVERAL GERMAN TANKS CAME RUMBLING ACROSS THE BRIDGE WHICH SHOULD HAVE BEEN DEMOLISHED...
GET GOING, 'D' PLATOON. IT'S NO USE STAYING!
SCARPER, 'B' PLATOON. JERRY'S BEATEN US TO IT!

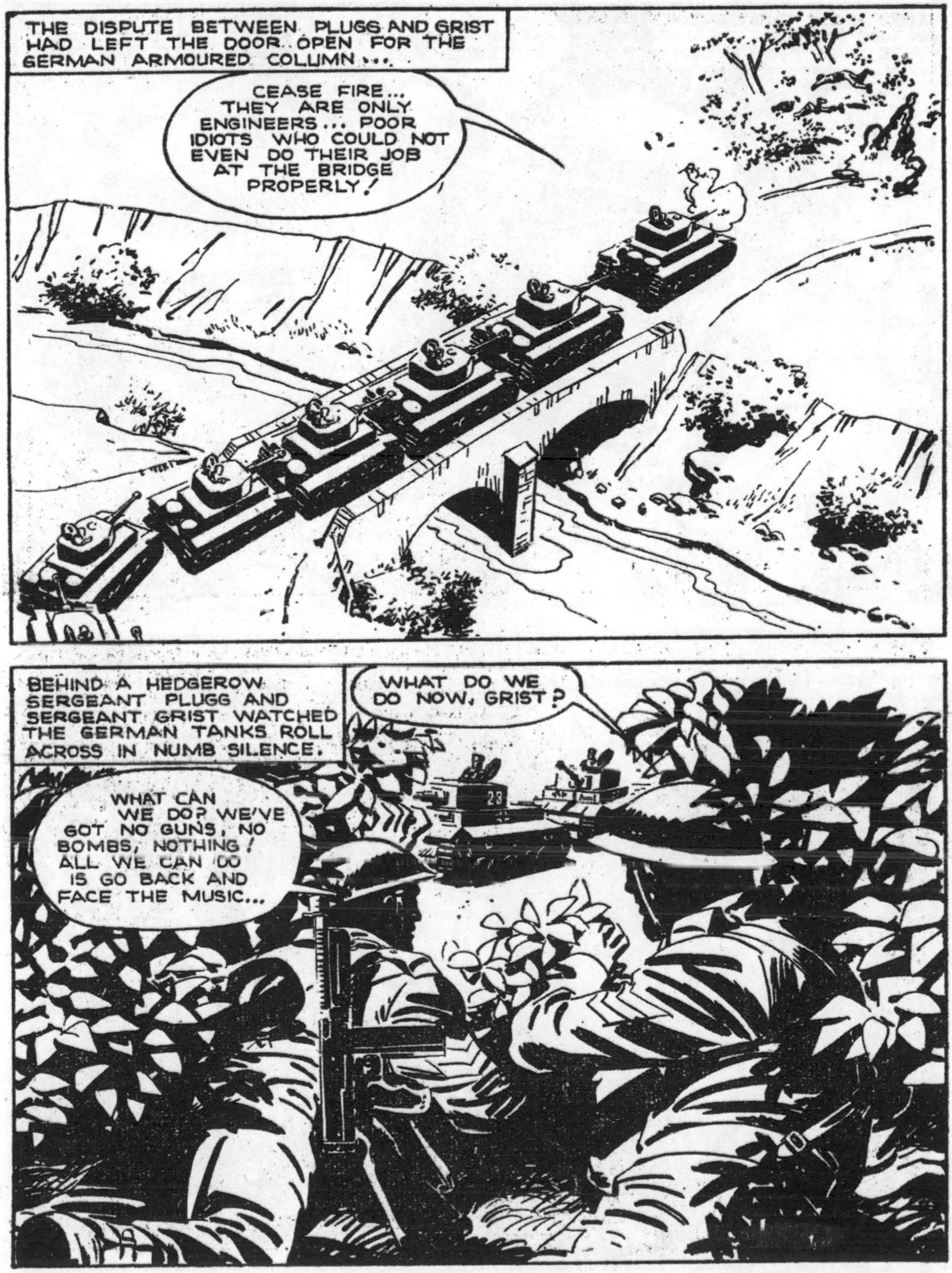
THE DISPUTE BETWEEN PLUGG AND GRIST HAD LEFT THE DOOR OPEN FOR THE GERMAN ARMOURED COLUMN ...
CEASE FIRE... THEY ARE ONLY ENGINEERS... POOR IDIOTS WHO COULD NOT EVEN DO THEIR JOB AT THE BRIDGE PROPERLY!
BEHIND A HEDGEROW SERGEANT PLUGG AND SERGEANT GRIST WATCHED THE GERMAN TANKS ROLL ACROSS IN NUMB SILENCE.
WHAT DO WE DO NOW, GRIST?
WHAT CAN WE DO? WE'VE GOT NO GUNS, NO BOMBS, NOTHING! ALL WE CAN DO IS GO BACK AND FACE THE MUSIC...
23

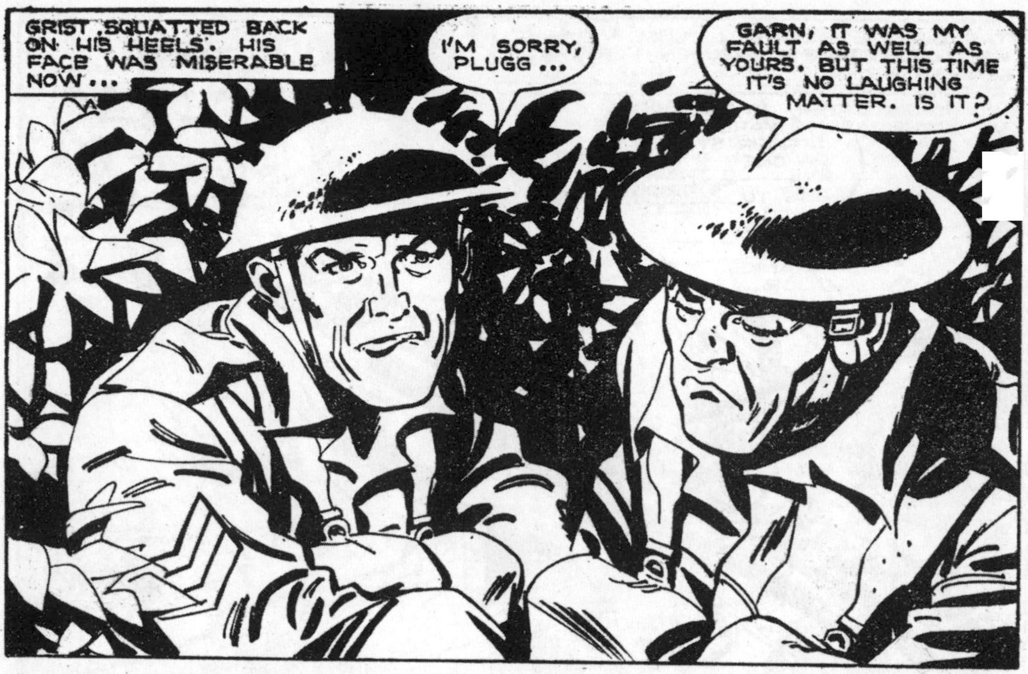
GRIST SQUATTED BACK ON HIS HEELS. HIS FACE WAS MISERABLE NOW ...
I'M SORRY, PLUGG ...
GARN, IT WAS MY FAULT AS WELL AS YOURS. BUT THIS TIME IT'S NO LAUGHING MATTER. IS IT?

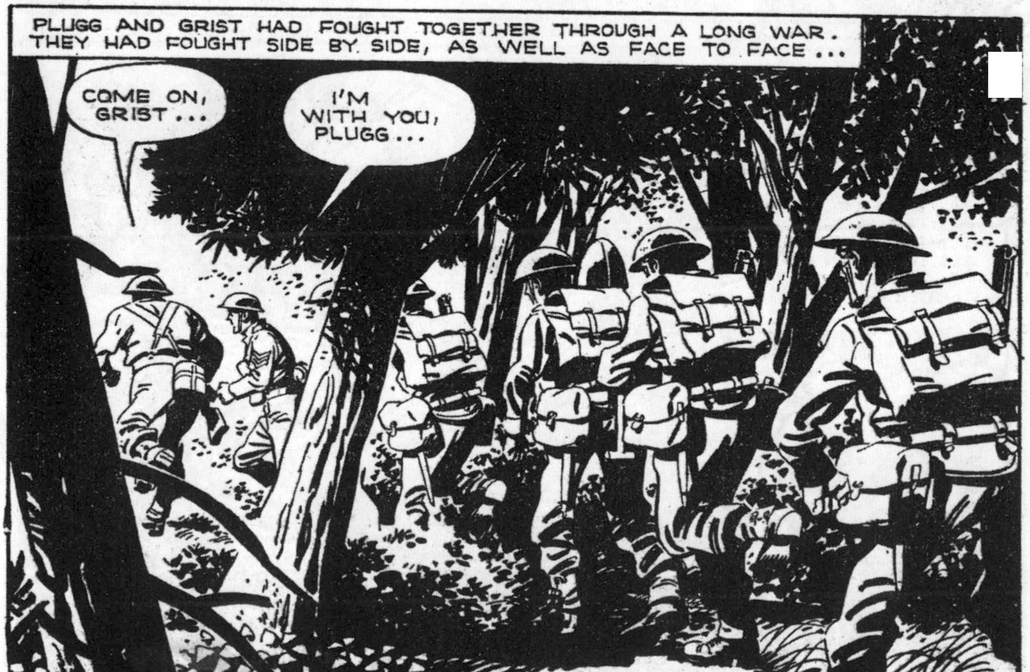
PLUGG AND GRIST HAD FOUGHT TOGETHER THROUGH A LONG WAR. THEY HAD FOUGHT SIDE BY SIDE, AS WELL AS FACE TO FACE ...
COME ON, GRIST ...
I'M WITH YOU, PLUGG ...

Chapter 4. The Doomed Town

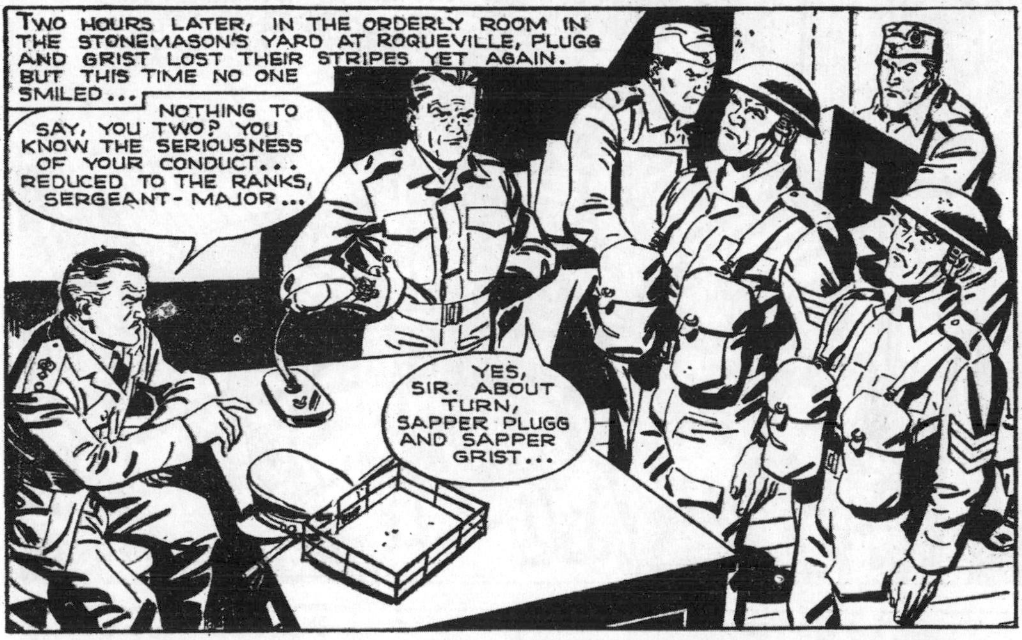
TWO HOURS LATER, IN THE ORDERLY ROOM IN THE STONEMASON'S YARD AT ROQUEVILLE, PLUGG AND GRIST LOST THEIR STRIPES YET AGAIN. BUT THIS TIME NO ONE SMILED...
NOTHING TO SAY, YOU TWO? YOU KNOW THE SERIOUSNESS OF YOUR CONDUCT... REDUCED TO THE RANKS, SERGEANT-MAJOR...
YES, SIR. ABOUT TURN, SAPPER PLUGG AND SAPPER GRIST...

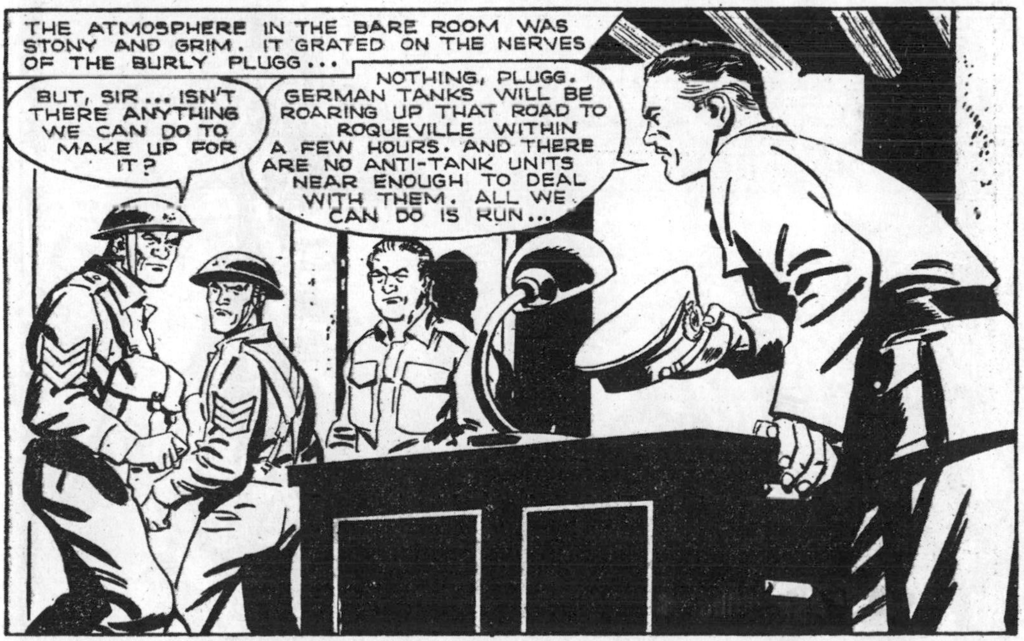
THE ATMOSPHERE IN THE BARE ROOM WAS STONY AND GRIM. IT GRATED ON THE NERVES OF THE BURLY PLUGG...
BUT, SIR... ISN'T THERE ANYTHING WE CAN DO TO MAKE UP FOR IT?
NOTHING, PLUGG. GERMAN TANKS WILL BE ROARING UP THAT ROAD TO ROQUEVILLE WITHIN A FEW HOURS. AND THERE ARE NO ANTI-TANK UNITS NEAR ENOUGH TO DEAL WITH THEM. ALL WE CAN DO IS RUN...

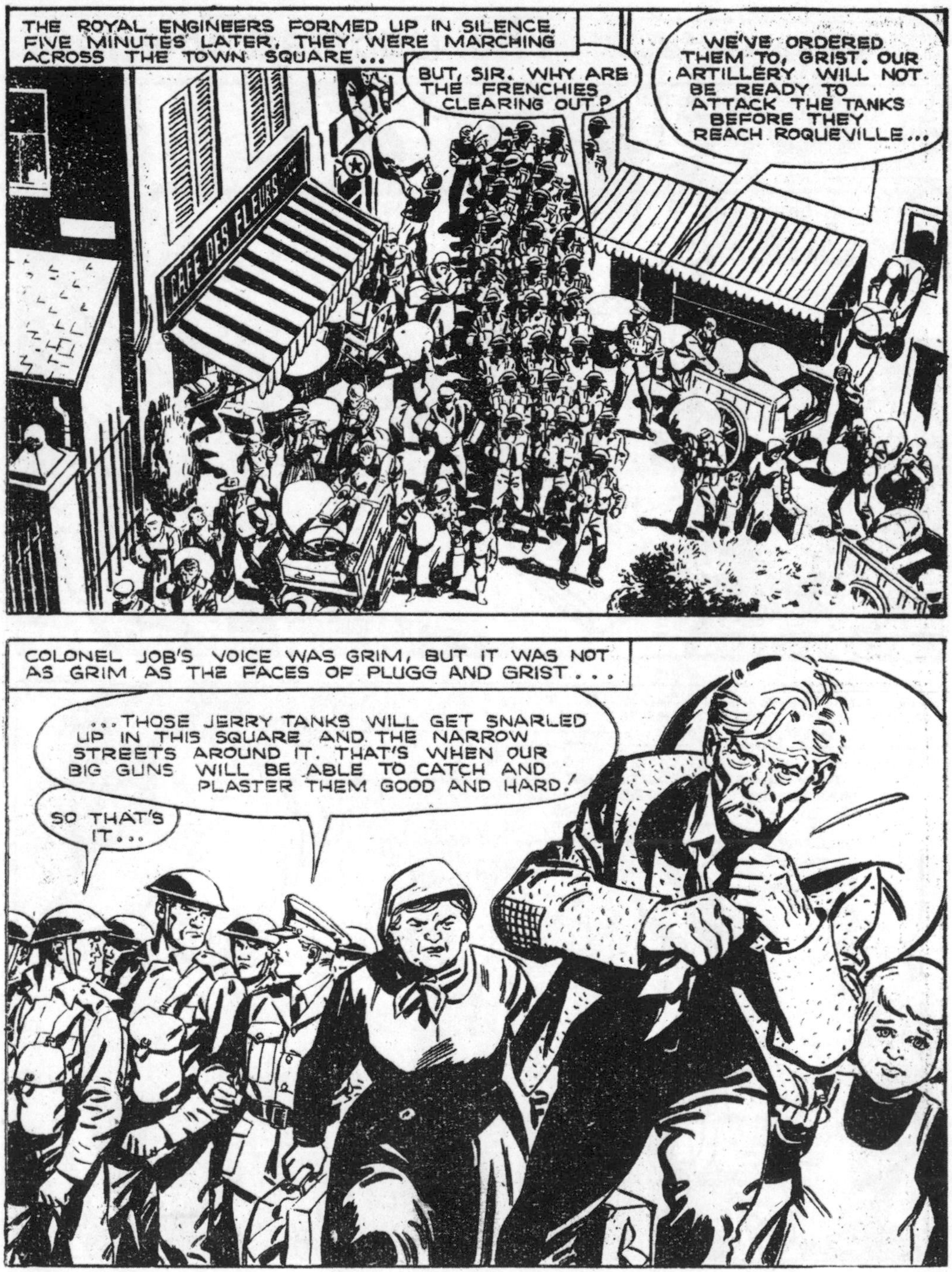
THE ROYAL ENGINEERS FORMED UP IN SILENCE. FIVE MINUTES LATER, THEY WERE MARCHING ACROSS THE TOWN SQUARE...
BUT, SIR. WHY ARE THE FRENCHIES CLEARING OUT?
WE'VE ORDERED THEM TO, GRIST. OUR ARTILLERY WILL NOT BE READY TO ATTACK THE TANKS BEFORE THEY REACH ROQUEVILLE...
CAFE DES FLEURS
COLONEL JOB'S VOICE WAS GRIM, BUT IT WAS NOT AS GRIM AS THE FACES OF PLUGG AND GRIST...
...THOSE JERRY TANKS WILL GET SNARLED UP IN THIS SQUARE AND THE NARROW STREETS AROUND IT. THAT'S WHEN OUR BIG GUNS WILL BE ABLE TO CATCH AND PLASTER THEM GOOD AND HARD!
SO THAT'S IT...

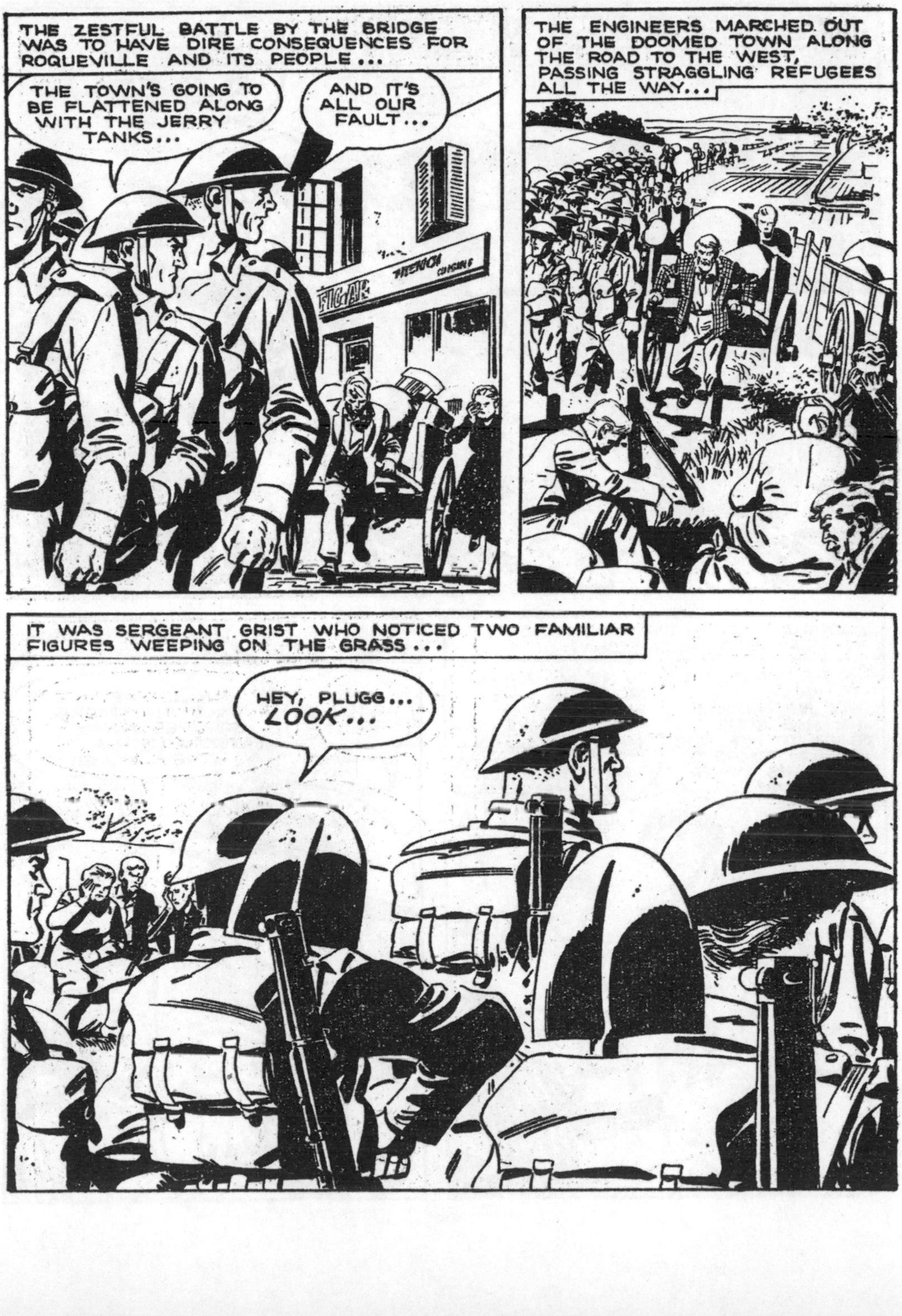
THE ZESTFUL BATTLE BY THE BRIDGE WAS TO HAVE DIRE CONSEQUENCES FOR ROQUEVILLE AND ITS PEOPLE ...
THE TOWN'S GOING TO BE FLATTENED ALONG WITH THE JERRY TANKS...
AND IT'S ALL OUR FAULT...
THE ENGINEERS MARCHED OUT OF THE DOOMED TOWN ALONG THE ROAD TO THE WEST, PASSING STRAGGLING REFUGEES ALL THE WAY...
IT WAS SERGEANT GRIST WHO NOTICED TWO FAMILIAR FIGURES WEEPING ON THE GRASS ...
HEY, PLUGG... *LOOK*...

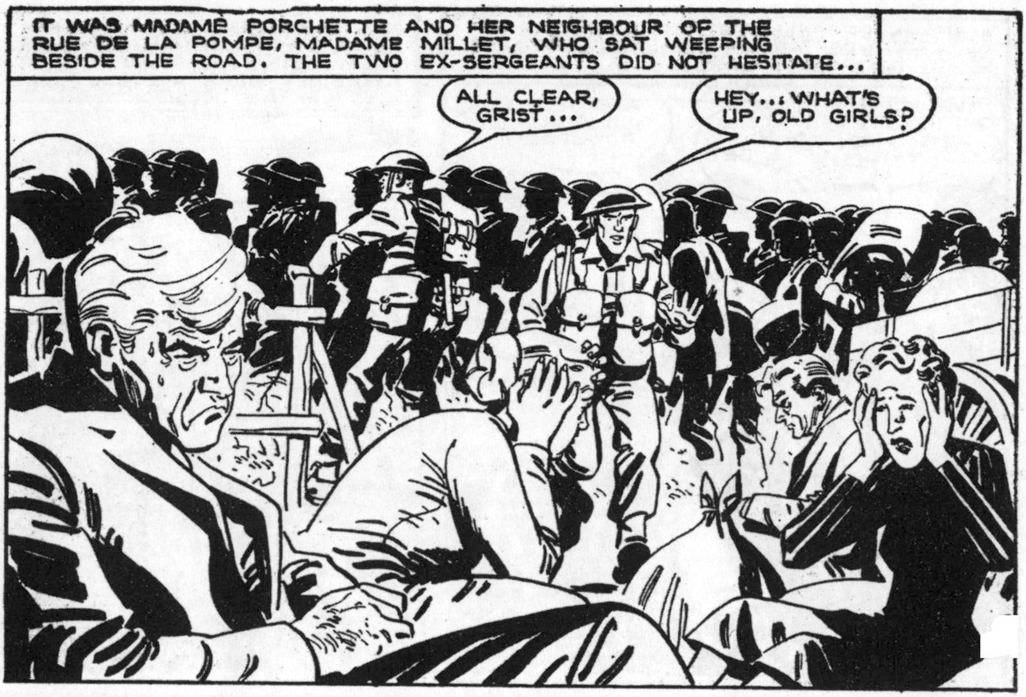
IT WAS MADAME PORCHETTE AND HER NEIGHBOUR OF THE RUE DE LA POMPE, MADAME MILLET, WHO SAT WEEPING BESIDE THE ROAD. THE TWO EX-SERGEANTS DID NOT HESITATE...
ALL CLEAR, GRIST...
HEY...: WHAT'S UP, OLD GIRLS?

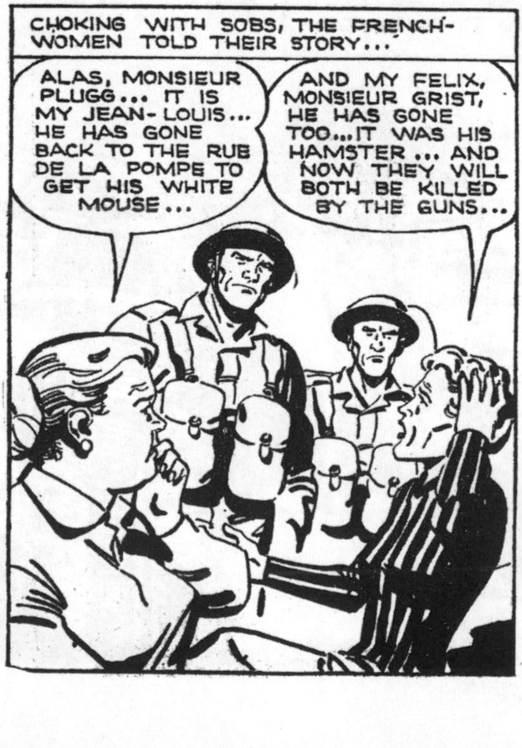
CHOKING WITH SOBS, THE FRENCH-WOMEN TOLD THEIR STORY...
ALAS, MONSIEUR PLUGG... IT IS MY JEAN-LOUIS... HE HAS GONE BACK TO THE RUE DE LA POMPE TO GET HIS WHITE MOUSE...
AND MY FELIX, MONSIEUR GRIST, HE HAS GONE TOO...IT WAS HIS HAMSTER ... AND NOW THEY WILL BOTH BE KILLED BY THE GUNS...

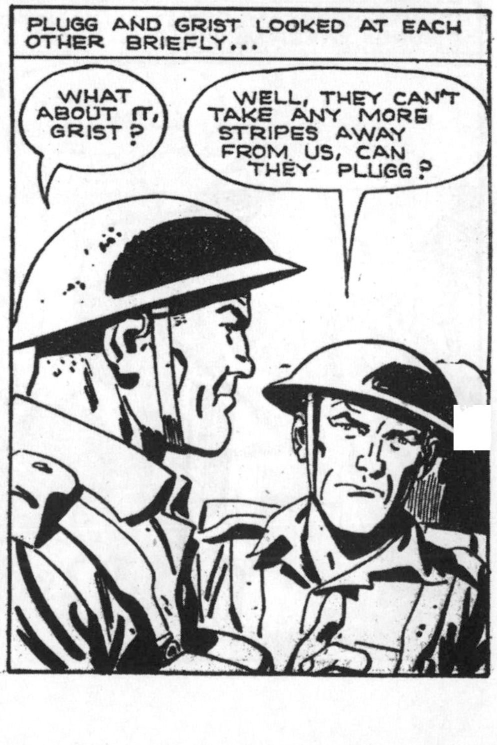
PLUGG AND GRIST LOOKED AT EACH OTHER BRIEFLY...
WHAT ABOUT IT, GRIST?
WELL, THEY CAN'T TAKE ANY MORE STRIPES AWAY FROM US, CAN THEY PLUGG?

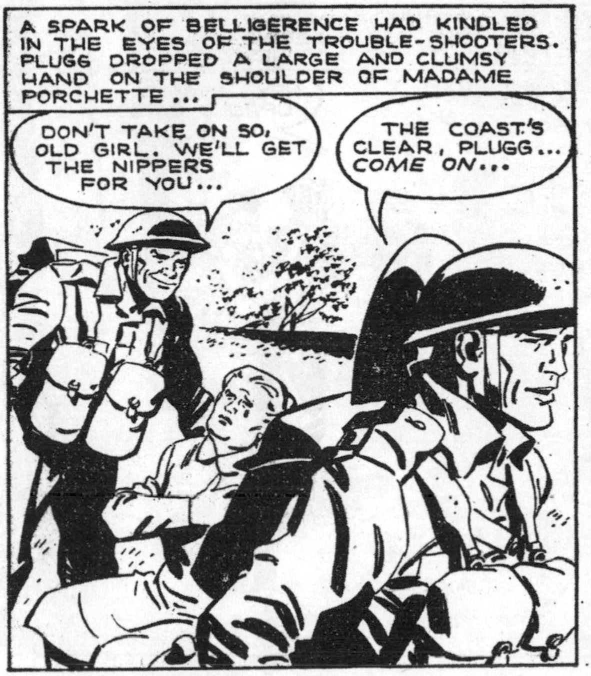
A SPARK OF BELLIGERENCE HAD KINDLED IN THE EYES OF THE TROUBLE-SHOOTERS. PLUGG DROPPED A LARGE AND CLUMSY HAND ON THE SHOULDER OF MADAME PORCHETTE ...
DON'T TAKE ON SO, OLD GIRL. WE'LL GET THE NIPPERS FOR YOU...
THE COAST'S CLEAR, PLUGG... COME ON...

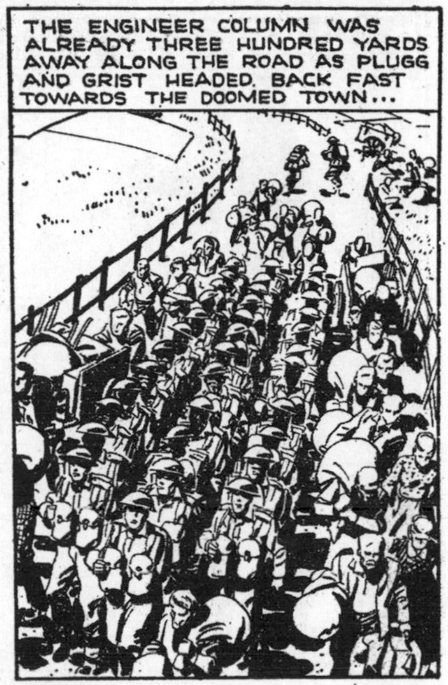
THE ENGINEER COLUMN WAS ALREADY THREE HUNDRED YARDS AWAY ALONG THE ROAD AS PLUGG AND GRIST HEADED BACK FAST TOWARDS THE DOOMED TOWN...

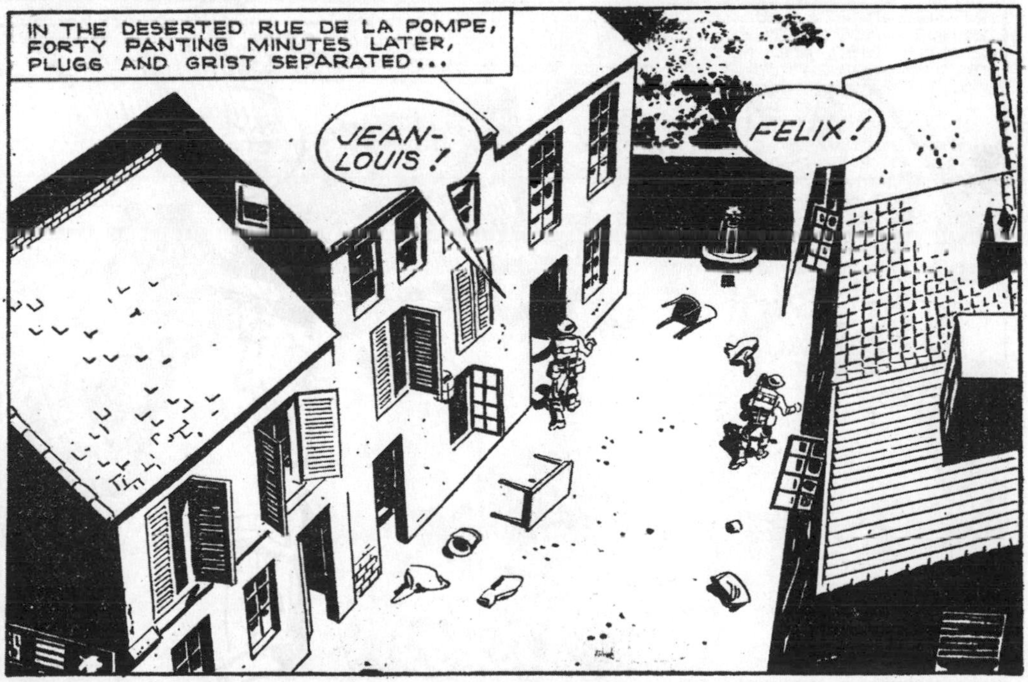
IN THE DESERTED RUE DE LA POMPE, FORTY PANTING MINUTES LATER, PLUGG AND GRIST SEPARATED...
JEAN-LOUIS!
FELIX!

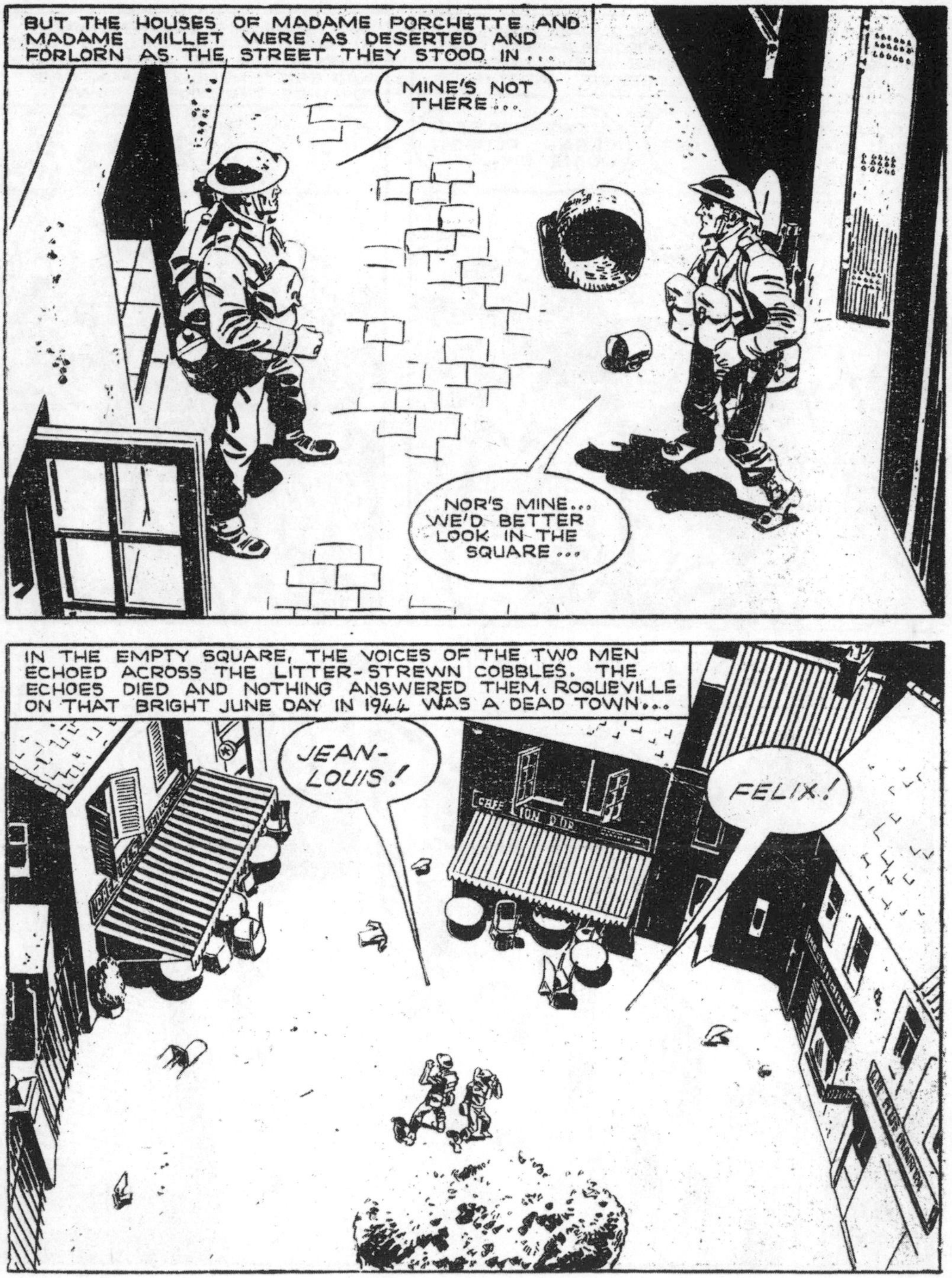
BUT THE HOUSES OF MADAME PORCHETTE AND MADAME MILLET WERE AS DESERTED AND FORLORN AS THE STREET THEY STOOD IN...
MINE'S NOT THERE...
NOR'S MINE... WE'D BETTER LOOK IN THE SQUARE...
IN THE EMPTY SQUARE, THE VOICES OF THE TWO MEN ECHOED ACROSS THE LITTER-STREWN COBBLES. THE ECHOES DIED AND NOTHING ANSWERED THEM. ROQUEVILLE ON THAT BRIGHT JUNE DAY IN 1944 WAS A DEAD TOWN...
JEAN-LOUIS!
FELIX!

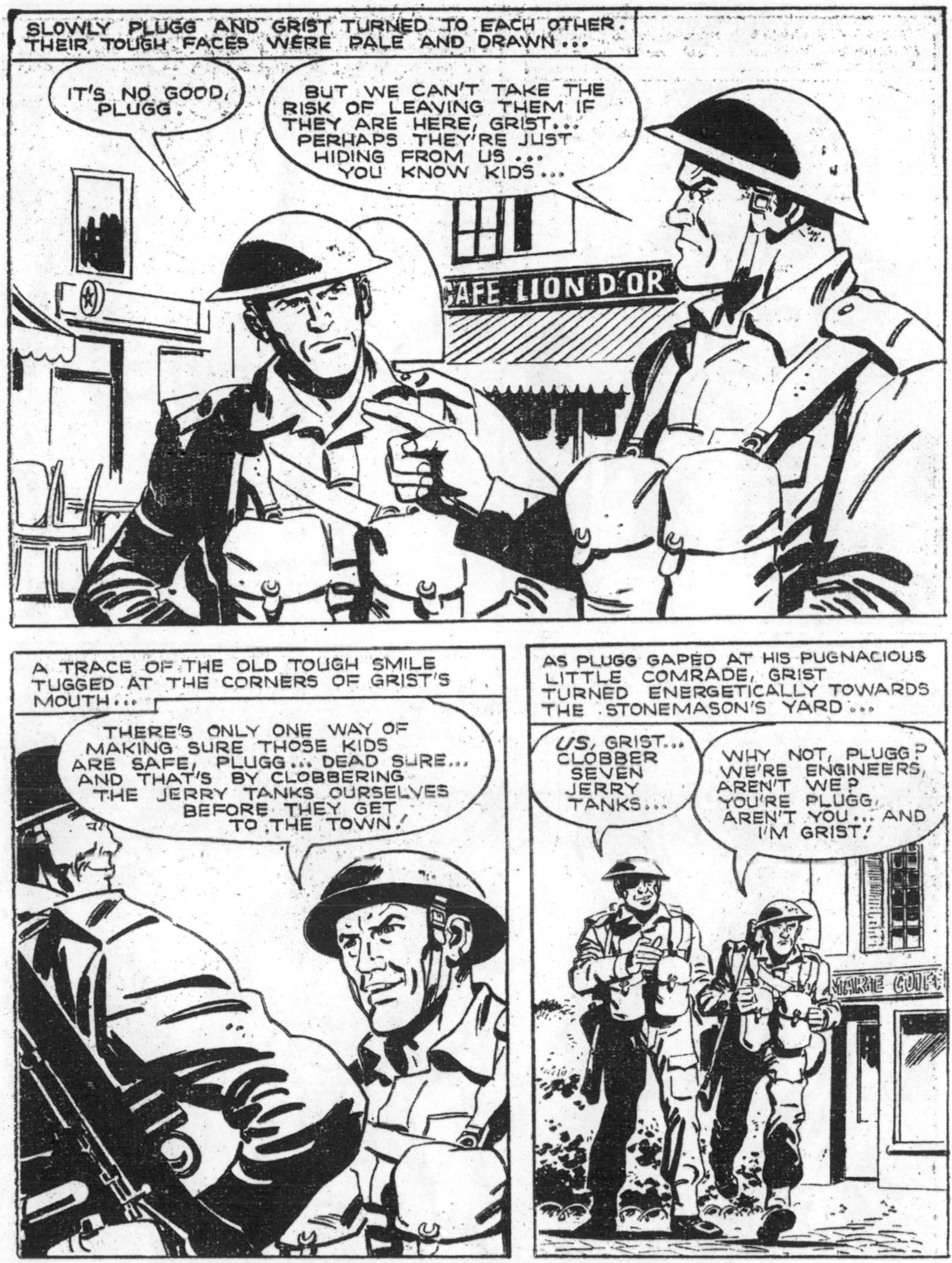
SLOWLY PLUGG AND GRIST TURNED TO EACH OTHER. THEIR TOUGH FACES WERE PALE AND DRAWN...
IT'S NO GOOD, PLUGG.
BUT WE CAN'T TAKE THE RISK OF LEAVING THEM IF THEY ARE HERE, GRIST... PERHAPS THEY'RE JUST HIDING FROM US ... YOU KNOW KIDS...
AFE LION D'OR
A TRACE OF THE OLD TOUGH SMILE TUGGED AT THE CORNERS OF GRIST'S MOUTH...
THERE'S ONLY ONE WAY OF MAKING SURE THOSE KIDS ARE SAFE, PLUGG... DEAD SURE... AND THAT'S BY CLOBBERING THE JERRY TANKS OURSELVES BEFORE THEY GET TO THE TOWN!
AS PLUGG GAPED AT HIS PUGNACIOUS LITTLE COMRADE, GRIST TURNED ENERGETICALLY TOWARDS THE STONEMASON'S YARD...
US, GRIST... CLOBBER SEVEN JERRY TANKS...
WHY NOT, PLUGG? WE'RE ENGINEERS, AREN'T WE? YOU'RE PLUGG, AREN'T YOU... AND I'M GRIST!

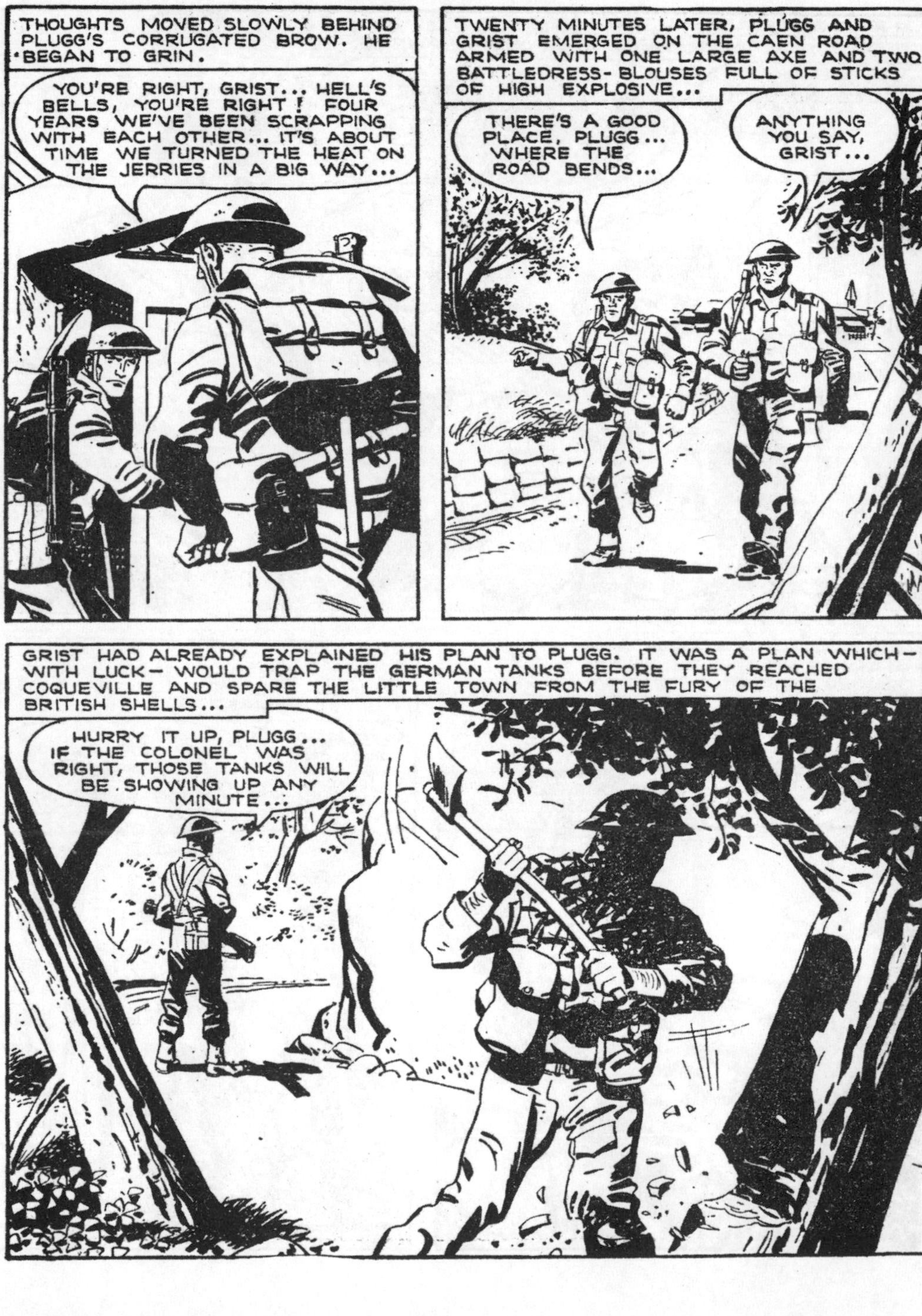
THOUGHTS MOVED SLOWLY BEHIND PLUGG'S CORRUGATED BROW. HE BEGAN TO GRIN.
YOU'RE RIGHT, GRIST... HELL'S BELLS, YOU'RE RIGHT! FOUR YEARS WE'VE BEEN SCRAPPING WITH EACH OTHER... IT'S ABOUT TIME WE TURNED THE HEAT ON THE JERRIES IN A BIG WAY...
TWENTY MINUTES LATER, PLUGG AND GRIST EMERGED ON THE CAEN ROAD ARMED WITH ONE LARGE AXE AND TWO BATTLEDRESS-BLOUSES FULL OF STICKS OF HIGH EXPLOSIVE...
THERE'S A GOOD PLACE, PLUGG... WHERE THE ROAD BENDS...
ANYTHING YOU SAY, GRIST...
GRIST HAD ALREADY EXPLAINED HIS PLAN TO PLUGG. IT WAS A PLAN WHICH—WITH LUCK—WOULD TRAP THE GERMAN TANKS BEFORE THEY REACHED COQUEVILLE AND SPARE THE LITTLE TOWN FROM THE FURY OF THE BRITISH SHELLS...
HURRY IT UP, PLUGG... IF THE COLONEL WAS RIGHT, THOSE TANKS WILL BE SHOWING UP ANY MINUTE...

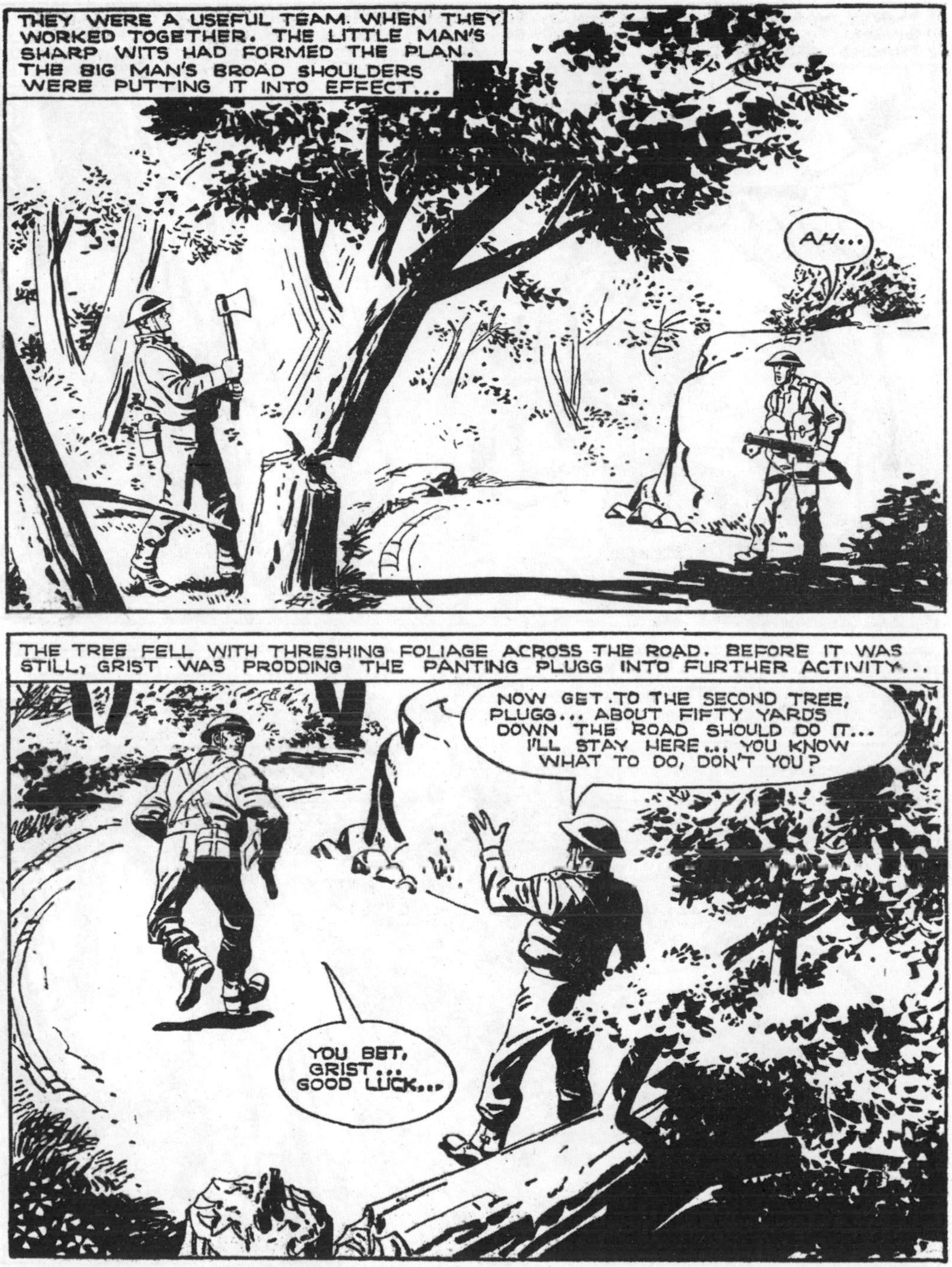
THEY WERE A USEFUL TEAM WHEN THEY WORKED TOGETHER. THE LITTLE MAN'S SHARP WITS HAD FORMED THE PLAN. THE BIG MAN'S BROAD SHOULDERS WERE PUTTING IT INTO EFFECT...
AH...
THE TREE FELL WITH THRESHING FOLIAGE ACROSS THE ROAD. BEFORE IT WAS STILL, GRIST WAS PRODDING THE PANTING PLUGG INTO FURTHER ACTIVITY...
NOW GET TO THE SECOND TREE, PLUGG... ABOUT FIFTY YARDS DOWN THE ROAD SHOULD DO IT... I'LL STAY HERE... YOU KNOW WHAT TO DO, DON'T YOU?
YOU BET, GRIST... GOOD LUCK...

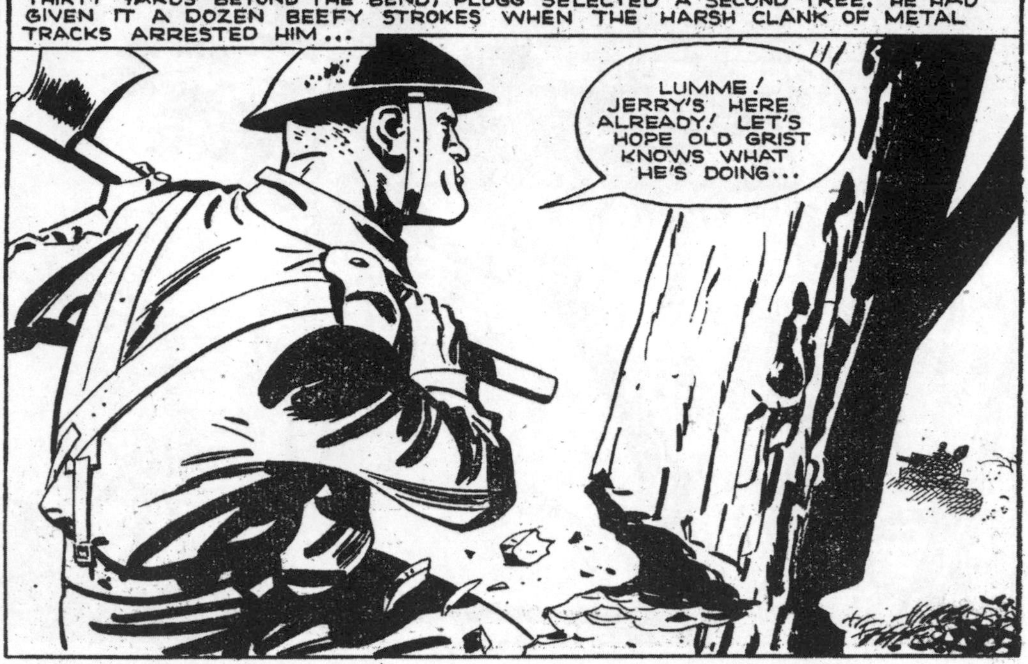
THIRTY YARDS BEYOND THE BEND, PLUGG SELECTED A SECOND TREE. HE HAD GIVEN IT A DOZEN BEEFY STROKES WHEN THE HARSH CLANK OF METAL TRACKS ARRESTED HIM...
LUMME! JERRY'S HERE ALREADY! LET'S HOPE OLD GRIST KNOWS WHAT HE'S DOING...

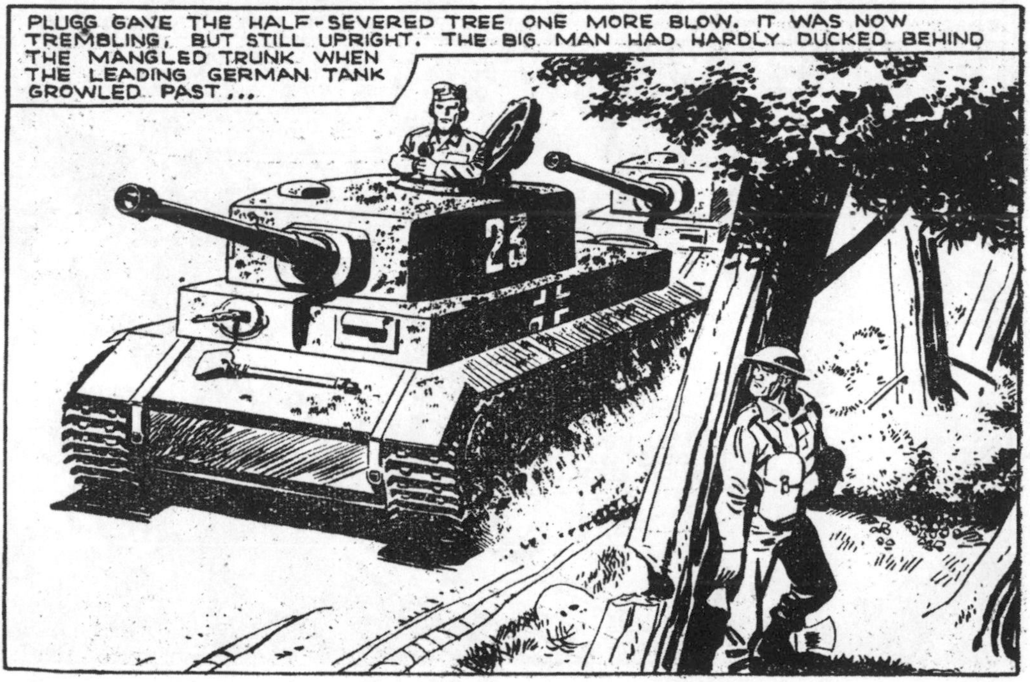
PLUGG GAVE THE HALF-SEVERED TREE ONE MORE BLOW. IT WAS NOW TREMBLING, BUT STILL UPRIGHT. THE BIG MAN HAD HARDLY DUCKED BEHIND THE MANGLED TRUNK WHEN THE LEADING GERMAN TANK GROWLED PAST...
23

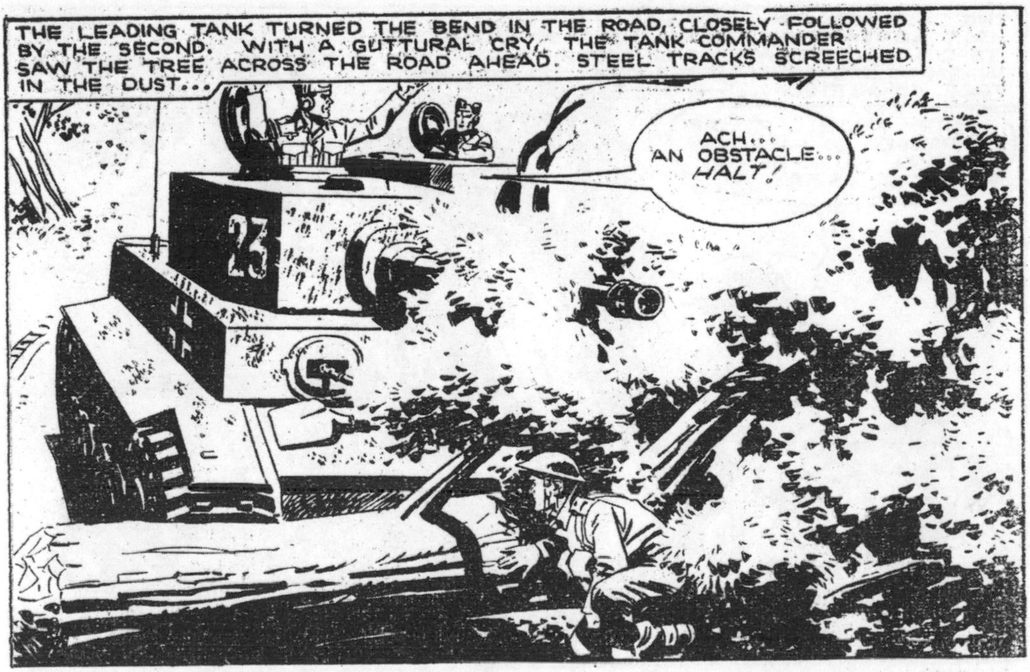
THE LEADING TANK TURNED THE BEND IN THE ROAD, CLOSELY FOLLOWED BY THE SECOND. WITH A GUTTURAL CRY, THE TANK COMMANDER SAW THE TREE ACROSS THE ROAD AHEAD. STEEL TRACKS SCREECHED IN THE DUST...
ACH... AN OBSTACLE... HALT!
23

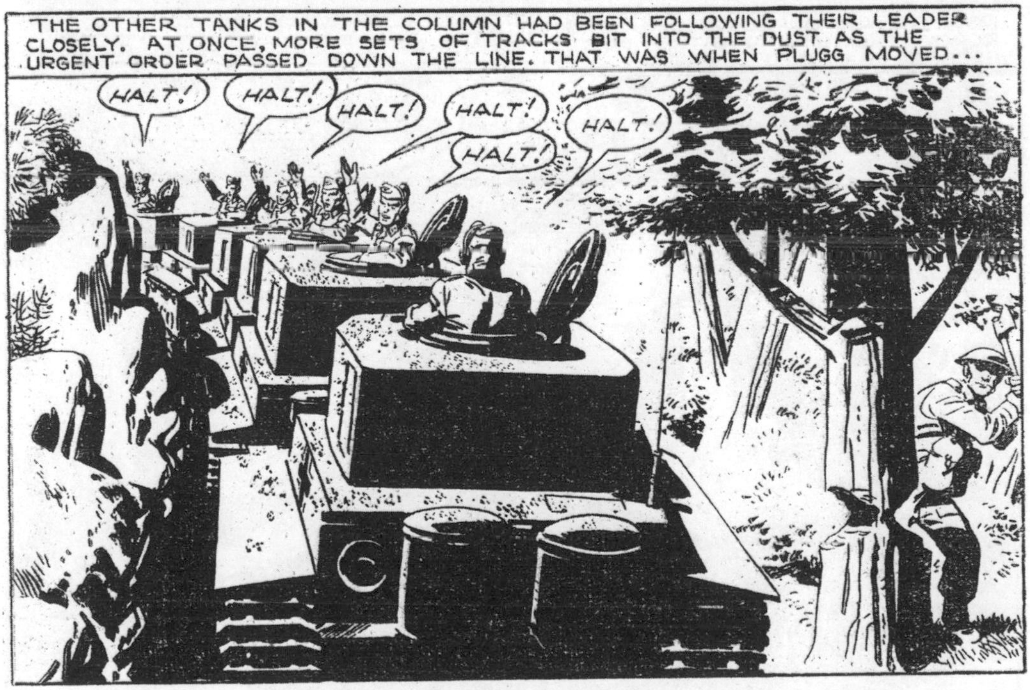
THE OTHER TANKS IN THE COLUMN HAD BEEN FOLLOWING THEIR LEADER CLOSELY. AT ONCE, MORE SETS OF TRACKS BIT INTO THE DUST AS THE URGENT ORDER PASSED DOWN THE LINE. THAT WAS WHEN PLUGG MOVED...
HALT!
HALT!
HALT!
HALT!
HALT!
HALT!

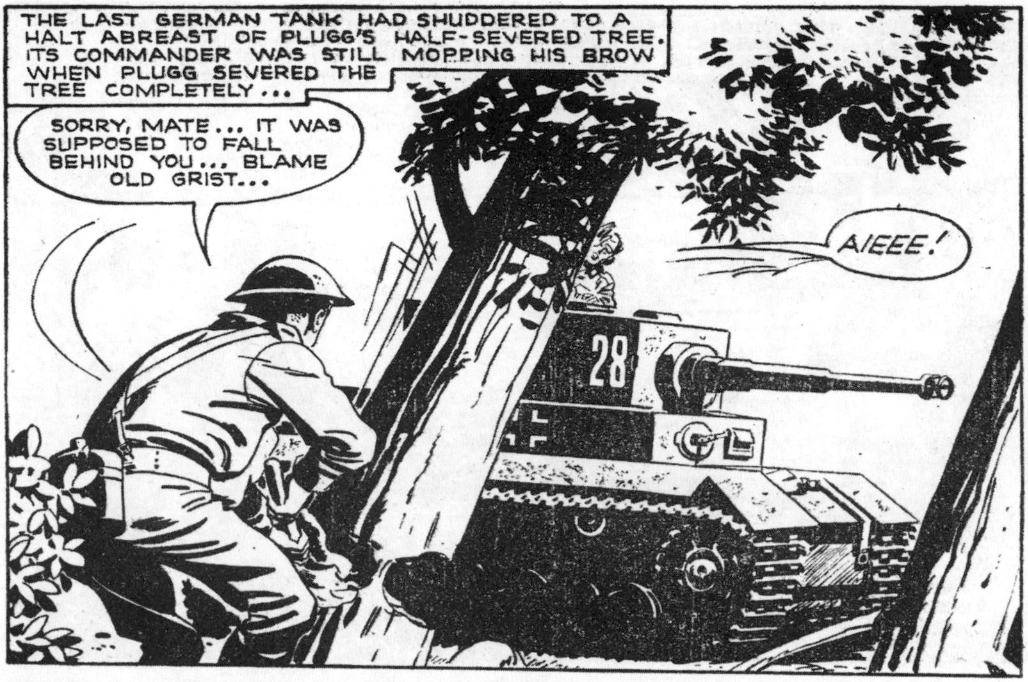
THE LAST GERMAN TANK HAD SHUDDERED TO A HALT ABREAST OF PLUGG'S HALF-SEVERED TREE. ITS COMMANDER WAS STILL MOPPING HIS BROW WHEN PLUGG SEVERED THE TREE COMPLETELY...
SORRY, MATE... IT WAS SUPPOSED TO FALL BEHIND YOU... BLAME OLD GRIST...
AIEEE!
28

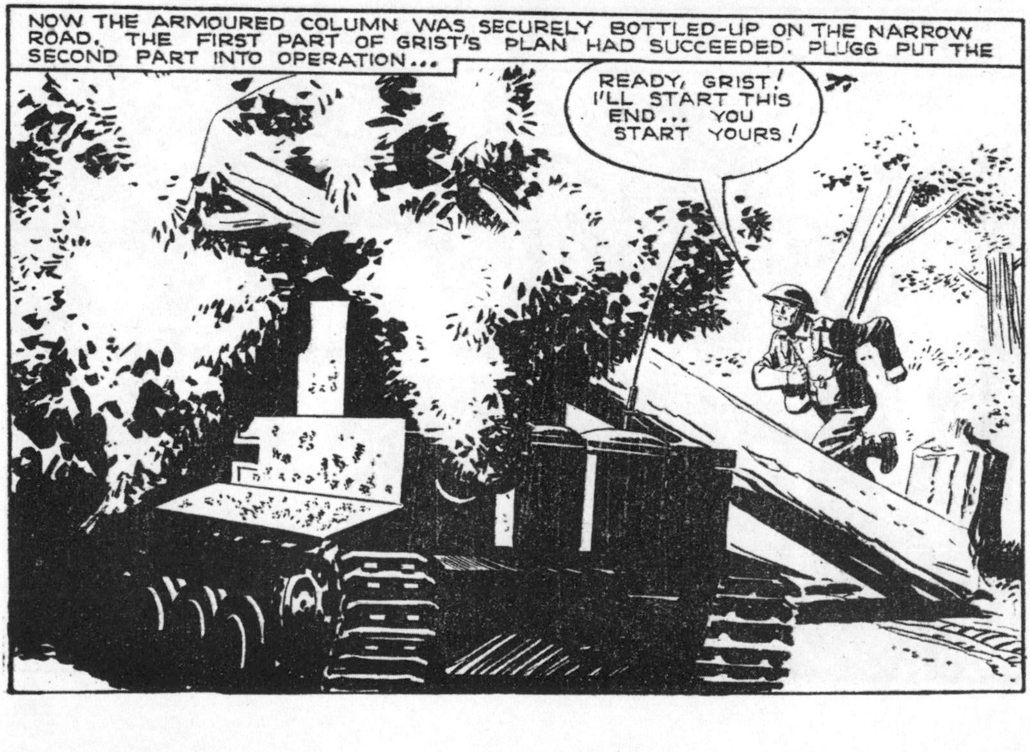
NOW THE ARMOURED COLUMN WAS SECURELY BOTTLED-UP ON THE NARROW ROAD. THE FIRST PART OF GRIST'S PLAN HAD SUCCEEDED. PLUGG PUT THE SECOND PART INTO OPERATION...
READY, GRIST! I'LL START THIS END... YOU START YOURS!

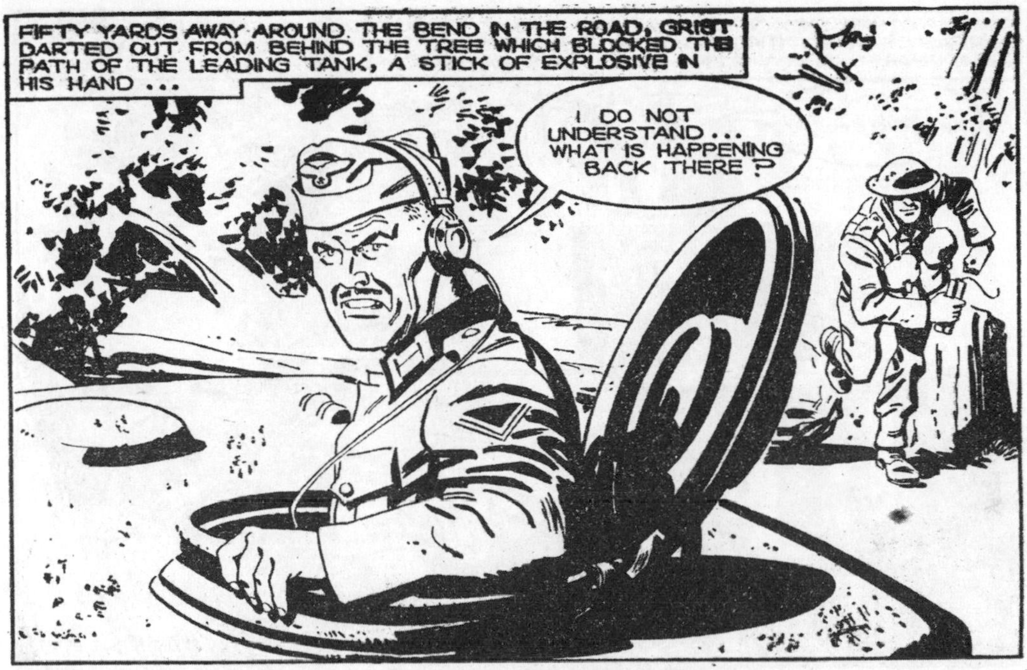
FIFTY YARDS AWAY AROUND THE BEND IN THE ROAD, GRIST DARTED OUT FROM BEHIND THE TREE WHICH BLOCKED THE PATH OF THE LEADING TANK, A STICK OF EXPLOSIVE IN HIS HAND ...
I DO NOT UNDERSTAND ... WHAT IS HAPPENING BACK THERE ?

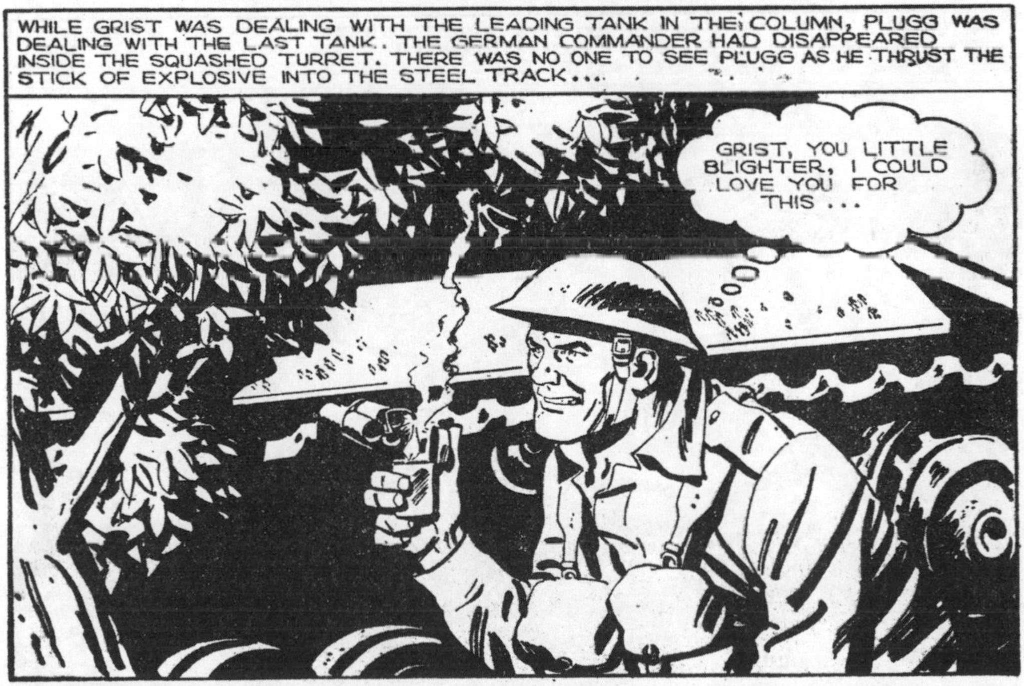
WHILE GRIST WAS DEALING WITH THE LEADING TANK IN THE COLUMN, PLUGG WAS DEALING WITH THE LAST TANK. THE GERMAN COMMANDER HAD DISAPPEARED INSIDE THE SQUASHED TURRET. THERE WAS NO ONE TO SEE PLUGG AS HE THRUST THE STICK OF EXPLOSIVE INTO THE STEEL TRACK ...
GRIST, YOU LITTLE BLIGHTER, I COULD LOVE YOU FOR THIS ...

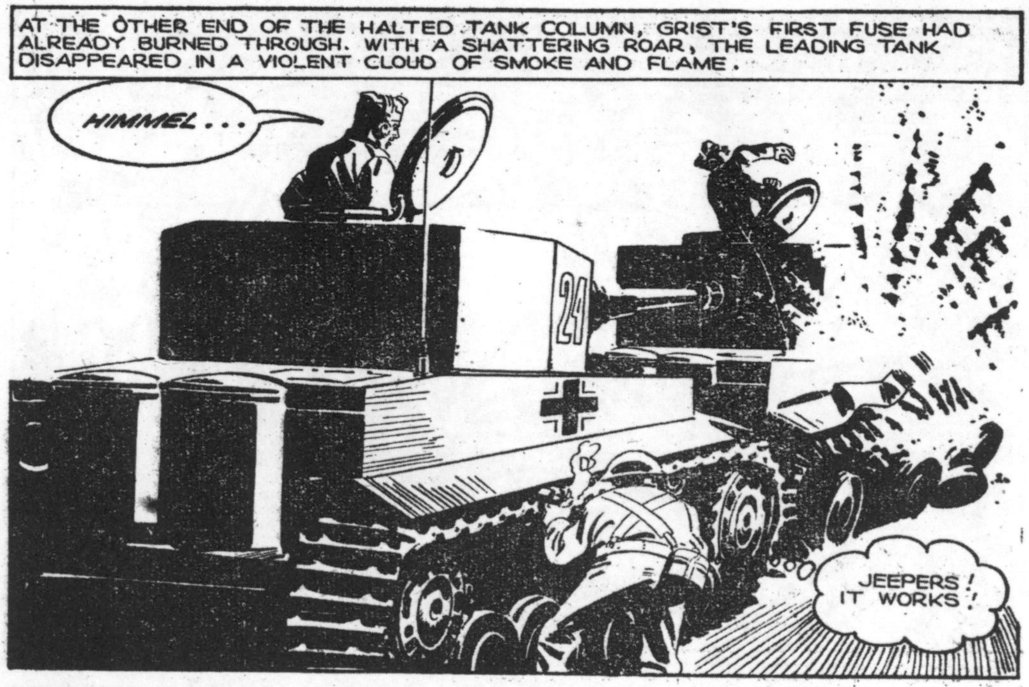
AT THE OTHER END OF THE HALTED TANK COLUMN, GRIST'S FIRST FUSE HAD ALREADY BURNED THROUGH. WITH A SHATTERING ROAR, THE LEADING TANK DISAPPEARED IN A VIOLENT CLOUD OF SMOKE AND FLAME.
HIMMEL . . .
24
JEEPERS! IT WORKS!

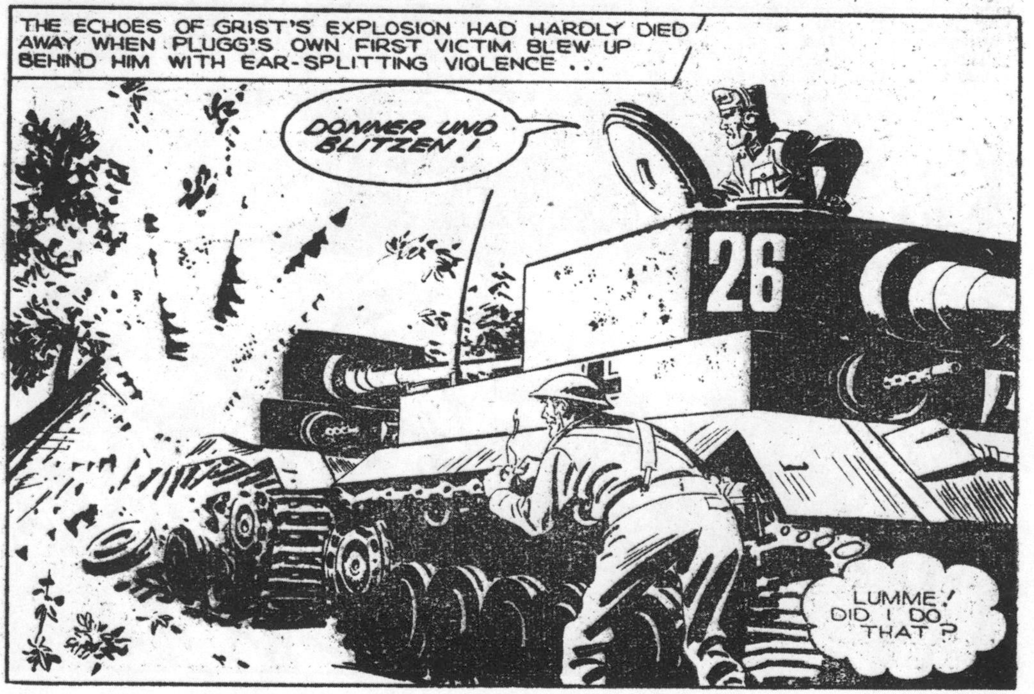
THE ECHOES OF GRIST'S EXPLOSION HAD HARDLY DIED AWAY WHEN PLUGG'S OWN FIRST VICTIM BLEW UP BEHIND HIM WITH EAR-SPLITTING VIOLENCE . . .
DONNER UND BLITZEN!
26
LUMME! DID I DO THAT?

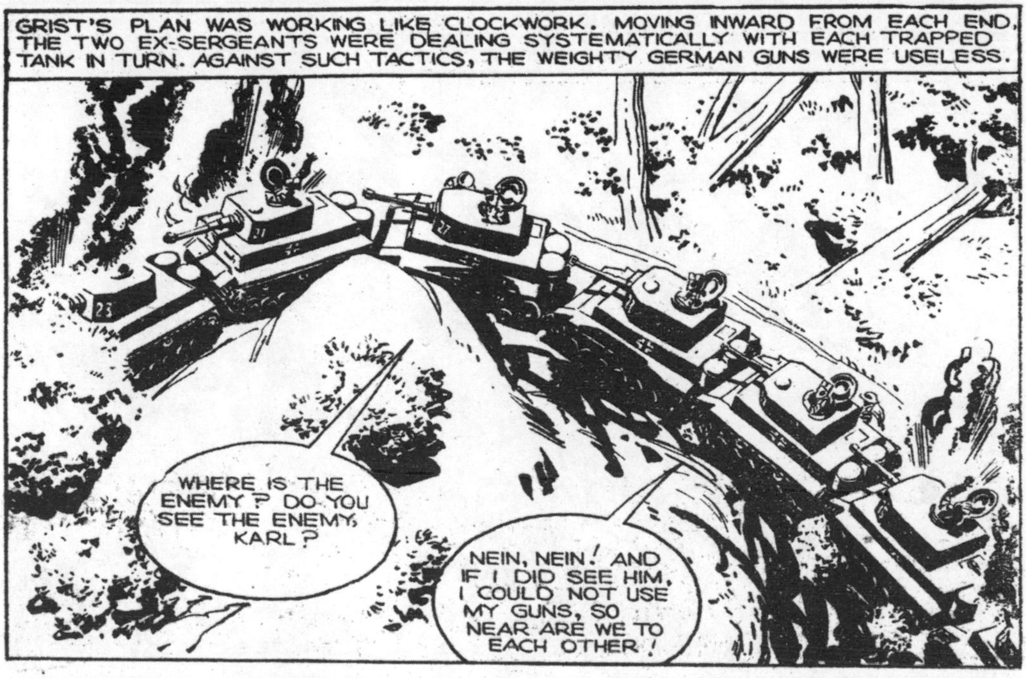
GRIST'S PLAN WAS WORKING LIKE CLOCKWORK. MOVING INWARD FROM EACH END, THE TWO EX-SERGEANTS WERE DEALING SYSTEMATICALLY WITH EACH TRAPPED TANK IN TURN. AGAINST SUCH TACTICS, THE WEIGHTY GERMAN GUNS WERE USELESS.
WHERE IS THE ENEMY? DO YOU SEE THE ENEMY, KARL?
NEIN, NEIN! AND IF I DID SEE HIM, I COULD NOT USE MY GUNS, SO NEAR ARE WE TO EACH OTHER!

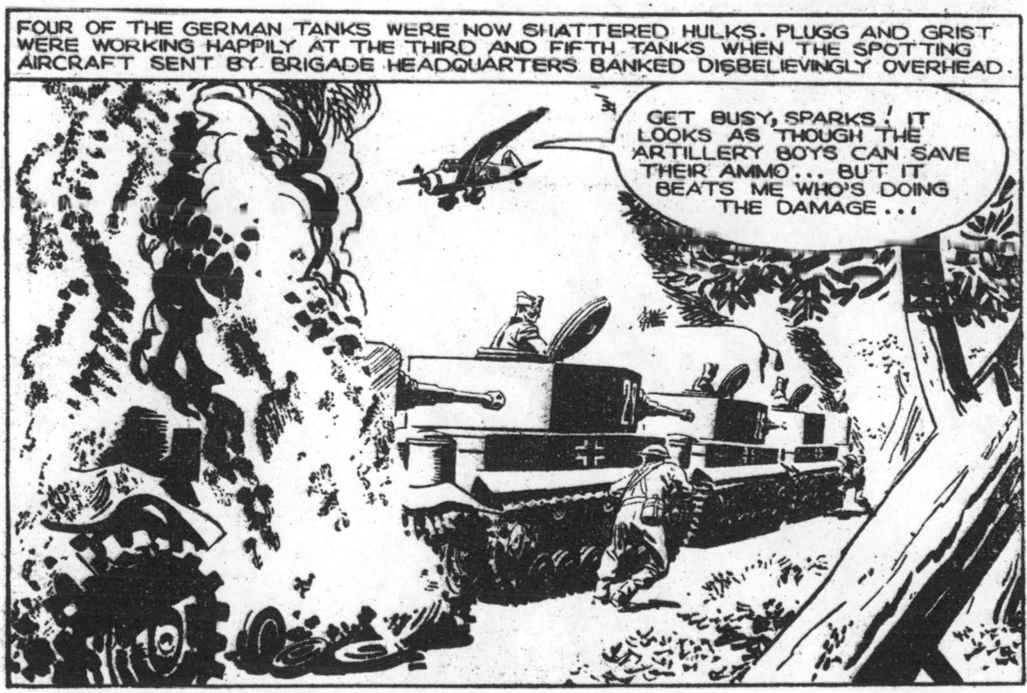
FOUR OF THE GERMAN TANKS WERE NOW SHATTERED HULKS. PLUGG AND GRIST WERE WORKING HAPPILY AT THE THIRD AND FIFTH TANKS WHEN THE SPOTTING AIRCRAFT SENT BY BRIGADE HEADQUARTERS BANKED DISBELIEVINGLY OVERHEAD.
GET BUSY, SPARKS! IT LOOKS AS THOUGH THE ARTILLERY BOYS CAN SAVE THEIR AMMO... BUT IT BEATS ME WHO'S DOING THE DAMAGE...

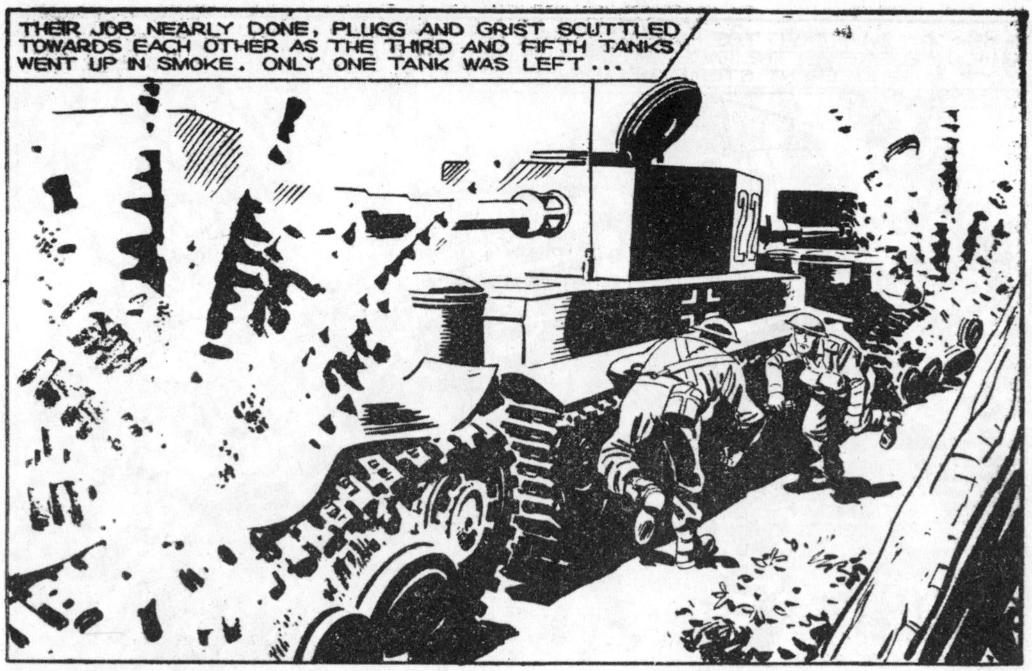
THEIR JOB NEARLY DONE, PLUGG AND GRIST SCUTTLED TOWARDS EACH OTHER AS THE THIRD AND FIFTH TANKS WENT UP IN SMOKE. ONLY ONE TANK WAS LEFT...

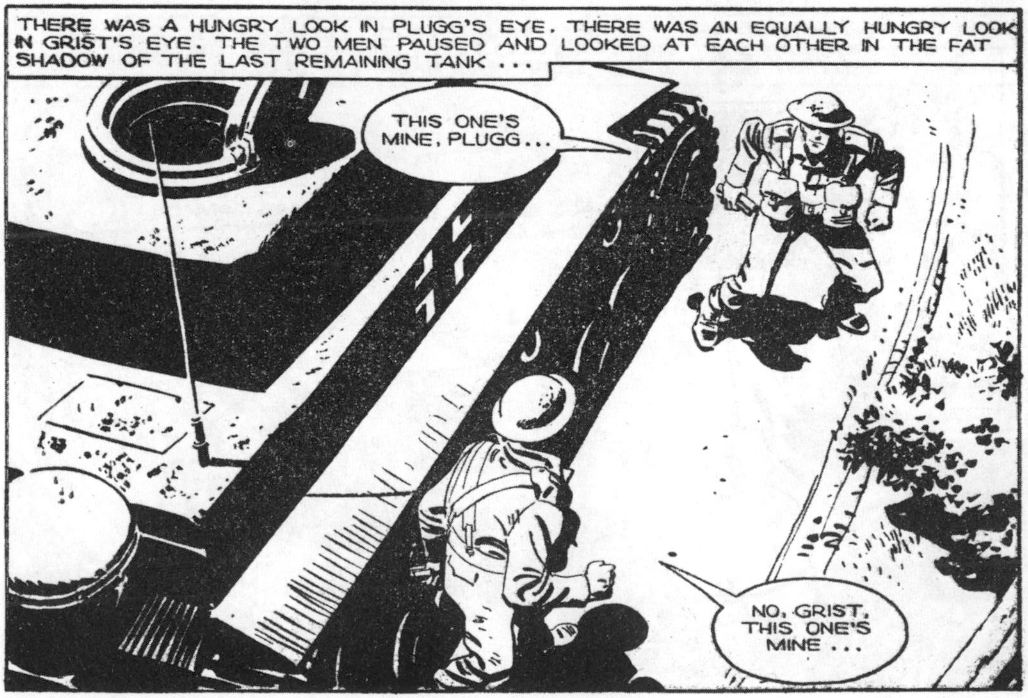
THERE WAS A HUNGRY LOOK IN PLUGG'S EYE. THERE WAS AN EQUALLY HUNGRY LOOK IN GRIST'S EYE. THE TWO MEN PAUSED AND LOOKED AT EACH OTHER IN THE FAT SHADOW OF THE LAST REMAINING TANK...
THIS ONE'S MINE, PLUGG...
NO, GRIST, THIS ONE'S MINE...

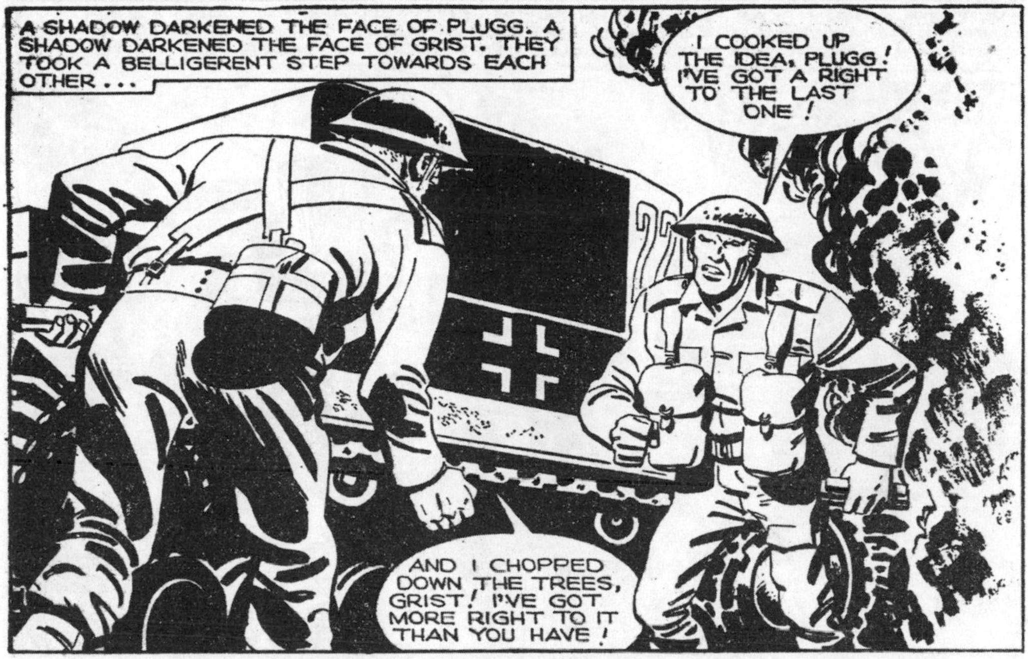
A SHADOW DARKENED THE FACE OF PLUGG. A SHADOW DARKENED THE FACE OF GRIST. THEY TOOK A BELLIGERENT STEP TOWARDS EACH OTHER ...
I COOKED UP THE IDEA, PLUGG! I'VE GOT A RIGHT TO THE LAST ONE!
AND I CHOPPED DOWN THE TREES, GRIST! I'VE GOT MORE RIGHT TO IT THAN YOU HAVE!

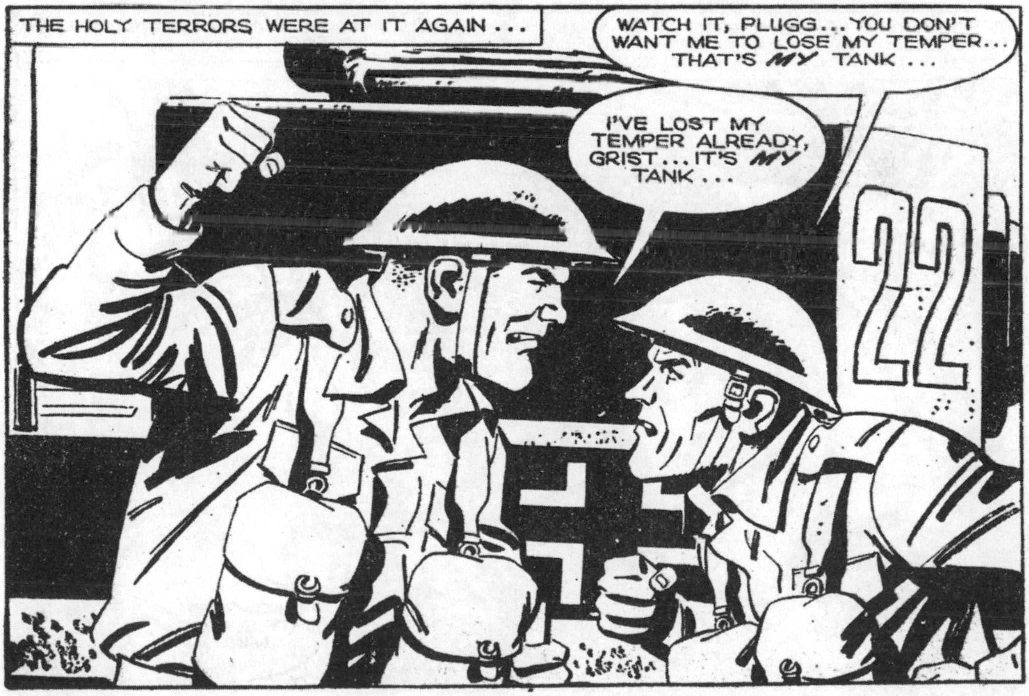
THE HOLY TERRORS WERE AT IT AGAIN ...
WATCH IT, PLUGG ... YOU DON'T WANT ME TO LOSE MY TEMPER ... THAT'S MY TANK ...
I'VE LOST MY TEMPER ALREADY, GRIST ... IT'S MY TANK ...
22

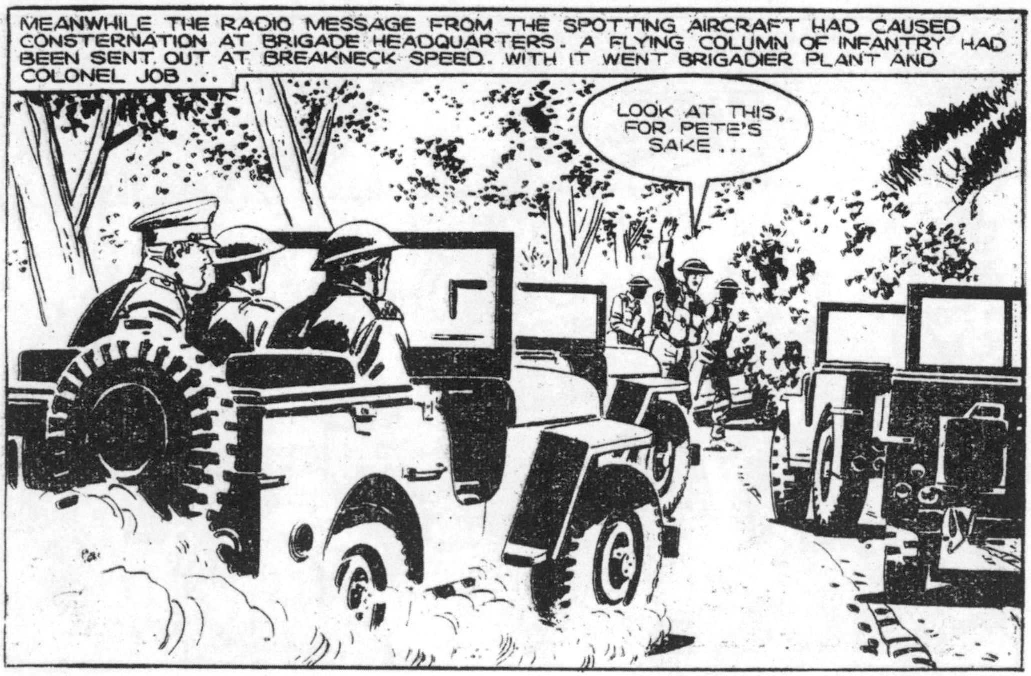
MEANWHILE THE RADIO MESSAGE FROM THE SPOTTING AIRCRAFT HAD CAUSED CONSTERNATION AT BRIGADE HEADQUARTERS. A FLYING COLUMN OF INFANTRY HAD BEEN SENT OUT AT BREAKNECK SPEED. WITH IT WENT BRIGADIER PLANT AND COLONEL JOB . . .
LOOK AT THIS, FOR PETE'S SAKE . . .

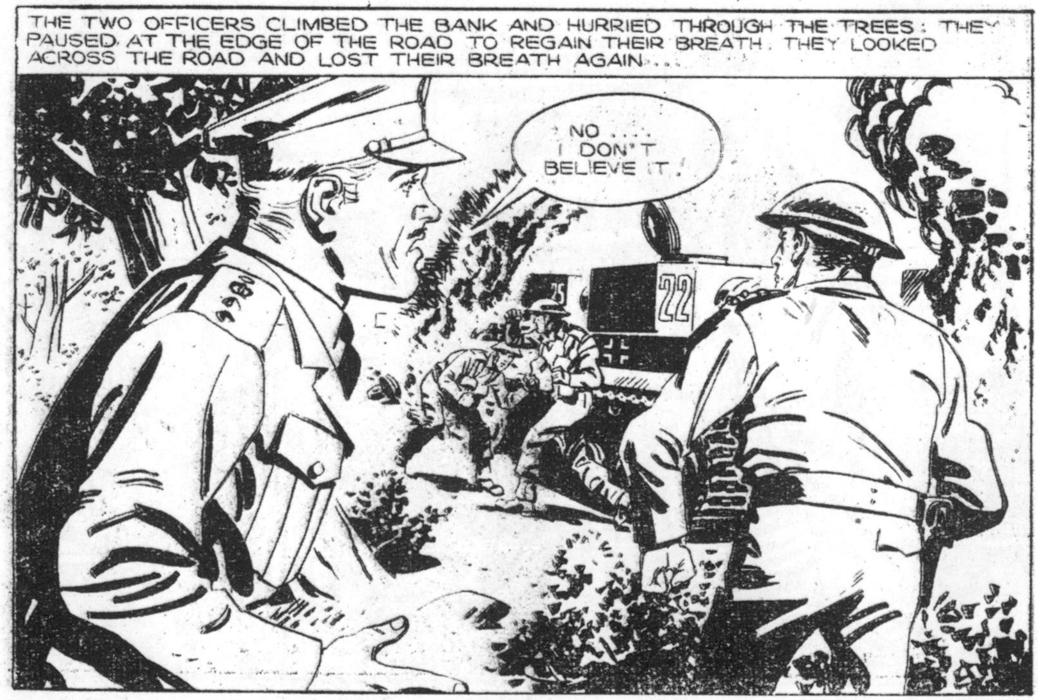
THE TWO OFFICERS CLIMBED THE BANK AND HURRIED THROUGH THE TREES: THEY PAUSED AT THE EDGE OF THE ROAD TO REGAIN THEIR BREATH. THEY LOOKED ACROSS THE ROAD AND LOST THEIR BREATH AGAIN . . .
NO . . . I DON'T BELIEVE IT.

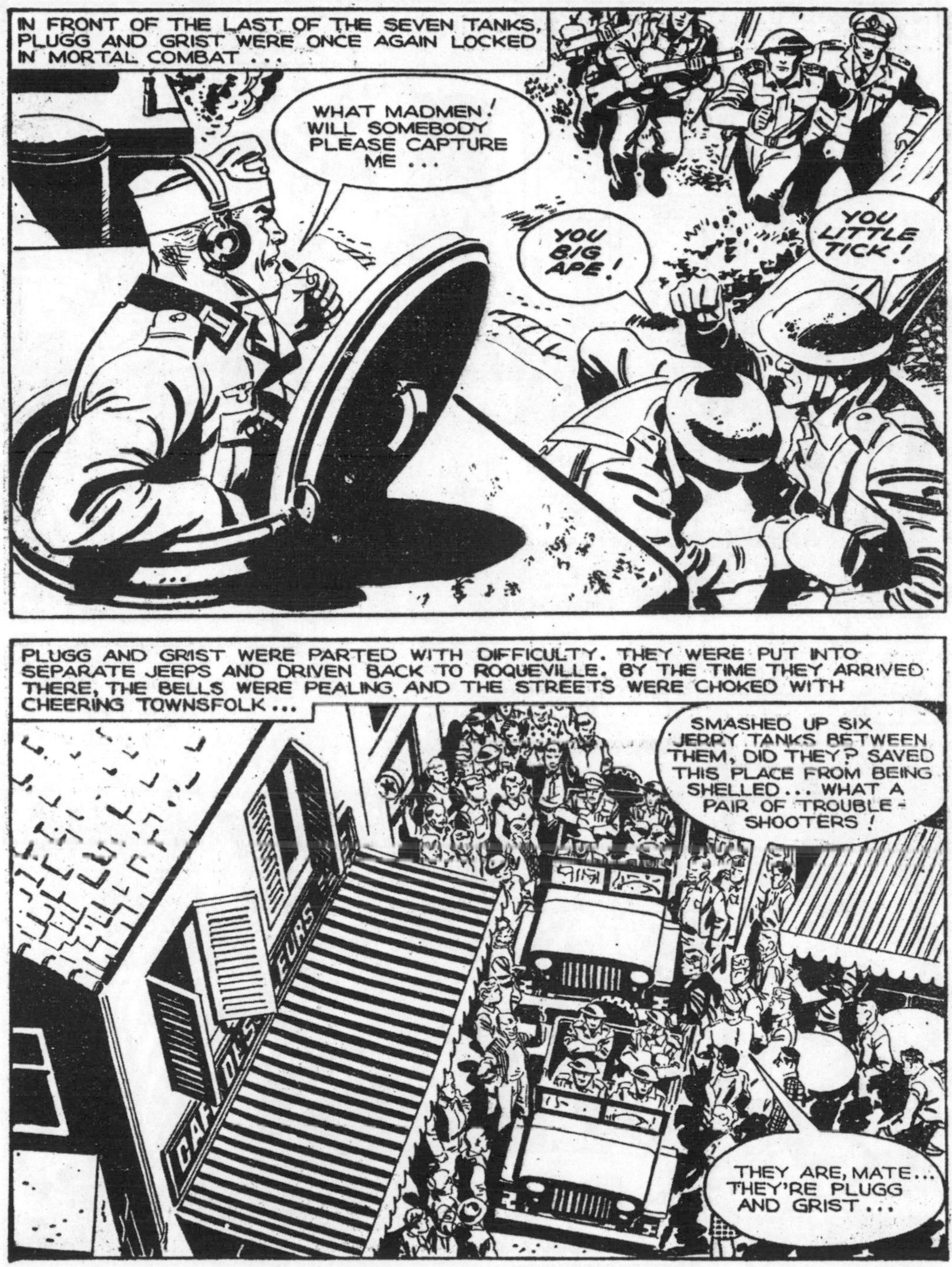
IN FRONT OF THE LAST OF THE SEVEN TANKS, PLUGG AND GRIST WERE ONCE AGAIN LOCKED IN MORTAL COMBAT . . .
WHAT MADMEN! WILL SOMEBODY PLEASE CAPTURE ME . . .
YOU BIG APE!
YOU LITTLE TICK!
PLUGG AND GRIST WERE PARTED WITH DIFFICULTY. THEY WERE PUT INTO SEPARATE JEEPS AND DRIVEN BACK TO ROQUEVILLE. BY THE TIME THEY ARRIVED THERE, THE BELLS WERE PEALING AND THE STREETS WERE CHOKED WITH CHEERING TOWNSFOLK . . .
SMASHED UP SIX JERRY TANKS BETWEEN THEM, DID THEY? SAVED THIS PLACE FROM BEING SHELLED . . . WHAT A PAIR OF TROUBLE-SHOOTERS!
THEY ARE, MATE . . . THEY'RE PLUGG AND GRIST . . .

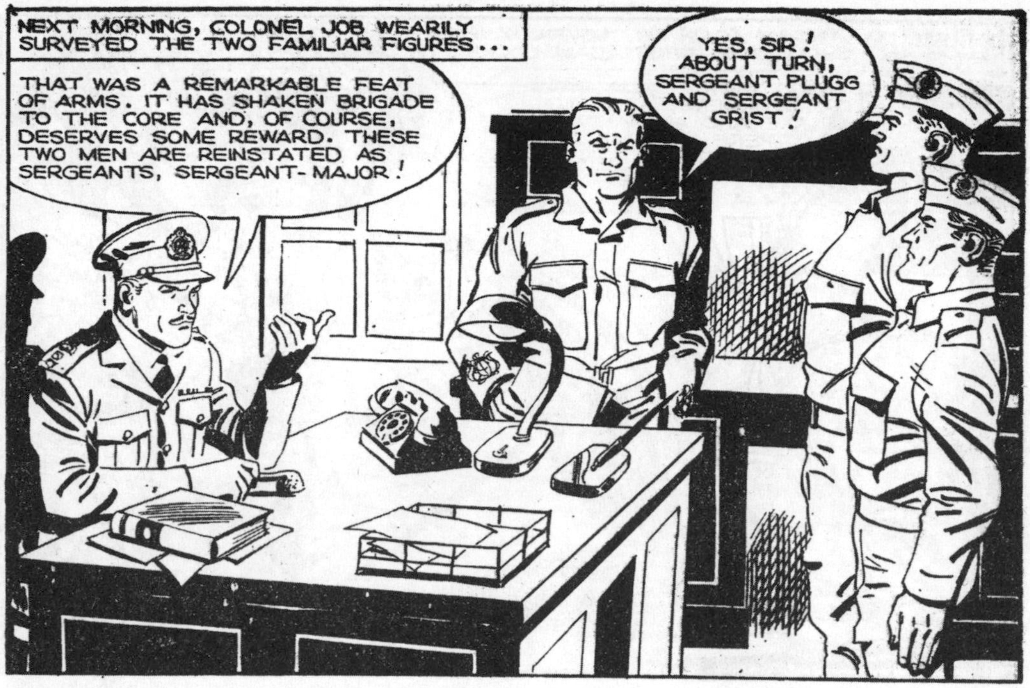
NEXT MORNING, COLONEL JOB WEARILY SURVEYED THE TWO FAMILIAR FIGURES...
THAT WAS A REMARKABLE FEAT OF ARMS. IT HAS SHAKEN BRIGADE TO THE CORE AND, OF COURSE, DESERVES SOME REWARD. THESE TWO MEN ARE REINSTATED AS SERGEANTS, SERGEANT-MAJOR!
YES, SIR! ABOUT TURN, SERGEANT PLUGG AND SERGEANT GRIST!

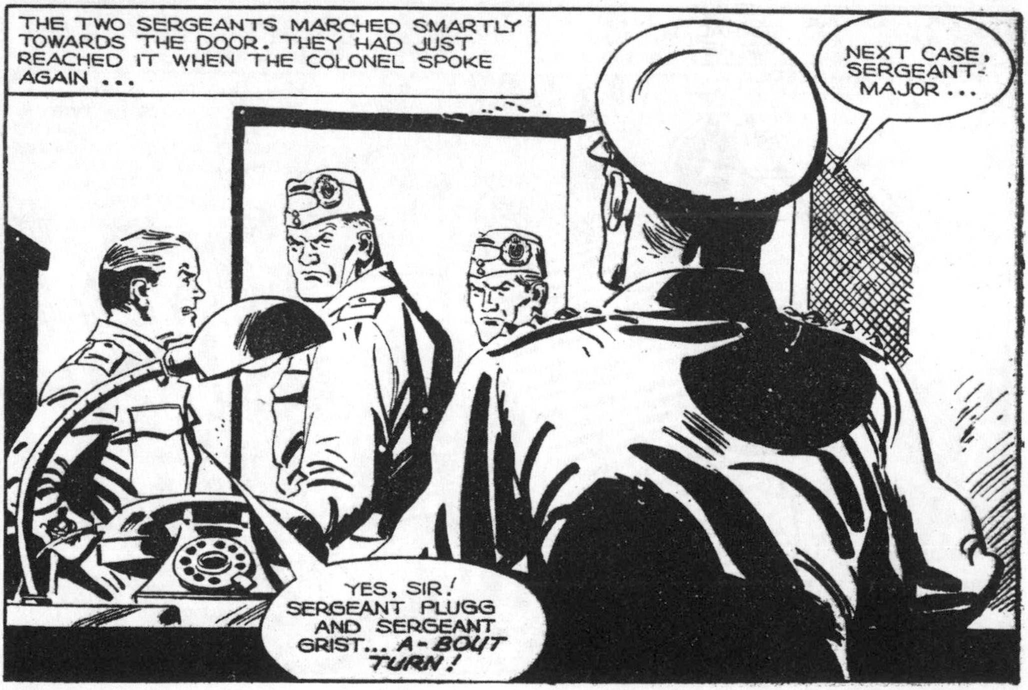
THE TWO SERGEANTS MARCHED SMARTLY TOWARDS THE DOOR. THEY HAD JUST REACHED IT WHEN THE COLONEL SPOKE AGAIN...
NEXT CASE, SERGEANT-MAJOR...
YES, SIR! SERGEANT PLUGG AND SERGEANT GRIST... A-BOUT TURN!

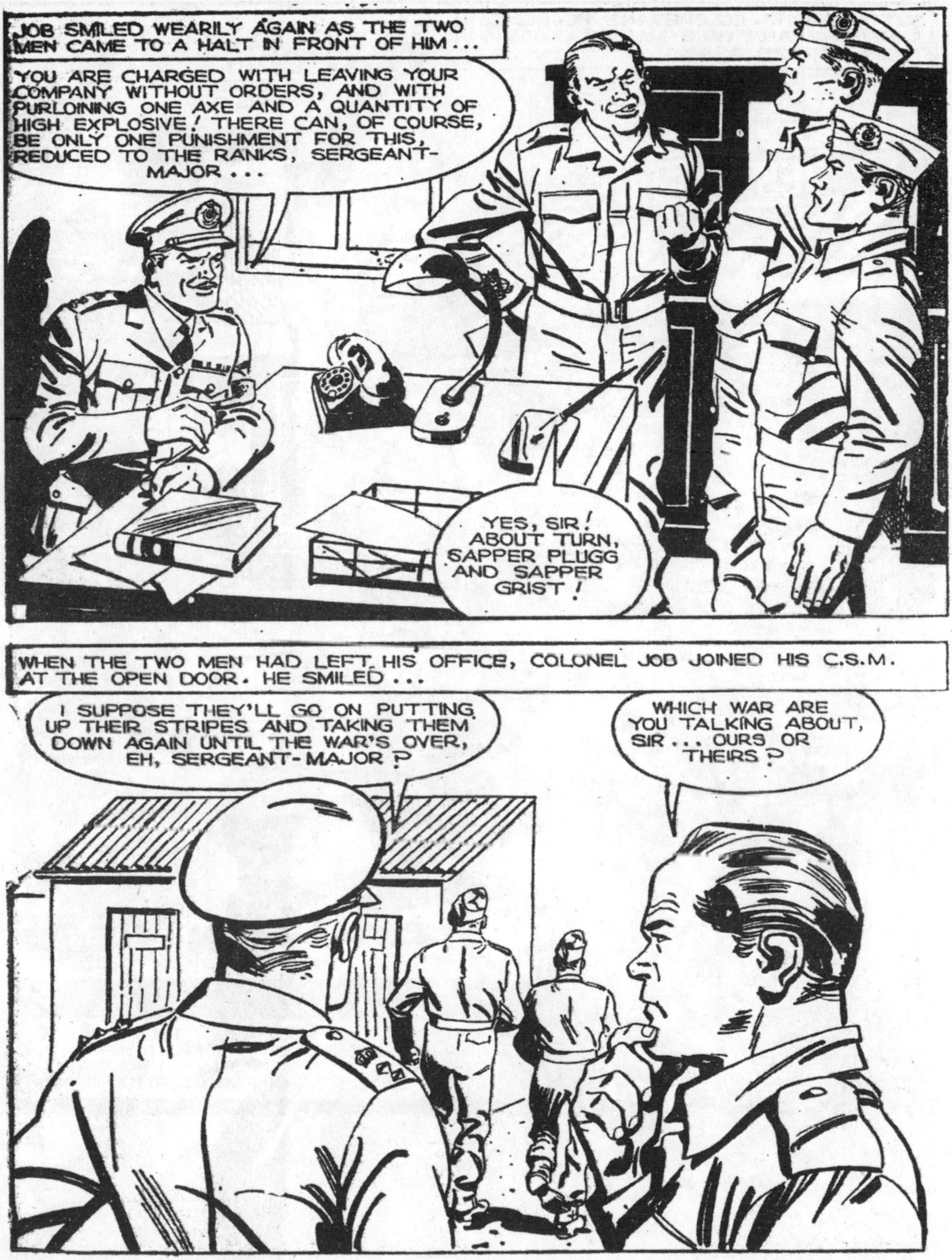
JOB SMILED WEARILY AGAIN AS THE TWO MEN CAME TO A HALT IN FRONT OF HIM...
YOU ARE CHARGED WITH LEAVING YOUR COMPANY WITHOUT ORDERS, AND WITH PURLOINING ONE AXE AND A QUANTITY OF HIGH EXPLOSIVE! THERE CAN, OF COURSE, BE ONLY ONE PUNISHMENT FOR THIS, REDUCED TO THE RANKS, SERGEANT-MAJOR...
YES, SIR! ABOUT TURN, SAPPER PLUGG AND SAPPER GRIST!
WHEN THE TWO MEN HAD LEFT HIS OFFICE, COLONEL JOB JOINED HIS C.S.M. AT THE OPEN DOOR. HE SMILED...
I SUPPOSE THEY'LL GO ON PUTTING UP THEIR STRIPES AND TAKING THEM DOWN AGAIN UNTIL THE WAR'S OVER, EH, SERGEANT-MAJOR?
WHICH WAR ARE YOU TALKING ABOUT, SIR... OURS OR THEIRS?

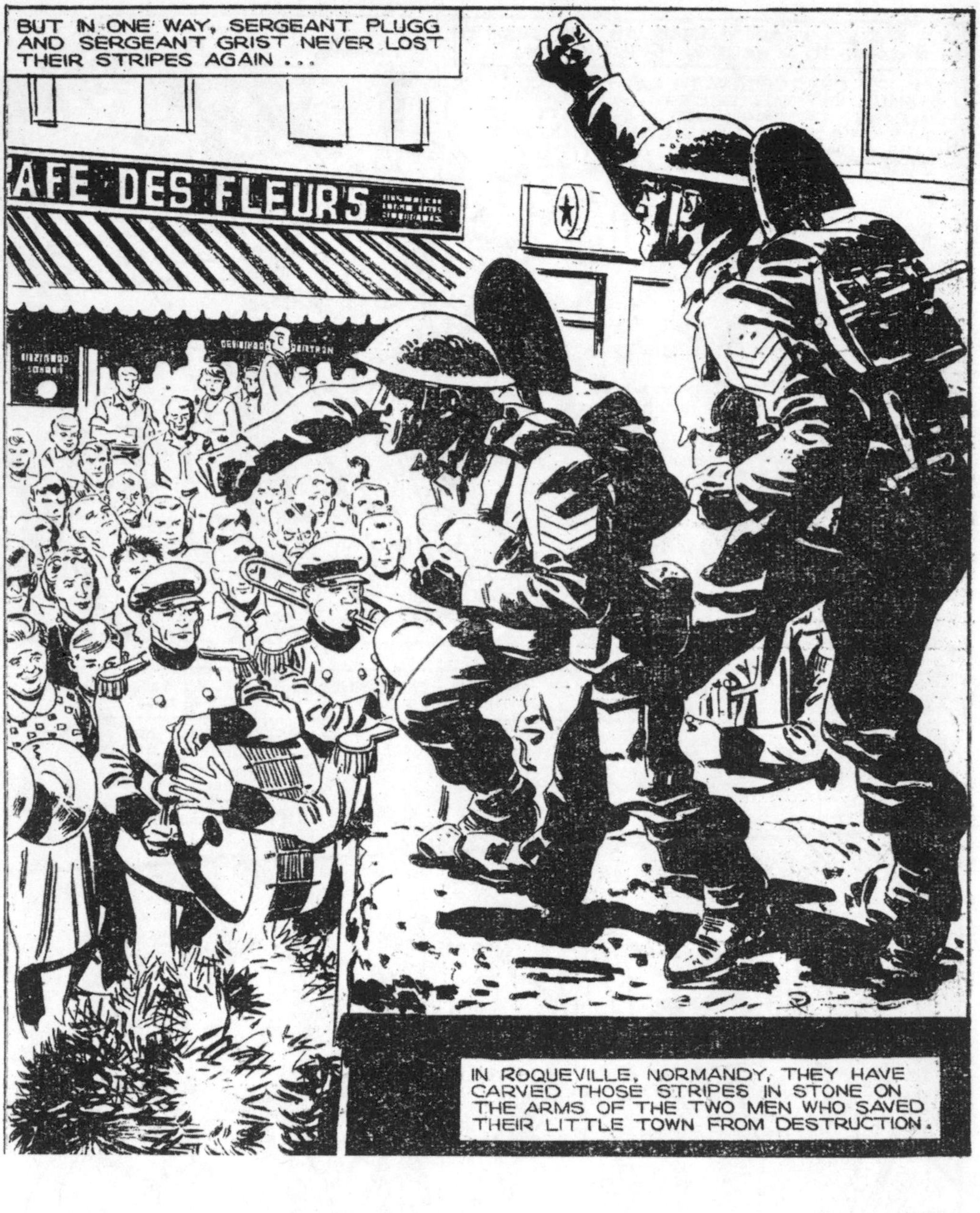
BUT IN ONE WAY, SERGEANT PLUGG AND SERGEANT GRIST NEVER LOST THEIR STRIPES AGAIN ...
AFE DES FLEURS
IN ROQUEVILLE, NORMANDY, THEY HAVE CARVED THOSE STRIPES IN STONE ON THE ARMS OF THE TWO MEN WHO SAVED THEIR LITTLE TOWN FROM DESTRUCTION.

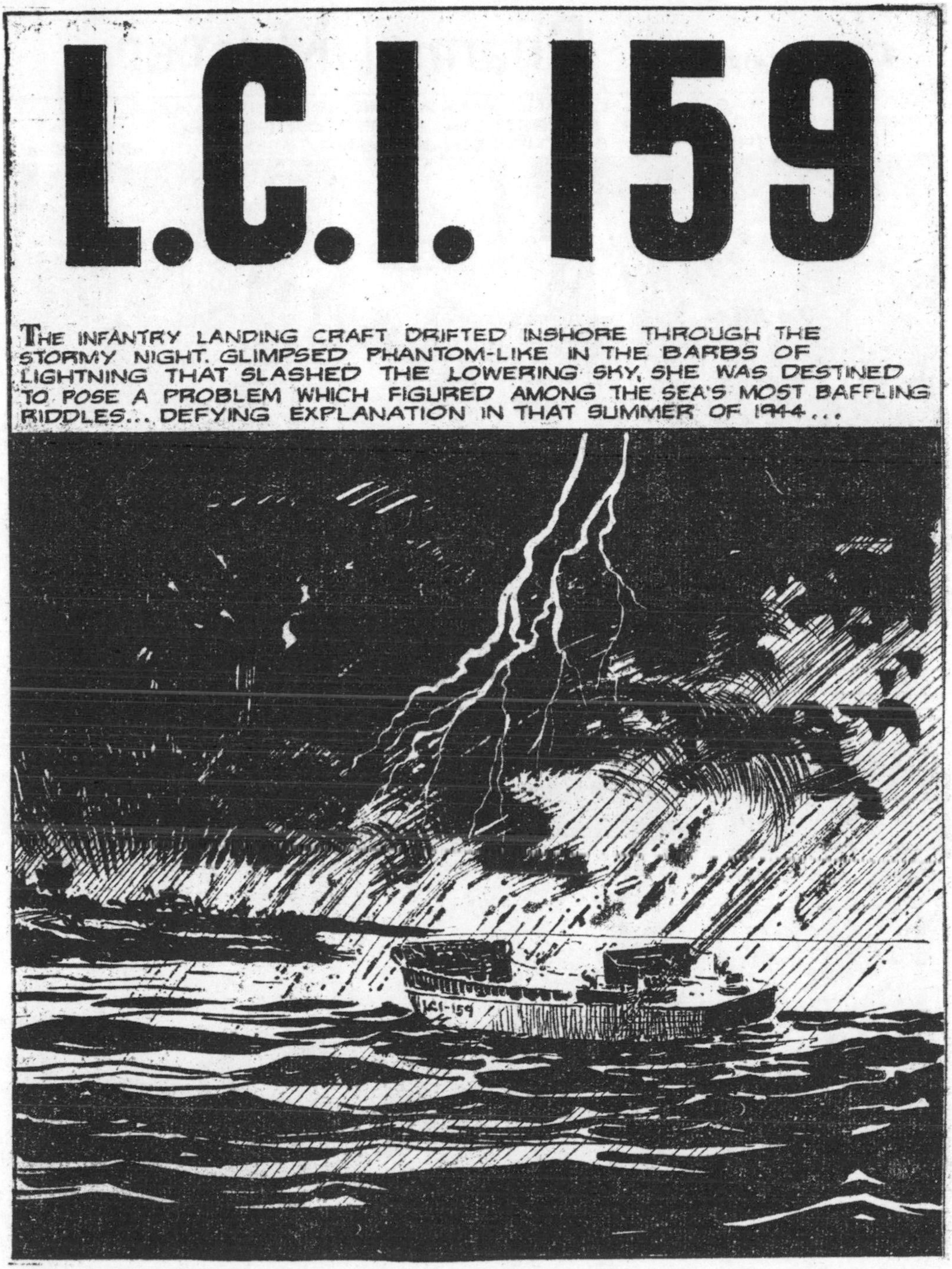
L.C.I. 159
THE INFANTRY LANDING CRAFT DRIFTED INSHORE THROUGH THE STORMY NIGHT. GLIMPSED PHANTOM-LIKE IN THE BARBS OF LIGHTNING THAT SLASHED THE LOWERING SKY, SHE WAS DESTINED TO POSE A PROBLEM WHICH FIGURED AMONG THE SEA'S MOST BAFFLING RIDDLES... DEFYING EXPLANATION IN THAT SUMMER OF 1944...
L.C.I-159

Chapter 1. Channel Mystery

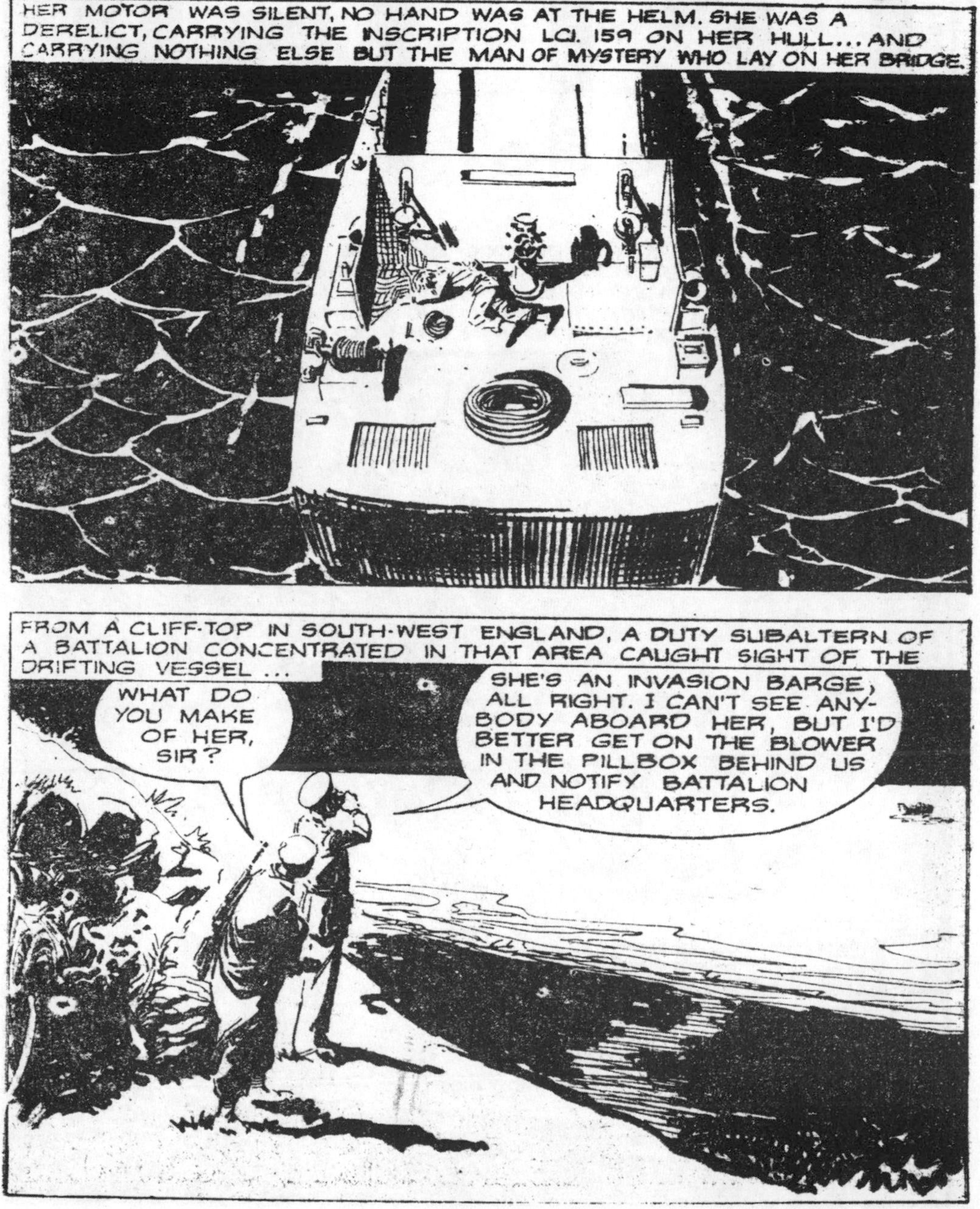
HER MOTOR WAS SILENT, NO HAND WAS AT THE HELM. SHE WAS A DERELICT, CARRYING THE INSCRIPTION L.C.I. 159 ON HER HULL... AND CARRYING NOTHING ELSE BUT THE MAN OF MYSTERY WHO LAY ON HER BRIDGE.
FROM A CLIFF-TOP IN SOUTH-WEST ENGLAND, A DUTY SUBALTERN OF A BATTALION CONCENTRATED IN THAT AREA CAUGHT SIGHT OF THE DRIFTING VESSEL ...
WHAT DO YOU MAKE OF HER, SIR?
SHE'S AN INVASION BARGE, ALL RIGHT. I CAN'T SEE ANYBODY ABOARD HER, BUT I'D BETTER GET ON THE BLOWER IN THE PILLBOX BEHIND US AND NOTIFY BATTALION HEADQUARTERS.

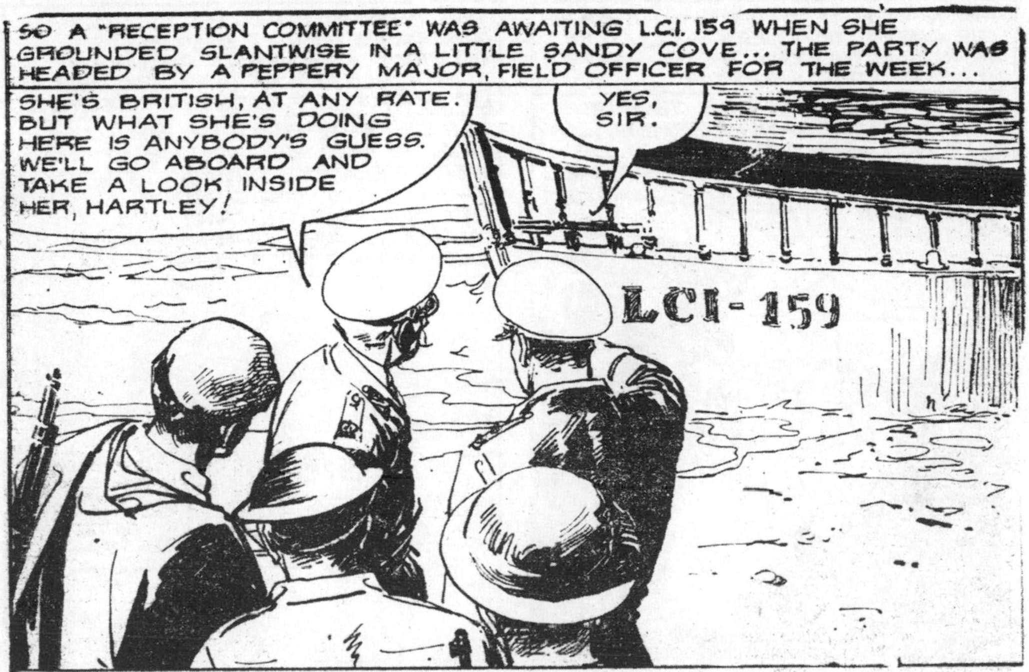
SO A "RECEPTION COMMITTEE" WAS AWAITING L.C.I. 159 WHEN SHE GROUNDED SLANTWISE IN A LITTLE SANDY COVE... THE PARTY WAS HEADED BY A PEPPERY MAJOR, FIELD OFFICER FOR THE WEEK...
SHE'S BRITISH, AT ANY RATE. BUT WHAT SHE'S DOING HERE IS ANYBODY'S GUESS. WE'LL GO ABOARD AND TAKE A LOOK INSIDE HER, HARTLEY!
YES, SIR.
LCI-159

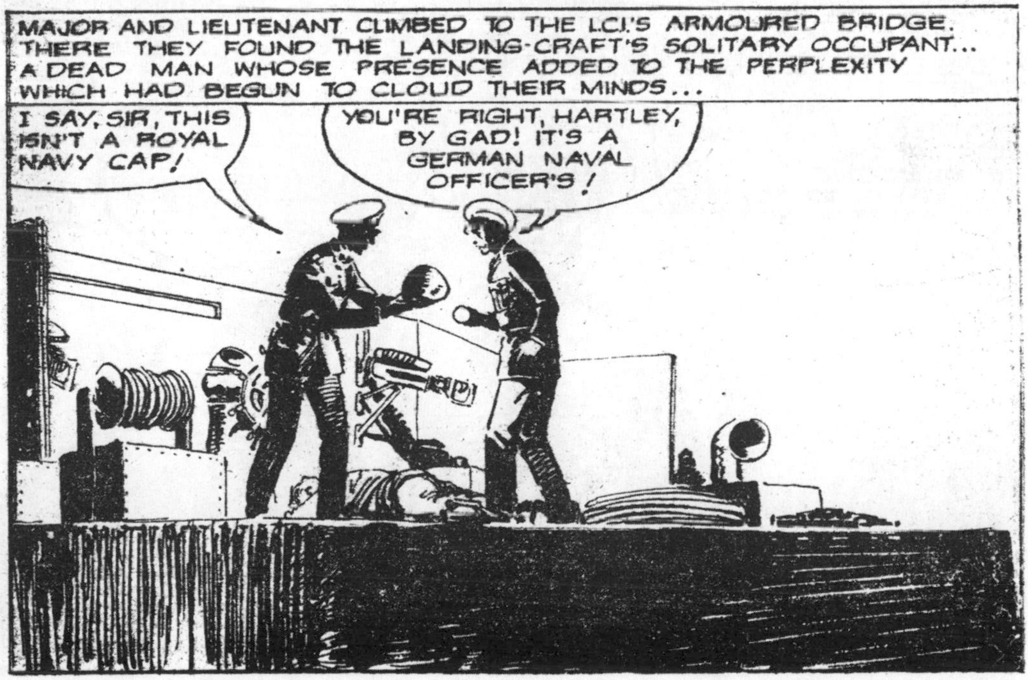
MAJOR AND LIEUTENANT CLIMBED TO THE L.C.I.'S ARMOURED BRIDGE. THERE THEY FOUND THE LANDING-CRAFT'S SOLITARY OCCUPANT... A DEAD MAN WHOSE PRESENCE ADDED TO THE PERPLEXITY WHICH HAD BEGUN TO CLOUD THEIR MINDS...
I SAY, SIR, THIS ISN'T A ROYAL NAVY CAP!
YOU'RE RIGHT, HARTLEY, BY GAD! IT'S A GERMAN NAVAL OFFICER'S!

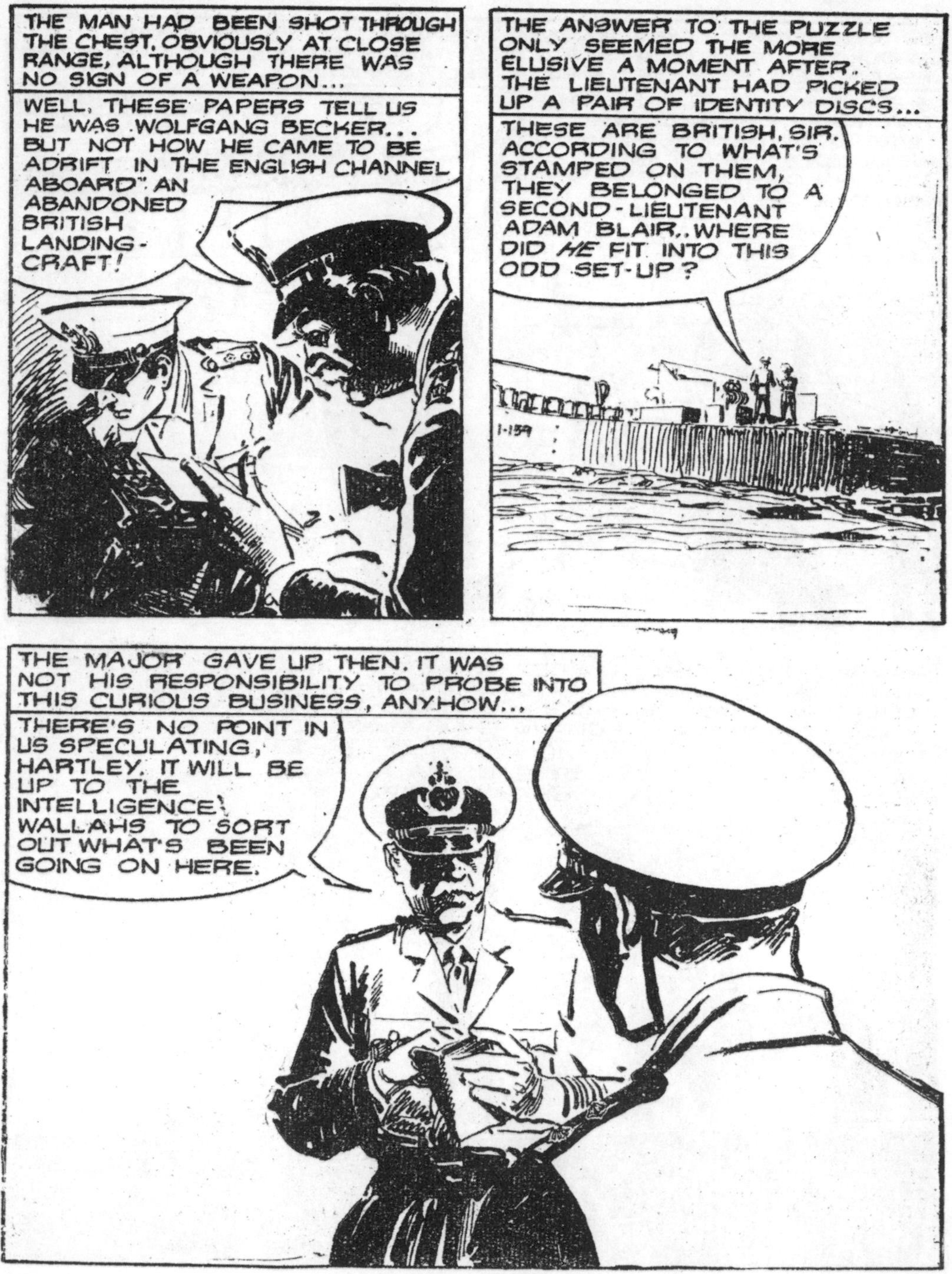
THE MAN HAD BEEN SHOT THROUGH THE CHEST, OBVIOUSLY AT CLOSE RANGE, ALTHOUGH THERE WAS NO SIGN OF A WEAPON...
WELL, THESE PAPERS TELL US HE WAS WOLFGANG BECKER... BUT NOT HOW HE CAME TO BE ADRIFT IN THE ENGLISH CHANNEL ABOARD AN ABANDONED BRITISH LANDING-CRAFT!
THE ANSWER TO THE PUZZLE ONLY SEEMED THE MORE ELUSIVE A MOMENT AFTER. THE LIEUTENANT HAD PICKED UP A PAIR OF IDENTITY DISCS...
THESE ARE BRITISH, SIR. ACCORDING TO WHAT'S STAMPED ON THEM, THEY BELONGED TO A SECOND-LIEUTENANT ADAM BLAIR.. WHERE DID *HE* FIT INTO THIS ODD SET-UP?
THE MAJOR GAVE UP THEN. IT WAS NOT HIS RESPONSIBILITY TO PROBE INTO THIS CURIOUS BUSINESS, ANYHOW...
THERE'S NO POINT IN US SPECULATING, HARTLEY. IT WILL BE UP TO THE INTELLIGENCE WALLAHS TO SORT OUT WHAT'S BEEN GOING ON HERE.

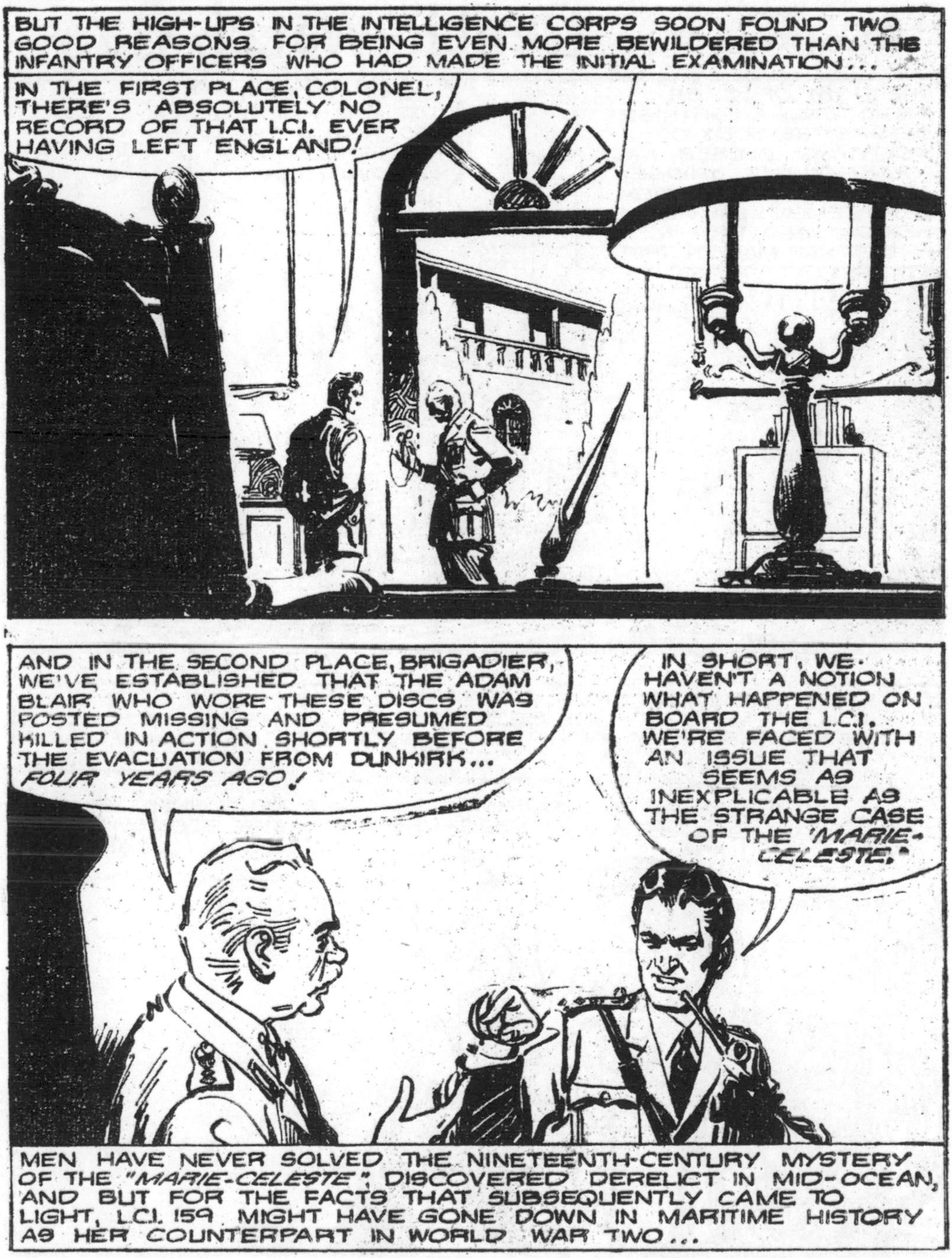
BUT THE HIGH-UPS IN THE INTELLIGENCE CORPS SOON FOUND TWO GOOD REASONS FOR BEING EVEN MORE BEWILDERED THAN THE INFANTRY OFFICERS WHO HAD MADE THE INITIAL EXAMINATION...
IN THE FIRST PLACE, COLONEL, THERE'S ABSOLUTELY NO RECORD OF THAT L.C.I. EVER HAVING LEFT ENGLAND!
AND IN THE SECOND PLACE, BRIGADIER, WE'VE ESTABLISHED THAT THE ADAM BLAIR WHO WORE THESE DISCS WAS POSTED MISSING AND PRESUMED KILLED IN ACTION SHORTLY BEFORE THE EVACUATION FROM DUNKIRK... *FOUR YEARS AGO!*
IN SHORT, WE HAVEN'T A NOTION WHAT HAPPENED ON BOARD THE L.C.I. WE'RE FACED WITH AN ISSUE THAT SEEMS AS INEXPLICABLE AS THE STRANGE CASE OF THE *'MARIE-CELESTE.'*
MEN HAVE NEVER SOLVED THE NINETEENTH-CENTURY MYSTERY OF THE *"MARIE-CELESTE"*, DISCOVERED DERELICT IN MID-OCEAN, AND BUT FOR THE FACTS THAT SUBSEQUENTLY CAME TO LIGHT, L.C.I. 159 MIGHT HAVE GONE DOWN IN MARITIME HISTORY AS HER COUNTERPART IN WORLD WAR TWO...

Chapter 2. Death-Watch Bay

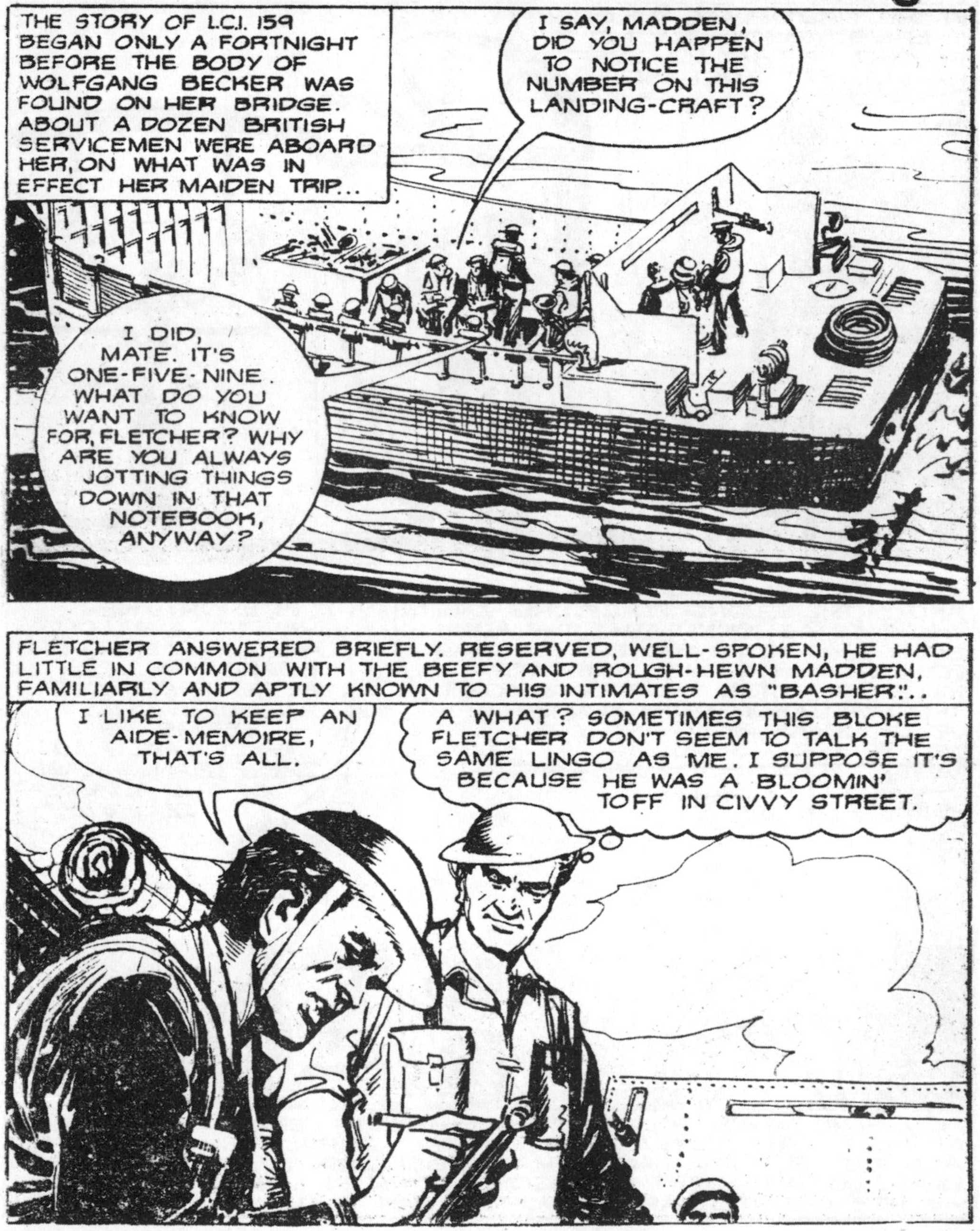
THE STORY OF L.C.I. 159 BEGAN ONLY A FORTNIGHT BEFORE THE BODY OF WOLFGANG BECKER WAS FOUND ON HER BRIDGE. ABOUT A DOZEN BRITISH SERVICEMEN WERE ABOARD HER, ON WHAT WAS IN EFFECT HER MAIDEN TRIP...
I SAY, MADDEN, DID YOU HAPPEN TO NOTICE THE NUMBER ON THIS LANDING-CRAFT?
I DID, MATE. IT'S ONE-FIVE-NINE. WHAT DO YOU WANT TO KNOW FOR, FLETCHER? WHY ARE YOU ALWAYS JOTTING THINGS DOWN IN THAT NOTEBOOK, ANYWAY?
FLETCHER ANSWERED BRIEFLY. RESERVED, WELL-SPOKEN, HE HAD LITTLE IN COMMON WITH THE BEEFY AND ROUGH-HEWN MADDEN, FAMILIARLY AND APTLY KNOWN TO HIS INTIMATES AS "BASHER"..
I LIKE TO KEEP AN AIDE-MEMOIRE, THAT'S ALL.
A WHAT? SOMETIMES THIS BLOKE FLETCHER DON'T SEEM TO TALK THE SAME LINGO AS ME. I SUPPOSE IT'S BECAUSE HE WAS A BLOOMIN' TOFF IN CIVVY STREET.

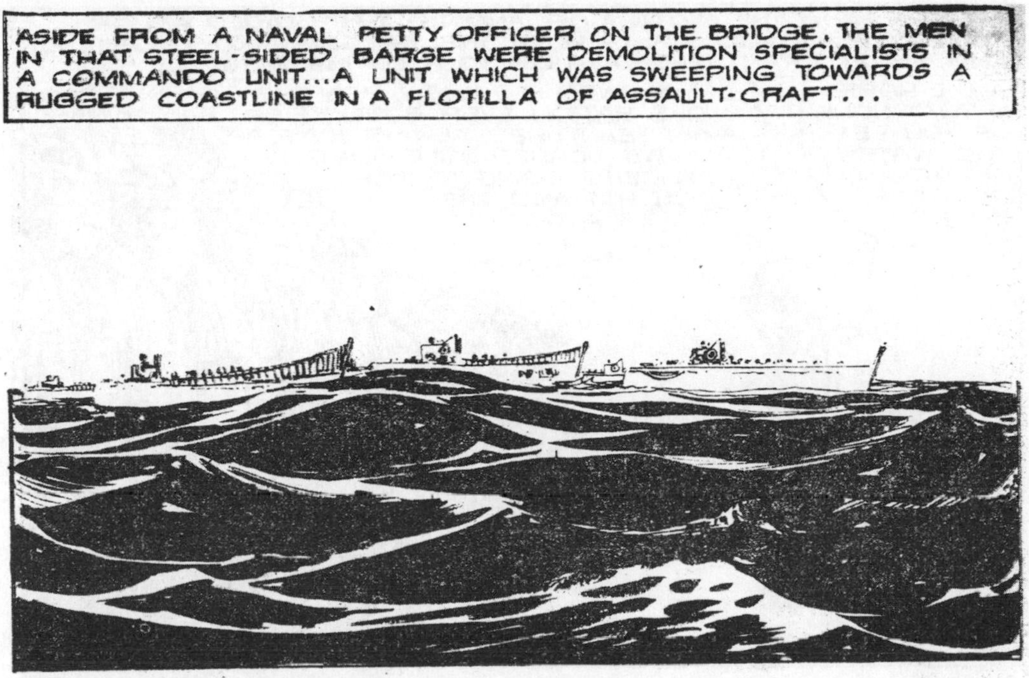
ASIDE FROM A NAVAL PETTY OFFICER ON THE BRIDGE, THE MEN IN THAT STEEL-SIDED BARGE WERE DEMOLITION SPECIALISTS IN A COMMANDO UNIT...A UNIT WHICH WAS SWEEPING TOWARDS A RUGGED COASTLINE IN A FLOTILLA OF ASSAULT-CRAFT...

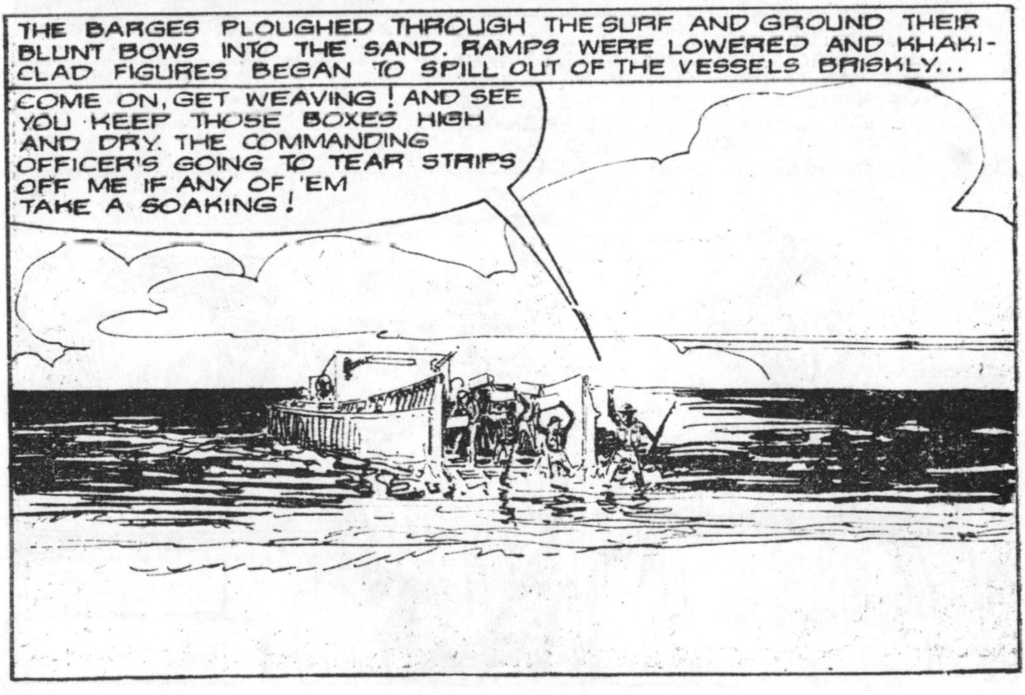
THE BARGES PLOUGHED THROUGH THE SURF AND GROUND THEIR BLUNT BOWS INTO THE SAND. RAMPS WERE LOWERED AND KHAKI-CLAD FIGURES BEGAN TO SPILL OUT OF THE VESSELS BRISKLY...
COME ON, GET WEAVING! AND SEE YOU KEEP THOSE BOXES HIGH AND DRY. THE COMMANDING OFFICER'S GOING TO TEAR STRIPS OFF ME IF ANY OF 'EM TAKE A SOAKING!

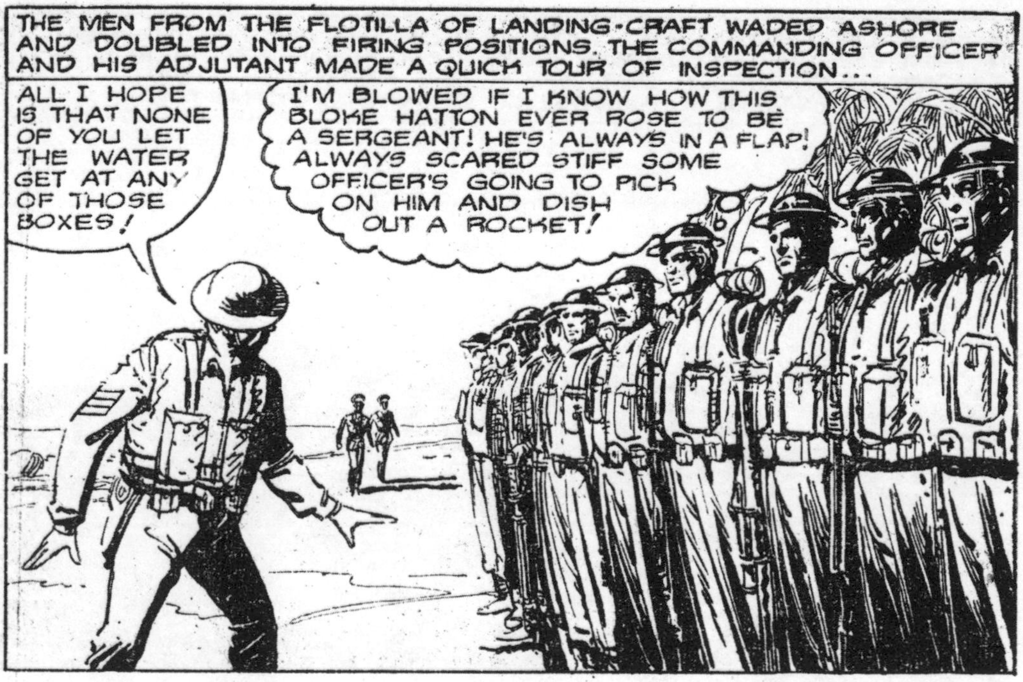
THE MEN FROM THE FLOTILLA OF LANDING-CRAFT WADED ASHORE AND DOUBLED INTO FIRING POSITIONS. THE COMMANDING OFFICER AND HIS ADJUTANT MADE A QUICK TOUR OF INSPECTION...
ALL I HOPE IS THAT NONE OF YOU LET THE WATER GET AT ANY OF THOSE BOXES!
I'M BLOWED IF I KNOW HOW THIS BLOKE HATTON EVER ROSE TO BE A SERGEANT! HE'S ALWAYS IN A FLAP! ALWAYS SCARED STIFF SOME OFFICER'S GOING TO PICK ON HIM AND DISH OUT A ROCKET!

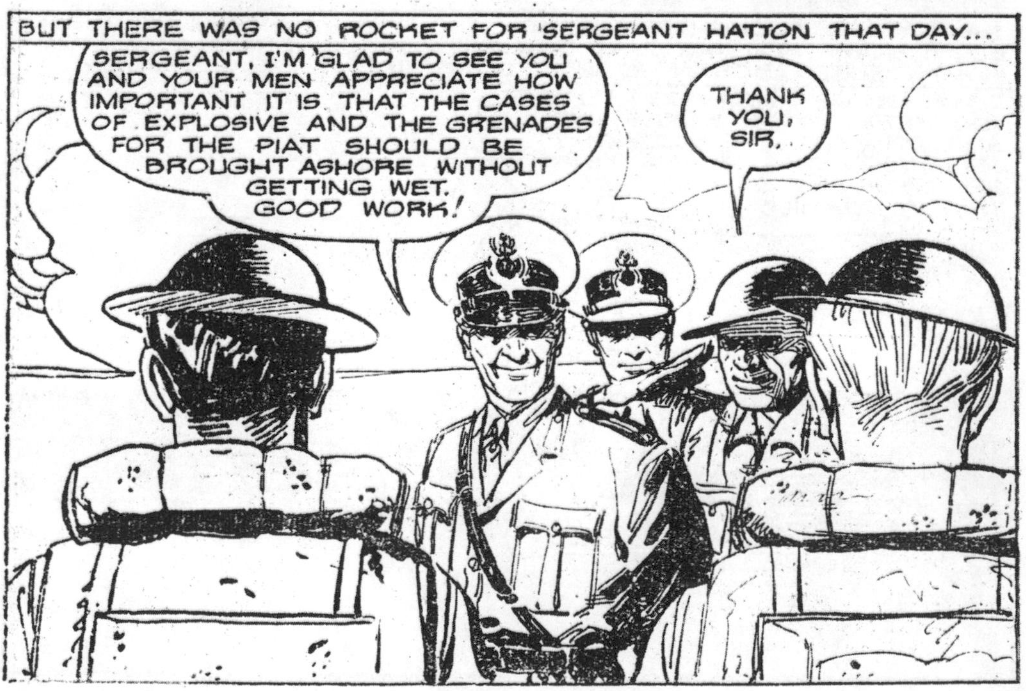
BUT THERE WAS NO ROCKET FOR SERGEANT HATTON THAT DAY...
SERGEANT, I'M GLAD TO SEE YOU AND YOUR MEN APPRECIATE HOW IMPORTANT IT IS THAT THE CASES OF EXPLOSIVE AND THE GRENADES FOR THE PIAT SHOULD BE BROUGHT ASHORE WITHOUT GETTING WET. GOOD WORK!
THANK YOU, SIR.

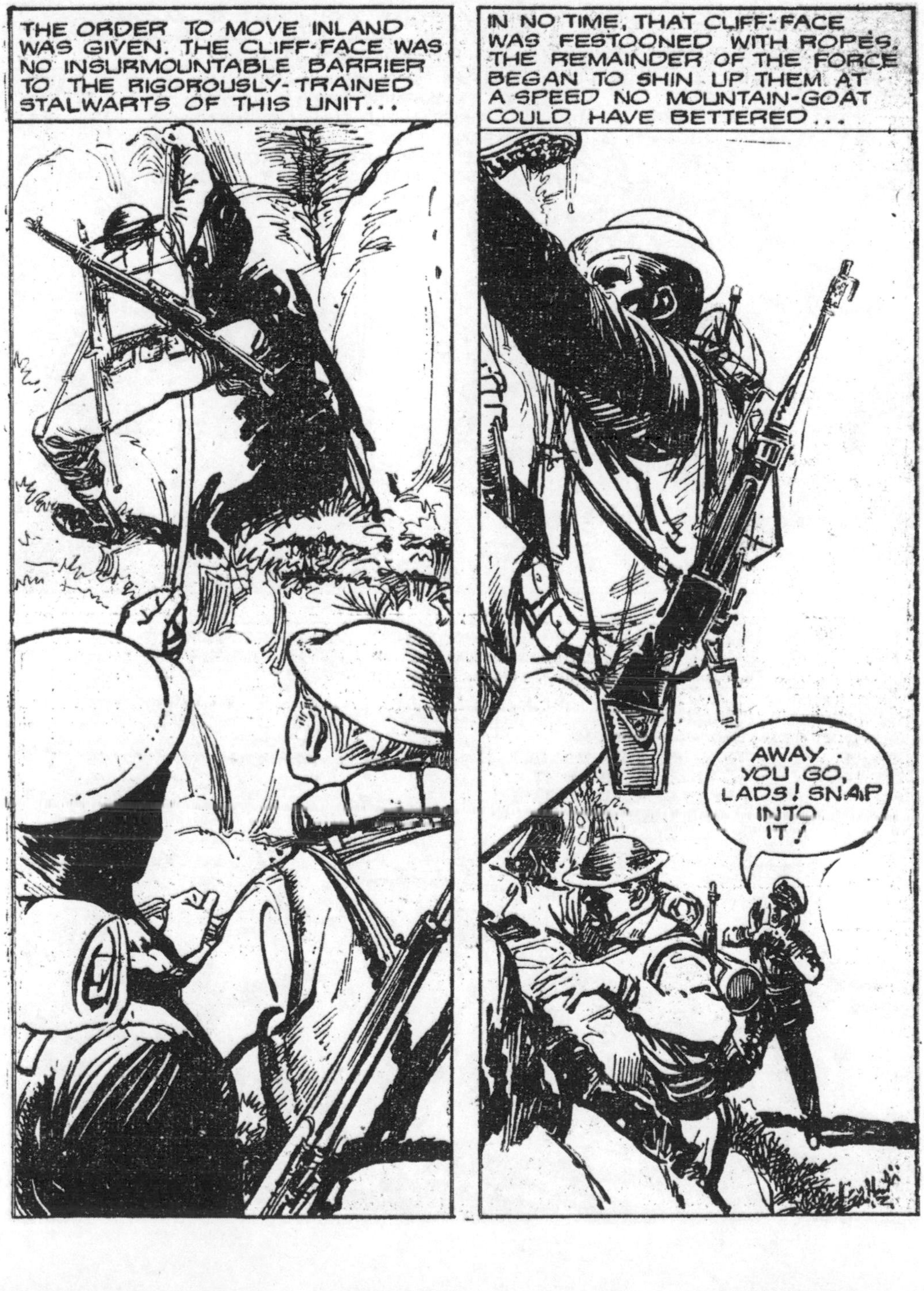
THE ORDER TO MOVE INLAND WAS GIVEN. THE CLIFF-FACE WAS NO INSURMOUNTABLE BARRIER TO THE RIGOROUSLY-TRAINED STALWARTS OF THIS UNIT...
IN NO TIME, THAT CLIFF-FACE WAS FESTOONED WITH ROPES. THE REMAINDER OF THE FORCE BEGAN TO SHIN UP THEM AT A SPEED NO MOUNTAIN-GOAT COULD HAVE BETTERED...
AWAY YOU GO, LADS! SNAP INTO IT!

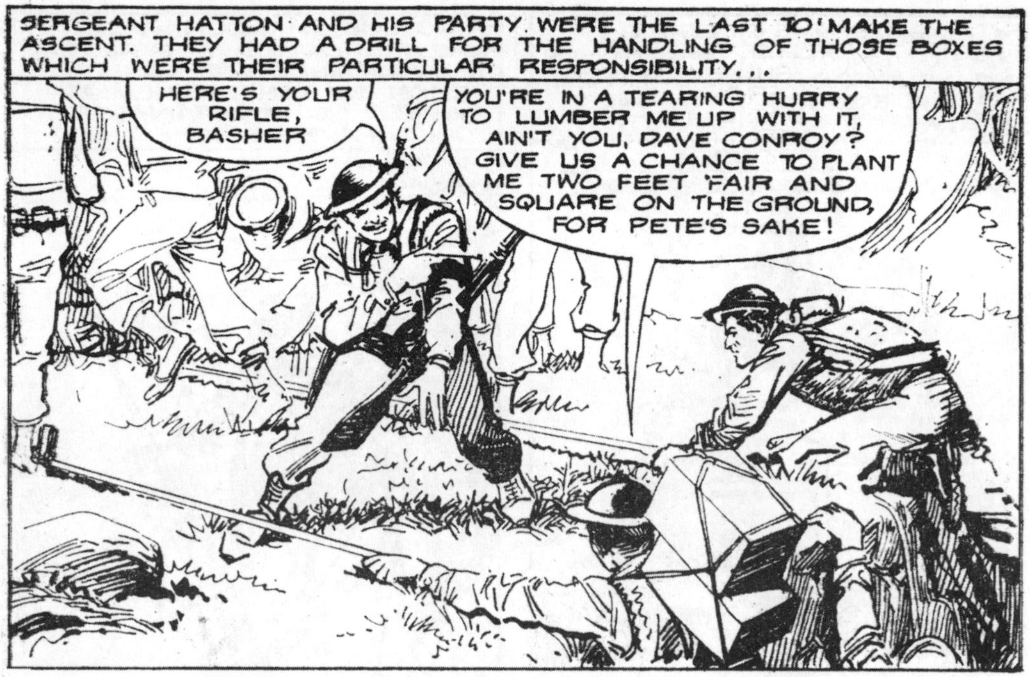
SERGEANT HATTON AND HIS PARTY WERE THE LAST TO MAKE THE ASCENT. THEY HAD A DRILL FOR THE HANDLING OF THOSE BOXES WHICH WERE THEIR PARTICULAR RESPONSIBILITY...
HERE'S YOUR RIFLE, BASHER
YOU'RE IN A TEARING HURRY TO LUMBER ME UP WITH IT, AIN'T YOU, DAVE CONROY? GIVE US A CHANCE TO PLANT ME TWO FEET FAIR AND SQUARE ON THE GROUND, FOR PETE'S SAKE!

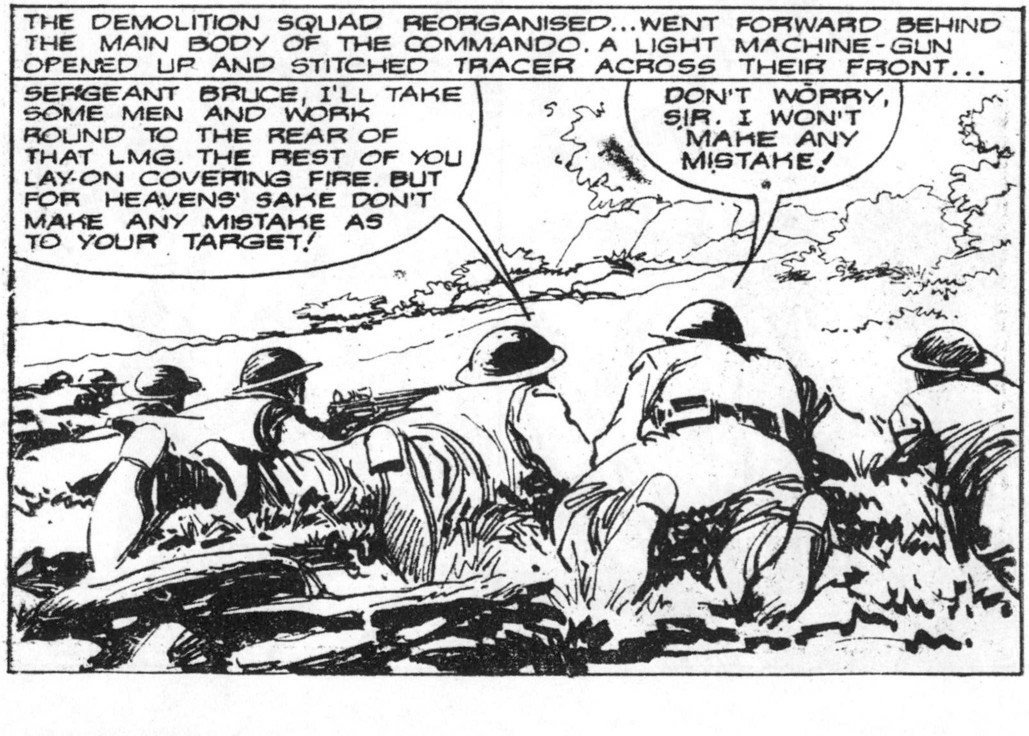
THE DEMOLITION SQUAD REORGANISED...WENT FORWARD BEHIND THE MAIN BODY OF THE COMMANDO. A LIGHT MACHINE-GUN OPENED UP AND STITCHED TRACER ACROSS THEIR FRONT...
SERGEANT BRUCE, I'LL TAKE SOME MEN AND WORK ROUND TO THE REAR OF THAT LMG. THE REST OF YOU LAY-ON COVERING FIRE. BUT FOR HEAVENS' SAKE DON'T MAKE ANY MISTAKE AS TO YOUR TARGET!
DON'T WORRY, SIR. I WON'T MAKE ANY MISTAKE!

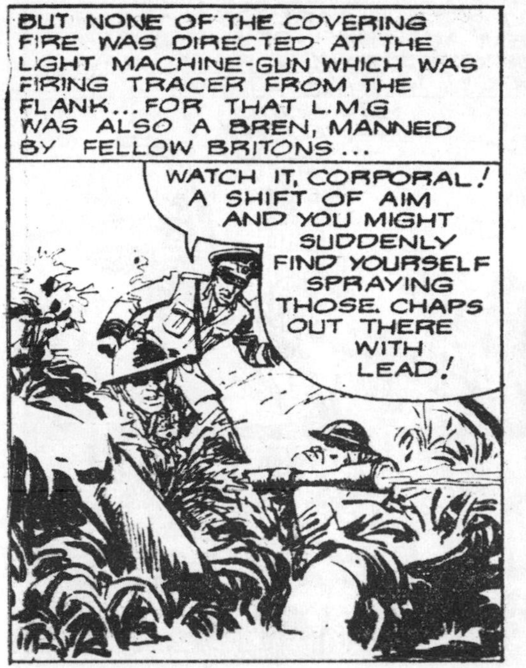
BUT NONE OF THE COVERING FIRE WAS DIRECTED AT THE LIGHT MACHINE-GUN WHICH WAS FIRING TRACER FROM THE FLANK... FOR THAT L.M.G WAS ALSO A BREN, MANNED BY FELLOW BRITONS...
WATCH IT, CORPORAL! A SHIFT OF AIM AND YOU MIGHT SUDDENLY FIND YOURSELF SPRAYING THOSE CHAPS OUT THERE WITH LEAD!

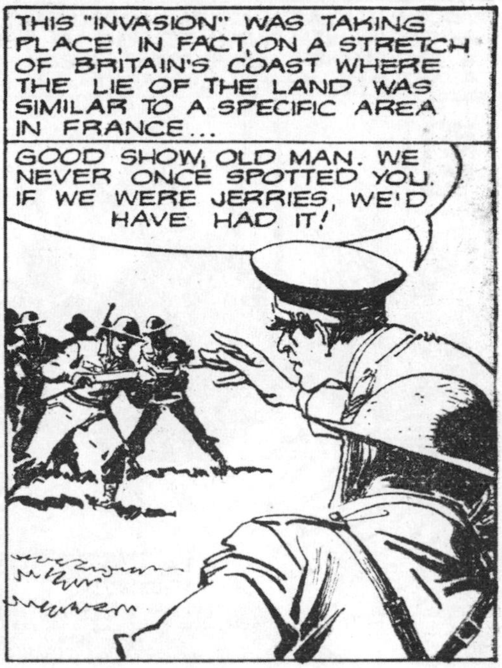
THIS "INVASION" WAS TAKING PLACE, IN FACT, ON A STRETCH OF BRITAIN'S COAST WHERE THE LIE OF THE LAND WAS SIMILAR TO A SPECIFIC AREA IN FRANCE...
GOOD SHOW, OLD MAN. WE NEVER ONCE SPOTTED YOU. IF WE WERE JERRIES, WE'D HAVE HAD IT!

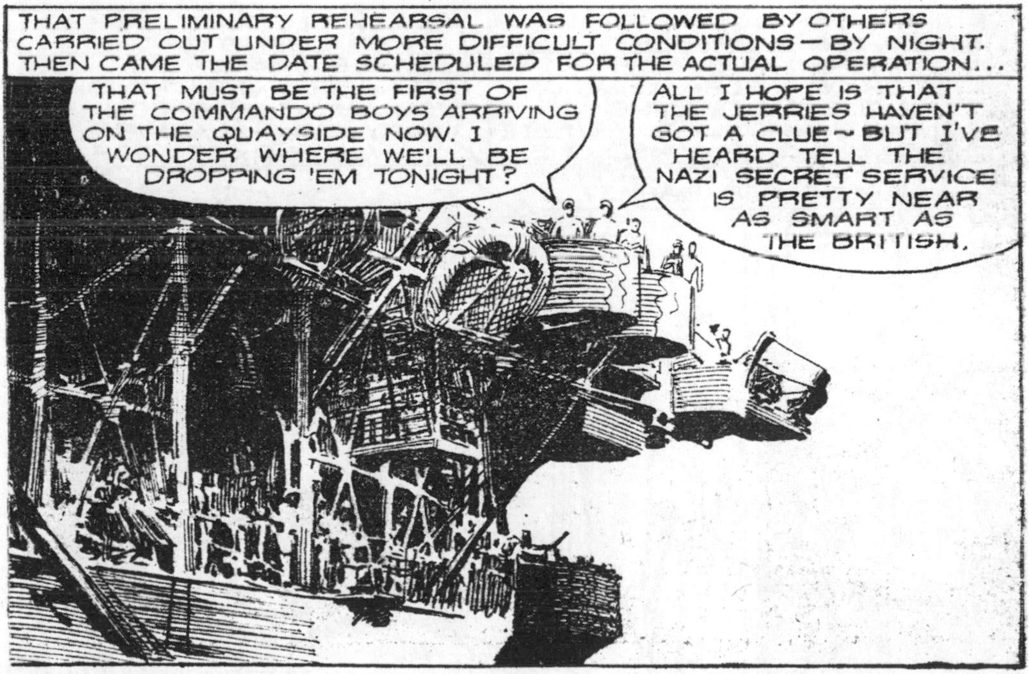
THAT PRELIMINARY REHEARSAL WAS FOLLOWED BY OTHERS CARRIED OUT UNDER MORE DIFFICULT CONDITIONS — BY NIGHT. THEN CAME THE DATE SCHEDULED FOR THE ACTUAL OPERATION...
THAT MUST BE THE FIRST OF THE COMMANDO BOYS ARRIVING ON THE QUAYSIDE NOW. I WONDER WHERE WE'LL BE DROPPING 'EM TONIGHT?
ALL I HOPE IS THAT THE JERRIES HAVEN'T GOT A CLUE ~ BUT I'VE HEARD TELL THE NAZI SECRET SERVICE IS PRETTY NEAR AS SMART AS THE BRITISH.

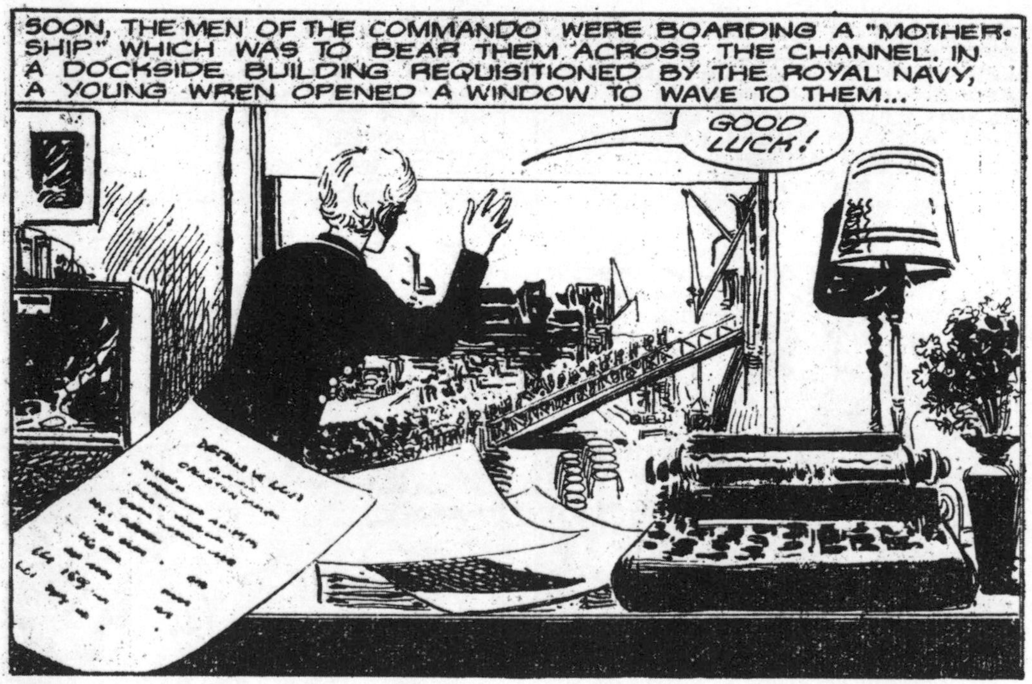
SOON, THE MEN OF THE COMMANDO WERE BOARDING A "MOTHER-SHIP" WHICH WAS TO BEAR THEM ACROSS THE CHANNEL. IN A DOCKSIDE BUILDING REQUISITIONED BY THE ROYAL NAVY, A YOUNG WREN OPENED A WINDOW TO WAVE TO THEM...
GOOD LUCK!

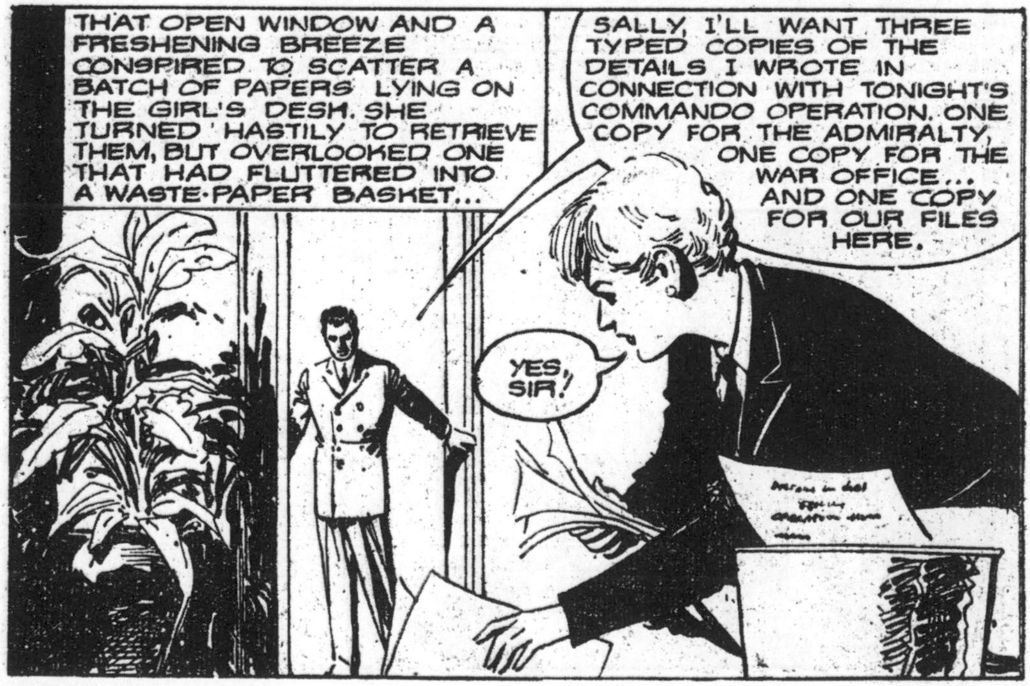
THAT OPEN WINDOW AND A FRESHENING BREEZE CONSPIRED TO SCATTER A BATCH OF PAPERS LYING ON THE GIRL'S DESK. SHE TURNED HASTILY TO RETRIEVE THEM, BUT OVERLOOKED ONE THAT HAD FLUTTERED INTO A WASTE-PAPER BASKET...
SALLY, I'LL WANT THREE TYPED COPIES OF THE DETAILS I WROTE IN CONNECTION WITH TONIGHT'S COMMANDO OPERATION. ONE COPY FOR THE ADMIRALTY, ONE COPY FOR THE WAR OFFICE... AND ONE COPY FOR OUR FILES HERE.
YES, SIR!

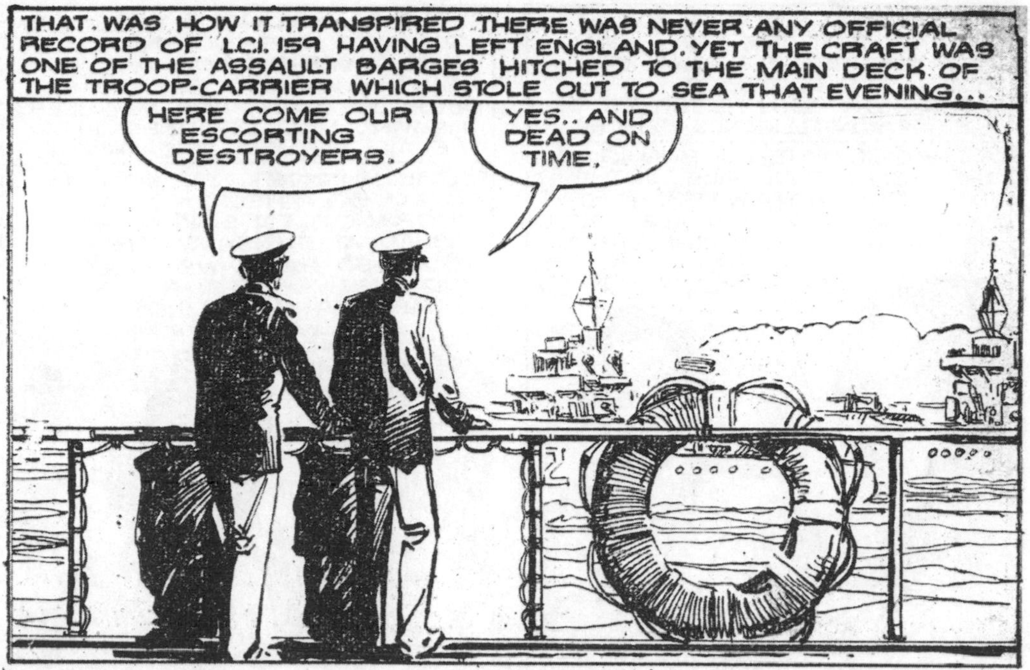
THAT WAS HOW IT TRANSPIRED THERE WAS NEVER ANY OFFICIAL RECORD OF L.C.I. 159 HAVING LEFT ENGLAND. YET THE CRAFT WAS ONE OF THE ASSAULT BARGES HITCHED TO THE MAIN DECK OF THE TROOP-CARRIER WHICH STOLE OUT TO SEA THAT EVENING...
HERE COME OUR ESCORTING DESTROYERS.
YES.. AND DEAD ON TIME.

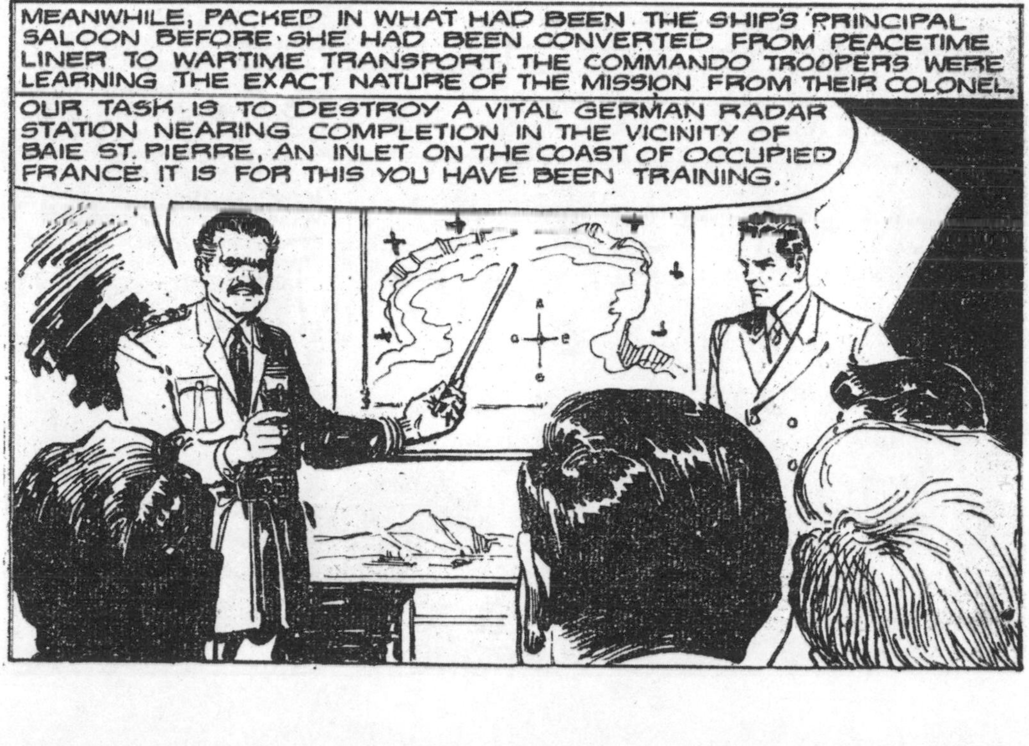
MEANWHILE, PACKED IN WHAT HAD BEEN THE SHIP'S PRINCIPAL SALOON BEFORE SHE HAD BEEN CONVERTED FROM PEACETIME LINER TO WARTIME TRANSPORT, THE COMMANDO TROOPERS WERE LEARNING THE EXACT NATURE OF THE MISSION FROM THEIR COLONEL.
OUR TASK IS TO DESTROY A VITAL GERMAN RADAR STATION NEARING COMPLETION IN THE VICINITY OF BAIE ST. PIERRE, AN INLET ON THE COAST OF OCCUPIED FRANCE. IT IS FOR THIS YOU HAVE BEEN TRAINING.

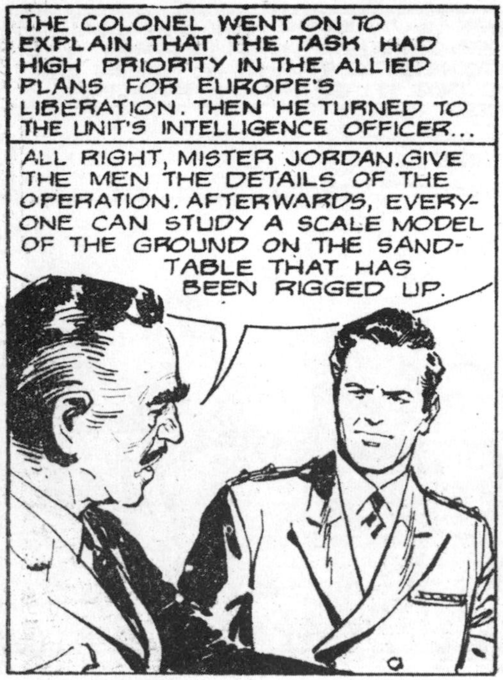
THE COLONEL WENT ON TO EXPLAIN THAT THE TASK HAD HIGH PRIORITY IN THE ALLIED PLANS FOR EUROPE'S LIBERATION. THEN HE TURNED TO THE UNIT'S INTELLIGENCE OFFICER...
ALL RIGHT, MISTER JORDAN. GIVE THE MEN THE DETAILS OF THE OPERATION. AFTERWARDS, EVERYONE CAN STUDY A SCALE MODEL OF THE GROUND ON THE SAND-TABLE THAT HAS BEEN RIGGED UP.

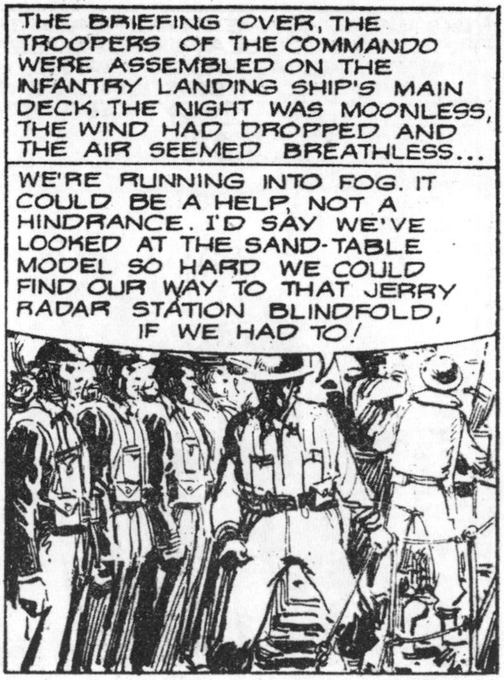
THE BRIEFING OVER, THE TROOPERS OF THE COMMANDO WERE ASSEMBLED ON THE INFANTRY LANDING SHIP'S MAIN DECK. THE NIGHT WAS MOONLESS, THE WIND HAD DROPPED AND THE AIR SEEMED BREATHLESS...
WE'RE RUNNING INTO FOG. IT COULD BE A HELP, NOT A HINDRANCE. I'D SAY WE'VE LOOKED AT THE SAND-TABLE MODEL SO HARD WE COULD FIND OUR WAY TO THAT JERRY RADAR STATION BLINDFOLD, IF WE HAD TO!

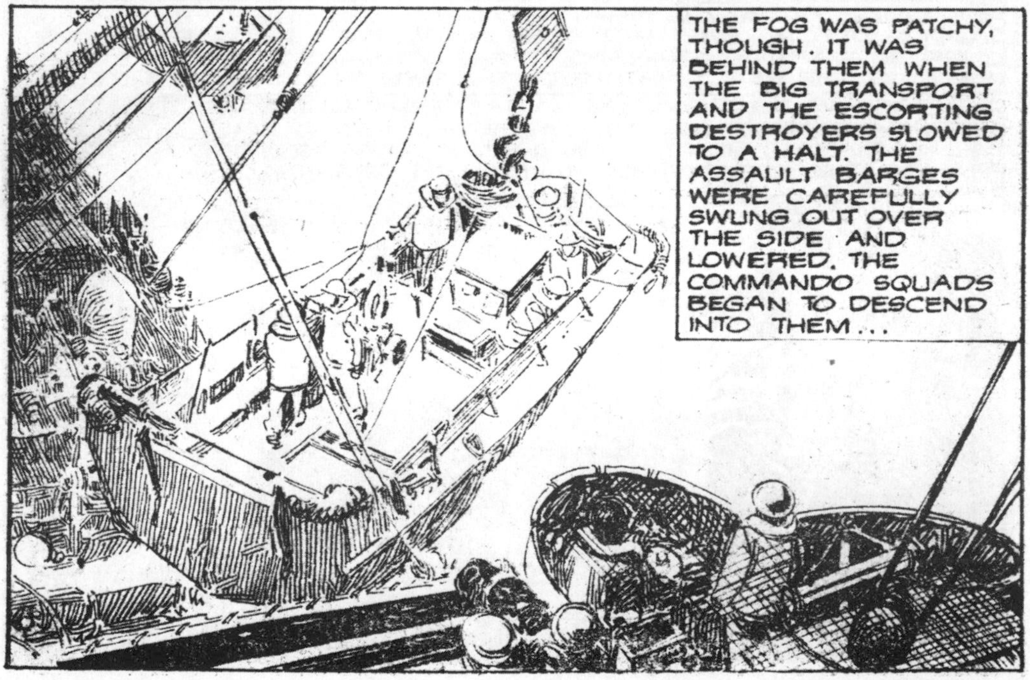
THE FOG WAS PATCHY, THOUGH. IT WAS BEHIND THEM WHEN THE BIG TRANSPORT AND THE ESCORTING DESTROYERS SLOWED TO A HALT. THE ASSAULT BARGES WERE CAREFULLY SWUNG OUT OVER THE SIDE AND LOWERED. THE COMMANDO SQUADS BEGAN TO DESCEND INTO THEM...

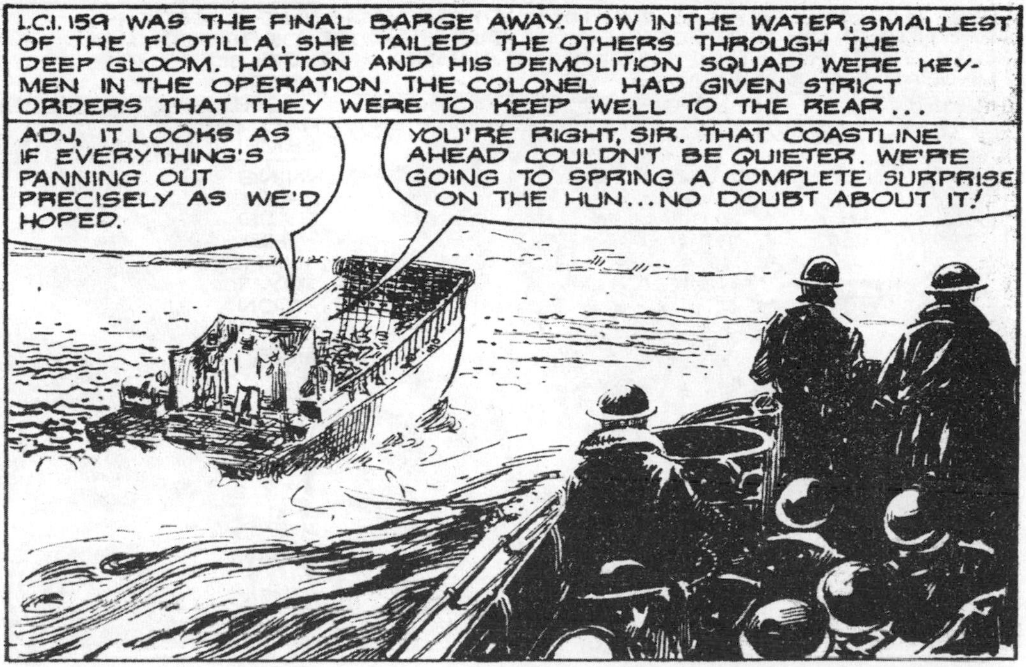
L.C.I. 159 WAS THE FINAL BARGE AWAY. LOW IN THE WATER, SMALLEST OF THE FLOTILLA, SHE TAILED THE OTHERS THROUGH THE DEEP GLOOM. HATTON AND HIS DEMOLITION SQUAD WERE KEY-MEN IN THE OPERATION. THE COLONEL HAD GIVEN STRICT ORDERS THAT THEY WERE TO KEEP WELL TO THE REAR...
ADJ, IT LOOKS AS IF EVERYTHING'S PANNING OUT PRECISELY AS WE'D HOPED.
YOU'RE RIGHT, SIR. THAT COASTLINE AHEAD COULDN'T BE QUIETER. WE'RE GOING TO SPRING A COMPLETE SURPRISE ON THE HUN... NO DOUBT ABOUT IT!

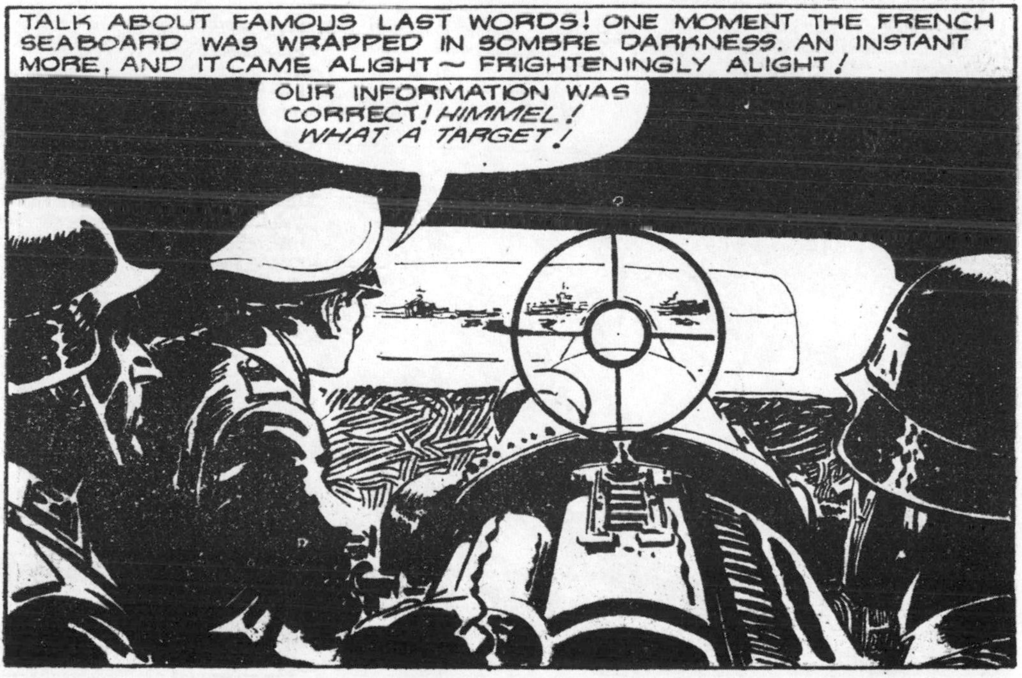
TALK ABOUT FAMOUS LAST WORDS! ONE MOMENT THE FRENCH SEABOARD WAS WRAPPED IN SOMBRE DARKNESS. AN INSTANT MORE, AND IT CAME ALIGHT ~ FRIGHTENINGLY ALIGHT!
OUR INFORMATION WAS CORRECT! HIMMEL! WHAT A TARGET!

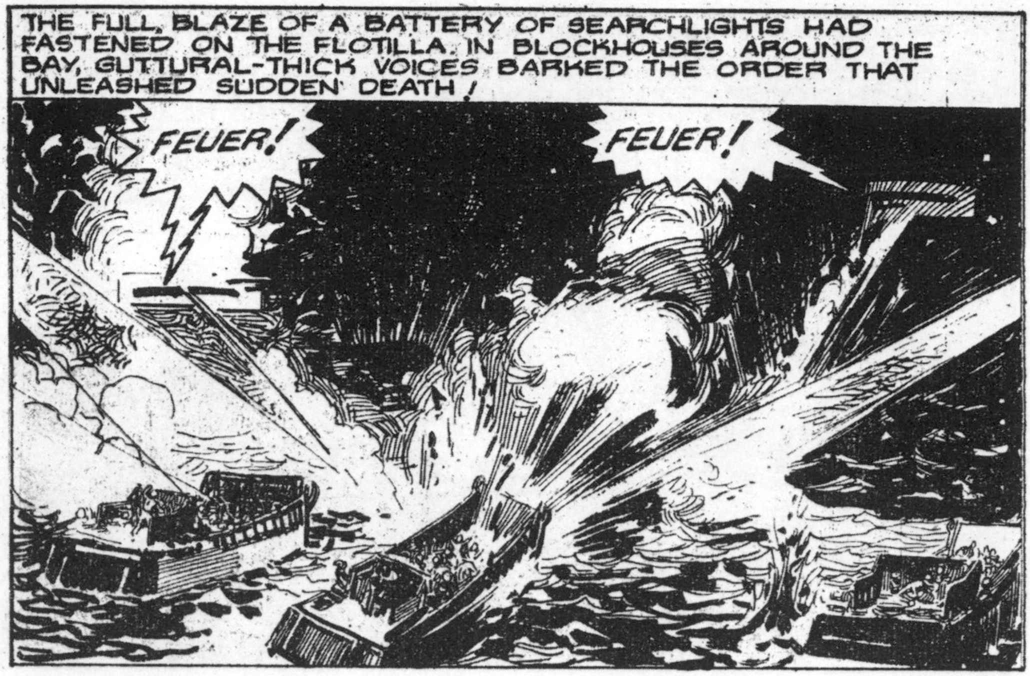
THE FULL BLAZE OF A BATTERY OF SEARCHLIGHTS HAD FASTENED ON THE FLOTILLA. IN BLOCKHOUSES AROUND THE BAY, GUTTURAL-THICK VOICES BARKED THE ORDER THAT UNLEASHED SUDDEN DEATH!
FEUER!
FEUER!

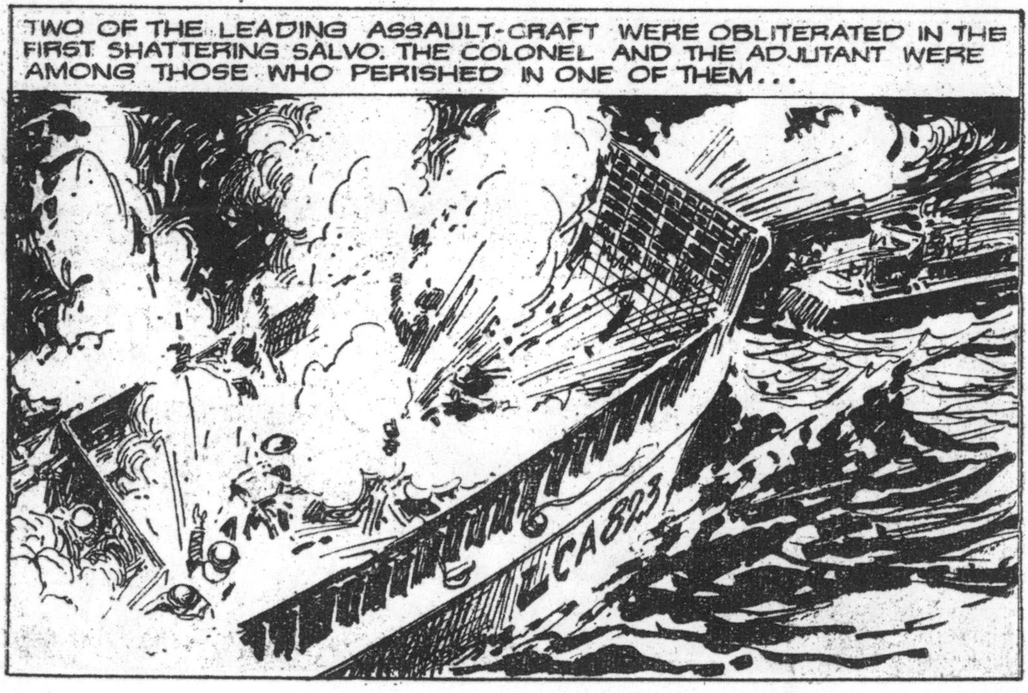
TWO OF THE LEADING ASSAULT-CRAFT WERE OBLITERATED IN THE FIRST SHATTERING SALVO. THE COLONEL AND THE ADJUTANT WERE AMONG THOSE WHO PERISHED IN ONE OF THEM...
LCA823

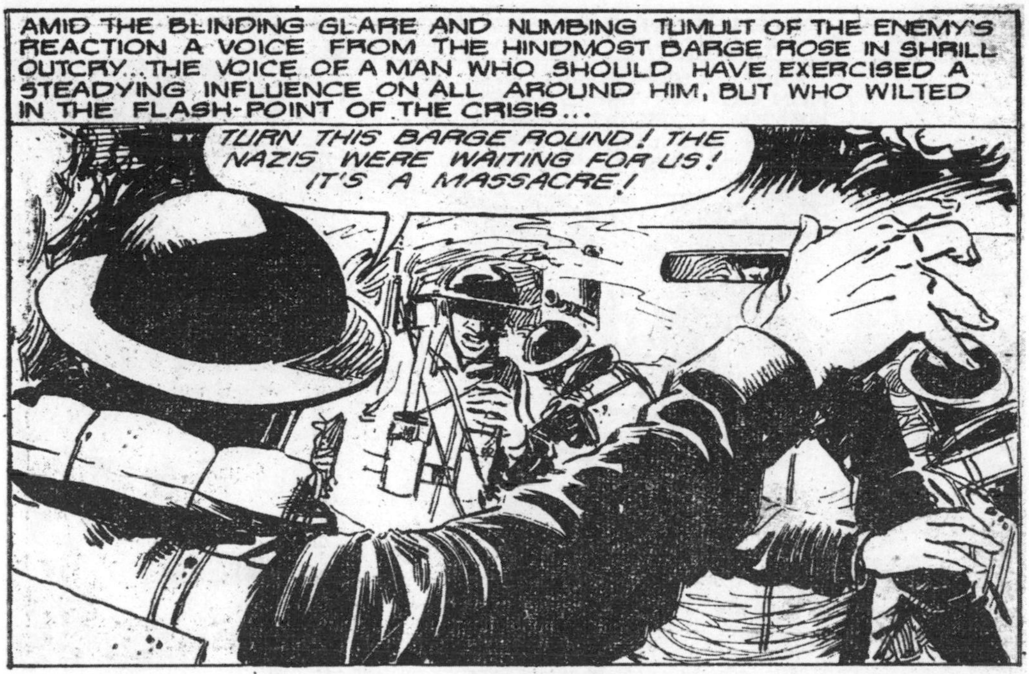
AMID THE BLINDING GLARE AND NUMBING TUMULT OF THE ENEMY'S REACTION A VOICE FROM THE HINDMOST BARGE ROSE IN SHRILL OUTCRY.. THE VOICE OF A MAN WHO SHOULD HAVE EXERCISED A STEADYING INFLUENCE ON ALL AROUND HIM, BUT WHO WILTED IN THE FLASH-POINT OF THE CRISIS...
TURN THIS BARGE ROUND! THE NAZIS WERE WAITING FOR US! IT'S A MASSACRE!

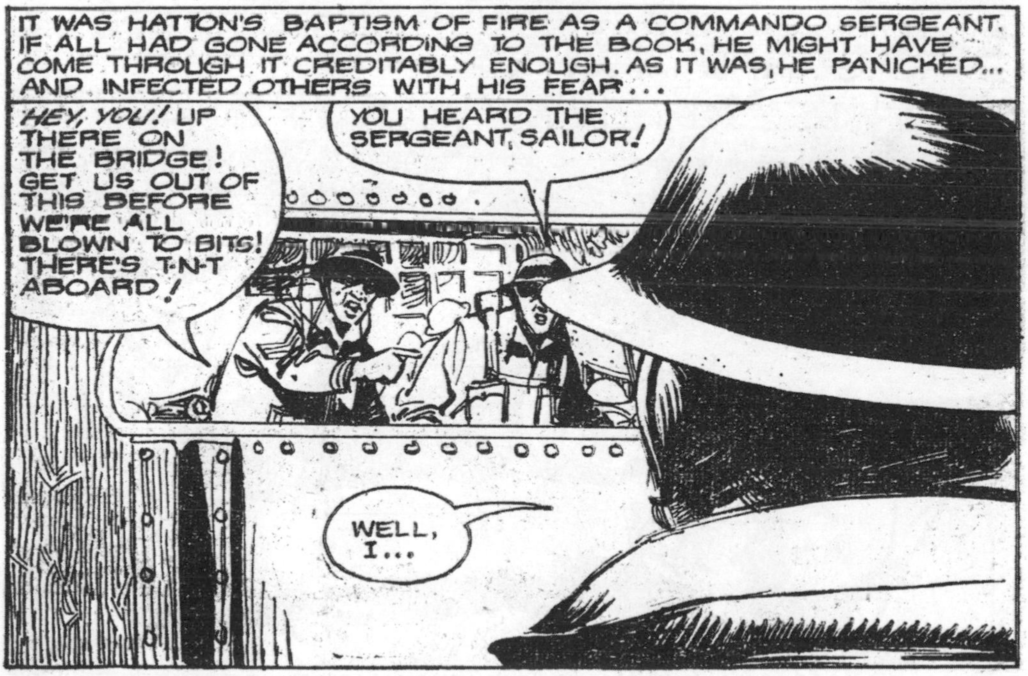
IT WAS HATTON'S BAPTISM OF FIRE AS A COMMANDO SERGEANT. IF ALL HAD GONE ACCORDING TO THE BOOK, HE MIGHT HAVE COME THROUGH IT CREDITABLY ENOUGH. AS IT WAS, HE PANICKED... AND INFECTED OTHERS WITH HIS FEAR...
HEY, YOU! UP THERE ON THE BRIDGE! GET US OUT OF THIS BEFORE WE'RE ALL BLOWN TO BITS! THERE'S T-N-T ABOARD!
YOU HEARD THE SERGEANT, SAILOR!
WELL, I...

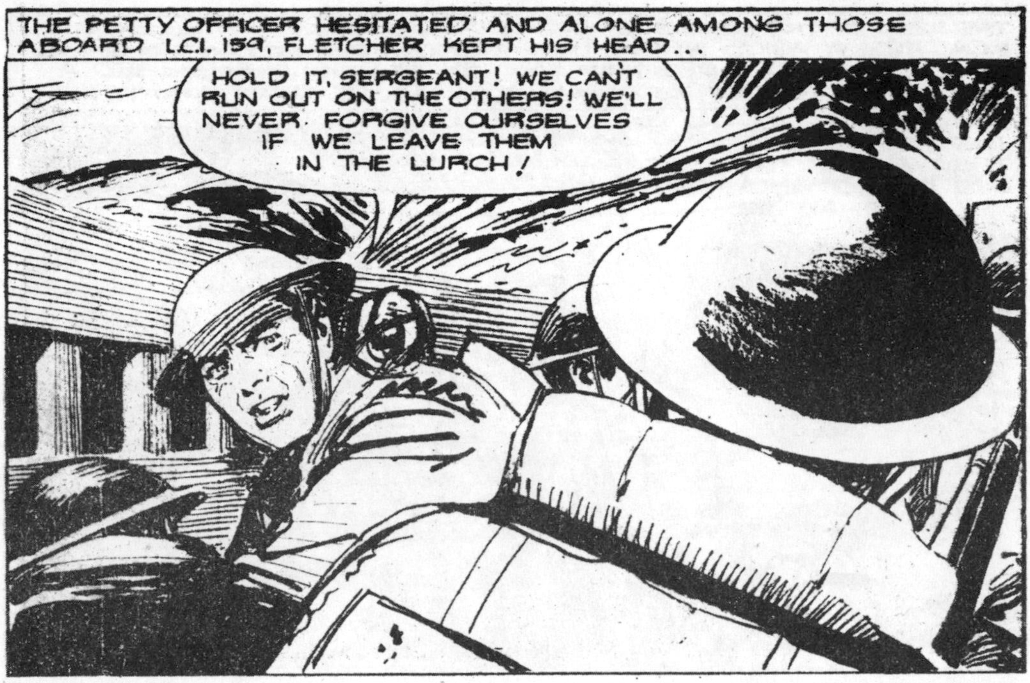
THE PETTY OFFICER HESITATED AND ALONE AMONG THOSE ABOARD L.C.I. 159, FLETCHER KEPT HIS HEAD...
HOLD IT, SERGEANT! WE CAN'T RUN OUT ON THE OTHERS! WE'LL NEVER FORGIVE OURSELVES IF WE LEAVE THEM IN THE LURCH!

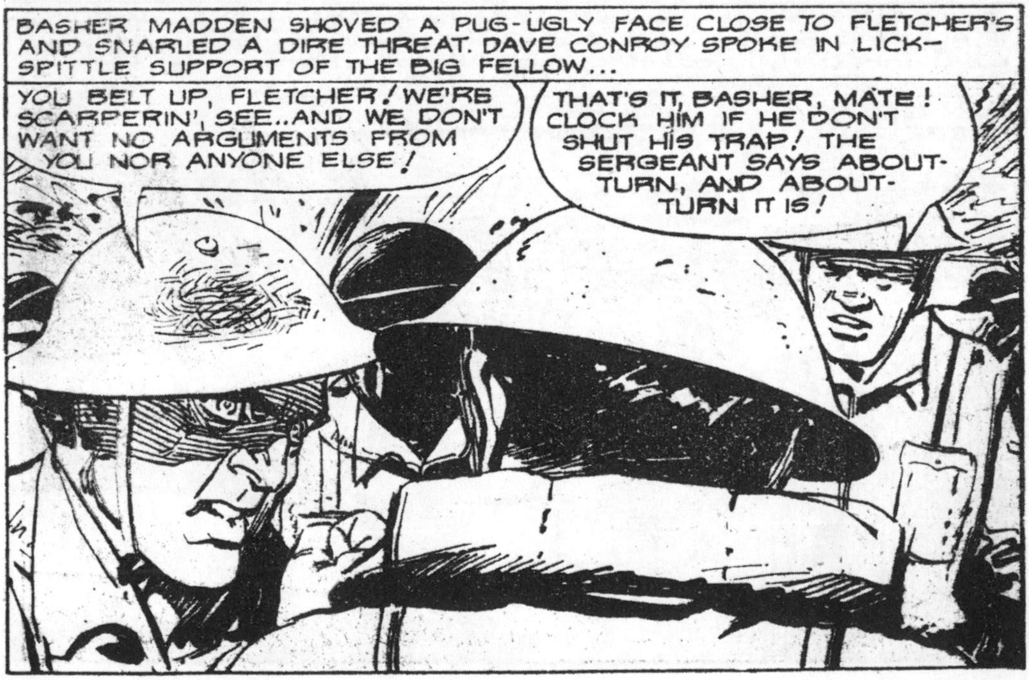
BASHER MADDEN SHOVED A PUG-UGLY FACE CLOSE TO FLETCHER'S AND SNARLED A DIRE THREAT. DAVE CONROY SPOKE IN LICK-SPITTLE SUPPORT OF THE BIG FELLOW...
YOU BELT UP, FLETCHER! WE'RE SCARPERIN', SEE..AND WE DON'T WANT NO ARGUMENTS FROM YOU NOR ANYONE ELSE!
THAT'S IT, BASHER, MATE! CLOCK HIM IF HE DON'T SHUT HIS TRAP! THE SERGEANT SAYS ABOUT-TURN, AND ABOUT-TURN IT IS!

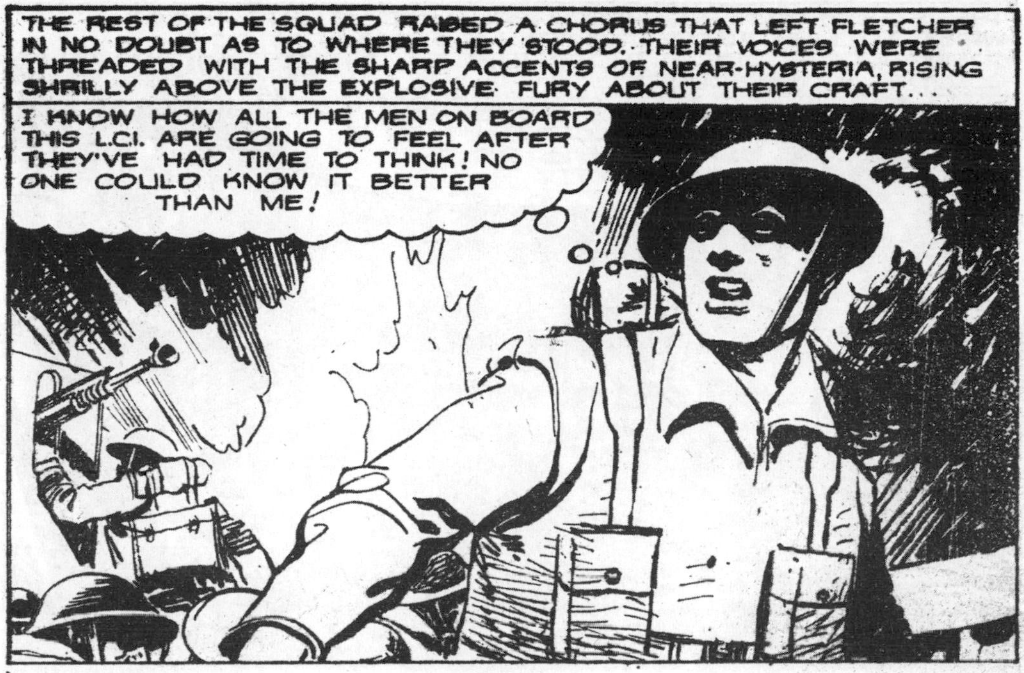
THE REST OF THE SQUAD RAISED A CHORUS THAT LEFT FLETCHER IN NO DOUBT AS TO WHERE THEY STOOD. THEIR VOICES WERE THREADED WITH THE SHARP ACCENTS OF NEAR-HYSTERIA, RISING SHRILLY ABOVE THE EXPLOSIVE FURY ABOUT THEIR CRAFT...
I KNOW HOW ALL THE MEN ON BOARD THIS L.C.I. ARE GOING TO FEEL AFTER THEY'VE HAD TIME TO THINK! NO ONE COULD KNOW IT BETTER THAN ME!

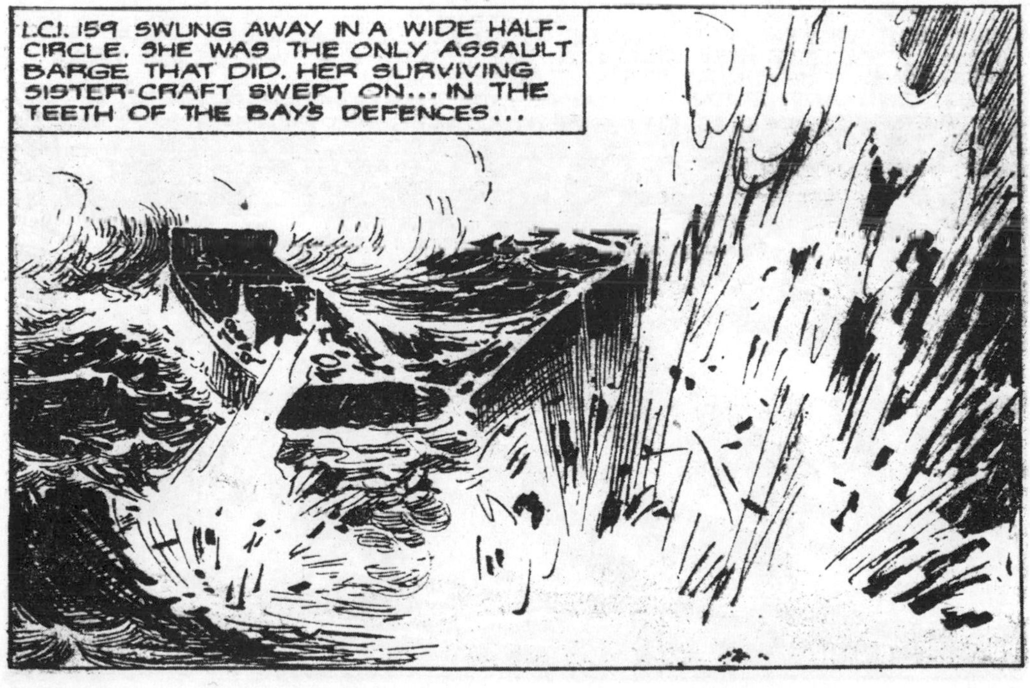
L.C.I. 159 SWUNG AWAY IN A WIDE HALF-CIRCLE. SHE WAS THE ONLY ASSAULT BARGE THAT DID. HER SURVIVING SISTER-CRAFT SWEPT ON... IN THE TEETH OF THE BAY'S DEFENCES...

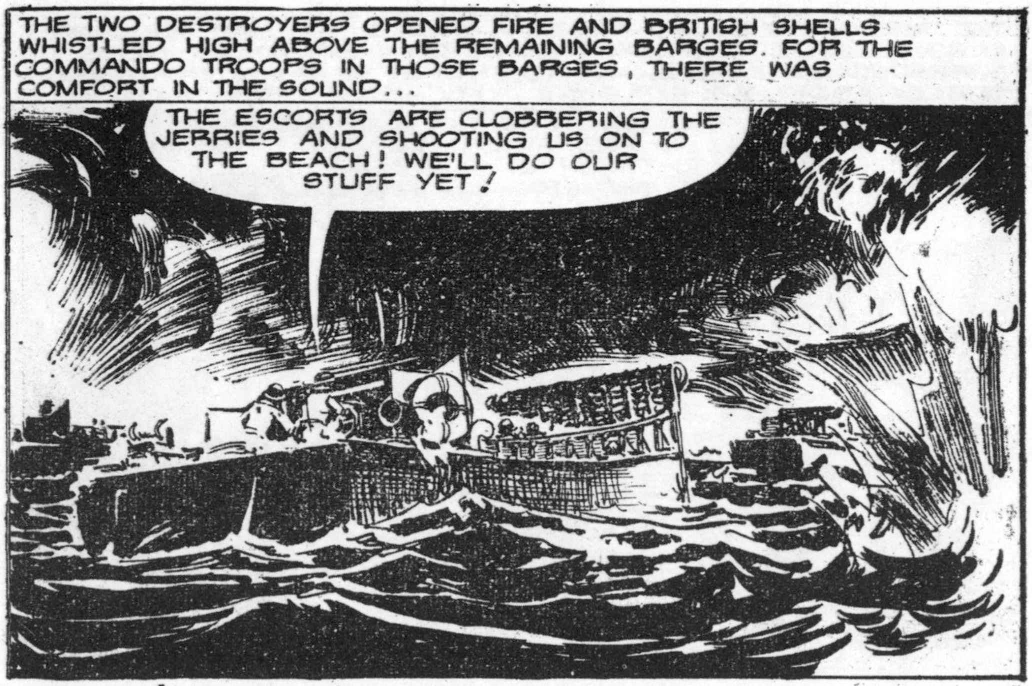
THE TWO DESTROYERS OPENED FIRE AND BRITISH SHELLS WHISTLED HIGH ABOVE THE REMAINING BARGES. FOR THE COMMANDO TROOPS IN THOSE BARGES, THERE WAS COMFORT IN THE SOUND...
THE ESCORTS ARE CLOBBERING THE JERRIES AND SHOOTING US ON TO THE BEACH! WE'LL DO OUR STUFF YET!

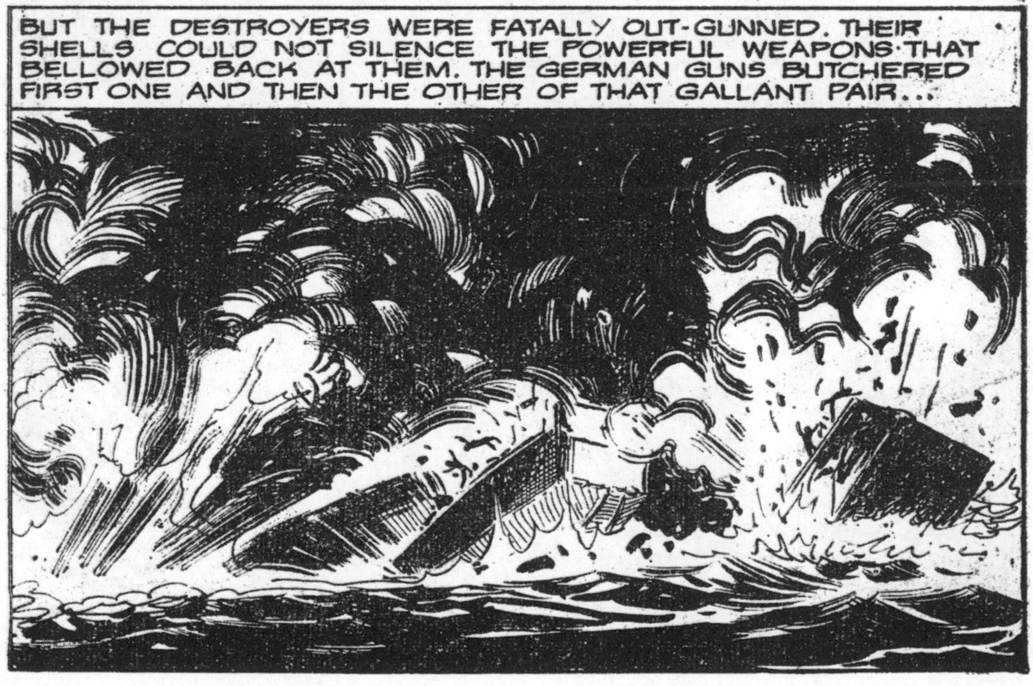
BUT THE DESTROYERS WERE FATALLY OUT-GUNNED. THEIR SHELLS COULD NOT SILENCE THE POWERFUL WEAPONS THAT BELLOWED BACK AT THEM. THE GERMAN GUNS BUTCHERED FIRST ONE AND THEN THE OTHER OF THAT GALLANT PAIR...

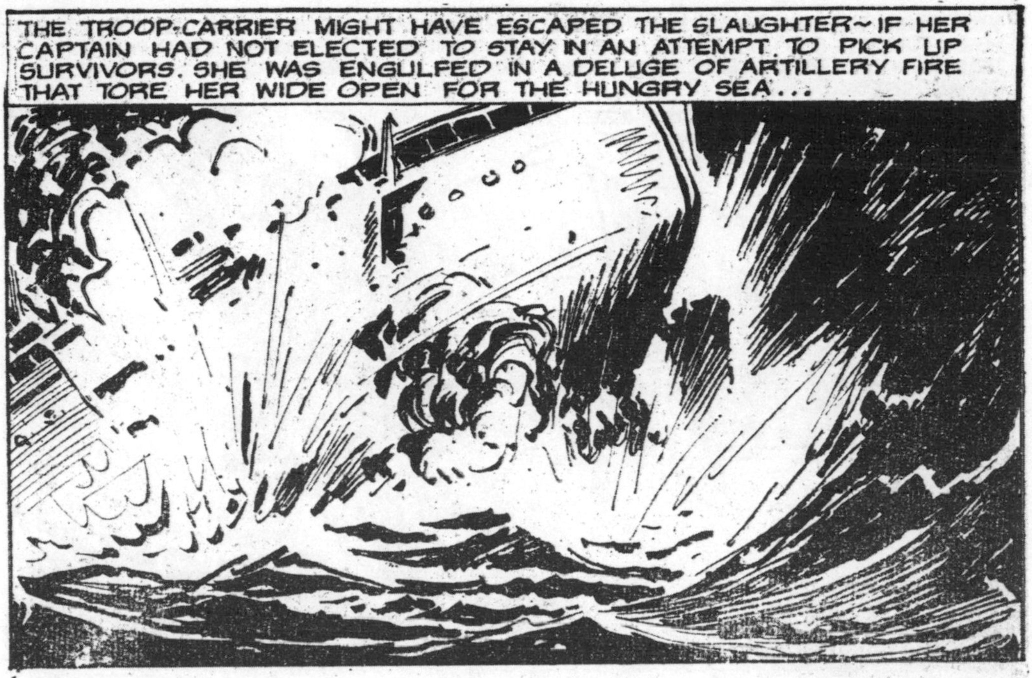
THE TROOP-CARRIER MIGHT HAVE ESCAPED THE SLAUGHTER~IF HER CAPTAIN HAD NOT ELECTED TO STAY IN AN ATTEMPT TO PICK UP SURVIVORS. SHE WAS ENGULFED IN A DELUGE OF ARTILLERY FIRE THAT TORE HER WIDE OPEN FOR THE HUNGRY SEA...

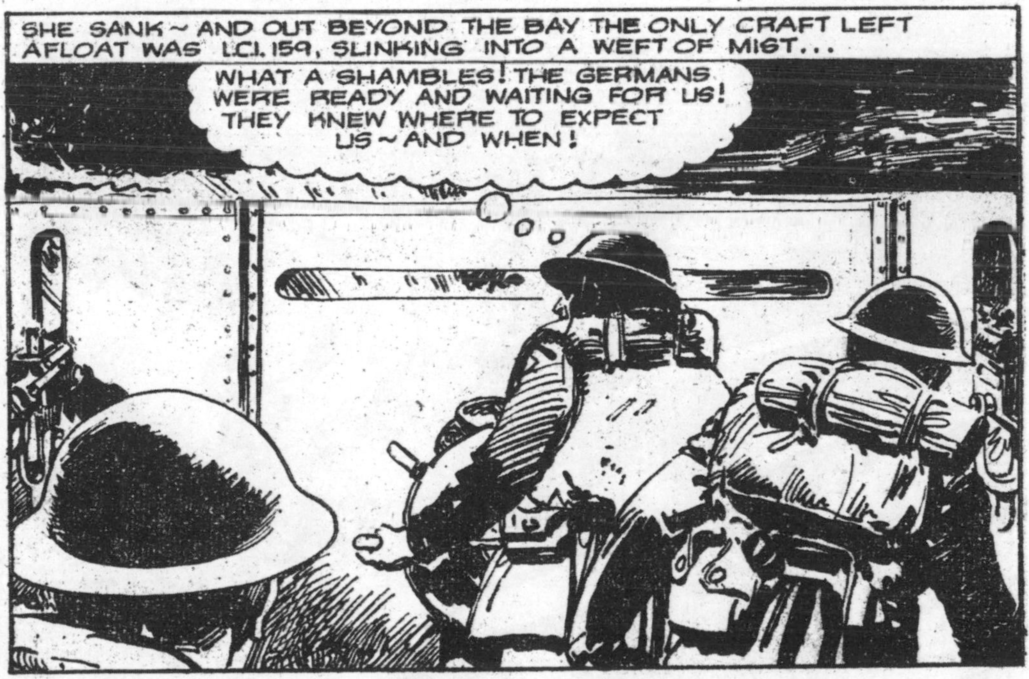
SHE SANK~AND OUT BEYOND THE BAY THE ONLY CRAFT LEFT AFLOAT WAS L.C.I. 159, SLINKING INTO A WEFT OF MIST...
WHAT A SHAMBLES! THE GERMANS WERE READY AND WAITING FOR US! THEY KNEW WHERE TO EXPECT US~AND WHEN!

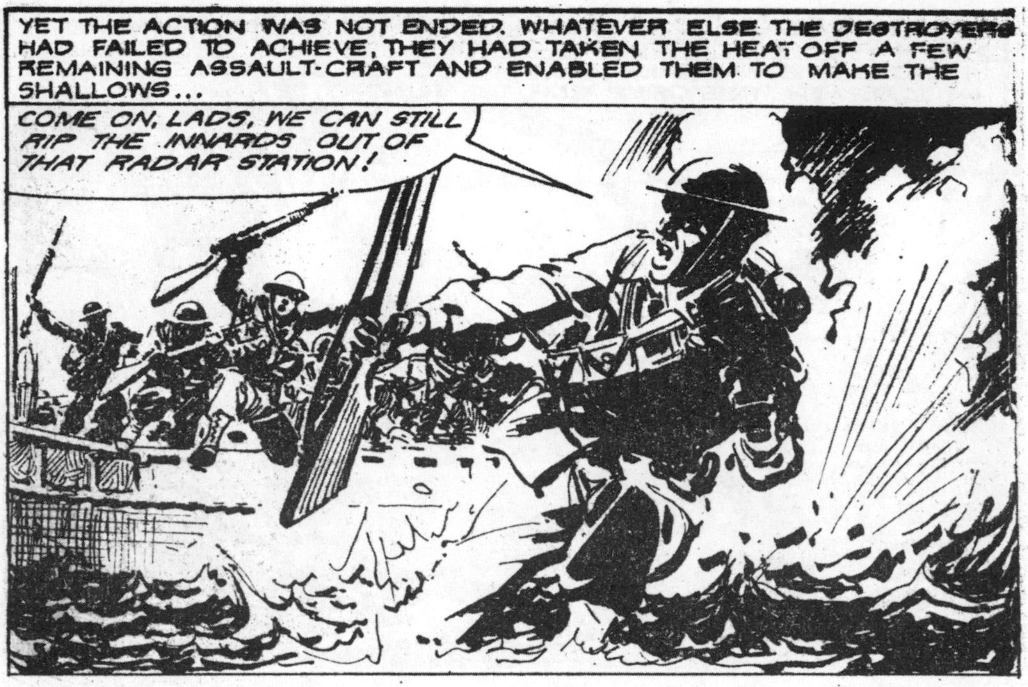
YET THE ACTION WAS NOT ENDED. WHATEVER ELSE THE DESTROYERS HAD FAILED TO ACHIEVE, THEY HAD TAKEN THE HEAT OFF A FEW REMAINING ASSAULT-CRAFT AND ENABLED THEM TO MAKE THE SHALLOWS...
COME ON, LADS, WE CAN STILL RIP THE INNARDS OUT OF THAT RADAR STATION!

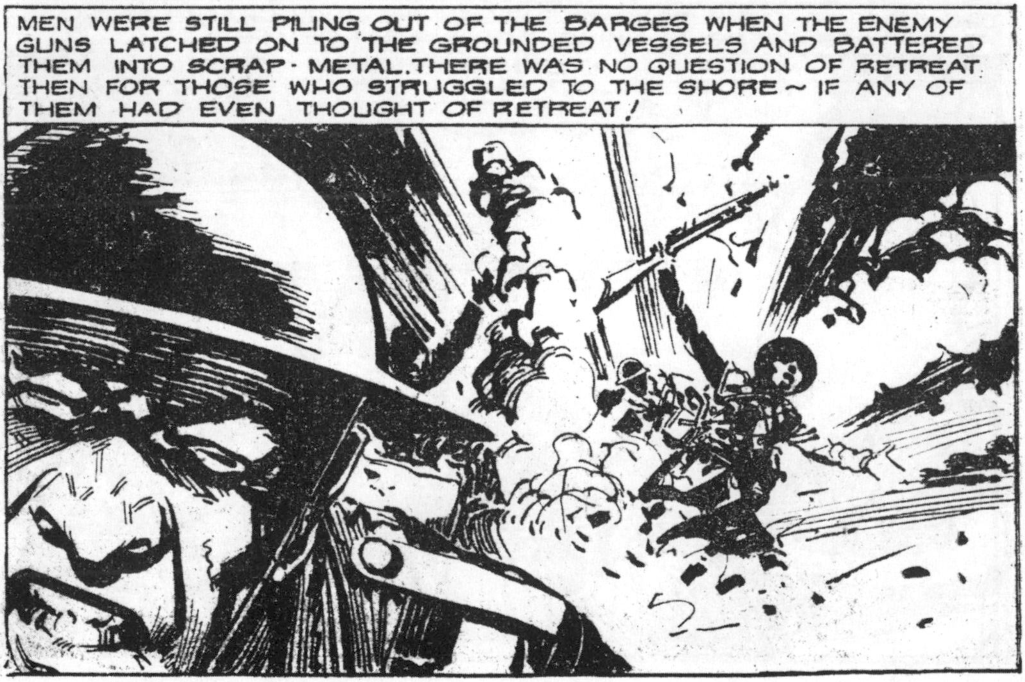
MEN WERE STILL PILING OUT OF THE BARGES WHEN THE ENEMY GUNS LATCHED ON TO THE GROUNDED VESSELS AND BATTERED THEM INTO SCRAP-METAL. THERE WAS NO QUESTION OF RETREAT THEN FOR THOSE WHO STRUGGLED TO THE SHORE ~ IF ANY OF THEM HAD EVEN THOUGHT OF RETREAT!

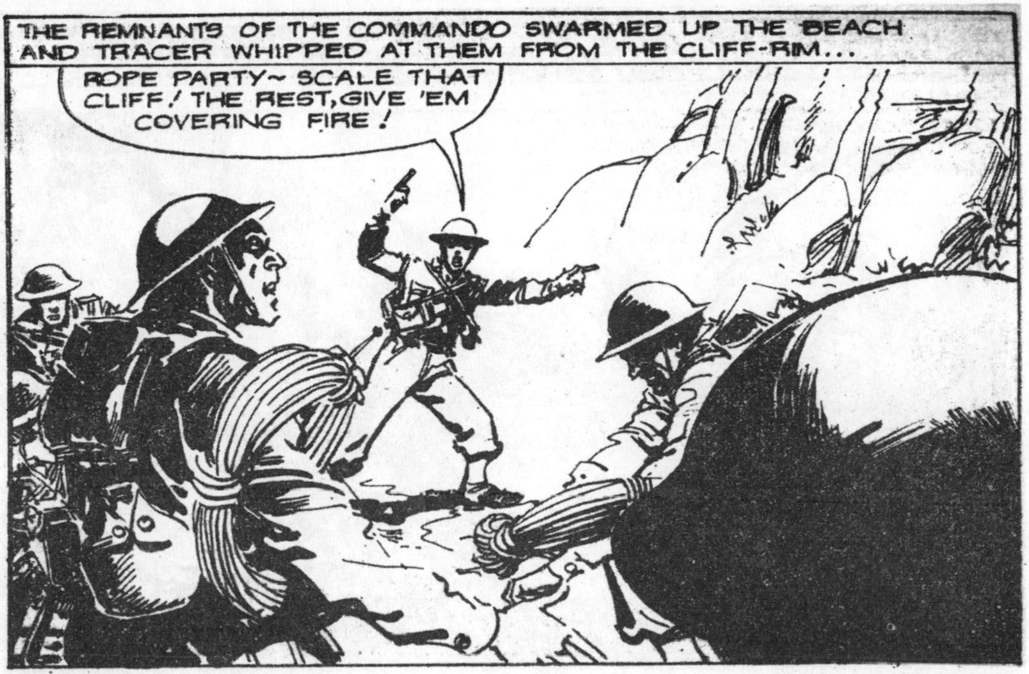
THE REMNANTS OF THE COMMANDO SWARMED UP THE BEACH AND TRACER WHIPPED AT THEM FROM THE CLIFF-RIM...
ROPE PARTY~ SCALE THAT CLIFF! THE REST, GIVE 'EM COVERING FIRE!

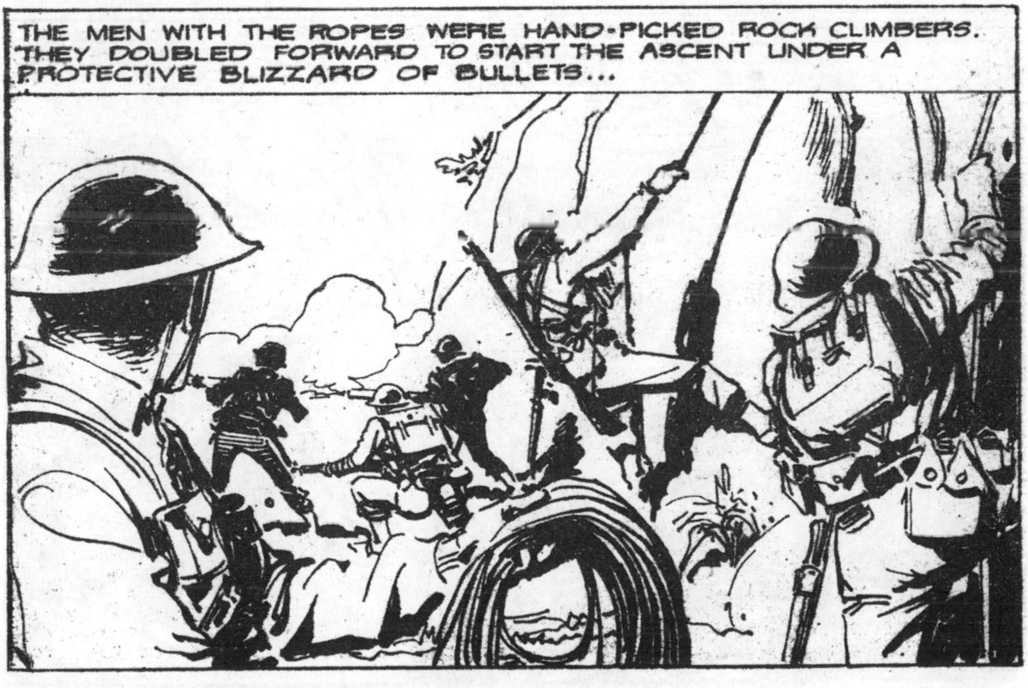
THE MEN WITH THE ROPES WERE HAND-PICKED ROCK CLIMBERS. THEY DOUBLED FORWARD TO START THE ASCENT UNDER A PROTECTIVE BLIZZARD OF BULLETS...

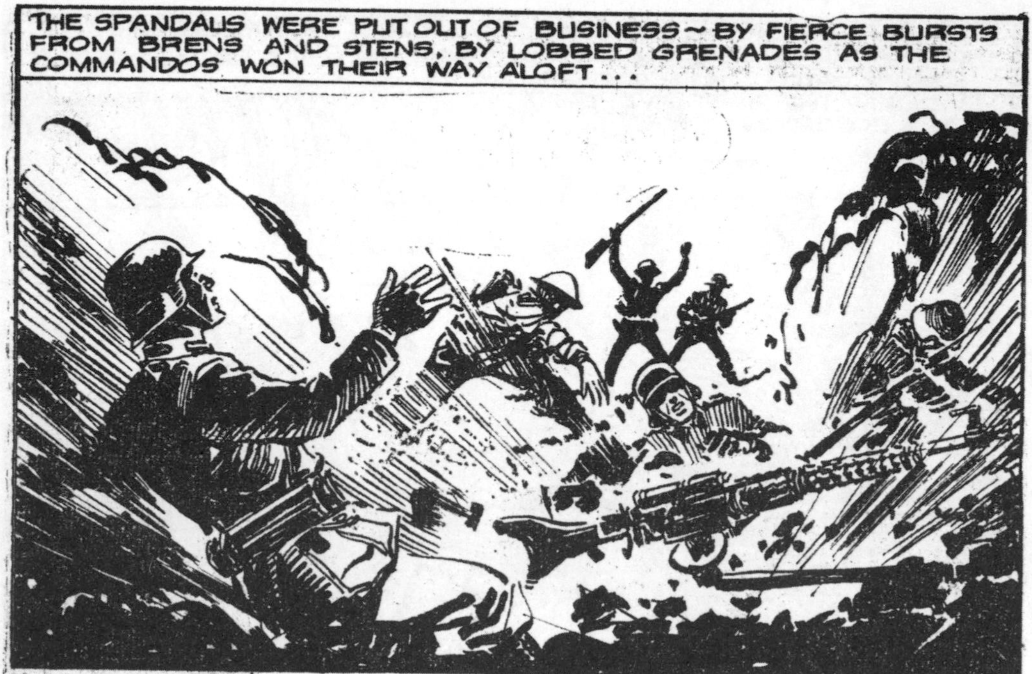
THE SPANDAUS WERE PUT OUT OF BUSINESS~BY FIERCE BURSTS FROM BRENS AND STENS, BY LOBBED GRENADES AS THE COMMANDOS WON THEIR WAY ALOFT...

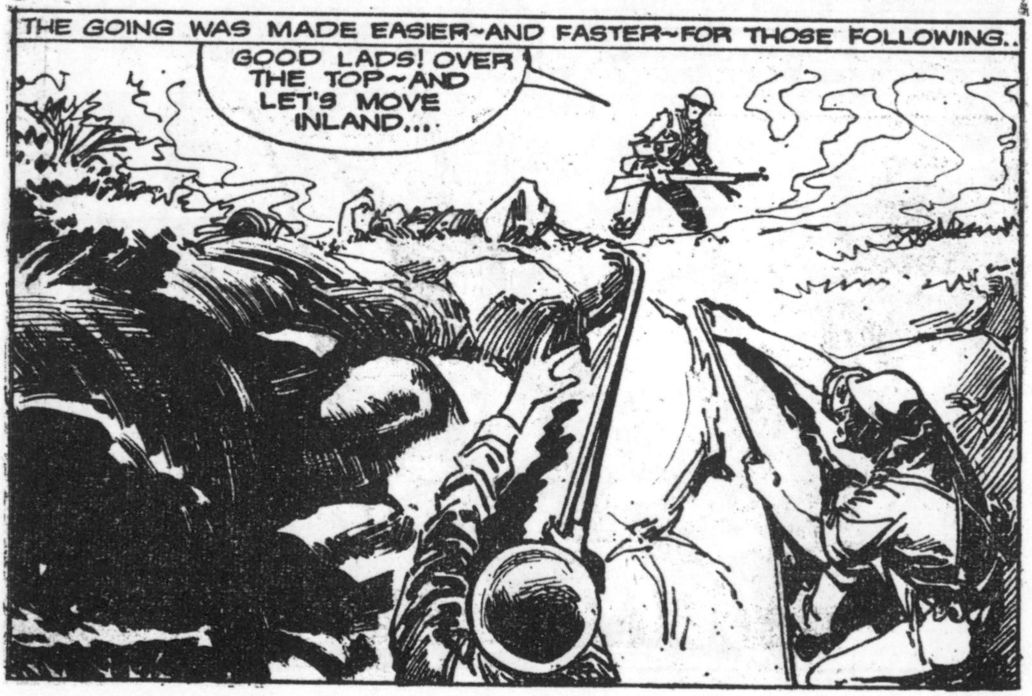
THE GOING WAS MADE EASIER~AND FASTER~FOR THOSE FOLLOWING..
GOOD LADS! OVER THE TOP~AND LET'S MOVE INLAND...

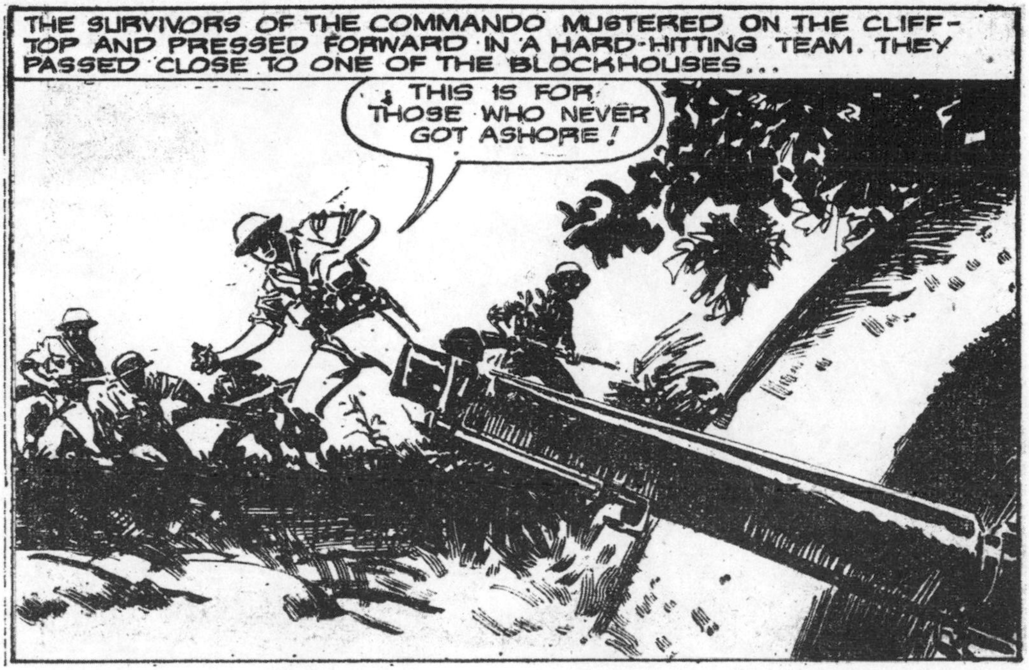
THE SURVIVORS OF THE COMMANDO MUSTERED ON THE CLIFF-TOP AND PRESSED FORWARD IN A HARD-HITTING TEAM. THEY PASSED CLOSE TO ONE OF THE BLOCKHOUSES...
THIS IS FOR THOSE WHO NEVER GOT ASHORE!

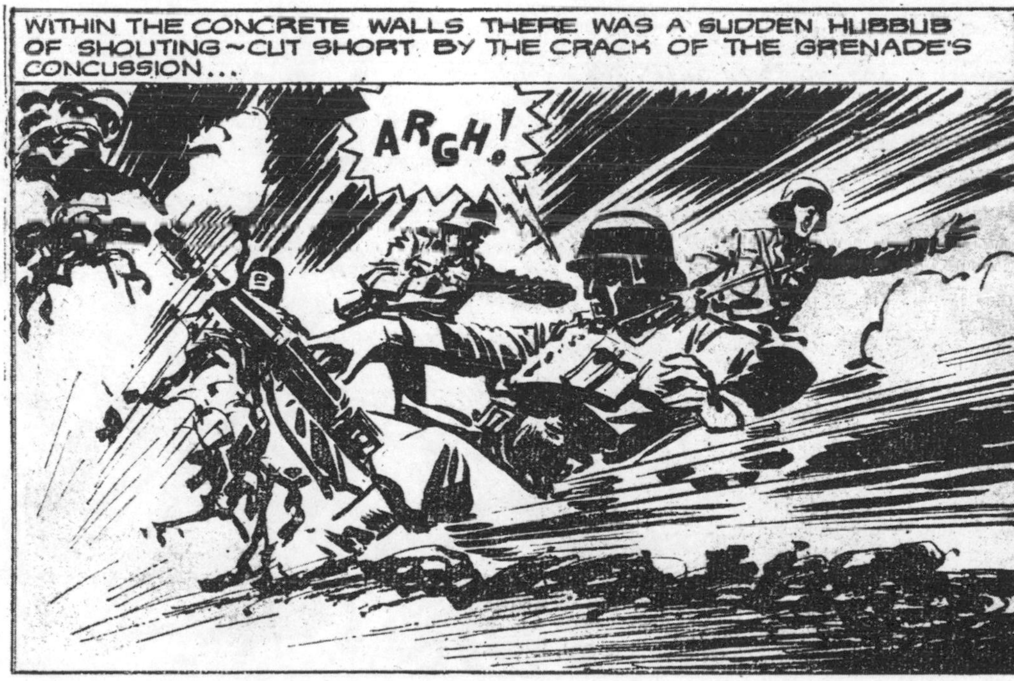
WITHIN THE CONCRETE WALLS THERE WAS A SUDDEN HUBBUB OF SHOUTING~CUT SHORT BY THE CRACK OF THE GRENADE'S CONCUSSION...
ARGH!

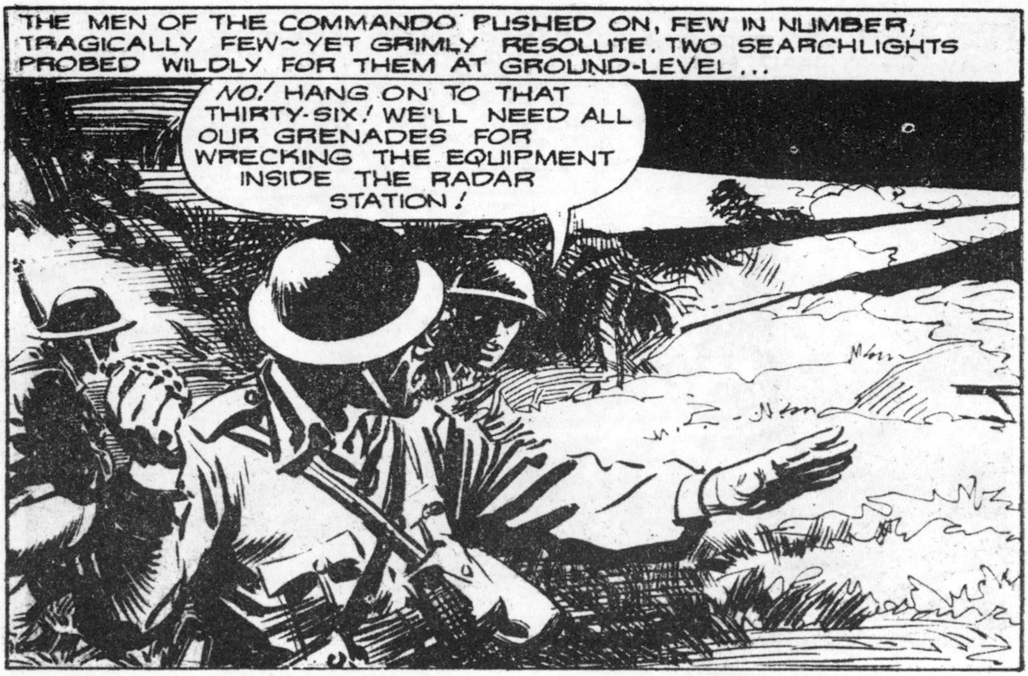
THE MEN OF THE COMMANDO PUSHED ON, FEW IN NUMBER, TRAGICALLY FEW~YET GRIMLY RESOLUTE. TWO SEARCHLIGHTS PROBED WILDLY FOR THEM AT GROUND-LEVEL...
NO! HANG ON TO THAT THIRTY-SIX! WE'LL NEED ALL OUR GRENADES FOR WRECKING THE EQUIPMENT INSIDE THE RADAR STATION!

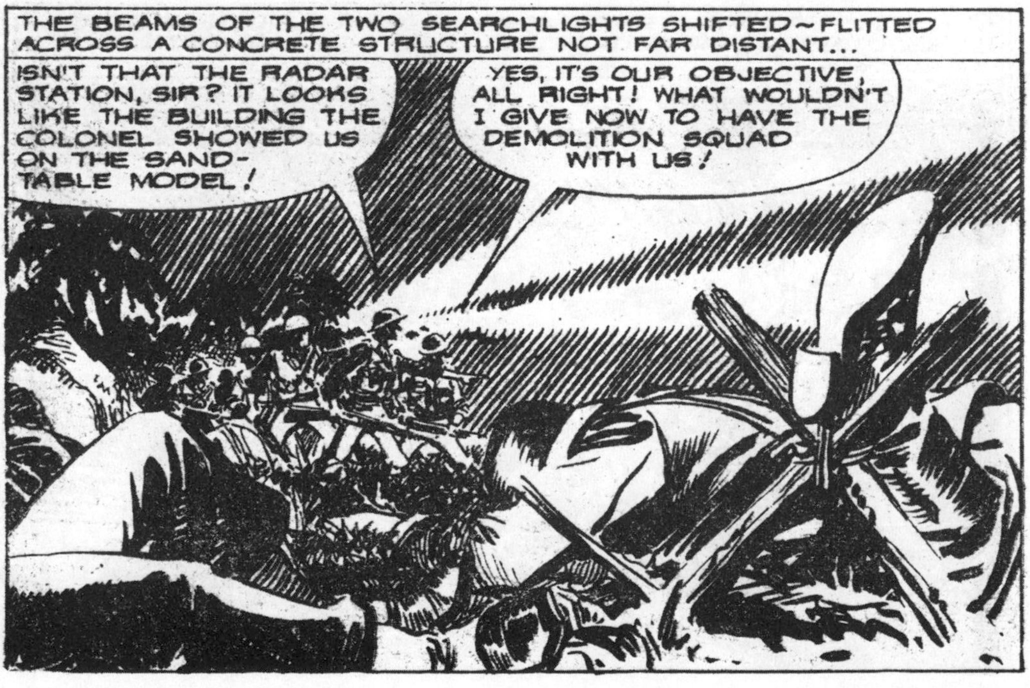
THE BEAMS OF THE TWO SEARCHLIGHTS SHIFTED~FLITTED ACROSS A CONCRETE STRUCTURE NOT FAR DISTANT...
ISN'T THAT THE RADAR STATION, SIR? IT LOOKS LIKE THE BUILDING THE COLONEL SHOWED US ON THE SAND-TABLE MODEL!
YES, IT'S OUR OBJECTIVE, ALL RIGHT! WHAT WOULDN'T I GIVE NOW TO HAVE THE DEMOLITION SQUAD WITH US!

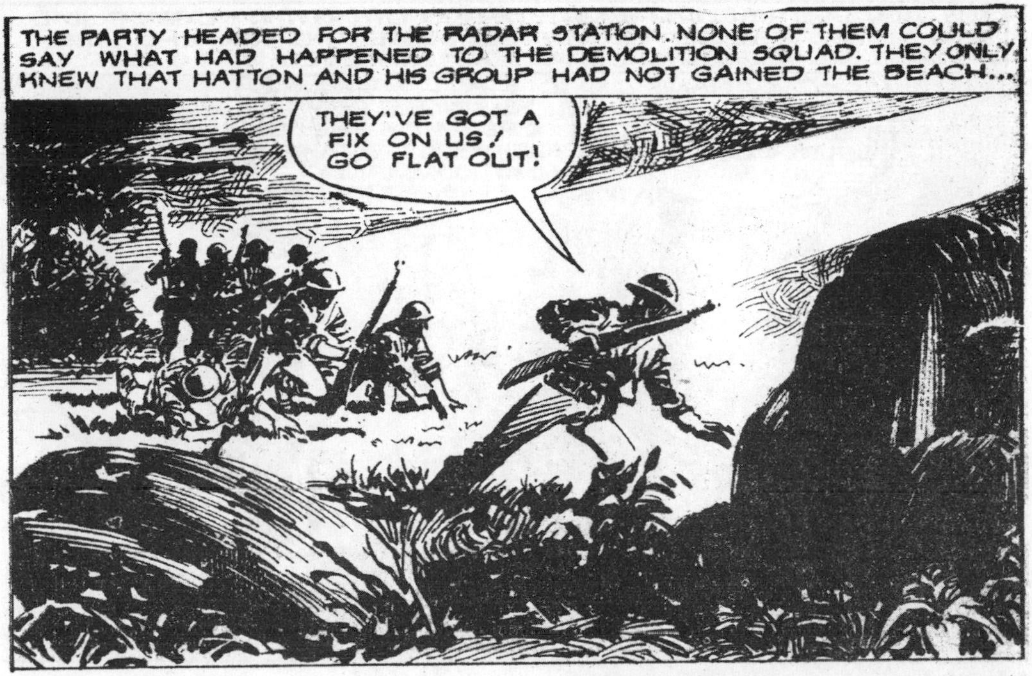
THE PARTY HEADED FOR THE RADAR STATION. NONE OF THEM COULD SAY WHAT HAD HAPPENED TO THE DEMOLITION SQUAD. THEY ONLY KNEW THAT HATTON AND HIS GROUP HAD NOT GAINED THE BEACH...
THEY'VE GOT A FIX ON US! GO FLAT OUT!

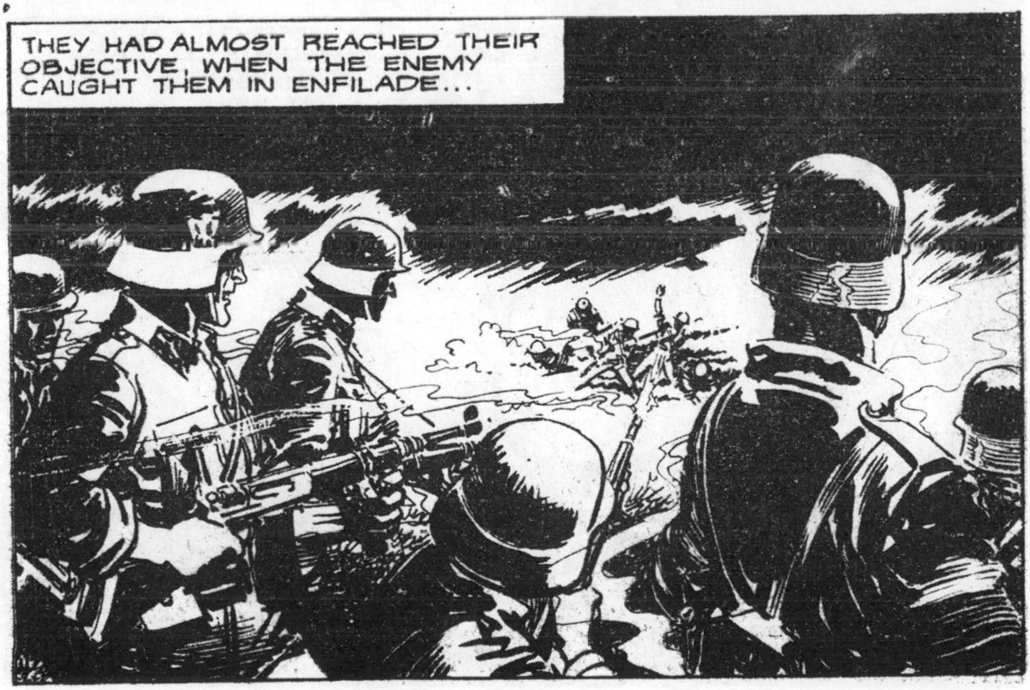
THEY HAD ALMOST REACHED THEIR OBJECTIVE, WHEN THE ENEMY CAUGHT THEM IN ENFILADE...

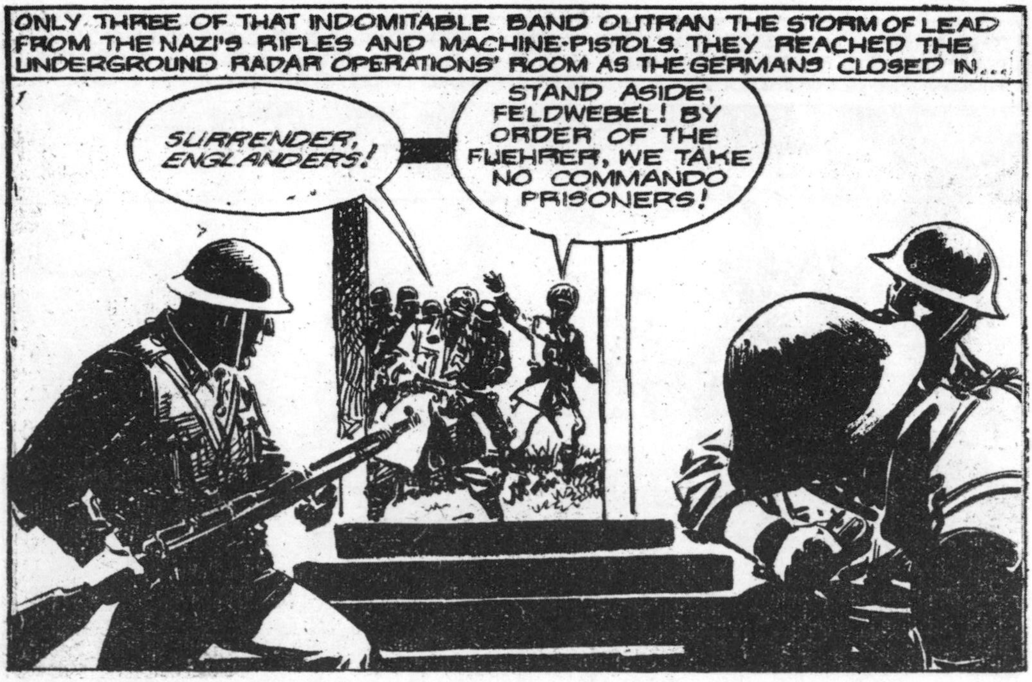
ONLY THREE OF THAT INDOMITABLE BAND OUTRAN THE STORM OF LEAD FROM THE NAZI'S RIFLES AND MACHINE-PISTOLS. THEY REACHED THE UNDERGROUND RADAR OPERATIONS' ROOM AS THE GERMANS CLOSED IN...
SURRENDER, ENGLANDERS!
STAND ASIDE, FELDWEBEL! BY ORDER OF THE FUEHRER, WE TAKE NO COMMANDO PRISONERS!

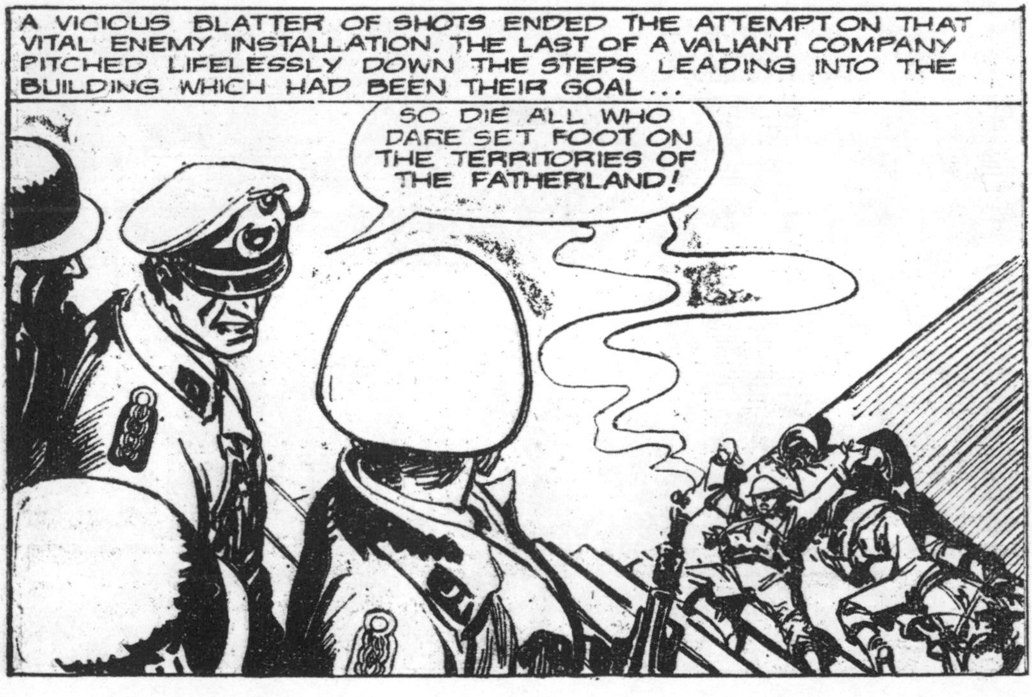
A VICIOUS BLATTER OF SHOTS ENDED THE ATTEMPT ON THAT VITAL ENEMY INSTALLATION. THE LAST OF A VALIANT COMPANY PITCHED LIFELESSLY DOWN THE STEPS LEADING INTO THE BUILDING WHICH HAD BEEN THEIR GOAL...
SO DIE ALL WHO DARE SET FOOT ON THE TERRITORIES OF THE FATHERLAND!

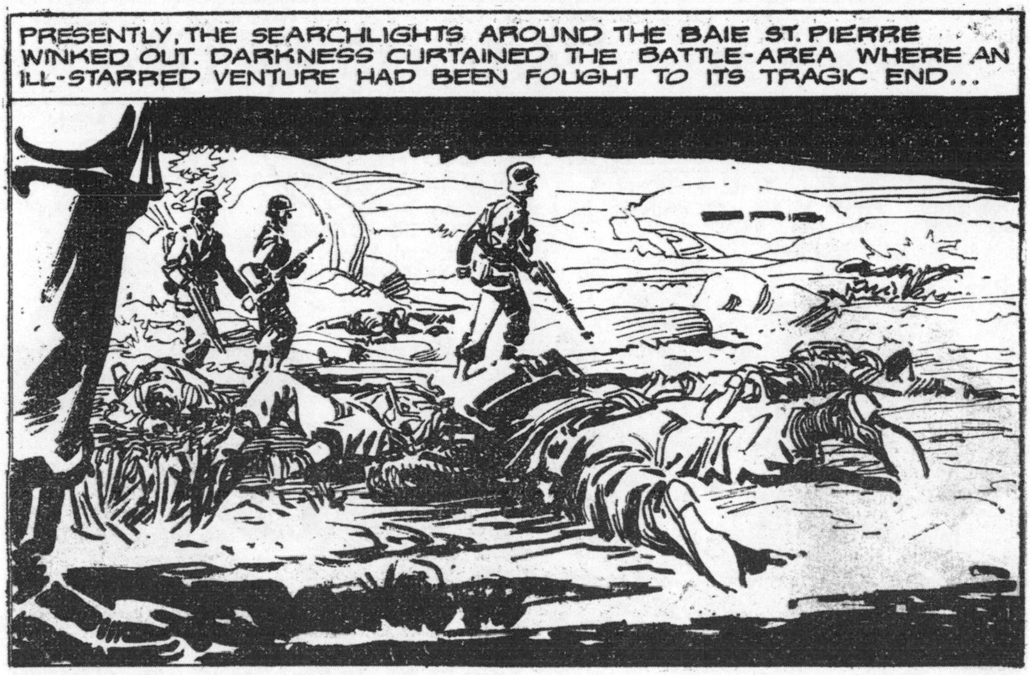
PRESENTLY, THE SEARCHLIGHTS AROUND THE BAIE ST. PIERRE WINKED OUT. DARKNESS CURTAINED THE BATTLE-AREA WHERE AN ILL-STARRED VENTURE HAD BEEN FOUGHT TO ITS TRAGIC END...

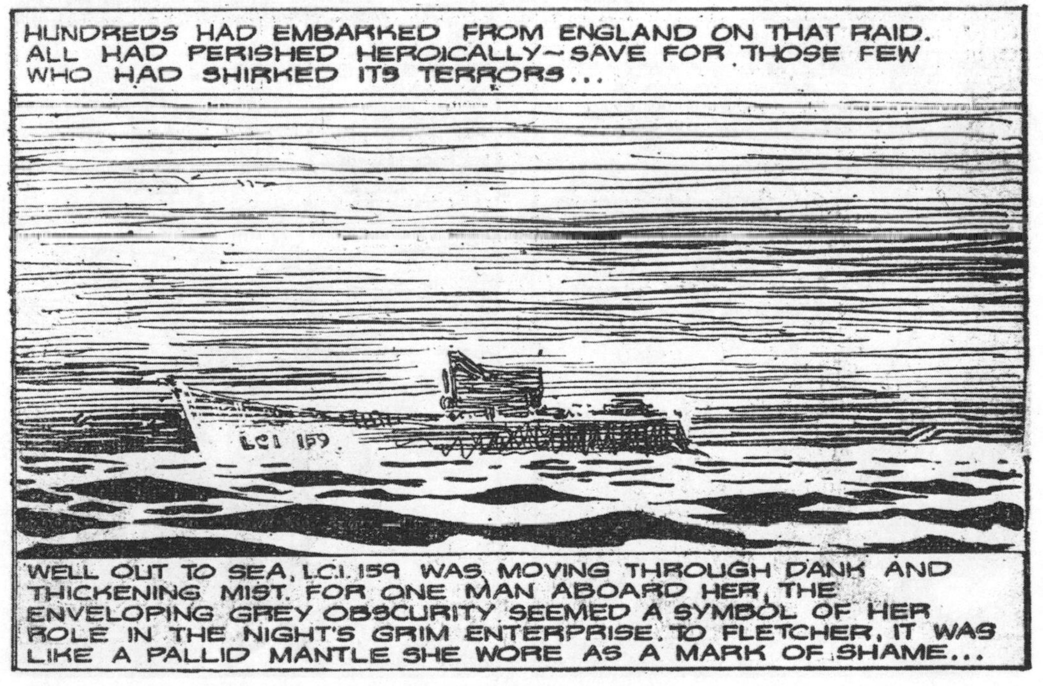
HUNDREDS HAD EMBARKED FROM ENGLAND ON THAT RAID. ALL HAD PERISHED HEROICALLY—SAVE FOR THOSE FEW WHO HAD SHIRKED ITS TERRORS...
LCI 159
WELL OUT TO SEA, L.C.I. 159 WAS MOVING THROUGH DANK AND THICKENING MIST. FOR ONE MAN ABOARD HER, THE ENVELOPING GREY OBSCURITY SEEMED A SYMBOL OF HER ROLE IN THE NIGHT'S GRIM ENTERPRISE. TO FLETCHER, IT WAS LIKE A PALLID MANTLE SHE WORE AS A MARK OF SHAME...

Chapter 3. Skirmish at Sea

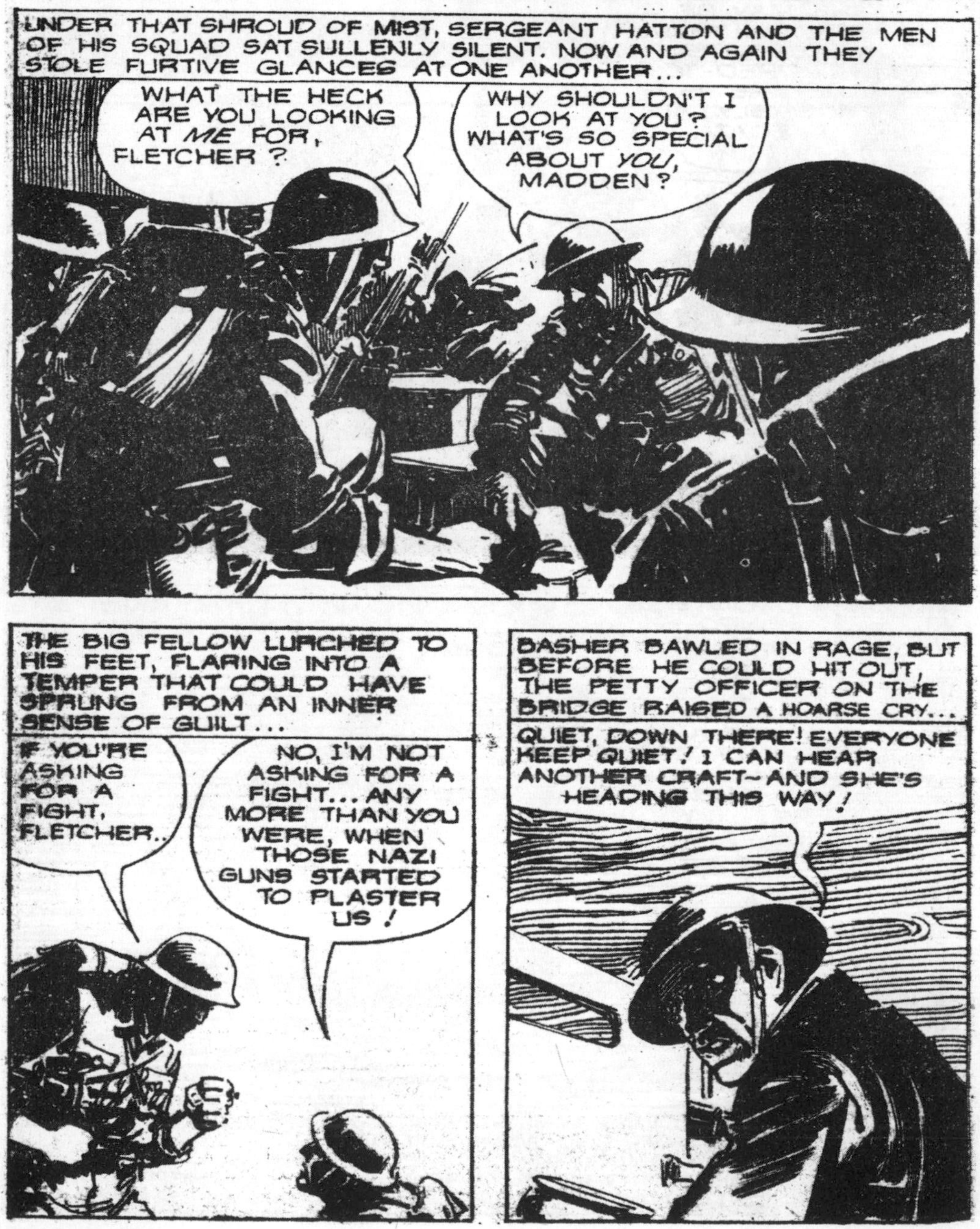
UNDER THAT SHROUD OF MIST, SERGEANT HATTON AND THE MEN OF HIS SQUAD SAT SULLENLY SILENT. NOW AND AGAIN THEY STOLE FURTIVE GLANCES AT ONE ANOTHER...
WHAT THE HECK ARE YOU LOOKING AT *ME* FOR, FLETCHER ?
WHY SHOULDN'T I LOOK AT YOU? WHAT'S SO SPECIAL ABOUT *YOU*, MADDEN?
THE BIG FELLOW LURCHED TO HIS FEET, FLARING INTO A TEMPER THAT COULD HAVE SPRUNG FROM AN INNER SENSE OF GUILT...
IF YOU'RE ASKING FOR A FIGHT, FLETCHER..
NO, I'M NOT ASKING FOR A FIGHT... ANY MORE THAN YOU WERE, WHEN THOSE NAZI GUNS STARTED TO PLASTER US !
BASHER BAWLED IN RAGE, BUT BEFORE HE COULD HIT OUT, THE PETTY OFFICER ON THE BRIDGE RAISED A HOARSE CRY...
QUIET, DOWN THERE! EVERYONE KEEP QUIET! I CAN HEAR ANOTHER CRAFT~AND SHE'S HEADING THIS WAY!

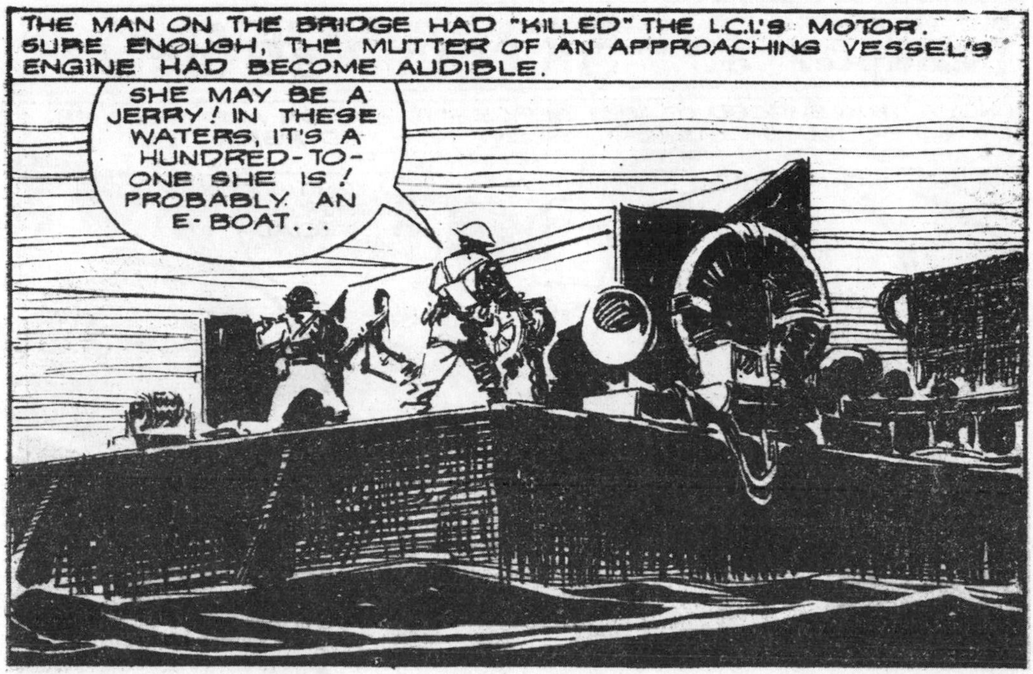
THE MAN ON THE BRIDGE HAD "KILLED" THE L.C.I.'S MOTOR. SURE ENOUGH, THE MUTTER OF AN APPROACHING VESSEL'S ENGINE HAD BECOME AUDIBLE.
SHE MAY BE A JERRY! IN THESE WATERS, IT'S A HUNDRED-TO-ONE SHE IS! PROBABLY AN E-BOAT...

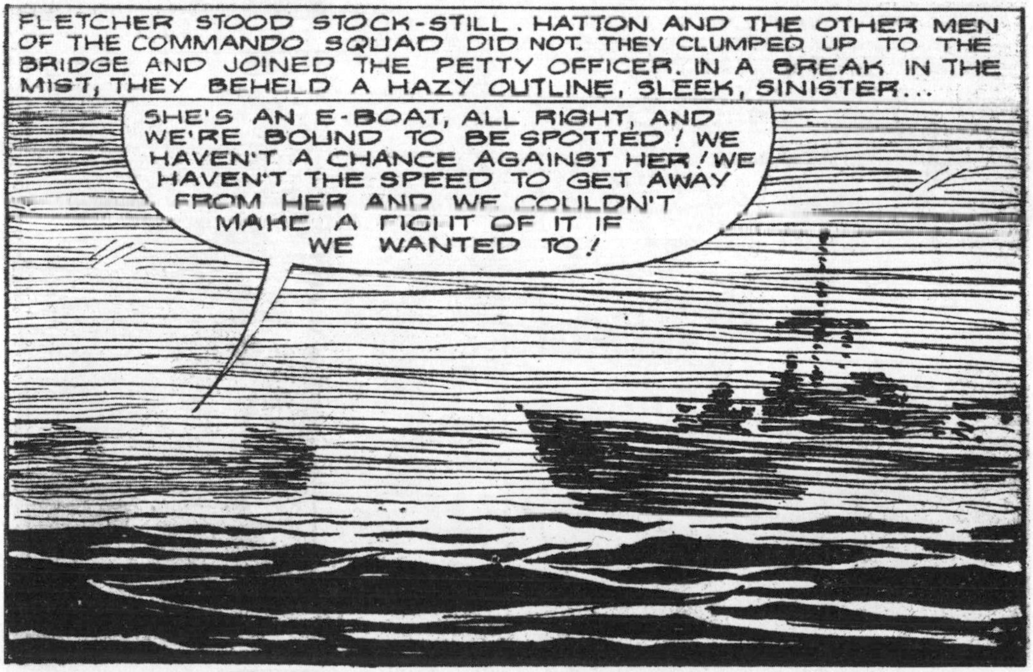
FLETCHER STOOD STOCK-STILL. HATTON AND THE OTHER MEN OF THE COMMANDO SQUAD DID NOT. THEY CLUMPED UP TO THE BRIDGE AND JOINED THE PETTY OFFICER. IN A BREAK IN THE MIST, THEY BEHELD A HAZY OUTLINE, SLEEK, SINISTER...
SHE'S AN E-BOAT, ALL RIGHT, AND WE'RE BOUND TO BE SPOTTED! WE HAVEN'T A CHANCE AGAINST HER! WE HAVEN'T THE SPEED TO GET AWAY FROM HER AND WE COULDN'T MAKE A FIGHT OF IT IF WE WANTED TO!

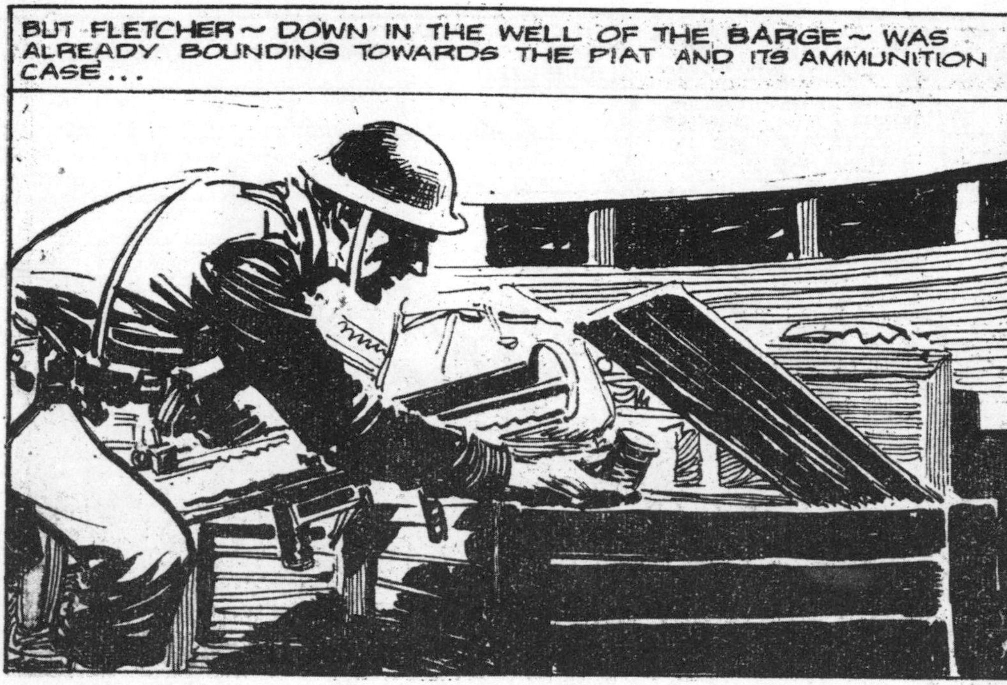
BUT FLETCHER ~ DOWN IN THE WELL OF THE BARGE ~ WAS ALREADY BOUNDING TOWARDS THE PIAT AND ITS AMMUNITION CASE...

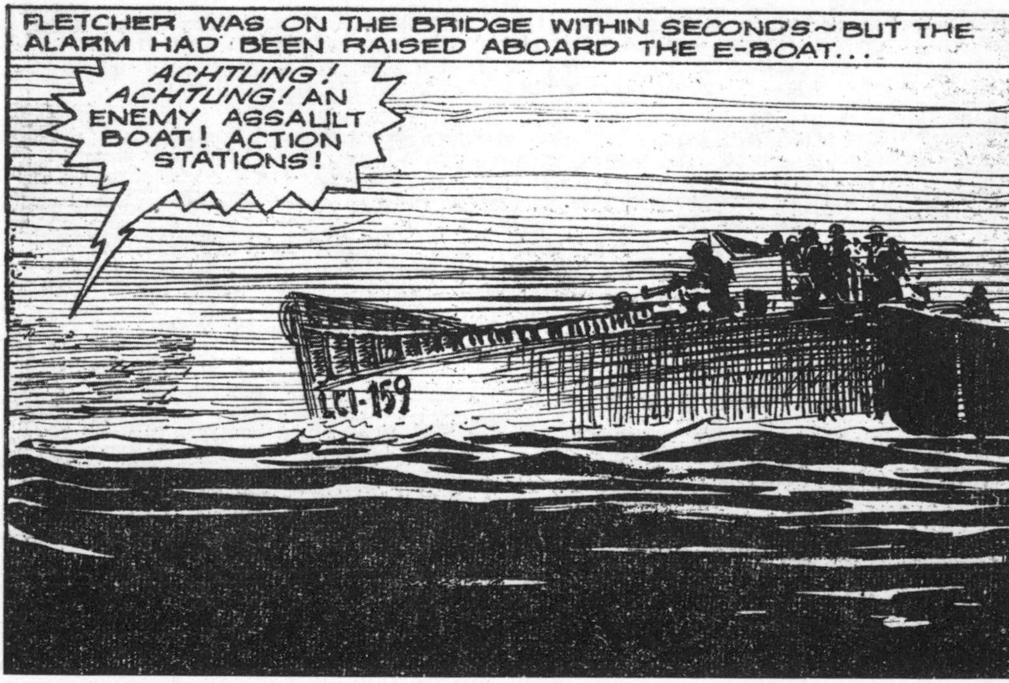
FLETCHER WAS ON THE BRIDGE WITHIN SECONDS ~ BUT THE ALARM HAD BEEN RAISED ABOARD THE E-BOAT...
ACHTUNG! ACHTUNG! AN ENEMY ASSAULT BOAT! ACTION STATIONS!
LCI-159

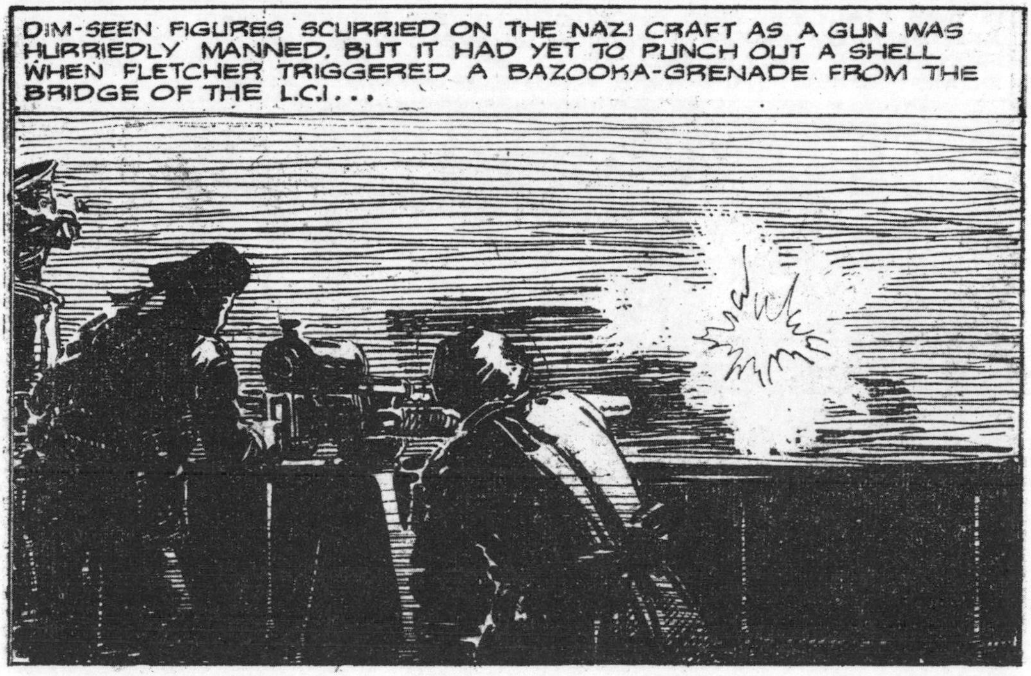
DIM-SEEN FIGURES SCURRIED ON THE NAZI CRAFT AS A GUN WAS HURRIEDLY MANNED. BUT IT HAD YET TO PUNCH OUT A SHELL WHEN FLETCHER TRIGGERED A BAZOOKA-GRENADE FROM THE BRIDGE OF THE L.C.I...

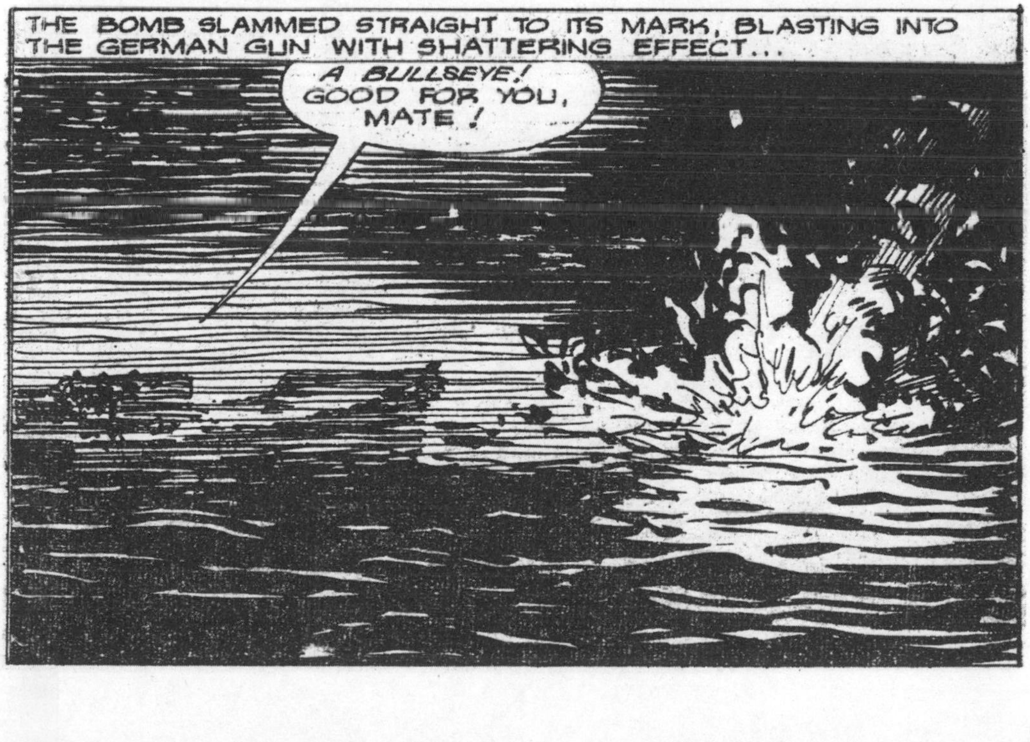
THE BOMB SLAMMED STRAIGHT TO ITS MARK, BLASTING INTO THE GERMAN GUN WITH SHATTERING EFFECT...
A BULLSEYE! GOOD FOR YOU, MATE!

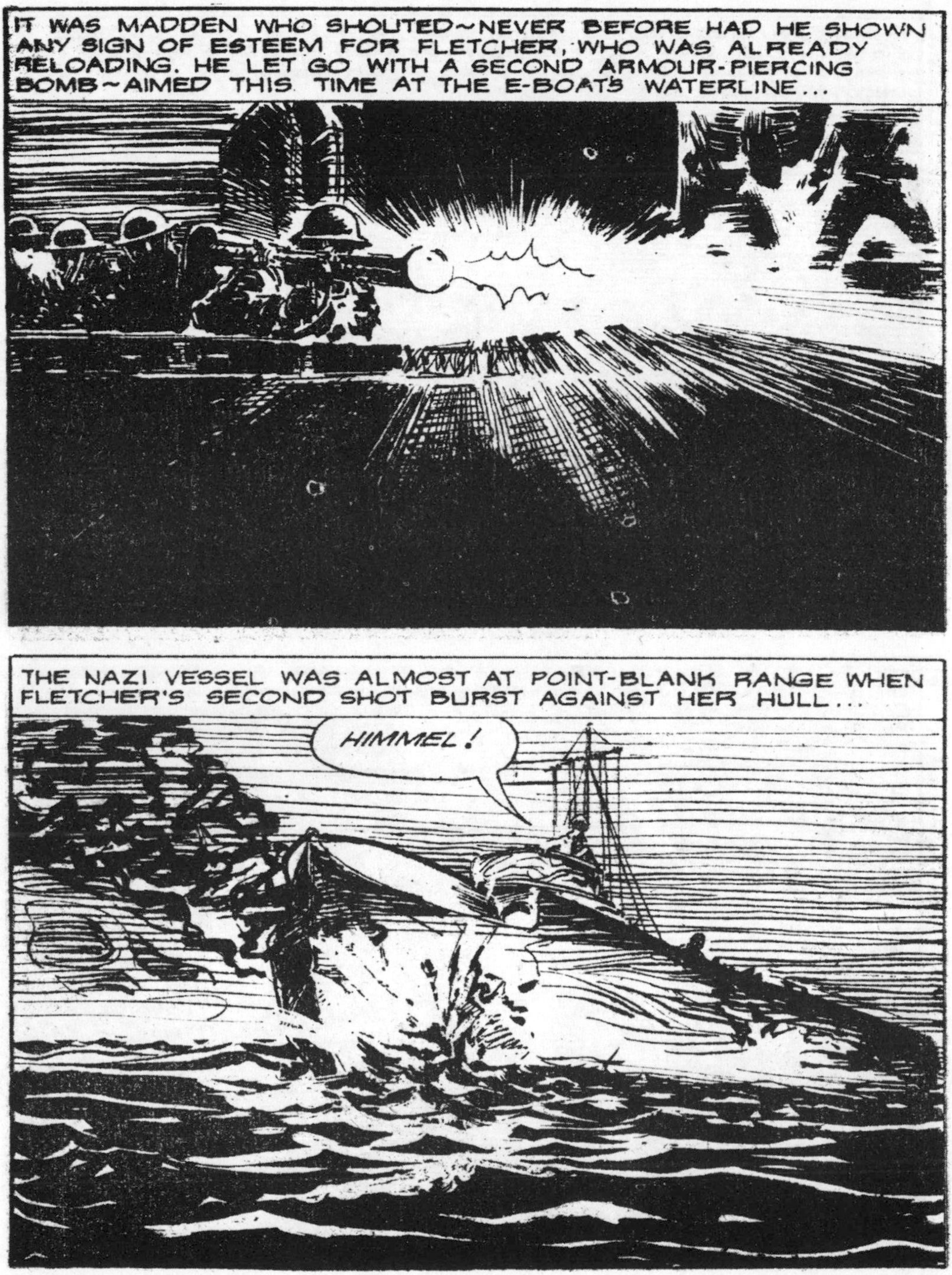
IT WAS MADDEN WHO SHOUTED~NEVER BEFORE HAD HE SHOWN ANY SIGN OF ESTEEM FOR FLETCHER, WHO WAS ALREADY RELOADING. HE LET GO WITH A SECOND ARMOUR-PIERCING BOMB~AIMED THIS TIME AT THE E-BOAT'S WATERLINE...
THE NAZI VESSEL WAS ALMOST AT POINT-BLANK RANGE WHEN FLETCHER'S SECOND SHOT BURST AGAINST HER HULL...
HIMMEL!

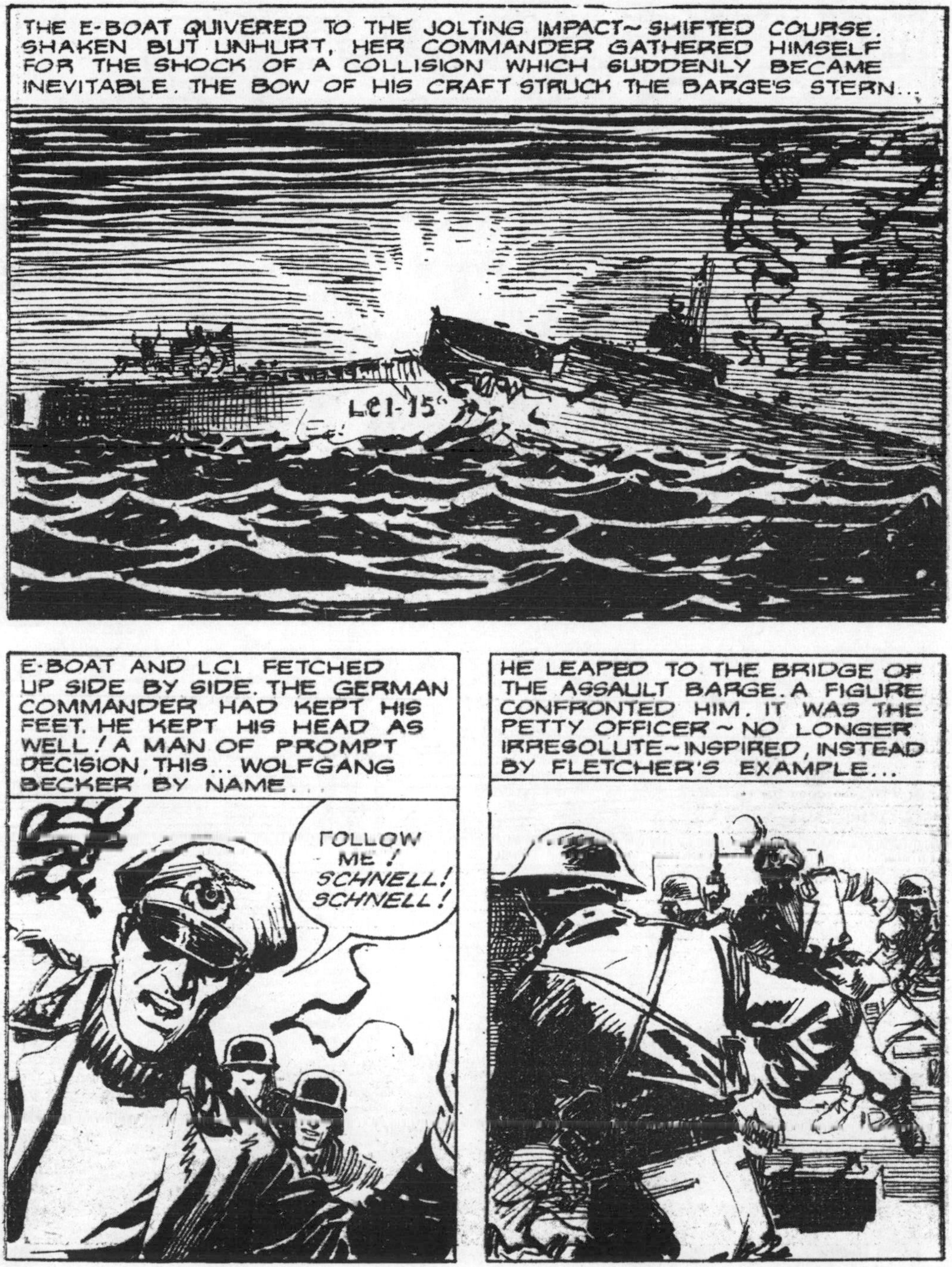
THE E-BOAT QUIVERED TO THE JOLTING IMPACT~ SHIFTED COURSE. SHAKEN BUT UNHURT, HER COMMANDER GATHERED HIMSELF FOR THE SHOCK OF A COLLISION WHICH SUDDENLY BECAME INEVITABLE. THE BOW OF HIS CRAFT STRUCK THE BARGE'S STERN...
E-BOAT AND L.C.I. FETCHED UP SIDE BY SIDE. THE GERMAN COMMANDER HAD KEPT HIS FEET. HE KEPT HIS HEAD AS WELL! A MAN OF PROMPT DECISION, THIS... WOLFGANG BECKER BY NAME...
FOLLOW ME! SCHNELL! SCHNELL!
HE LEAPED TO THE BRIDGE OF THE ASSAULT BARGE. A FIGURE CONFRONTED HIM. IT WAS THE PETTY OFFICER ~ NO LONGER IRRESOLUTE~ INSPIRED, INSTEAD BY FLETCHER'S EXAMPLE...

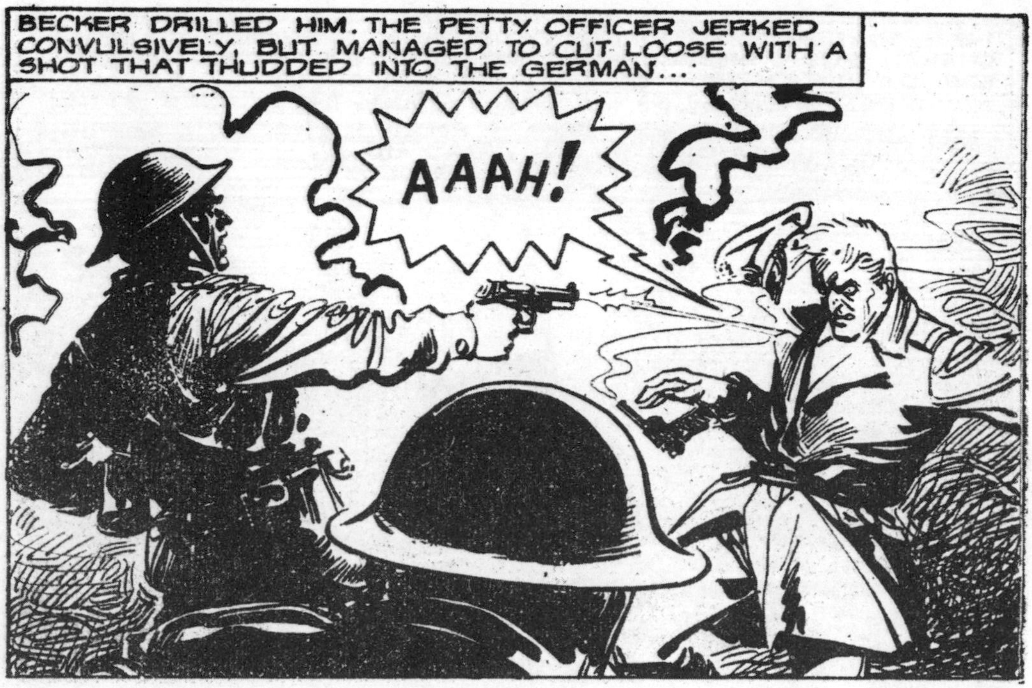
BECKER DRILLED HIM. THE PETTY OFFICER JERKED CONVULSIVELY, BUT MANAGED TO CUT LOOSE WITH A SHOT THAT THUDDED INTO THE GERMAN...
AAAH!

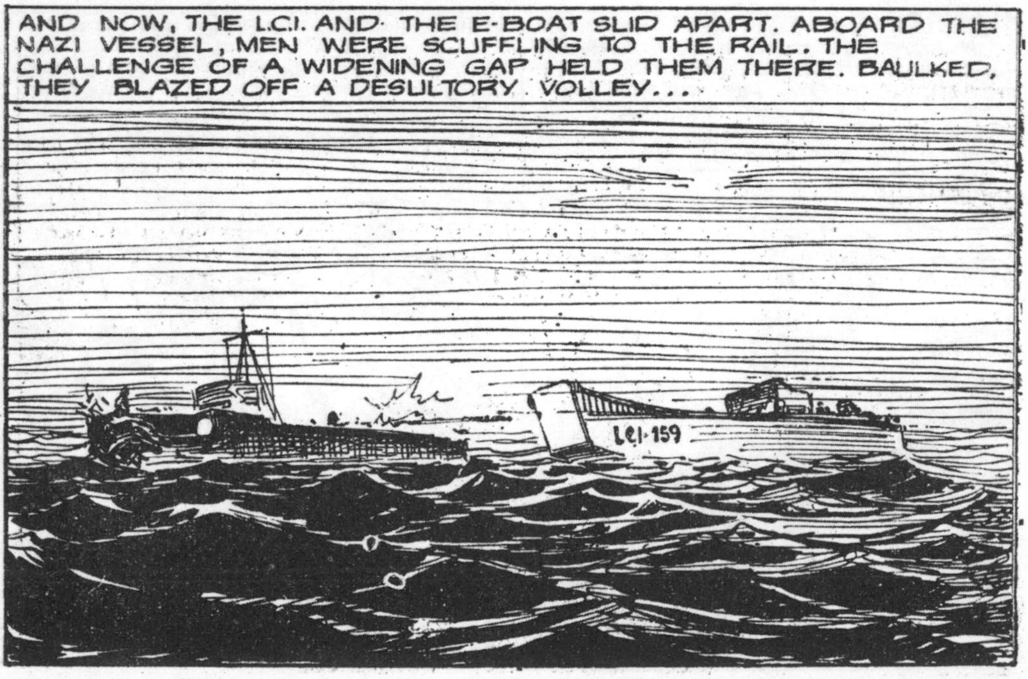
AND NOW, THE L.C.I. AND THE E-BOAT SLID APART. ABOARD THE NAZI VESSEL, MEN WERE SCUFFLING TO THE RAIL. THE CHALLENGE OF A WIDENING GAP HELD THEM THERE. BAULKED, THEY BLAZED OFF A DESULTORY VOLLEY...
LCI-159

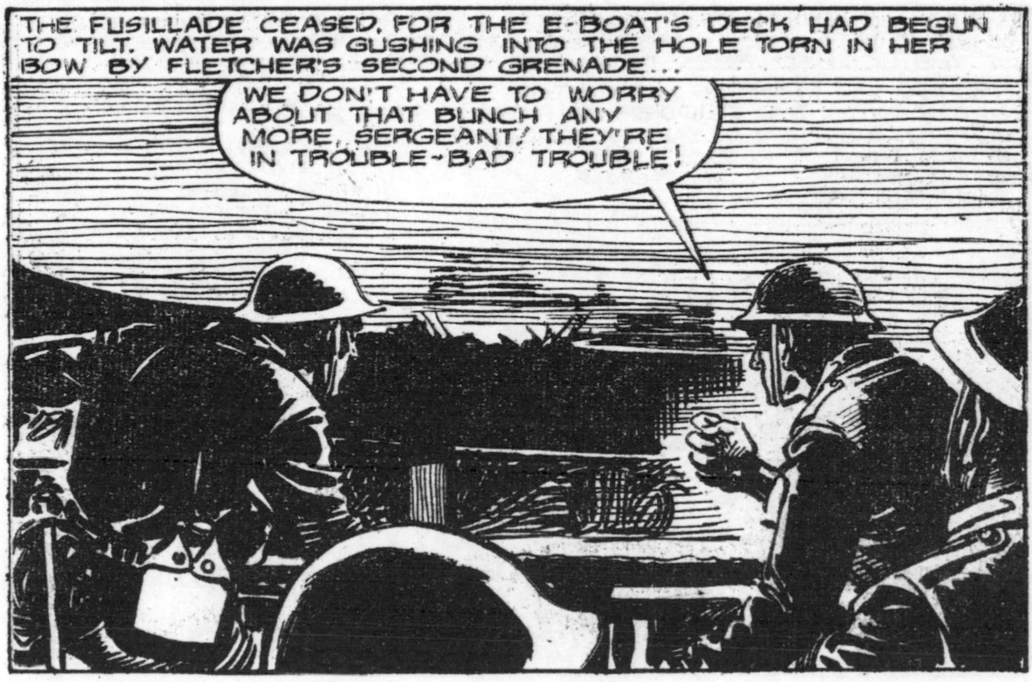
THE FUSILLADE CEASED, FOR THE E-BOAT'S DECK HAD BEGUN TO TILT. WATER WAS GUSHING INTO THE HOLE TORN IN HER BOW BY FLETCHER'S SECOND GRENADE...
WE DON'T HAVE TO WORRY ABOUT THAT BUNCH ANY MORE, SERGEANT! THEY'RE IN TROUBLE~BAD TROUBLE!

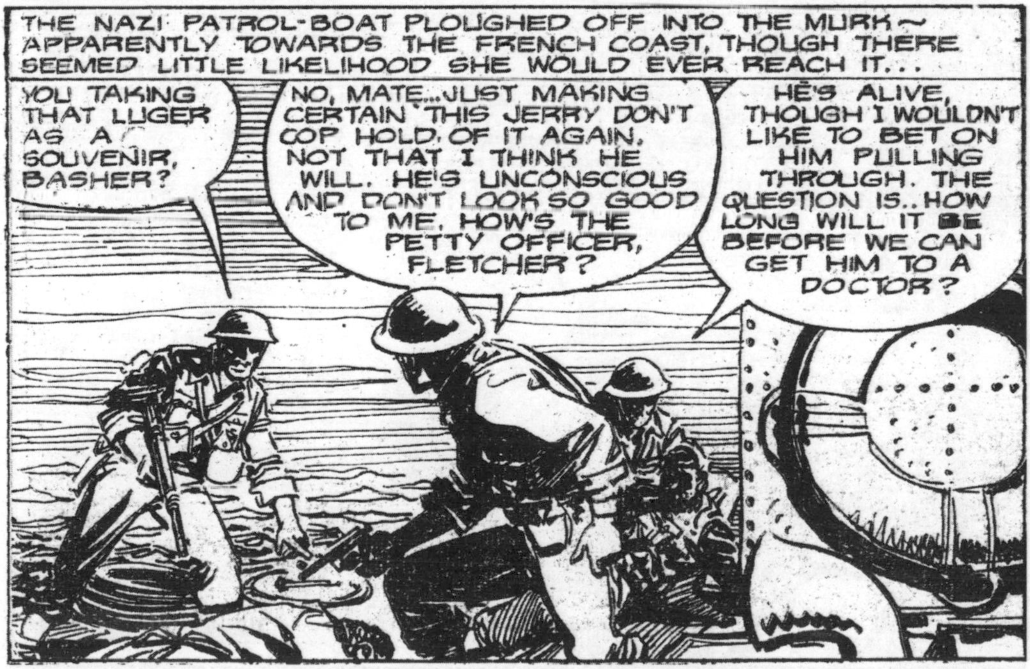
THE NAZI PATROL-BOAT PLOUGHED OFF INTO THE MURK~ APPARENTLY TOWARDS THE FRENCH COAST, THOUGH THERE SEEMED LITTLE LIKELIHOOD SHE WOULD EVER REACH IT...
YOU TAKING THAT LUGER AS A SOUVENIR, BASHER?
NO, MATE...JUST MAKING CERTAIN THIS JERRY DON'T COP HOLD OF IT AGAIN. NOT THAT I THINK HE WILL. HE'S UNCONSCIOUS AND DON'T LOOK SO GOOD TO ME. HOW'S THE PETTY OFFICER, FLETCHER?
HE'S ALIVE, THOUGH I WOULDN'T LIKE TO BET ON HIM PULLING THROUGH. THE QUESTION IS.. HOW LONG WILL IT BE BEFORE WE CAN GET HIM TO A DOCTOR?

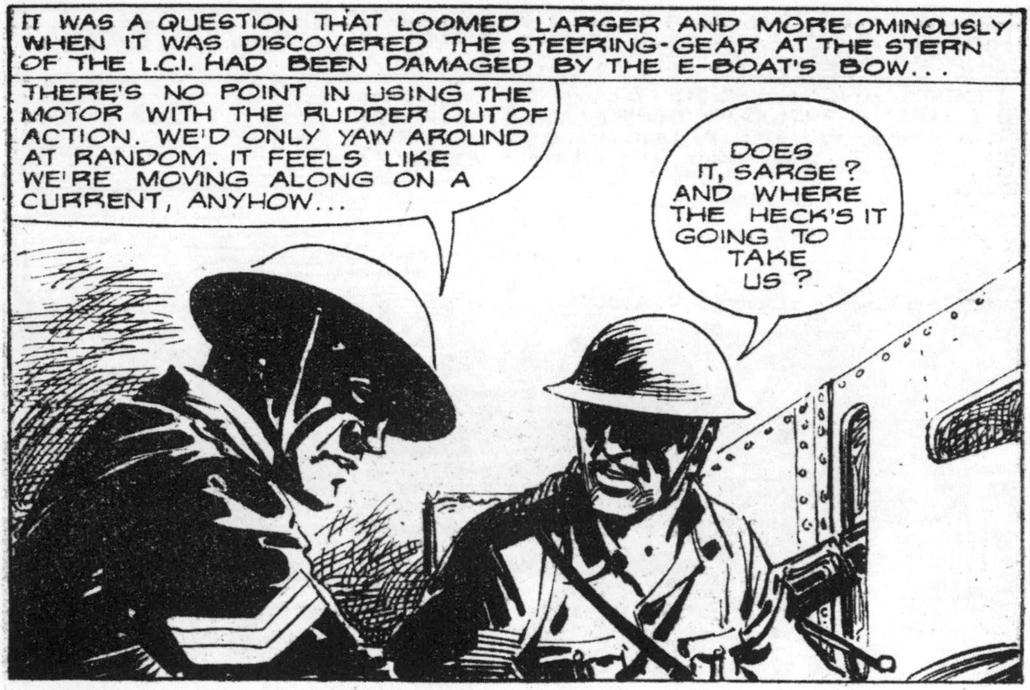
IT WAS A QUESTION THAT LOOMED LARGER AND MORE OMINOUSLY WHEN IT WAS DISCOVERED THE STEERING-GEAR AT THE STERN OF THE L.C.I. HAD BEEN DAMAGED BY THE E-BOAT'S BOW...
THERE'S NO POINT IN USING THE MOTOR WITH THE RUDDER OUT OF ACTION. WE'D ONLY YAW AROUND AT RANDOM. IT FEELS LIKE WE'RE MOVING ALONG ON A CURRENT, ANYHOW...
DOES IT, SARGE? AND WHERE THE HECK'S IT GOING TO TAKE US?

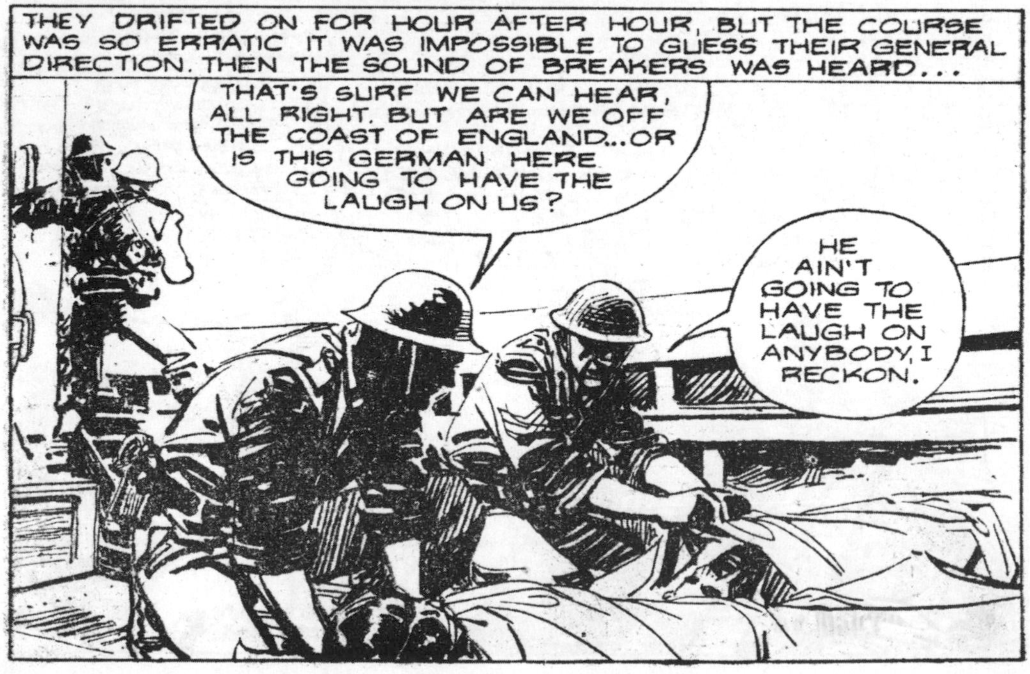
THEY DRIFTED ON FOR HOUR AFTER HOUR, BUT THE COURSE WAS SO ERRATIC IT WAS IMPOSSIBLE TO GUESS THEIR GENERAL DIRECTION. THEN THE SOUND OF BREAKERS WAS HEARD...
THAT'S SURF WE CAN HEAR, ALL RIGHT. BUT ARE WE OFF THE COAST OF ENGLAND...OR IS THIS GERMAN HERE GOING TO HAVE THE LAUGH ON US?
HE AIN'T GOING TO HAVE THE LAUGH ON ANYBODY, I RECKON.

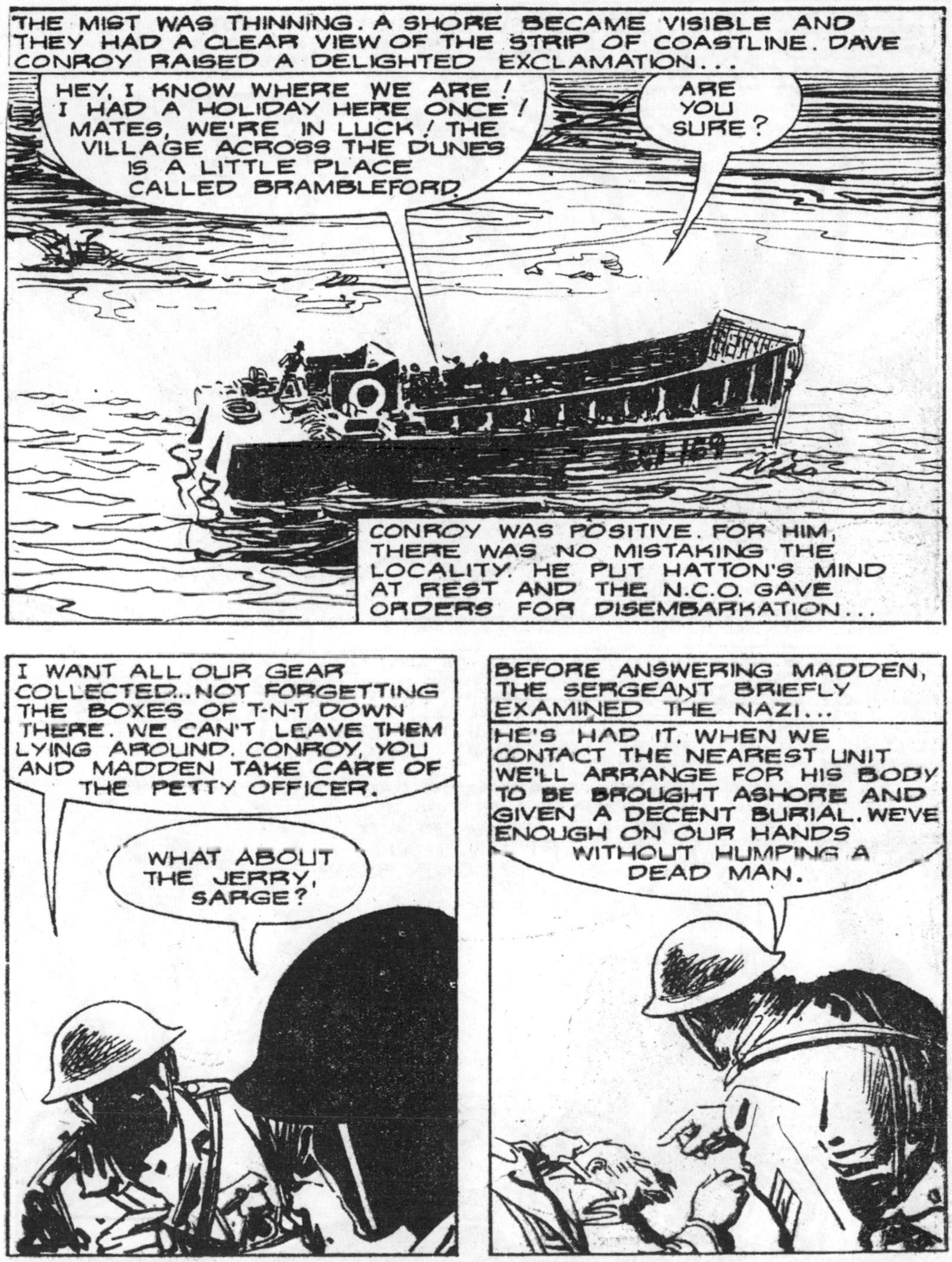
THE MIST WAS THINNING. A SHORE BECAME VISIBLE AND THEY HAD A CLEAR VIEW OF THE STRIP OF COASTLINE. DAVE CONROY RAISED A DELIGHTED EXCLAMATION...
HEY, I KNOW WHERE WE ARE! I HAD A HOLIDAY HERE ONCE! MATES, WE'RE IN LUCK! THE VILLAGE ACROSS THE DUNES IS A LITTLE PLACE CALLED BRAMBLEFORD.
ARE YOU SURE?
CONROY WAS POSITIVE. FOR HIM, THERE WAS NO MISTAKING THE LOCALITY. HE PUT HATTON'S MIND AT REST AND THE N.C.O. GAVE ORDERS FOR DISEMBARKATION...
I WANT ALL OUR GEAR COLLECTED...NOT FORGETTING THE BOXES OF T-N-T DOWN THERE. WE CAN'T LEAVE THEM LYING AROUND. CONROY, YOU AND MADDEN TAKE CARE OF THE PETTY OFFICER.
WHAT ABOUT THE JERRY, SARGE?
BEFORE ANSWERING MADDEN, THE SERGEANT BRIEFLY EXAMINED THE NAZI...
HE'S HAD IT. WHEN WE CONTACT THE NEAREST UNIT WE'LL ARRANGE FOR HIS BODY TO BE BROUGHT ASHORE AND GIVEN A DECENT BURIAL. WE'VE ENOUGH ON OUR HANDS WITHOUT HUMPING A DEAD MAN.

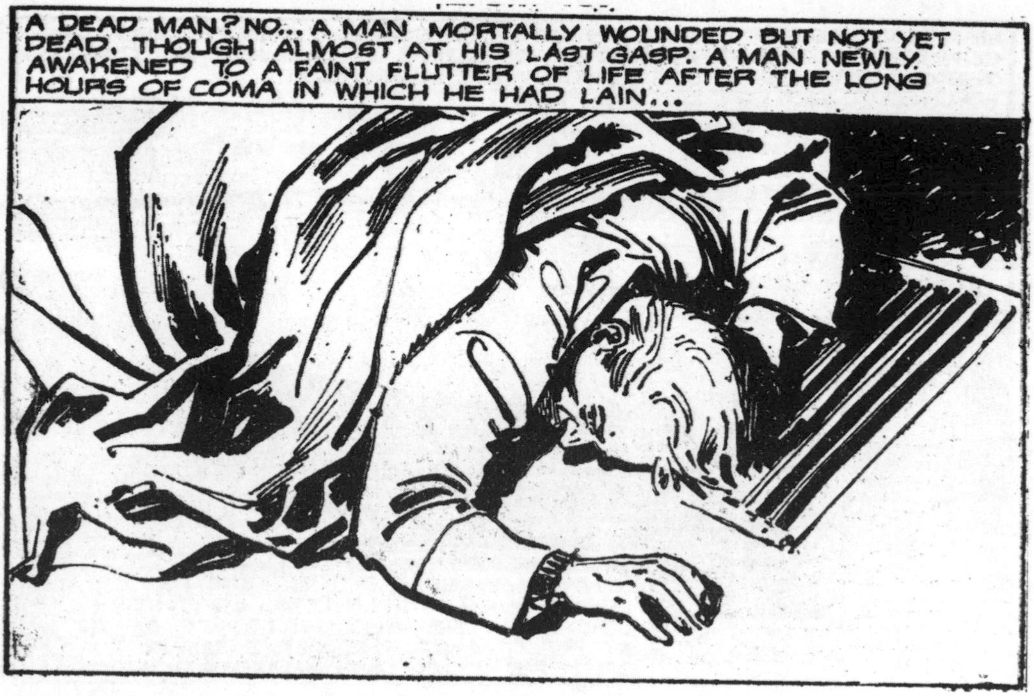
A DEAD MAN? NO... A MAN MORTALLY WOUNDED BUT NOT YET DEAD, THOUGH ALMOST AT HIS LAST GASP. A MAN NEWLY AWAKENED TO A FAINT FLUTTER OF LIFE AFTER THE LONG HOURS OF COMA IN WHICH HE HAD LAIN...

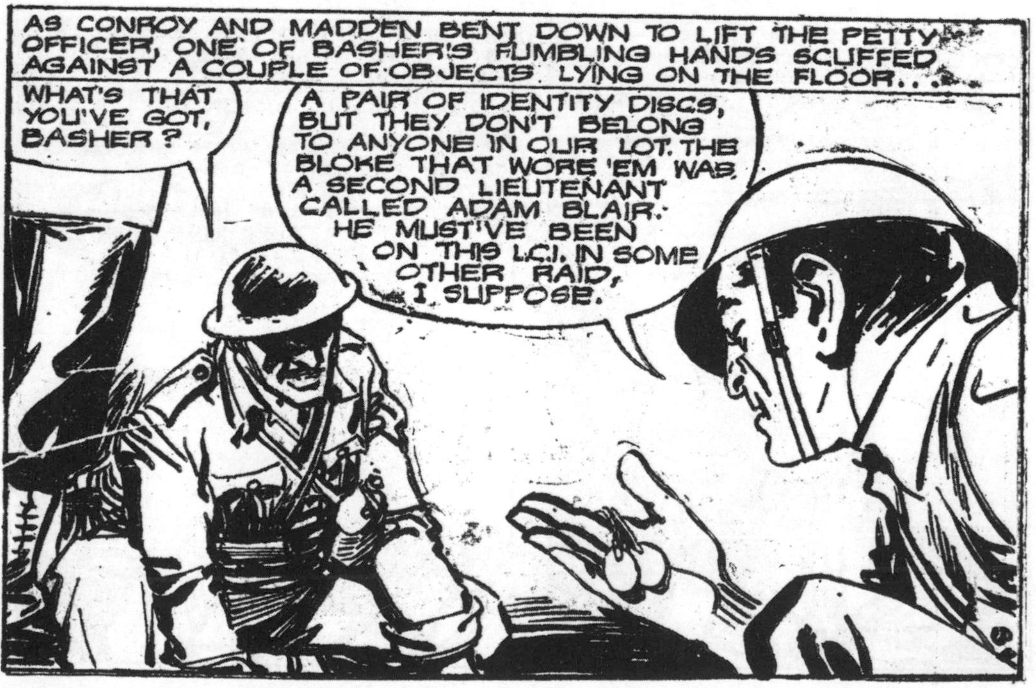
AS CONROY AND MADDEN BENT DOWN TO LIFT THE PETTY OFFICER, ONE OF BASHER'S FUMBLING HANDS SCUFFED AGAINST A COUPLE OF OBJECTS LYING ON THE FLOOR...
WHAT'S THAT YOU'VE GOT, BASHER?
A PAIR OF IDENTITY DISCS, BUT THEY DON'T BELONG TO ANYONE IN OUR LOT. THE BLOKE THAT WORE 'EM WAS A SECOND LIEUTENANT CALLED ADAM BLAIR. HE MUST'VE BEEN ON THIS L.C.I. IN SOME OTHER RAID, I SUPPOSE.

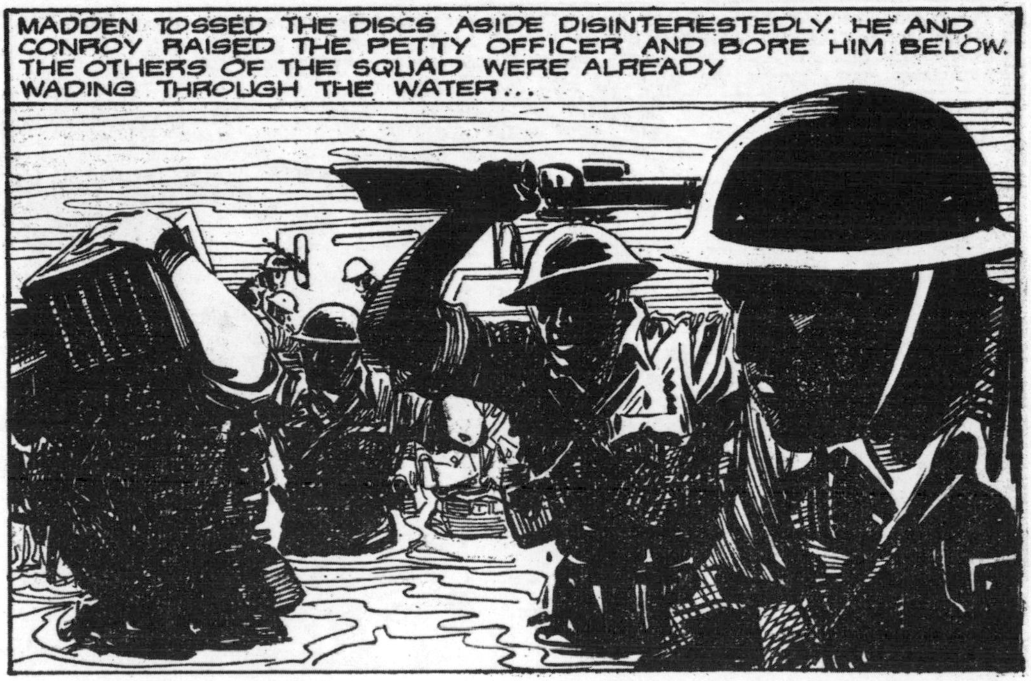
MADDEN TOSSED THE DISCS ASIDE DISINTERESTEDLY. HE AND CONROY RAISED THE PETTY OFFICER AND BORE HIM BELOW. THE OTHERS OF THE SQUAD WERE ALREADY WADING THROUGH THE WATER...

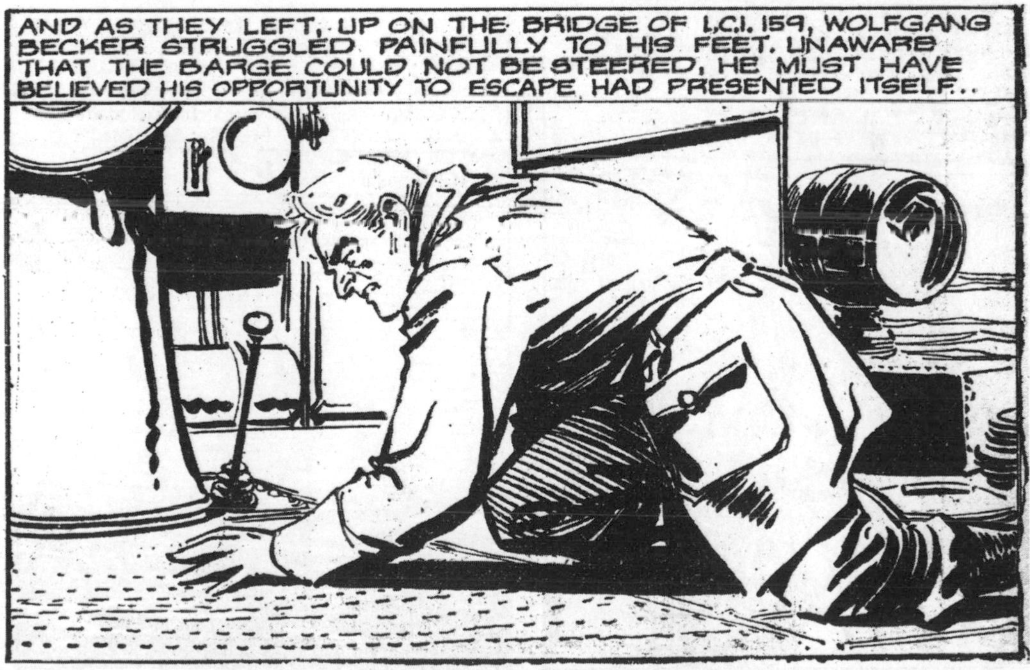
AND AS THEY LEFT, UP ON THE BRIDGE OF L.C.I. 159, WOLFGANG BECKER STRUGGLED PAINFULLY TO HIS FEET. UNAWARE THAT THE BARGE COULD NOT BE STEERED, HE MUST HAVE BELIEVED HIS OPPORTUNITY TO ESCAPE HAD PRESENTED ITSELF...

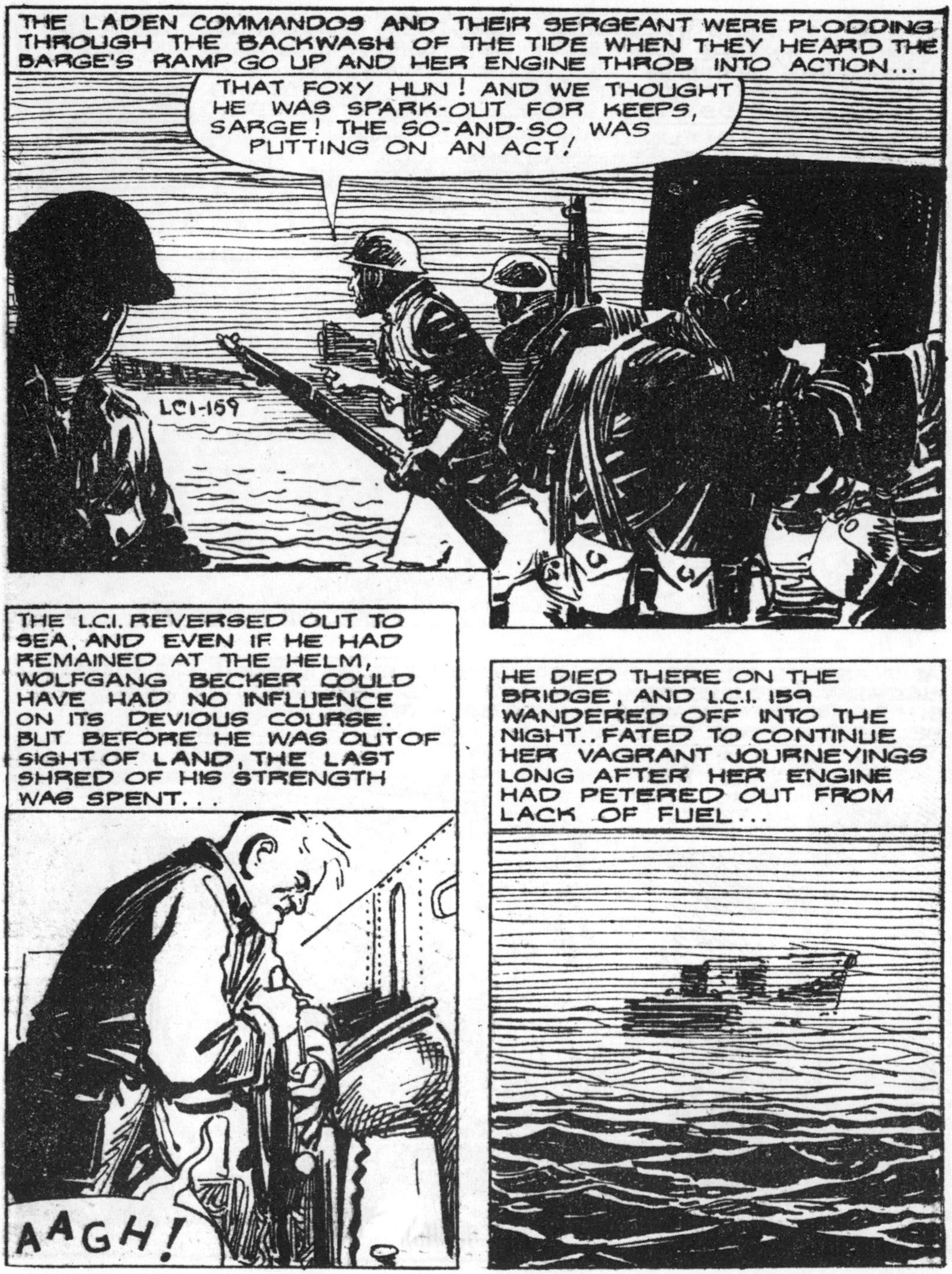
THE LADEN COMMANDOS AND THEIR SERGEANT WERE PLODDING THROUGH THE BACKWASH OF THE TIDE WHEN THEY HEARD THE BARGE'S RAMP GO UP AND HER ENGINE THROB INTO ACTION...
THAT FOXY HUN! AND WE THOUGHT HE WAS SPARK-OUT FOR KEEPS, SARGE! THE SO-AND-SO, WAS PUTTING ON AN ACT!
LCI-159
THE L.C.I. REVERSED OUT TO SEA, AND EVEN IF HE HAD REMAINED AT THE HELM, WOLFGANG BECKER COULD HAVE HAD NO INFLUENCE ON ITS DEVIOUS COURSE. BUT BEFORE HE WAS OUT OF SIGHT OF LAND, THE LAST SHRED OF HIS STRENGTH WAS SPENT...
AAGH!
HE DIED THERE ON THE BRIDGE, AND L.C.I. 159 WANDERED OFF INTO THE NIGHT.. FATED TO CONTINUE HER VAGRANT JOURNEYINGS LONG AFTER HER ENGINE HAD PETERED OUT FROM LACK OF FUEL...

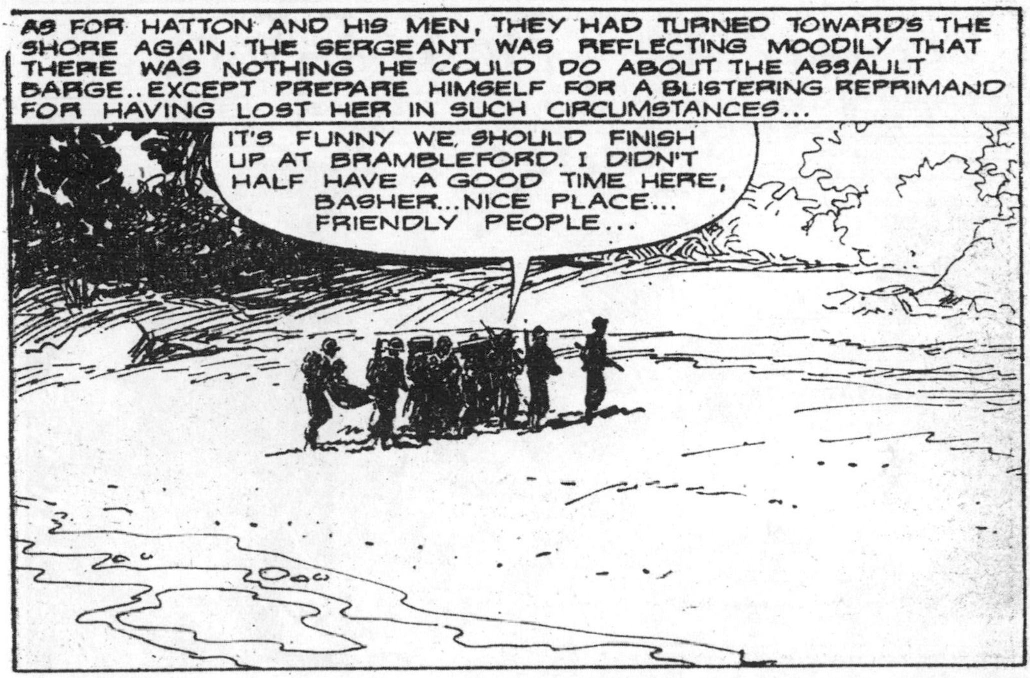
AS FOR HATTON AND HIS MEN, THEY HAD TURNED TOWARDS THE SHORE AGAIN. THE SERGEANT WAS REFLECTING MOODILY THAT THERE WAS NOTHING HE COULD DO ABOUT THE ASSAULT BARGE.. EXCEPT PREPARE HIMSELF FOR A BLISTERING REPRIMAND FOR HAVING LOST HER IN SUCH CIRCUMSTANCES...
IT'S FUNNY WE SHOULD FINISH UP AT BRAMBLEFORD. I DIDN'T HALF HAVE A GOOD TIME HERE, BASHER...NICE PLACE... FRIENDLY PEOPLE...

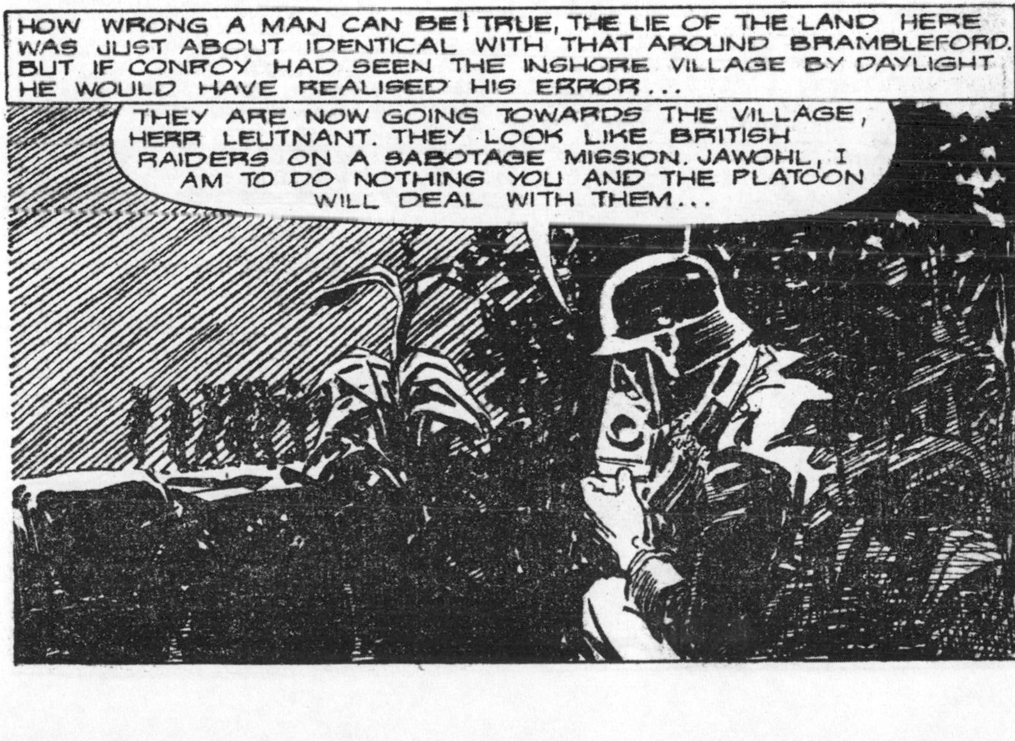
HOW WRONG A MAN CAN BE! TRUE, THE LIE OF THE LAND HERE WAS JUST ABOUT IDENTICAL WITH THAT AROUND BRAMBLEFORD. BUT IF CONROY HAD SEEN THE INSHORE VILLAGE BY DAYLIGHT HE WOULD HAVE REALISED HIS ERROR...
THEY ARE NOW GOING TOWARDS THE VILLAGE, HERR LEUTNANT. THEY LOOK LIKE BRITISH RAIDERS ON A SABOTAGE MISSION. JAWOHL, I AM TO DO NOTHING YOU AND THE PLATOON WILL DEAL WITH THEM...

Chapter 4. Final Effort

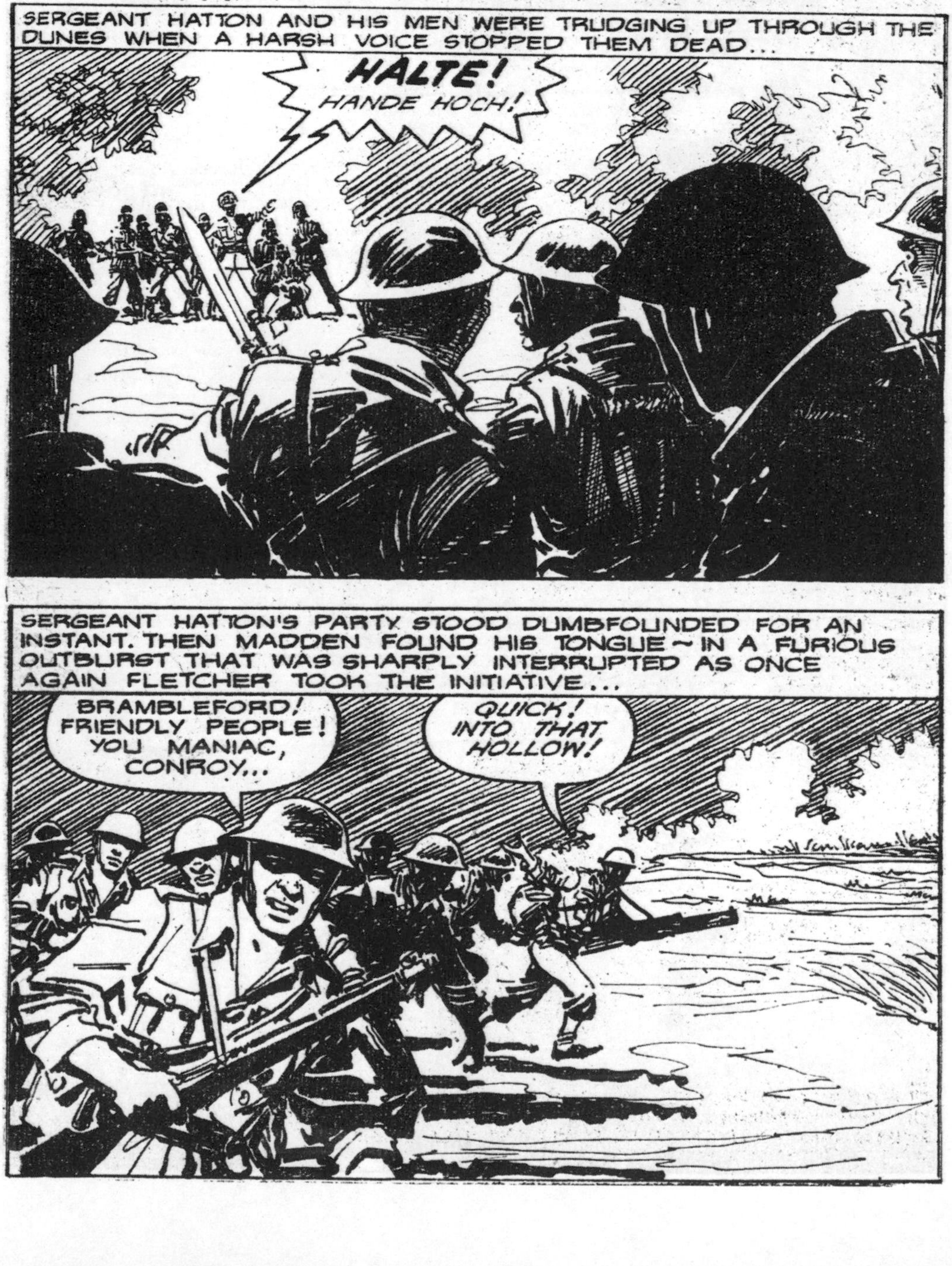
SERGEANT HATTON AND HIS MEN WERE TRUDGING UP THROUGH THE DUNES WHEN A HARSH VOICE STOPPED THEM DEAD...
HALTE! HANDE HOCH!
SERGEANT HATTON'S PARTY STOOD DUMBFOUNDED FOR AN INSTANT. THEN MADDEN FOUND HIS TONGUE ~ IN A FURIOUS OUTBURST THAT WAS SHARPLY INTERRUPTED AS ONCE AGAIN FLETCHER TOOK THE INITIATIVE...
BRAMBLEFORD! FRIENDLY PEOPLE! YOU MANIAC, CONROY...
QUICK! INTO THAT HOLLOW!

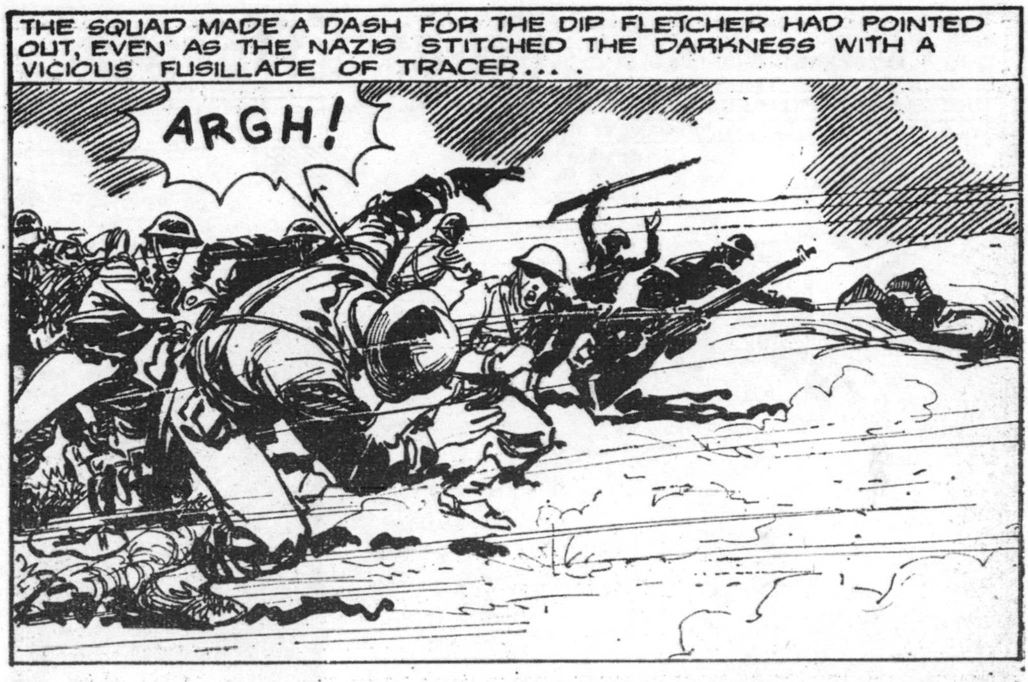
THE SQUAD MADE A DASH FOR THE DIP FLETCHER HAD POINTED OUT, EVEN AS THE NAZIS STITCHED THE DARKNESS WITH A VICIOUS FUSILLADE OF TRACER...
ARGH!

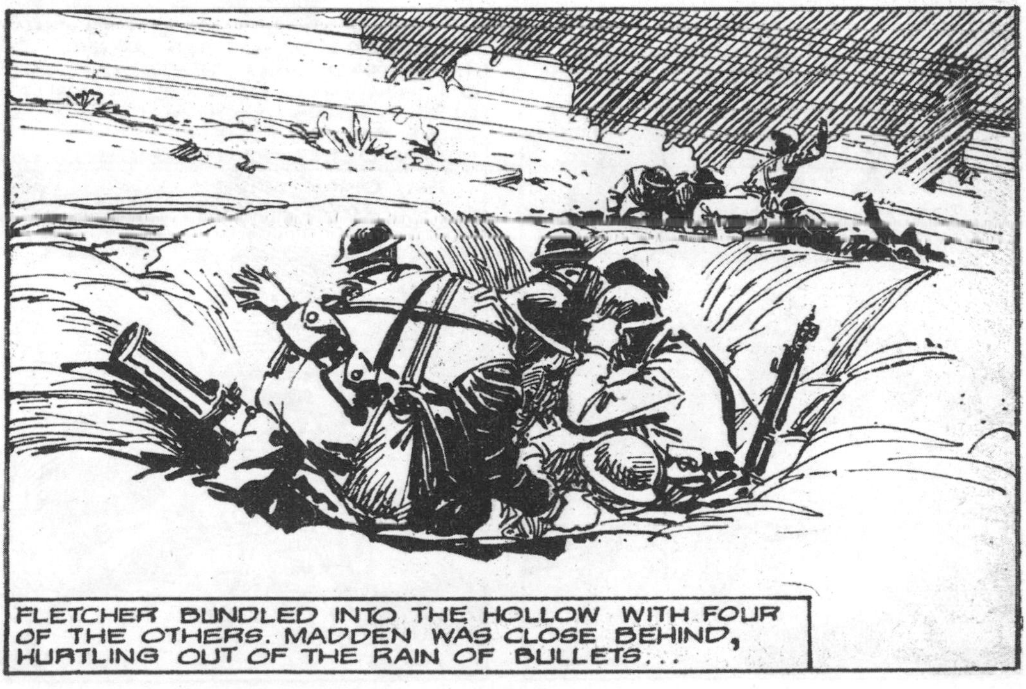
FLETCHER BUNDLED INTO THE HOLLOW WITH FOUR OF THE OTHERS. MADDEN WAS CLOSE BEHIND, HURTLING OUT OF THE RAIN OF BULLETS...

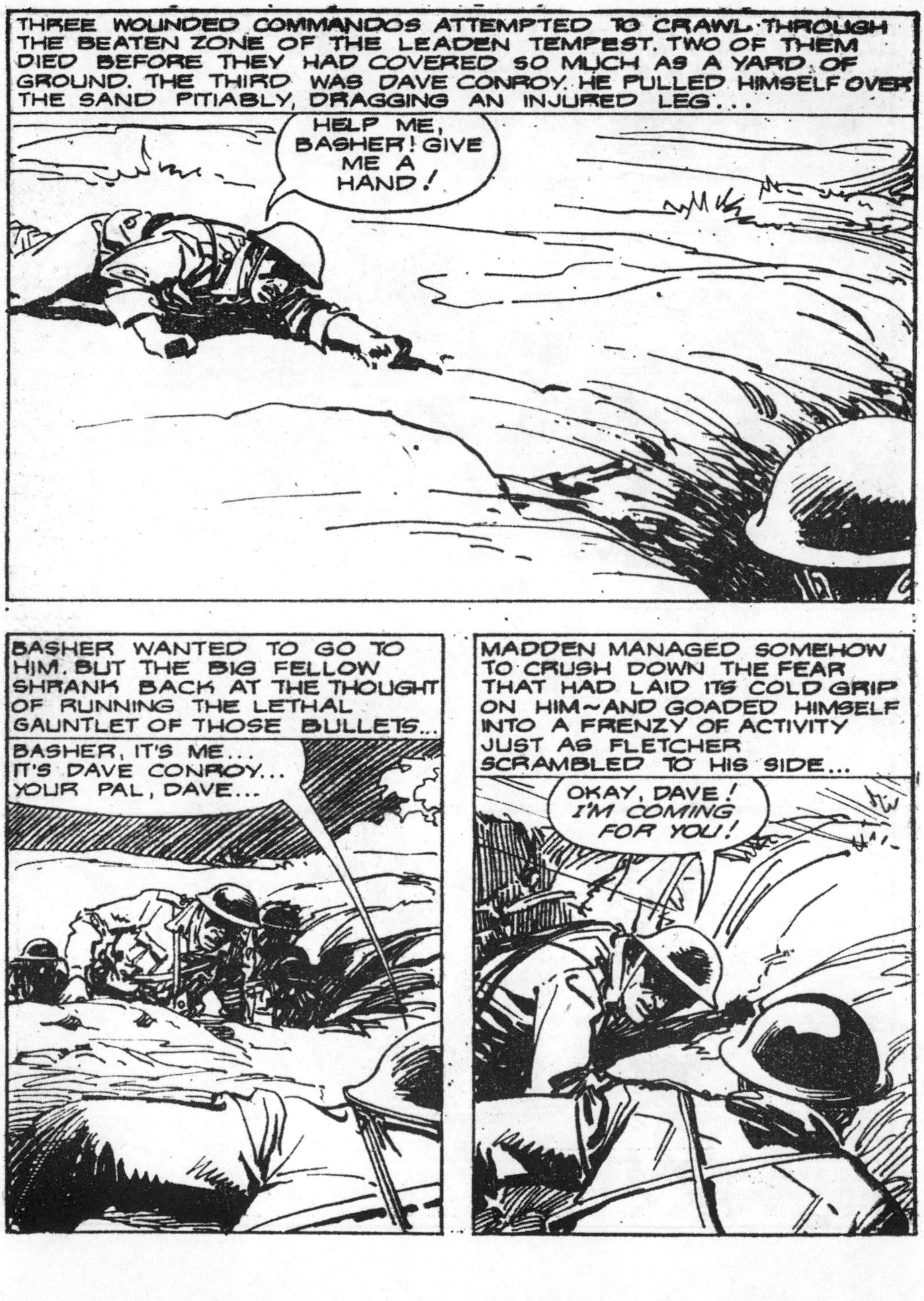
THREE WOUNDED COMMANDOS ATTEMPTED TO CRAWL THROUGH THE BEATEN ZONE OF THE LEADEN TEMPEST. TWO OF THEM DIED BEFORE THEY HAD COVERED SO MUCH AS A YARD OF GROUND. THE THIRD WAS DAVE CONROY. HE PULLED HIMSELF OVER THE SAND PITIABLY, DRAGGING AN INJURED LEG...
HELP ME, BASHER! GIVE ME A HAND!
BASHER WANTED TO GO TO HIM. BUT THE BIG FELLOW SHRANK BACK AT THE THOUGHT OF RUNNING THE LETHAL GAUNTLET OF THOSE BULLETS...
BASHER, IT'S ME... IT'S DAVE CONROY... YOUR PAL, DAVE...
MADDEN MANAGED SOMEHOW TO CRUSH DOWN THE FEAR THAT HAD LAID ITS COLD GRIP ON HIM~AND GOADED HIMSELF INTO A FRENZY OF ACTIVITY JUST AS FLETCHER SCRAMBLED TO HIS SIDE...
OKAY, DAVE! I'M COMING FOR YOU!

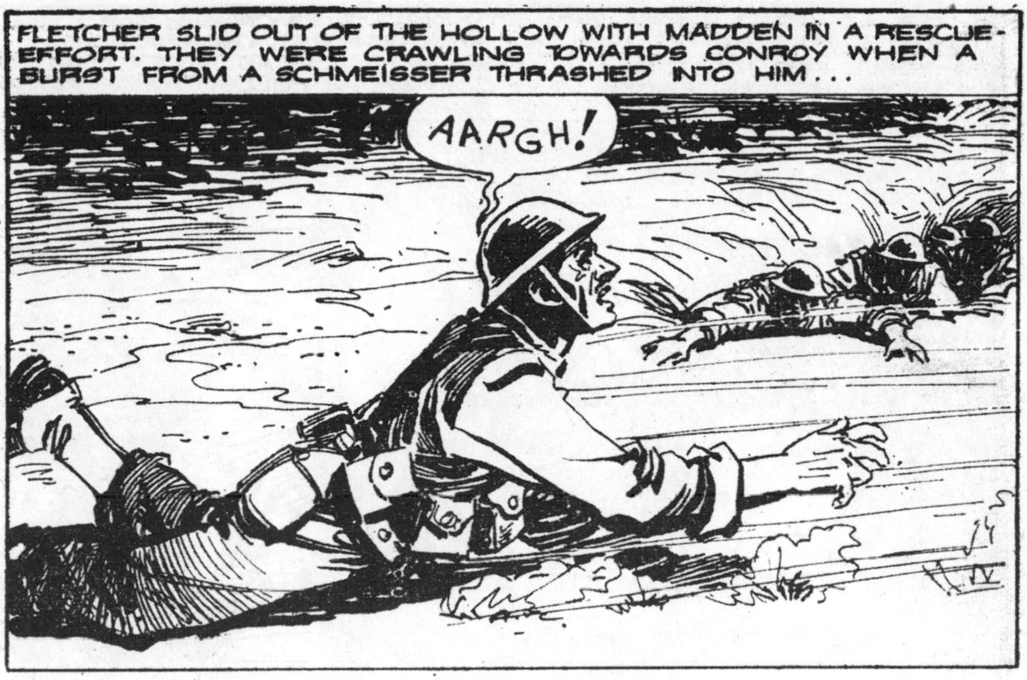
FLETCHER SLID OUT OF THE HOLLOW WITH MADDEN IN A RESCUE-EFFORT. THEY WERE CRAWLING TOWARDS CONROY WHEN A BURST FROM A SCHMEISSER THRASHED INTO HIM...
AARGH!

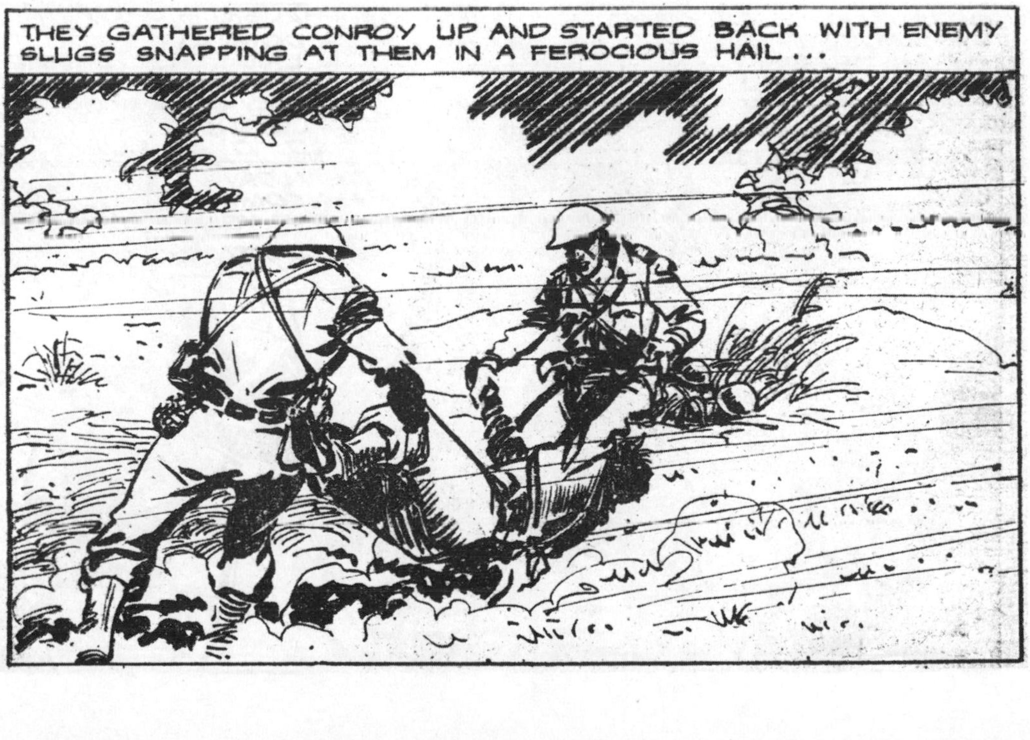
THEY GATHERED CONROY UP AND STARTED BACK WITH ENEMY SLUGS SNAPPING AT THEM IN A FEROCIOUS HAIL...

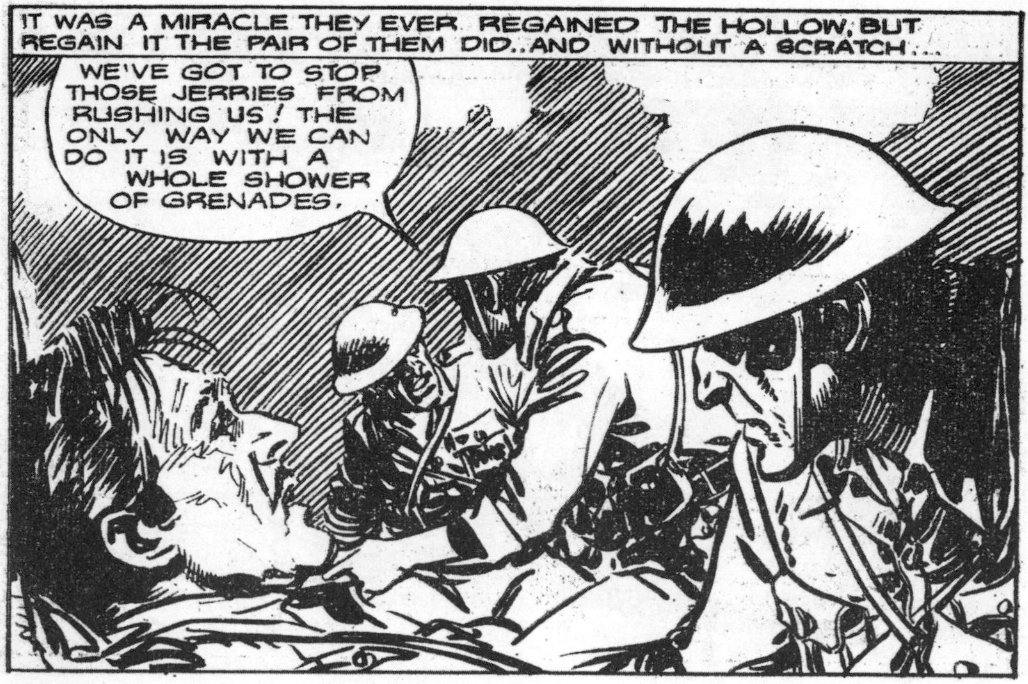
IT WAS A MIRACLE THEY EVER REGAINED THE HOLLOW, BUT REGAIN IT THE PAIR OF THEM DID.. AND WITHOUT A SCRATCH...
WE'VE GOT TO STOP THOSE JERRIES FROM RUSHING US! THE ONLY WAY WE CAN DO IT IS WITH A WHOLE SHOWER OF GRENADES.

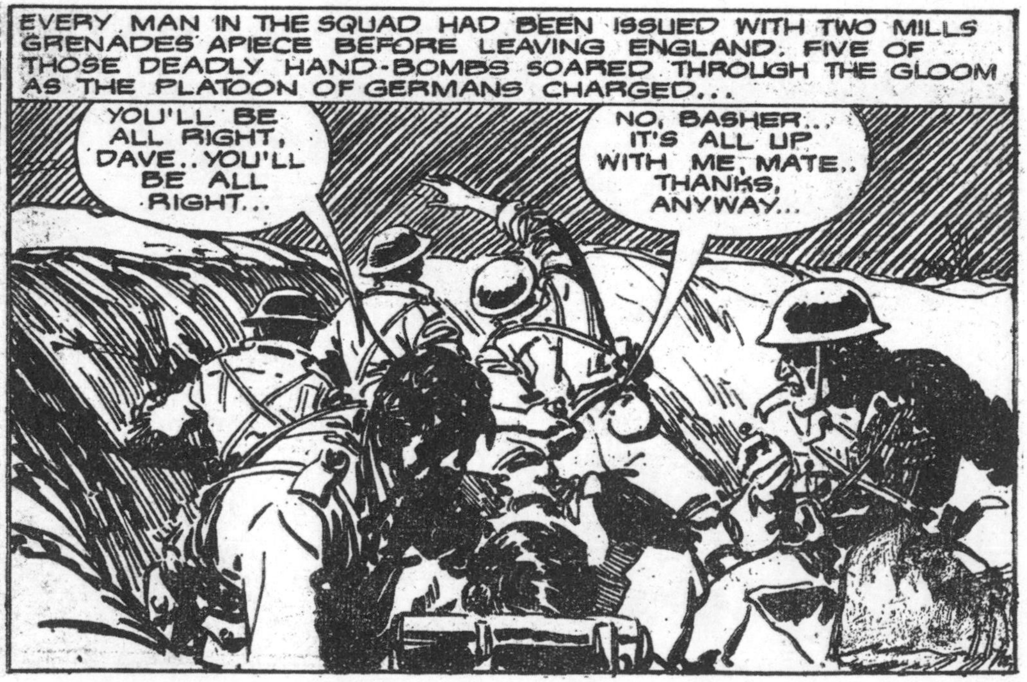
EVERY MAN IN THE SQUAD HAD BEEN ISSUED WITH TWO MILLS GRENADES APIECE BEFORE LEAVING ENGLAND. FIVE OF THOSE DEADLY HAND-BOMBS SOARED THROUGH THE GLOOM AS THE PLATOON OF GERMANS CHARGED...
YOU'LL BE ALL RIGHT, DAVE.. YOU'LL BE ALL RIGHT...
NO, BASHER... IT'S ALL UP WITH ME, MATE.. THANKS, ANYWAY...

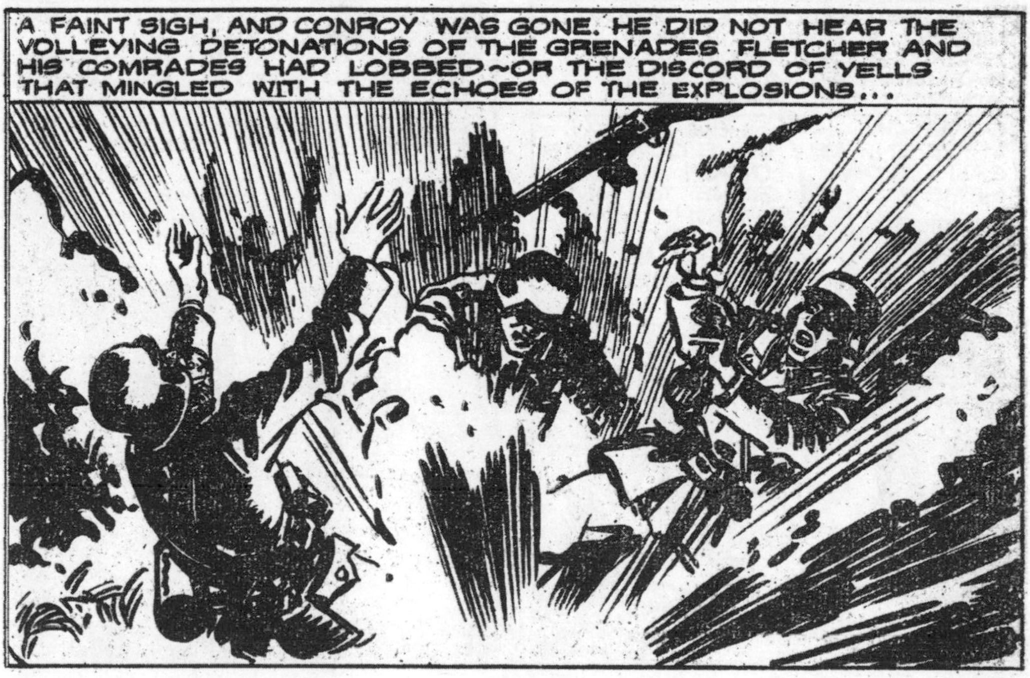
A FAINT SIGH, AND CONROY WAS GONE. HE DID NOT HEAR THE VOLLEYING DETONATIONS OF THE GRENADES FLETCHER AND HIS COMRADES HAD LOBBED~OR THE DISCORD OF YELLS THAT MINGLED WITH THE ECHOES OF THE EXPLOSIONS...

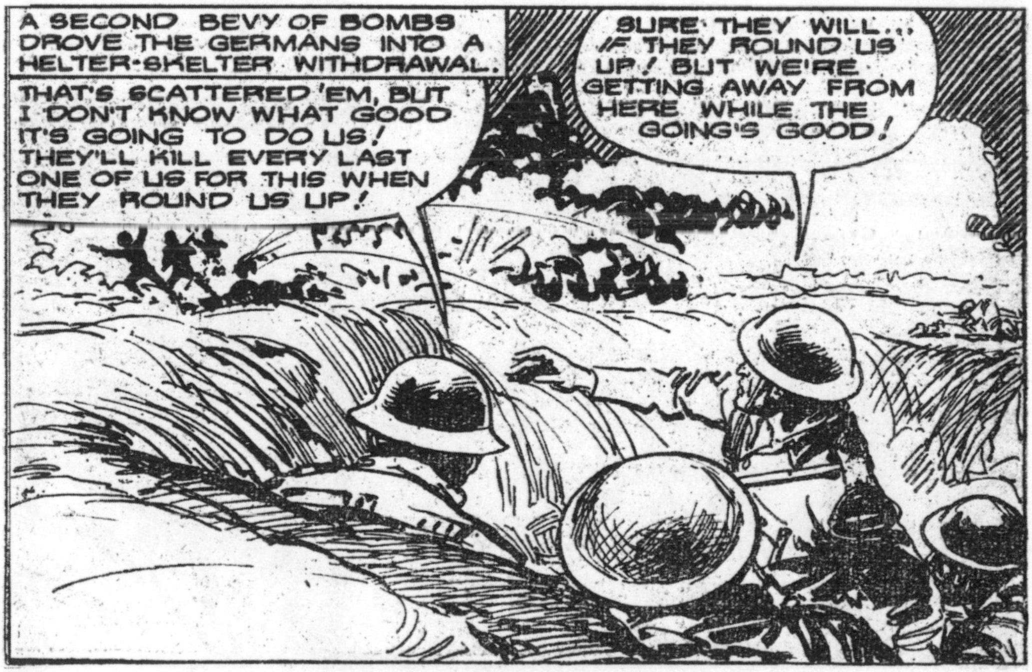
A SECOND BEVY OF BOMBS DROVE THE GERMANS INTO A HELTER-SKELTER WITHDRAWAL.
THAT'S SCATTERED 'EM, BUT I DON'T KNOW WHAT GOOD IT'S GOING TO DO US! THEY'LL KILL EVERY LAST ONE OF US FOR THIS WHEN THEY ROUND US UP!
SURE THEY WILL... IF THEY ROUND US UP! BUT WE'RE GETTING AWAY FROM HERE WHILE THE GOING'S GOOD!

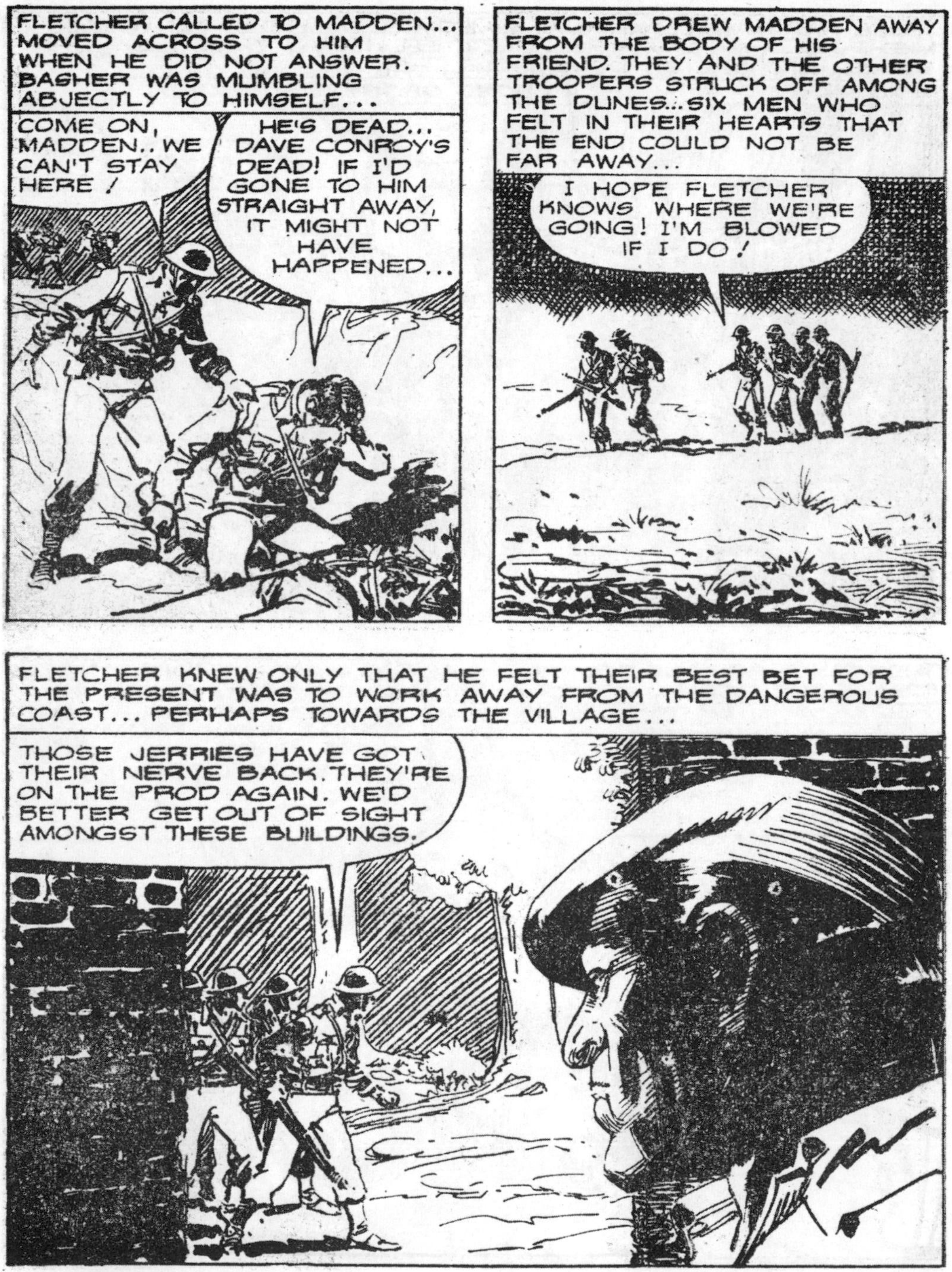
FLETCHER CALLED TO MADDEN... MOVED ACROSS TO HIM WHEN HE DID NOT ANSWER. BASHER WAS MUMBLING ABJECTLY TO HIMSELF...
COME ON, MADDEN.. WE CAN'T STAY HERE!
HE'S DEAD... DAVE CONROY'S DEAD! IF I'D GONE TO HIM STRAIGHT AWAY, IT MIGHT NOT HAVE HAPPENED...
FLETCHER DREW MADDEN AWAY FROM THE BODY OF HIS FRIEND. THEY AND THE OTHER TROOPERS STRUCK OFF AMONG THE DUNES...SIX MEN WHO FELT IN THEIR HEARTS THAT THE END COULD NOT BE FAR AWAY...
I HOPE FLETCHER KNOWS WHERE WE'RE GOING! I'M BLOWED IF I DO!
FLETCHER KNEW ONLY THAT HE FELT THEIR BEST BET FOR THE PRESENT WAS TO WORK AWAY FROM THE DANGEROUS COAST... PERHAPS TOWARDS THE VILLAGE...
THOSE JERRIES HAVE GOT THEIR NERVE BACK. THEY'RE ON THE PROD AGAIN. WE'D BETTER GET OUT OF SIGHT AMONGST THESE BUILDINGS.

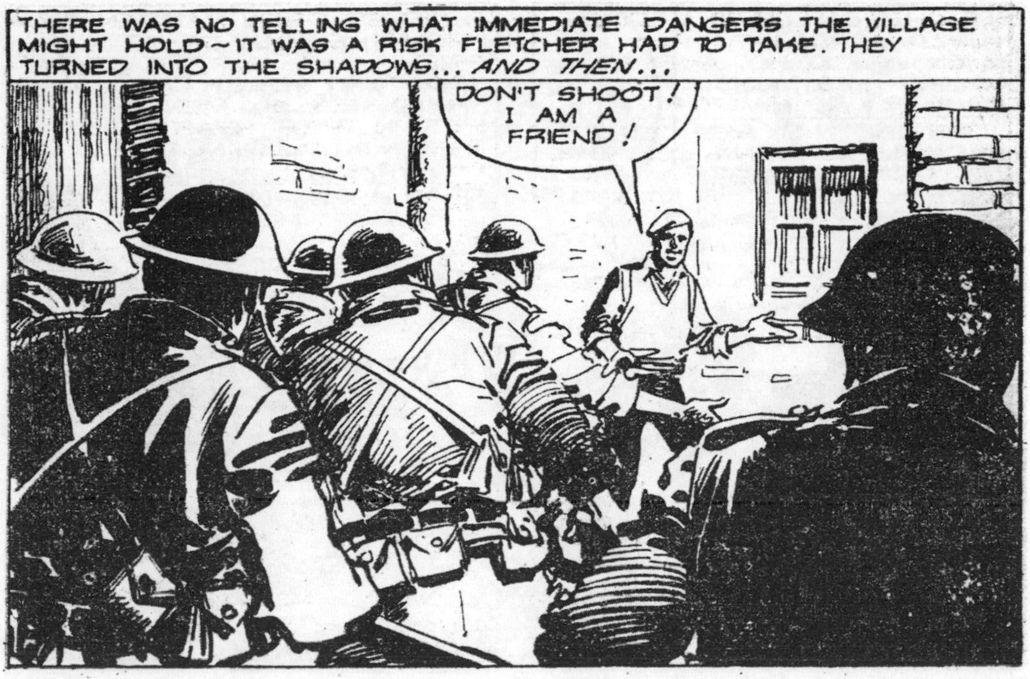
THERE WAS NO TELLING WHAT IMMEDIATE DANGERS THE VILLAGE MIGHT HOLD~IT WAS A RISK FLETCHER HAD TO TAKE. THEY TURNED INTO THE SHADOWS... AND THEN...
DON'T SHOOT! I AM A FRIEND!

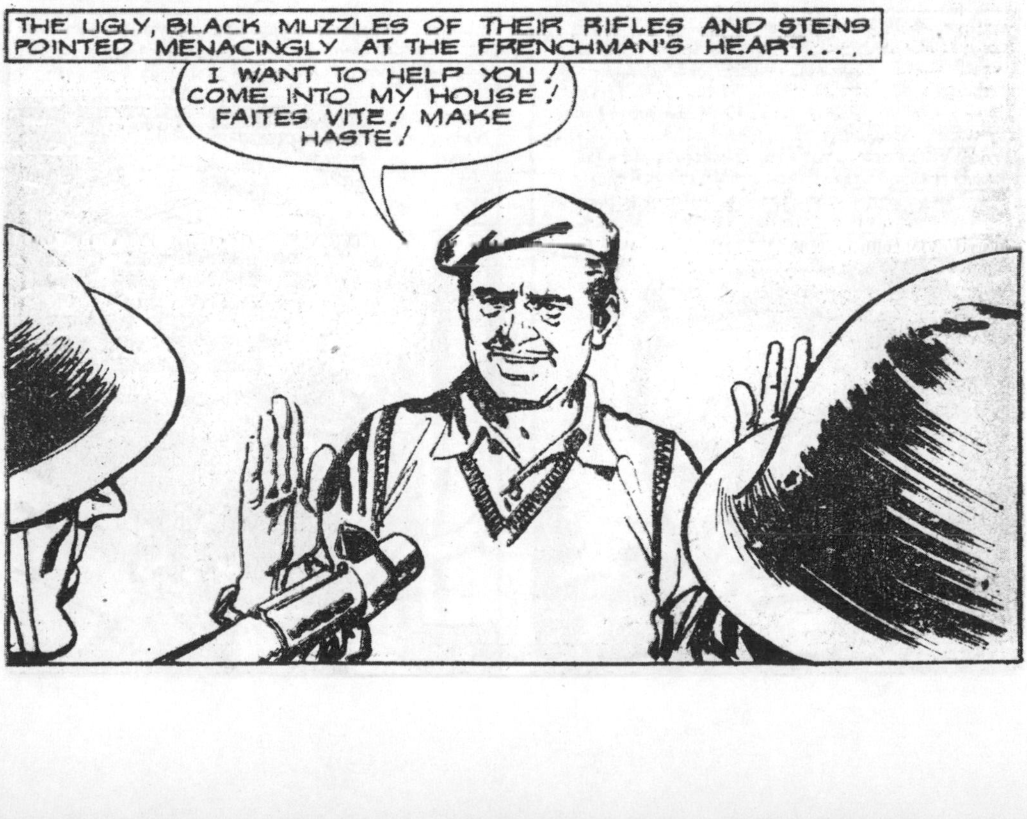
THE UGLY, BLACK MUZZLES OF THEIR RIFLES AND STENS POINTED MENACINGLY AT THE FRENCHMAN'S HEART....
I WANT TO HELP YOU! COME INTO MY HOUSE! FAITES VITE! MAKE HASTE!

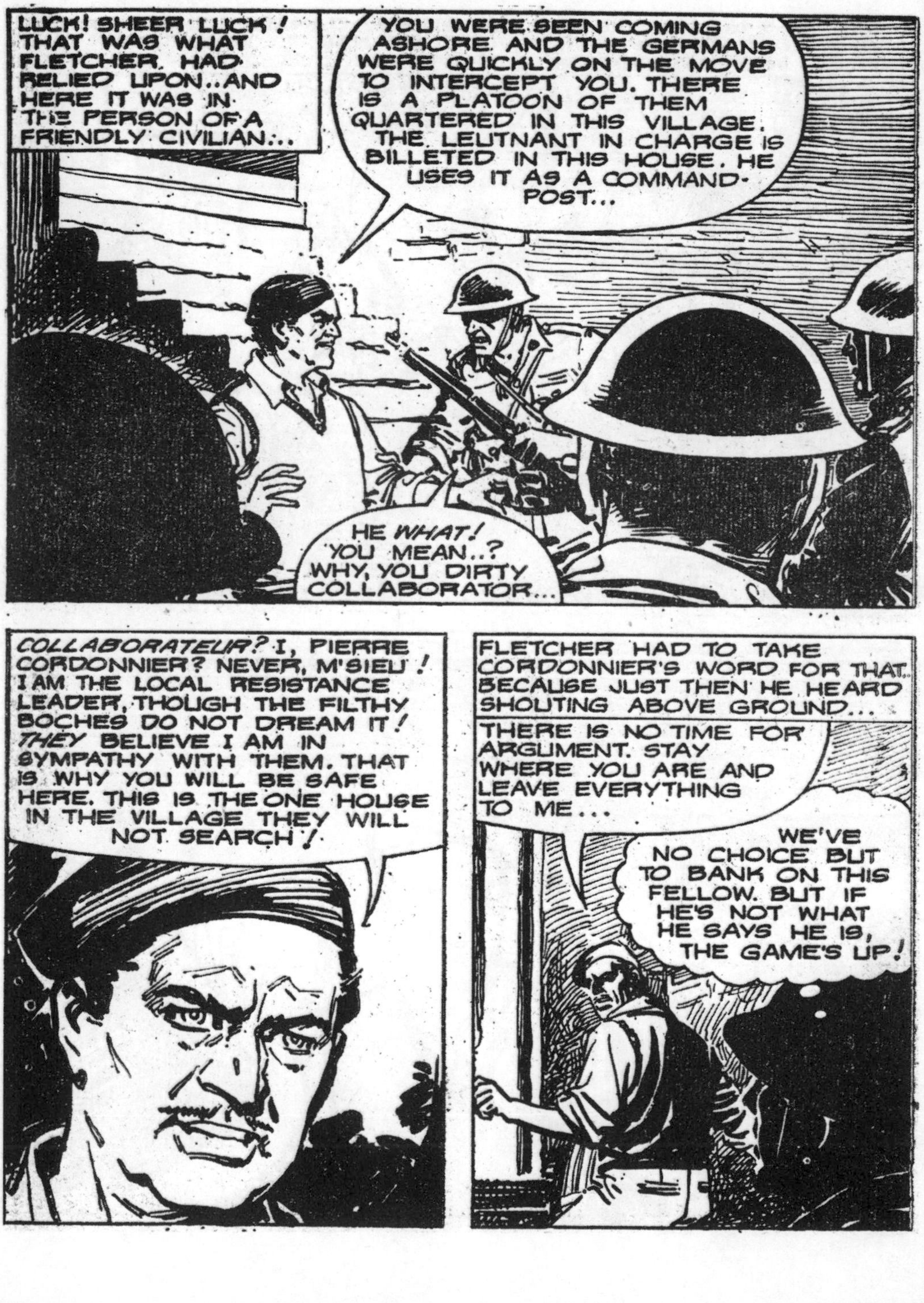
LUCK! SHEER LUCK! THAT WAS WHAT FLETCHER HAD RELIED UPON..AND HERE IT WAS IN THE PERSON OF A FRIENDLY CIVILIAN...
YOU WERE SEEN COMING ASHORE AND THE GERMANS WERE QUICKLY ON THE MOVE TO INTERCEPT YOU. THERE IS A PLATOON OF THEM QUARTERED IN THIS VILLAGE. THE LEUTNANT IN CHARGE IS BILLETED IN THIS HOUSE. HE USES IT AS A COMMAND-POST...
HE *WHAT!* YOU MEAN..? WHY, YOU DIRTY COLLABORATOR...
COLLABORATEUR? I, PIERRE CORDONNIER? NEVER, M'SIEU! I AM THE LOCAL RESISTANCE LEADER, THOUGH THE FILTHY BOCHES DO NOT DREAM IT! *THEY* BELIEVE I AM IN SYMPATHY WITH THEM. THAT IS WHY YOU WILL BE SAFE HERE. THIS IS THE ONE HOUSE IN THE VILLAGE THEY WILL NOT SEARCH!
FLETCHER HAD TO TAKE CORDONNIER'S WORD FOR THAT, BECAUSE JUST THEN HE HEARD SHOUTING ABOVE GROUND...
THERE IS NO TIME FOR ARGUMENT. STAY WHERE YOU ARE AND LEAVE EVERYTHING TO ME...
WE'VE NO CHOICE BUT TO BANK ON THIS FELLOW. BUT IF HE'S NOT WHAT HE SAYS HE IS, THE GAME'S UP!

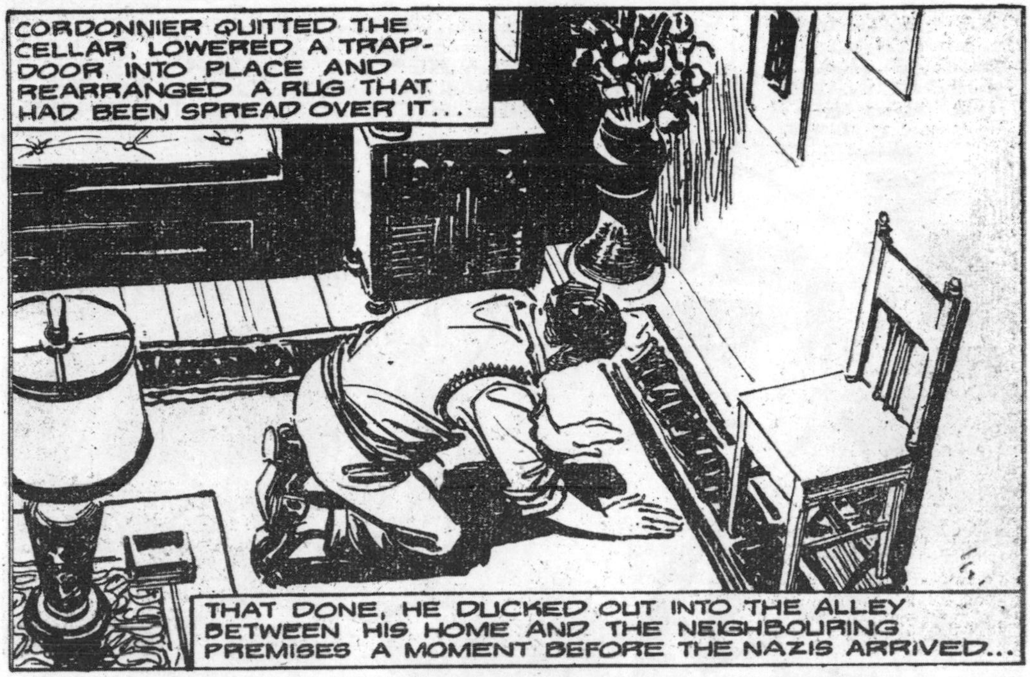
CORDONNIER QUITTED THE CELLAR, LOWERED A TRAP-DOOR INTO PLACE AND REARRANGED A RUG THAT HAD BEEN SPREAD OVER IT...
THAT DONE, HE DUCKED OUT INTO THE ALLEY BETWEEN HIS HOME AND THE NEIGHBOURING PREMISES A MOMENT BEFORE THE NAZIS ARRIVED...

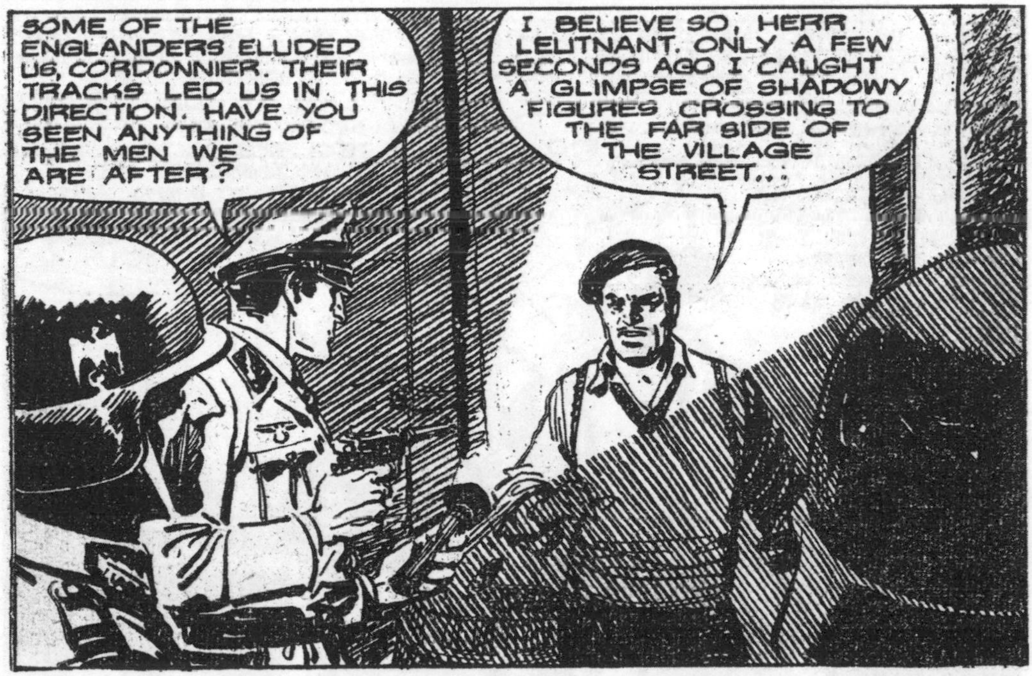
SOME OF THE ENGLANDERS ELUDED US, CORDONNIER. THEIR TRACKS LED US IN THIS DIRECTION. HAVE YOU SEEN ANYTHING OF THE MEN WE ARE AFTER?
I BELIEVE SO, HERR LEUTNANT. ONLY A FEW SECONDS AGO I CAUGHT A GLIMPSE OF SHADOWY FIGURES CROSSING TO THE FAR SIDE OF THE VILLAGE STREET...

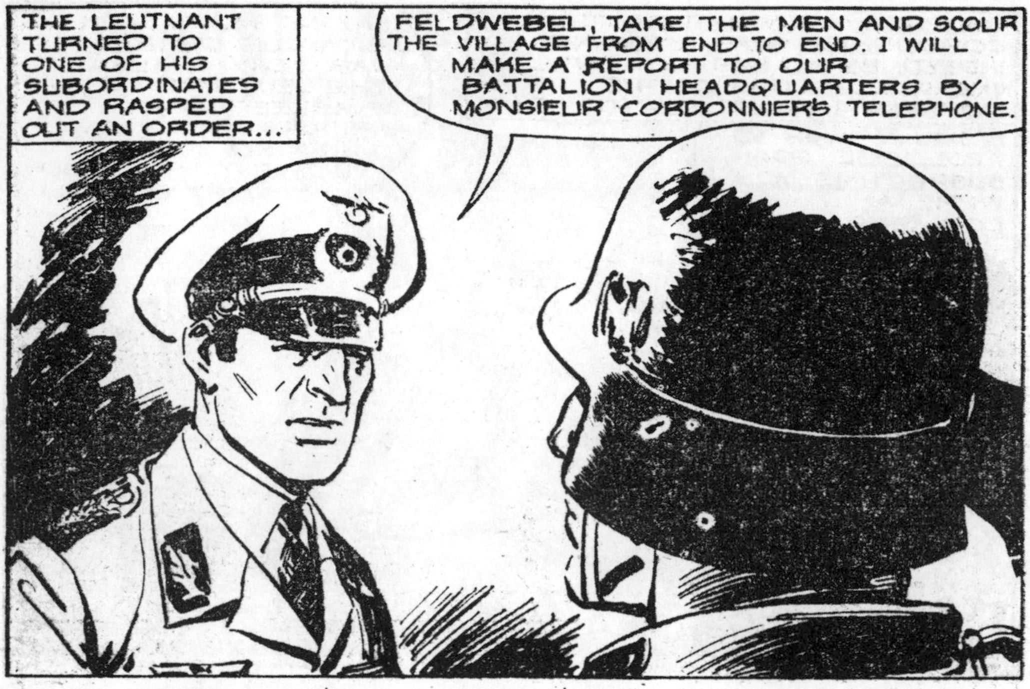
THE LEUTNANT TURNED TO ONE OF HIS SUBORDINATES AND RASPED OUT AN ORDER...
FELDWEBEL, TAKE THE MEN AND SCOUR THE VILLAGE FROM END TO END. I WILL MAKE A REPORT TO OUR BATTALION HEADQUARTERS BY MONSIEUR CORDONNIER'S TELEPHONE.

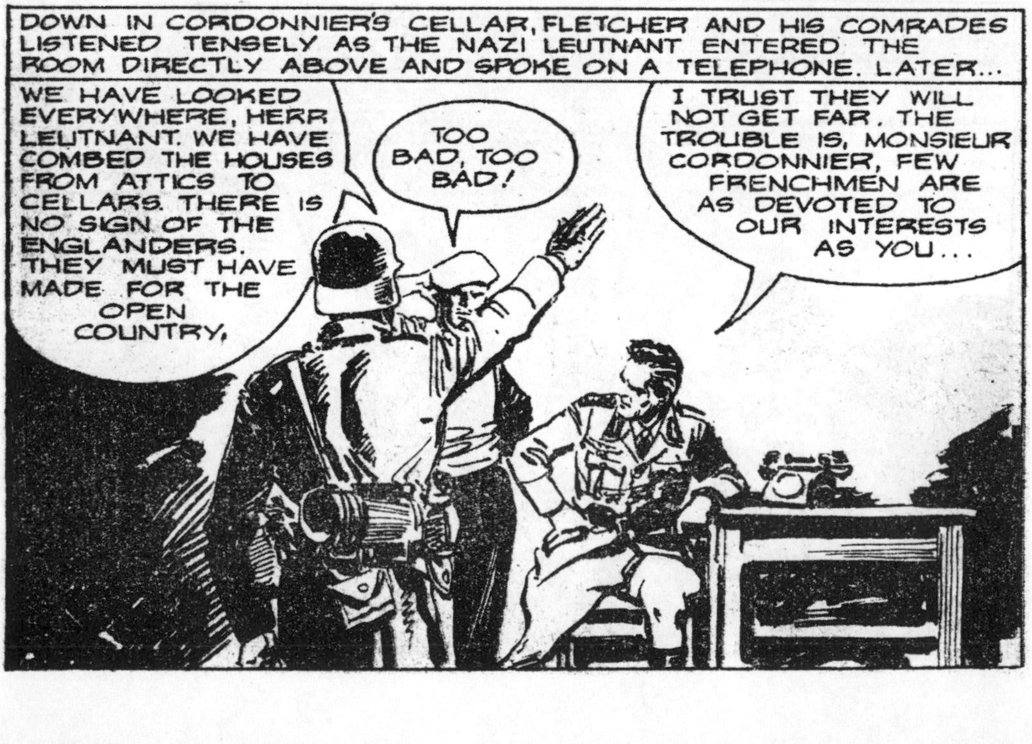
DOWN IN CORDONNIER'S CELLAR, FLETCHER AND HIS COMRADES LISTENED TENSELY AS THE NAZI LEUTNANT ENTERED THE ROOM DIRECTLY ABOVE AND SPOKE ON A TELEPHONE. LATER...
WE HAVE LOOKED EVERYWHERE, HERR LEUTNANT. WE HAVE COMBED THE HOUSES FROM ATTICS TO CELLARS. THERE IS NO SIGN OF THE ENGLANDERS. THEY MUST HAVE MADE FOR THE OPEN COUNTRY.
TOO BAD, TOO BAD!
I TRUST THEY WILL NOT GET FAR. THE TROUBLE IS, MONSIEUR CORDONNIER, FEW FRENCHMEN ARE AS DEVOTED TO OUR INTERESTS AS YOU...

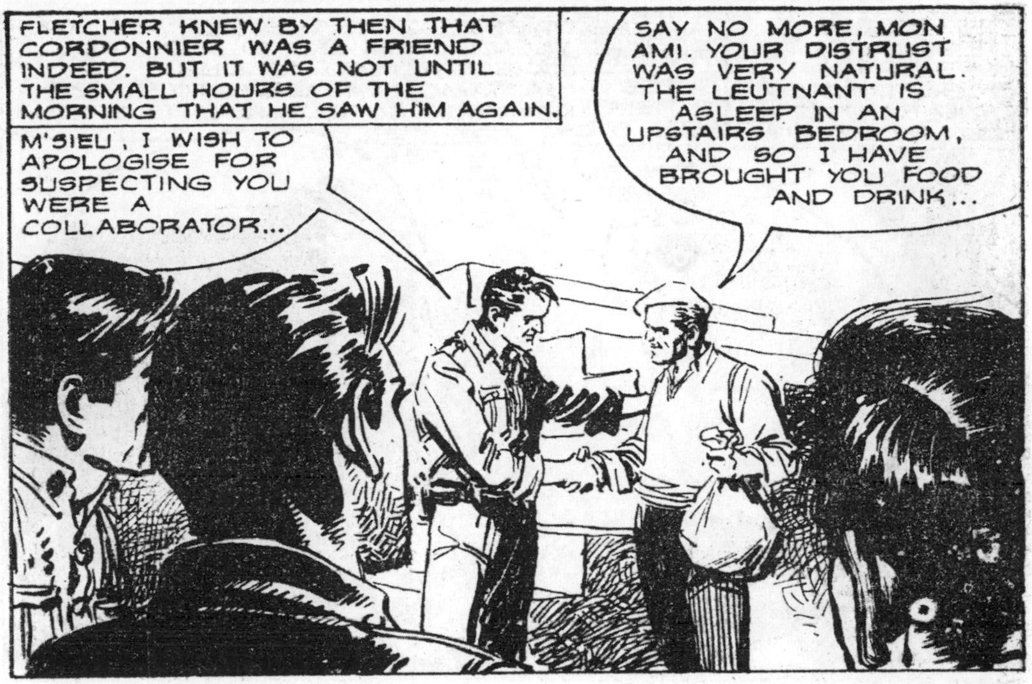
FLETCHER KNEW BY THEN THAT CORDONNIER WAS A FRIEND INDEED. BUT IT WAS NOT UNTIL THE SMALL HOURS OF THE MORNING THAT HE SAW HIM AGAIN.
M'SIEU, I WISH TO APOLOGISE FOR SUSPECTING YOU WERE A COLLABORATOR...
SAY NO MORE, MON AMI. YOUR DISTRUST WAS VERY NATURAL. THE LEUTNANT IS ASLEEP IN AN UPSTAIRS BEDROOM, AND SO I HAVE BROUGHT YOU FOOD AND DRINK...

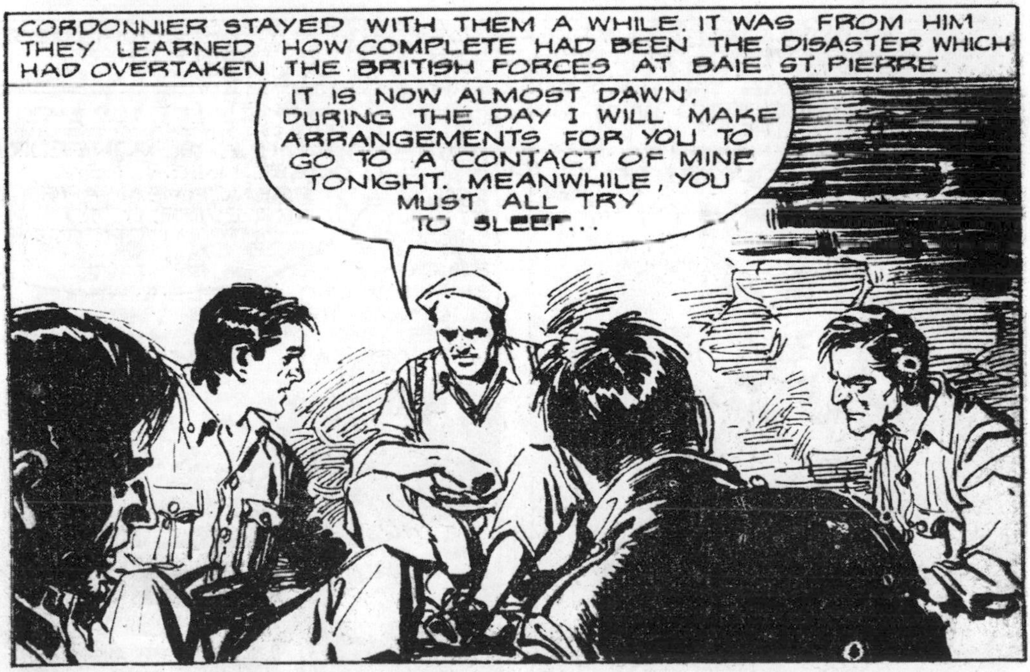
CORDONNIER STAYED WITH THEM A WHILE. IT WAS FROM HIM THEY LEARNED HOW COMPLETE HAD BEEN THE DISASTER WHICH HAD OVERTAKEN THE BRITISH FORCES AT BAIE ST. PIERRE.
IT IS NOW ALMOST DAWN. DURING THE DAY I WILL MAKE ARRANGEMENTS FOR YOU TO GO TO A CONTACT OF MINE TONIGHT. MEANWHILE, YOU MUST ALL TRY TO SLEEP...

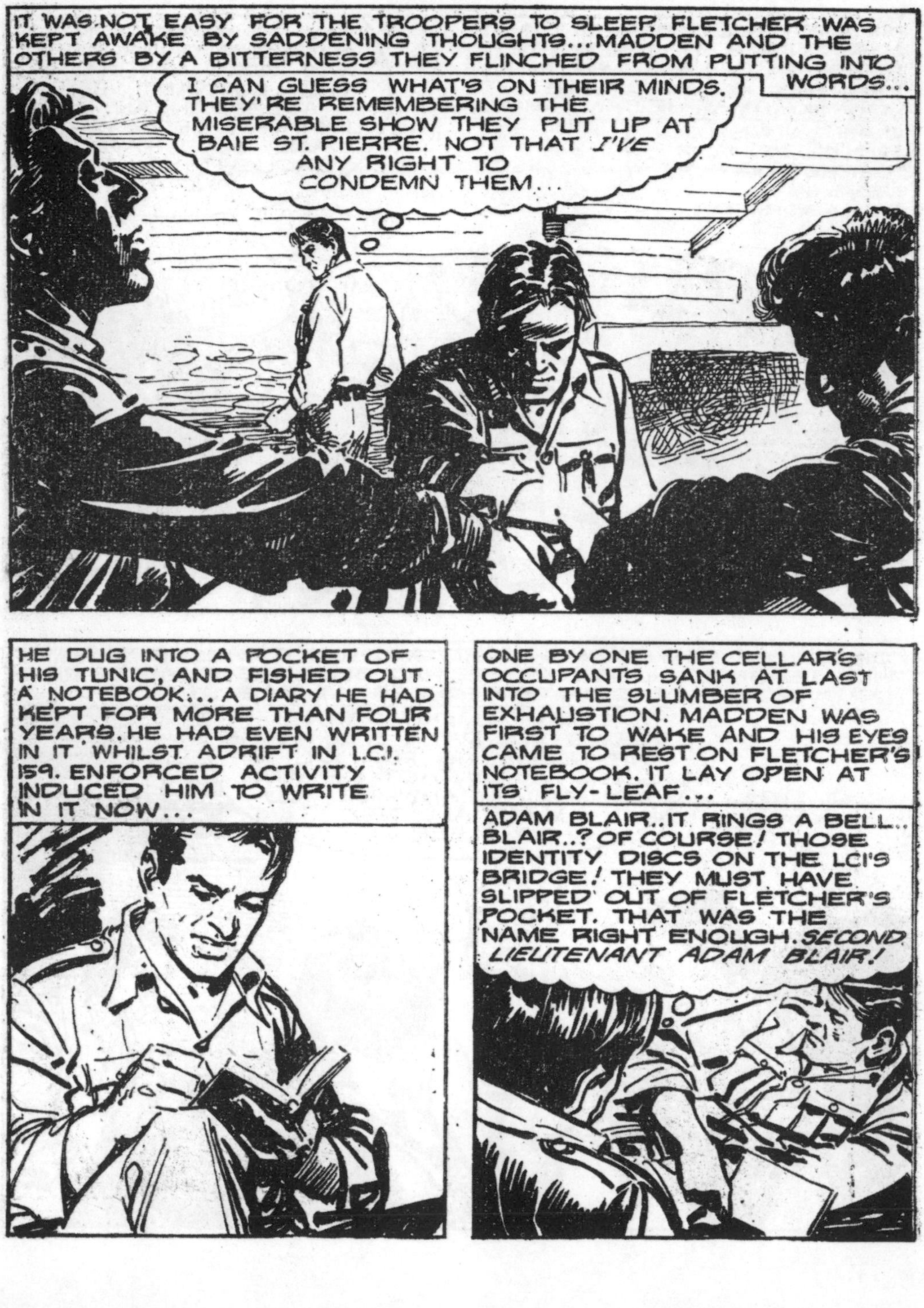
IT WAS NOT EASY FOR THE TROOPERS TO SLEEP. FLETCHER WAS KEPT AWAKE BY SADDENING THOUGHTS... MADDEN AND THE OTHERS BY A BITTERNESS THEY FLINCHED FROM PUTTING INTO WORDS...
I CAN GUESS WHAT'S ON THEIR MINDS. THEY'RE REMEMBERING THE MISERABLE SHOW THEY PUT UP AT BAIE ST. PIERRE. NOT THAT I'VE ANY RIGHT TO CONDEMN THEM...
HE DUG INTO A POCKET OF HIS TUNIC, AND FISHED OUT A NOTEBOOK... A DIARY HE HAD KEPT FOR MORE THAN FOUR YEARS. HE HAD EVEN WRITTEN IN IT WHILST ADRIFT IN L.C.I. 159. ENFORCED ACTIVITY INDUCED HIM TO WRITE IN IT NOW...
ONE BY ONE THE CELLAR'S OCCUPANTS SANK AT LAST INTO THE SLUMBER OF EXHAUSTION. MADDEN WAS FIRST TO WAKE AND HIS EYES CAME TO REST ON FLETCHER'S NOTEBOOK. IT LAY OPEN AT ITS FLY-LEAF...
ADAM BLAIR.. IT RINGS A BELL... BLAIR..? OF COURSE! THOSE IDENTITY DISCS ON THE LCI'S BRIDGE! THEY MUST HAVE SLIPPED OUT OF FLETCHER'S POCKET. THAT WAS THE NAME RIGHT ENOUGH. SECOND LIEUTENANT ADAM BLAIR!

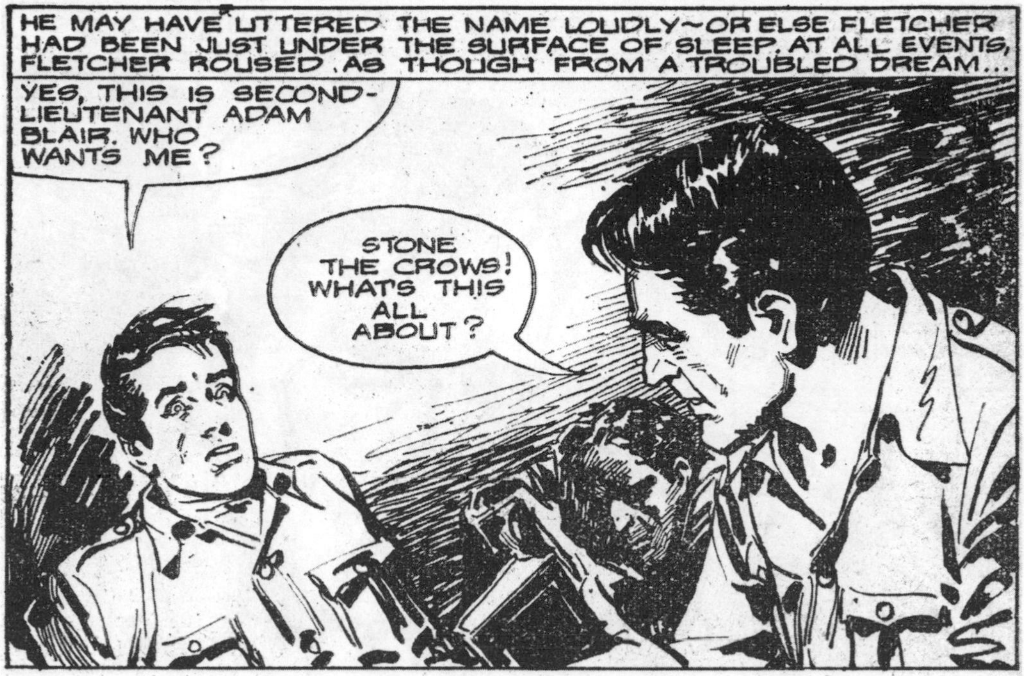
HE MAY HAVE UTTERED THE NAME LOUDLY~OR ELSE FLETCHER HAD BEEN JUST UNDER THE SURFACE OF SLEEP. AT ALL EVENTS, FLETCHER ROUSED AS THOUGH FROM A TROUBLED DREAM...
YES, THIS IS SECOND-LIEUTENANT ADAM BLAIR. WHO WANTS ME?
STONE THE CROWS! WHAT'S THIS ALL ABOUT?

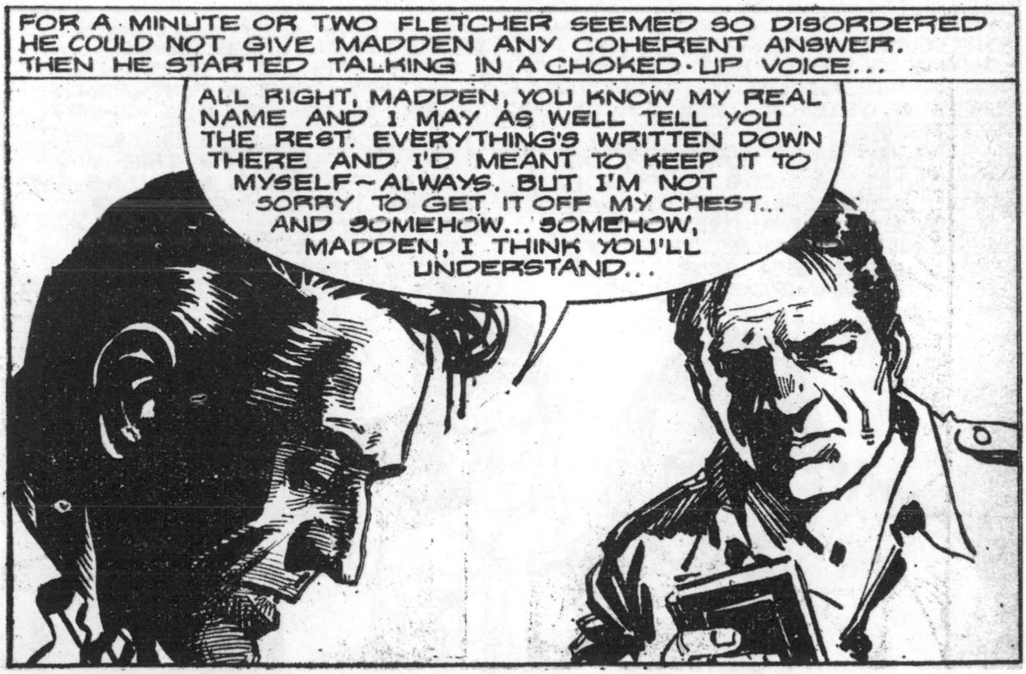
FOR A MINUTE OR TWO FLETCHER SEEMED SO DISORDERED HE COULD NOT GIVE MADDEN ANY COHERENT ANSWER. THEN HE STARTED TALKING IN A CHOKED-UP VOICE...
ALL RIGHT, MADDEN, YOU KNOW MY REAL NAME AND I MAY AS WELL TELL YOU THE REST. EVERYTHING'S WRITTEN DOWN THERE AND I'D MEANT TO KEEP IT TO MYSELF~ALWAYS. BUT I'M NOT SORRY TO GET IT OFF MY CHEST... AND SOMEHOW... SOMEHOW, MADDEN, I THINK YOU'LL UNDERSTAND...

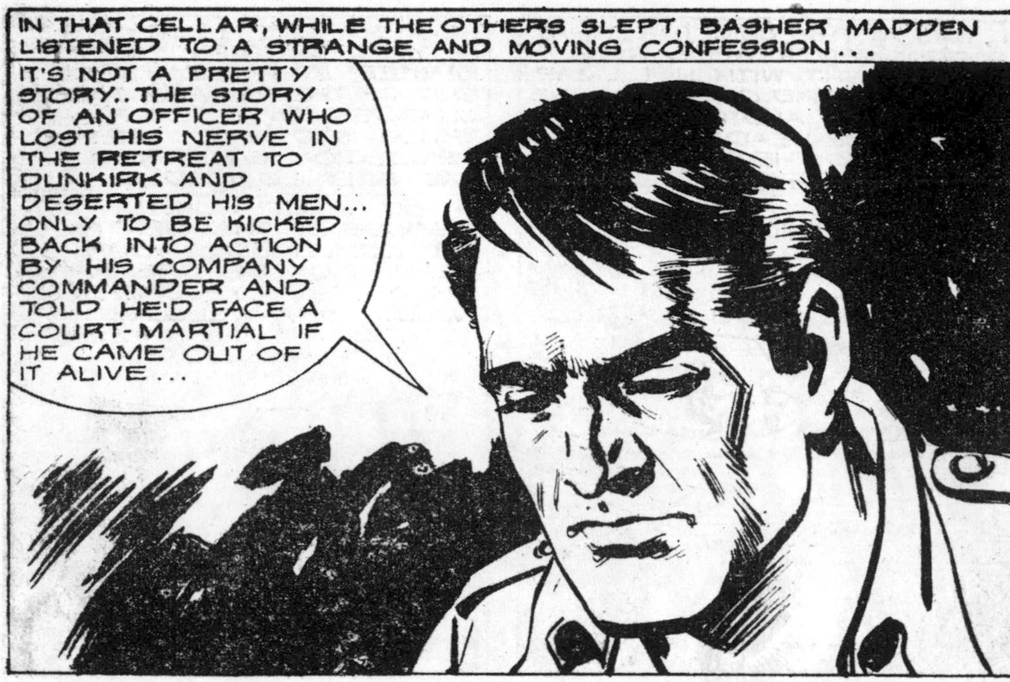
IN THAT CELLAR, WHILE THE OTHERS SLEPT, BASHER MADDEN LISTENED TO A STRANGE AND MOVING CONFESSION...
IT'S NOT A PRETTY STORY.. THE STORY OF AN OFFICER WHO LOST HIS NERVE IN THE RETREAT TO DUNKIRK AND DESERTED HIS MEN... ONLY TO BE KICKED BACK INTO ACTION BY HIS COMPANY COMMANDER AND TOLD HE'D FACE A COURT-MARTIAL IF HE CAME OUT OF IT ALIVE...

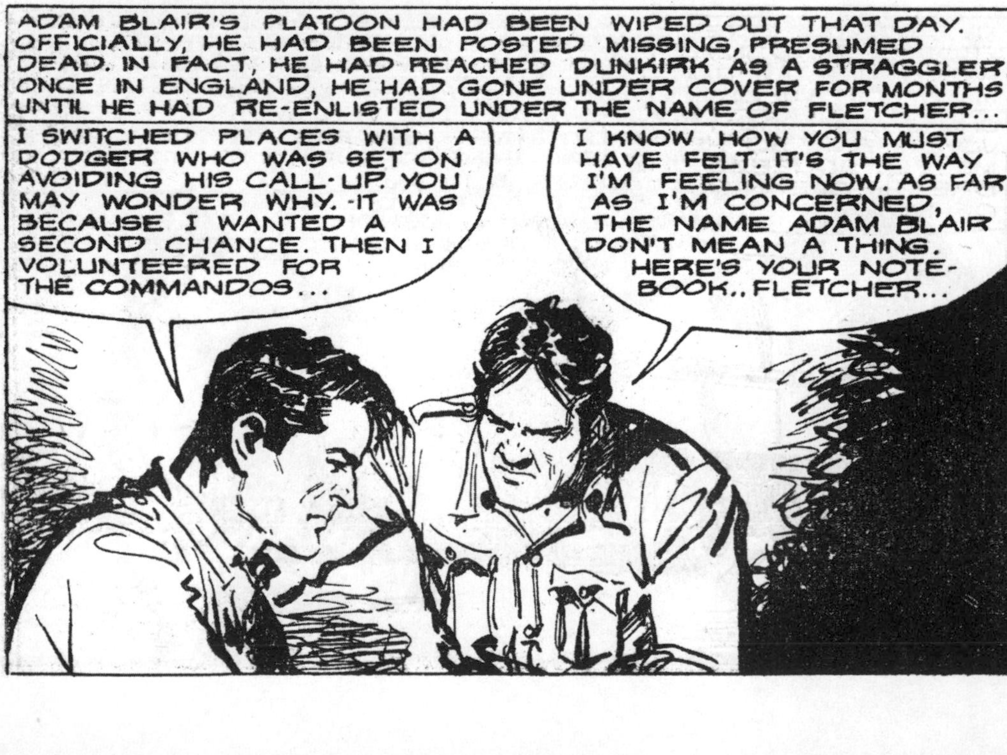
ADAM BLAIR'S PLATOON HAD BEEN WIPED OUT THAT DAY. OFFICIALLY, HE HAD BEEN POSTED MISSING, PRESUMED DEAD. IN FACT, HE HAD REACHED DUNKIRK AS A STRAGGLER. ONCE IN ENGLAND, HE HAD GONE UNDER COVER FOR MONTHS UNTIL HE HAD RE-ENLISTED UNDER THE NAME OF FLETCHER...
I SWITCHED PLACES WITH A DODGER WHO WAS SET ON AVOIDING HIS CALL-UP. YOU MAY WONDER WHY. IT WAS BECAUSE I WANTED A SECOND CHANCE. THEN I VOLUNTEERED FOR THE COMMANDOS...
I KNOW HOW YOU MUST HAVE FELT. IT'S THE WAY I'M FEELING NOW. AS FAR AS I'M CONCERNED, THE NAME ADAM BLAIR DON'T MEAN A THING. HERE'S YOUR NOTE-BOOK.. FLETCHER...

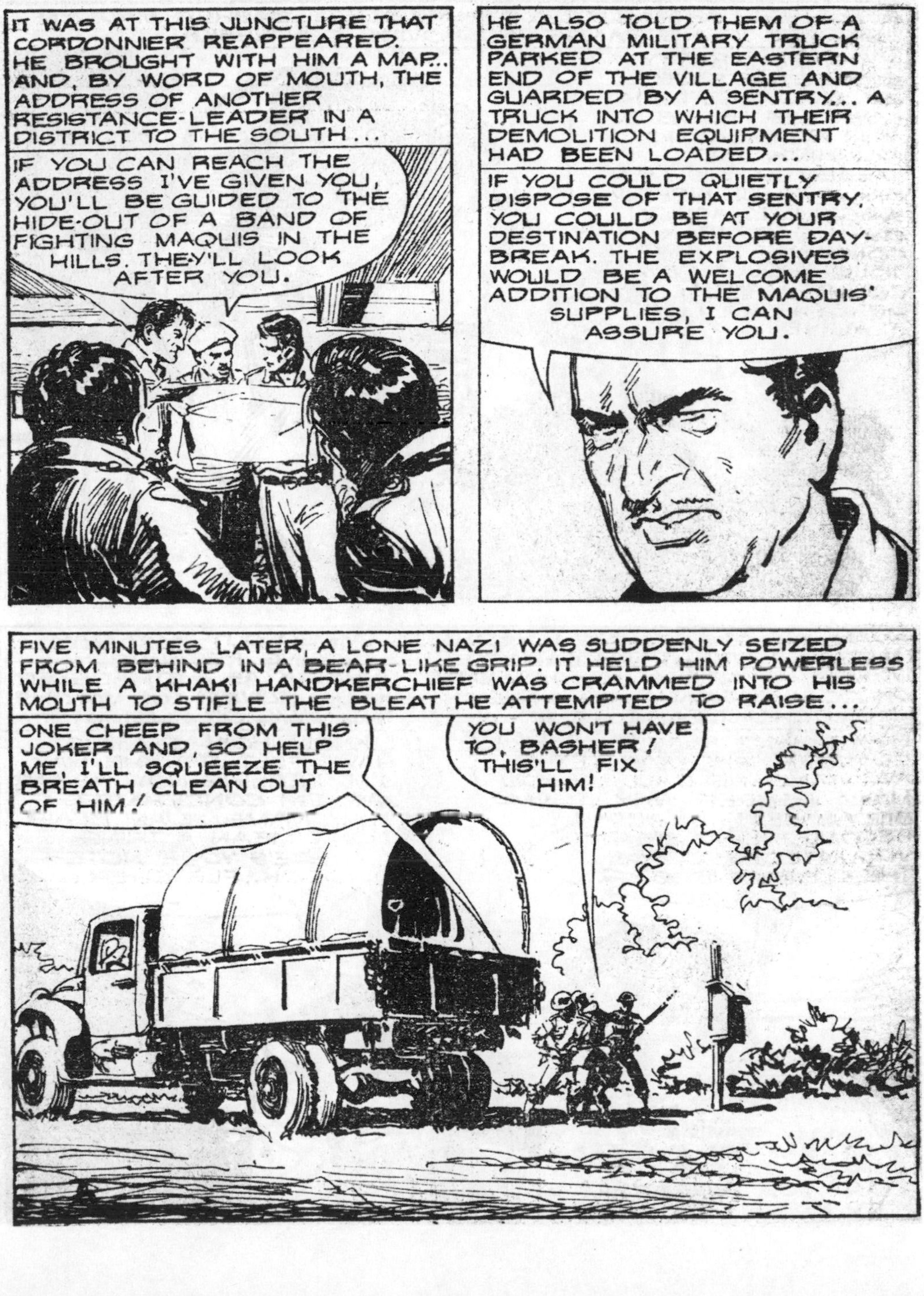
IT WAS AT THIS JUNCTURE THAT CORDONNIER REAPPEARED. HE BROUGHT WITH HIM A MAP... AND, BY WORD OF MOUTH, THE ADDRESS OF ANOTHER RESISTANCE-LEADER IN A DISTRICT TO THE SOUTH...
IF YOU CAN REACH THE ADDRESS I'VE GIVEN YOU, YOU'LL BE GUIDED TO THE HIDE-OUT OF A BAND OF FIGHTING MAQUIS IN THE HILLS. THEY'LL LOOK AFTER YOU.
HE ALSO TOLD THEM OF A GERMAN MILITARY TRUCK PARKED AT THE EASTERN END OF THE VILLAGE AND GUARDED BY A SENTRY... A TRUCK INTO WHICH THEIR DEMOLITION EQUIPMENT HAD BEEN LOADED...
IF YOU COULD QUIETLY DISPOSE OF THAT SENTRY, YOU COULD BE AT YOUR DESTINATION BEFORE DAY-BREAK. THE EXPLOSIVES WOULD BE A WELCOME ADDITION TO THE MAQUIS' SUPPLIES, I CAN ASSURE YOU.
FIVE MINUTES LATER, A LONE NAZI WAS SUDDENLY SEIZED FROM BEHIND IN A BEAR-LIKE GRIP. IT HELD HIM POWERLESS WHILE A KHAKI HANDKERCHIEF WAS CRAMMED INTO HIS MOUTH TO STIFLE THE BLEAT HE ATTEMPTED TO RAISE...
ONE CHEEP FROM THIS JOKER AND, SO HELP ME, I'LL SQUEEZE THE BREATH CLEAN OUT OF HIM!
YOU WON'T HAVE TO, BASHER! THIS'LL FIX HIM!

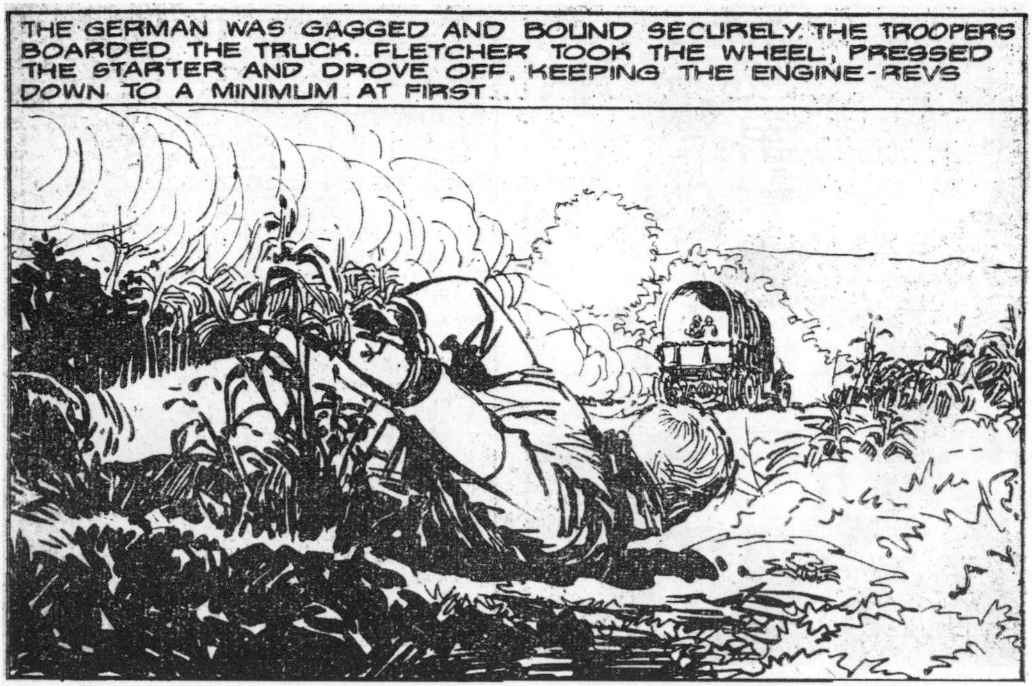
THE GERMAN WAS GAGGED AND BOUND SECURELY. THE TROOPERS BOARDED THE TRUCK. FLETCHER TOOK THE WHEEL, PRESSED THE STARTER AND DROVE OFF, KEEPING THE ENGINE-REVS DOWN TO A MINIMUM AT FIRST...

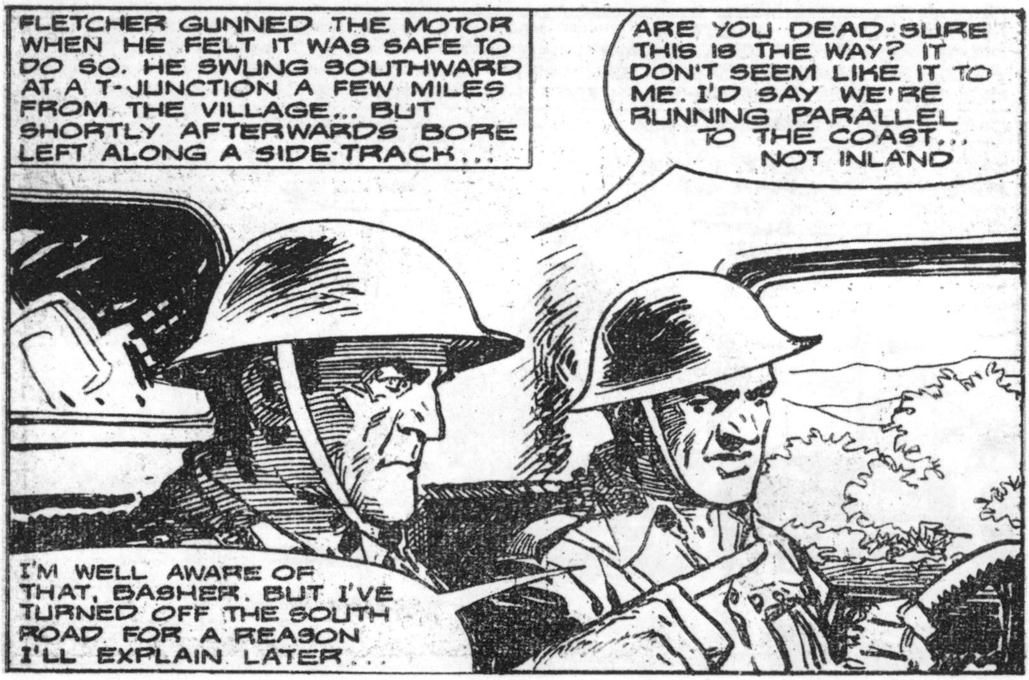
FLETCHER GUNNED THE MOTOR WHEN HE FELT IT WAS SAFE TO DO SO. HE SWUNG SOUTHWARD AT A T-JUNCTION A FEW MILES FROM THE VILLAGE... BUT SHORTLY AFTERWARDS BORE LEFT ALONG A SIDE-TRACK...
ARE YOU DEAD-SURE THIS IS THE WAY? IT DON'T SEEM LIKE IT TO ME. I'D SAY WE'RE RUNNING PARALLEL TO THE COAST... NOT INLAND
I'M WELL AWARE OF THAT, BASHER. BUT I'VE TURNED OFF THE SOUTH ROAD FOR A REASON I'LL EXPLAIN LATER...

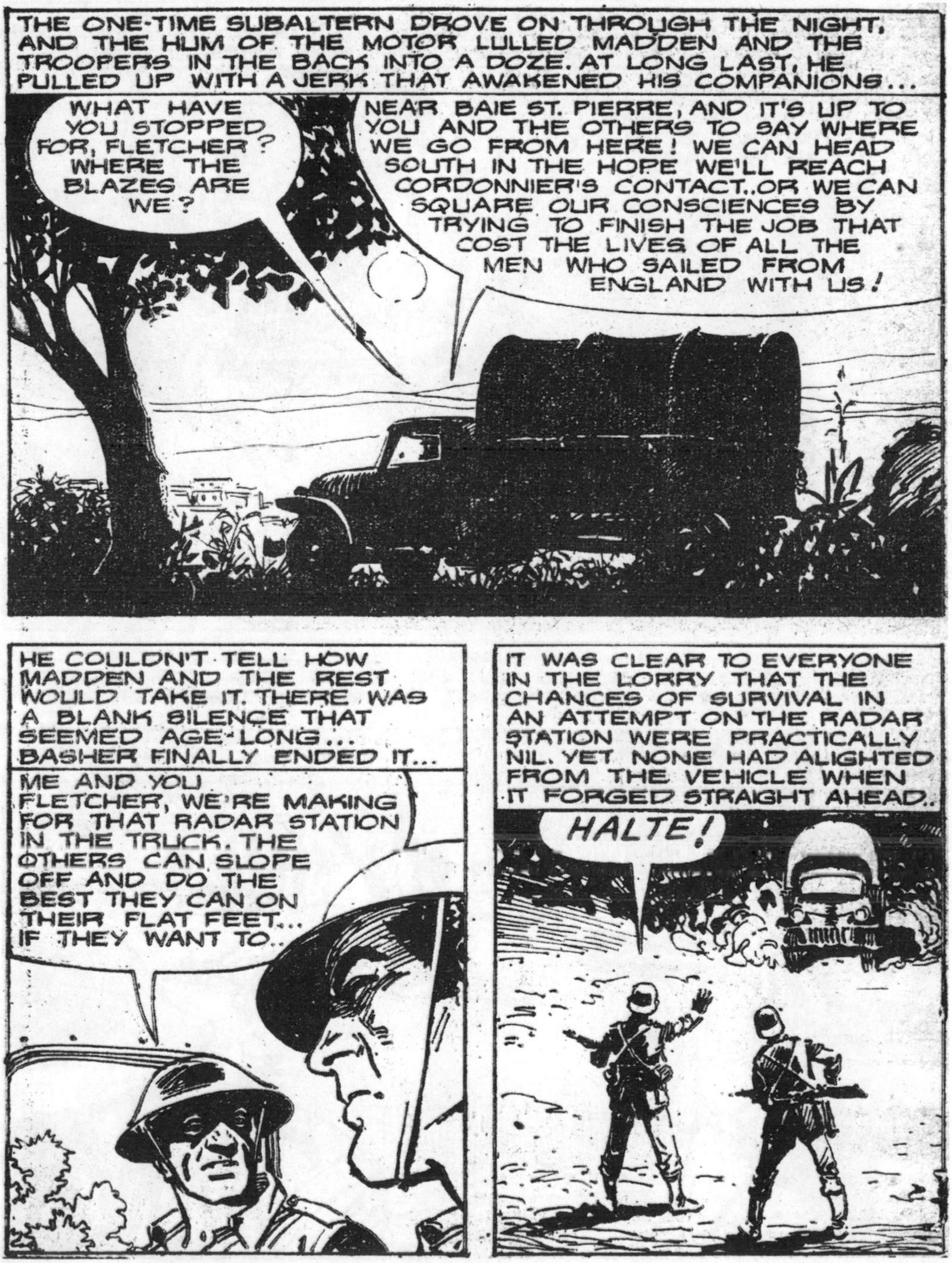
THE ONE-TIME SUBALTERN DROVE ON THROUGH THE NIGHT, AND THE HUM OF THE MOTOR LULLED MADDEN AND THE TROOPERS IN THE BACK INTO A DOZE. AT LONG LAST, HE PULLED UP WITH A JERK THAT AWAKENED HIS COMPANIONS...
WHAT HAVE YOU STOPPED FOR, FLETCHER? WHERE THE BLAZES ARE WE?
NEAR BAIE ST. PIERRE, AND IT'S UP TO YOU AND THE OTHERS TO SAY WHERE WE GO FROM HERE! WE CAN HEAD SOUTH IN THE HOPE WE'LL REACH CORDONNIER'S CONTACT..OR WE CAN SQUARE OUR CONSCIENCES BY TRYING TO FINISH THE JOB THAT COST THE LIVES OF ALL THE MEN WHO SAILED FROM ENGLAND WITH US!
HE COULDN'T TELL HOW MADDEN AND THE REST WOULD TAKE IT. THERE WAS A BLANK SILENCE THAT SEEMED AGE-LONG... BASHER FINALLY ENDED IT...
ME AND YOU FLETCHER, WE'RE MAKING FOR THAT RADAR STATION IN THE TRUCK. THE OTHERS CAN SLOPE OFF AND DO THE BEST THEY CAN ON THEIR FLAT FEET... IF THEY WANT TO..
IT WAS CLEAR TO EVERYONE IN THE LORRY THAT THE CHANCES OF SURVIVAL IN AN ATTEMPT ON THE RADAR STATION WERE PRACTICALLY NIL. YET NONE HAD ALIGHTED FROM THE VEHICLE WHEN IT FORGED STRAIGHT AHEAD..
HALTE!

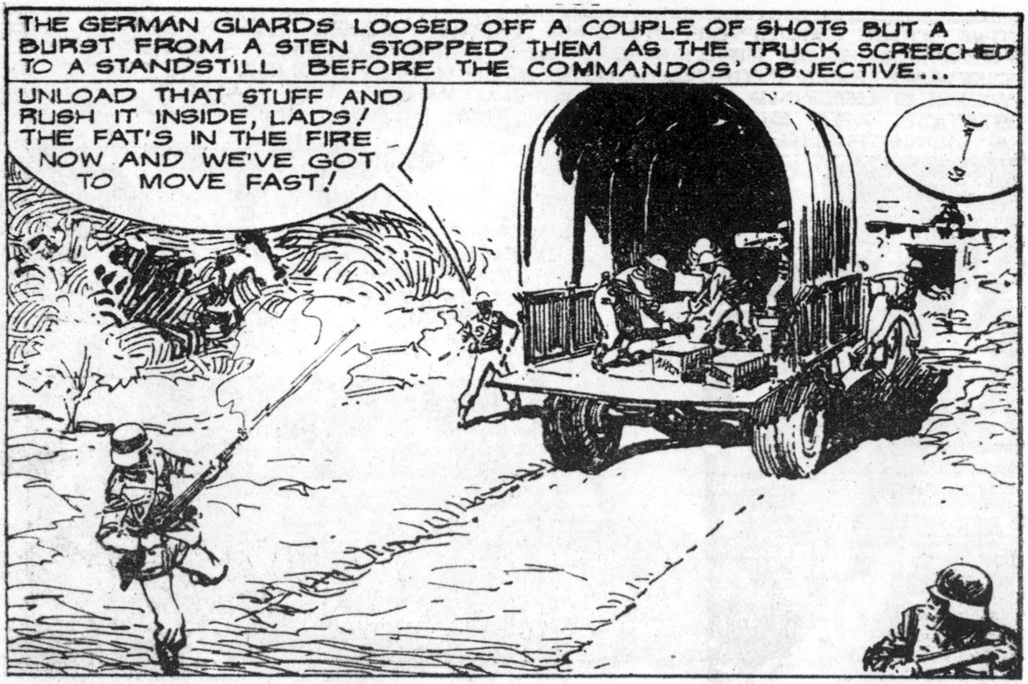
THE GERMAN GUARDS LOOSED OFF A COUPLE OF SHOTS BUT A BURST FROM A STEN STOPPED THEM AS THE TRUCK SCREECHED TO A STANDSTILL BEFORE THE COMMANDOS' OBJECTIVE...
UNLOAD THAT STUFF AND RUSH IT INSIDE, LADS! THE FAT'S IN THE FIRE NOW AND WE'VE GOT TO MOVE FAST!

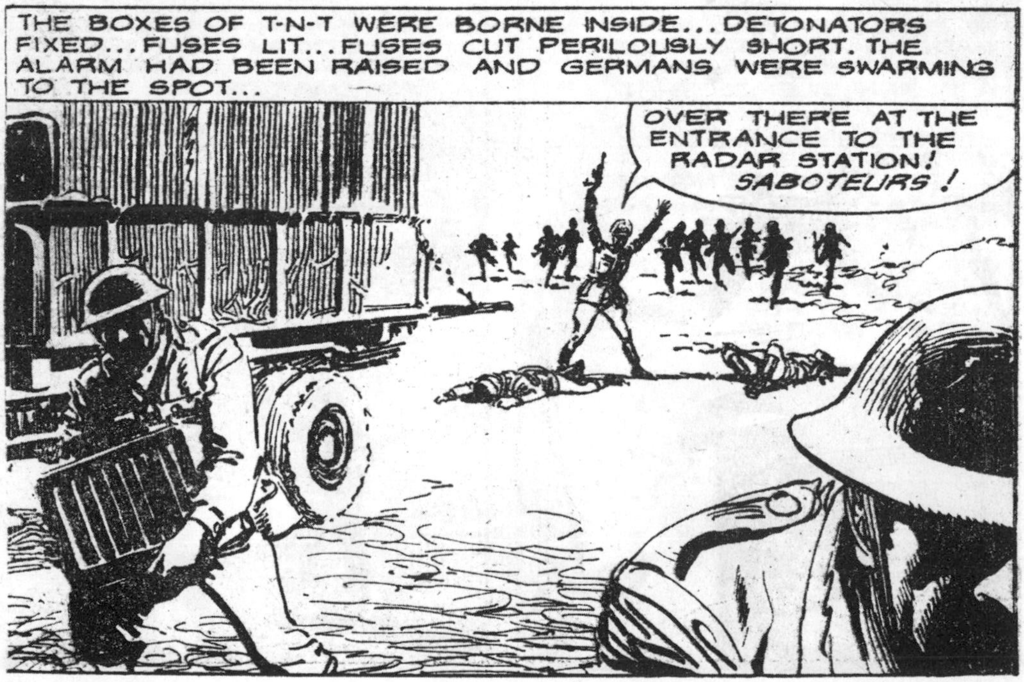
THE BOXES OF T-N-T WERE BORNE INSIDE... DETONATORS FIXED... FUSES LIT... FUSES CUT PERILOUSLY SHORT. THE ALARM HAD BEEN RAISED AND GERMANS WERE SWARMING TO THE SPOT...
OVER THERE AT THE ENTRANCE TO THE RADAR STATION! *SABOTEURS!*

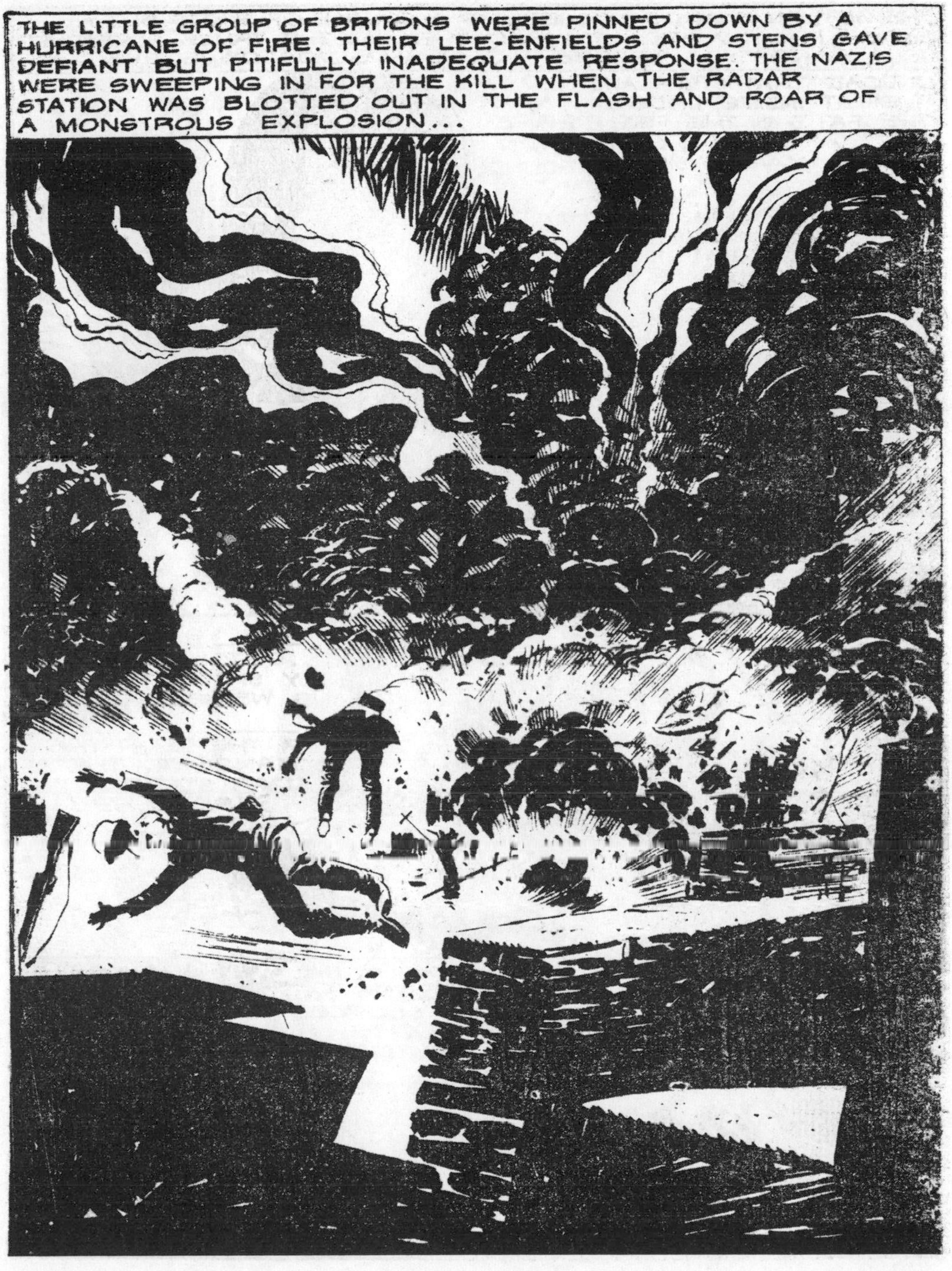
THE LITTLE GROUP OF BRITONS WERE PINNED DOWN BY A HURRICANE OF FIRE. THEIR LEE-ENFIELDS AND STENS GAVE DEFIANT BUT PITIFULLY INADEQUATE RESPONSE. THE NAZIS WERE SWEEPING IN FOR THE KILL WHEN THE RADAR STATION WAS BLOTTED OUT IN THE FLASH AND ROAR OF A MONSTROUS EXPLOSION...

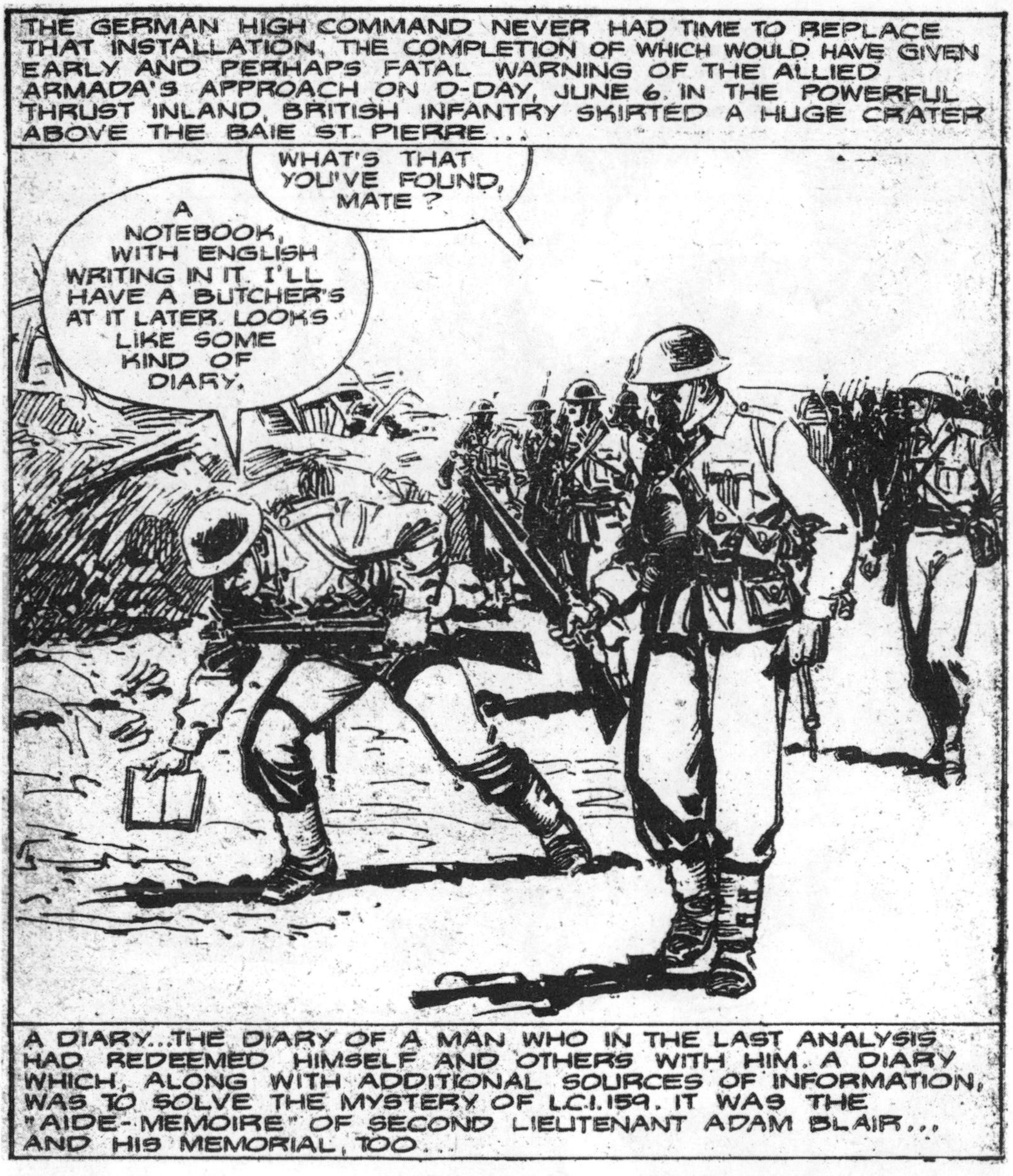
THE GERMAN HIGH COMMAND NEVER HAD TIME TO REPLACE THAT INSTALLATION, THE COMPLETION OF WHICH WOULD HAVE GIVEN EARLY AND PERHAPS FATAL WARNING OF THE ALLIED ARMADA'S APPROACH ON D-DAY, JUNE 6. IN THE POWERFUL THRUST INLAND, BRITISH INFANTRY SKIRTED A HUGE CRATER ABOVE THE BAIE ST. PIERRE...
WHAT'S THAT YOU'VE FOUND, MATE?
A NOTEBOOK, WITH ENGLISH WRITING IN IT. I'LL HAVE A BUTCHER'S AT IT LATER. LOOKS LIKE SOME KIND OF DIARY.
A DIARY...THE DIARY OF A MAN WHO IN THE LAST ANALYSIS HAD REDEEMED HIMSELF AND OTHERS WITH HIM. A DIARY WHICH, ALONG WITH ADDITIONAL SOURCES OF INFORMATION, WAS TO SOLVE THE MYSTERY OF L.C.I.159. IT WAS THE "AIDE-MEMOIRE" OF SECOND LIEUTENANT ADAM BLAIR... AND HIS MEMORIAL, TOO...

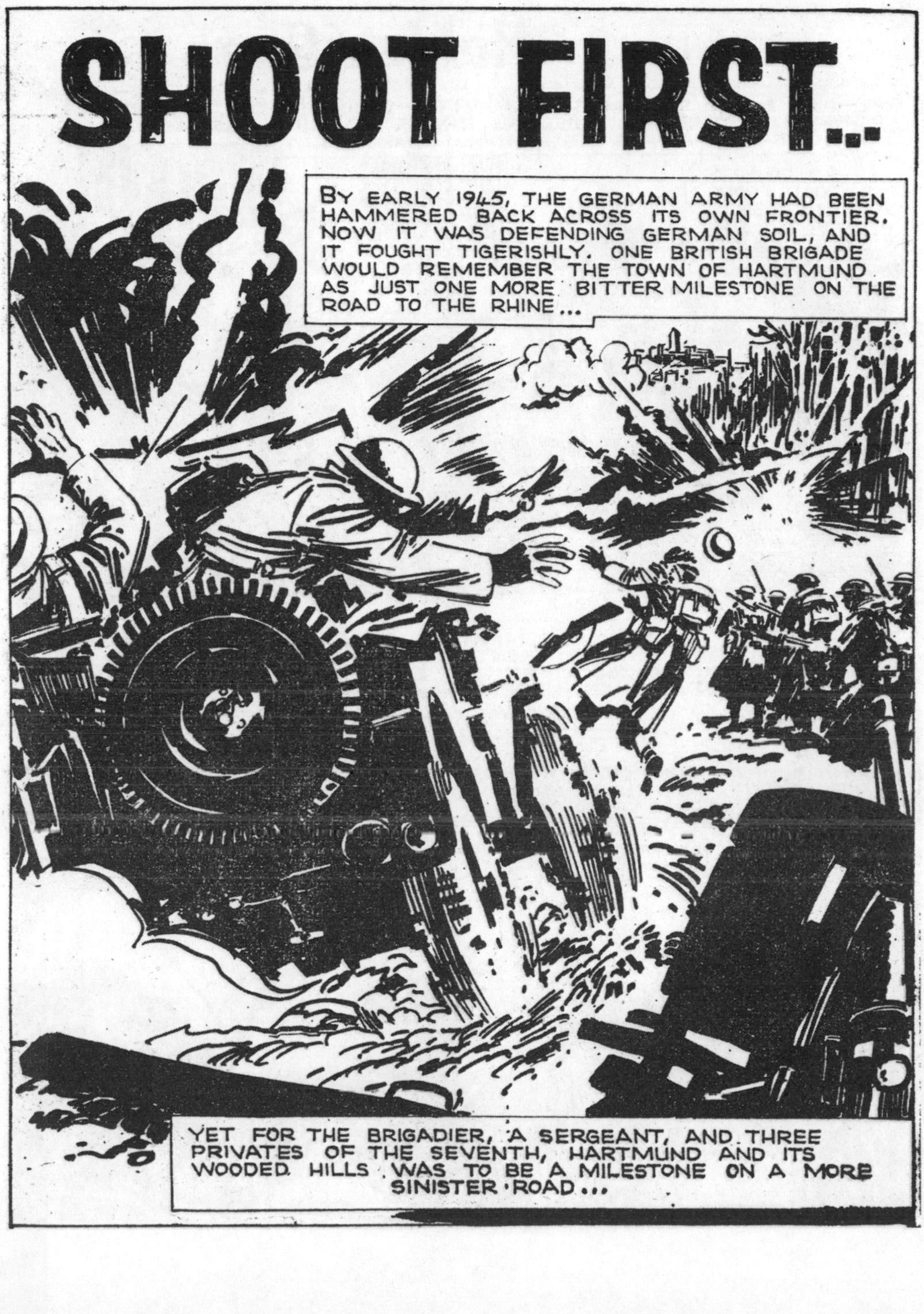
SHOOT FIRST...
BY EARLY 1945, THE GERMAN ARMY HAD BEEN HAMMERED BACK ACROSS ITS OWN FRONTIER. NOW IT WAS DEFENDING GERMAN SOIL, AND IT FOUGHT TIGERISHLY. ONE BRITISH BRIGADE WOULD REMEMBER THE TOWN OF HARTMUND AS JUST ONE MORE BITTER MILESTONE ON THE ROAD TO THE RHINE...
YET FOR THE BRIGADIER, A SERGEANT, AND THREE PRIVATES OF THE SEVENTH, HARTMUND AND ITS WOODED HILLS WAS TO BE A MILESTONE ON A MORE SINISTER ROAD...

Chapter 1. Hidden Guns

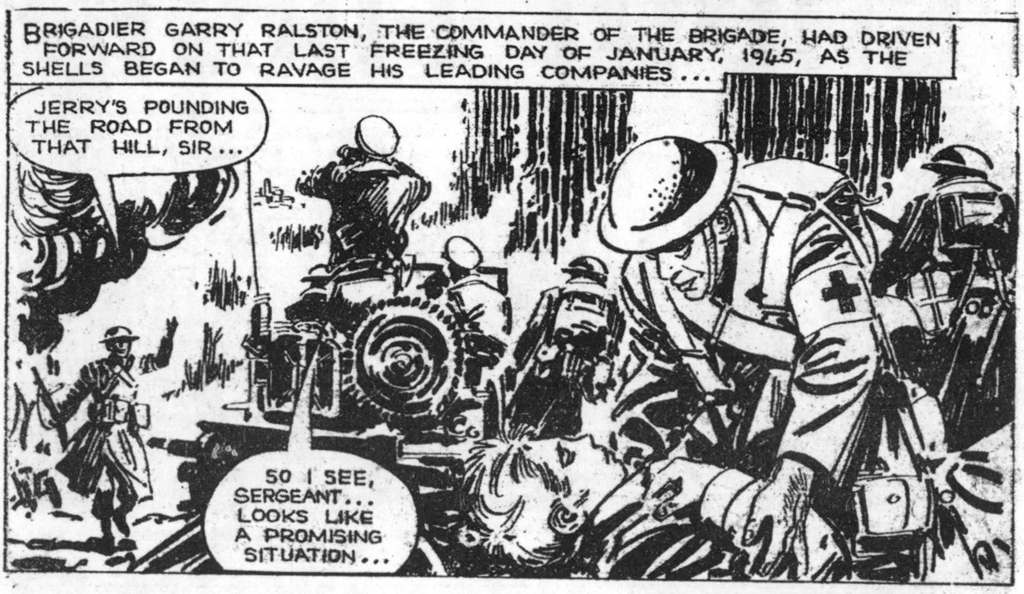
BRIGADIER GARRY RALSTON, THE COMMANDER OF THE BRIGADE, HAD DRIVEN FORWARD ON THAT LAST FREEZING DAY OF JANUARY, 1945, AS THE SHELLS BEGAN TO RAVAGE HIS LEADING COMPANIES...
JERRY'S POUNDING THE ROAD FROM THAT HILL, SIR...
SO I SEE, SERGEANT... LOOKS LIKE A PROMISING SITUATION...

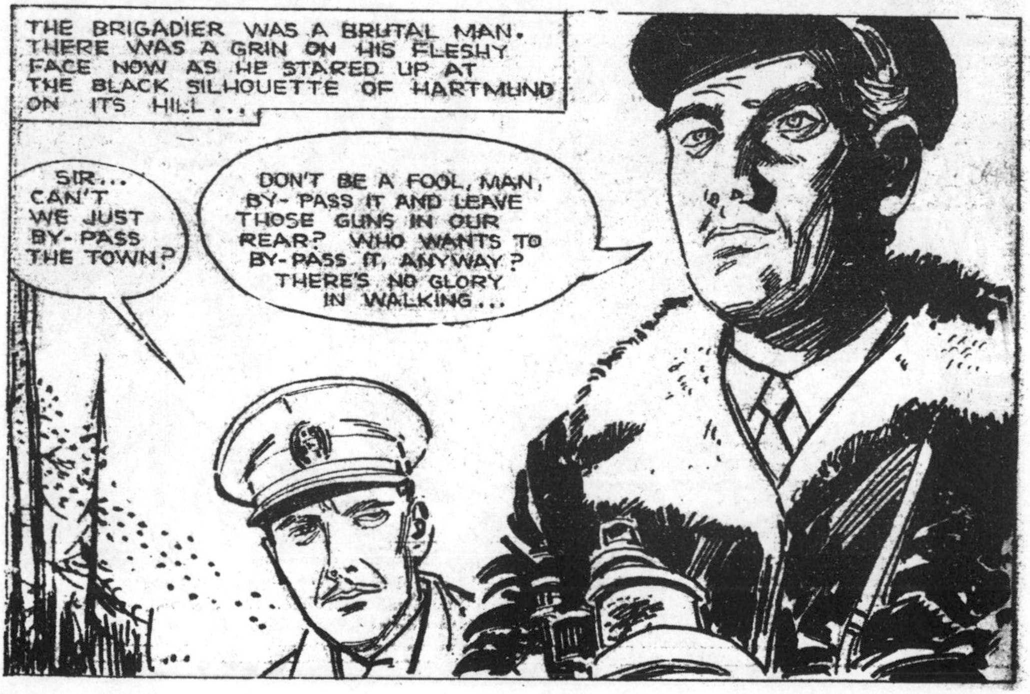
THE BRIGADIER WAS A BRUTAL MAN. THERE WAS A GRIN ON HIS FLESHY FACE NOW AS HE STARED UP AT THE BLACK SILHOUETTE OF HARTMUND ON ITS HILL...
SIR... CAN'T WE JUST BY-PASS THE TOWN?
DON'T BE A FOOL, MAN, BY-PASS IT AND LEAVE THOSE GUNS IN OUR REAR? WHO WANTS TO BY-PASS IT, ANYWAY? THERE'S NO GLORY IN WALKING...

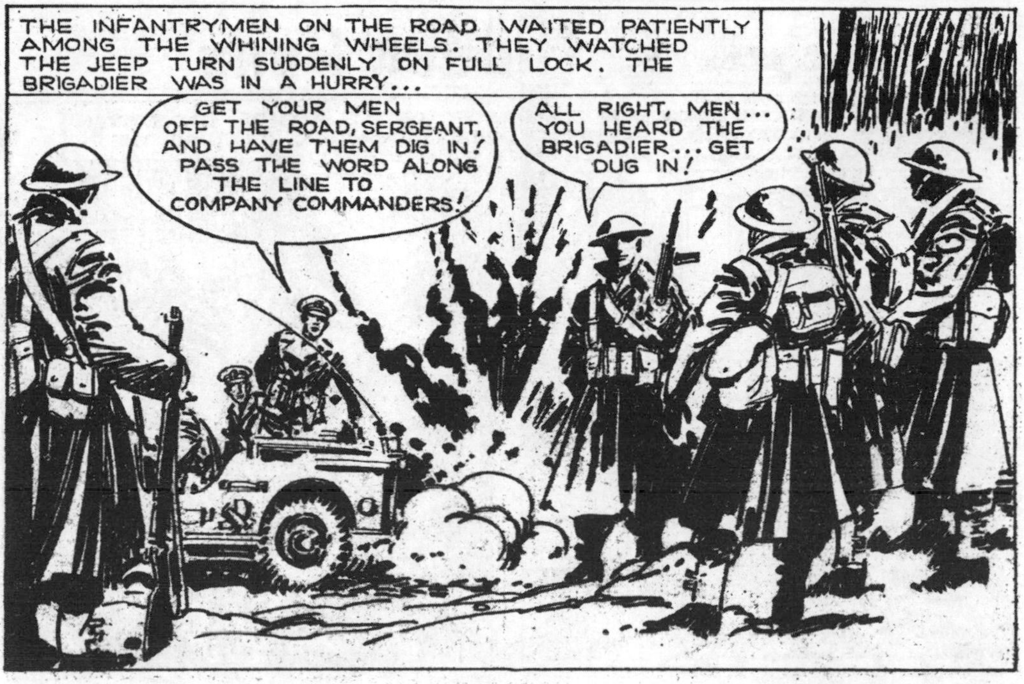
THE INFANTRYMEN ON THE ROAD WAITED PATIENTLY AMONG THE WHINING WHEELS. THEY WATCHED THE JEEP TURN SUDDENLY ON FULL LOCK. THE BRIGADIER WAS IN A HURRY...
GET YOUR MEN OFF THE ROAD, SERGEANT, AND HAVE THEM DIG IN! PASS THE WORD ALONG THE LINE TO COMPANY COMMANDERS!
ALL RIGHT, MEN... YOU HEARD THE BRIGADIER... GET DUG IN!

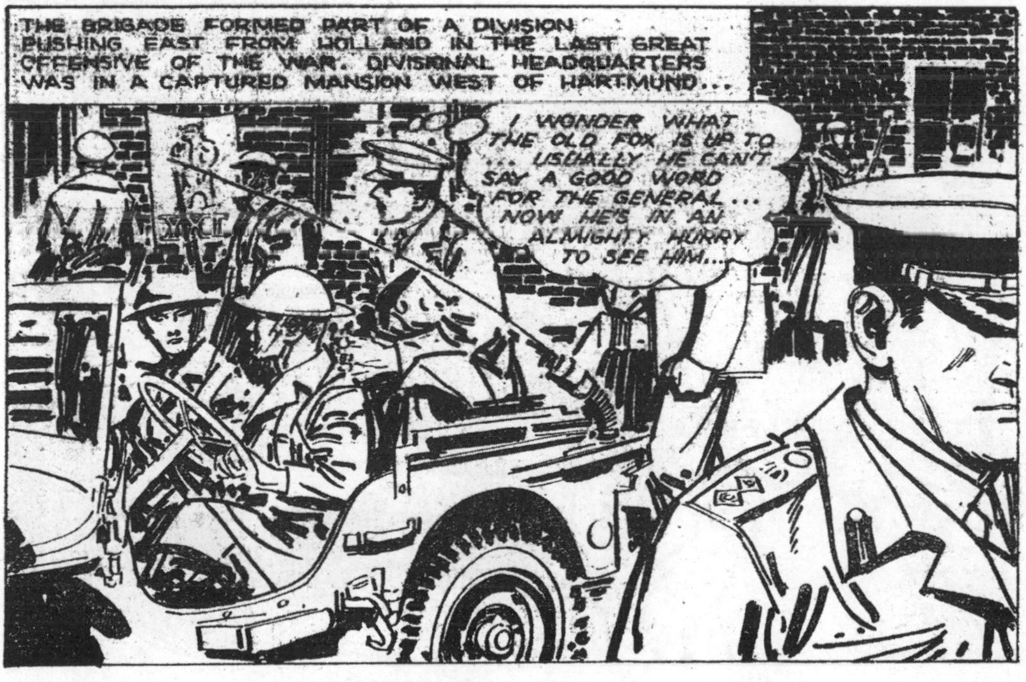
THE BRIGADE FORMED PART OF A DIVISION PUSHING EAST FROM HOLLAND IN THE LAST GREAT OFFENSIVE OF THE WAR. DIVISIONAL HEADQUARTERS WAS IN A CAPTURED MANSION WEST OF HARTMUND...
I WONDER WHAT THE OLD FOX IS UP TO ... USUALLY HE CAN'T SAY A GOOD WORD FOR THE GENERAL ... NOW HE'S IN AN ALMIGHTY HURRY TO SEE HIM....

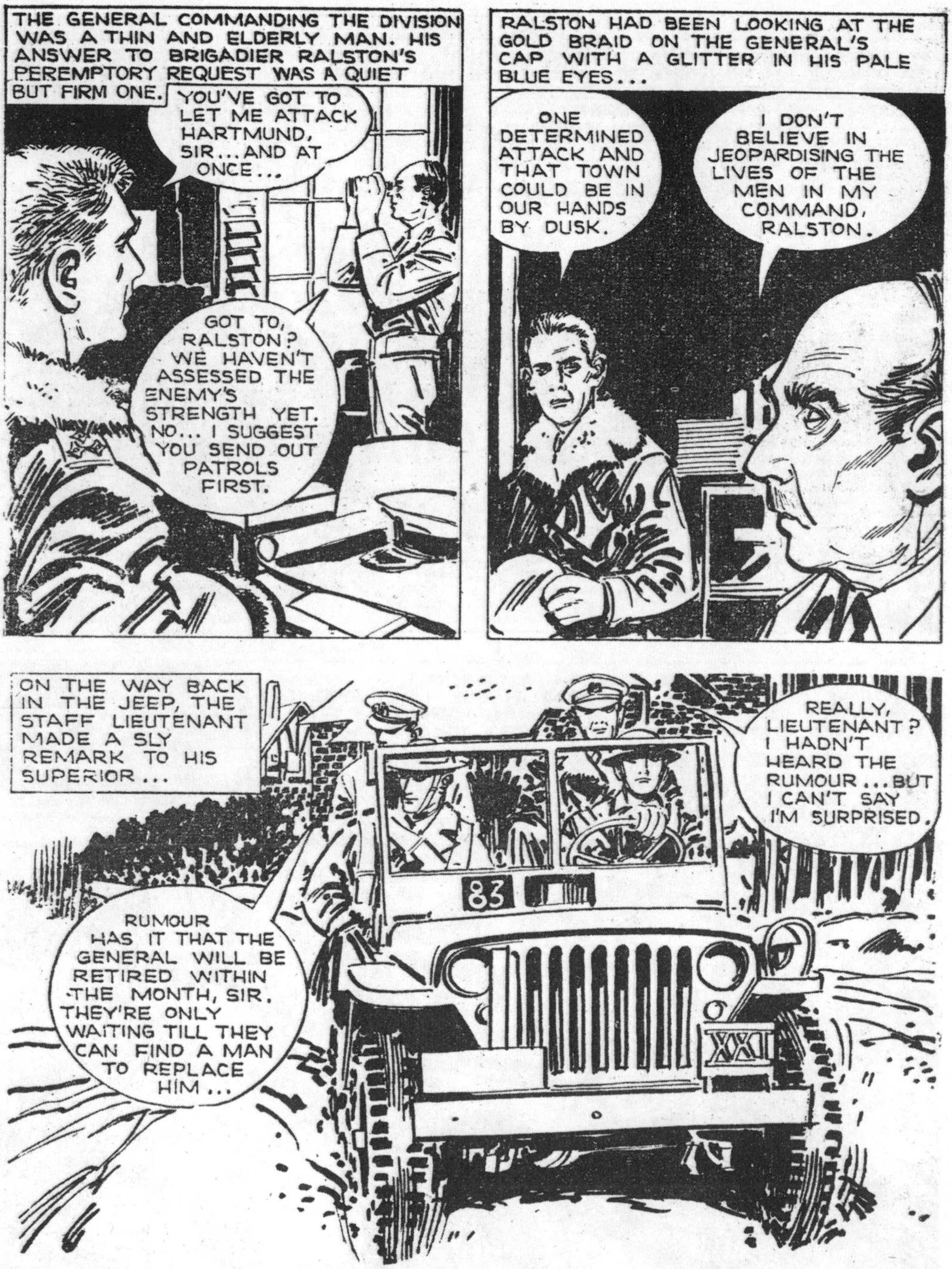
THE GENERAL COMMANDING THE DIVISION WAS A THIN AND ELDERLY MAN. HIS ANSWER TO BRIGADIER RALSTON'S PEREMPTORY REQUEST WAS A QUIET BUT FIRM ONE.
YOU'VE GOT TO LET ME ATTACK HARTMUND, SIR... AND AT ONCE...
GOT TO, RALSTON? WE HAVEN'T ASSESSED THE ENEMY'S STRENGTH YET. NO... I SUGGEST YOU SEND OUT PATROLS FIRST.
RALSTON HAD BEEN LOOKING AT THE GOLD BRAID ON THE GENERAL'S CAP WITH A GLITTER IN HIS PALE BLUE EYES...
ONE DETERMINED ATTACK AND THAT TOWN COULD BE IN OUR HANDS BY DUSK.
I DON'T BELIEVE IN JEOPARDISING THE LIVES OF THE MEN IN MY COMMAND, RALSTON.
ON THE WAY BACK IN THE JEEP, THE STAFF LIEUTENANT MADE A SLY REMARK TO HIS SUPERIOR...
RUMOUR HAS IT THAT THE GENERAL WILL BE RETIRED WITHIN THE MONTH, SIR. THEY'RE ONLY WAITING TILL THEY CAN FIND A MAN TO REPLACE HIM...
REALLY, LIEUTENANT? I HADN'T HEARD THE RUMOUR... BUT I CAN'T SAY I'M SURPRISED.
83
XXI

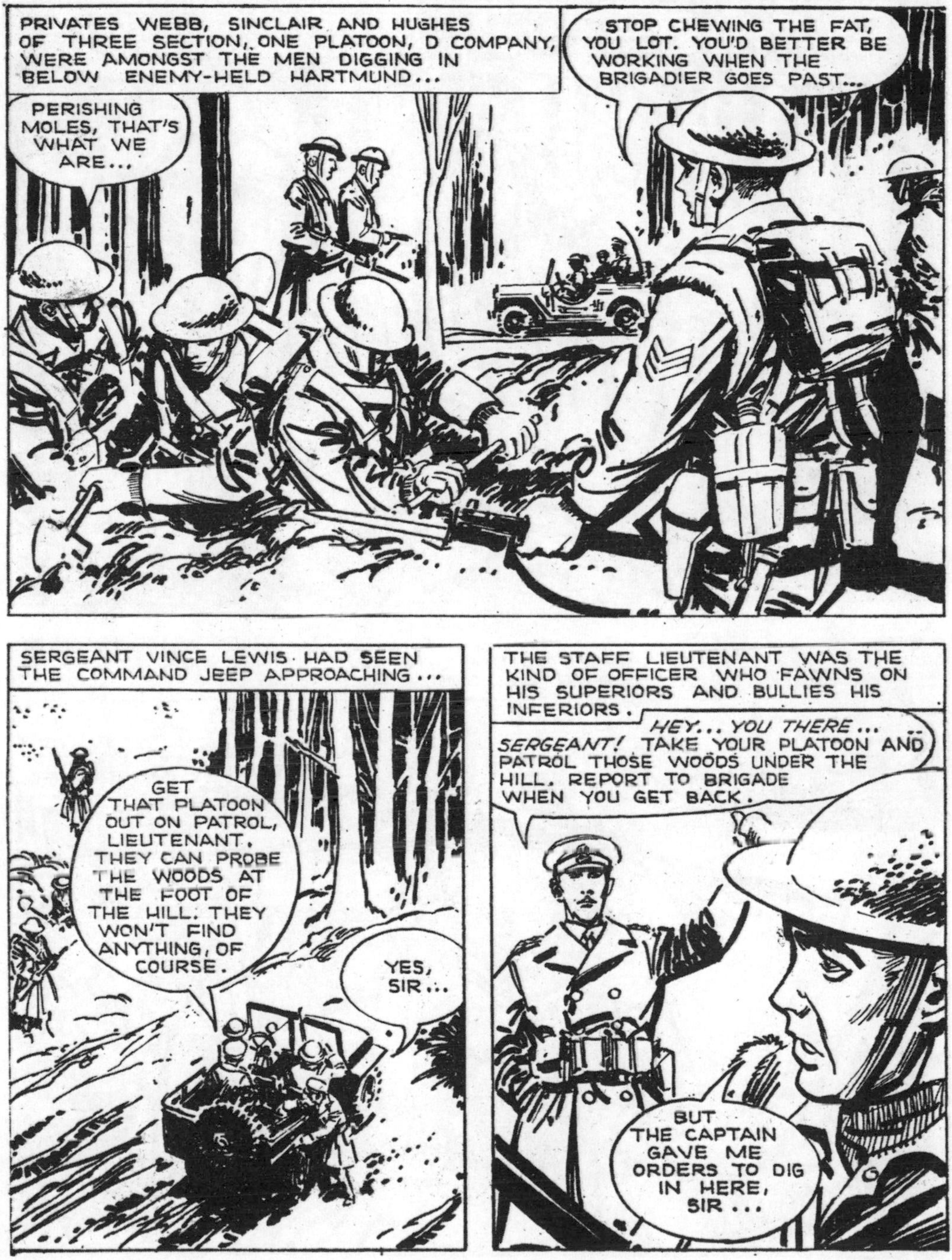
PRIVATES WEBB, SINCLAIR AND HUGHES OF THREE SECTION, ONE PLATOON, D COMPANY, WERE AMONGST THE MEN DIGGING IN BELOW ENEMY-HELD HARTMUND...
PERISHING MOLES, THAT'S WHAT WE ARE...
STOP CHEWING THE FAT, YOU LOT. YOU'D BETTER BE WORKING WHEN THE BRIGADIER GOES PAST...
SERGEANT VINCE LEWIS HAD SEEN THE COMMAND JEEP APPROACHING...
GET THAT PLATOON OUT ON PATROL, LIEUTENANT. THEY CAN PROBE THE WOODS AT THE FOOT OF THE HILL. THEY WON'T FIND ANYTHING, OF COURSE.
YES, SIR...
THE STAFF LIEUTENANT WAS THE KIND OF OFFICER WHO FAWNS ON HIS SUPERIORS AND BULLIES HIS INFERIORS.
HEY... YOU THERE... SERGEANT! TAKE YOUR PLATOON AND PATROL THOSE WOODS UNDER THE HILL. REPORT TO BRIGADE WHEN YOU GET BACK.
BUT THE CAPTAIN GAVE ME ORDERS TO DIG IN HERE, SIR...

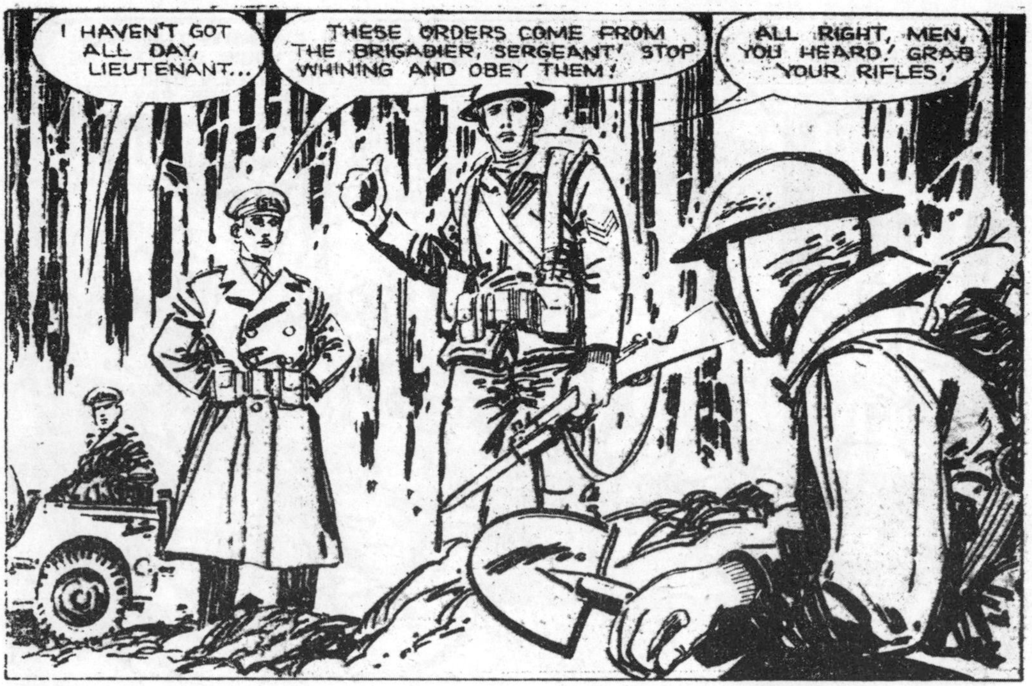
I HAVEN'T GOT ALL DAY, LIEUTENANT...
THESE ORDERS COME FROM THE BRIGADIER, SERGEANT! STOP WHINING AND OBEY THEM!
ALL RIGHT, MEN, YOU HEARD! GRAB YOUR RIFLES!

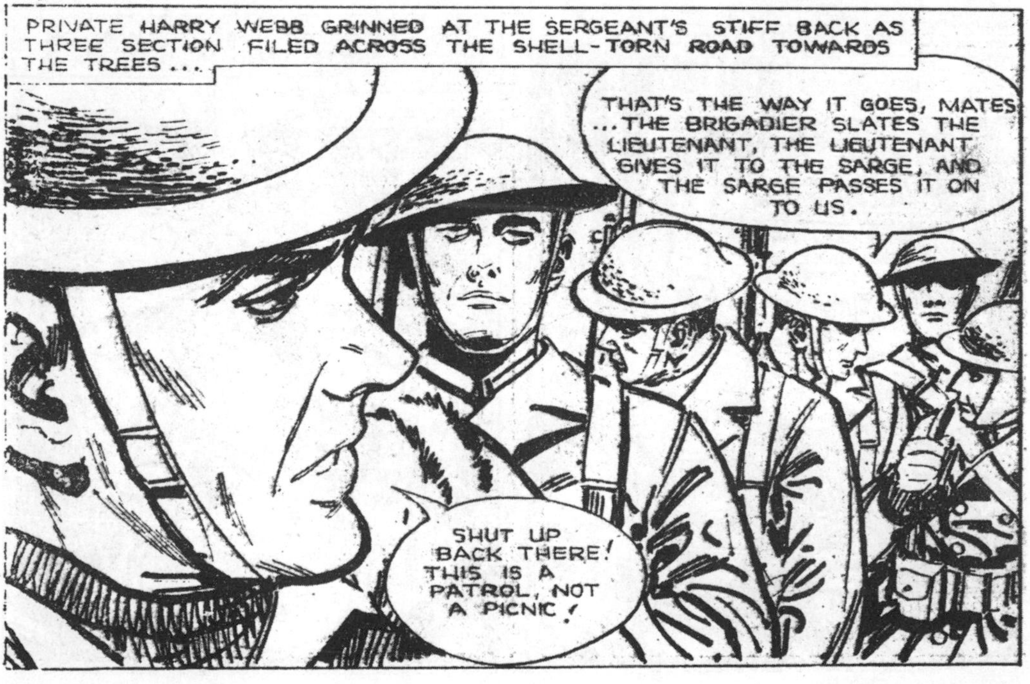
PRIVATE HARRY WEBB GRINNED AT THE SERGEANT'S STIFF BACK AS THREE SECTION FILED ACROSS THE SHELL-TORN ROAD TOWARDS THE TREES...
THAT'S THE WAY IT GOES, MATES ...THE BRIGADIER SLATES THE LIEUTENANT, THE LIEUTENANT GIVES IT TO THE SARGE, AND THE SARGE PASSES IT ON TO US.
SHUT UP BACK THERE! THIS IS A PATROL, NOT A PICNIC!

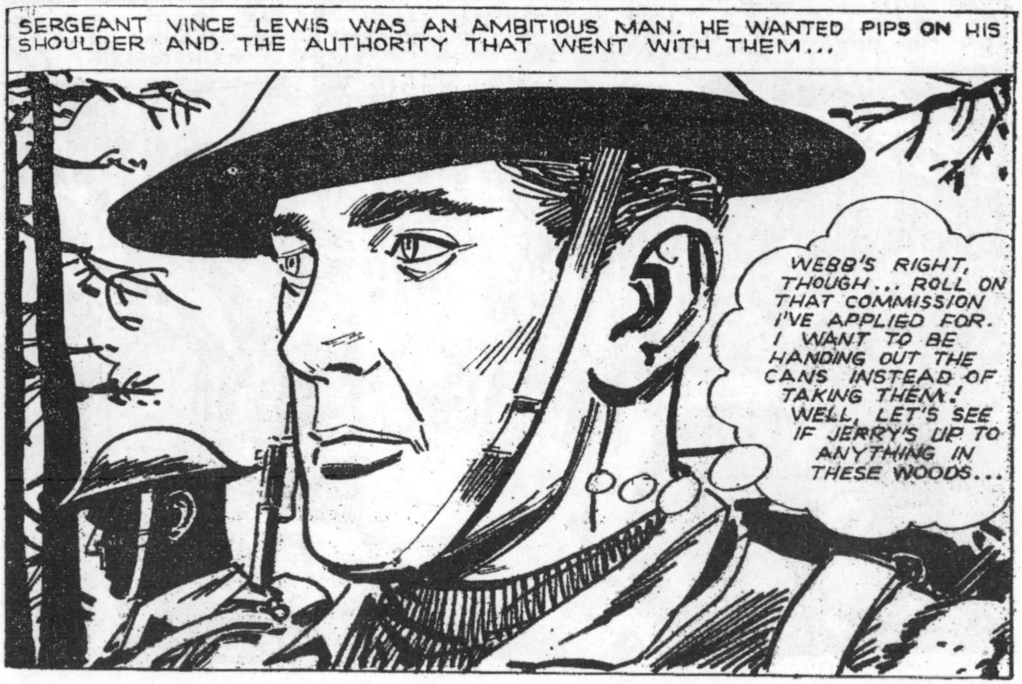
SERGEANT VINCE LEWIS WAS AN AMBITIOUS MAN. HE WANTED PIPS ON HIS SHOULDER AND THE AUTHORITY THAT WENT WITH THEM...
WEBB'S RIGHT, THOUGH... ROLL ON THAT COMMISSION I'VE APPLIED FOR. I WANT TO BE HANDING OUT THE CANS INSTEAD OF TAKING THEM! WELL, LET'S SEE IF JERRY'S UP TO ANYTHING IN THESE WOODS...

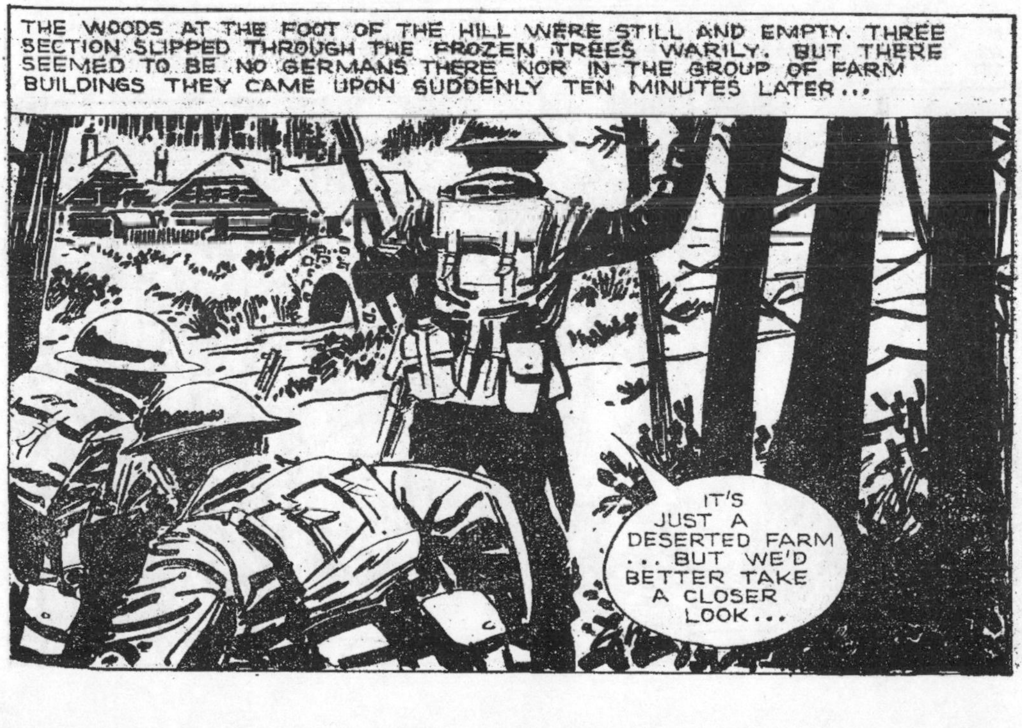
THE WOODS AT THE FOOT OF THE HILL WERE STILL AND EMPTY. THREE SECTION SLIPPED THROUGH THE FROZEN TREES WARILY. BUT THERE SEEMED TO BE NO GERMANS THERE NOR IN THE GROUP OF FARM BUILDINGS THEY CAME UPON SUDDENLY TEN MINUTES LATER...
IT'S JUST A DESERTED FARM ... BUT WE'D BETTER TAKE A CLOSER LOOK...

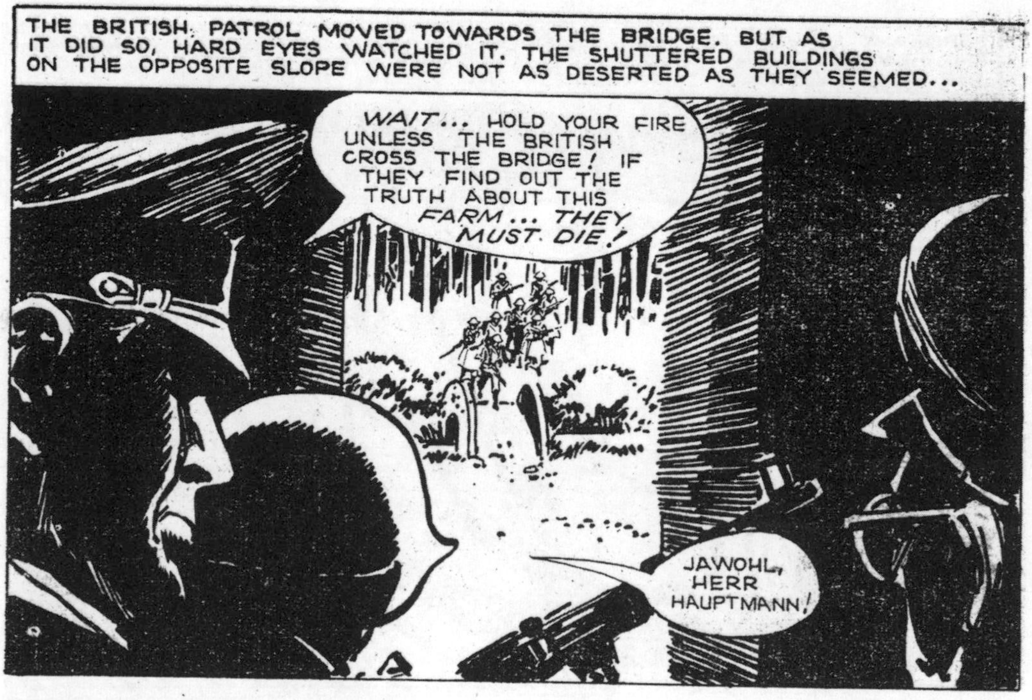
THE BRITISH PATROL MOVED TOWARDS THE BRIDGE. BUT AS IT DID SO, HARD EYES WATCHED IT. THE SHUTTERED BUILDINGS ON THE OPPOSITE SLOPE WERE NOT AS DESERTED AS THEY SEEMED...
WAIT... HOLD YOUR FIRE UNLESS THE BRITISH CROSS THE BRIDGE! IF THEY FIND OUT THE TRUTH ABOUT THIS FARM... THEY MUST DIE!
JAWOHL, HERR HAUPTMANN!

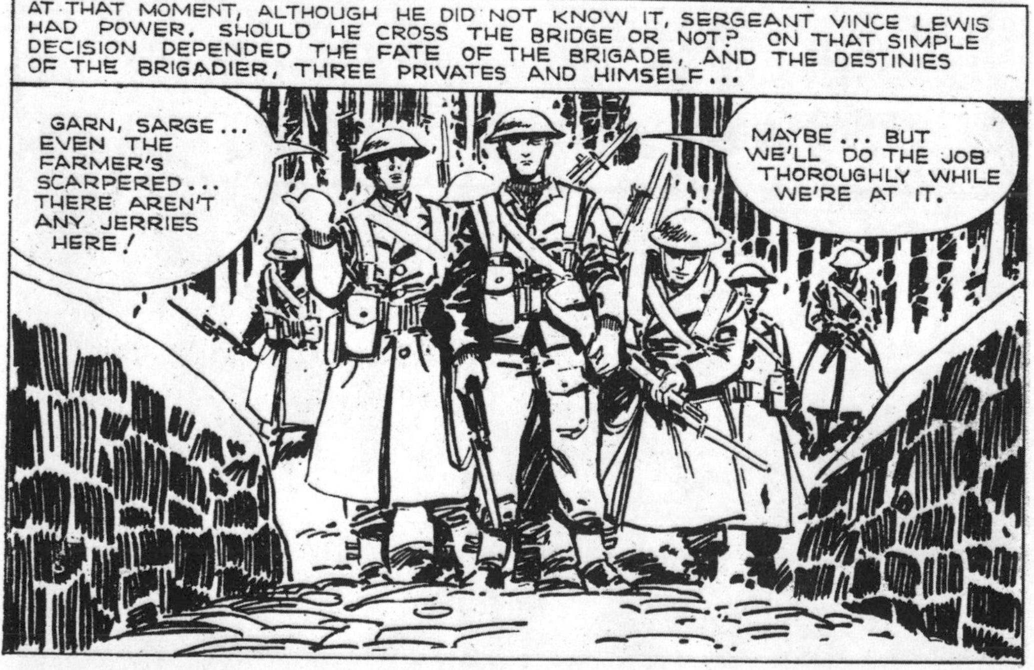
AT THAT MOMENT, ALTHOUGH HE DID NOT KNOW IT, SERGEANT VINCE LEWIS HAD POWER. SHOULD HE CROSS THE BRIDGE OR NOT? ON THAT SIMPLE DECISION DEPENDED THE FATE OF THE BRIGADE, AND THE DESTINIES OF THE BRIGADIER, THREE PRIVATES AND HIMSELF...
GARN, SARGE... EVEN THE FARMER'S SCARPERED... THERE AREN'T ANY JERRIES HERE!
MAYBE... BUT WE'LL DO THE JOB THOROUGHLY WHILE WE'RE AT IT.

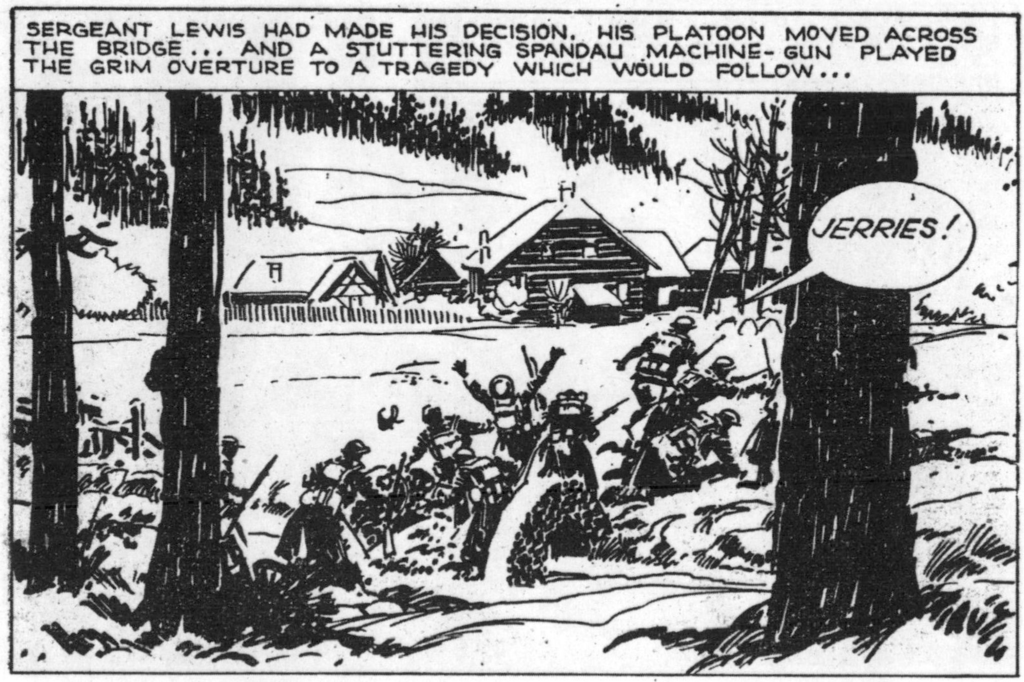
SERGEANT LEWIS HAD MADE HIS DECISION. HIS PLATOON MOVED ACROSS THE BRIDGE... AND A STUTTERING SPANDAU MACHINE-GUN PLAYED THE GRIM OVERTURE TO A TRAGEDY WHICH WOULD FOLLOW...
JERRIES!

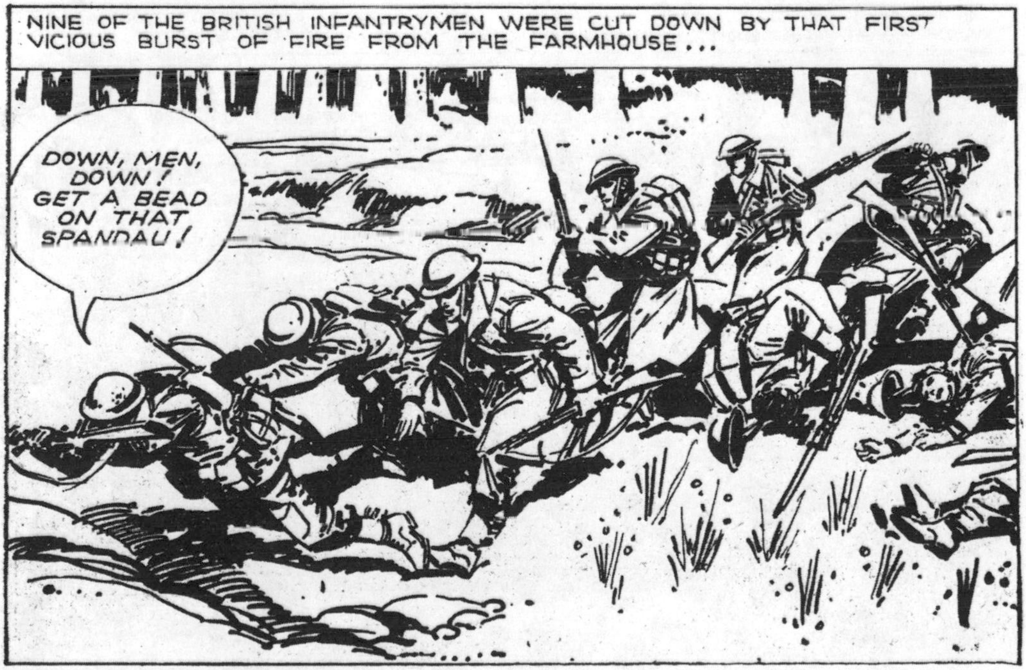
NINE OF THE BRITISH INFANTRYMEN WERE CUT DOWN BY THAT FIRST VICIOUS BURST OF FIRE FROM THE FARMHOUSE...
DOWN, MEN, DOWN! GET A BEAD ON THAT SPANDAU!

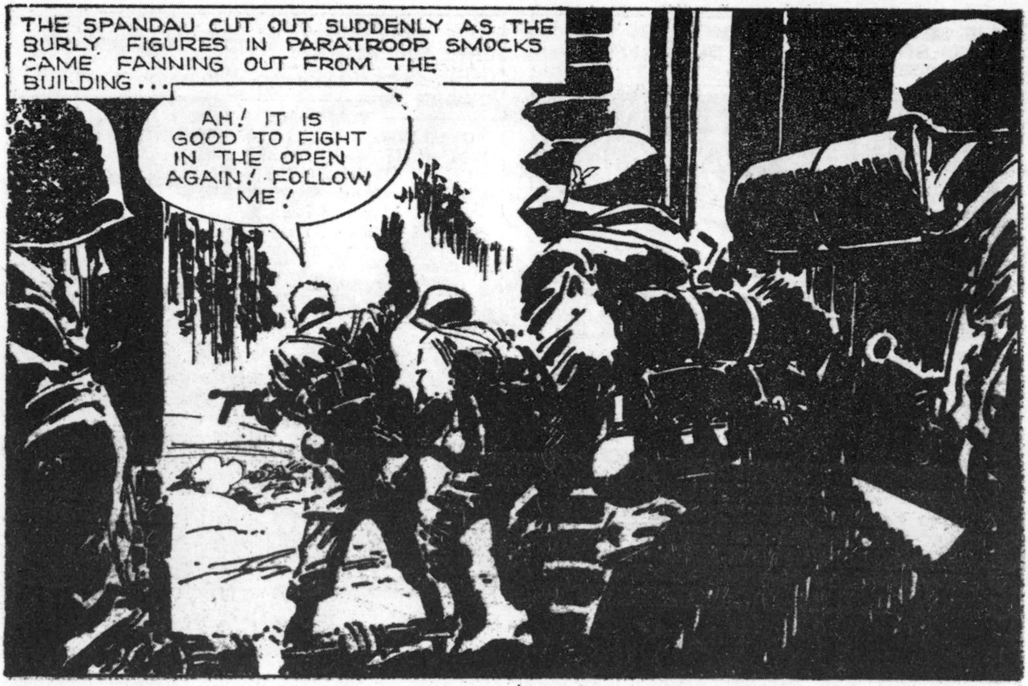
THE SPANDAU CUT OUT SUDDENLY AS THE BURLY FIGURES IN PARATROOP SMOCKS CAME FANNING OUT FROM THE BUILDING...
AH! IT IS GOOD TO FIGHT IN THE OPEN AGAIN! FOLLOW ME!

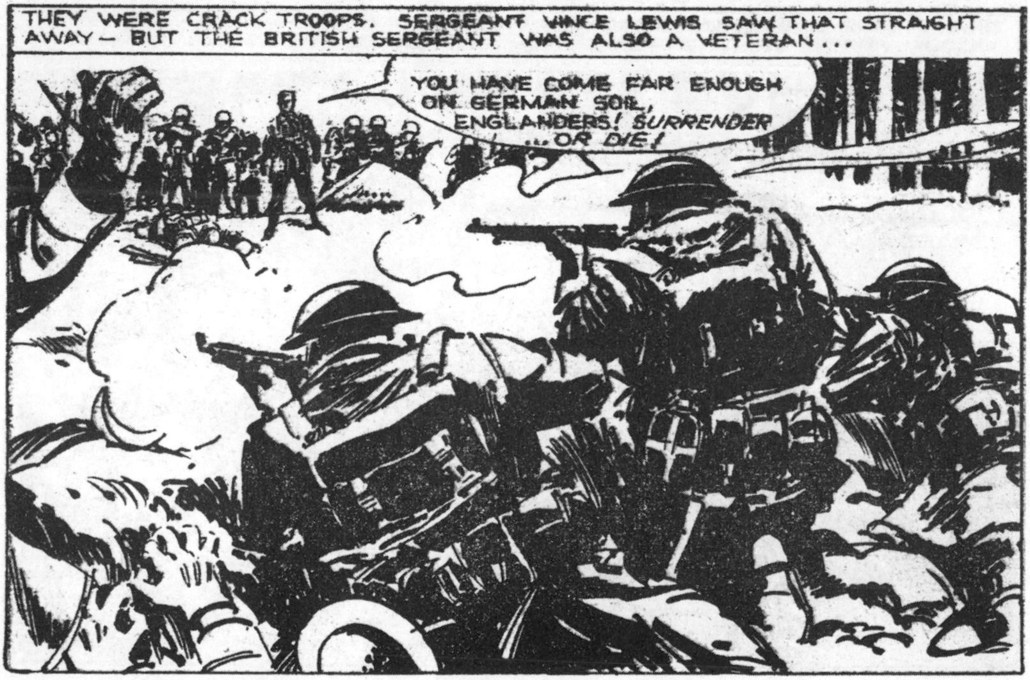
THEY WERE CRACK TROOPS. SERGEANT VINCE LEWIS SAW THAT STRAIGHT AWAY– BUT THE BRITISH SERGEANT WAS ALSO A VETERAN...
YOU HAVE COME FAR ENOUGH ON GERMAN SOIL, ENGLANDERS! SURRENDER ...OR DIE!

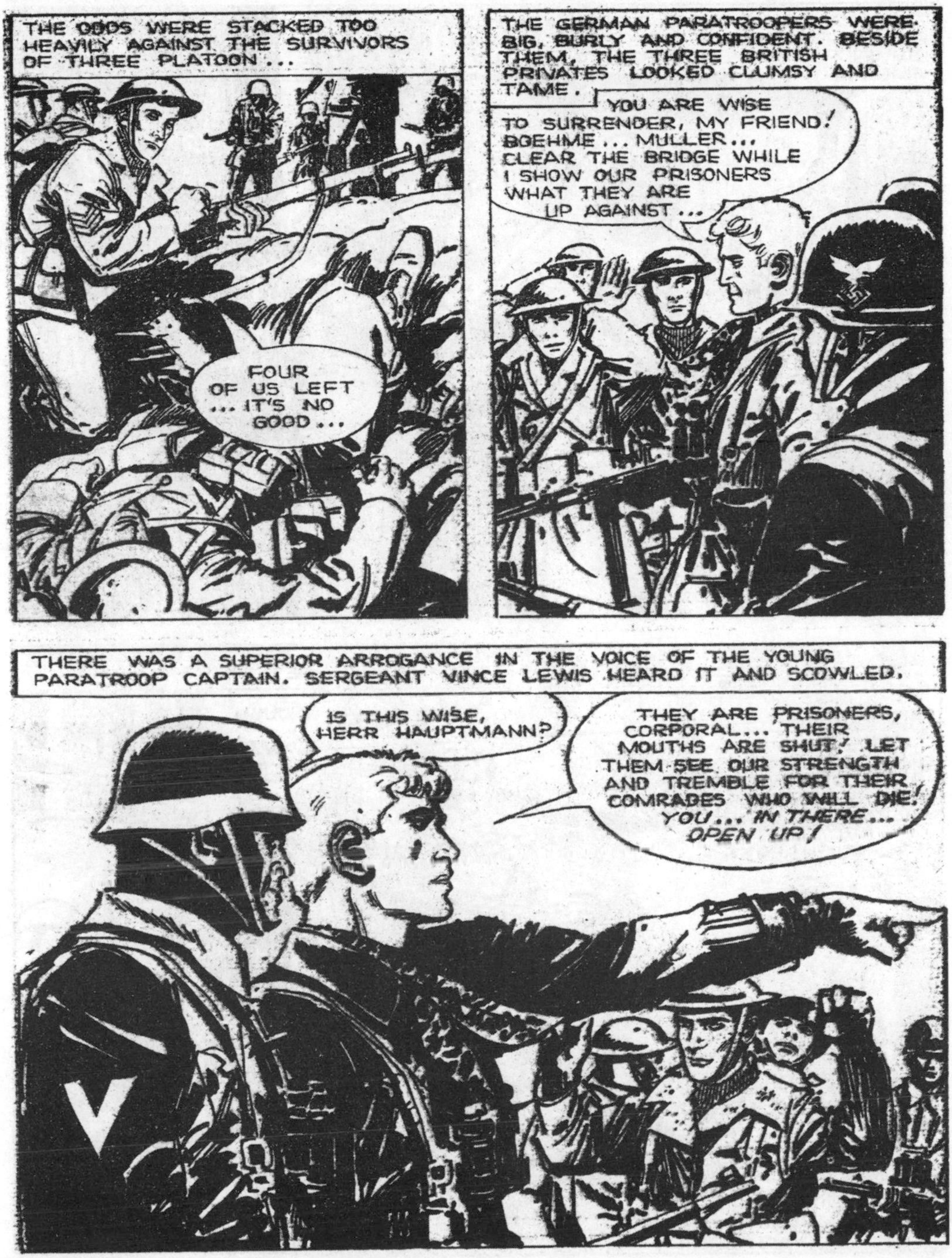
THE ODDS WERE STACKED TOO HEAVILY AGAINST THE SURVIVORS OF THREE PLATOON ...
FOUR OF US LEFT ... IT'S NO GOOD ...
THE GERMAN PARATROOPERS WERE BIG, BURLY AND CONFIDENT. BESIDE THEM, THE THREE BRITISH PRIVATES LOOKED CLUMSY AND TAME.
YOU ARE WISE TO SURRENDER, MY FRIEND! BOEHME ... MULLER ... CLEAR THE BRIDGE WHILE I SHOW OUR PRISONERS WHAT THEY ARE UP AGAINST ...
THERE WAS A SUPERIOR ARROGANCE IN THE VOICE OF THE YOUNG PARATROOP CAPTAIN. SERGEANT VINCE LEWIS HEARD IT AND SCOWLED.
IS THIS WISE, HERR HAUPTMANN?
THEY ARE PRISONERS, CORPORAL... THEIR MOUTHS ARE SHUT! LET THEM SEE OUR STRENGTH AND TREMBLE FOR THEIR COMRADES WHO WILL DIE! YOU... IN THERE... OPEN UP!

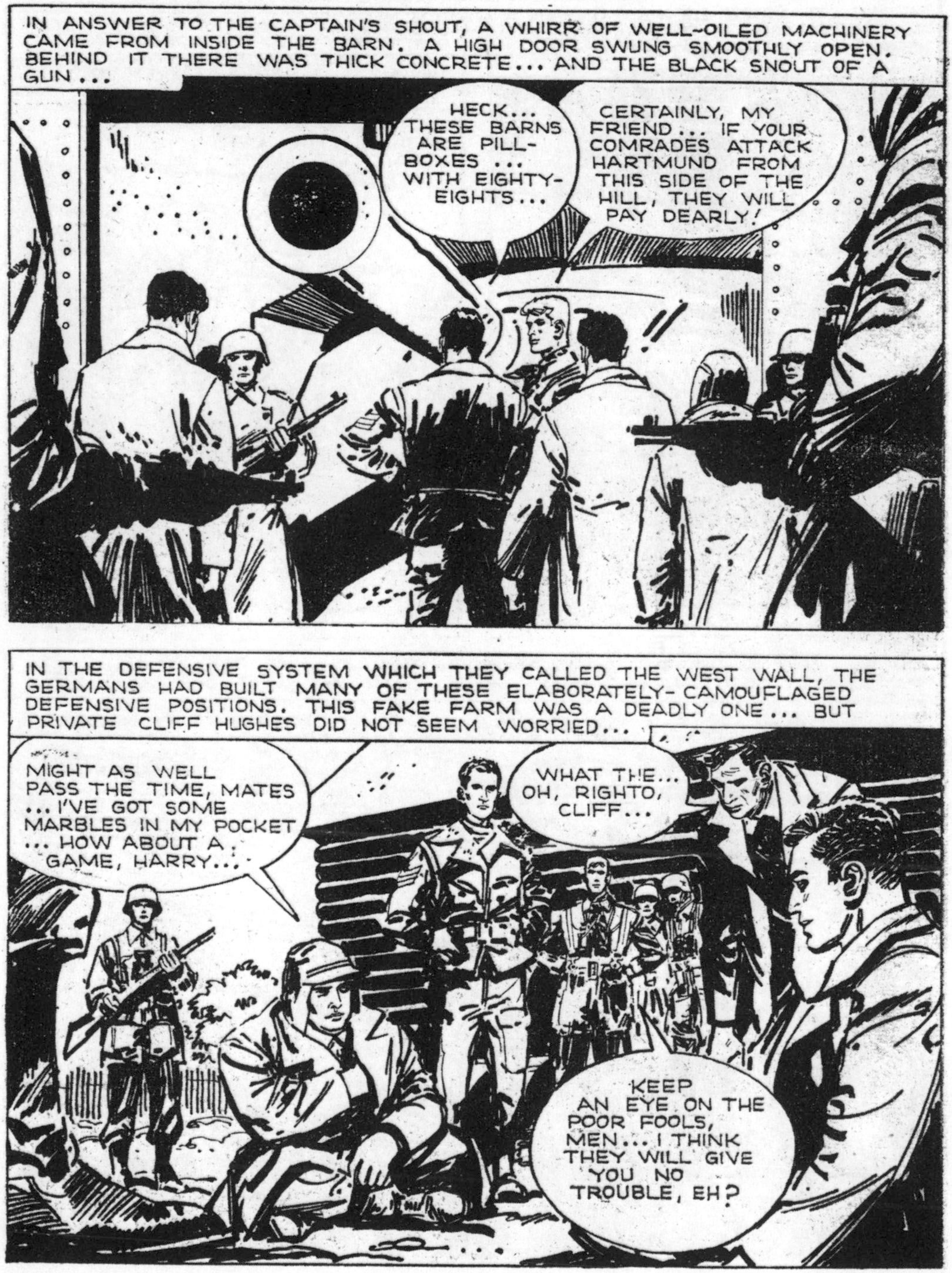
IN ANSWER TO THE CAPTAIN'S SHOUT, A WHIRR OF WELL-OILED MACHINERY CAME FROM INSIDE THE BARN. A HIGH DOOR SWUNG SMOOTHLY OPEN. BEHIND IT THERE WAS THICK CONCRETE... AND THE BLACK SNOUT OF A GUN...
HECK... THESE BARNS ARE PILL-BOXES ... WITH EIGHTY-EIGHTS...
CERTAINLY, MY FRIEND... IF YOUR COMRADES ATTACK HARTMUND FROM THIS SIDE OF THE HILL, THEY WILL PAY DEARLY!
IN THE DEFENSIVE SYSTEM WHICH THEY CALLED THE WEST WALL, THE GERMANS HAD BUILT MANY OF THESE ELABORATELY-CAMOUFLAGED DEFENSIVE POSITIONS. THIS FAKE FARM WAS A DEADLY ONE... BUT PRIVATE CLIFF HUGHES DID NOT SEEM WORRIED...
MIGHT AS WELL PASS THE TIME, MATES ... I'VE GOT SOME MARBLES IN MY POCKET ... HOW ABOUT A GAME, HARRY...
WHAT THE... OH, RIGHTO, CLIFF...
KEEP AN EYE ON THE POOR FOOLS, MEN... I THINK THEY WILL GIVE YOU NO TROUBLE, EH?

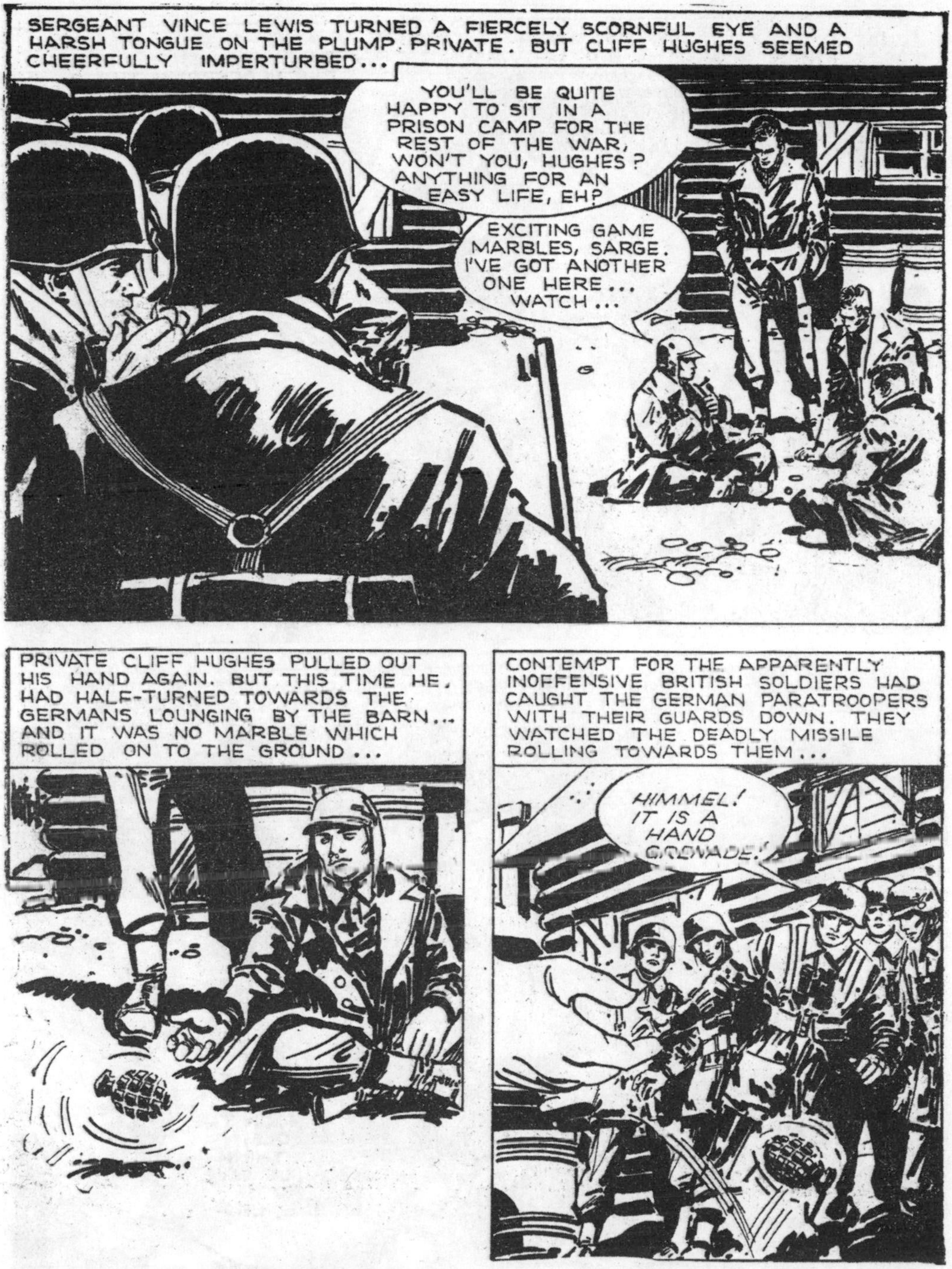
SERGEANT VINCE LEWIS TURNED A FIERCELY SCORNFUL EYE AND A HARSH TONGUE ON THE PLUMP PRIVATE. BUT CLIFF HUGHES SEEMED CHEERFULLY IMPERTURBED...
YOU'LL BE QUITE HAPPY TO SIT IN A PRISON CAMP FOR THE REST OF THE WAR, WON'T YOU, HUGHES? ANYTHING FOR AN EASY LIFE, EH?
EXCITING GAME MARBLES, SARGE. I'VE GOT ANOTHER ONE HERE... WATCH...
PRIVATE CLIFF HUGHES PULLED OUT HIS HAND AGAIN. BUT THIS TIME HE HAD HALF-TURNED TOWARDS THE GERMANS LOUNGING BY THE BARN... AND IT WAS NO MARBLE WHICH ROLLED ON TO THE GROUND...
CONTEMPT FOR THE APPARENTLY INOFFENSIVE BRITISH SOLDIERS HAD CAUGHT THE GERMAN PARATROOPERS WITH THEIR GUARDS DOWN. THEY WATCHED THE DEADLY MISSILE ROLLING TOWARDS THEM...
HIMMEL! IT IS A HAND

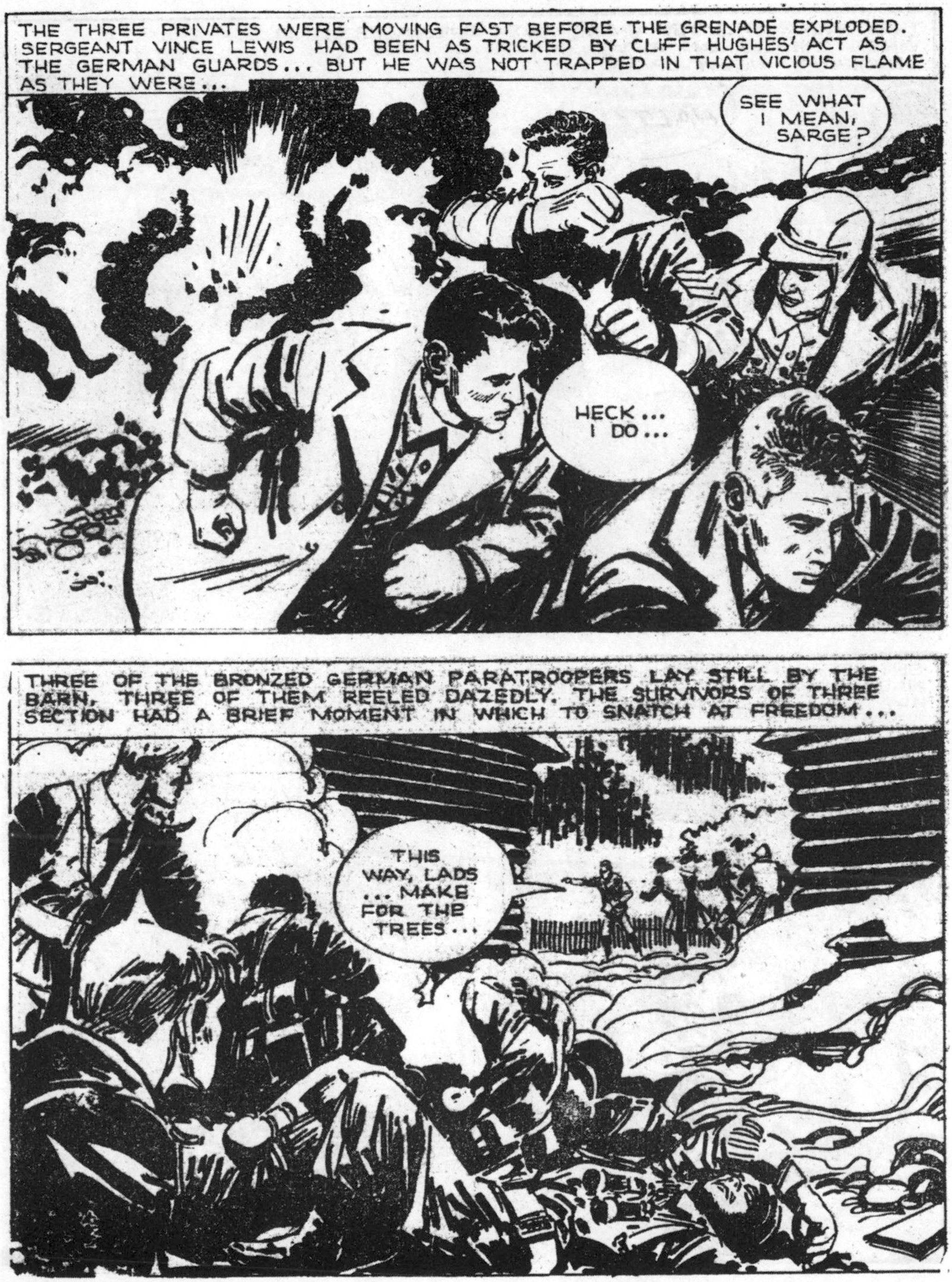
THE THREE PRIVATES WERE MOVING FAST BEFORE THE GRENADE EXPLODED. SERGEANT VINCE LEWIS HAD BEEN AS TRICKED BY CLIFF HUGHES' ACT AS THE GERMAN GUARDS... BUT HE WAS NOT TRAPPED IN THAT VICIOUS FLAME AS THEY WERE...
SEE WHAT I MEAN, SARGE?
HECK... I DO...
THREE OF THE BRONZED GERMAN PARATROOPERS LAY STILL BY THE BARN, THREE OF THEM REELED DAZEDLY. THE SURVIVORS OF THREE SECTION HAD A BRIEF MOMENT IN WHICH TO SNATCH AT FREEDOM...
THIS WAY, LADS ... MAKE FOR THE TREES...

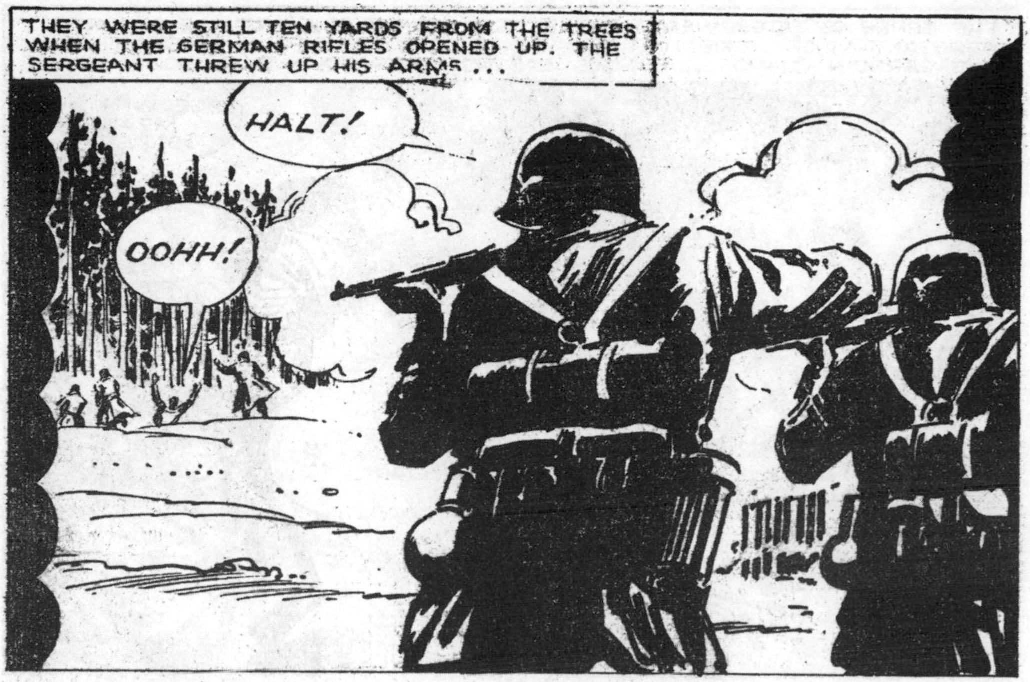
THEY WERE STILL TEN YARDS FROM THE TREES WHEN THE GERMAN RIFLES OPENED UP. THE SERGEANT THREW UP HIS ARMS ...
HALT!
OOHH!

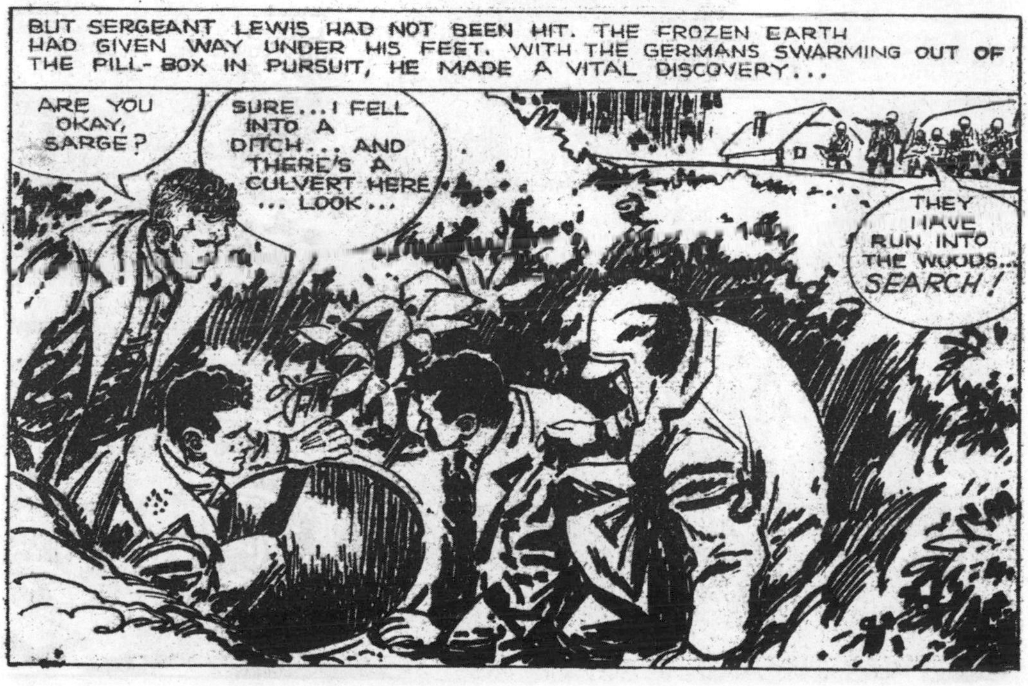
BUT SERGEANT LEWIS HAD NOT BEEN HIT. THE FROZEN EARTH HAD GIVEN WAY UNDER HIS FEET. WITH THE GERMANS SWARMING OUT OF THE PILL-BOX IN PURSUIT, HE MADE A VITAL DISCOVERY...
ARE YOU OKAY, SARGE?
SURE...I FELL INTO A DITCH... AND THERE'S A CULVERT HERE ... LOOK...
THEY HAVE RUN INTO THE WOODS... SEARCH!

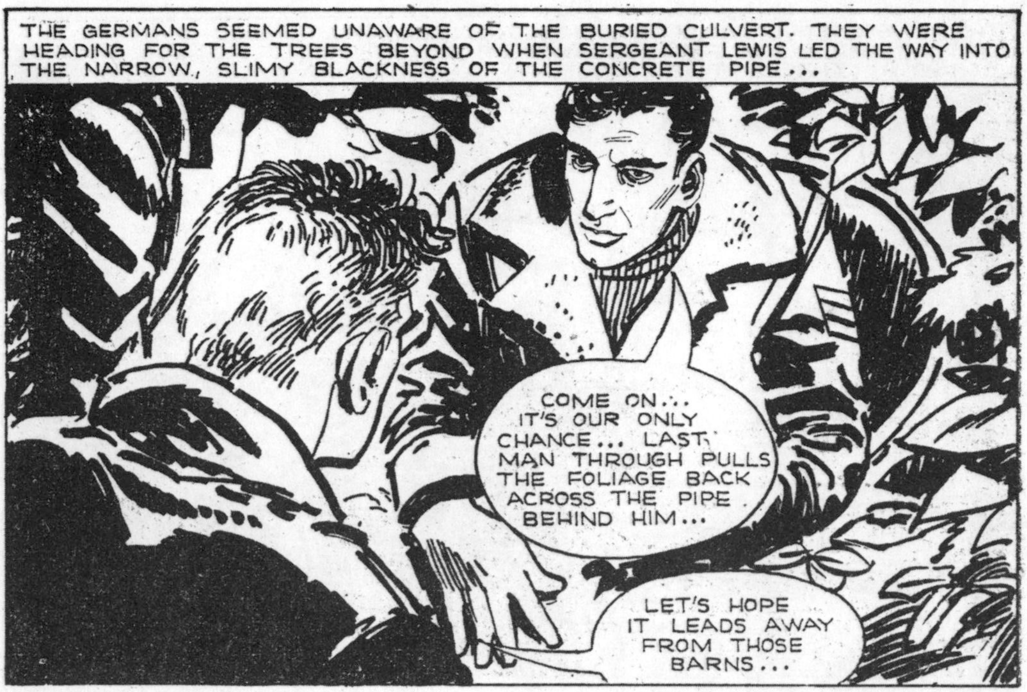
THE GERMANS SEEMED UNAWARE OF THE BURIED CULVERT. THEY WERE HEADING FOR THE TREES BEYOND WHEN SERGEANT LEWIS LED THE WAY INTO THE NARROW, SLIMY BLACKNESS OF THE CONCRETE PIPE...
COME ON... IT'S OUR ONLY CHANCE... LAST MAN THROUGH PULLS THE FOLIAGE BACK ACROSS THE PIPE BEHIND HIM...
LET'S HOPE IT LEADS AWAY FROM THOSE BARNS...

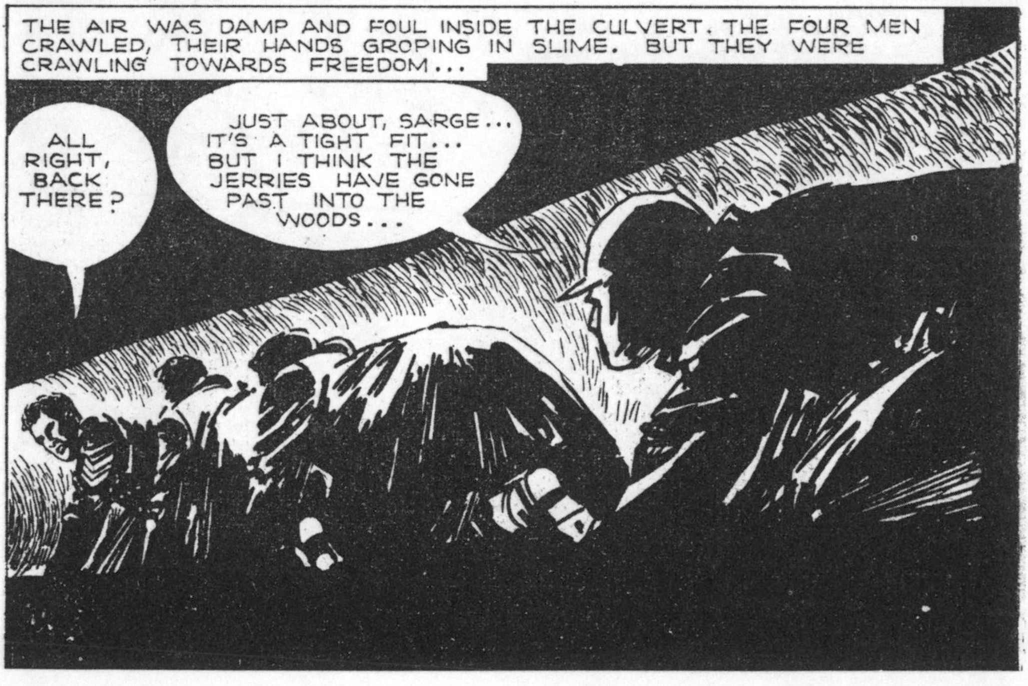
THE AIR WAS DAMP AND FOUL INSIDE THE CULVERT. THE FOUR MEN CRAWLED, THEIR HANDS GROPING IN SLIME. BUT THEY WERE CRAWLING TOWARDS FREEDOM...
ALL RIGHT, BACK THERE?
JUST ABOUT, SARGE... IT'S A TIGHT FIT... BUT I THINK THE JERRIES HAVE GONE PAST INTO THE WOODS...

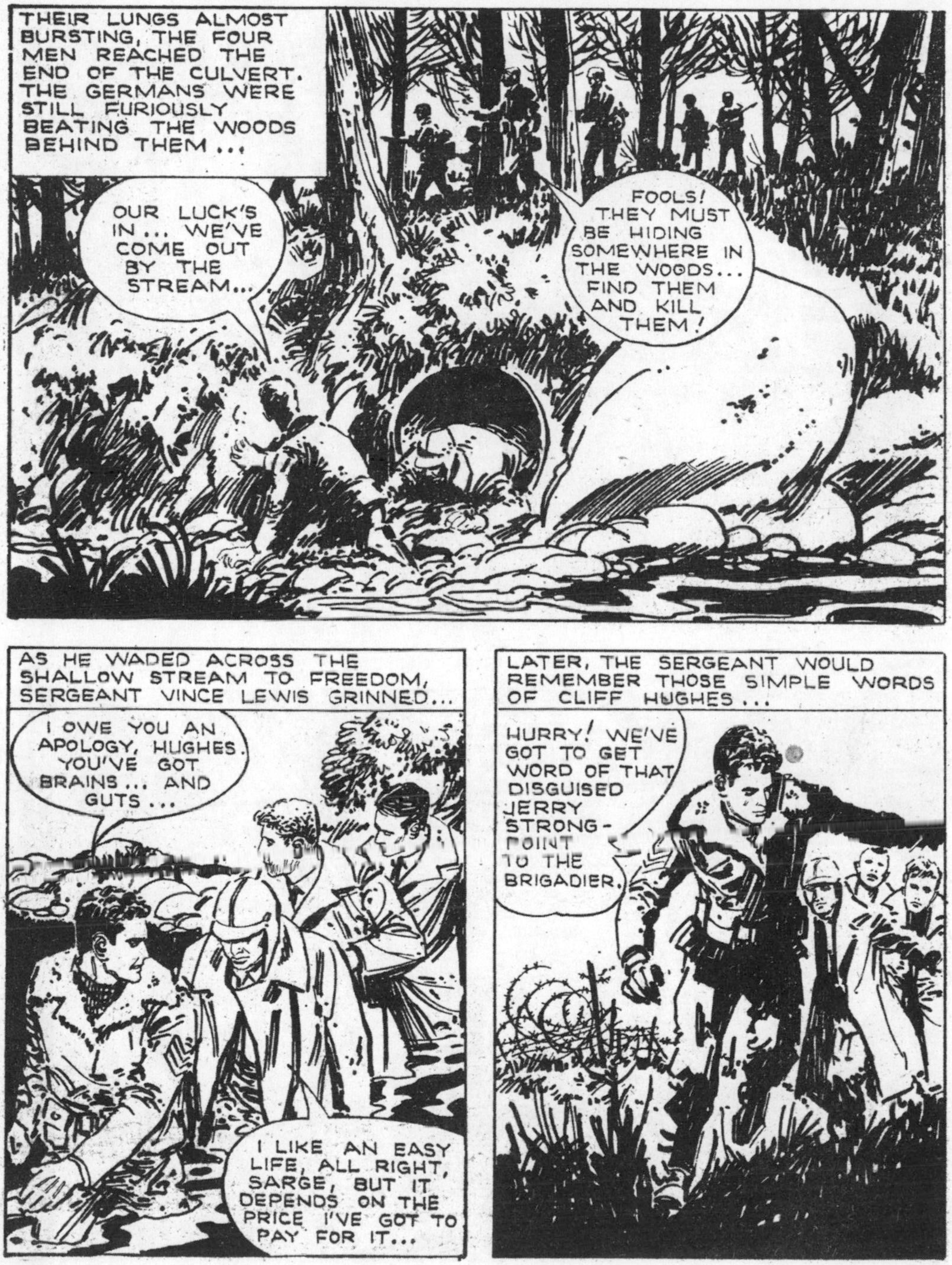
THEIR LUNGS ALMOST BURSTING, THE FOUR MEN REACHED THE END OF THE CULVERT. THE GERMANS WERE STILL FURIOUSLY BEATING THE WOODS BEHIND THEM...
OUR LUCK'S IN... WE'VE COME OUT BY THE STREAM...
FOOLS! THEY MUST BE HIDING SOMEWHERE IN THE WOODS... FIND THEM AND KILL THEM!
AS HE WADED ACROSS THE SHALLOW STREAM TO FREEDOM, SERGEANT VINCE LEWIS GRINNED...
I OWE YOU AN APOLOGY, HUGHES. YOU'VE GOT BRAINS... AND GUTS...
I LIKE AN EASY LIFE, ALL RIGHT, SARGE, BUT IT DEPENDS ON THE PRICE I'VE GOT TO PAY FOR IT...
LATER, THE SERGEANT WOULD REMEMBER THOSE SIMPLE WORDS OF CLIFF HUGHES...
HURRY! WE'VE GOT TO GET WORD OF THAT DISGUISED JERRY STRONG-POINT TO THE BRIGADIER.

Chapter 2. The Suppressed Report

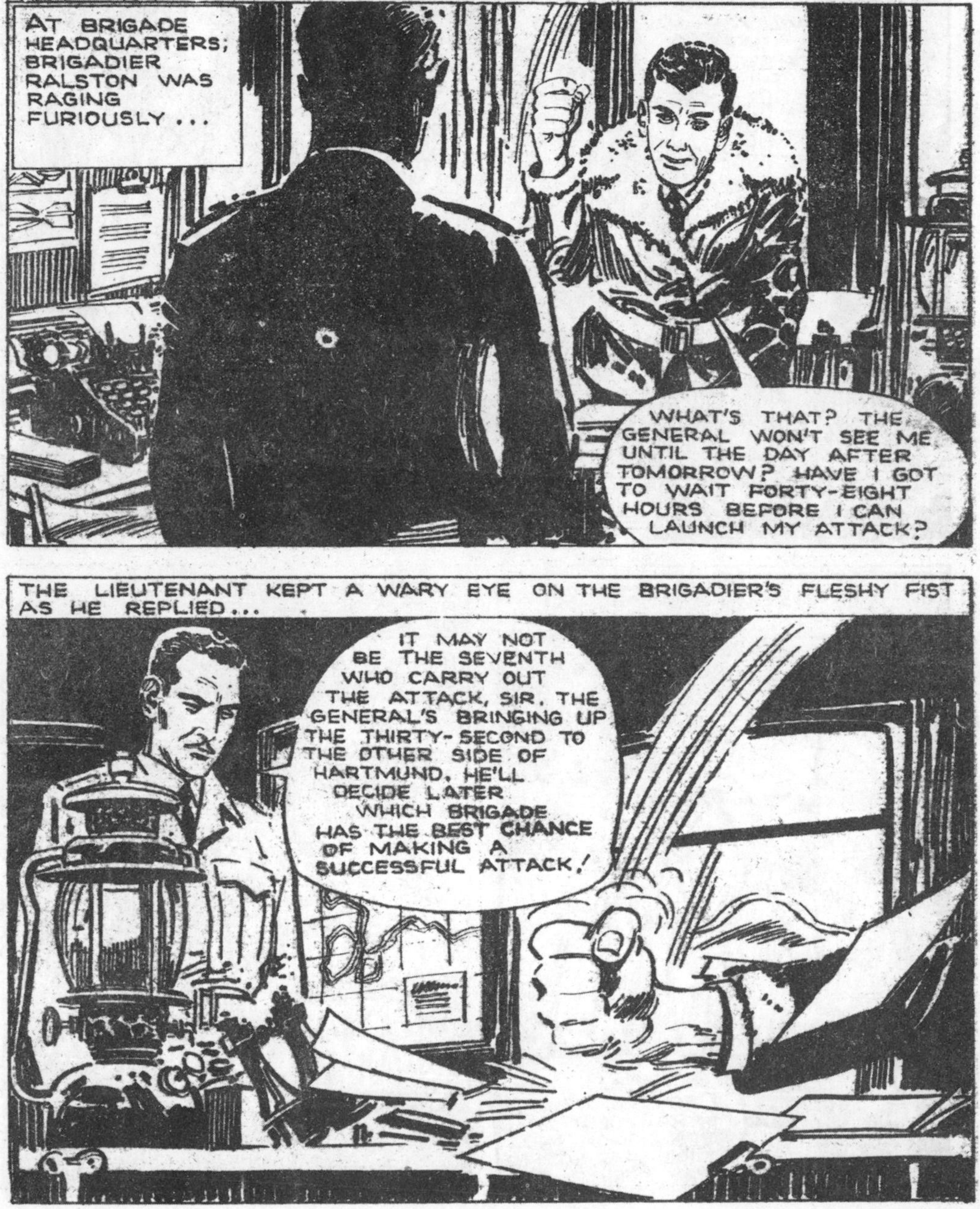
AT BRIGADE HEADQUARTERS; BRIGADIER RALSTON WAS RAGING FURIOUSLY ...
WHAT'S THAT? THE GENERAL WON'T SEE ME UNTIL THE DAY AFTER TOMORROW? HAVE I GOT TO WAIT FORTY-EIGHT HOURS BEFORE I CAN LAUNCH MY ATTACK?
THE LIEUTENANT KEPT A WARY EYE ON THE BRIGADIER'S FLESHY FIST AS HE REPLIED ...
IT MAY NOT BE THE SEVENTH WHO CARRY OUT THE ATTACK, SIR. THE GENERAL'S BRINGING UP THE THIRTY-SECOND TO THE OTHER SIDE OF HARTMUND. HE'LL DECIDE LATER WHICH BRIGADE HAS THE BEST CHANCE OF MAKING A SUCCESSFUL ATTACK!

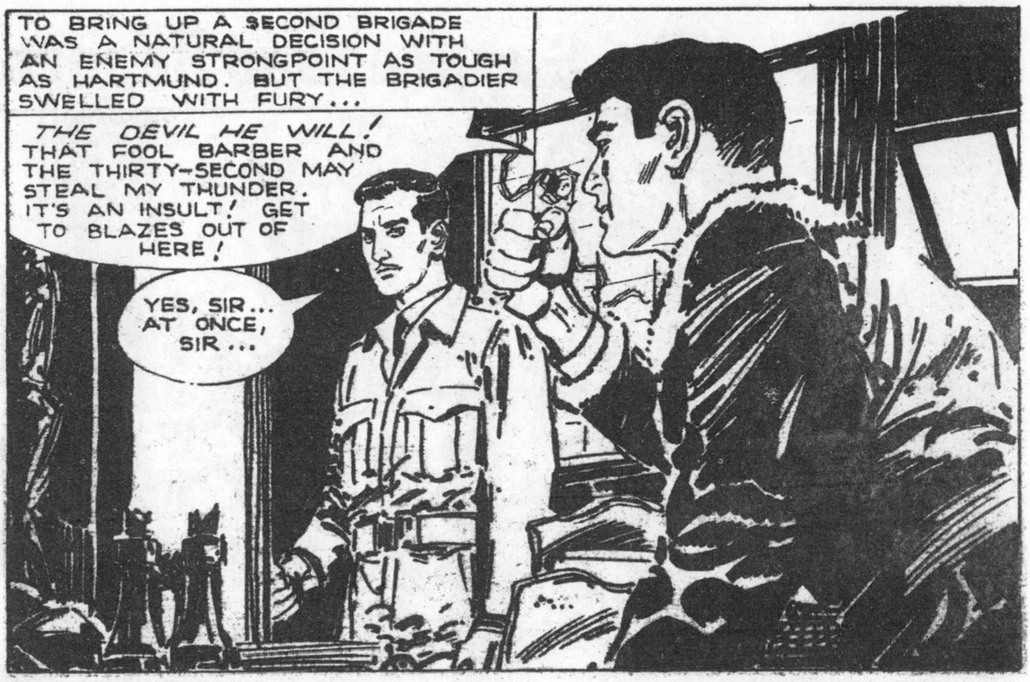
TO BRING UP A SECOND BRIGADE WAS A NATURAL DECISION WITH AN ENEMY STRONGPOINT AS TOUGH AS HARTMUND. BUT THE BRIGADIER SWELLED WITH FURY...
THE DEVIL HE WILL! THAT FOOL BARBER AND THE THIRTY-SECOND MAY STEAL MY THUNDER. IT'S AN INSULT! GET TO BLAZES OUT OF HERE!
YES, SIR... AT ONCE, SIR...

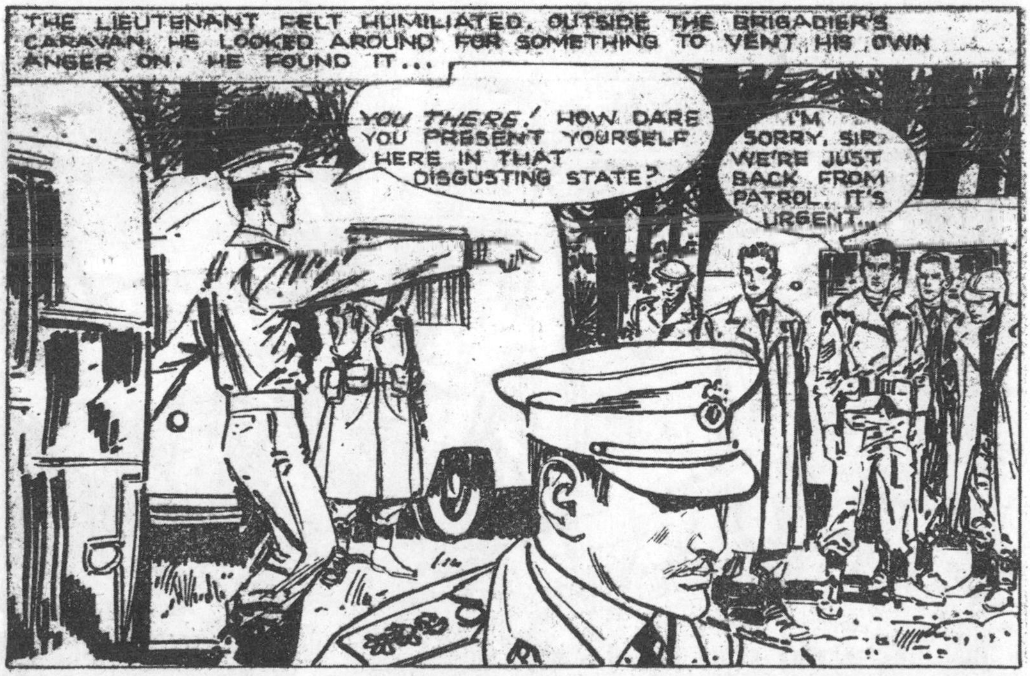
THE LIEUTENANT FELT HUMILIATED. OUTSIDE THE BRIGADIER'S CARAVAN HE LOOKED AROUND FOR SOMETHING TO VENT HIS OWN ANGER ON. HE FOUND IT...
YOU THERE! HOW DARE YOU PRESENT YOURSELF HERE IN THAT DISGUSTING STATE?
I'M SORRY, SIR. WE'RE JUST BACK FROM PATROL. IT'S URGENT...

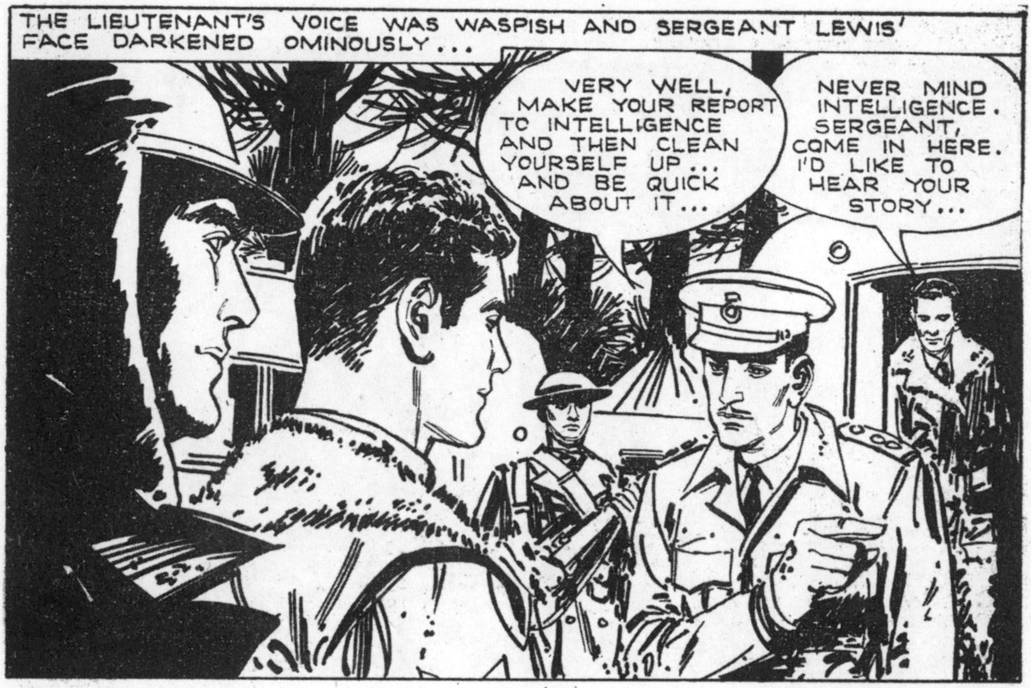
THE LIEUTENANT'S VOICE WAS WASPISH AND SERGEANT LEWIS' FACE DARKENED OMINOUSLY...
VERY WELL, MAKE YOUR REPORT TO INTELLIGENCE AND THEN CLEAN YOURSELF UP... AND BE QUICK ABOUT IT...
NEVER MIND INTELLIGENCE. SERGEANT, COME IN HERE. I'D LIKE TO HEAR YOUR STORY...

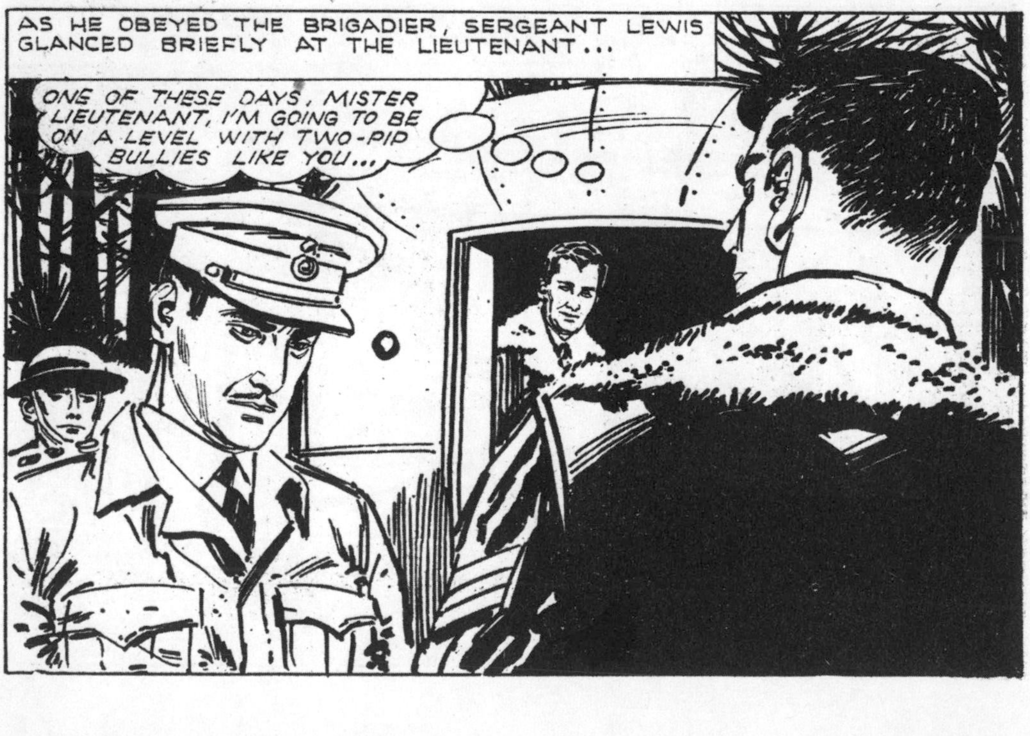
AS HE OBEYED THE BRIGADIER, SERGEANT LEWIS GLANCED BRIEFLY AT THE LIEUTENANT...
ONE OF THESE DAYS, MISTER LIEUTENANT, I'M GOING TO BE ON A LEVEL WITH TWO-PIP BULLIES LIKE YOU...

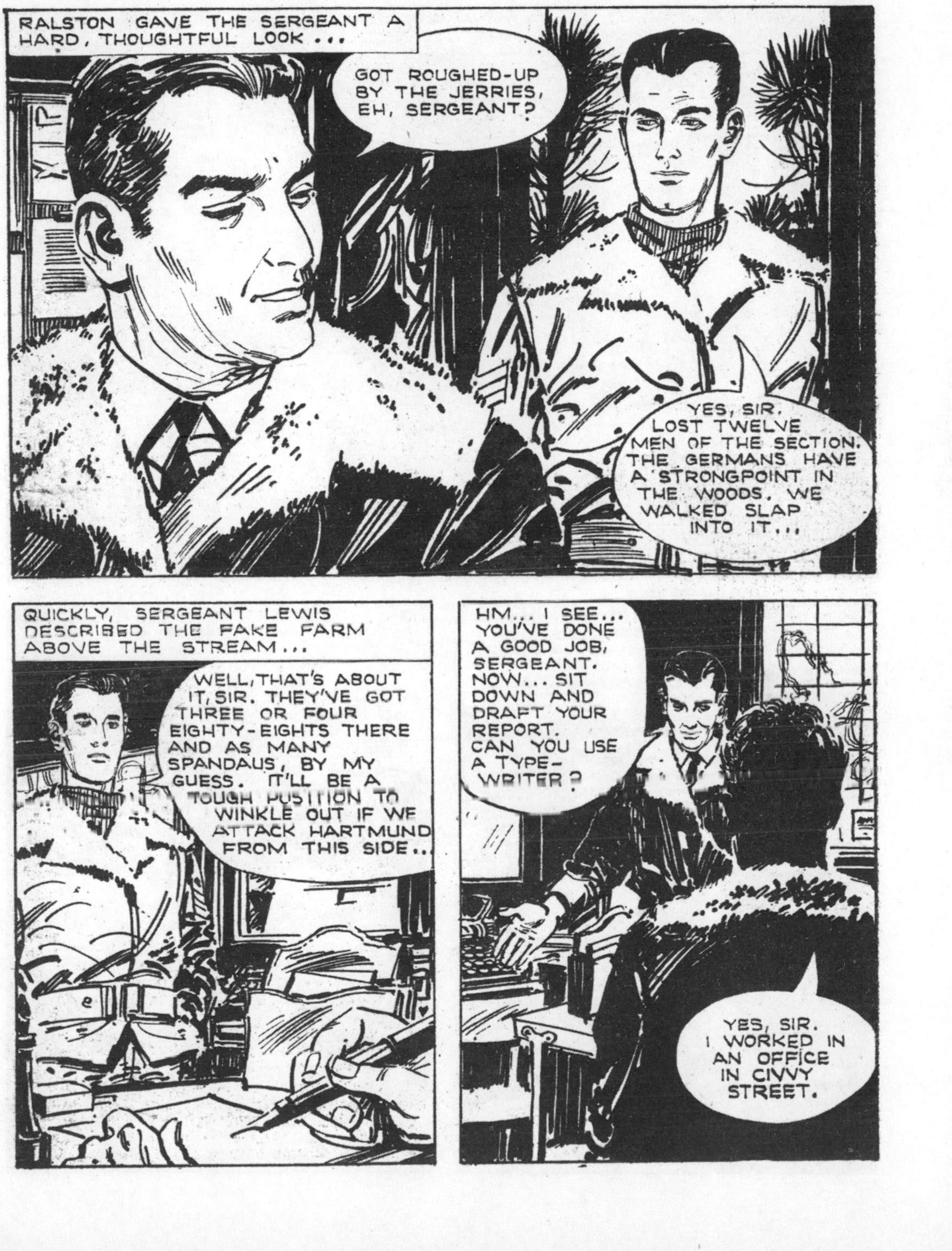
RALSTON GAVE THE SERGEANT A HARD, THOUGHTFUL LOOK ...
GOT ROUGHED-UP BY THE JERRIES, EH, SERGEANT?
YES, SIR. LOST TWELVE MEN OF THE SECTION. THE GERMANS HAVE A STRONGPOINT IN THE WOODS. WE WALKED SLAP INTO IT...
QUICKLY, SERGEANT LEWIS DESCRIBED THE FAKE FARM ABOVE THE STREAM...
WELL, THAT'S ABOUT IT, SIR. THEY'VE GOT THREE OR FOUR EIGHTY-EIGHTS THERE AND AS MANY SPANDAUS, BY MY GUESS. IT'LL BE A TOUGH POSITION TO WINKLE OUT IF WE ATTACK HARTMUND FROM THIS SIDE...
HM... I SEE... YOU'VE DONE A GOOD JOB, SERGEANT. NOW... SIT DOWN AND DRAFT YOUR REPORT. CAN YOU USE A TYPE-WRITER?
YES, SIR. I WORKED IN AN OFFICE IN CIVVY STREET.

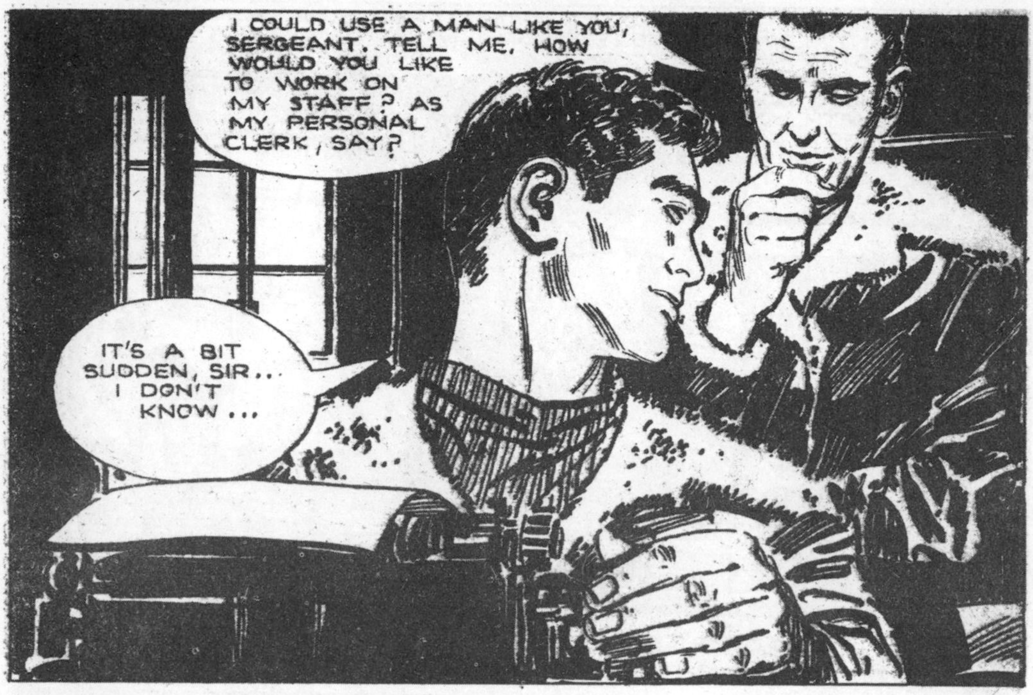
I COULD USE A MAN LIKE YOU, SERGEANT. TELL ME, HOW WOULD YOU LIKE TO WORK ON MY STAFF? AS MY PERSONAL CLERK, SAY?
IT'S A BIT SUDDEN, SIR... I DON'T KNOW...

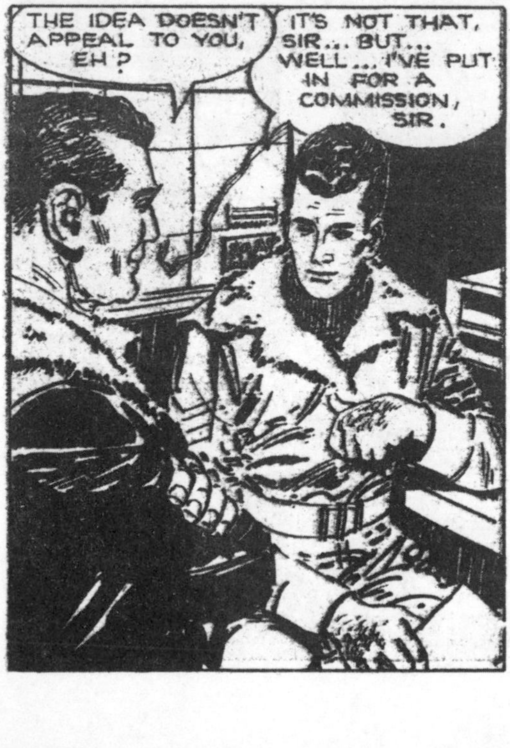
THE IDEA DOESN'T APPEAL TO YOU, EH?
IT'S NOT THAT, SIR... BUT... WELL... I'VE PUT IN FOR A COMMISSION, SIR.

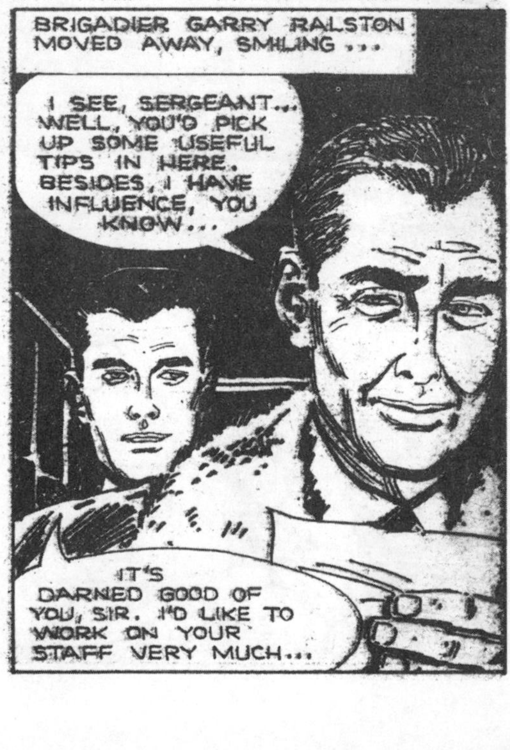
BRIGADIER GARRY RALSTON MOVED AWAY, SMILING...
I SEE, SERGEANT... WELL, YOU'D PICK UP SOME USEFUL TIPS IN HERE. BESIDES, I HAVE INFLUENCE, YOU KNOW...
IT'S DARNED GOOD OF YOU, SIR. I'D LIKE TO WORK ON YOUR STAFF VERY MUCH...

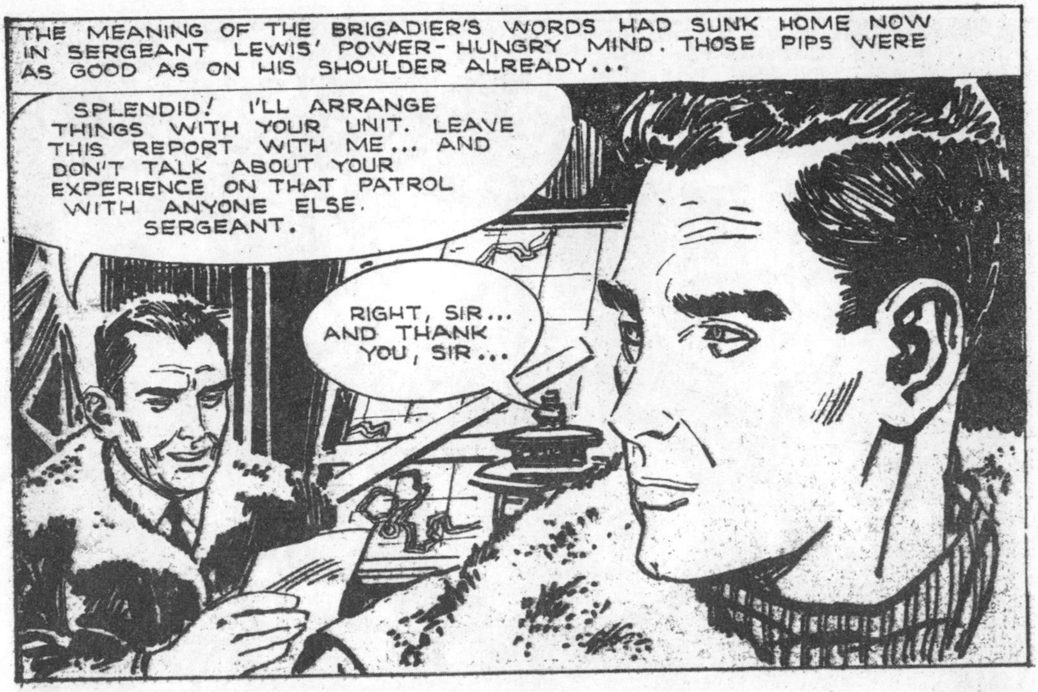
THE MEANING OF THE BRIGADIER'S WORDS HAD SUNK HOME NOW IN SERGEANT LEWIS' POWER-HUNGRY MIND. THOSE PIPS WERE AS GOOD AS ON HIS SHOULDER ALREADY...
SPLENDID! I'LL ARRANGE THINGS WITH YOUR UNIT. LEAVE THIS REPORT WITH ME... AND DON'T TALK ABOUT YOUR EXPERIENCE ON THAT PATROL WITH ANYONE ELSE. SERGEANT.
RIGHT, SIR... AND THANK YOU, SIR...

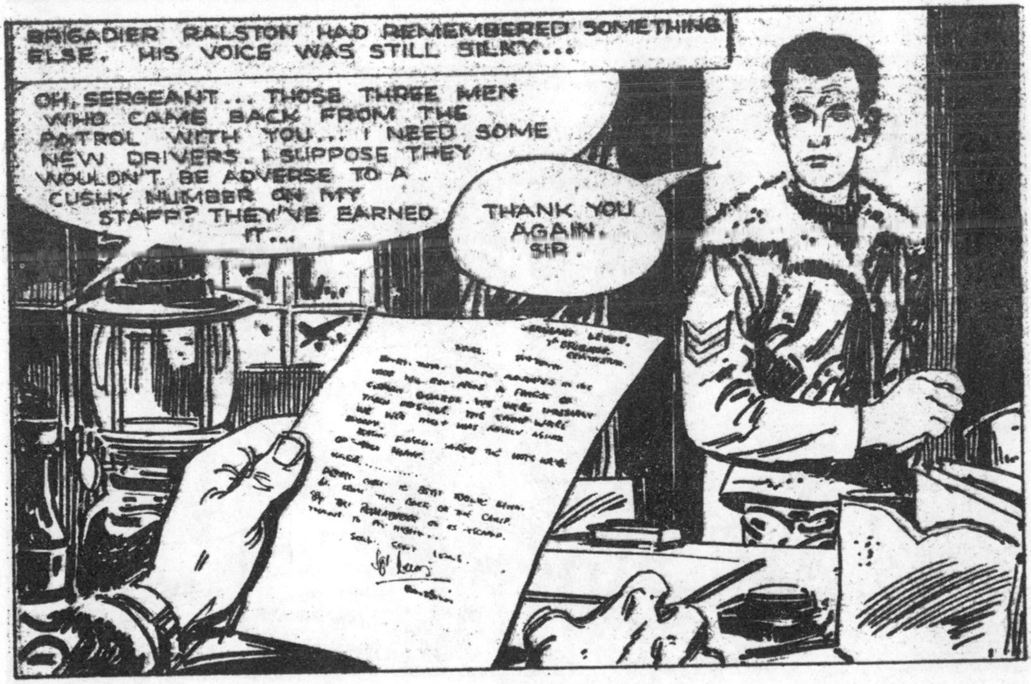
BRIGADIER RALSTON HAD REMEMBERED SOMETHING ELSE. HIS VOICE WAS STILL SILKY...
OH, SERGEANT... THOSE THREE MEN WHO CAME BACK FROM THE PATROL WITH YOU... I NEED SOME NEW DRIVERS. I SUPPOSE THEY WOULDN'T BE ADVERSE TO A CUSHY NUMBER ON MY STAFF? THEY'VE EARNED IT...
THANK YOU AGAIN. SIR.

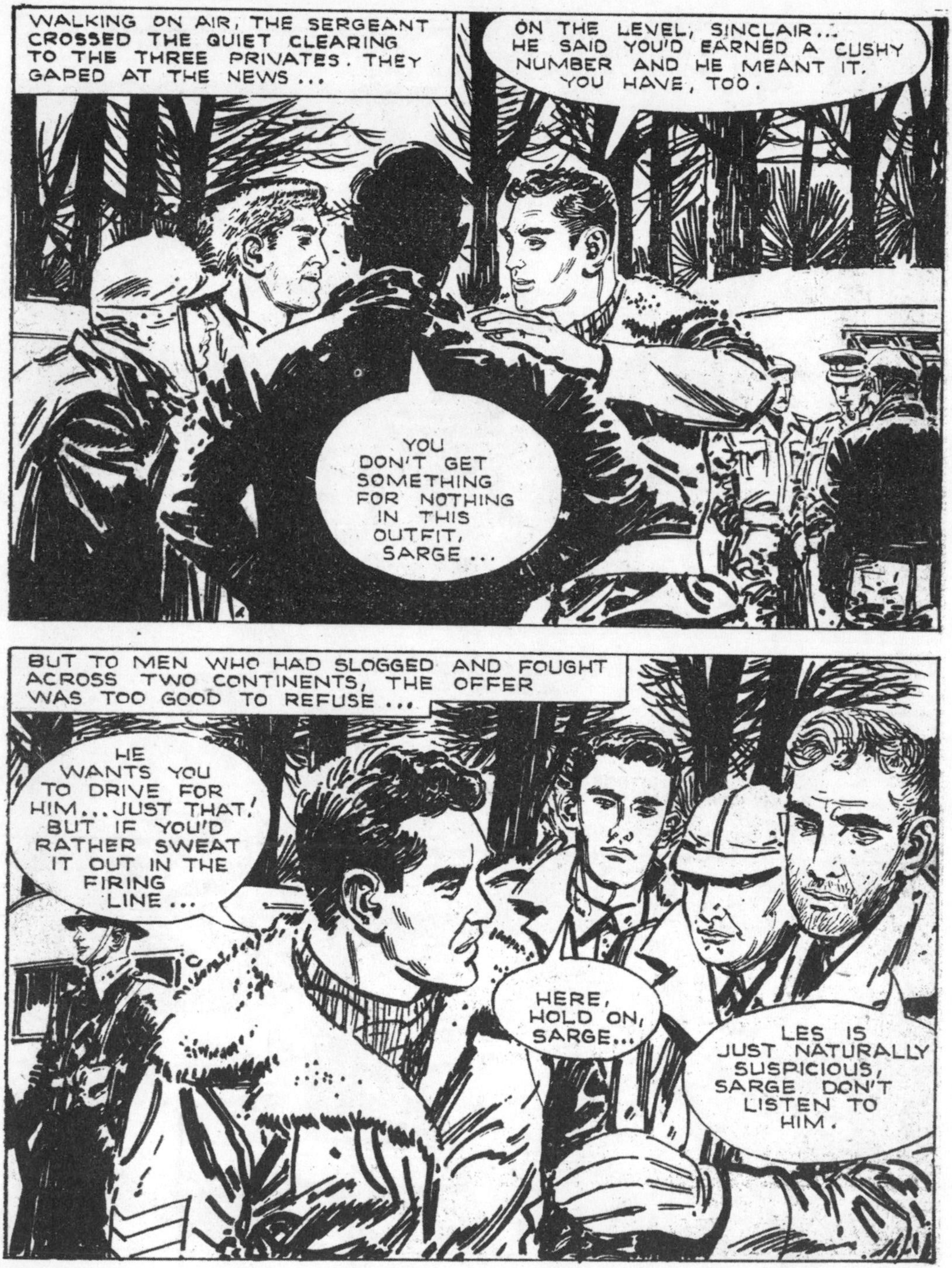
WALKING ON AIR, THE SERGEANT CROSSED THE QUIET CLEARING TO THE THREE PRIVATES. THEY GAPED AT THE NEWS ...
ON THE LEVEL, SINCLAIR... HE SAID YOU'D EARNED A CUSHY NUMBER AND HE MEANT IT. YOU HAVE, TOO.
YOU DON'T GET SOMETHING FOR NOTHING IN THIS OUTFIT, SARGE ...
BUT TO MEN WHO HAD SLOGGED AND FOUGHT ACROSS TWO CONTINENTS, THE OFFER WAS TOO GOOD TO REFUSE ...
HE WANTS YOU TO DRIVE FOR HIM... JUST THAT! BUT IF YOU'D RATHER SWEAT IT OUT IN THE FIRING LINE...
HERE, HOLD ON, SARGE...
LES IS JUST NATURALLY SUSPICIOUS, SARGE. DON'T LISTEN TO HIM.

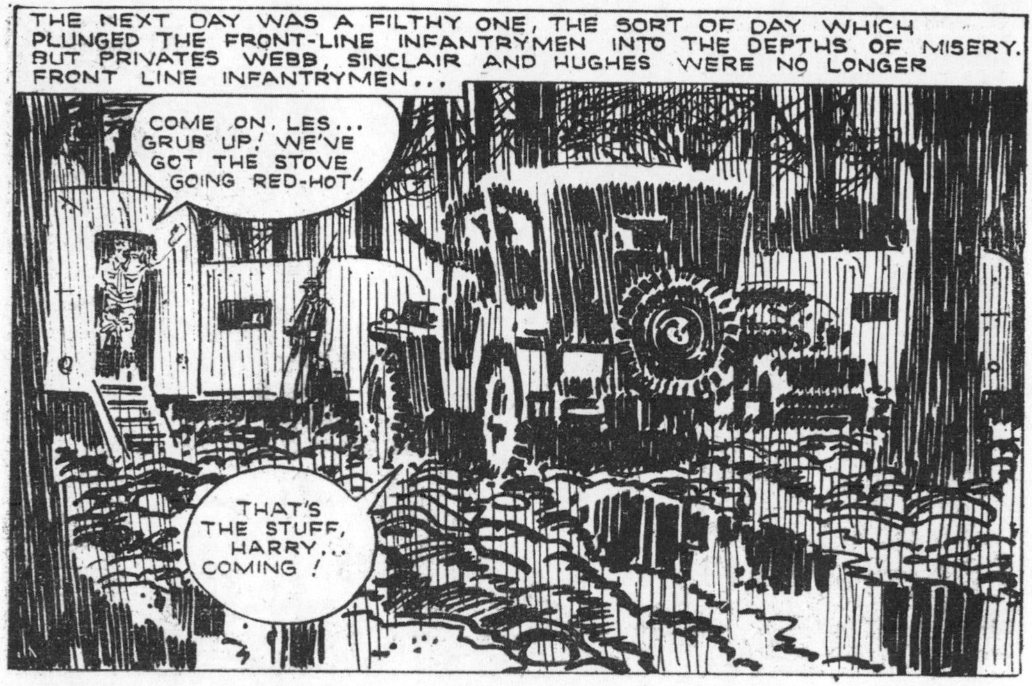
THE NEXT DAY WAS A FILTHY ONE, THE SORT OF DAY WHICH PLUNGED THE FRONT-LINE INFANTRYMEN INTO THE DEPTHS OF MISERY. BUT PRIVATES WEBB, SINCLAIR AND HUGHES WERE NO LONGER FRONT LINE INFANTRYMEN...
COME ON, LES... GRUB UP! WE'VE GOT THE STOVE GOING RED-HOT!
THAT'S THE STUFF, HARRY... COMING!

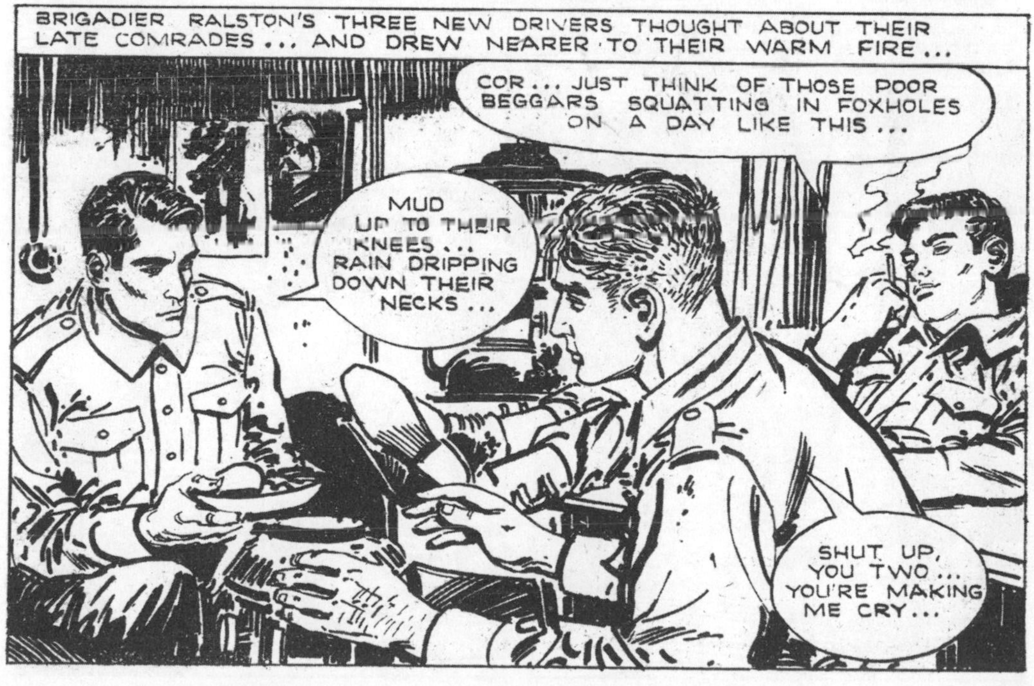
BRIGADIER RALSTON'S THREE NEW DRIVERS THOUGHT ABOUT THEIR LATE COMRADES... AND DREW NEARER TO THEIR WARM FIRE...
COR... JUST THINK OF THOSE POOR BEGGARS SQUATTING IN FOXHOLES ON A DAY LIKE THIS...
MUD UP TO THEIR KNEES... RAIN DRIPPING DOWN THEIR NECKS...
SHUT UP, YOU TWO... YOU'RE MAKING ME CRY...

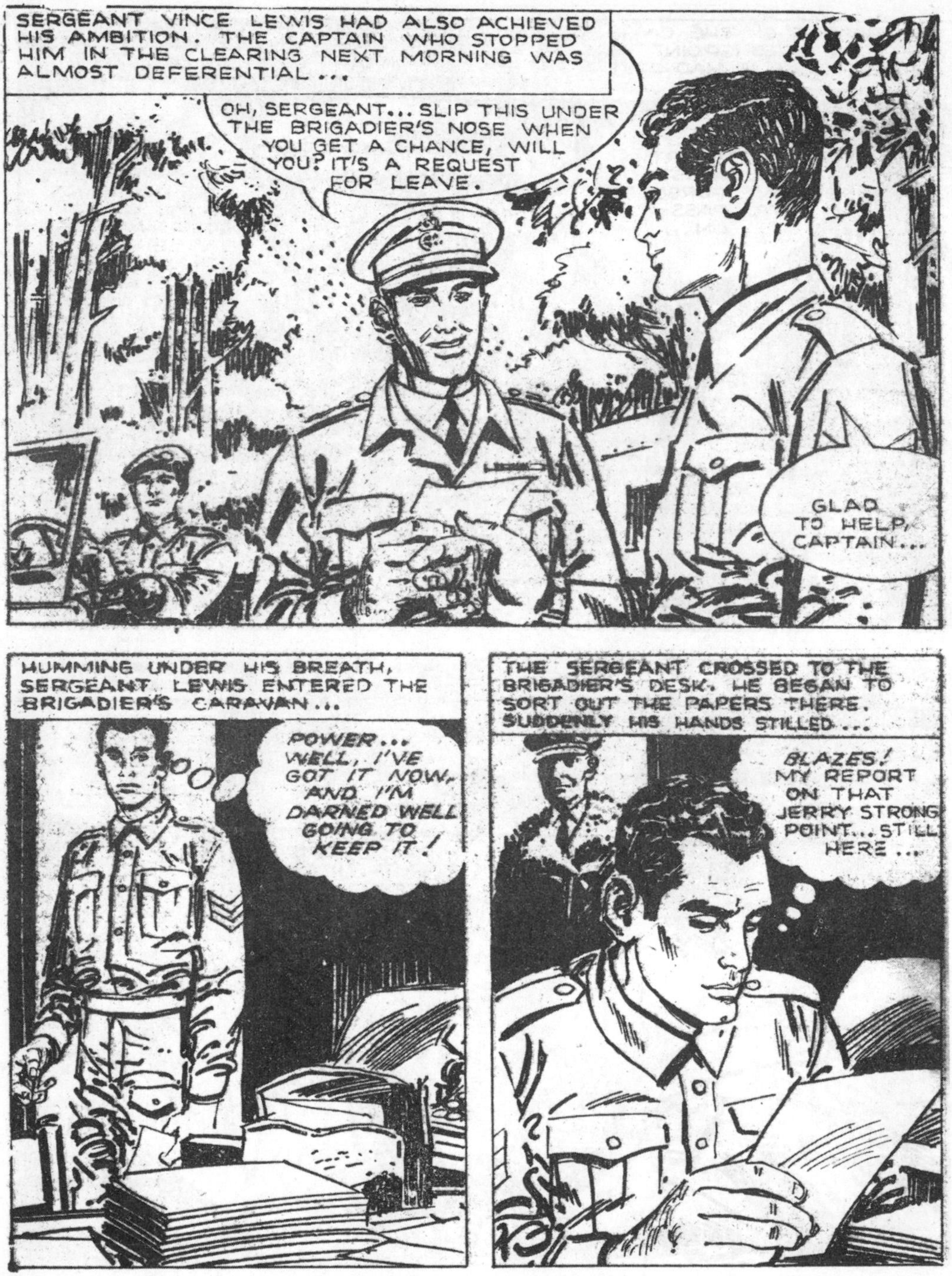
SERGEANT VINCE LEWIS HAD ALSO ACHIEVED HIS AMBITION. THE CAPTAIN WHO STOPPED HIM IN THE CLEARING NEXT MORNING WAS ALMOST DEFERENTIAL ...
OH, SERGEANT... SLIP THIS UNDER THE BRIGADIER'S NOSE WHEN YOU GET A CHANCE, WILL YOU? IT'S A REQUEST FOR LEAVE.
GLAD TO HELP, CAPTAIN ...
HUMMING UNDER HIS BREATH, SERGEANT LEWIS ENTERED THE BRIGADIER'S CARAVAN ...
POWER ... WELL, I'VE GOT IT NOW, AND I'M DARNED WELL GOING TO KEEP IT!
THE SERGEANT CROSSED TO THE BRIGADIER'S DESK. HE BEGAN TO SORT OUT THE PAPERS THERE. SUDDENLY HIS HANDS STILLED ...
BLAZES! MY REPORT ON THAT JERRY STRONG POINT... STILL HERE ...

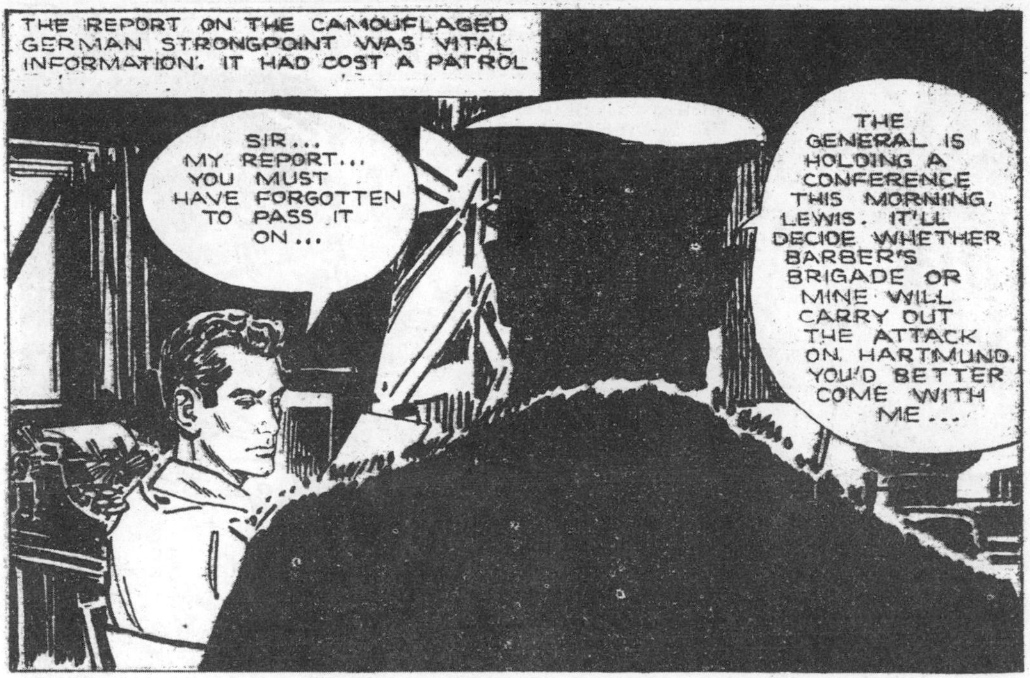
THE REPORT ON THE CAMOUFLAGED GERMAN STRONGPOINT WAS VITAL INFORMATION. IT HAD COST A PATROL
SIR... MY REPORT... YOU MUST HAVE FORGOTTEN TO PASS IT ON...
THE GENERAL IS HOLDING A CONFERENCE THIS MORNING, LEWIS. IT'LL DECIDE WHETHER BARBER'S BRIGADE OR MINE WILL CARRY OUT THE ATTACK ON HARTMUND. YOU'D BETTER COME WITH ME...

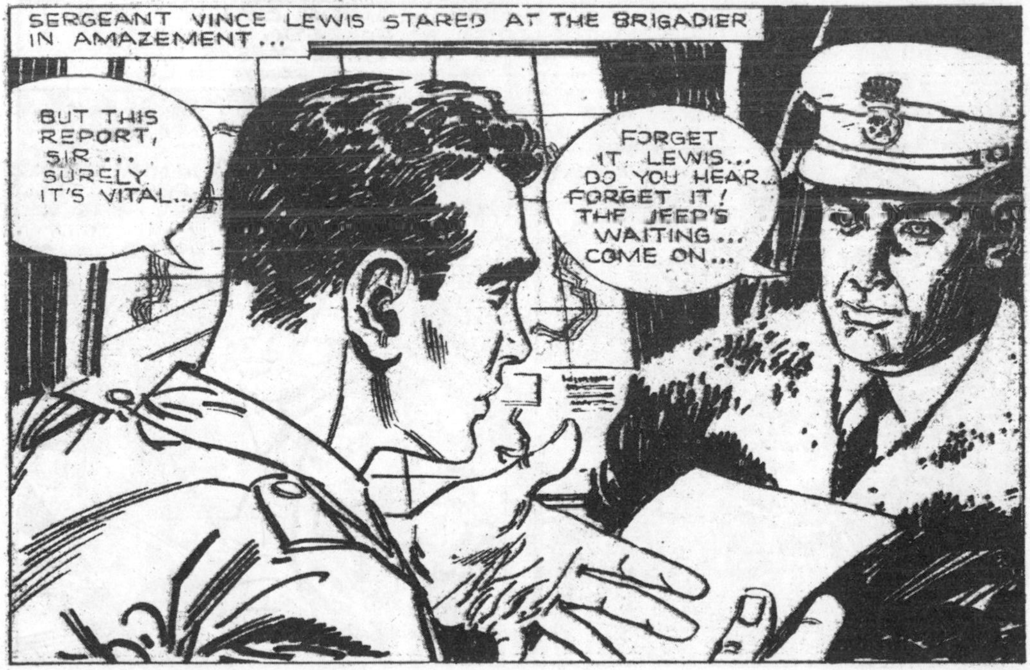
SERGEANT VINCE LEWIS STARED AT THE BRIGADIER IN AMAZEMENT...
BUT THIS REPORT, SIR... SURELY IT'S VITAL...
FORGET IT LEWIS... DO YOU HEAR... FORGET IT! THE JEEP'S WAITING... COME ON...

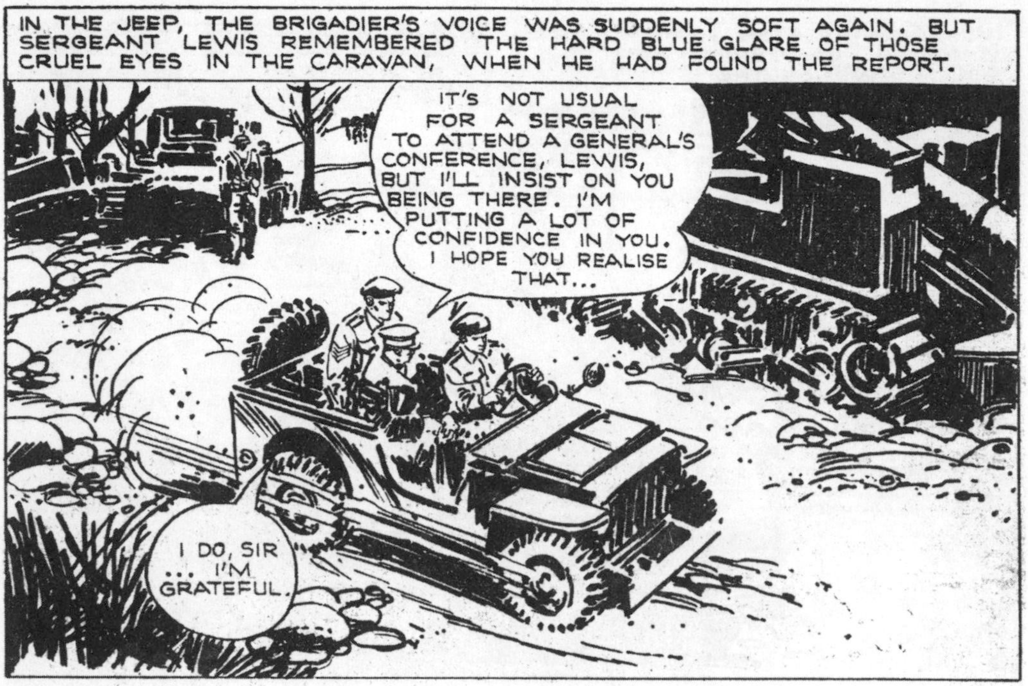
IN THE JEEP, THE BRIGADIER'S VOICE WAS SUDDENLY SOFT AGAIN. BUT SERGEANT LEWIS REMEMBERED THE HARD BLUE GLARE OF THOSE CRUEL EYES IN THE CARAVAN, WHEN HE HAD FOUND THE REPORT.
IT'S NOT USUAL FOR A SERGEANT TO ATTEND A GENERAL'S CONFERENCE, LEWIS, BUT I'LL INSIST ON YOU BEING THERE. I'M PUTTING A LOT OF CONFIDENCE IN YOU. I HOPE YOU REALISE THAT...
I DO, SIR ... I'M GRATEFUL.

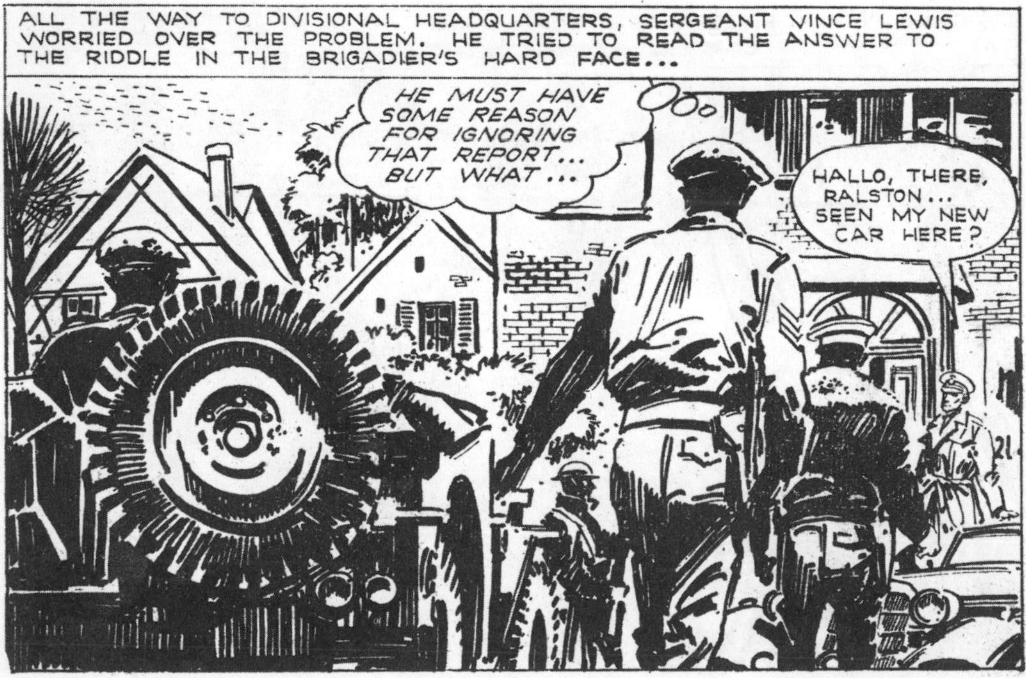
ALL THE WAY TO DIVISIONAL HEADQUARTERS, SERGEANT VINCE LEWIS WORRIED OVER THE PROBLEM. HE TRIED TO READ THE ANSWER TO THE RIDDLE IN THE BRIGADIER'S HARD FACE...
HE MUST HAVE SOME REASON FOR IGNORING THAT REPORT... BUT WHAT...
HALLO, THERE, RALSTON... SEEN MY NEW CAR HERE?

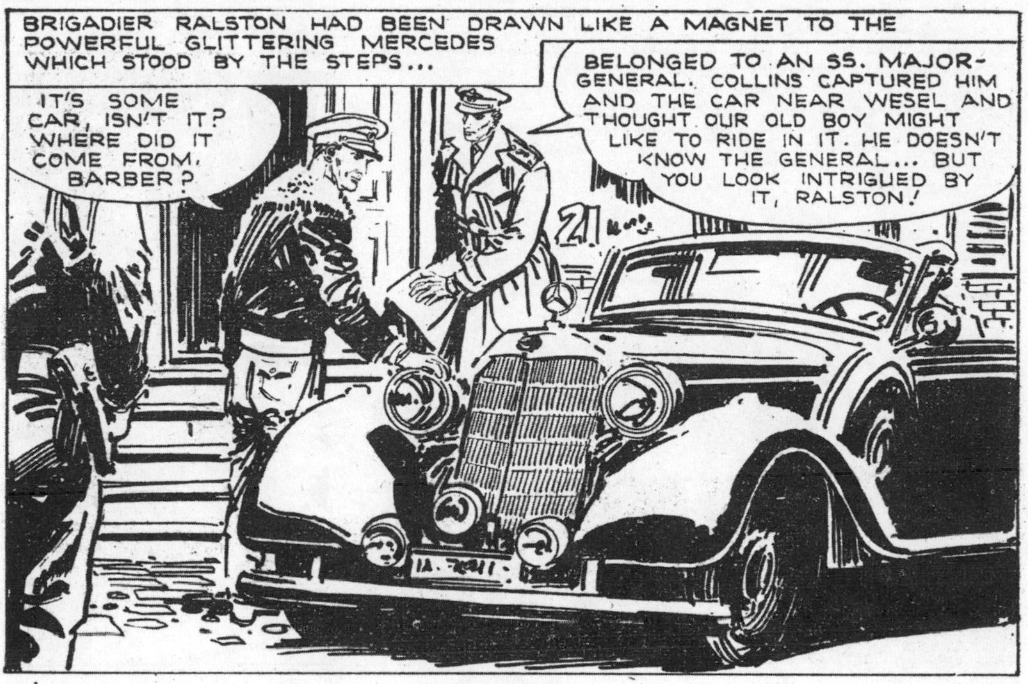
BRIGADIER RALSTON HAD BEEN DRAWN LIKE A MAGNET TO THE POWERFUL GLITTERING MERCEDES WHICH STOOD BY THE STEPS...
IT'S SOME CAR, ISN'T IT? WHERE DID IT COME FROM, BARBER?
BELONGED TO AN SS. MAJOR-GENERAL. COLLINS CAPTURED HIM AND THE CAR NEAR WESEL AND THOUGHT OUR OLD BOY MIGHT LIKE TO RIDE IN IT. HE DOESN'T KNOW THE GENERAL... BUT YOU LOOK INTRIGUED BY IT, RALSTON!

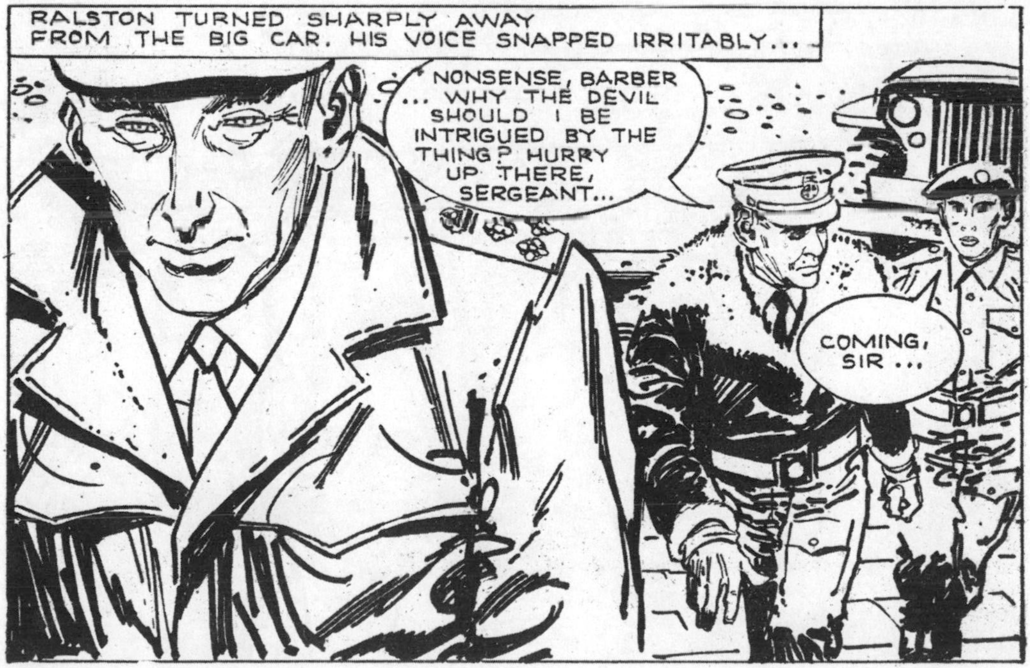
RALSTON TURNED SHARPLY AWAY FROM THE BIG CAR. HIS VOICE SNAPPED IRRITABLY...
NONSENSE, BARBER ... WHY THE DEVIL SHOULD I BE INTRIGUED BY THE THING? HURRY UP THERE, SERGEANT...
COMING, SIR ...

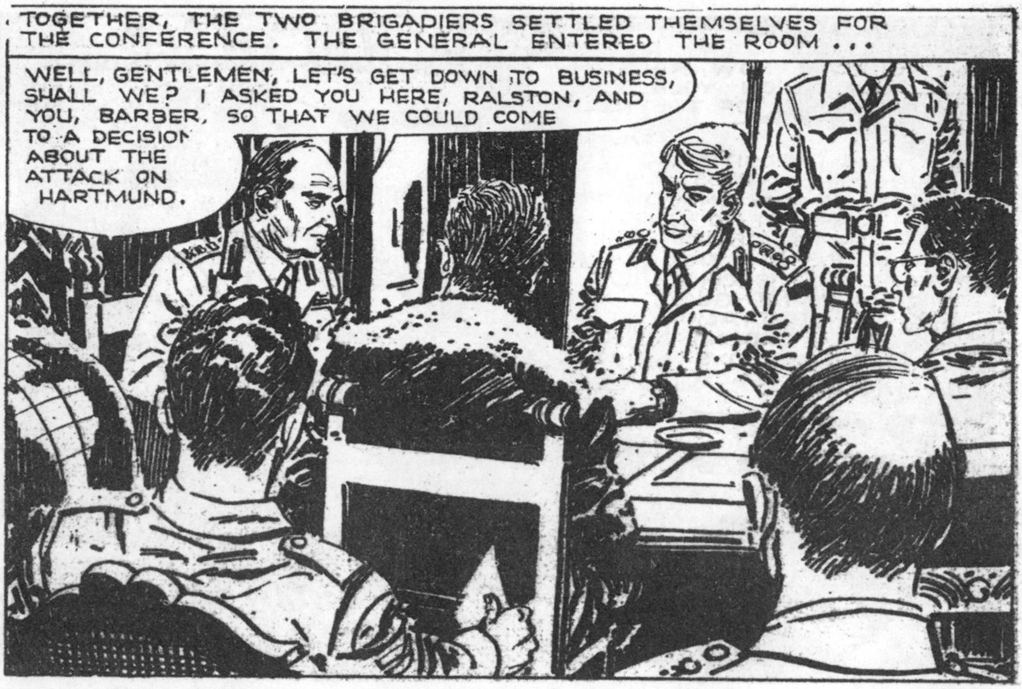
TOGETHER, THE TWO BRIGADIERS SETTLED THEMSELVES FOR THE CONFERENCE. THE GENERAL ENTERED THE ROOM . . .
WELL, GENTLEMEN, LET'S GET DOWN TO BUSINESS, SHALL WE? I ASKED YOU HERE, RALSTON, AND YOU, BARBER, SO THAT WE COULD COME TO A DECISION ABOUT THE ATTACK ON HARTMUND.

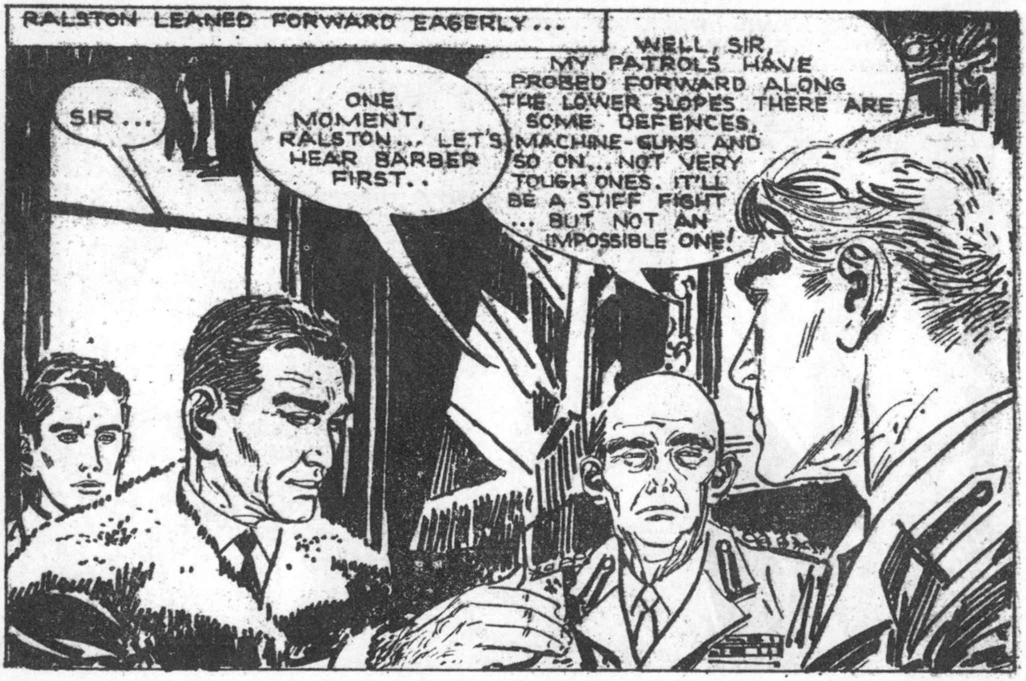
RALSTON LEANED FORWARD EAGERLY . . .
SIR . . .
ONE MOMENT, RALSTON . . . LET'S HEAR BARBER FIRST. .
WELL, SIR, MY PATROLS HAVE PROBED FORWARD ALONG THE LOWER SLOPES. THERE ARE SOME DEFENCES, MACHINE-GUNS AND SO ON . . . NOT VERY TOUGH ONES. IT'LL BE A STIFF FIGHT . . . BUT NOT AN IMPOSSIBLE ONE!

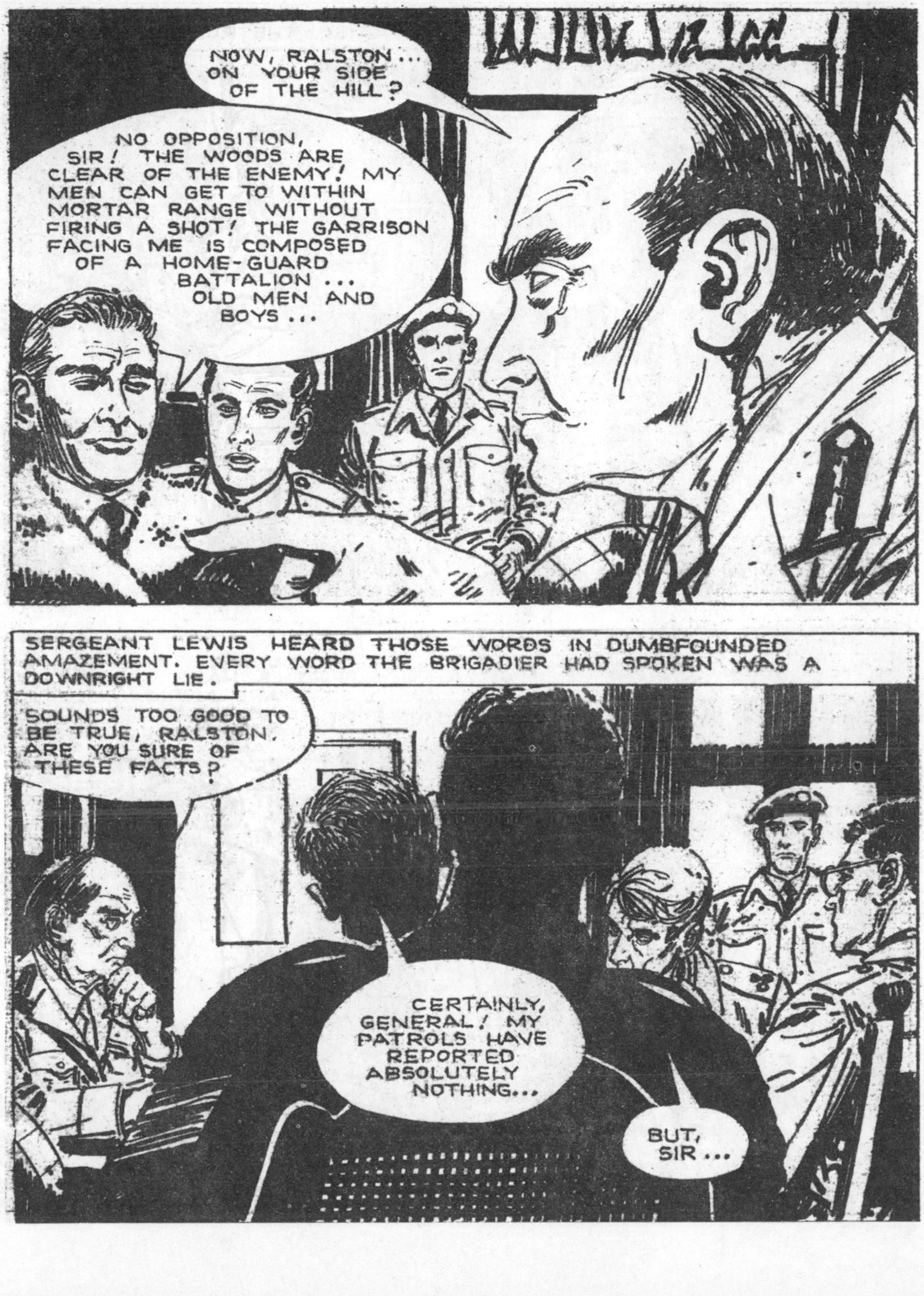
NOW, RALSTON... ON YOUR SIDE OF THE HILL?
NO OPPOSITION, SIR! THE WOODS ARE CLEAR OF THE ENEMY! MY MEN CAN GET TO WITHIN MORTAR RANGE WITHOUT FIRING A SHOT! THE GARRISON FACING ME IS COMPOSED OF A HOME-GUARD BATTALION ... OLD MEN AND BOYS ...
SERGEANT LEWIS HEARD THOSE WORDS IN DUMBFOUNDED AMAZEMENT. EVERY WORD THE BRIGADIER HAD SPOKEN WAS A DOWNRIGHT LIE.
SOUNDS TOO GOOD TO BE TRUE, RALSTON. ARE YOU SURE OF THESE FACTS?
CERTAINLY, GENERAL! MY PATROLS HAVE REPORTED ABSOLUTELY NOTHING...
BUT, SIR ...

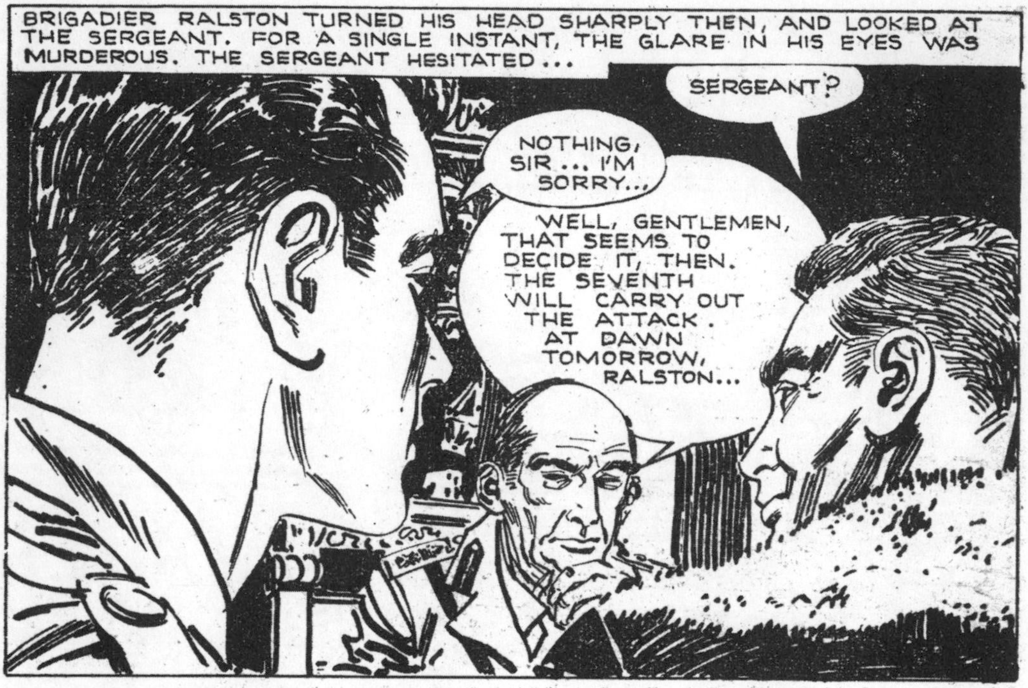
BRIGADIER RALSTON TURNED HIS HEAD SHARPLY THEN, AND LOOKED AT THE SERGEANT. FOR A SINGLE INSTANT, THE GLARE IN HIS EYES WAS MURDEROUS. THE SERGEANT HESITATED...
SERGEANT?
NOTHING, SIR ... I'M SORRY...
WELL, GENTLEMEN, THAT SEEMS TO DECIDE IT, THEN. THE SEVENTH WILL CARRY OUT THE ATTACK. AT DAWN TOMORROW, RALSTON...

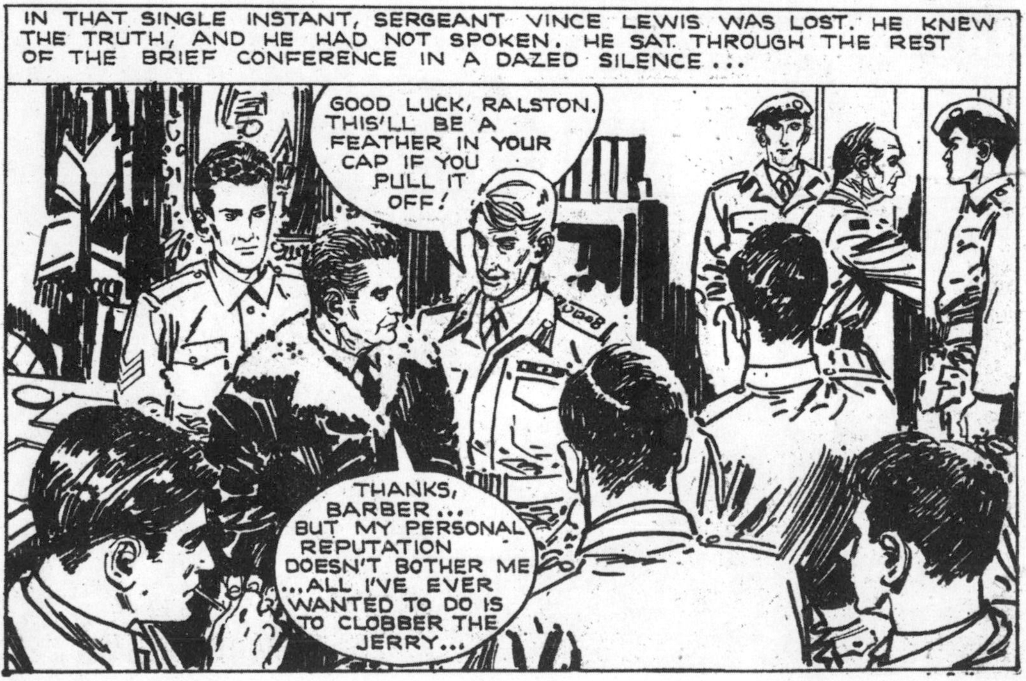
IN THAT SINGLE INSTANT, SERGEANT VINCE LEWIS WAS LOST. HE KNEW THE TRUTH, AND HE HAD NOT SPOKEN. HE SAT THROUGH THE REST OF THE BRIEF CONFERENCE IN A DAZED SILENCE...
GOOD LUCK, RALSTON. THIS'LL BE A FEATHER IN YOUR CAP IF YOU PULL IT OFF!
THANKS, BARBER... BUT MY PERSONAL REPUTATION DOESN'T BOTHER ME ...ALL I'VE EVER WANTED TO DO IS TO CLOBBER THE JERRY...

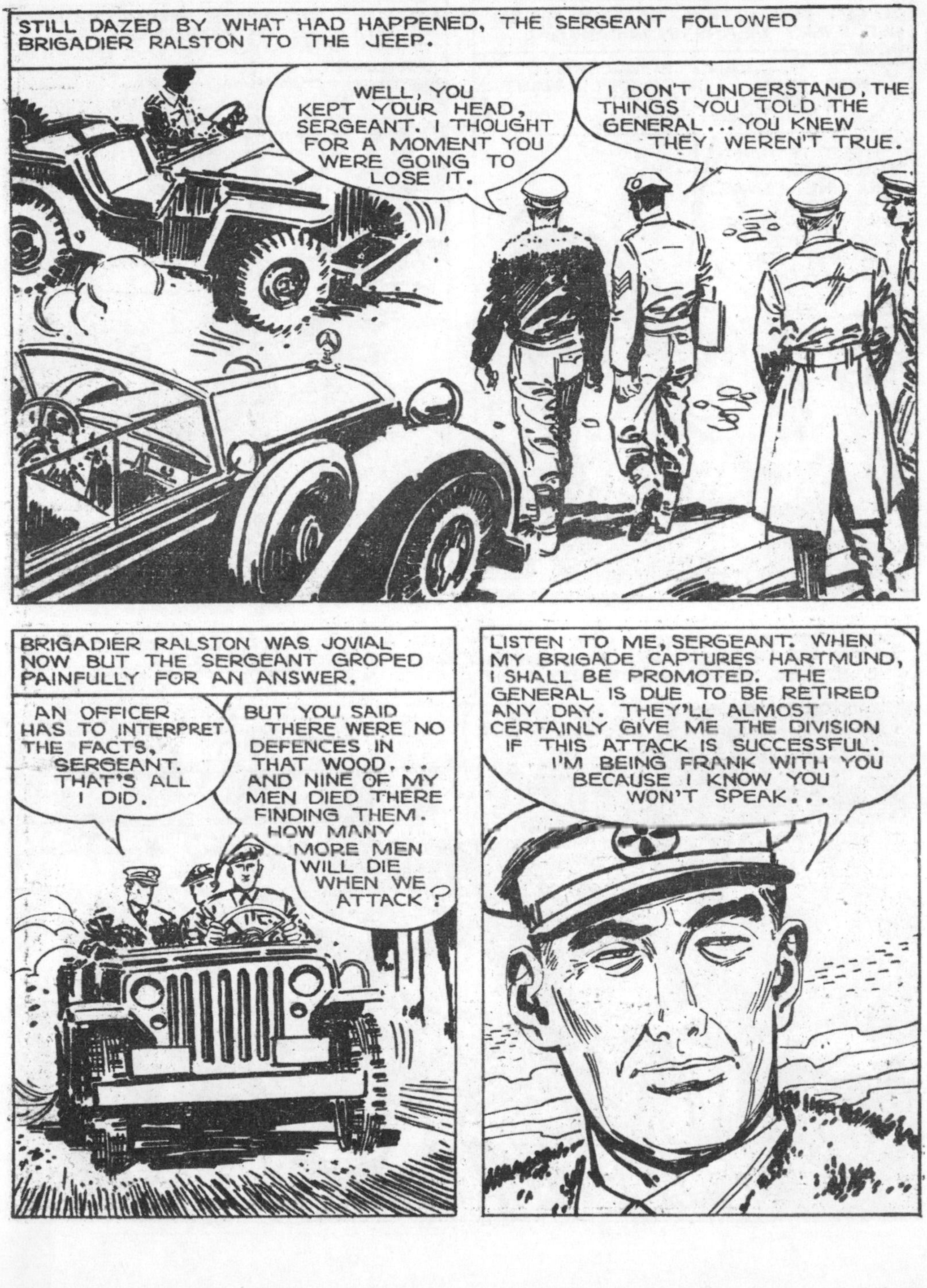
STILL DAZED BY WHAT HAD HAPPENED, THE SERGEANT FOLLOWED BRIGADIER RALSTON TO THE JEEP.
WELL, YOU KEPT YOUR HEAD, SERGEANT. I THOUGHT FOR A MOMENT YOU WERE GOING TO LOSE IT.
I DON'T UNDERSTAND, THE THINGS YOU TOLD THE GENERAL... YOU KNEW THEY WEREN'T TRUE.
BRIGADIER RALSTON WAS JOVIAL NOW BUT THE SERGEANT GROPED PAINFULLY FOR AN ANSWER.
AN OFFICER HAS TO INTERPRET THE FACTS, SERGEANT. THAT'S ALL I DID.
BUT YOU SAID THERE WERE NO DEFENCES IN THAT WOOD... AND NINE OF MY MEN DIED THERE FINDING THEM. HOW MANY MORE MEN WILL DIE WHEN WE ATTACK?
LISTEN TO ME, SERGEANT. WHEN MY BRIGADE CAPTURES HARTMUND, I SHALL BE PROMOTED. THE GENERAL IS DUE TO BE RETIRED ANY DAY. THEY'LL ALMOST CERTAINLY GIVE ME THE DIVISION IF THIS ATTACK IS SUCCESSFUL. I'M BEING FRANK WITH YOU BECAUSE I KNOW YOU WON'T SPEAK...

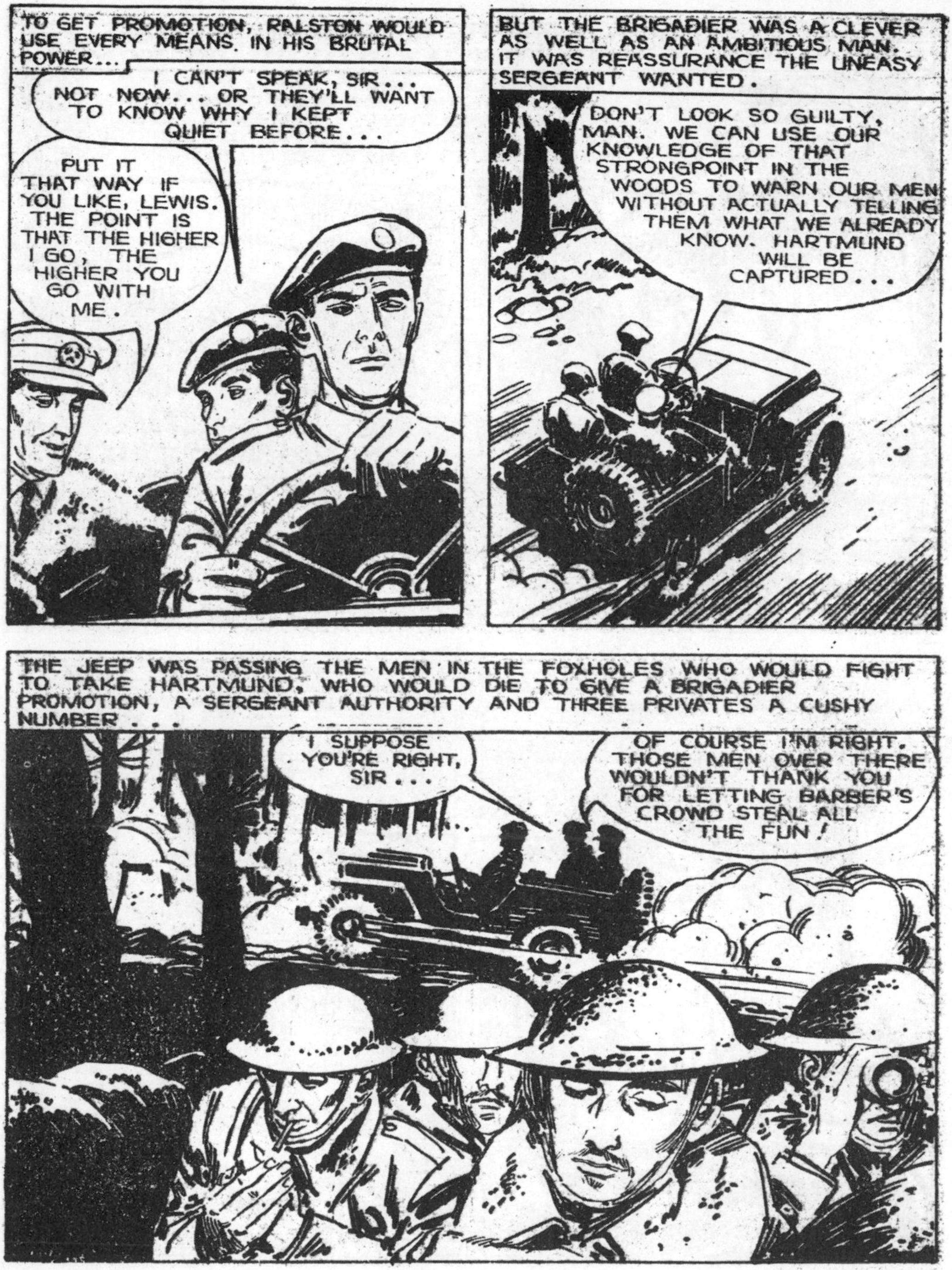
TO GET PROMOTION, RALSTON WOULD USE EVERY MEANS IN HIS BRUTAL POWER...
I CAN'T SPEAK, SIR... NOT NOW... OR THEY'LL WANT TO KNOW WHY I KEPT QUIET BEFORE...
PUT IT THAT WAY IF YOU LIKE, LEWIS. THE POINT IS THAT THE HIGHER I GO, THE HIGHER YOU GO WITH ME.
BUT THE BRIGADIER WAS A CLEVER AS WELL AS AN AMBITIOUS MAN. IT WAS REASSURANCE THE UNEASY SERGEANT WANTED.
DON'T LOOK SO GUILTY, MAN. WE CAN USE OUR KNOWLEDGE OF THAT STRONGPOINT IN THE WOODS TO WARN OUR MEN WITHOUT ACTUALLY TELLING THEM WHAT WE ALREADY KNOW. HARTMUND WILL BE CAPTURED...
THE JEEP WAS PASSING THE MEN IN THE FOXHOLES WHO WOULD FIGHT TO TAKE HARTMUND, WHO WOULD DIE TO GIVE A BRIGADIER PROMOTION, A SERGEANT AUTHORITY AND THREE PRIVATES A CUSHY NUMBER...
I SUPPOSE YOU'RE RIGHT, SIR...
OF COURSE I'M RIGHT. THOSE MEN OVER THERE WOULDN'T THANK YOU FOR LETTING BARBER'S CROWD STEAL ALL THE FUN!

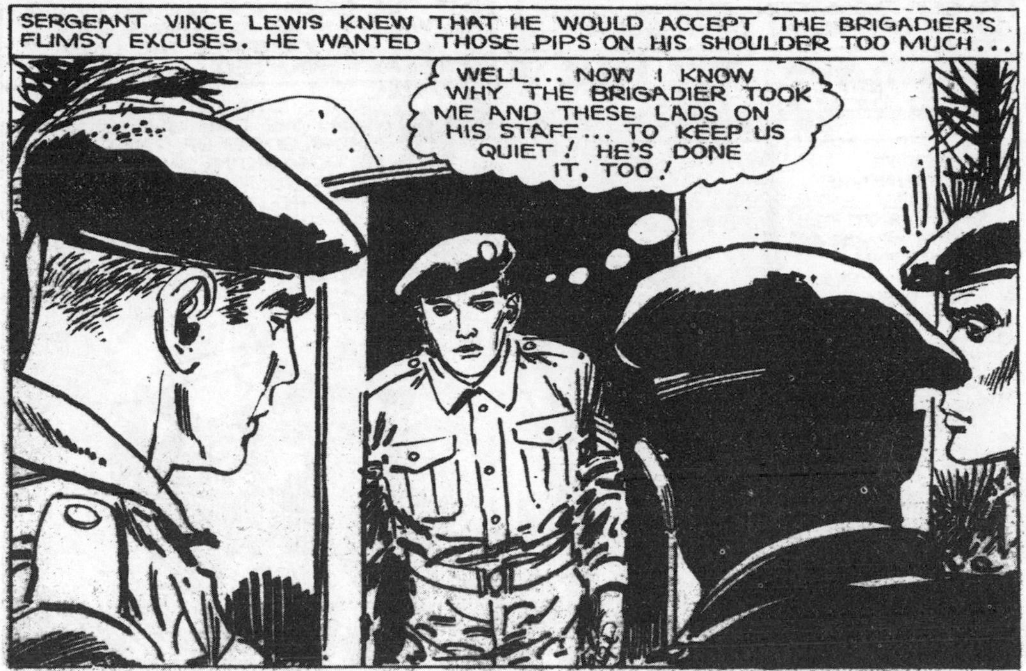
SERGEANT VINCE LEWIS KNEW THAT HE WOULD ACCEPT THE BRIGADIER'S FLIMSY EXCUSES. HE WANTED THOSE PIPS ON HIS SHOULDER TOO MUCH...
WELL... NOW I KNOW WHY THE BRIGADIER TOOK ME AND THESE LADS ON HIS STAFF... TO KEEP US QUIET! HE'S DONE IT, TOO!

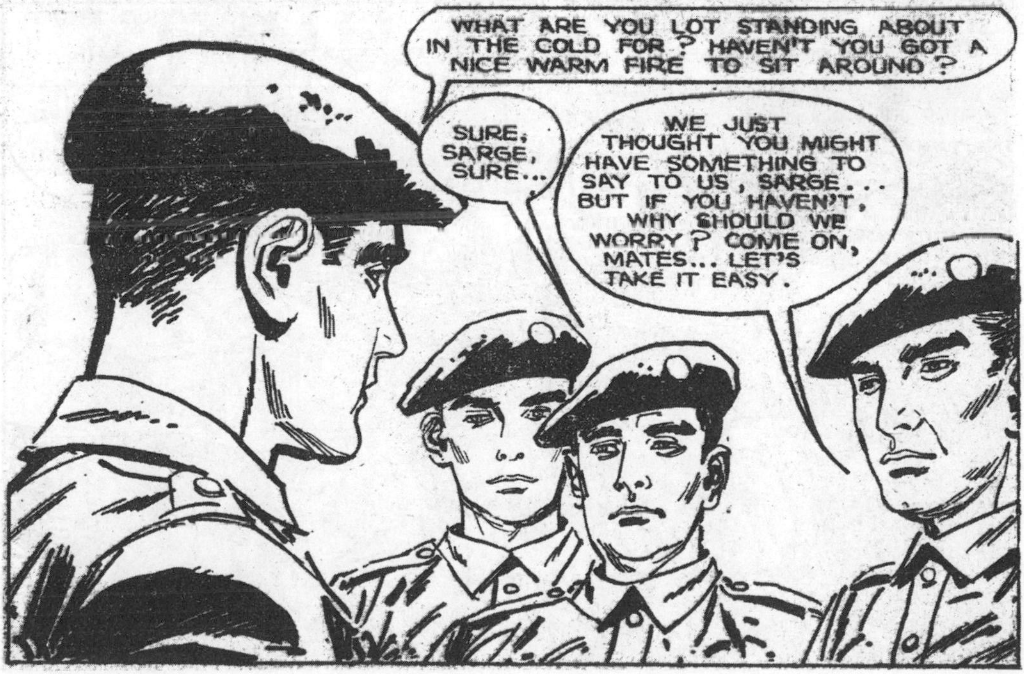
WHAT ARE YOU LOT STANDING ABOUT IN THE COLD FOR? HAVEN'T YOU GOT A NICE WARM FIRE TO SIT AROUND?
SURE, SARGE, SURE...
WE JUST THOUGHT YOU MIGHT HAVE SOMETHING TO SAY TO US, SARGE... BUT IF YOU HAVEN'T, WHY SHOULD WE WORRY? COME ON, MATES... LET'S TAKE IT EASY.

Chapter 3. The Price of Silence

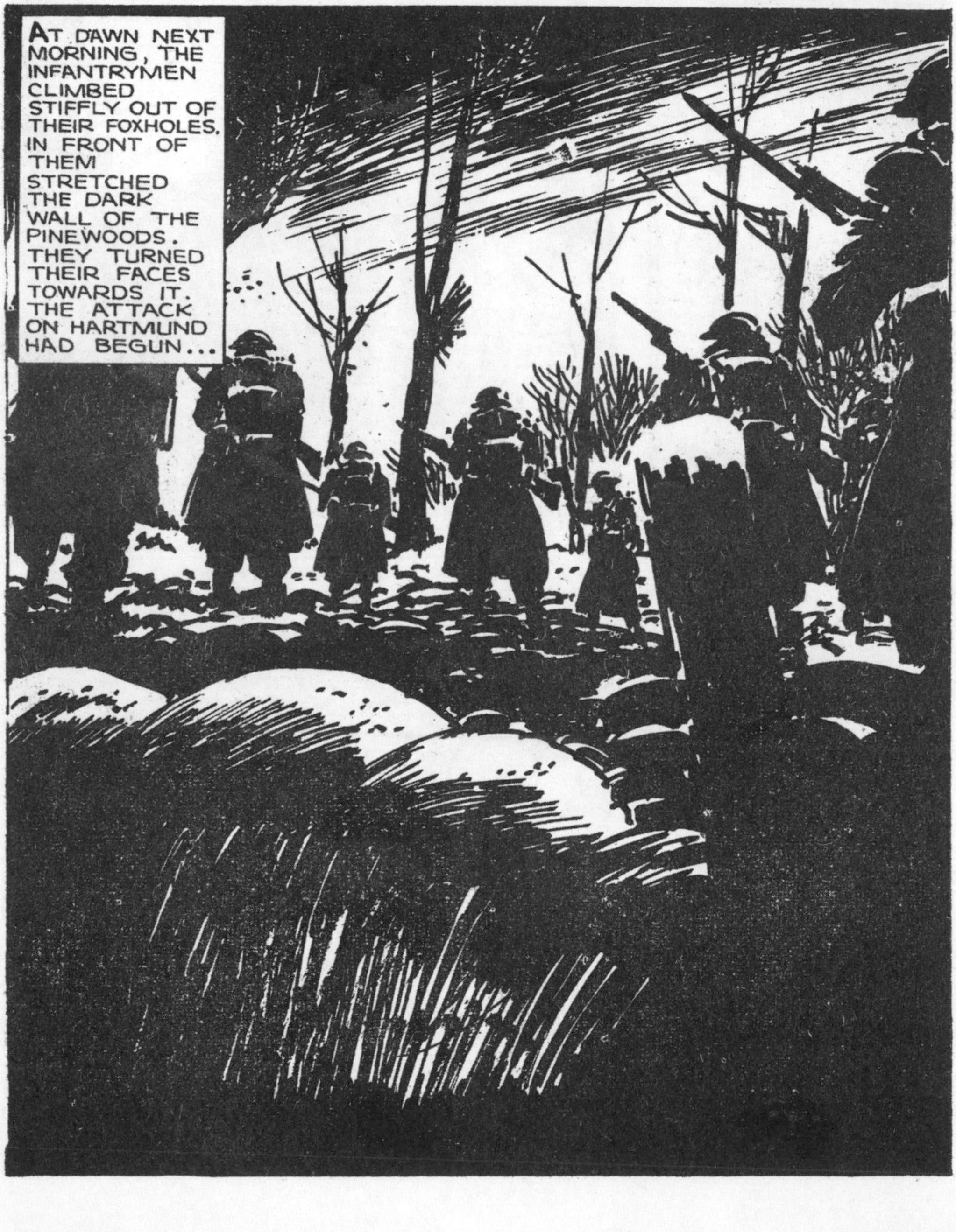
AT DAWN NEXT MORNING, THE INFANTRYMEN CLIMBED STIFFLY OUT OF THEIR FOXHOLES. IN FRONT OF THEM STRETCHED THE DARK WALL OF THE PINEWOODS. THEY TURNED THEIR FACES TOWARDS IT. THE ATTACK ON HARTMUND HAD BEGUN...

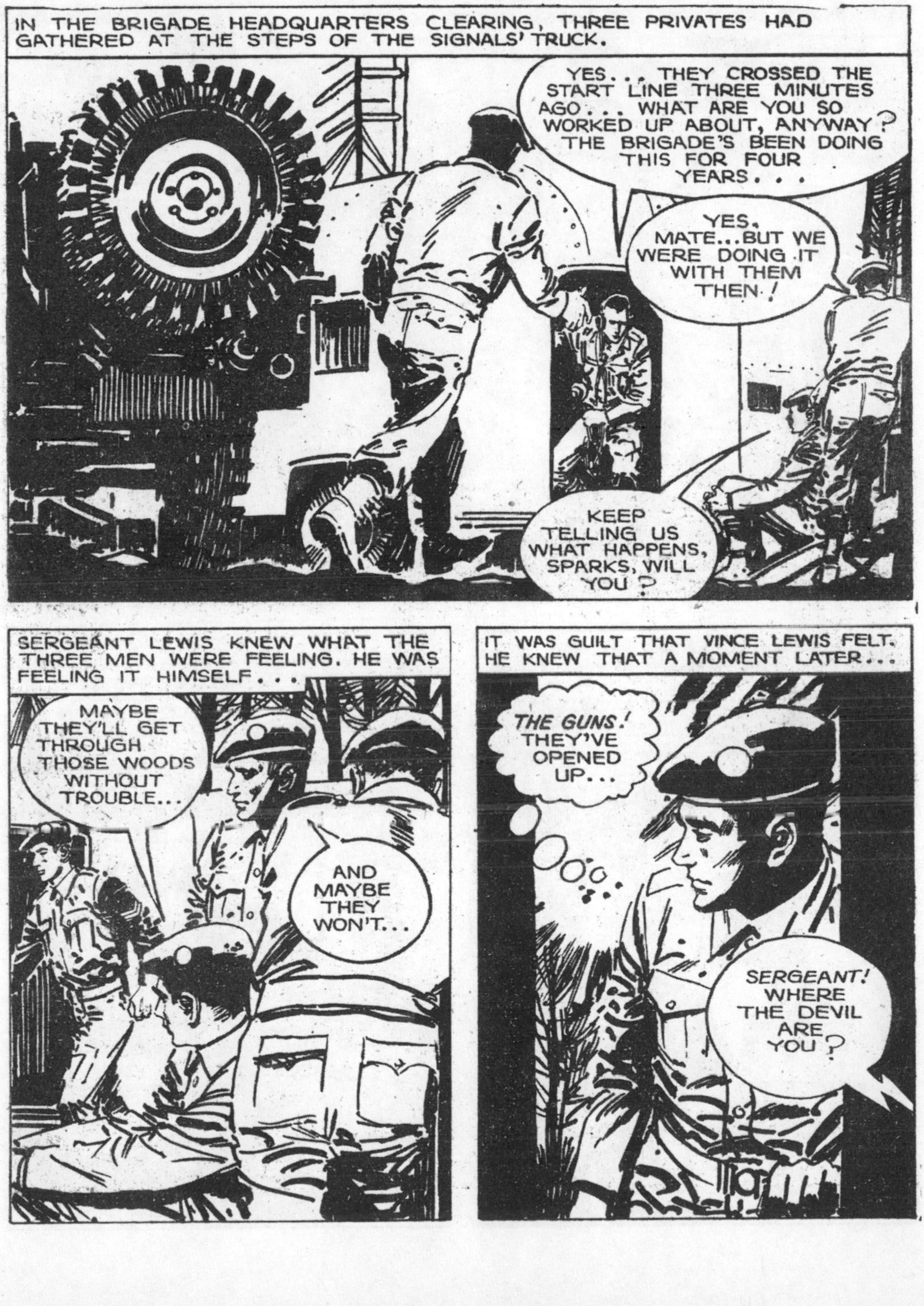
IN THE BRIGADE HEADQUARTERS CLEARING, THREE PRIVATES HAD GATHERED AT THE STEPS OF THE SIGNALS' TRUCK.
YES.. THEY CROSSED THE START LINE THREE MINUTES AGO.. WHAT ARE YOU SO WORKED UP ABOUT, ANYWAY? THE BRIGADE'S BEEN DOING THIS FOR FOUR YEARS...
YES, MATE...BUT WE WERE DOING IT WITH THEM THEN!
KEEP TELLING US WHAT HAPPENS, SPARKS, WILL YOU?
SERGEANT LEWIS KNEW WHAT THE THREE MEN WERE FEELING. HE WAS FEELING IT HIMSELF...
MAYBE THEY'LL GET THROUGH THOSE WOODS WITHOUT TROUBLE...
AND MAYBE THEY WON'T...
IT WAS GUILT THAT VINCE LEWIS FELT. HE KNEW THAT A MOMENT LATER...
THE GUNS! THEY'VE OPENED UP...
SERGEANT! WHERE THE DEVIL ARE YOU?

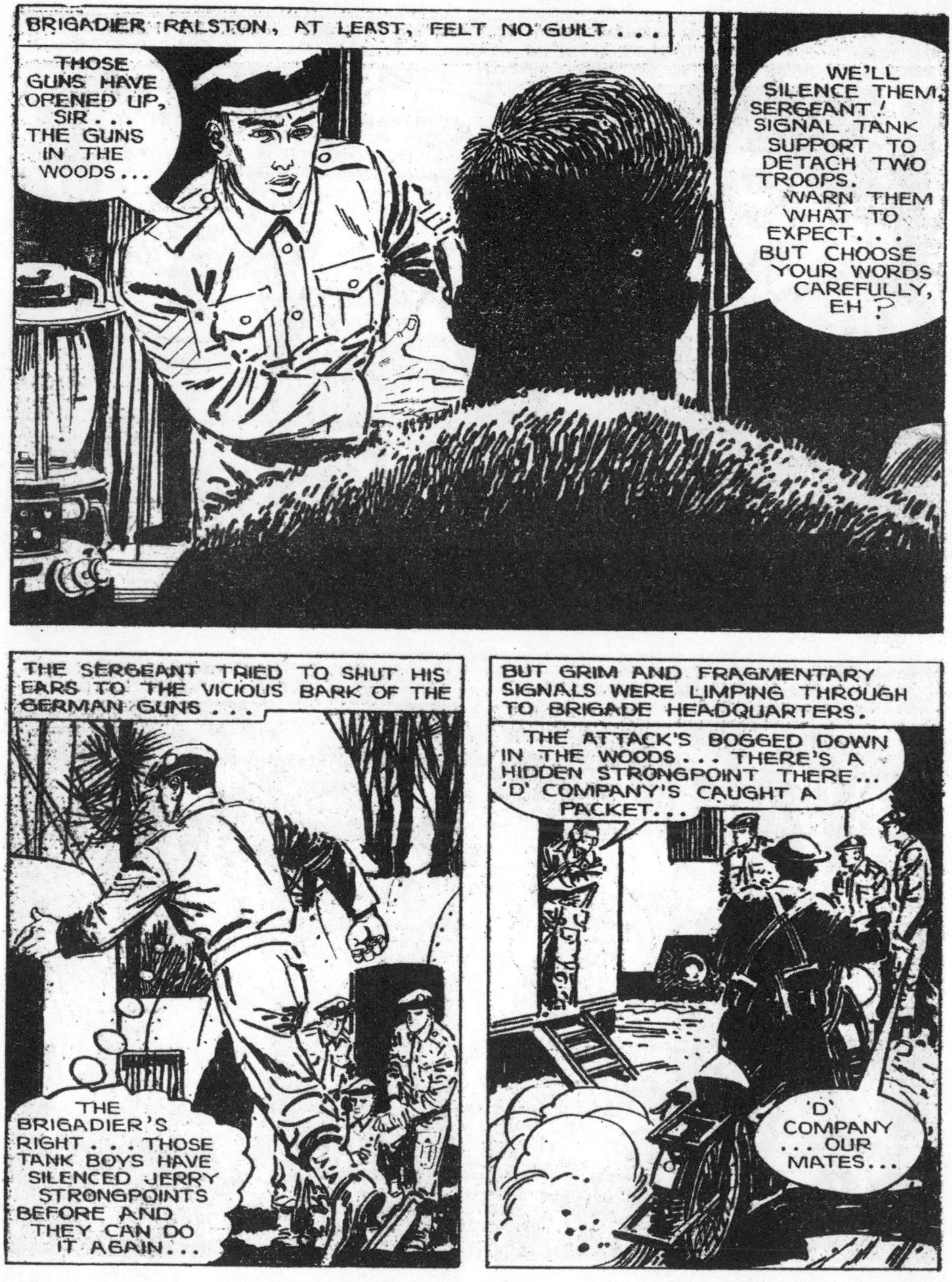
BRIGADIER RALSTON, AT LEAST, FELT NO GUILT . . .
THOSE GUNS HAVE OPENED UP, SIR . . . THE GUNS IN THE WOODS . . .
WE'LL SILENCE THEM, SERGEANT! SIGNAL TANK SUPPORT TO DETACH TWO TROOPS. WARN THEM WHAT TO EXPECT . . . BUT CHOOSE YOUR WORDS CAREFULLY, EH?
THE SERGEANT TRIED TO SHUT HIS EARS TO THE VICIOUS BARK OF THE GERMAN GUNS . . .
THE BRIGADIER'S RIGHT . . . THOSE TANK BOYS HAVE SILENCED JERRY STRONGPOINTS BEFORE AND THEY CAN DO IT AGAIN . . .
BUT GRIM AND FRAGMENTARY SIGNALS WERE LIMPING THROUGH TO BRIGADE HEADQUARTERS.
THE ATTACK'S BOGGED DOWN IN THE WOODS . . . THERE'S A HIDDEN STRONGPOINT THERE . . . 'D' COMPANY'S CAUGHT A PACKET . . .
'D' COMPANY . . . OUR MATES . . .

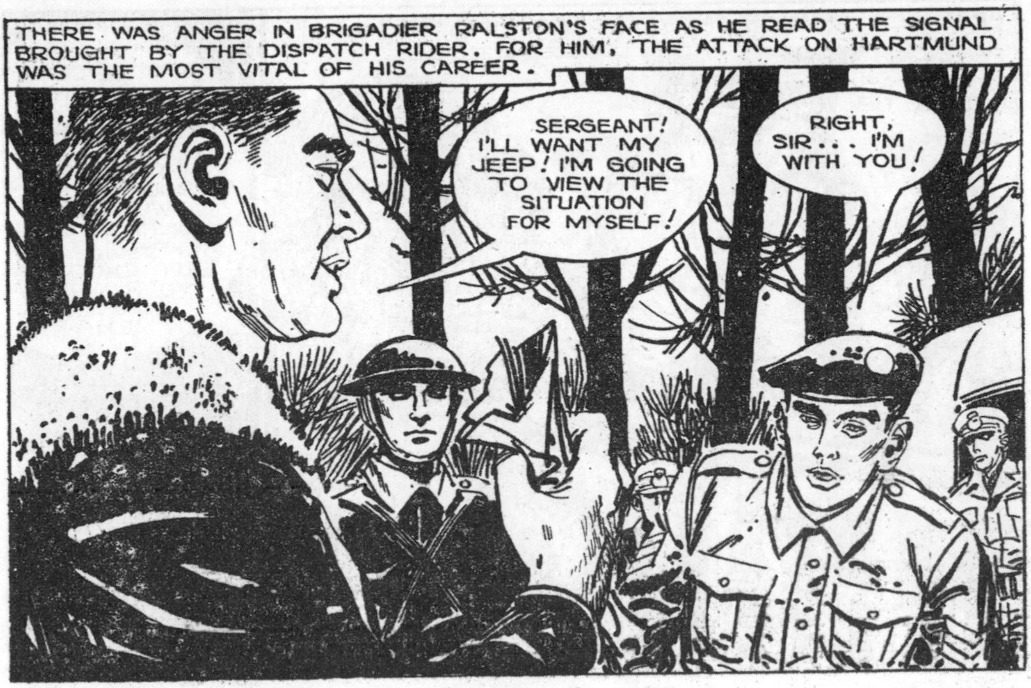
THERE WAS ANGER IN BRIGADIER RALSTON'S FACE AS HE READ THE SIGNAL BROUGHT BY THE DISPATCH RIDER. FOR HIM, THE ATTACK ON HARTMUND WAS THE MOST VITAL OF HIS CAREER.
SERGEANT! I'LL WANT MY JEEP! I'M GOING TO VIEW THE SITUATION FOR MYSELF!
RIGHT, SIR... I'M WITH YOU!

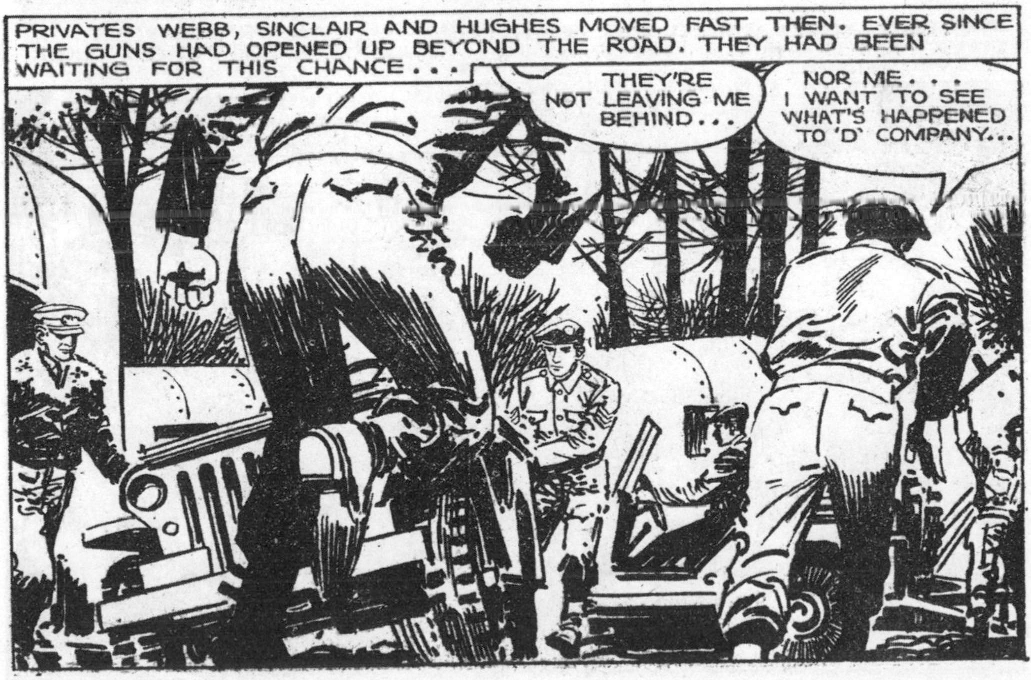
PRIVATES WEBB, SINCLAIR AND HUGHES MOVED FAST THEN. EVER SINCE THE GUNS HAD OPENED UP BEYOND THE ROAD, THEY HAD BEEN WAITING FOR THIS CHANCE...
THEY'RE NOT LEAVING ME BEHIND...
NOR ME... I WANT TO SEE WHAT'S HAPPENED TO 'D' COMPANY...

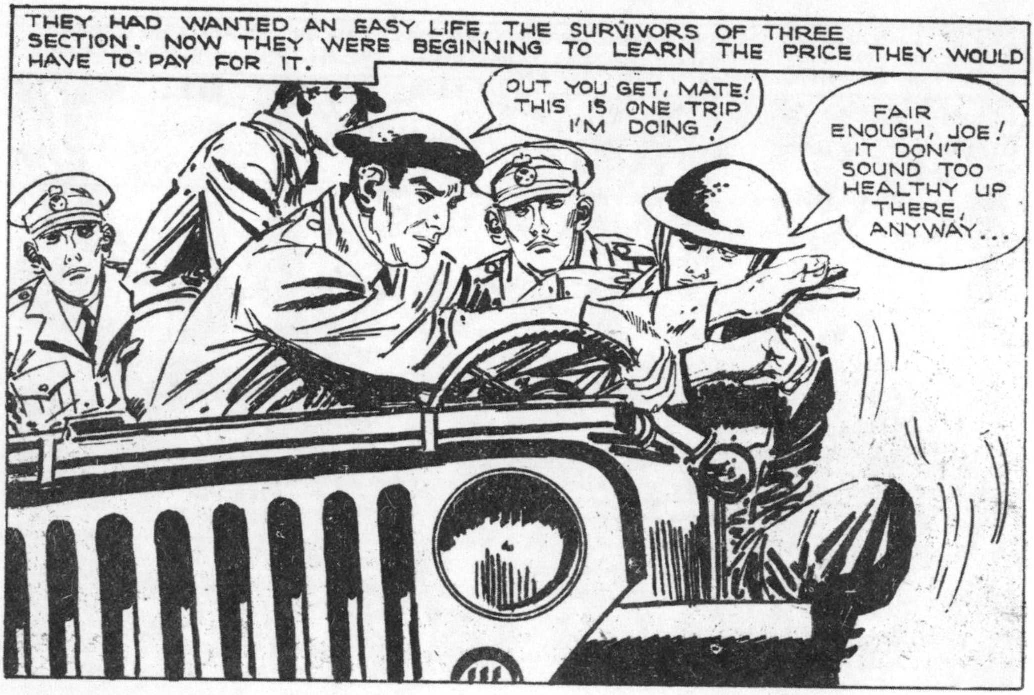
THEY HAD WANTED AN EASY LIFE, THE SURVIVORS OF THREE SECTION. NOW THEY WERE BEGINNING TO LEARN THE PRICE THEY WOULD HAVE TO PAY FOR IT.
OUT YOU GET, MATE! THIS IS ONE TRIP I'M DOING!
FAIR ENOUGH, JOE! IT DON'T SOUND TOO HEALTHY UP THERE, ANYWAY...

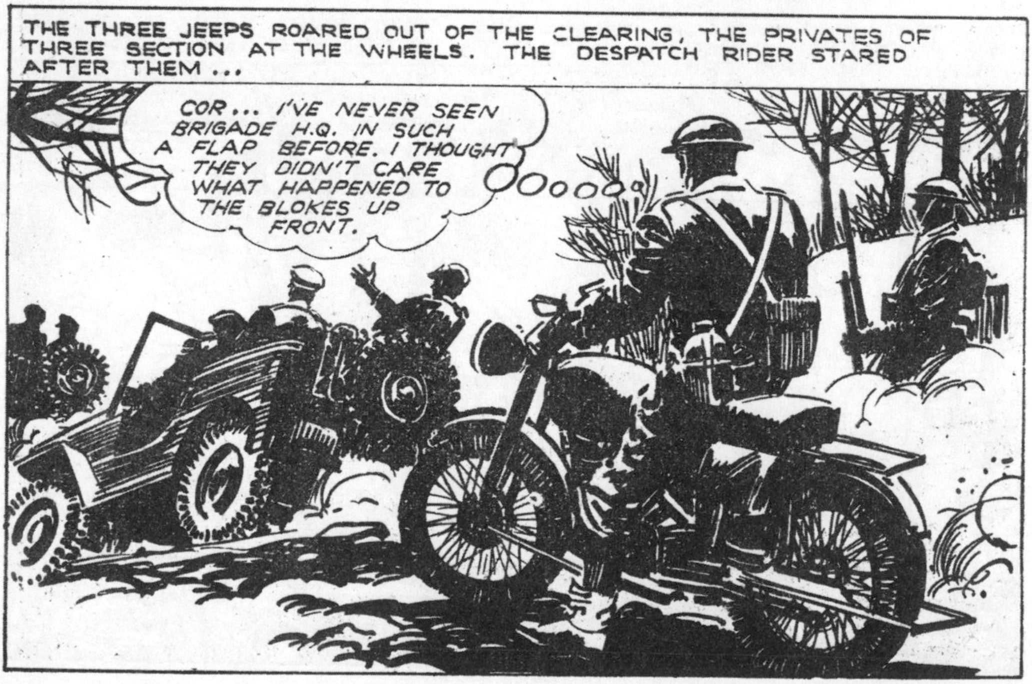
THE THREE JEEPS ROARED OUT OF THE CLEARING, THE PRIVATES OF THREE SECTION AT THE WHEELS. THE DESPATCH RIDER STARED AFTER THEM...
COR... I'VE NEVER SEEN BRIGADE H.Q. IN SUCH A FLAP BEFORE. I THOUGHT THEY DIDN'T CARE WHAT HAPPENED TO THE BLOKES UP FRONT.

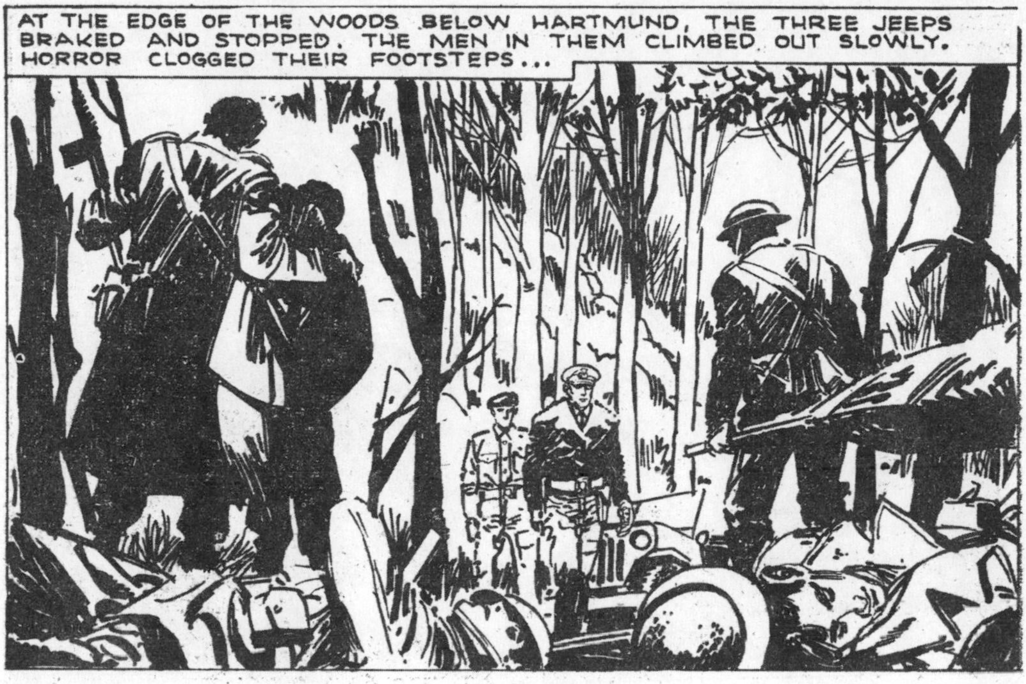
AT THE EDGE OF THE WOODS BELOW HARTMUND, THE THREE JEEPS BRAKED AND STOPPED. THE MEN IN THEM CLIMBED OUT SLOWLY. HORROR CLOGGED THEIR FOOTSTEPS...

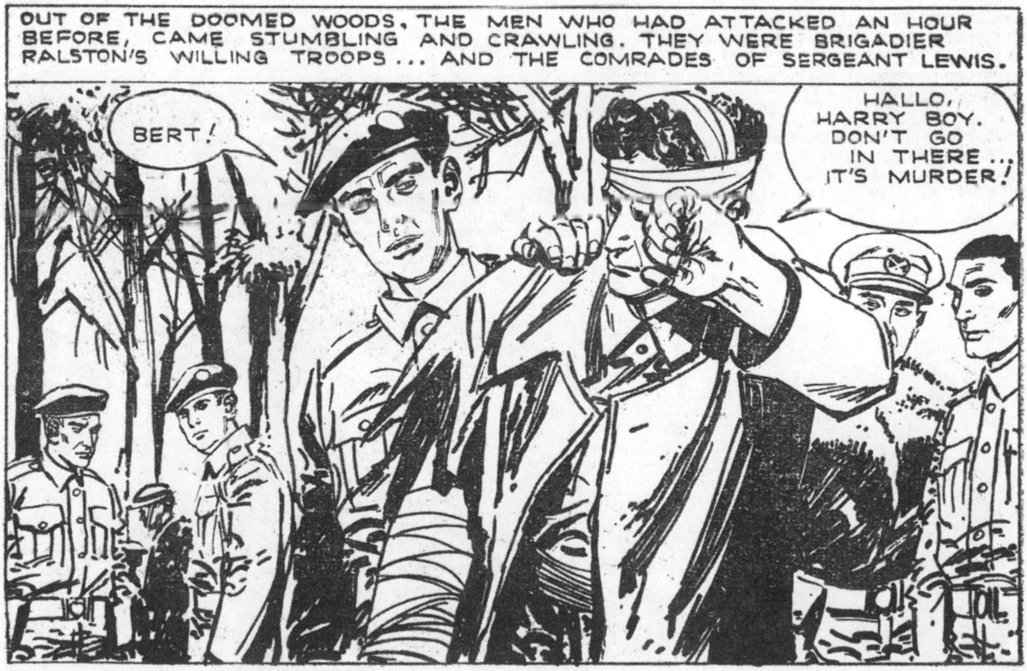
OUT OF THE DOOMED WOODS, THE MEN WHO HAD ATTACKED AN HOUR BEFORE, CAME STUMBLING AND CRAWLING. THEY WERE BRIGADIER RALSTON'S WILLING TROOPS... AND THE COMRADES OF SERGEANT LEWIS.
BERT!
HALLO, HARRY BOY. DON'T GO IN THERE... IT'S MURDER!

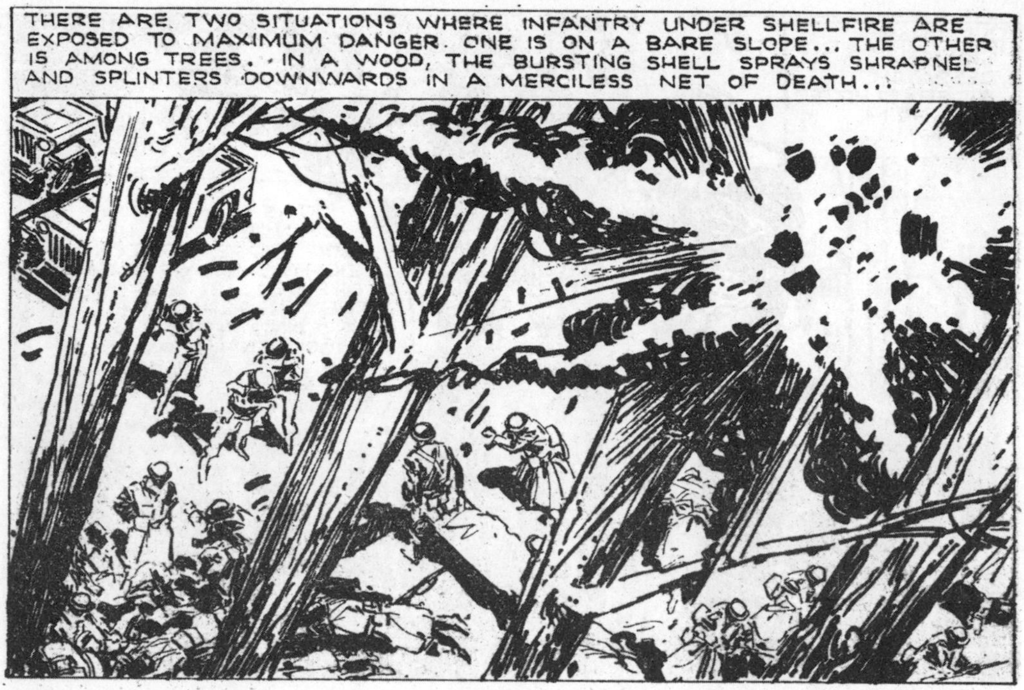
THERE ARE TWO SITUATIONS WHERE INFANTRY UNDER SHELLFIRE ARE EXPOSED TO MAXIMUM DANGER. ONE IS ON A BARE SLOPE... THE OTHER IS AMONG TREES. IN A WOOD, THE BURSTING SHELL SPRAYS SHRAPNEL AND SPLINTERS DOWNWARDS IN A MERCILESS NET OF DEATH...

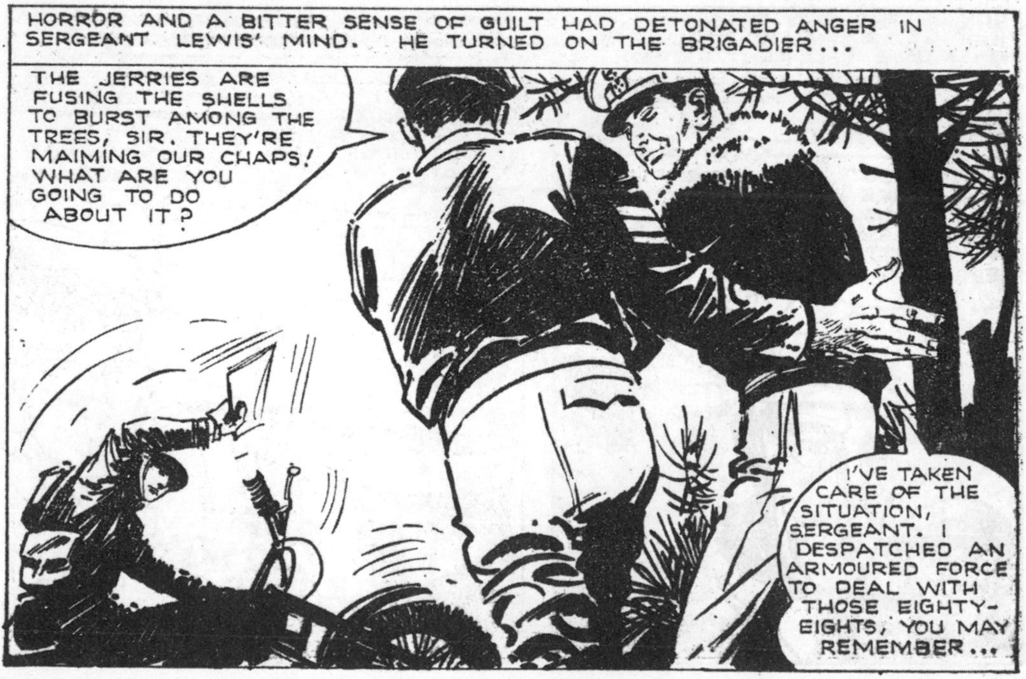
HORROR AND A BITTER SENSE OF GUILT HAD DETONATED ANGER IN SERGEANT LEWIS' MIND. HE TURNED ON THE BRIGADIER...
THE JERRIES ARE FUSING THE SHELLS TO BURST AMONG THE TREES, SIR. THEY'RE MAIMING OUR CHAPS! WHAT ARE YOU GOING TO DO ABOUT IT?
I'VE TAKEN CARE OF THE SITUATION, SERGEANT. I DESPATCHED AN ARMOURED FORCE TO DEAL WITH THOSE EIGHTY-EIGHTS, YOU MAY REMEMBER...

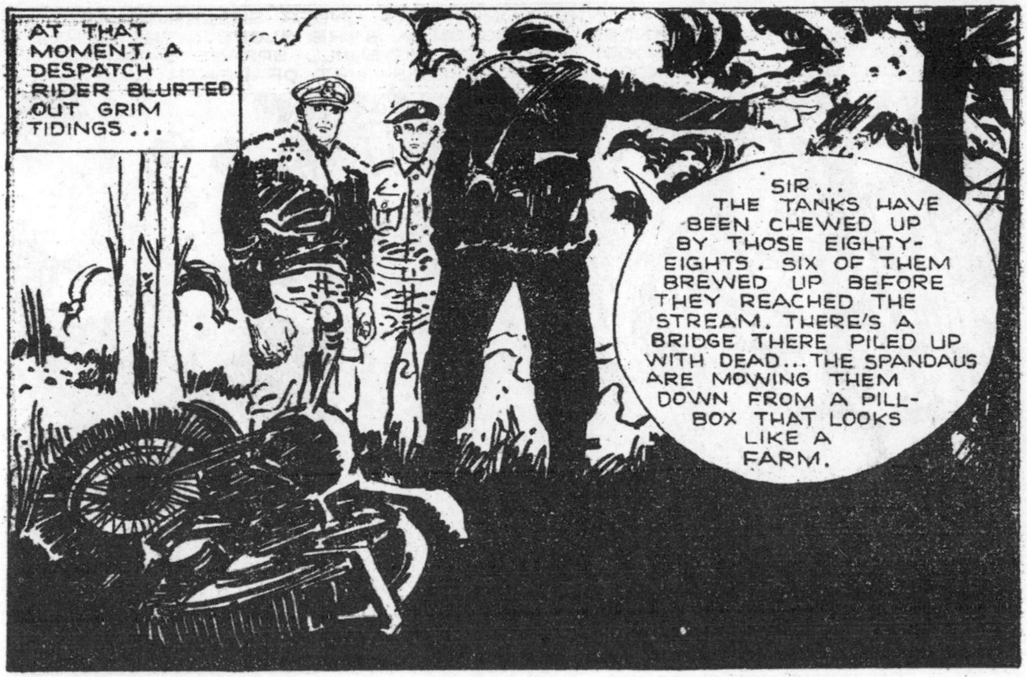
AT THAT MOMENT, A DESPATCH RIDER BLURTED OUT GRIM TIDINGS...
SIR... THE TANKS HAVE BEEN CHEWED UP BY THOSE EIGHTY-EIGHTS. SIX OF THEM BREWED UP BEFORE THEY REACHED THE STREAM. THERE'S A BRIDGE THERE PILED UP WITH DEAD... THE SPANDAUS ARE MOWING THEM DOWN FROM A PILL-BOX THAT LOOKS LIKE A FARM.

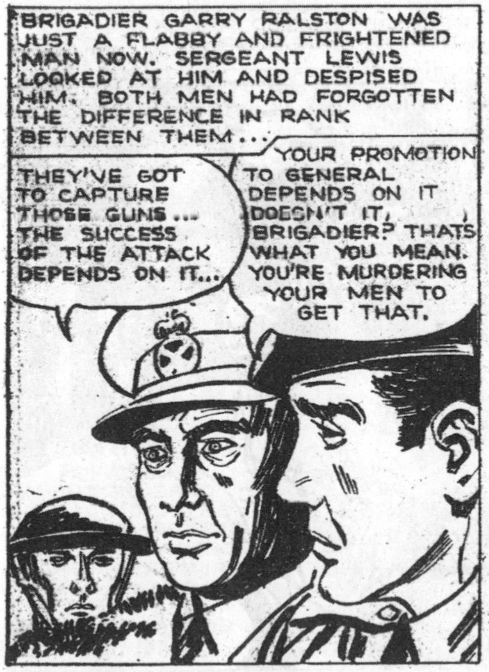
BRIGADIER GARRY RALSTON WAS JUST A FLABBY AND FRIGHTENED MAN NOW. SERGEANT LEWIS LOOKED AT HIM AND DESPISED HIM. BOTH MEN HAD FORGOTTEN THE DIFFERENCE IN RANK BETWEEN THEM...
THEY'VE GOT TO CAPTURE THOSE GUNS... THE SUCCESS OF THE ATTACK DEPENDS ON IT...
YOUR PROMOTION TO GENERAL DEPENDS ON IT DOESN'T IT, BRIGADIER? THATS WHAT YOU MEAN. YOU'RE MURDERING YOUR MEN TO GET THAT.

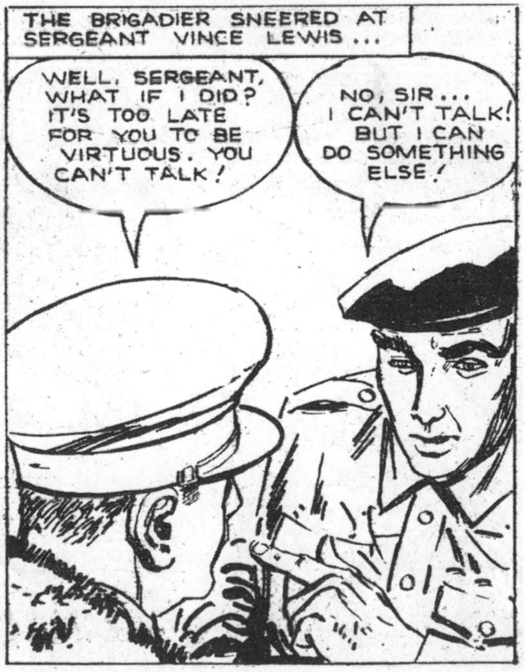
THE BRIGADIER SNEERED AT SERGEANT VINCE LEWIS...
WELL, SERGEANT, WHAT IF I DID? IT'S TOO LATE FOR YOU TO BE VIRTUOUS. YOU CAN'T TALK!
NO, SIR... I CAN'T TALK! BUT I CAN DO SOMETHING ELSE!

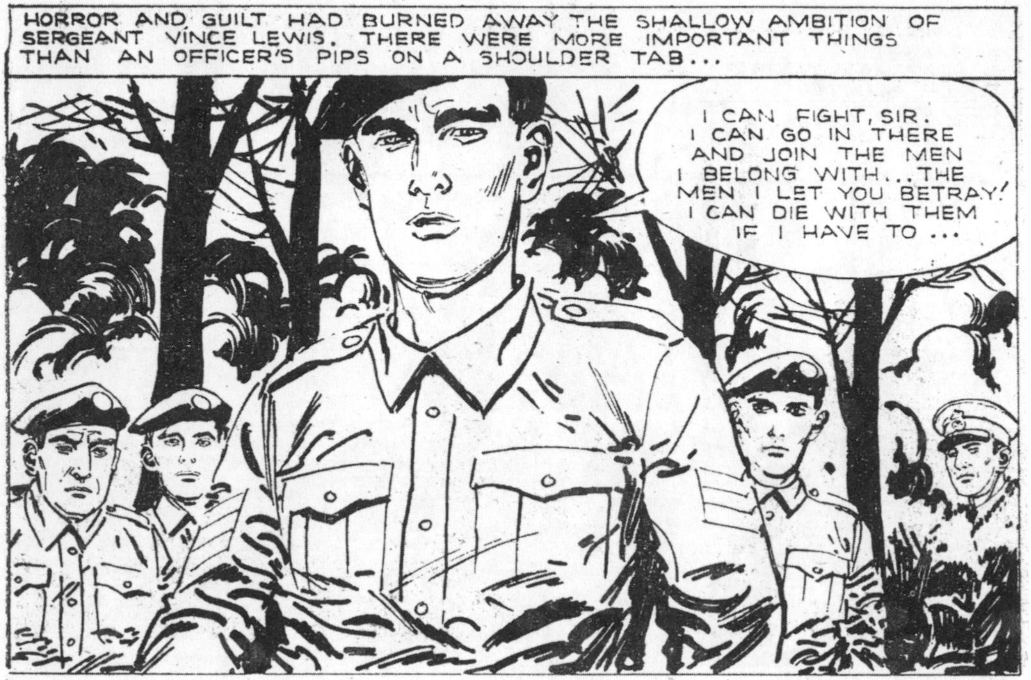
HORROR AND GUILT HAD BURNED AWAY THE SHALLOW AMBITION OF SERGEANT VINCE LEWIS. THERE WERE MORE IMPORTANT THINGS THAN AN OFFICER'S PIPS ON A SHOULDER TAB...
I CAN FIGHT, SIR. I CAN GO IN THERE AND JOIN THE MEN I BELONG WITH...THE MEN I LET YOU BETRAY! I CAN DIE WITH THEM IF I HAVE TO ...

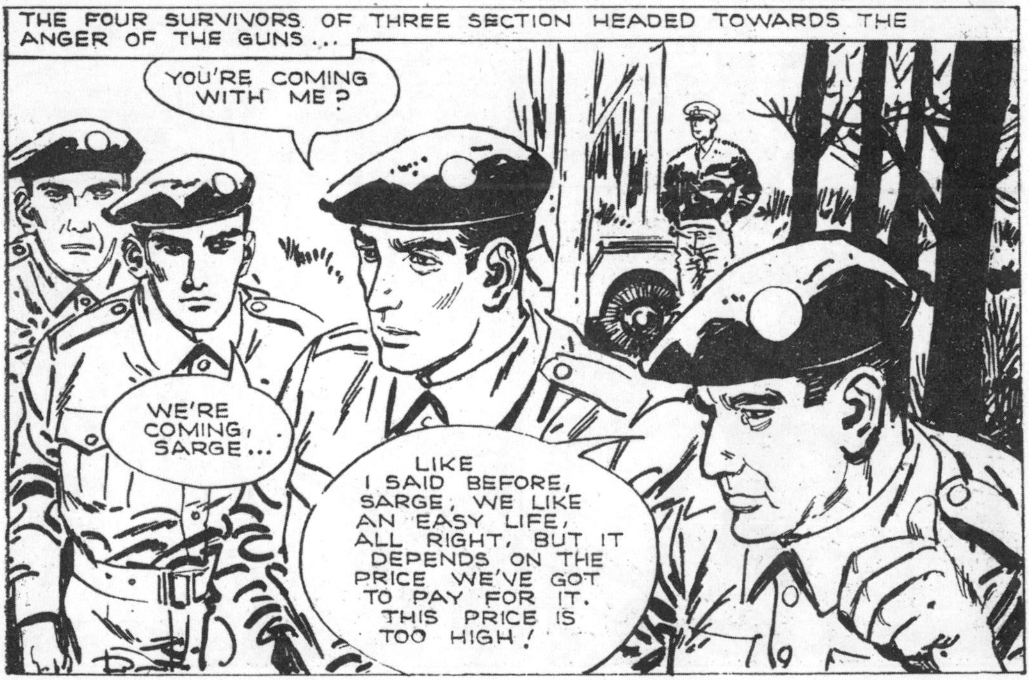
THE FOUR SURVIVORS OF THREE SECTION HEADED TOWARDS THE ANGER OF THE GUNS...
YOU'RE COMING WITH ME?
WE'RE COMING, SARGE...
LIKE I SAID BEFORE, SARGE, WE LIKE AN EASY LIFE, ALL RIGHT, BUT IT DEPENDS ON THE PRICE WE'VE GOT TO PAY FOR IT. THIS PRICE IS TOO HIGH!

Chapter 4. Out of the Wood

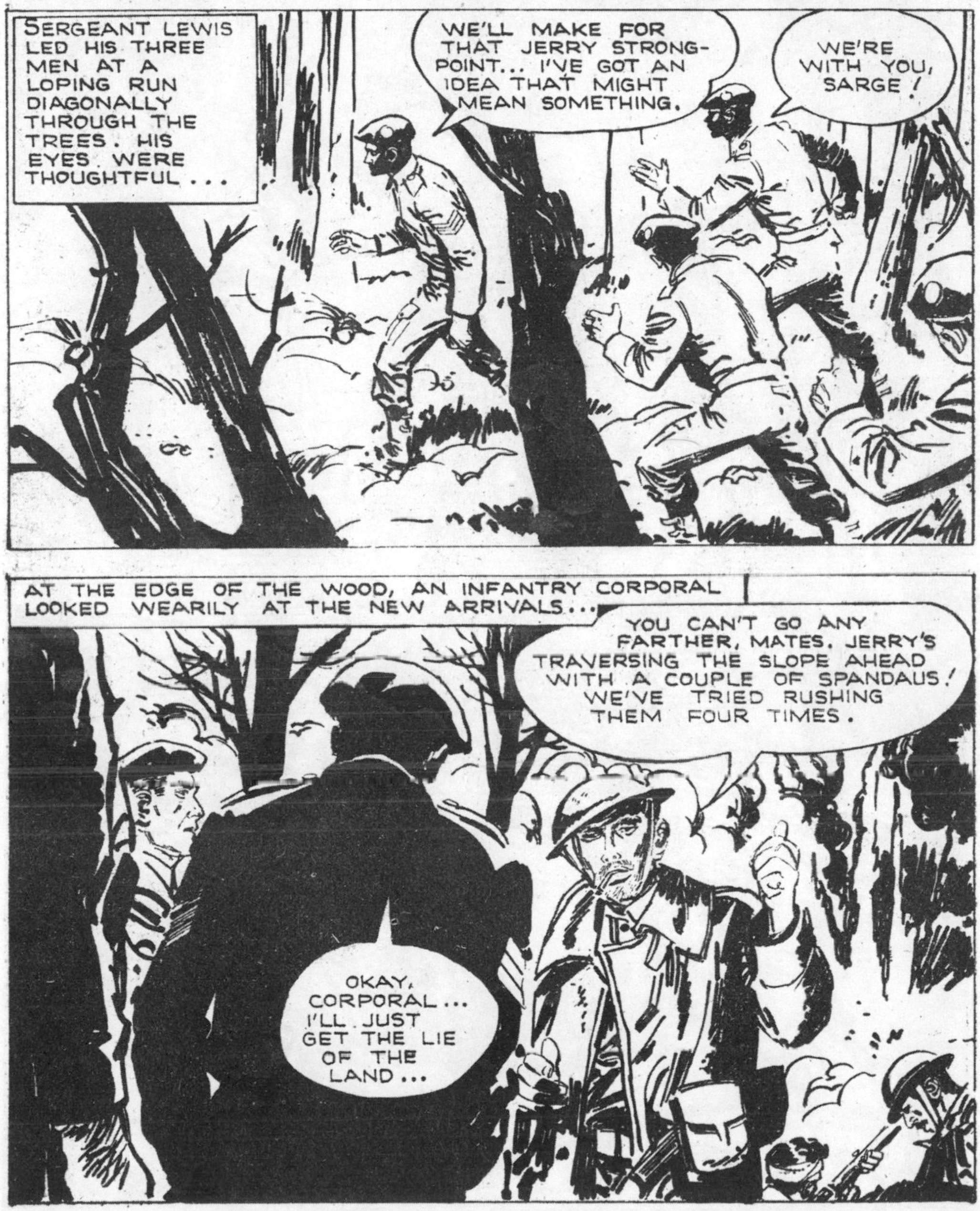
SERGEANT LEWIS LED HIS THREE MEN AT A LOPING RUN DIAGONALLY THROUGH THE TREES. HIS EYES WERE THOUGHTFUL ...
WE'LL MAKE FOR THAT JERRY STRONG-POINT... I'VE GOT AN IDEA THAT MIGHT MEAN SOMETHING.
WE'RE WITH YOU, SARGE!
AT THE EDGE OF THE WOOD, AN INFANTRY CORPORAL LOOKED WEARILY AT THE NEW ARRIVALS...
YOU CAN'T GO ANY FARTHER, MATES. JERRY'S TRAVERSING THE SLOPE AHEAD WITH A COUPLE OF SPANDAUS! WE'VE TRIED RUSHING THEM FOUR TIMES.
OKAY, CORPORAL... I'LL JUST GET THE LIE OF THE LAND ...

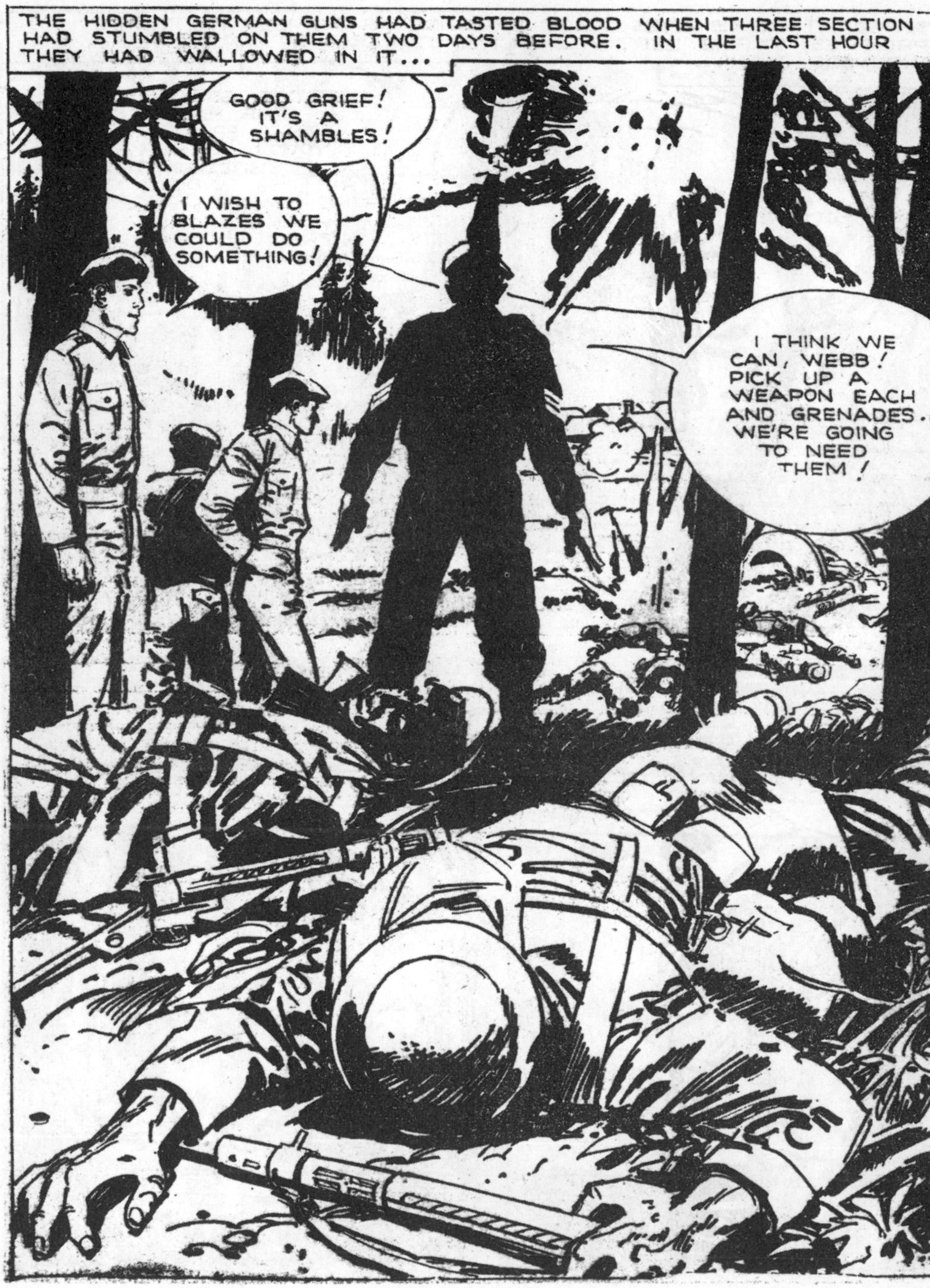
THE HIDDEN GERMAN GUNS HAD TASTED BLOOD WHEN THREE SECTION HAD STUMBLED ON THEM TWO DAYS BEFORE. IN THE LAST HOUR THEY HAD WALLOWED IN IT...
GOOD GRIEF! IT'S A SHAMBLES!
I WISH TO BLAZES WE COULD DO SOMETHING!
I THINK WE CAN, WEBB! PICK UP A WEAPON EACH AND GRENADES... WE'RE GOING TO NEED THEM!

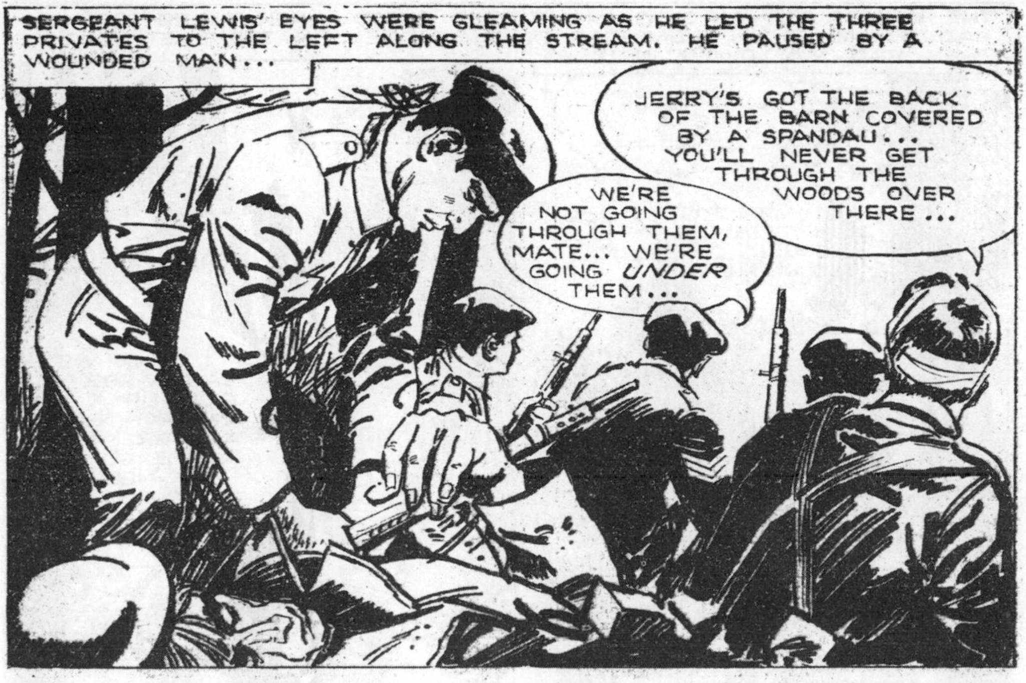
SERGEANT LEWIS' EYES WERE GLEAMING AS HE LED THE THREE PRIVATES TO THE LEFT ALONG THE STREAM. HE PAUSED BY A WOUNDED MAN...
JERRY'S GOT THE BACK OF THE BARN COVERED BY A SPANDAU... YOU'LL NEVER GET THROUGH THE WOODS OVER THERE...
WE'RE NOT GOING THROUGH THEM, MATE... WE'RE GOING *UNDER* THEM...

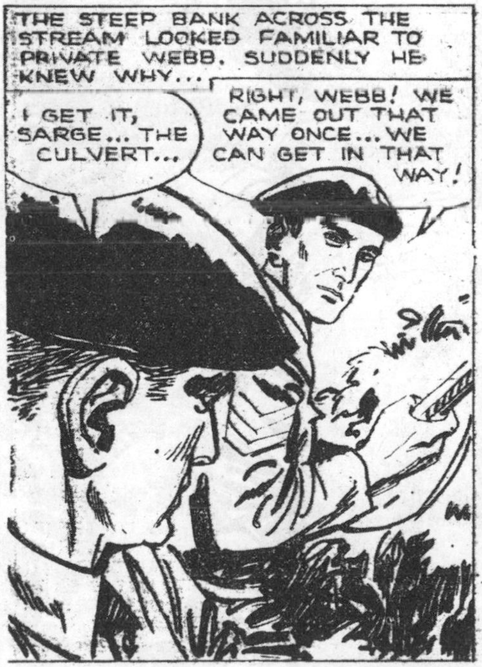
THE STEEP BANK ACROSS THE STREAM LOOKED FAMILIAR TO PRIVATE WEBB. SUDDENLY HE KNEW WHY...
I GET IT, SARGE... THE CULVERT...
RIGHT, WEBB! WE CAME OUT THAT WAY ONCE... WE CAN GET IN THAT WAY!

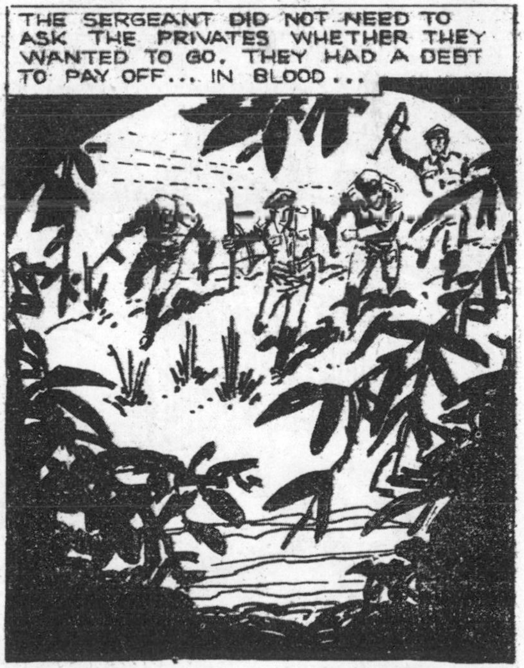
THE SERGEANT DID NOT NEED TO ASK THE PRIVATES WHETHER THEY WANTED TO GO. THEY HAD A DEBT TO PAY OFF... IN BLOOD...

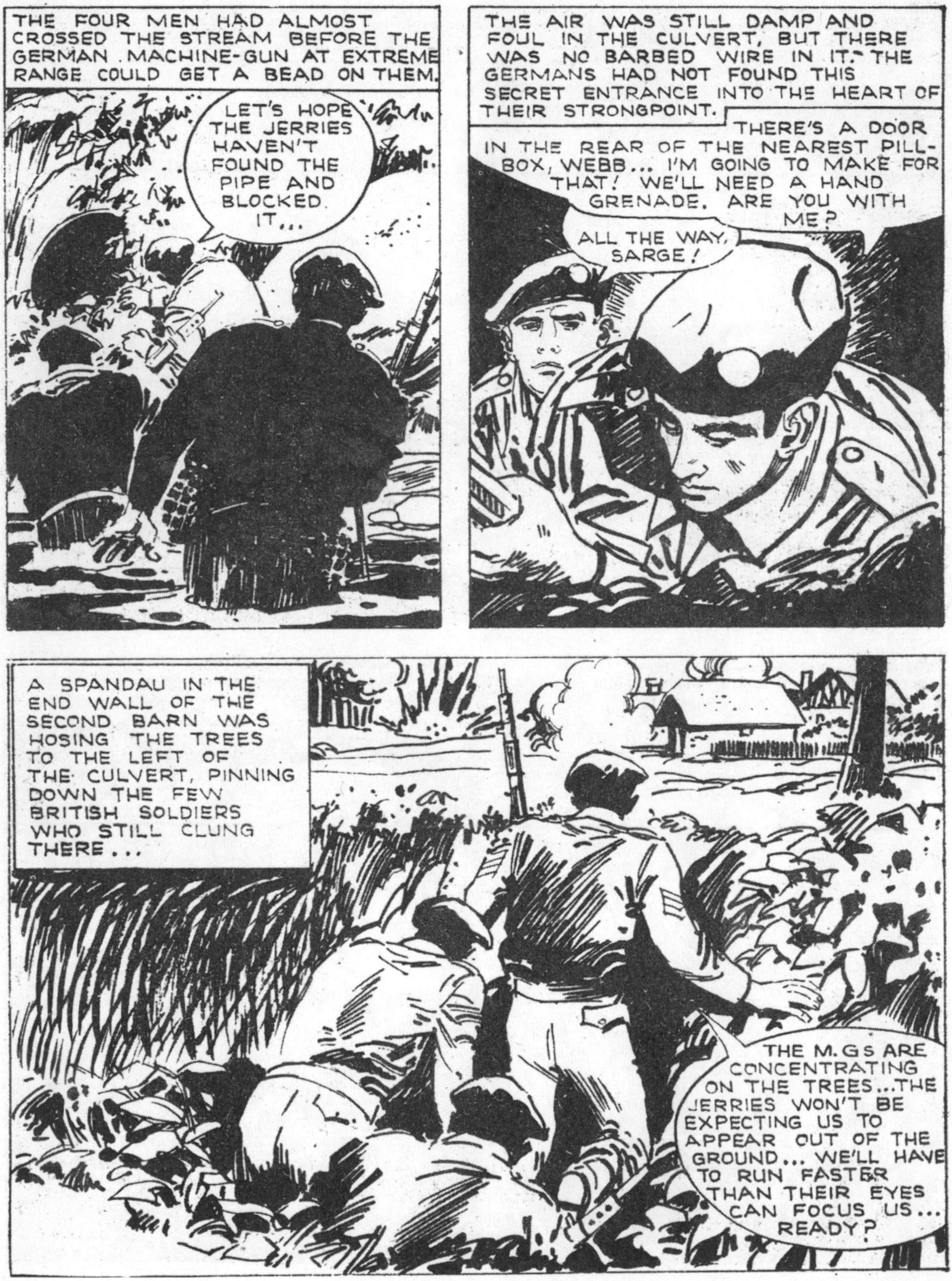
THE FOUR MEN HAD ALMOST CROSSED THE STREAM BEFORE THE GERMAN MACHINE-GUN AT EXTREME RANGE COULD GET A BEAD ON THEM.
LET'S HOPE THE JERRIES HAVEN'T FOUND THE PIPE AND BLOCKED IT...
THE AIR WAS STILL DAMP AND FOUL IN THE CULVERT, BUT THERE WAS NO BARBED WIRE IN IT. THE GERMANS HAD NOT FOUND THIS SECRET ENTRANCE INTO THE HEART OF THEIR STRONGPOINT.
THERE'S A DOOR IN THE REAR OF THE NEAREST PILL-BOX, WEBB... I'M GOING TO MAKE FOR THAT! WE'LL NEED A HAND GRENADE. ARE YOU WITH ME?
ALL THE WAY, SARGE!
A SPANDAU IN THE END WALL OF THE SECOND BARN WAS HOSING THE TREES TO THE LEFT OF THE CULVERT, PINNING DOWN THE FEW BRITISH SOLDIERS WHO STILL CLUNG THERE...
THE M.Gs ARE CONCENTRATING ON THE TREES...THE JERRIES WON'T BE EXPECTING US TO APPEAR OUT OF THE GROUND... WE'LL HAVE TO RUN FASTER THAN THEIR EYES CAN FOCUS US... READY?

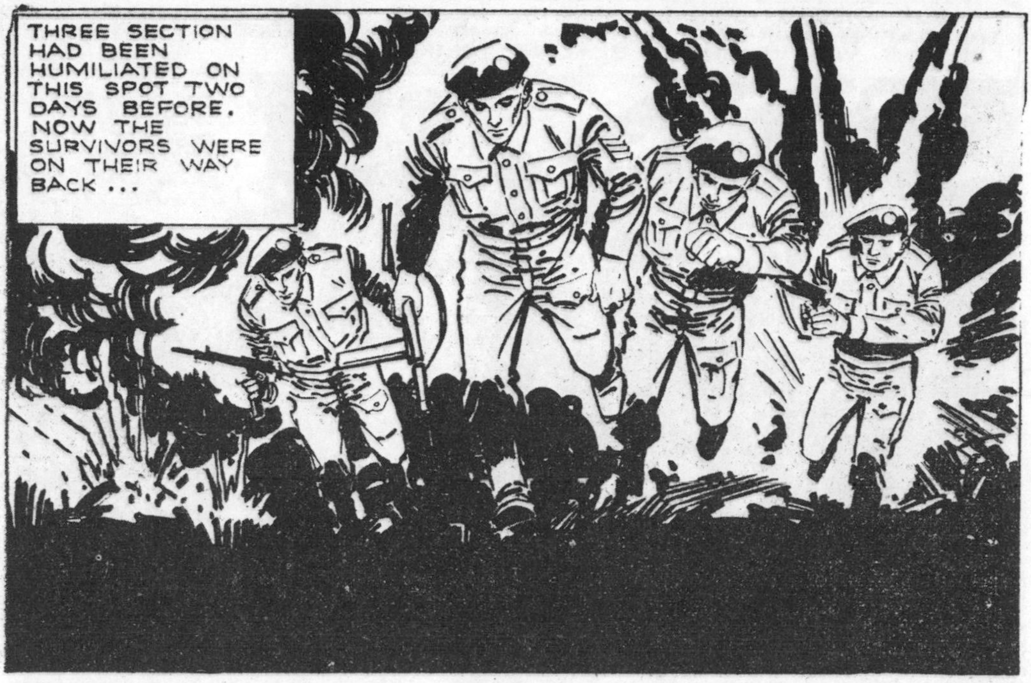
THREE SECTION HAD BEEN HUMILIATED ON THIS SPOT TWO DAYS BEFORE. NOW THE SURVIVORS WERE ON THEIR WAY BACK ...

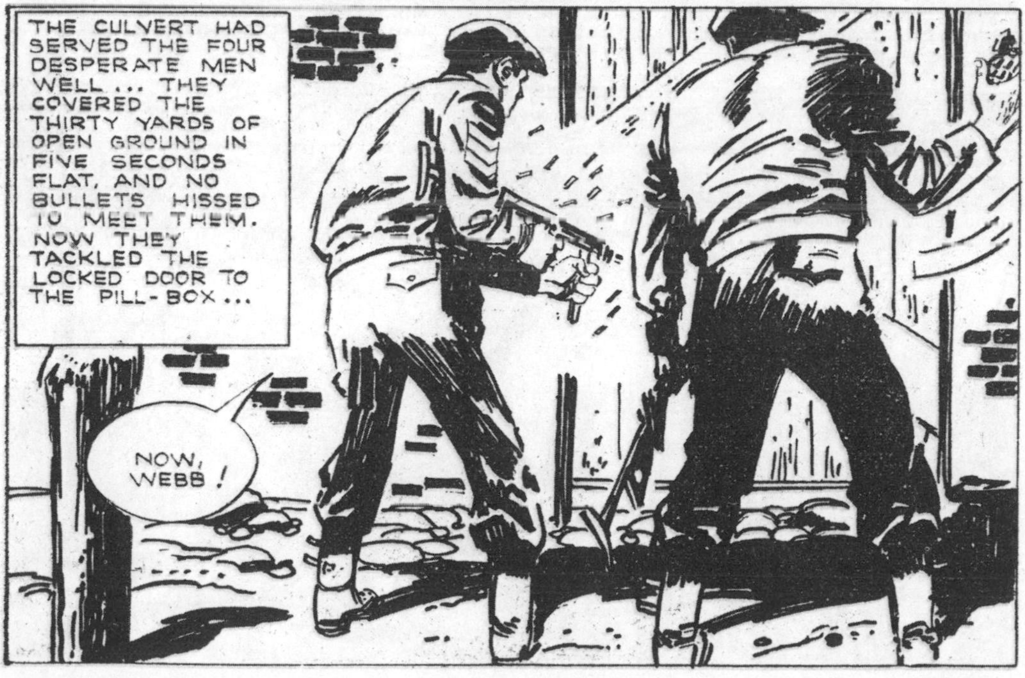
THE CULVERT HAD SERVED THE FOUR DESPERATE MEN WELL ... THEY COVERED THE THIRTY YARDS OF OPEN GROUND IN FIVE SECONDS FLAT, AND NO BULLETS HISSED TO MEET THEM. NOW THEY TACKLED THE LOCKED DOOR TO THE PILL-BOX ...
NOW, WEBB!

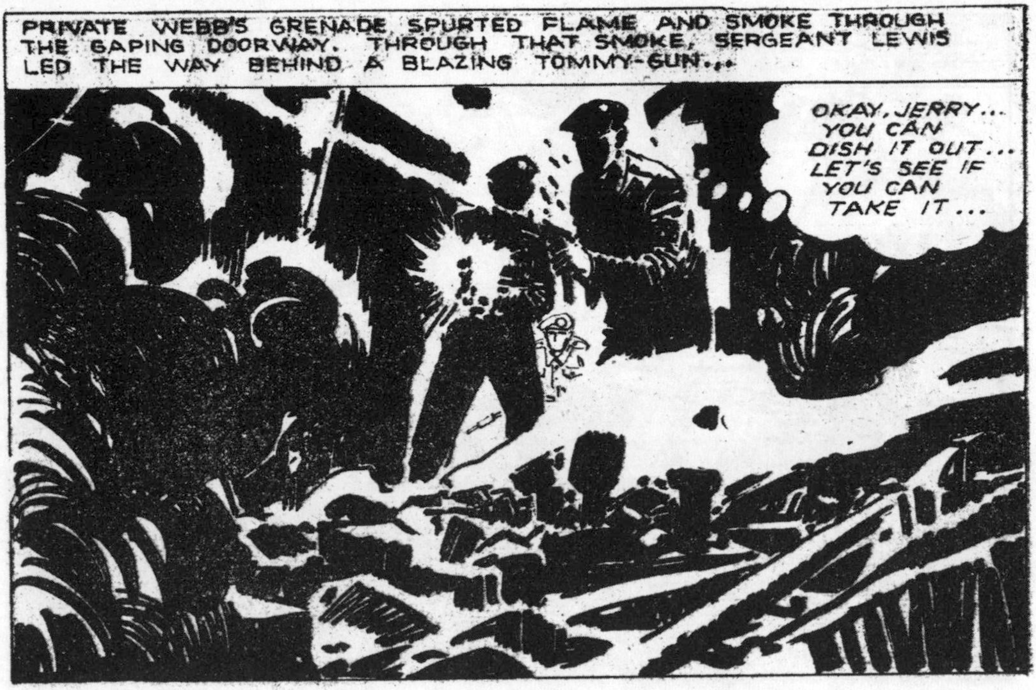
PRIVATE WEBB'S GRENADE SPURTED FLAME AND SMOKE THROUGH THE GAPING DOORWAY. THROUGH THAT SMOKE, SERGEANT LEWIS LED THE WAY BEHIND A BLAZING TOMMY-GUN...
OKAY, JERRY... YOU CAN DISH IT OUT... LET'S SEE IF YOU CAN TAKE IT...

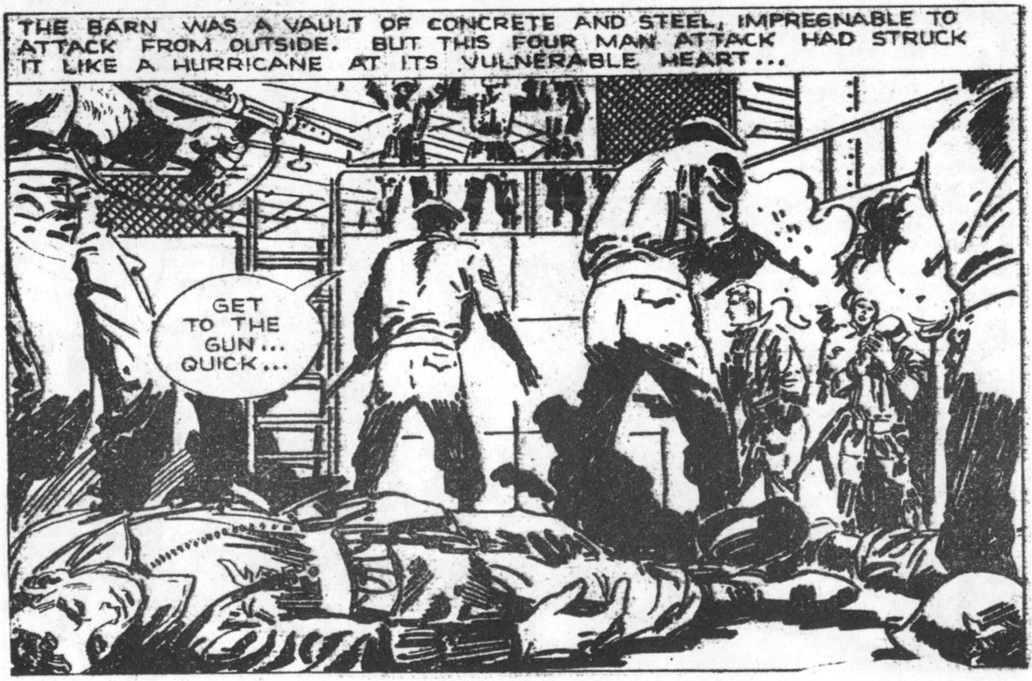
THE BARN WAS A VAULT OF CONCRETE AND STEEL, IMPREGNABLE TO ATTACK FROM OUTSIDE. BUT THIS FOUR MAN ATTACK HAD STRUCK IT LIKE A HURRICANE AT ITS VULNERABLE HEART...
GET TO THE GUN... QUICK...

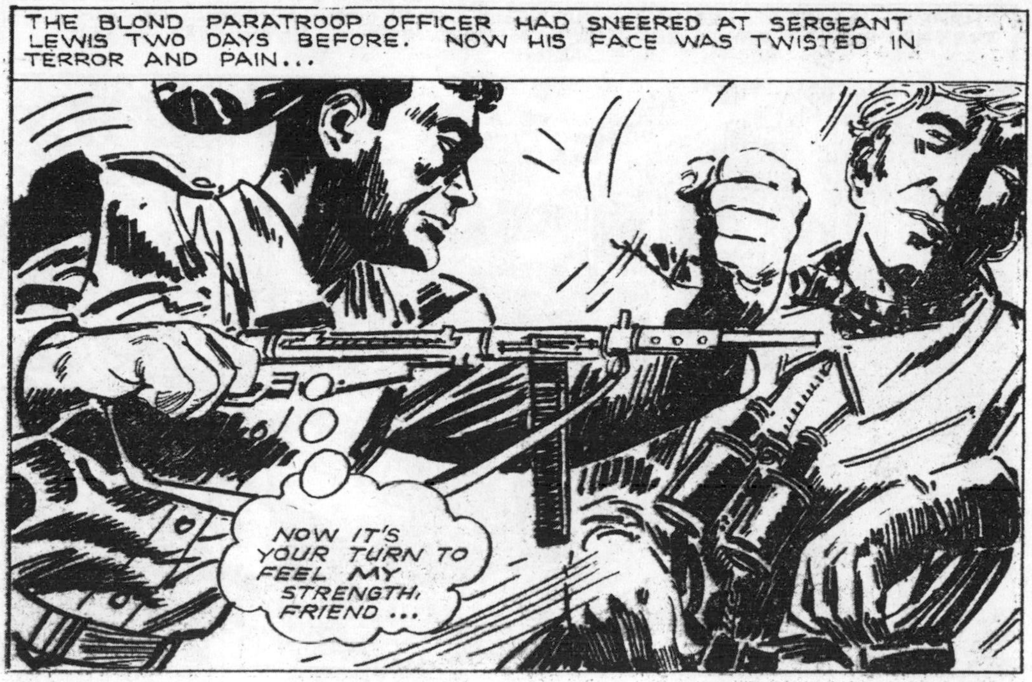
THE BLOND PARATROOP OFFICER HAD SNEERED AT SERGEANT LEWIS TWO DAYS BEFORE. NOW HIS FACE WAS TWISTED IN TERROR AND PAIN...
NOW IT'S YOUR TURN TO FEEL MY STRENGTH, FRIEND ...

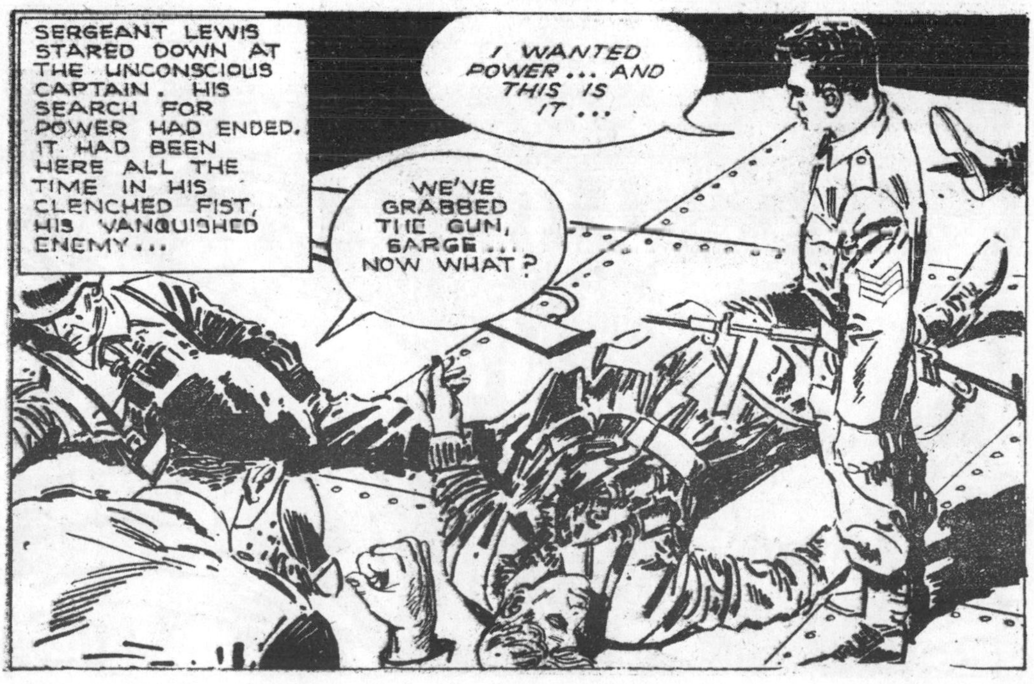
SERGEANT LEWIS STARED DOWN AT THE UNCONSCIOUS CAPTAIN. HIS SEARCH FOR POWER HAD ENDED. IT HAD BEEN HERE ALL THE TIME IN HIS CLENCHED FIST, HIS VANQUISHED ENEMY...
I WANTED POWER ... AND THIS IS IT ...
WE'VE GRABBED THE GUN, SARGE ... NOW WHAT?

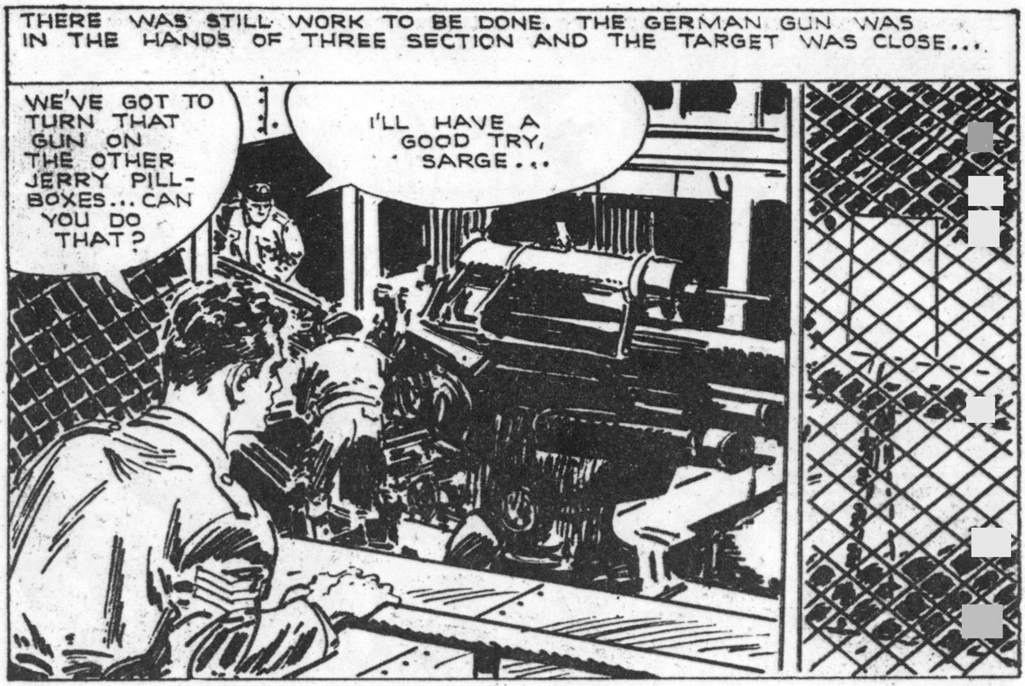
THERE WAS STILL WORK TO BE DONE. THE GERMAN GUN WAS IN THE HANDS OF THREE SECTION AND THE TARGET WAS CLOSE...
WE'VE GOT TO TURN THAT GUN ON THE OTHER JERRY PILL-BOXES... CAN YOU DO THAT?
I'LL HAVE A GOOD TRY, SARGE...

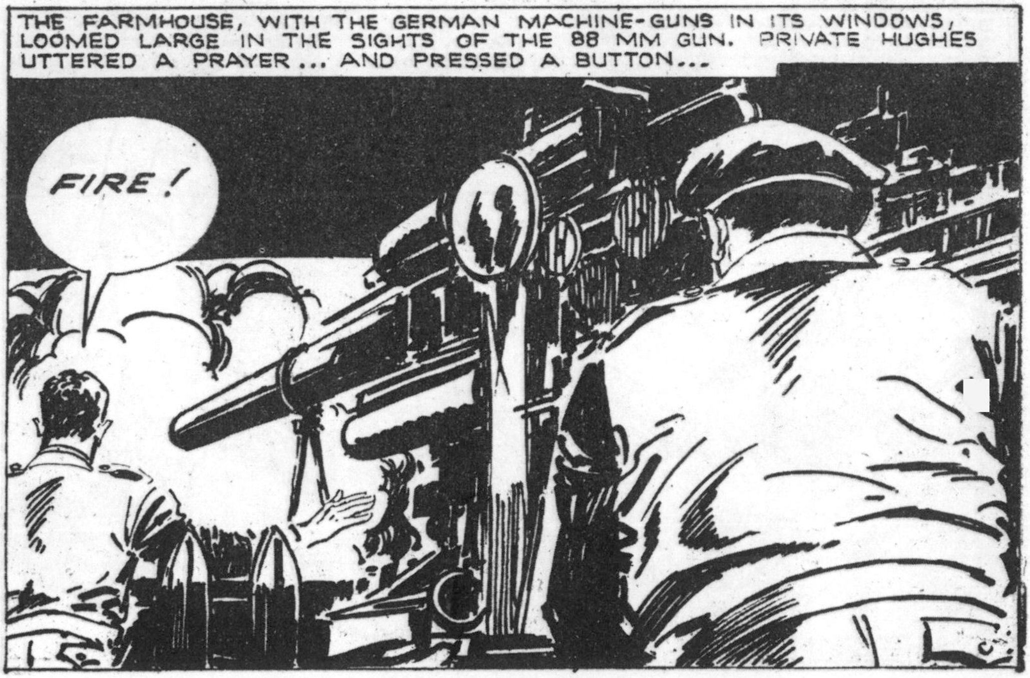
THE FARMHOUSE, WITH THE GERMAN MACHINE-GUNS IN ITS WINDOWS, LOOMED LARGE IN THE SIGHTS OF THE 88 MM GUN. PRIVATE HUGHES UTTERED A PRAYER... AND PRESSED A BUTTON...
FIRE!

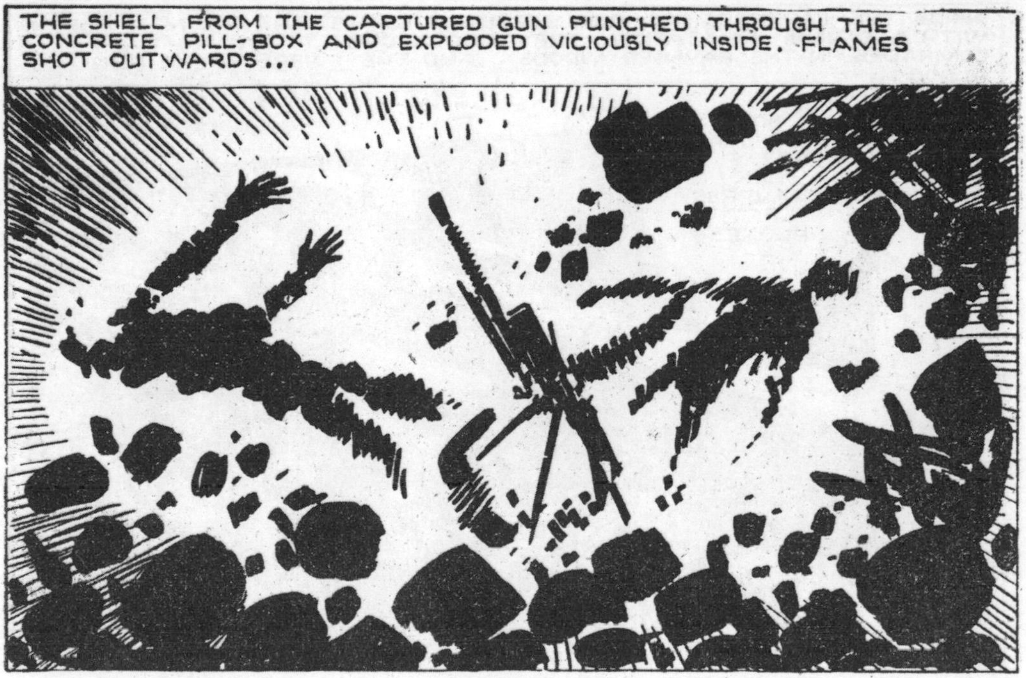
THE SHELL FROM THE CAPTURED GUN PUNCHED THROUGH THE CONCRETE PILL-BOX AND EXPLODED VICIOUSLY INSIDE. FLAMES SHOT OUTWARDS...

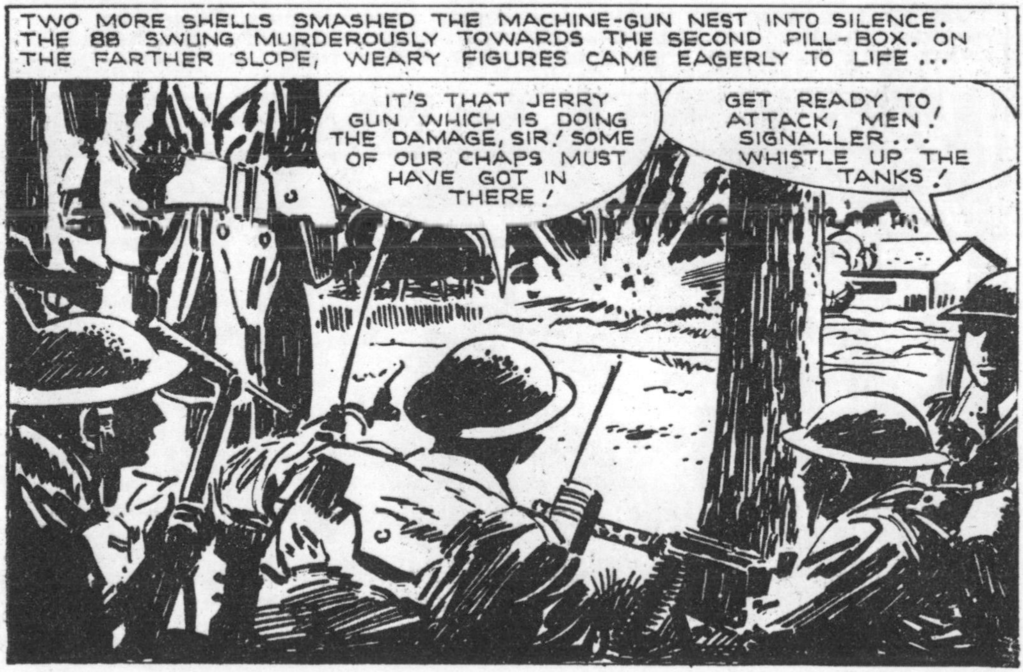
TWO MORE SHELLS SMASHED THE MACHINE-GUN NEST INTO SILENCE. THE 88 SWUNG MURDEROUSLY TOWARDS THE SECOND PILL-BOX. ON THE FARTHER SLOPE, WEARY FIGURES CAME EAGERLY TO LIFE...
IT'S THAT JERRY GUN WHICH IS DOING THE DAMAGE, SIR! SOME OF OUR CHAPS MUST HAVE GOT IN THERE!
GET READY TO ATTACK, MEN! SIGNALLER... WHISTLE UP THE TANKS!

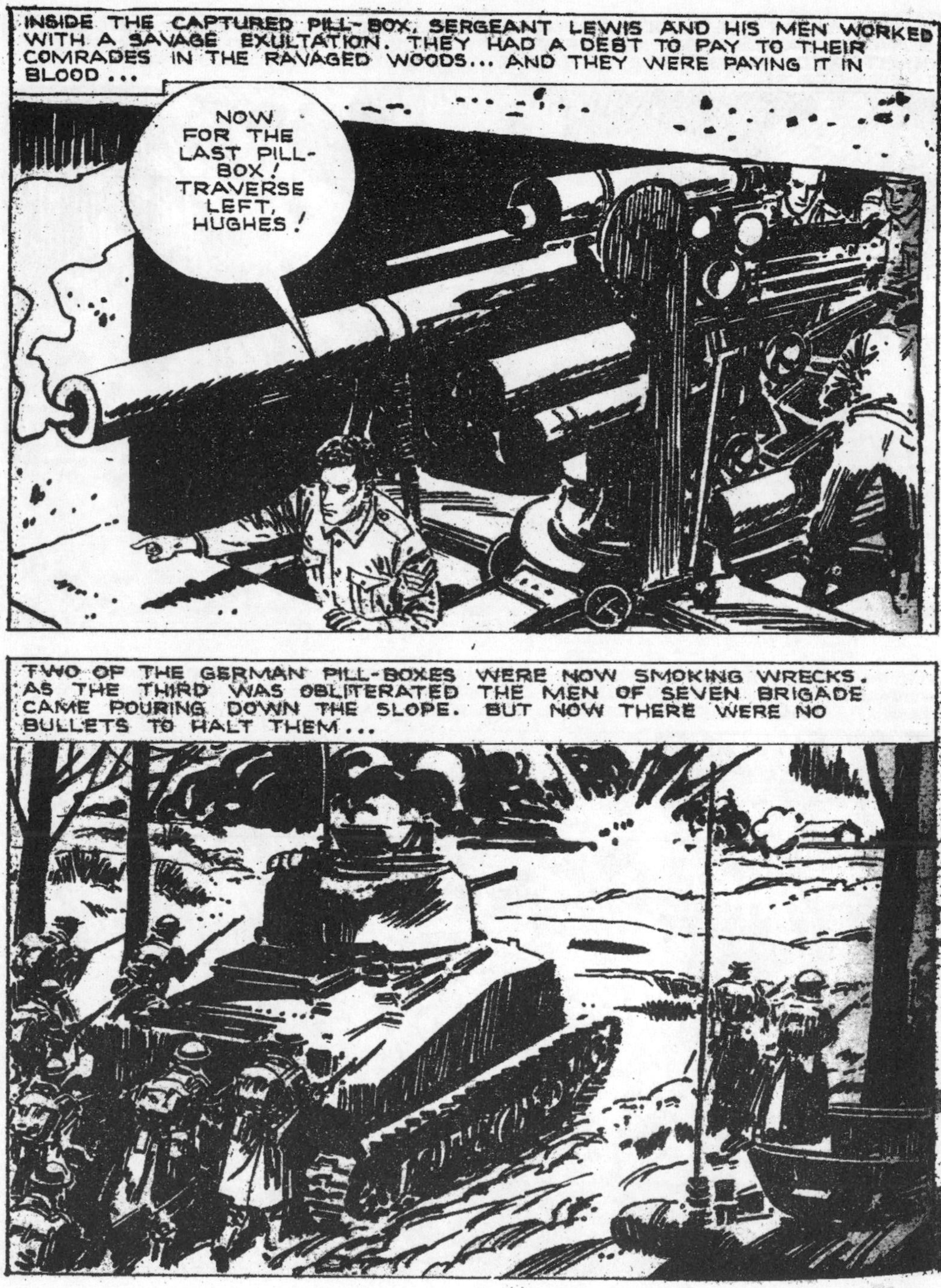
INSIDE THE CAPTURED PILL-BOX, SERGEANT LEWIS AND HIS MEN WORKED WITH A SAVAGE EXULTATION. THEY HAD A DEBT TO PAY TO THEIR COMRADES IN THE RAVAGED WOODS... AND THEY WERE PAYING IT IN BLOOD...
NOW FOR THE LAST PILL-BOX! TRAVERSE LEFT, HUGHES!
TWO OF THE GERMAN PILL-BOXES WERE NOW SMOKING WRECKS. AS THE THIRD WAS OBLITERATED THE MEN OF SEVEN BRIGADE CAME POURING DOWN THE SLOPE. BUT NOW THERE WERE NO BULLETS TO HALT THEM...

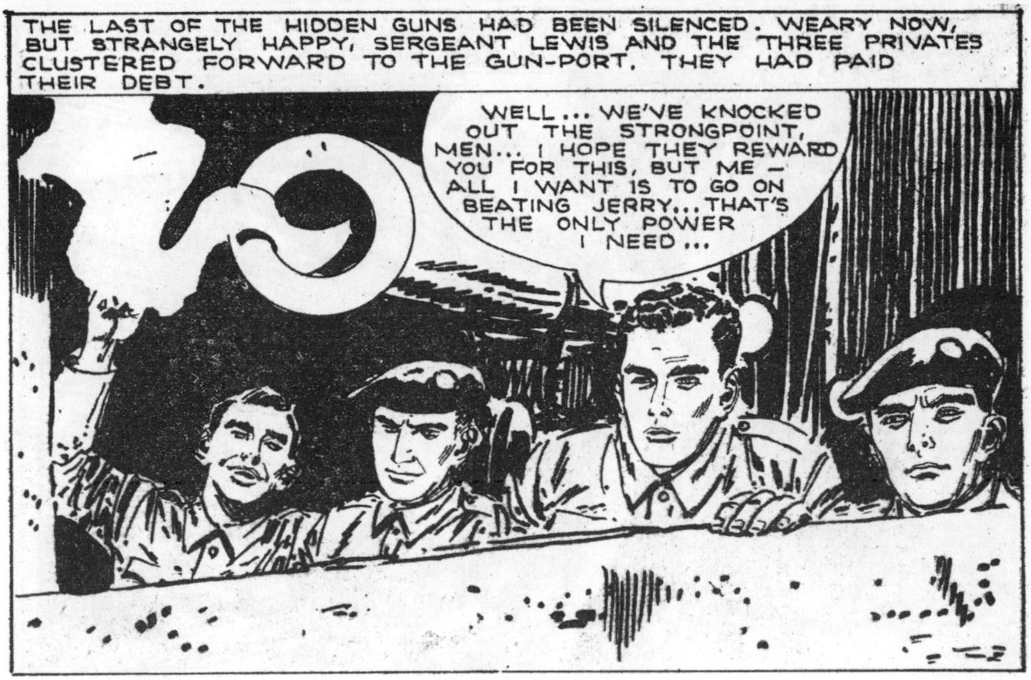
THE LAST OF THE HIDDEN GUNS HAD BEEN SILENCED. WEARY NOW, BUT STRANGELY HAPPY, SERGEANT LEWIS AND THE THREE PRIVATES CLUSTERED FORWARD TO THE GUN-PORT. THEY HAD PAID THEIR DEBT.
WELL... WE'VE KNOCKED OUT THE STRONGPOINT, MEN... I HOPE THEY REWARD YOU FOR THIS, BUT ME – ALL I WANT IS TO GO ON BEATING JERRY... THAT'S THE ONLY POWER I NEED...

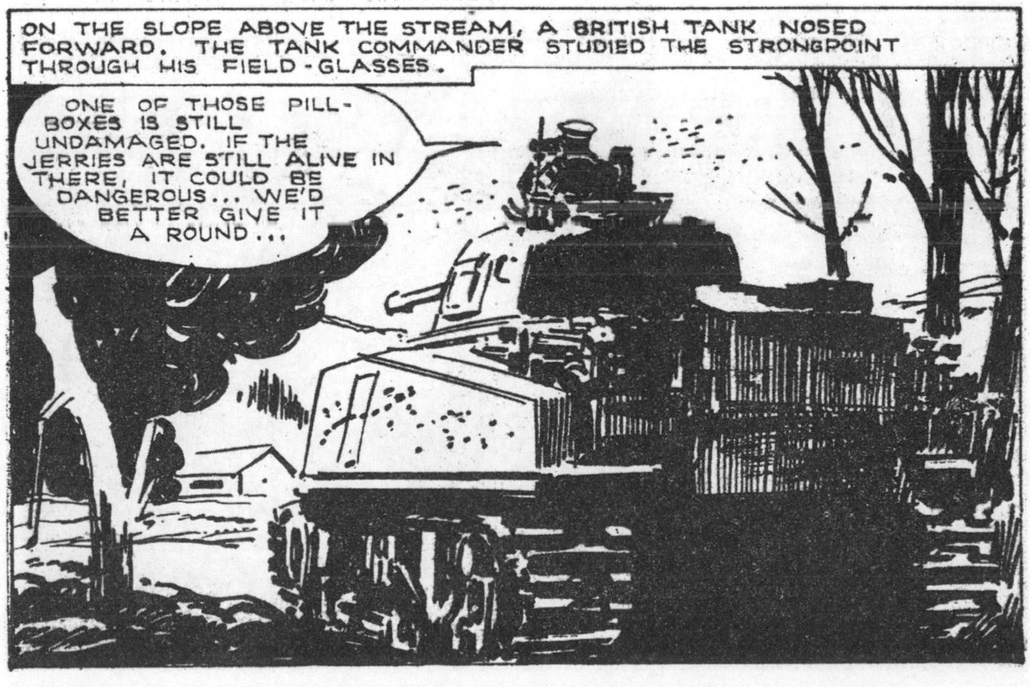
ON THE SLOPE ABOVE THE STREAM, A BRITISH TANK NOSED FORWARD. THE TANK COMMANDER STUDIED THE STRONGPOINT THROUGH HIS FIELD-GLASSES.
ONE OF THOSE PILL-BOXES IS STILL UNDAMAGED. IF THE JERRIES ARE STILL ALIVE IN THERE, IT COULD BE DANGEROUS... WE'D BETTER GIVE IT A ROUND...

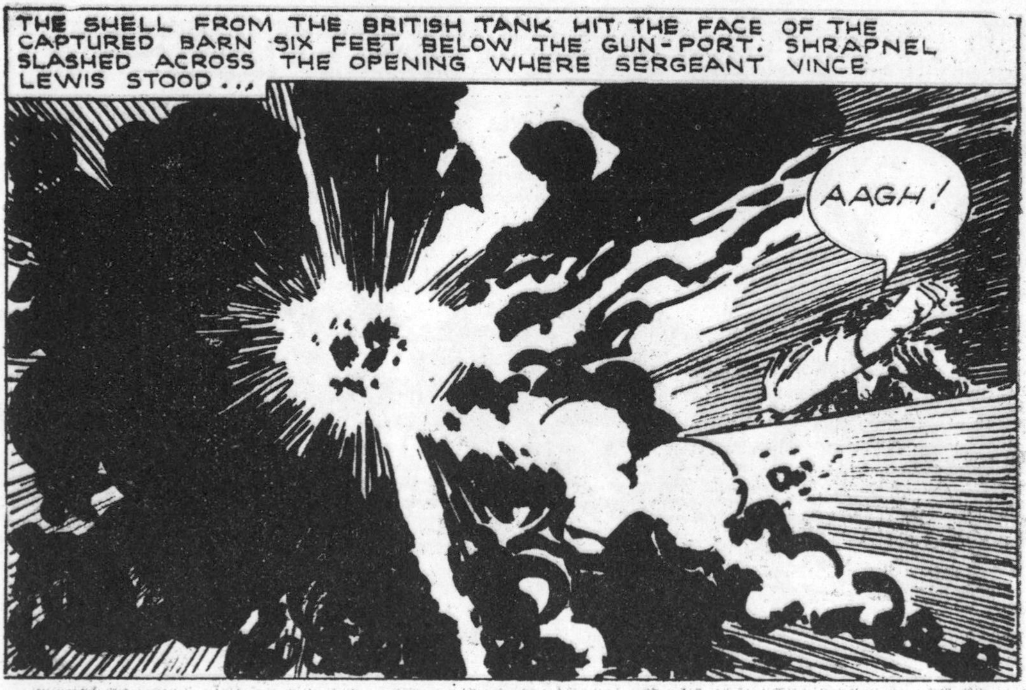
THE SHELL FROM THE BRITISH TANK HIT THE FACE OF THE CAPTURED BARN SIX FEET BELOW THE GUN-PORT. SHRAPNEL SLASHED ACROSS THE OPENING WHERE SERGEANT VINCE LEWIS STOOD...
AAGH!

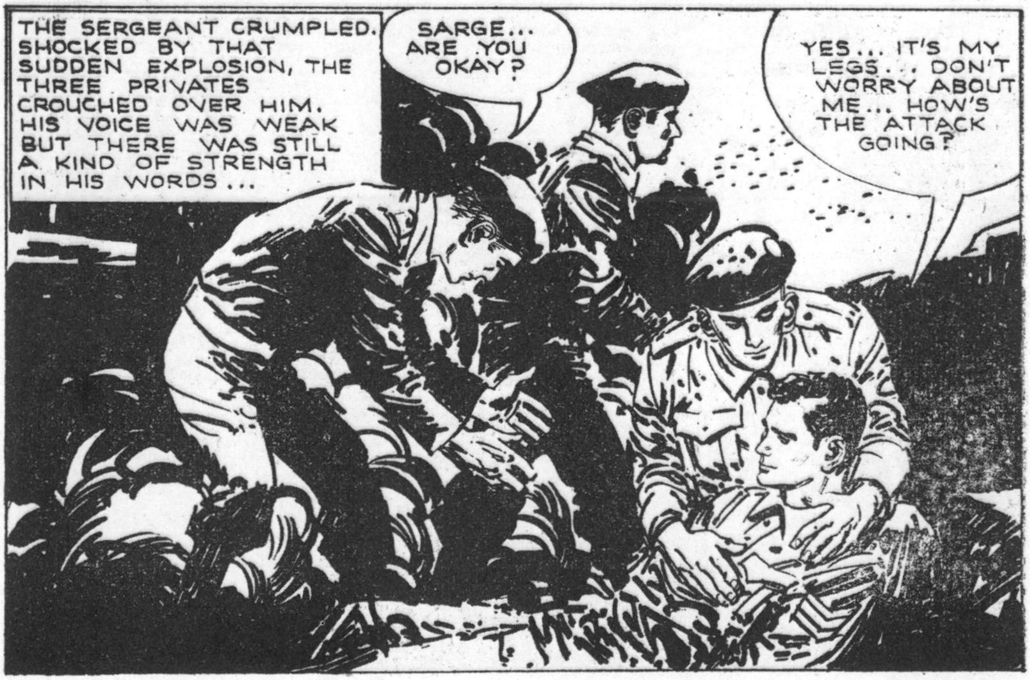
THE SERGEANT CRUMPLED. SHOCKED BY THAT SUDDEN EXPLOSION, THE THREE PRIVATES CROUCHED OVER HIM. HIS VOICE WAS WEAK BUT THERE WAS STILL A KIND OF STRENGTH IN HIS WORDS...
SARGE... ARE YOU OKAY?
YES... IT'S MY LEGS... DON'T WORRY ABOUT ME... HOW'S THE ATTACK GOING?

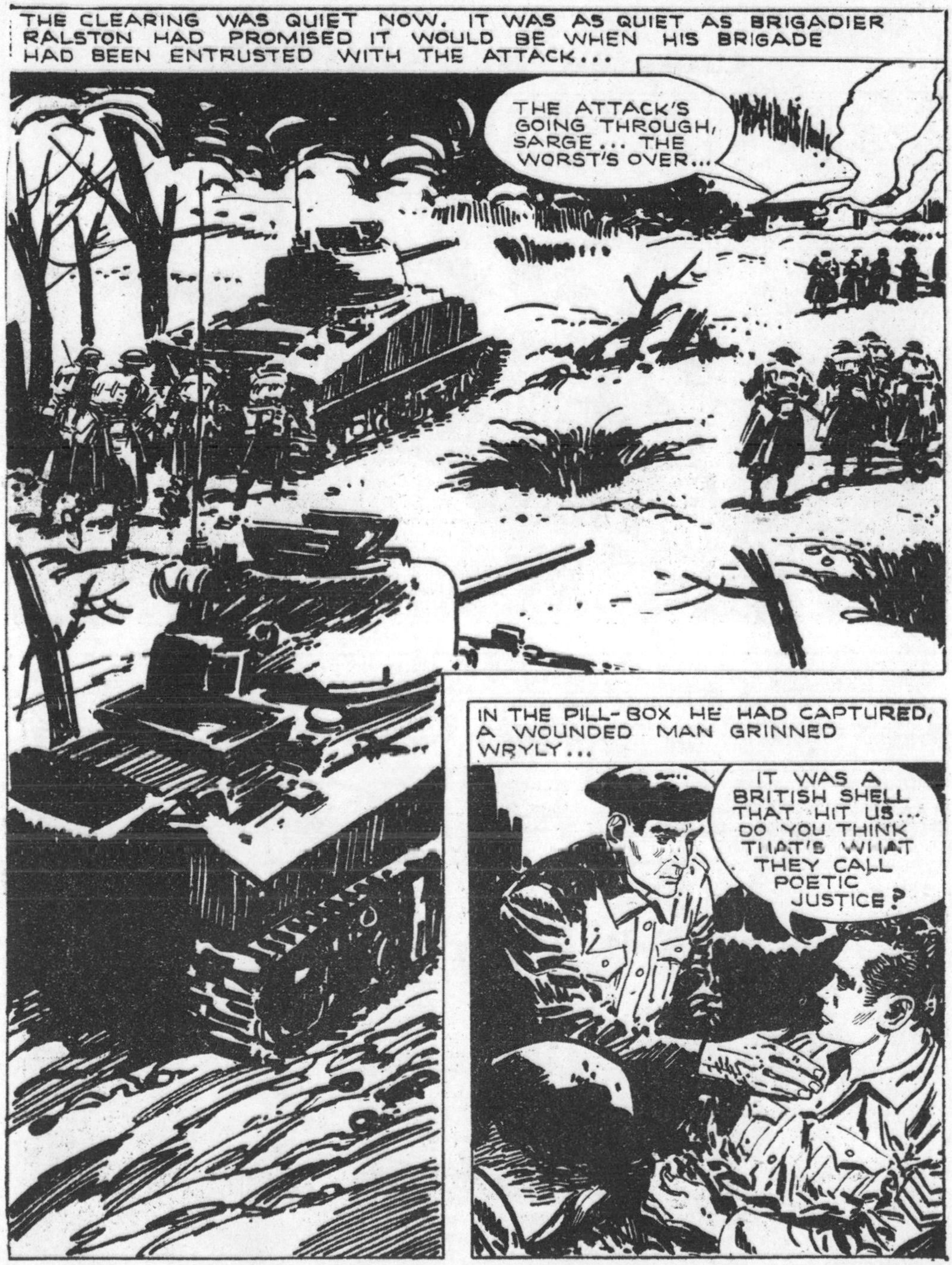
THE CLEARING WAS QUIET NOW. IT WAS AS QUIET AS BRIGADIER RALSTON HAD PROMISED IT WOULD BE WHEN HIS BRIGADE HAD BEEN ENTRUSTED WITH THE ATTACK...
THE ATTACK'S GOING THROUGH, SARGE ... THE WORST'S OVER...
IN THE PILL-BOX HE HAD CAPTURED, A WOUNDED MAN GRINNED WRYLY...
IT WAS A BRITISH SHELL THAT HIT US... DO YOU THINK THAT'S WHAT THEY CALL POETIC JUSTICE?

Chapter 5. Justice

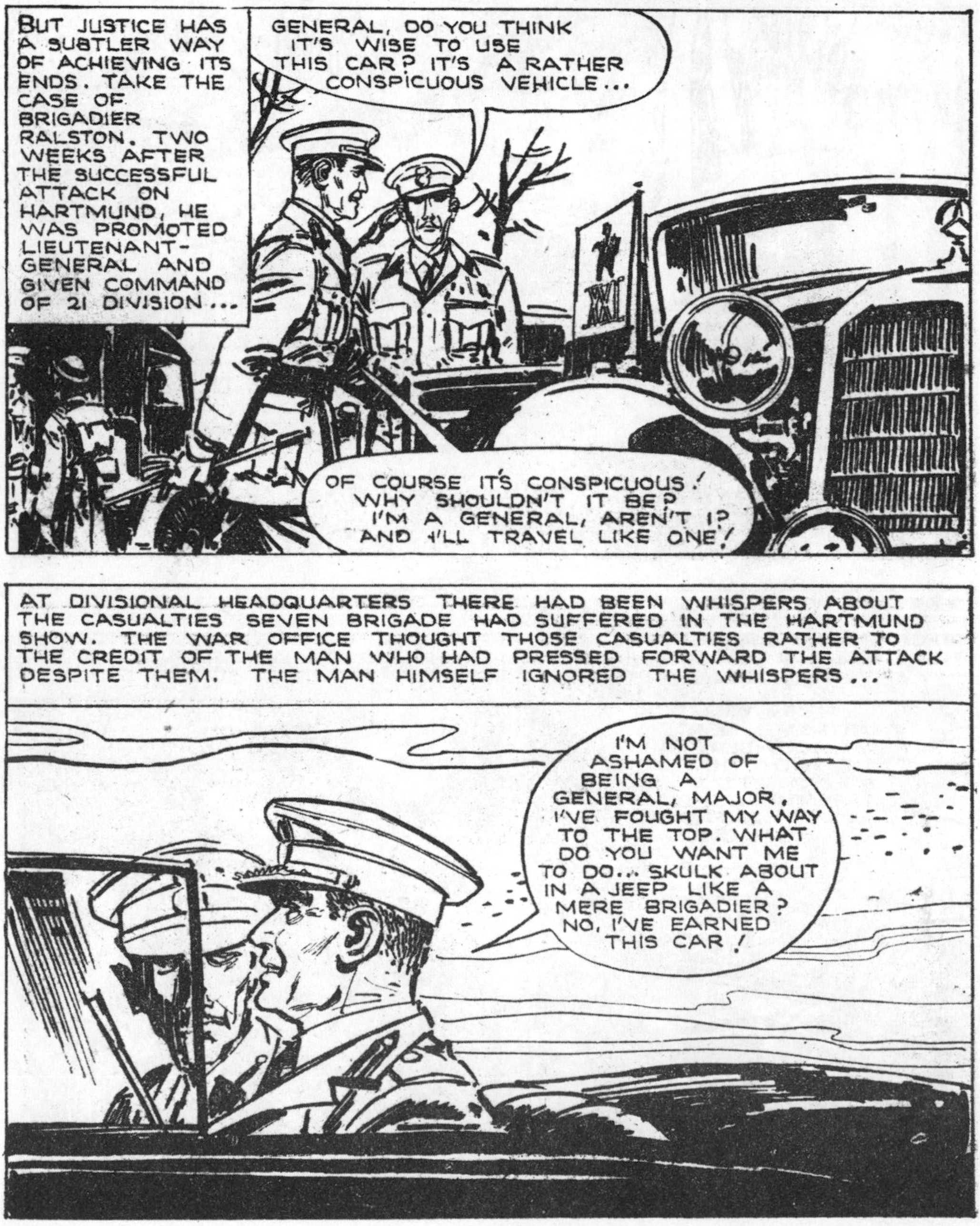
BUT JUSTICE HAS A SUBTLER WAY OF ACHIEVING ITS ENDS. TAKE THE CASE OF BRIGADIER RALSTON. TWO WEEKS AFTER THE SUCCESSFUL ATTACK ON HARTMUND, HE WAS PROMOTED LIEUTENANT-GENERAL AND GIVEN COMMAND OF 21 DIVISION...
GENERAL, DO YOU THINK IT'S WISE TO USE THIS CAR? IT'S A RATHER CONSPICUOUS VEHICLE...
XXI
OF COURSE IT'S CONSPICUOUS! WHY SHOULDN'T IT BE? I'M A GENERAL, AREN'T I? AND I'LL TRAVEL LIKE ONE!
AT DIVISIONAL HEADQUARTERS THERE HAD BEEN WHISPERS ABOUT THE CASUALTIES SEVEN BRIGADE HAD SUFFERED IN THE HARTMUND SHOW. THE WAR OFFICE THOUGHT THOSE CASUALTIES RATHER TO THE CREDIT OF THE MAN WHO HAD PRESSED FORWARD THE ATTACK DESPITE THEM. THE MAN HIMSELF IGNORED THE WHISPERS...
I'M NOT ASHAMED OF BEING A GENERAL, MAJOR. I'VE FOUGHT MY WAY TO THE TOP. WHAT DO YOU WANT ME TO DO... SKULK ABOUT IN A JEEP LIKE A MERE BRIGADIER? NO, I'VE EARNED THIS CAR!

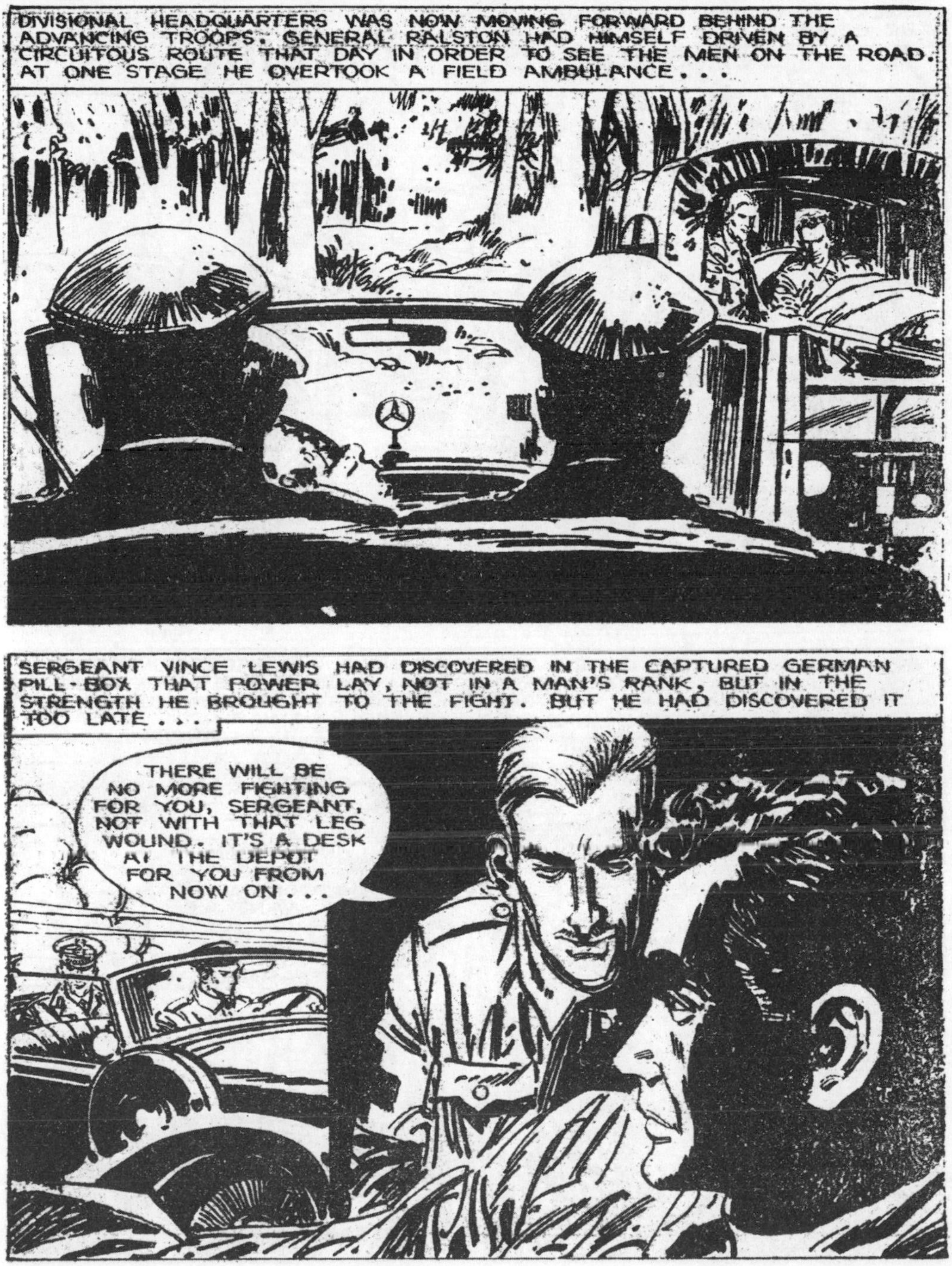
DIVISIONAL HEADQUARTERS WAS NOW MOVING FORWARD BEHIND THE ADVANCING TROOPS. GENERAL RALSTON HAD HIMSELF DRIVEN BY A CIRCUITOUS ROUTE THAT DAY IN ORDER TO SEE THE MEN ON THE ROAD. AT ONE STAGE HE OVERTOOK A FIELD AMBULANCE . . .
SERGEANT VINCE LEWIS HAD DISCOVERED IN THE CAPTURED GERMAN PILL-BOX THAT POWER LAY, NOT IN A MAN'S RANK, BUT IN THE STRENGTH HE BROUGHT TO THE FIGHT. BUT HE HAD DISCOVERED IT TOO LATE . . .
THERE WILL BE NO MORE FIGHTING FOR YOU, SERGEANT, NOT WITH THAT LEG WOUND. IT'S A DESK AT THE DEPOT FOR YOU FROM NOW ON . . .

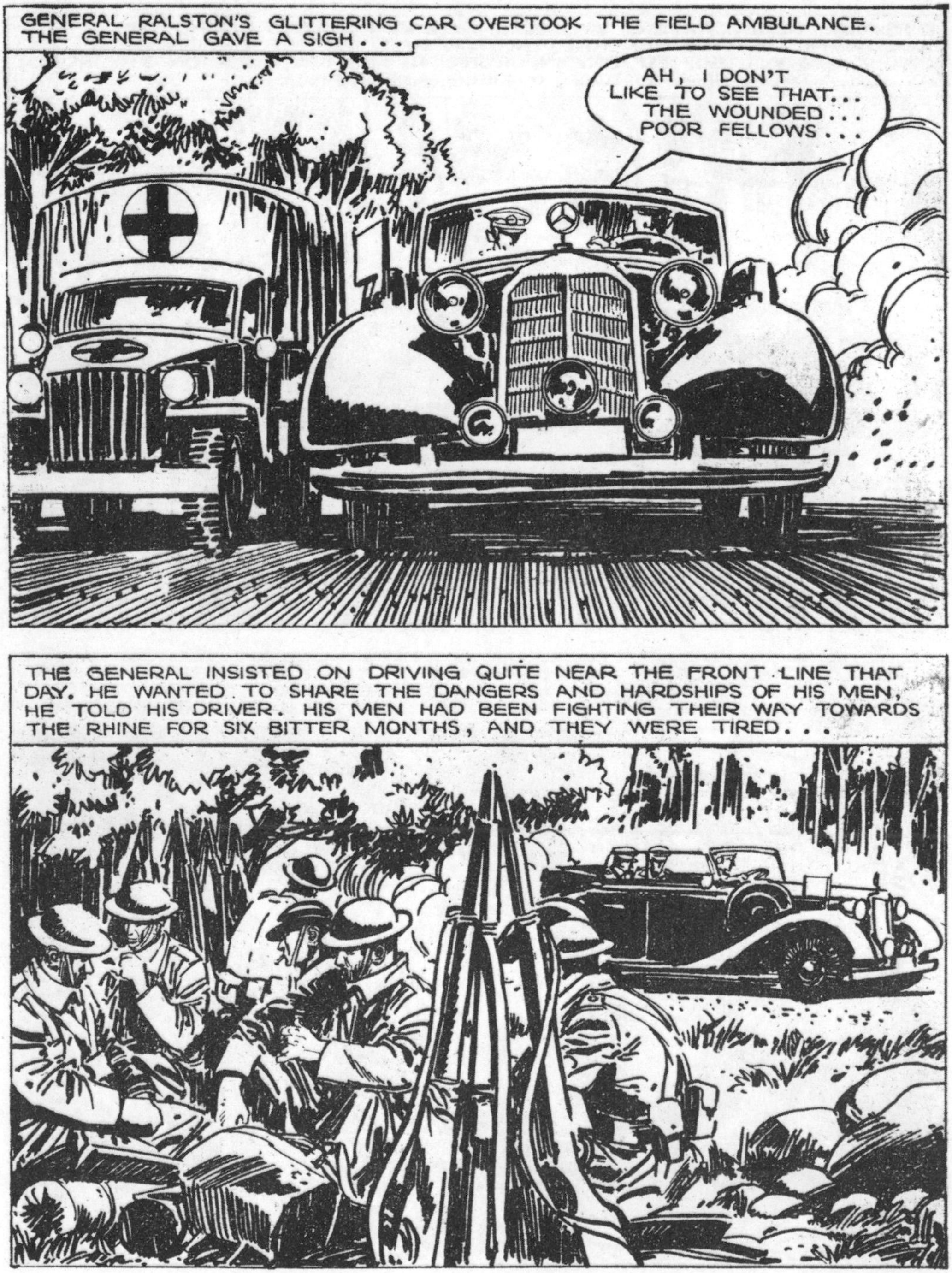
GENERAL RALSTON'S GLITTERING CAR OVERTOOK THE FIELD AMBULANCE. THE GENERAL GAVE A SIGH . . .
AH, I DON'T LIKE TO SEE THAT... THE WOUNDED... POOR FELLOWS . . .
THE GENERAL INSISTED ON DRIVING QUITE NEAR THE FRONT LINE THAT DAY. HE WANTED TO SHARE THE DANGERS AND HARDSHIPS OF HIS MEN, HE TOLD HIS DRIVER. HIS MEN HAD BEEN FIGHTING THEIR WAY TOWARDS THE RHINE FOR SIX BITTER MONTHS, AND THEY WERE TIRED . . .

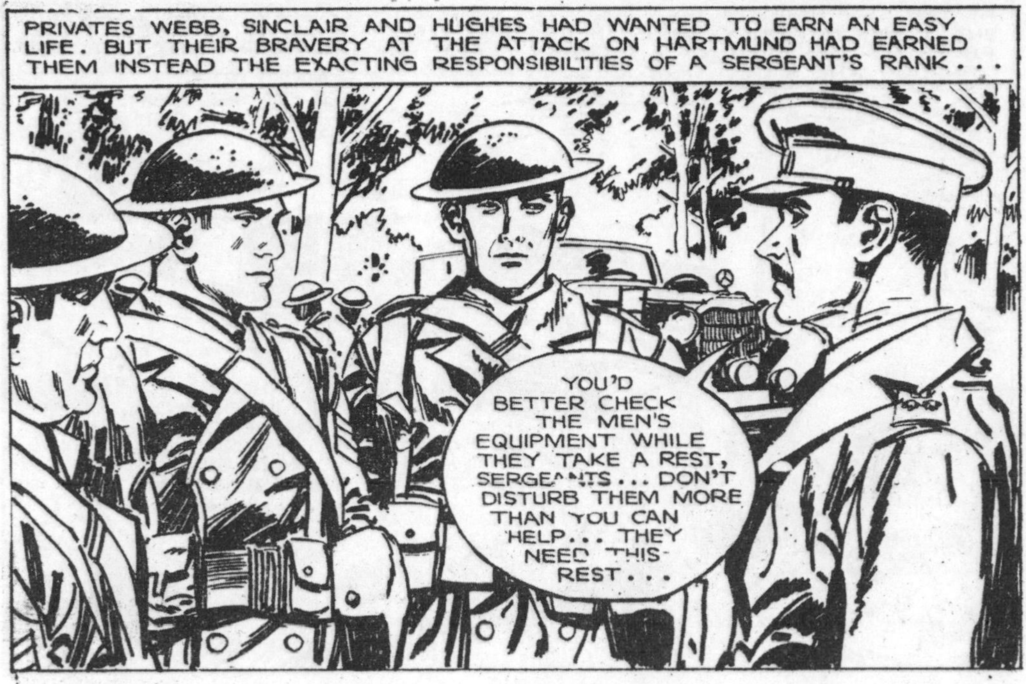
PRIVATES WEBB, SINCLAIR AND HUGHES HAD WANTED TO EARN AN EASY LIFE. BUT THEIR BRAVERY AT THE ATTACK ON HARTMUND HAD EARNED THEM INSTEAD THE EXACTING RESPONSIBILITIES OF A SERGEANT'S RANK . . .
YOU'D BETTER CHECK THE MEN'S EQUIPMENT WHILE THEY TAKE A REST, SERGEANTS . . . DON'T DISTURB THEM MORE THAN YOU CAN HELP . . . THEY NEED THIS REST . . .

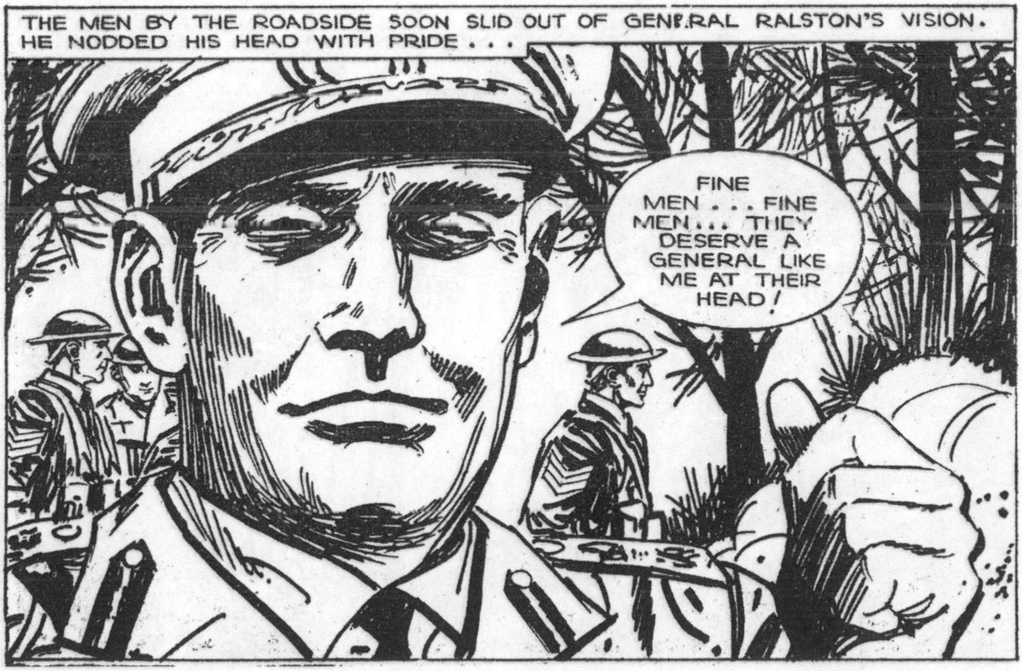
THE MEN BY THE ROADSIDE SOON SLID OUT OF GENERAL RALSTON'S VISION. HE NODDED HIS HEAD WITH PRIDE . . .
FINE MEN . . . FINE MEN . . . THEY DESERVE A GENERAL LIKE ME AT THEIR HEAD!

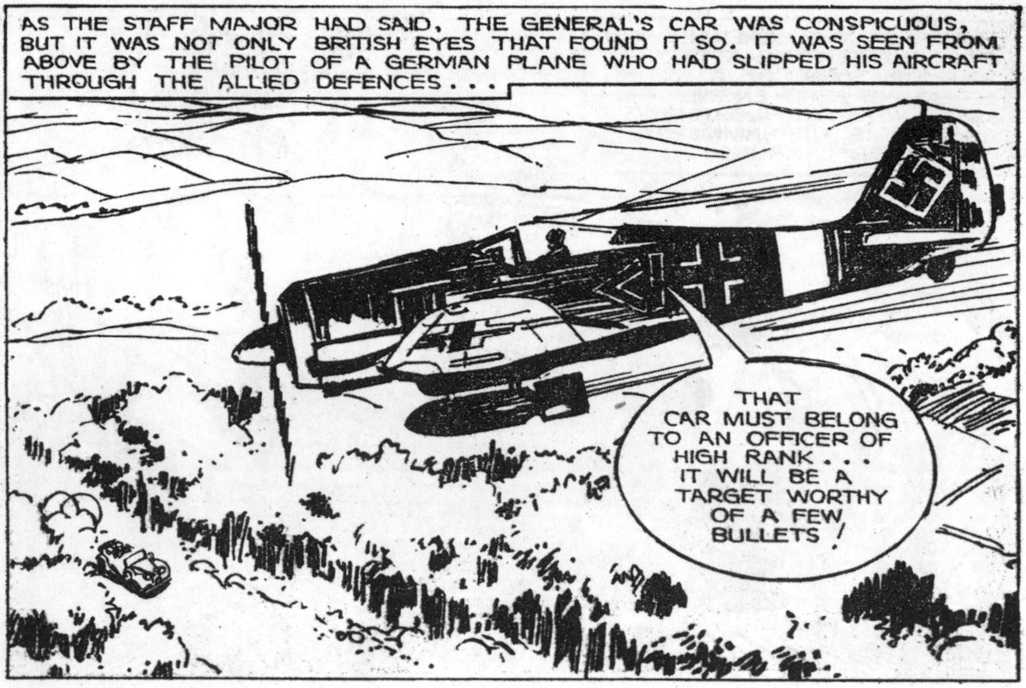
AS THE STAFF MAJOR HAD SAID, THE GENERAL'S CAR WAS CONSPICUOUS, BUT IT WAS NOT ONLY BRITISH EYES THAT FOUND IT SO. IT WAS SEEN FROM ABOVE BY THE PILOT OF A GERMAN PLANE WHO HAD SLIPPED HIS AIRCRAFT THROUGH THE ALLIED DEFENCES . . .
THAT CAR MUST BELONG TO AN OFFICER OF HIGH RANK . . . IT WILL BE A TARGET WORTHY OF A FEW BULLETS !

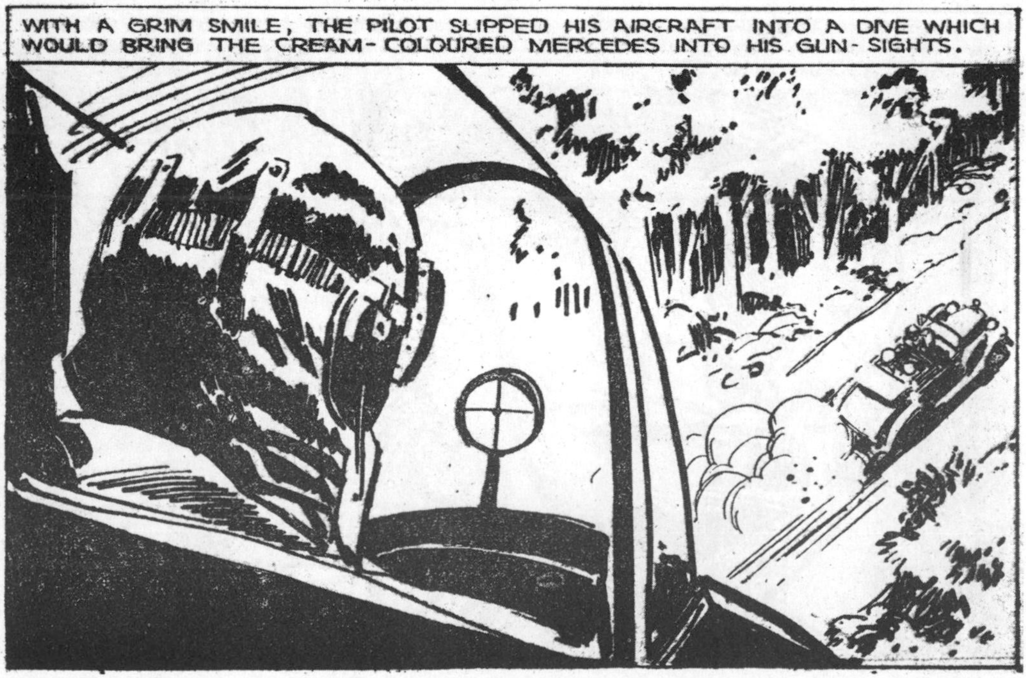
WITH A GRIM SMILE, THE PILOT SLIPPED HIS AIRCRAFT INTO A DIVE WHICH WOULD BRING THE CREAM-COLOURED MERCEDES INTO HIS GUN-SIGHTS.

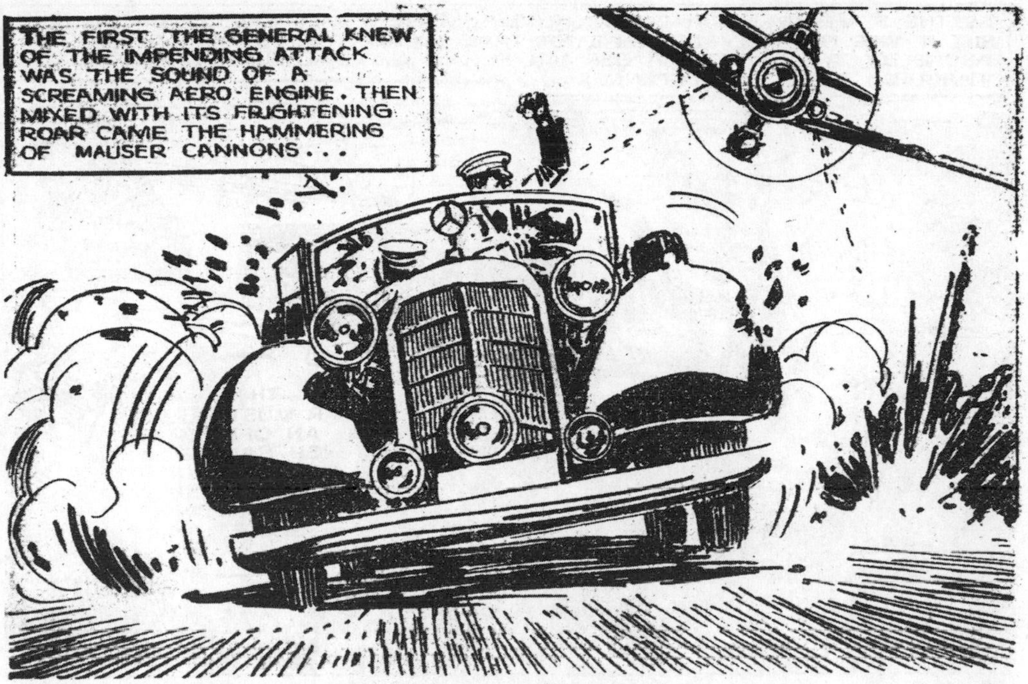
THE FIRST THE GENERAL KNEW OF THE IMPENDING ATTACK WAS THE SOUND OF A SCREAMING AERO-ENGINE. THEN MIXED WITH ITS FRIGHTENING ROAR CAME THE HAMMERING OF MAUSER CANNONS...

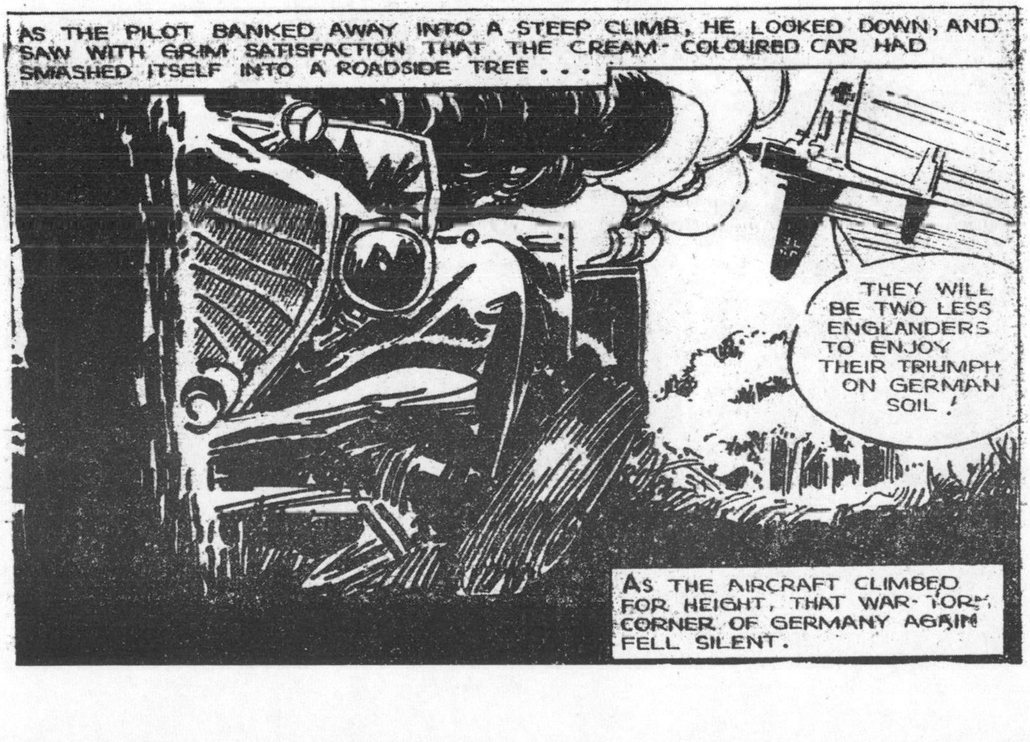
AS THE PILOT BANKED AWAY INTO A STEEP CLIMB, HE LOOKED DOWN, AND SAW WITH GRIM SATISFACTION THAT THE CREAM-COLOURED CAR HAD SMASHED ITSELF INTO A ROADSIDE TREE...
THEY WILL BE TWO LESS ENGLANDERS TO ENJOY THEIR TRIUMPH ON GERMAN SOIL!
AS THE AIRCRAFT CLIMBED FOR HEIGHT, THAT WAR-TORN CORNER OF GERMANY AGAIN FELL SILENT.

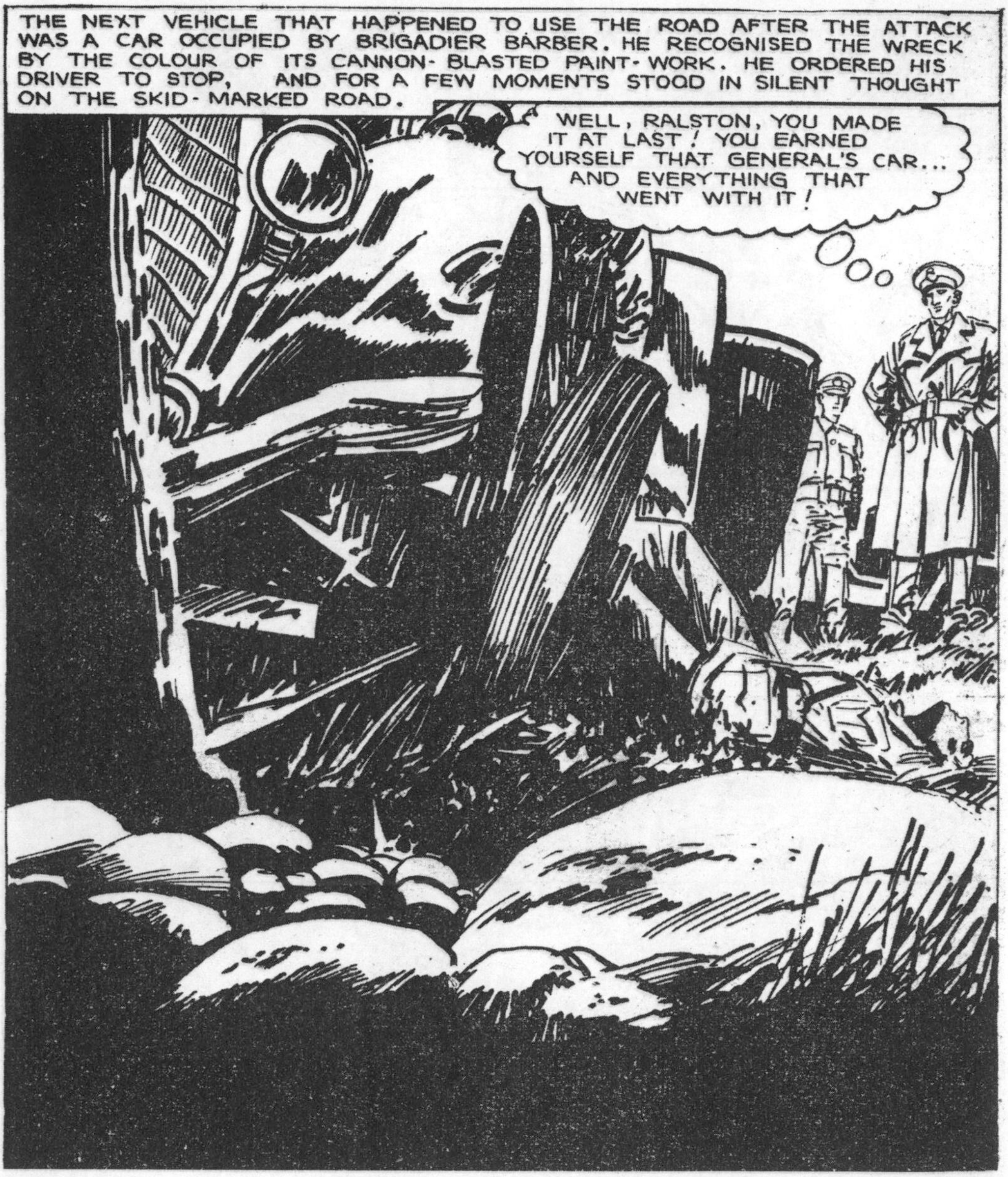
THE NEXT VEHICLE THAT HAPPENED TO USE THE ROAD AFTER THE ATTACK WAS A CAR OCCUPIED BY BRIGADIER BARBER. HE RECOGNISED THE WRECK BY THE COLOUR OF ITS CANNON-BLASTED PAINT-WORK. HE ORDERED HIS DRIVER TO STOP, AND FOR A FEW MOMENTS STOOD IN SILENT THOUGHT ON THE SKID-MARKED ROAD.
WELL, RALSTON, YOU MADE IT AT LAST! YOU EARNED YOURSELF THAT GENERAL'S CAR... AND EVERYTHING THAT WENT WITH IT!

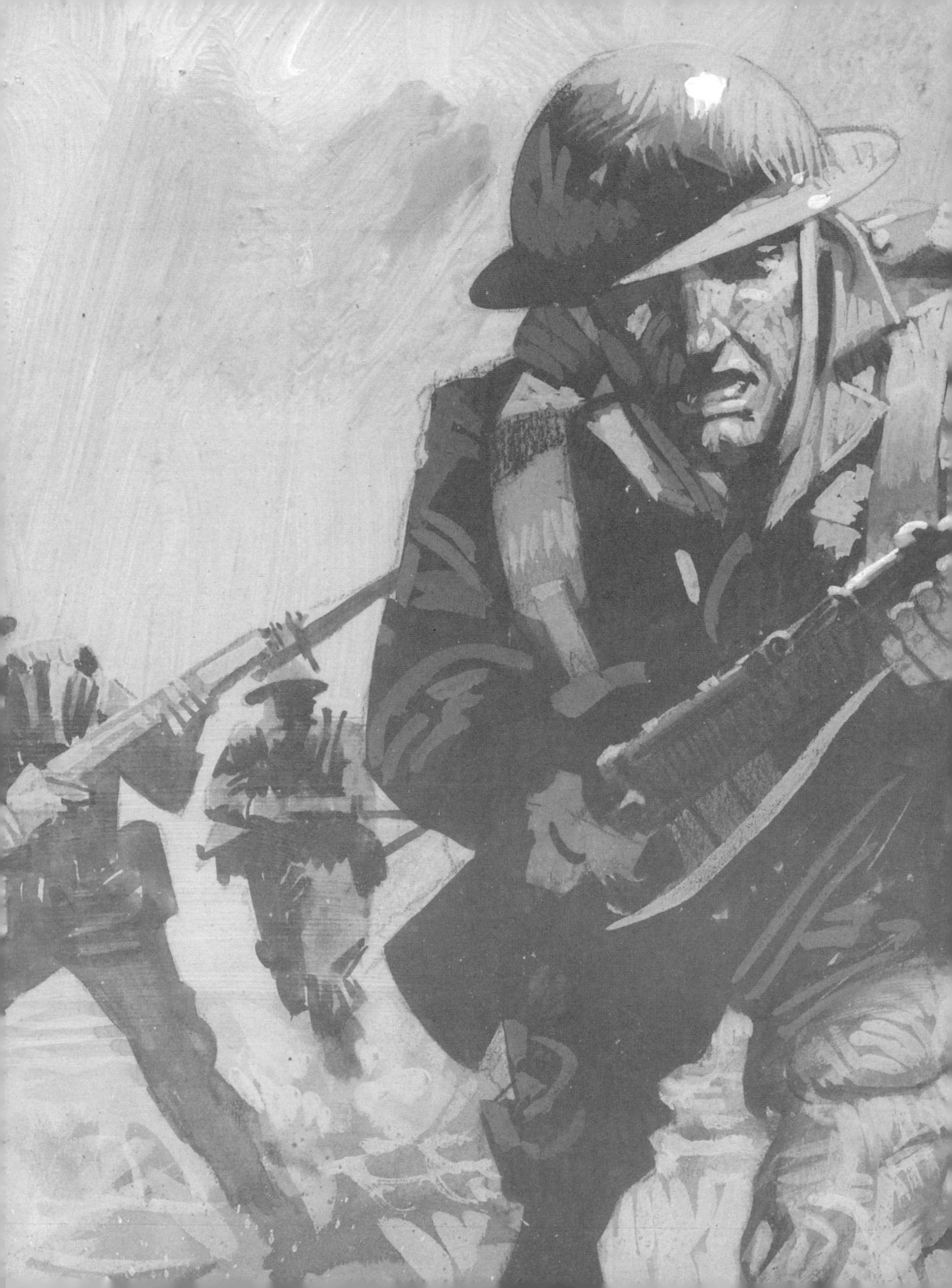